CHILTON®

EUROPEAN
SERVICE MANUAL
2012 EDITION
VOLUME I
AUDI
FIAT
MINI
VOLKSWAGEN

CENGAGE
Learning®

Australia • Brazil • Japan • Korea • Mexico • Singapore • Spain • United Kingdom • United States

CENGAGE
Learning·

CHILTON®
European Service Manual
2012 Edition
Volume I
Audi, Fiat, MINI, Volkswagen

Vice President,
Technology & Trades Professional
Business Unit:
Gregory L. Clayton

Publisher:
David Koontz

Director of Marketing:
Beth A. Lutz

Senior Production Director:
Wendy Troeger

Production Manager:
Sherondra Thedford

Senior Marketing Manager:
Jennifer Barbic

Associate Marketing Manager:
Rachael Torres

Chilton Content Specialist:
Paula Baillie

Graphical Designer:
Melinda Possinger

Art Director:
Benj Gleeksman

Sr. Content Project Manager:
William Tubbert

Senior Editors:
Eugene F. Hannon, Jr., A.S.E.
Ryan Lee Price
Richard J. Rivele
Christine L. Sheeky

Editors:
Dennis L. Bailey
Nick D'Andrea
Celia McCarty
Lance Williams

For product information and technology assistance, contact us at
Professional & Career Group customer Support, 1-800-648-7450.
For permission to use material from this text or product,
submit all requests online at
www.cengage.com/permissions.
Further permissions questions can be e-mailed to
permissionrequest@cengage.com

ISBN-13: 978-1-2854-7110-5
ISBN-10: 1-2854-7110-5
ISSN: 2161-7872

Chilton
5 Maxwell Drive
Clifton Park, NY 12065-2919
USA

Cengage Learning is a leading provider of customized learning solutions with office locations around the globe, including Singapore, the United Kingdom, Australia, Mexico, Brazil, and Japan. Locate your local office at: **international.cengage.com/region**

Chilton products are represented in Canada by Nelson Education, Ltd.

NOTICE TO THE READER

Publisher does not warrant or guarantee any of the products described herein or perform any independent analysis in connection with any of the product information contained herein. Publisher does not assume, and expressly disclaims, any obligation to obtain and include information other than that provided to it by the manufacturer.

The reader is expressly warned to consider and adopt all safety precautions that might be indicated by the activities described herein and to avoid all potential hazards. By following the instructions contained herein, the reader willingly assumes all risks in connection with such instructions.

The publisher makes no representations or warranties of any kind, including but not limited to, the warranties of fitness for particular purpose or merchantability, nor are any such representations implied with respect to the material set forth herein, and the publisher takes no responsibility with respect to such material. The publisher shall not be liable for any special, consequential, or exemplary damages resulting, in whole or part, from the readers' use of, or reliance upon, this material.

Printed in the United States of America
1 2 3 4 5 6 7 XX 17 16 15 14 13

Contents

Model Index

USING THIS INFORMATION

Organization

To find where a particular model section or procedure is located, look in the Table of Contents. Main topics are listed with the page number on which they may be found. Following the main topics is an alphabetical listing of all of the procedures within the section and their page numbers.

Manufacturer and Model Coverage

This product covers 2011-2012 European models that are produced in sufficient quantities to warrant coverage, and which have technical content available from the vehicle manufacturers before our publication date. Although this information is as complete as possible at the time of publication, some manufacturers may make changes which cannot be included here. While striving for total accuracy, the publisher cannot assume responsibility for any errors, changes, or omissions that may occur in the compilation of this data.

Part Numbers and Special Tools

Part numbers and special tools are recommended by the publisher and vehicle manufacturer to perform specific jobs. Before substituting any part or tool for the one recommended, you must be completely satisfied that neither your personal safety, nor the performance of the vehicle will be endangered.

ACKNOWLEDGEMENT

The publisher would like to express appreciation to the following vehicle manufacturers for their assistance in producing this manual: Audi of America, Inc., BMW of North America, LLC, Mercedes-Benz USA, LLC, MINI USA, Saab Cars USA, Inc., Volkswagen of America, Inc., Volvo Cars of North America, LLC.

Portions of materials contained herein have been reprinted under license from VWGoA, License Agreement **11503VWA**.

No further reproduction or distribution of the material in this manual is allowed without the expressed written permission of the vehicle manufacturers and the publisher.

PRECAUTIONS

Before servicing any vehicle, please be sure to read all of the following precautions, which deal with personal safety, prevention of component damage, and important points to take into consideration when servicing a motor vehicle:
- Always wear safety glasses or goggles when drilling, cutting, grinding or prying.
- Steel-toed work shoes should be worn when working with heavy parts. Pockets should not be used for carrying tools. A slip or fall can drive a screwdriver into your body.
- Work surfaces, including tools and the floor should be kept clean of grease, oil or other slippery material.
- When working around moving parts, don't wear loose clothing. Long hair should be tied back under a hat or cap, or in a hair net.
- Always use tools only for the purpose for which they were designed. Never pry with a screwdriver.
- Keep a fire extinguisher and first aid kit handy.
- Always properly support the vehicle with approved stands or lift.
- Always have adequate ventilation when working with chemicals or hazardous material.
- Carbon monoxide is colorless, odorless and dangerous. If it is necessary to operate the engine with vehicle in a closed area such as a garage, always use an exhaust collector to vent the exhaust gases outside the closed area.

- When draining coolant, keep in mind that small children and some pets are attracted by ethylene glycol antifreeze, and are quite likely to drink any left in an open container, or in puddles on the ground. This will prove fatal in sufficient quantity. Always drain the coolant into a sealable container.
- To avoid personal injury, do not remove the coolant pressure relief cap while the engine is operating or hot. The cooling system is under pressure; steam and hot liquid can come out forcefully when the cap is loosened slightly. Failure to follow these instructions may result in personal injury. The coolant must be recovered in a suitable, clean container for reuse. If the coolant is contaminated it must be recycled or disposed of correctly.
- When carrying out maintenance on the starting system be aware that heavy gauge leads are connected directly to the battery. Make sure the protective caps are in place when maintenance is completed. Failure to follow these instructions may result in personal injury.
- Do not remove any part of the engine emission control system. Operating the engine without the engine emission control system will reduce fuel economy and engine ventilation. This will weaken engine performance and shorten engine life. It is also a violation of Federal law.
- Due to environmental concerns, when the air conditioning system is drained, the refrigerant must be collected using refrigerant recovery/recycling equipment. Federal law requires that refrigerant be recovered into appropriate recovery equipment and the process be conducted by qualified technicians who have been certified by an approved organization, such as MACS, ASI, etc. Use of a recovery machine dedicated to the appropriate refrigerant is necessary to reduce the possibility of oil and refrigerant incompatibility concerns. Refer to the instructions provided by the equipment manufacturer when removing refrigerant from or charging the air conditioning system.
- Always disconnect the battery ground when working on or around the electrical system.
- Batteries contain sulfuric acid. Avoid contact with skin, eyes, or clothing. Also, shield your eyes when working near batteries to protect against possible splashing of the acid solution. In case of acid contact with skin or eyes, flush immediately with water for a minimum of 15 minutes and get prompt medical attention. If acid is swallowed, call a physician immediately. Failure to follow these instructions may result in personal injury.
- Batteries normally produce explosive gases. Therefore, do not allow flames, sparks or lighted substances to come near the battery. When charging or working near a battery, always shield your face and protect your eyes. Always provide ventilation. Failure to follow these instructions may result in personal injury.

• When lifting a battery, excessive pressure on the end walls could cause acid to spew through the vent caps, resulting in personal injury, damage to the vehicle or battery. Lift with a battery carrier or with your hands on opposite corners. Failure to follow these instructions may result in personal injury.

• Observe all applicable safety precautions when working around fuel. Whenever servicing the fuel system, always work in a well-ventilated area. Do not allow fuel spray or vapors to come in contact with a spark, open flame, or excessive heat (a hot drop light, for example). Keep a dry chemical fire extinguisher near the work area. Always keep fuel in a container specifically designed for fuel storage; also, always properly seal fuel containers to avoid the possibility of fire or explosion. Do not smoke or carry lighted tobacco or open flame of any type when working on or near any fuel-related components.

• Fuel injection systems often remain pressurized, even after the engine has been turned OFF. The fuel system pressure must be relieved before disconnecting any fuel lines. Failure to do so may result in fire and/or personal injury.

• The evaporative emissions system contains fuel vapor and condensed fuel vapor. Although not present in large quantities, it still presents the danger of explosion or fire. Disconnect the battery ground cable from the battery to minimize the possibility of an electrical spark occurring, possibly causing a fire or explosion if fuel vapor or liquid fuel is present in the area. Failure to follow these instructions can result in personal injury.

• The EPA warns that prolonged contact with used engine oil may cause a number of skin disorders, including cancer! You should make every effort to minimize your exposure to used engine oil. Protective gloves should be worn when changing oil. Wash your hands and any other exposed skin areas as soon as possible after exposure to used engine oil. Soap and water, or waterless hand cleaner should be used.

• Some vehicles are equipped with an air bag system, often referred to as a Supplemental Restraint System (SRS) or Supplemental Inflatable Restraint (SIR) system. The system must be disabled before performing service on or around system components, steering column, instrument panel components, wiring and sensors. Failure to follow safety and disabling procedures could result in accidental air bag deployment, possible personal injury and unnecessary system repairs.

• Always wear safety goggles when working with, or around, the air bag system. When carrying a non-deployed air bag, be sure the bag and trim cover are pointed away from your body. When placing a non-deployed air bag on a work surface, always face the bag and trim cover upward, away from the surface. This will reduce the motion of the module if it is accidentally deployed.

• Electronic modules are sensitive to electrical charges. The ABS module can be damaged if exposed to these charges.

• Brake pads and shoes may contain asbestos, which has been determined to be a cancer-causing agent. Never clean brake surfaces with compressed air. Avoid inhaling brake dust. Clean all brake surfaces with a commercially available brake cleaning fluid.

• When replacing brake pads, shoes, discs or drums, replace them as complete axle sets.

• When servicing drum brakes, disassemble and assemble one side at a time, leaving the remaining side intact for reference.

• Brake fluid often contains polyglycol ethers and polyglycols. Avoid contact with the eyes and wash your hands thoroughly after handling brake fluid. If you do get brake fluid in your eyes, flush your eyes with clean, running water for 15 minutes. If eye irritation persists, or if you have taken brake fluid internally, immediately seek medical assistance.

• Clean, high quality brake fluid from a sealed container is essential to the safe and proper operation of the brake system. You should always buy the correct type of brake fluid for your vehicle. If the brake fluid becomes contaminated, completely flush the system with new fluid. Never reuse any brake fluid. Any brake fluid that is removed from the system should be discarded. Also, do not allow any brake fluid to come in contact with a painted or plastic surface; it will damage the paint.

• Never operate the engine without the proper amount and type of engine oil; doing so will result in severe engine damage.

• Timing belt maintenance is extremely important! Many models utilize an interference- type, non freewheeling engine. If the timing belt breaks, the valves in the cylinder head may strike the pistons, causing potentially serious (also time-consuming and expensive) engine damage.

• Disconnecting the negative battery cable on some vehicles may interfere with the functions of the on-board computer system(s) and may require the computer to undergo a relearning process once the negative battery cable is reconnected.

• Steering and suspension fasteners are critical parts because they affect performance of vital components and systems and their failure can result in major service expense. They must be replaced with the same grade or part number or an equivalent part if replacement is necessary. Do not use a replacement part of lesser quality or substitute design. Torque values must be used as specified during reassembly.

SPECIFICATIONS AND MAINTENANCE CHARTS

ENGINE AND VEHICLE IDENTIFICATION

| | Engine | | | | | | Model Year | |
Code	Liters (cc)	Cu. In.	Cyl.	Fuel Sys.	Engine Type	Eng. Mfg.	Code ①	Year
CBEA	2.0 (1968)	120	4	TDI	DOHC	Audi	B	2011
CBFA	2.0 (1984)	121	4	TFSI	DOHC	Audi	C	2012
CCTA	2.0 (1984)	121	4	TFSI	DOHC	Audi		
CAEB	2.0 (1984)	121	4	TFSI	DOHC	Audi		

TFSI: Turbocharged Fuel Stratified Injection

TDI: Turbocharged Direct Injection

DOHC: Double Overhead Camshaft

① 10th digit of the Vehicle Identification Number (VIN)

71105_A3A4_C0001

GENERAL ENGINE SPECIFICATIONS

Year	Model	Engine Displacement Liters	Engine ID Code	Net Horsepower @ rpm	Net Torque@rpm (ft. lbs.)	Bore x Stroke (in.)	Com- pression Ratio	Oil Pressure @ rpm
2011	A3	2.0	CBEA	211@4,300	207@2000	3.18x3.75	16.5.1	29@2000
	A3	2.0	CBFA	208@6,000	258@1500	3.25x3.65	10.3.1	22@2000
	A3	2.0	CCTA	208@6,000	258@1500	3.25x3.65	9.6.1	22@2000
	A4, A5	2.0	CAEB	208@6,000	258@1500	3.25x3.65	9.6.1	22@2000
2012	A3	2.0	CBEA	211@4,300	207@2000	3.18x3.75	16.5.1	29@2000
	A3	2.0	CBFA	208@6,000	258@1500	3.25x3.65	10.3.1	22@2000
	A3	2.0	CCTA	208@6,000	258@1500	3.25x3.65	9.6.1	22@2000
	A4, A5	2.0	CAEB	208@6,000	258@1500	3.25x3.65	9.6.1	22@2000

① Minimum oil pressure

71105_A3A4_C0002

GASOLINE ENGINE TUNE-UP SPECIFICATIONS

| | | | | Ignition Timing (deg.) | | | Idle Speed (rpm) | | Valve Clearance | |
Year	Engine Displacement Liters	Engine ID/VIN	Spark Plug Gap (in.)	MT	AT	Fuel Pump (psi)	MT	AT	In.	Ex.
2011	2.0	①	0.028-0.031	②	②	101.5	640-800	640-800	HYD	HYD
2012	2.0	①	0.028-0.031	②	②	101.5	640-800	640-800	HYD	HYD

① Inspect timing cover for code.

② Ignition timing and idle speed is controlled electronically. Specification no longer provided.

HYD: Hydraulic

NOTE: The Vehicle Emission Control Information label reflects specification changes made during production and must be used if different from this chart.

NOTE: Fuel pump pressure specifications are with the fuel pressure regulator vacuum hose attached.

NOTE: The basic setting is controlled by the ECU and is not adjustable.

71105_A3A4_C0003

DIESEL ENGINE TUNE-UP SPECIFICATIONS

Year	Engine Displacement Liters	Engine ID/Code	Valve Clearance Intake (in.)	Exhaust (in.)	Intake Valve Opens (deg.)	Injection Pump Setting (deg.)	Injection Nozzle Pressure (psi) New	Used	Idle Speed (rpm)	Cranking Compression Pressure (psi)
2011	2.0	CBEA	HYD	HYD	NS	①	NS	NS	①	275.5
2012	2.0	CBEA	HYD	HYD	NS	①	NS	NS	①	275.5

Note: The Vehicle Emission Control Information label reflects specification changes made during production.

NS: Not Specified

① Injection pump timing and idle speed is controlled electronically. Specification no longer provided.

71105_A3A4_C0004

CAPACITIES

Year	Model	Engine Displacement Liters	Engine ID/VIN	Engine Oil with Filter	Transmission Manual (pts.)	Auto. (qts.)	Fuel Tank (gal.)	Cooling System (qts.)
2011	A3, A4, A5	2.0 (1984)	①	4.9	4.9	NA	14.5	7.7
	A3, A4	2.0 (1968)	②	4.3	4.9	5.5	14.5	8.5
2012	A3, A4, A5	2.0 (1984)	①	4.9	4.9	NA	14.5	7.7
	A3, A4	2.0 (1968)	②	4.3	4.9	5.5	14.5	8.5

Note: All capacities are approximate. Add fluid gradually and check often to avoid overfilling or under filling.

NA: Not Applicable

① Inspect timing cover for code.

② TDI: Turbocharged Direct Injection

71105_A3A4_C0006

FLUID SPECIFICATIONS

Year	Model	Engine Displacement Liters	Engine ID/VIN	Engine Oil	Man. Trans.	Auto. Trans.	Brake Master Cylinder	Cooling System
2011	A3, A4, A5	2.0 (1984)	①	5W-40	Synthetic MTF 75W-90	Synthetic ATF	DOT4	LLC
	A3, A4	2.0 (1968)	②	5W-40	Synthetic MTF 75W-90	Synthetic ATF	DOT4	LLC
2012	A3, A4, A5	2.0 (1984)	①	5W-40	Synthetic MTF 75W-90	Synthetic ATF	DOT4	LLC
	A3, A4	2.0 (1968)	②	5W-40	Synthetic MTF 75W-90	Synthetic ATF	DOT4	LLC

LLC: Long Life Coolant

NA: Not Applicable

① Inspect timing cover for code.

② TDI: Turbocharged Direct Injection

71105_A3A4_C0005

VALVE SPECIFICATIONS

Year	Engine Displacement Liters	Engine ID/VIN	Seat Angle (deg.)	Face Angle (deg.)	Head Diameter (in.)		Stem-to-Guide Clearance (in.)		Stem Diameter (in.)	
					Intake	Exhaust	Intake	Exhaust	Intake	Exhaust
2011	2.0	①	45	45	0.031	0.031	0.031	0.031	0.2354	0.2346
	2.0	②	45	45	1.106	1.023	0.050	0.050	0.2352	0.2348
2012	2.0	①	45	45	0.031	0.031	0.031	0.031	0.2354	0.2346
	2.0	②	45	45	1.106	1.023	0.050	0.050	0.2352	0.2348

NS: Not Specified

① Inspect timing cover for code.

② TDI: Turbocharged Direct Injection

71105_A3A4_C0009

CRANKSHAFT AND CONNECTING ROD SPECIFICATIONS

All measurements are given in inches.

Year	Engine Disp. Liters	Engine ID/VIN	Main Brg. Journal Dia.	Main Brg. Oil Clearance	Shaft End-play	Thrust on No.	Connecting Rod		
							Journal Diameter	Oil Clearance	Side Clearance
2011	2.0	①	2.1260	0.0007- 0.0015	0.0028- 0.0090	3	1.8819	0.0008- 0.0024	0.0039- 0.0138
	2.0	②	2.1060	NS	0.0027- 0.0066	3	1.8642	0.0031	0.0144
2012	2.0	①	2.1260	0.0007- 0.0015	0.0028- 0.0090	3	1.8819	0.0008- 0.0024	0.0039- 0.0138
	2.0	②	2.1060	NS	0.0027- 0.0066	3	1.8642	0.0031	0.0144

NS - Not Specified

① Inspect timing cover for code.

② TDI: Turbocharged Direct Injection

71105_A3A4_C0008

PISTON AND RING SPECIFICATIONS

All measurements are given in inches.

Year	Engine Disp. Liters	Engine ID/VIN	Piston Clearance	Ring Gap			Ring Side Clearance		
				Top Compression	Bottom Compression	Oil Control	Top Compression	Bottom Compression	Oil Control
2011	2.0	①	0.0177	0.008- 0.016	0.008- 0.016	0.010- 0.020	0.0024- 0.0035	0.0025- 0.0042	0.0011- 0.0027
	2.0	②	0.0177	0.008- 0.016	0.008- 0.016	0.010- 0.020	0.0024- 0.0035	0.0020- 0.0031	0.0011- 0.0023
2012	2.0	①	0.0177	0.008- 0.016	0.008- 0.016	0.010- 0.020	0.0024- 0.0035	0.0025- 0.0042	0.0011- 0.0027
	2.0	②	0.0177	0.008- 0.016	0.008- 0.016	0.010- 0.020	0.0024- 0.0035	0.0020- 0.0031	0.0011- 0.0023

① Inspect timing cover for code.

② TDI: Turbocharged Direct Injection

71105_A3A4_C0010

TORQUE SPECIFICATIONS
All readings in ft. lbs.

Year	Engine Displacement Liters	Engine ID/VIN	Cylinder Head Bolts	Main Bearing Bolts	Rod Bearing Bolts	Crankshaft Damper Bolt	Flywheel Bolts	Manifold Intake	Manifold Exhaust	Spark Plugs	Oil Pan Drain Plug
2011	2.0	①	②	③	④	⑤	⑥	7	15 ⑦	22	22
	2.0	①	⑧	⑨	④	⑩	⑥	16	17	22	22
2012	2.0	①	②	③	④	⑤	⑥	7	15 ⑦	22	22
	2.0	①	⑧	⑨	④	⑩	⑥	16	17	22	22

① Inspect timing cover for code.
② Torque in three steps. Use new bolts.
   Step 1: 30 ft. lbs.
   Step 2: plus 90 degrees
   Step 3: plus 90 degrees
③ Two Steps. 66 ft. lbs. Plus 90 degrees. Use new bolt.
④ Two Steps. 22 ft. lbs. plus 90 degrees. Use new bolts.
⑤ Two Steps. 66 ft. lbs. Plus 90 degrees. Use new bolt.
⑥ Two Steps. 44 ft. lbs. plus 90 degrees. Use new bolts.
⑦ Use new bolts.

⑧ Torque in four steps. Use new bolts.
   Step 1: 26 ft. lbs.
   Step 2: 44 ft. lbs.
   Step 3: plus 90 degrees
   Step 4: plus 90 degrees
⑨ Two Steps. 48 ft. lbs. plus 90 degrees. Use new bolts.
⑩ Two Steps. 89 inch lbs. plus 90 degrees. Use new bolts.

71105_A3A4_C0011

WHEEL ALIGNMENT

Year	Model		Caster Range (+/-Deg.)	Caster Preferred Setting (Deg.)	Camber Range (+/-Deg.)	Camber Preferred Setting (Deg.)	Toe-in (Deg.)
2011	A3, A4, A5	Front	0.50	+7.57	0.50	-0.50	1.63+/-0.33 ①
	Standard	Rear	—	—	0.50	-1.33	0.17+/-0.21 ②
	Sport	Front	0.50	+7.83	0.50	-0.68	1.67+/-0.33 ①
		Rear	—	—	0.50	-1.33	0.17+/-0.21 ②
2012	A3, A4, A5	Front	0.50	+7.57	0.50	-0.50	1.63+/-0.33 ①
	Standard	Rear	—	—	0.50	-1.33	0.17+/-0.21 ②
	Sport	Front	0.50	+7.83	0.50	-0.68	1.67+/-0.33 ①
		Rear	—	—	0.50	-1.33	0.17+/-0.21 ②

① Toe differential angle with 20 deg. steering lock to left and right
② Total toe at specified camber.

71105_A3A4_C0012

TIRE, WHEEL AND BALL JOINT SPECIFICATIONS

| Year | Model | OEM Tires | | Tire Pressures (psi) | | Wheel Size | Ball Joint Inspection | Lug Nut (ft. lbs.) |
		Standard	Optional	Front	Rear			
2011	A3	225/45R-17	225/40R-18	34	34	7-J, 8.5J	NS	89
	A4	225/45R-17	245/40R-18	34	34	7-J, 8.5J	NS	89
	A5	245/40R-18	245/35ZR-19	34	34	7-J, 8.5J	NS	89
2012	A3	225/45R-17	225/40R-18	34	34	7-J, 8.5J	NS	89
	A4	225/45R-17	245/40R-18	34	34	7-J, 8.5J	NS	89
	A5	245/40R-18	245/35ZR-19	34	34	7-J, 8.5J	NS	89

OEM: Original Equipment Manufacturer

PSI: Pounds Per Square Inch

NS: Not Specified by manufacturer

71105_A3A4_C0013

BRAKE SPECIFICATIONS

All measurements in inches unless noted

| Year | Model | | Brake Disc | | | Minimum Lining Thickness | Brake Caliper | |
			Original Thickness	Minimum Thickness	Maximum Run-out		Guide Pins (ft. lbs.)	Mounting Bolts (ft. lbs.)
2011	A3, A4, A5	Front	0.975	0.858	0.002	0.078	22	142
		Rear	0.486	0.390	0.002	0.078	NA	28 ①
2012	A3, A4, A5	Front	0.975	0.858	0.002	0.078	22	142
		Rear	0.486	0.390	0.002	0.078	NA	28 ①

NA: Not Applicable

NOTE: Use minimum thickness noted on disc if different from specification.

① Brake carrier 66 ft. lbs. Always use new bolts.

71105_A3A4_C0014

SCHEDULED MAINTENANCE INTERVALS
AUDI—A3, A4, A5

TO BE SERVICED	TYPE OF SERVICE	10	20	30	40	50	60	70	80	90	100	110	120
Auto Trans - fluid	R				✓				✓				✓
Battery - check	S/I		✓		✓		✓		✓		✓		✓
Body- inspect for corrosion	S/I		✓		✓		✓		✓		✓		✓
Brake Pad thickness - check	S/I	✓	✓	✓	✓	✓	✓	✓	✓	✓	✓	✓	✓
Brake system - inspection	S/I		✓		✓		✓		✓		✓		✓
Cooling System - level check	S/I				✓				✓				✓
CV Joints - leaks & damage	S/I				✓				✓				✓
Door Arresters - lubricate	S/I				✓				✓				✓
Engine Oil & Filter - replace	R	✓	✓	✓	✓	✓	✓	✓	✓	✓	✓	✓	✓
Engine Compartment - leaks & damage	S/I				✓				✓				✓
Exhaust System - inspection	S/I				✓				✓				✓
Fuel Filter (2.0L TDI) - replace	S/I		✓		✓		✓		✓		✓		✓
Headlights - Check and adjust	S/I				✓				✓				✓
Power Steering - level check	S/I				✓				✓				✓
Rotate wheels	S/I	✓	✓	✓	✓	✓	✓	✓	✓	✓	✓	✓	✓
Serpentine Belt - inspection	S/I				✓				✓				✓
Service Interval Display - reset	S/I	✓	✓	✓	✓	✓	✓	✓	✓	✓	✓	✓	✓
Spark Plugs (except 2.0L) - replace	R				✓				✓				✓
Spark Plugs (2.0L) - replace	R						✓						✓
Tie Rod Ends - play & boots	S/I				✓				✓				✓
Timing Belt (except 2.0L TDI) - replace	R											✓	
Timing Belt (2.0L TDI) - replace	R												✓
Tires/Spare - inspection	S/I		✓		✓		✓		✓		✓		✓
Washer - clean nozzles	S/I	✓	✓	✓	✓	✓	✓	✓	✓	✓	✓	✓	✓
Wiper Blades - check	S/I	✓	✓	✓	✓	✓	✓	✓	✓	✓	✓	✓	✓
Air Cleaner - replace	Every 72 months												
Airbag System - inspect	Every 12 months												
Brake Fluid - replace	At 36 months, then every 24 months												
Brake Fluid (New Beetle) - replace	Every 24 months												
Cabin Air Filter - replace	Every 24 months												
Convertible roof latch - inspect	Every 24 months												
Spark Plugs - replace	Every 72 months												
Tire Filler Bottle - inspect	Every 24 months												
Tire Filler Bottle - replace	Every 48 months												
Tire Pressure Sensors - replace	Every 72 months												

R: Replace   S/I: Service or Inspect

PRECAUTIONS

Before servicing any vehicle, please be sure to read all of the following precautions, which deal with personal safety, prevention of component damage, and important points to take into consideration when servicing a motor vehicle:

• Never open, service or drain the radiator or cooling system when the engine is hot; serious burns can occur from the steam and hot coolant.

• Observe all applicable safety precautions when working around fuel. Whenever servicing the fuel system, always work in a well-ventilated area. Do not allow fuel spray or vapors to come in contact with a spark, open flame, or excessive heat (a hot drop light, for example). Keep a dry chemical fire extinguisher near the work area. Always keep fuel in a container specifically designed for fuel storage; also, always properly seal fuel containers to avoid the possibility of fire or explosion. Refer to the additional fuel system precautions later in this section.

• Fuel injection systems often remain pressurized, even after the engine has been turned **OFF**. The fuel system pressure must be relieved before disconnecting any fuel lines. Failure to do so may result in fire and/or personal injury.

• Brake fluid often contains polyglycol ethers and polyglycols. Avoid contact with the eyes and wash your hands thoroughly after handling brake fluid. If you do get brake fluid in your eyes, flush your eyes with clean, running water for 15 minutes. If eye irritation persists, or if you have taken

brake fluid internally, IMMEDIATELY seek medical assistance.

• The EPA warns that prolonged contact with used engine oil may cause a number of skin disorders, including cancer. You should make every effort to minimize your exposure to used engine oil. Protective gloves should be worn when changing oil. Wash your hands and any other exposed skin areas as soon as possible after exposure to used engine oil. Soap and water, or waterless hand cleaner should be used.

• All new vehicles are now equipped with an air bag system, often referred to as a Supplemental Restraint System (SRS) or Supplemental Inflatable Restraint (SIR) system. The system must be disabled before performing service on or around system components, steering column, instrument panel components, wiring and sensors. Failure to follow safety and disabling procedures could result in accidental air bag deployment, possible personal injury and unnecessary system repairs.

• Always wear safety goggles when working with, or around, the air bag system. When carrying a non-deployed air bag, be sure the bag and trim cover are pointed away from your body. When placing a non-deployed air bag on a work surface, always face the bag and trim cover upward, away from the surface. This will reduce the motion of the module if it is accidentally deployed. Refer to the additional air bag system precautions later in this section.

• Clean, high quality brake fluid from a sealed container is essential to the safe and

proper operation of the brake system. You should always buy the correct type of brake fluid for your vehicle. If the brake fluid becomes contaminated, completely flush the system with new fluid. Never reuse any brake fluid. Any brake fluid that is removed from the system should be discarded. Also, do not allow any brake fluid to come in contact with a painted surface; it will damage the paint.

• Never operate the engine without the proper amount and type of engine oil; doing so WILL result in severe engine damage.

• Timing belt maintenance is extremely important. Many models utilize an interference-type, non-freewheeling engine. If the timing belt breaks, the valves in the cylinder head may strike the pistons, causing potentially serious (also time-consuming and expensive) engine damage. Refer to the maintenance interval charts for the recommended replacement interval for the timing belt, and to the timing belt section for belt replacement and inspection.

• Disconnecting the negative battery cable on some vehicles may interfere with the functions of the on-board computer system(s) and may require the computer to undergo a relearning process once the negative battery cable is reconnected.

• When servicing drum brakes, only disassemble and assemble one side at a time, leaving the remaining side intact for reference.

• Only an MVAC-trained, EPA-certified automotive technician should service the air conditioning system or its components.

BRACES

GENERAL INFORMATION

PRECAUTIONS

• Certain components within the ABS system are not intended to be serviced or repaired individually.

• Do not use rubber hoses or other parts not specifically specified for and ABS system. When using repair kits, replace all parts included in the kit. Partial or incorrect repair may lead to functional problems and require the replacement of components.

• Lubricate rubber parts with clean, fresh brake fluid to ease assembly. Do not use shop air to clean parts; damage to rubber components may result.

• Use only DOT 3 brake fluid from an unopened container.

• If any hydraulic component or line is removed or replaced, it may be necessary to bleed the entire system.

• A clean repair area is essential. Always clean the reservoir and cap thoroughly before removing the cap. The slightest amount of dirt in the fluid may plug an orifice and impair the system function. Perform repairs after components have been thoroughly cleaned; use only denatured alcohol to clean components. Do not allow ABS components to come into contact with any substance containing mineral oil; this includes used shop rags.

• The Anti-Lock control unit is a microprocessor similar to other computer units in the vehicle. Ensure that the ignition switch is **OFF** before removing or installing con-

ANTI-LOCK BRAKE SYSTEM (ABS)

troller harnesses. Avoid static electricity discharge at or near the controller.

• If any arc welding is to be done on the vehicle, the control unit should be unplugged before welding operations begin.

SPEED SENSORS

REMOVAL & INSTALLATION

Front

See Figure 1.

1. Raise the vehicle.
2. Separate speed sensor and speed sensor wiring connector.
3. Remove the bolt from wheel bearing housing.
4. Remove ABS speed sensor from wheel bearing housing.

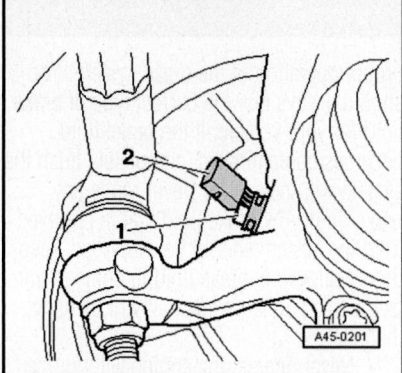

Fig. 1 Separate speed sensor and speed sensor wiring connector (1), Remove bolt (2)

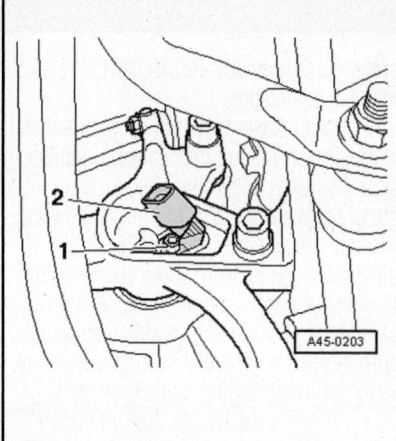

Fig. 2 Disconnect the connector (2); remove the bolt (1)

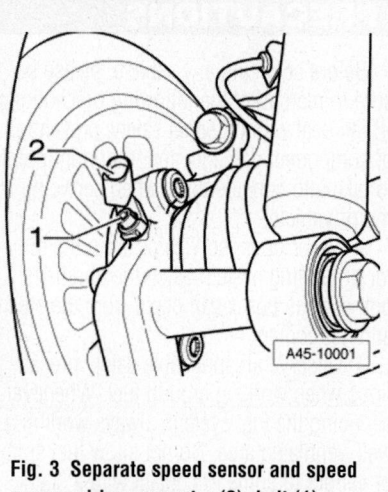

Fig. 3 Separate speed sensor and speed sensor wiring connector (2), bolt (1)

To install:

5. Before inserting speed sensor, clean hole inner surface and coat speed sensor all-round with hot bolt paste G 052 112 A3.

6. Insert the speed sensor into the hole in the wheel bearing housing and tighten the bolt to 71 inch lbs. (8 Nm).

7. Connect speed sensor to speed sensor wiring.

Rear

Disc—FWD

See Figure 2.

1. Raise the vehicle.
2. Disconnect the connector.
3. Remove the bolt.

4. Remove the wheel speed sensor 1 from the wheel bearing housing.

To install:

5. Before inserting the speed sensor, clean out the holes inner surface and coat speed sensor all-round with hot bolt paste G 052 112 A3.

6. Insert the speed sensor into the hole in the wheel bearing housing and tighten the bolt to 71 inch lbs. (8 Nm).

7. Connect speed sensor to speed sensor wiring.

Disc—AWD

See Figure 3.

1. Raise the vehicle.

2. Separate speed sensor and speed sensor wiring connector.

3. Remove bolt 2 from wheel bearing housing.

4. Remove ABS speed sensor from wheel bearing housing.

To install:

5. Before inserting the speed sensor, clean out the holes inner surface and coat speed sensor all-round with hot bolt paste G 052 112 A3.

6. Insert the speed sensor into the hole in the wheel bearing housing and tighten the bolt to 71 inch lbs. (8 Nm).

7. Connect speed sensor to speed sensor wiring.

BRAKES
BLEEDING THE BRAKE SYSTEM

BLEEDING PROCEDURE

BLEEDING PROCEDURE

1. Before servicing the vehicle, refer to the precautions.

✳✳ WARNING

Adhere strictly to work sequence when bleeding brake system.

2. Connect the brake charger/bleeder unit VAS 5234 or VAG 1869.

3. Open the bleeder valves in the prescribed sequence and bleed the brake calipers.

- Left front brake caliper
- Right front brake caliper
- Left rear brake caliper
- Right rear brake caliper

➡The bleeder hose must fit tightly on the bleeder valve so

that no air can enter the brake system.

4. With the bleeder bottle hose attached, leave the bleeder valve open long enough that brake fluid exits without bubbles.

5. Press the brake pedal forcefully and hold.

6. Open the bleeder valve at the brake caliper.

7. Press the brake pedal down until stopped.

8. Close the bleeder valve with the pedal pressed.

9. Release the brake pedal slowly.

✳✳ WARNING

This bleeding procedure must be performed 5 times per brake caliper.

10. Perform the bleeding sequence as follows:

- Left front brake caliper
- Right front brake caliper
- Left rear brake caliper
- Right rear brake caliper

✳✳ WARNING

A road test must be performed after bleeding. During this, at least one Anti-lock Brake System (ABS) stop must be performed!

PRESSURE BLEEDING PROCEDURE

See Figures 4 through 8.

1. Remove the cap from the brake fluid reservoir.

2. Use the hose from the brake charger/bleeder unit VAS 5234 to extract as much brake fluid as possible.

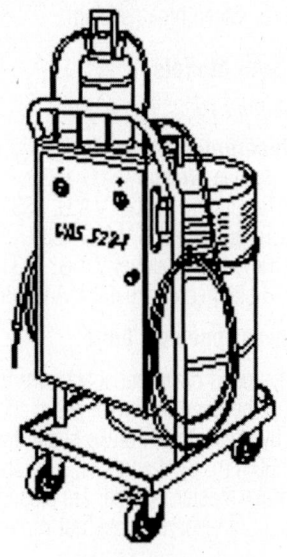

Fig. 4 Brake charger/bleeder unit VAS 5234

➡**Do not remove the strainer inside the brake fluid reservoir.**

➡**Do not use extracted brake fluid again!**

3. Attach the adapter to the brake fluid reservoir.

4. Please observe all operating instructions for the VAS 5234.

5. Set the correct pressure using a brake charger/bleeding unit VAS 5234.

6. Connect the hose from the brake charger/bleeding unit VAS 5234 to the adapter. Use a suitable bleed hose. It must seat tightly on the bleed valve so that no air can get into the brake system.

7. Remove the cap from the bleed valve on the left front brake caliper.

8. Connect collector bottle bleed hose to left front bleed valve. Then open the bleed valve and allow the corresponding quantity to flow out (see table). Close the bleed valve.

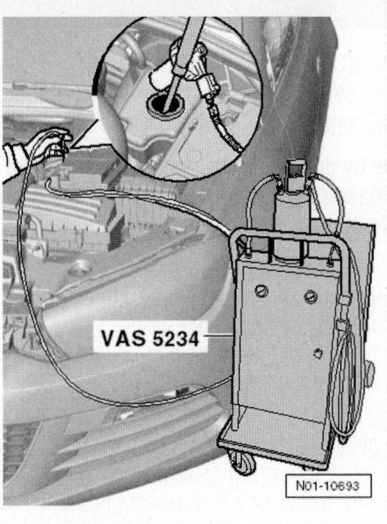

Fig. 5 Use the hose from the brake charger/bleeder unit VAS 5234

9. Install the cap on the left front brake caliper bleed valve.

10. Repeat the same procedure on the right front side of the vehicle.

11. Remove both rear wheels to access the bleed valve.

12. Remove the cap on the left rear brake caliper bleed valve.

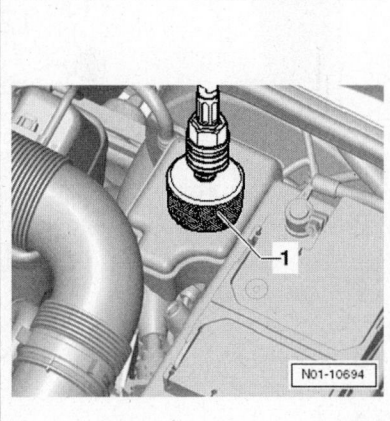

Fig. 6 Attach the adapter (1) to the brake fluid reservoir.

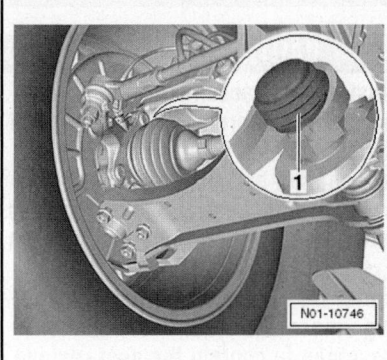

Fig. 7 Remove the cap (1) from the bleed valve

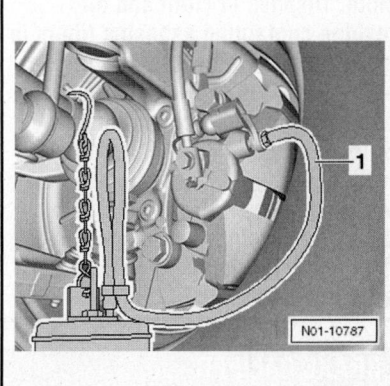

Fig. 8 Connect collector bottle bleed hose (1) to left front bleed valve

13. Open the bleed valve and let the corresponding amount of brake fluid (see table) flow out. Close the bleed valve.

14. Install the cap on the left rear brake caliper bleed valve.

15. Repeat the same procedure on the right rear side of the vehicle.

❋❋ **WARNING**

A road test must be performed after bleeding. During this, at least one Anti-lock Brake System (ABS) stop must be performed!

BRAKES   **FRONT DISC BRAKES**

⁑ CAUTION

Dust and dirt accumulating on brake parts during normal use may contain asbestos fibers from production or aftermarket brake linings. Breathing excessive concentrations of asbestos fibers can cause serious bodily harm. Exercise care when servicing brake parts. Do not sand or grind brake lining unless equipment used is designed to contain the dust residue. Do not clean brake parts with compressed air or by dry brushing. Cleaning should be done by dampening the brake components with a fine mist of water, then wiping the brake components clean with a dampened cloth. Dispose of cloth and all residue containing asbestos fibers in an impermeable container with the appropriate label. Follow practices prescribed by the Occupational Safety and Health Administration (OSHA) and the Environmental Protection Agency (EPA) for the handling, processing, and disposing of dust or debris that may contain asbestos fibers.

BRAKE CALIPER

REMOVAL & INSTALLATION

A3 Models

See Figure 9.

Recommended tools: brake pedal depressor V.A.G. 1869/2.
1. Remove the brake pads.
2. Install brake pedal loading device

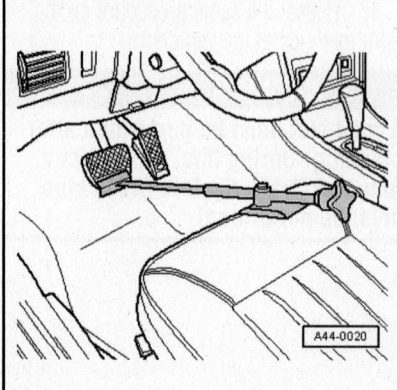

Fig. 9 Brake pedal loading device V.A.G 1869/2 between brake pedal and driver seat

V.A.G 1869/2 between brake pedal and driver seat. Depress brake pedal a minimum of 60 mm.

➡**By doing this, the valves in the brake master cylinder are closed and the brake fluid reservoir does not run empty.**

3. Connect hose of a bleeder bottle to bleeder screw of the removed brake caliper.
4. Open the bleeder screw.
5. Do not remove brake pedal loading device V.A.G 1869/2.
6. Remove brake hose from the brake caliper.
7. Remove the brake caliper.
8. Installation is in reverse order of removal, with special attention to the following:
9. Tighten the brake caliper mounting bolts to 18 ft. lbs. (25 Nm)

a. Install brake pads.
b. Bleed brake system.

A4 & A5 Models

See Figure 10.

Recommended tools:
- Torque Wrench V.A.G 1332
- Reversible ratchet V.A.G. 1332/1
- Torque Wrench V.A.G 1331
- Reversible ratchet V.A.G. 1331/1
- Brake pedal actuator V.A.G 1869/2

➡**Always use new bolts.**

1. Insert brake pedal actuator V.A.G 1869/2 between the brake pedal and driver seat by pressing the brake pedal down at least 60 mm. By doing this, the valves in the brake master cylinder are closed and the brake fluid reservoir does not run empty.

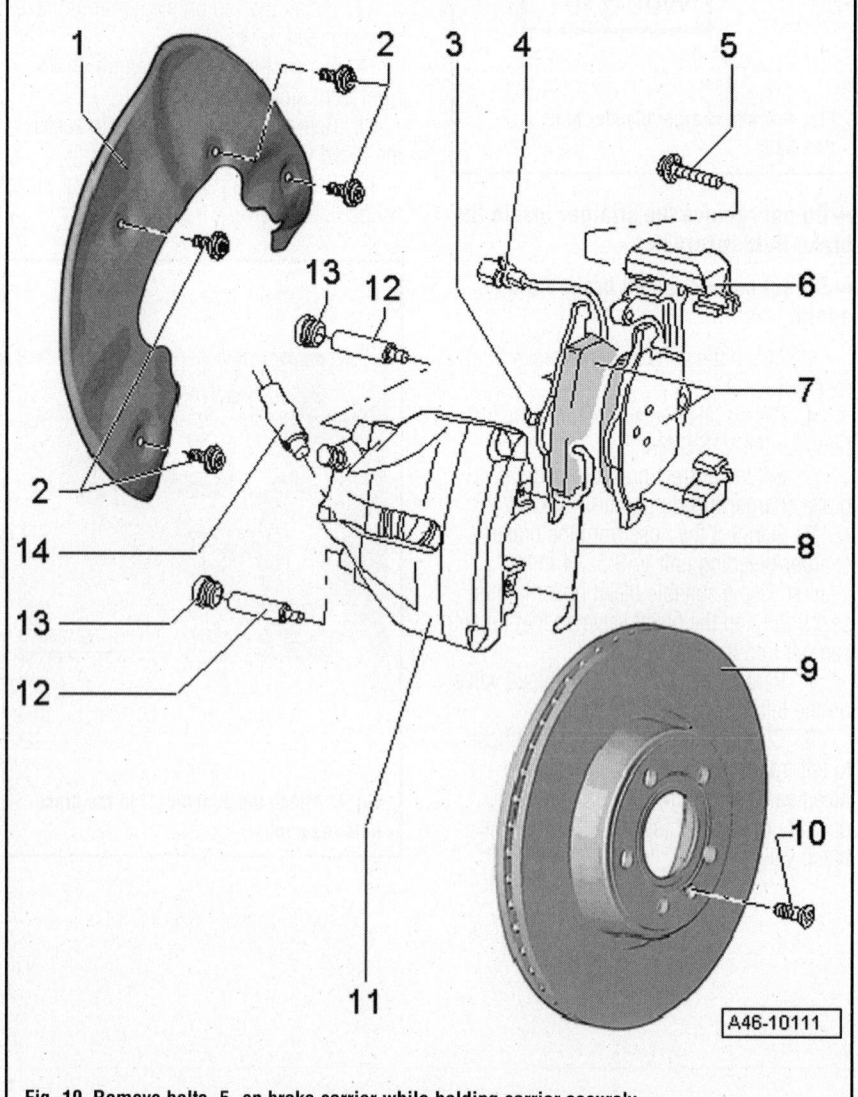

Fig. 10 Remove bolts, 5, on brake carrier while holding carrier securely

2. Raise the vehicle.

3. Remove the wheels.

4. Connect the hose from a bleeder bottle to one of the bleeder screws on the front caliper.

5. Open a bleeder screw on the front brake caliper to reduce the pressure from the brake system.

6. Close bleeder screw.

➡**Do not remove brake pedal loading device V.A.G. 1869/2.**

7. Remove brake pads.

➡**When removing, mark brake pads that will be used again. Install in the same position, otherwise braking effect will be uneven! The brake disc is secured with a bolt.**

8. Remove brake hose from brake caliper.

9. Remove brake caliper from vehicle.

10. Remove bolts, 5, on brake carrier while holding carrier securely.

11. Remove brake carrier.

To install:

12. Always use new bolts.

13. Position brake carrier.

14. Tighten brake carrier with 5 new bolts.

15. Install brake hose into brake caliper and tighten.

16. Install brake pads

➡**After replacing the brake pads, press the brake pedal firmly several times while the vehicle is stationary so that the brake pads are seated properly in their normal operating position.**

17. Remove brake pedal loading device V.A.G. 1869/2.

18. Bleed brake system.

19. Install wheels.

DISC BRAKE PADS

REMOVAL & INSTALLATION

A3 Models

See Figures 11 through 15.

Recommended tools: Torque wrench V.A.G 1331, Piston resetting tool T 10145.

➡**If reusing brake pads, mark location. Reinstall in same position, otherwise uneven braking will occur.**

1. Remove both front wheels.

2. Disconnect the connector, 1, for brake pad wear indicator, on left brake.

3. Remove caps.

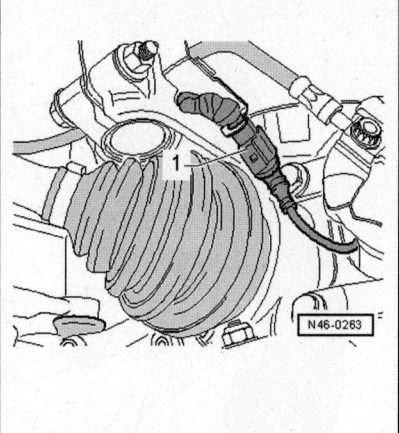

Fig. 11 Disconnect the connector, 1, for brake pad wear indicator, on left brake

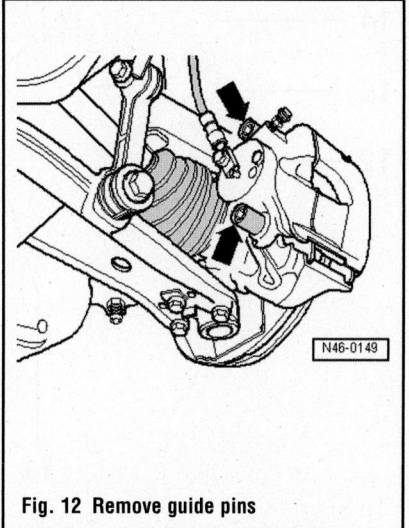

Fig. 12 Remove guide pins

4. Remove guide pins at the arrows.

5. Remove brake caliper and suspend it using bundling wire.

➡**Do not twist or kink the brake hose lines.**

➡**If reusing brake pads, mark location. Install in same position when installing, otherwise uneven braking will occur!**

6. Remove brake pads.

To install:

7. Installation is in reverse order of removal, with special attention to the following:

a. Clean brake caliper. Clean brake caliper with mineral spirits exclusively.

b. Press the piston back into the cylinder using the piston resetting tool. Before pressing the piston back, draw off brake fluid from the reservoir with a bleeder bottle. Otherwise fluid will over-

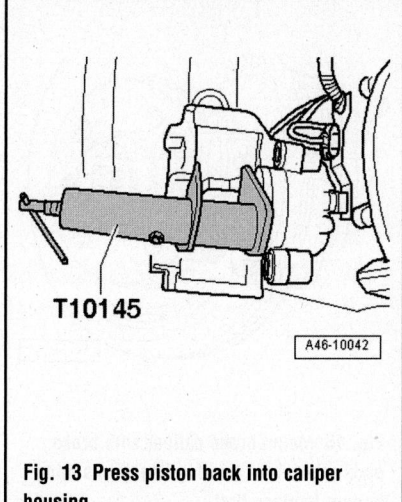

Fig. 13 Press piston back into caliper housing

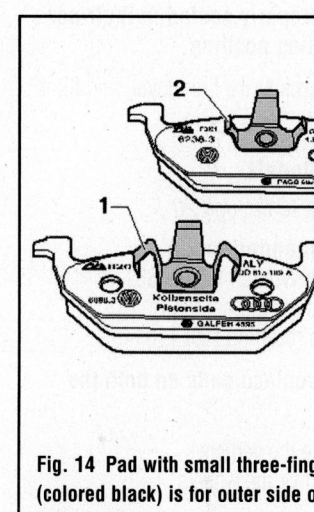

Fig. 14 Pad with small three-finger clip 2 (colored black) is for outer side of brake caliper.

flow and cause damage if the reservoir was topped off during repair work.

➡ **Brake fluid is poisonous and must never be extracted by mouth using a hose!**

c. Install brake pads, observing installation position:

• Pad with large three-finger clip 1 is for piston side.

• Pad with small three-finger clip (colored black) is for outer side of brake caliper.

d. Mount brake caliper with brake pads onto wheel bearing housing, setting bottom in place first.

➡**The tab arrow of brake caliper housing must be positioned behind guide of wheel bearing housing.**

➡**After installing brake pads, depress brake pedal firmly several times with vehicle stationary so that the brake**

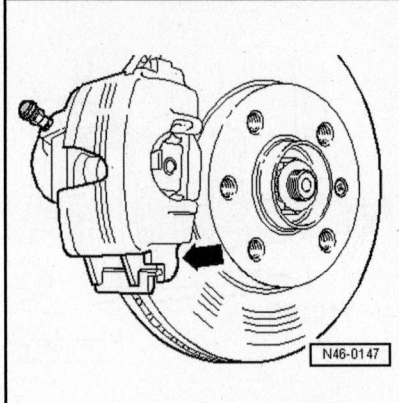

Fig. 15 Mount brake caliper with brake pads onto wheel bearing housing, setting bottom in place first

pads are properly seated in their normal operating position.

   e. Check brake fluid level, and fill if necessary.

A4 & A5 Models

See Figures 16 through 20.

Recommended tools:

- Torque Wrench V.A.G 1331
- Reversible ratchet V.A.G. 1331/1
- Piston resetting tool T10145

➡**Always replace pads on both the axles.**

   1. Raise the vehicle.
   2. Remove the wheels.

➡**When removing, mark brake pads that will be used again. Install in the same position, otherwise braking effect will be uneven!**

   3. Remove the cap.
   4. For vehicles with the brake wear pad indicator, disconnect the left front connector "4".
   5. Lift the securing strap slightly at bottom of connector and then rotate 90°.
   6. Remove lower part of the brake pad wear indicator connector from the bracket.
   7. Using screwdriver, pry off brake pad retaining spring from brake caliper housing and remove.
   8. Loosen and remove both guide pins from brake caliper.
   9. Secure the brake caliper to the vehicle with a suitable wire. Do not support the weight with the brake hose.
   10. Remove brake pads from brake caliper housing or from brake carrier.

➡**Do not press the brake pedal when the caliper is removed.**

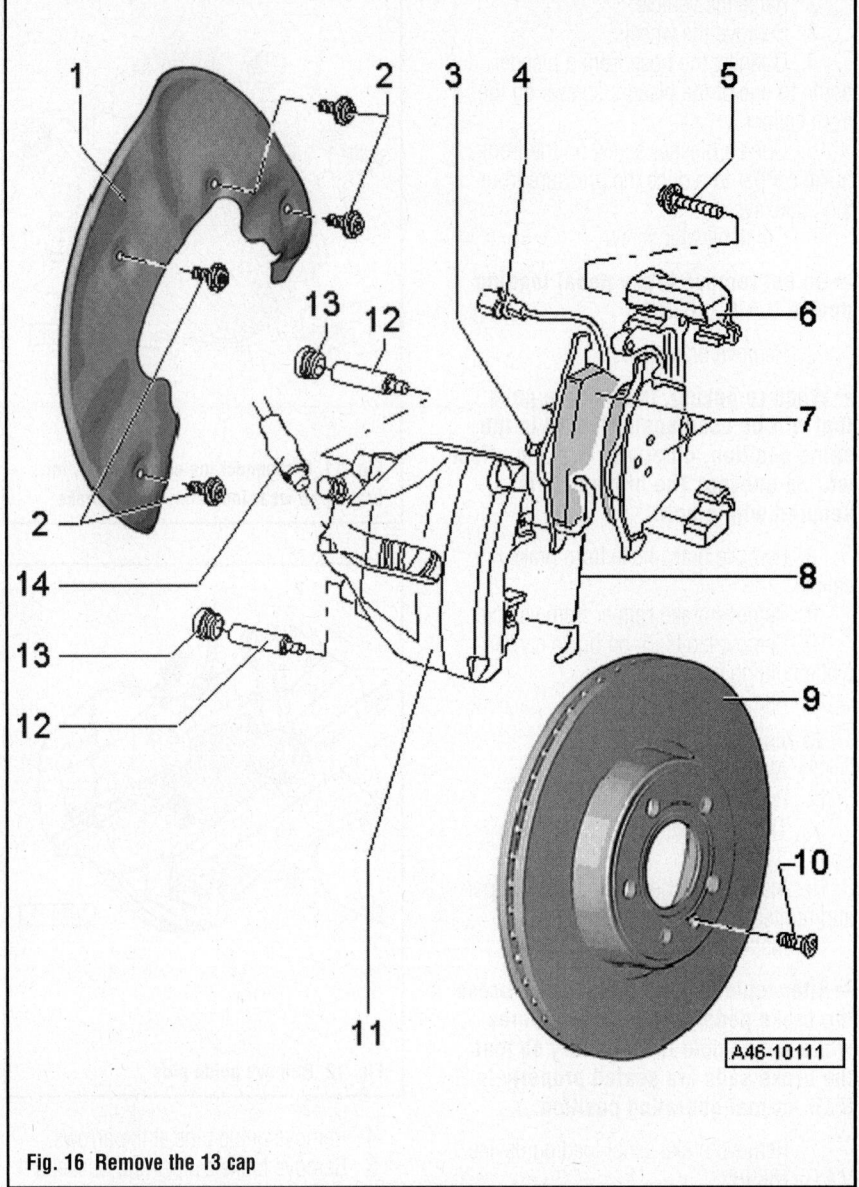

Fig. 16 Remove the 13 cap

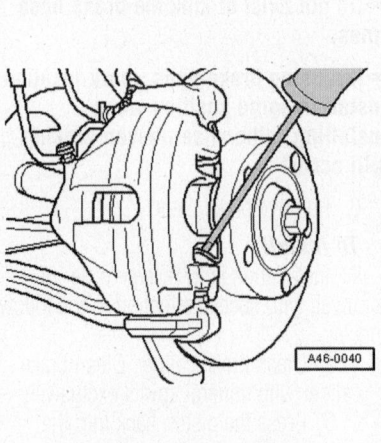

Fig. 17 Using tool, pry off brake pad retaining spring from brake caliper housing and remove.

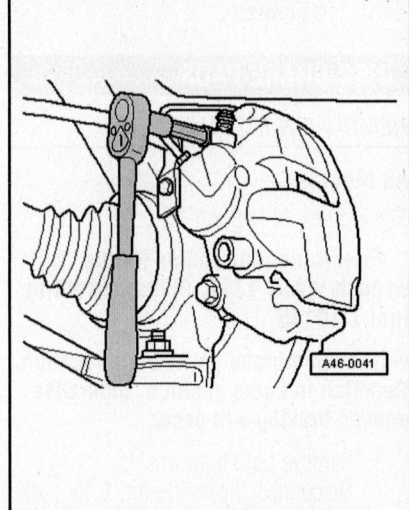

Fig. 18 Loosen and remove both guide pins 12 from brake caliper

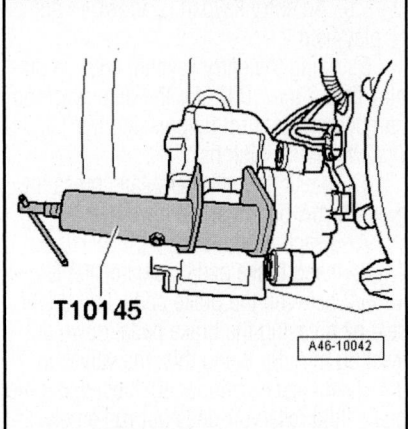

Fig. 19 Press piston back. Use Piston Resetting Tool T10145

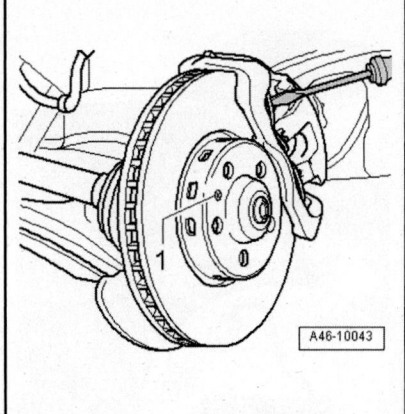

Fig. 20 Insert brake pad with retaining spring into brake caliper housing (piston)

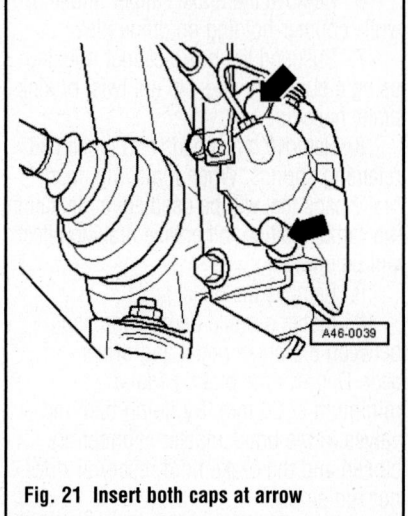

Fig. 21 Insert both caps at arrow

To install:

11. Clean brake caliper housing. Clean brake caliper with mineral spirits exclusively.

➡Press the piston back into caliper housing using resetting tool before inserting new brake pads. Before pushing back the piston, siphon some of the brake fluid out of the brake fluid reservoir. Otherwise brake fluid can leak out and cause damage.

➡Brake fluid is poisonous. NEVER siphon brake fluid with your mouth!

12. Press the piston back. Use Piston Resetting Tool T10145.

13. Insert brake pad with retaining spring into brake caliper housing (piston).

➡The inner surface (with tension spring) is indicated by an arrow. The arrow must point in the rotation direction of the brake rotor when driving forward. If improperly installed, noises could result.

14. Remove any protective film from the brake pad backing plate.
15. Install outer brake pad on brake carrier.
16. Install both guide pins in the brake caliper housing and tighten.

17. Insert both caps.
18. Install the retaining spring in brake caliper housing.

➡Retaining spring must be pressed under brake carrier after it is inserted in both holes. If improperly installed, the wear of the outer brake pad cannot be adjusted, thereby increasing brake pedal travel.

➡After installing brake pads, depress brake pedal several times firmly to properly seat brake pads in their normal operating position.

19. Check brake fluid level, and fill if necessary.

BRAKES

☀☀ CAUTION

Dust and dirt accumulating on brake parts during normal use may contain asbestos fibers from production or aftermarket brake linings. Breathing excessive concentrations of asbestos fibers can cause serious bodily harm. Exercise care when servicing brake parts. Do not sand or grind brake lining unless equipment used is designed to contain the dust residue. Do not clean brake parts with compressed air or by dry brushing. Cleaning should be done by dampening the brake components with a fine mist of water, then wiping the brake components clean with a dampened cloth. Dispose of cloth and all residue containing asbestos fibers in an impermeable container with the appropriate label. Follow practices prescribed by the Occupational

Safety and Health Administration (OSHA) and the Environmental Protection Agency (EPA) for the handling, processing, and disposing of dust or debris that may contain asbestos fibers.

BRAKE CALIPER

REMOVAL & INSTALLATION

A3 Models

See Figure 22.

1. Raise the vehicle.
2. Remove the wheels.
3. Pry off the securing clip for the brake cable.
4. Press brake lever in the direction of the arrow and disengage parking brake cable.
5. Press brake lever in and unhook parking brake cable.

REAR DISC BRAKES

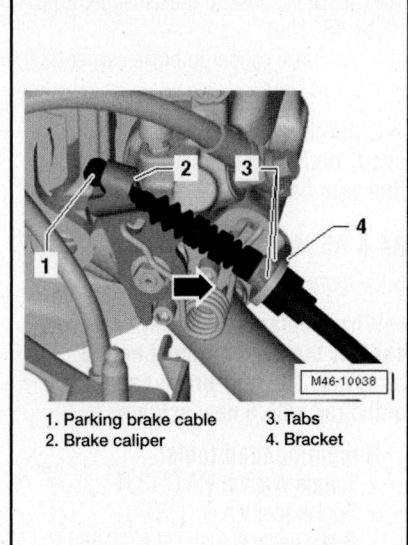

1. Parking brake cable   3. Tabs
2. Brake caliper   4. Bracket

Fig. 22 Press brake lever 2 in direction of arrow and unhook parking brake cable 3.

6. Remove the brake caliper housing, while counter-holding on guide pins.

7. Suspend the brake caliper housing using a bundling wire. Do not twist or kink brake hose line.

8. Remove brake pads and brake pad retaining springs. When removing, mark brake pads that will be used again. Install in the same position, otherwise braking effect will be uneven!

9. Remove the brake pads.

10. Install a brake pedal depressor between the brake pedal and driver seat. Depress the brake pedal a minimum of 60 mm. By doing this, the valves in the brake master cylinder are closed and the brake fluid reservoir does not run empty.

11. Connect the hose of a bleeder bottle to the bleeder screw of the removed rear brake caliper, as well as the front brake caliper on the same side of the vehicle.

12. Open the bleeder screws.

13. Close the front bleeder screw. Do not remove V.A.G 1869/2. Unfasten the brake hose from the brake caliper.

To install:

14. Installation is the reverse of removal, with special attention to the following:

15. Install brake pads.

16. Press brake lever in and engage parking brake cable. Press on the securing clip for the parking brake cable.

17. Install brake hose to brake caliper

18. After installing a serviced or new brake caliper, the parking brake must be adjusted.

19. Bleed the brake system.

20. Tightening Specifications:

a. Brake hose to brake caliper 26 ft. lbs. (35 Nm)

b. Brake caliper to brake carrier 28 ft. lbs. (38 Nm)

➡**Every time the banjo bolt is loosened, replace the brake hose/brake line with banjo bolt**

A4 & A5 Models

See Figures 9, 23 and 24..

➡**When replacing the rear brake caliper, the actuator must not be removed. The new brake caliper is delivered with a new actuator.**

Recommended tools:

• Torque Wrench V.A.G 1331
• Socket tool V.A.G. 1331/3
• Brake pedal actuator V.A.G 1869/2
• Vehicle diagnostic, test and information system

1. Connect vehicle diagnosis, testing

Fig. 23 Connect vehicle diagnosis, testing and information system VAS 5051B or VAS 5052

and information system VAS 5051B or VAS 5052 to the 16-pin Data Link Connector (DLC) in the vehicle with the ignition switched off.

a. Switch on ignition.

b. Parking brake released.

c. Coding check and reported if necessary.

d. DTC memory interrogated, errors shown corrected and DTC memory erased.

2. Select function *"053 - Parking brake"*.

3. Select function *"006 - Basic setting"*.

4. Display on vehicle diagnostic, test and information system:

a. The request to enter a display group number appears in display field 1.

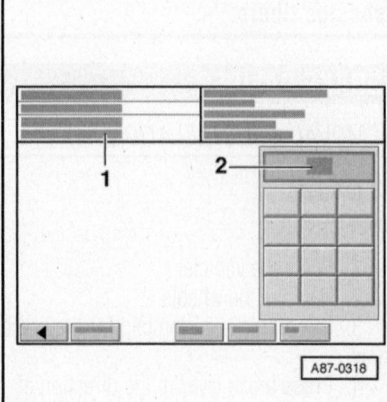

Fig. 24 Display on vehicle diagnostic, test and information system

b. An entry keypad is shown in display field 2.

5. Using the entry keypad, enter in display field 2 the " 007" for the display group number and confirm by pressing the *"Q button"*. (Reset pistons).

6. To exit the entry template, press the green Arrow button at the lower left.

7. Switch off ignition

8. Insert brake pedal actuator V.A.G 1869/2 between the brake pedal and driver seat by pressing the brake pedal down at least 60 mm. By doing this, the valves in the brake master cylinder are closed and the brake fluid reservoir does not run empty.

9. Raise the vehicle.

10. Remove the wheels.

11. Connect hose from a bleeder bottle to one of the bleeder screws on the rear caliper.

12. Open a bleeder screw on the rear brake caliper to reduce the pressure from the brake system.

13. Close the bleeder screw. Do not remove brake pedal loading device V.A.G 1869/2.

14. Disconnect the parking brake connector.

15. Remove brake hose and electrical wire from the bracket on the stub axle carrier.

16. Remove rear brake pads.

➡**When removing, mark brake pads that will be used again. Install in the same position, otherwise braking effect will be uneven! Operating the electromechanical parking brake again after a long drive is recommended. Brake pad play is automatically adjusted every 1000 km if the EPB is not operated in this distance.**

17. Remove brake pressure line from brake caliper.

18. Remove brake caliper from the vehicle.

➡**When replacing the rear brake caliper, the actuator must not be removed. The new brake caliper is delivered with a new actuator.**

To install:

➡ **Use new bolts.**

19. Install brake line in the brake caliper and tighten.

20. Install rear brake pads.

21. Tighten brake caliper with the new bolts "4". To tighten bolts 4 use torque wrench V.A.G 1331 and socket V.A.G 1331/3. Reconnect the parking brake connector only after tightening the bolts.

22. Connect the electrical connector to the parking brake.

23. Install brake hose and electrical wire into the bracket on the stub axle carrier.

➡**Make sure the brake hose is correctly installed and secured inside the bracket on the stub axle carrier. So that the brake hose does not come out of the bracket on its own. After replacing the brake pads, press the brake pedal firmly several times while the vehicle is stationary so that the brake pads are seated properly in their normal operating position.**

24. Remove brake pedal loading device V.A.G 1869/2.

25. Bleed brake system.

26. Install the wheels.

27. Lower the vehicle.

28. Switch on the ignition.

29. Display on vehicle diagnostic, test and information system:

    a. The request to enter a display group number appears in display field 1. An entry keypad is shown in display field 2.

30. Using the entry keypad, enter in display field 2 the *"006"* for the display group number and confirm by pressing the *"Q button".* (guide pistons together).

31. To exit the entry template, press the green Arrow button at the lower left.

➡**DTC memory interrogated, errors shown corrected and DTC memory erased.**

32. Disconnect the vehicle diagnostic, test and information system VAS 5051B or VAS 5052 from the 16-pin Data Link Connector (DLC) in the vehicle with the ignition switched off.

DISC BRAKE PADS

REMOVAL & INSTALLATION

A3 Models

See Figures 25 through 29.

Recommended tools: Torque wrench V.A.G 1331, Piston resetting tool T 10145.

➡**If reusing brake pads, mark location. Reinstall in same position, otherwise uneven braking will occur.**

1. Remove both front wheels.

2. Disconnect the connector, 1, for brake pad wear indicator, on left brake.

3. Remove caps.

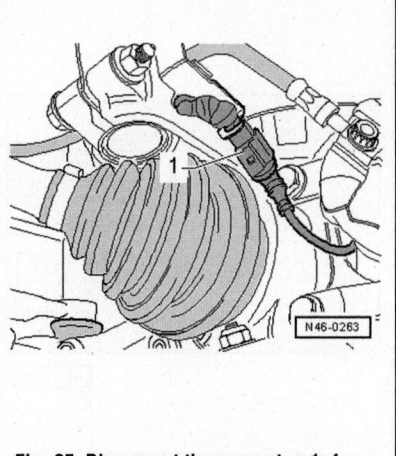

Fig. 25 Disconnect the connector, 1, for brake pad wear indicator, on left brake

4. Remove guide pins at the arrows.

5. Remove brake caliper and suspend it using bundling wire.

➡**Do not twist or kink the brake hose line.**

➡**If reusing brake pads, mark location. Install in same position when installing, otherwise uneven braking will occur!**

6. Remove brake pads.

To install:

7. Installation is in reverse order of removal, with special attention to the following:

    a. Clean brake caliper. Clean brake caliper with mineral spirits exclusively.

    b. Press the piston back into caliper housing.

➡**Before inserting new brake pads, press the piston back into the cylinder using the piston resetting tool. Before**

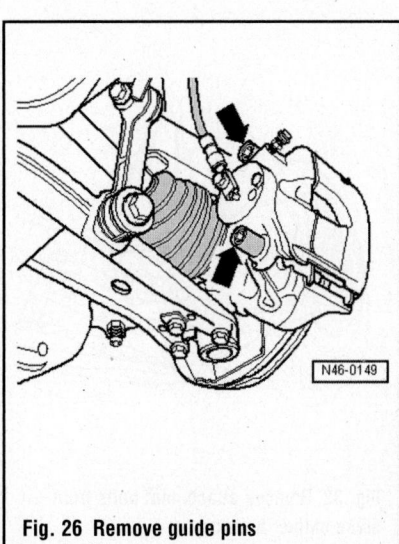

Fig. 26 Remove guide pins

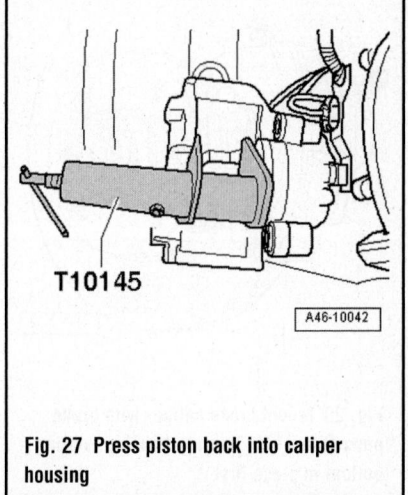

Fig. 27 Press piston back into caliper housing

pressing the piston back, draw off brake fluid from the reservoir with a bleeder bottle. Otherwise fluid will overflow and cause damage if the reservoir was topped off during repair work.

➡**Brake fluid is poisonous and must never be extracted by mouth using a hose!**

    c. Install brake pads, observing installation position:
- Pad with large three-finger clip is for piston side.
- Pad with small three-finger clip **2** (colored black) is for outer side of brake caliper.

    d. Mount brake caliper with brake pads onto wheel bearing housing, setting bottom in place first.

➡**The tab arrow of brake caliper housing must be positioned behind guide of wheel bearing housing.**

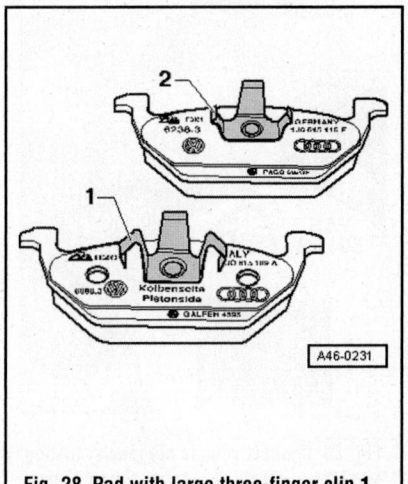

Fig. 28 Pad with large three-finger clip 1 is for piston side

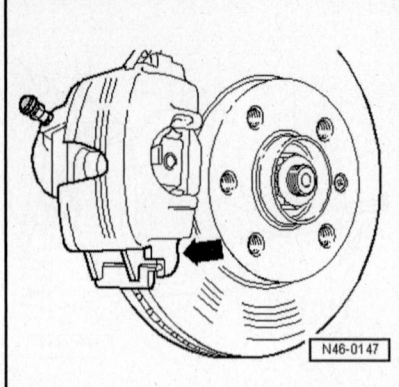

Fig. 29 Mount brake caliper with brake pads onto wheel bearing housing, setting bottom in place first

➡️**After installing brake pads, depress brake pedal firmly several times with vehicle stationary so that the brake pads are properly seated in their normal operating position.**

  e. Check brake fluid level, and fill if necessary.

A4 & A5 Models

See Figures 30 through 36.

Recommended tools:
• Torque wrench V.A.G 1331
• Piston resetting tool T 10145.
• Vehicle diagnostic, test and information system

➡️**When removing, mark brake pads that will be used again. Install in the same position, otherwise braking effect will be uneven! Operating the electromechanical**

Fig. 30 Connect vehicle diagnosis, testing and information system VAS 5051B or VAS 5052

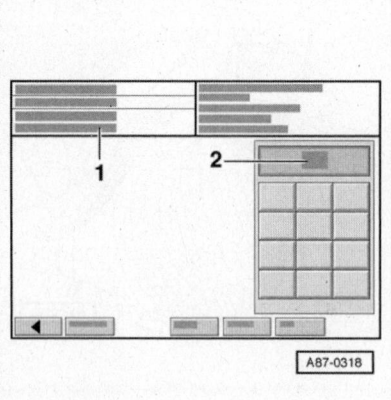

Fig. 31 Display on vehicle diagnostic, test and information system

parking brake again after a long drive is recommended. Brake pad play is automatically adjusted every 1000 km if the EPB is not operated in this distance.

  1. Connect the vehicle diagnosis, testing and information system vas 5051b or vas 5052 to the 16-pin Data Link Connector (DLC) in the vehicle with the ignition switched off.
    a. Switch on ignition
    b. Parking brake released
    c. Coding check and reported if necessary.
    d. DTC memory interrogated, errors shown corrected and DTC memory erased.
  2. Select function *"053 - Parking brake"*.
  3. Select function *"006 - Basic setting"*.
  4. Display on vehicle diagnostic, test and information system:
    a. The request to enter a display group number appears in display field 1.
    b. An entry keypad is shown in display field 2.

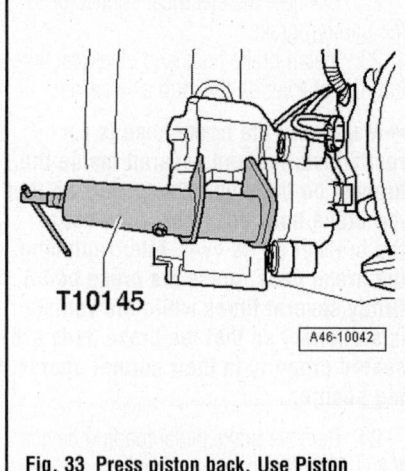

Fig. 33 Press piston back. Use Piston Resetting Tool T10145

  5. Using the entry keypad, enter in display field 2 the *"007"* for the display group number and confirm by pressing the *"Q button"*. (Reset pistons).
  6. To exit the entry template, press the green Arrow button at the lower left.
  7. Switch off ignition
  8. Raise the vehicle.
  9. Remove the tires.
  10. Remove brake hose and electrical wire from the bracket on the stub axle carrier.
  11. Remove attachment bolts from brake caliper housing, counter-hold guide pins to do so.

➡️**Do not pull on brake hose or electrical wiring.**

  12. Remove brake caliper. Do not let the brake caliper hang from the brake hose. Secure it to the body with suitable cable ties or wire. Do not support the weight with the brake hose.

Fig. 32 Remove attachment bolts from brake caliper housing

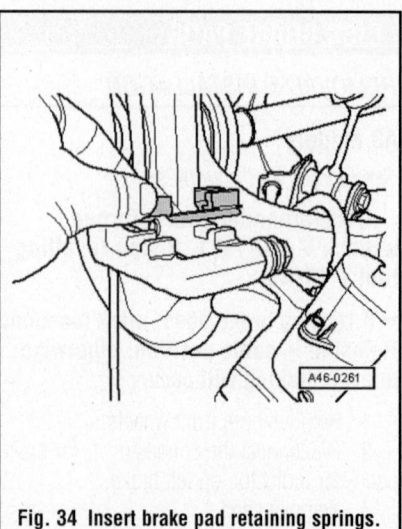

Fig. 34 Insert brake pad retaining springs.

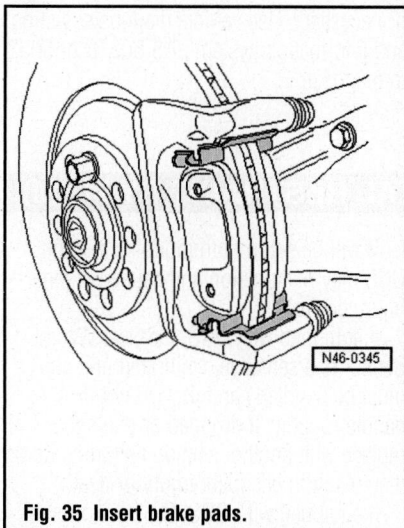

Fig. 35 Insert brake pads.

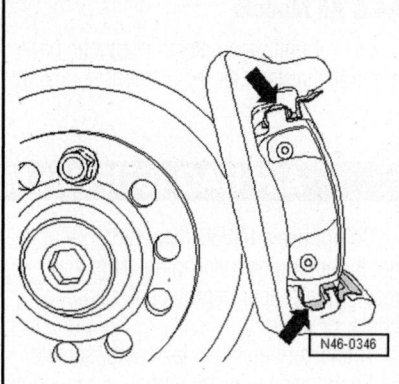

Fig. 36 Make sure that the brake pads are seated correctly in the retaining plates at arrows.

➡**Do not press the brake pedal when the caliper is removed.**

13. Remove brake pads.
14. Remove brake pad retaining plate.
15. Press the piston back. Use Piston Resetting Tool T10145. Do not tilt the brake piston when pressing it back.

To install:
16. Clean brake caliper with mineral spirits exclusively.
17. Insert brake pad retaining springs.
18. Remove any protective film from the brake pad backing plate.
19. Insert brake pads.
20. Make sure that the brake pads are

seated correctly in the retaining plates at arrows.

➡**The brake pads must be seated between both securing tabs on the pad retaining plate to provide the air gap between the brake disc and brake pad.**

21. Position brake caliper.

➡**The repair kit includes new self-locking hex that must be installed in all cases.**

22. Secure brake caliper using new self-locking bolts.
23. To tighten bolts use torque wrench V.A.G 1331 with socket V.A.G 1331/3.

24. Install brake hose and electrical wire into the bracket on the stub axle carrier.

➡**Make sure the brake hose is correctly installed and secured inside the bracket on the stub axle carrier. So that the brake hose does not come out of the bracket on its own.**

25. Install the wheels.
26. Lower the vehicle.
27. Check brake fluid level and fill if necessary.
28. Switch on the ignition.
29. Display on vehicle diagnostic, test and information system:
   a. The request to enter a display group number appears in display field 1.
   b. An entry keypad is shown in display field 2.
30. Using the entry keypad, enter in display field 2 the "006" for the display group number and confirm by pressing the "Q button". (guide pistons together).
31. To exit the entry template, press the green Arrow button at the lower left.

➡**DTC memory interrogated, errors shown corrected and DTC memory erased.**

32. Disconnect the vehicle diagnostic, test and information system VAS 5051B or VAS 5052 from the 16-pin Data Link Connector (DLC) in the vehicle with the ignition switched off.

BRAKES   PARKING BRAKE

PARKING BRAKE CABLES

ADJUSTMENT

A3 Models
See Figures 37 and 38.

➡**A new adjustment is necessary only after replacing brake cables, brake calipers or brake discs.**

1. Remove rear ashtray from center console.
2. Parking brake lever in rest position. Tighten adjustment nut "2" so far that the lever 1 on brake calipers lift off from their stops 2.
3. Distance "a" to stop "2" at left and right brake calipers together must not be less than 1 mm and not exceed 4 mm.

➡**The distance on one side must not exceed 3 mm and must be greater than 0 mm.**

4. Apply the parking brake 3 times and then release.
5. With parking brake released, check if both wheels can be turned freely. And dis-

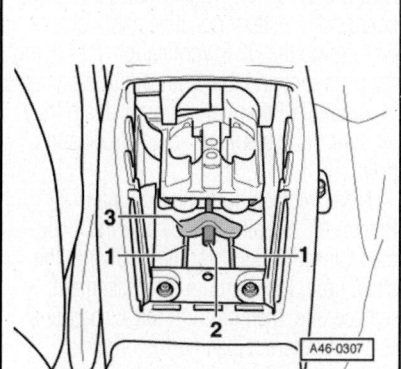

Fig. 37 Parking brake lever in rest position—1 of 2

tance A at calipers is maintained. Correct adjustment, if necessary, by adjusting adjustment nut.

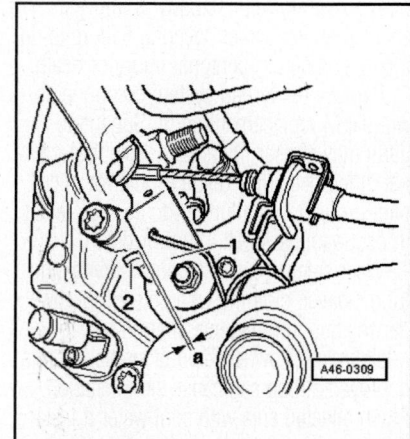

Fig. 38 Parking brake lever in rest position—1 of 2

➡Due to the automatic rear brake adjuster, there is no need to adjust the parking brake after making initial adjustment.

A4 & A5 Models

The A4 utilizes an electromagnetic parking brake system. No adjustment is possible

or necessary. Use vehicle diagnosis, testing and information system VAS 5051B or 5052 to diagnose

CHASSIS ELECTRICAL

AIR BAG (SUPPLEMENTAL RESTRAINT SYSTEM)

GENERAL INFORMATION

❄❄ CAUTION

These vehicles are equipped with an air bag system. The system must be disarmed before performing service on, or around, system components, the steering column, instrument panel components, wiring and sensors. Failure to follow the safety precautions and the disarming procedure could result in accidental air bag deployment, possible injury and unnecessary system repairs.

SERVICE PRECAUTIONS

Disconnect and isolate the battery negative cable before beginning any airbag system component diagnosis, testing, removal, or installation procedures. Allow system capacitor to discharge for two minutes before beginning any component service. This will disable the airbag system. Failure to disable the airbag system may result in accidental airbag deployment, personal injury, or death.

Do not place an intact undeployed airbag face down on a solid surface. The airbag will propel into the air if accidentally deployed and may result in personal injury or death.

When carrying or handling an undeployed airbag, the trim side (face) of the airbag should be pointing away from the body to minimize possibility of injury if accidental deployment occurs. Failure to do this may result in personal injury or death.

Replace the airbag system components with OEM replacement parts. Substitute parts may appear interchangeable, but internal differences may result in inferior occupant protection. Failure to do so may result in occupant personal injury or death.

Wear safety glasses, rubber gloves, and long sleeved clothing when cleaning powder residue from vehicle after an airbag deployment. Powder residue emitted from a deployed airbag can cause skin irritation. Flush affected area with cool water if irritation is experienced. If nasal or throat irritation is experienced, exit the vehicle for fresh air until the irritation ceases. If irritation continues, see a physician.

Do not use a replacement airbag that is not in the original packaging. This may result in improper deployment, personal injury, or death.

The factory installed fasteners, screws and bolts used to fasten airbag components have a special coating and are specifically designed for the airbag system. Do not use substitute fasteners. Use only original equipment fasteners listed in the parts catalog when fastener replacement is required.

During, and following, any child restraint anchor service, due to impact event or vehicle repair, carefully inspect all mounting hardware, tether straps, and anchors for proper installation, operation, or damage. If a child restraint anchor is found damaged in any way, the anchor must be replaced. Failure to do this may result in personal injury or death.

Deployed and non-deployed airbags may or may not have live pyrotechnic material within the airbag inflator.

Do not dispose of driver/passenger/curtain airbags or seat belt tensioners unless you are sure of complete deployment. Refer to the Hazardous Substance Control System for proper disposal.

Dispose of deployed airbags and tensioners consistent with state, provincial, local, and federal regulations.

After any airbag component testing or service, do not connect the battery negative cable. Personal injury or death may result if the system test is not performed first.

If the vehicle is equipped with the Occupant Classification System (OCS), do not connect the battery negative cable before performing the OCS Verification Test using the scan tool and the appropriate diagnostic information. Personal injury or death may result if the system test is not performed properly.

Never replace both the Occupant Restraint Controller (ORC) and the Occupant Classification Module (OCM) at the same time. If both require replacement, replace one, then perform the Airbag System test before replacing the other.

Both the ORC and the OCM store Occupant Classification System (OCS) calibration data, which they transfer to one another when one of them is replaced. If both are replaced at the same time, an irreversible

fault will be set in both modules and the OCS may malfunction and cause personal injury or death.

If equipped with OCS, the Seat Weight Sensor is a sensitive, calibrated unit and must be handled carefully. Do not drop or handle roughly. If dropped or damaged, replace with another sensor. Failure to do so may result in occupant injury or death.

If equipped with OCS, the front passenger seat must be handled carefully as well. When removing the seat, be careful when setting on floor not to drop. If dropped, the sensor may be inoperative, could result in occupant injury, or possibly death.

If equipped with OCS, when the passenger front seat is on the floor, no one should sit in the front passenger seat. This uneven force may damage the sensing ability of the seat weight sensors. If sat on and damaged, the sensor may be inoperative, could result in occupant injury, or possibly death.

DISARMING THE SYSTEM

➡The Anti-theft system must be deactivated before disconnecting the battery to avoid system engagement upon reconnecting the battery.

The Anti-theft system is deactivated when the vehicle is unlocked via the unlock button on the key fob, or when the vehicle is opened via Keyless Access, or when the ignition switch is turned **ON** (with a charged battery connected), or when the immobilizer registers an authorized key. Do not disconnect the positive battery terminal unless the battery is to be removed.

Disconnect the negative battery cable to disarm the airbag system. No waiting time is necessary before beginning work.

ARMING THE SYSTEM

➡The Anti-theft system must be deactivated before disconnecting the battery to avoid system engagement upon reconnecting the battery.

The Anti-theft system is deactivated when the vehicle is unlocked via the unlock button on the key fob, or when the vehicle is opened via Keyless Access, or when the ignition switch is turned **ON** (with a charged battery connected), or when the immobilizer registers an authorized key. Do not disconnect the positive battery terminal unless the battery is to be removed.

After reconnecting the airbag wiring, turn the ignition switch **ON** and make sure no one is inside the vehicle, then connect the battery cable.

1. Before servicing the vehicle, refer to the precautions.
2. When installing spiral spring, spiral spring must be in center position and wheels must be in the "straight ahead position".

3. The following depicts center position of spiral spring, which is dependent on the manufacturer.
   a. The color marked (black square) band must be located in viewing window.
   b. The color marked (yellow) band must be located in viewing window.

DRIVE TRAIN

AUTOMATIC TRANSAXLE FLUID

DRAIN AND REFILL

See Figures 39 through 41.

Use the Direct Shift Gearbox (DSG) transmission fluid as a replacement part. Refer to the Parts Catalog. Short Description

First, the fluid temperature is read out. If it is higher than 122° F), then let the transmission cool down.

Turn off the engine, remove the overflow tube and drain any transmission fluid. Install the overflow tube and overfill the transmission fluid.

Start the engine and drain any excess fluid until the level has reached the overflow tube.

Tools:
• Vehicle Diagnosis, Testing and Information System VAS 5051B
• Oil Collecting and Extracting Device V.A.G 1782
• Adapter for Oil Filling VAS 6262 A
Requirements
• The engine is off.
• The vehicle is level and all hoist supports are the same height.
• The noise insulation is removed if necessary
• The selector level is in the "P" position.
• The vehicle diagnosis, testing and information system VAS 5051B is connected.
• The transmission fluid should not be warmer than 45°C (113°F) when starting the procedure.
Procedure
1. Follow the rules of cleanliness when working on the transmission.
2. Only use the transmission fluid for the DSG available as a replacement part. Other fluids can cause malfunctions or transmission failure.

➡**Risk of injury due to hot transmission fluid.**

3. Connect the vehicle diagnosis, testing and information system VAS 5051B and identify the vehicle in Guided Functions.

4. Select DSG transmission.
5. Select Check Fluid Level.
6. Let the transmission cool down if the fluid temperature is higher than 113° F.

➡**Do not start the engine if there is no transmission fluid in the transmission.**

7. Engine off - do not start!

8. Remove the drain plug near the pendulum support.
9. A black plastic overflow tube is located in this hole (with an 8 mm hex socket head). Its length determines the oil level in the transmission.
10. Remove the overflow tube and let the fluid drain.

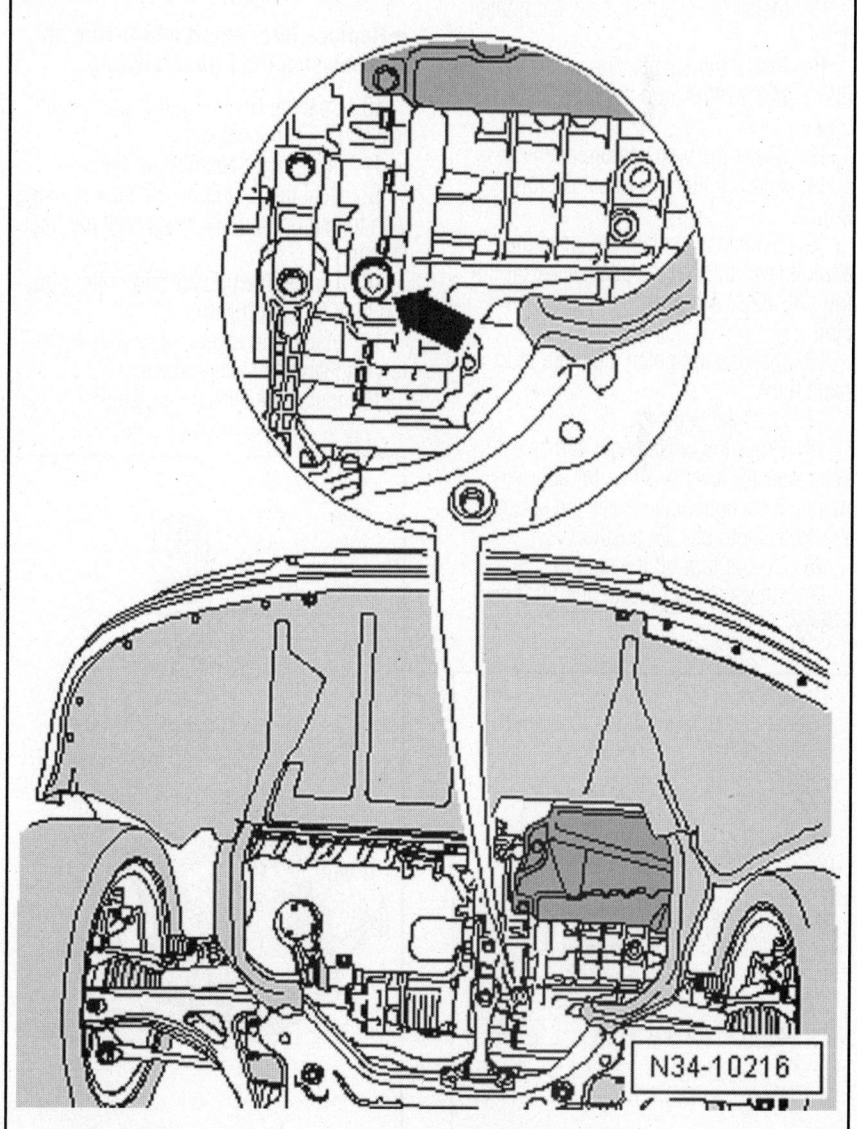

Fig. 39 Remove the drain plug (arrow) near the pendulum support

N34-10216

Fig. 40 Remove the overflow tube (arrow) and let the fluid drain

➡**About 5 liters of fluid will drain out.**

11. Install the overflow tube and tighten it.

12. Install the adapter for oil filling VAS 6262 A into the hole hand tight.

13. Shake the bottle before opening.

14. Add 5.5 liters of transmission fluid.

15. To change containers, close the shutoff lever or hold the adapter for oil filling VAS 6262 A higher than the transmission.

16. Install and tighten the drain plug hand tight.

17. Start the engine.

18. Press the brake pedal and select each selector lever position for approximately 3 seconds, then move the selector lever back into the "P" position.

19. Do not turn off the engine.

20. Check the fluid level and fill if necessary.

FILTER REPLACEMENT

See Figure 42.

1. Carefully remove the engine cover.
2. Remove the air filter housing.
3. Remove the battery.
4. Remove the mounting bolts and the battery tray.
5. Place a drain pan under the transmission.
6. Remove transmission oil filter housing.
7. To let gear oil from oil filter housing flow back into the transmission, tip housing slightly in its seat before removing.
8. Slowly pull filter insert up. If the O-ring on the filter insert intake collar was not removed, remove it from the transmission.

To install:

9. Install in reverse order, paying attention to the following:

➡**Replace filter insert and O-ring on transmission fluid filter housing.**

10. Coat the O-ring on the filter insert intake neck with gear oil.
11. Install the transmission filter.
12. Coat the O-ring on the filter housing with transmission fluid and install the filter housing.
13. Tighten the transmission filter housing to 15 ft. lbs. (20Nm).
14. Install the battery tray and the battery. Tighten the battery tray to
15. Install the air filter housing.

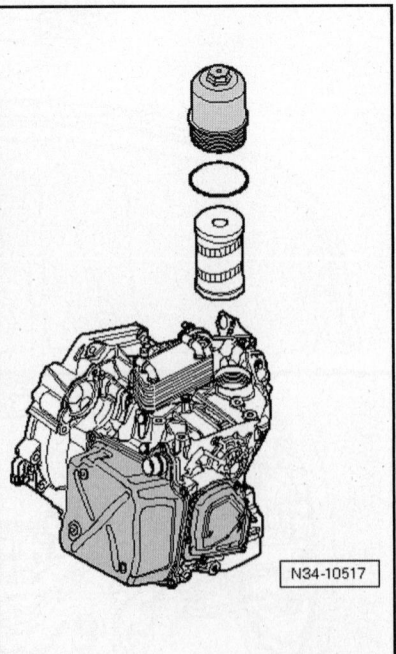

Fig. 42 Transmission filter & housing overview

16. Refill and check the transmission fluid.

MANUAL TRANSAXLE FLUID

FLUID CHECK

See Figure 43.

1. Remove the transmission fluid filler plug to check the transmission fluid.

2. Add the transmission fluid, as necessary. The level is correct when the transmission fluid comes up to the bottom edge of the oil filler hole.

3. Install the transmission fluid filler plug, tighten to 30 ft. lbs. (40 Nm)

CLUTCH

REMOVAL & INSTALLATION

A3 Models

Luk Clutch

See Figure 44.

Recommended tools:
• Retainer 3067
• Centering mandrel T10097
• Grease for clutch disc shaft splines G 000 100

1. Remove the transmission.
2. Insert flywheel retainer 3067 to loosen bolts.
3. When removing, loosen bolts as follows, so that pressure plate does not distort (causing shuddering on acceleration):
4. Loosen all 6 bolts clockwise, one after the other and in steps of 90° (1/4 turn) until pressure plate is free.
5. Remove pressure plate and clutch plate.

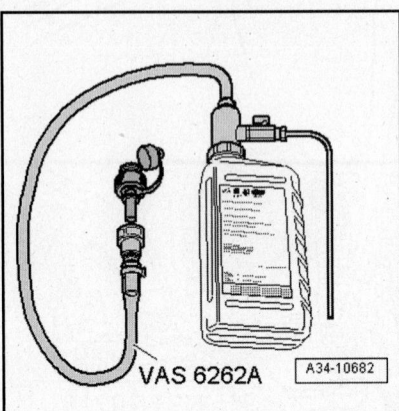

Fig. 41 Install the adapter for oil filling VAS 6262 A into the hole hand tight

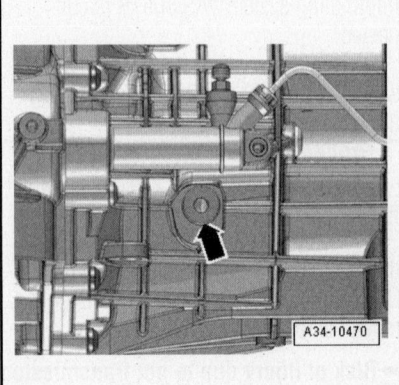

Fig. 43 Manual transmission fluid filler plug (arrow)

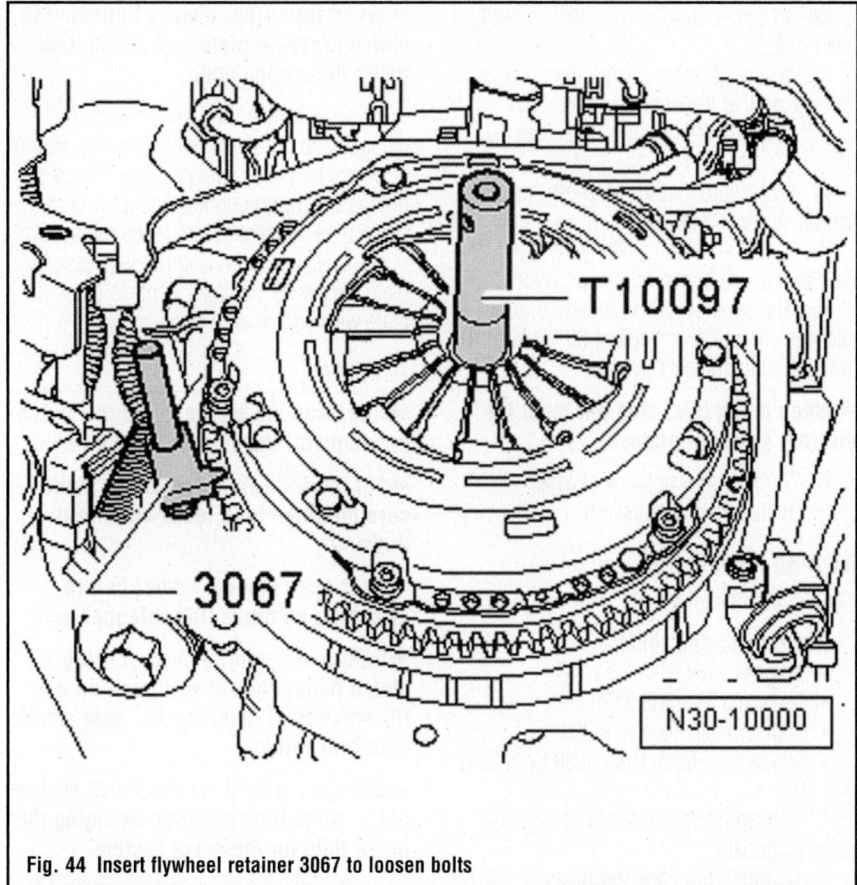

Fig. 44 Insert flywheel retainer 3067 to loosen bolts

To install:

6. Installation is in reverse order of removal, note the following:

a. Self-adjusting pressure plate adjusting ring, checking and resetting in LuK clutches.

b. Replace clutch plates and pressure plates with damaged or loose rivets.

c. Always replace clutch plate and pressure plate together.

d. Allocate clutch plate and pressure plate according to engine code via see: Electronic Parts Catalog

e. To reduce odor caused by a burnt clutch, thoroughly clean the clutch bell housing, the flywheel and side of the engine facing toward the transmission.

f. Clean input shaft splines and on a used clutch plate, the hub splines, remove corrosion and apply only a very thin coating of grease G 000 100 onto the splines. Then move clutch plate back and forth on input shaft until the hub moves freely on the shaft. Excess grease must be removed.

g. Pressure plates are corrosion-protected and greased. Only the contact surfaces may be cleaned, otherwise the service life of the clutch will be considerably reduced.

h. The pressure plate contact surface and clutch plate lining must make full contact with flywheel. Only then may the securing bolts be installed.

➡ **Make sure centering sleeves for engine to transmission are installed in cylinder block, install if necessary.**

➡ **If centering sleeves are not present, shifting difficulties, clutch problems and possibly noise in transmission (loose gear rattling) will occur.**

7. Note installed position of clutch plate: Marking *"Getriebeseite"* (transmission side) faces toward transmission.

8. Insert the flywheel retainer 3067.

9. Position pressure plate on alignment pins.

10. To center clutch plate, use centering pin T10097 .

11. When installing, fasten bolts as follows, so that the pressure plate does not distort (causing shuddering on acceleration):

12. Install all 6 bolts evenly, by hand, until bolt heads contact pressure plate.

13. Tighten all 6 bolts clockwise, one after the other and in steps of 90° (1/4 turn) until housing contacts flywheel.

14. Tighten all 6 bolts clockwise.

Sachs Clutch

See Figures 45 through 47.

Recommended tools:
- Retainer 3067
- Centering mandrel T10097
- Grease for clutch disc shaft splines G 000 100

1. Remove the transmission.

2. When removing, loosen bolts as follows, so that pressure plate does not distort (causing shuddering on acceleration):

3. Insert flywheel retainer 3067 to loosen bolts.

4. Loosen all 6 bolts clockwise, one after the other and in steps of 90° (1/4 turn) until pressure plate is free.

5. When removing, stop 2 must loosen together with pin 1.

6. If stop does not loosen: Press pin in direction of dual mass flywheel.

7. Remove the pressure plate and clutch plate.

To install:

8. Installation is in reverse order of removal, note the following:

a. Replace clutch plates and pressure plates with damaged or loose rivets.

b. Always replace clutch plate and pressure plate together.

c. Allocate clutch plate and pressure plate according to engine code via see: Electronic Parts Catalog

d. To reduce odor caused by a burnt clutch, thoroughly clean clutch bell housing, the flywheel and side of engine facing toward the transmission.

e. Clean the input shaft splines and on a used clutch plate, the hub splines, remove corrosion and apply only a very thin coating of grease G 000 100 onto the splines. Then move clutch plate back

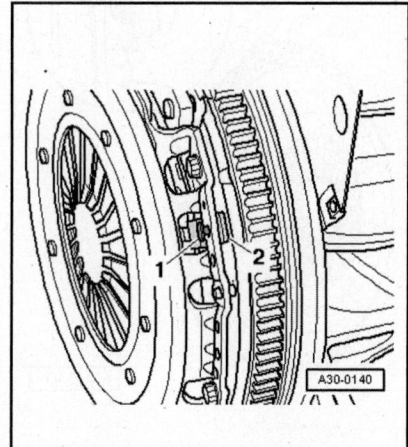

Fig. 45 When removing, stop 2 must loosen together with pin 1

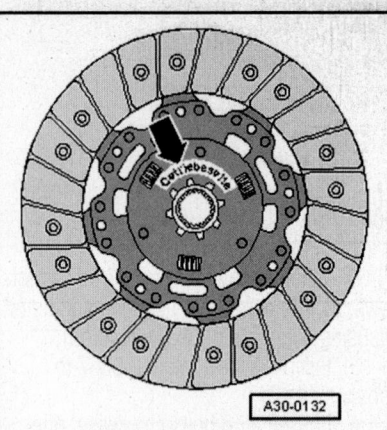

Fig. 46 Make sure *"Getriebeseite"* (transmission side) faces toward transmission

and forth on input shaft until the hub moves freely on the shaft. Excess grease must be removed.

f. Pressure plates are corrosion-protected and greased. Only the contact surfaces may be cleaned, otherwise the service life of the clutch will be considerably reduced.

g. The pressure plate contact surface and clutch plate lining must make full contact with flywheel. Only then may the securing bolts be installed.

9. Note installed position of clutch plate:

10. Insert the Flywheel Retainer 3067.

11. Position pressure plate on alignment pins.

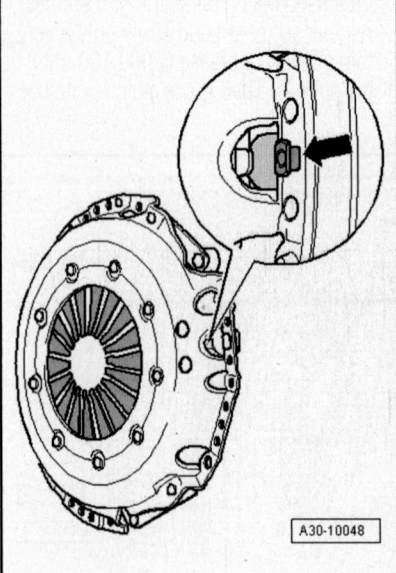

Fig. 47 Make sure that the stop pin (locator) can be easily moved

12. To center clutch plate, use centering pin T10097.

13. When installing, fasten the bolts as follows, so that the pressure plate does not distort (causing shuddering on acceleration):

14. Make sure that the stop pin (locator) can be easily moved.

15. Install all 6 bolts evenly, by hand, until bolt heads contact pressure plate.

16. Tighten all 6 bolts clockwise, one after the other and in steps of 90° (1/4 turn) until housing contacts flywheel.

➡**When doing this, stop pin must lift off from pressure plate.**

17. Tighten all 6 bolts clockwise.
18. Install the transmission.

A4 & A5 Models
See Figure 48 and 49.

Recommended tools:
• Retainer 3067
• Centering Mandrel 3176
• Counter Hold Tool 10 - 201
• Grease for Clutch Disc Shaft Splines G 000 100

1. Loosen or tighten the bolts in small steps diagonally.

2. Change from Flywheel Retainer 3067 to Counter Hold Tool 10 - 201 for removing.

3. Clutch plate installation location: Spring pack (coil springs) or marking *"Getriebeseite"* must face pressure plate and transmission.

4. Install the bolts only when the pressure plate contact surface and clutch plate lining make full contact with flywheel.

➡**Wear up to half the thickness of the diaphragm spring is permitted.**

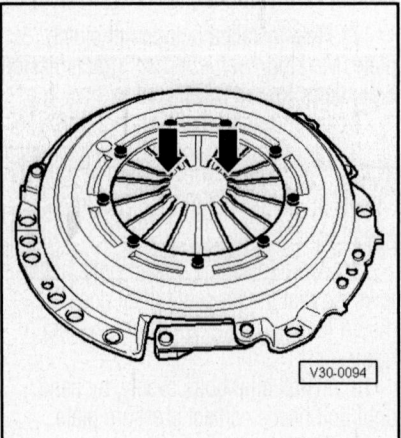

Fig. 48 Checking Ends of the Diaphragm Spring

➡**When repairing, always allocate the clutch pressure plate and clutch disc using the engine code.**

5. Check the spring connections for damage and the rivet connections for secure fit. Pressure plates with severely kinked or broken off spring connections as well as loose rivet connections must be replaced.

6. Check the wire ring in the pressure plate **arrow** for damage. Replace pressure plate with broken wire ring.

BLEEDING

➡**After working on the hydraulic clutch mechanism, the system must be bled.**

➡**For the following work step, make sure no brake fluid leaks onto transmission.**

➡**First open bleeder valve, before switching on brake filler/bleeder unit.**

➡**Before bleeding, you must bring clutch pedal back to rest position and fill brake fluid reservoir to *"max"* mark with brake fluid.**

➡**Change the fluid for the clutch system at the same interval when changing the brake fluid for the brake system.**

1. Connect brake charger/bleeder unit V.A.G 1869 or VAS 5234 but do not switch on yet.

2. Loosen the quick-release fasteners and remove the rear noise insulation.

3. Connect bleeder hose to clutch slave cylinder and open bleeder valve.

4. Connect the bleeder hose with the collector bottle vacuum hose.

5. Now switch on brake filler/bleeder unit and bleed approximately 100 cm3 of brake fluid.

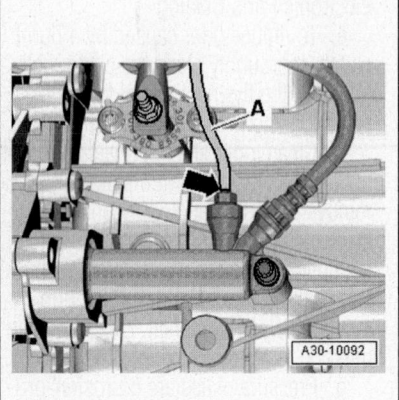

Fig. 49 Connect bleeder hose to clutch slave cylinder and open bleeder valve

- Working pressure 2.5 bar
- Ensure correct bleeder hose seating during bleeding process.

6. Tighten the bleeder valve.

7. Depress clutch pedal several times after completion of bleeding process.

8. Bleed the system again if necessary.

9. Install noise insulation.

FRONT HALFSHAFT

REMOVAL & INSTALLATION

A3 Models

See Figure 50.

1. Remove the noise insulation.

2. Loosen wheel side drive axle threaded connection.

3. Remove the wheel.

4. Remove drive axle from the transmission flange.

5. Remove hex nuts on the ball joint.

6. Remove nut from the level control system sensor linkage.

7. Disengage the transverse link from ball joint.

8. Tip the suspension strut outward while pressing drive axle out of wheel bearing unit with a brass drive.

9. Remove drive axle.

10. Installation is in reverse order of removal.

11. Tighten drive axle hex combination bolt to 147 ft. lbs. (200 Nm).

12. Tighten the 12-point bolt to 51 ft. lbs. (70 Nm). Lower the vehicle onto its wheels. Tighten 12-point bolt an additional 90°.

A4 & A5 Models

1. Remove wheel covers, remove cover cap on light-alloy wheels (removal hook in vehicle tool kit).

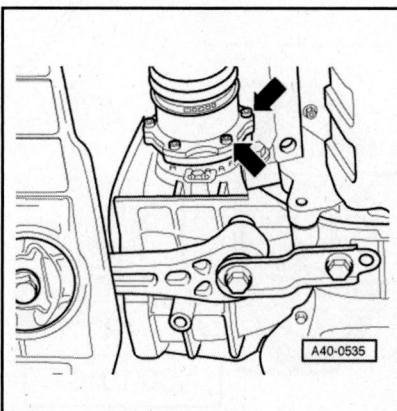

Fig. 50 Remove drive axle from the transmission flange

2. Loosen outer drive axle joint bolt a maximum of 90° (only loosen with vehicle resting on wheels risk of accident).

3. Remove the wheel.

4. Tighten all five wheel bolts by hand.

5. Remove drive axle outer joint bolt.

6. Remove drive axle from flange shaft/transmission.

7. If there is not enough room available to remove drive axle, perform following steps:

   a. Remove nut, remove hex bolt and lift out both control arms upward. The slits in the wheel bearing housing must not be widened using a chisel or similar tool!

➡**Do not loosen bolts 3 and 4, otherwise the adjustment of the front axle will change!**

   b. Swing wheel bearing housing to side.

   c. Remove the drive axle.

To install:

8. Insert drive axle in wheel bearing housing.

9. Insert both upper control arms, insert new bolt and tighten new nut. While tightening, press control arm as far as possible toward wheel bearing housing.

10. Fasten drive axle to flange shaft/transmission:

   a. First pre-tighten all bolt to 11 ft. lbs. (15 Nm), then tighten all bolts to specified torque.

   b. Tightening specifications: M8 bolt: 29 ft. lbs. (40 Nm). M10 bolt: 51 ft. lbs. (70 Nm).

11. Fasten drive axle outer joint.

➡**When tightening drive axle outer joint to pre-tightening specification, vehicle must not come in contact with floor; otherwise wheel bearing can be damaged.**

12. A second technician is needed for the next step:

   a. Technician 1: Sit in vehicle and operate foot brake.

   b. Technician 2: Tighten drive axle hex bolt to pre-tightening specification:
- Hex bolt M14: 84 ft. lbs. (115 Nm).
- Hex bolt M16: 147 ft. lbs. (200 Nm).

13. Install wheel and place vehicle on floor.

14. Turn drive axle bolt an additional 180°. (Only turn additional turn on vehicle resting on wheels risk of accident).

REAR AXLE FLUID

DRAIN & REFILL

1. Before servicing the vehicle, refer to the precautions.

2. Raise the vehicle.

3. Install a drain pan under the rear final drive.

4. Remove the lower rear final drive drain plug and drain the fluid.

To refill:

5. Install the lower rear final drive drain plug and tighten to 26 ft. lbs. (35 Nm).

6. Remove the top fill plug and refill the unit. The level is correct when the rear final drive is filled up to the lower edge of the opening.

7. Install the top fill plug and tighten to 26 ft. lbs. (35 Nm).

REAR DRIVESHAFT

REMOVAL & INSTALLATION

A3 Models

See Figures 51 through 54.

➡**Engine/transmission jack V.A.G 1383 A with universal support V.A.G 1359/2. A twin pillar vehicle hoist should be used when working on the driveshaft.**

➡**Before removing, mark the positions of all parts in relation to each other. Re-install in the same position otherwise imbalance will be excessive, the bearings could be damaged causing rumbling noises.**

➡**Do not kink driveshaft, only store and move when fully extended.**

1. Remove noise insulation.

2. Vehicles with 4-cylinder engine:

   a. Disconnect exhaust system at clamping sleeve and remove rear part of exhaust system.

3. Vehicles with 6-cylinder engine:

   a. Remove the entire exhaust system.

4. Support the driveshaft with Engine/transmission jack V.A.G 1383 A (use a wooden wedge for help).

5. Finally, remove heat shield.

6. After removing the heat shield, re-install the center bearing.

7. Remove the driveshaft with flexible disc from bevel box.

8. Remove bolts and then remove the pendulum support.

9. Check whether CV joint/driveshaft markings are present. If not, apply these with color.

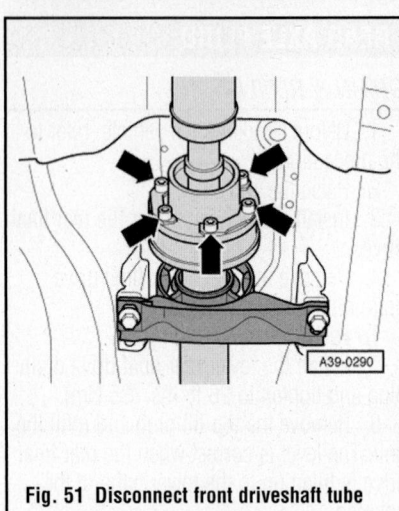

Fig. 51 Disconnect front driveshaft tube from rear driveshaft tube

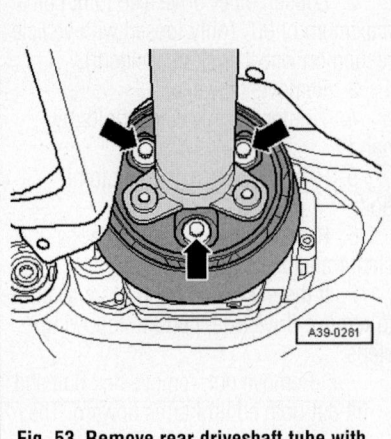

Fig. 53 Remove rear driveshaft tube with flexible disc and vibration damper from rear final drive

To install:

21. Install in reverse order of removal, note the following:

   a. Install all driveshaft parts marked in relation to each other in same position when reinstalling.

   b. Sealing rings in driveshaft flanges must not be damaged when removing and installing. If seals are damaged, driveshaft must be replaced.

   c. Slip the driveshaft horizontally onto the respective guide pin.

22. Installation position:

   a. Three projecting sleeves each on transmission flange or final drive flange and driveshaft flange engage in flexible disc mounting holes.

   b. Install the driveshaft on the final drive so that both markings align.

   • A: Small collar
   • B: Large collar

   c. Ensure CV joint/driveshaft markings align.

   d. Tighten front driveshaft tube on rear driveshaft tube.

23. Install center bearing free of tension as follows:

➡**All driveshaft bolts are tightened.**

10. Disconnect front driveshaft tube from rear driveshaft tube.

11. Press front driveshaft tube forwards and swivel it out of flange of rear driveshaft tube.

12. When swiveling, ensure front driveshaft tube is tilted downward as little as possible.

13. Carefully remove front driveshaft tube from centering pins on bevel box.

➡**Sealing ring in driveshaft flange must not be damaged. Detach driveshaft horizontally from guide pin.**

14. Swivel down and detach front driveshaft tube.

15. Check whether there is a marking (colored dot) on driveshaft and rear final drive driveshaft flange.

16. If not, identify position of flexible disc and flange/driveshaft to rear final drive

17. Remove rear driveshaft tube with flexible disc and vibration damper from rear final drive.

18. Remove driveshaft intermediate bearing from vehicle.

19. Carefully detach rear driveshaft tube from centering pin.

20. Do not damage the driveshaft when removing, pull off from centering pin in horizontal position. Sealing ring in centering bushing must not be damaged.

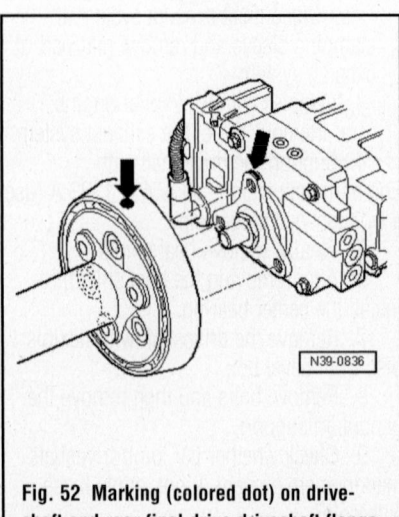

Fig. 52 Marking (colored dot) on driveshaft and rear final drive driveshaft flange

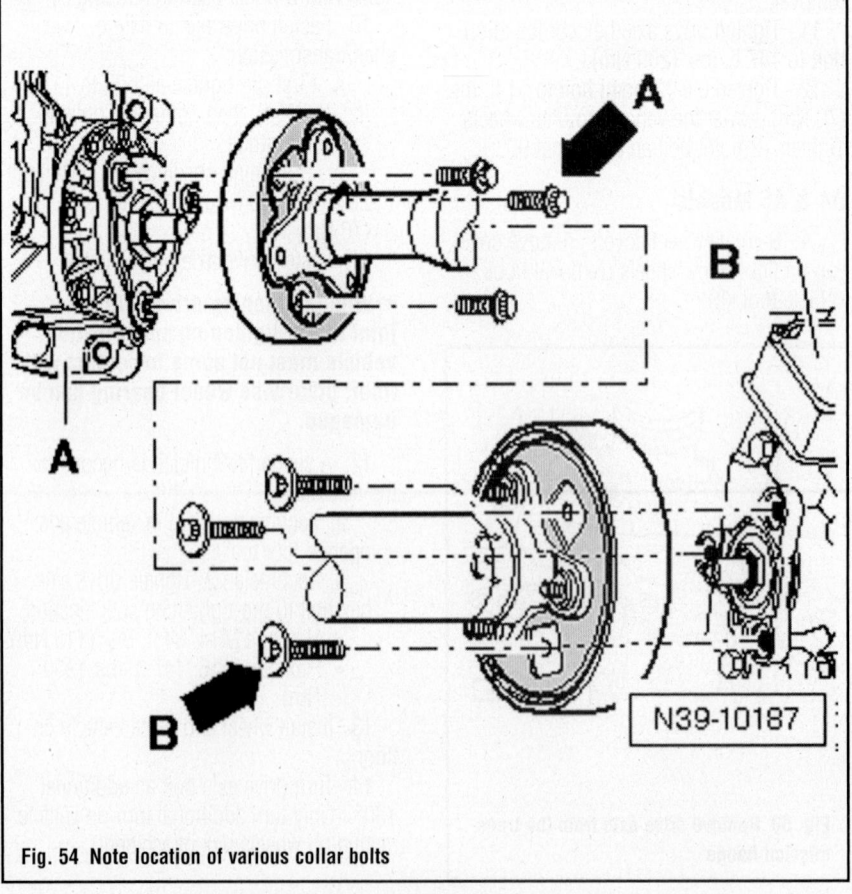

Fig. 54 Note location of various collar bolts

a. Align intermediate bearing on its longitudinal holes so that driveshaft or bearing is not under stress.

b. Tighten combination bolts. The combination-bolts must lie inside four heat shield centering tabs.

c. Tighten the pendulum support first to transmission and then to sub frame.

- Pendulum support first to transmission: 30 ft. lbs. (40 Nm) plus 90°.
- Pendulum support to sub frame: 74 ft. lbs. (100 Nm) plus 90°.

d. Install the exhaust system free of tension.

24. Install noise insulation. If droning noises are audible while driving, do the following:

a. Remove balance nut and balance washer.

b. Then, if necessary, remove driveshaft with flexible disc from flange/driveshaft on rear final drive and rotate one hole and reinstall.

c. If droning noises are still heard, the driveshaft must be bolted on again, offset by one more hole.

A4 & A5 Models

See Figure 55.

1. Remove rear section of exhaust system as from clamp(s).

2. Use pressing lever 80-200 to pry off rear attachments of heat shield for driveshaft.

3. Remove bolts for center bearing.

➡ **When removing the bolts support the driveshaft by hand. Do not bend driveshaft.**

4. Remove heat shield. Continue supporting driveshaft.

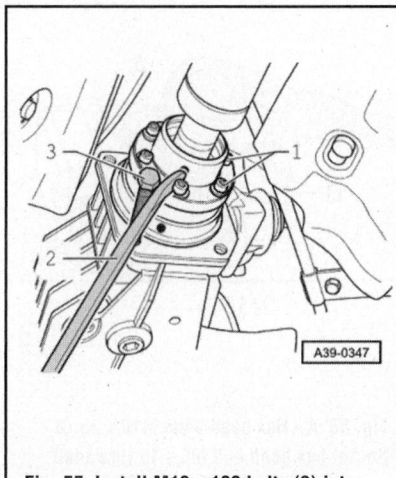

Fig. 55 Install M10 x 100 bolts (3) into rear final drive

5. Install bolts for center bearing again hand-tight.

6. Remove heat shield for driveshaft off transmission.

7. Check for a factory marking (colored dot), at the driveshaft/driveshaft flange and on the final drive at the rear. If no colored dot is present, mark the position of the driveshaft flange relative to the rear final drive with a colored dot.

8. Engage Assembly tool 3139 and tighten plastic nuts.

9. Never install assembly appliance onto balance plates.

10. Remove bolts for the center bearing.

11. Install M10 x 100 bolt into rear final drive.

12. To loosen bolts of the driveshaft, counter hold with an assembly lever.

13. Remove bolts at the front Constant Velocity (CV) joint, detach the driveshaft and support it using engine and transmission jack VAG1383A.

14. Remove bolts at rear CV joint and detach driveshaft.

➡ **Only transport and store the driveshaft when extended.**

To install:

15. Installation is carried out in reverse order. Note the following:

16. To avoid imbalance, the flanges of the driveshaft and of the rear final drive must be installed so that the factory color markings or the markings made subsequently are in line.

- If a new driveshaft is installed and if the factory color marking on the flange of the rear final drive is no longer visible, the radial run out on the driveshaft flange must be measured.
- Replace gaskets on flange shafts (detach protective foil and stick gasket onto flange shaft).
- Remove the old and dry high temperature grease from the CV joints and the flanges for the driveshaft. Replace with the exact same quantity of new high temperature grease G 000 633.
- Note the installation position of the driveshaft: The central CV joint is located behind the center bearing facing toward the rear final drive.
- After removing the driveshaft from the rear final drive, a thick washer that may be located between the shim and the bolt head must not be reinstalled.
- It is essential that the locking fluid remaining in the threads in the

flange shafts on the transmission and rear final drive is cleaned out after removing the driveshaft. Otherwise there is a danger that the new bolts will seize when they are installed and then shear if they have to removed later.

- The threaded holes can be cleaned with a thread tap.
- Replace driveshaft bolts (self-locking).

17. Install the driveshaft and bolts for CV joints.

18. Install bolts arrows for center bearing hand tight.

19. Install M10 x 100 bolt into rear final drive.

20. To tighten bolts for the driveshaft, counter hold with an assembly lever.

21. Remove assembly device 3139.

22. Remove bolts arrows for the center bearing. The driveshaft must be supported manually by a second mechanic.

23. When removing the bolts support the driveshaft by hand.

24. Install heat shield. Continue supporting driveshaft.

25. Install bolts for center bearing several turns.

26. Secure heat shield on right and left at the center bearing using bolts (M8 x 30).

27. When tightening the combination bolt make sure that the center plug is located at the securing bore.

28. Tighten bolts for the center bearing.

29. Install rear securing clips for the heat shield.

30. Remove the bolts.

31. Install exhaust system and align stress-free.

32. Tightening Specifications:

a. Intermediate bearing on body: 16 ft. lbs. (23 Nm).

b. Driveshaft to transmission: 40 ft. lbs. (55 Nm).

c. Driveshaft to rear final drive: 40 ft. lbs. (55 Nm).

d. Heat shield for driveshaft to transmission

REAR HALFSHAFT

REMOVAL & INSTALLATION

A3 Models

See Figure 56.

1. Loosen the drive axle threaded connection.

2. Remove the wheel.

3. Remove coil spring.

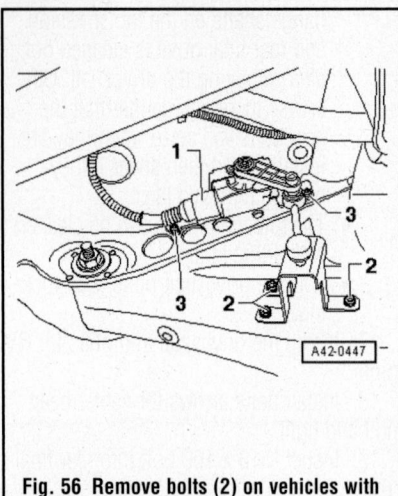

Fig. 56 Remove bolts (2) on vehicles with level control system sensor

4. Remove bolts on vehicles with level control system sensor.

5. Remove bolts for tie rod and lower transverse link from wheel bearing housing.

6. Remove the bolt and washer. The washer is installed on vehicles with an aluminum wheel bearing housing.

7. Loosen drive axle on the transmission side.

8. Swing wheel bearing housing upward and remove drive axle from wheel bearing splines.

9. Remove drive axle.

10. Installation is in reverse order of removal, noting the following:

11. Transmission Side Drive Axle Connection Tightening Specification:

   a. Always replace after removal.

   b. Pre-tightening torque: 7 ft. lbs. (10 Nm).

   c. Tightening torque M8: 29 ft. lbs. (40 Nm).

   d. Tightening torque M10: 51 ft. lbs. (70 Nm).

12. On vehicles with Audi magnetic ride, reprogram control position. Refer to see: Diagnostic Unit.

A4 & A5 Models

See Figure 57.

1. Remove wheel covers, remove cover cap on light-alloy wheels (removal hook in vehicle tool kit).

2. Loosen collar bolt only 90°, otherwise wheel bearing will be damaged.

➡**When loosening and tightening collar bolt, vehicle must stand on wheels. Risk of accident.**

3. Remove the wheel.

4. Install all 5 wheel bolts and tighten by hand.

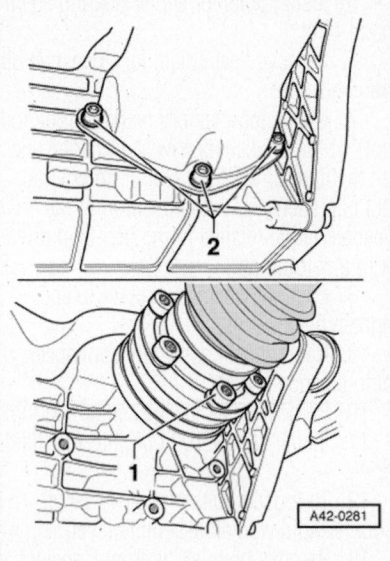

Fig. 57 Remove the combination bolts and cover (2) and bolts (1)

5. Engage the parking brake.

6. Remove collar bolt.

7. Remove coil spring.

8. Remove the combination bolts and cover.

9. Remove bolts.

10. Raise trapezoidal control arm with hand until drive axle can be taken forward out of flange shaft/transmission.

11. Press exhaust pipe downward slightly and slide drive axle inward until it can be removed from wheel hub.

12. Press exhaust pipe down again slightly and guide drive axle outward over cover plate.

13. Remove drive axle downward.

14. Make sure that cover plate and body are not damaged.

To install:

➡**Replace the screws and self-locking nuts.**

15. Installation is in reverse order of removal.

16. Insert drive axle from below and slide into wheel hub up to stop.

17. Align drive axle holes and flange shaft/transmission holes with each other, install bolts.

18. Insert cover, install combination-bolts and tighten to 81 ft. lbs (110 Nm). Always replace. Threads in body can be repaired according to DIN 8140 using wire thread inserts (Heli-Coil). Thread insert must be same length as thread in body.

19. Install coil spring.

20. Install new collar bolt and tighten to 147 ft. lbs. (200 Nm) plus an additional 180° without turning any farther.

21. Mount wheel and tighten.

22. Lower the vehicle onto its wheels.

23. Tighten the collar bolt to 59 ft. lbs. (80 Nm) plus 90°.

REAR PINION SEAL

REMOVAL & INSTALLATION

A3 Models

See Figures 58 and 59.

1. Remove the rear driveshaft.

2. Remove hex nut for flange / drive axle.

3. A - Hex head bolts M10 x 25. B - Socket hex head bolt M8 x 15 (installed from rear in bracket Counter Support 3415)

4. Pull off flange for driveshaft. Use three arm puller (e.g. Kukko 12-1) if difficult to access.

5. Remove seal using extractor lever VW 681.

To install:

6. Before installing, lightly coat new seal on outside circumference and between sealing lips with Haldex clutch high performance oil .

7. Drive in new sealing ring to stop using thrust piece T10019. Do not cant sealing ring when doing this.

8. Drive off flange/driveshaft with sleeve 30 - 20.

9. Insert new hex nut with locking compound D 000 600 and tighten.

10. Install the rear driveshaft.

11. Check oil level in Haldex clutch.

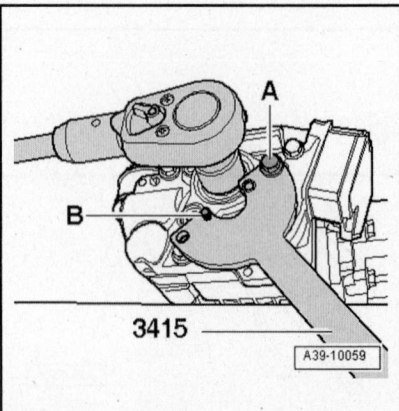

Fig. 58 A - Hex head bolts M10 x 25. B - Socket hex head bolt M8 x 15 (installed from rear in bracket Counter Support 3415)

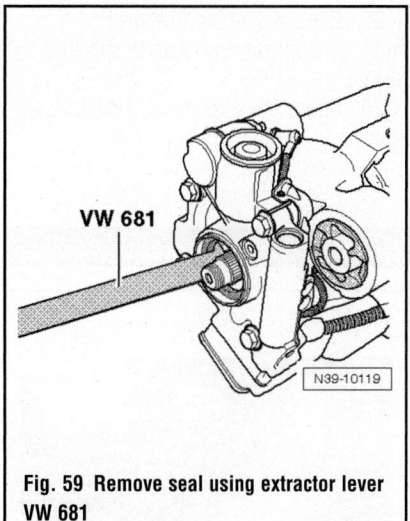

Fig. 59 Remove seal using extractor lever VW 681

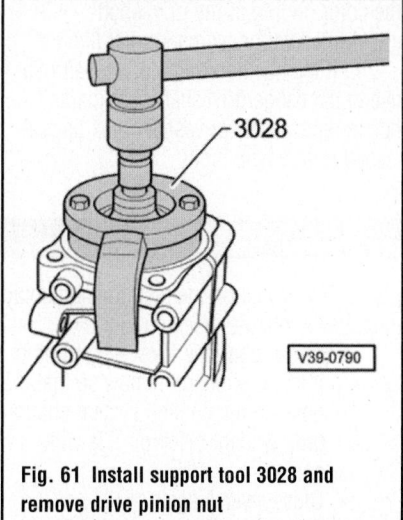

Fig. 61 Install support tool 3028 and remove drive pinion nut

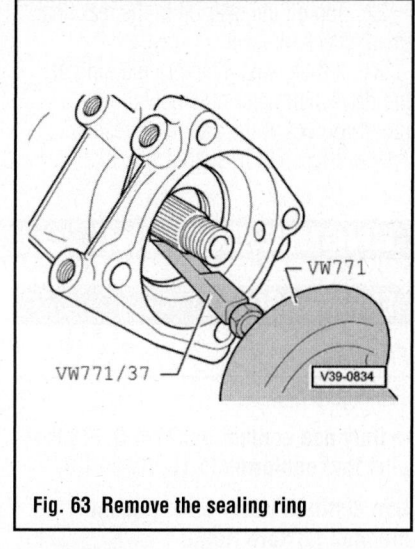

Fig. 63 Remove the sealing ring

A4 & A5 Models

See Figures 60 through 63.

1. Remove rear section of exhaust system as from clamp(s).

2. Check whether there is a factory marking (paint dot) on drive shaft. If you do not find one, mark the position of the Constant Velocity (CV) joint relative to the rear final drive with a colored dot.

3. Disconnect driveshaft from rear final drive and tie it up to exhaust system brackets.

4. Place engine and transmission jack VAG1383A with universal mounting 1359/2 under final drive and secure final drive.

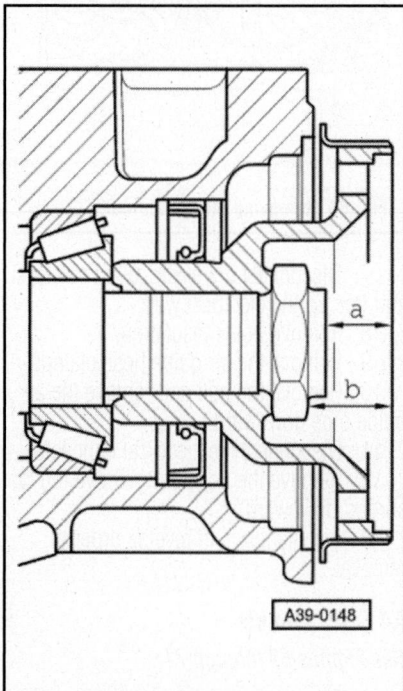

Fig. 60 Calculate dimension "a" and dimension "b"

5. Remove bolts of left final drive support.

6. Carefully lower final drive until flange is freely accessible.

7. Color mark the position of the securing nut for the drive pinion.

8. Calculate dimension "a" and dimension "b":

   a. Distance of flange to drive pinion = Dimension a

   b. Distance of flange to securing nut for the drive pinion = Dimension b

9. Note calculated dimensions.

10. Count turns when unscrewing the securing nut and make a note of them.

11. Install support tool 3028 and remove drive pinion nut.

12. Place drip tray underneath to collect oil.

13. Detach flange with removal tool VW391.

14. Install two M8 x 30 bolts into flange.

15. Remove the sealing ring.

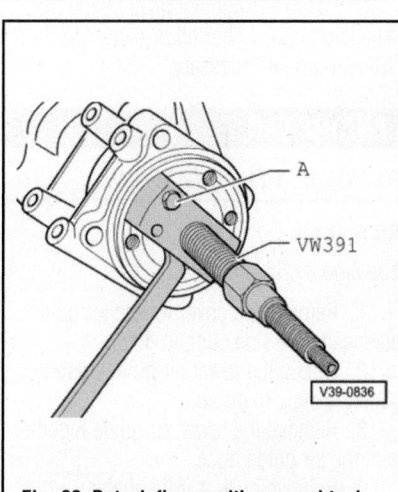

Fig. 62 Detach flange with removal tool VW391

To install:

16. Installation is carried out in reverse order. Note the following:

   a. Replace O-ring between drive pinion bearing and flange.

   b. Lightly oil O-ring before installing.

   c. Pack space between sealing and dust lips half full with sealing grease G 052 128 A1.

   d. Lightly oil outer circumference of seal.

   e. Drive in the seal for the drive shaft flange, onto the stop with drift 3026.

   f. Drive shaft flange onto drive pinion until securing nut can be mounted.

➡**Use the old nut to reattach the flange to the drive pinion. Otherwise the original installed position will not be relocated.**

17. Clean drive pinion nut and threads on drive pinion of oil and grease residues. Thinly coat the threads with locking fluid D 000 600.

➡**The number of turns when reattaching must be the same as during unscrewing.**

18. Perform control measurement - check dimension "a" and dimension "b".

   a. O-ring must be installed when measuring.

   b. The nut must be returned to exactly the marked position.

   c. Maximum permissible deviation from original measurements: ± 0.3 mm.

19. Install the lock nut.

20. Move final drive back to installation position.

21. Install the final drive to front mounting bracket.

22. Top off the gear oil in the rear final drive, check oil level.

23. If there was a factory marking at the driveshaft determine now the radial run out at the flange/driveshaft. Attach driveshaft in such a way that the color coding at the driveshaft are aligned with new marking at flange.

24. If the position of the driveshaft relative to the flange/driveshaft were marked before removal the driveshaft must be reattached at same position.

25. Replace seal on driveshaft flange and tighten driveshaft to specifications.

26. Stress free alignment of exhaust system.

ENGINE COOLING

ENGINE COOLANT

FILLING

See Figure 64.

➡**Only use coolant additive G 12 plus-plus that conforms to TL VW 774 G.**

Use distilled water only. Recommended Mixture Ratio:

1. Fill the coolant reservoir on the cooling system charge unit with at least 17 liters of premixed coolant of the proper mixture ratio: 40%-50%.

2. Install the adapter V.A.G 1274/8 onto the coolant expansion tank.

3. Connect the cooling system charge unit to the adapter.

4. Place the air outlet in a small container. A small amount of coolant which should be collected is drawn off with the discharged air.

5. Close the levers A and B by turning the levers at a right angle to the direction of flow.

6. Connect hose to compressed air. Pressure: 87-145 psi. (6-10 bars) pressure.

7. Open the lever B by turning it in the direction of flow.

8. Condition: A further vacuum is created in the cooling system by the suction jet pump. The needle on the instrument display must travel into the green region.

- Briefly open the lever A by turning it in the direction of flow so that the hose on the cooling system charge unit, coolant reservoir fills with coolant.
- Close lever A again.
- Leave lever B open another 2 minutes.

Condition: A further vacuum is created in the cooling system by the suction jet pump. The needle on the instrument display must still remain in the green region.

- Close lever B.

9. Condition:
- The needle on display must remain in the green range. Only then is there enough vacuum in the coolant system for the filling. If the pressure falls, check the coolant system for leaks.
- Remove the pressurized air hose.
- Open the lever A slowly.

10. Coolant is extracted from the cooling system charge unit coolant reservoir by pressure in the coolant system and the system is filled.

11. Remove the cooling system charge unit from the adapter on the coolant expansion tank.

12. Check the coolant level inside the expansion tank. Either fill or extract to the "MAX" mark, if necessary.

ENGINE FAN

REMOVAL & INSTALLATION

A3 Models

See Figures 65 and 66.

1. Remove the cover for the air guide; disengage the side clips to do so.

2. Unclip the lower air guide, disengage the clips to do so.

3. Remove the lower air guide together with the air guide hose.

4. Remove bolts 1 from above.

5. Loosen the hose clamp.

6. Remove bolt.

Fig. 65 Hose clamp (2), bolt (4) and electrical connector (arrow)

Fig. 66 Removing the fan shroud

7. Disconnect the electrical connectors and free up the electrical wire.

8. Remove noise insulation.

9. Remove the air guide hose clamps.

10. Remove the bolt and remove the air guide pipe downward.

11. Disconnect the electrical connector.

12. Remove the bolts and remove the fan shroud downward.

13. Installation is in reverse order of removal.

A4 & A5 Models

See Figures 67 through 71.

1. Remove both front wheels.

2. Loosen quick-release fasteners and remove front noise insulation.

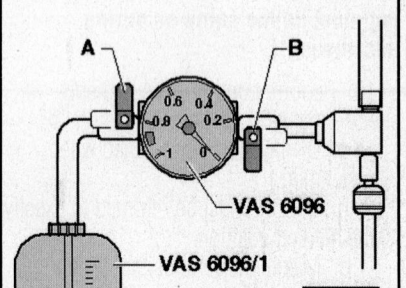

Fig. 64 Coolant charge unit VAS 6096, reservoir VAS 6096/1 and levers

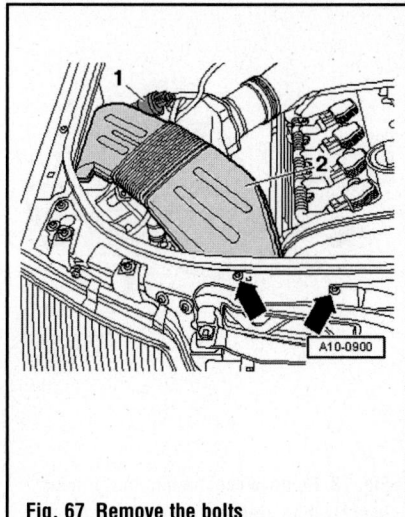

Fig. 67 Remove the bolts

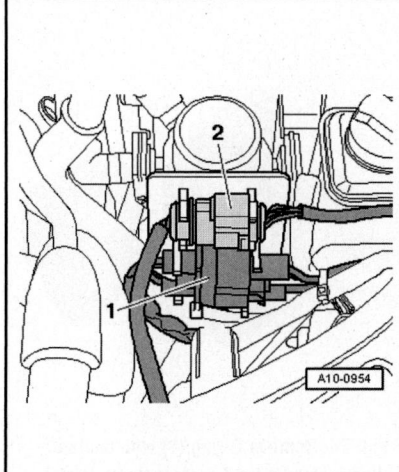

Fig. 68 Disconnect the connectors

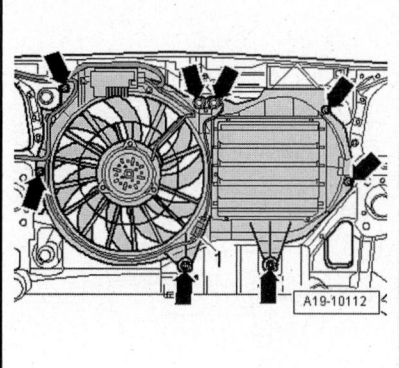

Fig. 69 Remove bolts and remove fan shroud upward and out

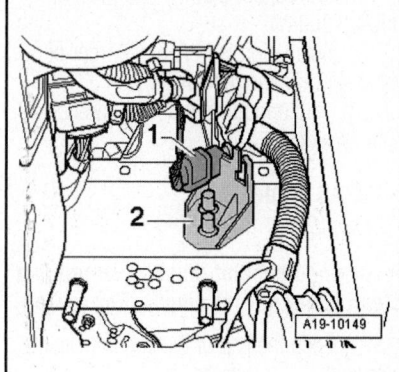

Fig. 70 Remove the retainer for cable connector (2), disconnect the electrical connector from hood lock (1)

3. Remove front bumper cover.

4. Remove air guide in front of the charge air cooler.

5. Remove cover arrow at power steering fluid reservoir.

6. Remove electrical harness connectors 1 and 2 from bracket.

7. Free up the electrical wires to lock carrier.

8. Remove right cover in the engine compartment, if equipped.

9. Disengage Evaporative Emission (EVAP) Canister Purge Regulator Valve N80 from air guide.

10. Remove bolts.

11. Remove air duct.

12. Remove bolts at left and right.

13. Remove hood seal on the lock carrier and on the bolted fender flanges.

14. Thread Support Tool 3369 into empty bores at left and right.

15. Remove bolts at left and right.

16. Carefully pull lock carrier toward front.

17. Disconnect the connectors.

18. Free up the electrical wiring.

19. Disconnect connector for the hood lock and free up the electrical wires.

20. Remove bolts and remove fan shroud upward and out.

21. Installation is in reverse order of removal, note the following:

22. Install lock carrier with attachments.

23. Place the torque support stop on the rubber buffer and tighten the nuts arrows.

24. Install front bumper cover.

25. Check the headlamp adjustment.

RADIATOR

REMOVAL & INSTALLATION

A3 Models

See Figures 70 and 71.

⁂ CAUTION

Never open, service or drain the radiator or cooling system when hot; serious burns can occur from the steam and hot coolant. Also, when draining engine coolant, keep in mind that cats and dogs are attracted to ethylene glycol antifreeze and could drink any that is left in an uncovered container or in puddles on the ground. This will prove fatal in sufficient quantities. Always drain coolant into a sealable container. Coolant should be reused unless it is contaminated or is several years old.

1. Open the cap to the coolant expansion tank.

2. Disconnect the intake connection using spring-type clip pliers VAS 5024 A.

3. Unscrew intake connection at lock carrier and remove it.

4. Remove the fan shroud.

5. Remove noise insulation.

6. Remove air duct for charge air cooler.

7. Separate the electrical connector.

8. Place a drip tray under engine.

9. Drain the coolant, by pulling off lower coolant hose.

10. Pull the connector at left longitudinal member out of retainer.

11. Remove the retainer for cable connector.

12. Disconnect the electrical connector from hood lock.

13. Disconnect upper coolant hose from radiator.

14. Remove bolts on rear side of radiator.

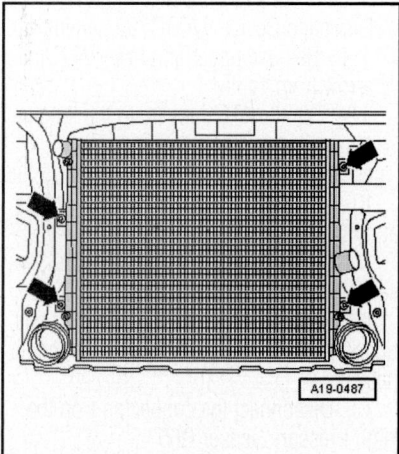

Fig. 71 Remove bolts on rear side of radiator

15. Lift radiator slightly and remove upward and off.

16. Installation is in reverse order of removal, note the following:

   a. Fill engine with coolant and check for leaks.

A4 & A5 Models

See Figure 72.

➥ **Drained coolant must be stored in a clean container for disposal or reuse.**

1. Open the cap of the coolant expansion tank.

2. Loosen quick-release fasteners and remove front noise insulation.

3. Remove front bumper cover.

4. Place Drip Tray For Workshop Crane VAS 6208 or Drip Tray V.A.G 1306 under engine.

5. Vehicles with coolant drain plug: Open coolant drain plug to coolant line at bottom of cooler.

6. Vehicles without coolant drain plug:

   a. Remove the retaining clip on the Engine Coolant Temperature (ECT) Sensor (on Radiator) G83.

   b. Remove the Engine Coolant Temperature (ECT) Sensor (on Radiator) G83 from its supports and drain the coolant.

7. Disconnect lower coolant hose from radiator.

8. Disconnect upper coolant hose from radiator.

9. Vehicles with Multitronic/automatic transmission 01V:

   a. Remove right cover 1 in the engine compartment, if equipped.

   b. Disengage Evaporative Emission (EVAP) Canister Purge Regulator Valve N80 from the air guide.

   c. Remove bolts.

   d. Remove air duct.

   e. Place Old Oil Collecting And Extracting Device V.A.G 1782 underneath.

   f. Remove upper and lower ATF lines arrow from cooler.

   g. Tie the ATF lines up to the longitudinal member to prevent fluid from escaping.

10. Remove the left and right air guides at radiator.

11. Unclip Outside Air Temperature Sensor G17 2 from the bracket.

12. Remove power steering cooling coil bolts 3 and 4 hydraulic hoses remain connected.

13. Disconnect the connector 1 on the High Pressure Sensor G65.

➥ **The air conditioning refrigerant circuit must not be opened.**

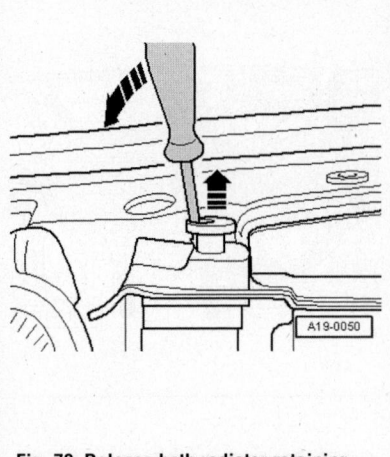

Fig. 72 Release both radiator retaining pins and remove by pulling upward

14. Remove bolts for the condenser.

15. Pivot condenser downward with lines connected.

➥ **To prevent damage to the refrigerant lines/hoses, ensure that the lines and hoses are not stretched, kinked or bent.**

16. Release both radiator retaining pins and remove by pulling upward.

17. Pivot radiator forward, pull up and remove.

18. Installation is in reverse order of removal.

19. Fill with coolant.

20. Vehicles with Multitronic/automatic transmission 01V:

   a. Check the ATF level.

THERMOSTAT

REMOVAL & INSTALLATION

A3 Models

See Figures 73 and 74.

1. Drained coolant must be stored in a clean container for disposal or reuse.

➥ **Cover the cap of the expansion tank with a rag and open carefully. Steam or hot coolant may escape when opening.**

2. Open the cap of coolant expansion tank.

3. Remove center noise insulation fasteners.

4. Place drip tray for workshop crane VAS 6208 under engine.

5. Vehicles with drain plug:

   a. Turn the drain plug arrow on radia-

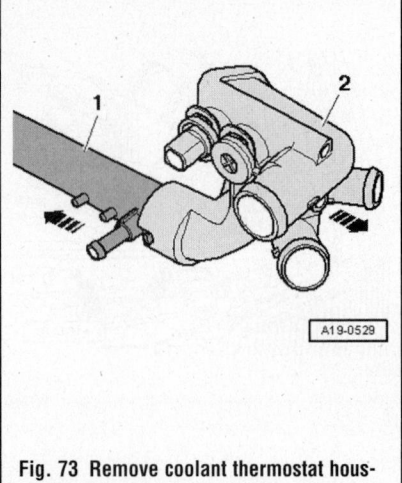

Fig. 73 Remove coolant thermostat housing (2) while pressing coolant pipe (1)

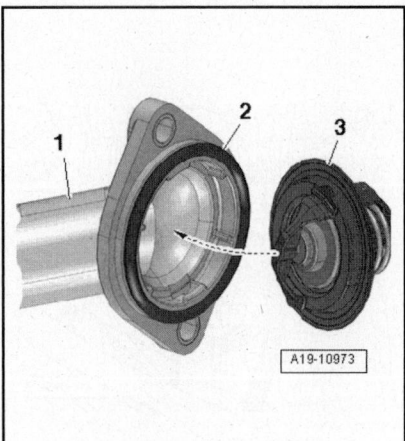

Fig. 74 Remove O-ring (3) with coolant thermostat (2) from coolant thermostat housing (1)

tor left, place assisting hose on supports if necessary.

6. Vehicles without drain plug:

   a. Remove the lower coolant hose from radiator by removing retaining clamps.

7. Disconnect the electrical connector 1 at Engine Coolant Temperature (ECT) Sensor (on Radiator) G83.

8. Also remove lower coolant hose to After-Run Coolant Pump V51 arrow and allow remaining coolant to drain.

9. Disconnect the battery.

10. If equipped, remove vacuum hose to air guide hose.

11. Disconnect air guide hose at Throttle Valve Control Module J338.

12. Remove the air filter.

13. Remove vacuum line at variable intake manifold actuator.

14. Remove bolts and remove vacuum actuator from intake manifold.

15. Disconnect the electrical connector

arrow at Engine Coolant Temperature (ECT) Sensor G62.

16. Disconnect the secondary air hose at position indicated by.

17. Free up the air hose at bracket.

18. Disconnect coolant hoses at positions indicated.

19. Remove bolts.

20. Pull the transmission oil cooler coolant pipe bracket toward left.

21. Swing Secondary Air Injection (AIR) system hose bracket forward.

22. Remove bolt at wiring harness bracket.

➡**Press coolant pipe in direction of coolant pump using pry bar when removing coolant thermostat housing so that is not pulled off.**

23. Remove the coolant thermostat housing while pressing coolant pipe toward coolant pump with pry bar.

24. Remove bolts and remove connecting pieces.

25. Remove O-ring with coolant thermostat from coolant thermostat housing.

26. Installation is in reverse order of removal, note the following:

    a. Always replace the gaskets and seals.

    b. Clean the O-ring sealing surfaces.

    c. Insert the coolant regulator.

    d. Coat new the O-ring 1 with coolant G12+.

    e. Attach the connecting pieces to coolant thermostat housing.

A4 & A5 Models

See Figure 75.

1. Drain the coolant.

2. Remove the intake manifold.

3. Remove the thermostat screws.

4. Remove the coolant hose.

5. Remove the connecting piece with thermostat.

6. Installation is performed in reverse order of removal, noting the following:

    a. Replace the O-ring.

    b. Clean or smooth the O-ring sealing surface.

    c. Fill with coolant.

A3 2.0L TDI Engines

See Figure 76.

1. Before servicing the vehicle, refer to the precautions.

2. Drain the coolant.

3. Remove throttle valve control module J338.

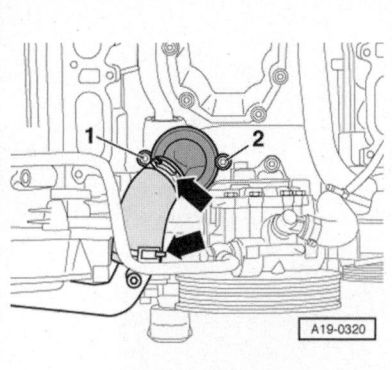

Fig. 75 Removing screws (1, 2) and hose clamps (arrows)

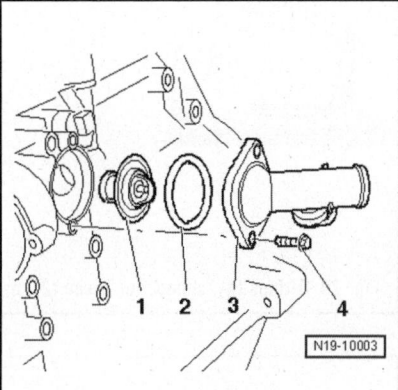

Fig. 76 Coat new O-ring (2) with coolant. Insert coolant thermostat (1) in the connecting piece (3) and tighten bolts (4)

4. Remove coolant hose from the connection.

5. Loosen bolts on connection with a 10 mm flex wrench 3185, remove with socket T10058 and remove connection with the coolant thermostat.

6. Rotate coolant thermostat 90° to the left and remove it from the connection.

To install:

7. Installation is in the reverse order of removal.

8. Always replace seals, sealing rings and O-rings.

9. Coat new O-ring with coolant.

10. Insert coolant thermostat in the connecting piece and turn it 90° turn to the right.

11. The clip of the thermostat must be positioned at approximately right angle.

12. Insert connection with coolant thermostat in the cylinder block.

13. Tighten bolts with a 10 mm flex wrench 3185.

14. Tightening specifications 11 ft. lbs. (15 Nm).

15. Secure connection coolant hose.

16. Install throttle valve control module J338.

WATER PUMP

REMOVAL & INSTALLATION

2.0L Gas Engines

See Figures 77 through 79.

1. Remove the small coolant pipe.

2. Remove coolant pump toothed belt.

3. Disconnect the electrical connector 1 on Throttle Valve Control Module J338.

4. Remove bolts arrows and remove Throttle Valve Control Module J338.

5. Disconnect the electrical connector 1 on the Engine Coolant Temperature (ECT) Sensor G62.

6. Lift clamps, remove the coolant hoses and move them to the side.

7. Remove bolts the water pump bolts.

8. Remove coolant pump from the centering pin and remove the engine oil cooler.

To install:

9. Installation is in reverse order of removal, note the following:

    a. Replace the seals and O-rings.

    b. Coat the O-rings with coolant.

    c. Make sure both centering pins are installed in the cylinder block.

    d. Install the connection piece into the engine oil cooler.

    e. Push the coolant pump onto the connection piece and onto the centering pins in the cylinder block.

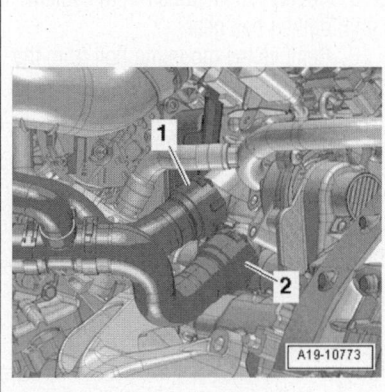

Fig. 77 Lift clamps 1 and 2, remove the coolant hoses and move them to the side

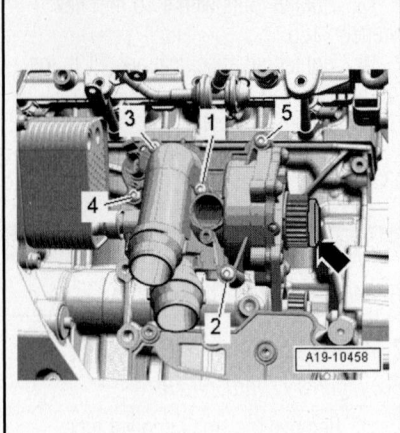

Fig. 78 Remove bolts the water pump bolts (1—5)

f. Tighten the water pump bolts to 7 ft. lbs. (9 Nm).

➡**If a new coolant pump was installed, then the protective cap must be removed.**

10. Fill with coolant.

2.0L TDI Engines

See Figure 80.

1. Always replace gaskets and seals.
2. The lower toothed belt guard can remain installed.
3. The toothed belt remains in position on the crankshaft sprocket.
4. Cover the toothed belt with a cloth to protect it from coolant before removing the coolant pump.
5. Drain the coolant.
6. Remove ribbed belt.
7. Remove the ribbed belt tensioning damper.
8. Remove the upper and center toothed belt guards.
9. Remove toothed belt from coolant pump toothed belt gear.
10. Remove the mounting bolt from the rear toothed belt guard.
11. Remove the coolant pump bolts and then remove the coolant pump.

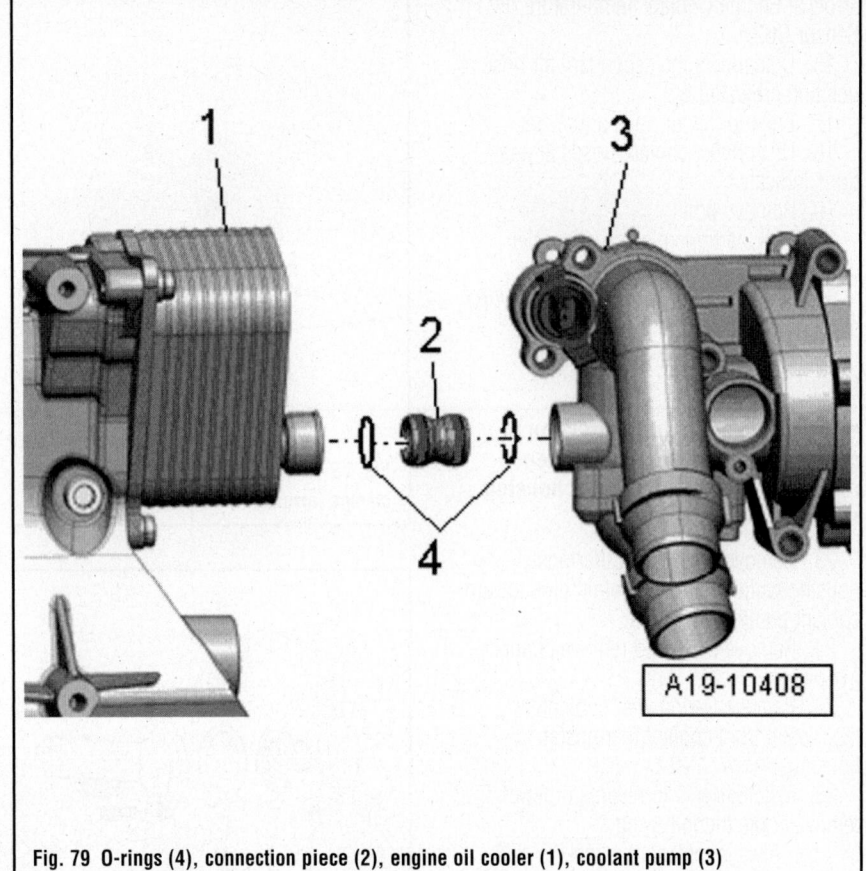

Fig. 79 O-rings (4), connection piece (2), engine oil cooler (1), coolant pump (3)

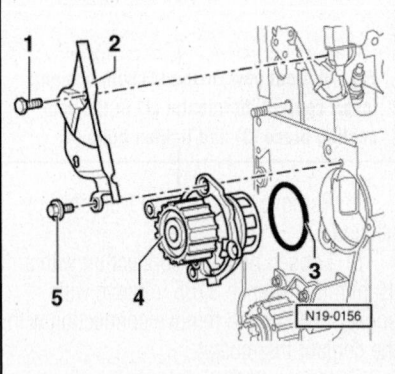

Fig. 80 Identifying the mounting bolt (1) from the rear toothed belt guard (2), O-ring (3), coolant pump bolts (5) and coolant pump (4)

To install:

12. Installation is performed in the reverse order of removal. When doing this note the following:
13. Moisten a new O-ring 3 with coolant.
14. Insert the coolant pump 4.
15. Installation position: Sealing plug in housing points downward.
16. Tighten the mounting bolts 5. Tightening specification: 11 ft. lbs. (15 Nm).
17. Tighten the mounting bolt 1 for the toothed belt guard 1 on the cylinder head. Tightening specification: 15 ft. lbs. (20 Nm)
18. Install toothed belt, installing.
19. Install the ribbed belt tensioning element. Tightening specification: 18 ft. lbs. (25 Nm)
20. Install the ribbed belt.
21. Fill the coolant.

ENGINE ELECTRICAL

BATTERY

See Figure 81.

1. Disconnect the battery.
2. Open the battery housing or the jacket in direction of and remove it from the battery.
3. Remove mounting screws and remove retaining bracket.
4. Fold handles arrows upward (if present) and take out battery.

➡ **If battery is not secured properly, the following risks are possible:**

- Shortened battery service life due to vibration damage (explosion hazard).
- If battery is not secured properly, the plates within the battery can be damaged.
- Damage to battery casing caused by bracket (possible electrolyte leakage, high subsequent costs).
- Reduced collision safety.

5. Install in reverse order of removal, noting the following:
6. Tighten the threaded connections.

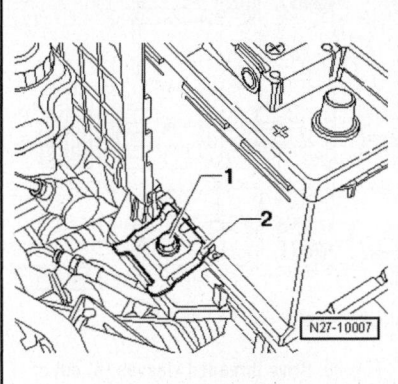

Fig. 81 Remove mounting screws (1) and remove retaining bracket (2)

7. After installing, verify battery is properly seated.
8. Connect battery.

BATTERY RECONNECT/RELEARN PROCEDURE

After connecting the battery and switching on the ignition, the ASR/ESP Control

Lamp K155 and Electro-mechanical Power Steering Indicator Lamp light up continuously. The indicator lamps switch off automatically after driving straight ahead at 15 to 20 km/h. This activates Steering Angle Sensor G85.

Work steps required after connecting battery:

1. Switch on ignition using ignition key or start button and switch off again.
2. Read the DTC memory: using Vehicle Diagnosis, Testing & Information System VAS5051B, and select "Guided Fault Finding".
3. Clock: Check clock time setting, set anew if necessary.
4. Electrical window regulators:
   a. Open and close windows to each end stop respectively.
   b. With window closed, then pull switch until relay switches audibly.
   c. Check comfort switching of power window. While comfort switching is operated, window must close without holding the switch.
5. Check function: all electrical consumers.

ENGINE ELECTRICAL

ALTERNATOR

REMOVAL & INSTALLATION

See Figure 82.

2.0L Gas Engine

1. With ignition switched off, disconnect battery Ground (GND) wire.
2. Disconnect the mass air flow (MAF) sensor G70 connector item 1.
3. Remove engine cover.
4. If equipped, remove the EVAP canister, with the lines still connected, upward and out of its mount arrow and lay it to the side.

➡ **Risk of destroying if the running direction of a used ribbed belt is reversed. Before removing ribbed belt, mark the running direction with chalk or a felt-tip pen for reinstallation.**

5. Swivel ribbed belt tensioner in direction of arrow to tension ribbed belt.
6. Secure the ribbed belt tensioner with the Locking Pin T10060 A.
7. Remove ribbed belt.
8. Remove ribbed belt tensioner.
9. Remove the bolts and remove the alternator on the accessories bracket.

➡ **If alternator sticks in holder, turn bolt back in again down to the last 2 turns. Tap carefully on screw heads with flat side of hammer to release alternator mount bushings.**

10. Tip alternator with electrical wires connected to right side of vehicle.
11. Disconnect the electrical connector.

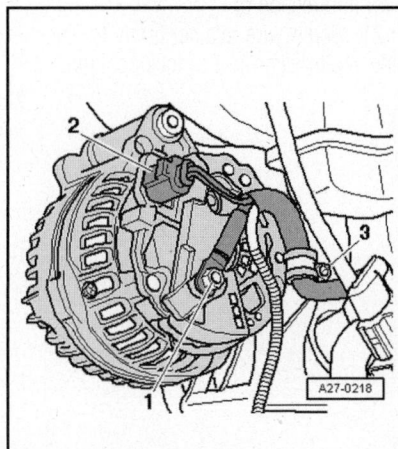

Fig. 82 Electrical wire (1), electrical connector (2) and clamp (3)

12. Disconnect the electric wire and clamp on the alternator.
13. Remove the alternator upward.
14. Install in reverse order of removal, noting the following:
    a. Slightly drive back sleeves for retaining bolts in order for easier installation of generator.
    b. Tight sleeves for alternator mount must be made smooth-running, otherwise clamping force of sleeve is too little despite correct torque.
    - Terminal 30/B+ to alternator: 12 ft. lbs. (16 Nm)
    - Alternator to the accessories bracket: 16 ft. lbs. (23 Nm)
    - Ribbed belt tensioner to the accessories bracket: 16 ft. lbs. (23 Nm)
    c. Route the ribbed belt on belt pulleys for the crankshaft and A/C compressor.
    d. Route the ribbed belts on the alternator belt pulley, release the tension on the tensioner.
    e. Check ribbed belt for correct seating.
15. Connect the battery.
16. Start engine and check belt routing.

2.0L TDI Engine

See Figures 85 and 86.

1. Before servicing the vehicle, refer to the precautions.
2. Disconnect the battery.
3. Pull the engine cover upward at the corners from the mounting points.
4. Bring the lock carrier into the service position.

WARNING

Before removing ribbed belt, mark the top side and direction of travel. When installing, pay attention to correct running direction and installation position. If the belt is installed in the opposite running direction or is positioned incorrectly, the belt will fail!

5. Remove ribbed belt.
6. Remove both A/C compressor screws.
7. Disengage and disconnect harness connector.
8. Remove the third screw and remove the A/C compressor downward from the accessories bracket.
9. Hoses on A/C compressor can remain connected.
10. Hang the A/C compressor with wire in a suitable place under the body until it is ready for installation.
11. Make sure the hoses are not pulled off or kinked.
12. Release and disconnect DF wire connector.
13. Pry off the protective cap.
14. Remove the nut and B+ wire below from alternator connector threads.
15. Remove nut and remove wiring bracket from alternator.
16. Remove both of the bolts and the nut for the fuel filter and lay them aside. The fuel hoses can remain connected.

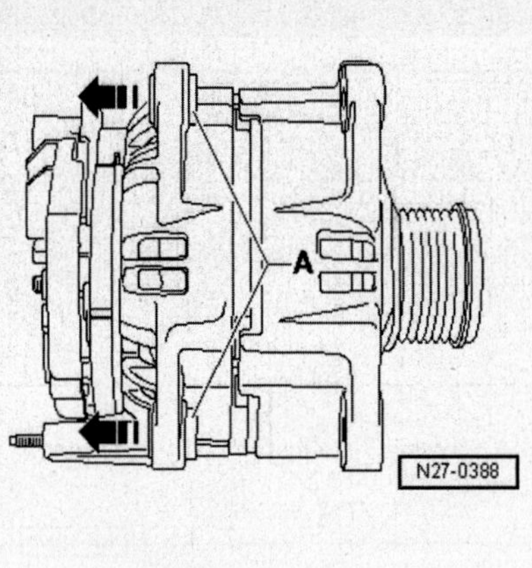

Fig. 83 Drive threaded sleeves (A) out of alternator housing approximately 0.156 in. (4 mm) in direction of

17. Remove both alternator mounting bolts.
18. Remove the alternator downward from vehicle.

To install:

19. Install in reverse order of removal, noting the following:

WARNING

When installing an already used ribbed belt, note direction of travel marked when it was removed! Before installing the ribbed belt, make sure all components (alternator, A/C compressor) are securely fastened. When installing the ribbed belt, make sure it is properly seated in the belt pulley!

20. Drive threaded sleeves out of alternator housing approximately 0.156 in. (4 mm) in direction of.
21. Screw wire retainer firmly to rear side of alternator in 3 o'clock position.

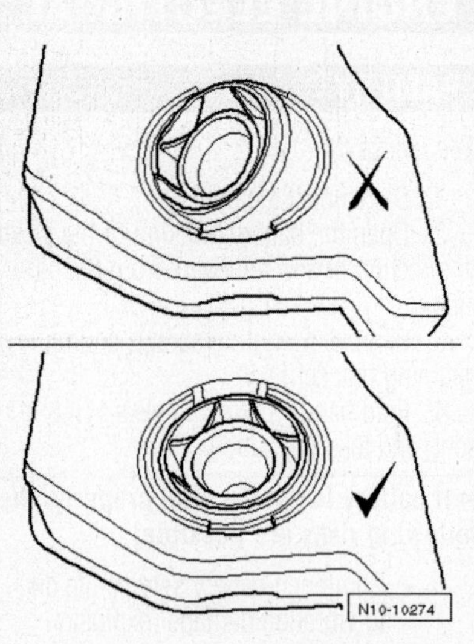

Fig. 84 Before installing the engine cover, make sure the four fasteners (ball sockets) are positioned correctly. Bring them into the correct position if necessary. Otherwise the engine cover will be damaged

WARNING

Before installing the engine cover, make sure the four fasteners (ball sockets) are positioned correctly. Bring them into the correct position if necessary. Otherwise the engine cover will be damaged.

22. Place the engine cover on the mounting points and press the corners into the retainers.
23. Reconnect the battery.
24. Start the engine and verify that the belt is running properly.
25. Turn off the engine.
26. Tighten bolts/nuts to specification as follows:
   - Alternator bolts: 15 ft. lbs. (20 Nm)
   - M5 Wire: 28 inch lbs. (3.2 Nm)

ENGINE ELECTRICAL

IGNITION SYSTEM

FIRING ORDER

2.0L engine firing order: 1–3–4–2 Distributor less ignition.

2.0L TDI engine firing order: 1–3–4–2.

IGNITION COIL

REMOVAL & INSTALLATION

2.0L Gas Engine

Standard

See Figures 85 and 86.

1. Disconnect the negative battery cable.

2. Disconnect electrical harness connectors to ignition coils, to do so attach assembly tool T10118 on release button and carefully disconnect harness connector.

3. Attach Puller For Ignition Coil T10095 A on ignition coils as depicted in the illustration and pull out ignition coils in succession.

4. Installation is in reverse order of removal, noting the following:

5. Insert ignition coil into corresponding spark plug shaft so that the straight connector sides fit with each other.

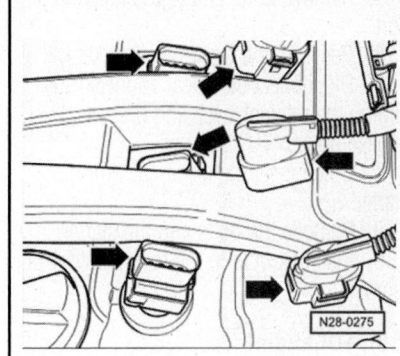

Fig. 86 Insert ignition coil into corresponding spark plug shaft so that the straight connector sides fit with each other

With Power Output Stages

See Figure 87.

1. Disconnect the negative battery cable.

2. Release electrical connectors on all ignition coils and remove them from the ignition coils.

3. Using ignition coil puller T40039, remove all ignition coils from spark plug shaft.

To install:

a. Insert all ignition coils loosely into each spark plug shaft.

b. Align ignition coils to connectors and then connect all of connectors simultaneously onto ignition coils.

c. Press the ignition coils uniformly onto spark plugs by hand (do not use an impact tool).

IGNITION TIMING

ADJUSTMENT

All gasoline engines are equipped with a Distributor less Ignition System (DIS). No adjustment is necessary.

SPARK PLUGS

REMOVAL & INSTALLATION

2.0L Gas Engine

See Figure 88.

1. Disconnect the negative battery cable.

2. Switch the ignition off.

3. Remove engine cover.

4. Remove the ignition coils.

5. Remove the spark plugs Spark plug wrench 3122B.

6. Install new spark plugs using Spark plug wrench 3122B. Tighten to 22 ft. lbs. (30 Nm).

7. Push ignition coils by hand into intended resources in cylinder head cover.

8. Install ignition coils by rotating slightly - they must engage noticeably.

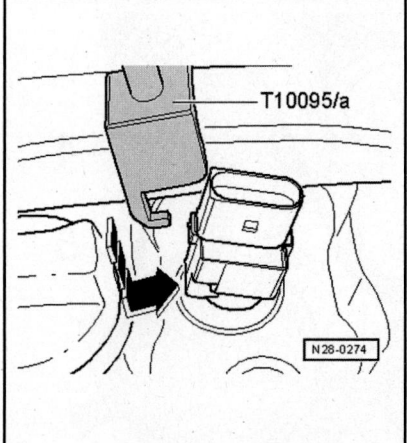

Fig. 85 Attach puller for ignition coil T10095 A on ignition coils

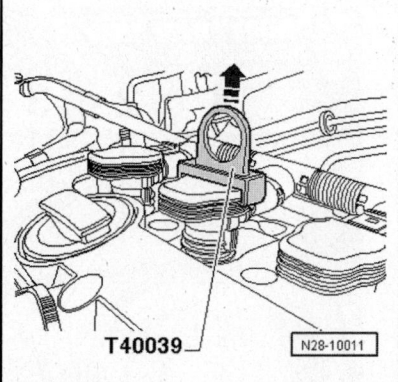

Fig. 87 Using ignition coil puller T40039, remove all ignition coils from spark plug shaft

Fig. 88 Remove the spark plugs Spark plug wrench 3122B

ENGINE ELECTRICAL

STARTING SYSTEM

STARTER

REMOVAL & INSTALLATION

2.0L Gas Engine

See Figure 89.

1. With ignition switched off, disconnect battery Ground (GND) cable.

2. Remove right engine mount.

3. Remove nut and free up Ground (GND) cable on the engine support.

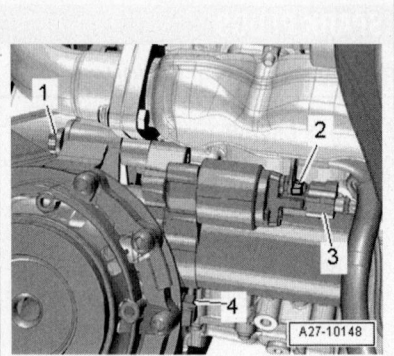

Fig. 89 Removing the starter: Bolt (1), electrical wire (2), connector (3) and bolt (4)

4. Remove bolts and right engine support.

5. Remove bolt for wiring bracket.

6. Disconnect electrical connector by sliding the retainer back and pressing release down.

7. Disconnect the electrical wire from starter.

8. Remove the bolts and the starter.

9. Installation is in the reverse order of removal.

2.0L TDI Engine

1. Before servicing the vehicle, refer to the precautions.

2. Disconnect the battery.

3. Pull engine cover upward and forward.

4. Loosen spring clamp using spring clamp pliers VAS 5024 and disconnect connector.

5. Remove screw.

6. Remove vacuum hose.

7. Pull air filter housing on the right side upward from its rubber mounting.

8. Remove air filter housing from vehicle.

9. Slide the protective cap in direction of downward from solenoid.

10. Remove positive wire and disconnect harness connector of terminal 50 2.

11. Remove the ground wire from the starter mounting bolt.

12. Remove the starter mounting bolt.

13. Remove the noise insulation.

14. Remove the nut from the lower starter mounting bolt.

15. Remove wire retainer.

16. Remove the starter mounting bolt.

17. Remove the starter.

To install:

18. Installation is in the reverse order of removal.

19. Tighten bolts/nuts to specification as follows:

- Starter to transmission M12: 56 ft. lbs. (75 Nm)
- Ground wire to Starter B mounting bolt M8: 11 ft. lbs. (15 Nm)
- Wire retainer to Starter B mounting bolt M8: 11 ft. lbs. (15 Nm)
- Positive wire to Starter B solenoid switch M8: 11 ft. lbs. (15 Nm)
- Air filter housing to body: 89 inch lbs. (10 Nm)
- GND wire to automatic transmission housing M8: 11 ft. lbs. (15 Nm)

ENGINE MECHANICAL

➡️**Disconnecting the negative battery cable may interfere with the functions of the on board computer systems and may require the computer to undergo a relearning process, once the negative battery cable is reconnected.**

ACCESSORY DRIVE BELTS

ACCESSORY BELT ROUTING

See Figure 90 and 91.

INSPECTION

1. Turn the engine at vibration damper/crankshaft pulley with a suitable socket wrench.

2. Raise the vehicle if necessary. Check the drive belt for:

    a. Sub-surface (deep) cracks

    b. Layer separation (top layer, cord strands)

    c. Traces of oil and grease

3. Replace the belt if any damage is found or if contaminated with oil or grease.

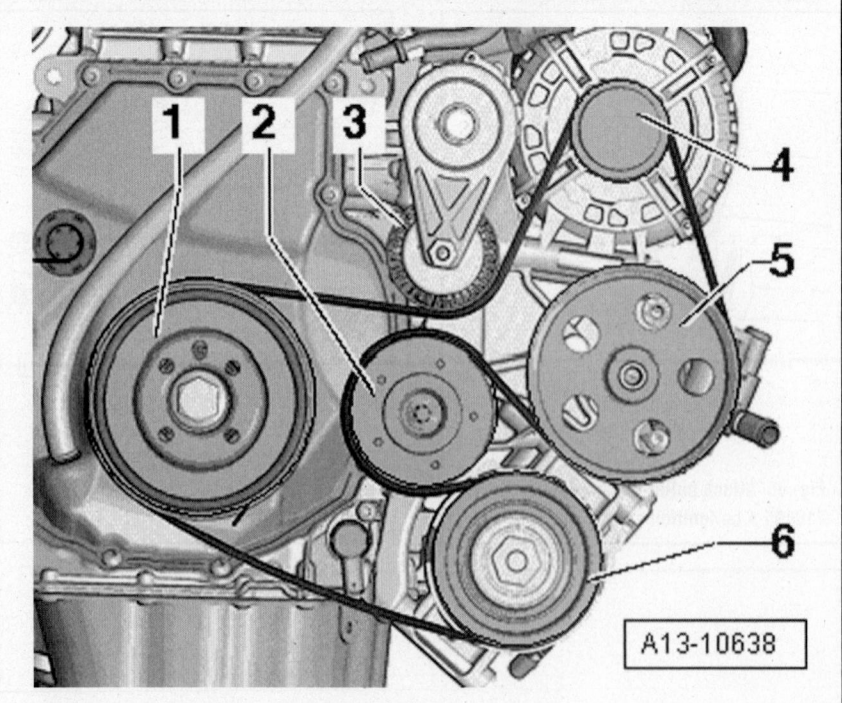

Fig. 90 Accessory drive belt routing: 2.0L Gas Engines

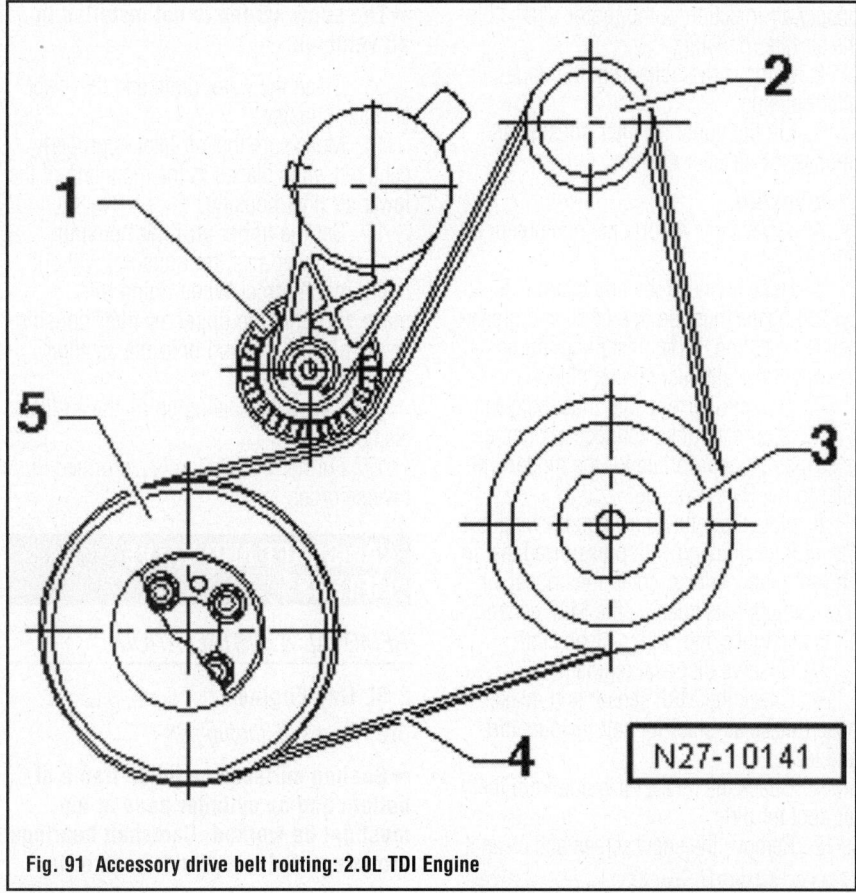

Fig. 91 Accessory drive belt routing: 2.0L TDI Engine

ADJUSTMENT

All models use an automatic (spring powered) tensioner. No adjustment is required.

REMOVAL & INSTALLATION

2.0L Gas Engine

1. Before servicing the vehicle, refer to the precautions.

> ※ **WARNING**
>
> **Risk of destroying due to reversed running direction on a used ribbed belt. Before removing the ribbed belt, mark the running direction with chalk or a felt-tip pen for reinstallation later.**

2. Remove the noise insulation.
3. Remove the right air guide hose.
4. To release the tension on the ribbed belt, turn the tensioner in direction of rotation from underneath.
5. Secure the tensioner with Drift T10060 A.
6. Remove ribbed belt.

To install:

7. Installation is performed in reverse order of removal.

> ※ **WARNING**
>
> **Before installing ribbed belt, generator, A/C compressor must be securely installed.**

8. First mount the ribbed belt on the crankshaft pulley, then on the A/C compressor and generator.
9. Turn the tensioner with a box-end wrench and remove the drift T10060 A.
10. Release the tensioner.
11. Check whether ribbed belt is routed correctly.
12. Start engine and check whether ribbed belt runs correctly.

2.0L TDI Engine

1. Before servicing the vehicle, refer to the precautions.
2. Remove noise insulation.
3. Remove engine cover.
   a. On one piece cover, pull the one piece front engine cover upward with a quick jerk and then pull the lower mount forward.
   b. On the two piece engine cover, first pull the outer cover upward with a quick jerk in the upper illustration, then pull the inner engine cover upward with a quick jerk in lower illustration.

4. To remove fuel filter fuel filter without the retaining plate:
   a. Release the retainers, pull the fuel filter with connected hoses upward and out of the retaining plate and lay it aside.
5. To remove fuel filter with the retaining plate:
   a. Loosen the bolt one turn.
   b. Remove the bolt and the nut.
   c. Lay the fuel filter, with the hoses still connected, to the side.
6. Mark the direction of rotation on the ribbed belt.
7. Pivot tensioner element in the correct direction as to relieve the tension on the ribbed belt.
8. Secure tensioner element using the drift T10060.
9. Remove ribbed belt.

To install:

10. Installation is performed in reverse order.
11. Before installing ribbed belt, make sure that all ancillaries (alternator, air conditioner compressor) are secured tightly.
12. Note previously marked direction of belt rotation and be sure that it is seated correctly on pulley.
13. Set the ribbed belt onto the generator lastly.
14. Start the engine and check the running belt.

AIR CLEANER

REMOVAL & INSTALLATION

2.0L Gas Engine

See Figure 92.

1. Remove the cover for the air guide; disengage the side clips to do so.

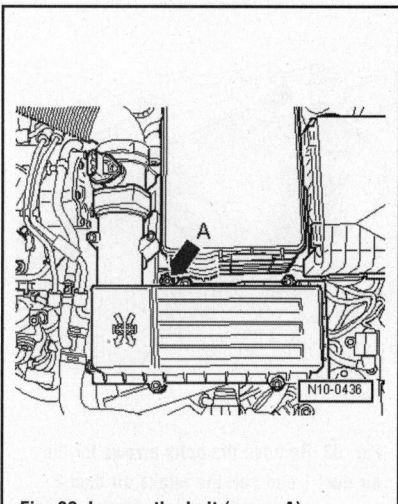

Fig. 92 Loosen the bolt (arrow A)

2. Unclip the lower air guide, disengage the clips to do so.

3. Remove both the lower air guide and the air guide hose.

4. Engine Code CBFA: Disconnect the hose leading to the secondary air injection pump motor V101 from the air filter housing.

5. Loosen the bolt and pull the air filter housing upward out of the bracket.

6. Remove the air filter housing together with the Mass Airflow (MAF) sensor and connecting pipe.

7. Installation is performed in reverse order.

2.0L TDI Diesel Engines

See Figures 93 and 94.

1. Release the tabs arrows and open the cover on the air duct.

2. Remove the bolts arrows for the air duct 1 and pull the intake air duct 2 from the air duct.

3. Press the tabs and remove the intake air duct from the lower air filter housing.

4. Disconnect the connector from the Mass Airflow (MAF) sensor G70 1 and the vacuum line 2.

5. Loosen the threaded connector on the lower air filter housing 3.

6. Open the clamp 4 and remove the intake hose to the turbocharger.

7. Remove the entire air filter housing.

8. Installation is performed in reverse order.

FILTER/ELEMENT REPLACEMENT

See Figure 00.

1. Removing for Engine Code CBFA: Disconnect the hose leading to the sec-ondary air injection pump motor V101 from the air filter housing.

2. Remove the bolts from the upper air filter housing.

3. Lift the upper air filter housing and remove the air filter element.

To install:

4. Always use an original equipment air filter element.

5. Hose connections and charge air system hoses must be free of oil and grease before installing. When installing, do not use any lubricants containing silicone.

6. The air filter housing must be clean.

7. Secure all hose connections using hose clamps appropriate for the model type, refer to the Parts Catalog.

8. Note the following when blowing out the air filter housing with pressurized air: To prevent malfunctions, cover the critical air flow components such as the MAF sensor, air intake tubes, etc. with a clean cloth.

9. Observe disposal regulations!

10. Check the MAF sensor and intake hose (intake air side) for salt residue, dirt, and leaves.

11. Check the intake air guide from the air duct for dirt.

12. Remove the snow screen and clean it.

➡The snow screen is not installed in all vehicles.

13. Clean the water drain and the lower air filter housing.

14. Make sure that air filter is properly centered when placed in the mounting of the lower air filter housing.

15. Set the upper air filter housing onto the lower air filter housing, without using much force. When doing this, make sure that the upper air filter housing is not placed crooked onto the air filter element.

16. Check the sealing lip on the air filter element.

17. Further installation is performed in reverse order.

CAMSHAFT AND VALVE LIFTERS

REMOVAL & INSTALLATION

2.0L Gas Engine

See Figures 95 through 98.

➡Sealing surfaces on guide frame at bottom and on cylinder head at top must not be worked. Camshaft bearings are integrated in cylinder head or in

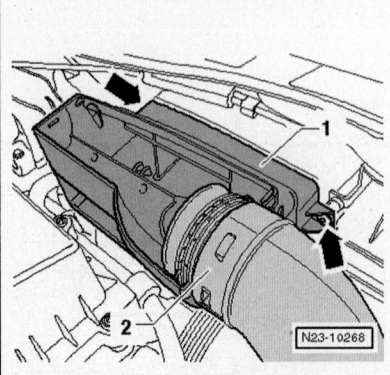

Fig. 93 Remove the bolts arrows for the air duct 1 and pull the intake air duct 2 from the air duct

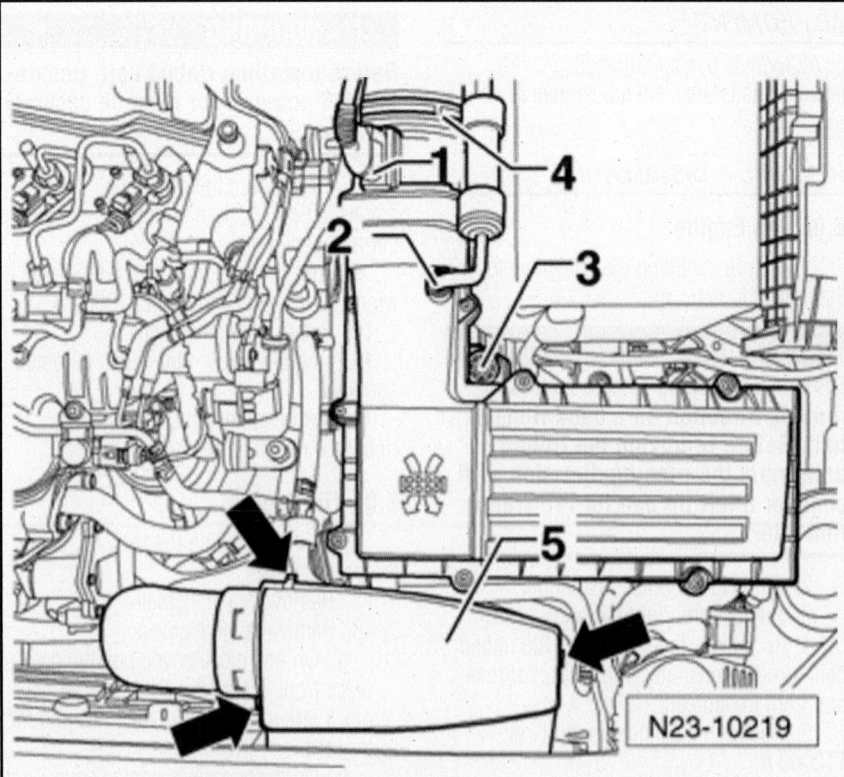

Fig. 94 Connector from the Mass Airflow (MAF) sensor G70 (10 and the vacuum line (2). Lower air filter housing (3) and clamp (4) to the intake hose to the turbocharger

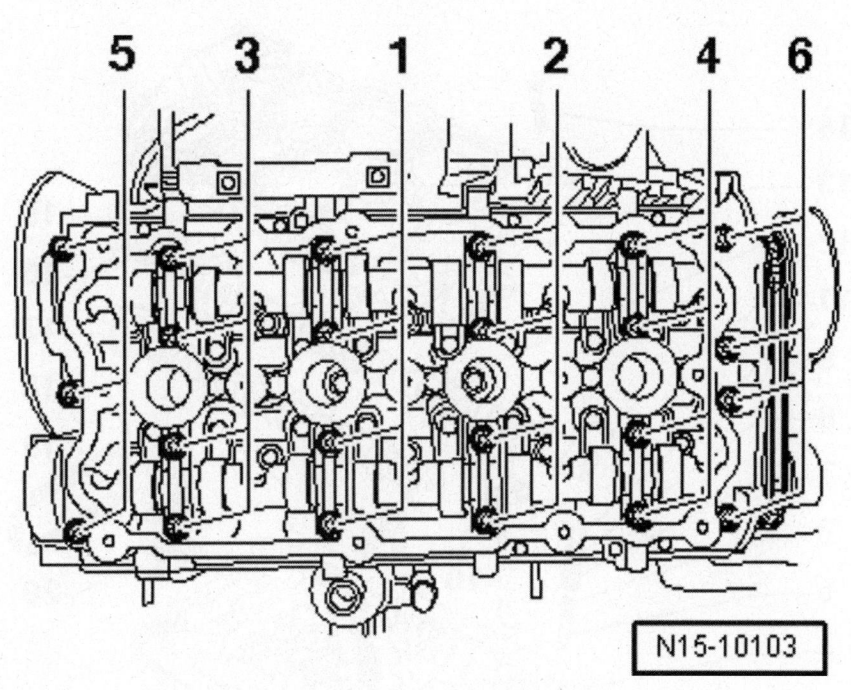

Fig. 95 Remove guide frame bolts in 6 to 1 sequence and carefully remove guide frame

guide frame. Before removing guide frame, tension on toothed belt must be released. If guide frame was loosened, camshaft sealing ring and sealing cap must be replaced.

1. Remove cylinder head cover.
2. Remove the camshaft adjuster.
3. Remove toothed belt.
4. Loosen the camshaft gear with Retainer 3036.
5. Pull off the camshaft gear using puller T40001, claw T40001/6 and claw T40001/7.
6. Remove toothed belt guard at rear of cylinder head.
7. Remove guide frame bolts in **6 to 1** sequence and carefully remove guide frame.
8. Remove the camshafts together with drive chain from cylinder head.
9. Prevent any dirt or adhesive residue from entering the cylinder head.

To install:

➡Sealing surfaces must be completely free of oil and grease. The pistons must not be positioned at TDC. Make sure that all roller cam followers make contact correctly on valve stem ends.

10. Refer to the illustration for torque values.

11. Remove the old sealant from the guide frame groove and from sealing surfaces.
12. Prevent any dirt or adhesive residue from entering the cylinder head. Pay special attention to oil journal surfaces of camshafts.
13. Place the drive chain onto the removed camshaft chain sprockets as follows:
   a. Oil journal surfaces of camshafts.
   b. Cams of cylinder must face each other.
   c. The notches on both camshafts must align.
   d. The side surfaces of the notches must be exactly vertical.
14. Place camshafts together with drive chain in cylinder head and in chain tensioner.
15. Verify TDC position of camshafts again.
   a. Cams of cylinder must face each other.
   b. The notches on both camshafts must align.
   c. The side surfaces of the notches must be exactly perpendicular to the cylinder head.
16. Oil journal surfaces of camshafts.
17. Apply an even, light sealant bead into the clean groove of the guide frame.

➡Sealant must not be applied too thickly. Attaching and bolting the guide frame should be performed without interruption because the sealant begins to harden immediately as soon as it contacts the sealing surfaces. Note the expiration date of the sealing compound.

18. Set the guide frame in place so that it can get by the EGR Vacuum Regulator Solenoid Valve N18.
19. Replace guide frame screws.
20. Gently tighten bolts from inside working toward outside in several stages.

➡Ensure guide frame is not tilted.

21. Check TDC position of camshafts by inserting Camshaft Clamp T10252 as far as stop.

➡Rotate the camshafts back and forth slightly if necessary to insert Camshaft Clamp T10252.

22. If the Camshaft Clamp T10252 cannot be inserted, remove guide frame again and repeat camshaft installation.
23. Remove Camshaft Clamp T10252.
24. Drive in the sealing cap with the thrust piece 3334 approximately 1 to 2 mm deep.

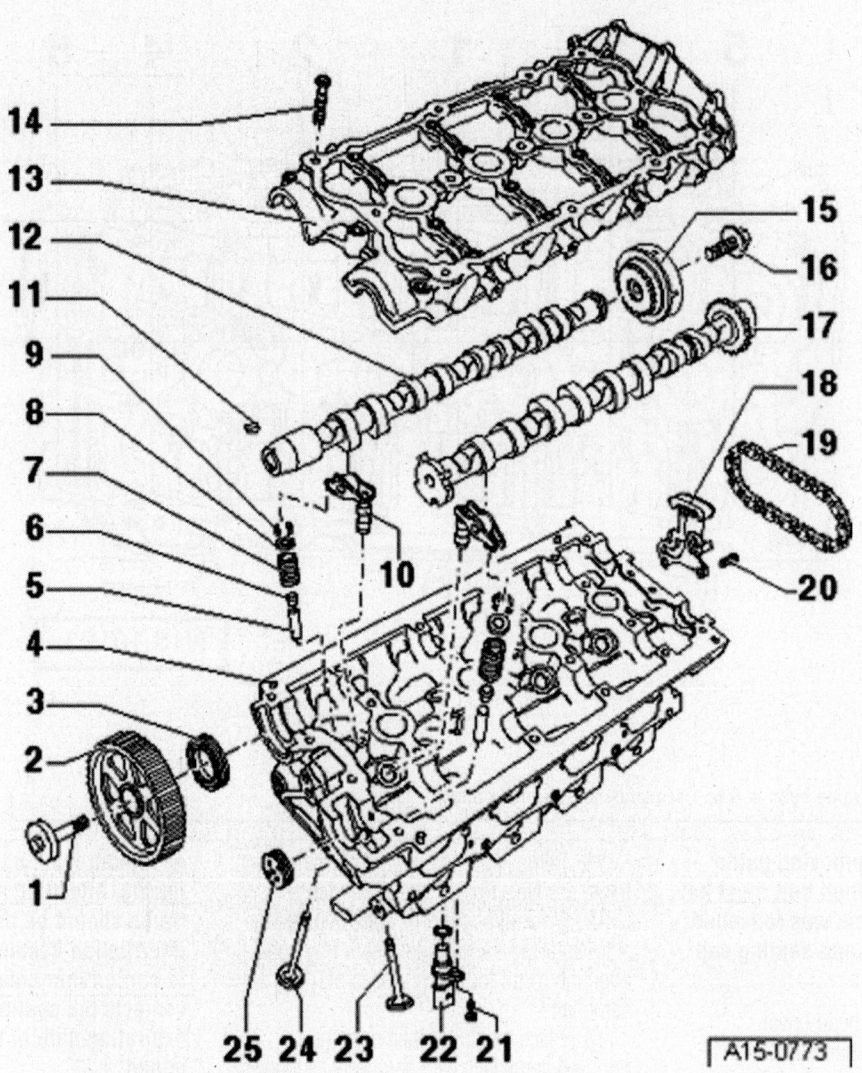

A15-0773

1. **Bolt** [36 ft. lbs. (50 Nm) plus an additional 180° turn further]
2. **Camshaft sprocket**
3. **Seal**
4. **Cylinder Head**
5. **Valve guide**
6. **Valve stem seal**
7. **Valve spring**
8. **Top valve spring retainer**
9. **Valve keepers**
10. **Hydraulic valve play balancing element** (Lubricate contact surface and do not interchange)
11. **Fitted key**
12. **Exhaust camshaft**
13. **Bearing bracket**
14. **Bolt**
15. **Camshaft adjuster**
16. **Bolt** [14 ft. lbs. (20 Nm) plus an additional 45° turn]
17. **Intake camshaft**
18. **Chain tensioner**
19. **Drive chain**
20. **Bolt** [7 ft. lbs. (10 Nm)]
21. **Bolt** [7 ft. lbs. (10 Nm)]
22. **Phase sensor**
23. **Exhaust valve**
24. **Intake valve**
25. **Sealing cap**

Fig. 96 Valve train assembly overview—2.0L Engines

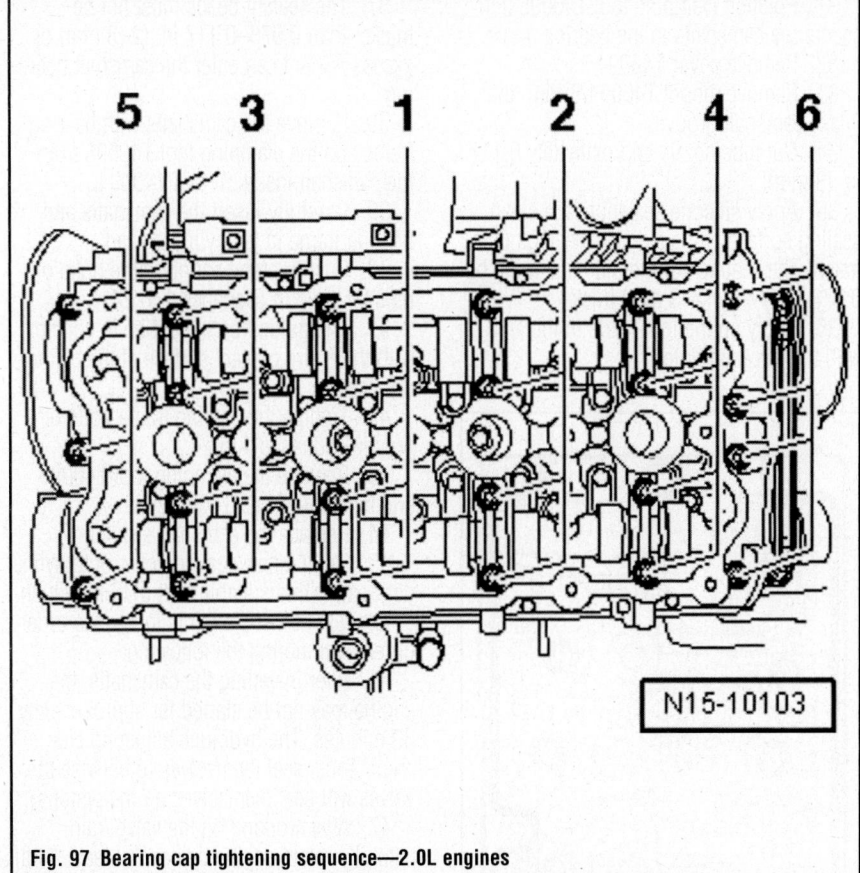

Fig. 97 Bearing cap tightening sequence—2.0L engines

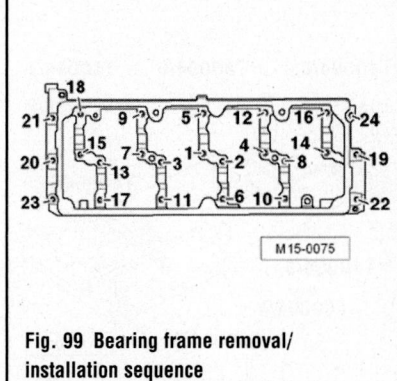

**Fig. 99 Bearing frame removal/
installation sequence**

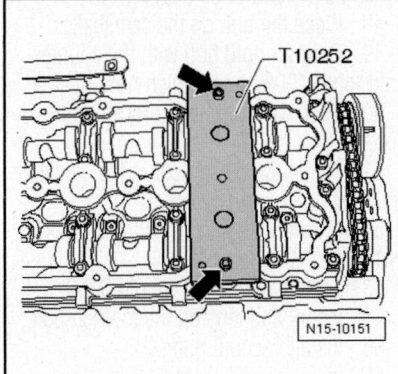

**Fig. 98 Check TDC position of camshafts
by inserting Camshaft Clamp T10252**

25. Install the camshaft sealing ring.
26. Install the rear toothed belt guard.
27. Insert the fitting key into camshaft.
28. Install the camshaft gear. To tighten bolt, hold camshaft gear in place using retainer 3036.
29. When turning camshaft, pistons may not be at TDC for any cylinder. Valves/pistons may be damaged.

30. Be sure fitting keys are properly seated.
31. To complete the installation, reverse the remaining removal procedure.

2.0L TDI Engine

See Figures 99 through 101.

➡**Only remove the plastic protectors installed to protect the open valves immediately before positioning the cylinder head.**

➡**When replacing the cylinder head or cylinder head gasket, the coolant must be completely replaced.**

➡**Cylinder heads with cracks between the valve seats can continue to be used without reducing service life, as long as the tears have a maximum width of 0.0195 in. (0.5 mm).**

➡**After installing the camshafts, the engine may not be started for approximately 30 minutes. The hydraulic adjusting elements must seat themselves (otherwise the valves will seat themselves on the pistons).**

➡**After working on the valve train and lifters, carefully rotate the crankshaft by hand at least 2 full revolutions**

before starting to be sure that valves do not strike the pistons.

Always replace gaskets and seals.
1. Before servicing the vehicle, refer to the precautions.
2. Remove toothed belt from the camshaft and high pressure fuel pump.
3. Remove cylinder head cover.
4. Remove bolts for camshaft sprocket.
5. Remove camshaft sprocket from the hub.
6. Counter hold hub with the counter hold tool T10051 and loosen hub bolt.
7. Remove bolt for hub by approximately 2 turns.
8. Position puller T10052 and align it to the bores in the hub.
9. Tighten mounting bolts.
10. Tension hub by tightening puller T10052 evenly until it can be removed from the camshaft taper.
11. Hold puller T10052 with a 30 mm wrench.
12. Remove hub from the cone of the camshaft.
13. Remove vacuum pump Vacuum Pump.
14. Remove bearing frame bolts or nuts in the sequence 24 to 1.
15. Remove bearing frame.
16. Carefully remove camshafts.

To install:
17. Seal separating surfaces between the bearing frame and cylinder head with silicone adhesive sealant D 176 501 A1.

❋❋ WARNING

Only install the camshafts with the camshaft insertion tool T40094 as described below. Otherwise the axial bearing in the bearing frame will be destroyed and the cylinder head will have to be replaced. Make sure that no sealant residue enters the cylinder head and bearings.

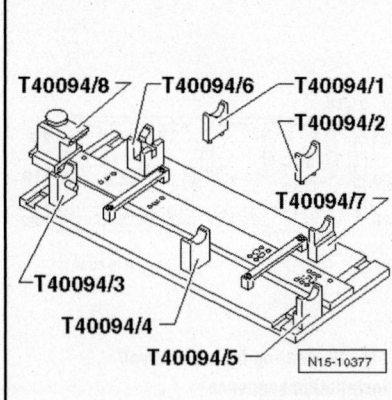

Fig. 100 Only install the camshafts with the camshaft insertion tool T40094 as described below

18. Using rotating plastic brush, remove any remaining sealant from cylinder head and guide frame.

19. Clean sealing surfaces, they must be free of oil and grease.

20. Oil journal surfaces of camshafts.

21. Assemble camshaft insertion tool T40094 as follows:

    a. Remove mounts T40094/3, T40094/4 and T40094/5 from base plate. Loosen threaded connections from below.

    b. If the mounts on the camshaft insertion tool T40094 are not marked, mark the removed mounts, for example with numbers, to ensure it can be assembled later.

    c. Install mounts T40094/9 and T40094/10 in the empty outer locations.

    d. Position mount T40094/2 on location "A" and mount T40094/1 on location "F".

22. Insert the intake camshaft first. Make sure the indentation for the cylinder head bolt faces "outward".

23. Position 0.0195 in. (0.50 mm) feeler gauge and slide the mount T40094/8 into groove on the intake camshaft.

24. Insert exhaust camshaft.

25. Secure exhaust camshaft at its groove with cover T40094/11.

26. Position the tensioning tool T40096/1 on the exhaust camshaft sprockets.

27. Tighten tensioning tool T40096/1 with thumb wheel until the tooth faces align. Use a 13 mm open end wrench if necessary.

28. Slide the intake camshaft toward the exhaust camshaft until the splines engage.

29. Position the bearing frame on the camshafts.

30. All the camshaft bearings must lie on the camshafts.

31. Position clamping tool T40095 and secure the camshafts in the bearing frame.

32. Remove cover T40094/11.

33. Remove mount T40094/8 from the intake camshaft groove.

34. Cut tube nozzle approximately 0.117 in. (3 mm).

35. Apply silicone sealant to the clean sealing surface of the cylinder head as illustrated. The sealing compound bead must be 0.078–0.117 in. (2–3 mm) thick

36. Apply on the inner side in the area with the threaded holes

Fig. 101 Apply silicone sealant to the clean sealing surface of the cylinder head as illustrated. The sealing compound bead must be 0.078–0.117 in. (2–3 mm) thick

37. The sealant beads must not be thicker than 0.078–0.117 in. (2–3 mm) or excess sealant can enter the camshaft bearing.

38. Remove the camshafts with bearing frame and the clamping tool T40095 from the camshaft insertion tool T40094.

39. Carefully insert the camshafts and bearing frame in the cylinder head.

40. First tighten bearing frame bolts or nuts by hand in sequence 1 to 24.

41. The guide frame must be in contact with the entire contact surface of the cylinder head.

42. Tighten the bearing frame bolts or nuts in sequence 1 to 24.

43. Remove the clamping tool T40095 and tensioning tool T40096/1.

44. Replace the camshaft seal.

45. Drive a new sealing cover onto cylinder head with a suitable drift until it is flush.

The rest of installation is in reverse order of removal, noting the following:

46. After installing the camshafts, the engine may not be started for approximately 30 minutes. The hydraulic adjusting elements must seat themselves (otherwise the valves will seat themselves on the pistons).

47. After working on the valve train, carefully rotate engine by hand at least 2 full revolutions to ensure that valves do not strike the pistons when starting.

48. Place the hub on the camshaft.

49. Counter hold hub with the counter hold tool T10051 and tighten hub bolt.

50. Push the camshaft sprocket onto hub.

51. The toothed segment of the camshaft sprocket must face upward.

52. Install bolts into camshaft sprocket by hand to eliminate play.

53. Lock the hub with rig pin 3359.

54. Install and tension the toothed belt.

55. Install vacuum pump.

56. Install cylinder head cover.

CATALYTIC CONVERTER

REMOVAL & INSTALLATION

A3 Models

See Figure 102.

1. Before servicing the vehicle, refer to the Precautions section.

2. Disconnect the electrical connector.

3. Disconnect the intake tube using spring type pliers.

4. Remove the engine cover with the air filter.

5. Disconnect the HO2S electrical connector.

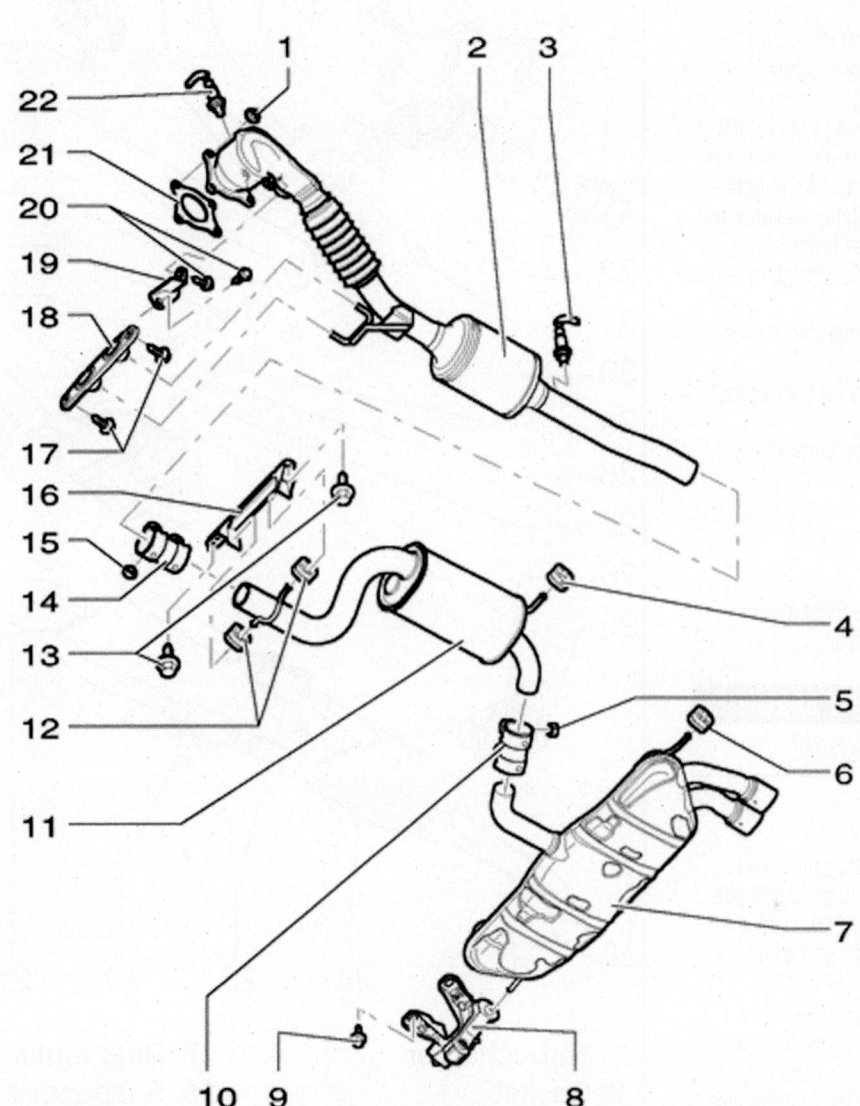

1. Nut
2. Catalytic converter
3. O2 sensor
4. Retaining loop
5. Nut
6. Retaining loop
7. Rear muffler
8. Suspended mount
9. Bolt
10. Rear clamping sleeve
11. Center muffler
12. Retaining loop
13. Screw
14. Front clamping sleeve
15. Nut
16. Suspended mount
17. Screws
18. Suspended mount
19. Support
20. Screws
21. Gasket
22. HO2S and O2S

41311_AUDI_G0083

Fig. 102 Exploded view of the exhaust and catalytic converter components—2.0L Engines

6. Remove the accessible nuts for the front exhaust pipe/turbocharger from above.

7. Remove the right cover for the vehicle floor.

8. Pull off the electrical connector for the O2S behind the three way catalytic converter to free up the wiring.

9. Remove the remaining nuts for the front exhaust pipe/turbocharger from below.

10. Remove the supports for the front exhaust pipe with the catalytic converter by unscrewing the bracket and bolts.

11. Disconnect the exhaust system at the clamping sleeve.

12. Remove the cross member for the vehicle floor.

13. Remove the bracket for the exhaust system.

14. Remove the catalytic converter with the front exhaust pipe.

A4 & A5 Models

See Figure 103.

Refer to the appropriate illustration to remove the catalytic converter.

CRANKSHAFT FRONT SEAL

REMOVAL & INSTALLATION

See Figures 104 and 105.

1. Remove ribbed belt.
2. Remove the accessory drive belt.
3. Loosen crankshaft toothed belt gear. To do this, lock toothed belt sprocket with counter support 3415. Refer to Timing Chain in this section.
4. Remove crankshaft-toothed belt sprocket center bolt and remove toothed belt sprocket.
5. Remove diamond disc from toothed belt gear.
6. To guide seal puller, thread center bolt into crankshaft by hand until stop.
7. Remove inner part of Seal Remover 3203 nine rotations (approximately 20 mm) from outer part and secure with knurled-head screw.
8. Grease threaded head of Seal Remover 3203, position and screw into oil seal as far as possible with forceful pressure.
9. Loosen knurled screw and turn inner portion against crankshaft until the oil seal is pulled out.
10. Secure seal remover in a vise at the flat spots. Remove seal using pliers.

To install:

11. Clean running and sealing surface.
12. Before installing, remove oil remains from end of crankshaft with a clean cloth.

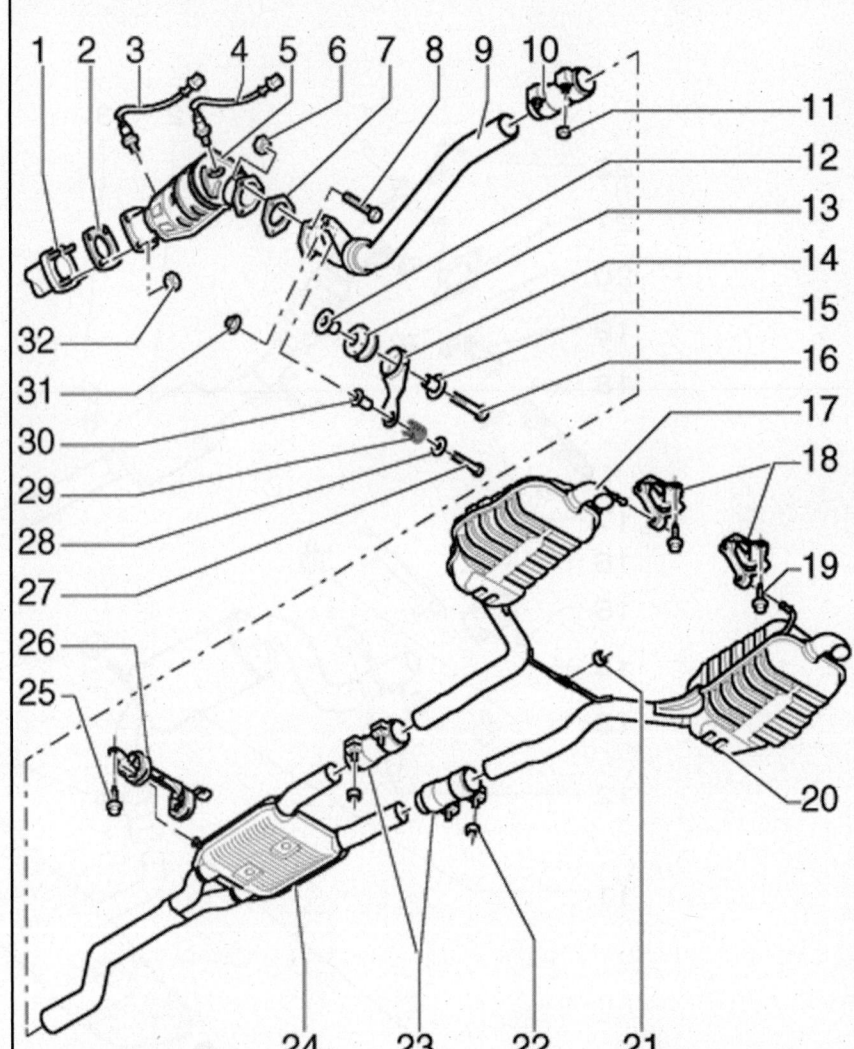

1. Turbocharger	17. Rear muffler
2. Gasket	18. Suspended mountings
3. HO2S (G39)	19. Bolt
4. O2S (G130)	20. Rear muffler
5. Catalytic converter	21. Nut
6. Nut	22. Nut
7. Gasket	23. Rear clamping sleeves
8. Bolt	24. Center muffler
9. Front exhaust pipe	25. Bolt
10. Front clamping sleeve	26. Suspended mount
11. Nut	27. Bolt
12. Spacer sleeve	28. Washer
13. Buffer	29. Spring
14. Tongue	30. Spacing sleeve
15. Spacer sleeve	31. Nut
16. Bolt	32. Nut

41311_AUDI_G0086

Fig. 103 Exploded view of the exhaust and catalytic converter components—2.0L Engines

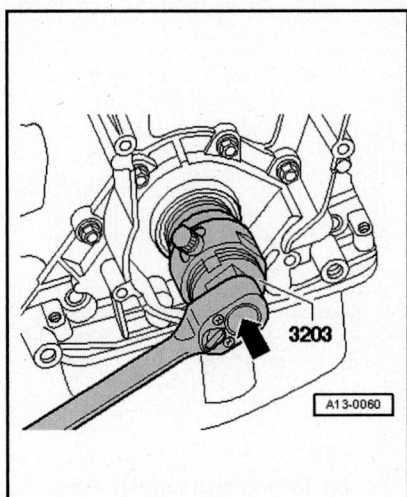

Fig. 104 Removing the crankshaft front seal—2.0L Engines

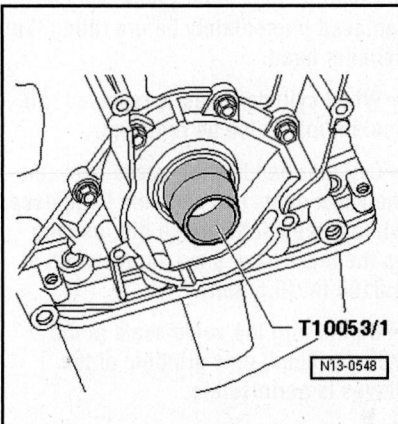

Fig. 105 Position guide sleeve T10053/1 of assembly tool T10053 on end of crankshaft

13. Position guide sleeve T10053/1 of assembly tool T10053 on end of crankshaft.

14. Slide oil seal over guide sleeve onto the crankshaft pin.

15. Press in seal using center bolt of toothed belt sprocket and pressure sleeve of assembly tool T10053 until it is flush.

16. Install crankshaft toothed belt gear with new diamond disc and new center bolt.

➡**Contact surface between toothed belt gear, diamond disc and crankshaft must be free of oil. Do not oil the bolt for crankshaft toothed belt sprocket.**

17. Use counter support 3415 to tighten crankshaft toothed belt gear.

18. Install toothed belt.

19. Install ribbed belt.

CYLINDER HEAD

REMOVAL & INSTALLATION

2.0L Gas Engine

See Figures 106 through 110.

1. Before servicing the vehicle, refer to the precautions section.

2. Disconnect the electrical connector.

3. Remove the engine cover upward and out in direction of

4. Remove the coolant expansion tank cap.

5. Remove the center sound insulation fasteners.

6. Remove the right sound insulation fasteners.

7. Drain and recycle the coolant.

8. Remove the wiper arms.

9. Unclip spray nozzles and push spray nozzles, with lines still attached, back through opening and into plenum chamber.

10. Remove the rubber seal for plenum chamber cover.

11. Remove the plenum chamber cover.

12. Loosen up the rear engine wiring harness at partition for plenum chamber.

13. Remove the electrical connector for oxygen sensor before catalytic converter from bracket, disconnect it and lay it aside.

14. Remove the partition for plenum chamber.

15. Disconnect the coolant line to coolant expansion tank.

16. Disconnect the coolant hose.

17. Disconnect the coolant hose.

18. Unscrew the ground wire.

19. Disconnect the electrical connector.

20. Disconnect the coolant hoses.

21. Remove the intake manifold

22. Remove the catalytic converter with front exhaust pipe

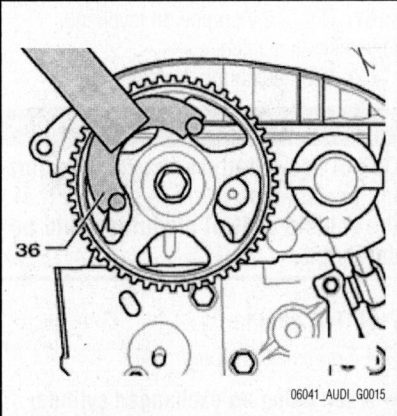

Fig. 106 Loosen the bolt for camshaft sprocket using retainer 3036—A3 with 2.0L engine

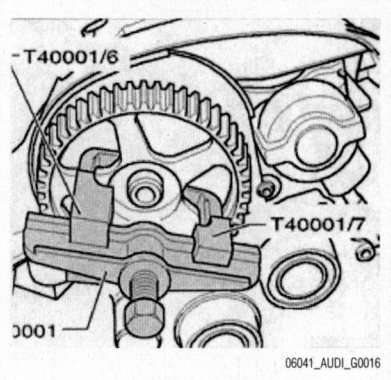

Fig. 107 Pull off camshaft sprocket using two-arm puller T40001 and claws T40001/6 and T40001/7—A3 with 2.0L engine

23. Remove the right driveshaft

24. Remove the heat shield for right driveshaft

25. Pull air duct off from charge air cooler.

26. Unfasten the air duct from turbocharger.

27. Disconnect the connector and loosen up cable.

28. Unscrew bolts and remove air duct.

29. Disconnect the oil supply line for turbocharger at cylinder block.

30. Remove the oil supply line for turbocharger.

31. Disconnect the coolant supply line for turbocharger at cylinder block.

32. Unscrew the coolant supply line to turbocharger.

33. Remove the coolant supply line for turbocharger at cylinder block.

34. Remove the oil return line at turbocharger.

35. Remove the bolts and remove turbocharger support.

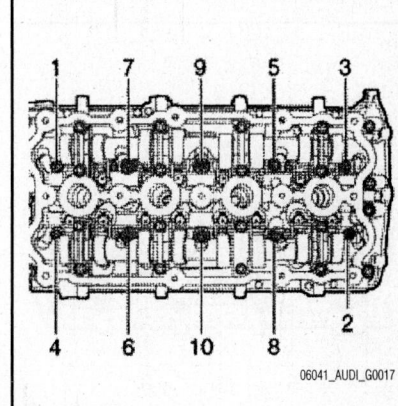

Fig. 108 Cylinder head bolt loosening sequence—A3 with 2.0L engine

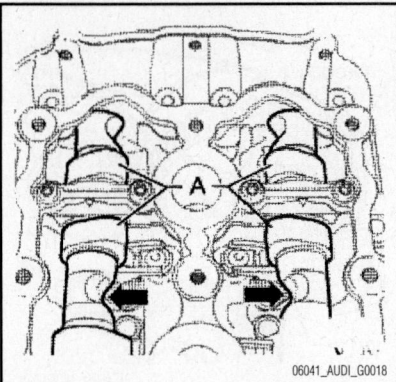

Fig. 109 Move marking on the camshaft sprocket so that it is across from the marking on the timing belt cover. The notches of camshafts should now face toward each other vertically—A3 with 2.0L engine

36. Remove the timing belt.

37. Loosen the bolt for camshaft sprocket using retainer 3036.

38. Pull off the camshaft sprocket using two-arm puller T40001 and claws T40001/6 and T40001/7.

39. Remove the rear the timing belt housing from cylinder head.

40. Remove the cylinder head cover.

41. Loosen the cylinder head bolts in the sequence illustrated.

➡Verify that all hose and line connections between engine, transmission and body have been disconnected.

42. Remove the cylinder head.

To install:

➡Use new cylinder head bolts.

43. Always replace self-locking nuts, bolts that have been tightened to tightening torque as well as gaskets and O-rings.

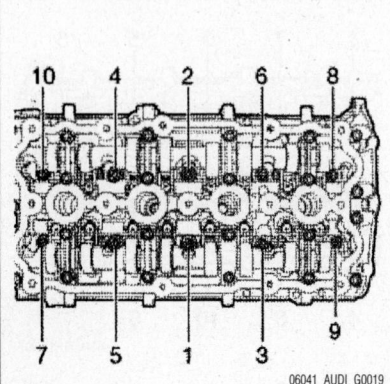

Fig. 110 Cylinder head bolt tightening sequence—A3 with 2.0L engine

44. Clean all gasket mating surfaces.

45. Only unpack new cylinder head gasket immediately prior to installation. Handle gasket carefully. Damages to the silicone layer and in areas of recesses may result in leaks.

46. There must be no oil or coolant in the blind holes for the cylinder head bolts in the cylinder block.

High-temperature lubricant Parts Catalog

➡Only turn over the engine at the crankshaft in direction of engine rotation (clockwise) using the crankshaft bolt.

47. Move marking on the camshaft sprocket so that it is across from the marking on the timing belt cover. The notches of camshafts should now face toward each other vertically.

48. If the crankshaft was turned in the meantime: set cyl1 to TDC and turn crankshaft back again slightly.

49. Set the cylinder head gasket in place.

50. Pay attention to the centering pins in the cylinder block.

51. Observe the installed position of the cylinder head gasket marking. The replacement part numbers must be legible from the intake side.

52. Install the cylinder head in place.

53. Insert cylinder head bolts and tighten by hand.

54. Tighten the cylinder head in the sequence illustrated as follows:

  a. Step 1: tighten to 30 ft. lbs. (40 Nm)

  b. Step 2: tighten and additional 180 degrees.

55. Install the cylinder head cover and tighten to 7 ft. lbs. (10 Nm).

56. Install the wiper arms.

57. Install the timing belt.

58. Install the accessory drive belt.

59. Install the intake manifold.

60. Connect the negative battery cable.

61. Check the engine oil level and replenish as needed.

62. Fill the cooling system.

✲✲ CAUTION

Do not use a battery charger for starting assistance! There is the risk that the vehicle control modules could be damaged.

2.0L TDI Engine

See Figures 111 through 113.

➡When using an exchanged cylinder head with camshaft installed, the contact surfaces between the lifters and cam lobes must be lubricated before installing the cylinder head cover.

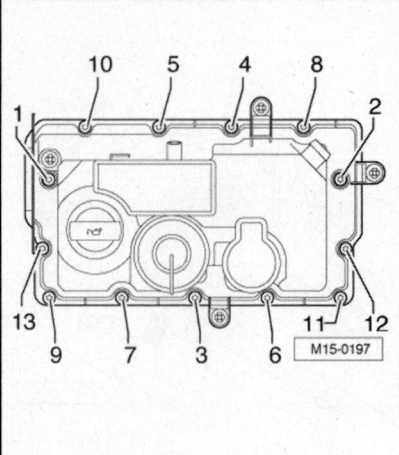

Fig. 111 Cylinder head cover loosening/ tightening sequence

➡The plastic protectors installed to protect the open valves must only be removed immediately before fitting the cylinder head.

➡When cylinder head is replaced, all coolant must also be replaced.

➡Cylinder heads with cracks between the valve seats can continue to be used without reducing service life, as long as the tears have a maximum width of 0.0195 in. (0.5 mm).

➡Do not mill the valve seats in the cylinder head; only grinding of the valves is permissible.

➡After installing the camshafts, the engine may not be started for approximately 30 minutes. The hydraulic equalization elements must seat themselves (otherwise the valves will crash into the pistons).

➡After working on the valve train and lifters, carefully rotate the crankshaft by hand at least 2 full revolutions before starting to be sure that valves do not strike the pistons.

➡Always replace gaskets and seals.

➡All cable ties which are opened or cut open when removing cylinder head, must be replaced in the same position when installing cylinder head.

✲✲ WARNING

When doing any repair work, especially in the engine compartment, pay attention to the following due to clearance issues. Route lines of all types (e.g. for fuel, hydraulic, coolant and refrigerant, brake fluid, vacuum) and electrical wiring so that

the original path is followed. Ensure sufficient clearance to all moving or hot components.

1. Before servicing the vehicle, refer to the precautions.

2. Before removing the cylinder head, extract the fuel with the hand vacuum pump and the draining container V.A.G 1390/1Tandem Pump.

3. Turn the ignition and all electrical consumers off and remove the ignition key.

4. Remove engine cover.

   a. On one piece engine cover. Pull the one piece front engine cover upward with a quick jerk and then pull the lower mount forward.

   b. On two piece engine cover, first pull the outer cover upward with a quick jerk in the upper illustration, then pull the inner engine cover upward with a quick jerk in lower illustration.

5. Remove plenum chamber bulkhead.

6. Disconnect the connector on the Mass Air Flow (MAF) sensor G70.

7. Disconnect the ventilation hose and disengage it from the bracket.

8. Open the spring-type clip3 using spring-type clip pliers VAS 5024A and disconnect the intake hose from the Mass Air Flow (MAF) sensor G70.

9. Disconnect the intake manifold from the air guide.

10. Unfasten bolt and remove air filter housing and mass air flow sensor.

11. Remove noise insulation.

12. Drain the coolant.

13. For safety reasons, pull the connector off the fuel delivery unit.

14. Disconnect the fuel supply and return lines, as well as the coolant line on the cylinder head.

15. Before removing the cylinder head, extract the fuel with the diesel extractor VAS 5226 or the hand vacuum pump and the breather reservoir V.A.G 1390/1 to the tandem pump Tandem Pump.

16. On fuel filter without the retaining plate, release the clips and remove the fuel filter with the hoses still connected from the retaining plate.

17. On fuel filter with the retaining plate

   a. Loosen the bolt one turn.

   b. Remove the bolt and the nut.

   c. Remove the fuel filter with the hoses still connected.

18. Remove the front exhaust pipe.

19. Remove the turbocharger support and the oil return from the turbocharger.

20. Remove the oil supply line and lay the oil supply line off to the side.

21. Remove toothed belt.

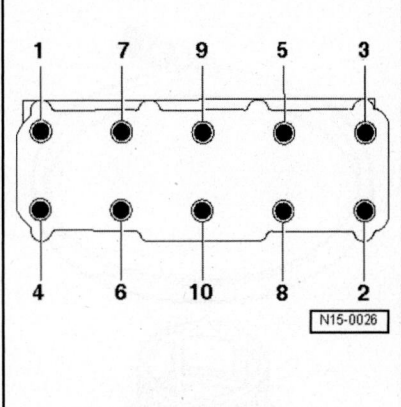

Fig. 112 Cylinder head loosening sequence

22. Remove the toothed belt tensioning roller.

23. Remove the hub for camshaft sprocket Camshaft.

24. Remove the bolts for the rear toothed belt guard.

25. Remove the Camshaft Position (CMP) sensor G40.

26. Remove the connecting pipe for exhaust gas recirculation.

27. Pull off/disconnect all remaining electrical wires required from cylinder head and set aside.

28. Disconnect all connections, coolant lines, vacuum hoses and intake hoses from the cylinder head.

29. Remove cylinder head cover.

30. Follow the sequence when loosening the cylinder head bolts.

31. Lift the cylinder head slightly and then remove it from the engine sideways, past the toothed belt guard.

32. The cylinder head must be carefully guided to prevent damages.

   Installing

33. Always replace cylinder head bolts.

34. Carefully remove residual sealant from cylinder head and cylinder block. Make sure that no long scrapes or scratches result. When using sand paper, grit must not be below 100.

35. Carefully remove all grinding and sanding residue.

36. Only unpack new cylinder head gasket immediately prior to installation.

37. Handle gasket carefully. Damages to the silicone layer and in areas of recesses may result in leaks.

38. Before installing cylinder head, position crankshaft to TDC marking.

39. Turn the crankshaft in opposite direction of engine rotation until all pistons are positioned almost evenly below TDC.

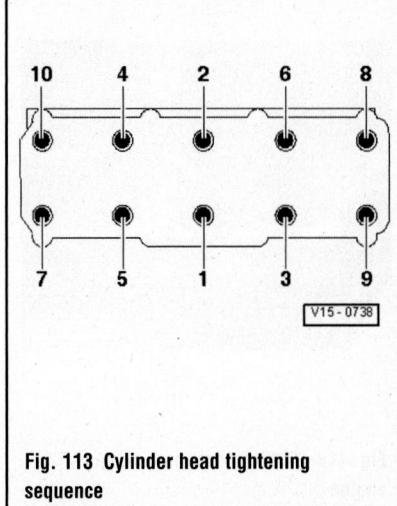

Fig. 113 Cylinder head tightening sequence

40. Position the cylinder head gasket.

✳✳ **WARNING**

Observe the cylinder head gasket identification.

41. Set cylinder head in place and tighten all cylinder head bolts hand tight.

42. Fasten the cylinder head in four steps according to the indicated tightening sequence.

   • Tighten to 26 ft. lbs. (35 Nm)
   • Tighten to 44 ft. lbs. (60 Nm)
   • Tighten 90° additional rotation.
   • Tighten 90° additional rotation.

43. There is no requirement to retighten the cylinder head bolts after repairs.

Further installation is performed in reverse order. When doing this note the following:

44. After fastening the cylinder head turn the camshaft sprocket so that the lobes for cylinder 1 point upward equally. Before installing the toothed belt, turn the crankshaft in engine rotation direction to TDC Toothed Belt.

45. Install the hub for camshaft sprocket.

46. Install toothed belt.

47. Install ribbed belt.

48. Install oil supply line.

49. Install noise insulation.

50. Install the plenum chamber bulkhead.

51. Fill with coolant.

52. Perform a test drive and afterwards check the fault memory Engine Control Module DTC Memory, Checking and Erasing.

ENGINE OIL & FILTER

REPLACEMENT

2.0L Gas Engine

See Figure 114.

1. Remove the noise insulation.

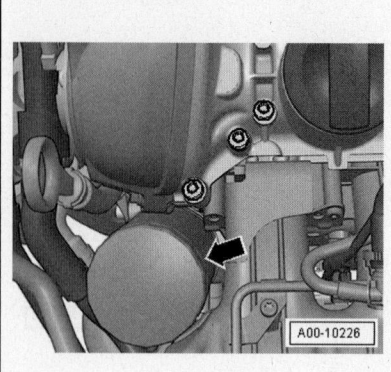

Fig. 114 Oil filter location 2.0L gas engine

2. Loosen oil filter and remove it.

3. Open oil drain plug or extract engine oil.

4. Clean oil filter sealing surface on engine. Lubricate rubber seal lightly with oil.

5. Install new filter and tighten.

6. Install oil drain plug with new gasket and tighten to 22 ft. lbs. (30 Nm)

7. Fill the engine with oil.

➡ Observe waste disposal regulations!

2.0L TDI Engine

See Figure 115.

1. To drain oil, remove noise insulation on drain plug.

2. Loosen the cap before draining/extracting, so that the engine oil can run out of the oil filter housing.

3. Open oil drain plug or extract engine oil.

4. Replace O-rings and oil filter insert.

5. Tighten cap with Socket AF 36.

6. Install oil drain plug with new gasket and tighten to 22 ft. lbs. (30 Nm)

7. Fill the engine with oil.

➡ Observe waste disposal regulations!

EXHAUST MANIFOLD

REMOVAL & INSTALLATION

2.0L Gas Engine

See Figure 116.

1. Before servicing the vehicle, refer to the precautions.

❊❊ WARNING

If mechanical damage is found on exhaust turbocharger, e.g. a destroyed compression wheel, it is

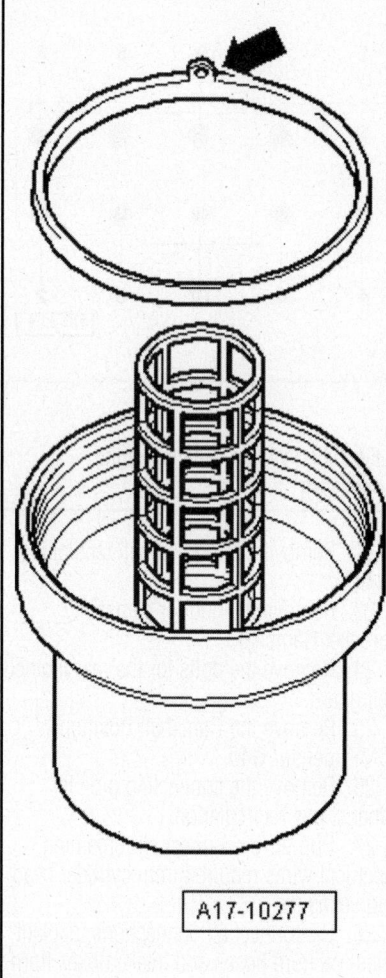

Fig. 115 Position of service flag on sealing ring (see arrow)

not enough to just replace the turbocharger. Perform the following steps to prevent subsequent damage. Check the air filter housing, the air filter insert and the intake hoses for contamination. Check entire charge air circuit and cooler for contamination. If contaminants are found in charge air circuit, circuit must be cleaned and cooler replaced if necessary.

2. Remove the air filter.

3. Remove the battery and battery tray.

4. Remove noise insulation.

5. Remove the front part of the right wheel housing liner and/or the front right wheel housing liner.

6. Drain the coolant.

7. Remove catalytic converters with front exhaust pipe.

8. Remove bolts.

9. Remove the air guide pipe by lifting the clamps items.

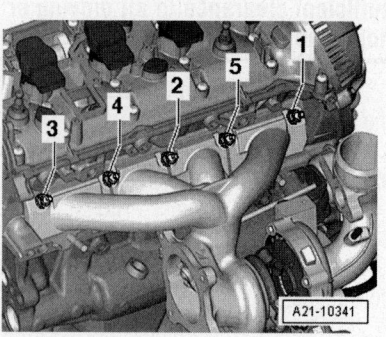

Fig. 116 Observe tightening sequence for exhaust manifold/turbocharger to the cylinder head

10. On vehicles with all-wheel drive remove the heat shield above the right driveshaft.

11. Disconnect electrical connectors and free up electrical wire.

12. On vehicles with auxiliary heater remove the bolts and swivel the coolant tubs to the left.

13. On vehicles with front wheel drive remove the right driveshaft heat shield.

14. Remove the bolt Socket XZN 10 T10154.

15. Remove the bolt.

16. Remove the banjo bolt and move the coolant line to the side.

17. On vehicles with front wheel drive remove the bolts on the oil return line.

18. On vehicles with all-wheel drive remove the oil return line bolts on the crankcase.

19. Remove the bolt on the oil supply line.

20. Remove engine cover.

21. Disconnect the connectors from the ignition coils and the wiring harness and lay them aside.

22. Disconnect the coolant line to the coolant reservoir.

23. Disconnect the vacuum line at the separating point and free up the wire.

24. Remove the coolant hoses from the coolant pipe.

25. Press the release buttons, remove the air guide hose and move them to the side.

26. Remove the air guide pipe bolt.

27. Remove the air guide pipe; to do this, loosen the hose clamp.

28. Remove the air guide pipe bolt.

29. Loose the hose clamp and lay the air guide pipe on the cylinder head.

30. Seal the turbocharger with the Engine bung set VAS 6122.

31. Remove the bolts and remove the heat shield together with the coolant pipe.

32. On 2.0L engines, remove the bolt from the heat shield with a 6 mm hex socket. The hex socket must be at least 5 cm long. A socket that is 6 mm at the tip is too wide.

33. Disconnect the oil supply line from the turbocharger.

34. Disconnect the coolant hose and move it to the side.

35. Remove the nuts.

36. Remove the turbocharger/exhaust manifold upward.

To install:

37. Installation is performed in the reverse order of removal, noting the following:

38. Always replace seals, gaskets and self-locking nuts.

39. Add oil to turbocharger through oil feed line connecting piece.

40. After installing turbocharger, let engine idle for approximately 1 minute to ensure adequate oil supply to the turbocharger.

41. Coolant return line must be installed together with turbocharger.

42. Hose connections and charge air system hoses must be free of oil and grease before installing. Sealing ring and sealing surfaces must only be lightly oiled with connector couplings.

43. Secure all hose connections using hose clamps appropriate for the model type.

44. Exhaust manifold/turbocharger to the cylinder head

- Tighten the bolts 1 through 5 in 4 stages as follows:
- Tighten the bolts to 44 inch lbs. (5 Nm)
- Tighten the bolts to 106 inch lbs. (12 Nm)
- Tighten the bolts to 12 ft. lbs. (16 Nm)
- Tighten the bolts to 19 ft. lbs. (25 Nm)

45. Tighten bolts/nuts to specification as follows:

- Oil supply line to exhaust turbocharger: 15 ft. lbs. (20 Nm) plus 45° additional rotations
- Oil return line to exhaust turbocharger: 80 inch lbs. (9 Nm)
- Coolant supply line to turbocharger: 15 ft. lbs. (20 Nm) plus 45° additional rotations
- Turbocharger bracket to cylinder block: 22 ft. lbs. (30 Nm)
- Turbocharger bracket to turbocharger: 22 ft. lbs. (30 Nm)

- Right charge air pipe to oil pan: 89 inch. lbs. (10 Nm)
- Heat shield to cylinder head (replace nuts and use hot bolt paste) M8 and M12: 15 ft. lbs. (20 Nm)

2.0L TDI Engine

1. Before servicing the vehicle, refer to the precautions.

❋❋ WARNING

If mechanical damage was found on the turbocharger, for example a destroyed compression wheel, just replacing the turbocharger is not enough. Perform the following steps to prevent subsequent damage. Check the air filter housing, the air filter insert and the intake hoses for contamination.

2. Remove particulate filter with NOx reduction catalytic converter.

3. Mark installation position of the exhaust gas temperature sensor and remove it.

4. Remove control wire between the exhaust gas recirculation housing and the exhaust pressure sensor.

5. Remove housing with the exhaust gas recirculation cooler.

6. Disconnect connector from the charge pressure actuator position sensor G581 at the turbocharger vacuum diaphragm.

7. Disconnect vacuum hose at the turbocharger vacuum diaphragm.

8. Disconnect "black" connector for the exhaust gas temperature sensor 1 G235 at the engine bulkhead.

9. Guide line out of the retainers on the engine bulkhead and the turbocharger.

10. Remove the connecting pipe.

11. Remove oil supply line.

12. Remove the banjo bolt from the turbocharger support.

13. Remove hex stud bolt from the turbocharger support.

14. Rotate the lower section of the support 90° and remove the support downward from the upper section.

15. Remove heat shield on the exhaust manifold.

16. Remove exhaust manifold nuts.

17. Remove turbocharger with the exhaust manifold, from the cylinder head and rotate it so the intake side faces down. Remove the turbocharger with the exhaust manifold downward.

To install:

❋❋ WARNING

Before installing, check if the oil return pipe decoupling element is bent and therefore stretched. If that is the case, tiny cracks can form that can lead to leaks. Replace the oil return pipe before installing the turbocharger if necessary.

18. Installation is in the reverse order of removal.

19. Always replace the self-locking nuts, seals, gaskets and clamps.

20. Insert the turbocharger with the pressure side upward.

21. Position charge air pipe connecting hose before securing the turbocharger.

➡ Note the exhaust gas temperature sensor 1 installation position.

22. Replace the banjo bolt with the turbocharger support gaskets and oil return pipe O-rings.

23. Do not stretch the oil return pipe decoupling element when installing the turbocharger support.

24. Tighten bolts/nuts to specification as follows:

- Turbocharger with exhaust manifold (Replace): 17 ft. lbs. (23 Nm)
- Oil return line: 11 ft. lbs. (15 Nm)

INTAKE MANIFOLD

REMOVAL & INSTALLATION

2.0L Gas Engine

1. Before servicing the vehicle, refer to the precautions section.

2. Relieve the fuel system pressure.

3. Remove the engine cover.

4. Disconnect the all necessary electrical harness connectors.

5. Disconnect the vacuum hose between intake manifold and vacuum pump from intake manifold.

6. Disconnect the hose connections from valve cover.

7. Loosen the fuel supply line and hose connection from EVAP canister and cap off open lines.

8. Open both fuel lines at high-pressure pump.

9. Disconnect the electrical connector from Fuel Pressure sensor.

10. Remove the oil dipstick and remove bolt for oil dipstick guide tube.

11. Remove the bolt for oil line from intake manifold.

12. Open hose clamps and pull intake

hose off from Throttle Valve Control Module and intake manifold.

13. Remove the nut from intake manifold bracket, if necessary, remove Throttle Valve Control Module.

14. Separate oil dipstick guide tube at separation point and remove bolt from intake manifold bracket.

15. Remove the bolts from intake manifold.

16. Carefully pull intake manifold with fuel rail off from cylinder head.

➡ **The fuel injectors could remain stuck in the fuel rail.**

To install:

17. Installation is the reverse of removal, please note the following:

   a. Intake manifold bolts are tightened to 5 ft. lbs. (9 Nm).

   b. Intake manifold support bolts are tightened to 16 ft. lbs. (23 Nm).

   c. Intake manifold support nuts are tightened to 7 ft. lbs (10 Nm).

   d. Fuel supply line to pump are tightened to 20 ft. lbs. (27 Nm).

   e. New fuel return line to pump are tightened to 13 ft. lbs. (17 Nm).

2.0L TDI Engine

➡ **Make sure no contaminants enter the fuel system when removing the intake manifold.**

➡ **Seal off the connections in the fuel system using the plugs from the engine bung set VAS 6122.**

1. Remove the engine cover.

2. Remove the protective strip, if equipped.

3. Loosen the high pressure line or fuel line bolts arrows on the intake manifold.

4. Disconnect the fuel injector A connectors, the exhaust pressure sensor 1 G450 connector B and the fuel pressure sensor G247 connector C.

5. Remove the coolant line bolts arrows from the intake manifold and lay the line in front of the intake manifold.

6. Unclip the wiring harness from the wiring guide for the glow plugs.

7. Disconnect the glow plug connectors.

8. Remove the high pressure line between the high pressure fuel pump and fuel rail.

9. Loosen the hose clip using hose clip pliers VAS 6362 and remove the line from the fuel rail.

10. Before removing, clean the return line connection on the fuel injectors (for example using a commercially available detergent).

11. Dry the return line connections.

12. Cover the return line connections with a cloth.

13. Remove the fuel return line connections from the fuel injectors. Pull them upward to release them.

➡ **Maintain clean working conditions. Dirt and contaminants must not enter the return lines and the connections on the fuel injectors.**

14. Loosen the hose clips using hose clip pliers VAS 6362 and remove the fuel return line.

15. Loosen the hose clip 4 using the hose clip pliers VAS 6362 and remove the fuel return line from the high pressure fuel pump.

16. Seal the lines so that the fuel system is not contaminated by dirt, etc.

17. Remove the fuel return lines.

18. Disconnect the EGR vacuum regulator solenoid valve N18 connector 1 and the throttle valve control module J338 connector 3.

19. Loosen the clamp 4 and remove the charge air hose.

20. Remove the oil dipstick bracket.

➡ **Make sure the connecting pipe decoupling element does not bend or stretch. Cracks could develop.**

21. Disconnect the connecting pipe 2.

22. Remove the intake manifold bolts using Socket XZN 8 T40159 in a diagonal sequence working from the outside to the inside.

23. Remove the intake manifold.

To install:

24. Installation is in the reverse order of removal. When doing this note the following:

25. Condition: Always replace seals.

26. When installing the high pressure line or fuel lines, make sure no dirt or contaminants enter the fuel system.

27. Only remove the sealing plugs right before installing the fuel lines.

28. Do not change the angles of the high pressure lines

29. Make sure lines connections are securely fastened.

30. Do not swap supply and return lines.

31. Tighten bolts/nuts to specification as follows:

- Intake manifold to cylinder head: 16 ft. lbs. (22 Nm)
- Engine lifting eyelet to cylinder head: 15 ft. lbs. (20 Nm)
- Bracket to intake manifold: 89 inch lbs. (10 Nm)
- Connecting pipe to intake manifold connection bolt: 16 ft. lbs. (22 Nm)
- EGR cooler to intake manifold: 89 inch lbs. (10 Nm)
- Intake Flap Motor V157 to intake manifold: 89 inch lbs. (10 Nm)

32. Install mounting supports and torque bolts to 18 ft. lbs. (25 Nm).

33. Tighten the high pressure line union nuts by hand.

34. Make sure the high pressure line is free of tension.

35. Use torque wrench (5-50 Nm) V.A.G 1331 with ratchet, reversible V.A.G 1331/1 and socket T40055 to tighten the high pressure line.

36. Fill the fuel system. Refer to Fuel System, Filling and Bleeding.

OIL PAN

REMOVAL & INSTALLATION

2.0L Gas Engine

See Figures 117 and 118.

1. Before servicing the vehicle, refer to the precautions section.

2. Disconnect the negative battery cable.

3. Disconnect the electrical connector.

4. Disconnect the intake connection using spring-type clip pliers.

5. Remove the engine cover upward and out in direction of.

6. Remove the center sound insulation fasteners.

7. Remove the right sound insulation fasteners.

8. Remove the air duct from charge air cooler.

9. Unfasten the air duct from turbocharger.

10. Remove the bolts and remove air duct.

11. Remove the air duct for charge air cooler.

12. Disconnect the charge air pressure sensor connector.

13. Remove the air duct.

14. Disconnect the oil Level thermal sensor connector.

15. Remove the oil return line from turbocharger.

16. Drain the engine oil.

17. Remove the bolts for oil pan/transmission.

18. Loosen the bolts in a diagonal sequence.

19. Remove the oil pan, if necessary loosen by applying light strikes with a rubber mallet.

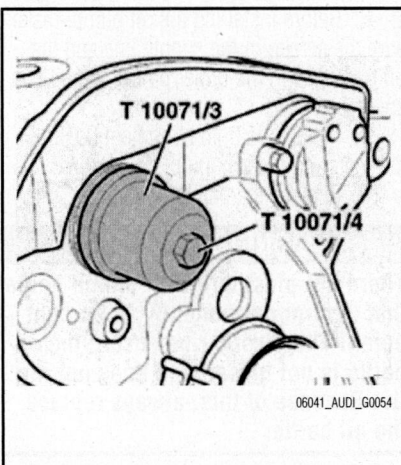

Fig. 117 Oil pan bolt loosening/tightening sequence—A3 with 2.0L engine

To install:

➡ The oil pan must be installed within 5 minutes after applying the silicone sealant.

20. Clean the oil pan mating surfaces.

21. Apply 2 to 3mm bead of silicone sealant as illustrated to the sealing surface of oil pan.

➡ The sealant bead may not be thicker than specified, otherwise excess sealant could enter the oil pan and clog the oil intake tube.

22. Apply a bead of sealant at the rear area of the sealing flange as shown in the illustration.

23. Install the oil pan immediately and tighten bolts in sequence as follows:

   a. Step 1: Bolts 1 through 20 to 5 Nm.

   b. Step 2: Oil pan to transmission bolts to 30 ft. lbs. (40 Nm).

   c. Step 3: Bolts 1 through 20 to 11 ft. lbs. (15 Nm).

➡ Make sure that the oil pan is positioned flush with the cylinder block on the flywheel side.

➡ After installing oil pan, allow sealant to dry for about 30 minutes, then fill the crankcase with oil.

24. Check and adjust the oil level.

25. Install the remaining components in the reverse order of removal.

2.0L TDI Engine

See Figure 119.

1. Before servicing the vehicle, refer to the precautions.

> ✳ **WARNING**
>
> If large quantities of metal particles or abraded material are detected during engine repairs, it may be an indication for a damaged crankshaft or rod bearings. To prevent further damage, perform the following steps after the repair: Carefully clean oil passages, replace oil cooler, replace oil filter insert,

2. Remove engine cover.

3. On one piece engine cover, pull the one piece front engine cover upward with a quick jerk and then pull the lower mount forward.

4. On two piece engine cover, first pull the outer cover upward with a quick jerkin the upper illustration, then pull the inner engine cover upward with a quick jerk.

5. Remove the air filter/turbocharger intake hose.

6. Carefully cut the cable tie.

7. Open the wiring bracket and disengage the wiring harness.

8. Disconnect the connector on the Mass Air Flow (MAF) sensor G70.

9. Disconnect the ventilation hose and disengage it from the bracket.

10. Open the spring-type clip3 using spring-type clip pliers VAS 5024A and disconnect the intake hose from the Mass Air Flow (MAF) sensor G70.

11. Disconnect the intake manifold from the air guide.

12. Unfasten bolt and remove air filter housing and mass air flow sensor.

13. Remove both bolts from the upper charge air pipe.

14. Remove noise insulation.

15. Remove the charge air pipe bolt from the oil pan.

16. Disconnect the connector, if

equipped, from the oil level thermal sensor G266.

17. Drain engine oil.

18. Remove the oil pan/transmission connecting bolts.

19. Loosen oil pan screws with 10 mm hex ball socket 3185. (Remove using 5 mm socket 3249 or T10058).

20. Remove the oil pan. Loosen oil pan with light blows of a rubber headed hammer if necessary.

21. Remove the sealant residue from cylinder block with a flat scraper.

22. Remove remaining sealant at oil pan using a rotating brush, e.g. a drill with plastic brush attachment (wear protective glasses).

23. Clean all sealing surfaces. They must be free of oil and grease.

To install:

> ✳ **WARNING**
>
> The oil pan must be installed within 5 minutes after application of silicone sealant.

24. Cut off the nozzle on the tube of sealant at the front mark approximately 0.117 in. (3 mm).

25. Apply silicone sealant to clean sealing surfaces of oil pan. Sealing compound beads must be 0.078–0.117 in. (2–3 mm thick and run on inside of bolt holes.

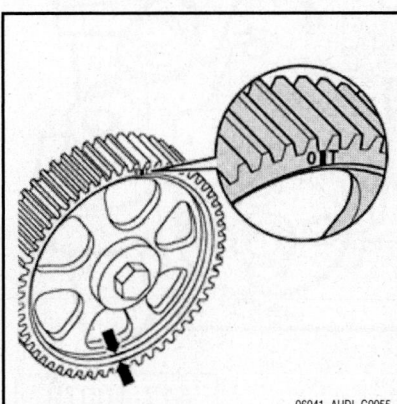

Fig. 118 Apply 2 to 3mm bead of silicone sealant to the sealing surface of oil pan — A3 with 2.0L engine

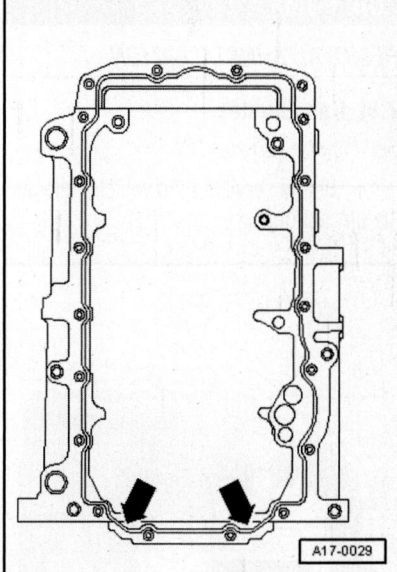

Fig. 119 Apply silicone sealant to clean sealing surfaces of oil pan. Sealing compound beads must be 0.078–0.117 in. (2–3 mm thick and run on inside of bolt holes

※ WARNING

Sealant bead must not be thicker than specified. Otherwise, excess sealant could get into oil pan and clog strainer in intake line of oil pump.

26. With transmission removed, oil pan must seal flush with cylinder block.

27. With transmission installed, oil pan must make contact on transmission.

28. Apply silicone sealing compound bead as illustrated to clean sealing surface of oil pan.

29. Install oil pan immediately and tighten all oil pan bolts lightly. Make sure that the oil pan is seated flush against the intermediate plate/transmission flange.

30. When installing the oil pan to a removed engine, make sure that the oil pan is positioned flush with the cylinder block on the flywheel side.

31. Tighten the oil pan bolts in a diagonal sequence to 11 ft. lbs. (15 Nm).

32. Tighten the oil pan/transmission bolts to 33 ft. lbs. (45 Nm).

33. After installing oil pan, allow sealant to dry for approximately 30 minutes. Only after then may the engine oil be replenished.

34. The rest of the assembly is basically a reverse of the disassembling sequence.

35. Install noise insulation.

OIL PUMP

REMOVAL & INSTALLATION

2.0L Gas Engines

See Figures 120 and 121.

1. Before servicing the vehicle, refer to the precautions.

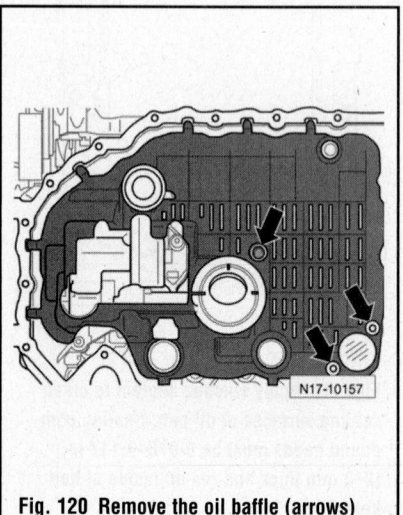

Fig. 120 Remove the oil baffle (arrows)

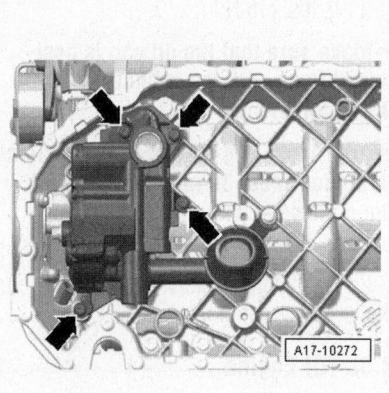

Fig. 121 Remove the oil pump bolts

2. Remove the lower oil pan section.

3. Remove the oil baffle.

4. The following must be performed in one sequence; technicians are necessary.

5. Remove the oil pump bolts.

6. Pull back the chain tensioner using the Assembly Tool T10118 and have a second technician remove the oil pump.

To install:

7. Installation is performed in reverse order of removal.

8. Before installing the oil pump, make sure the screen in the supply line and the oil passages in the upper part of the oil pan are clean.

9. Make sure both alignment bushings for centering the oil pump are in there.

10. Replace the baffle plate.

※ WARNING

There are plastic ribs on the oil baffle that deform permanently when tightening. The plastic ribs ensure the oil baffle is not loosen and does not rattle. Because of this, always replace the oil baffle.

2.0L TDI Engine

See Figure 122.

1. Before servicing the vehicle, refer to the precautions.

2. Remove the oil pan and the splash wall.

3. Remove the circlip with circlip pliers.

4. Install a M3 bolt and remove the input shaft from the oil pump.

5. Remove the bolt and remove the intake connection from the oil pump.

6. Remove the two bolts and the oil pump.

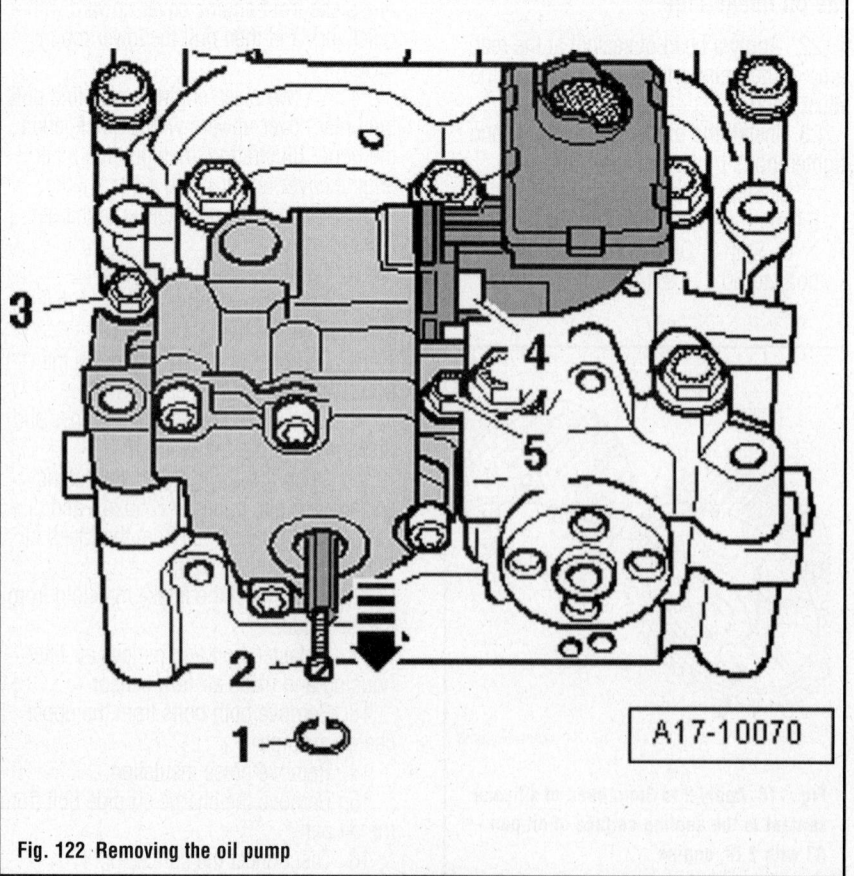

Fig. 122 Removing the oil pump

➡Do not loosen the bolt for the intermediate sprocket.

To install:

7. Installation is in the reverse order of removal. Note the following:

   a. Replace the O-ring.

   b. Replace damaged or stretched circlips.

   c. The circlip must lie in the base of the groove.

8. Before installing the oil pump, make sure both alignment sleeves for centering the pump on the balance shaft assembly are present.

9. Install the oil pan.

10. Tighten bolts/nuts to specification as follows:

   • Chain sprocket to oil pump shaft: 15 ft. lbs. (20 Nm) plus 90° rotations.

   • Oil pump to cylinder block: 15 ft. lbs. (20 Nm) plus 90° rotations.

PISTON AND RING

POSITIONING

See Figures 123 through 126.

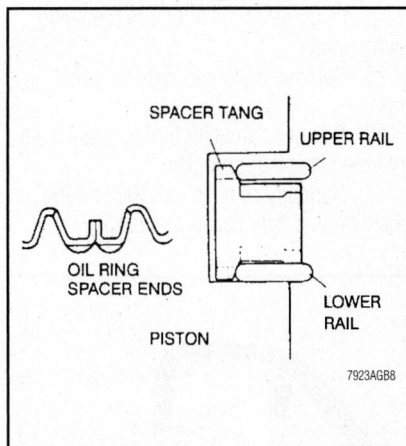

Fig. 123 Piston ring positioning mark and location—Audi engines

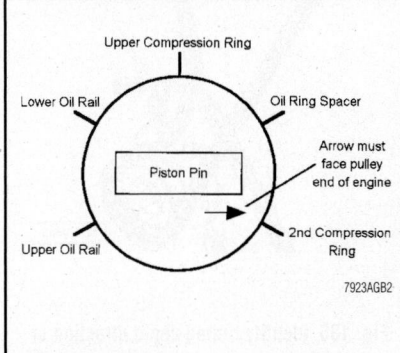

Fig. 124 Piston ring and end-gap spacing—Audi engines

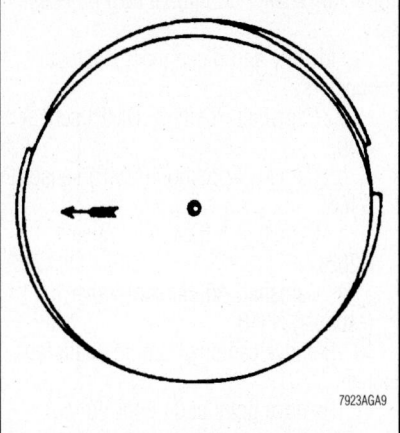

Fig. 125 Arrow on the piston crown must face the front of the engine—Audi engines

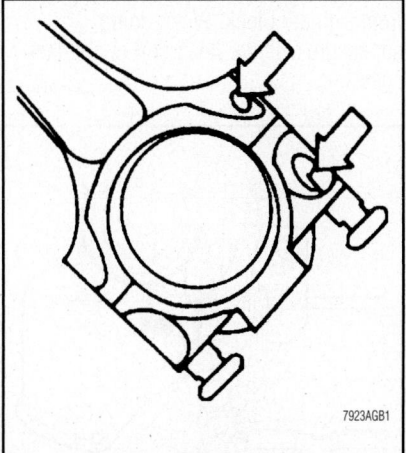

Fig. 126 Connecting rod to bearing cap assembly—Audi engines

REAR MAIN SEAL

REMOVAL & INSTALLATION

See Figures 127 through 131.

1. Before servicing the vehicle, refer to the precautions section.

2. Remove the transmission.

3. Remove the flywheel.

4. Disconnect the intermediate plate at sealing flange and at the alignment sleeves.

5. Remove the bolts and the rear sealing flange.

To install:

➡Lay a rag over the open portion of the oil pan.

6. Clean the gasket mating surfaces.

7. Apply a thin bead of sealant to edge between cylinder block and oil pan.

8. Lightly coat lower sealing surface of sealing flange with sealant.

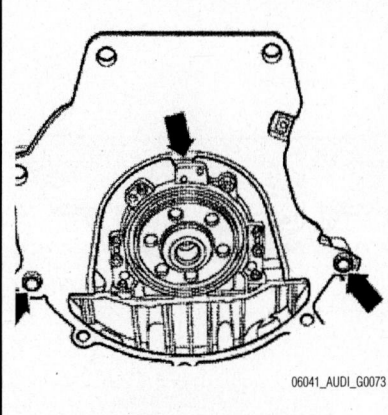

Fig. 127 Disconnect the intermediate plate at sealing flange and at the alignment sleeve

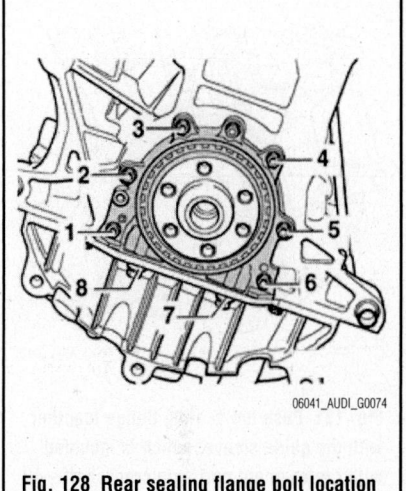

Fig. 128 Rear sealing flange bolt location

➡The sealing flange must be installed within 5 minutes of sealant being applied.

9. Push the sealing flange together with the guide sleeve, which is included with replacement part onto crankshaft.

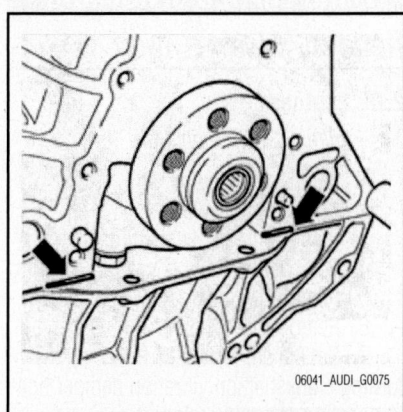

Fig. 129 Apply a thin bead of sealant to edge between cylinder block and oil pan

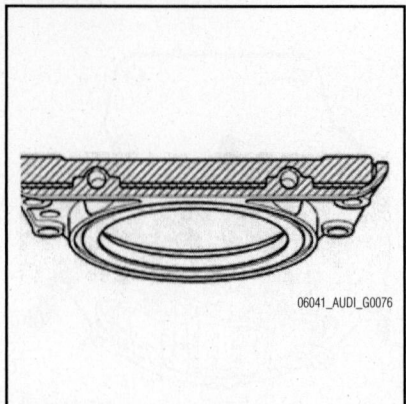

Fig. 130 Lightly coat lower sealing surface of sealing flange with sealant

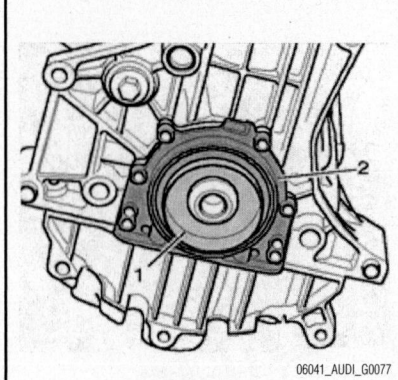

Fig. 131 Push the sealing flange together with the guide sleeve, which is included with replacement part onto crankshaft—A3

10. Carefully push the sealing flange onto the locating pins on cylinder block.

11. Fasten the bolts to 11 ft. lbs. (15 Nm).

12. Install the remaining components in the reverse order of removal.

TIMING CHAIN & SPROCKETS

REMOVAL & INSTALLATION

2.0L Engines

See Figures 132 through 144.

1. Remove the engine.
2. Remove the flywheel.
3. Remove the intake manifold.
4. Remove the valve cover.
5. Remove the thermostat housing,
6. Remove the oil pan.
7. Set the crankshaft to TDC mark by turning crankshaft on vibration damper bolt in direction of engine rotation.
8. At the same time, camshaft bar T10068 must engage in both shaft grooves.

Turn crankshaft 1 additional turn if necessary.

9. Identify and disconnect electrical connectors:
  a. Camshaft Position (CMP) sensor G40.
  b. Camshaft position (CMP) sensor 2 G163.
  c. Camshaft Adjustment Valve 1 N205.
  d. Camshaft Adjustment Valve 1 (exhaust) N318.

10. Remove camshaft timing chain tensioner.

11. Remove bolts and upper timing chain cover horizontally from cylinder head. When doing so, ensure cylinder bolt is not damaged.

12. Remove bolts and remove lower timing chain cover horizontally from cylinder block. When doing so, ensure cylinder head bolt is not damaged.

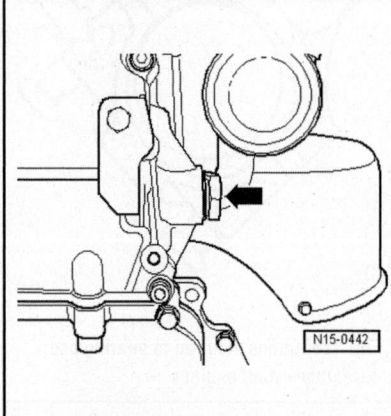

Fig. 132 Remove camshaft timing chain tensioner

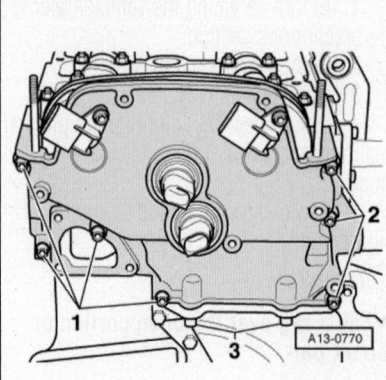

Fig. 133 Remove bolts and upper timing chain cover

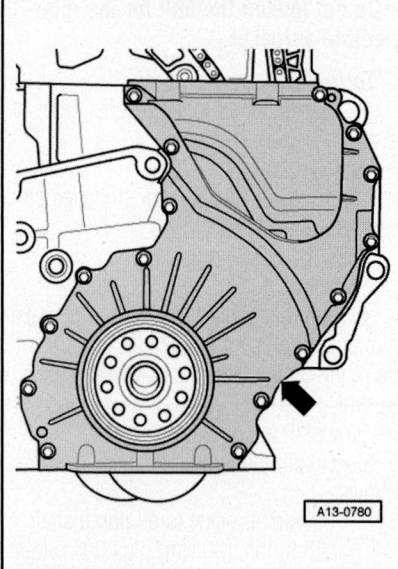

Fig. 134 Remove bolts and remove lower timing chain cover

13. Press crankshaft seal timing chain side out of cover.

➡**Do not mark chain with punch, notch or something similar!**

14. Identify timing chain direction of rotation with arrow mark before removing, using paint.

15. Remove bolts and remove guide track.

16. Remove camshaft timing chain from intermediate shaft sprocket.

17. Carefully remove camshaft timing chain behind cylinder head seal rib.

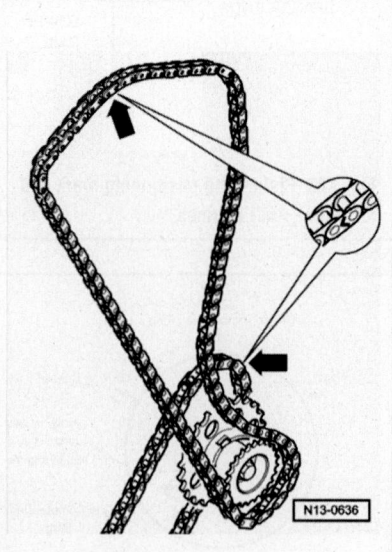

Fig. 135 Identify timing chain direction of rotation with arrow mark before removing, using paint

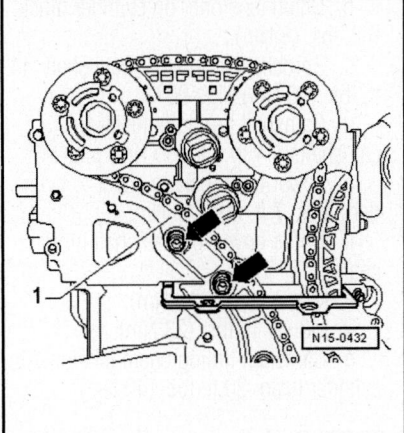
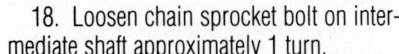

Fig. 136 Remove bolts and remove guide track

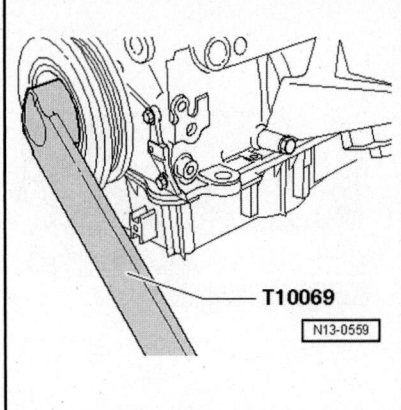
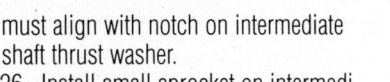

Fig. 138 Counter hold at vibration damper with counter hold T10069 when doing so

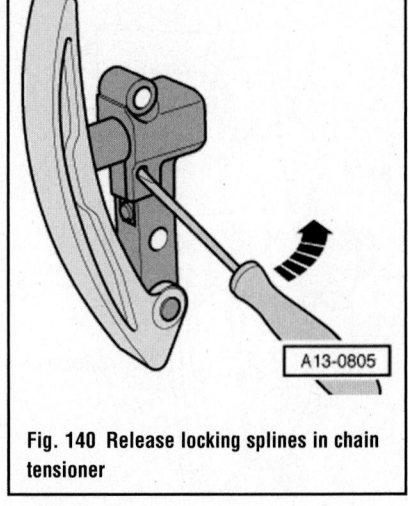

Fig. 140 Release locking splines in chain tensioner

18. Loosen chain sprocket bolt on intermediate shaft approximately 1 turn.

19. Counter hold at vibration damper with counter hold T10069 when doing so.

20. Remove the timing mechanism drive chain tensioner.

21. Remove bolt and remove drive chain together with chain sprockets from intermediate shaft.

To install:

22. When reinstalling a used timing mechanism drive chain, note running direction identification mark.

23. Install drive chain together with large sprocket.

24. Note location of sprocket: It can only be installed in one position in intermediate shaft. Turn intermediate shaft slightly if necessary.

25. Verify crankshaft TDC position:

   a. Milled drive chain sprocket tooth must align with bearing joint

   b. Tab on intermediate shaft sprocket must align with notch on intermediate shaft thrust washer.

26. Install small sprocket on intermediate shaft: It can only be installed in one position on intermediate shaft.

   a. Replace intermediate shaft sprocket securing bolt

   b. Tighten bolt by hand.

27. Release locking splines in chain tensioner with a small screwdriver and press tensioning rail against chain tensioner.

28. Tighten chain tensioner in this position.

29. Tighten sprocket securing bolt.

30. Counter hold at vibration damper with counter hold T10069 when doing so.

31. Route camshaft timing chain as follows:

   a. Yellow link (1) must align with marking (2) on smaller intermediate chain sprocket.

   b. Both copper-colored links (4) must align with arrows (3) at camshaft

adjusters and notch 5 on control housing.

   c. 16 chain rollers must now lie between arrows.

32. Insert guide track and tighten bolts

33. Remove the camshaft bar T10068.

34. When turning crankshaft, tensioning rail must be pressed strongly with hand (instead of chain tensioner) against camshaft timing chain to prevent chain from jumping off.

35. Set crankshaft to TDC mark by turning crankshaft on vibration damper bolt 2 turns in direction of engine rotation .

36. At the same time, the camshaft bar T10068 must engage in both shaft grooves.

37. If the camshaft bar cannot be inserted:

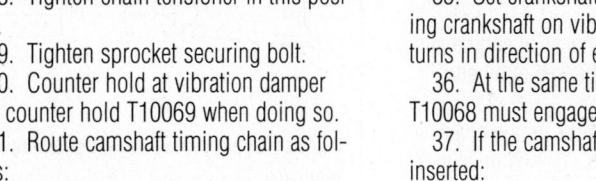

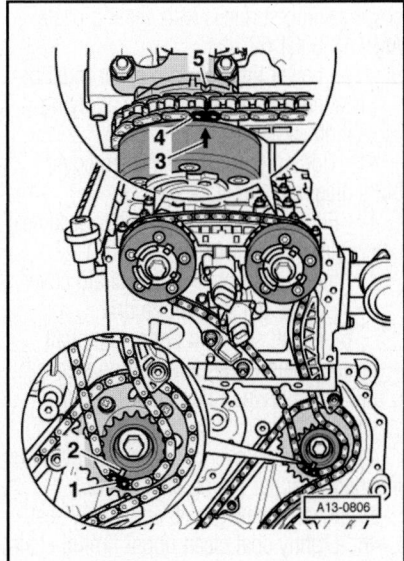

Fig. 141 Route camshaft timing chain as shown

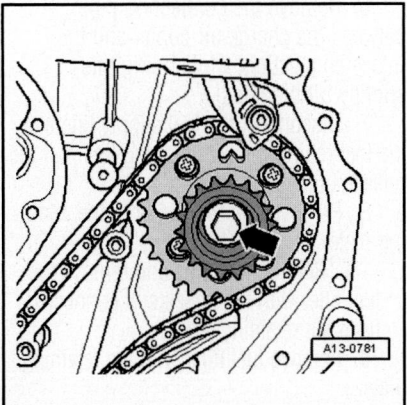

Fig. 137 Loosen chain sprocket bolt on intermediate shaft approximately 1 turn

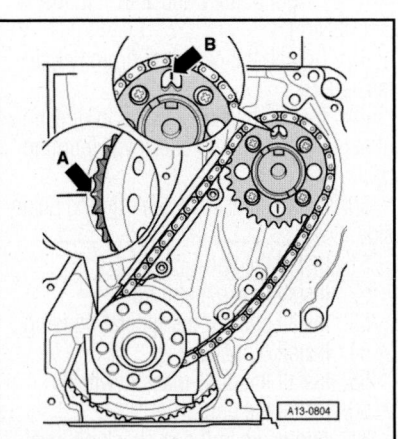

Fig. 139 Milled drive chain sprocket tooth must align with bearing joint

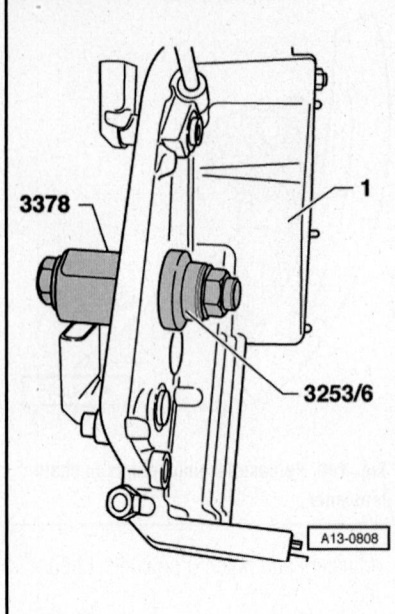

Fig. 142 Install seal into upper camshaft timing chain cover

a. Repeat valve timing adjustment.

b. Clean old sealant from 3 mm holes in cylinder head seal.

c. With the cylinder head installed only half of the holes in the cylinder head gasket are visible.

38. Clean sealing surfaces at engine and both covers; they must be free of oil and grease.

39. Check whether lower timing chain cover alignment pins are inserted in cylinder block.

40. Lightly coat clean lower timing chain cover sealing surfaces with sealing paste AMV 188 001 02.

a. Lower timing chain cover must be installed within 5 minutes of applying sealing paste.

41. Tighten lower timing chain cover bolts diagonally in stages.

42. Fill 3 mm holes in cylinder head seal using black sealant AMV 174 04 01.

43. Install the upper timing chain cover:

a. Drive out seal with a drift.

b. Install seal into upper camshaft timing chain cover using fitting sleeve 3378 and drive in flush using fitting sleeve 3253/6.

44. Check whether alignment sleeves are inserted in upper timing chain cover.

45. Insert a new gasket and a new seal.

46. Lightly coat clean upper timing chain cover sealing surfaces shown hatched with sealing paste AMV 188 001 02.

47. Set upper timing chain cover in place and tighten screws as follows:

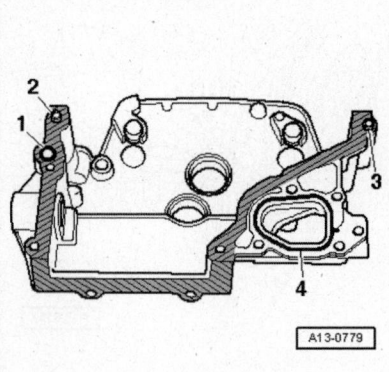

Fig. 143 Identifying alignment sleeves (2,3), new gasket (1) and a new seal (4)

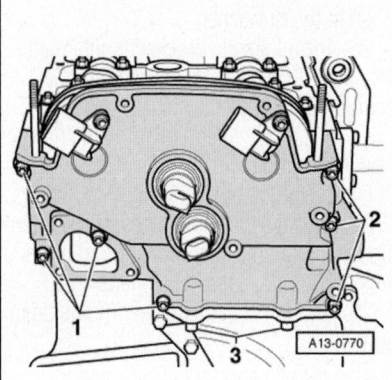

Fig. 144 Upper timing chain tightening sequence

a. Tighten the bolts **1** and **2** to 4 ft. lbs. (5 Nm.).

b. Tighten bolts **3** to 17 ft. lbs. (23 Nm.).

c. Tight bolts **1** and **2** to 7 ft. lbs. (10 Nm.).

48. Tighten the camshaft timing chain tensioner.

49. Turn crankshaft 2 times in direction of engine rotation and check valve timing again.

50. Install crankshaft seal, timing chain side.

51. Install the valve cover.

52. Install intake manifold

53. Install coolant thermostat housing.

54. Install oil pan

55. Install the dual-mass flywheel.

56. Install the engine.

57. Add engine oil and check oil level.

58. Tightening Specifications:

a. Guide rail bolts to cylinder block: 7 ft. lbs. (10 Nm).

b. Chain tensioner on cylinder block: 6 ft. lbs. (8 Nm).

c. Sprockets to intermediate shaft: 44 ft. lbs. (60 Nm) plus 90°.

d. Camshaft timing adjuster to camshafts: 44 ft. lbs. (60 Nm) plus 90°.

e. Lower timing chain cover to cylinder block: 7 ft. lbs. (10 Nm).

f. Upper cover for Camshaft timing chain:
- M6: 7 ft. lbs. (10 Nm).
- M8: 17 ft. lbs. (23 Nm).

g. Camshaft timing chain tensioner to cylinder head: 30 ft. lbs. (40 Nm).

2.0L TDI Engine

See Figures 145 through 148.

1. Before servicing the vehicle, refer to the precautions.

2. Remove engine cover.

a. One piece engine cover, pull the one piece front engine cover upward with a quick jerk and then pull the lower mount forward.

b. Two piece engine cover, first pull the outer cover upward with a quick jerk in the upper illustration, then pull the inner engine cover upward with a quick jerk in lower illustration.

✳✳ CAUTION

The temperature of the fuel lines, as well as the fuel, can be very hot on vehicles equipped with a TDI engine. Before opening any line connections, let the fuel cool down otherwise you could get burned. Wear protective gloves. Wear safety glasses.

3. Disconnect the fuel supply hose and the fuel return hose from the fuel lines.

4. Disconnect the coolant line.

5. Remove bolts.

6. Remove the connecting pipe between the charge air cooler and the intake connection; while doing this, slightly lift the clips.

7. Disconnect the fuel supply line and the fuel return line; while doing this pull the release buttons.

8. Remove fuel filter without the retaining plate.

a. Release the clips and remove the fuel filter with the hoses still connected from the retaining plate.

9. Remove fuel filter with the retaining plate.

a. Loosen the bolt one turn.

b. Remove the bolt and the nut.

c. Remove the fuel filter with the hoses still connected.

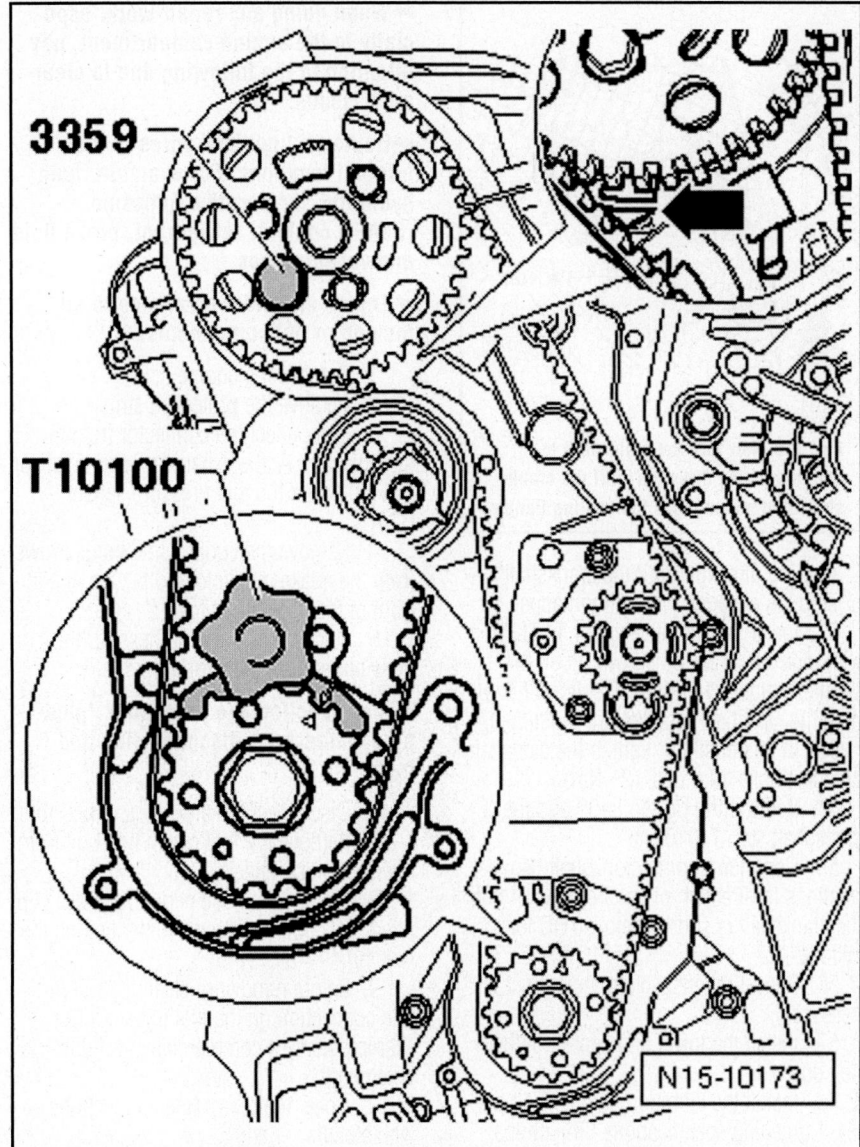

Fig. 145 Markings on toothed belt crankshaft sprocket and the crankshaft stop must be aligned. The tab of the crankshaft stop must engage in the bore of the sealing flange

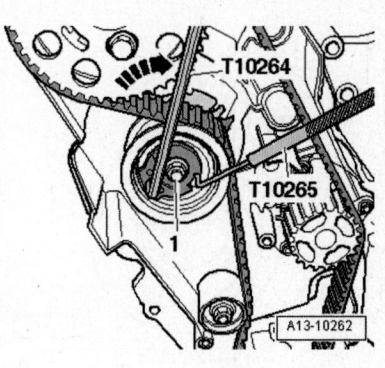

Fig. 146 Turn the tension roller eccentric pulley using socket wrench T10264 counterclockwise arrow, until the securing pin T10265 can lock the tension roller. Now turn the tensioning roller eccentric pulley clockwise all the way and tighten the nut by hand

10. Remove the bolt on the fuel filler tube for the washer fluid reservoir.

11. Remove the retaining plate for the fuel filter, if equipped.

12. Disconnect the electrical connectors on the coolant expansion tank.

13. Remove coolant expansion tank with the hoses still connected. Lay it on the engine.

14. Remove ribbed belt.

15. Remove the ribbed belt tensioning element.

16. Remove the upper toothed belt guard; to do this, loosen the clips.

17. Remove front right wheel housing liner.

18. Remove the vibration damper/belt pulley.

19. Remove the lower and center toothed belt guard.

20. Turn the crankshaft to set cylinder 1 at TDC.

21. When doing so, turn the crankshaft so that the marking on the crankshaft toothed belt gear and the tooth segment of the camshaft gear are positioned upward. The marking on the rear toothed belt guard must align with the marking on the camshaft sensor wheel.

22. Lock the hub with the rig pin 3359. To do this, push the rig pin through the left-sided empty slot in the bore of the cylinder head.

23. Also, lock the toothed belt crankshaft sprocket with the crankshaft stop T10100. Push the crankshaft stop from the front side of the toothed belt sprocket into the teeth.

24. Markings on toothed belt crankshaft sprocket and the crankshaft stop must be

aligned. The tab of the crankshaft stop must engage in the bore of the sealing flange.

25. Mark the rotational direction of toothed belt.

26. Loosen the bolts of the camshaft sprockets, until the camshaft sprocket can be turned in the slots.

27. Loosen the nut of the tensioning roller.

28. Turn the tension roller eccentric pulley using socket wrench T10264 counterclockwise arrow, until the securing pin T10265 can lock the tension roller.

29. Now turn the tensioning roller eccentric pulley clockwise all the way and tighten the nut by hand.

30. First, take the toothed belt from the coolant pump and then from the remaining toothed belt gears.

Installing

31. Camshaft is secured with the rig pin 3359.

32. Crankshaft locked with crankshaft stop T10100.

33. Tensioning roller secured with pin T10265 and seated on right stop with the nut.

34. Adjustments to toothed belt may generally only be performed when the engine is cold, because the indicator position of the tensioning element changes depending on engine temperature.

35. Turn the camshaft sprocket in its slots to middle position.

36. Install the toothed belt through the space between the engine mount and the engine.

37. Place the toothed belt onto the crankshaft sprocket, tensioning roller, camshaft sprocket and idler roller.

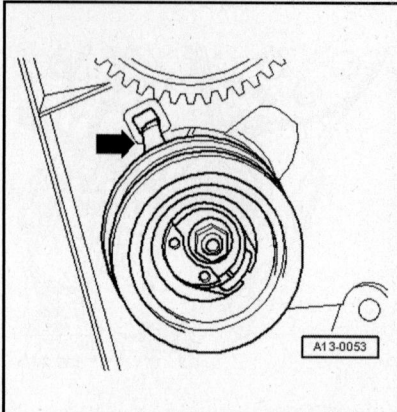

Fig. 147 Make sure the tensioning roller is properly positioned in the rear toothed belt guard (arrow)

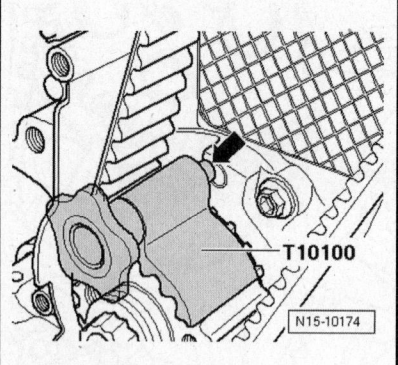

Fig. 148 Now turn the crankshaft in engine running direction until the crankshaft stop tab engages the sealing flange

38. Lastly, lay the toothed belt onto the toothed belt coolant pump sprocket.

39. Make sure the tensioning roller is properly positioned in the rear toothed belt guard.

40. Pull the locking pin T10265 out from the tensioning roller.

41. Loosen the nut of the tensioning roller.

42. Turn the tensioning roller eccentric pulley using the socket wrench T10264 clockwise, until the indicator is located centrally in the gap of the base plate.

43. Make sure that the nut does not turn along with it.

44. Hold the tensioner roller in this position and tighten the nut to 15 ft. lbs. (20 Nm) plus 45° rotations.

45. Mount the counter-holder tool T10172 with the bolt T10172/4 as shown in the illustration, and hold the toothed belt tensioned by pushing in direction of.

46. Tighten the camshaft sprocket bolts to 19 ft. lbs. (25 Nm).

47. Remove the rig pin 3359 and the crankshaft stop T10100.

48. Turn the crankshaft 2 turns in the direction of the engine, until the crankshaft is once again just in front of TDC.

49. Lock the hub with the rig pin 3359 from the rotating movement in engine rotation direction.

50. Check if the crankshaft can be locked with the crankshaft stop T10100.

51. If the crankshaft cannot be locked:

   a. Loosen the bolts of the camshaft sprocket.

   b. Turn the crankshaft against the engine running direction until the crankshaft stop tab is positioned shortly before the sealing flange bore.

   c. Now turn the crankshaft in engine running direction until the crankshaft stop tab engages the sealing flange.

52. Install the counter-holder T10172 with pins T10172/4 as shown. Push the counter-holder T10172 in direction of and hold the camshaft sprocket pre-tensioned.

53. In this position, tighten the camshaft sprocket bolts 19 ft. lbs. (25 Nm).

54. Remove the rig pin 3359 and the crankshaft stop T10100.

55. Continue turning crankshaft two rotations in direction of engine rotation until the crankshaft is shortly before TDC for cylinder 1.

56. Repeat the inspection and adjust if necessary.

57. Install the lower and center toothed belt guard.

58. Install the vibration damper/belt pulley. Tightening specifications 89 inch lbs. (10 Nm) plus 90° rotations.

59. Install ribbed belt.

60. Install the upper toothed belt guard.

61. Install the connecting tube between the charge air cooler and intake connection.

62. Install the front right wheel housing liner.

63. Install the coolant expansion tank.

64. Install the fuel filter.

65. Tighten the filler tube for the windshield washer.

66. Install the engine cover.

TURBOCHARGER

REMOVAL & INSTALLATION

Refer to Exhaust Manifold.

VALVE COVERS

REMOVAL & INSTALLATION

See Figure 149.

➡When doing any repair work, especially in the engine compartment, pay attention to the following due to clearance issues:

➡Route all lines and wires in their original locations. For example, fuel, hydraulic, Evaporative Emission (EVAP), coolant, refrigerant, brake fluid and vacuum lines.

➡Ensure sufficient clearance to all moving or hot components.

1. Remove the engine cover.

2. Remove the protective strip.

3. Disconnect the connector from the fuel injectors A, the exhaust pressure sensor 1 G450 B and the fuel pressure sensor G247 C.

4. Remove the coolant line bolts arrows from the intake manifold and lay the line in front of the intake manifold.

5. Unclip the wiring harness for the glow plugs from the wiring guide.

➡Always follow the procedure "glow plug connectors, disconnecting and installing".

6. Disconnect the glow plug connectors.

7. Remove the fuel return line bolt from the intake manifold.

8. Loosen the hose clip using hose clip pliers VAS 6362 and remove the line on the fuel rail.

9. Before removing, clean the return line connection on the fuel injectors (for example using a commercially available detergent).

10. Cover the return line connections with a cloth.

11. Remove the fuel return line connections on the fuel injectors. Pull them upward to release them.

12. Follow the rules of cleanliness.

13. Do not let any dirt to get into the disconnected return lines or into the connections for the fuel injection units.

14. Loosen the hose clip using hose clip pliers VAS 6362 and remove the fuel return line.

15. Loosen the hose clip 4 using hose clip pliers VAS 6362 and remove the fuel return line at the high pressure fuel pump.

16. Seal the lines so that the fuel system is not contaminated by dirt, etc.

17. Remove the fuel return line and lay the lines in front of the intake manifold.

18. Disconnect the connector from the charge pressure actuator position sensor G581 at the turbocharger vacuum diaphragm and guide the line out of the retainers.

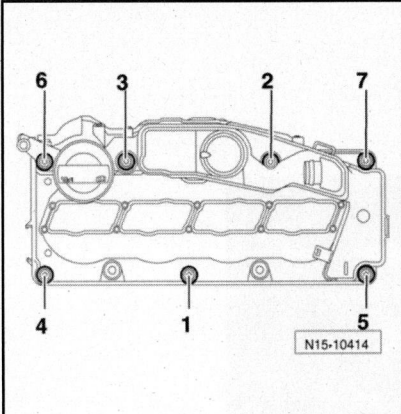

Fig. 149 Remove/install the cylinder head cover bolts in sequence 7 through 1

19. Disconnect the connector from the fuel pressure regulator valve N276.
20. Remove the line guide on the fuel rail and lay it aside.
21. Remove the vacuum hose from the cylinder head cover.
22. Remove the remaining vacuum hoses from the bracket on the cylinder head cover.
23. Disconnect the connector 1 from the engine coolant temperature sensor on radiator G83, open the clips arrows and remove the upper toothed belt guard.
24. Remove the crankcase ventilation hose between the intake tube and the cylinder head cover.
   The crankcase ventilation hose is destroyed when it is removed.
25. Remove the high pressure fuel line between the high pressure fuel pump and fuel rail.
26. Remove the high pressure fuel lines between the fuel rail and fuel injectors.
27. Remove the bolts arrows and the fuel rail.
28. Remove the fuel injectors.
29. Remove the cylinder head cover bolts in sequence 7 through 1.
30. Remove the cylinder head cover.
31. Remove the cylinder head cover.

To install:
32. Installation is in the reverse order of removal. Note the following:
   a. When installing the high pressure line or fuel lines, make sure no dirt or contaminants enter the fuel system.
   b. Only remove the sealing plugs right before installing the fuel lines.
   c. Do not change the angles of the high pressure lines
   d. Make sure line connections are securely fastened.
   e. Do not swap the supply and return lines.
33. First tighten the cylinder head cover bolts by hand in sequence 1 through 7.
34. Tighten the cylinder head cover bolts in sequence 1 through 7 to 44 inch lbs. (5 Nm).
35. Condition: Tightening specifications.
36. Install the upper toothed belt guard.
37. Make sure the upper toothed belt guard is clipped to the cylinder head cover correctly.
38. Press the upper toothed belt guard in the area with the clips arrows against the cylinder head cover until the clips engage with each other. Use a screwdriver to press the guard if necessary.
39. Check the clearance between the hub and the upper toothed belt guard.
40. Tighten the high pressure line union nuts by hand.
41. Make sure the high pressure line is free of tension.
42. Use torque wrench (5-50 Nm) V.A.G 1331 with ratchet, reversible V.A.G 1331/1 and socket T40055 to tighten the high pressure line.
43. Fill the fuel system, refer to Fuel System, Filling and Bleeding.

VALVE LASH

ADJUSTMENT

Audi engines are equipped with hydraulic lash adjusters. No adjustment is possible.

ENGINE PERFORMANCE & EMISSION CONTROLS

COMPONENT LOCATIONS

See Figure 150.

CAMSHAFT POSITION (CMP) SENSOR

REMOVAL & INSTALLATION

2.0L TDI Engine
See Figure 151.

1. Remove the ribbed belt.
2. Remove the vibration damper.
3. Remove the toothed belt.
4. Remove the EGR vacuum regulator solenoid valve.
5. Disconnect the connector from the camshaft position sensor and pull the connector out of the mount.
6. Remove the camshaft position sensor.
7. Remove the ribs with a screwdriver and remove the cover for the repair opening **arrows**.
8. Remove the camshaft position sensor from the cylinder head and guide the connector through the opening in the toothed belt guard.

To install:
9. Installation is in reverse order. Note the following:
   a. Seal off the opening in the toothed belt guard with a rubber plug.
   b. Mount the toothed belt and adjust the valve timing.
   c. Install the vibration damper.
   d. Install the ribbed belt.

ELECTRONIC CONTROL MODULE (ECM)

LOCATION

The ECM is located in the plenum chamber at the base of the windshield.

REMOVAL & INSTALLATION

➡**If it is desired to replace Engine Control Module (ECM), connect vehicle diagnosis, testing and information system VAS 5051 and perform the function "Replace Control Module".**

1. Before servicing the vehicle, refer to the precautions.
2. Switch off the ignition.
3. Remove the wiper arms and plenum chamber cover.
4. Remove plenum chamber bulkhead
5. On vehicles equipped with shear bolts proceed as follows:

❊❊ WARNING

Thread of shear bolts is equipped with locking compound. By heating the shear bolts using a hot air gun, inhibition effect of the locking compound is lowered.

➡**Cover wires, harness connectors and control modules in the close vicinity of Engine Control Module (ECM) to prevent damage from burning.**

   a. Unscrew shear bolt using pliers on bolt head.

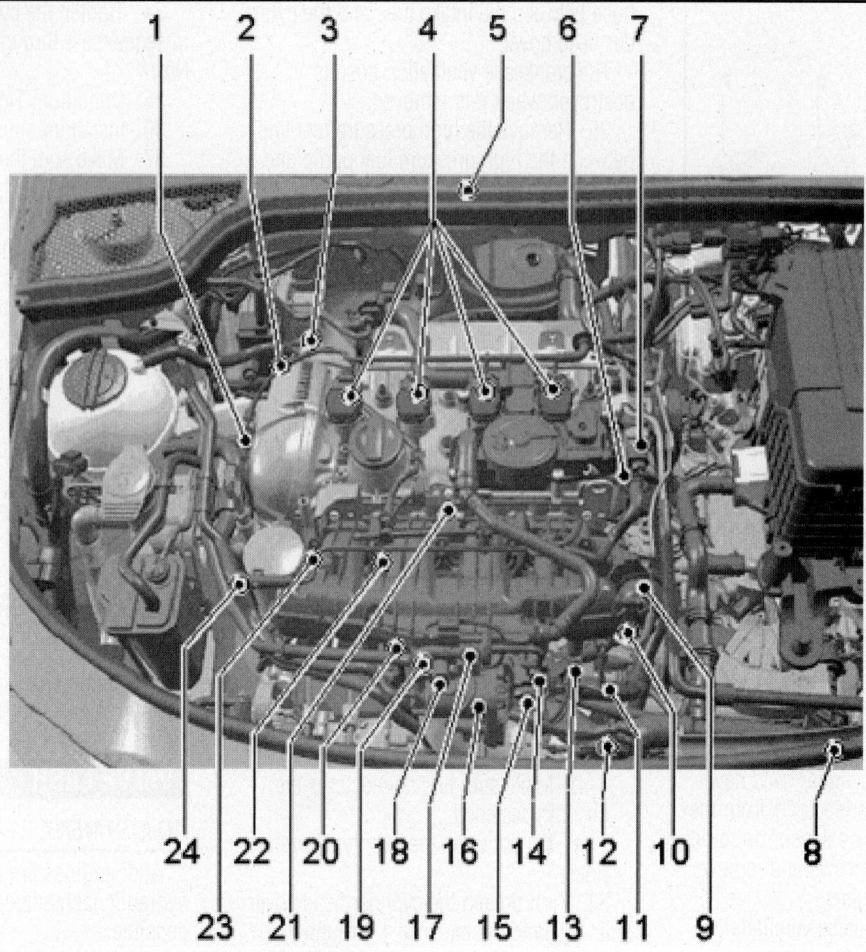

A24-10566

1. Camshaft adjustment valve 1
2. Wastegate bypass regulator valve
3. Turbocharger recalculating valve
4. Ignition coils with power output stages.
5. Engine control module
6. Mechanical single-piston high-pressure pump
7. Fuel pressure regulator valve
8. Engine Coolant Temperature (ECT) sensor (on radiator)
9. Vacuum diaphragm for the channel separating plate
10. Intake Manifold Runner Control (IMRC) valve
11. Engine speed (RPM) sensor
12. Charge air pressure sensor
13. Electrical connector from Knock Sensor (KS) 1
14. Electrical connector from Camshaft Position (CMP) sensor 2
15. 8 pin harness connector for fuel injectors
16. Throttle valve control module J338, throttle drive
     (for Electronic Power Control (EPC),
17. Evaporative Emission (EVAP) canister purge regulator valve N80
18. Intake Air Temperature (IAT) sensor (11 Nm)
19. Knock Sensor (KS) 1 (20 Nm)
20. Engine Coolant Temperature (ECT) sensor
21. Camshaft Position (CMP) sensor
22. Fuel pressure sensor (27 Nm)
23. Intake manifold runner position sensor
24. Oil pressure switch

Fig. 150 Engine bay component locations—2.0L Engines

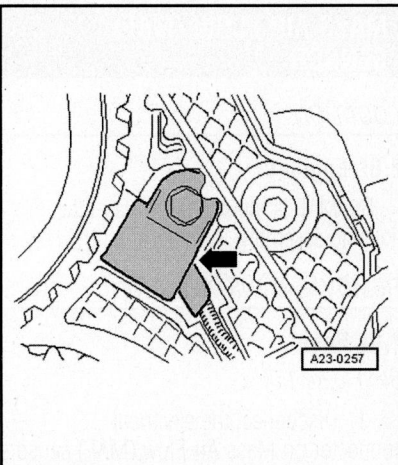

Fig. 151 Remove the camshaft position sensor (arrow)—2.0L Engines

☀☀ WARNING

If screws cannot be removed, saw into heads of shear bolts so that two parallel surfaces are formed and then unscrew them.

    b. Insert a screwdriver between protective housing and retaining plate.

    c. Pry protective housing upward using screwdriver and pull it off sideways from retaining plate.

    6. Disengage forward harness connector from Engine Control Module (ECM) and disconnect it.

    7. Pry-up the locking mechanism slightly.

    8. Then slide Engine Control Module (ECM) out of retainer.

    9. Now disengage rear harness connector from Engine Control Module (ECM) and disconnect it.

To install:

    10. Connect rear harness connector to Engine Control Module (ECM) and engage it.

    11. Slide Engine Control Module (ECM) on to retaining plate.

    12. Press the catch against the engine control module.

    13. Now connect front connector to Engine Control Module (ECM) and engage it.

    14. Slide protective housing on to retaining plate.

    15. Tighten new shear bolts uniformly until bolt heads shear off.

    16. Install the plenum chamber bulkhead.

    17. Install wiper arms and plenum chamber cover.

ENGINE COOLANT TEMPERATURE (ECT) SENSOR

REMOVAL & INSTALLATION

2.0L Engines

See Figures 152 and 153.

    1. With a cold engine briefly open the coolant reservoir cap to reduce the residual pressure in the coolant system.

    2. Remove the cover for the air guide; disengage the side clips to do so.

    3. Unclip the lower air guide, disengage the clips to do so.

    4. Remove the lower air guide together with the air guide hose.

    5. Remove the air guide hose.

    6. Disconnect the electrical connector on throttle valve control module J338.

    7. Remove bolts and remove throttle valve control module J338.

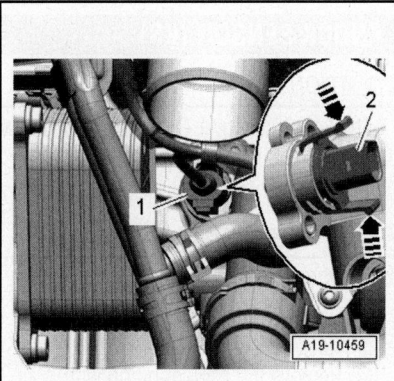

Fig. 152 Remove the Engine Coolant Temperature (ECT) sensor G62— Inserted Version

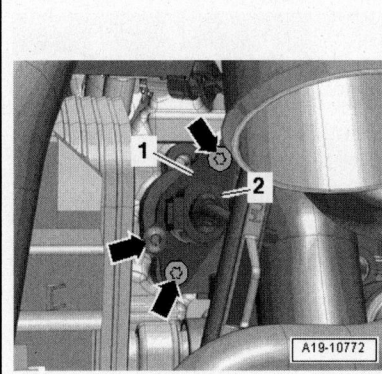

Fig. 153 Remove the coolant temperature sensor G62— Threaded Version

    8. Remove the intake manifold support; to do so, remove the nut and bolt.

➡**Different coolant temperature sensors G62 may be installed, depending on the version.**

    9. Inserted Version:

    a. Disconnect the electrical connector on the Engine Coolant Temperature (ECT) sensor G62.

➡**Lay a cloth below to catch leaking coolant.**

    b. Remove the clamp, to do so, press the latches.

    c. Remove the Engine Coolant Temperature (ECT) sensor G62.

    10. Threaded Version:

    a. Disconnect the electrical connector on the Engine Coolant Temperature (ECT) sensor G62.

➡**Lay a cloth below to catch leaking coolant.**

    b. Remove the bolts and the retaining plate.

    c. Remove the coolant temperature sensor G62.

To install:

    11. Installation is performed in the reverse order of removal, noting the following:

    a. Replace the O-ring.

    b. To prevent coolant loss, immediately insert new Engine Coolant Temperature (ECT) sensor G62 in connecting pieces.

    12. Check the coolant level.

HEATED OXYGEN (HO2S) SENSOR

LOCATION

2.0L Engines

The primary oxygen sensor is on the exhaust pipe at the turbocharger outlet. The secondary sensor is behind the catalytic converter.

2.0L TDI Engine

The primary oxygen sensor is on the exhaust pipe at the turbocharger outlet.

REMOVAL & INSTALLATION

2.0L Gas Engine

See Figures 154 and 155.

    1. Disconnect the electrical harness connector of Heated Oxygen Sensor (HO2S) G39 and Oxygen Sensor (O2S) heater Z19.

Fig. 154 Disconnect electrical harness connector (1) of Heated Oxygen Sensor (HO2S) G39 and Oxygen Sensor (O2S) heater Z19

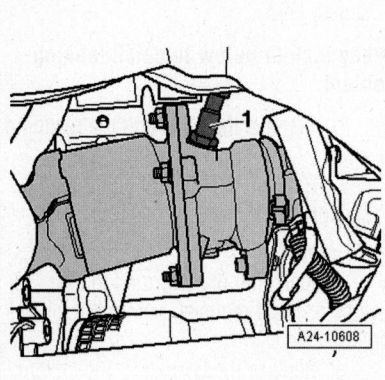

Fig. 155 Remove Heated Oxygen Sensor (HO2S) G39 (1) using a tool from the ring spanner 7 piece set 3337

2. Remove Heated Oxygen Sensor (HO2S) G39 using a tool from the ring spanner 7 piece set 3337.

3. When installing, note the following:

   a. New oxygen sensors are coated with assembly paste; the paste must not get into slots of oxygen sensor body.

   b. For a used oxygen sensor, only coat threads with hot bolt paste. This paste must not come into contact with sensor slots.

   c. Electrical wire of oxygen sensor must always be secured in the same position when installing so that contact with the exhaust pipe is avoided.

2.0L TDI Engine

1. Before servicing the vehicle, refer to the precautions.

2. Unplug the connector.

3. Remove the sensor and cover the hole to prevent dirt from getting into the engine.

To install:

4. Installation is the reverse of removal.

→Thread of new oxygen sensors is coated with hot bolt paste.

❊❊ WARNING

When re-using the previous oxygen sensor, grease only the threads with hot bolt paste G 052 112; the paste must not get into slots of oxygen sensor body

5. Tighten to 41 ft. lbs. (55 Nm).

INTAKE AIR TEMPERATURE (IAT) SENSOR

LOCATION

The IAT is built into the Mass Airflow Sensor (MAF) and cannot be removed separately.

KNOCK SENSOR (KS)

LOCATION

The knock sensor 1 G61 is located below the intake manifold behind the coolant pump.

REMOVAL & INSTALLATION

See Figure 156.

1. Remove the electrical connector 2 from knock sensor 1 G61.

2. Remove the coolant pump with coolant thermostat.

3. Remove knock sensor 1 G61.

4. Installation is in reverse order.

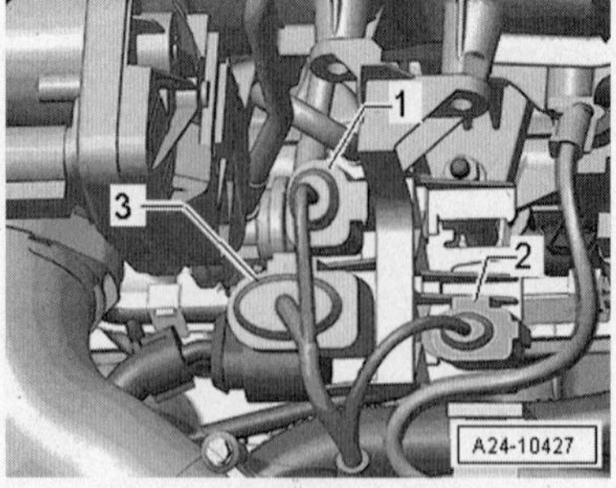

Fig. 156 Electrical connector (2), knock sensor (1) G61

MASS AIR FLOW (MAF) SENSOR

LOCATION

2.0L Engines

The MAF is mounted in the air filter housing assembly.

REMOVAL & INSTALLATION

2.0L Engine

See Figure 157.

1. Disconnect the electrical connector on Mass Air Flow (MAF) sensor G70.

2. Remove both bolts from Mass Air Flow (MAF) sensor G70 and carefully remove Mass Air Flow (MAF) sensor G70 from air filter housing guide.

To install:

3. For problem free operation of Mass Air Flow (MAF) sensor G70 it is very important to observe the following notes and procedures.

4. If the air filter element is very dirty or soaked, dirt particles or moisture may have contaminated the Mass Air Flow (MAF) sensor G70 and may be causing false mass air flow values. This results in a reduction of power, since a lower injection quantity is calculated.

5. Always use an original equipment air filter element.

6. Use a lubricant (silicone free) for installing the intake hose.

7. Secure all hose connections using hose clamps appropriate for the model type.

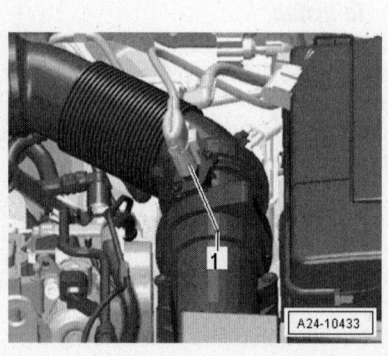

Fig. 157 Remove both bolts from Mass Air Flow (MAF) sensor (1) G70 and carefully remove Mass Air Flow (MAF) sensor G70 from air filter housing guide

8. Check the MAF sensor and intake hose (intake air side) for salt residue, dirt, and leaves.

9. Check the intake duct up to air filter element for dirt. If any contaminants are discovered, clean air filter housing (upper and lower sections) of salt residue, dirt and leaves (if necessary, clean by washing or vacuuming).

10. Further installation is in reverse order.

2.0L TDI Engine

1. Before servicing the vehicle, refer to the precautions.

2. Disconnect air intake hose from the air filter housing.

3. Disconnect the electrical connector on Mass Air Flow (MAF) Sensor G70.

4. Remove both bolts from the Mass Air Flow (MAF) Sensor G70 and carefully remove the Mass Air Flow (MAF) Sensor G70 from the air filter housing guide.

To install:

5. Installation is the reverse of removal.

6. If the air filter element is very dirty or soaked, dirt particles or moisture may have contaminated the Mass Air Flow (MAF) Sensor G70 and may be causing false mass air flow values. This results in a reduction of power, since a lower injection quantity is calculated.

7. Always use an original equipment air filter element.

8. Use a lubricant (silicone-free) for installing the intake hose.

9. Secure all the hose connections using hose clamps appropriate for the model type

10. Check the MAF sensor and intake hose (intake air side) for salt residue, dirt, and leaves.

11. Check the intake ducting to the air filter element for dirt. If any contaminants are discovered, clean the air filter housing (upper and lower parts) of salt residue, dirt and leaves (if necessary, clean by washing or vacuuming).

THROTTLE POSITION SENSOR (TPS)

LOCATION

2.0L & 2.5L Engines

The Throttle Position Sensor (TPS) is built into the electronic throttle valve control module (throttle body).

2.0L TDI Engine

The Throttle Position Sensor (TPS) is built into the intake flap motor V157 (throttle body).

REMOVAL & INSTALLATION

2.0L Gas Engine

See Figure 158.

1. Before servicing the vehicle, refer to the precautions.

2. Loosen the hose clamp.

3. Remove the bolt.

4. Disconnect the electrical connector.

5. Remove the noise insulation.

6. Remove the air guide pipe.

7. Remove the bolt and remove the air guide pipe downward.

8. Disconnect the electrical connector on Throttle Valve Control Module J338.

9. Remove bolts and remove Throttle Valve Control Module J338.

To install:

10. Installation is performed in reverse order of removal, noting the following:

11. Clean the O-ring sealing surface.

12. Replace the seal; when doing so, pay attention to the correct position of the service flag on the sealing ring.

13. Tighten bolts in criss-cross pattern to 31 inch lbs. (3.5 Nm).

※※ WARNING

If a new Throttle Valve Control Module J338 was installed, adapt the engine control module to the Throttle Valve Control Module J338.

2.0L TDI Engine

1. Before servicing the vehicle, refer to the precautions.

➡**When engine is switched off, the intake manifold flap is closed for approximately 3 seconds and then opens again. This reduces the stop jolt.**

Fig. 158 Disconnect electrical connector (1) and remove Throttle Valve Control Module J338 bolts (arrow)

2. Loosen the hose clamp.

3. Remove bolt.

4. Disconnect the electrical connector.

5. Remove the noise insulation.

6. Remove the air guide pipe.

7. Remove the bolt and remove the air guide pipe downward.

8. Disconnect the electrical connector on Intake flap motor V157.

9. Remove bolts and remove Intake flap motor V157.

To install:

10. Installation is performed in reverse order of removal, noting the following:

11. Clean the O-ring sealing surface.

12. Replace the seal; when doing so, pay attention to the correct position of the service flag on the sealing ring.

13. Tighten bolts in criss-cross pattern to 89 inch lbs. (10 Nm).

※※ WARNING

If a new Intake flap motor V157 was installed, adapt the engine control module to the Intake flap motor V157.

VEHICLE SPEED SENSOR (VSS)

LOCATION

The Vehicle Speed Sensor (VSS) is located in the transmission housing.

REMOVAL & INSTALLATION

See Figure 159.

1. Remove the engine cover.

2. Open the air guide pipe hose clamp.

3. Disconnect the electrical harness connector.

4. Remove the noise insulation. Refer to see Description and Operation.

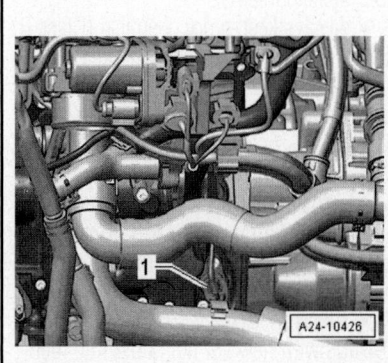

Fig. 159 Disconnect the electrical connector (1) from engine speed sensor

5. Remove the bolts and remove the charge air pipe downward from the throttle valve control module.

6. Remove the charge air hose from the charge air cooler and remove the charge air pipe downward.

7. Disconnect the electrical connector from engine speed sensor.

8. Remove the engine speed sensor bolt.

9. Installation is in the reverse order of removal.

FUEL   GASOLINE FUEL INJECTION SYSTEM

FUEL SYSTEM SERVICE PRECAUTIONS

Safety is the most important factor when performing not only fuel system maintenance but any type of maintenance. Failure to conduct maintenance and repairs in a safe manner may result in serious personal injury or death. Maintenance and testing of the vehicle's fuel system components can be accomplished safely and effectively by adhering to the following rules and guidelines.

• To avoid the possibility of fire and personal injury, always disconnect the negative battery cable unless the repair or test procedure requires that battery voltage be applied.

• Always relieve the fuel system pressure prior to disconnecting any fuel system component (injector, fuel rail, pressure regulator, etc.), fitting or fuel line connection. Exercise extreme caution whenever relieving fuel system pressure to avoid exposing skin, face and eyes to fuel spray. Please be advised that fuel under pressure may penetrate the skin or any part of the body that it contacts.

• Always place a shop towel or cloth around the fitting or connection prior to loosening to absorb any excess fuel due to spillage. Ensure that all fuel spillage (should it occur) is quickly removed from engine surfaces. Ensure that all fuel soaked cloths or towels are deposited into a suitable waste container.

• Always keep a dry chemical (Class B) fire extinguisher near the work area.

• Do not allow fuel spray or fuel vapors to come into contact with a spark or open flame.

• Always use a back-up wrench when loosening and tightening fuel line connection fittings. This will prevent unnecessary stress and torsion to fuel line piping.

• Always replace worn fuel fitting O-rings with new Do not substitute fuel hose or equivalent where fuel pipe is installed.

Before servicing the vehicle, make sure to also refer to the precautions in the beginning of this section as well.

RELIEVING FUEL SYSTEM PRESSURE

See Figures 160 and 161.

➡The fuel injection system is divided into a high pressure section (maximum approximately 150 bars) and a low pressure system (approximately 7 bars).

➡Before opening high pressure parts, e.g. removing high pressure pump, fuel rail, fuel injectors, fuel lines or fuel pressure sensor G247, fuel pressure in high pressure area must be reduced to a residual pressure of approximately 7 bar. The procedure for this is as follows.

1. Connect the vehicle diagnosis, testing and information system VAS 5051B or an ODBII scanner or equivalent.

2. Start engine and run at idle speed.

3. Select *"engine electronics"* in OBD.

4. Then select *"Measured values"* read out.

5. Select measured value block 140.

6. With engine running in idle, the fuel pressure will be displayed in display field 3. Specified value: between 35 and 45 bar.

7. Pry off the left cover on instrument panel using special hook 3370.

8. With engine at idle, pull fuse SC 27 in the fuse holder in driver's side instru-

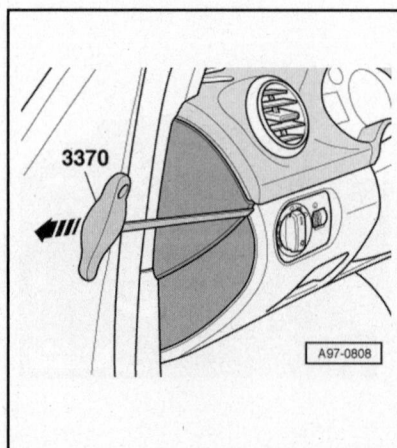

Fig. 160 Pry off left cover on instrument panel using special hook 3370

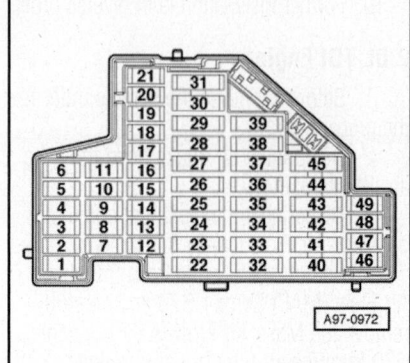

Fig. 161 Pull fuse SC 27 in the fuse holder in driver's side instrument panel— A3 Models only

ment panel from fuel pump control module J538.

9. Check fuel pressure on tester. The fuel pressure decreases rapidly because the mechanical high pressure pump is no longer supplied with fuel from transfer fuel pump G6.

10. Switch ignition off as soon as fuel pressure drops to approximately 8 bar. The fuel pressure must not drop below 6 bars, because otherwise the engine will shut off (risk of catalytic converter damage).

➡The fuel lines will continue to be filled with fuel, but will no longer be under high pressure. To open fuel system, wear protective eyewear and clothing to prevent injuries and contact with skin. Before opening the high pressure system, place a cloth around the connection.

11. After reducing fuel pressure, place a clean cloth around the connection and open the high pressure system immediately. Escaping fuel must be absorbed.

12. Perform the following steps are completing all work:

   a. Install the fuse.

   b. In *"Guided Functions"* operating mode, generate readiness code for the engine control module see: Diagnostic Unit.

FUEL FILTER

REMOVAL & INSTALLATION

A3 Models

MPI Systems, SFI and TFSI Systems

See Figures 162 and 163.

✴✴ CAUTION

Observe all the applicable safety precautions when working around fuel. Whenever servicing the fuel system, always work in a well-ventilated area. Do not allow fuel spray or vapors to come in contact with a spark or open flame. Keep a dry chemical fire extinguisher near the work area. Always keep fuel in a container specifically designed for fuel storage; also, always properly seal fuel containers to avoid the possibility of fire or explosion.

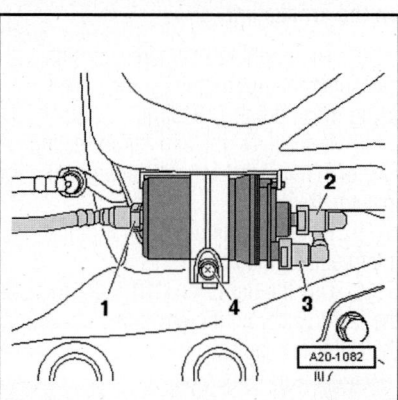

Fig. 162 Disconnect fuel lines (1, 2 and 3) by pressing release buttons and remove bolt (4)

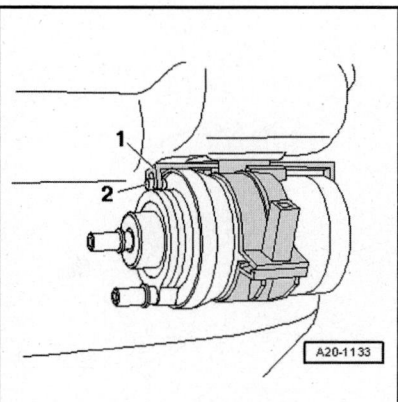

Fig. 163 Pin (2) on filter housing must engage in recess of guide (1) on filter bracket

➡**Before opening the fuel system, lay a clean cloth around the connection point and carefully loosen it, which lowers the pressure.**

1. Properly relieve the fuel system pressure.
2. Place drip tray under fuel filter.
3. Disconnect fuel lines 1, 2 and 3 by pressing release buttons.
4. Remove bolt.
5. Remove fuel filter.
6. Installation is in reverse order of removal, note the following:
   a. The direction of flow is marked on filter housing with arrows.
   b. The pin on filter housing must engage in recess of the guide on filter bracket.

FSI System

See Figure 164.

✴✴ CAUTION

Observe all the applicable safety precautions when working around fuel. Whenever servicing the fuel system, always work in a well-ventilated area. Do not allow fuel spray or vapors to come in contact with a spark or open flame. Keep a dry chemical fire extinguisher near the work area. Always keep fuel in a container specifically designed for fuel storage; also, always properly seal fuel containers to avoid the possibility of fire or explosion.

➡**Before opening the fuel system, lay a clean cloth around the connection point and carefully loosen it, which lowers the pressure.**

1. Properly relieve the fuel system pressure.

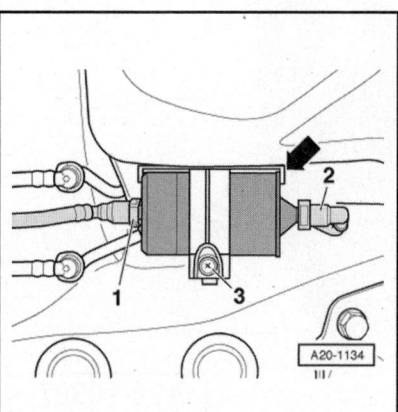

Fig. 164 Disconnect fuel lines (1 and 2) by pressing release buttons and remove bolt (3)

2. Place drip tray under fuel filter.
3. Disconnect the fuel lines 1 and 2 by pressing release buttons.
4. Remove the bolt.
5. Remove the fuel filter.
6. Installation is in reverse order of removal, note the following:
   a. The direction of flow is marked on filter housing with arrows.
   b. The pin on filter housing must engage in recess of the guide on filter bracket.

A4 & A5 Models

See Figures 165 and 166.

✴✴ CAUTION

Observe all the applicable safety precautions when working around fuel. Whenever servicing the fuel system, always work in a well-ventilated area. Do not allow fuel spray or vapors to come in contact with a spark or open flame. Keep a dry chemical fire extinguisher near the work area. Always keep fuel in a container specifically designed for fuel storage; also, always properly seal fuel containers to avoid the possibility of fire or explosion.

➡**Before opening the fuel system, lay a clean cloth around the connection point and carefully loosen it, which lowers the pressure.**

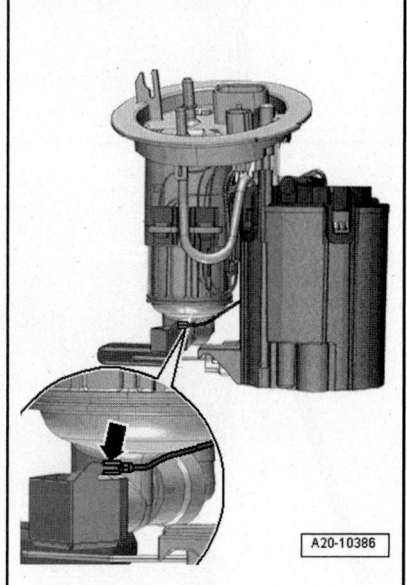

Fig. 165 Disconnect ground connection (arrow) on the fuel pressure regulator retaining plate

1. Remove fuel delivery unit.
2. Disconnect ground connection on the fuel pressure regulator retaining plate.
3. Remove fuel line by pressing the release button.
4. Disconnect the electrical connector for the fuel level sensor.
5. Disconnect the fuel pump electrical connector at the fuel pump.
6. Remove the locking flange with fuel filter upward out of the fuel delivery unit.
7. Release a total of 3 retaining tabs by sliding 3 release bars.
8. Pull the fuel filter down and out of the locking flange.
9. Installation is in reverse order of removal, noting the following:
   a. Replace the O-ring.
   b. Insert the fuel filter into the guides

on the locking flange and press it in until it engages.
   c. The fuel filter can only be inserted in one position.

FUEL INJECTORS

REMOVAL & INSTALLATION
See Figure 167.

1. Before servicing the vehicle, refer to the precautions.

➡**Puller T10133/2A is required to complete this operation.**

2. Remove the intake manifold with the fuel rail. If the injector valves remain attached in the fuel rail, then pull them out.

3. Cover the intake channels with a clean rag.
4. Remove the support element A downward and disconnect the connector from the fuel injectors.
5. Position the puller T10133/2A in the groove on the fuel injector.
6. Mount the removal tool T10133/16, turn the screw and remove the fuel injector.

➡**Pay attention to the intermediate rings.**

To install:

✳✳ WARNING
The combustion chamber seal must always be replaced before re-installing the fuel injector. The Teflon sealing ring of fuel injector may not be oiled or greased.

➡**If an opened intake valve hinders the cleaning, the engine must be turned further by hand using a screw wrench on the crankshaft.**

7. Thoroughly clean bores for high pressure fuel injectors in cylinder head using nylon brush T10133/4.
8. Replace O-ring and Teflon sealing ring of fuel injector Teflon Seal on Fuel Injector, Replacing.
9. Install the fuel injection with the intermediate ring again.
10. Use the Remover T10133/2A to push the fuel injector all the way into the hole in the cylinder head.

✳✳ WARNING
Make sure fuel injectors are positioned correctly in cylinder head.

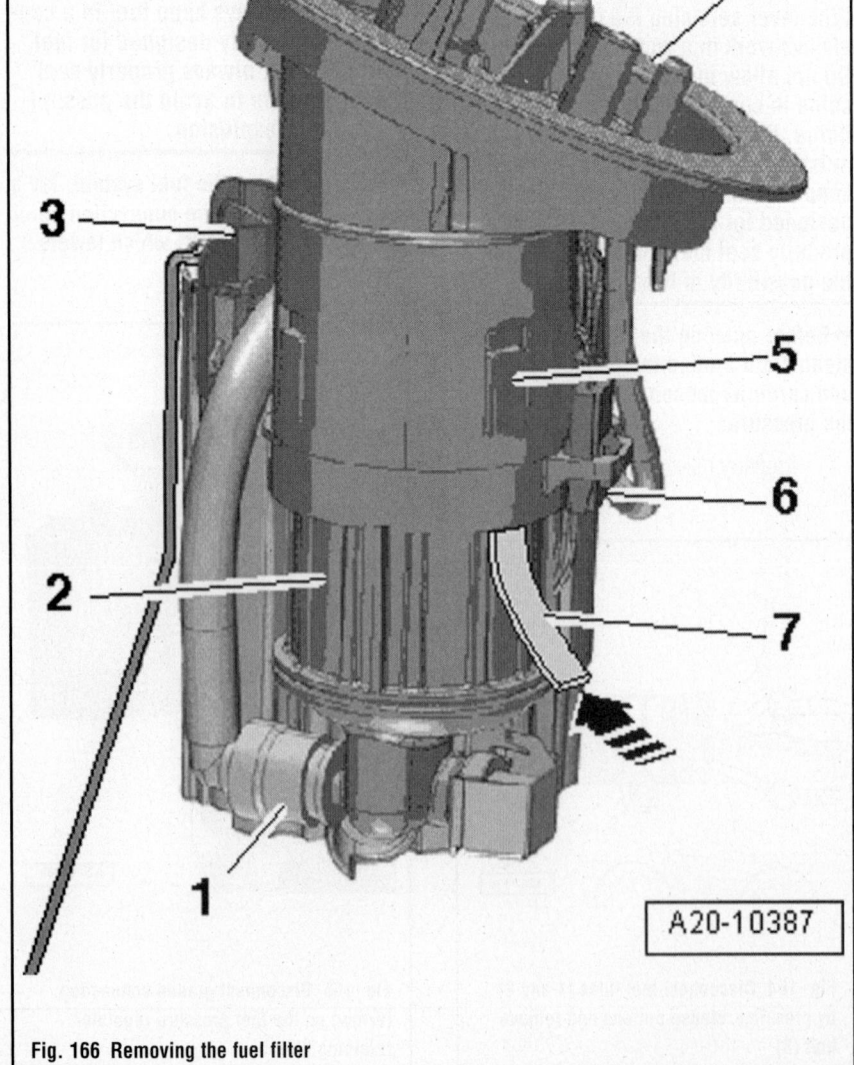

Fig. 166 Removing the fuel filter

A20-10387

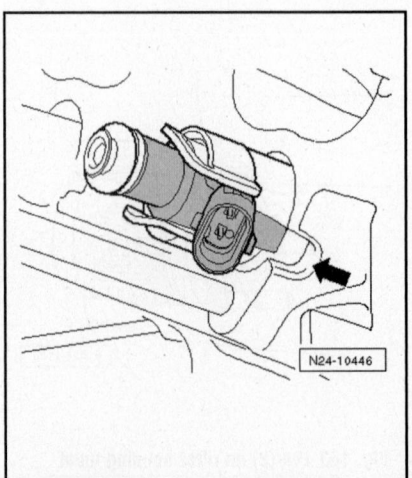

N24-10446

Fig. 167 Make sure fuel injectors are positioned correctly in cylinder head

11. Install the intake manifold with the fuel rail.

FUEL PUMP

REMOVAL & INSTALLATION

Bolt In High Pressure Pump

See Figures 168 through 170.

1. Before servicing the vehicle, refer to the precautions.

✳✳ CAUTION

Fuel system is under high pressure! Before opening the system, perform the procedure for releasing fuel pressure.

2. The removal and installation of the high-pressure fuel pump can only be performed on a cold engine.
3. Catch escaping fuel with a rag.
4. Remove engine cover.

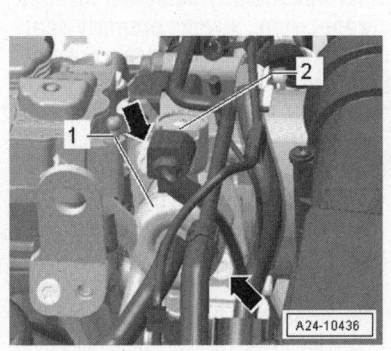

Fig. 168 Disconnect the electrical connector from the Fuel Pressure Regulator Valve N276

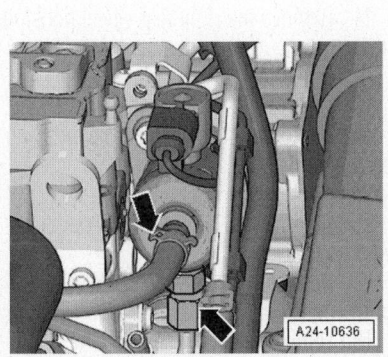

Fig. 169 Open both fuel lines

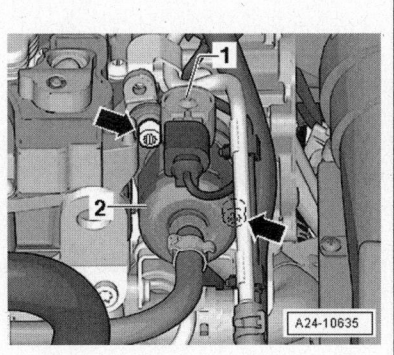

Fig. 170 Remove the two bolts

5. Disconnect the electrical connector from the Fuel Pressure Regulator Valve N276.
6. Open both fuel lines.
7. Remove the two bolts.
8. Carefully pull the high pressure fuel pump out. The roller tappet may stay in the cylinder head.

To install:

9. When installing the high-pressure fuel pump, make sure that no dirt enters the fuel system.
10. The O-ring must always be replaced.
11. High-pressure fuel lines must always be fastened free of tension.
12. Replace the O-ring for the high-pressure pump.
13. Carefully place high pressure pump with sleeve (pay attention to the groove) in opening in cylinder head (check sleeve for damage first).
14. Install new bolts and tighten by hand.
15. Before installing the fuel lines, check the torque of the connections on the high-pressure pump.
16. Tighten the bolts crosswise to 89 inch lbs. (10 Nm).
17. Hand tighten the fuel supply line union nut so that it is free of tension and then tighten it.
18. Connect the electrical connector from the Fuel Pressure Regulator Valve N276.
19. If the fuse was pulled, insert it again.
20. Check fuel system for leaks.

In Tank Lock Ring Pump

See Figures 171 through 173.

1. Condition: The fuel tank may be a maximum of 1/2 full.
2. Empty the fuel tank if necessary using the fuel extracting device VAS 5190.

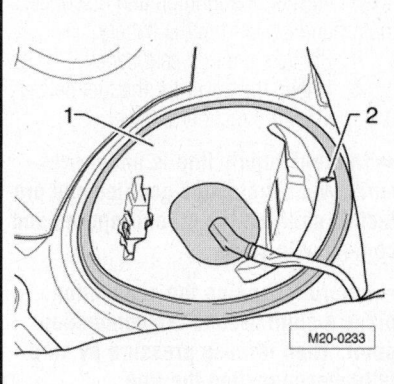

Fig. 171 Unclip the cover (1) for the fuel delivery unit. (2) points in direction of travel

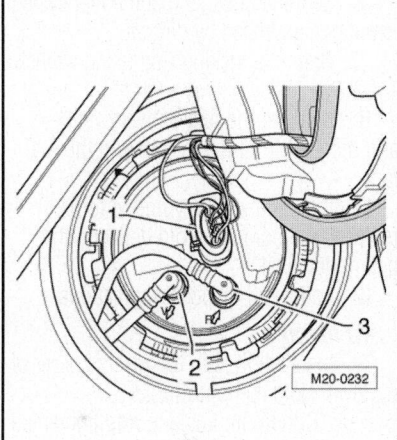

Fig. 172 Disconnect the connector 1, the black supply line 2 and the blue return line 3

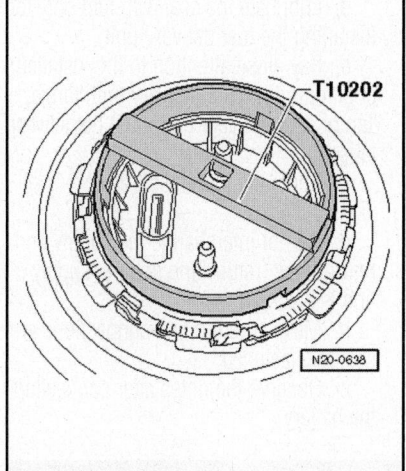

Fig. 173 Open the locking ring using wrench T10202

3. Turn off the ignition and disconnect the ground cable from the battery.

4. Remove the rear seat bench.

5. Unclip the cover for the fuel delivery unit. points in direction of travel.

➡ **The fuel supply line is under pressure! Wear protective goggles and protective clothing to prevent injuries and contact with skin.**

➡ **Before loosening the connection, place a cloth around the connection point. Then release pressure by carefully disconnecting the line.**

6. Disconnect the connector 1, the black supply line 2 and the blue return line 3.

7. Press in the securing ring to disengage the fuel lines.

8. Seal the lines so that the fuel system is not contaminated by dirt, etc.

9. Open the locking ring using wrench T10202.

10. Remove the fuel delivery unit and the seal from the opening in the fuel tank.

11. If the fuel delivery unit is to be replaced then drain the old delivery unit before disposal.

12. Follow all disposal regulations.

To install:

13. Installation is in the reverse order of removal. Note the following:

   a. Condition: Locking ring tightening specification: 81 ft. lbs. (110 Nm).

   b. Do not bend the fuel level sensor G when inserting the fuel delivery unit.

   c. Replace the fuel delivery unit seal if damaged and insert it in the fuel tank opening dry.

   d. Lubricate the seal with fuel only for installing the fuel delivery unit.

   e. Pay close attention to the installed position of the fuel delivery unit flange. Tab on fuel delivery unit must lie between tabs.

   f. Route the fuel lines free of kinks.

   g. Do not interchange the supply and return lines (return line is blue, supply line is black).

   h. Make sure the line connections are securely fastened.

   i. Observe the notes after connecting the battery.

FUEL TANK

DRAINING

See Figures 174 and 175.

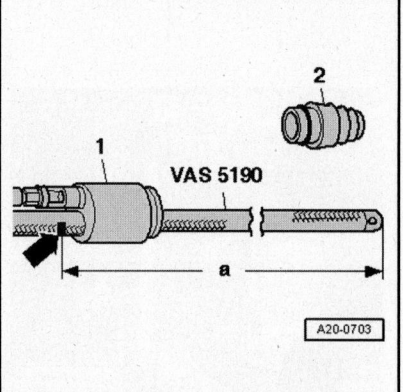

Fig. 174 Remove the cone piece 2 from the shaft piece 1 on the fuel extracting device VAS 5190

✳✳ CAUTION

Secure the fuel extracting device VAS 5190 ground strap to a bare area on the chassis.

---

1. Remove the cone piece from the shaft piece on the fuel extracting device VAS 5190.

2. Using insulating tape, apply a mark on the suction hose at a length of 1,500 mm (a) from the end of the hose.

3. Remove the cap from the fuel filler tube.

4. Install the shaft piece for the fuel extracting device VAS 5190 in on the fuel tank filler tube.

5. On vehicles equipped with a bayonet connection, the shaft piece of the fuel extracting device must be held accordingly.

6. Push the suction hose into the fuel tank until it reaches the mark on the suction hose made previously and extract the fuel. Refer to the operating instructions

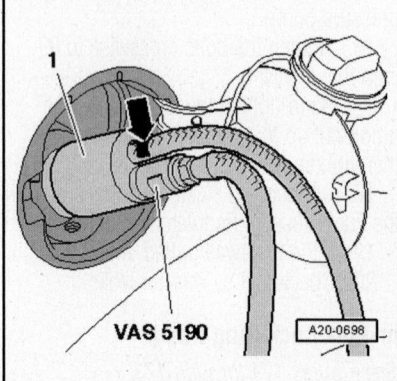

Fig. 175 Install the shaft piece 1 for the fuel extracting device VAS 5190 in on the fuel tank filler tube

---

that come with the fuel extracting device VAS 5190.

7. A pressure point can be sensed after approximately 120 cm. The check valve in the fuel tank must be pushed open. Pull out the hose slightly and slide it in using a light jerk.

8. The fuel tank is drained almost completely.

9. Remove the hose the same way.

REMOVAL & INSTALLATION

A3 Models

✳✳ CAUTION

Observe all the applicable safety precautions when working around fuel. Whenever servicing the fuel system, always work in a well-ventilated area. Do not allow fuel spray or vapors to come in contact with a spark or open flame. Keep a dry chemical fire extinguisher near the work area. Always keep fuel in a container specifically designed for fuel storage; also, always properly seal fuel containers to avoid the possibility of fire or explosion.

---

1. Before servicing the vehicle, refer to the Precautions section.

2. Ensure the tank is empty.

3. Disconnect the negative battery cable.

4. Remove the rear seat.

5. Release the fuel tank flap

6. Unclip the retainers of the fuel tank sending unit cover for the sealing flange.

7. Disconnect the electrical harness at the locking flange.

8. Open the fuel tank flap. Clean the area around the fuel filler tube.

9. Remove the fuel filler cap.

10. Close off the fuel filler tube with a clean rag to prevent dirt from falling in.

11. Remove the right rear wheel housing liner.

12. Disconnect the vent line.

13. Disconnect the electrical connector.

14. Disconnect the vent line by pressing the release buttons.

15. Remove the nuts.

16. Remove the leak detection pump with the bracket.

17. Remove the vent line to EVAP canister by pressing the release button.

18. Unclip the vent line from the bracket.

19. Remove the electrical wiring for the ABS speed sensor from the fuel filler tube bracket.

20. Unfasten the bolts for the fuel filler tube.

21. Disconnect the vent line to EVAP canister by pressing the release button.

22. Loosen the nuts of the double clamp.

23. Push the clamping sleeve rearward to separate the exhaust system.

24. Remove the rear cross member for vehicle floor, by removing the four nuts.

→**An assistant is required to help remove a rear portion of the exhaust system.**

25. Unhook the exhaust system at the retaining loops.

26. Unhook the rear muffler from the retaining loops and remove the rear portion of the exhaust system.

27. Separate the vent lines from the right front of the fuel tank by pressing the release button.

28. Disconnect the fuel line at the fuel filter by pressing the release button.

29. First remove the fuel tank bolts, place an engine or transmission jack underneath for support.

30. Remove the fuel tank straps.

31. By turning it accordingly, lower the fuel tank sideways and remove it.

To install:

32. Installation is in the reverse order of removal.

33. Check for leaks and proper grounding.

34. Check the metal ring electrical connection at the fuel filler tube to a blank portion of the chassis using an Ohm meter. Must read approximately 0 Ohms.

A4 & A5 Models

❊❊ CAUTION

Observe all applicable safety precautions when working around fuel. Whenever servicing the fuel system, always work in a well-ventilated area. Do not allow fuel spray or vapors to come in contact with a spark or open flame. Keep a dry chemical fire extinguisher near the work area. Always keep fuel in a container specifically designed for fuel storage; also, always properly seal fuel containers to avoid the possibility of fire or explosion.

1. Before servicing the vehicle, refer to the Precautions section.

2. Ensure the tank is empty.

3. Disconnect the negative battery cable.

4. For sedans, remove the carpeting in the luggage compartment. If necessary fold the right rear seat backrest.

5. For wagons, remove the 1/3 backrest. Remove the left side luggage compartment trim dirt tray.

6. Unbolt cover for the locking flange in the luggage compartment.

7. Disconnect the electrical harness connector at the locking flange.

8. Disconnect the electrical connector.

9. Disconnect the vent line.

10. For vehicles with connection coupling, disconnect the vent line by pressing the releasing ring downwards and pulling the vent line away.

11. Open the tank flap and clean area around the fuel filler tube.

12. Do not remove the fuel cap.

13. Pry the tensioning ring out from the rubber gaskets and press the rubber gasket through towards the inside.

14. Remove the right rear wheel.

15. Remove the right rear wheel housing liner.

16. Disconnect the vent line from the filler tube.

17. Remove the three EVAP canister cover bolts and cover at the bottom of the spare wheel well.

18. Remove the vent lines. Unclip the vent lines at the top of the bracket.

19. Remove the vehicle floor cover.

20. Remove the rear part of the exhaust system.

❊❊ CAUTION

Before remove the sub frame bolts, secure the vehicle against falling over. Load the luggage compartment with approximately 50 kg.

21. Remove the rear axle.

22. Disconnect the right parking brake cable at the front of the fuel tank.

❊❊ CAUTION

The fuel system is still under pressure. Before opening the system, place rags around the connection area. Then release pressure by carefully loosening the connection.

23. For fuel systems with a return line:

   a. Disconnect the fuel supply line from the fuel filter by pressing the release buttons. Catch the escaping fuel.

   b. Disconnect the fuel return line and vent line at the connection point by pressing the release buttons.

24. For fuel systems without a return line, separate the vent line and fuel line from the right front of the fuel tank by pressing the release buttons.

25. Place an engine or transmission jack under the fuel tank for support.

26. For FWD vehicles, remove the seven bolts securing the tank and lower it onto the jack.

27. For AWD vehicles, remove the 10 bolts securing the tank and lower it onto the jack.

To install:

28. Installation is in the reverse order of removal.

29. Check for leaks and proper grounding.

30. Check the metal ring electrical connection at the fuel filler tube to a blank portion of the chassis using an Ohm meter. Must read approximately 0 Ohms.

IDLE SPEED

ADJUSTMENT

Idle speed is automatically controlled by the Electronic Control Module (ECM). No adjustment is possible.

FUEL SYSTEM SERVICE PRECAUTIONS

Safety is the most important factor when performing not only fuel system maintenance but any type of maintenance. Failure to conduct maintenance and repairs in a safe manner may result in serious personal injury or death. Maintenance and testing of the vehicle's fuel system components can be accomplished safely and effectively by adhering to the following rules and guidelines.

• To avoid the possibility of fire and personal injury, always disconnect the negative battery cable unless the repair or test procedure requires that battery voltage be applied.

• Always relieve the fuel system pressure prior to disconnecting any fuel system component (injector, fuel rail, pressure regulator, etc.), fitting or fuel line connection. Exercise extreme caution whenever relieving fuel system pressure to avoid exposing skin, face and eyes to fuel spray. Please be advised that fuel under pressure may penetrate the skin or any part of the body that it contacts.

• Always place a shop towel or cloth around the fitting or connection prior to loosening to absorb any excess fuel due to spillage. Ensure that all fuel spillage (should it occur) is quickly removed from engine surfaces. Ensure that all fuel soaked cloths or towels are deposited into a suitable waste container.

• Always keep a dry chemical (Class B) fire extinguisher near the work area.

• Do not allow fuel spray or fuel vapors to come into contact with a spark or open flame.

• Always use a back-up wrench when loosening and tightening fuel line connection fittings. This will prevent unnecessary stress and torsion to fuel line piping.

• Always replace worn fuel fitting O-rings with new. Do not substitute fuel hose or equivalent where fuel pipe is installed.

Before servicing the vehicle, make sure to also refer to the precautions in the beginning of this section as well.

RELIEVING FUEL SYSTEM PRESSURE

Fuel pump is activated with switching on the ignition and by door contact switch of driver's door. For safety, disconnect the electrical connector from fuel delivery unit

before opening fuel supply system, if the battery is not disconnected.

FUEL FILTER

REMOVAL & INSTALLATION

See Figures 176 and 177.

1. Before servicing the vehicle, refer to the precautions.

✵ WARNING

Fuel pump is activated with switching on the ignition and by door contact switch of driver's door. For safety, disconnect the electrical connector from fuel delivery unit before opening fuel supply system, if the battery is not disconnected.

2. On fuel filter without the retaining plate, release the clips and remove the fuel filter with the hoses still connected from the retaining plate.

3. On fuel filter with the retaining plate
   a. Loosen the bolt one turn.
   b. Remove the bolt and the nut.
   c. Remove the fuel filter with the hoses still connected.

To install:

4. Installation is the reverse of removal.

FUEL SYSTEM PURGING

BLEEDING

1. Before servicing the vehicle, refer to the precautions.
2. Connect the diesel extractor VAS 5226 or the hand vacuum pump to the

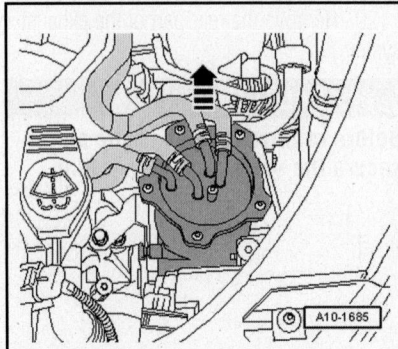

Fig. 176 On fuel filter without the retaining plate, release the clips and remove the fuel filter with the hoses still connected from the retaining plate (arrow)

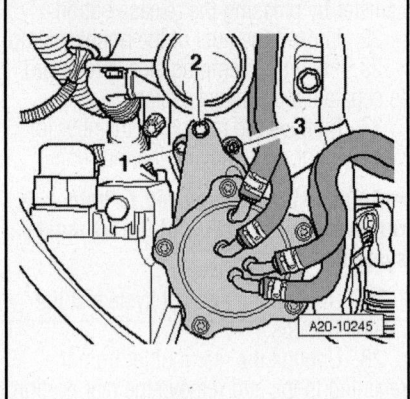

Fig. 177 Loosen the bolt (1) one turn, remove the bolt (2) and the nut (3)

draining container V.A.G 1390/1 on the return hose.

3. Operate the diesel extractor VAS 5226 or the hand vacuum pump, until fuel comes out of the return hose. Make sure no fuel gets into the hand vacuum pump.

When installing the high pressure pump, make sure that no dirt enters the fuel system. Only remove the sealing plugs right before installing the fuel lines.

The fuel tank must be filled.

4. To fill the high pressure fuel pump with fuel, proceed as follows:
   a. Turn on the ignition.
   b. Connect the vehicle diagnostic tester and perform the "bleed fuel system" Guided Function.

5. The fuel pump is activated for 3 minutes.

   a. Then start the engine.
   b. After filling the fuel system, let the engine run at a moderate speed for a few minutes and then turn it off.
   c. Check fuel system for leaks.
   d. Check the Diagnostic Trouble Code (DTC) memory and erase any DTC memory entries if necessary.
   e. Take the vehicle on a 20 km road test using full throttle at least one time. Then check the high pressure area one more time for leaks.

6. If there is still air in the fuel system, the engine may switch to emergency mode during the road test. Turn off the engine and erase the DTC memory. Then continue the road test.

7. Check the DTC memory again.

INJECTION TIMING

ADJUSTMENT

Injection timing is automatically controlled by the Electronic Control Module (ECM). No adjustment is possible.

INJECTION LINES

REMOVAL & INSTALLATION

Refer to Intake Manifold.

INJECTORS

REMOVAL & INSTALLATION

Refer to Intake Manifold.

FUEL SUPPLY PUMP

REMOVAL & INSTALLATION

See Figure 178.

➡**The fuel tank may be a maximum of 1/2 full. Empty the fuel tank if necessary using the fuel extracting device VAS 5190Fuel Tank, Draining.**

1. Before servicing the vehicle, refer to the precautions.
2. With the ignition switched off, disconnect Ground (GND) wire to the battery.
3. Remove seat bench.
4. Unclip cover for fuel delivery unit.

✳✳ CAUTION

The fuel supply line is under pressure. Wear protective goggles and protective clothing to prevent injuries and contact with skin. Before loosening line connections, place rags around the connection

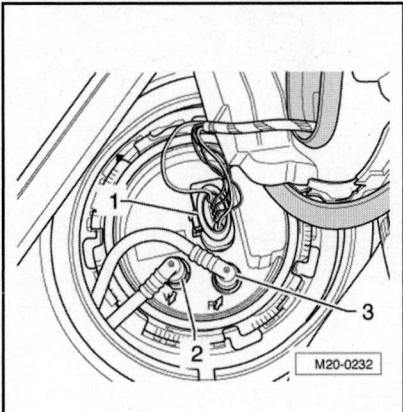

Fig. 178 Disconnect connector (1), black supply line (2) and blue return line (3)

point. Then release pressure by carefully pulling off the line.**

5. Disconnect the connector, black supply line and blue return line.
6. Press in on the securing ring to disengage the fuel lines.
7. Seal lines so that the fuel system is not contaminated by dirt etc.
8. Open the locking ring using wrench T10202.
9. Remove fuel delivery unit and gasket from the fuel tank opening.

➡**If the fuel delivery unit is to be replaced then drain old delivery unit before disposal.**

To install:

10. Installation is the reverse of removal.
11. When inserting fuel delivery unit into fuel tank, be sure not to bend Fuel Level Sensor.
12. Replace fuel delivery unit gasket if damaged and insert it in the fuel tank opening dry.
13. Only coat the seal with fuel when installing fuel delivery unit.
14. Note the installation position of fuel delivery unit flange.
15. Route fuel lines kink-free.
16. Do not interchange supply and return line (return line blue, supply line black).
17. Make sure lines connections are securely fastened.
18. Observe notes after connecting the battery.

INJECTION PUMP

REMOVAL & INSTALLATION

See Figure 179.

1. Before servicing the vehicle, refer to the precautions.
2. Turn the ignition and all electrical consumers off and remove the ignition key.
3. Remove engine cover.
   a. On one piece engine cover, pull the one piece front engine cover s upward with a quick jerk and then pull the lower mount forward.
   b. On the two piece engine cover, first pull the outer cover upward with a quick jerk s in the upper illustration, then pull the inner engine cover upward with a quick jerk s in lower illustration.
4. Disconnect electrical harness connector at Mass Air Flow (MAF) sensor G70.
5. Disconnect the ventilation hose and disengage it from the bracket.
6. Open the spring-type clip using

spring-type clip pliers VAS 5024A and disconnect the intake hose from the Mass Air Flow (MAF) sensor G70.
7. Disconnect the intake manifold from the air guide.
8. Unfasten bolt and remove air filter housing and mass air flow sensor.
9. Carefully cut the cable tie.
10. Open the wiring bracket and disengage the wiring harness.
11. Remove both bolts s from the upper charge air pipe.
12. Remove noise insulation.
13. Remove the charge air pipe bolt from the oil pan.

✳✳ CAUTION

The fuel or fuel lines in fuel system can become very hot. In addition, the fuel system is under pressure. Before opening the system, place rags around the connection area and release pressure by carefully loosening the connection. Wear protective goggles and protective gloves when working on the fuel system.

14. Pull off the supply hose (white marking) and the return hose (blue marking) from the fuel filter.
15. Connect the diesel extractor VAS 5226 or the hand vacuum pump to the draining container V.A.G 1390/1 on the return hose.
16. Operate the diesel extractor VAS 5226 or the hand vacuum pump, until fuel stops coming out of the return hose. Make sure no fuel gets into the hand vacuum pump.
17. Disconnect vacuum line of brake booster from tandem pump.

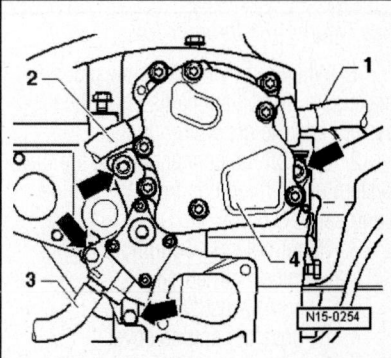

Fig. 179 Disconnect vacuum line of brake booster (1), disconnect supply hose (2) (white marking) and return hose (3) (blue marking) from tandem pump (4). Remove mounting bolts (arrows)

18. Disconnect supply hose (white marking) and return hose (blue marking) from tandem pump.

19. Remove the mounting bolts.

20. Remove the tandem pump from cylinder head.

To install:

21. Installation is performed in reverse order.

☀ WARNING

Make sure that tandem pump coupling has proper seating in camshaft.

➡️**Tandem pump gasket must always be replaced.**

22. Install the tandem pump and tighten the upper bolts to 15 ft. lbs. (20 Nm).

23. Tighten the lower bolts to 89 inch lbs. (10 Nm).

24. Connect the return hose (blue marking) to the return connection on the tandem pump.

25. Connect the supply hose (white marking) to supply connection and the vacuum line from the brake booster to the tandem pump.

26. Connect the supply hose (white marking) to the fuel filter.

27. Connect the diesel extractor VAS 5226 or the hand vacuum pump to the draining container V.A.G 1390/1 on the return hose.

28. Operate the diesel extractor VAS 5226 or the hand vacuum pump, until fuel comes out of the return hose. Make sure no fuel gets into the hand vacuum pump.

29. Connect the return hose (blue marking) to the fuel filter.

GLOW PLUGS

REMOVAL & INSTALLATION

See Figures 180 through 182.

1. When removing the glow plugs, make sure no contaminants enter the fuel system and the glow plug duct.

2. Seal off the connections in the fuel system using the plugs from the engine bung set VAS 6122.

3. Requirements: Condition:
   a. Ignition turned off.
   b. Engine must be cold.

4. Remove the engine cover.

5. Remove the protective strip, if equipped.

6. Remove the connectors from the fuel injectors, the exhaust pressure sensor 1 G450 and the fuel pressure sensor G247.

7. Remove the coolant line bolts arrows

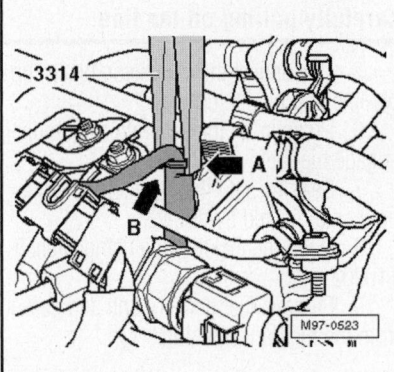

Fig. 180 Position the pliers 3314 with the groove A on the upper collar of the connector B

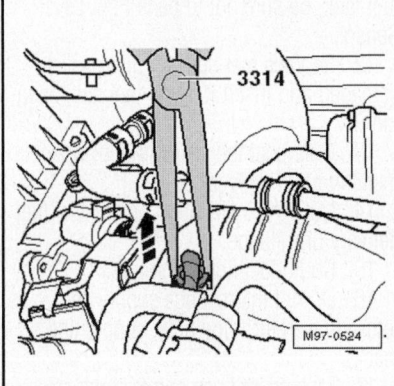

Fig. 181 Carefully pull the connector off the glow plug in the direction of the with the pliers 3314

from the intake manifold and lay the line in front of the intake manifold.

8. Remove the bolt on the intake manifold for the fuel return line.

9. Position the pliers 3314 with the groove on the upper collar of the connector and press together lightly.

➡️**Position the pliers so they do not touch or damage the cable.**

10. Only use suitable tools.

11. Other unsuitable tools can damage the connector.

12. If the connector is damaged when removing it, replace the complete wiring harness including the connector (a connector cannot be replaced separately).

13. Carefully pull the connector off the glow plug with the pliers 3314.

➡️**Do not pull abruptly on the connector.**

14. Do not damage the connector wire.

15. Do not press the pliers together too firmly or the connector will be damaged.

16. The connector is surround by a protective sleeve. Replace the protective sleeve if it is damaged.

17. Loosen the hose clip using the hose clip pliers VAS 6362 and remove the line from the fuel rail.

18. Before removing, clean the return line connection on the fuel injectors (for example using a commercially available detergent).

19. Dry the return line connections.

20. Cover the return line connections with a cloth.

21. Remove the fuel return line connections from the fuel injectors. Pull them upward to release them.

22. Pay attention to cleanliness. Do not let any dirt to get into the disconnected return lines or into the connections for the fuel injection units.

23. Loosen the hose clip using the hose clip pliers VAS 6362 and remove the fuel return line.

24. Loosen the hose clip 4 using the hose clip pliers VAS 6362 and remove the fuel return line at the high pressure fuel pump.

25. Seal the lines so that the fuel system is not contaminated by dirt etc.

26. Remove the fuel return lines and lay them in front of the intake manifold.

27. Remove the glow plug wiring guide and lay it aside.

28. When cleaning the glow plug duct, make sure no contaminants or cleaning solutions enter the connector contacts on the glow plugs.

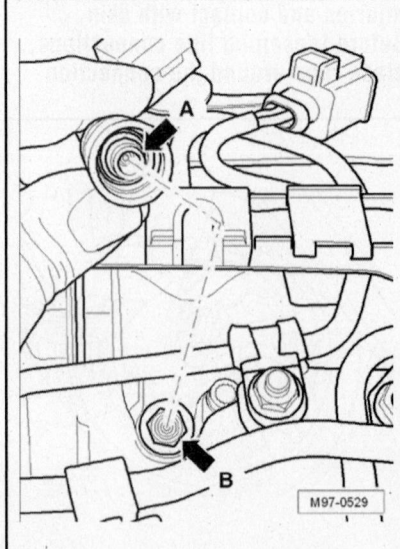

Fig. 182 Guide the center terminal on the connector A into the glow plug socket B by hand

29. Do not clean the connectors with cleaning solutions or compressed air.

30. Clean the glow plug duct in the cylinder head (contaminants must not fall into the cylinder).

31. Extract large contaminants with a vacuum cleaner.

32. Clean glow plugs with a commercially available detergent.

33. Dry the glow plugs with compressed air.

34. Then clean the glow plug duct with a rag dampened with oil.

35. Remove the glow plugs using the socket insert AF 12 for glow plugs . TDI CR VAS 6454.

To install:

36. Install is in the reverse order of removal. Note the following:

37. Condition: When installing the glow plugs, make sure no contaminants enter the fuel system and the glow plug duct.

38. Only remove the sealing plugs right before installing the fuel return line.

39. Make sure lines connections are securely fastened.

40. Install the glow plugs with the socket insert AF 12 for glow plugs 4 cyl. TDI CR VAS 6454.

41. Condition: Tightening specification: 9 ft. lbs. (12 Nm).

42. Secure the fuel return line to the intake manifold.

43. Condition: Tightening specification: 71 inch lbs. (8 Nm).

44. Guide the center terminal on the connector A into the glow plug socket B by hand.

45. Press the glow plug connector 1 on by hand until it engages.

46. Install the fuel return line.

47. Check the Engine Control Module (ECM) Diagnostic Trouble Code (DTC) memory and erase all DTC entries. Refer to "Guided Functions" in the vehicle diagnostic tester.

HEATING & AIR CONDITIONING SYSTEM

BLOWER MOTOR

REMOVAL & INSTALLATION

A3 Models

See Figure 183 and 184.

1. Disconnect the negative battery cable.
2. Remove the glove box.
3. Remove screw clips and remove insulation mat.

4. Remove the bolt (if present).
5. Disconnect the connector.

➡ Do not grasp fan wheel of Fresh Air Blower V2, force against the fan wheel or shifting the balancing weights fastened to fan wheel may cause imbalance and then problems during operation.

6. Disengage locking mechanism and

rotate fresh air blower housing in direction of

➡ Connection between fresh air blower housing and heater (heating & A/C unit of manually regulated A/C system) may be sealed with sealing compound, in this case a great use of force is required for rotating.

➡ Fresh Air Blower V2 is installed in

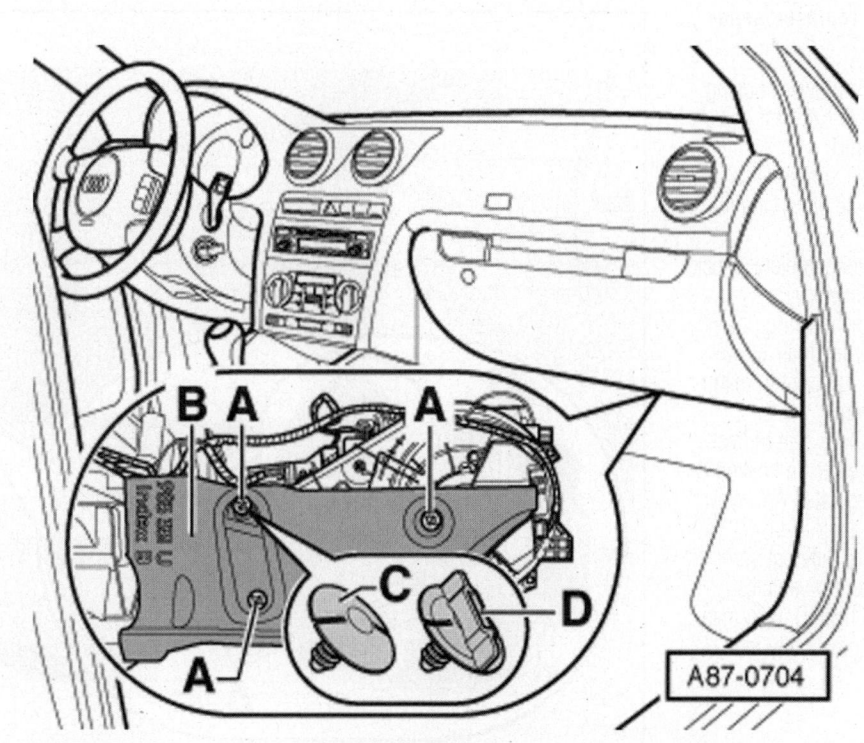

Fig. 183 Remove screw clips (A) (different versions (C) and (D)) and remove insulation mat (B)

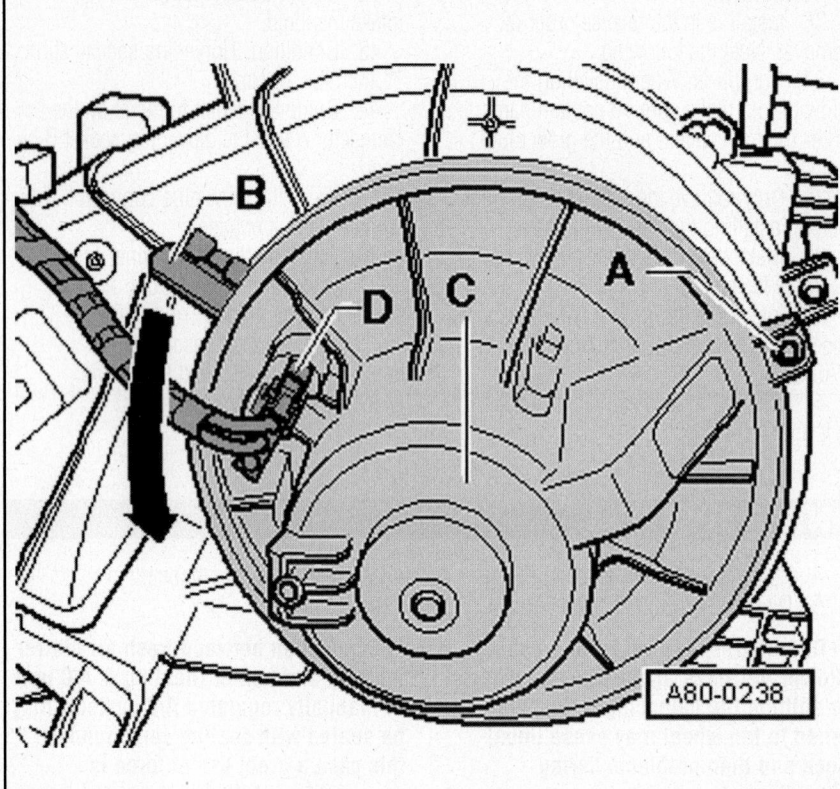

Fig. 184 Remove bolt (A) (if present), disconnect connector (D), disengage locking mechanism (B), rotate fresh air blower housing (C)

2. Remove the screw clips and remove the insulation mat.

3. Loosen the locking mechanism and turn the Fresh Air Blower V2 housing in the direction of the arrow.

➡**Do not grasp fan wheel of Fresh Air Blower V2, force against the fan wheel or shifting the balancing weights fastened to fan wheel may cause imbalance and then problems during operation.**

4. Installation is carried out in the reverse order, when doing this note the following:

a. If the locking mechanism breaks or can no longer hold, you can secure Fresh Air Blower V2 to the air intake housing using a screw.

b. When installing, make sure the Fresh Air Blower V2 fits correctly in the air intake housing.

c. Check DTC memory of A/C control head Climatronic Control Module J255 and erase any displayed malfunction if necessary. Refer to Vehicle Diagnosis, Testing and Information System VAS 5051 in "Guided Fault Finding" function.

d. To check the function, perform an output Diagnostic Test Mode (DTM) on the A/C system. Refer to Vehicle Diagno-

housing and cannot be replaced separately.

7. Remove the fresh air blower housing from heater (from heating & A/C unit of manually regulated A/C unit).

8. Reinstall all removed components in the opposite sequence while observing the following:

a. After installation is complete, check function of Fresh Air Blower V2.

b. Observe the correct seating position when installing the fresh air blower in heater (in heating & A/C unit in manually regulated A/C system).

c. After installing, check seat of fresh air blower housing in heater (in heating & A/C unit in manually regulated A/C system) and function of Fresh Air Blower V2.

d. Note that there are different versions of fresh air blower for vehicles without A/C (only with heater), with manually regulated and automatically regulated A/C system.

A4 & A5 Models

See Figures 185 and 186.

1. Remove the Fresh Air Blower Control Module J126.

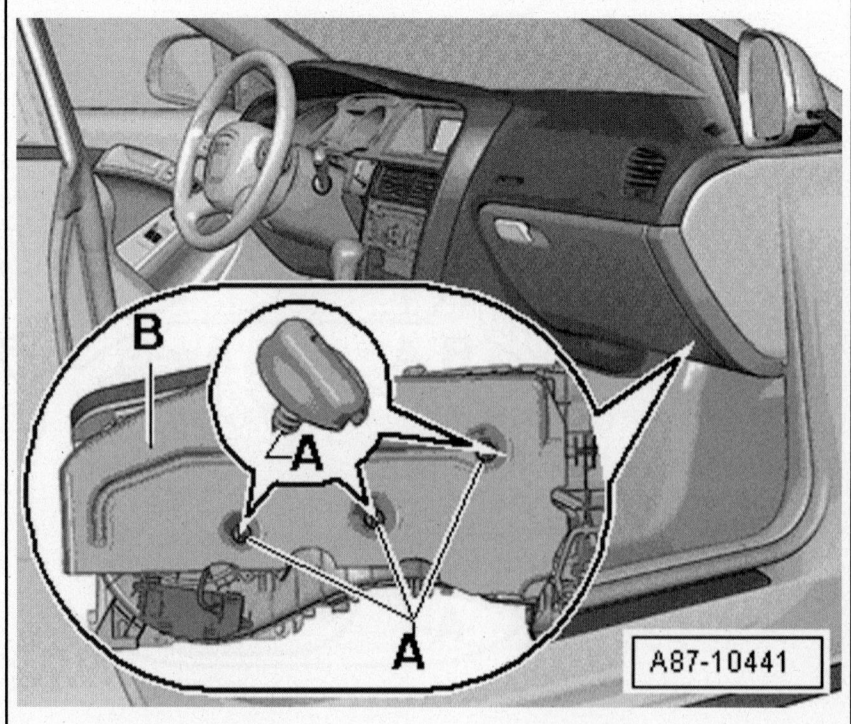

Fig. 185 Remove the screw clips (A) and remove the insulation mat (B)

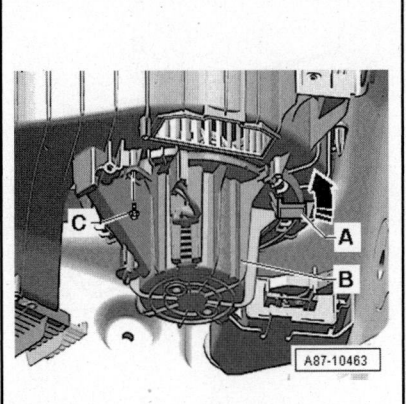

Fig. 186 Loosen the locking mechanism (A) and turn the Fresh Air Blower V2 (B)

sis, Testing and Information System VAS 5051 in "Guided Fault Finding" function.

HEATER CORE

REMOVAL & INSTALLATION

A3 Models

See Figures 187 and 188.

1. Before servicing the vehicle, refer to the Precautions section.
2. Disconnect the negative battery cable.
3. Drain and recycle the engine coolant.
4. Remove the following, if necessary, to gain access to the coolant hoses:
    a. Top engine cover.
    b. Air guide to throttle valve and possible the intake manifold.
    c. Air pipe to intake manifold.
    d. Heat protection cover for the connection area of the coolant hoses and expansion valve.
5. Before removing the hoses, mark the orientation. The top hose is the coolant supply hose from the cylinder head. The bottom hose is the return hose to the water pump.
6. Clamp the hoses off to heater core.
7. Connect a section of hose to the supply connection and hold a container under the return connection.
8. Using compressed air, carefully blow in the length of hose connected to the supply connector and catch the excess coolant in the container.
9. Remove the bolt from the hose connector flange.
10. Remove the storage compartment on the driver's side.
11. Remove the center console. Refer to Console in Interior under Body.

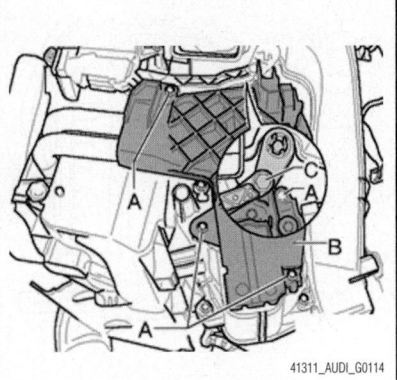

Fig. 187 Removing the four bolts (A), cover (B) and lever location (C)—A3 Models

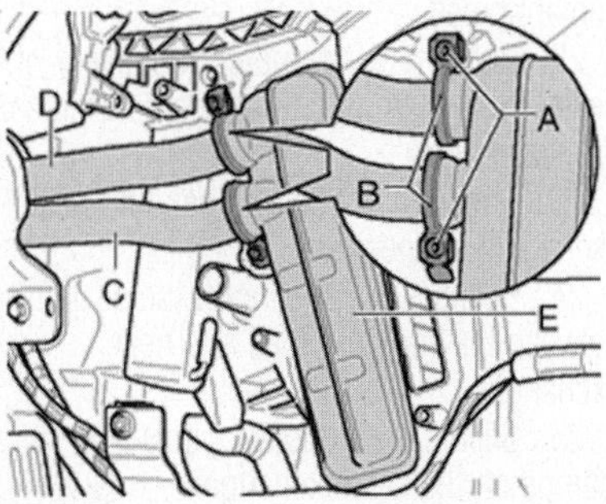

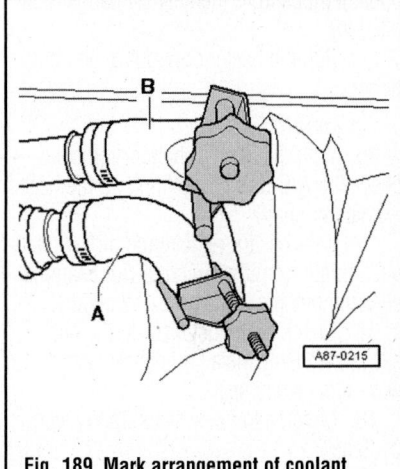

A. Bolts   D. Coolant pipes
B. Clamps   E. Heater core
C. Coolant pipes

Fig. 188 Removing the heater core—A3 Models

12. Remove the left footwall vent and remove the bracket.
13. Remove the four bolts and remove the cover.

➡**If the lever to the left of the temperature flap is located unfavorably so that the bolt is not accessible, switch the ignition on and select a different temperature setting on the climate controls, e.g. "Hi".**

14. Cover the floor mat in an area below the heater core with leak proof foil and absorbent paper.
15. Remove the bolts and the clamps from the connections of the coolant pipes and at the heater core.
16. Disconnect the coolant pipes from the heater core by sliding the pipes towards the bulkheads.
17. Pull the heater core out of the heating and A/C unit.
18. To install, reverse removal procedure.

19. Check the seals installed on the heater core, make sure that they are not damaged and replace as necessary.

A4 & A5 Models

See Figures 189 through 192.

1. Remove the plenum chamber cover.

➡**In vehicles with electrically adjustable seats, move the seats back as far as possible before disconnecting the battery.**

2. Remove the battery.
3. Dissipate pressure in coolant circuit by opening cap at coolant expansion tank.
4. Mark the arrangement of coolant hoses.
    • Connect the coolant hoses on the proper side:
    • Coolant hose (A) supply hose from the cylinder head.

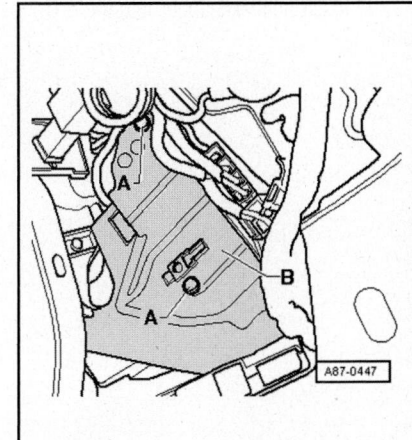

Fig. 189 Mark arrangement of coolant hoses A and B

Fig. 190 Remove screws (A) and remove cover (B) from the coolant pipes

- Coolant hose (B) return hose to water pump.
- Bleed the coolant circuit.

5. Clamp off both coolant hoses to the heat exchanger of the A/C unit (e.g. using hose clamps up to Ø 25 mm 3094) and remove them.

6. Place a container under supply hose from the cylinder head connection .

7. Attach a piece of hose to return hose to water pump connection and carefully blow the coolant with a compressed air gun out of the heat exchanger (into the container).

8. Remove the firewall grommet.

9. Remove the storage compartment on the driver side.

10. Remove the gas pedal module.

11. Remove screws and remove the cover from the coolant pipes.

12. Cover the carpet under the connections to the heat exchanger with absorbent paper.

13. Release clamps and remove both coolant pipes from the heat exchanger connections.

14. Pull the heater core out of air conditioner.

To install:

15. With the heat exchanger removed, check the A/C unit for soiling (via the heat exchanger shaft).

16. If necessary remove the dirt or residual coolant from the A/C unit (for example after removing a leaky heat exchanger).

17. Check seals installed on the heat exchanger. Only install a heat exchanger with undamaged seals.

18. Moisten the new seals lightly with coolant.

19. Insert the new seals (included in the delivery scope of the heat exchanger) in the connections of heat exchanger.

20. Insert heat exchanger into the A/C unit.

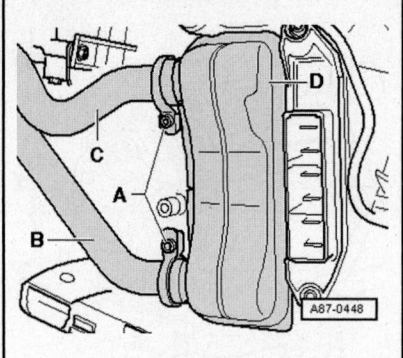

Fig. 191 Release clamps (A) and remove both coolant pipes (B) and (C) from the heat exchanger connections. Pull heater core (D) out of air conditioner

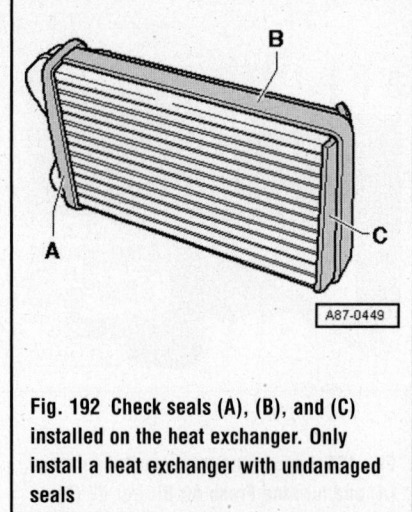

Fig. 192 Check seals (A), (B), and (C) installed on the heat exchanger. Only install a heat exchanger with undamaged seals

21. Remove the old clamps from both coolant pipes.

22. Install new (included in delivery of heater core) clamps on both coolant pipes for heater core.

23. Push both coolant pipes into heat exchanger connections.

24. Recheck the seating of the seals between the coolant pipes and heat exchanger.

25. Secure both coolant pipes with clamps on the heat exchanger.

26. Check the seating of both clamps. They must enclose the flange on the heat exchanger and coolant pipe completely and must not touch other components.

27. Tighten bolts on clamps to 2.5 Nm.

28. Connect the coolant hoses properly to heater core. Observe markings:

    a. A - Supply hose from cylinder head.

    b. B - Return hose to water pump.

29. Reinstall the removed components in reverse order of removal except the driver side storage compartment.

30. Bleed the cooling circuit.

31. The heat exchanger must be additionally bled by the arrangement of the coolant pipes to the heat exchanger of the A/C unit. Proceed as follows:

    a. Bleed the coolant circuit.

    b. Switch the ignition off.

    c. Carefully open the coolant reservoir cap (observe safety precautions when opening the cap).

    d. Release the clamp on coolant hose.

    e. Push hose back until the bore in the hose is no longer closed by the pipe.

    f. Increase the pressure in the coolant circuit e.g. using the hand pump of the cooling system tester V.A.G 1274.

    g. Bleed the heat exchanger via hose until the coolant is bubble-free.

    h. Connect coolant hose and secure it with the clamp.

    i. If necessary add coolant.

32. Check the coolant circuit for leaks, pay particular attention between coolant hoses and heater core.

33. Reinstall the driver's side storage compartment and remaining removed components.

STEERING

POWER STEERING GEAR

REMOVAL & INSTALLATION

A3 Models

See Figure 193.

1. Before servicing the vehicle, refer to the precautions section.
2. Disconnect the battery.
3. Remove the nuts and remove foot well trim.
4. Remove the bolt and pull universal joint from steering gear.
5. Remove the front wheels.
6. Loosen the nut from tie rod end but do not remove completely.
7. Press off tie rod end from wheel bearing housing using Ball Joint Puller 3287A.
8. Remove the sound insulation at bottom.
9. Remove the coupling rod from stabilizer bar.
10. Remove the bolts.
11. Remove the bolts and remove pendulum support from transmission.
12. Remove the bracket for exhaust system from sub frame.
13. Remove the bolts for heat shield.
14. Remove the heat shield from sub frame.
15. Loosen the bolts for steering gear and stabilizer bar.
16. Secure sub frame and consoles.
17. Position engine/transmission assembly jack under sub frame.
18. Place wooden block or similar between engine/transmission assembly jack and sub frame.

19. Loosen the bolts and lower sub frame and consoles slightly. Make sure all electrical connections are out of the way.
20. Remove the heat shield above steering gear.
21. Remove the bolts.
22. Remove the cable guide from sub frame.
23. Unclip all other cable fasteners from steering gear.
24. Disconnect the all electrical connections at steering gear.
25. Remove the stabilizer bar from sub frame, then remove steering gear.

To install:

➡**Threaded sleeves of steering gear must sit in holes of sub frame.**

➡**Coat seal on steering gear with lubricant, e.g. lubricating soap, before installing.**

26. After attaching steering gear to drive axle, make sure that seal on steering gear makes contact with mounting plate without kinking and seals opening to foot well prop-

erly. Otherwise, this may result in water leaks and/or noise.
27. Before positioning bolts for sub frame, position steering gear on sub frame and fasten bolts for steering gear and stabilizer bar.
28. Bolt on heat shields with steering gear.
29. Bolt on sub frame and consoles with body.
30. Bolt on steering gear with sub frame.
31. Bolt on ball joint with control arm. Always use new bolts.

➡**Make sure that boot is not damaged or twisted.**

32. Bolt on universal joint with steering gear.
33. After installation, position of steering wheel must be checked with a road test.

A4 & A5 Models

See Figure 194.

1. Before servicing the vehicle, refer to the precautions section.

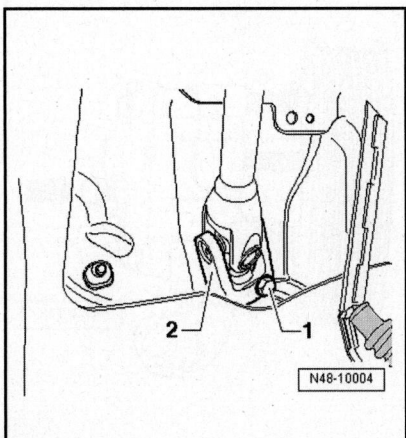

Fig. 193 Remove bolt (1) and remove the universal joint (2) from the steering gear

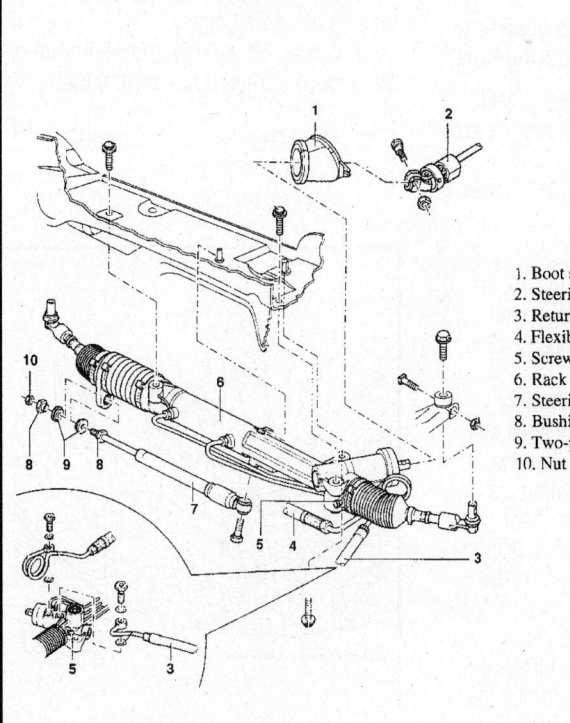

1. Boot seal
2. Steering column
3. Return hose
4. Flexible hose
5. Screw plug for centering the steering wheel
6. Rack and pinion steering gear
7. Steering damper
8. Bushing
9. Two-piece rubber bushing
10. Nut

Fig. 194 Exploded view of the steering gear mounting—A4 models

2. Remove or disconnect the following:
- Battery
- Battery box
- Steering column U-joint bolt

3. Release the eccentric by turning the Torx® T50 bolt clockwise, then remove the bolt.

➡ **Before removing the steering column from the steering gear, secure the steering column with safety wire.**

❊❊ WARNING

Be sure to lock the steering wheel, otherwise the air bag unit coil spring may be damaged.

4. Lock the steering wheel in the center position and do not move during the repairs.

➡ **The splines between the top and bottom part of the steering column must not be separated.**

5. Move the U-joint down and out of the way.

6. Using hose clamps tool 3094, pinch off the suction and return lines to the steering gear.

7. Remove or disconnect the following:
- Front wheels
- Left and right tie rods
- Tie rod opening cover

➡ **Place a drip tray under the vehicle to catch any residual power steering fluid.**

- Banjo bolts for the steering gear suction and return hydraulic hoses
- Steering gear mounting bolts
- Steering gear through the left side wheel opening

To install:

8. Remove the screw plug to lock the steering gear in the center position with locking tool VAG 1907 and torque to 13 ft. lbs. (18 Nm)

9. Install or connect the following:
- Steering gear through the left side wheel opening. Torque bolt No. 3 to 48 ft. lbs. (65 Nm) and bolts No. 1 and 2 to 48 ft. lbs. (65 Nm).
- Power steering gear hoses using new sealing gaskets. Torque the return hose banjo bolt to 37 ft. lbs. (50 Nm) and the suction hose banjo bolt to 30 ft. lbs. (40 Nm).
- Left and right tie rods. Torque the bolts to 33 ft. lbs. (45 Nm).
- Tie rod opening cover
- U-joint to the steering gear and the Torx® adjusting bolt by turning it clockwise

10. Remove the locking tool VAG 1907.

11. Install or connect the following:
- Screw plug. Torque it to 13 ft. lbs. (18 Nm)
- Adjusting bolt. Torque the nut to 30 ft. lbs. (40 Nm)

12. Remove the steering wheel lock

13. Remove the Hose Clamp tools 3094 and check the hydraulic fluid

14. Install or connect the following:
- Battery tray
- Battery

❊❊ WARNING

If the hydraulic fluid requires being topped of, use only an approved fluid, otherwise internal damage may occur.

15. Start the vehicle and check for leaks.

16. Check and/or adjust the wheel alignment.

POWER STEERING PUMP

REMOVAL & INSTALLATION

See Figures 195 through 198.

1. Remove noise insulation.
2. Tension ribbed belt.
3. Remove ribbed belt from power steering pump belt pulley.
4. Clamp off suction and return line using Hose clamps up to 25 mm dia. 3094.
5. Position drip tray underneath.
6. Remove suction line.
7. Remove pressure hose, SW 22 mm.

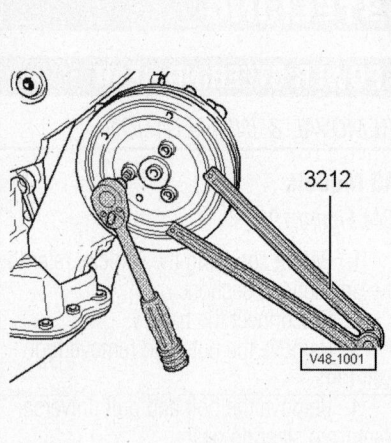

Fig. 196 Remove pulley of power steering pump using Spanner Wrench 3212

8. Remove pulley of power steering pump depending on version, counter hold using Spanner Wrench 3212 do to do.

9. Remove connections on back side of power steering pump.

10. Remove power steering pump.

To install:

11. Installation is in reverse order of removal, with special attention to the following:

a. Refer to the illustration for torque values.

b. Replace the seals and gaskets.

c. Before installing new pump on intake side, fill hydraulic oil and turn by hand until oil escapes on pressure side.

d. Secure all the hose connections using new hose clamps.

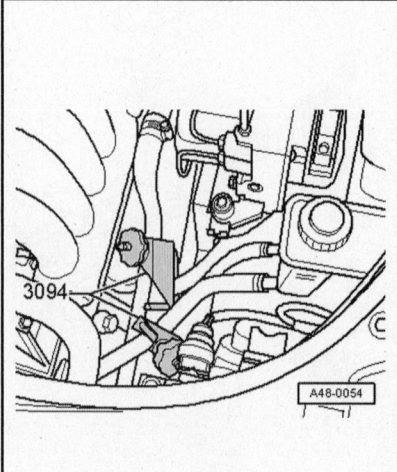

Fig. 195 Clamp off suction and return line using Hose clamps up to 25 mm dia. 3094

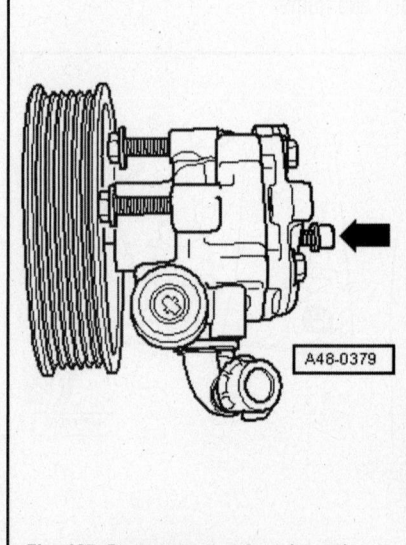

Fig. 197 Remove connections (arrow) on back side of power steering pump

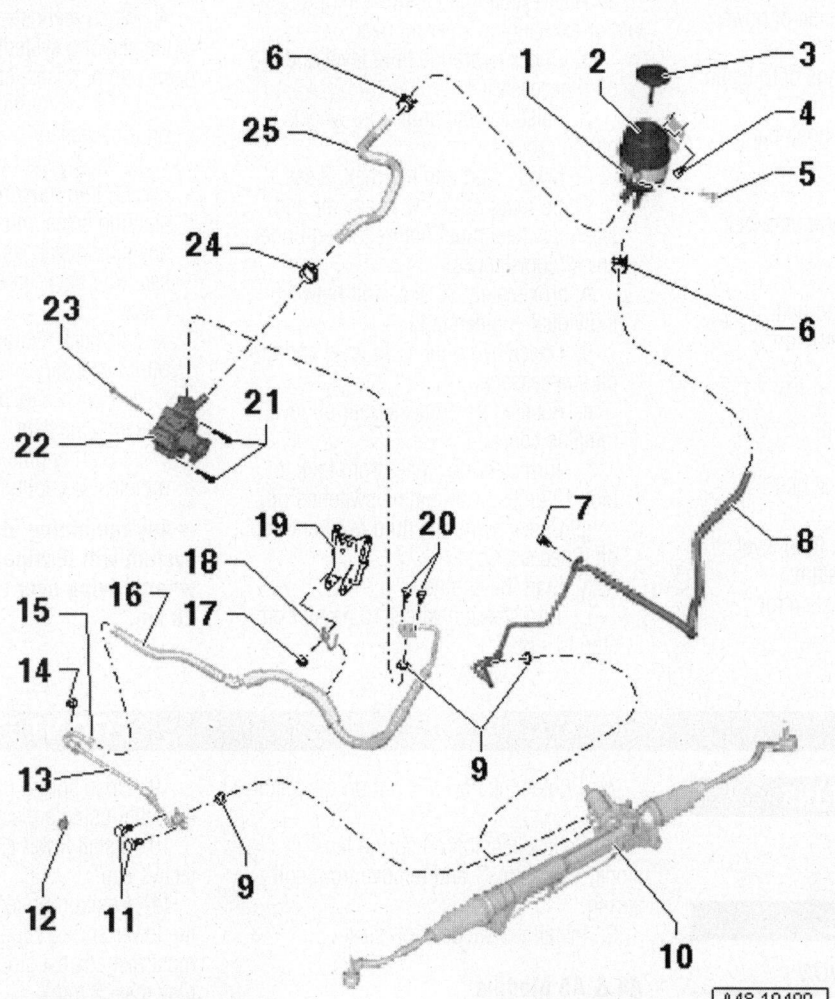

A48-10490

1. Tensioning Strap
2. Reservoir
3. Cap with Dip Stick
4. Bolt 7 ft. lbs. (9 Nm)
5. Bolt 7 ft. lbs. (9 Nm)
6. Spring Clamp
7. Bolt 7 ft. lbs. (9 Nm)
8. Return Line
9. Seal
10. Power-Assisted Steering Gear
11. Bolt 25 ft. lbs. (20 Nm)
12. Rubber Bushing 6 Nm
13. Pressurized Line

14. Nut 6 Nm
15. Union Nut 30 ft. lbs. (40 Nm)
16. Pressurized Line
17. Nut 7 ft. lbs. (9 Nm)
18. Retaining Bracket
19. Connector
20. Bolt 7 ft. lbs. (9 Nm)
21. Bolt 18 ft. lbs. (25 Nm)
22. Power Steering Pump
23. Bolt 18 ft. lbs. (25 Nm)
24. Clamp
25. Intake Hose

Fig. 198 Power steering pump overview

12. Turn hub by hand until oil runs out of the pressure side.

13. Fasten power steering pump to bracket.

14. Install and fasten bolts.

15. Tighten bolt on back side of power steering pump.

16. Install new sealing rings onto banjo bolt.

17. Tighten the pressure hose banjo bolt.

18. Install the intake line.

19. Tighten power steering pump belt pulley.

20. Install ribbed belt.

21. When installing ribbed belt, make sure it is seated correctly on pulleys.

22. Install lock carrier.

23. Install noise insulation.

24. Fill with hydraulic oil.

25. Start engine and check belt running.

26. Check power steering fluid level.

27. Bleed the steering system.

28. Check the steering system for leaks.

BLEEDING

1. After steering system reconstruction, system must be bled differently depending on extent of reconstruction.

2. After exchanging entire steering system or exchanging steering gear:

   a. Check hydraulic fluid level and top off if necessary.

   b. Raise vehicle until front wheels are off the ground.

   c. Briefly start engine (max. 2 sec.) Pump must not draw in any air and steering wheel must not be turned under any circumstances.

   Approximately 30 sec. wait between individual engine starts.

   d. Check hydraulic fluid level and top off if necessary.

   e. Repeat this process until oil level remains constant.

   f. Turn steering wheel from lock to lock 10 times, with engine switched off.

   g. Check hydraulic fluid level and top off if necessary.

   h. Start the engine.

   i. Turn steering wheel 10 times from stop to stop.

   j. Check hydraulic fluid level and top off if necessary.

3. Any remaining air in steering system will dissipate by itself when driving over the next 10 to 20 km.

4. When reconstruction of a component of the steering system besides the steering gear (pump, hoses, etc.):

   a. Check hydraulic fluid level and top off if necessary.

   b. Briefly start the engine (max. 2 sec.) Pump must not draw in any air and steering wheel must not be turned under any circumstances. Approximately 30 sec. wait between individual engine starts.

   c. Check hydraulic fluid level and top off if necessary.

   d. Repeat this process until oil level remains constant.

   e. Start engine and allow to run 2 - 3 minutes, do not turn steering wheel.

➡ **Any remaining air in steering system will dissipate by itself when driving over the next 10 to 20 km.**

SUSPENSION

COMPONENT LOCATIONS

See Figures 199 through 201.

COIL SPRING

REMOVAL & INSTALLATION

A3 Models

See Figures 202 and 203.

1. Pretension coil spring using spring compressor VAG 1752/1 until upper axial groove ball bearing is free.

2. Remove hex nut from piston rod.

3. Remove components of suspension strut and coil spring using spring compressor VAG 1752/1.

➡ **First preload spring far enough so that tension is relieved on upper spring retainer!**

4. Make sure the coil spring is properly seated in the spring holder VAG 1752/4 see.

To install:

5. Place coil spring with spring compressor VAG 1752/1 on lower spring plate.

6. End of spring coil must rest against stop

7. Tighten the new hex nut on the piston rod.

8. Relieve tension on spring tensioner VAG 1752/1 and remove from coil spring.

9. Install the suspension strut.

A4 & A5 Models

See Figures 204 through 207.

1. Clamp suspension strut in vise with shock absorber fork installed.

2. Mark installation location of the mounting bracket to the T-pin on the shock absorber tube (felt-tip pen).

3. Pretension coil spring using spring compressor V.A.G 1752/1 and spring holder V.A.G 1752/7 until upper suspension strut is free.

4. Make sure coil spring is seated in spring holder correctly.

5. Remove nut from piston rod using tools.

6. Remove individual components of suspension strut and pretensioned coil spring with spring compressor V.A.G 1752/1.

7. Remove protective cap 1 and bottom spring washer.

8. Loosen suspension strut 3 using plastic hammer and remove upward.

FRONT SUSPENSION

9. Drive spring plate onto new shock absorber using a plastic hammer.

10. Install lower spring support and protective cap.

11. Position pretensioned coil spring on the lower spring support. End of spring coil must rest against stop arrow (permissible play max. 2 mm).

12. Install mounting bracket with spring washer onto pre-loaded spring so that spring washer makes contact on end of spring coil arrow (permissible play max. 2 mm).

13. Position individual suspension strut components.

14. Tighten nut using special tools.

15. Align marking on mounting bracket to T-pin on shock absorber tube and release tension in the spring.

16. Mounting bracket installation position:

   a. Install spring mounting tool V.A.G 1752/2 as shown in the illustration.

17. Tension suspension strut with spring compressor vertically in the spring mounting tool V.A.G 1752/2.

18. Tension suspension strut so the pin engages in the clamping jaw opening.

19. When tensioning, make sure front damping adjustment valve or electrical

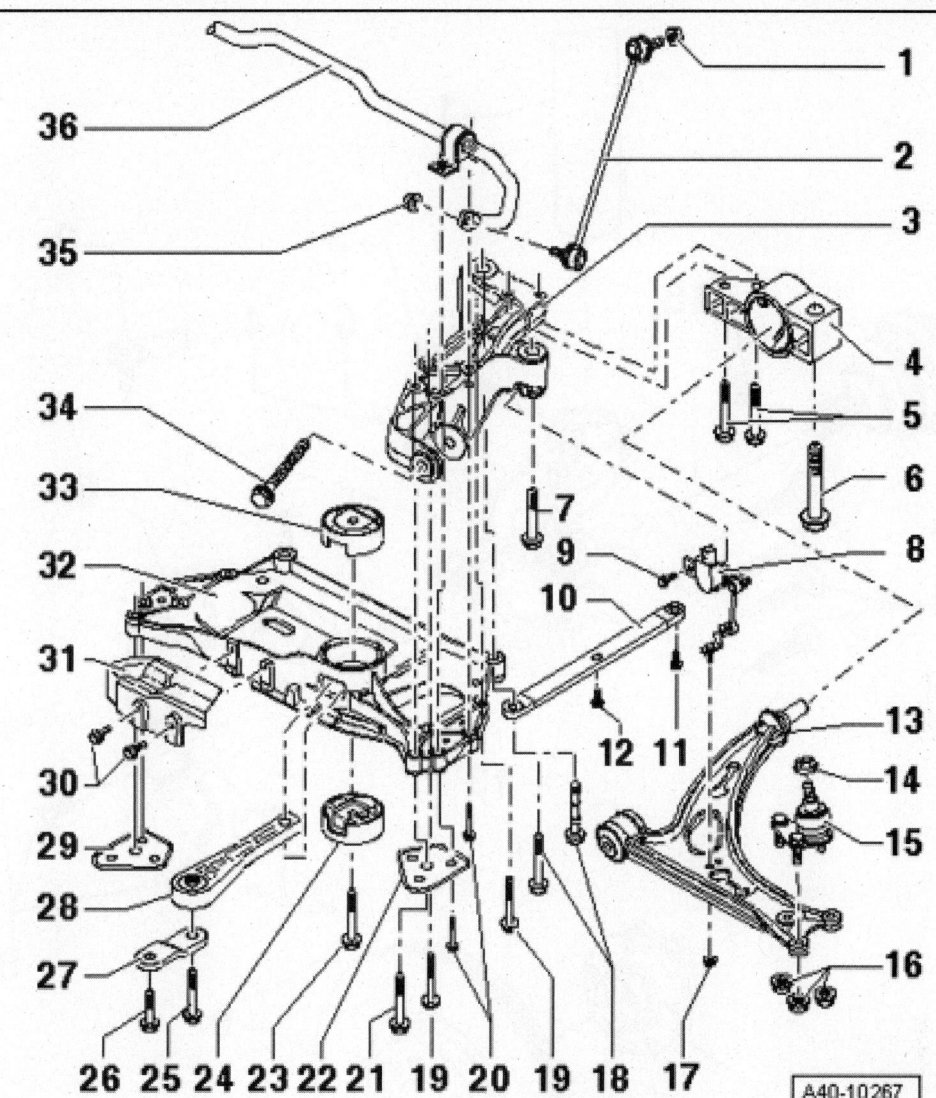

A40-10267

1. Nut (65 Nm)
2. Coupling Rod
3. Bracket
4. Mounting Bracket
5. Bolt (50 Nm plus an additional 90° turn)
6. Bolt (70 Nm plus an additional 90° turn)
7. Bolt (70 Nm plus an additional 90° turn)
8. Left Front Level Control System Sensor and Right Front Level Control Sensor
9. Hex head bolt (9 Nm)
10. Diagonal Brace (Only on Cabriolet)
11. Bolt (90 Nm plus an additional 45° turn)
12. Bolt (90 Nm plus an additional 45° turn)
13. Transverse Link
14. Nut (60 Nm)
15. Ball Joint
16. Nut (60 Nm)
17. Nut (9 Nm)
18. Bolt (70 Nm plus an additional 90° turn)
19. Threaded Connection on Steering Gear (50 Nm plus an additional 90° turn)

20. Threaded Connection on Stabilizer Bar (20 Nm plus an additional 90° turn)
21. Bolt (70 Nm plus an additional 90° turn)
22. Retainer Plate (Cabriolet only)
23. Bolt (100 Nm plus an additional 90° turn)
24. Lower Bonded Rubber Bushing for Pendulum Support
25. Bolt
26. Bolt
27. Bracket on Pendulum Support
28. Pendulum Support
29. Retainer Plate
30. Torx Bolt (6 Nm)
31. Shield
32. Subframe
33. Upper Bonded Rubber Bushing for Pendulum Support
34. Bolt (70 Nm plus an additional 90° turn)
35. Nut (65 Nm)
36. Stabilizer Bar

Fig. 199 Exploded view of the front suspension—A3 models

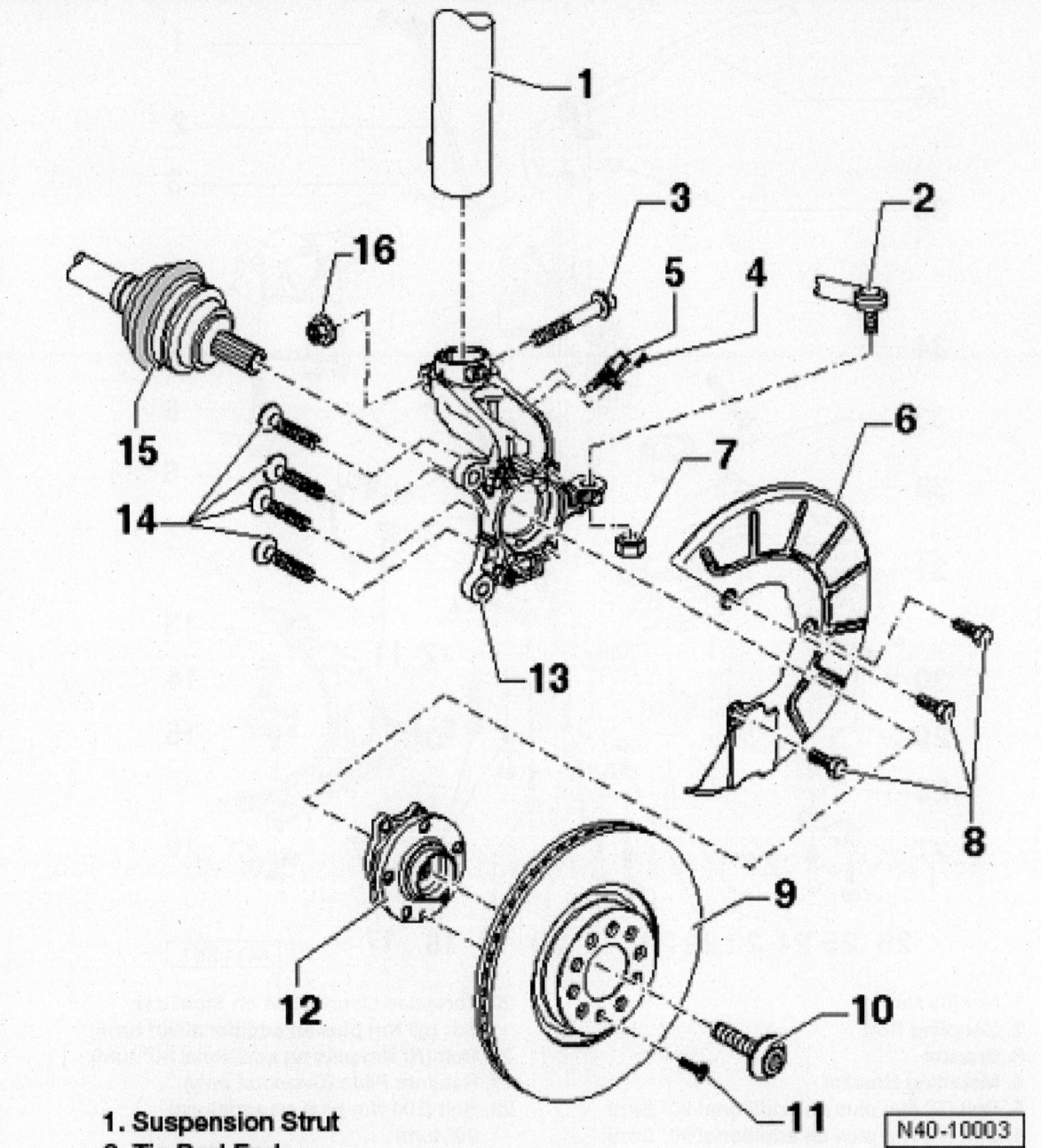

N40-10003

1. Suspension Strut
2. Tie Rod End
3. Bolt (70 Nm plus an additional 90° turn)
4. Bolt (M6 x 16. 8 Nm)
5. Left Front ABS Wheel Speed Sensor/Right Front ABS Wheel Speed Sensor
6. Cover Plate
7. Nut (20 Nm plus an additional 90° turn)
8. Bolt (M6 x 10. 12 Nm)
9. Ventilated Brake Disc (Hex bolt = 200 Nm plus an additional 180° turn,
   Twelve point bolt = 70 Nm plus an additional 90° turn)
10. Bolt (4 Nm)
11. Wheel Hub with Wheel Bearing
12. Wheel Bearing Housing (70 Nm plus an additional 90° turn)
13. Driveshaft

Fig. 200 Exploded view of the wheel bearing assembly—A3 Models

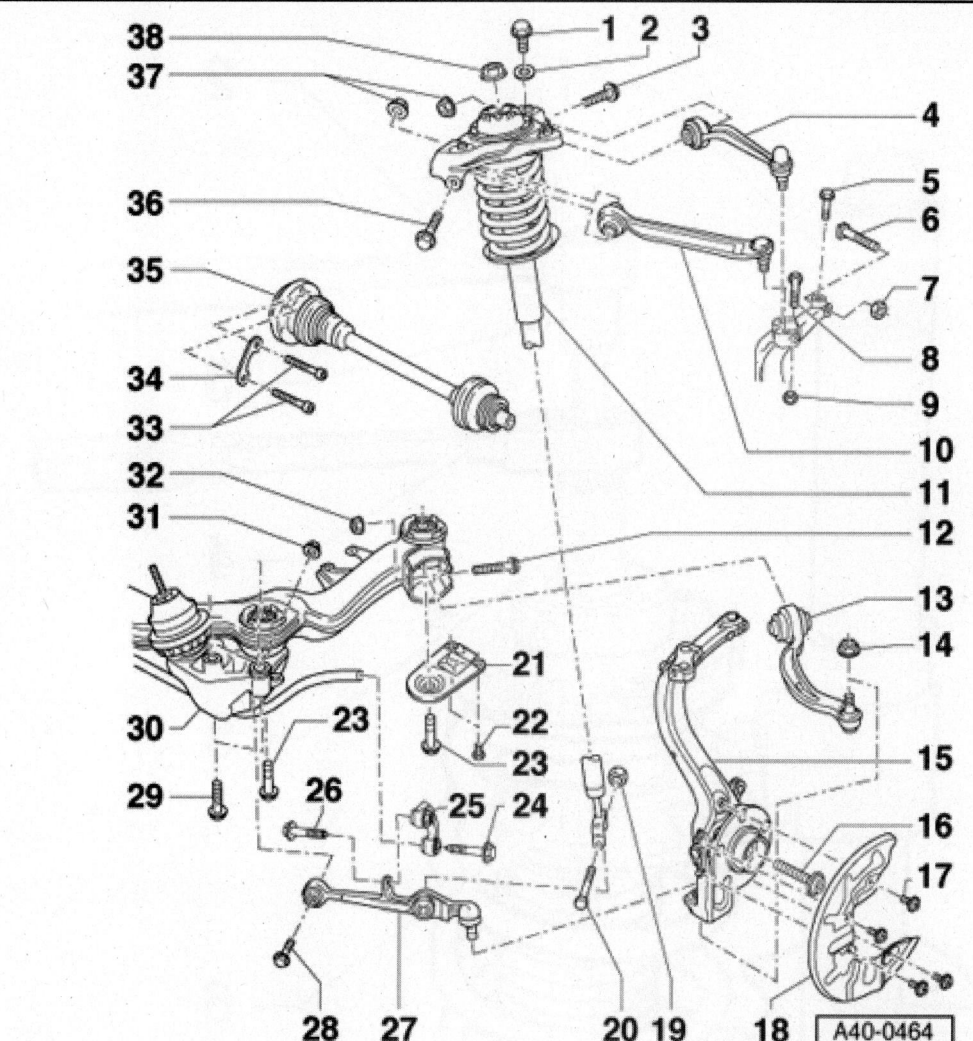

A40-0464

1. Hex bolt (75 Nm)
2. Washer
3. Hex bolt
4. Upper rear control arm
5. Hex bolt (7 Nm)
6. Bolt
7. Self-locking nut (45 Nm)
8. Hex bolt (40 Nm)
9. Self-locking nut
10. Upper front control arm
11. Suspension Strut
12. Hex bolt (70 Nm plus an add-
    itional 180° turn)
13. Lower guide link
14. Nut (110 Nm)
15. Wheel Bearing Housing
16. Collar bolt
17. Flange bolt (10 Nm)
18. Cover plate
19. Self-locking nut
20. Hex bolt (90 Nm)
21. Support for subframe
22. Hex bolt (55 Nm)

23. Hex bolt (110 Nm plus an add-
    itional 90° turn)
24. Hex bolt (40 Nm plus an add-
    itional 90° turn)
25. Coupling rod
26. Hex bolt (40 Nm plus an add-
    itional 90° turn)
27. Lower control arm
28. Hex bolt (70 Nm plus an add-
    itional 180° turn)
29. Hex bolt (75 Nm)
30. Subframe
31. Self-locking nut
32. Self-locking nut
33. Socket head bolt (M8 bolt.
    40 Nm, M10 bolt. 70 Nm)
34. Backing plate
35. Drive axle
36. Hex bolt
37. Self-locking nut (50 Nm plus an
    additional 90° turn)
38. Collar nut (50 Nm)

Fig. 201 Exploded view of the front suspension—A4 Models

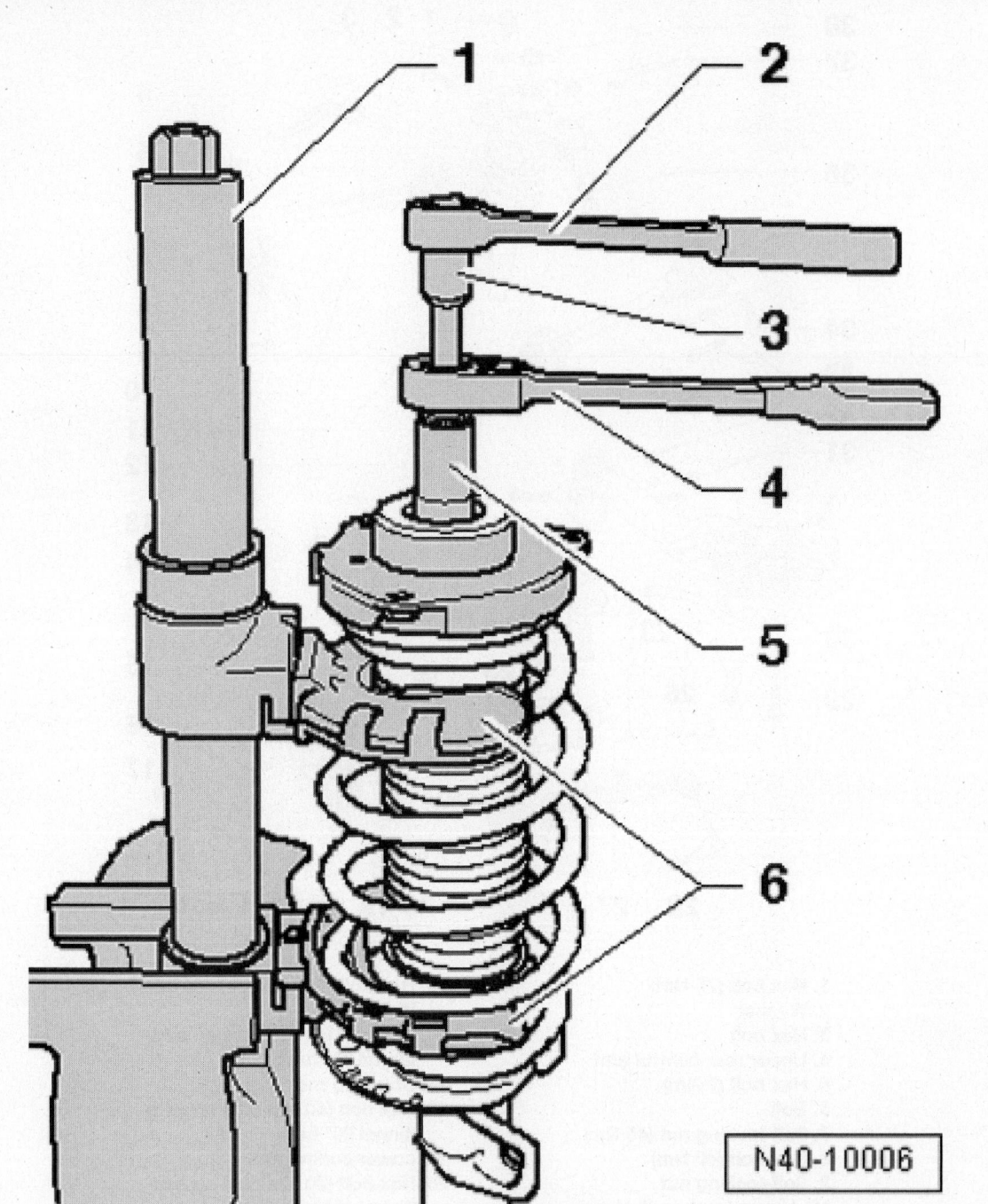

N40-10006

1. Spring Compressor VAG 1752/1
2. Torque Wrench VAG 1332
3. Ring Spanner Insert AF 21 T10001/8
4. Ratchet T10001/11
5. Ring Spanner Insert AF 21 T10001/5
6. Spring Holder VAG 1752/4

Fig. 202 Removing the spring

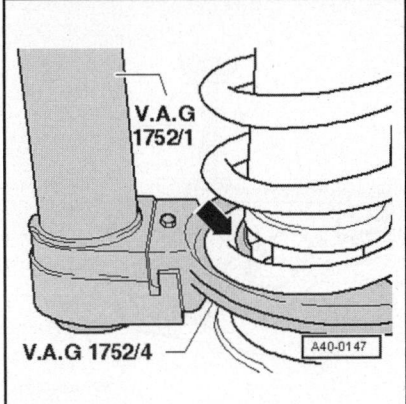

Fig. 203 Make sure the coil spring is properly seated in the spring holder VAG 1752/4 (arrow)

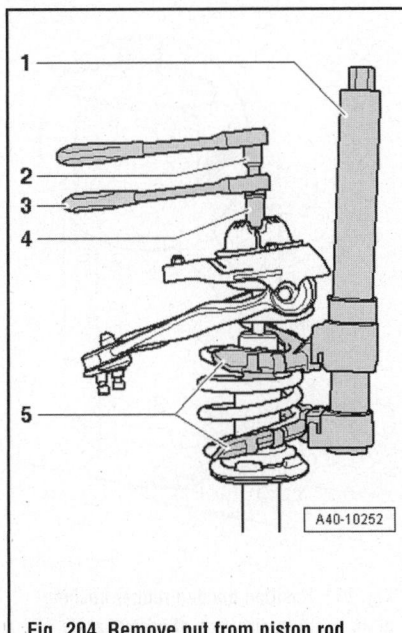

Fig. 204 Remove nut from piston rod using tools 2, 3 and 4.

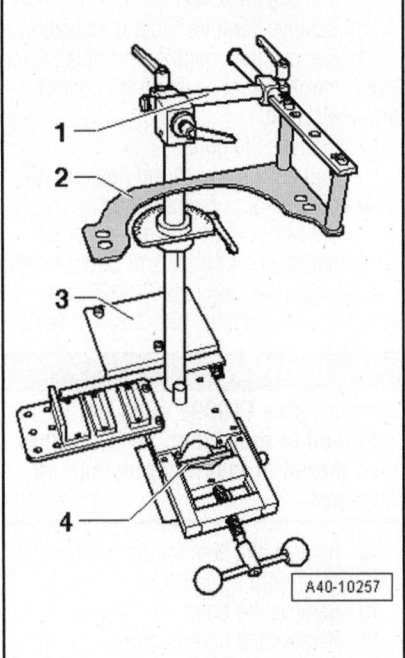

Fig. 205 Install spring mounting tool V.A.G 1752/2

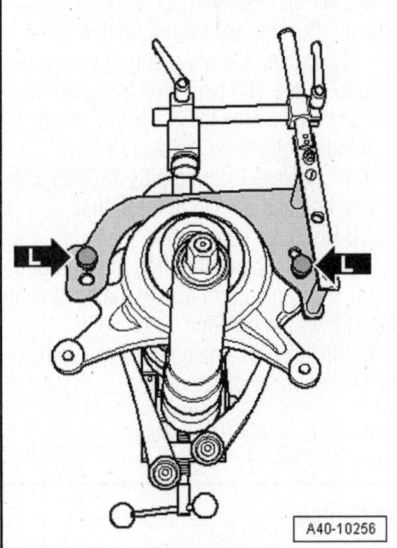

Fig. 206 Bolt adjust gage for suspension strut V.A.G 1752/19 on to mounting bracket (L)

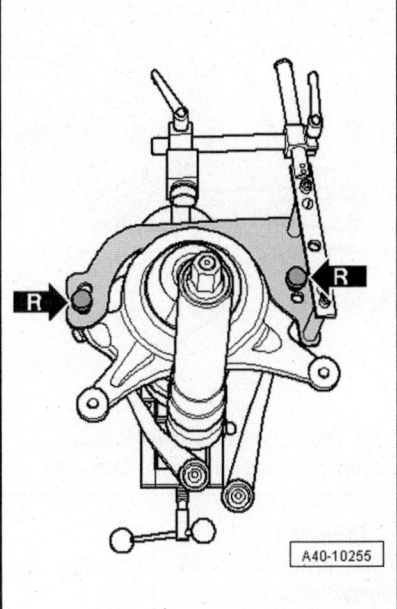

Fig. 207 Bolt adjust gage for suspension strut V.A.G 1752/19 to mounting bracket (R)

wiring connection does not sit on the suspension strut mount.

20. Disengage locking lever and set pointer to 0° position arrow and tighten locking lever.

21. Adjust mounting bracket so the suspension strut adjustment gauge V.A.G 1752/19 for the respective side of the vehicle can be bolted to the mounting bracket.

22. Left side:
  a. Bolt adjust gage for suspension strut V.A.G 1752/19 on to mounting bracket.

23. Right side:
  a. Bolt adjust gage for suspension strut V.A.G 1752/19 to mounting bracket.

24. Release tension in spring compressor V.A.G 1752/1 and remove it.

➡ **When releasing the tension, make sure the ends of the spring lie on the spring support stops in the mounting bracket and lower spring support.**

25. Check adjustment, repeat procedure if necessary.

26. Permissible deviation: ± 2°.

LOWER BALL JOINT

REMOVAL & INSTALLATION

A3 Models

See Figure 208.

1. Before servicing the vehicle, refer to the precautions section.

2. Remove the hex-combination bolt for drive axle

3. Remove the wheel.

4. Remove the hex nuts from ball joint.

5. Remove the hex nut from bracket for level control system sensor, if equipped on left side of vehicle.

6. Disengage control arm from ball joint.

7. Press constant velocity joint out of wheel bearing unit using a brass drift.

8. Swing suspension strut outward, at the same time guide drive axle out of wheel bearing.

➡ **Drive axle must not hang down, otherwise inner joint will be damaged by over bending. Tie up drive axle at body using wire.**

9. Position ball joint puller 3287 A at ball joint as shown in the accompanying illustration.

10. Press ball joint out of wheel bearing housing.

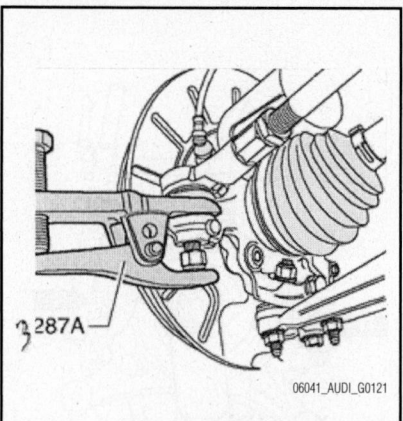

Fig. 208 Press ball joint out of wheel bearing housing using puller 3287 —A3

To install:

11. Installation is the reverse order of removal, please note the following:

a. Install the new self-locking nut, while holding with internal Torx T40. Tighten the ball joint nuts to 55 ft. lbs. (75 Nm).

➡**Instead of insertion tool V.A.G 1332/10 other commercially available 18mm ring-insertion tools may be used.**

b. Guide drive axle into wheel hub splines, tighten the bolt to 147 ft. lbs. (200 Nm) plus 180 degrees.

LOWER CONTROL ARM

REMOVAL & INSTALLATION

A3 Models

See Figure 209.

1. Before servicing the vehicle, refer to the precautions section.

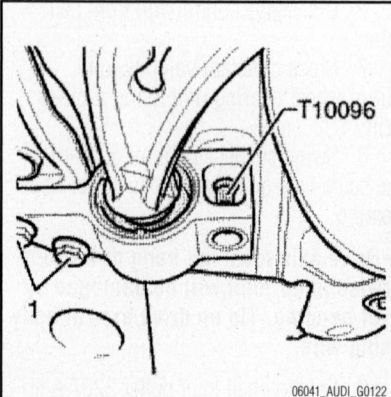

Fig. 209 Replace bolt for left side and the right side by using locating pins T10096—A3

2. Remove the wheel.

3. Remove the lower sound insulation

4. Remove the coupling rod of left front level control system sensor from control arm, if installed.

5. Remove the bolts.

6. Pull out wheel bearing housing with lower ball joint out of control arm.

7. Set position for mounting bracket.

8. Replace bolt for left side and the right side by using locating pins T10096 and tighten locating pins to 15 ft. lbs. (20 Nm).

✳✳CAUTION

Locating pins T10096 must not be tightened to more than 20 Nm, otherwise thread of locating pins can be damaged.

9. Remove the item for left vehicle side and item for right vehicle side.

10. Remove the bolts.

11. Remove the control arms.

To install:

12. Installation is the reverse order of removal, please note the following:

a. Insert control arm with mounting bracket into sub-frame.

b. Position but do not tighten yet.

c. Tighten the mounting bracket bolts to 37 ft. lbs. (50 Nm) plus 90 degrees.

d. Tighten the lower control arm to spindle bolts to 55 ft. lbs. (75 Nm)

e. Replace locating pins T10096 with new bolt and tighten to 52 ft. lbs. (70 Nm) plus 90 degrees.

13. Bolt the control arm to the ball joint.

14. Tighten control arm to the console in the curb weight position.

15. Install the remaining components in the reverse order of removal.

CONTROL ARM BUSHING REPLACEMENT

A3 Models

See Figures 210 through 214.

1. Before servicing the vehicle, refer to the precautions section.

2. Press out bonded rubber bushing, as shown in the accompanying illustration.

3. Pressing in bonded rubber bushing

➡**Bonded rubber bushing must be positioned at an angle when pressed in to avoid damage. When pressing in, bonded rubber bushing will straighten.**

4. Apply a suitable lubricant on outside of bonded rubber bushing.

5. Position bonded rubber bushing at an angle in direction of control arm. The lip

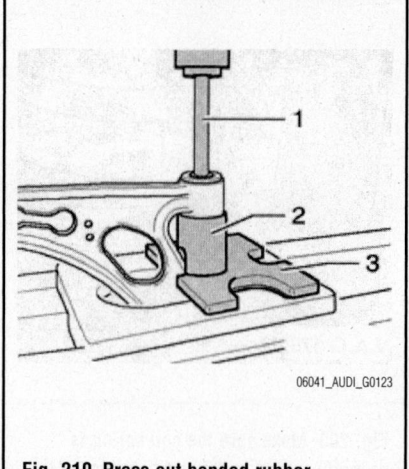

Fig. 210 Press out bonded rubber bushing—A3

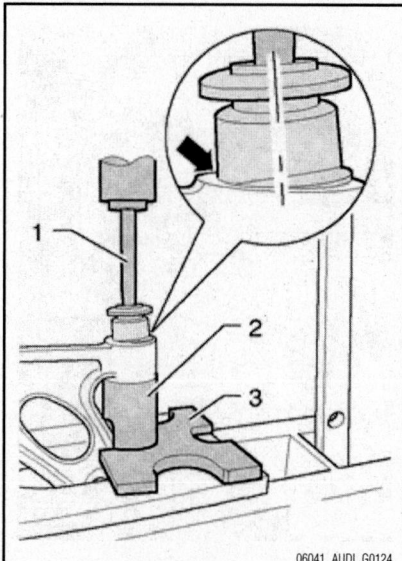

Fig. 211 Position bonded rubber bushing at an angle in direction of control arm. The lip (arrow) must slide into hole—A3

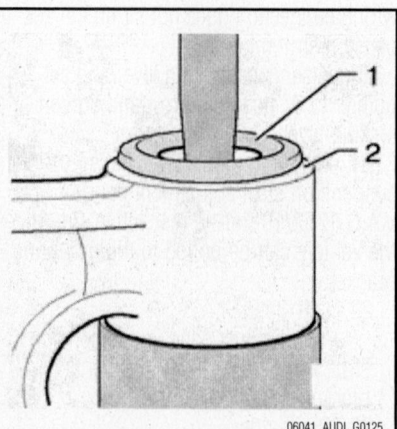

Fig. 212 Press in bonded rubber bushing until core and hole of control arm are at same level—A3

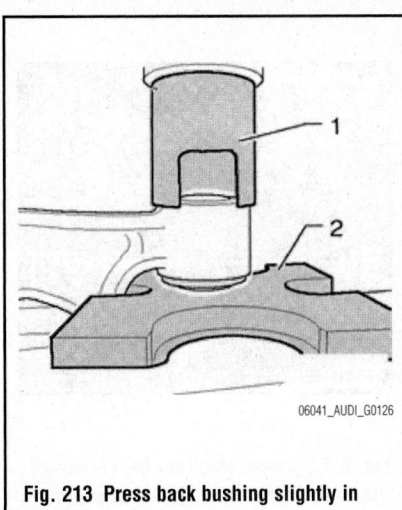

Fig. 213 Press back bushing slightly in control arm—A3

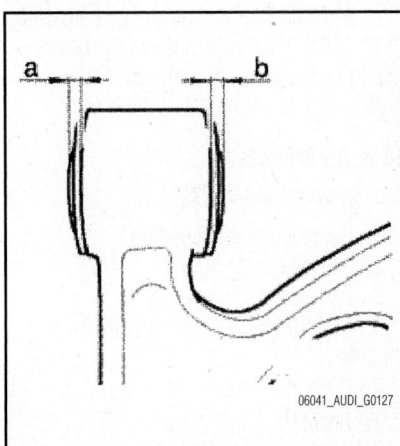

Fig. 214 The dimensions and must be the same as shown—A3

must slide into hole as shown in the accompanying illustration.

6. Press in bonded rubber bushing until core and hole of control arm are at same level.

7. Press back bushing slightly in control arm.

8. The dimensions and must be the same as shown.

A4 & A5 Models

Front Bushings

1. Before servicing the vehicle, refer to the precautions section.

2. Remove the lower control arm from the vehicle.

3. Press the front bushing out of the control arm.

To install:

4. Lubricate the front bushing with soap and press into the control arm.

5. Install the control arm to the vehicle.

6. Check and/or adjust the wheel alignment.

Rear Bushings

1. Before servicing the vehicle, refer to the precautions section.

2. Remove or disconnect the following:
   • Rear wheel
   • Rear control arm
   • Press the rear control arm bushing out

To install:

3. Lube the rear bushing with soap

4. Install or connect the following:
   • Rear bushing
   • Rear control arm
   • Front wheel

5. Check and/or adjust the wheel alignment.

LOWER BALL JOINT

REMOVAL & INSTALLATION

A3 Models

See Figure 215.

1. Before servicing the vehicle, refer to the precautions section.

2. Remove the hex-combination bolt for drive axle

3. Remove the wheel.

4. Remove the hex nuts from ball joint.

5. Remove the hex nut from bracket for level control system sensor, if equipped on left side of vehicle.

6. Disengage control arm from ball joint.

7. Press constant velocity joint out of wheel bearing unit using a brass drift.

8. Swing suspension strut outward, at the same time guide drive axle out of wheel bearing.

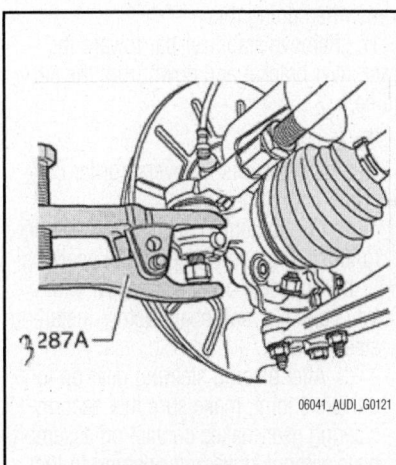

Fig. 215 Press ball joint out of wheel bearing housing using puller 3287 —A3

➡Drive axle must not hang down, otherwise inner joint will be damaged by over bending. Tie up drive axle at body using wire.

9. Position ball joint puller 3287 A at ball joint as shown in the accompanying illustration.

10. Press ball joint out of wheel bearing housing.

To install:

11. Installation is the reverse order of removal, please note the following:

a. Install the new self-locking nut, while holding with internal Torx T40. Tighten the ball joint nuts to 55 ft. lbs. (75 Nm).

➡Instead of insertion tool V.A.G 1332/10 other commercially available 18mm ring-insertion tools may be used.

b. Guide drive axle into wheel hub splines, tighten the bolt to 200 Nm plus 180 degrees.

A4 & A5 Models

➡The A4 and A6 models are equipped with 2 lower ball joints that are not serviceable. The control arms must be replaced if a joint is worn. The lower track control link ball joint stud faces down, and the guide link ball joint stud faces up.

Lower Track Control Link

1. Before servicing the vehicle, refer to the precautions section.

2. Remove or disconnect the following:
   • Front wheels
   • Nut from the lower track control link

3. Press the ball joint out of the tapered seat.

4. Support the wheel bearing housing to prevent excessive rebound travel in the suspension.

5. Remove or disconnect the following:
   • Stabilizer link and lower strut mounting bolt
   • Lower track control link-to-sub frame attaching bolt
   • Lower track control link

To install:

6. Install or connect the following:
   • Lower track control link
   • Sub frame attaching bolt. Torque the bolt to 74 ft. lbs. (100 Nm)

7. Install or connect the following:
   • Stabilizer link. Torque the upper bolt to 30 ft. lbs. (40 Nm) plus ¼ (90 degree) turn and the lower bolt to 74 ft. lbs. (100 Nm)

8. Load the suspension and torque the sub frame bolt to 59 ft. lbs. (80 Nm) plus ¼ (90 degree) turn.

9. Front wheels

10. Check and/or adjust the front suspension alignment.

Lower Guide Link

See Figure 216.

1. Before servicing the vehicle, refer to the precautions section.

2. Remove or disconnect the following:
   - Front wheels
   - Nut from the lower guide link joint and press the joint from the wheel bearing housing

3. Loosen lower guide link-to-sub frame attaching bolt

➡ **The sub frame must be lowered at the rear to remove the lower guide link-to-sub frame attaching bolt.**

4. Loosen the rear sub frame support plate bolts and sub frame bolts.

5. Remove or disconnect the following:
   - Lower guide link-to-sub frame bolt
   - Link from the vehicle

To install:

6. Install or connect the following:
   - Link into the vehicle
   - Guide link-to-sub frame mounting bolt

7. Torque the support plate bolts as follows:
   - Bolt type **A**: 18 ft. lbs. (25 Nm)
   - Bolt type **B**: 55 ft. lbs. (75 Nm)

8. Install or connect the following:
   - New sub frame bolts. Torque the bolts to 81 ft. lbs. (110 Nm) plus a ¼ (90 degree) turn
   - Joint end into the wheel bearing

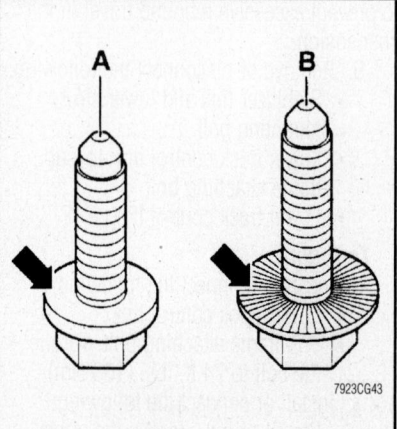

Fig. 216 Sub frame support bracket bolt identification—A4 model

housing. Torque the nut to 74 ft. lbs. (100 Nm)

9. Load the suspension. Torque the lower guide link-to-sub frame attaching bolt to 66 ft. lbs. (90 Nm) plus ¼ (90 degree) turn.

10. Install the front wheels.

11. Check and/or adjust the front suspension alignment.

STABILIZER BAR

REMOVAL & INSTALLATION

A3 Models

See Figure 217.

1. Remove front wheels.

2. Remove nuts and foot well trim.

3. Remove bolt and the universal joint from the steering gear.

4. Remove lower noise insulation.

5. Remove noise insulation if installed.

6. Remove diagonal brace if installed.

7. Remove bracket for exhaust system from the sub frame.

8. Remove coupling rods from stabilizer.

9. Remove the steering knuckle lower nuts.

10. Loosen nut of tie rod ball joint, but do not remove yet.

11. Press tie rod end off of wheel bearing housing using ball joint puller 3287 A.

12. Secure the sub frame.

13. Remove pendulum support from transmission, remove bolts.

14. Place engine/transmission jack VAG 1383 A below sub frame.

15. Place a block of wood 1 between engine/transmission jack VAG 1383 A and sub frame.

16. Loosen bolts and lower sub frame with brackets slightly. Observe electrical wires when doing this.

17. Remove stabilizer bar toward the front, over bracket and down from the sub frame.

To install:

18. Installation is in reverse order of removal, noting the following:

   a. For tightening specifications, refer to illustrations in Component Locations

   b. Coat seal on steering gear with lubricant, e.g. soft soap, before installing steering gear.

   c. After placing steering gear on to universal joint, make sure that seal on steering gear makes contact on assembly plate without kinks and opening to foot well is correctly sealed. Ingress of water and/or noises may be the result.

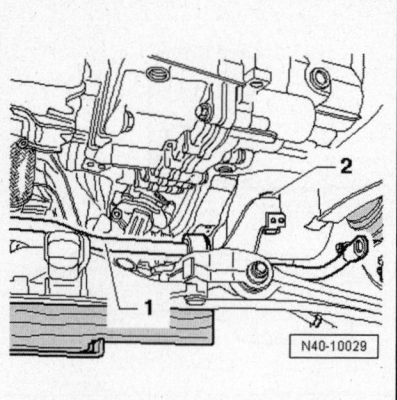

Fig. 217 Remove stabilizer bar (1) toward the front, over bracket (2) and down from the sub frame

   d. Make sure sealing surfaces are clean.

19. After installing, perform the basic setting on the steering angle sensor.

20. Vehicle alignment is required.

A4 & A5 Models

See Figures 218 and 219.

1. Remove noise insulation.

2. Remove bolt.

3. Remove the hex nut.

4. Perform the same procedure for the left side.

5. Remove stabilizer bar.

To install:

6. If you replace stabilizer, note chassis version.

7. Stabilizer and mounting must be free of grease.

8. To complete installation, reverse the removal procedure.

9. Upon installation, loosely tighten all bolts before tightening to specified torque. Refer to illustrations under Component Locations for torque values.

STEERING KNUCKLE

REMOVAL & INSTALLATION

Refer to Wheel Hub & Bearing in this section.

STRUT & SPRING ASSEMBLY

REMOVAL & INSTALLATION

A3 Models

See Figure 220 and 221.

1. Before servicing the vehicle, refer to the precautions section.

2. Loosen the hex-combination bolt for drive axle.

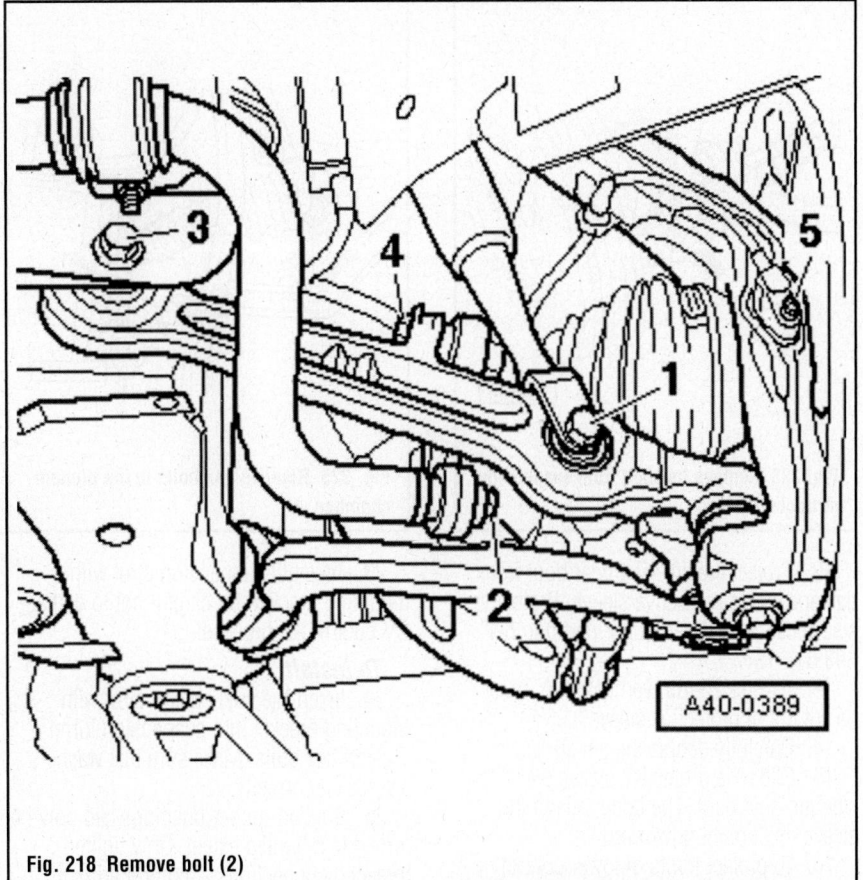

Fig. 218 Remove bolt (2)

3. Remove the wheel.

4. Remove the upper coupling rod hex nut from suspension strut.

5. Disengage wheel speed sensor wire from suspension strut.

6. Remove the bolts.

7. Pull out wheel bearing housing with lower ball joint out of control arm.

8. Fasten drive axle to body with wire.

➥**Drive axle must not hang down, otherwise inner joint will be damaged by over bending.**

9. Bolt ball joint to the control arm.

10. Secure Engine/transmission jack with wheel hub support T10149 to wheel hub using a wheel bolt.

11. Remove the wheel bearing housing/suspension strut bolt connection

12. Insert Spreader 3424 into slot of wheel bearing housing.

13. Turn ratchet 90 degrees and remove from spreader 3424.

14. Press brake disc by hand in direction of suspension strut. Otherwise strut tube may be canted in hole of wheel bearing housing.

15. Pull off wheel bearing housing downward from strut tube using engine/transmission jack and lower until strut tube hangs free.

16. Tie wheel bearing housing with wire at console/sub frame.

17. Remove the Engine/transmission jack under wheel bearing housing.

18. Remove the wiper arms and plenum chamber cover

19. Remove the hex bolts for top strut mounting and remove strut.

To install:

20. Insert strut, one of two markings must point in direction of travel.

21. Tighten hex bolts for top strut mounting to 11 ft. lbs. (15 Nm) plus 90 degrees.

22. Secure Engine/transmission jack with Wheel hub support T10149 to wheel hub using wheel bolt.

23. Place the suspension strut on to the wheel bearing housing.

24. Remove the wire on wheel bearing housing.

25. Install the remaining components in the reverse order of removal, please note the following:

a. Tighten the strut to wheel bearing housing to bolt/nut to 52 ft. lbs. (70 Nm) plus an additional 90 degrees.

b. Tighten the drive axle bolt to 200 Nm plus an additional 180 degrees.

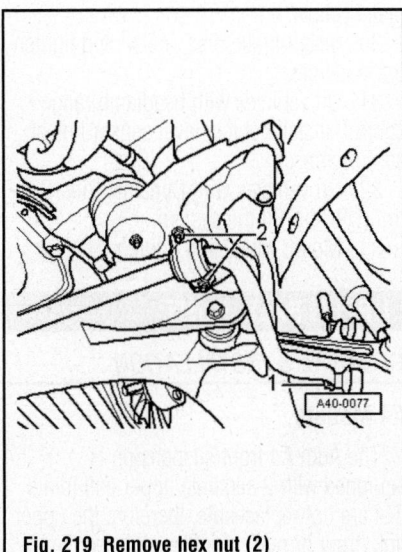

Fig. 219 Remove hex nut (2)

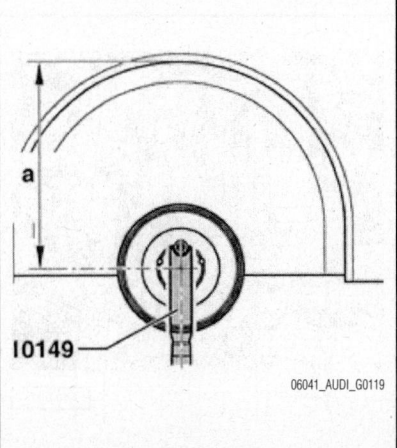

Fig. 220 Secure Engine/transmission jack with wheel hub support T10149 to wheel hub using a wheel bolt—A3

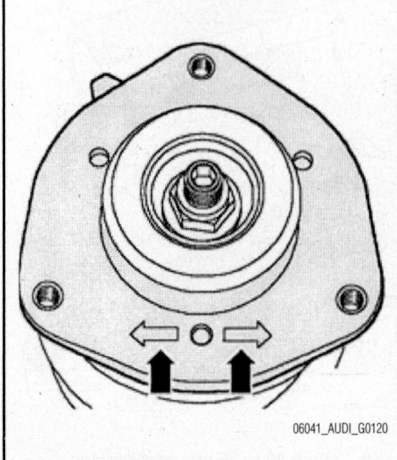

Fig. 221 Insert strut, one of two markings must point in direction of travel—A3

A4 & A5 Models

See Figures 222 through 225.

1. On vehicles with Dynamic Ride Control (DRC II), empty the system.

2. Remove wheel trim cap, remove cover cap on light-alloy wheels (removal hook in vehicle tool kit).

3. Remove the wheel.

4. Secure the brake disc with a wheel bolt.

5. Before removing left suspension strut, level control system sensor link must be loosened from control arm on vehicles with headlamp range control module by opening retaining clip.

6. Unclip ABS line from bracket at brake caliper.

7. Vehicles with brake caliper HP-2:

 a. Remove hex bolt and remove brake line bracket.

 b. Remove bolts for brake caliper and take off brake caliper.

 c. Reinstall brake line holder. Install and tighten hex bolt.

 d. Secure brake caliper to body so that the weight of the brake caliper does not stress or damage the brake line.

8. Remove brake caliper and secure to body so weight of caliper does not stress or damage brake hose or brake line.

9. Remove clip with a pair of pliers. This clip does not need to be inserted again.

10. Remove nut, remove hex bolt and remove both control arms upward.

11. The slits in the wheel bearing housing MUST NOT be widened using a chisel or similar tool.

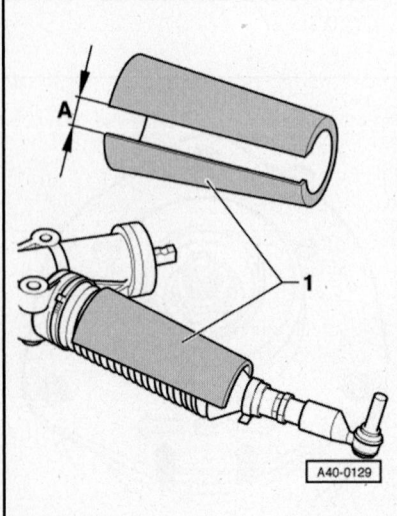

Fig. 222 A 20 to 25 mm vertical strip, dimension "A" must be cut out of protective sleeve

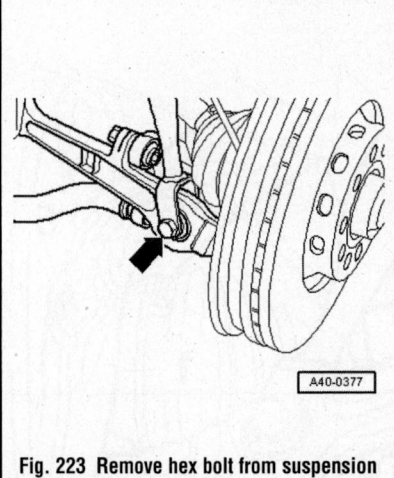

Fig. 223 Remove hex bolt from suspension strut/control link

12. Protect the steering gear boot from damage with a protective sleeve. Protective sleeve can be ordered under part number: 893 512 137.

13. A 20 to 25 mm vertical strip, must be cut out of protective sleeve.

14. Carefully deburr the cut surfaces.

15. Slide the protective sleeve over the steering gear boot. The open side of the sleeve must point downward.

16. To protect joints of lower control arms from damage, it is necessary to use e.g. Engine/Transmission Jack V.A.G 1383 A to brace against too strong rebound.

17. Remove hex bolt from suspension strut/control link.

18. Swing wheel bearing housing to side.

19. Loosen the coolant reservoir mount.

20. Remove the plenum chamber cover.

21. Remove cover of the bolt.

22. Remove hex bolts in the plenum chamber.

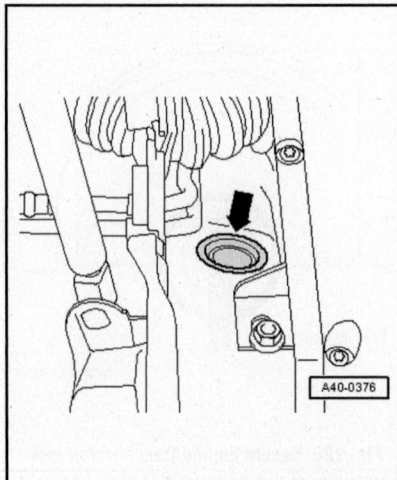

Fig. 224 Remove cover (arrow) of bolt.

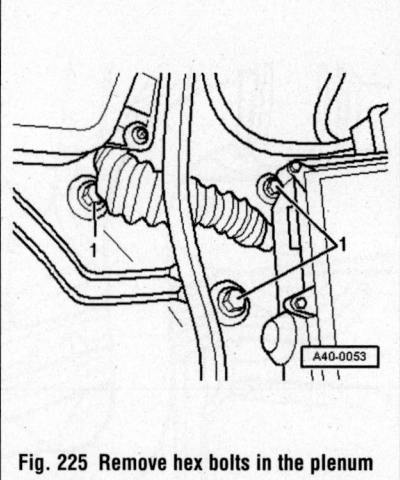

Fig. 225 Remove hex bolts in the plenum chamber

23. Take out suspension strut with mounting bracket. Be careful not to damage CV boot in the process!

To install:

24. Insert the suspension strut with mounting bracket into suspension turret. Tighten hex bolts. Make sure that washers are seated correctly.

25. Bonded rubber bushings can only be turned to a limited extent. Only tighten threaded connections at control arms if vehicle is in curb weight position.

26. Insert suspension strut forked head into the control arm and tighten the threaded connection. Bolt must be inserted opposite direction of travel.

27. Insert both upper control arm joint pins in the wheel bearing housing Bend downward as much as possible using Pliers T40067.

28. Insert new bolt and self-locking nut and tighten.

29. Insert ABS wiring into retainer on brake caliper.

30. Install brake disc, install and tighten brake caliper.

31. On vehicles with headlamp range control, install vehicle level sensor link at control arm.

32. On vehicles with Dynamic Ride Control (DRC II), fill the system.

33. Mount wheel and tighten.

UPPER BALL JOINT

REMOVAL & INSTALLATION

A4 Models

The Audi A4 front suspension is equipped with 2 separate upper ball joints that are not replaceable, therefore the upper link (front or rear) must be replaced. To

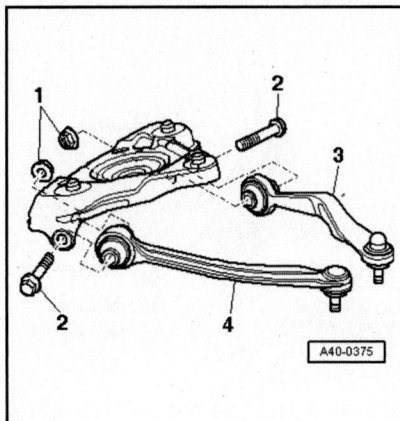

Fig. 226 Exploded view of the upper control arm

remove this link, perform the following procedures.

1. Before servicing the vehicle, refer to the precautions section.
2. Remove or disconnect the following:
   • Front wheels
   • Pinch bolt and pull both control arms upward and out
3. Cover the steering gear boot.
4. Remove or disconnect the following:
   • Guide link ball joint and press off the joint
   • Anti-lock Brake System (ABS) wheel speed sensor wire from the brake caliper bracket
5. Support the suspension from excessive rebound travel.
6. Remove or disconnect the following:
   • Lower strut bolt and swing the wheel bearing housing aside
   • Rubber grommets from the plenum chamber
   • Upper strut-to-body nuts
   • Strut together with the mounting bracket
7. Clamp the strut in a vise with the protective jaw covers.
8. Remove or disconnect the following:
   • Upper link bolts and detach both of the links
   • Bracket-to-strut nuts, then separate

To install:
9. Install or connect the following:
   • Brackets and links, as shown. Torque the bracket-to-strut mounting nuts to 15 ft. lbs. (20 Nm)
   • Links by aligning them, as shown. Torque to 37 ft. lbs. (50 Nm) plus a ¼ (90 degree) turn
   • Strut with mounting bracket. Torque the upper strut-to-body nuts to 48 ft. lbs. (75 Nm)

   • Lower strut bolt. Torque it to 66 ft. lbs. (90 Nm)
   • Nut on the ball joint. Torque to 74 ft. lbs. (100 Nm)
   • Upper links to the wheel bearing housing. Torque the pinch bolt to 30 ft. lbs. (40 Nm)
   • ABS wiring to the brake caliper bracket
   • Wheels
10. Check the front suspension alignment.

UPPER CONTROL ARM

REMOVAL & INSTALLATION
See Figure 226.

1. Before servicing the vehicle, refer to the precautions section.
2. Remove or disconnect the following:
   • Negative battery cable
   • Wheel
3. Loosen the upper strut mounting nuts.
4. Loosen, but do not remove, the upper strut rod nut.

❋❋ CAUTION

DO NOT completely remove the upper strut nut at this time.

5. Remove the brake caliper, leaving the line attached and secure it out of the way
6. Remove the Anti-lock Brake System (ABS) speed sensor and harness, if applicable
7. Remove the cotter pin and nut from the upper control arm
8. Remove the upper control arm from the steering knuckle
9. Remove the stabilizer bar from the link, if applicable

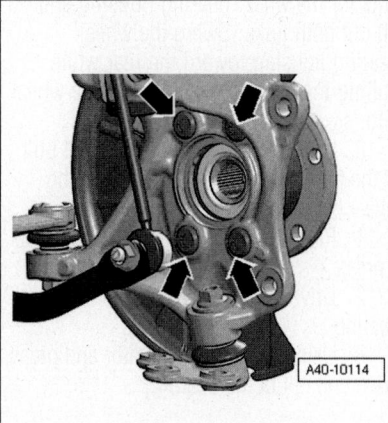

Fig. 227 Remove the wheel bearing unit bolts

10. Remove the cotter pin and nut from the lower control arm
11. Remove the strut
12. Remove the upper strut mounting nuts
13. Remove the strut
14. Remove the upper control arm

To install:
15. Install or connect the following:
   • Upper suspension arm
   • Strut. Torque the upper nuts to 42 ft. lbs. (56 Nm)
   • Strut to the lower arm
   • Stabilizer bar bracket
   • Stabilizer bar to the link
   • Upper suspension arm to the steering knuckle. Torque the nut to 64 ft. lbs. (87 Nm)
   • New cotter pin
   • ABS speed sensor. Torque the bolt to 69 inch lbs. (8 Nm)
   • Brake caliper
   • Front wheel
16. Bounce the vehicle several times to stabilize the suspension.
17. Tighten the lower strut bolt.
18. Check and/or adjust the front wheel alignment.

CONTROL ARM BUSHING REPLACEMENT

The upper control arm bushings are serviced with the control arm as an assembly.

WHEEL BEARINGS

REMOVAL & INSTALLATION

A3 Models
See Figures 227 and 228.

1. Before servicing the vehicle, refer to the precautions section.
2. Remove the hex-combination bolt for drive axle.
3. Remove the wheel.
4. Remove the brake caliper and hang on body using tie wire.
5. Remove the ABS wheel speed sensor
6. Remove the brake disc.
7. Loosen the nut from tie rod end but do not remove completely. Press off tie rod end from wheel bearing housing using Ball Joint Puller 3287A.
8. In vehicles with level control system sensor, remove nut.
9. On vehicles with Audi magnetic ride, disconnect connector from the strut tower. Remove the connector with both hands; use one hand to open the retainer and use the other hand to press it off; do not use tools.

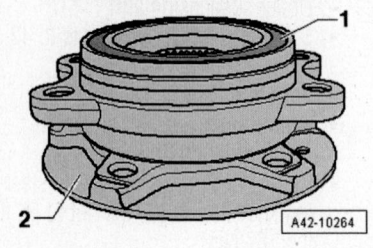

Fig. 228 The wheel bearing must always face up

10. Disconnect threaded connection of wheel bearing housing/suspension strut.

11. Insert Spreader 3424 into slot of wheel bearing housing.

12. Turn ratchet around 90 degrees and remove from the ratchet from spreader 3424.

13. Remove the lower control arm to spindle nuts.

14. Guide control arm out of wheel bearing housing with ball joint.

15. Remove the wheel bearing housing downward from strut tube and pull driveshaft out of wheel hub.

➡ **Drive axle must not hang down, otherwise inner joint will be damaged by over bending.**

16. Fasten drive axle to body with wire.

17. Remove the wheel bearing housing with ball joint.

18. Remove the wheel bearing unit bolts.

19. Remove wheel bearing unit from wheel bearing housing.

➡ **Avoid contaminating with dirt and damaging the seal when setting down/storing. The wheel bearing must always face up.**

To install:

20. Installation is the reverse order of removal, please note the following:

   a. Tighten the NEW wheel bearing

housing bolts to 51 ft. lbs. (70 Nm) plus 90 degrees.

   b. Tighten the tie rod end nut to 14 ft. lbs. (20 Nm) plus 90 degrees.

   c. Tighten the lower control arm to spindle bolts to 55 ft. lbs. (75 Nm).

   d. Tighten the drive axle bolts to 147 ft. lbs. (200 Nm) plus 180 degrees.

21. Refer to the illustrations under Component Locations for further torque specifications.

A4 & A5 Models

See Figure 229.

1. Before servicing the vehicle, refer to the precautions section.

2. Loosen the halfshaft retaining bolt.

3. Remove or disconnect the following:

- Front wheel, then reinstall all 5 wheel bolts at this time
- Anti-lock Brake System (ABS) wheel speed sensor
- Caliper (suspend by wire to body)
- Rotor
- Backing plate bolts

4. Pull ABS wheel speed sensor from wheel bearing housing

5. Loosen the mounting nuts for the lower guide and track links.

6. Remove ABS cable grommet and clips and feed the cable through the opening.

7. Remove the tie rod end from the wheel bearing housing (use care to not damage the CV joint boot).

8. Remove the mounting nuts for the lower guide and track links and press out the joints

➡ **If equipped with self-leveling control (for headlight aiming), disconnect or remove actuating arm.**

9. Remove the upper mounting nuts for the wheel bearing housing and lift out both links. Swing the wheel bearing housing toward the rear while pulling the drive axle end out of the wheel hub.

10. Unscrew the nut from the joint bolt of the track control link and remove the wheel bearing housing.

11. Place the wheel bearing housing on a press.

12. Drive out the hub with the wheel bearing.

13. Using a bearing separator and press, drive hub out of the bearing.

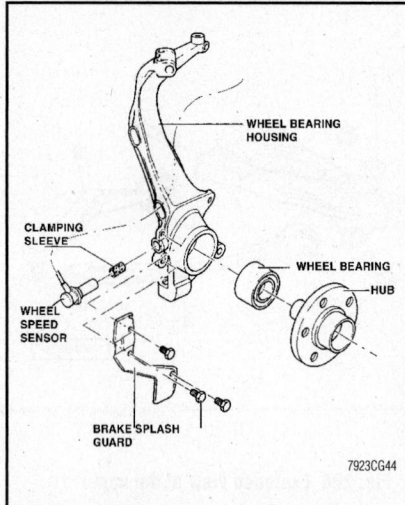

Fig. 229 Exploded view of the front wheel bearing housing—A4 models

To install:

14. Press the new wheel bearing into the bearing housing using the appropriate bearing driver.

15. Press the hub into the wheel bearing using the appropriate bearing driver.

16. Install or connect the following:

- CV-joint by sliding it through the wheel hub and hand-tighten the new nut
- Lower track control and guide link. Torque the new self-locking nut to 74 ft. lbs. (100 Nm)
- Both of the upper link ball joints into the wheel bearing. Torque the pinch bolt to 30 ft. lbs. (40 Nm)
- Socket-head bolt and self-locking nut for self-leveling control arm. Torque to 7 ft. lbs. (10 Nm)
- Tie rod end. Torque the new self-locking nut to 37 ft. lbs. (50 Nm) and the bolt to 44 inch lbs. (5 Nm)
- ABS wheel speed sensor
- Brake splash guard. Torque the bolts to 84 inch lbs. (10 Nm)
- Brake rotor
- Bake caliper. Torque the bolt to 89 ft. lbs. (120 Nm)
- Front wheel

17. Tighten the halfshaft retaining bolt as follows:

- M14 bolt: 85 ft. lbs. (115 Nm) plus ½ (180 degree) turn
- M16 bolt: 140 ft. lbs. (190 Nm) plus ½ (180 degree) turn

18. Check and/or adjust the front alignment, if necessary.

COMPONENT LOCATIONS

See Figure 230.

COIL SPRING

REMOVAL & INSTALLATION

A3 Models
See Figures 231 and 232.

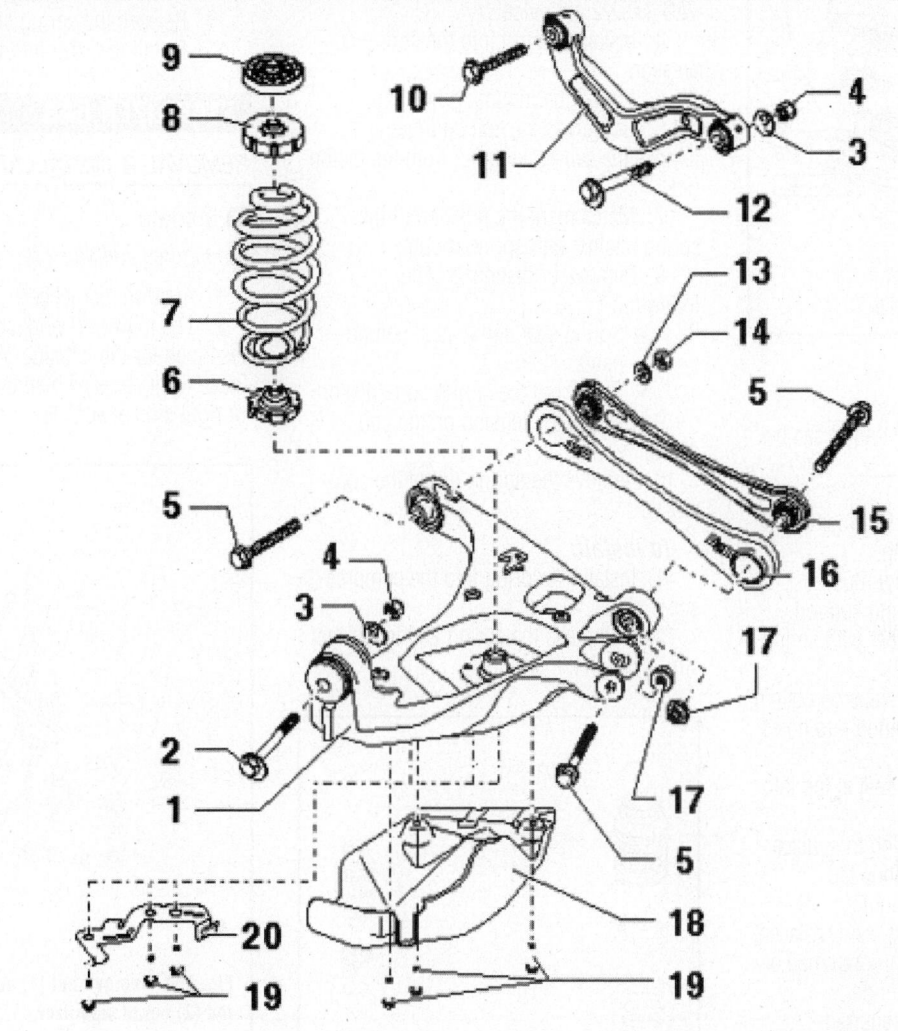

A42-0236

1. Trapezoidal Control Arm
2. Eccentric bolt (Do not turn more than 90° left or right)
3. Eccentric washer
4. Self-locking nut (95 Nm)
5. Combi-bolt (85 Nm plus an additional 90° turn)
6. Lower spring support
7. Coil spring
8. Upper spring support
9. Upper spring support
10. Combi-bolt (85 Nm plus an additional 90° turn)
11. Transverse Link
12. Eccentric bolt (Do not turn more than 90° left or right)
13. Washer
14. Self-locking nut (85 Nm plus an additional 90° turn)
15. Tie Rod
16. Stone protection plate
17. Collar nut, self-locking
18. Stone deflector for trapezoidal control arm
19. Collar bolt (25 Nm)
20. Bracket (for parking cable)

Fig. 230 Exploded view of the rear suspension—A4 models

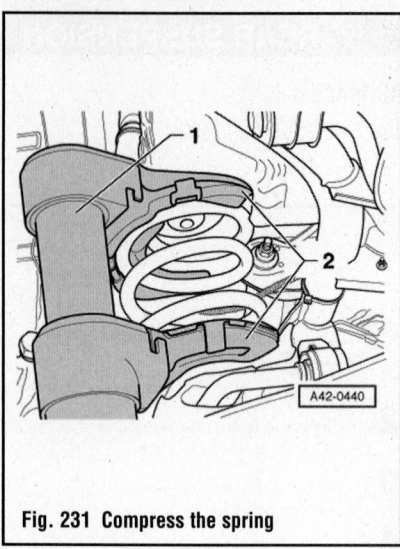

Fig. 231 Compress the spring

1. Remove the wheel.
2. Insert spring compressor.
3. Compress coil spring until it can be removed.
4. Remove spring.
5. Installation is in reverse order of removal, noting the following:
   a. End of spring **arrow** must rest against stop of lower spring support.
   b. Install spring together with spring seat.
   c. Spring seat has two pins on bottom.
   d. These pins are inserted into holes on lower transverse link.
   e. Then insert spring seat at top into upper spring end.
   f. Tension spring. To do this, place upper end of spring on body tab.
   g. Mount wheel and tighten.
6. If one or more springs were replaced, then the system must be reprogrammed on vehicles with Audi magnetic ride.
7. Vehicle alignment is required.

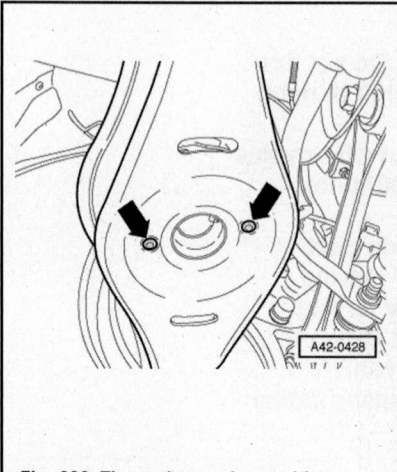

Fig. 232 These pins are inserted into holes on lower transverse link

A4 & A5 Models

See Figure 233.

1. Before servicing the vehicle, refer to the precautions section.
2. Remove the strut from the vehicle.
3. Clamp the spring compressor tool VAG 1752/2, in a vise.
4. Install the strut into the spring compressor.
5. Pry off the mounting bolt cap.
6. Compress the coil spring and remove the self-locking nut from the piston rod.
7. Match mark the position of the spring retainer and spring mount.
8. Remove or disconnect the following:
   • Spring seat and related components
   • Strut from the spring compressor
9. Release the tension on the coil spring.
10. Remove the spring out of the compressor.

To install:

11. Install the spring into the compressor.
12. Compress the spring and insert the strut through the spring.

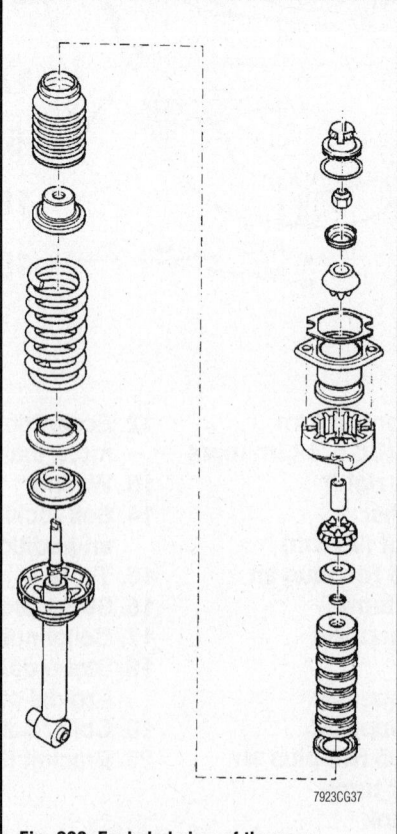

Fig. 233 Exploded view of the rear strut—A4 model

13. Install or connect the following:
   • Spring seat and related components in the reverse order as they were removed by aligning the match marks
   • New self-locking nut
   • Mounting bolt cap
14. Release the spring compressor.
15. Install the strut into the vehicle.

STABILIZER BAR

REMOVAL & INSTALLATION

A3 Models

See Figures 234 and 235.

1. Remove rear wheels.
2. The following work steps are described for the left side of the vehicle. These work steps also apply simultaneously for right side of vehicle.

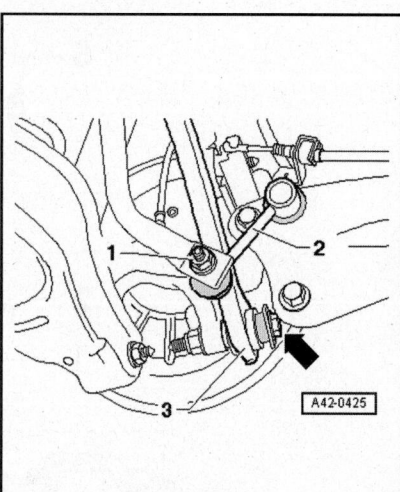

Fig. 234 Remove nut (1) and pull coupling rod (2) out of stabilizer.

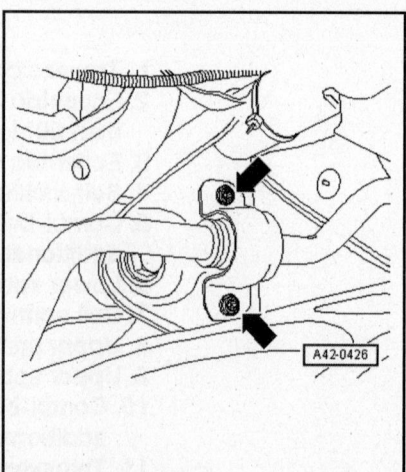

Fig. 235 Remove bolts (arrows) for stabilizer clamp

3. Remove nut and pull coupling rod out of stabilizer.

4. Remove bolts arrows for stabilizer clamp.

5. Installation is in reverse order of removal.

6. Refer to illustrations under Component Locations for torque values.

7. Vehicle alignment is required.

A4 & A5 Models

See Figure 236.

1. Remove rear underbody trim.

2. Convertible only:

　a. Remove rear diagonal brace.

3. Vehicles with exhaust system with 2 rear mufflers:

　a. Remove rear portion of the exhaust system.

4. Vehicles with heavy duty suspension:

　a. Remove stone impact protection from trapezoidal control arm.

5. Continuation for all vehicles:

6. Remove bolts (1).

7. Remove bolts (2). Counter hold joint with open-end wrench.

8. Remove bolts (3).

9. Remove stabilizer with mount.

To install:

10. Rubber bushing must rest on stabilizer bar collar.

11. Install all the bolts and hand tighten. Tighten all bolts to specified torque value. Refer to illustrations under Component Locations.

12. Place vehicle on wheels and bounce several times.

13. To complete installation, reverse the remaining removal procedure.

STRUT & SPRING ASSEMBLY

REMOVAL & INSTALLATION

A3 Models

See Figure 237.

1. Before servicing the vehicle, refer to the precautions section.

2. Remove the wheel.

3. Measure dimension from center of wheel to lower edge of wheel housing

4. Remove the wheel housing liner.

5. Remove the coil spring as follows:

　a. Compress the coil spring until it can be removed. Using spring compressor V.A.G 1752/1 and spring holders V.A.G 1752/3.

　b. Remove the spring.

6. Remove the upper strut bolts.

7. Remove the lower bolt.

8. Remove the shock absorber.

To install:

9. Installation is the reverse order of removal, please note the following:

　a. The end of the spring must rest against stop of lower spring support.

　b. Install the spring together with spring support.

　c. The spring support has two pins at bottom.

　d. Insert the pins into the bores of lower control arm.

　e. Insert the upper spring support into the upper end of spring.

　f. Release the spring. Position the upper spring support on lug of body while doing so.

WHEEL BEARINGS

REMOVAL & INSTALLATION

A3 Models

See Figures 238 through 241.

Wheel Bearing Housing

1. Measure dimension from center of wheel to lower edge of wheel housing.

2. Remove the wheel.

3. Remove the coil spring.

4. Remove brake carrier and brake caliper and tie to body with wire.

5. Remove ABS speed sensor from wheel bearing housing.

6. Remove cover plate.

7. Remove bolt and washer. The washer is installed on vehicles with an aluminum wheel bearing housing.

8. Remove bolt for tie rod, upper transverse link and lower transverse link from wheel bearing housing.

9. Remove connecting link from trailing arm.

10. Hold wheel bearing housing firmly and remove bolts.

11. Pull coupling rod out of trailing link.

12. Remove wheel bearing housing.

To install:

13. Refer to illustrations under Component Locations for torque values.

14. Installation is in reverse order of removal, noting the following:

15. Install tie rod bolt, upper transverse link and lower transverse link.

16. Tighten\connecting link to the trailing arm by hand.

17. Threaded connection of trailing link/ wheel bearing housing must only be tightened when all other components (spring and

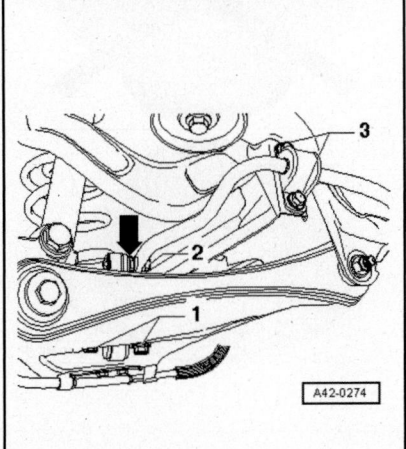

Fig. 236 Removing the stabilizer bar and components

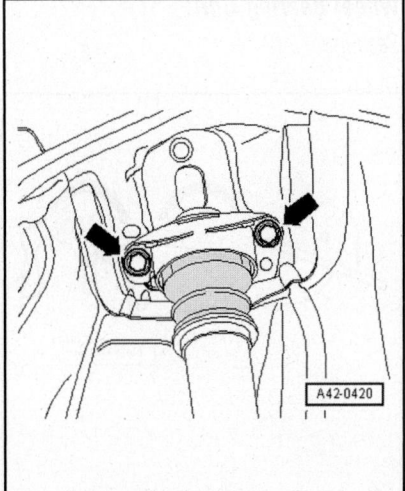

Fig. 237 Remove the upper strut bolts

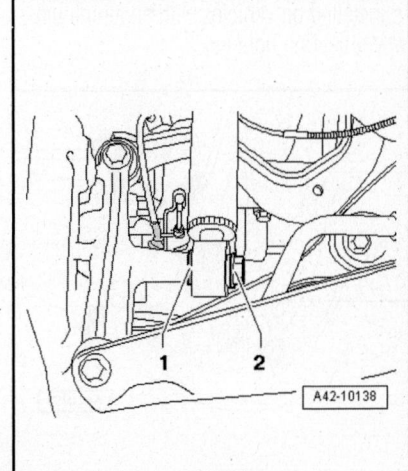

Fig. 238 Remove bolt (2) and washer (1)

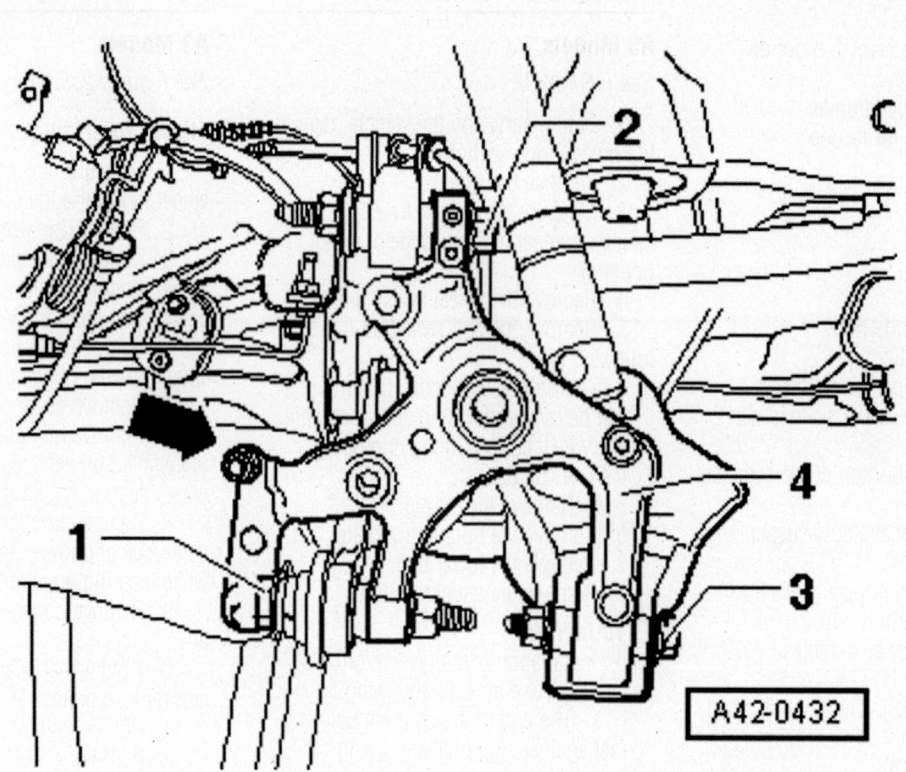

Fig. 239 Remove bolt for tie rod (1), upper transverse link (2) and lower transverse link (3) from wheel bearing housing (4)

strut always) of the respective wheel suspension have been already assembled. To tighten, suspension must be unladen. Only now do the trailing link and wheel bearing housing move into the position required.

18. Tighten bolt and washer. The washer is installed on vehicles with an aluminum wheel bearing housing.

19. Place trailing arm on wheel bearing housing with bolts but do not tighten yet.

20. Install coil spring.

21. To complete installation, reverse the remaining removal procedure.

22. Vehicle alignment is required.

Wheel Bearing Unit

See Figure 242.

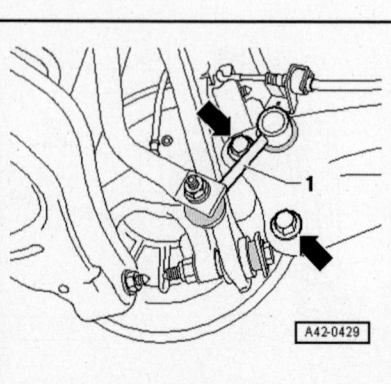

Fig. 240 Hold wheel bearing housing firmly and remove bolts

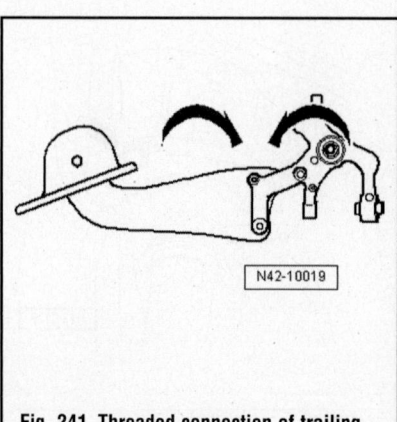

Fig. 241 Threaded connection of trailing link/wheel bearing housing

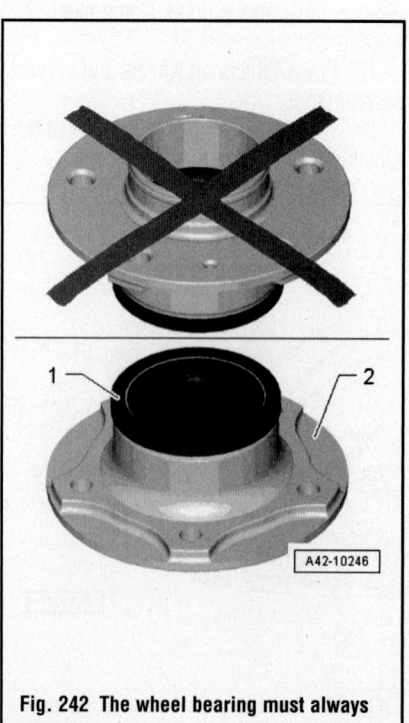

Fig. 242 The wheel bearing must always face up

1. Before servicing the vehicle, refer to the precautions section.

2. Remove the wheel.

3. Loosen dust cap from seat by tapping lightly on claw of grease cap puller VW 637/2.

4. Press off dust cap.

5. Remove the brake carrier

caliper and support to one side with a piece of wire.

6. Remove the brake rotor.

7. Remove the multipoint socket bolt with the socket AF 24 T10361.

8. Remove wheel bearing unit from stub axle.

9. The wheel bearing must always face up.

To install:

10. Installation is the reverse order of removal, tighten the bearing nut to 133 ft. lbs. (180 Nm) plus 180 degrees:

A4 & A5 Models

See Figures 243 and 244.

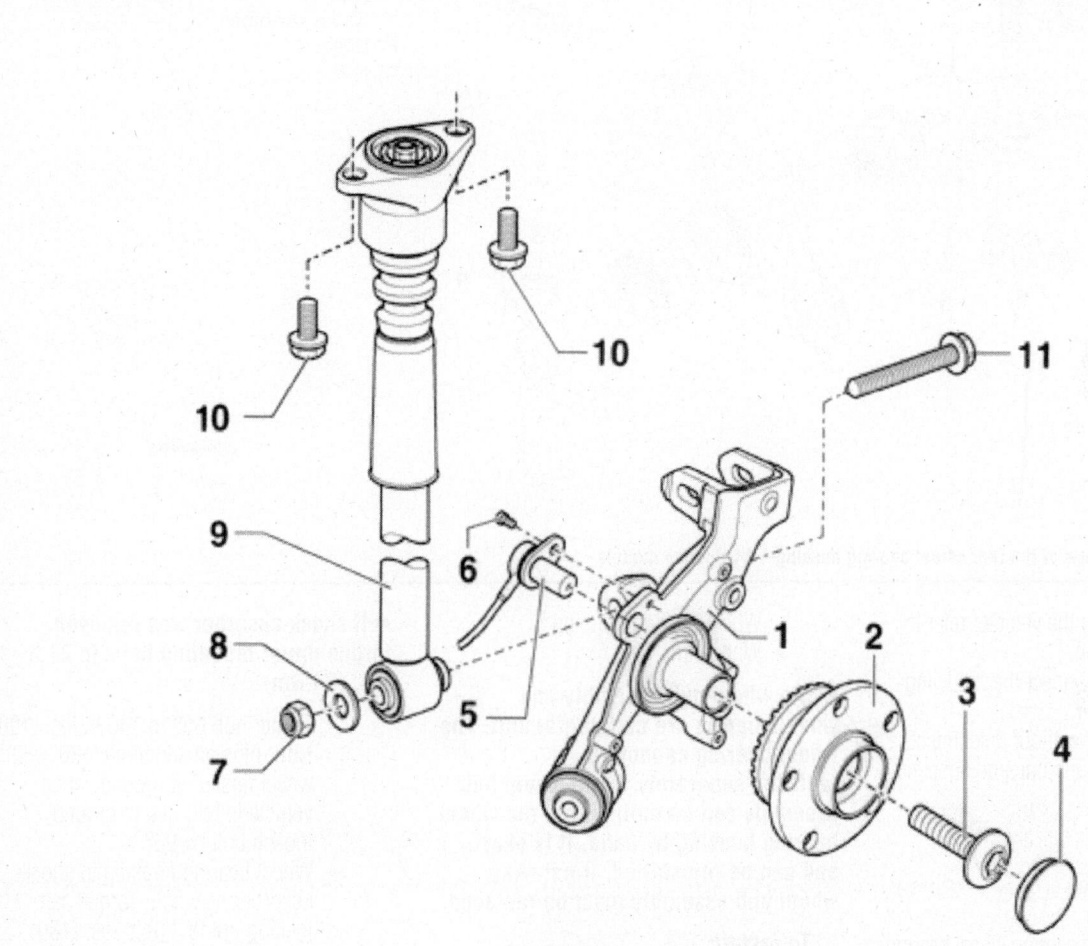

1. Wheel bearing housing
2. Wheel bearing hub
3. Bolt
4. Dust cap
5. Speed sensor
6. Bolt
7. Nut
8. Washer
9. Shock absorber
10. Combi bolts
11. Combi bolt

67200-A4A4-G02

Fig. 243 Exploded view of the rear wheel bearing—A4 with front wheel drive vehicles

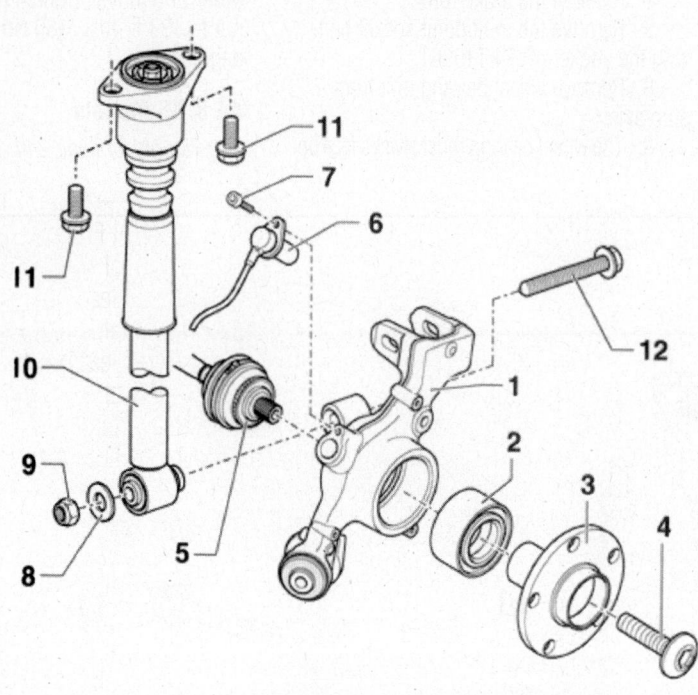

1. Wheel bearing housing
2. Wheel bearing
3. Hub
4. Center bolt
5. Drive axle
6. Speed sensor
7. Bolt
8. Washer
9. Nut
10. Shock absorber
11. Bolts
12. Bolt

67200-A4A4-G03

Fig. 244 Exploded view of the rear wheel bearing housing—A4 Quattro models

1. Before servicing the vehicle, refer to the precautions section.
2. Remove or disconnect the following:
   • Rear wheel
   • Brake caliper, without disconnecting the hydraulic line and suspend it on a wire.
   • Brake rotor
   • Dust cap
   • Center hub bolt
   • Speed sensor
   • Collared bolt securing wheel bearing housing to rear shock absorber (mark position for proper reinstallation)
   • Shock absorber, if necessary

   • Wheel bearing housing
   • Wheel hub

➡The wheel hub assembly and wheel bearing are an integral unit. The wheel bearing cannot be replaced separately. If the wheel hub assembly can be pulled from the wheel bearing housing by hand, it is okay and can be reinstalled. If not okay, wheel hub assembly must be replaced.

To install:
3. Clean and inspect mating surfaces for bearing races.
4. Install in reverse of the removal procedure, noting the following:

➡If shock absorber was removed, torque upper mounting bolts to 27 ft. lbs. (36 Nm).

   • Center hub bolt to 140 ft. lbs. (190 Nm), plus an additional 180° with wheel raised off ground; when vehicle is returned to ground, loosen bolt by 90°
   • Wheel bearing housing to shock absorber new bolt. Torque self-locking nut to 118 ft. lbs. (160 Nm), plus an additional 90°, with vehicle standing on ground.
5. Check the brakes for proper operation.

AUDI

TT

2

SPECIFICATIONS AND MAINTENANCE CHARTS

ENGINE AND VEHICLE IDENTIFICATION

		Engine						Model Year	
Code	Liters (cc)	Cu. In.	Cyl.	Fuel Sys.	Engine Type	Eng. Mfg.		Code ①	Year
CCTA	2.0 (1998)	121	4	FSI-Turbo	DOHC	Audi		B	2011
CCZA	2.0 (1998)	121	4	FSI-Turbo	DOHC	Audi		C	2012
CDMA	2.0 (1998)	121	4	FSI-Turbo	DOHC	Audi			
CBRA	3.2 (3200)	195	6	MFI	DOHC	Audi			

MFI: Multi-point Fuel Injection

FSI: Direct Fuel Induction

DOHC: Double Overhead Camshaft

① 10th digit of the Vehicle Identification Number (VIN)

71105_AUTT_C0001

GENERAL ENGINE SPECIFICATIONS

Year	Model	Engine Displacement Liters	Engine ID	Net Horsepower @ rpm	Net Torque@rpm (ft. lbs.)	Bore x Stroke (in.)	Compression Ratio	Oil Pressure @ rpm
2011	TT/S	2.0	CCTA	200@5100	207@5000	3.25x3.65	9.6:1	NA
		2.0	CCZA	265@6000	258@5000	3.25x3.65	9.8:1	NA
		2.0	CDMA	195@6000	350@2500	3.25x3.65	9.8:1	NA
		3.2	CBRA	250@6300	236@3200	3.31x3.78	10.85:1	NA
2012	TT/S	2.0	CCTA	200@5100	207@5000	3.25x3.65	9.6:1	NA
		2.0	CCZA	265@6000	258@5000	3.25x3.65	9.8:1	NA
		2.0	CDMA	195@6000	350@2500	3.25x3.65	9.8:1	NA
		3.2	CBRA	250@6300	236@3200	3.31x3.78	10.85:1	NA

71105_AUTT_C0002

ENGINE TUNE-UP SPECIFICATIONS

Year	Engine Displacement Liters	Engine ID/VIN	Spark Plug Gap (in.)	Ignition Timing (deg.) MT	Ignition Timing (deg.) AT	Fuel Pump (psi)	Idle Speed (rpm) MT	Idle Speed (rpm) AT	Valve Clearance In.	Valve Clearance Ex.
2011	2.0	CCTA	0.039	①	①	87	640-800	640-800	HYD	HYD
	2.0	CCZA	0.039	①	①	87	640-800	640-800	HYD	HYD
	2.0	CDMA	0.039	①	①	87	640-800	640-800	HYD	HYD
	3.2	CBRA	0.039	①	①	40	600-700	600-700	HYD	HYD
2012	2.0	CCTA	0.039	①	①	87	640-800	640-800	HYD	HYD
	2.0	CCZA	0.039	①	①	87	640-800	640-800	HYD	HYD
	2.0	CDMA	0.039	①	①	87	640-800	640-800	HYD	HYD
	3.2	CBRA	0.039	①	①	40	600-700	600-700	HYD	HYD

NOTE: The Vehicle Emission Control Information label reflects specification changes made during production and must be used if different from this chart.

NOTE: Fuel pump pressure specifications with the fuel pressure regulator vacuum hose attached.

HYD: Hydraulic

① The basic setting is controlled by the ECU and is not adjustable

71105_AUTT_C0003

CAPACITIES

Year	Model	Engine Displacement Liters	Engine ID	Engine Oil with Filter (qts.)	Transmission (pts.) 5-Spd	Auto	Fuel Tank (gal.)	Cooling System (qts.)
2011	TT/S	2.0	CCTA	4.8	4.8	12.6	14.5	8.5
		2.0	CCZA	4.8	4.8	12.6	14.5	8.5
		2.0	CDMA	4.8	4.8	12.6	14.5	8.5
		3.2	CBRA	NA	NA	NA	14.5	7.4
2012	TT/S	2.0	CCTA	4.8	4.8	12.6	14.5	8.5
		2.0	CCZA	4.8	4.8	12.6	14.5	8.5
		2.0	CDMA	4.8	4.8	12.6	14.5	8.5
		3.2	CBRA	NA	NA	NA	14.5	7.4

NOTE: All capacities are approximate. Add fluid gradually and ensure a proper fluid level is obtained. Always check levels against the dipstick or tank measurements when adding.

NA: Not Available

71105_AUTT_C0005

FLUID SPECIFICATIONS

Year	Model	Engine Displ. Liters	Engine Oil	Man. Trans.	Auto. Trans.	Drive Axle	Power Steering Fluid	Brake Master Cylinder
2011	TT/S	2.0	5W-30	SAE 75W	ATF Fluid	NA	ATF Fluid	DOT 3
		3.2	5W-30	SAE 75W	ATF Fluid	NA	ATF Fluid	DOT 3
2012	TT/S	2.0	5W-30	SAE 75W	ATF Fluid	NA	ATF Fluid	DOT 3
		3.2	5W-30	SAE 75W	ATF Fluid	NA	ATF Fluid	DOT 3

NA: Not Available

DOT: Department Of Transpotation

71105_AUTT_C0004

VALVE SPECIFICATIONS

Year	Engine Disp. Liters	Engine ID	Seat Angle (deg.)	Face Angle (deg.)	Spring Test Pressure (lbs. @ in.)	Spring Installed Height (in.)	Stem-to-Guide Clearance (in.) Intake	Exhaust	Stem Diameter (in.) Intake	Exhaust
2011	2.0	CCTA	45	45	NA	NA	NA	NA	0.235	0.234
	2.0	CCZA	45	45	NA	NA	NA	NA	0.235	0.234
	2.0	CDMA	45	45	NA	NA	NA	NA	0.235	0.234
	3.2	CBRA	45	45	NA	NA	0.031 ①	0.031 ①	0.2346	0.2343
2012	2.0	CCTA	45	45	NA	NA	NA	NA	0.235	0.234
	2.0	CCZA	45	45	NA	NA	NA	NA	0.235	0.234
	2.0	CDMA	45	45	NA	NA	NA	NA	0.235	0.234
	3.2	CBRA	45	45	NA	NA	0.031 ①	0.031 ①	0.2346	0.2343

NA: Not Available

① To measure: Insert a new valve into guide with end of valve flush with end of guide. Use a dial indicator to measure axial valve head movement.

71105_AUTT_C0008

CRANKSHAFT AND CONNECTING ROD SPECIFICATIONS

All measurements are given in inches.

Year	Engine Disp. Liters	Engine ID	Crankshaft				Connecting Rod		
			Main Brg. Journal Dia.	Main Brg. Oil Clearance	Shaft End-play	Thrust on No.	Journal Diameter	Oil Clearance	Side Clearance
2011	2.0	CCTA	2.126	NA	NA	NA	1.882	NA	NA
	2.0	CCZA	2.126	NA	NA	NA	1.882	NA	NA
	2.0	CDMA	2.126	NA	NA	NA	1.882	NA	NA
	3.2	CBRA	2.3606-2.3613	0.0008-0.0024	0.0003-0.009	5	2.1243-2.1251	0.0008-0.0028	NA
2012	2.0	CCTA	2.126	NA	NA	NA	1.882	NA	NA
	2.0	CCZA	2.126	NA	NA	NA	1.882	NA	NA
	2.0	CDMA	2.126	NA	NA	NA	1.882	NA	NA
	3.2	CBRA	2.3606-2.3613	0.0008-0.0024	0.0003-0.009	5	2.1243-2.1251	0.0008-0.0028	NA

NA: Not Available

71105_AUTT_C0007

PISTON AND RING SPECIFICATIONS

All measurements are given in inches

Year	Engine Disp. Liters	Engine ID	Piston Clearance	Ring Gap			Ring Side Clearance		
				Top Compression	Bottom Compression	Oil Control	Top Compression	Bottom Compression	Oil Control
2011	2.0	CCTA	0.001	NA	NA	NA	NA	NA	NA
	2.0	CCZA	0.001	NA	NA	NA	NA	NA	NA
	2.0	CDMA	0.001	NA	NA	NA	NA	NA	NA
	3.2	CBRA	NA	0.0078-0.0157	0.0078-0.0157	0.0098-0.0197	0.0016-0.0035	0.0012-0.0023	0.0008-0.0023
2012	2.0	CCTA	NA	NA	NA	NA	NA	NA	NA
	2.0	CCZA	NA	NA	NA	NA	NA	NA	NA
	2.0	CDMA	0.001	NA	NA	NA	NA	NA	NA
	3.2	CBRA	NA	0.0078-0.0157	0.0078-0.0157	0.0098-0.0197	0.0016-0.0035	0.0012-0.0023	0.0008-0.0023

Not Available.

71105_AUTT_C0009

TORQUE SPECIFICATIONS
All readings in ft. lbs.

Year	Engine Displacement Liters	Engine ID	Cylinder Head Bolts	Main Bearing Bolts	Rod Bearing Bolts	Manifold		Spark Plugs	Oil Drain Plug
						Intake	Exhaust		
2011	2.0	CCTA	①	②	③	NA	NA	22	22
	2.0	CCZA	①	②	③	NA	NA	22	22
	2.0	CDMA	①	②	③	NA	NA	22	22
	3.2	CBRA	①	NA	③	9	18	22	22
2012	2.0	CCTA	①	②	③	NA	NA	22	22
	2.0	CCZA	①	②	③	NA	NA	22	22
	2.0	CDMA	①	②	③	NA	NA	22	22
	3.2	CBRA	①	NA	③	9	18	22	22

NA: Not Available

① Refer to "Cylinder Head" in "ENGINE MECHANICAL" section.

② Step 1: 48 ft. lbs.

   Step 2: Plus 90 degrees

③ Step 1: 33 ft. lbs.

   Step 2: 90 degrees

71105_AUTT_C0010

WHEEL ALIGNMENT

Year	Model		Caster		Camber		Toe Setting (Deg.)
			Range (+/-Deg.)	Preferred Setting (Deg.)	Range (+/-Deg.)	Preferred Setting (Deg.)	
2011	TT/S	F	NA	NA	30'	-41'	0.10' +/- 0.10'
	All Suspensions	R	NA	NA	30'	-1° 20'	0.25' +/- 0.10'
2012	TT/S	F	NA	NA	30'	-41'	0.10' +/- 0.10'
	All Suspensions	R	NA	NA	30'	-1° 20'	0.25' +/- 0.10'

NA: Not Available

71105_AUTT_C0011

TIRE, WHEEL AND BALL JOINT SPECIFICATIONS

Year	Model	OEM Tires		Tire Pressures (psi)		Wheel Size	Ball Joint Inspection	Lug Nut (ft. lbs.)
		Standard	Optional	Front	Rear			
2011	TT	245/40/R18	①	②	②	①	NS	NS
	TTS	255/35/R19	①	②	②	①	NS	NS
2012	TT	245/40/R18	①	②	②	①	NS	NS
	TTS	255/35/R19	①	②	②	①	NS	NS

OEM: Original Equipment Manufacturer

PSI: Pounds Per Square Inch

NS: Not Specified by manufacturer

① Several optional size tires and wheels are available. Consult your local tire supplier.

② Refer to the door jamb label and/or tire dealer recommendations for pressure settings.

71105_AUTT_C0012

BRAKE SPECIFICATIONS

All measurements in inches unless noted

Year	Model		Brake Disc			Minimum Lining Thickness		Brake Caliper	
			Original Thickness	Minimum Thickness	Maximum Runout	Front	Rear	Bracket Bolts (ft. lbs.)	Mounting Bolts (Nm.)
2011	TT/S	F	①	②	NA	0.079	NA	144	22
		R	③	④	NA	NA	0.079	73	25
2012	TT/S	F	①	②	NA	0.079	NA	144	22
		R	③	④	NA	NA	0.079	73	25

① Brake disc PR number 1LJ: 0.984 in.
  Brake disc PR number 1LK: 1.181 in.

② Brake disc PR number 1LJ: 0.827 in.
  Brake disc PR number 1LK: 1.063 in.

③ Brake disc PR number 1KJ, 1KZ, 2ED, 2EE (non-ventilated): 0.472 in.
  Brake disc PR number 2EA, 2EF, 2EG (ventilated): 0.866 in.

④ Brake disc PR number 1KJ, 1KZ, 2ED, 2EE (non-ventilated): 0.354 in.
  Brake disc PR number 2EA, 2EF, 2EG (ventilated): 0.748 in.

71105_AUTT_C0013

SCHEDULED MAINTENANCE INTERVALS
Audi—TT & TTS

TO BE SERVICED	TYPE OF SERVICE	VEHICLE MILEAGE INTERVAL (x1000)												
		5	10	20	30	40	50	60	70	80	90	100	105	120
Engine oil & filter	R	✓	✓	✓	✓	✓	✓	✓	✓	✓	✓	✓	✓	✓
Service reminder reset	S/I	✓	✓	✓	✓	✓	✓	✓	✓	✓	✓	✓	✓	✓
Rotate wheels	S/I	✓												
Fluid levels	S/I	✓	✓	✓	✓	✓	✓	✓	✓	✓	✓	✓	✓	✓
Auto shift lock	S/I	✓	✓	✓	✓	✓	✓	✓	✓	✓	✓	✓	✓	✓
Brake system	S/I	✓	✓	✓	✓	✓	✓	✓	✓	✓	✓	✓	✓	✓
Brake fluid	R	Replace fluid every two years, regardless of mileage												
M/T shift & clutch interlock	S/I	✓	✓	✓	✓	✓	✓	✓	✓	✓	✓	✓	✓	✓
Cooling system	S/I		✓	✓	✓	✓	✓	✓	✓	✓	✓	✓	✓	✓
Exhaust system	S/I		✓	✓	✓	✓	✓	✓	✓	✓	✓	✓	✓	✓
ODB check for codes	S/I		✓	✓	✓	✓	✓	✓	✓	✓	✓	✓	✓	✓
Door hinges - lubricate	S/I		✓	✓	✓	✓	✓	✓	✓	✓	✓	✓	✓	✓
Battery level	S/I		✓	✓	✓	✓	✓	✓	✓	✓	✓	✓	✓	✓
Windshield washer fluid	S/I		✓	✓	✓	✓	✓	✓	✓	✓	✓	✓	✓	✓
Tire condition & pressure	S/I		✓	✓	✓	✓	✓	✓	✓	✓	✓	✓	✓	✓
Drive shaft boots	S/I		✓	✓	✓	✓	✓	✓	✓	✓	✓	✓	✓	✓
Road test	S/I		✓	✓	✓	✓	✓	✓	✓	✓	✓	✓	✓	✓
Lighting	S/I		✓	✓	✓	✓	✓	✓	✓	✓	✓	✓	✓	✓
Engine for leaks	S/I			✓		✓		✓		✓		✓		✓
Front axle dust seals on ball joints & tie rod ends	S/I			✓		✓		✓		✓		✓		✓
Haldex clutch oil & filter	R			✓		✓		✓		✓		✓		✓
Transmission for leaks	S/I			✓		✓		✓		✓		✓		
Multronic trans fluid	R					✓				✓				✓
MT final drive fluid	S/I			✓		✓		✓		✓		✓		✓
AT final drive fluid	S/I					✓				✓				✓
Dust/pollen filter	R			✓		✓		✓		✓		✓		✓
Sliding roof rails	S/I			✓		✓		✓		✓		✓		✓
PS fluid	S/I					✓				✓				✓
Air cleaner element	R					✓				✓				✓
Spark plugs	R					✓				✓				✓
Serpentine belt	R									✓				
Timing belt 2.0	R												✓	

R: Replace   S/I: Service or Inspect

71105_AUTT_C0014

PRECAUTIONS

Before servicing any vehicle, please be sure to read all of the following precautions, which deal with personal safety, prevention of component damage, and important points to take into consideration when servicing a motor vehicle:

• Never open, service or drain the radiator or cooling system when the engine is hot; serious burns can occur from the steam and hot coolant.

• Observe all applicable safety precautions when working around fuel. Whenever servicing the fuel system, always work in a well-ventilated area. Do not allow fuel spray or vapors to come in contact with a spark, open flame, or excessive heat (a hot drop light, for example). Keep a dry chemical fire extinguisher near the work area. Always keep fuel in a container specifically designed for fuel storage; also, always properly seal fuel containers to avoid the possibility of fire or explosion. Refer to the additional fuel system precautions later in this section.

• Fuel injection systems often remain pressurized, even after the engine has been turned **OFF**. The fuel system pressure must be relieved before disconnecting any fuel lines. Failure to do so may result in fire and/or personal injury.

• Brake fluid often contains polyglycol ethers and polyglycols. Avoid contact with the eyes and wash your hands thoroughly after handling brake fluid. If you do get brake fluid in your eyes, flush your eyes with clean, running water for 15 minutes. If eye irritation persists, or if you have taken brake fluid internally, IMMEDIATELY seek medical assistance.

• The EPA warns that prolonged contact with used engine oil may cause a number of skin disorders, including cancer. You should make every effort to minimize your exposure to used engine oil. Protective gloves should be worn when changing oil. Wash your hands and any other exposed skin areas as soon as possible after exposure to used engine oil. Soap and water, or waterless hand cleaner should be used.

• All new vehicles are now equipped with an air bag system, often referred to as a Supplemental Restraint System (SRS) or Supplemental Inflatable Restraint (SIR) system. The system must be disabled before performing service on or around system components, steering column, instrument panel components, wiring and sensors. Failure to follow safety and disabling procedures could result in accidental air bag deployment, possible personal injury and unnecessary system repairs.

• Always wear safety goggles when working with, or around, the air bag system. When carrying a non-deployed air bag, be sure the bag and trim cover are pointed away from your body. When placing a non-deployed air bag on a work surface, always face the bag and trim cover upward, away from the surface. This will reduce the motion of the module if it is accidentally deployed. Refer to the additional air bag system precautions later in this section.

• Clean, high quality brake fluid from a sealed container is essential to the safe and proper operation of the brake system. You should always buy the correct type of brake fluid for your vehicle. If the brake fluid becomes contaminated, completely flush the system with new fluid. Never reuse any brake fluid. Any brake fluid that is removed from the system should be discarded. Also, do not allow any brake fluid to come in contact with a painted surface; it will damage the paint.

• Never operate the engine without the proper amount and type of engine oil; doing so WILL result in severe engine damage.

• Timing belt maintenance is extremely important. Many models utilize an interference-type, non-freewheeling engine. If the timing belt breaks, the valves in the cylinder head may strike the pistons, causing potentially serious (also time-consuming and expensive) engine damage. Refer to the maintenance interval charts for the recommended replacement interval for the timing belt, and to the timing belt section for belt replacement and inspection.

• Disconnecting the negative battery cable on some vehicles may interfere with the functions of the on-board computer system(s) and may require the computer to undergo a relearning process once the negative battery cable is reconnected.

• When servicing drum brakes, only disassemble and assemble one side at a time, leaving the remaining side intact for reference.

• Only an MVAC-trained, EPA-certified automotive technician should service the air conditioning system or its components.

BRAKES

GENERAL INFORMATION

PRECAUTIONS

• Certain components within the ABS system are not intended to be serviced or repaired individually.

• Do not use rubber hoses or other parts not specifically specified for and ABS system. When using repair kits, replace all parts included in the kit. Partial or incorrect repair may lead to functional problems and require the replacement of components.

• Lubricate rubber parts with clean, fresh brake fluid to ease assembly. Do not use shop air to clean parts; damage to rubber components may result.

• Use only DOT 3 brake fluid from an unopened container.

• If any hydraulic component or line is removed or replaced, it may be necessary to bleed the entire system.

• A clean repair area is essential. Always clean the reservoir and cap thoroughly before removing the cap. The slightest amount of dirt in the fluid may plug an orifice and impair the system function. Perform repairs after components have been thoroughly cleaned; use only denatured alcohol to clean components. Do not allow ABS components to come into contact with any substance containing mineral oil; this includes used shop rags.

• The Anti-Lock control unit is a microprocessor similar to other computer units in the vehicle. Ensure that the ignition switch is **OFF** before removing or installing controller harnesses. Avoid

ANTI-LOCK BRAKE SYSTEM (ABS)

static electricity discharge at or near the controller.

• If any arc welding is to be done on the vehicle, the control unit should be unplugged before welding operations begin.

SPEED SENSORS

REMOVAL & INSTALLATION

Front

1. Release connector on speed sensor and disconnect.

2. Remove bolt and remove speed sensor from wheel bearing housing.

To install:

3. Installation is the reverse of removal, with special attention to the following:

a. Before inserting speed sensor, clean hole inner surface and coat speed sensor all-round with polycarbamide grease (G 000 650).

b. Turn the steering completely left and right, making sure that the speed sensor wiring has sufficient clearance.

Rear

1. Release connector on speed sensor and disconnect.

2. Remove bolt and remove speed sensor from stub axle.

To install:

3. Installation is the reverse of removal, with special attention to the following:

a. Before inserting speed sensor, clean hole inner surface and coat speed sensor all-round with polycarbamide grease (G 000 650).

BRAKES   BLEEDING THE BRAKE SYSTEM

BLEEDING PROCEDURE

BLEEDING PROCEDURE

Do not, under any circumstances, allow brake fluid to come into contact with any fluids containing mineral oil (oil, gasoline, cleaning solvents). Mineral oil damages the sealing plugs and boots of the brake system.

Brake fluid is poisonous. NEVER siphon brake fluid with your mouth! Also due to its corrosive effect, brake fluid must not come into contact with paintwork.

Brake fluid is hygroscopic, meaning that it absorbs moisture from the surrounding air, and must therefore be stored in air-tight containers.

Observe disposal regulations.

When filling with brake fluid using e.g. brake charger/bleeder unit VAS 5234 or brake filler/bleeder unit suction adapter V.A.G 1869/4, make sure that the filling pressure does not exceed 14.5 psi (1 bar). Regulate brake fluid pressure on brake charger/bleeder unit to 14.5 psi (1 bar). Refer to the VAS 5234 or V.A.G 1869/4 operating instructions.

Only use new brake fluid.

Rinse off any spilled brake fluid using plenty of water.

➡**A second person is needed to bleed the brake charger/bleeder unit. Make sure that brake fluid reservoir does not run empty.**

1. Remove protective cap on brake caliper bleeder screw.

2. Connect bleeder bottle hose to brake caliper bleeder valve.

3. Build pressure up in brake system by pumping brake pedal.

4. Slowly press brake pedal to prevent bubbles from forming.

5. As soon as pressure is built up, hold brake pedal in depressed position.

6. Open the bleeder screw, with bleeder bottle hose connected, until the pressure is relieved (pedal drops).

7. Hold pedal in completely depressed position and close the bleeder screw.

8. Release brake pedal and wait approximately 2 seconds so that brake fluid can flow out of the brake fluid reservoir.

9. Repeat the procedure until the brake fluid flows out clear and free of bubbles.

10. Tighten bleeder screw to 7 ft. lbs. (10 Nm).

11. Remove bleeder hose and install protective cap on bleeder screw.

12. Repeat bleeding process on remaining brake calipers.

13. Note the bleeding sequence:
   • Left front brake caliper
   • Right front brake caliper
   • Left rear brake caliper
   • Right rear brake caliper

14. Fill brake fluid reservoir up to "MAX" marking and install sealing cap.

15. Start engine to check brake pedal travel and pressure.

16. If pedal travel is too long and pressure is too weak, check brake system for possible leaks. Repeat bleeding procedure.

17. Make sure the brakes are working correctly before driving the vehicle for the first time.

FLUID FILL PROCEDURE

Fluid Level Checking

1. To prevent the brake fluid from overflowing from the reservoir, the level must not be over the MAX mark.

➡**When driving, fluid level drops slightly from use and automatic brake pad adjustment.**

2. Always check fluid level in conjunction with brake pad wear:

3. When brake pads are new or if there is still enough brake lining left, the brake fluid level must be between MIN and MAX marks on the brake fluid reservoir.

4. With brake fluid at MIN mark or slightly above, topping off brake fluid is not necessary when wear limit of brake pads has been almost reached.

5. If brake fluid level is below MIN mark, check brake system before adding brake fluid.

Fluid Changing

See Figure 1.

➡**Special tool required: Brake Fluid, Changing using Brake Charger/Bleeder Unit VAS 5234.**

The brake fluid level in the reservoir must be high enough so that air cannot get into the brake system.

➡**Do not remove the strainer inside the brake fluid reservoir.**

1. Follow VAS 5234 operating instructions!

2. Remove brake fluid reservoir cap.

3. Use the hose from the VAS 5234 to extract as much brake fluid as possible.

4. Install adapter to brake fluid reservoir. Connect filler hose on VAS 5234 to adapter.

5. On manual transmission models, do the following:

a. Pull cover cap off clutch slave cylinder bleed screw.

b. Place extractor bleeder hose 1 on clutch slave cylinder bleeder screw, open bleeder screw, and let about 100 ml drain

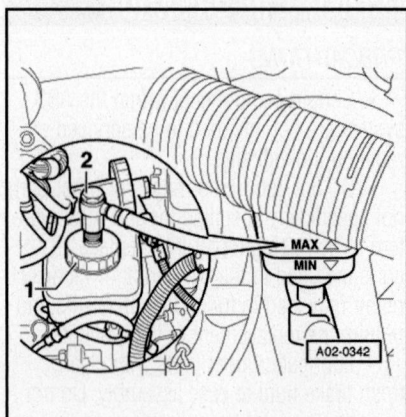

Fig. 1 Install adapter (1) to brake fluid reservoir. Connect filler hose (2) on VAS 5234 to adapter.

out. Close bleeder screw and install cover cap.

c. Operate clutch pedal several times.

6. For all vehicles, do the following:

a. Remove caps from the bleeder screws.

b. Connect extractor bleeder hose to front left bleeder screw, open bleeder screw and allow about 7 oz. (200 ml) to flow out. Close bleeder screw.

c. Repeat work sequence on other side of vehicle at front.

d. Connect extractor bleeder hose to rear left bleeder screw, open bleeder screw and allow about 7 oz. (200 ml) to flow out. Close bleeder screw.

e. Repeat procedure on opposite rear.

f. Install cover caps on brake caliper bleeder screws.

g. Move filler lever on VAS 5234 to position B.

h. Remove the filler hose from the adapter.

i. Remove the adapter from the brake fluid reservoir.

j. Install the brake fluid reservoir cap.

k. Check brake fluid level and fill if necessary.

l. Check pedal pressure and brake pedal free play. Free play: maximum 1/3 of pedal travel.

BRAKES

✳✳ CAUTION

Dust and dirt accumulating on brake parts during normal use may contain asbestos fibers from production or aftermarket brake linings. Breathing excessive concentrations of asbestos fibers can cause serious bodily harm. Exercise care when servicing brake parts. Do not sand or grind brake lining unless equipment used is designed to contain the dust residue. Do not clean brake parts with compressed air or by dry brushing. Cleaning should be done by dampening the brake components with a fine mist of water, then wiping the brake components clean with a dampened cloth. Dispose of cloth and all residue containing asbestos fibers in an impermeable container with the appropriate label. Follow practices prescribed by the Occupational Safety and Health Administration (OSHA) and the Environmental Protection Agency (EPA) for the handling, processing, and disposing of dust or debris that may contain asbestos fibers.

BRAKE CALIPER

REMOVAL & INSTALLATION

Front Brake Caliper, 16" FN3

See Figure 2.

➡**Recommended tools: brake pedal depressor V.A.G 1869/2.**

1. Remove the brake pads.

2. Install brake pedal loading device V.A.G 1869/2 between brake pedal and driver seat. Depress brake pedal a minimum of 60 mm.

➡**By doing this, the valves in the brake master cylinder are closed and the**

brake fluid reservoir does not run empty.

3. Connect hose of a bleeder bottle to bleeder screw of the removed brake caliper.

4. Open bleeder screw.

5. Do not remove brake pedal loading device V.A.G 1869/2.

6. Remove brake hose from the brake caliper.

7. Installation is in reverse order of removal, with special attention to the following:

a. Install brake pads.

b. Bleed brake system.

Front Brake Caliper, 17" FNR G57

➡**Special tool recommendations:**

- Brake pedal actuator V.A.G 1869/2
- Piston resetting tool T10145

1. Insert V.A.G 1869/2 between brake pedal and driver's seat by pressing brake pedal down at least 2.4 in. (60 mm).

➡**By doing this, the valves in the brake master cylinder are closed and the brake fluid reservoir does not run empty.**

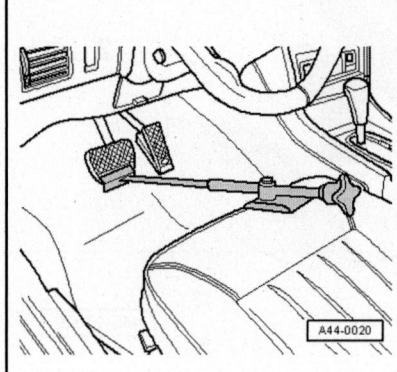

Fig. 2 Brake pedal loading device V.A.G 1869/2 between brake pedal and driver seat

2. Connect the hose of a bleeder bottle to the bleeder screw of the removed brake caliper.

3. Open bleeder screw.

4. Do not remove V.A.G 1869/2.

5. Close the bleed screws.

6. Remove brake hose from brake caliper.

7. Remove cover caps from the caliper guide pins and remove the guide pins.

8. Pull both guide pins out of brake caliper and bushings.

9. Remove brake pads, as described in this section.

To install:

10. Installation is the reverse of removal, with special attention to the following:

a. Remove V.A.G 1869/2.

b. Push the brake pistons back using the T10145 before installing the brake pads.

c. Make sure that brake fluid cannot leak out of the brake fluid reservoir because it will damage components and the paint.

d. When siphoning brake fluid, always use a bleeder bottle that is used exclusively for brake fluid.

e. Install brake pads, as described in this section.

f. Slide both guide pins through bushings into brake caliper.

g. Tighten brake caliper housing to brake carrier using both guide pins. Note required torque: 22 ft. lbs. (30 Nm).

h. Connect the brake line to the brake caliper. Tighten the hose connection to 10 ft. lbs. (14 Nm).

i. Bleed the brake system.

j. Check brake caliper for ease of movement by moving it sideways.

k. Mount the wheels.

l. Lower vehicle.

11. After installing brake pads, depress brake pedal several times firmly to properly seat brake pads in their normal operating position.

12. Make sure the brakes are working correctly before driving the vehicle for the first time.

DISC BRAKE PADS

REMOVAL & INSTALLATION

Front Brake Caliper, 16" FN3

See Figures 3 and 4.

➡Recommended tools: Torque wrench V.A.G 1331, Piston resetting tool T 10145.

➡If reusing brake pads, mark location. Reinstall in same position, otherwise uneven braking will occur.

1. Remove both front wheels.
2. Disconnect the connector, 1, for brake pad wear indicator, on left brake.
3. Remove guide pins.
4. Using screwdriver, pry off brake pad retaining spring from brake caliper housing and remove.
5. Remove brake caliper and suspend it using bundling wire.

➡Do not twist or kink brake hose line.

➡If reusing brake pads, mark location. Install in same position when installing, otherwise uneven braking will occur!

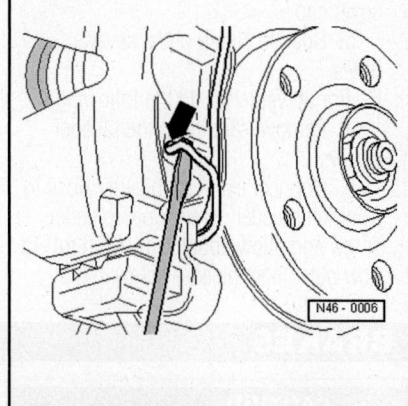

Fig. 4 Using screwdriver, pry off brake pad retaining spring from brake caliper housing (arrow) and remove

6. Remove brake pads.

To install:

7. Installation is in reverse order of removal, with special attention to the following:

    a. Clean brake caliper. Clean brake caliper with mineral spirits exclusively.

    b. Only push back brake piston when inserting new brake pads.

➡Before inserting new brake pads, press the piston back into the cylinder using the piston resetting tool. Before pressing the piston back, draw off brake fluid from the reservoir with a bleeder bottle. Otherwise fluid will overflow and cause damage if the reservoir was topped off during repair work.

8. When brake pads are installed correctly, arrow on backing plate points down.

➡Brake pad with wear indicator sits at front in left brake caliper on inner brake pad.

9. Remove protective foil on backing plate of outer brake pad.

➡Retaining spring must be pressed under brake carrier after it is inserted in both holes. If improperly installed, the wear of the outer brake pad cannot be adjusted, thereby increasing brake pedal travel.

➡After inserting brake pads and bleeding brake system, forcefully press brake pedal several times while vehicle is stationary so brake pads can be seated in their normal operating position.

10. Check brake fluid level, and fill if necessary.

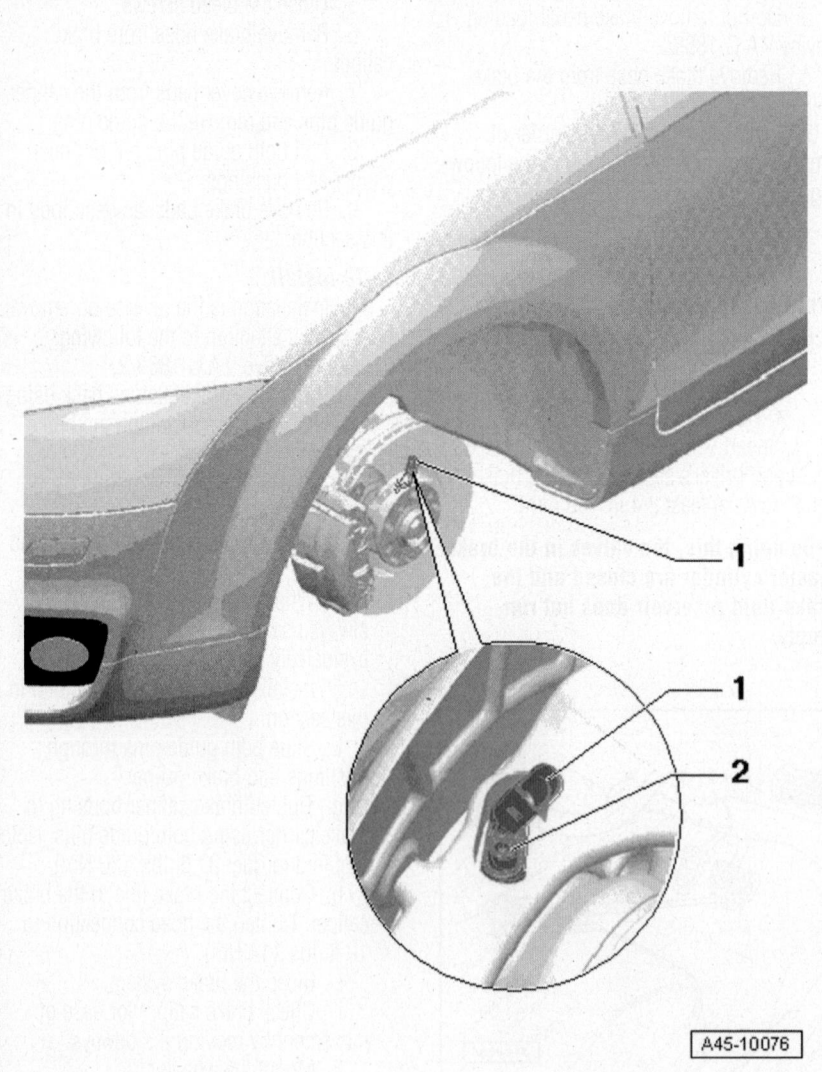

Fig. 3 Disconnect the connector, 1, for brake pad wear indicator, on left brake. Do not loosen bolt (2)

11. Mount wheels.

12. After installing brake pads, depress brake pedal several times firmly to properly seat brake pads in their normal operating position.

13. Make sure the brakes are working correctly before driving the vehicle for the first time.

Front Brake Caliper, 17" FNR G57

See Figures 5 and 6.

➡ **Recommended special tools:**

- Torque wrench V.A.G 1331
- Torque wrench V.A.G 1410
- Torque wrench V.A.G 1332
- Brake pedal actuator V.A.G 1869/2
- Piston resetting tool T10145

➡**When removing, mark brake pads that will be used again. Install in the same position, otherwise braking effect will be uneven!**

➡**Observe the direction of rotation when installing brake disc (arrow on brake disc) and installed location (left or right).**

1. Raise vehicle.

2. Remove wheels.

3. Using screwdriver, pry off brake pad retaining spring from brake caliper housing and remove.

4. Loosen the pad wear indicator retaining bolt only to remove brake disc. Disconnect brake pad wear indicator connector. Do not remove the bolt to the hub.

5. Remove brake pad wear indicator connector from bracket and disengage cable.

6. Remove spring clip from brake line bracket.

7. Unhook brake line from retainer.

8. Remove bolt and remove brake line bracket.

Remove brake caliper, as described in this section.

9. Remove brake caliper and hang so brake line cannot be damaged by the weight of the brake caliper.

➡**Do not twist or kink brake hose line.**

10. Remove brake pads from brake caliper housing or from brake carrier.

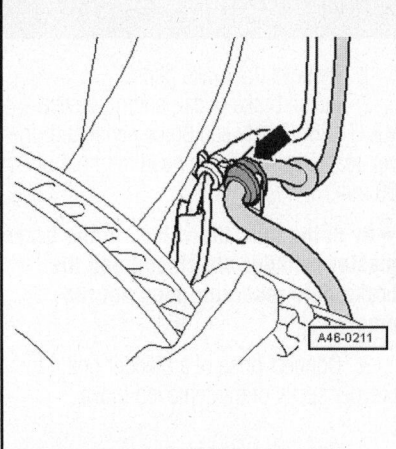

Fig. 5 Remove spring clip (arrow) from brake line bracket.

11. Clean brake caliper housing, in particular the adhesion surface for the brake pads. This must be free of adhesive residue and grease.

➡**Clean brake caliper with mineral spirits exclusively.**

To install:

12. Before installing the brake pads, clean the pad guide surface and coat it with a film of grease.

13. Push the brake pistons back using the piston resetting tool T10145 before installing the brake pads.

❋❋ CAUTION

Make sure that brake fluid cannot leak out of the brake fluid reservoir because it will damage components and the paint.

➡**When siphoning brake fluid, always use a bleeder bottle that is used exclusively for brake fluid.**

➡**Brake pad with wear indicator sits at front in left brake caliper on inner brake pad.**

14. Set the brake pad with retaining spring and wear indicator into the brake caliper housing (piston).

15. Set outer brake pad onto the brake caliper. Wear indicator wire is on inside of left front brake pad.

16. Position brake caliper with brake pads inserted on brake carrier or brake disc.

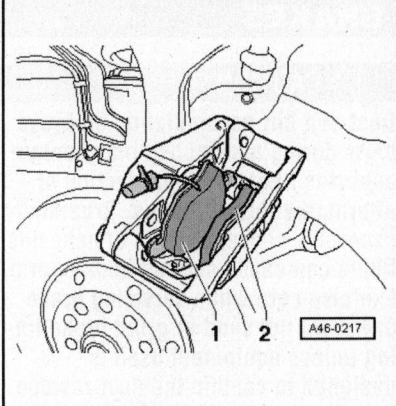

Fig. 6 Set outer brake pad (2) onto the brake caliper. Wear indicator wire is on inside of left front brake pad (1).

17. Tighten brake caliper housing to brake carrier using both guide pins to 22 ft. lbs. (30 Nm).

➡**Make sure that brake hose is installed without being twisted or pulled.**

18. Install both protective caps.

19. Attach brake line bracket.

20. Install retaining spring in brake caliper housing.

21. Engage brake line in bracket.

22. Press in spring clip.

23. Connect wear indicator connector.

24. Press wear indicator connector in bracket and engage line.

25. Mounting wheels, refer to see General Information.

26. After hooking into both studs, the retaining spring must be pressed under the brake carrier. If improperly installed, the wear of the outer brake pad cannot be adjusted, thereby increasing brake pedal travel.

27. Check brake caliper for ease of movement by moving it sideways.

28. Check brake fluid level, and fill if necessary.

29. After installing brake pads, depress brake pedal several times firmly to properly seat brake pads in their normal operating position.

30. Make sure the brakes are working correctly before driving the vehicle for the first time.

BRAKES

✳✳ CAUTION

Dust and dirt accumulating on brake parts during normal use may contain asbestos fibers from production or aftermarket brake linings. Breathing excessive concentrations of asbestos fibers can cause serious bodily harm. Exercise care when servicing brake parts. Do not sand or grind brake lining unless equipment used is designed to contain the dust residue. Do not clean brake parts with compressed air or by dry brushing. Cleaning should be done by dampening the brake components with a fine mist of water, then wiping the brake components clean with a dampened cloth. Dispose of cloth and all residue containing asbestos fibers in an impermeable container with the appropriate label. Follow practices prescribed by the Occupational Safety and Health Administration (OSHA) and the Environmental Protection Agency (EPA) for the handling, processing, and disposing of dust or debris that may contain asbestos fibers.

BRAKE CALIPER

REMOVAL & INSTALLATION

➡Recommended tools: brake pedal depressor V.A.G. 1869/2.

1. Remove the brake pads.
2. Install brake pedal loading device V.A.G 1869/2 between brake pedal and driver seat. Depress brake pedal a minimum of 60 mm.

➡By doing this, the valves in the brake master cylinder are closed and the brake fluid reservoir does not run empty.

3. Connect hose of a bleeder bottle to bleeder screw of the removed brake caliper.
4. Open bleeder screw.
5. Do not remove brake pedal loading device V.A.G 1869/2.
6. Remove brake hose from the brake caliper.
7. Installation is in reverse order of removal, with special attention to the following:
   a. Install brake pads.
   b. Bleed brake system.

DISC BRAKE PADS

REMOVAL & INSTALLATION

1. Raise vehicle.
2. Remove wheels.
3. Do not loosen parking brake cable from brake caliper.
4. Remove brake caliper housing while counter holding at guide pins.
5. Remove brake caliper housing from brake disc.

6. Hang brake caliper housing with wire so brake hose is not damaged by weight of brake caliper.
7. Remove brake pads and pad retaining springs from brake carrier
8. Remove brake pads.
9. When removing, mark brake pads that will be used again. Install in the same position, otherwise braking effect will be uneven!
10. Installation is in reverse order of removal, with special attention to the following:
    a. Clean brake caliper. Clean brake caliper with mineral spirits exclusively.
    b. Only push back brake piston when inserting new brake pads.
11. Remove protective foil on backing plate of brake pad.
12. Secure brake caliper housing using new self-locking bolts.
13. The repair kit includes four self-locking hex bolts which must be installed in all cases.
14. Check brake fluid level, and fill if necessary.

➡After installing brake pads, depress brake pedal several times firmly to properly seat brake pads in their normal operating position.

BRAKES

PARKING BRAKE CABLES

ADJUSTMENT

➡A new adjustment is necessary only after replacing brake cables, brake calipers or brake discs.

1. For parking brake cable zero adjustment, both rear wheels must run freely.
2. The parking brake lever must go below first catch by itself in zero position.
3. The adjusting nut on the compensator must be installed over the end of the relay rod.
4. Release parking brake.

5. Loosen cover in rear center console compartment with a hook and remove.
6. The parking brake cable must be routed without tension.
7. When adjusting parking brake, lever may be raised a maximum of 2 degrees.
8. Install adjusting nut on compensator lever until lever on brake caliper can be raised from stop.
9. With parking brake lever zero adjustment, distance between lever on brake caliper and stop together must be at least 0.039 in. (1 mm).

➡Distance to the stop on one side must be greater than zero and must not exceed 0.157 in. (4 mm).

10. Apply parking brake 3 times and then release.
11. With parking brake released, check if both wheels can be turned freely. And distance at calipers is maintained.
12. A light braking effect on rear wheels must be noticeable in first parking brake lever detent.
13. Correct adjustment, if necessary, by adjusting adjustment nut.
14. Due to the automatic rear brake adjuster, there is no need to adjust the parking brake after making initial adjustment.

GENERAL INFORMATION

✳✳ CAUTION

These vehicles are equipped with an air bag system. The system must be disarmed before performing service on, or around, system components, the steering column, instrument panel components, wiring and sensors. Failure to follow the safety precautions and the disarming procedure could result in accidental air bag deployment, possible injury and unnecessary system repairs.

SERVICE PRECAUTIONS

Disconnect and isolate the battery negative cable before beginning any airbag system component diagnosis, testing, removal, or installation procedures. Allow system capacitor to discharge for two minutes before beginning any component service. This will disable the airbag system. Failure to disable the airbag system may result in accidental airbag deployment, personal injury, or death.

Do not place an intact undeployed airbag face down on a solid surface. The airbag will propel into the air if accidentally deployed and may result in personal injury or death.

When carrying or handling an undeployed airbag, the trim side (face) of the airbag should be pointing away from the body to minimize possibility of injury if accidental deployment occurs. Failure to do this may result in personal injury or death.

Replace airbag system components with OEM replacement parts. Substitute parts may appear interchangeable, but internal differences may result in inferior occupant protection. Failure to do so may result in occupant personal injury or death.

Wear safety glasses, rubber gloves, and long sleeved clothing when cleaning powder residue from vehicle after an airbag deployment. Powder residue emitted from a deployed airbag can cause skin irritation. Flush affected area with cool water if irritation is experienced. If nasal or throat irritation is experienced, exit the vehicle for fresh air until the irritation ceases. If irritation continues, see a physician.

Do not use a replacement airbag that is not in the original packaging. This may result in improper deployment, personal injury, or death.

The factory installed fasteners, screws and bolts used to fasten airbag components have a special coating and are specifically designed for the airbag system. Do not use substitute fasteners. Use only original equipment fasteners listed in the parts catalog when fastener replacement is required.

During, and following, any child restraint anchor service, due to impact event or vehicle repair, carefully inspect all mounting hardware, tether straps, and anchors for proper installation, operation, or damage. If a child restraint anchor is found damaged in any way, the anchor must be replaced. Failure to do this may result in personal injury or death.

Deployed and non-deployed airbags may or may not have live pyrotechnic material within the airbag inflator.

Do not dispose of driver/passenger/curtain airbags or seat belt tensioners unless you are sure of complete deployment. Refer to the Hazardous Substance Control System for proper disposal.

Dispose of deployed airbags and tensioners consistent with state, provincial, local, and federal regulations.

After any airbag component testing or service, do not connect the battery negative cable. Personal injury or death may result if the system test is not performed first.

If the vehicle is equipped with the Occupant Classification System (OCS), do not connect the battery negative cable before performing the OCS Verification Test using the scan tool and the appropriate diagnostic information. Personal injury or death may result if the system test is not performed properly.

Never replace both the Occupant Restraint Controller (ORC) and the Occupant Classification Module (OCM) at the same time. If both require replacement, replace one, then perform the Airbag System test before replacing the other.

Both the ORC and the OCM store Occupant Classification System (OCS) calibration data, which they transfer to one another when one of them is replaced. If both are replaced at the same time, an irreversible fault will be set in both modules and the OCS may malfunction and cause personal injury or death.

If equipped with OCS, the Seat Weight Sensor is a sensitive, calibrated unit and must be handled carefully. Do not drop or handle roughly. If dropped or damaged, replace with another sensor. Failure to do so may result in occupant injury or death.

If equipped with OCS, the front passenger seat must be handled carefully as well. When removing the seat, be careful when setting on floor not to drop. If dropped, the sensor may be inoperative, could result in occupant injury, or possibly death.

If equipped with OCS, when the passenger front seat is on the floor, no one should sit in the front passenger seat. This uneven force may damage the sensing ability of the seat weight sensors. If sat on and damaged, the sensor may be inoperative, could result in occupant injury, or possibly death.

DISARMING THE SYSTEM

Disconnect the negative battery cable and wait at least 90 seconds.

ARMING THE SYSTEM

Connect the negative battery cable.

DRIVE TRAIN

AUTOMATIC TRANSMISSION FLUID

DRAIN AND REFILL

See Figures 7 through 9.

➡**The direct shift (S-Tronic) automatic transmission and front final drive have a shared gear oil fill.**

> ✲✲ **CAUTION**
>
> **Only the gear oil available as a replacement part may be used for the 02E direct shift automatic transmission. Other oils can cause malfunctions or transmission failure.**

1. Be sure the transmission not in emergency operation mode.
2. Move vehicle onto a 4-column lifting platform or over a work pit so that it stands absolutely horizontal.
3. Place selector lever in position P, engage parking brake.
4. The exhaust extraction system should be connected.
5. Run engine at normal idle.
6. Switch the air conditioning and heater OFF.

> ✲✲ **CAUTION**
>
> **The gear oil level changes with the gear oil temperature. Gear oil temperature that is too low leads to overfilling, too high a temperature leads to under-filling. An incorrect gear oil level affects transmission function.**

7. Connect the VAS 5051B, and select Vehicle Self-Diagnosis and vehicle system "02 - Transmission electronics".
   a. In selection 1, press the Measured Values Function and continue by pressing the right arrow button.
   b. In button field 1, press buttons 1 9 for "Display Group 019" and confirm entry by pressing Q button.
   c. Ensure the specified value at beginning of test is not higher than 86°F (30°C), otherwise let transmission cool.
8. Remove front 1 and rear 2 noise insulation.
9. Press and hold brake pedal.
10. With brake pressed, shift through all selector lever positions "P, R, N, D, S" at idle, retaining each position for at least 3 seconds.

11. Place a proper drain pan under the transmission.
12. Read gear oil temperature in display field 1. Specified value should be about 95°F (35°C).
13. When specified value is reached, remove inspection plug.
14. The collected gear oil will run out of the overflow tube.

➡**Some gear oil always leaks out when opening the inspection plug, regardless of the gear oil level.**

15. Check whether overflow tube is securely installed in inspection plug hole, as the gear oil level cannot be checked exactly if overflow tube is loose.

➡**If some gear oil still leaks out at a temperature between 35 and 45°C (due to additional warming), gear oil level is OK.**

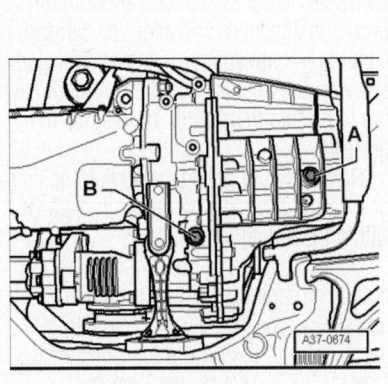

Fig. 7 When specified value is reached, remove inspection plug B (ignore A).

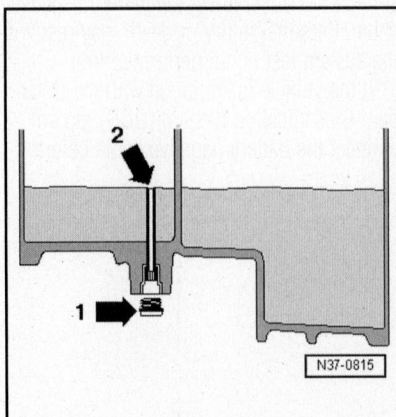

Fig. 8 The collected gear oil will run out of the overflow tube (2).

16. Regardless of the gear oil level, a small wave of fluid comes out of the overflow tube every 30 seconds due to the multi-plate clutch cooling oil pulse. This procedure is irrelevant for checking gear oil level.

➡**Leaked gear oil must not be reused.**

17. If no gear oil leaks out at the overflow tube between temperature range specified, top off gear oil as follows:

➡**Check whether VAS 6262 is clean. DSG transmission gear oil must not be mixed with other oils.**

   a. Install DSG transmission gear oil container on VAS 6262.
   b. Install VAS 6262 A in inspection plug opening and tighten by hand.
   c. Hold container with VAS 6262 as high as possible over DSG transmission and let gear oil run into transmission.
   d. To check whether DSG transmission is filled sufficiently, disconnect quick release coupling on VAS 6262 at regular intervals and seal with finger or clean plug.

➡**Regardless of the gear oil level, a small wave of fluid comes out of the overflow tube every 30 seconds due to the multi-plate clutch cooling oil pulse. This procedure is irrelevant for checking gear oil level.**

   e. Check gear oil temperature on VAS 5051B while filling oil. If 45°C is

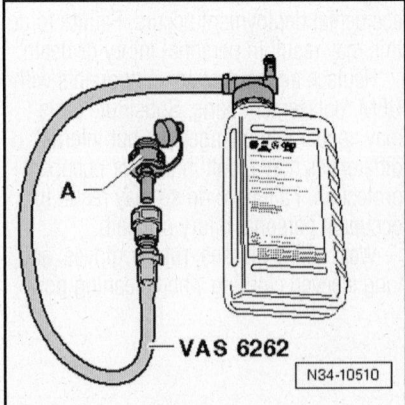

Fig. 9 Install DSG transmission gear oil container on VAS 6262. Install VAS 6262 A in inspection plug opening and tighten by hand. Hold container with VAS 6262 as high as possible over DSG transmission and let gear oil run into transmission.

exceeded, cancel procedure and let transmission cool.

18. Replace inspection plug gasket.

19. Remove VAS 6262 from transmission.

20. Tighten inspection plug.

21. Install the noise insulation.

22. End function Measured values by pressing left arrow button.

23. Press end output.

24. Switch ignition off and disconnect diagnostic connector.

FILTER REPLACEMENT

1. Remove upper and lower sections of air filter housing.

2. Place drain pan under transmission.

3. Remove transmission oil filter housing.

➡**To let gear oil from oil filter housing flow back into the transmission, tip housing slightly in its seat before removing.**

4. Slowly pull filter insert up.

5. If the O-ring on the filter insert intake collar was not removed when the filter insert was, O-ring must be removed from transmission.

To install:

6. Install in reverse order, noting the following:

a. Replace filter insert and O-ring on transmission oil filter housing.

b. Coat O-ring on filter insert intake neck with gear oil.

c. Insert filter insert with intake neck facing down.

d. Coat O-ring on transmission oil filter housing with gear oil.

e. Tighten filter housing to 15 ft. lbs. (20 Nm).

f. Check the gear oil level, as described above.

FRONT HALFSHAFT

REMOVAL & INSTALLATION

See Figure 10.

1. Remove the noise insulation.

2. Loosen wheel side drive axle threaded connection.

3. Remove wheel.

4. Remove drive axle from the transmission flange.

5. Remove hex nuts on the ball joint.

6. Remove nut from the level control system sensor linkage.

7. Disengage transverse link from ball joint.

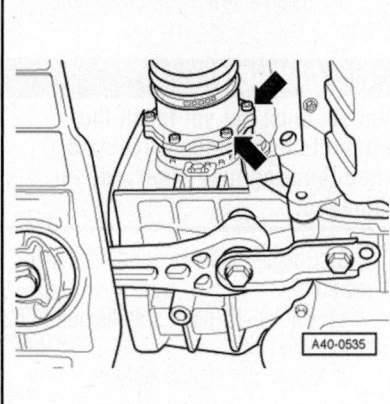

Fig. 10 Remove drive axle from the transmission flange

8. Tip the suspension strut outward while pressing drive axle out of wheel bearing unit with a brass drive.

9. Remove drive axle.

10. Installation is in reverse order of removal.

11. Tighten drive axle hex combi bolt to 147 ft. lbs. (200 Nm).

12. Tighten the 12-point bolt to 51 ft. lbs. (70 Nm). Lower the vehicle onto its wheels. Tighten 12-point bolt an additional 90°.

REAR DRIVE AXLE

REMOVAL & INSTALLATION

See Figures 11 and 12.

1. Loosen wheel side drive shaft threaded connection.

2. For hex bolt between drive axle and wheel hub, loosen the connection between the drive axle and wheel hub as follows:

a. Only loosen drive axle to wheel hub threaded connection a maximum of 90° when vehicle is resting on its wheels, otherwise wheel bearing will be damaged.

b. Raise vehicle enough that wheels hang freely.

c. Operate brake (second mechanic required).

d. Remove the spindle bolt.

3. For 12-point bolt between drive axle and wheel hub, loosen the connection between the drive axle and wheel hub as follows:

➡**The wheel bearing must not be under a load while the drive axle threaded connection on the wheel side is loose.**

If the bearings are loaded by the vehicle's own weight the wheel bearing will be damaged. This reduces the service life of the wheel bearings. Therefore, observe the following:

a. Vehicles without a drive axle must not be moved, otherwise the wheel bearing will be damaged.

b. If vehicle must be moved, install an outer joint in place of the drive axle. Tighten the outer joint to 88.5 ft. lbs. (120 Nm).

c. With vehicle still resting on wheels, loosen 12-point bolt with T10361 maximum 90°, otherwise, wheel bearing will be damaged.

d. Raise vehicle enough that wheels hang freely.

e. Operate brake (second mechanic required).

f. Remove 12-point spindle bolt.

4. For all vehicles, perform the following:

a. Remove wheel.

b. Remove coil spring.

c. Remove bracket bolts on vehicles with level control system sensor.

d. Remove bolts for tie rod and lower transverse link from wheel bearing housing.

e. Remove the lower strut bolt and washer.

f. Loosen the drive axle on the transmission side.

g. Swing wheel bearing housing upward and remove drive shaft from wheel bearing splines.

h. Remove drive axle.

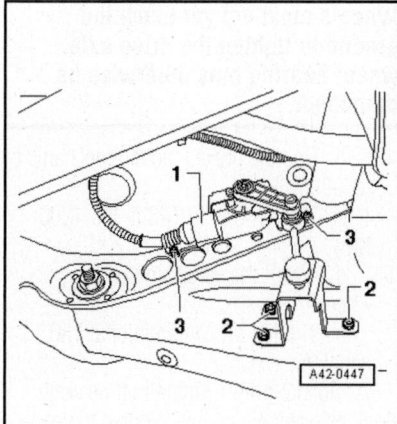

Fig. 11 Remove bracket bolts (2) on vehicles with level control system sensor (1)—(sensor retaining bolts (3)).

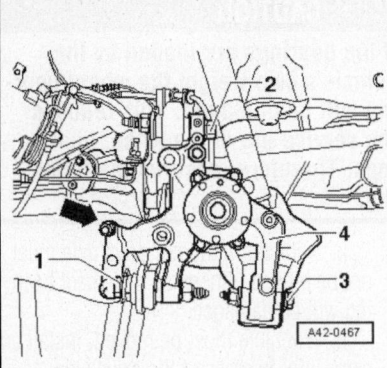

Fig. 12 Remove bolts for tie rod (1) and lower transverse link (3) from wheel bearing housing (4)—item (2) not identified.

To install:

5. Installation is performed in the reverse order of removal. Observe the following when doing so:

a. Lightly coat the splines on the outer joint with assembly paste before installing the outer joint into the wheel hub.

b. Connections to wheel bearing housing may only be carried out of dimension between wheel hub center and lower edge of wheel housing, measured before assembly, is achieved.

6. For hex spindle bolt between drive axle and wheel hub, tighten the connection between the drive axle and wheel hub as follows:

a. Install a new hex spindle bolt.

➡**Before installing, threads in constant velocity joint should be cleaned with a tap.**

❈❈ CAUTION

Wheels must not yet touch the ground to tighten the drive axle, wheel bearing may otherwise be damaged.

b. Operate brake (second mechanic required).

c. Tighten bolt to 148 ft. lbs. (200 Nm).

d. Lower the vehicle onto its wheels.

e. Tighten bolt an additional 180 degrees.

7. For 12-point spindle bolt between drive axle and wheel hub, tighten the connection between the drive axle and wheel hub as follows:

➡**Before installing, clean the threads in the constant velocity joint with a tap.**

a. Install a new 12-point spindle bolt.

❈❈ CAUTION

Wheels must not yet touch the ground to tighten the drive axle, wheel bearing may otherwise be damaged.

b. Operate brake (second mechanic required).

c. Tighten 12-point spindle bolt to 52 ft. lbs. (70 Nm).

d. Lower the vehicle onto its wheels.

e. Tighten 12-point bolt an additional 90 degrees.

8. For all vehicles:

a. Install lower strut bolt with washer and tighten securely.

➡**Tightening specification not available; contact local dealer.**

b. On vehicles with electronically-controlled damping (Audi magnetic ride), reprogram control position with VAS 5051B.

c. On vehicles with automatic headlamp range control, perform headlamp basic setting.

REAR DRIVESHAFT

REMOVAL & INSTALLATION
See Figures 13 through 18.

➡**Service notes:**

- Perform work on driveshaft on a two-column lift if possible.
- Before removing, mark the positions of all parts in relation to each other. Install in the same position otherwise imbalance will be excessive, the bearings could be damaged causing rumbling noises.
- Do not kink driveshaft, only store and move when fully extended.
- Do not allow driveshaft to hang down when removing, always support.
- Always remove or install driveshaft horizontally on drive flange.

1. Remove the front noise insulation plate.

2. On TT Roadster with 4-cylinder engine. remove the bolts and remove the cross brace.

3. On all vehicles with 4-cylinder engine:

a. Remove the crossmember for the underbody, if equipped.

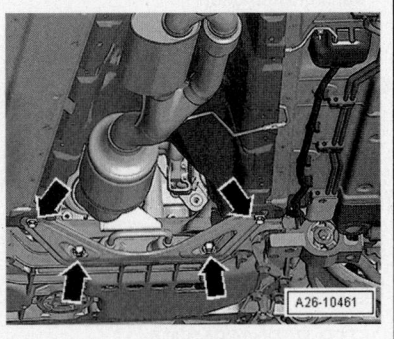

Fig. 13 On TT Roadster with 4-cylinder engine. remove the bolts and remove the cross brace.

b. Separate the front exhaust system from the rear part of the system at the clamping sleeve.

c. Tie the front exhaust pipe to the underbody.

d. Remove the exhaust system rear section.

4. On vehicles with 6-cylinder engine, remove entire exhaust system.

➡**The rest of this procedure applies to all vehicles:**

5. Counterhold the rear final drive with the T10172 and T10172/5 when loosening or tightening the driveshaft.

6. Remove the driveshaft bolts from the flange connection.

7. Remove pendulum support bolts.

8. Press engine and transmission forward and secure position with a suitable wood block.

9. Carefully remove front driveshaft tube from centering pins on flange.

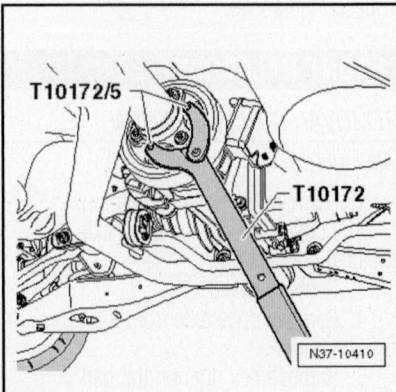

Fig. 14 Counterhold the rear final drive with the T10172 and T10172/5 when loosening or tightening the driveshaft.

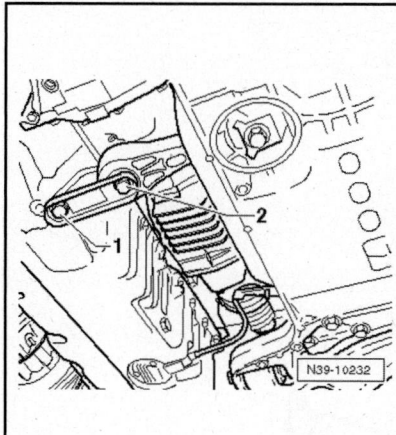

Fig. 15 Remove pendulum support bolts (1, 2).

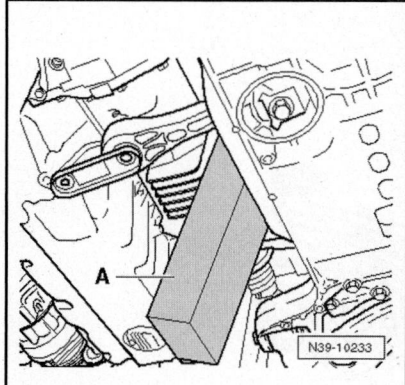

Fig. 16 Press engine and transmission forward and secure position with a suitable wood block (A).

Detach driveshaft horizontally from guide pin.

※ CAUTION

Sealing ring in driveshaft flange must not be damaged.

10. Support the rear section of the driveshaft with the V.A.G 1383 A.

11. Secure driveshaft against falling down with strap from universal transmission support and wood block to retain its in-car position.

12. Remove the bolts for the center bearing and the heat shield. Remove the heat shield.

13. Check whether there is an alignment marking (colored dot) on driveshaft and rear final drive driveshaft flange. If not, identify position of flexible disc and flange/driveshaft to rear final drive.

14. Remove the driveshaft bolts on the rear final drive. Remove the driveshaft from

the rear final drive and lower it onto the support.

➡ **When removing and installing the driveshaft, be careful not to damage the center bushing. Do not cant driveshaft when removing, pull off from centering pin in horizontal position. Sealing ring in center bushing must not be damaged.**

➡ **To prevent damaging the protective boot in the center bearing, remove and install the driveshaft in its fully extended position; likewise, store it in this position. Two technicians are needed to remove the driveshaft.**

15. Remove the driveshaft toward the rear and fully extended, if possible.

To install:

16. Install in reverse sequence; note the following points:

   a. Install all parts marked to each other in original positions.

   b. Install driveshaft on final drive so that both markings align. Tighten the driveshaft bolts.

   c. Align the intermediate bearing in its elongated holes so the driveshaft or bearing is not under stress.

   d. Tighten combi-bolt. The combi-bolts must lie inside the heat shield centering tabs.

   e. Tighten pendulum support with new bolts to 30 ft. lbs. (40 Nm), plus 90 degrees.

   f. Install the exhaust system.

   g. Install the crossmember for the underbody, if equipped.

   h. Install the noise insulation.

REAR FINAL DRIVE

REMOVAL & INSTALLATION

See Figures 19 through 26.

1. Remove the spare wheel if present. Remove spare wheel well or foam inserts.

2. Remove two rubber plugs or adhesive strips in luggage compartment floor.

3. Remove both transmission mount bolts from above through these holes.

4. Separate the exhaust system at the clamping sleeves. Tie the front exhaust pipe to the underbody.

※ CAUTION

There is a risk of damaging decoupling elements. Do not bend decoupling elements in front exhaust pipe more than 10°.

5. Remove the exhaust system rear section.

6. Remove rear flexible disc.

7. Tie driveshaft sideways onto underbody.

8. For TT Roadster, remove the diagonal braces, the lower stabilizer clamp bolts, and remove the crossmember.

➡ **The remainder of this procedure applies to all vehicles.**

9. Remove stabilizer bar.

10. Remove left and right drive axles from rear final drive.

11. If equipped with crossmember, remove both front bolts on subframe, while the rear bolts on subframe remain installed!

12. Remove crossmember.

13. Place V.A.G 1383 A (jack) with V.A.G 1359/2 (support) and a wood block under rear final drive and secure final drive. Remove the front bolt and washer.

14. Disconnect the connector on the all wheel drive control module J492. Remove the vent lines from the final drive.

15. Slide final drive to the right as far as possible. Press final drive upward and to right side.

16. Guide left drive axle out of flange shaft.

17. Lower final drive slightly and carefully remove from right drive axle and rear subframe carrier with V.A.G 1383 A.

18. Lower final drive past the driveshaft.

To install:

19. Place rear final drive on engine/transmission jack V.A.G 1383 A with universal mount V.A.G 1359/2 and a wooden block. Secure final drive against falling down with strap from V.A.G 1359/2.

20. Before installing the final drive, make sure the washers are placed on the two rear bonded rubber bushings.

21. Raise rear final drive. Guide right drive axle into flange shaft. Slide final drive to the right as far as possible. Press final drive upward on the right side.

22. Guide left drive axle into flange shaft. Connect the connector and slide the ventilation lines onto the ventilation pipes. Place the washer with the chamfer facing up between the bonded rubber bushing and subframe. Install mount through-bolt hand-tight.

23. Remove the jack and support from final drive.

24. Install and tighten both bolts for the rear final drive. Seal off both holes in the luggage compartment floor panel. Install spare wheel well or foam inserts. Install spare wheel if present.

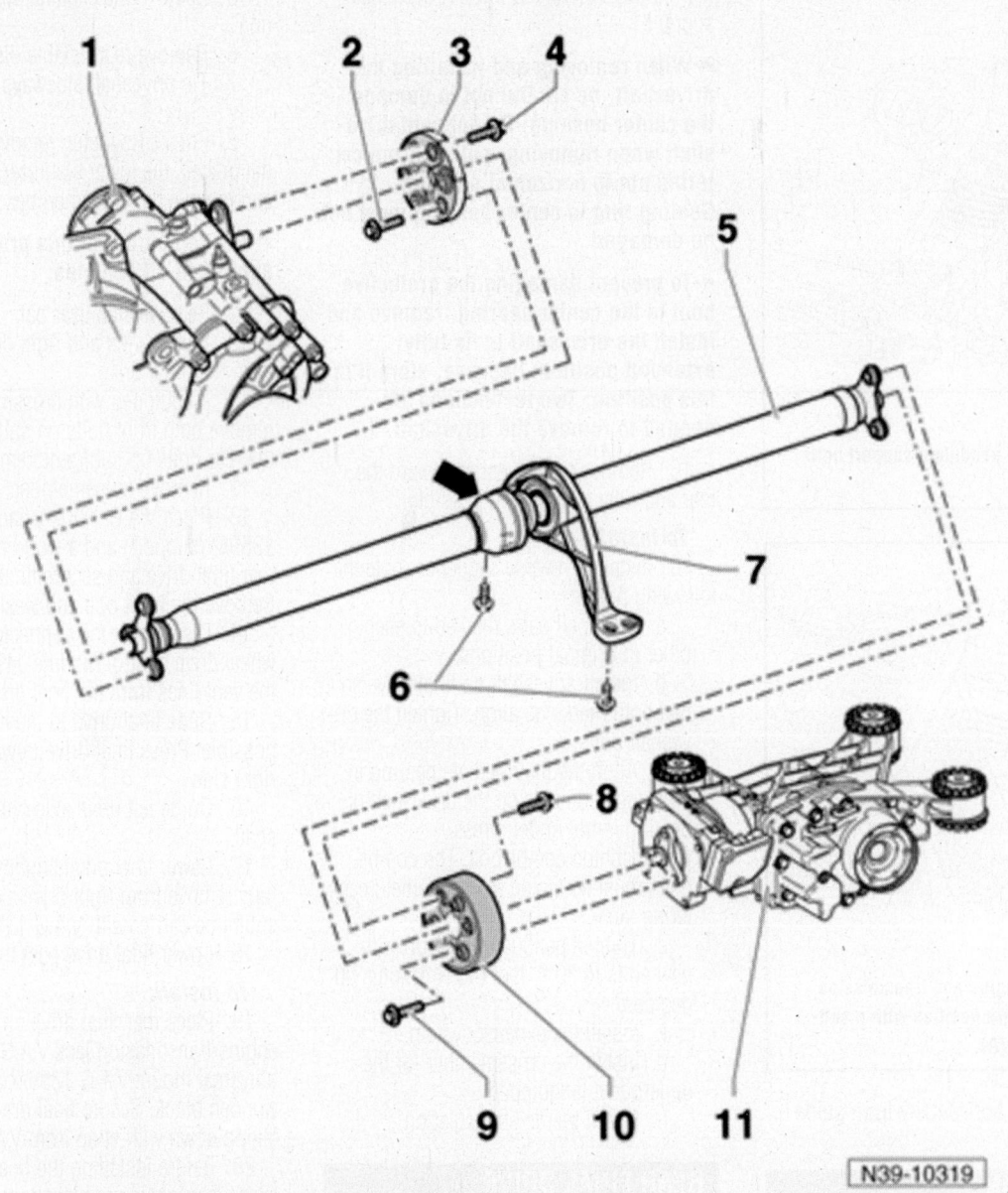

N39-10319

1. Transmission with bevel box
2. Front flexible disc to the driveshaft: 37 ft. lbs. (50 Nm)
   plus an additional 90°rotation
3. Front flexible disc (Open side of heat shield faces toward transmission)
4. Flexible disc to the bevel box: 44 ft. lbs. (60 Nm)
5. Driveshaft (Cannot be separated at the joint arrow)
6. Bolt: 19 ft. lbs. (25 Nm)
7. Center bearing (Align it without tension)
8. Rear flexible disc to the driveshaft (Always replace): 37 ft. lbs. (50 Nm)
   plus an additional 90°
9. Flexible disc to the rear final drive: 44 ft. lbs. (60 Nm).
10. Flexible disc with vibration dampener (Heat shield faces the driveshaft)
11. Rear final drive

Fig. 17 Install driveshaft on final drive so that both markings align. Tighten the driveshaft bolts.

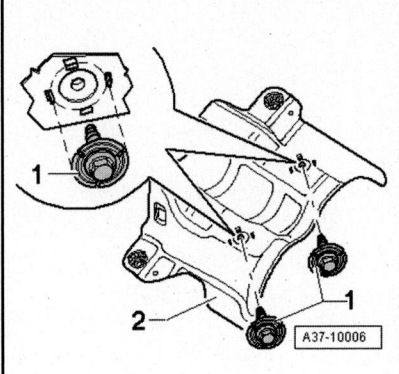

Fig. 18 Tighten combi-bolt (1). The combi-bolts must lie inside the heat shield centering tabs (2).

Fig. 21 Remove crossmember.

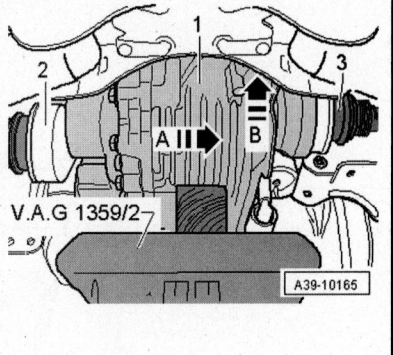

Fig. 24 Slide final drive right (A) in direction of arrow as far as possible. Press final drive (1) upward (B). Guide left drive axle (2) out of flange shaft. Lower final drive slightly and carefully remove from right drive axle (3) and rear subframe carrier with V.A.G 1383 A. Lower final drive past the driveshaft.

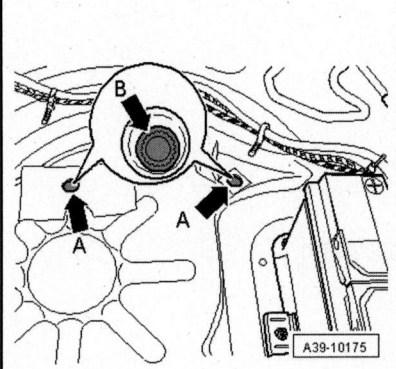

Fig. 19 Remove two rubber plugs or adhesive strips in luggage compartment floor. Remove both transmission mount bolts (B) from above through holes (A).

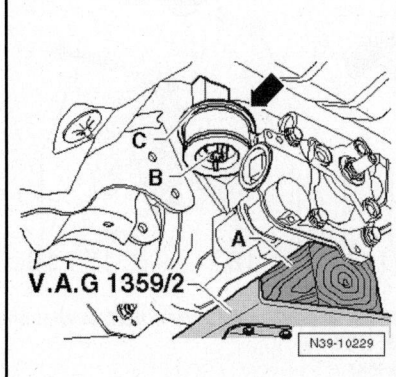

Fig. 22 Place V.A.G 1383 A with V.A.G 1359/2 and a wood block (A) under rear final drive and secure final drive. Remove the front bolt (B). and washer (C).

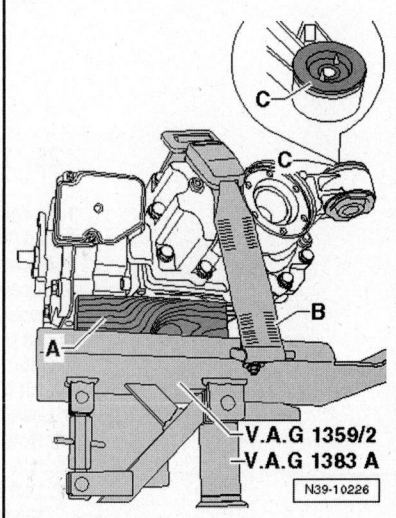

Fig. 25 Place rear final drive on engine/transmission jack V.A.G 1383 A with universal mount V.A.G 1359/2 and a wooden block (A). Secure final drive against falling down with strap (B) from V.A.G 1359/2. Before installing the final drive, make sure the washers (C) are placed on the two rear bonded rubber bushings.

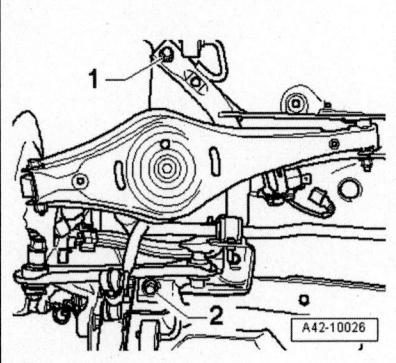

Fig. 20 If equipped with crossmember, remove both front bolts (1) on subframe, while the rear bolts (2) on subframe remain installed!

Fig. 23 Disconnect the connector (A) on the all wheel drive control module J492. Remove the vent lines (arrows) from the final drive.

25. Tighten final drive mounting bolts from below to 37 ft. lbs. (50 Nm), plus 90 degrees.

26. Install the crossmember, if equipped and tighten the bolts.

27. Tighten the rear subframe.

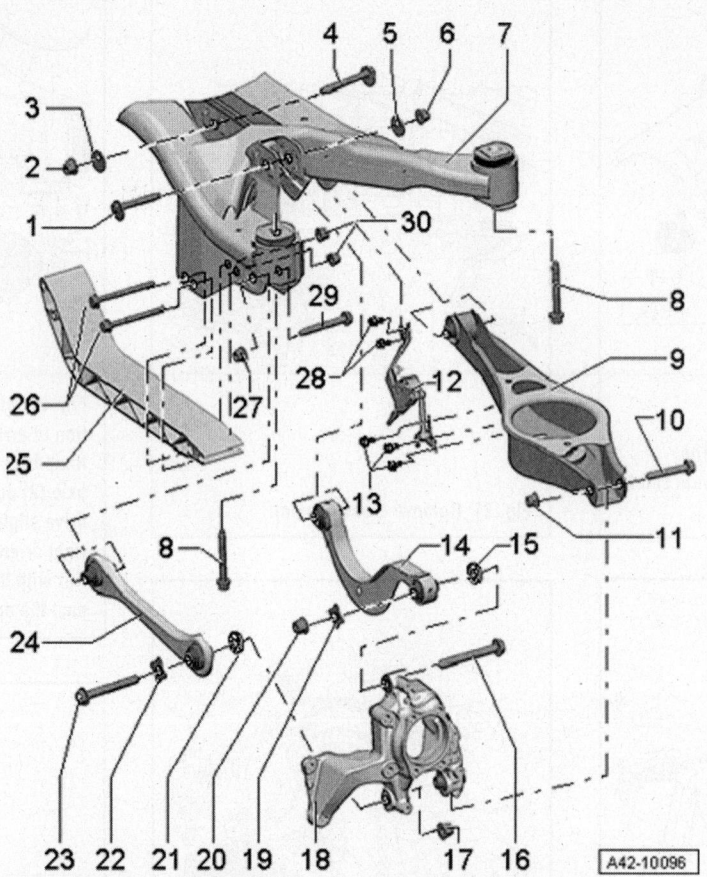

1. Eccentric bolt (after loosening, perform vehicle alignment)
2. Nut [70 ft. lbs. (95 Nm)]
3. Eccentric washer
4. Eccentric bolt (after loosening, perform vehicle alignment)
5. Eccentric washer
6. Nut [70 ft. lbs. (95 Nm)]
7. Subframe
8. Bolt [66 ft. lbs. (90 Nm) plus an additional 90° turn]
9. Lower transverse link
10. Bolt
11. Nut [66 ft. lbs. (90 Nm) plus an additional 90° turn]
12. Left Rear Level Control System Sensor and Right Rear Level Control System Sensor
13. Bolt [3 ft. lbs. (5 Nm)]
14. Upper control arm
15. Washer
16. Bolt [95 ft. lbs. (130 Nm) plus an additional 90° turn]
17. Nut
18. Wheel Bearing Housing
19. Washer
20. Nut
21. Washer
22. Washer
23. Bolt [95 ft. lbs. (130 Nm) plus an additional 90° turn]
24. Tie Rod
25. Crossmember
26. Bolt
27. Nut [66 ft. lbs. (90 Nm) plus an additional 90° turn]
28. Bolt [3 ft. lbs. (5 Nm)]
29. Bolt
30. Bolt [37 ft. lbs. (50 Nm) plus an additional 180° turn]

Fig. 26 Tighten the rear subframe.

28. Tighten the stabilizer bar bolts to 18 ft. lbs. (25 Nm), plus 90 degrees.

29. Tighten drive axle bolts. See "Rear Drive Axle" in this section.

30. Install rear flexible disc.

31. Install exhaust system and then align it free of tension.

32. For TT Roadster, do the following:

a. Install crossmember and tighten bolts.

b. Install diagonal braces and tighten bolts.

33. When replacing rear final drive, you must check axle oil level. Remove the plug and check that level is even with bottom of plug opening.

34. Check the Haldex clutch oil and top off, if necessary. Remove the plug and check that level is even with bottom of plug opening.

ENGINE COOLING

ENGINE COOLANT

DRAIN & REFILL PROCEDURE

1. Open the coolant reservoir cap.

2. Remove the undercar noise insulation and the frame for the noise insulation

3. Remove the clamps from the air guide hose.

➡ **Drained coolant must be stored in a clean container for disposal or reuse.**

4. Place a collection pan under engine.

5. Remove the lower coolant hose from the radiator and let the coolant drain.

6. Remove lower coolant hose to after-run coolant pump and allow coolant to drain.

➡ **Only use coolant according to the manufacturer recommendations. Other coolant additives may above all reduce the corrosion protection effect significantly. The damage resulting from this may lead to loss of coolant and consequently to severe engine damage.**

Use the refractometer T10007 (or equivalent) to determine the level of freeze protection in the coolant system:

- Coolant (40%) and distilled water (60%) for freeze protection down to -13°F (-25°C)
- Coolant (50%) and distilled water (50%) for freeze protection down to -31°F (-35°C)
- Coolant (60%) and distilled water (40%) for freeze protection down to -40°F (-40°C)

7. Connect the lower coolant hose to the radiator.

8. Connect coolant hose to after-run coolant pump.

9. Fill VAS 6069/1 coolant reservoir on with 10.6 qts. (10 liters) of premixed coolant with the proper mixture ratio.

10. Attach the V.A.G 1274/8 to the reservoir. Install the VAS 6096 on V.A.G 1274/8.

11. Place air outlet hose in a small container.

➡ **A small amount of coolant which should be collected is drawn off with the discharged air.**

12. Close both valves by turning lever at a right angle to direction of flow.

13. Connect hose to compressed air.

➡ **Pressure from compressed air should be87–145 psi (6–10 bar).**

14. Open valve on side of two hoses by turning lever in direction of flow.

➡ **The suction jet pump generates pressure in the coolant system; indicator on display instrument must move into green area.**

15. Briefly open the valve from the reservoir side by turning lever in direction of flow so that the hose on coolant reservoir fills with coolant. Close the valve.

➡ **Leave the other valve open another 2 minutes. More pressure is generated in the coolant system by the suction jet pump; indicator on display instrument must stay in green area.**

16. Close the valve on the compressed air side.

17. Needle in the display instrument must remain in the green region, then sufficient vacuum in the cooling system is obtained for the upcoming filling.

a. If needle stands below the green area, repeat procedure.

b. If pressure falls, check coolant system for leaks.

18. Remove pressurized air hose.

19. Open valve on the reservoir side.

➡ **Coolant is extracted from the coolant reservoir by pressure in the coolant system and the system is filled.**

20. Check the coolant level. Fill coolant up to "max" marking.

21. Start engine and run at approximately 1500 RPM for a maximum of 2 minutes.

22. With engine running, fill coolant up to overflow hole on coolant expansion tank.

23. Close the cap on the coolant reservoir.

24. Start the engine and let it run at approximately 3000 RPM until the coolant fan starts running.

25. Check coolant level.

➡ **With warm engine, coolant level must be at "max" marking, with cold engine, between "min" and "max" marking.**

26. If necessary, fill with coolant again.

27. Shut off engine.

28. The rest of the assembly is basically a reverse of the disassembling sequence.

a. The hose supports, air guide pipes and hoses must be free of oil and grease before installing.

b. Secure all hose connections with hose clamps appropriate for the model.

➡ **To mount the charge hoses on their connectors securely, spray the bolts on the used clamps with rust remover before installing.**

ENGINE FAN

REMOVAL & INSTALLATION

See Figure 27.

1. Remove the cover for the air guide; disengage the side clips to do so.

2. Unclip the lower air guide, disengage the clips to do so.

3. Remove the lower air guide together with the air guide hose.

4. Remove bolts from above.

5. Loosen the hose clamp.

6. Remove bolt.

7. Disconnect the electrical connectors and free up the electrical wire.

8. Remove noise insulation.

9. Remove the air guide hose clamps.

10. Remove the bolt and remove the air guide pipe downward.

11. Disconnect electrical connector.

12. Remove the bolts and remove the fan shroud downward.

13. Installation is in reverse order of removal.

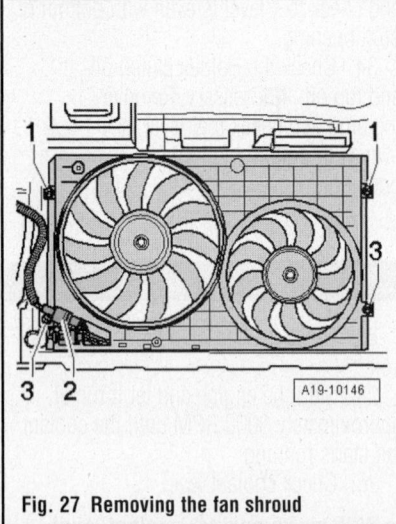

Fig. 27 Removing the fan shroud

RADIATOR

REMOVAL & INSTALLATION
See Figure 28.

✻✻ CAUTION

Never open, service or drain the radiator or cooling system when hot; serious burns can occur from the steam and hot coolant. Also, when draining engine coolant, keep in mind that cats and dogs are attracted to ethylene glycol antifreeze and could drink any that is left in an uncovered container or in puddles on the ground. This will prove fatal in sufficient quantities. Always drain coolant into a sealable container. Coolant should be reused unless it is contaminated or is several years old.

1. Open cap of coolant expansion tank.
2. Disconnect intake connection using spring-type clip pliers.
3. Unscrew intake connection at lock carrier and remove it.
4. Remove the fan shroud.
5. Remove noise insulation.
6. Remove air duct for charge air cooler.
7. Separate the electrical connector.
8. Place a drip tray under engine.
9. Drain the coolant, by pulling off lower coolant hose.
10. Pull the connector at left longitudinal member out of retainer.
11. Remove the retainer for cable connector.
12. Disconnect the electrical connector from hood lock.
13. Disconnect upper coolant hose from radiator.

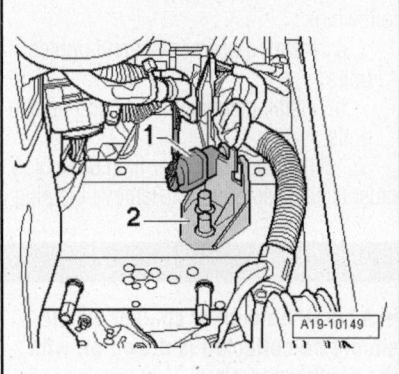

Fig. 28 Remove the retainer for cable connector (2), disconnect the electrical connector from hood lock (1)

14. Remove bolts on rear side of radiator.
15. Lift radiator slightly and remove upward and off.
16. Installation is in reverse order of removal, note the following:
   a. Fill engine with coolant and check for leaks.

THERMOSTAT

REMOVAL & INSTALLATION
See Figure 29.

1. Drained coolant must be stored in a clean container for disposal or reuse.

➡**Cover the cap of the expansion tank with a rag and open carefully. Steam or hot coolant may escape when opening.**

2. Open the cap of coolant expansion tank.
3. Remove center noise insulation fasteners.
4. Place drip tray for workshop crane VAS 6208 under engine.
5. Vehicles with drain plug:
   a. Turn the drain plug on radiator left, place assisting hose on supports if necessary.
6. Vehicles without drain plug:
   a. Remove the lower coolant hose from radiator by removing retaining clamps.
7. Disconnect the electrical connector at Engine Coolant Temperature (ECT) Sensor (on Radiator).
8. Also remove lower coolant hose to After-Run Coolant Pump and allow remaining coolant to drain.
9. Disconnect the battery.
10. If equipped, remove vacuum hose to air guide hose.

11. Disconnect air guide hose at Throttle Valve Control Module J338.
12. Remove the air filter.
13. Remove vacuum line at variable intake manifold actuator.
14. Remove bolts and remove vacuum actuator from intake manifold.
15. Disconnect the electrical connector at Engine Coolant Temperature (ECT) Sensor.
16. Disconnect the secondary air hose at position indicated by.
17. Free up the air hose at bracket.
18. Disconnect coolant hoses at positions indicated.
19. Remove bolts.
20. Pull the transmission oil cooler coolant pipe bracket toward left.
21. Swing Secondary Air Injection (AIR) system hose bracket forward.
22. Remove bolt at wiring harness bracket.

➡**Press coolant pipe in direction of coolant pump using pry bar when removing coolant thermostat housing so that is not pulled off.**

23. Remove the coolant thermostat housing while pressing coolant pipe toward coolant pump with pry bar.
24. Remove bolts and remove connecting pieces.
25. Remove O-ring with coolant thermostat from coolant thermostat housing 1.
26. Installation is in reverse order of removal, note the following:
   a. Always replace the gaskets and seals.
   b. Clean the O-ring sealing surfaces.
   c. Insert the coolant regulator.
   d. Coat new the O-ring with coolant.

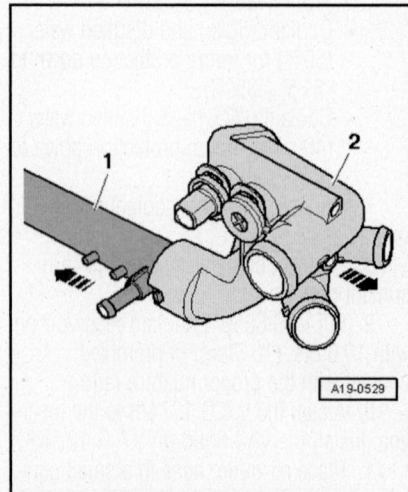

Fig. 29 Remove coolant thermostat housing (2) while pressing coolant pipe (1)

e. Attach the connecting pieces to coolant thermostat housing.

WATER PUMP

REMOVAL & INSTALLATION

2.0L Engines

See Figure 30.

1. Remove small coolant pipe.
2. Remove coolant pump toothed belt.
3. Disconnect electrical connector on Throttle Valve Control Module and remove the bolts.
4. Disconnect the electrical connector on the Engine Coolant Temperature (ECT) Sensor.
5. Lift clamps, remove the coolant hoses and move them to the side.
6. Remove bolts the water pump bolts.
7. Remove coolant pump from the centering pin and remove the engine oil cooler.

To install:

8. Installation is in reverse order of removal, note the following:
   a. Replace the seals and O-rings.
   b. Coat the O-rings with coolant.
   c. Make sure both centering pins are installed in the cylinder block.
   d. Install the connection piece into the engine oil cooler.

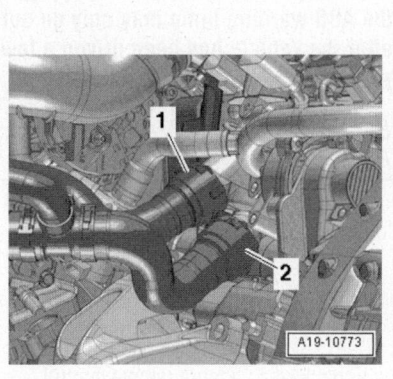

Fig. 30 Lift clamps 1 and 2, remove the coolant hoses and move them to the side

e. Push the coolant pump onto the connection piece and onto the centering pins in the cylinder block.
   f. Tighten the water pump bolts to 7 ft. lbs. (9 Nm).

➡**If a new coolant pump was installed, then the protective cap must be removed.**

9. Fill with coolant.

3.2L Engines

See Figure 31.

1. Remove the engine cover.
2. Drain coolant.

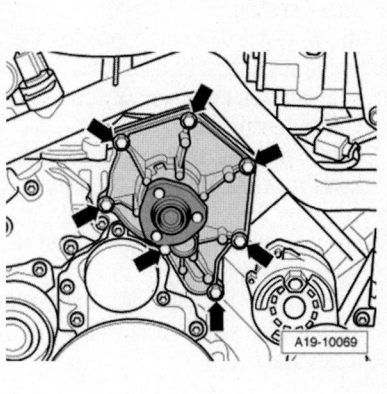

Fig. 31 Remove coolant pump bolts and the coolant pump

3. Remove ribbed belt.
4. Remove bolts for the coolant pump ribbed belt pulley, using a Spanner Wrench 3212 to counterhold.
5. Remove coolant pump bolts and the coolant pump.
6. Installation is in reverse order of removal, note the following:
   a. Tighten the water pump bolts to 7 ft. lbs. (9 Nm).
7. Clean sealing surfaces, must be free of oil and grease.
8. Install ribbed belt.
9. Fill with coolant.

ENGINE ELECTRICAL

BATTERY SYSTEM

BATTERY

REMOVAL & INSTALLATION

1. Switch off ignition and remove ignition key.
2. Remove luggage compartment floor cover.
3. Release clips and remove cover from negative terminal.

➡**If the battery negative terminal cover is under the rear lid trim, trim must be removed.**

4. Connect the battery charger for battery assistance mode.
5. Loosen nut a few turns and remove ground wire terminal clamp from battery terminal.
6. Loosen nut a few turns and remove positive wire terminal clamp with main fuse box from battery terminal.
7. Disconnect central gas venting system hose.

8. Remove the screw at battery bracket.
9. Remove battery from battery mount.
10. Lift battery out of right side of luggage compartment.

✳ CAUTION

Pollution risk: Battery and sulfuric acid disposal regulations must be followed when disposing of batteries.

To install:

➡**Installation Notes:**

- Only maintenance-free batteries conforming to standards "VW75073" (as of August 2001) may be installed.
- If the vehicle was originally equipped with a deep cycle resistant and leak-proof AGM battery, another AGM battery must be installed when replacing.
- Batteries from the Audi Parts Program have a bottom strip-adapter

for adapting to different grip channels. Whether and how bottom strip-adapter is used, refer to operating instructions for battery.

11. Insert battery in battery mount so that base strip engages in battery mount retaining strips. It should no longer be possible to move the battery.
12. Attach battery bracket. Lug at battery bracket must engage in recess at battery base strip.
13. Tighten nut for battery bracket.
14. Connect central venting system hose.
15. With ignition switched off and electrical consumers switched off, connect battery in the following sequence:
   a. Connect positive cable terminal clamp 1 by hand to battery positive terminal "+" and tighten nut.
   b. Connect pole shoe of ground cable by hand to battery negative terminal "-" and tighten nut.

c. Check battery after installation for secure seating.

16. When the battery is connected, the following steps must be performed:

a. Activate the power window regulator one-touch up/down function.

b. Synchronize secondary and additional keys to ensure remote control operation. To do so, insert key into ignition lock, switch the ignition on and off again and remove key.

c. Check DTC memories of all control modules and erase "Undervoltage" DTC, if necessary.

➡**After connecting the power supply, the ABS warning lamp may only go out after the vehicle has been driven a few yards.**

BATTERY RECONNECT/RELEARN PROCEDURE

1. When the battery is connected, the following steps must be performed:

a. Activate the power window regulator one-touch up/down function.

b. Synchronize secondary and additional keys to ensure remote control

operation. To do so, insert key into ignition lock, switch the ignition on and off again and remove key.

c. Check DTC memories of all control modules and erase "Undervoltage" DTC.

d. If necessary, perform vehicle diagnosis, testing and information system with VAS 5051.

e. After connecting the power supply, the ABS warning lamp may only go out after the vehicle has been driven a few yards.

ENGINE ELECTRICAL

ALTERNATOR

REMOVAL & INSTALLATION

2.0L Engines

See Figure 32.

1. With ignition switched off, disconnect battery ground wire.

2. Disconnect the mass air flow (MAF) sensor connector.

3. Remove engine cover.

4. If equipped, remove the EVAP canister, with the lines still connected, upward and out of its mount arrow and lay it to the side.

➡**Risk of destroying if the running direction of a used ribbed belt is reversed. Before removing ribbed belt, mark the running direction with chalk or a felt-tip pen for reinstallation.**

5. Swivel ribbed belt tensioner in direction of arrow to tension ribbed belt.

6. Secure the ribbed belt tensioner with the Locking Pin T10060 A.

7. Remove ribbed belt.

8. Remove ribbed belt tensioner.

9. Remove the bolts and remove the generator on the accessories bracket.

➡**If alternator sticks in holder, turn bolt back in again down to the last two turns. Tap carefully on screw heads with flat side of hammer to release alternator mount bushings.**

10. Tip alternator with electrical wires connected to right side of vehicle.

11. Disconnect electrical connector.

12. Disconnect the electric wire and clamp on the alternator.

13. Remove alternator upward.

14. Install in reverse order of removal, noting the following:

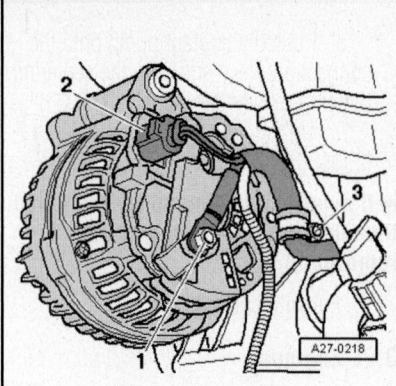

Fig. 32 Electrical wire (1), electrical connector (2) and clamp (3)

a. Slightly drive back sleeves for retaining bolts in order for easier installation of generator.

b. Tight sleeves for generator mount must be made smooth-running, otherwise clamping force of sleeve is too little despite correct torque.

- Terminal 30/B+ to generator: 12 ft. lbs. (16 Nm)
- Generator to the accessories bracket: 16 ft. lbs. (23 Nm)
- Ribbed belt tensioner to the accessories bracket: 16 ft. lbs. (23 Nm)

c. Route the ribbed belt on belt pulleys for the crankshaft and A/C compressor.

d. Route the ribbed belts on the generator belt pulley, release the tension on the tensioner.

e. Check ribbed belt for correct seating.

15. Connect battery.

16. Start engine and check belt routing.

CHARGING SYSTEM

3.2L Engines

1. With ignition switched off, disconnect battery ground wire.

2. Remove the EVAP canister vacuum line while pressing the release button.

3. Remove the vacuum hose on the coolant pipe.

4. Remove the EVAP canister with the line still connected out of its bracket while lifting the release strap.

5. Move the EVAP canister to the side.

➡**If alternator sticks in holder, turn bolt back in again down to the last two turns. Tap carefully on screw heads with flat side of hammer to release alternator mount bushings.**

6. To release the tension on the ribbed belt, turn the tensioning element clockwise.

7. Secure the tensioning element with the drift T10060 A.

8. Remove ribbed belt.

9. Disconnect the electrical connectors.

10. Remove the bolts and remove the generator from the accessories bracket.

11. Tip generator with electrical wires connected to right side of vehicle.

12. Disconnect the electrical connector.

13. Pry off the cap and disconnect the 30/B+ terminal on the generator.

14. Remove the generator upward.

15. Install in reverse order of removal, observing the following:

a. Mount the ribbed belt onto the ribbed belt pulley and then onto the generator belt pulley.

b. Hold the tensioning element and open end wrench and remove the drift T10060 A.

c. Release the tension on the tensioner.

d. Connect battery.

e. Terminal 30/B+ to generator: 11 ft. lbs. (16 Nm)

f. Alternator: 16 ft. lbs. (23 Nm)

16. Start the engine and check the ribbed belt routing.

ENGINE ELECTRICAL | IGNITION SYSTEM

FIRING ORDER

For 4 cylinder engines: 1-3-4-2.
For 6 cylinder engines: 1-5-3-6-2-4.

IGNITION COIL

REMOVAL & INSTALLATION

1. Disconnect the negative battery cable.

2. Release electrical connectors on all ignition coils and remove them from the ignition coils.

3. Using ignition coil puller T40039, remove all ignition coils from spark plug shaft.

4. To install:

a. Insert all ignition coils loosely into each spark plug shaft.

b. Align ignition coils to connectors and then connect all of connectors simultaneously onto ignition coils.

c. Press the ignition coils uniformly onto spark plugs by hand (do not use an impact tool).

IGNITION TIMING

ADJUSTMENT

Ignition timing is not possible or necessary.

SPARK PLUGS

REMOVAL & INSTALLATION

1. Disconnect the negative battery cable.

2. Switch the ignition off.

3. Remove engine cover.

4. Remove the ignition coils.

5. Remove the spark plugs using Spark plug wrench 3122B.

6. Install new spark plugs using Spark plug wrench 3122B. Tighten as follows:

a. For 2.0L engines: 22 ft. lbs. (30 Nm).

b. For 3.2L engines: 15 ft. lbs. (20 Nm).

7. Push ignition coils by hand into intended resources in cylinder head cover.

8. Install ignition coils by rotating slightly - they must engage noticeably.

ENGINE ELECTRICAL | STARTING SYSTEM

STARTER

REMOVAL & INSTALLATION

TT Model

See Figure 33.

➡**When installing, reinstall all cable ties that were loosened or cut during removal in the same locations.**

1. With ignition switched off, disconnect battery ground cable.

2. Remove protective boot cable tie.

3. Disconnect electrical connector.

4. Fold protective boot back and remove B+ wire from solenoid switch.

5. Remove ground wire.

6. Remove lower starter bolt (accessible from above).

7. Remove upper starter bolt and remove starter.

8. Install in reverse order of removal.

9. Tighten starter bolts to 30 ft. lbs. (40 Nm).

10. Connect battery.

TTS Model

See Figure 34.

1. With ignition switched off, disconnect battery Ground (ND) wire.

2. Disconnect Mass Air Flow (MAF) Sensor electrical connector.

Fig. 33 Remove protective boot cable tie (arrow). Disconnect electrical connector (2). Fold protective boot (1) back and remove B+ wire from solenoid switch. Remove ground wire (3) (disregard item 4).

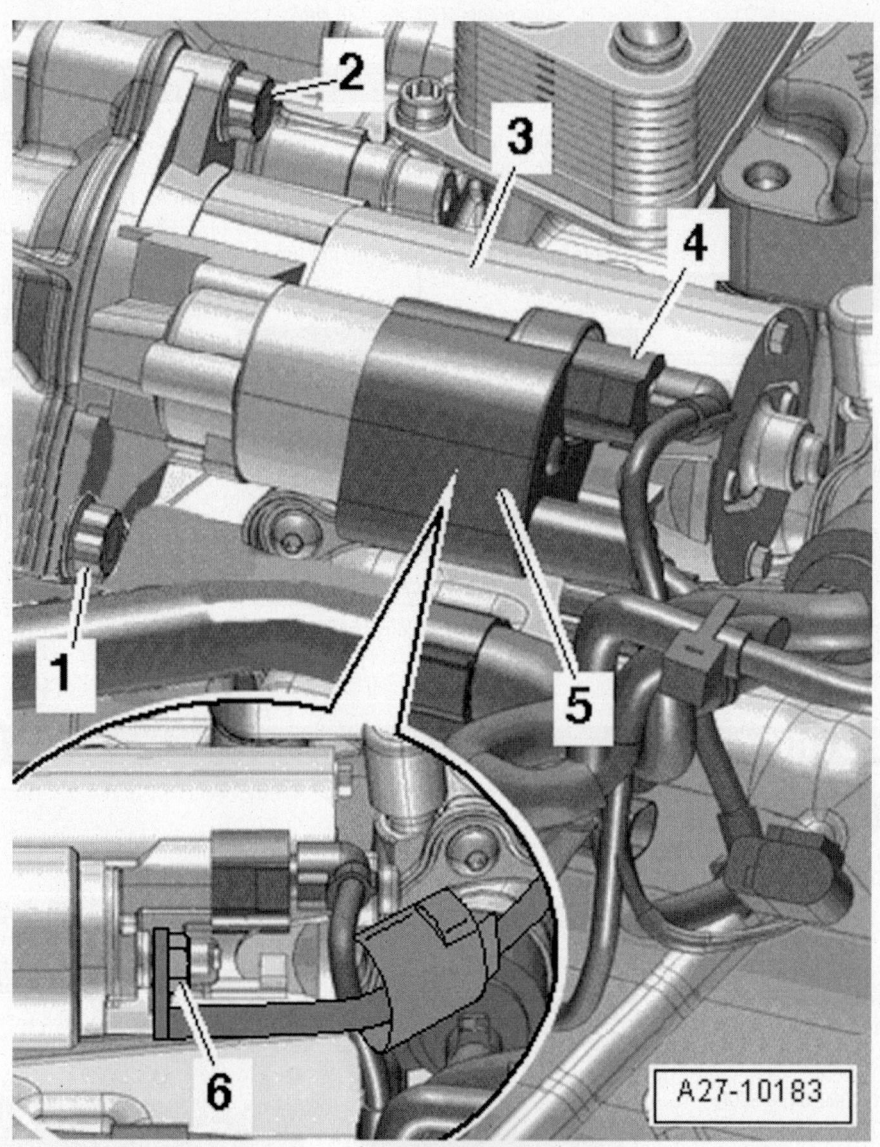

1. Screws   4. Electrical connector
2. Screws   5. Boot
3. Starter   6. B+ wire

A27-10183

Fig. 34 Showing starter and component locations

3. Remove the air guide hose.

4. Remove upper part of air filter housing and remove air filter insert.

5. Remove bolts and remove air duct.

6. Remove lower part of air filter housing.

7. If equipped, remove the cable tie for the protective boot.

8. Disconnect the electrical connector by sliding the retainer back and pressing the release down.

9. Fold back the boot and disconnect the B+ wire from the solenoid switch.

10. Remove the screws and then remove the starter upward.

11. Install in reverse order of removal.

ENGINE MECHANICAL

➡Disconnecting the negative battery cable may interfere with the functions of the on board computer systems and may require the computer to undergo a relearning process, once the negative battery cable is reconnected.

ACCESSORY DRIVE BELTS

ADJUSTMENT

➡The ribbed belt system uses an automatic tensioner that does not require adjustment.

REMOVAL & INSTALLATION

2.0L Engine

See Figure 35.

1. To release the belt tension, rotate tensioner clockwise with a suitable wrench.
2. Belt can be removed or installed.

3.2L Engine

See Figure 36.

1. Move the tensioner in a clockwise direction to relieve belt tension.
2. Secure the tensioning element with the T10060 A pin.
3. Remove the belt.
4. Install in reverse of the removal procedure.

AIR CLEANER

REMOVAL & INSTALLATION

2.0L Engine

1. Remove the bolts from the air filter upper section.

Fig. 35 To release the belt tension, rotate tensioner clockwise with a suitable wrench.

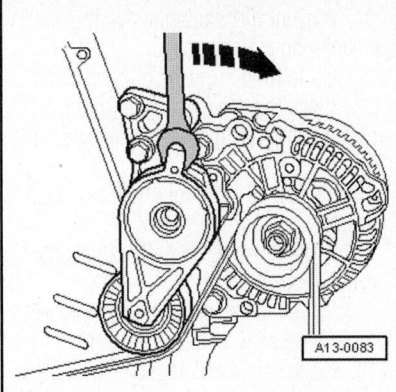

Fig. 36 Move the tensioner in a clockwise direction to relieve belt tension.

2. Lift the upper section of the air filter housing and remove the air filter element.
3. Remove the air guide from the lock carrier to the air filter housing.
4. Open the bolt.
5. Carefully remove the air filter housing lower section.

To install:

6. Remove the snow screen and clean it (the snow screen is not installed on all vehicles).
7. Clean the water drain and the air filter lower section.
8. Disconnect the water drain hose from the lower air filter housing section and clean any dirt and leaves from the connection and the hose.
9. Make sure that the air filter is properly centered when placed in the mounting of the air filter housing lower section.
10. Set the upper section of air filter housing onto lower section of air filter housing, without using much force. When doing this, make sure that the upper section of air filter housing is not placed crooked onto the air filter (observe sealing lip of air filter).
11. Further installation is performed in reverse order.

3.2L Engine

See Figure 37.

1. Remove air filter element, as described in this section.
2. Remove bolts and remove air duct.

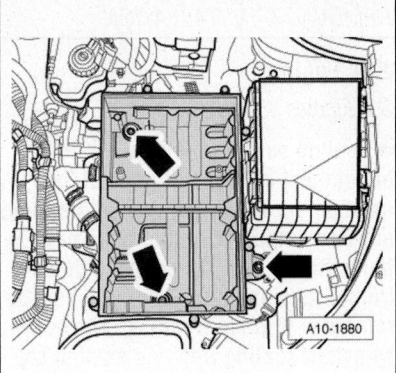

Fig. 37 Remove lower section of air filter housing.

3. Remove lower section of air filter housing.

To install:

4. Installation is in reverse order of removal, note the following.

a. Air filter housing must always be clean.

b. Secure all hose connections with hose clamps appropriate for the model.

c. Note the following when blowing out air filter housing with compressed air: To prevent malfunctions, cover critical air-flow engine components such as Mass Air Flow sensor, air duct pipes etc. with a clean cloth.

d. Blow out water drain (small hole in lower section of air filter housing) with compressed air.

e. Clean air filter housing (upper and lower sections) of salt residue, dirt or leaves (use vacuum cleaner if necessary).

f. Check Mass Air Flow sensor and air duct hose (clean air side) for salt residue, dirt and leaves.

g. Check the air duct from lock carrier to air filter housing for dirt and leaves.

h. Place upper section of air filter housing on to lower section or air filter housing carefully and without using excessive force. When doing this, make sure that upper section of air filter housing is not placed tilted on the air filter element (pay attention to sealing lip of air filter element).

CAMSHAFT AND VALVE LIFTERS

REMOVAL & INSTALLATION

2.0L Engines

See Figures 38 and 39.

➡Sealing surfaces on guide frame at bottom and on cylinder head at top must not be worked. Camshaft bearings are integrated in cylinder head or in guide frame. Before removing guide frame, tension on toothed belt must be released. If guide frame was loosened, camshaft sealing ring and sealing cap must be replaced.

1. Remove cylinder head cover.
2. Remove camshaft adjuster.
3. Remove toothed belt.
4. Loosen camshaft gear with Retainer 3036.
5. Pull off camshaft gear using puller T40001, claw T40001/6 and claw T40001/7.
6. Remove toothed belt guard at rear of cylinder head.
7. Remove guide frame bolts and carefully remove guide frame.
8. Remove camshafts together with drive chain from cylinder head.
9. Prevent dirt and adhesive residue from entering cylinder head.

To install:

➡Sealing surfaces must be completely free of oil and grease. The pistons must not be positioned at TDC. Make sure that all roller cam followers make contact correctly on valve stem ends.

➡Refer to illustration for torque values.

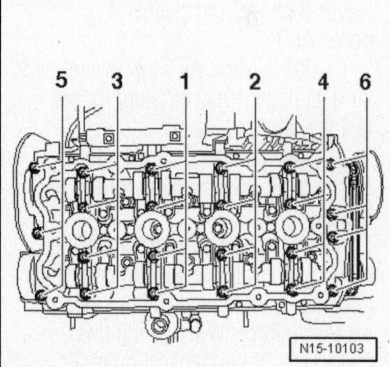

Fig. 38 Remove guide frame bolts in 6 to 1 sequence and carefully remove guide frame

10. Remove the old sealant from the guide frame groove and from sealing surfaces.
11. Prevent dirt and adhesive residue from entering cylinder head.
12. Oil journal surfaces of camshafts.
13. Place the drive chain onto the removed camshaft chain sprockets as follows:
    a. Cams of cylinder must face each other.
    b. The notches on both camshafts must align.
    c. The side surfaces of the notches must be exactly vertical.
14. Place camshafts together with drive chain in cylinder head and in chain tensioner.
15. Verify TDC position of camshafts again.
    a. Cams of cylinder must face each other.
    b. The notches on both camshafts must align.
    c. The side surfaces of the notches must be exactly perpendicular to the cylinder head.
16. Apply an even, light sealant bead into the clean groove of the guide frame.

➡Sealant must not be applied too thickly. Attaching and bolting the guide frame should be performed without interruption because the sealant begins to harden immediately as soon as it contacts the sealing surfaces. Note the expiration date of the sealing compound.

17. Set the guide frame in place so that it can get by the EGR Vacuum Regulator Solenoid Valve N18.
18. Replace guide frame screws.
19. Gently tighten bolts from inside working toward outside in several stages.

➡Ensure guide frame is not tilted.

20. Then check TDC position of camshafts by inserting Camshaft Clamp T10252 as far as stop.

➡Rotate camshafts back and forth slightly if necessary to insert Camshaft Clamp T10252.

21. If the Camshaft Clamp T10252 cannot be inserted, remove guide frame again and repeat camshaft installation.
22. Remove Camshaft Clamp T10252.
23. Drive in the sealing cap with the thrust piece 3334 approximately 1 to 2 mm deep.
24. Install camshaft sealing ring.
25. Install the rear toothed belt guard.

26. Insert fitting key into camshaft.
27. Install camshaft gear. To tighten bolt, hold camshaft gear in place using retainer 3036.
28. When turning camshaft, pistons may not be at TDC for any cylinder.

✳✳ CAUTION

Always rotate in direction of normal engine rotation or valves/pistons may be damaged.

29. Be sure fitting keys are properly seated.
30. To complete the installation, reverse the remaining removal procedure.

3.2L Engines

See Figures 40 through 45.

1. Remove the valve cover.
2. Remove the timing chain.
3. To remove the camshafts in the left cylinder head, remove the brake booster vacuum pump.
4. To remove the camshafts in the right cylinder head, remove the high pressure pump and pump motor housing.
5. Remove the bolts and the camshaft adjuster valves.
6. Loosen guide frame bolts in sequence.
7. Carefully remove the guide frame and lay it on a soft surface on the workbench.
8. Remove Locking Pin T40133.
9. Mark camshafts and remove.

To install:

➡Refer to illustration for torque values.

10. Secure crankshaft using Locking Pin T40069.
11. Replace the seals and gaskets.

➡Cover the open parts of engine. There is risk of contaminating the lubricating system and bearing.

➡Wear safety glasses.

12. Using a rotating plastic brush, remove any remaining ealant from the cylinder head and guide frame.
13. lean sealing surfaces, must be free of oil and grease.
14. Check the screen for dirt and clean it if necessary.
15. Oil running surfaces of both camshafts.
16. Insert the camshafts in the guide frame.

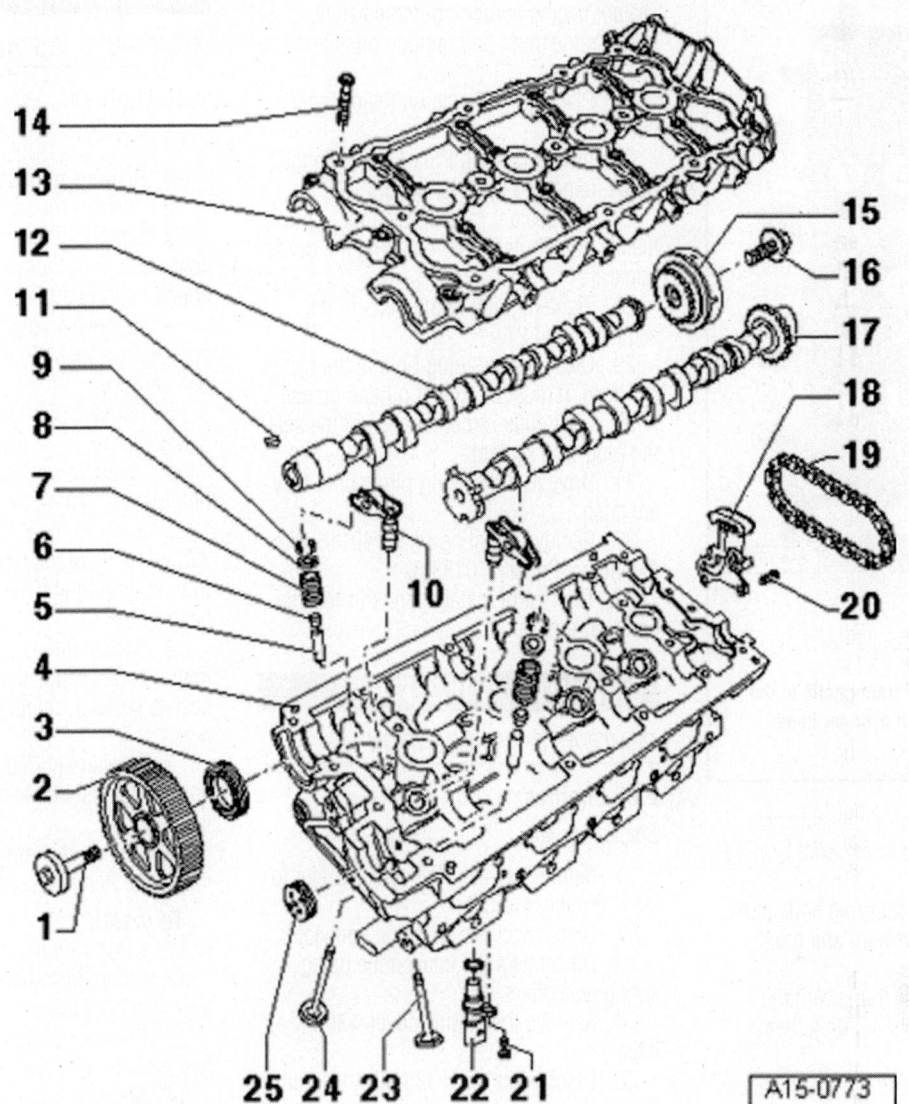

A15-0773

1. Bolt [36 ft. lbs. (50 Nm) plus an
   additional 180° turn further]
2. Camshaft sprocket
3. Seal
4. Cylinder Head
5. Valve guide
6. Valve stem seal
7. Valve spring
8. Top valve spring retainer
9. Valve keepers
10. Hydraulic valve play balancing
    element (Lubricate contact
    surface and do not interchange)
11. Fitted key
12. Exhaust camshaft
13. Bearing bracket
14. Bolt
15. Camshaft adjuster
16. Bolt [14 ft. lbs. (20 Nm)
    plus an additional 45° turn]
17. Intake camshaft
18. Chain tensioner
19. Drive chain
20. Bolt [7 ft. lbs. (10 Nm)]
21. Bolt [7 ft. lbs. (10 Nm)]
22. Phase sensor
23. Exhaust valve
24. Intake valve
25. Sealing cap

Fig. 39 Valve train assembly overview—2.0L Engines

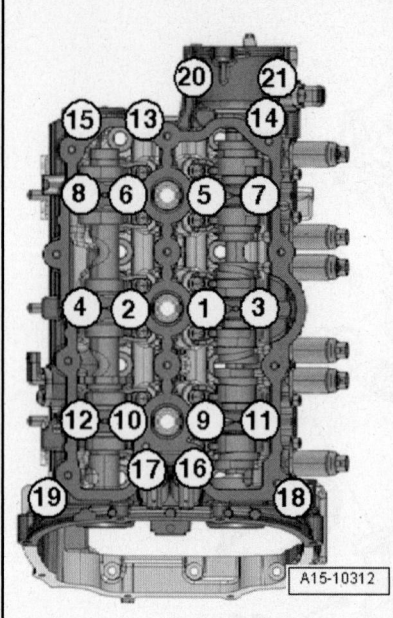

Fig. 40 Loosen guide frame bolts in the sequence 21 to 1—left cylinder head application shown.

a. The placement of the camshafts must be exactly within the axial bearings of the guide frame.

b. The compression ring ends must face upward or downward and must never face sideways.

17. Rotate the guide frame with the camshafts inserted while holding them securely in the frame.

18. Rotate camshafts until the threaded holes face upward.

19. Check if the camshafts still lie in the guide frame axial bearings.

20. Install the Camshaft Locator T40133 and tighten the bolts to 18 ft. lbs. (25 Nm).

➡Note the expiration date of the sealing compound.

21. Cut the tube nozzle at the front marking (nozzle diameter approximately 2.0 mm).

22. Rotate guide frame again.

➡The lubrication system could be plugged with excess sealant. Do not apply sealant beads thicker than specified.

23. Apply sealant beads to the clean sealing surfaces on the guide frame. Thickness of sealant bead: 2.0 mm.

24. Apply sealant beads to the clean sealing surfaces on the guide frame. Thick-

ness of sealant bead: 2.5 mm. Because the sealant begins hardening immediately, guide frame must be promptly positioned and tightened.

25. Place guide frame on the cylinder head.

26. Insert Locating Pins T40116 in the guide frame and cylinder head.

27. The sealant must harden for approximately 30 minutes after installing the guide frame.

28. Tighten guide frame bolts in the sequence 1 to 21.

29. Clean sealing plug hole in the cylinder head. It must be free of oil and grease.

30. Coat outer circumference of the sealing plug with sealant.

31. Drive in the sealing plugs until they are flush.

32. Remove Locating Pins T40116 with the Impact Puller T10133/3.

33. The rest of installation is in reverse order of removal.

CATALYTIC CONVERTER

REMOVAL & INSTALLATION

2.0L Engines

See Figure 46.

1. Before servicing the vehicle, refer to the Precautions section.

2. Disconnect the electrical connector.

3. Disconnect the intake tube using spring type pliers.

4. Remove the engine cover with the air filter.

5. Disconnect the HO2S electrical connector.

6. Remove the accessible nuts for the front exhaust pipe/turbocharger from above.

7. Remove the right cover for the vehicle floor.

8. Pull off the electrical connector for the O2S behind the three way catalytic converter to free up the wiring.

9. Remove the remaining nuts for the front exhaust pipe/turbocharger from below.

10. Remove the supports for the front exhaust pipe with the catalytic converter by unscrewing the bracket and bolts.

11. Disconnect the exhaust system at the clamping sleeve.

12. Remove the cross member for the vehicle floor.

13. Remove the bracket for the exhaust system.

14. Remove the catalytic converter with the front exhaust pipe.

CRANKSHAFT FRONT SEAL

REMOVAL & INSTALLATION

2.0L Engines

See Figure 47.

1. Remove ribbed belt.

2. Remove the accessory drive belt.

3. Loosen crankshaft toothed belt gear. To do this, lock toothed belt sprocket with counter support 3415.

4. Remove crankshaft-toothed belt sprocket center bolt and remove toothed belt sprocket.

5. Remove diamond disc from toothed belt gear.

6. To guide seal puller, thread center bolt into crankshaft by hand until stop.

7. Remove inner part of Seal Remover 3203 nine rotations (approximately 20 mm) from outer part and secure with knurled-head screw.

8. Grease threaded head of Seal Remover 3203, position and screw into oil seal as far as possible with forceful pressure.

9. Loosen knurled screw and turn inner portion against crankshaft until the oil seal is pulled out.

10. Secure seal remover in a vise at the flat spots. Remove seal using pliers.

To install:

11. Clean running and sealing surface.

12. Before installing, remove oil remains from end of crankshaft with a clean cloth.

13. Position guide sleeve T10053/1 of assembly tool T10053 on end of crankshaft.

14. Slide oil seal over guide sleeve onto the crankshaft pin.

15. Press in seal using center bolt of toothed belt sprocket and pressure sleeve of assembly tool T10053 until it is flush.

16. Install crankshaft toothed belt gear with new diamond disc and new center bolt.

➡Contact surface between toothed belt gear, diamond disc and crankshaft must be free of oil. Do not oil the bolt for crankshaft toothed belt sprocket.

17. Use counter support 3415 to tighten crankshaft toothed belt gear.

18. Install toothed belt.

19. Install ribbed belt.

3.2L Engines

See Figure 48.

1. Remove both front wheels.

2. Loosen quick-release fasteners and remove front noise insulation.

3. Remove front bumper cover.

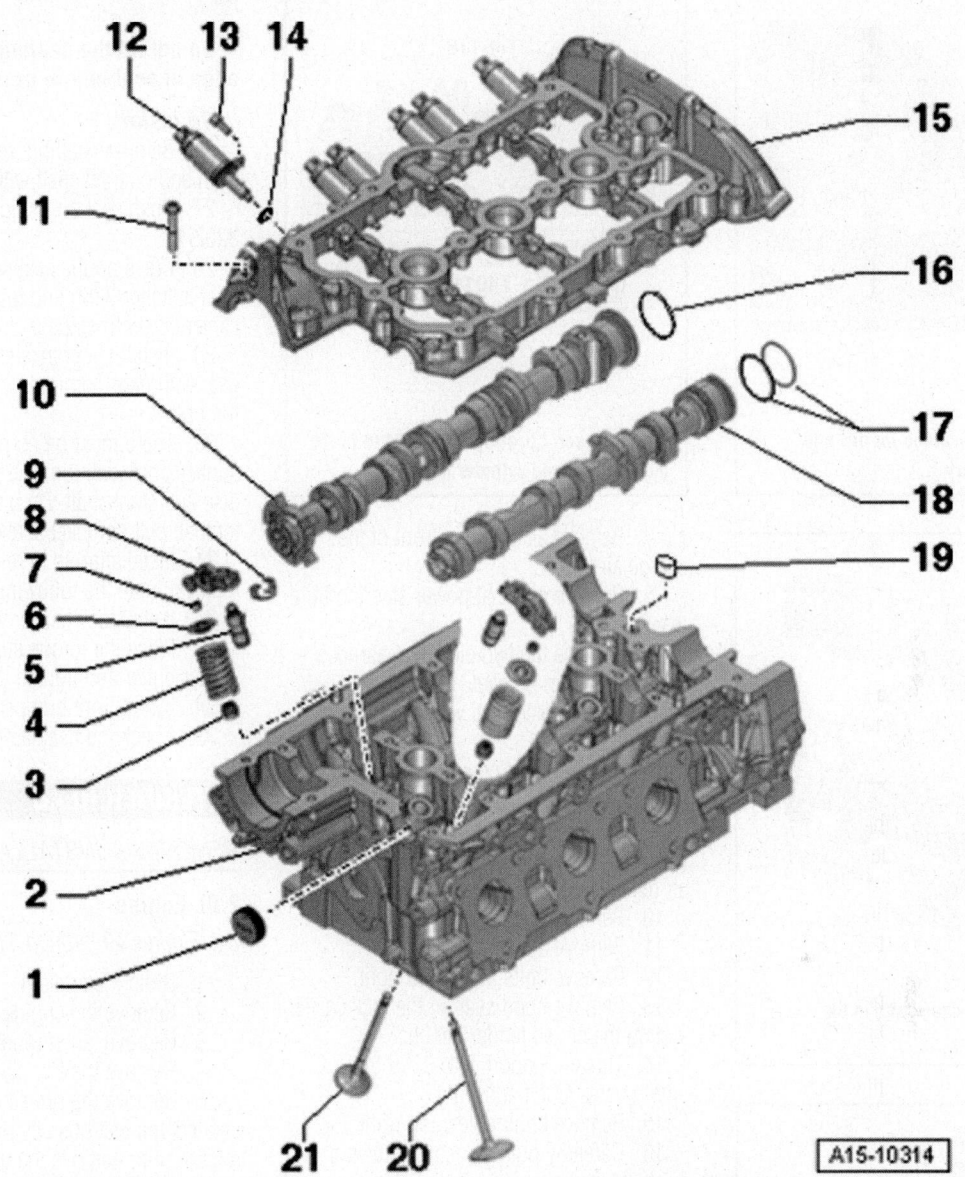

12 13 14

11

15

16

10

17

9
8
7
6
5
4
3

18

19

2

1

21 20

A15-10314

1. Sealing plug
2. Cylinder Head
3. Valve stem seal
4. Valve spring
5. Hydraulic adjusting elements
6. Valve spring plate
7. Valve keys
8. Roller rocker lever
9. Securing clip (different clips for intake and exhaust side)
10. Intake camshaft (Maximum run-out. 0.04 mm)
11. Bolt

12. Camshaft adjuster actuator
13. Bolt (5 Nm)
14. O-ring
15. Bearing bracket (With integrated camshaft bearings)
16. Compression ring
17. Compression ring
18. Exhaust camshaft (Maximum run-out. 0.04 mm)
19. Oil strainer
20. Intake valve
21. Exhaust valve

Fig. 41 Overview of the valve train assembly—3.2L engines

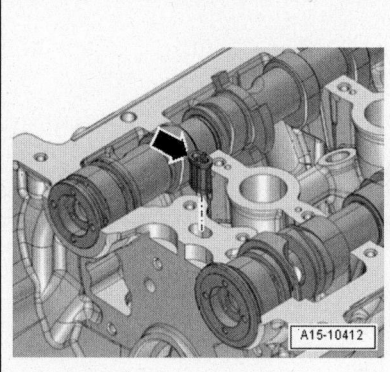

Fig. 42 Check the screen for dirt and clean it if necessary

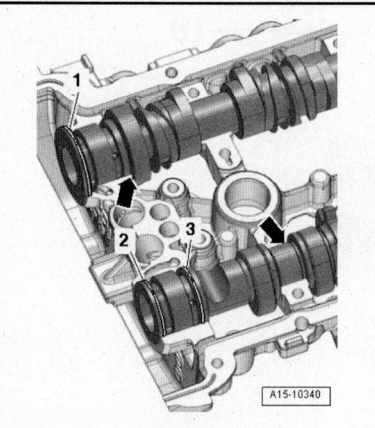

Fig. 43 Insert the camshafts in the guide frame

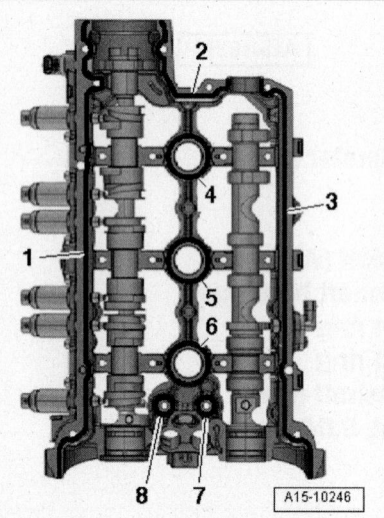

Fig. 44 Apply sealant beads (4 through 8) to the clean sealing surfaces on the guide frame

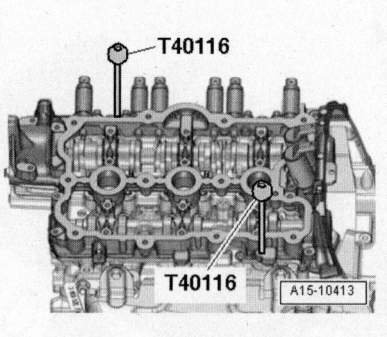

Fig. 45 Insert Locating Pins T40116 in the guide frame and cylinder head

4. Remove air guide in front of the charge air cooler.

5. Remove cover at power steering fluid reservoir.

6. Remove the two electrical harness connectors from bracket.

7. Free up electrical wires to lock carrier.

8. Remove right cover in the engine compartment, if equipped.

9. Disengage Evaporative Emission (EVAP) Canister Purge Regulator Valve from air guide.

10. Remove bolts.

11. Remove air duct.

12. Remove bolts at left and right.

13. Remove hood seal on the lock carrier and on the bolted fender flanges.

14. Thread Support Tool 3369 into empty bores at left and right.

15. Remove bolts at left and right.

16. Carefully pull lock carrier toward front.

17. Remove toothed belt.

18. Remove center bolt for crankshaft toothed belt gear and remove toothed belt gear.

19. Remove diamond disc from toothed belt gear.

20. Remove inner portion of Seal Remover 3203 6 rotations from outer portion and secure with knurled-head bolt.

21. Lubricate the threaded head of the seal remover, place against seal, and with strong force screw into the seal as far as possible.

22. Loosen knurled screw and turn inner portion against crankshaft until the oil seal is pulled out.

23. Clamp seal extractor at mounting points in a vise.

24. Remove seal using pliers.

25. Clean the running and sealing surfaces.

➡**Do not oil the sealing lip and outer edge of seal before pressing in.**

To install:

26. Before installing, remove oil remains from end of crankshaft with a clean cloth.

27. Push seal on using fitting sleeve 3202/1.

28. Press on the sealing ring using the Seal Installer 3265 and toothed belt gear center screw to stop.

29. Install the crankshaft toothed belt gear with new diamond disc and new central bolt.

30. There must be no oil on the contact surfaces between toothed belt gear, diamond disc and crankshaft. Do not oil crankshaft toothed belt sprocket screw additionally.

31. Installation is in reverse order of removal, note the following:

32. Install lock carrier with attachments.

33. Place the torque support stop on the rubber buffer and tighten the nuts.

34. Install front bumper cover.

35. Check the headlamp adjustment.

CYLINDER HEAD

REMOVAL & INSTALLATION

2.0L Engine

See Figures 49 through 51.

1. Drain the coolant.

2. Remove the engine cover.

3. Remove fan shroud.

4. Remove the turbocharger.

5. Remove the protective boot and disconnect the fuel hose by pressing the release ring. Remove the hose.

6. Release the EVAP canister, then remove it upward and lay it aside.

7. Remove the bolt and nut and then push the front right coolant pipe to the side with the coolant hoses still connected.

8. Remove the double bolt for the oil dipstick guide tube.

9. Disconnect the connector 3.

10. Remove bolt.

11. Remove the hose.

12. Loosen the hose clamp and then remove the turbocharger recirculating valve with the hose still connected from the air guide pipe and lay it to the side.

13. Disconnect the connector on the charge air pressure sensor.

14. Remove the bolt 1 and nut 4.

15. Loosen the hose clamp 2 and remove the air guide pipe.

Ignore 3.

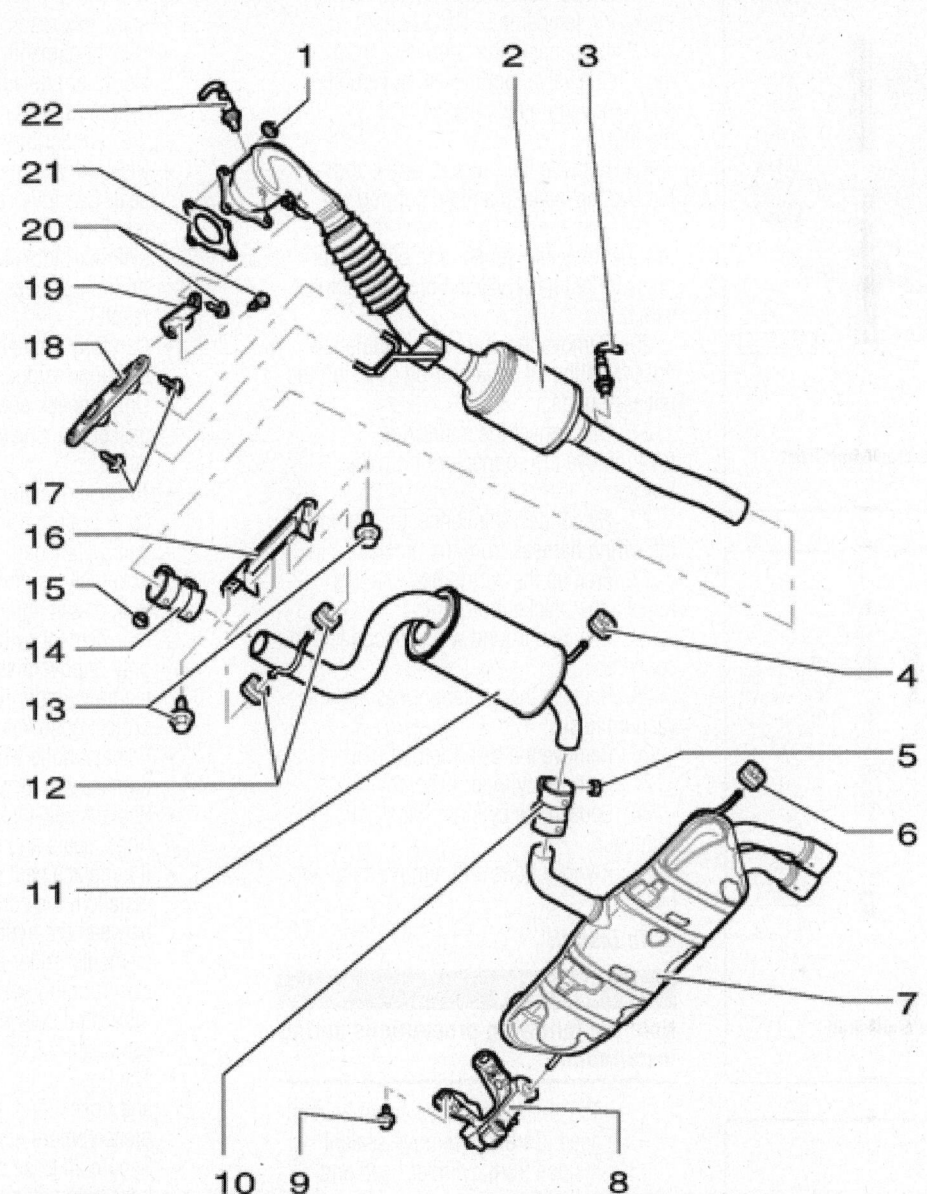

1. Nut
2. Catalytic converter
3. O2 sensor
4. Retaining loop
5. Nut
6. Retaining loop
7. Rear muffler
8. Suspended mount
9. Bolt
10. Rear clamping sleeve
11. Center muffler
12. Retaining loop
13. Screw
14. Front clamping sleeve
15. Nut
16. Suspended mount
17. Screws
18. Suspended mount
19. Support
20. Screws
21. Gasket
22. HO2S and O2S

41311_AUDI_G0083

Fig. 46 Exploded view of the exhaust and catalytic converter components—2.0L Engines

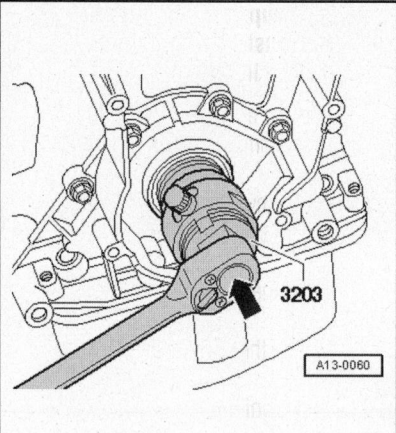

Fig. 47 Removing the crankshaft front seal—2.0L Engines

Fig. 48 Removing the crankshaft front seal

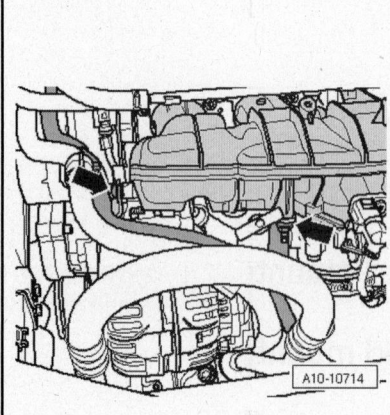

Fig. 49 Remove the bolt and nut (arrows) and then push the front right coolant pipe to the side with the coolant hoses still connected.

16. Disconnect the connector on the Intake Air Temperature (IAT) Sensor.

17. Disconnect the connector from the throttle valve module. Remove bolts and remove throttle valve control module.

18. Remove the nut and screw and remove the intake manifold support.

19. Disconnect the connectors on the low fuel pressure sensor and on the fuel pressure regulator valve. Free up electrical wires.

20. Remove the crankcase ventilation hose from the oil separator by pressing the release buttons.

21. Disconnect the connectors, then remove the connectors from the bracket.

22. Disconnect the connector. Remove the wiring harness from the bracket..

23. Free up the wiring harness and remove the bracket bolt.

24. Remove ground wire. Disconnect the connector.

25. Remove the coolant hoses and the vacuum hoses.

26. Remove the cam toothed belt.

27. Remove cylinder head cover.

28. Loosen the cylinder head bolts in sequence.

29. Remove bolts and remove cylinder head.

To install:

❋❋ CAUTION

Note the following precautions during installation:

- The sealing surfaces could be damaged. Carefully remove sealant residue from cylinder head and cylinder block.

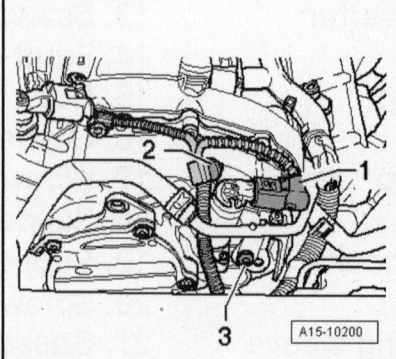

Fig. 50 Disconnect the connector (1). Remove the wiring harness (2) from the bracket (ignore 3).

- Make sure that no long scrapes or scratches result.
- Risk of damaging cylinder block. No oil or coolant must be in the cylinder head bolt blind holes in the cylinder block.
- Risk of leaks in cylinder head seal. Carefully remove sealant residue from cylinder head and cylinder block. Make sure that no long scrapes or scratches result.
- Carefully remove all grinding and sanding residue.
- Only unpack new cylinder head gasket immediately prior to installation.
- To prevent cylinder head seal silicone layer and recessed area from being damaged, always handle seal extremely carefully.
- Risk of damaging open valves. If a replacement cylinder is installed, only remove plastic base right before cylinder head is installed to protect open valves.
- Replace bolts which have been tightened to torque.
- Replace self-locking nuts, sealing rings, seals and O-rings.
- If a replacement cylinder is installed, the contact surfaces between the hydraulic adjusting elements, roller rocker levers and cam running surfaces must be lubricated before installing the camshaft housing.
- The hose supports, air guide pipes and hoses must be free of oil and grease before installing.
- Secure all hose connections with hose clamps appropriate for the model.
- To mount the charge hoses on their connectors securely, spray the bolts on the used clamps with rust remover before installing.
- When replacing the cylinder head or cylinder head seal, all of the coolant and engine oil must be replaced.

30. Align the marking on the toothed belt camshaft pulley with the marking on the toothed belt guard top.

31. Ensure the cams on both camshafts are symmetrical to each other. The notches on both camshafts must align.

32. Clean the sealing surfaces; they must be free of oil and grease.

33. Make sure the crankshaft is still at "TDC" and then turn it back 45° opposite the engine rotation.

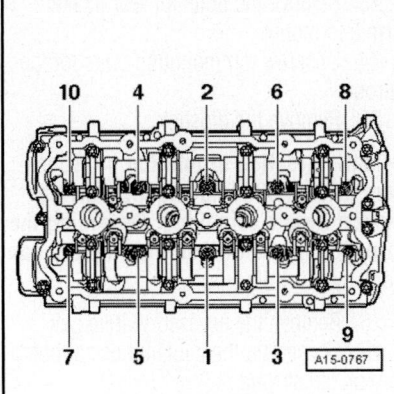

Fig. 51 Cylinder head bolt tightening sequence

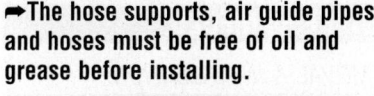
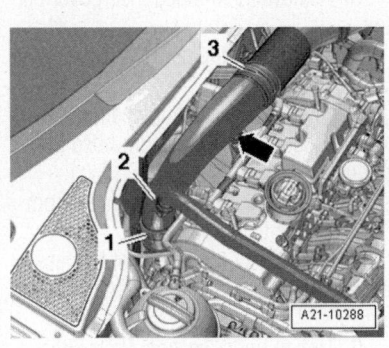

Fig. 52 Remove bolt (arrow). Loosen the hose clamps (1 and 3) and move the air guide pipe to the side with the hose still connected (2).

34. Set cylinder head gasket in place. In its installed position, it must be possible to read the part number. Note the sleeves in the cylinder block.
35. Set cylinder head in place. Tighten the cylinder head bolts, in sequence. Tighten in 3 steps:
    a. Step 1: 30 ft. lbs. (40 Nm)
    b. Step 2: Additional 90 degrees
    c. Step 3: Additional 90 degrees

➡**Do not tighten cylinder head bolts after repairs.**

36. Install cylinder head cover.
37. Rotate the crankshaft back to "TDC".
38. Install toothed belt (adjust timing).
39. Install the intake manifold support and throttle valve control module J338.
40. Tighten the oil dipstick guide tube.
41. Install the air guide pipe.
42. Install the right front coolant pipe.
43. Install the turbocharger.
44. Install fan shroud.
45. Change engine oil.
46. Replace coolant. See "ENGINE COOLING" section.

CYLINDER HEAD COVER

REMOVAL & INSTALLATION

See Figures 52 and 53.

1. Remove the engine cover.
2. Remove the two upper bolts and move the toothed belt cover to the side.
3. Remove ignition coils.
4. Remove bolt. Loosen the hose clamps and move the air guide pipe to the side with the hose still connected.
5. Remove the vacuum line from the cylinder head cover.

6. Remove the bolts and then remove the crankcase housing ventilation pressure regulator valve.
7. Remove the Evaporative Emission (EVAP) canister line from the cylinder head cover.
8. Remove the bolts and then remove the crankcase ventilation tube and heat shield from the cylinder head cover by loosening the hose clamp.
9. Loosen the cylinder head cover bolts in sequence.
10. Remove the bolts and the cylinder head cover.

To install:

11. Installation is done is reverse order, observe the following:
    a. Replace the cylinder head seal if it is damaged.
    b. Replace the cylinder head cover bolts when replacing the damaged seal.

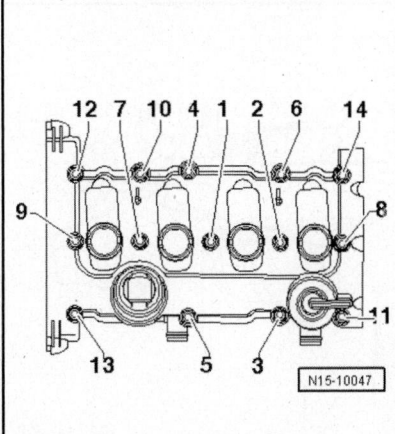

Fig. 53 Loosen/tighten the cylinder head cover bolts in sequence.

➡The hose supports, air guide pipes and hoses must be free of oil and grease before installing.

    c. Secure all hose connections with hose clamps appropriate for the model.
12. Tighten cylinder head cover bolts, in sequence, to 7 ft. lbs. (10 Nm).
13. Install the crankcase ventilation line.
14. Tighten the upper toothed belt guard.
15. Install ignition coils.

EXHAUST MANIFOLD

REMOVAL & INSTALLATION

3.2L Engine

See Figure 54.

1. Before servicing the vehicle, refer to the precautions section.
2. Remove or disconnect the following:
- Negative battery cable
- Intake manifold
- Heat shield
- Remove 7 nuts and washers on both exhaust manifolds
- Pull exhaust manifolds towards the rear and remove

To install:

3. Installation is the reverse of the removal procedure, using the following torque values:
- Exhaust manifold to cylinder head 17 ft. lbs (23 Nm)
- Exhaust pipe to manifold 29 ft. lbs (40 NM)

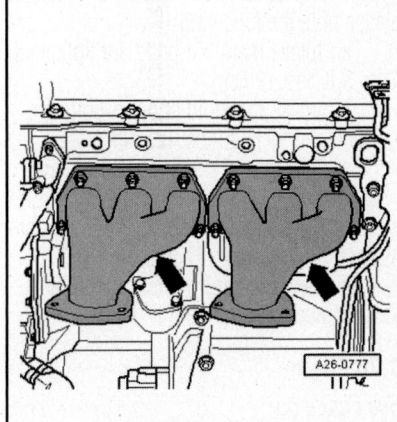

Fig. 54 Remove 7 nuts and washers on both exhaust manifolds

INTAKE MANIFOLD

REMOVAL & INSTALLATION

2.0L Engine

1. Relieve the fuel system pressure.
2. Remove the engine cover.
3. Disconnect the all necessary electrical harness connectors.
4. Disconnect the vacuum hose between intake manifold and vacuum pump from intake manifold.
5. Disconnect the hose connections from valve cover.
6. Loosen the fuel supply line and hose connection from EVAP canister and cap off open lines.
7. Open both fuel lines at high-pressure pump.
8. Disconnect the electrical connector from Fuel Pressure sensor.
9. Remove the oil dipstick and remove bolt for oil dipstick guide tube.
10. Remove the bolt for oil line from intake manifold.
11. Open hose clamps and pull intake hose off from Throttle Valve Control Module and intake manifold.
12. Remove the nut from intake manifold bracket, if necessary, remove Throttle Valve Control Module.
13. Separate oil dipstick guide tube at separation point and remove bolt from intake manifold bracket.
14. Remove the bolts from intake manifold.
15. Carefully pull intake manifold with fuel rail off from cylinder head.

➡The fuel injectors could remain stuck in the fuel rail.

To install:

16. Installation is the reverse of removal, please note the following:
   a. Intake manifold bolts are tightened to 5 ft. lbs. (9 Nm).
   b. Intake manifold support bolts are tightened to 16 ft. lbs. (23 Nm).
   c. Intake manifold support nuts are tightened to 7 ft. lbs (10 Nm).
   d. Fuel supply line to pump are tightened to 20 ft. lbs. (27 Nm).
   e. New fuel return line to pump are tightened to 13 ft. lbs. (17 Nm).

3.2L Engine

See Figure 55.

1. Remove the molded insert for tools under luggage compartment floor cover.
2. Unscrew cover for battery compartment.

3. Remove the molded insert over battery.
4. Disconnect the negative battery cable.
5. Remove the noise insulation.
6. Disconnect the vacuum hose from air duct hose.
7. Disconnect the air duct hose from Throttle Valve Control Module.
8. Disconnect the electrical harness connector at Mass Air Flow (MAF) sensor.
9. Unbolt upper section of air filter housing.
10. Remove the filter element.
11. Unbolt lower section of air duct.
12. Unbolt lower section of air filter housing.
13. Disconnect the secondary air hose at position indicated by.
14. Loosen up the air hose to Secondary Air Injection (AIR) pump.
15. Disconnect the electrical harness connectors and.
16. Disconnect the crankcase ventilation hose.
17. Unscrew Throttle Valve Control Module from the intake manifold and lay it aside with coolant hoses connected.
18. Disconnect the electrical connectors from the ignition coils.
19. Attach Puller for ignition coil tool T10095A on ignition coils as shown in the illustration and pull out ignition coils in succession.
20. Remove the ignition wiring harness strip and set it aside.
21. Disconnect the vacuum hoses at rear from intake manifold.
22. Remove the line union from intake manifold and place it in the rear with hoses connected.

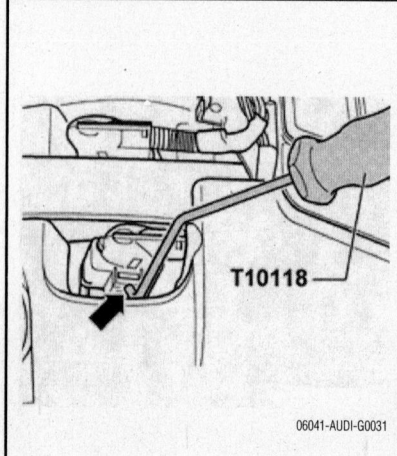

```
06041-AUDI-G0031
```

Fig. 55 Disconnect the electrical connectors from the ignition coils—3.2L engine

23. Remove the bolts for rear intake manifold mount.
24. Unscrew top mounting bolts for fan shroud.
25. Remove the dipstick.

➡Mark direction of rotation of accessory drive belt using chalk or felt-tip marker before removing. Reversing the direction of rotation of a run-in belt can destroy the belt

26. Remove the accessory drive belt.
27. Loosen up the coolant hose at bottom on fan shroud.
28. Disconnect the electrical harness connector at Secondary Air Injection (AIR) pump motor.
29. Unscrew bracket for coolant pipe.
30. Remove the bolts.
31. Loosen the bolt and remove Secondary Air Injection (AIR) pump with bracket.
32. Disconnect the electrical harness connectors for coolant fans at bottom on fan shroud.
33. Unscrew mounting bolts for fan shroud at the bottom.
34. Pull out fan shroud downward with both fans.
35. Disconnect the electrical harness connector for A/C clutch on A/C compressor and loosen up electrical wire.
36. Remove the bolts for A/C compressor. Securely tie the A/C compressor with connected coolant hoses at front on the longitudinal member.
37. Unscrew electrical wire on alternator.
38. Disconnect the electrical harness connector.
39. Remove the upper idler roller.
40. Remove the mounting bolts and for alternator.

➡The alternator can be removed from bracket only with the upper mounting bolt still installed.

41. Remove the alternator with electrical wires connected from bracket for assemblies.
42. Remove the alternator downward and to the left.
43. Disconnect the electrical harness connector at the after-run coolant pump.
44. Remove the bolts and remove bracket for assemblies.
45. Pull the after-run coolant pump with coolant hoses connected, downward out of rubber loops of retainer. Spray rubber loops with silicon-free lubricant if necessary.

➡The water pump remains on the engine with the coolant hoses connected.

46. Disengage harness connector for Engine Speed (RPM) sensor from bracket on oil dipstick guide tube.

47. Unscrew bolt and pull out oil dipstick guide tube.

48. Unscrew bolt and pull off vacuum reservoir from intake manifold.

49. Set aside vacuum reservoir with lines still connected.

50. Remove the bolts at front on intake manifold.

51. Disconnect the vacuum line from actuator for intake manifold change-over.

➡**Protect intake manifold from damage with a clean cloth.**

52. Swivel intake manifold forward and then pull slightly toward left.

➡**Seal intake channels in cylinder head with clean rags or foam pieces so that small pieces cannot fall in.**

53. Remove the bracket for right fuel line at cylinder head cover.

54. Expose electrical wiring harness on cylinder head cover.

55. Remove the bolts.

56. Pull off fuel rail pipe with fuel injectors from cylinder head and set aside with fuel line connected.

57. Swivel intake manifold back into installation position and remove.

To install:

58. Installation is the reverse of removal, please note the following:

➡**Replace all gaskets.**

a. Intake manifold to cylinder head retainers are tightened to 13 Nm.

b. Intake manifold support to intake manifold are tightened to 20 Nm.

c. Throttle Valve Control Module to intake manifold retainers are tightened to 10 Nm.

OIL PAN

REMOVAL & INSTALLATION

See Figures 56 through 58.

1. Drain engine oil.
2. Remove the right noise insulation.
3. On the TTS Roadster, remove the noise insulation frame with the rear noise insulation.
4. Remove the air guide pipe.
5. Remove the side air tube lower bolt from the pan.
6. Disconnect the connector from the oil level thermal sensor.
7. Remove the turbocharger oil return line bolts.

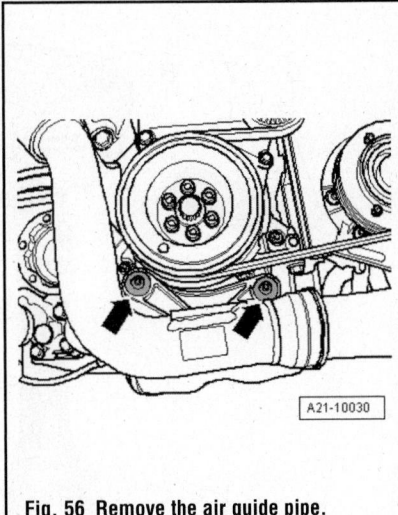

Fig. 56 Remove the air guide pipe.

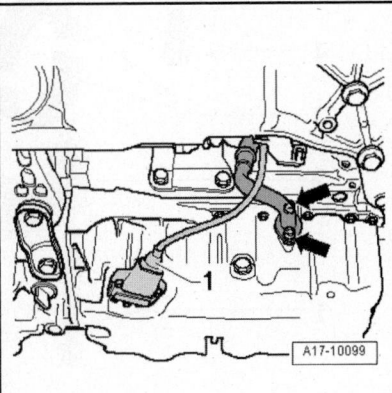

Fig. 57 Disconnect the connector from the oil level thermal sensor.

8. Remove the three bolts from the oil pan to the transmission.

9. Remove the 20 bolts from the oil pan to the cylinder block in a diagonal sequence.

10. Carefully loosen the oil pan from the bond without bending it.

To install:

11. Remove the sealant residue on the cylinder block and the oil pan, for example using a rotating plastic brush.

12. Clean the sealing surfaces; they must be free of oil and grease.

➡**Note the expiration date of the sealing compound.**

13. Apply a sealant bead to the clean sealing edge surface on the oil pan (avoid the bolt holes). Thickness of sealant bead should be only 2 to 3 mm.

14. Carefully apply a sealant bead in the sealing flange area.

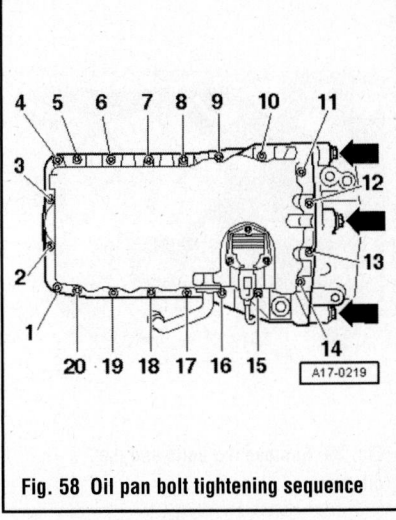

Fig. 58 Oil pan bolt tightening sequence

➡**The oil pan must be installed within 5 minutes after applying the sealant.**

15. Position the oil pan and tighten the bolts:
- Oil pan to transmission bolts: 30 ft. lbs. (40 Nm).
- Oil pan to engine block bolts: 15 ft. lbs. (20 Nm).

➡**When installing the oil pan on an engine that has been removed, make sure the transmission side of the oil pan seals flush with the cylinder block.**

16. Allow the sealant to dry for approximately 30 minutes after installing the oil pan. Only after then may the engine oil be replenished.

17. The rest of the installation is performed in reverse order of removal, noting the following:
a. Install the air guide pipe.
b. Install the noise insulation frame.

18. Fill the engine oil and check the oil level.

OIL PUMP

REMOVAL & INSTALLATION

2.0L Engine

See Figure 59.

1. Before servicing the vehicle, refer to the precautions section.
2. Remove the noise insulation panel from undercar and the insulation frame.
3. Disconnect the connector from the oil level thermal sensor.
4. Drain the engine oil, then remove the oil pan, removing the pan bolts in a crisscross pattern.
5. Remove the oil baffle.
6. Remove the bolts and the oil pump.

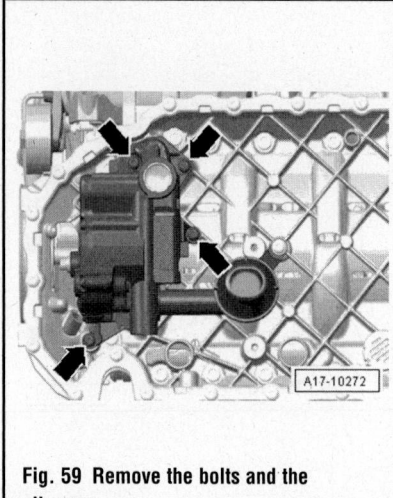

Fig. 59 Remove the bolts and the oil pump.

7. Pull the chain tensioner in the direction of the using the T10118 and remove the oil pump with the chain sprocket.

To install:

8. Installation is the reverse of removal, please note the following:

   a. Make sure both alignment bushings for centering the oil pump are in there.

   b. Replace the baffle plate.

   c. Install oil pan.

9. Refill the engine oil and replace the filter.

PISTON AND RING

POSITIONING

See Figure 60.

REAR MAIN SEAL

REMOVAL & INSTALLATION

See Figures 61 and 62.

1. Remove the transmission.
2. Remove the flywheel.
3. Disconnect the intermediate plate at sealing flange and at the alignment sleeves.
4. Remove the bolts and the rear sealing flange.

To install:

➡**Lay a rag over the open portion of the oil pan.**

5. Clean the gasket mating surfaces.
6. Apply a thin bead of sealant to edge between cylinder block and oil pan.
7. Lightly coat lower sealing surface of sealing flange with sealant.

➡**The sealing flange must be installed within 5 minutes of sealant being applied.**

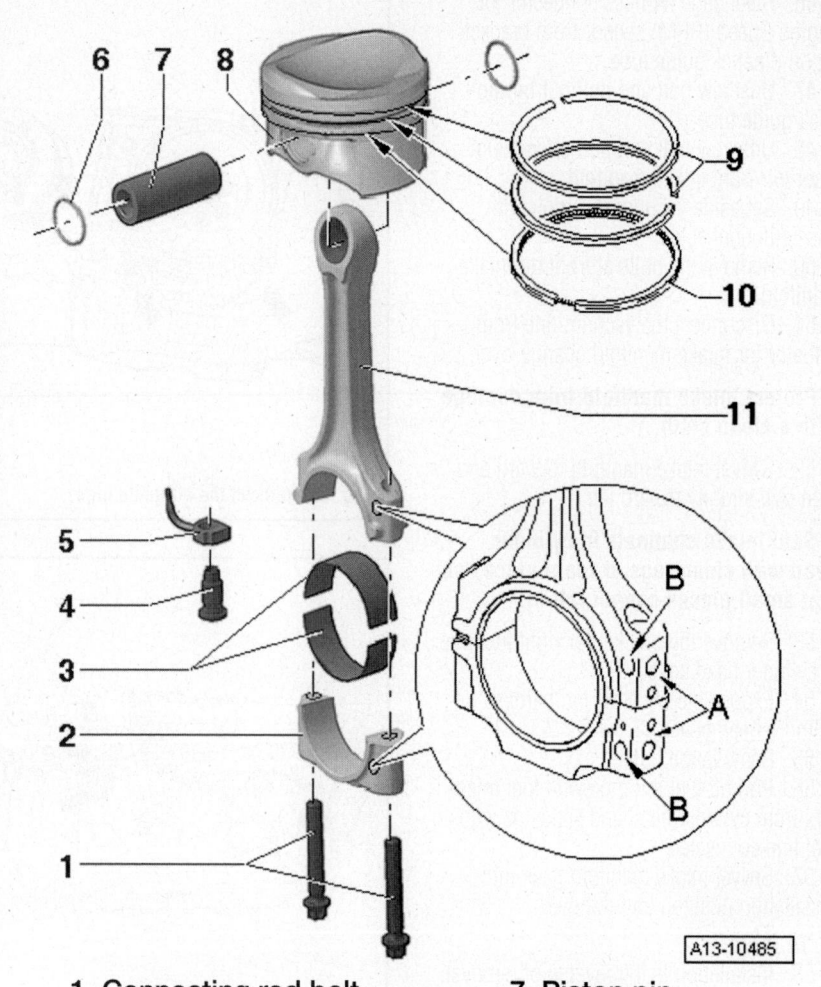

1. Connecting rod bolt
2. Connecting rod bearing cap
3. Bearing shells
4. Pressure relief valve
5. Oil spray jet
6. Circlip
7. Piston pin
8. Piston
9. Compression rings
10. Oil scraping ring
11. Connecting rod

Fig. 60 Piston assembly, showing ring positioning

8. Push the sealing flange together with the guide sleeve, which is included with replacement part onto crankshaft.

9. Carefully push the sealing flange onto the locating pins on cylinder block.

10. Fasten the bolts to 15 Nm.

11. Install the remaining components in the reverse order of removal.

TIMING CHAIN COVERS

REMOVAL & INSTALLATION

Upper Cover

See Figure 63.

1. Release the EVAP canister, remove it upward and lay it aside.

2. Disconnect the connector from the camshaft adjustment valve.

3. Remove the bolts and then the camshaft adjustment valve.

4. Remove the bolts and the timing chain guard upper section.

To install:

5. Installation is performed in the reverse order of removal, noting the following:

   a. Replace O-ring.

   b. Coat the seal and the O-ring with engine oil.

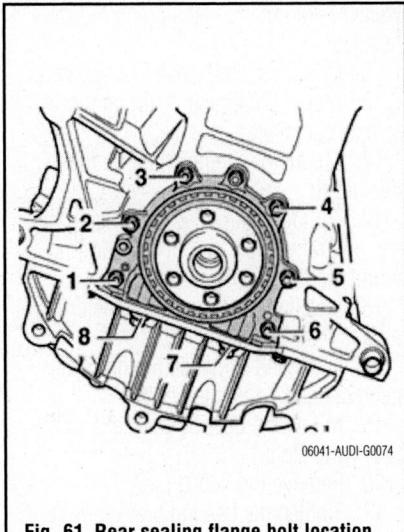

Fig. 61 Rear sealing flange bolt location

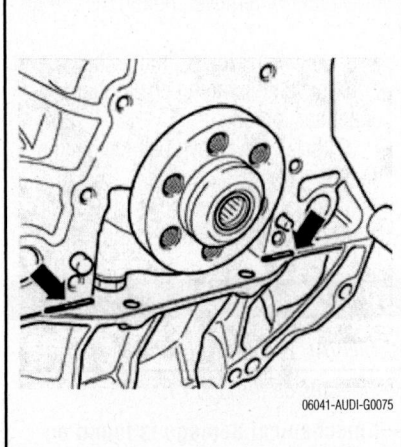

Fig. 62 Apply a thin bead of sealant to edge between cylinder block and oil pan

c. Install the upper timing chain cover.

d. Install the camshaft adjustment valve.

Lower Cover

See Figures 64 through 66.

1. Release the EVAP canister, remove it upward and lay it aside; then, remove the EVAP canister bracket.

2. Free up the electrical wiring harness on the coolant reservoir.

3. Disconnect the electrical connector on the engine coolant level (ECL) warning switch.

4. Remove the bolts and lay the coolant reservoir aside with the coolant hoses attached.

5. Remove the undercar noise insulation and the right noise insulation from the wheel well area. Remove the frame for the noise insulation.

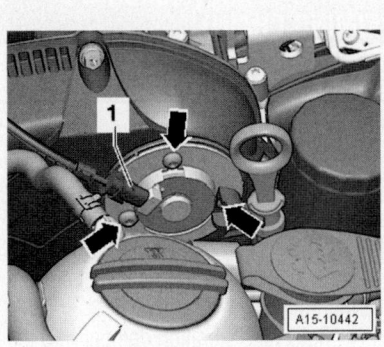

Fig. 63 Disconnect the connector from the camshaft adjustment valve (1). Remove the bolts (arrows) and then the camshaft adjustment valve.

6. Remove the bolts and lift the clamps to remove the air guide pipe from across the lower front of the engine.

7. Release ribbed belt (drive belt) tension by rotating the tensioner clockwise. Then, secure tensioner with a pin or holding device (T10060 A). Remove ribbed belt from vibration damper ribbed belt pulley.

8. Rotate the vibration damper, in normal engine rotation direction only, into the "TDC" position. The notch on the vibration damper must line up with the arrow marking on the timing chain lower cover. Remove vibration damper bolt and the vibration damper.

9. Install the vibration damper bolt and the thrust piece (T10368) again. Remove the idler roller.

10. Remove the engine cover.

11. Install the engine lift assembly (10 - 222 A, engine brackets 10 - 222 A /1, spindle 10 - 222 A /11). Engage the spindle in the engine lifting eye and tension the engine.

12. Remove the bolts and the connecting brace. Remove the bolts and the engine mount.

13. Lift the engine approximately 2 inches (50 mm) and loosen the upper bolt for the engine support. Now lower the engine approximately 4 inches (100 mm).

14. Free up electrical wiring harness. Remove the bolt and remove the ribbed belt tensioner from the accessory assembly bracket.

15. Remove the lower bolts for the engine support, then remove the engine support and the bolts.

16. Remove the bolts and remove the oil dipstick guide tube from the timing chain cover.

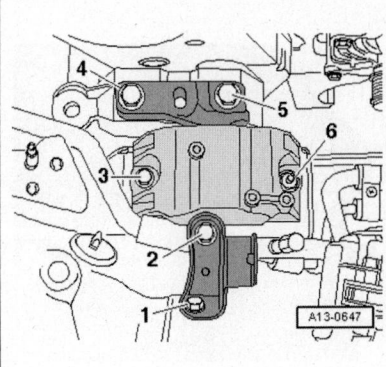

Fig. 64 Remove the bolts (1 and 2) and the connecting brace. Remove the bolts (3 to 6) and the engine mount.

17. Disconnect the wastegate bypass regulator valve from the turbocharger. Remove the turbocharger support.

18. Remove the lower timing chain cover bolts, in a criss-cross pattern. Pry off the lower timing chain cover; when doing this, beginning at the left middle edge and the left upper corner.

➡**To avoid deformation, do not hold between the bolting points.**

To install:

➡**Installation notes:**

- The cover must be installed within 5 minutes after application of silicone sealant.
- Replace the bolts which are being tightened with an additional turn.
- Replace sealing rings, seals and self-locking nuts.

19. Spray the sealing surface with sealant remover and allow it to work. Remove any sealant residue on the cylinder block using a flat blade scraper. Seal off both sides of the seal with tape to prevent contamination. Remove residual sealant on the cover for example with a rotating plastic brush. Clean sealing surfaces, must be free of oil and grease.

20. Install the cover using the old bolts and tighten to 6 ft. lbs. (8 Nm).

21. Check between the cover and crankcase using a feeler gauge; the gap must not exceed 0.0001 in. (0.2 mm). If the gap exceeds this measurement, replace the cover.

➡**It is not possible to measure between the cover the upper section of the oil pan, however check the sealing surface for evenness.**

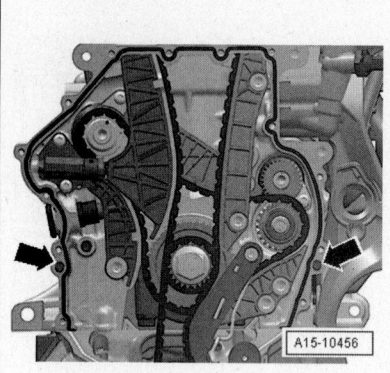

Fig. 65 Make sure both alignment bushings for centering the cover are present.

22. Make sure both alignment bushings for centering the cover are present.

23. Apply the silicone sealant, not thicker than 0.3 mm, on the clean sealing surface of the cover (not over any bolt holes).

24. The cover must be installed within 5 minutes after application of silicone sealant.

25. Mount the cover immediately and tighten the bolts in two steps, following the tightening sequence.
   - Step 1: 6 ft. lbs. (8 Nm)
   - Step 2: Additional 45 degrees

26. After installing cover, allow sealant to dry for approximately 30 minutes. Only after then may the engine oil be replenished.

27. Check and adjust engine oil level.

28. Installation remaining components in the reverse order of removal.

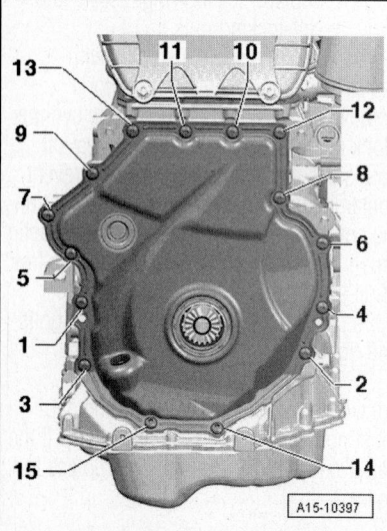

Fig. 66 Mount the cover immediately and tighten the bolts in two steps, following the tightening sequence

TIMING CHAIN (CAMSHAFT TIMING CHAIN)

REMOVAL & INSTALLATION

See Figures 67 and 68.

1. Remove timing chain upper cover.

2. Remove the control valve, noting the left-hand thread, using a proper socket (T10352 or T10352/1).

3. Remove the bolts and remove the bearing bracket.

4. Rotate the vibration damper into the "TDC" position. The notch on the vibration damper must line up with the marking on the timing chain lower cover. The markings on the camshafts must point upward.

5. Remove the lower timing chain cover, as described in this section.

6. Press the oil pump chain tensioner to the right and secure it with a T40011. Remove the oil pump chain tensioner.

7. Lift the chain tensioner locking wedge by inserting a scriber or a suitable screwdriver into the hole in the chain tensioner as shown. Press the timing chain tensioning rail to the left and secure it with the T40011. Remove the camshaft timing chain from the cylinder head. The intake camshaft switches in the engine direction of rotation.

Remove the timing chain tensioning rail. Remove the guide rail for the camshaft timing chain. Remove the timing chain.

To install:

➡**The following procedure must be performed in one step. A second technician is needed.**

8. When installing, the painted links of the timing chain must be positioned on the markings on the chain sprockets. Hold the

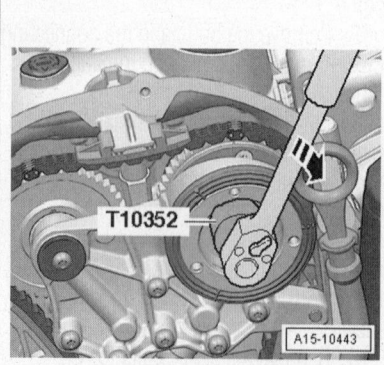

Fig. 67 Remove the control valve, noting the left-hand thread, using a proper socket (T10352 or T10352/1).

wrench tight until the tensioning rail is installed.

9. Check the crankshaft TDC position.

10. Mount the timing chain on the exhaust camshaft.

11. Mount the timing chain on the crankshaft.

12. Turn the intake camshaft using the wrench in the direction of the arrow and mount the timing chain.

13. Install the timing chain tensioning rail and tighten the bolt.

14. Install the camshaft timing chain guide rail and tighten the bolts.

15. Mount the bearing bracket and the bolts hand-tight.

16. Remove the T40011.

17. Tighten the bearing bracket bolts.

18. Install the control valve.

19. Further installation is performed in reverse order of removal, noting the following:
   a. Install the lower timing chain cover.
   b. Install the timing chain guard upper section.
   c. Install the ribbed belt tensioning damper.
   d. Install the ribbed belt (drive belt).
   e. Adjust the subframe mount.

TURBOCHARGER

REMOVAL & INSTALLATION

See Figures 69 through 71.

➡**If mechanical damage is found on exhaust turbocharger, for example a destroyed compression wheel, it is not enough to just replace the turbocharger. Perform the following steps to prevent subsequent damage.**

   - Check the air filter housing, the air filter insert and the intake hoses for contamination.
   - Check entire charge air circuit and cooler for contamination.
   - If contaminants are found in charge air circuit, circuit must be cleaned and cooler replaced if necessary.

1. Remove the undercar and the right engine/fenderwell noise insulations. Remove the frame for the noise insulation.

2. Drain the coolant.

3. Remove front exhaust pipe with catalytic converter.

4. Remove the bolts, lift the clamps and remove the air guide pipe from across the lower front of the engine.

5. Disconnect electrical connectors and free up electrical wire.

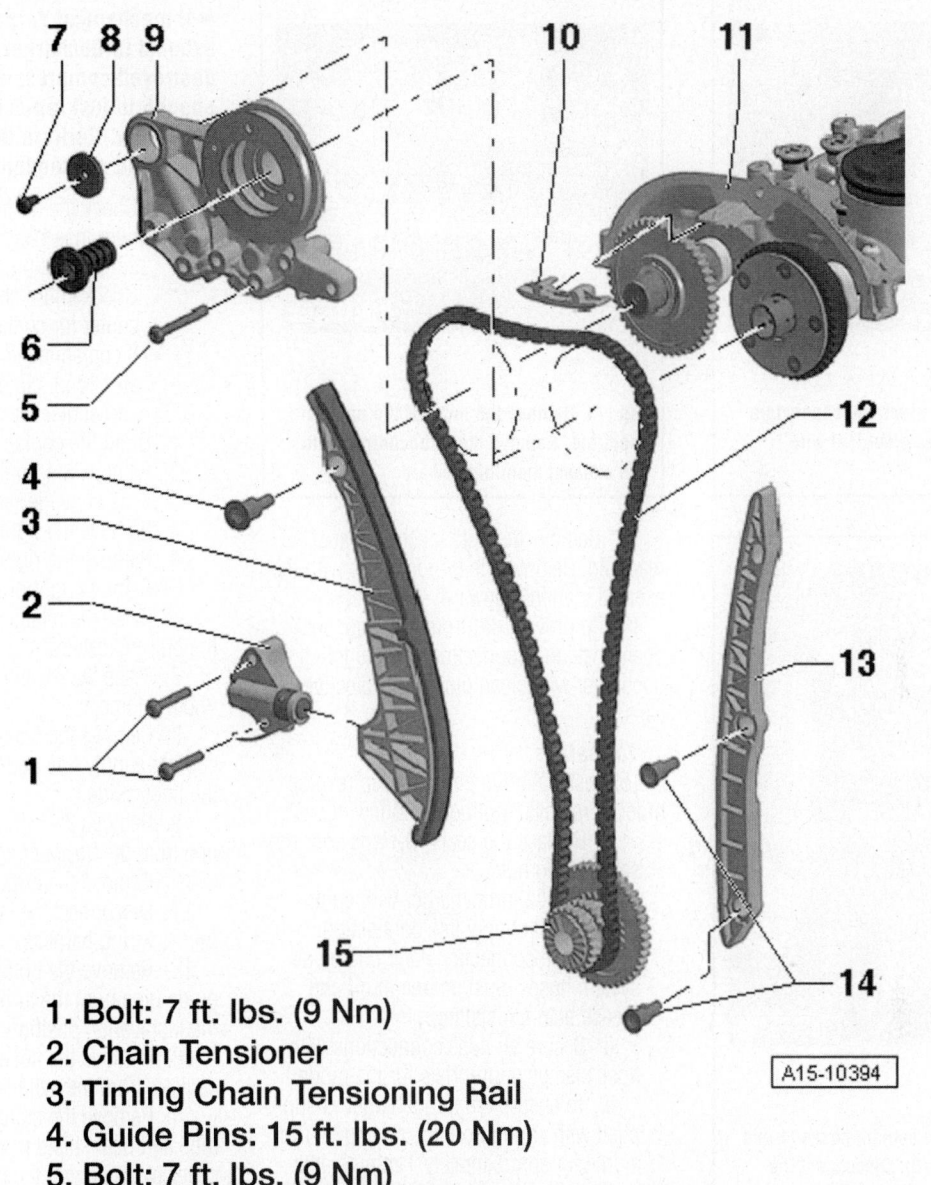

A15-10394

1. Bolt: 7 ft. lbs. (9 Nm)
2. Chain Tensioner
3. Timing Chain Tensioning Rail
4. Guide Pins: 15 ft. lbs. (20 Nm)
5. Bolt: 7 ft. lbs. (9 Nm)
6. Left thread: 26 ft. lbs. (35 Nm)
7. Bolt (replace):
a. M6: 5 ft. lbs. (8 Nm) plus an additional 90 degrees
b. M8: 15 ft. lbs. (20 Nm) plus an additional 90 degrees
8. Washer
9. Bearing Bracket
10. Camshaft Timing Chain Guide Rail
11. Camshaft Housing
12. Camshaft Timing Chain
13. Camshaft Timing Chain Guide Rail
14. Guide Pins: 15 ft. lbs. (20 Nm)
15. Chain Sprocket

Fig. 68 Exploded view of the timing chain and components

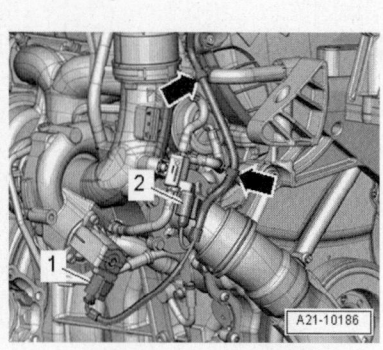

Fig. 69 Disconnect electrical connectors (1 and 2) and free up electrical wire (arrows).

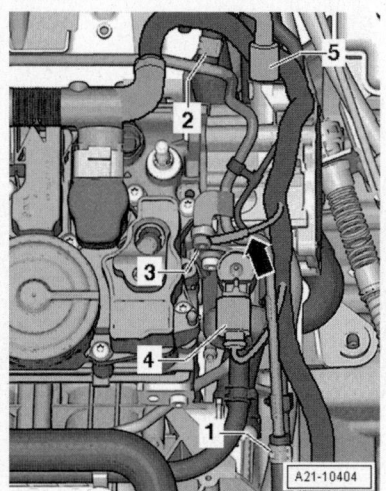

Fig. 70 Remove the coolant hoses (1 and 2) and coolant line (3). Disconnect the coolant hose and move it to the side (ignore item 4).

6. Remove the bolts and remove the turbocharger support.

7. Remove the banjo bolt and move the turbocharger coolant line to the side.

8. Remove the bolts attaching the oil return line to the turbocharger.

9. Remove the engine cover.

10. Remove the air guide pipe bolt, then remove the air guide pipe; to do this, loosen the hose clamp. Press the release buttons and remove the air guide hose.

11. Remove the coolant hoses and coolant line. Disconnect the coolant hose and move it to the side.

12. Remove the heat shield above the turbocharger. Disconnect the oil supply line from the turbocharger.

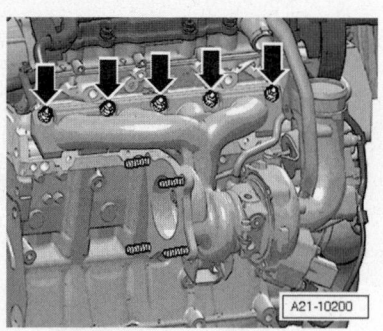

Fig. 71 Remove the nuts for the exhaust manifold. Remove the turbocharger with the exhaust manifold upward.

13. Remove the nuts for the exhaust manifold. Remove the turbocharger with the exhaust manifold upward.

14. To prevent dirt from entering, seal open lines and connections on the turbocharger with clean plugs or protective caps.

To install:

15. Installation is performed in reverse order of removal, noting the following:

a. Replace the seals, O-rings and the self-locking nuts.

b. Fill the turbocharger with engine oil at the oil supply line connection.

c. Hose connections and charge air system hoses must be free of oil and grease before installing.

d. Secure all hose connections with hose clamps appropriate for the model.

e. To ensure the turbocharger is supplied with enough oil, let the engine run at idle for approximately 1 minute after installing the turbocharger. Do not increase the engine speed during this time.

16. Install the turbocharger and exhaust manifold; use an alternating tightening sequence as follows:

a. Step 1: Tighten the bolts to 3 ft. lbs. (5 Nm).

b. Step 2: Tighten the bolts to 9 ft. lbs. (12 Nm).

c. Step 3: Tighten the bolts to 12 ft. lbs. (16 Nm).

d. Step 4: Tighten the bolts to 18 ft. lbs. (25 Nm).

17. Install the front exhaust pipe with the catalytic converter and front muffler.

18. Install exhaust system free of stress.

19. Air guides, installing with connector.

20. Fill with coolant.

21. Check oil level.

3.2L Engine

➡ If mechanical damage is found on exhaust turbocharger, for example a destroyed compression wheel, it is not enough to just replace the turbocharger. Perform the following steps to prevent subsequent damage.

- Check the air filter housing, the air filter insert and the intake hoses for contamination.
- Check entire charge air circuit and cooler for contamination.
- If contaminants are found in charge air circuit, circuit must be cleaned and cooler replaced if necessary.

1. Drain the coolant.

2. Remove the front exhaust pipe with the catalytic converter and front muffler.

3. Remove the right front wheel.

4. Remove the right noise insulation

5. Remove right drive axle heat shield.

6. Raise the retaining clip and remove the bolt indicated.

7. Place the engine support (VAS 6208) under engine.

8. Remove the banjo bolt for the coolant supply line and oil supply line. Lay the lines aside.

9. Remove the bolts and the oil supply line from the turbocharger.

10. Remove the turbocharger support.

11. Disconnect the connector and free up the wiring harness.

12. Remove the bolts and remove the air guide pipe from the turbocharger leave it in the installation position.

13. Remove the hose from the EVAP canister from the cylinder head cover.

14. Remove the crankcase ventilation tube and heat shield from the cylinder head cover by loosening the hose clamp.

15. Disconnect the connectors from the ignition coils.

16. Move the electrical wiring harness to the left.

17. Disconnect the coolant hose from the coolant reservoir.

18. Remove the coolant hoses. Remove the bolt and the coolant ventilation line.

19. Remove the coolant hose.

20. Remove the nuts and remove the turbocharger with the exhaust manifold upward.

➡ To prevent dirt from entering, seal open lines and connections on the turbocharger with clean plugs or protective caps.

To install:

21. Installation is done is reverse order, observe the following:

a. Replace the seals, O-rings and the self-locking nuts.

b. Fill the turbocharger with engine oil at the oil supply line connection.

c. The hose supports, air guide pipes and hoses must be free of oil and grease before installing.

d. Secure all hose connections with hose clamps appropriate for the model.

e. To ensure the turbocharger is supplied with enough oil, let the engine run at idle for approximately 1 minute after installing the turbocharger. Do not increase the engine speed during this time.

22. Install the turbocharger and exhaust manifold; use an alternating tightening sequence as follows:

a. Step 1: Tighten the bolts to 3 ft. lbs. (5 Nm).

b. Step 2: Tighten the bolts to 9 ft. lbs. (12 Nm).

c. Step 3: Tighten the bolts to 12 ft. lbs. (16 Nm).

d. Step 4: Tighten the bolts to 18 ft. lbs. (25 Nm).

23. Install the coolant ventilation line.

24. Install the air guide pipes and hoses with connector couplings.

25. Install the front exhaust pipe with the catalytic converter and front muffler.

26. Check engine oil level.

27. Install the noise insulation.

28. Fill with coolant.

ENGINE PERFORMANCE & EMISSION CONTROLS

CAMSHAFT ADJUSTMENT VALVE

REMOVAL & INSTALLATION

2.0L Engine

See Figure 72.

1. Remove the engine cover
2. Disconnect the connector
3. Remove the wiring harness bracket
4. Remove the camshaft adjustment valve bolt.

✳✳ CAUTION

Do not pull out camshaft adjustment valve with the connector.

5. Remove the bolts and camshaft adjustment valve from the drive chain housing.

To install:

6. Clean the camshaft adjustment valve and the drive chain housing.

➡**Protect the camshaft adjustment valve from shocks and impact stress.**

7. Coal the sealing ring with engine oil.

8. Carefully install the camshaft adjustment valve into the drive chain housing and push it all the way by hand horizontally to the valve axle.

9. The rest of the installation is performed in reverse order of removal.

3.2L Engine

See Figure 73.

1. Disconnect the connector from the camshaft adjustment valve.

2. Remove the bolts and then the camshaft adjustment valve.

To install:

3. Installation is performed in reverse order of removal, noting the following:

a. Replace O-ring.

b. Coat the seal and the O-ring with engine oil.

ELECTRONIC CONTROL MODULE (ECM)

REMOVAL & INSTALLATION
See Figures 74 and 75.

1. Turn ignition and remove ignition key.

2. Pry off caps on wiper arms using a screwdriver.

3. Loosen nuts by several turns.

4. Loosen wiper arms from the wiper axle by tilting slightly.

5. Then, remove nuts completely and remove wiper arms from wiper axles.

6. If wiper arm cannot be removed in this way, use a standard puller.

7. Remove rubber seal and remove plenum chamber cover.

8. Open clamp and remove engine control module.

9. Cover painted surfaces with a cloth to protect against scratches.

10. To increase difficulty with which the ECM connectors can be accessed, the ECM is secured in a metal housing with retaining tabs and shear bolts.

11. The threads of the shear bolts (that are not installed in ECM) are coated with a locking compound. For this reason, the threads must be heated with the heat gun to remove both bolts.

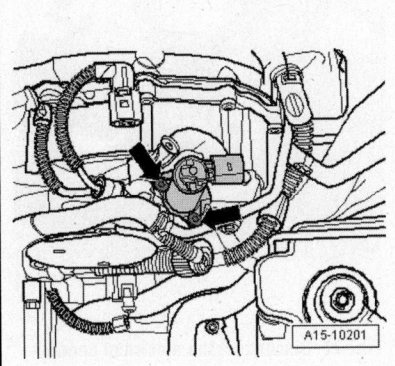

Fig. 72 Remove the bolts (arrows) and camshaft adjustment valve (1) from the drive chain housing.

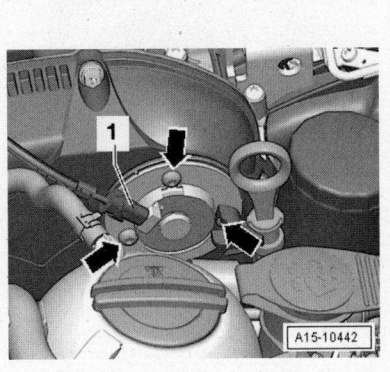

Fig. 73 Disconnect the connector from the camshaft adjustment valve (1).

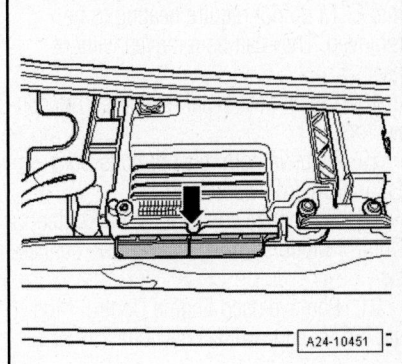

Fig. 74 Open clamp and remove engine control module

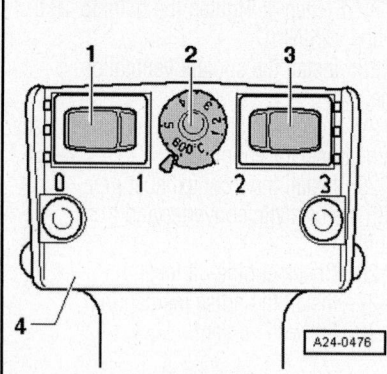

Fig. 75 Temperature potentiometer (2) set to maximum heat and the two-stage air flow switch (3) set to level 3

12. The threads of both shear bolts (that are installed in ECM) are not coated with a locking compound. The threads in the ECM housing must not be heated and do not require to be heated (unintentional heating of the ECM).

13. Set adjustment on the heat gun, with the temperature potentiometer set to maximum heat and the two-stage air flow switch set to level 3.

➡**By heating the threads, the retaining tabs, shear bolts and parts of the metal housing become very hot. Do not burn yourself on this! Make sure that only the threads are heated as much as possible, and not any of the surrounding parts. Possibly cover these parts.**

14. Warm threads on connector side of shear bolts.

15. Switch on heat gun and heat bolt for approximately 20 to 30 seconds.

16. Remove shear bolts with suitable locking pliers.

17. Both shear bolts that are screwed into ECM do not require heating to be removed. They can be removed without heat.

18. Disconnect metal retainers from connectors.

19. Remove both retainer bolts from Engine Control Module (ECM).

20. Disengage connector from Engine Control Module (ECM) and remove connector.

21. Remove used Engine Control Module (ECM) and connect new one.

To install:

22. Installation is in reverse order.

23. After that, the Engine Control Module (ECM) must be equipped with the metal retainer.

24. Clean threaded holes for shear bolts of locking compound residue. Cleaning can be performed with a thread cutter (tap).

25. Always use new shear bolts.

26. Activate engine control module in "Guided Functions" operating mode under "Replace engine control module" on the vehicle diagnosis and service system VAS 5051B.

ENGINE COOLANT TEMPERATURE (ECT) SENSOR

REMOVAL & INSTALLATION

2.0L Engine

See Figure 76.

➡**Engine cold.**

1. Remove the engine cover.

2. Disconnect the connector 1 from the Engine Coolant Temperature (ECT) Sensor.

➡**Lay a cloth below to catch escaping coolant.**

3. Remove the retaining clip and the engine coolant temperature sensor.

To install:

4. Installation is done is reverse order, observe the following:

    a. Replace O-ring.

    b. To prevent coolant loss, immediately insert new engine coolant temperature sensor in support.

    c. Check the coolant level

3.2L Engines

See Figure 77.

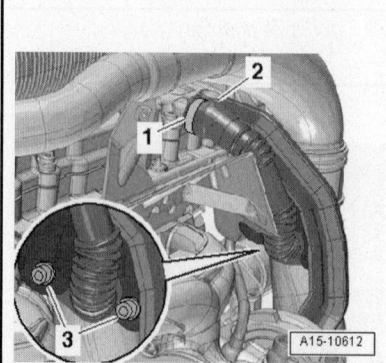

Fig. 76 Disconnect the connector 1 from the Engine Coolant Temperature (ECT) Sensor (ignore item 2). Remove the retaining clip and the engine coolant temperature sensor.

1. Remove the two front bolts and air intake guide.

2. Remove both the lower air guide and the air guide hose.

3. Remove the air guide hose from the side of the engine.

4. Disconnect electrical connector from throttle valve control module on the throttle body. Remove the bolts and remove the throttle valve control module.

5. Remove the intake manifold support.

6. Disconnect the electrical connector on the engine coolant temperature (ECT) sensor. Lay a cloth below to catch escaping coolant. Remove the clamp, then remove the engine coolant temperature (ECT) sensor.

To install:

7. Installation is performed in reverse order of removal, noting the following:

    a. Replace O-ring.

    b. To prevent coolant loss, immediately insert a new engine coolant temperature (ECT) sensor in the connecting pieces.

    c. Check the coolant level

ENGINE SPEED SENSOR

REMOVAL & INSTALLATION

See Figure 78.

1. Remove engine cover.

2. Remove the cover for the air guide, then remove the air guide pipe (air guide does not have to be removed).

3. Remove the side air guide pipe hose clamp. Disconnect electrical harness connector from the air guide pipe.

Fig. 77 Disconnect the electrical connector (1) on the engine coolant temperature (ECT) sensor. Lay a cloth below to catch escaping coolant. Remove the clamp, then remove the engine coolant temperature (ECT) sensor (2).

Fig. 78 Disconnect electrical connector (1) on engine speed sensor. Remove the engine speed sensor.

4. Remove the undercar noise insulation.

5. Remove the bolts and remove the air guide hose downward from the throttle valve control module.

6. Remove the air guide hose from the charge air cooler and remove the air guide pipe downward.

7. Disconnect electrical connector on engine speed sensor. Remove the engine speed sensor.

8. Installation is in reverse order of removal

EVAPORATIVE EMISSIONS (EVAP) CANISTER

REMOVAL & INSTALLATION

See Figure 79.

1. Remove the rear part of the exhaust system.

2. Remove the rear muffler heat shield.

3. Disconnect the vent and connecting lines by pressing the release buttons.

4. Remove the bolts, then release the retaining tabs with a screwdriver and remove the EVAP canister.

To install:

5. Installation is performed in the reverse order of removal, noting the following:

    a. Press on the vent and connecting lines until they engage audibly.

    b. Install the rear muffler heat shield.

    c. Install the exhaust system

FUEL PRESSURE SENSOR

REMOVAL & INSTALLATION

See Figure 80.

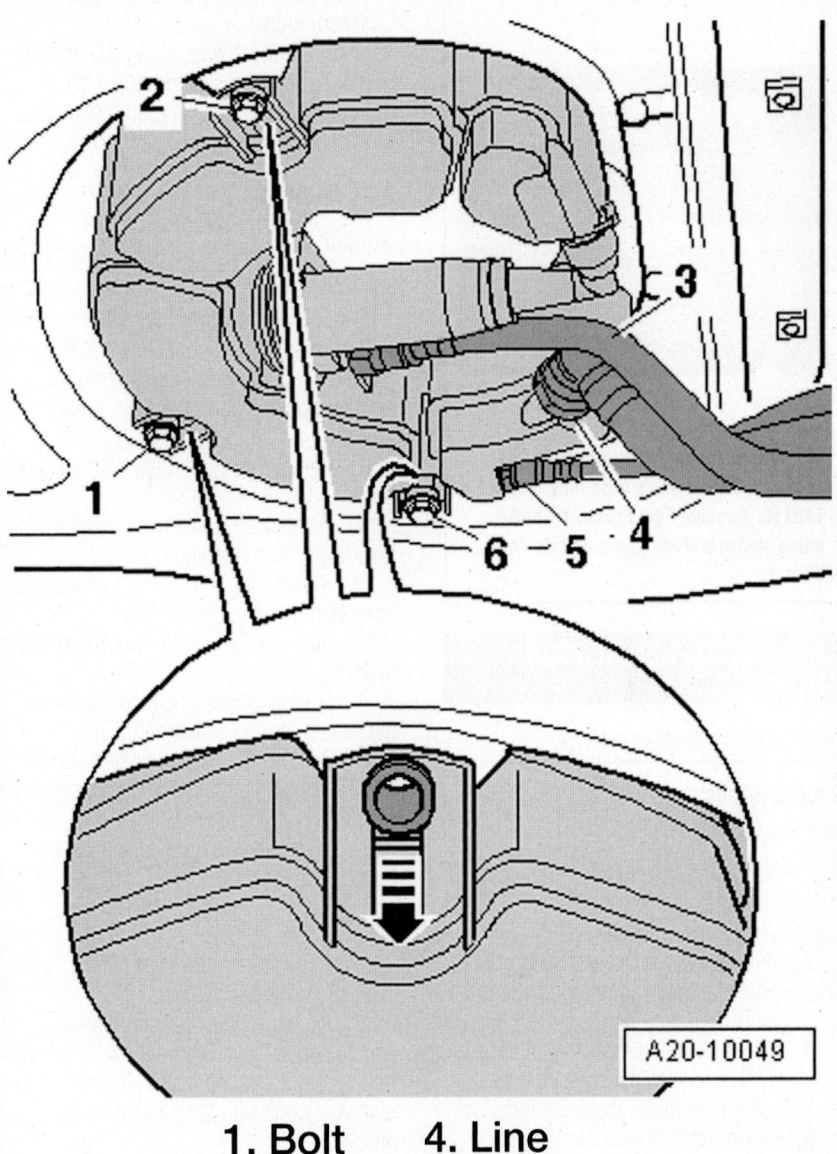

1. Bolt	4. Line
2. Bolt	5. Line
3. Line	6. Bolt

Fig. 79 Disconnect the vent and connecting lines by pressing the release buttons. Remove the bolts, then release the retaining tabs with a screwdriver and remove the EVAP canister.

➡**Fuel system is under pressure! Fuel pressure must be reduced to a residual pressure before opening high pressure area of injection system.**

1. For 2.0L engines, disconnect coolant pipe and oil dipstick guide from intake manifold and pull off oil dipstick guide upward from engine.

2. For 3.2L engines, remove the upper engine cover, the loosen the coolant pipe from the intake manifold.

3. Disengage connector from Fuel Pressure Sensor using assembly tool T10118.

4. Remove Fuel Pressure Sensor using socket wrench insert 27 mm VAS 5301/7.

To install:

5. Installation is in reverse order of removal.

6. Tighten connection to 20 ft. lbs. (30 Nm) on fuel line before installing Fuel Pressure Sensor.

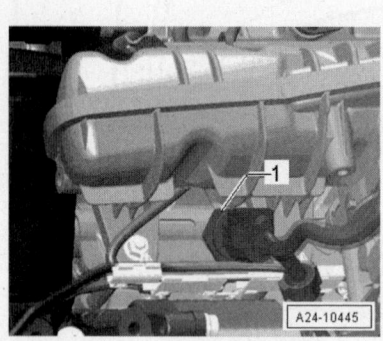

Fig. 80 Disengage connector from Fuel Pressure Sensor using assembly tool T10118. Remove Fuel Pressure Sensor using socket wrench insert 27 mm VAS 5301/7.

HEATED OXYGEN SENSOR (HO2S)

REMOVAL & INSTALLATION

2.0L Engines

See Figure 81.

1. Disconnect the electrical harness connector of Heated Oxygen Sensor (HO2S) and Oxygen Sensor (O2S) heater.
2. Remove Heated Oxygen Sensor (HO2S) using a tool from the ring spanner 7 piece set (3337).
3. When installing, note the following:
    a. New oxygen sensors are coated with assembly paste; the paste must not get into slots of oxygen sensor body.
    b. For a used oxygen sensor, only coat threads with hot bolt paste. This paste must not come into contact with sensor slots.
    c. Electrical wire of oxygen sensor must always be secured in the same position when installing so that contact with the exhaust pipe is avoided.

3.2L Engines

Sensor 1

See Figure 82.

1. Pull rear engine cover off.
2. Free up fuel supply line and hose connection to the EVAP canister on the air filter housing and on the air guide tube.
3. Remove vacuum hose from air guide hose.
4. Remove air guide hose by loosening hose clamp and opening clips.
5. Remove air guide hose by loosening hose clamp and opening clips.
6. Remove lower section of the air filter housing.
7. Disconnect electrical connector for the heated oxygen sensor (HO2S) 1.
8. Remove the heated oxygen sensor (HO2S) 1 using a tool from the ring spanner set (3337).
9. Installation is in reverse order of removal.

Sensor 2

1. Pull rear engine cover off.
2. Remove coolant reservoir.
3. Disconnect electrical connector to engine coolant level warning switch on the bottom of the coolant reservoir and lay the reservoir aside with the coolant hoses attached.
4. Disconnect the electrical connector for heated oxygen sensor (HO2S) 2.
5. Remove heated oxygen sensor (HO2S) 2 (1) using a tool from ring spanner set (3337).
6. Installation is in reverse order of removal.

KNOCK SENSOR (KS)

REMOVAL & INSTALLATION

See Figure 83.

1. Remove electrical connector from knock sensor.
2. Remove coolant pump with coolant thermostat.
3. Remove knock sensor.
4. Installation is in reverse order.

MASS AIR FLOW (MAF) SENSOR

REMOVAL & INSTALLATION

See Figure 84.

1. On 2.0L engines, do the following:
    a. Separate the electrical connector for mass air flow (MAF) sensor from the air intake duct.
    b. Remove air guide hose by opening the hose clamp.
    c. Remove bolts and remove the top of the air cleaner housing, and carefully pull Mass Air Flow (MAF) Sensor out of guide at upper section of air filter housing.
2. On 3.2L engine, remove the electrical connector, remove the mounting bolts and remove the Mass Air Flow (MAF) Sensor from the air intake duct.

To install:

3. Installation is in reverse order of removal, note the following:

Fig. 81 Disconnect electrical harness connector (1) of Heated Oxygen Sensor (HO2S) and Oxygen Sensor (O2S) heater

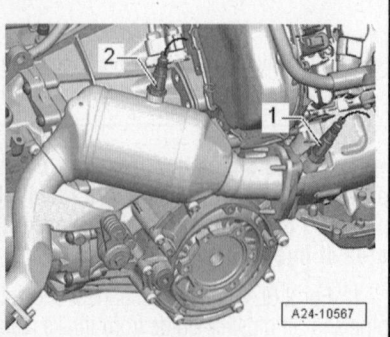

Fig. 82 Remove the heated oxygen sensor (HO2S) 1 (1)

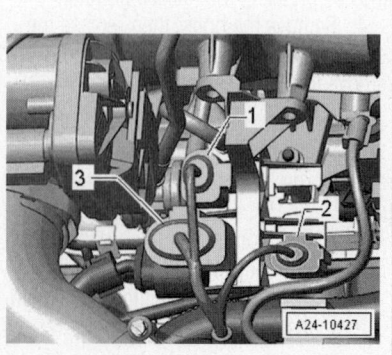

Fig. 83 Electrical connector (2), knock sensor (1)

Fig. 84 On 3.2L engine, remove the electrical connector, remove the mounting bolts and remove the Mass Air Flow (MAF) Sensor from the air intake duct.

a. For trouble-free function of the Mass Air Flow sensor, it is important to observe the following notes and perform the work procedures exactly.

b. Replace O-ring.

c. In the event the air filter element is severely contaminated or completely saturated, dirt particles or moisture may penetrate the MAF sensor and falsify the measured air mass value. This results in a reduction of power, since a lower injection quantity is calculated.

d. Always use an original equipment air filter element.

e. Use a silicon-free lubricant to install the air duct hose.

f. Secure all hose connections with hose clamps appropriate for the model.

FUEL   **GASOLINE FUEL INJECTION SYSTEM**

FUEL SYSTEM SERVICE PRECAUTIONS

Safety is the most important factor when performing not only fuel system maintenance but any type of maintenance. Failure to conduct maintenance and repairs in a safe manner may result in serious personal injury or death. Maintenance and testing of the vehicle's fuel system components can be accomplished safely and effectively by adhering to the following rules and guidelines.

• To avoid the possibility of fire and personal injury, always disconnect the negative battery cable unless the repair or test procedure requires that battery voltage be applied.

• Always relieve the fuel system pressure prior to disconnecting any fuel system component (injector, fuel rail, pressure regulator, etc.), fitting or fuel line connection. Exercise extreme caution whenever relieving fuel system pressure to avoid exposing skin, face and eyes to fuel spray. Please be advised that fuel under pressure may penetrate the skin or any part of the body that it contacts.

• Always place a shop towel or cloth around the fitting or connection prior to loosening to absorb any excess fuel due to spillage. Ensure that all fuel spillage (should it occur) is quickly removed from engine surfaces. Ensure that all fuel soaked cloths or towels are deposited into a suitable waste container.

• Always keep a dry chemical (Class B) fire extinguisher near the work area.

• Do not allow fuel spray or fuel vapors to come into contact with a spark or open flame.

• Always use a back-up wrench when loosening and tightening fuel line connection fittings. This will prevent unnecessary stress and torsion to fuel line piping.

• Always replace worn fuel fitting O-rings with new Do not substitute fuel hose or equivalent where fuel pipe is installed.

Before servicing the vehicle, make sure to also refer to the precautions in the beginning of this section as well.

RELIEVING FUEL SYSTEM PRESSURE

✴✴ CAUTION

The fuel injection system is divided into a high pressure section (maximum approximately 150 bar) and a low pressure system (approximately 7 bar). Before opening high pressure parts; e.g. removing high pressure pump, fuel rail, fuel injectors, fuel pipes or Fuel Pressure Sensor, fuel pressure in high pressure area must be reduced to a residual pressure of approximately 7 bar. The procedure for this is as follows.

1. Connect Vehicle Diagnosis system, VAS 5051B.
2. Start engine and run at idle speed.

3. Select "engine electronics" in OBD.
4. Then select "Measured Values" read out.
5. Select measured value block 140.
6. With the engine running at idle, the fuel pressure will be displayed in display field. Specified value should be between 653–798 psi (45–55 bar).

➡**The fuse is located in the fuse holder in the right of the luggage compartment.**

7. With the engine running at idle, pull out SF 6 fuse from the fuel pump control module.

➡**By removing fuse SF 6, the voltage supply to terminal 30 for the Fuel Pump (FP) Control Module is interrupted.**

8. Check the fuel pressure on the tester.

➡**The fuel pressure decreases rapidly because the mechanical high pressure pump is no longer supplied with fuel from the transfer fuel pump.**

9. Switch ignition off as soon as the fuel pressure drops to approximately 116 psi (8 bar).

✴✴ CAUTION

The fuel pressure must not drop below 87 psi (6 bar), because otherwise the engine will shut off (risk of catalytic converter damage).

10. After reducing fuel pressure, place a clean cloth around the connection and open

the high pressure system immediately. Escaping fuel must be absorbed.

11. Perform the following steps before completing all work:

   a. Install fuse.

   b. Erase the DTC memory and, using "Guided Fault Finding", generate the readiness code in the engine control module Vehicle Diagnosis and Service System VAS 5052 A.

FUEL FILTER

REMOVAL & INSTALLATION

See Figure 85.

✳✳ CAUTION

Observe all applicable safety precautions when working around fuel. Whenever servicing the fuel system, always work in a well ventilated area. Do not allow fuel spray or vapors to come in contact with a spark or open flame. Keep a dry chemical fire extinguisher near the work area. Always keep fuel in a container specifically designed for fuel storage; also, always properly seal fuel containers to avoid the possibility of fire or explosion.

➡ **Before opening the fuel system, lay a clean cloth around the connection point and carefully loosen it, which lowers the pressure.**

1. Properly relieve the fuel system pressure.

2. Place drip tray under fuel filter.

3. Disconnect fuel lines 1, 2 and 3 by pressing release buttons.

4. Remove bolt.

5. Remove fuel filter.

6. Installation is in reverse order of removal, note the following:

   a. The direction of flow is marked on filter housing with arrows.

   b. The pin on filter housing must engage in recess of the guide on filter bracket.

FUEL INJECTORS

REMOVAL & INSTALLATION

✳✳ CAUTION

Observe all applicable safety precautions when working around fuel. Whenever servicing the fuel system, always work in a well ventilated area. Do not allow fuel spray or vapors to come in contact with a

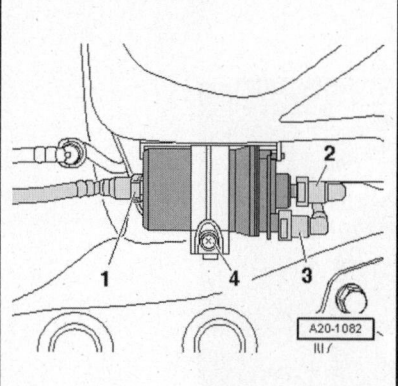

Fig. 85 Disconnect fuel lines (1, 2 and 3) by pressing release buttons and remove bolt (4)

spark or open flame. Keep a dry chemical fire extinguisher near the work area. Always keep fuel in a container specifically designed for fuel storage; also, always properly seal fuel containers to avoid the possibility of fire or explosion.**

1. Before servicing the vehicle, refer to the precautions section.

2. Properly relieve the fuel system pressure.

3. Remove the intake manifold and fuel rail.

4. Carefully pull fuel injectors out of fuel rail.

➡**With fuel injector installed, the radial adjustment is clipped into the support ring. To remove the fuel injector, the support ring must be separated from the fuel injector in order to install the puller T10133/2 into the indentation on the fuel injector.**

5. Cover open intake channels with a clean rag.

6. Disconnect the electrical harness connector at fuel injector that is to be removed.

7. Using a screwdriver, bend the retaining tabs of the radial adjustment aside and pull support ring off from fuel injector.

8. Screw together slide hammer T10133/3 with puller T10133/2. Then, guide puller T10133/2 into the groove on the fuel injector and carefully drive the fuel injector out. By doing this, it is possible that the radial adjustment will be damaged by breaking the retaining tabs. These must be replaced when re-installing the fuel injector.

➡**The combustion chamber seal must always be replaced before re-installing the high-pressure fuel injector.**

9. Clean off the old Teflon seal, make sure not to damage the groove and rib in groove base.

➡**If the groove is damaged, the fuel injector must be replaced.**

To install:

10. Before installing new Teflon seal, the seal groove and shaft of the fuel injector must be clean.

11. Place assembly cone T10133/5 with new Teflon seal onto fuel injector.

12. Using the assembly sleeve T10133/6, push Teflon seal further onto assembly cone T10133/5 until the Teflon seal is engaged in seal groove. Do not use any lubricants.

13. By pushing the Teflon seal onto the fuel injector, the Teflon seal is expanded. For this reason, the Teflon seal must be contracted again, once it has been pushed on as follows:

   a. Using calibration sleeve T10133/7, a 180 degree rotating motion and light pressure, push calibration sleeve T10133/7 over the fuel injector up to stop. Pull calibration sleeve T10133/7 off again, rotating it in the opposite direction.

   b. Using calibration sleeve T10133/8, 180 degree rotating motion and light pressure, push calibration sleeve T10133/8 over the fuel injector up to stop. Pull calibration sleeve T10133/8 off again, rotating it in the opposite direction.

14. Replace O-ring on the fuel injector and on spacer sleeve. Moisten O-ring with clean engine oil before installing.

➡**The Teflon seal must not get oil on it.**

15. Clean the bores for the high-pressure fuel injectors in the cylinder head before installing the fuel injectors.

➡**An open intake valve could possibly hinder the cleaning process. In this case, turn the engine further by hand using a socket wrench at the crankshaft.**

16. Equip the fuel injector again with support ring and clip the radial adjustment in at the support ring.

17. Using the assembly drift T10133/9, press the fuel injector into its bore in the cylinder head until it stops. Make sure fuel injectors are correctly positioned in cylinder head.

18. Install the remaining components in the reverse order of removal.

FUEL PUMP

REMOVAL & INSTALLATION

See Figures 86 and 87.

✷✷ CAUTION

Observe all applicable safety precautions when working around fuel. Whenever servicing the fuel system, always work in a well ventilated area. Do not allow fuel spray or vapors to come in contact with a spark or open flame. Keep a dry chemical fire extinguisher near the work area. Always keep fuel in a container specifically designed for fuel storage; also, always properly seal fuel containers to avoid the possibility of fire or explosion.

➡ **To prevent large quantities of fuel from leaking from the fuel delivery unit when removing, the fuel tank may only be a maximum of 1/4 full.**

1. Properly relieve the fuel system pressure.
2. Empty the fuel tank if necessary.
3. TT Roadster: Removing fuel tank with front wheel drive.
4. TT Coupe: Disconnect battery.
5. Empty fuel tank if necessary with front wheel drive.
6. Remove rear seat bench.
7. Unclip retainers of cover for sealing flange.
8. Disconnect electrical harness connector at the locking flange.
9. Mark fuel supply line and fuel return line.

➡ **To reduce pressure in fuel system, lay a clean cloth around the connector and carefully loosen connector.**

10. Pull both lines from locking flange, by pressing release buttons.
11. TT Roadster: Mark fuel supply line and fuel return line on removed fuel tank. Pull both lines from locking flange, by pressing release buttons.

➡ **To prevent large quantities of fuel from coming out of the fuel delivery unit when removing, fuel tank may only be a maximum of 3/4 full.**

12. Remove locking ring with wrench T10202.
13. Pull fuel delivery unit and seal out of opening in fuel tank.

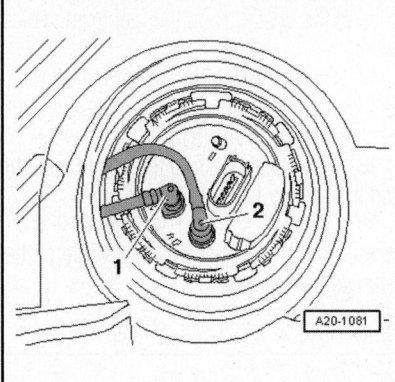

Fig. 86 Identifying the fuel supply line (1) and fuel return line (2)

14. When removing fuel delivery unit, be sure not to bend floater arm of fuel level sensor Fuel Level Sensor G.
15. Be aware that fuel is still in the fuel delivery unit.
16. Installation is in reverse order of removal, note the following:
   a. Replace seal.
   b. When inserting fuel delivery unit, be sure not to bend floater arm of fuel level sensor Fuel Level Sensor G.
17. Insert fuel delivery unit into fuel tank.
18. Install new locking flange seal dry.
19. Fill vehicle with at least 5 liters of fuel after installing fuel level sensor.
20. On vehicles with TFSI engine with toothed belt drive, a fuel pump adaptation must be performed after replacing the fuel delivery unit.

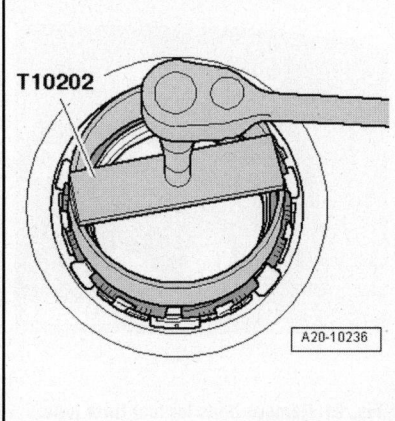

Fig. 87 Remove locking ring with wrench T10202

FUEL TANK

DRAINING

See Figures 88 through 90.

1. Open the fuel filler door.

✷✷ CAUTION

There is a danger of causing damage to electrical components when disconnecting the battery. Use caution and complete the steps for disconnecting the battery.

2. Disconnect the battery.

✷✷ WARNING

There is a risk of explosion due to electrostatic charge. Secure the fuel extracting device VAS 5190 ground wire to a bare area on the chassis.

3. Remove the cone piece 2 from the shaft piece 1 on the fuel extracting device VAS 5190.
4. Using insulating tape, apply a mark 54 in. (1370 mm) from the end of the suction hose.
5. Remove the fuel cap from the fuel filler tube.
6. Install the fuel extracting device VAS 5190 shaft piece into the fuel tank filler tube.
7. Slide the suction hose into the fuel tank until the mark applied earlier aligns with the shaft piece.
   a. If using a fuel siphoning device without the shaft piece, proceed principally in the same manner.
   b. In this case, apply a mark using insulating tape on the hose 51 in. (1305 mm) from the end of the hose. The hose is inserted correctly when

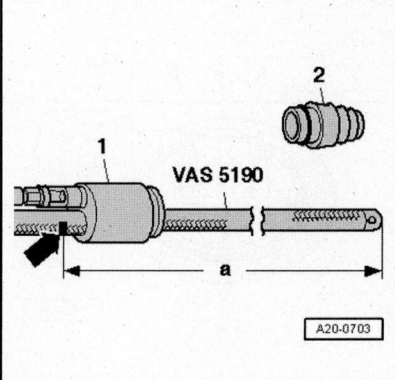

Fig. 88 Remove the cone piece 2 from the shaft piece 1 on the fuel extracting device VAS 5190.

the mark aligns with the lip of the fuel filler neck.

c. If the hose can only be inserted with difficulty, coat it lightly with engine oil. Never use lubricants containing silicon.

8. Empty the fuel tank as much as possible via the fuel filler tube.

9. Carefully pull out the hose.

10. For TT Coupe, remove the rear seat bench.

11. For TT Roadster, remove the left side rear panel trim panel.

12. Unclip the retainers for the left sealing flange cover.

13. Disconnect the electrical connector from the locking flange.

14. Disengage the electrical connector and lay it aside.

15. Remove the locking ring using the wrench T10202.

16. Carefully pull the fuel level sensor 2 and suction jet pump partially out of the fuel

tank opening. When removing, be sure not to bend the float arm on the fuel level sensor 2.

17. Extract the fuel in the left half of the fuel tank through the opening using the fuel extracting device VAS 5190.

18. Push the hose into the right chamber and extract any fuel still there.

19. Reinstall the fuel level sensor 2 and reassemble all components in reverse of the removal procedure.

REMOVAL & INSTALLATION

See Figures 91 through 93.

1. Release fuel tank flap.
2. Disconnect battery.
3. Drain the fuel tank.
4. TT Coupe: Remove rear seat bench.
5. TT Roadster: Remove right rear panel side trim.
6. Unclip retainers of cover for sealing flange.
7. Disconnect electrical harness connector at locking flange.
8. Clean area around fuel filler tube.
9. Remove fuel filler cap.
10. Close off opening of the fuel filler tube with a clean piece of foam to prevent dirt from falling in.
11. Remove right rear wheel housing liner.
12. Remove bolts for fuel filler tube.
13. Remove ventilation line to EVAP canister by pressing release button.
14. Remove electrical wiring for ABS speed sensor from fuel filler tube bracket.
15. Free up overflow hose on fuel filler tube.
16. Remove spreader pins.
17. Disengage stone impact protection on right of longitudinal member remove it.

18. TT Roadster: Remove bolts and remove pendulum support.
19. Disconnect vent line to EVAP canister by pressing release button.
20. Separate exhaust system at clamping sleeve.
21. Tie up front part of exhaust system with a chain. To do this, engage hooks in openings on vehicle floor (remove plugs if necessary).
22. Push clamping sleeve rearward to separate exhaust system.
23. Unhook rear muffler from retaining loops and remove rear portion of exhaust system.
24. Disconnect right front vent line on fuel tank by pressing release button.
25. Disconnect right front fuel line on fuel tank by pressing release buttons.
26. First, remove bolts, then place the Engine/Transmission Jack (V.A.G 1383 A) under fuel tank for support.
27. Remove the remaining two bolts.
28. Installation is in reverse order of removal.

IDLE SPEED

ADJUSTMENT

➡ **Idle speed cannot be adjusted, it is regulated by idle stabilization.**

THROTTLE VALVE CONTROL MODULE

REMOVAL & INSTALLATION

See Figure 94.

1. Remove engine cover.
2. Remove the noise insulation.
3. Loosen screws and clamps and remove charge air pipe and hose downward.

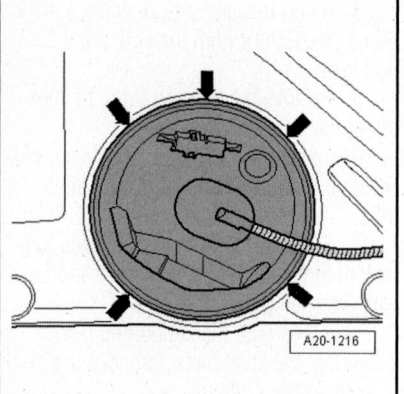

Fig. 89 Unclip the retainers (arrows) for the left sealing flange cover.

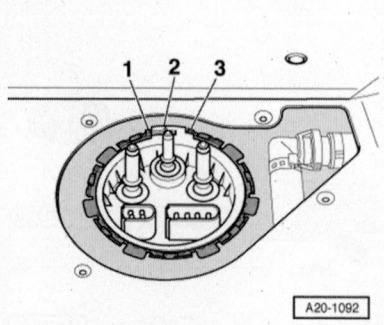

Fig. 90 Disconnect the electrical connector (1) from the locking flange. Disengage the electrical connector (2) and lay it aside.

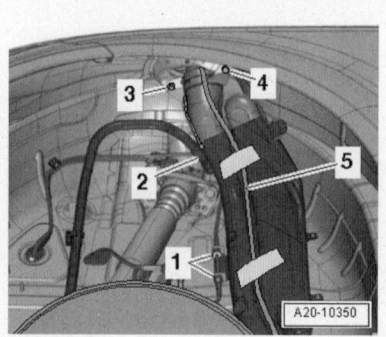

Fig. 91 Remove bolts for fuel filler tube, remove ventilation line to EVAP canister, then remove electrical wiring for ABS speed sensor from fuel filler tube bracket.

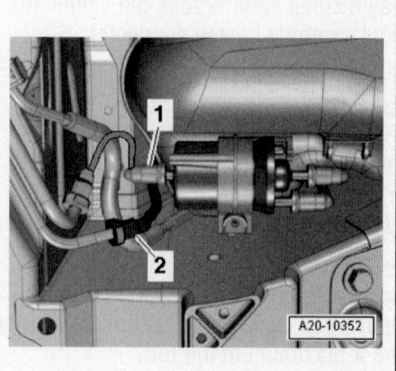

Fig. 92 Disconnect right front vent line (2) on fuel tank by pressing release button

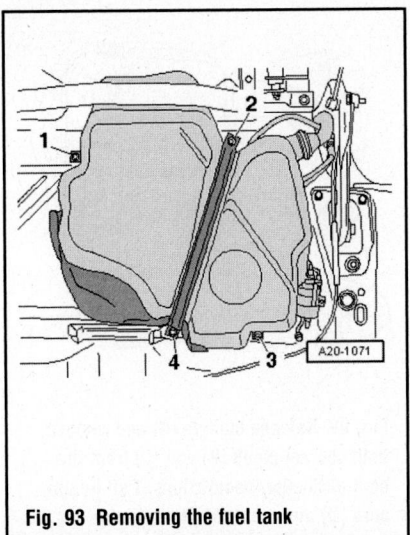

Fig. 93 Removing the fuel tank

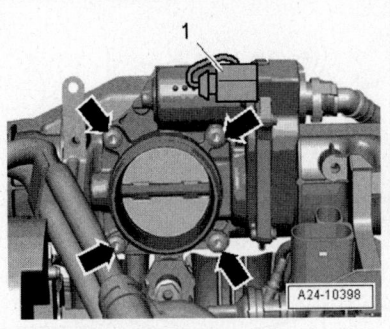

Fig. 94 Disconnect the electrical connector (1) from the throttle valve control module. Remove the four bolts on the throttle valve control module and then remove the throttle valve control module.

4. Disconnect the electrical connector 1 from the throttle valve control module.

5. Remove the four bolts on the throttle valve control module and then remove the throttle valve control module.

To install:

6. Installation is performed in reverse order.

7. Clean the sealing ring surface.

8. Replace seal.

9. The throttle valve control module must be adapted to the engine control module after it is replaced. Use a vehicle diagnosis tester for this.

HEATING & AIR CONDITIONING SYSTEM

BLOWER MOTOR

REMOVAL & INSTALLATION

See Figures 95 and 96.

1. Remove glove box.

2. Remove screw clips and remove insulating mat.

3. Disconnect connectors.

4. Remove bolt.

5. Reinstall all removed components in opposite sequence while observing the following:

   a. When installing, check Fresh Air Blower Control Module for proper seating in mount of Fresh Air Blower.

   b. After installing, check function of Fresh Air Blower Control Module and of Fresh Air Blower.

   c. Check DTC memory of Climatronic Control Module A/C control head

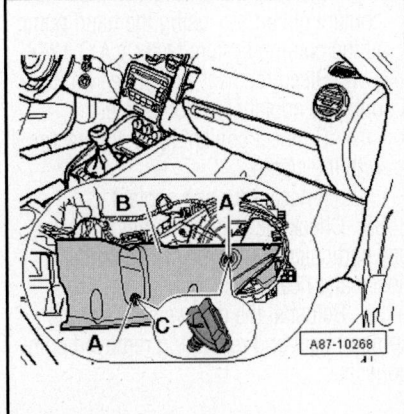

Fig. 95 Remove screw clips (A) and remove insulating mat (B).

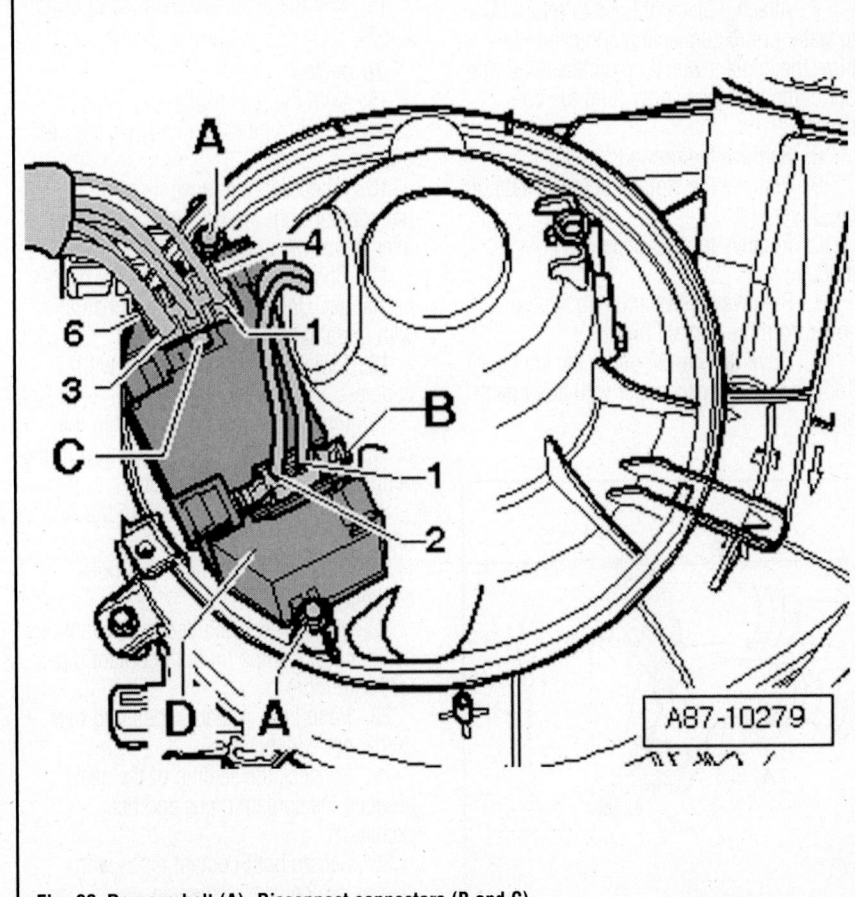

Fig. 96 Remove bolt (A). Disconnect connectors (B and C).

and erase any malfunctions displayed.

   d. Perform Basic Setting and output Diagnostic Test Mode (DTM) of A/C (heating) system and check DTC memory again.

HEATER CORE

REMOVAL & INSTALLATION

See Figures 97 through 99.

1. Remove the plenum chamber cover.

➡ **In vehicles with electrically adjustable seats, move the seats back as far as possible before disconnecting the battery.**

2. Remove the battery.

3. Dissipate pressure in coolant circuit by opening cap at coolant expansion tank.

4. Mark arrangement of coolant hoses.

- Connect the coolant hoses on the proper side:
- Coolant hose supply hose from the cylinder head.
- Coolant hose return hose to water pump.
- Bleed coolant circuit.

5. Clamp off both coolant hoses to the heat exchanger of the A/C unit and remove them.

6. Place a container under supply hose from the cylinder head connection.

7. Attach a piece of hose to return hose to water pump connection and carefully blow the coolant with a compressed air gun out of the heat exchanger (into the container).

8. Remove the firewall grommet.

9. Remove the storage compartment on the driver side.

10. Remove the gas pedal module.

11. Remove screws and remove the cover from the coolant pipes.

12. Cover the carpet under the connections to the heat exchanger with absorbent paper.

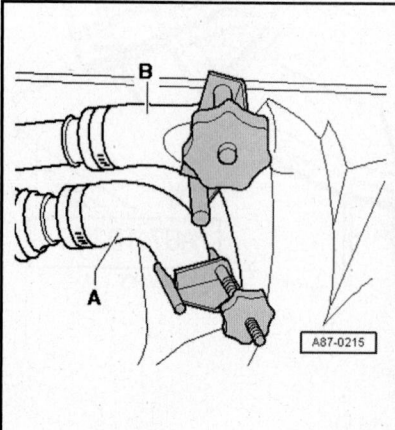

Fig. 97 Mark arrangement of coolant hoses (A and B)

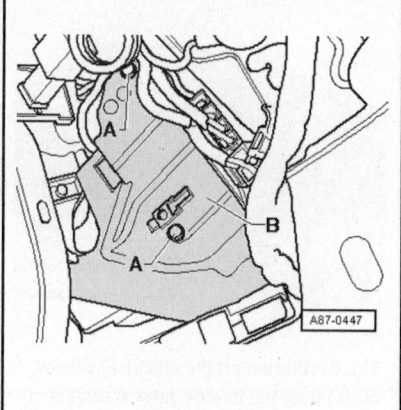

Fig. 98 Remove screws (A) and remove cover (B) from the coolant pipes

13. Release clamps and remove both coolant pipes from the heat exchanger connections.

14. Pull the heater core out of air conditioner.

To install:

15. With the heat exchanger removed, check the A/C unit for soiling (via the heat exchanger shaft).

16. If necessary remove the dirt or residual coolant from the A/C unit (for example after removing a leaky heat exchanger).

17. Check seals installed on the heat exchanger. Only install a heat exchanger with undamaged seals.

18. Moisten new seals lightly with coolant.

19. Insert new seals (included in the delivery scope of the heat exchanger) in the connections of heat exchanger.

20. Insert heat exchanger into the A/C unit.

21. Remove old clamps from both coolant pipes.

22. Install new (included in delivery of heater core) clamps on both coolant pipes for heater core.

23. Push both coolant pipes into heat exchanger connections.

24. Recheck the seating of the seals between the coolant pipes and heat exchanger.

25. Secure both coolant pipes with clamps on the heat exchanger.

26. Check the seating of both clamps. They must enclose the flange on the heat exchanger and coolant pipe completely and must not touch other components.

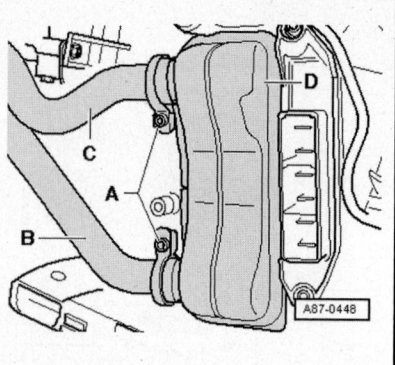

Fig. 99 Release clamps (A) and remove both coolant pipes (B) and (C) from the heat exchanger connections. Pull heater core (D) out of air conditioner

27. Tighten bolts on clamps to 2 ft. lbs. (2.5 Nm).

28. Connect coolant hoses properly to heater core. Observe markings:

    a. A - Supply hose from cylinder head.

    b. B - Return hose to water pump.

29. Reinstall the removed components in reverse order of removal except the driver side storage compartment.

30. Bleed the cooling circuit.

31. The heat exchanger must be additionally bled by the arrangement of the coolant pipes to the heat exchanger of the A/C unit. Proceed as follows:

    a. Bleed the coolant circuit.

    b. Switch the ignition off.

    c. Carefully open the coolant reservoir cap (observe safety precautions when opening the cap).

    d. Release the clamp on coolant hose.

    e. Push hose back until the bore in the hose is no longer closed by the pipe.

    f. Increase the pressure in the coolant circuit e.g. using the hand pump of the cooling system tester V.A.G 1274.

    g. Bleed the heat exchanger via hose until the coolant is bubble-free.

    h. Connect coolant hose and secure it with the clamp.

    i. If necessary add coolant.

32. Check the coolant circuit for leaks, pay particular attention between coolant hoses and heater core.

33. Reinstall the driver's side storage compartment and remaining removed components.

STEERING

POWER STEERING GEAR

REMOVAL & INSTALLATION

See Figures 100 through 108.

➡ **Special tools required:**

- Ball joint puller 3287 A
- Torque wrench V.A.G 1331
- Torque wrench V.A.G 1332
- Engine/transmission jack V.A.G 1383 A
- Locating pins T10096
- Vehicle diagnosis, testing and information system VAS 5051B

➡ **The steering gear is removed together with the subframe, stabilizer bar and transverse links.**

1. Set the wheels to the straight ahead position.

2. Disconnect the battery.

3. Remove the nuts and the steering column universal joint cover.

4. Remove the pinch bolt and remove the universal joint from the steering gear.

5. Disconnect indicated connector and electrical wires. Unclip wiring harness from wiring shaft.

6. Remove the front wheels.

7. Remove lower noise insulation.

8. Remove noise insulation frame.

9. Loosen tie rod end nut, but do not remove yet.

10. Press tie rod end off of wheel bearing housing using 3287 A.

11. Remove the four exhaust system bracket bolts.

12. Remove the nut from the stabilizer link to stabilizer bar connection.

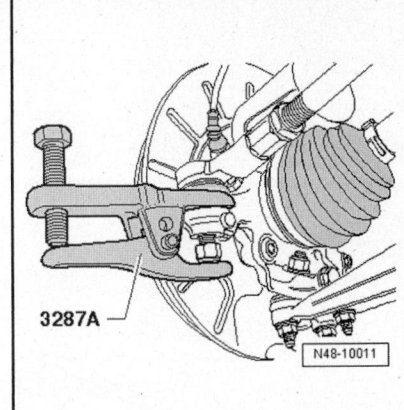

Fig. 101 Loosen tie rod end nut, but do not remove yet. Press tie rod end off of wheel bearing housing using 3287 A.

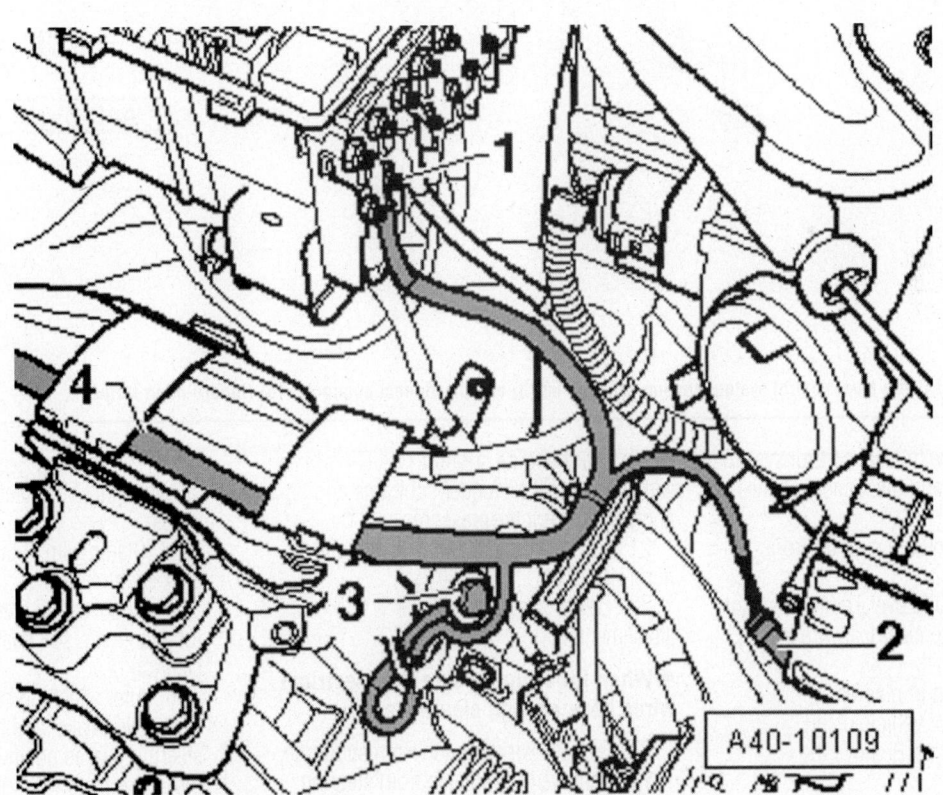

1. Wire   3. Wire
2. Connector   4. Wiring harness

Fig. 100 Disconnect the connector (2) and remove the indicated electrical wires (1 and 3). Unclip wiring harness (4) from wiring shaft.

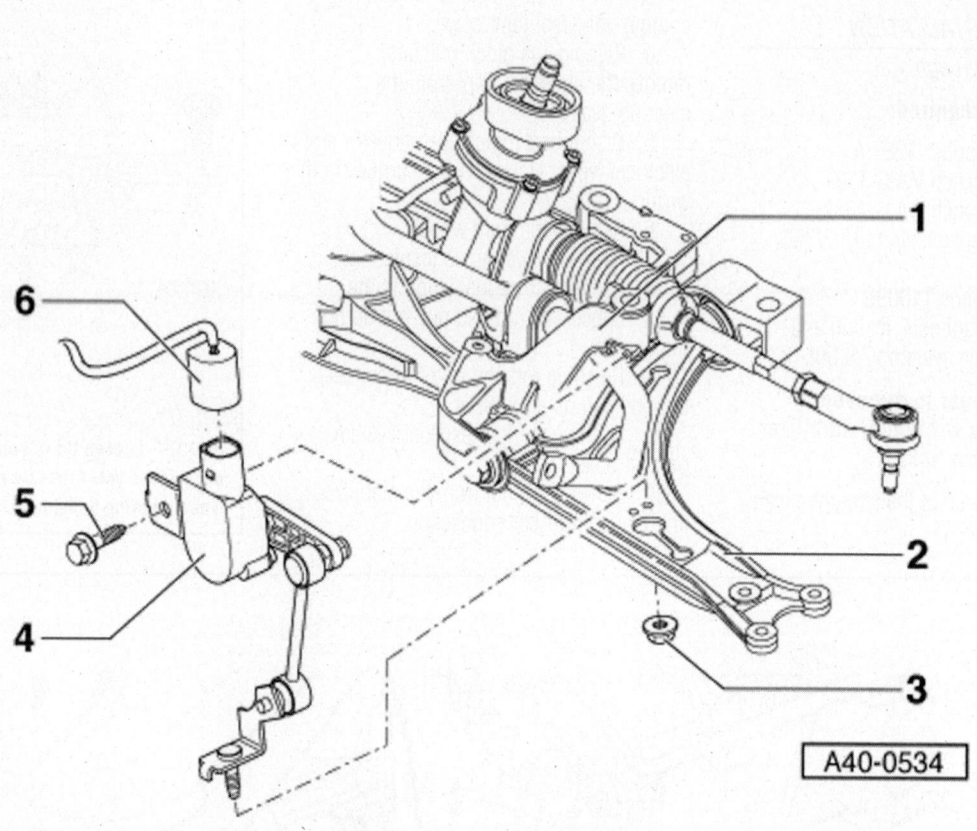

Fig. 102 On vehicles with level control system sensor, remove nut (3) and disconnect connector (6) (ignore other items)

13. On vehicles with level control system sensor, remove nut and disconnect connector, as noted.

14. Remove pendulum support from transmission.

15. Disconnect Oil Level Thermal Sensor connector and unclip electrical wire from bracket.

16. Mark location of nuts on left and right sides of vehicle using a marking pen or paint. Remove the nuts.

17. Remove transverse link from ball joint.

18. Secure the subframe to the transverse links, using T10096 bolted to items "1", "8", "9" and "16", one after the other.

19. Replace bolts with T10096 and tighten to 15 ft. lbs. (20 Nm).

20. Place engine support (V.A.G 1383 A) with wood blocks 1 under subframe and apply slight counter-pressure.

21. Remove bolts 4 and 5 (see illustration N40-10181).

22. Lower subframe with attachments.

➡**When lowering, ensure the electrical wires have enough clearance.**

23. Remove wiring guide from subframe.

24. Remove heat shields from steering gear.

25. Remove steering gear bolts 3 and 6 (see illustration N40-10181).

26. Remove steering gear from subframe.

To install:

27. Installation is the reverse of removal, with special attention to the following:

a. The steering gear threaded sleeves must be seated in the subframe holes.

b. Clamp with nuts must be replaced after each removal.

c. Coat seal on steering gear with lubricant, e.g. soft soap, before installing steering gear.

d. After attaching steering gear to drive axle, make sure that seal on steering gear is positioned to mounting plate without kinks and opening to foot well is sealed correctly. Ingress of water and/or noises may be the result.

e. Make sure sealing surfaces are clean.

f. Make sure that the ball joint boot is not damaged or twisted.

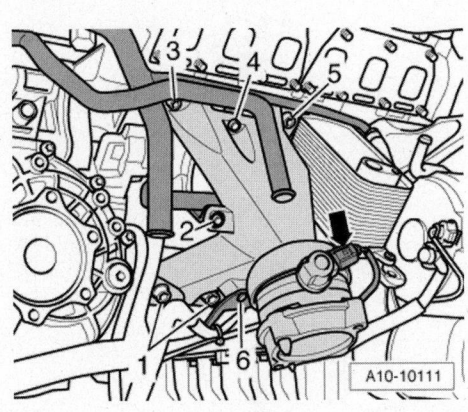

Fig. 103 Mark location of nuts (arrows) on left and right sides of vehicle using a marking pen or paint. Remove the nuts.

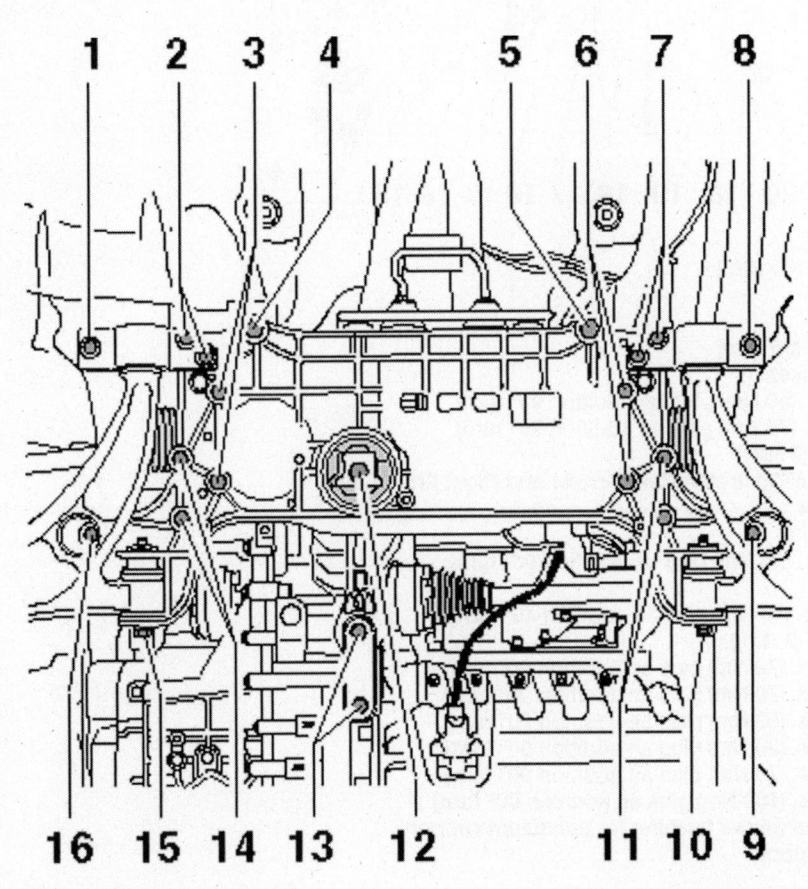

Fig. 104 Secure the subframe to the transverse links, using T10096 bolted to items "1", "8", "9" and "16", one after the other.

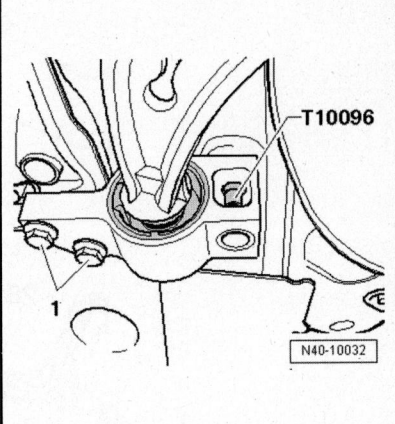

Fig. 105 Replace bolts with T10096 and tighten to 15 ft. lbs. (20 Nm)—view 1 of 2

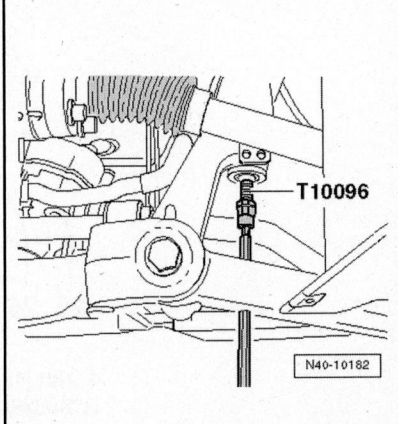

Fig. 106 Replace bolts with T10096 and tighten to 15 ft. lbs. (20 Nm)—view 2 of 2

g. Replace locking element after each removal.

h. Align transverse link nuts according to markings made earlier and tighten.

i. Install noise insulation frame and noise insulation.

j. Connect the battery.

28. Applies to Vehicles with Generation II Steering Gear: If a new steering gear was installed, the power steering control module J500 must be programmed with the VAS 5051B and the characteristic lines must be downloaded in "Guided Fault Finding".

29. Applies to Vehicles with Generation III Steering Gear: If new steering box was installed, the power steering control module J500 must be adapted with the VAS 5051B in "Guided Fault Finding".

30. Affects All Vehicles:

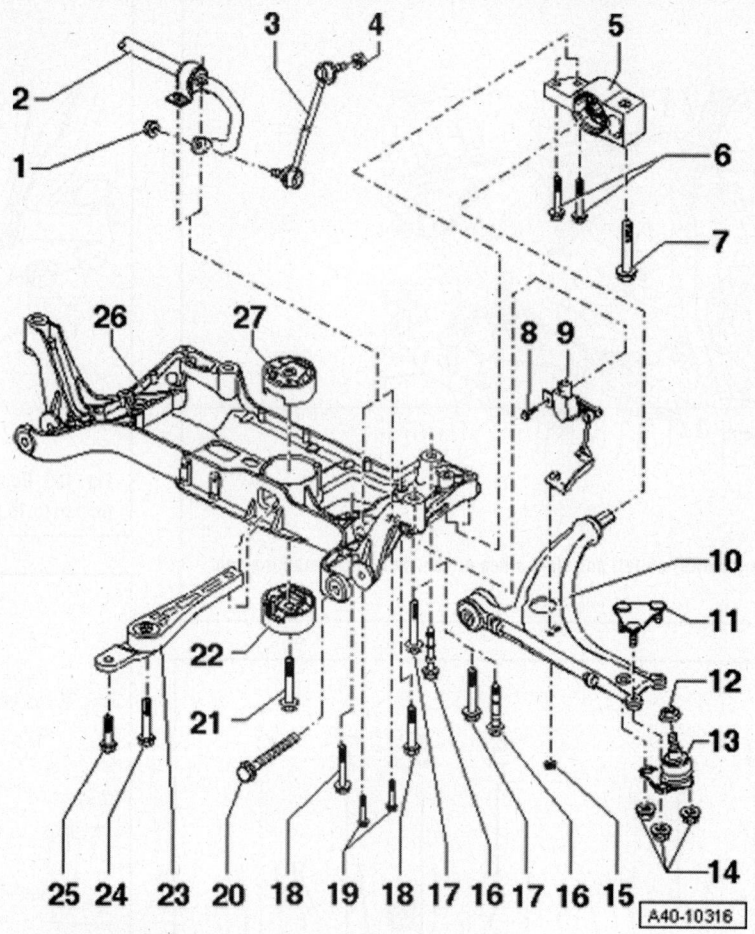

1. Nut [48 ft. lbs. (65 Nm)]
2. Stabilizer bar
3. Coupling rod
4. Nut [48 ft. lbs. (65 Nm)]
5. Mounting bracket
6. Bolt [37 ft. lbs. (50 Nm) plus an addition 90° turn]
7. Bolt [52 ft. lbs. (70 Nm) plus an addition 90° turn]
8. Bolt [7 ft. lbs. (9 Nm)]
9. Left Front Level Control System Sensor and Right Front Level Control Sensor
10. Transverse Link
12. Nut [15 ft. lbs. (20 Nm) plus an addition 90° turn]
13. Ball joint
14. Nut [29 ft. lbs. (40 Nm) plus an addition 45° turn]
15. Nut [7 ft. lbs. (9 Nm)]
16. Bolt [52 ft. lbs. (70 Nm) plus an addition 90° turn]
17. Bolt [52 ft. lbs. (70 Nm) plus an addition 90° turn]
18. Bolt [37 ft. lbs. (50 Nm) plus an addition 90° turn]
19. Bolt [15 ft. lbs. (20 Nm) plus an addition 90° turn]
20. Bolt [52 ft. lbs. (70 Nm) plus an addition 90° turn]
21. Bolt [74 ft. lbs. (100 Nm) plus an addition 90° turn]
22. Lower bonded rubber bushing for pendulum support.
23. Pendulum support
24. Bolt
25. Bolt
26. Subframe
27. Upper bonded rubber bushing for pendulum support

Fig. 107 Exploded view of subframe and related components, with torque specifications

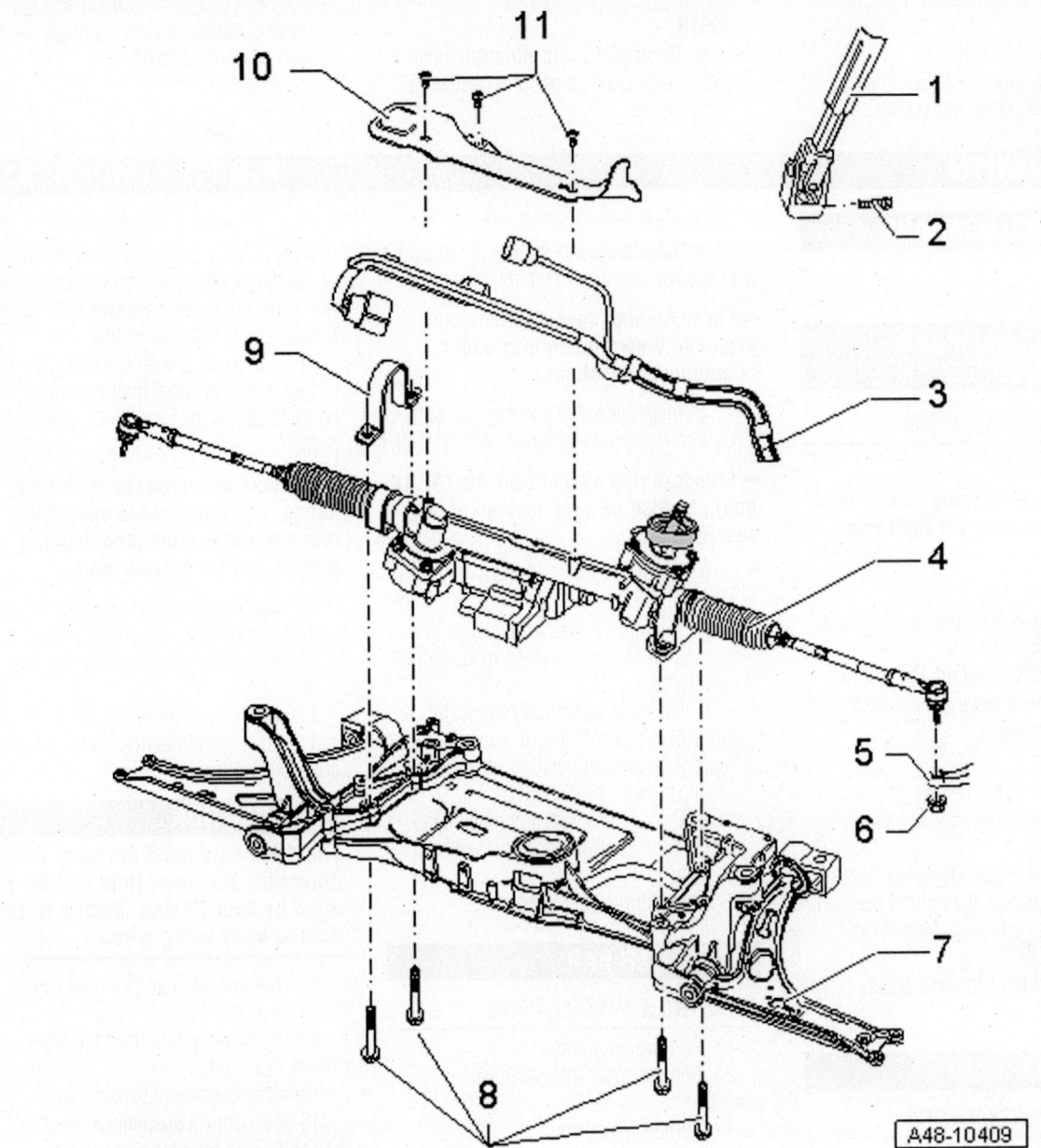

A48-10409

1. Universal Joint
2. Pinch bolt: 15 ft. lbs. (20 Nm), plus 90 degrees
3. Electrical Wiring
4. Power Steering Gear
5. Wheel Bearing Housing
6. Nut: 15 ft. lbs. (20 Nm), plus 90 degrees
7. Subframe with Brackets
8. Subframe mounting bolts: 37 ft. lbs. (50 Nm), plus 90 degrees
9. Clamp with Nuts
10. Shield
11. Shield screws: 4.5 ft. lbs. (6 Nm)

Fig. 108 Exploded view of steering gear and related components

a. Vehicle alignment required, see table.

b. On vehicles with electronically-controlled damping (Audi magnetic ride), reprogram control position using VAS 5051B.

c. On vehicles with automatic headlamp range control, perform headlamp basic setting.

d. If a vehicle alignment was performed, calibrate Steering Angle Sensor G85 with VAS 5051B.

SUSPENSION

COMPONENT LOCATIONS

See Figure 109.

ELECTRONIC DAMPING CONTROL MODULE

REMOVAL & INSTALLATION

See Figures 110 and 111.

➡**The electronic damping control module is installed under the right front seat.**

1. Remove the right front seat.
2. Cut carpet at markings shown, using a standard carpet knife.
3. Fold carpet up and unclip control module. Disconnect electrical connector and remove control module.

To install:
4. Installation is the reverse of removal, with special attention to the following:

a. If the Electronic Damping Control Module is replaced, the control position must be reprogrammed using VAS 5051B.

b. Insert control module access carpet frame.

LOWER BALL JOINT

REMOVAL & INSTALLATION

See Figures 112 and 113.

1. Remove the front wheel(s).
2. On vehicles with a level control system sensor, remove the nut from the linkage on the transverse link.
3. Mark the installed reference location of the ball joint nuts with marking pen or paint. Remove the nuts.
4. Disengage the transverse link from the ball joint.
5. Position the ball joint remover (3287 A) on the ball joint.

✳✳ CAUTION

When pressing off, the ball joint loosens itself from the wheel bearing housing abruptly - risk of accident!

6. Press ball joint out of wheel bearing housing.

To install:
7. Installation is the reverse of removal, with special attention to the following:

➡**For tightening specifications, see Exploded View illustrations under "Component Locations".**

a. Install new self-locking nut, and counter-hold using Internal Torx Bit T40.

➡**Standard ring spanner inserts (AF 18 mm) can also be used instead of the specified tool.**

b. Replace locking element after each removal.

c. Align ball joint to transverse link nuts according to markings made earlier and tighten.

d. On vehicles with electronically-controlled damping (Audi magnetic ride), reprogram control position using the diagnostic tool (VAS 5051B).

e. On vehicles with automatic headlamp range control, perform headlamp basic setting.

f. Perform wheel alignment.

STABILIZER BAR

REMOVAL & INSTALLATION

1. Remove subframe.
2. Remove stabilizer bar from subframe.
3. Remove stabilizer.
4. Installation is the reverse of removal.
5. Refer to illustrations under Component Locations for torque values.

STRUT & SPRING ASSEMBLY

REMOVAL & INSTALLATION

See Figures 114 and 115.

1. Loosen the drive axle spindle nut on the wheel side.
2. Remove the wheel.
3. Remove the brake caliper and secure it to the body using wire.
4. Remove brake line and electrical line bracket from wheel bearing housing.
5. Remove the ABS speed sensor.
6. Remove coupling rod upper hex nut from suspension strut.
7. Loosen tie rod end nut, but do not remove yet. Press off track rod ball joint

from wheel bearing housing using a separator tool (3287A) and now unscrew nut.

8. On vehicles with a level control system sensor, remove the lower nut from the linkage on the transverse link.
9. On vehicles with electronically-controlled damping (Audi magnetic ride), disconnect connector near the drive axle boot.

➡**Remove the connector with both hands. Use one hand to open the retainer and use the other hand to press it off. Do not use tools.**

10. Mark location of ball joint to transverse link nuts with a marking pen or paint, for installation reference. Remove the nuts.
11. Guide transverse link out of ball joint and remove wheel bearing housing from drive axle splines.

✳✳ CAUTION

The drive axle must not hang down, otherwise the inner joint will be damaged by over-flexing. Secure drive axle to body using wire.

12. Remove plenum chamber cover (cowl cover).
13. Remove upper shock absorber mount hex bolts.
14. Remove the suspension strut.
15. Disconnect suspension strut to wheel bearing housing connection.
16. Insert 3424 into slot of wheel bearing housing. Using a ratchet and the 3424, open the wheel bearing housing slot.
17. Remove suspension strut from wheel bearing housing.

To install:
18. Installation is the reverse of removal, with special attention to the following:

a. Tighten the lower strut pinch bolt to 56 ft. lbs. (70 Nm), plus additional 90 degrees.

b. When tightening the spindle bolt, tighten as follows:

- Hex bolt: 148 ft. lbs. (200 Nm), plus an additional 180 degrees when vehicle is resting on ground.
- 12-point bolt: 56 ft. lbs. (70 Nm), plus an additional 90 degrees when vehicle is resting on ground.

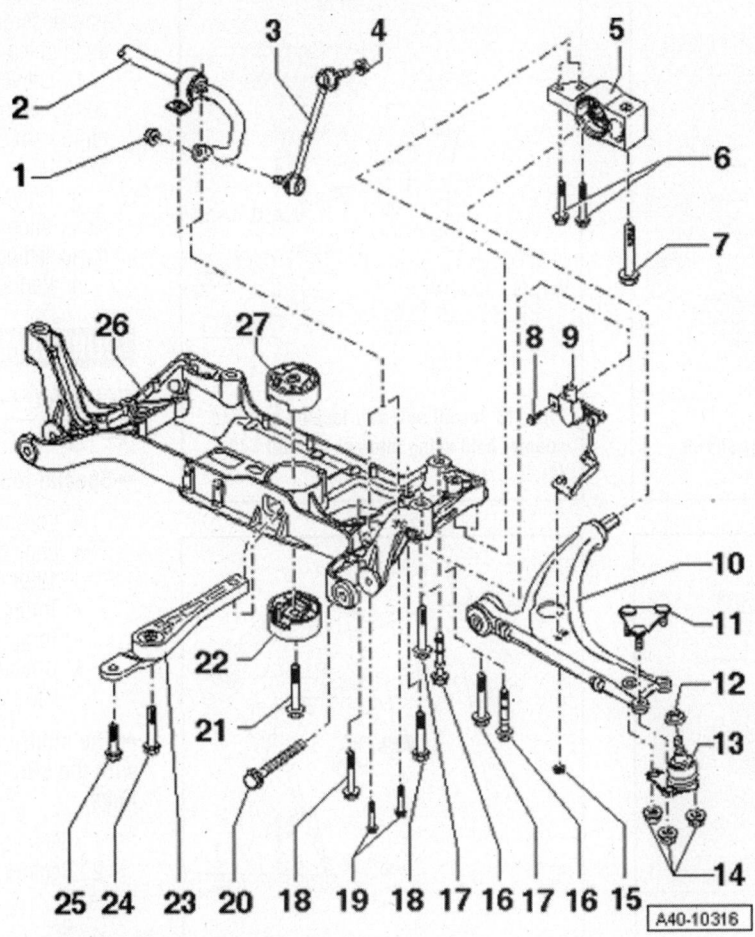

1. Nut [48 ft. lbs. (65 Nm)]
2. Stabilizer bar
3. Coupling rod
4. Nut [48 ft. lbs. (65 Nm)]
5. Mounting bracket
6. Bolt [37 ft. lbs. (50 Nm) plus an addition 90° turn]
7. Bolt [52 ft. lbs. (70 Nm) plus an addition 90° turn]
8. Bolt [7 ft. lbs. (9 Nm)]
9. Left Front Level Control System Sensor and Right Front Level Control Sensor
10. Transverse Link
12. Nut [15 ft. lbs. (20 Nm) plus an addition 90° turn]
13. Ball joint
14. Nut [29 ft. lbs. (40 Nm) plus an addition 45° turn]
15. Nut [7 ft. lbs. (9 Nm)]
16. Bolt [52 ft. lbs. (70 Nm) plus an addition 90° turn]
17. Bolt [52 ft. lbs. (70 Nm) plus an addition 90° turn]
18. Bolt [37 ft. lbs. (50 Nm) plus an addition 90° turn]
19. Bolt [15 ft. lbs. (20 Nm) plus an addition 90° turn]
20. Bolt [52 ft. lbs. (70 Nm) plus an addition 90° turn]
21. Bolt [74 ft. lbs. (100 Nm) plus an addition 90° turn]
22. Lower bonded rubber bushing for pendulum support.
23. Pendulum support
24. Bolt
25. Bolt
26. Subframe
27. Upper bonded rubber bushing for pendulum support

Fig. 109 Exploded view of the subframe, stabilizer bar, transverse link, ball joint and level control sensor assembly

Fig. 110 Cut carpet at markings shown, using a standard carpet knife.

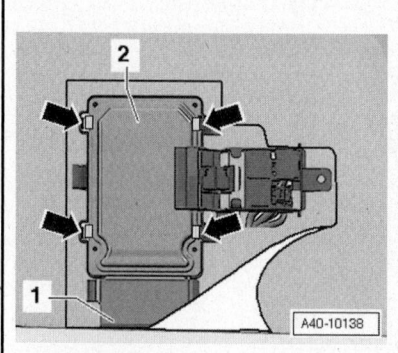

Fig. 111 Fold carpet up and unclip control module (2). Disconnect electrical connector (1) and remove control module.

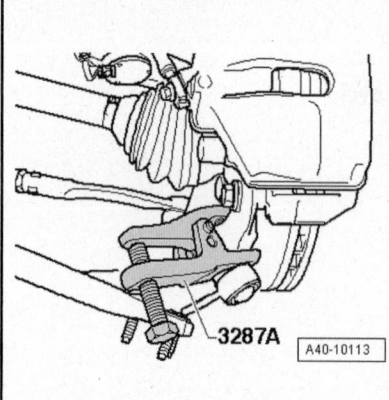

Fig. 112 Position the ball joint remover (3287 A) on the ball joint.

c. Insert suspension strut with one of the two markings pointing in direction of travel.

d. Replace locking element after each removal.

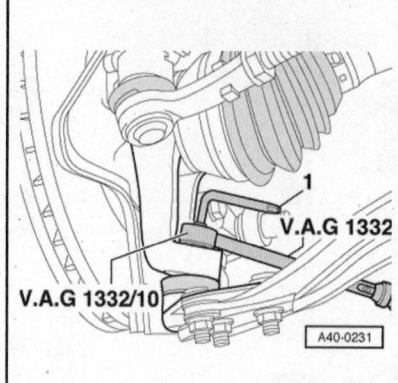

Fig. 113 Install new self-locking nut, and counter-hold using Internal Torx Bit T40 (1).

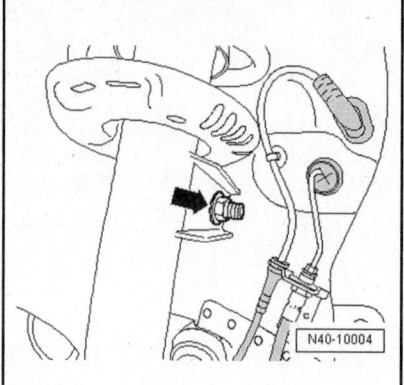

Fig. 114 Remove coupling rod upper hex nut from suspension strut.

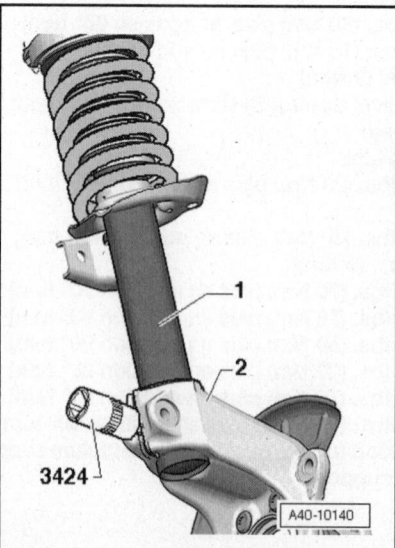

Fig. 115 Insert 3424 into slot of wheel bearing housing. Using a ratchet and the 3424, open the wheel bearing housing slot.

e. Align ball joint to transverse link nuts according to markings made earlier and tighten.

f. On vehicles with electronically-controlled damping (Audi magnetic ride), reprogram control position using VAS 5051B.

g. On vehicles with automatic headlamp range control, perform headlamp basic setting.

h. Perform wheel alignment.

SUBFRAME

REMOVAL & INSTALLATION

See Figures 116 through 119.

➡**Special tools required:**

- Locating pins T10096
- Engine/transmission jack V.A.G 1383 A
- Torque wrench V.A.G 1331
- Torque wrench V.A.G 1332
- Vehicle Diagnostic, Testing and Information System VAS 5051B

➡**The subframe is removed together with the stabilizer bar and transverse links.**

1. Remove wheels.
2. Remove lower noise insulation and frame.
3. Remove exhaust system bracket bolts.
4. Remove stabilizer link nut.

➡**When numbered bolts are referenced in this procedure, refer to bolt numbering graphic in this procedure.**

5. On vehicles with a level control system sensor, disconnect the connector and remove the nut from the linkage on the transverse link.

6. Remove pendulum support from transmission, unscrew bolts "13" to do so.

7. Disconnect Oil Level Thermal Sensor connector and unclip electrical wire from bracket.

8. Mark location of transverse link to ball joint nuts on left and right sides of vehicle using a felt-tip pen. Remove the nuts.

9. Remove transverse link from ball joint.

10. Secure the subframe to the transverse links, using T10096 bolted to items "1", "8", "9" and "16", one after the other.

11. Replace bolts with T10096 and tighten to 15 ft. lbs. (20 Nm).

12. Remove steering gear bolts "3" and "6".

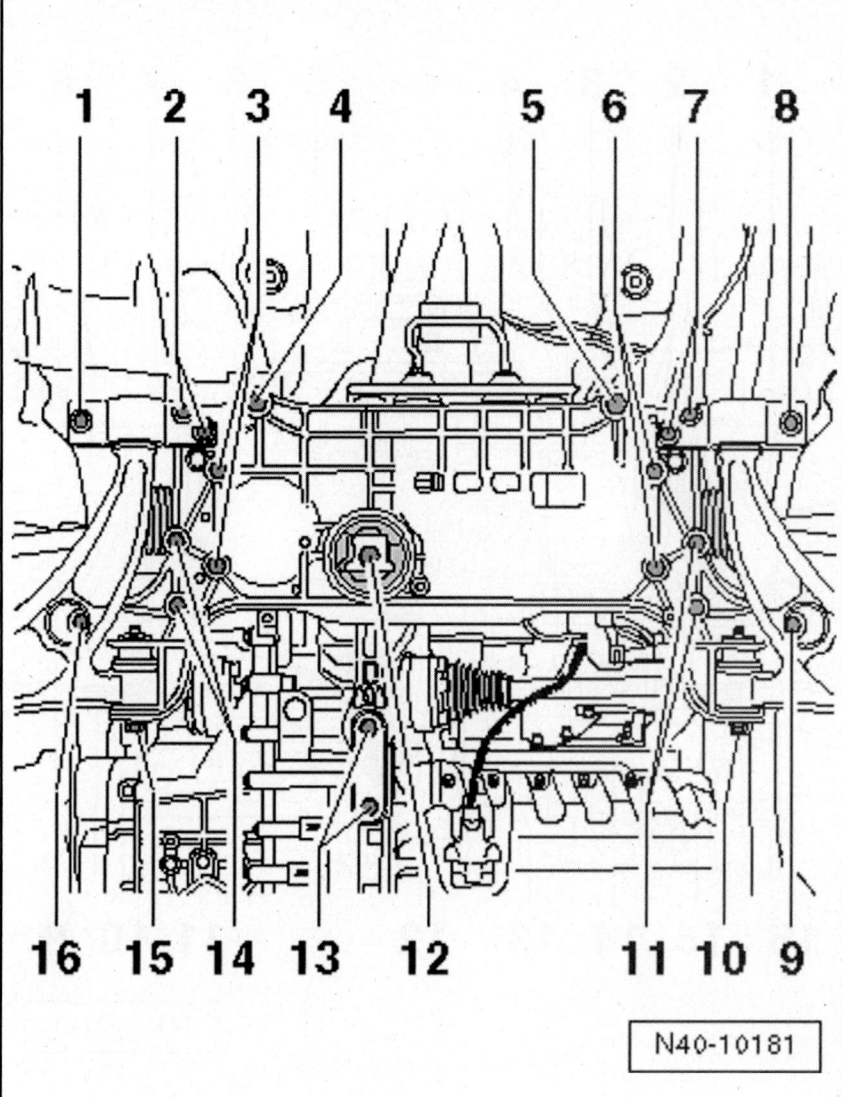

Fig. 116 Secure the subframe to the transverse links, using T10096 bolted to items "1", "8", "9" and "16", one after the other.

N40-10181

13. Place the engine support jack (V.A.G 1383 A) with wood blocks under subframe and apply slight counter-pressure.

14. Remove bolts "4" and "5".

15. Lower subframe with attachments approximately 30 mm and pry steering gear threaded sleeves out of holes in subframe.

16. Secure steering gear on body.

17. Remove cable guide from subframe.

18. Lower the subframe with attachments.

To install:

19. Installation is the reverse of removal, with special attention to the following:

   a. For tightening specifications, see "Exploded View" graphic under "Component Locations" in this section. Also see "Steering Gear" in "STEERING" section for steering-related tightening specifications.

➡**The steering gear threaded sleeves must be seated in the subframe holes.**

   b. Replace locking element after each removal.

   c. Align nuts according to markings made earlier and tighten.

   d. Install noise insulation frame and insulation.

   e. On vehicles with electronically-controlled damping (Audi magnetic ride), reprogram control position using VAS 5051B.

   f. On vehicles with automatic headlamp range control, perform headlamp basic setting.

20. Perform wheel alignment.

TRANSVERSE LINK

REMOVAL & INSTALLATION

See Figures 120 and 104

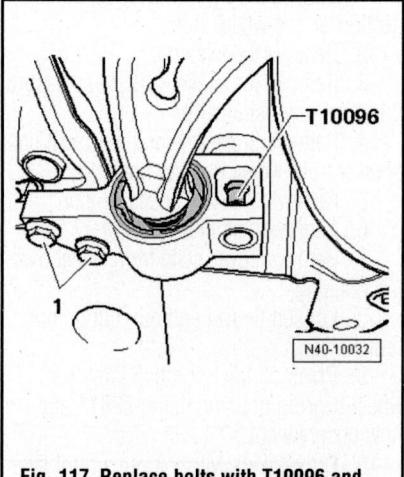

Fig. 117 Replace bolts with T10096 and tighten to 15 ft. lbs. (20 Nm)—view 1 of 2

N40-10032

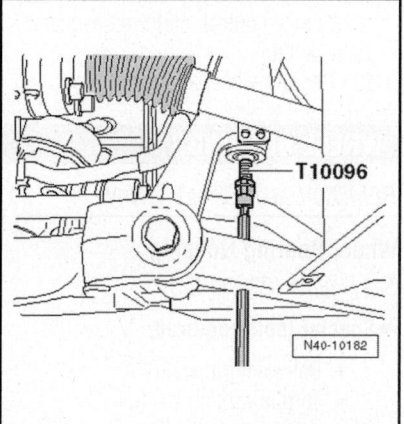

Fig. 118 Replace bolts with T10096 and tighten to 15 ft. lbs. (20 Nm)—view 2 of 2

N40-10182

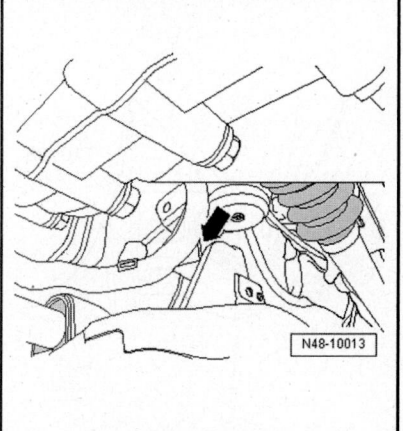

Fig. 119 Remove cable guide from subframe.

N48-10013

1. Remove the wheel.

2. Remove lower noise insulation.

3. On vehicles with a level control system sensor, remove the nut from the linkage on the transverse link.

4. Mark location of ball joint to transverse link nuts with felt-tip pen. Remove the nuts.

5. Pull wheel bearing housing with ball joint out of transverse link.

6. Replace bolt "1" for left side or "8" for right side using T10096 and tighten locating pins to 15 ft. lbs. (20 Nm).

7. Remove bolts.

8. Remove left side bolt "15" or right side bolt "10".

9. On vehicles where bolt "15" or "10" is not to be removed, the subframe must be removed.

10. Remove left side bolt "15" or right side bolt "10".

To install:

11. Installation is the reverse of removal, with special attention to the following:

   a. For tightening specifications, see "Exploded View" illustration under "Component Locations".

   b. Install left side bolt "15" or right side bolt "10" and tighten by hand.

   c. Replace locking element after each removal.

   d. Align transverse link nuts according to markings made earlier and tighten.

   e. Bonded rubber bushings can only be turned to a limited extent. Only tighten suspension screws when vehicle is in curb weight or control position.

   f. Tighten left side bolt "15" or right side bolt "10" in curb weight position.

   g. On vehicles with electronically-controlled damping (Audi magnetic ride),

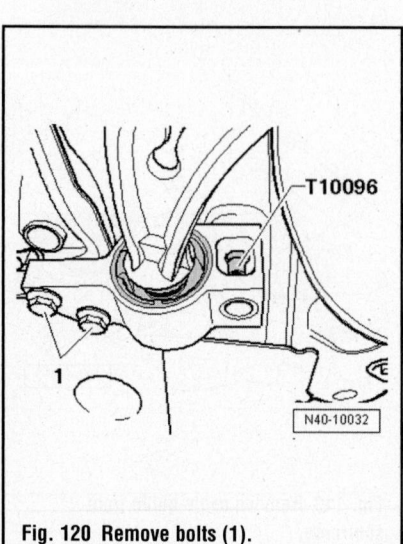

Fig. 120 Remove bolts (1).

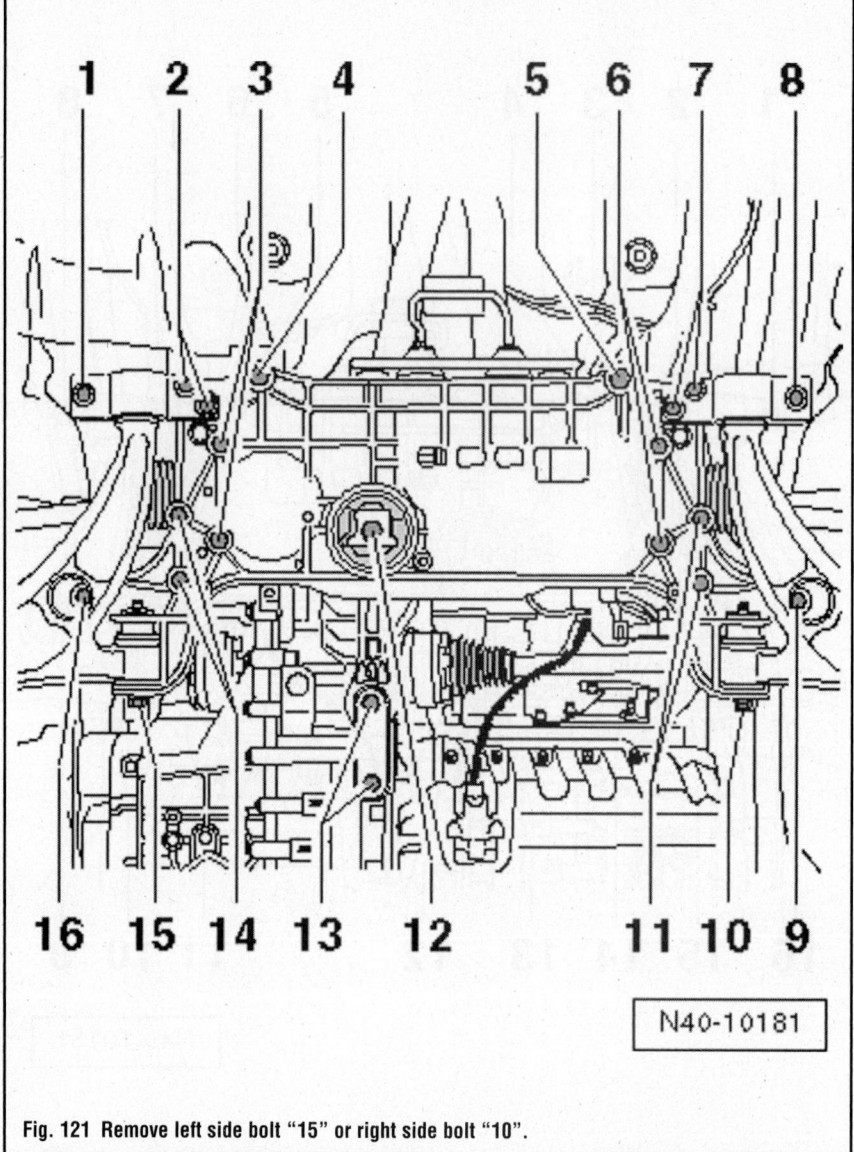

Fig. 121 Remove left side bolt "15" or right side bolt "10".

reprogram control position using VAS 5051B.

   h. On vehicles with automatic headlamp range control, perform headlamp basic setting

12. Perform wheel alignment.

WHEEL BEARINGS

REMOVAL & INSTALLATION

Wheel Bearing Housing

See Figures 122 and 123.

➡**Special tools required:**

- Ball joint puller 3287A
- Torque wrench V.A.G 1332
- Engine/transmission jack V.A.G 1383 A
- Angle wrench V.A.G 1756
- Spreader 3424

- Vehicle Diagnostic, Testing and Information System VAS 5051B

1. Loosen the drive axle threaded connection on the wheel side.

2. Remove the wheel.

3. Remove the brake caliper and secure it to the body using wire.

4. Remove brake line and electrical line bracket from wheel bearing housing.

5. Remove the ABS speed sensor.

6. Remove disc brake.

7. Remove cover plate from wheel bearing housing.

8. Loosen tie rod end nut, but do not remove yet.

9. Press off track rod ball joint from wheel bearing housing using 3287A and now unscrew nut.

10. On vehicles with a level control system sensor, remove the nut from the linkage on the transverse link.

11. On vehicles with electronically-controlled damping (Audi magnetic ride), disconnect connector. Remove the connector with both hands. Use one hand to open the retainer and use the other hand to press it off. Do not use tools.

12. Mark location of transverse link nuts with felt-tip pen. Remove the nuts.

13. Guide transverse link out of wheel bearing housing with ball joint.

14. Remove wheel bearing housing from drive axle splines.

➡**The drive axle must not hang down, otherwise the inner joint will be damaged by over-flexing. Secure drive axle to body using wire.**

15. Separate wheel bearing housing/suspension strut threaded connection.

16. Insert 3424 into slot of wheel bearing housing. Using a ratchet and the spreaders socket, open the wheel bearing housing slot.

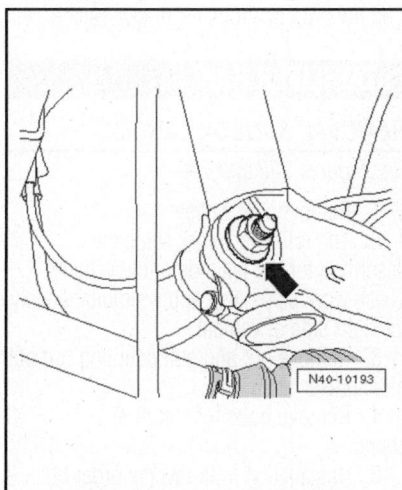

Fig. 122 Separate wheel bearing housing/suspension strut threaded connection.

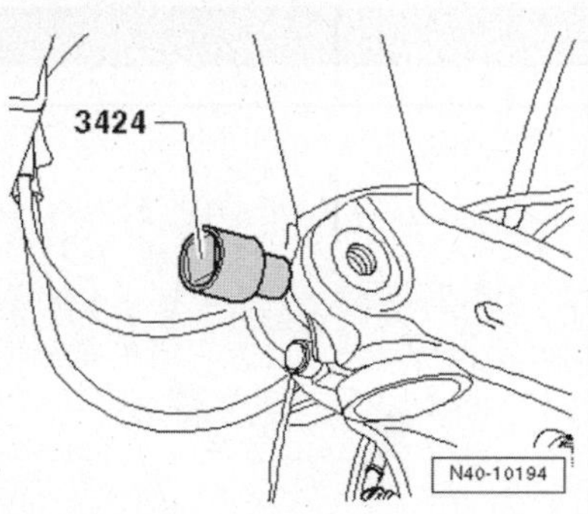

Fig. 123 Insert 3424 into slot of wheel bearing housing. Using a ratchet and the spreaders socket, open the wheel bearing housing slot.

17. Pull wheel bearing housing with ball joint down from shock absorber tube and remove.

To install:

18. Installation is the reverse of removal, with special attention to the following:

a. For tightening specifications, see "Exploded View" illustration under "Component Locations".

b. Replace locking element after each removal.

c. Align transverse link nuts according to markings made earlier and tighten.

d. Tighten drive axle to wheel hub threaded connection.

e. On vehicles with electronically-controlled damping (Audi magnetic ride), reprogram control position using VAS 5051B.

f. On vehicles with automatic headlamp range control, perform headlamp basic setting.

19. Perform wheel alignment.

Wheel Bearing Unit

➡**Special tools required:**

- Angle wrench V.A.G 1756
- Torque wrench V.A.G 1332
- Vehicle Diagnostic, Testing and Information System VAS 5051B

1. Remove drive axle. See "DRIVE TRAIN" section.

2. Remove the brake caliper and secure it to the body using wire.

3. Remove the ABS speed sensor.

4. Remove disc brake.

5. Remove wheel bearing housing to wheel bearing unit (hub) bolts. Remove wheel bearing unit from wheel bearing housing.

➡**Avoid contaminating with dirt and damaging the seal when setting down/storing. The wheel bearing must always face up. Always set the wheel bearing unit down on the wheel hub.**

To install:

6. Installation is the reverse of removal, with special attention to the following:

a. For tightening specifications, see "Exploded View" illustration under "Component Locations".

b. Replace locking element after each removal.

c. Align transverse link nuts according to markings made earlier and tighten.

d. Tighten drive axle to wheel hub threaded connection.

e. On vehicles with electronically-controlled damping (Audi magnetic ride), reprogram control position using VAS 5051B.

f. On vehicles with automatic headlamp range control, perform headlamp basic setting.

7. Perform wheel alignment.

COIL SPRING

REMOVAL & INSTALLATION

See Figures 124 and 125.

1. Remove wheel.
2. Insert spring compressor.
3. Compress coil spring until it can be removed.
4. Remove spring.
5. Installation is in reverse order of removal, noting the following:
   a. End of spring must rest against stop of lower spring support.
   b. Install spring together with spring seat.
   c. Spring seat has two pins on bottom.
   d. These pins are inserted into holes on lower transverse link.
   e. Then insert spring seat at top into upper spring end.
   f. Tension spring. To do this, place upper end of spring on body tab.
   g. Mount wheel and tighten.
6. If one or more springs were replaced, then the system must be reprogrammed on vehicles with Audi magnetic ride.
7. Vehicle alignment is required.

LOWER CONTROL ARM (TRANSVERSE LINK)

REMOVAL & INSTALLATION

See Figures 126 and 127.

1. Determine dimension from center of wheel to lower edge of wheel housing before starting work while vehicle is resting on its wheels.

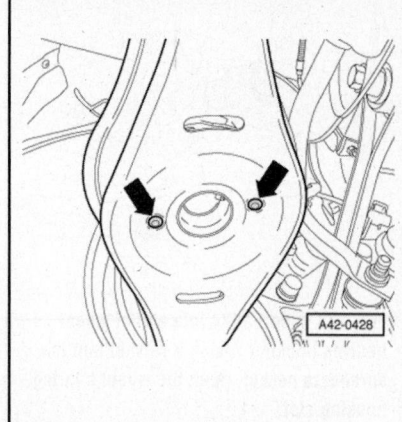

Fig. 125 These pins are inserted into holes on lower transverse link

2. Place vehicle on a hoist.
3. Remove wheel.
4. Remove coil spring.
5. Remove bolt for lower transverse link.
6. Remove bolts on vehicles with level control system sensor.
7. Mark, e.g. using felt-tip marker, position of eccentric bolt to subframe.
8. Disengage rear exhaust system and lower.
9. Remove bolt.
10. Remove lower transverse link.
11. Installation is in reverse of removal.
12. On vehicles with automatic headlamp range control, perform headlamp basic setting.
13. On vehicles with electronically-controlled damping (Audi magnetic ride), reprogram control position.

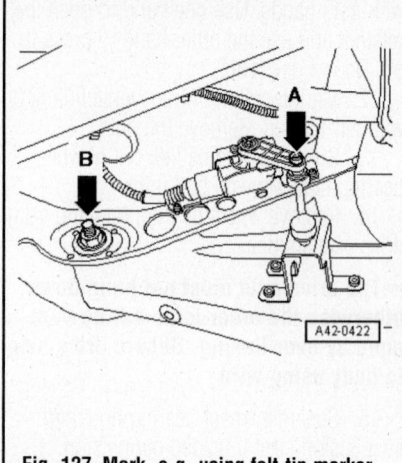

Fig. 127 Mark, e.g. using felt-tip marker, position of eccentric bolt "B" to subframe

14. Vehicle alignment required.
15. Refer to illustrations under Component Locations for torque values.

STABILIZER BAR

REMOVAL & INSTALLATION

See Figures 128 and 129.

1. Remove rear wheels.
2. The following work steps are described for the left side of the vehicle. These work steps also apply simultaneously for right side of vehicle.
3. Remove nut and pull coupling rod out of stabilizer.
4. Remove bolts for stabilizer clamp.
5. Installation is in reverse order of removal.

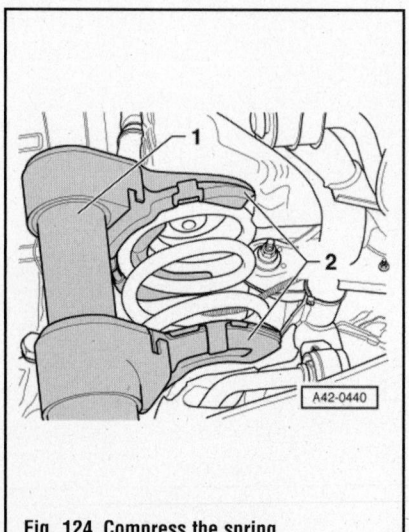

Fig. 124 Compress the spring

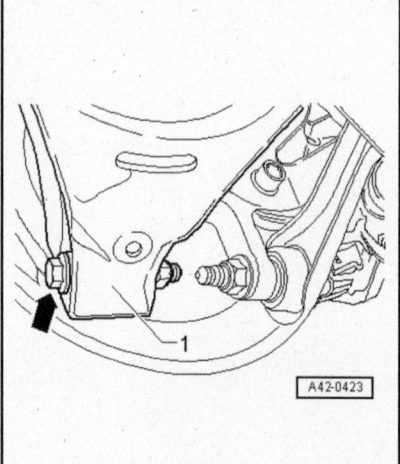

Fig. 126 Remove bolt for lower transverse link (1)

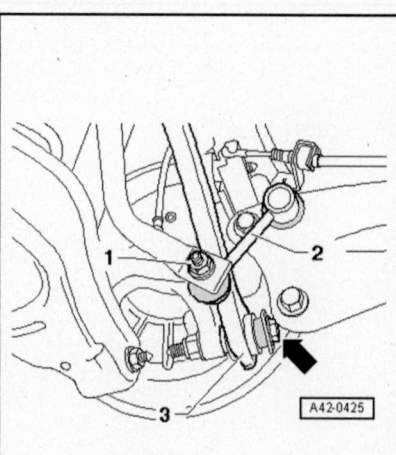

Fig. 128 Remove nut (1) and pull coupling rod (2) out of stabilizer.

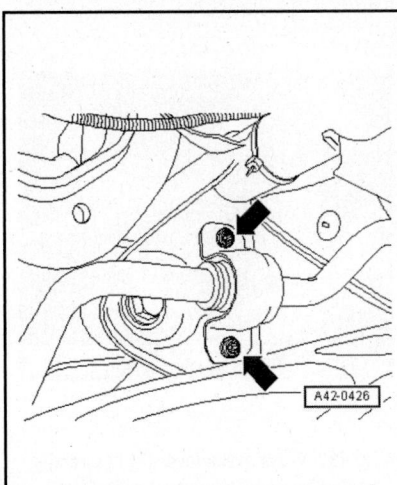

Fig. 129 Remove bolts (arrows) for stabilizer clamp

6. Refer to illustrations under Component Locations for torque values.

7. Vehicle alignment is required.

SHOCK ABSORBER

REMOVAL & INSTALLATION

See Figure 130.

1. Measure dimension from center of wheel to lower edge of wheel housing.

2. Remove the wheel.

3. Remove wheel housing liner.

4. Remove coil spring.

5. On vehicles with electronically-controlled damping (Audi magnetic ride), disconnect connector.

6. Remove the bolts.

7. Remove the shock absorber lower mounting bolt and washer.

8. Remove shock absorber.

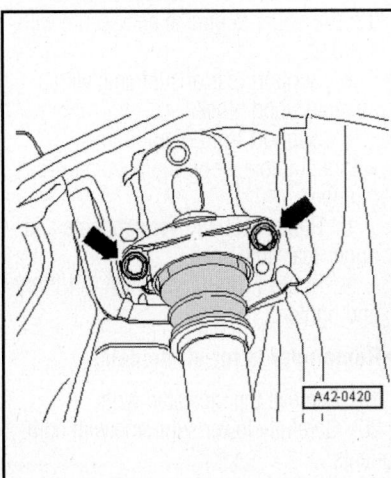

Fig. 130 Remove the bolts.

To install:

9. Installation is performed in the reverse order of removal. Observe the following when doing so:

a. Bolting bumper to wheel bearing housing must only occur after dimension measured before installation between the wheel hub center and the lower edge of wheel housing has been attained.

b. Install the shock absorber lower mounting bolt and washer and tighten.

c. For tightening specifications, refer to illustrations for:

- Subframe, Lower Transverse Link, Upper Transverse Link, Tie Rod and Level Control System Sensor Assembly Overview—Coupe.
- Subframe, Diagonal Braces, Crossmember, Lower Transverse Link, Upper Transverse Link, Tie Rod and Level Control System Sensor Assembly Overview—Roadster.
- Wheel Bearing Housing, Wheel Bearing Unit and Trailing Arm with Mounting Bracket Assembly Overview.
- Tighten the upper shock absorber bolts to 37 ft. lbs. (50 Nm), plus an additional 45 degrees, and the lower shock absorber mounting bolt (with washer) to 133 ft. lbs. (180 Nm).
- Stabilizer Bar Assembly, see "Stabilizer Bar" in this section.

10. On vehicles with electronically-controlled damping (Audi magnetic ride), the control position must be reprogrammed each time a shock absorber is replaced using Vehicle Diagnosis, Testing and Information System VAS 5051B.

STABILIZER BAR

REMOVAL & INSTALLATION

See Figure 131.

1. Remove rear wheels.

➡**The following work steps are described for the left side of the vehicle. These work steps also apply simultaneously for right side of vehicle.**

2. Remove the nut and pull coupling rod (link) out of stabilizer.

3. Remove bolts for stabilizer clamp.

4. Remove the stabilizer bar.

To install:

5. Installation is the reverse of removal, with special attention to the following:

a. For tightening specifications, refer to:

- Subframe, Lower Transverse Link, Upper Transverse Link, Tie Rod and Level Control System Sensor Assembly Overview—Coupe.
- Subframe, Diagonal Braces, Crossmember, Lower Transverse Link, Upper Transverse Link, Tie Rod and Level Control System Sensor Assembly Overview—Roadster.
- Wheel Bearings in this section.
- Shock absorber and/or Coil Spring Assembly in this section.
- Stabilizer bar bracket mounting bolts: 18 ft. lbs. (25 Nm), plus 90 degrees when vehicle is at curb weight.
- Stabilizer bar to link nut: 30 ft. lbs. (40 Nm).

SUBFRAME

REMOVAL & INSTALLATION

See Figures 132 through 135.

➡**Special tools required:**

- Torque wrench V.A.G 1332
- Engine-/transmission jack V.A.G 1383 A with universal transmission support V.A.G 1359/2
- Tensioning strap T10038
- Vehicle Diagnosis, Testing and Information System VAS 5051B

➡**For later reassembly work where the drive axle to wheel hub threaded connection must be loosened, note that it must not be done while the vehicle is resting on its wheels.**

1. Remove wheels.

2. Remove coil springs. See "Coil Springs" in this section.

3. On Roadster model, remove the diagonal braces.

4. Remove exhaust system rear muffler.

5. Disconnect electrical wires to Haldex clutch, ABS speed sensor and, on vehicles with level control system sensor, connectors and unclip.

6. Remove the shock absorber low bolt and washer.

7. Press brake lever in away from axle and unhook parking brake cable.

8. Press retaining tabs together and remove parking brake cable.

9. Remove parking brake cable from bracket.

10. Remove brake caliper. Secure the brake caliper to the body so that the weight

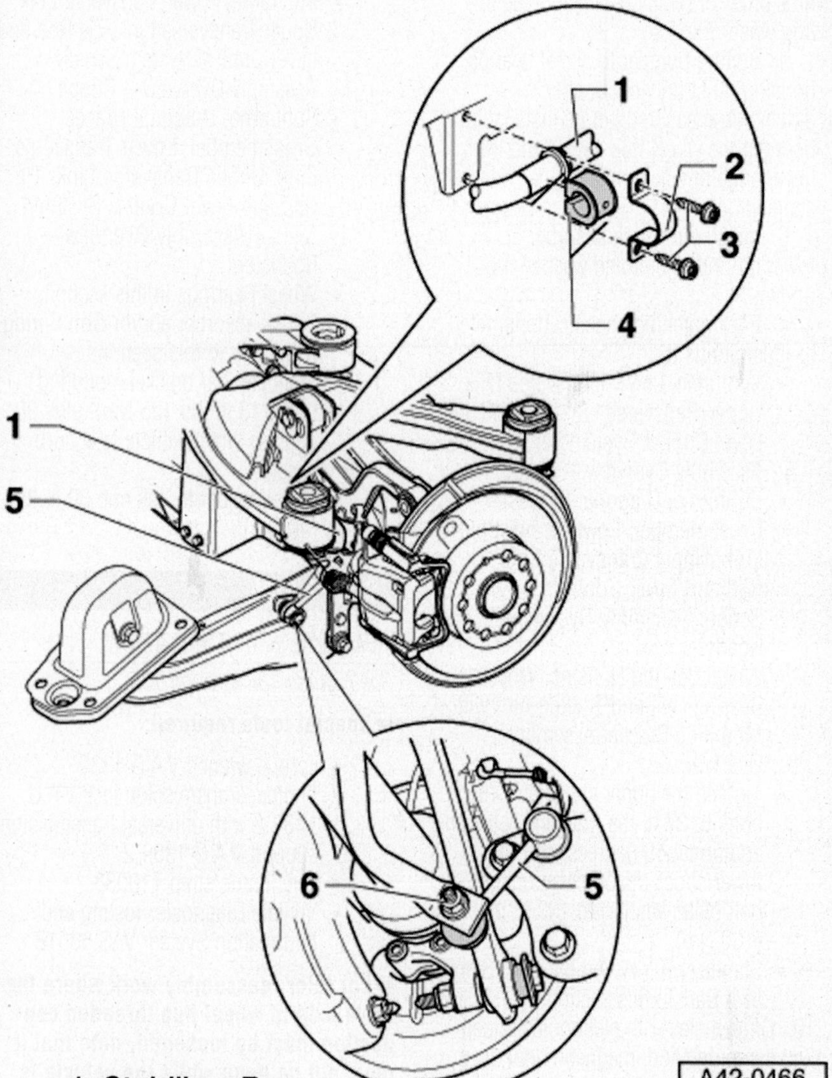

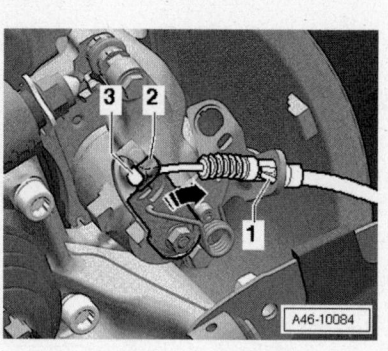

Fig. 132 Press brake lever (2) in direction of arrow and unhook parking brake cable (3).

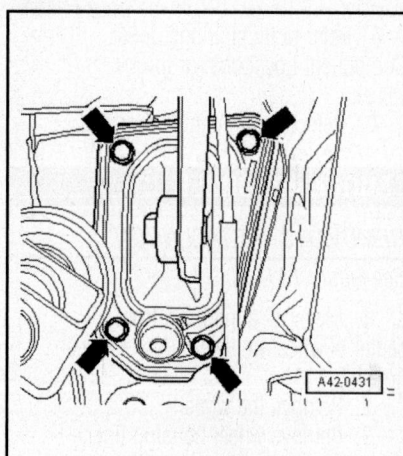

Fig. 133 Mark installation position of mounting bracket on body. Remove bolts.

1. Stabilizer Bar
2. Clamp
3. Bolt: 18 ft. lbs. (25 Nm), plus 90 degrees
4. Rubber Mount
5. Coupling Rod (Stabilizer Link)
6. Nut: 30 ft. lbs. (40 Nm)

A42-0466

Fig. 131 Stabilizer bar assembly overview

of the caliper does not stress or damage the brake hose or brake line.

11. Remove brake splash deflector.

12. Mark installation position of mounting bracket on body. Remove bolts.

13. Check for a factory-applied marking (colored dot) on the joint washer and Haldex clutch flange. If there is not one, mark location of joint washer and Haldex clutch flange to each other.

14. Remove rear driveshaft tube from rear final drive with joint washer and vibration damper.

15. Remove the driveshaft center bracket bolts two turns. Secure driveshaft to exhaust system bracket with a wire.

16. Move rear driveshaft tube as far as possible in direction of transmission.

17. For Coupe models, place V.A.G 1383

A with V.A.G 1359/2 under subframe and secure with T10038.

18. Fro Roadster models, do the following:

   a. Place V.A.G 1383 A with V.A.G 1359/2 under subframe and secure with T10038.

   b. Support rear of subframe with a suitable wood block.

   c. Support front of subframe with a suitable wood block under crossmember.

   d. Route T10038 over subframe and under rear final drive.

   e. Route T10038 under V.A.G 1359/2 and tighten.

➡**Remainder is for all models.**

19. Remove the indicated bolts.

20. Carefully lower subframe with components.

21. When lowering, ensure there is enough clearance between the brake lines,

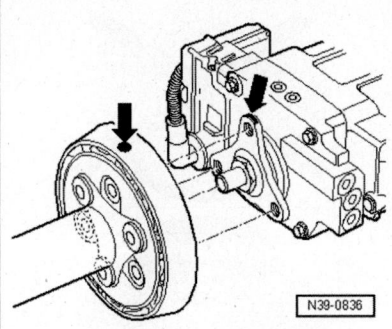

Fig. 134 Check for a factory-applied marking (colored dot) on the joint washer and Haldex clutch flange. If there is not one, mark location of joint washer and Haldex clutch flange to each other.

electrical lines and centering pints to driveshaft.

To install:

22. Installation is performed in the reverse order of removal. Observe the following when doing so:

a. Driveshaft, attaching to rear final drive. See "DRIVE TRAIN" section.

b. The center of the subframe mount holes must be aligned to the bolting points on the body.

c. For tightening specifications not given here, refer to applicable component heading.

d. On vehicles with electronically-controlled damping (Audi magnetic ride), reprogram control position using VAS 5051B.

e. On vehicles with automatic headlamp range control, perform headlamp basic setting.

23. Perform wheel alignment.

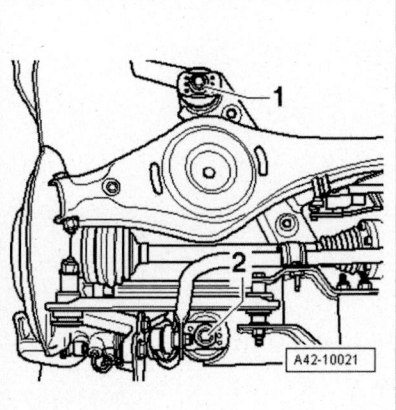

Fig. 135 Remove the indicated bolts (1 and 2).

UPPER CONTROL ARM

REMOVAL & INSTALLATION

See Figure 136.

1. Determine dimension from center of wheel to lower edge of wheel housing before starting work while vehicle is resting on its wheels.
2. Place vehicle on a hoist.
3. Remove wheels.
4. Remove coil spring.
5. Completely disengage wire from bracket.
6. Remove nut and washer.
7. Remove bolt and washer.
8. Mark, e.g. using felt-tip marker, position of eccentric bolt to subframe.
9. Remove bolt and remove the upper transverse link.
10. Installation is in reverse order of removal.
11. Transverse link connections may only be carried out of dimension between wheel hub center and lower edge of wheel housing, measured before assembly, is achieved.
12. Vehicle alignment required.
13. Refer to illustrations under Component Locations for torque values.

WHEEL BEARINGS

REMOVAL & INSTALLATION

Wheel Bearing Housing

See Figures 137 through 140.

1. Measure dimension from center of wheel to lower edge of wheel housing.
2. Remove wheel.
3. Remove coil spring.
4. Remove brake carrier and brake caliper and tie to body with wire.

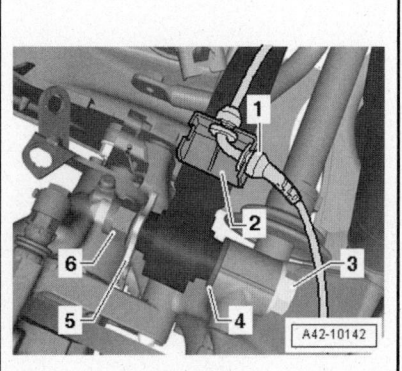

Fig. 136 Completely disengage wire (1) from bracket (2)

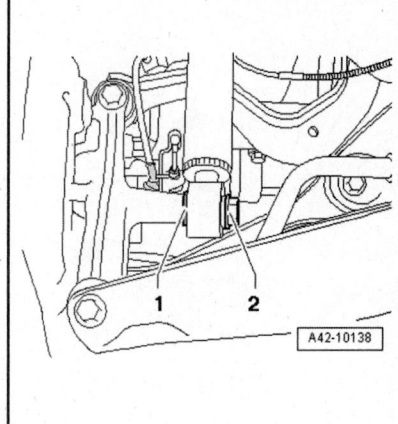

Fig. 137 Remove bolt (2) and washer (1)

5. Remove ABS speed sensor from wheel bearing housing.
6. Remove cover plate.
7. Remove bolt and washer. The washer is installed on vehicles with an aluminum wheel bearing housing.
8. Remove bolt for tie rod, upper transverse link and lower transverse link from wheel bearing housing.
9. Remove connecting link from trailing arm.
10. Hold wheel bearing housing firmly and remove bolts.
11. Pull coupling rod out of trailing link.
12. Remove wheel bearing housing.

To install:

13. Refer to illustrations under Component Locations for torque values.
14. Installation is in reverse order of removal, noting the following:
15. Install tie rod bolt, upper transverse link and lower transverse link.

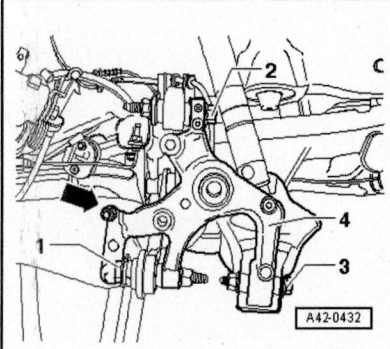

Fig. 138 Remove bolt for tie rod (1), upper transverse link (2) and lower transverse link (3) from wheel bearing housing (4)

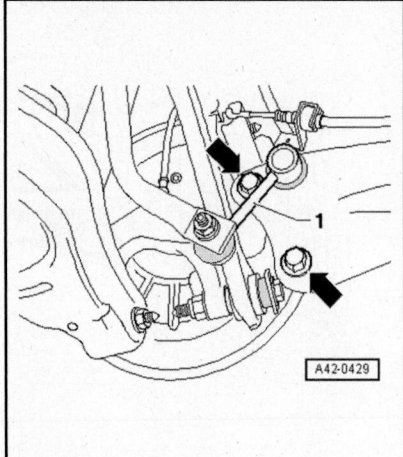

Fig. 139 Hold wheel bearing housing firmly and remove bolts

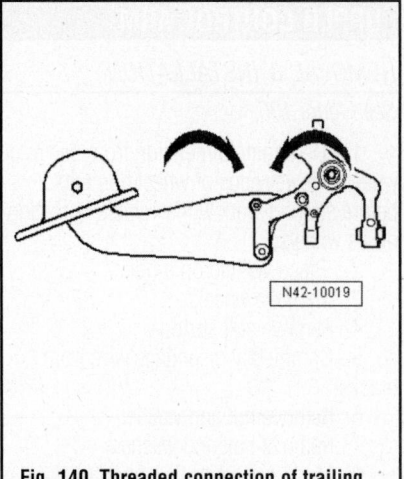

Fig. 140 Threaded connection of trailing link/wheel bearing housing. . .

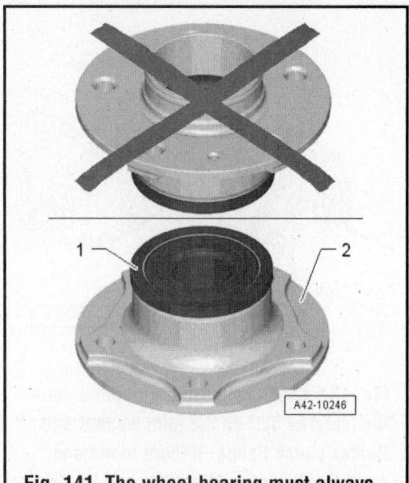

Fig. 141 The wheel bearing must always face up

16. Tighten\connecting link to the trailing arm by hand.

17. Threaded connection of trailing link/wheel bearing housing must only be tightened when all other components (spring and strut always) of the respective wheel suspension have been already assembled. To tighten, suspension must be relaxed. Only now do the trailing link and wheel bearing housing move into the position required.

18. Tighten bolt and washer. The washer is installed on vehicles with an aluminum wheel bearing housing.

19. Place trailing arm on wheel bearing housing with bolts but do not tighten yet.

20. Install coil spring.

21. To complete installation, reverse the remaining removal procedure.

22. Vehicle alignment is required.

Wheel Bearing Unit

See Figure 141.

1. Before servicing the vehicle, refer to the precautions section.

2. Remove the wheel.

3. Loosen dust cap from seat by tapping lightly on claw of grease cap puller VW 637/2.

4. Press off dust cap.

5. Remove the brake carrier caliper and support to one side with a piece of wire.

6. Remove the brake rotor.

7. Remove the multipoint socket bolt with the socket AF 24 T10361.

8. Remove wheel bearing unit from stub axle.

9. The wheel bearing must always face up.

10. Installation is the reverse order of removal, tighten the bearing nut to 180 Nm plus 180 degrees:

AUDI

Q5 • Q7

SPECIFICATIONS AND MAINTENANCE CHARTS

ENGINE AND VEHICLE IDENTIFICATION

| | | Engine | | | | | | Model Year | |
Code	Liters	Cu. In.	Cyl.	Fuel Sys.	Engine Type	Eng. Mfg.		Code ②	Year
CAEB (Q5)	2.0	121	4	FSI-Turbo	DOHC	Audi		B	2011
CALB (Q5)	3.2	190	6	FSI	DOHC	Audi		C	2012
BHK (Q7)	3.6	220	6	FSI	DOHC	Audi			
BAR (Q7)	4.2	256	8	FSO	DOHC	Audi			
CATA (Q7)	3.0	195	6	TDI	DOHC	Audi			

DOHC: Double Overhead Camshafts

TDI: Turbocharged Diesel Injection

FSI: Direct Fuel Induction

71105_Q5Q7_C0001

GENERAL ENGINE SPECIFICATIONS

Year	Model	Engine Displacement Liters	Engine Code	Net Horsepower @ rpm	Net Torque@rpm (ft. lbs.)	Bore x Stroke (in.)	Compression Ratio	Oil Pressure @ rpm
2011	Q5	2.0	CAEB	220@6300	243@5000	3.25x3.65	9.6:1	21.8@2000
	Q5	3.2	CALB	270@6000	243@5000	3.37x3.65	12.5:1	39-65@2000
	Q7	3.0 TDI	CATA	221@4500	407@2000	3.23x3.56	16.4:1	29@2000
	Q7	3.0T	BHK	276@6200	266@2800	3.50x3.80	10.85:1	44-80@2000
	Q7	3.0T S	BAR	306@6200	302@3200	3.33x3.66	11.0:1	44-80@2000
2012	Q5	2.0	CAEB	220@6300	243@5000	3.25x3.65	9.6:1	21.8@2000
	Q5	3.2	CALB	270@6000	243@5000	3.37x3.65	12.5:1	39-65@2000
	Q7	3.0 TDI	CATA	221@4500	407@2000	3.23x3.56	16.4:1	29@2000
	Q7	3.6	BHK	276@6200	266@2800	3.50x3.80	10.85:1	44-80@2000
	Q7	4.2	BAR	306@6200	302@3200	3.33x3.66	11.0:1	44-80@2000

71105_Q5Q7_C0002

ENGINE TUNE-UP SPECIFICATIONS

Year	Engine Displacement Liters	Engine Code	Spark Plug Gap (in.)	Ignition Timing (deg.) AT	Fuel Pump (psi)	Idle Speed (rpm) AT	Valve Clearance Intake	Valve Clearance Exhaust
2011	2.0	CAEB	NA	①	NA	640-800	HYD	HYD
	3.2	CALB	0.039	①	40	600-700	HYD	HYD
	3.6	BHK	0.043	①	58 ②	670-730	HYD	HYD
	4.2	BAR	0.043	①	58 ②	670-730	HYD	HYD
2012	2.0	CAEB	NA	①	NA	640-800	HYD	HYD
	3.2	CALB	0.039	①	40	600-700	HYD	HYD
	3.6	BHK	0.043	①	58 ②	600-800	HYD	HYD
	4.2	BAR	0.043	①	58 ②	670-730	HYD	HYD

Note: The Vehicle Emission Control Information label reflects specification changes made during production.

The label figures must be used if they differ from those in this chart.

HYD: Hydraulic

NA: Information not available

① The ignition timing is controlled by the ECM and is not adjustable.

② System pressure at idle.

71105_Q5Q7_C0003

DIESEL ENGINE TUNE-UP SPECIFICATIONS

Year	Engine Displacement Liters	Engine Code	Valve Clearance Intake (in.)	Valve Clearance Exhaust (in.)	Intake Valve Opens (deg.)	Injection Pump Setting (deg.)	Idle Speed (rpm)	Cranking Compression Pressure (psi)
2011	3.0	CATA	HYD	HYD	NS	①	①	NS
2012	3.0	CATA	HYD	HYD	NS	①	①	NS

Note: The Vehicle Emission Control Information label reflects specification changes made during production.

NS: Not Specified

① Injection pump timing/idle speed controlled electronically. Specification no longer provided.

71105_Q5Q7_C0003A

CAPACITIES

Year	Model	Engine Displacement Liters	Engine Code	Engine Oil with Filter	Transmission (qts.) Automatic	Final Drive (pts.)	Fuel Tank (gal.)	Cooling System (qts.)
2011	Q7	3.0TDI	CATA	8.8	9.6	①	26.4	16.3
	Q7	3.6	BHK	6.7	9.6	①	26.4	18
	Q7	4.2	BAR	9.0	9.6	①	26.4	10.6
2012	Q7	3.0TDI	CATA	8.8	9.6	①	26.4	16.3
	Q7	3.6	BHK	6.7	9.6	①	26.4	18
	Q7	4.2	BAR	9.0	9.6	①	26.4	10.6

Note: All capacities are approximate. Add fluid gradually and check often to avoid overfilling.

NA: Not applicable

① Transfer case: 2 pts.; Front final drive: 2.2 pts..; Rear final drive w/o EDL: 2.6 pts.; Rear final drive w/ EDL: 3.4 pts

71105_Q5Q7_C0004

FLUID SPECIFICATIONS

Year	Model	Engine Displacement Liters	Engine Code	Engine Oil	Auto. Trans.	Power Steering Fluid	Brake Master Cylinder
2011	Q5	3.2	BKH	5W-40	VW ATF	①	DOT 4
	Q7	3.0 TDI	CATA	5W-40	VW ATF	①	DOT 4
	Q7	3.6	BHK	5W-40	VW ATF	①	DOT 4
	Q7	4.2	BAR	5W-40	VW ATF	①	DOT 4
2012	Q5	3.2	BKH	5W-40	VW ATF	①	DOT 4
	Q7	3.0 TDI	CATA	5W-40	VW ATF	①	DOT 4
	Q7	3.6	BHK	5W-40	VW ATF	①	DOT 4
	Q7	4.2	BAR	5W-40	VW ATF	①	DOT 4

NA: Not Applicable

DOT: Department Of Transportation

① VW G002 000 (do not use ATF)

71105_Q5Q7_C0005

VALVE SPECIFICATIONS

Year	Model	Engine Displacement Liters	Engine Code	Seat Angle (deg.)	Face Angle (deg.)	Stem Diameter (in.)	
						Intake	Exhaust
2011	Q5	2.0	CAEB	45	45	0.2354	0.2346
		3.2	CALB	45	45	0.2346	0.2343
	Q7	3.0 TDI	CATA	45	45	0.232-0.233	0.232-0.233
		3.6	BHK	45	45	0.233	0.232
		4.2	BAR	45	45	0.233	0.232
2012	Q5	2.0	CAEB	45	45	0.2354	0.2346
		3.2	CALB	45	45	0.2346	0.2343
	Q7	3.0 TDI	CATA	45	45	0.232-0.233	0.232-0.233
		3.6	BHK	45	45	0.233	0.232
		4.2	BAR	45	45	0.233	0.232

NS: Not Specified

71105_Q5Q7_C0006

CAMSHAFT AND BEARING SPECIFICATIONS CHART

All measurements are given in inches.

Year	Model	Engine Displ. Liters	Engine Code	Journal Dia.	Brg. Oil Clearance	Shaft End-play	Runout	Journal Bore
2011	Q5	2.0	CAEB	NS	NS	NS	NS	NS
		3.2	CALB	NS	NS	NS	NS	NS
	Q7	3.0 TDI	CATA	NS	NS	0.0058	NS	NS
		3.6	BHK	NS	NS	0.0157	NS	NS
		4.2	BAR	NS	NS	0.0079	NS	NS
2012	Q5	2.0	CAEB	NS	NS	NS	NS	NS
		3.2	CALB	NS	NS	NS	NS	NS
	Q7	3.0 TDI	CATA	NS	NS	0.0058	NS	NS
		3.6	BHK	NS	NS	0.0157	NS	NS
		4.2	BAR	NS	NS	0.0079	NS	NS

NS: Not Specified

71105_Q5Q7_C0007

PISTON AND RING SPECIFICATIONS

All measurements are given in inches.

Year	Model	Engine Disp. Liters	Engine Code	Piston Clearance	Ring Gap			Ring Side Clearance		
					Top Compression	Bottom Compression	Oil Control	Top Compression	Bottom Compression	Oil Control
2011	Q5	2.0	CAEB	0.002	0.0138-0.0197	0.0236-0.0315	0.0010-0.0197	0.0008-0.0032	0.0008-0.0032	0.0008-0.0032
		3.2	CALB	NA	0.0078-0.0157	0.0078-0.0157	0.0098-0.0197	0.0016-0.0035	0.0012-0.0023	0.0008-0.0035
	Q7	3.0 TDI	CATA	0.0025-0.0026	0.010-0.014	0.027-0.035	0.0150	0.0047-0.0062	0.0008-0.0035	0.0008-0.0035
		3.6	BHK	0.0025	0.008-0.015	0.008-0.015	0.009-0.019	0.0015-0.0035	0.0012-0.0024	0.0008-0.0024
		4.2	BAR	0.0027	0.008-0.014	0.008-0.016	0.008-0.016	0.0014-0.0034	0.0002-0.0018	0.0004-0.0020
2012	Q5	2.0	CAEB	0.002	0.0138-0.0197	0.0236-0.0315	0.0010-0.0197	0.0008-0.0032	0.0008-0.0032	0.0008-0.0032
		3.2	CALB	NA	0.0078-0.0157	0.0078-0.0157	0.0098-0.0197	0.0016-0.0035	0.0012-0.0023	0.0008-0.0035
	Q7	3.0 TDI	CATA	0.0025-0.0026	0.010-0.014	0.027-0.035	0.0150	0.0047-0.0062	0.0008-0.0035	0.0008-0.0035
		3.6	BHK	0.0025	0.008-0.015	0.008-0.015	0.009-0.019	0.0015-0.0035	0.0012-0.0024	0.0008-0.0024
		4.2	BAR	0.0027	0.008-0.014	0.008-0.016	0.008-0.016	0.0014-0.0034	0.0002-0.0018	0.0004-0.0020

71105_Q5Q7_C0008

CRANKSHAFT AND CONNECTING ROD SPECIFICATIONS

All measurements are given in inches.

Year	Model	Engine Disp. Liters	Engine Code	Crankshaft				Connecting Rod		
				Main Brg. Journal Dia.	Main Brg. Oil Clearance	Shaft End-play	Thrust on No.	Journal Diameter	Oil Clearance	Side Clearance
2011	Q5	2.0	CAEB	2.5590	NS	0.006-0.0100	NS	2.2830	NS	0.0004-0.0020
		3.2	CALB	2.3606-2.3613	0.0008-0.0024	0.0003-0.0090	5	2.1243-2.1251	0.0008-0.0028	NS
	Q7	3.0 TDI	BHK	2.5350	0.0007-0.0017	0.0035-0.0083	NS	2.3400	0.0006-0.0024	NS
		3.6	BAR	2.3605	0.0007-0.0023	0.0027-0.0090	5	2.1243	0.0007-0.0027	0.0019-0.0122
		4.2	CALB	2.558-2.5600	0.0007-0.0017	0.0035-0.0100	4	2.1251-2.1276	0.0008-0.0027	NS
2012	Q5	2.0	CAEB	2.5590	NS	0.006-0.0100	NS	2.2830	NS	0.0004-0.0020
		3.2	CALB	2.3606-2.3613	0.0008-0.0024	0.0003-0.0090	5	2.1243-2.1251	0.0008-0.0028	NS
	Q7	3.0 TDI	BHK	2.5350	0.0007-0.0017	0.0035-0.0083	NS	2.3400	0.0006-0.0024	NS
		3.6	BAR	2.3605	0.0007-0.0023	0.0027-0.0090	5	2.1243	0.0007-0.0027	0.0019-0.0122
		4.2	CALB	2.558-2.5600	0.0007-0.0017	0.0035-0.0100	4	2.1251-2.1276	0.0008-0.0027	NS

NS: Not specified

71105_Q5Q7_C0009

TORQUE SPECIFICATIONS
All readings in ft. lbs.

Year	Model	Engine Disp. Liters	Engine Code	Cylinder Head Bolts	Main Bearing Bolts	Rod Bearing Bolts	Crankshaft Damper Bolt	Flywheel Bolts	Manifold Intake	Manifold Exhaust	Spark Plugs	Oil Pan Drain Plug
2011	Q5	2.0	CAEB	①	②	③	④	NS	⑤	⑥	22	22
		3.2	CALB	⑦	⑧	⑧	⑨	NS	10	17	22	22
	Q7	3.0L TDI	CATA	⑩	⑪	③	⑫	⑧	⑤	17	NS	22
		3.6	BHK	⑪	⑬	⑧	⑩	⑪	⑫	NS	15	22
		4.2	BAR	⑬	⑧	⑭	⑮	⑯	⑫	NS	22	37
2012	Q5	2.0	CAEB	①	②	③	④	NS	⑤	⑥	22	22
		3.2	BKH	⑯	③	③	⑩	NS	10	17	22	22
	Q7	3.0L TDI	CATA	⑩	⑪	③	⑫	⑧	⑤	17	NS	22
		3.6	BHK	⑪	⑬	⑧	⑩	⑪	⑫	NS	15	22
		4.2	BAR	⑬	⑧	⑭	⑮	⑯	⑫	NS	22	37

NS: Not specified

① Torque in three steps: (use new bolts)

   Step 1: 30 ft. lbs., in sequence

   Step 2: plus 90 degrees, in sequence

   Step 3: plus 90 degrees, in sequence

② Torque in three steps: (use new bolts)

   Step 1: Hand tight, in sequence

   Step 2: 48 ft. lbs., in sequence

   Step 3: plus 90 degrees, in sequence

③ Use new bolts: 30 ft. lbs. plus 90 degrees

④ Use new bolts: 150 ft. lbs. plus 90 degrees

⑤ Lower intake manifold with fuel rail: 7 ft. lbs.

   Upper intake manifold: 6 ft. lbs.

⑥ Torque in four steps: (use new nuts)

   Step 1: 4 ft. lbs., in sequence

   Step 2: 9 ft. lbs., in sequence

   Step 3: 12 ft. lbs., in sequence

   Step 4: 18 ft. lbs., in sequence

⑧ Use new bolts: 22 ft. lbs. plus 90 degrees

⑨ Use new bolts: 74 ft. lbs. plus 90 degrees

⑩ Torque in four steps: (use new bolts)

   Step 1: 22 ft. lbs.

   Step 2: 44 ft. lbs.

   Step 3: plus 90 degrees

   Step 4: plus 90 degrees

⑪ Torque in four steps: (use new bolts)

   Step 1: 22 ft. lbs.

   Step 2: 37 ft. lbs.

   Step 3: plus 90 degrees

   Step 4: plus 90 degrees

⑫ Use new bolts: 15 ft. lbs. plus 90 degrees

⑬ Use new bolts: 22 ft. lbs. plus 180 degrees

⑭ Use new bolts: 44 ft. lbs. plus 90 degrees

⑮ M8 nuts: 18 ft. lbs

   M10 nuts: 30 ft. lbs.

71105_Q5Q7_C0010

WHEEL ALIGNMENT

Year	Model		Caster Range (+/-Deg.)	Caster Preferred Setting (Deg.)	Camber Range (+/-Deg.)	Camber Preferred Setting (Deg.)	Toe-in (Deg.)
2011	Standard	F	0.16	8.16	0.33	0.00	0.04 +/- 0.04
	Suspension	R	—	—	0.33	1.00	0.16 +/- 0.08
	Sport	F	0.16	8.58	0.33	-0.16	0.08 +/- 0.04
	Suspension	R	—	—	0.33	1.00	0.16 +/- 0.08
	Air Springs	F	0.50	8.45	0.1	-0.20	0.10 +/- 0.30
	Suspension	R	—	—	0.2	-1.20	0.10 +/- 0.05
2012	Standard	F	0.16	8.16	0.33	0.00	0.04 +/- 0.04
	Suspension	R	—	—	0.33	1.00	0.16 +/- 0.08
	Sport	F	0.16	8.58	0.33	-0.16	0.08 +/- 0.04
	Suspension	R	—	—	0.33	1.00	0.16 +/- 0.08
	Air Springs	F	0.50	8.45	0.1	-0.20	0.10 +/- 0.30
	Suspension	R	—	—	0.2	-1.20	0.10 +/- 0.05

NOTE: Alignment specifications are dependent on proger vehicle ride height.

71105_Q5Q7_C0011

TIRE, WHEEL AND BALL JOINT SPECIFICATIONS

Year	Model	OEM Tires Standard	OEM Tires Optional	Tire Pressures (psi) Front	Tire Pressures (psi) Rear	Lug Nut (ft. lbs.)
2011	Q5 2.0L	235/60-18	235/55-19	①	①	103
	Q5 3.2L	235/55-19	255/45-20	①	①	103
	Q7 3.0L TDI	②	NS	①	①	133
	Q7 3.6L	②	NS	①	①	118
	Q7 4.2L	P275/45-19	NS	①	①	133
2012	Q5 2.0L	235/60-18	235/55-19	①	①	103
	Q5 3.2L	235/55-19	255/45-20	①	①	103
	Q7 3.0L TDI	②	NS	①	①	133
	Q7 3.6L	②	NS	①	①	118
	Q7 4.2L	P275/45-19	NS	①	①	133

NS: Not specified

OEM: Original Equipment Manufacturer

PSI: Pounds Per Square Inch

① All models equipped with TPMS; consult vehicle tag or owner's handbook for specific pressures.

② 255/60-17, 275/45-19, 275/40-20

71105_Q5Q7_C0012

BRAKE SPECIFICATIONS
All measurements in inches unless noted

Year	Model		Brake Disc Original Thickness	Brake Disc Minimum Thickness	Brake Disc Maximum Run-out	Minimum Lining Thickness	Brake Caliper Guide Pins (ft. lbs.)	Brake Caliper Mounting Bolts (ft. lbs.)
2011	Q5/Q7	F	①	NA	NA	0.07	22	145
		R	②	NA	NA	0.07	26	③
2012	Q5/Q7	F	①	NA	NA	0.07	22	145
		R	②	NA	NA	0.07	26	③

NA: Information not available
① 17" 1LC, 1LE: 1.26"
   18" 1LF: 1.34"
② 17" 1KF, 1KQ: 1.10"
③ 74 ft. lbs., plus 90 degrees additional

71105_Q5Q7_C0013

SCHEDULED MAINTENANCE INTERVALS
Audi Q5 & Q7 Gasoline Engines

TO BE SERVICED	TYPE OF SERVICE	5	10	20	30	40	45	50	60	70	75	80	90	100
Engine oil & filter	R	✔	✔	✔	✔	✔		✔	✔	✔		✔	✔	✔
Brake pad thickness	S/I		✔	✔	✔	✔		✔	✔	✔		✔	✔	✔
Dust seals on ball joints, tie rod ends & tie rods	S/I			✔		✔			✔			✔		✔
Battery	S/I		✔	✔	✔	✔		✔	✔	✔		✔	✔	✔
Brake system	S/I		✔	✔	✔	✔		✔	✔	✔		✔	✔	✔
Cooling system	S/I			✔		✔			✔			✔		✔
Driveshaft boots	S/I			✔		✔			✔			✔		✔
Engine (check for leaks)	S/I			✔		✔			✔			✔		✔
Engine exhaust	S/I			✔		✔			✔			✔		✔
Power steering fluid level	S/I			✔		✔			✔			✔		✔
Underbody	S/I						✔					✔		
Timing belt (V8)	R											✔		
Transmission fluid level	S/I			✔		✔			✔			✔		✔
Air filter element	R			✔								✔		
Spark plugs (V6)	R			✔								✔		
Spark plugs (V8)	R							✔				✔		
Passenger compartment air filter	R		✔			✔			✔			✔		✔
Drive belts	S/I					✔						✔		
Brake fluid ①	R													

R: Replace   S/I: Service or Inspect
① Replace every two years regardless of mileage.

FREQUENT OPERATION MAINTENANCE (SEVERE SERVICE)
If a vehicle is operated under any of the following conditions it is considered severe service:
- Extremely dusty areas.
- 50% or more of the vehicle operation is in 32°C (90°F) or higher temperatures, or constant operation in temperatures below 0°C (32°F).
- Prolonged idling (vehicle operation in stop and go traffic).
- Frequent short running periods (engine does not warm to normal operating temperatures).
- Police, taxi, delivery usage or trailer towing usage.

Oil & oil filter change: change every 3750 miles.
Air filter element: service or inspect every 15,000 miles.
Automatic transaxle fluid & filter: replace every 30,000 miles.

71105_Q5Q7_C0014

PRECAUTIONS

Before servicing any vehicle, please be sure to read all of the following precautions, which deal with personal safety, prevention of component damage, and important points to take into consideration when servicing a motor vehicle:

• Never open, service or drain the radiator or cooling system when the engine is hot; serious burns can occur from the steam and hot coolant.

• Observe all applicable safety precautions when working around fuel. Whenever servicing the fuel system, always work in a well-ventilated area. Do not allow fuel spray or vapors to come in contact with a spark, open flame, or excessive heat (a hot drop light, for example). Keep a dry chemical fire extinguisher near the work area. Always keep fuel in a container specifically designed for fuel storage; also, always properly seal fuel containers to avoid the possibility of fire or explosion. Refer to the additional fuel system precautions later in this section.

• Fuel injection systems often remain pressurized, even after the engine has been turned **OFF**. The fuel system pressure must be relieved before disconnecting any fuel lines. Failure to do so may result in fire and/or personal injury.

• Brake fluid often contains polyglycol ethers and polyglycols. Avoid contact with the eyes and wash your hands thoroughly after handling brake fluid. If you do get brake fluid in your eyes, flush your eyes with clean, running water for 15 minutes. If eye irritation persists, or if you have taken brake fluid internally, IMMEDIATELY seek medical assistance.

• The EPA warns that prolonged contact with used engine oil may cause a number of skin disorders, including cancer. You should make every effort to minimize your exposure to used engine oil. Protective gloves should be worn when changing oil. Wash your hands and any other exposed skin areas as soon as possible after exposure to used engine oil. Soap and water, or waterless hand cleaner should be used.

• All new vehicles are now equipped with an air bag system, often referred to as a Supplemental Restraint System (SRS) or Supplemental Inflatable Restraint (SIR) system. The system must be disabled before performing service on or around system components, steering column, instrument panel components, wiring and sensors. Failure to follow safety and disabling procedures could result in accidental air bag deployment, possible personal injury and unnecessary system repairs.

• Always wear safety goggles when working with, or around, the air bag system. When carrying a non-deployed air bag, be sure the bag and trim cover are pointed away from your body. When placing a non-deployed air bag on a work surface, always face the bag and trim cover upward, away from the surface. This will reduce the motion of the module if it is accidentally deployed. Refer to the additional air bag system precautions later in this section.

• Clean, high quality brake fluid from a sealed container is essential to the safe and proper operation of the brake system. You should always buy the correct type of brake fluid for your vehicle. If the brake fluid becomes contaminated, completely flush the system with new fluid. Never reuse any brake fluid. Any brake fluid that is removed from the system should be discarded. Also, do not allow any brake fluid to come in contact with a painted surface; it will damage the paint.

• Never operate the engine without the proper amount and type of engine oil; doing so WILL result in severe engine damage.

• Timing belt maintenance is extremely important. Many models utilize an interference-type, non-freewheeling engine. If the timing belt breaks, the valves in the cylinder head may strike the pistons, causing potentially serious (also time-consuming and expensive) engine damage. Refer to the maintenance interval charts for the recommended replacement interval for the timing belt, and to the timing belt section for belt replacement and inspection.

• Disconnecting the negative battery cable on some vehicles may interfere with the functions of the on-board computer system(s) and may require the computer to undergo a relearning process once the negative battery cable is reconnected.

• When servicing drum brakes, only disassemble and assemble one side at a time, leaving the remaining side intact for reference.

• Only an MVAC-trained, EPA-certified automotive technician should service the air conditioning system or its components.

BRAKES   ANTI-LOCK BRAKE SYSTEM (ABS)

GENERAL INFORMATION

PRECAUTIONS

• Certain components within the ABS system are not intended to be serviced or repaired individually.

• Do not use rubber hoses or other parts not specifically specified for and ABS system. When using repair kits, replace all parts included in the kit. Partial or incorrect repair may lead to functional problems and require the replacement of components.

• Lubricate rubber parts with clean, fresh brake fluid to ease assembly. Do not use shop air to clean parts; damage to rubber components may result.

• Use only DOT 3 brake fluid from an unopened container.

• If any hydraulic component or line is removed or replaced, it may be necessary to bleed the entire system.

• A clean repair area is essential. Always clean the reservoir and cap thoroughly before removing the cap. The slightest amount of dirt in the fluid may plug an orifice and impair the system function. Perform repairs after components have been thoroughly cleaned; use only denatured alcohol to clean components.

Do not allow ABS components to come into contact with any substance containing mineral oil; this includes used shop rags.

• The Anti-Lock control unit is a microprocessor similar to other computer units in the vehicle. Ensure that the ignition switch is **OFF** before removing or installing controller harnesses. Avoid static electricity discharge at or near the controller.

• If any arc welding is to be done on the vehicle, the control unit should be unplugged before welding operations begin.

SPEED SENSORS

REMOVAL & INSTALLATION

➥**The sensor ring/rotor is installed in the respective wheel bearing unit and cannot be replaced.**

1. Raise vehicle.

2. Unlock and disconnect connector on speed sensor.

3. Remove the retaining bolt.

4. Remove speed sensor from wheel bearing housing.

To install:

5. Installation is in reverse order of removal, with special attention to the following:

a. Before inserting speed sensor, clean hole inner surface and coat speed sensor all-round with Polycarbamide grease.

b. Turn the steering completely left and right after installation, making sure the speed sensor wiring has sufficient clearance.

BRAKES

BLEEDING THE BRAKE SYSTEM

BLEEDING PROCEDURE

BLEEDING PROCEDURE

1. Do not, under any circumstances, allow brake fluid to come into contact with any fluids containing mineral oil (oil, gasoline, cleaning solvents). Mineral oil damages the sealing plugs and boots of the brake system.

2. Brake fluid is poisonous. NEVER siphon brake fluid with your mouth! Also due to its corrosive effect, brake fluid must not come into contact with paintwork.

3. Brake fluid is hygroscopic, meaning that it absorbs moisture from the surrounding air, and must therefore be stored in airtight containers.

4. When bleeding, brake fluid that has been flushed through must not be reused and must be disposed of properly.

5. Observe the disposal regulations.

Q5

Only use new brake fluid conforming to US-Norm FMVSS 116 DOT 4.

Genuine VW/Audi brake fluid conforms to this specification.

Do not use any silicone-based fluid.

Avoid contaminating brake fluid with particles or lint (e.g. from cleaning cloths).

Rinse off spills, by using plenty of water.

Do not work with compressed air and do not move vehicle while the system is open.

During the final road test, ensure that an

ABS-controlled brake test is performed at least once (pulsation must be felt at the brake pedal).

The brake system indicator light blinks when the brake fluid is too low or the ABS system or parking brake is malfunctioning.

1. Bleeding, with Electronic Stability Program:

➥**There must be a positive pressure of 2 bar to bleed the hydraulic unit N55. Pressure setting must be checked at bleeder device.**

➥**Only place brake pedal load device on brake system during assembly, then bleed.**

➥**Tools Needed:**

- Brake filler/bleeder unit VAS 5234
- Adapter VAS 5234/1A

Bleed brake system with brake filler/bleeder unit VAS 5234 with adapter VAS 5234/1A

Follow VAS 5234 operating instructions.

2. Raise vehicle.

3. Connect VAS 5234 with adapter VAS 5234/1A.

4. Open bleeder screws in specified sequence and bleed (support with pedal pressure if necessary).

Bleeding sequence:

➥**Each brake caliper has two bleeder screws. To achieve optimum brake sys-**

tem bleeding, bleed the respective brake caliper at both bleeder screws. Always bleed the outer screw first, then the inner one.**

a. Left front brake caliper.
b. Right front brake caliper.
c. Left rear brake caliper.
d. Right rear brake caliper.

5. Bleed until the brake fluid comes out with no bubbles and foam.

6. Close the bleeder screws.

7. Lower the vehicle.

Q7

Adhere strictly to work sequence when bleeding brake system.

a. There are two bleeder valves installed on Brembo brake calipers. Always bleed at both bleeder valves.

b. Bleed at outer bleeder valve first.

1. Connect Brake filler/bleeder unit VAS 5234.

2. Open bleeder valves in the prescribed sequence and bleed brake caliper.

- Right rear brake caliper
- Left rear brake caliper
- Right front brake caliper
- Left front brake caliper

3. Use a suitable bleeder hose. It must fit tightly on bleeder valve so that no air gets into brake system.

4. With bleeder bottle hose attached, leave bleeder valves open long enough that brake fluid exits without bubbles.

✳✳ CAUTION

Dust and dirt accumulating on brake parts during normal use may contain asbestos fibers from production or aftermarket brake linings. Breathing excessive concentrations of asbestos fibers can cause serious bodily harm. Exercise care when servicing brake parts. Do not sand or grind brake lining unless equipment used is designed to contain the dust residue. Do not clean brake parts with compressed air or by dry brushing. Cleaning should be done by dampening the brake components with a fine mist of water, then wiping the brake components clean with a dampened cloth. Dispose of cloth and all residue containing asbestos fibers in an impermeable container with the appropriate label. Follow practices prescribed by the Occupational Safety and Health Administration (OSHA) and the Environmental Protection Agency (EPA) for the handling, processing, and disposing of dust or debris that may contain asbestos fibers.

BRAKE CALIPER

REMOVAL & INSTALLATION

Q5

Type FN-3

See Figure 1.

➡**Tools needed:**

- Torque Wrench V.A.G 1332
- Reversible ratchet V.A.G. 1332/1
- Torque Wrench V.A.G 1331
- Reversible ratchet V.A.G. 1331/1
- Brake pedal actuator V.A.G 1869/2
- Piston resetting tool T10145

1. Insert brake pedal actuator V.A.G 1869/2 between the brake pedal and driver seat by pressing the brake pedal down at least 60 mm. By doing this, the valves in the brake master cylinder are closed and the brake fluid reservoir does not run empty.

2. Raise the vehicle.

3. Remove the wheels.

4. Connect hose from a bleeder bottle to one of the bleeder screws on the front caliper.

5. Open a bleeder screw on the front brake caliper to reduce the pressure from the brake system.

6. Close bleeder screw.

   a. Do not remove brake pedal loading device V.A.G 1869/2.

7. Remove brake pressure line from brake caliper.

8. Remove brake pads.

   a. When removing, mark brake pads that will be used again. Install in the same position or braking effect will be uneven.

9. Remove brake caliper from the vehicle.

10. Remove bolts on the brake carrier while holding the carrier securely.

11. Remove brake carrier.

to install:

Use new bolts.

12. Position brake carrier.

13. Tighten brake carrier with new bolts.

14. Install brake pads.

➡After replacing the brake pads, press the brake pedal firmly several times while the vehicle is stationary so that the brake pads are seated properly in their normal operating position.

15. Install the brake pressure line **5** in the brake caliper and tighten.

16. Remove brake pedal loading device V.A.G 1869/2.

17. Bleed brake system.

18. Install the wheels. For wheel bolt tightening specifications refer to Specifications.

Except FN-3

➡**Tools Needed:**

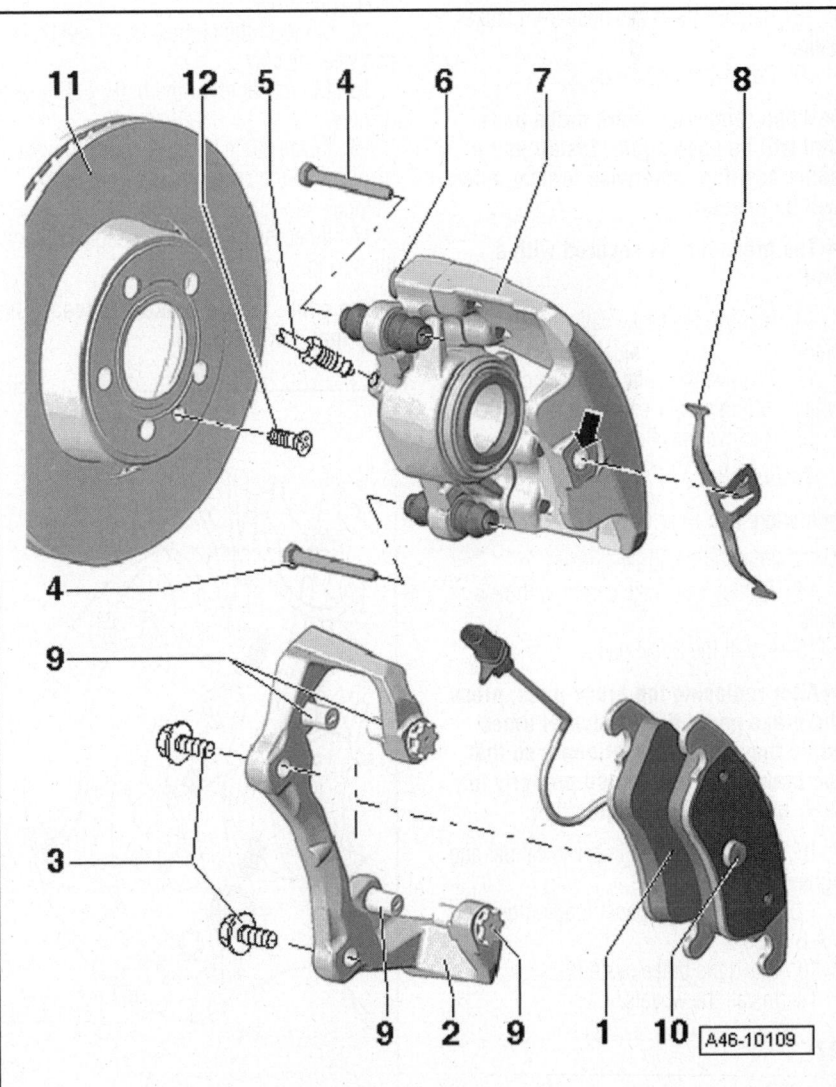

Fig. 1 Removing the brake caliper—Never remove bolts 6 and 9.

- Torque wrench V.A.G 1332
- Reversible ratchet V.A.G. 1332/1
- Torque wrench V.A.G 1331
- Reversible ratchet V.A.G. 1331/1
- Brake pedal actuator V.A.G 1869/2

1. Piston resetting tool T10145
2. Insert brake pedal actuator V.A.G 1869/2 between brake pedal and driver seat by pressing brake pedal down at least 2.35 in. (60 mm). By doing this, the valves in the brake master cylinder are closed and brake fluid reservoir does not run empty.
3. Raise the vehicle.
4. Remove the wheels.
5. Connect the hose from a bleeder bottle to one of bleeder screws on front caliper.
6. Open a bleeder screw on the front brake caliper to reduce pressure from the brake system.
7. Close the bleeder screw.

➡**Do not remove brake pedal loading device V.A.G 1869/2.**

8. Remove the brake hose from brake caliper.
9. Remove the brake pads.

➡**When removing, mark brake pads that will be used again. Install in the same position, otherwise braking effect will be uneven.**

➡**The brake disc is secured with a bolt.**

10. Remove the brake caliper from vehicle.
11. Remove the bolts on brake carrier while holding carrier securely.
12. Remove brake carrier.

To install:

➡**Always use new bolts.**

13. Position the brake carrier.
14. Tighten the brake carrier with new bolts.
15. Install the brake pads.

➡**After replacing the brake pads, press the brake pedal firmly several times while the vehicle is stationary so that the brake pads are seated properly in their normal operating position.**

16. Install brake line in brake caliper and tighten.
17. Remove brake pedal loading device V.A.G 1869/2.
18. Bleed the brake system.
19. Install the wheels.

Q7

18"Plus

See Figure 2.

1. Remove wheels.
2. Connect bleeder bottle hose to bleeder valve of brake caliper and then open bleeder valve.
3. Insert brake pedal depressor V.A.G 1869/2.
4. Close bleeder valve and remove bleeder bottle.
5. Disconnect brake line from the brake caliper.
6. Remove brake pads.
7. Remove brake caliper from the vehicle.

To install:

8. Install brake pads.
9. Clean bolt ribbing.
10. Replace damaged bolts.
11. Tighten bolts on the brake caliper to 199 ft. lbs. (270 Nm).
12. Install brake line in the brake caliper. Tighten to 10 ft. lbs. (14 Nm).
13. Press brake hose into mount on the stub axle carrier.
14. Connect the connector for the brake pad wear display.
15. Mount cable for the brake pad wear display.
16. Install cable for the brake pad wear display into the spring in the front brake caliper.
17. If necessary, close the cable clips on the spring.

➡**The cable for the brake pad wear display may not lay open.**

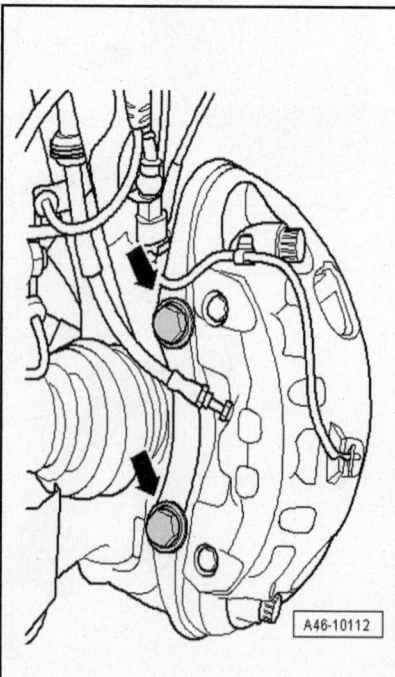

Fig. 2 Tightening the brake caliper bolts

18. Install the wheels. Tighten to 199 ft. lbs. (270 Nm).
19. Remove brake pedal loading device V.A.G 1869/2.
20. Bleed brake system.
21. Install the wheels. Before moving vehicle, depress brake pedal several times firmly to properly seat brake pads in their normal operating position.
    a. Check brake fluid level.

DISC BRAKE PADS

REMOVAL & INSTALLATION

Q5

FBC-57

See Figure 3.

➡**Tools needed:**

- Torque Wrench V.A.G 1331
- Reversible ratchet V.A.G. 1331/1
- Piston resetting tool T10145

➡**The 4 retaining pins for the brake pads on the brake carrier must not be loosened under any circumstances.**

1. Raise the vehicle.
2. Remove the wheels.
    a. When removing, mark brake pads that will be used again. Install in the same position, otherwise braking effect will be uneven.
3. Free the brake hose on the bracket.
4. Release electrical wire from the bracket toward the left and remove.

➡**The four retaining pins for the brake pads in the brake caliper must not be loosened under any circumstances.**

5. Press the retaining spring in the center.

FBC-3

See Figure 4.

Always replace on both axles.

➡**Tools Needed:**

- Torque wrench V.A.G 1331
- Reversible ratchet V.A.G. 1331/1
- Piston resetting tool T10145

1. Raise the vehicle.
2. Remove the wheels.

➡**When removing, mark brake pads that will be used again. Install in the same position, otherwise braking effect will be uneven.**

3. Remove the caps (#13 in the illustration).

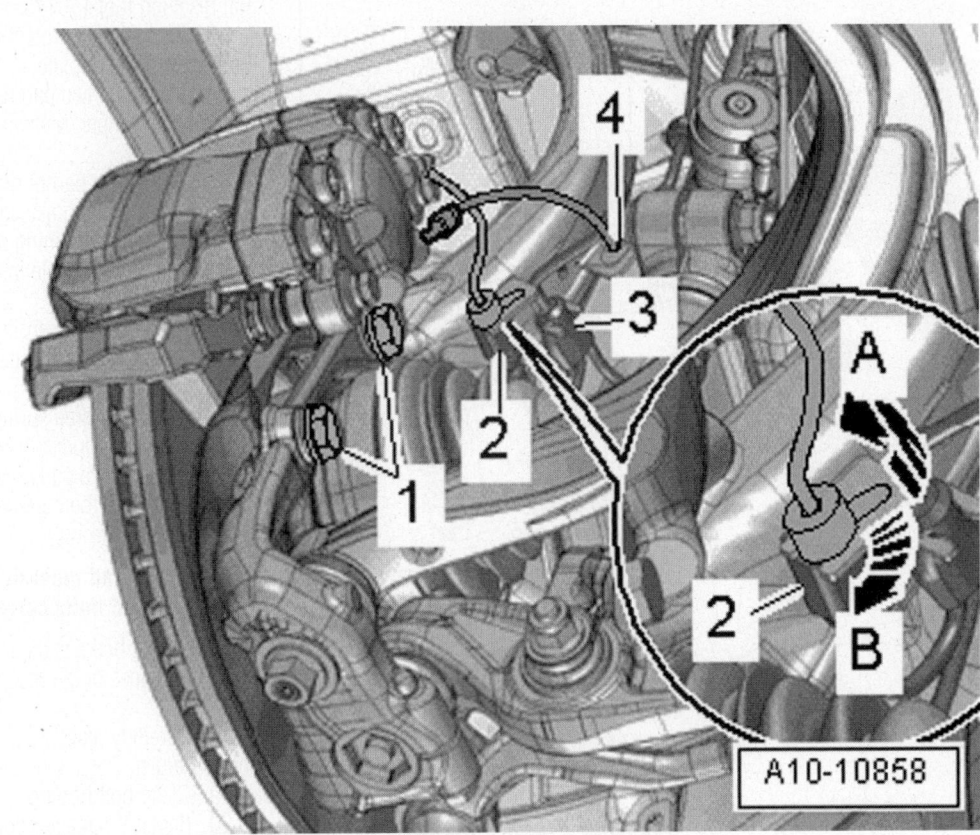

Fig. 3 Freeing up the brake hose on the bracket

4. For vehicles with the brake wear pad indicator, disconnect the left front connector.

5. Lift securing strap slightly at bottom of connector and then rotate 90°.

6. Remove lower part of the brake pad wear indicator connector from the bracket.

7. Using a screwdriver, pry off brake pad retaining spring from brake caliper housing and remove.

8. Loosen and remove both guide pins from brake caliper.

Secure brake caliper to the vehicle with a suitable wire. Do not support weight with the brake hose.

9. Remove brake pads from brake caliper housing or from brake carrier.

To install:

10. Clean brake caliper housing.

➡**Clean brake caliper with mineral spirits exclusively.**

➡**Press piston back into caliper housing using resetting tool before inserting new brake pads. Before pushing back the piston, siphon some of the brake**

fluid out of the brake fluid reservoir. **Otherwise, especially if reservoir has been topped off, fluid will overflow and cause damage.**

❊❊ WARNING

Brake fluid is poisonous. NEVER siphon brake fluid with your mouth.

11. Press piston back. Use piston resetting tool T10145.

12. Insert brake pad with retaining spring into brake caliper housing (piston).

➡**The inner surface (with tension spring) is indicated by an arrow. The arrow must point in the rotation direction of the brake rotor when driving forward. If improperly installed, noises could result.**

13. Remove any protective film from the brake pad backing plate.

14. Install the outer brake pad on brake carrier.

15. Install both guide pins in the brake caliper housing and tighten.

16. Insert both caps.

17. Install the retaining spring in brake caliper housing.

➡**Retaining spring must be pressed under brake carrier after it is inserted in both holes. If improperly installed, the wear of the outer brake pad cannot be adjusted, thereby increasing brake pedal travel.**

➡**After installing the brake pads, depress brake pedal several times firmly to properly seat brake pads in their normal operating position.**

18. Check the brake fluid level, and fill if necessary.

Q7

See Figure 5.

➡**Tools needed:**

- Torque Wrench V.A.G 1576
- Piston resetting tool T10145

➡**When removing, mark brake pads that will be used again. Install in the same position, otherwise braking effect will be uneven.**

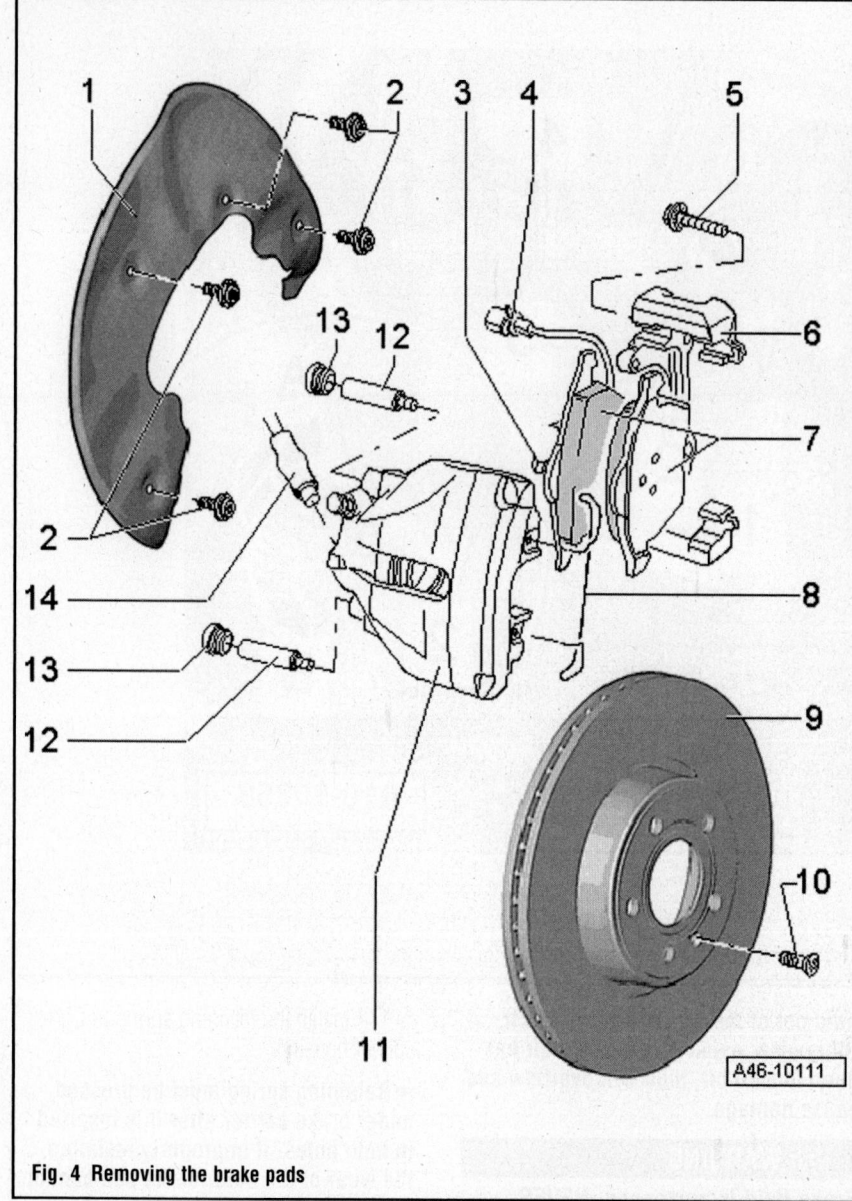

Fig. 4 Removing the brake pads

1. Remove the wheels.
2. Separate connector for brake pad wear indicator.
3. Unclip cable for the brake pad wear display from the spring in the brake caliper.
4. Remove brake hose from its mount on the stub axle carrier.
5. Using pliers, slightly push the brake piston on the installed brake pads.
   a. Do not loosen the brake hose.
6. Loosen brake caliper at the bolts.

➡**Never mount the brake caliper on the adapter plate. The radial bolted multi-point head cap bolt must never be loosened.**

7. Pull brake caliper from brake disc.
8. Hang brake caliper on the body using a suitable wire.

9. Pry brake pads out of the brake caliper with a screwdriver; be sure not to damage the dust caps.
10. Remove brake pads from the retaining springs.

To install:
11. Clean brake caliper.
   a. Only use commercially available brake cleaner to clean the brake caliper housing.

➡**Before pressing the pistons into cylinder using piston resetting tool, brake fluid must be extracted from brake fluid reservoir. Otherwise, especially if reservoir has been topped off, fluid will overflow and cause damage.**

➡**Brake fluid is poisonous. NEVER siphon brake fluid with your mouth.**

12. Press the piston back. Use the Piston resetting tool T10145.
13. Remove any protective film from the brake pad backing plate.
14. Install the two pad retaining springs in the brake caliper. Make sure they fit correctly.
   a. The long part of the springs faces the center of the brake caliper.
15. Install the retaining spring for the brake wear display cable into the center of the brake caliper.
   a. The retaining spring for the brake wear display cable faces outward.
   b. In total, three springs are installed in the brake caliper.
16. Install brake pads inside the brake caliper and push them onto the 4 pad retaining bolts arrows.

➡**The brake pad must fit in the retaining spring and bolts correctly.**

17. Mount brake pads on the 4 contact surfaces of the brake retaining springs.
18. Carefully place the brake caliper over the brake disc.
19. Clean bolt ribbing.
20. Replace damaged bolts.
21. Tighten bolts on the brake caliper to 199 ft. lbs. (270 Nm).
22. Press brake hose into the mount on the stub axle carrier.
23. Connect the connector for the brake pad wear display.
24. Mount cable for the brake pad wear display.
25. Install cable for the brake pad wear display into the retaining spring in the front brake caliper.
26. If necessary, close the cable clip on the retaining spring.

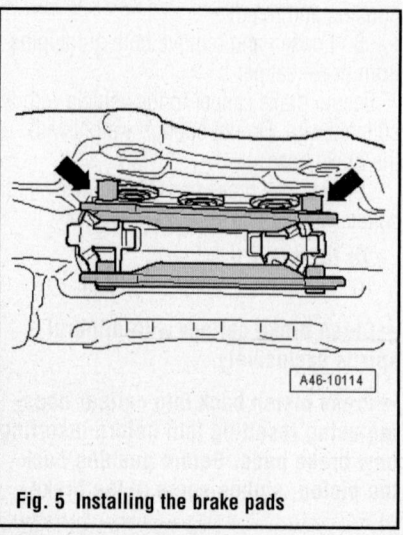

Fig. 5 Installing the brake pads

a. The cable for the brake pad wear display may not lay open.

27. Install the wheels.

BRAKES

BRAKE CALIPER

REMOVAL & INSTALLATION

Q5

See Figure 6.

Use new bolts.

➡ **When replacing the rear brake caliper, the actuator must not be removed. The new brake caliper is delivered with a new actuator.**

➡ **Tools Needed:**

- Torque wrench V.A.G 1332
- Reversible ratchet V.A.G. 1332/1
- Torque wrench V.A.G 1331
- Reversible ratchet V.A.G. 1331/1
- Brake pedal actuator V.A.G 1869/2

1. Insert brake pedal actuator V.A.G 1869/2 between brake pedal and driver seat by pressing brake pedal down at least 2.35 in. (60 mm). By doing this, the valves in the brake master cylinder are closed and the brake fluid reservoir does not run empty.

2. Raise the vehicle.

3. Remove the wheels.

4. Connect hose from a bleeder bottle to one of the bleeder screws on the rear caliper.

5. Open a bleeder screw on the rear brake caliper to reduce the pressure from the brake system.

6. Close the bleeder screw.

➡ **Do not remove brake pedal loading device V.A.G 1869/2.**

a. After replacing brake pads and before moving vehicle, always depress brake pedal several times firmly to properly seat brake pads

in their normal operating position.

b. Check brake fluid level after replacing brake pad.

REAR DISC BRAKES

7. Remove brake pressure line from brake caliper.

8. Remove rear brake pads.

9. Disconnect electrical connector to electronic parking brake.

10. Remove bolts on brake carrier while holding carrier securely.

11. Remove the brake carrier.

➡ **When replacing the rear brake caliper, the actuator must not be removed. The new brake caliper is delivered with a new actuator.**

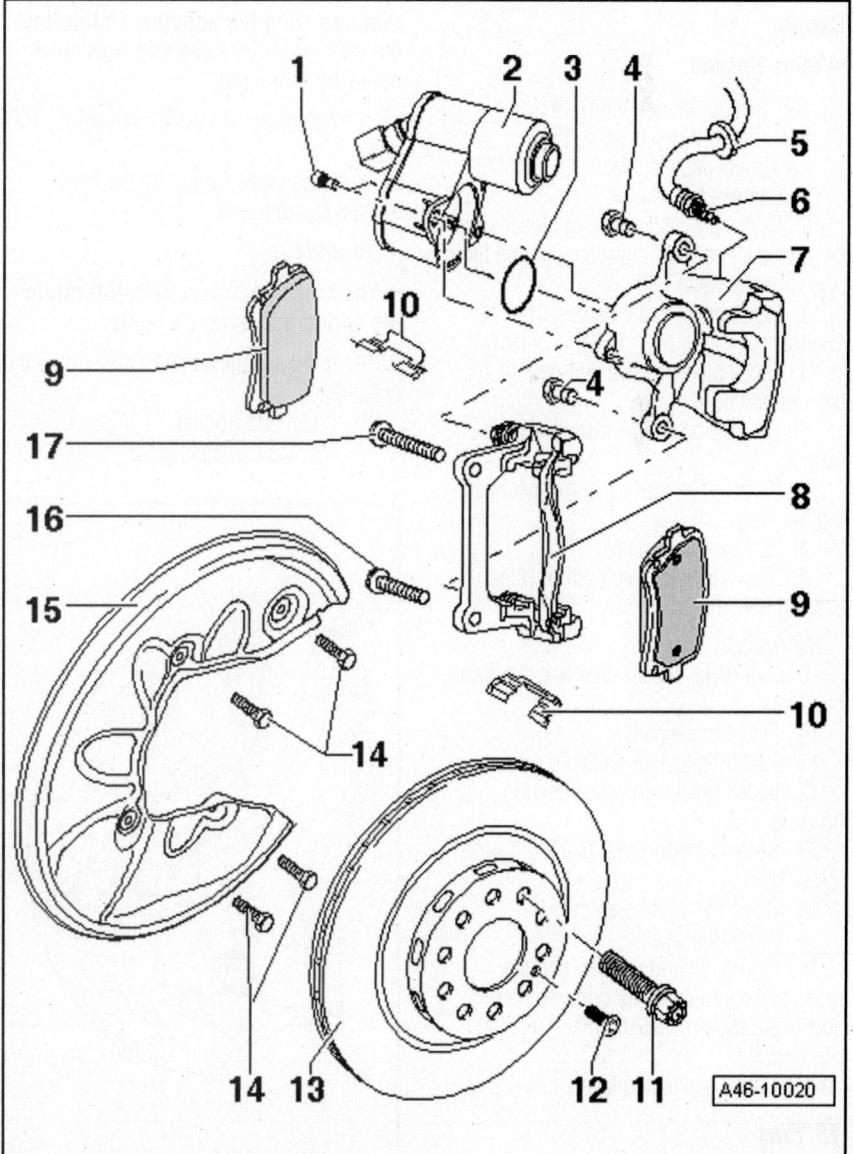

Fig. 6 Removing the rear brake caliper

To install:

12. Position the brake carrier.
13. Tighten the brake carrier with new bolts.
14. Install the brake pads.
15. Connect electrical connector to parking brake.

➡ **After replacing the brake pads, press brake pedal firmly several times while the vehicle is stationary so that the brake pads are seated properly in their normal operating position.**

16. Install the brake line in brake caliper and tighten.
17. Remove the brake pedal loading device V.A.G 1869/2.
18. Bleed the brake system.
19. Install the wheels.

Q7

Caliper

➡ **Tools Needed:**

- Torque Wrench V.A.G 1410
- Torque Wrench V.A.G 1576
- Brake pedal actuator V.A.G 1869/2

1. Remove the wheels.
2. Connect bleeder hose of bleeder bottle to bleeder valve of brake caliper and then open bleeder valve.
3. Insert brake pedal depressor V.A.G 1869/2.
4. Close bleeder valve and remove bleeder bottle.
5. Remove brake line from brake caliper.
6. Remove the bracket from wheel bearing housing.
7. Remove brake pads.
8. Remove brake caliper from wheel bearing housing.

To install:

9. Bolt brake caliper onto wheel bearing housing.
10. Install brake pads.
11. Install brake line on brake caliper.
12. Install bracket to wheel bearing housing.
13. Remove brake pedal loading device V.A.G 1869/2.
14. Bleed the brake system.
15. Install the wheels.
16. Before moving vehicle, depress brake pedal several times firmly to properly seat brake pads in their normal operating position.
17. Check brake fluid level.

18"Plus

See Figure 7.

➡ **Tools Needed: Torque Wrench V.A.G 1576**

➡ **When removing, mark brake pads that will be used again. Install in the same position, otherwise braking effect will be uneven.**

1. Remove wheels.
2. Separate the connector for brake pad wear indicator.
3. Unclip the cable for the brake pad wear display from the spring in the brake caliper.
4. Remove the brake hose from its mount on the stub axle carrier.
5. Using pliers, slightly push the brake piston on the installed brake pads.

➡ **Do not loosen the brake hose.**

6. Loosen brake caliper at the bolts.

➡ **The brake caliper must never be removed from the adapter. The radial bolted multipoint head cap bolt must never be loosened.**

7. Pull brake caliper from brake disc.
8. Hang brake caliper on the body using a suitable wire.

To install:

➡ **The brake pad must fit in the retaining spring and bolts correctly.**

9. Carefully place brake caliper over the brake disc.
10. Clean bolt ribbing.
11. Replace damaged bolts.

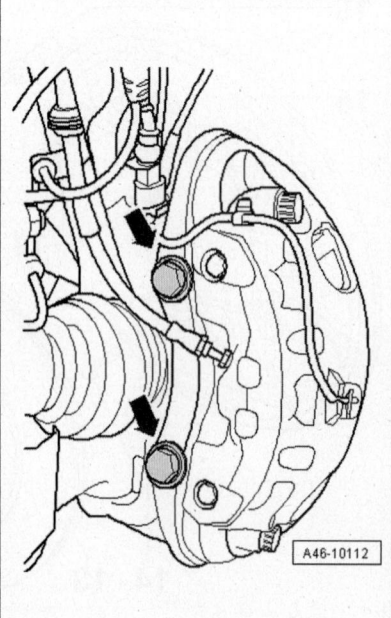

Fig. 7 Loosening the brake caliper bolts

12. Tighten bolts on brake caliper to 199 ft. lbs. (270 Nm).
13. Press brake hose into the mount on the stub axle carrier.
14. Connect the connector for the brake pad wear display.
15. Mount cable for the brake pad wear display.
16. Install cable for the brake pad wear display into the spring in the front brake caliper.
17. If necessary, close the cable clip on the spring.
  a. The cable for the brake pad wear display may not lay open.
18. Install the wheels.
  a. After installing a brake caliper, depress brake pedal several times firmly to properly seat the brake pads in their normal operating position.

DISC BRAKE PADS

REMOVAL & INSTALLATION

Q5

➡ **Tools Needed:**

- Torque wrench V.A.G 1331
- Vehicle diagnostic, test and information system VAS 5051A

➡ **When removing, mark brake pads that will be used again. Install in the same position, otherwise braking effect will be uneven.**

➡ **Operating the electromechanical parking brake again after a long drive is recommended.**

➡ **Brake pad play is automatically adjusted every 1000 km if the EPB is not operated in this distance.**

1. Connect vehicle diagnosis, testing and information system VAS 5051B or VAS 5052 to 16-pin Data Link Connector (DLC) in vehicle with ignition switched off.
2. Select parking brake with "address word" 53.
  a. Ignition on.
  b. Release parking brake.
  c. Coding check and report if necessary.
  d. DTC memory interrogated, errors shown corrected and DTC memory erased.
3. Select function "53 - Parking brake".
4. Select function "06 - Basic setting".
  a. The request to enter a display group number appears in display field 1.
  b. An entry keypad is shown in display field 2.

5. Using entry keypad, enter in display field the "7" for display group number and confirm by pressing "Q button". (Reset pistons).

6. To exit entry template, press green arrow button at lower left.

7. Raise vehicle.

8. Dismount tires.

9. Remove attachment bolts from brake caliper housing, counter-hold guide pins to do so.

    a. Actuator or brake system connector must not be disconnected (otherwise, a fault will be saved).

    b. Do not pull on brake hose or electrical wiring.

10. Remove brake caliper.

➡**Do not let brake caliper hang from brake hose. Secure it to the body with suitable cable ties or wire. Do not support weight with the brake hose.**

➡**Do not press the brake pedal when the caliper is removed.**

11. Remove the brake pads.

12. Remove the brake pad retaining plate.

13. Press the brake piston back into cylinder by hand.

➡**Do not tilt brake piston when pressing it back.**

To install:

➡**Clean brake caliper with mineral spirits exclusively.**

14. Insert the brake pad retaining springs.

15. Insert the brake pads.

16. Make sure the brake pads are seated correctly in retaining plates.

➡**The brake pads must be seated between both securing tabs on the pad retaining plate to provide the air gap between the brake disc and brake pad.**

17. Position the brake caliper.

18. Secure the brake caliper using new self-locking bolts.

➡**The repair kit includes new self-locking hex that must be installed in all cases.**

19. Using entry keypad, enter in display field the "06" or for display group number and confirm by pressing "Q button "(guide pistons together).

20. To exit entry template, press green arrow button at lower left.

21. Install the wheels.

22. Check the brake fluid level and fill if necessary.

Q7

See Figure 8.

➡**Tools Needed: Piston resetting tool T10145**

➡**When removing, mark brake pads that will be used again. Install in the same position, otherwise braking effect will be uneven.**

1. Remove the wheels.

2. Separate connector from the brake pad wear indicator.

3. Remove the securing cotter pin from pad retaining pin.

4. Press retaining spring down and remove pad retaining pin at the same time.

5. Remove the brake pad wear indicator wire from brake caliper housing and from retaining spring.

6. Remove the retaining spring.

7. Press brake pads off brake disc and remove from brake caliper.

8. If brake pads are to be replaced, carefully remove contact sensor with brake pad wear indicator wire from brake pads and check for damage.

    a. Reuse undamaged contact sensors and wires.

To install:

➡**Press the piston back into caliper housing using resetting tool before inserting new brake pads.**

➡**Before pressing pistons into cylinder using piston resetting tool, brake fluid must be extracted from brake fluid**

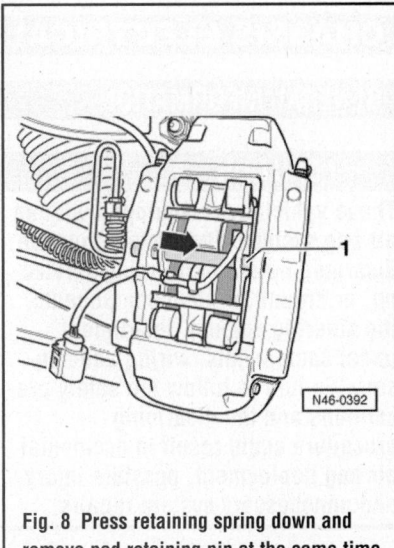

Fig. 8 Press retaining spring down and remove pad retaining pin at the same time

reservoir. Otherwise, especially if reservoir has been topped off, fluid will overflow and cause damage.

9. Press the pistons back.

10. Carefully install brake pad wear indicator wire contact sensor in new brake pads.

11. Insert brake pads into brake caliper housing.

12. Insert the retaining spring.

13. Install wire for brake pad wear indicator below tab of retaining spring and in brake caliper housing.

14. Press retaining spring down and press pad retaining pin in until stop.

15. Secure pad retaining pin using securing cotter pin.

16. Connect the connectors of the brake pad wear indicator in the bracket of brake caliper housing.

17. Install the wheels.

    a. After replacing brake pads and before moving vehicle, always depress brake pedal several times firmly to properly seat brake pads in their normal operating position.

    b. Check brake fluid level after replacing brake pad.

CHASSIS ELECTRICAL   **AIR BAG (SUPPLEMENTAL RESTRAINT SYSTEM)**

GENERAL INFORMATION

✳✳ CAUTION

These vehicles are equipped with an air bag system. The system must be disarmed before performing service on, or around, system components, the steering column, instrument panel components, wiring and sensors. Failure to follow the safety precautions and the disarming procedure could result in accidental air bag deployment, possible injury and unnecessary system repairs.

SERVICE PRECAUTIONS

Disconnect and isolate the battery negative cable before beginning any airbag system component diagnosis, testing, removal, or installation procedures. Allow system capacitor to discharge for two minutes before beginning any component service. This will disable the airbag system. Failure to disable the airbag system may result in accidental airbag deployment, personal injury, or death.

Do not place an intact undeployed airbag face down on a solid surface. The airbag will propel into the air if accidentally deployed and may result in personal injury or death.

When carrying or handling an undeployed airbag, the trim side (face) of the airbag should be pointing away from the body to minimize possibility of injury if accidental deployment occurs. Failure to do this may result in personal injury or death.

Replace airbag system components with OEM replacement parts. Substitute parts may appear interchangeable, but internal differences may result in inferior occupant protection. Failure to do so may result in occupant personal injury or death.

Wear safety glasses, rubber gloves, and long sleeved clothing when cleaning powder residue from vehicle after an airbag deployment. Powder residue emitted from a deployed airbag can cause skin irritation. Flush affected area with cool water if irritation is experienced. If nasal or throat irritation is experienced, exit the vehicle for fresh air until the irritation ceases. If irritation continues, see a physician.

Do not use a replacement airbag that is not in the original packaging. This may result in improper deployment, personal injury, or death.

The factory installed fasteners, screws and bolts used to fasten airbag components have a special coating and are specifically designed for the airbag system. Do not use substitute fasteners. Use only original equipment fasteners listed in the parts catalog when fastener replacement is required.

During, and following, any child restraint anchor service, due to impact event or vehicle repair, carefully inspect all mounting hardware, tether straps, and anchors for proper installation, operation, or damage. If a child restraint anchor is found damaged in any way, the anchor must be replaced. Failure to do this may result in personal injury or death.

Deployed and non-deployed airbags may or may not have live pyrotechnic material within the airbag inflator.

Do not dispose of driver/passenger/curtain airbags or seat belt tensioners unless you are sure of complete deployment. Refer to the Hazardous Substance Control System for proper disposal.

Dispose of deployed airbags and tensioners consistent with state, provincial, local, and federal regulations.

After any airbag component testing or service, do not connect the battery negative cable. Personal injury or death may result if the system test is not performed first.

If the vehicle is equipped with the Occupant Classification System (OCS), do not connect the battery negative cable before performing the OCS Verification Test using the scan tool and the appropriate diagnostic information. Personal injury or death may result if the system test is not performed properly.

Never replace both the Occupant Restraint Controller (ORC) and the Occupant Classification Module (OCM) at the same time. If both require replacement, replace one, then perform the Airbag System test before replacing the other.

Both the ORC and the OCM store Occupant Classification System (OCS) calibration data, which they transfer to one another when one of them is replaced. If both are replaced at the same time, an irreversible fault will be set in both modules and the OCS may malfunction and cause personal injury or death.

If equipped with OCS, the Seat Weight Sensor is a sensitive, calibrated unit and must be handled carefully. Do not drop or handle roughly. If dropped or damaged, replace with another sensor. Failure to do so may result in occupant injury or death.

If equipped with OCS, the front passenger seat must be handled carefully as well. When removing the seat, be careful when setting on floor not to drop. If dropped, the sensor may be inoperative, could result in occupant injury, or possibly death.

If equipped with OCS, when the passenger front seat is on the floor, no one should sit in the front passenger seat. This uneven force may damage the sensing ability of the seat weight sensors. If sat on and damaged, the sensor may be inoperative, could result in occupant injury, or possibly death.

DISARMING THE SYSTEM

Disconnect the negative battery cable and wait at least 90 seconds.

ARMING THE SYSTEM

Connect the negative battery cable.

DRIVE TRAIN

FRONT HALFSHAFT

REMOVAL & INSTALLATION

Q7

See Figures 9 and 10.

➡**Special tools needed:**

- Counterhold tool T10172 with adapters T10172/6
- Final drive support T10337
- Engine/transmission jack V.A.G 1383 A
- Thread locking compound D 154 100 A1

1. Place selector lever in position "N".

2. Remove screws and remove rear noise insulation.

3. If equipped, remove right heat shield from front final drive.

4. Check whether there is a factory marking (colored marking) on front driveshaft and at driveshaft flange. If not, identify position of driveshaft CV joint to driveshaft flange at front final drive with paint.

5. Remove bolts from front output drive/front driveshaft connection.

6. Use the counterhold tool T10172 with the adapters T10172/6 to do this.

7. Remove bolts at transfer case/front driveshaft connection.

8. Use the counterhold tool T10172 with the adapters T10172/6.

9. With 4.2L FSI engine, remove bolts at left main catalytic converter bracket.

10. Remove bolts at right main catalytic converter bracket.

11. Mount engine/transmission jack V.A.G 1383 A thrust plate together with the lower transmission support T10337 on the transfer case.

12. Lift the transfer case slightly using engine/transmission jack V.A.G 1383 A.

✳✳ CAUTION

There is the risk of an accident. The engine/transmission jack V.A.G 1383 A may only be used during assembly and must not sit unsupervised under the vehicle.

13. Remove transmission carrier bolts.

14. Remove bolts and remove transmission carrier.

15. Slide driveshaft forward and together. CV joints can be moved axially.

16. Remove front driveshaft.

To install:
Install in reverse order, paying attention to the following:

a. To avoid imbalance, driveshaft and driveshaft flange must be installed on front final drive so that factory markings or markings applied later on driveshaft CV joint A and driveshaft flange at front final drive B align.

b. Always replace driveshaft bolts.

c. If a new driveshaft is installed and factory marking on driveshaft flange at front final drive is no longer visible, install driveshaft in any position. If droning noises occur when driving, remove front driveshaft from flange at front final drive, rotate one hole relative to flange and attach again.

d. If droning sounds can still be heard, front driveshaft can be removed from front final drive, rotated one hole and attached again a maximum of 5 times.

17. If equipped, fasten right heat shield to front final drive with locking fluid D 154 100 A1.

18. For 4.2L FSI engine, install transmission carrier.
Tightening Specifications:
- Front driveshaft to transfer case: 22 ft. lbs. (30 Nm), plus 90°
- Front final drive: 22 ft. lbs. (30 Nm), plus 90°
- Right heat shield to front final drive: 7 ft. lbs. (10 Nm)

REAR HALFSHAFT

REMOVAL & INSTALLATION

Q5

See Figure 11.

1. Loosen the connection between the drive axle and wheel hub.

2. Remove wheel.

3. Remove coil spring.

4. Remove the rear muffler.

5. Remove rear final drive.

6. Remove the rear speed sensor. Remove bolt to do so.

7. Remove the drive axle toward the inside.

To install:

8. Installation is performed in the reverse order of removal. Observe the following when doing so:

a. Install rear final drive.

b. Install the exhaust system rear muffler.

c. Install coil spring.

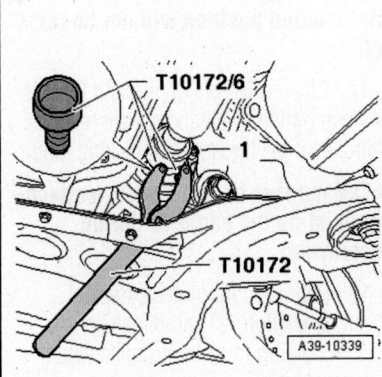

Fig. 9 Removing the bolts from the front output drive/front driveshaft connection

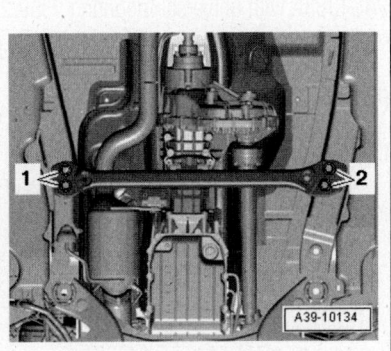

Fig. 10 Removing the transmission carrier bolts

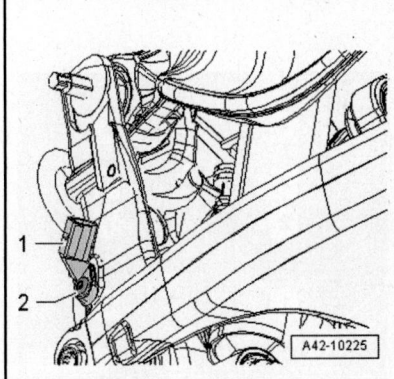

Fig. 11 Remove the rear speed sensor (1). Remove bolt (2) to do so. Remove the drive axle toward the inside.

d. Install the rear speed sensor.

e. Install the rear wheel.

f. Tighten the drive axle to wheel hub threaded connection new nut to 148 ft. lbs. (200 Nm), plus 180°.

Q7

See Figure 12.

➡**Special tools needed: Counterhold tool T10172 with adapters T10172/6**

1. Place selector lever in position "N".

2. Check whether there is a factory marking (colored marking) on rear driveshaft and at driveshaft flange. If not, identify position of driveshaft CV joint to driveshaft flange at rear final drive with paint.

3. Remove bolts at rear final drive/rear driveshaft connection; leave one bolt installed hand-tight.

4. Use the counterhold tool T10172 with the adapters T10172/6.

5. Remove the bolts at transfer case/rear driveshaft connection; leave one bolt installed hand-tight.

6. Use the counterhold tool T10172 with the adapters T10172/6 to do this.

a. A second technician is needed to hold the rear driveshaft to avoid damage from bending it.

7. Remove bolts 2 to 7 and remove tunnel bridge.

8. Remove bolts 1 and 8 at driveshaft center bearing bracket.

9. Remove rear driveshaft.

10. Position rear driveshaft with center bearing bracket facing upward.

a. The round hole on tunnel bridge faces in direction of travel.

To install:

Install in reverse order, paying attention to the following:

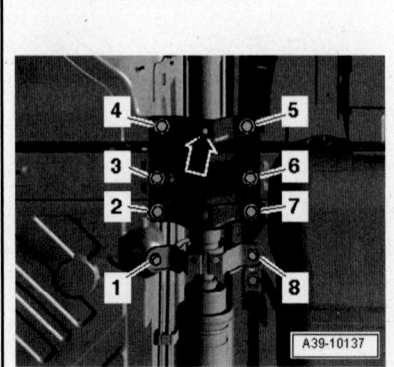

Fig. 12 Remove bolts 2 to 7 and remove tunnel bridge.

11. Always replace driveshaft bolts.

12. To avoid imbalance, driveshaft and driveshaft flange must be installed on rear final drive so that factory markings or markings applied later on driveshaft CV joint and driveshaft flange at rear final drive align.

13. If a new driveshaft is installed and factory marking on driveshaft flange at rear final drive is no longer visible, install driveshaft in any position. If droning noises occur when driving, remove rear driveshaft from flange at rear final drive, rotate one hole relative to flange and attach again.

14. If droning sounds can still be heard, the rear driveshaft can be rotated from rear final drive and rotated back in offset by one hole a total of 5 times.

Tightening Specifications:

• Rear driveshaft to transfer case: 22 ft. lbs. (30 Nm) + 90°

• Rear final drive: 22 ft. lbs. (30 Nm) + 90°

• Driveshaft center bearing bracket to body: 20 Nm

• Tunnel bridge to body: 44 ft.lbs. (60 Nm)

REAR PINION SEAL

REMOVAL & INSTALLATION

Q5

See Figure 13.

1. Remove rear section of exhaust system as from clamp(s).

2. Check whether there is a factory marking (paint dot) on drive shaft. If you do not find one, mark the position of the Constant Velocity (CV) joint relative to the rear final drive with a colored dot.

3. Disconnect driveshaft from rear final drive and tie it up to exhaust system brackets.

4. Place engine and transmission jack VAG1383A with universal mounting 1359/2 under final drive and secure final drive.

5. Remove bolts of left final drive support.

6. Carefully lower final drive until flange is freely accessible.

7. Color mark the position of the securing nut for the drive pinion.

8. Calculate the indicated dimension "a" and dimension "b":

a. Distance of flange to drive pinion = Dimension a

b. Distance of flange to securing nut for the drive pinion = Dimension b

9. Note calculated dimensions.

10. Count turns when unscrewing the securing nut and make a note of them.

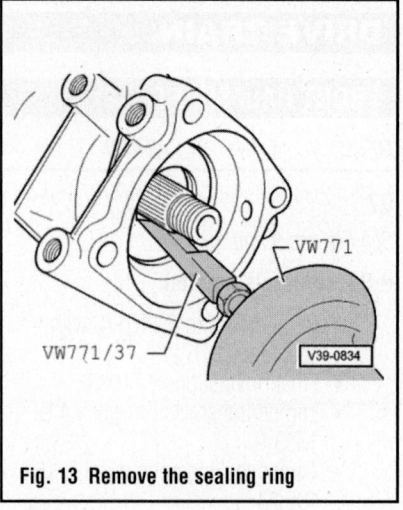

Fig. 13 Remove the sealing ring

11. Install support tool 3028 and remove drive pinion nut.

12. Place drip tray underneath to collect oil.

13. Detach flange with removal tool VW391.

14. Install two M8 x 30 bolts into flange.

15. Remove the sealing ring.

to install:

16. Installation is carried out in reverse order. Note the following:

a. Replace O-ring between drive pinion bearing and flange.

b. Lightly oil O-ring before installing.

c. Pack space between sealing and dust lips half full with sealing grease G 052 128 A1.

d. Lightly oil outer circumference of seal.

e. Drive in seal for drive shaft flange onto stop with drift 3026.

f. Drive shaft flange onto drive pinion until securing nut can be mounted.

➡**Use the old nut to reattach the flange to the drive pinion. Otherwise the original installed position will not be relocated.**

17. Clean drive pinion nut and threads on drive pinion of oil and grease residues. Thinly coat the threads with locking fluid.

➡**The number of turns when reattaching must be the same as during unscrewing.**

18. Perform control measurement - check dimension "a" and dimension "b".

a. O-ring must be installed when measuring.

b. The nut must be returned to exactly the marked position.

c. Maximum permissible deviation from original measurements: ± 0.3 mm.

19. Install the lock nut.

20. Move final drive back to installation position.

21. Install the final drive to front mounting bracket.

22. Top off the gear oil in the rear final drive and check oil level.

23. If there was a factory marking at the driveshaft determine now the radial run out at the flange/driveshaft. Attach driveshaft in such a way that the color coding at the driveshaft are aligned with new marking at flange.

24. If the position of the driveshaft relative to the flange/driveshaft were marked

before removal the driveshaft must be reattached at same position.

25. Replace seal on driveshaft flange and tighten driveshaft to specifications.

26. Stress free alignment of exhaust system.

ENGINE COOLING

ENGINE COOLANT

DRAIN & REFILL PROCEDURE

Draining

1. Open coolant reservoir cap.
2. Remove front noise insulation.
3. Remove drain plug and drain coolant.
4. Loosen hose clamp arrow, allow any remaining coolant drain out and then remove the coolant hose from the oil cooler.

Filling

1. Ignition switched off.

➡**Refill notes:**

- The cooling system is filled all year round with a mixture of frost and corrosion protection additives and water.
- Only use one of the frost and corrosion additives approved for this vehicle.
- Other coolant additives may above all reduce the corrosion protection effect significantly. The damage resulting from this may lead to loss of coolant and consequently to severe engine damage.
- Frost and corrosion protection additives prevent freezing and corrosion damage and scaling. They also raise the boiling point. For this reason the system must be filled all year round with frost and corrosion protection additives.
- Because of its high boiling point, the coolant improves engine reliability under heavy loads, particularly in countries with tropical climates.
- Protection against frost must be assured to about -25 °C (in arctic climatic countries to about -35 °C).
- The coolant concentration must not be reduced by adding water even in warmer seasons and in warmer countries. The coolant additive portion must be at least 40%.
- If increased freeze protection is needed because of the climate, the

amount of anti-freeze can be increased, but only up to 60% (freeze protection to about -40 °C. Otherwise the freeze protection and cooling effectiveness will be reduced.

- Only use clean drinking water for mixing coolant.
- Use a Refractometer (T10007) to determine the level of freeze protection in the coolant system.

2. Close drain plug.

3. Install coolant hose on the oil cooler.

4. Fill coolant reservoir on VAS 6096 with at least 12 liters of premixed coolant with the proper mixture ratio.

5. Attach Adapter V.A.G 1274/8 to coolant reservoir.

6. Install cooling system charge unit VAS 6096 on the adapter V.A.G 1274/8.

7. Place air outlet in a small container.

➡**A small amount of coolant which should be collected is drawn off with the discharged air.**

8. Close the valves by turning lever at a right angle to direction of flow.

9. Connect a hose to compressed air, with 87–147 psi positive pressure.

10. Open valve B by turning level in direction of flow.

➡**The suction jet pump generates pressure in the coolant system; indicator on display instrument must move into green area.**

11. Briefly open valve A by turning lever in direction of flow so that hose on VAS 6096 coolant reservoir fills with coolant.

12. Close valve A again.

13. Leave valve B open another 2 minutes.

➡**More pressure is generated in the coolant system by the suction jet pump; indicator on display instrument must stay in green area.**

14. Close valve B.

➡**Needle in display must remain in green region, then vacuum in cooling**

system is sufficient for subsequent filling.

15. If needle stands below the green area, repeat procedure.

16. If pressure falls, check coolant system for leaks.

17. Remove pressurized air hose.

18. Open valve A.

➡**Coolant is extracted from VAS 6096 coolant reservoir by pressure in the coolant system and the system is filled.**

19. Remove Cooling System Charge Unit VAS 6096 form adapter V.A.G 1274/8 on coolant reservoir.

20. Connect tube V.A.G 1274/10 to the adapter V.A.G 1274/8.

21. Fill coolant until coolant system tester tube is full. Fill again during bleeding procedure if necessary.

22. Remove gasket from front of the plenum chamber in engine compartment. Open clips and remove the plenum chamber cover.

23. Open clamp and remove heat exchanger coolant hose.

24. As soon as coolant starts to come out of the vent hole arrow, attach coolant hose to the connection and tighten the clamp.

25. If vehicle has an auxiliary heater, switch it on for about 30 seconds.

26. Close cap on the coolant reservoir until it latches.

27. Start engine.

28. Set temperature to "HI" for all zones and set the fan speed as low as possible (0).

29. Switch A/C compressor off by pressing AC button.

➡**The LED in button must not come on.**

30. Run engine at 2000 RPM for 3 minutes.

31. Run engine at idle until both large coolant hoses on the radiator are warm.

32. Run engine at 2000 RPM for 2 minutes.

33. Turn off engine and allow it to cool off.

34. Install noise insulation.
35. Check coolant level.

ENGINE FAN

REMOVAL & INSTALLATION

Q5

See Figures 14 and 15.

1. Remove both front wheels.
2. Loosen quick-release fasteners and remove front noise insulation.
3. Remove front bumper cover.
4. Remove air guide in front of the charge air cooler.
5. Remove cover arrow at power steering fluid reservoir.
6. Remove electrical harness connectors 1 and 2 from bracket.
7. Free up electrical wires to lock carrier.
8. Remove right cover in the engine compartment, if equipped.
9. Disengage Evaporative Emission (EVAP) Canister Purge Regulator Valve N80 from air guide.
10. Remove bolts.
11. Remove air duct.
12. Remove bolts at left and right.
13. Remove hood seal on the lock carrier and on the bolted fender flanges.
14. Thread Support Tool 3369 into empty bores at left and right.
15. Remove bolts at left and right.
16. Carefully pull lock carrier toward front.
17. Disconnect the connectors.
18. Free up the electrical wiring.
19. Disconnect connector for the hood lock and free up the electrical wires.
20. Remove bolts and remove fan shroud upward and out.

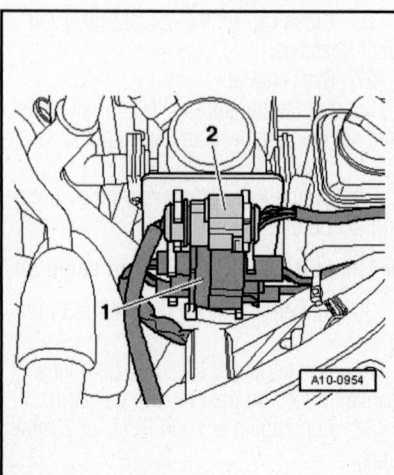

Fig. 14 Disconnect the connectors

Fig. 15 Remove bolts and remove fan shroud upward and out

21. Installation is in reverse order of removal, note the following:
22. Install lock carrier with attachments.
23. Place the torque support stop on the rubber buffer and tighten the nuts arrows.
24. Install front bumper cover.
25. Check the headlamp adjustment.

Q7

3.6L Engine

See Figure 16.

1. Remove fan shroud.
2. Free up electrical wires.
3. Remove Coolant Fan with Coolant Fan Control (FC) Control Module. Remove bolts and remove Coolant Fan with Coolant Fan Control (FC) Control Module.

   to install:

   Installation is in reverse order of removal, note the following:

4. Install fan shroud.

4.2L & 3.0L Engines

See Figure 17.

1. Remove fan shroud.
2. Free up electrical wires.
3. Remove Coolant Fan with Coolant Fan Control (FC) Control Module. Remove bolts and remove Coolant Fan V7 with Coolant Fan Control (FC) Control Module J293.

   To install:

   Installation is in reverse order of removal, note the following:

4. Install the fan shroud.

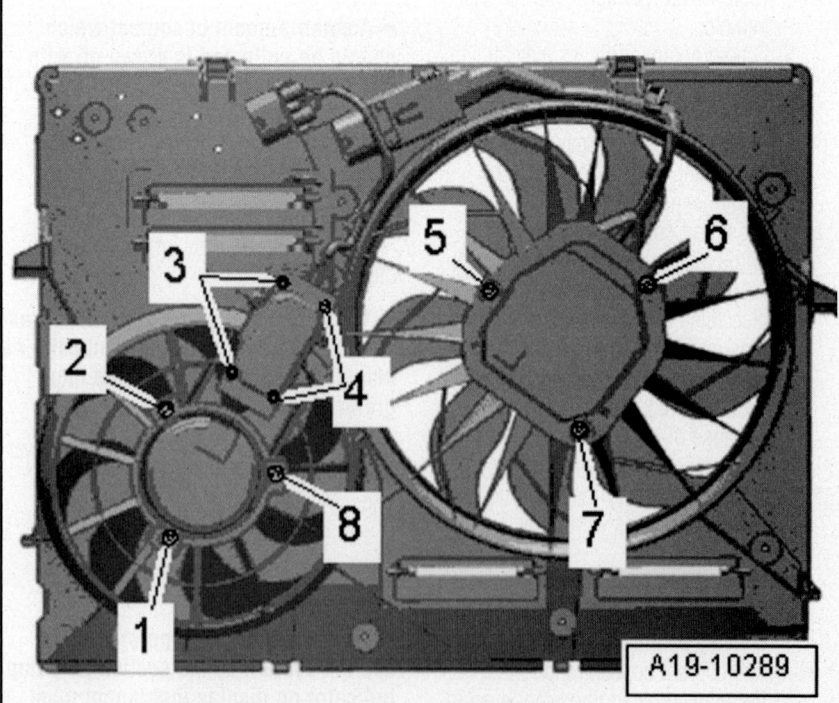

Fig. 16 Remove bolts 1, 2, 3, 4, 8 and remove Coolant Fan with Coolant Fan Control (FC) Control Module. Remove bolts 5, 6, 7 and remove Coolant Fan with Coolant Fan Control (FC) Control Module.

RADIATOR

REMOVAL & INSTALLATION

Q5

See Figure 17.

➡**Drained coolant must be stored in a clean container for disposal or reuse.**

1. Open the cap of the coolant expansion tank.
2. Loosen quick-release fasteners and remove front noise insulation.
3. Remove front bumper cover.
4. Place Drip Tray For Workshop Crane VAS 6208 or Drip Tray V.A.G 1306 under engine.
5. Vehicles with coolant drain plug: Open coolant drain plug to coolant line at bottom of cooler.
6. Vehicles without coolant drain plug:
   a. Remove the retaining clip on the Engine Coolant Temperature (ECT) Sensor (on radiator).
   b. Remove the Engine Coolant Temperature (ECT) Sensor (on radiator) from its supports and drain the coolant.
7. Disconnect lower coolant hose from radiator.
8. Disconnect upper coolant hose from radiator.
9. Vehicles with Multitronic/automatic transmission:
   a. Remove right cover in the engine compartment, if equipped.
   b. Disengage EVAP canister purge regulator valve from the air guide.
   c. Remove bolts.
   d. Remove air duct.
   e. Place Old Oil Collecting And Extracting Device V.A.G 1782 underneath.
   f. Remove upper and lower ATF lines arrow from cooler.
   g. Tie the ATF lines up to the longitudinal member to prevent fluid from escaping.
10. Remove the left and right air guides at radiator.
11. Unclip outside air temperature sensor from the bracket.
12. Remove power steering cooling coil bolts hydraulic hoses remain connected.
13. Disconnect the connector on the High Pressure Sensor.

➡**The air conditioning refrigerant circuit must not be opened.**

14. Remove bolts for the condenser.
15. Pivot condenser downward with lines connected.

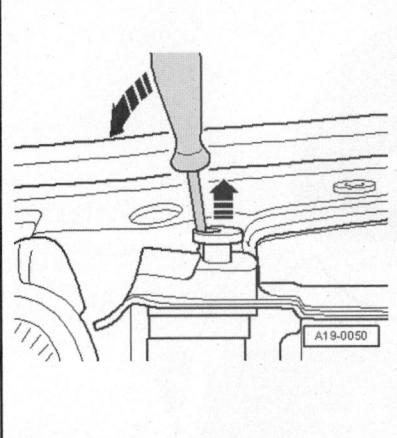

Fig. 17 Release both radiator retaining pins and remove by pulling upward

➡**To prevent damage to the refrigerant lines/hoses, ensure that the lines and hoses are not stretched, kinked or bent.**

16. Release both radiator retaining pins and remove by pulling upward.
17. Pivot radiator forward, pull up and remove.

To install:

18. Installation is in reverse order of removal.
19. Fill with coolant.
20. Vehicles with Multitronic/automatic transmission:
   a. Check ATF level.

Q7

3.0L Engine

See Figures 18 through 21.

Tools Needed:
• Hose clamp pliers V.A.G 1921

➡**When assembled correctly, the radiator and condenser may have slight indentations on their fins. This is not damage. Radiators or condensers should not be replaced because of slight impressions like these.**

1. Discharge the refrigerant circuit.
2. Drain the coolant.
3. Remove fan shroud.
4. Remove air guide hose to Secondary Air Injection (AIR) pump from upper section of air filter housing.
5. Disconnect the electrical connector at Engine Coolant Temperature (ECT) Sensor (on Radiator).
6. Lift the retaining clip and remove upper coolant hose from the radiator.
7. Remove the coolant hose to radiator from right coolant pipe.

8. Separate the electrical connector.

Risk of damaging coolant lines and hoses. Do not stretch, kink or bend coolant lines and hoses.

9. Remove the refrigerant lines from condenser.
   a. Remove air intake grille in upper section of bumper cover.
   b. Remove left and right radiator locking mechanism by pressing down against clamps.
   c. Remove bolts on rear side of radiator.
   d. Disengage power steering cooler at A/C system condenser.
   e. Remove bolts on rear side of radiator.
   f. Press off the retaining clips.
   g. Remove ATF cooler from radiator.

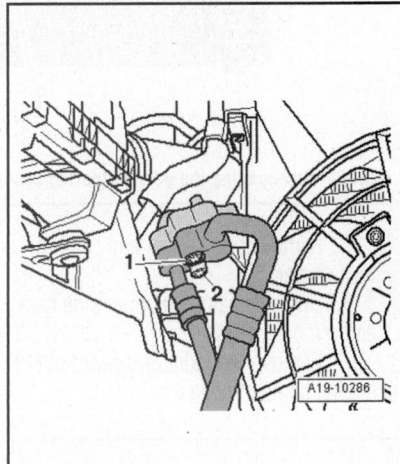

Fig. 18 Removing the refrigerant lines—ignore 2 and 3

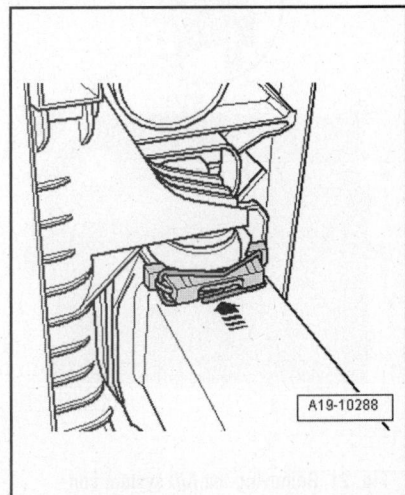

Fig. 19 Identifying the locking mechanism

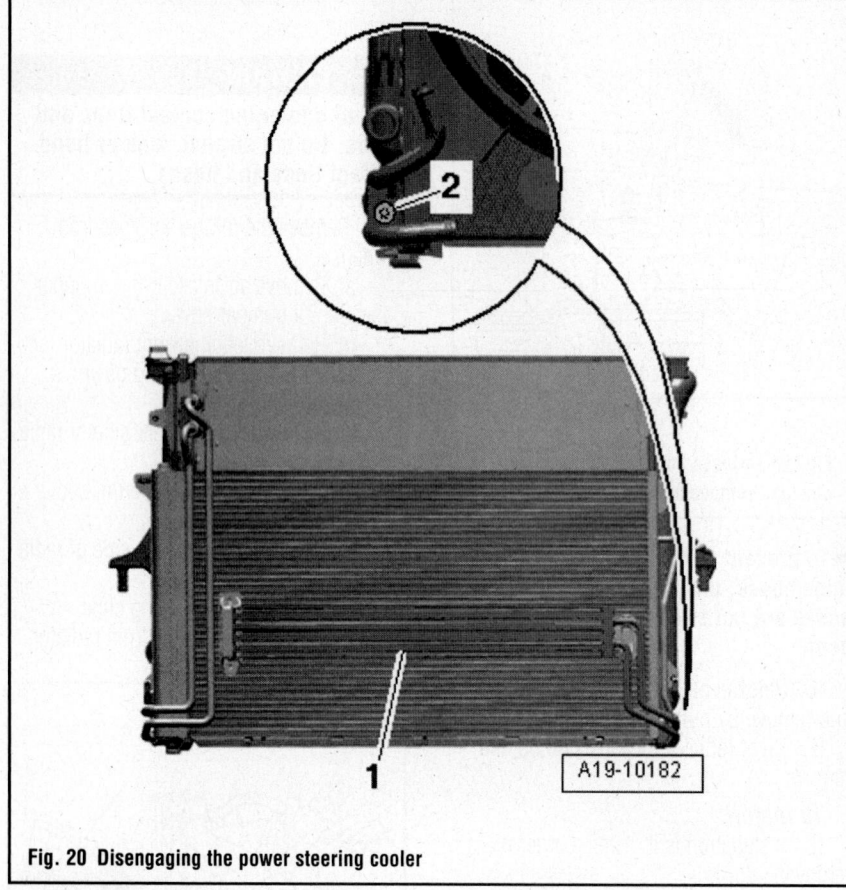

Fig. 20 Disengaging the power steering cooler

h. Remove bolts at left and right of lock carrier.

i. Swing radiator on upper side back and remove coolant hose.

j. Remove the radiator upward out of engine compartment.

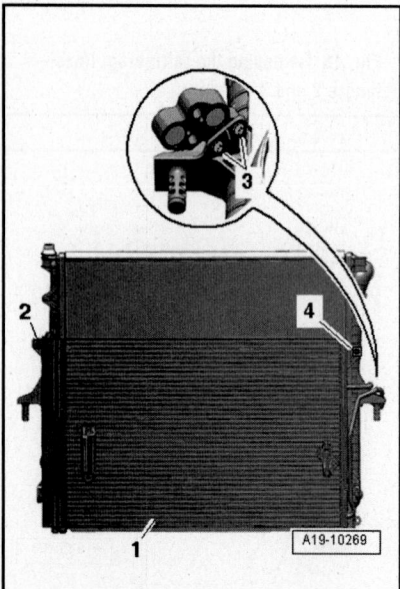

Fig. 21 Removing the A/C system condenser from the radiator

k. Remove bolts on rear side of radiator.

l. Press off the retaining.

m. Remove the A/C system condenser from radiator.

To install:

Installation is in reverse order of removal, note the following:

a. Connect the coolant hose with the connector coupling.

b. Install the refrigerant lines.

c. Install fan shroud.

d. Tighten the ATF lines.

e. Fill the radiator with coolant.

f. Complete coolant must be replaced if the radiator was replaced.

g. Check the ATF level.

3.6L Engine

See Figures 22 through 24.

➡ When assembled correctly, the radiator and condenser can show slight impressions on fins. This is not damage. Radiators or condensers should not be replaced because of slight impressions like these.

h. Evacuate the A/C system.

i. Drain the coolant.

j. Remove the fan shroud.

k. Remove upper coolant hose from the radiator.

l. Remove upper coolant hose from front coolant pipe and remove coolant pipe.

m. Ignore the other hose clamp.

n. Disconnect the electrical connector on Engine Coolant Temperature (ECT) sensor (on radiator).

o. Remove the lower coolant hose from radiator.

➡ Risk of damaging the coolant lines and hoses. Do not stretch, kink or bend the coolant lines and hoses.

p. Remove the refrigerant lines from condenser.

q. Remove left and right radiator locking mechanism by pressing down against clamps.

r. Remove the bolt on rear side of radiator.

s. Disengage power steering cooler on climate control system condenser.

t. Remove the bolt on rear side of radiator.

u. Press the retaining clips.

v. Remove ATF cooler from the radiator

w. Remove the bolts at left and right on lock carrier.

x. Tilt the top of the radiator back and remove it upward out of engine compartment.

y. Ignore the hose clamp.

z. Remove the bolt on rear side of radiator.

aa. Press of retaining clips.

bb. Remove the climate control condenser from radiator.

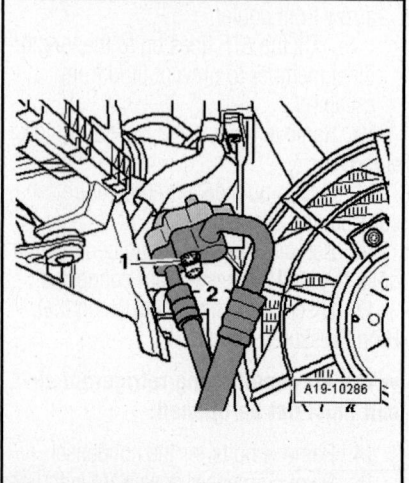

Fig. 22 Removing the refrigerant lines from the condenser

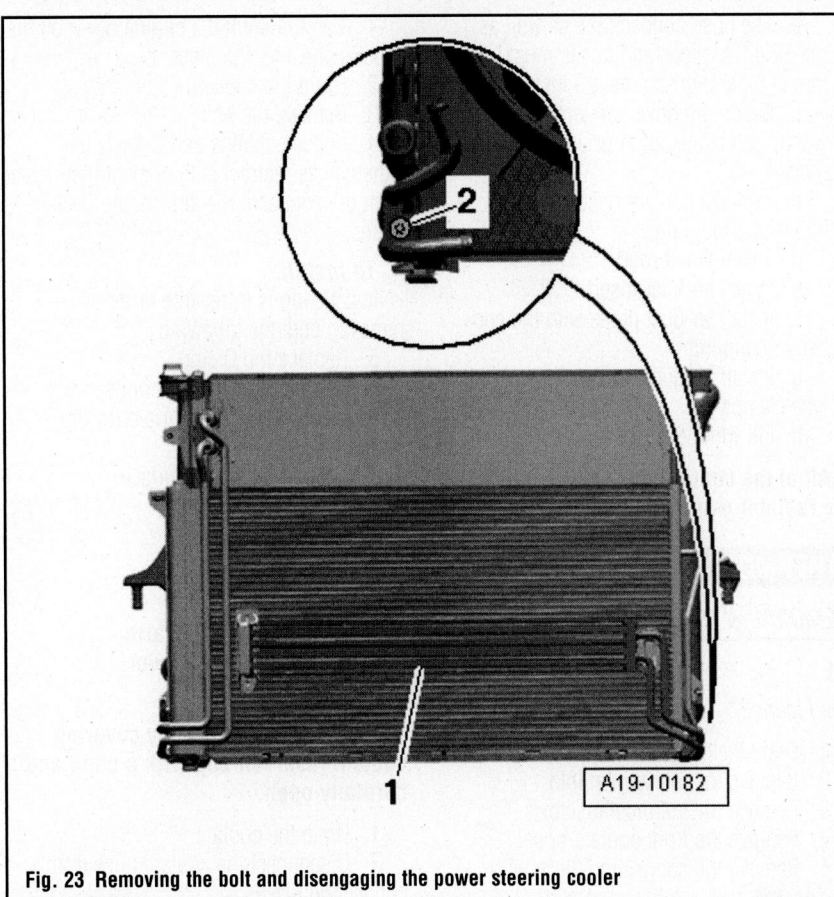

Fig. 23 Removing the bolt and disengaging the power steering cooler

d. Tighten the ATF lines.
e. Tighten the power steering hydraulic lines.
f. Charge the A/C system.
g. Fill the radiator with coolant.
h. If the radiator was replaced, coolant must be changed.

4.2L Engine

See Figures 25 and 26.

➡ **If there are small impressions on the fins. This is not damage. Radiators or condensers should not be replaced because of slight impressions like these.**

1. Drain coolant.
2. Disconnect electrical connector.
3. Remove bolts.
4. Lift clips, loosen the clamp, and remove the air duct hoses.

➡ **The lower air duct pipe is removed later.**

5. Remove air filter insert.
6. Remove fan shroud.
7. Remove air duct hoses by loosening the hose clamps.
8. Free up the coolant hose on the front air duct in the center.

To install:

Installation is in reverse order of removal, note the following:
a. Install the refrigerant lines.
b. Install the fan shroud.
c. Install the front coolant pipe.

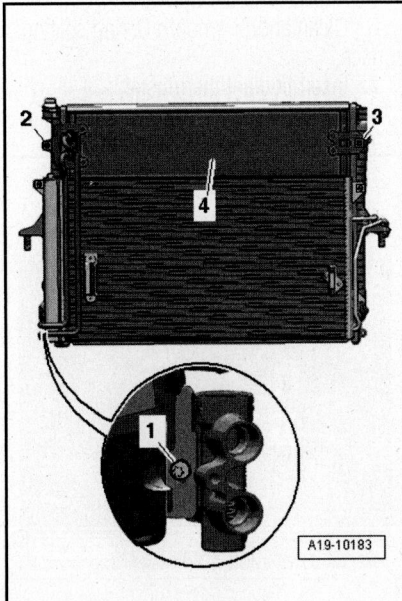

Fig. 24 Removing the bolt, pressing the clips and removing the ATF cooler

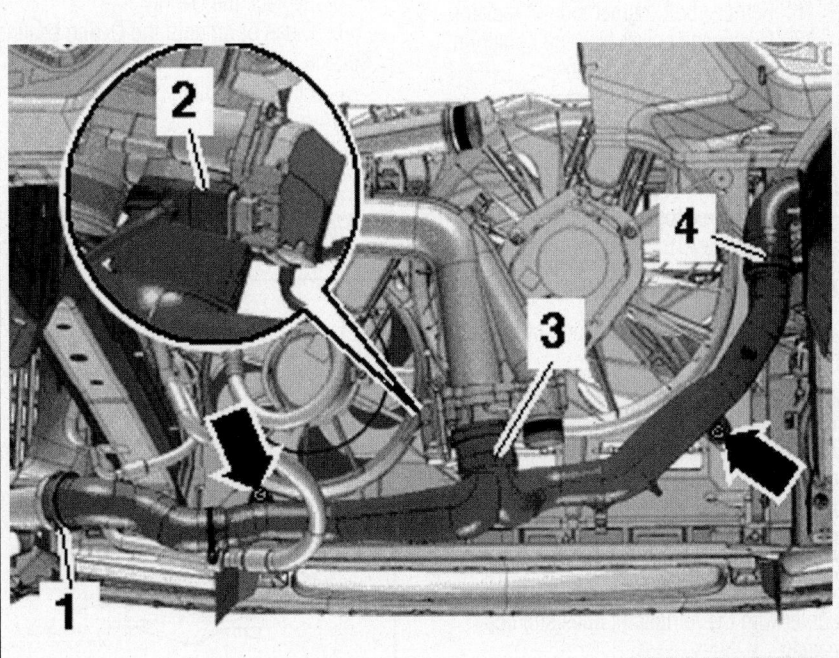

Fig. 25 Lift clips 1, loosen the clamp 3 and 4 and remove the air duct hoses.

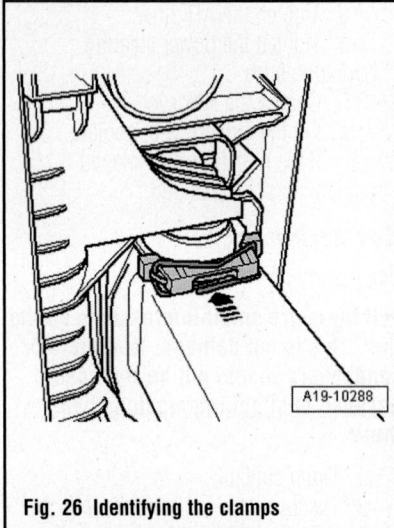

Fig. 26 Identifying the clamps

9. Disconnect the connector on the Charge Air Pressure Sensor.

10. Remove coolant hose by loosening the hose clamp.

11. Remove front air duct pipe in the center and the intake flap motor.

12. Remove lower air duct pipe.

13. Disconnect coolant hose from the radiator by raising the retaining clip arrow.

14. Remove left and right radiator locking mechanism by pressing down against clamps.

15. Remove bolts at left and right on lock carrier. Disengage cooler and move it toward the rear.

16. Remove bolt on rear side of radiator.

17. Disengage power steering cooler on climate control system condenser.

The hydraulic hose lines remain connected.

18. Remove bolt on rear side of radiator.

19. Remove clips.

20. Remove ATF cooler from radiator.

➡ **The ATF hose line remain connected.**

21. Remove bolt on rear side of radiator.

22. Remove clips.

❊ CAUTION

There is a risk of damaging the condenser and refrigerant lines and hoses. Do not stretch, kink or bend coolant lines and hoses.

23. Remove A/C condenser from the cooler with the refrigerant lines still connected.

24. Remove radiator downward.

To install:

25. Installation is in reverse order of removal, note the following:

a. The hose connections as well as the air guide pipes and hoses must be free of oil and grease before installing.

b. Secure all hose connections with hose clamps appropriate for the model.

c. Connect coolant hoses with the connector coupling.

d. Install fan shroud.

e. Install air filter insert.

f. Install air duct pipes with the connector coupling.

g. Install air duct hoses and screw-type clamps.

h. Fill with coolant.

➡ **All of the coolant must be changed if the radiator was replaced.**

THERMOSTAT

REMOVAL & INSTALLATION

Q5

See Figure 27.

1. Drain the coolant.

2. Remove the intake manifold.

3. Remove the thermostat screws.

4. Remove the front coolant hose.

5. Remove the connecting piece with thermostat.

6. Installation is performed in reverse order of removal, noting the following:

a. Replace the O-ring.

b. Clean or smooth the O-ring sealing surface.

c. Fill with coolant.

Q7

3.0L Engine

See Figure 28.

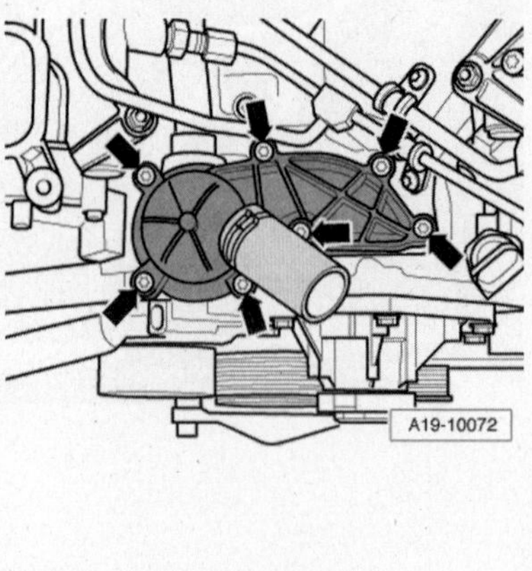

Fig. 27 Removing screws and hose clamps

1. Carefully pull the engine cover off the 4 bolts one after the other.

2. Drain the coolant.

3. Remove the bolt.

4. Loosen clamps and remove the exhaust gas recirculation coolant thermostat from the connection and from the coolant hoses.

To install:

Installation is in reverse order of removal, note the following:

5. Replace the O-ring.

6. Secure all the hose connections with hose clamps appropriate for the model.

7. Clean the sealing surface.

8. Fill with coolant.

3.6L Engine

See Figure 29.

➡ **When the engine is warm the cooling system is under pressure.**

➡ **Reduce the pressure by covering coolant reservoir cap with a cloth and carefully open.**

1. Drain the coolant.

2. Disconnect the coolant hose from connecting pieces.

3. Remove bolts and the connecting pieces.

4. Remove the coolant thermostat from mount on coolant pipe.

To install:

Installation is in reverse order of removal, note the following:

5. Replace the O-ring.

6. Clean and/or smooth O-ring sealing surface.

7. Insert coolant thermostat.

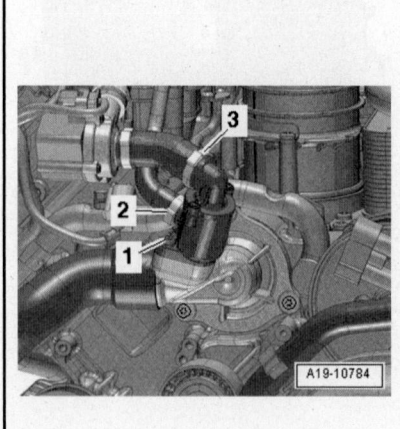

Fig. 28 Removing the thermostat

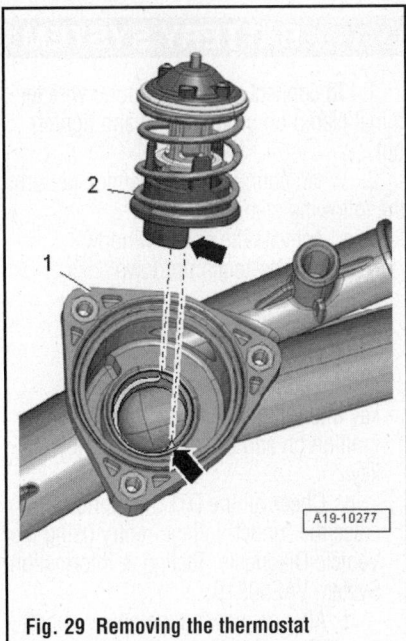

Fig. 29 Removing the thermostat

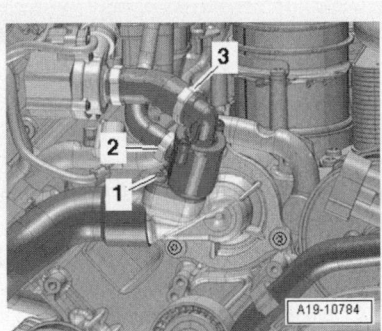

Fig. 30 Remove bolt (1) and disconnect the exhaust gas recirculation coolant thermostat and connection from the connection. Ignore 2 and 3.

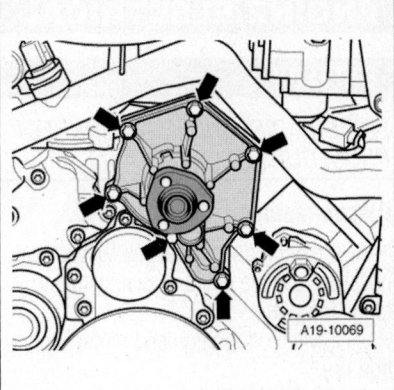

Fig. 31 Remove coolant pump bolts and the coolant pump

➡**Installed location: Edges arrows on coolant thermostat and housing must align.**

8. Coat O-ring with proper coolant additive.
9. Fill with coolant.

4.2L Engine
See Figure 30.

1. Drain coolant.
2. Remove ribbed belt from the tensioning element.
3. Remove bolt and disconnect the exhaust gas recirculation coolant thermostat and connection from the connection.
4. Remove coolant hose; to do so, loosen the hose clamp.
5. Remove bolts and the coolant thermostat with the connection.

To install:
Installation is in reverse order of removal, note the following:

➡**Replace O-rings.**

➡**Secure all hose connections with hose clamps appropriate for the model.**

6. Clean the sealing surface.
7. Install ribbed belt.

8. Fill with coolant.

WATER PUMP

REMOVAL & INSTALLATION

Q5
See Figure 31.

1. Remove the engine cover.
2. Drain coolant.
3. Remove ribbed belt.
4. Remove bolts for the coolant pump ribbed belt pulley, using a Spanner Wrench 3212 to counterhold.
5. Remove coolant pump bolts and the coolant pump.

To install:
6. Installation is in reverse order of removal, note the following:
   a. Tighten the water pump bolts to 7 ft. lbs. (9 Nm).
   b. Clean sealing surfaces, must be free of oil and grease.
7. Install ribbed belt.
8. Fill with coolant.

Q7

3.0L Diesel Engine
See Figure 32.

1. Drain the coolant.
2. Remove the ribbed belt from the tensioning element.

3. Tilt the toothed belt guard forward and disengage the pins on the underside of the guard.
4. Using a 3212 as a counterholder, remove the bolts and remove the coolant pump ribbed belt pulley.
5. Remove the bolts and remove the coolant pump.

To install:
6. Install in reverse order of removal. Note the following:
   a. Clean the sealing surface.
   b. Tighten the coolant pump bolts.
7. Install the ribbed belt.
8. Fill with coolant

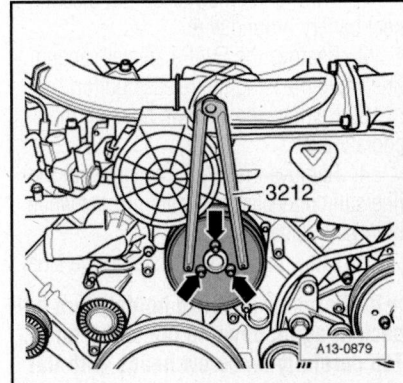

Fig. 32 Using a 3212 as a counterholder, remove the bolts and remove the coolant pump ribbed belt pulley.

ENGINE ELECTRICAL
BATTERY SYSTEM

BATTERY

BATTERY DISCONNECT/RECONNECT PROCEDURE

Disconnecting

1. Position driver's seat as far back as possible. use the entire seat adjustment range to do this.

2. Switch off ignition and remove ignition key.

3. On TDI (SCR) vehicles:

   a. After the ignition is switched off, the reducing agent goes from the metering line to the Reducing agent injector and back into the reducing agent active chamber.

   b. Wait until all the reducing agent has been returned before working in this area. This could take up to 10 minutes after switching off the ignition.

   c. Only after this is complete can the battery be disconnected. Again, this could take up to 10 minutes after switching off the ignition.

4. On all engines, reach under seat and release retaining clips on back side of cover. Then, remove cover from driver's seat console.

5. Pry cover from floor covering.

6. Raise floor covering slightly in ground wire area.

7. Remove nut and remove ground wire from ground point.

Reconnecting

➡**The connector must be connected when connecting the ground wire to the ground point on vehicles with Battery monitoring control module.**

➡**If the connector on the battery monitoring control module comes loosen when connecting the battery, wait 30 seconds before connecting it again.**

1. To connect, position ground wire terminal clamp on ground point and tighten nut.

2. When connecting the battery, perform the following steps:

   a. Activate the power window regulator one-touch up/down function.

   b. Synchronize the spare and additional keys to ensure remote control operation. To do so, insert key into ignition lock, switch the ignition on and off again and remove key.

   c. Check all the DTC memories and erase the "under-voltage" entry using the Vehicle Diagnosis, Testing & Information System VAS5051B.

   d. After connecting the power supply, the ABS warning lamp may only go out after the vehicle has been driven a few yards.

ENGINE ELECTRICAL
CHARGING SYSTEM

ALTERNATOR

REMOVAL & INSTALLATION

Q5

See Figure 33.

1. With ignition switched off, disconnect battery ground wire.

2. Remove the EVAP canister vacuum line while pressing the release button.

3. Remove the vacuum hose on the coolant pipe.

4. Remove the EVAP canister with the line still connected out of its bracket while lifting the release strap.

5. Move the EVAP canister to the side.

➡**If alternator sticks in holder, turn bolt back in again down to the last 2 turns. Tap carefully on screw heads with flat side of hammer to release alternator mount bushings.**

6. To release the tension on the ribbed belt, turn the tensioning element clockwise.

7. Secure the tensioning element with the drift T10060.

8. Remove ribbed belt.

9. Disconnect the electrical connectors.

10. Remove the bolts and remove the generator from the accessories bracket.

11. Tip generator with electrical wires connected to right side of vehicle.

12. Disconnect the electrical connector.

Fig. 33 Remove the bolts and remove the generator from the accessories bracket

13. Pry off the cap and disconnect the 30/B+ terminal on the generator.

14. Remove the generator upward.

15. Install in reverse order of removal, observing the following:

    a. Mount the ribbed belt onto the ribbed belt pulley and then onto the generator belt pulley.

    b. Hold the tensioning element and open end wrench and remove the drift T10060.

    c. Release the tension on the tensioner.

    d. Connect battery.

    e. Terminal 30/B+ to generator: 11 ft. lbs. (16 Nm)

    f. Alternator: 16 ft. lbs. (23 Nm)

16. Start the engine and check the ribbed belt routing.

Q7

3.0L Engine

See Figures 34 and 35.

➡ **Tools needed: Torx T 60 socket T40087**

➡ **When installing, reinstall all cable ties that were loosened or cut during removal in the same locations.**

1. With ignition switched off, disconnect battery ground wire.

2. Carefully remove engine cover successively from the 4 locking bolts.

> ☀☀ **CAUTION**
>
> **Risk of destroying if the running direction of a used ribbed belt is reversed. Before removing the ribbed belt, mark running direction with chalk or a felt-tip pen for reinstallation.**

3. To release the tension the ribbed belt, move the tensioner using the T 60 Torx socket T40087.

4. Remove ribbed belt from tensioning roller.

5. Remove right front wheel.

6. Remove the screws and the front and rear noise insulation.

7. Remove stabilizer bar.

8. Remove the screw and move the fuel cooler pump with coolant hoses and electrical connector still connected to the side.

9. Detach the wiring harnesses from generator.

10. Free the electrical wiring harness.

11. Unscrew bolts and remove generator.

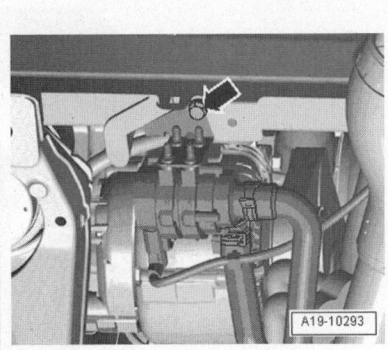

Fig. 34 Remove the screw and move the fuel cooler pump with coolant hoses and electrical connector still connected to the side.

➡ **If alternator sticks in holder, install screw again down as far as the last 2 turns.**

➡ **Carefully strike on bolt heads using flat side of hammer; doing this loosens sleeves of generator mount.**

To install:

Install in reverse order of removal, observing the following:

➡ **Replace the self-locking nuts.**

12. Slightly drive back sleeves for retaining bolts in order for easier installation of generator.

    a. Tight sleeves for generator mount must be made smooth-running, otherwise clamping force of sleeve is too little despite correct torque.

13. Install stabilizer bar.

14. Fit the poly V-belt over pulleys.

➡ **When installing the ribbed belt, be sure that it is seated correctly on belt pulleys.**

15. Connect the battery.

16. Start the engine and verify that the belt is running properly.

Tightening Specifications:

- Generator to engine: 14 ft. lbs. (22 Nm)
- Terminal 30/B+ to generator: 11 ft. lbs. (16 Nm)
- After-Run Coolant Pump V51 bracket to longmember: 14 ft. lbs. (22 Nm)

3.6L Engine

See Figures 36 and 37.

➡ **Tools needed:**

- Hose clamps up to 25mm 3094
- Workshop crane drip tray VAS 6208

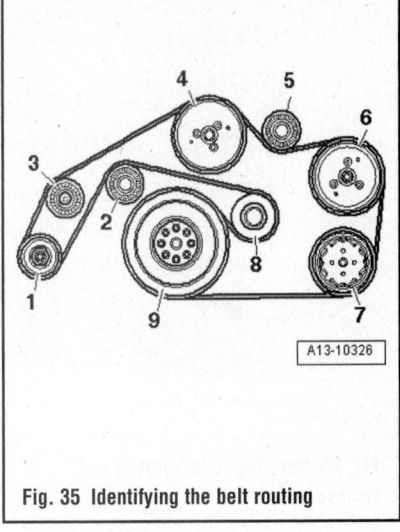

Fig. 35 Identifying the belt routing

- Bolt: M8x50

1. With ignition switched off, disconnect battery ground wire.

➡ **Hot vapor/hot coolant may escape when opening expansion tank. Cover cap with cloth and open carefully.**

2. Open the cap of coolant expansion tank.

3. Remove the bolts and the front noise insulation.

> ☀☀ **CAUTION**
>
> **Risk of destroying if the running direction of a used ribbed belt is reversed. Before removing the ribbed belt, mark the running direction with chalk or a felt-tip pen for reinstallation.**

4. Pivot the tensioner clockwise to release tension on ribbed belt.

5. To secure ribbed belt tensioner, install an M8x50 bolt in the threaded hole. Only install M8x50 bolt far enough so that ribbed belt can be removed from the tensioner without force, otherwise the tensioner will be damaged.

6. Remove the ribbed belt.

7. Remove the bolts.

8. Remove ribbed belt tensioner.

9. Disconnect the electrical connector.

10. Remove B+ line protective cap.

11. Remove nut and remove B+ line.

12. Remove the bolt 3 and clamp off the coolant hoses using hose clamps 3094.

13. Place Workshop Crane Drip Tray VAS 6208 under engine.

14. Detach the coolant hoses at generator.

15. Unscrew bolts Unscrew bolts arrows and remove generator and remove generator.

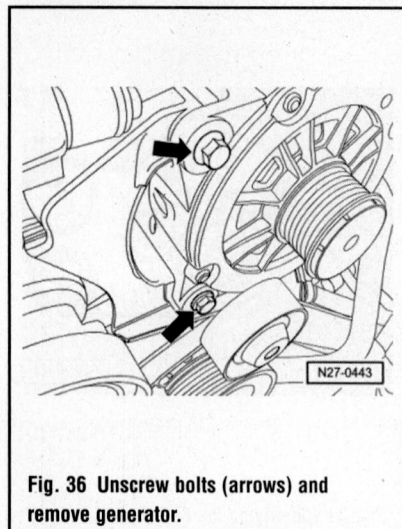

Fig. 36 Unscrew bolts (arrows) and remove generator.

➡If generator is stuck in its bracket, screw in mounting bolts again except 2 rotations.

➡Carefully strike on bolt heads using flat side of hammer - doing this loosens sleeves of generator mount.

To install:

Install in reverse order of removal, observing the following:

16. Secure all the hose connections using standard hose clamps.

17. Slightly drive back sleeves for retaining bolts in order for easier installation of generator.

➡Tight sleeves for generator mount must be made smooth-running, otherwise clamping force of sleeve is too little despite correct torque.

18. Position ribbed belt over pulleys in stated sequence.

➡Replace O-ring

➡When installing ribbed belt, be sure that it is seated correctly on belt pulleys.

19. Install ribbed belt tensioner and ribbed belt.

20. Connect the battery.

21. Check the coolant level.

22. Start engine and check belt routing. Tightening Specifications:
• Bracket for coolant lines to generator: 7 ft. lbs. (9 Nm)
• Generator to engine: 17 ft. lbs. (23 Nm)
• Terminal 30/B+ to generator: 12 ft. lbs. (16 Nm)

4.2L Engine

See Figure 38.

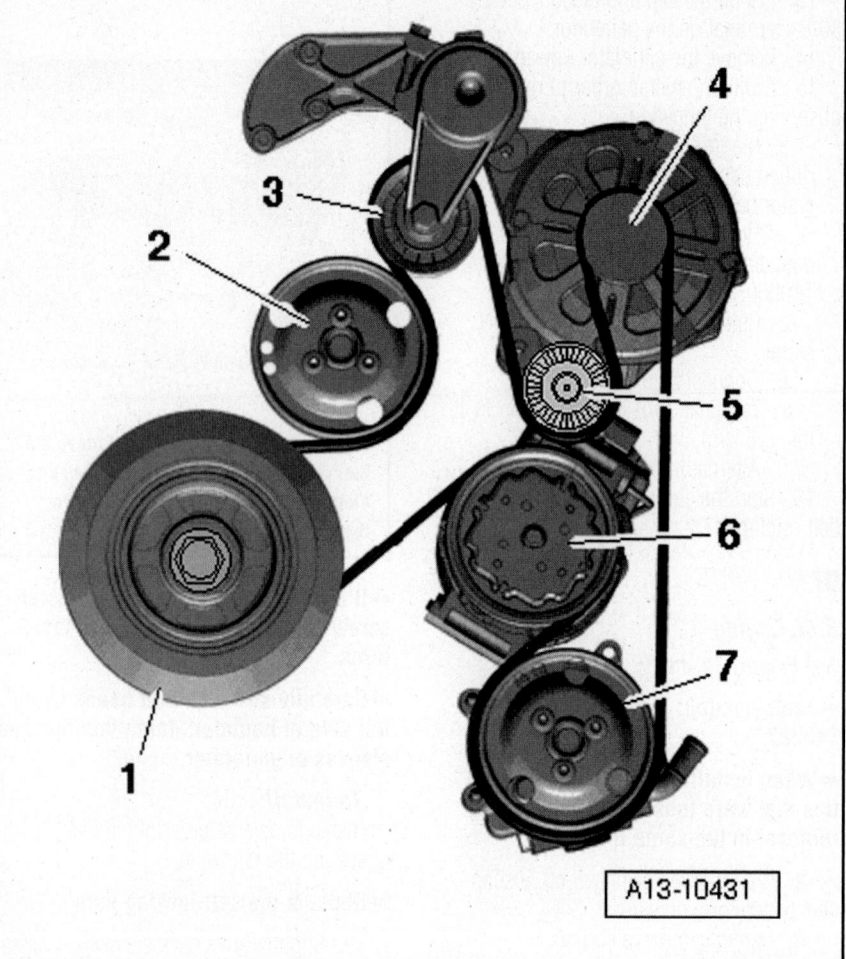

Fig. 37 Positioning the ribbed belt over the pulleys

➡Tools needed: Hose clamp pliers V.A.G 1921

1. With ignition switched off, disconnect battery ground wire.
2. Drain the coolant.
3. Remove the coolant hose to radiator from right coolant pipe.
4. Remove bolt.

➡Risk of destroying if the running direction of a used ribbed belt is reversed.

➡Before removing ribbed belt, marking running direction with chalk or a felt-tip pen for reinstallation.

5. Pivot the tensioner in direction of arrow to release tension on ribbed belt.
6. Remove ribbed belt and release tensioner.
7. Remove screws and remove ribbed belt tensioner from upper part of oil pan.
8. Remove fan shroud.
9. Cut through cable ties and remove air guide hose to secondary air injection combi-valves upper.

10. Remove right air filter housing.
11. Unscrew bolts and remove generator.
   a. If alternator sticks in holder, install screw again down as far as the last 2 turns.

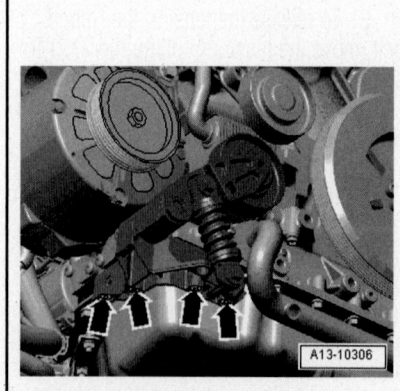

Fig. 38 Remove screws and remove ribbed belt tensioner from upper part of oil pan.

b. Carefully strike on bolt heads using flat side of hammer - doing this loosens threaded sleeves of generator mount.

12. Remove screw and remove coolant pipe bracket.

　a. Place a rag under separating point to catch escaping coolant.

13. Remove the coolant pipes from generator.

14. Disconnect the electrical connector from the generator.

15. Remove terminal 30/B+ item.

To install:

Install in reverse order of removal, observing the following:

16. Replace the self-locking nuts.

17. Replace the O-ring.

18. Secure all the hose connections using standard hose clamps.

19. Slightly drive back sleeves for retaining bolts in order for easier installation of generator.

　a. Tight sleeves for generator mount must be made smooth-running, otherwise clamping force of sleeve is too little despite correct torque.

20. Place ribbed belt over belt pulleys in the specified sequence.

➡**When installing ribbed belt, be sure that it is seated correctly on belt pulleys.**

21. Connect the battery.

22. Install right air filter housing.

23. Install fan shroud.

24. Secure the ATF lines.

25. Fill the coolant.

26. Check the ATF level.

27. Start the engine and verify that the belt is running properly.

Tightening Specifications:

• Bracket for coolant lines to generator: 7 ft. lbs. (9 Nm)

• Generator to engine: 17 ft. lbs. (23 Nm)

• Terminal 30/B+ to generator: 12 ft. lbs. (16 Nm)

• Tensioner for ribbed belt to upper part of oil pan: 7 ft. lbs. (9 Nm)

ENGINE ELECTRICAL

FIRING ORDER

The 2.0L engine firing order is 1-3-4-2.

The 3.0L diesel engine firing order is 1-4-3-6-2-5.

The 3.6L engines the firing order is 1-5-3-6-2-4.

The 4.2L engine the firing order is 1-5-4-8-6-3-7-2.

IGNITION COIL

REMOVAL & INSTALLATION

Q5

2.0L Engine

See Figure 39.

1. Remove engine cover.

2. Open both bolts on the connector strip.

3. Pull all the ignition coils out approximately 30 mm from the spark plug holes using the T40039.

4. Release the connectors and pull all connectors simultaneously off from the ignition coils.

To install:

5. Insert all ignition coils loosely into spark plug shaft.

6. Align the ignition coils to the connectors and then connect all of the connectors simultaneously onto the ignition coils.

7. Press the ignition coils uniformly onto the spark plugs by hand (do not use an impact tool).

3.2L Engine—Standard

See Figure 40.

1. Remove front engine cover.

2. Remove rear engine cover.

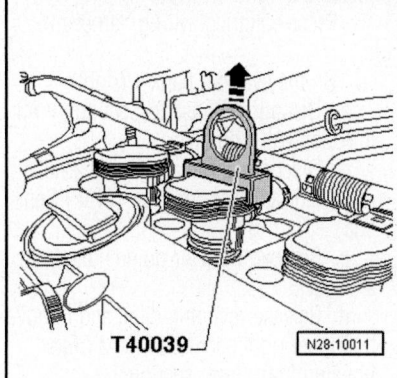

Fig. 39 Pull all the ignition coils out approximately 30 mm from the spark plug holes using the T40039.

3. On cylinder bank 1 (right):

　a. Remove bolts.

　b. Remove air ducts.

　c. Disconnect check valve from air duct hose.

　d. Remove air duct hose, thereby loosening hose clamp and opening clips.

　e. Disconnect the electrical connectors at Engine Coolant Temperature (ECT) Sensor and Intake Manifold Flap Change-over Valve.

　f. Disconnect the electrical harness connectors.

　g. Remove the bolts and disconnect the electrical connections at ignition coils.

　h. Set electrical wiring harness aside.

4. On cylinder bank 2 (left):

　a. Remove the coolant expansion tank.

　b. Disconnect electrical connection from Engine Coolant Level (ECL) Warn-

IGNITION SYSTEM

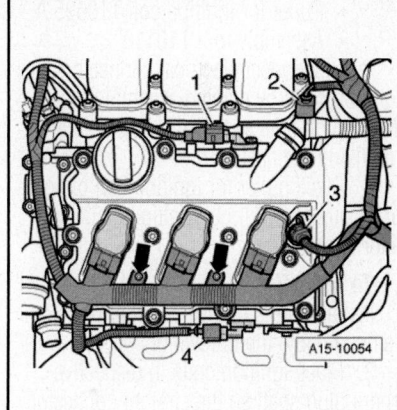

Fig. 40 Disconnect the electrical connectors—Bank 1

ing Switch at bottom of coolant reservoir and set aside coolant reservoir with coolant hoses connected.

　c. Disconnect the electrical connectors on Intake Manifold Tuning (IMT) Valve Position Sensor.

　d. Disconnect the electrical harness connectors.

　e. Remove the bolts and disconnect the electrical connections at ignition coils.

　f. Set electrical wiring harness aside.

5. Continued for both sides:

　a. Remove ignition coils using ignition coil puller T40039.

　b. Installation is in reverse order of removal.

3.2L Engine—With Power Output Stages

1. Disconnect the negative battery cable.

2. Release electrical connectors on all ignition coils and remove them from the ignition coils.

3. Using ignition coil puller, remove all ignition coils from spark plug shaft.

4. To install:

a. Insert all ignition coils loosely into each spark plug shaft.

b. Align ignition coils to connectors and then connect all of connectors simultaneously onto ignition coils.

c. Press the ignition coils uniformly onto spark plugs by hand (do not use an impact tool).

Q7

3.6L Engine

See Figure 41.

➡**Tools needed:**

- Puller for ignition coil T10095 A
- Assembly tool T10118

1. Disconnect electrical connectors at ignition coils by placing assembly tool T10118 on release button and carefully removing connector.

2. Place puller for ignition coil on ignition coils and pull out ignition coils one after another.

To install:

Installation is in reverse order of removal, note the following:

3. Place ignition coils in respective spark plug shaft so the straight connector sides fit with each other.

4.2L & 3.0L Engines

See Figure 42.

➡**Tools needed: Ignition Coil Puller T40039**

1. On cylinder bank 2 (left):

a. Disconnect the electrical connector at Mass Air Flow (MAF) Sensor.

b. Remove left air guide hose from air duct.

c. Release retaining clips and remove upper left section of air filter housing.

2. Remove the oil dipstick from guide tube.

3. Remove the bolts.

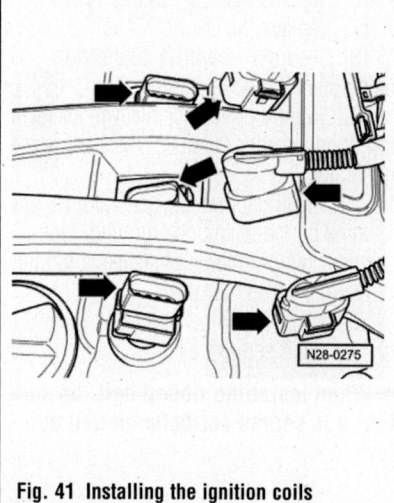

Fig. 41 Installing the ignition coils

4. Disconnect the electrical harness connectors at ignition coils.

5. Press electrical wiring harness to side.

6. On the cylinder bank 1 (right):

a. Disconnect hose to Secondary Air Injection (AIR) pump.

b. Disconnect the electrical harness connector at Mass Air Flow (MAF) Sensor.

c. Remove right air guide hose from air duct.

d. Release retaining clips and remove the upper right section of the air filter housing from lower section.

7. For vehicles with air suspension:

➡**If necessary, remove electrical connector for Heated Oxygen Sensor (HO2S) from bracket at right strut tower for better access.**

a. Press the circlip forward from hose coupling.

b. Press release ring down and remove vent hose from the upper section of air filter.

8. Remove the bolts.

9. Disconnect the electrical harness connectors at ignition coils.

10. Press the electrical wiring harness to side.

Continued for both sides: Remove ignition coils using puller.

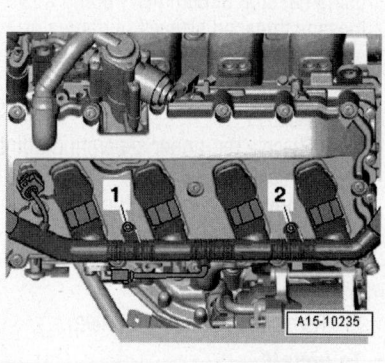

Fig. 42 Disconnecting the electrical harness connectors

To install:

Installation is in reverse order of removal. Tighten the wiring for the ignition coils at the cylinder head cover to 5 Nm.

IGNITION TIMING

ADJUSTMENT

Ignition timing is regulated by control module. It is not possible to adjust the ignition timing.

SPARK PLUGS

REMOVAL & INSTALLATION

1. Disconnect the negative battery cable.

2. Switch the ignition off.

3. For 3.2L, remove the lower air filter housing cover.

4. Remove engine cover.

5. Remove the ignition coils.

6. Remove the spark plugs Spark plug wrench.

7. Install new sparks plugs using Spark plug wrench 3122B.

8. Tighten to:

- 2.0L: 22 ft. lbs. (30 Nm)
- 3.2L: 15 ft. lbs. (20 Nm)

9. Push ignition coils by hand into intended resources in cylinder head cover.

10. Install ignition coils by rotating slightly - they must engage noticeably.

ENGINE ELECTRICAL | **STARTING SYSTEM**

STARTER

REMOVAL & INSTALLATION

Q5

2.0L Engine

See Figure 43.

1. With ignition switched off, disconnect battery ground wire.

2. Loosen the clamping sleeve 1, push it toward the rear and tie up the left front muffler.

3. Remove the right engine mount:
   a. Remove the nut and free up the ground wire on the engine support.
   b. Remove the bolts and the right engine support.

4. Disconnect the electrical connector by sliding the retainer back and pressing the release down.

5. Disconnect electrical wire from starter.

6. Remove the bolt (from above) and the rear extension from the transmission.

7. Remove the bolt and remove the starter.

To install:

8. Install in reverse order of removal, observing the following:
   a. Install the engine support and the right engine mount.
   b. Align the exhaust system so that there is no tension.
   c. Connect battery.

3.2L Engine

See Figure 44.

1. Remove front right wheel.
2. Remove the alternator.
3. Remove heat shield for right halfshaft.
4. Disconnect cable for terminal B+.

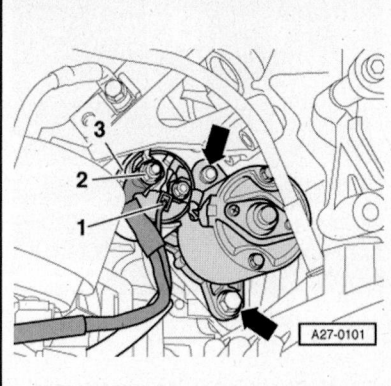

Fig. 44 Disconnect cable for terminal B+ (2), disconnect the connector for terminal 50 (1), remove heat shield from solenoid switch (3)

5. Disconnect the connector for terminal 50.

6. Remove heat shield from solenoid switch.

7. Remove starter mounting bolts, detach starter.

8. Installation is reverse of removal, paying attention to the following torque specifications:
   a. Starter to engine: 33 ft. lbs. (45 Nm).
   b. Terminal B+ to starter: 11 ft. lbs. (16 Nm).
   c. Heat shield for drive shaft to transmission: 17 ft. lbs. (23 Nm).

Q7

3.0L Engine

See Figure 45.

➡**Tool needed: 16 mm open end wrench T10388.**

1. With ignition switched off, disconnect battery Ground wire.
2. Remove the generator.
3. Remove the bolt.
4. Remove the bolt.
5. Leave ATF line in installation location.
6. Disconnect the electrical connector.
7. Remove B+ wire.
8. Remove engine support screw. Remove the bolt using the 16 mm open end wrench T10388. Remove the bolt and remove the starter.

To install:

Install in reverse order of removal, observing the following:

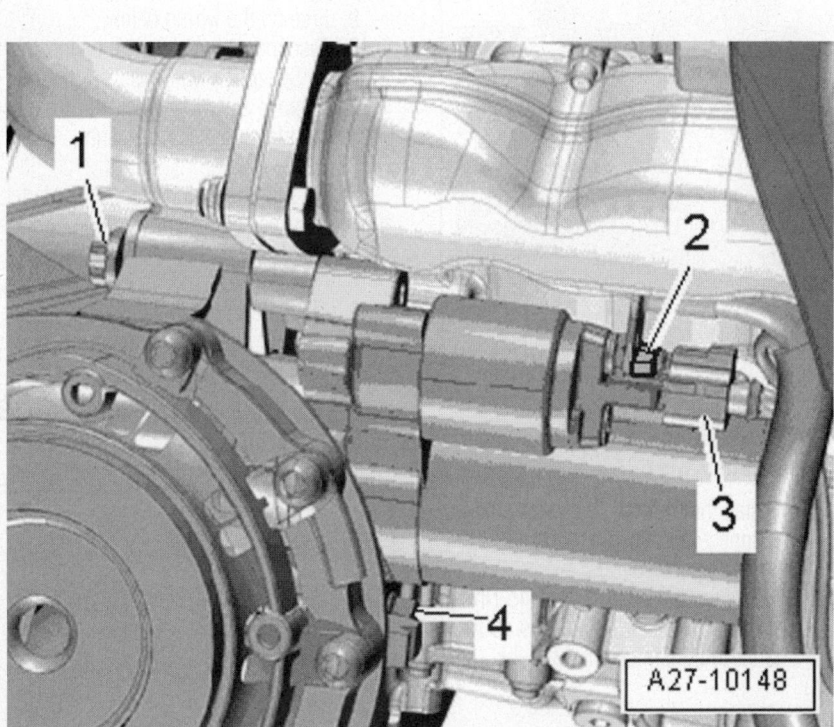

1. Rear extension bolt
2. Electrical wire
3. Electrical connector
4. Starter bolt

Fig. 43 Disconnect the electrical connector by sliding the retainer back and pressing the release down. Disconnect electrical wire from starter. Remove the bolt and the rear extension from the transmission. Remove the bolt and remove the starter.

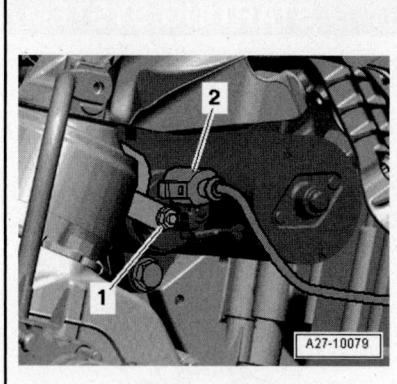

Fig. 45 Disconnecting the connector and removing the B+ wire

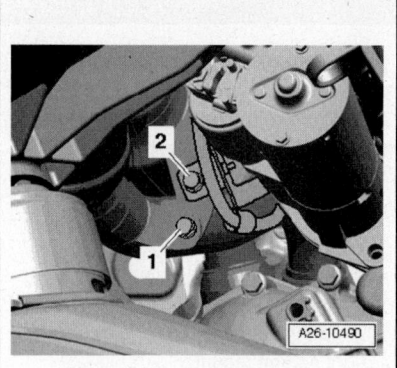

Fig. 46 Removing the catalytic converter bolts. Disregard item 1.

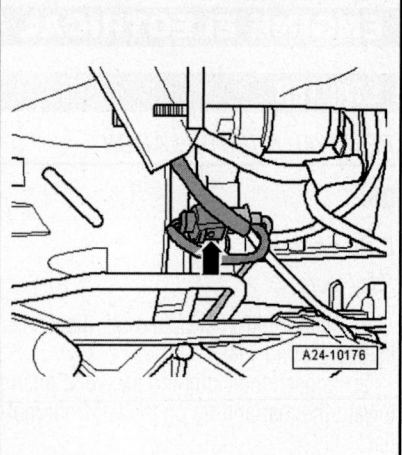

Fig. 48 Disconnecting the electrical connector

9. Install the engine support.
10. Install the generator.
11. Connect the battery.
Tightening Specifications:
• Starter to transmission–upper bolt; without 16 mm open end wrench T10388: 48 ft. lbs. (65 Nm).
• Starter to transmission–upper bolt; with 16 mm open end wrench T10388 and torque wrench V.A.G 1332: 39 ft. lbs. (53 Nm)
• Starter to transmission–upper bolt; with 16 mm open end wrench T10388 and torque wrench VAS 5820: 37 ft. lbs. (50 Nm)
• Starter to transmission–lower bolt: 48 ft. lbs. (65 Nm)
• B+ wire to starter: 12 ft. lbs. (16 Nm)
• ATF line to the upper part of the oil pan: 7 ft. lbs. (9 Nm)
• ATF line to the transmission: 7 ft. lbs. (9 Nm)

3.6L Engine

See Figures 46 and 47.

1. With ignition switched off, disconnect battery ground wire.
2. Remove screws and remove the front and rear noise insulation.
3. Remove catalytic converter bolts.
4. Remove the bolt and nuts.
5. Remove B+ line bracket and catalytic converters.
6. Remove heat shield on starter.
7. Remove the protective caps.
8. Remove the wires.
9. Remove bolts and remove starter.

To install:

Install in reverse order of removal, observing the following:

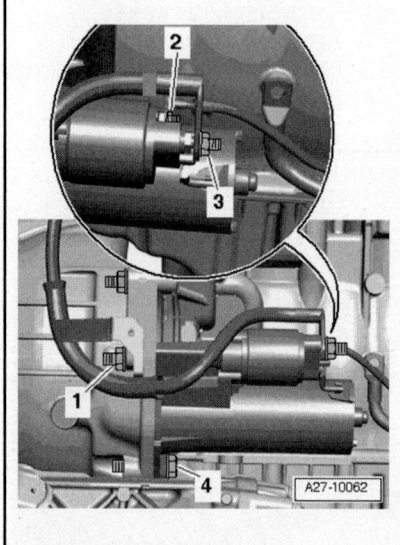

Fig. 47 Removing the starter

➡When installing, install cable ties at same location.

10. Install the catalytic converter bracket.
11. Connect the battery.
Tightening Specifications:
• B+ wire to starter: 11 ft. lbs. (15 Nm)
• Terminal 50 to starter: 6 ft. lbs. (8 Nm)
• Starter to transmission: 48 ft. lbs. (65 Nm)

4.2L Engine

See Figures 48 through 50.

➡When installing, reinstall all cable ties that were loosened or cut during removal in the same locations.

1. With ignition switched off, disconnect battery ground wire.
2. Drain the coolant.

3. Remove primary catalytic converter.
4. Remove right coolant pipe.
5. Remove the generator.
6. Remove oil cooler.
7. Remove heat shield from steering gear.
8. Remove heat shield.
9. Free up the wiring below.
10. Disconnect the electrical connector to Engine Speed (RPM) Sensor.
11. Remove electrical connector from bracket and free up electrical wiring.
12. Remove bolts.
13. Free up the wiring harness to starter at wiring harness bracket by cutting through cable ties.
14. Remove bolt.
15. Tip starter to side slightly so that engine support cut-out allows access to release terminal 50 connector.

➡Release lever is not visible and must be felt with fingers.

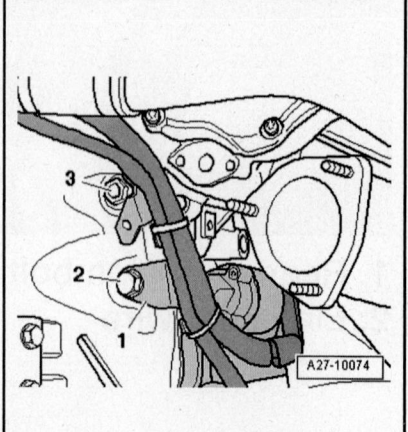

Fig. 49 Freeing up the wiring harness to the starter at the bracket

16. Disconnect electrical connector by sliding locking mechanism back and pressing release down.

➡**The B+ line can only be removed after disconnecting terminal 50 electrical connector.**

17. Remove nut and remove B+ wire from solenoid switch.

18. Remove the starter.

To install:

19. Bring the starter into installation position.

20. Install upper starter screw only 2 turns.

➡**It must be possible to pivot starter lightly.**

21. Tighten B+ wire.

22. Have a 2nd person hold terminal 50 electrical connector from front through engine support and back into installation position.

23. Position the terminal 50 electrical connector on starter.

Install in reverse order of removal, observing the following:

When installing, install cable ties at same location.

24. Install oil cooler.

25. Install the generator.

26. Install right coolant pipe.

27. Install primary catalytic converter.

28. Fill the coolant.

29. Connect the battery.

Tightening Specifications:

• B+ wire to starter: 12 ft. lbs. (16 Nm)

• Starter to transmission: 32 ft. lbs. (45 Nm)

• Heat shield to steering gear: 8 ft. lbs. (10 Nm)

• Heat shield to engine: 7 ft. lbs. (9 Nm)

• Heat shield to bracket: 7 ft. lbs. (9 Nm)

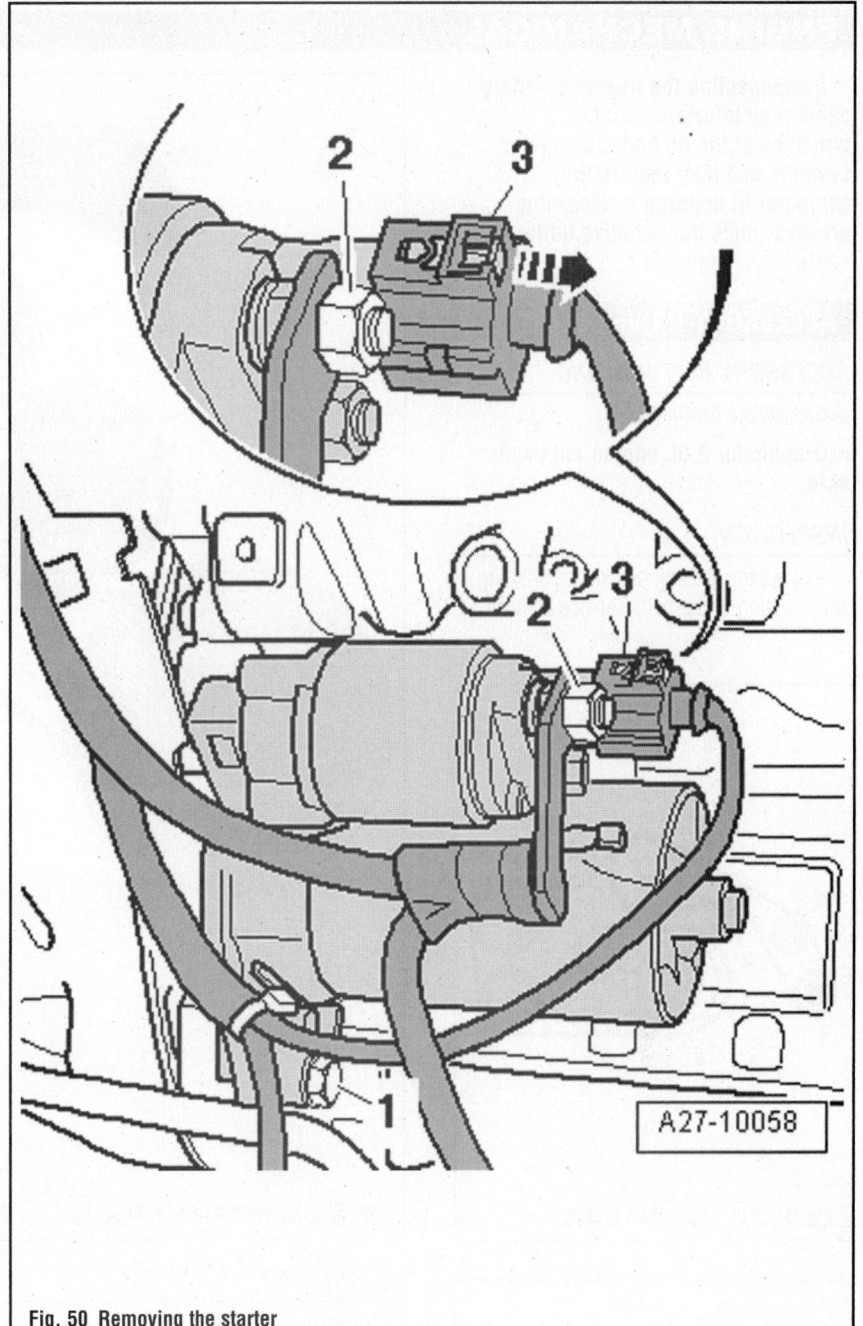

Fig. 50 Removing the starter

ENGINE MECHANICAL

➡Disconnecting the negative battery cable may interfere with the functions of the on board computer systems and may require the computer to undergo a relearning process, once the negative battery cable is reconnected.

ACCESSORY DRIVE BELTS

ACCESSORY BELT ROUTING

See Figures 51 through 54.

➡Graphic for 2.0L engine not available.

INSPECTION

Inspect for glazing, cracking, perishing and slacking in the belt. Replace as necessary.

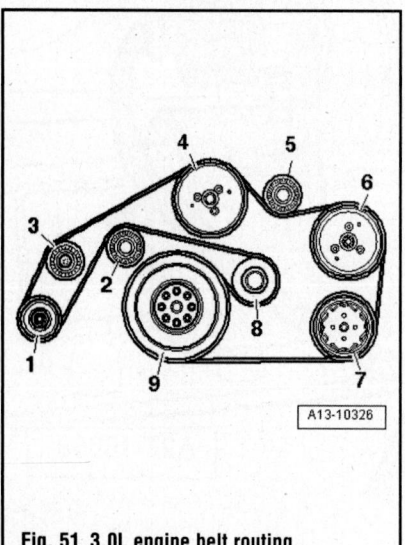

Fig. 51 3.0L engine belt routing

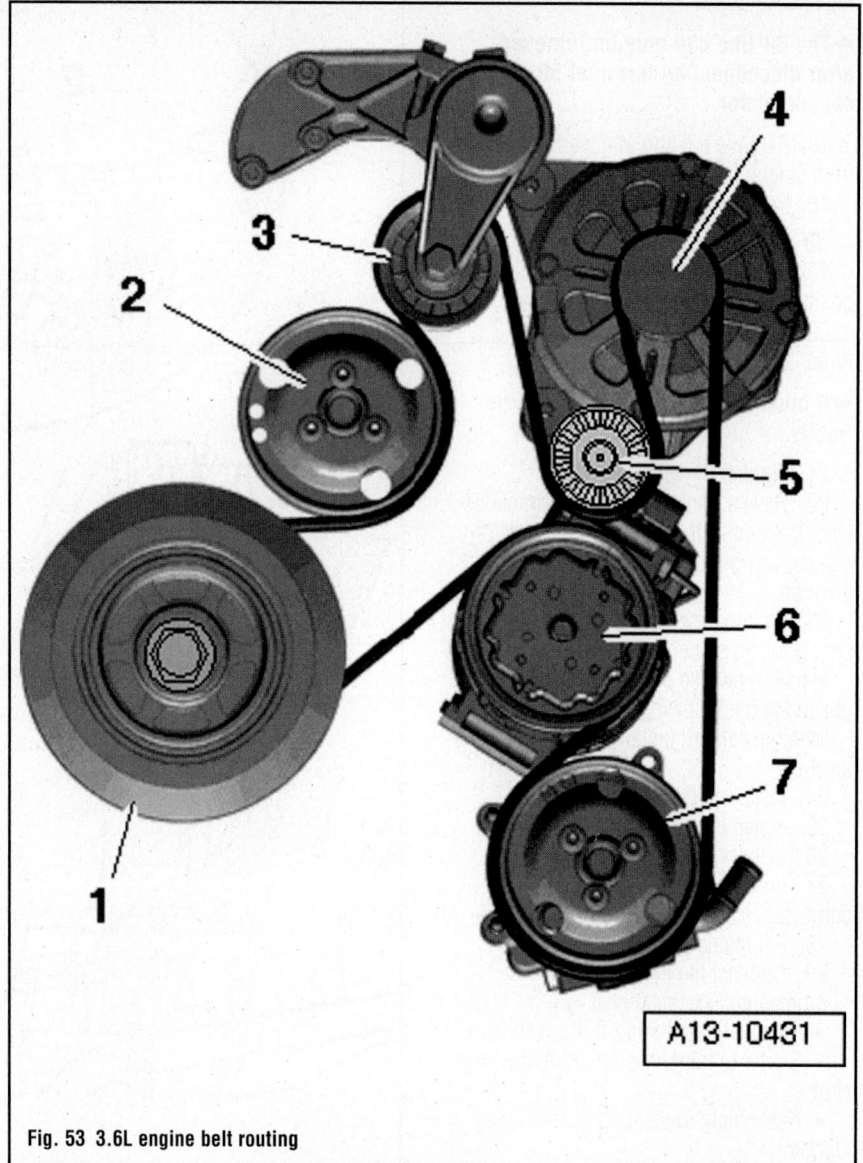

Fig. 53 3.6L engine belt routing

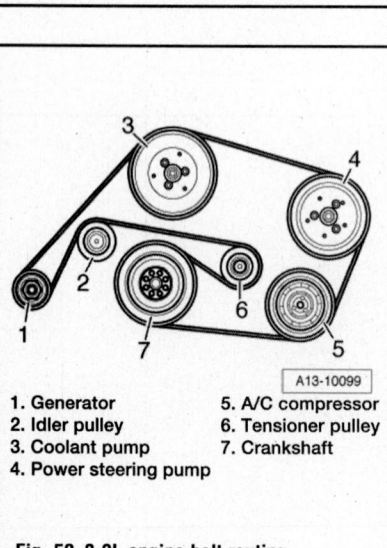

1. Generator
2. Idler pulley
3. Coolant pump
4. Power steering pump
5. A/C compressor
6. Tensioner pulley
7. Crankshaft

Fig. 52 3.2L engine belt routing

ADJUSTMENT

These engines utilize a belt tensioner. No adjustment is necessary.

REMOVAL & INSTALLATION

Q5

1. If necessary, remove the front noise insulation.
2. To release ribbed belt tension, rotate tensioner clockwise.
3. Before removing ribbed belt, mark the turning direction on it with chalk or a felt tip pen. A reversed turning direction can cause damage to the ribbed belt under operating conditions.
4. To remove tension, swing tensioner ribbed belt clockwise using Ribbed Belt

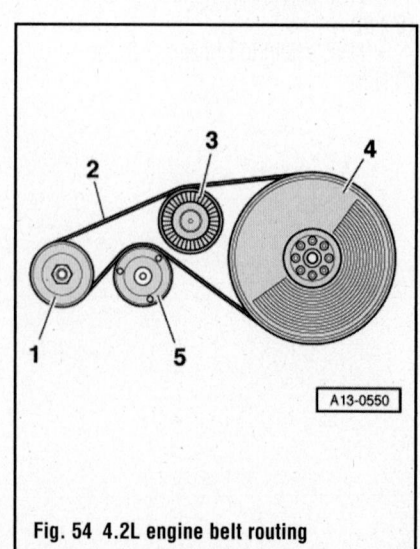

Fig. 54 4.2L engine belt routing

Install. Tool 3299 and Claw For Tensioner 3299/1.

    a. Remove ribbed belt from power steering pump belt pulley and release tensioning device.

    5. Remove ribbed belt.

    6. Installation is in reverse order of removal, note the following:

    a. When installing the ribbed belt, make sure it is seated correctly on the pulleys.

    b. Start the engine and check the belt routing.

    c. Install the front noise insulation.

Q7

3.6L Engine

See Figure 55.

➡ **Tools Needed: M8 x 50 bolt**

➡ **Risk of destroying due to reversed running direction on a used ribbed belt. Before removing the ribbed belt, mark the running direction with chalk or felt-tip pen for reinstallation later.**

    1. To release ribbed belt tension, rotate tensioner clockwise.

➡ **Risk of destroying tensioner. Only install bolt for securing tensioner far enough so that ribbed belt can be removed.**

    2. Secure tensioner with M8 x 50 bolt.
    3. Remove ribbed belt.

To install:

Installation is in reverse order of removal, note the following:

    a. Before installing ribbed belt, generator, A/C compressor and power steering pump must be securely installed.

    4. Route ribbed belt as follows:

➡ **When installing ribbed belt, make sure it is seated correctly on the pulleys.**

    5. Release tensioner by removing bolt.

    6. Check whether ribbed belt is routed correctly.

    7. Start engine and check whether ribbed belt runs correctly.

3.0L Engine

See Figure 56.

    1. On a vehicle with air suspension, activate vehicle lift mode.

    2. Carefully pull the engine cover off the 4 bolts one after the other.

    3. Loosen hose clamp, remove the air duct hose and move it to the side.

    4. Remove front noise insulation.

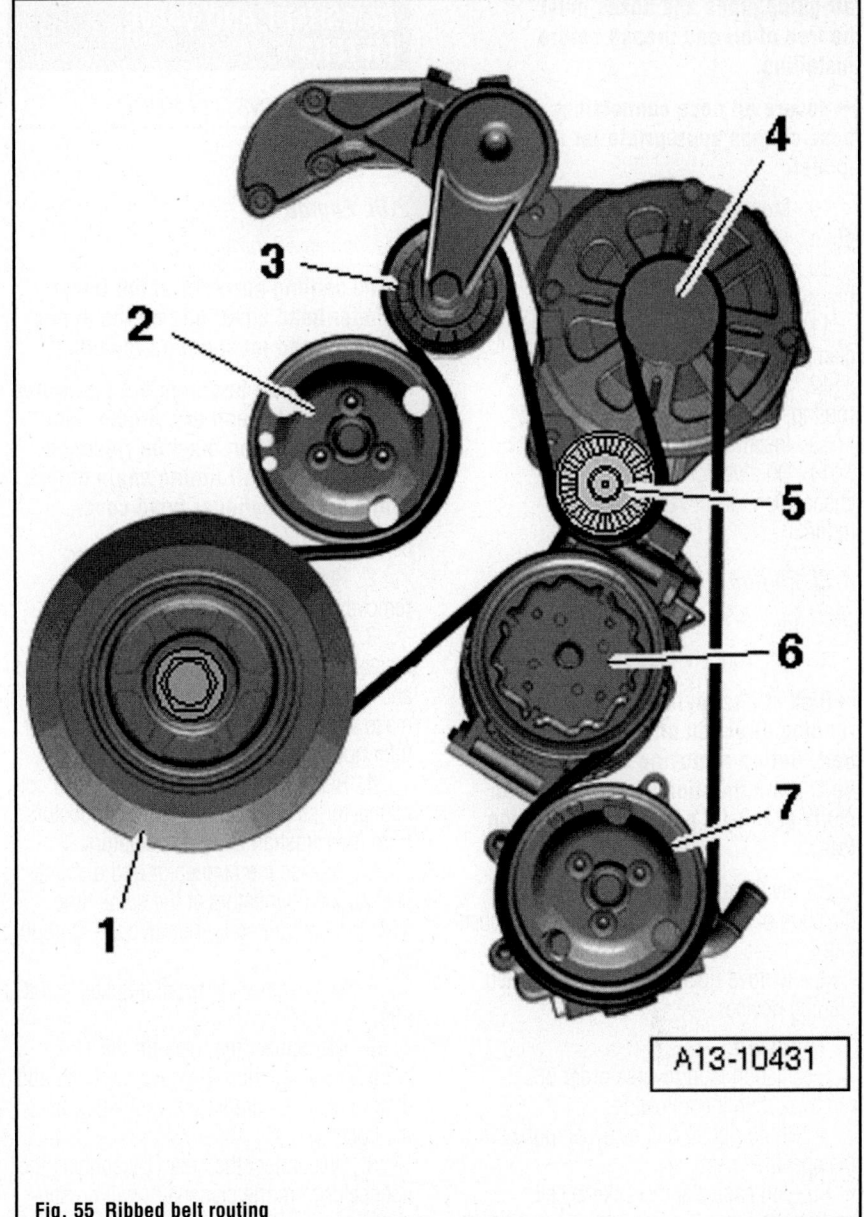

Fig. 55 Ribbed belt routing

    5. Disconnect the electrical connectors.

    6. Remove the bolt and move the bracket and wiring harness to the side.

➡ **Risk of destroying due to reversed running direction on a used ribbed belt. Before removing the ribbed belt, mark the running direction with chalk or felt-tip pen for reinstallation later.**

    7. Turn the tensioning element clockwise using the T60 Torx® socket T40087 to release the tension on the ribbed belt.

    8. Remove ribbed belt and release tension on the tensioning element.

To install:

Installation is in reverse order of removal, note the following:

➡ **The hose connections as well as the**

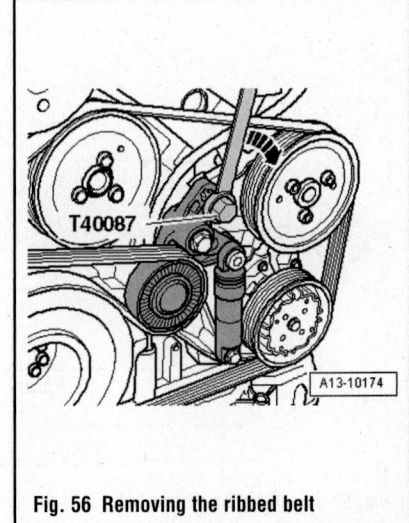

Fig. 56 Removing the ribbed belt

air guide pipes and hoses must be free of oil and grease before installing.

→Secure all hose connections with hose clamps appropriate for the model.

9. Mount ribbed belt over the pulley.

10. Install the wiring harness bracket.

11. Install air duct hose and screw-type clamps.

12. Start engine and check belt routing.

13. Install noise insulation.

14. On a vehicle with air suspension, deactivate vehicle lift mode.

4.2L Engine

See Figure 57.

1. Pull front engine cover off.

→Risk of destroying due to reversed running direction on a used ribbed belt. Before removing the ribbed belt, mark the running direction with chalk or felt-tip pen for reinstallation later.

2. Pivot the tensioning device in direction of arrow to relieve tension on ribbed belt.

3. Remove ribbed belt and release tensioning device.

To install:

Installation is in reverse order of removal, note the following:

4. Route ribbed belt over belt pulley in the specified sequence.

5. Start engine and check the belt routing.

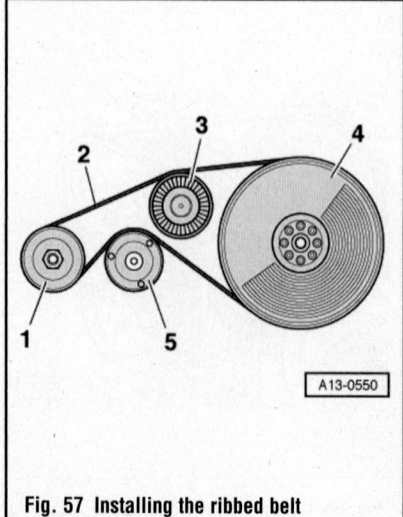

Fig. 57 Installing the ribbed belt

CAMSHAFT AND VALVE LIFTERS

REMOVAL & INSTALLATION

Q5

2.0L Engine

See Figures 58 through 63.

→The sealing surfaces of the lower cylinder head cover and on the upper cylinder head must not be reworked.

→The camshaft bearings are integrated in the cylinder head or cylinder head cover. The tension must be released from the camshaft timing chain before removing the cylinder head cover.

1. Perform a service position.

2. Remove the engine cover, then remove the intake air duct.

3. Disconnect the connector from the mass airflow (MAF) sensor. Open the clamp and remove the air guide tube from the mass airflow (MAF) sensor. Remove the air filter housing upward.

4. Remove the bolts on the ignition coil connector strip. Disconnect the connectors from the camshaft adjuster actuators.

5. Release the connector and disconnect all the connectors at the same time from the ignition coils. Remove the ignition coils.

6. Remove the camshaft adjuster actuators.

7. Disconnect the hose for the crankcase ventilation. Remove the bolts and then remove the crankcase ventilation from the hose.

8. Disconnect the hose. Disconnect the connector from the camshaft position sensor.

9. Disconnect the connector from camshaft adjustment valve. Remove the bolts arrows and the camshaft adjustment valve.

10. Remove the timing chain upper cover.

11. Remove the camshaft control valve, in a clockwise direction, using the assembly tool T10352/1.

12. Remove the bolts and remove the bearing bracket.

13. Turn the vibration damper to "TDC" using the socket T10355. The notch on the vibration damper must line up with the arrow marking on the timing chain lower cover.

14. To avoid engine damage, install T40196 plugs into the camshaft adjuster actuator holes.

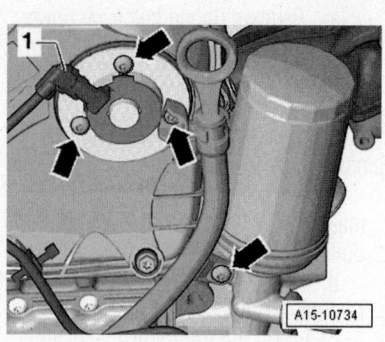

Fig. 58 Disconnect the connector from camshaft adjustment valve (1). Remove the bolts arrows and the camshaft adjustment valve.

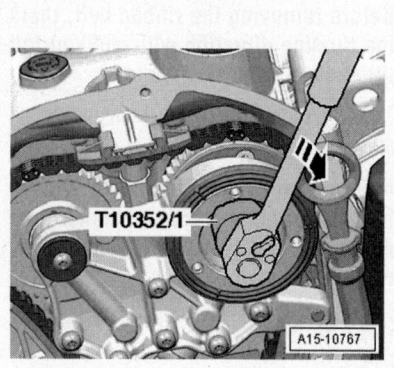

Fig. 59 Remove the camshaft control valve (in direction of arrow) using the assembly tool T10352/1.

15. Turn the crankshaft two complete turns in the direction of engine rotation (the engine should be back at "TDC"), then remove the T40196 plugs.

16. Mark the camshaft timing chain and the cylinder head to match the marking on the chain sprockets with a waterproof marker.

17. Remove the lower timing cover plug (left of the crankshaft).

18. Lift the chain tensioner locking wedge by inserting a scriber or a suitable screwdriver into the hole in the chain tensioner to the right.

19. Turn the crankshaft opposite the engine direction of rotation and secure it with a securing pin T40011. The intake camshaft switches in the engine direction of rotation.

20. Remove the bolt and guide the tensioning rail downward. Remove the upper

guide track by unlocking the latch with a screwdriver and pushing the guide track forward. Remove camshaft timing chain from chain sprockets.

> ※※ **CAUTION**

Risk of damaging valves and piston crowns: if the camshaft timing chain was removed from the cylinder head, then the crankshaft may not be turned further.

21. Remove the high pressure pump.
22. Remove vacuum pump.
23. Remove the cylinder head cover bolts in sequence. Remove the cylinder head cover.
24. Remove the camshafts.

➡**Cover open parts of the engine until reinstallation.**

To install:

➡**The pistons must not be positioned at TDC.**

➡**If the cylinder head cover was loosened, the sealing cap must be replaced.**

25. Make sure that all roller cam followers make contact correctly on valve stem ends.
26. Remove any sealant residue on the cylinder head using the flat blade scraper.
27. Remove any seal out of the groove in the cylinder head cover as well as from any sealing surface using, for example, a rotating plastic brush. Clean sealing surfaces, must be free of oil and grease.
28. Lubricate the running surfaces of both camshafts.
29. Install the camshaft with the T40191, move the spacers into the correct position if necessary. If necessary, use a second set of T40191 or T40191/1.
30. Install the camshafts into the cylinder head; the markings arrows must be properly located, as marked during removal.
31. Place a straightedge across the camshaft sprockets to check the alignment of the camshafts.
32. Apply the silicone sealant on the clean sealing surface of the cylinder head cover to about 2 to 3 mm. The cylinder head cover must be installed within 5 minutes after application of silicone sealant. Do not make the sealant bead any thicker than needed.
33. Mount the cylinder head cover on the cylinder head, replace the cylinder head cover bolts, then tighten the bolts in several steps.

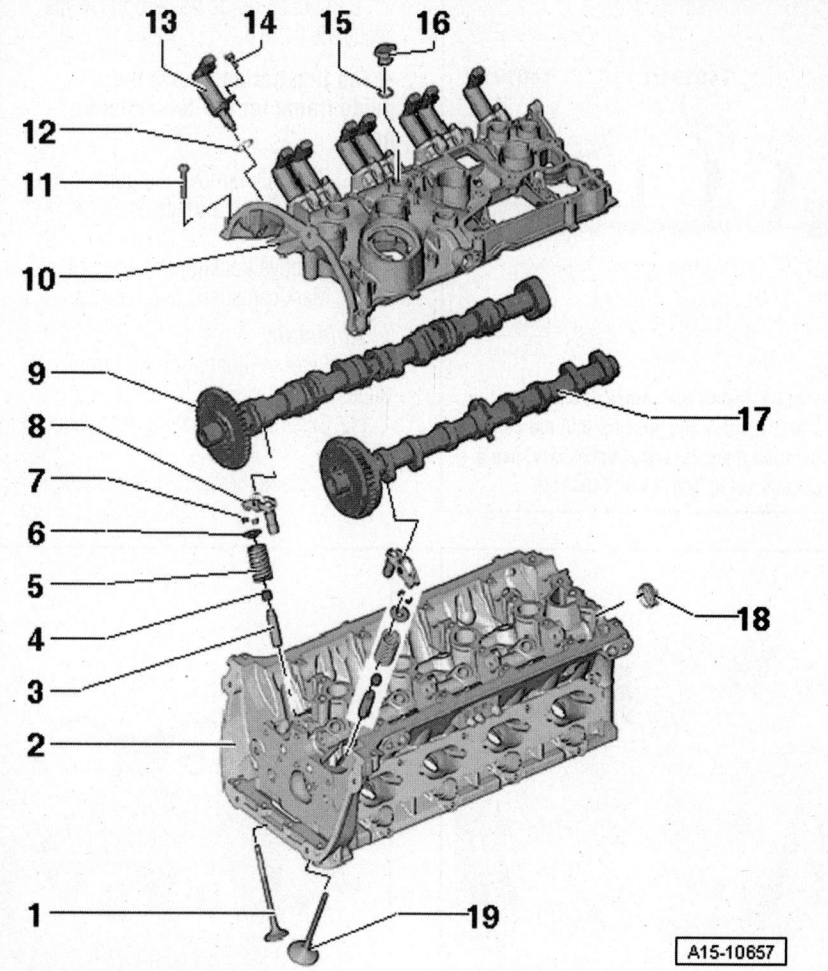

1. Exhaust Valve
2. Cylinder Head
3. Valve Guide
4. Valve Stem Seal
5. Valve Spring
6. Valve Spring Plate
7. Valve Retainers
8. Hydraulic Adjusting Element
9. Exhaust Camshaft
10. Cylinder Head Cover
11. Bolts: 6 ft. lbs. (8 Nm) plus 90°
12. O-ring
13. Camshaft Adjuster Actuator
14. Bolt: 4 ft. lbs. (5 Nm)
15. O-ring
16. Sealing Plugs
17. Intake Camshaft
18. Cap
19. Intake Valve

Fig. 60 Exploded view of the camshaft and valve assemblies

➡**Make sure the cylinder head cover is not tilted.**

34. Install the cap in the side of the cylinder head using the T10174 and without sealant to a depth of 1 to 2 mm.
35. Turn the vibration damper to "TDC". The notch on the vibration damper must line up with the arrow marking on the timing chain lower cover. The marked links of the camshaft timing chain must be positioned on the markings on the chain sprockets.

36. Turn the intake camshaft in direction of arrow with the wrench and install the camshaft timing chain. The markings on the camshaft timing chain and on the cylinder head must line up with the markings on the chain sprockets, as marked during removal.
37. Mount the bearing bracket and the bolts hand-tight. Remove the T40011. Tighten the bolts to 7 ft. lbs. (9 Nm).
38. Install the control valve
39. Install the T40196 in control valve actuator holes, as illustrated during

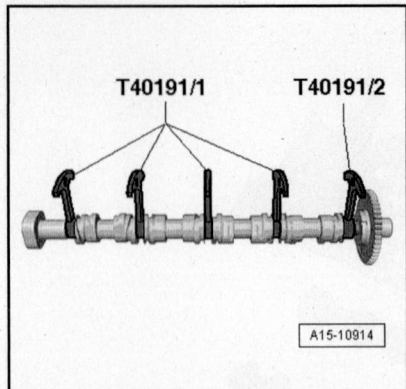

Fig. 61 Install the camshaft with the T40191, move the spacers into the correct position if necessary. If necessary, use a second set of T40191 or T40191/1.

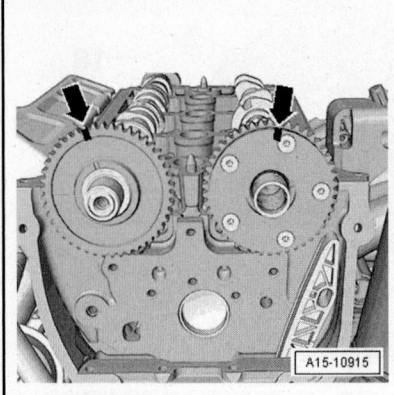

Fig. 62 Install the camshafts into the cylinder head; the markings arrows must be located as shown in the illustration.

removal. Turn the crankshaft 4 complete turns in the direction of engine rotation. Remove the T40196.

40. Install timing chain upper cover.
41. Install the vacuum pump.
42. Install the high pressure pump.
43. Install the service position.
44. Install air filter housing.
45. The rest of the assembly is basically a reverse of the disassembling sequence.

3.2L Engine

See Figures 63 and 64.

1. Remove the valve cover.
2. Remove the timing chain.
3. To remove the camshafts in the left cylinder head, remove the brake booster vacuum pump.
4. To remove the camshafts in the right cylinder head, remove the high pressure pump and pump motor housing.
5. Remove the bolts and the camshaft adjuster valves.

6. Loosen guide frame bolts in the sequence 21 to 1.

➡ **The illustration shows the guide frame for the left cylinder head.**

7. Carefully remove the guide frame and lay it on a soft surface on the workbench.
8. Remove Locking Pin T40133.
9. Mark camshafts and remove.

To install:

10. Refer to illustration for torque values.
11. Secure crankshaft using Locking Pin T40069.
12. Replace the seals and gaskets.

➡ **Cover the open parts of engine. There is risk of contaminating the lubricating system and bearing.**

➡ **Wear safety glasses.**

13. Using a rotating plastic brush, remove any remaining sealant from the cylinder head and guide frame.
14. lean sealing surfaces must be free of oil and grease.
15. Check the screen for dirt and clean it if necessary.
16. Oil running surfaces of both camshafts.
17. Insert the camshafts in the guide frame.

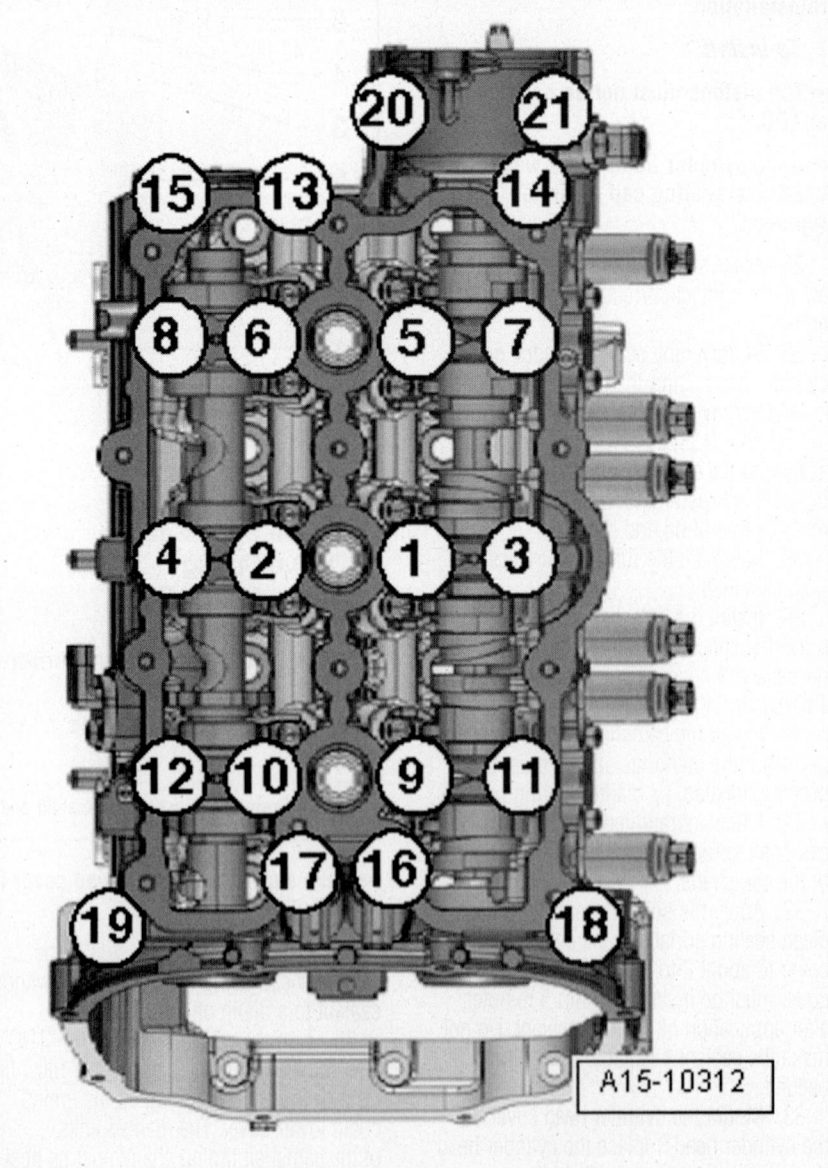

Fig. 63 Loosen guide frame bolts in the sequence 21 to 1

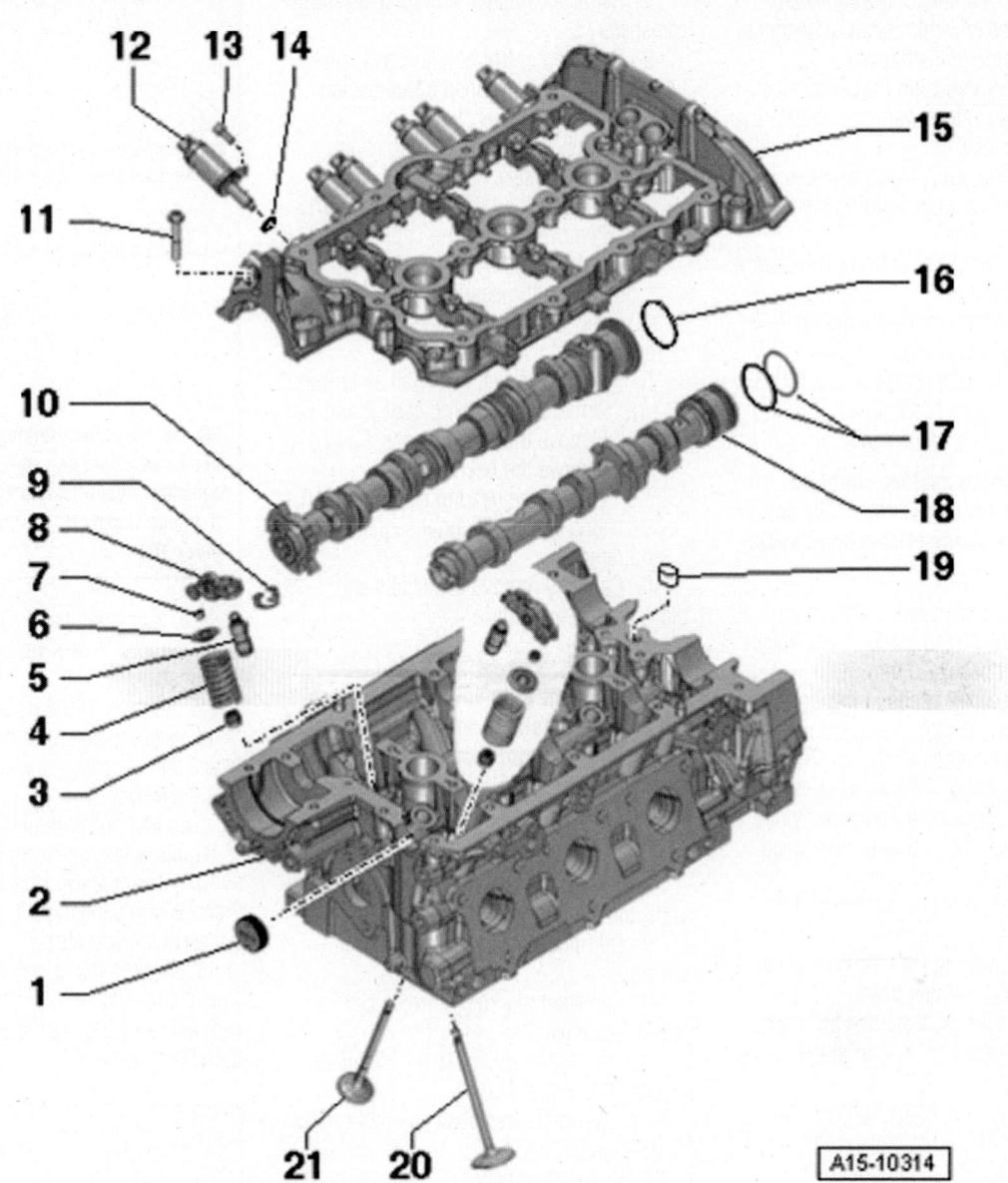

1. Sealing plug
2. Cylinder Head
3. Valve stem seal
4. Valve spring
5. Hydraulic adjusting elements
6. Valve spring plate
7. Valve keys
8. Roller rocker lever
9. Securing clip (different clips-for intake and exhaust side)
10. Intake camshaft (Maximum run-out. 0.04 mm)
11. Bolt
12. Camshaft adjuster actuator
13. Bolt (5 Nm)
14. O-ring
15. Bearing bracket (With integrated camshaft bearings)
16. Compression ring
17. Compression ring
18. Exhaust camshaft (Maximum run-out. 0.04 mm)
19. Oil strainer
20. Intake valve
21. Exhaust valve

A15-10314

Fig. 64 Overview of the valvetrain assembly—3.2L engines

a. The placement of the camshafts must be exactly within the axial bearings (arrows) of the guide frame.

b. The compression ring ends must face upward or downward and must never face sideways.

18. Rotate the guide frame with the camshafts inserted while holding them securely in the frame.

19. Rotate camshafts until the threaded holes face upward.

20. Check if the camshafts still lie in the guide frame axial bearings.

21. Install the Camshaft Locator T40133 and tighten the bolts to 18 ft. lbs. (25 Nm).

22. Rotate guide frame again.

➡The lubrication system could be plugged with excess sealant. Do not apply sealant beads thicker than specified.

23. Apply sealant beads to the clean sealing surfaces on the guide frame. Thickness of sealant bead: 2.0 mm.

24. Apply sealant beads (1 through 3) to the clean sealing surfaces on the guide frame as shown in the illustration. Thickness of sealant bead: 2.5 mm. Because the sealant begins hardening immediately, guide frame must be promptly positioned and tightened.

25. Place guide frame on the cylinder head.

26. Insert Locating Pins T40116 in the guide frame and cylinder head.

27. The sealant must harden for approximately 30 minutes after installing the guide frame.

28. Tighten guide frame bolts in the sequence 1 to 21.

29. Clean sealing plug hole in the cylinder head. It must be free of oil and grease.

30. Coat outer circumference of the sealing plug arrow with sealant.

31. Drive in the sealing plugs until they are flush.

32. Remove Locating Pins T40116 with the Impact Puller T10133/3.

33. The rest of installation is in reverse order of removal.

Q7

3.6L Engine

See Figures 65 through 68.

➡Tools needed: Adhesive lubricating paste

➡During installation, all cable ties must be reinstalled at the same location.

1. Remove camshaft timing chain from camshafts

2. Remove control housing and carefully remove from camshaft compression rings.

3. Lay aside camshaft timing chain.

4. Remove intake camshaft as follows:

a. Remove the bearing caps 1 and 13.

b. Remove the bearing caps 3 and 11.

c. Remove the bearing cap 7.

d. Loosen the bearing caps 5 and 9 alternately and in diagonal sequence, and remove.

5. Remove exhaust camshaft as follows:

a. Remove the bearing caps 2 and 14.

b. Remove the bearing caps 4 and 12.

c. Remove the bearing cap 8.

d. Loosen the bearing caps 6 and 10 alternating and in diagonal sequence, and remove.

6. Carefully remove camshafts and place on a clean surface.

To install:

➡Risk of damaging valves and piston crowns. If camshafts are rotated, crankshaft may not rest with any piston at "TDC".

7. Insert support elements in cylinder head.

8. Lay roller rocker lever on valve stem ends and clip in support elements.

9. Oil running surfaces of both camshafts.

10. Camshaft marking between cylinder 4 and 5 cam pair:

a. A - Exhaust camshaft - Identification 022 - Index 101

b. B - Intake camshaft - Identification 022 - Index 102

11. Place the camshafts in cylinder head camshaft bearing so that they stand at "TDC".

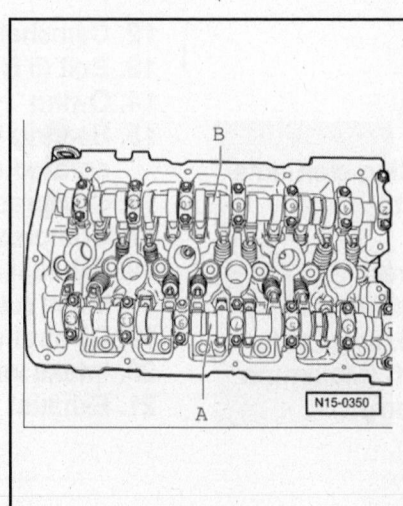

Fig. 65 Removing the camshafts

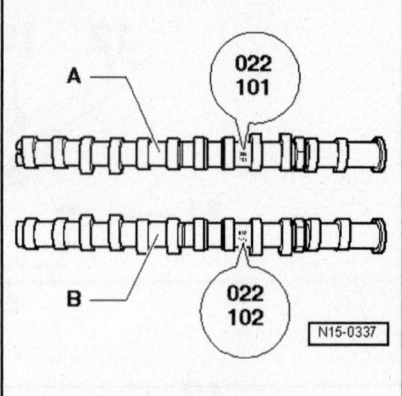

Fig. 66 Camshaft marking between cylinder 4 and 5 cam pair: A–Exhaust camshaft, identification 022, index 101; B–Intake camshaft, identification 022, index 102

a. Camshaft bar T10068 A must be situated in grooves in both camshafts.

12. Remove the camshaft bar T10068 A.

13. Bearing cap location: Points of intake and exhaust camshaft bearing caps face outwards.

a. Identification on bearing caps is legible when read from intake side.

14. Coat contact surface on bearing cap 7 and 8 with adhesive lubricating paste; adhesive lubricating paste.

15. Tighten the camshaft bearing cap. Coat contact surface on bearing cap 7 and 8 with adhesive lubricating paste; adhesive lubricating paste.

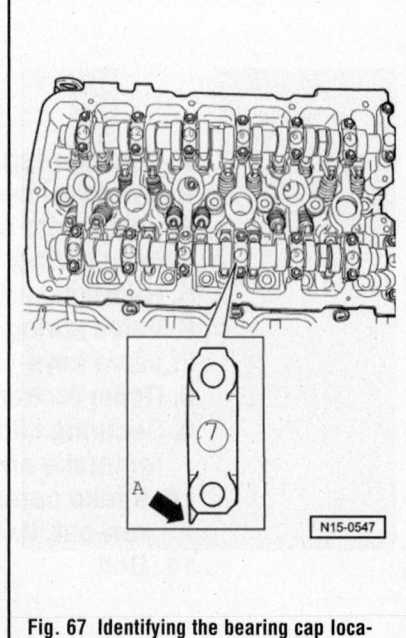

Fig. 67 Identifying the bearing cap locations

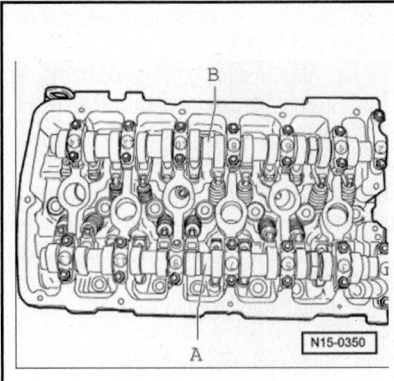

Fig. 68 Intake camshaft A tightening sequence

16. Tighten nuts in 5 stages as follows:
   a. Install the bearing cap 5 and 9 nuts alternating and diagonally as far as stop.
   b. Tighten bearing cap 5 and 9 nuts to 4 ft. lbs. (5 Nm) plus 45 degrees.
   c. Tighten bearing cap 1 and 13 nuts to 4 ft. lbs. (5 Nm) plus 45 degrees.
   d. Tighten bearing cap 7 nuts to 4 ft. lbs. (5 Nm) plus 45 degrees.
   e. Tighten bearing cap 3 and 11 nuts to 4 ft. lbs. (5 Nm) plus 45 degrees.
17. Tighten nuts in 5 stages as follows:
   a. Install the bearing cap 6 and 10 nuts alternately and diagonally as far as stop.
   b. Tighten bearing cap 6 and 10 nuts to 4 ft. lbs. (5 Nm) plus 45 degrees.
   c. Tighten bearing cap 2 and 14 nuts to 4 ft. lbs. (5 Nm) plus 45 degrees.
   d. Tighten bearing cap 8 nuts to 4 ft. lbs. (5 Nm) plus 45 degrees.
   e. Tighten bearing cap 4 and 12 nuts to 4 ft. lbs. (5 Nm) plus 45 degrees.
18. Position the camshafts at "TDC".
   a. Camshaft bar T10068 A must be situated in grooves in both camshafts.
   b. Turn the camshaft back and forth slightly with an open end wrench if necessary to insert camshaft bar T10068 A.
19. Unclip screen on back side of control housing and clean.
20. Lightly lubricate camshaft compression ring contact surface in control housing.
21. Lightly oil camshaft compression ring contact surfaces and carefully slide control housing over camshaft compression rings.
22. Tighten control housing.
23. Install camshaft timing chain.

➡**Risk of damaging valves and piston heads after working on valve train. The motor must not be started for about 30** minutes after installing camshafts because the hydraulic equalization elements must seat themselves. To ensure valves do not strike pistons when starting, carefully rotate engine at least 2 full revolutions.

3.0L Engine

See Figures 69 through 74.

➡**Tools needed:**

- Puller T10320
- Camshaft insertion tool T40094
- Camshaft insertion tool T40095
- Camshaft insertion tool T40096
- Pry lever 80 - 200
- Counter-holder tool 3036
- Hand drill with plastic brush attachment
- Protective eyewear
   a. Sealant

1. Remove affected camshaft timing chain from the camshaft.
2. Remove the upper section of the intake manifold.
3. Remove high pressure pump toothed belt.
4. Loosen toothed belt drive sprocket bolt 2 turns using the retainer 3036.
5. Remove toothed belt drive sprocket using puller T10320.
6. Remove left cylinder head cover.
7. Remove exhaust gas recirculation cooler switch-over valve from the bracket.
8. Remove bolt and engine cover bolts.
9. Free the wiring harness on top of the coolant pipe on the left side.
10. Remove the high pressure line union nut.
11. Remove bolts and remove rail element from the left cylinder head.
12. Remove right cylinder head cover.
13. Remove union nuts.
14. Remove bolts and lay the rail element aside with the fuel hoses attached to the side.
15. Free up the wiring harness using the Pry Lever.
16. Loosen the guide frame bolts and nuts in the sequence 18 to 1.

➡**When removing the camshafts, pay special attention to the roller rocker lever and the balance elements.**

17. Carefully remove the bearing bracket and camshafts.

To install:

18. Replace the front cover in the cylinder head on the right side.

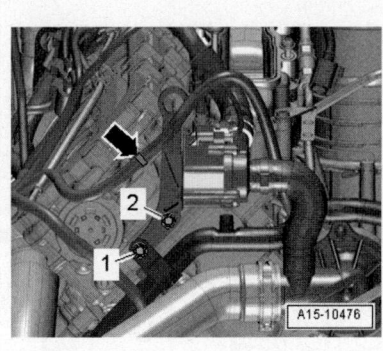

Fig. 69 Freeing up the wiring harness—Ignore 1 and 2 in the illustration.

➡**Risk of contaminating lubricating system. Cover any open parts in the cylinder head.**

19. Remove the sealant residue on the cylinder head and guide frame and the upper section of the oil pan, for example using a rotating plastic brush.
20. Clean the sealing surfaces; they must be free of oil and grease.
21. Lubricate the running surfaces of both camshafts.
22. Set up the camshaft insertion tool T40094 as follows:
   a. On the left cylinder head, install bracket T40094/2 in A and bracket T40094/1 in D.
   b. On the right cylinder head, install bracket T40094/2 in B and bracket T40094/1 in C.

➡**The following describe the work procedure on the left cylinder head. The procedure for the right cylinder head follows the same sequence.**

23. Install the exhaust camshaft into the bracket T40094/1 and T40094/2.
24. Turn the exhaust camshaft so that it can be locked with the straight-edge in the "TDC" position.
25. Mount the camshaft insertion tool T40096 onto the teeth of the exhaust camshaft so that one arm of the clamping device engages in one sprocket half.
26. Tension the clamping devise with the thumb wheel until the tooth faces align.
27. Place the intake camshaft into the camshaft insertion tool T40094. The securing pin must engage in the groove on the intake camshaft.
28. Push the exhaust camshaft toward the intake camshaft until the splines engage.

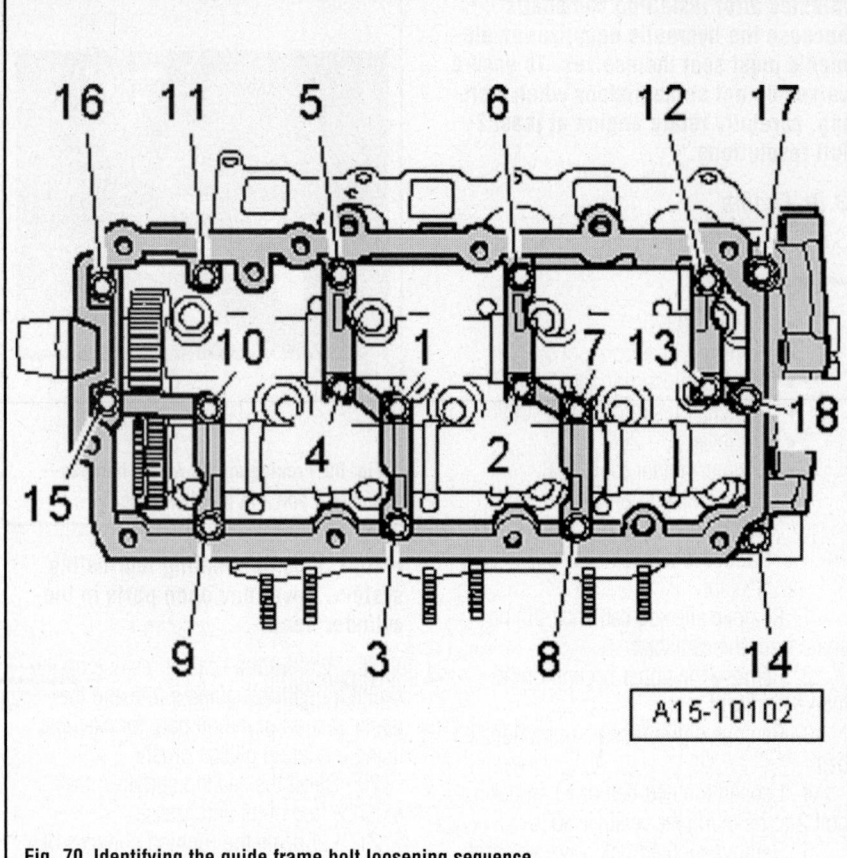

Fig. 70 Identifying the guide frame bolt loosening sequence

36. Remove the camshaft insertion tool T40095 and T40096.

   a. After installing the guide frame, let the sealant harden for approximately 30 minutes.

The rest of installation is in reverse order of removal, note the following:

37. Install the rail elements and the high pressure lines.

38. Install the left cylinder head cover.

39. Install the camshaft seal.

40. Install the high pressure pump toothed belt and the upper section of the intake manifold.

41. Install right cylinder head cover, with a suitable drift so that it is flush.

42. For both sides, install camshaft timing chains

➡**Risk of damaging valves and piston heads after working on valve train. The motor must not be started for about 30 minutes after installing camshafts because the hydraulic equalization elements must seat themselves. To ensure valves do not strike pistons when starting, carefully rotate engine at least 2 full revolutions.**

29. Place the bearing brackets on both camshafts. All the camshaft bearings must lie on the camshafts.

30. Mount the camshaft insertion tool T40095 onto the camshafts by aligning the pliers and tension with the knurled nuts.

   a. Note that the intake and exhaust camshafts have different shapes.

31. Turn the guide frame around.

➡**The lubrication system could be plugged with excess sealant. Do not apply sealant beads thicker than needed.**

32. Apply sealant beads to the clean sealing surfaces on the guide frame.

   a. The grooves of sealing surface must be completely filled with sealant.

   b. The sealant beads must be 1.5 to 2.0 mm above the sealing surface.

   c. The guide frame must be installed within 5 minutes after applying the sealant.

33. Make sure all the roller rocker levers contact the valve shaft ends and on the balance elements correctly.

34. Mount the guide frame together with both camshaft and the camshaft insertion tool T40095 to the cylinder head.

35. Tighten guide frame bolts.

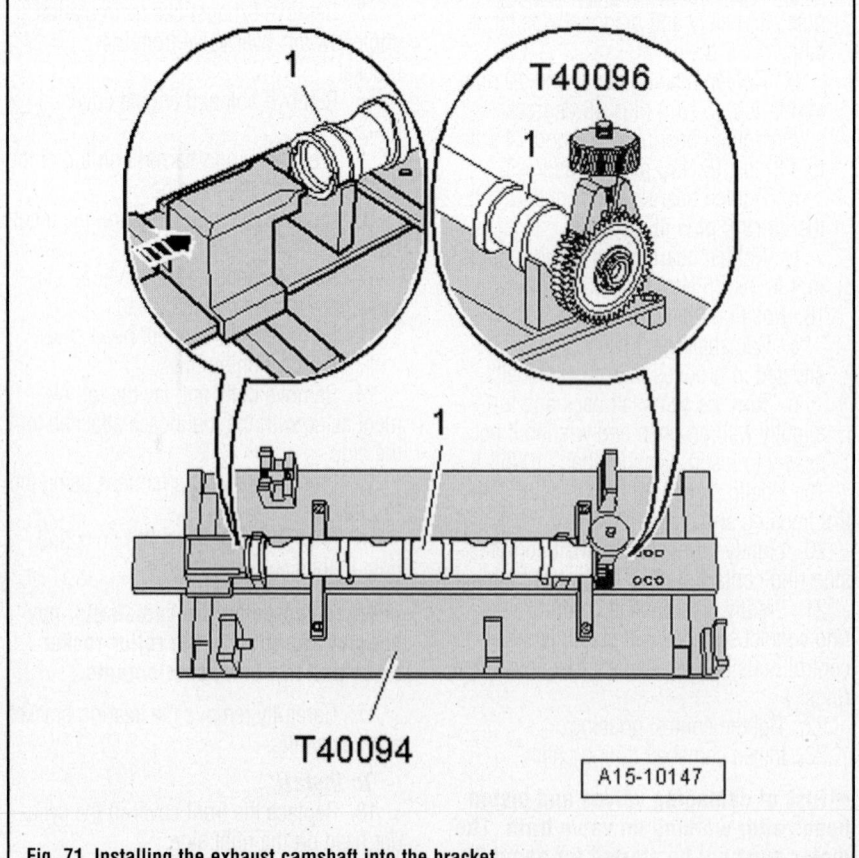

Fig. 71 Installing the exhaust camshaft into the bracket

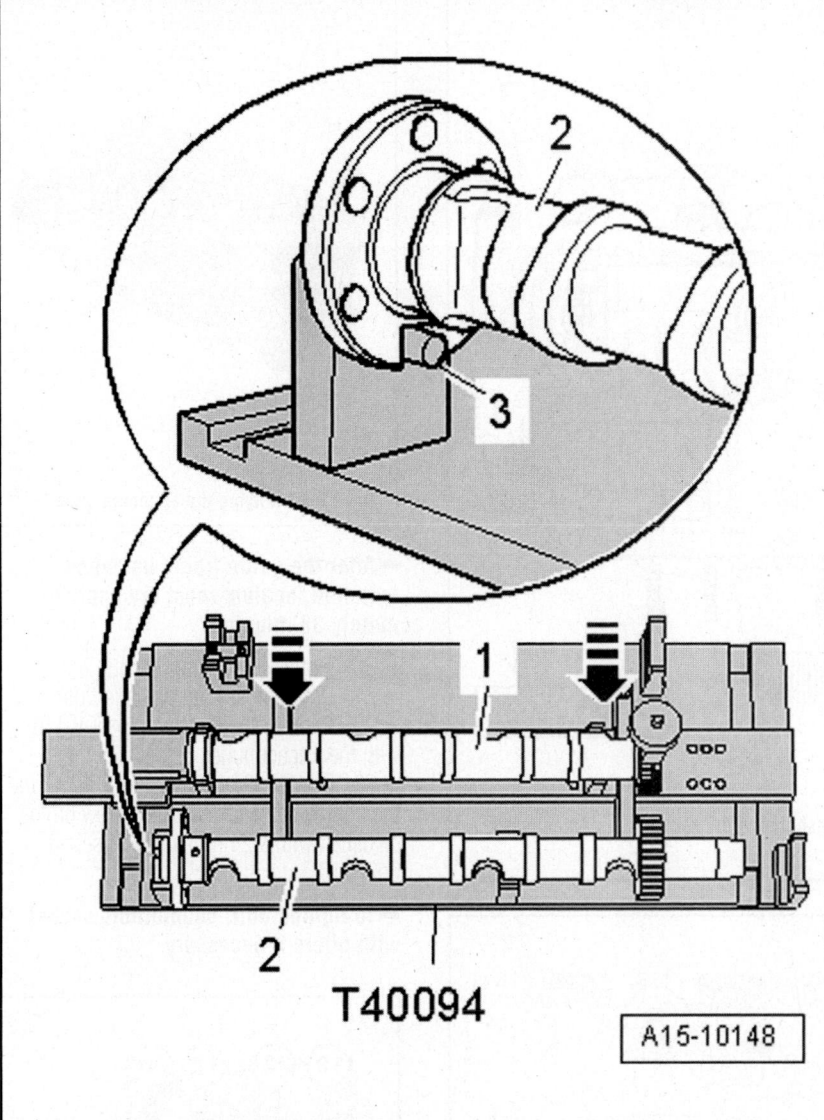

Fig. 72 Place the intake camshaft into the camshaft insertion tool T40094. The securing pin must engage in the groove on the intake camshaft.

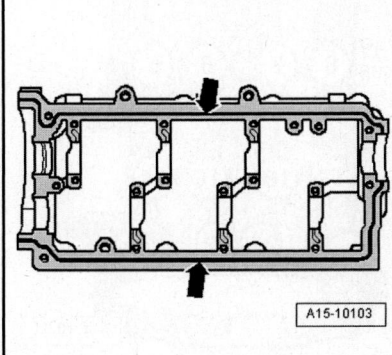

Fig. 73 Apply sealant beads to the clean sealing surfaces on the guide frame as shown in the illustration.

4.2L Engine

See Figures 75 through 78.

➡**Tools needed:**

- Multi-point socket T10035
- Impact puller T10133/3 from the tool set T10133
- Adapter T40058
- Guide frame securing pins T40116
- Hand drill with plastic brush attachment
- Protective eyewear
- Sealant

➡**The following procedure is depicted at the left cylinder head.**

1. Remove camshaft timing chains from camshafts.

2. Disconnect the electrical connector at intake camshaft position sensor.

3. Remove high-pressure pump.

➡**Risk of damaging valves and piston crowns. In the course of the following steps, the crankshaft must not stand with any piston at "TDC".**

4. Remove Crankshaft Holder 3242 from upper section of oil pan.

5. Insert Socket T40058 guide pins as follows:

a. Small diameter points to engine.

b. Large diameter points to socket.

6. Rotate the crankshaft with Socket T40058 opposite engine rotation direction 40° out of "TDC" position.

7. Remove Camshaft Clamp T40070 at cylinder head.

8. Loosen guide frame bolts in sequence 24 to 1.

a. Proceed in the same way with the right guide frame.

9. Carefully remove guide frame.

10. Mark camshafts and remove them.

➡**Because the special tool cannot be used during installation, the alignment pins on an engine with alignment pins must be driven out with a cotter pin driver.**

To install:

➡**Always replace the gaskets and seals.**

➡**Risk of contaminating lubricating system and bearing. Cover open parts of the engine.**

11. Remove sealant residue on cylinder head and guide frame, e.g. with rotating plastic brush.

12. Clean sealing surfaces, they must be free of oil and grease.

13. Oil journal surfaces of the camshafts.

14. Place camshafts in cylinder head, note position of camshafts so that guide frame can be installed without tension.

a. Groove on end of shaft must lie in proper position and direction.

15. On both sides, check the location of compression ring ends, insert the locating pins T40116 in the guide frame and cylinder head.

➡**Note the expiration date of the sealing compound.**

16. Lay a new seal in guide frame groove.

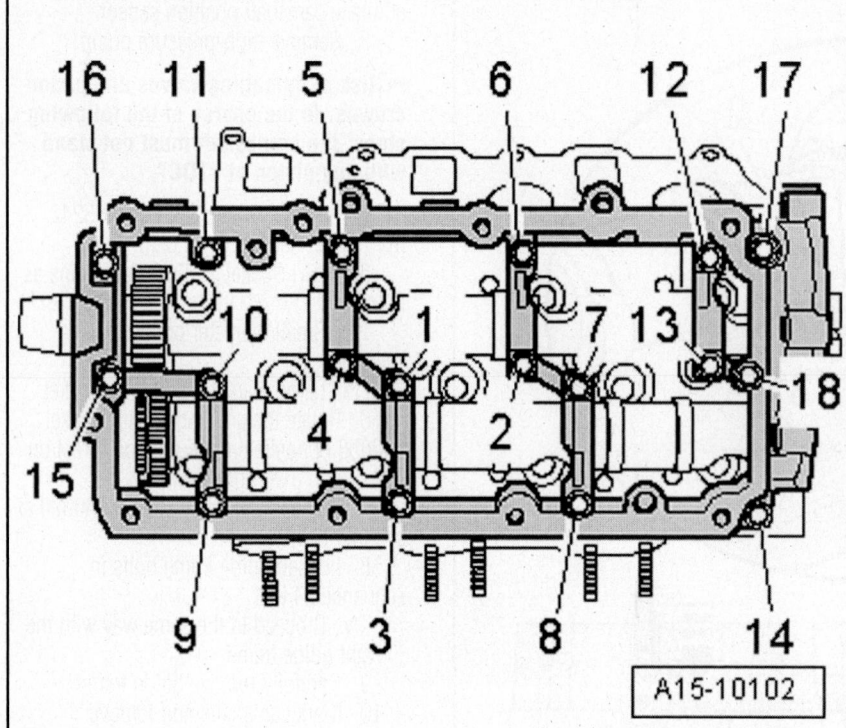

Fig. 74 Mount the guide frame together with both camshaft and the camshaft insertion tool T40095 to the cylinder head.

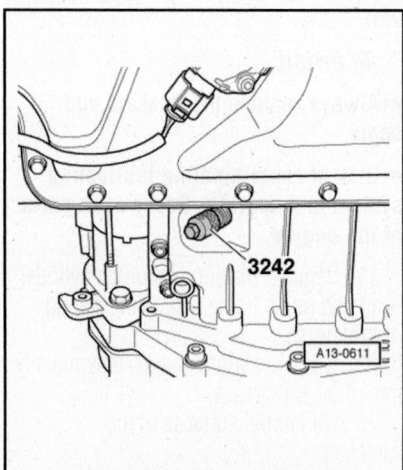

Fig. 75 Removing the crankshaft holder from the upper section of the oil pan

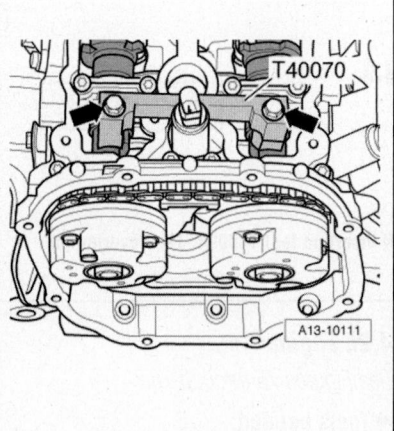

Fig. 76 Removing the camshaft clamp

✳✳ CAUTION

Risk of contaminating camshaft bearing with excess sealant. Do not apply sealant beads thicker than specified.

17. Apply sealant beads on clean guide frame sealing surfaces.
  a. Thickness of sealant beads: 2.5 mm.
18. Immediately place guide frame on cylinder head.

  a. Ensure camshafts can be inserted in guide frame axial bearing without force.
19. Insert the locating pins T40116 in the guide frame and cylinder head.

➡ **Because the sealant begins hardening immediately, guide frame must be promptly positioned and tightened.**

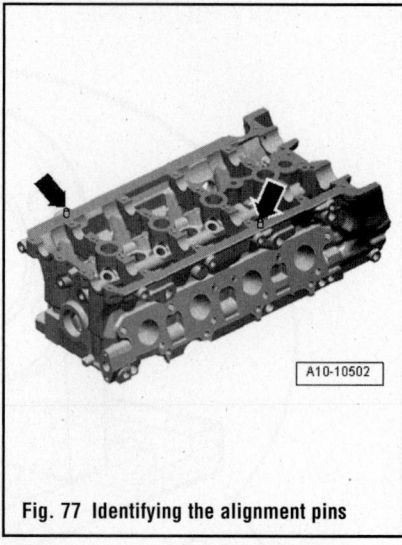

Fig. 77 Identifying the alignment pins

➡ **After the guide frame has been installed, sealant must dry approximately 30 minutes.**

20. Tighten guide frame bolts.
21. Drive the sealing plugs in flush.
22. Remove the locating pins T40116 with the impact puller T10133/3.
23. Rotate intake camshaft to "TDC" and the tighten camshaft adjuster screw on the camshaft with a 24 mm socket inserted between.

➡ **To tighten bolt, counterhold socket with pliers if necessary.**

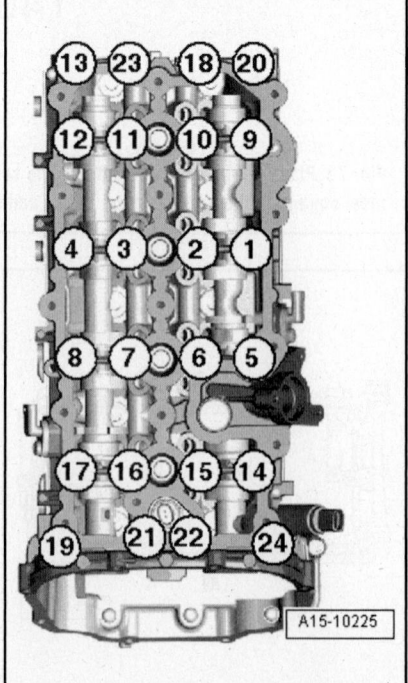

Fig. 78 Identifying the guide frame bolt tightening sequence

24. Position a lever or ratchet with Socket on bolt and rotate camshaft until threaded holes for Camshaft Clamp face up.

25. Next, loosely fasten Camshaft Clamp to intake camshaft.

The camshaft locating tool T40070 is correctly positioned when the holes for the cylinder head bolts remain free.

26. Adapt camshaft adjuster screw and socket to exhaust camshaft.

27. Rotate exhaust camshaft until threaded hole for Camshaft Clamp faces up.

28. At the same time, position a counter-hole SW 24 on Camshaft Clamp and swing Camshaft Clamp against exhaust camshaft to install.

29. Tighten Camshaft Clamp by hand onto exhaust camshaft to avoid damaging threads (2nd technician needed).

30. Tighten Camshaft Clamp bolts to 25 Nm.

31. Using Socket T40058, rotate crankshaft in direction of engine rotation to "TDC".

✳✳ CAUTION

Risk of injury when touching "TDC" hole with finger. Do not rotate crankshaft.

32. Install crankshaft holder 3242 into hole to 20 Nm, if necessary rotate crankshaft very slightly back and forth to completely center the holder.

33. The rest of installation is in reverse order of removal, note the following:

34. Position the camshaft timing chains on camshafts.

✳✳ CAUTION

Risk of damaging valves and piston heads after working on valve train. The motor must not be started for about 30 minutes after installing camshafts because the hydraulic equalization elements must seat themselves. To ensure valves do not strike pistons when starting, carefully rotate engine at least 2 full revolutions.

CATALYTIC CONVERTER

REMOVAL & INSTALLATION

Q5

2.0L Engine

See Figure 79.

1. Disconnect the connectors from the oxygen sensor after three way catalytic con-

verter and heater for oxygen sensor after catalytic converter and free up the wires.

2. Disconnect the connector from the heated oxygen sensor and oxygen sensor heater and free up the wire.

3. Remove the intake air duct.

4. Disconnect the connector from the mass airflow (MAF) sensor. Open the clamp and remove the air guide hose from the mass airflow (MAF) sensor. Remove the air filter housing upward.

5. Remove the undercar noise insulation.

6. Remove the front muffler.

7. Disconnect the threaded connection, remove the bolt and remove the catalytic converter mounting.

8. Remove the right drive axle heat shield.

9. Remove the catalytic converter upward.

To install:

10. Installation is performed in the reverse order of removal, noting the following:

    a. Replace seals and self-locking nuts.

    b. Install the front muffler.

3.2L Engine

See Figure 80.

Refer to the appropriate illustration to remove the catalytic converter.

Q7

3.6L Engine—Main

See Figures 81 and 82.

➡**Tools Needed:**

- Engine/transmission jack V.A.G 1383 A

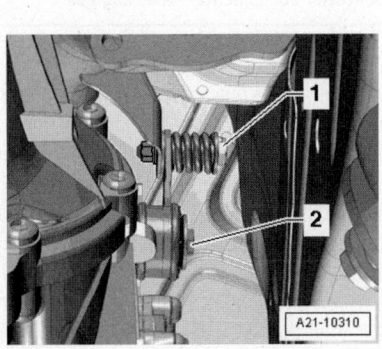

Fig. 79 Disconnect the threaded connection (1), remove the bolt (2) and remove the catalytic converter mounting.

- Gearbox support T10337

1. On a vehicle with air suspension, activate vehicle lift mode.

2. Remove bolt and remove rear noise insulation.

3. Remove the bolts on main catalytic converter brackets.

✳✳ CAUTION

Risk of accident. Engine/transmission jack V.A.G 1383 A may only be used during assembly and not stand unsupervised under vehicle.

4. Support transmission with Engine/transmission jack V.A.G 1383 A and connected gearbox support T10337.

5. Remove transmission carrier bolts.

6. Remove bolts and remove transmission carrier.

7. Loosen the clamping sleeves.

✳✳ CAUTION

Risk of damaging decoupling elements. Do not bend decoupling element in front exhaust pipe more than 10°.

8. Remove bolts and main catalytic converters from clamping sleeves.

To install:

Installation is in reverse order of removal, note the following:

➡**Replace the seals**

9. Align transmission carrier and tighten.

10. Install the exhaust system free of stress.

11. On a vehicle with air suspension, deactivate vehicle lift mode.

3.6L Engine—Primary

See Figures 83 and 84.

1. On a vehicle with air suspension, activate vehicle lift mode.

➡**During installation, all cable ties must be reinstalled at the same location.**

2. Disconnect vacuum hose.

3. Remove air guide pipe.

4. Disconnect the electrical connector on throttle valve control module.

5. Remove bolts and remove throttle valve control module.

Without Mechanical Vacuum Pump

6. Remove vacuum lines on intake manifold as follows:

- EVAP canister, press release buttons

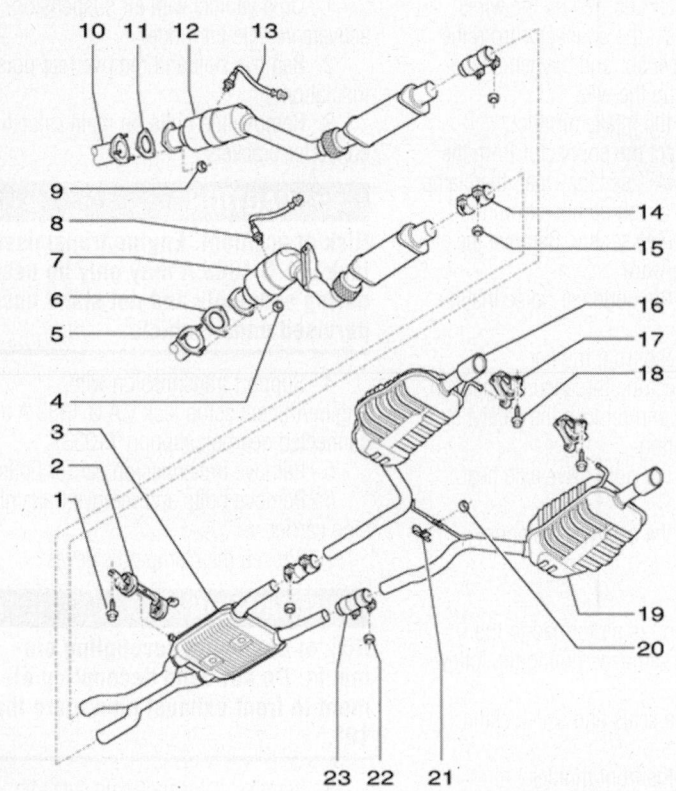

1. Screw
2. Suspended mount
3. Center muffler
4. Nut
5. Exhaust manifold
6. Gasket
7. Front exhaust pipe with
    catalytic converter and from muffler
8. O2S
9. Nut
10. Exhaust manifold
11. Gasket

12. Front exhaust pipe with
    catalytic converter and from muffler
13. O2S
14. Front clamping sleeves
15. Nut
16. Rear muffler
17. Suspended mount
18. Bolt
19. Rear muffler
20. Nut
21. Bracket
22. Nut
23. Rear clamping sleeves

Fig. 80 Exploded view of the exhaust and catalytic converter components—3.2L Engines

- Brake booster, remove suction jet pump arrow from bracket and press release buttons
- To Leak Detection Pump (LDP), press release buttons

With Mechanical Vacuum Pump:

7. Remove vacuum lines on intake manifold as follows:

- EVAP canister, press release buttons
- For brake booster

Continuation for all vehicles:

8. Remove bolts and remove bracket.

9. Remove bolts and remove heat shield.

10. Remove the oxygen sensors.

11. Remove nuts on connection between primary catalytic converters and exhaust manifold.

12. Remove the bolt and remove rear noise insulation.

13. Remove noise insulation bracket.

14. Remove bolts on primary catalytic converter bracket.

15. Remove front driveshaft heat shield.

16. Remove bolts on connection between driveshaft and final drive and lay driveshaft aside.

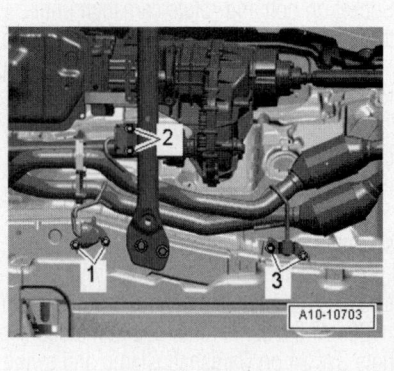

Fig. 81 Removing the bolts on the main catalytic converter brackets

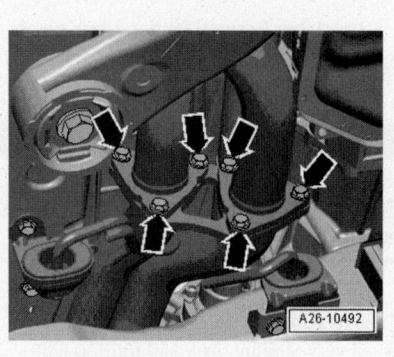

Fig. 82 Loosen the clamping sleeves (1 and 2). Remove bolts and main catalytic converters from clamping sleeves.

✳✳ CAUTION

Risk of damaging decoupling elements. Do not bend decoupling element in front exhaust pipe more than 10°.

17. Remove primary catalytic converters from main catalytic converters.

18. Remove primary catalytic converters downward.

To install:

Installation is in reverse order of removal, note the following:

a. Replace the seals and self-locking nuts.

b. Secure all hose connections using hose clamps appropriate for the model type.

➡During the installation, all cable ties must be reinstalled at the same location.

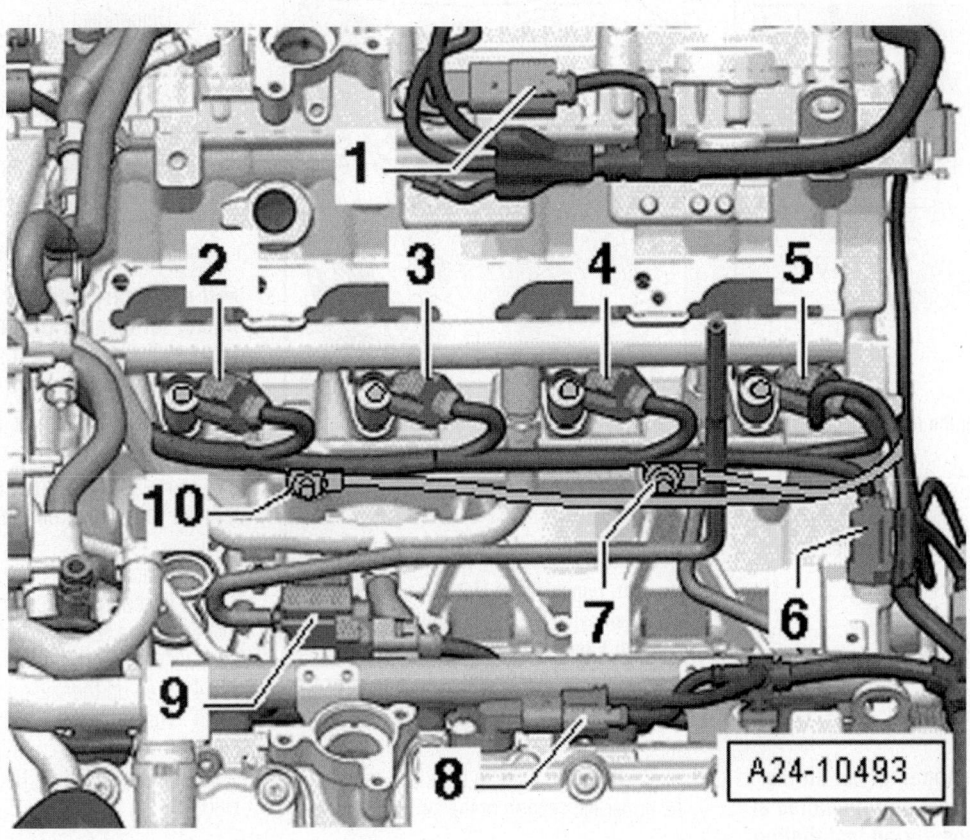

Fig. 83 Removing the nuts on the connection between the primary catalytic converters and the exhaust manifold

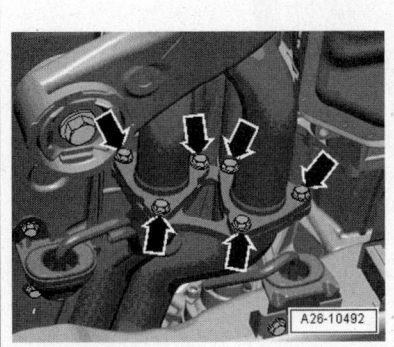

Fig. 84 Removing the primary catalytic converters from the main catalytic converters

19. Fasten driveshaft on front final drive.
20. Install driveshaft heat shield.
21. Install the oxygen sensors.
22. Install throttle valve control module.
23. Install the exhaust system free of stress.

24. On a vehicle with air suspension, deactivate vehicle lift mode.

4.2L Engine—Left Main

See Figures 85 and 86.

1. On a vehicle with air suspension, activate vehicle lift mode.
2. Remove screws and remove the rear noise insulation.

✳✳ CAUTION

Risk of damaging decoupling elements. Do not bend the flex joints in the front muffler more than 10°.

3. Separate the exhaust system at clamping sleeve.

➡️**Ignore 2 in the illustration.**

4. Remove left main catalytic converter bracket bolts.
5. Remove nuts and remove left main catalytic converter.

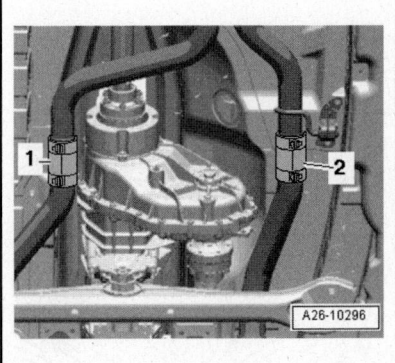

Fig. 85 Separating the exhaust system at the clamping sleeve

To install:

Installation is in reverse order of removal, note the following:

➡️**Replace the gaskets and self-locking nuts.**

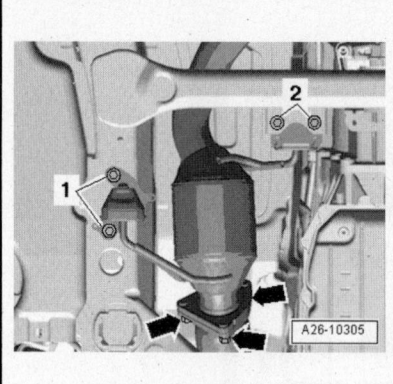

Fig. 86 Removing the left main catalytic converter

6. Align exhaust system free of tension.
7. On a vehicle with air suspension, deactivate vehicle lift mode.

4.2L Engine—Left Primary

See Figures 87 through 96.

1. On a vehicle with air suspension, activate vehicle lift mode.

➡**All cable ties opened or cut during engine removal must be reinstalled at the same locations during installation.**

2. Pull rear engine cover off.
3. Pull front engine cover off.
4. Disconnect the electrical connector at the Mass Air Flow (MAF) Sensor 2.

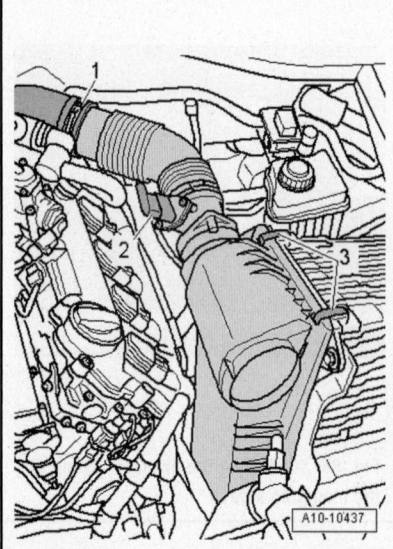

Fig. 87 Disconnecting the electrical connector, removing the air guide hose and removing the upper left section of the air filter housing

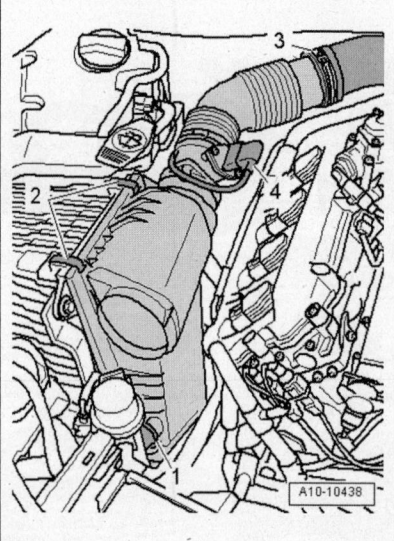

Fig. 88 Disconnecting the electrical connector, removing the right air guide hose and removing the upper right section of the air filter housing

5. Remove left air guide hose from air duct.
6. Release retaining clips and remove the upper left section of the air filter housing.

7. Disconnect hose from the Secondary Air Injection (AIR) pump.
8. Disconnect the electrical harness connector at Mass Air Flow (MAF) Sensor.
9. Remove right air guide hose from air duct.
10. Release retaining clips and remove the upper right section of the air filter housing from lower section.

Vehicles with air suspension:

➡**If necessary, remove electrical connector for Heated Oxygen Sensor (HO2S) 2 from bracket at right strut tower for better access.**

11. Press the circlip forward from hose coupling.
12. Press release ring down and remove vent hose from upper section of air filter.

All Vehicles

13. Disconnect vacuum hose to Evaporative Emission (EVAP) Canister Purge Regulator Valve by pressing release button.
14. Free up the vacuum hose.
15. Disconnect the electrical harness connector from Evaporative Emission (EVAP) Canister Purge Regulator Valve N80.

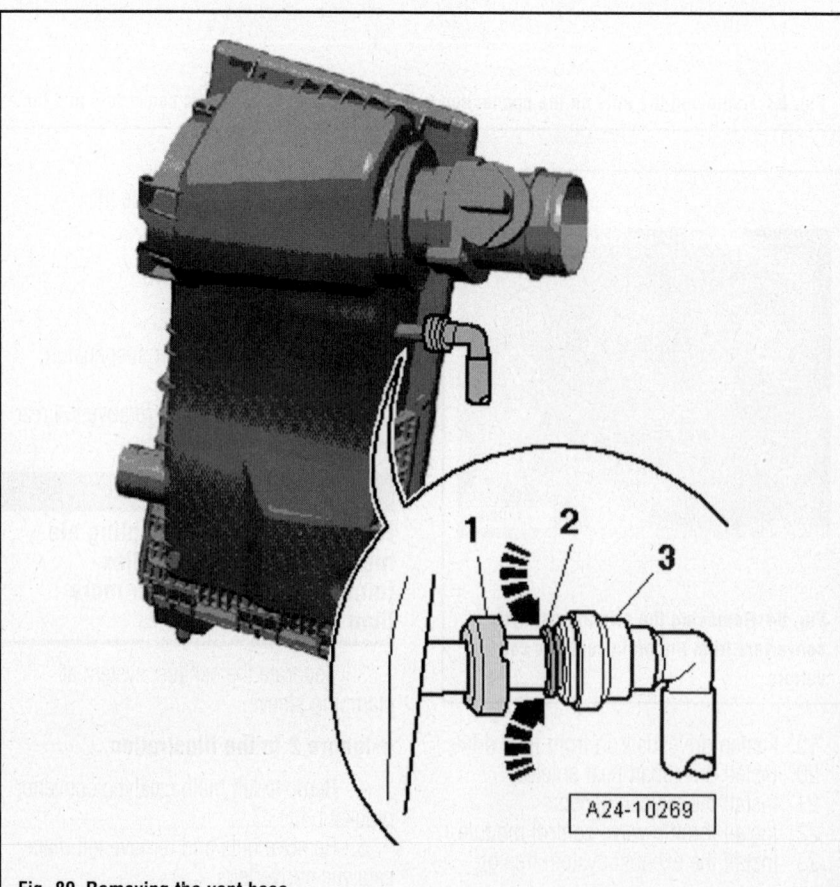

Fig. 89 Removing the vent hose

16. Remove Evaporative Emission (EVAP) Canister Purge Regulator Valve from bracket and lay aside.

17. Disconnect vacuum hose.

➡**Risk of violating emissions legislation. Do not open hose connection!**

18. Lay air guide hose aside with the vacuum hose connected.

19. Loosen hose clamp and remove bolts.

20. Remove air guide pipe to right.

21. Remove the electrical connectors for Oxygen Sensor (O2S) 2 Behind Three Way Catalytic Converter (TWC) and Heated Oxygen Sensor (HO2S) 2 from bracket on right strut tower.

22. Disconnect electrical connections and free up electrical wiring to Heated Oxygen Sensor (HO2S) 2 and Oxygen Sensor (O2S) Behind Three Way Catalytic Converter (TWC).

23. Remove bolts and remove the front and rear noise insulation.

24. Remove bracket for noise insulation.

➡**Risk of damaging decoupling elements. Do not bend the flex joints in the front muffler more than 10°.**

25. Separate the exhaust system at clamping sleeve.

26. Remove left main catalytic converter bracket bolts.

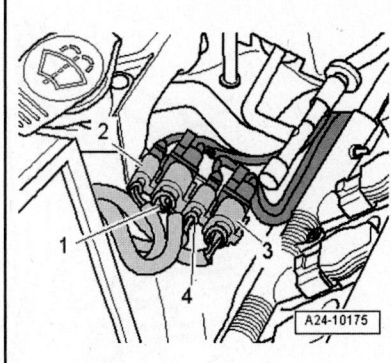

Fig. 91 Remove the electrical connectors for Oxygen Sensor (O2S) (2) Behind Three Way Catalytic Converter (TWC) and Heated Oxygen Sensor (HO2S) 2 from bracket on right strut tower. Disconnect electrical connections and free up electrical wiring to Heated Oxygen Sensor (HO2S) (2) and Oxygen Sensor (O2S) Behind Three Way Catalytic Converter (TWC).

27. Remove the bolts and the left primary catalytic converter strap.

28. Remove the nuts and the remove left primary catalytic converter.

To install:

Installation is in reverse order of removal, note the following:

➡**Replace the gaskets and self-locking nuts.**

➡**Secure all hose connections with hose clamps appropriate for the model.**

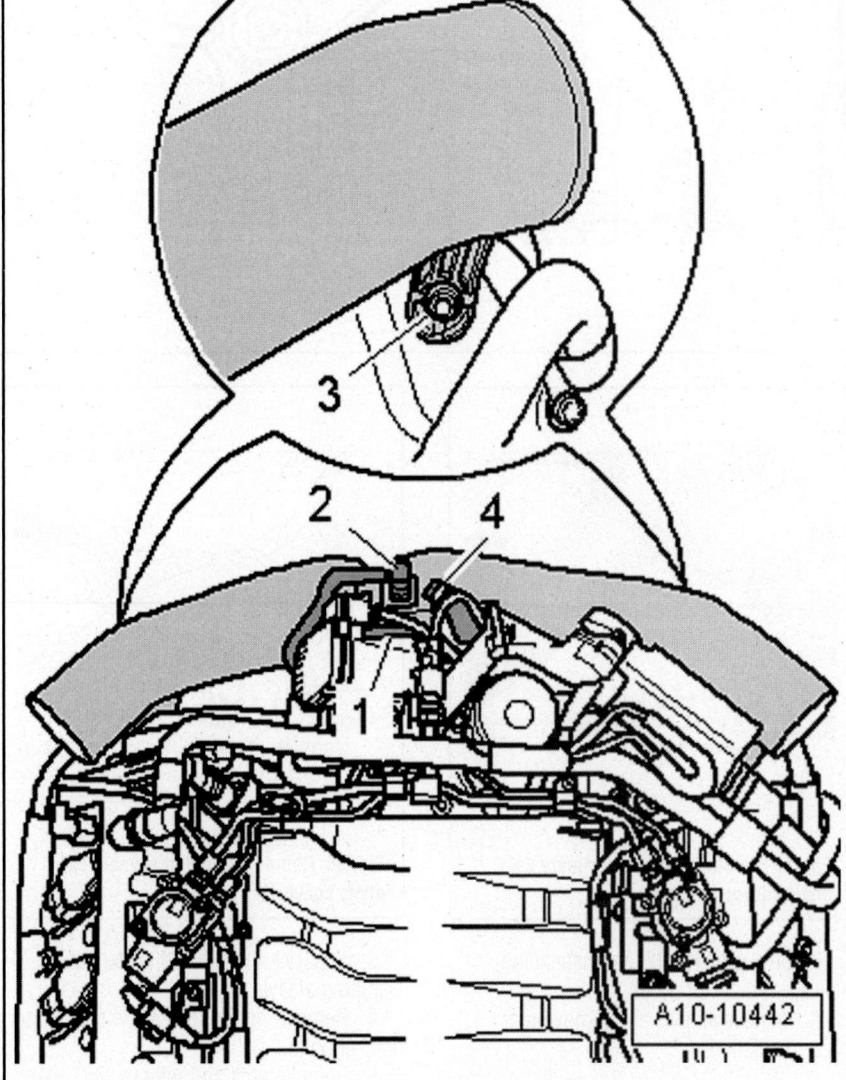

Fig. 90 Disconnecting the hose, moving the guide hose, loosening the hose clamp and removing the bolts

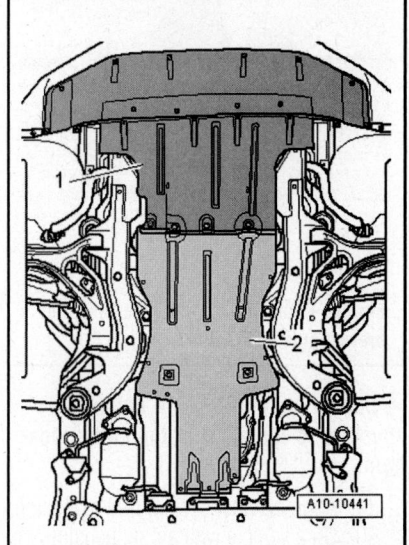

Fig. 92 Removing the noise insulation

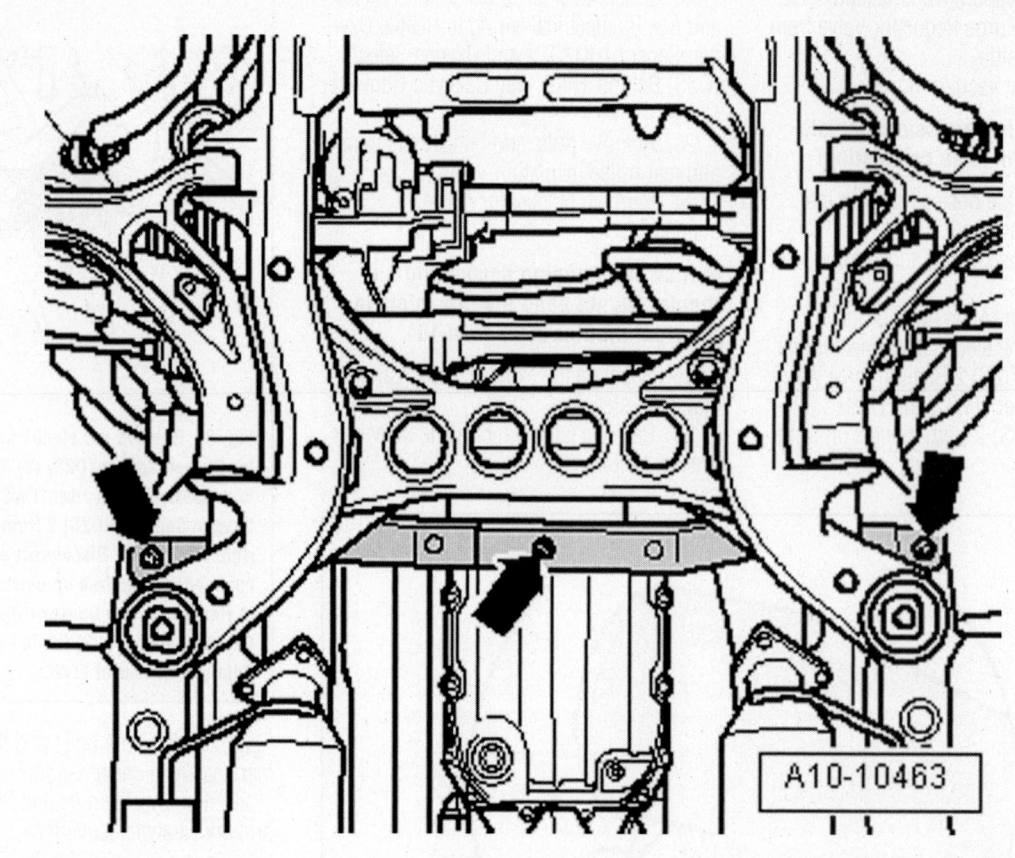

Fig. 93 Removing the noise insulation bracket

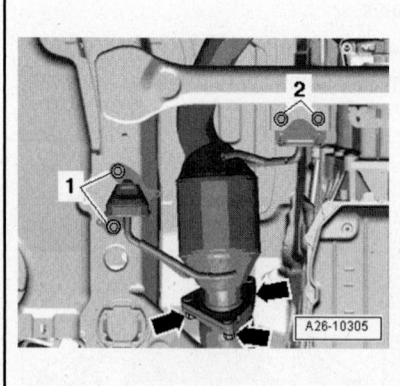

Fig. 94 Removing the catalytic converter bracket nuts and bolts

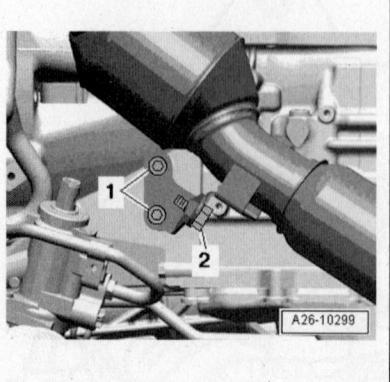

Fig. 95 Removing the left primary catalytic converter strap

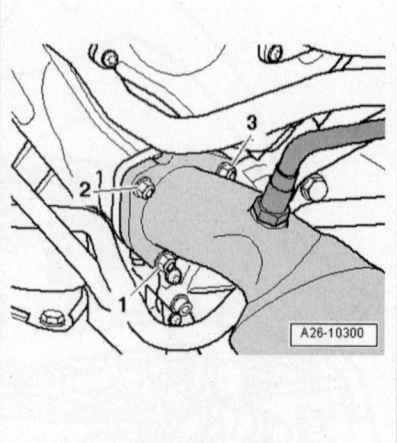

Fig. 96 Removing the left primary catalytic converter

➡**During installation, all cable ties must be re-installed at the same location.**

29. Align exhaust system free of tension.
30. On a vehicle with air suspension, deactivate vehicle lift mode.

4.2L Engine—Right Main

See Figure 97.

1. On a vehicle with air suspension, activate vehicle lift mode.
2. Remove screws and remove rear noise insulation.

➡**Risk of damaging decoupling elements. Do not bend the flex joints in the front muffler more than 10°.**

3. Separate the exhaust system at clamping sleeve.
4. Remove right main catalytic converter bracket bolts.
5. Remove nuts and remove right main catalytic converter.

To install:
Installation is in reverse order of removal, note the following:

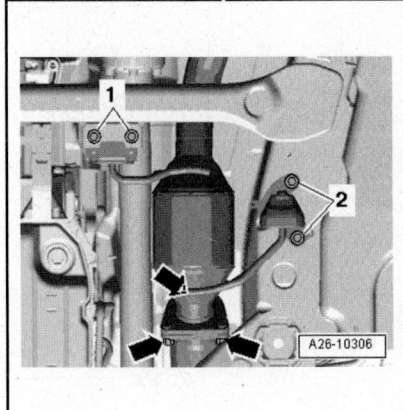

Fig. 97 Removing the right main catalytic converter

➡**Replace the gaskets and self-locking nuts.**

6. Align exhaust system free of tension.
7. On a vehicle with air suspension, deactivate vehicle lift mode.

4.2L Engine—Right Primary

See Figures 98 through 105.

1. On a vehicle with air suspension, activate vehicle lift mode.

➡**All cable ties opened or cut during engine removal must be reinstalled at the same locations during installation.**

2. Pull rear engine cover off.
3. Pull front engine cover off.
4. Disconnect the electrical connector at Mass Air Flow (MAF) Sensor.
5. Remove left air guide hose from air duct.
6. Release retaining clips and remove upper left section of air filter housing.
7. Disconnect hose to Secondary Air Injection (AIR) pump.
8. Disconnect the electrical harness connector at Mass Air Flow (MAF) Sensor.
9. Remove right air guide hose from air duct.
10. Release retaining clips and remove upper right section of air filter housing from lower section.
Vehicles with air suspension:

➡**If necessary, remove electrical connector for Heated Oxygen Sensor (HO2S) 2 from bracket at right strut tower for better access.**

11. Press the circlip forward from hose coupling.
12. Press release ring down and remove vent hose from upper section of air filter.
All Vehicles

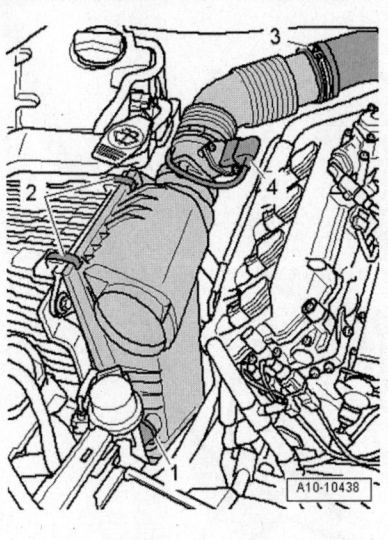

Fig. 98 Removing the upper right section of the air filter housing from the lower section

13. Disconnect vacuum hose to Evaporative Emission (EVAP) Canister Purge Regulator Valve by pressing release button.
14. Disconnect the electrical harness connector from Evaporative Emission (EVAP) Canister Purge Regulator Valve.
15. Remove Evaporative Emission (EVAP) Canister Purge Regulator Valve from bracket and lay aside.
16. Disconnect vacuum hose.

➡**Risk of violating emissions legislation. Do not open hose connection in the illustration.**

17. Lay the air guide hose aside with the vacuum hose connected.
18. Loosen hose clamp and remove screws.
19. Remove air guide pipe to right.
20. Remove electrical connectors for Heated Oxygen Sensor (HO2S) and for Oxygen Sensor (O2S) Behind Three Way

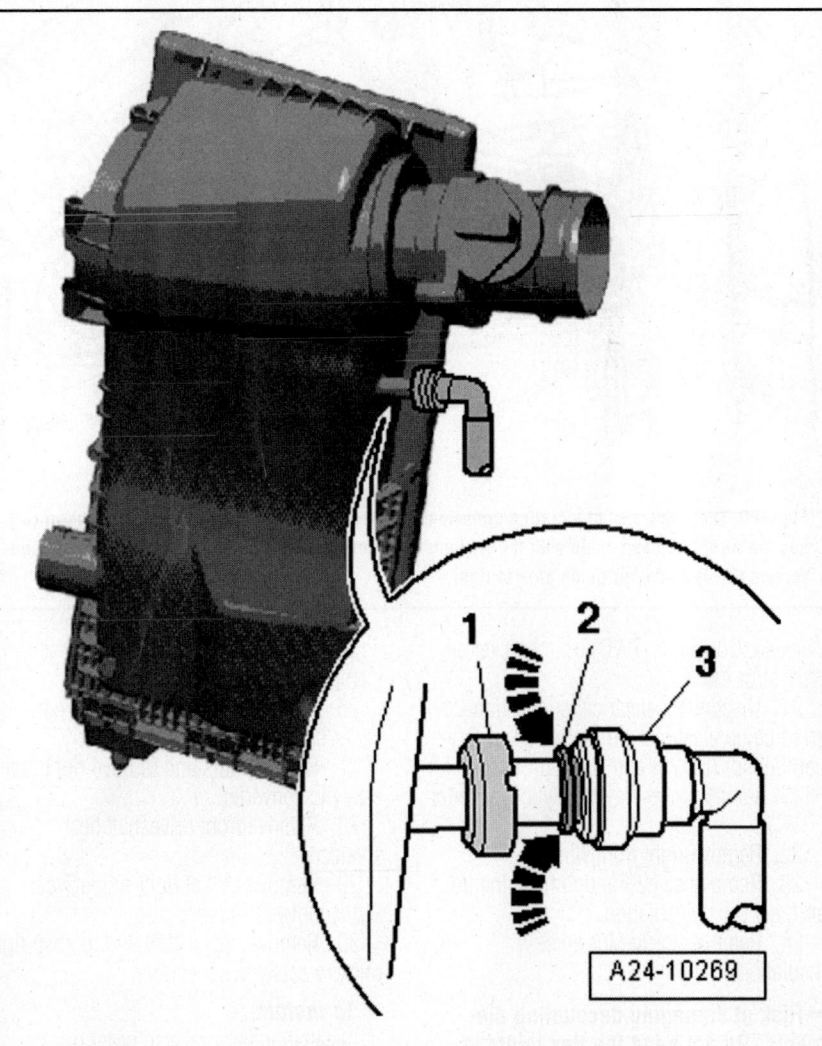

Fig. 99 Removing the vent hose from the upper section of the air filter

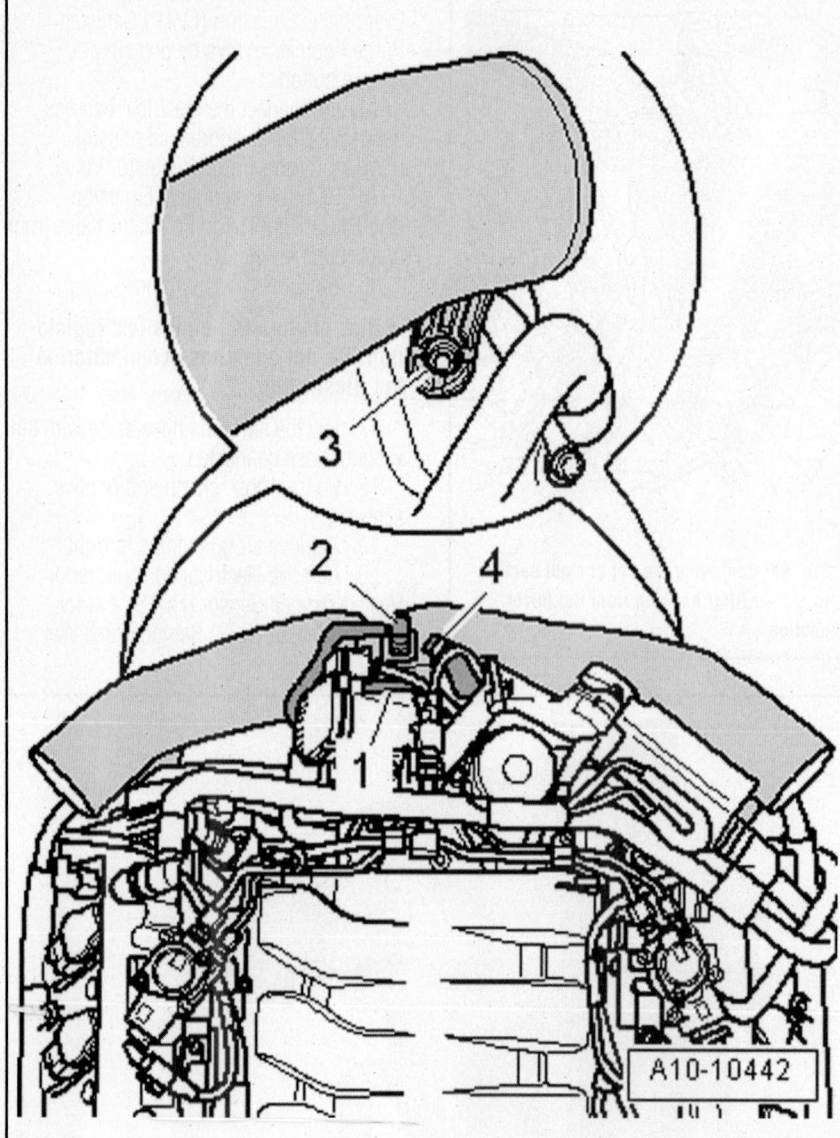

Fig. 100 There is a risk of violating emissions legislation, so do not open hose connection (2). Lay the air guide hose aside with the vacuum hose connected. Loosen hose clamp and remove screws (3). Remove air guide pipe to right.

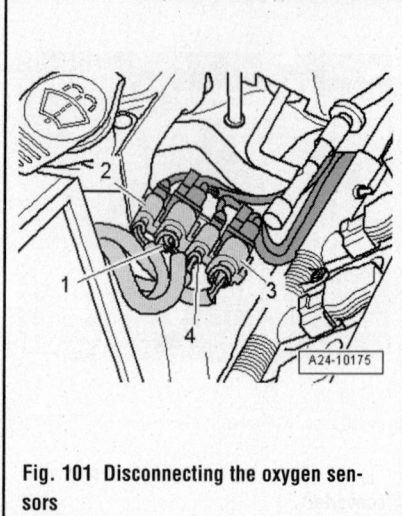

Fig. 101 Disconnecting the oxygen sensors

➡ Replace the gaskets and self-locking nuts.

➡ Secure all hose connections with hose clamps appropriate for the model.

➡ During the installation, all cable ties must be re-installed at the same location.

31. Align exhaust system free of tension.
32. On a vehicle with air suspension, deactivate vehicle lift mode.

3.0L Engine—Primary

See Figures 106 through 110.

1. On a vehicle with air suspension, activate vehicle lift mode.
2. Remove noise insulation.
3. Drain the coolant.
4. Remove bolts and noise insulation bracket.
5. Remove the particulate filter.
6. Remove heated oxygen sensor (HO2S).
7. Remove bolts, loosen the bolt and remove the turbocharger heat shield.
8. Remove nuts.
9. Remove the sensor (accessible from above).
10. Remove the exhaust gas temperature sensor 3 accessible from underneath.
11. Remove bolt.
12. Remove the left rear coolant pipe from the exhaust gas recirculation auxiliary cooler.
13. Remove heat shield from the steering gear.

Catalytic Converter (TWC) from bracket on right strut tower.

21. Disconnect electrical connections and free up electrical wiring to Heated Oxygen Sensor (HO2S) and Oxygen Sensor (O2S) Behind Three Way Catalytic Converter (TWC).
22. Remove right front wheel.
23. Remove screws and remove the front and rear noise insulation.
24. Remove bracket for noise insulation.

➡ Risk of damaging decoupling elements. Do not bend the flex joints in the front muffler more than 10°.

25. Separate the exhaust system at clamping sleeve.
26. Remove right main catalytic converter bracket bolts.
27. Remove nuts and remove right main catalytic converter.
28. Remove front driveshaft heat shield.
29. Remove bolt at right primary catalytic converter strap.
30. Remove nuts 1 to 3 and remove right primary catalytic converter.

To install:

Installation is in reverse order of removal, note the following:

❋❋ CAUTION

Risk of distorting airbag spiral spring. Separate universal joint from steering gear only when front wheels

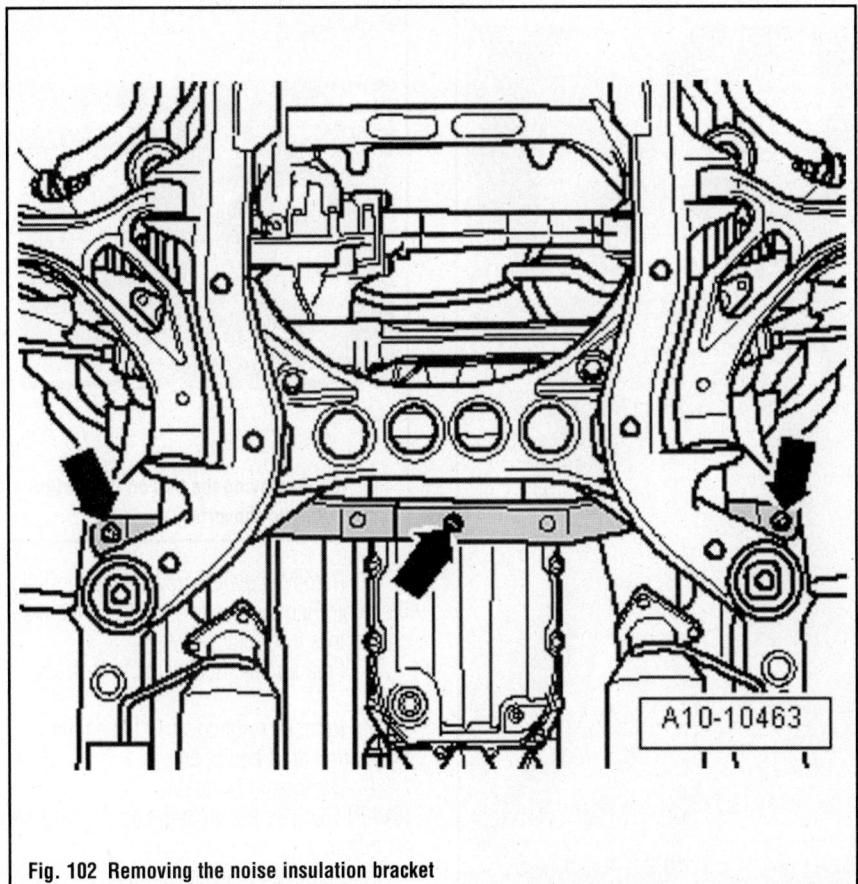

Fig. 102 Removing the noise insulation bracket

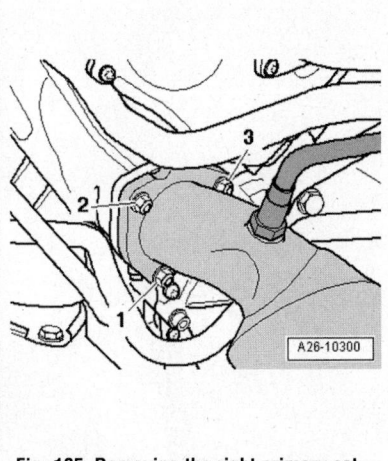

Fig. 105 Removing the right primary catalytic converter

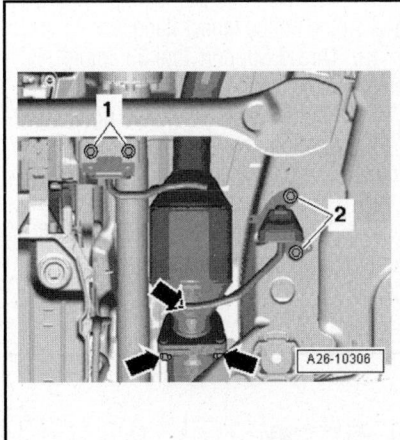

Fig. 103 Removing the right main catalytic converter

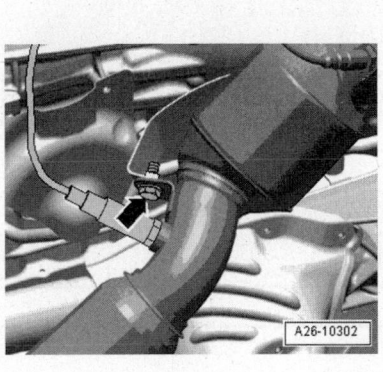

Fig. 104 Removing the bolt at the right primary catalytic converter strap

are in straight ahead position. **Secure steering wheel with adhesive tape to prevent position of steering wheel and steering gear from changing.**

14. Remove the universal joint bolt.
15. Remove universal joint from steering gear.
16. Remove bolt on the preliminary catalytic converter strap.

✳✳ CAUTION

The subframe could cause an accident if it is not secured. Do not loosen the subframe bolts 1, 3 and 4.

17. Remove only bolts to be able to lower the rear subframe.
18. Remove primary catalytic converter toward the rear.

To install:

Installation is in reverse order of removal, note the following:

➡**Replace the seals and self-locking nuts.**

➡**During installation, all cable ties must be re-installed at the same location.**

19. Install subframe.
20. Install universal joint on steering gear.
21. Install exhaust gas temperature sensor 3.
22. Install exhaust gas temperature sensor 2.
23. Install turbocharger heat shield.
24. Install the NOx sensor and the heated oxygen sensor (HO2S).
25. Install the particulate filter.
26. Install the exhaust system free of stress.
27. Fill with coolant.
28. Install noise insulation bracket and noise insulation.
29. On a vehicle with air suspension, deactivate vehicle lift mode.

CRANKSHAFT FRONT SEAL

REMOVAL & INSTALLATION

Q5

3.2L Engine

See Figures 111 through 112.

1. Remove both front wheels.
2. Loosen quick-release fasteners and remove front noise insulation.
3. Remove front bumper cover.
4. Remove air guide in front of the charge air cooler.

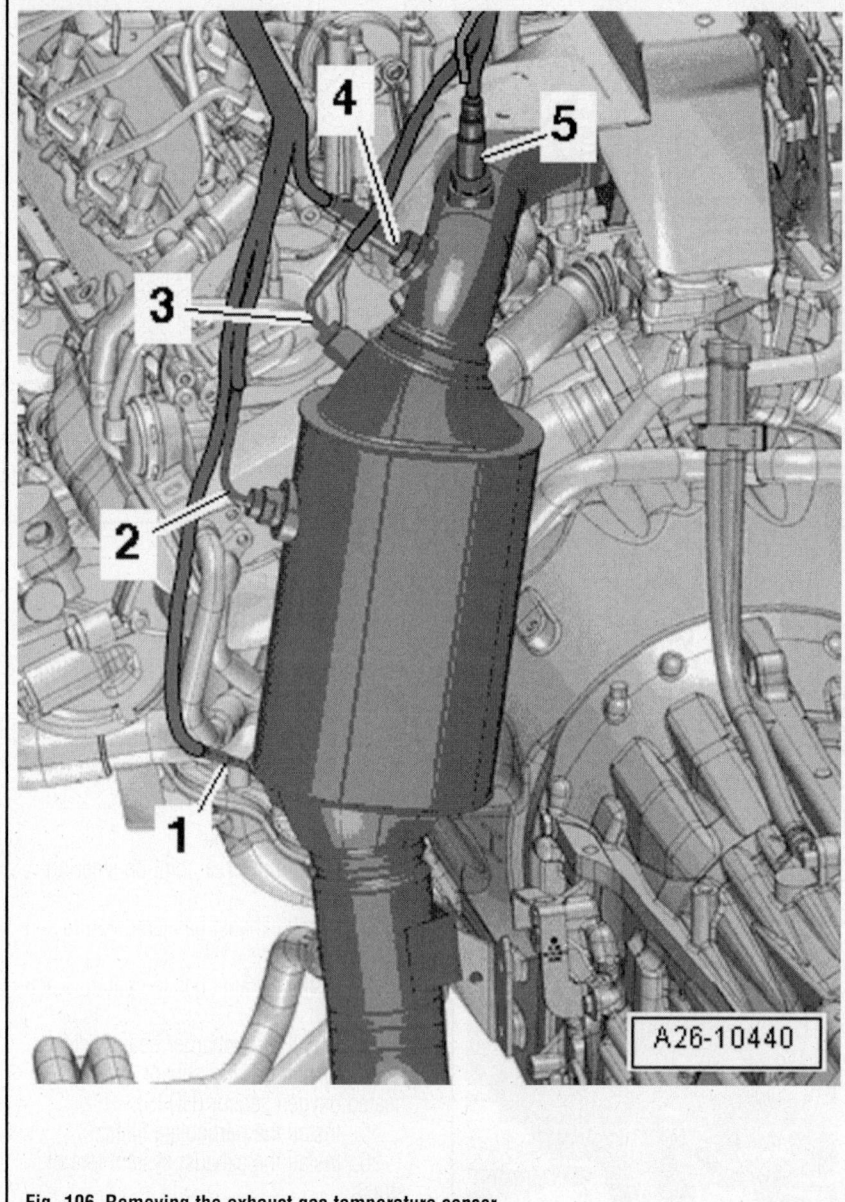

Fig. 106 Removing the exhaust gas temperature sensor

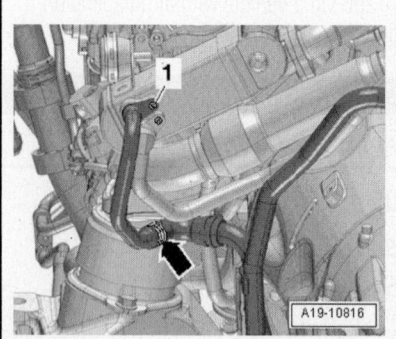

Fig. 107 Removing the left rear coolant pipe from the exhaust gas recirculation auxiliary cooler

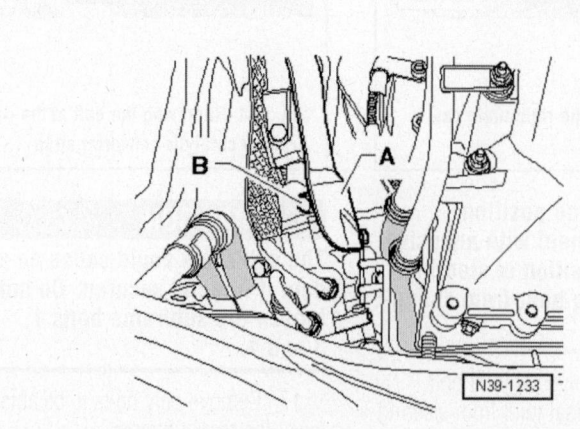

Fig. 108 Removing the heat shield and universal joint from the steering gear

Fig. 109 Removing the bolt on the preliminary catalytic converter

5. Remove cover at power steering fluid reservoir. Remove the two electrical harness connectors from bracket.

6. Free up electrical wires to lock carrier.

7. Remove right cover in the engine compartment, if equipped.

8. Disengage Evaporative Emission (EVAP) Canister Purge Regulator Valve from air guide.

9. Remove the intake air duct.

10. Remove bolts at left and right.

11. Remove hood seal on the lock carrier and on the bolted fender flanges.

12. Thread Support Tool 3369 into empty bores at left and right.

13. Remove bolts at left and right.

14. Carefully pull lock carrier toward front.

15. Remove toothed belt.

16. Remove center bolt for crankshaft toothed belt gear and remove toothed belt gear.

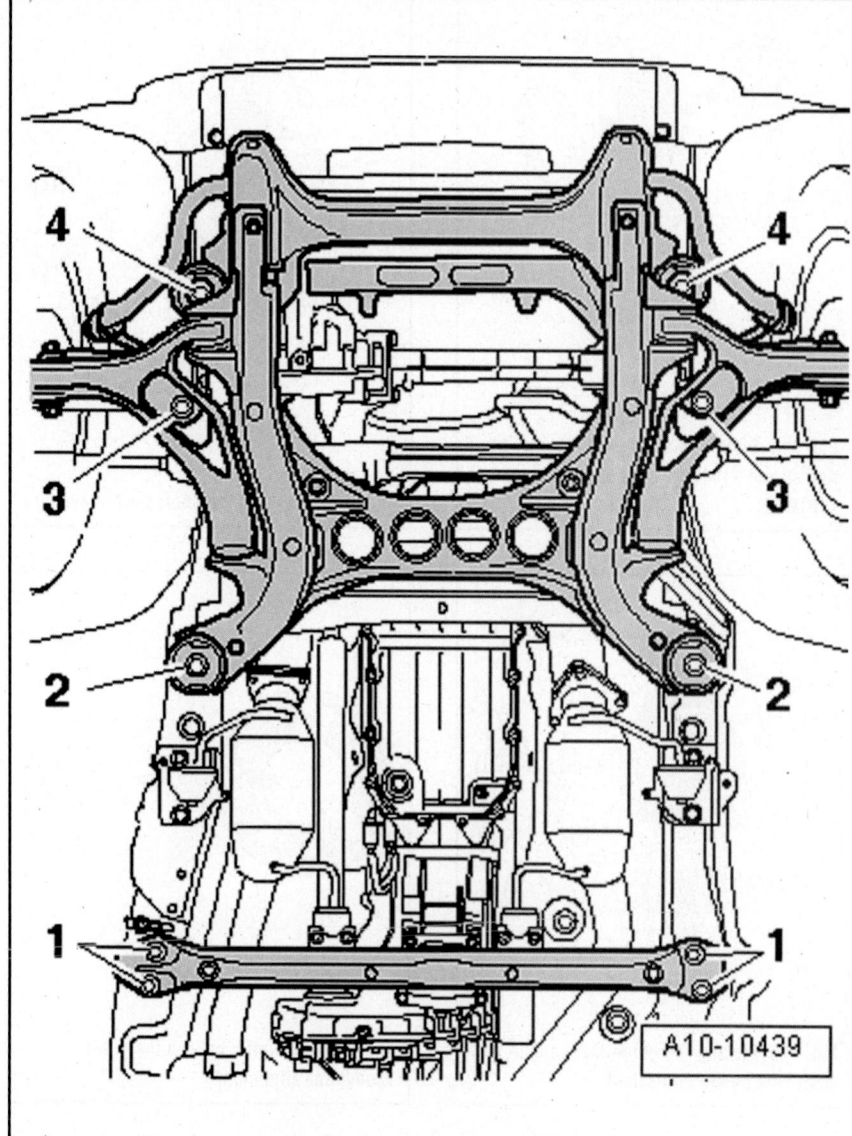

Fig. 110 The subframe could cause an accident if it is not secured. Do not loosen the subframe bolts 1, 3 and 4. Remove bolts (2) to be able to lower the rear subframe.

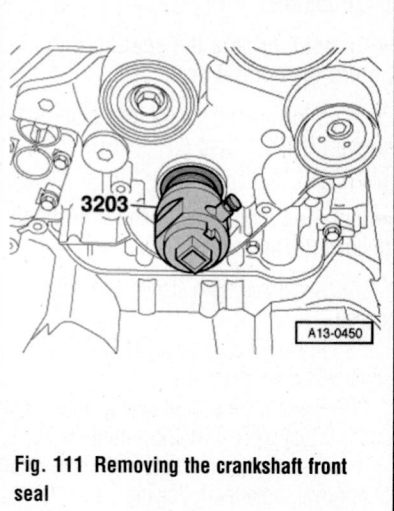

Fig. 111 Removing the crankshaft front seal

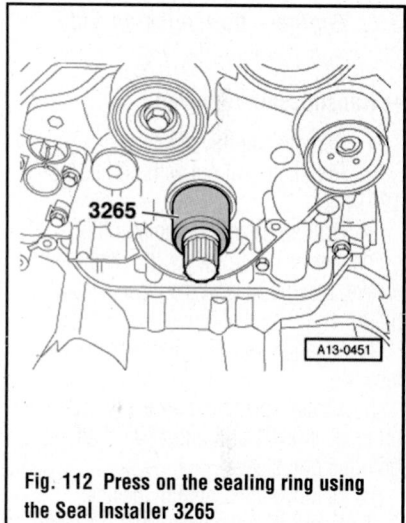

Fig. 112 Press on the sealing ring using the Seal Installer 3265

17. Remove diamond disc from toothed belt gear.

18. Remove inner portion of Seal Remover 3203 6 rotations from outer portion and secure with knurled-head bolt.

19. Lubricate the threaded head of the seal remover, place against seal, and with strong force screw into the seal as far as possible.

20. Loosen knurled screw and turn inner portion against crankshaft until the oil seal is pulled out.

21. Clamp seal extractor at mounting points in a vise.

22. Remove seal using pliers.

23. Clean the running and sealing surfaces.

➡**Do not oil the sealing lip and outer edge of seal before pressing in.**

To install:

24. Before installing, remove oil remains from end of crankshaft with a clean cloth.

25. Push seal on using fitting sleeve 3202/1.

26. Press on the sealing ring using the Seal Installer 3265 and toothed belt gear center screw to stop.

27. Install the crankshaft toothed belt gear with new diamond disc and new central bolt.

28. There must be no oil on the contact surfaces between toothed belt gear, diamond disc and crankshaft. Do not oil crankshaft toothed belt sprocket screw additionally.

29. Installation is in reverse order of removal, note the following:

30. Install lock carrier with attachments.

31. Place the torque support stop on the rubber buffer and tighten the nuts arrows.

32. Install front bumper cover.

33. Check the headlamp adjustment.

Q7

3.6L Engine

See Figures 113 through 116.

➡**Tools Needed:**

- Pulling fixture T10122
- Extractor hook T20143

➡**Transmission removed.**

1. On a vehicle with automatic transmission, remove drive plate.

2. Position the pulling hook T20143/2 behind sealing lip on shaft seal.

3. Support the pulling hook T20143/2 on sealing flange and pry out shaft seal.

4. Clean the running and sealing surface.

5. Remove oil residue on crankshaft pins.

To install:

➡**Do not lubricate the sealing ring before pressing it in.**

6. Slide new shaft seal over fitting sleeve T10122/1 onto guide sleeve T10122/2.

➡**Installed location: Closed side faces toward fitting sleeve.**

7. Separate fitting sleeve and guide sleeve.

8. Place guide sleeve T10122/2 with shaft seal on crankshaft.

9. Press shaft seal in evenly all around using thrust piece T10122/3 until flush.

The rest of installation is in reverse order of removal, note the following:

10. Install the drive plate.

3.0L Engine—Transmission Side

See Figures 117 through 120.

➡**Transmission removed.**

1. Remove the drive plate.

2. Pry shaft seal out with pulling hook T20143/2.

3. Drill an 8 mm dia. hole in the guide sleeve T10122/2 for the alignment sleeve; use the hole in the washer as a template.

4. Clean the running and sealing surface.

5. Place assembly device T10122/1 on pull sleeve T10122/2 and slide shaft seal onto the pull sleeve.

6. Remove the assembly device.

7. Position pull sleeve T10122/2 with shaft seal on the crankshaft.

8. Press shaft seal in, evenly and flush, using T10122/3 pressure sleeve.

9. Install the drive plate.

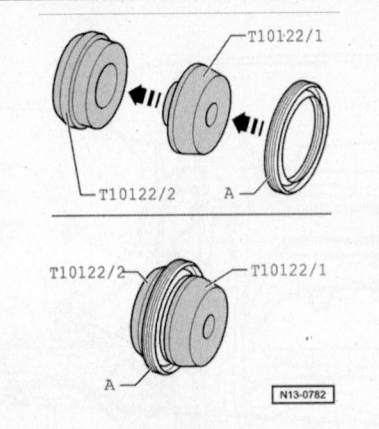

Fig. 114 Slide new shaft seal (A) over fitting sleeve T10122/1 onto guide sleeve T10122/2.

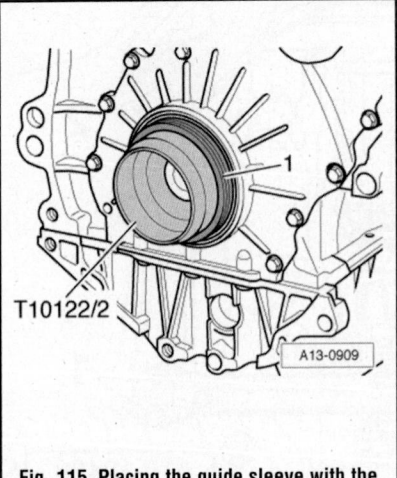

Fig. 115 Placing the guide sleeve with the shaft seal on the crankshaft

4.2L Engine—Transmission Side

See Figures 121 through 124.

➡**Tools Needed:**

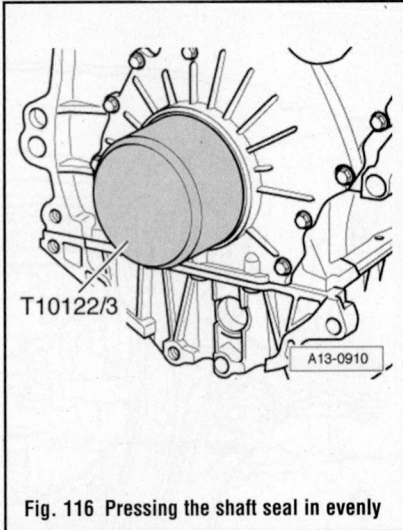

Fig. 116 Pressing the shaft seal in evenly

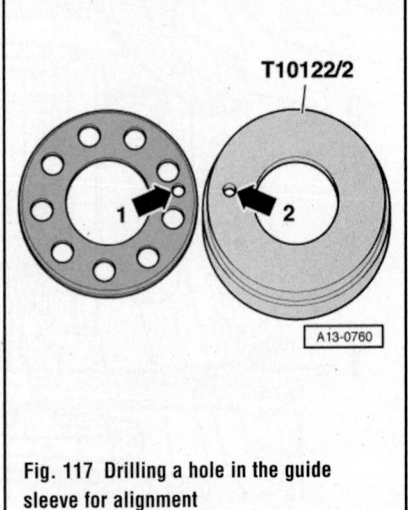

Fig. 117 Drilling a hole in the guide sleeve for alignment

• Pulling fixture T10122
• Extractor hook T20143

➡**Engine-transmission assembly should be removed and separated on the scissor lift table VAS 6131 A.**

1. Remove driveplate.

2. Pry shaft seal out with pulling hook T20143/2.

3. Clean operating and sealing surfaces.

4. Position assembly tool T10122/1 on the pulling sleeve T10122/2 and slide shaft seal onto the pulling sleeve.

5. Remove the assembly device.

6. Position pull sleeve T10122/2 with shaft seal on the crankshaft.

7. Press shaft seal in, evenly and flush, using pressure sleeve T10122/3.

The rest of installation is in reverse order of removal, note the following:

8. Install the driveplate.

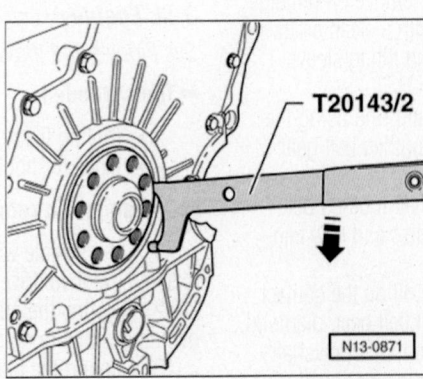

Fig. 113 Position the pulling hook T20143/2 behind sealing lip on shaft seal as shown in the illustration.

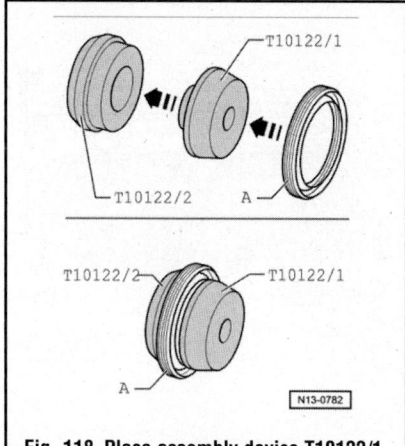

Fig. 118 Place assembly device T10122/1 on pull sleeve T10122/2 and slide shaft seal (A) onto the pull sleeve.

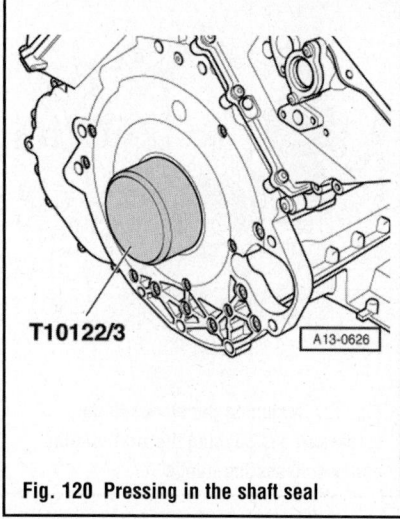

Fig. 120 Pressing in the shaft seal

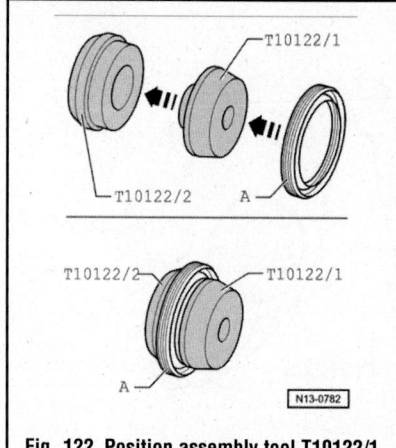

Fig. 122 Position assembly tool T10122/1 on the pulling sleeve T10122/2 and slide shaft seal (A) onto the pulling sleeve.

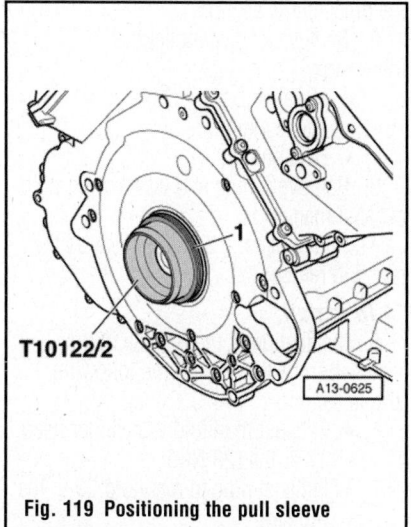

Fig. 119 Positioning the pull sleeve

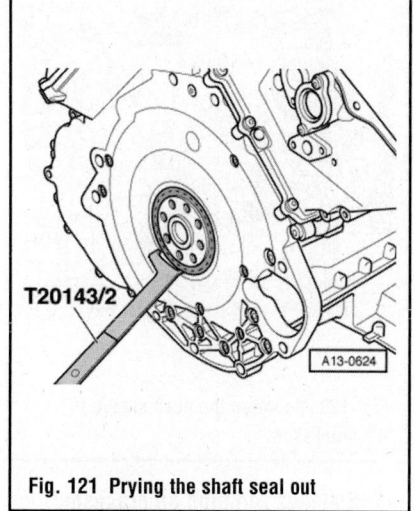
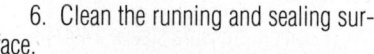

Fig. 121 Prying the shaft seal out

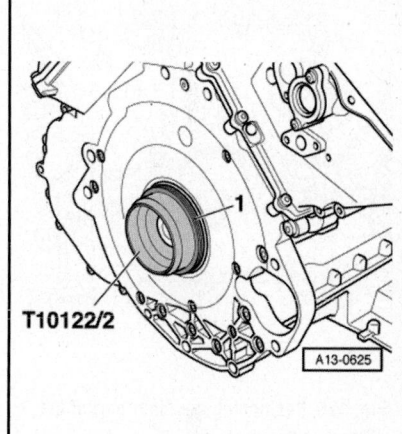

Fig. 123 Positioning the pull sleeve with the shaft seal on the crankshaft

3.0L Engine—Belt Pullley Side

See Figures 125 through 127.

➡**Tools Needed:**

- Seal remover T40019
- Assembly device T40048 with T40048/4
- M8 x 55 mm bolt, quantity: 2

1. Remove the vibration damper with the ribbed belt pulley.

2. Position the inner part of the oil seal extractor T40019 flush with inner part and secure it with the knurled screw.

3. Lubricate the seal remover threaded head, position it, and screw it into the shaft seal as far as possible using strong force.

4. Loosen knurled screw and turn the inner portion against the crankshaft until the seal is pulled out.

5. Secure the seal remover in a vise at the flat spots and remove the seal using pliers.

6. Clean the running and sealing surface.

7. Place assembly device T40048/1 on the pull sleeve T40048/2 and slide shaft seal onto the pull sleeve.

8. Remove the assembly device.

9. Mount sleeve T40048/2 to the crankshaft and push the seal into the pulley side sealing flange.

➡**Leave pull sleeve T40048/2 for pressing onto the crankshaft.**

10. Mount push sleeve T40048/4 (depth 5 mm) to the crankshaft with M8 x 55 mm bolts arrows.

11. Install bolts by hand.

12. Tighten bolts 1/2 turn each, alternating sides, to press the shaft seal in as far as the stop.

The rest of installation is in reverse order of removal, note the following:

13. Install vibration damper with ribbed belt pulley.

4.2L Engine—Belt Pulley Side

➡**Tools Needed:**

- Seal remover T40019
- Assembly tool T40048

1. Remove the vibration damper.

2. Position the inner section of the oil seal extractor T40019 so it is flush with outer section and secure it with the knurled screw.

3. Lubricate seal remover threaded head, position it, and screw it into the shaft seal as far as possible using strong force.

4. Loosen the knurled screw and turn the inner portion against the crankshaft until the seal is pulled out.

5. Secure the seal remover in a vise at the flat spots and remove the seal using pliers.

6. Clean operating and sealing surfaces.

7. Place assembly device T40048/1 on

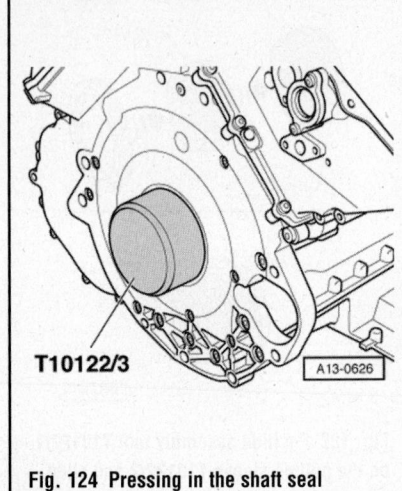

Fig. 124 Pressing in the shaft seal

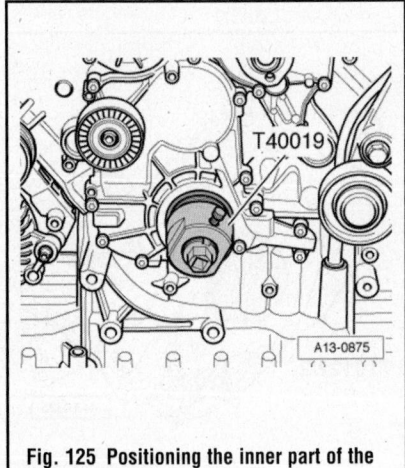

Fig. 125 Positioning the inner part of the oil seal extractor

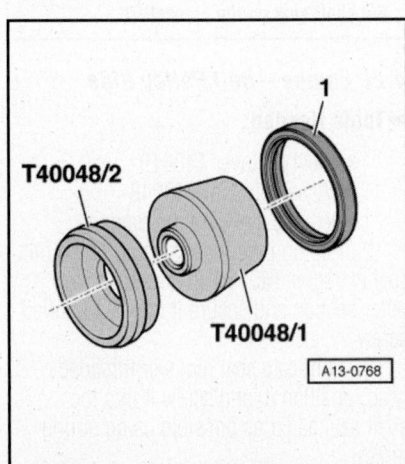

Fig. 126 Placing the pull sleeve and slide shaft seal (1) onto the pull sleeve

the pull sleeve T40048/2 and slide the shaft seal onto the pull sleeve.

8. Remove the assembly device.
9. Place pull sleeve T40048/2 on the crankshaft and slide the shaft seal into the sealing surface on the engine.

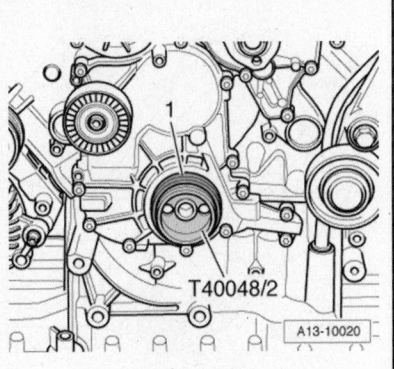

Fig. 127 Mounting the sleeve to the crankshaft and pushing the seal into the pulley side sealing flange

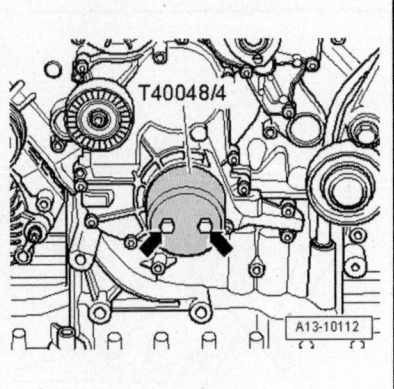

Fig. 128 Mounting the push sleeve to the crankshaft

➡ **Pull sleeve remains on crankshaft for pressing in.**

10. Position pressure sleeve T40048/3 with 2 M8-55 mm bolts on crankshaft.
11. Screw in the bolts by hand.
12. Tighten bolts 1/2 turn each, alternating sides, to press the shaft seal in as far as the stop.
13. The rest of installation is in reverse order of removal.
14. Install the vibration damper.

EXHAUST MANIFOLD

REMOVAL & INSTALLATION

Q5

2.0L Engine

➡ **The exhaust manifold and turbocharger are one component; removing and installing.**

3.2L Engine

See Figure 129.

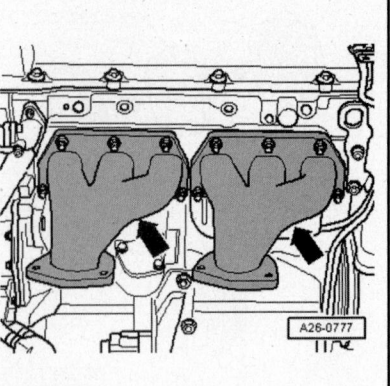

Fig. 129 Remove 7 nuts and washers on both exhaust manifolds

1. Before servicing the vehicle, refer to the precautions section.
2. Remove or disconnect the following:
   • Negative battery cable
   • Intake manifold
   • Heat shield
3. Remove 7 nuts and washers on both exhaust manifolds.
4. Pull exhaust manifolds towards the rear and remove.

To install:

5. Installation is the reverse of the removal procedure, using the following torque values:
   • Exhaust manifold to cylinder head 17 ft. lbs (23 Nm)
   • Exhaust pipe to manifold 29 ft. lbs (40 Nm)

Q7

3.6L Engine

See Figures 130 through 134.

➡ **During installation, all cable ties must be reinstalled at the same location.**

1. Disconnect vacuum hose.
2. Remove air guide pipe.
3. Disconnect electrical connector on throttle valve control module.
4. Remove bolts and remove throttle valve control module.

Without Mechanical Vacuum Pump:

5. Remove vacuum lines on intake manifold as follows:
   a. 1 - For EVAP canister, press release buttons
   b. 3 - For brake booster, remove suction jet pump arrow from bracket and press release buttons
   c. 4 - To Leak Detection Pump (LDP), press release buttons

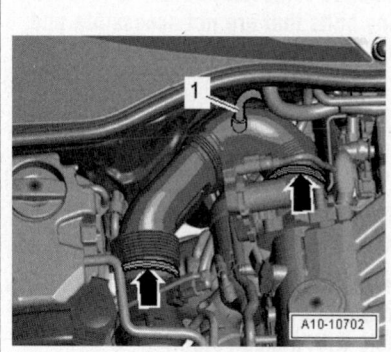

Fig. 130 Disconnecting the vacuum hose and removing the air guide pipe

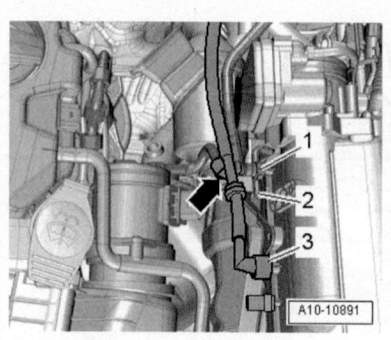

Fig. 132 Removing the vacuum lines on the intake manifold

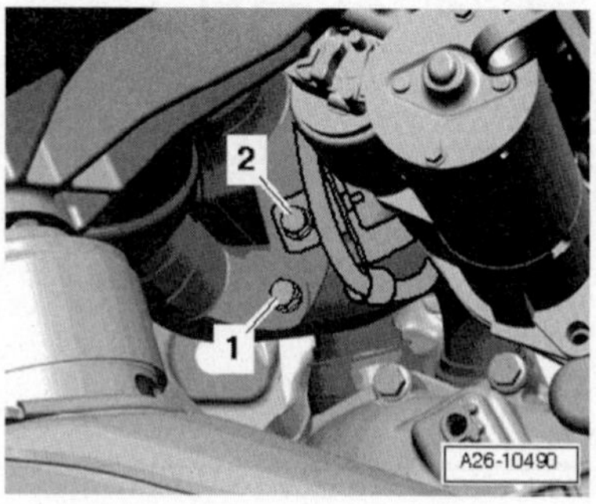

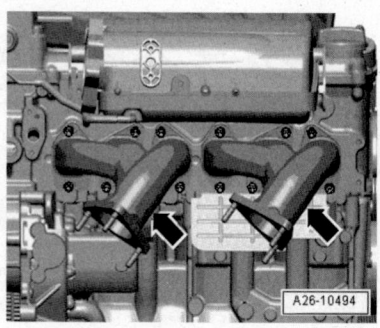

Fig. 134 Removing the exhaust manifolds

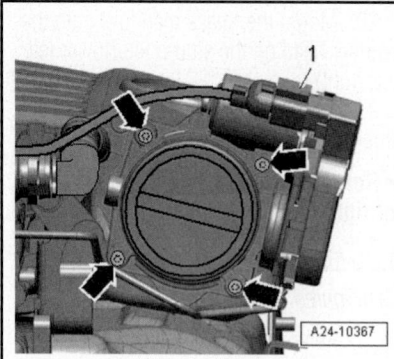

Fig. 131 Disconnecting the electrical connector and removing the throttle valve control module

Fig. 133 Removing the heat shield

With Mechanical Vacuum Pump:
6. Remove vacuum lines on intake manifold as follows:
   a. 1 - For EVAP canister, press release buttons
   b. 3 - For brake booster arrow
   c. Ignore 2.
Continuation for All:
7. Remove bolts and remove bracket.
8. Remove bolts and heat shield.
9. Remove bolts on primary converter brackets.
10. Remove nuts and remove primary catalytic converters from exhaust manifolds.
11. Remove 6 nuts each on both exhaust manifolds and pull manifold toward right.

To install:
Installation is in reverse order of removal, note the following:
   a. Replace seals and self-locking nuts.
12. Install primary catalytic converters.
13. Install throttle valve control module.

3.0L Engine—Left
➡**Tools Needed:**

- Hose clamps up to 25 mm diameter 3094
- Engine bung set VAS 6122
1. Remove left intermediate pipe.
   a. To collect escaping power steering fluid, lay a cloth under the separating point.
2. Clamp off power steering fluid hose with hose clamps.
3. Loosen hose clamp and remove power steering fluid hose.
4. Remove banjo bolt and lay the power steering fluid line to the side.
5. Seal off the open lines and connections with clean plugs taken from the engine bung set VAS 6122.
6. Remove nuts and the exhaust manifold.

To install:
Installation is in reverse order of removal, note the following:
   a. Replace seals, O-rings and the self-locking nuts.

b. Secure all hose connections with hose clamps appropriate for the model.
7. Install power steering fluid line.
8. Install left intermediate pipe.

4.2L Engine—Left
See Figure 135.

1. Drain coolant.
2. Remove left primary catalytic converter.
3. Remove left coolant pipe.
4. Remove nuts 6 to 1 and remove left exhaust manifold.
   a. Both securing strips can remain installed when removing exhaust manifold.

To install:
Installation is in reverse order of removal, note the following:
   a. Replace gasket and self-locking nuts.
5. Place new gasket onto stud bolts.
6. Insert exhaust manifold in securing strips and tighten.
7. Install left coolant pipe.
8. Install left primary catalytic converter.
9. Align exhaust system free of tension.
10. Fill with coolant.

INTAKE MANIFOLD

REMOVAL & INSTALLATION

Q5

2.0L Engine
See Figure 136.

➡**If the fuel rail is removed or replaced, the intake manifold runner position sensor must be adapted to the engine control module. To do this, use vehicle diagnosis, testing and information system VAS 5051B guided functions.**

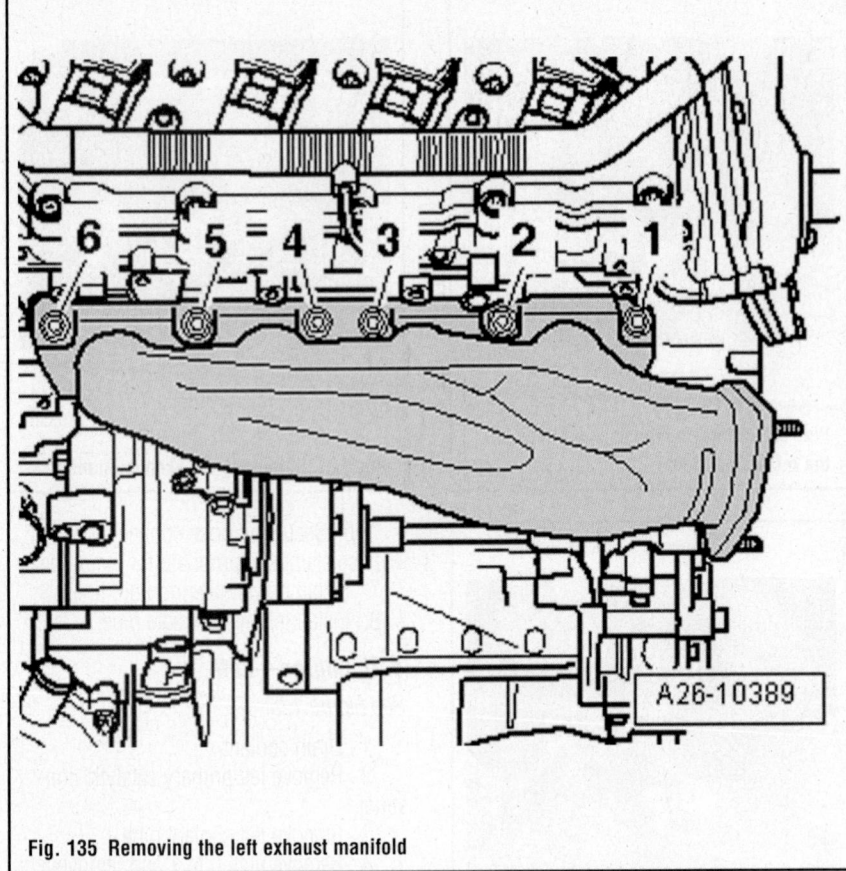

Fig. 135 Removing the left exhaust manifold

➡**Special tools:**

- Assembly Tool T10118
- Hose Clip Pliers V.A.G 1921
- Multipoint Socket T10347

➡**Removal notes:**

- It is necessary to remove the intake manifold and fuel rail in order to be able to get to the fuel injectors.
- The combustion chamber seal (Teflon) and the O-ring must be replaced.

❄❄ CAUTION

Fuel system is under pressure! Fuel pressure must be reduced to a residual pressure before opening high pressure area of injection system.

1. Disconnect the battery at the negative terminal.
2. Remove engine cover.
3. Disconnect the vacuum line to the EVAP canister.
4. Disconnect the electrical connectors from the side of the intake manifold area.
5. Disconnect the electrical connector from the camshaft position sensor

6. Remove the air guide hose from the throttle valve control module.
7. Disconnect the vacuum line at the separating point. Remove the crankcase ventilation hose.
8. Remove the fuel supply line from the high pressure pump.
9. Open the high pressure fuel line union nut lower on the high pressure pump.

➡**The fuel system must have no pressure. Use a clean rag to absorb exiting fuel. Seal the open connections with clean caps and make sure no dirt has entered the fuel system.**

10. Remove the vacuum line from the intake manifold runner control valve.
11. Remove the coolant line bolt arrow from the intake manifold.
12. Disconnect the electrical connector from the fuel pressure sensor to the left of the coolant line bolt just removed.
13. Loosen the mounting nut slightly and remove the bolt completely.
14. Remove the oil filter with a proper oil filter wrench (2171-1 or an oil filter wrench 3417).
15. Remove the intake manifold bolts using socket wrench (T10347).

➡**The throttle valve control module**

must be removed in order to remove any bolts that are not accessible and not using the T10347.

16. Carefully pull the intake manifold with fuel rail away from the cylinder head slightly.
17. Disconnect the electrical connector 1 from the intake manifold runner position sensor and remove the intake manifold.

➡**The fuel injectors could remain stuck in the fuel rail. Seal the intake channels with a clean cloth.**

18. Disconnect the intake manifold from the fuel rail.

To install:

19. Make sure the fuel injectors are installed correctly.
20. Mount the intake manifold onto the cylinder head on the stud bolts (lower left and right).
21. Further installation is in reverse order.

➡**Refer to exploded view illustration for tightening specifications.**

3.2L Engine

See Figures 137 and 138.

1. Remove the molded insert for tools under luggage compartment floor cover.
2. Unscrew cover for battery compartment.
3. Remove the molded insert over battery.
4. Disconnect the negative battery cable.
5. Remove the noise insulation.
6. Disconnect the vacuum hose from air duct hose.
7. Disconnect the air duct hose from Throttle Valve Control Module.
8. Disconnect the electrical harness connector at Mass Air Flow (MAF) sensor.
9. Unbolt upper section of air filter housing.
10. Remove the filter element.
11. Unbolt lower section of air duct.
12. Unbolt lower section of air filter housing.
13. Disconnect the secondary air hose at position indicated by.
14. Loosen up the air hose to Secondary Air Injection (AIR) pump.
15. Disconnect the electrical harness connectors and.
16. Disconnect the crankcase ventilation hose.
17. Unscrew Throttle Valve Control Module from the intake manifold and lay it aside with coolant hoses connected.

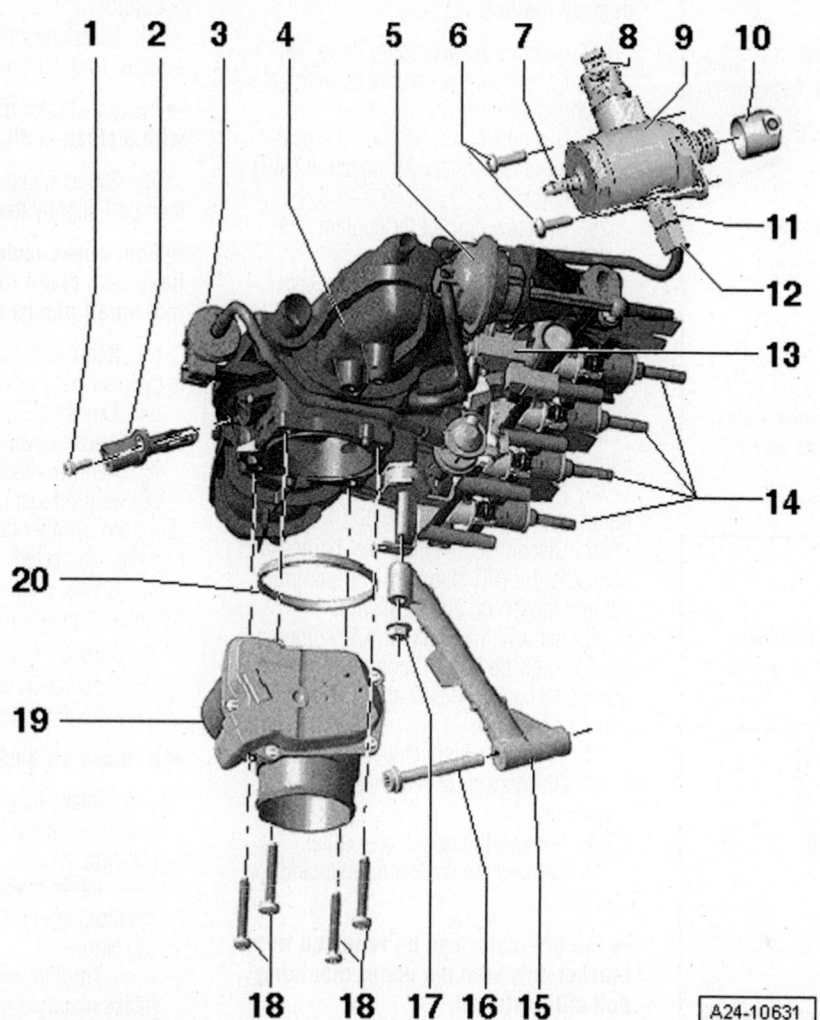

1. Intake Air Temperature Sensor Bolt: 4 ft. lbs. (5 Nm)
2. Intake Air Temperature Sensor
3. EVAP Canister Purge Regulator Valve
4. Intake Manifold
5. Channel Separating Plate Vacuum Diaphragm (intake manifold flaps)
6. High Pressure Pump Bolts: 15 ft. lbs. (20 Nm)
7. Fuel Supply Line Connectors
8. Fuel Pressure Regulator Valve
9. High Pressure Pump
10. Roller Tappet
11. Fuel Supply Line Connectors: 30 ft. lbs. (40 Nm)
12. High Pressure Fuel Line: 20 ft. lbs. (27 Nm)
13. Intake Manifold Runner Control Valve
14. Fuel Injector
15. Intake Manifold Support
16. Intake Manifold Support Bolt: 17 ft. lbs. (23 Nm)
17. Intake Manifold Support Nut: 7 ft. lbs. (10 Nm)
18. Throttle Valve Control Module Bolts: 4 ft. lbs. (5 Nm)
19. Throttle Valve Control Module, EPC Throttle Drive

Fig. 136 Exploded view of the intake manifold assembly

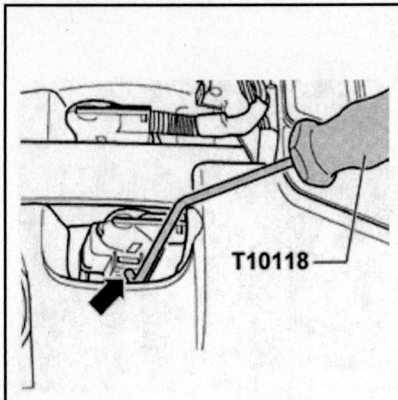

Fig. 137 Disconnect the electrical connectors from the ignition coils—A3 with 3.2L engine

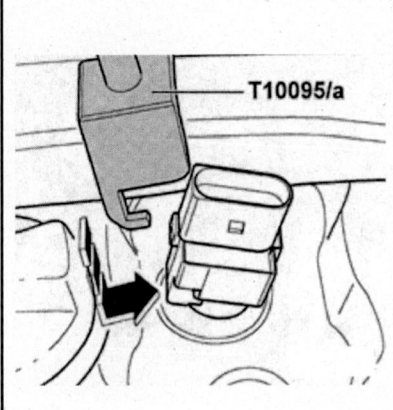

Fig. 138 Attach Puller for ignition coil tool T10095A on ignition coils and pull out ignition coils in succession—A3 with 3.2L engine

18. Disconnect the electrical connectors from the ignition coils.

19. Attach Puller for ignition coil tool T10095A on ignition coils as shown in the illustration and pull out ignition coils in succession.

20. Remove the ignition wiring harness strip and set it aside.

21. Disconnect the vacuum hoses at rear from intake manifold.

22. Remove the line union from intake manifold and place it in the rear with hoses connected.

23. Remove the bolts for rear intake manifold mount.

24. Unscrew top mounting bolts for fan shroud.

25. Remove the dipstick.

➡**Mark direction of rotation of accessory drive belt using chalk or felt-tip marker before removing. Reversing the direction of rotation of a run-in belt can destroy the belt**

26. Remove the accessory drive belt.

27. Loosen up the coolant hose at bottom on fan shroud.

28. Disconnect the electrical harness connector at Secondary Air Injection (AIR) pump motor.

29. Unscrew bracket for coolant pipe.

30. Remove the bolts.

31. Loosen the bolt and remove Secondary Air Injection (AIR) pump with bracket.

32. Disconnect the electrical harness connectors for coolant fans at bottom on fan shroud.

33. Unscrew mounting bolts for fan shroud at the bottom.

34. Pull out fan shroud downward with both fans.

35. Disconnect the electrical harness connector for A/C clutch on A/C compressor and loosen up electrical wire.

36. Remove the bolts for A/C compressor. Securely tie the A/C compressor with connected coolant hoses at front on the longitudinal member.

37. Unscrew electrical wire on alternator.

38. Disconnect the electrical harness connector.

39. Remove the upper idler roller.

40. Remove the mounting bolts and for alternator.

➡**The alternator can be removed from bracket only with the upper mounting bolt still installed.**

41. Remove the alternator with electrical wires connected from bracket for assemblies.

42. Remove the alternator downward and to the left.

43. Disconnect the electrical harness connector at the after-run coolant pump.

44. Remove the bolts and remove bracket for assemblies.

45. Pull the after-run coolant pump with coolant hoses connected, downward out of rubber loops of retainer. Spray rubber loops with silicon-free lubricant if necessary.

➡**The water pump remains on the engine with the coolant hoses connected.**

46. Disengage harness connector for Engine Speed (RPM) sensor from bracket on oil dipstick guide tube.

47. Unscrew bolt and pull out oil dipstick guide tube.

48. Unscrew bolt and pull off vacuum reservoir from intake manifold.

49. Set aside vacuum reservoir with lines still connected.

50. Remove the bolts at front on intake manifold.

51. Disconnect the vacuum line from actuator for intake manifold change-over.

➡**Protect intake manifold from damage with a clean cloth.**

52. Swivel intake manifold forward and then pull slightly toward left.

➡**Seal intake channels in cylinder head with clean rags or foam pieces so that small pieces cannot fall in.**

53. Remove the bracket for right fuel line at cylinder head cover.

54. Expose electrical wiring harness on cylinder head cover.

55. Remove the bolts.

56. Pull off fuel rail pipe with fuel injectors from cylinder head and set aside with fuel line connected.

57. Swivel intake manifold back into installation position and remove.

To install:

58. Installation is the reverse of removal, please note the following:

➡**Replace all gaskets.**

   a. Intake manifold to cylinder head retainers are tightened to 10 ft. lbs. (13 Nm)

   b. Intake manifold support to intake manifold are tightened to 15 ft. lbs. (20 Nm).

   c. Throttle Valve Control Module to intake manifold retainers are tightened to 89 inch lbs. (10 Nm).

Q7

3.0L TDI Engine—Left

1. Before servicing the vehicle, refer to the precautions.

2. Carefully remove the engine cover from the 4 studs one after the other.

3. Loosen the air guide hose clamps and remove the air guide hose.

4. Place a cloth under the separating point to catch any leaking hydraulic fluid.

5. Clamp off the power steering pump hydraulic hose using 3094.

6. Remove the hydraulic hose 1 from the power steering pump.

7. Remove the banjo bolt 2 and lay the pressure line aside.

8. Remove the power steering pump.

9. Remove the bolts 1 through 8 and remove the exhaust manifold.

To install:

10. Installation is performed in reverse order of removal, noting the following:

11. Replace seals, gaskets, O-rings and self-locking nuts.

12. Secure all hose connections using hose clamps appropriate for the model type.

13. Tighten the connection between the intermediate pipe and exhaust manifold as follows:

14. Tighten bolts/nuts to specification as follows:

- Tighten the nut to 89 inch lbs. (10 Nm)
- Tighten the nut to 22 ft. lbs. (30 Nm)
- Then, tighten the nut an additional 90°

15. Align the exhaust system so it is free of tension.

16. Check the power steering hydraulic fluid level.

17. Tighten bolts/nuts to specification as follows:

- Exhaust manifold to cylinder head: 22 ft. lbs. (30 Nm) plus 90°
- Intermediate pipe to exhaust manifold: 19 ft. lbs. (25 Nm)
- Pressure line banjo bolt to power steering pump: 37 ft. lbs. (50 Nm)
- Hose clamps 13 mm wide: 49 inch lbs. (5.5 Nm)

3.0L TDI Engine—Right

1. Before servicing the vehicle, refer to the precautions.

2. Carefully remove the engine cover from the studs one after the other.

3. Drain the cooling system.

4. Remove the differential ventilation hose from the upper air filter housing.

5. Disconnect the electrical connector for the Mass Air Flow sensor.

6. Loosen the air guide hose clamp at the turbocharger and remove the air guide hose from the turbocharger.

7. Release the clips and remove the upper air filter housing.

8. On vehicles with Air Suspension:

a. If necessary, remove the electrical connector for the Heated Oxygen Sensor (HO2S) 2 from the bracket at the right strut tower for better access.

b. Press circlip forward from hose coupling.

c. Press the release ring down and remove the ventilation hose from the upper air filter housing.

9. Remove the connector from the bracket and disconnect it.

10. Remove the connector bracket from the cylinder head cover.

11. Remove the coolant hose from the coolant reservoir.

12. Remove the bolts.

13. Remove the air duct pipe from the hoses and remove the pipe downward.

14. Remove the bolts and the exhaust manifold.

To install:

15. Installation is performed in reverse order of removal, noting the following:

16. Replace gaskets and self-locking nuts.

17. Tighten bolts/nuts to specification as follows:

- Exhaust manifold to cylinder head: 22 ft. lbs. (30 Nm) plus 90°
- Intermediate pipe to exhaust manifold: 19 ft. lbs. (25 Nm)
- Pressure line banjo bolt to power steering pump: 37 ft. lbs. (50 Nm)
- Hose clamps 13 mm wide: 49 inch lbs. (5.5 Nm)

18. Hose connections and charge air system hoses must be free of oil and grease before installing.

19. Secure all hose connections using hose clamps appropriate for the model type.

20. Fill the cooling system.

3.6L Engine

1. Before servicing the vehicle, refer to the precautions.

2. Disconnect the batteries.

3. If equipped with one-piece intake manifold:

a. Remove the four vacuum hoses from intake manifold.

b. Remove air filter housing with intake hose to throttle valve control module.

c. Remove throttle valve control module from intake manifold.

4. If equipped with a two-piece intake manifold, remove the upper manifold.

5. Disconnect the four oxygen sensor connectors.

6. Using a ring spanner (3337), remove the Heated Oxygen sensors (HO2S) in front of catalytic converters.

7. Remove heat shield with intake manifold support.

8. Remove the oxygen sensor (O2S) behind both three-way catalytic (TWC) converters.

9. Raise the vehicle.

10. Identify both exhaust pipe flanges, this makes assembly later easier.

11. Remove nuts on flanges.

12. Remove support to transmission.

13. Unbolt flange to exhaust manifold.

➡**To loosen or tighten nuts more easily, shorten a commercially available**

16 mm open end wrench to approximately 11 cm handle length.

14. First, remove exhaust pipe with catalytic converter from cylinders 4 to 6, then from cylinders 1 to 3.

15. Remove exhaust manifold.

To install:

16. When installing exhaust pipes, ensure that the flange connection after the catalytic converter seals tightly. Leaks in this area produce pulsations in the exhaust. This allows ambient air to reach the lambda probe after catalytic converter and the lambda regulation will be disturbed.

17. Tighten the new exhaust manifold nuts to:

- M8: 18 ft. lbs. (25 Nm)
- M10: 30 ft. lbs. (40 Nm)

18. Adjust the exhaust system so that there is sufficient clearance to the transmission and subframe.

19. The rest of the assembly is basically a reverse of the disassembling sequence.

4.2L Engine

1. Remove the applicable main catalytic converter.

2. Remove the applicable primary catalytic converter.

3. Drain coolant.

4. Remove coolant pipe.

5. Remove six nuts and remove exhaust manifold.

➡**Both securing strips can remain installed when removing exhaust manifold.**

To install:

6. Installation is in reverse order of removal, note the following:

a. Replace gasket and self-locking nuts.

b. Grease studs and bolts with hot-bolt paste.

c. Place new gasket onto stud bolts.

d. Insert exhaust manifold in securing strips and hand tighten nuts.

e. Tighten exhaust manifold nuts in two steps as follows:

- Step 1: Tighten nuts, from back to front, to 15 ft. lbs. (20 Nm).
- Step 2: Tighten nuts in same sequence 22 ft. lbs. (30 Nm).

f. Install left coolant pipe.

g. Install left primary catalytic converter.

h. Align exhaust system free of tension.

i. Fill with coolant.

OIL PAN

REMOVAL & INSTALLATION

Q5

2.0L Engine

See Figure 139.

→**Special tools:**

- Oil Collection and Extraction Device V.A.G 1782
- Hand drill with plastic brush attachment
- Protective eyewear
- Silicone sealant

1. Remove the undercar noise insulation panels.
2. Remove the crossbrace and then the stabilizer bar.
3. Remove the steering gear mounting bolts and the nuts, and move the steering gear slightly to the right, lower it approximately 4 in. (10 cm) and then tie it up.

→**Use care to not stretch, kink or bend oil lines and hoses.**

※※ CAUTION

Never rest the vehicle on its wheels if the subframe mount, steering gear or subframe crossbrace are not installed correctly. Do not support the vehicle on the subframe or the subframe crossbrace, for example, by a floor jack or similar device.

4. Remove steering gear to column pinch bolt, then separate the steering column from the steering gear.
5. Disconnect the connector from the oil level thermal sensor. Remove the oil level thermal sensor.

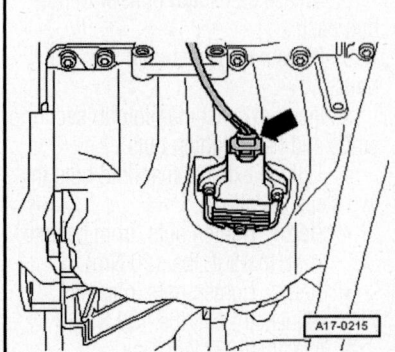

Fig. 139 Disconnect the connector from the oil level thermal sensor. Remove the oil level thermal sensor.

6. Remove the oil pan 19 bolts in a criss-cross pattern.
7. Remove oil pan, if necessary loosen by applying light strikes with a rubber hammer.

To install:

→**Note the following:**

- Replace the bolts which are being tightened with an additional turn.
- Replace sealing rings, seals and self-locking nuts.

8. Spray the sealing surface with sealant remover and allow it to work.
9. Remove any sealant residue on the upper section of the oil pan using a flat blade scraper.
10. Remove sealant residue on the lower section of the oil pan, for example with a rotating plastic brush.
11. Clean sealing surfaces, must be free of oil and grease.
12. Apply silicon sealant to clean sealing surfaces of the oil pan (lower section), but not excessively or over the bolt holes. The sealant bead should be no more than 2 to 3 mm.

→**The oil pan must be installed within 5 minutes after application of silicon sealant.**

13. Position the lower section of the oil pan immediately, in a criss-cross pattern and tighten the bolts in two steps to:
   - Step 1: 7 ft. lbs. (8 Nm)
   - Step 2: additional 45 degrees

→**After installing oil pan, allow sealant to dry for approximately 30 minutes. Only after then may the engine oil be replenished.**

14. Fill engine oil and check oil level.
15. Install the steering gear.
16. Install stabilizer bar and the crossbrace.
17. Install the noise insulation panels.
18. The rest of the assembly is basically a reverse of the disassembling sequence.

3.2L Engine

See Figures 140 and 141.

→**Removal of the upper section of the oil pan is only done after the transmission is removed.**

1. Before servicing the vehicle, refer to the precautions section.
2. Disconnect the negative battery cable.
3. Disconnect the secondary air injection hose.

4. Remove the center noise insulation fasteners.
5. Remove the right noise insulation fasteners.
6. Drain the engine oil.
7. Disconnect the lower coolant hose at fan shroud.
8. Disconnect the electrical connector at Secondary Air Injection (AIR) pump.
9. Remove the coolant pipe bracket to transmission oil cooler.
10. Remove the bolts.
11. Loosen the bolt and remove Secondary Air Injection (AIR) pump with bracket.
12. Disconnect the oil level thermal sensor connector.
13. Remove the bolts for oil pan/transmission.
14. Loosen the oil pan bolts diagonally and remove.
15. Remove the oil pan, and if necessary loosen by applying light strikes with a rubber mallet.

To install:

→**The oil pan must be installed within 5 minutes after applying the silicone sealant.**

16. Clean the oil pan mating surfaces.
17. Apply 2 to 3mm bead of silicone sealant as illustrated to the sealing surface of oil pan.

→**The sealant bead may not be thicker than specified, otherwise excess sealant could enter the oil pan and clog the oil intake tube.**

18. Install the oil pan immediately and tighten bolts in sequence as follows:
   a. Step 1: Oil pan bolts to 5 Nm.

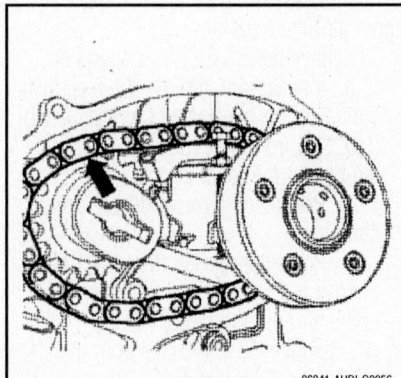

Fig. 140 Apply 2 to 3mm bead of silicone sealant to the sealing surface of oil pan— 3.2L engine

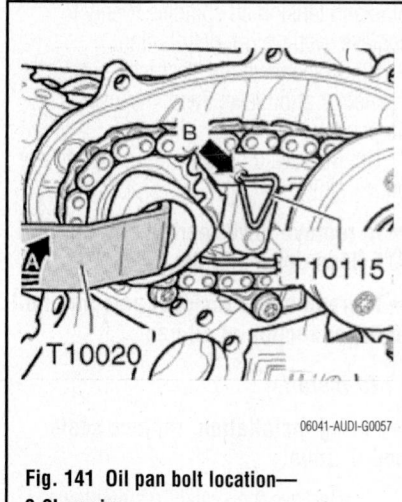

**Fig. 141 Oil pan bolt location—
3.2L engine**

   b. Step 2: New oil pan to transmission bolts to 30 ft. lbs. (40 Nm).

   c. Step 3: Oil pan bolts to 9 ft. lbs. (12 Nm).

➡**Make sure that the oil pan is positioned flush with the cylinder block on the flywheel side.**

➡**After installing oil pan, allow sealant to dry for about 30 minutes, then fill the crankcase with oil.**

   19. Check and adjust the oil level.

   20. Install the remaining components in the reverse order of removal.

Q7

3.0L TDI Engine—Lower

➡**The manufacturer does not provide a specific procedure for oil pan removal. Except for the torque specifications, this procedure should be used as a guide only.**

   1. Before servicing the vehicle, refer to the precautions.

   2. Remove the ribbed belt.

   3. Remove the ribbed belt tensioner.

   4. Remove the left coolant pipe.

   5. Remove the air filter housing.

   6. Remove the left and right engine mount bracket to engine mount nuts.

   7. Remove the left front wheel housing liner.

   8. Remove the nuts and bolts from the coolant line clamps.

   9. With the nuts and bolts removed, the coolant lines can be moved aside slightly to position the 10-222 A /19 on the longitudinal members.

   10. Position the 10-222A on the bolted fender flanges with the T40091/3 and two spindles.

   11. The spindles are positioned forward.

   12. Engage both spindles in both rear engine lifting eyes.

   13. Install additional parts of the 10-222A. Position 10 - 222 A /19 on the notches in the longitudinal members.

   14. Slide the support T40091/2 with the slide T40093/5 into both T40093/4.

✳✳ WARNING

Secure the T40091/2 with the pins to the T40093/4.

   15. Install the T10014 in the mounting hole for the ribbed belt tensioner.

   16. Remove the 2024 A eyes.

   17. Insert bolts 1 in the center bore of 2024 A again and secure with a cotter pin.

   18. Engage the pins on the 2024 A in the front spindle on the 10-222A.

   19. Install the 2024 A/1 on the left side of the 2024 A.

   20. Engage the 2024 A in the right front engine lifting eye and on the T10014.

✳✳ WARNING

Lifting hooks and alignment pins on 2024 A must be secured with securing pinss.

   21. Raise engine until engine mount bracket are above threaded studs of the engine mounts and tension all spindles evenly to achieve even weight distribution.

   22. Position the VAG 1383A on the bottom of the subframe.

   23. Remove the bolts 4 and carefully lower the subframe using the VAG 1383A.

   24. Remove the engine carrier bolts 3 and place the engine carrier on the subframe.

   25. Disconnect the electrical connector item 1 for the oil level thermal sensor.

   26. Place the VAG 1782 under the engine.

   27. Drain the engine oil.

   28. Remove the oil level thermal sensor.

   29. Remove the lower oil pan bolts and pan.

   30. Rotate the lower oil pan 180°and remove it toward the front.

   31. When removing the lower oil pan, keep in mind that there is still some oil in it.

To install:

   32. Replace seals.

   33. Remove any sealant residue on the upper and lower oil pans with a rotating plastic brush.

   34. Clean sealing surfaces so they are completely free of any oil or grease.

   35. Cut the tube nozzle at the front marking (nozzle diameter approximately 1.5 mm).

   36. Apply sealant bead on clean sealing surface of lower oil pan as shown in illustration.

   37. Apply the sealant in a 0.078 in (2 mm) bead on the lower oil pan so it seals corrected with the tapered base on the upper oil pan.

   38. The sealant bead must not be thicker than specified or sealant could enter the oil pan and clog the oil pump strainer.

   39. The lower oil pan must be installed within 5 minutes after application of sealant.

   40. Position the lower oil pan and tighten all the bolts in a diagonal sequence to 5 Nm.

   41. Install the oil level thermal sensor.

   42. Install the subframe.

   43. If the subframe was not secured to the body, perform an alignment after installing.

   44. Install the air filter housing.

   45. Install the left coolant pipe.

   46. Install the ribbed belt tensioner.

   47. Install the ribbed belt.

   48. Add engine oil and check the oil level.

   49. Tighten bolts/nuts to specification as follows:

- Lower oil pan bolts: 71 inch lbs. (8 Nm)

3.0L TDI Engine—Upper

➡**The manufacturer does not provide a specific procedure for oil pan removal. Except for the torque specifications, this procedure should be used as a guide only.**

   1. Before servicing the vehicle, refer to the precautions.

   2. Remove the engine.

   3. Separate the engine and transmission.

   4. Secure the engine to the assembly stand.

   5. Remove the drive plate.

   6. Remove the shim behind it.

   7. Remove the timing chain covers.

   8. Remove the balance shaft and oil pump timing chain.

   9. Remove the sealing flange.

   10. Remove the lower oil pan.

   11. Remove the oil pump.

   12. Remove the bolts for the upper oil pan.

   13. Separate the upper oil pan from the alignment pins in the cylinder block.

To install:

   14. Replace the gaskets, seals and O-rings.

15. Remove any sealant from the grooves in the upper oil pan and from the sealing surfaces.

16. Remove any remaining sealant on the oil pan using a rotating brush, e.g. a drill with plastic brush attachment (wear protective glasses).

17. Clean sealing surfaces so they are completely free of any oil or grease.

18. Cut the tube nozzle at the front marking 0.117 (3 mm).

19. Insert the seals in the upper oil pan.

20. Apply the sealant beads to the clean sealing surface on the upper oil pan as illustrated.

21. The grooves of the sealing surfaces must be completely filled with sealant.

22. Sealant beads must be 0.058–0.078 in (1.5–2.0 mm) above the sealing surface.

23. The sealant bead must not be thicker than specified or sealant could enter the oil pan and clog the oil pump strainer.

24. The upper oil pan must be installed within 5 minutes after application of sealant.

25. Position the upper oil pan in place and tighten the bolts.

26. Tighten bolts/nuts to specification as follows:

- Upper oil pan bolts: 71 inch lbs. (8 Nm)

3.6L Engine

1. Before servicing the vehicle, refer to the precautions.

2. Drain engine oil.

3. Disconnect wire connection to air suspension compressor at air filter.

4. Completely remove air filter with Mass Air Flow (MAF) sensor.

5. Remove nuts on right and left engine bracket.

6. Position an engine support/lifting device to the engine.

7. With the lifting device in place, pre-tension engine slightly.

8. Remove the subframe.

9. Remove engine carrier. Engine mounts can remain attached to engine carrier.

10. Disconnect 3-pin connector from oil level thermal sensor.

11. Remove the oil pan.

12. Loosen oil pan with light blows of a rubber headed hammer if necessary.

13. Remove sealant residue from cylinder block with a flat scraper.

14. Remove sealant residue at oil pan using a rotating brush, e.g. a drill with plastic brush attachment (wear protective glasses).

15. Clean the sealing surfaces, they must be free of oil and grease.

To install:

➡ **The oil pan must be installed within 5 minutes after application of silicone sealant.**

16. Apply silicone sealant to clean sealing surfaces of oil pan. The sealing compound bead must be about 0.078–0.117 in. (2–3 mm) thick, and running on the inside of bolt holes.

➡ **Sealant bead must not be thicker than specified. Otherwise, excess sealant could get into oil pan and clog strainer in intake line of oil pump.**

17. Apply silicone sealant to clean oil pan sealing surfaces.

18. Install oil pan immediately and tighten all oil pan bolts lightly.

19. Repeat tightening sequence to 9 ft. lbs. (12 Nm).

20. After installing oil pan, allow sealant to dry for approximately 30 minutes, before installing any new engine oil.

21. The rest of the assembly is basically a reverse of the disassembling sequence.

4.2L Engine—Lower Oil Pan

1. Before servicing the vehicle, refer to the precautions.

2. Remove rear and front engine covers.

3. Remove noise insulation.

4. Remove front wheels.

5. Remove both front wheel housing liners.

6. Remove left and right air filter housing.

7. Remove engine bracket nuts at left and right.

8. Rotate A/C line nuts down. Carefully press lines off long member and position support adapter (10 - 222 A /19) on longitudinal member.

9. Install an engine support bridge (10 - 222 A) and tension engine slightly.

10. Drain engine oil.

11. Drain the coolant.

12. Remove bolts from front coolant pipe running across the lower part of the block.

13. Remove the coolant pipe from engine and from coolant pump.

14. Remove ATF line bolt at right of transmission.

15. Remove ATF line from transmission.

16. Remove bolt in front of right side of long member.

➡ **Leave ATF lines in installation location.**

17. Raise engine until the engine supports are above threaded engine bracket pins and tension all spindles evenly to achieve even weight distribution.

18. Disconnect the electrical connector at oil level thermal sensor on pan.

19. Remove oil pan (lower part) and pry out carefully.

➡ **To remove lower part of oil pan, pull ATF lines down slightly.**

➡ **There is still a residual amount of oil in lower section of oil pan.**

To install:

➡ **During installation, replace seals and O-rings.**

20. Remove the sealant residue lower part and upper part of oil pan, e.g. with rotating plastic brush.

21. Clean sealing surfaces, they must be free of oil and grease.

22. Apply sealant bead on clean, oil-free sealing surface of lower section of oil pan, keeping the sealant on the inside of the bolt holes. Sealant bead should be no more than 2.5 mm thick.

23. Sealing surface on upper part of oil pan must be free of oil and grease.

24. The oil pan (lower part) must be installed within 5 minutes after application of sealant.

25. Position lower part of oil pan and hand tighten all bolts.

26. Tighten bolts for lower part of oil pan in 2 stages as follows.

   a. Pre-tighten all bolts in a diagonal sequence to 3 ft. lbs. (5 Nm).

   b. Tighten all bolts in a diagonal sequence to 6 ft. lbs. (9 Nm).

27. The rest of installation is in reverse order of removal, note the following:

   a. Install front coolant pipe.

   b. Tighten the ATF lines.

   c. Add engine oil and check oil level. Ensure the drain plug is tightened to 18 ft. lbs. (25 Nm).

   d. Install left and right air filter housing.

   e. Fill with coolant.

4.2L Engine—Upper Oil Pan

See Figure 142.

1. Before servicing the vehicle, refer to the precautions.

➡ **The upper part of the oil pan can only be removed or installed with the engine removed.**

2. Remove the engine.

3. Separate the engine and transmission.

4. Remove the drive plate.

5. Remove left and right timing chain covers.

6. Remove the intake manifold.

7. Remove oil filter housing.

8. Remove lower timing chain cover.

➡**Before removing ribbed belt, mark the turning direction on it with chalk or a felt tip pen. A reversed turning direction can cause damage to the ribbed belt under operating conditions.**

9. Pivot the belt tensioning device downward to relieve tension on ribbed belt. Remove ribbed belt and release tensioning device.

10. Remove bolts holding tensioning device and remove ribbed belt tensioner from upper part of oil pan.

11. Remove the electrical connections from rear of alternator.

12. Remove the alternator.

13. Remove bolts and remove air alternator bracket.

14. Remove bolts and remove front coolant pipe from engine and from coolant pump.

15. Remove lower section of oil pan.

16. Remove oil pump.

17. Remove bolts (1 through 7) for upper section of oil pan.

18. Press the upper part of oil pan from alignment pins of cylinder block.

To install:

➡**During installation, replace seals and O-rings.**

19. Using rotating plastic brush, remove any remaining sealant from oil pan (upper part) and at cylinder block.

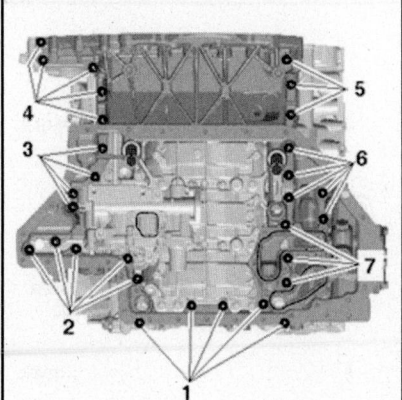

Fig. 142 Locations of upper oil pan bolts—4.2L engine

20. Clean sealing surfaces, they must be free of oil and grease.

21. Insert new seals into grooves on cylinder block.

22. Apply sealant beads on clean sealing surfaces of upper part of oil pan, as shown in illustration. Thickness of sealant beads: 2.5 mm.

➡**The oil pan (upper part) must be installed within 5 minutes after application of sealant.**

23. Position upper part of oil pan and tighten bolts in two steps, using a diagonal tightening sequence:

    a. Pre-tighten bolts to diagonally to 3 ft. lbs. (5 Nm).

    b. Tighten bolts diagonally to 10 ft. lbs. (14 Nm).

24. The rest of installation is in reverse order of removal, note the following:

    a. Add engine oil and check oil level.

OIL PUMP

REMOVAL & INSTALLATION

Q5

2.0L Engine

See Figures 143 through 145.

1. Remove the lower oil pan section, as described in this section.

2. Remove the oil baffle.

3. Remove the bolts and the oil pump.

4. Pull the chain tensioner with the assembly tool T10118 and remove the oil pump and the chain sprocket.

To install:

5. Installation is performed in the reverse order of removal, noting the following:

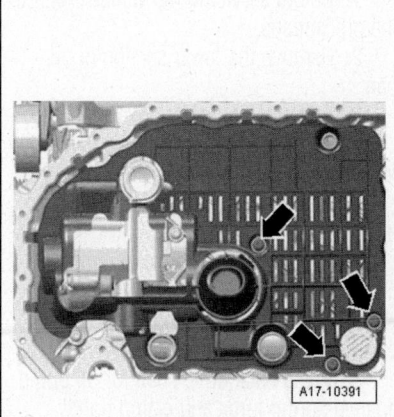

Fig. 143 Remove the oil baffle (arrows).

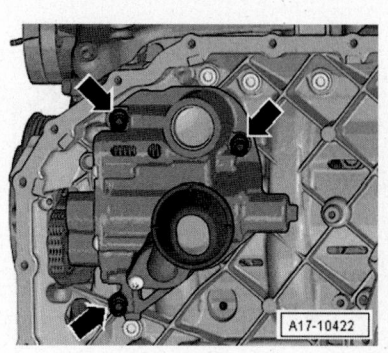

Fig. 144 Remove the bolts (arrows) and the oil pump.

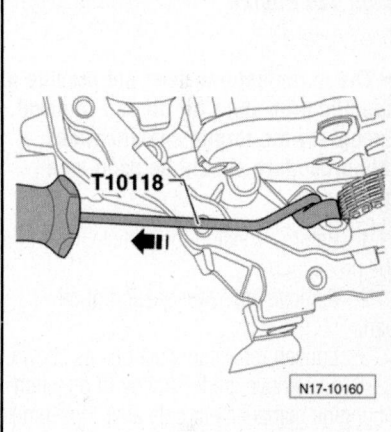

Fig. 145 Pull the chain tensioner in direction of arrow with the assembly tool T10118 and remove the oil pump and the chain sprocket.

6. Install the oil pump, tightening the bolts to 15 ft. lbs. (20 Nm).

7. Replace the baffle plate.

8. Make sure both alignment bushings for centering the oil pump are in there.

9. Install oil pan lower section, as described in this section.

10. Fill engine oil and check oil level.

3.2L Engine

See Figure 146.

1. Remove lowers oil pan section.

2. Remove bolts.

3. Installation is in reverse order of removal, note the following:

4. Replace O-rings.

5. Fill the engine oil and check the oil level.

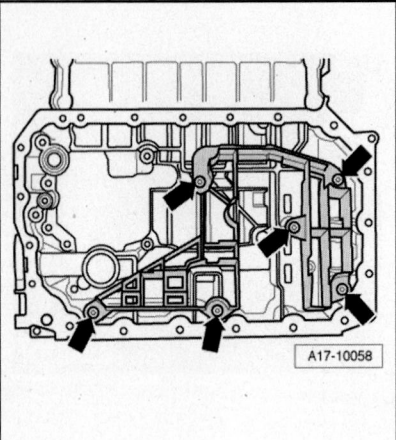

Fig. 146 Remove bolts, remove oil pump forward from the input shaft

3.0L TDI Engine

See Figure 147.

➡The manufacturer does not provide a specific procedure for oil pan removal. Except for the torque specifications, this procedure should be used as a guide only.

1. Before servicing the vehicle, refer to the precautions.
2. Remove the lower section of oil pan.
3. Loosen return connections as shown.
4. To remove, slide slightly in direction of engine management side after loosening all mounts and remove.

To install:

➡During installation, replace all seals and O-rings.

5. Install the oil pump and tighten the bolts to 6 ft. lbs. (8 Nm), plus an additional 90°.

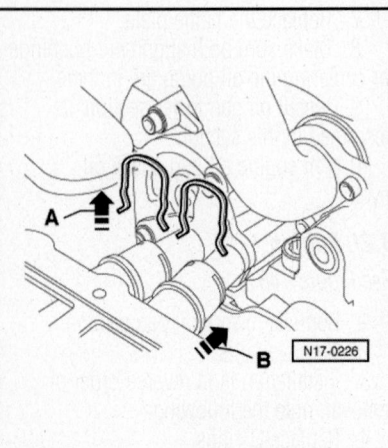

Fig. 147 Loosen return connections as shown

6. The rest of installation is in reverse order of removal, note the following:
7. Install lowers section of oil pan.
8. Add engine oil and check oil level.

3.6L Engine

1. Before servicing the vehicle, refer to the precautions.
2. Remove the engine.
3. Separate the transmission from engine.
4. Remove the timing chain cover from cylinder head.
5. Remove drive plate and sealing flange from engine.
6. Remove the chain tensioner and then remove the camshaft control chain from the front chain sprocket for the oil pump.
7. Loosen the bolt and remove the chain sprockets, together with the timing chain from the oil pump.
8. Remove the bolts of oil pump.
9. Install a threaded bolt M10 x 30 (standard) into oil pump shaft.
10. Install a slide hammer onto the threaded bolt.
11. Pull oil pump out of cylinder block using light knocking motions.

To install:

12. Installation is performed in the reverse of removal.
   a. O-ring as well as mounting bolts for oil pump and chain sprockets must always be replaced.
   b. Install oil pump with new bolts. Tighten the bolts to 6 ft. lbs. (8 Nm).
   c. Install chain sprockets with a new bolt. Tighten the bolt to 47 ft. lbs. (60 Nm), plus an additional 90°.
   d. Install the camshaft adjustor with timing chain for camshaft drive.

4.2L Engine

1. Before servicing the vehicle, refer to the precautions.
2. Remove the lower section of oil pan.
3. Remove the coolant (water) pump.
4. Remove drive shaft for coolant pump from bore in oil pump.
5. Remove bolts and remove oil pipe from the side of the engine.
6. Remove three bolts and remove intake tube.
7. Remove oil pipe together with oil check valve housing.
8. Press back drive shaft for oil pump against spring force and clamp tightly, using long-nose pliers.
9. Remove bolts and remove oil pump.

To install:

➡During installation, replace all seals and O-rings.

10. Check whether two alignment bushings are present in cylinder block, install if necessary.
11. Install the oil pump and tighten the bolts to 6 ft. lbs. (8 Nm), plus an additional 90°.
12. Unlock long-nose gripping pliers and let drive shaft glide into oil pump.
13. Check whether drive shaft is friction locked to oil pump. To do so, reach into intake opening of oil pump and try to rotate oil pump gears. Toothed gears must not be able to be rotated.
14. The rest of installation is in reverse order of removal, note the following:
   a. Install the coolant pump. Tighten all bolts to 7 ft. lbs. (9 Nm).
   b. Install the lower section of oil pan.
   c. Add engine oil and check oil level.
   d. Fill with coolant.

PISTON AND RING

POSITIONING

See Figures 148 through 153.

REAR MAIN SEAL

REMOVAL & INSTALLATION

Q5

See Figures 154 through 157.

1. Before servicing the vehicle, refer to the precautions section.
2. Remove the transmission.
3. Remove the flywheel.

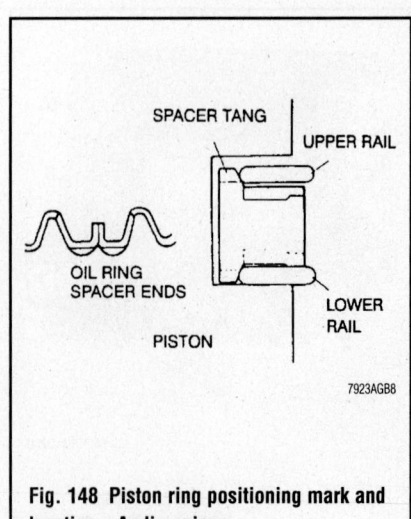

Fig. 148 Piston ring positioning mark and location—Audi engines

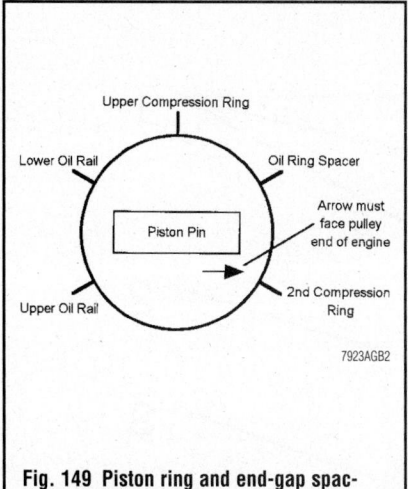

Fig. 149 Piston ring and end-gap spacing—Audi engines

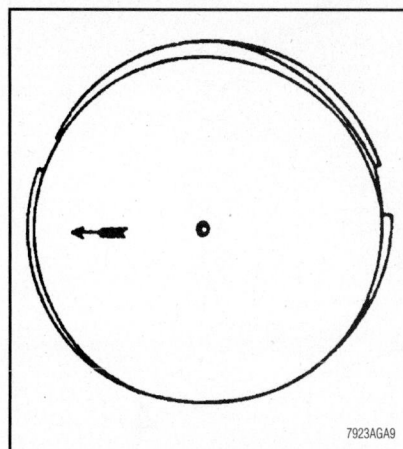

Fig. 150 Arrow on the piston crown must face the front of the engine—Audi engines

4. Disconnect the intermediate plate at sealing flange and at the alignment sleeves.
5. Remove the bolts and the rear sealing flange.

To install:

➡ **Lay a rag over the open portion of the oil pan.**

6. Clean the gasket mating surfaces.
7. Apply a thin bead of sealant to edge between cylinder block and oil pan.
8. Lightly coat lower sealing surface of sealing flange with sealant.

➡ **The sealing flange must be installed within 5 minutes of sealant being applied.**

9. Push the sealing flange together with the guide sleeve, which is included with replacement part onto crankshaft.
10. Carefully push the sealing flange onto the locating pins on cylinder block.
11. Fasten the bolts to 15 Nm.

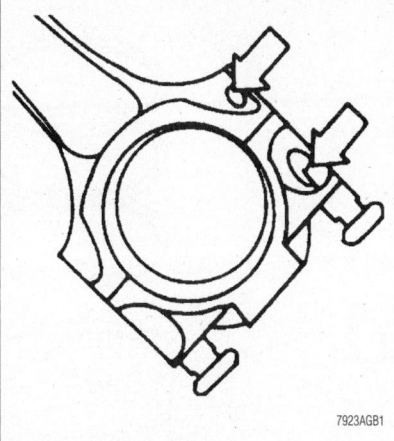

Fig. 151 Connecting rod to bearing cap assembly—Audi engines

12. Install the remaining components in the reverse order of removal.

Q7

3.0L TDI Engine

1. Before servicing the vehicle, refer to the precautions.
2. Remove the engine and transmission.
3. Be careful not to damage sealing surface when removing sealing ring.
4. Carefully remove old sealing ring from its seat using hook T20143/2.

To install:

5. Remove oil remains from end of crankshaft with a clean cloth.
6. Join assembly sleeve T10207/1 and assembly sleeve T10207/2. Slide sealing ring A to stop on assembly sleeve T10207/2.
7. Separate both assembly sleeves.
8. Place assembly sleeve T10207/2 together with sealing ring on crankshaft flange and tighten knurled bolts A hand tight.
9. Press in seal up to stop using pressure sleeve T1207/3.
10. The rest of the assembly is basically a reverse of the removal sequence.

3.6L Engine

1. Before servicing the vehicle, refer to the precautions.
2. Remove the engine and separate the transmission.
3. Place the pulling hook (T20143/2) behind sealing lip of rear main sealing ring.
4. Support the pulling hook on sealing flange and pry out sealing ring.

To install:

5. Pull the sealing ring with its outside over the sleeve and onto a proper assembly/installer tool.
6. Place the assembly tool with dry sealing ring onto crankshaft pin.
7. Knock it into sealing flange until it stops.
8. Attach transmission to engine and install the assembly.

4.2L Engine

1. Before servicing the vehicle, refer to the precautions.
2. Remove the engine.
3. Separate the engine from transmission.
4. Remove the drive plate (flywheel).
5. Remove oil pan.
6. Remove the sealing flange from cylinder block.
7. Remove and discard old gasket.

To install:

➡ **If repairs are required, the complete sealing flange with seal must be replaced. Then to install, use the supplied support sleeve.**

8. Clean sealing surfaces of sealing flange and cylinder block. Sealing surfaces must be free of oil and grease.
9. Before installing, remove oil remains from end of crankshaft with a clean cloth.
10. Place a new gasket onto alignment bushings of the cylinder head.
11. Pull seal and sealing flange with outer side over sleeve (T10122/1) onto assembly tool (T10122/2).
12. Separate both assembly sleeves.
13. Place assembly tool (T10122/2) with dry seal and sealing flange onto crankshaft flange.
14. Fasten sealing flange to cylinder block and tighten bolts to 7 ft. lbs. (10 Nm).
15. Install oil pan.
16. Install the drive plate (flywheel).
17. Install the engine and transmission assembly.

TURBOCHARGER

REMOVAL & INSTALLATION

2.0L Engine

See Figures 158 through 161.

1. Remove the engine cover.
2. Drain the cooling system.
3. Remove the front air intake duct.

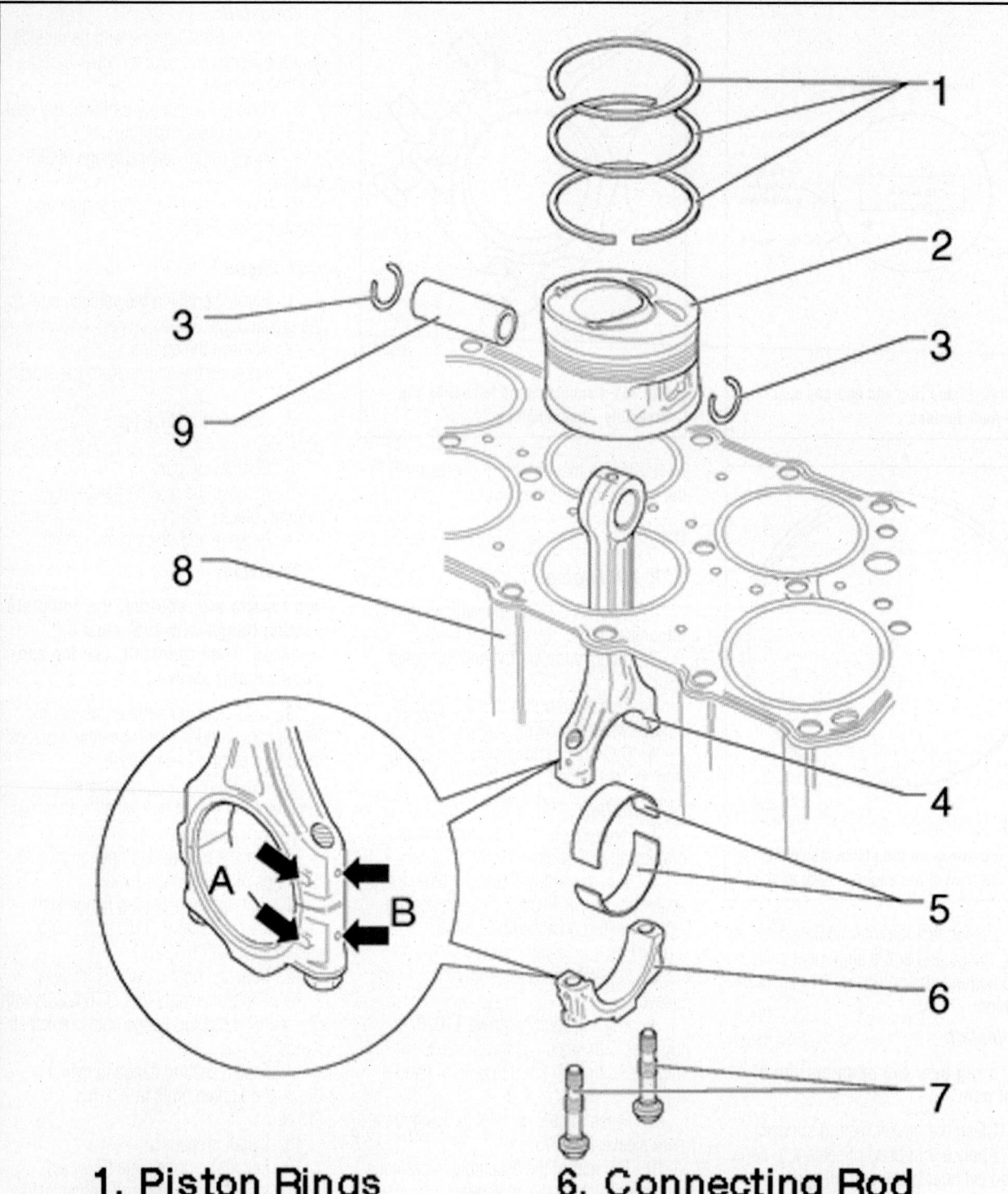

1. Piston Rings
2. Piston
3. Circlip
4. Connecting Rod
5. Bearing Shell
6. Connecting Rod Bearing Cap
7. Bearing Cap Bolts
8. Cylinder Block
9. Piston Pin

22205_TOUA_G0127

Fig. 155 Exploded view of the piston and rod assembly—note positions of ring end gaps on piston—3.6L engine

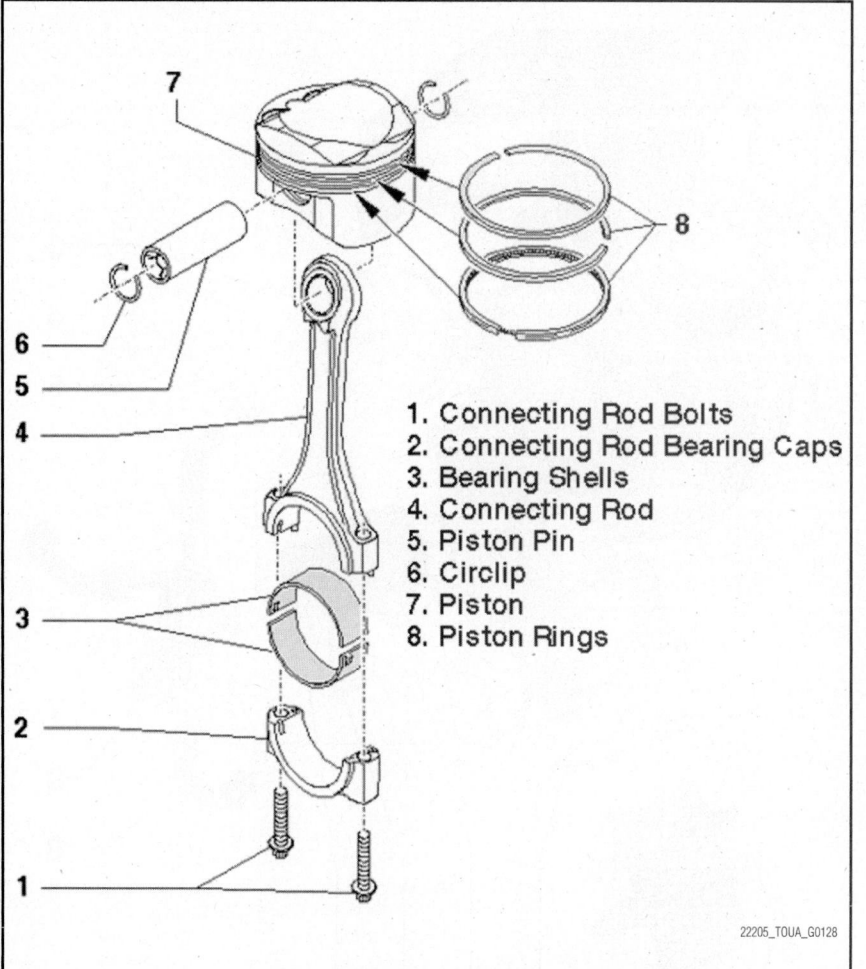

1. Connecting Rod Bolts
2. Connecting Rod Bearing Caps
3. Bearing Shells
4. Connecting Rod
5. Piston Pin
6. Circlip
7. Piston
8. Piston Rings

22205_TOUA_G0128

Fig. 153 Exploded view of the piston and rod assembly—note positions of ring end gaps on piston—4.2L engine

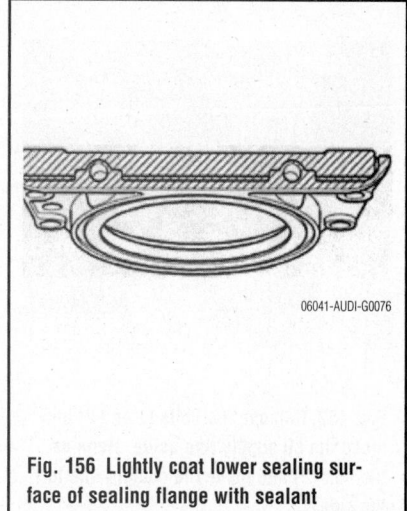

06041-AUDI-G0076

Fig. 156 Lightly coat lower sealing surface of sealing flange with sealant

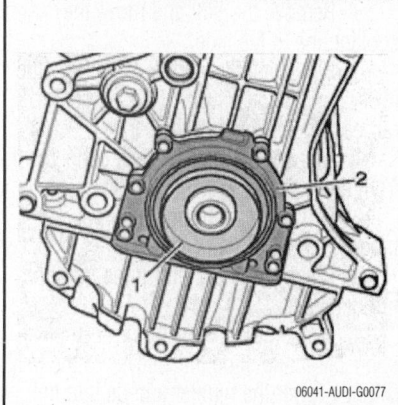

06041-AUDI-G0077

Fig. 157 Push the sealing flange together with the guide sleeve, which is included with replacement part onto crankshaft—A3

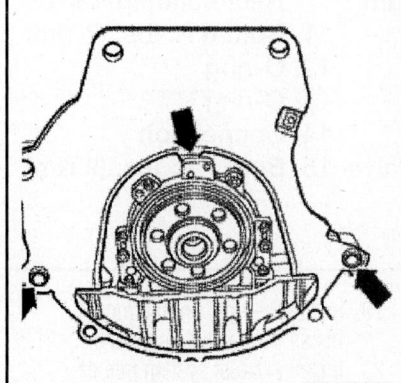

06041-AUDI-G0073

Fig. 154 Disconnect the intermediate plate at sealing flange and at the alignment sleeve

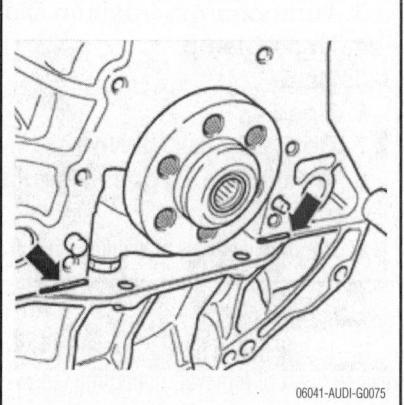

06041-AUDI-G0075

Fig. 155 Apply a thin bead of sealant to edge between cylinder block and oil pan

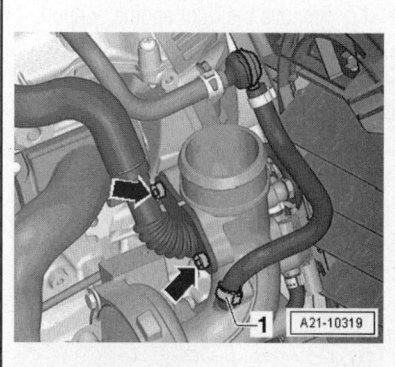

A21-10319

Fig. 158 Remove the crankcase housing ventilation from the turbocharger. Remove the hose (1).

4. Remove the connector from the MAF sensor, remove the air guide tube and remove the upper part of the air cleaner housing.

5. Disconnect the coolant hose.

6. Remove the heat shield above the exhaust manifold.

7. Remove the crankcase housing ventilation from the turbocharger. Remove the hose.

8. Remove the bolts and move the oil supply line aside.

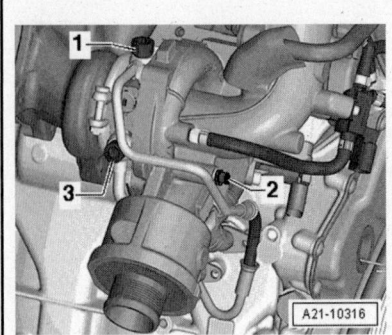

Fig. 159 Remove the bolts (1 and 2) and move the oil supply line aside. Remove the bolt (3) and move the coolant line to the side.

9. Remove the bolt and move the coolant line to the side.

10. Remove the air guide hose from the lower connection on the turbocharger (accessible from under the car).

11. Disconnect the electrical connectors from the turbocharger.

12. Remove the turbocharger support brace.

13. Remove the oil return line from the turbocharger.

14. Loosen the exhaust pipe-to-muffler connection and slide the sleeves to the rear. Slightly lower the muffler and tie it to the crossbrace.

15. Remove the catalytic converter-to-turbocharger flange nuts and push the catalytic converter rearward.

16. Remove the right engine mount (be sure engine is properly supported).

17. Remove the right engine support.

18. Remove the exhaust manifold-to-block nuts, then remove the turbocharger and exhaust manifold assembly upward.

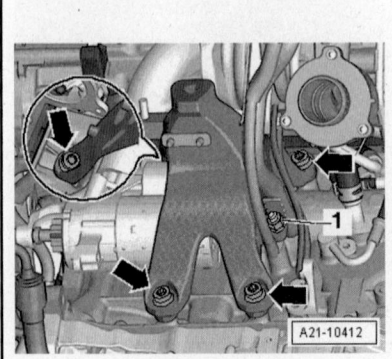

Fig. 160 Remove the right engine support.

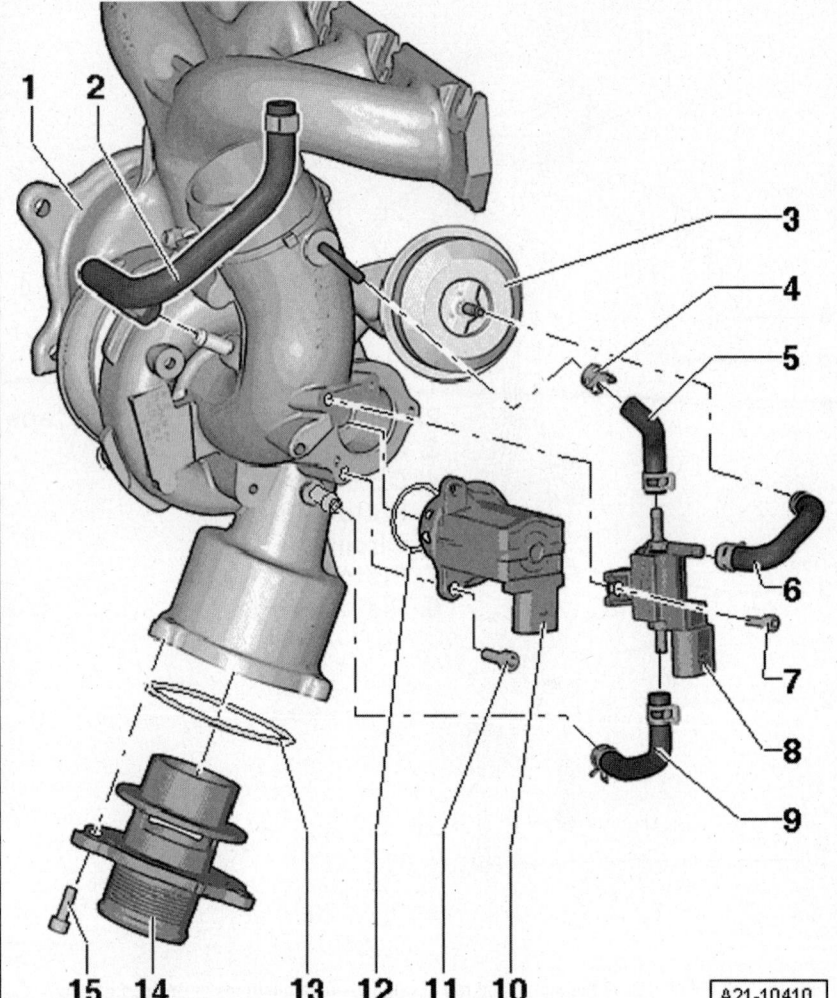

1. Turbocharger
2. Hose
3. Turbocharger Vacuum Diaphragm
4. Hose Clamp
5. Hose
6. Hose
7. Bolt: 2 ft. lbs. (3 Nm)
8. Wastegate Bypass Regulator Valve
9. Hose
10. Turbocharger Recirculating Valve
11. Bolt: 6 ft. lbs. (7 Nm)
12. O-ring
13. O-ring
14. Connection
15. Bolt: 7 ft. lbs. (9 Nm)

Fig. 161 Exploded view of the turbocharger assembly

To install:
19. Installation is performed in the reverse order of removal, noting the following:

    a. Replace the seals, O-rings and the self-locking nuts.

    b. Fill the turbocharger with engine oil at the oil supply line connection.

    c. Hose connections and charge air system hoses must be free of oil and grease before installing.

    d. Secure all hose connections with hose clamps appropriate for the model.

20. Install the right engine mount.

21. Install the catalytic converter.

22. Install exhaust system free of stress.

23. Install air filter housing.

24. Fill with coolant.

25. Check oil level.

➥After installing turbocharger, let engine idle for approximately 1 minute without increasing engine speed. This ensures adequate oil supply to the turbocharger.

ENGINE PERFORMANCE & EMISSION CONTROLS

COMPONENT LOCATIONS

See Figure 162.

➡ **For other engine applications and component locations, see individual headings in this section.**

CAMSHAFT POSITION (CMP) SENSOR

REMOVAL & INSTALLATION

3.0L Diesel Engine

See Figures 163 and 164.

1. Remove the engine cover.
2. Detach the electrical connector from the CMP sensor. Remove the CMP sensor.

To install:
3. Install the sensor(s) and tighten retaining bolt to 7 ft. lbs. (9 Nm).
4. Attach electrical connector.
5. Install the engine cover.

3.2L Engine

1. Disconnect electrical connector on the respective camshaft position sensor.
2. Remove lower air filter housing section to remove the camshaft position (CMP) sensor on cylinder bank 1. Removing lower section of air filter housing.
3. Remove coolant reservoir to remove the camshaft position (CMP) sensor 4 on cylinder bank 2.
4. Disconnect electrical connector to the engine coolant level warning switch on the bottom of the coolant reservoir and lay the reservoir aside with the three coolant hoses attached.

To install:
5. Replace O-ring and lubricate it with clean engine oil.
6. Press camshaft position sensor in carefully by hand.
7. Tighten camshaft position sensor and connect electrical connector.
8. Further installation is in reverse order.

3.6L Engines

See Figure 165.

1. Unplug the connector.
2. Remove the screw and then the sensor

✳✳ WARNING

Cover the hole to prevent dirt from getting into the engine.

To install:
3. Installation is the reverse of removal.
4. When installing, use a new seal as necessary.

CRANKSHAFT POSITION (CKP) SENSOR

LOCATION

See Figure 166.

REMOVAL & INSTALLATION

4.2L Engine

1. Before servicing the vehicle, refer to the precautions.
2. Unplug the connector.
3. Remove the screw and then the sensor

✳✳ WARNING

Cover the hole to prevent dirt from getting into the engine.

To install:
4. Installation is the reverse of removal.
5. When installing, use a new seal as necessary.

ELECTRONIC CONTROL MODULE (ECM)

LOCATION

See Figures 167 and 168.

REMOVAL & INSTALLATION

Q5

2.0L Engine

See Figure 169.

➡ **Some engine control modules are not equipped with a protective housing. The removal and installation of the protective housing depends on the engine and transmission combination.**

The Engine Control Module (ECM) 1 is bolted to a protective housing 5. To make removing the shear bolts for the retaining tabs more difficult, the threads are coated with locking compound.

➡ **To disconnect the connectors from the ECM (for example to connect the test box or to replace the ECM), the protective housing must be removed.**

➡ **If engine control module was replaced, use the diagnostic tool and select diagnostic object.**

1. Turn the ignition and remove the ignition key.
2. Remove the filler neck with the filler tube from the washer fluid reservoir and the opening in the body arrow.
3. Remove the bolts and the cover from the E-box.
4. Release the retainers and remove the engine control module.
5. Additional steps if there is a protective housing installed:

   a. The engine control module is secured in a protective housing with retaining tabs and shear bolts to make it harder to access it. The threads of the shear bolts (that are not screwed into the ECM) are coated with a locking compound. For this reason, the threads must be heated with the heat gun to remove both bolts.

   b. The threads of both shear bolts, that are screwed into the ECM, are not coated with a locking compound. The threads in the ECM housing must not be heated and do not require to be heated (unintentional heating of the ECM).

   c. Set the adjustment on the heat gun, with the temperature potentiometer set to maximum heat and the two-stage airflow switch set to level 3.

   d. When heating threads of locking mechanism, shear bolts and components of protective housing are also heated intensely. Do not burn yourself on this! Make sure that only the threads are heated as much as possible, and not any of the surrounding parts. Possibly cover these parts.

   e. Warm threads on connector side of shear bolts.

   f. Switch on heat gun and heat the bolt for approximately 20 to 30 seconds.

   g. Remove shear bolts with locking pliers.

➡ **The shear bolts installed in the engine control module do not need to be heated for removal. They can be removed without heat.**

   h. Separate the protective housing from the control module connectors.

   i. Disengage the connectors from the engine control module and disconnect the connector.

   j. Remove old engine control module and install the engine control module.

To install:
6. Install in reverse order of removal.

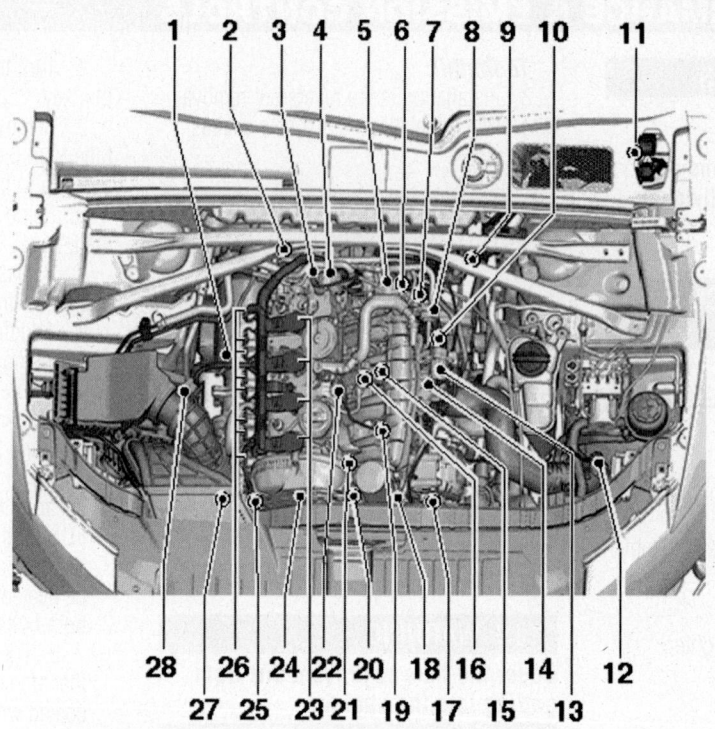

1. Heated Oxygen Sensor and Oxygen Sensor Heater
2. Oxygen Sensor after Three Way Catalytic Converter
   and Heater for Oxygen Sensor 1 after Catalytic Converter

A24-10629

3. Fuel Pressure Regulator Valve
4. High Pressure Pump
5. Channel Separating Plate for the Intake Manifold
   Flaps (vacuum diaphragm)
6. Intake Manifold Runner Control Valve
7. Engine Speed Sensor
8. EVAP Canister Purge Regulator Valve
9. 6-Pin Connectors
10. Electrical Harness Connectors
11. Engine Control Module
12. Charge Air Pressure Sensor
13. Throttle Valve Control Module, EPC Throttle Drive
14. Intake Air Temperature Sensor
15. Knock Sensor 1
16. Engine Coolant Temperature Sensor
17. Fuel Pressure Sensor
18. Oil Pressure Regulation Valve
19. Reduced Oil Pressure Switch
20. Oil Pressure Switch
21. Intake Manifold Runner Position Sensor
22. Camshaft Position Sensor
23. Ignition Coils with Power Output Stages
24. Camshaft Adjustment Valve
25. Turbocharger Recirculating Valve
26. Camshaft Adjuster Actuators
27. Wastegate Bypass Regulator Valve
28. Mass Air Flow Sensor
A. Data Link Connector (DLC)
B. Fuel Pump Control Module
C. Brake Light Switch and Brake Pedal Switch
D. Clutch Position Sensor
E. Throttle Position Sensor and Accelerator Pedal Position Sensor 2
F. Coolant Fan Control Module
G. Fuel Injector
H. After-Run Coolant Pump
I. Left Electro-Hydraulic Engine Mount Solenoid Valve

Fig. 162 Engine performance and emission control component locations—3.2L engine

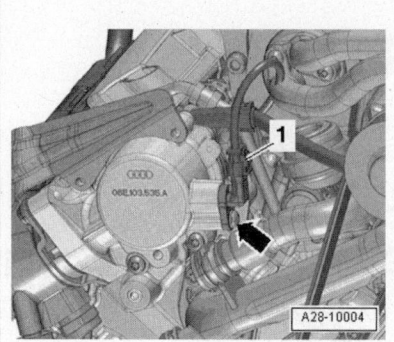

Fig. 163 Detach the electrical connector from the CMP sensor. Remove the CMP sensor—Cylinder bank 1

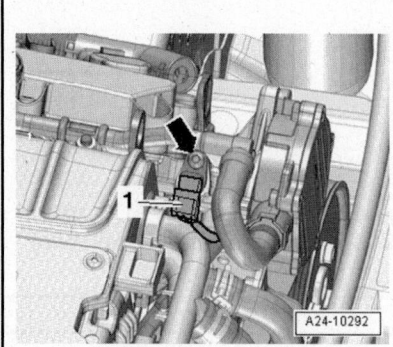

Fig. 164 Detach the electrical connector from the CMP sensor. Remove the CMP sensor—Cylinder bank 2

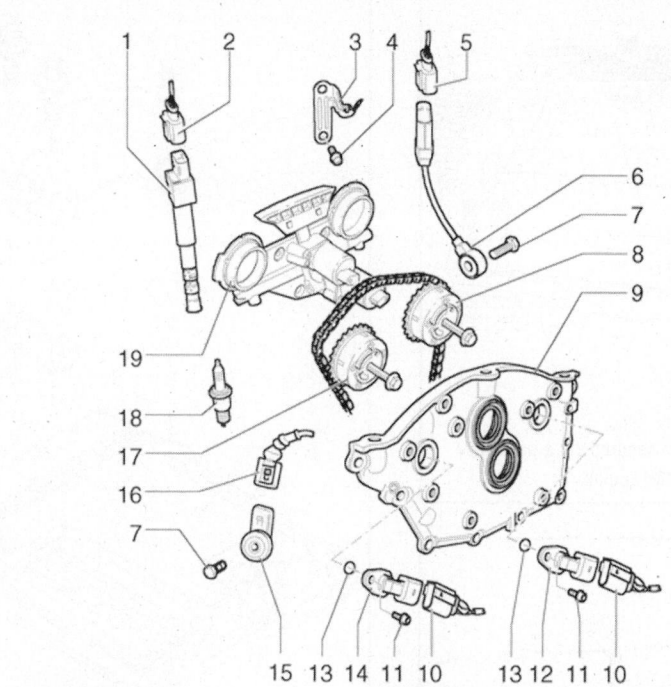

1. Ignition Coil
2. Connector
3. Bracket
4. Bolt
5. Connector
6. Knock Sensor 1
7. Bolt
8. Exhaust Camshaft Adjuster
9. Cover
10. Connector
11. Bolt
12. Camshaft Position (CMP) Sensor 2
13. Seal
14. Camshaft Position (CMP) Sensor 1
15. Knock Sensor 2
16. Connector
17. Intake Camshaft Adjuster
18. Spark Plug
19. Control Housing

22205_TOUA_G0157

Fig. 165 CMP sensor (1) and CMP sensor (2) locations—3.6L engine

a. Thereafter, the engine control module must be equipped with the protective housing.

b. Clean threaded holes for shear bolts of locking compound residue. Cleaning can be performed with a thread cutter (tap).

c. Always use new shear bolts.

d. Activate the engine control module in guided functions under replace engine control module. Use a vehicle diagnosis tester for this.

3.2L Engine

See Figures 170 and 171.

1. If Engine Control Module (ECM) was replaced, select diagnostic object *"Replacing Engine Control Module (ECM)"in "Guided Functions"; see:* Diagnostic Unit.

2. Turn ignition and remove ignition key.

3. Pry off caps on wiper arms using a screwdriver.

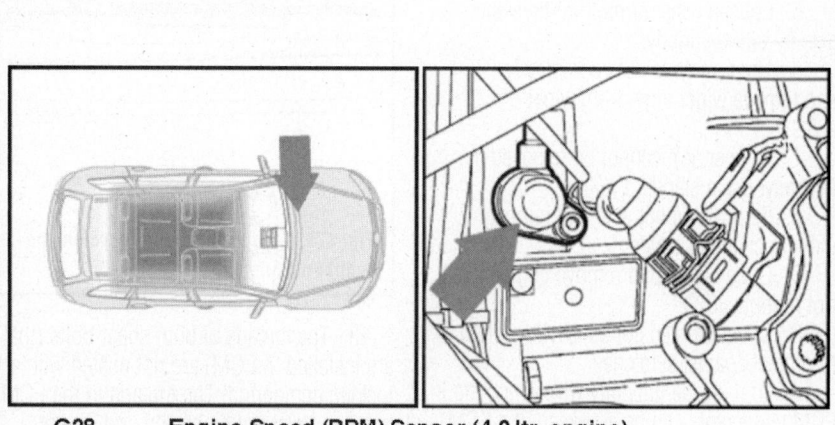

G28   Engine Speed (RPM) Sensor (4.2 ltr. engine)

• on transmission, left–side
• to rear of flange for engine

22205_TOUA_G0278

Fig. 166 CKP sensor location—4.2L engine

Fig. 167 ECM is secured via a protective housing (1)—3.6L engine

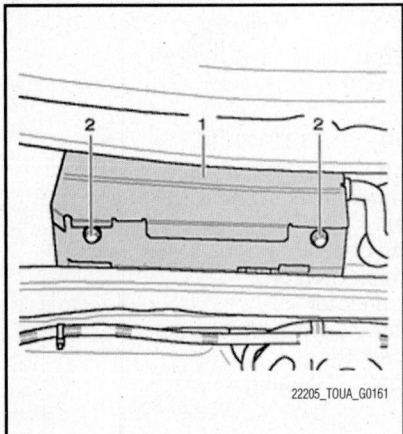

Fig. 168 ECM is secured via a protective housing—3.0L TDI engine and 4.2L engine

4. Loosen nuts by several turns.

5. Loosen wiper arms from the wiper axle by tilting slightly.

6. Then, remove nuts completely and remove wiper arms from wiper axles.

7. If wiper arm cannot be removed in this way, use a standard puller.

8. Remove rubber seal and remove plenum chamber cover.

9. Open clamp and remove engine control module J623.

10. Cover painted surfaces with a cloth to protect against scratches.

11. To increase difficulty with which the ECM connectors can be accessed, the ECM is secured in a metal housing with retaining tabs and shear bolts.

12. The threads of the shear bolts (that are not installed in ECM) are coated with a locking compound. For this reason, the threads must be heated with the heat gun to remove both bolts.

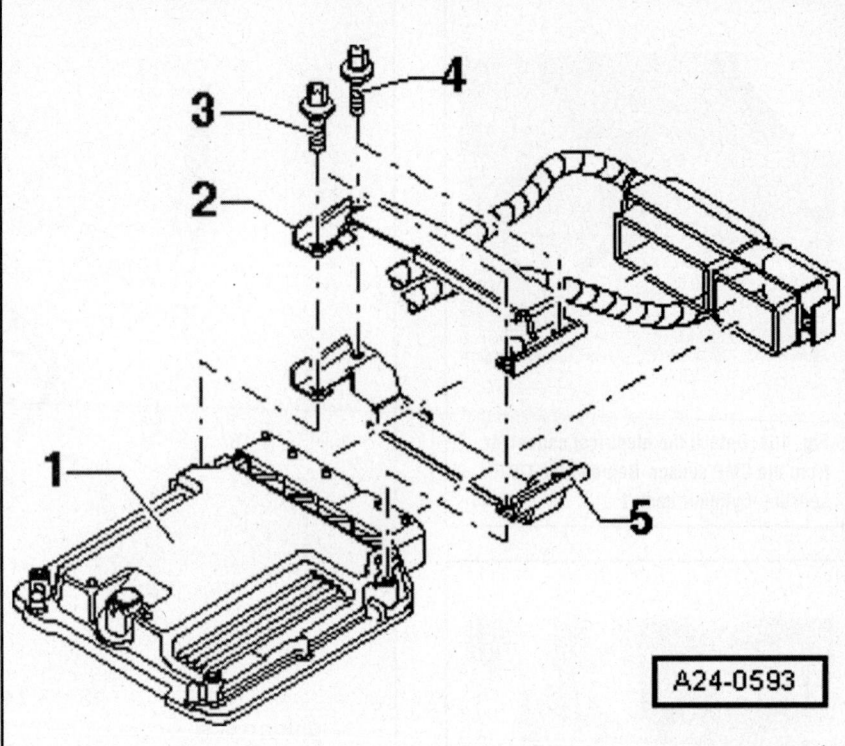

Fig. 169 The Engine Control Module (ECM) (1) is bolted to a protective housing (5). To make removing the shear bolts (3, 4) for the retaining tabs (2) more difficult, the threads are coated with locking compound.

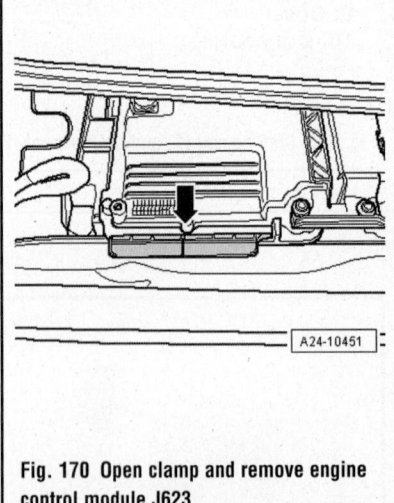

Fig. 170 Open clamp and remove engine control module J623

13. The threads of both shear bolts (that are installed in ECM) are not coated with a locking compound. The threads in the ECM housing must not be heated and do not require to be heated (unintentional heating of the ECM).

14. Set adjustment on the heat gun as shown in the illustration, with the temperature potentiometer **2** set to maximum heat and the two-stage air flow switch **3** set to level 3.

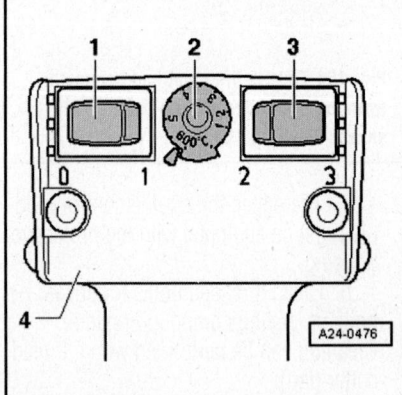

Fig. 171 Temperature potentiometer (2) set to maximum heat and the two-stage air flow switch (3) set to level 3

➡ **By heating the threads, the retaining tabs, shear bolts and parts of the metal housing become very hot. Do not burn yourself on this! Make sure that only the threads are heated as much as possible, and not any of the surrounding parts. Possibly cover these parts.**

15. Warm threads on connector side of shear bolts.

16. Switch on heat gun and heat bolt for approximately 20 to 30 seconds.

17. Remove shear bolts with suitable locking pliers.

18. Both shear bolts that are screwed into ECM do not require heating to be removed. They can be removed without heat.

19. Disconnect metal retainers from connectors.

20. Remove both retainer bolts from Engine Control Module (ECM) J623.

21. Disengage connector from Engine Control Module (ECM) J623 and remove connector.

22. Remove used Engine Control Module (ECM) J623 and connect new one.

23. Installation is in reverse order.

24. After that, the Engine Control Module (ECM) J623 must be equipped with the metal retainer.

25. Clean threaded holes for shear bolts of locking compound residue. Cleaning can be performed with a thread cutter (tap).

26. Always use new shear bolts.

27. Activate engine control module in *"Guided Functions"* operating mode under *"Replace engine control module"* on the vehicle diagnosis and service system VAS 5051B.

Q7

3.6L Engine

1. Switch off ignition.
2. Remove windshield wiper arms.
3. Remove plenum chamber cover.
4. Disengage connector from control module and then disconnect it.
5. Remove the old control unit and insert the new one.
6. Recode the control unit and adapt to electronic immobilizer and throttle valve control unit. If necessary, enable cruise control system "Guided Function", using scan tool.
7. Read fault memory of new engine control module and, if necessary, erase fault memory using scan tool.
8. Perform test drive.
9. Check control modules DTC memory again.

3.0L TDI Engine & 4.2L Engine

➡When the Motronic Engine Control Module (ECM) electrical harness connectors are disconnected, the adaptation values are erased and the DTC memory content remains intact.

1. Connect the scan tool.
2. Switch the ignition on.
3. Using the scan tool, select "Vehicle information".

4. Select "Calibration Identification" in vehicle information. The electronic control module identification number will be displayed, e.g.: 06A906032NA 4983.

5. Record the electronic control module identification number.

6. End diagnosis and switch the ignition off.

7. Switch the ignition on.

8. Actuate the touch-wipe function to allow the wipers to move to the end position.

➡The wiper arms will now move into the line of view on the windshield (service position).

9. Remove the wiper arms caps.

10. Loosen the wiper arm nuts several turns.

11. Loosen the wiper arms from the wiper axle by rocking slightly.

12. Remove the wiper arms nuts and the wiper arms from the wiper axles.

13. Remove the spray nozzles.

14. Press the spray nozzles, with the water lines attached, through the plenum chamber opening.

15. Remove the rubber seal and the plenum chamber cover.

➡The threads of the shear bolts have been coated with a locking compound and must be heated to be removed.

➡The Motronic Engine Control Module (ECM) is secured via a protective housing and shear bolts.

16. Using a heat gun set at its lowest setting, heat the shear bolt for approx. 20 to 25 seconds.

17. Remove the shear bolt with locking pliers. Discard the used shear bolts.

18. Repeat the previous steps for the second shear bolt.

19. Remove the protective housing from the Motronic Engine Control Module (ECM).

20. Remove the front electrical harness connector from the Motronic Engine Control Module (ECM).

21. Remove the Motronic Engine Control Module (ECM) from the retainer.

22. Remove the rear electrical harness connector from the Motronic Engine Control Module (ECM).

To install:

23. Installation is performed in reverse order of removal. Note the following:

a. The Motronic Engine Control Module (ECM) must be installed with the protective housing.

b. Use New shear bolts when installing the Motronic Engine Control Module (ECM).

c. Motronic Engine Control Module (ECM) reprogramming is required.

d. The new Engine Control Module (ECM) and immobilizer must be activated.

e. After repair work, the following work steps must be performed in the following sequence:

- Check the DTC memory.
- If necessary, erase the DTC memory.
- If the DTC memory was erased, generate readiness code.

ENGINE COOLANT TEMPERATURE (ECT) SENSOR

LOCATION

Q7

3.6L Engine

The Engine Coolant Temperature (ECT) sensor is located on the lower radiator outlet.

4.2L Engine

The Engine Coolant Temperature (ECT) sensor is located on the cooling line from the thermostat and is near the back side of the engine.

REMOVAL & INSTALLATION

Q5

2.0L Engine

See Figures 172 and 173.

1. Briefly open the coolant reservoir cap to reduce the residual pressure in the coolant system.

2. Remove the air guide tube.

3. Disconnect electrical connector from the throttle valve control module. Remove the throttle valve control module.

4. Remove the intake manifold support.

➡Different engine coolant temperature sensor may be installed, depending on the version.

Inserted Version

5. Disconnect the connector 1 from the engine coolant temperature sensor.

6. Lay a cloth below to catch escaping coolant.

7. Remove the clamp, to do so, press the latches and remove the engine coolant temperature sensor.

Fig. 172 Disconnect the connector 1 from the engine coolant temperature sensor. Lay a cloth below to catch escaping coolant. Remove the clamp, to do so, press the latches and remove the engine coolant temperature sensor—inserted version

Threaded Version

8. Disconnect the connector from the engine coolant temperature sensor.

9. Lay a cloth below to catch escaping coolant.

10. Remove the bolts and the sensor retaining plate. Remove the engine coolant temperature sensor.

To install:

11. Installation is performed in reverse order of removal, noting the following:

a. Replace O-rings.

b. To prevent coolant loss, install the engine coolant temperature sensor immediately.

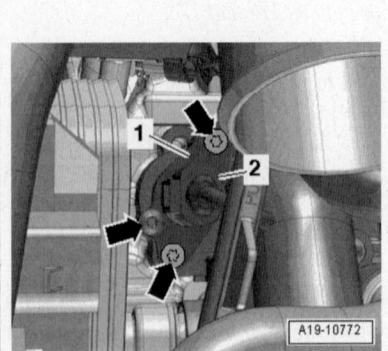

Fig. 173 Disconnect the connector from the engine coolant temperature sensor. Lay a cloth below to catch escaping coolant. Remove the bolts and the sensor retaining plate. Remove the engine coolant temperature sensor—threaded version

c. The hose connections as well as the air guide pipes and hoses must be free of oil and grease before installing.

d. In order to be able to securely mount the air guide hoses on their connectors, spray the screws on the previously used clamps with a rust remover.

12. Install the intake manifold support.

13. Install the throttle valve control module.

14. Check coolant level

3.2L Engine

See Figure 174.

1. Briefly open the coolant reservoir cap to reduce the residual pressure in the coolant system.

2. Remove front engine cover.

3. Disconnect electrical connector on the Engine Coolant Temperature (ECT) Sensor.

➡**Lay a cloth below to catch escaping coolant.**

4. Remove the retaining clip and Engine Coolant Temperature (ECT) Sensor.

5. Installation is in reverse order of removal, note the following:

a. Replace O-ring.

b. To prevent coolant loss, immediately insert new Engine Coolant Temperature (ECT) Sensor in support.

6. Check coolant level.

Q7

3.6L Engine

1. Before servicing the vehicle, refer to the precautions.

2. Drain the cooling system.

3. Disconnect electrical connector from the Engine Coolant Temperature (ECT) sensor.

Fig. 174 Electrical connector (1) and ECT sensor (2)

4. Unscrew and remove the ECT sensor from the radiator lower outlet connection.

To install:

5. Installation is the reverse of the removal procedure.

4.2L Engine

1. Before servicing the vehicle, refer to the precautions.

2. Remove rear engine cover.

3. Remove connector on Mass Air Flow (MAF) sensor on intake air assembly.

4. Release tension from spring clips and remove right air intake hose.

5. Disconnect breather line to Evaporative Emission (EVAP) canister purge regulator valve in engine compartment.

6. Remove connector from camshaft adjustment valve 1, then remove right crankcase housing ventilation, unclip hose from clamp and pull it forward in direction shown, with coolant line attached.

7. Remove connector from EVAP canister purge regulator valve, pull valve down from bracket, and lay it aside.

✳✳ WARNING

Hot steam may escape when opening expansion tank. Wear protective goggles and protective clothing to prevent damage to eyes and scalding. Cover cap with a rag and open carefully.

8. Open and seal reservoir to remove pressure from cooling system.

9. Remove bracket to obtain better access. Now, remove Engine Coolant Temperature (ECT) sensor.

To install:

10. Installation is in reverse order of removal, note the following:

a. Replace O-ring.

b. Secure all hose connections with hose clamps appropriate for the model.

c. Insert ECT sensor as quickly as possible so that coolant does not escape unnecessarily.

d. Ensure sensor retaining clip is seated securely.

e. Check coolant level.

HEATED OXYGEN (HO2S) SENSOR

LOCATION

See Figures 175 and 176.

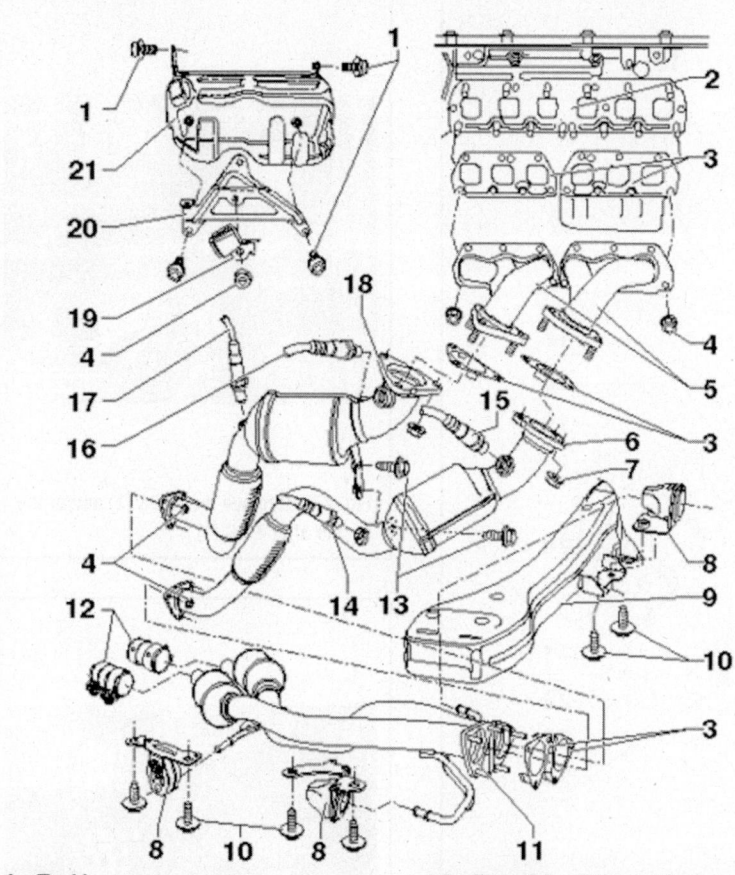

1. Bolt
2. Cylinder Head
3. Gasket
4. Nuts
5. Exhaust Manifold
6. Primary Catalytic Converter
7. Nuts
8. Suspended Mount
9. Transmission Bracket
10. Bolts
11. Catalytic Converters
12. Double Pipe Clamp
13. Bolts
14. Oxygen Sensor 1
15. Heated Oxygen Sensor 1
16. Heated Oxygen Sensor 2
17. Oxygen Sensor 2
18. Primary Catalytic Converter
19. Bracket
20. Intake Manifold Support
21. Heat Shield

22205_TOUA_G0165

Fig. 175 Heated Oxygen (HO2S) sensors and Oxygen Sensors location—3.6L engine

REMOVAL & INSTALLATION

Q5

2.0L Engine

See Figure 177.

1. Detach the HO2S electrical connector.
2. Remove the HO2S.
3. Installation is the reverse of the removal steps.
4. Tighten the sensor to 41 ft. lbs. (55 Nm).

3.2L Engine—Sensor 1

See Figures 178 and 179.

1. Pull rear engine cover off.
2. Free up fuel supply line and hose connection to the EVAP canister on the air filter housing and on the air guide tube.
3. Remove vacuum hose from air guide hose.
4. Remove air guide hose by loosening hose clamp and opening clips.
5. Remove air guide hose by loosening hose clamp and opening clips.
6. Remove lowers section of the air filter housing.
7. Disconnect electrical connector for the heated oxygen sensor (HO2S).

8. Remove the heated oxygen sensor (HO2S) G39 using a tool from the ring spanner set 3337.
9. Installation is in reverse order of removal.

3.2L Engine—Sensor 2

See Figures 180 and 181.

1. Pull rear engine cover off.
2. Remove coolant reservoir.
3. Disconnect electrical connector to engine coolant level warning switch F66 on the bottom of the coolant reservoir and lay the reservoir aside with the coolant hoses attached.
4. Disconnect the electrical connector for heated oxygen sensor (HO2S) 2 G108.
5. Remove heated oxygen sensor (HO2S) G108 1 using a tool from ring spanner set 3337.
6. Installation is in reverse order of removal.

Q7

1. Before servicing the vehicle, refer to the precautions.
2. Unplug the connector.
3. Remove the sensor and cover the hole to prevent dirt from getting into the engine.

To install:

4. Installation is the reverse of removal.

➡**Thread of new oxygen sensors is coated with hot bolt paste.**

✳✳ WARNING

When re-using the previous oxygen sensor, grease only the threads with hot bolt paste G 052 112; the paste must not get into slots of oxygen sensor body

5. Tighten to 41 ft. lbs. (55 Nm).

KNOCK SENSOR (KS)

LOCATION

See Figure 182.

REMOVAL & INSTALLATION

Q5

2.0L Engine

See Figure 183.

1. Detach the electrical connector (2) and remove the knock sensor.
2. Installation is the reverse of the removal procedure.

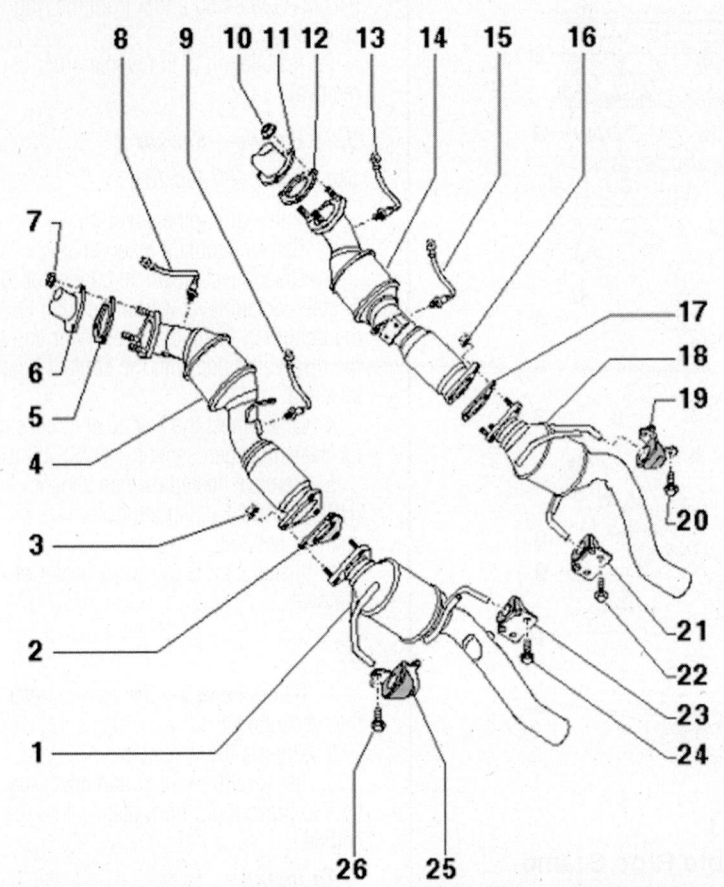

1. Main Catalytic Converter
2. Gasket
3. Bolt
4. Primary Catalytic Converter
5. Gasket
6. Exhaust Manifold
7. Bolt
8. Heated Oxygen Sensor 1
9. Oxygen Sensor 1
10. Bolt
11. Exhaust Manifold
12. Gasket
13. Heated Oxygen Sensor 2
14. Primary Catalytic Converter
15. Oxygen Sensor 2
16. Bolt
17. Gasket
18. Main Catalytic Converter
19. Suspended Mount
20. Bolt
21. Suspended Mount
22. Bolt
23. Suspended Mount
24. Bolt
25. Suspended Mount
26. Bolt

22205_TOUA_G0168

Fig. 176 Heated Oxygen (HO2S) sensors and Oxygen Sensors location—4.2L engine

3.2L Engine

See Figures 184 and 185.

⁑ WARNING

Fuel system is under high pressure! Before opening high pressure components of the fuel injection system, pressure must be relieved to residual pressure.

➡ Wrap a clean rag around the connection and relieve residual pressure by carefully loosening the connection.

1. Remove upper and lower intake manifold.

2. Remove lower right intake manifold section with the fuel rail.

3. Right cylinder: Remove fuel injector to reach the bolt for the knock sensor (KS).

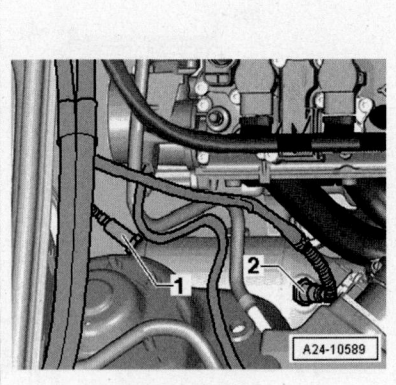

Fig. 177 Remove the HO2S (2) and/or the sensor after TWC (1)

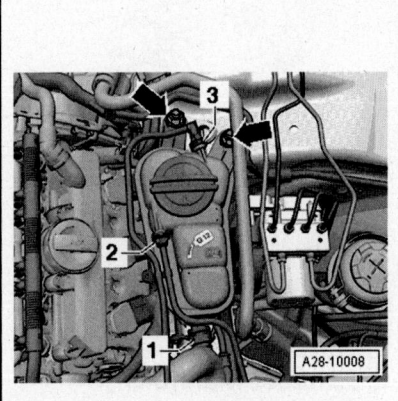

Fig. 178 Disconnect electrical connector for the heated oxygen sensor (HO2S) G39

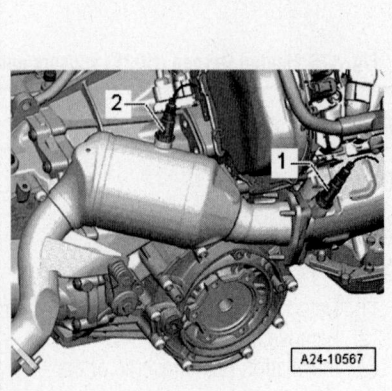

Fig. 179 Remove the heated oxygen sensor (HO2S) (1)

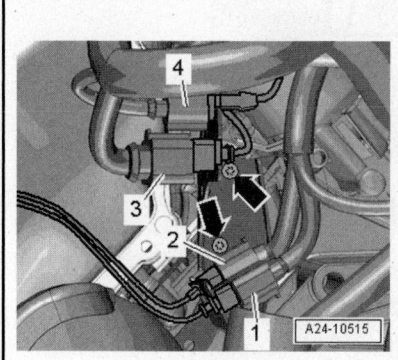

Fig. 180 Disconnect the electrical connector (2) for heated oxygen sensor (HO2S) 2 G108

Fig. 181 heated oxygen sensor (HO2S) (2) G108 1 using a tool from ring spanner set 3337

4. Left cylinder:

To install:

5. Install removed knock sensor.

6. Tightening specifications affects function of Knock Sensor (KS).

7. To complete installation, reverse the removal procedure.

Q7

4.2L Engine

1. Before servicing the vehicle, refer to the precautions.

2. Remove intake manifold

3. Then, according to need, remove Knock Sensor (KS).

4. Remove the KS 3 or KS 4.

To install:

5. Attach the respective removed knock sensor in its installation location.

6. Install the intake manifold.

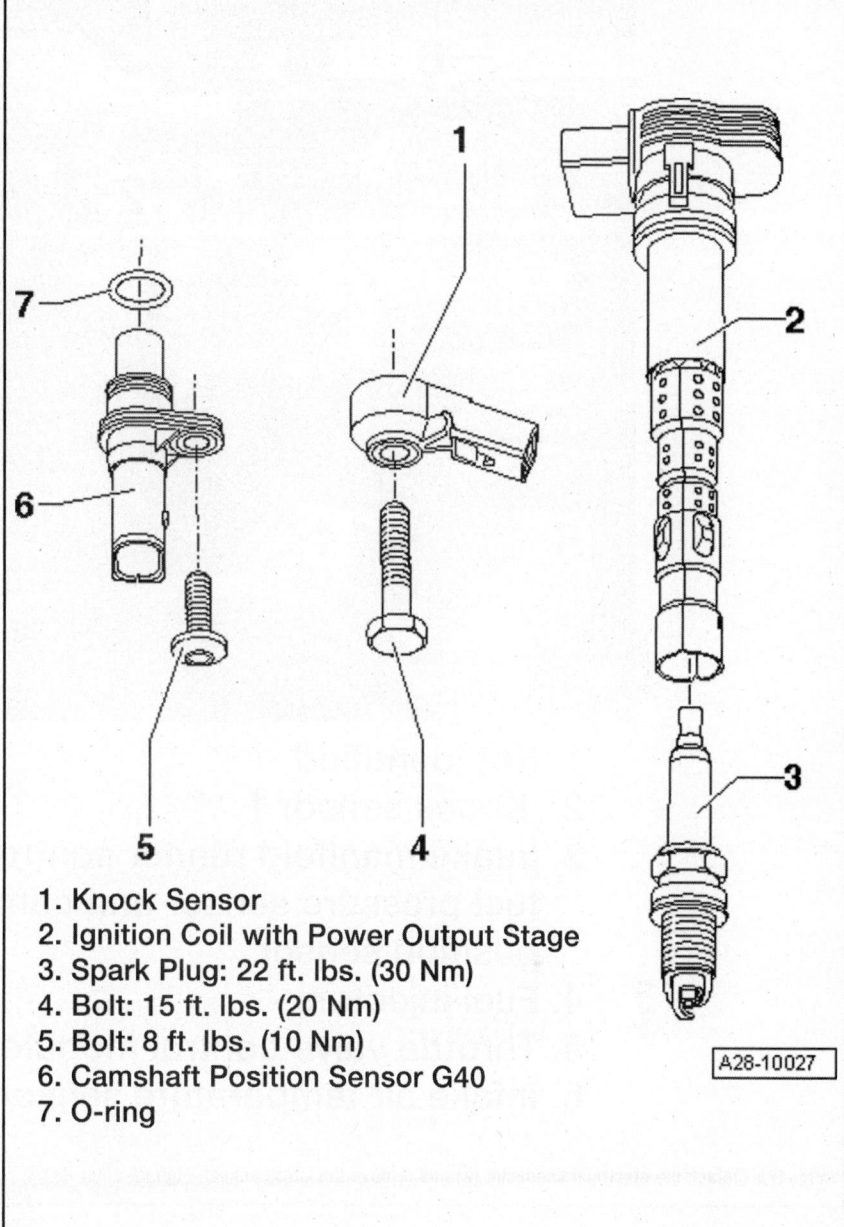

1. Knock Sensor
2. Ignition Coil with Power Output Stage
3. Spark Plug: 22 ft. lbs. (30 Nm)
4. Bolt: 15 ft. lbs. (20 Nm)
5. Bolt: 8 ft. lbs. (10 Nm)
6. Camshaft Position Sensor G40
7. O-ring

Fig. 182 Showing the knock sensor and related ignition components

✴✴ WARNING

Tightening specifications affects function of KS.

7. Tighten bolts/nuts to specification as follows:

- Knock sensor to cylinder block: 15 ft. lbs. (20 Nm)

MASS AIR FLOW (MAF) SENSOR

LOCATION

See Figures 186 and 187.

REMOVAL & INSTALLATION

Q5

2.0L Engine

See Figure 188.

1. Separate the electrical connector 1 from mass airflow sensor G70.

2. Open the hose clamp on air duct hose to turbocharger and pull it off at mass airflow sensor.

3. Remove both bolts from mass airflow sensor. Carefully pull the mass airflow sensor out of the guide from air filter housing.

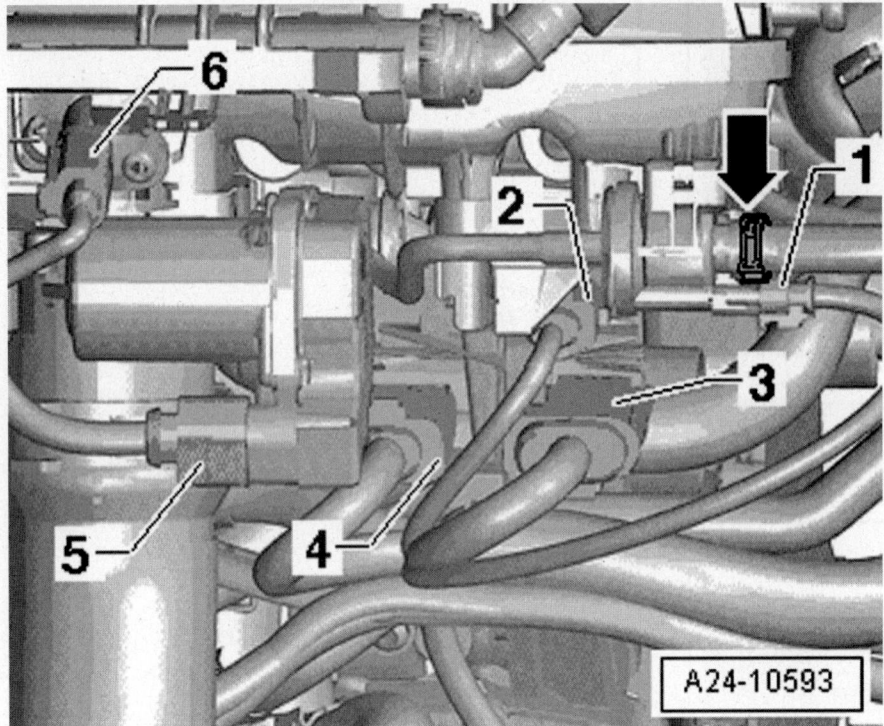

1. Not identified
2. Knock sensor 1
3. Intake manifold runner control valve, fuel pressure sensor and camshaft position sensor
4. Fuel injectors
5. Throttle valve control module
6. Intake air temperature sensor

Fig. 183 Detach the electrical connector (2) and remove the knock sensor—ignore other items

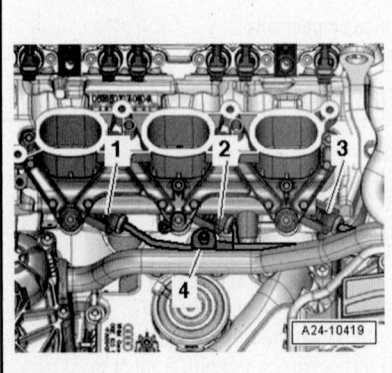

Fig. 184 Remove fuel injector (2) to reach the bolt for the knock sensor (KS) 1 (4)—Right cylinder

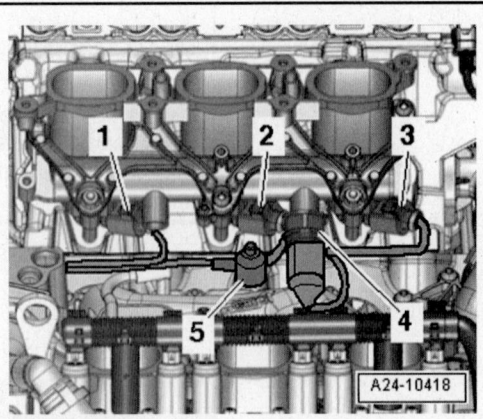

Fig. 185 Remove fuel injector (2) to reach the bolt for the knock sensor (KS) 1 (4)—Right cylinder

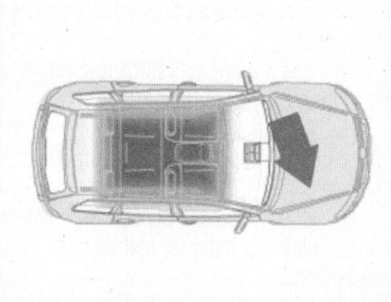

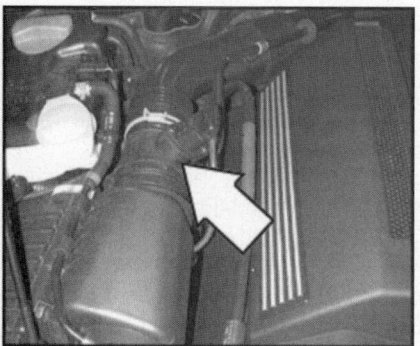

G70   Mass Air Flow (MAF) Sensor (4.2 liter engine)
G42 - Intake Air Temperature Sensor integrated

• on right side of engine compartment

22205_TOUA_G0287

Fig. 186 MAF sensor location—4.2L engine (right side)

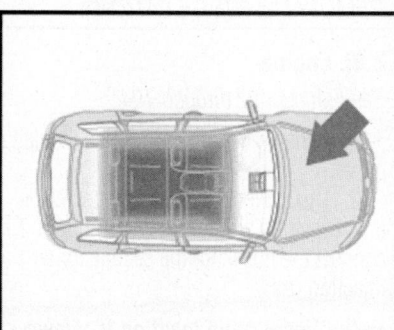

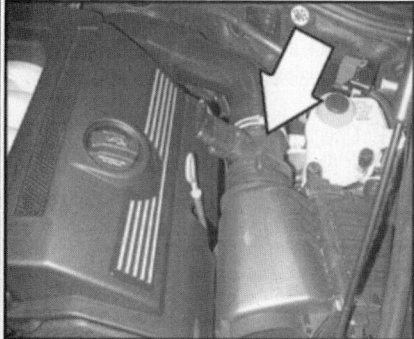

G246   Mass Air Flow (MAF) Sensor 2 (4.2 liter engine)

• left side of engine

22205_TOUA_G0289

Fig. 187 MAF sensor 2 location—4.2L engine (left side)

To install:

➡**For problem-free operation of the mass airflow sensor it is very important to observe the following notes and procedures.**

4. If the air filter is very dirty or soaked, dirt particles or moisture may

have contaminated the mass airflow sensor and may be causing false mass airflow values. This results in a reduction of power, since a lower injection quantity is calculated.

5. Always use an original air filter.

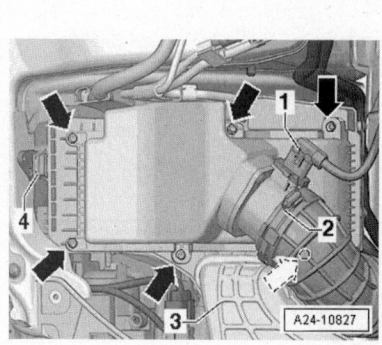

Fig. 191 Separate the electrical connector 1 from mass airflow sensor G70. Open the hose clamp on air duct hose to turbocharger and pull it off at mass airflow sensor. Remove both bolts from mass airflow sensor. Carefully pull the mass airflow sensor out of the guide from air filter housing.

6. Use a silicone-free lubricant for installing the air guide hose.

7. Check the mass airflow sensor and air duct hose (intake air side) for salt residue, dirt, and leaves.

8. Check the intake channels up to the air filter for dirt. If any contaminants are discovered, clean the air filter housing upper and lower section of salt residue, dirt and leaves. Wash or vacuum if necessary.

9. Further installation is performed in reverse order.

3.2L Engine

See Figures 189 and 190.

1. Disconnect the electrical connector from mass air flow (MAF) sensor.

2. Remove both bolts arrows of the air duct at the lock carrier.

3. Disconnect air duct from air filter housing.

4. Open hose clamp on air duct hose to turbocharger and pull it off at Mass Air Flow (MAF) Sensor G70.

5. Remove both bolts from Mass Air Flow (MAF) Sensor.

6. Carefully pull the Mass Air Flow (MAF) Sensor out of the guide from air filter housing.

To install:

7. For problem-free operation of the Mass Air flow (MAF) Sensor it is very important to observe the following notes and procedures.

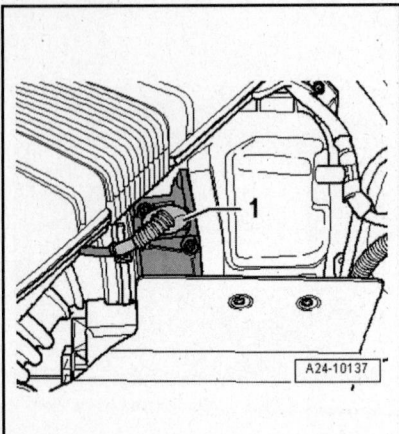

Fig. 189 Disconnect electrical connector (1) from mass air flow (MAF) sensor (2)

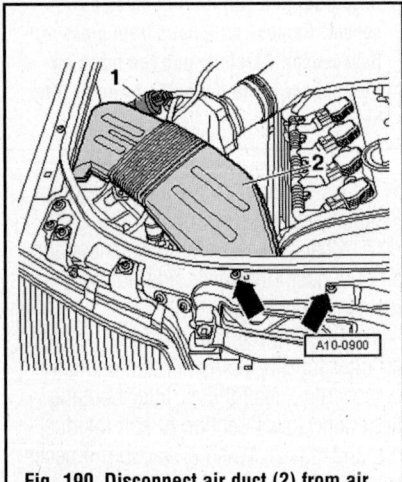

Fig. 190 Disconnect air duct (2) from air filter housing

8. If the air filter element is very dirty or soaked, dirt particles or moisture may have contaminated the Mass Air Flow (MAF) Sensor and may be causing false mass air flow values. This results in a reduction of power, since a lower injection quantity is calculated.

9. Always use an original equipment air filter element.

10. Use a lubricant (silicone-free) for installing the air duct hose.

11. Secure all those connections using hose clamps appropriate for the model type.

12. Check (MAF) Sensor and air duct hose (intake air side) for salt residue, dirt, and leaves.

13. Check intake duct up to the air filter element for dirt. If any contaminants are discovered, clean the air filter housing (upper and lower parts) of salt residue, dirt and leaves (if necessary, clean by washing or vacuuming).

14. Installation is in reverse order of removal.

Q7

3.6L Engine

1. Before servicing the vehicle, refer to the precautions.

2. Disconnect air intake hose from the air filter housing.

3. Disconnect the electrical connector on Mass Air Flow (MAF) Sensor.

4. Remove both bolts from the Mass Air Flow (MAF) Sensor and carefully remove the Mass Air Flow (MAF) Sensor from the air filter housing guide.

To install:

5. Installation is the reverse of removal.

6. If the air filter element is very dirty or soaked, dirt particles or moisture may have contaminated the Mass Air Flow (MAF) Sensor and may be causing false mass air flow values. This results in a reduction of power, since a lower injection quantity is calculated.

7. Always use an original equipment air filter element.

8. Use a lubricant (silicone-free) for installing the intake hose.

9. Secure all hose connections using hose clamps appropriate for the model type.

10. Check the MAF sensor and intake hose (intake air side) for salt residue, dirt, and leaves.

11. Check the intake ducting up to the air filter element for dirt. If any contaminants are discovered, clean the air filter housing (upper and lower parts) of salt residue, dirt and leaves (if necessary, clean by washing or vacuuming).

4.2L Engine

1. Before servicing the vehicle, refer to the precautions.

2. Disconnect air intake hose from the air filter housing.

3. Disconnect the electrical connector on Mass Air Flow (MAF) Sensor.

4. Remove both bolts from the Mass Air Flow (MAF) Sensor and carefully remove the Mass Air Flow (MAF) Sensor from the air filter housing guide.

To install:

5. Installation is the reverse of removal.

6. If the air filter element is very dirty or soaked, dirt particles or moisture may have contaminated the Mass Air Flow (MAF) Sensor and may be causing false mass air flow values. This results in a reduction of power, since a lower injection quantity is calculated.

7. Always use an original equipment air filter element.

8. Use a lubricant (silicone-free) for installing the intake hose.

9. Secure all hose connections using hose clamps appropriate for the model type.

10. Check the MAF sensor and intake hose (intake air side) for salt residue, dirt, and leaves.

11. Check the intake ducting up to the air filter element for dirt. If any contaminants are discovered, clean the air filter housing (upper and lower parts) of salt residue, dirt and leaves (if necessary, clean by washing or vacuuming).

12. Tighten clamps/screws to 80 inch lbs. (9 Nm).

SECONDARY AIR INJECTION (AIR) SYSTEM PUMP

LOCATION
See Figure 191.

REMOVAL & INSTALLATION

2.0L Engine
See Figures 192 through 194.

1. Remove the undercar noise insulation panel.

2. Disconnect electrical connector on the secondary air injection (AIR) pump. Disconnect the hoses for the secondary air injection (AIR).

➡**The installation location is shown with the wheel housing lining removed.**

3. Open hook with a screwdriver. Remove air grille from bumper cover. Remove bolts and remove bumper cover noise insulation toward the rear.

4. Remove bolts and remove secondary air pump.

➡**The installed location is shown with the bumper cover removed.**

To install:

5. Installation is in reverse order of removal, note the following:

  a. Replace O-rings.

  b. Install bumper cover insulation.

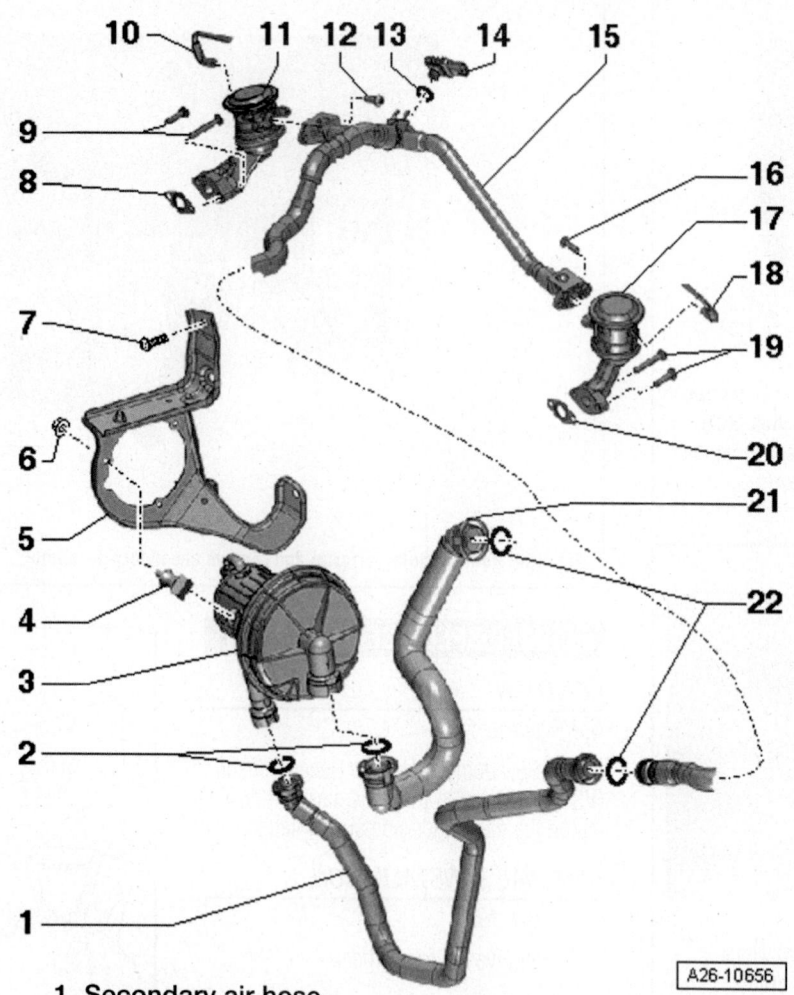

1. Secondary air hose
2. O-rings
3. Secondary Air Injection (AIR) Pump Motor V101
4. Bonded rubber bushing
5. Bracket
6. Nut: 7 ft. lbs. (9 Nm)
7. Bolt: 7 ft. lbs. (9 Nm)
8. Gasket
9. Bolts: 7 ft. lbs. (9 Nm)
10. Vacuum hose
11. Right secondary air injection (AIR) combination valve
12. Bolt: 7 ft. lbs. (9 Nm)
13. O-ring
14. Secondary Air Injection Sensor 1 G609
15. Secondary Air Injection (AIR) pipe
16. Bolt: 7 ft. lbs. (9 Nm)
17. Left secondary air injection (AIR) combination valve
18. Vacuum hose
19. Bolts: 7 ft. lbs. (9 Nm)
20. Gasket
21. Secondary air hose
22. O-rings

Fig. 191 Exploded view of the AIR pump and related system components—2.0L engine

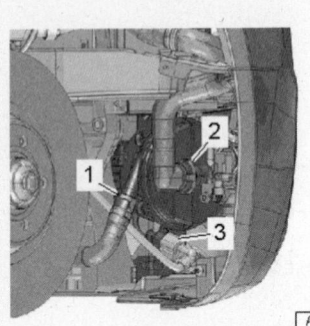

Fig. 192 Disconnect electrical connector (3) on the secondary air injection (AIR) pump. Disconnect hoses (1 and 2) for the secondary air injection (AIR).

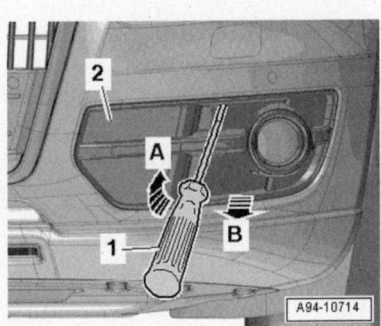

Fig. 193 Open hook (arrow A) with a screwdriver (1). Remove air grille (2) from bumper cover (arrow B). Remove the bolts and remove bumper cover noise insulation toward the rear.

c. Install noise insulation.

THROTTLE POSITION SENSOR (TPS)

LOCATION

TPS is located above the accelerator pedal.

REMOVAL & INSTALLATION

The throttle position sensor is an integral part of the throttle body and is not serviced separately.

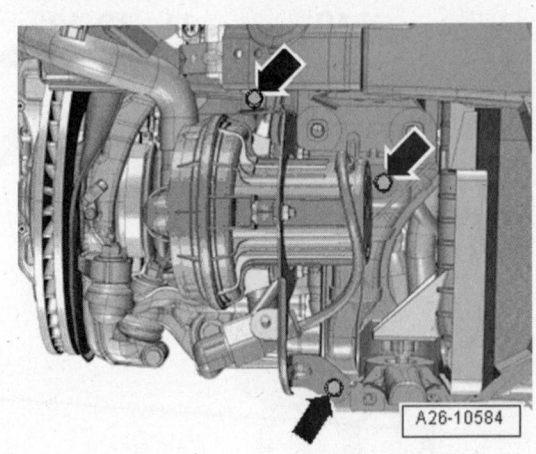

Fig. 194 Remove bolts (arrows) and remove secondary air pump.

VEHICLE SPEED SENSOR (VSS)

LOCATION

See Figure 195.

The Speedometer Vehicle Speed Sensor (VSS) is located in the transmission housing on the passenger side output flange.

REMOVAL & INSTALLATION

See Figure 196.

1. Remove left front wheel.

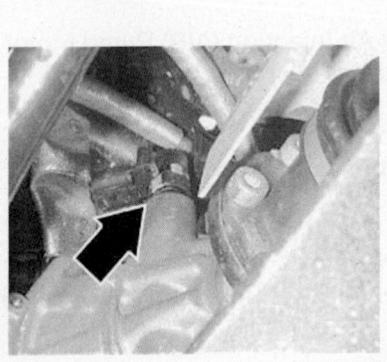

Fig. 195 Speedometer Vehicle Speed Sensor location for all engines

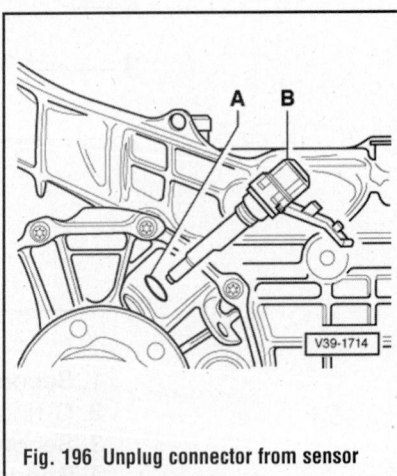

Fig. 196 Unplug connector from sensor (B), Replace O-ring "A"

2. Remove splash plate above left drive axle if installed.

3. Unplug connector from sensor.

4. Press retaining clip down, turn sensor sideways and pull out upward.

To install:

5. Replace O-ring.

6. Handle sender carefully. If it is damaged it is possible that the speedometer will not indicate exactly.

7. Reverse remaining removal procedure to complete the installation.

FUEL SYSTEMS

GASOLINE FUEL INJECTION SYSTEM

FUEL SYSTEM SERVICE PRECAUTIONS

Safety is the most important factor when performing not only fuel system maintenance but any type of maintenance. Failure to conduct maintenance and repairs in a safe manner may result in serious personal injury or death. Maintenance and testing of the vehicle's fuel system components can be accomplished safely and effectively by adhering to the following rules and guidelines.

• To avoid the possibility of fire and personal injury, always disconnect the negative battery cable unless the repair or test procedure requires that battery voltage be applied.

• Always relieve the fuel system pressure prior to disconnecting any fuel system component (injector, fuel rail, pressure regulator, etc.), fitting or fuel line connection. Exercise extreme caution whenever relieving fuel system pressure to avoid exposing skin, face and eyes to fuel spray. Please be advised that fuel under pressure may penetrate the skin or any part of the body that it contacts.

• Always place a shop towel or cloth around the fitting or connection prior to loosening to absorb any excess fuel due to spillage. Ensure that all fuel spillage (should it occur) is quickly removed from engine surfaces. Ensure that all fuel soaked cloths or towels are deposited into a suitable waste container.

• Always keep a dry chemical (Class B) fire extinguisher near the work area.

• Do not allow fuel spray or fuel vapors to come into contact with a spark or open flame.

• Always use a back-up wrench when loosening and tightening fuel line connection fittings. This will prevent unnecessary stress and torsion to fuel line piping.

• Always replace worn fuel fitting O-rings with new Do not substitute fuel hose or equivalent where fuel pipe is installed.

Before servicing the vehicle, make sure to also refer to the precautions in the beginning of this section as well.

RELIEVING FUEL SYSTEM PRESSURE

1. Before servicing the vehicle, refer to the precautions.

2. Remove electrical connector from fuel pressure regulator valve.

3. Allow engine to idle approximately 10 seconds.

➡**When the fuel pressure regulator valve N276 electrical connector is disconnected during idle, pressure in high pressure area decreases to approximately 87 psi (6 bar).**

4. After high pressure has been released, high pressure system must be opened immediately. Otherwise, the pressure increases again due to the warming of the fuel.

5. Switch off ignition.

> ⁑ **CAUTION**
>
> **Fuel lines are pressurized! Wear protective goggles and protective clothing to prevent injuries and contact with skin. Before opening the high pressure system, place a cloth around the connection.**

6. Place a clean cloth around the connection point and carefully open to release the residual pressure of approximately 87 psi (6 bar). Escaping fuel must be absorbed.

7. To conclude work, check DTC memory of Engine Control Module (ECM), erase all DTC entries which may have occurred from removing the connector.

Q5

➡**The fuel injection system is divided into a high pressure section (maximum approximately 150 bar) and a low pressure system (approximately 7 bar).**

➡ **Before opening high pressure parts, e.g. removing high pressure pump, fuel rail, fuel injectors, fuel lines or fuel pressure sensor, fuel pressure in high pressure area must be reduced to a residual pressure of approximately 7 bar. The procedure for this is as follows.**

1. Connect the vehicle diagnosis, testing and information system VAS 5051B or an ODBII scanner or equivalent.

2. Start engine and run at idle speed.

3. Select "engine electronics" in OBD.

4. Then select "Measured values read out.

5. Select measured value block 140.

6. With engine running in idle, the fuel pressure will be displayed in display field 3. Specified value: between 35 and 45 bar.

7. Pry off left cover on instrument panel using special hook 3370.

8. With engine at idle, pull fuse SC 27 in the fuse holder in driver's side instrument panel from fuel pump control module J538.

9. Check fuel pressure on tester. The fuel pressure decreases rapidly because the mechanical high pressure pump is no longer supplied with fuel from transfer fuel pump G6.

10. Switch ignition off as soon as fuel pressure drops to approximately 8 bar. The fuel pressure must not drop below 6 bar, because otherwise the engine will shut off (risk of catalytic converter damage).

➡**The fuel lines will continue to be filled with fuel, but will no longer be under high pressure. To open fuel system, wear protective eyewear and clothing to prevent injuries and contact with skin. Before opening the high pressure system, place a cloth around the connection.**

11. After reducing fuel pressure, place a clean cloth around the connection and open the high pressure system immediately. Escaping fuel must be absorbed.

12. Perform the following steps are completing all work:

a. Install fuses.

b. In *"Guided Functions"* operating mode, generate readiness code for the engine control module see: Diagnostic Unit.

Q7

4.2L Engine

1. Before servicing the vehicle, refer to the precautions.

2. Disconnect connector from fuel metering valve on right high pressure pump. Then, disconnect connector from fuel metering valve 2 on left high pressure pump.

3. Allow engine to idle approximately 10 seconds.

➡**If the fuel metering valve electrical connectors are disconnected at idle, the pressure in the high pressure area drops to approximately 87 psi (6 bar).**

4. After high pressure has been released, high pressure system must be opened immediately. Otherwise, the pressure increases again due to the warming of the fuel.

5. Switch off ignition.

6. Place a clean cloth around connection point and carefully open to release the residual pressure of approximately 87 psi (6 bar). Escaping fuel must be absorbed.

7. To conclude work, check DTC memory of Engine Control Module (ECM), erase all DTC entries which may have occurred from removing the connector.

FUEL FILTER

REMOVAL & INSTALLATION

Q5

See Figures 197 and 198.

➡Before opening the fuel system, lay a clean cloth around the connection point and carefully loosen it, which lowers the pressure.

1. Remove fuel delivery unit.
2. Disconnect ground connection on the fuel pressure regulator retaining plate.
3. Remove fuel line by pressing the release button.
4. Disconnect the electrical connector 6 for the fuel level sensor.
5. Disconnect fuel pump electrical connector at the fuel pump.
6. Remove locking flange 4 with fuel filter upward out of the fuel delivery unit 3.
7. Release a total of 3 retaining tabs 5 by sliding 3 release bars 7 (with the fuel filter parts set) arrow.
8. Pull the fuel filter 2 down and out of the locking flange.
9. Installation is in reverse order of removal, noting the following:

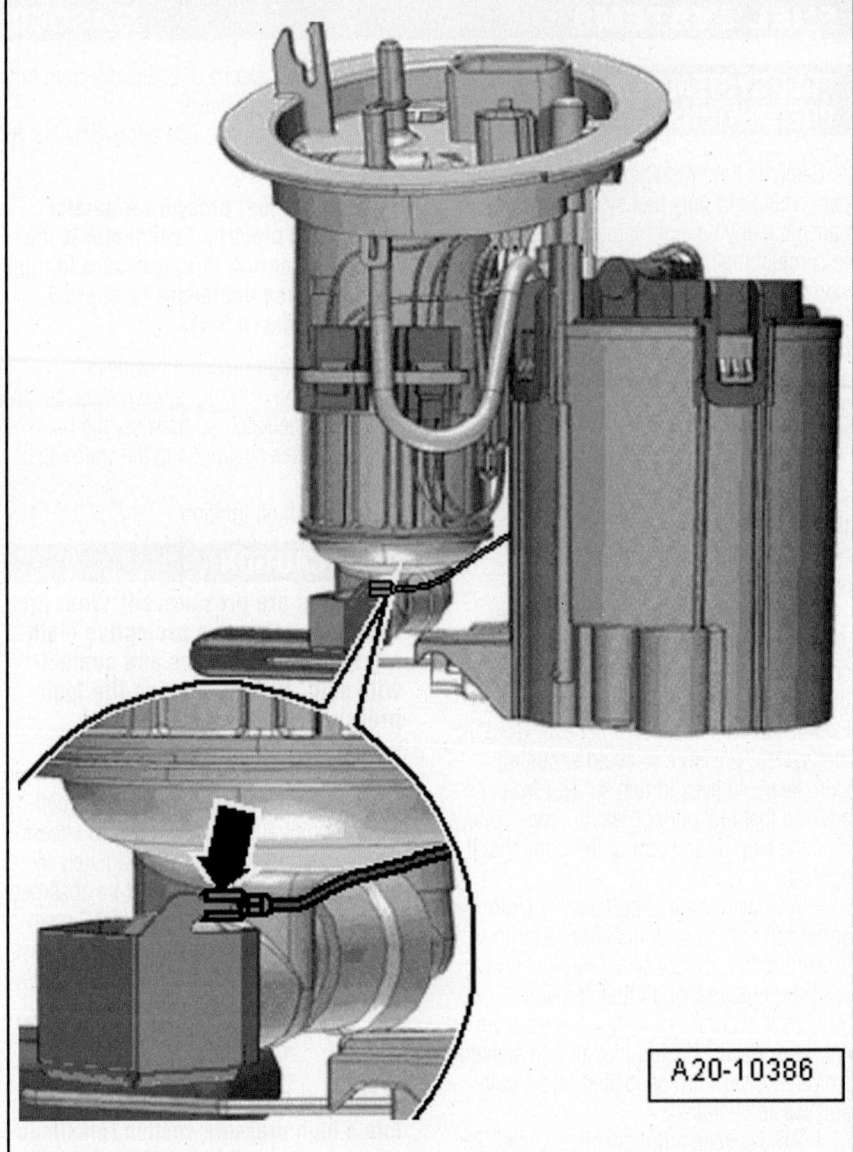

Fig. 197 Disconnect ground connection (arrow) on the fuel pressure regulator retaining plate

a. Replace the O-ring.
b. Insert the fuel filter into the guides on the locking flange and press it in until it engages.
c. The fuel filter can only be inserted in one position.

Q7

3.6L & 4.2L Engines

Fuel filter is located in left fuel tank opening, when viewed in direction of travel.

1. Before beginning work, read the "Fuel System Service Precautions" in this section.
2. Locate and remove fuel system fuses from fuse panel.
3. Drain the fuel tank.
4. Remove rear seat bench.

5. Cut a circular opening in the carpet, at the pre-cut area, on the left side near the seat attaching bracket (feel through carpet to determine location of access cover).
6. Remove bolts for seat mounting bracket and press it up slightly. Loosen bolts for the fuel access cover and remove cover.
7. Remove vent line and connector from flange.

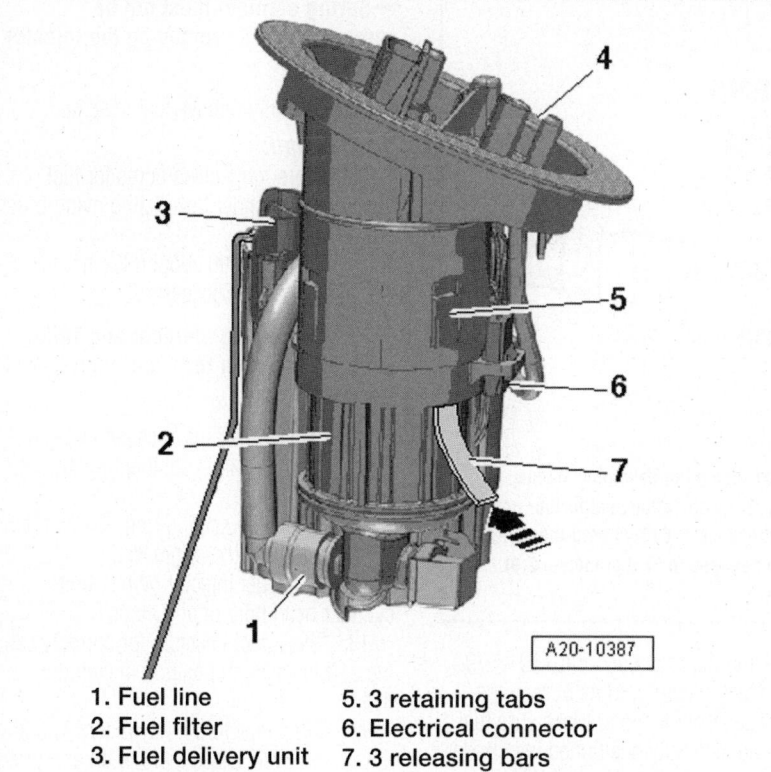

1. Fuel line
2. Fuel filter
3. Fuel delivery unit
4. Locking flange
5. 3 retaining tabs
6. Electrical connector
7. 3 releasing bars
   (with the fuel filter parts set) arrow

A20-10387

Fig. 198 Removing the fuel filter

the connection. Then release pressure by carefully pulling hose off connection.

➡ **When breather line is pulled off, hose coupling button often cannot be pressed in. In that case, use special assembly tool (T10118).**

8. Remove the locking ring from left flange using locking ring wrench (T10202).
9. Remove flange with fuel filter housing from fuel tank.
10. Remove the connector from fuel level sensor and fuel lines from fuel filter housing.

➡ **Release line connections by pressing button on hose coupling.**

11. Empty the fuel filter housing.
12. Mark installation position of filter cover, using colored felt tip marker pen.
13. Disconnect ground wire and unbolt filter cover from housing.

➡ **If filter insert is to be replaced, ensure that the ground connection contacts are not bent and have sufficient pretension.**

FUEL INJECTORS

REMOVAL & INSTALLATION

Q5

3.2L Engine
See Figures 199 through 203.

✳✳ CAUTION

Observe all applicable safety precautions when working around fuel. Whenever servicing the fuel system, always work in a well ventilated area. Do not allow fuel spray or vapors to come in contact with a spark or open flame. Keep a dry chemical fire extinguisher near the work area. Always keep fuel in a container specifically designed for fuel storage; also, always properly seal fuel containers to avoid the possibility of fire or explosion.

1. Before servicing the vehicle, refer to the precautions section.
2. Properly relieve the fuel system pressure.
3. Remove the intake manifold and fuel rail.

4. Carefully pull fuel injectors out of fuel rail.

➡ **With fuel injector installed, the radial adjustment is clipped into the support ring. To remove the fuel injector, the support ring must be separated from the fuel injector in order to install the puller T10133/2 into the indentation on the fuel injector.**

5. Cover open intake channels with a clean rag.
6. Disconnect the electrical harness connector at fuel injector that is to be removed.
7. Using a screwdriver, bend the retaining tabs of the radial adjustment aside and pull support ring off from fuel injector.
8. Screw together slide hammer T10133/3 with puller T10133/2. Then, guide puller T10133/2 into the groove on the fuel injector and carefully drive the fuel injector out. By doing this, it is possible that the radial adjustment will be damaged by breaking the retaining tabs. These must be replaced when re-installing the fuel injector.

➡ **The combustion chamber seal must always be replaced before re-installing the high-pressure fuel injector.**

9. Clean off the old Teflon seal, make sure not to damage the groove and rib in groove base.

➡ **If the groove is damaged, the fuel injector must be replaced.**

To install:
10. Before installing new Teflon seal, the seal groove and shaft of the fuel injector must be clean.

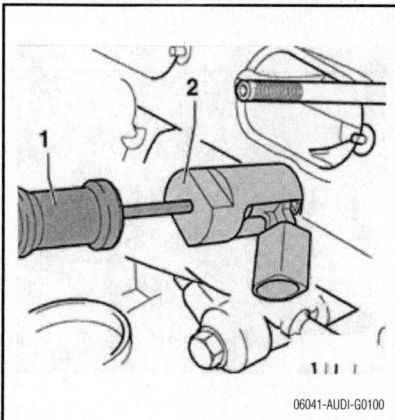

06041-AUDI-G0100

Fig. 199 Screw together slide hammer T10133/3 (1) with puller T10133/2 (2). Then, guide puller T10133/2 into the groove on the fuel injector and carefully drive the fuel injector out—2.0L engine

11. Place assembly cone T10133/5 with new Teflon seal onto fuel injector.

12. Using the assembly sleeve T10133/6, push Teflon seal further onto assembly cone T10133/5 until the Teflon seal is engaged in seal groove. Do not use any lubricants.

13. By pushing the Teflon seal onto the fuel injector, the Teflon seal is expanded. For this reason, the Teflon seal must be contracted again, once it has been pushed on as follows:

   a. Using calibration sleeve T10133/7, a 180 degree rotating motion and light pressure, push calibration sleeve T10133/7 over the fuel injector up to stop. Pull calibration sleeve T10133/7 off again, rotating it in the opposite direction.

   b. Using calibration sleeve T10133/8, 180 degree rotating motion and light pressure, push calibration sleeve T10133/8 over the fuel injector up to stop. Pull calibration sleeve T10133/8 off again, rotating it in the opposite direction.

14. Replace O-ring on the fuel injector and on spacer sleeve. Moisten O-ring with clean engine oil before installing.

➡ **The Teflon seal must not get oil on it.**

15. Clean the bores for the high-pressure fuel injectors in the cylinder head before installing the fuel injectors.

➡ **An open intake valve could possibly hinder the cleaning process. In this case, turn the engine further by hand using a socket wrench at the crankshaft.**

16. Equip the fuel injector again with support ring and clip the radial adjustment in at the support ring.

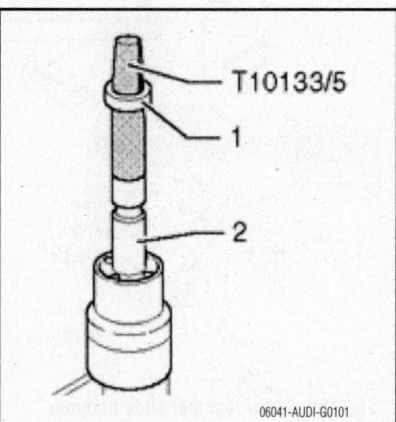

Fig. 200 Place assembly cone T10133/5 with new Teflon seal onto fuel injector— 2.0L engine

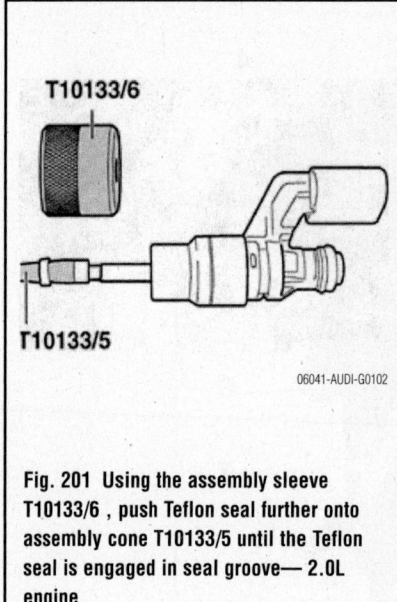

Fig. 201 Using the assembly sleeve T10133/6 , push Teflon seal further onto assembly cone T10133/5 until the Teflon seal is engaged in seal groove— 2.0L engine

17. Using the assembly drift T10133/9, press the fuel injector into its bore in the cylinder head until it stops. Make sure fuel injectors are correctly positioned in cylinder head.

18. Install the remaining components in the reverse order of removal.

Q7

3.6L Engine

1. Before servicing the vehicle, refer to the precautions.

2. Remove the intake manifold.

3. If fuel injectors for cylinders 1, 3 and 5 are to be removed, remove fuel rail.

4. Push the O-ring upward by hand and remove it from fuel injector.

5. Assemble a slide hammer/puller assembly (T10133/3 and T10133/15).

6. Guide the puller onto the groove on the fuel injector.

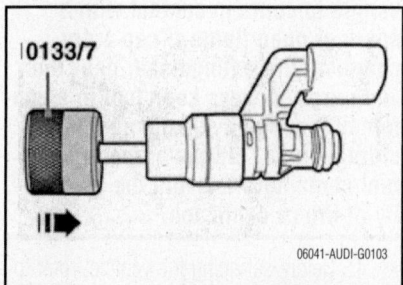

Fig. 202 Using calibration sleeve T10133/7, a 180 degree rotating motion and light pressure, push calibration sleeve T10133/7 over the fuel injector up to a stop— 2.0L engine

➡ **Spring element must not be removed prior to removing the injector valves.**

7. Carefully remove fuel injector.

To install:

8. Thoroughly clean bores for fuel injectors in cylinder head using nylon brush T10133/4.

9. Check plastic support washer for damage, replace if necessary.

➡ **Replace spring element and Teflon sealing ring each time fuel injector is removed.**

10. Replace O-rings between fuel injectors and fuel rail and coat them lightly with clean motor oil.

11. The Teflon sealing ring of fuel injector may not be oiled or greased.

12. Press fuel injector by hand into cylinder head bore until it stops.

13. Check fuel injectors for correct seating and installation position in cylinder head.

14. If fuel injectors for cylinders 1, 3 and 5 were removed, place fuel rail on and press evenly on to fuel injectors.

15. Tighten the fuel rail with new bolts, uniformly, to 22 ft. lbs. (30 Nm), plus an additional 90°.

16. Install the union nut for fuel supply line tightly to supply line of fuel rail. To do so, counter hold on fuel supply line using a wrench. Tighten to 16 ft. lbs. (22 Nm).

17. Install the intake manifold.

4.2L Engine

See Figure 204.

✲✲ CAUTION

Fuel system is under high pressure! Before opening high pressure components of the fuel injection system, pressure must be relieved to residual pressure. Wrap a clean rag around

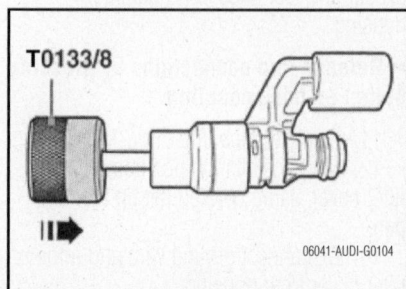

Fig. 203 Using calibration sleeve T10133/8 , 180 degree rotating motion and light pressure, push calibration sleeve T10133/8 over the fuel injector up to a stop— 2.0L engine

connection and relieve residual pressure by carefully loosening connection.

1. Remove the intake manifold.
2. Seal the intake channels in cylinder heads with clean cloths.
3. Disconnect the electrical harness connectors at fuel injectors.
4. Remove high pressure lines from connector on fuel rail. To do this, counter hold at hex head with and open-end wrench and loosen union nut.
5. Remove bolts "1", "2", "3", "4", "6"and "8"as shown.
6. Do not change bent shape of high pressure lines.
7. Remove fuel rail with fuel injectors.
8. If fuel injectors cannot be pulled out of cylinder head by hand, proceed as follows:
  a. Using a screwdriver, bend retaining tabs of radial adjustment aside and pull support ring from fuel injector.
  b. Remove O-ring from fuel injector.
  c. Attach slide wrench and adapter (T10133/3 and T10133/10) to injector.
  d. Guide puller adapter into groove on fuel injector and carefully drive fuel injector out.

➡**When setting the puller in place, the radial adjustment can be destroyed, because the retaining tabs break.**

9. Carefully remove old combustion chamber seal by cutting seal open with a knife or spreading seal open with a small screwdriver and pulling it forward and off.
10. Make sure that the groove of fuel injector does not become damaged. If groove is damage, fuel injector must be replaced.

To install:

➡**During installation, replace combustion chamber seal and O-ring.**

11. Replace the spacer ring if damaged.
12. Lightly moisten fuel injector O-rings with clean engine oil.
13. Re-insert the injector lines at same cylinder.
14. Clean bore in cylinder head with nylon cylinder brush T10133/4.
15. Clip the radial adjustment to support ring on injector.
16. When re-installing a fuel injector, use a clean cloth to clean combustion residue from groove for combustion chamber seal and shaft of fuel injector.
17. Place the assembly tool (cone

Fig. 204 Remove bolts "1", "2", "3", "4", "6" and "8"—4.2L engine

22205_TOUA_G0175

T10133/5), with new combustion chamber seal, on fuel injector.
18. Slide the combustion chamber seal as far possible onto installer assembly tool (cone T10133/5).
19. Slide the combustion chamber seal into groove.
20. When pushing combustion chamber seal onto the fuel injector, the seal spreads open. Therefore after pushing it on, it must be tightened again in 2 steps, as follows.
  a. Press a sleeve with a slight turning motion (approximately 180°) onto fuel injector until it stops.
  b. Pull the sizing sleeve (T10133/7) off again, turning it in opposite direction.
  c. Press sizing sleeve (T10133/8) with a slight turning motion (approximately 180°) onto fuel injector until it stops.
  d. Pull the sizing sleeve off again, turning it in opposite direction.
21. Moisten new O-ring with clean engine oil before installing.

✳✳ **CAUTION**

The combustion chamber seal must not be oiled.

22. Slide fuel injector into bore cylinder head as far as stop, using a proper assembly drift (T10133/9).

➡**The fuel injector must not be difficult to install. If necessary, wait as the combustion chamber seal continues to pull itself together.**

23. Make sure fuel injectors are correctly positioned in cylinder head.
24. The electrical connection of fuel injector must engage in intended recess of cylinder head.

25. Press fuel rail onto fuel injectors with uniform pressure.
26. Tighten the removed bolts diagonally in stages to 6 ft. lbs. (9 Nm).

➡**High pressure line connections must not show any signs of damage.**

✳✳ **CAUTION**

Do not change bent shape of high pressure lines.

27. Hand-tighten union nuts for high-pressure lines.
28. Make sure high-pressure lines are seated free of stress.
29. To tighten the union nut on the high pressure line, use a torque wrench (VAG 1331) with a socket insert (AF 14, open ring VAG 1331/8 or 1331/6).
30. Tighten the high pressure line nuts to 18 ft. lbs. (25 Nm).
31. Only install retaining tabs after high pressure lines have been tightened.
32. Install the intake manifold.
33. Fill with coolant, if necessary.

FUEL PUMP

REMOVAL & INSTALLATION

Q5

See Figures 205 through 209.

✳✳ **CAUTION**

Observe all applicable safety precautions when working around fuel. Whenever servicing the fuel system, always work in a well ventilated area. Do not allow fuel spray or vapors to come in contact with a spark or open flame. Keep a dry chemical fire extinguisher near the work area. Always keep fuel in a container specifically designed for fuel storage; also, always properly seal fuel containers to avoid the possibility of fire or explosion.

➡**To prevent large quantities of fuel from leaking from the fuel delivery unit when removing, the fuel tank may only be a maximum of 1/ 4 full.**

1. Properly relieve the fuel system pressure.
2. Empty the fuel tank if necessary.
3. Move passenger seat all the way forward if necessary.
4. Disconnect the battery.
5. Remove rear bench seat.
6. Remove the locking flange cover.

7. Disconnect electrical connector on the locking flange.

8. If necessary, disengage the electrical connector to the auxiliary heater metering pump at the locking flange and lay it aside.

➡ **To reduce pressure in fuel system, lay a clean cloth around the connector and carefully loosen connector.**

9. Disconnect fuel line at the locking flange by pressing the release button.

10. Disconnect fuel line to the auxiliary heater metering pump at the locking flange by pressing the release button.

11. Use a union nut tool T40068 A to remove the union nut.

➡ **When union nut is loosened, plastic catch on threaded ring breaks off. Ignore this.**

12. Remove locking flange with fuel filter from the fuel tank and tip it slightly to the left side of the vehicle.

13. Remove seal.

14. Pull locking flange with fuel filter away from the fuel delivery unit slightly.

15. At the same time, tilt the locking flange with fuel filter out of the fuel tank, being especially careful of the retaining plate with the ground connection and the fuel line.

➡ **Lay cloths below to catch the leaking fuel.**

16. Pull the locking flange with fuel filter away from the fuel delivery unit slightly again.

17. Tilt fuel delivery unit to the left side of the vehicle and pull it out of the fuel tank slightly.

➡ **When removing fuel delivery unit, be**

sure not to bend float arm on the fuel level sensor.

18. Guide fuel level sensor out of the fuel tank opening and remove the fuel delivery unit with suction line from the fuel tank.

To install:

19. Note the following:

   a. Replace the sealing ring and the union nut.

   b. When inserting the fuel delivery unit, do not bend the float arm on the fuel level sensor.

   c. Check the fuel lines for secure seating.

20. Make sure the ground wire is connected securely to the fuel pressure regulator retaining plate.

21. Tilt the suction line on the fuel delivery unit down.

22. First, guide the suction line into the fuel tank.

23. Then insert the float on the fuel level sensor into the fuel tank.

24. Pull the locking flange with fuel filter away from the fuel delivery unit slightly again.

25. Bend the fuel delivery unit to the left side of the vehicle and tilt it into the fuel tank while being careful of the fuel level sensor.

26. Pull the locking flange with the fuel filter away from the fuel delivery unit slightly.

27. At the same time, tilt the locking flange with fuel filter into the fuel tank, being especially careful of the retaining plate with the ground connection and the fuel line.

28. Stretch the new sealing ring over the locking flange and insert it in the groove on the fuel tank.

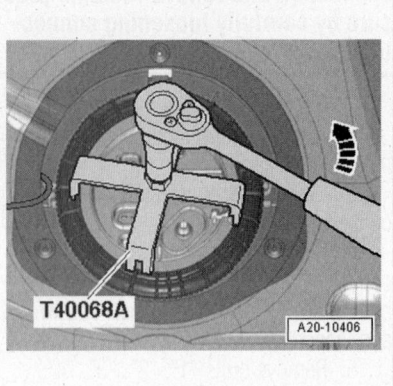

Fig. 207 Use a union nut tool T40068 A to remove the union nut

29. Place the union nut on your left arm and push the locking flange forcefully into installation position with your left hand.

30. The tab on locking flange must lie between tabs and on threaded ring.

31. Slide the union nut off your left arm using your right hand while your left hand keeps holding the locking flange down firmly.

32. Position union nut with your right hand so the double ridge on the ribs is over the plug on the locking flange (approximately *"10 o'clock"* position). This makes sure the union nut engages at the beginning of the threads immediately when tightening it.

33. Press locking flange down firmly with a screwdriver.

34. Turn the union nut approximately 480° with your right hand until the double ridge is in approximately *"2 o'clock position"* while keeping the locking flange pressed down firmly with your left hand.

➡ **There is a risk of the locking flange threaded connection leaking. Press the locking flange down firmly when tightening the union nut so it does not rotate too.**

35. Tighten union nut using a union nut tool T40068 A.

36. Verification: The double ridge must now be between *"7 and 8 o'clock"*.

37. Connect fuel lines.

38. Remaining installation is in reverse order of removal.

39. After installing fuel delivery unit, fill vehicle with at least 5 liters of fuel.

Q7

3.6L Engine

1. Before servicing the vehicle, refer to the precautions.

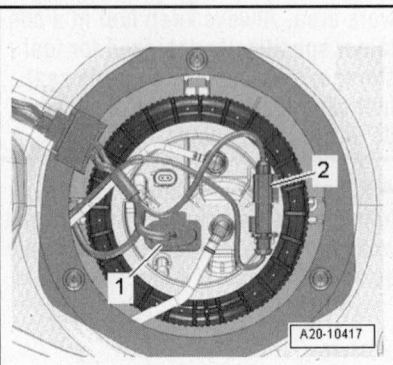

Fig. 205 Disconnect electrical connector (1) on the locking flange and/or the electrical connector (2) to the auxiliary heater metering pump

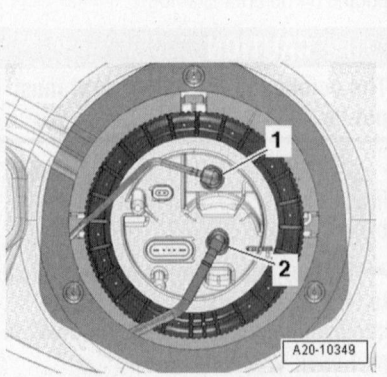

Fig. 206 Disconnect fuel line (2) and Disconnect fuel line (1) to the auxiliary heater metering pump

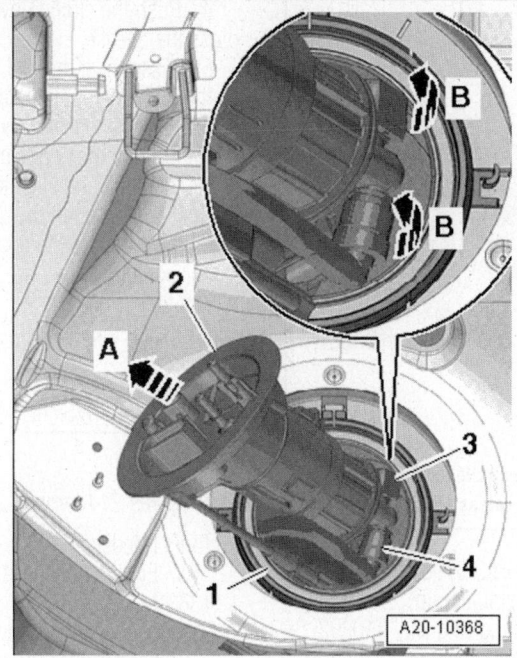

Fig. 208 Remove seal (1). Pull locking flange with fuel filter away from the fuel delivery unit slightly (arrow A). At the same time, tilt the locking flange with fuel filter out of the fuel tank (arrows B). retaining plate with the ground connection (3) and the fuel line (4).

✳✳ CAUTION

Follow safety measures for releasing fuel pressure in high pressure area. Fuel pipes are under pressure! Wear protective goggles and protective clothing to prevent injuries and contact with skin. Before loosening the fuel pipe, place a cloth around the connection point. Then release pressure by carefully loosening.

2. Before beginning work, read the "Fuel System Service Precautions" in this section.

3. Lay a cloth around threaded connection and loosen union nut from fuel supply hose. To do so, counter hold on fuel supply line using a wrench.

4. Remove connector and remove low pressure line and high pressure line. When doing this, counter hold on connection of high pressure pump using a wrench.

5. Disconnect connector, remove bolts, and remove high pressure pump from engine.

To install:

6. Check plunger, for damage; replace if necessary.

7. Insert oiled lifter with guide perpendicularly into cylinder head.

8. Rotate the engine at vibration damper slowly in direction of engine rota-tion. When doing this, press plunger in until it reaches the deepest point in cylinder head.

9. Replace the high pressure pump O-ring.

10. Install high pressure pump and evenly tighten bolts to 7 ft. lbs. (10 Nm).

➡**O-ring of high pressure pump must always be replaced.**

11. Before installing fuel lines, first tighten connection for fuel lines on high pressure pump.

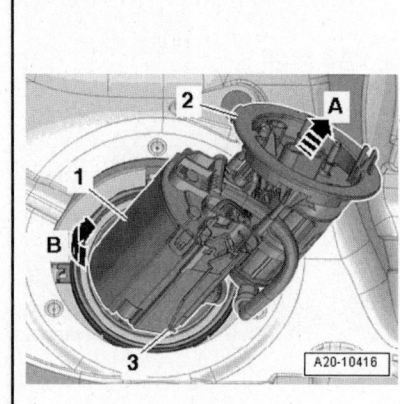

Fig. 209 fuel delivery unit (1), locking flange (2) and fuel level sensor (3)

- Connection for high pressure line: 30 ft. lbs. (40 Nm)
- Connection for low pressure line: 21 ft. lbs. (28 Nm)

4.2L Engine

1. Before servicing the vehicle, refer to the precautions.

2. Before opening high pressure components of the fuel injection system, pressure must be relieved to residual pressure.

3. With ignition switched off, disconnect battery ground cable.

4. Remove rear engine cover.

5. Disconnect electrical connector, loosen union nuts, and remove mounting bolts.

➡**Do not change bent shape of high pressure lines.**

6. Carefully remove high pressure pump.

7. Remove the roller tappet from cylinder head.

To install:

8. Installation is in reverse order of removal, note the following:

   a. Replace the O-ring.

   b. Insert the roller tappet in cylinder head.

   c. To set high pressure pump in place, lift high pressure lines only slightly.

   d. Insert high pressure pump in cylinder head and tighten.

➡**High pressure line connections must not show any signs of damage. Do not change bent shape of high pressure lines.**

   e. Hand-tighten the union nuts for high-pressure lines.

   f. Make sure high-pressure lines are seated free of stress.

   g. Tighten the union nuts on high pressure lines to 18 ft. lbs. (25 Nm).

   h. Reconnect the battery.

FUEL TANK

DRAINING

Emptying A Fuel Tank More Than 3/4 Filled

See Figures 210 through 213.

If the VAS 5190 has a suction hose with a mounted tip, then replace this with one that has a tip which screws on.

1. Disconnect the battery.

2. Remove the tip from the fuel extraction unit suction hose VAS 5190. Connect the fuel extraction adapter VAS 5190 /1

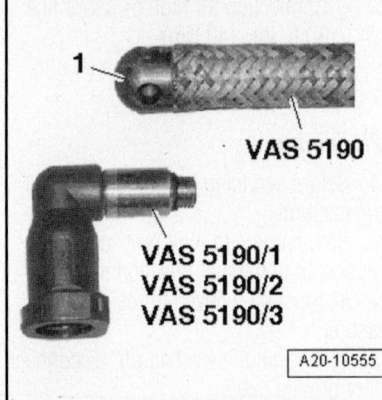

Fig. 210 Remove the tip (1) from the fuel extraction unit suction hose VAS 5190. Connect the fuel extraction adapter VAS 5190 /1 from the fuel extraction adapter set VAS 5190 /10 on the suction hose.

from the fuel extraction adapter set VAS 5190 /10 on the suction hose.

3. Remove the right 1/3 rear seat.

4. Remove the bolts arrows and remove the locking flange cover.

5. Disconnect the electrical connector on the locking flange.

6. Push the circlip upward and compress the release.

7. Disconnect the fuel line at the locking flange by pressing the release button.

8. Press the release button and disconnect the metering pump fuel line at the locking flange on vehicles with an auxiliary heater.

9. Connect the suction hose with the VAS 5190 /1 to the locking flange supply connection.

10. Extract approximately 10 liters of fuel.

11. Press the release button and disconnect the VAS 5190 /1 on the locking flange.

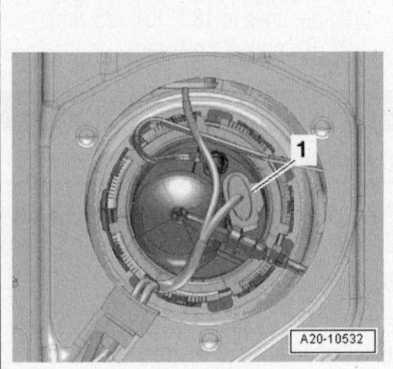

Fig. 211 Disconnect the electrical connector (1) on the locking flange.

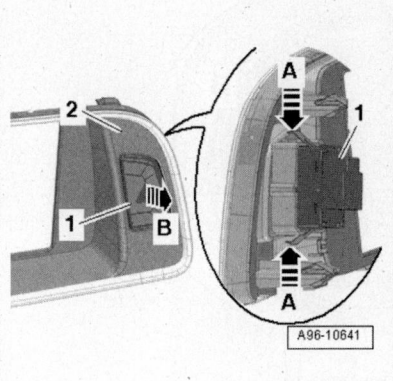

Fig. 212 Push the circlip (1) upward (A) and compress the release (B).

12. Remove the VAS 5190 /1 on the suction hose and re-install the tip.

13. Remove locking ring with T10202.

14. Pull the locking flange a little bit out of the fuel tank and slide the VAS 5190 into the fuel tank through the gap between the locking flange and the opening.

15. Extract any remaining fuel through the opening for the fuel delivery unit.

16. Install the locking flange for the fuel delivery unit..

Emptying a Fuel Tank Less Than 3/4 Filled

1. Remove the right 1/3 rear seat.

2. Remove the bolts arrows and remove the locking flange cover.

3. Disconnect the electrical connector 1 on the locking flange.

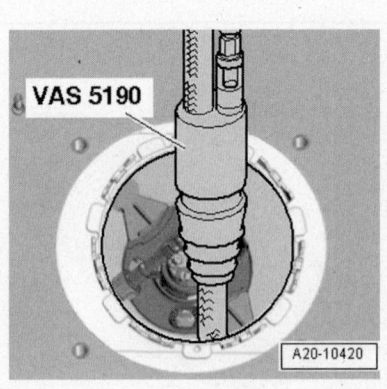

Fig. 213 Pull the locking flange a little bit out of the fuel tank and slide the VAS 5190 into the fuel tank through the gap between the locking flange and the opening.

4. Push the circlip upward and compress the release.

5. Disconnect the fuel line at the locking flange by pressing the release button.

6. Remove locking ring with T10202.

7. Pull the locking flange a little bit out of the fuel tank and slide the VAS 5190 into the fuel tank through the gap between the locking flange and the opening.

8. Extract the fuel through the opening for the fuel delivery unit.

9. Install the locking flange for the fuel delivery unit.

REMOVAL & INSTALLATION

Q5

See Figures 214 through 217.

Tools Needed:
a. Engine/transmission jack V.A.G 1383 A

1. Observe safety precautions.

2. Observe rules for cleanliness.

3. Move passenger seat all the way forward if necessary.

➡**Risk of accident due to fuel tank weight. Fuel tank must be empty when removing. Empty fuel tank if necessary.**

➡**Risk of destroying electrical components when battery is disconnected. Observe measures when disconnecting battery.**

4. Disconnect battery.

5. Remove right 1/3 rear seat.

6. Remove bolts the locking flange cover.

7. Disconnect electrical connector on the locking flange.

8. Pull locks upward and press, disconnect connector.

9. Open tank door.

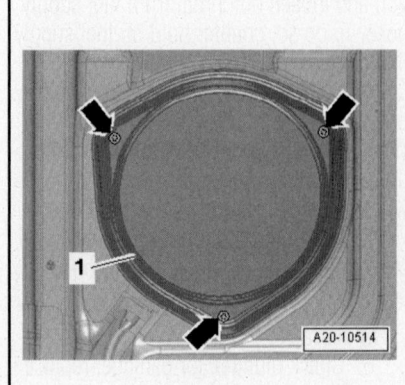

Fig. 214 Removing the locking flange cover

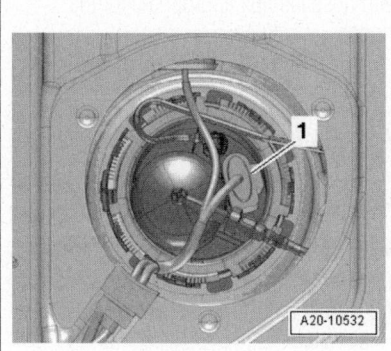

Fig. 215 Disconnecting the electrical connector

10. Clean area around the fuel filler tube.

11. Remove locking cap from fuel filler tube.

   a. To prevent dirt from entering the fuel tank, seal the opening with a clean foam piece.

12. Remove right rear wheel.

13. Remove right rear wheel housing liner.

14. Remove fuel filler tube bolts.

15. Remove rear section of exhaust system.

➡**Risk of vehicle tipping on hoist with rear axle removed. Secure the vehicle on a hoist before loosening the subframe bolts (for example, load the luggage compartment with about 50 kg).**

16. Remove rear axle.

17. Remove right floor panel in the center.

18. Remove nuts and remove bracket.

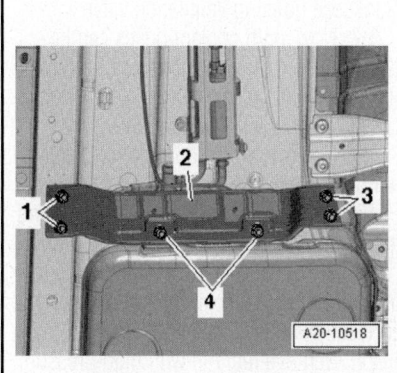

Fig. 216 Remove nuts (1, 3 and 4) and remove bracket (2).

➡**There is a risk of injury because the fuel is under high pressure. To reduce pressure in fuel system, lay a clean cloth around the connector and carefully loosen connector.**

19. Disconnect fuel line on the right front of the fuel tank by pressing release button.

20. Press release button and disconnect the EVAP canister vent line.

21. Place engine/transmission jack V.A.G 1383 A under the fuel tank for support.

22. Support fuel tank using engine/transmission jack V.A.G 1383 A.

➡**Risk of accident due to fuel tank weight. Fuel tank must be empty when removing.**

23. Remove bolts the exhaust system bracket.

24. Remove bolts and lower fuel tank with the Engine/Transmission jack V.A.G 1383 A while guiding it by hand.

To install:

Installation is in reverse order of removal, note the following:

25. Make sure the fuel and vent lines are clipped to the fuel tank properly.

26. Check if the Ground wiring on both connections show signs of oxidation. If necessary, remove.

27. Make sure the filler tube threaded connections are free of corrosion so the ground connection to the body is not affected.

28. Route Ground connection.

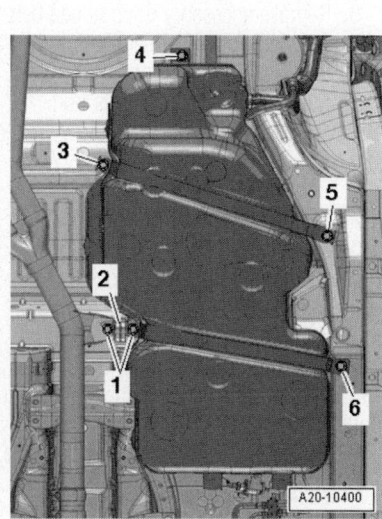

Fig. 217 Removing the fuel tank

29. Engage Ground connection contact into the opening in fuel tank and then install the spacer bushing.

30. Make sure the ground connector fits securely on the fuel filler tube metal ring.

31. Position fuel tank with mounting straps on the vehicle underbody using the Engine/Transmission Jack V.A.G 1383 A.

32. Make sure the fuel tank is positioned so that the filler tube can be guided into the opening of the body correctly.

33. Install the exhaust system bracket and tighten the bolts.

34. Tighten fuel filler tube bolts.

➡**Risk of explosion due to electrostatic charge. After installing, check electrical connection on fuel filler neck metal ring to an empty spot on the body using an Ohm meter. Specified value: About 0 Ω**

35. Install bracket.

36. Install rear axle.

37. Install floor panel.

38. Install rear section of the exhaust system.

39. Install right rear wheel housing liner.

40. Mount right rear wheel.

41. Install right locking flange cover.

42. Install right 1/3 rear seat.

43. Connect battery and observe safety precautions after connecting battery.

Q7

1. Before servicing the vehicle, refer to the precautions.

❋❋ CAUTION

During all repair procedures on the fuel tank, be aware of the following:

- Route all the various lines (e.g. for fuel, EVAP system, or vacuum) and electrical wiring so that the original routing positions are restored.
- Make sure that the ground (-) strap between the fuel filler tube and body is securely fastened, to prevent electrostatic charging.
- Ensure sufficient clearance to all moving or hot components.

2. Drain the fuel tank.

3. Remove rear seat bench.

4. Cut open carpet on right side in pre cut area (feel near seat bracket for fuel tank access panel before cutting).

5. Remove the nuts on the right side of the fuel delivery unit cover. If necessary, remove backrest support or mounting bracket.

Fuel supply lines are under pressure! Wear protective goggles and protective gloves to avoid damage and contact with skin. Before removing from hose connection wrap a cloth around the connection. Then release pressure by carefully pulling hose off connection.

6. Remove fuel supply line, auxiliary heater fuel line, fuel pump connector, vent line, and fuel pump (FP) control module connector from fuel sending unit.

7. Press in securing ring to disengage the fuel line.

8. Remove mufflers and mountings.

9. Remove driveshaft.

10. Remove rear axle.

11. Open fuel flap and remove fuel tank cap.

12. Pull rubber gasket off filler neck.

13. Remove bolts on filler neck and pull off ground wire.

14. Remove right rear wheel housing liner.

15. Unbolt fuel line cover plate.

16. Unclip fuel tank breather lines at securing clip attached on longitudinal member.

17. Remove bolts for filler pipe and EVAP canister in wheel housing.

18. Bend filler neck slightly downward and pull off breather line connections to EVAP canister.

➡**Release connection by pressing button on hose coupling.**

19. Disconnect ground wire clipped to EVAP canister and remove canister.

20. Separate fuel pump connectors, on left next to fuel tank.

21. Remove securing straps with covers on left and right below fuel tank.

22. Support fuel tank using engine/transmission jack, and remove securing strap at center of fuel tank.

23. Carefully lower fuel tank about 12 inches (30 cm).

24. Grab between fuel tank and vehicle floor and disconnect vent line from left sensor flange.

➡**This step eliminates having to cut open the carpeting in the vehicle interior in the vicinity of sender flange cover.**

25. Lower the fuel tank.

To install:
26. Installation is performed in the reverse order of removal.

a. Connections for breather and fuel lines must engage audibly when joined.

b. Make sure ventilation and fuel lines are not kinked when installed.

c. The flange seal should be replaced each time it is opened.

d. Secure fuel hoses with spring-type clamps.

e. Ensure fuel hoses are seated securely.

f. The ground strap at the fuel filler tube must be securely connected to the body.

g. Before fastening the fuel tank, check that the supply and ventilation lines are still clipped onto the fuel tank.

IDLE SPEED

ADJUSTMENT

➡**Idle speed is electronically controlled through the engine control module and is not manually adjustable.**

THROTTLE BODY

REMOVAL & INSTALLATION

Q7

3.6L Engine

1. Before servicing the vehicle, refer to the precautions.

2. Disconnect battery ground strap with ignition switched off.

3. Drain the coolant.

4. Remove the coolant hoses from the straps on the manifold.

5. Remove bolt from oil dipstick guide tube. Remove guide tube with oil dipstick.

6. Remove accessory drive ribbed belt.

7. Remove ribbed belt tensioner.

8. Remove the alternator.

9. Remove the coolant hoses from coolant pipe on the intake manifold/cylinder head.

10. Remove vacuum hoses from Intake Manifold Runner Control (IMRC) valve.

11. Loosen bolts from coolant pipe approximately 1 turn, then remove bolt and remove coolant pipe from intake manifold.

12. Remove the connecting hose to throttle valve control module.

13. Disconnect harness connector from throttle valve control module.

14. Remove throttle valve control module.

To install:
15. Installation is performed in the reverse order of removal.

16. Replace O-rings between fuel injectors and fuel rail and coat them lightly with clean motor oil.

17. Secure all hose connections with hose clamps appropriate for the model.

18. During installation, all cable ties must be reinstalled at the same location.

4.2L Engine

1. Before servicing the vehicle, refer to the precautions.

➡**All cable ties opened or cut during engine removal must be reinstalled at the same locations during installation.**

2. With ignition switched off, disconnect battery ground cable.

3. Remove front engine cover.

4. Remove rear engine cover.

5. Disconnect vent hose to Evaporative Emission (EVAP) canister purge regulator valve by pressing release button.

6. Free up the ventilation hose.

7. Disconnect the connector on EVAP canister purge regulator valve.

8. Remove the ventilation hose from intake manifold.

9. Remove the EVAP canister purge regulator valve down from bracket.

Fuel system is under pressure! Always follow safety measures before opening the system.

10. Place a rag around threaded connection and relieve fuel pressure by briefly opening the line.

11. Now remove fuel supply line on distribution piece.

12. Remove air filter pipe.

13. Remove bolts and place crankcase ventilation pressure regulation valve slightly to side. The hose can remain connected.

14. Clamp off the coolant hose above intake manifold.

15. Clamp off the coolant hose on crankcase housing ventilation valve.

16. Now, both coolant hoses can be removed from throttle valve control module.

17. Remove the crankcase ventilation hoses together with coolant line.

18. Remove bolt and union nut and remove fuel supply line.

19. Disconnect electrical connector and remove the bracket.

20. Carefully, open union nuts at high pressure lines. Place a rag around each connection as it is opened.

21. Remove fuel rail with high pressure lines.

22. Remove vacuum hose from intake manifold.

23. Disconnect connector on throttle

valve control module by pulling the rubber cover over release button.

24. Remove throttle valve control module, ensure seal does not fall down.

To install:

25. Installation is in reverse order of removal, note the following:

26. Replace the gaskets and O-rings.

27. Secure all hose connections with hose clamps appropriate for the model.

28. During installation, all cable ties must be reinstalled at the same location.

FUEL — DIESEL FUEL INJECTION SYSTEM

FUEL SYSTEM SERVICE PRECAUTIONS

Safety is the most important factor when performing not only fuel system maintenance but any type of maintenance. Failure to conduct maintenance and repairs in a safe manner may result in serious personal injury or death. Maintenance and testing of the vehicle's fuel system components can be accomplished safely and effectively by adhering to the following rules and guidelines.

- To avoid the possibility of fire and personal injury, always disconnect the negative battery cable unless the repair or test procedure requires that battery voltage be applied.
- Always relieve the fuel system pressure prior to disconnecting any fuel system component (injector, fuel rail, pressure regulator, etc.), fitting or fuel line connection. Exercise extreme caution whenever relieving fuel system pressure to avoid exposing skin, face and eyes to fuel spray. Please be advised that fuel under pressure may penetrate the skin or any part of the body that it contacts.
- Always place a shop towel or cloth around the fitting or connection prior to loosening to absorb any excess fuel due to spillage. Ensure that all fuel spillage (should it occur) is quickly removed from engine surfaces. Ensure that all fuel soaked cloths or towels are deposited into a suitable waste container.
- Always keep a dry chemical (Class B) fire extinguisher near the work area.
- Do not allow fuel spray or fuel vapors to come into contact with a spark or open flame.
- Always use a back-up wrench when loosening and tightening fuel line connection fittings. This will prevent unnecessary stress and torsion to fuel line piping.
- Always replace worn fuel fitting O-rings with new. Do not substitute fuel hose or equivalent where fuel pipe is installed.

Before servicing the vehicle, make sure to also refer to the precautions in the beginning of this section as well.

FUEL FILTER

REMOVAL & INSTALLATION

Q7

3.0L TDI Engine

See Figure 218.

The manufacturer does not provide a specific removal& installation procedure for this component. Refer to the illustration.

DRAINING WATER FROM THE SYSTEM

Q7

3.0L TDI Engine

See Figure 218

To drain the water, remove and extract approximately 100 cm 3 of fluid using the hand vacuum pump VAG 1390 and draining container VAG 1390/1. Tighten locking bolt to 44 inch lbs. (5 Nm).

INJECTION TIMING

ADJUSTMENT

Ignition timing is electronically controlled and cannot be adjusted manually.

INJECTION LINES

REMOVAL & INSTALLATION

Q7

3.0L TDI Engine

1. Before servicing the vehicle, refer to the precautions.
2. When reusing the high pressure line, pay attention to the cylinder marking.
3. The high pressure lines can be reused only after the following checks:
4. Check the sealing cone on each high pressure line for deformation and cracks.
5. The bores for the lines must not be deformed, narrowed or damaged.
6. Do not reuse corroded lines.
7. Remove any dirt from the sealing cone on the rail.
8. Clean the fuel line and line head with detergent and dry it with compressed air.
9. Coat the threads on the union nut with fuel.
10. Tighten the high pressure line union nuts by hand, making sure they are seated without tension.
11. Final tighten to 19 ft. lbs. (25 Nm).
12. Tighten the high pressure lines using the VAG 1331 with the VAG 1331/1 and a T40055.
13. Tighten the high pressure lines using a VAG 1331 with the VAG 1331/6 or the VAG 1331/5.
14. Perform the fuel system leak test.

INJECTORS

REMOVAL & INSTALLATION

Q7

3.0L TDI Engine

1. Before servicing the vehicle, refer to the precautions.
2. Remove the engine cover.

⁂ WARNING

Mark the allocation of the injectors to the cylinder.

3. On cylinder bank 1, remove the upper air filter housing with the Mass Air Flow sensor.
4. Pull the release pins upward and remove the return line connections from the injectors.
5. Disconnect the electrical connector from the injector to be removed.
6. Loosen the union nuts for the injector lines at the injectors using the T40055.
7. Loosen the union nuts for the injector lines at the high pressure reservoir (rail element) using the 3150 or the VAG 1331/5.
8. Remove the fuel injector cover bolts and covers.
9. Pull the covers upward and turn them 1/4 turn.
10. Remove the fuel injector tensioning bracket nuts and brackets.
11. Remove the injectors using the T10055 and T10055/1.
12. Place the injectors on a clean cloth.
13. Replace the following components and seals or O-rings with each removal and installation

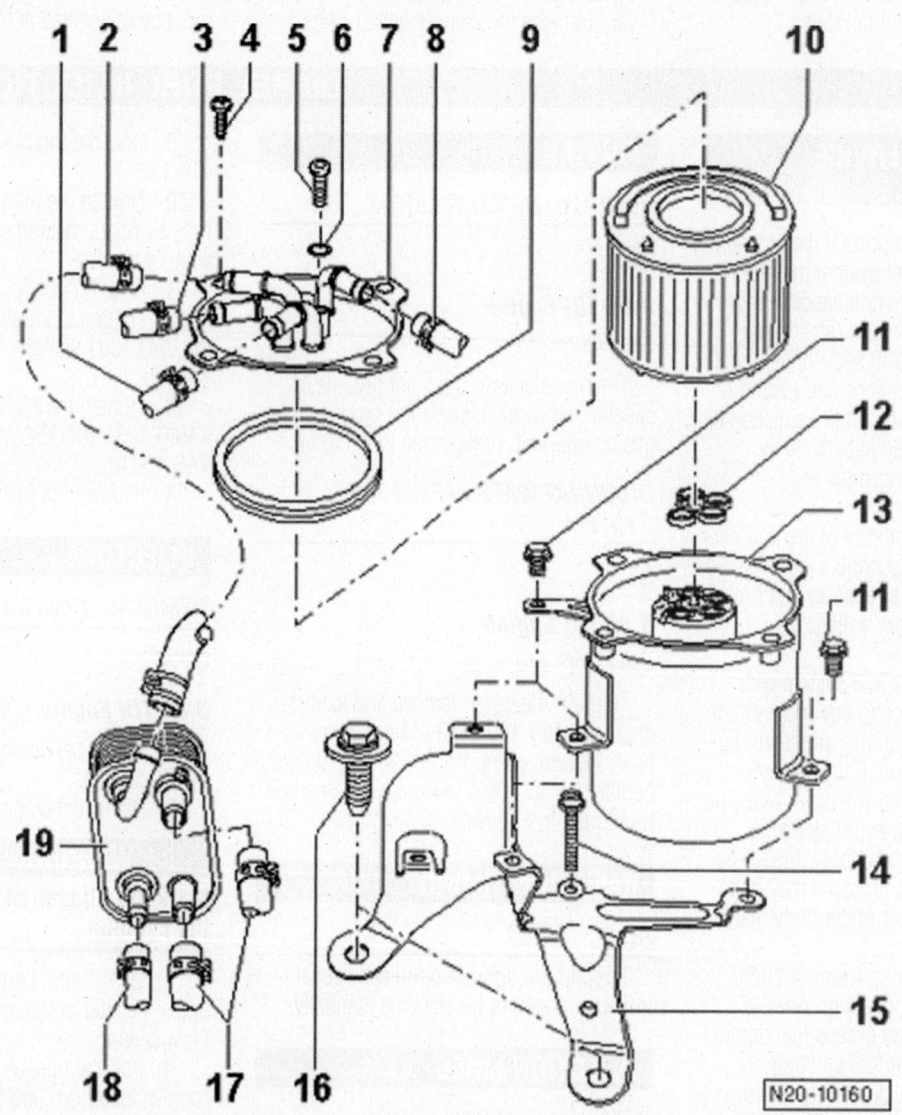

1. Fuel return line
2. Fuel return line
3. Fuel supply line
4. Bolt, 89 inch lbs (10 Nm)
5. Locking bolt,
   44 inch lbs. (5 Nm)
6. Seal
7. Fuel filter cover
8. Fuel supply line
9. Seal
10. Fuel filter element

11. Bolt, 89 inch lbs (10 Nm)
12. Gasket
13. Fuel filter housing
14. Bolt, 71 inch lbs. (8 Nm)
15. Bracket
16. Bolt, 37 ft. lbs. (50 Nm)
    plus 90° turn
17. Coolant hoses
18. Fuel return line
19. Fuel cooler

Fig. 218 Fuel filter and cooler assembly

- Copper washer
- Injector shaft O-ring
- Injector return O-ring

14. Replace the following components, seals and/or O-rings each time an injector is replaced.

- Tensioning bracket
- Injection line
- Copper washer
- Injector shaft O-ring
- Injector return O-ring

15. When installing, the fuel injectors and injection lines may only be installed on the same cylinder as before.

16. Check the fuel injectors and installation locations for contamination before assembling.

17. The fuel injectors must not have any damage.

18. Lubricate all of the O-rings with assembly oil or engine oil before installing.

19. If a used fuel injector is installed:

a. Spray the tip of the fuel injector with a rust removing spray. Remove the rust or oil particles with a cloth after approximately 5 minutes.

b. If an injector is very dirty, clean the tips of the injection around the copper sealing ring with a soft brush (do not let the brush come in contact with the holes for the jets).

c. To remove the used copper sealing ring from the fuel injector, clamp the sealing ring carefully in a vise until the clamping jaws on the vise prevent the ring from turning. Pull the fuel injector out of the copper sealing ring by hand with slight twisting and pulling motions.

d. Use a scraper to remove any deposits under the copper sealing ring.

e. Install the new copper sealing ring with a plastic bushing.

f. To avoid damaging the O-ring, slide the new O-ring for the fuel return line connection over the assembly drift.

g. To remove rust particles on the fuel injector sealing surface, clean the fuel injector duct in the cylinder head with a cloth dampened with engine oil or rust remover. Do not damage the sealing flanges.

20. Install the fuel injectors.

21. First tighten the union nuts on the high pressure or injection lines by hand.

22. Make sure the lines are seated correctly without tension.

23. Tighten the high pressure lines to 19 ft. lbs. (25 Nm).

24. Press the return line connections carefully over the sealing ring onto the injector (check the sealing ring first for damage). The connection must engage audibly. Then press the release pin down carefully.

➡The "injector quantity calibration" and the "injection pressure calibration" for the new injectors must be must be programmed into the engine control module after replacing one or more injectors.

➡Check all the other injectors as well regarding their "injector quantity calibration" and "injection pressure calibration "to make sure all comparison values have been entered correctly. If the correct comparison value have been stored in the engine control module, then these comparison value must never be reentered.

25. Let the engine run a few minutes at idle and then stop it.

26. Switch off the ignition.

27. Check the entire fuel system and the six return line connections for leaks.

If there are leaks despite correct tightening specifications, replace the affected component.

28. The return lines may only be replaced completely with the pressure retention valve.

29. Test drive the vehicle a minimum of 20 km/h and using full throttle at least one time. Then check the high pressure area one more time for leaks.

30. If there is still air in the fuel system, the engine may switch to emergency mode during the road test.

31. Stop the engine and erase the Diagnostic Trouble Code memory. Then continue the road test.

FUEL SUPPLY PUMP

REMOVAL & INSTALLATION

Q7

3.0L TDI Engine

1. Before servicing the vehicle, refer to the precautions.

2. Drain the fuel tank.

3. Disconnect wires for the left and right sensor flanges.

4. Remove the locking rings for the left and right sensor flanges.

5. Read the safety precautions before beginning work.

6. Disconnect the electrical connectors and the fittings below the right sensor flange.

7. Remove the sensor flanges.

8. Unclip the black filler hose from the fuel delivery unit on the left and right sides of the fuel tank.

9. Remove the supply line to the suction jet pumps at the fuel delivery unit on the right and left sides of the fuel tank.

10. Disconnect the supply and return lines between both fuel delivery units on the left side of the fuel tank.

11. Rotate the fuel delivery unit approximately 90 degrees to the left and remove it from the bottom of the fuel tank.

✳✳ WARNING

The fuel delivery unit housing is filled with fuel. Fuel may run out if the housing is tipped or tilted.

12. Unclip the fuel level sensors on each side of fuel tank and pull them out.

13. Unclip the suction jet pumps from the bottom on each side and remove with a slight turn.

14. Pull out hose ends through left and right sensor openings.

To install:

15. Installation is the reverse of removal.

16. Tighten fuel tank lock ring to 107 ft. lbs. (143 Nm).

INJECTION PUMP

REMOVAL & INSTALLATION

Q7

3.0L TDI Engine

1. Before servicing the vehicle, refer to the precautions.

2. Remove the upper intake manifold.

3. Remove the high pressure pump toothed belt.

4. Remove the bolts and the high pressure line protective plate.

5. Remove the union nuts and free up the high pressure lines.

6. Disconnect the electrical connector.

7. Remove the fuel supply line and return line.

8. Remove the bolts and remove the high pressure pump.

To install:

9. Installation is performed in reverse order of removal, noting the following:

✳✳ WARNING

The high pressure pump will be destroyed if it runs dry. The high pressure pump must be filled with fuel before starting the engine for the first time.

10. Replace the gaskets and seals.

11. The fuel return line must not be bent, damaged or plugged

12. Install the high pressure pump toothed belt.

13. Install the high pressure lines.

14. Install the upper intake manifold.

15. Bleed the fuel system after installing the high pressure pump.

16. Tighten bolts/nuts to specification as follows:
- Pump bolt M6: 80 inch lbs. (9 Nm)
- Pump bolt M8: 17 ft. lbs. (23 Nm)
- High pressure pump bracket bolt: 80 inch lbs. (9 Nm)
- High pressure line union nut: 19 ft. lbs. (25 Nm)

INJECTION TIMING

Ignition timing is electronically controlled and cannot be adjusted manually.

FUEL PRESSURE REGULATOR

REMOVAL & INSTALLATION

Q7

3.0L TDI Engine

➡The fuel pressure regulator valve is located in the right high pressure reservoir for cylinder bank 1 and maintains a constant pressure in the reservoir and the injector lines.

➡If the pressure in the fuel high pressure circuit is too high, the regulator valve will open so that some of the fuel flows from the rail back into the fuel tank via a return line.

➡If the pressure is too low, then the check valve closes and seals off the high pressure side from the low pressure side.

✳✳ WARNING

The fuel pressure regulator valve cannot be reused.

1. Before servicing the vehicle, refer to the precautions.

✳✳ WARNING

Follow the guidelines for clean working conditions when working on the fuel system.

2. Remove the engine cover.

3. Before removing, clean the threaded area around the fuel pressure regulator valve with a commercially available detergent. Dirt must not enter the hole in the high pressure reservoir.

4. Clean carefully, cleaner must not enter the connector.

5. Dry the fuel pressure regulator valve.

6. Disconnect the electrical connector for the fuel pressure regulator valve.

7. Counter hold at the housing bolt and loosen the union nut. Then remove it by hand.

8. Suction any dirt out of the hole in the high pressure reservoir, the threads and the sealing surface. Do not use mechanical tools.

9. Seal the hole in the high pressure reservoir with a plug to prevent dirt from entering.

Installing

10. The fuel pressure regulator valve does not have a sealing ring, but rather a biting edge and cannot be reused.

11. Check the new fuel pressure regulator valve sealing surface and threads for damage.

12. Check the sealing surface on the hole in the high pressure reservoir.

13. The threads on the fuel pressure regulator valve must be free of oil and grease.

14. Tighten the union nut by hand.

15. Align the fuel pressure regulator valve so the connecting line is not taut after connecting the connector.

16. Tighten the union nut in 2 steps:
- Step 1: 44 ft. lbs. (60 Nm), counter hold the housing bolt while doing this
- Then rotate the union nut back 1/4 turn while counter holding at the housing nut.
- Step 2: 59 ft. lbs. (80 Nm), counter hold the housing bolt while doing this

17. After installing, let the engine run at a moderate speed for a few minutes and then stop it.

18. Check the fuel system for leaks.

19. Check the Diagnostic Trouble Code memory.

20. Perform a road test where the accelerator pedal is pressed all the way down at least one time. Then check the high pressure area again for leaks.

21. Check the DTC memory again.

GLOW PLUGS

REMOVAL & INSTALLATION

Q7

3.0L TDI Engine

1. Before servicing the vehicle, refer to the precautions.

2. Observe visual characteristics of ceramic sheathed element glow plugs.

3. When removing and installing, do not cant ceramic sheathed element glow plugs. Remove components which hinder installation.

4. Remove the intake manifolds.

5. Disconnect the connectors from the ceramic sheathed element glow plugs using the pliers 6275.

6. Remove ceramic sheathed element glow plugs using flex wrench 3220.

To install:

7. Installation is performed in the reverse order of removal, noting the following:

8. Cylinder head bore and thread must be completely cleaned of deposits before installing.

9. Never oil or grease thread of bore in cylinder head and ceramic sheathed element glow plugs.

10. Install ceramic sheathed element glow plugs into cylinder head by hand using flex wrench 3220.

11. Then tighten 11 ft. lbs. (15 Nm) ceramic sheathed element glow plugs.

✳✳ WARNING

After installing and before first engine start with a cold engine, always perform a resistance test at all ceramic sheathed element glow plugs. Specified value: max. 1.0 ohms.

12. If specified value is exceeded, replace malfunctioning ceramic sheathed element glow plug.

13. If the malfunctioning ceramic sheathed element glow plug is broken, remove all broken pieces from engine, otherwise they can cause damage to engine.

HEATING & AIR CONDITIONING SYSTEM

BLOWER MOTOR

REMOVAL & INSTALLATION

Q5

See Figures 219 and 220.

➡The fresh air blower as a replacement part is available in different versions, make sure of the correct application.

➡The fresh air blower V2 A with a revised housing (optimized motor with a revised motor mount) is being installed. With the introduction of the revised fresh air blower the foam jacket around the housing has been discontinued, a revised noise insulation in being installed because the engine mount is larger.

1. Remove the fresh air blower control module.
2. Remove the screw clips the insulation mat.
3. Loosen the locking mechanism and turn the fresh air blower housing to the right.

➡Do not grasp fan wheel of fresh air blower, force against the fan wheel or shifting the balancing weights fastened to fan wheel may cause imbalance and then problems during operation.

To install:

Installation is carried out in the reverse order, when doing this note the following.

4. If the locking mechanism A breaks or can no longer hold, you can secure fresh air blower to the air intake housing using a screw .

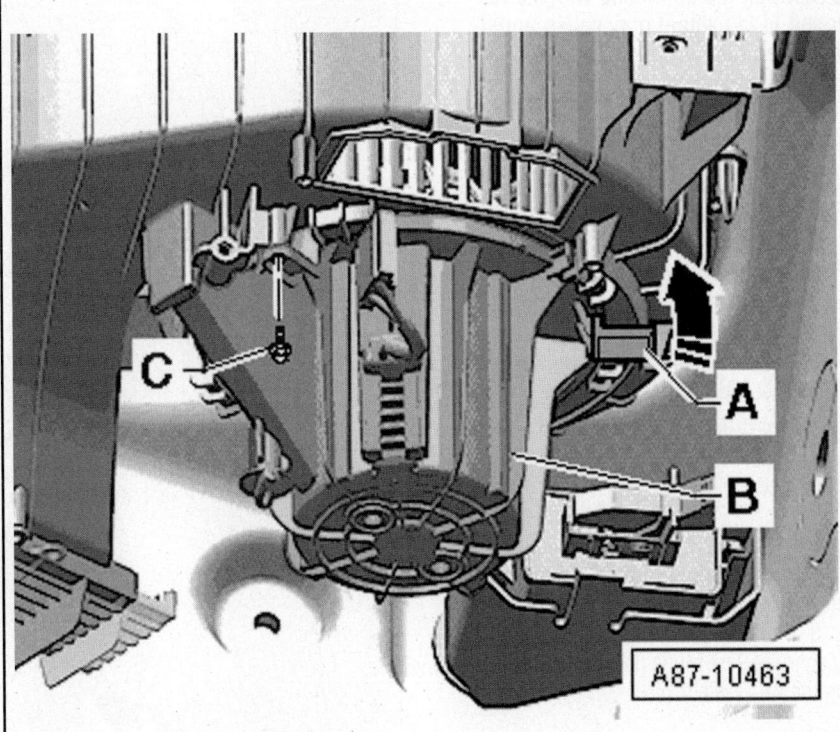

Fig. 220 Loosen the locking mechanism (A) and turn the fresh air blower housing in the direction of the arrow.

5. When installing, make sure the fresh air blower fits correctly in the air intake housing.
6. Check Diagnostic Trouble Code (DTC) memory of Air Conditioning (A/C) control head Climatronic control module and erase any displayed malfunction if necessary.
7. To check the function, perform an output Diagnostic Test Mode (DTM) on the A/C system.

Q7

Front

See Figure 221.

1. Switch ignition off.
2. Remove lower right instrument panel trim.
3. Remove glove compartment.
4. Disconnect connector from Fresh Air Blower.
5. Remove bolts.
6. Take out Fresh Air Blower downward.

To install:

7. Insert Fresh Air Blower carefully into heating & A/C unit from below.

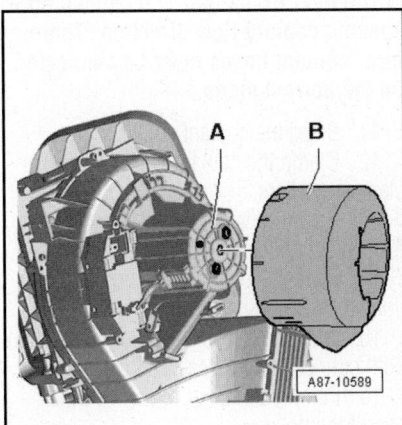

Fig. 219 Blower motor

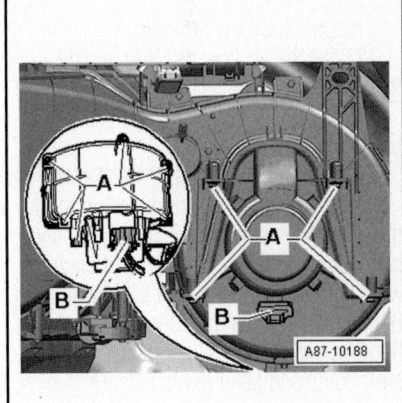

Fig. 221 Disconnecting the connector (B)

8. Install the remaining removed components again in reverse order.
9. Check DTC memory of front A/C control head Climatronic Control Module and erase DTCs displayed if necessary.
10. Perform basic setting (and output Diagnostic Test Mode (DTM) if necessary) on the A/C system.

Rear

➡Do not grasp fan wheel of Rear Fresh Air Blower, force against the fan wheel or shifting the balancing weights fastened to fan wheel may cause imbalance and then problems during operation.

1. Switch ignition off
2. Bring rear heating & A/C unit into service position Rear Heating and A/C Unit, Service Position
3. Disconnect electrical connection from Rear Fresh Air Blower.
4. Gently lift the tab and rotate Rear Fresh Air Blower.
5. Remove Rear Fresh Air Blower from heating & A/C unit

To install:

6. Install the removed components again in reverse order.
7. Check DTC memory of front A/C control head Climatronic Control Module and of Rear A/C Control Head (Climatronic) and erase DTCs displayed if necessary.
8. Perform basic setting (and output Diagnostic Test Mode (DTM) if necessary) on the A/C system.

HEATER CORE

REMOVAL & INSTALLATION

Q5

See Figures 222 and 223.

1. Switch on the ignition.
2. Set the air flow direction to DEF on the Climatronic Control Module.
3. Move the passenger seats as far back as possible.
4. Switch off ignition.
5. Disconnect the ground cable from the battery. Disconnect the battery ground connection so that it cannot short circuit when the jumper cable post is removed. Remove the jumper cable post cover. Remove the jumper cable post from the strut dome and lay it to the side.
6. Remove the air intake housing.
7. Disconnect the connector from the Evaporator Vent Temperature Sensor.
8. Remove the right radiator housing.

➡Due to space limitation when the instrument panel is installed, it is not possible to install the factory-installed heat exchanger and the hose clamps again. If a factory installed heat exchanger (original part) must be installed again, remove the instrument panel and the air guide leading to the

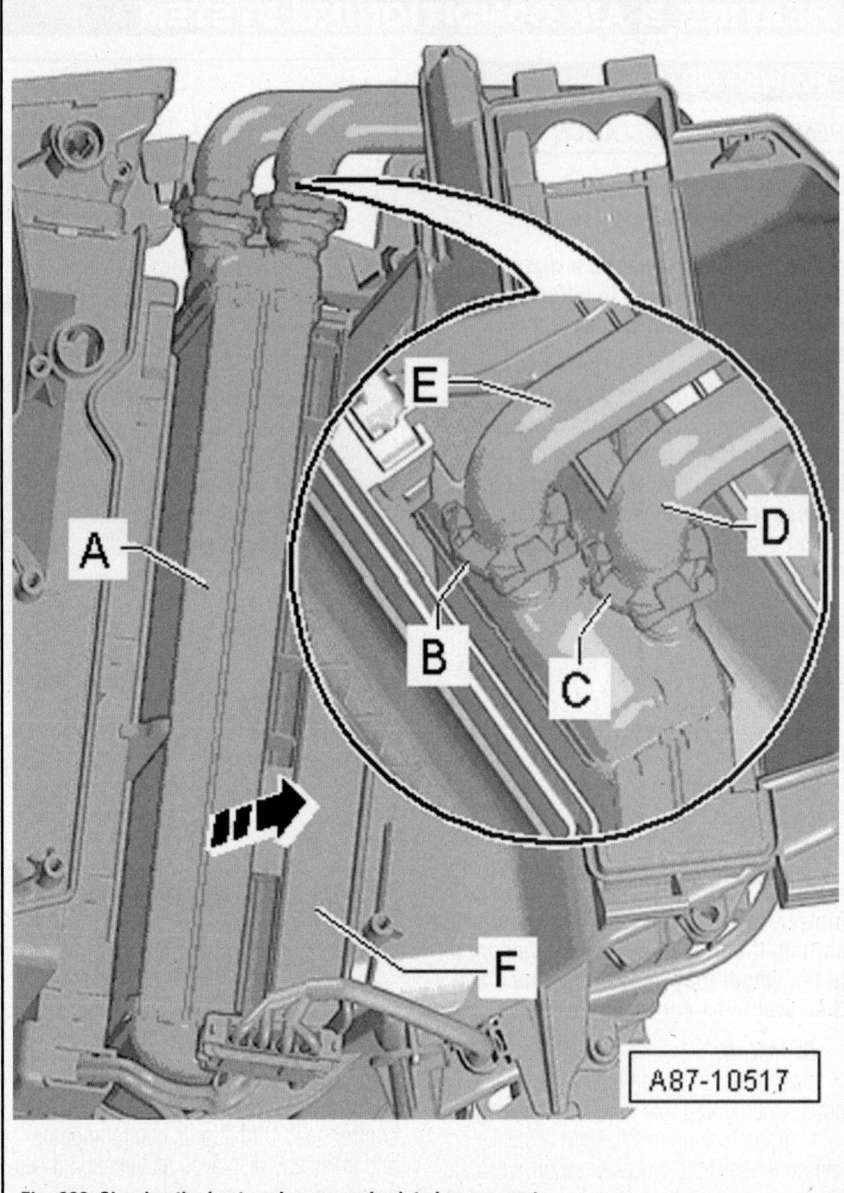

Fig. 222 Showing the heat exchanger and related components

A87-10517

Defrost vent. Coat the O-rings with coolant (as described for installing an exchange part - heat exchanger) and mount them on the coolant pipes and then push the coolant pipes (with the O-rings) from the top into the connections on the heat exchanger. Hold the coolant pipes in the heat exchanger and install the clamps. Further assembly is performed as described for installing a replacement part - heat exchanger.

9. Release pressure in cooling circuit by opening cap on coolant expansion tank.
10. Mark the arrangement of coolant hoses (supply to cylinder head) and (return to coolant pump).

➡The heat exchanger is designed for a specific coolant flow direction. Therefore, coolant hoses must be connected on the correct sides.

11. Bleed the coolant circuit.
12. Clamp the coolant hoses with hose clamps or pliers.
13. Cover the area beneath connections for coolant hoses with absorbent paper.
14. Remove coolant hoses from connections to A/C unit heat exchanger.
15. Insert one section each of hose on to both connections to heater core.
16. Place a container under the other end of the hose.
17. Using a compressed air gun, carefully blow coolant out of heater core (into container) via the hose.

18. Remove the clamps from the heat exchanger connectors.

19. Loosen both coolant pipes from the heat exchanger connectors.

20. Remove the heat exchanger outward.

To install:

21. Installation is carried out in the reverse order, when doing this note the following:

   a. Depending on the A/C version, cover the heat exchanger with the foam seal provided A through D.

   b. Check the seals on the heat exchanger; only install a heat exchanger with seals that are not damaged and are secured glued on.

➡**If the vehicle has the Comfort A/C system, then there are different temperature settings for the right and left sides as well as for the rear. The seals separate the air guides in the air conditioner from each other.**

➡**The heat exchanger has a color mark that shows where to affix the seal. The seal must be applied to the center of the heat exchanger.**

➡**The seal may have different lengths (a short version as illustrated or a long version which reaches all the way around the heat exchanger). If the heat exchanger is delivered with the longer seal, then attach it all the way around the exchanger.**

※※ CAUTION

Seal may curl up on insertion if not correctly bonded on. If the seal is damaged or installed incorrectly, cold air can flow over the heat exchanger; on vehicles equipped with the Comfort A/C system, it is possible that there is no clear separation between the various areas.

---

22. Check the A/C unit and the evaporator F with the heat exchanger removed A(via heater core opening) for dirt.

23. Remove any dirt or coolant which has leaked out of the A/C unit (for example, after removing a leaking heat exchanger).

24. Check both connections on the heat exchanger for damage and dirt, then grease both connections on the heat exchanger with silicone grease.

25. Lightly moisten the seals (contained in the heat exchanger delivery) with coolant (or lightly with silicone grease).

26. Install the new seals on both heat exchanger coolant pipes.

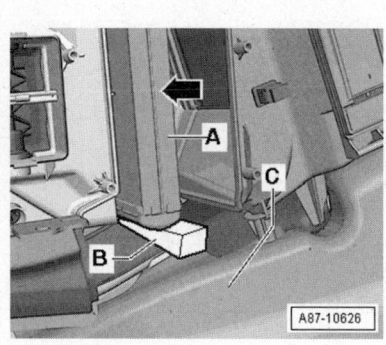

Fig. 223 Support the heat exchanger, for example, with a plastic wedge on the center tunnel so that it cannot slip down when attaching the coolant pipes.

27. Push the heat exchanger into the A/C unit.

28. Support the heat exchanger, for example, with a plastic wedge on the center tunnel so that it cannot slip down when attaching the coolant pipes.

29. Install a longer screw (with a M5 thread) all the way to the stop in the bracket.

30. Install and push both coolant pipes with each seal into the heat exchanger connector flange all the way.

➡**Do not bend the coolant pipes when pushing them into the connections on the heat exchanger.**

31. Make sure the seals between the coolant pipes and the flange connection on the heat exchanger fit securely.

➡**Seals that are incorrectly installed or jammed will leak. The seals must be installed completely into both the coolant pipe connections and the flange connections.**

32. Secure both coolant pipes with the bracket on the heat exchanger flange.

33. Insert the screw and the washer and tighten the screw.

34. Remove the installation assist screw.

35. Make sure the grommet fits correctly in the back of the plenum chamber.

36. Properly connect the coolant hoses to the heat exchanger, pay attention to the marking:

   • A: Supply hose from cylinder head
   • B: Return to the coolant pump

37. Connect the coolant hose to the heat exchanger coolant pipe (pay attention to the marking) and secure it with the clamp.

38. Attach the coolant hose for the heat exchanger onto the coolant pipe just far enough as to not cover the bleed hole.

39. Remove the hose clamp from the coolant hose.

40. Fill the coolant overflow reservoir with coolant.

41. Carefully force the coolant out of the coolant overflow reservoir into the heat exchanger using, for example, the hand pump from the Cooling System Tester V.A.G 1274.

42. As soon as the coolant comes out the ventilation hole, install the coolant hose on to the coolant pipe at the marking.

43. Secure the coolant hose with the clamp on the marked location.

44. Remove the hose clamp from the coolant hose.

45. If necessary, add more coolant to the overflow reservoir.

➡**By this procedure, the cooling system is not completely bled. If, for some other reason, there still should be some air in the cooling system, install all the components and bleed the system once again..**

46. Check the connections on the heat exchanger for leaks as follows:

   a. Carefully increase the pressure in the cooling system by using, for example, the hand pump from the Cooling System Tester V.A.G 1274

   b. Check coolant circuit for leaks, pay particular attention to the connection between coolant hoses and heater core..

➡**When bleeding coolant circuit, take special care to ensure complete bleeding of heat exchangers. If there are still air bubbles in the heater core, it may cause the customer to complain of insufficient heating performance in winter or different air temperature from vents at same setting in regulated mode.**

➡**Depending on vehicle equipment and on engine, heat insulation has been applied to coolant hoses, these must not be damaged and must be re-applied after installing.**

47. Install all the remaining components in reverse sequence.

48. Reconnect the battery ground connection.

49. Perform a basic setting and the output Diagnostic Test Mode (DTM) on the A/C system using Vehicle Diagnosis, Testing and Information System VAS 5051 under Guided Fault Finding.

➡On this vehicle, the control motors are equipped with electronics, during the first basic setting, a new control motor learns its position on the air conditioner and can then be controlled by the Climatronic Control Module (currently all control motors are identical). Check using Vehicle Diagnosis, Testing and Information System VAS 5051 under Guided Fault Finding. During the basic adjustment, the control motors are assigned and adapted corresponding to the switching sequence of the wiring. If this sequence does not conform the specification, the control motors will adapt incorrectly and the door control will be wrong.

50. Check the Climatronic control module DTC memory and erase any displayed malfunction if necessary using Vehicle Diagnosis, Testing and Information System VAS 5051 in Guided Fault Finding function.

51. Adjust and check the air flow direction on the different air ducts via Climatronic control module, making sure the quantity of air actually changes at each setting.

Q7

Front

See Figures 224 through 226.

➡Heater core can also be removed and re-installed with the heating & A/C unit installed.

1. Remove front heating & A/C unit. Remove the two bolts.

2. Disengage cover from mounts and from wiring harness secured to upper side. Remove bolt.

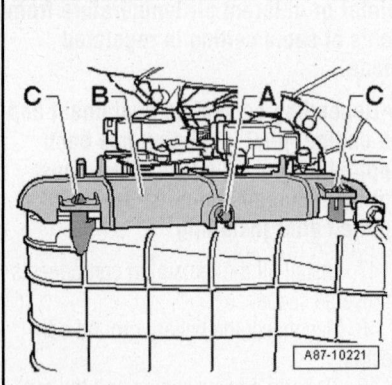

Fig. 224 Disengage cover (D) from mounts (C) and from wiring harness secured to upper side. Remove bolt (A).

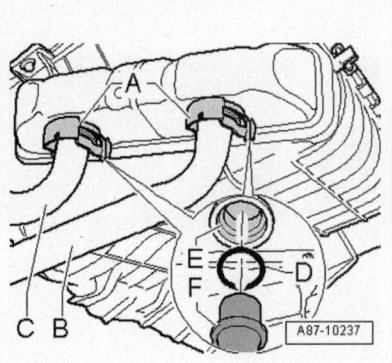

Fig. 225 Disengage cover (B) from mounts (C) and from wiring harness secured to upper side. Pull off retaining clips (A) from coolant lines (B and C).

3. Disengage cover from mounts and from wiring harness secured to upper side.

4. Pull off retaining clips from coolant lines.

5. Pull the coolant lines out of heater core. Remove the bolts.

6. Turn retaining pin out of locking mechanism.

7. Pull retaining pin out of lower air duct and heating & A/C unit.

8. Release catches of lower air guide.

9. Fold lower air duct and remove lower air duct and heater core.

To install:

10. Clean front heating & A/C unit and lower air duct (e.g. of residual coolant).

11. Check foam seals at heater core, they must be glued all around without gaps and must not be damaged.

12. Insert the heater core on proper side into lower air duct.

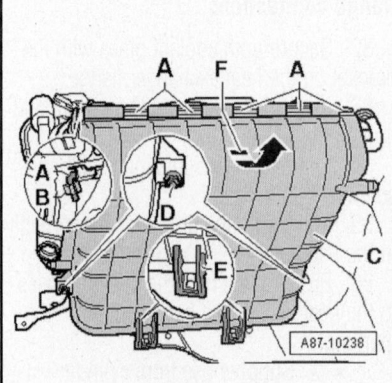

Fig. 226 Pull the coolant lines (B and C) out of heater core. Remove bolts (D).

13. Install the heater core with lower air duct into heating & A/C unit.

➡While inserting, make sure that groove/spring connection between heating & A/C unit and lower air guide is joined correctly.

14. Insert the retaining pin for connecting lower air duct to heating & A/C unit.

15. Turn the retaining pin into locking mechanism.

16. Install bolts.

17. Moisten new O-ring seals (included in heater core delivery casing) lightly with coolant.

18. Insert new seals on to coolant pipe connections.

19. Push both coolant pipes into heater core connections.

20. Insert the retaining clips on proper side on to coolant lines and heater core connections.

➡Only use retaining clips of standard used in series production.

21. Check retaining clips on coolant pipes and heater core connections again for secure fit.

22. Re-install both left and right covers on heater core and the remaining removed components in reverse order.

23. Install front heating & A/C unit.

Rear Hvac Unit Installed

See Figures 227 and 228.

➡Tools Needed:

- Hose clamps up to ⌀ 25 mm 3094
- Cooling system tester V.A.G 1274 (hand pump and corresponding adapter)

1. Switch off ignition.

2. Release pressure in cooling circuit by opening cap on coolant expansion tank.

3. Bring rear heating & A/C unit into service position.

4. Remove Left Rear Air Flap Motor V239.

5. Remove Right Rear Air Flap Motor V240.

6. Remove bolts and the upper cover.

7. Mark both coolant hoses to rear heater core (risk of interchange).

8. Clamp off both coolant hoses to rear heater core (e.g. using hose clamps up to 25 mm dia. 3094).

9. Pull heater core out of heating & A/C unit.

10. Cover the area below heating & A/C unit, where any coolant flowing out may reach, with absorbent paper (so that any

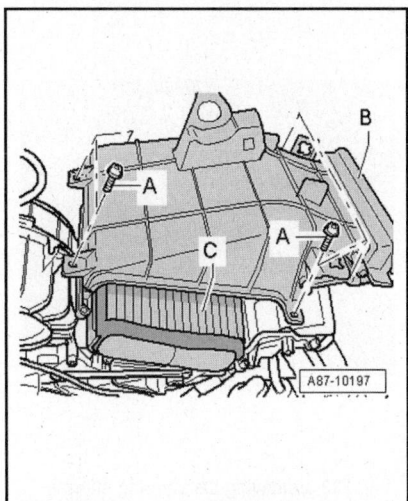

Fig. 227 Removing the upper cover

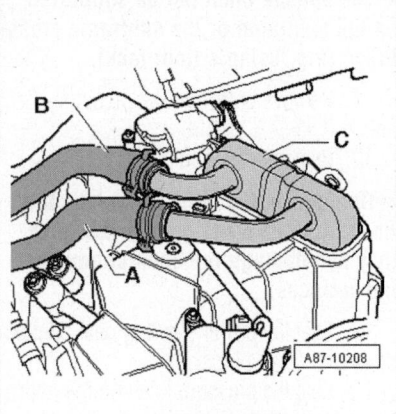

Fig. 228 Mark both coolant hoses A and B to rear heater core C (risk of interchange).

17. Cover the area below heating & A/C unit, where any coolant flowing out may reach, with absorbent paper (so that any coolant still present will not flow on and into heating & A/C unit or on to floor mat).

18. Place a container under connection to heater core.

19. Open hose clamps up to 1 in. (25 mm) dia. 3094 on coolant hose far enough that coolant can flow slowly into heater core (to pre-bleed heater core).

➡ **If coolant does not flow into heater core on its own, pressure can be built up in coolant expansion tank using hand pump of cooling system tester V.A.G 1274 and thereby accelerate the flow.**

➡ **By pre-bleeding the cooling circuit, bleeding of the cooling system after installation is greatly simplified on first starting in operation.**

20. Wait until coolant exits from coolant hose connection on coolant pipe to heater core.

21. Connect the coolant hose at coolant pipe to heater core.

22. Install the removed components again in reverse order.

23. Bleed the cooling circuit.

coolant flowing out will not flow on and into heating & A/C unit or on to floor mat).

11. Place a container under both connections to heater core C and disconnect both coolant hoses.

To install:

12. Clean rear heating & A/C unit (e.g. of coolant residue).

13. Check foam seals at heater core, they must be glued on without gaps and must not be damaged.

14. Insert the heater core into heating & A/C unit.

15. Connect coolant hose to coolant pipe to heater core (other coolant hose is not connected for the time being).

➡ **Connect coolant hoses on proper side, coolant hose supply from engine (via pipe group under left fender) and coolant hose return to engine (via pipe group under left fender).**

16. Fill coolant into coolant expansion tank up to top marking.

STEERING

POWER STEERING GEAR

REMOVAL & INSTALLATION

Q5

See Figures 229 through 233.

➡ **Tools Needed:**

- Hose Clamps Up to 25 mm dia. 3094
- Torque Wrench V.A.G 1331
- Torque Wrench V.A.G 1332
- Ball Joint Puller T40010 A
- Ring Spanner Insert VAG 1332/10 V.A.G 1332/10

1. Install or connect the following:
   a. Ring Spanner Insert VAG 1332/10 V.A.G 1332/7
   b. Sealing Plug Set VAS 6122
2. Place the vehicle on a hoist.
3. Clamp off the suction hose and return hose using the Hose Clamps 1 in. (25 mm) dia..

➡ **The Hose Clamps Up to 1 in. (25 mm) dia. must not be secured on the return hose in the check valve area.**

Otherwise, check valve will be damaged.

➡ **The check valve is located in the return hose between the hose clamps.**

4. Remove front wheels.
5. Remove the nut from the tie rod end joint pin until it is flush with the joint pin threads. Counterhold when loosening if necessary.
   a. To protect thread, screw nut on pin a few turns.
6. Press tie rod end off wheel bearing housing using Ball Joint Puller T40010 A. Remove the nut.

➡ **Make sure that both puller lever arms are parallel to each other when using greatest force, adjust if necessary.**

7. Remove noise insulation.
8. Remove nut from the rubber bushing.
9. Remove stabilizer bar.
10. Remove crossbrace.

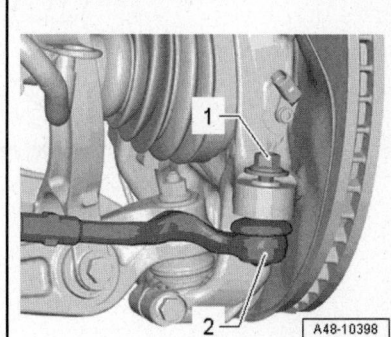

Fig. 229 Remove the nut from the tie rod end joint pin until it is flush with the joint pin threads. Counterhold when loosening if necessary.

➡ **The suspension components could be damaged. If the subframe mount, the steering gear or the subframe crossbrace are not installed correctly, do not rest the vehicle on its wheels.**

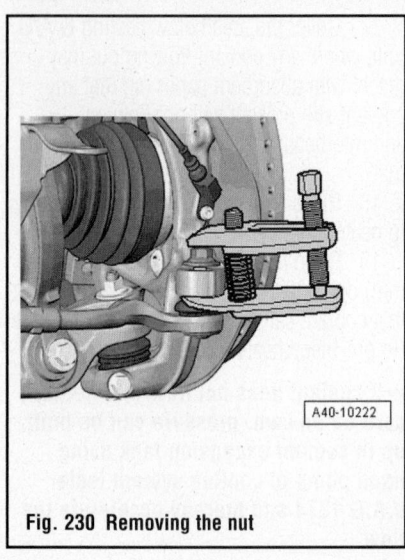

Fig. 230 Removing the nut

➡The vehicle must not be supported on the subframe or the subframe cross-brace (e.g. using a floor jack).

11. Remove bolts and the pressure line.

12. Remove return line.

➡Do not use any tools to remove the lines from the steering gear because they can damage the contact and sealing surfaces.

13. Seal the power steering gear connections with clean plugs.

14. Seal the pressure line and the return line with clean sealing plugs.

15. Remove bolt.

16. Remove the steering intermediate shaft from the steering gear.

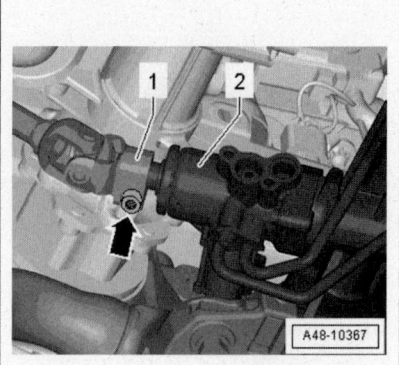

Fig. 232 Removing the steering intermediate shaft from the steering gear

Applies to vehicles with Servotronic Solenoid Valve.

17. Disconnect the connector and remove it from the Servotronic Solenoid Valve.

Continued for all engines:

18. Remove bolts and nuts.

19. Guide the steering gear to the right slightly and remove it.

To install:

Installation is in reverse order of removal. Observe the following when doing so:

20. Lightly coat the seals with Hydraulic Oil before installing.

21. Insert the pressure line and return line completely when installing.

22. Install stabilizer bar.

23. Install both bolts loosely at first and then tighten them.

24. Install the crossbrace.

25. Remove the Hose Clamps Up to 1 in. (25 mm) dia. from the intake hose and from the return hose.

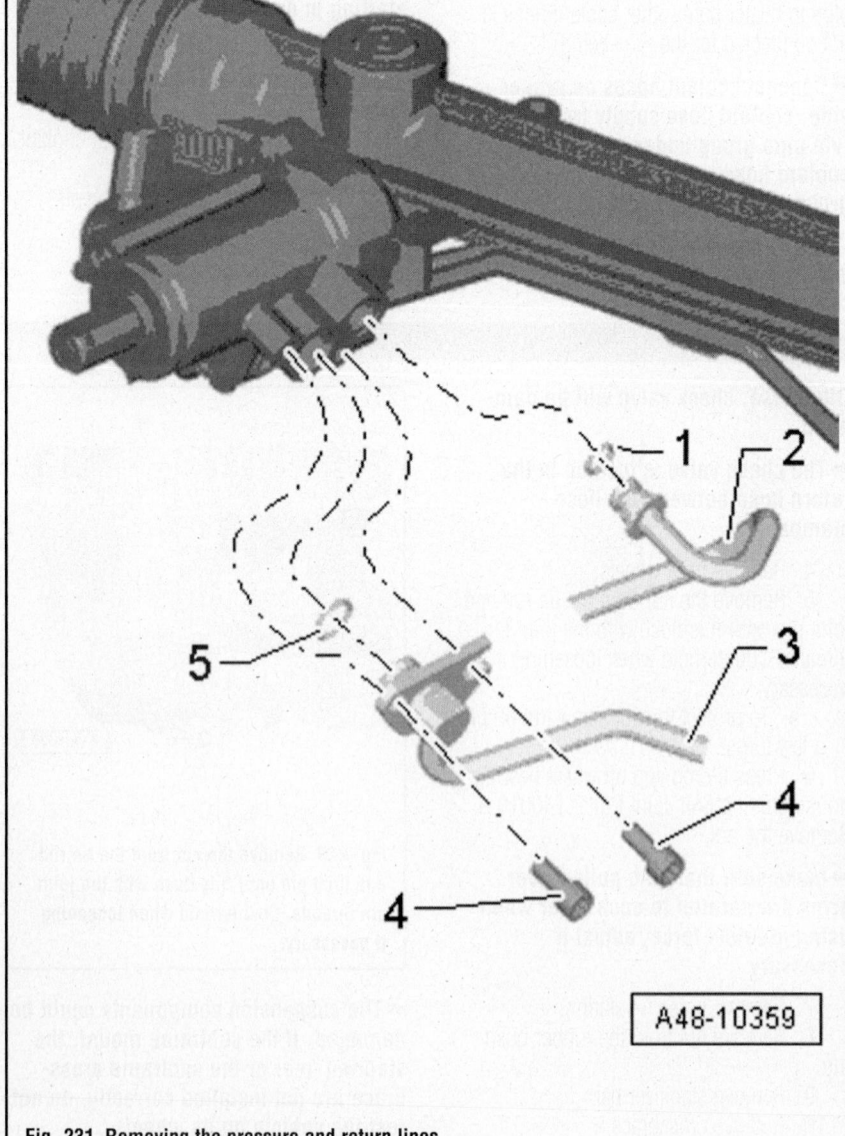

Fig. 231 Removing the pressure and return lines

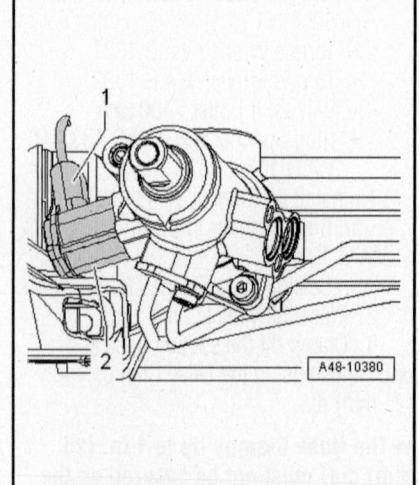

Fig. 233 Disconnecting the connector (1)

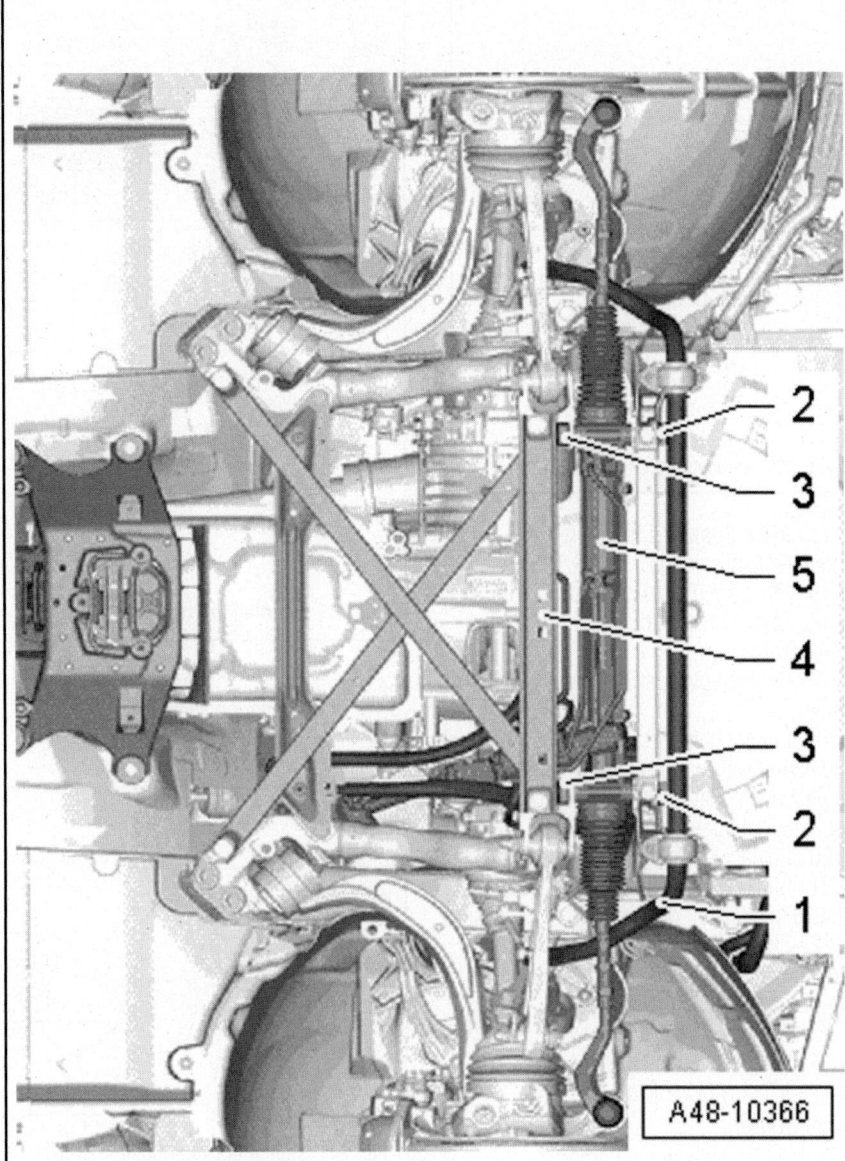

Fig. 234 Guide the steering gear (5) to the right slightly and remove it. (Ignore other numbered items).

26. Bring the steering gear into the center position.
27. Bleed the steering.
28. Check power steering fluid level.
29. Check all open line connections for leaks.
30. Perform an axle alignment.

Q7

See Figures 235 through 242.

➡**Tools Needed:**

- Hose clamps up to 25 mm dia. 3094
- Torque wrench V.A.G 1331
- Insert tool 17 V.A.G 1331/6
- Torque wrench V.A.G 1332
- Engine/transmission jack V.A.G 1383 A
- Support T10031
- Vehicle Diagnosis, Testing and Information System VAS 5051 B
- Ball joint puller T10187
- Wood block

➡**In order to remove steering gear, rear subframe must be removed and supported.**

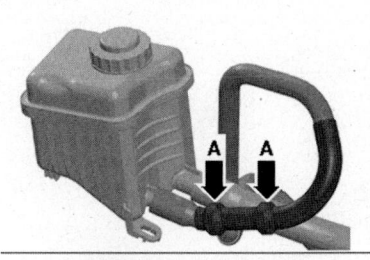
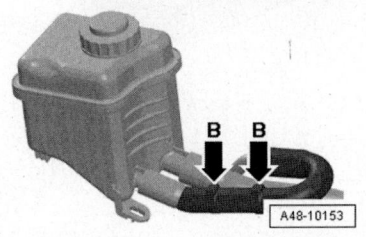

Fig. 235 The check valve is in the return hose between the cambers (A) arrows or between hose clamps (B) arrows.

1. Vehicles with air suspension, place vehicle on hoist Positioning Vehicle on Hoist.

➡**Hose clamps up to 1 in. (25 mm) dia. may not be secured on return hose in check valve area. Otherwise, check valve will be damaged.**

➡**The check valve is in the return hose between the cambers or between hose clamps.**

2. Clamp off suction and return line at reservoir with Hose Clamps up to 1 in. (25 mm) dia.
3. Remove front noise insulation.
4. Remove wheels.
5. Rotate steering gear toward left until stop.

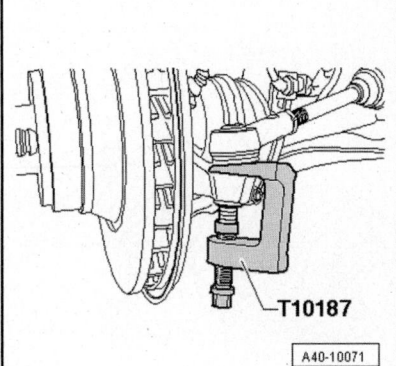

Fig. 236 Pressing the tie rod off of the wheel bearing housing

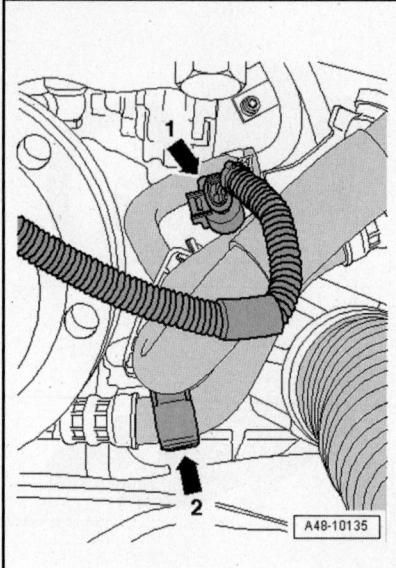

Fig. 237 Removing the connector and coolant hose bracket

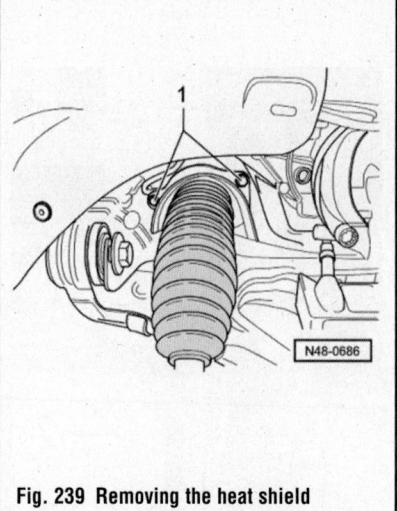

Fig. 239 Removing the heat shield

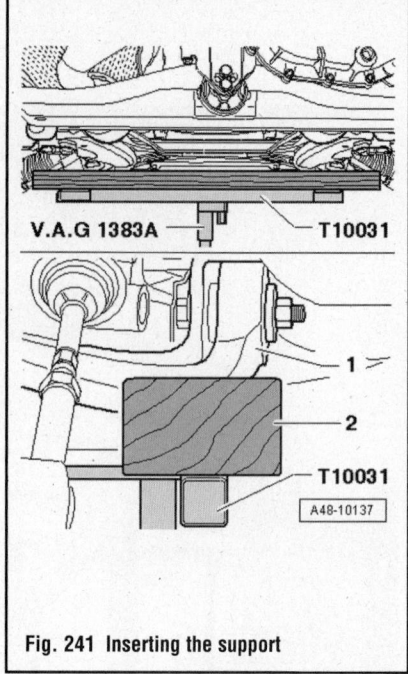

Fig. 241 Inserting the support

6. Remove nut and press tie rod off of wheel bearing housing.

7. Remove connector from Servotronic Solenoid Valve.

8. Remove coolant hose bracket from return line. Place coolant hoses on front final drive.

9. Remove the shield from steering gear (2 screws).

10. Remove bolt for universal joint at steering gear and remove universal joint from steering gear.

11. Remove bracket for hydraulic lines.

12. Remove pressure line and return line from steering gear.

13. Remove heat shield.

14. Remove bolts from steering gear.

15. Insert Support T10031 in Engine/transmission jack V.A.G 1383 A.

16. Place wood block on Support T10031.

17. Support rear subframe in lower control arm area.

18. Only remove rear bolts from subframe.

19. Lower subframe with Engine/transmission jack V.A.G 1383 only far enough so that it supports subframe. Do not allow subframe to hang freely.

20. Remove steering gear from mounts.

21. Slide steering gear to right side of vehicle in direction of arrow 1.

22. Skirt Servotronic Solenoid Valve around coolant hoses and rotate the steering gear forward.

23. Swing left tie rod downward.

24. Remove steering gear downward toward left side of vehicle.

To install:

Installation is in reverse order of removal. Observe the following:

25. Tighten new bolts for subframe.

26. Bleed steering system.

27. Check steering system for leaks.

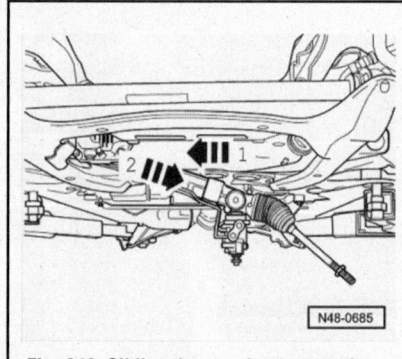

Fig. 242 Sliding the steering gear to the right

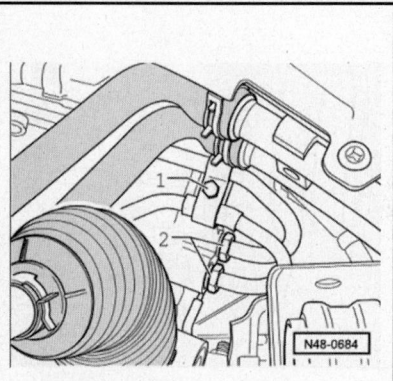

Fig. 238 Removing the bracket for the hydraulic lines and the pressure and return lines from the steering gear

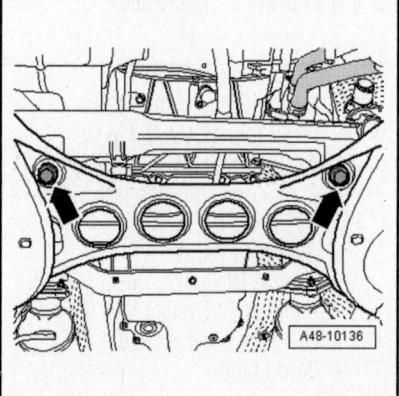

Fig. 240 Removing the bolts from the steering gear

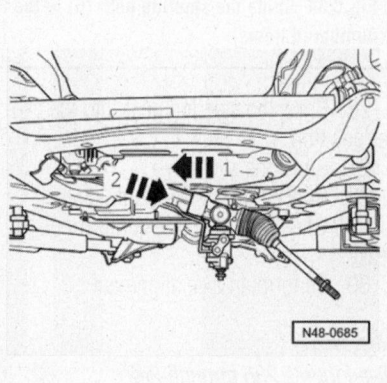

Fig. 243 Remove steering gear downward toward left side of vehicle in direction of arrow (2).

28. Check hydraulic fluid level and top off, if necessary.

29. After installation, a vehicle alignment must be performed.

30. Perform Steering Angle Sensor basic setting with Diagnostic Unit.

POWER STEERING PUMP

Q5

See Figures 243 through 250.

➡**Tools Needed:**

- Hose Clamps Up to 25 mm dia. 3094
- Spanner Wrench 3212
- Hose Clamp Pliers V.A.G 1275
- Torque Wrench V.A.G 1331
- Ratchet V.A.G 1331/1
- 17 mm ring spanner insert, open V.A.G 1331/10
- Used Oil Collection and Extraction Device V.A.G 1782
- Shop Crane Drip Tray VAS 6208
- Torque Wrench V.A.G 1410
- Pawl V.A.G 1410/3
- Sealing plug set VAS 6122

The power steering pump is not designed to be serviced. If there are customer complaints, the cause must be determined using a pressure and leak test. If there is a malfunction, replace the pump.

a. If there is no fluid in the reservoir, then the steering system must always be checked for leaks.

b. If there are leaks in the area of the line connections, the lines/connections must first be inspected for leaks, tightened as necessary and wiped dry.

c. Power steering pump is delivered without oil. Therefore, Hydraulic Oil must be filled before installation and turned by hand. Otherwise, noises when driving or damage to power steering pump may occur.

1. Place the vehicle on a hoist.

2. Remove engine cover upward.

3. Extract hydraulic oil from reservoir using Old Oil Collecting and Extracting Device V.A.G 1782.

4. Clamp off the suction hose and return hose using the Hose Clamps Up to 25 mm Diameter 3094.

➡**The hose clamps, up to 1 in. (25 mm) dia., must not be secured on the return hose in the check valve area. Otherwise, check valve will be damaged.**

5. Remove noise insulation.

6. Remove nuts and the coolant reservoir with the lines attached.

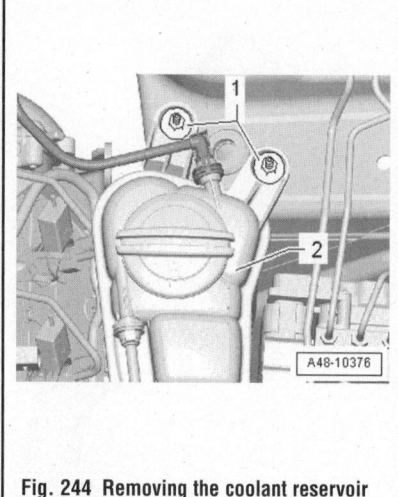

Fig. 244 Removing the coolant reservoir

7. Release and disconnect the connector on the coolant reservoir.

➡**Identify direction of travel before removing ribbed belt. Reversed direction of travel with a used belt can lead to malfunctions. When installing ribbed belt, make sure it is seated correctly on pulleys.**

8. Move the tensioner in direction of arrow to release the tension on the ribbed belt.

9. Remove the ribbed belt from the power steering pump belt pulley.

10. Release tensioner and remove the tool.

11. Mark the position of the belt pulley to the hub.

➡**If the power steering pump will be replaced, transfer the marking from the hub on the old pump to the new one.**

➡**Because of space restrictions, it is not possible to see the position of the belt pulley holes to the holes in the hub when installing.**

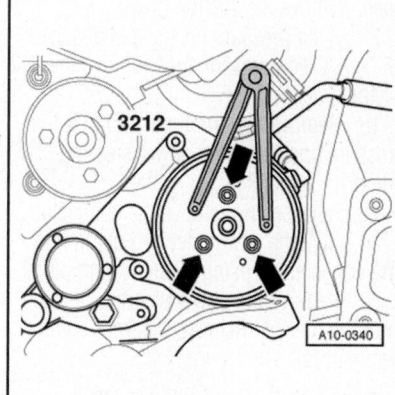

Fig. 246 Removing the belt pulley for the power steering pump

12. Remove bolts. Use Spanner Wrench 3212 as counterhold.

13. Remove belt pulley for power steering pump.

14. Place the Drip Tray under the power steering pump.

15. Carefully cut through the cable ties for the wiring harness if applicable.

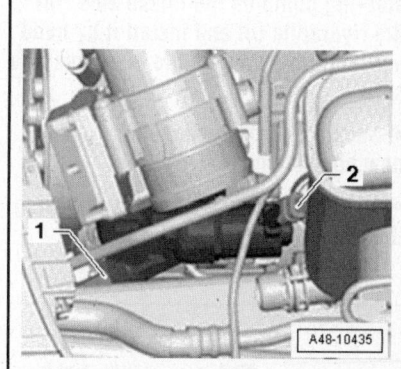

Fig. 247 Removing the union nut and the connector

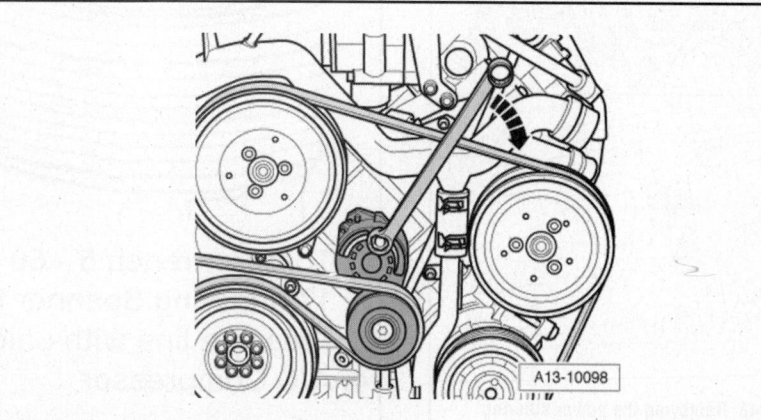

Fig. 245 Releasing the tension on the ribbed belt

16. Remove the clamp from the intake hose. Remove the suction hose.

17. If the pressure line is also attached to the A/C compressor, then remove the bolt for the bracket.

18. Remove the union nut and pull the pressure line out of the power steering pump.

19. Release and remove the connector.

20. Seal the power steering pump and line connections using clean sealing plugs.

21. Remove the power steering pump from the bracket. Remove the front bolts and rear bolt.

➡**The bolt cannot be seen in the bracket. The illustration shows it unscrewed.**

22. Remove power steering pump.

To install:

Installation is in reverse order of removal. Observe the following when doing so:

23. Drive the sleeve in the bracket back slightly to install the power steering pump.

➡**Replace seals and gaskets.**

➡**Before installing the new power steering pump on the intake side, fill the Hydraulic Oil and install it by hand until oil drains out on the high pressure side.**

➡**Secure all hose connections with new hose clamps.**

➡**The clamp cannot be tightened using the Hose Clamp Pliers V.A.G 1275**

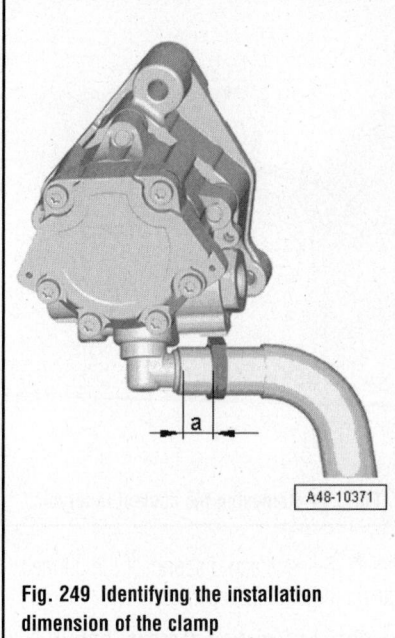

Fig. 249 Identifying the installation dimension of the clamp

when the power steering pump is installed due to restricted space.

24. Before installing the power steering pump, connect the intake hose and align the marking on the power steering pump with the "P" marking.

25. Secure the suction hose with the new clamp.

26. Secure the wiring harness on the supports using a new cable tie, where applicable.

27. Note the installation dimension of the clamp; it must be 4 mm.

28. Insert the power steering pump in the bracket.

29. First install bolts loosely.

30. Then install the rear bolt loosely.

31. Install and tighten the bolts.

➡**Make sure the intake hose is installed correctly and is not twisted or bent.**

32. Turn the hub by hand until oil runs out of the pressure side.

33. Press the pressure line into the power steering pump as far as the stop. Then install the union nut.

34. Connect connector.

35. Tighten the union nut with the 17 mm Ring Spanner Insert V.A.G 1331/10.

36. If the pressure line is also attached to the A/C compressor, then tighten the bolt for the bracket.

37. Clean oiled places in engine compartment.

38. Align the marking made on the belt pulley to the marking made on the hub.

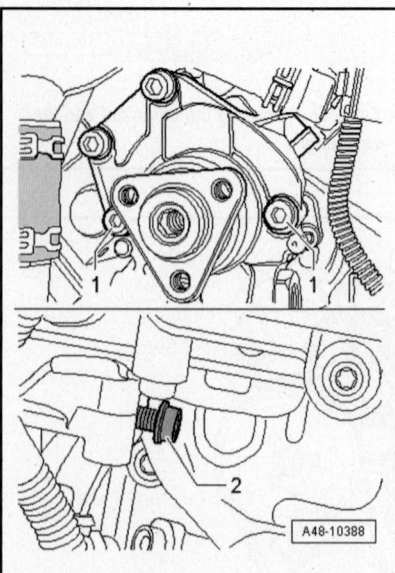

Fig. 248 Removing the power steering pump from the bracket

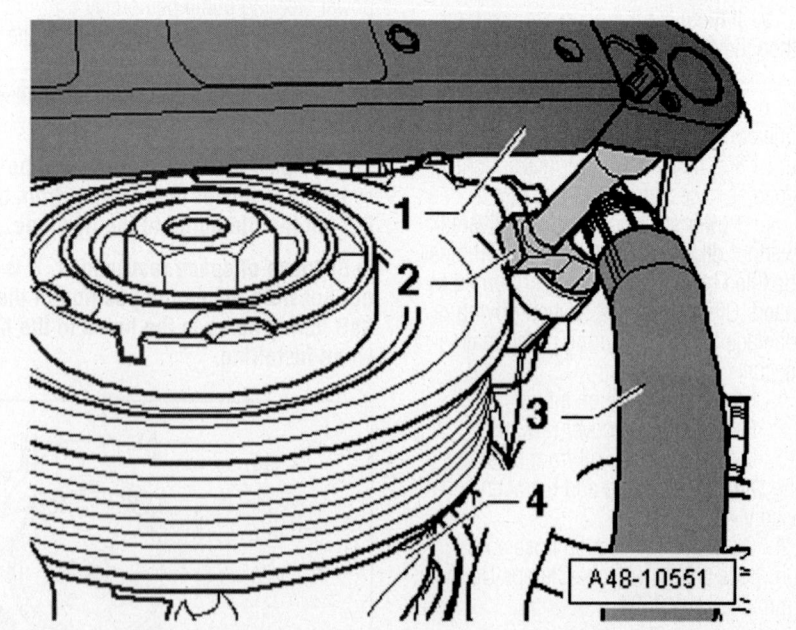

1. Torque wrench 5 - 50 Nm V.A.G 1331 with extension
2. 17 mm Ring Spanner Insert, Open V.A.G 1331/10
3. Pressure line with union nut
4. A/C Compressor

Fig. 250 Tightening the union nut

39. Tighten the belt pulley bolts.
   a. Install power steering pump ribbed belt.
40. Check power steering fluid level.
41. Bleed the steering.
42. Check the steering for leaks.
43. Install noise insulation.
44. Install ribbed belt and check alignment of ribbed belt.

➡**When installing ribbed belt, ensure it is correctly seated in ribbed belt pulley.**

Q7

3.6L Engine

See Figures 251 through 256.

➡**Tools Needed:**

- Hose clamps up to 25 mm dia. 3094
- Spanner wrench 3212
- Torque wrench V.A.G 1331
- Used Oil Collection and Extraction Device V.A.G 1782
- Spring type clip pliers VAS 5024 A
- Hydraulic fluid

Power steering pump is not designed to be serviced. If there are customer complaints, the cause must be determined using a pressure and leak test. If there is a malfunction, replace power steering pump.

➡**If fluid is missing in reservoir, check steering system for leaks.**

➡**If there are leaks in the area of the line connections, the lines/connections must first be inspected for leaks, tightened as necessary and wiped dry.**

➡**Pump is delivered without oil. Therefore, hydraulic oil must be filled before installation and turned by hand. Otherwise, noises when driving or damage to pump may occur.**

1. With vehicles with air suspension, place vehicle on hoist.
2. Only remove front noise insulation.
3. Extract hydraulic oil from reservoir with Used Oil Collection and Extraction Device V.A.G 1782.
4. Mark ribbed belt running direction
5. Remove ribbed belt.
6. Remove bolts. Counter hold belt pulley with Spanner Wrench 3212 when doing so.
7. Clamp off intake and return line in area of long member with Hose clamps up to 1 in. (25 mm) dia..
8. Lay cloths beneath and remove banjo bolt.

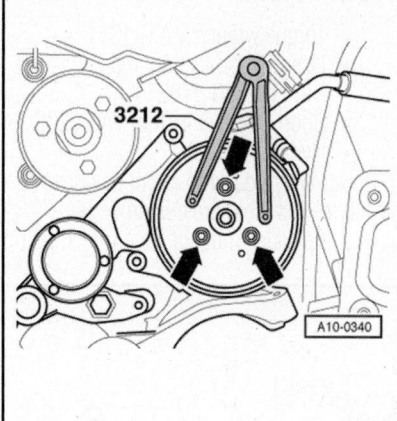

Fig. 251 Removing the bolts and counter holding the belt pulley

9. Open spring clip and disconnect intake hose.
10. Remove bolts and remove power steering pump.

To install:

11. Install intake hose so the markings on support align.
12. Installation is in reverse order of removal. Observe the following:
   a. Clean oiled places in engine compartment.
   b. Replace sealing rings.
   c. Before installing new pump on intake side, fill hydraulic oil and turn by hand until oil escapes on pressure side.
   d. Charge air system hose supports and hoses must be free of oil and grease before installation.
   e. Secure all hose connections with hose clamps appropriate to the model.
13. Turn hub by hand until oil runs out of pressure side.

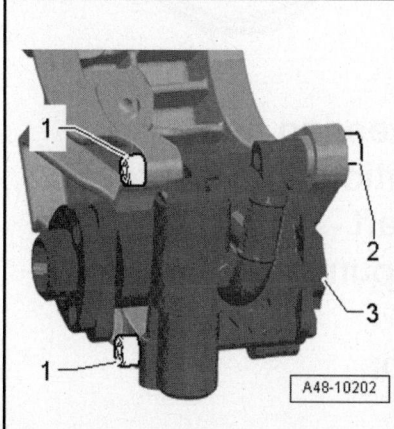

Fig. 252 Remove bolts (1, 2) and remove power steering pump (3).

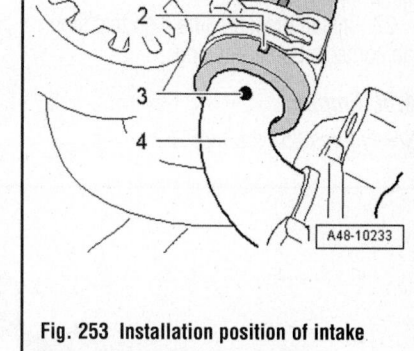

Fig. 253 Installation position of intake hose and pressure line at power steering pump

14. To mark positioning of power steering pump easier, drive threaded bushings for bolts back slightly into bracket.
15. Insert power steering pump.
16. First tighten front bolts, then tighten rear bolt.
17. Tighten belt pulley on power steering pump.
18. Secure suction hose with new hose clamp. Note location of suction hose on power steering pump.
19. Install new sealing rings onto banjo bolt. Tighten pressure line banjo bolt.
20. Clean oiled places in engine compartment.
21. On vehicles with air suspension, position vehicle on wheels.
22. Top off hydraulic oil.
23. Check power steering fluid level.
24. Bleed steering system.
25. Check steering system for leaks.

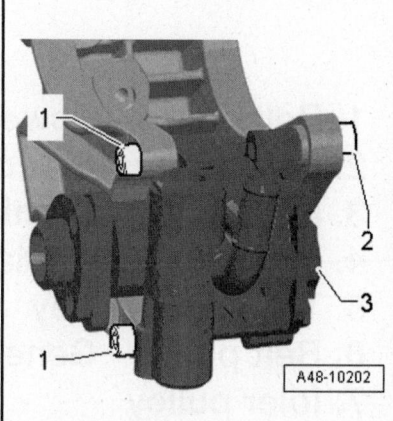

Fig. 254 Installing the power steering pump

→When installing ribbed belt, ensure it is correctly seated in ribbed belt pulley

26. Install ribbed belt and check alignment.

27. Install pressure line 3 so that stop tab contacts pump housing.

4.6L Engine

See Figures 257 through 262.

→Tools Needed:

- Torque wrench V.A.G 1331
- Used Oil Collection and Extraction Device V.A.G 1782
- Shop Crane Drip Tray VAS 6208
- Hydraulic fluid

Power steering pump is not designed to be serviced. If there are customer complaints, the cause must be determined using

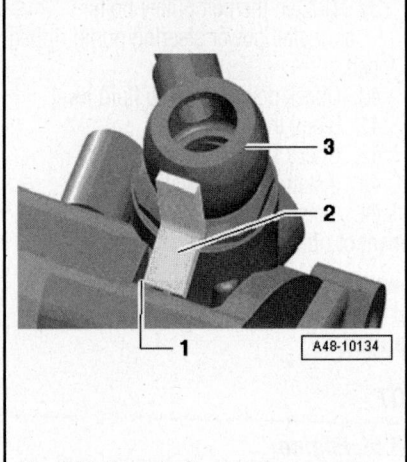

Fig. 256 Pressure line location on power steering pump

a pressure and leak test. If there is a malfunction, replace power steering pump.

→If fluid is missing in reservoir, check steering system for leaks.

→If there are leaks in the area of the line connections, the lines/connections must first be inspected for leaks, tightened as necessary and wiped dry.

→Pump is delivered without oil. Therefore, hydraulic oil must be filled before installation and turned by hand. Otherwise, noises when driving or damage to pump may occur.

1. With vehicles with air suspension, place vehicle on hoist Positioning Vehicle on Hoist.

2. Extract hydraulic oil from reservoir with Used Oil Collection and Extraction Device V.A.G 1782.

3. Remove left front wheel.

4. Remove front noise insulation.

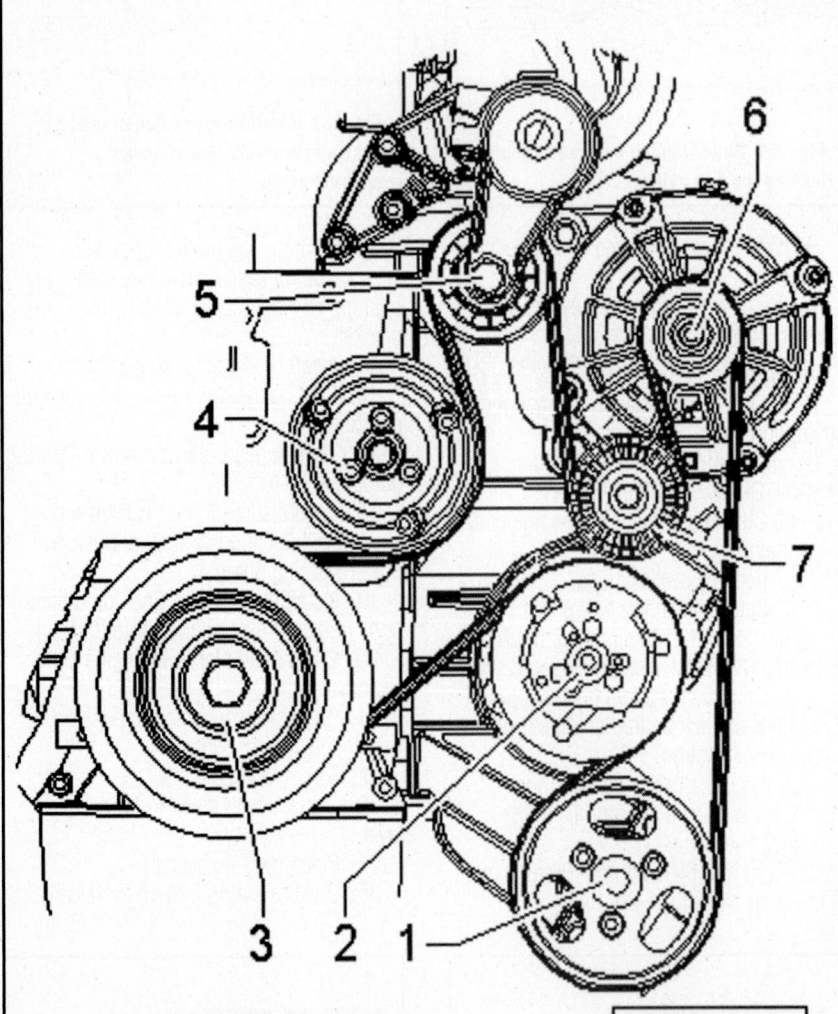

A48-10201

1. Belt pulley - Power steering pump
2. Belt pulley - Air conditioning compressor
3. Belt pulley - Crankshaft
4. Belt pulley - Coolant pump
5. Tensioner pulley
6. Belt pulley - Generator
7. Idler pulley

Fig. 255 Checking belt installation

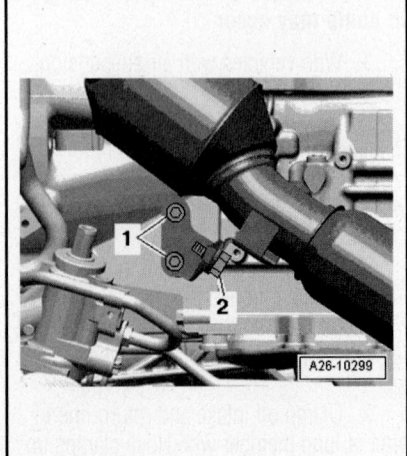

Fig. 257 Removing the left primary catalytic converter strap

5. Remove the noise insulation bracket.
6. Remove head shield from steering gear.
7. Remove the bolts and the left primary catalytic converter strap.

➡**Place a cloth under separation point to absorb escaping hydraulic oil.**

8. Remove hose from reservoir.

➡**Place a cloth under separation point to absorb escaping hydraulic oil.**

9. Remove bolts and nut to remove the suction line.
10. Remove pressure line banjo bolt.
11. Remove bolts and remove power steering pump.

➡**When removing power steering pump, note location of input shaft.**

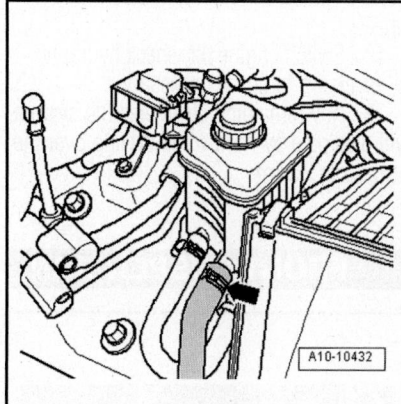

Fig. 258 Removing the hose from the reservoir

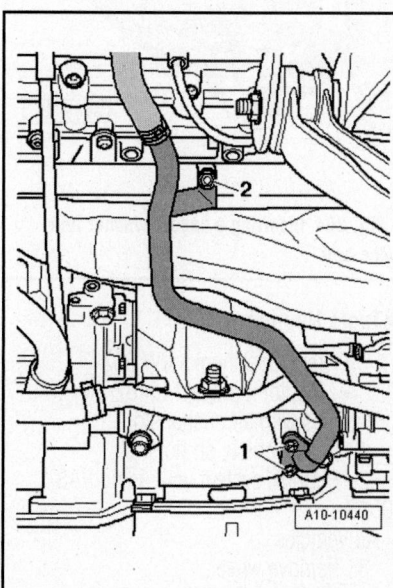

Fig. 259 Removing the suction line

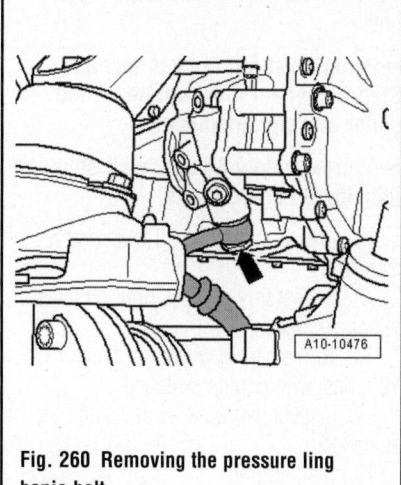

Fig. 260 Removing the pressure ling banjo bolt

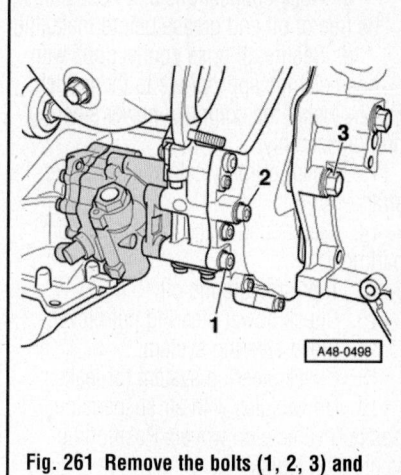

Fig. 261 Remove the bolts (1, 2, 3) and remove the power steering pump

To install:

Installation is in reverse order of removal. Observe the following:

a. Clean oiled places in engine compartment.

b. Always replace seal on power steering pump input shaft and suction line.

c. Before installing new power steering pump on intake side, fill hydraulic oil and turn by hand until oil escapes on pressure side.

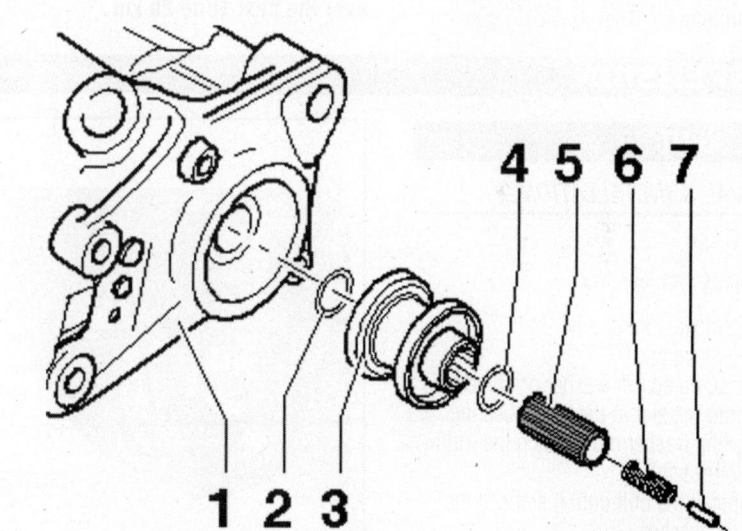

1. **Power steering pump**
2. **Sealing ring**
3. **Lightly coat sleeve, splines with lithium grease G 052 150 A2**
4. **Sealing ring**
5. **Lightly coat input shaft, splines with lithium grease**
6. **Lightly coat spring with lithium grease before inserting input shaft**
7. **Buffer stop**

Fig. 262 Install the complete power steering pump assembly.

d. Hose connections and hoses must be free of oil and grease before installing

e. Secure all hose connections with hose clamps appropriate to the model.

12. Install the complete power steering pump assembly.

13. Install primary catalytic converter strap.

14. Clean oiled places in engine compartment.

15. Top off hydraulic oil.

16. Check power steering fluid level.

17. Bleed steering system.

18. Check steering system for leaks.

19. On vehicles with air suspension, position vehicle on wheels Positioning Vehicle on Hoist.

BLEEDING

1. After steering system assembly, system must be bled differently depending on extent of reassembly.

2. Bleed after replacing entire steering system or replacing steering gear:

3. Inspect hydraulic oil level and top off as needed.

4. Raise vehicle until front wheels are off the ground.

5. Briefly start engine (max. 2 seconds).

➡ **Pump must not draw in any air. Steering wheel must not be turned under any circumstances.**

➡ **Approximately 30 sec. wait between individual engine starts.**

6. Inspect hydraulic oil level and top off as needed.

7. Repeat this process until oil level remains constant.

8. Turn steering wheel from lock to lock 10 times, with engine switched off.

9. Inspect hydraulic oil level and top off as needed.

10. Start engine.

11. Turn steering wheel 10 times from stop to stop.

12. Switch off engine and wait 2 - 3 minutes until foam on hydraulic oil in reservoir has dissipated.

13. Inspect hydraulic oil level and top off as needed.

➡ **Any remaining air in steering system will dissipate by itself when driving over the next 10 to 20 km.**

➡ **Bleed after assembling component of the steering system, besides the steering gear (pump, hoses, etc.):**

14. Inspect hydraulic oil level and top off as needed.

15. Briefly start engine (max. 2 seconds).

➡ **Pump must not draw in any air and steering wheel must not be turned under any circumstances.**

➡ **Approximately 30 sec. wait between individual engine starts.**

16. Inspect hydraulic oil level and top off as needed.

17. Repeat this process until oil level remains constant.

18. Start engine and allow to run 2 3 minutes, do not turn steering wheel.

19. Switch engine off, check hydraulic oil level and top off if necessary.

20. Any remaining air in steering system will dissipate by itself when driving over the next 10 to 20 km.

SUSPENSION   FRONT SUSPENSION

BALL JOINT

REMOVAL & INSTALLATION

Q5

See Figures 263 and 264.

1. Remove control arm.

2. Remove bolt.

3. Insert a spacer washer or something similar into the slot in the wheel bearing housing (the washer must match the width of the slot exactly).

4. Install the bolt until it stops at the back of the washer.

5. Side the wheel bearing housing slot by installing the bolt further (one half turn).

6. Remove ball joint from the wheel bearing housing.

To install:

Installation is in reverse order of removal. Observe the following when doing so:

7. Install ball joint into the wheel bearing housing as far as the contact surface.

➡ **If the ball joint is not inserted up to the contact surface arrows then the threaded connection on the wheel bearing housing could get damaged.**

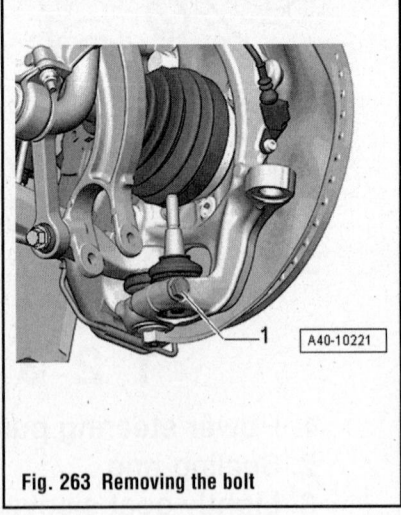

Fig. 263 Removing the bolt

8. Install control arm.

9. Tighten wheel.

10. Vehicle alignment required.

LOWER CONTROL ARM

REMOVAL & INSTALLATION

Q7

See Figures 265 through 267.

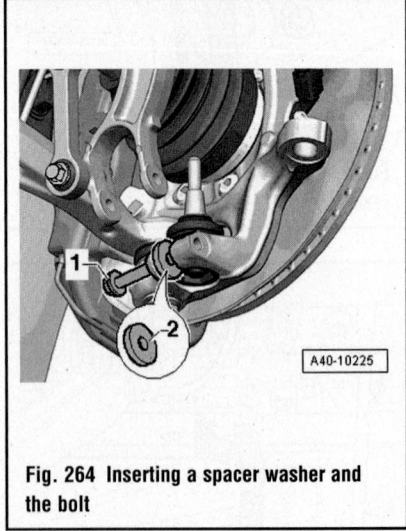

Fig. 264 Inserting a spacer washer and the bolt

➡ **Tools Needed:**

- Tensioner hooks VW 552
- Ball joint puller T10187

Vehicles with air suspension:

1. Place vehicle on hoist.

2. Perform system vent using VAS 5051B.

All vehicles:

3. Remove wheel.

4. Wheel housing liner.

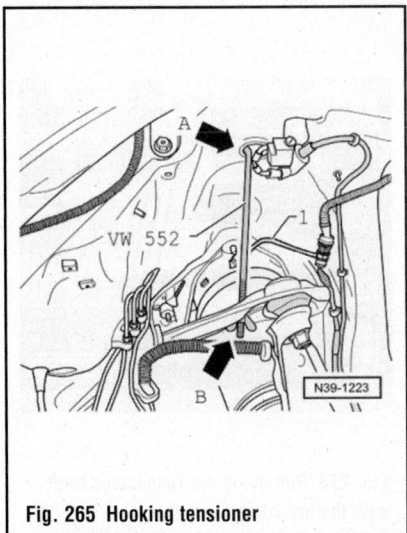

Fig. 265 Hooking tensioner

5. Hook in tensioner hooks VW 552 in upper opening of wheel housing arrow A and in upper control arm arrow B.

6. Lightly pre-tension control arm to prevent damage to ball stud caused by ball joint.

7. Remove suspension strut from lower control arm.

8. Loosen nut on lower control arm and press off ball stud using ball joint puller T10187.

9. Remove nut.

10. Disconnect connections and remove lower control arm from wheel bearing housing.

To install:

Installation is in reverse order of removal, with special attention to the following:

➡**Bonded rubber bushings can only be turned to a limited extent. Only tighten suspension bolts when**

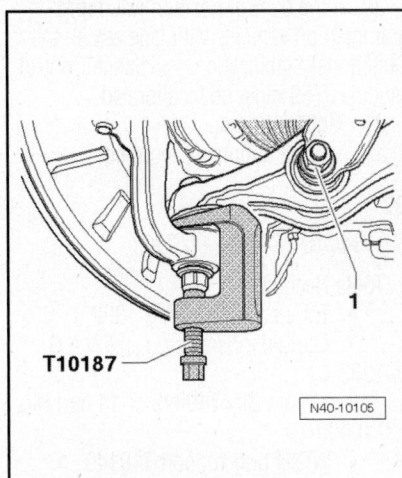

Fig. 266 Removing the strut from the lower control arm

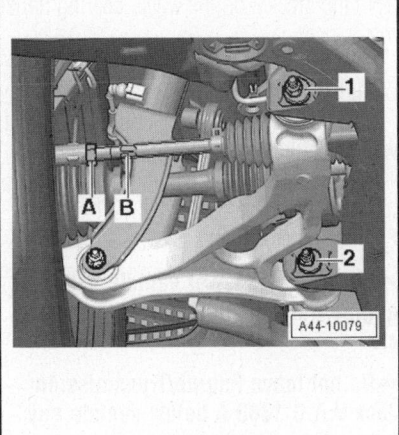

Fig. 267 Removing the lower control arm

vehicle is in curb weight or control position.

➡**Wheel bearing, lifting to curb weight position on vehicles with coil springs.**

➡**Wheel bearing, lifting to control position on vehicles with air suspension.**

11. Wheel housing liner, installing.

12. Mount wheel and tighten.

13. On vehicles with air suspension, position vehicle on wheels.

14. Perform vehicle alignment.

Checking and aligning front/rear axle must take place on a VW/Audi recommended alignment stand.

STABILIZER BAR

REMOVAL & INSTALLATION

Q5

See Figure 268.

1. Remove noise insulation.

2. Disconnect left and right connectors.

3. Remove left and right nuts and the clamp.

4. Remove stabilizer bar.

To install:

Installation is in the reverse order of removal. Observe the following when doing so:

➡**Bonded rubber bushings can only be turned to a limited extent. Only tighten suspension bolts when vehicle is in curb weight or control position.**

➡**Wheel bearing, lifting to curb weight position on vehicles with coil springs.**

➡**If you replace stabilizer, note chassis version.**

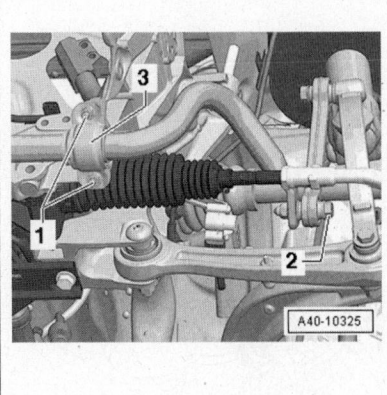

Fig. 268 Removing the stabilizer bar

➡**Stabilizer and mounting must be free of grease.**

➡**Install the rubber bushing opening in the direction of the subframe contact surface.**

5. Install the nuts but do not tighten them.

6. Install left and right threaded connections but do not tighten them.

7. Wheel bearing, lifting to curb weight position on vehicles with coil springs.

8. Tighten connections.

STRUT & SPRING ASSEMBLY

REMOVAL & INSTALLATION

Q5

See Figures 269 through 273.

Tools Needed:
a. Spreader 3424
b. Torque Wrench V.A.G 1331
c. Torque Wrench V.A.G 1332
d. Wheel Hub Support T10149
e. Engine/Transmission Jack V.A.G 1383 A

1. Remove wheel.

2. Remove additional reinforcement.

3. Remove plenum chamber cover.

Applies to vehicles with electronically controlled damping:

4. Release and remove the connector.

5. Remove the brackets and free up the wire.

Continuation for all vehicles:

6. Remove the shock absorber fork.

7. Remove nuts and the cover.

8. Remove bolts from the flange shaft/transmission.

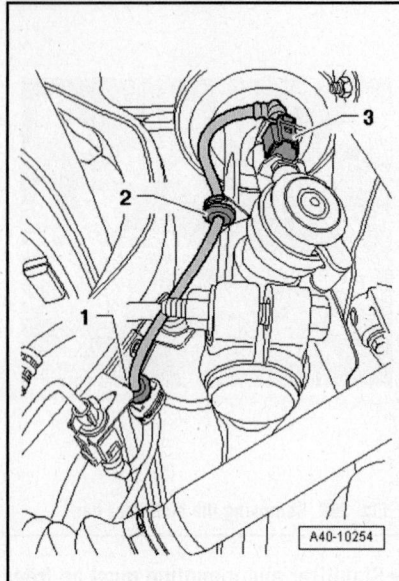

Fig. 269 Removing the connector and freeing up the wire

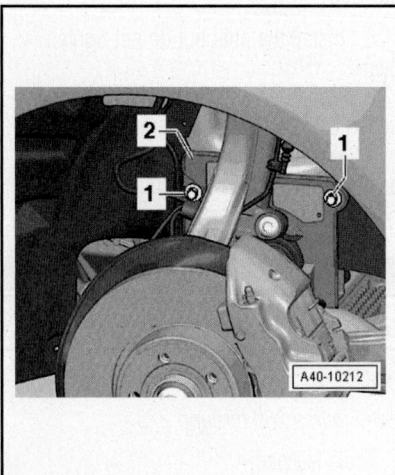

Fig. 270 Removing the cover

Fig. 271 Removing the bolts from the flange shaft/transmission

9. Remove the brake line and wires from the bracket on the wheel bearing housing.

10. Turn wheel hub far enough until one of the holes for wheel bolts is on top.

11. Install Wheel Hub Support T10149 1 with wheel bolt on wheel hub.

12. Support wheel bearing housing over the Wheel Hub Support T10149 1 with Engine/Transmission Jack V.A.G 1383 A.

➡ **Do not lift or lower vehicle with engine/transmission jack below vehicle.**

➡ **Do not leave Engine/Transmission Jack V.A.G 1383 A below vehicle any longer than necessary.**

13. Remove bolt.

➡ **The slits in the wheel bearing housing must not be widened using a chisel or similar tool.**

14. Remove booth joint pins in the upper control arm from the wheel bearing housing.

➡ **Do not lower wheel bearing housing more than necessary.**

15. Remove bolts 1 through 4 and remove the suspension strut with mounting bracket.

To install:

Installation is in the reverse order of removal. Observe the following when doing so:

a. Always observe the tightening sequence for the mounting bracket threaded connection with the suspension strut to the suspension strut tower.

b. Tightening specification of threaded connection depicted as numbered is mandatory.

Fig. 272 Installing the wheel hub support

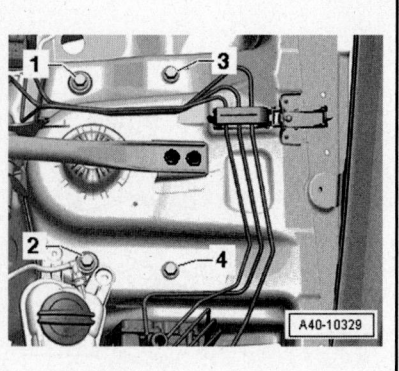

Fig. 273 Removing the suspension strut with the mounting bracket

c. Push the upper control arms down as far as possible while tightening the bolts.

16. Tighten threaded connection.

➡ **On vehicles with electronic damper control, make sure the T-pin arrow fits into the groove in the shock absorber fork when being installed.**

➡ **Bonded rubber bushings can only be turned to a limited extent. Only tighten suspension bolts when vehicle is in curb weight or control position.**

17. Wheel bearing, lifting to curb weight position on vehicles with coil springs.

18. On vehicles with automatic headlamp range control system, perform basic setting of headlamps.

19. If the Vehicle Level Sensor was removed and installed on a vehicle with electronic damper regulation or if the linkage was loosened, the control position must be reprogrammed.

20. If the control position was reprogrammed on vehicles with lane assist, the Directional Stabilization Assistance Control Module J759 must be recalibrated.

21. Tighten wheel.

22. Vehicle alignment required.

Q7

See Figures 274 through 280.

Tools Needed:
- Torque wrench V.A.G 1332
- Engine/transmission jack V.A.G 1383 A
- 12 mm Bits T10099 or 14 mm Bits T10099/1
- Wheel hub support T10149
- Ball joint puller T10187

1. Remove wheel.

2. Remove bolt 2.

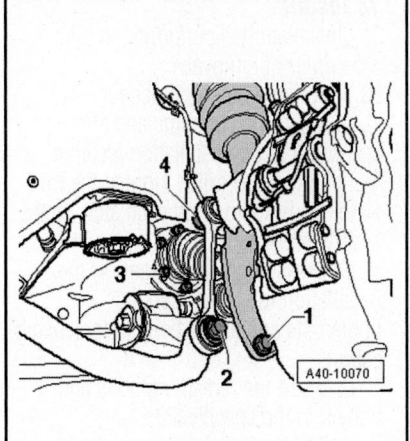

Fig. 274 Disconnecting the driveshaft from the rear final drive

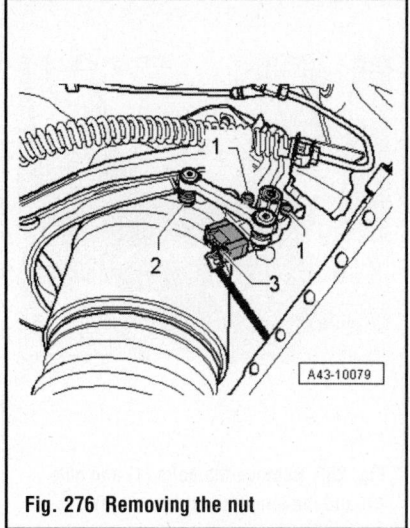

Fig. 276 Removing the nut

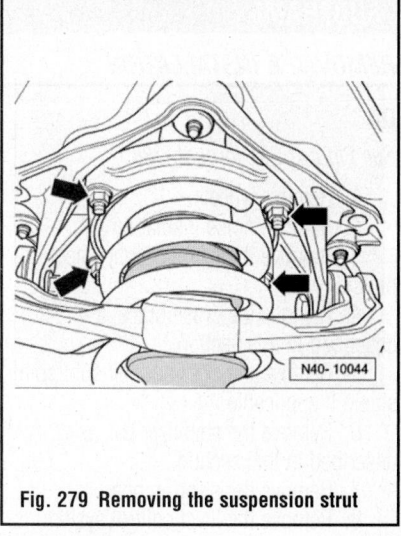

Fig. 279 Removing the suspension strut

3. Disconnect the driveshaft from rear final drive. Use 12 mm Bits T10099 or 14 mm Bits T10099/1 to loosen bolts 3.

4. Remove nut from tie rod end and press tie rod end off of wheel bearing housing.

5. In vehicles with level control system sensor, remove nut.

6. Remove brake hose with bracket from wheel bearing housing.

7. Turn wheel hub far enough until one of the holes for wheel bolts is on top.

8. Install wheel hub support T10149 with wheel bolt on wheel hub.

9. Support wheel bearing housing over Wheel Hub Support T10149 with Engine/transmission jack V.A.G 1383 A.

➡ **Do not lift or lower vehicle with engine/transmission jack below vehicle.**

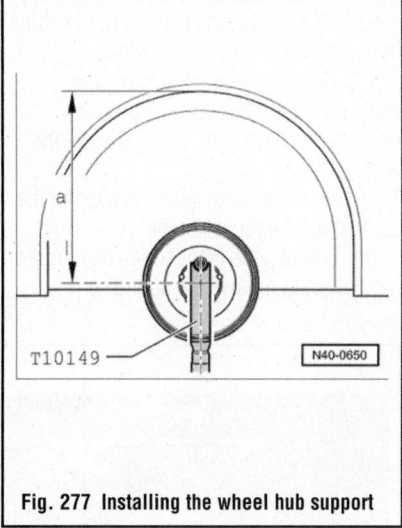

Fig. 277 Installing the wheel hub support

➡ **Do not leave engine/transmission jack V.A.G 1383 A below vehicle any longer than necessary.**

10. Remove nut from upper control arm and press arm off.

11. Remove the suspension strut from body.

12. Remove the connector nut, suspension strut to lower control arm.

13. Do not the lower wheel bearing housing more than necessary.

14. Remove bolt from lower control arm and remove suspension strut.

To install:

Installation is in reverse order of removal, with special attention to the following:

15. Wheel bearing, lifting to curb weight position on vehicles with coil springs.

16. On vehicles with automatic headlamp range control, perform headlamp basic setting.

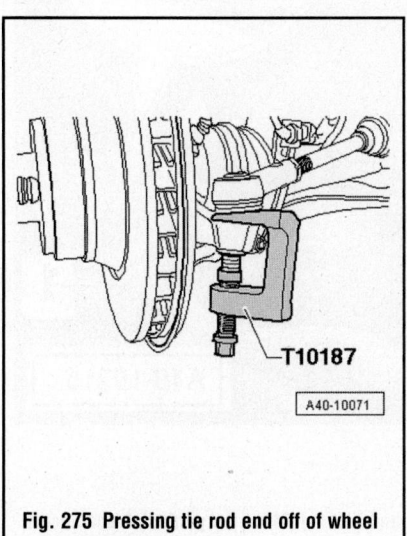

Fig. 275 Pressing tie rod end off of wheel bearing housing

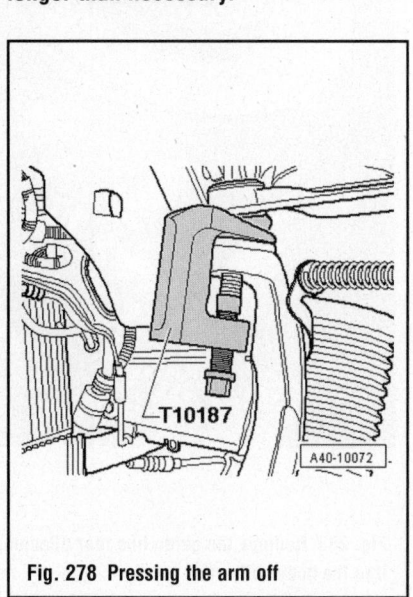

Fig. 278 Pressing the arm off

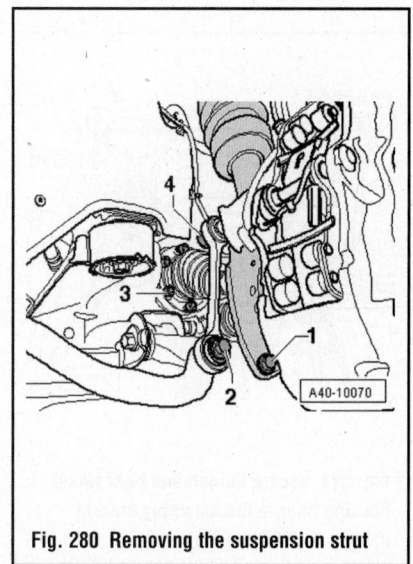

Fig. 280 Removing the suspension strut

SUBFRAME

REMOVAL & INSTALLATION

Q5

See Figures 281 through 288.

1. Remove wheels.

2. Remove noise insulation.

3. Remove the left and right wheel housing liner.

4. Remove the cross brace, as described in this section.

5. Remove the right and left subframe shield if applicable.

6. Remove the stabilizer bar, as described in this section.

7. Remove the steering gear.

8. Remove the level control system sensor, if applicable.

9. Secure the left and right wheel housing liner to the mounting bracket using a T10038.

10. Remove the left and right control arms, as described in this section.

11. Support the engine entirely using the engine support bridge.

12. Remove the bolts and nuts and the longitudinal braces.

13. Remove the guide line rear attaching nut and bolt. Move the guide link and secure it to the body with wire.

14. On vehicles with electro-hydraulic engine mounts, disconnect the left electro-hydraulic engine mount solenoid valve and right electro-hydraulic engine mount solenoid valve connector.

15. Depending on the engine version, remove the nut for the electrical wiring bracket on the right side of the vehicle.

16. Remove the bolt for the power steering line bracket.

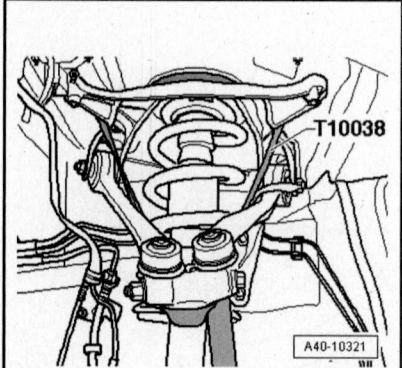

Fig. 281 Secure the left and right wheel housing liner to the mounting bracket using a T10038 as illustrated.

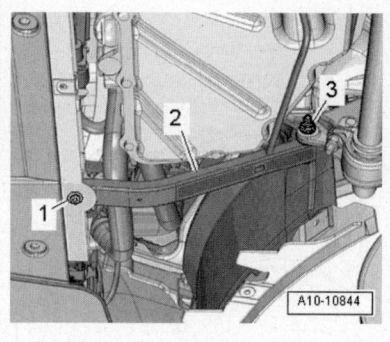

Fig. 282 Remove the bolts (1) and nuts (3) and the longitudinal braces (2).

17. Remove the left and right engine mount bolts. Move the left and right engine mount retaining plate to the side.

18. Before lowering the subframe, make sure all the electrical wiring connections have been disconnected and removed.

19. Mark the installation location of the subframe, using a felt-tip pen.

20. Remove the eight subframe mounting bolts and remove the subframe.

To install:

21. Installation is performed in the reverse order of removal.

22. Subframe bolting procedure:

a. Insert the subframe and align according to the installation location markings made earlier. Tighten the forward two bolts (one on each side) to the specification.

b. Press the rear subframe at the installation reference markings and tighten the applicable bolts to the specification.

c. Insert the remaining bolts and tighten to the specification.

d. Tighten the eight screws to the additional tightening angle after performing axle alignment.

➡**Bonded rubber bushings can only be turned to a limited extent. Only tighten suspension screws when vehicle is in curb weight or control position.**

23. On vehicles with automatic headlamp range control system, perform a basic setting on the headlamps.

24. If the vehicle level sensor was removed and installed on a vehicle with electronically controlled damping or if the

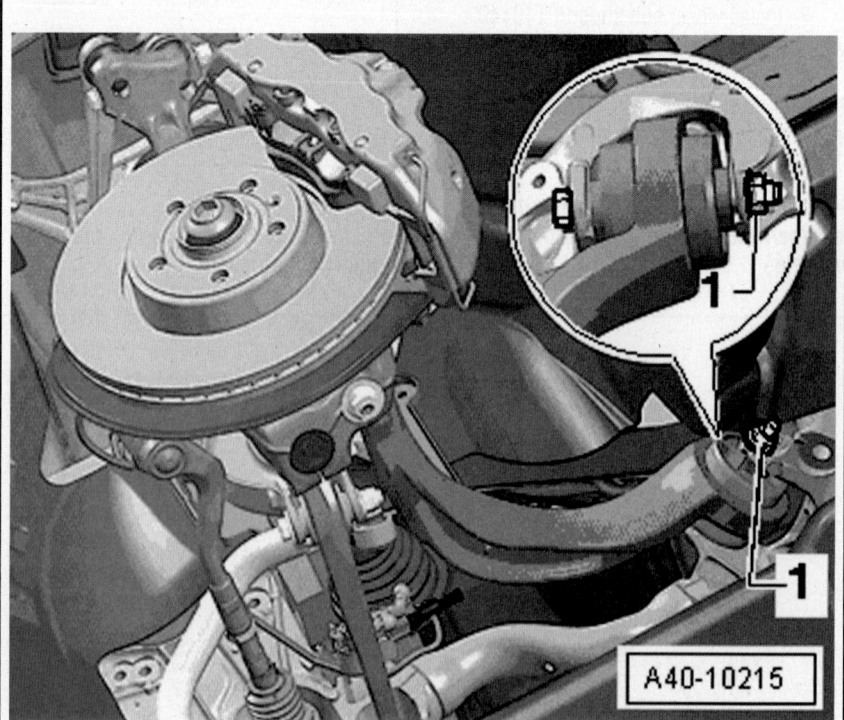

Fig. 283 Remove the guide line rear attaching nut and bolt (1). Move the guide link and secure it to the body with wire.

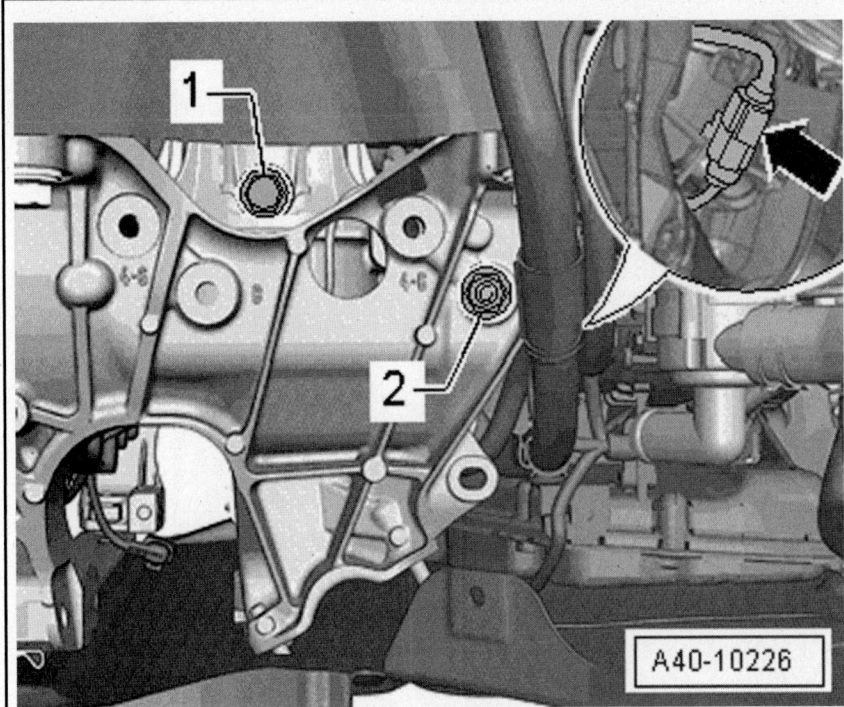

Fig. 284 On vehicles with electro-hydraulic engine mounts, disconnect the left electro-hydraulic engine mount solenoid valve (1) and right electro-hydraulic engine mount solenoid valve connector (arrow). Depending on the engine version, remove the nut (2) for the electrical wiring bracket on the right side of the vehicle.

1. Vehicle Diagnosis, Testing & Info. System VAS5051B

➡Subframe is removed using scissor lift table. Front mounting points of engine carrier must be secured using shorter bolts. Subframe is removed together with the following: Steering gear, front axle drive, lower control arm and wheel bearing housing. The suspension struts with mounting brackets and upper control arms remain on vehicle.

2. For vehicles with air suspension (this step only), place vehicle on hoist and perform a System Vent using VAS 5051B.

3. Remove the front wheels.

4. Remove noise insulation.

5. Remove the left front wheel housing liner.

6. Remove coolant line retaining clamp nuts and screws arrows.

7. With connectors removed, coolant lines may be laid aside slightly in order to position supports 10 - 222 A /19 on longitudinal members.

8. Support engine entirely with engine support bridge.

9. For vehicles with 3.6L FSI engine, do the following:

linkage was loosened, the control position must be reprogrammed.

25. If the control position was reprogrammed on vehicles with lane assist, the lane assist control module must be recalibrated.

26. Tighten wheel.

27. Axle alignment is required.

Q7

See Figures 289 through 300.

➡**Tools needed:**

- Engine support bridge 10 - 222 A
- Adapter 10 - 222 A /22
- Bracket with spindle and hook 10 - 222 A /10
- Engine Sling 2024 A
- Engine Support Basic Set T40091
- Engine Support Supplement Set T40093
- Engine Support T10014 (only needed with 3.0L TDI)
- Ball joint puller T10187
- Hose clamps up to 25 mm diameter 3094
- Scissor lift table VAS 6131
- Support Set VAS 6131/10, VAS 6131/11, VAS 6131/13

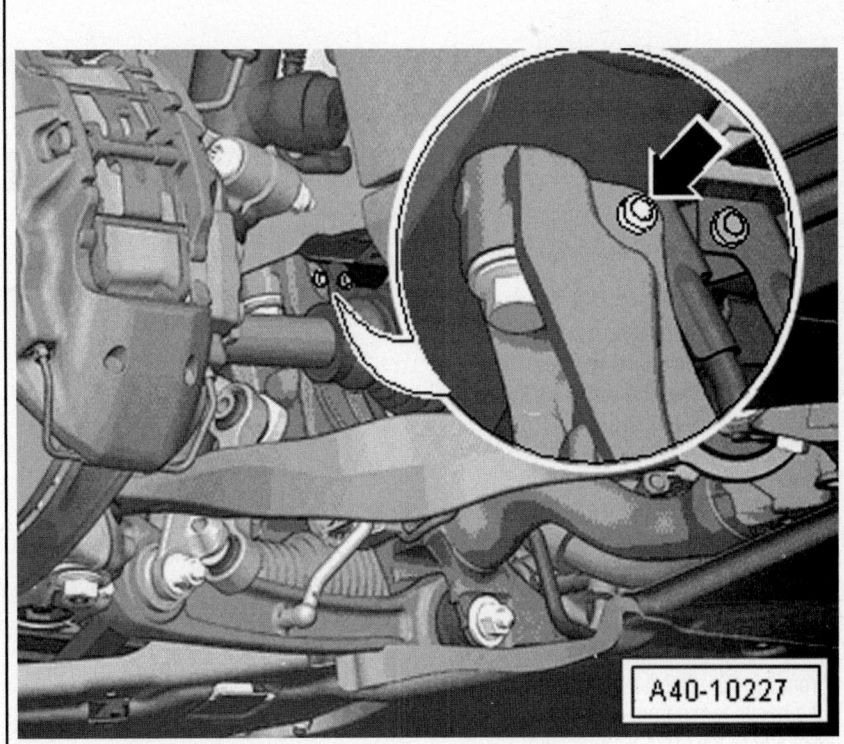

Fig. 285 Remove the bolt for the power steering line bracket (arrow).

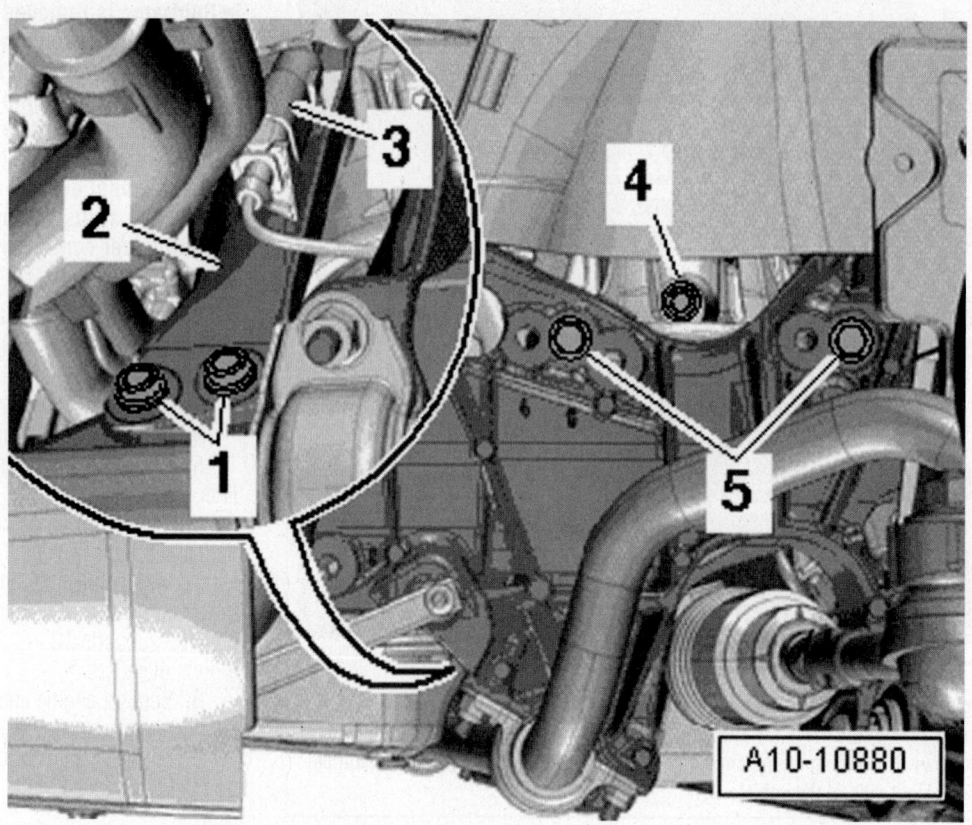

Fig. 286 Remove the left and right engine mount bolts (1 and 5). Move the left and right engine mount retaining plate (2) to the side. (Ignore items 3 and 4.)

a. Remove bolt from the outside edge of the belt tensioner.

b. Attach the engine sling 2024 A /2 with an M8 x 35 bolt to the belt tensioner bolt hole.

c. Mount the 10 - 222 A, the 10 - 222 A /22 and the supplement set T40091/3 on the fender bolting edges. Attach the parts from the T40091 and from the T40093 axially across the engine compartment. Mount the adapter T40093/3 to the notches on the longitudinal member. Push the left refrigerant lines to the side and out of the way. Push the support T40091/2 with both slides T40093/5 into both mounts T40093/4.

d. Install the long spindles from the 10 - 222 A and engage the hooks to the front engine lifting eye and to the 2024 A /2. Secure the support T40091/2 with the connector pins and splints T40093/4.

⁂ CAUTION

Loose parts on the engine support bridge can cause serious personal injury.

e. Tension engine by tightening 2 spindles evenly.

10. For vehicles with 4.2L FSI engine, do the following:

a. Remove rear and then the front engine covers.

b. Remove left and right air filter housing.

c. Assemble and mount the engine support/lift assembly components: 10-222 A, 10-222 A/22, T40091/3, 10-222 A, 10 - 222 A /19.

d. Mount the 10 - 222 A /19 to the notches on the longitudinal member. Push the left refrigerant lines to the side and out of the way.

e. Engage hooks on both short spindles 10 - 222 A /10 at rear engine lifting eyes.

f. Slide support T40091/2 with both slides T40093/5 in both mounts T40093/4.

g. Install long spindles from 10-222 A and engage spindle hooks at both front engine lifting eyes.

h. Secure support T40091/2 with connector pins and splints T40093/4.

i. Tension engine by tightening 4 spindles evenly.

11. For vehicles with 3.0L TDI engine, do the following:

a. Carefully remove engine cover from 4 retaining pins in succession.

b. Remove air filter housing.

c. Remove air guide hose.

d. Remove ribbed belt and belt tensioner.

e. Install T10014 in ribbed belt tensioner securing hole.

f. Assemble and position the engine support/lifting assembly components: 10-222 A, T40091/3 and 2, 10-222 A, 10 - 222 A /19

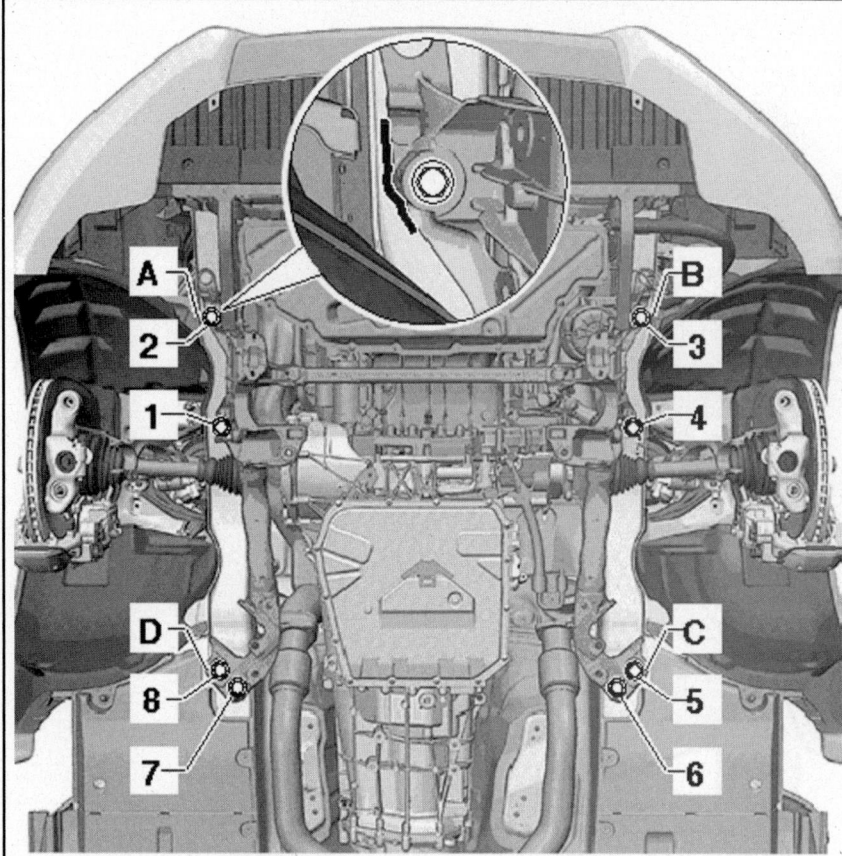

A. — D. Installation locations
1. — 8. Bolts

Fig. 287 Mark the installation location of the subframe (A to D, for example), using a felt-tip pen. Remove the eight bolts and remove the subframe.

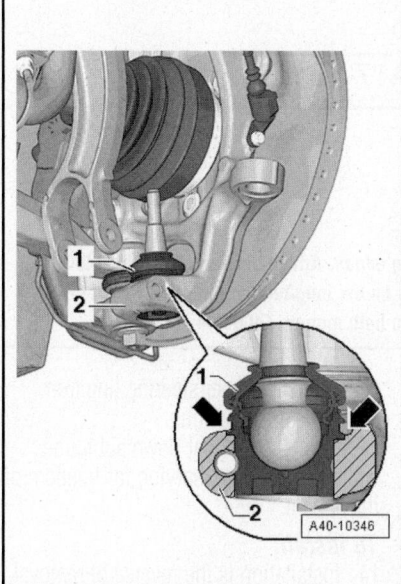

Fig. 288 Exploded view of the subframe assembly and related components

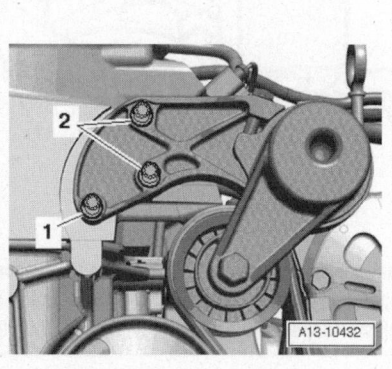

Fig. 289 Remove bolt (1) from the outside edge of the belt tensioner (ignore item 2)—3.6L FSI engine

➡ **Engage both spindles at rear engine lifting eyes.**

   g. Slide support T40091/2 with slide T40093/5 into both connectors T40093/4.

h. Secure support T40091/2 with connector pins and splints T40093/4.

   i. Remove 2024 A eyes.

   j. Insert pins in center Engine Sling eye and secure with a splint.

   k. Engage engine sling pins at front engine support bridge spindle.

   l. Install 2024 A/1 on left side of engine sling. Engage 2024 A at front right engine lifting eye and at T10014. Hooks and pins on engine sling must be secured with connectors arrows. Tension engine by tightening the spindles evenly.

12. For all vehicles, do the following:

   a. Remove both brackets with ABS speed sensor and brake wear indicator electrical lines at wheel bearing housing and disconnect connectors.

   b. Remove brake caliper and secure to body so that weight of caliper does not stress or damage brake hose or brake line..

13. The hose clamping device (3094) must not be secured on return hose in check valve area. The check valve is in the return hose between the cambers or between hose clamps.

   a. Clamp the intake hose and the return line on the reservoir.

   b. Remove bracket for hydraulic lines, then remove pressure line and return line from steering gear.

   c. Disconnect and free up the coolant hoses.

   d. Disengage the power steering hydraulic line from the left brackets on the subframe.

   e. Remove the driveshaft from front final drive and tie it up.

➡ **Only remove universal joint from steering gear with front wheels in straight ahead position. Do not change steering wheel position and steering gear position.**

   f. Remove steering column to gear pinch bolt for universal joint at steering gear and remove universal joint from steering gear.

   g. Disconnect the connector at Servotronic Solenoid Valve.

   h. Remove nut from upper control arm and press arm off.

   i. Position VAS 6131 horizontally.

➡ **Note bubble level indicator.**

   j. Guide scissor lift table under engine/transmission assembly.

   k. Attach mounting elements from VAS 6131/10 and VAS 6131/11 at front of subframe.

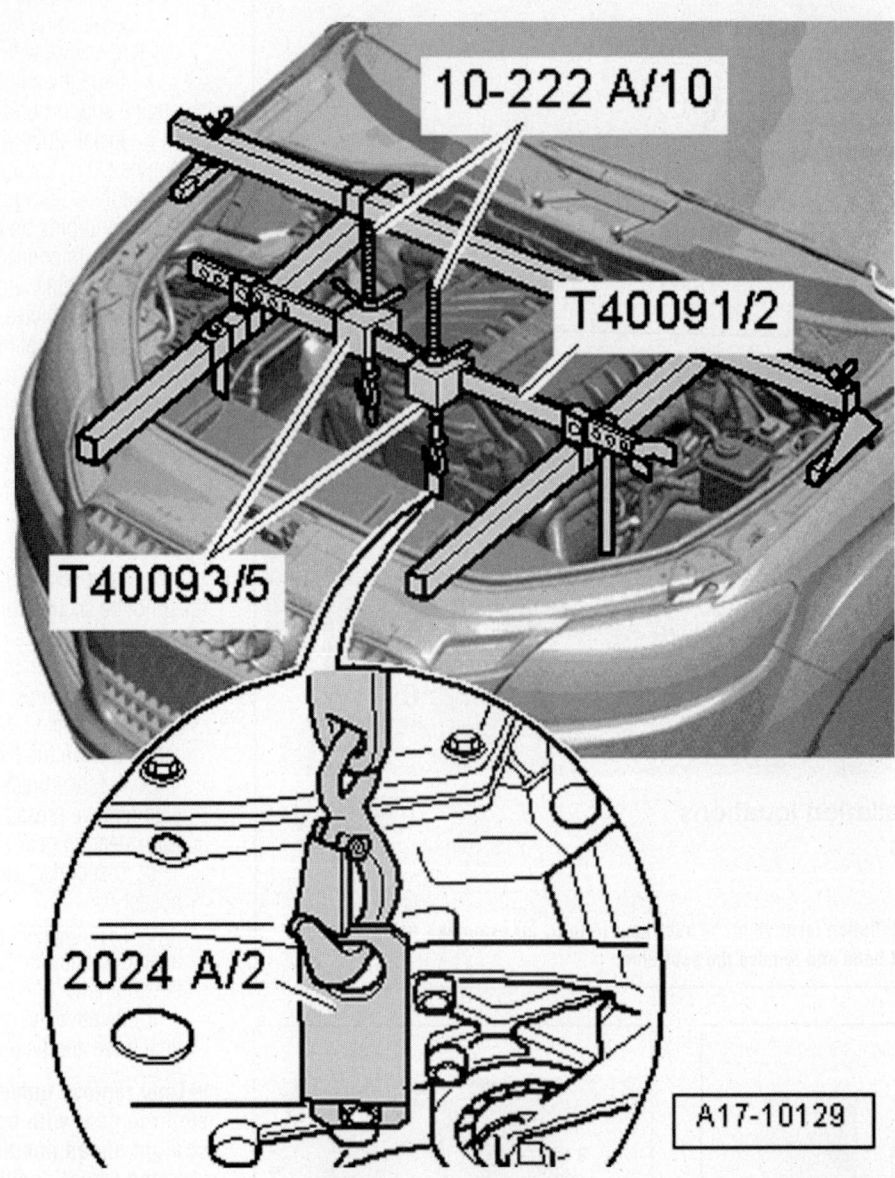

Fig. 290 Mount the 10 - 222 A, the 10 - 222 A /22 and the supplement set T40091/3 on the fender bolting edges. Attach the parts from the T40091 and from the T40093 axially across the engine compartment. Mount the adapter T40093/3 to the notches on the longitudinal member. Push the left refrigerant lines to the side and out of the way. Push the support T40091/2 with both slides T40093/5 into both mounts T40093/4.

l. Position supporting elements from VAS 6131/13 under the lower control arm at the strut supports.

m. Attach mounting elements from VAS 6131/10 at rear of subframe.

n. Rotate support element spindles upward enough so that all mounting pins contact mounting points.

o. Attach the support element base plates to the VAS 6131 and tighten to 15 ft. lbs. (20 Nm).

p. Disconnect left and right lower bolts from the steering knuckle and the stabilizer bar link. Ensure the subframe is secure. Remove upper bolt from the stabilizer bar link.

q. Lower subframe approximately 50 mm and carefully remove breather line from front final drive.

r. Unclip power steering line from subframe and free it up.

s. Now, slowly let down subframe while constantly observing for freedom of movement.

To install:
14. Installation is the reverse of removal, with special attention to the following:
    a. Tightening specifications.
    b. Tighten the driveshaft.

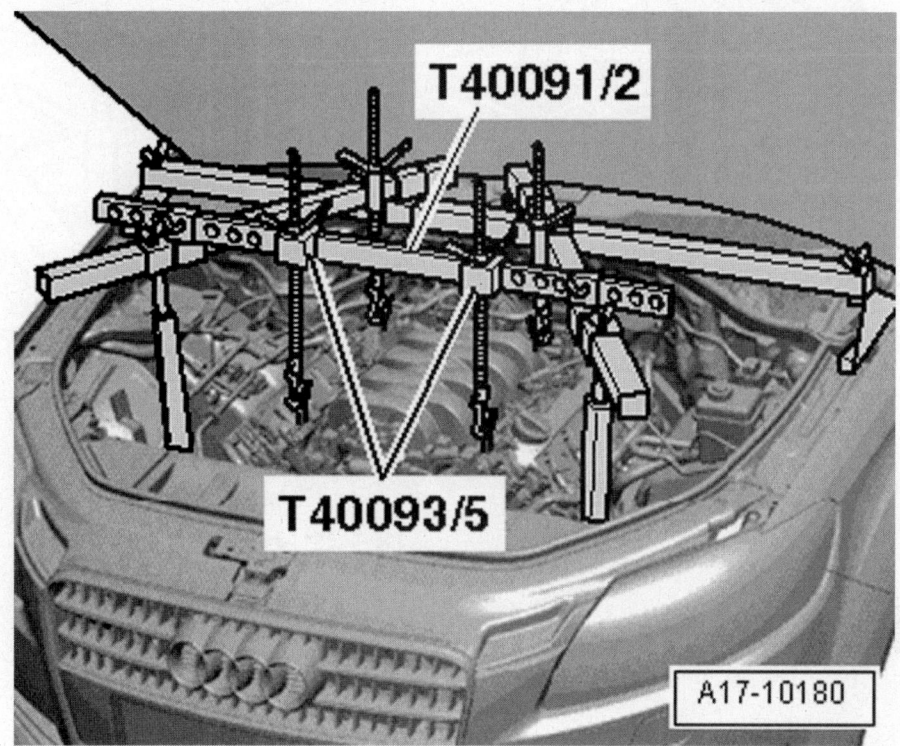

Fig. 291 Assemble and mount the engine support/lift assembly components: 10-222 A, 10-222 A/22, T40091/3, 10-222 A, 10 - 222 A /19.

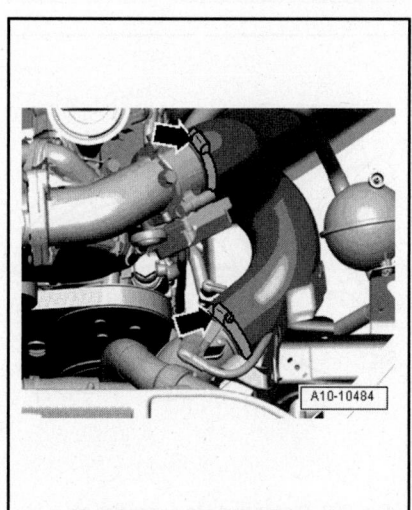

Fig. 292 Remove air guide hose.

c. On vehicles with air suspension, position vehicle on wheels.

d. Install the wheels.

15. Bleed steering system.

16. Check power steering fluid level.

17. Check the steering system for leaks.

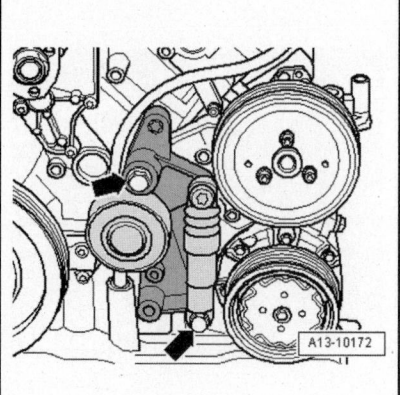

Fig. 293 Remove ribbed belt and belt tensioner.

UPPER CONTROL ARM

REMOVAL & INSTALLATION

Q5

See Figures 301 through 303.

1. Remove wheel.

2. Turn wheel hub far enough until one of the holes for wheel bolts is on top.

3. Install Wheel Hub Support T10149 with wheel bolt on wheel hub.

4. Support wheel bearing housing over the Wheel Hub Support T10149 with Engine/Transmission Jack V.A.G 1383 A.

➡**Do not lift or lower vehicle with engine/transmission jack below vehicle.**

➡**Do not leave Engine/Transmission Jack V.A.G 1383 A below vehicle any longer than necessary.**

5. Remove bolt 1.

6. Remove booth joint pins in the upper control arm 2 from the wheel bearing housing.

➡**Do not lower wheel bearing housing more than necessary.**

➡**The slits in the wheel bearing housing must not be widened using a chisel or similar tool.**

7. Remove nuts 3 and 6.

8. Remove bolts 4 and 5 and remove the upper control arm upward.

To install:

Installation is in reverse order of removal. Observe the following when doing so:

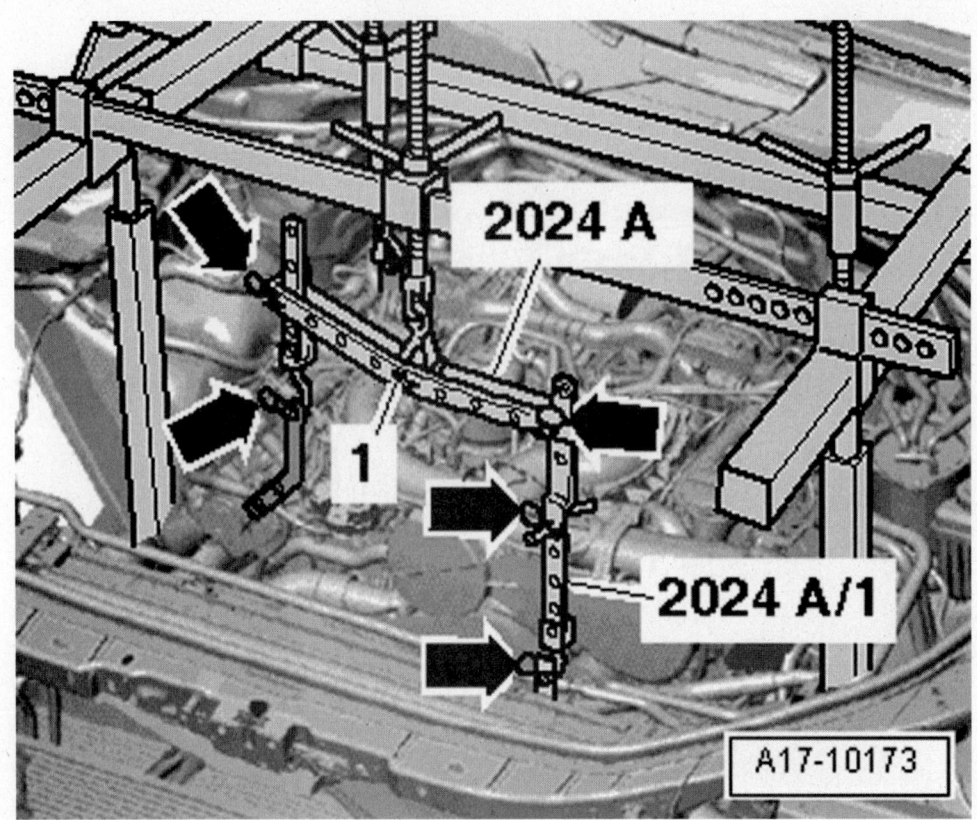

Fig. 294 Remove 2024 A eyes. Insert pins in center Engine Sling eye and secure with a splint.

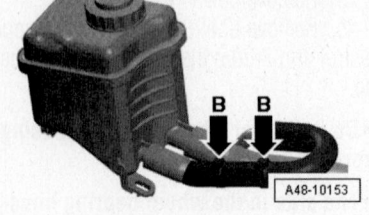

Fig. 295 The hose clamping device must not be secured on return hose in check valve area. The check valve is in the return hose between the cambers (A arrows) or between hose clamps (B arrows).

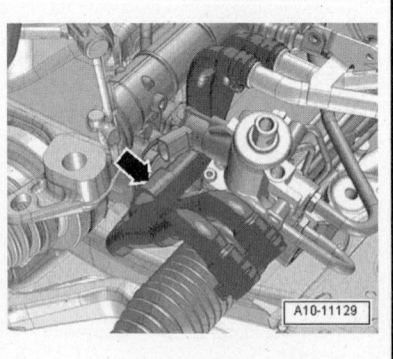

Fig. 296 Disconnect and free up the coolant hoses.

➡ Bonded rubber bushings can only be turned to a limited extent. Only tighten suspension bolts when vehicle is in curb weight or control position.

9. Insert upper control arm and the bolts.

10. Install nuts 3 and 6 and tighten by hand.

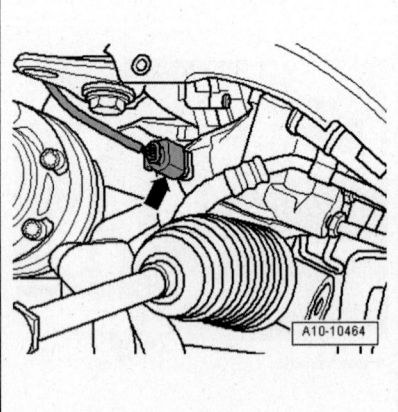

Fig. 297 Disconnect the connector at Servotronic Solenoid Valve.

11. Insert both of upper control arm joint pins in the wheel bearing housing and insert the bolt.

➡ Push the upper control arms down as far as possible while tightening the bolts!

12. Tighten threaded connection.

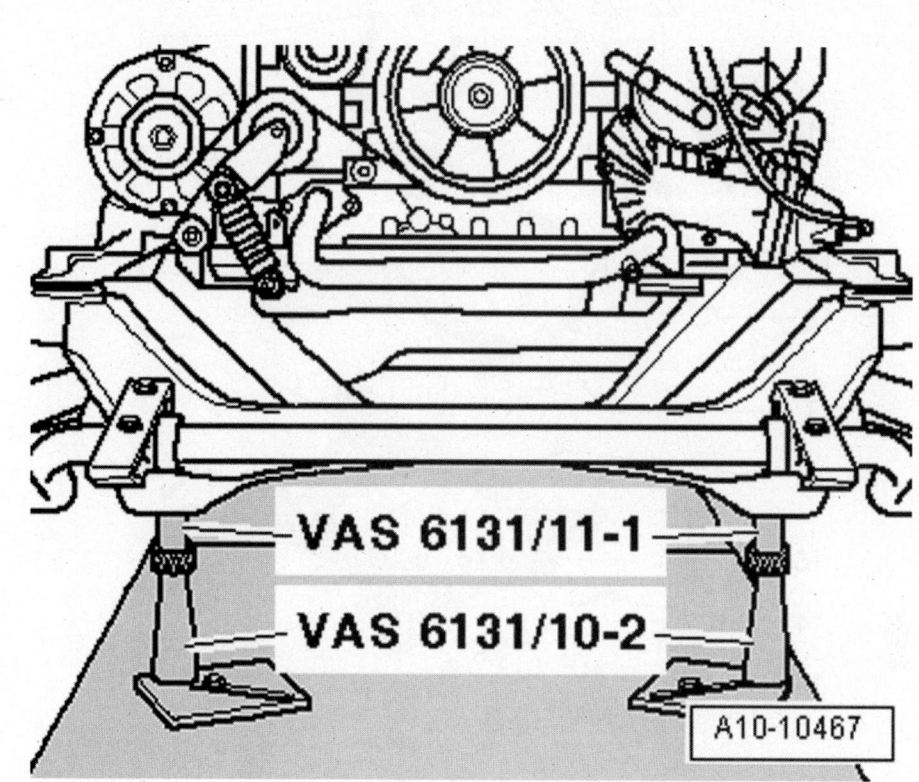

Fig. 298 Attach mounting elements from VAS 6131/10 and VAS 6131/11 at front of subframe as shown in illustration.

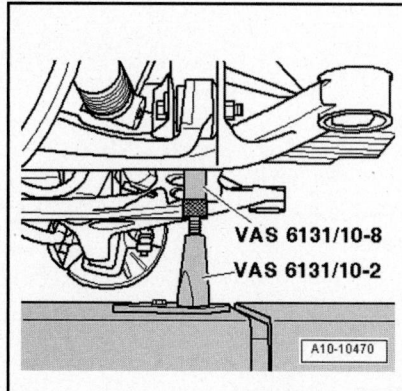

Fig. 299 Attach mounting elements from VAS 6131/10 at rear of subframe as shown in illustration.

13. Wheel bearing, lifting to curb weight position on vehicles with coil springs.

➡**The upper control arm must be pressed toward the inside of the vehicle when tightening the nuts.**

14. Tighten wheel.

15. Vehicle alignment required.

Q7

See Figures 304 and 305.

1. Remove the suspension strut (coil spring).

2. Disconnect connections and remove upper control arm.

To install:

Installation is in reverse order of removal, with special attention to the following:

3. Hand tighten the connections.

4. Set the dimension.

➡**For illustrative purposes, control arm adjuster is shown removed.**

5. Tighten the connections.

6. Install the Suspension strut (coil spring).

WHEEL BEARINGS

REMOVAL & INSTALLATION

Q5

See Figure 306.

Tools Needed:

a. Torque Wrench V.A.G 1331
b. Torque Wrench V.A.G 1332
c. Torque Wrench V.A.G 1576

1. Remove drive axle.

2. Insert both of the upper control arm joint pins in the wheel bearing housing and insert bolt.

➡**This step is necessary to avoid damage to suspension components when loosening and tightening the bolts.**

3. Remove brake caliper and secure to body so that the weight of the brake caliper does not stress or damage brake hose or brake line.

4. Remove disc brake.

5. Remove front wheel speed sensor.

6. Remove cap bolts.

7. Remove wheel bearing unit.

➡**Avoid contaminating with dirt and damaging the seal when setting down/storing.**

➡**The wheel bearing must always face up.**

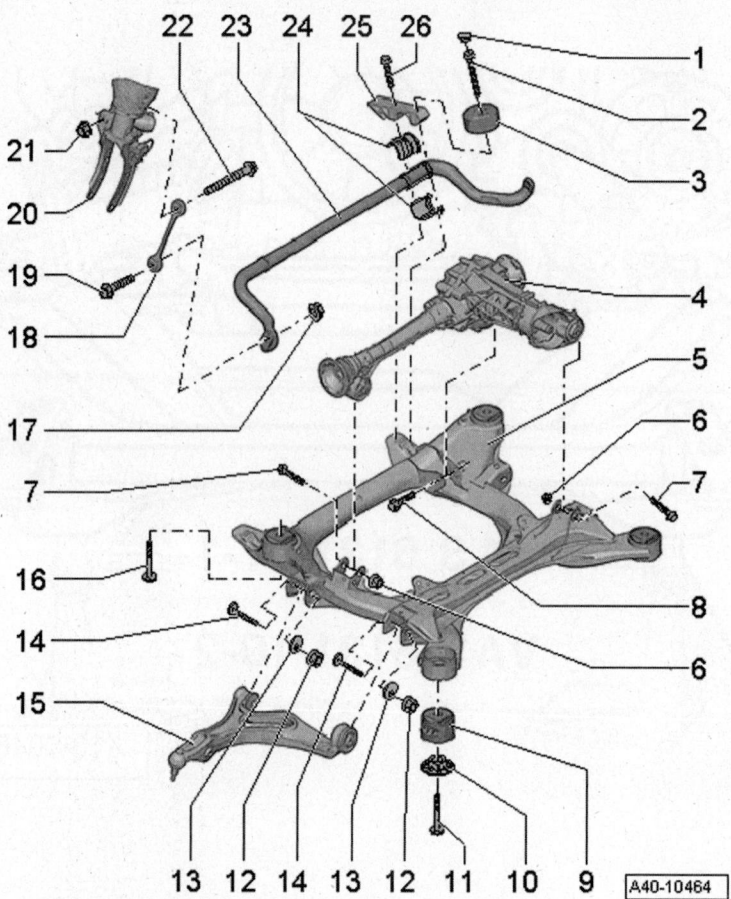

1. Cap (on V6 TDI Generation II)
2. Bolt: 48 ft. lbs. (60 Nm); (on V6 TDI Generation II)
3. Vibration Damper (on V6 TDI Generation II)
4. Front Final Drive
5. Subframe
6. Nut, self-locking
7. Bolt: 48 ft. lbs. (90 Nm), plus additional 90 degrees
8. Bolt: 48 ft. lbs. (90 Nm), plus additional 90 degrees
9. Bonded Rubber Mount
10. Thrust Washer (V8 TDI)
11. Bolt: 89 ft. lbs. (120 Nm), plus additional 180 degrees
12. Nut, self-locking: 133 ft. lbs. (180 Nm)
13. Eccentric Washer
14. Eccentric Bolt
15. Lower Control Arm
16. Bolt: 89 ft. lbs. (120 Nm), plus additional 180 degrees
17. Nut, self-locking: 81 ft. lbs. (110 Nm)
18. Coupling Rod
19. Bolt
20. Suspension Strut
21. Nut, self-locking: 81 ft. lbs. (110 Nm)
22. Bolt
23. Stabilizer Bar
24. Stabilizer Bar Mount
25. Clamp
26. Bolt

Fig. 300 Exploded view of the subframe, stabilizer bar, and coupling rod assembly

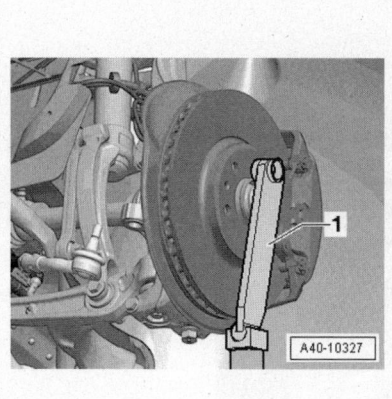

Fig. 301 Installing the wheel hub support

8. Always set the wheel bearing down on the wheel hub.

9. Servicing wheel bearing unit.

To install:

Installation is in reverse order of removal. Observe the following when doing so:

10. Install drive axle.

11. Tighten wheel.

12. On vehicles with automatic headlamp range control system, perform basic setting of headlamps.

13. If the Vehicle Level Sensor was removed and installed on a vehicle with electronic damper regulation or if the linkage was loosened, the control position must be reprogrammed.

14. If the control position was reprogrammed on vehicles with lane assist, the Directional Stabilization Assistance Control Module J759 must be recalibrated.

Q7

See Figures 307 through 314.

➡ **During the entire work procedure, always ensure proper seating of tools and components (wheel bearing/wheel hub).**

➡ **Always place engine/transmission jack V.A.G 1383 A beneath wheel bearing housing during entire work procedure (danger of accident if parts fall off).**

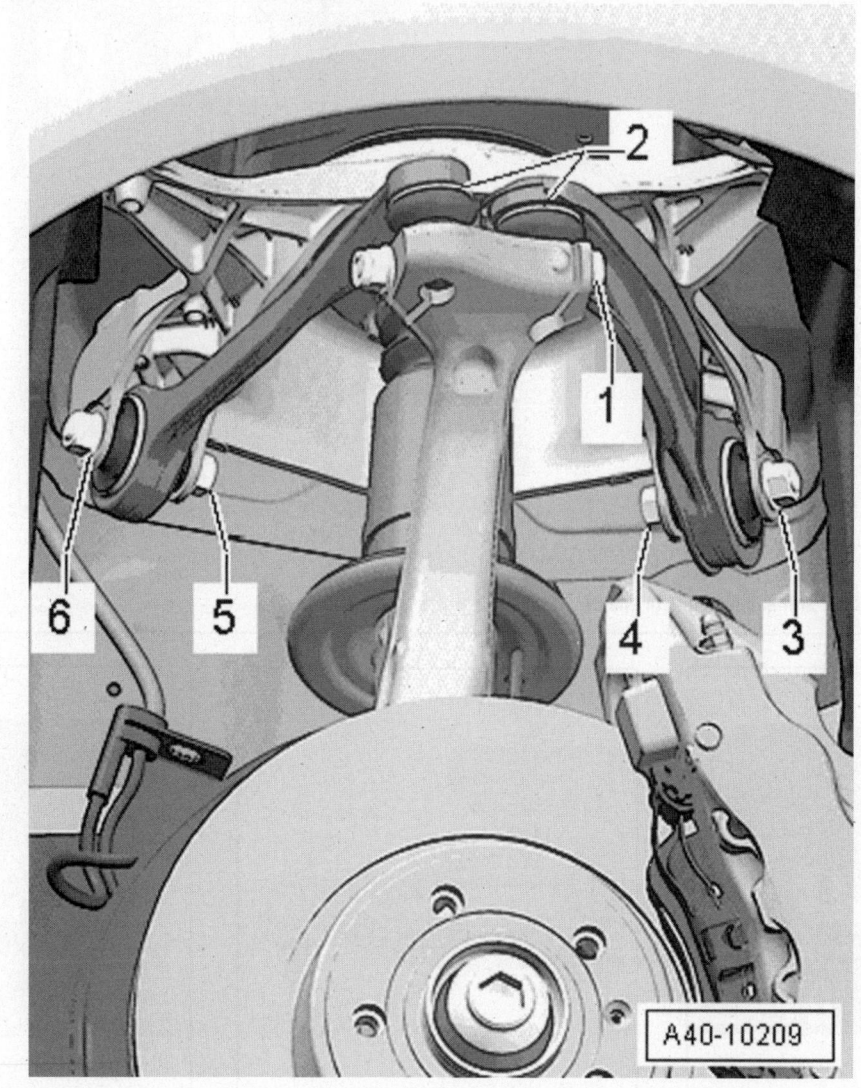

Fig. 302 Removing the upper control arm

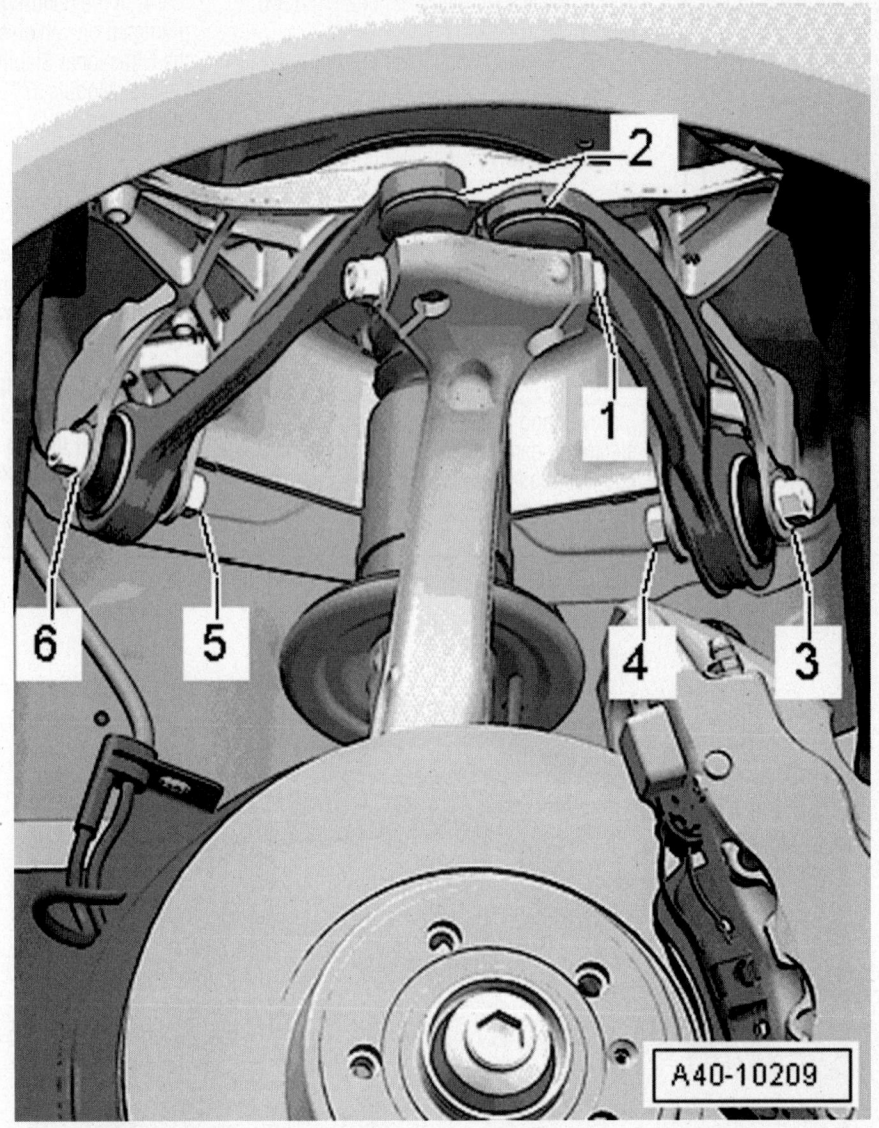

Fig. 303 Insert upper control arm and the bolts (4 and 5).

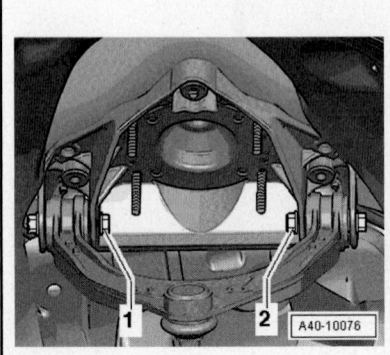

Fig. 304 Disconnect connections (1 and 2) and remove upper control arm.

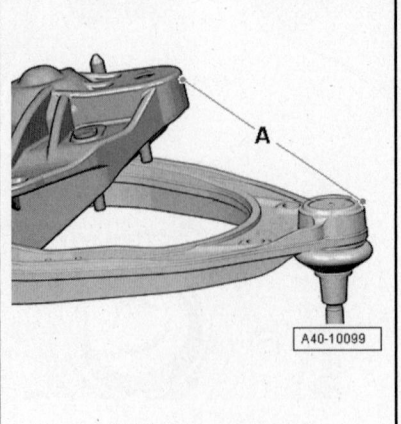

Fig. 305 Setting dimension A to 6.1 in. (155 mm)

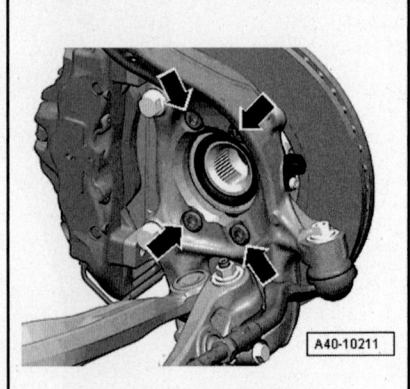

Fig. 306 Removing the cap bolts and wheel bearing unit

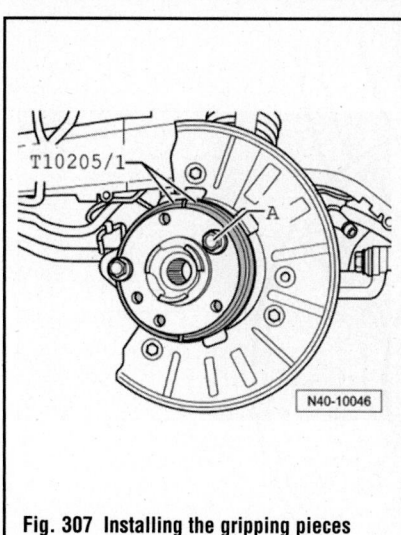

Fig. 307 Installing the gripping pieces

➡**Tools Needed:**

- Hydraulic cylinder VAS 6178
- Engine/Transmission Jack V.A.G 1383 A with Universal Transmission Support V.A.G 1359/2
- Separating tool - Kukko 15/3
- Assembly tool T10205
- Hollow piston cylinder VAS 6179

- Pliers for circlips, 180 mm internal circlip VAS 5498, not depicted
- Pressure gauge w/connection VAS 6179/1, not depicted

1. First remove driveshaft.

2. Install the upper control arm on wheel bearing housing.

3. Remove brake disc and backing plate.

4. Unclip wire for wheel speed sensor from retainer.

5. Remove ABS wheel speed sensor.

Wheel Hub, Pulling Out:

6. Install gripping pieces T10205/1 with wheel bolts A onto wheel hub.

➡**Wheel bolts must not protrude on rear side of attachments T10205/1.**

7. Mount tools as depicted.

8. Mount tools as depicted.

9. Pull out wheel hub, hold tool securely.

Wheel Bearing, Pulling Out:

10. Remove the securing ring.

11. Mount tools as depicted in illustration.

➡**Offset of thrust piece T10205/6 must point toward rear final drive.**

12. Pull out the wheel bearing while holding the device securely.

Pulling bearing inner race off of wheel hub:

13. Install the separating tool behind bearing inner ring.

➡**Beveled parts of blades face bearing inner ring.**

➡**When pulling off, hold tool so that bearing inner ring points downward (danger of accident if bearing inner ring jumps off at end of pulling process).**

14. Pull off the wheel hub from the bearing inner ring.

Wheel Bearing, Pressing in:

15. Make sure that rubberized sensor ring for ABS points toward rear final drive.

➡**If no rubberized ring is visible, check, for example using a paper clip, which of the sides is magnetic. This side must face rear final drive when installed.**

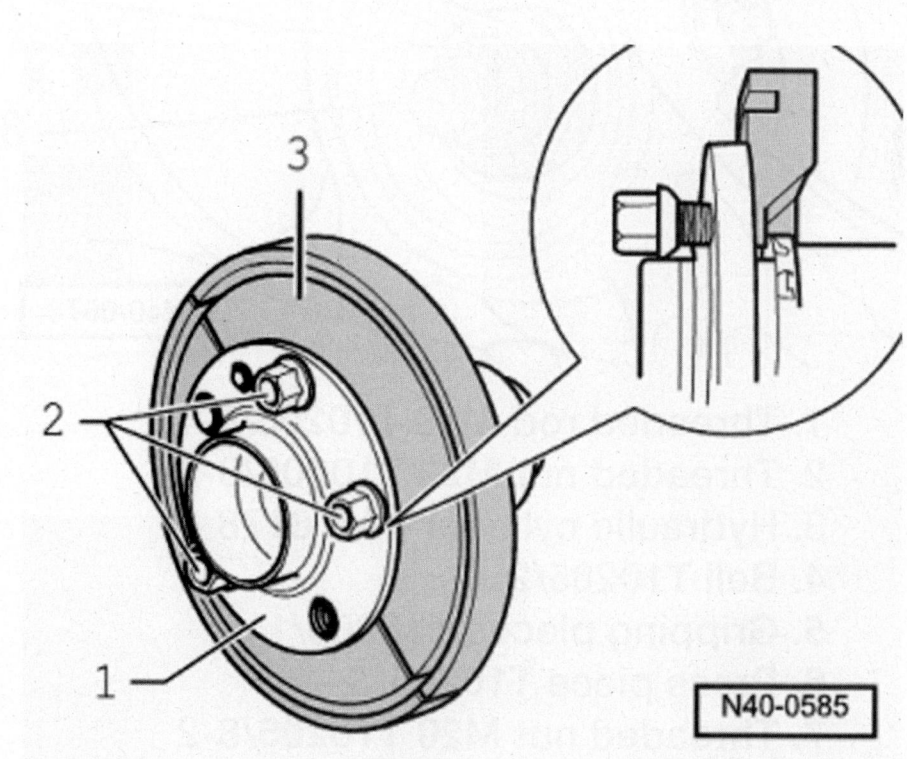

Fig. 308 Checking bolt (2) protrusion

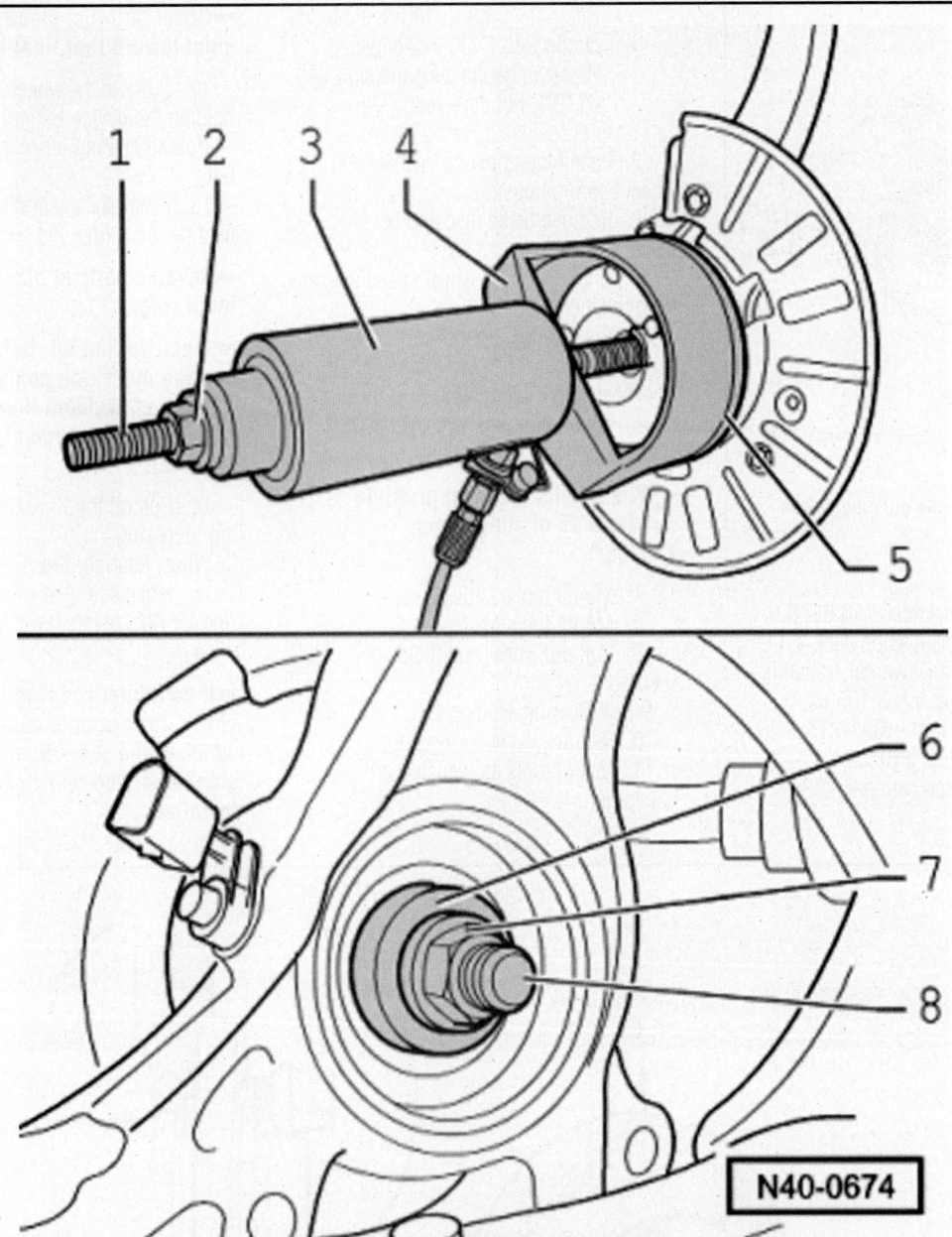

N40-0674

1. Threaded rod M20 T10205/8-1
2. Threaded nut M20 T10205/8-2
3. Hydraulic cylinder VAS 6178
4. Bell T10205/2
5. Gripping pieces T10205/1
6. Press piece T10205/3
7. Threaded nut M20 T10205/8-2
8. Threaded rod M20 T10205/8-1

Fig. 309 Mount tools as depicted.

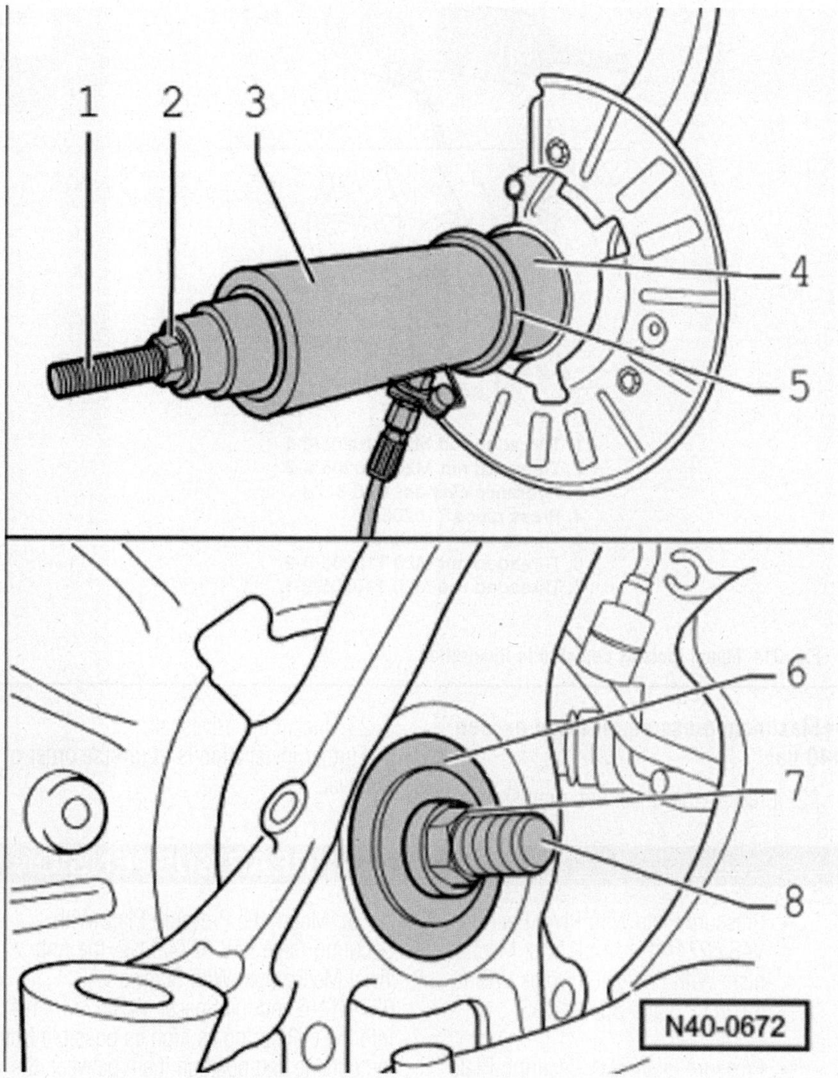

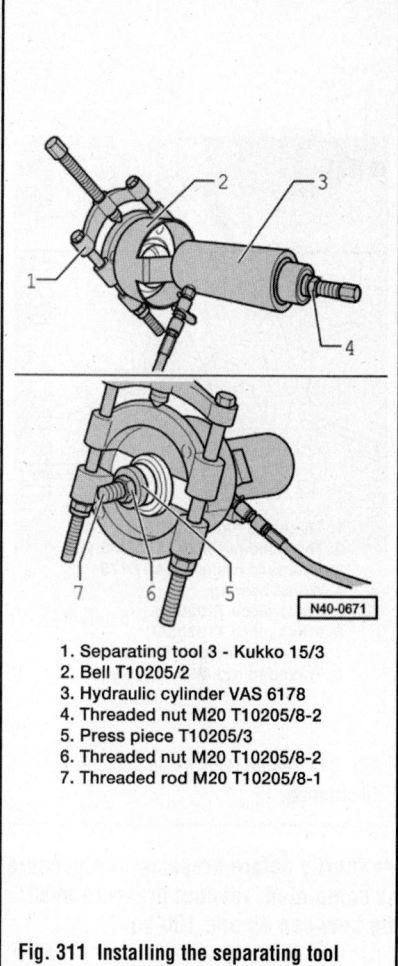

Fig. 310 Mounting the tools

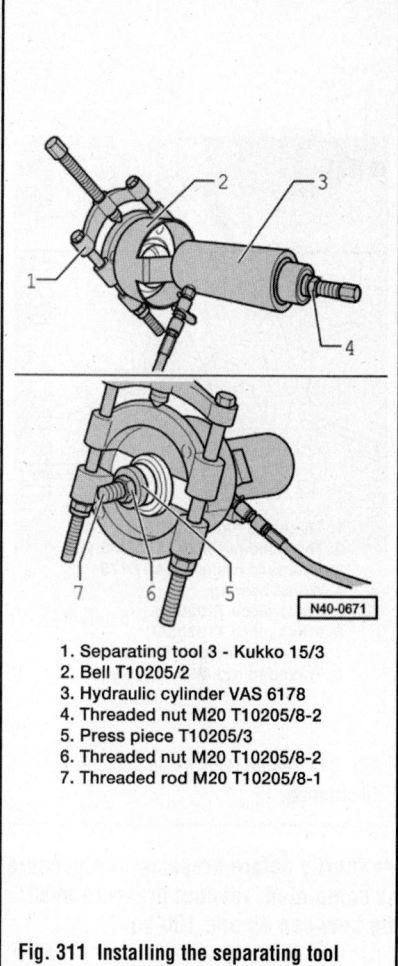

1. Separating tool 3 - Kukko 15/3
2. Bell T10205/2
3. Hydraulic cylinder VAS 6178
4. Threaded nut M20 T10205/8-2
5. Press piece T10205/3
6. Threaded nut M20 T10205/8-2
7. Threaded rod M20 T10205/8-1

Fig. 311 Installing the separating tool

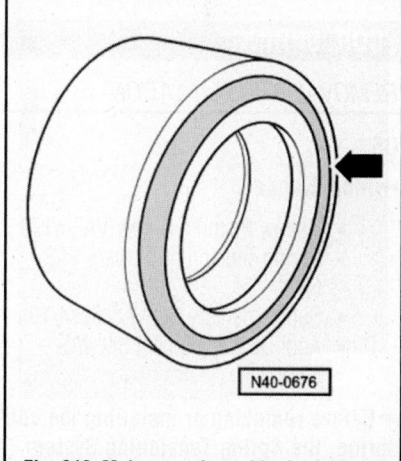

Fig. 312 Make sure that rubberized sensor ring for ABS points toward rear final drive.

16. Mount tools as depicted.

➡**Offset of thrust piece T10205/9 must point toward wheel bearing housing.**

17. Connect pressure gauge w/connection VAS 6179/1 between hydraulic cylinder VAS 6178 and hydraulic line of hydraulic cylinder VAS 6178.

➡**Pressures, described in the following, apply only to hydraulic cylinder VAS 6178.**

➡**Shortly before pressing-in procedure is completed, readout pressure must be between 1450–2756 psi (100–190 bar.**

Maximum pressure must not exceed 4496 psi (310 bar).
18. Press wheel bearing in until stop.
19. Install the circlip.
Wheel Hub, Pressing in:
20. Mount tools as depicted.

➡**Offset of thrust piece T10205/6 must point toward rear final drive.**

21. Connect pressure gauge w/connection VAS 6179/1 between hydraulic cylinder VAS 6178 and hydraulic line of hydraulic cylinder VAS 6178.

➡**Pressures, described in the following, apply only to hydraulic cylinder VAS 6178.**

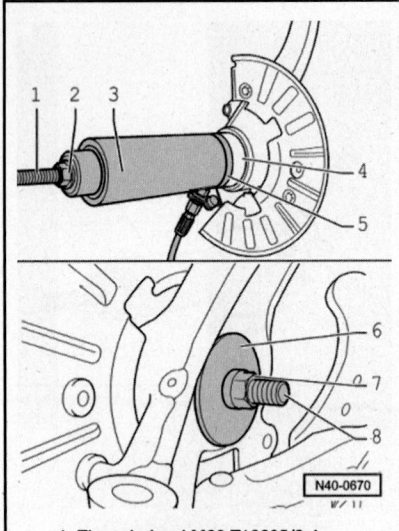

1. Threaded rod M20 T10205/8-1
2. Threaded nut M20 T10205/8-2
3. Hydraulic cylinder VAS 6178
4. Wheel bearing
5. Press piece T10205/7
6. Press piece T10205/9
7. Threaded nut M20 T10205/8-2
8. Threaded rod M20 T10205/8-1

Fig. 313 Mount tools as depicted in illustration.

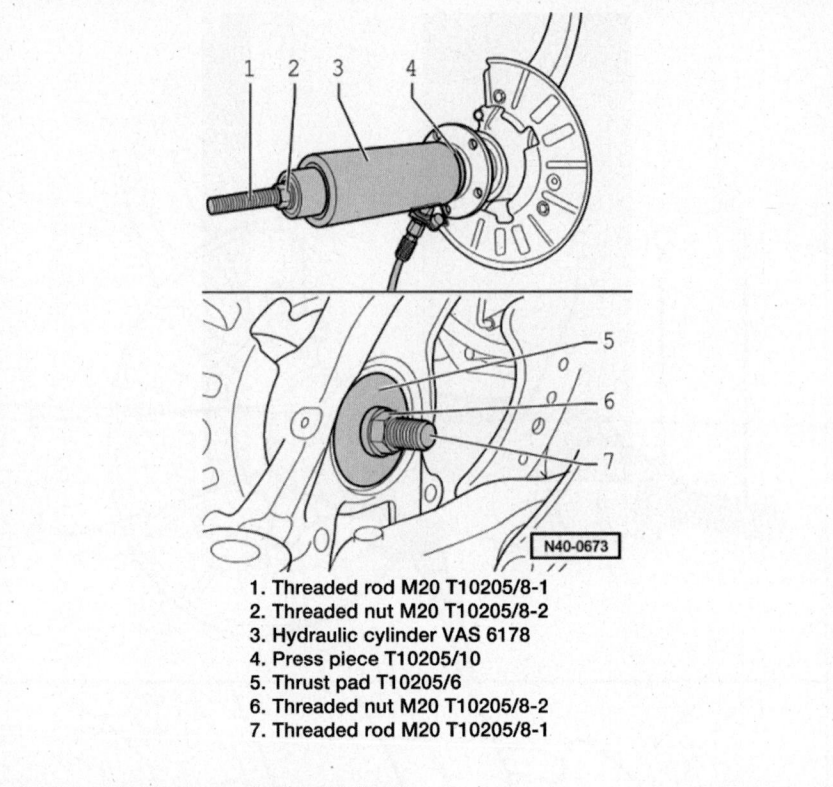

1. Threaded rod M20 T10205/8-1
2. Threaded nut M20 T10205/8-2
3. Hydraulic cylinder VAS 6178
4. Press piece T10205/10
5. Thrust pad T10205/6
6. Threaded nut M20 T10205/8-2
7. Threaded rod M20 T10205/8-1

Fig. 314 Mount tools as depicted in illustration.

➡**Shortly before pressing-in procedure is completed, readout pressure must be between 30 and 100 bar.**

➡**Maximum pressure must not exceed 140 bar.**

22. Press in the wheel hub until stop.

23. Install the driveshaft.
Further installation is in reverse order of removal.

SUSPENSION

REAR SUSPENSION

COIL SPRING

REMOVAL & INSTALLATION

Q5

➡**Tools Needed:**

- Hollow Piston Cylinder VAS 6179
- Spring Tensioning System VAS 6274
- Supplementary Set VAS 6274/10
- Audi Q5 Supplement Set VAS 6274/11

➡**Before removing or installing the coil spring, the Spring Tensioning System VAS 6274 with the Supplement Set VAS 6274/10 and Audi Q5 Supplement Set VAS 6274/11 must be changed over.**

➡**Convert the Spring Tensioning System VAS 6274 using the Supplementary Set VAS 6274/10Spring Tensioning System VAS 6274, Converting.**

➡**Additional tools from Supplement Set VAS 6274/10 and Audi Q5 Supplement Set VAS 6274/11 will be needed later.**

- Pressure Plate With Pivot Bearing VAS 6274/11-1, Anti-Twist Mechanism With Elongated Holes VAS 6274/11-5 and Spacer VAS 6274/11-4
- Pressure Plate With Securing Plate VAS 6274/11-2, Anti-Twist Mechanism With Guide Bolts VAS 6274/11-6 and Spacer VAS 6274/11-4
- Bolts for the anti-twist mechanism bracket, contained in the Audi Q5 Supplement Set VAS 6274/11
- Spindle VAS 6274/10-4
- Sleeve
- Pistons VAS 6274/4

1. Before starting, align the anti-twist mechanisms and the spacers on the thrust plates near the markings and then tighten them with the bolts supplied.

- Spacer VAS 6274/11-4

2. Place vehicle on a hoist.
3. Remove wheels.
4. Slide securing lever back if necessary.

5. Mount the Pressure Plate With Securing Plate VAS 6274/11-2, the Anti-Twist Mechanism With Screws VAS 6274/11-6 and the Spacer VAS 6274/11-4 into the coil spring as high as possible from the outside and position them between the lower transverse link and the tie rod.

➡**If it is not possible to install the Pressure Plate With Securing Plate VAS 6274/11-2, the Anti-Twist Mechanism With Screws VAS 6274/11-6 and the Spacer VAS 6274/11-4 because there is not enough space, then the tools must be taken apart, installed individually and be assembled in their final installation position.**

6. Install the Piston VAS 6274/4 2 and the T Handle VAS 6274/5 3 into the pressure plate. Slide the locking lever on the pressure plate back toward the outside (open).

7. Press the locking lever in the direction to secure the piston.

8. Turn the Pressure Plate With Securing Plate VAS 6274/11-2, the Anti-Twist

Mechanism With Screws VAS 6274/11-6 and the Spacer VAS 6274/11-4 all the way up.

9. Install the Pressure Plate With Securing Plate VAS 6274/11-1, the Anti-Twist Mechanism With Oblong Holes VAS 6274/11-5 and the Spacer VAS 6274/11-4 into the coil spring from the inside as far down as possible between the transverse line and the tie rod. Move the stone protection plate to the side if necessary.

➡ **If it is not possible to install the Pressure Plate With Swivel Bearing VAS 6274/11-1, the Anti-Twist Mechanism Oblong Holes VAS 6274/11-5 and the Spacer VAS 6274/11-4 because there is not enough space, then the tools must be taken apart, installed individually and be assembled in their final installation position.**

10. Rotate the Pressure Plate With Pivot Bearing all the way down.
   a. The anti-twist mechanism bracket must be located between the tie rod and the lower transverse link.

➡ **Coat the front area of the spindle lightly with the accompanying grease before removal and installation of each spring.**

➡ **Only grease the spindle with the accompanying grease. The spindle will be damaged if a different grease is used.**

11. Coat the front area of the Spindle VAS 6274/10-4 lightly with the appropriate grease.

12. Install the Spindle VAS 6274/10-4 1 and the Socket VAS 6274/6 2 by hand.

13. Attach the locking devices on both pressure plates to each other.

14. Install the bolts from the Audi Q5 Supplement Set VAS 6274/11 by hand.

➡ **The coil spring may only be tensioned or released if both locking device brackets are connected to each other using both bolts.**

15. Lightly tension the pressure plates using the Spindle VAS 6274/10-4.

16. Check to see if both coil springs are seated correctly in the pressure plates.
   a. The anti-twist mechanism bracket must be positioned between the lower transverse line and the tie rod when the coil spring is being tensioned.

17. Tension the coil spring using the Socket VAS 6274/6 3. If necessary, use the Counterhold Tool VAS 6274/7 on the bracket.

➡ **Do not use an impact wrench to tighten the coil spring.**

➡ **Use a commercially available ratchet to tighten.**

18. Tension the coil spring just enough until it is possible to remove the stone protection plate and the lower spring plate. Use a screwdriver to tension the spring further.

➡ **When tightening, make sure the bolts do not lie on the pressure plate stop.**

➡ **The pressure plate locking device must not lie on the stop on the pressure plate.**

19. Remove the coil spring forward and down.

➡ **If is it not possible to this because there is not enough space even though the coil spring is sufficiently pre-tensioned, then a second technician will be needed to pull the suspension down slightly.**

➡ **Use the Spring Tensioning System VAS 6274 and its accessories to tension the coil spring. Otherwise personal injury can occur.**

20. Turn the spindle back slightly but do not remove it all the way. The spindle must not project over the end of the coil spring.

21. Insert the pre-tensioned coil into the Spring Tensioning System VAS 6274.

22. Insert the left coil spring on the spring plate so the stop aligns with the marking "L". Only applies to the left coil spring.
   a. For the right coil spring, the stop must align with the "R" marking.

23. Position the bottom side of the end of the left coil spring in the Spring Tensioning System VAS 6274 at the "L" marking.

24. Position the bottom side of the end of the right coil spring in the Spring Tensioning System VAS 6274 at the "R" marking.
   a. On a left coil spring the anti-twist mechanisms face the 10 o'clock position and on the right coil spring the 2 o'clock position.

25. Release the coil spring using the Socket VAS 6274/6. Release the tension at the same time using the Spring Tensioning System VAS 6274 and Pneumatic/Hydraulic Foot Pump VAS 6179.

26. After the tension has been released on the coil spring, remove the Spindle VAS 6274/10-4 3.

27. Remove the screws for the anti-twist mechanism bracket and remove the Pres-

sure Plate with Swivel Bearing VAS 6274/11-1, the Anti-Twist Mechanism Oblong Holes VAS 6274/11-5 and the Spacer VAS 6274/11-4.

28. Slide the locking lever back.

29. Remove the Piston VAS 6274/4 2 and the T-Handle VAS 6274/5 3 and remove the Pressure Plate with Securing Plate VAS 6274/11-2, the Anti-Twist Mechanism with Screws VAS 6274/11-6 and the Spacer VAS 6274/11-4 from the coil spring.

30. Release the coil spring completely.

To install:

Installation is in reverse order of removal. Observe the following when doing so:

➡ **It takes more than 4 turns to tension the coil spring with the pressure plates.**

31. Insert the bottom side of the coil spring in the Spring Tensioning System VAS 6274.

32. Install the lower spring end (identified with the color points) on the left coil spring in the Spring Tensioning System VAS 6274 on the "L" marking arrow in the spring plate.

33. Install the lower spring end (identified with the color points) on the right coil spring in the Spring Tensioning System VAS 6274 on the "R" marking in the spring plate.

34. Install the Pressure Plate With Securing Plate VAS 6274/11-2, the Anti-Twist Mechanism With Screws VAS 6274/11-6 and the Spacer VAS 6274/11-4 and then install the Piston VAS 6274/4 2 together with the T-Handle VAS 6274/5 3.

35. Secure the piston with the securing lever.

36. Install the Pressure Plate With Pivot Bearing VAS 6274/11-1, the Anti-Twist Mechanism With Elongated Holes VAS 6274/11-5 and the Spacer VAS 6274/11-4 5.

37. Install the locking device bolts loosely.

38. Install the Spindle VAS 6274/10-4 6.

39. Install the sleeve all the way.
Applies to the left coil spring:

40. Tighten the locking device bolts lightly by hand. Align the anti-twist mechanism and pressure plates in the Spring Tensioning System VAS 6274 so that the left coil spring points in the 10 o'clock. While doing this make sure the lower end of the coil spring fits into the spring plate on the "L" marking.

41. Tighten the coil spring using the Socket VAS 6274/6 3. Tighten at the same

time using the Spring Tensioning System VAS 6274 and Pneumatic/Hydraulic Foot Pump VAS 6179.

Applies to the right coil spring:

42. Tighten the locking device bolts lightly by hand. Align the anti-twist mechanism and pressure plates in the Spring Tensioning System VAS 6274 so that the right coil spring points in the 2 o'clock position. While doing this make sure the lower end of the coil spring fits into the spring plate on the "R" marking.

43. Tighten the coil spring using the Socket VAS 6274/6 3. Tighten at the same time using the Spring Tensioning System VAS 6274 and Pneumatic/Hydraulic Foot Pump VAS 6179.

Applies to both coil springs:

➡ **When tightening, make sure the locking mechanism bolts do not lie on the Pressure Plate with Pivot Bearing VAS 6274/11-1 stop.**

➡ **The Pressure Plate with Lock VAS 6274/11-2 locking device must not lie on the Pressure Plate with Pivot Bearing VAS 6274/11-1 stop.**

The anti-twist mechanisms points to the 10 o'clock position on the left coil spring and to the 2 o'clock position on the right coil spring.

44. When tightening using the spindle, make sure the sleeve does not slip out of the Pressure Plate With Pivot Bearing VAS 6274/11-1.

45. Release Spring Tensioning System VAS 6274 and remove the coil spring with the tensioner.

46. Tension the coil spring slightly using spindle if necessary.

The spindle must only project far enough over the coil spring that the upper spring plate can still rest completely on the coil spring.

47. Position the coil spring with the lower spring plate and stone deflector on the wheel bearing housing.

48. Make sure the upper spring plate is installed.

49. Insert the lower spring plate with the pins in the wheel bearing housing hole.

50. Install the coil spring in the lower spring plate as far as the stop.

51. Then release the coil spring.

52. Tighten wheel.

53. Vehicle alignment required.

➡ **If one or both coil springs have been replaced, then is it necessary to adapt the control position..**

54. If the Vehicle Level Sensor was removed and installed on a vehicle with electronic damper regulation or if the linkage was loosened, the control position must be reprogrammed.

55. If the control position was reprogrammed on vehicles with lane assist, the Directional Stabilization Assistance Control Module J759 must be recalibrated.

LOWER CONTROL ARM

REMOVAL & INSTALLATION

Q7

See Figure 315.

➡ **Tools Needed: Torque wrench V.A.G 1332**

➡ **If lower control arm is replaced, axle alignment should be performed after installation.**

1. Vehicles with air suspension, place vehicle on hoist.

2. Remove the wheel.

3. If equipped, remove stone impact protection from lower control arm.

4. Mark the eccentric bolt position to subframe and remove.

5. Remove bolt.

6. Remove bolt through opening in subframe. Pry bolt out of subframe with a small screwdriver.

7. Pry lower control arm out of subframe with a screwdriver.

To install:

Installation is in reverse order of removal. Observe the following:

➡ **Bonded rubber bushings can only be turned to a limited extent. Only tighten suspension bolts when vehicle is in curb weight or control position.**

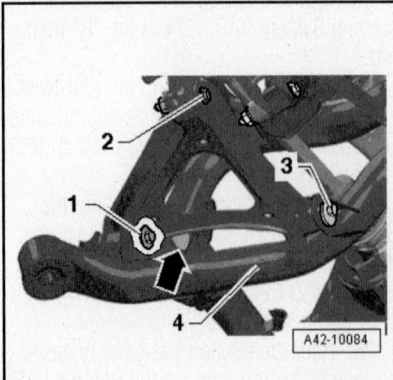

Fig. 315 Removing the lower control arm

➡ **Wheel bearing, lifting to curb weight position on vehicles with coil springs.**

➡ **Wheel bearing, lifting to control position on vehicles with air suspension.**

8. On vehicles with air suspension, position vehicle on wheels.

9. Tighten the wheels.

10. On vehicles with automatic headlamp range control, perform headlamp basic setting.

STABILIZER BAR & COUPLING ROD

REMOVAL & INSTALLATION

Q5

See Figures 316 through 318.

➡ **Before starting work, determine dimension from the center of the wheel to the lower edge of the wheel housing while the vehicle is resting on its wheels. Make a note of this dimension.**

1. Place the vehicle on a hoist.

2. Remove the rear wheels.

✷✷ CAUTION

Do not damage the paint on the stabilizer bar when removing and installing.

3. Remove the exhaust system rear muffler as applicable.

4. Remove the right and left bolts from the stabilizer bar coupling rod mounting at the body.

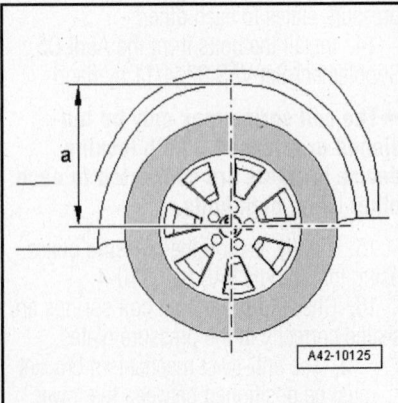

Fig. 316 Before starting work, determine dimension (a) from the center of the wheel to the lower edge of the wheel housing while the vehicle is resting on its wheels. Make a note of this dimension.

5. Remove the left and right stabilizer bar bracket bolts

6. Remove the stabilizer bar and coupling rods.

➡ **The stabilizer bar is completely removed and installed with the rubber bushings and clamps. Do not remove the clamps and rubber bushings.**

7. Detach the coupling rod from the stabilizer bar.

To install:

8. Installation is performed in the reverse order of removal. Observe the following when doing so:

a. Bonded rubber bushings can only be turned to a limited extent. Only tighten suspension screws when vehicle is in curb weight or control position.

b. Wheel bearing, lifting to curb weight position on vehicles with coil springs.

c. Attach the coupling rod to the stabilizer bar and tighten the threaded connection hand tight.

d. Insert the stabilizer bar and tighten the right and left bolts so that they are still loose.

e. Install the left and right bracket bolts so that they are still loose, then tighten the left and right bolts evenly.

f. Tighten the stabilizer bar to coupling rod left and right bolts and nuts.

g. Tighten the left and right coupling rod mounting bolts.

9. Install the wheels.

10. Axle alignment is required.

Q7

See Figures 319 through 321.

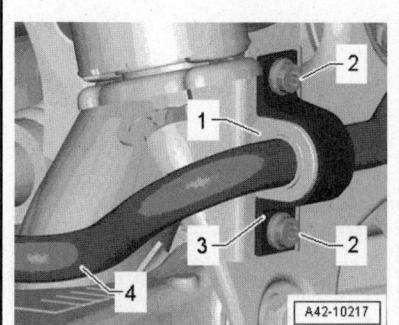

1. Bushing   3. Bracket
2. Bracket bolts   4. Stabilizer bar

Fig. 317 Remove the left and right stabilizer bar bracket bolts. Remove the stabilizer bar and coupling rods.

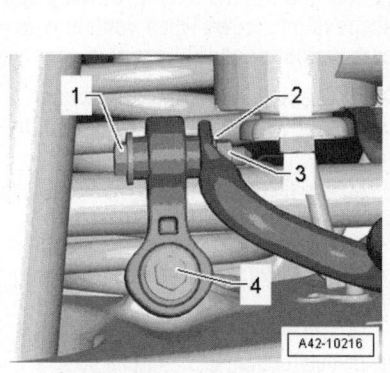

1. Stabilizer bar to coupling rod bolt
2. Stabilizer bar
3. Nut
4. Coupling rod mounting bolt

Fig. 318 Tighten the left and right coupling rod mounting bolts.

➡**Before starting work, determine dimension from the center of the wheel to the lower edge of the wheel housing while the vehicle is resting on its wheels. Make a note of this dimension.**

1. Place vehicle on hoist.

2. Remove the rear wheels.

3. Insert wood block between underbody and upper rear control arm. Wood block is needed to press wheel bearing housing down.

4. Remove nut on lower strut mounting. Push the wheel bearing housing downward using a block of wood until it is possible to remove the bolt.

5. Remove upper mounting nut from left and right coupling rod.

6. Mark the installed location of stabilizer bar mount and bushing to the stabilizer bar.

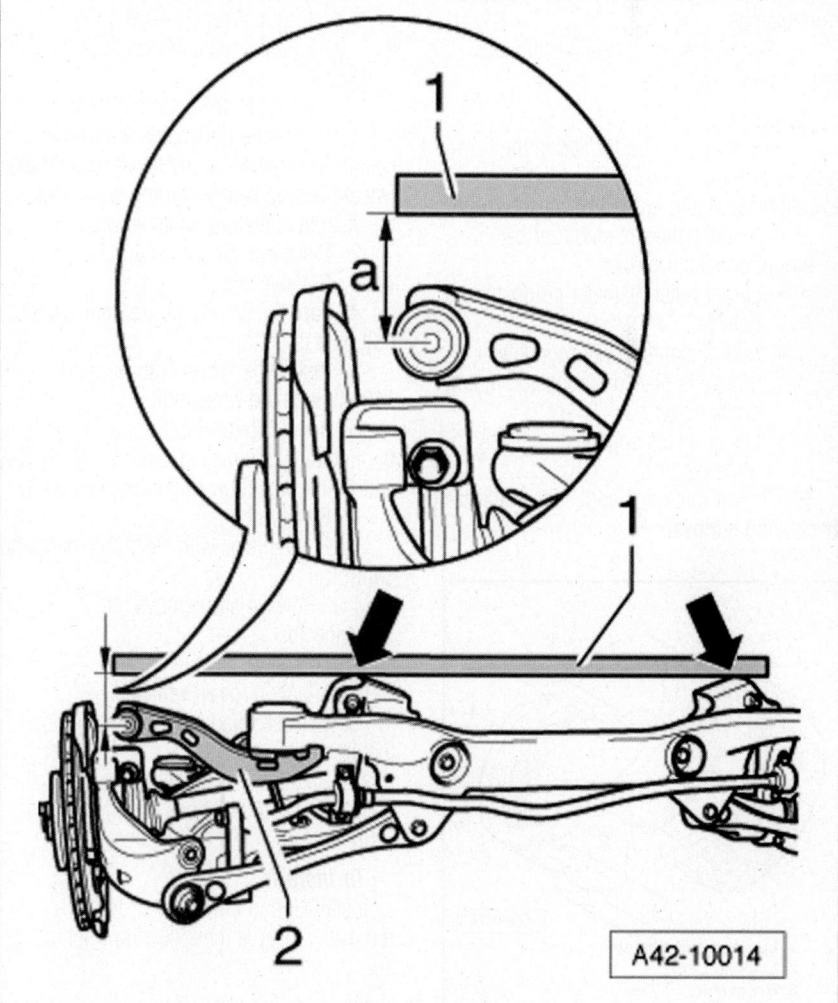

Fig. 319 Insert wood block between underbody (arrow A) and upper rear control arm (arrow B). Wood block is needed to press wheel bearing housing down.

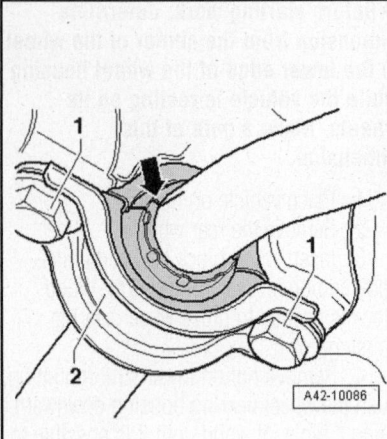

Fig. 320 Mark the installed location of stabilizer bar mount on left and right stabilizer bar (arrow). Remove bolts (1) and remove left and right clamps (2).

7. Remove bolts and remove left and right clamps.

8. Remove the stabilizer bar mounts and the stabilizer bar.

To install:

9. Installation is performed in the reverse order of removal. Observe the following when doing so:

   a. Install halves of stabilizer bar mount on stabilizer bar:

- Larger outer diameter points toward outside.
- Half of stabilizer bar mount with groove is placed on octagon mount on stabilizer bar.
- Locking tabs engage completely in recesses.

10. Follow markings applied to stabilizer bar during removal.

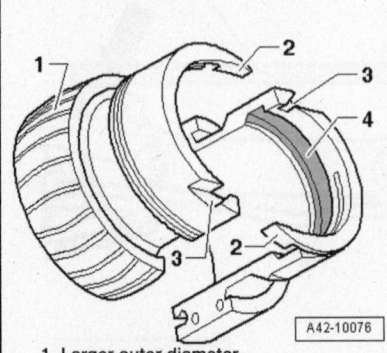

1. Larger outer diameter
2. Locking tabs
3. Recesses
4. Half of stabilizer bar mount with groove

Fig. 321 Install halves of stabilizer bar mount on stabilizer bar

➡**Bonded rubber bushings can only be turned to a limited extent. Only tighten suspension screws when vehicle is in curb weight or control position.**

11. Measure and ensure curb weight position of vehicle is as measured prior to removal.

12. Tighten the wheels. Refer to Specifications.

13. Measure and ensure curb weight position of vehicle is as measured prior to removal.

14. On vehicles with automatic headlamp range control system, perform a basic setting on the headlamps.

SHOCK ABSORBER

REMOVAL & INSTALLATION

Q5

Tools Needed:
   a. Torque Wrench V.A.G 1331
   b. Torque Wrench V.A.G 1332
   c. Engine/Transmission Jack V.A.G 1383 A
   d. Wheel Hub Support T10149

1. Determine dimension a from the center of the wheel to the lower edge of the wheel housing before starting work while the vehicle is resting on its wheels.

2. Place the vehicle on a hoist.

3. Remove wheel.

4. Turn the wheel hub up until a wheel bolt hole is on top.

5. Install the Wheel Hub Support T10149 with the wheel bolt.

6. Insert Wheel Hub Support T10149 in the Engine/Transmission Jack V.A.G 1383 A and lift the wheel bearing housing slightly.

7. Remove bolts.

8. For vehicles with electronic damping control:

   a. Release and remove the connector.

   b. Remove fastener.

Continuation for all vehicles:

9. Release retaining tabs and remove the stone deflector.

10. Remove bolt and washer.

11. Remove the shock absorber downward.

To install:

Installation is in reverse order of removal. Observe the following when doing so:

➡**Bonded rubber bushings can only be turned to a limited extent. Only tighten suspension bolts when vehicle is in curb weight or control position.**

➡**Wheel bearing, lifting to curb weight position on vehicles with coil springs.**

12. Tighten wheel.

STRUT & SPRING ASSEMBLY

REMOVAL & INSTALLATION

Q7

See Figures 322 through 324.

➡**Tools Needed:**

- Torque wrench V.A.G 1332
- Wood block (hardwood) 30 x 50 x 1300 mm

1. With vehicles with air suspension, place vehicle on hoist.

2. Remove the wheel.

3. Remove the suspension strut.

4. Insert wood block between underbody and rear upper link.

➡**Wood block is needed to press wheel bearing housing down.**

5. Remove nut from bolt.

6. Using the wood block, press the wheel bearing housing down far enough to remove bolt.

7. Remove the suspension strut.

To install:

Installation is in reverse order of removal. Observe the following:

➡**Bonded rubber bushings can only be turned to a limited extent. Only tighten suspension bolts when vehicle is in curb weight or control position.**

➡**Wheel bearing, lifting to curb weight position on vehicles with coil springs.**

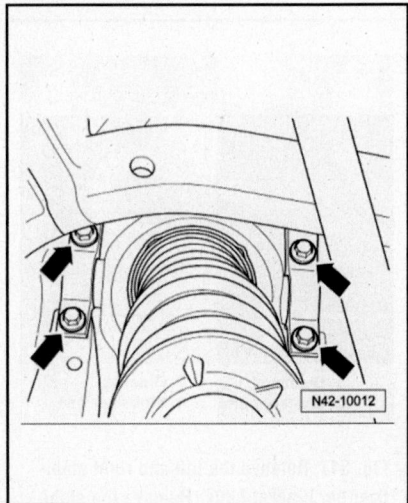

Fig. 322 Removing the suspension strut

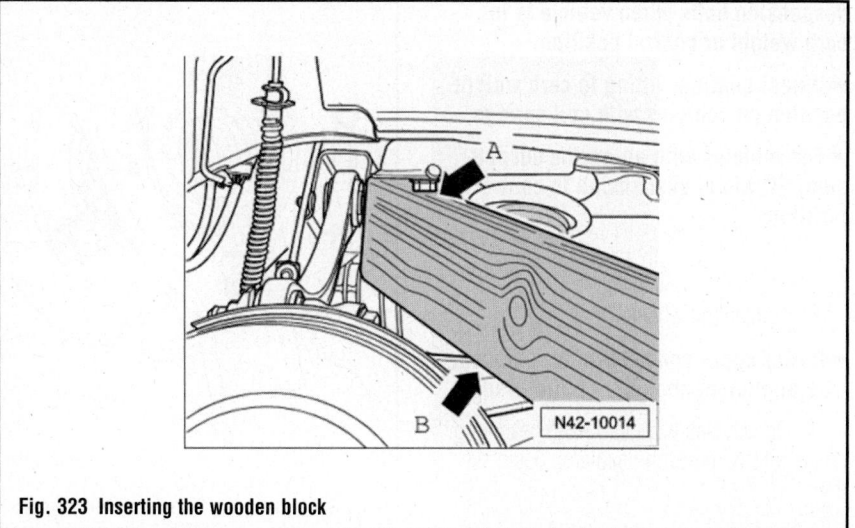

Fig. 323 Inserting the wooden block

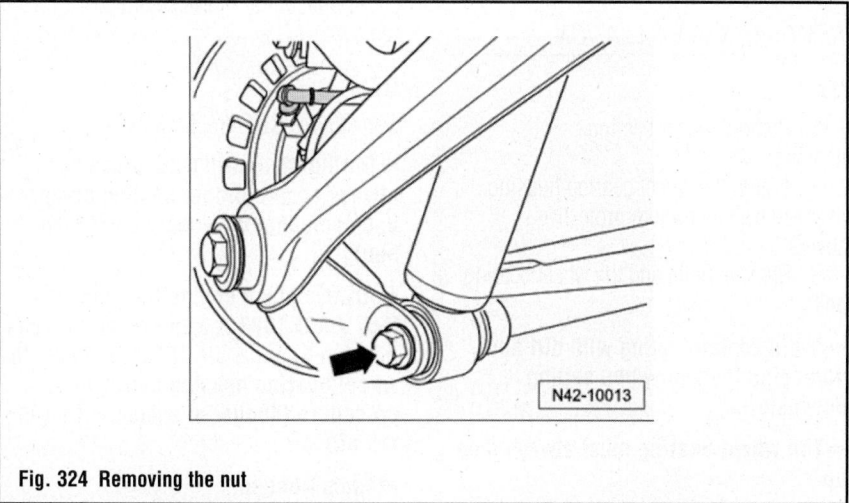

Fig. 324 Removing the nut

➡**For vehicles with air spring suspension, lift wheel suspension in control position.**

8. Install suspension strut on cross member and tighten to 44 ft. lbs. (60 Nm).
9. On vehicles with air suspension, position vehicle on wheels.
10. Tighten the wheels.
11. On vehicles with automatic headlamp range control, perform headlamp basic setting.

UPPER CONTROL ARM

REMOVAL & INSTALLATION

Q5

➡**Tools Needed:**

Torque Wrench V.A.G 1332

➡**Due to the inaccessibility of the inner threaded connection, the upper control arm can only be removed when the subframe has been removed.**

1. Determine dimension a from the center of the wheel to the lower edge of the wheel housing before starting work while the vehicle is resting on its wheels.
2. Place the vehicle on a hoist.
3. Remove wheels.
4. Remove subframe.
5. Mark the position of the eccentric bolt the wheel bearing housing, for example using a felt-tip pen.
6. Separate connections.
7. Remove upper transverse link.

To install:

➡**Replace the bolts and the self-locking nuts.**

Installation position of the transverse link to the subframe.

8. Install the upper control arm on the threaded connection by hand.
9. Lay a ruler or straight edge flat against the upper control arm.
10. Position the upper control

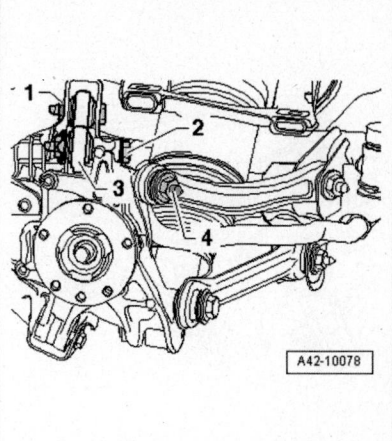

Fig. 325 Removing the front upper control arm

arm so the dimension between the straight edge and the stamping burr on the upper control arm is about 0.32 in. (8 mm).

11. Tighten the upper control arm on the subframe.
12. Screw wheel bearing housing on control arm and tighten new nut to 15 ft. lbs. (20 Nm). Note the installation position of the centering washer.
13. Install subframe.
14. Loosen threaded connection.
15. Lift the wheel bearing hub into curb weight position.
16. Tighten wheel.
17. Perform vehicle alignment.

Q7

Front

See Figure 325.

➡**Tools Needed:**

- Torque wrench V.A.G 1332
- Torque wrench V.A.G 1410

1. With vehicles with air suspension, place vehicle on hoist.
2. Remove the wheel.
3. Remove rear level control system sensor.
4. If front upper control arm is to be replaced, remove bracket.
5. Remove bolt and press rear upper link back slightly.
6. Remove bolt.
7. Remove nut and remove screw.
8. Remove front upper control arm.

To install:

Installation is in reverse order of removal. Observe the following:

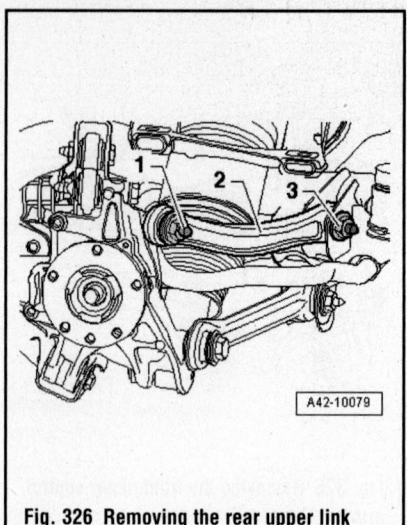

Fig. 326 Removing the rear upper link

➡Bonded rubber bushings can only be turned to a limited extent. Only tighten suspension bolts when vehicle is in curb weight or control position.

➡Wheel bearing, lifting to curb weight position on vehicles with coil springs.

➡For vehicles with air spring suspension, lift wheel suspension in control position.

9. On vehicles with air suspension, position vehicle on wheels.
10. Tighten the wheels.
11. Adapt control position again on vehicles with air spring suspension.

➡If front upper control arm is replaced, axle alignment should be performed.

12. On vehicles with automatic headlamp range control, perform headlamp basic setting.

Rear

See Figure 326.

➡Tool needed: Torque wrench V.A.G 1332

1. With vehicles with air suspension, place vehicle on hoist.
2. Remove the wheel.
3. Remove bolt.
4. Remove nut and remove bolt.
5. Remove rear upper link.

To install:
Installation is in reverse order of removal. Observe the following:

➡Bonded rubber bushings can only be turned to a limited extent. Only tighten

suspension bolts when vehicle is in curb weight or control position.

➡Wheel bearing, lifting to curb weight position on vehicles with coil springs.

➡For vehicles with air spring suspension, lift wheel suspension in control position.

6. On vehicles with air suspension, position vehicle on wheels.
7. Tighten the wheels.

➡If rear upper control arm is replaced, axle alignment should be performed.

8. On vehicles with automatic headlamp range control, perform headlamp basic setting.

WHEEL BEARINGS

REMOVAL & INSTALLATION

Q5

1. Remove wheel bearing housing.
2. Clamp the wheel bearing housing in a vise with aluminum protective covers.
3. Remove bolts and the wheel bearing unit.

➡Avoid contaminating with dirt and damaging the seal when setting down/storing.

➡The wheel bearing must always face up.

4. Always set the wheel bearing down on the wheel hub.

➡The same procedure also applies to the wheel bearing without a wheel hub.

To install:

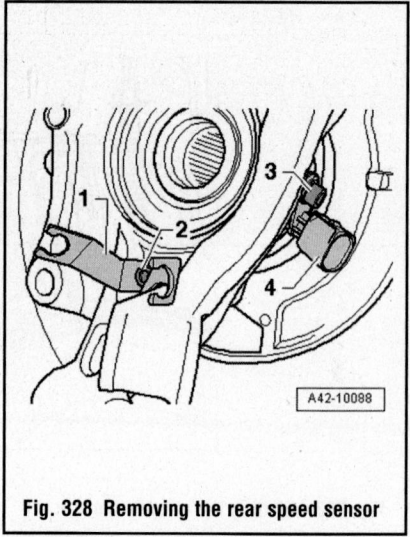

Fig. 328 Removing the rear speed sensor

Installation is in reverse order of removal.

Q7

See Figures 327 through 336.

➡During the entire work procedure, always ensure proper seating of tools and components (wheel bearing/wheel hub).

➡Always place engine/transmission jack V.A.G 1383 A with Universal Transmission Support V.A.G 1359/2 beneath wheel bearing housing during entire procedure (danger of accident if parts fall off).

➡Tools Needed:

- Hydraulic cylinder VAS 6178
- Engine/Transmission Jack V.A.G 1383 A with Universal Transmission Support V.A.G 1359/2

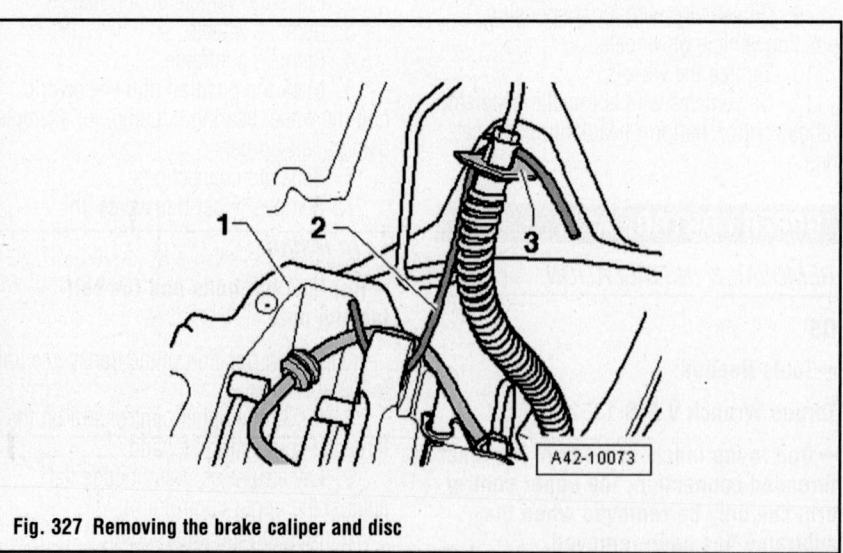

Fig. 327 Removing the brake caliper and disc

- Separating tool 3 - Kukko 15/3
- Assembly tool T10205
- Hollow piston cylinder VAS 6179
- Pliers for circlips, 180 mm internal circlip VAS 5498
- Pressure gauge w/connection VAS 6179/1

1. Remove the driveshaft.
2. Remove brake caliper and tie it with a wire at brake line bracket.
3. Remove brake disc.
4. Remove bolt and rear speed sensor.
5. Remove the wiring harness from bracket.
6. Disengage the parking brake cable at wheel bearing housing.
7. Remove the parking brake shoes.
8. Install attachment T10205/1 with wheel bolts onto wheel hub.

Wheel bolts 2 must not protrude on rear side of attachment T10205/1.

9. Mount tools as depicted in illustration.

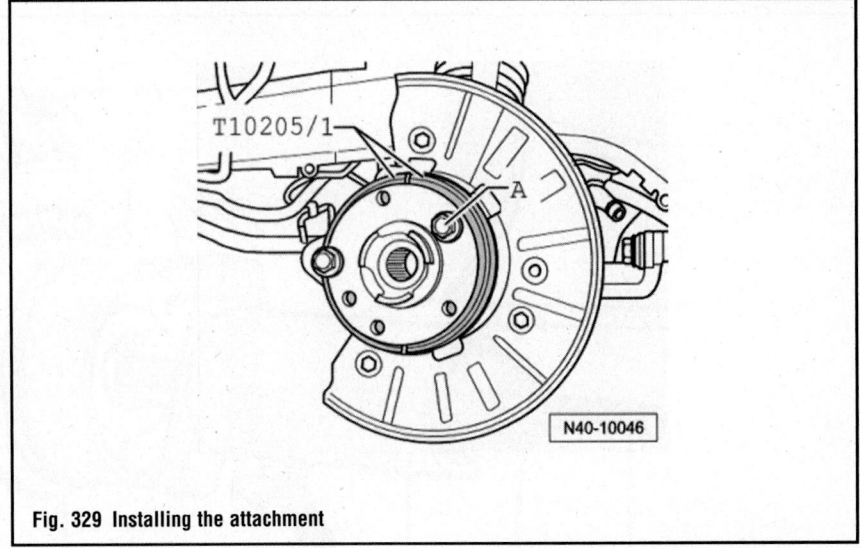

Fig. 329 Installing the attachment

10. Remove wheel hub while counter holding Hydraulic Press VAS 6178.
11. Remove the circlip.
12. Mount tools as depicted in illustration.

➡**Ensure Pressure Piece T10205/6 should faces toward rear final drive.**

13. Remove wheel bearing while counter holding Hydraulic Press VAS 6178.

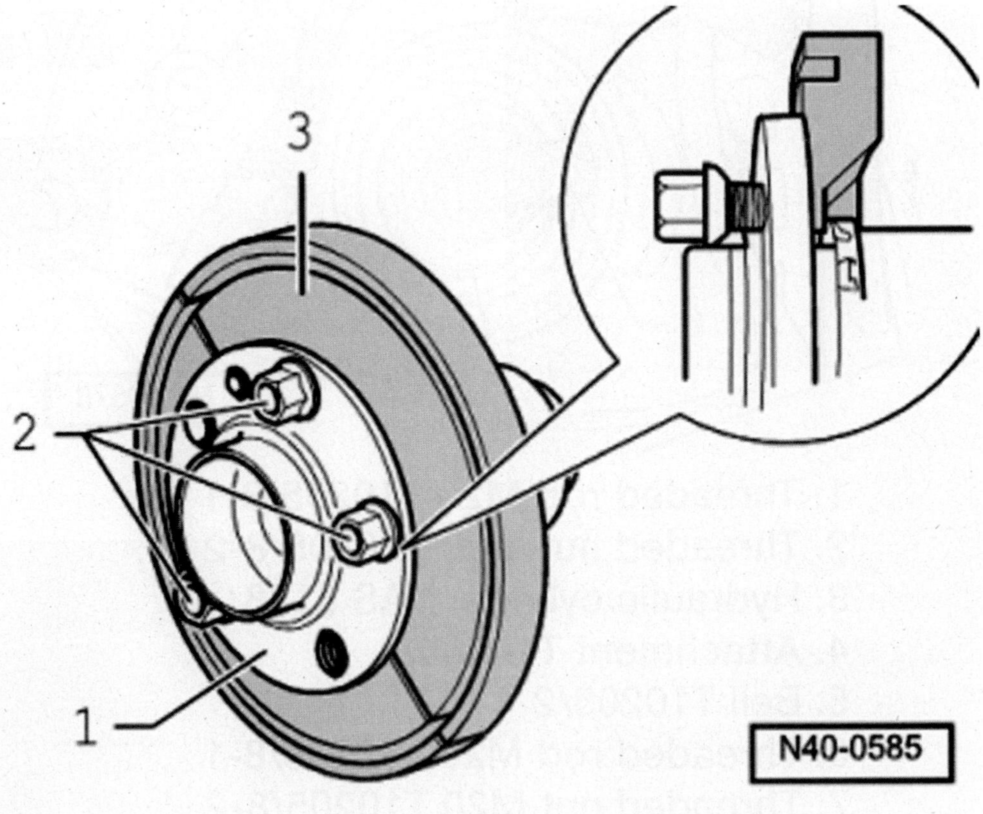

Fig. 330 Checking the bolts

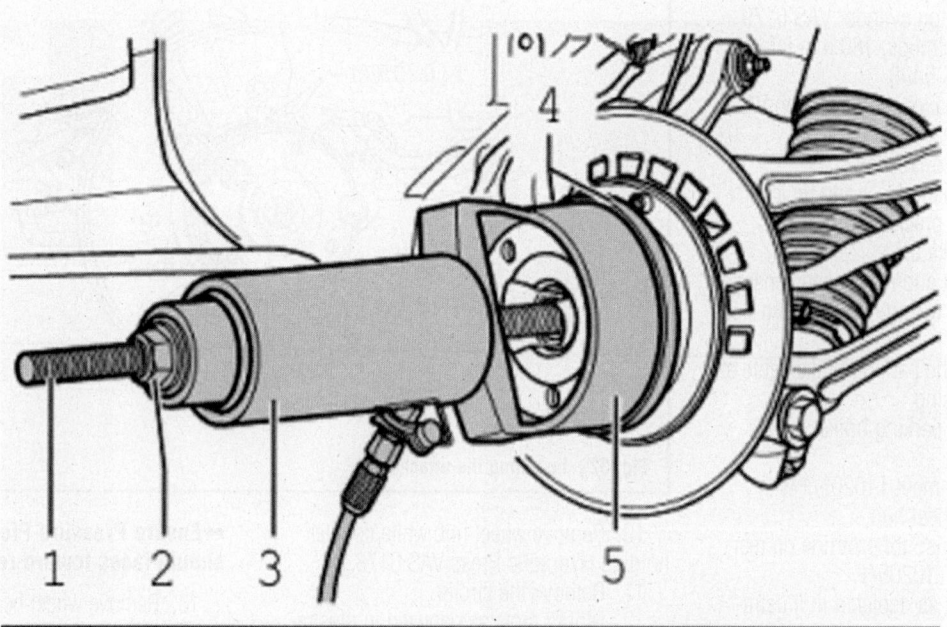

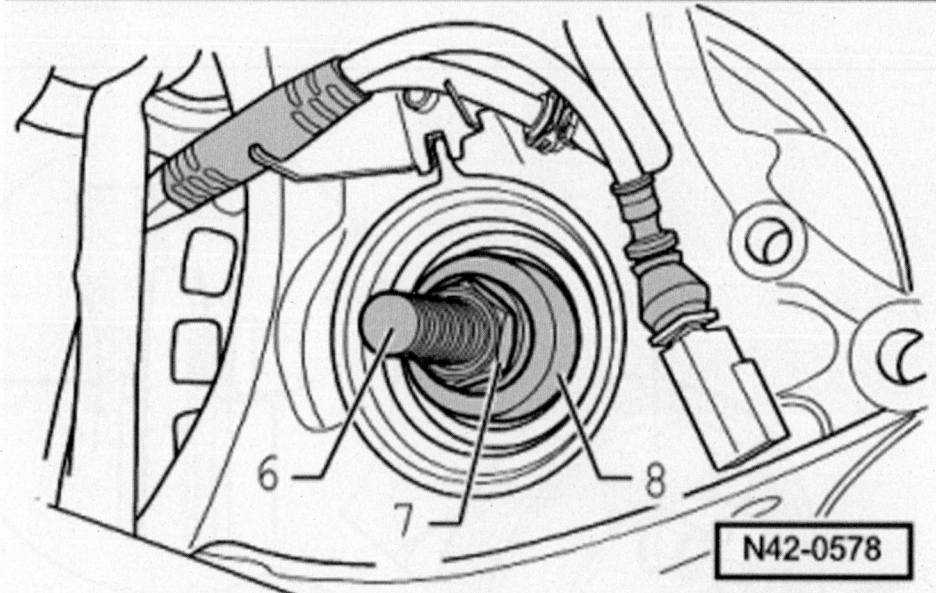

N42-0578

1. Threaded rod M20 T10205/8-1
2. Threaded nut M20 T10205/8-2
3. Hydraulic cylinder VAS 6178
4. Attachment T10205/1
5. Bell T10205/2
6. Threaded rod M20 T10205/8-1
7. Threaded nut M20 T10205/8-2
8. Press piece T10205/3

Fig. 331 Mounting tools

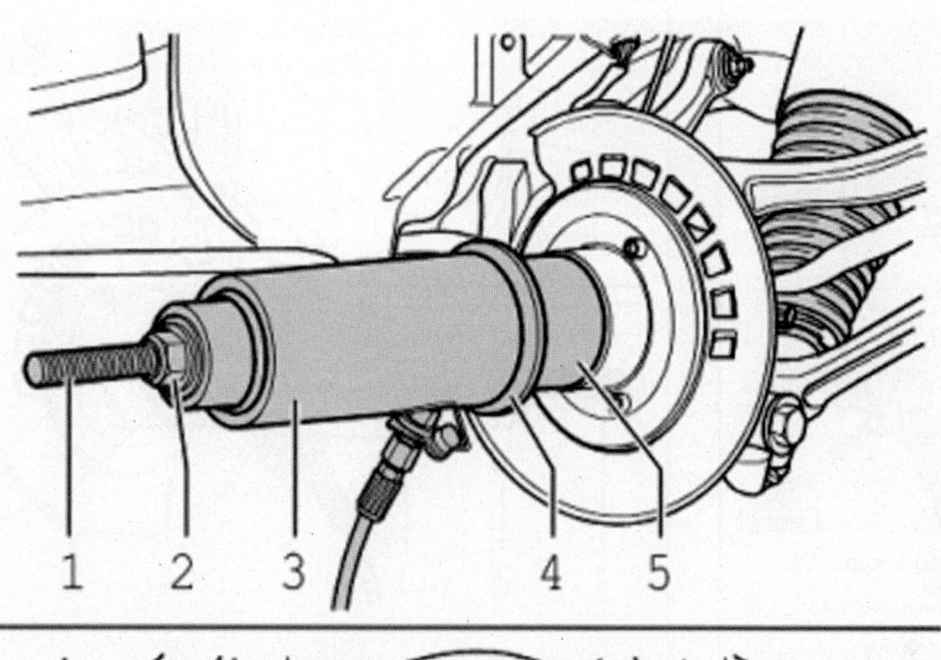

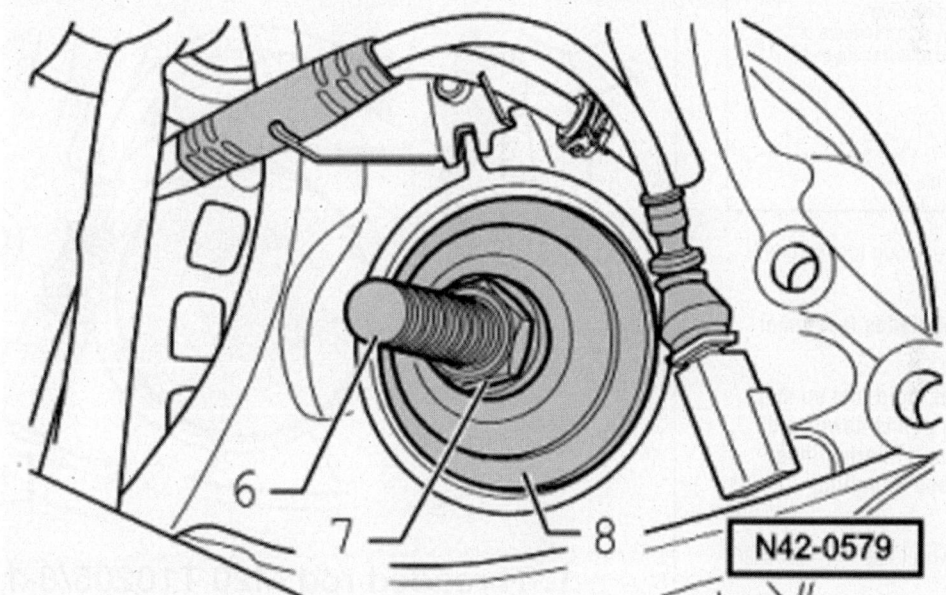

1. Threaded rod M20 T10205/8-1
2. Threaded nut M20 T10205/8-2
3. Hydraulic cylinder VAS 6178
4. Wheel hub support T10205/4
5. Mounting tube T10205/5
6. Threaded rod M20 T10205/8-1
7. Threaded nut M20 T10205/8-2
8. Thrust pad T10205/6

Fig. 332 Mounting tools

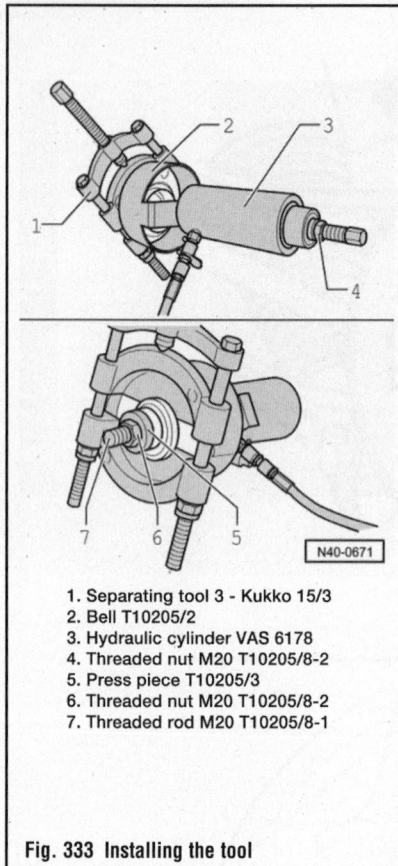

1. Separating tool 3 - Kukko 15/3
2. Bell T10205/2
3. Hydraulic cylinder VAS 6178
4. Threaded nut M20 T10205/8-2
5. Press piece T10205/3
6. Threaded nut M20 T10205/8-2
7. Threaded rod M20 T10205/8-1

Fig. 333 Installing the tool

14. Install the separating tool behind bearing inner ring.

➡ Beveled parts of blades face inner bearing race.

➡ When pulling off, hold tool so that bearing inner ring points downward (danger of accident if bearing inner ring jumps off at end of pulling process).

15. Pull off the wheel hub from the bearing inner ring.

16. Ensure rubberized ABS sensor ring faces toward rear final drive.

➡ If no rubberized ring is visible, check, using a paper clip, which of the sides is magnetic. When installed, this must face toward rear final drive.

17. Mount tools as depicted in illustration.

➡ Offset of thrust piece T10205/9 must point toward wheel bearing housing.

18. Connect pressure gauge w/connection VAS 6179/1 between hydraulic cylinder VAS 6178 and hydraulic line of hydraulic cylinder VAS 6178.

Pressures, described in the following, apply only to hydraulic cylinder VAS 6178.

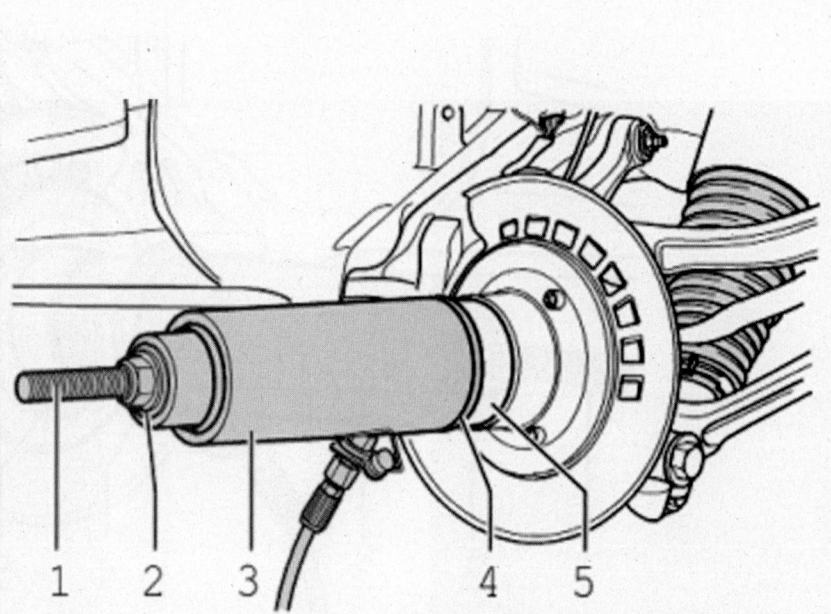

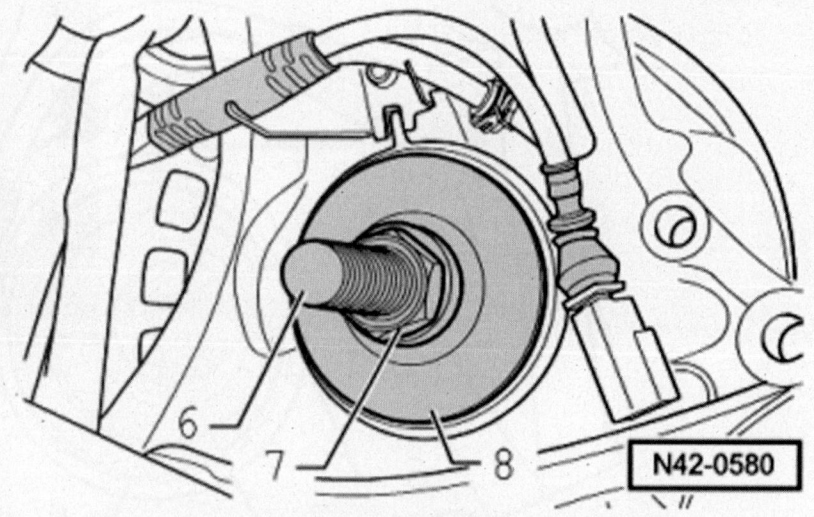

1. **Threaded rod M20 T10205/8-1**
2. **Threaded nut M20 T10205/8-2**
3. **Hydraulic cylinder VAS 6178**
4. **Press piece T10205/7**
5. **Wheel bearing**
6. **Threaded rod M20 T10205/8-1**
7. **Threaded nut M20 T10205/8-2**
8. **Press piece T10205/9**

Fig. 334 Mounting tool

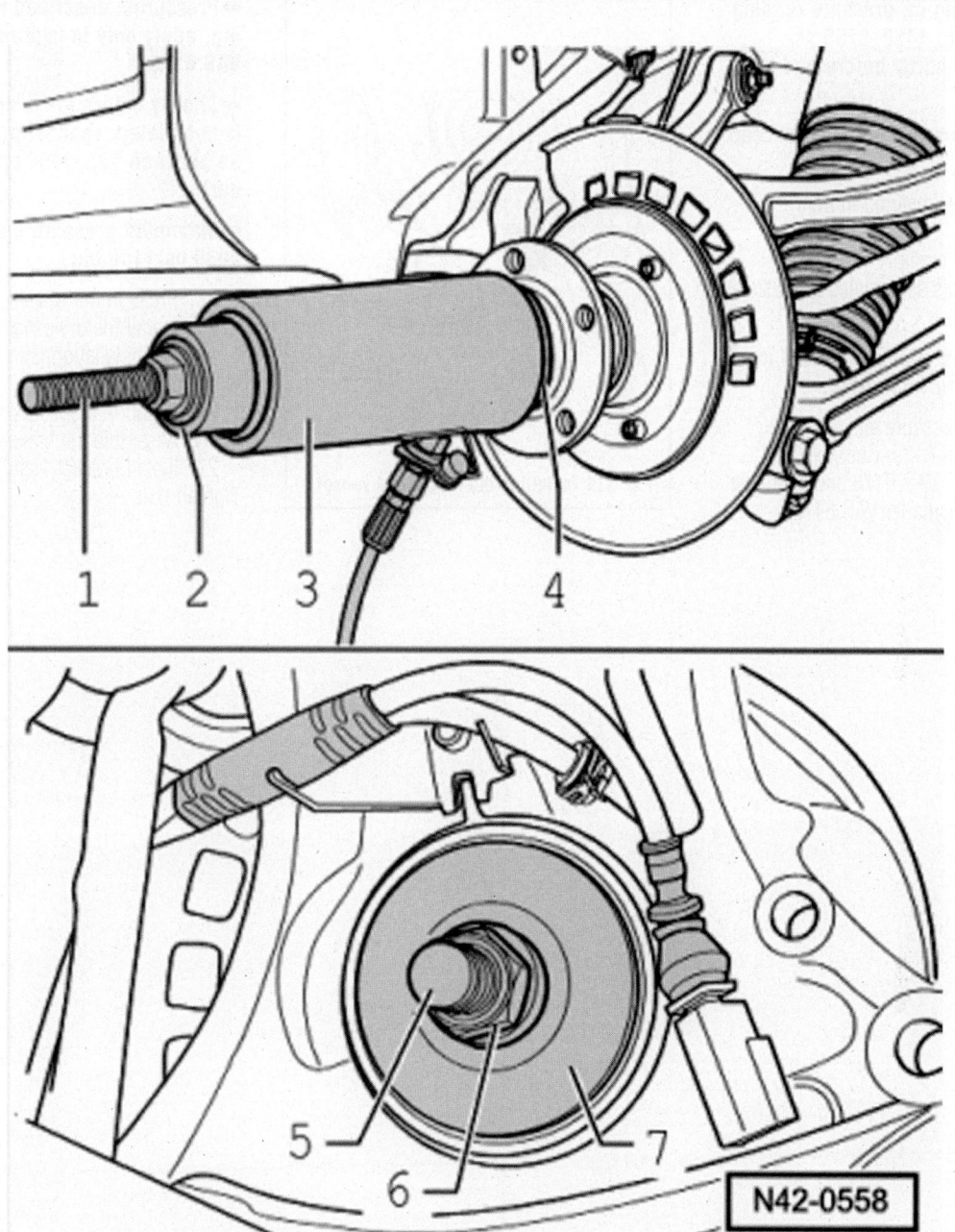

1. Threaded rod M20 T10205/8-1
2. Threaded nut M20 T10205/8-2
3. Hydraulic cylinder VAS 6178
4. Press piece T10205/10
5. Threaded rod M20 T10205/8-1
6. Threaded nut M20 T10205/8-2
7. Thrust pad T10205/6

Fig. 335 Mounting tools

➡**While pressing in, pressure reading must be between 1450–2755 psi (100–190 bar) shortly before end of pressing in.**

➡**Maximum pressure must not exceed 310 bar.**

19. Press wheel bearing in until stop.

20. Install the circlip.

21. Mount tools as depicted in illustration.

➡**Offset of thrust piece T10205/6 must point toward rear final drive.**

22. Connect pressure gauge w/connection VAS 6179/1 between hydraulic cylinder VAS 6178 and hydraulic line of hydraulic cylinder VAS 6178.

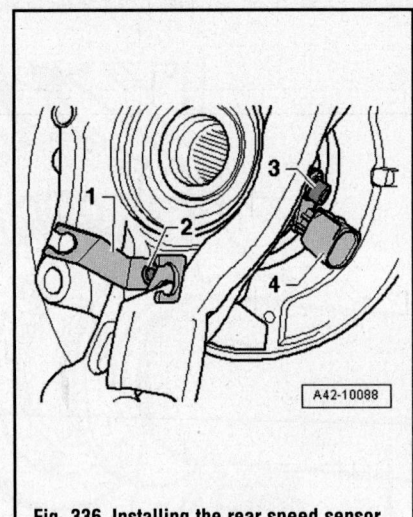

Fig. 336 Installing the rear speed sensor

➡**Pressures, described in the following, apply only to hydraulic cylinder VAS 6178.**

➡**Shortly before pressing-in procedure is completed, readout pressure must be between 435–1450 psi (30–100 bar).**

➡**Maximum pressure must not exceed 2030 psi (140 bar).**

23. Press in the wheel hub until stop.

24. Install the driveshaft.

Further installation is in reverse order of removal.

25. Install rear speed sensor.

26. Assemble the brakes.

27. Install bracket 1 and wiring harness. Tighten bolt.

AUDI

Diagnostic Trouble Codes

DIAGNOSTIC TROUBLE CODES

OBD II VEHICLE APPLICATIONS

AUDI

A3, A4, A5
2011–2012
- 2.0L L4 TDI . . . . .Engine Code: CBEA
- 2.0L L4 TFSI. . . . .Engine Code: CCTA
- 2.0L L4 TFSI. . . . .Engine Code: CBFA
- 2.0L L4 TFSI. . . . .Engine Code: CAEB

TT/TTS
2011–2012
- 2.0L L4 TFSI. . . . .Engine Code: CCZA
- 2.0L L4 TFSI. . . . .Engine Code: CCTA
- 2.0L L4 TFSI. . . .Engine Code: CDMA
- 3.2L V6 MFI . . . . .Engine Code: CBRA

Q5, Q7
2011–2012
- 2.0L L4 TFSI. . . . .Engine Code: CBFA
- 3.0L V6 TDI . . . . .Engine Code: CATA

OBD II Trouble Code List (P0XXX Codes)

DTC	Trouble Code Title, Conditions, Possible Causes
DTC: P0001 **1T ECM, MIL: Yes** **Year:** 2011, 2012 **Model:** TTS, Q7 **Engine:** 3.0L V6, 3.2L V6 **Transmission:** All	**FUEL QUANTITY CONTROL CIRCUIT/OPEN:** With the ignition on and the ECM command of the Fuel Quantity Solenoid off. The ECM does not detect voltage on the Fuel Quantity Solenoid Control circuit for 0.2 seconds.
DTC: P0003 **1T ECM, MIL: Yes** **Year:** 2011, 2012 **Model:** TTS, Q7 **Engine:** 3.0L V6, 3.2L V6 **Transmission:** All	**FUEL QUANTITY CONTROL CIRCUIT LOW:** With the ignition on and the ECM command of the Fuel Quantity Solenoid off. The ECM detects that the Fuel Quantity Solenoid Control circuit voltage is shorted to ground for 0.2 seconds.
DTC: P0004 **1T ECM, MIL: Yes** **Year:** 2011, 2012 **Model:** TTS, Q7 **Engine:** 3.0L V6, 3.2L V6 **Transmission:** All	**FUEL QUANTITY CONTROL CIRCUIT HIGH:** With the ignition on and the ECM command of the Fuel Quantity Solenoid on. The ECM detects excessive current on the Fuel Quantity Solenoid Control circuit for 0.2 seconds.
DTC: P000A **2T ECM, MIL: Yes** **Year:** 2012 **Model:** A3, A4, A5, TT, TTS, Q5, Q7, TTS, **Engine:** 2.0L L4, V6 **Transmission:** All	**BANK 1 CAMSHAFT (A or 1) POSITION SLOW RESPONSE:** The actual camshaft phasing position does not match the desired camshaft phasing position during camshaft phasing position changes. * Engine speed, 600 - 6320 RPM * Engine oil temp -48 to 180 °C * ECT -48 to 143 °C * Time after engine start > 1.5 to 3 Sec. * Number of checks 4
DTC: P000B **2T ECM, MIL: Yes** **Year:** 2011, 2012 **Model:** A3, A4, A5, TT, TTS, Q5, Q7, TTS, **Engine:** 2.0L L4, V6 **Transmission:** All	**BANK 1 CAMSHAFT (B or 2) POSITION SLOW RESPONSE:** Variable Valve Timing (VVT) rationality is monitored under the following conditions: (1) Cam phasing is commanded off of the default (lock-pin) position; (2) Oil temperature is between -12° C to 139° C (10° F to 282° F); (3) Battery voltage is greater than 10 Volts; Engine speed is at least 650 to 1400 rpm, depending on oil temperature. (4) No CMP sensor, CKP sensor or OBDI plausibility errors. Before VVT can be enabled, reference adaptation must be completed. The actual camshaft phasing position does not match the desired camshaft phasing position during camshaft phasing position changes.
DTC: P000C **2T ECM, MIL: Yes** **Year:** 2011, 2012 **Model:** TTS, Q7 **Engine:** 3.0L V6, 3.2L V6 **Transmission:** All	**BANK 2 CAMSHAFT (A or 1) POSITION SLOW RESPONSE :** Variable Valve Timing (VVT) rationality is monitored under the following conditions: (1) Cam phasing is commanded off of the default (lock-pin) position; (2) Oil temperature is between -12° C to 139° C (10° F to 282° F); (3) Battery voltage is greater than 10 Volts; Engine speed is at least 650 to 1400 rpm, depending on oil temperature; (4) No CMP sensor, CKP sensor or OBDI plausibility errors. Before VVT can be enabled, reference adaptation must be completed. The actual camshaft phasing position does not match the desired camshaft phasing position during camshaft phasing position changes.
DTC: P000D **2T ECM, MIL: Yes** **Year:** 2011, 2012 **Model:** TTS, Q7 **Engine:** 3.0L V6, 3.2L V6 **Transmission:** All	**BANK 2 CAMSHAFT (B or 2) POSITION SLOW RESPONSE:** Variable Valve Timing (VVT) rationality is monitored under the following conditions: (1) Cam phasing is commanded off of the default (lock-pin) position; (2) Oil temperature is between -12° C to 139° C (10° F to 282° F); (3) Battery voltage is greater than 10 Volts; Engine speed is at least 650 to 1400 RPM, depending on oil temperature; (4) No CMP sensor, CKP sensor or OBDI plausibility errors. Before VVT can be enabled, reference adaptation must be completed. The actual camshaft phasing position does not match the desired camshaft phasing position during camshaft phasing position changes.
DTC: P000E **2T PCM, MIL: Yes** **Year:** 2011, 2012 **Model:** A3, A4, A5, TT, TTS, Q5, Q7 **Engine:** 2.0L L4 **Transmission:** All	**Fuel Volume Regulator Control Exceeded Learning Limit:** Number of learning points at adaptation limits >= 8 of 64 Upper limit > 1.2 Monitoring Time Length: 100 m Sec.

DTC	Trouble Code Title, Conditions, Possible Causes
DTC: P0010 **2T ECM, MIL: Yes** **Year:** 2011, 2012 **Model:** A3, A4, A5, TT, TTS, Q5, Q7 **Engine:** 2.0L L4, 3.0L V6, 3.2L V6 **Transmission:** All	**"A or 1" Camshaft Position Actuator Circuit / Open (Bank 1):** The Powertrain Control Module (PCM) detects that the actual state of the VVT Intake Solenoid does not match the intended state. * Camshaft valve, commanded off * Engine speed, >80 RPM
DTC: P0011 **2T ECM, MIL: Yes** **Year:** 2011, 2012 **Model:** A3, A4, A5, TT, TTS, Q5, Q7 **Engine:** 2.0L L4, 3.0L V6, 3.2L V6 **Transmission:** All	**"A or 1" Camshaft Position Timing - Over-Advanced (Bank 1):** * Time after engine start > 10 to 300 Sec. * Oil temperature -48 to 143.30 °C * Frequency 4 times * Frequency cold 2 times
DTC: P0012 **2T ECM, MIL: Yes** **Year:** 2011, 2012 **Model:** A3, A4, A5, TT, TTS, Q5, Q7 **Engine:** 2.0L L4, 3.0L V6, 3.2L V6 **Transmission:** All	**"A or 1" Camshaft Position Over-Retarded (Bank 1):** Engine started and driven at an engine speed of more than 400rpm; and the ECM detected the camshaft timing exceeded the minimum calibrated retarded value, or the camshaft remained in the retarded position during the CCM test. The valve timing did not change from the current valve timing or it remained fixed during the testing. **NOTE: The camshaft adjustment is load- and RPM dependent. The electrical camshaft adjustment valve 1 switches oil pressure onto camshaft adjuster (mechanical adjustment mechanism), which adjusts the camshaft.**
DTC: P0013 **2T ECM, MIL: Yes** **Year:** 2011, 2012 **Model:** A3, A4, A5, TT, TTS, Q5, Q7 **Engine:** 2.0L L4, 3.0L V6, 3.2L V6 **Transmission:** All	**"B or 2" Camshaft Position - Actuator Circuit Bank 1:** With the engine running and battery voltage greater than 10.4 Volts. The Powertrain Control Module (PCM) detects that the actual state of the VVT intake solenoid, does not match the intended state. • Battery voltage below 11.5 volts * Camshaft valve, Off * Engine speed, >80 RPM
DTC: P0014 **2T ECM, MIL: Yes** **Year:** 2011, 2012 **Model:** A3, A4, A5, TT, TTS, Q5, Q7 **Engine:** 2.0L L4, 3.0L V6, 3.2L V6 **Transmission:** All	**"B or 2" Camshaft Position - Timing Over-Advanced or System Performance Bank 1:** The Powertrain Control Module (PCM) detects that the CPS circuit is open, shorted to ground or shorted to power. * Time after engine start, >30 Sec. * Engine speed, 800-6400 RPM * Modeled oil Temperature, -10.5–105 °C * ECT -20.3–114.8 °C * Frequency, 3 times
DTC: P0016 **1T ECM, MIL: Yes** **Year:** 2011, 2012 **Model:** A3, A4, A5, TT, TTS, Q5, Q7 **Engine:** 2.0L L4, 3.0L V6, 3.2L V6 **Transmission:** All	**CRANKSHAFT/CAMSHAFT TIMING MISALIGNMENT:** Engine cranking and Engine running Powertrain Control Module (PCM) detects an error when the camshaft position is out of phase with the crankshaft position. One Trip Fault. Three good trips to turn off the MIL.
DTC: P0017 **1T ECM, MIL: Yes** **Year:** 2011, 2012 **Model:** A3, A4, A5, TT, TTS, Q5, Q7 **Engine:** 2.0L L4, 3.0L V6, 3.2L V6 **Transmission:** All	**Crankshaft Position – Camshaft Position Correlation Bank 1 Sensor (B or2):** The Powertrain Control Module (PCM) detects an error when the camshaft position is out of phase with the crankshaft position. One Trip Fault. Three good trips to turn off the MIL. * Engine speed, <1000 RPM * Engine load, <30% * ECT, -15–110° C * Time after engine start, >5 Sec.
DTC: P0018 **1T ECM, MIL: Yes** **Year:** 2011, 2012 **Model:** TTS, Q7 **Engine:** 3.0L V6, 3.2L V6 **Transmission:** All	**Crankshaft Position – Camshaft Position Correlation Bank 2 Sensor A:** The Powertrain Control Module (PCM) detects an error when the camshaft position is out of phase with the crankshaft position. One Trip Fault. Three good trips to turn off the MIL. * Engine speed, <1000 RPM * Engine load, <30% * ECT, -15–110° C * Time after engine start, >5 Sec.

DTC	Trouble Code Title, Conditions, Possible Causes
DTC: P0019 **1T ECM, MIL: Yes** **Year:** 2011, 2012 **Model:** TTS, Q7 **Engine:** 3.0L V6, 3.2L V6 **Transmission:** All	**-CRANKSHAFT/CAMSHAFT TIMING MISALIGNMENT:** The Powertrain Control Module (PCM) detects an error when the camshaft position is out of phase with the crankshaft position. One Trip Fault. Three good trips to turn off the MIL. * Engine speed, <1000 RPM * Engine load, <30% * ECT, -15–110° C * Time after engine start, >5 Sec.
DTC: P0020 **Year:** 2011, 2012 **Model:** TTS, Q7 **Engine:** 3.0L V6, 3.2L V6 **Transmission:** All	**-BANK 2CAMSHAFT 1 POSITION ACTUATOR CIRCUIT OPEN:** With the engine running and battery voltage greater than 10.4 Volts. The Powertrain Control Module (PCM) detects that the actual state of the VVT Intake Solenoid does not match the intended state. * Engine speed, >550 RPM * ECT, -7.5° C * Time after engine start, >3.5 Sec. * Number of checks 3 * Time length for more than 1.5 Sec.
DTC: P0021 **1T ECM, MIL: Yes** **Year:** 2011, 2012 **Model:** TTS, Q7 **Engine:** 3.0L V6, 3.2L V6 **Transmission:** All	**Intake (A) Camshaft Position Timing - Over-Advanced (Bank 2):** The Powertrain Control Module (PCM) detects that the actual state of the VVT Intake Solenoid does not match the intended state. * Engine speed, >550 RPM * ECT, -7.5° C * Time after engine start, >3.5 Sec. * Number of checks 3 * Time length for more than 1.5 Sec.
DTC: P0023 **1T ECM, MIL: Yes** **Year:** 2011, 2012 **Model:** TTS, Q7 **Engine:** 3.0L V6, 3.2L V6 **Transmission:** All	**"B or 2" Camshaft Position - Actuator Circuit Bank 2:** With the engine running and battery voltage greater than 10.4 Volts. The Powertrain Control Module (PCM) detects that the actual state of the VVT Intake Solenoid does not match the intended state. * Camshaft valve, Off * Engine speed, >80 RPM
DTC: P0024 **1T ECM, MIL: Yes** **Year:** 2011, 2012 **Model:** TTS, Q7 **Engine:** 3.0L V6, 3.2L V6 **Transmission:** All	**"B" Camshaft Position - Timing Over-Advanced or System Performance Bank 2:** The Powertrain Control Module (PCM) detects that the actual state of the VVT Intake Solenoid does not match the intended state. * Engine speed, >550 RPM * ECT, -7.5° C * Time after engine start, >3.5 Sec. * Number of checks 3 * Time length for more than 1.5 Sec.
DTC: P0030 **1T ECM, MIL: Yes** **Year:** 2011, 2012 **Model:** A3, A4, A5, TT, TTS, Q5, Q7 **Engine:** 2.0L L4, 3.0L V6, 3.2L V6 **Transmission:** All	**HO2S Heater Control Circuit (Bank 1, Sensor 1):** With the ignition on and the Oxygen Sensor Heater command on. The ECM detects an implausible voltage on the bank 1, sensor 1heater control circuit for 2.0 seconds. * Heater, Commanded off * Time after engine start, >10 Sec.
DTC: P0031 **1T ECM, MIL: Yes** **Year:** 2011, 2012 **Model:** A3, A4, A5, TT, TTS, Q5, Q7 **Engine:** 2.0L L4, 3.0L V6, 3.2L V6 **Transmission:** All	**HO2S Heater Control Circuit Low (Bank 1, Sensor 1) Short to ground:** Continuously during O2 heater operation with battery voltage between 10.4 and 15.75 Volts. The Powertrain Control Module (PCM) detects that the O2 sensor heater element input is below the minimum acceptable voltage. One trip fault. Three good trips to turn off the MIL.

DTC	Trouble Code Title, Conditions, Possible Causes
DTC: P0032 **1T ECM, MIL: Yes** **Year:** 2011, 2012 **Model:** A3, A4, A5, TT, TTS, Q5, Q7 **Engine:** 2.0L L4, 3.0L V6, 3.2L V6 **Transmission:** All	**HO2S Heater Control Circuit High (Bank 1, Sensor 1):** The Powertrain Control Module (PCM) detects that the O2 sensor heater element input is above the maximum acceptable voltage. One trip fault. Three good trips to turn off the MIL. * Continuously during O2 heater operation with battery voltage between 10.4 and 15.75 Volts. * Heater, Commanded On * Time after engine start, > 5 seconds
DTC: P0036 **2T ECM, MIL: Yes** **Year:** 2011, 2012 **Model:** A3, A4, A5, TT, Q5 **Engine:** 2.0L L4 **Transmission:** All	**HO2S Heater Circuit (Bank 1, Sensor 3) Open Circuit** The Powertrain Control Module (PCM) detects that the O2 sensor heater element input is above the maximum acceptable voltage. * Engine speed, >80 RPM * Heater commanded off
DTC: P0036 **1T ECM, MIL: Yes** **Year:** 2011, 2012 **Model:** A3, A4, A5, TT, TTS, Q5, Q7 **Engine:** 2.0L L4, 3.0L V6, 3.2L V6 **Transmission:** All	**HO2S Heater Control Circuit (Bank 1, Sensor 2):** With the ignition on and the Oxygen Sensor Heater command on. The ECM detects an implausible voltage on the bank 1, sensor 2heater control circuit for 2.0 seconds. * Heater, Commanded off * Engine speed, >80 RPM
DTC: P0037 **1T ECM, MIL: Yes** **Year:** 2011, 2012 **Model:** A3, A4, A5, TT, TTS, Q5, Q7 **Engine:** 2.0L L4, 3.0L V6, 3.2L V6 **Transmission:** All	**O2 SENSOR 1/2 HEATER CIRCUIT LOW:** Continuously during O2 heater operation with battery voltage between 10.4 and 15.75 Volts. The Powertrain Control Module (PCM) detects that the O2 sensor heater element input is below the minimum acceptable voltage. One trip fault. Three good trips to turn off the MIL.
DTC: P0038 **1T ECM, MIL: Yes** **Year:** 2011, 2012 **Model:** A3, A4, A5, TT, TTS, Q5, Q7 **Engine:** 2.0L L4, 3.0L V6, 3.2L V6 **Transmission:** All	**HO2S Heater Control Circuit High (Bank 1, Sensor 2):** The Powertrain Control Module (PCM) detects that the O2 sensor heater element input is above the maximum acceptable voltage. One trip fault. Three good trips to turn off the MIL. Continuously during O2 heater operation with battery voltage between 10.4 and 15.75 Volts.
DTC: P0040 **2T PCM, MIL: Yes** **Year:** 2011, 2012 **Model:** TTS, Q7 **Engine:** 3.0L V6, 3.2L V6 **Transmission:** All	**O2 Sensor Signals Swapped Bank 1 Sensor 1/ Bank 2 Sensor 1:** The Powertrain Control Module (PCM) detects that the O2 sensor harness connectors are swapped or shorted. One trip fault. Three good trips to turn off the MIL. * Lambda control, Closed loop * VVT, Ready, no fault
DTC: P0042 **2T ECM, MIL: Yes** **Year:** 2011, 2012 **Model:** A3, A4, A5, TT, Q5, **Engine:** 2.0L L4 **Transmission:** All	**HO2S Heater Control Circuit (Bank 1 Sensor 3):** The Powertrain Control Module (PCM) detects that the O2 sensor signal circuit is shorted. One trip fault. Three good trips to turn off the MIL. * Heater, Commanded off * Engine speed, > 80 RPM
DTC: P0043 **Year:** 2011, 2012 **Model:** A3, A4, A5, TT, Q5, **Engine:** 2.0L L4 **Transmission:** All	**HO2S Heater Control Circuit Low Bank 1 Sensor 3:** The Powertrain Control Module (PCM) detects that the O2 sensor signal circuit is shorted. * Engine speed > 80 RPM * Heater commanded off
DTC: P0043 **2T PCM, MIL: Yes** **Year:** 2011, 2012 **Model:** TTS, Q7 **Engine:** 3.0L V6, 3.2L V6 **Transmission:** All	**HO2S Heater Control Circuit Low (Bank 1, Sensor 2) short to ground:** * SULEV Time after engine start, >5 Sec * Heater commanded off * ULEV engine speed >80 RPM * Heater, commanded off

DTC	Trouble Code Title, Conditions, Possible Causes
DTC: P0044 **2T PCM, MIL: Yes** **Year:** 2011, 2012 **Model:** TTS, Q7 **Engine:** 3.0L V6, 3.2L V6 **Transmission:** All	**HO2S Heater Control Circuit High (Bank 1, Sensor 2) Short to B+:** With the ignition on and the Oxygen Sensor Heater command on. The ECM detects an implausible signal on the bank 1, sensor 2 control circuit for 2.0 seconds.
DTC: P0044 **2T ECM, MIL: Yes** **Year:** 2011, 2012 **Model:** A3, A4, A5, TT, Q5, **Engine:** 2.0L L4 **Transmission:** All	**HO2S Heater Control Circuit High (Bank 1 Sensor 3):** The Powertrain Control Module (PCM) detects that the O2 sensor control circuit is shorted.
DTC: P0045 **2T ECM, MIL: Yes** **Year:** 2011, 2012 **Model:** A3, A4, A5, TT, TTS, Q5, Q7 **Engine:** 2.0L L4, 3.2L V6 **Transmission:** All	**Turbocharger Boost Control Solenoid "A" Circuit Open:** With the ignition on and the Boost Pressure Servo Motor command off. The ECM detects that the Boost Pressure Servo Motor Control circuit is open for 0.5 second.
DTC: P0046 **2T ECM, MIL: Yes** **Year:** 2011, 2012 **Model:** A3, A4, A5, TT, TTS, Q5, Q7 **Engine:** 2.0L L4, 3.0L V6, 3.2L V6 **Transmission:** All	**TURBOCHARGER BOOST CONTROL CIRCUIT/EXCESSIVE CURRENT:** With the ignition on and the Boost Pressure Servo Motor command off. The Boost Pressure Servo Motor reports an internal error to the ECM.
DTC: P0047 **2T ECM, MIL: Yes** **Year:** 2011, 2012 **Model:** A3, A4, A5, TT, TTS, Q5, Q7 **Engine:** 2.0L L4, 3.0L V6, 3.2L V6 **Transmission:** All	**Turbocharger Boost Control Solenoid "A" Circuit Low:** With the ignition on and the Boost Pressure Servo Motor command off. The ECM detects that the (K137) Boost Pressure Servo Motor Control circuit is shorted to ground for 0.5 second.
DTC: P0048 **2T ECM, MIL: Yes** **Year:** 2011, 2012 **Model:** A3, A4, A5, TT, TTS, Q5, Q7 **Engine:** 2.0L L4, 3.0L V6, 3.2L V6 **Transmission:** All	**Turbocharger Boost Control Solenoid "A" Circuit High:** With the ignition on and the Boost Pressure Servo Motor command on. The ECM detects that the Boost Pressure Servo Motor Control circuit is shorted to voltage for 0.5 second.
DTC: P0050 **2T ECM, MIL: Yes** **Year:** 2011, 2012 **Model:** A3, A4, A5, TT, TTS, Q5, Q7 **Engine:** 2.0L L4, 3.0L V6, 3.2L V6 **Transmission:** All	**HO2S Heater Control Circuit Bank 2 Sensor 1:** * Time after engine start, >5 Sec. * Heater, Commanded off
DTC: P0051 **2T ECM, MIL: Yes** **Year:** 2011, 2012 **Model:** A3, A4, A5, TT, TTS, Q5, Q7 **Engine:** 2.0L L4, 3.0L V6, 3.2L V6 **Transmission:** All	**HO2S SENSOR 2/1 HEATER CIRCUIT LOW:** Continuously during O2 heater operation with battery voltage between 10.4 and 15.75 Volts. The Powertrain Control Module (PCM) detects that the O2 sensor heater element input is below the minimum acceptable voltage. One trip fault. Three good trips to turn off the MIL.

DTC	Trouble Code Title, Conditions, Possible Causes
DTC: P0052 **2T ECM, MIL: Yes** **Year:** 2011, 2012 **Model:** A3, A4, A5, TT, TTS, Q5, Q7 **Engine:** 2.0L L4, 3.0L V6, 3.2L V6 **Transmission:** All	**HO2S SENSOR 2/1 HEATER CIRCUIT HIGH:** Continuously during O2 heater operation with battery voltage between 10.4 and 15.75 Volts. The Powertrain Control Module (PCM) detects that the O2 sensor heater element input is above the maximum acceptable voltage. One trip fault. Three good trips to turn off the MIL.
DTC: P0053 **2T ECM, MIL: Yes** **Year:** 2011, 2012 **Model:** A3, A4, A5, TT, TTS, Q5, Q7 **Engine:** 2.0L L4, 3.0L V6, 3.2L V6 **Transmission:** All	**HO2S SENSOR 1/1 HEATER RESISTANCE:** With the ignition on and the Oxygen Sensor Heater command on. The ECM detects an implausible voltage on the (K79) O2 1/1 Heater Control circuit for 2.0 seconds.
DTC: P0056 **2T ECM, MIL: Yes** **Year:** 2011, 2012 **Model:** A3, A4, A5, TT, TTS, Q5, Q7 **Engine:** 2.0L L4, 3.0L V6, 3.2L V6 **Transmission:** All	**HO2S Heater Control Circuit Bank 2 Sensor 2:** * Time after engine start, >5 Sec. * Heater, Commanded off
DTC: P0057 **2T ECM, MIL: Yes** **Year:** 2011, 2012 **Model:** A3, A4, A5, TT, TTS, Q5, Q7 **Engine:** 2.0L L4, 3.0L V6, 3.2L V6 **Transmission:** All	**HO2S SENSOR 2/2 HEATER CIRCUIT LOW:** Continuously during O2 heater operation with battery voltage between 10.4 and 15.75 volts. The Powertrain Control Module (PCM) detects that the O2 sensor heater element input is below the minimum acceptable voltage. One trip fault. Three good trips to turn off the MIL.
DTC: P0058 **2T ECM, MIL: Yes** **Year:** 2011, 2012 **Model:** A3, A4, A5, TT, TTS, Q5, Q7 **Engine:** 2.0L L4, 3.0L V6, 3.2L V6 **Transmission:** All	**HO2S SENSOR 2/2 HEATER CIRCUIT HIGH:** Continuously during O2 heater operation with battery voltage between 10.4 and 15.75 Volts. The Powertrain Control Module (PCM) detects that the O2 sensor heater element input is above the maximum acceptable voltage. One trip fault. Three good trips to turn off the MIL.
DTC: P0068 **2T ECM, MIL: Yes** **Year:** 2011, 2012 **Model:** A3, A4, A5, TT, TTS, Q5, Q7 **Engine:** 2.0L L4, 3.0L V6, 3.2L V6 **Transmission:** All	**MAP/MAF – Throttle Position Correlation:** * Fuel system monitor, running * Fuel adaptation, active, no fault * Lambda control, closed loop * Mass air flow, > 45 * Manifold to ambient pressure ratio, <0.82
DTC: P0069 **2T ECM, MIL: Yes** **Year:** 2011, 2012 **Model:** A3, A4, A5, TT, TTS, Q5, Q7 **Engine:** 2.0L L4, 3.0L V6, 3.2L V6 **Transmission:** All	**MANIFOLD PRESSURE/BAROMETRIC PRESSURE CORRELATION:** With the ignition on and at engine idle. There are no Sensor Reference Voltage DTC's. There are no other Boost Pressure related DTC's. There are no Inlet Pressure Sensor DTC's. The difference between the Boost Pressure Sensor Signal and the Inlet Pressure Sensor Signal is greater than 100 hpa (1.45 psi) for 4.0 seconds.
DTC: P0070 **2T ECM, MIL: Yes** **Year:** 2011, 2012 **Model:** A3, A4, A5, TT, Q5 **Engine:** 2.0L L4 **Transmission:** All	**Ambient Air Temp Sensor Short To B+:** * CAN active, Sensor signal circuit is shorted to B+

DTC	Trouble Code Title, Conditions, Possible Causes
DTC: P0070 **2T ECM, MIL: Yes** **Year:** 2011, 2012 **Model:** A3, A4, A5, TT, TTS, Q5, Q7 **Engine:** 2.0L L4, 3.0L V6, 3.2L V6 **Transmission:** All	**Ambient Air Temperature:** * CAN active, signal circuit is shorted to ground or to sensor ground.
DTC: P0071 **2T ECM, MIL: Yes** **Year:** 2011, 2012 **Model:** A3, A4, A5, TT, TTS, Q5, Q7 **Engine:** 2.0L L4, 3.0L V6, 3.2L V6 **Transmission:** All	**Ambient Air Temperature Sensor Range/Performance:** Engine off time is greater than 480 minutes and the vehicle has been driven for one Minute, over 35 mph. Ambient temperature is greater than -64° C (-83°F). The PCM compares the ambient, engine coolant and intake air temperature sensor values. If engine coolant and intake air temperature sensors agree with each other, but ambient air temperature does not agree, the ambient air temperature sensor is declared as irrational. Two Trip Fault. Three good trips to turn off the MIL.
DTC: P0072 **1T ECM, MIL: Yes** **Year:** 2011, 2012 **Model:** A3, A4, A5, TT, TTS, Q5, Q7 **Engine:** 2.0L L4, 3.0L V6, 3.2L V6 **Transmission:** All	**AMBIENT AIR TEMPERATURE SENSOR CIRCUIT LOW:** With the ignition on. Battery voltage greater than 10.4 volts. The Ambient Air Temperature (AAT) sensor circuit voltage at the TIPM is less than 0.078, of a volt for more than 2.8 seconds. One Trip Fault. Three good trips to clear the MIL.
DTC: P0073 **1 T ECM, MIL: Yes** **Year:** 2011, 2012 **Model:** A3, A4, A5, TT, TTS, Q5, Q7 **Engine:** 2.0L L4, 3.0L V6, 3.2L V6 **Transmission:** All	**AMBIENT AIR TEMPERATURE SENSOR CIRCUIT HIGH:** With the ignition on. Battery voltage greater than 10.4 volts. The Ambient Air Temperature (AAT) sensor circuit voltage at the TIPM is greater than 4.98 volts for more than 2.8 seconds. One Trip Fault. Three good trips to turn off the MIL.
DTC: P0087 **2T ECM, MIL: Yes** **Year:** 2011, 2012 **Model:** A3, A4, A5, TT, TTS, Q5, Q7 **Engine:** 2.0L L4, 3.0L V6, 3.2L V6 **Transmission:** All	**FUEL RAIL PRESSURE TOO LOW:** With the engine running. The ECM determines that the fuel rail pressure is too low for a given engine speed and load.
DTC: P0088 **2T ECM, MIL: Yes** **Year:** 2011, 2012 **Model:** A3, A4, A5, TT, TTS, Q5, Q7 **Engine:** 2.0L L4, 3.0L V6, 3.2L V6 **Transmission:** All	**FUEL RAIL PRESSURE TOO HIGH:** With the engine running. The ECM determines that the fuel rail pressure is too high for a given engine speed and load.
DTC: P0089 **2T ECM, MIL: Yes** **Year:** 2011, 2012 **Model:** A3, A4, A5, TT, TTS, Q5, Q7 **Engine:** 2.0L L4, 3.0L V6, 3.2L V6 **Transmission:** All	**Fuel Pressure Regulator 1 Performance:** * Time after engine start, 60 Sec. * Time after engine start, 60 Sec. * Fuel cut off, Not active * Time after fuel cut off, 20 Sec. * Time after engine start, 60 Sec.
DTC: P008A **2T ECM, MIL: Yes** **Year:** 2011, 2012 **Model:** A3, A4, A5, TT, TTS, Q5, Q7 **Engine:** 2.0L L4, 3.0L V6, 3.2L V6 **Transmission:** All	**Fuel System Pressure Sensor Low pressure system:** Actual pressure <40 kPa, monitoring time length 2 seconds.

DTC	Trouble Code Title, Conditions, Possible Causes
DTC: P008B **2T ECM, MIL:** Yes **Year:** 2011, 2012 **Model:** A3, A4, A5, TT, TTS, Q5, Q7 **Engine:** 2.0L L4, 3.0L V6, 3.2L V6 **Transmission:** All	**Low Pressure Fuel System Pressure - Too High:** Actual pressure> 780 kPa, monitoring time length 2 seconds.
DTC: P0090 **2T ECM, MIL:** Yes **Year:** 2011, 2012 **Model:** A3, A4, A5, TT, TTS, Q5, Q7 **Engine:** 2.0L L4, 3.0L V6, 3.2L V6 **Transmission:** All	**FUEL PRESSURE 1 CONTROL CIRCUIT/OPEN:** With the ignition on and the Fuel Pressure Solenoid command off. The ECM detects that the (K370) Fuel Pressure Solenoid Control circuit is open for 0.28 seconds.
DTC: P0091 **2T ECM, MIL:** Yes **Year:** 2011, 2012 **Model:** A3, A4, A5, TT, TTS, Q5, Q7 **Engine:** 2.0L L4, 3.0L V6, 3.2L V6 **Transmission:** All	**-FUEL PRESSURE 1 CONTROL CIRCUIT LOW:** With the ignition on and the Fuel Pressure Solenoid command off. The ECM detects that the Fuel Pressure Solenoid Control circuit is shorted to ground for 0.22 seconds.
DTC: P0092 **2T ECM, MIL:** Yes **Year:** 2011, 2012 **Model:** A3, A4, A5, TT, TTS, Q5, Q7 **Engine:** 2.0L L4, 3.0L V6, 3.2L V6 **Transmission:** All	**Fuel Pressure Regulator 1 Control Circuit High:** With the ignition on and the Fuel Pressure Solenoid command on. The ECM detects excessive current on the Fuel Pressure Solenoid Control circuit for 0.28 seconds.
DTC: P0097 **2T ECM, MIL:** Yes **Year:** 2011, 2012 **Model:** A3, A4, A5, TT, TTS, Q5, Q7 **Engine:** 2.0L L4, 3.0L V6, 3.2L V6 **Transmission:** All	**Intake Air Temperature Sensor 2 Circuit Low:** * Time after engine start * Engine speed * No fuel cut off
DTC: P0098 **2T ECM, MIL:** Yes **Year:** 2011, 2012 **Model:** A3, A4, A5, TT, TTS, Q5, Q7 **Engine:** 2.0L L4, 3.0L V6, 3.2L V6 **Transmission:** All	**Intake Air Temperature Sensor 2 circuit high:** The ECM detects an Open in IAT sensor circuit. * Time after engine start * Engine speed * No fuel cut off
DTC: P00AF **2T ECM, MIL:** Yes **Year:** 2011, 2012 **Model:** A3, A4, A5, TT, TTS, Q5, Q7 **Engine:** 2.0L L4, 3.0L V6, 3.2L V6 **Transmission:** All	**Turbocharger Boost Control "A" Module Performance:** Boost pressure actuator stuck on or off. Control deviation > 15% or < -15% Time after engine start > 96000 m Sec
DTC: P00D1 **2T ECM, MIL:** Yes **Year:** 2011, 2012 **Model:** A3, A4, A5, TT, TTS, Q5, Q7 **Engine:** 2.0L L4, 3.0L V6, 3.2L V6 **Transmission:** All	**HO2S Bank 1 Sensor 1 Heater Output Warm Up Time Exceeded:** * Sensor temperature < 720 °C * Ambient temperature > -10 °C * Baro > 750 hPa * Battery voltage > 10.7 V * LSU heater control active, 20 min. up and down

DTC	Trouble Code Title, Conditions, Possible Causes
DTC: P00D2 **2T ECM, MIL: Yes** **Year:** 2011, 2012 **Model:** A3, A4, A5, TT, TTS, Q5, Q7 **Engine:** 2.0L L4, 3.0L V6, 3.2L V6 **Transmission:** All	**HO2S Bank 1 Sensor 2 Heater Output Warm Up Time Exceeded:** * Sensor temperature < 720 °C * Ambient temperature > -10 °C * Baro > 750 hPa * Battery voltage > 10.7 V * LSU heater control active, 20 min. up and down
DTC: P00D5 **2T ECM, MIL: Yes** **Year:** 2011, 2012 **Model:** A3, A4, A5, TT, TTS, Q5, Q7 **Engine:** 2.0L L4, 3.0L V6, 3.2L V6 **Transmission:** All	**HO2S Bank 1 Sensor 1 to O2S Bank 1 Sensor 2 Implausible:** * Battery voltage > 10.7 V * LSU heater control active, modeled dew-point exceeded * Offset air fuel ratio > 0.05
DTC: P0100 **1 T ECM, MIL: Yes** **Year:** 2011, 2012 **Model:** A3, A4, A5, TT, TTS, Q5, Q7 **Engine:** 2.0L L4, 3.0L V6, 3.2L V6 **Transmission:** All	**Mass or Volume Air Flow A Circuit:** The ECM detects an open or short in the Mass Air Flow (MAF) sensor circuit. * Engine speed, >80 U/min * Battery voltage, >8 V
DTC: P0101 **1T ECM, MIL: Yes** **Year:** 2011, 2012 **Model:** A3, A4, A5, TT, TTS, Q5, Q7 **Engine:** 2.0L L4, 3.0L V6, 3.2L V6 **Transmission:** All	**Mass or Volume Air Flow A Circuit Range/Performance:** Mass air (Depending on engine speed, and throttle angle).>60.8-890 kg/h upper threshold map, <0-197 kg/h lower threshold map. Time after engine start, 150 Rev.
DTC: P0102 **1 T ECM, MIL: Yes** **Year:** 2011, 2012 **Model:** A3, A4, A5, TT, TTS, Q5, Q7 **Engine:** 2.0L L4, 3.0L V6, 3.2L V6 **Transmission:** All	**MASS AIR FLOW SENSOR CIRCUIT LOW:** No reference Voltage DTC's present. With the engine running and engine speed below 5100 rpm. The Mass Air Flow Sensor Signal is below the valid operating range for 0.5 Seconds.
DTC: P0103 **1 T ECM, MIL: Yes** **Year:** 2011, 2012 **Model:** A3, A4, A5, TT, TTS, Q5, Q7 **Engine:** 2.0L L4, 3.0L V6, 3.2L V6 **Transmission:** All	**MASS AIR FLOW SENSOR CIRCUIT HIGH:** No reference Voltage DTC's present. With the engine running and engine speed below 5100 rpm. The Mass Air Flow Sensor Signal is above the valid operating range for 0.5 seconds.
DTC: P0105 **1 T ECM, MIL: Yes** **Year:** 2011, 2012 **Model:** A3, A4, A5, TT, TTS, Q5, Q7 **Engine:** 2.0L L4, 3.0L V6, 3.2L V6 **Transmission:** All	**Manifold Absolute Pressure/Barometric Pressure Circuit:** Engine started, the temperature must be at least 185-degrees (F) and all electrical equipment (A/C, lights, etc.) must be off. The ECM detected the BARO sensor was out of range during the test. Boost pressure sensor supply voltage 5.10 - 4.89 V, 480 m Sec.
DTC: P0106 **2T ECM** **Year:** 2011, 2012 **Model:** A3, A4, A5, TT, Q5 **Engine:** 2.0L L4 **Transmission:** All	**Manifold Absolute Pressure/Barometric Pressure Circuit Range/Performance:** * Engine speed, 0 RPM * Atm. pressure sensor, Not defective * Boost pres. sensor, Not defective

DTC	Trouble Code Title, Conditions, Possible Causes
DTC: P0106 **1 T ECM, MIL: Yes** **Year:** 2011, 2012 **Model:** A3, A4, A5, TT, TTS, Q5, Q7 **Engine:** 2.0L L4, 3.0L V6, 3.2L V6 **Transmission:** All	**Manifold Absolute Pressure/BARO Sensor, range/performance:** * Time engine start, > 25 Revs * EVAP purge system, No fault * IAT, No fault * Ambient pressure sensor, No fault * Camshaft position sensor, No fault * Throttle, No fault * Time after engine start, 10 camshaft Revs
DTC: P0107 **1 T ECM, MIL: Yes** **Year:** 2011, 2012 **Model:** A3, A4, A5, TT, TTS, Q5, Q7 **Engine:** 2.0L L4, 3.0L V6, 3.2L V6 **Transmission:** All	**Manifold Absolute Pressure/Barometric Pressure Sensor Circuit Low Input:** Engine started, the temperature must be at least 185-degrees (F) and all electrical equipment (A/C, lights, etc.) must be off. The ECM detected the BARO sensor was out of range during the CCM test. The BARO sensor signal should be in 4.5v. The BARO sensor is a variable capacitance unit used to detect altitude.
DTC: P0108 **1 T ECM, MIL: Yes** **Year:** 2011, 2012 **Model:** A3, A4, A5, TT, TTS, Q5, Q7 **Engine:** 2.0L L4, 3.0L V6, 3.2L V6 **Transmission:** All	**Manifold Absolute Pressure/Barometric Pressure Circuit High/Low Input:** Engine started, the temperature must be at least 185-degrees (F) and all electrical equipment (A/C, lights, etc.) must be off. The ECM detected the BARO sensor was out of range during the test. The BARO sensor signal should be in 4.5v. The BARO sensor is a variable capacitance unit used to detect altitude.
DTC: P010B **1 T ECM, MIL: Yes** **Year:** 2011, 2012 **Model:** A3, A4, A5, TT, TTS, Q5, Q7 **Engine:** 2.0L L4, 3.0L V6, 3.2L V6 **Transmission:** All	**Mass or Volume Air Flow "B" Circuit Range/Performance:** * DTC P1009 (Map), Detected * Engine speed, 1400-4000 RPM * Throttle position, >15% * Vehicle speed, 19-75 MPH
DTC: P010C **1 T ECM, MIL: Yes** **Year:** 2011, 2012 **Model:** A3, A4, A5, TT, TTS, Q5, Q7 **Engine:** 2.0L L4, 3.0L V6, 3.2L V6 **Transmission:** All	**Mass or Volume Air Flow "B" Circuit Low:** * Engine speed, 1400-4000 RPM * Throttle position, >15% * Vehicle speed, 19-75 MPH
DTC: P010D **1 T ECM, MIL: Yes** **Year:** 2011, 2012 **Model:** A3, A4, A5, TT, TTS, Q5, Q7 **Engine:** 2.0L L4, 3.0L V6, 3.2L V6 **Transmission:** All	**Mass or Volume Air Flow "B" Circuit High:** * Engine speed, 1400-4000 RPM * Throttle position, >15% * Vehicle speed, 19-75 MPH
DTC: P0111 **2 T ECM, MIL: Yes** **Year:** 2011, 2012 **Model:** A3, A4, A5, TT, TTS, Q5, Q7 **Engine:** 2.0L L4, 3.0L V6, 3.2L V6 **Transmission:** All	**Intake Air Temperature Circuit Range/Performance:** The engine off time is greater than 480 minutes. Ambient Temperature if greater than -64° C (-83° F). Once the vehicle is soaked for a calibrated engine off time and then driven over calibrated speed and load conditions for some calibrated time, the PCM compares the ambient, engine coolant and intake air temperature sensor values. If engine coolant and ambient air temperature sensors agree with each other but intake air temperature does not agree with them, the intake air temperature sensor is declared as irrational. Two Trip Fault. Three good trips to turn off the MIL.
DTC: P0111 **2T** **Year:** 2011, 2012 **Model:** A3, A4, A5, TT, Q5 **Engine:** 2.0L L4 **Transmission:** All	**Intake Air Temperature Sensor 1 Circuit Low Input:** Key on or engine running, the temperature must be at least 185-degrees (F) and all electrical equipment (A/C, lights, etc.) must be off; and the ECM detected the IAT sensor signal was less than the self-test minimum. This is a thermistor-type sensor with a variable resistance that changes when exposed to different temperatures. This means: the higher the temperature, the lower the resistance value.

DTC	Trouble Code Title, Conditions, Possible Causes
DTC: P0112 **1 T ECM, MIL: Yes** **Year:** 2011, 2012 **Model:** A3, A4, A5, TT, TTS, Q5, Q7 **Engine:** 2.0L L4, 3.0L V6, 3.2L V6 **Transmission:** All	**INTAKE AIR TEMPERATURE SENSOR CIRCUIT LOW:** With the ignition on and battery voltage greater than 10.4 Volts. When the Inlet Air Temp Sensor Signal circuit voltage is less than the minimum acceptable value. One trip failure. Three good trips to clear the MIL.
DTC: P0112 **2T ECM, MIL: Yes** **Year:** 2011, 2012 **Model:** A3, A4, A5, TT, TTS, Q5, Q7 **Engine:** 2.0L L4 **Transmission:** All	**Intake Air Temperature Sensor 1 Circuit Low Input:** * Time after start, 180 sec. * Engine cranking range, 120 – 320 rpm * Fuel cutoff not active
DTC: P0113 **2 T ECM, MIL: Yes** **Year:** 2011, 2012 **Model:** A3, A4, A5, TT, TTS, Q5, Q7 **Engine:** 2.0L L4, 3.0L V6, 3.2L V6 **Transmission:** All	**Intake Air Temperature Sensor 1 Circuit high:** * Time after engine start 240 Sec * Engine speed, n.a. * Fuel cutoff, not active
DTC: P0113 **2T ECM, MIL: Yes** **Year:** 2012 **Model:** A3, A4, A5, TT, Q5 A3, A4, A5, TT, Q5, **Engine:** 2.0L L4 **Transmission:** All	**Intake Air Temperature Sensor Circuit High Input:** Time after engine start 240 Sec. and no fuel cutoff. * * No fuel cut off
DTC: P0116 **2 T ECM, MIL: Yes** **Year:** 2011, 2012 **Model:** A3, A4, A5, TT, TTS, Q5, Q7 **Engine:** 2.0L L4, 3.0L V6, 3.2L V6 **Transmission:** All	**ENGINE COOLANT TEMPERATURE SENSOR CIRCUIT PERFORMANCE:** Engine off time is greater than 480 minutes and the vehicle has been driven for one minute over 35 mph. Ambient temperature is greater than -64° C (-83° F). Once the vehicle is soaked for a calibrated engine off time and then driven over calibrated speed and load conditions for some calibrated time, the PCM compares the ambient, engine coolant and intake air temperature sensor values. If ambient air and intake air temperature sensors agree with each other but engine coolant temperature does not agree with them, the engine coolant temperature sensor is declared as irrational. Two Trip Fault. Three good trips to turn off the MIL.
DTC: P0117 **1 T ECM, MIL: Yes** **Year:** 2011, 2012 **Model:** A3, A4, A5, TT, TTS, Q5, Q7 **Engine:** 2.0L L4, 3.0L V6, 3.2L V6 **Transmission:** All	**ENGINE COOLANT TEMPERATURE SENSOR CIRCUIT LOW:** With the ignition on. Battery voltage greater than 10.4 Volts. The Powertrain Control Module (PCM) detects that the Engine Coolant Temperature Sensor input voltage is below the minimum acceptable value. One Trip Fault. Three good trips to clear the MIL. The MIL and ETC light will illuminate if equipped.
DTC: P0118 **1 T ECM, MIL: Yes** **Year:** 2011, 2012 **Model:** A3, A4, A5, TT, TTS, Q5, Q7 **Engine:** 2.0L L4, 3.0L V6, 3.2L V6 **Transmission:** All	**ENGINE COOLANT TEMPERATURE SENSOR CIRCUIT HIGH:** With the ignition on. Battery voltage greater than 10.4 Volts. The Powertrain Control Module (PCM) detects that the Engine Coolant Temperature Sensor input voltage is above the maximum acceptable value. One Trip Fault. Three good trips to turn off the MIL. The MIL and ETC light will illuminate if equipped.
DTC: P0120 **1 T ECM, MIL: Yes** **Year:** 2011, 2012 **Model:** A3, A4, A5, TT, TTS, Q5, Q7 **Engine:** 2.0L L4, 3.0L V6, 3.2L V6 **Transmission:** All	**Throttle/Pedal Position Sensor (A) Circuit Malfunction:** Engine started, at idle, the temperature must be 80 degrees Celsius. The throttle position sensor supplies implausible signal to the ECM. The throttle valve activation occurs via an electric motor (throttle drive) in the throttle valve control module. It is activated by the Engine Control Module (ECM) according to specifications of the two sensors, Throttle Position (TP) Sensor and Accelerator Pedal Position Sensor 2.

DTC	Trouble Code Title, Conditions, Possible Causes
DTC: P0121 **2 T ECM, MIL: Yes** **Year:** 2011, 2012 **Model:** A3, A4, A5, TT, TTS, Q5, Q7 **Engine:** 2.0L L4, 3.0L V6, 3.2L V6 **Transmission:** All	**THROTTLE POSITION SENSOR 1 PERFORMANCE:** Ignition on and No MAP Sensor DTCs set. The Powertrain Control Module (PCM) detects that the sensor input voltage does not fall within a valid range based on engine speed and load. Two Trip Fault. (Electronic Throttle Control) ETC light will illuminate.
DTC: P0121 **2T ECM, MIL: Yes** **Year:** 2011, 2012 **Model:** A3, A4, A5, TT, TTS, Q5, Q7 **Engine:** 2.0L L4 **Transmission:** All	**Throttle/Pedal Position Sensor A Circuit Range/Performance:** * Engine speed > 480 RPM
DTC: P0122 **1 T ECM, MIL: Yes** **Year:** 2011, 2012 **Model:** A3, A4, A5, TT, TTS, Q5, Q7 **Engine:** 2.0L L4, 3.0L V6, 3.2L V6 **Transmission:** All	**TPS/APP CIRCUIT LOW:** Continuously with the ignition on and engine running. This DTC will set if the monitored TPS voltage drops below .078 of a volt for the period of 0.48 of a second.
DTC: P0123 **1 T ECM, MIL: Yes** **Year:** 2011, 2012 **Model:** A3, A4, A5, TT, TTS, Q5, Q7 **Engine:** 2.0L L4, 3.0L V6, 3.2L V6 **Transmission:** All	**TPS/APP CIRCUIT HIGH:** Continuously with the ignition on and engine running. This DTC will set if the monitored TPS voltage rises above 4.94 volts for the period of 0.48 of a second.
DTC: P0123 **1T ECM, MIL: Yes** **Year:** 2012 **Model:** A3, A4, A5, TT, Q5 A3, A4, A5, TT, Q5, **Engine:** 2.0L L4 **Transmission:** All	**Throttle/Pedal Position Sensor "A" Circuit High:** With the ignition on and battery voltage greater than 10 Volts. Throttle Position Sensor No.1 voltage is greater than 4.8 Volts for 25 ms. One Trip Fault. ETC light will illuminate.
DTC: P0124 **1 T ECM, MIL: Yes** **Year:** 2011, 2012 **Model:** A3, A4, A5, TT, TTS, Q5, Q7 **Engine:** 2.0L L4, 3.0L V6, 3.2L V6 **Transmission:** All	**TPS/APP INTERMITTENT:** Continuously with the ignition on and engine running. This DTC will set if the monitored TPS throttle angle is between 6° and 120° and the value changes by more than 5° in a period of 7.0 ms or less.
DTC: P0125 **2 T ECM, MIL: Yes** **Year:** 2011, 2012 **Model:** A3, A4, A5, TT, TTS, Q5, Q7 **Engine:** 2.0L L4, 3.0L V6, 3.2L V6 **Transmission:** All	**COOLANT TEMP FOR CLOSED-LOOP FUEL CONTROL:** With battery voltage greater than 10.4 Volts and after engine is started. The engine temperature does not go above -10° C (15° F). Failure time depends on start-up coolant temperature and ambient temperature. (i.e. two minutes for a start temp of -10° C (15° F) or up to 10 minutes for a vehicle with a start-up temp of -28° C (5° F). Two Trip Fault. Three good trips to turn off the MIL.
DTC: P0128 **2 T ECM, MIL: Yes** **Year:** 2011, 2012 **Model:** A3, A4, A5, TT, TTS, Q5, Q7 **Engine:** 2.0L L4, 3.0L V6, 3.2L V6 **Transmission:** All	**Coolant Thermostat / Valve Temperature below control range:** With the engine running, ambient temperature between -8° C (17.6° F) and 50° C (122° F), start up coolant temperature less than 50° C (122° F) and average vehicle speed greater than 16 kph (10 mph) until coolant temperature reaches 85° C (185° F). The PCM detects that the actual engine coolant temperature falls too far below the predicted engine coolant temperature and the predicted coolant temperature reaches the predicted target value before the actual coolant temperature reaches the actual coolant temperature target value. Two trip fault. Three good trips to turn off the MIL.

DTC	Trouble Code Title, Conditions, Possible Causes
DTC: P0129 **1 T ECM, MIL: Yes** **Year:** 2011, 2012 **Model:** A3, A4, A5, TT, TTS, Q5, Q7 **Engine:** 2.0L L4, 3.0L V6, 3.2L V6 **Transmission:** All	**BAROMETRIC PRESSURE OUT-OF-RANGE LOW:** With the ignition key on. No Cam or Crank signal within 75 ms. Engine speed less than 250 RPM. The Powertrain Control Module (PCM) senses the voltage from the MAP sensor to be less than 2.2 Volts but above 0.04 of a Volt for 300 milliseconds. One Trip Fault. Three good trips to turn off the MIL. MIL is illuminated and the ETC lamp will flash.
DTC: P0130 **2 T ECM, MIL: Yes** **Year:** 2011, 2012 **Model:** A3, A4, A5, TT, TTS, Q5, Q7 **Engine:** 2.0L L4, 3.0L V6, 3.2L V6 **Transmission:** All	**HO2S Sensor Circuit (Bank 1, Sensor 1):** * Modeled exhaust temp>300° C * Fuel cut-off not active * Heater control active
DTC: P0131 **2 T ECM, MIL: Yes** **Year:** 2011, 2012 **Model:** A3, A4, A5, TT, TTS, Q5, Q7 **Engine:** 2.0L L4, 3.0L V6, 3.2L V6 **Transmission:** All	**HO2S SENSOR 1/1 CIRCUIT LOW:** Engine running for less than 30 seconds and the O2 Sensor Heater Temperature is less than 251° C (484° F) with battery voltage greater 10.4 Volts. The Powertrain Control Module (PCM) detects that the 1/1 Oxygen Sensor signal voltage is below the minimum acceptable value. The DTC will set as Pending after one trip and Active after two trips. Three good trips to turn off the MIL.
DTC: P0132 **2 T ECM, MIL: Yes** **Year:** 2011, 2012 **Model:** A3, A4, A5, TT, TTS, Q5, Q7 **Engine:** 2.0L L4, 3.0L V6, 3.2L V6 **Transmission:** All	**HO2S Sensor Circuit, Bank 1 - Sensor 1 High Voltage:** With the ignition on and the O2 1/1 Sensor at operating temperature. The ECM detects a short to voltage on the (K902) O2 1/1 Negative Current Control circuit for 2.0 seconds.
DTC: P0133 **2 T ECM, MIL: Yes** **Year:** 2011, 2012 **Model:** A3, A4, A5, TT, TTS, Q5, Q7 **Engine:** 2.0L L4, 3.0L V6, 3.2L V6 **Transmission:** All	**HO2S Circuit Slow Response (Bank 1, Sensor 1):** With the ECT above 70° C (158° F), engine RPM between 1400 and 2300, vehicle speed between 64 and 96 kph (40 and 60 mph), and engine run time greater than three minutes. The Powertrain Control Module (PCM) detects that the oxygen sensor signal does not switch adequately during monitoring. Two Trip Fault. Three good trips to turn off the MIL.
DTC: P0134 **1 T ECM, MIL: Yes** **Year:** 2011, 2012 **Model:** A3, A4, A5, TT, TTS, Q5, Q7 **Engine:** 2.0L L4, 3.0L V6, 3.2L V6 **Transmission:** All	**HO2S (Bank 1 Sensor 1) Circuit No Activity:** Engine running, battery voltage 11.5, all electrical components off, ground between engine and chassis well connected and the exhaust system must be properly sealed between catalytic converter and the cylinder head. The ECM detected the HO2S signal failed to meet the maximum or minimum voltage levels (i.e., it failed the voltage range check).
DTC: P0135 **2 T ECM, MIL: Yes** **Year:** 2011, 2012 **Model:** A3, A4, A5, TT, TTS, Q5, Q7 **Engine:** 2.0L L4, 3.0L V6, 3.2L V6 **Transmission:** All	**HO2S SENSOR 1/1 HEATER PERFORMANCE:** Engine running and heater duty cycle greater than 0%. Battery voltage greater than 11.0 Volts. The Powertrain Control Module (PCM) detects no temperature change in the O2 sensor heater element when the heater circuit is active. The heater temperature is obtained by measuring the heater resistance and calculating the heater temperature. Two trip fault. Three good trips to turn off the MIL.
DTC: P0136 **2 T ECM, MIL: Yes** **Year:** 2011, 2012 **Model:** A3, A4, A5, TT, TTS, Q5, Q7 **Engine:** 2.0L L4, 3.0L V6, 3.2L V6 **Transmission:** All	**HO2S Circuit (Bank 1, Sensor 2) Malfunction:** * Battery voltage, >11 V * Engine speed, >25 RPM * O2S rear dew-point, Exceeded * O2S rear, fully heated up * Modeled exhaust gas temp. 200-800° C for 60 Sec. * Heater rear, Commanded on for >0.04 Sec.

DTC	Trouble Code Title, Conditions, Possible Causes
DTC: P0137 **1 T ECM, MIL: Yes** **Year:** 2011, 2012 **Model:** A3, A4, A5, TT, TTS, Q5, Q7 **Engine:** 2.0L L4, 3.0L V6, 3.2L V6 **Transmission:** All	**HO2S SENSOR (Bank 1, Sensor 2) CIRCUIT LOW:** Engine running for less than 30 seconds and the O2 Sensor Heater Temperature is less than 251° C (484° F) with battery voltage greater 10.99 Volts The Powertrain Control Module (PCM) detects that the 1/2 Oxygen Sensor signal voltage is below minimum acceptable value. The DTC will set as Pending after one trip, and Active after two trips. Three good trips to turn off the MIL.
DTC: P0138 **1 T ECM, MIL: Yes** **Year:** 2011, 2012 **Model:** A3, A4, A5, TT, TTS, Q5, Q7 **Engine:** 2.0L L4, 3.0L V6, 3.2L V6 **Transmission:** All	**HO2S Circuit High Voltage (Bank 1, Sensor 2):** Continuously with the engine running, no O2 sensor heater DTCs present, 1/2 Oxygen Sensor heater temperature within a specific range and battery voltage greater than 10.4 Volts. The Powertrain Control Module (PCM) detects that the 1/2 Oxygen Sensor voltage is greater than the maximum acceptable value for a specific amount of time, based on O2 sensor heater temperature. The DTC will set as Pending after one trip and Active after two trips. Three good trips to turn off the MIL.
DTC: P0139 **1 T ECM, MIL: Yes** **Year:** 2011, 2012 **Model:** A3, A4, A5, TT, TTS, Q5, Q7 **Engine:** 2.0L L4, 3.0L V6, 3.2L V6 **Transmission:** All	**HO2S Circuit Slow Response (Bank 1, Sensor 2):** With the engine running, vehicle speed above 96 kph (60 mph), throttle open for a minimum of 120 seconds, ECT greater than 70° C (158° F), catalytic converter temperature greater than 600° C (1112° F) and downstream oxygen sensor in a rich state during a decel fuel shutoff event, the downstream oxygen sensor should switch from rich to lean within a specific time. The Powertrain Control Module (PCM) monitors the downstream O2 Sensor. If the PCM does not detect a rich to lean switch within a specific time during a decal, fuel shutoff event, the monitor will fail. One trip fault. Three good trips to turn off the MIL.
DTC: P013B **1T ECM, MIL: Yes** **Year:** 2011, 2012 **Model:** A3, Q7 **Engine:** 2.0L L4 **Transmission:** All	**O2 Sensor Bank 1 Sensor 2 Slow Response Lean to Rich:** * Regeneration demand for NOx trap = on * Adaptation of oxygen sensor pre and post NOx trap = realized * Dew point release oxygen sensor signals pre and post NOx trap = on * Temperature of upstream turbine < 850 °C * Fuel temp < 90 °C * APP > 1 and < 100%
DTC: P0140 **2 T ECM, MIL: Yes** **Year:** 2011, 2012 **Model:** A3, A4, A5, TT, TTS, Q5, Q7 **Engine:** 2.0L L4, 3.0L V6, 3.2L V6 **Transmission:** All	**HO2S Circuit No Activity Detected (Bank 1, Sensor 2):**With the engine running, vehicle speed between 32 and 88 kph (20 and 55 mph), throttle open for a minimum of 120 seconds, ECT greater than 70° C (158° F), Catalytic Converter Temperature greater than 600° C (1112° F) and EVAP Purge active. The Powertrain Control Module (PCM) detects that the oxygen sensor signal switches from lean to rich less than 16 times within 20 seconds during monitoring. Two Trip fault. Three good trips to turn off the MIL.
DTC: P0141 **2 T ECM, MIL: Yes** **Year:** 2011, 2012 **Model:** A3, A4, A5, TT, TTS, Q5, Q7 **Engine:** 2.0L L4, 3.0L V6, 3.2L V6 **Transmission:** All	**-O2 SENSOR 1/2 HEATER PERFORMANCE:** Continuously during O2 sensor heater operation with battery voltage between 10.4 and 15.75 Volts and no O2 sensor circuit DTCs present. The Powertrain Control Module (PCM) detects no temperature change in the O2 sensor heater element when the heater circuit is active. The heater temperature is obtained by measuring the heater resistance and calculating the heater temperature. Two trip fault. Three good trips to turn off the MIL.
DTC: P0142 **2T ECM, MIL: Yes** **Year:** 2011, 2012 **Model:** A3, A4, A5, TT, Q5CC, A3, Q7 **Engine:** 2.0L L4 **Transmission:** All	**O2 circuit Bank 1 Sensor 3 heater check:** * Modeled exhaust gas temp. 200-800° C * Dew-point exceeded and lower exhaust gas temp limit exceeded for 60 Sec.
DTC: P0143 **2T ECM, MIL: Yes** **Year:** 2011, 2012 **Model:** A3, A4, A5, TT, Q5CC, A3, Q7 **Engine:** 2.0L L4 **Transmission:** All	**O2 Sensor Circuit Low Voltage Bank 1 Sensor 3:** * Sensor voltage <= 0.40 V or 0.50 to 1.08 V * Modeled exhaust gas temp. 700 °C for > 10 Sec. * Heater power >= 50% for > 10 Sec.

DTC	Trouble Code Title, Conditions, Possible Causes
DTC: P0144 **2T** **Year:** 2012 **Model:** A3, A4, A5, TT, Q5 **Engine:** 2.0L L4 **Transmission:** All	**O2 Sensor Circuit High Voltage Bank 1 Sensor 3:** * Sensor voltage <= 0.40 V or 0.50 to 1.08 V * Modeled exhaust gas temp. 700 °C for > 10 Sec. * Heater power >= 50% for > 10 Sec.
DTC: P0145 **2 T ECM, MIL: Yes** **Year:** 2011, 2012 **Model:** A3, A4, A5, TT, TTS, Q5, Q7 **Engine:** 3.0L V6, 3.2L V6 **Transmission:** All	**O2 Circuit Slow Response (Bank 1, Sensor 2):** * Rich voltage, >=547.9 mV * Lean voltage <=152.3 mV * Max O2 mass flow (disable), >=6000 mg * HO2S rear, ready * Fuel cut-off, active * Front O2 sensor, lambda signal, >2.00 * Modeled exhaust gas temp. >400° C
DTC: P0145 **2T ECM, MIL: Yes** **Year:** 2011, 2012 **Model:** A3, A4, A5 **Engine:** 2.0L L4 **Transmission:** All	**O2 Sensor Circuit Slow Response Bank 1 Sensor 3:** * O2S rear, Fully heated up * Rich voltage enable > = 548 mV * Modeled exhaust temp. > 480 °C * No other O2 sensor faults set.
DTC: P0146 **2T ECM, MIL: Yes** **Year:** 2011, 2012 **Model:** A3, A4, A5 **Engine:** 2.0L L4 **Transmission:** All	**O2 Sensor Circuit No Activity Detected Bank 1 Sensor 3:** * Sensor voltage <= 0.40 V or 0.50 to 1.08 V * Modeled exhaust gas temp. 700 °C for > 10 Sec. * Heater power >= 50% for > 10 Sec.
DTC: P0147 **2T ECM, MIL: Yes** **Year:** 2011, 2012 **Model:** A3, A4, A5 **Engine:** 2.0L L4 **Transmission:** All	**O2 Sensor Heater Circuit Bank 1 Sensor 3:** * Modeled exhaust gas temp 250 - 650 °C * Engine shutoff time > 60 Sec. * Fuel cutoff not active * Heater commanded on
DTC: P0147 **2T ECM, MIL: Yes** **Year:** 2011, 2012 **Model:** A3, A4, A5, TT, Q5 **Engine:** 2.0L L4 **Transmission:** All	**O2 circuit Bank 1 Sensor 3 heater check SULEV:** * Modeled exhaust gas temp, 250-650.1° C * Engine shutoff time, >300 Sec. * Fuel cut-off not active * Heater commanded on
DTC: P014D **2T ECM, MIL: Yes** **Year:** 2011, 2012 **Model:** A3, A4, A5, TT, TTS, Q5, Q7 **Engine:** 2.0L L4, 3.0L V6, 3.2L V6 **Transmission:** All	**O2 Sensor Bank 1 Sensor 1 Slow Response Lean to Rich:** * Regeneration demand for NOx trap = on * Adaptation of oxygen sensor pre and post NOx trap = realized * Dew point release oxygen sensor signals pre and post NOx trap = on * Temperature of upstream turbine < 850 °C * Fuel temp < 90 °C * APP > 1 and < 100% * Gear = 2 * Engine run time > 240 Sec. * Exhaust gas flow > 100 and < 200 kg/h
DTC: P0150 **1T ECM, MIL: Yes** **Year:** 2011, 2012 **Model:** A3, A4, A5, TT, TTS, Q5, Q7 **Engine:** 2.0L L4, 3.0L V6, 3.2L V6 **Transmission:** All	**HO2S Sensor Circuit, Bank 2 Sensor 1 Low Voltage:** * Modeled exhaust gas temp, >170° C * Fuel cut off, Not active

DTC	Trouble Code Title, Conditions, Possible Causes
DTC: P0151 **1T ECM, MIL: Yes** **Year:** 2011, 2012 **Model:** A3, A4, A5, TT, TTS, Q5, Q7 **Engine:** 2.0L L4, 3.0L V6, 3.2L V6 **Transmission:** All	**HO2S Sensor Circuit Low Voltage Bank 2 Sensor 1:** Engine running for less than 30 seconds and the O2 Sensor Heater Temperature is less than 251° C (484° F) with the battery voltage greater 10.99 Volts. The Powertrain Control Module (PCM) detects that the 2/1 Oxygen Sensor signal voltage is below the minimum acceptable value. The DTC will set as Pending after one trip and Active after two trips. Three good trips to turn off the MIL.
DTC: P0152 **2T ECM, MIL: Yes** **Year:** 2011, 2012 **Model:** **Engine:** 3.0L V6, 3.2L V6 **Transmission:** All	**O2 Sensor Circuit High Voltage Bank 2 Sensor 1:** Engine speed, >25 RPM
DTC: P0152 **2T ECM, MIL: Yes** **Year:** 2011, 2012 **Model:** TTS **Engine:** 3.0L V6, 3.2L V6 **Transmission:** All	**HO2S Sensor Circuit High Voltage Bank 2 Sensor 1:** Continuously with the engine running, no O2 sensor heater DTCs present, 2/1 Oxygen Sensor heater temperature within a specific range and battery voltage greater than 10.4 Volts. The Powertrain Control Module (PCM) detects that the 2/1 Oxygen Sensor voltage is greater than the maximum acceptable value for a specific amount of time, based on O2 sensor heater temperature. The DTC will set as Pending after one trip and Active after two trips. Three good trips to turn off the MIL.
DTC: P0153 **2T ECM, MIL: Yes** **Year:** 2011, 2012 **Model:** TTS **Engine:** 3.0L V6, 3.2L V6 **Transmission:** All	**O2 Sensor Circuit Slow Response Bank 2 Sensor 1:** With the ECT above 70 °C (158 °F), engine RPM between 1400 and 2300, vehicle speed between 64 and 96 kph (40 and 60 mph) and engine run time greater than three minutes. The Powertrain Control Module (PCM) detects that the oxygen sensor signal does not switch adequately during monitoring. Two Trip Fault. Three good trips to turn off the MIL.
DTC: P0155 **2T ECM, MIL: Yes** **Year:** 2011, 2012 **Model:** A3, A4, A5, TT, Q5 **Engine:** 2.0L L4 **Transmission:** All	**O2 Sensor Heater Circuit Bank 2 Sensor 1:** * Modeled exhaust gas temp., > 250 °C * Heater control, Active * ECT at start, >48 °C * Engine shut off time, >120 Sec. * During ECM keep alive time after ign off, <950 Sec.
DTC: P0155 **2T ECM, MIL: Yes** **Year:** 2011, 2012 **Model:** TTS **Engine:** 3.2L V6 **Transmission:** All	**O2 Sensor Heater Circuit Bank 2 Sensor 1:** Engine running and heater duty cycle greater than 0%. Battery voltage greater than 11.0 Volts. No sensor output is received when the Powertrain Control Module (PCM) powers up the sensor heater. Two trip fault. Three good trips to turn off the MIL.
DTC: P0156 **1T ECM, MIL: Yes** **Year:** 2011, 2012 **Model:** A3, A4, A5, TT, TTS, Q5, Q7 **Engine:** 2.0L L4, 3.0L V6, 3.2L V6 **Transmission:** All	**O2 Sensor Circuit Bank 2 Sensor 2:** * O2S rear, Ready * Modeled exhaust gas temp. 250-800 °C for >90 Sec. * Engine speed, >25 RPM
DTC: P0156 **2T ECM, MIL: Yes** **Year:** 2011, 2012 **Model:** A3, A4, A5, TT, Q5 **Engine:** L5 **Transmission:** All	**O2 Sensor Circuit Bank 2 Sensor 2:** * Modeled exhaust gas temp. 250-700° C * Dew point exceeded and lower exhaust gas temp exceeded, 30 Sec.
DTC: P0157 **1T ECM, MIL: Yes** **Year:** 2011, 2012 **Model:** A3, A4, A5, TT, TTS, Q5, Q7 **Engine:** 2.0L L4, 3.0L V6, 3.2L V6 **Transmission:** All	**HO2S Sensor Circuit Low Voltage Bank 2 Sensor 2:** The Powertrain Control Module (PCM) detects that the 2/2 Oxygen Sensor signal voltage is below the minimum acceptable value. The DTC will set as Pending after one trip and Active after two trips. Three good trips to turn off the MIL.

DTC	Trouble Code Title, Conditions, Possible Causes
DTC: P0158 **1T ECM, MIL: Yes** **Year:** 2011, 2012 **Model:** A3, A4, A5, TT, TTS, Q5, Q7 **Engine:** 2.0L L4, 3.0L V6, 3.2L V6 **Transmission:** All	**HO2S Sensor Circuit High Voltage Bank 2 Sensor 2:** Continuously with the engine running, no O2 sensor heater DTCs present, 2/2 Oxygen Sensor heater temperature within a specific range and battery voltage greater than 10.4 Volts. The Powertrain Control Module (PCM) detects that the 2/2 Oxygen Sensor voltage is greater than the maximum acceptable value for a specific amount of time, based on O2 sensor heater temperature. The DTC will set as Pending after one trip and Active after two trips. Three good trips to turn off the MIL.
DTC: P0159 **1T ECM, MIL: Yes** **Year:** 2011, 2012 **Model:** A3, A4, A5, TT, TTS, Q5, Q7 **Engine:** 2.0L L4, 3.0L V6, 3.2L V6 **Transmission:** All	**HO2S Sensor Circuit Slow Response Bank 2 Sensor 2:** With the engine running, vehicle speed above 96 kph (60 mph), throttle open for a minimum of 120 seconds, ECT greater than 70° C (158° F), catalytic converter temperature greater than 600° C (1112° F), and downstream oxygen sensor in a rich state. During a decel fuel shutoff event, the downstream oxygen sensor should switch from rich to lean within a specific time. The Powertrain Control Module (PCM) monitors the downstream O2 sensor. If the PCM does not detect a rich to lean switch within a specific time during a decel fuel shutoff event, the monitor will fail. One trip fault. Three good trips to turn off the MIL.
DTC: P0160 **2T ECM, MIL: Yes** **Year:** 2011, 2012 **Model:** A3, A4, A5, TT, TTS, Q5, Q7 **Engine:** 2.0L L4, 3.0L V6, 3.2L V6 **Transmission:** All	**HO2S Sensor Circuit No Activity Detected Bank 2 Sensor 2:** Vehicle is started and driven between 32 and 88.5 km/h (20 and 55 mph) with the Throttle open for a minimum of 120 seconds. Coolant greater than 70° C (158° F). Catalytic Converter Temp greater than 600° C (1112° F) and EVAP Purge are active. The oxygen sensor signal voltage switches less than 16 times from lean to rich within 20 seconds during monitoring. Two Trip Fault. Three good trips to turn off the MIL
DTC: P0161 **2T ECM, MIL: Yes** **Year:** 2011, 2012 **Model:** A3, A4, A5, TT, TTS, Q5, Q7 **Engine:** 2.0L L4, 3.0L V6, 3.2L V6 **Transmission:** All	**HO2S Sensor Heater Circuit Bank 2 Sensor 2 Malfunction:** Engine running and heater duty cycle greater than 0%. Battery voltage greater than 11.0 Volts. No sensor output is received when the Powertrain Control Module (PCM) powers up the sensor heater. Two trip fault. Three good trips to turn off the MIL.
DTC: P0169 **2T ECM, MIL: Yes** **Year:** 2011, 2012 **Model:** A3, A4, A5, TT, TTS, Q5, Q7 **Engine:** 2.0L L4 **Transmission:** All	**Incorrect Fuel Composition:** **NOTE: Use of a high concentration of ethanol may cause DTCs P0169. Other contamination such as water and salts may cause this DTC to set.** * Engine speed > 1200 RPM
DTC: P0170 **2T ECM, MIL: Yes** **Year:** 2011, 2012 **Model:** A3, A4, A5, TT, Q5 **Engine:** 2.0L L4 **Transmission:** All	**Fuel System Malfunction (Cylinder Bank 1):** The engine is running in a closed loop at a stable engine speed, and the ECM detected the lean or rich fuel trim correction valve was more than or less than a calibrated limit.
DTC: P0171 **1T ECM, MIL: Yes** **Year:** 2011, 2012 **Model:** A3, A4, A5, TT, TTS, Q5, Q7 **Engine:** 2.0L L4, 3.0L V6, 3.2L V6 **Transmission:** All	**-FUEL SYSTEM 1/1 LEAN:** With the engine running in closed loop mode, the ambient/battery temperature above -6.7°C (20°F) and altitude below 2590.8 m (8500 ft). If the Powertrain Control Module (PCM) multiplies short term compensation by long term adaptive and a certain percentage is exceeded for two trips, a freeze frame is stored, the MIL illuminates and a trouble code is stored. Two Trip Fault. Three good trips to turn off the MIL.
DTC: P0172 **2T ECM, MIL: Yes** **Year:** 2011, 2012 **Model:** A3, A4, A5, TT, TTS, Q5, Q7 **Engine:** 2.0L L4, 3.0L V6, 3.2L V6 **Transmission:** All	**System Too Rich (Bank 1):** With the engine running in closed loop mode, the ambient/battery temperature above -6.7°C (20°F) and altitude below 2590.8 m (8500 ft). If the Powertrain Control Module (PCM) multiplies short term compensation by long term adaptive and a purge fuel multiplier and the result is below a certain value for 30 seconds over two trips, a freeze frame is stored, the MIL illuminates and a trouble code is stored. Two Trip Fault. Three good trips to turn off the MIL.

DTC	Trouble Code Title, Conditions, Possible Causes
DTC: P0174 **2T ECM, MIL: Yes** **Year:** 2011, 2012 **Model:** A3, A4, A5, TT, TTS, Q5, Q7 **Engine:** 2.0L L4, 3.0L V6, 3.2L V6 **Transmission:** All	**System Too Lean Bank 2:** With the engine running in closed loop mode, the ambient/battery temperature above -6.7°C (20°F) and altitude below 2590.8 m (8500 ft). If the Powertrain Control Module (PCM) multiplies short term compensation by long term adaptive and a certain percentage is exceeded for two trips, a freeze frame is stored, the MIL illuminates and a trouble code is stored. Two Trip Fault. Three good trips to turn off the MIL.
DTC: P0175 **2T ECM, MIL: Yes** **Year:** 2011, 2012 **Model:** A3, A4, A5, TT, TTS, Q5, Q7 **Engine:** 2.0L L4, 3.0L V6, 3.2L V6 **Transmission:** All	**System Too Rich Bank 2:** With the engine running in closed loop mode, the ambient/battery temperature above -6.7°C (20°F) and altitude below 2590.8 m (8500 ft). If the Powertrain Control Module (PCM) multiplies short term compensation by long term adaptive and a purge fuel multiplier and the result is below a certain value for 30 seconds over two trips, a freeze frame is stored, the MIL illuminates and a trouble code is stored. Two Trip Fault. Three good trips to turn off the MIL.
DTC: P0181 **2T ECM, MIL: Yes** **Year:** 2011, 2012 **Model:** A3, A4, A5, TT, TTS, Q5, Q7 **Engine:** 2.0L L4, 3.0L V6, 3.2L V6 **Transmission:** All	**Fuel Temperature Sensor A Circuit Range/Performance:** * Engine off time > 9 hr * Decrease of IAT and T2 < 5 °K at > 25 mph for 20 Sec. * Decrease of AAT after engine start < 5 °K for 60 Sec.
DTC: P0182 **2T ECM, MIL: Yes** **Year:** 2011, 2012 **Model:** A3 **Engine:** 2.0L L4 **Transmission:** All	**Engine Fuel Temperature Sensor 'A' Circuit Low Input:** Key on or engine running; and the ECM detected the Engine Fuel Temperature (EFT) Sensor 'A' signal was under the required voltage in the self-test.
DTC: P0183 **2T ECM, MIL: Yes** **Year:** 2011, 2012 **Model:** A3, Q7 **Engine:** 2.0L L4, 3.0L V6, 3.2L V6 **Transmission:** All	**Fuel Temperature Sensor A Circuit High:** With the ignition on and engine running, the ECM detected the fuel temperature sensor was out of range.
DTC: P0190 **2T ECM, MIL: Yes** **Year:** 2011, 2012 **Model:** A3, A4, A5, TT, TTS, Q5, Q7 **Engine:** 2.0L L4, 3.0L V6, 3.2L V6 **Transmission:** All	**Fuel Rail Pressure Sensor A Circuit:** With the ignition on and engine running, the ECM detected the fuel temperature sensor was out of range. Malfunction Criteria and Threshold Value: 4.8V
DTC: P0191 **2T ECM, MIL: Yes** **Year:** 2011, 2012 **Model:** A3, A4, A5, TT, TTS, Q5, Q7 **Engine:** 2.0L L4, 3.0L V6, 3.2L V6 **Transmission:** All	**Fuel Rail Pressure Sensor Circuit Range/Performance:** With the ignition on and engine running, the ECM detected the fuel temperature sensor was out of range. * Time after engine start > 10 Sec. * Engine speed > 90 RPM
DTC: P0192 **2T ECM, MIL: Yes** **Year:** 2011, 2012 **Model:** A3, A4, A5, TT, TTS, Q5, Q7 **Engine:** 2.0L L4, 3.0L V6, 3.2L V6 **Transmission:** All	**Fuel Rail Pressure Sensor A Circuit Low Input:** With the ignition on and engine running, the ECM detected the fuel temperature sensor was out of range. Malfunction Criteria and Threshold Value: Signal voltage < 2.0 V.

DTC	Trouble Code Title, Conditions, Possible Causes
DTC: P0193 **2T ECM, MIL: Yes** **Year:** 2011, 2012 **Model:** A3, A4, A5, TT, TTS, Q5, Q7 **Engine:** 2.0L L4, 3.0L V6, 3.2L V6 **Transmission:** All	**Fuel Rail Pressure Sensor Circuit High Input:** With the ignition on and engine running, the ECM detected the fuel temperature sensor was out of range. * Key On engine Off * Fuel temperature > 5 and < 60 °C * Fuel rail pressure set point > 500 hpa * Voltage deviation in pressure control valve < 2%
DTC: P0196 **2T ECM, MIL: Yes** **Year:** 2011, 2012 **Model:** A3, A4, A5, TT, TTS, Q5, Q7 **Engine:** 2.0L L4, 3.0L V6, 3.2L V6 **Transmission:** All	**ENGINE OIL TEMPERATURE SENSOR CIRCUIT PERFORMANCE:** With engine off time greater than 480 minutes and ambient temperature greater than -7°C (19.4°F). After a calibrated amount of cool down time, the Powertrain Control Module (PCM) compares the AAT, ECT and IAT Sensor values. If the general temperature rationality passes, the PCM compares the Oil Temperature Sensor value to a threshold based on the other temp sensor values. If the difference is greater than a calibrated value, the diagnostic fails.
DTC: P0197 **2T ECM, MIL: Yes** **Year:** 2011, 2012 **Model:** A3, A4, A5, TT, TTS, Q5, Q7 **Engine:** 2.0L L4, 3.0L V6, 3.2L V6 **Transmission:** All	**ENGINE OIL TEMPERATURE SENSOR CIRCUIT LOW:** With the ignition on. Battery voltage greater than 10.4 Volts. The Engine Oil Temperature sensor circuit voltage at the Powertrain Control Module (PCM) is less than the calibrated amount. One Trip Fault. Three good trips to clear the MIL.
DTC: P0198 **1T ECM, MIL: Yes** **Year:** 2011, 2012 **Model:** A3, A4, A5, TT, TTS, Q5, Q7 **Engine:** 2.0L L4, 3.0L V6, 3.2L V6 **Transmission:** All	**ENGINE OIL TEMPERATURE SENSOR CIRCUIT HIGH:** With the ignition on. Battery voltage greater than 10.4 Volts. The Engine Oil Temperature Sensor circuit voltage at the Powertrain Control Module (PCM) is greater than the calibrated amount. One Trip Fault. Three good trips to turn off the MIL.
DTC: P0201 **2T ECM, MIL: Yes** **Year:** 2011, 2012 **Model:** A3, A4, A5, TT, TTS, Q5, Q7 **Engine:** 2.0L L4, 3.0L V6, 3.2L V6 **Transmission:** All	**Injector Circuit / Open - Cylinder 1:** With battery voltage greater than 10 Volts. Auto Shutdown Relay energized. Engine speed less than 3000 RPM. The Powertrain Control Module (PCM) monitors the continuity of the injector circuits, as well as the voltage spike created by the collapse of the magnetic field in the injector coil. Any condition that reduces the maximum current flow or the magnitude of the voltage spike can cause this DTC to set.
DTC: P0202 **2T ECM, MIL: Yes** **Year:** 2011, 2012 **Model:** A3, A4, A5, TT, TTS, Q5, Q7 **Engine:** 2.0L L4, 3.0L V6, 3.2L V6 **Transmission:** All	**Injector Circuit / Open - Cylinder 2:** With battery voltage greater than 10 Volts. Auto Shutdown Relay energized. Engine speed less than 3000 RPM. The Powertrain Control Module (PCM) monitors the continuity of the injector circuits, as well as the voltage spike created by the collapse of the magnetic field in the injector coil. Any condition that reduces the maximum current flow or the magnitude of the voltage spike can cause this DTC to set.
DTC: P0203 **2T ECM, MIL: Yes** **Year:** 2011, 2012 **Model:** A3, A4, A5, TT, TTS, Q5, Q7 **Engine:** 2.0L L4, 3.0L V6, 3.2L V6 **Transmission:** All	**Injector Circuit / Open - Cylinder 3:** With battery voltage greater than 10 Volts. Auto Shutdown Relay energized. Engine speed less than 3000 RPM. The Powertrain Control Module (PCM) monitors the continuity of the injector circuits, as well as the voltage spike created by the collapse of the magnetic field in the injector coil. Any condition that reduces the maximum current flow or the magnitude of the voltage spike can cause this DTC to set.
DTC: P0204 **2T ECM, MIL: Yes** **Year:** 2011, 2012 **Model:** A3, A4, A5, TT, TTS, Q5, Q7 **Engine:** 2.0L L4, 3.0L V6, 3.2L V6 **Transmission:** All	**Injector Circuit / Open - Cylinder 4:** With battery voltage greater than 10 Volts. Auto Shutdown Relay energized. Engine speed less than 3000 RPM. The Powertrain Control Module (PCM) monitors the continuity of the injector circuits as well as the voltage spike created by the collapse of the magnetic field in the injector coil. Any condition that reduces the maximum current flow or the magnitude of the voltage spike can cause this DTC to set.

DTC	Trouble Code Title, Conditions, Possible Causes
DTC: P0205 **2T ECM, MIL: Yes** **Year:** 2011, 2012 **Model:** A3, A4, A5, TT, TTS, Q5, Q7 **Engine:** L5, 3.0L V6, 3.2L V6 **Transmission:** All	**Injector Circuit / Open - Cylinder 5:** With battery voltage greater than 10 Volts. Auto Shutdown Relay energized. Engine speed less than 3000 RPM. The Powertrain Control Module (PCM) monitors the continuity of the injector circuits as well as the voltage spike created by the collapse of the magnetic field in the injector coil. Any condition that reduces the maximum current flow or the magnitude of the voltage spike can cause this DTC to set.
DTC: P0206 **2T ECM, MIL: Yes** **Year:** 2011, 2012 **Model:** TTS, Q7 **Engine:** 3.0L V6, 3.2L V6 **Transmission:** All	**Injector Circuit / Open - Cylinder 6:** With battery voltage greater than 10 Volts. Auto Shutdown Relay energized. Engine speed less than 3000 RPM. The Powertrain Control Module (PCM) monitors the continuity of the injector circuits as well as the voltage spike created by the collapse of the magnetic field in the injector coil. Any condition that reduces the maximum current flow or the magnitude of the voltage spike can cause this DTC to set.
DTC: P020A **2T ECM, MIL: Yes** **Year:** 2011, 2012 **Model:** A3, A4, A5, TT, TTS, Q5, Q7 **Engine:** 2.0L L4 **Transmission:** All	**Cylinder 1 Injection Timing:** * Engine running * ECM in closed loop * BARO pressure > 750 hPa * ECT > 50 °C * Time since engine start > 30 Sec. * Regeneration = off
DTC: P020B **2T ECM, MIL: Yes** **Year:** 2011, 2012 **Model:** A3, A4, A5, TT, TTS, Q5, Q7 **Engine:** 2.0L L4 **Transmission:** All	**Cylinder 2 Injection Timing:** * Engine running * ECM in closed loop * ECT > 50 °C * Time since engine start > 30 Sec.
DTC: P020C **2T ECM, MIL: Yes** **Year:** 2011, 2012 **Model:** A3, A4, A5, TT, TTS, Q5, Q7 **Engine:** 2.0L L4 **Transmission:** All	**Cylinder 3 Injection Timing:** * Engine running * ECM in closed loop * ECT > 50 °C * Time since engine start > 30 Sec.
DTC: P0216 **2T ECM, MIL: Yes** **Year:** 2011, 2012 **Model:** A3, A4, A5, TT, Q5, **Engine:** 2.0L L4 **Transmission:** All	**Injector/Injection Timing Control Malfunction:** Engine started, and the ECM has detected a malfunction in the injector timing control.
DTC: P0218 **2T ECM, MIL: Yes** **Year:** 2011, 2012 **Model:** TTS **Engine:** 3.2L V6 **Transmission:** All	**-HIGH TEMPERATURE OPERATION ACTIVATED:** Whenever the engine is running. Immediately when an Overheat shift schedule is activated when the Transmission Oil Temperature reaches 115° C (240° F).
DTC: P0221 **2T ECM, MIL: Yes** **Year:** 2011, 2012 **Model:** A3, A4, A5, TT, TTS, Q5, Q7 **Engine:** 2.0L L4, 3.0L V6, 3.2L V6 **Transmission:** All	**Throttle/Pedal Position Sensor/Switch B Circuit Range/Performance:** Ignition on and No MAP Sensor DTCs set. The TP Sensor signals do not correlate to the MAP Sensor signal. Two Trip Fault. ETC light will illuminate. P2135 should set with this code. Engine speed, >1200 RPM.
DTC: P0222 **1T ECM, MIL: Yes** **Year:** 2011, 2012 **Model:** A3, A4, A5, TT, TTS, Q5, Q7 **Engine:** 2.0L L4, 3.0L V6, 3.2L V6 **Transmission:** All	**Throttle/Pedal Position Sensor/Switch B Circuit Low Input:** With the ignition on and the battery voltage greater than 10 Volts. Throttle Position Sensor voltage at the Powertrain Control Module (PCM) is less than 0.16 of a Volt for 0.7 of a second. One Trip Fault. Three good trips to turn off the MIL. ETC light will illuminate.

DTC	Trouble Code Title, Conditions, Possible Causes
DTC: P0223 **1T ECM, MIL: Yes** **Year:** 2011, 2012 **Model:** A3, A4, A5, TT, TTS, Q5, Q7 **Engine:** 2.0L L4, 3.0L V6, 3.2L V6 **Transmission:** All	**Throttle/Pedal Position Sensor B Circuit High:** With the ignition on. Throttle Position Sensor No.2 Signal circuit voltage is greater than 4.9 Volts for 25ms. One Trip Fault. ETC light will illuminate.
DTC: P0225 **1T ECM, MIL: Yes** **Year:** 2011, 2012 **Model:** A3 **Engine:** 2.0L L4 **Transmission:** All	**Throttle/Pedal Position Sensor/Switch "C" Circuit Voltage Supply:** Supply voltage for accelerator pedal position sensor -4.89 - 5.10 V.
DTC: P0226 **1T ECM, MIL: Yes** **Year:** 2011, 2012 **Model:** A3 **Engine:** 2.0L L4 **Transmission:** All	**Throttle/Pedal Position Sensor/Switch "C" Circuit Range/Performance:** * Idle switch, idle * Idle switch, not idle
DTC: P0228 **1T ECM, MIL: Yes** **Year:** 2011, 2012 **Model:** A3, A4, A5, TT, Q5, **Engine:** 2.0L L4 **Transmission:** All	**Throttle/Pedal Position Sensor/Switch "C" Circuit High:** Accelerator pedal position sensor voltage > 4.76 V.
DTC: P022A **2T ECM, MIL: Yes** **Year:** 2011, 2012 **Model:** Q7 **Engine:** 3.0L TDI V6 **Transmission:** All	**Charge Air Cooler Bypass Control "A" Circuit Open:** * Power stage commanded Off * Ignition Off
DTC: P022B **2T ECM** **Year:** 2011, 2012 **Model:** Q7 **Engine:** 3.0L TDI V6 **Transmission:** All	**Charge Air Cooler Bypass Control "A" Circuit Low:** * Power stage commanded Off * Ignition Off
DTC: P022C **2T ECM, MIL: Yes** **Year:** 2011, 2012 **Model:** Q7 **Engine:** 3.0L TDI V6 **Transmission:** All	**Charge Air Cooler Bypass Control "A" Circuit High:** * Power stage commanded On
DTC: P0230 **2T ECM, MIL: Yes** **Year:** 2011, 2012 **Model:** A3, A4, A5, TT, Q5, Q7 **Engine:** 2.0L TDI L4 **Transmission:** All	**Fuel Pump Primary Circuit Malfunction:** Engine started, battery voltage at least 11.5v, all electrical components off, ground connections between engine and chassis well connected, coolant temperature at least 80-degrees celcius. The ECM detected high current in fuel pump or fuel shutoff valve (FSV) circuit, or it detected voltage with the valve off, or it did not detect voltage on the circuit. The circuit is used to energize the fuel pump relay at key on or while running. Fuel pressure value should be 3000 to 5000 kPa at idle.
DTC: P0234 **2T ECM, MIL: Yes** **Year:** 2011, 2012 **Model:** Q7 **Engine:** 3.0L TDI V6, **Transmission:** All	**Turbo Charger Over-boost Condition limit exceeded:** * Boost pressure control mode = closed loop * RPM > 1650* Fuel quantity > 15 mg/stroke

DTC	Trouble Code Title, Conditions, Possible Causes
DTC: P0234 **2T ECM, MIL: Yes** **Year:** 2011, 2012 **Model:** A3, A4, A5, TT, TTS, Q5, Q7 **Engine:** 2.0L TDI L4 **Transmission:** All	**Turbocharger/Supercharger Over-boost Condition Rationality check high:** Malfunction Criteria and Threshold Value: * Negative system deviation high>300-1275 hPa * Engine speed > 2400 . . . 3000 RPM.
DTC: P0235 **1T ECM, MIL: Yes** **Year:** 2011, 2012 **Model:** A3, A4, A5, TT, Q5 **Engine:** 2.0L TDI L4 **Transmission:** All	**Turbocharger Boost Sensor (A) Circ Control Limit Not Reached:** Engine started, battery voltage at least 11.5v, all electrical components off, ground connections between engine and chassis well connected, coolant temperature at least 80-degrees celsius. The ECM detected an operating condition that could harm the engine or automatic transmission.
DTC: P0236 **2T ECM, MIL: Yes** **Year:** 2011, 2012 **Model:** Q7 **Engine:** 3.0L TDI V6 **Transmission:** All	**Turbocharger Boost Sensor (A) Circuit Performance:** * Engine started, battery voltage at least 11.5v * Engine speed < 600 rpm
DTC: P0236 **1T ECM, MIL: Yes** **Year:** 2011, 2012 **Model:** A3, A4, A5, TT, TTS, Q5, Q7 **Engine:** 2.0L TDI L4 **Transmission:** All	**Turbocharger Boost Sensor (A) Circ Control Range/Performance:** Engine started, battery voltage at least 11.5v, all electrical components off, ground connections between engine and chassis well connected, coolant temperature at least 80-degrees Celsius. The ECM detected an operating condition that could harm the engine or automatic transmission.
DTC: P0237 **2T ECM, MIL: Yes** **Year:** 2011, 2012 **Model:** A3, A4, A5, TT, TTS, Q5, Q7 **Engine:** 2.0L L4 **Transmission:** All	**Turbocharger/Supercharger Boost Sensor A Circuit Low:** Malfunction Criteria and Threshold Value: * Signal voltage, < 0.2 V
DTC: P0238 **2T ECM, MIL: Yes** **Year:** 2011, 2012 **Model:** A3, A4, A5, TT, TTS, Q5, Q7 **Engine:** 2.0L TDI L4 **Transmission:** All	**Turbocharger/Supercharger Boost Sensor A Circuit High:** Malfunction Criteria and Threshold Value: * Short to battery + 4.88 V.
DTC: P0243 **2T ECM, MIL: Yes** **Year:** 2011, 2012 **Model:** A3, A4, A5, TT, TTS, Q5, Q7 **Engine:** 2.0L TDI L4 **Transmission:** All	**Turbocharger/Supercharger Wastegate Solenoid A:** * Charge pressure control valve, commanded off * Engine speed, > 80 RPM * Battery voltage, 9.04-16 V
DTC: P0245 **2T ECM, MIL: Yes** **Year:** 2011, 2012 **Model:** A3, A4, A5, TT, TTS, Q5, Q7 **Engine:** 2.0L TDI L4 **Transmission:** All	**Turbocharger/Supercharger Wastegate Solenoid A Low:** * Charge pressure control valve, commanded off * Engine speed, > 80 RPM

DTC	Trouble Code Title, Conditions, Possible Causes
DTC: P0246 **2T ECM, MIL: Yes** **Year:** 2011, 2012 **Model:** A3, A4, A5, TT, TTS, Q5, Q7 **Engine:** 2.0L TDI L4 **Transmission:** All	**Turbocharger/Supercharger Wastegate Solenoid A High:** * Charge (boost) pressure control valve, commanded on * Engine speed, > 80 RPM
DTC: P025A **2T ECM, MIL: Yes** **Year:** 2011, 2012 **Model:** A3, A4, A5, TT, TTS, Q5, Q7, **Engine:** 2.0L TDI L4, 3.0L TDI V6 **Transmission:** All	**Fuel Pump Module Control Circuit/Open:** * Engine speed, > 80 RPM
DTC: P025C **2T ECM, MIL: Yes** **Year:** 2011, 2012 **Model:** A3, A4, A5, TT, TTS, Q5, Q7, **Engine:** 2.0L TDI L4, 3.0L TDI V6 **Transmission:** All	**Fuel Pump Module Control Circuit Low:** Engine speed, >40 RPM
DTC: P025D **2T ECM, MIL: Yes** **Year:** 2011, 2012 **Model:** A3, A4, A5, TT, TTS, Q5, Q7, **Engine:** 2.0L TDI L4, 3.0L TDI V6 **Transmission:** All	**Fuel Pump Module Control Circuit High:** Engine speed, >40 RPM
DTC: P0261 **2T ECM, MIL: Yes** **Year:** 2011, 2012 **Model:** A3, A4, A5, TT, TTS, Q5, Q7 **Engine:** 2.0L L4, 3.0L V6, 3.2L V6 **Transmission:** All	**Cylinder 1 Injector Circuit Low:** With the engine cranking or running. The ECM detects a fault on a Fuel Injector Control circuit. * Engine speed,> 80 RPM * Injection valves, Switched off * High side signal current, > 4.20 A
DTC: P0262 **2T ECM, MIL: Yes** **Year:** 2011, 2012 **Model:** A3, A4, A5, TT, TTS, Q5, Q7 **Engine:** 2.0L L4, 3.0L V6, 3.2L V6 **Transmission:** All	**Cylinder 1 Injector Circuit High:** With the engine cranking or running. The ECM detects a fault on a Fuel Injector Control circuit. * Engine speed, > 80 RPM * Injection valve, switched on.
DTC: P0263 **2T ECM, MIL: Yes** **Year:** 2011, 2012 **Model:** A3, A4, A5, TT, TTS, Q5, Q7 **Engine:** 2.0L L4, 3.0L V6, 3.2L V6 **Transmission:** All	**Cylinder 1 Contribution/Balance:** With the engine cranking or running. The ECM detects a fault on a Fuel Injector Control circuit. * Engine speed > 1400 and < 2200 RPM * Fuel temperature > 0 and < 80 °C * Intake air temp > 0 °C * Coolant temp > 70 °C * Boost pressure > 80 hpa
DTC: P0264 **2T ECM, MIL: Yes** **Year:** 2011, 2012 **Model:** A3, A4, A5, TT, TTS, Q5, Q7 **Engine:** 2.0L L4, 3.0L V6, 3.2L V6 **Transmission:** All	**Cylinder 2 Injector Circuit Low:** With the engine cranking or running. The ECM detects a fault on a Fuel Injector Control circuit. * Injection valve, commanded OFF * Engine speed, > 80 RPM

DTC	Trouble Code Title, Conditions, Possible Causes
DTC: P0265 **2T ECM, MIL: Yes** **Year:** 2011, 2012 **Model:** A3, A4, A5, TT, TTS, Q5, Q7 **Engine:** 2.0L L4, 3.0L V6, 3.2L V6 **Transmission:** All	**Cylinder 2 Injector Circuit High:** With the engine cranking or running. The ECM detects a fault on a Fuel Injector Control circuit. * Injection valve, Commanded on * Engine speed, > 80 RPM * Battery voltage, 9.04-16 V
DTC: P0266 **2T ECM, MIL: Yes** **Year:** 2011, 2012 **Model:** A3, A4, A5, TT, TTS, Q5, Q7 **Engine:** 2.0L L4, 3.0L V6, 3.2L V6 **Transmission:** All	**Cylinder 2 Contribution/Balance:** With the engine cranking or running. The ECM detects a fault on a Fuel Injector Control circuit. * Engine speed > 1600 and < 2500 RPM * Fuel temperature > 0 and < 80 °C * Intake air temp > 0 °C * Boost pressure > 90000 Pa * Gear > 2 * Fuel cutoff active
DTC: P0267 **2T ECM, MIL: Yes** **Year:** 2011, 2012 **Model:** A3, A4, A5, TT, TTS, Q5, Q7 **Engine:** 2.0L L4, 3.0L V6, 3.2L V6 **Transmission:** All	**Cylinder 3 Injector Circuit Low:** With the engine cranking or running. The ECM detects a fault on a Fuel Injector Control circuit. * Injection valve, commanded OFF * Engine speed, > 80 RPM
DTC: P0268 **2T ECM, MIL: Yes** **Year:** 2011, 2012 **Model:** A3, A4, A5, TT, TTS, Q5, Q7 **Engine:** 2.0L L4, 3.0L V6, 3.2L V6 **Transmission:** All	**Cylinder 3 Injector Circuit High:** With the engine cranking or running. The ECM detects a fault on a Fuel Injector Control circuit. * Injection valve, Commanded on * Engine speed, > 80 RPM
DTC: P0269 **2T ECM, MIL: Yes** **Year:** 2011, 2012 **Model:** A3, A4, A5, TT, TTS, Q5, Q7 **Engine:** 2.0L L4, 3.0L V6, 3.2L V6 **Transmission:** All	**Cylinder 3 Contribution/Balance:** With the ignition on. The Engine Control Module (ECM) is unable to stabilize fuel quantity in cylinder 3. * Engine speed > 1400 and < 2200 RPM * Fuel temperature > 0 and < 80 °C * Intake air temp > 0 °C * Coolant temp > 70 °C
DTC: P026A **2T ECM, MIL: Yes** **Year:** 2011, 2012 **Model:** A3, A4, A5, TT, TTS, Q5, Q7 **Engine:** 2.0L L4, 3.0L V6, 3.2L V6 **Transmission:** All	**Charge Air Cooler Efficiency Below Threshold:** * ECT > 60 °C * vehicle speed > 40 km/h * Ratio (boost pressure/baro) > 1.20 * Charge air flow rate > 50 and < 400 kg/h
DTC: P0270 **2T ECM, MIL: Yes** **Year:** 2011, 2012 **Model:** A3, A4, A5, TT, TTS, Q5, Q7 **Engine:** 2.0L L4, 3.0L V6, 3.2L V6 **Transmission:** All	**Cylinder 4 Injector Circuit Low:** With the engine cranking or running. The ECM detects a fault on a Fuel Injector Control circuit. * Injection valve, Commanded on * High pressure system current, >4.2 A * Engine speed, > 80 RPM
DTC: P0271 **2T ECM, MIL: Yes** **Year:** 2011, 2012 **Model:** A3, A4, A5, TT, TTS, Q5, Q7 **Engine:** 2.0L L4, 3.0L V6, 3.2L V6 **Transmission:** All	**Cylinder 4 Injector Circuit High:** With the engine cranking or running. The ECM detects a fault on a Fuel Injector Control circuit. * Injection valve, switched on * Engine speed > 80 RPM

DTC	Trouble Code Title, Conditions, Possible Causes
DTC: P0272 **2T ECM, MIL: Yes** **Year:** 2011, 2012 **Model:** A3, A4, A5, TT, TTS, Q5, Q7 **Engine:** 2.0L L4, 3.0L V6, 3.2L V6 **Transmission:** All	**Cylinder 4 Contribution/Balance:** With the engine cranking or running. The ECM detects a fault on a Fuel Injector Control circuit. * Engine speed > 1600 and < 2500 RPM * Fuel temperature > 0 and < 80 °C * Intake air temp > 0 °C * Boost pressure > 90000 Pa * Gear > 2 * Fuel cutoff active
DTC: P0273 **2T ECM, MIL: Yes** **Year:** 2011, 2012 **Model:** A3, A4, A5, TT, TTS, Q5, Q7 **Engine:** L5, 3.0L V6, 3.2L V6 **Transmission:** All	**Cylinder 5 Injector Circuit Low:** With the engine cranking or running. The ECM detects a fault on a Fuel Injector Control circuit. * Injection valve, switched off * Engine speed > 80 RPM
DTC: P0274 **2T ECM, MIL: Yes** **Year:** 2011, 2012 **Model:** A3, A4, A5, TT, TTS, Q5, Q7 **Engine:** L5, 3.0L V6, 3.2L V6 **Transmission:** All	**Cylinder 5 Injector Circuit High:** With the engine cranking or running. The ECM detects a fault on a Fuel Injector Control circuit. * Engine speed,> 80 RPM * Injection valves, Switched on
DTC: P0275 **2T ECM, MIL: Yes** **Year:** 2011, 2012 **Model:** A3, A4, A5, TT, TTS, Q5, Q7 **Engine:** L5, 3.0L V6, 3.2L V6 **Transmission:** All	**Cylinder 5 Contribution/Balance:** With the engine cranking or running. The ECM detects a fault on a Fuel Injector Control circuit. * Engine speed > 1600 and < 2500 RPM * Fuel temperature > 0 and < 80 °C * Intake air temp > 0 °C * Boost pressure > 90000 Pa * Gear > 2 * Fuel cutoff active
DTC: P0276 **2T ECM, MIL: Yes** **Year:** 2011, 2012 **Model:** TTS, Q7 **Engine:** 3.0L V6, 3.2L V6 **Transmission:** All	**Cylinder 6 Injector Circuit Low:** With the engine cranking or running. The ECM detects a fault on a Fuel Injector Control circuit. * Injection valve, Commanded on * High pressure system current, >4.2 A * Engine speed, > 80 RPM
DTC: P0277 **2T ECM, MIL: Yes** **Year:** 2011, 2012 **Model:** TTS, Q7 **Engine:** 3.0L V6, 3.2L V6 **Transmission:** All	**Cylinder 6- Injector Circuit High:** With the engine cranking or running. The ECM detects a fault on a Fuel Injector Control circuit. * Injection valve, Commanded on * Engine speed, > 80 RPM
DTC: P0278 **2T ECM, MIL: Yes** **Year:** 2011, 2012 **Model:** TTS, Q7 **Engine:** 3.0L V6, 3.2L V6 **Transmission:** All	**Cylinder 6 Contribution/Balance:** With the engine cranking or running. The ECM detects a fault on a Fuel Injector Control circuit. * Engine speed > 1600 and < 2500 RPM * Fuel temperature > 0 and < 80 °C * Intake air temp > 0 °C * Boost pressure > 90000 Pa * Gear > 2 * Fuel cutoff active
DTC: P0290 **2T ECM, MIL: Yes** **Year:** 2011, 2012 **Model:** A3, A4, A5, TT, Q5, Q7 **Engine:** 2.0L L4 **Transmission:** All	**"B" Camshaft Position Actuator Control Circuit Low Bank 1:** * Camshaft valve, commanded off * Engine speed, >80 RPM

DTC	Trouble Code Title, Conditions, Possible Causes
DTC: P0298 **2T ECM, MIL: Yes** **Year:** 2011, 2012 **Model:** TTS **Engine:** 3.2L V6 **Transmission:** All	**ENGINE OIL TEMPERATURE TOO HIGH:** The engine oil temperature has dropped below a calibrated value. Engine start up. The Engine Oil temperature rises faster than a calibrated modeled temperature. When the actual oil temperature exceeds the high boundary of the calibrated modeled temperature for three minutes the fault is set. Two trip fault. Three good trips to turn off the MIL.
DTC: P0299 **2T ECM, MIL: Yes** **Year:** 2011, 2012 **Model:** A3, A4, A5, TT, TTS, Q5, Q7 **Engine:** 2.0L L4 **Transmission:** All	**Turbocharger/Supercharger Under-boost:** * Difference of set value boost pressure vs. basic boost pressure value > 250 hPa * Engine speed, 2400-3000 RPM * Basic boost pressure * Ambient pressure, +450 hPa > 700 hPa
DTC: P0300 **2T ECM, MIL: Yes** **Year:** 2011, 2012 **Model:** A3, A4, A5, TT, TTS, Q5, Q7 **Engine:** 2.0L L4, 3.0L V6, 3.2L V6 **Transmission:** All	**Random Misfire Detected:** Engine running under positive torque conditions, and the ECM detected a misfire or uneven engine running in two or more cylinders. **NOTE: If the misfire is severe, the MIL will flash on/off on the first trip!** * Engine speed range, 440-6800 RPM * IAT, >-48° C * ECT at start, > 10.50° C * Fuel cutoff, Not active * rough road not detected * internal CAN no fault
DTC: P0301 **2T ECM, MIL: Yes** **Year:** 2011, 2012 **Model:** A3, A4, A5, TT, TTS, Q5, Q7 **Engine:** 2.0L L4, 3.0L V6, 3.2L V6 **Transmission:** All	**Cylinder 1 Misfire Detected:** Engine running under positive torque conditions, and the ECM detected a misfire or uneven engine function. **NOTE: If the misfire is severe, the MIL will flash on/off on the 1st trip!** * IAT, > -48° C * Time after engine start, Idle - 150 RPM * Engine torque, > 5.47-23.4% * Camshaft revolutions 1 * Engine speed range, 480-6800 RPM * Fuel cutoff, Not active * ECT at start, > -10.50 °C
DTC: P0302 **2T ECM, MIL: Yes** **Year:** 2011, 2012 **Model:** A3, A4, A5, TT, TTS, Q5, Q7 **Engine:** 2.0L L4, 3.0L V6, 3.2L V6 **Transmission:** All	**Cylinder 2 Misfire Detected:** Engine running under positive torque conditions, and the ECM detected a misfire or uneven engine function. **NOTE: If the misfire is severe, the MIL will flash on/off on the 1st trip!** * IAT, > -48° C * Time after engine start, Idle - 150 RPM * Engine torque, > 5.47-23.4% * Camshaft revolutions 1 * Engine speed range, 480-6800 RPM * Fuel cutoff, Not active * ECT at start, > -10.50 °C
DTC: P0303 **2T ECM, MIL: Yes** **Year:** 2011, 2012 **Model:** A3, A4, A5, TT, TTS, Q5, Q7 **Engine:** 2.0L L4, 3.0L V6, 3.2L V6 **Transmission:** All	**Cylinder 3 Misfire Detected:** Engine running under positive torque conditions, and the ECM detected a misfire or uneven engine function. **NOTE: If the misfire is severe, the MIL will flash on/off on the 1st trip!** * IAT, > -48° C * Time after engine start, Idle - 150 RPM * Engine torque, > 5.47-23.4% * Camshaft revolutions 1 * Engine speed range, 480-6800 RPM * Fuel cutoff, Not active * ECT at start, > -10.50 °C

DTC	Trouble Code Title, Conditions, Possible Causes
DTC: P0304 **2T ECM, MIL: Yes** **Year:** 2011, 2012 **Model:** A3, A4, A5, TT, TTS, Q5, Q7 **Engine:** 2.0L L4, 3.0L V6, 3.2L V6 **Transmission:** All	**Cylinder 4 Misfire Detected:** Engine running under positive torque conditions, and the ECM detected a misfire or uneven engine function. **NOTE: If the misfire is severe, the MIL will flash on/off on the 1st trip!** * IAT, > -48° C * Time after engine start, Idle - 150 RPM * Engine torque, > 5.47-23.4% * Camshaft revolutions 1 * Engine speed range, 480-6800 RPM * Fuel cutoff, Not active * ECT at start, > -10.50 °C
DTC: P0305 **2T ECM, MIL: Yes** **Year:** 2011, 2012 **Model:** A3, A4, A5, TT, TTS, Q5, Q7 **Engine:** L5, 3.0L V6, 3.2L V6 **Transmission:** All	**Cylinder 5 Misfire Detected:** Engine running under positive torque conditions, and the ECM detected a misfire or uneven engine function. **NOTE: If the misfire is severe, the MIL will flash on/off on the 1st trip!** * IAT, > -48° C * Time after engine start, Idle - 150 RPM * Engine torque, > 5.47-23.4% * Camshaft revolutions 1 * Engine speed range, 480-6800 RPM * Fuel cutoff, Not active * ECT at start, > -10.50 °C
DTC: P0306 **2T ECM, MIL: Yes** **Year:** 2011, 2012 **Model:** A3, A4, A5, TT, TTS, Q5, Q7 **Engine:** 3.0L V6, 3.2L V6 **Transmission:** All	**Cylinder Number 6 Misfire Detected:** Engine running under positive torque conditions, and the ECM detected a misfire or uneven engine function. **NOTE: If the misfire is severe, the MIL will flash on/off on the 1st trip!** * IAT, > -48° C * Time after engine start, Idle - 150 RPM * Engine torque, > 5.47-23.4% * Camshaft revolutions 1 * Engine speed range, 480-6800 RPM * Fuel cutoff, Not active * ECT at start, > -10.50 °C
DTC: P0315 **2T ECM, MIL: Yes** **Year:** 2011, 2012 **Model:** A3, A4, A5, TT, TTS, Q5, Q7 **Engine:** 2.0L L4, 3.0L V6, 3.2L V6 **Transmission:** All	**NO CRANK SENSOR LEARNED:** Under closed throttle decel and A/C off. ECT above 75° C (167° F). Engine start time is greater than 50 seconds. One of the CKP sensor target windows has more than 2% variance from the reference. One Trip Fault. Three good trips to turn off the MIL.
DTC: P0318 **2T ECM, MIL: Yes** **Year:** 2011, 2012 **Model:** A3, A4, A5, TT, TTS, Q5, Q7 **Engine:** 2.0L L4, 3.0L V6, 3.2L V6 **Transmission:** All	**Rough Road Sensor:** Engine running, and the ECM detected an implausible signal from the rough road sensor.
DTC: P0321 **2T ECM, MIL: Yes** **Year:** 2011, 2012 **Model:** A3, A4, A5, TT, TTS, Q5, Q7 **Engine:** 2.0L L4, 3.2L V6 **Transmission:** All	**Ignition/Distributor Engine Speed Input Circuit Range/Performance:** * Engine speed, >0 RPM * Crankshaft revolutions, 2 revs
DTC: P0322 **2T ECM, MIL: Yes** **Year:** 2011, 2012 **Model:** A3, A4, A5, TT, TTS, Q5, Q7 **Engine:** 2.0L L4, 3.2L V6 **Transmission:** All	**Ignition/Distributor Engine Speed Input Circuit No Signal:** * No engine speed signal but phase signals during 4.5 cam shaft revs. * Engine speed signal partly interrupted, Phase sensor, No DTC.

DTC	Trouble Code Title, Conditions, Possible Causes
DTC: P0324 **2T ECM, MIL: Yes** **Year:** 2011, 2012 **Model:** A3, A4, A5, TT, TTS, Q5, Q7 **Engine:** 2.0L L4, 3.0L V6, 3.2L V6 **Transmission:** All	**Knock control System Error Malfunction:** * ECT >39° C * Knock control, Active * Engine load, >30% * Engine speed, 1200-5040 RPM
DTC: P0325 **2T ECM, MIL: Yes** **Year:** 2011, 2012 **Model:** A3, A4, A5, TT, TTS, Q5, Q7 **Engine:** 2.0L L4, 3.0L V6, 3.2L V6 **Transmission:** All	**Knock Sensor 1 Circuit Malfunction:** The Powertrain Control Module (PCM) detects that the Knock Sensor input voltage is: Above 4.0 Volts, less than or equal to 1.0 Volt with engine RPM at or above 2200 or equal to 0.0 Volts with engine RPM below 2200. Two Trip Fault. Three good trips to turn off the MIL.
DTC: P0327 **2T ECM, MIL: Yes** **Year:** 2011, 2012 **Model:** A3, A4, A5, TT, TTS, Q5, Q7 **Engine:** 2.0L L4, 3.0L V6, 3.2L V6 **Transmission:** All	**Knock Sensor 1 Circuit Low Input (Bank 1):** * Engine speed, > 2400 RPM * ECT, > 40.5 °C * Engine load, > 30% * Signal range check, No DTC
DTC: P0328 **2T ECM, MIL: Yes** **Year:** 2011, 2012 **Model:** A3, A4, A5, TT, TTS, Q5, Q7 **Engine:** 2.0L L4, 3.0L V6, 3.2L V6 **Transmission:** All	**Knock Sensor 1 Circuit High Input (Bank 1):** * Engine speed, > 1000 RPM * ECT > 40.5° C * Engine load > 35 - 60% * Engine speed > 2000 RPM
DTC: P0330 **2T ECM, MIL: Yes** **Year:** 2011, 2012 **Model:** A3, A4, A5, TT, TTS, Q5, Q7 **Engine:** 2.0L L4, 3.0L V6, 3.2L V6 **Transmission:** All	**KNOCK SENSOR 2 CIRCUIT:** This monitor runs above 2000 RPM, under open throttle conditions. The Knock diagnostic does not run at idle or during decelerations. The high voltage test runs all the times the engine is running. The Powertrain Control Module (PCM) detects that the Knock Sensor input voltage is: Above 4.0 Volts, less than or equal to 1.0 Volt with engine RPM at or above 2200 or equal to 0.0 Volts with engine RPM below 2200. Two Trip Fault. Three good trips to turn off the MIL.
DTC: P0332 **2T ECM, MIL: Yes** **Year:** 2011, 2012 **Model:** A3, A4, A5, TT, TTS, Q5, Q7 **Engine:** L5, 3.0L V6, 3.2L V6 **Transmission:** All	**Knock Sensor 2 Circuit Low Input (Bank 2):** * Signal or 5 V reference circuit > 1000 RPM * Signal range check > 2000 RPM * ECT > 40.5 °C * Engine load 30 to 33.8 %
DTC: P0333 **2T ECM, MIL: Yes** **Year:** 2011, 2012 **Model:** A3, A4, A5, TT, TTS, Q5, Q7 **Engine:** L5, 3.0L V6, 3.2L V6 **Transmission:** All	**Knock Sensor 2 Circuit High Input (Bank 2):** * Signal or 5 V reference circuit > 1000 RPM * Signal range check > 2000 RPM * ECT > 40.5 °C * Engine load 30 to 33.8 %
DTC: P0335 **1T ECM, MIL: Yes** **Year:** 2011, 2012 **Model:** A3, A4, A5, TT, TTS, Q5, Q7 **Engine:** 2.0L L4, 3.0L V6, 3.2L V6 **Transmission:** All	**CRANKSHAFT POSITION SENSOR CIRCUIT:** With the engine cranking, No CKP signal is present during engine cranking and at least eight camshaft position sensor signals have occurred. One Trip Fault. Three good trips to turn off the MIL.

DTC	Trouble Code Title, Conditions, Possible Causes
DTC: P0339 **1T ECM, MIL: Yes** **Year:** 2011, 2012 **Model:** A3, A4, A5, TT, TTS, Q5, Q7 **Engine:** 2.0L L4, 3.0L V6, 3.2L V6 **Transmission:** All	**CRANKSHAFT POSITION SENSOR INTERMITTENT:** While cranking the engine and with the engine running. When the CKP Sensor failure counter reaches 20. One Trip Fault. Three good trips to turn off the MIL.
DTC: P0340 **1T ECM, MIL: Yes** **Year:** 2011, 2012 **Model:** A3, A4, A5, TT, TTS, Q5, Q7 **Engine:** 2.0L L4, 3.0L V6, 3.2L V6 **Transmission:** All	**Camshaft Position Sensor A Circuit (Bank 1 or single sensor):** During engine cranking and with the engine running. Battery voltage greater than 10 Volts. At least five seconds or 2.5 engine revolutions have elapsed with crankshaft position sensor signals present but no camshaft position sensor signal. One Trip Fault. Three good trips to turn off the MIL.
DTC: P0341 **1T ECM, MIL: Yes** **Year:** 2011, 2012 **Model:** A3, A4, A5, TT, TTS, Q5, Q7 **Engine:** 2.0L L4, 3.0L V6, 3.2L V6 **Transmission:** All	**Camshaft Position Sensor A Circuit Range / Performance (Bank 1 or single sensor):** Signals compared to engine speed sensor signals. No alternating signal at reference gap.
DTC: P0342 **1T ECM, MIL: Yes** **Year:** 2011, 2012 **Model:** A3, A4, A5, TT, TTS, Q5, Q7 **Engine:** 2.0L L4, 3.0L V6, 3.2L V6 **Transmission:** All	**Camshaft Position Sensor A Circuit Low Input (Bank 1 or single sensor):** Irregular number of phase changes Incorrect for 12 crank revs. Engine speed signal and phase signal synchronized.
DTC: P0343 **1T ECM, MIL: Yes** **Year:** 2011, 2012 **Model:** A3, A4, A5, TT, TTS, Q5, Q7 **Engine:** 2.0L L4, 3.0L V6, 3.2L V6 **Transmission:** All	**Camshaft Position Sensor A Circuit High Input (Bank 1 or single sensor):** Irregular number of phase changes Incorrect for 12 crank revs. Engine speed signal and phase signal synchronized.
DTC: P0344 **1T ECM, MIL: Yes** **Year:** 2011, 2012 **Model:** A3, A4, A5, TT, TTS, Q5, Q7 **Engine:** 2.0L L4, 3.0L V6, 3.2L V6 **Transmission:** All	**CAMSHAFT POSITION SENSOR INTERMITTENT:** While cranking the engine and engine running. When the failure counter reaches 20. One Trip Fault. Three good trips to turn off the MIL.
DTC: P0345 **1T ECM, MIL: Yes** **Year:** 2011, 2012 **Model:** A3, A4, A5, TT, TTS, Q5, Q7 **Engine:** 2.0L L4, 3.0L V6, 3.2L V6 **Transmission:** All	**CAMSHAFT 1/3 POSITION SENSOR CIRCUIT:** During engine cranking and with the engine running. Battery voltage greater than 10 Volts. At least five seconds or 2.5 engine revolutions have elapsed with crankshaft position sensor signals present but no camshaft position sensor signal. One Trip Fault. Three good trips to turn off the MIL.
DTC: P0346 **1T ECM, MIL: Yes** **Year:** 2011, 2012 **Model:** A3, A4, A5, TT, TTS, Q5, Q7 **Engine:** L5, 3.0L V6, 3.2L V6 **Transmission:** All	**Camshaft Position Sensor "A" Circuit Range/Performance Bank 2:** During engine cranking and with the engine running. Battery voltage greater than 10 Volts. At least five seconds or 2.5 engine revolutions have elapsed with crankshaft position sensor signals present but no camshaft position sensor signal. One Trip Fault. Three good trips to turn off the MIL.

DTC	Trouble Code Title, Conditions, Possible Causes
DTC: P0347 **1T ECM, MIL: Yes** **Year:** 2011, 2012 **Model:** A3, A4, A5, TT, TTS, Q5, Q7 **Engine:** L5, 3.0L V6, 3.2L V6 **Transmission:** All I	**Camshaft Position Sensor "A" Circuit Low Bank 2:** During engine cranking and with the engine running. Battery voltage greater than 10 Volts. At least five seconds or 2.5 engine revolutions have elapsed with crankshaft position sensor signals present but no camshaft position sensor signal. One Trip Fault. Three good trips to turn off the MIL.
DTC: P0348 **1T ECM, MIL: Yes** **Year:** 2011, 2012 **Model:** A3, A4, A5, TT, TTS, Q5, Q7 **Engine:** L5, 3.0L V6, 3.2L V6 **Transmission:** All I	**Camshaft Position Sensor "A" Circuit High Bank 2:** During engine cranking and with the engine running. Battery voltage greater than 10 Volts. At least five seconds or 2.5 engine revolutions have elapsed with crankshaft position sensor signals present but no camshaft position sensor signal. One Trip Fault. Three good trips to turn off the MIL.
DTC: P0349 **1T ECM, MIL: Yes** **Year:** 2011, 2012 **Model:** A3, A4, A5, TT, TTS, Q5, Q7 **Engine:** 2.0L L4, 3.0L V6, 3.2L V6 **Transmission:** All	**-CAMSHAFT 1/3 POSITION SENSOR INTERMITTENT:** While cranking the engine and engine running. When the failure counter reaches 20. One Trip Fault. Three good trips to turn off the MIL.
DTC: P0351 **1T ECM, MIL: Yes** **Year:** 2011, 2012 **Model:** A3, A4, A5, TT, TTS, Q5, Q7 **Engine:** 2.0L L4, 3.0L V6, 3.2L V6 **Transmission:** All	**Ignition Coil A Primary/Secondary Circuit:** * Battery voltage, 9-16 V * Engine speed, 1400-7000 RPM * SW ignition counter diagnose, Not active
DTC: P0352 **1T ECM, MIL: Yes** **Year:** 2011, 2012 **Model:** A3, A4, A5, TT, TTS, Q5, Q7 **Engine:** 2.0L L4, 3.0L V6, 3.2L V6 **Transmission:** All	**Ignition Coil B Primary/Secondary Circuit:** * Battery voltage, 9-16 V * Engine speed, 1400-7000 RPM * SW ignition counter diagnose, Not active
DTC: P0353 **1T ECM, MIL: Yes** **Year:** 2011, 2012 **Model:** A3, A4, A5, TT, TTS, Q5, Q7 **Engine:** 2.0L L4, 3.0L V6, 3.2L V6 **Transmission:** All	**Ignition Coil C Primary/Secondary Circuit:** * Battery voltage, 9-16 V * Engine speed, 1400-7000 RPM * SW ignition counter diagnose, Not active
DTC: P0354 **1T ECM, MIL: Yes** **Year:** 2011, 2012 **Model:** A3, A4, A5, TT, TTS, Q5, Q7 **Engine:** 2.0L L4, 3.0L V6, 3.2L V6 **Transmission:** All	**Ignition Coil D Primary/Secondary Circuit:** * Battery voltage, 9-16 V * Engine speed, 1400-7000 RPM * SW ignition counter diagnose, Not active
DTC: P0355 **1T ECM, MIL: Yes** **Year:** 2011, 2012 **Model:** A3, A4, A5, TT, TTS, Q5, Q7 **Engine:** 2.0L L4, 3.0L V6, 3.2L V6 **Transmission:** All	**Ignition Coil "E" Primary/Secondary Circuit:** * Battery voltage, 9-16 V * Engine speed, 1400-7000 RPM * SW ignition counter diagnose, Not active

DTC	Trouble Code Title, Conditions, Possible Causes
DTC: P0356 **1T ECM, MIL: Yes** **Year:** 2011, 2012 **Model:** A3, A4, A5, TT, TTS, Q5, Q7 **Engine:** L5, 3.0L V6, 3.2L V6 **Transmission:** All	**Coil "F" Primary/Secondary Circuit:** * Battery voltage, 9-16 V * Engine speed, 1400-7000 RPM * SW ignition counter diagnose, Not active
DTC: P0365 **1T ECM, MIL: Yes** **Year:** 2011, 2012 **Model:** A3, A4, A5, TT, TTS, Q5, Q7 **Engine:** 2.0L L4, 3.0L V6, 3.2L V6 **Transmission:** All	**-CAMSHAFT 1/2 POSITION SENSOR CIRCUIT:** During engine cranking and with the engine running. Battery voltage greater than 10 volts. At least five seconds or 2.5 engine revolutions have elapsed with crankshaft position sensor signals present but no camshaft position sensor signal. One Trip Fault. Three good trips to turn off the MIL.
DTC: P0366 **2T ECM, MIL: Yes** **Year:** 2011, 2012 **Model:** A3, A4, A5, TT, TTS, Q5, Q7 **Engine:** 2.0L L4, 3.0L V6, 3.2L V6 **Transmission:** All	**Camshaft Position Sensor "B" Circuit Range/Performance Bank 1:** While cranking the engine and with the engine running. The ECM/PCM has detected an open or short in the circuit.
DTC: P0367 **2T ECM, MIL: Yes** **Year:** 2011, 2012 **Model:** A3, A4, A5, TT, TTS, Q5, Q7 **Engine:** 2.0L L4, 3.0L V6, 3.2L V6 **Transmission:** All	**Camshaft Position Sensor "B" Circuit Low Bank 1:** While cranking the engine and with the engine running. The ECM/PCM has detected an open or short in the circuit.
DTC: P0368 **2T ECM, MIL: Yes** **Year:** 2011, 2012 **Model:** A3, A4, A5, TT, TTS, Q5, Q7 **Engine:** 2.0L L4, 3.0L V6, 3.2L V6 **Transmission:** All	**Camshaft Position Sensor "B" Circuit High Bank 1:** While cranking the engine and with the engine running. The ECM/PCM has detected an open or short in the circuit.
DTC: P0369 **2T ECM, MIL: Yes** **Year:** 2011, 2012 **Model:** A3, A4, A5, TT, TTS, Q5, Q7 **Engine:** 2.0L L4, 3.0L V6, 3.2L V6 **Transmission:** All	**CAMSHAFT 1/2 POSITION SENSOR INTERMITTENT:** While cranking the engine and engine running. When the failure counter reaches 20. One Trip Fault. Three good trips to turn off the MIL.
DTC: P0381 **2T ECM, MIL: Yes** **Year:** 2011, 2012 A3, A4, A5, TT, Q5, Q7 **Engine:** 2.0L TDI L4, 3.0L TDI V6 **Transmission:** All	**Glow Plug/Heater Indicator Circuit:** While cranking the engine. The ECM/PCM has detected an open or short in the circuit. * Battery voltage > 9 V * Glow system active
DTC: P0383 **2T ECM, MIL: Yes** **Year:** 2011, 2012 A3, A4, A5, TT, Q5, Q7 **Engine:** 2.0L TDI L4, 3.0L TDI V6 **Transmission:** All	**Glow Plug Control Module Control Circuit Low:** While cranking the engine. The ECM/PCM has detected an open or short in the circuit. * Battery voltage > 9 V * Glow system active
DTC: P0384 **2T ECM, MIL: Yes** **Year:** 2011, 2012 A3, A4, A5, TT, Q5, Q7 **Engine:** 2.0L TDI L4, 3.0L TDI V6 **Transmission:** All	**Glow Plug Control Module Control Circuit High:** While cranking the engine. The ECM/PCM has detected an open or short in the circuit. * Battery voltage > 9 V * Glow system active

DTC	Trouble Code Title, Conditions, Possible Causes
DTC: P0390 **1T ECM, MIL: Yes** **Year:** 2011, 2012 **Model:** TTS, **Engine:** 3.0L V6, 3.2L V6 **Transmission:** All	**-CAMSHAFT 1/4 POSITION SENSOR CIRCUIT:** During engine cranking and with the engine running. Battery voltage greater than 10 Volts. At least five seconds or 2.5 engine revolutions have elapsed with crankshaft position sensor signals present but no camshaft position sensor signal. One Trip Fault. Three good trips to turn off the MIL.
DTC: P0391 **1T ECM, MIL: Yes** **Year:** 2011, 2012 **Model:** TTS, **Engine:** 3.0L V6, 3.2L V6 **Transmission:** All	**Camshaft Position Sensor "B" Circuit Range/Performance Bank 2:** No camshaft position sensor signal detected.
DTC: P0392 **1T ECM, MIL: Yes** **Year:** 2011, 2012 **Model:** TTS, **Engine:** 3.0L V6, 3.2L V6 **Transmission:** All	**Camshaft Position Sensor "B" Circuit Low Bank 2:** No camshaft position sensor signal detected.
DTC: P0393 **1T ECM, MIL: Yes** **Year:** 2011, 2012 **Model:** TTS, **Engine:** 3.0L V6, 3.2L V6 **Transmission:** All	**Camshaft Position Sensor "B" Circuit High Bank 2:** No camshaft position sensor signal detected.
DTC: P0394 **1T ECM, MIL: Yes** **Year:** 2011, 2012 **Model:** TTS, **Engine:** 3.0L V6, 3.2L V6 **Transmission:** All	**-CAMSHAFT 1/4 POSITION SENSOR INTERMITTENT:** While cranking the engine and engine running. When the failure counter reaches 20. One Trip Fault. Three good trips to turn off the MIL.
DTC: P0401 **2T ECM, MIL: Yes** **Year:** 2011, 2012 **Model:** A3, A4, A5, TT, TTS, Q5, Q7 **Engine:** 2.0L L4, 3.0L V6, 3.2L V6 **Transmission:** All	**Exhaust Gas Recirculation Flow Insufficient Detected:** Malfunction Criteria and Threshold Value: * EGR mode, closed loop * Fuel quantity, >6 mg/stroke * Fuel quantity, <22 mg/stroke * Engine speed, >1300 rpm * Engine speed, <2,000 rpm
DTC: P0402 **2T ECM, MIL: Yes** **Year:** 2011, 2012 **Model:** A3, A4, A5, TT, TTS, Q5, Q7 **Engine:** 2.0L L4, 3.0L V6, 3.2L V6 **Transmission:** All	**Exhaust Gas Recirculation Excessive Flow Detected:** Malfunction Criteria and Threshold Value: * EGR valve closed = 100% * Throttle valve signal > 94% * Engine speed, > 1100 - 2500 rpm * Boost pressure = 50 - 200 kPa * ECT = 60 - 110 °C * Ambient pressure > 50 kPa * Fuel quantity > 0.5 mg/stroke
DTC: P0403 **2T ECM, MIL: Yes** **Year:** 2011, 2012 **Model:** A3, A4, A5, TT, TTS, Q5, Q7 **Engine:** 2.0L L4, 3.0L V6, 3.2L V6 **Transmission:** All	**Exhaust gas recirculation valve -N18 Malfunction:** Power stage = On or Off (dependent on diagnostic run).

DTC	Trouble Code Title, Conditions, Possible Causes
DTC: P0404 **2T ECM, MIL: Yes** **Year:** 2011, 2012 **Model:** A3, A4, A5, TT, TTS, Q5, Q7 **Engine:** 2.0L L4, 3.0L V6, 3.2L V6 **Transmission:** All	**Exhaust Gas Recirculation Contr. Circuit Range/Performance:** The ECM/PCM detected an unexpected low or high condition on the control circuit during testing. * Engine running 480 mSec.
DTC: P040B **2T ECM, MIL: Yes** **Year:** 2011, 2012 **Model:** A3, A4, A5, TT, TTS, Q5, Q7 **Engine:** 2.0L L4, 3.0L V6, 3.2L V6 **Transmission:** All	**Exhaust Gas Recirculation Temperature Sensor Circuit Range/Performance:** Condition 1: Engine run time > 3 min. ECT > 70 °C. Simulated sensor temp > 85 °C Elapsed time since EGR valve opens > 30 Sec. Condition 2: Engine off time > 32400 Sec. Decrease of intake air temp after engine start < 5 °K. Decrease of ambient air temp after engine start < 5°K
DTC: P040C **2T ECM, MIL: Yes** **Year:** 2011, 2012 **Model:** A3, A4, A5, TT, TTS, Q5, Q7 **Engine:** 2.0L L4, 3.0L V6, 3.2L V6 **Transmission:** All	**Exhaust Gas Recirculation Temperature Sensor Circuit Low:** The ECM/PCM detected an unexpected low condition on the control circuit during testing. * Signal sensor voltage < 0.06 V, * Engine running 480 mSec.
DTC: P040D **2T ECM, MIL: Yes** **Year:** 2011, 2012 **Model:** A3, A4, A5, TT, TTS, Q5, Q7 **Engine:** 2.0L L4, 3.0L V6, 3.2L V6 **Transmission:** All	**Exhaust Gas Recirculation Temperature Sensor Circuit High:** The ECM/PCM detected an unexpected high condition on the control circuit during testing.
DTC: P0410 **2T ECM, MIL: Yes** **Year:** 2011, 2012 **Model:** A3, A4, A5, TT, TTS, Q5, Q7 **Engine:** 2.0L L4 **Transmission:** All	**Secondary Air Injection System:** Malfunction Criteria and Threshold Value: * Mass airflow 7 to 120 kg/h * Delta engine load -10 to 10 % * ECT 5 to 108 °C * Altitude < 2700 m * IAT 5 to 100 °C * SAI pressure sensor - ready
DTC: P0411 **2T ECM, MIL: Yes** **Year:** 2011, 2012 **Model:** A3, A4, A5, TT, TTS, Q5, Q7 **Engine:** 2.0L L4 **Transmission:** All	**Secondary Air Injection System Upstream Flow Detected:** Engine started, battery voltage must be at least 11.5v, all electrical components must be off, parking brake must be engaged (to keep daytime driving lights off), automatic transmission selector must be in park and the ground between the engine and the chassis must be well connected. The ECM detected the Secondary AIR pump airflow was not diverted correctly when requested during the self-test. The pump is functioning but the quantity of air is recognized as insufficient by HO2S. **NOTE: The solenoid valve is closed when no voltage is present.**
DTC: P0412 **2T ECM, MIL: Yes** **Year:** 2011, 2012 **Model:** A3, A4, A5, TT, TTS, Q5, Q7 **Engine:** 2.0L L4 **Transmission:** All	**Secondary Air Injection Solenoid Circuit Malfunction:** Engine started, battery voltage must be at least 11.5v, all electrical components must be off, parking brake must be engaged (to keep daytime driving lights off), automatic transmission selector must be in park and the ground between the engine and the chassis must be well connected. The ECM detected an unexpected low or high voltage condition on the AIR solenoid control circuit during testing.
DTC: P0413 **2T ECM, MIL: Yes** **Year:** 2011, 2012 **Model:** A3, A4, A5, TT, TTS, Q5, Q7 **Engine:** 2.0L L4 **Transmission:** All	**Secondary Air Injection Solenoid Circuit Open:** Engine started, battery voltage must be at least 11.5v, all electrical components must be off, parking brake must be engaged (to keep daytime driving lights off), automatic transmission selector must be in park and the ground between the engine and the chassis must be well connected. The ECM detected an unexpected low or high voltage condition on the AIR solenoid control circuit during testing.

DTC	Trouble Code Title, Conditions, Possible Causes
DTC: P0414 **2T ECM, MIL: Yes** **Year:** 2011, 2012 **Model:** A3, A4, A5, TT, TTS, Q5, Q7 **Engine:** 2.0L L4 **Transmission:** All	**Secondary Air Injection Solenoid Circuit Short:** Engine started, battery voltage must be at least 11.5v, all electrical components must be off, parking brake must be engaged (to keep daytime driving lights off), automatic transmission selector must be in park and the ground between the engine and the chassis must be well connected. The ECM detected an unexpected low or high voltage condition on the AIR solenoid control circuit during testing.
DTC: P0415 **2T ECM, MIL: Yes** **Year:** 2011, 2012 **Model:** A3, A4, A5, TT, TTS, Q5, Q7 **Engine:** 2.0L L4 **Transmission:** All	**Secondary Air Injection System Switching Valve "B" Circuit Malfunction:** The ECM/PCM detected an unexpected low or high voltage condition on the valve B control circuit during testing. * Engine started * Battery voltage must be at least 11.5v
DTC: P0416 **2T ECM, MIL: Yes** **Year:** 2011, 2012 **Model:** A3, A4, A5, TT, TTS, Q5, Q7 **Engine:** 2.0L L4 **Transmission:** All	**Secondary Air Injection System Switching Valve "B" Circuit Open:** The ECM/PCM detected an unexpected low or high voltage condition on the valve B control circuit during testing. * Engine started * Battery voltage must be at least 11.5v
DTC: P0417 **2T ECM, MIL: Yes** **Year:** 2011, 2012 **Model:** A3, A4, A5, TT, TTS, Q5, Q7 **Engine:** 2.0L L4 **Transmission:** All	**Secondary Air Injection System Switching Valve "B" Circuit Shorted:** The ECM/PCM detected an unexpected high voltage condition on the valve B control circuit during testing. * Air valve, commanded off * Engine speed, >80 RPM * Air valve, commanded on * Engine speed, >80 RPM
DTC: P0418 **2T ECM, MIL: Yes** **Year:** 2011, 2012 **Model:** A3, A4, A5, TT, TTS, Q5, Q7 **Engine:** 2.0L L4, 3.0L V6, 3.2L V6 **Transmission:** All	**Secondary Air Injection Relay (A) Circuit Malfunction:** Engine started, battery voltage must be at least 11.5v, all electrical components must be off, parking brake must be engaged (to keep daytime driving lights off), automatic transmission selector must be in park and the ground between the engine and the chassis must be well connected. The ECM detected an unexpected low or high voltage condition on the AIR solenoid control circuit during testing.
DTC: P0420 **2T ECM, MIL: Yes** **Year:** 2011, 2012 **Model:** A3, A4, A5, TT, TTS, Q5, Q7 **Engine:** 2.0L L4, 3.0L V6, 3.2L V6 **Transmission:** All	**Catalyst System Efficiency (Bank 1) Below Threshold:** Engine started, battery voltage must be at least 11.5v, all electrical components must be off, parking brake must be engaged (to keep daytime driving lights off), automatic transmission selector must be in park, the exhaust system must be properly sealed between the catalytic converter and the cylinder head, coolant temperature must be at least 80 degrees Celsius and oxygen sensor heaters for oxygen sensors before the catalytic converter must be functioning properly and the ground between the engine and the chassis must be well connected. The ECM detected the switch rate of the rear HO2S-12 was close to the switch rate of front HO2S (it should be much slower).
DTC: P0421 **1T ECM, MIL: Yes** **Year:** 2011, 2012 **Model:** A3, A4, A5, TT, TTS, Q5, Q7 **Engine:** 2.0L L4, 3.0L V6, 3.2L V6 **Transmission:** All	**Warm Up Catalyst, Bank 1 Efficiency Below Threshold:** Malfunction Criteria and Threshold Value: * Catalyst temperature -385 - 665°C * engine start temperature-> -10°C * Misfire rate-< 2.3 %
DTC: P0422 **2T ECM, MIL: Yes** **Year:** 2011, 2012 **Model:** A3, A4, A5, TT, TTS, Q5, Q7 **Engine:** 2.0L L4, 3.0L V6, 3.2L V6 **Transmission:** All	**Main Catalyst (Bank 1) Efficiency Below Threshold:** Engine started, battery voltage must be at least 11.5v, all electrical components must be off, parking brake must be engaged (to keep daytime driving lights off), automatic transmission selector must be in park, the exhaust system must be properly sealed between the catalytic converter and the cylinder head, coolant temperature must be at least 80 degrees Celsius and oxygen sensor heaters for oxygen sensors before the catalytic converter must be functioning properly and the ground between the engine and the chassis must be well connected. The ECM detected the switch rate of the rear HO2S-12 was close to the switch rate of front HO2S (it should be much slower).

DTC	Trouble Code Title, Conditions, Possible Causes
DTC: P0430 **2T ECM, MIL: Yes** **Year:** 2011, 2012 **Model:** A3, A4, A5, TT, TTS, Q5, Q7 **Engine:** 2.0L L4, 3.0L V6, 3.2L V6 **Transmission:** All	**Catalyst System Efficiency Below Threshold Bank 2:** The monitor will run at between 1400 and 2300 RPM and MAP vacuum between 40 to 70 kPa (15.0 and 21.0 (Hg)).If the final State of Change index is within the calibrated fail threshold. Two trip fault. Three good trips to turn off the MIL.
DTC: P0431 **2T ECM, MIL: Yes** **Year:** 2011, 2012 **Model:** A3, A4, A5, TT, TTS, Q5, Q7 **Engine:** 2.0L L4, 3.0L V6, 3.2L V6 **Transmission:** All	**Warm Up Catalyst, Bank 2 Efficiency Below Threshold:** Malfunction Criteria and Threshold Value: * Catalyst temperature -385 - 665°C * engine start temperature-> -10°C * Misfire rate-< 2.3 %
DTC: P0440 **2T ECM, MIL: Yes** **Year:** 2011, 2012 **Model:** A3, A4, A5, TT, TTS, Q5, Q7 **Engine:** 2.0L L4, 3.0L V6, 3.2L V6 **Transmission:** All	**EVAP System General Malfunction:** Engine running after a cold start with the difference between ECT and AAT is less than 10° C (19° F). Fuel Level between 12% and 88% full. Manifold vacuum greater than a calculated minimum value. Ambient Temperature between 4° C and 32° C (39° F and 89° F). When the monitor conditions are met, the Powertrain Control Module (PCM) will ramp in purge flow. If the PCM does not sense an ESIM Switch closure after a calculated amount of purge flow accumulation, an error is detected. Two Trip Fault. Three good trips to turn off the MIL.
DTC: P0441 **1T ECM, MIL: Yes** **Year:** 2011, 2012 **Model:** A3, A4, A5, TT, TTS, Q5, Q7 **Engine:** 2.0L L4, 3.0L V6, 3.2L V6 **Transmission:** All	**Evaporative Emission System Incorrect Purge Flow:** After the Evaporative System small leak test has passed, with the engine running, ambient temperature between 4° C (39° F) and 35° (95° F), with the engine at idle after a calibrated amount of drive time has accumulated. If the Powertrain Control Module (PCM) detects that the purge vapor ratio and the ESIM switch closed ratio are below a calculated value, the PCM commands the purge solenoid to flow at a specified rate to update the purge vapor ratio. If the ratio remains below a specified value, a one trip failure is recorded. Two Trip Fault. Three good trips to turn off the MIL.
DTC: P0442 **1T ECM, MIL: Yes** **Year:** 2011, 2012 **Model:** A3, A4, A5, TT, TTS, Q5, Q7 **Engine:** 2.0L L4, 3.0L V6, 3.2L V6 **Transmission:** All	**Evaporative Emission System Leak found (Small Leak):** Malfunction Criteria and Threshold Value: * Time after engine start, 5–1200 Sec. * ECT, 4.5-105.80° C * IAT, > 4.5-60.00° C * IAT drop after engine start, < 6.00 K * Intake manifold vacuum, >140 hPa * Altitude, <2700 m * Vehicle speed, 22 km/h * Selected gear, Any drive * Restart temperature difference, >45K * EVAP purge valve, Closed
DTC: P0443 **1T ECM, MIL: Yes** **Year:** 2011, 2012 **Model:** A3, A4, A5, TT, TTS, Q5, Q7 **Engine:** 2.0L L4, 3.0L V6, 3.2L V6 **Transmission:** All	**EVAP Vapor Management Valve Circuit Malfunction:** Engine started, battery voltage must be at least 11.5v, all electrical components must be off, parking brake must be engaged (to keep daytime driving lights off), automatic transmission selector must be in park, the exhaust system must be properly sealed between the catalytic converter and the cylinder head, coolant temperature must be at least 80 degrees Celsius and oxygen sensor heaters for oxygen sensors before the catalytic converter must be functioning properly and the ground between the engine and the chassis must be well connected. The ECM/PCM detected an unexpected high or low voltage condition on the Vapor Management Valve (VMV) circuit when the device was cycled On/Off during testing.
DTC: P0444 **1T ECM, MIL: Yes** **Year:** 2011, 2012 **Model:** A3, A4, A5, TT, TTS, Q5, Q7 **Engine:** 2.0L L4, 3.0L V6, 3.2L V6 **Transmission:** All	**Evaporative Emission System Purge Control Valve Circuit Open:** The ignition on or engine running. Battery voltage greater than 10 volts. The Powertrain Control Module (PCM) will set a trouble code if the actual state of the solenoid does not match the intended state. One Trip Fault. Three good trips to turn off the MIL. Malfunction Criteria and Threshold Value: * EVAP purge valve Commanded Off * Engine speed > 80 RPM

DTC	Trouble Code Title, Conditions, Possible Causes
DTC: P0445 **1T ECM, MIL: Yes** **Year:** 2011, 2012 **Model:** A3, A4, A5, TT, TTS, Q5, Q7 **Engine:** 2.0L L4, 3.0L V6, 3.2L V6 **Transmission:** All	**Evaporative Emission System Purge Control Valve Circuit Shorted:** Engine started, battery voltage must be at least 11.5v, all electrical components must be off, parking brake must be engaged (to keep daytime driving lights off), automatic transmission selector must be in park, the exhaust system must be properly sealed between the catalytic converter and the cylinder head, coolant temperature must be at least 80 degrees Celsius and oxygen sensor heaters for oxygen sensors before the catalytic converter must be functioning properly and the ground between the engine and the chassis must be well connected. The ECM detected an unexpected voltage condition on the EVAP circuit when the device was cycled On/Off during testing.
DTC: P0449 **1T ECM, MIL: Yes** **Year:** 2011, 2012 **Model:** A3, A4, A5, TT, TTS, Q5, Q7 **Engine:** 2.0L L4, 3.0L V6, 3.2L V6 **Transmission:** All	**Evaporative Emission System Vent Valve/Solenoid Circuit:** Engine started, battery voltage must be at least 11.5v, all electrical components must be off, parking brake must be engaged (to keep daytime driving lights off), automatic transmission selector must be in park, the exhaust system must be properly sealed between the catalytic converter and the cylinder head, coolant temperature must be at least 80 degrees Celsius and oxygen sensor heaters for oxygen sensors before the catalytic converter must be functioning properly and the ground between the engine and the chassis must be well connected. The ECM detected an unexpected voltage condition on the EVAP circuit when the device was cycled On/Off during testing.
DTC: P0452 **2T ECM, MIL: Yes** **Year:** 2011, 2012 **Model:** A3, A4, A5, TT, TTS, Q5, Q7 **Engine:** 2.0L L4, 3.0L V6, 3.2L V6 **Transmission:** All	**EVAP PRESSURE SWITCH STUCK CLOSED:** Immediately after the ignition has been turned off. At key off, the Powertrain Control Module (PCM) energizes the Purge Solenoid for a calibrated amount of time (30 seconds maximum) and stores the state of the ESIM switch. The state is evaluated again at the next key on. If the PCM does not detect that the ESIM switch is open, an error is detected. Two Trip Fault. Three good trips to turn off the MIL.
DTC: P0455 **2T ECM, MIL: Yes** **Year:** 2011, 2012 **Model:** A3, A4, A5, TT, TTS, Q5, Q7 **Engine:** 2.0L L4, 3.0L V6, 3.2L V6 **Transmission:** All	**Evaporative Emission System Leak Detected (large leak/no flow):** With the engine running, during a cold start test with the fuel level above 12%, ambient temperature between 4° C and 32° C (39° F and 89° F) and the fuel system in closed loop. The test runs when the small leak test is maturing. The Powertrain Control Module (PCM) activates the Evap Purge solenoid to pull the Evaporative system into a vacuum to close the ESIM switch. Once the ESIM switch is closed, the PCM turns the Evap Purge solenoid off to seal the Evaporative system. If the ESIM switch reopens before the calibrated amount of time, a large leak error is detected. Two Trip Fault. Three good trips to turn off the MIL.
DTC: P0456 **1T ECM, MIL: Yes** **Year:** 2011, 2012 **Model:** A3, A4, A5, TT, TTS, Q5, Q7 **Engine:** 2.0L L4, 3.0L V6, 3.2L V6 **Transmission:** All	**Evaporative Emission System Leak Detected (very small leak):** With the ignition off, fuel level less than 88%, ambient temperature between 4° C and 43° C (39° F and 109° F) and the fuel system in closed loop. As temperatures change, a vacuum is created in the fuel tank and Evaporative system. With the Evaporative system sealed, the PCM monitors the ESIM Switch. If the ESIM Switch does not close within a calibrated time, an error is detected by the PCM. One Trip Fault. Three good trips to turn off the MIL.
DTC: P0457 **2T ECM, MIL: Yes** **Year:** 2011, 2012 **Model:** A3, A4, A5, TT, TTS, Q5, Q7 **Engine:** 2.0L L4, 3.0L V6, 3.2L V6 **Transmission:** All	**LOOSE FUEL CAP:** Ignition on. Ambient Temperature between 4° C and 32° C (39° F and 89° F) Close Loop fuel system. Test runs after the medium leak test is inconclusive and the PCM senses a fuel increase. If a leak greater than .090" is detected by the Powertrain Control Module (PCM) for two consecutive cold start trips after a significant fuel level change, this DTC will set. One good trip turns off the MIL.
DTC: P0458 **2T ECM, MIL: Yes** **Year:** 2011, 2012 **Model:** A3, A4, A5, TT, TTS, Q5, Q7 **Engine:** 2.0L L4, 3.0L V6, 3.2L V6 **Transmission:** All	**Evaporative Emission System Purge Control Valve Circuit Low:** The ECM detected an unexpected voltage condition on the EVAP circuit when the device was cycled On/Off during testing. * EVAP purge valve, Commanded off * Engine speed, >80 RPM
DTC: P0459 **2T ECM, MIL: Yes** **Year:** 2011, 2012 **Model:** A3, A4, A5, TT, TTS, Q5, Q7 **Engine:** 2.0L L4, 3.0L V6, 3.2L V6 **Transmission:** All	**Evaporative Emission System Purge Control Valve Circuit High:** The ECM detected an unexpected voltage condition on the EVAP circuit when the device was cycled On/Off during testing. * EVAP purge valve, Commanded on * Engine speed, >80 RPM

DTC	Trouble Code Title, Conditions, Possible Causes
DTC: P045A **2T ECM, MIL: Yes** **Year:** 2011, 2012 **Model:** A3, A4, A5, TT, TTS, Q5, Q7 **Engine:** 2.0L L4 **Transmission:** All	**Exhaust Gas Recirculation "B" Control Circuit:** With the engine running and the engine temperature at 120 °C. The ECM/PCM has detected an open or short in the control circuit.
DTC: P045B **2T ECM, MIL: Yes** **Year:** 2011, 2012 **Model:** A3, A4, A5, TT, TTS, Q5, Q7 **Engine:** 2.0L L4 **Transmission:** All	**Exhaust Gas Recirculation "B" Control Circuit Range/Performance:** With the engine running and the engine temperature at 120 °C. The ECM/PCM has detected an open or short in the control circuit.
DTC: P045C **2T ECM, MIL: Yes** **Year:** 2011, 2012 **Model:** A3, A4, A5, TT, TTS, Q5, Q7 **Engine:** 2.0L L4 **Transmission:** All	**Exhaust Gas Recirculation "B" Control Circuit Low:** With the engine running and the engine temperature at 120 °C. The ECM/PCM has detected an open or short in the control circuit.
DTC: P045D **2T ECM, MIL: Yes** **Year:** 2011, 2012 **Model:** A3, A4, A5, TT, TTS, Q5, Q7 **Engine:** 2.0L L4 **Transmission:** All	**Exhaust Gas Recirculation "B" Control Circuit High:** With the engine running and the engine temperature at 120 °C. The ECM/PCM has detected an open or short in the control circuit.
DTC: P045E **2T ECM, MIL: Yes** **Year:** 2011, 2012 **Model:** A3, A4, A5, TT, TTS, Q5, Q7 **Engine:** 2.0L L4 **Transmission:** All	**Exhaust Gas Recirculation "B" Control Stuck Open:** With the engine running and the engine temperature at 120 °C. The ECM/PCM has detected an open or short in the control circuit.
DTC: P0461 **2T ECM, MIL: Yes** **Year:** 2011, 2012 **Model:** A3, A4, A5, TT, TTS, Q5, Q7 **Engine:** 2.0L L4, 3.0L V6, 3.2L V6 **Transmission:** All	**FUEL LEVEL SENSOR 1 PERFORMANCE:** If the PCM does not see a difference in fuel level of greater than 0.1 Volt the test will fail. If the PCM does not see a change in the fuel level over a set amount of miles the test will fail. Two trip fault. Three good trips to turn off the MIL.
DTC: P0462 **1T ECM, MIL: Yes** **Year:** 2011, 2012 **Model:** A3, A4, A5, TT, TTS, Q5, Q7 **Engine:** 2.0L L4, 3.0L V6, 3.2L V6 **Transmission:** All	**FUEL LEVEL SENSOR 1 CIRCUIT LOW:** With the ignition on and battery voltage above 10.4 Volts. The fuel level sensor signal voltage goes below the minimum acceptable value. One Trip Fault. Three good trips to turn off the MIL.
DTC: P0463 **1T ECM, MIL: Yes** **Year:** 2011, 2012 **Model:** A3, A4, A5, TT, TTS, Q5, Q7 **Engine:** 2.0L L4, 3.0L V6, 3.2L V6 **Transmission:** All	**-FUEL LEVEL SENSOR 1 CIRCUIT HIGH:** With the ignition on and battery voltage above 10.4 Volts. The fuel level sensor input voltage is above the maximum acceptable value. One Trip Fault. Three good trips to turn off the MIL.

DTC	Trouble Code Title, Conditions, Possible Causes
DTC: P046C **2T ECM, MIL: Yes** **Year:** 2011, 2012 **Model:** **Engine:** 3.0L V6, 3.2L V6 **Transmission:** All	**Exhaust Gas Recirculation Sensor "A" Circuit Range/Performance:** * ECT > -20 °C
DTC: P0471 **2T ECM, MIL: Yes** **Year:** 2011, 2012 **Model:** **Engine:** 3.0L V6, 3.2L V6 **Transmission:** All	**Exhaust Pressure Sensor "A" Range/Performance:** * ECT > 69.96 °C * Engine = after run * Engine run time > 720 Sec.
DTC: P0472 **2T ECM, MIL: Yes** **Year:** 2011, 2012 **Model:** A3, Q7 **Engine:** 2.0L L4 **Transmission:** All	**Exhaust Pressure Sensor A Low:** Exhaust Pressure Sensor A Low
DTC: P0473 **2T ECM, MIL: Yes** **Year:** 2011, 2012 **Model:** A3, Q7 **Engine:** 2.0L L4 **Transmission:** All	**Exhaust Pressure Sensor A High:** Exhaust Pressure Sensor A High
DTC: P0475 **2T ECM, MIL: Yes** **Year:** 2011, 2012 **Model:** A3, Q7 **Engine:** 2.0L L4 **Transmission:** All	**Exhaust Pressure Control Valve "A":** Engine Running
DTC: P0477 **2T ECM, MIL: Yes** **Year:** 2011, 2012 **Model:** A3, Q7 **Engine:** 2.0L L4 **Transmission:** All	**Exhaust Pressure Control Valve "A" Low:** Engine running
DTC: P0478 **2T ECM, MIL: Yes** **Year:** 2011, 2012 **Model:** A3, Q7 **Engine:** 2.0L L4 **Transmission:** All	**Exhaust Pressure Control Valve "A" High:** Engine running and circuit high.
DTC: P047C **2T ECM, MIL: Yes** **Year:** 2011, 2012 **Model:** A3, Q7 **Engine:** 2.0L L4 **Transmission:** All	**Exhaust Pressure Sensor "B" Low:** Engine running and circuit low.
DTC: P047D **2T ECM, MIL: Yes** **Year:** 2011, 2012 **Model:** A3, Q7 **Engine:** 2.0L L4 **Transmission:** All	**Exhaust Pressure Sensor "B" High:** Engine running and circuit high.

DTC	Trouble Code Title, Conditions, Possible Causes
DTC: P047F **2T ECM, MIL: Yes** **Year:** 2011, 2012 **Model:** A3, Q7 **Engine:** 2.0L L4 **Transmission:** All	**Exhaust Pressure Control Valve "A" Stuck Open:** Engine running, control deviation > 10%
DTC: P0480 **1 T ECM, MIL: Yes** **Year:** 2011, 2012 **Model:** A3, A4, A5, TT, TTS, Q5, Q7 **Engine:** 2.0L L4, 3.0L V6, 3.2L V6 **Transmission:** All	**Cooling Fan 1 Control Circuit:** With the ignition on. Battery voltage greater than 10 Volts. The ECM/PCM) is requesting the Totally Integrated Power Module (TIPM) to turn on the Cooling Fan On and it is not operating.
DTC: P0481 **1 T ECM, MIL: Yes** **Year:** 2011, 2012 **Model:** A3, A4, A5, TT, TTS, Q5, Q7 **Engine:** 2.0L L4, 3.0L V6, 3.2L V6 **Transmission:** All	**Cooling Fan 2 Control Circuit:** With the ignition on. Battery voltage greater than 10 Volts. The ECM/PCM) is requesting the Totally Integrated Power Module (TIPM) to turn on the Cooling Fan On and it is not operating.
DTC: P048B **2T ECM, MIL: Yes** **Year:** 2011, 2012 **Model:** A3, Q7 **Engine:** 2.0L L4 **Transmission:** All	**Exhaust Pressure Control Valve Position Sensor Circuit Low:** Engine running
DTC: P048E **2T ECM, MIL: Yes** **Year:** 2011, 2012 **Model:** A3, Q7 **Engine:** 2.0L L4 **Transmission:** All	**Exhaust Pressure Control Valve Position Sensor Circuit High:** Engine running
DTC: P0491 **1 T ECM, MIL: Yes** **Year:** 2011, 2012 **Model:** A3, A4, A5, TT, TTS, Q5, Q7 **Engine:** 2.0L L4, 3.0L V6, 3.2L V6 **Transmission:** All	**Secondary Air Injection System Insufficient Flow:** * Mass air flow 7 to 120 kg/h * ECT 4.5 to 108 °C * IAT 4.5 to * Altitude < 2700
DTC: P0492 **1 T ECM, MIL: Yes** **Year:** 2011, 2012 **Model:** A3, A4, A5, TT, TTS, Q5, Q7 **Engine:** 2.0L L4, 3.0L V6, 3.2L V6 **Transmission:** All	**Secondary Air Injection System Insufficient Flow Bank 2:** * Mass air flow, 12–140 kg/h * ECT, 5.3–60° C * IAT, >5.3° C * Altitude, <2600 m
DTC: P0501 **2T ECM, MIL: Yes** **Year:** 2011, 2012 **Model:** A3, A4, A5, TT, TTS, Q5, Q7 **Engine:** 2.0L L4, 3.0L V6, 3.2L V6 **Transmission:** All	**Vehicle Speed Sensor A Range/Performance:** With the engine running, transmission not in park or neutral, brakes not applied. Engine rpm greater than 1500. This code will set if no vehicle speed signal is received from the ABS Module up to 120 seconds for two consecutive trips. Two Trip Fault. Three good trips to turn off the MIL.
DTC: P0503 **1 T ECM, MIL: Yes** **Year:** 2011, 2012 **Model:** A3, A4, A5, TT, TTS, Q5, Q7 **Engine:** 2.0L L4, 3.0L V6, 3.2L V6 **Transmission:** All	**Vehicle Speed Sensor "A" Intermittent/Erratic/High:** With the engine running, transmission not in park or neutral, brakes not applied. Engine rpm greater than 1500. This code will set if no vehicle speed signal is received from the ABS Module up to 120 seconds for two consecutive trips. Two Trip Fault. Three good trips to turn off the MIL.

DTC	Trouble Code Title, Conditions, Possible Causes
DTC: P0504 **1 T ECM, MIL: Yes** **Year:** 2011, 2012 **Model:** TTS **Engine:** 3.2L V6 **Transmission:** All	**BRAKE SWITCH A/B CORRELATION:** With the ignition on. VSS indicates increasing and decreasing vehicle speed. APP Sensor indicates increasing and decreasing acceleration demand. The ECM determines that the brakes have been applied without the receiving an input from the Primary Brake Switch Signal and Secondary Brake Switches.
DTC: P0506 **1 T ECM, MIL: Yes** **Year:** 2011, 2012 **Model:** A3, A4, A5, TT, TTS, Q5, Q7 **Engine:** 2.0L L4, 3.0L V6, 3.2L V6 **Transmission:** All	**Idle Air Control System RPM Lower Than Expected:** Engine speed is 100 RPM or more below idle speed for 7 seconds. Two Trip Fault. Three good trips to turn off the MIL. * Engine speed, idle * Accelerator PP, 0% * Vehicle speed, 0 MPH * EVAP purge valve, Closed * Altitude, < 2600 m * IAT, >-7 °C * ECT, >60 °C
DTC: P0507 **2 T ECM, MIL: Yes** **Year:** 2011, 2012 **Model:** A3, A4, A5, TT, TTS, Q5, Q7 **Engine:** 2.0L L4, 3.0L V6, 3.2L V6 **Transmission:** All	**-IDLE SPEED PERFORMANCE HIGHER THAN EXCEPTED:** Engine speed is 200 RPM or more above idle speed for 7 seconds. Two Trip Fault. Three good trips to turn off the MIL. * Engine speed, idle * Vehicle speed 0 MPH * Altitude < 2700 m * IAT, > -48 °C * ECT, > -48 °C * Time after engine start > 0 Sec. * Lambda control active * EVAP purge adaptation < 22
DTC: P050A **2 T ECM, MIL: Yes** **Year:** 2011, 2012 **Model:** A3, A4, A5, TT, TTS, Q5, Q7 **Engine:** 2.0L L4, 3.0L V6, 3.2L V6 **Transmission:** All	**Cold Start Idle Air Control System Performance:** * Time after engine start > 0 Sec. * Driver torque demand - none * Veh speed 0 km/h * Altitude < 2700 m * IAT > -48.0 °C * Catalyst heating active * Man. trans engine load < 40 - 75% * Time after engine start > 0 Sec.
DTC: P050B **2 T ECM, MIL: Yes** **Year:** 2011, 2012 **Model:** A3, A4, A5, TT, TTS, Q5, Q7 **Engine:** 2.0L L4, 3.0L V6, 3.2L V6 **Transmission:** All	**-COLD START IGNITION TIMING PERFORMANCE:** Cold start condition. Ambient Air temperature between -7° C and 50° C (19.4° F and 122° F). Engine Coolant temperature between -7° C and 50° C (19.4° F and 122° F). The difference between the Ambient Air temp and ECT temp at Start is equal to and less than 10° C (50° F). Engine running at idle only. Engine RPM is 50 RPM or more (depending on vehicle specifications), below idle speed for at least 3 seconds and the average spark advance is above the threshold, too much spark advance, for a specified time limit. Two trip fault. Three good trips to turn off the MIL.
DTC: P0510 **2 T ECM, MIL: Yes** **Year:** 2011, 2012 **Model:** A3, A4, A5, TT, TTS, Q5, Q7 **Engine:** 2.0L L4, 3.0L V6, 3.2L V6 **Transmission:** All	**Closed Throttle Position Switch:** Throttle potentiometer – Engine is running at idle/coasting condition Throttle actuator potentiometer – Coasting condition /under load condition switch has to be open
DTC: P0513 **2 T ECM, MIL: Yes** **Year:** 2011, 2012 **Model:** A3, A4, A5, TT, TTS, Q5, Q7 **Engine:** 2.0L L4, 3.0L V6, 3.2L V6 **Transmission:** All	**INVALID SKIM KEY:** With the ignition on. The Engine Control Module (ECM) receives an invalid message from the Wireless Ignition Node (WIN).

DTC	Trouble Code Title, Conditions, Possible Causes
DTC: P0520 **2 T ECM, MIL: Yes** **Year:** 2011, 2012 **Model:** A3, A4, A5, TT, TTS, Q5, Q7 **Engine:** 2.0L L4, 3.0L V6, 3.2L V6 **Transmission:** All	**ENGINE OIL PRESSURE SENSOR CIRCUIT:** Ignition on, engine not running. The Powertrain Control Module (PCM) senses the oil pressure is out of the calibrated range. Two Trip fault.
DTC: P0521 **1 T ECM, MIL: Yes** **Year:** 2011, 2012 **Model:** A3, A4, A5, TT, TTS, Q5, Q7 **Engine:** 2.0L L4, 3.0L V6, 3.2L V6 **Transmission:** All	**ENGINE OIL PRESSURE SENSOR PERFORMANCE:** Engine running. The Engine Oil pressure never reaches the calibrated specification with the engine RPM at 1250. One trip fault.
DTC: P0522 **2 T ECM, MIL: Yes** **Year:** 2011, 2012 **Model:** A3, A4, A5, TT, TTS, Q5, Q7 **Engine:** 2.0L L4, 3.0L V6, 3.2L V6 **Transmission:** All	**OIL PRESSURE SENSOR CIRCUIT LOW:** With the ignition key on and battery voltage above 10.4 Volts. The oil pressure sensor voltage at Powertrain Control Module (PCM) goes below the minimum acceptable value. One Trip Fault. Three good trips to turn off the MIL.
DTC: P0523 **1 T ECM, MIL: Yes** **Year:** 2011, 2012 **Model:** A3, A4, A5, TT, TTS, Q5, Q7 **Engine:** 2.0L L4, 3.0L V6, 3.2L V6 **Transmission:** All	**ENGINE OIL PRESSURE SENSOR CIRCUIT HIGH:** With the ignition on. Battery voltage greater than 10.4 Volts. The Engine Oil pressure signal is greater than the calibrated amount. One Trip Fault.
DTC: P0524 **1 T ECM, MIL: Yes** **Year:** 2011, 2012 **Model:** A3, A4, A5, TT, TTS, Q5, Q7 **Engine:** 2.0L L4, 3.0L V6, 3.2L V6 **Transmission:** All	**ENGINE OIL PRESSURE IS TOO LOW:** With the engine running. The Oil Pressure Sensor indicates low oil pressure for 5 seconds.
DTC: P052A **1 T ECM, MIL: Yes** **Year:** 2011, 2012 **Model:** A3, A4, A5, TT, TTS, Q5, Q7 **Engine:** 2.0L L4, 3.0L V6, 3.2L V6 **Transmission:** All	**Cold Start "A" Camshaft Position Timing Over-Advanced:** * Time after engine start >= 15 Sec. * Engine speed >= 0 RPM * Modeled oil temperature >= -13 °C * Catalyst heating active
DTC: P0532 **1 T ECM, MIL: Yes** **Year:** 2011, 2012 **Model:** A3, A4, A5, TT, TTS, Q5, Q7 **Engine:** 2.0L L4, 3.0L V6, 3.2L V6 **Transmission:** All	**-A/C PRESSURE SENSOR CIRCUIT LOW:** Engine running, AC is learned and AC Clutch Relay energized. The A/C pressure transducer signal voltage received by the PCM from the TIPM is below the minimum acceptable value. One Trip Fault. Three good trips to turn off the MIL.
DTC: P0533 **1 T ECM, MIL: Yes** **Year:** 2011, 2012 **Model:** A3, A4, A5, TT, TTS, Q5, Q7 **Engine:** 2.0L L4, 3.0L V6, 3.2L V6 **Transmission:** All	**A/C PRESSURE SENSOR CIRCUIT HIGH:** Engine running and the A/C Clutch Relay energized. The A/C pressure transducer signal the PCM received from the TIPM is above the maximum acceptable value. One trip Fault. Three good trips to turn off the MIL.

DTC	Trouble Code Title, Conditions, Possible Causes
DTC: P0534 **2 T ECM, MIL: Yes** **Year:** 2011, 2012 **Model:** A3, A4, A5, TT, TTS, Q5, Q7 **Engine:** 2.0L L4, 3.0L V6, 3.2L V6 **Transmission:** All	**Vehicle Speed Sensor "A" Intermittent/Erratic/High:** * Engine speed 1500-4500 RPM
DTC: P053F **2 T ECM, MIL: Yes** **Year:** 2011, 2012 **Model:** A3, A4, A5, TT, TTS, Q5, Q7 **Engine:** 2.0L L4, 3.0L V6, 3.2L V6 **Transmission:** All	**Cold Start Fuel Pressure Performance:** * Time after engine start 3 Sec. * Fuel cutoff not active * Catalyst heating active
DTC: P0544 **2 T ECM, MIL: Yes** **Year:** 2011, 2012 **Model:** A3, A4, A5, TT, TTS, Q5, Q7 **Engine:** 2.0L L4 **Transmission:** All	**Exhaust Gas Temperature Sensor Circuit - Bank 1:** Engine running
DTC: P0545 **2 T ECM, MIL: Yes** **Year:** 2011, 2012 **Model:** A3, A4, A5, TT, TTS, Q5, Q7 **Engine:** 2.0L L4 **Transmission:** All	**Exhaust Gas Temperature Sensor Circuit - Bank 1 Low:** Engine running
DTC: P054A **2 T ECM, MIL: Yes** **Year:** 2011, 2012 **Model:** A3, A4, A5, TT, TTS, Q5, Q7 **Engine:** 2.0L L4, 3.0L V6, 3.2L V6 **Transmission:** All	**CAMSHAFT POSITION TIMING OVER - ADVANCED-BANK1:** Engine cranking and engine running If the Camshaft Position Signal (angular variation) is more than 15° of the Crankshaft Position Signal, this DTC is set.
DTC: P054C **2 T ECM, MIL: Yes** **Year:** 2011, 2012 **Model:** A3, A4, A5, TT, TTS, Q5, Q7 **Engine:** 2.0L L4, 3.0L V6, 3.2L V6 **Transmission:** All	**-CAMSHAFT POSITION TIMING OVER - ADVANCED-BANK 2:** Engine cranking and engine running If the Camshaft Position Signal (angular variation) is more than 15° of the Crankshaft Position Signal, this DTC is set.
DTC: P0562 **1 T ECM, MIL: Yes** **Year:** 2011, 2012 **Model:** A3, A4, A5, TT, TTS, Q5, Q7 **Engine:** 2.0L L4, 3.0L V6, 3.2L V6 **Transmission:** All	**BATTERY VOLTAGE LOW:** With the engine running and the PCM has commanded the TIPM to energize the Transmission Control Output. If the battery voltage of the Transmission Control Output Sense circuit(s) to the PCM is less than 10.0 volts for the period of 15 seconds.
DTC: P0563 **1 T ECM, MIL: Yes** **Year:** 2011, 2012 **Model:** A3, A4, A5, TT, TTS, Q5, Q7 **Engine:** 2.0L L4, 3.0L V6, 3.2L V6 **Transmission:** All	**BATTERY VOLTAGE HIGH:** With the ignition on. Engine RPM greater than 1000 RPM. With no other charging system codes set. Battery voltage is one Volt greater than desired voltage for more than 10 seconds. Battery voltage greater than 15.75 Volts. One Trip Fault. Three good trips to turn off the MIL.

DTC	Trouble Code Title, Conditions, Possible Causes
DTC: P0568 **1 T ECM, MIL: Yes** **Year:** 2011, 2012 **Model:** A3, A4, A5, TT, TTS, Q5, Q7 **Engine:** 2.0L L4, 3.0L V6, 3.2L V6 **Transmission:** All	**Cruise Control Set Signal:** Engine running and vehicle speed above 8 mph.
DTC: P0571 **1 T ECM, MIL: Yes** **Year:** 2011, 2012 **Model:** A3, A4, A5, TT, TTS, Q5, Q7 **Engine:** 2.0L L4, 3.0L V6, 3.2L V6 **Transmission:** All	**-BRAKE SWITCH 1 PERFORMANCE:** With the gear selector in drive, vehicle speed above a minimum value, and battery voltage greater than 10.4 volts. The PCM detects that the actual state of Brake Signal 1 or Brake Signal 2 does not match the desired state during monitoring.
DTC: P0572 **1 T ECM, MIL: Yes** **Year:** 2011, 2012 **Model:** A3, A4, A5, TT, TTS, Q5, Q7 **Engine:** 2.0L L4, 3.0L V6, 3.2L V6 **Transmission:** All	**-BRAKE SWITCH 1 STUCK ON:** With the gear selector in drive, vehicle speed above a minimum value, and battery voltage greater than 10.4 volts. The PCM detects that the actual state of Brake Signal 1 or Brake Signal 2 does not match the desired state during monitoring.
DTC: P0573 **1 T ECM, MIL: Yes** **Year:** 2011, 2012 **Model:** A3, A4, A5, TT, TTS, Q5, Q7 **Engine:** 2.0L L4, 3.0L V6, 3.2L V6 **Transmission:** All	**BRAKE SWITCH STUCK OFF:** With the ignition on. VSS indicates increasing and decreasing vehicle speed. APP Sensor indicates increasing and decreasing acceleration demand. The ECM determines that the brakes have been applied without the receiving an input from the Primary Brake Switch Signal and Secondary Brake Switches.
DTC: P0579 **1 T ECM, MIL: Yes** **Year:** 2011, 2012 **Model:** A3, A4, A5, TT, TTS, Q5, Q7 **Engine:** 2.0L L4, 3.0L V6, 3.2L V6 **Transmission:** All	**SPEED CONTROL SWITCH 1 PERFORMANCE:** With the ignition switch on and no other S/C Switch DTCs present. The S/C Switch Signal 2 voltage is not within a valid switch signal range.
DTC: P0580 **1 T ECM, MIL: Yes** **Year:** 2011, 2012 **Model:** A3, A4, A5, TT, TTS, Q5, Q7 **Engine:** 2.0L L4, 3.0L V6, 3.2L V6 **Transmission:** All	**SPEED CONTROL SWITCH 1 CIRCUIT LOW:** With the ignition on and battery voltage greater than 10.4 Volts. The S/C Signal 1 voltage is below a calibrated threshold for 0.06 second.
DTC: P0581 **1 T ECM, MIL: Yes** **Year:** 2011, 2012 **Model:** A3, A4, A5, TT, TTS, Q5, Q7 **Engine:** 2.0L L4, 3.0L V6, 3.2L V6 **Transmission:** All	**SPEED CONTROL SWITCH 1 CIRCUIT HIGH:** With the ignition on. The S/C Signal 1 is above a calibrated threshold for 0.06 second.
DTC: P0585 **1 T ECM, MIL: Yes** **Year:** 2011, 2012 **Model:** A3, A4, A5, TT, TTS, Q5, Q7 **Engine:** 2.0L L4, 3.0L V6, 3.2L V6 **Transmission:** All	**SPEED CONTROL SWITCH 1/2 CORRELATION:** With the ignition on and no other S/C Switch DTCs present. The S/C Signal 1 and (V72) S/C Signal 2 do not indicate the same S/C Switch position.

DTC	Trouble Code Title, Conditions, Possible Causes
DTC: P0591 **1 T ECM, MIL: Yes** **Year:** 2011, 2012 **Model:** A3, A4, A5, TT, TTS, Q5, Q7 **Engine:** 2.0L L4, 3.0L V6, 3.2L V6 **Transmission:** All	**SPEED CONTROL SWITCH 2 PERFORMANCE:** With the ignition on and battery voltage greater than 10.4 Volts. The Powertrain Control Module (PCM) detects that the Speed Control signal voltage is implausible.
DTC: P0592 **1 T ECM, MIL: Yes** **Year:** 2011, 2012 **Model:** A3, A4, A5, TT, TTS, Q5, Q7 **Engine:** 2.0L L4, 3.0L V6, 3.2L V6 **Transmission:** All	**SPEED CONTROL SWITCH 2 CIRCUIT LOW:** With the ignition on. The S/C Signal 2 voltage is below a calibrated threshold for 0.06 second.
DTC: P0593 **1 T ECM, MIL: Yes** **Year:** 2011, 2012 **Model:** A3, A4, A5, TT, TTS, Q5, Q7 **Engine:** 2.0L L4, 3.0L V6, 3.2L V6 **Transmission:** All	**SPEED CONTROL SWITCH 2 CIRCUIT HIGH:** With the ignition on. The S/C Signal 2 voltage is below a calibrated threshold for 0.06 second.
DTC: P0600 **1 T ECM, MIL: Yes** **Year:** 2011, 2012 **Model:** A3, A4, A5, TT, TTS, Q5, Q7 **Engine:** 2.0L L4, 3.0L V6, 3.2L V6 **Transmission:** All	**Serial Communication Link (Data Bus) Message Missing:** With the ignition on. Internal Bus communication failure between processors. One Trip Fault. Three good trips to clear. * Engine condition-running Battery voltage-> 9 V
DTC: P0601 **1 T ECM, MIL: Yes** **Year:** 2011, 2012 **Model:** A3, A4, A5, TT, TTS, Q5, Q7 **Engine:** 2.0L L4, 3.0L V6, 3.2L V6 **Transmission:** All	**INTERNAL MEMORY CHECKSUM INVALID:** With the ignition on. Internal checksum for software failed, it does not match the calculated value. One Trip Fault, Three Good Trips to clear.
DTC: P0602 **1 T ECM, MIL: Yes** **Year:** 2011, 2012 **Model:** A3, A4, A5, TT, TTS, Q5, Q7 **Engine:** 2.0L L4, 3.0L V6, 3.2L V6 **Transmission:** All	**CONTROL MODULE PROGRAMMING ERROR/NOT PROGRAMMED:** Check for generic software is made at power-up. If generic software is found , the MIL will light immediately. This DTC is designed to signal the technician that the controller still has generic software installed. * Re-programming not completed
DTC: P0604 **2 T ECM, MIL: Yes** **Year:** 2011, 2012 **Model:** A3, A4, A5, TT, TTS, Q5, Q7 **Engine:** 2.0L L4, 3.0L V6, 3.2L V6 **Transmission:** All	**Internal Control Module Random Access Memory (RAM) Error:** Internal logic and checksum control error. Write ability check, failed.
DTC: P0605 **2 T ECM, MIL: Yes** **Year:** 2011, 2012 **Model:** A3, A4, A5, TT, TTS, Q5, Q7 **Engine:** 2.0L L4, 3.0L V6, 3.2L V6 **Transmission:** All	**Internal Control Module Read Only Memory (ROM) Error:** ECM/PCM detected a ROM test error, Wrong check sum.

DTC	Trouble Code Title, Conditions, Possible Causes
DTC: P0606 **2 T ECM, MIL: Yes** **Year:** 2011, 2012 **Model:** A3, A4, A5, TT, TTS, Q5, Q7 **Engine:** 2.0L L4, 3.0L V6, 3.2L V6 **Transmission:** All	**INTERNAL ECM/PCM PROCESSOR:** Engine running. When the ECM/PCM recognizes an internal failure to communicate with the ECM or the CMP and CKP Sensor count periods are too short. One trip fault. ETC light is flashing.
DTC: P0607 **2 T ECM, MIL: Yes** **Year:** 2011, 2012 **Model:** A3, A4, A5, TT, TTS, Q5, Q7 **Engine:** 2.0L L4, 3.0L V6, 3.2L V6 **Transmission:** All	**Control Module Performance:** * With the ignition ON * Fuel quantity-> 0 mg/stroke * Engine condition –running * Battery voltage-> 9 V
DTC: P060B **1 T ECM, MIL: Yes** **Year:** 2011, 2012 **Model:** A3, A4, A5, TT, TTS, Q5, Q7 **Engine:** 2.0L L4, 3.0L V6, 3.2L V6 **Transmission:** All	**ETC A/D GROUND PERFORMANCE:** When the Throttle Motor is powered. When A2D reading does not return to ground within a set period of time of test activation, this fault sets. The test typically runs a couple of times per second, and is the reason why APP2 signal spikes to ground a couple of times per second in normal running. Reprogramming the module may not always fix this fault. One trip fault. ETC lamp is illuminated.
DTC: P060D **1 T ECM, MIL: Yes** **Year:** 2011, 2012 **Model:** A3, A4, A5, TT, TTS, Q5, Q7 **Engine:** 2.0L L4, 3.0L V6, 3.2L V6 **Transmission:** All	**ETC LEVEL 2 APP PERFORMANCE:** Throttle motor is powered and no matured faults related to APP Sensors. When secondary software determines that APPS 1 and APPS 2 signals do not match for a period of time. One trip fault. ETC lamp will flash.
DTC: P060E **1 T ECM, MIL: Yes** **Year:** 2011, 2012 **Model:** A3, A4, A5, TT, TTS, Q5, Q7 **Engine:** 2.0L L4, 3.0L V6, 3.2L V6 **Transmission:** All	**ETC LEVEL 2 TPS PERFORMANCE:** Throttle motor is powered and no matured faults related to TP Sensors. When secondary software determines that TPS 1 and TPS 2 signals do not match for a period of time. One trip fault. ETC lamp will flash.
DTC: P060F **1 T ECM, MIL: Yes** **Year:** 2011, 2012 **Model:** A3, A4, A5, TT, TTS, Q5, Q7 **Engine:** 2.0L L4, 3.0L V6, 3.2L V6 **Transmission:** All	**ETC LEVEL 2 ECT PERFORMANCE:** Throttle motor is powered and no matured faults related to the Engine Coolant Temp Sensor. When secondary software determines that the Coolant Temperature is implausible for a period of time. One trip fault. ETC lamp will flash.
DTC: P0613 **2 T ECM, MIL: Yes** **Year:** 2011, 2012 **Model:** A3, A4, A5, TT, TTS, Q5, Q7 **Engine:** 2.0L L4, 3.0L V6, 3.2L V6 **Transmission:** All	**INTERNAL TRANSMISSION PROCESSOR:** After the ignition switch is turned to the run position and 60 seconds thereafter. The fault conditions occur 3 times in less than 590 milliseconds: * The watchdog line remains high after the watchdog test or the transmission relay coil is energized and remains on after the watchdog delay expires.
DTC: P0614 **2 T ECM, MIL: Yes** **Year:** 2011, 2012 **Model:** A3, A4, A5, TT, TTS, Q5, Q7 **Engine:** 2.0L L4, 3.0L V6, 3.2L V6 **Transmission:** All	**Transmission Control Module (TCM) Incorrect Software Version:** CAN communication valid. Replacement control module ID doesn't match old control module ID.

DTC	Trouble Code Title, Conditions, Possible Causes
DTC: P061A **1 T ECM, MIL: Yes** **Year:** 2011, 2012 **Model:** A3, A4, A5, TT, TTS, Q5, Q7 **Engine:** 2.0L L4, 3.0L V6, 3.2L V6 **Transmission:** All	**ETC LEVEL 2 TORQUE PERFORMANCE:** Throttle motor is powered. When secondary software determines that the customer requested output is not being achieved by the engine for a period of time. One trip fault. ETC lamp will flash.
DTC: P061C **1 T ECM, MIL: Yes** **Year:** 2011, 2012 **Model:** A3, A4, A5, TT, TTS, Q5, Q7 **Engine:** 2.0L L4, 3.0L V6, 3.2L V6 **Transmission:** All	**ETC LEVEL 2 RPM PERFORMANCE:** Throttle motor is powered and no camshaft or crankshaft electrical signal related DTCs are set. When secondary software determines that the engine speed is implausible for a period of time. One trip fault. ETC lamp will flash.
DTC: P0622 **1 T ECM, MIL: Yes** **Year:** 2011, 2012 **Model:** A3, A4, A5, TT, TTS, Q5, Q7 **Engine:** 2.0L L4, 3.0L V6, 3.2L V6 **Transmission:** All	**GENERATOR FIELD CONTROL CIRCUIT:** With the ignition on and the engine running. The Powertrain Control Module (PCM) tries to regulate the generator field with no result during monitoring. One Trip Fault. Three good trips to turn off the MIL.
DTC: P0627 **1 T ECM, MIL: Yes** **Year:** 2011, 2012 **Model:** A3, A4, A5, TT, TTS, Q5, Q7 **Engine:** 2.0L L4, 3.0L V6, 3.2L V6 **Transmission:** All	**FUEL PUMP RELAY CIRCUIT:** With the engine running and the battery voltage greater than 10.4 Volts. The Powertrain Control Module (PCM) detects that the actual state of the fuel pump control does not match the intended state.
DTC: P0629 **1 T ECM, MIL: Yes** **Year:** 2011, 2012 **Model:** A3, A4, A5, TT, TTS, Q5, Q7 **Engine:** 2.0L L4, 3.0L V6, 3.2L V6 **Transmission:** All	**Fuel Pump "A" Control Circuit High:** * Pump relay, Commanded on * Engine speed, >80 RPM * Faulty activation of Fuel Pump (FP) Relay
DTC: P062B **2T ECM, MIL: Yes** **Year:** 2011, 2012 **Model:** A3, A4, A5, TT, TTS, Q5, Q7Q7 **Engine:** 2.0L L4, 3.0L V6, **Transmission:** All	**Injector Valves Communication CPU:** Engine speed, >80 RPM
DTC: P062C **1 T ECM, MIL: Yes** **Year:** 2011, 2012 **Model:** A3, A4, A5, TT, TTS, Q5, Q7 **Engine:** 2.0L L4, 3.0L V6, 3.2L V6 **Transmission:** All	**ETC LEVEL 2 MPH PERFORMANCE:** Throttle motor is powered and no vehicle speed related DTCs have matured. When secondary software determines that the vehicle speed is implausible for a period of time. One trip fault. ETC lamp will flash.
DTC: P0630 **1 T ECM, MIL: Yes** **Year:** 2011, 2012 **Model:** A3, A4, A5, TT, TTS, Q5, Q7 **Engine:** 2.0L L4, 3.0L V6, 3.2L V6 **Transmission:** All	**VIN NOT PROGRAMMED IN PCM:** At initialization. The VIN has not been programmed into the PCM. One Trip Fault. Three good trips to turn off the MIL.

DTC	Trouble Code Title, Conditions, Possible Causes
DTC: P0632 **1 T ECM, MIL: Yes** **Year:** 2011, 2012 **Model:** A3, A4, A5, TT, TTS, Q5, Q7 **Engine:** 2.0L L4, 3.2L V6 **Transmission:** All	**ODOMETER NOT PROGRAMMED IN PCM:** Ignition on. The Odometer is not programmed into the Powertrain Control Module (PCM). One Trip Fault. Three good trips to turn off the MIL.
DTC: P0632 **2 T ECM, MIL: Yes** **Year:** 2011, 2012 **Model:** Q7 **Engine:** 3.0L TDI V6 **Transmission:** All	**ECM/PCM Injection Valves Communication:** Engine running. The ECM/PCM recognizes a communication failure with the injection valve circuit.
DTC: P0633 **2 T ECM, MIL: Yes** **Year:** 2011, 2012 **Model:** A3, A4, A5, TT, TTS, Q5, Q7 **Engine:** 2.0L L4, 3.0L V6, 3.2L V6 **Transmission:** All	**SKIM SECRET KEY NOT STORED IN PCM:** Ignition on. The Secret Key information has not been programmed into the Powertrain Control Module (PCM). One Trip Fault. Three good trips to turn off the MIL.
DTC: P0634 **2 T ECM, MIL: Yes** **Year:** 2011, 2012 **Model:** A3, A4, A5, TT, TTS, Q5, Q7 **Engine:** 2.0L L4, 3.0L V6, 3.2L V6 **Transmission:** All	**ECM Internal Temperature Too High:** Output driver On state OR not applicable.
DTC: P0638 **2 T ECM, MIL: Yes** **Year:** 2011, 2012 **Model:** A3, A4, A5, TT, TTS, Q5, Q7 **Engine:** 2.0L L4, 3.0L V6, 3.2L V6 **Transmission:** All	**Throttle Actuator Control Range/Performance - Bank 1:** * Ignition on * Engine speed 0 RPM * ECT > -20.3 to 114.8 °C * IAT > -20.3 to 143.3 °C * Vehicle speed 0 km/h * Engine shutoff time 5 Sec. * Number of checks = 2
DTC: P063A **1 T ECM, MIL: Yes** **Year:** 2011, 2012 **Model:** A3, A4, A5, TT, TTS, Q5, Q7 **Engine:** 2.0L L4, 3.0L V6, 3.2L V6 **Transmission:** All	**GENERATOR VOLTAGE SENSE CIRCUIT:** With the engine running and the speed greater than 1157 RPM. The Powertrain Control Module (PCM) recognizes the alternator output voltage is less than the Battery feed circuit voltage. One trip failure. The Generator light will illuminate. The fault will be checked again on the next key cycle.
DTC: P0641 **1 T ECM, MIL: Yes** **Year:** 2011, 2012 **Model:** A3, A4, A5, TT, TTS, Q5, Q7 **Engine:** 2.0L L4, 3.0L V6, 3.2L V6 **Transmission:** All	**Sensor Reference Voltage A Circuit/Open:** Threshold values depending on internal 5 V rev voltage. Internal communication failed.
DTC: P0642 **1 T ECM, MIL: Yes** **Year:** 2011, 2012 **Model:** A3, A4, A5, TT, TTS, Q5, Q7 **Engine:** 2.0L L4, 3.0L V6, 3.2L V6 **Transmission:** All	**SENSOR REFERENCE VOLTAGE 1 CIRCUIT LOW:** With the ignition on. The ECM detects low voltage on the Sensor Supply 1 circuit for 0.10 seconds.

DTC	Trouble Code Title, Conditions, Possible Causes
DTC: P0643 **1 T ECM, MIL: Yes** **Year:** 2011, 2012 **Model:** A3, A4, A5, TT, TTS, Q5, Q7 **Engine:** 2.0L L4, 3.0L V6, 3.2L V6 **Transmission:** All	**SENSOR REFERENCE VOLTAGE 1 CIRCUIT HIGH:** Ignition on, the Powertrain Control Module (PCM) recognizes the Primary 5-Volt Supply circuit voltage is too high. One Trip Fault. ETC light is flashing.
DTC: P0645 **1 T ECM, MIL: Yes** **Year:** 2011, 2012 **Model:** A3, A4, A5, TT, TTS, Q5, Q7 **Engine:** 2.0L L4, 3.0L V6, 3.2L V6 **Transmission:** All	**A/C CLUTCH RELAY CIRCUIT:** With the ignition on. And the battery voltage greater than 10 Volts. The A/C is being requested. An open or shorted condition is detected in the A/C Clutch Relay control circuit. One Trip Fault. Three good trips to turn off the MIL.
DTC: P064C **2T ECM, MIL: Yes** **Year:** 2011, 2012 **Model:** A3, Q7 **Engine:** 2.0L TDI L4, 3.0L TDI V6 **Transmission:** All	**Glow Plug Control Module:** Glow system = Active
DTC: P0651 **1 T ECM, MIL: Yes** **Year:** 2011, 2012 **Model:** A3, A4, A5, TT, TTS, Q5, Q7 **Engine:** 2.0L L4, 3.0L V6, 3.2L V6 **Transmission:** All	**Sensor Reference Voltage B Circuit/Open:** Internal communication failed. Faulty reference signal.
DTC: P0652 **1 T ECM, MIL: Yes** **Year:** 2011, 2012 **Model:** A3, A4, A5, TT, TTS, Q5, Q7 **Engine:** 2.0L L4, 3.0L V6, 3.2L V6 **Transmission:** All	**SENSOR REFERENCE VOLTAGE 2 CIRCUIT LOW:** Ignition on. When the Powertrain Control Module (PCM) recognizes the (K856) 5-Volt Supply circuit voltage is too low. One Trip Fault. ETC light is flashing.
DTC: P0653 **1 T ECM, MIL: Yes** **Year:** 2011, 2012 **Model:** A3, A4, A5, TT, TTS, Q5, Q7 **Engine:** 2.0L L4, 3.0L V6, 3.2L V6 **Transmission:** All	**SENSOR REFERENCE VOLTAGE 2 CIRCUIT HIGH:** Ignition on. When the Powertrain Control Module (PCM) recognizes the Auxiliary 5-Volt Supply circuit voltage is too high. One Trip Fault. ETC light is flashing.
DTC: P0657 **2 T ECM, MIL: Yes** **Year:** 2011, 2012 **Model:** A3, A4, A5, TT, TTS, Q5, Q7 **Engine:** 2.0L L4, 3.0L V6, 3.2L V6 **Transmission:** All	**Actuator Supply Voltage A Circuit / Open:** * Relay, commanded off * Engine speed, > 80 RPM * Battery voltage test counter, 9.04-16 V>3
DTC: P0658 **2 T ECM, MIL: Yes** **Year:** 2011, 2012 **Model:** A3, A4, A5, TT, TTS, Q5, Q7 **Engine:** 2.0L L4, 3.0L V6, 3.2L V6 **Transmission:** All	**Actuator Supply Voltage A Circuit Low:** * Relay, commanded off (Key on engine off) * Engine speed, < 80 RPM * Battery voltage test counter, 9.04-16 V>3

DTC	Trouble Code Title, Conditions, Possible Causes
DTC: P0659 **2 T ECM, MIL: Yes** **Year:** 2011, 2012 **Model:** A3, A4, A5, TT, TTS, Q5, Q7 **Engine:** 2.0L L4, 3.0L V6, 3.2L V6 **Transmission:** All	**Actuator Supply Voltage "A" Circuit High:** * Relay, commanded off * Engine speed, < 80 RPM * Battery voltage test counter, 9.04-16 V>3
DTC: P065A **1 T ECM, MIL: Yes** **Year:** 2011, 2012 **Model:** A3, A4, A5, TT, TTS, Q5, Q7 **Engine:** 2.0L L4, 3.0L V6, 3.2L V6 **Transmission:** All	**GENERATOR PERFORMANCE:** With the engine running. The ECM detects that the Generator output is not within specifications.
DTC: P066A **2 T ECM, MIL: Yes** **Year:** 2011, 2012 **Model:** A3, Q7 **Engine:** 2.0L TDI, L4, 3.0L TDI V6 **Transmission:** All	**CYLINDER 1 GLOW PLUG CIRCUIT LOW:** With the ignition on and the Glow Plug Module Glow Plug command on. The ECM detects an open or short to ground on the Cylinder 1 Glow Plug circuit for 0.5 second.
DTC: P066C **2 T ECM, MIL: Yes** **Year:** 2011, 2012 **Model:** A3, Q7 **Engine:** 2.0L TDI, L4, 3.0L TDI V6 **Transmission:** All	**CYLINDER 2 GLOW PLUG CIRCUIT LOW:** With the ignition on and the Glow Plug Module Glow Plug command on. The ECM detects an open or short to ground on the Cylinder 2 Glow Plug circuit for 0.5 second.
DTC: P066E **2 T ECM, MIL: Yes** **Year:** 2011, 2012 **Model:** A3, Q7 **Engine:** 2.0L TDI, L4, 3.0L TDI V6 **Transmission:** All	**CYLINDER 3 GLOW PLUG CIRCUIT LOW:** With the ignition on and the Glow Plug Module Glow Plug command off. The ECM detects an open or short to ground on the Cylinder 3 Glow Plug circuit.
DTC: P0670 **2 T ECM, MIL: Yes** **Year:** 2011, 2012 **Model:** A3, Q7 **Engine:** 2.0L TDI, L4, 3.0L TDI V6 **Transmission:** All	**Glow Plug Module 1 Control Circuit electrical malfunction electrical circuit:** Open or short in glow plug control circuit * Glow system = not active * Glow system = active
DTC: P0671 **2 T ECM, MIL: Yes** **Year:** 2011, 2012 **Model:** A3, Q7 **Engine:** 2.0L TDI, L4, 3.0L TDI V6 **Transmission:** All	**Cylinder 1 Glow Plug Circuit:** Key on, and the ECM detected an unexpected voltage condition on the Glow Plug Lamp circuit during the CCM test. The Glow Plug Lamp remains "on" for 1-12 seconds (depending on the Glow Plug relay on-time which can vary from 1 and 120 seconds).
DTC: P0672 **2 T ECM, MIL: Yes** **Year:** 2011, 2012 **Model:** A3, Q7 **Engine:** 2.0L TDI, L4, 3.0L TDI V6 **Transmission:** All	**-CYLINDER 2 GLOW PLUG CIRCUIT:** With the ignition on and the Glow Plug Module Glow Plug command on. The ECM detects an open or short on the Cylinder 2 Glow Plug circuit for 0.5 second.
DTC: P0673 **2 T ECM, MIL: Yes** **Year:** 2011, 2012 **Model:** A3, Q7 **Engine:** 2.0L TDI, L4, 3.0L TDI V6 **Transmission:** All	**-CYLINDER 3 GLOW PLUG CIRCUIT:** With the ignition on and the Glow Plug Module Glow Plug command off. The ECM detects an open or shorted on the Cylinder 3 Glow Plug circuit.

DTC	Trouble Code Title, Conditions, Possible Causes
DTC: P0674 **2 T ECM, MIL: Yes** **Year:** 2011, 2012 **Model:** A3, Q7 **Engine:** 2.0L TDI, L4, 3.0L TDI V6 **Transmission:** All	**CYLINDER 4 GLOW PLUG CIRCUIT:** With the ignition on and the Glow Plug Module Glow Plug command on. The ECM detects an open or short on the Cylinder 4 Glow Plug circuit for 0.5 seconds.
DTC: P0675 **2 T ECM, MIL: Yes** **Year:** 2011, 2012 **Model:** Q7 **Engine:** 3.0L TDI V6 **Transmission:** All	**Cylinder 5 Glow Plug Circuit:** With the ignition on and the Glow Plug Module Glow Plug command on. The ECM detects an open or short on the Cylinder 5 Glow Plug circuit for 0.5 seconds.
DTC: P0676 **2 T ECM, MIL: Yes** **Year:** 2011, 2012 **Model:** Q7 **Engine:** 3.0L TDI V6 **Transmission:** All	**Cylinder 6 Glow Plug Circuit:** With the ignition on and the Glow Plug Module Glow Plug command on. The ECM detects an open or short on the Cylinder 6 Glow Plug circuit for 0.5 seconds.
DTC: P067A **2 T ECM, MIL: Yes** **Year:** 2011, 2012 **Model:** A3, Q7 **Engine:** 2.0L TDI, L4, 3.0L TDI V6 **Transmission:** All	**Cylinder 4 Glow Plug Control Circuit Low:** With the ignition on and the Glow Plug Module Glow Plug command on. The ECM detects an open or short on the Cylinder 4 Glow Plug circuit for 0.5 seconds.
DTC: P067C **2 T ECM, MIL: Yes** **Year:** 2011, 2012 **Model:** Q7 **Engine:** 3.0L TDI V6 **Transmission:** All	**Cylinder 5 Glow Plug Control Circuit Low:** With the ignition on and the Glow Plug Module Glow Plug command on. The ECM detects an open or short on the Cylinder 5 Glow Plug circuit for 0.5 seconds.
DTC: P067E **2 T ECM, MIL: Yes** **Year:** 2011, 2012 **Model:** Q7 **Engine:** 3.0L TDI V6 **Transmission:** All	**Cylinder 6 Glow Plug Control Circuit Low:** With the ignition on and the Glow Plug Module Glow Plug command on. The ECM detects an open or short on the Cylinder 6 Glow Plug circuit for 0.5 seconds.
DTC: P0684 **2T PCM, MIL: Yes** **Year:** 2011, 2012 **Model:** A3, Q7 **Engine:** 2.0L L4 **Transmission:** All	**Glow Plug Control Module to PCM Communication Circuit Range/Performance:** With the ignition on and the Glow Plug Module Glow Plug command on. The ECM detects an open or short in the Glow Plug circuit for 0.5 seconds.
DTC: P0685 **1 T ECM, MIL: Yes** **Year:** 2011, 2012 **Model:** A3, A4, A5, TT, TTS, Q5, Q7 **Engine:** 2.0L L4, 3.0L V6, 3.2L V6 **Transmission:** All	**AUTO SHUTDOWN RELAY CONTROL CIRCUIT OPEN:** With ignition on. Battery voltage above 10.0 Volts. The actual ASD state is not equal to the desired ASD state. One Trip Fault. Three good trips to turn off the MIL.
DTC: P0686 **1 T ECM, MIL: Yes** **Year:** 2011, 2012 **Model:** A3, A4, A5, TT, TTS, Q5, Q7 **Engine:** 2.0L L4, 3.0L V6, 3.2L V6 **Transmission:** All	**ECM/PCM Power Relay Control Circuit Low:** With ignition on. Battery voltage above 10.0 Volts. The power relay state is not equal to the desired state. One Trip Fault. Three good trips to turn off the MIL.

DTC	Trouble Code Title, Conditions, Possible Causes
DTC: P0687 **1 T ECM, MIL: Yes** **Year:** 2011, 2012 **Model:** A3, A4, A5, TT, TTS, Q5, Q7 **Engine:** 2.0L L4, 3.0L V6, 3.2L V6 **Transmission:** All	**ECM/PCM Power Relay Control Circuit High:** With ignition on. Battery voltage above 10.0 Volts. The power relay state is not equal to the desired state. One Trip Fault. Three good trips to turn off the MIL. * Main relay, Commanded on * ECM keep alive time
DTC: P0688 **1 T ECM, MIL: Yes** **Year:** 2011, 2012 **Model:** A3, A4, A5, TT, TTS, Q5, Q7 **Engine:** 2.0L L4, 3.0L V6, 3.2L V6 **Transmission:** All	**ECM Power Relay Sense Circuit Open:** With ignition on. Battery voltage above 10.0 Volts. The power relay state is not equal to the desired state. One Trip Fault. Three good trips to turn off the MIL. * Main relay, Commanded on * Engine speed > 80 RPM
DTC: P068A **1 T ECM, MIL: Yes** **Year:** 2011, 2012 **Model:** A3, A4, A5, TT, TTS, Q5, Q7 **Engine:** 2.0L L4, 3.0L V6, 3.2L V6 **Transmission:** All	**ECM/PCM RELAY OFF TOO EARLY:** When the ignition is turned off, during after-run mode of operation. The internal ECM/PCM timer determines that the ASD Relay has shut off before the AFTER-RUN mode of operation has been completed.
DTC: P068B **1 T ECM, MIL: Yes** **Year:** 2011, 2012 **Model:** A3, A4, A5, TT, TTS, Q5, Q7 **Engine:** 2.0L L4, 3.0L V6, 3.2L V6 **Transmission:** All	**ECM/PCM RELAY OFF TOO LATE:** When the ignition is turned off, during AFTER-RUN mode of operation. The internal ECM timer determines that the ASD Relay remained on for 2.0 seconds once AFTER-RUN mode of operation has been completed.
DTC: P0691 **1 T ECM, MIL: Yes** **Year:** 2011, 2012 **Model:** A3, A4, A5, TT, TTS, Q5, Q7 **Engine:** 2.0L L4, 3.0L V6, 3.2L V6 **Transmission:** All	**COOLING FAN 1 CIRCUIT LOW:** With the engine running, battery voltage is greater than 10.4 volts, and the Cooling Fan 1 control is active. The Totally Integrated Power Module (TIPM) detects an open or shorted condition in the Cooling Fan 1 control circuit.
DTC: P0692 **1 T ECM, MIL: Yes** **Year:** 2011, 2012 **Model:** A3, A4, A5, TT, TTS, Q5, Q7 **Engine:** 2.0L L4, 3.0L V6, 3.2L V6 **Transmission:** All	**COOLING FAN 1 CIRCUIT HIGH:** With the engine running, battery voltage greater than 10.4 volts, and the Cooling Fan 1 control active. The Totally Integrated Power Module (TIPM) detects an open or shorted condition in the Cooling Fan 1 control circuit.
DTC: P0693 **1 T ECM, MIL: Yes** **Year:** 2011, 2012 **Model:** A3, A4, A5, TT, TTS, Q5, Q7 **Engine:** 2.0L L4, 3.0L V6, 3.2L V6 **Transmission:** All	**-COOLING FAN 2 CIRCUIT LOW - GAS:** With the engine running, battery voltage greater than 10.4 volts, and the Cooling Fan 2 control is active. The Totally Integrated Power Module (TIPM) detects an open or shorted condition in the Cooling Fan 2 control circuit.
DTC: P0694 **1 T ECM, MIL: Yes** **Year:** 2011, 2012 **Model:** A3, A4, A5, TT, TTS, Q5, Q7 **Engine:** 2.0L L4, 3.0L V6, 3.2L V6 **Transmission:** All	**COOLING FAN 2 CIRCUIT HIGH:** With the engine running, battery voltage greater than 10.4 volts, and the Cooling Fan 2 control is active. The Totally Integrated Power Module (TIPM) detects an open or shorted condition in the Cooling Fan 2 control circuit.

DTC	Trouble Code Title, Conditions, Possible Causes
DTC: P0697 **2 T ECM, MIL: Yes** **Year:** 2011, 2012 **Model:** A3, A4, A5, TT, TTS, Q5, Q7 **Engine:** 2.0L L4, 3.0L V6, 3.2L V6 **Transmission:** All	**Sensor Reference Voltage C Circuit Open:** With the ignition on. The ECM detects a low voltage on the sensor circuit for 0.10 seconds * Threshold values dep. on internal 5 V rev voltage.
DTC: P0698 **2 T ECM, MIL: Yes** **Year:** 2011, 2012 **Model:** A3, A4, A5, TT, TTS, Q5, Q7 **Engine:** 2.0L L4, 3.0L V6, 3.2L V6 **Transmission:** All	**SENSOR REFERENCE VOLTAGE 3 CIRCUIT LOW:** With the ignition on. The ECM detects a low voltage on the Sensor Supply 3 circuit for 0.10 seconds
DTC: P0699 **2 T ECM, MIL: Yes** **Year:** 2011, 2012 **Model:** A3, A4, A5, TT, TTS, Q5, Q7 **Engine:** 2.0L L4, 3.0L V6, 3.2L V6 **Transmission:** All	**SENSOR REFERENCE VOLTAGE 3 TOO HIGH:** With the ignition on. The ECM detects a short to voltage on the Sensor Supply 3 circuit for 0.10 seconds.
DTC: P06A3 **2 T ECM, MIL: Yes** **Year:** 2011, 2012 **Model:** A3, Q7 **Engine:** 2.0L L4 **Transmission:** All	**Sensor Reference Voltage "D" Circuit/Open:** With the ignition on. The ECM detects an Open condition on the sensor voltage D circuit.
DTC: P06B9 **2 T ECM, MIL: Yes** **Year:** 2011, 2012 **Model:** A3, Q7 **Engine:** 2.0L TDI, L4, 3.0L TDI V6 **Transmission:** All	**Cylinder 1 Glow Plug Circuit Range/Performance:** The ECM/PCM has detected an open or short in the glow plug control circuit. * Glow system active * Demand signal 8 - 95%
DTC: P06BA **2 T ECM, MIL: Yes** **Year:** 2011, 2012 **Model:** A3, Q7 **Engine:** 2.0L TDI, L4, 3.0L TDI V6 **Transmission:** All	**Cylinder 2 Glow Plug Circuit Range/Performance:** The ECM/PCM has detected an open or short in the glow plug control circuit. * Glow system active * Demand signal 8 - 95%
DTC: P06BB **2 T ECM, MIL: Yes** **Year:** 2011, 2012 **Model:** A3, Q7 **Engine:** 2.0L TDI, L4, 3.0L TDI V6 **Transmission:** All	**Cylinder 3 Glow Plug Circuit Range/Performance:** The ECM/PCM has detected an open or short in the glow plug control circuit. * Glow system active * Demand signal 8 - 95%
DTC: P06BC **2 T ECM, MIL: Yes** **Year:** 2011, 2012 **Model:** A3, Q7 **Engine:** 2.0L TDI, L4, 3.0L TDI V6 **Transmission:** All	**Cylinder 4 Glow Plug Circuit Range/Performance:** The ECM/PCM has detected an open or short in the glow plug control circuit. * Glow system active * Demand signal 8 - 95%
DTC: P06BD **2 T ECM, MIL: Yes** **Year:** 2011, 2012 **Model:** Q7 **Engine:** 3.0L TDI V6 **Transmission:** All	**Cylinder 5 Glow Plug Circuit Range/Performance:** The ECM/PCM has detected an open or short in the glow plug control circuit. * Glow system active * Demand signal 8 - 95%

DTC	Trouble Code Title, Conditions, Possible Causes
DTC: P06BE **2 T ECM, MIL: Yes** **Year:** 2011, 2012 **Model:** Q7 **Engine:** 3.0L TDI V6 **Transmission:** All	**Cylinder 6 Glow Plug Circuit Range/Performance:** The ECM/PCM has detected an open or short in the glow plug control circuit. * Glow system active * Demand signal 8 - 95%
DTC: P06C5 **2T ECM, MIL: Yes** **Year:** 2011, 2012 **Model:** A3, Q7 **Engine:** 2.0L TDI L4 **Transmission:** All	**Cylinder 1 Glow Plug Incorrect:** * Glow System = active * ECT < 18 * ECU off time > or = to 900 Sec. * Demand signal = 95%
DTC: P06C6 **2T ECM, MIL: Yes** **Year:** 2011, 2012 **Model:** A3, Q7 **Engine:** 2.0L TDI L4 **Transmission:** All	**Cylinder 2 Glow Plug Incorrect:** * Glow System = active * ECT < 18 * ECU off time > or = to 900 Sec. * Demand signal = 95%
DTC: P06C7 **2T ECM, MIL: Yes** **Year:** 2011, 2012 **Model:** A3, Q7 **Engine:** 2.0L TDI L4 **Transmission:** All	**Cylinder 3 Glow Plug Incorrect:** * Glow System = active * ECT < 18 * ECU off time > or = to 900 Sec. * Demand signal = 95%
DTC: P06C8 **2T ECM, MIL: Yes** **Year:** 2011, 2012 **Model:** A3, Q7 **Engine:** 2.0L TDI L4 **Transmission:** All	**Cylinder 4 Glow Plug Incorrect:** * Glow System = active * ECT < 18 * ECU off time > or = to 900 Sec. * Demand signal = 95%
DTC: P06DA **1T ECM, MIL: Yes** **Year:** 2011, 2012 **Model:** TTS **Engine:** 3.2L V6 **Transmission:** All	**DUAL STAGE OIL PUMP CIRCUIT:** With the battery voltage is between 11 and 18 Volts with the engine running. The Powertrain Control Module (PCM) detects that the actual voltage of the oil pump solenoid control circuit does not match the intended state. One Trip Fault. Three good trips to turn off the MIL.
DTC: P06DD **1T ECM, MIL: Yes** **Year:** 2011, 2012 **Model:** TTS **Engine:** 3.2L V6 **Transmission:** All	**-DUAL STAGE OIL PUMP STUCK LOW:** Based upon the engine oil temperature, the monitor runs when engine speed (RPM) is over a calibrated value. The cooler the engine oil, the lower is the enable engine speed (Minimum 1000rpm). To evaluate the dual stage oil pump, fully warm up the engine. To run DUAL STAGE OIL PUMP STUCK LOW (P06DD), drive vehicle with engine speed over 3500 rpm. The Powertrain Control Module (PCM) senses the oil pressure is less than a low Threshold for five (5) seconds. One Trip fault.
DTC: P06DE **1T ECM, MIL: Yes** **Year:** 2011, 2012 **Model:** TTS **Engine:** 3.2L V6 **Transmission:** All	**DUAL STAGE OIL PUMP STUCK HIGH:** Based upon Engine oil temperature, the monitor runs when engine speed (RPM) is over a calibrated value. The cooler the engine oil, the lower is the enable engine speed (Minimum 1000rpm). To evaluate dual stage oil pump, fully warm up the engine. To run DUAL STAGE OIL PUMP STUCK HIGH (P06DE), drive vehicle over 2500 rpm. The Powertrain Control Module (PCM) senses the oil pressure is more than a high threshold for (50) seconds . One Trip fault.
DTC: P0700 **2T ECM, MIL: Yes** **Year:** 2011, 2012 **Model:** A3, A4, A5, TT, TTS, Q5, Q7 **Engine:** 2.0L L4 **Transmission:** All	**Transmission Control System (MIL Request):** With the battery voltage is between 11 and 18 Volts with the engine running. The ECM/PCM detects a malfunction

DTC	Trouble Code Title, Conditions, Possible Causes
DTC: P0701 **2T ECM, MIL: Yes** **Year:** 2011, 2012 **Model:** A3, A4, A5, TT, TTS, Q5, Q7 **Engine:** 2.0L L4 **Transmission:** All	**Transmission control system range/performance:** The TCM has detected a concern with the operational strategy.
DTC: P0702 **2T ECM, MIL: Yes** **Year:** 2011, 2012 **Model:** A3, A4, A5, TT, TTS, Q5, Q7 **Engine:** 2.0L L4 **Transmission:** All	**Transmission control system electrical:** The TCM has detected a concern with the operational strategy. *Battery voltage > 9 V for more than 500 ms
DTC: P0703 **1 T ECM, MIL: Yes** **Year:** 2011, 2012 **Model:** A3, A4, A5, TT, TTS, Q5, Q7 **Engine:** 2.0L L4, 3.0L V6, 3.2L V6 **Transmission:** All	**BRAKE SWITCH 2 PERFORMANCE:** With the gear selector in drive, vehicle speed above a minimum value, and battery voltage greater than 10.4 volts. The PCM detects that the actual state of Brake Signal 1 or Brake Signal 2 does not match the desired state during monitoring.
DTC: P0705 **1 T ECM, MIL: Yes** **Year:** 2011, 2012 **Model:** A3, A4, A5, TT, TTS, Q5, Q7 **Engine:** 2.0L L4, 3.0L V6, 3.2L V6 **Transmission:** All	**Transmission Range Sensor Circuit Malfunction (PRNDL Input):** The DTC will set if an invalid PRNDL code exists for more than 100 milliseconds within one second of power-up
DTC: P0706 **1 T ECM, MIL: Yes** **Year:** 2011, 2012 **Model:** A3, A4, A5, TT, TTS, Q5, Q7 **Engine:** 2.0L L4, 3.0L V6, 3.2L V6 **Transmission:** All	**TRANSMISSION RANGE SENSOR RATIONALITY:** The DTC will set if an invalid PRNDL code exists for more than 100 milliseconds within one second of power-up or if the PRNDL code error does not correct itself when (or before) the shift lever is moved to a different position (P, R, N, or OD), or if the PCM sees the PRNDL code rapidly (within 7 ms) jump across more than three shift lever detent positions.
DTC: P0711 **1 T ECM, MIL: Yes** **Year:** 2011, 2012 **Model:** A3, A4, A5, TT, TTS, Q5, Q7 **Engine:** 2.0L L4, 3.0L V6, 3.2L V6 **Transmission:** All	**TRANSMISSION TEMPERATURE SENSOR PERFORMANCE:** This DTC will set when the transmission temperature does not reach a normal operating temperature within a given time frame. Time is variable due to ambient temperature. Approximate DTC set time is 10 to 35 minutes. The following are starting temperature to warm up times to set this DTC: starting temperature -40° C (-40° F) warm up time 35 minutes, starting temperature -28° C (-20° F) 25 minutes, starting temperature -6.6° C (20° F) 20 minutes, starting temperature 15.5 ° C (60° F) 10 minutes. When the fault is set, calculated temperature is substituted for measured temperature, however the DTC is stored only after three consecutive occurrences.
DTC: P0712 **1 T ECM, MIL: Yes** **Year:** 2011, 2012 **Model:** A3, A4, A5, TT, TTS, Q5, Q7 **Engine:** 2.0L L4, 3.0L V6, 3.2L V6 **Transmission:** All	**TRANSMISSION TEMPERATURE SENSOR LOW:** Continuously with the ignition on and engine running. The DTC will set when the monitored Temperature Sensor voltage drops below 0.078 of a volt for the period of 1.45 seconds. When the fault is set, calculated temperature is substituted for measured temperature, however the fault code is stored only after three consecutive occurrences of the fault.
DTC: P0713 **1 T ECM, MIL: Yes** **Year:** 2011, 2012 **Model:** A3, A4, A5, TT, TTS, Q5, Q7 **Engine:** 2.0L L4, 3.0L V6, 3.2L V6 **Transmission:** All	**TRANSMISSION TEMPERATURE SENSOR HIGH:** Continuously with the ignition on and engine running. The DTC will set when the monitored Temperature voltage rises above 4.94 volts for the period of 1.45 seconds. When the fault is set, calculated temperature is substituted for measured temperature, however the fault code is stored only after three consecutive occurrences of the fault.

DTC	Trouble Code Title, Conditions, Possible Causes
DTC: P0714 **1 T ECM, MIL: Yes** **Year:** 2011, 2012 **Model:** A3, A4, A5, TT, TTS, Q5, Q7 **Engine:** 2.0L L4, 3.0L V6, 3.2L V6 **Transmission:** All	**TRANSMISSION TEMPERATURE SENSOR INTERMITTENT:** Continuously with the ignition on and engine running. The DTC will set when the monitored Temperature Sensor voltage fluctuates or changes abruptly within a predetermined period of time.
DTC: P0715 **2T TCM** **Year:** 2011, 2012 **Model:** A3, A4, A5, TT, TTS, Q5, Q7 **Engine:** 2.0L L4, 3.0L V6, 3.2L V6 **Transmission:** All	**Input/Turbine Speed Sensor "A" Circuit:** Input sensor, No failure decision for input sensor no pulse failure.
DTC: P0716 **1 T ECM, MIL: Yes** **Year:** 2011, 2012 **Model:** A3, A4, A5, TT, TTS, Q5, Q7 **Engine:** 2.0L L4, 3.0L V6, 3.2L V6 **Transmission:** All	**Input Turbine/Speed Sensor (A) Circuit Range/Performance:** The transmission gear ratio is monitored continuously while the transmission is in gear. If there is an excessive change in the Input RPM in any valid gears this DTC will set.
DTC: P0720 **2 T ECM, MIL: Yes** **Model:** A3, A4, A5, TT, TTS, Q5, Q7 **Engine:** 2.0L L4, 3.0L V6, 3.2L V6 **Transmission:** All	**Output Speed Sensor Circuit:** Output sensor, No failure decision for output sensor no pulse.
DTC: P0721 **2 T ECM, MIL: Yes** **Model:** A3, A4, A5, TT, TTS, Q5, Q7 **Engine:** 2.0L L4, 3.0L V6, 3.2L V6 **Transmission:** All	**Output Speed Sensor Circuit Range/Performance:** The transmission gear ratio is monitored continuously while the transmission is in gear. If there is an excessive change in the Output rpm in any gear.
DTC: P0722 **2 T ECM, MIL: Yes** **Model:** A3, A4, A5, TT, TTS, Q5, Q7 **Engine:** 2.0L L4, 3.0L V6, 3.2L V6 **Transmission:** All	**Output Speed Sensor Circuit No Signal:** The transmission gear ratio is monitored continuously while the transmission is in gear. If there is an excessive change in the Output rpm in any gear. Comparison with reference voltage-VSS = 0 mph and U < 2.2 V.
DTC: P0725 **2T TCM** **Year:** 2011, 2012 **Model:** A3, A4, A5, TT, TTS, Q5, Q7 **Engine:** 2.0L L4, 3.0L V6, 3.2L V6 **Transmission:** All	**Engine Speed Input Circuit:** Whenever the engine is running. The ECM detects a malfunction with the transmission input speed sensor.
DTC: P0726 **2 T ECM, MIL: Yes** **Year:** 2011, 2012 **Model:** A3, A4, A5, TT, TTS, Q5, Q7 **Engine:** 2.0L L4, 3.0L V6, 3.2L V6 **Transmission:** All	**Engine Speed Input Circuit Range/ Performance:** The Engine Speed (RPM) Sensor detects engine speed and reference marks. Without an engine speed signal, the engine will not start. If the engine speed signal fails while the engine is running, the engine will stop immediately.
DTC: P0729 **2 T TCM, MIL: Yes** **Year:** 2011, 2012 **Model:** A3, A4, A5, TT, TTS, Q5, Q7 **Engine:** 2.0L L4, 3.0L V6, 3.2L V6 **Transmission:** All	**GEAR RATIO ERROR IN 6TH:** The Transmission gear ratio is monitored continuously while the transmission is in gear. If the ratio of the Input RPM to the Output RPM does not match the current gear ratio when compared to the known gear ratio.

DTC	Trouble Code Title, Conditions, Possible Causes
DTC: P0730 **2 T TCM, MIL: Yes** **Year:** 2011, 2012 **Model:** A3, A4, A5, TT, TTS, Q5, Q7 **Engine:** 2.0L L4, 3.0L V6, 3.2L V6 **Transmission:** All	**Gear Incorrect Ratio:** The Transmission gear ratio is monitored continuously while the transmission is in gear. If the ratio of the Input RPM to the Output RPM does not match the current gear ratio when compared to the known gear ratio.
DTC: P0731 **2 T TCM, MIL: Yes** **Year:** 2011, 2012 **Model:** A3, A4, A5, TT, TTS, Q5, Q7 **Engine:** 2.0L L4, 3.0L V6, 3.2L V6 **Transmission:** All	**Gear 1 incorrect ratio:** The Transmission gear ratio is monitored continuously while the transmission is in gear. If the ratio of the Input RPM to the Output RPM does not match the current gear ratio when compared to the known gear ratio.
DTC: P0732 **2 T TCM, MIL: Yes** **Year:** 2011, 2012 **Model:** A3, A4, A5, TT, TTS, Q5, Q7 **Engine:** 2.0L L4, 3.0L V6, 3.2L V6 **Transmission:** All	**Gear 2 incorrect ratio:** The Transmission gear ratio is monitored continuously while the transmission is in gear. If the ratio of the Input RPM to the Output RPM does not match the current gear ratio when compared to the known gear ratio.
DTC: P0733 **2 T TCM, MIL: Yes** **Year:** 2011, 2012 **Model:** A3, A4, A5, TT, TTS, Q5, Q7 **Engine:** 2.0L L4, 3.0L V6, 3.2L V6 **Transmission:** All	**Gear 3 Incorrect Ratio:** The Transmission gear ratio is monitored continuously while the transmission is in gear. If the ratio of the Input RPM to the Output RPM does not match the current gear ratio, when compared to the known gear ratio.
DTC: P0734 **2 T TCM, MIL: Yes** **Year:** 2011, 2012 **Model:** A3, A4, A5, TT, TTS, Q5, Q7 **Engine:** 2.0L L4, 3.0L V6, 3.2L V6 **Transmission:** All	**Gear 4 Incorrect Ratio:** The Transmission gear ratio is monitored continuously while the transmission is in gear. If the ratio of the Input RPM to the Output RPM does not match the current gear ratio when compared to the known gear ratio.
DTC: P0735 **2 T TCM, MIL: Yes** **Year:** 2011, 2012 **Model:** A3, A4, A5, TT, TTS, Q5, Q7 **Engine:** 2.0L L4, 3.0L V6, 3.2L V6 **Transmission:** All	**Gear 5 Incorrect Ratio:** The Transmission gear ratio is monitored continuously while the transmission is in gear. If the ratio of the Input RPM to the Output RPM does not match the current gear ratio when compared to the known gear ratio.
DTC: P0736 **2 T TCM, MIL: Yes** **Year:** 2011, 2012 **Model:** A3, A4, A5, TT, TTS, Q5, Q7 **Engine:** 2.0L L4, 3.0L V6, 3.2L V6 **Transmission:** All	**GEAR RATIO ERROR IN REVERSE:** The Transmission gear ratio is monitored continuously while the transmission is in gear. If the ratio of the Input RPM to the Output RPM does not match the current gear ratio when compared to the known gear ratio.
DTC: P0740 **3 T TCM, MIL: Yes** **Year:** 2011, 2012 **Model:** TTS **Engine:** 3.2L V6 **Transmission:** All	**TCC OUT OF RANGE:** This DTC is set after the period of 10 seconds and three occurrences of either: FEMCC - with slip greater than 100 RPM or PEMCC - duty cycle greater than 85%.

DTC	Trouble Code Title, Conditions, Possible Causes
DTC: P0743 **2 T TCM, MIL: Yes** **Year:** 2011, 2012 **Model:** A3, A4, A5, TT, TTS, Q5, Q7 **Engine:** 2.0L L4, 3.0L V6, 3.2L V6 **Transmission:** All	**Torque Converter Clutch Circuit Electrical Malfunction:** * Main Solenoid, ON * Linear feedback current, >23 mA (AD:15) < 1333 mA (AD:1000)
DTC: P0746 **2 T TCM, MIL: Yes** **Year:** 2011, 2012 **Model:** A3, A4, A5, TT, TTS, Q5, Q7 **Engine:** 2.0L L4, 3.0L V6, 3.2L V6 **Transmission:** All	**Pressure control solenoid A performance or stuck off:** * Desired pressure <= adapted clutch slipping point + 1 bar * Standing vehicle with accelerator pedal < 1.5% * Battery voltage > 9 V for more than 500 ms * Engine speed >600 RPM for more than 500 ms
DTC: P0747 **2 T TCM, MIL: Yes** **Year:** 2011, 2012 **Model:** A3, A4, A5, TT, TTS, Q5, Q7 **Engine:** 2.0L L4, 3.0L V6, 3.2L V6 **Transmission:** All	**Pressure Control Solenoid A (Stuck On):** * Common high-side switch 1 on and not defective, gearbox subsystem 1 active * Common high-side switches not deactivated by module 2 * Terminal 15 voltage >4 V for more than 500 ms
DTC: P0748 **2 T TCM, MIL: Yes** **Year:** 2011, 2012 **Model:** A3, A4, A5, TT, TTS, Q5, Q7 **Engine:** 2.0L L4, 3.0L V6, 3.2L V6 **Transmission:** All	**Pressure Control Solenoid "A" Electrical:** * Main Solenoid, ON * Linear feedback current, >23 mA (AD:15) < 1333 mA (AD:1000)
DTC: P0748 **2 T TCM, MIL: Yes** **Year:** 2011, 2012 **Model:** A3, A4, A5, TT, TTS, Q5, Q7 **Engine:** 2.0L L4, 3.0L V6, 3.2L V6 **Transmission:** All	**Pressure Control Solenoid 'A" Electrical:** * Main solenoid switch, On * Linear feedback current, > 23 mA (AD:15) < 1333 mA (AD:1000)
DTC: P0750 **2 T TCM, MIL: Yes** **Year:** 2011, 2012 **Model:** A3, A4, A5, TT, TTS, Q5, Q7 **Engine:** 2.0L L4, 3.0L V6, 3.2L V6 **Transmission:** All	**L/R SOLENOID CIRCUIT:** Initially at ignition on, then every 10 seconds thereafter. The solenoids will also be tested immediately after a gear ratio error or pressure switch error is detected. Three consecutive solenoid continuity test failures, or one failure if test is run in response to a gear ratio or pressure switches error.
DTC: P0751 **2 T TCM, MIL: Yes** **Year:** 2011, 2012 **Model:** A3, A4, A5, TT, TTS, Q5, Q7 **Engine:** 2.0L L4, 3.0L V6, 3.2L V6 **Transmission:** All	**Shift solenoid A performance or stuck off:** * Common high-side switches 1 and 3 on and no defects gearbox subsystem 1 active. * Common high-side switches not deactivated by module 2. * Duty factor change of safety valve 1 (control of safety valve 1 is stable) <= 5% duty factor change of gearshift fork valve 2 (control of gearshift fork valve 2 is stable) <= 5% duty factor of control gearshift fork valve 1 >70% and steady state time >= 50 ms terminal 15 voltage > 4 V for more than 500 ms
DTC: P0753 **2 T TCM, MIL: Yes** **Year:** 2011, 2012 **Model:** A3, Q7 **Engine:** 2.0L L4, 3.0L V6, 3.2L V6 **Transmission:** All	**Shift Solenoid "A" Electrical:** Engine started, vehicle driven with the solenoid applied, and the ECM detected an unexpected voltage condition on the SS1/A solenoid circuit was incorrect during the test.

DTC	Trouble Code Title, Conditions, Possible Causes
DTC: P0755 **2 T TCM, MIL: Yes** **Year:** 2011, 2012 **Model:** A3, A4, A5, TT, TTS, Q5, Q7 **Engine:** 2.0L L4, 3.0L V6, 3.2L V6 **Transmission:** All	**2/4 SOLENOID CIRCUIT:** Initially at ignition on, then every 10 seconds thereafter. The solenoids will also be tested immediately after a gear ratio error or pressure switch error is detected. Three consecutive solenoid continuity test failures, or one failure if test is run in response to a gear ratio or pressure switches error.
DTC: P0756 **2 T TCM, MIL: Yes** **Year:** 2011, 2012 **Model:** A3, A4, A5, TT, TTS, Q5, Q7 **Engine:** 2.0L L4 **Transmission:** All	**Shift solenoid B performance or stuck off:** * Common high-side switch 1 and 3 on and no defects * Gearbox subsystem 1 active * Common high-side switches not deactivated by module 2 * Duty factor change of safety valve 1 (control of safety valve 1 is stable) <= 5% * Duty factor change of gearshift fork valve 1 (control of gearshift fork valve 1 is stable) <= 5%
DTC: P0758 **2 T TCM, MIL: Yes** **Year:** 2011, 2012 **Model:** A3, A4, A5, TT, TTS, Q5, Q7 **Engine:** 2.0L L4 **Transmission:** All	**Shift Solenoid "B" Electrical:** Engine started, vehicle driven with the solenoid applied, and the ECM detected an unexpected voltage condition.
DTC: P075A **3 T TCM, MIL: Yes** **Year:** 2011, 2012 **Model:** TTS **Engine:** 3.2L V6 **Transmission:** All	**LC SOLENOID CIRCUIT:** Initially at ignition on, then every 10 seconds thereafter. The solenoids will also be tested immediately after a gear ratio error or pressure switch error is detected. Three consecutive solenoid continuity test failures, or one failure if test is run in response to a gear ratio or pressure switch error.
DTC: P0760 **3 T TCM, MIL: Yes** **Year:** 2011, 2012 **Model:** TTS **Engine:** 3.2L V6 **Transmission:** All	**OD SOLENOID CIRCUIT:** Initially at ignition on, then every 10 seconds thereafter. The solenoids will also be tested immediately after a gear ratio error or pressure switch error is detected. Three consecutive solenoid continuity test failures, or one failure if test is run in response to a gear ratio or pressure switches error.
DTC: P0761 **2 T TCM, MIL: Yes** **Year:** 2011, 2012 **Model:** A3, A4, A5, TT, TTS, Q5, Q7 **Engine:** 2.0L L4, 3.0L V6, 3.2L V6 **Transmission:** All	**Shift solenoid C performance or stuck off:** * Common high-side switch 2 and 3 on, and no defects * Gearbox subsystem 2 active * Common high-side switches not deactivated by module 2 * Duty factor change of safety valve 2 (control of safety valve 2 is stable) <= 5% * Duty factor change of gearshift fork valve 4 (control of gearshift fork valve 4 is stable) <= 5% * Duty factor of control gearshift fork valve 3 >70% and steady state time >= 50 ms * Terminal 15 voltage > 4 V for more than 500 ms
DTC: P0763 **2 T TCM, MIL: Yes** **Year:** 2011, 2012 **Model:** A3, A4, A5, TT, TTS, Q5, Q7 **Engine:** 2.0L L4, 3.0L V6, 3.2L V6 **Transmission:** All	**Shift Solenoid "C" Electrical:** Engine started, vehicle driven with the solenoid applied, and the ECM detected an unexpected voltage condition on the SS3/C solenoid circuit was incorrect during the test.
DTC: P0765 **2 T TCM, MIL: Yes** **Year:** 2011, 2012 **Model:** A3, A4, A5, TT, TTS, Q5, Q7 **Engine:** 2.0L L4, 3.0L V6, 3.2L V6 **Transmission:** All	**UD SOLENOID CIRCUIT:** Ignition on, then every 10 seconds thereafter. The solenoids will also be tested immediately after a gear ratio error or pressure switch error is detected. Three consecutive solenoid continuity test failures, or one failure if test is run in response to a gear ratio or pressure switches error.

DTC	Trouble Code Title, Conditions, Possible Causes
DTC: P0766 **2 T TCM, MIL: Yes** **Year:** 2011, 2012 **Model:** A3, A4, A5, TT, TTS, Q5, Q7 **Engine:** 2.0L L4, 3.0L V6, 3.2L V6 **Transmission:** All	**Shift solenoid D performance or stuck off:** * Common high-side switch 2 and 3 on, and no defects * Gearbox subsystem 2 active * Common high-side switches not deactivated by module 2 * Duty factor change of safety valve 2 (control of safety valve 2 is stable) <= 5% * Duty factor change of gearshift fork valve 3 (control of gearshift fork valve 3 is stable) <= 5% * Duty factor of control gearshift fork valve 4 >70% and steady state time >= 50 ms * Terminal 15 voltage > 4 V for more than 500 ms
DTC: P0768 **2 T TCM, MIL: Yes** **Year:** 2011, 2012 **Model:** A3, A4, A5, TT, TTS, Q5, Q7 **Engine:** 2.0L L4, 3.0L V6, 3.2L V6 **Transmission:** All	**Shift Solenoid "D" Electrical:** Engine started, vehicle driven with the solenoid applied, and the ECM detected an unexpected voltage condition on the SS3/D solenoid circuit was incorrect during the test.
DTC: P076A-DC **3 T TCM, MIL: Yes** **Year:** 2011, 2012 **Model:** TTS, **Engine:** 3.2L V6 **Transmission:** All	**SOLENOID CIRCUIT:** With the ignition on, then every 10 seconds thereafter. The solenoids will also be tested immediately after a gear ratio error or pressure switch error is detected. Three consecutive solenoid continuity test failures, or one failure if test is run in response to a gear ratio or pressure switches error.
DTC: P0771 **1 T TCM, MIL: Yes** **Year:** 2011, 2012 **Model:** A3, A4, A5, TT, TTS, Q5, Q7 **Engine:** 2.0L L4, 3.0L V6, 3.2L V6 **Transmission:** All	**Shift solenoid E performance or stuck off:** * Common high-side switch 3 on and no defects * Common high-side switches not deactivated by module 2 * Multiplexer valve is controlled and steady state time (>= 50 ms) * Terminal 15 voltage >4 V for more than 500 ms
DTC: P0773 **1 T TCM, MIL: Yes** **Year:** 2011, 2012 **Model:** A3, A4, A5, TT, TTS, Q5, Q7 **Engine:** 2.0L L4, 3.0L V6, 3.2L V6 **Transmission:** All	**Shift Solenoid "E" Electrical:** Engine started, vehicle driven with the solenoid applied, and the ECM detected an unexpected voltage condition on the SS3/D solenoid circuit was incorrect during the test.
DTC: P0776 **1 T TCM, MIL: Yes** **Year:** 2011, 2012 **Model:** A3, A4, A5, TT, TTS, Q5, Q7 **Engine:** 2.0L L4, 3.0L V6, 3.2L V6 **Transmission:** All	**Pressure control solenoid B performance or stuck off:** * Desired pressure <= adapted clutch slipping point + 1 bar * Standing vehicle with accelerator pedal < 1.5% * Battery voltage > 9 V for more than 500 ms * Engine speed > 600 RPM for more than 500 ms
DTC: P0777 **1 T TCM, MIL: Yes** **Year:** 2011, 2012 **Model:** A3, A4, A5, TT, TTS, Q5, Q7 **Engine:** 2.0L L4, 3.0L V6, 3.2L V6 **Transmission:** All	**Pressure Control Solenoid B (Stuck On):** Common high-side switch 2 on and not defective gearbox subsystem 2 active common high-side switches not deactivated by module 2 terminal 15 voltage > 4 V for more than 500 ms.
DTC: P0781 **1 T TCM, MIL: Yes** **Year:** 2011, 2012 **Model:** A3, A4, A5, TT, TTS, Q5, Q7 **Engine:** 2.0L L4, 3.0L V6, 3.2L V6 **Transmission:** All	**1-2 shift:** * Control safety valve 1 (on) >=20% * Multiplexer position ==0 * desired main pressure > 2 bars * Terminal 15 V > 4 V for more than 500 ms * Battery voltage > 9 V for more than 500 ms * Engine speed > 600 RPM for more than 500 ms

DTC	Trouble Code Title, Conditions, Possible Causes
DTC: P0782 **1 T TCM, MIL: Yes** **Year:** 2011, 2012 **Model:** A3, A4, A5, TT, TTS, Q5, Q7 **Engine:** 2.0L L4, 3.0L V6, 3.2L V6 **Transmission:** All	**2-3 shift:** * Control safety valve 1 (on) >=20% * Multiplexer position ==0 * desired main pressure > 2 bars * Terminal 15 V > 4 V for more than 500 ms * Battery voltage > 9 V for more than 500 ms * Engine speed > 600 RPM for more than 500 ms
DTC: P0783 **1 T TCM, MIL: Yes** **Year:** 2011, 2012 **Model:** A3, A4, A5, TT, TTS, Q5, Q7 **Engine:** 2.0L L4, 3.0L V6, 3.2L V6 **Transmission:** All	**3-4 shift:** * Control safety valve 1 (on) >=20% * Multiplexer position ==0 * desired main pressure > 2 bars * Terminal 15 V > 4 V for more than 500 ms * Battery voltage > 9 V for more than 500 ms * Engine speed > 600 RPM for more than 500 ms
DTC: P0784 **1 T TCM, MIL: Yes** **Year:** 2011, 2012 **Model:** A3, A4, A5, TT, TTS, Q5, Q7 **Engine:** 2.0L L4, 3.0L V6, 3.2L V6 **Transmission:** All	**4-5 shift:** * Control safety valve 2 (on) >=20% * Multiplexer position ==1 * Desired main pressure > 2 bars * Terminal 15 V > 4 V for more than 500 ms * Battery voltage > 9 V for more than 500 ms * Engine speed > 600 RPM for more than 500 ms
DTC: P0785 **1 T TCM, MIL: Yes** **Year:** 2011, 2012 **Model:** A3, A4, A5, TT, TTS, Q5, Q7 **Engine:** 2.0L L4, 3.0L V6, 3.2L V6 **Transmission:** All	**Shift/Timing Solenoid:** Engine running and vehicle driven, the ECM detected a malfunction within the transmission.
DTC: P0791 **1 T TCM, MIL: Yes** **Year:** 2011, 2012 **Model:** TTS **Engine:** 3.2L V6 **Transmission:** All	**TRANSFER SPEED SENSOR CIRCUIT:** The transmission gear ratio is monitored continuously while the transmission is in gear. If there is an excessive change in the Transfer RPM in any gear.
DTC: P0792 **1 T TCM, MIL: Yes** **Year:** 2011, 2012 **Model:** TTS **Engine:** 3.2L V6 **Transmission:** All	**COMPOUNDER SPEED RATIO ERROR:** The transmission gear ratio is monitored continuously while the transmission is in gear. If there is an excessive change in the Output RPM in any gear.
DTC: P0797 **1 T TCM, MIL: Yes** **Year:** 2011, 2012 **Model:** A3, A4, A5, TT, TTS, Q5, Q7 **Engine:** 2.0L L4, 3.0L V6, 3.2L V6 **Transmission:** All	**Pressure control solenoid C stuck on:** * Common high-side switch 3 on and not defective * Common high-side switches not deactivated by module 2 * Terminal 15 voltage > 4 V for more than 500 ms
DTC: P0798 **1 T TCM, MIL: Yes** **Year:** 2011, 2012 **Model:** A3, A4, A5, TT, TTS, Q5, Q7 **Engine:** 2.0L L4, 3.0L V6, 3.2L V6 **Transmission:** All	**Pressure Control Solenoid "C" Electrical:** * Main Solenoid, ON * Linear feedback current, >23 mA (AD:15) < 1333 mA (AD:1000)

DTC	Trouble Code Title, Conditions, Possible Causes
DTC: P0811 **1 T TCM, MIL: Yes** **Year:** 2011, 2012 **Model:** A3, A4, A5, TT, TTS, Q5, Q7 **Engine:** 2.0L L4, 3.0L V6, 3.2L V6 **Transmission:** All	**Excessive Clutch Slippage:** * Engine speed, 400 RPM * Shift lever, D or S * Engine speed, < 4000 RPM * Estimated engine torque, > 0 Nm * Revolution sensor, No back up condition * SLU target current, > 1000 mA* Model oil temp, > 20° C
DTC: P0811 **1 T TCM, MIL: Yes** **Year:** 2011, 2012 **Model:** A3, A4, A5, TT, TTS, Q5, Q7 **Engine:** 2.0L L4, 3.0L V6, 3.2L V6 **Transmission:** All	**Excessive Clutch Slippage:** * Engine speed, >400 RPM * Shift lever, D,S * Engine speed, < 4000 RPM * Estimated engine torque, >=0 Nm * Revolution sensor, No back up condition * SLU target current, > 1000 mA * Model oil temp, >=20° C
DTC: P0829 **1 T TCM, MIL: Yes** **Year:** 2011, 2012 **Model:** A3, A4, A5, TT, TTS, Q5, Q7 **Engine:** 2.0L L4, 3.0L V6, 3.2L V6 **Transmission:** All	**5-6 shift:** * Control safety valve 1 (on) >=20% * Multiplexer position ==1 * Desired main pressure > 2 bars * Terminal 15 V > 4 V for more than 500 ms * Battery voltage > 9 V for more than 500 ms * Engine speed > 600 RPM for more than 500 ms
DTC: P083A **1 T TCM, MIL: Yes** **Year:** 2011, 2012 **Model:** TTS **Engine:** 3.2L V6 **Transmission:** All	**LC HYDRAULIC PRESSURE TEST:** In any forward gear with engine speed above 1000 rpm, shortly after a shift and every minute thereafter. After a shift into a forward gear, with engine speed greater than 1000 rpm, the PCM momentarily turns on element pressure to the clutch circuits that don't have pressure to verify that the correct pressure switch closes. If the pressure switch does not close 2 times the DTC will set.
DTC: P083B **1 T TCM, MIL: Yes** **Year:** 2011, 2012 **Model:** TTS **Engine:** 3.2L V6 **Transmission:** All	**LC PRESSURE SWITCH RATIONALITY:** Whenever the engine is running. The DTC is set if one of the pressure switches is open or closed at the wrong time in a given gear. If the problem is identified for three successive key starts, the transmission will go into Limp-in mode and the MIL will turn on after 10 seconds of vehicle operation.
DTC: P0840 **1 T TCM, MIL: Yes** **Year:** 2011, 2012 **Model:** A3, A4, A5, TT, TTS, Q5, Q7 **Engine:** 2.0L L4, 3.0L V6, 3.2L V6 **Transmission:** All	**Transmission Fluid Pressure Sensor/Switch "A" Circuit:** * Engine speed, > 400 rpm * Shift Lever, D or S * Current Gear, 5th or 6th * Line pressure, > 6.0 kg/cm2 * Oil pressure No.1, No fault * Model oil temp, > 20°C * Common parameter, common condition
DTC: P0841 **1 T TCM, MIL: Yes** **Year:** 2011, 2012 **Model:** A3, A4, A5, TT, TTS, Q5, Q7 **Engine:** 2.0L L4, 3.0L V6, 3.2L V6 **Transmission:** All	**Transmission Fluid Pressure Sensor/Switch "A" Circuit Range/Performance:** Whenever the engine is running. The DTC is set if the L/R pressure switch is open or closed at the wrong time in a given gear. If the problem is identified for three successive key starts, the transmission will go into Limp-in mode and the MIL will turn on after 10 seconds of vehicle operation.
DTC: P0845 **1 T TCM, MIL: Yes** **Year:** 2011, 2012 **Model:** A3, A4, A5, TT, TTS, Q5, Q7 **Engine:** 2.0L L4, 3.0L V6, 3.2L V6 **Transmission:** All	**2/4 HYDRAULIC PRESSURE TEST:** In any forward gear with engine speed above 1000 RPM, shortly after a shift and every minute thereafter. After a shift into a forward gear, with engine speed greater than 1000 RPM, the Powertrain Control Module (PCM) momentarily turns on element pressure to the clutch circuits that don't have pressure to verify that the correct pressure switch closes. If the pressure switch does not close two times the DTC will set.

DTC	Trouble Code Title, Conditions, Possible Causes
DTC: P0846 **1 T TCM, MIL: Yes** **Year:** 2011, 2012 **Model:** A3, A4, A5, TT, TTS, Q5, Q7 **Engine:** 2.0L L4, 3.0L V6, 3.2L V6 **Transmission:** All	**2/4 PRESSURE SWITCH RATIONALITY:** Whenever the engine is running. The DTC is set if the 2/4 pressure switch is open or closed at the wrong time in a given gear. If the problem is identified for three successive ignition starts, the transmission will go into Limp-in mode and the MIL will turn on after 10 seconds of vehicle operation.
DTC: P084A-DC **1 T TCM, MIL: Yes** **Year:** 2011, 2012 **Model:** TTS **Engine:** 3.2L V6 **Transmission:** All	**HYDRAULIC PRESSURE TEST:** In any forward gear with engine speed above 1000 rpm, shortly after a shift and every minute thereafter. After a shift into a forward gear, with engine speed greater than 1000 rpm, the PCM momentarily turns on element pressure to the clutch circuits that don't have pressure to verify that the correct pressure switch closes. If the pressure switch does not close 2 times the DTC sets
DTC: P084B-DC **1 T TCM, MIL: Yes** **Year:** 2011, 2012 **Model:** TTS **Engine:** 3.2L V6 **Transmission:** All	**PRESSURE SWITCH RATIONALITY:** Whenever the engine is running. The DTC is set if one of the pressure switches is open or closed at the wrong time in a given gear. If the problem is identified for 3 successive key starts, the transmission will go into Limp-in mode and the MIL will turn on after 10 seconds of vehicle operation.
DTC: P0850 **1 T TCM, MIL: Yes** **Year:** 2011, 2012 **Model:** TTS **Engine:** 3.2L V6 **Transmission:** All	**PARK/NEUTRAL SWITCH PERFORMANCE:** Continuously with the transmission in Park, Neutral, or Drive and not in Limp-in mode. This code will set if the Powertrain Control Module (PCM) detects an irrational Park/Neutral switch state. Two trip fault. Three good trips to turn off the MIL.
DTC: P0863 **1 T TCM, MIL: Yes** **Year:** 2011, 2012 **Model:** A3, A4, A5, TT, TTS, Q5, Q7 **Engine:** 2.0L L4, 3.0L V6, 3.2L V6 **Transmission:** All	**Communication to Transmission Control Module Electrical Malfunction:** CAN bus okay 500 mSec after ignition on.
DTC: P0864 **1 T TCM, MIL: Yes** **Year:** 2011, 2012 **Model:** A3, A4, A5, TT, TTS, Q5, Q7 **Engine:** 2.0L L4, 3.0L V6, 3.2L V6 **Transmission:** All	**Communication to Transmission Control Module Range Performance:** CAN bus okay 500 mSec after ignition on
DTC: P0865 **2 T ECM, MIL: Yes** **Year:** 2011, 2012 **Model:** A3, A4, A5, TTS, **Engine:** 2.0L L4, 3.0L V6, 3.2L V6 **Transmission:** All	**TCM Communication Circuit Low:** * Time, 500 ms after IGN on
DTC: P0868 **2 T TCM, MIL: Yes** **Year:** 2011, 2012 **Model:** A3, A4, A5, TTS, **Engine:** 2.0L L4, 3.0L V6, 3.2L V6 **Transmission:** All	**LINE PRESSURE LOW:** Continuously while driving in a forward gear. The Powertrain Control Module (PCM) continuously monitors Actual Line Pressure and compares it to Desired Line Pressure. If the Actual Line Pressure is more than 5 psi below Desired Line Pressure while the PCS duty cycle is at or near its minimum value, this DTC will set.
DTC: P0869 **2 T TCM, MIL: Yes** **Year:** 2011, 2012 **Model:** A3, A4, A5, TTS, **Engine:** 2.0L L4, 3.0L V6, 3.2L V6 **Transmission:** All	**LINE PRESSURE HIGH:** Continuously while driving in a forward gear. The Powertrain Control Module (PCM) continuously monitors Actual Line Pressure. If the Actual Line Pressure reading is greater than the highest Desired Line Pressure ever used in the current gear, while the Pressure Control Solenoid duty cycle is at or near its maximum value (which should result in minimum line pressure), the DTC will set.

DTC	Trouble Code Title, Conditions, Possible Causes
DTC: P0870 **2 T TCM, MIL: Yes** **Year:** 2011, 2012 **Model:** A3, A4, A5, TTS, **Engine:** 2.0L L4, 3.0L V6, 3.2L V6 **Transmission:** All	**OD HYDRAULIC PRESSURE TEST:** In any forward gear with engine speed above 1000 RPM, shortly after a shift and every minute thereafter. After a shift into a forward gear, with engine speed greater than 1000 RPM, the Powertrain Control Module (PCM) momentarily turns on element pressure to the clutch circuits that don't have pressure to identify the correct pressure switch closes. If the pressure switch does not close two times the DTC sets.
DTC: P0871 **2 T TCM, MIL: Yes** **Year:** 2011, 2012 **Model:** A3, A4, A5, TTS, **Engine:** 2.0L L4, 3.0L V6, 3.2L V6 **Transmission:** All	**OD PRESSURE SWITCH RATIONALITY:** Whenever the engine is running. The DTC is set if the OD pressure switch is open or closed at the wrong time in a given gear. If the P0706 fault condition is also present, the transmission will go into Limp-in mode and the MIL will turn on.
DTC: P0882 **2 T TCM, MIL: Yes** **Year:** 2011, 2012 **Model:** A3, A4, A5, TTS, **Engine:** 2.0L L4, 3.0L V6, 3.2L V6 **Transmission:** All	**TCM POWER INPUT LOW:** When the ignition is turned from "OFF" position to "RUN" position and/or the ignition is turned from "START" position to "RUN" position. This DTC is set when there is less than 3.0 volts present at the transmission control output circuits located in the Powertrain Control Module (PCM) when the Transmission Control System request the power up of those circuits. **NOTE: Due to the integration of the Transmission Control Module and the Powertrain Control Module, both systems have their own power and ground circuits.**
DTC: P0883 **2 T TCM, MIL: Yes** **Year:** 2011, 2012 **Model:** A3, A4, A5, TTS, **Engine:** 2.0L L4, 3.0L V6, 3.2L V6 **Transmission:** All	**TCM POWER INPUT HIGH:** When the ignition is turned from "OFF" position to "RUN" position and/or the ignition is turned from "START" position to "RUN" position. This DTC is set if the Powertrain Control Module senses greater than 3.0 volts on the Transmission Control Relay Output circuits prior to a request from the PCM to TIPM to energize the Transmission Output circuits.
DTC: P0884 **2 T TCM, MIL: Yes** **Year:** 2011, 2012 **Model:** A3, A4, A5, TTS, **Engine:** 2.0L L4, 3.0L V6, 3.2L V6 **Transmission:** All	**POWER UP AT SPEED:** This DTC will set if the PCM powers up and senses the vehicle in a valid forward gear (no PRNDL DTCs) with an output speed above 800 rpm, approximately 32 km/h or 20 mph.
DTC: P0888 **2 T TCM, MIL: Yes** **Year:** 2011, 2012 **Model:** A3, A4, A5, TTS, **Engine:** 2.0L L4, 3.0L V6, 3.2L V6 **Transmission:** All	**TRANSMISSION RELAY ALWAYS OFF:** This DTC is set when there is less than 3.0 volts present at the transmission control output circuits located in the Powertrain Control Module (PCM) when the Transmission Control System request the power up of those circuits. **NOTE: Due to the integration of the Transmission Control Module and the Powertrain Control Module, both systems have their own power and ground circuits.**
DTC: P0890 **2 T TCM, MIL: Yes** **Year:** 2011, 2012 **Model:** A3, A4, A5, TT, TTS, Q5, Q7 **Engine:** 2.0L L4 **Transmission:** All	**TCM Power Relay Sense Circuit Low:** Terminal 15 voltage > 4 V for more than 500 ms
DTC: P0890 **2 T TCM, MIL: Yes** **Year:** 2011, 2012 **Model:** A3, A4, A5, TTS, **Engine:** 2.0L L4, 3.0L V6, 3.2L V6 **Transmission:** All	**SWITCHED BATTERY:** One time after a reset (ignition key turned to the RUN position or after cranking engine). A fault is set if voltage greater than 4.5 volts is detected for 7 msec on any of the pressure switch circuits before the relay is energized. The transmission is placed in Limp-In. The MIL is on after 10 seconds of vehicle operation.
DTC: P0891 **2 T TCM, MIL: Yes** **Year:** 2011, 2012 **Model:** A3, A4, A5, TTS, **Engine:** 2.0L L4, 3.0L V6, 3.2L V6 **Transmission:** All	**TRANSMISSION RELAY ALWAYS ON:** When the ignition is turned from "OFF" position to "RUN" position and/or the ignition is turned from "START" position to "RUN" position. This DTC is set if the Powertrain Control Module senses greater than 3.0 volts on the Transmission Control Relay Output circuits prior to a request from the PCM to TIPM to energize the Transmission Output circuits.

DTC	Trouble Code Title, Conditions, Possible Causes
DTC: P0892 2 T TCM, MIL: Yes Year: 2011, 2012 Model: A3, A4, A5, TTS, Engine: 2.0L L4, 3.0L V6, 3.2L V6 Transmission: All	**TCM Power Relay Sense Circuit Intermittent:** * Filtered battery voltage, > 7 V * High side and low side FET, enabled * Status counter initialization, 0 or 1
DTC: P0897 2 T TCM, MIL: Yes Year: 2011, 2012 Model: A3, A4, A5, TTS, Engine: 2.0L L4, 3.0L V6, 3.2L V6 Transmission: All	**TRANSMISSION FLUID DETERIORATED:** Each transition from full EMCC to partial EMCC for A/C bump prevention. DTC set if 20 occurrences of turbine acceleration sum. Fault Set Time: 20 transitions from full EMCC to partial EMCC. Transmission will not use partial EMCC. Established for A/C bump prevention.
DTC: P0914 2 T TCM, MIL: Yes Year: 2011, 2012 Model: A3, A4, A5, TTS, Engine: 2.0L L4, 3.0L V6, 3.2L V6 Transmission: All	**Gear shift position circuit:** * Gear message for selector lever is transmittable and selector lever message is receivable * No failure of selector lever CAN messages * Terminal 15 voltage > 4 V for more than 500 ms
DTC: P0919 2 T TCM, MIL: Yes Year: 2011, 2012 Model: A3, A4, A5, TTS, Engine: 2.0L L4, 3.0L V6, 3.2L V6 Transmission: All	**Gear shift position control error:** * No failure of selector lever CAN messages * Terminal 15 voltage > 4 V for more than 500 ms * Battery voltage > 9 V for more than 500 ms
DTC: P0928 2 T TCM, MIL: Yes Year: 2011, 2012 Model: A3, A4, A5, TTS, Engine: 2.0L L4, 3.0L V6, 3.2L V6 Transmission: All	**BTSI CONTROL CIRCUIT:** When the ignition is in accessory, run or start position. This DTC will set if the WIN module detects a problem with the BTSI solenoid control circuit. The DTC will remain active until the WIN module no longer detects a failure of the BTSI control circuit.
DTC: P0929 2 T TCM, MIL: Yes Year: 2011, 2012 Model: A3, A4, A5, TTS, Engine: 2.0L L4, 3.0L V6, 3.2L V6 Transmission: All	**Gear shift lock solenoid control circuit range/performance:** * No failure of selector lever CAN messages * terminal 15 voltage > 4 V for more than 500 ms
DTC: P0932 2 T TCM, MIL: Yes Year: 2011, 2012 Model: A3, A4, A5, TTS, Engine: 2.0L L4, 3.0L V6, 3.2L V6 Transmission: All	**LINE PRESSURE SENSOR CIRCUIT:** Continuously with the ignition on, engine running, with the transmission in gear. The PCM continuously monitors Actual Line Pressure and compares it to Desired Line Pressure. If the Actual Line Pressure reading is more than 172.4 kPa (25 psi) higher than the Desired Line Pressure, but is less than the highest Line Pressure ever used in the current gear, the DTC sets.
DTC: P0934 2 T TCM, MIL: Yes Year: 2011, 2012 Model: A3, A4, A5, TTS, Engine: 2.0L L4, 3.0L V6, 3.2L V6 Transmission: All	**LINE PRESSURE SENSOR CIRCUIT LOW:** Continuously with the ignition on and engine running. This DTC will set when the monitored Line Pressure Sensor voltage is less than or equal to 0.35 of a volt for 0.18 of a second.
DTC: P0935 2 T TCM, MIL: Yes Year: 2011, 2012 Model: A3, A4, A5, TTS, Engine: 2.0L L4, 3.0L V6, 3.2L V6 Transmission: All	**LINE PRESSURE SENSOR CIRCUIT HIGH:** Continuously with ignition on and engine running. This DTC will set if the monitored Line Pressure Sensor voltage is greater than or equal to 4.75 volts for the period of 0.18 of a second.

DTC	Trouble Code Title, Conditions, Possible Causes
DTC: P0944 **2T TCM** **Year:** 2011, 2012 **Model:** A3, A4, A5, TTS, **Engine:** 2.0L L4, 3.0L V6, 3.2L V6 **Transmission:** All	**LOSS OF HYDRAULIC PUMP PRIME:** Every 350 msec If the transmission begins to slip in any forward gear, and the pressure switch or switches that should be closed for a given gear are open, a loss of prime test begins. All available elements (in 1st gear LR, 2/4 and OD, in 2nd, 3rd, and 4th gear 2/4 and OD) are turned on by the Powertrain Control Module (PCM) to see if pump prime exists. The code is set if none of the pressure switches respond. The PCM will continue to run the loss of prime test until pump pressure returns. The vehicle will not move or the transmission will slip. Normal operation will continue if pump prime returns.
DTC: P0957 **2T TCM** **Year:** 2011, 2012 **Model:** A3, A4, A5, TTS, **Engine:** 2.0L L4, 3.0L V6, 3.2L V6 **Transmission:** All	**AUTOSTICK CIRCUIT LOW:** Whenever the engine is running. The transmission is not in the AutoStick® position and the up shift or downshift is reporting closed - below 0.71 of a volt or if both switches are reported closed at the same time.
DTC: P0992 **2T TCM** **Year:** 2011, 2012 **Model:** A3, A4, A5, TTS, **Engine:** 2.0L L4, 3.0L V6, 3.2L V6 **Transmission:** All	**2/4/OD HYDRAULIC PRESSURE TEST:** In any forward gear with engine speed above 1000 RPM, shortly after a shift and every minute thereafter. After a shift into a forward gear, with engine speed greater than 1000 RPM, the Powertrain Control Module (PCM) momentarily turns on element pressure to the clutch circuits that do not have pressure to identify that the correct pressure switch closes. If the pressure switch does not close two times the DTC sets.

VW

Eos • Golf • GTI • Tiguan

4

SPECIFICATIONS AND MAINTENANCE CHARTS

ENGINE AND VEHICLE IDENTIFICATION

		Engine						Model Year	
ENG Code	Liters (cc)	Cu. In.	Cyl.	Fuel Sys.	Engine Type	Eng. Mfg.		Code ②	Year
CBFA	2.0 (1984)	121	4	FSI	DOHC	Volkswagen		B	2011
CCTA	2.0 (1984)	121	4	FSI	DOHC	Volkswagen		C	2012
CBUA	2.5 (2412)	147	5	ME 7.1	DOHC	Volkswagen			
CBTA	2.5 (2412)	147	5	ME 7.1	DOHC	Volkswagen			
CJAA	2.0 (1984)	121	5	TDI	DOHC	Volkswagen			

DOHC: Double Overhead Camshafts

SOHC: Single Overhead Camshaft

① Bosch Motronic

② 10th digit of VIN

71105_VWCA_C0001

GENERAL ENGINE SPECIFICATIONS

Year	Model	Engine Displacement Liters	Engine ID/VIN	Net Horsepower @ rpm	Net Torque@rpm (ft. lbs.)	Bore x Stroke (in.)	Compression Ratio	Oil Pressure @ rpm
2011	Eos, Golf	2.0 (1984)	CBFA, CCTA	200@5700	207@1800	3.21x3.62	9.6:1	36-65@2000
	Golf	2.5 (2412)	CBTA, CBUA	170@5700	177@4250	3.21x3.62	10.0:1	36-65@2000
	Golf TDI	2.0L (1984)	CJAA	NA	NA	NA	NA	NA
	Tiguan	2.0 (1855)	CCTA	200@5700	207@1800	3.21x3.62	9.6:1	36-65@2000
2012	Eos, Golf	2.0 (1984)	CBFA, CCTA	200@5700	207@1800	3.21x3.62	9.6:1	36-65@2000
	Golf	2.5 (2412)	CBTA, CBUA	170@5700	177@4250	3.21x3.62	10.0:1	36-65@2000
	Golf TDI	2.0L (1984)	CJAA	NA	NA	NA	NA	NA
	Tiguan	2.0 (1855)	CCTA	200@5700	207@1800	3.21x3.62	9.6:1	36-65@2000

71105_VWCA_C0002

GASOLINE ENGINE TUNE-UP SPECIFICATIONS

Year	Engine Displacement Liters	Engine ID/VIN	Spark Plug Gap (in.)	Ignition Timing (deg.) MT	AT	Fuel Pump (psi)	Idle Speed (rpm) MT	AT	Valve Clearance Intake	Exhaust
2011	2.0 (1984)	CBFA, CCTA	0.028-0.031	②	②	101.5	②	②	HYD	HYD
	2.5 (2412)	CBTA/CBUA	0.039-0.043	②	②	58	②	②	HYD	HYD
2012	2.0 (1984)	CBFA, CCTA	0.028-0.031	②	②	101.5	②	②	HYD	HYD
	2.5 (2412)	CBTA/CBUA	0.039-0.043	②	②	58	②	②	HYD	HYD

Note: The Vehicle Emission Control Information label reflects specification changes made during production.

HYD: Hydraulic

① Inspect timing cover for code.

② Ignition timing/idle speed controlled electronically. Specification no longer provided.

71105_VWCA_C0003

DIESEL ENGINE TUNE-UP SPECIFICATIONS

Year	Engine Displacement Liters	Engine ID/VIN	Valve Clearance Intake (in.)	Valve Clearance Exhaust (in.)	Intake Valve Opens (deg.)	Injection Pump Setting (deg.)	Injection Nozzle Pressure (psi) New	Injection Nozzle Pressure (psi) Used	Idle Speed (rpm)	Cranking Compression Pressure (psi)
2011	2.0 (1855)	CJAA	HYD	HYD	NS	①	NS	NS	①	275.5
2012	2.0 (1855)	CJAA	HYD	HYD	NS	①	NS	NS	①	275.5

Note: The Vehicle Emission Control Information label reflects specification changes made during production.

NS: Not Specified

① Injection pump timing/idle speed controlled electronically. Specification no longer provided.

71105_VWCA_C0003A

CAPACITIES

Year	Model	Engine Displacement Liters	Engine ID/VIN	Engine Oil with Filter	Transmission Manual (pts.)	Transmission DSG ① (qts.)	Transmission Auto. (qts.)	Fuel Tank (gal.)	Cooling System (qts.)
2011	Eos, Golf	2.0 (1984)	CBFA, CCTA	4.9	4.8	5.5	NA	14.5	7.7
	Golf	2.5 (2412)	CBTA, CBUA	6.3	4.8	NA	7.4	NS	10.0
	Golf TDI	2.0 (1984)	CJAA	5.9	4.8	7.4	NA	14.5	10.1
	Tiguan	2.0 (1855)	CCTA	4.9	4.8	NA	5.5	14.5	7.7
2012	Eos, Golf	2.0 (1984)	CBFA, CCTA	4.9	4.8	5.5	NA	14.5	7.7
	Golf	2.5 (2412)	CBTA, CBUA	6.3	4.8	NA	7.4	NS	10.0
	Golf TDI	2.0 (1984)	CJAA	5.9	4.8	7.4	NA	14.5	10.1
	Tiguan	2.0 (1855)	CCTA	4.9	4.8	NA	5.5	14.5	7.7

Note: All capacities are approximate. Add fluid gradually and check often to avoid overfilling or underfilling.

NA: Not Applicable

NS: Not Specified

① DSG: Direct Shift Gear (Auto Trans.)

71105_VWCA_C0004

FLUID SPECIFICATIONS

Year	Model	Engine Displacement Liters	Engine ID/VIN	Engine Oil	Man. Trans.	Auto. Trans.	Brake Master Cylinder	Cooling System
2011	Eos, Golf	2.0 (1984)	CBFA, CCTA	5W-40	Synthetic MTF 75W-90	Synthetic ATF	DOT4	LLC
	Golf	2.5 (2412)	CBTA, CBUA	5W-40	Synthetic MTF 75W-90	Synthetic ATF	DOT4	LLC
	Golf TDI	2.0 (1984)	CJAA	①	Synthetic MTF 75W-90	Synthetic ATF	DOT4	LLC
	Tiguan	2.0 (1855)	CCTA	5W-40	Synthetic MTF 75W-90	Synthetic ATF	DOT4	LLC
2012	Eos, Golf	2.0 (1984)	CBFA, CCTA	5W-40	Synthetic MTF 75W-90	Synthetic ATF	DOT4	LLC
	Golf	2.5 (2412)	CBTA, CBUA	5W-40	Synthetic MTF 75W-90	Synthetic ATF	DOT4	LLC
	Golf TDI	2.0 (1984)	CJAA	①	Synthetic MTF 75W-90	Synthetic ATF	DOT4	LLC
	Tiguan	2.0 (1855)	CCTA	5W-40	Synthetic MTF 75W-90	Synthetic ATF	DOT4	LLC

DOT: Department Of Transpotation

LLC: Long Life Coolant

NA: Not Applicable

① Refer to Owner's Manual for proper oil type.

71105_VWCA_C0005

VALVE SPECIFICATIONS

Year	Engine Displacement Liters	Engine ID/VIN	Seat Angle (deg.)	Face Angle (deg.)	Spring Test Pressure (lbs. @ in.)	Spring Installed Height (in.)	Stem-to-Guide Clearance (in.)		Stem Diameter (in.)	
							Intake	Exhaust	Intake	Exhaust
2009	2.0	CBFA, CCTA	45	45	NS	NS	0.031	0.031	0.235	0.234
	2.5	CBTA, CBUA	45	45	NS	NS	NS	NS	0.234	0.234
	2.0 TDI	CJAA	45	45	NS	NS	0.050	0.050	0.2722	0.2712
2010	2.0	CBFA, CCTA	45	45	NS	NS	0.031	0.031	0.235	0.234
	2.5	CBTA, CBUA	45	45	NS	NS	NS	NS	0.234	0.234
	2.0 TDI	CJAA	45	45	NS	NS	0.050	0.050	0.2722	0.2712

NS: Not Specified

① Inspect timing cover for code.

71105_VWCA_C0006

CAMSHAFT AND BEARING SPECIFICATIONS

All measurements are given in inches.

Year	Engine Displacement Liters	Engine VIN	Journal Diameter	Brg. Oil Clearance	Shaft End-play	Runout	Journal Bore	Lobe Lift	
								Intake	Exhaust
2011	2.0	CBFA, CCTA	NS	NS	NS	NS	NS	NS	NS
	2.5	CBTA, CBUA	NS	0.0014-0.0033	0.002-0.005	NS	NS	NS	NS
	2.0 TDI	CJAA	NS	NS	0.016	NS	NS	NS	NS
2012	2.0	CBFA, CCTA	NS	NS	NS	NS	NS	NS	NS
	2.5	CBTA, CBUA	NS	0.0014-0.0033	0.002-0.005	NS	NS	NS	NS
	2.0 TDI	CJAA	NS	NS	0.016	NS	NS	NS	NS

NS: Not specified

71105_VWCA_C0007

CRANKSHAFT AND CONNECTING ROD SPECIFICATIONS

All measurements are given in inches.

Year	Engine Displacemnet Liters	Engine ID/VIN	Main Brg. Journal Dia.	Main Brg. Oil Clearance	Shaft End-play	Thrust on No.	Connecting Rod		
							Journal Diameter	Oil Clearance	Side Clearance
2011	2.0	CBFA, CCTA	2.2834	0.0007-0.0015	0.0028-0.0090	3	1.8819	0.0008-0.0024	0.0039-0.0138
	2.0 TDI	CJAA	2.1060	NS	0.0027-0.0066	3	1.8642	0.0031	0.0144
	2.5	CBTA, CBUA	2.2834	0.0007-0.0015	0.0007-0.0015	3	1.8819	0.0008-0.0024	0.0039-0.0138
2012	2.0	CBFA, CCTA	2.2834	0.0007-0.0015	0.0028-0.0090	3	1.8819	0.0008-0.0024	0.0039-0.0138
	2.0 TDI	CJAA	2.1060	NS	0.0027-0.0066	3	1.8642	0.0031	0.0144
	2.5	CBTA, CBUA	2.2834	0.0007-0.0015	0.0007-0.0015	3	1.8819	0.0008-0.0024	0.0039-0.0138

NS - Not Specified

71105_VWCA_C0008

PISTON AND RING SPECIFICATIONS
All measurements are given in inches.

| Year | Engine Disp. Liters | Engine ID/VIN | Piston Clearance | Ring Gap | | | Ring Side Clearance | | |
				Top Compression	Bottom Compression	Oil Control	Top Compression	Bottom Compression	Oil Control
2011	2.0	CBFA, CCTA	0.0008	0.008-0.016	0.008-0.016	0.010-0.020	0.0024-0.0035	0.0024-0.0035	0.0012-0.0024
	2.0 TDI	CJAA	0.0008	0.008-0.015	0.008-0.015	0.010-0.020	0.0020-0.0030	0.0020-0.0030	0.001-0.002
	2.5	CBTA, CBUA	0.0177	0.008-0.016	0.008-0.016	0.010-0.020	0.0024-0.0035	0.0024-0.0035	0.0011-0.0027
2010	2.0	CBFA, CCTA	0.0008	0.008-0.016	0.008-0.016	0.010-0.020	0.0024-0.0035	0.0024-0.0035	0.0012-0.0024
	2.0 TDI	CJAA	0.0008	0.008-0.015	0.008-0.015	0.010-0.020	0.0020-0.0030	0.0020-0.0030	0.001-0.002
	2.5	CBTA, CBUA	0.0177	0.008-0.016	0.008-0.016	0.010-0.020	0.0024-0.0035	0.0024-0.0035	0.0011-0.0027

71105_VWCA_C0009

TORQUE SPECIFICATIONS
All readings in ft. lbs.

| Year | Engine Disp. Liters | Engine ID/VIN ① | Cylinder Head Bolts | Main Bearing Bolts | Rod Bearing Bolts | Crankshaft Damper Bolt | Flywheel Bolts | Manifold | | Spark Plugs | Oil Pan Drain Plug |
								Intake	Exhaust		
2011	2.0	CBFA/CCTA	②	③	④	⑤	⑥	7	15 ⑦	18	22
	2.0 TDI	CJAA	⑧	⑨	④	⑩	⑥	6	18 ⑦	13 ⑪	22
	2.5	CNNA/CBUA	⑫	⑬	④	⑭	⑥	7	17 ⑦	18	22
2012	2.0	CBFA/CCTA	②	③	④	⑤	⑥	7	15 ⑦	18	22
	2.0 TDI	CJAA	⑧	⑨	④	⑩	⑥	6	18 ⑦	13 ⑪	22
	2.5	CNNA/CBUA	⑫	⑬	④	⑭	⑥	7	17 ⑦	18	22

① Inspect timing cover for code.

② Torque in three steps. Use new bolts.
   Step 1: 30 ft. lbs.
   Step 2: plus 90 degrees
   Step 3: plus 90 degrees

③ Two Steps. 66 ft. lbs. Plus 90 degrees. Use new bolt.

④ Two Steps. 22 ft. lbs. plus 90 degrees. Use new bolts.

⑤ Two Steps. 66 ft. lbs. Plus 90 degrees. Use new bolt.

⑥ Two Steps. 44 ft. lbs. plus 90 degrees. Use new bolts.

⑦ Use new bolts.

⑧ Torque in four steps, using new bolts:
   Step 1: Tighten the bolts using a torque wrench, first time to 20 ft. lbs. (30 Nm)
   Step 2: Tighten the bolts using a torque wrench a second pass to 37 ft. lbs. (50 Nm).
   Step 3: Using a ratchet, tighten each bolt, in sequence an additional 90<deg.> (1/4 turn).
   Step 4: Repeat this process, tightening each bolt with a ratchet another 90<deg.> (1/4 turn).

⑨ 48 ft. lbs., plus 90 degrees. Use new bolts.

⑩ Torque setting unclear; contact dealer for information.

⑪ Glow plugs

⑫ Torque in three steps, using new bolts:
   Step 1: Using a torque wrench, tighten the bolts to 30 ft. lbs. (40 Nm).
   Step 2: Using a ratchet, tighten the bolts an additional 90<deg.> (1/4) turn.
   Step 3: Using a ratchet. tighten the bolts an additional 90<deg.> (1/4) turn.

⑬ 30 ft. lbs., plus 90 degrees. Use new bolts.

⑭ 37 ft. lbs., plus 90 degrees. Use new bolts.

71105_VWCA_C0010

WHEEL ALIGNMENT

Year	Model		Caster Range (+/-Deg.)	Caster Preferred Setting (Deg.)	Camber Range (+/-Deg.)	Camber Preferred Setting (Deg.)	Toe-in (Deg.)
2011	Eos	Front	0.50	+7.57	0.50	-0.60	1.63+/-0.33 ①
		Rear	—	—	0.50	-1.75	0.17+/-0.17 ②
	Golf GLI	Front	0.50	+7.83	0.50	-0.58	1.67+/-0.33 ①
		Rear	—	—	0.50	-1.33	0.17+/-0.21 ②
	Golf GTI	Front	0.50	+7.78	0.50	-0.73	1.63+/-0.33 ①
		Rear	—	—	0.17	-1.45	0.17+/-0.21 ②
	Tiguan	Front	0.50	+7.56	0.50	-0.45	1.60+/-0.33 ①
		Rear	—	—	0.50	-1.33	0.67+/-0.67 ②
2012	Eos	Front	0.50	+7.57	0.50	-0.60	1.63+/-0.33 ①
		Rear	—	—	0.50	-1.75	0.17+/-0.17 ②
	Golf GLI	Front	0.50	+7.83	0.50	-0.58	1.67+/-0.33 ①
		Rear	—	—	0.50	-1.33	0.17+/-0.21 ②
	Golf GTI	Front	0.50	+7.78	0.50	-0.73	1.63+/-0.33 ①
		Rear	—	—	0.17	-1.45	0.17+/-0.21 ②
	Tiguan	Front	0.50	+7.56	0.50	-0.45	1.60+/-0.33 ①
		Rear	—	—	0.50	-1.33	0.67+/-0.67 ②

① Toe differential angle with 20 deg. steering lock to left and right

② Total toe at specified camber.

71105_VWCA_C0011

TIRE, WHEEL AND BALL JOINT SPECIFICATIONS

Year	Model	OEM Tires Standard	OEM Tires Optional	Tire Pressures (psi) Front	Tire Pressures (psi) Rear	Wheel Size	Lug Nut (ft. lbs.)
2011	Eos	215/55-16	235/45-17-234/40-18	②	②	NS	89
	Golf	225/45-17	225/40-18	②	②	NS	89
	Tiguan	215/65-16	235/55-17-235/50-18	②	②	NS	89
2012	Eos	215/55-16	235/45-17-234/40-18	②	②	NS	89
	Golf	225/45-17	225/40-18	②	②	NS	89
	Tiguan	215/65-16	235/55-17-235/50-18	②	②	NS	89

NS: Not Specified

① 215/55-16, 235/45-17, 235/40-18

② See Vehicle Tire Information Sticker for correct inflation values.

71105_VWCA_C0012

BRAKE SPECIFICATIONS

All measurements in inches unless noted

| Year | Model | | Brake Disc | | | Drum Diameter | | Minimum Lining Thickness | Brake Caliper | |
			Original Thickness	Minimum Thickness	Maximum Run-out	Original Inside Diameter	Maximum Machine Diameter		Guide Pins (ft. lbs.)	Mounting Bolts (ft. lbs.)
2011	Eos	F	0.975	0.858	0.002	—	—	0.078	22	—
		R	0.486	0.390	0.002	—	—	0.078	—	35
	Golf GLI	F	0.975	0.858	0.002	—	—	0.078	22	—
		R	0.486	0.390	0.002	—	—	0.078	—	35
	Golf GTI	F	0.975	0.858	0.002	—	—	0.078	22	—
		R	0.486	0.390	0.002	—	—	0.078	—	35
	Tiguan	F	0.975	0.858	0.002	—	—	0.078	22	—
		R	0.486	0.390	0.002	—	—	0.078	—	35
2012	Eos	F	0.975	0.858	0.002	—	—	0.078	22	—
		R	0.486	0.390	0.002	—	—	0.078	—	35
	GLI	F	0.975	0.858	0.002	—	—	0.078	22	—
		R	0.486	0.390	0.002	—	—	0.078	—	35
	GTI	F	0.975	0.858	0.002	—	—	0.078	22	—
		R	0.486	0.390	0.002	—	—	0.078	—	35
	Tiguan	F	0.975	0.858	0.002	—	—	0.078	22	—
		R	0.486	0.390	0.002	—	—	0.078	—	35

F: Front

R: Rear

NS: Not Specified

NOTE: Use minimum thickness noted on disc if different from specification.

NOTE: Always use new bolts.

71105_VWCA_C0013

SCHEDULED MAINTENANCE INTERVALS
VOLKSWAGEN—EOS, GOLF, TIGUAN

TO BE SERVICED	TYPE OF SERVICE	10	20	30	40	50	60	70	80	90	100	110	120
Auto Trans - fluid	R				✓				✓				✓
Battery - check	S/I		✓		✓		✓		✓		✓		✓
Body- inspect for corrosion	S/I		✓		✓		✓		✓		✓		✓
Brake Pad thickness - check	S/I	✓	✓	✓	✓	✓	✓	✓	✓	✓	✓	✓	✓
Brake system - inspection	S/I		✓		✓		✓		✓		✓		✓
Cooling System - level check	S/I				✓				✓				✓
CV Joints - leaks & damage	S/I				✓				✓				✓
Door Arresters - lubricate	S/I				✓				✓				✓
Engine Oil & Filter - replace	R	✓	✓	✓	✓	✓	✓	✓	✓	✓	✓	✓	✓
Engine Compartment - leaks & damage	S/I				✓				✓				✓
Exhaust System - inspection	S/I				✓				✓				✓
Fuel Filter (2.0L TDI) - replace	S/I		✓		✓		✓		✓		✓		✓
Headlights - Check and adjust	S/I				✓				✓				✓
Power Steering - level check	S/I				✓				✓				✓
Rotate wheels	S/I	✓	✓	✓	✓	✓	✓	✓	✓	✓	✓	✓	✓
Serpentine Belt - inspection	S/I				✓				✓				✓
Service Interval Display - reset	S/I	✓	✓	✓	✓	✓	✓	✓	✓	✓	✓	✓	✓
Spark Plugs (except 2.0L) - replace	R				✓				✓				✓
Spark Plugs (2.0L) - replace	R						✓						✓
Tie Rod Ends - play & boots	S/I				✓				✓				✓
Timing Belt (except 2.0L TDI) - replace	R											✓	
Timing Belt (2.0L TDI) - replace	R												✓
Tires/Spare - inspection	S/I		✓		✓		✓		✓		✓		✓
Washer - clean nozzles	S/I	✓	✓	✓	✓	✓	✓	✓	✓	✓	✓	✓	✓
Wiper Blades - check	S/I	✓	✓	✓	✓	✓	✓	✓	✓	✓	✓	✓	✓
Air Cleaner - replace	Every 72 months												
Airbag System - inspect	Every 12 months												
Brake Fluid - replace	At 36 months, then every 24 months												
Brake Fluid (New Beetle) - replace	Every 24 months												
Cabin Air Filter - replace	Every 24 months												
Convertible roof latch - inspect	Every 24 months												
Spark Plugs - replace	Every 72 months												
Tire Filler Bottle - inspect	Every 24 months												
Tire Filler Bottle - replace	Every 48 months												
Tire Pressure Sensors - replace	Every 72 months												

R: Replace   S/I: Service or Inspect

PRECAUTIONS

Before servicing any vehicle, please be sure to read all of the following precautions, which deal with personal safety, prevention of component damage, and important points to take into consideration when servicing a motor vehicle:

• Never open, service or drain the radiator or cooling system when the engine is hot; serious burns can occur from the steam and hot coolant.

• Observe all applicable safety precautions when working around fuel. Whenever servicing the fuel system, always work in a well-ventilated area. Do not allow fuel spray or vapors to come in contact with a spark, open flame, or excessive heat (a hot drop light, for example). Keep a dry chemical fire extinguisher near the work area. Always keep fuel in a container specifically designed for fuel storage; also, always properly seal fuel containers to avoid the possibility of fire or explosion. Refer to the additional fuel system precautions later in this section.

• Fuel injection systems often remain pressurized, even after the engine has been turned **OFF**. The fuel system pressure must be relieved before disconnecting any fuel lines. Failure to do so may result in fire and/or personal injury.

• Brake fluid often contains polyglycol ethers and polyglycols. Avoid contact with the eyes and wash your hands thoroughly after handling brake fluid. If you do get brake fluid in your eyes, flush your eyes with clean, running water for 15 minutes. If eye irritation persists, or if you have taken brake fluid internally, IMMEDIATELY seek medical assistance.

• The EPA warns that prolonged contact with used engine oil may cause a number of skin disorders, including cancer. You should make every effort to minimize your exposure to used engine oil. Protective gloves should be worn when changing oil. Wash your hands and any other exposed skin areas as soon as possible after exposure to used engine oil. Soap and water, or waterless hand cleaner should be used.

• All new vehicles are now equipped with an air bag system, often referred to as a Supplemental Restraint System (SRS) or Supplemental Inflatable Restraint (SIR) system. The system must be disabled before performing service on or around system components, steering column, instrument panel components, wiring and sensors. Failure to follow safety and disabling procedures could result in accidental air bag deployment, possible personal injury and unnecessary system repairs.

• Always wear safety goggles when working with, or around, the air bag system. When carrying a non-deployed air bag, be sure the bag and trim cover are pointed away from your body. When placing a non-deployed air bag on a work surface, always face the bag and trim cover upward, away from the surface. This will reduce the motion of the module if it is accidentally deployed. Refer to the additional air bag system precautions later in this section.

• Clean, high quality brake fluid from a sealed container is essential to the safe and proper operation of the brake system. You should always buy the correct type of brake fluid for your vehicle. If the brake fluid becomes contaminated, completely flush the system with new fluid. Never reuse any brake fluid. Any brake fluid that is removed from the system should be discarded. Also, do not allow any brake fluid to come in contact with a painted surface; it will damage the paint.

• Never operate the engine without the proper amount and type of engine oil; doing so WILL result in severe engine damage.

• Timing belt maintenance is extremely important. Many models utilize an interference-type, non-freewheeling engine. If the timing belt breaks, the valves in the cylinder head may strike the pistons, causing potentially serious (also time-consuming and expensive) engine damage. Refer to the maintenance interval charts for the recommended replacement interval for the timing belt, and to the timing belt section for belt replacement and inspection.

• Disconnecting the negative battery cable on some vehicles may interfere with the functions of the on-board computer system(s) and may require the computer to undergo a relearning process once the negative battery cable is reconnected.

• When servicing drum brakes, only disassemble and assemble one side at a time, leaving the remaining side intact for reference.

• Only an MVAC-trained, EPA-certified automotive technician should service the air conditioning system or its components.

BRAKES

GENERAL INFORMATION

PRECAUTIONS

• Certain components within the ABS system are not intended to be serviced or repaired individually.

• Do not use rubber hoses or other parts not specifically specified for and ABS system. When using repair kits, replace all parts included in the kit. Partial or incorrect repair may lead to functional problems and require the replacement of components.

• Lubricate rubber parts with clean, fresh brake fluid to ease assembly. Do not use shop air to clean parts; damage to rubber components may result.

• Use only DOT 3 brake fluid from an unopened container.

• If any hydraulic component or line is removed or replaced, it may be necessary to bleed the entire system.

• A clean repair area is essential. Always clean the reservoir and cap thoroughly before removing the cap. The slightest amount of dirt in the fluid may plug an orifice and impair the system function. Perform repairs after components have been thoroughly cleaned; use only denatured alcohol to clean components. Do not allow ABS components to come into contact with any substance containing mineral oil; this includes used shop rags.

• The Anti-Lock control unit is a

ANTI-LOCK BRAKE SYSTEM (ABS)

microprocessor similar to other computer units in the vehicle. Ensure that the ignition switch is **OFF** before removing or installing controller harnesses. Avoid static electricity discharge at or near the controller.

• If any arc welding is to be done on the vehicle, the control unit should be unplugged before welding operations begin.

SPEED SENSORS

REMOVAL & INSTALLATION

1. Raise and safely support the vehicle and remove the wheel.

2. Unplug the speed sensor wiring connector.

3. Remove the bolt and remove the

speed sensor from the wheel bearing housing.

4. Before inserting speed sensor, clean the mounting hole inner surface.

5. Coat the sensor with hot bolt paste G 052 112 A3 or equivalent anti-seize paste.

6. Insert the speed sensor into the hole

in the wheel bearing housing and tighten the bolt to 71 in. lbs. (8 Nm).

7. Connect the wiring.

BRAKES

BLEEDING PROCEDURE

BLEEDING PROCEDURE

✵✵ CAUTION

Adhere strictly to work sequence when bleeding brake system.

1. Connect the brake charger/bleeder unit VAS 5234 or VAG 1869.

2. Open the bleeder valves in the prescribed sequence and bleed the brake calipers.

- Left front brake caliper
- Right front brake caliper

- Left rear brake caliper
- Right rear brake caliper

➡**The bleeder hose must fit tightly on the bleeder valve so that no air can enter the brake system.**

3. With the bleeder bottle hose attached, leave the bleeder valve open long enough that brake fluid exits without bubbles.

4. Press the brake pedal forcefully and hold.

5. Open the bleeder valve at the brake caliper.

6. Press the brake pedal down until stopped.

BLEEDING THE BRAKE SYSTEM

7. Close the bleeder valve with the pedal pressed.

8. Release the brake pedal slowly.

➡**This bleeding procedure must be performed 5 times per brake caliper.**

9. Perform the bleeding sequence as follows:

- Left front brake caliper
- Right front brake caliper
- Left rear brake caliper
- Right rear brake caliper

➡**A road test must be performed after bleeding. During this, at least one Anti-lock Brake System (ABS) stop must be performed!**

BRAKES

BRAKE CALIPER

REMOVAL & INSTALLATION

FN3 Type

➡**Work procedure applies only for replacing or when performing subsequent service work on brake caliper.**

1. Remove the wheels.

2. Using screwdriver, pry off the brake pad retaining spring from the brake caliper and remove it.

3. Disconnect the connector for brake pad wear indicator.

4. Connect the bleeder hose from the bleeder bottle to the bleeder valve of the brake caliper and then open bleeder valve.

5. Install the brake pedal actuator VAG 1869/2.

6. Close the bleeder valve and remove the bleeder hose.

7. Remove the brake hose.

8. Remove the caps.

9. Loosen both guide pins and remove them from the brake caliper.

10. Pull off the brake caliper from the brake carrier.

11. Remove the brake pads from the brake caliper.

To install:

12. Piston is pressed back into caliper.

13. Outer brake pad sits on brake carrier.

14. Insert the inner brake pad with retaining spring into the brake caliper.

✵✵ CAUTION

When installing the brake caliper, make sure that brake pad is not affixed to the brake caliper before the correct installation position has been reached. Do not damage the adhesion surface.

➡**Install brake caliper housing at bottom first. Brake caliper housing pin must be behind wheel bearing housing guide.**

15. Tighten the brake caliper to brake carrier using both guide pins.

16. Install both protective caps.

17. Install the brake hose to the brake caliper.

18. Remove the brake pedal actuator VAG 1869/2.

19. Install the retaining spring to the brake caliper.

20. Connect the brake pad wear indicator connector.

21. Bleed the brake system.

22. Install the wheels.

23. Before moving the vehicle, press the brake pedal firmly several times to properly seat the brake pads in their normal operating position.

24. Check the brake fluid level.

25. Tighten bolts/nuts to specification as follows:

- Guide pin to brake carrier: 21–22 ft. lbs. (28–30 Nm)

FRONT DISC BRAKES

- Brake line to brake caliper: 26 ft. lbs. (35 Nm)

FS III Type

See Figures 1 and 5.

1. Remove wheel.

2. Disconnect harness connector on vehicles with brake pad wear indicator.

3. Attach bleeder bottle bleeder hose onto bleeder valve of brake caliper housing and open bleeder valve.

4. Install brake pedal actuator V.A.G 1869/2.

5. Close bleeder valve and remove bleeder bottle.

6. Remove brake hose.

7. Remove protective caps.

8. Using screwdriver, pry off brake pad retaining spring from brake caliper housing and remove.

9. Unscrew and remove both guide pins s from brake caliper housing.

10. Remove brake caliper housing from brake carrier.

11. Remove brake pads from brake caliper housing.

To install:

12. The piston is pushed back.

✵✵ CAUTION

Brake pads are unidirectional. When installed, on the backing plate arrow of brake pad must face downward. Make certain of this!

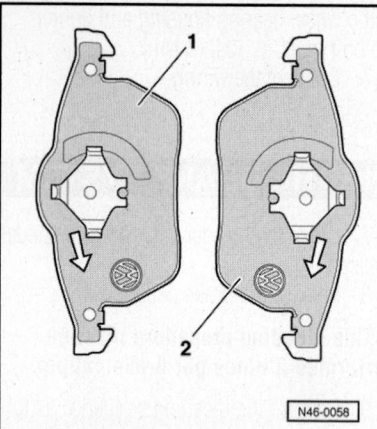

Fig. 1 Right brake pad, piston side (1) and Left brake pad, piston side; vehicles with wear indicator (2)

13. Insert brake pads.

14. Install outer brake pad on brake carrier.

15. Remove protective foil on backing plate of outer brake pad.

16. Tighten brake caliper housing to brake carrier using both guide pins.

17. Install both protective caps.

18. Install retaining spring in brake caliper housing.

19. Attach brake hose to brake caliper housing.

20. Remove brake pedal actuator V.A.G 1869/2.

21. Insert connector for brake pad wear indicator into bracket at suspension strut.

22. Bleeding brake system:

23. Mount wheel.

24. Depress brake pedal several times firmly before moving vehicle to properly seat brake pads in their normal operating position.

25. Check brake fluid level.

26. Tighten bolts/nuts to specification as follows:

- Guide pin to brake carrier: 21–22 ft. lbs. (28–30 Nm)
- Brake line to brake caliper: 26 ft. lbs. (35 Nm)

DISC BRAKE PADS

REMOVAL & INSTALLATION

FN3 Type

See Figures 2 through 4.

➡ **When removing, mark the brake pads in case they will be used again. Install in the same position, otherwise braking effect will be uneven!**

1. Remove the wheels.

2. Using a screwdriver, pry off the brake pad retaining spring from the brake caliper and remove.

3. Disconnect the connector for the brake pad wear indicator.

4. Remove the caps.

5. Loosen both guide pins and remove them from the brake caliper.

6. Remove the brake caliper and secure it with wire so that the weight of the caliper does not burden or damage the brake hose.

7. Remove the brake pads.

> ✳✳ **CAUTION**
>
> **Do not use compressed air to blow on the brake system components, the dust produced is harmful to health!**

8. Thoroughly clean the contact surfaces for the brake pads at the brake carrier, removing any corrosion.

9. Clean the brake caliper, especially the adhesive contact surface for the brake pads, it must be free of residual adhesive and grease.

➡ **Use only appropriate solvents for cleaning the brake caliper.**

To install:

> ✳✳ **CAUTION**
>
> **Before pressing the piston into the cylinder bore, some brake fluid must be extracted from the brake fluid reservoir. Otherwise, especially if the reservoir has been topped off, fluid will overflow and cause damage.**

10. Press the piston into the bore using the piston resetting tool T 10145.

11. On Eos, remove the protective foil on the backing plate of the outer brake pad. Install the outer brake pad to the brake carrier. Insert the inner brake pad with retaining spring in the brake caliper.

> ✳✳ **CAUTION**
>
> **When installing the brake caliper, make sure that brake pad is not affixed to the brake caliper before the correct installation position has been reached. Do not damage the adhesion surface.**

12. Insert inner brake pad (piston side) with large three finger clip and outer brake pad with small three finger clip.

13. Place the brake caliper with brake pads on the brake carrier first at the bottom.

14. Tighten guide pins and install both protective caps.

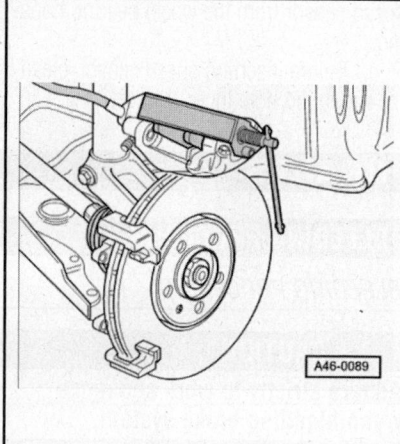

Fig. 2 Press the piston into the bore using the piston resetting tool T 10145

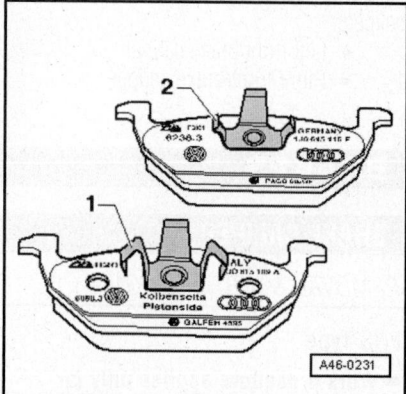

Fig. 3 Inner brake pad (piston side) with large three finger clip (1) and Outer brake pad with small three finger clip (2) (colored black)

15. Install retaining spring to the brake caliper.

16. Connect the brake pad wear indicator connector.

17. Install the wheels.

18. After replacing the brake pads, press the brake pedal firmly several times with the vehicle stationary so that the brake pads are properly seated in their normal operating position.

19. Check the brake fluid level after replacing the brake pads.

20. Tighten bolts/nuts to specification as follows:

- Guide pin to brake carrier: 21–22 ft. lbs. (28–30 Nm)

FS III Type

See Figures 1 and 5.

1. Remove wheels.

2. Disconnect harness connector on vehicles with brake pad wear indicator.

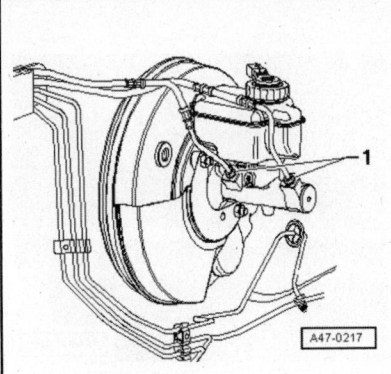

Fig. 4 Place the brake caliper with brake pads on the brake carrier first at the bottom

3. Remove protective caps.

4. Using screwdriver, pry off brake pad retaining spring from brake caliper housing and remove.

5. Unscrew and remove both guide pins from brake caliper housing.

6. Remove brake caliper housing and secure with wire so that the weight of the brake caliper housing does not stress or damage the brake hose.

7. Remove brake pads from brake caliper housing or from brake carrier.

8. Clean brake caliper housing, especially the adhesive surface for the brake

pad, it must be free of residual adhesive and grease.

➡**Use only appropriate solvents for cleaning brake caliper housing.**

To install:

9. Press piston back into caliper housing using resetting tool before inserting new brake pads. Before pushing back the piston, siphon some of the brake fluid out of brake fluid reservoir. Otherwise, if reservoir has been topped off, fluid will overflow and cause damage.

10. Press piston back.

11. Insert brake pads.

※※ **CAUTION**

Brake pads are unidirectional. When installed, on the backing plate arrow of brake pad must face downward. Make certain of this!

12. Install outer brake pad on brake carrier.

13. Remove protective foil on backing plate of outer brake pad.

14. Tighten brake caliper housing to brake carrier using both guide pins.

15. Install both protective caps.

16. Install retaining spring in brake caliper housing.

17. Insert connector for brake pad wear indicator into bracket at suspension strut.

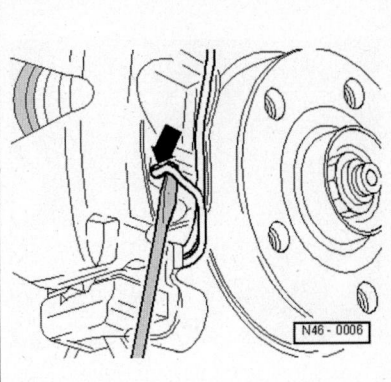

Fig. 5 Using screwdriver, pry off brake pad retaining spring from brake caliper housing and remove

18. Mount wheels.

19. After replacing brake pads and before moving vehicle, always depress brake pedal several times firmly to properly seat brake pads in their normal operating position.

20. Check brake fluid level after replacing brake pad.

21. Tighten bolts/nuts to specification as follows:

- Guide pin to brake carrier: 21–22 ft. lbs. (28–30 Nm)

BRAKES   **REAR DISC BRAKES**

BRAKE CALIPER

REMOVAL & INSTALLATION

Bosch Type

See Figures 6 through 8.

1. Raise the vehicle.

2. Remove rear wheels.

3. Push the lever on the brake caliper.

4. Disengage the parking brake cable from the lever on the brake caliper.

5. Squeeze the tabs and remove the parking brake cable from the bracket on the brake caliper.

6. Connect the bleed hose from the bleeder bottle to the brake caliper bleed valve and open the bleed valve.

7. Install a brake pedal holding tool (V.A.G 1869/2).

8. Close the bleed valve and remove the bleeder bottle.

9. Remove the brake hose connection and the banjo bolt from the brake caliper.

10. Counterhold the guide bolt and remove the bolts from the brake caliper.

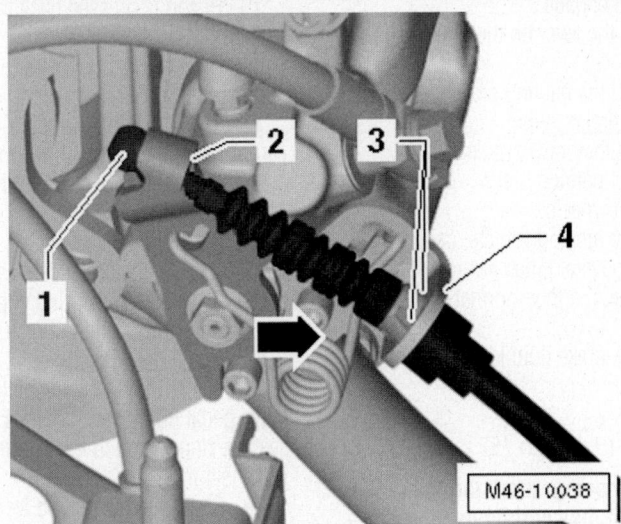

1. Parking brake cable   3. Tabs
2. Brake caliper   4. Bracket

Fig. 6 Push the lever on the brake caliper. Disengage the parking brake cable from the lever on the brake caliper. Squeeze the tabs and remove the parking brake cable from the bracket on the brake caliper.

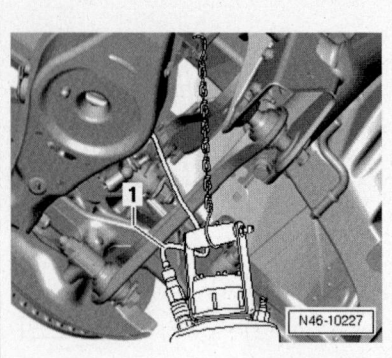

Fig. 7 Connect the bleed hose (1) from the bleeder bottle to the brake caliper bleed valve and open the bleed valve.

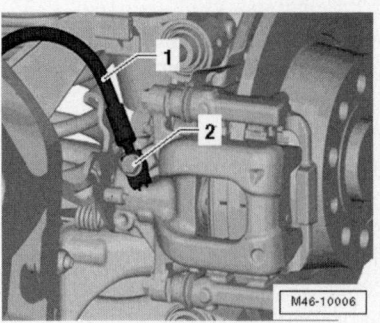

Fig. 8 Remove the brake hose connection (1) and the banjo bolt (2) from the brake caliper.

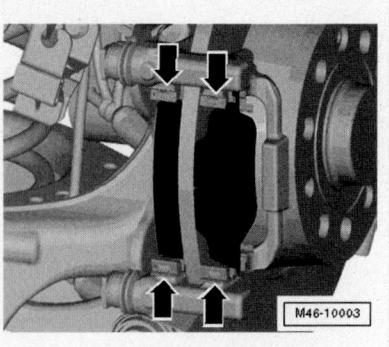

Fig. 9 Remove brake pads and anti-rattle springs.

11. Remove the brake caliper from the brake carrier.

To install:

12. Install in reverse order of removal. Note the following:

a. Piston is pressed back.

b. Brake pads sit in retaining springs on the brake carrier.

c. Secure brake caliper on brake carrier using new self-locking bolts. Tighten to 26 ft. lbs. (35 Nm).

13. Attach the brake hose and banjo bolt to the brake caliper. Tighten to 26 ft. lbs. (35 Nm).

14. Remove the pedal holding tool.

15. Guide the parking brake cable through the bracket on the brake caliper until the tabs engage.

16. Push the lever on the brake caliper back.

17. Attach the parking brake cable to the lever on the brake caliper.

18. Bleed the brake system.

19. Adjust parking brake

20. Install wheels.

21. Before moving vehicle, depress brake pedal several times firmly to properly seat brake pads in their normal operating position.

22. Check brake fluid level.

C38 Type

See Figures 13 through 15.

➡When removing, mark the brake pads in case they will be used again. Install in the same position, otherwise braking effect will be uneven!

1. Remove the wheels.

2. Unhook the brake cable from the lever on the brake caliper.

3. Remove the spring clip and pull the

brake cable from the holder on the brake caliper.

4. Connect the bleeder hose from the bleeder bottle to the bleeder valve on the brake caliper and then open the bleeder valve.

5. Install the brake pedal actuator VAG 1869/2.

6. Close the bleeder valve and remove the bleeder bottle.

7. Remove the brake line.

8. Remove both bolts from the brake caliper, counter hold on the guide pins when doing this.

9. Pull off the brake caliper from brake carrier.

To install:

10. Piston is pressed back into caliper.

11. Brake pads sit in the anti-rattle springs in the brake carrier.

12. Secure the brake caliper to the brake carrier using the new self-locking bolts.

13. Install the brake line to the brake caliper.

14. Bleed the brake system.

15. Hook in the brake cable and secure it to the holder with the spring clip.

16. Adjust the parking brake.

17. Install the wheels.

18. Before moving the vehicle, press the brake pedal firmly several times to properly seat the brake pads in their normal operating position.

19. Check the brake fluid level.

20. Tighten bolts/nuts to specification as follows:

- Bolt, brake caliper to brake carrier (use new bolts): 26 ft. lbs. (35 Nm)
- Brake line to brake caliper: 10 ft. lbs. (14 Nm)

DISC BRAKE PADS

REMOVAL & INSTALLATION

Bosch Type

See Figures 9 through 12.

➡When removing, mark brake pads that will be used again. Install in the same position, otherwise braking effect will be uneven!

1. Raise the vehicle and remove rear wheels.

2. Counterhold the guide bolt and remove the bolts from the brake caliper.

3. Remove brake caliper and secure with wire so that the weight of the brake caliper does not burden or damage the brake hose.

4. Remove brake pads and anti-rattle springs.

To install:

5. Install the (T10165) so that the collar on the (T10165/1) is touching.

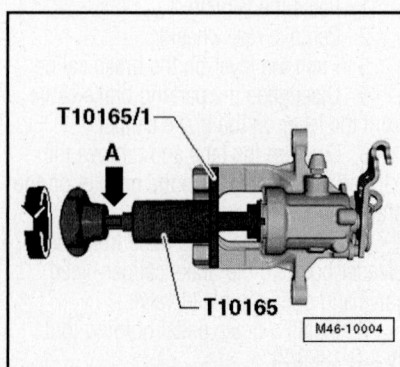

Fig. 10 Install the (T10165) so that the collar on the (T10165/1) is touching. For pistons that are difficult to move, an open-end wrench (13 mm) can be applied at the appropriate wrench surface (A).

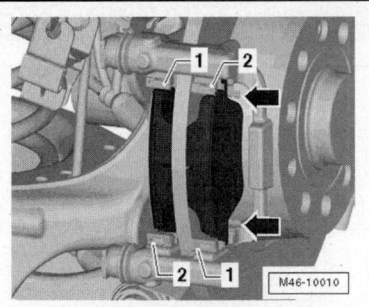

Fig. 11 Insert the brake pad retaining plates (1 and 2) in the brake carrier. The brake pad retaining plates are different. They can only be installed diagonally to each other. Install the brake pad retaining plates so that the guides on both sides of the brake carrier face out.

6. For pistons that are difficult to move, an open-end wrench (13 mm) can be applied at the appropriate wrench surface.

7. Insert the brake pad retaining plates in the brake carrier.

➡**The brake pad retaining plates are different. They can only be installed diagonally to each other.**

8. Install the brake pad retaining plates so that the guides on both sides of the brake carrier face out.

9. Insert brake pads in brake carrier.

10. Make sure the brake pads are seated in the brake pad retaining plates.

11. Secure brake caliper using new self-locking bolts. Tighten to 26 ft. lbs. (35 Nm).

12. Install wheels.

13. The repair kit has 4 self-locking screws for installing the brake caliper. Always use these.

14. After replacing brake pads, depress brake pedal firmly several times with vehicle stationary so that the brake pads are properly seated in their normal operating position.

15. Check brake fluid level after replacing brake pad.

C38 Type

See Figures 13 through 15.

➡**When removing, mark the brake pads in case they will be used again. Install in the same position, otherwise braking effect will be uneven!**

1. Remove the wheels.

2. Counter hold the guide pins and remove the bolts for the brake caliper.

3. Remove the brake caliper and secure it with wire so that the weight of the brake caliper does not burden or damage the brake hose.

Fig. 12 Insert brake pads in brake carrier. Make sure the brake pads are seated in the brake pad retaining plates.

4. Remove the brake pads and anti-rattle springs.

✳✳ CAUTION

Do not use compressed air to blow on the brake system components, the dust produced is harmful to health!

5. Contact surfaces between the brake pads and brake carrier must be cleaned, removing any corrosion.

6. Clean the brake caliper.

➡**Use only appropriate solvents for cleaning brake caliper.**

To install:

✳✳ CAUTION

Before pressing the piston into the cylinder bore, some brake fluid must be extracted from the brake fluid reservoir. Otherwise, especially if the reservoir has been topped off, fluid will overflow and cause damage.

7. Press the piston into the bore using the resetting & extracting tool T 10165 and 1065/1. Do not damage the protective caps.

➡**For pistons that are difficult to press in, a 13 mm open end wrench can be used on the resetting & extracting tool T 10165.**

8. Insert the brake pad anti-rattle springs and brake pads to the brake carrier.

9. Make sure that the brake pads are located correctly in the anti-rattle springs.

10. Secure the brake caliper using the new self-locking bolts to 26 ft. lbs. (35 Nm)

11. Install the wheels.

12. After replacing the brake pads, press the brake pedal firmly several times with the vehicle stationary so that the brake pads are

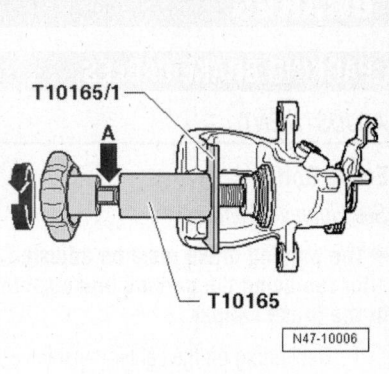

Fig. 13 Press the piston into the bore using the resetting & extracting tool T 10165 and 1065/1. Do not damage the protective caps

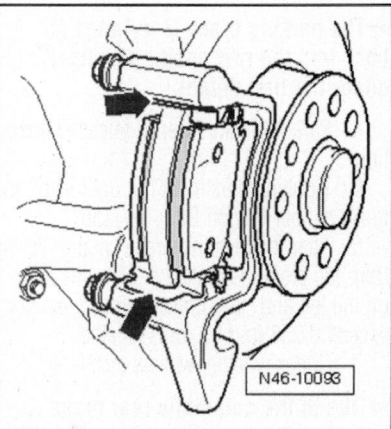

Fig. 14 Insert the brake pad anti-rattle springs and brake pads to the brake carrier

properly seated in their normal operating position.

13. Check the brake fluid level after replacing brake pad.

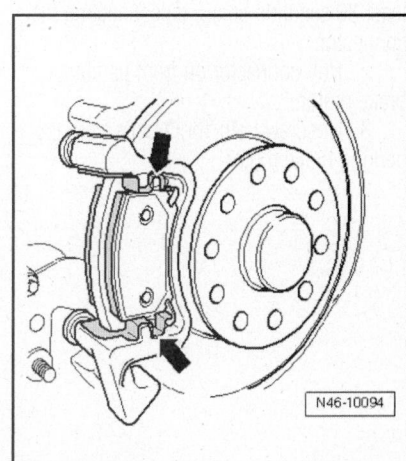

Fig. 15 Make sure that the brake pads are located correctly in the anti-rattle springs

PARKING BRAKE CABLES

ADJUSTMENT

Eos & Golf

See Figures 16 and 17.

➡The parking brake must be adjusted after replacing the parking brake cable or the brake caliper.

1. Depending on the center console version, either remove only the cup holder, the rear cover or the entire center console.
2. Press the brake forcefully at least three times.
3. Engage the parking brake three times and release it.

➡The parking brake lever must go back into the rest position by itself under the first detent.

4. Parking brake lever in released position.
5. Tighten adjustment nut until lever on brake caliper lifts off from the stop.
6. After the lever on brake caliper lifts off from the stop, the distance "a" to the stop on the left and right brake caliper must not exceed 0.056 in. (1.5 mm) together.
7. Check whether wheels turn freely.

➡Due to the automatic rear brake adjuster, there is no need to adjust the parking brake after making the initial adjustment.

Tiguan

See Figure 18.

The parking brake on this vehicle is operated by a motor and not cables.

1. Ignition must be switched off for at least 30 seconds before disconnecting the connector.
2. Pull connector off from parking brake motor.
3. Unscrew both Torx® bolts from the parking brake motor.

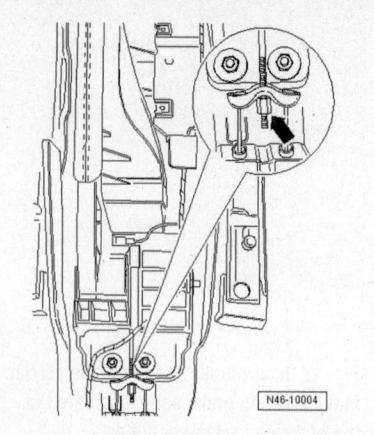

Fig. 16 Tighten adjustment nut until lever on brake caliper lifts off from the stop

4. Pull off parking brake motor from brake caliper.
5. Remove the seal.

✳✳ CAUTION

Make sure that the ring groove of the seal and the contact surface of the parking brake motor do not become damaged.

6. Clean the ring groove and the contact surface of the parking brake motor.

To install:

7. Lightly coat the new gasket with brake fluid and then install it.
8. Rotate the spindle back slightly with an 8 mm multi-point socket until the parking brake motor can be positioned correctly.

➡Do not remove the gasket when assembling the parking brake motor.

9. Carefully set the parking brake motor in place, paying attention to the seat of the seal.
10. Rotate the parking brake motor until the bolt hole and threads are aligned.

Make sure that the parking brake motor is seated flush against the brake caliper. Do

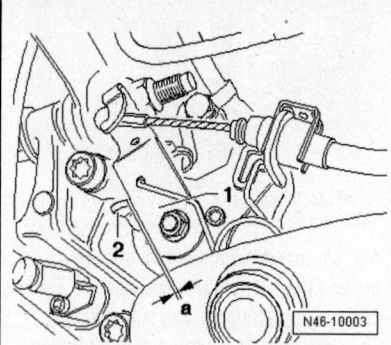

Fig. 17 After the lever 1 on brake caliper lifts off from the stop, the distance "a" to the stop 2 on the left and right brake caliper must not exceed 0.056 in. (1.5 mm) together

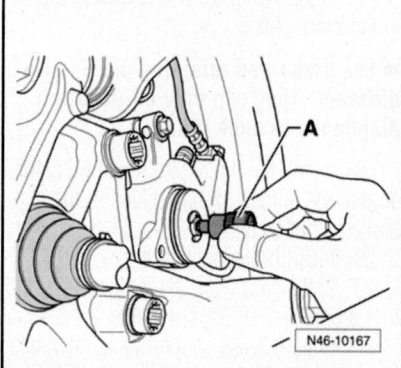

Fig. 18 Rotate the spindle back slightly with an 8 mm multi-point socket until the parking brake motor can be positioned correctly

not, under any circumstances, pull the parking brake motor against the brake caliper using the bolts.

11. Set the Torx® bolts in place by hand and then tighten.
12. Install connector.
13. Perform the brake system basic setting.

CHASSIS ELECTRICAL | **AIR BAG (SUPPLEMENTAL RESTRAINT SYSTEM)**

GENERAL INFORMATION

❊❊ CAUTION

These vehicles are equipped with an air bag system. The system must be disarmed before performing service on, or around, system components, the steering column, instrument panel components, wiring and sensors. Failure to follow the safety precautions and the disarming procedure could result in accidental air bag deployment, possible injury and unnecessary system repairs.

SERVICE PRECAUTIONS

Disconnect and isolate the battery negative cable before beginning any airbag system component diagnosis, testing, removal, or installation procedures. Allow system capacitor to discharge for two minutes before beginning any component service. This will disable the airbag system. Failure to disable the airbag system may result in accidental airbag deployment, personal injury, or death.

Do not place an intact undeployed airbag face down on a solid surface. The airbag will propel into the air if accidentally deployed and may result in personal injury or death.

When carrying or handling an undeployed airbag, the trim side (face) of the airbag should be pointing away from the body to minimize possibility of injury if accidental deployment occurs. Failure to do this may result in personal injury or death.

Replace airbag system components with OEM replacement parts. Substitute parts may appear interchangeable, but internal differences may result in inferior occupant protection. Failure to do so may result in occupant personal injury or death.

Wear safety glasses, rubber gloves, and long sleeved clothing when cleaning powder residue from vehicle after an airbag deployment. Powder residue emitted from a deployed airbag can cause skin irritation. Flush affected area with cool water if irritation is experienced. If nasal or throat irritation is experienced, exit the vehicle for fresh air until the irritation ceases. If irritation continues, see a physician.

Do not use a replacement airbag that is not in the original packaging. This may

result in improper deployment, personal injury, or death.

The factory installed fasteners, screws and bolts used to fasten airbag components have a special coating and are specifically designed for the airbag system. Do not use substitute fasteners. Use only original equipment fasteners listed in the parts catalog when fastener replacement is required.

During, and following, any child restraint anchor service, due to impact event or vehicle repair, carefully inspect all mounting hardware, tether straps, and anchors for proper installation, operation, or damage. If a child restraint anchor is found damaged in any way, the anchor must be replaced. Failure to do this may result in personal injury or death.

Deployed and non-deployed airbags may or may not have live pyrotechnic material within the airbag inflator.

Do not dispose of driver/passenger/curtain airbags or seat belt tensioners unless you are sure of complete deployment. Refer to the Hazardous Substance Control System for proper disposal.

Dispose of deployed airbags and tensioners consistent with state, provincial, local, and federal regulations.

After any airbag component testing or service, do not connect the battery negative cable. Personal injury or death may result if the system test is not performed first.

If the vehicle is equipped with the Occupant Classification System (OCS), do not connect the battery negative cable before performing the OCS Verification Test using the scan tool and the appropriate diagnostic information. Personal injury or death may result if the system test is not performed properly.

Never replace both the Occupant Restraint Controller (ORC) and the Occupant Classification Module (OCM) at the same time. If both require replacement, replace one, then perform the Airbag System test before replacing the other.

Both the ORC and the OCM store Occupant Classification System (OCS) calibration data, which they transfer to one another when one of them is replaced. If both are replaced at the same time, an irreversible fault will be set in both modules and the OCS may malfunction and cause personal injury or death.

If equipped with OCS, the Seat Weight Sensor is a sensitive, calibrated unit and

must be handled carefully. Do not drop or handle roughly. If dropped or damaged, replace with another sensor. Failure to do so may result in occupant injury or death.

If equipped with OCS, the front passenger seat must be handled carefully as well. When removing the seat, be careful when setting on floor not to drop. If dropped, the sensor may be inoperative, could result in occupant injury, or possibly death.

If equipped with OCS, when the passenger front seat is on the floor, no one should sit in the front passenger seat. This uneven force may damage the sensing ability of the seat weight sensors. If sat on and damaged, the sensor may be inoperative, could result in occupant injury, or possibly death.

DISARMING THE SYSTEM

➡**The Anti-theft system must be deactivated before disconnecting the battery to avoid system engagement upon reconnecting the battery.**

The Anti-theft system is deactivated when the vehicle is unlocked via the unlock button on the key fob, or when the vehicle is opened via Keyless Access, or when the ignition switch is turned **ON** (with a charged battery connected), or when the immobilizer registers an authorized key. Do not disconnect the positive battery terminal unless the battery is to be removed.

Disconnect the negative battery cable to disarm the airbag system. No waiting time is necessary before beginning work.

ARMING THE SYSTEM

➡**The Anti-theft system must be deactivated before disconnecting the battery to avoid system engagement upon reconnecting the battery.**

The Anti-theft system is deactivated when the vehicle is unlocked via the unlock button on the key fob, or when the vehicle is opened via Keyless Access, or when the ignition switch is turned **ON** (with a charged battery connected), or when the immobilizer registers an authorized key. Do not disconnect the positive battery terminal unless the battery is to be removed.

After reconnecting the airbag wiring, turn the ignition switch **ON** and make sure no one is inside the vehicle, then connect the battery cable.

CLOCKSPRING CENTERING

See Figures 19 and 20.

1. When installing spiral spring, spiral spring must be in center position and wheels must be in the straight-ahead position.

2. The following depicts center position of spiral spring, which is dependent on the manufacturer.

    a. The color marked (black square) band must be located in viewing window.

    b. The color marked (yellow) band must be located in viewing window.

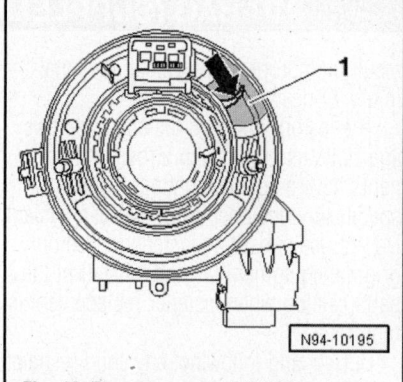

Fig. 19 The color marked (black square) band must be located in viewing window (1)

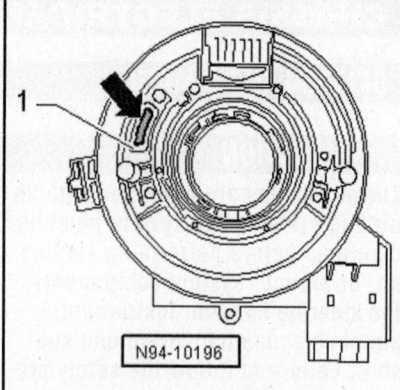

Fig. 20 The color marked (yellow) band must be located in viewing window (1)

DRIVE TRAIN

AUTOMATIC TRANSAXLE FLUID

DRAIN AND REFILL

See Figure 21.

Shortening The Pipe On The Adapter For Oil Filling (VAS 6262 A)

1. Shorten the pipe to 210 mm. This assures the pipe on the adapter for oil filling will not touch the bottom of some fluid containers.

➡**Dimension is measured starting from the green surface on the adapter for oil filling.**

2. Make a mark on the pipe at dimension -a-, and cut it using the pipe cutter (VAS 6056/2).

Checking Fluid

➡**When checking the transmission fluid level, always replace the seal on the plug.**

1. Turn off the engine.

➡**The transmission fluid temperature must not be more than approximately 86°F (30°C) at the start of the test.**

2. Make sure the transmission is not in emergency running mode, and the fluid temperature is not higher than 86°F (30°C) and check that the following conditions are met:

    a. The vehicle is horizontal

    b. The selector level is in the "P" position.

3. Connect the tester and move through the selections until it is ready for operation:

    a. Press the right button "Guided Functions".

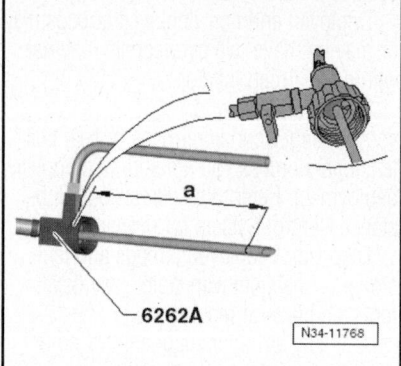

Fig. 21 Make a mark on the pipe at dimension (a), and cut it using the pipe cutter (VAS 6056/2).

    b. Select the vehicle, the transmission and check ATF level.

    c. Press the right arrow button.

4. Start the engine.

5. Lift the vehicle.

6. Place a drip tray under the transmission.

7. On the tester, press the right arrow button.

8. If the test temperature is 95 to 113°F (35 to 45°C), remove the plug from the oil pan.

➡**If the fluid flows out of the overflow tube and continues to drip out of hole, the fluid does not need to be topped off.**

9. Install and tighten the plug with a new seal to 20 ft. lbs. (27 Nm). The level check is now completed.

10. If no fluid drips out of the hole, fill with transmission fluid.

Filling

1. Install the adapter for oil filling (VAS 6291/2, VAS 6262/2) into the oil pan hole, hand tight while the engine is running.

2. Fill with 1 liter fluid.

3. Connect the oil filler adapter (VAS 6262) to the quick release coupling and check:

    a. If fluid flows out of the hole, the fluid does not need to be topped off.

    b. Allow the fluid to drain until it drips.

    c. Install and tighten the plug with a new seal to 20 ft. lbs. (27 Nm). The fluid level check is now completed.

4. If the fluid does not drip, fill with another liter of fluid.

✳✳ CAUTION

Too little or too much transmission fluid will impair the transmission. If 2 liters are missing, you should check the transmission more closely. There is probably a larger leak.

FILTER REPLACEMENT

1. Remove the transmission fluid pan.

2. Remove the transmission fluid filter bolts.

3. Remove the filter from the valve body.

To install:

4. Lightly coat the seals on the filter suction collar with transmission fluid.

5. Replace the filter if the seals are loose or faulty.

6. Install the filter and tighten the bolts.

7. Install the transmission fluid pan.

8. Fill with fluid and check the level.

DIRECT SHIFT GEAR TRANSAXLE

DRAINING AND REFILLING

See Figures 22 through 24.

1. Allow the transmission to cool down.
2. Turn off the engine, remove the overflow tube and drain any oil.
3. Reinstall the overflow tube and "overfill" the oil.
4. Start the engine and drain any excess oil until the level has reached the overflow tube.
5. Turn the engine off.
6. Make sure the vehicle is level and all hoist supports are the same height.
7. The noise insulation is removed, if necessary.
8. The selector level is in the "P" position.
9. The vehicle diagnostic tester is connected.

➡ **Only use the DSG® oil available as a replacement part. Other oils can cause malfunctions or transmission failure.**

10. Connect the vehicle diagnostic tester and identify the vehicle in "Guided Functions".
11. Select "DSG Transmission".
12. Select "Check Fluid Level".
13. Remove the oil drain and check plug.

➡ **A black plastic overflow tube is located in the plug hole (with 8 mm hex socket head). Its length determines the oil level in the transmission.**

14. Remove the overflow tube and allow the oil to drain.

➡ **About 5 liters of oil will drain out.**

15. Reinstall the overflow tube and tighten it to 2 ft. lbs. (3 Nm).
16. Install the quick release coupling from the adapter for oil filling (VAS 6262 A) into the plug hole hand-tight.
17. Shake the container before opening.
18. Connect the container to the adapter for oil filling. Connect the oil filler adapter to the quick release coupling.
19. Fill with 5.5 liters of oil.
20. To change containers, close the shut off valve or hold the adapter for oil filling higher than the transmission.
21. Install and tighten the oil drain and check plug hand-tight only.
22. Start the engine.
23. Press the brake pedal and select

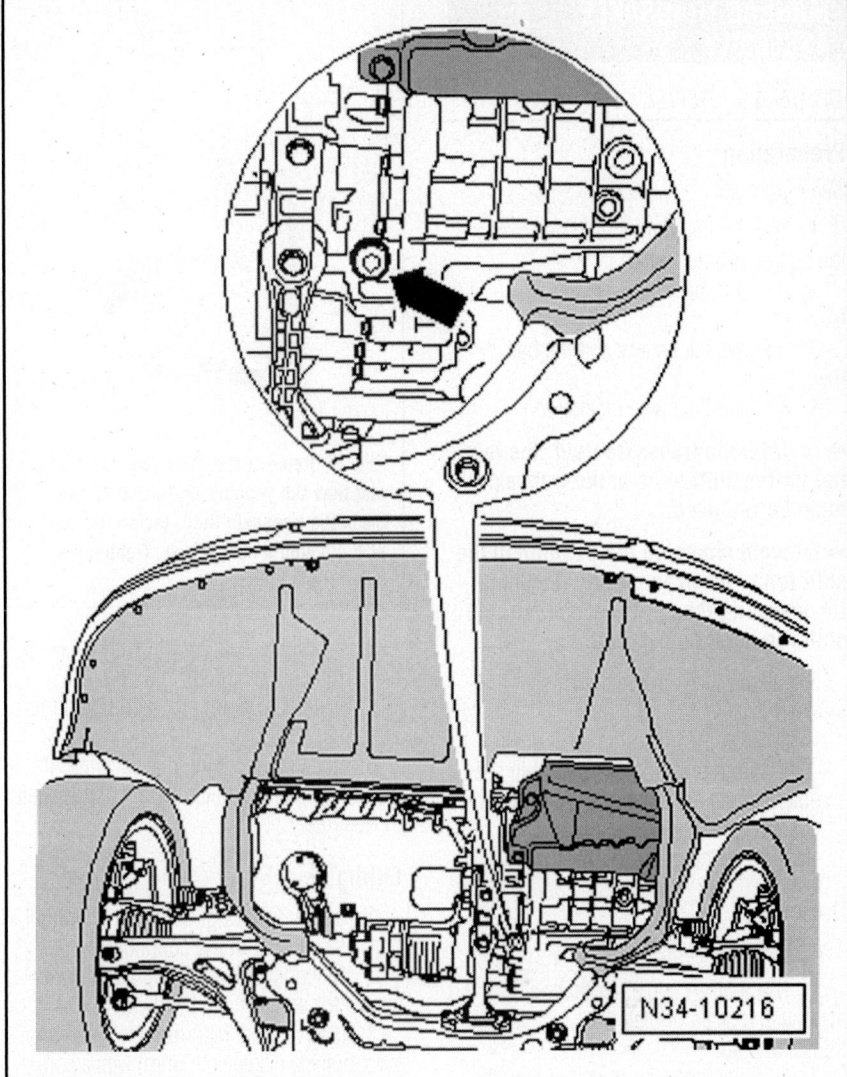

Fig. 22 Remove the oil drain and check plug.

each selector lever position for approximately 3 seconds, then move the selector lever back into the "P" position.

24. Do not turn off the engine.
25. Check the oil level and add oil as necessary.

Fig. 23 Remove the overflow tube and allow the oil to drain.

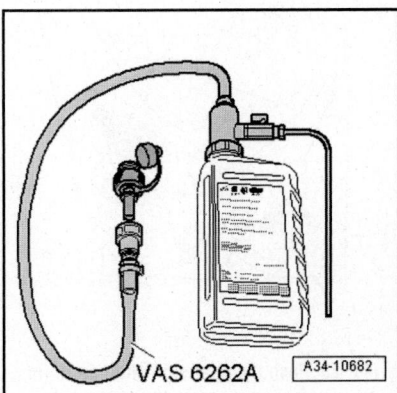

VAS 6262A

Fig. 24 Install the quick release coupling from the adapter for oil filling (VAS 6262 A) into the plug hole hand-tight.

MANUAL TRANSAXLE ASSEMBLY

DRAIN AND REFILL

Preparation

See Figure 25.

1. Turn off the ignition and disconnect the battery ground cable.
2. Remove the engine cover with air filter.
3. Remove the battery and the battery tray.
4. Remove the noise insulation.

➡ **To drain the transaxle fluid, the journal for the shift forks in the transaxle must be removed.**

➡ **To avoid changing the position of the shift forks, for example, by involuntarily operating the shift mechanism, the shift rod must be secured.**

5. Secure the gear shift shaft as follows:
   a. Push the gear shift shaft down.
   b. While pressing the gear shift shaft down, rotate the locking pin upward and simultaneously press it in until it engages in the gear shift shaft.

Draining

See Figures 26 and 27.

1. Use a clean container that holds 3 liters with a scale printed on it to catch the transaxle fluid.
2. Remove the drain plug and then the support pin and drain the transaxle fluid.

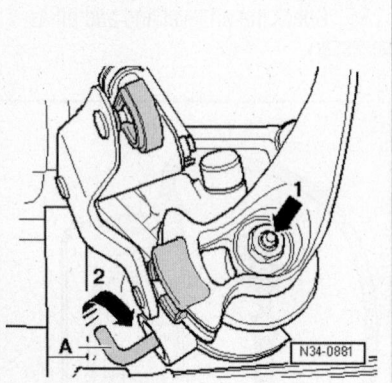

Fig. 25 Push the gear shift shaft down (in the direction of arrow 1). While pressing the gear shift shaft down, rotate the locking pin (A in the direction of arrow 2) upward and simultaneously press it in until it engages in the gear shift shaft.

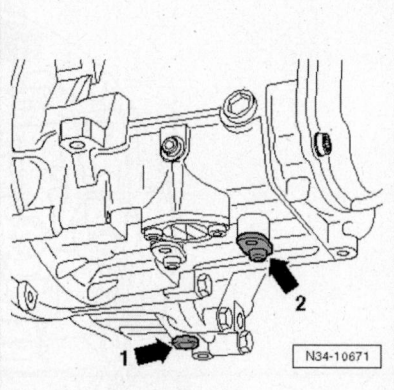

Fig. 26 Remove the drain plug (arrow 1) and then the support pin (arrow 2) and drain the transaxle fluid. Install the support pin with a new O-ring. Tighten the support pin bolt.

3. Install the support pin with a new O-ring. Tighten the support pin bolt.
4. Install the drain plug and tighten it to 26 ft. lbs. (35 Nm).
5. Rotate the locking pin back into its starting position so that the gear shift shaft moves freely.

Filling

1. Add 1.7 liters of fluid to the amount of transaxle fluid in the container.
2. Disconnect the backup lamp switch connector and remove the switch.
3. Insert a hose (approximately 600 mm long, outside diameter 10 mm) with a commercially available funnel into the hole backup lamp switch hole and fill the transaxle fluid.
4. Install the backup lamp switch and connect the connector.
5. Make sure the shift mechanism works correctly.
6. Install the battery tray and the battery.
7. Install the engine cover with air filter.
8. Connect the battery and follow the procedure regarding what to do after connecting the battery.
9. Install the noise insulation.

CLUTCH

BLEEDING

Except Pressure Bleeder

1. Before servicing the vehicle, refer to the Precautions Section.
2. The clutch and brakes share the same reservoir. Clean all dirt and grease from the cap to be sure no foreign substances enter the system.

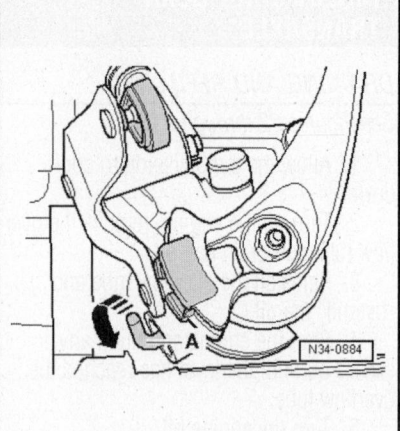

Fig. 27 Rotate the locking pin (A) back into its starting position (in the direction of the arrow) so that the gear shift shaft moves freely.

3. Remove the cap and diaphragm and fill the reservoir to the top with the approved DOT 4 brake fluid. Fully loosen the bleed screw which is in the slave cylinder body next to the inlet connection.
4. At this point bubbles of air will appear at the bleed screw outlet. When the slave cylinder is full and a steady stream of fluid comes out of the slave cylinder bleeder, tighten the bleed screw.
5. Refill the reservoir and cap it. Exert a light load of about 20 lbs. (9 kg) to the slave cylinder piston by pushing the release lever towards the cylinder and loosen the bleed screw. Maintain a constant light load; fluid and any air that is left will be expelled through the bleed port. Tighten the bleed screw when a steady flow of fluid with no air is being expelled.
6. Fill the reservoir fluid level back to normal capacity, if necessary repeat Step 4.
7. Exert a light load to the release lever but do not open the bleeder screw as the piston in the slave cylinder will move slowly down the bore. Repeat this operation 2–3 times; the fluid movement will force any air left in the system into the reservoir. The hydraulic system should now be fully bled.
8. Check the operation of the clutch hydraulic system and repeat this procedure, if necessary.

Pressure Bleeder

1. Remove entire air filter housing if bleeder is not accessible through it.
2. Connect brake filler/bleeder unit VAS 5234 or V.A.G 1869.

➡**If necessary, use bleeder hose (670 mm long) V.A.G 1238/B3 to bleed system.**

3. Connect bleeder hose to collector bottle of brake bleeder unit.

4. Connect bleeder hose to bleeder.

5. Pressurize the system to 29 psi (2 bar).

6. Open bleeder valve approximately 1/4 rotation.

7. Move the clutch pedal 15 to 20 times rapidly by hand from stop to stop.

8. Close bleeder valve and switch bleeder device off.

9. After completing the bleeding procedure, if a pressure of 29 psi (2 bar) has been released, operate brake pedal 10 times using the foot.

10. If removed, install entire air filter housing.

TRANSFER CASE ASSEMBLY

REMOVAL & INSTALLATION

Tiguan

See Figure 28.

This model does not use a traditional transfer case assembly. It uses a Haldex clutch that is attached in-line with the driveshaft at the rear differential.

1. Support the front exhaust pipe using the tensioning strap T10038 at the driveshaft center bearing.

2. Disconnect the exhaust system at the clamping sleeve when removing the rear exhaust system components.

3. Remove the noise insulation below the engine/transmission.

4. Remove pendulum support bolts.

5. Loosen driveshaft intermediate bearing bolts approximately 2 turns.

6. Press the engine and transmission forward and secure position with a suitable wood block.

7. So that noises due to imbalance do not occur later, if there are no markings present, then mark the position of the driveshaft flexible disc to the rear final drive flange.

8. Remove the driveshaft flexible disc bolts from the rear final drive.

9. Place a cloth on the tunnel brace.

10. Remove the driveshaft from the rear final drive and place it on the tunnel brace.

11. In order to remove the clutch, it is necessary to have sufficient clearance to the flexible disc.

12. When doing this, only loosen the tunnel brace, do not remove it.

13. Place the drip tray VAS 6208 under the rear final drive.

14. Remove drain plug and completely drain the high performance clutch oil.

15. Disconnect the connector from the all-wheel drive control module.

16. Install drain plug with new seal and tighten to 22 ft. lbs. (30 Nm).

17. Remove bolts and remove clutch from rear final drive.

To install:

18. Install in reverse sequence.

19. Install all parts marked to each other in original positions.

20. Insert new O-ring and lightly lubricate with high performance clutch oil.

21. Insert the clutch in the rear final drive.

22. Connect connector 2 to the all-wheel drive control module.

23. Tighten the driveshaft.

24. Align center bearing free of tension and tighten.

25. Tighten the tunnel brace.

26. Tighten pendulum support with new bolts.

27. Install the exhaust system and align it without tension.

28. Install noise insulation.

29. Fill with new high performance clutch oil and check oil level in clutch.

30. Tighten bolts/nuts to specification as follows:

- Clutch to rear final drive: 37 ft. lbs. (50 Nm)
- Flexible disc to rear final drive: 44 ft. lbs. (60 Nm)

FRONT HALFSHAFT

REMOVAL & INSTALLATION

Eos & Golf

See Figure 29.

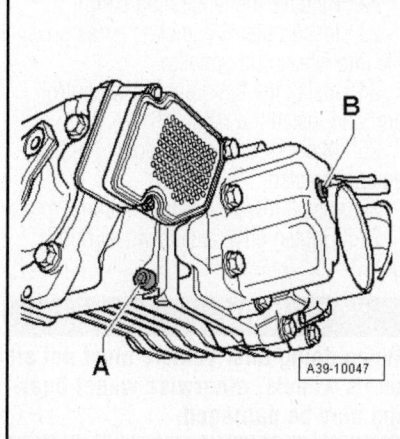

Fig. 28 Haldex clutch drain plug (A) and fill plug (B)

1. Loosen drive axle bolt to wheel hub

✳✳ CAUTION

When doing this, vehicle must not stand on wheels, otherwise wheel bearing may be damaged.

2. Remove wheel.

3. Remove lower noise insulation.

4. Remove nuts and pull wheel bearing housing with ball joint out of control arm.

5. Pull drive axle out of wheel hub and secure to body.

6. Attach wedge tool T10161 between transmission housing and triple roller joint.

7. Press inner joint out of transmission by tapping with hammer onto wedge tool.

8. Remove drive axle.

To install:

9. Insert new securing ring into groove of joint piece pin.

10. Mesh outer and inner splines of joint piece and transmission.

11. Grasp drive axle by hand and slide into joint piece until stop.

12. Slide joint piece into transmission with a "jerk".

➡**Do not pull drive axle out of joint piece too far when doing this.**

✳✳ CAUTION

Do not use hammer or other knocking tool under any circumstance!

13. Check drive axle in transmission for proper seating by pulling joint piece against resistance from circlip.

➡**For this check, do not pull drive axle but pull joint piece only.**

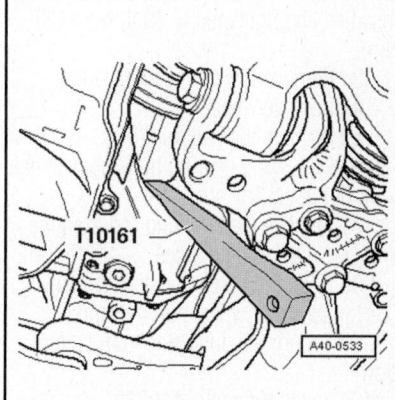

Fig. 29 Press inner joint out of transmission by tapping with hammer onto wedge tool T10161

14. Insert outer joint as far as possible into wheel hub splines.

15. Remove lower noise insulation.

16. Bolt on ball joint with control arm.

17. Ensure that boot is not damaged or twisted.

18. Tighten drive axle bolt to wheel hub.

19. When doing this, vehicle must not stand on wheels, otherwise wheel bearing may be damaged.

20. Install wheel.

21. Tighten bolts/nuts to specification as follows:

- Ball joint to control arm (Use new nut): 44 ft. lbs. (60 Nm)
- Drive axle to wheel hub "hex head bolt" (use new bolt): 148 ft. lbs. (200 Nm), plus 180° additional rotation
- Drive axle to wheel hub "12-point bolt" (use new bolt): 52 ft. lbs. (70 Nm), plus 90° additional rotation
- Drive axle to wheel hub "hex head bolt" (use new bolt): 148 ft. lbs. (200 Nm), plus 180° additional rotation
- Drive axle to wheel hub "12-point bolt" (use new bolt): 52 ft. lbs. (70 Nm), plus 90° additional rotation

Tiguan

CV Joint

1. Loosen the drive axle to wheel hub bolt.

➡**Vehicle must not sit on its wheels when doing so.**

2. With bolt loosened, wheel bearing can be damaged by vehicle's own weight. If a vehicle needs to be moved when the drive axle is removed, an outer joint must be installed and tightened to 89 ft. lbs. (120 Nm).

3. Remove lower noise insulation.

4. Remove wheel.

5. Remove the ball joint nuts.

6. Pull wheel bearing housing with ball joint out of control arm.

7. Remove the coupling rod from the stabilizer bar on both sides.

8. Slide the outer Constant Velocity (CV) joint out of wheel hub by hand.

9. Secure the drive axle from falling down.

10. Install the puller T10382.

➡**For the inner CV joint, the opening in the removing plate T10382/1 must face the spindles T10382/1.**

11. Attach the puller to the slide hammer VW 771.

12. In order to remove the drive axle from the transmission using the puller, the strut and all its components must be pulled toward the rear of the vehicle.

13. Pull the strut and its components using the tensioning strap T10038 as far as possible towards the rear of the vehicle, for example on the workshop hoist arm, until the puller can be installed parallel to the drive axle.

14. Install the puller and remove the drive axle.

15. Remove the drive axle from the vehicle.

To install:

16. Remove any paint residue and/or corrosion from the threads/splines of the outer CV joint.

17. Install the new circlip into the stub shaft groove on the transmission.

18. Lightly lubricate the stub shaft splines with universal grease G 060 735 A2.

19. Bring the inner splines of the CV joint and outer splines of the transmission stub shaft into engagement.

20. Grasp drive axle by hand and firmly push it into the CV joint until seated.

✳✳ CAUTION

Do not use a hammer under any circumstances.

21. Make sure the CV joint is securely installed by pulling the CV joint against the circlip resistance.

➡**For this check, do not pull on the drive axle, but rather only on the CV joint.**

22. Remove the tensioning strap.

23. Insert outer CV joint as far as possible into wheel hub splines.

24. Install the ball joint to the control arm and install the nuts.

25. Make sure that the boot is not damaged or twisted.

26. Install lower noise insulation.

27. Tighten drive axle to wheel hub bolt.

✳✳ CAUTION

When doing this, vehicle must not sit on its wheels, otherwise wheel bearing may be damaged.

28. Install wheel and tire.

29. Tighten bolts/nuts to specification as follows:

- Ball joint to control arm (use new nut): 44 ft. lbs. (60 Nm)
- Drive axle to wheel hub (use new bolt): 52 ft. lbs. (70 Nm), plus 90° additional turn

Triple Roller Joint

1. Loosen the drive axle to wheel hub bolt.

2. Remove wheel.

3. Remove lower noise insulation.

4. Remove the ball joint nuts.

5. Pull wheel bearing housing with ball joint out of control arm.

6. Pull drive axle out of wheel hub and secure to body.

7. Insert the wedge tool T10161 between transmission housing and joint piece.

8. Remove the joint piece from the transmission by tapping the wedge tool with a hammer.

9. Remove drive axle.

To install:

10. Insert a new circlip into the groove of joint piece stub.

11. Bring the outer splines of the joint piece and the inner splines of the transmission into engagement.

12. Grasp the drive axle by hand and firmly slide the joint piece in until seated.

✳✳ CAUTION

Do not use a hammer under any circumstances!

13. Check drive axle in transmission for proper seating by pulling triple roller joint against resistance from circlip.

➡**For this check, do not pull drive axle but pull triple roller joint only.**

14. Insert outer CV joint as far as possible into wheel hub splines.

15. Install the ball joint to the control arm and install the nuts.

16. Make sure that the boot is not damaged or twisted.

17. Install lower noise insulation.

18. Tighten the drive axle to wheel hub bolt.

19. When doing this, vehicle must not sit on its wheels, otherwise wheel bearing may be damaged.

20. Install wheel and tire.

21. Tighten bolts/nuts to specification as follows:

- Ball joint to control arm (Use new nut): 44 ft. lbs. (60 Nm)
- Drive axle to wheel hub (Use new bolt) 52 ft. lbs. (70 Nm), plus 90° additional turn.

FRONT FLANGE SHAFT SEAL

REMOVAL & INSTALLATION

Eos & Golf

Left

See Figure 30.

1. Remove left wheel.
2. Remove noise insulation.
3. Remove the lower part of the left front wheel housing liner.
4. Remove left drive axle.
5. Place appropriate receptacle underneath transmission.
6. Remove bolts for flange shaft, by screwing two bolts into the flange and counter-holding flange shaft using a pry bar.
7. Pull out flange shaft with spring.
8. Pull out flange shaft oil seal.

To install:

9. Drive new seal in as far as the stop; be sure not to distort seal.
10. Fill area between sealing lip and dust lip halfway with sealing grease G 052 128 A1.
11. Insert flange shaft.
12. Secure flange shaft with countersunk bolt.
13. Install left drive axle.
14. Install lower section of the left front wheel housing liner.
15. Install wheel.
16. Check gear oil.
17. Install noise insulation.

RIGHT

See Figure 30.

1. Remove noise insulation.
2. Remove drive axle heat shield from the engine, if equipped bolts.

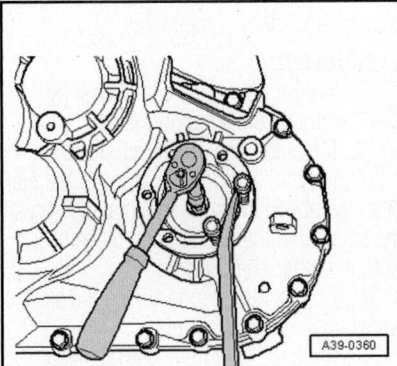

Fig. 31 Remove bolts for flange shaft, by screwing two bolts into the flange and counter-holding flange shaft using a pry bar

3. Remove left drive axle from transmission and tie it up high.
4. On some engines, the drive axle cannot be tied up so that the flange shaft can be removed.
5. Remove drive axle.
6. Remove bolts for flange shaft, by installing two bolts into the flange and counter-holding flange shaft using a pry bar.
7. Place appropriate receptacle underneath transmission.
8. Pull out flange shaft with spring.
9. Pry out seal with a lever.

To install:

10. Drive new seal in as far as stop; be sure not to distort seal.
11. Fill area between sealing lip and dust lip halfway with sealing grease.
12. Secure flange shaft with countersunk bolt.
13. Install right drive axle.
14. Install drive axle heat shield to the engine, if equipped bolts.
15. Check gear oil.
16. Install noise insulation.

Tiguan

Automatic Transaxle

1. Remove the noise insulation.
2. Set the drip tray for workshop crane VAS 6208 underneath.
3. Mark the position of the nuts securing lower control arm to the strut.
4. Separate the lower control arm from strut.
5. Press the drive axle off of the transmission.
6. On Left side, remove the drive axle.
7. On Right side, secure the right drive axle as high as possible on the strut.
8. Seal the opening of drive axle at the transmission using a clean cloth.
9. Grease the drill bit so that drill shavings remain held.
10. Drill only through the metal ring, otherwise the transmission may be damaged.
11. Carefully drill a hole 0.078–0.156 in. (2–4 mm) in diameter in the outer metal ring of the oil seal.
12. Install a small metal bolt of approximately 0.156 in. (4 mm) in diameter into the drilled hole of the oil seal.
13. Do not install the bolt too deep in order to avoid damage to the bearing lying behind it.
14. Remove the seal using puller T10055 and adapter T10055/2.
15. Remove the cloth and clean this area.

✳✳ CAUTION

There must be no metal shavings in the transmission of in the flange shaft, vacuum up any as necessary.

16. On Left side, if only the metal ring of the sealing ring could be pulled out, carefully pry out the remainder of the sealing ring using a screwdriver.

To install:

17. Installation is performed in the reverse order of removal.
18. Lubricate the outer circumference and sealing lips of the seal with ATF.

➡**The open side of the sealing ring faces the transmission.**

19. Press in the seal by hand evenly and as far as possible.
20. On left side, drive in the seal until it seats using thrust piece T10105, do not tilt the thrust piece while doing this.
21. On right side, drive in the seal until it seats using thrust piece T10176, do not tilt the thrust piece while doing this.
22. Install the drive axle.
23. Check the ATF level and top off, as necessary.
24. Install the noise insulation.

Manual Transaxle (Left)

1. Raise vehicle.
2. Remove the noise insulation under the engine/transmission assembly.
3. Remove the left drive axle.
4. Remove the circlip and the O-ring from the stub shaft.
5. Remove the stub shaft bolt; when doing this, counter-hold the stub shaft using the counter holder T10371.
6. Place appropriate receptacle underneath transmission.
7. Remove the stub shaft.
8. Remove the stub shaft seal using the slide hammer VW 771 and pulling hook VW 771/37.

To install:

9. Lightly lubricate the new seal on the outer circumference and install it all the way in without bending it.
10. Fill half of volume between sealing lip and dust lip with radial shaft seal sealing grease G 052 128 A1.
11. Tighten the stub shaft countersunk bolt; when doing this, counter-hold the stub shaft using the counter holder T10371.
12. Then install the new circlip and the new O-ring.

➡**Lubricate the stub shaft splines with grease G 000 100**

13. Install the left drive axle.

14. Check gear oil level in manual transmission.

15. Install the noise insulation under the engine/transmission assembly.

Manual Transaxle (Right)

1. Raise vehicle.

2. Remove the noise insulation under the engine/transmission assembly.

3. Remove the right drive axle from the transmission and tie up.

4. Remove the circlip and the O-ring from the stub shaft.

5. Remove the stub shaft bolt; when doing this, counter-hold the stub shaft using the counter holder.

6. Place appropriate receptacle underneath transmission.

7. Remove the stub shaft.

8. Remove the stub shaft seal using the slide hammer VW 771 and pulling hook VW 771/37.

To install:

9. Lightly lubricate outer edge of the new seal and fill the space between sealing lips halfway with radial shaft seal sealing grease G 052 128 A1.

➡ **The sealing ring must be flush with the sealing ring seat. It must not be installed too deep.**

10. Fill half of volume between sealing lip and dust lip with radial shaft seal sealing grease.

11. Tighten the stub shaft countersunk bolt; when doing this, counter-hold the stub shaft using the counter holder T10371.

12. Then install the circlip and the O-ring.

➡ **Lubricate the stub shaft splines with grease G 000 100**

13. Mount the right drive axle to the transmission.

14. Check gear oil level in manual transmission.

15. Install the noise insulation under the engine/transmission assembly.

REAR FINAL DRIVE

REMOVAL & INSTALLATION

Tiguan

See Figure 31.

1. Raise floor covering in luggage compartment.

2. Remove the spare wheel; now you have access to the markings on the luggage compartment floor.

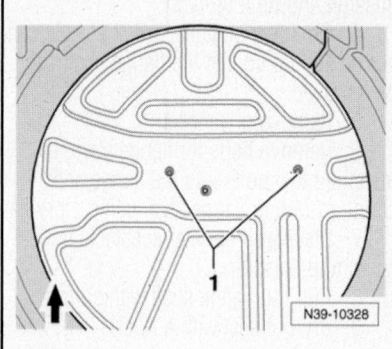

Fig. 31 Remove the spare wheel; now you have access to the markings on the luggage compartment floor

3. Drill 2 holes at the markings to dimension of 1.01 in. (26 mm) diameter. Remove drill shavings while drilling, if possible.

4. De-burr holes and remove shavings carefully.

5. Loosen and remove both bolts.

6. Raise vehicle.

7. Remove the stabilizer bar.

8. Support the front exhaust pipe using the tensioning strap T10038 on the driveshaft center bearing.

9. Remove the exhaust pipe bracket bolt from the subframe.

10. Disconnect the exhaust system at the clamping sleeve when removing the rear exhaust system components.

11. Remove the noise insulation below engine/transmission.

12. Remove pendulum support bolts.

13. In order not to damage the left rear level control system sensor, disconnect the connector, remove the sensor and lay it on the control arm.

14. Just loosen the driveshaft center bearing bracket bolts, do not remove it.

15. Press engine and transmission forward by hand and secure this position with a suitable wood block.

16. So that noises due to imbalance do not occur later, check whether there is a marking (colored dot) on the driveshaft flexible disc and rear final drive flange. If not, mark the position of the flexible disc to the flange.

17. Remove the driveshaft flexible disc bolts from the rear final drive.

18. Remove the driveshaft from the final drive, and guide it upward in the center until it is under the fuel tank. In this position, support the tunnel brace using a piece of wood.

✳✳ CAUTION

When doing this, be careful not to push in the fuel tank.

➡ **When removing and installing the drive axles, the final drive must be moveable in the rear area.**

19. To do this, do not loosen the bolt on the front mounting bracket more than 5 turns.

20. Disconnect the left drive axle from the final drive.

21. Lift the final drive in the rear and push it as far as possible to the right.

22. Remove the left drive axle out of the flange and carefully lower it.

23. Put the final drive back into its installation position.

24. Disconnect the right drive axle from the final drive.

25. Lift the final drive in the rear and push it as far as possible to the left.

26. Remove the right drive axle out of the flange and carefully lower it.

27. Put the final drive back into its installed position.

28. Support the final drive using the engine and transmission holder V.A.G 1383 A and secure it to the universal support with the belt to keep it from falling.

29. Remove the bolt on the front mounting bracket.

30. Remove the washer on top of the mounting bracket.

31. Position the final drive in the vehicle on the proper angle while lowering it at the same time.

32. Disconnect the connector on the all-wheel drive control module.

33. Remove the vent lines from the final drive.

34. To remove, lower final drive more and pull forward, ensuring there is sufficient clearance to other components.

To install:

35. Secure final drive against falling down with universal support strap.

36. Move the final drive into position.

37. Lift the final drive, and move the rear bearings above the subframe making sure at the same time there is enough clearance from the other components.

38. Connect the connector on the all-wheel drive control module.

39. Slide the vent lines onto the final drive vent tubes.

40. Lift the final drive using the transmission jack into the installation position.

41. Place the washer on the front mounting bracket.

➡**When removing and installing the drive axles, the final drive must be moveable in the rear area.**

42. Loosen the front mounting bolt by hand; do not loosen it more than 5 turns.

43. Remove the transmission jack from under the vehicle.

44. Lift the final drive in the rear and push it as far as possible to the left.

45. Carefully move the right drive axle upward into the flange.

46. Put the final drive back into its installation position.

47. Connect the right drive axle on the final drive.

48. Lift the final drive in the rear and push it as far as possible to the right.

49. Carefully move the left drive axle upward into the flange.

50. Put the final drive back into its installation position.

51. Connect the left drive axle on the final drive.

52. Tighten the driveshaft to the final drive.

53. Tighten final drive from below.

54. Tighten drive axles.

55. Tighten pendulum support with new bolts.

56. Install noise insulation.

57. Align center bearing free of tension and tighten.

58. Install the left rear level control system sensor.

59. Adjust the headlamps.

60. Install the exhaust system.

61. Install the stabilizer bar.

62. Insert two new bolts through the holes in the luggage compartment floor and tighten.

63. Seal holes. To do this, use the caps N 908 572 01.

64. If the final drive is replaced, check the oil level in the Haldex clutch, top off if necessary.

65. check the oil level in the final drive, top off if necessary.

REAR AXLE STUB SHAFT BEARING AND SEAL

REMOVAL & INSTALLATION

Tiguan

➡**The marking on the bottom side of the rear final drive identifies which final drive is installed.**

1. Do not remove the rear final drive for this.

2. This procedure applies to both sides.

3. Remove the drive axle.

4. Place the drip tray under rear final drive.

5. Install the plate from the puller T10037 on the flange and tighten the two M8 x 30 bolts by hand.

➡**The sections for the larger flange diameter face outward.**

6. Tighten one turn each in an alternating sequence until the flange contacts the plate and then stop tightening.

➡**Wear gloves to get a good grip on the flange.**

7. Drive the flange out of the final drive by tapping lightly on the plate.

➡**Only use a plastic mallet so the final drive and tool are not damaged.**

8. Pry out the flange shaft seal with the extractor lever VW 681.

To install:

9. Lightly lubricate the outer diameter of the new seal and drive in, without tilting until seated using the thrust piece T10049.

10. Fill the area between sealing lip and dust lip halfway with sealing grease G 052 128 A1.

11. Clamp the flange shaft using jaw protectors in a vise.

12. Press the previous circlip out of flange shaft groove with the new circlip.

13. Drive in the flange shaft with a plastic hammer and possibly drift.

14. Install the drive axle.

15. Check the oil level in the rear final drive.

REAR DRIVESHAFT

REMOVAL & INSTALLATION

Tiguan

✳✳ CAUTION

Before removing, mark the positions of all parts in relation to each other. Reinstall in the same position otherwise imbalance will be excessive, the bearings could be damaged causing rumbling noises.

1. Remove noise insulation.

2. Remove pendulum support bolts.

3. Press engine and transmission forward and secure position with a suitable wood block.

4. Support the front part of the exhaust system using the engine and transmission holder V.A.G 1383 A.

5. Disconnect the exhaust system at the clamping sleeve when removing the rear exhaust system components.

6. Remove the tunnel brace.

7. Loosen the bolts for the center bearing two turns.

8. Loosen the driveshaft front and rear bolts, but do not remove them.

9. Counter hold the rear final drive to loosen and tighten the driveshaft bolts.

10. So that noises due to imbalance do not occur later, if there are no markings present, then mark the position of the driveshaft flexible disc to the rear final drive flange.

11. Also mark the position of the driveshaft flexible disc to the bevel box output flange.

12. Remove the driveshaft from the rear final drive and lower it onto the engine and transmission holder.

13. When removing and installing the driveshaft, be careful not to damage the bushing.

➡**Two technicians are needed to remove the driveshaft.**

14. Remove the driveshaft from the bevel box.

➡**To prevent damaging the protective boot in the center bearing, remove and install the driveshaft in its fully extended position; likewise, store it in this position.**

15. Remove the center bearing and if possible, remove it to the rear in its fully extended length.

To install:

16. Install in reverse sequence.

17. Install all parts marked to each other in original positions.

18. Tighten the driveshaft bolts for the flexible disc to the bevel box/rear final drive to 50 ft. lbs. (60 Nm).

19. Install the pendulum support with new bolts.

20. Install exhaust system.

21. Install noise insulation.

22. Install the tunnel brace.

REAR HALFSHAFT

REMOVAL & INSTALLATION

Tiguan

1. Loosen the drive axle bolt.

2. Remove wheel.

3. Remove coil spring.

4. Remove the bolts for the lower transverse link and tie rod from the wheel bearing housing.

5. Remove bolt.

6. Loosen input shaft at transmission flange.

7. Swing wheel bearing housing upward and remove drive axle from inner splines.

8. Remove drive axle.

To install:

9. Installation is the reverse of removal.

➡**Any connection to the wheel bearing housing may only be carried out if the vehicle is in the normal ride height position.**

10. Place drive axle inner Constant Velocity (CV) joint in position and pre-tighten the socket head bolts diagonally to 89 inch lbs. (10 Nm).

11. Then, tighten the socket head bolts diagonally to 30 ft. lbs. (40 Nm).

12. Tighten bolts/nuts to specification as follows:

- Drive axle to wheel hub (Use new bolt) 52 ft. lbs. (70 Nm) plus 90° additional turn

- Drive axle to rear final drive flange shaft (Use new bolts): Pre-tighten to 89 inch lbs. (10 Nm) in diagonal sequence then to 30 ft. lbs. (40 Nm)

REAR PINION SEAL

REMOVAL & INSTALLATION

Tiguan

1. Disconnect the exhaust system at the clamping sleeve when removing the rear exhaust system components.

2. The flex joint of the exhaust system must not be bent more than 10 degrees, otherwise it may be damaged.

3. Remove the rear flexible disc:

➡**Secure the vehicle on the hoist with the tensioning straps T10038. If the vehicle is not secured, there is the risk that it could slip from the hoist.**

4. Remove the rear final drive flange nut.

5. Remove the rear final drive flange. Use a slide hammer Kukko 12/1 if it is difficult.

6. Remove rear final drive flange seal using the extractor lever VW 681.

To install:

7. Before installing, lightly coat new seal on outside circumference and between sealing lips with high performance Haldex clutch oil.

8. Drive in new seal to until seated using thrust piece T10019. Do not tilt seal when doing this.

9. Drive in rear final drive flange with sleeve 30 - 20.

10. Insert new nut with locking fluid D 000 600.

11. Install the rear flexible disc.

12. Install the exhaust system and align it without tension.

13. Check the oil level in the Haldex clutch.

14. Tighten the rear final drive flange nut 155 ft. lbs. (210 Nm)

ENGINE COOLING

ENGINE COOLANT

DRAIN & REFILL PROCEDURE

1. Open the coolant expansion tank cap.

2. Remove the noise insulation.

3. Remove the coolant hose from the charge air cooling pump.

4. Release the clamp and remove coolant hose from the quick release coupling on the radiator for the air charge coolant circuit.

5. Release the coolant hose clamp and remove the coolant hose from the quick release couplings for the radiator.

6. In addition, to draining the coolant from the engine, remove the coolant hose from the engine oil cooler.

7. If equipped with an engine preheating element, loosen the spring clamps. Disconnect the coolant hoses from the engine preheating element. Allow any remaining coolant to drain.

➡**Coolant Notes:**

- The water portion of the coolant influences the effectiveness of the coolant. Volkswagen has decided to define the water quality used in the cooling system based on the different mixtures and country and regional requirements. For this reason, we recommend using distilled

water for older models when adding coolant or filling coolant for the first time. On newer models (from MY 2010), distilled water is required. Do not mix distilled water with coolant additives. Using distilled water provides optimum corrosion protection.

- Because of its high boiling point, the coolant improves engine reliability under heavy loads, particularly in countries with tropical climates.

- Protection against frost must be assured down to approximately (13°F (25°C); in arctic climatic counties down to approximately (31°F (35°C).

- The coolant concentration must not be reduced by adding water even in warmer seasons and in warmer countries. The coolant additive portion must be at least 40%.

- If a lower freeze protection is necessary due to the climatic conditions, increase the amount of coolant additives.

- Increase the ratio only up to 60%; freeze protection down to approximately (40°F (40°C). Otherwise the freeze protection and cooling effect are reduced.

- Do not use the old coolant again if replacing the radiator, heater core, cylinder head or cylinder head gasket.

- The refractometer (T10007) is recommended for determining freeze protection density.

8. Install the lower coolant hose and secure it with the retaining clamp.

9. Install the coolant hose to the radiator for the air charge coolant circuit and secure it with the clamp.

10. Connect the coolant hoses to the engine oil cooler and the charge air cooling pump.

11. Install the noise insulation.

Filling Using the Cooling System Charge Unit (VAS 6096)

1. Install the adapter (V.A.G 1274/8) onto the coolant expansion tank.

2. Fill the coolant circuit using the cooling system charge unit. Refer to the operating instructions.

Filling Without Using the Cooling System Charge Unit

1. Slowly add coolant until it reaches the upper mark on the expansion tank.

2. Install the expansion tank cap.

3. Start the engine and maintain an engine speed of approximately 2000 RPM for approximately 3 minutes.

4. Let the engine run at idle until the coolant fan turns on.

5. Check the coolant level and fill if necessary. With the engine at operating temperature, the coolant level must be at the top mark, with the engine cold, it must be in the center of hatched area.

ENGINE FAN

REMOVAL & INSTALLATION

Eos & Golf

Except 2.0L TDI Engine
See Figure 32.

1. Remove the cover for the air guide; disengage the side clips to do so.

2. Unclip the lower air guide, disengage the clips to do so.

3. Remove the lower air guide together with the air guide hose.

4. Remove the bolts from the top.

5. Remove noise insulation.

6. Disconnect electrical connector.

7. Remove the bolts and remove the fan shroud downward.

8. Disconnect electrical connector.

9. Free up electrical wires.

10. Remove nuts and remove coolant fan.

To install:

11. Installation is performed in reverse order of removal.

12. Tightening radiator fan shroud to 44 inch lbs. (5 Nm).

2.0L TDI Engine

1. Move lock carrier into service position.

2. Drain coolant.

3. Remove upper coolant hose clip and remove coolant hose from radiator quick-release coupling.

4. Disconnect coolant fan connector.

5. Remove radiator bolts and remove radiator upward with the coolant fan.

To install:

6. Install in reverse order of removal.

7. Fill with coolant.

Tiguan

1. Remove the cover for the air guide; disengage the side clips.

2. Unclip the lower air guide, disengage the clips.

3. Remove the lower air guide together with the air guide hose.

4. Remove the bolts from the top.

5. Remove noise insulation.

6. Disconnect electrical connector.

7. Remove the bolts and remove the fan shroud downward.

To install:

8. Installation is performed in reverse order of removal

9. Tighten bolts to 44 inch lbs. (5 Nm).

RADIATOR

REMOVAL & INSTALLATION

Eos & Golf

EXCEPT 2.0L TDI ENGINE
See Figure 32.

1. Drain coolant.

2. Remove fan shroud.

3. Remove the upper coolant hose from the radiator.

4. Detach the air duct at the lock carrier and remove the air duct.

5. Remove the bolts and remove the radiator upward.

To install:

6. Installation is performed in reverse order.

7. Tightening radiator fasteners to 89 inch lbs. (10 Nm)

➡ **When installing a new radiator, old coolant must not be reused.**

8. Fill with coolant.

2.0L TDI Engine

1. Move lock carrier into service position.

2. Drain coolant.

3. Remove upper coolant hose clip and remove coolant hose from radiator quick-release coupling.

4. Disconnect coolant fan connector.

5. Remove radiator bolts and remove radiator upward with the coolant fan.

To install:

6. Install in reverse order of removal.

7. Fill with coolant.

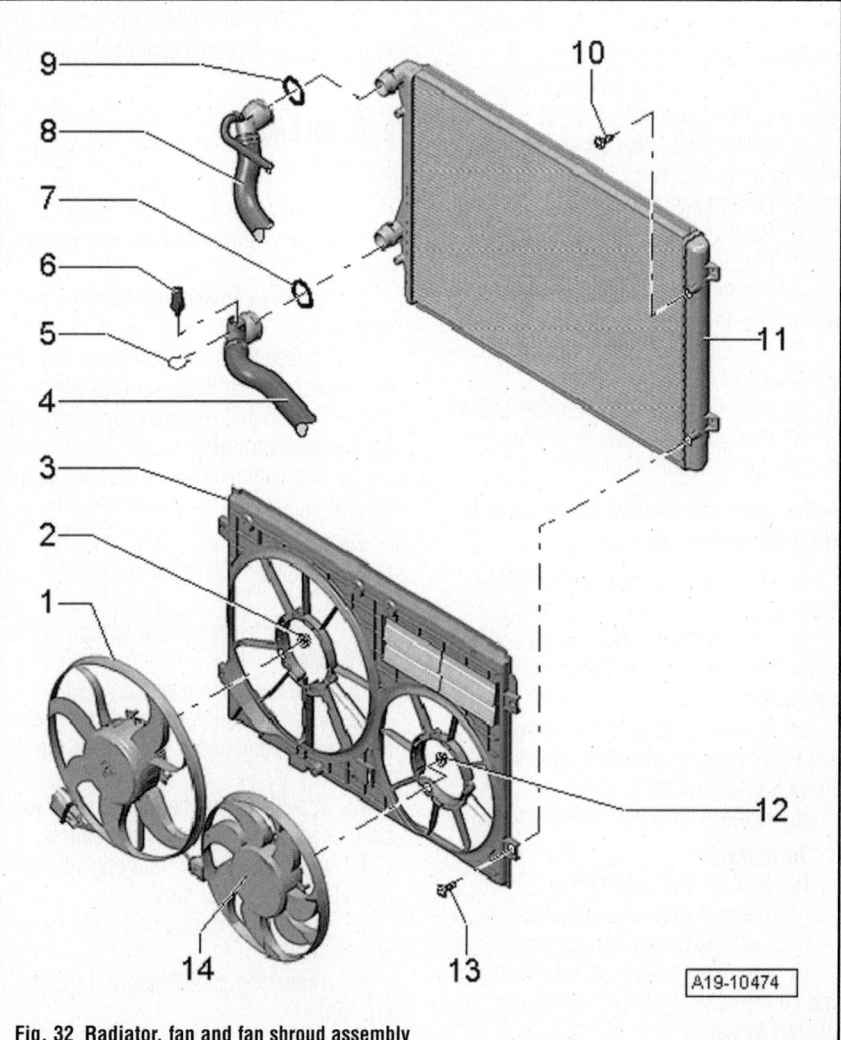

Fig. 32 Radiator, fan and fan shroud assembly

A19-10474

Tiguan

1. Drain coolant.
2. Remove fan shroud.
3. Remove air guide hose.
4. Remove the bracket by removing the mounting screws.
5. Disengage the clamps and remove the connection from the radiator.
6. Likewise, disconnect the connection on the right radiator.
7. Remove the mounting bolt.
8. Remove the bolts and remove the radiator downward.

To install:

9. Installation is performed in reverse order.
10. Tighten bolts to 44 inch lbs. (5 Nm).

THERMOSTAT

REMOVAL & INSTALLATION

2.0L Engines

See Figure 33.

1. Drain coolant.
2. Remove the cover for the air guide; disengage the side clips to do so.
3. Unclip the lower air guide, disengage the clips to do so.
4. Remove the lower air guide together with the air guide hose.
5. Loosen the hose clamp.
6. Remove bolt.
7. Disconnect electrical connector.
8. Remove the bolt and remove the air guide pipe downward.
9. Lay aside the coolant hose and electrical wiring harness.
10. Remove the bolt and remove bracket.
11. If installed, remove the bolt on the bracket for the after-run coolant pump.

➡**The after-run coolant pump stays in the installation position.**

12. Remove the coolant hoses and lay them aside.
13. Loosen the nut, remove the bolt and move the support for the intake manifold to the right.
14. Remove bolts and remove connecting pieces. For the right bolt, the Multi-Point Socket T10058 is useful.
15. Remove the coolant thermostat.

To install:

16. Replace seals and O-rings.
17. Clean O-ring sealing surface.
18. Coat the O-ring with coolant.
19. Install the thermostat into the housing for the coolant pump and move it slightly forward.

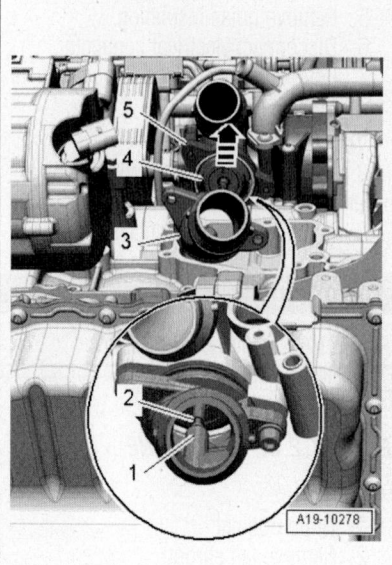

Fig. 33 Thermostat assembly

20. Tighten the bolts to 80 inch lbs. (9 Nm).
21. Carefully mount the connector ; while doing so, insert the centering pin into the guide.

2.0L TDI Engine

See Figure 34.

1. Drain coolant.
2. Remove throttle valve control module.
3. Remove coolant hose from the connection.
4. Loosen bolts on connection with a 10 mm flex wrench 3185, remove with socket T10058 and remove connection with the coolant thermostat.
5. Rotate coolant thermostat 90° to the left and remove it from the connection.

To install:

6. Install in reverse order of removal.
7. Always replace seals, sealing rings and O-rings.
8. Coat new O-ring with coolant.
9. Insert coolant thermostat in the connecting piece and turn it 90° turn to the right.
10. The clip of the thermostat must be positioned at approximately right angle.
11. Insert connection with coolant thermostat in the cylinder block.
12. Tighten bolts with a 10 mm flex wrench 3185.
13. Tightening specifications 11 ft. lbs. (15 Nm).
14. Secure connection coolant hose.

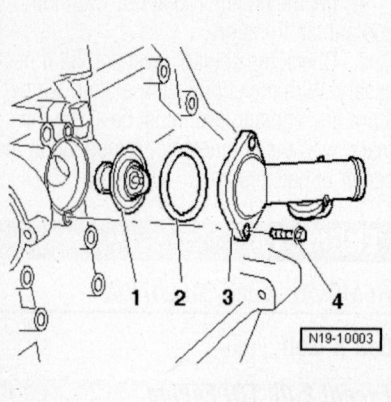

Fig. 34 Coat new O-ring (2) with coolant. Insert coolant thermostat (1) in the connecting piece (3) and tighten bolts (4)

15. Install throttle valve control module J338.
16. Fill with coolant.

2.5L Engine

See Figure 35.

1. Drain the cooling system
2. Remove the engine cover/air filter housing.
3. Remove the intake manifold.
4. Reinstall the oil dipstick tube so no escaping coolant can run into the engine.
5. Place a suitable container under coolant regulator housing to catch coolant flowing out.
6. Remove the bolts to remove the coolant regulator and thermostat.

To install:

7. Fit the thermostat into place with the jiggle valve at the top.
8. Install the housing and bolts. Torque the bolts to 44 in. lbs. (5 Nm)

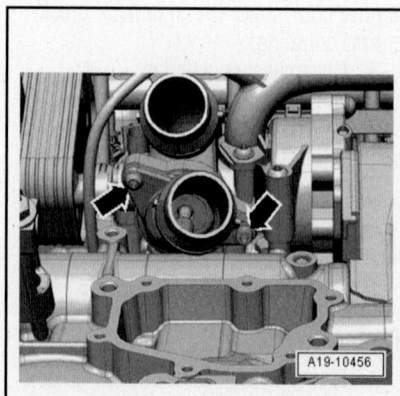

Fig. 35 Remove the bolts to remove the coolant regulator and thermostat—2.5L engine

9. Install the intake manifold and dipstick tube.

10. Refill the cooling system with coolant and install the cap. Run the engine at 2000 rpm for three minutes or until the fan runs and check coolant level.

WATER PUMP

REMOVAL & INSTALLATION

2.0L Engines

See Figures 36 and 37.

1. Remove coolant pipes.
2. Remove the coolant pump toothed belt.
3. Disconnect electrical connector on throttle valve control module.
4. Remove bolts and remove throttle valve control module.
5. Disconnect the electrical connector on the Engine Coolant Temperature (ECT) sensor.
6. Remove bolts.
7. Remove the coolant pump from the centering pin and remove the oil cooler.

To install:

8. Replace seals and O-rings.
9. Coat the O-rings with coolant.
10. Make sure both centering pins are installed in the cylinder block.
11. Install the connection piece into the oil cooler.
12. Push the coolant pump onto the connection piece and onto the centering pins in the cylinder block.
13. Tighten bolts in sequence.
14. If a new coolant pump was installed, then the protective cap must be removed.
15. The rest of the installation follows the reverse of the removal procedures.

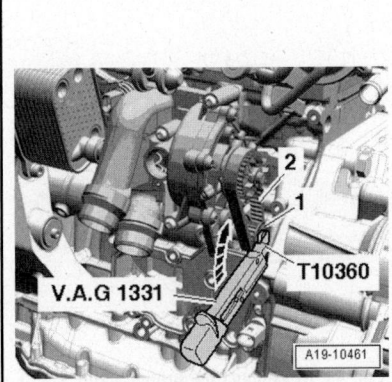

Fig. 36 Remove the coolant pump drive gear (1) and toothed belt (2)

Fig. 37 Tighten bolts in 1 to 5 sequence

2.0L TDI Engine

See Figure 38.

1. Drain coolant.
2. Remove toothed belt.
3. Remove bolts of coolant pump and carefully take out coolant pump.

To install:

4. Install in reverse order of removal.
5. Always replace seals, sealing rings and O-rings.
6. Coat new O-ring with coolant.
7. Insert coolant pump in cylinder block and tighten bolts and tighten to 11 ft. lbs. (15 Nm).

➡**The sealing plug of the coolant pump faces downward.**

8. Install and tension toothed belt.
9. Fill with coolant.

2.5L Engine

See Figure 39.

➡**This procedure requires removal of the front engine mount. New bolts will be needed.**

1. Remove the engine cover/air filter assembly.
2. Remove the battery and battery box.
3. Drain the cooling system by disconnecting the bottom radiator hose.
4. Remove air inlet tube guide above the fans.
5. Remove the air intake hose by disconnecting the smaller air hoses and removing the spring clamp.
6. Remove right inner fender.
7. Remove the coolant pump drive belt.
8. Disconnect the exhaust pipe from the

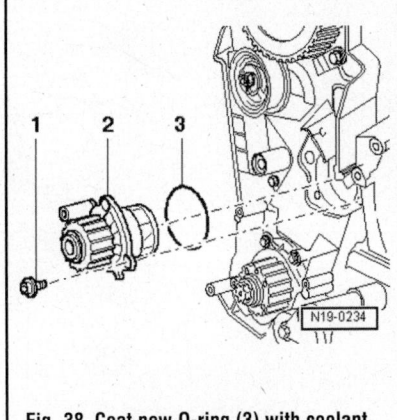

Fig. 38 Coat new O-ring (3) with coolant. Install bolts (1) of coolant pump (2) and carefully take out coolant pump

manifold and remove the bracket bolts. Tie the pipe out of the way.

✳✳ CAUTION

The flex joint in the front exhaust pipe must not be bent more than 10 degrees, otherwise it may be damaged.

9. Remove the pendulum support (under car engine mount).
10. Disconnect the shift control cables at the transaxle.
11. Install engine support bridge 10-222A with adapters 10-222A/8 and support engine/transaxle assembly in installation position using adapter 10-222A/3 and shackle 10-222 A/12.
12. Remove the bolt that holds the windshield washer reservoir and move it towards the front.
13. Remove the coolant reservoir bolts and disconnect the wiring. Set the reservoir out of the way without disconnecting the hoses.
14. Remove the bolts to remove the front engine mount. The rear bolt in cylinder block is accessible above wheel housing liner.
15. Remove the two transaxle mount bolts.
16. Slide the engine as far as possible toward the front and left.
17. Remove the three mounting bolts and swivel the coolant pump out.

To install:

18. Install the pump and torque the bolts to 7 ft. lbs. (10 Nm).
19. Install the engine mounts using new bolts.

• Torque the two pendulum support bracket bolts to 30 ft. lbs. (40 Nm),

Fig. 39 Swivel the pump to remove it from the engine compartment—2.5L engine

plus 90°. Install a new pendulum support center bolt and torque it to 75 ft. lbs. (100 Nm), plus 90°.
- Install two new transaxle mount bolts and torque to 45 ft. lbs. (60 Nm), plus 90°.

20. Remove the engine support bridge and adapter brackets.

21. Connect the shift cables and adjust as necessary.

22. Connect the exhaust pipe and install the bracket bolts.

23. Install the remaining components and connect all wiring and hoses.

24. Refill the coolant reservoir with G 12 coolant and install the cap. Run the engine at 2000 rpm for three minutes or until the fan runs and check coolant level.

ENGINE ELECTRICAL

BATTERY

DISCONNECTING & CONNECTING

Disconnecting

See Figures 40 and 41.

➡**Service Notes:**

- Deactivate the anti-theft alarm system first and then disconnect the battery.
- By removing the battery negative terminal clamp (current disruption), safe work on the electrical system is guaranteed.
- Disconnecting the battery positive (B+) terminal must only be performed as required to remove battery from vehicle, and must only be carried out after the negative (-) terminal is disconnected.

- Always follow the instructions for connecting the battery.

1. Turn off the ignition and all electrical consumers.

2. Remove the key.

3. Unclip the service cover off the side trim panel.

4. Disconnect the ground cable from the battery negative pole.

5. Open the terminal cover on the battery positive pole.

6. Disconnect the positive cable from the battery positive pole.

Connecting

After connecting the battery and switching on the ignition, the ASR/ESP Control Lamp and Electro-mechanical Power Steering Indicator Lamp light up continuously. The indicator lamps switch off automatically after driving straight ahead at 15 to 20 mph. This activates Steering Angle Sensor.

1. Connect the battery terminal clip of the positive wire to the positive terminal of the battery and tighten the bolt.

2. Turn positive cable/terminal in driving direction.

3. Connect the battery terminal clip of the ground wire to the negative terminal of the battery and tighten the bolt.

4. Close the terminal cover.

5. Perform the work steps listed:

    a. Turn on the ignition using either the key or start system button and then turn it off again.

    b. Read the DTC memory using the Vehicle Diagnostic Tester in "Guided Fault Finding".

    c. Check clock time setting, set anew if necessary.

CHARGING SYSTEM

    d. For the electrical window regulators, open and close all windows all the way. Then, with the windows closed, pull the window regulator switch until the relay audibly switches.

    e. Check the convenience switching for the window regulators. While comfort switching is operated, window must close without holding the switch.

    f. Check function of all electrical consumers.

REMOVAL & INSTALLATION

1. Disconnect the battery, as described above.

2. Remove the battery jacket.

3. Remove the bolt and clamping plate.

4. Fold the handles up (if equipped) and remove the battery.

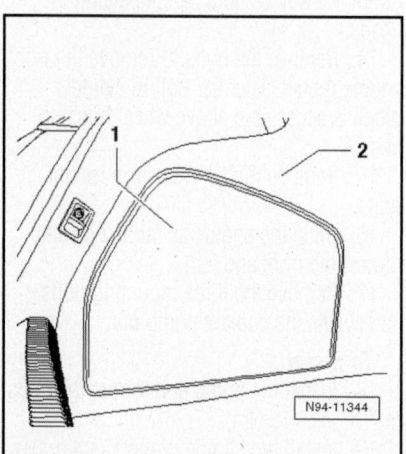

Fig. 40 Unclip the service cover (1) off the side trim panel (2).

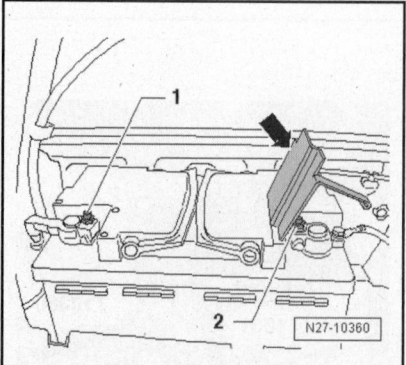

Fig. 41 Disconnect the ground cable (1) from the battery negative pole. Open the terminal cover on the battery positive pole. Disconnect the positive cable (2) from the battery positive pole.

To install:

> ※※ **CAUTION**
>
> **If the battery is not secured properly, the following risks are possible:**

- Shortened battery service life due to vibration damage (explosion hazard).
- If the battery is not secured properly, the plates inside the battery can get damaged.
- Damage to battery casing caused by bracket (possible electrolyte leakage, high subsequent costs).
- Inadequate crash safety.

5. Install in reverse order of removal. Note the following:

    a. Tighten the threaded connections.

    b. Make sure the battery is secure after installing it.

    c. Connect the battery.

ALTERNATOR

REMOVAL & INSTALLATION

2.0L Engines

See Figure 42.

➡**When disconnecting and connecting battery, the procedure must be followed as described in the repair manual.**

1. Disconnect battery.

> ※※ **CAUTION**
>
> **Before removing ribbed belt, mark the top side and direction of travel. When installing, pay attention to correct running direction and installation position. If the belt is installed in the opposite running direction or is positioned incorrectly, the belt will fail!**

2. Remove the ribbed belt.

3. Disengage and disconnect harness connector.

4. Remove the oil pressure switch.

5. Remove the generator bolts.

6. Turn the generator slightly to the left in order to be able to access the connections on the back of the generator.

7. Release and disconnect DF wire connector.

8. Pry off protective cap.

9. Remove the nut and B+ wire below from generator connector threads.

10. Remove both screws and move the pipes and the hose upward so that there is enough space to remove the generator.

Fig. 42 Remove the connector (2) from oil pressure switch (1) and the generator bolts (arrows)

➡**The pipes and the hose can remain connected.**

11. Remove the generator upward and out of the vehicle.

To install:

12. Install in reverse order of removal, noting the following:

➡**When installing an already used ribbed belt, note direction of travel marked when it was removed! Before installing the ribbed belt, make sure all components (generator, A/C compressor) are securely fastened. When installing the ribbed belt, make sure it is properly seated in the belt pulley!**

13. Tighten the threaded connections to the specification given in the assembly overview.

➡**When disconnecting and connecting battery, the procedure must be followed as described in the repair manual.**

2.0L TDI Engine

See Figures 43 and 44.

1. Disconnect battery.

2. Pull the engine cover upward at the corners from the mounting points.

3. Bring the lock carrier into the service position.

> ※※ **CAUTION**
>
> **Before removing ribbed belt, mark the top side and direction of travel. When installing, pay attention to correct running direction and installation position. If the belt is installed in the opposite running direction or is positioned incorrectly, the belt will fail!**

4. Remove ribbed belt.

5. Remove both A/C compressor screws.

6. Disengage and disconnect harness connector.

7. Remove the third screw and remove the A/C compressor downward from the accessories bracket.

8. Hoses on A/C compressor can remain connected.

9. Hang the A/C compressor with wire in a suitable place under the body until it is ready for installation.

➡**Make sure the hoses are not pulled off or kinked.**

10. Release and disconnect DF wire connector.

11. Pry off protective cap.

12. Remove nut and B+ wire below from generator connector threads.

13. Remove nut and remove wiring bracket from generator.

14. Remove both of the bolts and the nut for the fuel filter and lay them aside. The fuel hoses can remain connected.

15. Remove both generator mounting bolts.

16. Remove generator downward from vehicle.

To install:

17. Install in reverse order of removal, noting the following:

> ※※ **CAUTION**
>
> **When installing an already used ribbed belt, note direction of travel marked when it was removed! Before installing the ribbed belt, make sure all components (generator, A/C compressor) are securely fastened. When installing the ribbed belt, make sure it is properly seated in the belt pulley!**

18. Drive threaded sleeves out of generator housing approximately 0.156 in. (4 mm).

19. Screw wire retainer firmly to rear side of generator in 3 o'clock position.

> ※※ **CAUTION**
>
> **Before installing the engine cover, make sure the four fasteners (ball sockets) are positioned correctly. Bring them into the correct position if necessary. Otherwise the engine cover will be damaged.**

20. Place the engine cover on the mounting points and press the corners into the retainers.

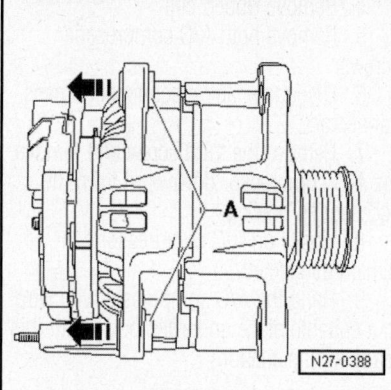

Fig. 43 Drive threaded sleeves (A) out of generator housing approximately 0.156 in. (4 mm) in direction of arrow

21. Reconnect battery.
22. Start the engine and verify that the belt is running properly.
23. Turn off the engine.
24. Tighten bolts/nuts to specification as follows:
   • Alternator bolts: 15 ft. lbs. (20 Nm)
   • M5 Wire: 28 inch lbs. (3.2 Nm)

2.5L Engine

1. Disconnect the battery.
2. Pull off engine cover upward and forward.
3. Bring the lock carrier into the service position.

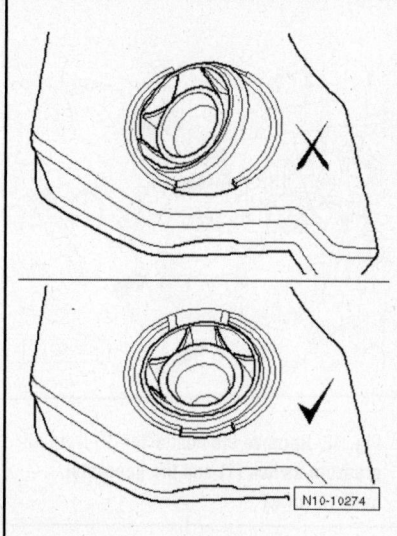

Fig. 44 Before installing the engine cover, make sure the four fasteners (ball sockets) are positioned correctly. Bring them into the correct position if necessary. Otherwise the engine cover will be damaged

4. Remove ribbed belt.
5. Separate the connector for the DF-lead and remove the protective cap.
6. Remove the B+ wire from the generator.

✴✴ CAUTION

Before removing ribbed belt, mark the top side and direction of travel.

When installing, pay attention to correct running direction and installation position. If the belt is installed in the opposite running direction or is positioned incorrectly, the belt will fail!

7. Remove the upper idler pulley, lower idler pulley and the generator ribbed belt pulley tensioning roller and coolant pump.
8. Remove the generator mounting bolts.
9. Remove the wire retainer from the generator.
10. Remove the generator upward.

To install:

11. Install in reverse order of removal.
12. Drive the threaded sleeves out of the generator housing approximately 4 mm.
13. Install the wire retainer securely on the rear side of the generator in the 9 o'clock position.
14. Tighten mounting bolts to 19 ft. lbs. (25 Nm).

➡**Observe notes for threaded connections of battery terminals.**

15. Connect the battery.
16. Start the engine and verify that the belt is running properly.
17. Turn off the engine.

ENGINE ELECTRICAL

FIRING ORDER

2.0L Engines

1–3–4–2

2.0L TDI Engines

1–3–4–2

2.5L Engines

1–2–4–5–3

GENERATOR

2.0L Engine

See Figure 45.

➡**When disconnecting and connecting battery, the procedure must be followed as described in the repair manual.**

1. Disconnect battery.

✴✴ CAUTION

Before removing ribbed belt, mark the top side and direction of travel. When installing, pay attention to correct running direction and installation position. If the belt is installed in the opposite running direction or is positioned incorrectly, the belt will fail!

2. Remove the ribbed belt.
3. Disengage and disconnect harness connector.
4. Remove the oil pressure switch.
5. Remove the generator bolts.
6. Turn the generator slightly to the left in order to be able to access the connections on the back of the generator.
7. Release and disconnect DF wire connector.
8. Pry off protective cap.
9. Remove the nut and B+ wire below from generator connector threads.
10. Remove both screws and move the

IGNITION SYSTEM

pipes and the hose upward so that there is enough space to remove the generator.

➡**The pipes and the hose can remain connected.**

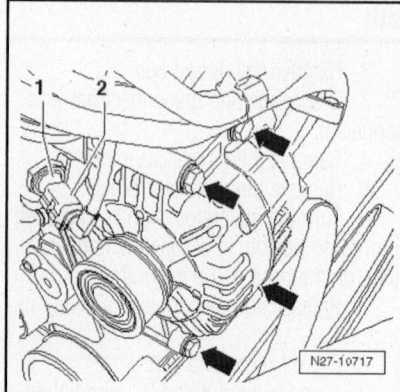

Fig. 45 Remove the connector (2) from oil pressure switch (1) and the generator bolts (arrows)

11. Remove the generator upward and out of the vehicle.

To install:

12. Install in reverse order of removal, noting the following:

➡ **When installing an already used ribbed belt, note direction of travel marked when it was removed! Before installing the ribbed belt, make sure all components (generator, A/C compressor) are securely fastened. When installing the ribbed belt, make sure it is properly seated in the belt pulley!**

13. Tighten the threaded connections to the specification given in the assembly overview.

➡ **When disconnecting and connecting battery, the procedure must be followed as described in the repair manual.**

2.0L TDI Engine

See Figure 46.

1. Disconnect the battery.
2. Remove the noise insulation.
3. Remove the right front wheel housing liner.
4. Mark the direction of travel of the ribbed belt.
5. Swivel the tensioner in a counterclockwise direction, using a 16 mm wrench to release the tension.
6. Lock the tensioner in place using T10060 A. Remove ribbed belt.
7. Remove the A/C compressor from its mounting and tie to the body using wire. Do not disconnect the A/C lines.
8. Remove the nut from the wire holder on the back of the generator.
9. Disconnect the other terminal connector.
10. Remove the wire cap. Open the retainer and remove the line from the retainer.
11. Remove the nut on the B+ wire from the generator and then move the B+ wire to the side.
12. Remove the bolt from the tensioning roller and then remove the tensioning roller.
13. Unscrew the mounting bolts of the generator and remove the generator downward from the vehicle.

To install:

14. Installation is performed in the reverse order of removal. Note the following:
   a. Drive the threaded sleeves out of

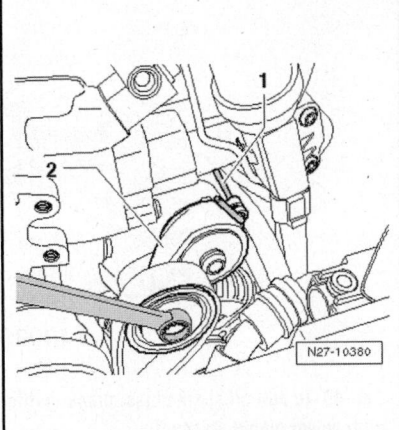

Fig. 46 Lock the tensioner (2) in place using T10060 A (1). Remove ribbed belt.

the Generator housing approximately 2 mm to the rear.
   b. Attach the wire holder on the back of the generator in the 9 o'clock position.
   c. Install the idler roller and ribbed belt tensioning roller for the generator.
   d. Tighten the nuts for the refrigerant lines on the longitudinal member to 7 ft. lbs. (10 Nm).
   e. Install the ribbed belt.
   f. Install the fan shroud.
   g. Install the battery.
15. Start the engine and make sure the generator is running.

2.5L Engine

See Figures 47 and 48.

1. Disconnect the battery as described in this section.
2. Remove the fan shroud.
3. Mark the top of the ribbed belt and the running direction before removal. Make sure the belt is installed correctly and pay attention to the running direction.

⁂ CAUTION

If the belt is installed in the opposite running direction or is positioned incorrectly, the belt will fail!

4. Remove the ribbed belt and then the idler roller for the generator.
5. Disconnect the connector from the A/C compressor.
6. If attached to the compressor, remove the refrigerant line attachment (do not disconnect the A/C lines).
7. Remove the A/C compressor bolts.

Fig. 47 Remove the idler roller (1) for the generator.

➡ **The hoses on the A/C compressor can remain connected.**

8. Tie the A/C compressor to a suitable place on the vehicle with wire until it is time to install it again. Make sure the hoses are not pulled off or kinked.
9. Release the connector (DF lead) and remove the cap.
10. Disconnect the B+ wire from the generator.
11. Remove the wire holder on the back of the generator.
12. Remove the bolts from the generator.
13. Remove the generator.

To install:

14. Installation is performed in the reverse order of removal. Note the following:
   a. Drive the threaded sleeves out of the generator housing approximately 2 mm to the rear.

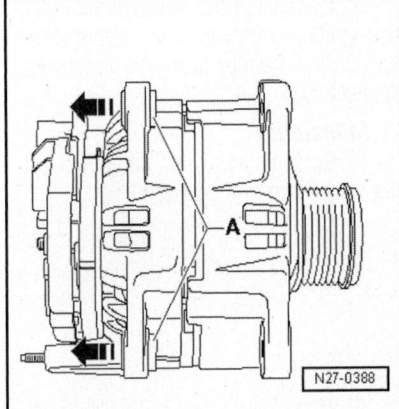

Fig. 48 Drive the threaded sleeves out of the generator housing approximately 2 mm in direction of arrow.

b. Attach the wire holder on the back of the generator in the 9 o'clock position.

15. Tighten the threaded connections.

a. Install the idler roller and ribbed belt tensioning roller for the generator.

b. Tighten the nuts for the refrigerant lines on the longitudinal member to 7 ft. lbs. (10 Nm).

c. Install the ribbed belt.

d. Install the fan shroud.

e. Install the battery.

16. Start the engine and make sure the generator is running.

IGNITION COIL

REMOVAL & INSTALLATION

2.0L & 2.5L Engines

See Figure 49.

1. To pull off spark plugs, place ignition coil puller T40039 on topmost thick rib of ignition coils with power output stages.

> ☀☀ **CAUTION**
>
> **If lower ribs are used, these can be damaged.**

2. Remove engine covers.

➡ **Spark plugs are located under ignition coils with power output stages.**

3. Remove both bolts.

➡ **Note installation position of ignition coils with power output stages.**

4. Pull all ignition coils approximately 1.17 in (30 mm) out of cylinder head in direction of rotation using ignition coil puller.

5. Push connector in direction of rotation ignition coils with power output stages, press catch down by hand and disconnect connectors.

To install:

6. Guide ignition coils with power output stages into cylinder head.

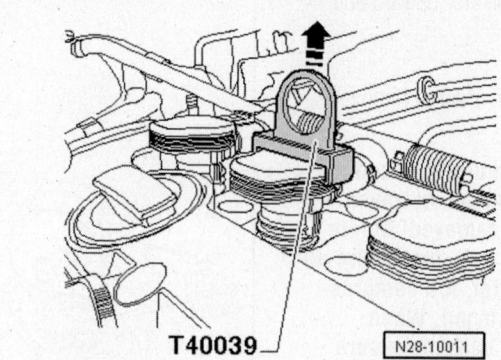

T40039— [N28-10011]

Fig. 49 To pull off spark plugs, place ignition coil puller on topmost thick rib of ignition coils with power output stages

7. Align ignition coils with power output stages into designated recesses of cylinder head cover.

8. Connect all connectors to ignition coils.

9. Press ignition coils with power output stages onto spark plugs by hand until stop. They must engage audibly.

10. Secure wiring using bolts.

11. Install engine cover.

IGNITION TIMING

ADJUSTMENT

All gasoline engines are equipped with a Distributorless Ignition System (DIS). No adjustment is necessary.

SPARK PLUGS

REMOVAL & INSTALLATION

2.0L & 2.5L Engines

See Figure 49.

1. To pull off spark plugs, place ignition coil puller T40039 on topmost thick rib of ignition coils with power output stages.

> ☀☀ **CAUTION**
>
> **If lower ribs are used, these can be damaged.**

2. Remove engine covers.

➡ **Spark plugs are located under ignition coils with power output stages.**

3. Remove both bolts.

➡ **Note installation position of ignition coils with power output stages.**

4. Pull all ignition coils approximately 1.17 in (30 mm) out of cylinder head in direction of rotation using ignition coil puller T40039.

5. Push connector in direction of rotation ignition coils with power output stages, press catch down by hand and disconnect connectors.

6. Remove spark plugs using spark plug wrench 3122 B.

To install:

7. Install new spark plugs using spark plug wrench.

8. Guide ignition coils with power output stages into cylinder head.

9. Align ignition coils with power output stages into designated recesses of cylinder head cover.

10. Connect all connectors to ignition coils.

11. Press ignition coils with power output stages onto spark plugs by hand until stop. They must engage audibly.

12. Secure wiring using bolts.

13. Install engine cover.

STARTER

REMOVAL & INSTALLATION

2.0L & 2.5L Engines

Manual Transmission

1. Disconnect battery.
2. Remove screws.
3. Disconnect hose after the clips have been opened.
4. Disconnect harness connector and free up line to air filter housing.
5. Pull off engine cover upward.
6. Remove the ground (GND) wire from starter mounting bolt.
7. Remove upper starter mounting bolt.
8. Slide protective cap downward from magnetic switch.
9. Remove the positive wire and disconnect harness connector of terminal.
10. Remove noise insulation.
11. All hose connections for charge air system are secured by spring-type clamps or by connector couplings. The following must be observed with connector couplings:
    a. Release connection by pulling locking clip.
    b. Disconnect hose/pipe without tools.
    c. Open screw-type clamp and disconnect connector coupling.
12. Remove charge air hose from vehicle.
13. Remove the nut from lower mounting bolt of starter.
14. Remove wire retainer.
15. Remove lower starter mounting bolt
16. Remove the starter downward and out from the vehicle.

To install:

17. Install in reverse order of removal.
18. All hose connections for charge air system are secured by spring-type clamps or by connector couplings. The following must be observed with connector couplings:
19. Connect hose/pipe without tools.
20. Make sure retaining tabs lock securely.
21. Tighten bolts/nuts to specification as follows:

- Starter to transmission M12: 59 ft. lbs. (80 Nm)
- Starter to transmission M10: 30 ft. lbs. (40 Nm)
- Ground (GND) wire to starter mounting bolt M8: 11 ft. lbs. (15 Nm)
- Ground wire to transmission M8: 11 ft. lbs. (15 Nm)
- Wire retainer to starter mounting bolt M8: 11 ft. lbs. (15 Nm)
- Positive wire to starter solenoid switch M8: 11 ft. lbs. (15 Nm)
- Air filter housing to body: 89 inch lbs. (10 Nm)

Automatic Transmission

1. Disconnect battery.
2. Pull off engine cover upward.
3. Disconnect harness connector, loosen spring-type clamp using Spring Type Clip Pliers VAS 5024 and disconnect vacuum hose.
4. Remove mounting bolt for air filter housing.
5. Release retaining tabs and remove cover.
6. Disconnect hose from air filter housing and remove it.
7. Pull off air filter housing upward out of brackets and remove it.
8. Slide protective cap downward from magnetic switch.
9. Remove the positive wire and disconnect harness connector of terminal.
10. Unclip wire from wiring harness.
11. Remove upper starter mounting bolt.
12. Remove lower mounting bolt for starter.
13. Remove starter upward and out of vehicle.

To install:

14. Install in reverse order of removal.
15. Tighten bolts/nuts to specification as follows:

- Starter to transmission M12: 59 ft. lbs. (80 Nm)
- Starter to transmission M10: 30 ft. lbs. (40 Nm)
- Ground (GND) wire to starter mounting bolt M8: 11 ft. lbs. (15 Nm)

- Ground wire to transmission M8: 11 ft. lbs. (15 Nm)
- Wire retainer to starter mounting bolt M8: 11 ft. lbs. (15 Nm)
- Positive wire to starter solenoid switch M8: 11 ft. lbs. (15 Nm)
- Air filter housing to body: 89 inch lbs. (10 Nm)

2.0L TDI Engine

1. Disconnect the battery.
2. Pull engine cover upward and forward.
3. Loosen spring clamp using spring clamp pliers VAS 5024 and disconnect connector.
4. Remove screw.
5. Remove vacuum hose.
6. Pull air filter housing on the right side upward from its rubber mounting.
7. Remove air filter housing from vehicle.
8. Slide protective cap downward from solenoid.
9. Remove positive wire and disconnect harness connector of terminal.
10. Remove the ground wire from the starter mounting bolt.
11. Remove the starter mounting bolt.
12. Remove the noise insulation.
13. Remove the nut from the lower starter mounting bolt.
14. Remove wire retainer.
15. Remove the starter mounting bolt.
16. Remove the starter.

To install:

17. Install in reverse order of removal.
18. Tighten bolts/nuts to specification as follows:

- Starter to transmission M12: 56 ft. lbs. (75 Nm)
- Ground wire to Starter B mounting bolt M8: 11 ft. lbs. (15 Nm)
- Wire retainer to Starter B mounting bolt M8: 11 ft. lbs. (15 Nm)
- Positive wire to Starter B solenoid switch M8: 11 ft. lbs. (15 Nm)
- Air filter housing to body: 89 inch lbs. (10 Nm)
- GND wire to automatic transmission housing M8: 11 ft. lbs. (15 Nm)

ENGINE MECHANICAL

➡Disconnecting the negative battery cable may interfere with the functions of the on board computer systems and may require the computer to undergo a relearning process, once the negative battery cable is reconnected.

ACCESSORY DRIVE BELTS

ACCESSORY BELT ROUTING

See Figures 50 through 52.

INSPECTION

1. Turn the engine at vibration damper/crankshaft pulley with a suitable socket wrench.
2. Raise the vehicle if necessary. Check the drive belt for:
   a. Sub-surface (deep) cracks
   b. Layer separation (top layer, cord strands)
   c. Traces of oil and grease
3. Replace the belt if any damage is found or if contaminated with oil or grease.

ADJUSTMENT

All models use an automatic (spring powered) tensioner. No adjustment is required.

REMOVAL & INSTALLATION

2.0L Engines, Except TDI

✳✳ CAUTION

Risk of destroying due to reversed running direction on a used ribbed belt. Before removing ribbed belt, marking running direction with chalk or felt-tip pen for reinstallation later.

1. Remove the noise insulation.
2. Remove the right air guide hose.
3. To release the tension on the ribbed belt, turn the tensioner in direction of rotation from underneath.
4. Secure tensioner with Drift T10060 A.
5. Remove ribbed belt.

To install:

6. Installation is performed in reverse order of removal.

➡**Before installing ribbed belt, generator, A/C compressor must be securely installed.**

7. First mount the ribbed belt on the crankshaft pulley, then on the A/C compressor and generator.

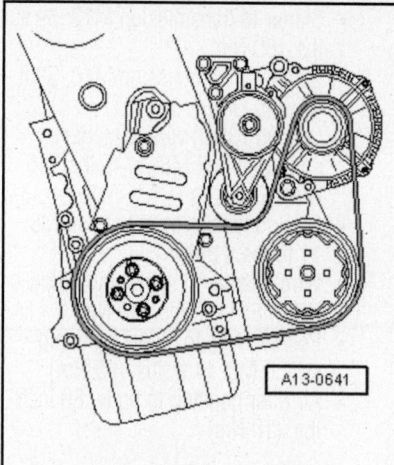

Fig. 50 Accessory drive belt routing— 2.0L Engine, except TDI

8. Turn the tensioner with a box-end wrench and remove the drift T10060 A.
9. Release tensioner.

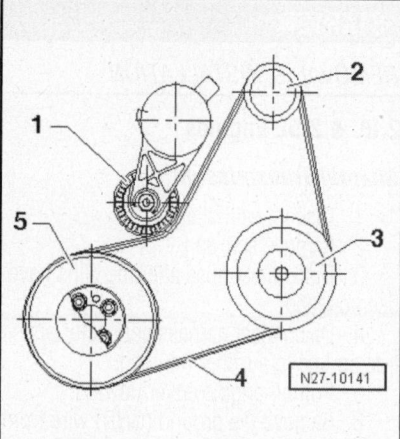

Fig. 52 Accessory drive belt routing— 2.0L TDI Engine

10. Check whether ribbed belt is routed correctly.
11. Start engine and check whether ribbed belt runs correctly.

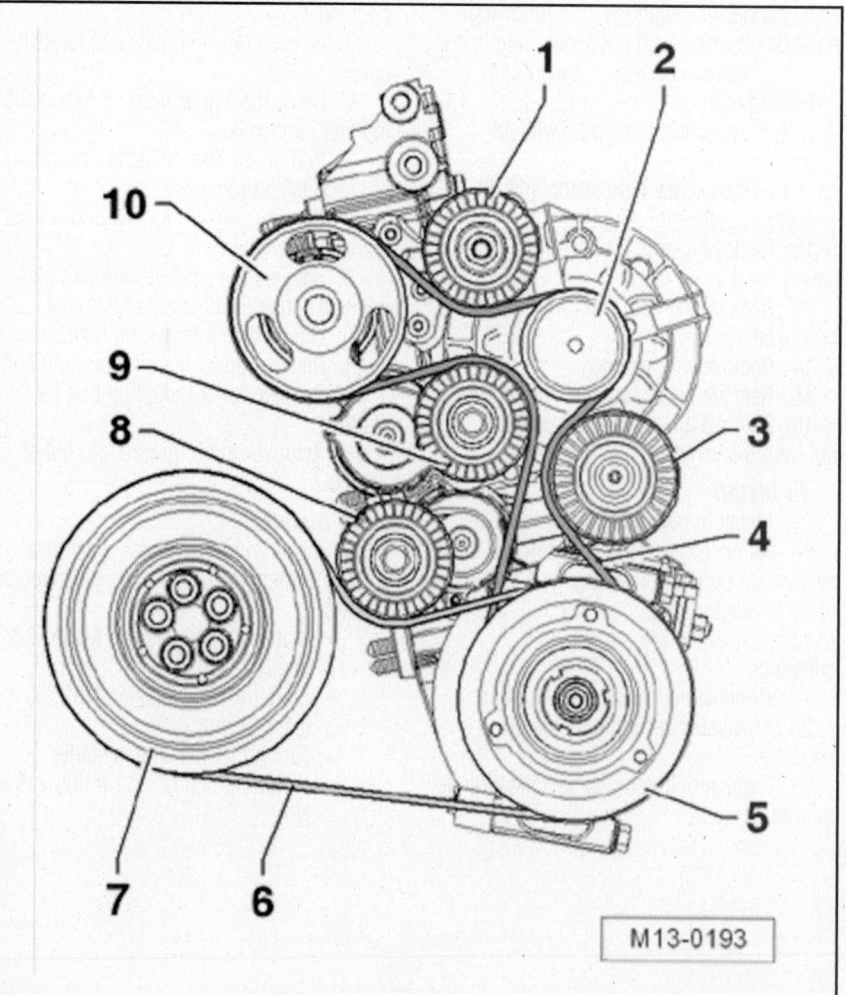

Fig. 51 Accessory drive belt routing—2.5L Engine

2.0L TDI Engine

1. Remove noise insulation.
2. Remove engine cover:

   a. On one piece cover, pull the one piece front engine cover upward with a quick jerk and then pull the lower mount forward.

   b. On the two piece engine cover, first pull the outer cover upward with a quick jerk, then pull the inner engine cover upward with a quick jerk.

3. To remove fuel filter fuel filter without the retaining plate, release the retainers, pull the fuel filter with connected hoses upward and out of the retaining plate and lay it aside.

4. To remove fuel filter with the retaining plate:

   a. Loosen the bolt one turn.

   b. Remove the bolt and the nut.

   c. Lay the fuel filter, with the hoses still connected, to the side.

5. Mark direction of rotation of ribbed belt.

6. Pivot tensioner element to relieve tension on ribbed belt.

7. Secure tensioner element using the drift T10060.

8. Remove ribbed belt.

To install:

9. Installation is performed in reverse order.

10. Before installing ribbed belt, make sure that all ancillaries (alternator, air conditioner compressor) are secured tightly.

11. Note previously marked direction of belt rotation and be sure that it is seated correctly on pulley.

12. Set the ribbed belt onto the generator lastly.

13. Start the engine and check the running belt.

2.5L Engine

See Figure 53.

1. Raise and safely support the front of the vehicle.

2. Remove front part of right front inner fender.

3. Put a 15mm wrench on the A/C belt tensioner and push towards the rear of the vehicle.

4. Insert a pin to hold the wrench in place.

5. Remove the compressor belt and mark its running direction for installation. Do not leave the wrench and pin in place if moving on to other work.

6. Mark the running direction of the alternator belt.

7. Move the tensioner and insert a pin to hold it in place.

8. Remove the belt. Do not leave the wrench and pin in place if moving on to other work.

To install:

9. Place the alternator belt on the alternator and coolant pump pulleys, then lastly on the idler pulley.

Fig. 53 Move the tensioner and insert a pin to hold it in place

10. Before releasing the tensioner, check ribbed for correct seating in the pulleys.

11. Secure the other tensioner and install the A/C compressor belt. Be sure that it is seated correctly on pulley before releasing the tensioner.

12. Start engine and check belt running.

AIR CLEANER

REMOVAL & INSTALLATION

2.0L Engine

Housing Assembly

See Figure 54.

1. Remove the cover for the intake air duct: disengage the side clips to do so.

2. Unclip the lower intake air duct, disengage the clips to do so.

3. Remove both the lower air duct and the air duct hose.

4. If equipped with engine code CBFA, disconnect the hose leading to the secondary air injection pump motor from the air filter housing.

5. Loosen the bolt and pull the air filter housing upward off of the bracket.

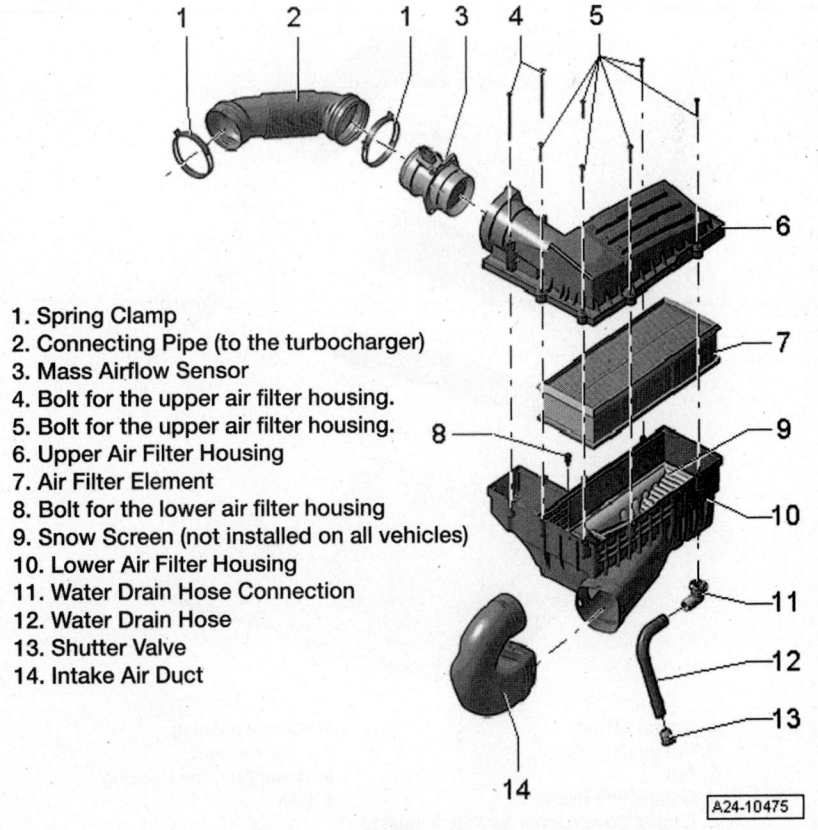

1. Spring Clamp
2. Connecting Pipe (to the turbocharger)
3. Mass Airflow Sensor
4. Bolt for the upper air filter housing.
5. Bolt for the upper air filter housing.
6. Upper Air Filter Housing
7. Air Filter Element
8. Bolt for the lower air filter housing
9. Snow Screen (not installed on all vehicles)
10. Lower Air Filter Housing
11. Water Drain Hose Connection
12. Water Drain Hose
13. Shutter Valve
14. Intake Air Duct

Fig. 54 Exploded view of the air intake and air cleaner assembly—2.0L engine

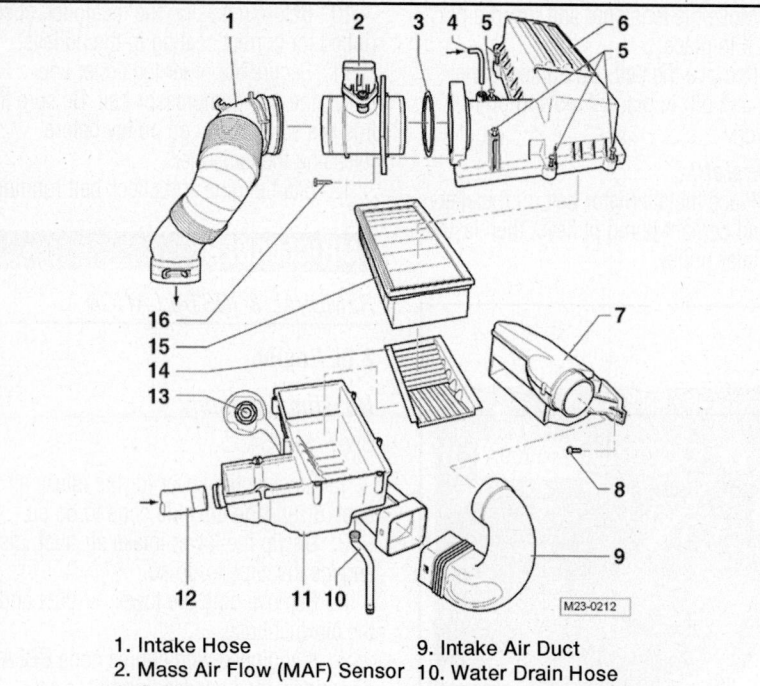

1. Intake Hose
2. Mass Air Flow (MAF) Sensor
3. O-Ring
4. Vacuum Hose
5. Bolt
6. Upper Air Filter Housing
7. Intake Air Duct
8. Bolt
9. Intake Air Duct
10. Water Drain Hose
11. Lower Air Filter Housing
12. Intake Hose
13. Bolt
14. Snow Screen
15. Air Filter Element
16. Bolt

Fig. 55 Exploded view of the air intake and air cleaner assembly—2.0L TDI engine

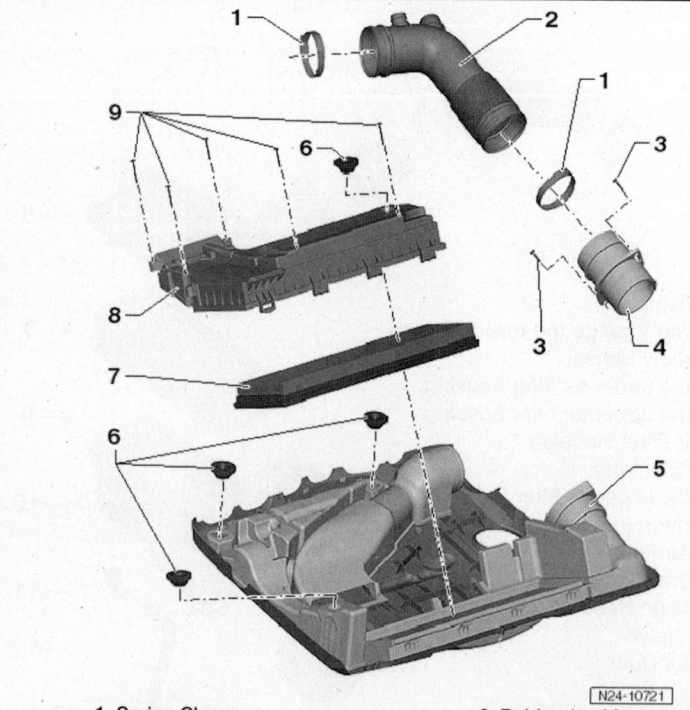

1. Spring Clamp
2. Connecting Pipe
3. Bolt
4. Connecting Piece
5. Engine Cover/Upper Air Filter Housing
6. Rubber bushing
7. Filter Element
8. Lower Air Filter Housing
9. Bolt

Fig. 56 Exploded view of the air intake and air cleaner assembly—2.5L engine

6. Remove air filter housing together with the Mass Airflow (MAF) sensor and connecting pipe.

7. Install in the reverse order of removal.

FILTER ELEMENT

1. If equipped with engine code CBFA, disconnect the hose leading to the secondary air injection pump motor from the air filter housing.

2. Remove the bolts from the upper air filter housing.

3. Lift the upper air filter housing and remove the air filter element.

4. Install a new element and replace the housing cover.

2.0L TDI Engine

Housing Assembly

See Figure 55.

1. Release the tabs and remove the cover from the intake air duct.

2. Remove the bolts for the intake air duct and pull the intake air duct from the lock carrier.

3. Press the tabs and remove the hose from the air filter housing.

4. Disconnect the connector from the Mass Airflow (MAF) sensor and the vacuum line.

5. Loosen the bolt on the air filter housing.

6. Open the clamp and remove the intake hose to the adapter.

7. Remove the entire air filter housing.

8. Install in the reverse order of removal.

2.5L Engine

Engine Cover with Air Filter

See Figure 56.

1. Disconnect the connector, if equipped, reposition the clamp and disconnect the connecting pipe.

2. Remove the screws and disconnect intake air duct.

3. Pull the engine cover up, with a jerking motion off of the mounts, first at the front, then at the right rear and finally at the left rear.

4. Carefully swivel the engine cover out of the rear area.

To install:

➡The rubber bushings must not be treated with lubricant, neither for assembly to the cover or for assembly to the engine.

5. Position the engine cover correctly on the mounts and press down by hand.

6. he rest of the installation follows the reverse of the removal procedure.

BALANCE SHAFT TIMING CHAIN

REMOVAL & INSTALLATION

2.0L Engine

See Figures 57 through 60.

➡ Always replace the intermediate shaft sprocket. Otherwise the backlash will not adjust itself and it could result in engine damage. The new intermediate shaft sprocket has an anti-friction coating that wears off after a short period of use, which automatically adjusts the backlash.

1. Remove timing chain upper cover.
2. Remove the lower timing chain cover.
3. Remove the camshaft timing chain.
4. Remove the balance shaft timing chain.
   a. Remove the guide rail for the camshaft timing chain.
   b. Remove chain tensioner for camshaft timing chain.
   c. Remove the balance shaft chain tensioner.
   d. Remove the tensioning rail.
   e. Remove the guide rail.
   f. Remove the guide rail.
   g. Remove the timing chain.
5. Remove the coolant pump toothed belt.
   a. Remove small coolant pipe.
   b. Lay aside the coolant hose and electrical wiring harness.
   c. Remove the bolt and remove bracket.
   d. Remove the bolt on the bracket for the after-run coolant pump.
   e. Remove the coolant hoses and lay them aside.

Fig. 58 Mark the tooth face on the intermediate sprocket (arrow)

   f. Remove the front right wheel housing liner.
   g. Remove bolts.
   h. Remove the air guide pipe by lifting the clamps items.
   i. Pull off the Intake Manifold Runner Control (IMRC) Valve.
   j. Remove the bolts and remove the toothed belt cover.

➡ The drive gear bolt has a left thread.

   k. Remove the bolt on the coolant pump drive gear using Torque Wrench V.A.G 1331 clockwise and Insert Tool T10360; at the same time, counterhold the vibration damper.
   l. Remove the drive gear and toothed belt.
6. Mark the tooth face on the intermediate sprocket.
7. Remove the intermediate sprocket.
8. Remove the intake camshaft balance shaft.

To install:

9. Lubricate the balance shaft bearing with engine oil.
10. Install the intake camshaft balance shaft.
11. Replace the O-ring and coat with engine oil.
12. Coat the bearing pin with engine oil and install it; the bearing pin must engage in the hole in the cylinder block.
13. Mark the tooth face on the intermediate sprocket.
14. Install the intermediate sprocket; the marking on the balance shaft must be between the markings on the tooth faces.
15. Tighten the chain sprocket bolt.
16. Check the markings on the intermediate shaft sprocket/balance shaft.

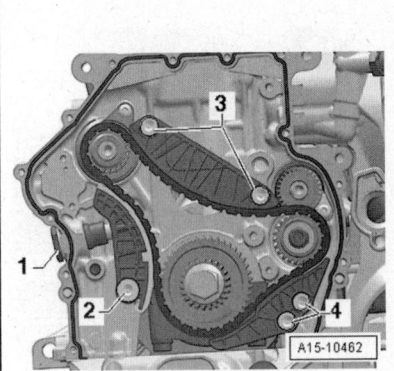

Fig. 57 Timing chain and guide positioning

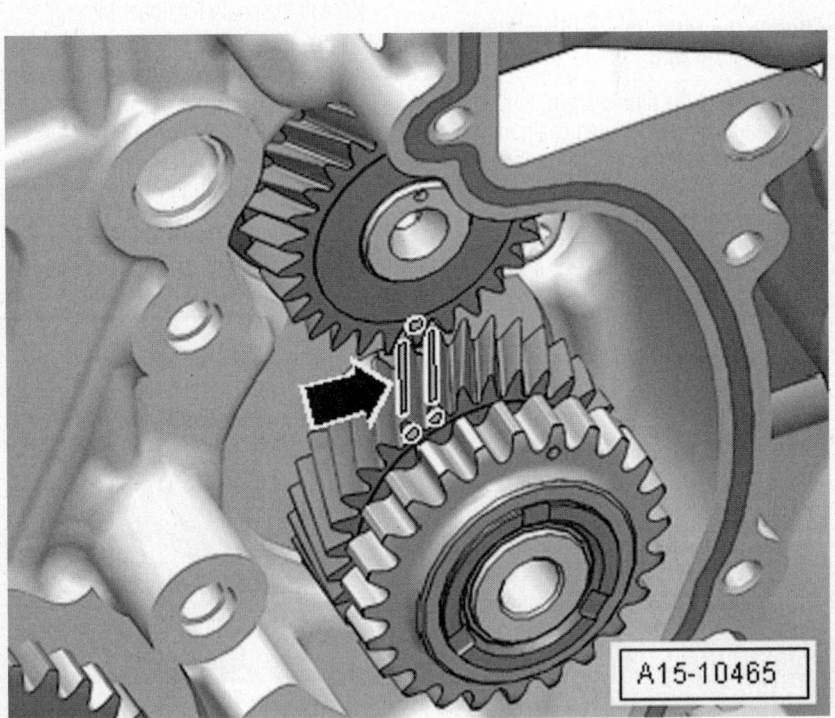

Fig. 59 Install the intermediate sprocket; the marking on the balance shaft must be between the markings on the tooth faces (arrow)

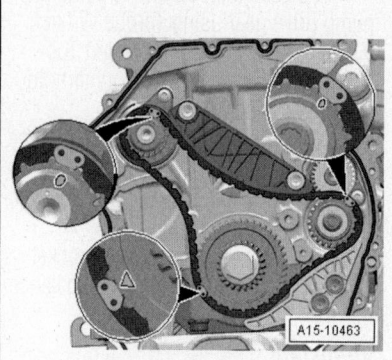

Fig. 60 Mount the timing chain; the painted links of the timing chain must be positioned on the markings on the chain sprockets

➡**Due to the ratio, the marking align only every 7th turn.**

17. Replace the coolant pump drive seal.
18. Install the coolant pump toothed belt.
   a. Replace the drive gear bolt.
   b. Replace seals and O-rings.
19. Make sure the drive gear installed position is with the collar on the drive gear faces the transmission.
20. Install the balance shaft timing chain.
   a. Turn the intermediate shaft sprocket/balance shaft to the marking.

➡**Due to the ratio, the marking align only every 7th turn.**

   b. Mount the timing chain; the painted links of the timing chain must be positioned on the markings on the chain sprockets.
   c. Install the timing chain tensioning rail and tighten the bolt.
   d. Install the timing chain guide rail and tighten the bolts.
   e. Install the timing chain guide rail and tighten the bolts.
   f. Insert the timing chain tensioner with locking compound.
   g. Check this adjustment one more time.
   h. Check the markings on the intermediate shaft sprocket/balance shaft
21. The rest of the assembly is basically a reverse of the disassembling sequence.

CAMSHAFT AND VALVE LIFTERS

REMOVAL & INSTALLATION

2.0L Engines

See Figures 61 through 68.

1. Remove the engine cover.
2. Remove the vacuum pump.
3. Remove the noise insulation.
4. Remove the front part of the right wheel housing liner and/or the front right wheel housing liner.
5. Remove bolts.
6. Remove the air guide pipe by lifting the clamps items.
7. Disconnect the connector from the Camshaft Adjustment Valve N205.
8. Remove the bolts and then the camshaft adjustment valve N205.
9. Remove the upper timing chain cover.

➡**The control valve has a left thread.**

10. Remove the control valve using Assembly Tool 10352 T10352 in the direction of.
11. Remove the bolts and remove the bearing bracket.
12. Rotate the vibration damper using the Counter Hold Tool T10355 into the "OT" position.

➡**The notch on the vibration damper must line up with the marking on the timing chain lower cover.**

13. Mark the drive chain/chain sprockets with a waterproof marker. These marks are necessary for reinstallation.
14. Remove the plug.
15. Lift the chain tensioner locking wedge by inserting a scriber or a suitable screwdriver into the hole in the chain tensioner direction.
16. Turn the crankshaft opposite the engine direction of rotation direction and secure it with a Securing Pin T40011.

➡**The intake camshaft switches in the engine direction of rotation.**

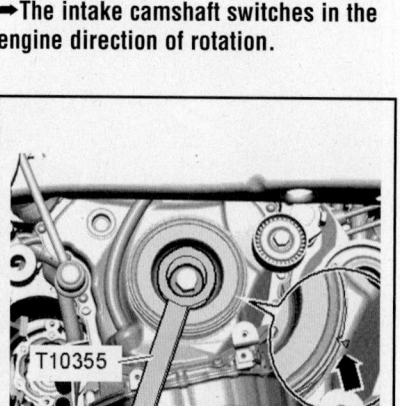

Fig. 61 Rotate the vibration damper using the Counter Hold Tool T10355 into the "OT" position

Fig. 62 Mark the drive chain/chain sprockets with a waterproof marker. These marks are necessary for reinstallation

17. Remove the bolt and guide the tensioning rail downward.
18. Remove the upper guide rail by unlocking the latch (located in the center) with a screwdriver and pushing the guide rail forward.

➡**When the lower timing chain cover is installed, the loose chain on the crankshaft cannot jump off.**

19. Remove camshaft timing chain from chain sprockets.

➡**If the camshaft timing chain was removed from the cylinder head, then the crankshaft may not be turned further. On this engine, when the valves are mounted, there is the danger that there are panels attached to the lower timing chain cover, which could fall and interfere with the chain; also a loose chain turned by the crankshaft can bend the panels. The panels can**

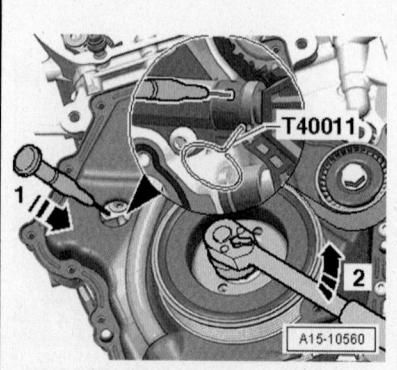

Fig. 63 Lift the chain tensioner locking wedge by inserting a scriber or a suitable screwdriver into the hole in the chain tensioner direction

bend if the crankshaft is rotated when the chain is loose.

20. Disconnect the electrical connectors on the ignition coils and free up the wiring harness.

21. Remove the ignition coils with the puller T40039.

22. Disconnect the crankcase ventilation hoses.

23. Remove the bolts and remove the crankcase ventilation.

24. Remove the bolts.

25. Remove the air guide pipe bolt.

26. Loosen the hose clamp and remove the air guide pipe together with the crankcase ventilation.

27. Disconnect the vacuum line and free up the wire.

28. Disconnect the electrical connector from the Camshaft Position (CMP) Sensor.

➡ **The sealing surfaces of the lower cylinder head cover and on the upper cylinder head must not be reworked.**

➡ **If the cylinder head cover was loosened, then the cover must be replaced.**

➡ **The camshaft bearings are integrated in the cylinder head or cylinder head cover. The tension must be released from the camshaft timing chain before removing the cylinder head cover.**

29. Remove the cylinder head cover bolts in 1 to 6 sequence.

30. Remove the cylinder head cover.

31. Remove the camshafts.

32. Prevent dirt and adhesive residue from entering cylinder head.

To install:

➡ **During installation, cable ties must be re-installed at the same location. Sealing surfaces must be completely free of oil and grease.**

✷✷ CAUTION

The pistons must not be positioned at TDC.

33. Make sure that all roller cam followers make contact correctly on valve stem ends.

➡ **The cover must be installed within 5 minutes after application of silicone sealant.**

34. Remove any sealant residue on the cylinder head using the flat blade scraper.

➡ **Prevent dirt and adhesive residue from entering cylinder head.**

35. Remove any seal out of the groove in the cylinder head cover as well as from any sealing surface using, for example, a rotating plastic brush.

36. Clean sealing surfaces, must be free of oil and grease.

37. Cut tube nozzle at front marking approximately 0.078 in. (2 mm).

38. Lubricate the running surfaces of both camshafts.

39. Place the camshaft into the cylinder head; the recesses must be perpendicular to each other.

40. Replace the cylinder head cover bolts.

41. Apply the silicone sealant D 154 103 A1 on the clean sealing surface of the cylinder head cover. Thickness of sealant bead: 0.078–0.117 in. (2–3 mm).

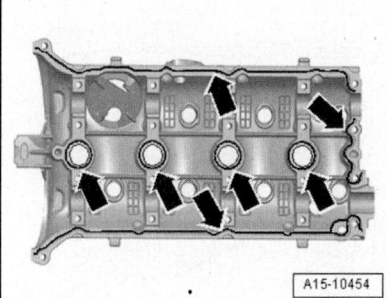

Fig. 66 Apply the silicone sealant D 154 103 A1 on the clean sealing surface of the cylinder head cover as shown. Thickness of sealant bead: 0.078–0.117 in. (2–3 mm)

➡ **The cylinder head cover must be installed within 5 minutes after application of silicone sealant. The sealant bead may not be thicker than specified, otherwise excess sealant could enter the oil pan and clog the oil intake tube.**

42. Tighten bolts in several stages.
  • Replace bolts
  • Hand-tighten bolts in several stages in 1 to 6 sequence
  • Tighten the bolts in a 1 to 6 sequence to 71 inch lbs. (8 Nm) using a torque wrench
  • Tighten the bolts an additional 90° using a rigid wrench in the sequence 1 to 6

➡ **Make sure the cylinder head cover is not tilted.**

43. Insert the cover without sealing using Thrust Piece T10174. Measurement A should be 0.039–0.078 in. (1–2 mm).

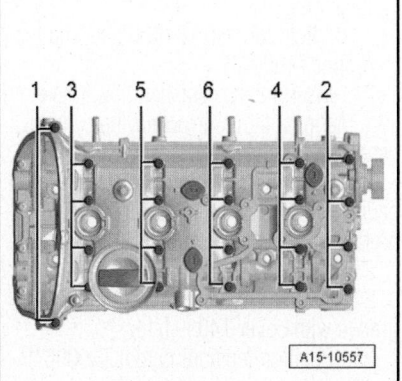

Fig. 64 Remove the cylinder head cover bolts in 1 to 6 sequence

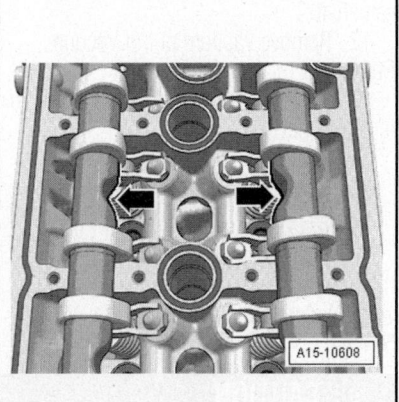

Fig. 65 Remove the cylinder head cover bolts in 1 to 6 sequence

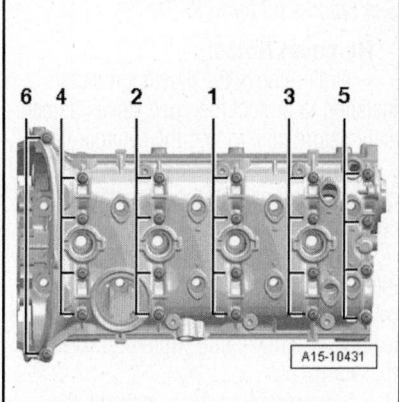

Fig. 67 Tighten bolts in several stages using the sequence shown

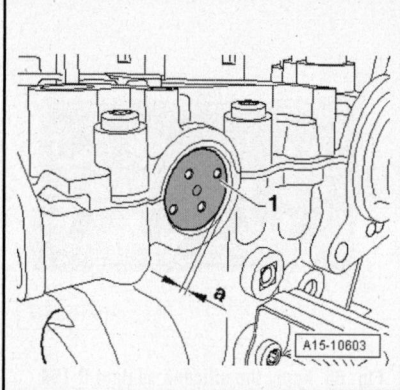

Fig. 68 Insert the cover without sealing using Thrust Piece T10174. Measurement A should be 0.039–0.078 in. (1–2 mm)

❈❈ CAUTION

When turning the crankshaft, make sure the timing chain cannot damage any other components.

44. Rotate the vibration damper using the Counter Hold Tool T10355 into the "OT" position.

45. The notch on the vibration damper must line up with the marking on the timing chain lower cover.

46. The marked links of the timing chain must be positioned on the markings on the chain sprockets.

47. Mount the camshaft timing chain: The markings drive chain/chain sprockets must align.

48. Turn the intake camshaft using the wrench in the direction of the and mount the timing chain.

49. The rest of the assembly is basically a reverse of the disassembling sequence.

2.0L TDI Engine

See Figures 69 through 71.

Removal Notes:

• Only remove the plastic protectors installed to protect the open valves immediately before positioning the cylinder head.

• When replacing the cylinder head or cylinder head gasket, the coolant must be completely replaced.

• Cylinder heads with cracks between the valve seats can continue to be used without reducing service life, as long as the tears have a maximum width of 0.0195 in. (0.5 mm).

• After installing the camshafts, the engine may not be started for approximately 30 minutes. The hydraulic adjusting elements must seat themselves (otherwise the

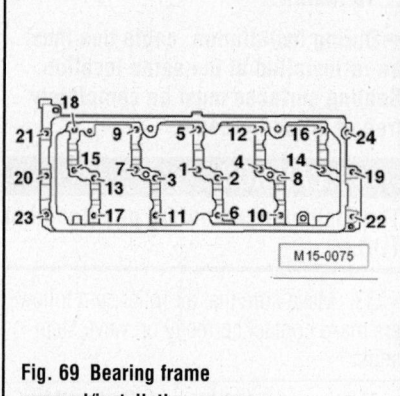

Fig. 69 Bearing frame removal/installation sequence

valves will seat themselves on the pistons).

• After working on the valve train and lifters, carefully rotate the crankshaft by hand at least 2 full revolutions before starting to be sure that valves do not strike the pistons.

Always replace gaskets and seals.

1. Remove toothed belt from the camshaft and high pressure fuel pump.

2. Remove cylinder head cover.

3. Remove bolts for camshaft sprocket.

4. Remove camshaft sprocket from the hub.

5. Counterhold hub with the counterhold tool T10051 and loosen hub bolt.

6. Remove bolt for hub by approximately 2 turns.

7. Position puller T10052 and align it to the bores in the hub.

8. Tighten mounting bolts.

9. Tension hub by tightening puller T10052 evenly until it can be removed from the camshaft taper.

10. Hold puller T10052 with a 30 mm wrench.

11. Remove hub from the cone of the camshaft.

12. Remove vacuum pump Vacuum Pump.

13. Remove bearing frame bolts or nuts in sequence.

14. Remove bearing frame.

15. Carefully remove camshafts.

To install:

16. Seal separating surfaces between the bearing frame and cylinder head with silicone adhesive sealant D 176 501 A1.

❈❈ CAUTION

Only install the camshafts with the camshaft insertion tool T40094 as described below. Otherwise the axial

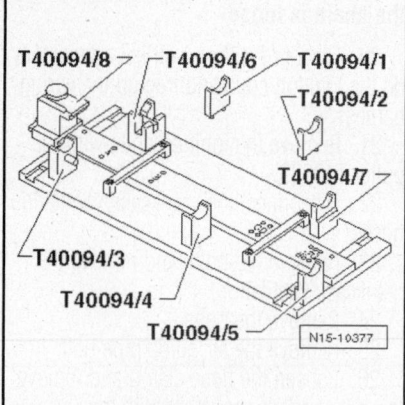

Fig. 70 Only install the camshafts with the camshaft insertion tool T40094 as described below

bearing in the bearing frame will be destroyed and the cylinder head will have to be replaced. Make sure that no sealant residue enters the cylinder head and bearings.

17. Using rotating plastic brush, remove any remaining sealant from cylinder head and guide frame.

18. Clean sealing surfaces, they must be free of oil and grease.

19. Oil journal surfaces of camshafts.

20. Assemble camshaft insertion tool T40094 as follows:

   a. Remove mounts T40094/3, T40094/4 and T40094/5 from base plate. Loosen threaded connections from below.

   b. If the mounts on the camshaft insertion tool T40094 are not marked, mark the removed mounts, for example with numbers, to ensure it can be assembled later.

   c. Install mounts T40094/9 and T40094/10 in the empty outer locations.

   d. Position mount T40094/2 and the mount T40094/1.

21. Insert intake camshaft first. Make sure the indentation arrow for the cylinder head bolt faces "outward".

22. Position 0.0195 in. (0.50 mm) feeler gauge and slide the mount T40094/8 into groove on the intake camshaft.

23. Insert exhaust camshaft.

24. Secure exhaust camshaft at its groove with cover T40094/11.

25. Position tensioning tool T40096/1 on the exhaust camshaft sprockets.

➡ Make sure the clamping jaw marked with an arrow is on the wider sprocket.

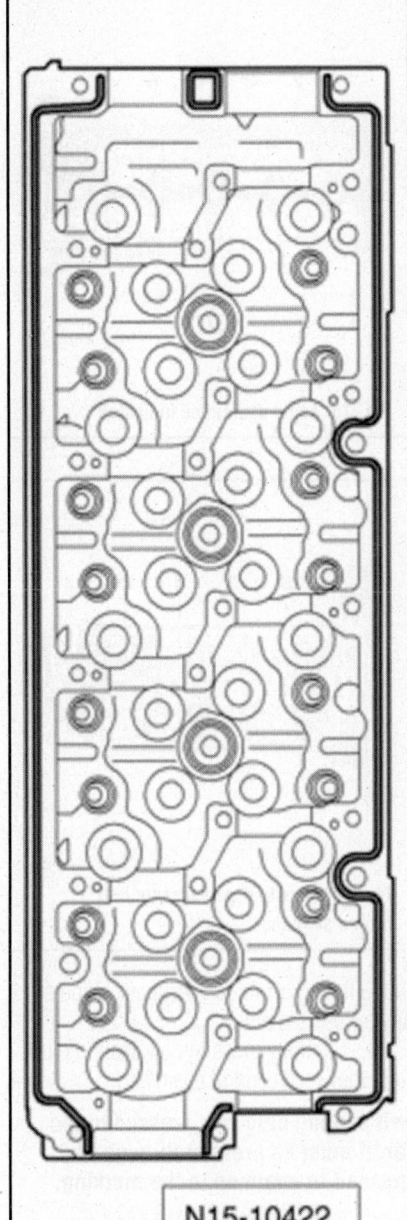

Fig. 71 Apply silicone sealant to the clean sealing surface of the cylinder head as illustrated. The sealing compound bead must be 0.078–0.117 in. (2–3 mm) thick

26. Tighten tensioning tool with thumb wheel until the tooth faces align. Use a 13 mm open end wrench if necessary.

27. Slide intake camshaft toward the exhaust camshaft until the splines engage.

28. Position bearing frame on the camshafts.

29. All the camshaft bearings must lie on the camshafts.

30. Position clamping tool T40095 and secure the camshafts in the bearing frame.

31. Remove cover T40094/11.

32. Remove mount T40094/8 from the intake camshaft groove.

33. Cut tube nozzle approximately 0.117 in. (3 mm).

34. Apply silicone sealant to the clean sealing surface of the cylinder head. The sealing compound bead must be 0.078–0.117 in. (2–3 mm) thick.

35. Apply on the inner side in the area with the threaded holes

36. The sealant beads must not be thicker than 0.078–0.117 in. (2–3 mm) or excess sealant can enter the camshaft bearing.

37. Remove camshafts with bearing frame and the clamping tool from the camshaft insertion tool T40094.

38. Carefully insert the camshafts and bearing frame in the cylinder head.

39. First tighten bearing frame bolts or nuts by hand in sequence 1 to 24.

40. The guide frame must be in contact with the entire contact surface of the cylinder head.

41. Tighten bearing frame bolts or nuts in sequence.

42. Remove clamping tool and tensioning tool.

43. Replace camshaft seal.

44. Drive a new sealing cover onto cylinder head with a suitable drift until it is flush.

The rest of installation is in reverse order of removal, noting the following:

45. After installing the camshafts, the engine may not be started for approximately 30 minutes. The hydraulic adjusting elements must seat themselves (otherwise the valves will seat themselves on the pistons).

46. After working on the valvetrain, carefully rotate engine by hand at least 2 full revolutions to ensure that valves do not strike the pistons when starting.

47. Place hub on the camshaft.

48. Counterhold hub with the counterhold tool T10051 and tighten hub bolt.

49. Push camshaft sprocket onto hub.

50. The toothed segment of the camshaft sprocket must face upward.

51. Install bolts into camshaft sprocket by hand to eliminate play.

52. Lock hub with rig pin 3359.

53. Install and tension the toothed belt.

54. Install vacuum pump.

55. Install cylinder head cover.

2.5L Engine

See Figures 72 through 76.

1. Remove the battery and battery holder.

2. Remove engine cover/air filter assembly.

3. Disconnect PCV hose from cylinder head cover. If equipped, remove the secondary air tube.

4. Remove the ignition coils.

5. Remove bolts for cylinder head cover in reverse of the tightening sequence.

6. Remove the timing chain cover. This requires removing the intake manifold.

7. Remove the brake booster vacuum pump.

➡ **The 4 cover bolts must not be loosened under any circumstances!**

8. If valve timing is correct:
   - Secure the crankshaft as if for removing the timing chain.
   - Install the camshaft locator T40070 on the camshafts and tighten bolts to 15 ft. lbs. (20 Nm). If the bolts could not be screwed in easily, rotate exhaust camshaft slightly using an open-end wrench.
   - Relieve tension on timing chain. To do so, pry between piston of chain tensioner and tensioning track. Secure completely pressed in piston using Locking Pins T03006. Locking pin must be inserted until it stops.

9. If valve timing is not correct:
   - Remove timing chain case cover
   - Rotate crankshaft to TDC cylinder 5 but do not lock it into place.
   - Rotate crankshaft so that camshaft locator can be screwed easily on to camshafts.

10. Remove the bolts to remove the sprockets. It may be necessary to gently pry them off.

11. Remove the camshaft locking tool and loosen the guide frame bolts a little at a time from the outside towards the center.

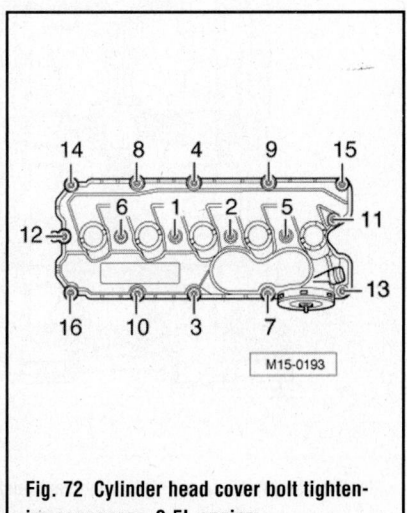

Fig. 72 Cylinder head cover bolt tightening sequence—2.5L engine

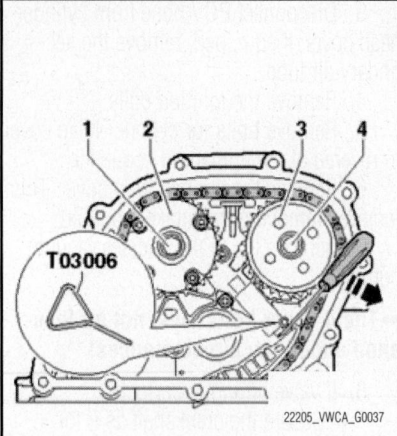

Fig. 73 Pry the chain tensioner to retract the piston and insert a locking pin. Remove bolts (1 and 4) to remove sprockets (2 and 3)

12. Remove the bolts and guide frame and lift the camshafts out of the cylinder head.

To install:

13. Make sure all sealing surfaces are clean and dry. Oil the camshaft bearing surfaces in the guide frame and cylinder head.

14. Fit the camshafts into the guide frame, not the cylinder head.

15. Make sure the sealing ends point up or down, not to the sides. Turn the guide frame over while holding camshafts firmly in place and fit the assembly onto the cylinder head.

16. Rotate camshafts until threaded holes point upward.

17. Check whether camshafts still lie correctly in the bearings, then install the holding tool T40070.

18. Carefully apply sealant.

✳✳ CAUTION

Do not use too much sealant or it will get into the cam bearings and prevent proper lubrication.

19. Install the bolts and tighten them in several stages. Torque all bolts in sequence to 71 in. lbs. (8 Nm), then repeat the sequence turning each bolt an additional 90°.

20. Sealant must bulge outward slightly

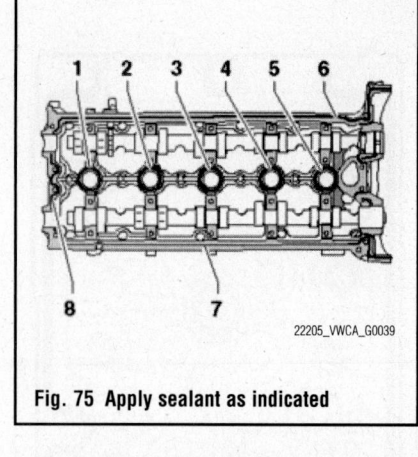

Fig. 75 Apply sealant as indicated

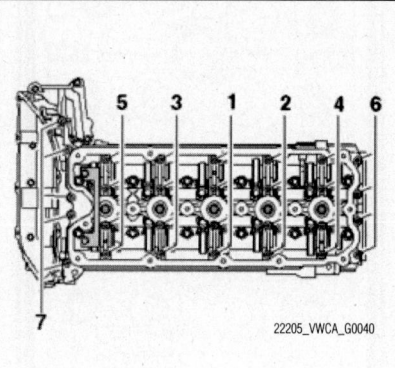

Fig. 76 Camshaft guide frame bolt torque sequence

in the timing chain compartment. Wipe off any excess sealant.

21. Carefully press in new sealing plugs until they reach end of chamfer.

➡**If sealing plug was pressed in too far, it must be pressed through and pressed in again up to the marking.**

22. Install the timing chain and remove the crankshaft locking pin from the cylinder block.

23. Install the remaining components.

CATALYTIC CONVERTER

REMOVAL & INSTALLATION

2.0L & 2.5L Engines

1. Remove the air filter.

2. Disconnect Heated Oxygen Sensor (HO2S) harness connector and free up cable.

3. From above, remove the nuts on the front exhaust pipe connection to the turbocharger.

4. Remove nuts accessible from below from front exhaust pipe to the turbocharger connection.

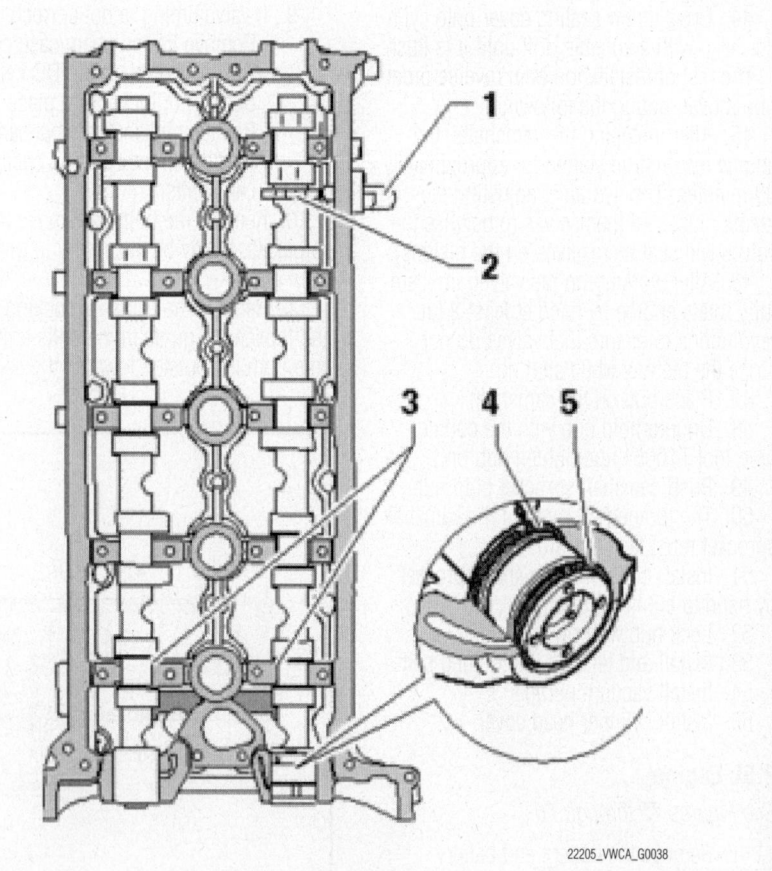

Fig. 74 The intake camshaft has the cam position sensor wheel (2) that aligns with the sensor (1)—make sure the sealing ring ends (4 and 5) point up or down, not towards the sides

5. Remove the nuts and slightly pull the vehicle floor cover downward.

6. Disconnect the electrical connector on the right side of the underbody.

7. Remove the electrical connector out of the bracket and free up the electrical wire to the oxygen sensor.

8. Unclip the wires, remove the bracket and disconnect the connectors.

9. Remove exhaust system bracket.

10. Remove the front cross member for the vehicle floor.

✳✳ CAUTION

Risk of damaging decoupling elements. Do not bend decoupling element in front exhaust pipe more than 10°.

11. Loosen clamping sleeve and push it rearward.

12. Remove the catalytic converters with the front exhaust pipe.

To install:

13. Installation is performed in the reverse order of removal.

14. Coat turbocharger stud bolts with hot bolt paste G 052 112 A3.

15. Replace gaskets and self-locking nuts.

16. Install exhaust system free of stress.

17. Tighten tunnel bridge to body bolts/nuts to 19 ft. lbs. (25 Nm).

CRANKSHAFT FRONT SEAL

REMOVAL & INSTALLATION

2.0L Engines

1. Remove the vibration damper and mount the Thrust Piece T10368.

2. Pry out the sealing ring.

To install:

3. Clean running and sealing surface.

4. Disconnect the thrust piece.

5. Pull the sealing ring using the thrust piece and the vibration damper bolt in all the way.

➡**Replace the vibration damper bolt and O-ring.**

6. The rest of the assembly is basically a reverse of the disassembling sequence.

2.0L TDI Engine

1. Remove toothed belt.

2. Remove toothed belt crankshaft sprocket. Secure toothed belt sprocket with the counterhold tool 3415.

3. To guide seal remover 3203, install the center bolt manually into the crankshaft all the way.

4. Rotate inner section of the seal remover two turns, approximately 0.117 in. (3 mm), out of the outer section and secure it with the knurled bolt.

5. Lubricate threaded head of the seal remover.

6. Using considerable force, screw seal remover as far as possible into the seal.

7. Loosen knurled screw and turn inner portion against crankshaft until the oil seal is pulled out.

To install:

8. The sealing lip of the sealing ring may not be additionally oiled or greased.

9. Before installing, remove oil remains from end of crankshaft with a clean cloth.

10. Place guide sleeve T10053/1 on crankshaft pin.

11. Push seal over the guide sleeve onto the end of the crankshaft.

12. Press seal in to the limit stop using the assembly tool T10053 and the center bolt.

13. Install crankshaft toothed belt sprocket and tighten to 15 ft. lbs. (20 Nm)

2.5L Engine

See Figures 77 and 78.

1. Raise and safely support the vehicle and remove the engine undercover.

2. Remove the front part of the right inner fender.

3. Remove the A/C compressor drive belt. Mark the belt's direction of rotation for reinstallation.

4. Remove the belt tensioner.

5. Set the engine to TDC of cylinder No. 5 and insert the crankshaft locking tool at the rear of the engine block.

6. Remove the bolts that hold the front seal flange to the engine block.

7. Starting at the alignment pins, carefully pry off the sealing flange. Take care to prevent damaging the cylinder block. The sealing flange will be damaged while removing.

✳✳ CAUTION

To prevent injuries from shavings, wear protective goggles and protective clothing.

8. Remove sealant from cylinder block. Make sure that no sealant residue enters the engine.

9. Clean sealing surface of cylinder block and the crankshaft; they must be clean and dry.

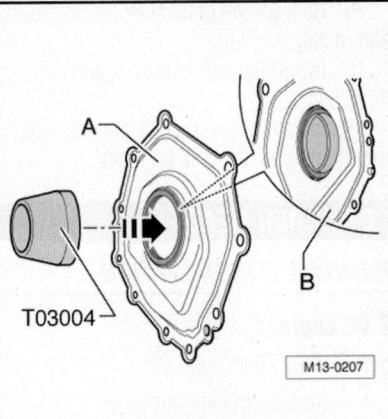

Fig. 77 Use the assembly sleeve to widen the seal enough to fit over the crankshaft–do not use any lubricants

To install:

➡**The following steps must be followed so that the sealing lip of sealing flange does not roll itself up when installing. Do not use any lubricants!**

10. Widen sealing lip of new sealing flange using the tapered end of assembly sleeve T03004.

11. After a short time, remove the assembly sleeve and insert the wide end into sealing ring. Assembly sleeve must protrude approximately 0.020 in. (3 mm) on the engine side of the seal.

12. Apply sealant bead into groove of sealing flange. Insert sealing flange sleeve T03004 over the crankshaft and press the flange plate uniformly into place.

13. Start all the bolts, then tighten uniformly in diagonal sequence. Torque to 7 ft. lbs. (10 Nm).

14. Install the crankshaft pulley and torque the bolt to 37 ft. lbs. (50 Nm), plus 90°.

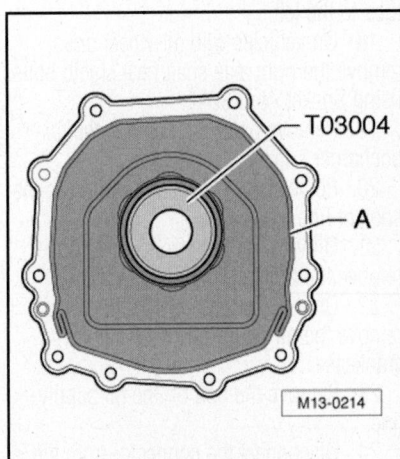

Fig. 78 Apply a bead of sealant and immediately install the sealing flange

15. Remove the crankshaft locking tool and install the plug.

16. Install the belt tensioner and A/C drive belt.

17. Install remaining components and run the engine to check for leaks.

CYLINDER HEAD

REMOVAL & INSTALLATION

2.0L Engines

See Figures 79 through 81.

1. Remove the engine cover.
2. Remove the air filter.
3. Loosen the hose clamp.
4. Remove bolt.
5. Disconnect the electrical connectors and free up the electrical wire.

> ✳✳ **CAUTION**
>
> **Reduce pressure by covering coolant reservoir cap with a cloth and carefully opening.**

6. Open coolant reservoir cap.
7. Remove front exhaust pipe with catalytic converter
8. Remove the right front wheel.
9. Remove the noise insulation.
10. Remove the front right wheel housing liner.
11. Remove the air guide pipe items.
12. Drain coolant.
13. Remove the bolt and remove the air guide pipe downward.
14. Remove bolts.
15. Remove the air guide pipe by lifting the clamps.
16. Disconnect electrical connectors and free up electrical wire.
17. On vehicles with auxiliary heater remove the bolts and swivel the coolant tubs to the left.
18. On vehicles with all-wheel drive, remove the right axle shaft heat shield bolts using Socket AF 8 3247.
19. Remove bolts and remove the turbocharger support.
20. Remove the banjo bolt and move the coolant line to the side.
21. On vehicles with front wheel drive, remove the bolts on the oil return line.
22. On vehicles with all-wheel drive, remove the oil return line bolts on the crankcase.
23. Remove the bolt on the oil supply line.
24. Disconnect the connector from the Camshaft Adjustment Valve.
25. Disconnect the electrical connectors

on the ignition coils and free up the wiring harness.

26. Remove the ignition coils with the puller T40039.
27. Remove the air guide pipe bolt.
28. Remove the air guide pipe; to do this, loosen the hose clamp.
29. Disconnect the hose for the crankcase ventilation.
30. Remove the bolts and remove the crankcase ventilation.
31. Disconnect the hose for the crankcase ventilation.
32. Remove the bolts.
33. Remove the air guide pipe bolt.
34. Loosen the hose clamp and remove the air guide pipe together with the crankcase ventilation.

> ✳✳ **CAUTION**
>
> **Fuel supply line is under pressure! Wear protective goggles and protective clothing to prevent injuries and contact with skin. Before removing from hose connection wrap a cloth around the connection. Then release pressure by carefully pulling hose off connection.**

35. Disconnect the wires from the fuel transfer.
36. Disconnect the coolant line to the coolant reservoir.
37. Remove the coolant hoses from the coolant pipe.
38. Disconnect the ground wire (GND) and remove the bolt.
39. Disconnect the vacuum hoses.
40. Loosen the bolts and remove the heat shield together with the coolant pipe.
41. Disconnect the oil supply line from the turbocharger.
42. Remove the bolt from the heat shield using a 6 mm hex multi-point socket. The hex socket must be at least 5 cm long. Socket that is 6 mm at the tip is too wide.
43. Disconnect the electrical connector from the Fuel Pressure Regulator Valve.
44. Loosen the coolant pipe; remove the bolts.
45. Disconnect the coolant hose from the side connection on the cylinder head.
46. Disconnect the electrical connectors.
47. Free up the electrical cable.
48. Disconnect the vacuum hose leading to the EVAP filter.
49. Disconnect the electrical connectors and pull the connectors out of the retainer.
50. Disconnect the electrical connectors.
51. Disconnect the coolant line from the intake manifold, when doing this, remove the bolts.

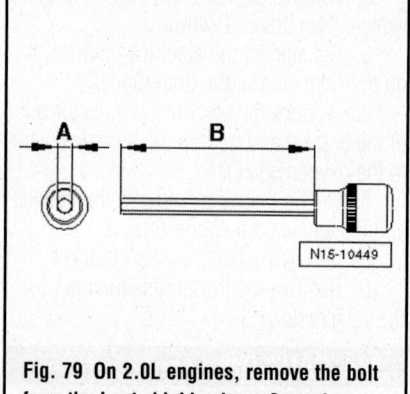

Fig. 79 On 2.0L engines, remove the bolt from the heat shield using a 6 mm hex multi-point socket. The hex socket must be at least 5 cm long. Socket that is 6 mm at the tip is too wide

52. Remove the intake manifold bracket by removing the mounting nut.
53. Remove the oil filter.
54. Disconnect the coolant hoses and move them to the side.
55. Remove the bolts and remove Camshaft Adjustment Valve
56. Remove timing chain upper cover.

➡ **The control valve has a left thread.**

57. Remove the control valve using Assembly Tool 10352 T10352.
58. Remove the bolts and remove the bearing bracket.
59. Rotate the vibration damper using the Counter Hold Tool T10355 into the "OT" position.
60. The notch on the vibration damper must line up with the marking on the timing chain lower cover.
61. Carefully mark the drive chain/chain sprockets with a waterproof marker. These marks are necessary for reinstallation.
62. Remove the plug.
63. Lift the chain tensioner locking wedge by inserting a scriber or a suitable screwdriver into the hole in the chain tensioner direction.
64. In order to tension the chain tensioner, turn the crankshaft opposite the direction of the engine rotation direction and secure it using Securing Pin T40011.
65. The intake camshaft switches in the engine direction of rotation.
66. Remove the bolt and guide the tensioning rail downward.
67. Remove the upper guide rail by unlocking the latch (located in the center) with a screwdriver and pushing the guide rail forward.
68. When the lower timing chain cover is

installed, the loose chain on the crankshaft cannot jump off.

69. Remove camshaft timing chain from chain sprockets.

※ CAUTION

Danger of damaging the valves, piston head and lower timing chain cover. If the camshaft timing chain was removed from the cylinder head, then the crankshaft may not be turn further. Panels are installed on the lower timing chain cover to prevent the chain from falling down. The panels can bend if the crankshaft is rotated when the chain is loose.

70. Turn the sealing plug counterclockwise 90° and remove it.

71. Remove the ball head.

72. Remove the oil filler cap.

73. Remove the bolts

74. Remove the cylinder head bolts in sequence 1 through 5 using Polydrive bit and drive socket T10070 until 2 are left.

75. To remove the cylinder head bolts, turn the camshaft with a wrench if necessary.

76. Make sure all wires and cables are disconnected.

77. Pay attention the tension and guide rails when lifting the cylinder head.

78. Install the Engine Support T10014 each of the two small and large washers.

79. Connect the Engine Sling 2024 in the Engine Support T10014 and in the front left lifting eye on the cylinder head.

80. Mount the Engine Sling 2024 into the workshop crane and gently lift the cylinder head.

81. Remove the last two cylinder head bolts.

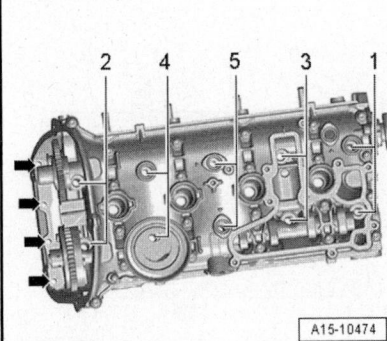

Fig. 80 Remove the cylinder head bolts in sequence 1 through 5 using Polydrive bit and drive socket T10070 until 2 are left

➡**Carefully lift the cylinder head until the guide rail for the camshaft timing chain is free. The tension- and guide rail must not be damaged.**

82. Lay the cylinder head on a soft surface, such as foam.

To install:

➡**The sealing surfaces could be damaged. Carefully remove sealant residue from cylinder head and cylinder block. Make sure that no long scrapes or scratches result.**

※ CAUTION

Risk of damaging cylinder block. There must be no oil or coolant in the blind holes for the cylinder head bolts in the cylinder block.

※ CAUTION

Risk of cylinder head seal leaking. Carefully remove all grinding and sanding residue. Only unpack new cylinder head gasket immediately prior to installation. To prevent cylinder head seal silicone layer and recessed area from being damaged, always handle seal extremely carefully.

※ CAUTION

Risk of damaging open valves. If a replacement cylinder is installed, only remove plastic base right before cylinder head is installed to protect open valves. Risk of damaging valves and piston heads after working on valvetrain. To ensure valves do not strike pistons when starting, carefully rotate engine at least 2 full revolutions.

83. Replace bolts which have been tightened to torque.

84. Replace sealing rings, seals and self-locking nuts.

85. Note different sealant for cylinder head sealing surfaces and bolts.

86. Secure all hose connections with hose clamps appropriate for the model.

87. When installing a replacement cylinder head, turn the camshaft to OT and mark the new chain sprockets exactly the same as on the old chain sprockets (note the factory color marking on the chain sprockets).

88. If an exchange cylinder head is installed, all contact surfaces between bearing elements, roller rocker levers and cam

running surfaces of camshafts must be oiled before installing cylinder head cover.

89. The engine oil and coolant must be changed if the cylinder head or cylinder head seal are replaced.

90. Hang the cylinder head on the workshop crane and position it above the cylinder block.

➡**Carefully lower the cylinder head. The tension- and guide rail must not be damaged. Pay attention to centering pins in cylinder block. Observe cylinder head seal location, identification: Replacement part number must be visible from intake side.**

➡**When turning the crankshaft, make sure the timing chain cannot damage any other components.**

91. In the event the crankshaft has been rotated in the meantime: Set piston of cylinder 1 to TDC and turn crankshaft back again slightly.

92. Set cylinder head in place.

93. Insert cylinder head bolts and tighten by hand.

94. In order to be able to turn the cylinder head bolts, the intake camshaft must be turned with a wrench.

95. There is no requirement to retighten the cylinder head bolts after repairs.

96. Tighten cylinder head bolts in sequence to the following specification:

- Tighten to 30 ft. lbs. (40 Nm) using a torque wrench
- Tighten further 90° using a rigid wrench
- Tighten further 90° using a rigid wrench
- Pre-tighten the bolts to 71 inch lbs. (8 Nm)
- Tighten the bolts 90° further using a rigid wrench

➡**When turning the crankshaft, make sure the timing chain cannot damage any other components.**

97. Rotate the vibration damper using the Counter Hold Tool T10355 into the "OT" position.

98. The notch on the vibration damper must line up with the marking on the timing chain lower cover.

99. The marked links of the timing chain must be positioned on the markings on the chain sprockets.

100. Mount the camshaft timing chain: The markings drive chain/chain sprockets must align.

101. Turn the intake camshaft using the wrench and mount the timing chain.

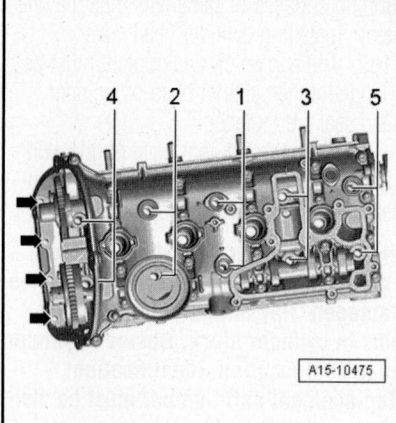

Fig. 81 Cylinder head bolt tightening sequence

102. The rest of the installation is performed in reverse order of removal.

103. During installation, cable ties must be re-installed at the same location.

104. Change the engine oil

105. Replace the coolant.

2.0L TDI Engine

See Figures 82 through 84.

Removal Notes:

• When using an exchanged cylinder head with camshaft installed, the contact surfaces between the lifters and cam lobes must be lubricated before installing the cylinder head cover.

• The plastic protectors installed to protect the open valves must only be removed immediately before fitting the cylinder head.

• When cylinder head is replaced, all coolant must also be replaced.

• Cylinder heads with cracks between the valve seats can continue to be used without reducing service life, as long as the tears have a maximum width of 0.0195 in. (0.5 mm).

• Do not mill the valve seats in the cylinder head; only grinding of the valves is permissible.

• After installing the camshafts, the engine may not be started for approximately 30 minutes. The hydraulic equalization elements must seat themselves (otherwise the valves will crash into the pistons).

• After working on the valvetrain and lifters, carefully rotate the crankshaft by hand at least 2 full revolutions before starting to be sure that valves do not strike the pistons.

• Always replace gaskets and seals.

• All cable ties which are opened or cut open when removing cylinder head, must be replaced in the same position when installing cylinder head.

❊❊ CAUTION

When doing any repair work, especially in the engine compartment, pay attention to the following due to clearance issues. Route lines of all types (e.g. for fuel, hydraulic, coolant and refrigerant, brake fluid, vacuum) and electrical wiring so that the original path is followed. Ensure sufficient clearance to all moving or hot components.

1. Before removing the cylinder head, extract the fuel with the hand vacuum pump and the draining container and Tandem Pump.

2. Turn the ignition and all electrical consumers off and remove the ignition key.

3. Remove engine cover as follows:

   a. On one piece engine cover. Pull the one piece front engine cover upward with a quick jerk and then pull the lower mount forward.

   b. On two piece engine cover, first pull the outer cover upward with a quick jerk, then pull the inner engine cover upward with a quick jerk.

4. Remove plenum chamber bulkhead.

5. Disconnect the connector on the Mass Air Flow (MAF) sensor.

6. Disconnect the ventilation hose and disengage it from the bracket.

7. Open the spring-type clip3 using spring-type clip pliers VAS 5024A and disconnect the intake hose from the Mass Air Flow (MAF) sensor.

8. Disconnect the intake manifold from the air guide.

9. Unfasten bolt and remove air filter housing and mass air flow sensor.

10. Remove noise insulation.

11. Drain the coolant.

12. For safety reasons, pull the connector off the fuel delivery unit.

13. Disconnect the fuel supply and return lines, as well as the coolant line on the cylinder head.

14. Before removing the cylinder head, extract the fuel with the diesel extractor VAS 5226 or the hand vacuum pump and the breather reservoir V.A.G 1390/1 to the tandem pump.

15. On fuel filter without the retaining plate, release the clips and remove the fuel filter with the hoses still connected from the retaining plate.

16. On fuel filter with the retaining plate

   a. Loosen the bolt one turn.

   b. Remove the bolt and the nut.

   c. Remove the fuel filter with the hoses still connected.

17. Remove the front exhaust pipe.

18. Remove the turbocharger support and the oil return from the turbocharger.

19. Remove the oil supply line and lay the oil supply line off to the side.

20. Remove toothed belt.

21. Remove the toothed belt tensioning roller.

22. Remove hub for camshaft sprocket.

23. Remove the bolts for the rear toothed belt guard.

24. Remove the Camshaft Position (CMP) sensor.

25. Remove the connecting pipe for exhaust gas recirculation.

26. Pull off/disconnect all remaining electrical wires required from cylinder head and set aside.

27. Disconnect all connections, coolant lines, vacuum hoses and intake hoses from the cylinder head.

28. Remove cylinder head cover.

29. Follow the sequence when loosening the cylinder head bolts.

30. Lift the cylinder head slightly and then remove it from the engine sideways, past the toothed belt guard.

31. The cylinder head must be carefully guided to prevent damages.

To install:

32. Always replace cylinder head bolts.

33. Carefully remove residual sealant from cylinder head and cylinder block. Make sure that no long scrapes or scratches result.

➡ **When using sand paper, grit must not be below 100.**

34. Carefully remove all grinding and sanding residue.

35. Only unpack new cylinder head gasket immediately prior to installation.

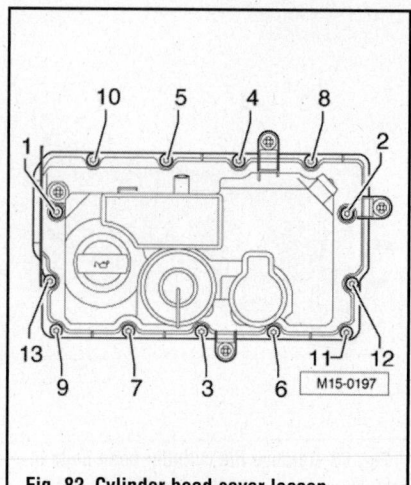

Fig. 82 Cylinder head cover loosening/tightening sequence

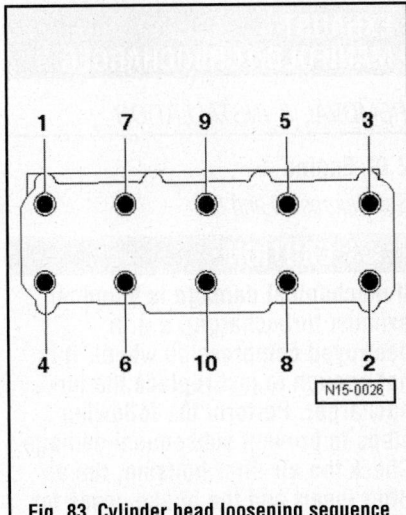

Fig. 83 Cylinder head loosening sequence

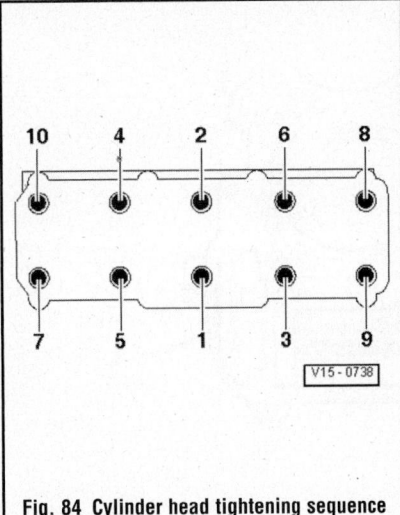

Fig. 84 Cylinder head tightening sequence

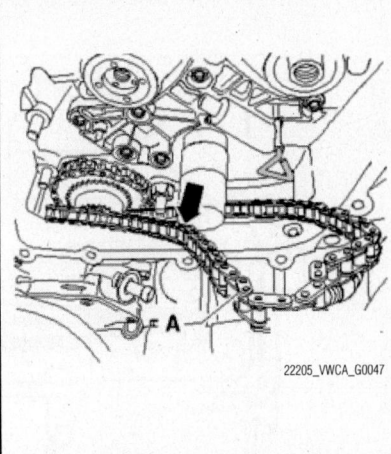

Fig. 85 Hold timing chain at "A" and lay it under the pipe connection

36. Handle gasket carefully. Damages to the silicone layer and in areas of recesses may result in leaks.

37. Before installing cylinder head, position crankshaft to TDC marking.

38. Turn the crankshaft in opposite direction of engine rotation until all pistons are positioned almost evenly below TDC.

39. Position cylinder head gasket.

➡**Observe cylinder head gasket identification.**

40. Set cylinder head in place and tighten all cylinder head bolts hand tight.

41. Fasten the cylinder head in four steps according to the indicated tightening sequence.
- Tighten to 26 ft. lbs. (35 Nm)
- Tighten to 44 ft. lbs. (60 Nm)
- Tighten 90° additional rotation
- Tighten 90° additional rotation

42. There is no requirement to retighten the cylinder head bolts after repairs.

Further installation is performed in reverse order. When doing this note the following:

43. After fastening the cylinder head turn the camshaft sprocket so that the lobes for cylinder 1 point upward equally. Before installing the toothed belt, turn the crankshaft in engine rotation direction to TDC Toothed Belt.

44. Install hub for camshaft sprocket.

45. Install toothed belt.

46. Install ribbed belt.

47. Install oil supply line.

48. Install noise insulation.

49. Install plenum chamber bulkhead.

50. Fill with coolant.

51. Perform a test drive and afterwards check the fault memory Engine Control Module DTC Memory, Checking and Erasing.

2.5L Engine

See Figures 85 through 87.

➡**Two people are needed to remove the cylinder head.**

1. If a coded radio is installed, obtain the anti-theft coding.

2. Remove the battery and battery holder.

3. Drain the cooling system.

4. Remove the engine cover/air filter housing.

5. Remove the intake manifold.

6. Install transport strap on cylinder head to better hold the head during removal.

7. Remove timing chain case cover.

8. Remove cylinder head cover.

9. Secure camshafts and remove chain sprockets for camshafts. See Camshaft Removal and Installation.

10. Disconnect the exhaust pipe and remove the bracket bolts. Move the pipe aside.

➡**Flex joint must not be bent more than 10° or it will be damaged.**

11. Disconnect the oxygen sensor wiring at the bulkhead.

12. Remove cable bracket at air injection valve.

13. Remove cylinder head bolts in reverse of tightening sequence.

➡**If bolt 12 could not be pulled out using a magnet, loosen bolts of camshaft locator T40070 one rotation, slide camshaft locator toward right front of vehicle and tighten bolts again.**

14. Carefully remove the cylinder head.

To install:

➡**Only remove the new cylinder head gasket from its packing immediately**

before installing. **Handle the new gasket with extreme care. Damage will lead to leaks. Install new cylinder head bolts.**

15. Clean all cylinder block sealing surfaces. There must be no oil or coolant in the blind holes for the cylinder head bolts in the cylinder block. Stuff clean rags into cylinders so no dirt or abrasive material can get between cylinder wall and piston. Do not allow dirt or abrasives to get into coolant either.

16. Carefully clean cylinder head and avoid introducing scratches or scoring (do not use sandpaper with grit below 100).

17. Carefully remove metal particles, emery remains and cloths.

18. Apply a bead of sealant on the block as illustrated.

19. Install new cylinder head gasket and apply sealant to the same places on the gasket.

20. Install cylinder head.

21. Guide timing chain over pipe connection.

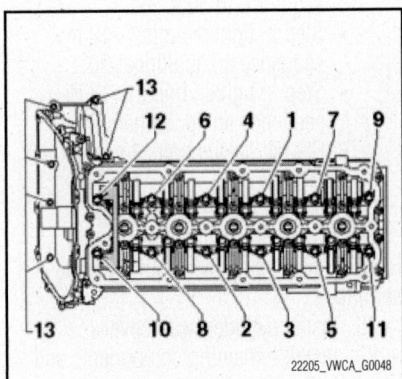

Fig. 86 Cylinder head bolt torque sequence

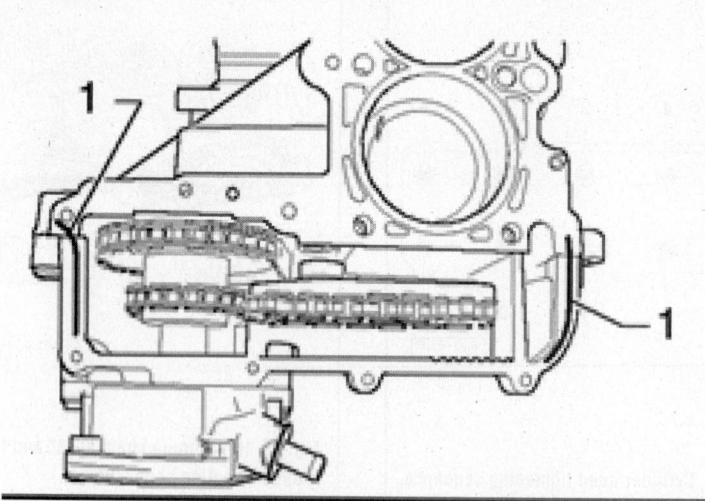

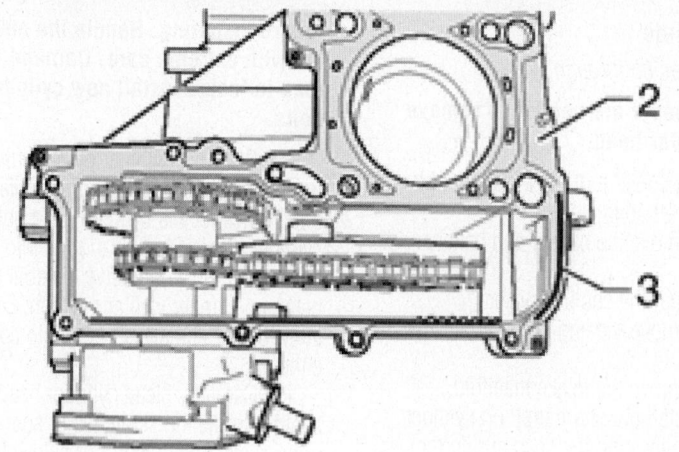

22205_VWCA_G0049

Fig. 87 Apply sealant to the block at location 1, then install the gasket (2) and apply sealant to location 3

22. Insert cylinder head bolts and tighten them hand-tight.

23. Torque cylinder head bolts in sequence as follows:
- Step 1: torque bolts 1–12 in sequence to 30 ft. lbs.
- Step 2: tighten bolts 1–12 in sequence an additional 90°
- Step 3: tighten bolts 1–12 in sequence an additional 90°
- Step 4: torque bolts 13 to 7 ft. lbs. (10 Nm).

24. Wipe off any excess sealant.

25. Install camshaft sprockets and rotate crankshaft to check timing mark alignment.

26. Install cylinder head cover.

27. Install remaining components and connect all wiring and hoses.

28. Refill with new coolant and engine oil.

29. Run the engine to check for leaks.

ENGINE OIL & FILTER

REMOVAL & INSTALLATION

2.5L Engine

➡**When installing the oil drain adapter (T40057), a valve in the oil filter housing is opened. If the oil drain adapter is removed, the valve is closed again.**

1. Remove the cap from the oil filter housing.

2. Hold the oil drain adapter hose in a drip tray and install the oil drain adapter all the way onto the oil filter housing.

3. Allow the engine oil to drain.

4. Remove the hose, close the valve and refill the engine with oil.

EXHAUST MANIFOLD/TURBOCHARGER

REMOVAL & INSTALLATION

2.0L Engine

See Figures 79 and 88.

✳✳ CAUTION

If mechanical damage is found on exhaust turbocharger, e.g. a destroyed compression wheel, it is not enough to just replace the turbocharger. Perform the following steps to prevent subsequent damage. Check the air filter housing, the air filter insert and the intake hoses for contamination. Check entire charge air circuit and cooler for contamination. If contaminants are found in charge air circuit, circuit must be cleaned and cooler replaced if necessary.

1. Remove the air filter.

2. Remove the battery and battery tray.

3. Remove noise insulation.

4. Remove the front part of the right wheel housing liner and/or the front right wheel housing liner.

5. Drain the coolant.

6. Remove catalytic converters with front exhaust pipe.

7. Remove bolts.

8. Remove the air guide pipe by lifting the clamps items.

9. On vehicles with all-wheel drive remove the heat shield above the right driveshaft.

10. Disconnect electrical connectors and free up electrical wire.

11. On vehicles with auxiliary heater remove the bolts and swivel the coolant tubs to the left.

12. On vehicles with front wheel drive remove the right driveshaft heat shield.

13. Remove the bolt with socket XZN 10 T10154.

14. Remove the bolt.

15. Remove the banjo bolt and move the coolant line to the side.

16. On vehicles with front wheel drive remove the bolts on the oil return line.

17. On vehicles with all-wheel drive remove the oil return line bolts on the crankcase.

18. Remove the bolt on the oil supply line.

19. Remove engine cover.

20. Disconnect the connectors from the

ignition coils and the wiring harness and lay them aside.

21. Disconnect the coolant line to the coolant reservoir.

22. Disconnect the vacuum line at the separating point and free up the wire.

23. Remove the coolant hoses from the coolant pipe.

24. Press the release buttons, remove the air guide hose and move them to the side.

25. Remove the air guide pipe bolt.

26. Remove the air guide pipe; to do this, loosen the hose clamp.

27. Remove the air guide pipe bolt.

28. Loose the hose clamp and lay the air guide pipe on the cylinder head.

29. Seal the turbocharger with the Engine bung set VAS 6122.

30. Remove the bolts and remove the heat shield together with the coolant pipe.

31. Remove the bolt from the heat shield with a 6 mm hex socket. The hex socket must be at least 5 cm long. A socket that is 6 mm at the tip is too wide.

32. Disconnect the oil supply line from the turbocharger.

33. Disconnect the coolant hose and move it to the side.

34. Remove the nuts.

35. Remove the turbocharger/exhaust manifold upward.

To install:

36. Installation is performed in the reverse order of removal, noting the following:

37. Always replace seals, gaskets and self-locking nuts.

38. Add oil to turbocharger through oil feed line connecting piece.

39. After installing turbocharger, let engine idle for approximately 1 minute to ensure adequate oil supply to the turbocharger.

40. Coolant return line must be installed together with turbocharger.

41. Hose connections and charge air system hoses must be free of oil and grease before installing. Sealing ring and sealing surfaces must only be lightly oiled with connector couplings.

42. Secure all hose connections, using hose clamps appropriate for the model type.

43. Tighten the exhaust manifold/turbocharger to the cylinder head bolts 1 through 5 in 4 stages as follows:
- Tighten the bolts to 44 inch lbs. (5 Nm)
- Tighten the bolts to 106 inch lbs. (12 Nm)

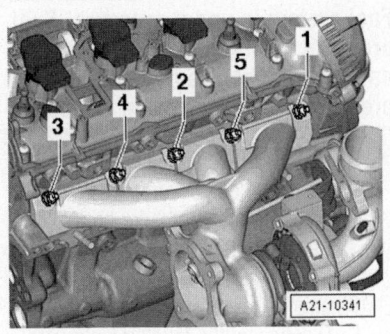

Fig. 88 Observe tightening sequence for exhaust manifold/turbocharger to the cylinder head

- Tighten the bolts to 12 ft. lbs. (16 Nm)
- Tighten the bolts to 19 ft. lbs. (25 Nm)

44. Tighten bolts/nuts to specification as follows:
- Oil supply line to exhaust turbocharger: 15 ft. lbs. (20 Nm), plus 45° additional rotation
- Oil return line to exhaust turbocharger: 80 inch lbs. (9 Nm)
- Coolant supply line to turbocharger: 15 ft. lbs. (20 Nm), plus 45° additional rotation
- Turbocharger bracket to cylinder block: 22 ft. lbs. (30 Nm)
- Turbocharger bracket to turbocharger: 22 ft. lbs. (30 Nm)
- Right charge air pipe to oil pan: 89 inch. lbs. (10 Nm)
- Heat shield to cylinder head (replace nuts and use hot bolt paste) M8 and M12: 15 ft. lbs. (20 Nm)

2.5L Engine

1. Remove the engine cover.
2. Remove the wiper arms.
3. Remove the outer plenum chamber cover and plenum chamber end plate.
4. Remove the heat shield.
5. Remove the protective cap for the right inner Constant Velocity (CV) joint from the engine.
6. Remove bolt and nut and remove the brace for the exhaust manifold.
7. Loosen the nuts for the double clamp.
8. Remove the nuts and bolts.
9. Remove the front exhaust pipe from the exhaust manifold and tie up firmly to the side.

✹✹ CAUTION

The flex joint in the front exhaust pipe must not be bent more than 10°; otherwise it may be damaged.

10. Disconnect the electrical connector for the oxygen sensor.

11. Remove the heat shield at the top of the front exhaust pipe and free up the wiring harness of the oxygen sensor in the exhaust manifold.

12. Remove the exhaust manifold bolts and remove it downward.

To install:

13. Installation is performed in reverse order.

14. Gaskets and self-locking nuts must be replaced.

15. Install the exhaust manifold.

16. Install the front exhaust pipe with catalytic converter,

17. Check the Diagnostic Trouble code (DTC) memory of the engine control module, repair any stored malfunctions and then erase the DTC memory.

18. Tighten bolts/nuts to specification as follows:
- Exhaust manifold nut: 19 ft. lbs. (25 Nm)
- Heat shield bolt: 89 inch lbs. (10 Nm)
- Exhaust nut/bolt: 19 ft. lbs. (25 Nm)

2.0L TDI Engine

✹✹ CAUTION

If mechanical damage was found on the turbocharger, for example a destroyed compression wheel, just replacing the turbocharger is not enough. Perform the following steps to prevent subsequent damage. Check the air filter housing, the air filter insert and the intake hoses for contamination.

1. Remove particulate filter with NOx reduction catalytic converter.

2. Mark installation position of the exhaust gas temperature sensor 1 and remove it.

3. Remove control wire between the exhaust gas recirculation housing and the exhaust pressure sensor 2.

4. Remove housing with the exhaust gas recirculation cooler.

5. Disconnect connector from the charge pressure actuator position sensor at the turbocharger vacuum diaphragm.

6. Disconnect vacuum hose at the turbocharger vacuum diaphragm.

7. Disconnect "black" connector for the exhaust gas temperature sensor 1 at the engine bulkhead.

8. Guide line out of the retainers on the engine bulkhead and the turbocharger.

9. Remove connecting pipe.

10. Remove oil supply line.

11. Remove banjo bolt from the turbocharger support.

12. Remove hex stud bolt from the turbocharger support.

13. Rotate the lower section of the support 90° and remove the support downward from the upper section.

14. Remove heat shield on the exhaust manifold.

15. Remove exhaust manifold nuts.

16. Remove turbocharger with the exhaust manifold from the cylinder head and rotate it so the intake side faces down. Remove the turbocharger with the exhaust manifold downward.

To install:

➡**Before installing, check if the oil return pipe decoupling element is bent and therefore stretched. If that is the case, tiny cracks can form that can lead to leaks. Replace the oil return pipe before installing the turbocharger if necessary.**

17. Install in reverse order of removal.

18. Always replace self-locking nuts, seals, gaskets and clamps.

19. Insert turbocharger with the pressure side upward.

20. Position charge air pipe connecting hose before securing the turbocharger.

➡**Note the exhaust gas temperature sensor 1 installation position.**

21. Replace the banjo bolt with the turbocharger support gaskets and oil return pipe O-rings.

22. Do not stretch the oil return pipe decoupling element when installing the turbocharger support.

23. Tighten bolts/nuts to specification as follows:

- Turbocharger with exhaust manifold (Replace): 17 ft. lbs. (23 Nm)
- Oil return line: 11 ft. lbs. (15 Nm)

INTAKE MANIFOLD

REMOVAL & INSTALLATION

2.0L Engines

See Figure 89.

Fuel system is under pressure! Fuel pressure must be reduced to a residual pressure before opening high pressure area of injection system.

1. Remove the engine cover.

2. Clean the contact surface from the intake manifold to the cylinder head.

3. Remove the air filter.

4. Separate the vacuum line to the EVAP canister.

5. Disconnect the following electrical connections:

- Intake Air Temperature Sensor
- throttle valve control module
- Evaporative Emission (EVAP) Canister Purge Regulator Valve
- Camshaft Position sensor

6. Disconnect the vacuum line at the separating point and remove the crankcase ventilation hose.

7. Remove the bolts for the fuel supply line and lay the line to the side.

8. The fuel system must have no pressure.

9. Open the fuel line union nut lower.

10. Disconnect the vacuum line from the Intake Manifold Runner Control (IMRC) Valve.

11. Remove the bolts for the coolant line from the intake manifold.

12. Disconnect the electrical connector from the Fuel Pressure Sensor.

13. Loosen the hose clamp.

14. Remove bolt.

15. Disconnect electrical connector.

16. Remove the noise insulation.

17. Remove the air guide pipe items.

18. Remove the bolt and remove the air guide pipe downward.

19. Disconnect the electrical connectors and remove the bracket from the intake manifold.

20. Remove the intake manifold bracket by removing the mounting nut.

21. Remove the oil filter.

22. Loosen the wiring bracket.

23. Loosen the wire from the intake manifold.

24. Remove the nuts and loosen the bolts from the intake manifold using the multi-point socket T10347.

25. Carefully pull the intake manifold and fuel rail away from the cylinder head just a little.

26. Disconnect the electrical connector from the Intake Manifold Runner Position Sensor and remove the intake manifold.

27. Cover the intake channels with a clean rag.

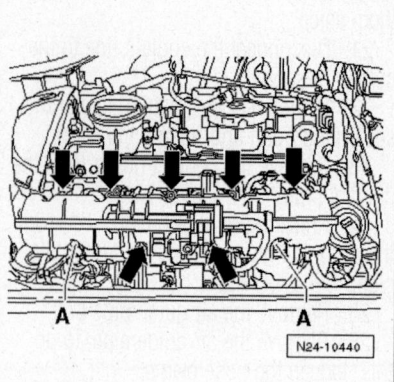

Fig. 89 Remove the nuts (A) and loosen the bolts from the intake manifold using the Multi-point socket

28. The fuel injectors could remain stuck in the fuel rail.

29. Disconnect the fuel rail from the intake manifold.

30. To access the fuel injectors, the intake manifold and the fuel rail with intake manifold runner control valve must be removed. The fuel injectors sit in the cylinder head.

To install:

31. The combustion chamber seal (Teflon) and the O-ring must always be replaced.

32. Mount the intake manifold onto the cylinder head on the stud bolts (lower left and right).

33. Make sure the fuel injectors are installed correctly and pay attention to the wiring bracket when mounting the intake manifold (located under the intake manifold).

34. When installing the intake manifold, the manifold must be pulled out slightly and the fuel injectors will stick in the fuel rail. Pull the fuel injectors out of the fuel rail and insert them in the cylinder head again.

35. The rest of the installation follows the reverse of the removal procedures.

36. When attaching the wiring bracket onto the intake manifold, make sure it clips into both latches.

Tightening specifications:

- High pressure pump bolts (replace): 89 inch lbs. (10 Nm)
- Fuel high pressure line connection (replace): 16 ft. lbs. (22 Nm)
- Fuel line to the fuel rail: 13 ft. lbs. (18 Nm)
- Bolt for the intake manifold support: 17 ft. lbs. (23 Nm)
- Nut for the intake manifold support: 89 inch lbs. (10 Nm)

2.0L TDI Engine

1. Remove engine cover.

  a. On one piece engine cover. Pull the one piece front engine cover upward with a quick jerk and then pull the lower mount forward.

  b. On two piece engine cover, first pull the outer cover upward with a quick jerk upward, then pull the inner engine cover upward with a quick jerk downward.

➡**The hoses remain connected.**

2. Remove air duct. To do this slightly lift the clips and remove the bolt from the transport strap.

3. Disconnect connector at intake flap motor.

4. Remove bolts and remove intake flap motor.

5. Remove intake connection with EGR potentiometer and EGR vacuum regulator solenoid valve.

6. Remove the turbocharger.

7. Remove intake manifold.

To install:

8. Installation is performed in reverse order.

9. Always replace gaskets and seals.

10. Observe installed position of intake manifold gasket.

11. Secure all hose connections with hose clamps.

12. Fill with coolant.

13. Tighten bolts/nuts to specification as follows:

- Intake manifold to cylinder head: 16 ft. lbs. (22 Nm)
- Engine lifting eyelet to cylinder head: 15 ft. lbs. (20 Nm)
- Bracket to intake manifold: 89 inch lbs. (10 Nm)
- Connecting pipe to intake manifold connection bolt: 16 ft. lbs. (22 Nm)
- EGR cooler to intake manifold: 89 inch lbs. (10 Nm)
- Intake Flap Motor V157 to intake manifold: 89 inch lbs. (10 Nm)

2.5L Engine

See Figure 90.

1. First, check whether a coded radio is installed. If necessary, obtain the anti-theft coding.

2. Disconnect the negative battery cable.

3. Remove engine cover/air filter assembly.

※ CAUTION

Fuel supply line is under pressure! Wear protective goggles and protective clothing to prevent injuries and contact with skin. Before loosening the fuel lines, place a rag around the connection point. Then release pressure by carefully pulling hose off connection.

4. Disconnect the three under-hood fuel lines. To release wires, press the circlip in. On the fuel supply line, the retainer must be pressed upward in the housing.

5. Disconnect connectors. Remove wiring harness from transport strap. Pull clamps and retaining ring out of locking mechanism. Remove bolts and remove transport strap.

6. Remove throttle valve control module (throttle body). The coolant hoses remain attached.

7. Disconnect manifold wiring and hose for crankcase ventilation.

8. Remove wiring harness by carefully pressing off clips.

9. Pull oil dipstick out and press dipstick tube retaining ring downward.

10. Raise and safely support the vehicle and remove the engine undercover.

11. Loosen bolts or nuts on the bottom side of the intake manifold.

12. Loosen bolt for intake manifold support and dipstick tube. Lay tube aside.

13. Open clip on leak detection pump (LDP) vacuum hose.

14. Loosen intake manifold bolts using tool T10107A. Bolts remain in intake manifold.

15. Remove intake manifold upward at an angle. Make sure that no bolts fall out.

16. Seal intake ports in cylinder head using a clean rag.

17. If manifold must be replaced:

- Remove fuel rail with injectors.
- Disconnect vacuum hose for Leak Detection Pump (LDP).
- Remove Manifold Absolute Pressure (MAP) sensor.

To install:

18. Make sure all sealing surfaces are clean and dry. Fit new sealing rings to the intake manifold runners.

19. If the injectors were removed, fit new O-rings, lubricate them with engine oil and install the injectors.

20. Replace oil dipstick tube seal.

21. Fit the manifold into place and torque the screws to 6 ft. lbs. (9 Nm) working from the middle and working towards the ends in a diagonal sequence.

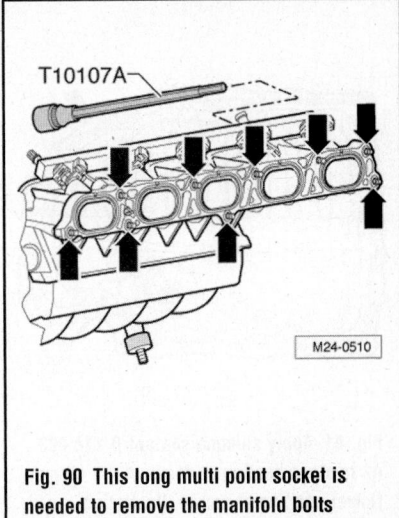

Fig. 90 This long multi point socket is needed to remove the manifold bolts

22. Install mounting supports and torque bolts to 18 ft. lbs. (25 Nm).

23. Install the dipstick tube and insert the dipstick.

24. Install the throttle body.

25. Connect all wires, hoses and tubes using new seals or gaskets as needed.

26. Connect the battery

27. Bleed fuel supply system

28. Run the engine to check for leaks.

OIL PAN

REMOVAL & INSTALLATION

2.0L Engines

Lower Pan

See Figures 91 and 92.

1. Remove noise insulation.

2. If present, disconnect the electrical connector for the Oil Level Thermal Sensor.

3. Drain engine oil.

4. Remove the screws.

5. Remove oil pan, if necessary loosen by applying light strikes with a rubber hammer.

To install:

6. Remove sealant residue from upper part of the oil pan with a flat scraper.

7. Remove sealant residue on the lower part of the oil pan, e.g. with a rotating plastic brush.

8. Clean sealing surfaces, must be free of oil and grease.

9. Cut tube nozzle at front nozzle approximately 0.117 in. (3 mm).

10. Apply silicone sealant D 174 003 A2 to clean sealing surfaces of the oil pan (lower part).

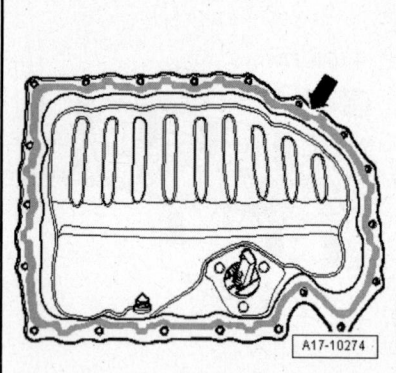

Fig. 91 Apply silicone sealant D 174 003 A2 to clean sealing surfaces of the oil pan (lower part) as shown in illustration

✳✳ CAUTION

The oil pan must be installed within 5 minutes after application of silicone sealant.

➡ **The sealant bead may not be thicker than 0.078–0.117 in. (2–3 mm), otherwise excess sealant could enter the oil pan and clog the oil intake tube.**

11. Immediately mount the lower part of the oil pan and tighten the screws 1 through 20 in two steps.

12. Tighten bolts/nuts to specification as follows:

- Tighten the bolts to 71 inch lbs. (8 Nm)
- Tighten the bolts an additional 90°

13. After installing oil pan, allow sealant to dry for approximately 30 minutes. Only after then may the engine oil be replenished.

14. Fill the engine oil, oil capacities.

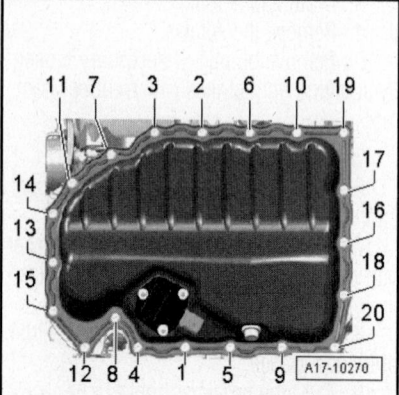

Fig. 92 Immediately mount the lower part of the oil pan and tighten the screws 1 through 20 in two steps as shown

15. The rest of the assembly is basically a reverse of the disassembling sequence.

Upper Pan

See Figures 93 through 95.

1. Remove the transmission.
2. Remove the oil pump.
3. Remove the transmission-side sealing flange.
4. Remove the front right wheel housing liner.
5. Remove bolts.
6. Remove the air guide pipe by lifting the clamps.
7. Remove the bolts 14 and 15.
8. Disconnect the wiring bracket mount next to the after-run coolant pump from the upper part of the oil pan.

✳✳ CAUTION

To prevent leaks in the future, do not bend the lower timing chain cover and do not reach between the mounting points.

✳✳ CAUTION

When removing the oil pan upper section, the chain tensioner spring for the oil pump motor will jump from the oil pan upper section to the lower timing chain cover. When removing the oil pan upper section, do not reach between the section and the lower timing chain cover.

9. Remove the bolts 1 through 14 and the upper section of the oil pan. When loosening, start on the transmission side.

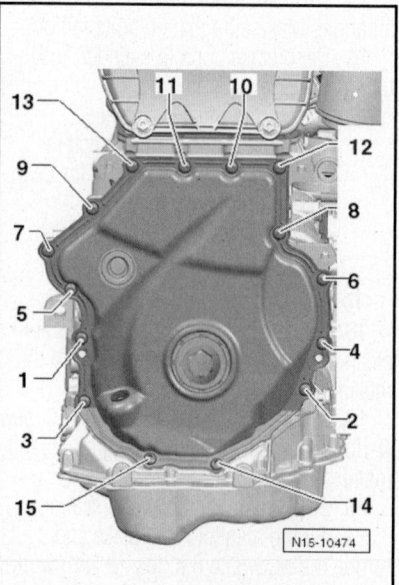

Fig. 93 Remove the bolts 14 and 15

To install:

10. Mount the Assembly Tool T10118 and pull the spring in the chain tensioner for the oil pump drive in the direction of the.

11. Secure the spring by inserting the gauge VW 136 into the 2.2 mm hole.

12. Remove sealant residue from engine block with a flat scraper.

13. Remove the remaining sealant on the upper part of the oil an on the lower timing chain cover with a rotating plastic brush.

14. See if the timing chain cover is deformed. Then mount the top section of the oil pan without any sealant and check the gap between the cover and the top section. If a deformation is found, do not try to re-align it, replace the cover.

15. Clean sealing surfaces, must be free of oil and grease.

16. Make sure the oil passages in the upper part of the oil pan and in the cylinder crankcase clean.

17. Cut tube nozzle at front to 0.117 in. (3 mm).

18. Apply the silicone sealant D 174 003 A2 in a bead of 0.078–0.117 in. (2–3 mm) on the clean sealing surface of the upper oil pan section.

✳✳ CAUTION

The oil pan (upper part) must be installed within 5 minutes after application of silicone sealant.

➡ **The sealant bead may not be thicker than specified, otherwise excess sealant could enter the oil pan and clog the oil intake tube.**

19. On the transmission side, the upper part of the oil pan and the crankcase must align.

20. Immediately mount the upper part of

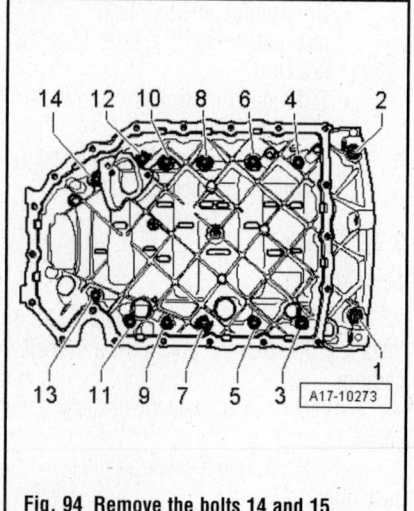

Fig. 94 Remove the bolts 14 and 15

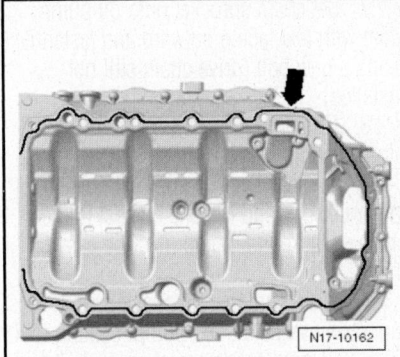

Fig. 95 Apply the silicone sealant D 174 003 A2 in a bead of 0.078–0.117 in. (2–3 mm) on the clean sealing surface of the upper oil pan section as shown

the oil pan and tighten the screws 1 through 14 in two steps as follows:

21. Tighten bolts/nuts to specification as follows:

- Tighten the bolts to 11 ft. lbs. (15 Nm)
- Tighten the bolts an additional 90°
- Install the bolts 14 and 15

22. The rest of the assembly is basically a reverse of the disassembling sequence.

2.0L TDI Engine

See Figure 96.

> ☀ **CAUTION**
>
> **If large quantities of metal particles or abraded material are detected during engine repairs, it may be an indication for a damaged crankshaft or rod bearings. To prevent further damage, perform the following steps after the repair: Carefully clean oil passages, replace oil cooler, replace oil filter insert.**

1. Remove engine cover.
2. On one piece engine cover, pull the one piece front engine cover upward with a quick jerk and then pull the lower mount forward.
3. On two piece engine cover, first pull the outer cover upward with a quick jerk, then pull the inner engine cover upward with a quick jerk.
4. Remove the air filter/turbocharger intake hose.
5. Carefully cut the cable tie.
6. Open the wiring bracket and disengage the wiring harness.
7. Disconnect the connector on the Mass Air Flow (MAF) sensor.
8. Disconnect the ventilation hose and disengage it from the bracket.

9. Open the spring-type clip using spring-type clip pliers VAS 5024A and disconnect the intake hose from the Mass Air Flow (MAF) sensor.
10. Disconnect the intake manifold from the air guide.
11. Unfasten bolt and remove air filter housing and mass air flow sensor.
12. Remove both bolts from the upper charge air pipe.
13. Remove noise insulation.
14. Remove the charge air pipe bolt from the oil pan. ·
15. Disconnect the connector, if equipped, from the oil level thermal sensor.
16. Drain engine oil.
17. Remove the oil pan/transmission connecting bolts.
18. Loosen oil pan screws with 10 mm hex ball socket 3185. (Remove using 5 mm socket 3249 or T10058).
19. Remove the oil pan. Loosen oil pan with light blows of a rubber headed hammer if necessary.
20. Remove sealant residue from cylinder block with a flat scraper.
21. Remove remaining sealant at oil pan using a rotating brush, e.g. a drill with plastic brush attachment (wear protective glasses).
22. Clean sealing surfaces. They must be free of oil and grease.

To install:

> ☀ **CAUTION**
>
> **The oil pan must be installed within 5 minutes after application of silicone sealant.**

23. Cut off the nozzle on the tube of sealant at the front mark approximately 0.117 in. (3 mm).
24. Apply silicone sealant to clean sealing surfaces of oil pan. Sealing compound beads must be 0.078–0.117 in. (2–3 mm thick and run on inside of bolt holes.

➡**Sealant bead must not be thicker than specified. Otherwise, excess sealant could get into oil pan and clog strainer in intake line of oil pump.**

25. With transmission removed, oil pan must seal flush with cylinder block.
26. With transmission installed, oil pan must make contact on transmission.
27. Apply silicone sealing compound bead as illustrated to clean sealing surface of oil pan.
28. Install oil pan immediately and tighten all oil pan bolts lightly. Make sure that the oil pan is seated flush against the intermediate plate/transmission flange.

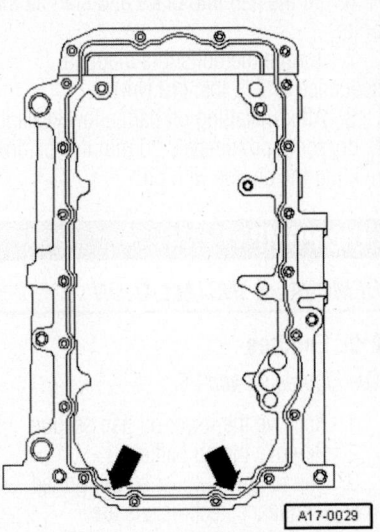

Fig. 96 Apply silicone sealant to clean sealing surfaces of oil pan. Sealing compound beads must be 0.078–0.117 in. (2–3 mm thick and run on inside of bolt holes

29. When installing the oil pan to a removed engine, make sure that the oil pan is positioned flush with the cylinder block on the flywheel side.
30. Tighten the oil pan bolts in a diagonal sequence to 11 ft. lbs. (15 Nm).
31. Tighten the oil pan/transmission bolts to 33 ft. lbs. (45 Nm).
32. After installing oil pan, allow sealant to dry for approximately 30 minutes. Only after then may the engine oil be replenished.
33. The rest of the assembly is basically a reverse of the disassembling sequence.
34. Install noise insulation.

2.5L Engine

Lower Oil Pan

1. Raise and safely support the vehicle and remove the engine undercover.
2. Drain the oil.
3. Remove the bolts to remove the lower oil pan. There are several recesses around the edge to pry without damaging the sealing surfaces.

To install:

4. Make sure all sealing surfaces are clean and dry.
5. Apply a bead of silicone sealant to the lower oil pan. The bead should run inside the bolt holes.

➡**Sealant bead must not be more than 0.080 in. (2 mm) thick to prevent excess sealant from getting into the oil pan and clogging the oil pump intake screen.**

6. Fit the pan into place and start all the bolts.

7. Torque the bolts in a diagonal sequence to 7 ft. lbs. (10 Nm).

8. After installing oil pan, allow sealant to dry for approximately 30 minutes before refilling the engine with oil.

OIL PUMP

REMOVAL & INSTALLATION

2.0L Engines

See Figures 97 and 98.

1. Remove the lower oil pan section.
2. Remove the oil baffle.
3. The following must be performed in one sequence; technicians are necessary.
4. Remove the oil pump bolts.
5. Pull back the chain tensioner using the assembly tool T10118 and have a second technician remove the oil pump.

To install:

6. Installation is performed in reverse order of removal.

7. Before installing the oil pump, make sure the screen in the supply line and the oil passages in the upper part of the oil pan are clean.

8. Make sure both alignment bushings for centering the oil pump are in there.

9. Replace the baffle plate.

✴✴ CAUTION

There are plastic ribs on the oil baffle that deform permanently when tightening. The plastic ribs ensure the oil baffle is not loosen and does not rattle. Because of this, always replace the oil baffle.

2.0L TDI Engine

1. Remove the oil pan and the splash wall.
2. Remove bolt.
3. Pull off chain sprocket from oil pump shaft.
4. Unscrew bolts and remove oil pump.

To install:

5. Installation is performed in reverse order.

6. Insert the alignment sleeves at the top of the oil pump.

➡**Pump shaft/chain sprocket can only be installed in one position.**

7. Install oil pan.
8. Tighten bolts/nuts to specification as follows:

- Chain sprocket to oil pump shaft: 15 ft. lbs. (20 Nm), plus 90° rotation
- Oil pump to cylinder block: 15 ft. lbs. (20 Nm), plus 90° rotation

2.5L Engine

See Figure 99.

The flywheel must be removed to remove the upper oil pan.

1. Remove upper oil pan.
2. Tension chain tensioner, secure it with locking pin T10115 and remove it.
3. Remove bolts and hold chain sprocket tightly with counterhold tool T10172.
4. Remove chain sprocket from oil pump and remove oil pump.

To install:

5. Secure crankshaft.
6. Replace O-ring and hand tighten bolts for oil pump to cylinder block.

7. Set chain sprocket onto oil pump shaft with text facing outward and fasten it using a new bolt (drive chain still not installed).

8. Tighten bolts to 14 ft. lbs. (20 Nm), plus an additional 90°.

9. Loosen the oil pump bolt closest to the crankshaft and the one closest to the chain sprocket; oil pump must be easy to move.

10. Make sure that no shavings are found on magnets of oil pump locating tool T03005. Contact surfaces of crankshaft and chain sprocket must be clean.

11. Place oil pump locating tool T03005 onto end of crankshaft and fasten it with two of the vibration damper/belt pulley bolts.

12. Tighten to 21 ft. lbs. (30 Nm). Oil pump is pulled into place by magnets.

13. Remove the chain tensioner locking pin T40069.

14. Push crankshaft, as for checking axial bearing play, toward pulley drive.

➡**This work step is important to guarantee the correct positioning of the chain sprockets to one another.**

15. In this position, first tighten the bolt closest to the crankshaft, the one closest to the chain sprocket, and then the remaining bolt to 17 ft. lbs. (25 Nm).

16. Install locking pin T40069 again. Crankshaft may only be moved minimally around TDC point. Otherwise, there is a risk that valves will contact piston.

17. Remove oil pump locating tool T03005.

18. If a new oil pump is installed, fill oil pump with some clean engine oil via suction pipe and turn pump shaft a several times.

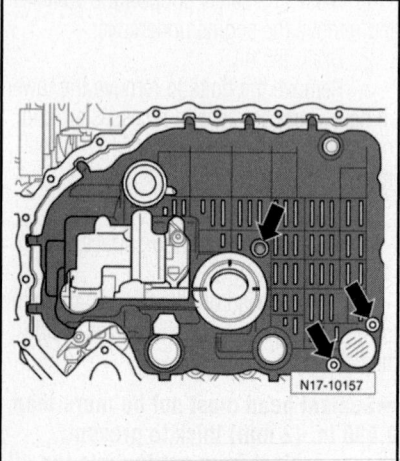

Fig. 97 Remove the oil baffle (arrows)

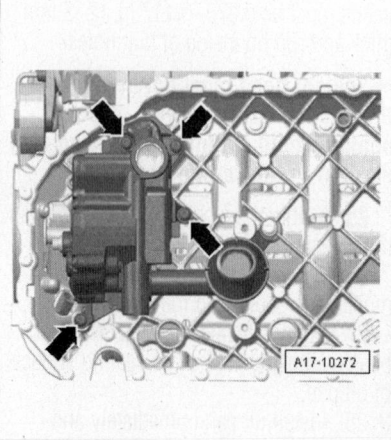

Fig. 98 Remove the oil pump bolts

Fig. 99 This tool aligns the chain sprockets using magnets to position the oil pump—2.5L engine

19. Place drive chain onto chain sprocket of oil pump.

20. Install oil pan.

21. Install guide rail, release tension on chain tensioner and pull out locking pin T10115.

➡**Make sure that the drive chain is correctly positioned in the guide rail and in the tensioning rail.**

22. Adjust valve timing.

23. Further assembly is performed in reverse order of removal. Note the following:

a. Remove locking pin T40069 from rear of cylinder block and screw in locking bolt. Tighten to 21 ft. lbs. (30 Nm).

b. Refill the engine cooling system.

PISTON AND RING

POSITIONING

See Figure 100.

TIMING CHAIN, SPROCKETS, FRONT COVER AND SEAL

REMOVAL & INSTALLATION

2.0L Engines

See Figures 101 through 107.

1. Remove timing chain upper cover.

a. Remove the Camshaft Adjustment Valve.

b. Remove five bolts and remove the upper timing chain cover.

➡**The control valve has a left thread.**

2. Remove the control valve using assembly tool.

3. Remove the bolts and remove the bearing bracket.

4. Rotate the vibration damper using the counter-hold the assembly tool T10355 into the "OT" position.

5. The notch on the vibration damper must line up with the marking on the timing chain lower cover.

6. The markings on the camshafts must point upward.

7. Remove the lower timing chain cover.

8. Remove the noise insulation.

9. Remove the front part of the right wheel housing liner.

10. Drain engine oil.

11. On vehicles with auxiliary heater, loosen the clamp, remove the bolt and remove the auxiliary heater muffler.

12. Remove bolts.

13. Remove the air guide pipe by lifting the clamps.

14. Remove the right air guide hose.

15. To release the tension on the ribbed belt, turn the tensioner in direction of rotation from underneath.

16. Secure tensioner with Drift T10060 A.

17. Remove ribbed belt from vibration damper ribbed belt pulley.

18. Rotate the vibration damper using the counter-hold tool into the "OT" position.

19. The notch on the vibration damper must line up with the marking on the timing chain lower cover.

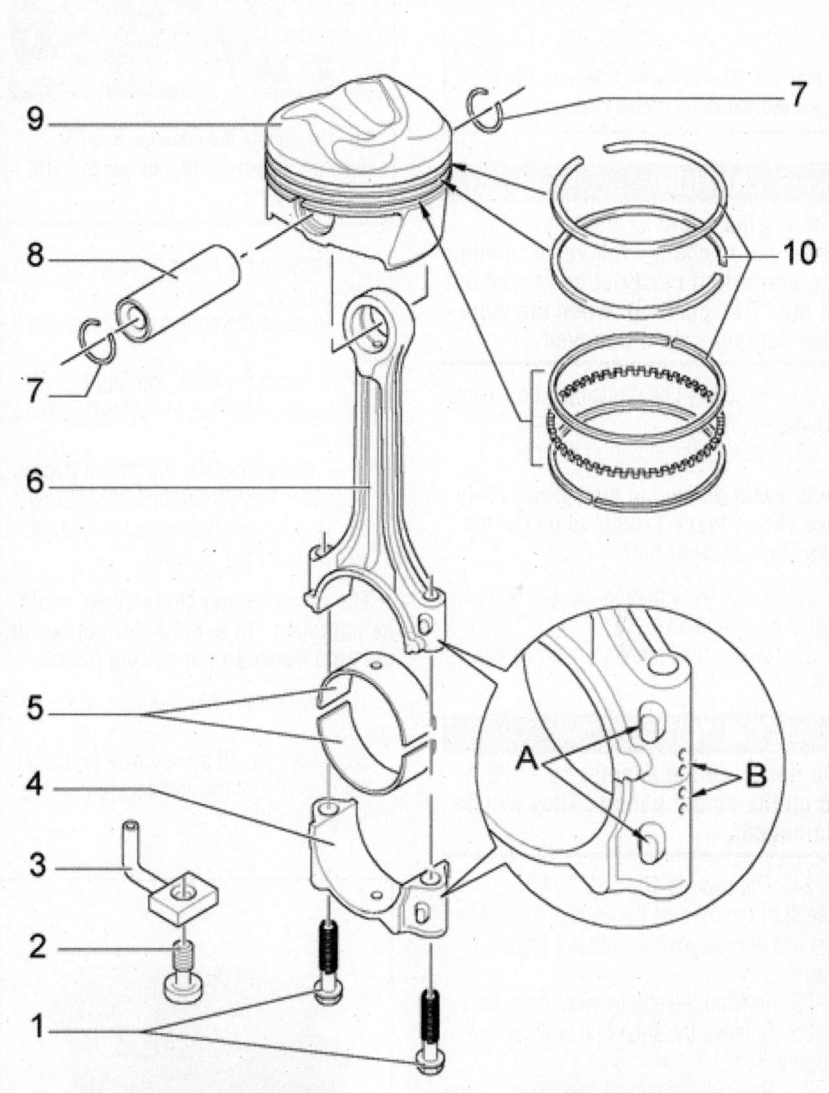

1. Connecting rod bolt
2. Bolt with pressure relief valve
3. Oil spray jet
4. Connecting rod bearing cap
5. Bearing shell
6. Connecting rod
7. Circlip
8. Piston pin
9. Piston
10. Piston rings

22205_VWCA_G0070

Fig. 100 Off set ring gaps by 120°—2.0L and 2.5L engine

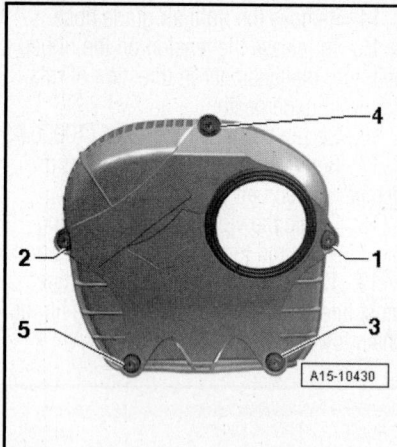

Fig. 101 Remove bolts 1 through 5 and remove the upper timing chain cover

> ⁂ **CAUTION**
>
> **The engine could be destroyed. In order not to change the valve timing, the crankshaft must not be moved out of the "OT" position. when the vibration damper bolt is removed.**

20. Remove vibration damper bolt using counter-hold tool.
21. Remove the vibration damper.

➡️**To avoid damaging the splines, only use Thrust Piece T10368 to install the vibration damper bolt.**

22. Install the vibration damper bolt and thrust piece again.
23. Mount the Engine Support Bridge 10 - 222 A.

> ⁂ **CAUTION**
>
> **Do not place the adapter 10 - 222 A /8 on the fender panels. They will be damaged.**

24. The shackle 10 - 222 A /12 is needed to make sure the engine is lifted in the installation position and not tipped away.
25. Tension the engine with the spindle.
26. Remove the subframe bolts on the engine.
27. Remove the engine bracket subframe mount.
28. Lift the engine approximately 1.95 in. (50 mm) and loosen the upper bolt for the engine support.
29. Now lower the engine approximately 3.9 in. (100 mm).
30. Free up electrical wiring harness.
31. Remove the bolt and remove the ribbed belt tensioner from the accessory assembly bracket.

Fig. 102 Rotate the vibration damper using the Counter Hold Tool into the "OT" position.

32. Remove the lower bolts for the engine support.
33. Remove the engine support and the bolts.
34. Remove the bolts and pull the oil dipstick guide tube out of the lower timing chain cover.
    a. Disconnect the Wastegate Bypass Regulator Valve from the turbocharger.
35. Remove the turbocharger support.
36. Remove the 15 bolts.

➡️**The lower timing chain cover could be damaged. To avoid deformation, do not hold between the bolting points.**

37. Pry off the lower timing chain cover.
38. Press the oil pump chain tensioner in the direction of the and secure it with a locking pin T40011.

Fig. 103 Pry off the lower timing chain cover starting with bolts 1 & 2 as shown

39. Remove the oil pump chain tensioner.
40. Using a screwdriver, lift the chain tensioner locking wedge in the direction of, press the timing chain tensioning rail in the direction of and secure it with locking pin.
41. Remove the timing chain tensioning rail.
42. The intake camshaft switches in the engine direction of rotation
43. Remove the timing chain.

To install:

➡️**The following must be performed in one sequence; technicians are necessary.**

44. The painted links of the timing chain must be positioned on the markings on the chain sprockets.
45. Hold the wrench until the tensioning rail is installed.
46. Mount the timing chain on the exhaust camshaft and crankshaft.
47. Turn the intake camshaft using the wrench and mount the timing chain.
48. Install the timing chain tensioning rail and tighten the bolt.
49. Mount the bearing bracket and hand tighten the bolts.
50. Remove the locking pin.
51. Tighten the bearing bracket bolts
52. Install the lower timing chain cover:

➡️**Replace bolts which have been tightened to torque. Replace sealing rings, seals and self-locking nuts.**

   a. Remove any sealant residue on the engine block using the flat blade scraper.

Fig. 104 Mount the timing chain on the exhaust camshaft and crankshaft

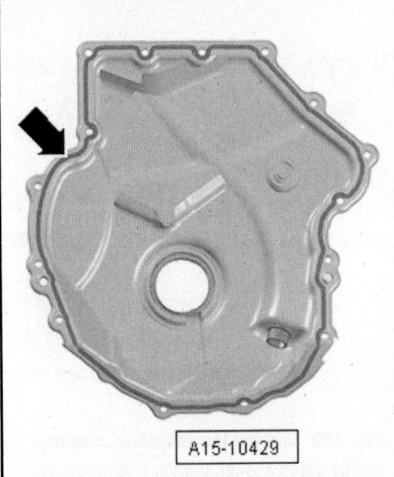

Fig. 105 Apply the silicone sealant D 174 003 A3 in a bead of 0.078–0.117 in. (2–3 mm) on the clean sealing surface of the cover as shown

b. Seal off both side of the seal with tape to prevent soiling

c. Remove residual sealant on the cover, e.g. with a rotating plastic brush.

d. Clean sealing surfaces must be free of oil and grease.

e. Install the cover using the old bolts and tighten to 71 inch lbs. (8 Nm).

f. Check between the cover and housing using a feeler gauge; the gap must not exceed 0.0078 in. (0.2 mm).

g. If the gap exceed 0.0078 in. (0.2 mm), replace the cover.

h. It is not possible to measure between the cover the upper part of the oil pan, however check the sealing surface for evenness.

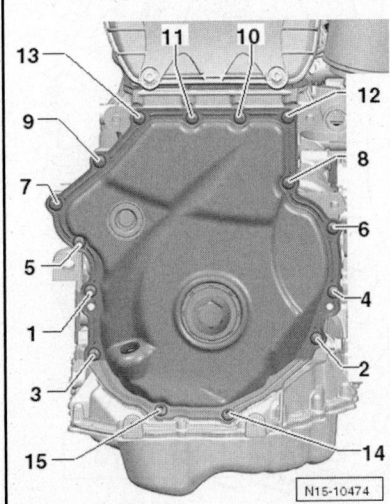

Fig. 106 Tighten the bolts 1 through 15 in 2 stages in the sequence shown

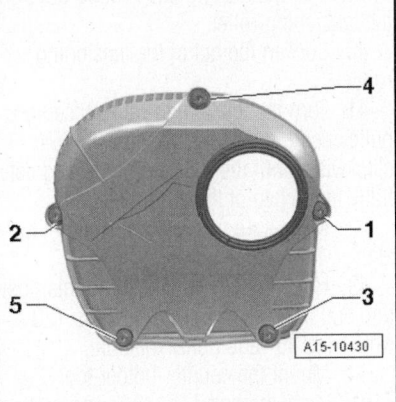

Fig. 107 Tighten the bolts 1 through 5 by hand in the illustrated sequence

i. Make sure both alignment bushings for centering the cover are present.

j. Cut tube nozzle at front marking to approximately 0.117 in. (3 mm).

k. Apply the silicone sealant D 174 003 A3 in a bead of 0.078–0.117 in. (2–3 mm) on the clean sealing surface of the cover.

l. The cover must be installed within 5 minutes after application of silicone sealant.

m. The sealant bead may not be thicker than specified, otherwise excess sealant could enter the oil pan and clog the oil intake tube.

n. Install the lid immediately and all the bolts.

o. Tighten the bolts in 2 stages.

p. Tighten the bolts to 71 inch lbs. (8 Nm), then tighten the bolts an additional 90°.

q. After installing cover, allow sealant to dry for approximately 30 minutes. Only after then may the engine oil be replenished.

53. Install timing chain upper cover:

a. Coat the sealing ring and the O-ring with engine oil.

b. Tighten the five bolts by hand in sequence.

c. Tighten the bolt to 80 inch lbs. (9 Nm) by using the torque wrench V.A.G 1783 and the open end spanner insert AF 10 V.A.G 1783/1.

54. The rest of the assembly is basically a reverse of the disassembling sequence.

55. Fill the engine oil.

56. Check oil level.

2.0L TDI Engine

See Figures 108 through 112.

1. Remove engine cover.

a. One piece engine cover, pull the one piece front engine cover upward with a quick jerk and then pull the lower mount forward.

b. Two piece engine cover, first pull the outer cover upward with a quick jerk, then pull the inner engine cover upward with a quick jerk.

✳✳ CAUTION

The temperature of the fuel lines as well as the fuel can be very hot on vehicles equipped with a TDI engine. Before opening any line connections, let the fuel cool down otherwise you could get burned. Wear protective gloves. Wear safety glasses.

2. Disconnect the fuel supply hose and the fuel return hose from the fuel lines.

3. Disconnect the coolant line.

4. Remove bolts.

5. Remove the connecting pipe between the charge air cooler and the intake connection; while doing this, slightly lift the clips.

6. Disconnect the fuel supply line and the fuel return line; while doing this pull the release buttons.

7. Remove fuel filter without the retaining plate. Release the clips and remove the fuel filter with the hoses still connected from the retaining plate.

8. Remove fuel filter with the retaining plate;

a. Loosen the bolt one turn.

b. Remove the bolt and the nut.

c. Remove the fuel filter with the hoses still connected.

9. Remove the bolt on the fuel filler tube for the washer fluid reservoir.

10. Remove the retaining plate for the fuel filter, if equipped.

11. Disconnect the electrical connectors on the coolant expansion tank.

12. Remove coolant expansion tank with the hoses still connected. Lay it on the engine.

13. Remove ribbed belt.

14. Remove the ribbed belt tensioning element.

15. Remove the upper toothed belt guard; to do this, loosen the clips.

16. Remove front right wheel housing liner.

17. Remove vibration damper/belt pulley.

18. Remove the lower and center toothed belt guard.

19. Turn crankshaft to set cylinder 1 at TDC.

20. When doing so, turn the crankshaft so that the marking on the crankshaft

toothed belt gear and the tooth segment of the camshaft gear are positioned upward. The marking on the rear toothed belt guard must align with the marking on the camshaft sensor wheel.

21. Lock the hub with the rig pin 3359. To do this, push the rig pin through the left-sided empty slot in the bore of the cylinder head.

22. Also, lock the toothed belt crankshaft sprocket with the crankshaft stop T10100. Push the crankshaft stop from the front side of the toothed belt sprocket into the teeth.

23. Markings on toothed belt crankshaft sprocket and the crankshaft stop must be aligned. The tab of the crankshaft stop must engage in the bore of the sealing flange.

24. Mark rotational direction of toothed belt.

25. Loosen the bolts of the camshaft sprockets, until the camshaft sprocket can be turned in the slots.

26. Loosen the nut of the tensioning roller.

27. Turn the tension roller eccentric pulley using socket wrench T10264 counter-clockwise, until the securing pin T10265 can lock the tension roller.

28. Now turn the tensioning roller eccentric pulley clockwise all the way and tighten the nut by hand.

29. First, take the toothed belt from the coolant pump and then from the remaining toothed belt gears.

To install:

30. Camshaft is secured with the rig pin 3359.

31. Crankshaft locked with crankshaft stop T10100.

32. Tensioning roller secured with pin T10265 and seated on right stop with the nut.

33. Adjustments to toothed belt may generally only be performed when the engine is cold, because the indicator position of the tensioning element changes depending on engine temperature.

34. Turn the camshaft sprocket in its slots to middle position.

35. Install the toothed belt through the space between the engine mount and the engine.

36. Place the toothed belt onto the crankshaft sprocket, tensioning roller, camshaft sprocket and idler roller.

37. Lastly, lay the toothed belt onto the toothed belt coolant pump sprocket.

38. Make sure the tensioning roller is properly positioned in the rear toothed belt guard.

39. Pull the locking pin T10265 out from the tensioning roller.

40. Loosen the nut of the tensioning roller.

41. Turn the tensioning roller eccentric pulley using the socket wrench T10264 clockwise, until the indicator is located centrally in the gap of the base plate.

42. Make sure that the nut does not turn along with it.

43. Hold the tensioner roller in this position and tighten the nut to 15 ft. lbs. (20 Nm), plus 45° additional rotation.

44. Mount the counter-holder tool T10172 with the bolt T10172/4, and hold the toothed belt, tensioning it by pushing it.

45. Tighten the camshaft sprocket bolts to 19 ft. lbs. (25 Nm).

46. Remove the rig pin 3359 and the crankshaft stop T10100.

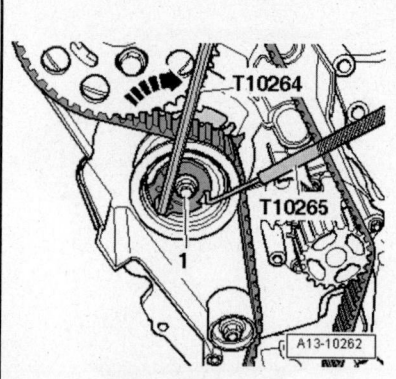

Fig. 109 Turn the tension roller eccentric pulley using socket wrench counterclockwise, until the securing pin can lock the tension roller. Now turn the tensioning roller eccentric pulley clockwise all the way and tighten the nut by hand

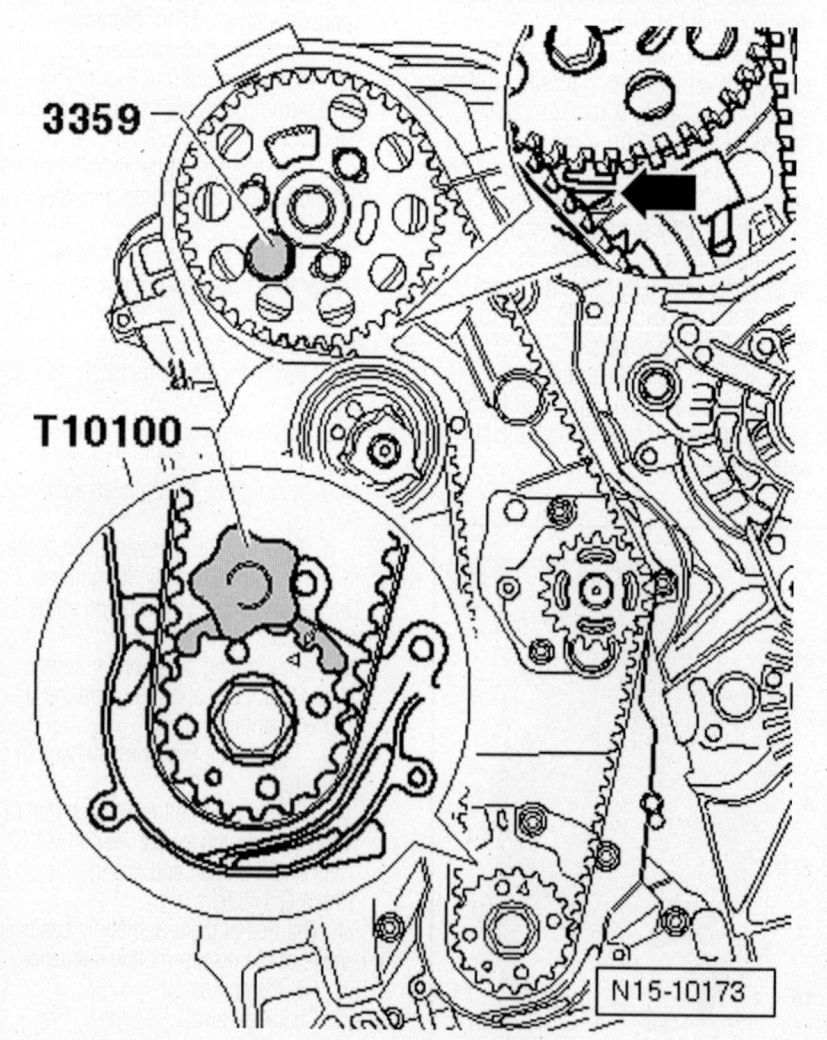

Fig. 108 Markings on toothed belt crankshaft sprocket and the crankshaft stop must be aligned. The tab of the crankshaft stop must engage in the bore of the sealing flange

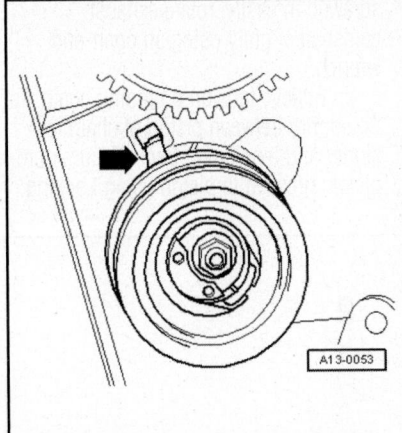

Fig. 110 Make sure the tensioning roller is properly positioned in the rear toothed belt guard (arrow)

47. Turn the crankshaft 2 turns in the direction of the engine, until the crankshaft is once again just in front of TDC.

48. Lock the hub with the rig pin 3359 from the rotating movement in engine rotation direction.

49. Check if the crankshaft can be locked with the crankshaft stop T10100.

50. If the crankshaft cannot be locked:

a. Loosen the bolts of the camshaft sprocket.

b. Turn the crankshaft against the engine running direction until the crankshaft stop tab is positioned shortly before the sealing flange bore.

c. Now turn the crankshaft in engine running direction until the crankshaft stop tab engages the sealing flange.

51. Install the counter-holder T10172 with pins T10172/4. Push the counter-holder T10172 and hold the camshaft sprocket pre-tensioned.

52. In this position, tighten the camshaft sprocket bolts 19 ft. lbs. (25 Nm).

53. Remove the rig pin and the crank-shaft stop.

54. Continue turning crankshaft two rotations in direction of engine rotation until the crankshaft is shortly before TDC for cylinder 1.

55. Repeat the inspection and adjust if necessary.

56. Install the lower and center toothed belt guard.

57. Install the vibration damper/belt pulley. Tightening specifications 89 inch lbs. (10 Nm), plus 90° additional rotation.

58. Install ribbed belt.

59. Install upper toothed belt guard.

60. Install the connecting tube between the charge air cooler and intake connection.

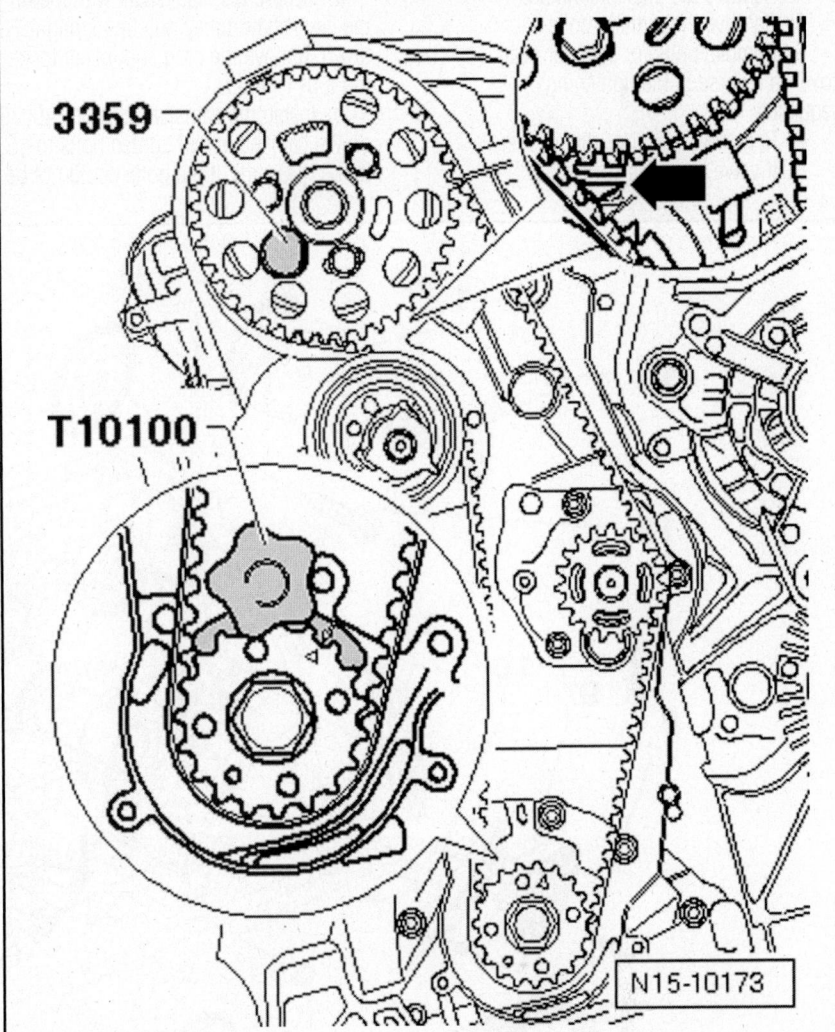

Fig. 111 Lock the hub with the rig pin 3359 and check if the crankshaft can be locked with the crankshaft stop

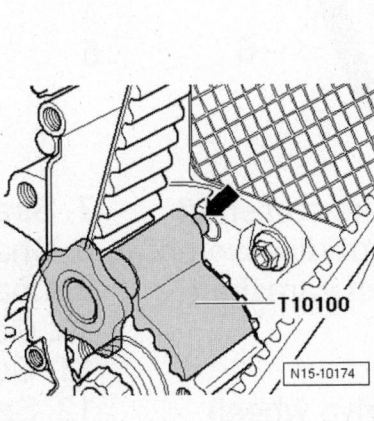

Fig. 112 Now turn the crankshaft in engine running direction until the crank-shaft stop tab engages the sealing flange

61. Install the front right wheel housing liner.

62. Install the coolant expansion tank.

63. Install the fuel filter.

64. Tighten the filler tube for the wind-shield washer.

65. Install the engine cover.

2.5L Engine

Upper Timing Chain

See Figures 113 through 117.

➡ **The upper timing chain can be removed with the engine installed.**

1. Remove the battery and battery holder.

2. Remove engine cover/air filter assembly.

3. Disconnect PCV hose from cylinder head cover. If equipped, remove the secondary air tube.

4. Remove the intake manifold.

5. Remove the ignition coils

6. Remove bolts for cylinder head cover in reverse of the tightening sequence.

7. Remove the timing chain cover.

8. If valve timing is correct:

a. Secure the crankshaft: with the on the crankshaft pulley pointing straight down, remove the plug and install locking tool T40069.

b. Install the camshaft locator T40070 on the camshafts and tighten bolts to 15 ft. lbs. (20 Nm). If the bolts could not be screwed in easily, rotate exhaust camshaft slightly using an open-end wrench.

c. Relieve tension on timing chain. To do so, pry between piston of chain tensioner and tensioning track. Secure completely pressed in piston using Locking

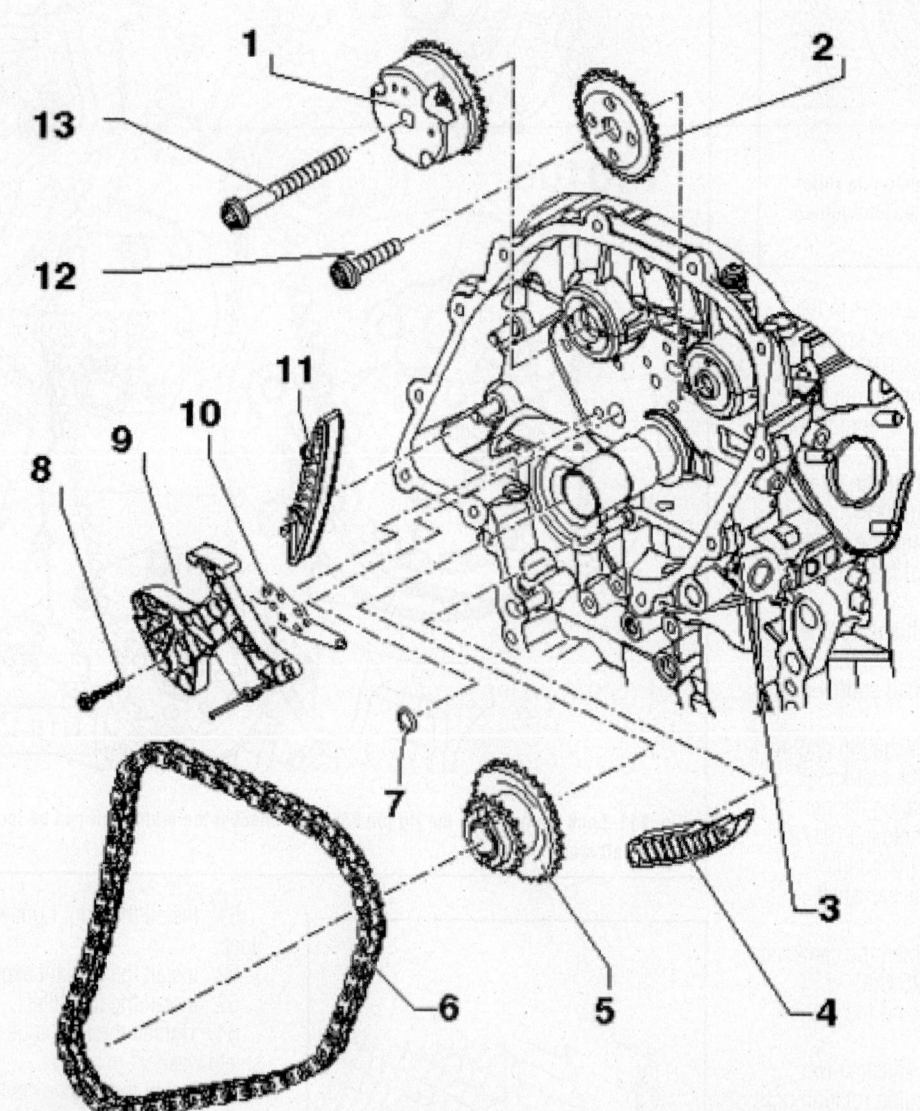

1. Camshaft adjuster for intake camshaft with chain sprocket: Do not disassemble
2. Chain sprocket for exhaust camshaft
3. Cylinder Head
4. Tensioning rail
5. Double chain sprocket (drive wheel)
6. Timing Chain
7. Strainer
8. Chain tensioner screw
9. Chain tensioner
10. Gasket
11. Guide rail
12. Sprocket bolt: always replace
13. Sprocket bolt: always replace

22205_VWCA_G0077

Fig. 113 Upper timing chain components—2.5L engine

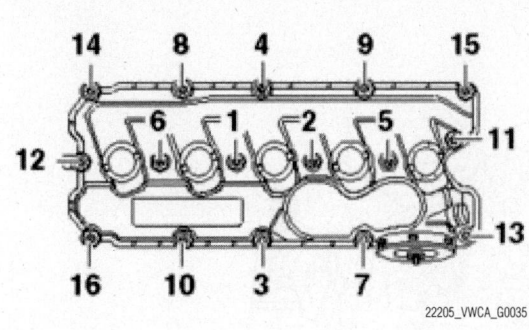

Fig. 114 Cylinder head cover bolt tightening sequence

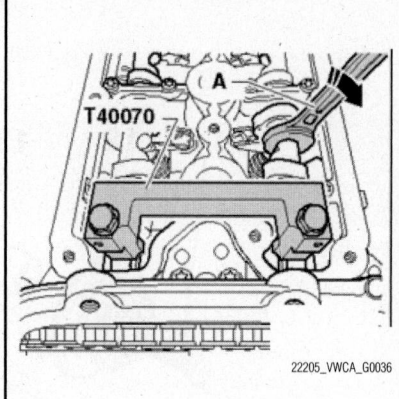

Fig. 116 Lock the camshafts in place with this tool. Rock camshaft slightly if needed.

Pins T03006. Locking pin must be inserted until it stops.

9. If valve timing is not correct:
    *   Remove timing chain case cover
    *   Rotate crankshaft to TDC cylinder 5 but do not lock it into place.
    *   Rotate crankshaft so that camshaft locator T40070 can be screwed easily on to camshafts.

10. Mark the direction of travel and remove the timing chain.

11. If necessary, remove the bolts to remove the sprockets. It may be necessary to gently pry them off. New bolts are required for installation.

To install:

12. Make sure all sealing surfaces are clean and dry.

13. Install the timing chain in the original direction of travel.

14. If removed, install the tensioner. Remove the tensioner lock pin.

15. Remove the camshaft locator tool.

16. Remove the crankshaft locking pin from the cylinder block. Rotate the crankshaft two full turns to make sure camshaft timing marks still align properly.

17. Install the remaining components.

Lower Timing Chain

See Figure 118.

1. Remove engine.
2. Remove control housing cover.
3. Remove timing chain. Mark direction of travel.
4. Remove chain tensioner.

➡**If reinstalling the original chain, place on in original direction of travel.**

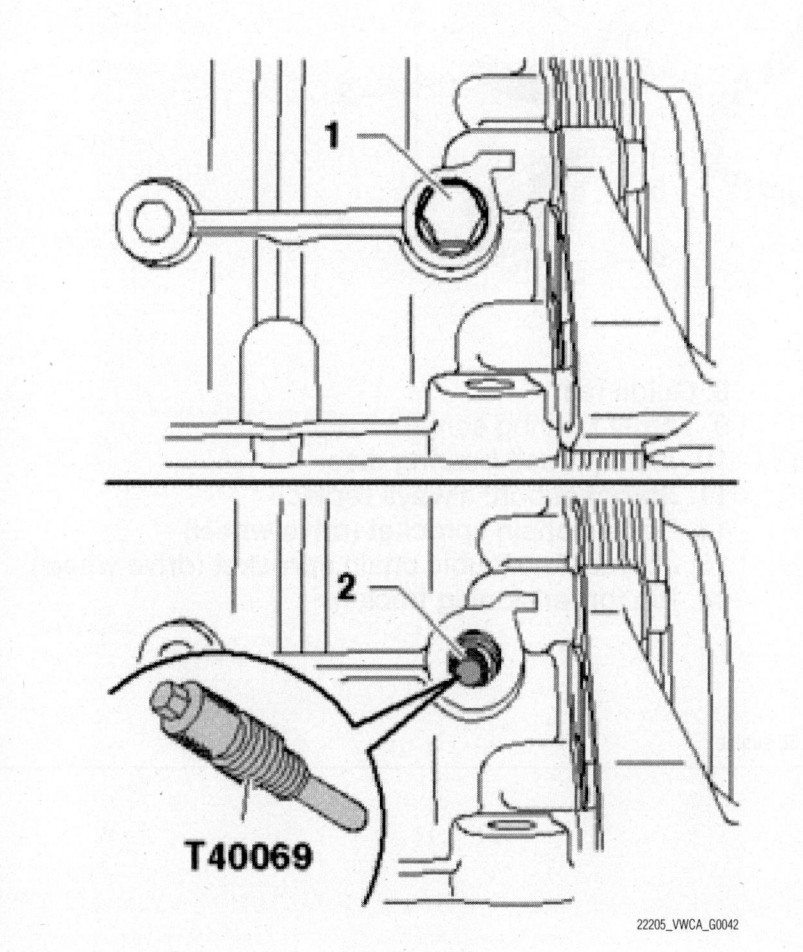

Fig. 115 Install tool T40069 to lock crankshaft in place

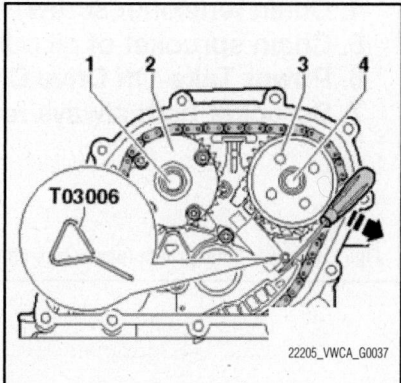

Fig. 117 Pry the chain tensioner to retract the piston and insert a locking pin. Remove bolts (1 and 4) to remove sprockets (2 and 3)

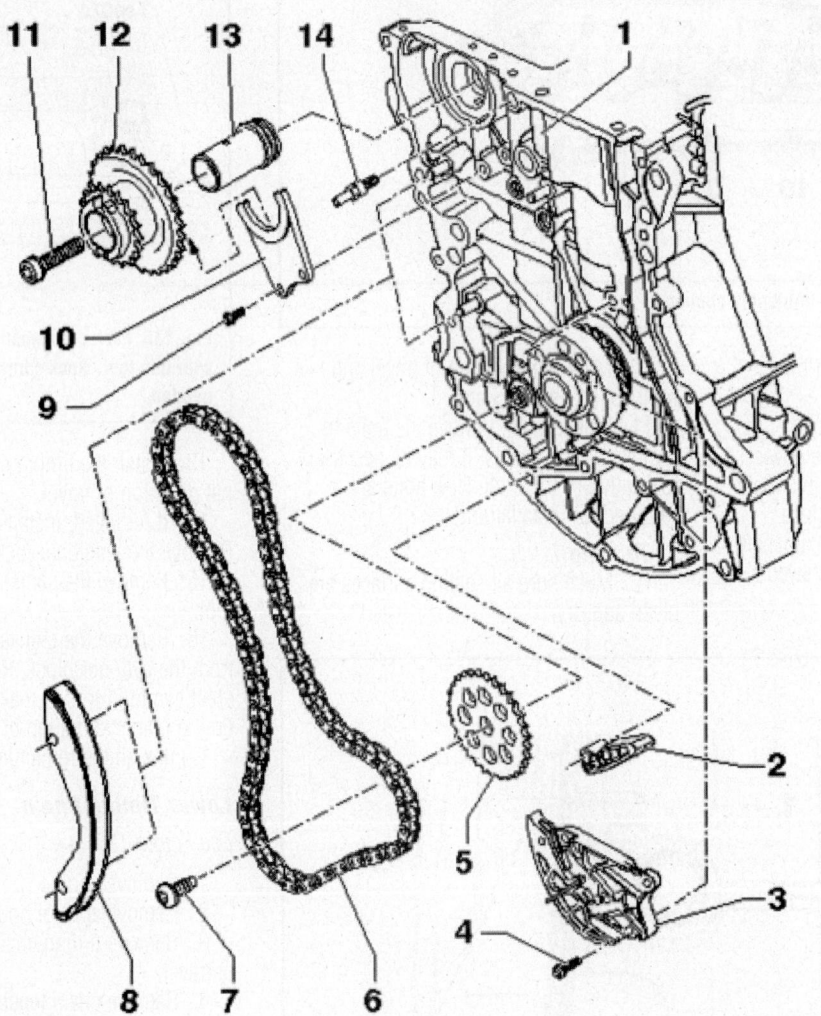

1. Cylinder block
2. Guide rail
3. Chain tensioner
4. Chain tensioner screw
5. Chain sprocket of oil pump
6. Power Take-Off Drive Chain
7. Sprocket bolt: always replace
8. Guide rail
9. Thrust bearing screw
10. Axial (thrust) bearing disc
11. Sprocket bolt: always replace
12. Double chain sprocket (drive wheel)
13. Journal for double chain sprocket (drive wheel)
14. Pin for tensioning track

22205_VWCA_G0078

Fig. 118 Lower timing chain (power take-off chain)—2.5L engine

ENGINE PERFORMANCE & EMISSION CONTROLS

CAMSHAFT POSITION (CMP) SENSOR

LOCATION

See Figures 119 and 120.

The CMP sensor is on the intake side of the cylinder head above the cylinder No. 1 intake runner on the 2.5L engine. Refer to the graphics for other engines.

REMOVAL & INSTALLATION

1. Unplug the connector.
2. Remove the screw and then the sensor

➡**Cover the hole to prevent dirt from getting into the engine.**

3. Installation is the reverse of removal.
4. When installing, use a new seal as necessary.

CRANKSHAFT POSITION (CKP) SENSOR

LOCATION

See Figures 121 and 122.

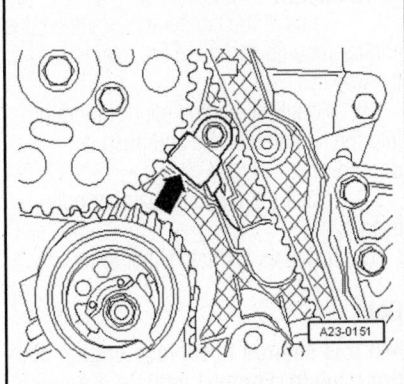

Fig. 120 Camshaft position sensor—2.0L TDI engine

The CKP sensor is the same as the Engine Speed Sensor and is mounted on the timing chain cover at the flywheel end, on the 2.5L engine. Refer to the graphics for other engines.

REMOVAL & INSTALLATION

1. Unplug the connector.
2. Remove the screw and then the sensor

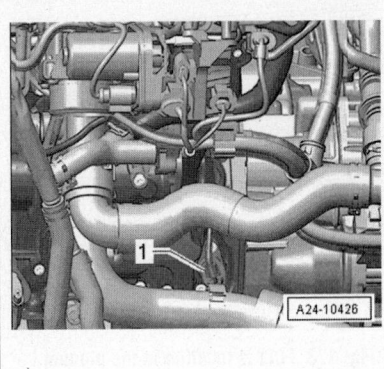

Fig. 121 Crankshaft Position (CKP) sensor connector (1)—2.0L engine

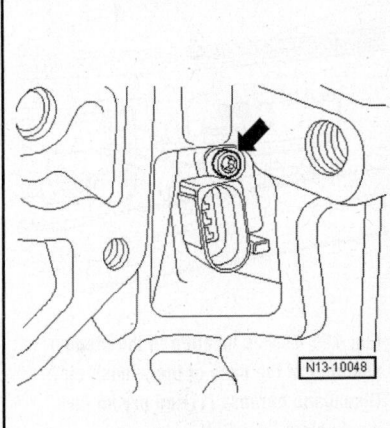

Fig. 122 Crankshaft Position (CKP) sensor connector (arrow)—2.0L TDI engine

➡**Cover the hole to prevent dirt from getting into the engine.**

3. When installing, use a new seal as necessary.

ELECTRONIC CONTROL MODULE (ECM)

LOCATION

See Figures 123 through 125.

REMOVAL & INSTALLATION

Eos

1. If it is desired to replace engine control module, connect Vehicle Diagnosis, Testing and Information System VAS 5051B and perform the guided function "Replace Engine Control Module".
2. Switch off ignition.

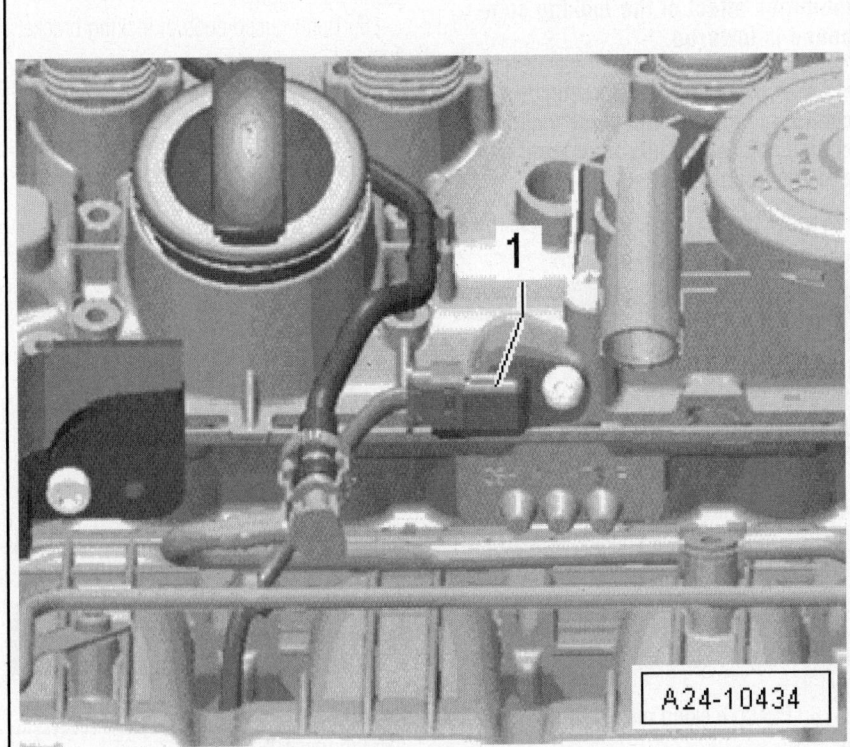

Fig. 119 Camshaft position sensor (1) with knock sensor (2) and fuel injector connector (3)—2.0L engine

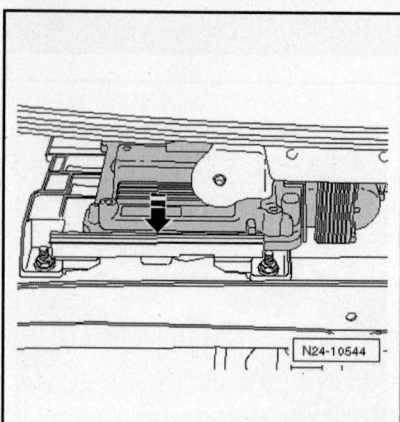

Fig. 123 ECM is location in the plenum chamber at the base of the windshield—Eos

Fig. 124 ECM is location in the plenum chamber at the base of the windshield. Disengage harness (1) and pry up lock mechanism (2)—Golf

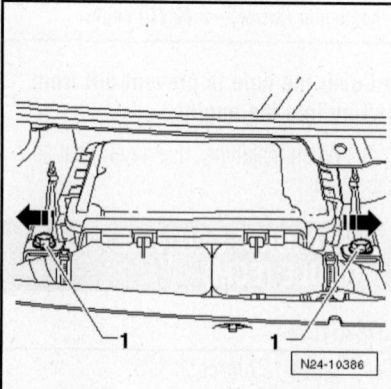

Fig. 125 ECM location in the plenum chamber at the base of the windshield showing retaining bolts (1)—Tiguan

3. Remove windshield wiper arms.
4. Remove plenum chamber bulkhead.
5. Push the retaining frame downward and remove the engine control module.

6. Push the retainers and disconnect the connector.

To install:

7. Connect the connector on the engine control module and push the retainers all the way in.
8. Mount the engine control module into the retaining frame and push it upward.
9. Install the plenum chamber bulkhead.
10. Install windshield wiper arms.

Golf

➡If it is desired to replace engine control module, connect vehicle diagnosis, testing and information system VAS 5051 and perform the function "Replace engine control module".

1. Switch off ignition.
2. Remove wiper arms and plenum chamber cover.
3. Remove plenum chamber bulkhead
4. On vehicles equipped with shear bolts proceed as follows:

✳✳ CAUTION

Thread of shear bolts is equipped with locking compound. By heating the shear bolts using a hot air gun, inhibition effect of the locking compound is lowered.

➡Cover wires, harness connectors and control modules in the close vicinity of engine control module to prevent damage from burning.

a. Unscrew shear bolt using pliers on bolt head.

✳✳ CAUTION

If screws cannot be removed, saw into heads of shear bolts so that two parallel surfaces are formed and then unscrew them.

b. Insert a screwdriver between protective housing and retaining plate.
c. Pry protective housing upward using screwdriver and pull it off sideways from retaining plate.
5. Disengage forward harness connector from engine control module and disconnect it.
6. Pry up locking mechanism slightly.
7. Then slide engine control module out of retainer.
8. Now disengage rear harness connec-

tor from engine control module and disconnect it.

To install:

9. Connect rear harness connector to engine control module and engage it.
10. Slide engine control module on to retaining plate.
11. Press the catch against the engine control module.
12. Now connect front connector to engine control module and engage it.
13. Slide protective housing on to retaining plate.
14. Tighten new shear bolts uniformly until bolt heads shear off.
15. Install plenum chamber bulkhead.
16. Install wiper arms and plenum chamber cover.

Tiguan

1. Switch off ignition.
2. Remove windshield wiper arms.
3. Remove plenum chamber cover.
4. Remove bolts.
5. Cover plenum chamber with a clean cloth so that it does not get scratched.
6. Raise engine control module with retaining mounting slightly.
7. Release engine control module and pull it out slightly.
8. Bend raised ends of locking bracket outward.
9. Remove shear bolts with locking pliers and remove locking bracket.
10. Slide connector release catches on engine control module outward and disconnect both harness connectors.
11. Remove engine control module.

To install:

12. Slide engine control module into mounting frame until it engages.
13. Tighten mounting frame to 53 inch lbs. (6 Nm).
14. Connect harness connectors to engine control module and slide release catches inward.
15. Take a new locking bracket and tighten new shear bolts evenly until bolt heads shear off.

ENGINE COOLANT TEMPERATURE (ECT) SENSOR

LOCATION

See Figures 126 and 127.

The ECT is on the upper radiator hose connection on the cylinder head—2.5L engine

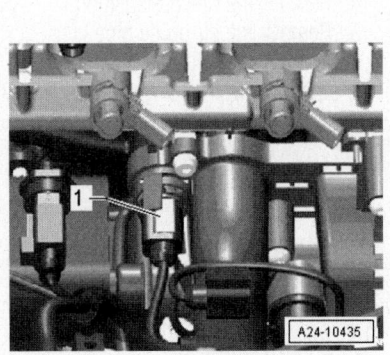

Fig. 126 Coolant temperature sensor—2.0L engine

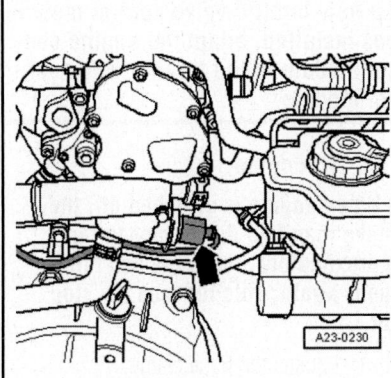

Fig. 127 Coolant temperature sensor—2.0L TDI engine

REMOVAL & INSTALLATION

1. Drain the coolant.
2. Unplug the connector.
3. Remove the sensor.

To install:
4. Installation is the reverse of removal.
5. When installing, use a new seal and/or retaining clip, as necessary.

HEATED OXYGEN (HO2S) SENSOR

LOCATION

2.0L Engines

The primary oxygen sensor is on the exhaust pipe at the turbocharger outlet. The secondary sensor is behind the catalytic converter.

2.0L TDI Engine

The primary oxygen sensor is on the exhaust pipe at the turbocharger outlet.

2.5L Engines

The primary oxygen sensor is on the exhaust pipe. The secondary sensor is behind the catalytic converter.

REMOVAL & INSTALLATION

2.0L & 2.5L Engines

1. Unplug the connector.
2. Remove the sensor and cover the hole to prevent dirt from getting into the engine.

To install:
3. Installation is the reverse of removal.

➡ Thread of new oxygen sensors is coated with hot bolt paste.

> **✳✳ CAUTION**
>
> When re-using the previous oxygen sensor, grease only the threads with hot bolt paste G 052 112; the paste must not get into slots of oxygen sensor body

4. Tighten to 41 ft. lbs. (55 Nm).

2.0L TDI Engine

1. Unplug the connector.
2. Remove the sensor and cover the hole to prevent dirt from getting into the engine.

To install:
3. Installation is the reverse of removal.

➡ Thread of new oxygen sensors is coated with hot bolt paste.

> **✳✳ CAUTION**
>
> When re-using the previous oxygen sensor, grease only the threads with hot bolt paste G 052 112; the paste must not get into slots of oxygen sensor body

4. Tighten to 41 ft. lbs. (55 Nm).

INTAKE AIR TEMPERATURE (IAT) SENSOR

LOCATION

2.0L Engines

1. The IAT is mounted in the center of the intake manifold plenum near the throttle body.

2.5L Engine

The IAT is built into the Mass Airflow (MAF) sensor and cannot be removed separately.

REMOVAL & INSTALLATION

2.0L Engines

1. Unplug the connector.
2. Remove the screw and the sensor and cover the hole to prevent dirt from getting into the engine.
3. Installation is the reverse of removal.
4. When installing, use a new seal as necessary.

KNOCK SENSOR (KS)

LOCATION

2.0L Engines

Knock sensor 1 is bolted to the cylinder block below the thermostat housing. Knock sensor 2 is bolted to the block below the oil filter bracket.

2.5L Engine

Two knock sensors are mounted on the engine block below the intake manifold.

REMOVAL & INSTALLATION

2.0L Engines

Knock Sensor 1

1. Drain the coolant.
2. Remove the thermostat.
3. Remove the bolt to remove the knock sensor.

To install:
4. Installation is the reverse of removal.
5. Torque the knock sensor bolt to 15 ft. lbs. (20 Nm). Do not over-tighten or the sensor will not work properly.

Knock Sensor 2

1. Drain the coolant.
2. Remove the intake manifold.
3. Disconnect the coolant hoses from the oil cooler.
4. Remove the oil cooler.
5. Disconnect the oil pressure switch.
6. Remove the four bolts to remove the oil filter bracket.
7. Remove the bolt to remove the knock sensor.

To install:
8. Install the sensor and torque the bolt to 15 ft. lbs. (20 Nm). Do not over-tighten or the sensor will not work properly.
9. Install the baffle plate, and then install the oil filter bracket using new gaskets. Torque the bolts to 11 ft. lbs. (15 Nm).
10. Install oil cooler and connect coolant hoses.
11. Install the intake manifold.

12. Refill the cooling system and run the engine to check for leaks.

2.5L Engine

1. Remove the intake manifold.
2. Remove the bolt to remove the knock sensor.

To install:

3. Installation is the reverse of removal.
4. Torque the knock sensor bolt to 15 ft. lbs. (20 Nm).

➡**Do not over-tighten or the sensor will not work properly.**

MASS AIR FLOW (MAF) SENSOR

LOCATION

2.0L Engines

The MAF sensor is mounted in the air filter housing assembly behind the opening for the oil filler cap.

2.0L TDI Engine

The MAF sensor is mounted in the air filter housing assembly

2.5L Engine

The MAF sensor is in the intake air tube next to the battery.

REMOVAL & INSTALLATION

2.0L & 2.5L Engines

1. Disconnect air intake hose from the air filter housing.
2. Disconnect electrical connector on Mass Air Flow (MAF) sensor.
3. Remove both bolts from the Mass Air Flow (MAF) sensor and carefully remove the Mass Air Flow (MAF) sensor from the air filter housing guide.

To install:

4. Installation is the reverse of removal.
5. If the air filter element is very dirty or soaked, dirt particles or moisture may have contaminated the Mass Air Flow (MAF) sensor and may be causing false mass air flow values. This results in a reduction of power, since a lower injection quantity is calculated.
6. Always use an original equipment air filter element.
7. Use a lubricant (silicone-free) for installing the intake hose.
8. Secure all hose connections using hose clamps appropriate for the model type.
9. Check the MAF sensor and intake hose (intake air side) for salt residue, dirt, and leaves.

10. Check the intake ducting up to the air filter element for dirt. If any contaminants are discovered, clean the air filter housing (upper and lower parts) of salt residue, dirt and leaves (if necessary, clean by washing or vacuuming).
11. Tighten clamps/screws to 13 inch lbs. (1.5 Nm).

2.0L TDI Engine

1. Disconnect air intake hose from the air filter housing.
2. Disconnect electrical connector on Mass Air Flow (MAF) sensor.
3. Remove both bolts from the Mass Air Flow (MAF) sensor and carefully remove the Mass Air Flow (MAF) sensor from the air filter housing guide.

To install:

4. Installation is the reverse of removal.
5. If the air filter element is very dirty or soaked, dirt particles or moisture may have contaminated the Mass Air Flow (MAF) Sensor and may be causing false mass air flow values. This results in a reduction of power, since a lower injection quantity is calculated.
6. Always use an original equipment air filter element.
7. Use a lubricant (silicone-free) for installing the intake hose.
8. Secure all hose connections using hose clamps appropriate for the model type.
9. Check the MAF sensor and intake hose (intake air side) for salt residue, dirt, and leaves.
10. Check the intake ducting up to the air filter element for dirt. If any contaminants are discovered, clean the air filter housing (upper and lower parts) of salt residue, dirt and leaves (if necessary, clean by washing or vacuuming).

THROTTLE POSITION SENSOR (TPS)

LOCATION

2.0L & 2.5L Engines

The Throttle Position Sensor (TPS) is built into the electronic throttle valve control module (throttle body).

2.0L TDI Engine

The Throttle Position Sensor (TPS) is built into the intake flap motor (throttle body).

REMOVAL & INSTALLATION

2.0L & 2.5L Engines

1. Loosen the hose clamp.
2. Remove bolt.

3. Disconnect electrical connector.
4. Remove the noise insulation.
5. Remove the air guide pipe.
6. Remove the bolt and remove the air guide pipe downward.
7. Disconnect electrical connector on throttle valve control module.
8. Remove bolts and remove throttle valve control module.

To install:

9. Installation is performed in reverse order of removal.
10. Clean O-ring sealing surface.
11. Replace the seal; when doing so, pay attention to the correct position of the service flag on the sealing ring.
12. Tighten bolts in crisscross pattern to 31 inch lbs. (3.5 Nm).

✷✷ CAUTION

If a new throttle valve control module was installed, adapt the engine control module to the throttle valve control module.

2.0L TDI Engine

➡**When engine is switched off, the intake manifold flap is closed for approximately 3 seconds and then opens again. This reduces the stop jolt.**

1. Loosen the hose clamp.
2. Remove bolt.
3. Disconnect electrical connector.
4. Remove the noise insulation.
5. Remove the air guide pipe.
6. Remove the bolt and remove the air guide pipe downward.
7. Disconnect electrical connector on intake flap motor.
8. Remove bolts and remove intake flap motor.

To install:

9. Installation is performed in reverse order of removal.
10. Clean O-ring sealing surface.
11. Replace the seal; when doing so, pay attention to the correct position of the service flag on the sealing ring.
12. Tighten bolts in crisscross pattern to 89 inch lbs. (10 Nm).

✷✷ CAUTION

If a new Intake flap motor was installed, adapt the engine control module to the intake flap motor.

FUEL

GASOLINE FUEL INJECTION SYSTEM

FUEL SYSTEM SERVICE PRECAUTIONS

Safety is the most important factor when performing not only fuel system maintenance but any type of maintenance. Failure to conduct maintenance and repairs in a safe manner may result in serious personal injury or death. Maintenance and testing of the vehicle's fuel system components can be accomplished safely and effectively by adhering to the following rules and guidelines.

• To avoid the possibility of fire and personal injury, always disconnect the negative battery cable unless the repair or test procedure requires that battery voltage be applied.

• Always relieve the fuel system pressure prior to disconnecting any fuel system component (injector, fuel rail, pressure regulator, etc.), fitting or fuel line connection. Exercise extreme caution whenever relieving fuel system pressure to avoid exposing skin, face and eyes to fuel spray. Please be advised that fuel under pressure may penetrate the skin or any part of the body that it contacts.

• Always place a shop towel or cloth around the fitting or connection prior to loosening to absorb any excess fuel due to spillage. Ensure that all fuel spillage (should it occur) is quickly removed from engine surfaces. Ensure that all fuel soaked cloths or towels are deposited into a suitable waste container.

• Always keep a dry chemical (Class B) fire extinguisher near the work area.

• Do not allow fuel spray or fuel vapors to come into contact with a spark or open flame.

• Always use a back-up wrench when loosening and tightening fuel line connection fittings. This will prevent unnecessary stress and torsion to fuel line piping.

• Always replace worn fuel fitting O-rings with new. Do not substitute fuel hose or equivalent where fuel pipe is installed.

Before servicing the vehicle, make sure to also refer to the precautions in the beginning of this section as well.

RELIEVING FUEL SYSTEM PRESSURE

☀ CAUTION

The fuel injection system is divided into a high pressure section (maxi-

mum approximately 1740 psi or 120 bar) and a low pressure system (approximately 87psi or 6 bar). Before opening high pressure area - e.g. removing high pressure pump, fuel rail, fuel injectors, fuel pipes or Fuel Pressure Sensor - fuel pressure in high pressure area must be reduced to a residual pressure of approximately 87psi (6 bar).

1. Remove electrical connector from Fuel Pressure Regulator Valve using the Assembly Tool T10118.
2. Allow engine to idle approximately 10 seconds.
   a. When the Fuel Pressure Regulator Valve electrical connector is disconnected during idle, pressure in high pressure area decreases to approximately 6 bar.
   b. After high pressure has been released, high pressure system must be opened, otherwise the pressure increases again due to the warming of the fuel.
3. Switch off ignition.

☀ CAUTION

Fuel lines are pressurized! Wear protective goggles and protective clothing to prevent injuries and contact with skin. Before opening the high pressure system, place a cloth around the connection.

4. Place a clean cloth around the connection point and carefully open to release the residual pressure of approximately 87psi (6 bar). Escaping fuel must be absorbed.
5. To conclude work, check DTC memory of engine control module, erase all DTC entries which may have occurred from removing the connector. If DTC memory was erased, generate readiness code.

FUEL FILTER

REMOVAL & INSTALLATION

Internal Fuel Filter

If the fuel filter is not located on the frame rail near the fuel tank then it is located in the tank mounted to the fuel delivery unit.

External Fuel Filter

See Figure 128.

On some models the fuel filter is located on the frame rail near the fuel tank.

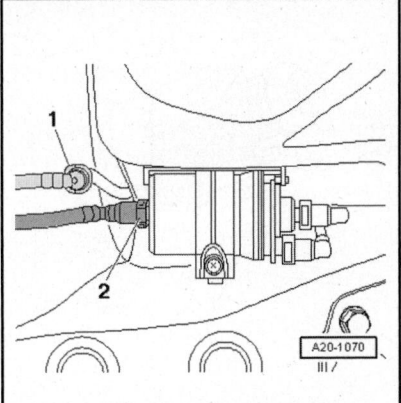

Fig. 128 Disconnect the white vent line 1 from the vent line and the black supply line 2 from the fuel filter

1. Remove the heat shield.

☀ CAUTION

The fuel supply line is under pressure. Wear protective goggles and protective clothing to prevent injuries and contact with skin.

2. Before disconnecting, place a cloth around the connection point. Then release pressure by carefully disconnecting the connection.
3. Disconnect the white vent line from the vent line and the black supply line from the fuel filter.
4. Remove the clamp bolt.
5. Remove the filter.

To install:
6. Installation is the reverse of removal.
7. Check for leaks.

FUEL INJECTORS

REMOVAL & INSTALLATION

2.0L Engines
See Figure 131.

➡**Puller T10133/2A is required to complete this operation.**

1. Remove the intake manifold with the fuel rail. If the injector valves remain attached in the fuel rail, then pull them out.
2. Cover the intake channels with a clean rag.
3. Remove the support element A downward and disconnect the connector from the fuel injectors.
4. Position the puller T10133/2A in the groove on the fuel injector.

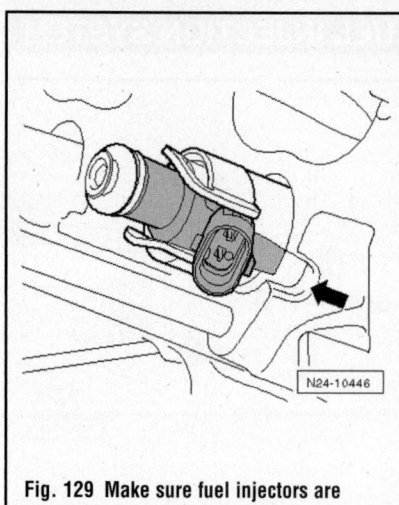

Fig. 129 Make sure fuel injectors are positioned correctly in cylinder head

5. Mount the removal tool T10133/16, turn the screw and remove the fuel injector.

➡**Pay attention to the intermediate rings.**

To install:

✻✻ CAUTION

The combustion chamber seal must always be replaced before re-installing the fuel injector. The Teflon sealing ring of fuel injector may not be oiled or greased.

➡**If an opened intake valve hinders the cleaning, the engine must be turned further by hand using a screw wrench on the crankshaft.**

6. Thoroughly clean bores for high pressure fuel injectors in cylinder head using nylon brush T10133/4.

7. Replace O-ring and Teflon sealing ring of fuel injector.

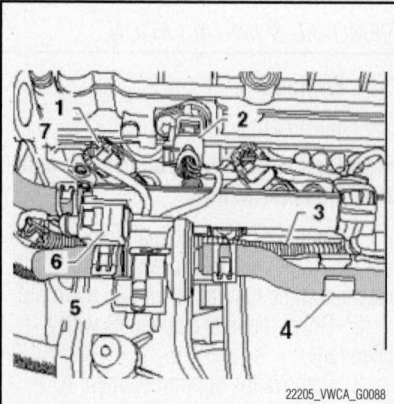

Fig. 130 Disconnect as indicated (1, 2 and 6)

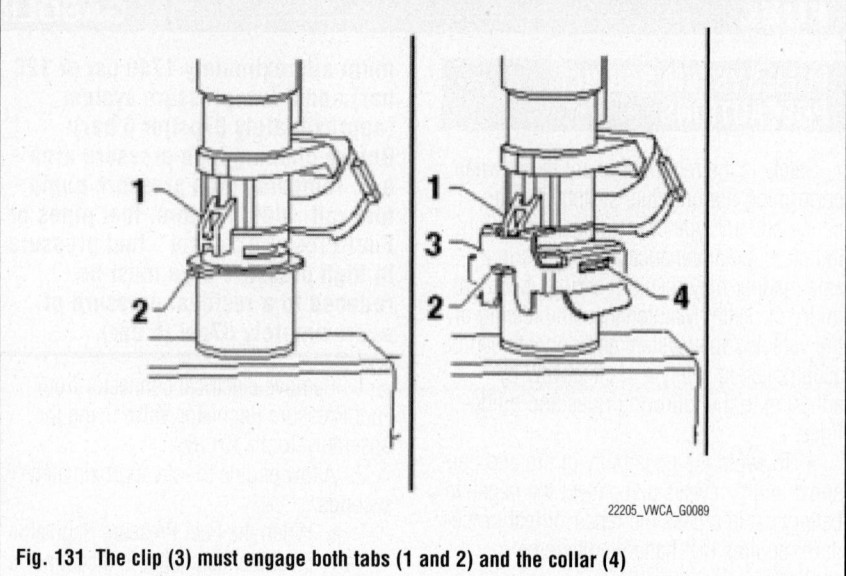

Fig. 131 The clip (3) must engage both tabs (1 and 2) and the collar (4)

8. Install the fuel injection with the intermediate ring again.

9. Use the Remover T10133/2A to push the fuel injector all the way into the hole in the cylinder head.

➡**Make sure fuel injectors are positioned correctly in cylinder head.**

10. Install the intake manifold with the fuel rail.

2.5L Engine

See Figures 132 and 133.

1. First, check whether a coded radio is installed. If necessary, obtain the anti-theft coding.

2. Disconnect the negative battery cable.

3. Remove engine cover/air filter housing.

✻✻ CAUTION

Fuel supply line is under pressure! Wear protective goggles and protective clothing to prevent injuries and contact with skin. Before loosening the fuel lines, place a rag around the connection point. Then release pressure by carefully pulling hose off connection.

4. Disconnect the fuel tank vent line and the fuel supply line. To release the connectors, press the circlip in. On the fuel supply line, the retainer must be pressed upward in the housing.

5. Disconnect connectors.

6. Remove wiring harness from transport strap.

7. Pull clamps and retaining ring out of locking mechanism.

8. Remove bolts and remove transport strap.

9. Remove bolts and pull fuel rail with fuel injectors evenly out of intake manifold.

10. Seal or cover openings in intake manifold.

11. Pull of retaining clips and then remove fuel injectors from fuel rail.

To install:

12. Install new O-rings for fuel injectors and coat them lightly with clean engine oil.

13. Press fuel injectors into fuel rail so that tabs align.

14. Slide retaining clip into groove of fuel injector. Collar must be located correctly in cutout of retaining clip on both sides.

15. After assembling, check all fuel injectors for correct fitting.

16. Fit fuel rail/injector assembly on intake manifold and press it in uniformly.

17. Bolt fuel rail to intake manifold.

18. Connect all wiring and the fuel lines.

19. Connect the battery and bleed the fuel system.

FUEL DELIVERY UNIT

REMOVAL & INSTALLATION

Bolt-In Type

✻✻ CAUTION

Fuel system is under high pressure! Before opening the system, perform the procedure for releasing fuel pressure.

1. The removal and installation of the high-pressure fuel pump can only be performed on a cold engine.

2. Catch escaping fuel with a rag.

3. Remove engine cover.

4. Disconnect the electrical connector from the Fuel Pressure Regulator Valve.

5. Open both fuel lines.

6. Remove the bolts.

7. Carefully pull the high pressure fuel pump out. The roller tappet may stay in the cylinder head.

To install:

8. When installing the high-pressure fuel pump, make sure that no dirt enters the fuel system.

9. The O-ring must always be replaced.

10. High-pressure fuel lines must always be fastened free of tension.

11. Replace the O-ring for the high-pressure pump.

12. Carefully place high pressure pump with sleeve (pay attention to the groove) in opening in cylinder head (check sleeve for damage first).

13. Install new bolts and tighten by hand.

14. Before installing the fuel lines, check the torque of the connections on the high-pressure pump.

15. Tighten the bolts crosswise to 89 inch lbs. (10 Nm).

16. Hand tighten the fuel supply line union nut so that it is free of tension and then tighten it.

17. Connect the electrical connector from the Fuel Pressure Regulator Valve.

18. If the fuse was pulled, insert it again.

19. Check fuel system for leaks.

Lock-Ring Type

See Figure 132.

1. Fuel tank may be a maximum of ¼ full.

2. Empty the fuel tank if necessary using the fuel extracting device VAS 5190.

3. Switch off ignition, switch off all electrical consumers and remove ignition key.

4. Remove seat bench.

5. Unclip cover with Fuel Pump (FP) Control Module.

6. On vehicles with an auxiliary heater, the connector for the metering pump must also be disconnected and the connector with the rubber grommet must be guided through cover.

✳✳ CAUTION

The fuel supply line is under pressure. Wear protective goggles and

protective clothing to prevent injuries and contact with skin. Before loosening line connections, place rags around the connection point. Then release pressure by carefully pulling off the line.

7. Disconnect 5-pin connector, black supply line and blue return line.

8. Press in securing ring to disengage the lines.

9. On vehicles with an auxiliary heater, the Metering Pump intake line must also be removed (open lower clamp).

10. Open locking ring using wrench T10202.

11. Pull fuel delivery unit with sealing ring out of fuel tank opening.

12. When removing fuel delivery unit, be sure not to bend fuel gauge sender.

To install:

13. Installation of fuel delivery unit is reverse order of removal.

14. Insert dry new sealing ring of fuel delivery unit into opening of fuel tank.

15. Only coat seal with fuel on the inside when installing fuel delivery unit.

16. When inserting fuel delivery unit into fuel tank, be sure not to bend fuel gauge sender.

17. Note installation position of fuel delivery unit. Tab on fuel delivery unit must lie between tabs.

18. Tighten locking ring to 81 ft. lbs. (110 Nm).

19. Do not interchange black supply line and blue return line (arrows on flange of fuel delivery unit).

20. Make sure fuel lines are securely fastened.

21. After installing fuel delivery unit,

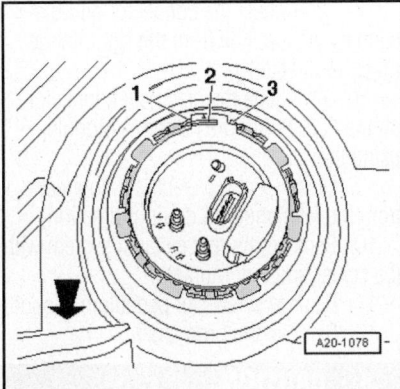

Fig. 132 Tab (2) on fuel delivery unit must lie between tabs (1) and (3). Arrow points in direction of travel.

check whether supply and return lines are still clipped in at fuel tank.

22. If the fuel delivery unit was replaced, adapt the engine control module to the fuel pump.

FUEL TANK

REMOVAL & INSTALLATION

Eos

1. Empty the fuel tank if necessary using the fuel extracting device VAS 5190.

2. Remove seat bench.

3. Remove cover from fuel delivery unit.

4. On vehicles with auxiliary heater, harness connector of Metering Pump must also be disconnected.

5. Disconnect 5-pin connector from flange.

6. Unscrew mounting bolt for fuel flap unit and remove fuel flap unit.

7. Remove tension struts.

8. Remove center and rear mufflers.

9. Remove center muffler heat shield.

10. Remove right rear wheel.

11. Remove rear right wheel housing liner.

12. Unclip electrical wire on filler connection.

13. Disconnect the ventilation line.

14. Unscrew fuel filler tube from body.

15. Disconnect ventilation line (white) and vacuum line (green) for Leak Detection Pump (LDP) behind fuel tank by pressing in circlip.

✳✳ CAUTION

Fuel system is under pressure! Wear protective goggles and protective clothing to prevent injuries and contact with skin. Before removing from hose connection wrap a cloth around the connection. Then release pressure by carefully pulling hose off connection.

16. Disconnect vent line (white) and fuel line (black) at connecting point.

17. Press in securing ring to disengage the fuel lines.

18. On vehicles with auxiliary heater, fuel line of Metering Pump must also be disconnected.

19. As necessary, also disconnect the leak detection pump (LDP) vacuum line (green).

20. Unscrew tension strap and mounting bolts. Support fuel tank using Engine/Transmission Jack V.A.G 1383 while doing so.

21. Carefully lower fuel tank.

To install:

22. Install in reverse order of removal. When doing this note the following:

23. To mount the fuel tank tension straps, only screws with loose washers may be used. If other screws are used, the tension straps could twist when the screws are tightened.

24. Make sure vent and fuel lines are not kinked.

25. Do not interchange supply and return line (return line blue, supply line black).

26. Make sure lines connections are securely fastened.

27. Check Ground (GND) connection of fuel tank/chassis at filler tube.

28. Install tension struts.

29. Tighten bolts/nuts to specification as follows:

- Fuel tank to chassis - bolts M6: 89 inch lbs. (10 Nm)
- Fuel tank to chassis - bolts M8: 19 ft. lbs. (25 Nm)

Golf

1. With the ignition off, disconnect the ground cable from the battery.

2. Clean the surrounding area around the fuel filler tube.

3. Drain the fuel tank as necessary using the VAS 5190.

4. Remove the rear seat bench.

5. Remove the cover with the fuel pump control module from the fuel delivery unit.

6. When installing the cover be sure to pay attention to the installed position.

7. Disconnect the electrical connector from the fuel delivery unit.

8. Remove the right rear wheel.

9. Remove the right rear wheel housing liner.

10. Remove the fuel tank door unit.

11. Disconnect the hoses.

12. Remove the fuel filler tube bolts from the body.

13. Unclip the wheel speed sensor wire from the filler tube bracket.

14. Remove the center and rear mufflers.

15. Remove the heat shield.

❊❊ CAUTION

The fuel supply line is under pressure. Wear protective goggles and protective clothing to prevent injuries and contact with skin. Before disconnecting, place a cloth around the connection point. Then release pressure by carefully disconnecting the connection.

16. Disconnect the white vent line from the vent line and the black supply line from the fuel filter.

17. Press the securing ring to disengage the lines.

18. Disconnect the green Leak Detection Pump (LDP) vacuum line as well.

19. Seal the lines so that the fuel system is not contaminated by dirt etc.

20. Remove the tensioning straps and bolts. Support the fuel tank using the VAG 1383A while doing so.

21. Lower the fuel tank.

To install:

22. Install in reverse order of removal.

23. Make sure the vent and fuel lines are not kinked.

24. Do not interchange the supply and return line (return line = blue, supply line = black).

25. Make sure the line connections are securely seated.

26. Check the ground connection for the fuel tank/chassis at the filler tube.

27. After installing the fuel tank, check to be sure the lines are still clipped to the fuel tank.

28. Observe the notes after connecting the battery.

29. Tighten bolts/nuts to specification as follows:

- Fuel tank to chassis (Replace bolts): 19 ft. lbs. (25 Nm)

Tiguan

1. First, check whether a coded radio is installed. If necessary, obtain the anti-theft coding.

2. With the ignition switched off disconnect battery ground strap.

3. Remove the mounting bolt for fuel flap and remove fuel flap unit.

4. Drain fuel tank and clean fuel filler tube and surrounding area.

5. Remove the seat bench.

6. Remove cover from fuel delivery unit.

7. Disconnect the connector and disconnect the fuel line from the right flange (in drive direction).

8. Disengage the electrical connector on the Fuel Pump (FP) Control Module using the

9. Disconnect the electrical connector 1 from the left flange (in driving direction).

10. Remove the rear exhaust system with the center and rear mufflers.

11. Remove screws for pendulum support.

12. Remove the prop shaft.

❊❊ CAUTION

Fuel supply lines are under pressure! Wear protective goggles and protective gloves to avoid damage and contact with skin. Before removing from

hose connection wrap a cloth around the connection. Then release pressure by carefully pulling hose off connection.

13. Disconnect the fuel line (black) and the ventilation line (white) at the connecting point.

14. If an auxiliary heater is installed, disconnect the fuel line as well.

15. Press in securing ring to disengage the fuel lines.

16. Remove right rear wheel.

17. Remove right rear wheel housing liner.

18. Disconnect vent lines and vacuum line from EVAP canister.

19. Unclip the wheel sensor wire from the retainer on the filler neck.

20. Remove the fuel tank flap and the fuel cap for the tank filler tube.

21. Disconnect the ground wire on the tank filler tube.

22. Unscrew fuel filler tube from body s.

23. Remove bolts.

24. Remove the tensioning strap and bolts s. Support the fuel tank with the engine/transmission jack V.A.G 1383 A

To install:

25. With a second mechanic assisting, guide fuel filler tube between rear axle and chassis. Then place fuel tank on to engine and transmission jack V.A.G 1383 A.

26. Lift fuel tank slowly up to installation position and secure it.

27. To mount the fuel tank tension straps, only screws with loose washers may be used. If other screws are used, the tension straps could twist when the screws are tightened.

28. Tighten the new screws on the tension straps and the new screw to 19 ft. lbs. (25 Nm).

29. Tighten the bolts for the fuel filler tube to 71 inch lbs. (8 Nm) plus 90° further.

30. Installation is performed in reverse order of removal.

31. Make sure vent and fuel lines are not kinked.

32. Check Ground (GND) connection of tank/chassis at filler tube.

33. Make sure lines connections are securely fastened.

34. After installing fuel tank, check that the supply and breather lines are still clipped onto the fuel tank.

IDLE SPEED

ADJUSTMENT

Idle speed is automatically controlled by the Electronic Control Module (ECM). No adjustment is possible.

THROTTLE BODY

REMOVAL & INSTALLATION

2.0L & 2.5L Engines

1. Loosen the hose clamp.
2. Remove bolt.
3. Disconnect electrical connector.
4. Remove the noise insulation.
5. Remove the air guide pipe.
6. Remove the bolt and remove the air guide pipe downward.
7. Disconnect electrical connector on throttle valve control module.
8. Remove bolts and remove throttle valve control module.

To install:

9. Installation is performed in reverse order of removal.
10. Clean O-ring sealing surface.
11. Replace the seal; when doing so, pay attention to the correct position of the service flag on the sealing ring.
12. Tighten bolts in crisscross pattern to 31 inch lbs. (3.5 Nm).

> ❊❊ **CAUTION**
>
> **If a new throttle valve control module was installed, adapt the engine control module to the throttle valve control module.**

FUEL   DIESEL FUEL INJECTION SYSTEM

FUEL SYSTEM SERVICE PRECAUTIONS

Safety is the most important factor when performing not only fuel system maintenance but any type of maintenance. Failure to conduct maintenance and repairs in a safe manner may result in serious personal injury or death. Maintenance and testing of the vehicle's fuel system components can be accomplished safely and effectively by adhering to the following rules and guidelines.

• To avoid the possibility of fire and personal injury, always disconnect the negative battery cable unless the repair or test procedure requires that battery voltage be applied.

• Always relieve the fuel system pressure prior to disconnecting any fuel system component (injector, fuel rail, pressure regulator, etc.), fitting or fuel line connection. Exercise extreme caution whenever relieving fuel system pressure to avoid exposing skin, face and eyes to fuel spray. Please be advised that fuel under pressure may penetrate the skin or any part of the body that it contacts.

• Always place a shop towel or cloth around the fitting or connection prior to loosening to absorb any excess fuel due to spillage. Ensure that all fuel spillage (should it occur) is quickly removed from engine surfaces. Ensure that all fuel soaked cloths or towels are deposited into a suitable waste container.

• Always keep a dry chemical (Class B) fire extinguisher near the work area.

• Do not allow fuel spray or fuel vapors to come into contact with a spark or open flame.

• Always use a back-up wrench when loosening and tightening fuel line connection fittings. This will prevent unnecessary stress and torsion to fuel line piping.

• Always replace worn fuel fitting O-rings with new. Do not substitute fuel hose or equivalent where fuel pipe is installed.

Before servicing the vehicle, make sure to also refer to the precautions in the beginning of this section as well.

RELIEVING FUEL SYSTEM PRESSURE

Fuel pump is activated with switching on the ignition and by door contact switch of driver's door. For safety, disconnect the electrical connector from fuel delivery unit before opening fuel supply system, if the battery is not disconnected.

FUEL FILTER

REMOVAL & INSTALLATION

2.0L TDI Engine

See Figures 133 and 134.

> ❊❊ **CAUTION**
>
> **Fuel pump is activated with switching on the ignition and by door contact switch of driver's door. For safety, disconnect the electrical connector from fuel delivery unit before opening fuel supply system, if the battery is not disconnected.**

1. On fuel filter without the retaining plate, release the clips and remove the fuel filter with the hoses still connected from the retaining plate.
2. On fuel filter with the retaining plate:
   a. Loosen the bolt one turn.
   b. Remove the bolt and the nut.
   c. Remove the fuel filter with the hoses still connected.

To install:

3. Installation is the reverse of removal.

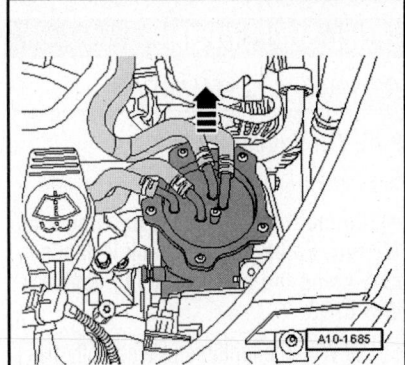

Fig. 133 On fuel filter without the retaining plate, release the clips and remove the fuel filter with the hoses still connected from the retaining plate (arrow)

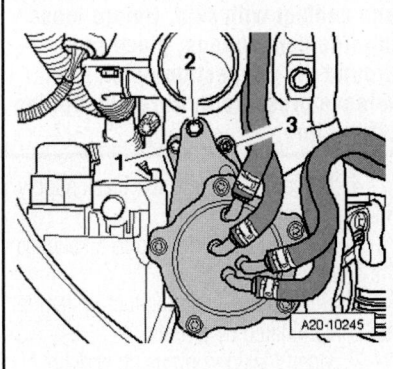

Fig. 134 Loosen the bolt (1) one turn, remove the bolt (2) and the nut (3)

FUEL SYSTEM PURGING

BLEEDING

2.0L TDI Engine

See Figure 136.

1. Connect the diesel extractor VAS 5226 or the hand vacuum pump to the

draining container V.A.G 1390/1 on the return hose.

2. Operate the diesel extractor or the hand vacuum pump, until fuel comes out of the return hose. Make sure no fuel gets into the hand vacuum pump.

INJECTION TIMING

ADJUSTMENT

2.0L TDI Engine

Injection timing is automatically controlled by the Electronic Control Module (ECM). No adjustment is possible.

FUEL SUPPLY PUMP

REMOVAL & INSTALLATION

2.0L TDI Engine

See Figure 135.

➡The fuel tank may be a maximum of 1/2 full. Empty the fuel tank if necessary using the fuel extracting device VAS 5190.

1. With the ignition switched off, disconnect Ground (GND) wire to the battery.
2. Remove seat bench.
3. Unclip cover for fuel delivery unit.

✳✳ CAUTION

The fuel supply line is under pressure. Wear protective goggles and protective clothing to prevent injuries and contact with skin. Before loosening line connections, place rags around the connection point. Then release pressure by carefully pulling off the line.

4. Disconnect connector, black supply line and blue return line.
5. Press in securing ring to disengage the fuel lines.
6. Seal lines so that the fuel system is not contaminated by dirt etc.
7. Open locking ring using wrench T10202.
8. Remove fuel delivery unit and gasket from the fuel tank opening.

➡If the fuel delivery unit is to be replaced then drain old delivery unit before disposal.

To install:

9. Install in order of removal.
10. When inserting fuel delivery unit into fuel tank, be sure not to bend Fuel Level Sensor.
11. Replace fuel delivery unit gasket if

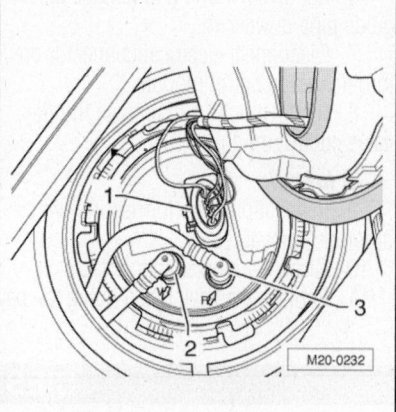

Fig. 135 Disconnect connector (1), black supply line (2) and blue return line (3)

damaged and insert it in the fuel tank opening dry.

12. Only coat seal with fuel when installing fuel delivery unit.
13. Note installation position of fuel delivery unit flange.
14. Route fuel lines kink-free.
15. Do not interchange supply and return line (return line blue, supply line black).
16. Make sure lines connections are securely fastened.
17. Observe notes after connecting the battery.

INJECTION PUMP

REMOVAL & INSTALLATION

2.0L TDI Engine

See Figure 136.

1. Turn the ignition and all electrical consumers off and remove the ignition key.
2. Remove engine cover.
   a. On one piece engine cover, pull the one piece front engine cover upward with a quick jerk and then pull the lower mount forward.
   b. On the two piece engine cover, first pull the outer cover upward with a quick jerk, then pull the inner engine cover upward with a quick jerk.
3. Disconnect electrical harness connector at Mass Air Flow (MAF) sensor.
4. Disconnect the ventilation hose and disengage it from the bracket.
5. Open the spring-type clip using spring-type clip pliers VAS 5024A and disconnect the intake hose from the Mass Air Flow (MAF) sensor.
6. Disconnect the intake manifold from the air guide.

7. Unfasten bolt and remove air filter housing and mass air flow sensor.
8. Carefully cut the cable tie.
9. Open the wiring bracket and disengage the wiring harness.
10. Remove both bolts s from the upper charge air pipe.
11. Remove noise insulation.
12. Remove the charge air pipe bolt from the oil pan.

✳✳ CAUTION

The fuel or fuel lines in fuel system can become very hot. In addition, the fuel system is under pressure. Before opening the system, place rags around the connection area and release pressure by carefully loosening the connection. Wear protective goggles and protective gloves when working on the fuel system.

13. Pull off the supply hose (white marking) and the return hose (blue marking) from the fuel filter.
14. Connect the diesel extractor VAS 5226 or the hand vacuum pump to the draining container V.A.G 1390/1 on the return hose.
15. Operate the diesel extractor or the hand vacuum pump, until fuel stops coming out of the return hose. Make sure no fuel gets into the hand vacuum pump.
16. Disconnect vacuum line of brake booster from tandem pump.
17. Disconnect supply hose (white marking) and return hose (blue marking) from tandem pump.
18. Remove mounting bolts.
19. Remove tandem pump from cylinder head.

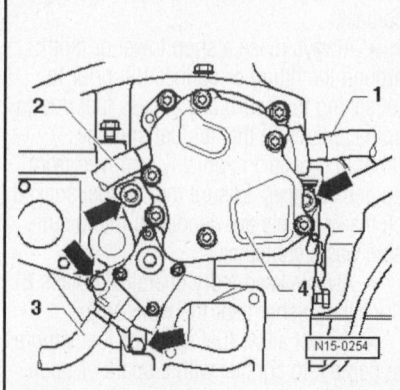

Fig. 136 Disconnect vacuum line of brake booster (1), disconnect supply hose (2) (white marking) and return hose (3) (blue marking) from tandem pump (4). Remove mounting bolts (arrows)

To install:

20. Installation is performed in reverse order.

❄❄ CAUTION

Make sure that tandem pump coupling has proper seating in camshaft.

➡**Tandem pump gasket must always be replaced.**

21. Install the tandem pump and tighten the upper bolts to 15 ft. lbs. (20 Nm).
22. Tighten the lower bolts to 89 inch lbs. (10 Nm).
23. Connect the return hose (blue marking) to the return connection on the tandem pump.
24. Connect the supply hose (white marking) to supply connection and the vacuum line from the brake booster to the tandem pump.
25. Connect the supply hose (white marking) to the fuel filter.
26. Connect the diesel extractor VAS 5226 or the hand vacuum pump to the draining container V.A.G 1390/1 on the return hose.
27. Operate the diesel extractor or the hand vacuum pump, until fuel comes out of the return hose. Make sure no fuel gets into the hand vacuum pump.
28. Connect the return hose (blue marking) to the fuel filter.

INJECTION TIMING

2.0L TDI Engine

Injection timing is automatically controlled by the Electronic Control Module (ECM). No adjustment is possible.

GLOW PLUGS

REMOVAL & INSTALLATION

2.0L TDI Engine

Ceramic

1. Turn the ignition and all electrical consumers off and remove the ignition key.
2. Remove engine cover.
   a. On one piece engine cover, pull the one piece front engine cover s upward with a quick jerk and then pull the lower mount forward.
   b. On the two piece engine cover, first pull the outer cover upward with a quick jerk, then pull the inner engine cover upward with a quick jerk.
3. Disconnect glow plug connectors from glow plugs.
4. Remove ceramic sheathed element glow plugs using flex wrench 3220.

To install:

5. Installation is performed in reverse order.
6. Cylinder head bore and thread must be completely cleaned of deposits before installing.

➡**Never oil or grease thread of bore in cylinder head and ceramic sheathed element glow plugs.**

7. Screw ceramic sheathed element glow plugs into cylinder head by hand using flex wrench.
8. Install the glow plugs with the hinged socket 3220 and tighten them to 11 ft. lbs. (15 Nm).

Metal

1. Turn the ignition and all electrical consumers off and remove the ignition key.
2. Remove engine cover.
   a. On one piece engine cover, pull the one piece front engine cover s upward with a quick jerk and then pull the lower mount forward.
   b. On the two piece engine cover, first pull the outer cover upward with a quick jerk, then pull the inner engine cover upward with a quick jerk.
3. Disconnect glow plug connectors from glow plugs.
4. Remove the glow plugs using flex wrench 3220.

To install:

5. Installation is the reverse of removal.
6. Install the glow plugs with the hinged socket
7. Tighten 11 ft. lbs. (15 Nm).

HEATING & AIR CONDITIONING SYSTEM

BLOWER MOTOR

REMOVAL & INSTALLATION

➡**Fresh Air Blower is accessible from foot well on front passenger side.**

1. Remove partition from heating unit.
2. Unscrew plastic screws and remove partition.
3. Disconnect harness connector from Fresh Air Blower.
4. Unscrew bolts for Fresh Air Blower.
5. Release catch and rotate Fresh Air Blower.
6. Remove Fresh Air Blower from heating unit.

To install:

7. Install in reverse order of removal.
8. Tighten bolts/nuts.

HEATER CORE

REMOVAL & INSTALLATION

1. Remove facing wall in plenum chamber.
2. Place drip tray under the engine.

❄❄ CAUTION

Contact with hot engine coolant can cause severe scalding. Coolant temperature can be above 212°F (100°C) with a warm engine. The cooling system is under pressure. If necessary, reduce pressure and temperature before repairs.

3. Clamp off coolant hoses using hose clamps and disconnect coolant hoses to heater core.
4. Connect a section of hose onto upper connection of heater core.
5. Hold a container under the lower connection.

6. Using a compressed air gun, carefully blow coolant out of heater core into container.
7. Loosen (do not unscrew completely) bolt out of connection flange between heater core connections.
8. This allows the coolant pipes to move for removing the heater core.
9. Remove driver side foot well trim.
10. Remove left foot well vent.
11. Remove screws and remove heater core trim.
12. Cover floor carpet in area below heater core with leak-proof foil and absorbent paper.
13. Open hose clamps A and disconnect coolant pipes.
14. Remove heater core from heating unit.

To install:

15. Installation is carried out in the reverse order.

16. Check seals installed on heater core, only install a heater core with undamaged seals.

17. An incorrectly glued seal can roll up into heating unit when sliding in the heater core.

18. Cold air may flow past heat exchanger if seal is damaged or not properly installed.

19. With the heater core removed, check heating unit for soiling (via heater core opening).

20. If necessary, remove dirt or coolant from heating unit, for example after removing leaky heater core.

21. Push heater core into heating unit.

22. Coat sealing rings with coolant before installing.

23. Insert sealing rings into connection on coolant pipe.

24. If hose clamps are deformed, replace them.

25. Connect coolant pipes.

26. Hose clamps must be able to be twisted slightly when installing onto the coolant pipes.

27. Tighten hose clamps.

28. Check seating of both clamps after tightening bolts, clamps must enclose the flange on coolant pipe completely and must not touch other components.

29. Tighten the screw from the connecting flange between heater core connections.

30. Check position of grommet in bulkhead for proper seating.

31. Seal the flange for coolant pipes to heater core and for expansion valve (to evaporator, only in vehicles with A/C system) at pass-through of grommet with silicone adhesive sealant if necessary (to prevent water from penetrating).

32. Sealing rings must always be replaced.

33. If hose clamps are deformed, replace them.

34. After replacing heater core, coolant must be replaced completely.

35. Check coolant circuit for leaks, pay particular attention between coolant pipes and heater core.

36. Tighten bolts/nuts to specification as follows:
   - Hose clamps: 18 inch lbs. (2.0 Nm)
   - Heater core connections to: 18 inch lbs. (2.0 Nm)

STEERING

POWER STEERING GEAR

REMOVAL & INSTALLATION

Eos & Golf

See Figure 137.

1. Disconnect battery.

2. Remove foot well trim, remove nuts to do so.

3. Remove bolt and pull off universal joint from steering gear.

4. Remove front wheels.

5. Loosen tie rod end nut, but do not remove yet.

❋❋ CAUTION

To protect thread, screw nut on pin a few turns.

6. Press tie rod end off of wheel bearing housing using Ball Joint Puller 3287A.

7. Remove lower noise insulation.

8. Remove pendulum support from transmission.

9. Remove bracket for exhaust system from subframe.

10. Remove bolts from heat shield.

11. Remove heat shield from subframe.

12. Now remove the indicated bolts for the steering gear and stabilizer bar.

13. Locate subframe and brackets. Subframe and Brackets, Securing

14. Place Engine/Transmission Jack VAG1383A under subframe.

15. Place a block of wood between the jack and the subframe.

16. Loosen bolts and lower subframe with brackets slightly. Observe electrical wires, when doing so.

17. Remove heat shield above steering gear.

18. Remove bolts.

19. Remove cable guide from subframe.

20. Unclip all other cable securing points on steering gear.

21. Disconnect all electrical connections from steering gear.

22. Lower subframe with the jack until steering gear can be removed.

23. Lay steering gear aside. This avoids damages on control module.

To install:

24. Installation is in reverse order of removal.

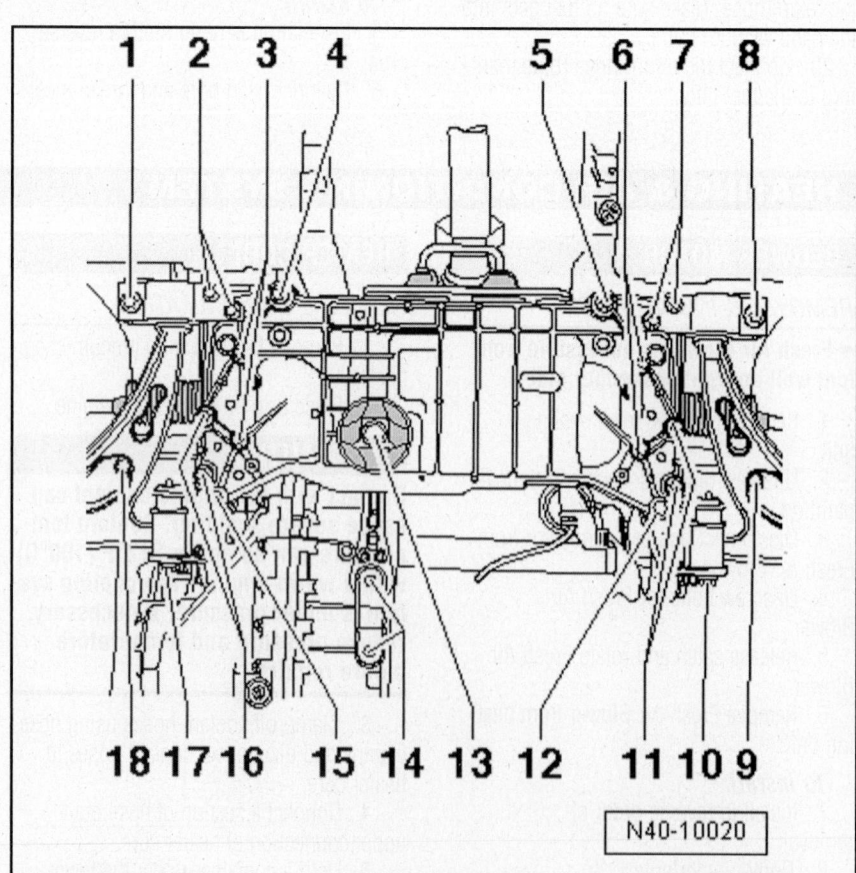

N40-10020

Fig. 137 Remove bolts 3, 6, 11 and 16 (as shown) for the steering gear and stabilizer bar.

➡**The steering gear threaded sleeves must be seated in the bracket holes.**

25. Coat seal on steering gear with lubricant, e.g. soft soap, before installing steering gear.

26. After attaching steering gear to drive shaft, make sure that seal on steering gear is positioned to mounting plate without kinks and opening to foot well is sealed correctly. Ingress of water and/or noises may be the result.

27. Make sure sealing surfaces are clean.

Before fastening the bolts for subframe, position steering gear on subframe and fasten bolts for steering gear and stabilizer.

28. Clamp off electrical connections to the steering gear.

29. Install lower noise insulation.

30. Ensure that boot is not damaged or twisted.

31. Universal joint to steering gear.

32. Connect battery.

33. Perform Steering Angle Sensor basic setting with the Vehicle Diagnosis, Testing and Information System VAS 5051

34. After installation, position of steering wheel must be checked with a road test.

35. If the steering wheel is crooked or new steering gear was installed, the toe on the front axle must be checked and adjusted if necessary.

36. Align vehicle.

37. If new steering gear was installed, Power Steering Control Module must be adapted using Vehicle Diagnosis, Testing and Information System.

38. If parking assist is installed in the vehicle, the Power Steering Control Module must be recoded after installing new steering gear.

➡**Parking assist is only in installed vehicles with Generation II steering gear.**

39. Tighten bolts/nuts to specification as follows:

- Subframe to body (Use new bolts): 52 ft. lbs. (70 Nm), plus 90° rotation
- Stabilizer bar to subframe (Use new bolts): 15 ft. lbs. (20 Nm), plus 90° rotation
- Stabilizer bar to connecting link (Use new bolts and counterhold at joint pin inner multi-point fitting): 48 ft. lbs. (65 Nm)
- Ball joint to control arm (Use new nut): 44 ft. lbs. (60 Nm)
- Shield to subframe (M6 bolt is self-tapping) 53 inch lbs. (6 Nm)

- Steering gear to subframe (Use new bolts) 37 ft. lbs. (50 Nm), plus 90° rotation
- Universal joint to steering gear (Use new bolt): 22 ft. lbs. (30 Nm)
- Shield to steering gear (M6 bolt is self-tapping) 53 inch lbs. (6 Nm)
- Tie rod end to wheel bearing housing (Use new nut): 15 ft. lbs. (20 Nm), plus 90° rotation

Tiguan

See Figure 138.

1. Disconnect battery.

2. Remove nuts and remove foot well trim.

3. Remove the bolt and remove the universal joint from the steering gear.

4. Remove front wheels.

5. Loosen the tie rod to wheel bearing housing nut, but do not remove yet.

➡**To protect threads, leave nut on stud a few turns.**

6. Press tie rod end off wheel bearing housing using ball joint puller 3287A and remove nut.

7. Remove lower noise insulation.

8. Remove coupling rods from stabilizer bar.

9. Remove the ball joint nuts.

10. Remove pendulum support from transmission.

11. Remove exhaust system bracket bolts and bracket from the subframe.

12. On vehicles with FWD, remove the heat shield bolts.

13. Remove heat shield from subframe.

14. Remove steering gear bolts.

15. Remove the stabilizer bar bolts.

16. Locate the subframe.

17. Disconnect the connector for the service interval extension to the oil pan.

18. Place the engine and transmission jack V.A.G 1383 A under the subframe.

19. Place, for example, a piece of wood 1 between the engine and transmission jack and subframe.

20. Remove the bolts and slightly lower the subframe. Pay attention the electrical wiring while doing this.

21. Remove the heat shield bolts and shield from above exhaust system.

22. Remove bolts.

23. Remove cable guide from subframe.

24. Unclip all other cable mounting points on steering gear.

25. Disconnect the connectors from the steering gear.

26. Carefully lower subframe using the engine and transmission jack.

27. Lift stabilizer bar toward the front, over the subframe and down, and slightly turn stabilizer bar while doing so.

28. Lift steering gear down from subframe.

29. Lay steering gear aside, as to not damage the control module.

To install:

30. Installation is performed in the reverse order of removal.

31. Make sure the white pressure membrane is clean and not damaged.

32. If necessary, carefully clean the pressure membrane.

33. If the pressure membrane is damaged, then the steering gear must be replaced.

34. Connect the connectors so that they audibly click into place.

➡**The threaded sleeve must seat in subframe hole.**

35. Coat seal on steering gear with lubricant, e.g. soft soap, before installing steering gear.

36. After placing steering gear on to universal joint, make sure that seal on steering gear makes contact on assembly plate without kinks and opening to foot well is correctly sealed. Ingress of water and/or noises may be the result.

37. Make sure sealing surfaces are clean.

➡**Before attaching the subframe bolts, position the steering gear on the subframe and attach the steering gear bolts and stabilizer bar.**

38. Install lower noise insulation.

39. Install the universal joint to steering gear.

40. Connect battery.

41. Perform a basic setting on the steering angle sensor using the vehicle diagnosis, testing and information system.

42. After installation, position of steering wheel must be checked with a road test.

43. If steering wheel is crooked or new steering gear was installed, vehicle alignment must be performed.

44. If the vehicle is equipped with park assist, then the power steering control module must be re-coded.

45. Tighten bolts/nuts to specification as follows:

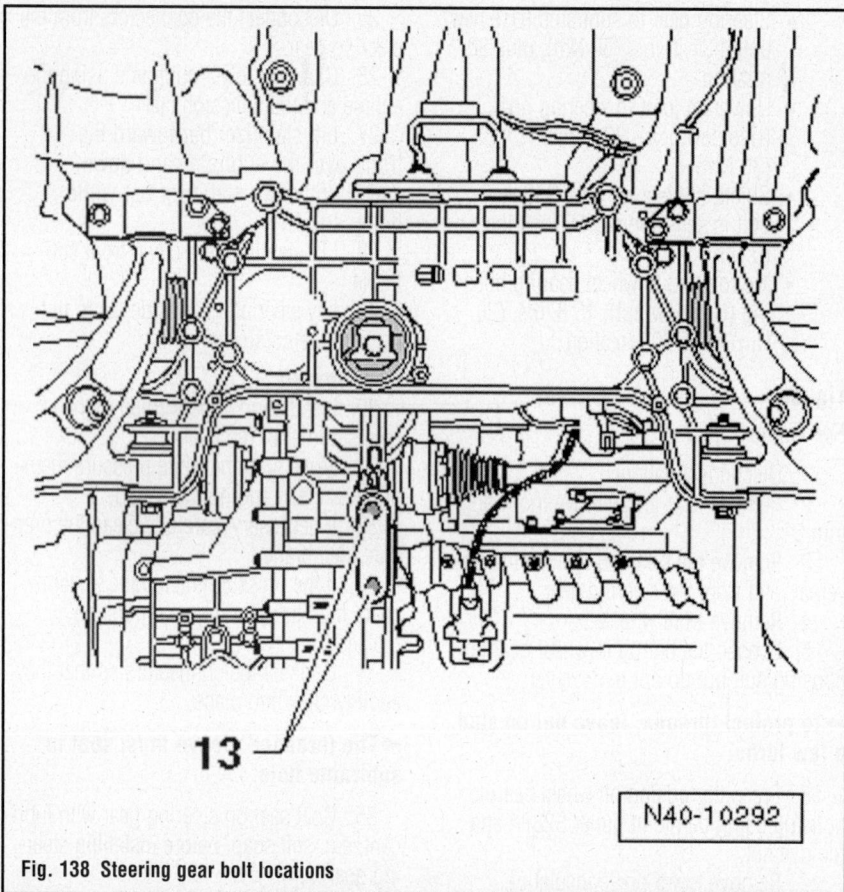

Fig. 138 Steering gear bolt locations

N40-10292

- Mounting bracket to body (use new bolts): 52 ft. lbs. (70 Nm), plus 180° additional turn
- Stabilizer bar to subframe (use new bolts): 15 ft. lbs. (20 Nm), plus 90° additional turn
- Stabilizer bar to coupling rod (use new nut and counter hold at joint pin inner multi point fitting): 48 ft. lbs. (65 Nm)
- Ball joint to control arm (use new nut): 44 ft. lbs. (60 Nm)
- Shield to subframe (M6 bolt is self-tapping): 53 inch lbs. (6 Nm)
- Steering gear to subframe (use new bolts): 37 ft. lbs. (50 Nm), plus 90° additional turn
- Universal joint to steering gear (use new bolt): 22 ft. lbs. (30 Nm)
- Shield to steering gear (M6 bolt is self-tapping): 53 inch lbs. (6 Nm)
- Tie rod end to wheel bearing housing (use new nut): 37 ft. lbs. (50 Nm)

POWER STEERING PUMP

REMOVAL & INSTALLATION

The power steering pump is electro-mechanical and is an integral part of the power steering gear.

SUSPENSION

LOWER BALL JOINT

REMOVAL & INSTALLATION

1. Loosen the drive axle to wheel hub bolt.
2. Remove the wheel.
3. Remove the ball joint nuts.
4. Pull the drive axle out of the wheel hub slightly.
5. Remove the ball joint from the control arm and at the same time swivel the wheel bearing housing to the outside.
6. Move the control arm downward as far as possible.
7. Install the ball joint remover VAG 3287A and press out the ball joint.

➡Place the remover, underneath (risk of accident if components fall off when pressing out ball joint).

➡To protect the ball joint threads, leave the nut on a few turns.

To install:

8. Tighten bolts/nuts to specification as follows:
   - Ball joint to steel control arm (use new nuts): 44 ft. lbs. (60 Nm)

- Ball joint to sheet steel or aluminum control arm (use new nuts): 74 ft. lbs. (100 Nm)
- Ball joint to wheel bearing housing (use new nut): 44 ft. lbs. (60 Nm)
- Drive axle to wheel hub "hex head bolt" (use new bolt): 148 ft. lbs. (200 Nm), plus an additional 180° rotation
- Drive axle to wheel hub "12-point bolt" (use new bolt): 52 ft. lbs. (70 Nm), plus an additional 90° rotation

9. Pull the drive axle out of the wheel hub.
10. Install the ball joint into the wheel bearing housing.
11. Install a new self-locking nut, counter hold the stud using a T40 Torx®.
12. Install the drive axle to the wheel hub.
13. Install and tighten the ball joint nuts.

➡Make sure that the ball joint boot is not damaged or twisted.

14. Install the wheel.
15. Tighten the drive axle to wheel hub bolt.

FRONT SUSPENSION

LOWER CONTROL ARM

REMOVAL AND & INSTALLATION

See Figure 137.

1. Remove wheel.
2. Remove lower noise insulation.
3. Remove nuts.
4. Pull control arm out of lower ball joint.
5. Locate position for mounting bracket.
6. Replace bolts 1 and 8 using locating pins T10096 and tighten locating pins to 15 ft. lbs. (20 Nm).

✱✱ CAUTION

Locating pins must only be tightened to maximum of 15 ft. lbs. (20 Nm); otherwise threads of locating pins may be damaged.

7. Remove bolts 10 and 17.

To install:

8. Install control arm with mounting bracket into subframe.
9. Install items 10 and 17, but do not tighten.

10. Install bolts and tighten.

11. Now replace locating pin with a new bolt and tighten it to tightening torque.

12. Bolt control arm onto ball joint.

13. Bolt control arm onto bracket in curb weight position.

14. Further installation is in reverse sequence to removal.

15. Ensure that boot is not damaged or twisted.

16. Install lower noise insulation.

17. Install wheel.

18. Tighten bolts/nuts to specification as follows:

- Mounting bracket to body (use new bolts): 52 ft. lbs. (70 Nm), plus an additional 90° rotation
- Mounting bracket to body (use new bolts) : 52 ft. lbs. (70 Nm), plus an additional 90° rotation
- Ball joint to control arm (use new nuts): 44 ft. lbs. (60 Nm)
- Control arm to bracket (use new bolt and tighten bolts at normal ride height): 52 ft. lbs. (70 Nm), plus 180° rotation

MACPHERSON STRUT

REMOVAL & INSTALLATION

1. Loosen the drive axle to wheel hub bolt.

2. Remove the wheel.

3. Remove the level control system sensor from the control arm.

4. Remove the coupling rod nut and remove the coupling rod from the strut.

5. Remove the ball joint nuts.

6. Remove the wheel bearing housing with ball joint from the control arm.

7. Remove the drive axle from the wheel hub.

8. Secure the drive axle to body using wire.

✳✳ CAUTION

The drive axle must not hang down; otherwise the inner Constant Velocity (CV) joint may be damaged when bent too far.

9. Install the ball joint to the control arm again.

10. Secure the VAG 1383 with the T10149 to the wheel hub using one wheel bolt.

11. Remove the wheel bearing housing/strut pinch bolt nut.

12. Insert the 3424 into the slot in the wheel bearing housing.

13. Install a ratchet to the 3424 and turn it 90°, opening the slot in the wheel bearing

housing, then remove the ratchet from the 3424.

14. Press the brake disc in the direction of the strut by hand.

Otherwise the strut tube may be tilted in the wheel bearing housing.

15. Pull the wheel bearing housing downward from the strut tube and lower using the VAG 1383A until the strut tube hangs free.

16. Secure the wheel bearing housing to the subframe with wire.

17. Remove the VAG 1383A from the below wheel bearing housing.

18. When removing the left strut, remove the wiper arms.

19. Remove the plenum chamber cover.

20. Remove the bolts from the strut dome and remove the strut.

To install:

21. Secure the VAG 1383A with the T10149 to the wheel hub using one wheel bolt.

22. Install the strut to the wheel bearing housing and secure the strut using and a new pinch bolt and nut.

➡ **Bolt tip must point in direction of rotation vehicle travel.**

23. Remove the 3424 from the wheel bearing housing.

➡ **One of two markings on the strut bearing must point in direction of rotation vehicle travel.**

24. Remove the wire securing the wheel bearing housing.

25. Carefully lift the wheel bearing housing using the VAG 1383A far enough until the bolts for the strut can be installed.

➡ **If necessary, use ladder, for example VAS 5085 to install the bolts.**

26. Tighten the strut to strut dome bolts.

27. Remove the T10149.

28. Tighten the wheel bearing housing/strut pinch bolt nut.

29. Remove the ball joint nuts again.

30. Install the drive axle to the wheel hub.

31. Install the wheel bearing housing with ball joint to the control arm.

32. Install the ball joint to control arm nuts.

➡ **Make sure that the ball joint boot is not damaged or twisted.**

33. Tighten the drive axle to wheel hub bolt.

➡ **When doing this, the vehicle must not rest on the ground, otherwise the wheel bearing could be damaged.**

34. Install the plenum chamber cover.

35. Install the wiper arms, if required.

36. Install the wheel.

37. Tighten bolts/nuts to specification as follows:

- Strut to wheel bearing housing (use new nut): 52 ft. lbs. (70 Nm), plus 90° additional rotation
- Strut to body (strut dome) (use new bolts): 11 ft. lbs. (15 Nm), plus 90° additional rotation
- Ball joint to steel control arm (use new nuts): 44 ft. lbs. (60 Nm)
- Coupling rod to strut (use new nut and counter hold at inner joint multi point stud): 48 ft. lbs. (65 Nm)
- Drive axle to wheel hub "hex head bolt" (use new bolt): 148 ft. lbs. (200 Nm), plus an additional 180° rotation
- Drive axle to wheel hub "12-point bolt" (use new bolt): 52 ft. lbs. (70 Nm), plus an additional 90° rotation

OVERHAUL

1. Fit the strut into spring compressor V.A.G 1752/1 and compress the spring until upper axial groove ball bearing is free.

✳✳ CAUTION

First pre-load spring far enough so that tension is relieved on upper spring retainer!

2. Make sure that coil spring is seated correctly in the tool.

3. Remove hex nut from top of piston rod.

4. Remove components of suspension strut and coil spring.

To install:

5. Place coil spring with spring compressor V.A.G 1752/1 on lower spring plate. End of spring coil must rest against the stop in the spring seat.

6. Install a new self-locking hex nut onto piston rod and torque to 45 ft. lbs. (60 Nm).

7. Carefully relieve tension on spring compressor V.A.G 1752/1 and remove from coil spring.

STABILIZER BAR

REMOVAL & INSTALLATION

1. Remove front wheels.

2. Remove foot well trim, remove nuts to do so.

3. Remove bolt and pull off universal joint from steering gear.

4. Remove lower noise insulation.
5. Remove coupling rods from stabilizer.
6. Remove nuts.
7. Loosen tie rod end nut on both sides, but do not remove yet.

➡ **To protect thread, screw nut on pin a few turns.**

8. Press off tie rod end from wheel bearing housing using ball joint puller 3287A.
9. Secure subframe with brackets.
10. Remove stabilizer from subframe.
11. Remove pendulum support from transmission.
12. Place engine/transmission jack V.A.G 1383 A below subframe.
13. Place, for example, a piece of wood between engine/transmission jack V.A.G 1383 A and subframe.
14. Loosen bolts and lower subframe with brackets slightly. Observe electrical wires, when doing so.
15. Now, lift stabilizer bar toward front, over bracket and down from subframe.

To install:
16. Installation is in reverse order of removal.
17. Coat seal on steering gear with lubricant, e.g. soft soap, before installing steering gear.
18. After attaching steering gear to drive axle, make sure that seal on steering gear is positioned to mounting plate without kinks and opening to foot well is sealed correctly. Ingress of water and/or noises may be the result.
19. Make sure sealing surfaces are clean.
20. Install lower noise insulation
21. Install front wheels.
22. Tighten bolts/nuts to specification as follows:
- Subframe to body (use new bolts): 52 ft. lbs. (70 Nm), plus 90° rotation
- Bracket to body (use new bolts): 52 ft. lbs. (70 Nm), plus 90° rotation
- Mounting bracket to body (use new bolts): 52 ft. lbs. (70 Nm), plus 90° rotation
- Subframe to bracket (use new bolts): 52 ft. lbs. (70 Nm), plus 90° rotation
- Ball joint to control arm (use new nut): 44 ft. lbs. (60 Nm)
- Stabilizer bar to subframe (use new bolts): 15 ft. lbs. (20 Nm), plus 90° rotation
- Stabilizer bar to connecting link (use new bolts and counterhold at joint pin inner multi-point fitting): 48 ft. lbs. (65 Nm)

- Control arm to bracket (use new bolts and tighten bracket in curb weight position): 52 ft. lbs. (70 Nm), plus 90° rotation
- Steering gear to subframe (use new bolts): 37 ft. lbs. (50 Nm) plus 90° rotation
- Universal joint to steering gear (use new bolt): 22 ft. lbs. (30 Nm)

STEERING KNUCKLE

REMOVAL & INSTALLATION

1. Loosen drive axle bolt to wheel hub.

✳✳ CAUTION

When doing this, vehicle must not stand on wheels, otherwise wheel bearing may be damaged.

2. Remove wheel.
3. Remove brake caliper and engage on body with wire.
4. Remove ABS wheel speed sensor.
5. Remove disc brake.
6. Remove cover plate from wheel bearing housing.
7. Loosen tie rod end nut, but do not remove yet.

➡ **To protect thread, screw nut on pin a few turns.**

8. Press off tie rod end from wheel bearing housing with ball joint puller 3287A and then remove nut.
9. Press drive axle out of wheel hub (in direction of transmission) as far as possible.
10. Remove wheel bearing housing/suspension strut bolt connection.
11. Insert spreader 3424 into wheel bearing housing slot.
12. Turn ratchet around 90° and remove from spreader 3424.
13. Loosen nuts.
14. Place engine/transmission jack V.A.G 1383 beneath wheel bearing housing.
15. First, press off ball joint from control arm, then pull off wheel bearing housing from suspension strut.

To install:
16. Installation is reverse of removal.
17. Tighten drive axle bolt to wheel hub. When doing this, vehicle must not stand on wheels; otherwise wheel bearing may be damaged.

➡ **If wheel bearing housing was replaced, vehicle alignment must be performed.**

18. Install wheel.

19. Tighten bolts/nuts to specification as follows:
- Strut to wheel bearing housing (use new nut): 52 ft. lbs. (70 Nm), plus 90° additional rotation
- Ball joint to steel control arm (use new nuts): 44 ft. lbs. (60 Nm)
- Tie rod end to wheel bearing housing (use new nuts): 15 ft. lbs. (20 Nm), plus 90° additional rotation
- Drive axle to wheel hub "hex head bolt" (use new bolt): 148 ft. lbs. (200 Nm), plus an additional 180° rotation
- Drive axle to wheel hub "12-point bolt" (use new bolt): 52 ft. lbs. (70 Nm), plus an additional 90° rotation

WHEEL BEARINGS

REMOVAL & INSTALLATION

1. Loosen drive axle bolt to wheel hub.

✳✳ CAUTION

When doing this, vehicle must not stand on wheels, otherwise wheel bearing may be damaged.

2. Remove wheel.
3. Remove brake caliper and engage on body with wire.
4. Remove ABS wheel speed sensor.
5. Remove disc brake.
6. Press drive axle out of wheel hub (in direction of transmission) as far as possible.
7. Remove bolts.
8. Remove wheel bearing unit from wheel bearing housing.

To install:
9. Installation is in reverse order of removal.
10. Install brake caliper.
11. Tighten drive axle bolt to wheel hub.
12. When doing this, vehicle must not stand on wheels, otherwise wheel bearing may be damaged.
13. Install ABS wheel speed sensor.
14. Install wheel.
15. Tighten bolts/nuts to specification as follows:
- Drive axle to wheel hub "hex head bolt" (Use new bolt): 148 ft. lbs. (200 Nm) plus an additional 180° rotation
- Drive axle to wheel hub "12-point bolt" (Use new bolt): 52 ft. lbs. (70 Nm) plus an additional 90° rotation
- Wheel hub with wheel bearing to wheel bearing housing (Use new nut): 52 ft. lbs. (70 Nm) plus 90° additional rotation

SUSPENSION

COIL SPRING

REMOVAL & INSTALLATION

See Figure 139.

1. Remove wheel.
2. Insert spring compressor.

✳✳ CAUTION

Be sure coil spring is properly seated in spring holder V.A.G 1752/4 2.

3. Use wrench or ratchet for tightening spring compressor.
4. Compress coil spring until it can be removed.
5. Remove spring using the following:
   - Spring holder V.A.G 1752/4
   - Adapter V.A.G 1752/9
   - Spring compressor V.A.G 1752/1

To install:

✳✳ CAUTION

The spring start must touch bottom of spring seat.

6. Install spring together with spring seat.
7. Lower spring support has a pin.
8. Insert this pin into hole of lower transverse link.
9. Then insert upper spring support into upper end of spring.
10. Release tension of spring, guiding upper spring support onto tab of body.
11. Remove spring tensioner.
12. Install wheel.

LOWER CONTROL ARM

REMOVAL & INSTALLATION

1. Measure the dimension from the wheel center to the lower edge of the wheel housing.
2. Remove the wheel.
3. Remove the coil spring.
4. Remove lower transverse link to wheel bearing housing bolt and nut.
5. With dynamic vertical headlamp aim control, remove the level control system sensor bolts from the lower transverse link.
6. Using a felt tip marker, mark the position of the eccentric bolt to the subframe.
7. Disengage and lower the rear exhaust system.
8. Remove the bolt, nut and washer.
9. Remove the lower transverse link.

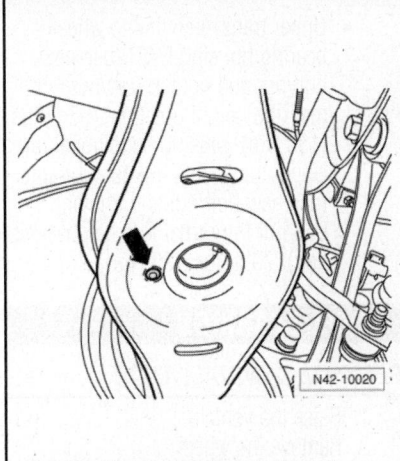

Fig. 139 The spring start must touch bottom of spring seat

To install:

10. Position the lower transverse link to the vehicle and install the bolts hand tight.

➡**Only tighten the lower transverse link bolts in normal ride height position.**

11. Install a new upper transverse link to subframe nut.
12. Align the eccentric bolt to the previously made mark on the subframe and tighten the nut.
13. Raise and engage the rear exhaust system.
14. With dynamic vertical headlight aim control, position and install the level control system sensor and bolts to the lower transverse link. Then tighten to 44 inch lbs. (5 Nm).
15. Hold the lower transverse link bolt and tighten the nut.
16. Install the coil spring.
17. Install the wheel.
18. Perform a vehicle alignment.
19. Tighten bolts/nuts to specification as follows:
   - Lower transverse link to wheel bearing housing (use new bolt/nut and tighten bolt/nut in normal ride height position): 66 ft. lbs. (90 Nm), plus 90° additional turn
   - Lower transverse link to subframe (use new bolt/nut and tighten bolt/nut in normal ride height position): 70 ft. lbs. (95 Nm)

STABILIZER BAR

REMOVAL & INSTALLATION

1. Remove the rear wheels.
2. Remove the coupling rod nut and

pull the coupling rod out of the stabilizer bar.

➡**Do NOT loosen the bolt for the tie rod.**

3. Remove the stabilizer bar clamp bolts.
4. Remove the stabilizer bar.

To install:

5. Tighten bolts/nuts to specification as follows:
   - Stabilizer bar clamp to subframe (use new bolts): 19 ft. lbs. (25 Nm), plus 45° additional turn
   - Stabilizer bar to coupling rod (use new nut): 33 ft. lbs. (45 Nm)
6. Install the stabilizer bar to the vehicle.
7. Tighten the stabilizer bar clamp bolts evenly.
8. Install the wheel.
9. Install the coupling rod to the stabilizer bar and tighten the nut.

SHOCK ABSORBER

REMOVAL & INSTALLATION

1. Remove wheel.
2. Remove wheel housing liner.
3. Remove coil spring.
4. Remove bolts.
5. Remove shock absorber.

To install:

6. Installation is in reverse order of removal.

➡**Only bolt on shock absorber to wheel bearing housing when vehicle is at normal ride height.**

7. Install shock absorber and tighten bolts.
8. Install coil spring.
9. Install wheel housing liner.
10. Install wheel.
11. Tighten bolts/nuts to specification as follows:
   - Shock absorber to body (use new bolt): 37 ft. lbs. (50 Nm), plus 45° additional rotation
   - Shock absorber to wheel bearing housing: 133 ft. lbs. (180 Nm)

UPPER CONTROL ARM

REMOVAL & INSTALLATION

1. Remove the wheel.
2. Remove the coil spring.
3. Remove the wire for the speed sensor from the upper transverse link.

4. Remove the upper transverse link to wheel bearing housing bolt.

5. Using a felt tip marker, mark the position of the eccentric bolt to the subframe.

6. Remove the bolt, nut and washer.

7. Remove upper transverse link.

To install:

8. Position the upper transverse link to the vehicle and install the bolts hand tight.

✳✳ CAUTION

Only tighten the upper transverse link bolts tighten bolt/nut in normal ride height position.

9. Install the new upper transverse link to subframe nut.

10. Align the eccentric bolt to the previously applied mark on the subframe and tighten the nut.

11. Tighten the new upper transverse link to wheel bearing housing bolt and nut.

✳✳ CAUTION

Make sure that washer is installed between the bolt and wheel bearing housing.

12. Secure the wire for the speed sensor to the upper transverse link.

13. Install the coil spring.

14. Install the wheel.

15. Perform a vehicle alignment.

16. Tighten bolts/nuts to specification as follows:

- Upper transverse link to wheel bearing housing FWD (use new bolt/nut and tighten bolt/nut in normal ride height position): 96 ft. lbs. (130 Nm), plus 90° additional turn
- Upper transverse link to subframe (use new bolt/nut and tighten bolt/nut in normal ride height position): 70 ft. lbs. (95 Nm)

WHEEL BEARINGS

REMOVAL & INSTALLATION

1. Raise the vehicle.
2. Remove the wheel.

➡**Loosen the dust cap by lightly tapping on the claw of the VW 637/2.**

3. Pry off the dust cap.

4. Remove the brake carrier with caliper and secure to the body using wire.

➡**Suspend the brake caliper from body.**

5. Remove the brake disc bolt and remove the brake disc.

6. Remove the wheel hub and bearing bolt using the T10162.

7. Pull the wheel hub and bearing off the stub axle.

To install:

8. Carefully slide the wheel hub and bearing onto the stub axle.

Make sure that wheel hub and bearing do not tilt!

9. Install a new wheel hub and bearing bolt and tighten.

➡**Tighten the bolt to specification using a torque wrench. Use a regular wrench for the additional torque angle.**

10. Install the dust cap using the 3241/4.

➡**Always replace the dust cap. Damaged dust caps allow moisture to enter. Therefore, always use the special tools indicated.**

11. Rest of the installation is the reverse of removal.

12. Install the wheel.

13. Tighten bolts/nuts to specification as follows:

- Except Tiguan wheel hub with bearing to wheel bearing housing (use new bolt): 148 ft. lbs. (200 Nm), plus 180° additional rotation
- Tiguan wheel hub with bearing to wheel bearing housing (use new bolt): 133 ft. lbs. (180 Nm), plus 180° additional rotation
- Brake disc to wheel bearing housing: 35 inch lbs. (4 Nm)

VOLKSWAGEN

GLI • Jetta

5

SPECIFICATIONS AND MAINTENANCE CHARTS

ENGINE AND VEHICLE IDENTIFICATION

ENG Code	Liters (cc)	Cu. In.	Cyl.	Fuel Sys. ①	Engine Type	Eng. Mfg.
					Engine	
BPY	2.0 (1984)	121	4	ME 9.1	DOHC	Volkswagen
CBFA	2.0 (1984)	121	4	FSI	DOHC	Volkswagen
CCTA	2.0 (1984)	121	4	FSI	DOHC	Volkswagen
CBEA	2.0 (1984)	121	4	TDI	DOHC	Volkswagen
BRM	2.0 (1855)	112	4	TDI	SOHC	Volkswagen
CJAA	2.0 (1855)	112	4	TDI	SOHC	Volkswagen
BGP	2.5 (2412)	147	5	ME 7.1	DOHC	Volkswagen
BGQ	2.5 (2412)	147	5	ME 7.1	DOHC	Volkswagen
CBUA	2.5 (2412)	147	5	ME 7.1	DOHC	Volkswagen
CBTA	2.5 (2412)	147	5	ME 7.1	DOHC	Volkswagen

Model Year	
Code ②	Year
B	2011
C	2012

DOHC: Double Overhead Camshafts

SOHC: Single Overhead Camshaft

① Bosch Motronic

② 10th digit of VIN

71105_VWJE_C0001

GENERAL ENGINE SPECIFICATIONS

Year	Model	Engine Displacement Liters	Engine ID/VIN	Net Horsepower @ rpm	Net Torque@rpm (ft. lbs.)	Bore x Stroke (in.)	Com- pression Ratio	Oil Pressure @ rpm
2011	Jetta	2.0 (1984)	①	200@5700	207@1800	3.21x3.62	9.6:1	36-65@2000
	Jetta	2.0 (1855)	BRM	140@4000	236@1750	3.10x3.72	19.0:1	36-65@2000
	Jetta	2.5 (2412)	①	170@5700	177@4250	3.21x3.62	10.0:1	36-65@2000
2012	GLI	2.0 (1984)	①	200@5700	207@1800	3.21x3.62	9.6:1	36-65@2000
	Jetta	2.0 (1984)	①	200@5700	207@1800	3.21x3.62	9.6:1	36-65@2000
	Jetta	2.0 (1855)	BRM	140@4000	236@1750	3.10x3.72	19.0:1	36-65@2000
	Jetta	2.5 (2412)	①	170@5700	177@4250	3.21x3.62	10.0:1	36-65@2000

① Inspect timing cover for code.

71105_VWJE_C0002

GASOLINE ENGINE TUNE-UP SPECIFICATIONS

Year	Engine Displacement Liters	Engine ID/VIN	Spark Plug Gap (in.)	Ignition Timing (deg.) MT	AT	Fuel Pump (psi)	Idle Speed (rpm) MT	AT	Valve Clearance Intake	Exhaust
2011	2.0 (1984)	①	0.028-0.031	②	②	101.5	②	②	HYD	HYD
	2.5 (2412)	①	0.039-0.043	②	②	58	②	②	HYD	HYD
2012	2.0 (1984)	①	0.028-0.031	②	②	101.5	②	②	HYD	HYD
	2.5 (2412)	①	0.039-0.043	②	②	58	②	②	HYD	HYD

Note: The Vehicle Emission Control Information label reflects specification changes made during production.

HYD: Hydraulic

① Inspect timing cover for code.

② Ignition timing/idle speed controlled electronically. Specification no longer provided.

71105_VWJE_C0003

DIESEL ENGINE TUNE-UP SPECIFICATIONS

Year	Engine Displacement Liters	Engine ID/VIN	Valve Clearance Intake (in.)	Valve Clearance Exhaust (in.)	Intake Valve Opens (deg.)	Injection Pump Setting (deg.)	Injection Nozzle Pressure (psi) New	Injection Nozzle Pressure (psi) Used	Idle Speed (rpm)	Cranking Compression Pressure (psi)
2011	2.0 (1855)	BRM	HYD	HYD	NS	①	NS	NS	①	275.5
	2.0 (1855)	CBEA	HYD	HYD	NS	①	NS	NS	①	275.5
	2.0 (1855)	CJAA	HYD	HYD	NS	①	NS	NS	①	275.5
2012	2.0 (1855)	BRM	HYD	HYD	NS	①	NS	NS	①	275.5
	2.0 (1855)	CBEA	HYD	HYD	NS	①	NS	NS	①	275.5
	2.0 (1855)	CJAA	HYD	HYD	NS	①	NS	NS	①	275.5

Note: The Vehicle Emission Control Information label reflects specification changes made during production.

NS: Not Specified

① Injection pump timing/idle speed controlled electronically. Specification no longer provided.

71105_VWJE_C0003A

CAPACITIES

Year	Model	Engine Displacement Liters	Engine ID/VIN	Engine Oil with Filter	Transmission Manual (pts.)	Transmission Auto. (qts.)	Fuel Tank (gal.)	Cooling System (qts.)
2011	Jetta	2.0 (1984)	①	4.9	4.9	NA	14.5	7.7
	Jetta	2.0 (1855)	②	4.3	4.9	5.5	14.5	8.5
	Jetta	2.5 (2412)	①	5.9	4.1	NA	14.5	10.1
2012	GLI	2.0 (1984)	①	4.9	4.9	NA	14.5	7.7
	Jetta	2.0 (1984)	①	4.9	4.9	NA	14.5	7.7
	Jetta	2.0 (1855)	②	4.3	4.9	5.5	14.5	8.5
	Jetta	2.5 (2412)	①	5.9	4.1	NA	14.5	10.1

Note: All capacities are approximate. Add fluid gradually and check often to avoid overfilling or underfilling.

NA: Not Applicable

① Inspect timing cover for code.

② TDI

71105_VWJE_C0004

FLUID SPECIFICATIONS

Year	Model	Engine Displacement Liters	Engine ID/VIN	Engine Oil	Man. Trans.	Auto. Trans.	Brake Master Cylinder	Cooling System
2011	Jetta	2.0 (1984)	①	5W-40	Synthetic MTF 75W-90	Synthetic ATF	DOT4	LLC
	Jetta	2.0 (1855)	②	5W-40	Synthetic MTF 75W-90	Synthetic ATF	DOT4	LLC
	Jetta	2.5 (2412)	①	5W-40	Synthetic MTF 75W-90	Synthetic ATF	DOT4	LLC
2012	GLI	2.0 (1855)	①	5W-40	Synthetic MTF 75W-90	Synthetic ATF	DOT4	LLC
	Jetta	2.0 (1984)	①	5W-40	Synthetic MTF 75W-90	Synthetic ATF	DOT4	LLC
	Jetta	2.0 (1855)	②	5W-40	Synthetic MTF 75W-90	Synthetic ATF	DOT4	LLC
	Jetta	2.5 (2412)	①	5W-40	Synthetic MTF 75W-90	Synthetic ATF	DOT4	LLC

DOT: Department Of Transpotation

LLC: Long Life Coolant

NA: Not Applicable

① Inspect timing cover for code.

② TDI

71105_VWJE_C0005

VALVE SPECIFICATIONS

Year	Engine Displacement Liters	Engine ID/VIN	Seat Angle (deg.)	Face Angle (deg.)	Spring Test Pressure (lbs. @ in.)	Spring Installed Height (in.)	Stem-to-Guide Clearance (in.)		Stem Diameter (in.)	
							Intake	Exhaust	Intake	Exhaust
2011	2.0 (1984)	①	45	45	NS	NS	0.031	0.031	NS	NS
	2.0 (1855)	②	45	45	NS	NS	0.050	0.050	0.2722	0.2712
	2.5 (2412)	①	45	45	NS	NS	0.031	0.031	NS	NS
2012	2.0 (1984)	①	45	45	NS	NS	0.031	0.031	NS	NS
	2.0 (1855)	②	45	45	NS	NS	0.050	0.050	0.2722	0.2712
	2.5 (2412)	①	45	45	NS	NS	0.031	0.031	NS	NS

NS: Not Specified

① Inspect timing cover for code.

② TDI

71105_VWJE_C0006

CRANKSHAFT AND CONNECTING ROD SPECIFICATIONS

All measurements are given in inches.

Year	Engine Disp. Liters	Engine ID/VIN	Main Brg. Journal Dia.	Main Brg. Oil Clearance	Shaft End-play	Thrust on No.	Connecting Rod		
							Journal Diameter	Oil Clearance	Side Clearance
2011	2.0	①	2.1260	0.0007-0.0015	0.0028-0.0090	3	1.8819	0.0008-0.0024	0.0039-0.0138
	2.0	②	2.1060	NS	0.0027-0.0066	3	1.8642	0.0031	0.0144
	2.5	①	2.2834	0.0007-0.0015	0.0007-0.0015	3	1.8819	0.0008-0.0024	0.0039-0.0138
2012	2.0	①	2.1260	0.0007-0.0015	0.0028-0.0090	3	1.8819	0.0008-0.0024	0.0039-0.0138
	2.0	②	2.1060	NS	0.0027-0.0066	3	1.8642	0.0031	0.0144
	2.5	①	2.2834	0.0007-0.0015	0.0007-0.0015	3	1.8819	0.0008-0.0024	0.0039-0.0138

NS - Not Specified

① Inspect timing cover for code.

② TDI

71105_VWJE_C0008

PISTON AND RING SPECIFICATIONS

All measurements are given in inches.

Year	Engine Disp. Liters	Engine ID/VIN	Piston Clearance	Ring Gap			Ring Side Clearance		
				Top Compression	Bottom Compression	Oil Control	Top Compression	Bottom Compression	Oil Control
2011	2.0	①	0.0177	0.008-0.016	0.008-0.016	0.010-0.020	0.0024-0.0035	0.0025-0.0042	0.0011-0.0027
	2.0	②	0.0177	0.008-0.016	0.008-0.016	0.010-0.020	0.0024-0.0035	0.0020-0.0031	0.0011-0.0023
	2.5	①	0.0177	0.008-0.016	0.008-0.016	0.010-0.020	0.0024-0.0035	0.0025-0.0042	0.0011-0.0027
2012	2.0	①	0.0177	0.008-0.016	0.008-0.016	0.010-0.020	0.0024-0.0035	0.0025-0.0042	0.0011-0.0027
	2.0	②	0.0177	0.008-0.016	0.008-0.016	0.010-0.020	0.0024-0.0035	0.0020-0.0031	0.0011-0.0023
	2.5	①	0.0177	0.008-0.016	0.008-0.016	0.010-0.020	0.0024-0.0035	0.0025-0.0042	0.0011-0.0027

① Inspect timing cover for code.

② TDI

71105_VWJE_C0007

TORQUE SPECIFICATIONS

All readings in ft. lbs.

Year	Engine Displacement Liters	Engine ID/VIN	Cylinder Head Bolts	Main Bearing Bolts	Rod Bearing Bolts	Crankshaft Damper Bolt	Flywheel Bolts	Manifold		Spark Plugs	Oil Pan Drain Plug
								Intake	Exhaust		
2011	2.0 (1984)	①	②	③	④	⑤	⑥	7	15 ⑦	18	22
	2.0 (1855)	①	⑧	⑨	④	⑩	⑥	16	17	15	22
	2.5 (2412)	①	②	⑪	④	⑫	⑥	7	18 ⑦	18	22
2012	2.0 (1984)	①	②	③	④	⑤	⑥	7	15 ⑦	18	22
	2.0 (1855)	①	⑧	⑨	④	⑩	⑥	16	17	15	22
	2.5 (2412)	①	②	⑪	④	⑫	⑥	7	18 ⑦	18	22

① Inspect timing cover for code.

② Torque in three steps. Use new bolts.
  Step 1: 30 ft. lbs.
  Step 2: plus 90 degrees
  Step 3: plus 90 degrees

③ Two Steps. 66 ft. lbs. Plus 90 degrees. Use new bolt.

④ Two Steps. 22 ft. lbs. plus 90 degrees. Use new bolts.

⑤ Two Steps. 66 ft. lbs. Plus 90 degrees. Use new bolt.

⑥ Two Steps. 44 ft. lbs. plus 90 degrees. Use new bolts.

⑦ Use new bolts.

⑧ Torque in four steps. Use new bolts.
  Step 1: 26 ft. lbs.
  Step 2: 44 ft. lbs.
  Step 3: plus 90 degrees
  Step 4: plus 90 degrees

⑨ Two Steps. 48 ft. lbs. plus 90 degrees. Use new bolts.

⑩ Two Steps. 89 inch lbs. plus 90 degrees. Use new bolts.

⑪ Two Steps. 30 ft. lbs. plus 90 degrees. Use new bolts.

⑫ Two Steps. 37 ft. lbs. plus 90 degrees. Use new bolts.

71105_VWJE_C0009

WHEEL ALIGNMENT

Year	Model		Caster Range (+/-Deg.)	Caster Preferred Setting (Deg.)	Camber Range (+/-Deg.)	Camber Preferred Setting (Deg.)	Toe-in (Deg.)
2011	Jetta	Front	0.50	+7.57	0.50	-0.50	1.63+/-0.33 ①
	Standard	Rear	—	—	0.50	-1.33	0.17+/-0.21 ②
	Sport	Front	0.50	+7.83	0.50	-0.68	1.67+/-0.33 ①
		Rear	—	—	0.50	-1.33	0.17+/-0.21 ②
2012	GLI	Front	0.50	+7.83	0.50	-0.58	1.67+/-0.33 ①
		Rear	—	—	0.50	-1.33	0.17+/-0.21 ②
	Jetta	Front	0.50	+7.57	0.50	-0.50	1.63+/-0.33 ①
	Standard	Rear	—	—	0.50	-1.33	0.17+/-0.21 ②
	Sport	Front	0.50	+7.83	0.50	-0.68	1.67+/-0.33 ①
		Rear	—	—	0.50	-1.33	0.17+/-0.21 ②

① Toe differential angle with 20 deg. steering lock to left and right

② Total toe at specified camber.

71105_VWJE_C0010

TIRE, WHEEL AND BALL JOINT SPECIFICATIONS

Year	Model	OEM Tires Standard	OEM Tires Optional	Tire Pressures (psi) Front	Tire Pressures (psi) Rear	Wheel Size	Lug Nut (ft. lbs.)
2011	Jetta	205/55-16	225/45-17	①	①	NS	89
2012	GLI	225/45-17	225/40-18	①	①	NS	89
	Jetta	205/55-16	225/45-17	①	①	NS	89

NS: Not Specified

① See Vehicle Tire Information Sticker for correct inflation values.

71105_VWJE_C0011

BRAKE SPECIFICATIONS

All measurements in inches unless noted

Year	Model		Brake Disc Original Thickness	Brake Disc Minimum Thickness	Brake Disc Maximum Run-out	Drum Diameter Original Inside Diameter	Drum Diameter Maximum Machine Diameter	Minimum Lining Thickness	Brake Caliper Guide Pins (ft. lbs.)	Brake Caliper Mounting Bolts (ft. lbs.)
2011	Jetta	Front	0.975	0.858	0.002	NS	NS	0.078	22	NS
		Rear	0.486	0.390	0.002	NS	NS	0.078	NS	35
2012	GLI	Front	0.975	0.858	0.002	NS	NS	0.078	22	NS
		Rear	0.486	0.390	0.002	NS	NS	0.078	NS	35
	Jetta	Front	0.975	0.858	0.002	NS	NS	0.078	22	NS
		Rear	0.486	0.390	0.002	NS	NS	0.078	NS	35

NS: Not Specified

NOTE: Use minimum thickness noted on disc if different from specification.

Always use new bolts.

71105_VWJE_C0012

SCHEDULED MAINTENANCE INTERVALS
VOLKSWAGEN—Jetta, Jetta Sportwagen & GLI

TO BE SERVICED	TYPE OF SERVICE	10	20	30	40	50	60	70	80	90	100	110	120
Auto Trans - fluid	R				✓				✓				✓
Battery - check	S/I		✓		✓		✓		✓		✓		✓
Body- inspect for corrosion	S/I		✓		✓		✓		✓		✓		✓
Brake Pad thickness - check	S/I	✓	✓	✓	✓	✓	✓	✓	✓	✓	✓	✓	✓
Brake system - inspection	S/I		✓		✓		✓		✓		✓		✓
Cooling System - level check	S/I				✓				✓				✓
CV Joints - leaks & damage	S/I				✓				✓				✓
Door Arresters - lubricate	S/I				✓				✓				✓
Engine Oil & Filter - replace	R	✓	✓	✓	✓	✓	✓	✓	✓	✓	✓	✓	✓
Engine Compartment - leaks & damage	S/I				✓				✓				✓
Exhaust System - inspection	S/I				✓				✓				✓
Fuel Filter (2.0L TDI) - replace	S/I		✓		✓		✓		✓		✓		✓
Headlights - Check and adjust	S/I				✓				✓				✓
Power Steering - level check	S/I				✓				✓				✓
Rotate wheels	S/I	✓	✓	✓	✓	✓	✓	✓	✓	✓	✓	✓	✓
Serpentine Belt - inspection	S/I				✓				✓				✓
Service Interval Display - reset	S/I	✓	✓	✓	✓	✓	✓	✓	✓	✓	✓	✓	✓
Spark Plugs (except 2.0L) - replace	R				✓				✓				✓
Spark Plugs (2.0L) - replace	R						✓						✓
Tie Rod Ends - play & boots	S/I				✓				✓				✓
Timing Belt (except 2.0L TDI) - replace	R											✓	
Timing Belt (2.0L TDI) - replace	R												✓
Tires/Spare - inspection	S/I		✓		✓		✓		✓		✓		
Washer - clean nozzles	S/I	✓	✓	✓	✓	✓	✓	✓	✓	✓	✓	✓	✓
Wiper Blades - check	S/I	✓	✓	✓	✓	✓	✓	✓	✓	✓	✓	✓	✓
Air Cleaner - replace	Every 72 months												
Airbag System - inspect	Every 12 months												
Brake Fluid - replace	At 36 months, then every 24 months												
Brake Fluid (New Beetle) - replace	Every 24 months												
Cabin Air Filter - replace	Every 24 months												
Convertible roof latch - inspect	Every 24 months												
Spark Plugs - replace	Every 72 months												
Tire Filler Bottle - inspect	Every 24 months												
Tire Filler Bottle - replace	Every 48 months												
Tire Pressure Sensors - replace	Every 72 months												

R: Replace   S/I: Service or Inspect

71105_VWJE_C0014

PRECAUTIONS

Before servicing any vehicle, please be sure to read all of the following precautions, which deal with personal safety, prevention of component damage, and important points to take into consideration when servicing a motor vehicle:

• Never open, service or drain the radiator or cooling system when the engine is hot; serious burns can occur from the steam and hot coolant.

• Observe all applicable safety precautions when working around fuel. Whenever servicing the fuel system, always work in a well-ventilated area. Do not allow fuel spray or vapors to come in contact with a spark, open flame, or excessive heat (a hot drop light, for example). Keep a dry chemical fire extinguisher near the work area. Always keep fuel in a container specifically designed for fuel storage; also, always properly seal fuel containers to avoid the possibility of fire or explosion. Refer to the additional fuel system precautions later in this section.

• Fuel injection systems often remain pressurized, even after the engine has been turned **OFF**. The fuel system pressure must be relieved before disconnecting any fuel lines. Failure to do so may result in fire and/or personal injury.

• Brake fluid often contains polyglycol ethers and polyglycols. Avoid contact with the eyes and wash your hands thoroughly after handling brake fluid. If you do get brake fluid in your eyes, flush your eyes with clean, running water for 15 minutes. If eye irritation persists, or if you have taken brake fluid internally, IMMEDIATELY seek medical assistance.

• The EPA warns that prolonged contact with used engine oil may cause a number of skin disorders, including cancer. You should make every effort to minimize your exposure to used engine oil. Protective gloves should be worn when changing oil. Wash your hands and any other exposed skin areas as soon as possible after exposure to used engine oil. Soap and water, or waterless hand cleaner should be used.

• All new vehicles are now equipped with an air bag system, often referred to as a Supplemental Restraint System (SRS) or Supplemental Inflatable Restraint (SIR) system. The system must be disabled before performing service on or around system components, steering column, instrument panel components, wiring and sensors. Failure to follow safety and disabling procedures could result in accidental air bag deployment, possible personal injury and unnecessary system repairs.

• Always wear safety goggles when working with, or around, the air bag system. When carrying a non-deployed air bag, be sure the bag and trim cover are pointed away from your body. When placing a non-deployed air bag on a work surface, always face the bag and trim cover upward, away from the surface. This will reduce the motion of the module if it is accidentally deployed. Refer to the additional air bag system precautions later in this section.

• Clean, high quality brake fluid from a sealed container is essential to the safe and proper operation of the brake system. You should always buy the correct type of brake fluid for your vehicle. If the brake fluid becomes contaminated, completely flush the system with new fluid. Never reuse any brake fluid. Any brake fluid that is removed from the system should be discarded. Also, do not allow any brake fluid to come in contact with a painted surface; it will damage the paint.

• Never operate the engine without the proper amount and type of engine oil; doing so WILL result in severe engine damage.

• Timing belt maintenance is extremely important. Many models utilize an interference-type, non-freewheeling engine. If the timing belt breaks, the valves in the cylinder head may strike the pistons, causing potentially serious (also time-consuming and expensive) engine damage. Refer to the maintenance interval charts for the recommended replacement interval for the timing belt, and to the timing belt section for belt replacement and inspection.

• Disconnecting the negative battery cable on some vehicles may interfere with the functions of the on-board computer system(s) and may require the computer to undergo a relearning process once the negative battery cable is reconnected.

• When servicing drum brakes, only disassemble and assemble one side at a time, leaving the remaining side intact for reference.

• Only an MVAC-trained, EPA-certified automotive technician should service the air conditioning system or its components.

BRAKES

GENERAL INFORMATION

PRECAUTIONS

• Certain components within the ABS system are not intended to be serviced or repaired individually.

• Do not use rubber hoses or other parts not specifically specified for and ABS system. When using repair kits, replace all parts included in the kit. Partial or incorrect repair may lead to functional problems and require the replacement of components.

• Lubricate rubber parts with clean, fresh brake fluid to ease assembly. Do not use shop air to clean parts; damage to rubber components may result.

• Use only DOT 3 brake fluid from an unopened container.

• If any hydraulic component or line is removed or replaced, it may be necessary to bleed the entire system.

• A clean repair area is essential. Always clean the reservoir and cap thoroughly before removing the cap. The slightest amount of dirt in the fluid may plug an orifice and impair the system function. Perform repairs after components have been thoroughly cleaned; use only denatured alcohol to clean components. Do not allow ABS components to come into contact with any substance containing mineral oil; this includes used shop rags.

• The Anti-Lock control unit is a microprocessor similar to other computer units in the vehicle. Ensure that the ignition switch is **OFF** before removing or

ANTI-LOCK BRAKE SYSTEM (ABS)

installing controller harnesses. Avoid static electricity discharge at or near the controller.

• If any arc welding is to be done on the vehicle, the control unit should be unplugged before welding operations begin.

SPEED SENSORS

REMOVAL & INSTALLATION

Front
See Figure 1.

1. Raise the vehicle.
2. Separate speed sensor and speed sensor wiring connector.
3. Remove the bolt from wheel bearing housing.

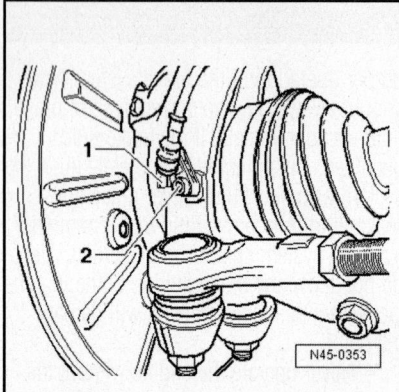

Fig. 1 Separate speed sensor and speed sensor wiring connector (1), Remove bolt (2)

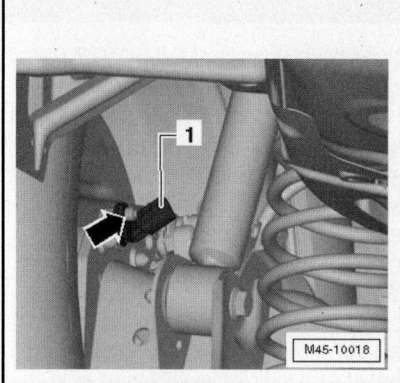

Fig. 2 Disconnect the connector (1), remove the bolt (arrow)

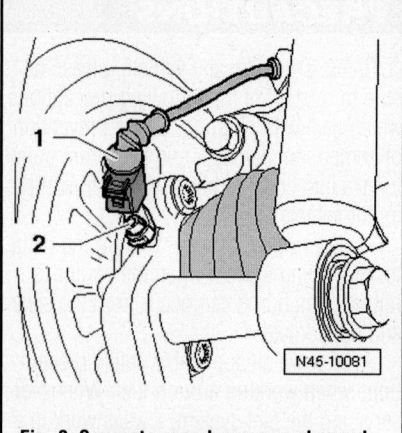

Fig. 3 Separate speed sensor and speed sensor wiring connector (1), Remove bolt (2)

4. Remove ABS speed sensor from wheel bearing housing.

To install:

5. Before inserting speed sensor, clean hole inner surface and coat speed sensor all-round with hot bolt paste G 052 112 A3.

6. Insert the speed sensor into the hole in the wheel bearing housing and tighten the bolt to 8 Nm.

7. Connect speed sensor to speed sensor wiring.

Rear

DISC—FWD

See Figure 2.

1. Raise vehicle.
2. Disconnect the connector.
3. Remove the bolt.
4. Remove the wheel speed sensor 1 from the wheel bearing housing.

To install:

5. Installation is performed in the reverse order of removal. Observe the following when doing so:

6. Clean the inside of the hole and coat it with hot bolt paste G 052 112 A3 before installing the wheel speed sensor.

7. Install the speed sensor into the hole in the rear axle and tighten it.

DISC—AWD

See Figure 3.

1. Raise vehicle.
2. Separate speed sensor and speed sensor wiring connector.
3. Remove bolt 2 from wheel bearing housing.
4. Remove ABS speed sensor from wheel bearing housing.

To install:

5. Before inserting speed sensor, clean hole inner surface and coat speed sensor all-round with hot bolt paste G 052 112 A3.

6. Insert the speed sensor into the hole in the wheel bearing housing and tighten the bolt to 8 Nm.

7. Connect speed sensor to speed sensor wiring.

DRUM

See Figure 4.

1. Raise the vehicle.
2. Disconnect the connector 1.
3. Remove the bolt.
4. Remove the wheel speed sensor 1 from the rear axle.

To install:

5. Installation is performed in the reverse order of removal. Observe the following when doing so:

6. Clean the inside of the hole and coat it with hot bolt paste G 052 112 A3 before installing the wheel speed sensor.

7. Install the wheel speed sensor into the hole in the rear axle and tighten it.

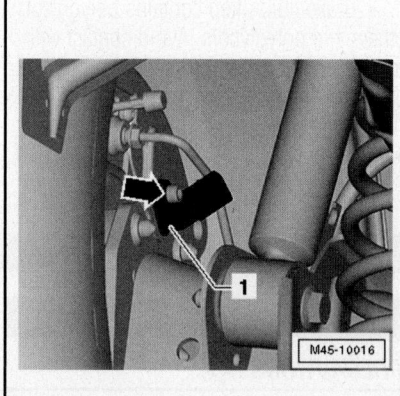

Fig. 4 Disconnect the connector (1), Remove the bolt (arrow)

BRAKES   **BLEEDING THE BRAKE SYSTEM**

BLEEDING PROCEDURE

BLEEDING PROCEDURE

1. Before servicing the vehicle, refer to the precautions.

※ WARNING

Adhere strictly to work sequence when bleeding brake system.

2. Connect the brake charger/bleeder unit VAS 5234 or VAG 1869.

3. Open the bleeder valves in the prescribed sequence and bleed the brake calipers.

- Left front brake caliper
- Right front brake caliper
- Left rear brake caliper
- Right rear brake caliper

➡ **The bleeder hose must fit tightly on the bleeder valve so that no air can enter the brake system.**

4. With the bleeder bottle hose attached, leave the bleeder valve open long enough that brake fluid exits without bubbles.

5. Press the brake pedal forcefully and hold.

6. Open the bleeder valve at the brake caliper.

7. Press the brake pedal down until stopped.

8. Close the bleeder valve with the pedal pressed.

9. Release the brake pedal slowly.

※ WARNING

This bleeding procedure must be performed 5 times per brake caliper.

10. Perform the bleeding sequence as follows:

- Left front brake caliper
- Right front brake caliper
- Left rear brake caliper
- Right rear brake caliper

※ WARNING

A road test must be performed after bleeding. During this, at least one Anti-lock Brake System (ABS) stop must be performed!

POST BLEEDING

1. A second mechanic is required to assist:

a. Depress brake pedal forcefully and hold.

b. Open bleeder valve at brake caliper.

c. Press brake pedal down onto stop.

d. Close bleeder screw with pedal depressed.

e. Release brake pedal slowly.

2. This bleeding procedure must be performed 5 times per brake caliper.

3. Bleeding sequence:

a. Front left brake caliper
b. Front right brake caliper
c. Left rear brake caliper
d. Right rear brake caliper

4. A road test must be performed after bleeding. During this, at least one ABS regulation must be performed!

5. Install rear wheels.

6. Torque specification for wheel bolts.

FLUID CHANGE & FILL PROCEDURE

See Figures 5 through 12.

1. Remove the cap from the brake fluid reservoir.

2. Use the hose from the brake charger/bleeder unit VAS 5234 to extract as much brake fluid as possible.

➡ **Do not remove the strainer inside the brake fluid reservoir.**

➡ **Do not use extracted brake fluid again!**

3. Attach the adapter to the brake fluid reservoir.

4. Observe operating instructions for VAS 5234.

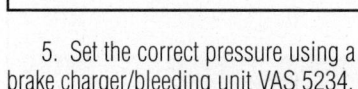

V.A.G 1869/2

W00-0679

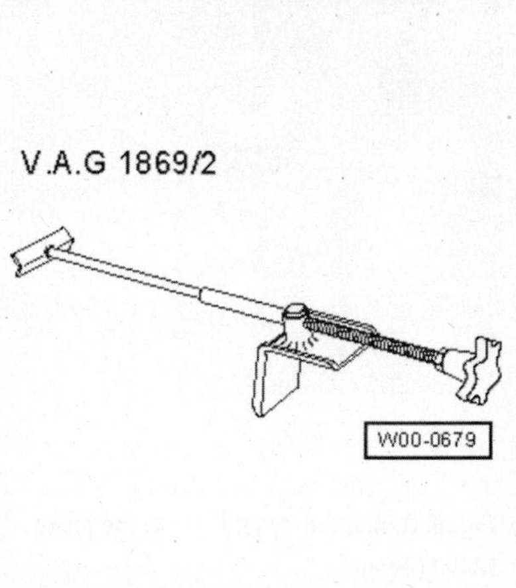

Fig. 6 Brake pedal depressor V.A.G 1869/2

5. Set the correct pressure using a brake charger/bleeding unit VAS 5234.

6. Connect the hose from the brake charger/bleeding unit VAS 5234 to the adapter. Use a suitable bleed hose. It must seat tightly on the bleed valve so that no air can get into the brake system.

7. Remove the cap from the bleed valve on the left front brake caliper.

8. Connect collector bottle bleed hose to left front bleed valve. Then open the bleed valve and allow the corresponding quantity to flow out. Close the bleed valve.

9. Install the cap on the left front brake caliper bleed valve.

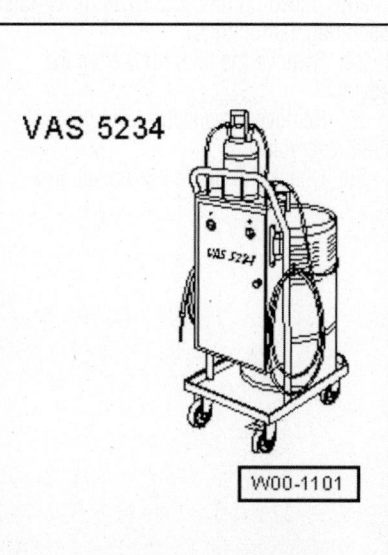

VAS 5234

W00-1101

Fig. 5 Brake charger/bleeder unit VAS 5234

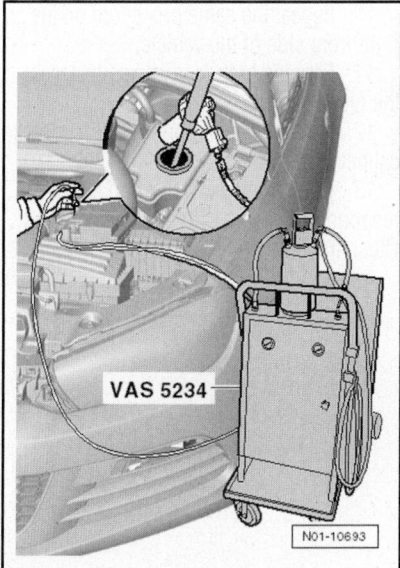

VAS 5234

N01-10693

Fig. 7 Use the hose from the brake charger/bleeder unit VAS 5234

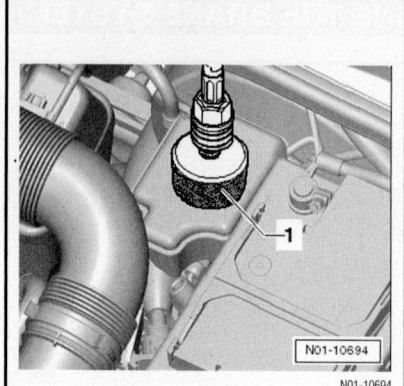

Fig. 8 Attach the adapter (1) to the brake fluid reservoir.

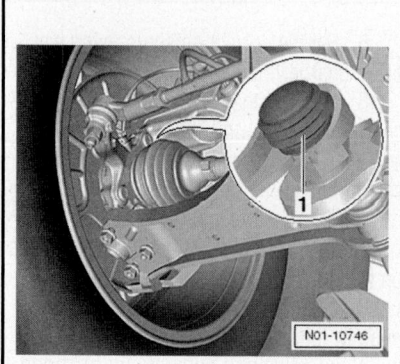

Fig. 9 Remove the cap (1) from the bleed valve

10. Repeat the same procedure on the right front side of the vehicle.

11. Remove both rear wheels to access the bleed valve.

12. Remove the cap on the left rear brake caliper bleed valve.

13. Open the bleed valve and let the corresponding amount of brake fluid flow out. Close the bleed valve.

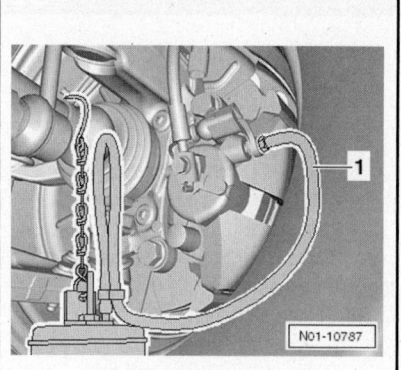

Fig. 10 Connect collector bottle bleed hose (1) to left front bleed valve

14. Install the cap on the left rear brake caliper bleed valve.

15. Repeat the same procedure on the right rear side of the vehicle.

Manual Transmission

16. Remove the air filter housing.

17. Attach the bleed hose to the bleed valve on the clutch slave cylinder 1.

18. Open the valve and drain approximately 100 ml brake fluid.

19. Close the value and press the clutch pedal quickly 10 to 15 times.

20. Open the valve again and drain approximately 50 ml brake fluid.

21. Close the valve, remove the bleed hose and press the clutch pedal several times.

22. Install the air filter housing in reverse order of removal.

23. Move filler lever on brake charger/bleeding unit VAS 5234 to "B" (see operating instructions).

24. Remove the filler hose from the adapter.

25. Remove the adapter from the brake fluid reservoir.

26. Check the brake fluid level and

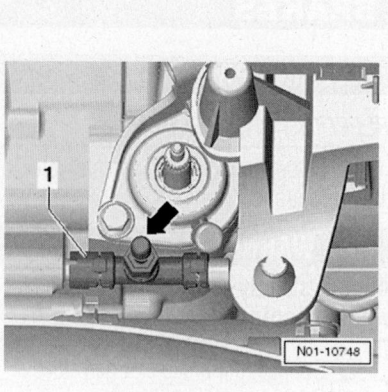

Fig. 11 Attach the bleed hose to the bleed valve on the clutch slave cylinder 1

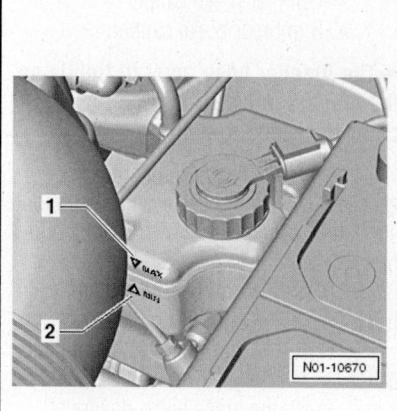

Fig. 12 Check the brake fluid level

fill if necessary. It must be between 1 and 2.

27. Screw in cap for brake fluid reservoir.

28. Install the rear wheels, if necessary.

29. Perform a function test during the test drive.

BRAKES

FRONT DISC BRAKES

BRAKE CALIPER

REMOVAL & INSTALLATION

FN 3

See Figures 13 through 16.

Special Tools:
- Torque wrench V.A.G 1331
- Brake pedal depressor V.A.G 1869/2

➡ **Work procedure applies only for replacing or when performing subsequent service work on brake caliper.**

1. Loosen wheel bolts.
2. Raise vehicle.
3. Remove wheel.
4. Pry the spring for the brake pads off the brake caliper with a screwdriver and remove it.
5. Remove the caps arrows.
6. Attach the bleeder bottle bleed hose to the brake caliper bleed valve.
7. Open the bleed valve.
8. Install the V.A.G 1869/2.
9. Close the bleed valve and remove the bleeder bottle.
10. Remove the brake hose threaded connection with the banjo bolt from the brake caliper.

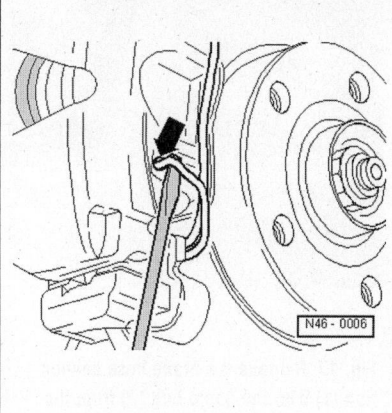

Fig. 13 Pry the spring for the brake pads off the brake caliper

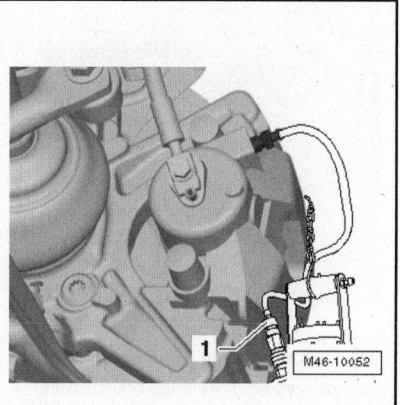

Fig. 14 Attach the bleeder bottle bleed hose (1) to the brake caliper bleed valve

11. Seal off the brake line and the threaded hole immediately with plugs 1H0 698 311 A.
12. Remove the guide pins arrows from the brake caliper.
13. Remove the brake caliper from the brake carrier.

➡ **Do not blow brake system using compressed air, the dust produced is harmful to health!**

14. Cleaning: Clean brake caliper with mineral spirits exclusively.

To install:

15. Installation is performed in the reverse order of removal. Observe the following when doing so:
16. Before installing, clean carefully and check for wear and damage.
17. Thoroughly clean the contact sur-

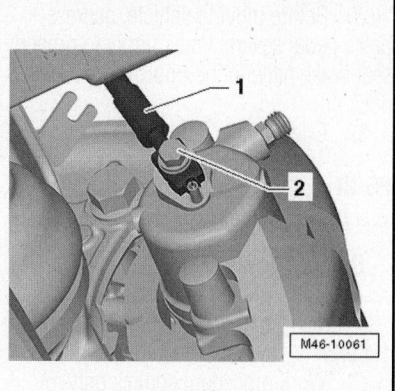

Fig. 15 Remove the brake hose threaded connection (1) with the banjo bolt (2)

Fig. 16 Remove the guide pins arrows from the brake caliper 1

faces on the brake carrier for the brake pads and remove any corrosion.
18. Condition: Piston is pressed back. Outer brake pad sits on brake carrier.
19. Insert inner brake pad with retaining spring in brake caliper (piston).
20. When installing brake caliper, make sure that brake pad is not affixed to brake caliper before the correct installation position has been reached.
21. Do not damage the adhesion surface.
22. Attach the brake caliper guide pins arrows and tighten them to 30 Nm.
23. Install both protective caps.
24. Attach the brake hose connection with the banjo bolt to the brake caliper and tighten it to 30 Nm.
25. Remove the V.A.G 1869/2.
26. Install the retaining spring in brake caliper.

27. Bleed the brake system. Refer to Brake System, Bleeding.

28. Install the wheel and tighten it.

29. Before moving vehicle, depress brake pedal several times firmly to properly seat brake pads in their normal operating position.

30. Check brake fluid level.

FS III

See Figures 17 through 20.

Special Tools:
• Torque wrench V.A.G 1331
• Brake pedal depressor V.A.G 1869/2

1. Work procedure applies only for replacing or when performing subsequent service work on brake caliper.

2. Loosen wheel bolts.

3. Raise vehicle.

4. Remove wheel.

5. Install the V.A.G 1869/2.

6. Attach the bleeder bottle bleed hose to the brake caliper bleed valve.

7. Open the bleed valve.

8. Close the bleed valve and remove the bleeder bottle.

9. Remove the caps arrows from the brake caliper bearing bushings.

10. Remove the brake hose connection with the banjo bolt from the brake caliper.

11. Seal off the brake line and the threaded hole immediately with plugs 1H0 698 311 A.

12. Loosen both guide pins arrows and remove them from the brake caliper.

13. Remove the brake caliper from the brake carrier.

14. Remove the brake pads from the brake caliper.

To install:

15. Installation is performed in the reverse order of removal. Observe the following when doing so:

16. Before installing, clean carefully and check for wear and damage.

17. Condition: Piston is pressed back.

18. Insert inner brake pad (piston side) and outer brake pad with retaining springs into brake caliper.

   a. Inside brake pad (piston side) with large 3-Finger clip.

   b. Outside brake pad with small 3-finger clip (black).

19. Install the brake caliper 1 with the brake pads 3 first at the bottom A of the brake carrier 2.

20. Condition: The pin B on the brake caliper 1 must be behind the brake carrier guide 2!

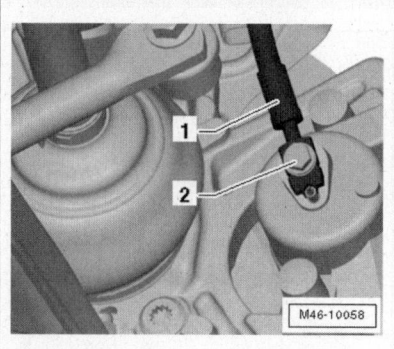

Fig. 17 Remove the brake hose connection (1) with the banjo bolt (2) from the brake caliper

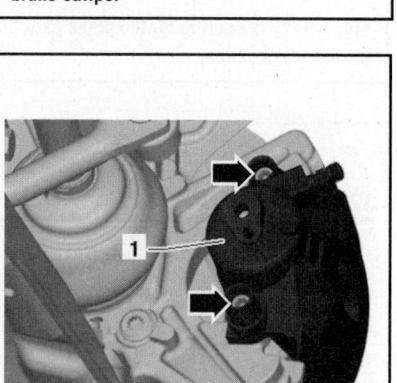

Fig. 18 Loosen both guide pins arrows and remove them from the brake caliper (1)

21. Attach the brake caliper to the brake carrier with both guide pins arrows and tighten.

22. Install both protective caps.

23. Attach the brake hose connection 1 with the banjo bolt 2 to the brake caliper.

24. Remove the V.A.G 1869/2.

25. Bleed the brake system. Refer to Brake System, Bleeding.

26. Install the wheels and tighten them.

27. Before moving vehicle, depress brake pedal several times firmly to properly seat brake pads in their normal operating position.

28. Check brake fluid level.

29. Tighten bolts/nuts to specification as follows:

• Guide pin to brake carrier (Use new bolts): 21 ft. lbs. (30 Nm)
• Brake line to brake caliper: 26 ft. lbs. (35 Nm)

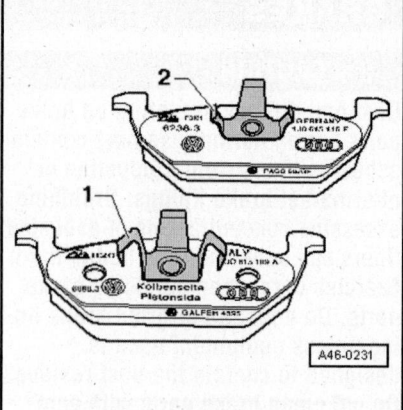

Fig. 19 Insert inner brake pad (piston side) (1) and outer brake pad (2)

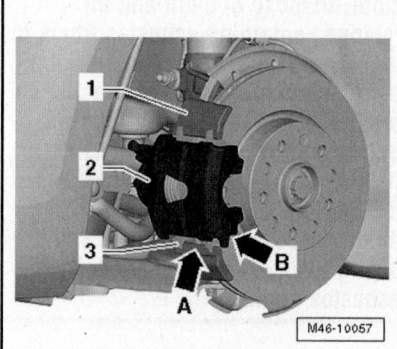

Fig. 20 Install the brake caliper (1) with the brake pads (3) first at the bottom (arrow A) of the brake carrier 2

DISC BRAKE PADS

REMOVAL & INSTALLATION

FN3 Type

See Figure 21.

➡**When removing, mark the brake pads in case they will be used again. Install in the same position, otherwise braking effect will be uneven!**

1. Remove the wheels.

2. Using a screwdriver, pry off the brake pad retaining spring from the brake caliper and remove.

3. Disconnect the connector for the brake pad wear indicator.

4. Remove the caps.

5. Loosen both guide pins and remove them from the brake caliper.

6. Remove the brake caliper and secure it with wire so that the weight of the caliper does not burden or damage the brake hose.

7. Remove the brake pads.

Do not use compressed air to blow on the brake system components, the dust produced is harmful to health!

8. Thoroughly clean the contact surfaces for the brake pads at the brake carrier, removing any corrosion.

9. Clean the brake caliper, especially the adhesive contact surface for the brake pads, it must be free of residual adhesive and grease.

❊❊ **WARNING**

Use only appropriate solvents for cleaning the brake caliper.

To install:

❊❊ **WARNING**

Before pressing the piston into the cylinder bore, some brake fluid must be extracted from the brake fluid reservoir. Otherwise, especially if the reservoir has been topped off, fluid will overflow and cause damage.

10. Press the piston into the bore using the piston resetting tool T 10145.

11. On Eos, remove the protective foil on the backing plate of the outer brake pad. Install the outer brake pad to the brake carrier. Insert the inner brake pad with retaining spring in the brake caliper.

❊❊ **WARNING**

When installing the brake caliper, make sure that brake pad is not affixed to the brake caliper before the correct installation position has been reached. Do not damage the adhesion surface.

12. Insert inner brake pad (piston side) with large three finger clip and outer brake pad with small three finger clip.

13. Place the brake caliper with brake pads on the brake carrier first at the bottom.

14. Tighten guide pins and install both protective caps.

15. Install retaining spring to the brake caliper.

16. Connect the brake pad wear indicator connector.

17. Install the wheels.

18. After replacing the brake pads, press the brake pedal firmly several times with the vehicle stationary so that the brake pads are

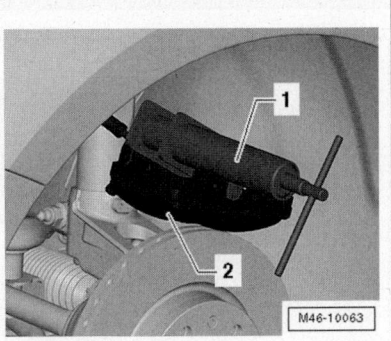

Fig. 21 Press the piston into the bore using the piston resetting tool T 10145

properly seated in their normal operating position.

19. Check the brake fluid level after replacing the brake pads.

20. Tighten bolts/nuts to specification as follows:
   • Guide pin to brake carrier: 22 ft. lbs. (30 Nm)

FS III Type

See Figure 22.

1. Before servicing the vehicle, refer to the precautions.

2. Remove wheels.

3. Disconnect harness connector 1 on vehicles with brake pad wear indicator.

4. Remove protective caps.

5. Using screwdriver, pry off brake pad retaining spring from brake caliper housing and remove.

6. Unscrew and remove both guide pins from brake caliper housing.

7. Remove brake caliper housing and secure with wire so that the weight of the brake caliper housing does not stress or damage the brake hose.

8. Remove brake pads from brake caliper housing or from brake carrier.

9. Clean brake caliper housing, especially the adhesive surface for the brake pad, it must be free of residual adhesive and grease.

❊❊ **WARNING**

Use only appropriate solvents for cleaning brake caliper housing.

To install:

10. Press piston back into caliper housing using resetting tool before inserting new

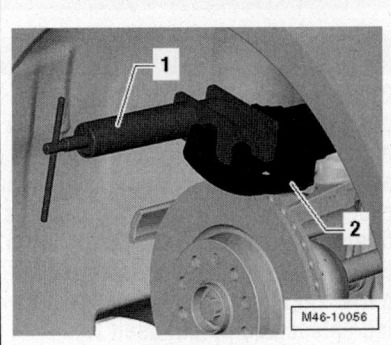

Fig. 22 Install the T10145 (1) into the brake caliper (2) and push the brake piston back

brake pads. Before pushing back the piston, siphon some of the brake fluid out of brake fluid reservoir. Otherwise, if reservoir has been topped off, fluid will overflow and cause damage.

11. Install the T10145 into the brake caliper and push the brake piston back.

12. Insert brake pads.

❊❊ **WARNING**

Brake pads are unidirectional. When installed, on the backing plate of brake pad must face downward. Make certain of this!

13. Install outer brake pad on brake carrier.

14. Remove protective foil on backing plate of outer brake pad.

15. Tighten brake caliper housing to brake carrier using both guide pins.

16. Install both protective caps.

17. Install retaining spring in brake caliper housing.

18. Insert connector for brake pad wear indicator into bracket at suspension strut.

19. Mount wheels.

20. After replacing brake pads and before moving vehicle, always depress brake pedal several times firmly to properly seat brake pads in their normal operating position.

21. Check brake fluid level after replacing brake pad.

22. Tighten bolts/nuts to specification as follows:
   • Guide pin to brake carrier: 21–22 ft. lbs. (28–30 Nm)

❋❋ CAUTION

Dust and dirt accumulating on brake parts during normal use may contain asbestos fibers from production or aftermarket brake linings. Breathing excessive concentrations of asbestos fibers can cause serious bodily harm. Exercise care when servicing brake parts. Do not sand or grind brake lining unless equipment used is designed to contain the dust residue. Do not clean brake parts with compressed air or by dry brushing. Cleaning should be done by dampening the brake components with a fine mist of water, then wiping the brake components clean with a dampened cloth. Dispose of cloth and all residue containing asbestos fibers in an impermeable container with the appropriate label. Follow practices prescribed by the Occupational Safety and Health Administration (OSHA) and the Environmental Protection Agency (EPA) for the handling, processing, and disposing of dust or debris that may contain asbestos fibers.

BRAKE CALIPER

REMOVAL & INSTALLATION

C38 Type

See Figure 23.

➡All other brake caliper types are similar in removal and installation.

➡When removing, mark the brake pads in case they will be used again. Install in the same position, otherwise braking effect will be uneven!

  1. Remove the wheels.
  2. Unhook the brake cable from the lever on the brake caliper.
  3. Remove the spring clip and pull the brake cable from the holder on the brake caliper.
  4. Connect the bleeder hose from the bleeder bottle to the bleeder valve on the brake caliper and then open the bleeder valve.
  5. Install the brake pedal actuator VAG 1869/2.
  6. Close the bleeder valve and remove the bleeder bottle.
  7. Remove the brake line.
  8. Remove both bolts from the brake

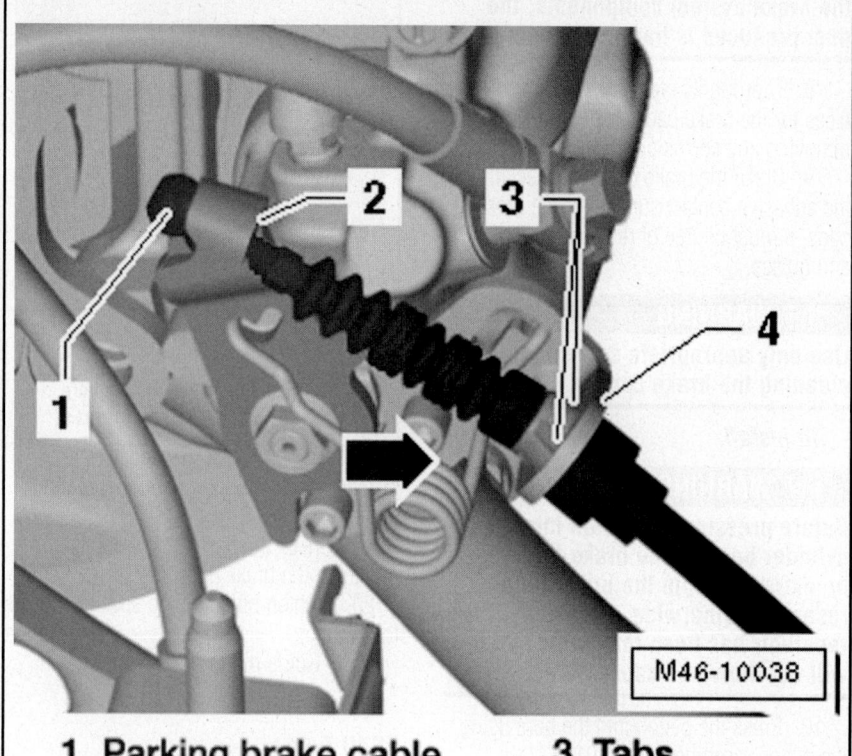

1. Parking brake cable   3. Tabs
2. Brake caliper   4. Bracket

Fig. 23 Push the lever on the brake caliper 2 in direction of.

caliper, counter hold on the guide pins when doing this.
  9. Pull off the brake caliper from brake carrier.

   To install:
  10. Piston is pressed back into caliper.
  11. Brake pads sit in the anti-rattle springs in the brake carrier.
  12. Secure the brake caliper to the brake carrier using the new self-locking bolts.
  13. Install the brake line to the brake caliper.
  14. Bleed the brake system.
  15. Hook in the brake cable and secure it to the holder with the spring clip.
  16. Adjust the parking brake.
  17. Install the wheels.
  18. Before moving the vehicle, press the brake pedal firmly several times to properly seat the brake pads in their normal operating position.
  19. Check the brake fluid level.
  20. Tighten bolts/nuts to specification as follows:

- Bolt, brake caliper to brake carrier (Use new bolts): 26 ft. lbs. (35 Nm)
- Brake line to brake caliper: 26 ft. lbs. (35 Nm)

DISC BRAKE PADS

REMOVAL & INSTALLATION

C38 Type

See Figures 24 and 25.

➡All other brake pad types are similar in removal and installation.

➡When removing, mark the brake pads in case they will be used again. Install in the same position, otherwise braking effect will be uneven!

  1. Remove the wheels.
  2. Counter hold the guide pins and remove the bolts for the brake caliper.
  3. Remove the brake caliper and secure it with wire so that the weight of the brake caliper does not burden or damage the brake hose.
  4. Remove the brake pads and anti-rattle springs.

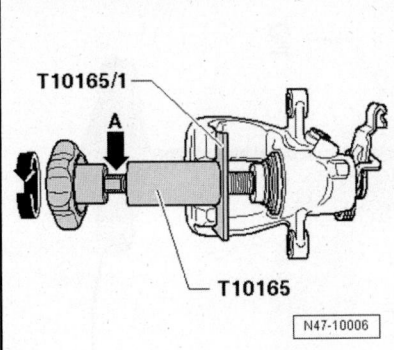

Fig. 24 Press the piston into the bore using the resetting & extracting tool T 10165 and 1065/1. Do not damage the protective caps

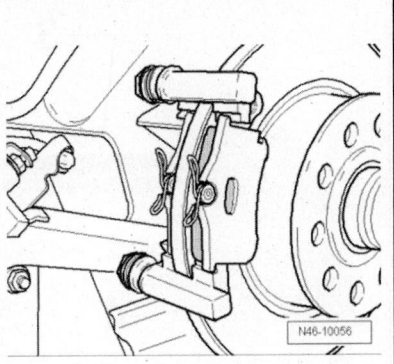

Fig. 25 Make sure that the brake pads are located correctly in the anti-rattle springs

be extracted from the brake fluid reservoir. Otherwise, especially if the reservoir has been topped off, fluid will overflow and cause damage.

7. Press the piston into the bore using the resetting & extracting tool T 10165 and 1065/1. Do not damage the protective caps.

➡ **For pistons that are difficult to press in, a 13 mm open end wrench can be used on the resetting & extracting tool T 10165.**

8. Insert the brake pad anti-rattle springs and brake pads to the brake carrier.

9. Make sure that the brake pads are located correctly in the anti-rattle springs.

10. Secure the brake caliper using the new self-locking bolts to 26 ft. lbs. (35 Nm)

11. Install the wheels.

12. After replacing the brake pads, press the brake pedal firmly several times with the vehicle stationary so that the brake pads are properly seated in their normal operating position.

13. Check the brake fluid level after replacing brake pad.

✳✳ CAUTION

Do not use compressed air to blow on the brake system components, the dust produced is harmful to health!

5. Contact surfaces between the brake pads and brake carrier must be cleaned, removing any corrosion.

6. Clean the brake caliper.

✳✳ WARNING

Use only appropriate solvents for cleaning brake caliper.

To install:

✳✳ WARNING

Before pressing the piston into the cylinder bore, some brake fluid must

---

BRAKES

✳✳ CAUTION

Dust and dirt accumulating on brake parts during normal use may contain asbestos fibers from production or aftermarket brake linings. Breathing excessive concentrations of asbestos fibers can cause serious bodily harm. Exercise care when servicing brake parts. Do not sand or grind brake lining unless equipment used is designed to contain the dust residue. Do not clean brake parts with compressed air or by dry brushing. Cleaning should be done by dampening the brake components with a fine mist of water, then wiping the brake components clean with a dampened cloth. Dispose of cloth and all residue containing asbestos fibers in an impermeable container with the appropriate label. Follow practices prescribed by the Occupational Safety and Health Administration (OSHA) and the Environmental Protection Agency (EPA) for the handling, processing, and disposing of dust or debris that may contain asbestos fibers.

BRAKE DRUM

REMOVAL & INSTALLATION
See Figure 26.

1. Loosen wheel bolts.
2. Raise vehicle.
3. Remove wheel.
4. Push the brake back with a screwdriver.
5. Remove the bolt.
6. Remove the brake drum evenly.

➡ **Do not blow brake system using compressed air, the dust produced is harmful to health!**

7. Use only appropriate solvents for cleaning brake system.

To install:

8. Installation is performed in the reverse order of removal. Observe the following when doing so:

9. Clean carefully and check for wear and damage, make sure the dimensions are correct and that the brake surface is perfect.

10. Install the brake drum evenly over the brake pads. Be careful not to tilt the brake drum.

REAR DRUM BRAKES

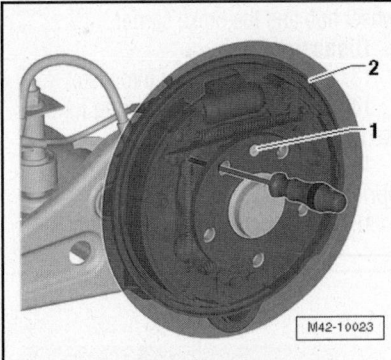

Fig. 26 Remove the bolt (1). Remove the brake drum (2)

11. Install the wheel and tighten it.

12. Adjust the parking brake. Refer to Parking Brake, Adjusting, with Rear Drum Brakes.

BRAKE SHOES

REMOVAL & INSTALLATION
See Figures 27 through 30.

After replacing the brake cylinder, the brake pads and the brake shoes, press the brake pedal once so that the brake shoes are properly seated.

Use the brake charger/bleeder unit VAS 5234 to extract the brake fluid form the brake fluid reservoir.

Before removing a brake cylinder, a brake carrier or disconnecting a brake hose from the brake cylinder, the brake pedal loading device V.A.G 1869/2 should be installed (relieve pressure).

- Bracket with spindle and hook 3438
- Torque wrench V.A.G 1331

Removing

1. Loosen wheel bolts.
2. Raise vehicle.
3. Remove wheel.
4. Reset the brake. Refer to Reset Brake, Rear Drum Brakes.
5. Remove the brake drum. Refer to Brake Drum.
6. Remove the spring plate and pressure springs.
7. Press against the spring and twist 90°.
8. Disengage the return spring downward using the special tool 3438.
9. Pry out the lower brake shoe with a screwdriver.
10. Lay the brake shoe on the support plate.
11. Disengage the parking brake cable.
12. Remove the brake shoes between the wheel hub and the brake carrier.

Disassembling

13. Clamp brake shoes into vise.
14. Remove the tension spring for the wedge.
15. Disengage the upper return spring.
16. Disengage the contact spring.

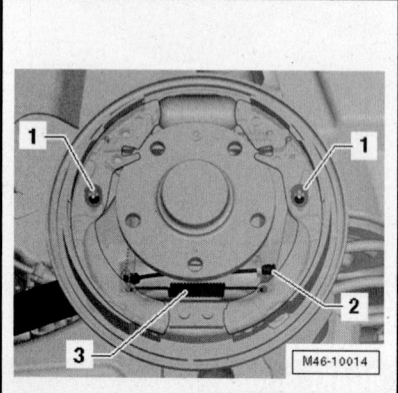

Fig. 27 Remove the spring plate (1) and pressure springs, disengage the return spring (3) and disengage the parking brake cable (2)

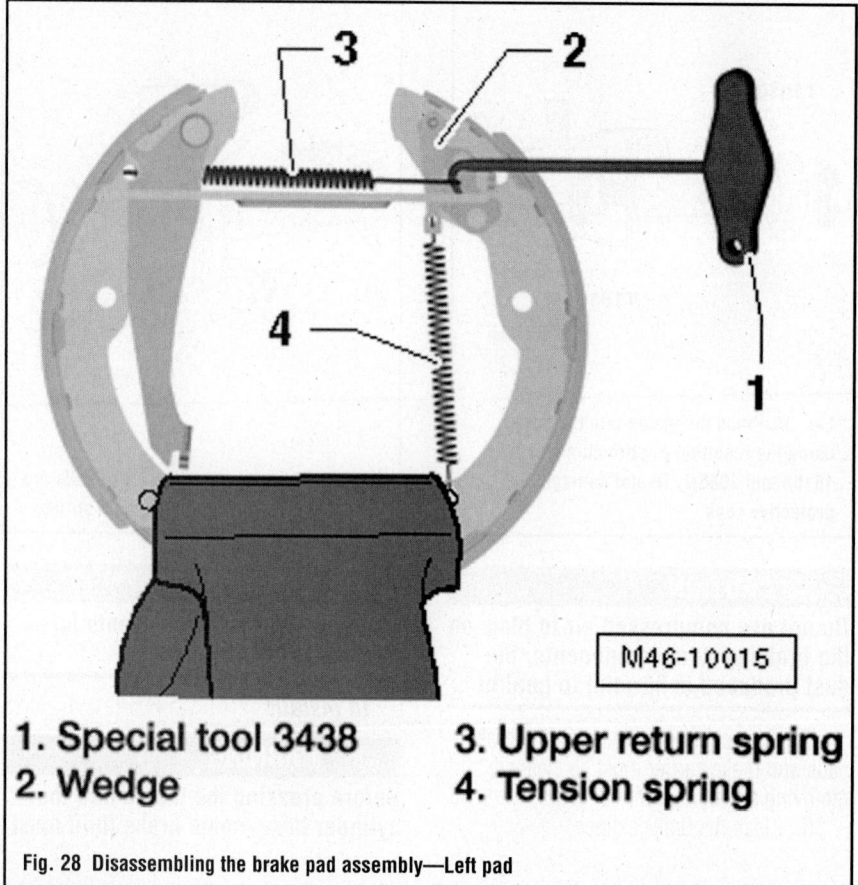

M46-10015

1. Special tool 3438
2. Wedge
3. Upper return spring
4. Tension spring

Fig. 28 Disassembling the brake pad assembly—Left pad

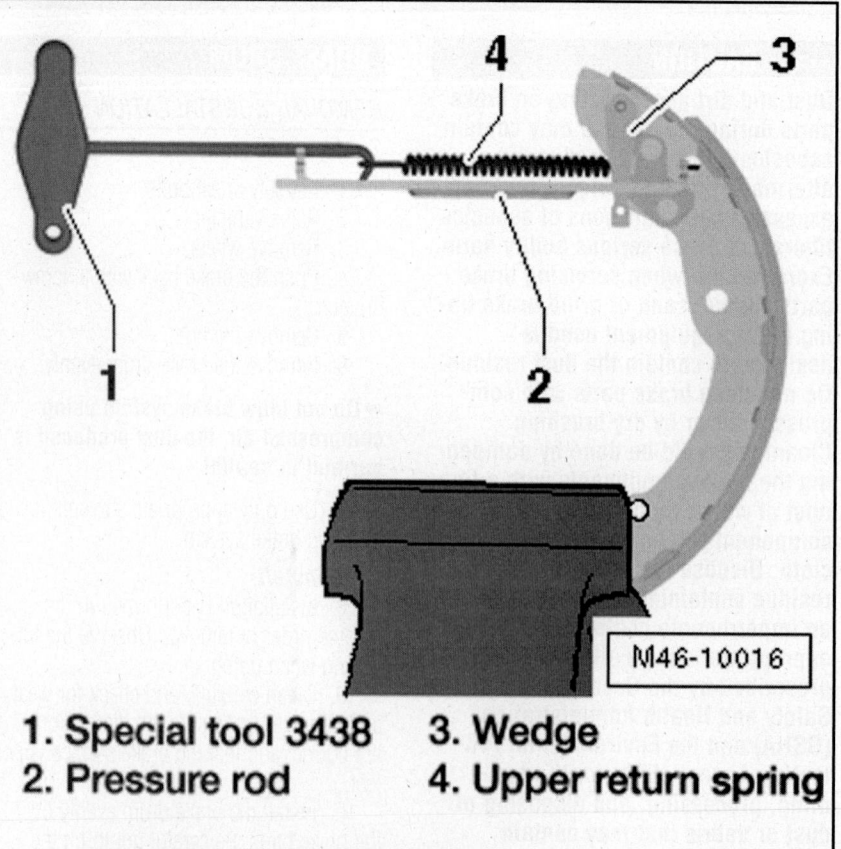

M46-10016

1. Special tool 3438
2. Pressure rod
3. Wedge
4. Upper return spring

Fig. 29 Disassembling the brake pad assembly—Right pad

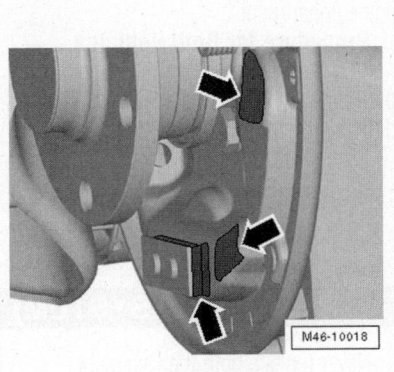

Fig. 30 Identifying lubrication contact surfaces

17. Remove the pressure rod and wedge from the brake shoe.

➡**Do not blow brake system using**

compressed air, the dust produced is harmful to health!

18. Cleaning: Use only appropriate solvents for cleaning brake system.

To install:

19. Installation is performed in the reverse order of removal. Observe the following when doing so:

20. Hook the contact spring into the pressure rod.

21. Engage the wedge at the same time.

Installation position:

22. The elevation must be visible when installing.

23. Attach the brake shoe with the parking brake lever to the pressure rod.

24. Attach the return spring.

25. Engage the tension spring for the wedge. Lubricate the contact surfaces for the brake shoes on the support plate and on the brake carrier (distributed on the circumference; 6 places) with adhesive lubricating paste G 000 650.

26. Install the brake shoes between the wheel hub and the brake carrier.

27. Mount the brake shoes on the brake cylinder piston.

28. Attach the parking brake cable to the parking brake lever.

29. Install the return spring at the bottom using the 3438.

30. Pry the brake shoe behind the lower support.

31. Install the spring plate with the pressure spring and turn it 90°.

32. Install the brake drum. Refer to Brake Drum.

33. Install the wheels and tighten them.

34. Adjust the parking brake. Refer to Parking Brake, Adjusting, with Rear Drum Brakes.

BRAKES

PARKING BRAKE

PARKING BRAKE CABLES

ADJUSTMENT

Disc

See Figure 31.

A new adjustment is necessary only after replacing brake cables, brake calipers or brake discs.

1. Raise vehicle.

2. Press the brake pedal forcefully at least three times.

3. Apply the parking brake 3 times and then release.

4. The parking brake lever must go back into the rest position by itself under the first detent.

5. Condition: Parking brake lever in released position.

Vehicles with the Highline Center Console

6. Open the cover on the rear storage compartment.

7. Remove the mat from the storage compartment.

Vehicles with the Basic Center Console

8. Remove the mat from the rear storage compartment.

Procedure for Both Vehicles

9. Tighten the adjusting nut until the levers on the brake calipers start to lift.

10. The distance a between the lever 1 to

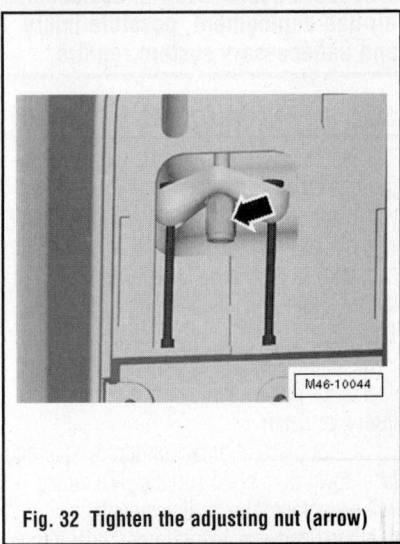

Fig. 32 Tighten the adjusting nut (arrow)

the stop 2 on the left and right brake calipers may be ≤ 1.5 mm together.

11. Check whether wheels turn freely.

12. Due to the automatic rear brake adjuster, there is no need to adjust the parking brake after making initial adjustment.

Drum

See Figure 32.

It is not necessary to adjust the parking brake due to automatic adjustment of the drum brakes on the rear axle.

An adjustment is necessary only after replacing parking brake cables, brake drums, brake carriers or brake pads.

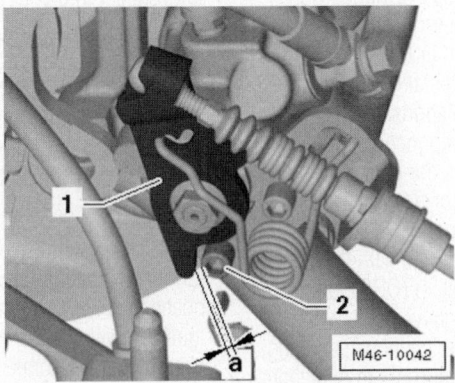

Fig. 31 The distance a between the lever 1 to the stop 2 on the left and right brake calipers may be ≤ 1.5 mm together

1. Raise vehicle.
2. Press the brake pedal forcefully at least three times.
3. Apply the parking brake 3 times and then release.
4. The parking brake lever must go back into the rest position by itself under the first detent.
5. Condition: Parking brake lever in released position.

6. Engage parking brake 4 teeth.

Vehicles with the Highline Center Console

7. Open the cover on the rear storage compartment.
8. Remove the mat from the storage compartment.

Vehicles with the Basis Center Console

9. Remove the mat from the rear storage compartment.

Procedure for Both Vehicles

10. Tighten the adjusting nut enough until both wheels can only be moved with difficulty by hand.
11. Release the parking brake.
12. Condition: Parking brake lever in released position.

CHASSIS ELECTRICAL

AIR BAG (SUPPLEMENTAL RESTRAINT SYSTEM)

GENERAL INFORMATION

✳✳ CAUTION

These vehicles are equipped with an air bag system. The system must be disarmed before performing service on, or around, system components, the steering column, instrument panel components, wiring and sensors. Failure to follow the safety precautions and the disarming procedure could result in accidental air bag deployment, possible injury and unnecessary system repairs.

SERVICE PRECAUTIONS

Disconnect and isolate the battery negative cable before beginning any airbag system component diagnosis, testing, removal, or installation procedures. Allow system capacitor to discharge for two minutes before beginning any component service. This will disable the airbag system. Failure to disable the airbag system may result in accidental airbag deployment, personal injury, or death.

Do not place an intact undeployed airbag face down on a solid surface. The airbag will propel into the air if accidentally deployed and may result in personal injury or death.

When carrying or handling an undeployed airbag, the trim side (face) of the airbag should be pointing away from the body to minimize possibility of injury if accidental deployment occurs. Failure to do this may result in personal injury or death.

Replace airbag system components with OEM replacement parts. Substitute parts may appear interchangeable, but internal differences may result in inferior occupant protection. Failure to do so may result in occupant personal injury or death.

Wear safety glasses, rubber gloves, and long sleeved clothing when cleaning powder residue from vehicle after an airbag deployment. Powder residue emitted from a deployed airbag can cause skin irritation. Flush affected area with cool water if irritation is experienced. If nasal or throat irritation is experienced, exit the vehicle for fresh air until the irritation ceases. If irritation continues, see a physician.

Do not use a replacement airbag that is not in the original packaging. This may result in improper deployment, personal injury, or death.

The factory installed fasteners, screws and bolts used to fasten airbag components have a special coating and are specifically designed for the airbag system. Do not use substitute fasteners. Use only original equipment fasteners listed in the parts catalog when fastener replacement is required.

During, and following, any child restraint anchor service, due to impact event or vehicle repair, carefully inspect all mounting hardware, tether straps, and anchors for proper installation, operation, or damage. If a child restraint anchor is found damaged in any way, the anchor must be replaced. Failure to do this may result in personal injury or death.

Deployed and non-deployed airbags may or may not have live pyrotechnic material within the airbag inflator.

Do not dispose of driver/passenger/curtain airbags or seat belt tensioners unless you are sure of complete deployment. Refer to the Hazardous Substance Control System for proper disposal.

Dispose of deployed airbags and tensioners consistent with state, provincial, local, and federal regulations.

After any airbag component testing or service, do not connect the battery negative cable. Personal injury or death may result if the system test is not performed first.

If the vehicle is equipped with the Occupant Classification System (OCS), do not connect the battery negative cable before performing the OCS Verification Test using the scan tool and the appropriate diagnostic information. Personal injury or death may result if the system test is not performed properly.

Never replace both the Occupant Restraint Controller (ORC) and the Occupant Classification Module (OCM) at the same time. If both require replacement, replace one, then perform the Airbag System test before replacing the other.

Both the ORC and the OCM store Occupant Classification System (OCS) calibration data, which they transfer to one another when one of them is replaced. If both are replaced at the same time, an irreversible fault will be set in both modules and the OCS may malfunction and cause personal injury or death.

If equipped with OCS, the Seat Weight Sensor is a sensitive, calibrated unit and must be handled carefully. Do not drop or handle roughly. If dropped or damaged, replace with another sensor. Failure to do so may result in occupant injury or death.

If equipped with OCS, the front passenger seat must be handled carefully as well. When removing the seat, be careful when setting on floor not to drop. If dropped, the sensor may be inoperative, could result in occupant injury, or possibly death.

If equipped with OCS, when the passenger front seat is on the floor, no one should sit in the front passenger seat. This uneven force may damage the sensing ability of the seat weight sensors. If sat on and damaged, the sensor may be inoperative, could result in occupant injury, or possibly death.

DISARMING THE SYSTEM

➡**The Anti-theft system must be deactivated before disconnecting the battery to avoid system engagement upon reconnecting the battery.**

The Anti-theft system is deactivated when the vehicle is unlocked via the unlock button on the key fob, or when the vehicle is opened via Keyless Access, or when the ignition switch is turned **ON** (with a charged battery connected), or when the immobilizer registers an authorized key. Do not disconnect the positive battery terminal unless the battery is to be removed.

Disconnect the negative battery cable to disarm the airbag system. No waiting time is necessary before beginning work.

ARMING THE SYSTEM

➡**The Anti-theft system must be deactivated before disconnecting the battery to avoid system engagement upon reconnecting the battery.**

The Anti-theft system is deactivated when the vehicle is unlocked via the unlock button on the key fob, or when the vehicle is opened via Keyless Access, or when the ignition switch is turned **ON** (with a charged battery connected), or when the immobilizer registers an authorized key. Do not disconnect the positive battery terminal unless the battery is to be removed.

After reconnecting the airbag wiring, turn the ignition switch **ON** and make sure no one is inside the vehicle, then connect the battery cable.

CLOCKSPRING CENTERING

1. Before servicing the vehicle, refer to the precautions.

2. When installing spiral spring, spiral spring must be in center position and wheels must be in the "straight ahead position".

3. The following depicts center position of spiral spring, which is dependent on the manufacturer.

    a. The color marked (black square) band must be located in viewing window.

    b. The color marked (yellow) band must be located in viewing window.

DRIVE TRAIN

AUTOMATIC TRANSAXLE FLUID

DRAIN AND REFILL

See Figures 33 through 35.

Use the Direct Shift Gearbox (DSG) transmission fluid as a replacement part. Refer to the Parts Catalog. Short Description

First, the fluid temperature is read out. If it is higher than 122° F, then let the transmission cool down.

Turn off the engine, remove the overflow tube and drain any transmission fluid. Install the overflow tube and overfill the transmission fluid.

Start the engine and drain any excess fluid until the level has reached the overflow tube.

Tools:
• Vehicle Diagnosis, Testing and Information System VAS 5051B
• Oil Collecting and Extracting Device V.A.G 1782
• Adapter for Oil Filling VAS 6262 A

Requirements
• The engine is off.
• The vehicle is level and all hoist supports are the same height.
• The noise insulation is removed if necessary
• The selector level is in the "P" position.
• The vehicle diagnosis, testing and information system VAS 5051B is connected.
• The transmission fluid should not be warmer than 45°C (113°F) when starting the procedure.

Procedure
1. Follow the rules of cleanliness when working on the transmission.
2. Only use the transmission fluid for the DSG available as a replacement part. Other fluids can cause malfunctions or transmission failure.

➡**Risk of injury due to hot transmission fluid.**

3. Connect the vehicle diagnosis, testing and information system VAS 5051B and identify the vehicle in Guided Functions.

4. Select DSG transmission.

5. Select Check Fluid Level.

6. Let the transmission cool down if the fluid temperature is higher than 113° F.

➡**Do not start the engine if there is no transmission fluid in the transmission.**

7. Engine off - do not start!

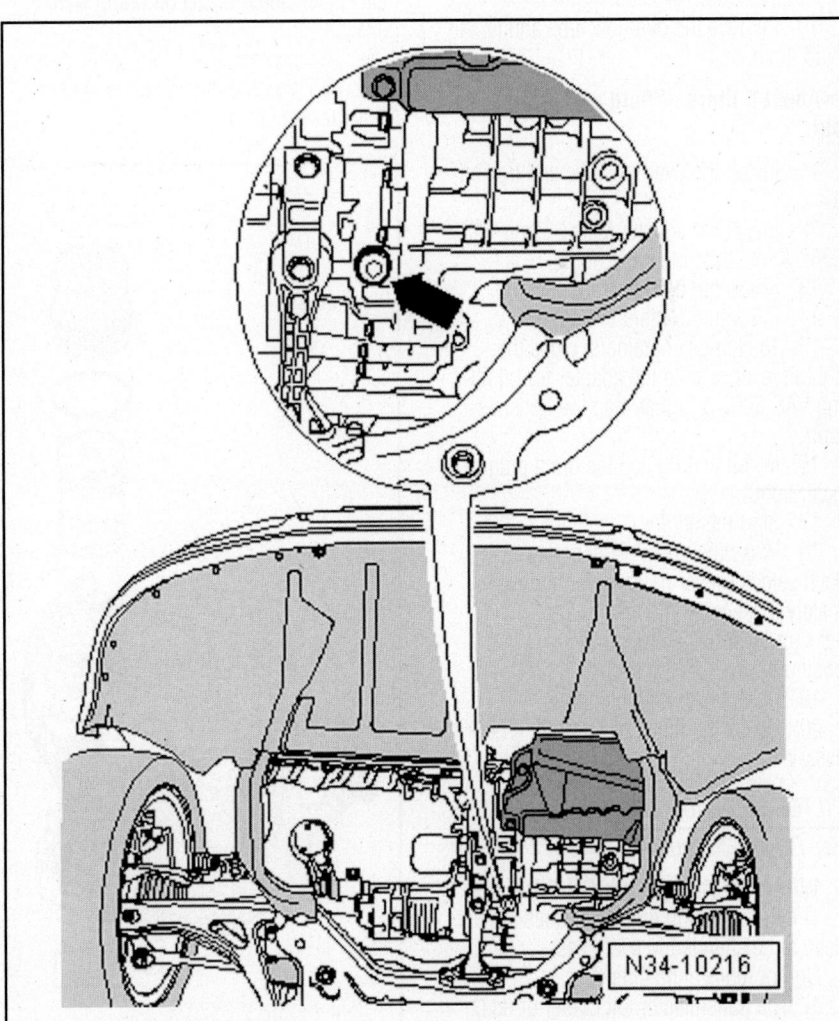

Fig. 33 Remove the drain plug (arrow) near the pendulum support

Fig. 34 Remove the overflow tube (arrow) and let the fluid drain

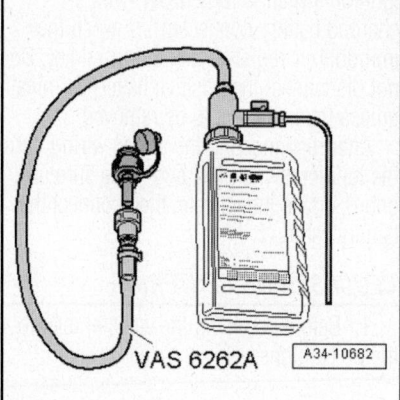

Fig. 35 Install the adapter for oil filling VAS 6262 A into the hole hand tight

8. Remove the drain plug near the pendulum support.

9. A black plastic overflow tube is located in this hole (with a 8 mm hex socket head). Its length determines the oil level in the transmission.

10. Remove the overflow tube and let the fluid drain.

➡**About 5 liters of fluid will drain out.**

11. Install the overflow tube and tighten it.

12. Install the adapter for oil filling VAS 6262 A into the hole hand tight.

13. Shake the bottle before opening.

14. Fill with 5.5 liters of fluid.

15. To change containers, close the shutoff lever or hold the adapter for oil filling VAS 6262 A higher than the transmission.

16. Install and tighten the drain plug hand tight.

17. Start the engine.

18. Press the brake pedal and select each selector lever position for approximately 3 seconds, then move the selector lever back into the "P" position.

19. Do not turn off the engine.

20. Check the fluid level and fill if necessary.

FILTER REPLACEMENT

See Figures 36 and 37.

When To Change the Oil Filter

The transmission fluid filter does not need to be changed in every case.

Do not replace the filter if:

1. The transmission oil cooler or its O-rings were replaced and no coolant has gotten into the fluid.

2. The selector shaft seal was replaced.

3. The flange or stub shaft seal was replaced.

4. Leaking Mechatronic covers, the multi-plate clutch or the oil pump were replaced.

5. The transmission input speed sensor G182 with clutch oil temperature sensor G509 was replaced.

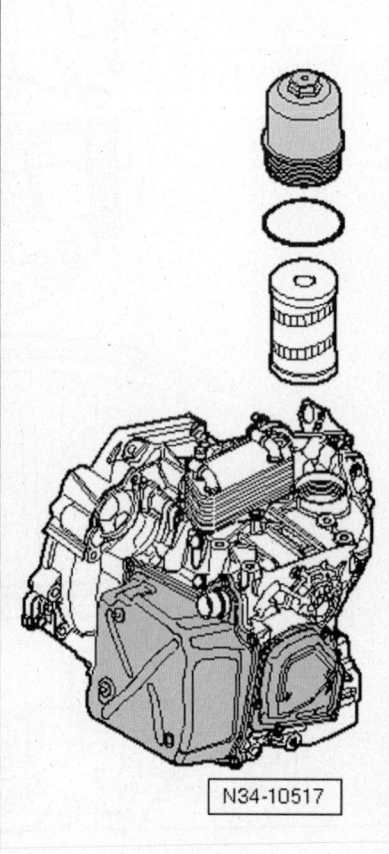

Fig. 36 Replacing the filter

The filter must be replaced if:

6. The 60,000 km maintenance interval was reached.

7. Coolant has entered the fluid.

8. Metal shavings were found in the fluid.

9. The clutch is burned or has a mechanical fault.

MANUAL TRANSAXLE FLUID

DRAIN AND REFILL

See Figure 38.

1. For the correct transmission fluid, refer to the Parts Catalog.

2. Remove the noise insulation.

3. Remove the oil fill plug in order to check the transmission fluid level.

4. The level is correct when the transmission fluid comes up to the bottom edge of hole.

5. Install the plug with a new seal.

6. Tighten the plug to specification.

7. Note the following when filling for the first time:

   a. Remove the oil fill plug.

   b. Add transmission fluid until it reaches the lower edge of the hole.

   c. Install the plug with a new seal.

   d. Tighten the plug to specification.

   e. Install the noise insulation.

   f. I - Plug with a multi-point socket head, 45 Nm (see accompanying graphic).

   g. II - Plug with hex socket head, 30 Nm (see accompanying graphic)

FILTER

Refer to Automatic Transmission filter replacement.

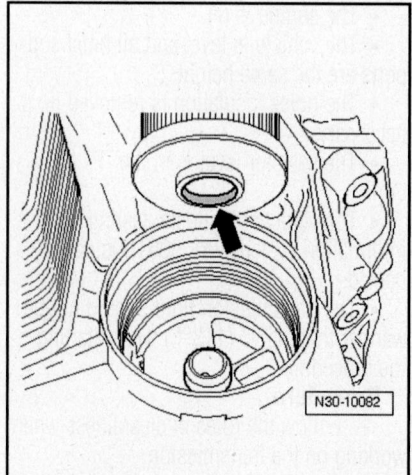

Fig. 37 Install the new filter with the seat facing downward and tighten the housing to 20 Nm

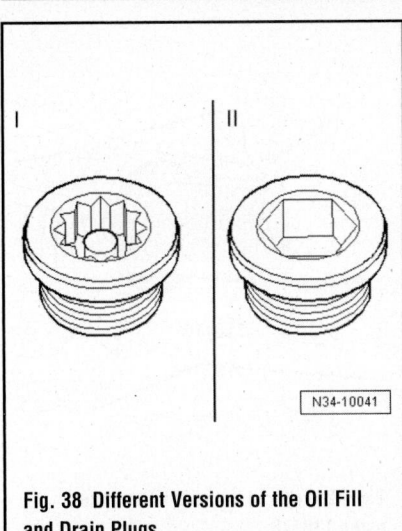

Fig. 38 Different Versions of the Oil Fill and Drain Plugs

CLUTCH

BLEEDING

Except Pressure Bleeder

1. Before servicing the vehicle, refer to the Precautions Section.

2. The clutch and brakes share the same reservoir. Clean all dirt and grease from the cap to be sure no foreign substances enter the system.

3. Remove the cap and diaphragm and fill the reservoir to the top with the approved DOT 3 or 4 brake fluid. Fully loosen the bleed screw which is in the slave cylinder body next to the inlet connection.

4. At this point bubbles of air will appear at the bleed screw outlet. When the slave cylinder is full and a steady stream of fluid comes out of the slave cylinder bleeder, tighten the bleed screw.

5. Refill the reservoir and cap it. Exert a light load of about 20 lbs. (9 kg) to the slave cylinder piston by pushing the release lever towards the cylinder and loosen the bleed screw. Maintain a constant light load; fluid and any air that is left will be expelled through the bleed port. Tighten the bleed screw when a steady flow of fluid with no air is being expelled.

6. Fill the reservoir fluid level back to normal capacity, if necessary repeat Step 4.

7. Exert a light load to the release lever but do not open the bleeder screw as the piston in the slave cylinder will move slowly down the bore. Repeat this operation 2–3 times; the fluid movement will force any air left in the system into the reservoir. The hydraulic system should now be fully bled.

8. Check the operation of the clutch hydraulic system and repeat this procedure, if necessary.

Pressure Bleeder

1. Before servicing the vehicle, refer to the precautions.

2. Remove entire air filter housing if bleeder is not accessible through it.

3. Connect brake filler/bleeder unit VAS 5234 or V.A.G 1869.

➡**If necessary, use bleeder hose (670 mm long) V.A.G 1238/B3 to bleed system.**

4. Connect bleeder hose to collector bottle of brake bleeder unit.

5. Connect bleeder hose to bleeder.

6. Pressurize the system to 29 psi (2 bar).

7. Open bleeder valve approximately 1/4 rotation.

8. Move the clutch pedal 15 to 20 times rapidly by hand from stop to stop.

9. Close bleeder valve and switch bleeder device off.

10. After completing the bleeding procedure, if a pressure of 29 psi (2 bar) has been released, operate brake pedal 10 times using the foot.

11. If removed, install entire air filter housing.

FLUID FILL PROCEDURE

Refer to Brakes.

FRONT HALFSHAFT

REMOVAL & INSTALLATION

See Figure 39.

1. Before servicing the vehicle, refer to the precautions.

2. Loosen drive axle bolt to wheel hub

3. When doing this, vehicle must not stand on wheels, otherwise wheel bearing may be damaged.

4. Remove wheel.

5. Remove lower noise insulation.

6. Remove nuts.

7. Pull wheel bearing housing with ball joint out of control arm.

8. Pull drive axle out of wheel hub and secure to body.

9. Attach wedge tool T10161 between transmission housing and triple roller joint.

10. Press inner joint out of transmission by tapping with hammer onto wedge tool T10161.

11. Remove drive axle.

To install:

12. Insert new securing ring into groove of joint piece pin.

13. Mesh outer and inner splines of joint piece and transmission.

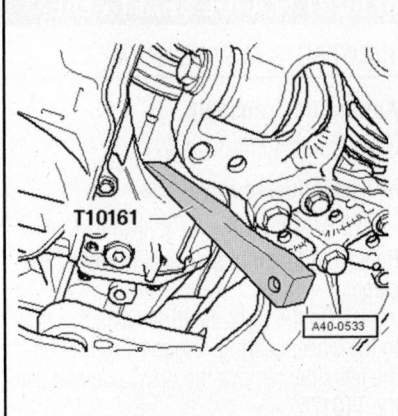

Fig. 39 Press inner joint out of transmission by tapping with hammer onto wedge tool T10161

14. Grasp drive axle by hand and slide into joint piece until stop.

15. Slide joint piece into transmission with a "jerk".

Sliding part in joint piece can be used for this "jerk". Do not pull drive axle out of joint piece too far when doing this.

16. Do not use hammer or other knocking tool under any circumstance!

17. Check drive axle in transmission for proper seating by pulling joint piece against resistance from circlip.

➡**For this check, do not pull drive axle but pull joint piece only.**

18. Insert outer joint as far as possible into wheel hub splines.

19. Remove lower noise insulation.

20. Bolt on ball joint with control arm.

21. Ensure that boot is not damaged or twisted.

22. Tighten drive axle bolt to wheel hub.

23. When doing this, vehicle must not stand on wheels, otherwise wheel bearing may be damaged.

24. Install wheel.

25. Tighten bolts/nuts to specification as follows:

- Ball joint to control arm (Use new nut): 44 ft. lbs. (60 Nm)
- Drive axle to wheel hub "hex head bolt" (Use new bolt): 148 ft. lbs. (200 Nm) 180° additional rotation
- Drive axle to wheel hub "12-point bolt" (Use new bolt): 52 ft. lbs. (70 Nm) plus 90° additional rotation
- Drive axle to wheel hub "hex head bolt" (Use new bolt): 148 ft. lbs. (200 Nm) 180° additional rotation
- Drive axle to wheel hub "12-point bolt" (Use new bolt): 52 ft. lbs. (70 Nm) plus 90° additional rotation

FRONT FLANGE SHAFT SEAL

REMOVAL & INSTALLATION

Automatic Transaxle

See Figures 40 through 43.

➡**Transmission in vehicle.**

1. Only the left side is described here. Replacing the right side seal is almost the same.

2. On the right, the drive axle remains in the wheel bearing, use the T10177, on the left side, remove the drive axle and use the T10176.

3. Necessary tools:
   - Drip tray V.A.G 1306
   - Puller T10055
   - Thrust piece T10176

4. Remove the noise insulation.

5. Place the VAG 1306 underneath.

6. Remove the left ball joint lower nuts arrows from the control arm.

7. Press the drive axle out of the transmission.

Right Side

8. Place the right drive axle as far upward as possible and secure it in this position.

Left Side

➡**Do not set the vehicle on the floor.**

9. Press the brake in order to remove the left drive axle bolt.

10. Remove the left drive axle.

11. Seal the opening of the drive axle at the transmission using clean cloth.

12. Carefully drill a hole B (2 to 4 millimeters (mm) in size) into the outer metal ring C of the seal.
   a. Grease the drill bit B so that the drill shavings remain held.

b. Drill only through the metal ring C, otherwise the transmission may be damaged.

13. Install a screw (approximately 4 mm in diameter) into the drilled hole in the seal. Do not install the screw too deeply to prevent damage to bearing lying behind it.

14. Pull out the seal using T10055 and T10055/2.

15. Remove the cloth and thoroughly clean the transmission and opening for the drive axle.

16. Metal shavings must not get into the transmission or into the opening for the drive axle, vacuum up the shavings if necessary.

17. If only the metal ring of the seal could be removed, carefully pry out the remaining seal using screwdriver.

To install:

18. Installation is performed in the reverse order of removal. Pay attention to the following:

19. Lubricate the outer circumference and sealing lips of the seal with Automatic Transmission Fluid (ATF).

20. Installed position: The open side of the seal faces the transmission.

21. Install the seal by hand as far as possible.

Left Side

Drive in the seal until seated using T10176, do not tilt the seal while doing this.

Right Side

22. Drive in the seal until seated using T10177, do not tilt the seal while doing this.

23. Install the drive axle.

24. Check the ATF level and top off.

25. Install the noise insulation.

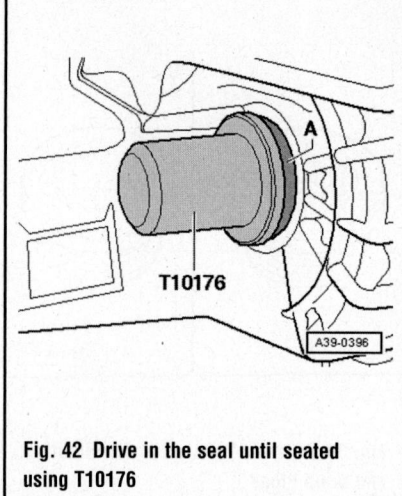

Fig. 42 Drive in the seal until seated using T10176

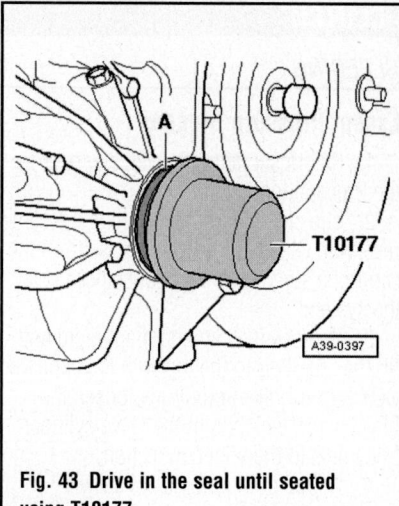

Fig. 43 Drive in the seal until seated using T10177

DSG Transaxle

Left Side

See Figures 44 and 45.

➡**Do not remove both bolts in the right and left flange shafts or the right stub shaft at the same time. If the differential bevel gears rotate, it will be difficult to install the bolts.**

Necessary tools:
- Slide Hammer-Complete Set VW 771
- Additional Part for VW 771 VW 771/37
- Thrust Piece 3305
- Torque Wrench (5-50 Nm) V.A.G 1331
- Torque Wrench (40-200 Nm) V.A.G 1332
- Sealing Grease for Seal G 052 128 A1
- Drip Tray for VAS 6100 VAS 6208

1. Remove the left wheel.
2. Remove the noise insulation.

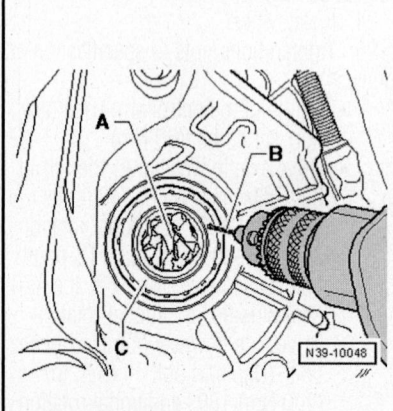

Fig. 40 Drill a hole (B) (2 to 4 millimeters (mm) in size) into the outer metal ring (C) of the seal

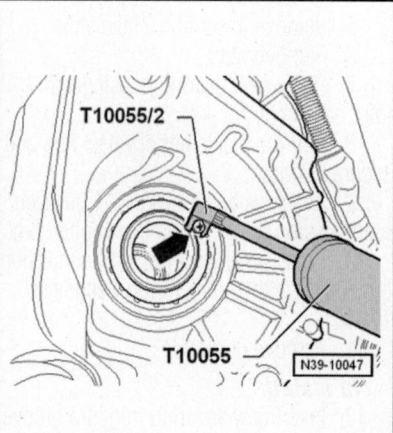

Fig. 41 Pull out the seal using T10055 and T10055/2

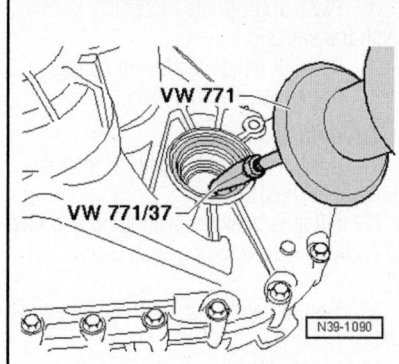

Fig. 44 Pull out the seal for the flange shaft using the slide hammer-complete set VW 771 and additional part for VW 771 VW 771/37

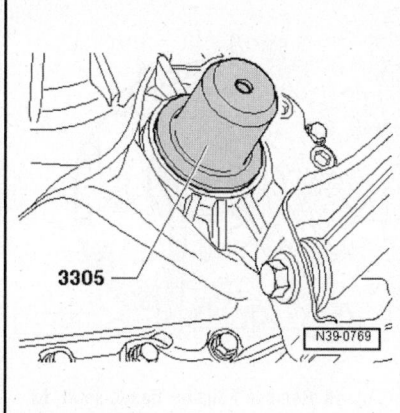

Fig. 45 Install the seal until seated and without tilting it using thrust piece 3305

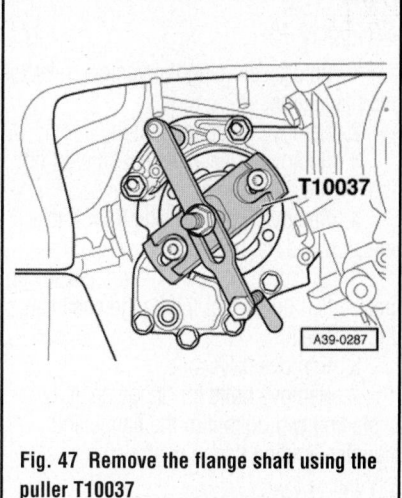

Fig. 47 Remove the flange shaft using the puller T10037

3. Remove the lower section of the left front wheel housing liner.

4. Remove the left drive axle.

5. Place the drip tray for VAS 6100 VAS 6208 under the transmission.

6. Remove bolt for the flange shaft, by installing two bolts into the flange and counter holding the flange shaft using a pry bar.

7. Remove the flange shaft together with the spring.

8. Pull out the seal for the flange shaft using the slide hammer-complete set VW 771 and additional part for VW 771 VW 771/37.

9. Lightly lubricate the new seal on the outer circumference.

10. Fill the space between the sealing and dust lips halfway with sealing grease for seal G 052 128.

11. Install the seal until seated and without tilting it using thrust piece 3305.

12. Install the flange shaft.

13. Tighten the new bolt to 30 Nm. Push the flange shaft against the transmission so that the bolt engages in the thread.

14. Install the left drive axle.

15. Install the left front wheel housing liner.

16. Install the left wheel.

17. Check the transmission fluid level and fill if necessary.

18. Install the noise insulation.

Right Side—with AWD

See Figures 46 and 47.

1. Remove the right drive axle.

2. Remove the right drive axle heat shield bolts arrows and shield from the bevel box.

3. Place the oil collecting and extracting device V.A.G 1782 under the transmission.

4. Remove right flange shaft countersunk bolt using the socket and extended bit T10107 by installing 2 bolts in the flange and counter holding the flange shaft with a pry bar.

5. Remove the flange shaft using the puller T10037.

6. Install in reverse order of removal. Pay attention to the following:

7. Replace the flange shaft countersunk bolt.

8. Remove the seal from the groove and replace it.

9. Carefully install the flange shaft while rotating it at the same time.

10. Secure the flange shaft with new countersunk bolt, tightening specification, refer to Flange Shaft and Bevel Box Seals Overview.

11. Install the right drive axle.

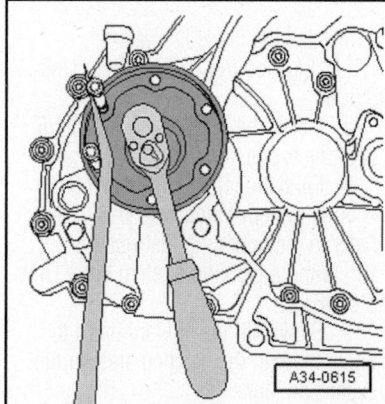

Fig. 46 Remove right flange shaft countersunk bolt using the socket and extended bit T10107

12. Check the fluid level in the bevel box, fill if necessary. Refer to Bevel Box Fluid Level, Checking and Filling.

Right Side

Refer to Automatic Transaxle.

Manual Transaxle

Left

See Figure 48.

1. Before servicing the vehicle, refer to the precautions.

2. Remove left wheel.

3. Remove noise insulation.

4. Remove the lower part of the left front wheel housing liner.

5. Remove left drive axle.

6. Place appropriate receptacle underneath transmission.

7. Remove bolts for flange shaft, by screwing two bolts into the flange and counter-holding flange shaft using a pry bar.

8. Pull out flange shaft with spring.

9. Pull out flange shaft oil seal.

To install:

10. Drive new seal in as far as the stop; be sure not to distort seal.

11. Fill area between sealing lip and dust lip halfway with sealing grease G 052 128 A1.

12. Insert flange shaft.

13. Secure flange shaft with countersunk bolt.

14. Install left drive axle.

15. Install lower section of the left front wheel housing liner.

16. Install wheel.

17. Check gear oil.

18. Install noise insulation.

Right

See Figure 48

1. Before servicing the vehicle, refer to the precautions.
2. Remove noise insulation.
3. Remove drive axle heat shield from the engine, if equipped bolts 1.
4. Remove left drive axle from transmission and tie it up high.
5. On some engines, the drive axle cannot be tied up so that the flange shaft can be removed.
6. Remove drive axle.
7. Remove bolts for flange shaft, by installing two bolts into the flange and counter-holding flange shaft using a pry bar.

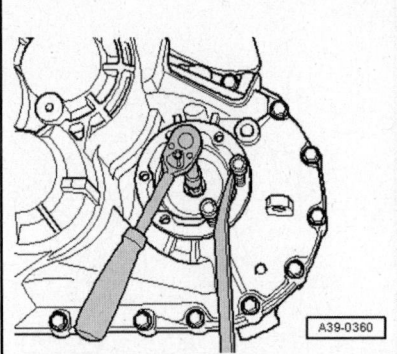

Fig. 48 Remove bolts for flange shaft, by screwing two bolts into the flange and counter-holding flange shaft using a pry bar

8. Place appropriate receptacle underneath transmission.
9. Pull out flange shaft with spring.
10. Pry out seal with a lever.

To install:

11. Drive new seal in as far as stop; be sure not to distort seal.
12. Fill area between sealing lip and dust lip halfway with sealing grease G 052 128 A1.
13. Secure flange shaft with countersunk bolt.
14. Install right drive axle.
15. Install drive axle heat shield to the engine, if equipped bolts.
16. Check gear oil.
17. Install noise insulation.

ENGINE COOLING

ENGINE COOLANT

DRAIN & REFILL PROCEDURE

2.0L Engine

See Figure 49.

Draining

1. Open the coolant expansion tank cap.
2. Remove the noise insulation.
3. Remove the coolant hose clip downward and remove the coolant hose from the radiator quick-release coupling.
4. In addition, to drain the coolant from the engine, disconnect the coolant hose at the oil cooler.

➡Observe disposal regulations!

➡Only use tap water for mixing. Well water does not have the quality needed to ensure the coolant will function correctly.

Filling

5. Only use coolant additive G12 plus-plus that conforms to TL VW 774 G.
6. G12 plus-plus prevents frost and corrosion damage, scaling and also raises the boiling point. The cooling system must be filled with coolant additive year-round.
7. Because of its high boiling point, the coolant improves engine reliability under heavy loads, particularly in countries with tropical climates.
8. Protection against frost must be assured down to approximately -13 ° F (in arctic climatic countries down to approximately -31 ° F).

9. The coolant concentration must not be reduced by adding water even in warmer seasons and in warmer countries. The coolant additive portion must be at least 40%.
10. The amount of G12 plus-plus can be increased if more freeze protection is needed. However, it may only be increased up to 60%, which provides freeze protection down to approximately -40 ° F.
11. Otherwise the freeze protection and cooling effect are reduced.
12. If the radiator, heater core, cylinder head or cylinder head gasket is replaced, do not reuse the old coolant.
13. The refractometer T10007 is recommended for determining freeze protection density.
14. Install the lower coolant hose and secure with the retaining clamp.
15. Connect the coolant hoses to the oil cooler and to the engine coolant circulation pump 2.
16. Install the noise insulation.
17. Using Cooling System Filler Unit VAS 6096:
    a. Install the adapter V.A.G 1274/8 onto the expansion tank.
    b. Fill the coolant circuit using the cooling system filling unit VAS 6096. Refer to the operating instructions.
18. Without Cooling System Filler Unit VAS 6096:
    a. Slowly fill the coolant up to the upper mark in the hatched area on the expansion tank.
    b. Close the expansion tank.
19. Start the engine and maintain an engine speed of about 2000 RPM for approximately 3 minutes.

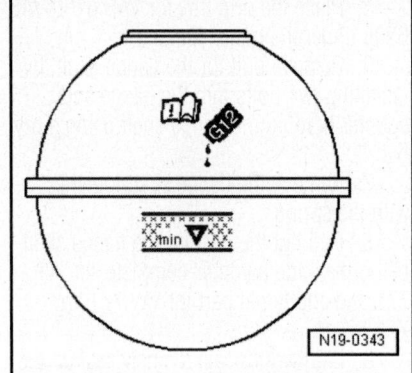

Fig. 49 Slowly fill the coolant up to the upper mark in the hatched area on the expansion tank

20. Let the engine run at idle until the coolant fan turns on.
21. Check the coolant level and fill if necessary. With the engine at operating temperature, the coolant level must be at the top mark, with the engine cold, it must be in the center of the hatched area.

2.5L Engine

Draining

- Drained coolant must be stored in a clean container for disposal or reuse.
- Follow all disposal regulations.
- Risk of scalding due to hot steam and hot coolant.
- The coolant system is under pressure when the engine is warm.
- Wear protective goggles and protective clothing to prevent damage to eyes and scalding.

• Reduce pressure by covering the coolant expansion tank cap with a cloth and carefully opening.

1. Open the coolant expansion tank cap.

2. Remove the noise insulation.

3. Place the drip tray under the radiator.

4. Open the spring clamp and remove the coolant hose.

Filling

5. Only use distilled water for mixing with G12 plus-plus. Using distilled water provides optimum corrosion protection.

6. Only use coolant additive G12 plus-plus that conforms to TL VW 774 G.

7. Coolant additives with the note "conforming to TL VW 774 G" prevent frost, corrosion damage and scaling. They also increase the boiling point. For this reason the system must be filled all year round with frost and corrosion protection additives.

8. Because of its high boiling point, the coolant improves engine reliability under heavy loads, particularly in countries with tropical climates.

9. Protection against frost must be assured down to approximately -13 ° F) (in arctic climatic countries down to approximately -31° F.

10. The coolant concentration must not be reduced by adding water even in warmer seasons and in warmer countries. The coolant additive portion must be at least 40%.

11. If a lower freeze protection is necessary due to the climatic conditions, increase the amount of coolant additive. Increase the coolant additive only up to 60% (freeze protection down to approximately -40 ° F). Otherwise the freeze protection and cooling effect are reduced.

12. The refractometer T10007 is recommended for determining freeze protection density.

13. If the radiator, heater core, cylinder head or cylinder head gasket is replaced, do not reuse the old coolant.

14. Using Cooling System Filler Unit VAS 6096:

   a. Install the adapter V.A.G 1274/8 onto the expansion tank.

   b. Fill the coolant circuit using the cooling system filling unit VAS 6096. Refer to the operating instructions.

15. Without Cooling System Filler Unit VAS 6096:

   a. Slowly fill the coolant up to the upper mark in the hatched area on the expansion tank.

   b. Close the expansion tank.

16. Turn off the heater and air conditioning.

17. Start the engine and maintain an engine speed of about 2000 RPM for approximately 3 minutes.

18. Let the engine run at idle until the coolant fan turns on.

19. Check the coolant level and fill if necessary. With the engine at operating temperature, the coolant level must be at the top mark, with the engine cold, it must be in the center of the hatched area.

ENGINE FAN

REMOVAL & INSTALLATION

2.0L Engines

See Figures 50 and 51.

1. Remove the bolts upper arrows at the top of the fan shroud.

2. Remove the noise insulation.

3. Remove the hot side hose for the charge air pipe. Loosen the hose clamp and lift the circlip.

4. Disconnect the connector.

5. Remove the bottom bolts lower arrows.

6. Remove the fan shroud and fans.

7. Disconnect the connector and (if equipped) and free up the wires.

8. Remove the nuts arrows and remove the fans.

9. Installation is performed in the reverse order of removal.

2.5L Engines

See Figure 52.

1. Remove the noise insulation.

2. Unclip the lower coolant hose from fan shroud.

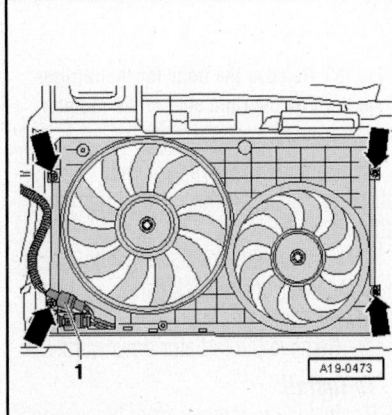

Fig. 50 Fan shroud bolts and electrical connector (1)

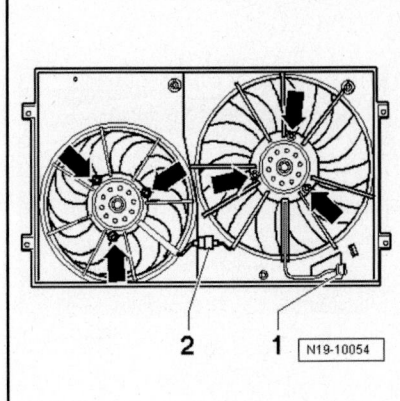

Fig. 51 Locating fan bolts and fan connectors (1 and 2)

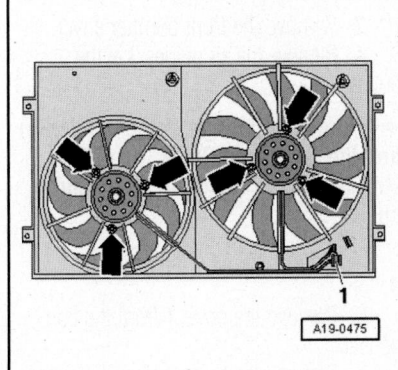

Fig. 52 Locating fan bolts and fan connector (1)

3. Disconnect the connector from the engine coolant temperature sensor on radiator G83.

4. Disconnect the electrical harness connector 1 and remove the fan shroud bolts arrows.

5. Move the fan shroud downward and to the left side.

6. Disconnect the electrical harness connector 1 and lay the wire free.

7. Remove the nuts arrows and remove the fans.

8. Installation is performed in the reverse order of removal.

RADIATOR

REMOVAL & INSTALLATION

2.0L Engine

See Figure 53.

1. Remove the air shroud with the radiator fans.

   a. Drain the coolant.

2. Open the spring clamps and remove the coolant hoses from the radiator.

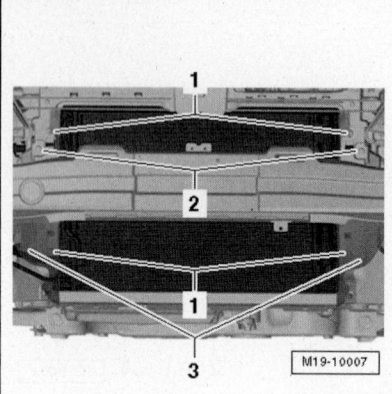

Fig. 53 Locating the bolts from the condenser (1), bolts from the radiator mounts and air guides (3)

3. Remove the front bumper cover.

4. Remove the air guides 3 at the bottom.

➡ **To prevent damage to the condenser and the refrigerant lines, do not stretch, kink or bend the pipes and hoses.**

5. Remove the air guides 3 at the bottom.

6. Remove the bolts 1 from the condenser.

7. Remove the bolts 2 from the radiator mounts.

8. Push the radiator to the rear and remove the radiator mounts.

9. Remove the radiator from its mounts in the lock carrier.

10. Installation is performed in the reverse order of removal. When doing this note the following:

11. Fill the coolant.

2.5L Engine

See Figures 54 and 55.

1. Remove the front bumper.
2. Remove the fan shroud.
3. Drain the coolant.
4. Disconnect the coolant hoses from radiator.

➡ **To prevent damage to the condenser and the refrigerant lines, do not stretch, kink or bend the pipes and hoses.**

5. Remove the bolts arrows from the radiator brackets.

6. Move the radiator and condenser toward the rear and out of the lower support. While doing this, pull the lock carrier on the left support slightly downward.

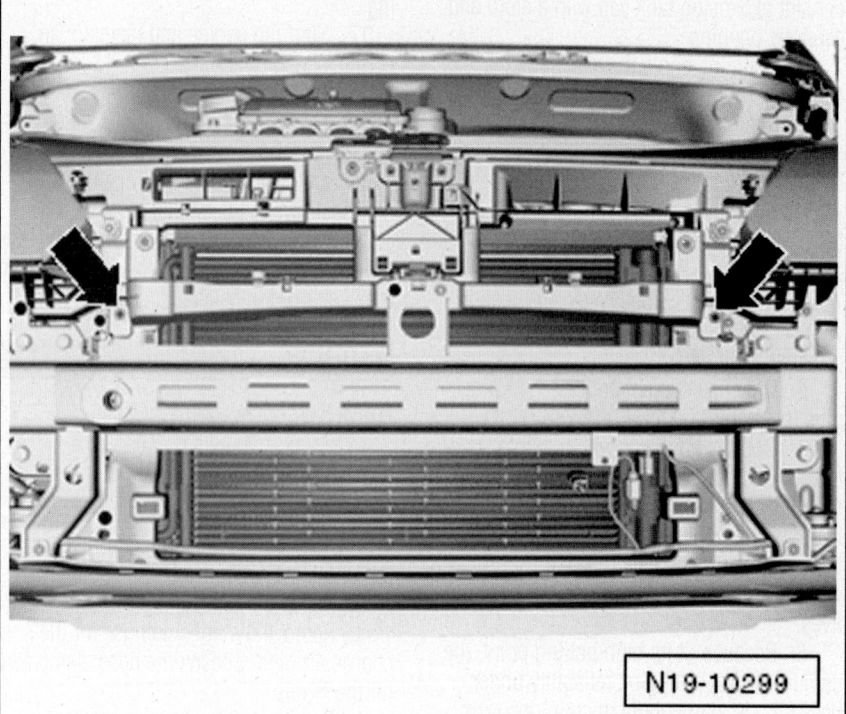

Fig. 54 Remove the bolts arrows from the radiator brackets

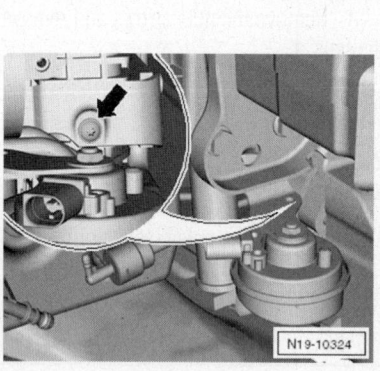

Fig. 55 Remove the bolts for the refrigerant lines on the right side of the radiator

7. Remove the bolts for the refrigerant lines on the right side of the radiator.

8. Remove the condenser bolts. Secure the condenser on the lock carrier using cable ties, for example.

9. Remove the radiator downward.

To install:

10. Install the radiator from below and secure it to the condenser.

11. Install the radiator and condenser in the lower supports.

12. Place the upper radiator mount on the radiator and secure it with the lock carrier arrows.

13. Install the front bumper.

14. Install the fan shroud.

15. Installation is performed in reverse order of removal. When doing this note the following:

16. Replace coolant if a new radiator was installed.

17. Fill with coolant.

THERMOSTAT

REMOVAL & INSTALLATION

2.0L Engines

See Figure 56.

1. Before servicing the vehicle, refer to the precautions.

2. Drain coolant.

3. Remove the cover for the air guide; disengage the side clips to do so.

4. Unclip the lower air guide, disengage the clips to do so.

5. Remove the lower air guide together with the air guide hose.

6. Loosen the hose clamp.

7. Remove bolt.

8. Disconnect electrical connector.

9. Remove the bolt and remove the air guide pipe downward.

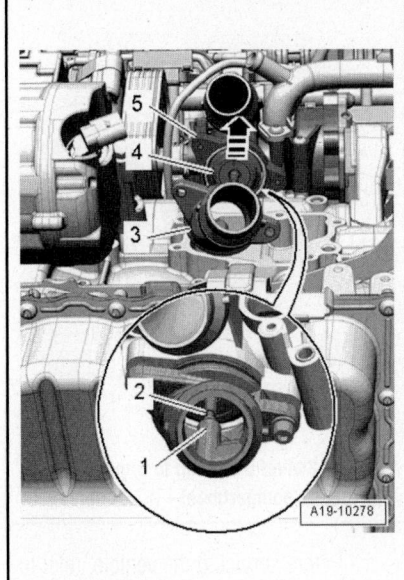

Fig. 56 Thermostat assembly

10. Lay aside the coolant hose and electrical wiring harness.

11. Remove the bolt and remove bracket.

12. If installed, remove the bolt on the bracket for the After-Run Coolant Pump V51.

➡ **The After-Run Coolant Pump V51 stays in the installation position.**

13. Remove the coolant hoses and lay them aside.

14. Loosen the nut , remove the bolt and move the support for the intake manifold to the right.

15. Remove bolts and remove connecting pieces. For the right bolt, the Multi-Point Socket T10058 is useful.

16. Remove the coolant thermostat.

To install:

17. Replace seals and O-rings.

18. Clean O-ring sealing surface.

19. Coat the O-ring with coolant G12 plus-plus.

20. Install the thermostat into the housing for the coolant pump and move it slightly forward.

21. Tighten the bolts to 80 inch lbs. (9 Nm).

22. Carefully mount the connector; while doing so, insert the centering pin into the guide.

2.0L TDI Engine

See Figure 57.

1. Before servicing the vehicle, refer to the precautions.

2. Drain coolant.

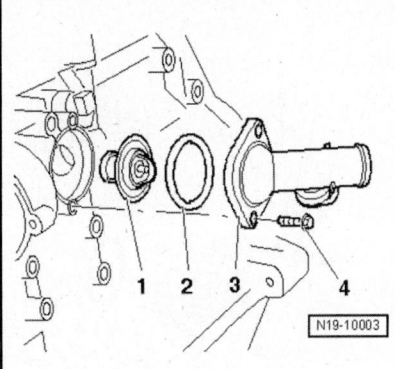

Fig. 57 Coat new O-ring (2) with coolant. Insert coolant thermostat (1) in the connecting piece (3) and tighten bolts (4)

3. Remove throttle valve control module J338.

4. Remove coolant hose from the connection.

5. Loosen bolts on connection with a 10 mm flex wrench 3185, remove with socket T10058 and remove connection with the coolant thermostat.

6. Rotate coolant thermostat 90° to the left and remove it from the connection.

To install:

7. Install in reverse order of removal.

8. Always replace seals, sealing rings and O-rings.

9. Coat new O-ring with coolant.

10. Insert coolant thermostat in the connecting piece and turn it 90° turn to the right.

11. The clip of the thermostat must be positioned at approximately right angle.

12. Insert connection with coolant thermostat in the cylinder block.

13. Tighten bolts with a 10 mm flex wrench 3185.

14. Tightening specifications 11 ft. lbs. (15 Nm).

15. Secure connection coolant hose.

16. Install throttle valve control module J338.

2.5L Engine

See Figure 58.

1. Drain the coolant.

2. Remove the engine cover with air filter.

3. Remove the intake manifold. Refer to Intake Manifold.

4. Insert the guide tube for the oil dipstick into the cylinder block again and secure it tightly so that no leaking coolant can run into the engine.

5. Place a suitable container under the

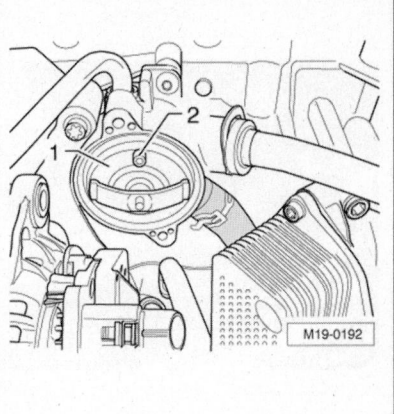

Fig. 58 Thermostat (1) and valve (2) installation orientation

coolant thermostat housing to catch coolant leaking out.

6. Remove the bolts arrows, the cover A and the thermostat

To install:

7. Installation is performed in the reverse order of removal. When doing this note the following:

8. Replace the seal and O-ring.

➡ **Note the installed position of the thermostat, the valve must point upward.**

WATER PUMP

REMOVAL & INSTALLATION

2.0L Engines

See Figures 59 and 60.

1. Before servicing the vehicle, refer to the precautions.

2. Remove coolant pipes.

3. Remove the coolant pump toothed belt.

4. Disconnect electrical connector on Throttle Valve Control Module J338.

5. Remove bolts and remove Throttle Valve Control Module J338.

6. Disconnect the electrical connector on the engine coolant temperature (ECT) sensor G62.

7. Remove bolts.

8. Remove the coolant pump from the centering pin and remove the oil cooler.

To install:

9. Replace seals and O-rings.

10. Coat the O-rings with coolant.

11. Make sure both centering pins are installed in the cylinder block.

12. Install the connection piece into the oil cooler.

Fig. 59 Remove the coolant pump drive gear (1) and toothed belt (2)

Fig. 60 Tighten bolts in 1 to 5 sequence

13. Push the coolant pump onto the connection piece and onto the centering pins in the cylinder block.

14. Tighten bolts in 1 to 5 sequence as shown.

15. If a new coolant pump was installed, then the protective cap must be removed.

16. The rest of the installation follows the reverse of the removal procedures.

2.0L TDI Engines

See Figure 61.

1. Always replace gaskets and seals.

2. The lower toothed belt guard can remain installed.

3. The toothed belt remains in position on the crankshaft sprocket.

4. Cover the toothed belt with a cloth to protect it from coolant before removing the coolant pump.

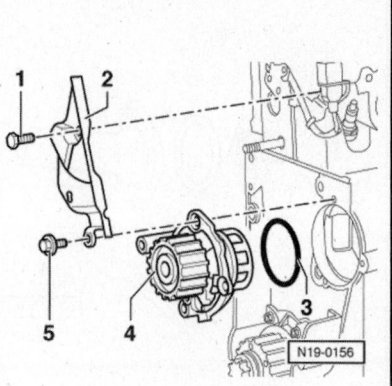

Fig. 61 Identifying the mounting bolt (1) from the rear toothed belt guard (2), O-ring (3), coolant pump bolts (5) and coolant pump (4)

5. Drain the coolant.

6. Remove ribbed belt.

7. Remove the ribbed belt tensioning damper.

8. Remove the upper and center toothed belt guards.

9. Remove toothed belt from coolant pump toothed belt gear.

10. Remove the mounting bolt from the rear toothed belt guard.

11. Remove the coolant pump bolts and then remove the coolant pump.

To install:

12. Installation is performed in the reverse order of removal. When doing this note the following:

13. Moisten a new O-ring 3 with coolant.

14. Insert the coolant pump 4.

15. Installation position: Sealing plug in housing points downward.

16. Tighten the mounting bolts 5. Tightening specification: 15 Nm

17. Tighten the mounting bolt 1 for the toothed belt guard 1 on the cylinder head. Tightening specification: 20 Nm

18. Install toothed belt, installing.

19. Install the ribbed belt tensioning element. Tightening specification: 25 Nm

20. Install the ribbed belt.

21. Fill the coolant.

2.5L Engine

See Figure 62.

➡This procedure requires removal of the front engine mount. New bolts will be needed.

Fig. 62 Swivel the pump to remove it from the engine compartment—2.5L engine

1. Before servicing the vehicle, refer to the precautions.

2. Remove the engine cover/air filter assembly.

3. Remove the battery and battery box.

4. Drain the cooling system by disconnecting the bottom radiator hose.

5. Remove air inlet tube guide above the fans.

6. Remove the air intake hose by disconnecting the smaller air hoses and removing the spring clamp.

7. Remove right inner fender.

8. Remove the coolant pump drive belt.

9. Disconnect the exhaust pipe from the manifold and remove the bracket bolts. Tie the pipe out of the way. The flex joint in the front exhaust pipe must not be bent more than 10 degrees, otherwise it may be damaged.

10. Remove the pendulum support (under car engine mount).

11. Disconnect the shift control cables at the transaxle.

12. Install engine support bridge 10-222A with adapters 10-222A/8 and support engine/transaxle assembly in installation position using adapter 10-222A/3 and shackle 10-222 A/12.

13. Remove the bolt that holds the windshield washer reservoir and move it towards the front.

14. Remove the coolant reservoir bolts and disconnect the wiring. Set the reservoir out of the way without disconnecting the hoses.

15. Remove the bolts to remove the front engine mount. The rear bolt in cylinder block is accessible above wheel housing liner.

16. Remove the two transaxle mount bolts.

17. Slide the engine as far as possible toward the front and left.

18. Remove the three mounting bolts and swivel the coolant pump out.

To install:

19. Install the pump and torque the bolts to 7 ft. lbs. (10 Nm).

20. Install the engine mounts using new bolts.

- Torque the two pendulum support bracket bolts to 30 ft. lbs. (40 Nm) plus 90°. Install a new pendulum support center bolt and torque it to 75 ft. lbs. (100 Nm) plus 90°.
- Install two new transaxle mount bolts and torque to 45 ft. lbs. (60 Nm) plus 90°.

21. Remove the engine support bridge and adapter brackets.

22. Connect the shift cables and adjust as necessary (See Transaxle Removal and Installation).

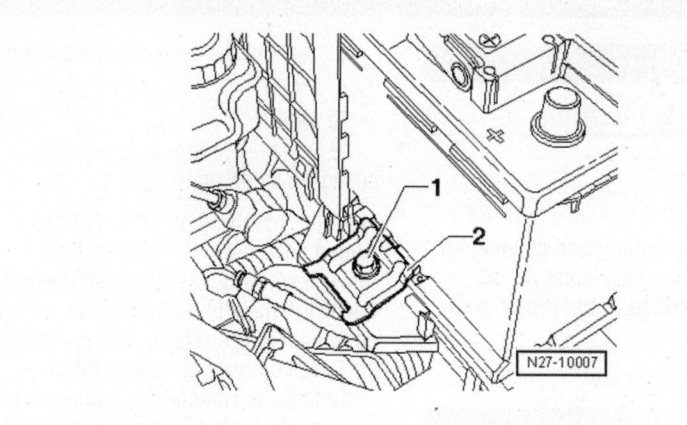

Fig. 63 Remove mounting screws (1) and remove retaining bracket (2)

23. Connect the exhaust pipe and install the bracket bolts.

24. Install the remaining components and connect all wiring and hoses.

25. Refill the coolant reservoir with G12 coolant and install the cap. Run the engine at 2000 rpm for three minutes or until the fan runs and check coolant level.

ENGINE ELECTRICAL

BATTERY

REMOVAL & INSTALLATION

See Figure 63.

1. Disconnect the battery.

2. Open the battery housing or the jacket in direction of and remove it from the battery.

3. Remove mounting screws and remove retaining bracket.

4. Fold handles arrows upward (if present) and take out battery.

➡**If battery is not secured properly, the following risks are possible:**

- Shortened battery service life due to vibration damage (explosion hazard).
- If battery is not secured properly, the plates within the battery can be damaged.

- Damage to battery casing caused by bracket (possible electrolyte leakage, high subsequent costs).
- Reduced collision safety.

5. Install in reverse order of removal, noting the following:

6. Tighten the threaded connections.

7. After installing, verify battery is properly seated.

8. Connect battery.

BATTERY RECONNECT/RELEARN PROCEDURE

After connecting the battery and switching on the ignition, the ASR/ESP Control Lamp K155 and Electro-mechanical Power Steering Indicator Lamp light up continuously. The indicator lamps switch off automatically after driving straight ahead at 15 to 20 km/h. This activates Steering Angle Sensor G85.

BATTERY SYSTEM

Work steps required after connecting battery:

1. Switch on ignition using ignition key or start button and switch off again.

2. Read the DTC memory: using Vehicle Diagnosis, Testing & Information System VAS5051B, select "Guided Fault Finding".

3. Clock: Check clock time setting, set anew if necessary.

4. Electrical window regulators:

   a. Open and close windows to each end stop respectively.

   b. With window closed, then pull switch until relay switches audibly.

   c. Check comfort switching of power window. While comfort switching is operated, window must close without holding the switch.

5. Check function: all electrical consumers.

ALTERNATOR

REMOVAL & INSTALLATION

2.0L Engines

See Figure 64.

➡ **When disconnecting and connecting battery, the procedure must be followed as described in the repair manual.**

1. Disconnect battery.

✳ WARNING

Before removing ribbed belt, mark the top side and direction of travel. When installing, pay attention to correct running direction and installation position. If the belt is installed in the opposite running direction or is positioned incorrectly, the belt will fail!

2. Remove the ribbed belt.
3. Disengage and disconnect harness connector.
4. Remove the oil pressure switch.
5. Remove the generator bolts.
6. Turn the generator slightly to the left in order to be able to access the connections on the back of the generator.
7. Release and disconnect DF wire connector.
8. Pry off protective cap.
9. Remove the nut and B+ wire below from generator connector threads.
10. Remove both screws and move the pipes and the hose upward so that there is enough space to remove the generator.

➡ **The pipes and the hose can remain connected.**

11. Remove the generator upward and out of the vehicle.

To install:

12. Install in reverse order of removal, noting the following:

➡ **When installing an already used ribbed belt, note direction of travel marked when it was removed! Before installing the ribbed belt, make sure all components (generator, A/C compressor) are securely fastened. When installing the ribbed belt, make sure it is properly seated in the belt pulley!**

13. Tighten the threaded connections to the specification given in the assembly overview.

➡ **When disconnecting and connecting battery, the procedure must be followed as described in the repair manual.**

2.0L TDI Engine

See Figures 65 and 66.

1. Before servicing the vehicle, refer to the precautions.
2. Disconnect battery.
3. Pull the engine cover upward at the corners from the mounting points.
4. Bring the lock carrier into the service position.

✳ WARNING

Before removing ribbed belt, mark the top side and direction of travel. When installing, pay attention to correct running direction and installation position. If the belt is installed in the opposite running direction or is positioned incorrectly, the belt will fail!

5. Remove ribbed belt.
6. Remove both A/C compressor screws.
7. Disengage and disconnect harness connector.
8. Remove the third screw and remove the A/C compressor downward from the accessories bracket.
9. Hoses on A/C compressor can remain connected.
10. Hang the A/C compressor with wire in a suitable place under the body until it is ready for installation.
11. Make sure the hoses are not pulled off or kinked.
12. Release and disconnect DF wire connector.

13. Pry off protective cap.
14. Remove nut and B+ wire below from generator connector threads.
15. Remove nut and remove wiring bracket from generator.
16. Remove both of the bolts and the nut for the fuel filter and lay them aside. The fuel hoses can remain connected.
17. Remove both generator mounting bolts.
18. Remove generator downward from vehicle.

To install:

19. Install in reverse order of removal, noting the following:

✳ WARNING

When installing an already used ribbed belt, note direction of travel marked when it was removed! Before installing the ribbed belt, make sure all components (generator, A/C compressor) are securely fastened. When installing the ribbed belt, make sure it is properly seated in the belt pulley!

20. Drive threaded sleeves out of generator housing approximately 0.156 in. (4 mm) in direction of.
21. Screw wire retainer firmly to rear side of generator in 3 o'clock position.

✳ WARNING

Before installing the engine cover, make sure the four fasteners (ball sockets) are positioned correctly. Bring them into the correct position if necessary. Otherwise the engine cover will be damaged.

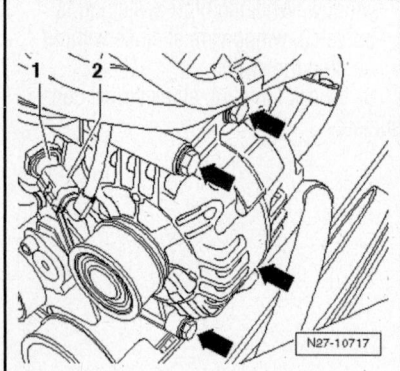

Fig. 64 Remove the connector (2) from oil pressure switch (1) and the generator bolts (arrows)

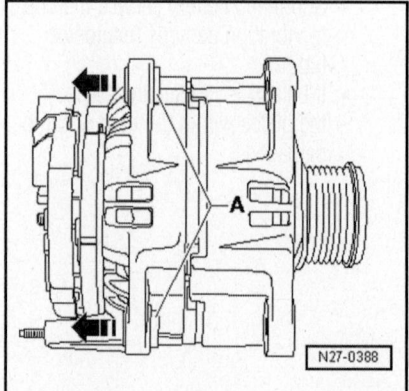

Fig. 65 Drive threaded sleeves (A) out of generator housing approximately 0.156 in. (4 mm) in direction of

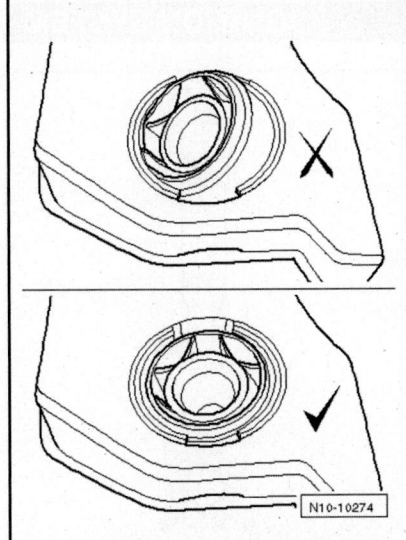

Fig. 66 Before installing the engine cover, make sure the four fasteners (ball sockets) are positioned correctly. Bring them into the correct position if necessary. Otherwise the engine cover will be damaged

22. Place the engine cover on the mounting points and press the corners into the retainers.

23. Reconnect battery.

24. Start the engine and verify that the belt is running properly.

25. Turn off the engine.

26. Tighten bolts/nuts to specification as follows:

- Alternator bolts: 15 ft. lbs. (20 Nm)
- M5 Wire: 28 inch lbs. (3.2 Nm)

2.5L Engine

See Figures 67 and 68.

1. Before servicing the vehicle, refer to the precautions.

2. Disconnect the battery.

3. Pull off engine cover upward and forward.

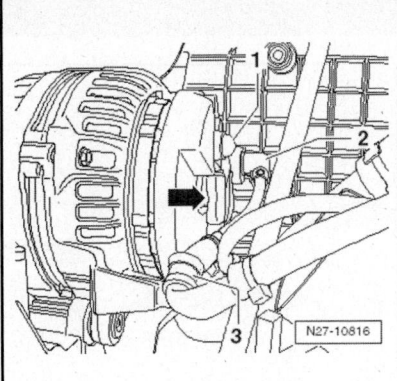

Fig. 67 Separate the connector for the DF-lead (2) and remove the protective cap (1), remove the B+ wire (arrow)

4. Bring the lock carrier into the service position.

5. Remove ribbed belt.

6. Remove the A/C compressor, but do not disconnect the hoses.

7. Remove the both bolts and then remove the lower idler roller from the auxiliary component bracket.

8. Remove the 3 bolts and then remove the upper idler roller from the auxiliary component bracket.

9. Separate the connector for the DF-lead and remove the protective cap.

10. Remove the B+ wire from the generator.

✴✴ WARNING

Before removing ribbed belt, mark the top side and direction of travel. When installing, pay attention to correct running direction and installation position. If the belt is installed in the opposite running direction or is positioned incorrectly, the belt will fail!

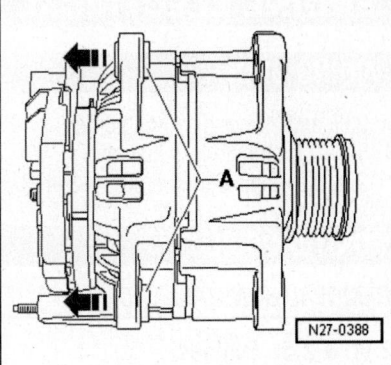

Fig. 68 Drive the threaded sleeves out of the generator housing approximately 4 mm

11. Remove the bolts and then remove the tensioning rollers

12. Remove the generator mounting bolts.

13. Remove the wire retainer from the generator.

14. Remove the generator upward.

To install:

15. Install in reverse order of removal.

16. Drive the threaded sleeves out of the generator housing approximately 4 mm.

17. Install the wire retainer securely on the rear side of the generator in the 8 o'clock position.

18. Tighten mounting bolts to 19 ft. lbs. (25 Nm).

✴✴ WARNING

Observe notes for threaded connections of battery terminals.

19. Connect the Battery.

20. Start the engine and verify that the belt is running properly.

21. Turn off the engine.

ENGINE ELECTRICAL

FIRING ORDER

2.0L and 2.5L engine firing order:
1–3–4–2 Distributorless ignition.
2.0L TDI engine firing order: 1–3–4–2.

IGNITION COIL

REMOVAL & INSTALLATION

2.0L & 2.5L Engines
See Figures 69 and 70.

1. Before servicing the vehicle, refer to the precautions.
2. To pull off spark plugs, place ignition coil puller T40039 on topmost thick rib of ignition coils with power output stages.

> **※ WARNING**
>
> **If lower ribs are used, these can be damaged**

3. Remove engine covers.

➡ **Spark plugs are located under ignition coils with power output stages.**

4. Remove both bolts.

➡ **Note installation position of ignition coils with power output stages.**

5. Pull all ignition coils approximately 1.17 in (30 mm) out of cylinder head in direction of rotation using ignition coil puller T40039.
6. Push connector in direction of rotation ignition coils with power output stages, press catch down by hand and disconnect connectors.

To install:
7. The ignition coils with power output stages must be greased with special lubricant G 052 141 A2 to install new spark plugs. This prevents the sealing hose on the ignition coil from sticking on the spark plug. The special lubricant must spread onto the spark plug when installing the ignition coil.
8. New ignition coils with power output stages are already greased when delivered.
9. Apply a thin bead of special lubricant G 052 141 A2 around the ignition sealing hose. The bead must be 1 to 2 mm thick.
10. Guide ignition coils with power output stages into cylinder head.

Fig. 69 To pull off spark plugs, place ignition coil puller T40039 on topmost thick rib of ignition coils with power output stages

11. Align ignition coils with power output stages into designated recesses of cylinder head cover.
12. Connect all connectors to ignition coils.
13. Press ignition coils with power output stages onto spark plugs by hand until stop. They must engage audibly.
14. Secure wiring using bolts.
15. Install engine cover.

IGNITION TIMING

ADJUSTMENT

All gasoline engines are equipped with a Distributorless Ignition System (DIS). No adjustment is necessary.

SPARK PLUGS

REMOVAL & INSTALLATION

2.0L & 2.5L Engines
See Figure 69.

1. Before servicing the vehicle, refer to the precautions.
2. To pull off spark plugs, place ignition coil puller T40039 on topmost thick rib of ignition coils with power output stages.

> **※ WARNING**
>
> **If lower ribs are used, these can be damaged**

IGNITION SYSTEM

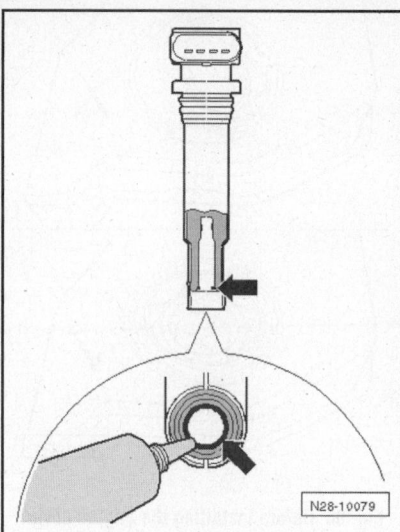

Fig. 70 Apply a thin bead of special lubricant G 052 141 A2 around the ignition sealing hose (arrow)

3. Remove engine covers.

➡ **Spark plugs are located under ignition coils with power output stages.**

4. Remove both bolts.

➡ **Note installation position of ignition coils with power output stages.**

5. Pull all ignition coils approximately 1.17 in (30 mm) out of cylinder head in direction of rotation using ignition coil puller T40039.
6. Push connector in direction of rotation ignition coils with power output stages, press catch down by hand and disconnect connectors.
7. Remove spark plugs using spark plug wrench 3122 B.

To install:
8. Install new spark plugs using spark plug wrench 3122 B.
9. Guide ignition coils with power output stages into cylinder head.
10. Align ignition coils with power output stages into designated recesses of cylinder head cover.
11. Connect all connectors to ignition coils.
12. Press ignition coils with power output stages onto spark plugs by hand until stop. They must engage audibly.
13. Secure wiring using bolts.
14. Install engine cover.

STARTER

REMOVAL & INSTALLATION

2.0L & 2.5L Engines

Manual Transaxle

See Figures 71 and 72.

1. Before servicing the vehicle, refer to the precautions.
2. Disconnect battery.
3. Remove screws.
4. Disconnect hose after the clips have been opened.
5. Disconnect harness connector and free up line to air filter housing.
6. Pull off engine cover upward.
7. Remove the Ground (GND) wire from starter mounting bolt.
8. Remove upper starter mounting bolt.
9. Slide protective cap downward from magnetic switch.
10. Remove the positive wire and disconnect harness connector of terminal 50.
11. Remove noise insulation.
12. All hose connections for charge air system are secured by spring-type clamps or by connector couplings. The following must be observed with connector couplings:
13. Release the connection by pulling locking clip.
14. Disconnect hose/pipe without tools.
15. Open screw-type clamp and disconnect connector coupling.
16. Remove charge air hose from vehicle.
17. Remove the nut from lower mounting bolt of starter.
18. Remove wire retainer.

19. Remove lower starter mounting bolt
20. Remove the starter downward and out from the vehicle.

To install:

21. Install in reverse order of removal.
22. All hose connections for charge air system are secured by spring-type clamps or by connector couplings. The following must be observed with connector couplings:
23. Connect hose/pipe without tools.
24. Make sure retaining tabs lock securely.
25. Tighten bolts/nuts to specification as follows:
   - Starter to transmission M12: 59 ft. lbs. (80 Nm)
   - Starter to transmission M10: 30 ft. lbs. (40 Nm)
   - Ground (GND) wire to starter mounting bolt M8: 11 ft. lbs. (15 Nm)
   - Ground wire to transmission M8: 11 ft. lbs. (15 Nm)
   - Wire retainer to starter mounting bolt M8: 11 ft. lbs. (15 Nm)
   - Positive wire to starter solenoid switch M8: 11 ft. lbs. (15 Nm)
   - Air filter housing to body: 89 inch lbs. (10 Nm)

Automatic Transaxle

1. Before servicing the vehicle, refer to the precautions.
2. Disconnect battery.
3. Pull off engine cover upward.
4. Disconnect harness connector, loosen spring-type clamp using Spring Type Clip Pliers VAS 5024 and disconnect vacuum hose.

5. Remove mounting bolt for air filter housing.
6. Release retaining tabs and remove cover.
7. Disconnect hose from air filter housing and remove it.
8. Pull off air filter housing upward out of brackets and remove it.
9. Slide protective cap in direction of downward from magnetic switch.
10. Remove the positive wire and disconnect harness connector of terminal 50.
11. Unclip wire from wiring harness.
12. Remove upper starter mounting bolt.
13. Remove lower mounting bolt for starter.
14. Remove starter upward and out of vehicle.

To install:

15. Install in reverse order of removal.
16. Tighten bolts/nuts to specification as follows:
   - Starter to transmission M12: 59 ft. lbs. (80 Nm)
   - Starter to transmission M10: 30 ft. lbs. (40 Nm)
   - Ground (GND) wire to starter mounting bolt M8: 11 ft. lbs. (15 Nm)
   - Ground wire to transmission M8: 11 ft. lbs. (15 Nm)
   - Wire retainer to starter mounting bolt M8: 11 ft. lbs. (15 Nm)
   - Positive wire to starter solenoid switch M8: 11 ft. lbs. (15 Nm)
   - Air filter housing to body: 89 inch lbs. (10 Nm)

2.0L TDI Engine

1. Before servicing the vehicle, refer to the precautions.
2. Disconnect the battery.
3. Pull engine cover upward and forward.
4. Loosen spring clamp using spring clamp pliers VAS 5024 and disconnect connector.
5. Remove screw.
6. Remove vacuum hose.
7. Pull air filter housing on the right side upward from its rubber mounting.
8. Remove air filter housing from vehicle.
9. Slide protective cap in direction of downward from solenoid.
10. Remove positive wire and disconnect harness connector of terminal 50 2.
11. Remove the ground wire from the starter mounting bolt.

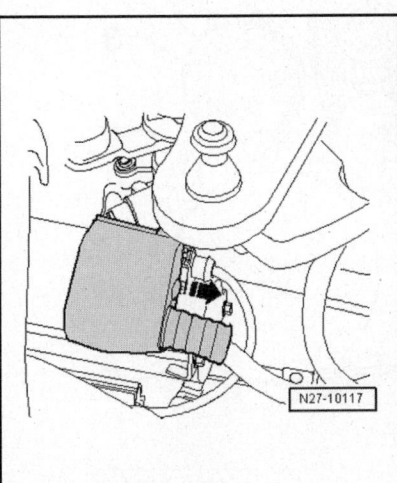

Fig. 71 Slide protective cap in direction of arrow

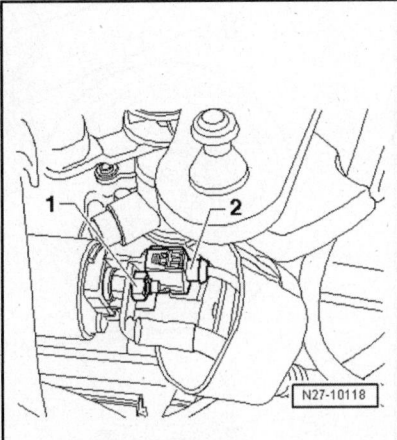

Fig. 72 Remove the positive wire and disconnect harness connector of terminal 50

12. Remove the starter mounting bolt.
13. Remove the noise insulation.
14. Remove the nut from the lower starter mounting bolt.
15. Remove wire retainer.
16. Remove the starter mounting bolt.
17. Remove the starter.

To install:
18. Install in reverse order of removal.
19. Tighten bolts/nuts to specification as follows:
  • Starter to transmission M12: 56 ft. lbs. (75 Nm)
  • Ground wire to Starter B mounting bolt M8: 11 ft. lbs. (15 Nm)

  • Wire retainer to Starter B mounting bolt M8: 11 ft. lbs. (15 Nm)
  • Positive wire to Starter B solenoid switch M8: 11 ft. lbs. (15 Nm)
  • Air filter housing to body: 89 inch lbs. (10 Nm)
  • GND wire to automatic transmission housing M8: 11 ft. lbs. (15 Nm)

ENGINE MECHANICAL

➡️**Disconnecting the negative battery cable may interfere with the functions of the on board computer systems and may require the computer to undergo a relearning process, once the negative battery cable is reconnected.**

ACCESSORY DRIVE BELTS

ACCESSORY BELT ROUTING
See Figures 73 through 75.

INSPECTION

1. Turn the engine at vibration damper/crankshaft pulley with a suitable socket wrench.
2. Raise the vehicle if necessary. Check the drive belt for:
  a. Sub-surface (deep) cracks
  b. Layer separation (top layer, cord strands)
  c. Traces of oil and grease
3. Replace the belt if any damage is found or if contaminated with oil or grease.

ADJUSTMENT

All models use an automatic (spring powered) tensioner. No adjustment is required.

REMOVAL & INSTALLATION

2.0L Engines
1. Before servicing the vehicle, refer to the precautions.

❊❊ WARNING
Risk of destroying due to reversed running direction on a used ribbed belt. Before removing ribbed belt, marking running direction with chalk or felt-tip pen for reinstallation later.

2. Remove the noise insulation.
3. Remove the right air guide hose.
4. To release the tension on the ribbed belt, turn the tensioner in direction of rotation from underneath.
5. Secure tensioner with Drift T10060 A.

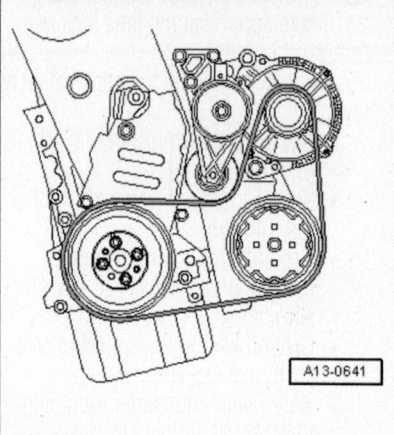

Fig. 73 Accessory drive belt routing: 2.0L Engine

6. Remove ribbed belt.

To install:
7. Installation is performed in reverse order of removal.

❊❊ WARNING
Before installing ribbed belt, generator, A/C compressor must be securely installed.

8. First mount the ribbed belt on the crankshaft pulley, then on the A/C compressor and generator.
9. Turn the tensioner with a box-end wrench and remove the drift T10060 A.
10. Release tensioner.
11. Check whether ribbed belt is routed correctly.

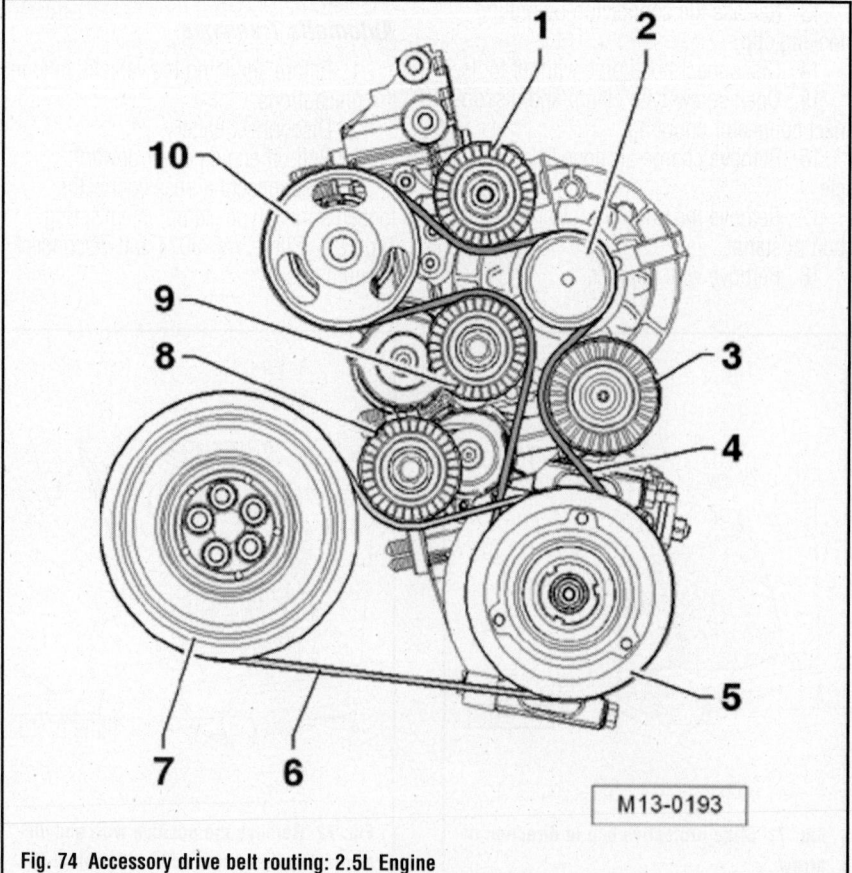

Fig. 74 Accessory drive belt routing: 2.5L Engine

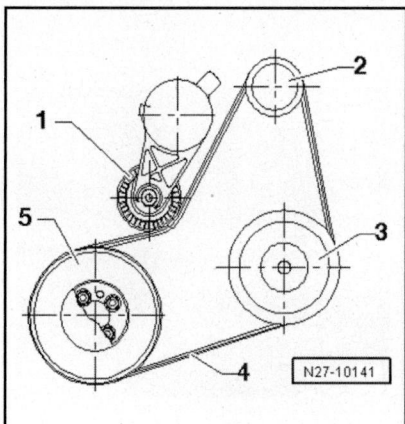
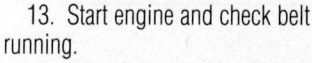

Fig. 75 Accessory drive belt routing: 2.0L TDI Engine

12. Start engine and check whether ribbed belt runs correctly.

2.0L TDI Engine

1. Before servicing the vehicle, refer to the precautions.

2. Remove noise insulation.

3. Remove engine cover.

   a. On one piece cover, pull the one piece front engine cover upward with a quick jerk and then pull the lower mount forward.

   b. On the two piece engine cover, first pull the outer cover upward with a quick jerk in the upper illustration, then pull the inner engine cover upward with a quick jerk in lower illustration.

4. To remove fuel filter fuel filter without the retaining plate:

   a. Release the retainers, pull the fuel filter with connected hoses upward and out of the retaining plate and lay it aside.

5. To remove fuel filter with the retaining plate:

   a. Loosen the bolt one turn.

   b. Remove the bolt and the nut.

   c. Lay the fuel filter, with the hoses still connected, to the side.

6. Mark direction of rotation of ribbed belt.

7. Pivot tensioner element in direction of to relieve tension on ribbed belt.

8. Secure tensioner element using the drift T10060.

9. Remove ribbed belt.

To install:

10. Installation is performed in reverse order.

11. Before installing ribbed belt, make sure that all ancillaries (alternator, air conditioner compressor) are secured tightly.

12. Note previously marked direction of belt rotation and be sure that it is seated correctly on pulley.

13. Set the ribbed belt onto the generator lastly.

14. Start the engine and check the running belt.

2.5L Engine

See Figure 76.

1. Before servicing the vehicle, refer to the precautions.

2. Raise and safely support the front of the vehicle.

3. Remove front part of right front inner fender.

4. Put a 15mm wrench on the A/C belt tensioner and push towards the rear of the vehicle.

5. Insert a pin to hold the wrench in place.

6. Remove the compressor belt and mark its running direction for installation. Do not leave the wrench and pin in place if moving on to other work.

7. Mark the running direction of the alternator belt.

8. Move the tensioner and insert a pin to hold it in place.

9. Remove the belt. Do not leave the wrench and pin in place if moving on to other work.

To install:

10. Place the alternator belt on the alternator and coolant pump pulleys, then lastly on the idler pulley.

11. Before releasing the tensioner, check ribbed for correct seating in the pulleys.

12. Secure the other tensioner and install the A/C compressor belt. Be sure that it is seated correctly on pulley before releasing the tensioner.

Fig. 76 Move the tensioner and insert a pin to hold it in place

13. Start engine and check belt running.

AIR CLEANER

REMOVAL & INSTALLATION

2.0L & 2.5L Gas Engines

See Figure 77.

1. Remove the cover for the air guide; disengage the side clips to do so.

2. Unclip the lower air guide, disengage the clips to do so.

3. Remove both the lower air guide and the air guide hose.

4. Engine Code CBFA: Disconnect the hose leading to the secondary air injection pump motor V101 from the air filter housing.

5. Loosen the bolt and pull the air filter housing upward out of the bracket.

6. Remove the air filter housing together with the Mass Airflow (MAF) sensor and connecting pipe.

7. Installation is performed in reverse order.

2.0L TDI Diesel Engines

See Figures 78 and 79.

1. Release the tabs arrows and open the cover on the air duct.

2. Remove the bolts arrows for the air duct 1 and pull the intake air duct 2 from the air duct.

3. Press the tabs and remove the intake air duct from the lower air filter housing.

4. Disconnect the connector from the Mass Airflow (MAF) sensor G70 1 and the vacuum line 2.

5. Loosen the threaded connector on the lower air filter housing 3.

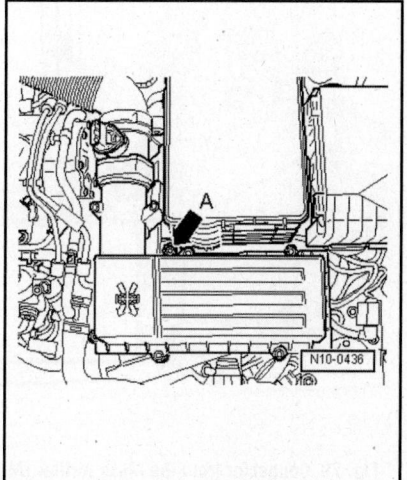

Fig. 77 Loosen the bolt (arrow A)

Fig. 78 Remove the bolts arrows for the air duct 1 and pull the intake air duct 2 from the air duct

6. Open the clamp 4 and remove the intake hose to the turbocharger.

7. Remove the entire air filter housing.

8. Installation is performed in reverse order.

FILTER/ELEMENT REPLACEMENT

See Figure 80.

1. Removing for Engine Code CBFA: Disconnect the hose leading to the sec-

---

ondary air injection pump motor V101 from the air filter housing.

2. Remove the bolts from the upper air filter housing.

3. Lift the upper air filter housing and remove the air filter element.

To install:

4. Always use an original equipment air filter element.

5. Hose connections and charge air system hoses must be free of oil and grease before installing. When installing, do not use any lubricants containing silicone.

6. The air filter housing must be clean.

7. Secure all hose connections using hose clamps appropriate for the model type, refer to the Parts Catalog.

8. Note the following when blowing out the air filter housing with pressurized air: To prevent malfunctions, cover the critical air flow components such as the MAF sensor, air intake tubes, etc. with a clean cloth.

9. Observe disposal regulations!

10. Check the MAF sensor and intake hose (intake air side) for salt residue, dirt, and leaves.

11. Check the intake air guide from the air duct for dirt.

12. Remove the snow screen and clean it.

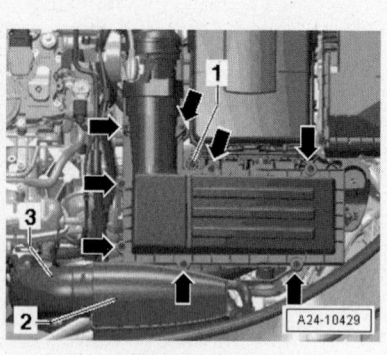

Fig. 80 Removing the upper air filter element housing bolts (arrows)

➡**The snow screen is not installed in all vehicles.**

13. Clean the water drain and the lower air filter housing.

14. Make sure that air filter is properly centered when placed in the mounting of the lower air filter housing.

15. Set the upper air filter housing onto the lower air filter housing, without using much force. When doing this, make sure that the upper air filter housing is not placed crooked onto the air filter element.

16. Check the sealing lip on the air filter element.

17. Further installation is performed in reverse order.

CAMSHAFT AND VALVE LIFTERS

REMOVAL & INSTALLATION

2.0L Engines

See Figures 81 through 88.

1. Before servicing the vehicle, refer to the precautions.

2. Remove the engine cover.

3. Remove the vacuum pump.

4. Remove the noise insulation.

5. Remove the front part of the right wheel housing liner and/or the front right wheel housing liner.

6. Remove bolts.

7. Remove the air guide pipe by lifting the clamps items.

8. Disconnect the connector from the Camshaft Adjustment Valve N205.

9. Remove the bolts and then the camshaft adjustment valve N205.

10. Remove the upper timing chain cover.

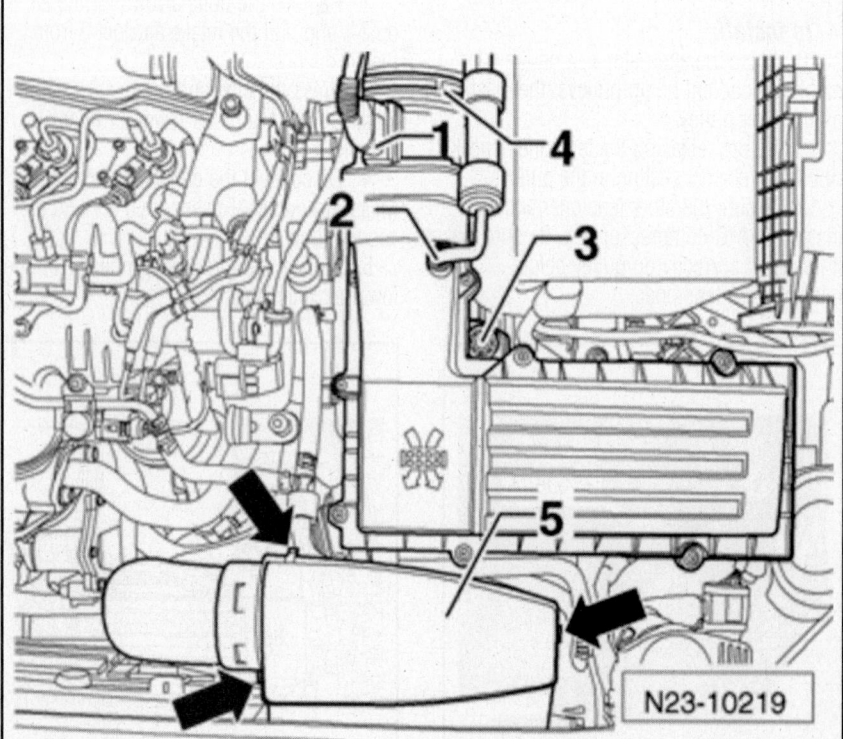

Fig. 79 Connector from the Mass Airflow (MAF) sensor G70 (10 and the vacuum line (2). Lower air filter housing (3) and clamp (4) to the intake hose to the turbocharger

The control valve has a left thread.

11. Remove the control valve using Assembly Tool T10352 in the direction of.

12. Remove the bolts and remove the bearing bracket.

13. Rotate the vibration damper using the Counter Hold Tool T10355 into the "OT" position.

➡**The notch on the vibration damper must line up with the marking on the timing chain lower cover.**

14. Mark the drive chain/chain sprockets with a waterproof marker. These marks are necessary for reinstallation.

15. Remove the plug.

16. Lift the chain tensioner locking wedge by inserting a scriber or a suitable screwdriver into the hole in the chain tensioner direction.

Fig. 81 Rotate the vibration damper using the Counter Hold Tool T10355 into the "OT" position

Fig. 82 Mark the drive chain/chain sprockets with a waterproof marker. These marks are necessary for reinstallation

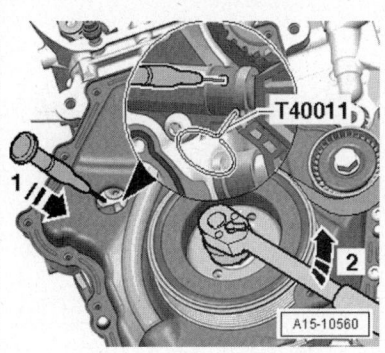

Fig. 83 Lift the chain tensioner locking wedge by inserting a scriber or a suitable screwdriver into the hole in the chain tensioner direction

17. Turn the crankshaft opposite the engine direction of rotation direction and secure it with a Securing Pin T40011.

➡**The intake camshaft switches in the engine direction of rotation.**

18. Remove the bolt and guide the tensioning rail downward.

19. Remove the upper guide rail by unlocking the latch (located in the center) with a screwdriver and pushing the guide rail forward.

➡**When the lower timing chain cover is installed, the loose chain on the crankshaft cannot jump off.**

20. Remove camshaft timing chain from chain sprockets.

❊❊ **WARNING**

If the camshaft timing chain was removed from the cylinder head, then the crankshaft may not be turn further. On this engine, when the valves are mounted, there is the danger that there are panels attached to the lower timing chain cover, which could fall and interfere with the chain; also a loose chain turned by the crankshaft can bend the panels. The panels can bend if the crankshaft is rotated when the chain is loose.

21. Disconnect the electrical connectors on the ignition coils and free up the wiring harness.

22. Remove the ignition coils with the puller T40039.

23. Disconnect the crankcase ventilation hoses.

24. Remove the bolts and remove the crankcase ventilation.

25. Remove the bolts.

26. Remove the air guide pipe bolt.

27. Loosen the hose clamp and remove the air guide pipe together with the crankcase ventilation.

28. Disconnect the vacuum line and free up the wire.

29. Disconnect the electrical connector from the Camshaft Position (CMP) Sensor G40.

➡**The sealing surfaces of the lower cylinder head cover and on the upper cylinder head must not be reworked.**

❊❊ **WARNING**

If the cylinder head cover was loosened, then the cover must be replaced.

❊❊ **WARNING**

The camshaft bearings are integrated in the cylinder head or cylinder head cover. The tension must be released from the camshaft timing chain before removing the cylinder head cover.

30. Remove the cylinder head cover bolts in 1 to 6 sequence.

31. Remove the cylinder head cover.

32. Remove the camshafts.

33. Prevent dirt and adhesive residue from entering cylinder head.

To install:

➡**During installation, cable ties must be re-installed at the same location. Sealing surfaces must be completely free of oil and grease.**

❊❊ **WARNING**

The pistons must not be positioned at TDC.

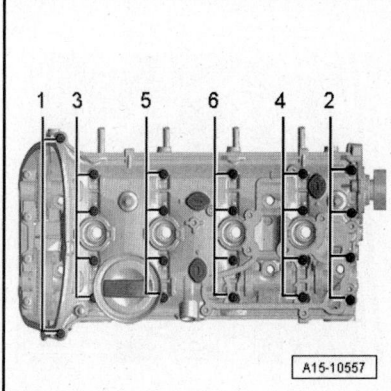

Fig. 84 Remove the cylinder head cover bolts in 1 to 6 sequence

34. Make sure that all roller cam followers make contact correctly on valve stem ends.

✳✳ WARNING
The cover must be installed within 5 minutes after application of silicone sealant.

35. Remove any sealant residue on the cylinder head using the flat blade scraper.

✳✳ WARNING
Prevent dirt and adhesive residue from entering cylinder head.

36. Remove any seal out of the groove in the cylinder head cover as well as from any sealing surface using, for example, a rotating plastic brush.
37. Clean sealing surfaces, must be free of oil and grease.
38. Cut tube nozzle at front marking approximately 0.078 in. (2 mm).
39. Lubricate the running surfaces of both camshafts.
40. Place the camshaft into the cylinder head; the recesses must be perpendicular to each other.
41. Replace the cylinder head cover bolts.
42. Apply the silicone sealant D 154 103 A1 on the clean sealing surface of the cylinder head cover as shown. Thickness of sealant bead: 0.078–0.117 in. (2–3 mm).

✳✳ WARNING
The cylinder head cover must be installed within 5 minutes after application of silicone sealant. The

Fig. 85 Remove the cylinder head cover bolts in 1 to 6 sequence

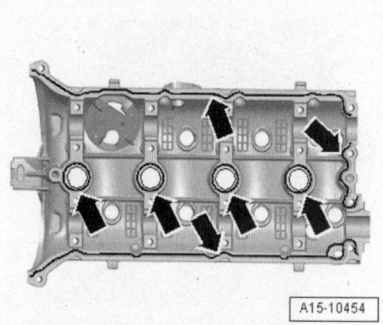

Fig. 86 Apply the silicone sealant D 154 103 A1 on the clean sealing surface of the cylinder head cover as shown. Thickness of sealant bead: 0.078–0.117 in. (2–3 mm)

sealant bead may not be thicker than specified, otherwise excess sealant could enter the oil pan and clog the oil intake tube.

43. Tighten bolts in several stages.
- Replace bolts
- Hand-tighten bolts in several stages in 1 to 6 sequence
- Tighten the bolts in a 1 to 6 sequence to 71 inch lbs. (8 Nm) using a torque wrench
- Tighten the bolts an additional 90° using a rigid wrench in the sequence 1 to 6

✳✳ WARNING
Make sure the cylinder head cover is not tilted.

44. Insert the cover without sealing using Thrust Piece T10174. Measurement A should be 0.039–0.078 in. (1–2 mm).

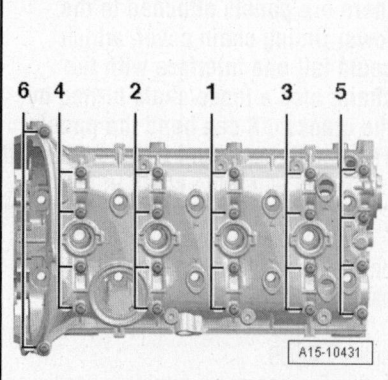

Fig. 87 Tighten bolts in several stages using the sequence shown

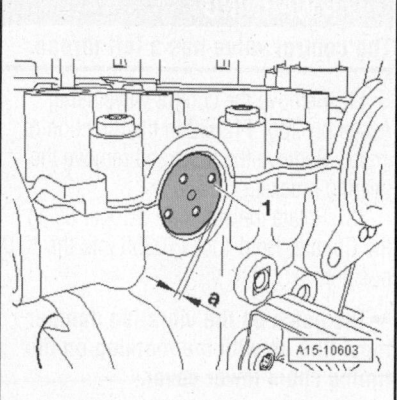

Fig. 88 Insert the cover without sealing using Thrust Piece T10174. Measurement A should be 0.039–0.078 in. (1–2 mm)

✳✳ WARNING
When turning the crankshaft, make sure the timing chain cannot damage any other components.

45. Rotate the vibration damper using the Counter Hold Tool T10355 into the "OT" position.
46. The notch on the vibration damper must line up with the marking on the timing chain lower cover.
47. The marked links of the timing chain must be positioned on the markings on the chain sprockets.
48. Mount the camshaft timing chain: The markings drive chain/chain sprockets must align.
49. Turn the intake camshaft using the wrench in the direction of the and mount the timing chain.
50. The rest of the assembly is basically a reverse of the disassembling sequence.

2.0L TDI Engine
See Figures 89 through 91.

➡Only remove the plastic protectors installed to protect the open valves immediately before positioning the cylinder head.

➡When replacing the cylinder head or cylinder head gasket, the coolant must be completely replaced.

➡Cylinder heads with cracks between the valve seats can continue to be used without reducing service life, as long as the tears have a maximum width of 0.0195 in. (0.5 mm).

➡After installing the camshafts, the engine may not be started for approximately 30 minutes. The hydraulic

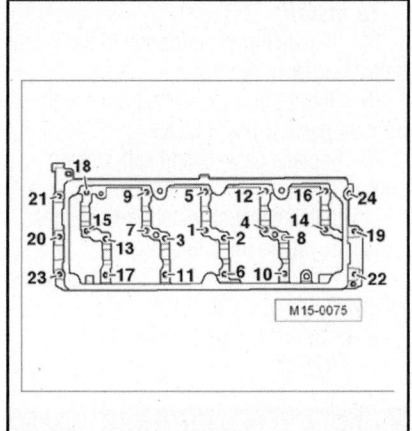

Fig. 89 Bearing frame removal/ installation sequence

adjusting elements must seat themselves (otherwise the valves will seat themselves on the pistons).

➡**After working on the valvetrain and lifters, carefully rotate the crankshaft by hand at least 2 full revolutions before starting to be sure that valves do not strike the pistons.**

Always replace gaskets and seals.
1. Before servicing the vehicle, refer to the precautions.
2. Remove toothed belt from the camshaft and high pressure fuel pump.
3. Remove cylinder head cover.
4. Remove bolts for camshaft sprocket.
5. Remove camshaft sprocket from the hub.
6. Counterhold hub with the counterhold tool T10051 and loosen hub bolt.
7. Remove bolt for hub by approximately 2 turns.
8. Position puller T10052 and align it to the bores in the hub.
9. Tighten mounting bolts.
10. Tension hub by tightening puller T10052 evenly until it can be removed from the camshaft taper.
11. Hold puller T10052 with a 30 mm wrench.
12. Remove hub from the cone of the camshaft.
13. Remove vacuum pump Vacuum Pump.
14. Remove bearing frame bolts or nuts in the sequence 24 to 1.
15. Remove bearing frame.
16. Carefully remove camshafts.

To install:
17. Seal separating surfaces between the bearing frame and cylinder head with silicone adhesive sealant D 176 501 A1.

Only install the camshafts with the camshaft insertion tool T40094 as described below. Otherwise the axial bearing in the bearing frame will be destroyed and the cylinder head will have to be replaced. Make sure that no sealant residue enters the cylinder head and bearings.

18. Using rotating plastic brush, remove any remaining sealant from cylinder head and guide frame.
19. Clean sealing surfaces, they must be free of oil and grease.
20. Oil journal surfaces of camshafts.
21. Assemble camshaft insertion tool T40094 as follows:
    a. Remove mounts T40094/3, T40094/4 and T40094/5 from base plate. Loosen threaded connections from below.
    b. If the mounts on the camshaft insertion tool T40094 are not marked, mark the removed mounts, for example with numbers, to ensure it can be assembled later.
    c. Install mounts T40094/9 and T40094/10 in the empty outer locations.
    d. Position mount T40094/2 on location "A" and mount T40094/1 on location "F".
22. Insert intake camshaft first. Make sure the indentation for the cylinder head bolt faces "outward".
23. Position 0.0195 in. (0.50 mm) feeler gauge and slide the mount T40094/8 into groove on the intake camshaft.
24. Insert exhaust camshaft.
25. Secure exhaust camshaft at its groove with cover T40094/11.

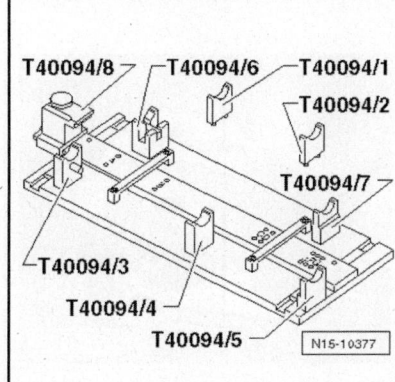

Fig. 90 Only install the camshafts with the camshaft insertion tool T40094 as described below

26. Position tensioning tool T40096/1 on the exhaust camshaft sprockets.

Make sure the clamping jaw marked with an is on the wider sprocket.

27. Tighten tensioning tool T40096/1 with thumb wheel until the tooth faces align. Use a 13 mm open end wrench if necessary.
28. Slide intake camshaft toward the exhaust camshaft until the splines engage.

Fig. 91 Apply silicone sealant to the clean sealing surface of the cylinder head as illustrated. The sealing compound bead must be 0.078–0.117 in. (2–3 mm) thick

29. Position bearing frame on the camshafts.

30. All the camshaft bearings must lie on the camshafts.

31. Position clamping tool T40095 and secure the camshafts in the bearing frame.

32. Remove cover T40094/11.

33. Remove mount T40094/8 from the intake camshaft groove.

34. Cut tube nozzle approximately 0.117 in. (3 mm).

35. Apply silicone sealant to the clean sealing surface of the cylinder head as illustrated. The sealing compound bead must be 0.078–0.117 in. (2–3 mm) thick

36. Apply on the inner side in the area with the threaded holes

37. The sealant beads must not be thicker than 0.078–0.117 in. (2–3 mm) or excess sealant can enter the camshaft bearing.

38. Remove camshafts with bearing frame and the clamping tool T40095 from the camshaft insertion tool T40094.

39. Carefully insert the camshafts and bearing frame in the cylinder head.

40. First tighten bearing frame bolts or nuts by hand in sequence 1 to 24.

41. The guide frame must be in contact with the entire contact surface of the cylinder head.

42. Tighten bearing frame bolts or nuts in sequence 1 to 24.

43. Remove clamping tool T40095 and tensioning tool T40096/1.

44. Replace camshaft seal.

45. Drive a new sealing cover onto cylinder head with a suitable drift until it is flush.

The rest of installation is in reverse order of removal, noting the following:

46. After installing the camshafts, the engine may not be started for approximately 30 minutes. The hydraulic adjusting elements must seat themselves (otherwise the valves will seat themselves on the pistons).

47. After working on the valvetrain, carefully rotate engine by hand at least 2 full revolutions to ensure that valves do not strike the pistons when starting.

48. Place hub on the camshaft.

49. Counterhold hub with the counterhold tool T10051 and tighten hub bolt.

50. Push camshaft sprocket onto hub.

51. The toothed segment of the camshaft sprocket must face upward.

52. Install bolts into camshaft sprocket by hand to eliminate play.

53. Lock hub with rig pin 3359.

54. Install and tension the toothed belt.

55. Install vacuum pump.

56. Install cylinder head cover.

CATALYTIC CONVERTER

REMOVAL & INSTALLATION

2.0L & 2.5L Engines

See Figure 92.

1. Before servicing the vehicle, refer to the precautions.

2. Remove the air filter.

3. Disconnect Heated Oxygen Sensor (HO2S) G39 harness connector and free up cable.

4. From above, remove the nuts on the front exhaust pipe connection to the turbocharger.

5. Remove nuts accessible from below from front exhaust pipe to the turbocharger connection.

6. Remove the nuts and slightly pull the vehicle floor cover downward.

7. Disconnect the electrical connector on the right side of the underbody.

8. Remove the electrical connector out of the bracket and free up the electrical wire to the oxygen sensor.

9. Unclip the wires, remove the bracket and disconnect the connectors.

10. Remove exhaust system bracket.

11. Remove the front cross member for the vehicle floor.

✳✳ WARNING

Risk of damaging decoupling elements. Do not bend decoupling element in front exhaust pipe more than 10°.

12. Loosen clamping sleeve and push it rearward.

13. Remove the catalytic converters with the front exhaust pipe.

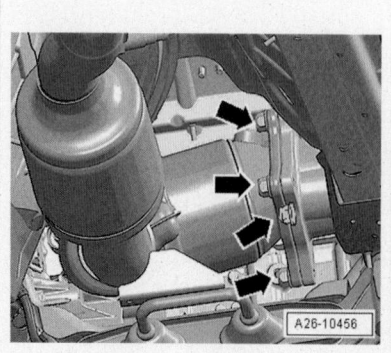

Fig. 92 From above, remove the nuts on the front exhaust pipe connection to the turbocharger

To install:

14. Installation is performed in the reverse order of removal.

15. Coat turbocharger stud bolts with hot bolt paste G 052 112 A3.

16. Replace gaskets and self-locking nuts.

17. Install exhaust system free of stress Exhaust System, Installing.

18. Tighten bolts/nuts to specification as follows:

• Tunnel bridge to body: 19 ft. lbs. (25 Nm)

CRANKSHAFT FRONT SEAL

REMOVAL & INSTALLATION

2.0L Engine

See Figures 93 through 95.

1. Before servicing the vehicle, refer to the precautions.

2. Remove toothed belt.

3. Remove toothed belt crankshaft sprocket. Secure toothed belt sprocket with the counterhold tool 3415

4. To guide seal remover 3203, install the center bolt manually into the crankshaft all the way.

5. Rotate inner section of the seal remover two turns, approximately 0.117 in. (3 mm), out of the outer section and secure it with the knurled bolt.

6. Lubricate threaded head of the seal remover.

7. Using considerable force, screw seal remover as far as possible into the seal.

8. Loosen knurled screw and turn inner portion against crankshaft until the oil seal is pulled out.

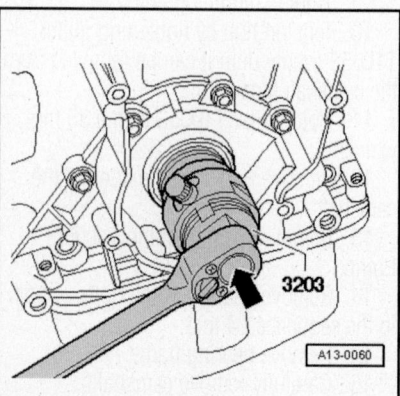

Fig. 93 To guide seal remover 3203, install the center bolt manually into the crankshaft all the way

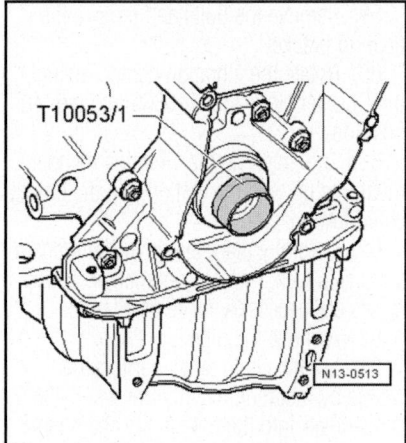

Fig. 94 Place guide sleeve T10053/1 on crankshaft pin

To install:

9. The sealing lip of the sealing ring may not be additionally oiled or greased.

10. Before installing, remove oil remains from end of crankshaft with a clean cloth.

11. Place guide sleeve T10053/1 on crankshaft pin.

12. Push seal over the guide sleeve onto the end of the crankshaft.

13. Press seal in to the limit stop using the assembly tool T10053 and the center bolt.

14. Install crankshaft toothed belt sprocket and tighten to 15 ft. lbs. (20 Nm).

2.5L Engine

See Figures 96 and 97.

1. Raise and safely support the vehicle and remove the engine undercover.

2. Remove the front part of the right inner fender.

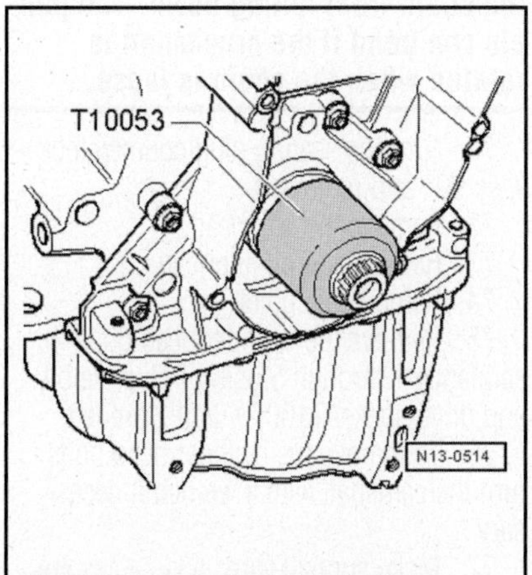

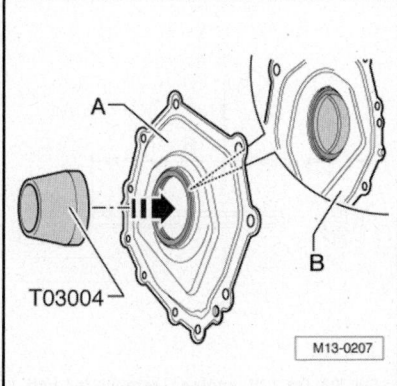

Fig. 95 Press seal in to the limit stop using the assembly tool T10053 and the center bolt

3. Remove the A/C compressor drive belt. Mark the belt's direction of rotation for reinstallation.

4. Remove the belt tensioner.

5. Set the engine to TDC of cylinder No. 5 and insert the crankshaft locking tool at the rear of the engine block.

6. Remove the bolts that hold the front seal flange to the engine block.

7. Starting at the alignment pins, carefully pry off the sealing flange. Take care to prevent damaging the cylinder block. The sealing flange will be damaged while removing.

✷✷ WARNING

To prevent injuries from shavings, wear protective goggles and protective clothing.

8. Remove sealant from cylinder block. Make sure that no sealant residue enters the engine.

9. Clean sealing surface of cylinder block and the crankshaft; they must be clean and dry.

To install:

➡**The following steps must be followed so that the sealing lip of sealing flange does not roll itself up when installing. Do not use any lubricants!**

10. Widen sealing lip of new sealing flange using the tapered end of assembly sleeve T03004.

11. After a short time, remove the assembly sleeve and insert the wide end into sealing ring. Assembly sleeve must protrude approximately 0.020 in. (3 mm) on the engine side of the seal.

12. Apply sealant bead into groove of sealing flange. Insert sealing flange sleeve

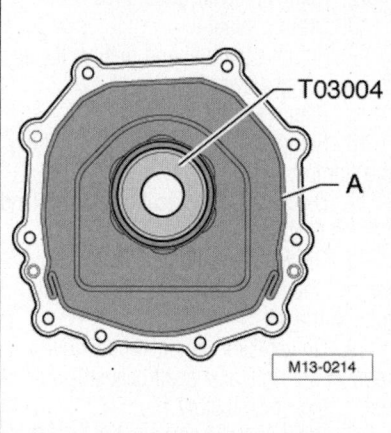

Fig. 97 Apply a bead of sealant and immediately install the sealing flange

T03004 over the crankshaft and press the flange plate uniformly into place.

13. Start all the bolts, then tighten uniformly in diagonal sequence. Torque to 7 ft. lbs. (10 Nm).

14. Install the crankshaft pulley and torque the bolt to 37 ft. lbs. (50 Nm) plus 90°.

15. Remove the crankshaft locking tool and install the plug.

16. Install the belt tensioner and A/C drive belt.

17. Install remaining components and run the engine to check for leaks.

CYLINDER HEAD

REMOVAL & INSTALLATION

2.0L & 2.5L Engines

See Figures 98 through 100.

1. Before servicing the vehicle, refer to the precautions.

2. Remove the engine cover.

3. Remove the air filter.

4. Loosen the hose clamp.

5. Remove bolt.

6. Disconnect the electrical connectors and free up the electrical wire.

✷✷ CAUTION

Reduce pressure by covering coolant reservoir cap with a cloth and carefully opening.

7. Open coolant reservoir cap.

8. Remove front exhaust pipe with catalytic converter

9. Remove the right front wheel.

10. Remove the noise insulation.

11. Remove the front right wheel housing liner.

Fig. 96 Use the assembly sleeve to widen the seal enough to fit over the crankshaft–do not use any lubricants

12. Remove the air guide pipe items.

13. Drain coolant.

14. Remove the bolt and remove the air guide pipe downward.

15. Remove bolts.

16. Remove the air guide pipe by lifting the clamps.

17. Disconnect electrical connectors and free up electrical wire.

18. On vehicles with auxiliary heater remove the bolts and swivel the coolant tubs to the left.

19. On vehicles with all-wheel drive, remove the right axle shaft heat shield bolts using Socket AF 8 3247.

20. Remove bolts and remove the turbocharger support.

21. Remove the banjo bolt and move the coolant line to the side.

22. On vehicles with front wheel drive, remove the bolts on the oil return line.

23. On vehicles with all-wheel drive, remove the oil return line bolts on the crankcase.

24. Remove the bolt on the oil supply line.

25. Disconnect the connector from the Camshaft Adjustment Valve N205 1.

26. Disconnect the electrical connectors on the ignition coils and free up the wiring harness.

27. Remove the ignition coils with the puller T40039.

28. Remove the air guide pipe bolt.

29. Remove the air guide pipe; to do this, loosen the hose clamp.

30. Disconnect the hose for the crankcase ventilation.

31. Remove the bolts and remove the crankcase ventilation.

32. Disconnect the hose for the crankcase ventilation.

33. Remove the bolts.

34. Remove the air guide pipe bolt.

35. Loosen the hose clamp and remove the air guide pipe together with the crankcase ventilation.

➡**Fuel supply line is under pressure! Wear protective goggles and protective clothing to prevent injuries and contact with skin. Before removing from hose connection wrap a cloth around the connection. Then release pressure by carefully pulling hose off connection.**

36. Disconnect the wires from the fuel transfer.

37. Disconnect the coolant line to the coolant reservoir.

38. Remove the coolant hoses from the coolant pipe.

39. Disconnect the ground wire (GND) and remove the bolt.

40. Disconnect the vacuum hoses.

41. Loosen the bolts and remove the heat shield together with the coolant pipe.

42. Disconnect the oil supply line from the turbocharger.

43. On 2.0L engines, remove the bolt from the heat shield using a 6 mm hex multi-point socket. The hex socket must be at least 5 cm long. Socket that is 6 mm at the tip is too wide.

44. Disconnect the electrical connector from the Fuel Pressure Regulator Valve N276.

45. Loosen the coolant pipe; remove the bolts.

46. Disconnect the coolant hose from the side connection on the cylinder head.

47. Disconnect the electrical connectors.

48. Free up the electrical cable.

49. Disconnect the vacuum hose leading to the EVAP filter.

50. Disconnect the electrical connectors and pull the connectors out of the retainer.

51. Disconnect the electrical connectors.

52. Disconnect the coolant line from the intake manifold, when doing this, remove the bolts.

53. Remove the intake manifold bracket by removing the mounting nut.

54. Remove the oil filter.

55. Disconnect the coolant hoses and move them to the side.

56. Remove the bolts and remove Camshaft Adjustment Valve N205

57. Remove timing chain upper cover.

➡**The control valve has a left thread.**

58. Remove the control valve using Assembly Tool 10352 T10352 in the direction of.

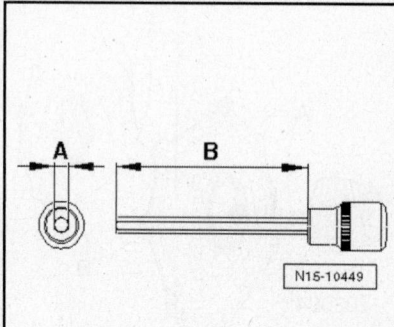

Fig. 98 On 2.0L engines, remove the bolt from the heat shield using a 6 mm hex multi-point socket. The hex socket must be at least 5 cm long. Socket that is 6 mm at the tip is too wide

59. Remove the bolts and remove the bearing bracket.

60. Rotate the vibration damper using the Counter Hold Tool T10355 into the "OT" position.

61. The notch on the vibration damper must line up with the marking on the timing chain lower cover.

62. Carefully mark the drive chain/chain sprockets with a waterproof marker. These marks are necessary for reinstallation.

63. Remove the plug.

64. Lift the chain tensioner locking wedge by inserting a scriber or a suitable screwdriver into the hole in the chain tensioner direction.

65. In order to tension the chain tensioner, turn the crankshaft opposite the direction of the engine rotation direction and secure it using Securing Pin T40011.

66. The intake camshaft switches in the engine direction of rotation.

67. Remove the bolt and guide the tensioning rail downward.

68. Remove the upper guide rail by unlocking the latch (located in the center) with a screwdriver and pushing the guide rail forward.

69. When the lower timing chain cover is installed, the loose chain on the crankshaft cannot jump off.

70. Remove camshaft timing chain from chain sprockets.

✳✳ WARNING

Danger of damaging the valves, piston head and lower timing chain cover. If the camshaft timing chain was removed from the cylinder head, then the crankshaft may not be turn further. Panels are installed on the lower timing chain cover to prevent the chain from falling down. The panels can bend if the crankshaft is rotated when the chain is loose.

71. Turn the sealing plug counterclockwise 90° and remove it.

72. Remove the ball head.

73. Remove the oil filler cap.

74. Remove the bolts

75. Remove the cylinder head bolts in sequence 1 through 5 using Polydrive bit and drive socket T10070 until 2 are left.

76. To remove the cylinder head bolts, turn the camshaft with a wrench if necessary.

77. Make sure all wires and cables are disconnected!

78. Pay attention the tension and guide rails when lifting the cylinder head.

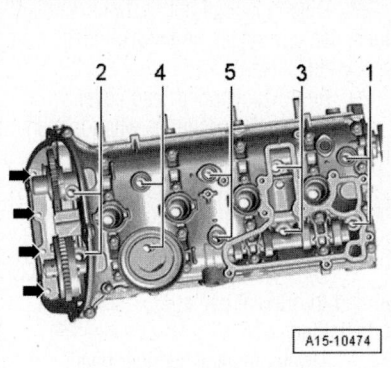

Fig. 99 Remove the cylinder head bolts in sequence 1 through 5 using Polydrive bit and drive socket T10070 until 2 are left

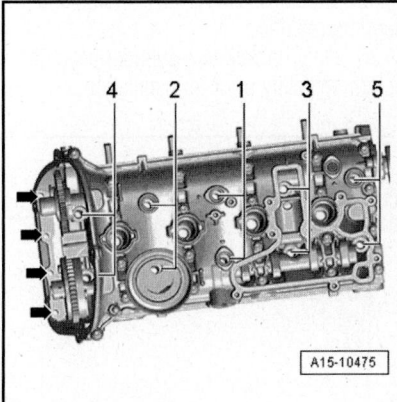

Fig. 100 Cylinder head bolt tightening sequence

79. Install the Engine Support T10014 each of the two small and large washers.

80. Connect the Engine Sling 2024 in the Engine Support T10014 and in the front left lifting eye on the cylinder head.

81. Mount the Engine Sling 2024 into the workshop crane and gently lift the cylinder head.

82. Remove the last two cylinder head bolts.

➡**Carefully lift the cylinder head until the guide rail for the camshaft timing chain is free. The tension- and guide rail must not be damaged.**

83. Lay the cylinder head on a soft surface, such as foam.

To install:

➡**The sealing surfaces could be damaged. Carefully remove sealant residue from cylinder head and cylinder block. Make sure that no long scrapes or scratches result.**

※※ **WARNING**

Risk of damaging cylinder block. There must be no oil or coolant in the blind holes for the cylinder head bolts in the cylinder block.

※※ **WARNING**

Risk of cylinder head seal leaking. Carefully remove all grinding and sanding residue. Only unpack new cylinder head gasket immediately prior to installation. To prevent cylinder head seal silicone layer and recessed area from being damaged, always handle seal extremely carefully.

※※ **WARNING**

Risk of damaging open valves. If a replacement cylinder is installed, only remove plastic base right before cylinder head is installed to protect open valves. Risk of damaging valves and piston heads after working on valvetrain. To ensure valves do not strike pistons when starting, carefully rotate engine at least 2 full revolutions.

84. Replace bolts which have been tightened to torque.

85. Replace sealing rings, seals and self-locking nuts.

86. Note different sealant for cylinder head sealing surfaces and bolts.

87. Secure all hose connections with hose clamps appropriate for the model.

88. When installing a replacement cylinder head, turn the camshaft to OT and mark the new chain sprockets exactly the same as on the old chain sprockets -arrows- (note the factory color marking on the chain sprockets).

89. If an exchange cylinder head is installed, all contact surfaces between bearing elements, roller rocker levers and cam running surfaces of camshafts must be oiled before installing cylinder head cover.

90. The engine oil and coolant must be changed if the cylinder head or cylinder head seal are replaced.

91. Hang the cylinder head on the workshop crane and position it above the cylinder block.

➡**Carefully lower the cylinder head. The tension- and guide rail must not be damaged. Pay attention to centering pins in cylinder block. Observe cylinder**

head seal location, identification: Replacement part number must be visible from intake side.

➡**When turning the crankshaft, make sure the timing chain cannot damage any other components.**

92. In the event the crankshaft has been rotated in the meantime: Set piston of cylinder 1 to TDC and turn crankshaft back again slightly.

93. Set cylinder head in place.

94. Insert cylinder head bolts and tighten by hand.

95. In order to be able to turn the cylinder head bolts, the intake camshaft must be turned with a wrench.

96. There is no requirement to retighten the cylinder head bolts after repairs.

97. Tighten cylinder head bolts in sequence to the following specification:
   - Tighten the cylinder head bolts in 1 to 5 sequence.
   - Tighten to 30 ft. lbs. (40 Nm) using a torque wrench
   - Tighten further 90° using a rigid wrench
   - Tighten further 90° using a rigid wrench
   - Pre-tighten the bolts (arrows) to 71 inch lbs. (8 Nm)
   - Tighten the bolts (arrows) 90° further using a rigid wrench

➡**When turning the crankshaft, make sure the timing chain cannot damage any other components.**

98. Rotate the vibration damper using the Counter Hold Tool T10355 into the "OT" position.

99. The notch on the vibration damper must line up with the marking on the timing chain lower cover.

100. The marked links of the timing chain must be positioned on the markings on the chain sprockets.

101. Mount the camshaft timing chain: The markings drive chain/chain sprockets must align.

102. Turn the intake camshaft using the wrench and mount the timing chain.

103. The rest of the installation is performed in reverse order of removal, noting the following:

104. During installation, cable ties must be re-installed at the same location.

105. Change the engine oil

106. Replace coolant.

2.0L TDI Engine

See Figures 101 through 103.

➡When using an exchanged cylinder head with camshaft installed, the contact surfaces between the lifters and cam lobes must be lubricated before installing the cylinder head cover.

➡The plastic protectors installed to protect the open valves must only be removed immediately before fitting the cylinder head.

➡When cylinder head is replaced, all coolant must also be replaced.

➡Cylinder heads with cracks between the valve seats can continue to be used without reducing service life, as long as the tears have a maximum width of 0.0195 in. (0.5 mm).

➡Do not mill the valve seats in the cylinder head; only grinding of the valves is permissible.

➡After installing the camshafts, the engine may not be started for approximately 30 minutes. The hydraulic equalization elements must seat themselves (otherwise the valves will crash into the pistons).

➡After working on the valvetrain and lifters, carefully rotate the crankshaft by hand at least 2 full revolutions before starting to be sure that valves do not strike the pistons.

➡Always replace gaskets and seals.

➡All cable ties which are opened or cut open when removing cylinder head, must be replaced in the same position when installing cylinder head.

✳✳ WARNING

When doing any repair work, especially in the engine compartment, pay attention to the following due to clearance issues. Route lines of all types (e.g. for fuel, hydraulic, coolant and refrigerant, brake fluid, vacuum) and electrical wiring so that the original path is followed. Ensure sufficient clearance to all moving or hot components.

1. Before servicing the vehicle, refer to the precautions.
2. Before removing the cylinder head, extract the fuel with the hand vacuum pump and the draining container V.A.G 1390/1 Tandem Pump.
3. Turn the ignition and all electrical consumers off and remove the ignition key.
4. Remove engine cover.

   a. On one piece engine cover. Pull the one piece front engine cover upward with a quick jerk and then pull the lower mount forward.
   b. On two piece engine cover, first pull the outer cover upward with a quick jerk in the upper illustration, then pull the inner engine cover upward with a quick jerk in lower illustration.
5. Remove plenum chamber bulkhead.
6. Disconnect the connector on the Mass Air Flow (MAF) sensor G70.
7. Disconnect the ventilation hose and disengage it from the bracket.
8. Open the spring-type clip3 using spring-type clip pliers VAS 5024A and disconnect the intake hose from the Mass Air Flow (MAF) sensor G70.
9. Disconnect the intake manifold from the air guide.
10. Unfasten bolt and remove air filter housing and mass air flow sensor.
11. Remove noise insulation.
12. Drain the coolant.
13. For safety reasons, pull the connector off the fuel delivery unit.
14. Disconnect the fuel supply and return lines, as well as the coolant line on the cylinder head.
15. Before removing the cylinder head, extract the fuel with the diesel extractor VAS 5226 or the hand vacuum pump and the breather reservoir V.A.G 1390/1 to the tandem pump Tandem Pump.
16. On fuel filter without the retaining plate, release the clips and remove the fuel filter with the hoses still connected from the retaining plate.
17. On fuel filter with the retaining plate
   a. Loosen the bolt one turn.
   b. Remove the bolt and the nut.
   c. Remove the fuel filter with the hoses still connected.
18. Remove the front exhaust pipe.
19. Remove the turbocharger support and the oil return from the turbocharger.
20. Remove the oil supply line and lay the oil supply line off to the side.
21. Remove toothed belt.
22. Remove the toothed belt tensioning roller.
23. Remove hub for camshaft sprocket Camshaft.
24. Remove the bolts for the rear toothed belt guard.
25. Remove the Camshaft Position (CMP) sensor G40.
26. Remove the connecting pipe for exhaust gas recirculation.
27. Pull off/disconnect all remaining electrical wires required from cylinder head and set aside.

28. Disconnect all connections, coolant lines, vacuum hoses and intake hoses from the cylinder head.
29. Remove cylinder head cover.
30. Follow the sequence when loosening the cylinder head bolts.
31. Lift the cylinder head slightly and then remove it from the engine sideways, past the toothed belt guard.
32. The cylinder head must be carefully guided to prevent damages.
Installing
33. Always replace cylinder head bolts.
34. Carefully remove residual sealant from cylinder head and cylinder block. Make sure that no long scrapes or scratches result. When using sand paper, grit must not be below 100.
35. Carefully remove all grinding and sanding residue.
36. Only unpack new cylinder head gasket immediately prior to installation.

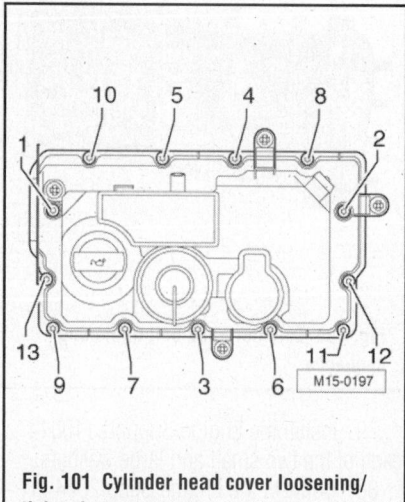

Fig. 101 Cylinder head cover loosening/tightening sequence

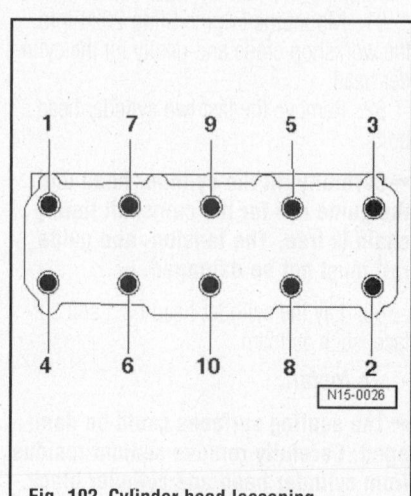

Fig. 102 Cylinder head loosening sequence

37. Handle gasket carefully. Damages to the silicone layer and in areas of recesses may result in leaks.

38. Before installing cylinder head, position crankshaft to TDC marking.

39. Turn the crankshaft in opposite direction of engine rotation until all pistons are positioned almost evenly below TDC.

40. Position cylinder head gasket.

✳✳ WARNING

Observe cylinder head gasket identification.

41. Set cylinder head in place and tighten all cylinder head bolts hand tight.

42. Fasten the cylinder head in four steps according to the indicated tightening sequence.
  • Tighten to 26 ft. lbs. (35 Nm)
  • Tighten to 44 ft. lbs. (60 Nm)
  • Tighten 90° additional rotation
  • Tighten 90° additional rotation

43. There is no requirement to retighten the cylinder head bolts after repairs.

Further installation is performed in reverse order. When doing this note the following:

44. After fastening the cylinder head turn the camshaft sprocket so that the lobes for cylinder 1 point upward equally. Before installing the toothed belt, turn the crankshaft in engine rotation direction to TDC Toothed Belt.

45. Install hub for camshaft sprocket.

46. Install toothed belt.

47. Install ribbed belt.

48. Install oil supply line.

49. Install noise insulation.

50. Install plenum chamber bulkhead.

51. Fill with coolant.

52. Perform a test drive and afterwards

check the fault memory Engine Control Module DTC Memory, Checking and Erasing.

▌EXHAUST MANIFOLD

REMOVAL & INSTALLATION

2.0L Engine

See Figures 98 and 104

1. Before servicing the vehicle, refer to the precautions.

✳✳ WARNING

If mechanical damage is found on exhaust turbocharger, e.g. a destroyed compression wheel, it is not enough to just replace the turbocharger. Perform the following steps to prevent subsequent damage. Check the air filter housing, the air filter insert and the intake hoses for contamination. Check entire charge air circuit and cooler for contamination. If contaminants are found in charge air circuit, circuit must be cleaned and cooler replaced if necessary.

2. Remove the air filter.

3. Remove the battery and battery tray.

4. Remove noise insulation.

5. Remove the front part of the right wheel housing liner and/or the front right wheel housing liner.

6. Drain the coolant.

7. Remove catalytic converters with front exhaust pipe.

8. Remove bolts.

9. Remove the air guide pipe by lifting the clamps items.

10. On vehicles with all-wheel drive remove the heat shield above the right driveshaft.

11. Disconnect electrical connectors and free up electrical wire.

12. On vehicles with auxiliary heater remove the bolts and swivel the coolant tubs to the left.

13. On vehicles with front wheel drive remove the right driveshaft heat shield.

14. Remove the bolt Socket XZN 10 T10154.

15. Remove the bolt.

16. Remove the banjo bolt and move the coolant line to the side.

17. On vehicles with front wheel drive remove the bolts on the oil return line.

18. On vehicles with all-wheel drive remove the oil return line bolts on the crankcase.

19. Remove the bolt on the oil supply line.

20. Remove engine cover.

21. Disconnect the connectors from the ignition coils and the wiring harness and lay them aside.

22. Disconnect the coolant line to the coolant reservoir.

23. Disconnect the vacuum line at the separating point and free up the wire.

24. Remove the coolant hoses from the coolant pipe.

25. Press the release buttons, remove the air guide hose and move them to the side.

26. Remove the air guide pipe bolt.

27. Remove the air guide pipe; to do this, loosen the hose clamp.

28. Remove the air guide pipe bolt.

29. Loose the hose clamp and lay the air guide pipe on the cylinder head.

30. Seal the turbocharger with the Engine bung set VAS 6122.

31. Remove the bolts and remove the heat shield together with the coolant pipe.

32. On 2.0L engines, remove the bolt from the heat shield with a 6 mm hex socket. The hex socket must be at least 5 cm long. A socket that is 6 mm at the tip is too wide.

33. Disconnect the oil supply line from the turbocharger.

34. Disconnect the coolant hose and move it to the side.

35. Remove the nuts.

36. Remove the turbocharger/exhaust manifold upward.

To install:

37. Installation is performed in the reverse order of removal, noting the following:

38. Always replace seals, gaskets and self-locking nuts.

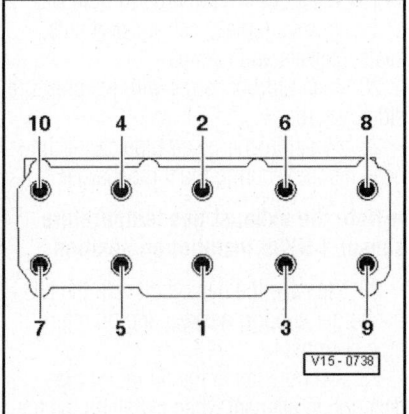

Fig. 103 Cylinder head tightening sequence

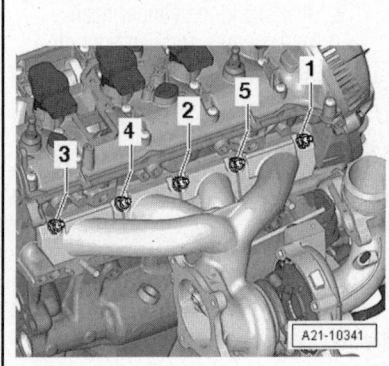

Fig. 104 Observe tightening sequence for exhaust manifold/turbocharger to the cylinder head

39. Add oil to turbocharger through oil feed line connecting piece.

40. After installing turbocharger, let engine idle for approximately 1 minute to ensure adequate oil supply to the turbocharger.

41. Coolant return line must be installed together with turbocharger.

42. Hose connections and charge air system hoses must be free of oil and grease before installing. Sealing ring and sealing surfaces must only be lightly oiled with connector couplings.

43. Secure all hose connections using hose clamps appropriate for the model type.

44. Exhaust manifold/turbocharger to the cylinder head
  - Tighten the bolts 1 through 5 in 4 stages as follows:
  - Tighten the bolts to 44 inch lbs. (5 Nm)
  - Tighten the bolts to 106 inch lbs. (12 Nm)
  - Tighten the bolts to 12 ft. lbs. (16 Nm)
  - Tighten the bolts to 19 ft. lbs. (25 Nm)

45. Tighten bolts/nuts to specification as follows:
  - Oil supply line to exhaust turbocharger: 15 ft. lbs. (20 Nm) plus 45° additional rotation
  - Oil return line to exhaust turbocharger: 80 inch lbs. (9 Nm)
  - Coolant supply line to turbocharger: 15 ft. lbs. (20 Nm) plus 45° additional rotation
  - Turbocharger bracket to cylinder block: 22 ft. lbs. (30 Nm)
  - Turbocharger bracket to turbocharger: 22 ft. lbs. (30 Nm)
  - Right charge air pipe to oil pan: 89 inch. lbs. (00 Nm)
  - Heat shield to cylinder head (replace nuts and use hot bolt paste) M8 and M12: 15 ft. lbs. (20 Nm)

2.5L Engine

1. Before servicing the vehicle, refer to the precautions.

2. Remove the engine cover.

3. Remove the wiper arms.

4. Remove the outer plenum chamber cover and plenum chamber end plate.

5. Remove the heat shield.

6. Remove the protective cap for the right inner Constant Velocity (CV) joint from the engine.

7. Remove bolt and nut and remove the brace for the exhaust manifold.

8. Loosen the nuts for the double clamp.

9. Remove the nuts and bolts.

10. Remove the front exhaust pipe from the exhaust manifold and tie up firmly to the side.

11. The flex joint in the front exhaust pipe must not be bent more than 10°, otherwise it may be damaged.

12. Disconnect the electrical connector for the oxygen sensor.

13. Remove the heat shield at the top of the front exhaust pipe and free up the wiring harness of the oxygen sensor in the exhaust manifold.

14. Remove the exhaust manifold bolts and remove it downward.

To install:

15. Installation is performed in reverse order.

16. Gaskets and self-locking nuts must be replaced.

17. Install the exhaust manifold.

18. Install the front exhaust pipe with catalytic converter,

19. Check the Diagnostic Trouble code (DTC) memory of the Engine Control Module (ECM), repair any stored malfunctions and then erase the DTC memory.

20. Tighten bolts/nuts to specification as follows:
  - Exhaust manifold nut: 19 ft. lbs. (25Nm)
  - Heat shield bolt: 89 inch lbs. (10 Nm)
  - Exhaust nut/bolt: 19 ft. lbs. (25Nm)

2.0L TDI Engine

1. Before servicing the vehicle, refer to the precautions.

✳✳ WARNING

If mechanical damage was found on the turbocharger, for example a destroyed compression wheel, just replacing the turbocharger is not enough. Perform the following steps to prevent subsequent damage. Check the air filter housing, the air filter insert and the intake hoses for contamination.

2. Remove particulate filter with NOx reduction catalytic converter.

3. Mark installation position of the exhaust gas temperature sensor 1 G235 and remove it.

4. Remove control wire between the exhaust gas recirculation housing and the exhaust pressure sensor 2 G451.

5. Remove housing with the exhaust gas recirculation cooler.

6. Disconnect connector from the charge pressure actuator position sensor G581 at the turbocharger vacuum diaphragm.

7. Disconnect vacuum hose at the turbocharger vacuum diaphragm.

8. Disconnect "black" connector for the exhaust gas temperature sensor 1 G235 at the engine bulkhead.

9. Guide line out of the retainers on the engine bulkhead and the turbocharger.

10. Remove connecting pipe.

11. Remove oil supply line.

12. Remove banjo bolt from the turbocharger support.

13. Remove hex stud bolt from the turbocharger support.

14. Rotate the lower section of the support 90° and remove the support downward from the upper section.

15. Remove heat shield on the exhaust manifold.

16. Remove exhaust manifold nuts.

17. Remove turbocharger with the exhaust manifold from the cylinder head and rotate it so the intake side faces down. Remove the turbocharger with the exhaust manifold downward.

To install:

✳✳ WARNING

Before installing, check if the oil return pipe decoupling element is bent and therefore stretched. If that is the case, tiny cracks can form that can lead to leaks. Replace the oil return pipe before installing the turbocharger if necessary.

18. Install in reverse order of removal.

19. Always replace self-locking nuts, seals, gaskets and clamps.

20. Insert turbocharger with the pressure side upward.

21. Position charge air pipe connecting hose before securing the turbocharger.

➡ **Note the exhaust gas temperature sensor 1 G235 installation position.**

22. Replace the banjo bolt with the turbocharger support gaskets and oil return pipe O-rings.

23. Do not stretch the oil return pipe decoupling element when installing the turbocharger support.

24. Tighten bolts/nuts to specification as follows:

- Turbocharger with exhaust manifold (Replace): 17 ft. lbs. (23 Nm)
- Oil return line: 11 ft. lbs. (15 Nm)

INTAKE MANIFOLD

REMOVAL & INSTALLATION

2.0L Engines

See Figure 105.

1. Before servicing the vehicle, refer to the precautions.

❊❊ WARNING

Fuel system is under pressure! Fuel pressure must be reduced to a residual pressure before opening high pressure area of injection system.

2. Remove the engine cover.
3. Clean the contact surface from the intake manifold to the cylinder head.
4. Remove the air filter.
5. Separate the vacuum line to the EVAP canister.
6. Disconnect the following electrical connections:
   - Intake Air Temperature Sensor G42
   - Throttle Valve Control Module J338
   - Evaporative Emission (EVAP) Canister Purge Regulator Valve N80
   - Camshaft Position sensor G40
7. Disconnect the vacuum line at the separating point and remove the crankcase ventilation hose.
8. Remove the bolts for the fuel supply line and lay the line to the side.
9. The fuel system must have no pressure.
10. Open the fuel line union nut lower.
11. Disconnect the vacuum line from the Intake Manifold Runner Control (IMRC) Valve N316.
12. Remove the bolts for the coolant line from the intake manifold.
13. Disconnect the electrical connector from the Fuel Pressure Sensor G247.
14. Loosen the hose clamp.
15. Remove bolt.
16. Disconnect electrical connector.
17. Remove the noise insulation.
18. Remove the air guide pipe items.
19. Remove the bolt and remove the air guide pipe downward.
20. Disconnect the electrical connectors and remove the bracket from the intake manifold.
21. Remove the intake manifold bracket by removing the mounting nut.
22. Remove the oil filter.
23. Loosen the wiring bracket.

24. Loosen the wire from the intake manifold.
25. Remove the nuts and loosen the bolts from the intake manifold using the Multi-point socket T10347.
26. Carefully pull the intake manifold and fuel rail away from the cylinder head just a little.
27. Disconnect the electrical connector from the Intake Manifold Runner Position Sensor G336 and remove the intake manifold.
28. Cover the intake channels with a clean rag.
29. The fuel injectors could remain stuck in the fuel rail.
30. Disconnect the fuel rail from the intake manifold.
31. To access the fuel injectors, the intake manifold and the fuel rail with intake manifold runner control valve must be removed. The fuel injectors sit in the cylinder head.

To install:

32. The combustion chamber seal (Teflon) and the O-ring must always be replaced.
33. Mount the intake manifold onto the cylinder head on the stud bolts (lower left and right).
34. Make sure the fuel injectors are installed correctly and pay attention to the wiring bracket when mounting the intake manifold (located under the intake manifold).
35. When installing the intake manifold, the manifold must be pulled out slightly and the fuel injectors will stick in the fuel rail. Pull the fuel injectors out of the fuel rail and insert them in the cylinder head again.
36. The rest of the installation follows the reverse of the removal procedures.

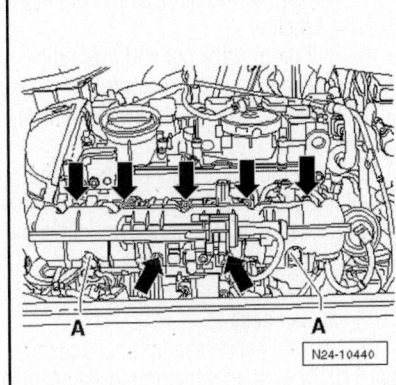

Fig. 105 Remove the nuts A and loosen the bolts from the intake manifold using the Multi-point socket T10347

37. When attaching the wiring bracket onto the intake manifold, make sure it clips into both latches.
38. Note the following tightening specifications:
   - High pressure pump bolts (Replace): 89 inch lbs. (10 Nm)
   - Fuel high pressure line connection (Replace): 16 ft. lbs. (22 Nm)
   - Fuel line to the fuel rail: 13 ft. lbs. (18 Nm)
   - Bolt for the intake manifold support: 17 ft. lbs. (23 Nm)
   - Nut for the intake manifold support: 89 inch lbs. (10 Nm)

2.0L TDI Engine

➡**Make sure no contaminants enter the fuel system when removing the intake manifold.**

➡**Seal off the connections in the fuel system using the plugs from the engine bung set VAS 6122.**

1. Remove the engine cover.
2. Remove the protective strip, if equipped.
3. Loosen the high pressure line or fuel line bolts arrows on the intake manifold.
4. Disconnect the fuel injector A connectors, the exhaust pressure sensor 1 G450 connector B and the fuel pressure sensor G247 connector C.
5. Remove the coolant line bolts arrows from the intake manifold and lay the line in front of the intake manifold.
6. Unclip the wiring harness from the wiring guide for the glow plugs.
7. Disconnect the glow plug connectors.
8. Remove the high pressure line between the high pressure fuel pump and fuel rail.
9. Loosen the hose clip using hose clip pliers VAS 6362 and remove the line from the fuel rail.
10. Before removing, clean the return line connection on the fuel injectors (for example using a commercially available detergent).
11. Dry the return line connections.
12. Cover the return line connections with a cloth.
13. Remove the fuel return line connections from the fuel injectors. Pull them upward to release them.

➡**Maintain clean working conditions. Dirt and contaminants must not enter the return lines and the connections on the fuel injectors.**

14. Loosen the hose clips using hose clip pliers VAS 6362 and remove the fuel return line.

15. Loosen the hose clip 4 using the hose clip pliers VAS 6362 and remove the fuel return line from the high pressure fuel pump.

16. Seal the lines so that the fuel system is not contaminated by dirt, etc.

17. Remove the fuel return lines.

18. Disconnect the EGR vacuum regulator solenoid valve N18 connector 1 and the throttle valve control module J338 connector 3.

19. Loosen the clamp 4 and remove the charge air hose.

20. Remove the oil dipstick bracket.

➡ **Make sure the connecting pipe decoupling element does not bend or stretch. Cracks could develop.**

21. Disconnect the connecting pipe 2.

22. Remove the intake manifold bolts using Socket XZN 8 T40159 in a diagonal sequence working from the outside to the inside.

23. Remove the intake manifold.

To install:

24. Install in reverse order of removal. When doing this note the following:

25. Condition: Always replace seals.

26. When installing the high pressure line or fuel lines, make sure no dirt or contaminants enter the fuel system.

27. Only remove the sealing plugs right before installing the fuel lines.

28. Do not change the angles of the high pressure lines

29. Make sure lines connections are securely fastened.

30. Do not swap supply and return lines.

31. Tighten bolts/nuts to specification as follows:

- Intake manifold to cylinder head: 16 ft. lbs. (22 Nm)
- Engine lifting eyelet to cylinder head: 15 ft. lbs. (20 Nm)
- Bracket to intake manifold: 89 inch lbs. (10 Nm)
- Connecting pipe to intake manifold connection bolt: 16 ft. lbs. (22 Nm)
- EGR cooler to intake manifold: 89 inch lbs. (10 Nm)
- Intake Flap Motor V157 to intake manifold: 89 inch lbs. (10 Nm)

32. Install mounting supports and torque bolts to 18 ft. lbs. (25 Nm).

33. Tighten the high pressure line union nuts by hand.

34. Make sure the high pressure line is free of tension.

35. Use torque wrench (5-50 Nm) V.A.G 1331 with ratchet, reversible V.A.G 1331/1 and socket T40055 to tighten the high pressure line.

36. Fill the fuel system. Refer to Fuel System, Filling and Bleeding.

2.5L Engine

See Figure 106.

1. Before servicing the vehicle, refer to the precautions.

2. First, check whether a coded radio is installed. If necessary, obtain the anti-theft coding.

3. Disconnect the negative battery cable.

4. Remove engine cover/air filter assembly.

> ✳✳ **CAUTION**
>
> **Fuel supply line is under pressure! Wear protective goggles and protective clothing to prevent injuries and contact with skin. Before loosening the fuel lines, place a rag around the connection point. Then release pressure by carefully pulling hose off connection.**

5. Disconnect the three under-hood fuel lines. To release wires, press the circlip in. On the fuel supply line, the retainer must be pressed upward in the housing.

6. Disconnect connectors. Remove wiring harness from transport strap. Pull clamps and retaining ring out of locking mechanism. Remove bolts and remove transport strap.

7. Remove throttle valve control module (throttle body). The coolant hoses remain attached.

8. Disconnect manifold wiring and hose for crankcase ventilation.

9. Remove wiring harness by carefully pressing off clips.

10. Pull oil dipstick out and press dipstick tube retaining ring downward.

11. Raise and safely support the vehicle and remove the engine undercover.

12. Loosen bolts or nuts on the bottom side of the intake manifold.

13. Loosen bolt for intake manifold support and dipstick tube. Lay tube aside.

14. Open clip on leak detection pump (LDP) vacuum hose.

15. Loosen intake manifold bolts using Tool T10107A. Bolts remain in intake manifold.

16. Remove intake manifold upward at an angle. Make sure that no bolts fall out.

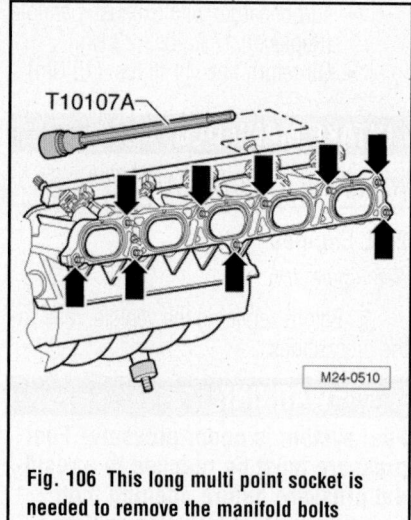

Fig. 106 This long multi point socket is needed to remove the manifold bolts

17. Seal intake ports in cylinder head using a clean rag.

18. If manifold must be replaced:
- Remove fuel rail with injectors.
- Disconnect vacuum hose for Leak Detection Pump (LDP).
- Remove Manifold Absolute Pressure (MAP) sensor.

To install:

19. Make sure all sealing surfaces are clean and dry. Fit new sealing rings to the intake manifold runners.

20. If the injectors were removed, fit new O-rings, lubricate them with engine oil and install the injectors.

21. Replace oil dipstick tube seal.

22. Fit the manifold into place and torque the screws to 6 ft. lbs. (9 Nm) working from the middle and working towards the ends in a diagonal sequence.

23. Install mounting supports and torque bolts to 18 ft. lbs. (25 Nm).

24. Install the dipstick tube and insert the dipstick.

25. Install the throttle body.

26. Connect all wires, hoses and tubes using new seals or gaskets as needed.

27. Connect the battery

28. Bleed fuel supply system.

29. Run the engine to check for leaks.

OIL PAN

REMOVAL & INSTALLATION

2.0L & 2.5L Engines

Lower Pan

See Figures 107 and 108.

1. Before servicing the vehicle, refer to the precautions.

2. Remove noise insulation.

3. If present, disconnect the electrical connector for the Oil Level Thermal Sensor G266.

4. Drain engine oil.

5. Remove the screws.

6. Remove oil pan, if necessary loosen by applying light strikes with a rubber hammer.

To install:

7. Remove sealant residue from upper part of the oil pan with a flat scraper.

8. Remove sealant residue on the lower part of the oil pan, e.g. with a rotating plastic brush.

9. Clean sealing surfaces, must be free of oil and grease.

10. Cut tube nozzle at front nozzle approximately 0.117 in. (3 mm).

11. Apply silicon sealant D 174 003 A2 to clean sealing surfaces of the oil pan (lower part) as shown in illustration.

✳✳ WARNING

The oil pan must be installed within 5 minutes after application of silicon sealant.

➡**The sealant bead may not be thicker than 0.078–0.117 in. (2–3 mm), otherwise excess sealant could enter the oil pan and clog the oil intake tube.**

12. Immediately mount the lower part of the oil pan and tighten the screws 1 through 20 in two steps as shown.

13. Tighten bolts/nuts to specification as follows:

- Tighten the bolts to 71 inch lbs. (8 Nm)
- Tighten the bolts an additional 90°

14. After installing oil pan, allow sealant to dry for approximately 30 minutes. Only after then may the engine oil be replenished.

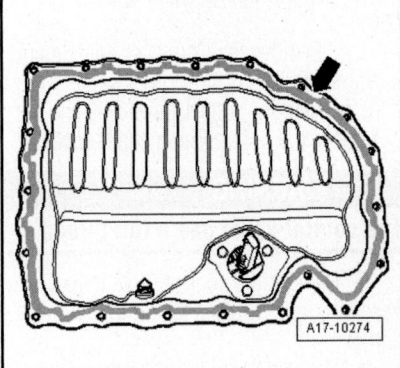

Fig. 107 Apply silicon sealant D 174 003 A2 to clean sealing surfaces of the oil pan (lower part) as shown in illustration

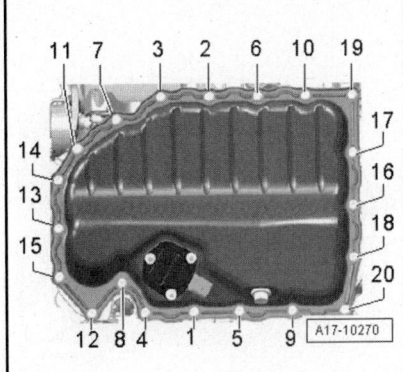

Fig. 108 Immediately mount the lower part of the oil pan and tighten the screws 1 through 20 in two steps as shown

15. Fill the engine oil, oil capacities Engine Oil.

16. The rest of the assembly is basically a reverse of the disassembling sequence.

2.0L TDI Engine

See Figure 109.

1. Before servicing the vehicle, refer to the precautions.

✳✳ WARNING

If large quantities of metal particles or abraded material are detected during engine repairs, it may be an indication for a damaged crankshaft or rod bearings. To prevent further damage, perform the following steps after the repair: Carefully clean oil passages, replace oil cooler, replace oil filter insert,

2. Remove engine cover.

3. On one piece engine cover, pull the one piece front engine cover upward with a quick jerk and then pull the lower mount forward.

4. On two piece engine cover, first pull the outer cover upward with a quick jerk in the upper illustration, then pull the inner engine cover upward with a quick jerk.

5. Remove the air filter/turbocharger intake hose.

6. Carefully cut the cable tie.

7. Open the wiring bracket and disengage the wiring harness.

8. Disconnect the connector on the Mass Air Flow (MAF) sensor G70.

9. Disconnect the ventilation hose and disengage it from the bracket.

10. Open the spring-type clip3 using spring-type clip pliers VAS 5024A and dis-

connect the intake hose from the Mass Air Flow (MAF) sensor G70.

11. Disconnect the intake manifold from the air guide.

12. Unfasten bolt and remove air filter housing and mass air flow sensor.

13. Remove both bolts from the upper charge air pipe.

14. Remove noise insulation.

15. Remove the charge air pipe bolt from the oil pan.

16. Disconnect the connector, if equipped, from the oil level thermal sensor G266.

17. Drain engine oil.

18. Remove the oil pan/transmission connecting bolts.

19. Loosen oil pan screws with 10 mm hex ball socket 3185. (Remove using 5 mm socket 3249 or T10058).

20. Remove the oil pan. Loosen oil pan with light blows of a rubber headed hammer if necessary.

21. Remove sealant residue from cylinder block with a flat scraper.

22. Remove remaining sealant at oil pan using a rotating brush, e.g. a drill with plastic brush attachment (wear protective glasses).

23. Clean sealing surfaces. They must be free of oil and grease.

To install:

✳✳ WARNING

The oil pan must be installed within 5 minutes after application of silicone sealant.

24. Cut off the nozzle on the tube of sealant at the front mark approximately 0.117 in. (3 mm).

25. Apply silicone sealant to clean sealing surfaces of oil pan. Sealing compound beads must be 0.078–0.117 in. (2–3 mm) thick and run on inside of bolt holes.

✳✳ WARNING

Sealant bead must not be thicker than specified. Otherwise, excess sealant could get into oil pan and clog strainer in intake line of oil pump.

26. With transmission removed, oil pan must seal flush with cylinder block.

27. With transmission installed, oil pan must make contact on transmission.

28. Apply silicone sealing compound bead as illustrated to clean sealing surface of oil pan.

29. Install oil pan immediately and tighten all oil pan bolts lightly. Make sure

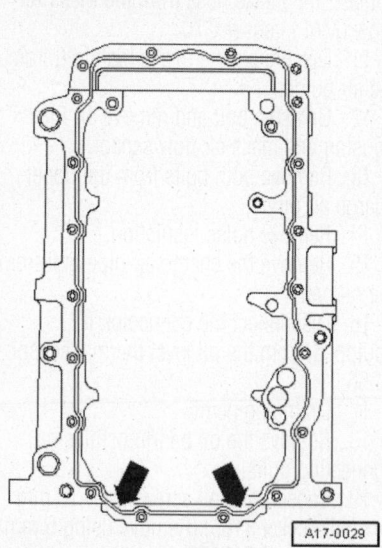

Fig. 109 Apply silicone sealant to clean sealing surfaces of oil pan. Sealing compound beads must be 0.078–0.117 in. (2–3 mm thick and run on inside of bolt holes

that the oil pan is seated flush against the intermediate plate/transmission flange.

30. When installing the oil pan to a removed engine, make sure that the oil pan is positioned flush with the cylinder block on the flywheel side.

31. Tighten the oil pan bolts in a diagonal sequence to 11 ft. lbs. (15 Nm).

32. Tighten the oil pan/transmission bolts to 33 ft. lbs. (45 Nm).

33. After installing oil pan, allow sealant to dry for approximately 30 minutes. Only after then may the engine oil be replenished.

34. The rest of the assembly is basically a reverse of the disassembling sequence.

35. Install noise insulation.

OIL PUMP

REMOVAL & INSTALLATION

2.0L & 2.5L Engines

See Figures 110 and 111.

1. Before servicing the vehicle, refer to the precautions.

2. Remove the lower oil pan section.

3. Remove the oil baffle.

4. The following must be performed in one sequence; technicians are necessary.

5. Remove the oil pump bolts.

6. Pull back the chain tensioner using the Assembly Tool T10118 and have a second technician remove the oil pump.

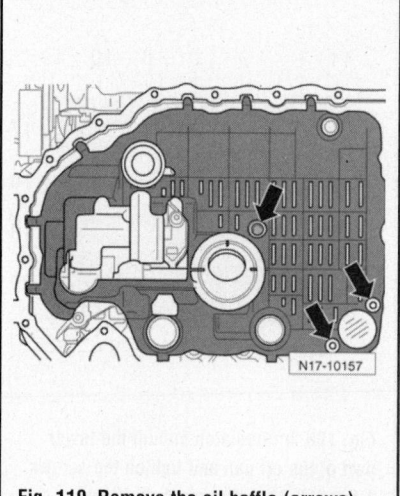

Fig. 110 Remove the oil baffle (arrows)

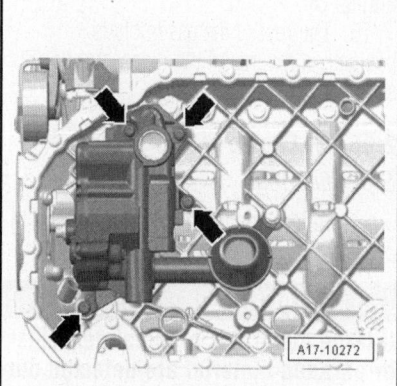

Fig. 111 Remove the oil pump bolts

To install:

7. Installation is performed in reverse order of removal.

8. Before installing the oil pump, make sure the screen in the supply line and the oil passages in the upper part of the oil pan are clean.

9. Make sure both alignment bushings for centering the oil pump are in there.

10. Replace the baffle plate.

✳✳ WARNING

There are plastic ribs on the oil baffle that deform permanently when tightening. The plastic ribs ensure the oil baffle is not loosen and does not rattle. Because of this, always replace the oil baffle.

2.0L TDI Engine

See Figure 112.

1. Before servicing the vehicle, refer to the precautions.

2. Remove the oil pan and the splash wall.

3. Remove the circlip with circlip pliers.

4. Install a M3 bolt and remove the input shaft from the oil pump.

5. Remove the bolt and remove the intake connection from the oil pump.

6. Remove the two bolts and the oil pump.

➥**Do not loosen the bolt for the intermediate sprocket.**

To install:

7. Install in reverse order of removal. When doing this note the following:

8. Condition: Replace the O-ring.

9. Replace damaged or stretched circlips.

10. The circlip must lie in the base of the groove.

11. Before installing the oil pump, make sure both alignment sleeves for centering the pump on the balance shaft assembly are present.

12. Install the oil pan.

13. Tighten bolts/nuts to specification as follows:

- Chain sprocket to oil pump shaft: 15 ft. lbs. (20 Nm) plus 90° rotation
- Oil pump to cylinder block: 15 ft. lbs. (20 Nm) plus 90° rotation

TIMING CHAIN, SPROCKETS, FRONT COVER AND SEAL

REMOVAL & INSTALLATION

2.0L & 2.5L Engines

See Figures 113 through 119.

1. Before servicing the vehicle, refer to the precautions.

2. Remove timing chain upper cover.

　a. Remove the Camshaft Adjustment Valve N205.

　b. Remove bolts 1 through 5 and remove the upper timing chain cover.

✳✳ WARNING

The control valve has a left thread.

3. Remove the control valve using Assembly Tool 10352 T10352 in the direction of.

4. Remove the bolts and remove the bearing bracket.

5. Rotate the vibration damper using the Counter Hold Tool T10355 into the "OT" position.

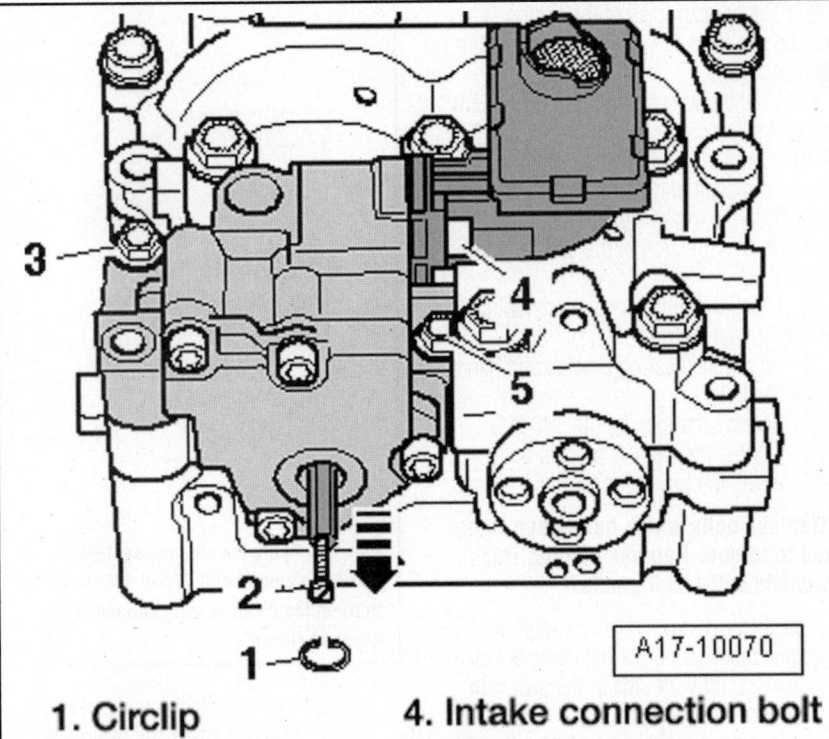

1. Circlip
2. M3 bolt
3. Oil pump bolt
4. Intake connection bolt
5. Oil pump bolt

Fig. 112 Removing the oil pump

6. The notch on the vibration damper must line up with the marking on the timing chain lower cover.

7. The markings on the camshafts must point upward.

8. Remove the lower timing chain cover.

  a. Remove the noise insulation.

  b. Remove the front part of the right wheel housing liner.

  c. Drain engine oil.

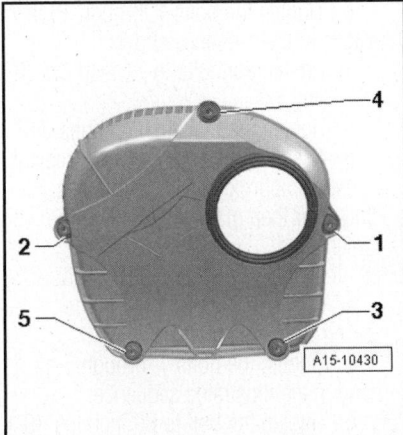

Fig. 113 Remove bolts 1 through 5 and remove the upper timing chain cover

  d. On vehicles with auxiliary heater, loosen the clamp, remove the bolt and remove the auxiliary heater muffler.

  e. Remove bolts.

  f. Remove the air guide pipe by lifting the clamps.

※※ WARNING

Risk of destroying due to reversed running direction on a used ribbed belt. Before removing ribbed belt, marking running direction with chalk or felt-tip pen for reinstallation later.

  g. Remove the right air guide hose.

  h. To release the tension on the ribbed belt, turn the tensioner in direction of rotation from underneath.

  i. Secure tensioner with Drift T10060 A.

  j. Remove ribbed belt from vibration damper ribbed belt pulley.

  k. Rotate the vibration damper using the Counter Hold Tool T10355 into the "OT" position.

  l. The notch on the vibration damper must line up with the marking on the timing chain lower cover.

※※ WARNING

The engine could be destroyed. 1.In order not to change the valve timing, the crankshaft must not be moved out of the "OT" position when the vibration damper bolt is removed.

  m. Remove vibration damper bolt using Counterhold T10355.

  n. Remove the vibration damper.

※※ WARNING

To avoid damaging the splines, only use Thrust Piece T10368 to install the vibration damper bolt.

  o. Install the vibration damper bolt and thrust piece T10368 again.

  p. Mount the Engine Support Bridge 10 - 222 A.

  q. Do not place the adapter 10 - 222 A /8 on the fender panels. They will be damaged.

  r. The shackle 10 - 222 A /12 is needed to make sure the engine is lifted in the installation position and not tipped away.

  s. Tension the engine with the spindle.

  t. Remove the subframe bolts on the engine.

  u. Remove the engine bracket subframe mount.

  v. Lift the engine approximately 1.95 in. (50 mm) and loosen the upper bolt for the engine support.

  w. Now lower the engine approximately 3.9 in. (100 mm).

  x. Free up electrical wiring harness.

  y. Remove the bolt and remove the ribbed belt tensioner from the accessory assembly bracket.

  z. Remove the lower bolts for the engine support using Bits T10099.

  aa. Remove the engine support and the bolts.

  bb. Remove the bolts and pull the oil dipstick guide tube out of the lower timing chain cover.

  cc. Disconnect the Wastegate Bypass Regulator Valve N75 from the turbocharger.

  dd. Remove the turbocharger support.

  ee. Remove the bolts 1 through 15.

※※ WARNING

The lower timing chain cover could be damaged. To avoid deformation, do not hold between the bolting points.

Fig. 114 Rotate the vibration damper using the Counter Hold Tool T10355 into the "OT" position

ff. Pry off the lower timing chain cover starting with bolts shown.

9. Press the oil pump chain tensioner in the direction of the and secure it with a locking pin T40011.

10. Remove the oil pump chain tensioner.

11. Using a screwdriver, lift the chain tensioner locking wedge in the direction of, press the timing chain tensioning rail in the direction of and secure it with Locking Pin T40011.

12. Remove the timing chain tensioning rail.

13. The intake camshaft switches in the engine direction of rotation

14. Remove the timing chain.
Installing

15. The following must be performed in one sequence; technicians are necessary.

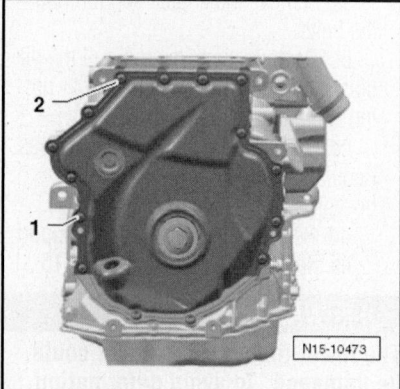

Fig. 115 Pry off the lower timing chain cover starting with bolts 1 & 2 as shown

16. The painted links of the timing chain must be positioned on the markings on the chain sprockets.

17. Hold the wrench until the tensioning rail is installed.

18. Mount the timing chain on the exhaust camshaft and crankshaft as shown.

19. Turn the intake camshaft using the wrench in the direction of the and mount the timing chain.

20. Install the timing chain tensioning rail and tighten the bolt.

21. Mount the bearing bracket and hand tighten the bolts.

22. Remove the locking pin T40011.

23. Tighten the bearing bracket bolts

24. Install the lower timing chain cover.

➡**Replace bolts which have been tightened to torque. Replace sealing rings, seals and self-locking nuts.**

a. Remove any sealant residue on the engine block using the flat blade scraper.

b. Seal off both side of the seal with tape to prevent soiling

c. Remove residual sealant on the cover e.g. with a rotating plastic brush.

d. Clean sealing surfaces, must be free of oil and grease.

e. Install the cover using the old bolts and tighten to 71 inch lbs. (8 Nm).

f. Check between the cover and housing using a feel gauge; the gap must not exceed 0.0078 in. (0.2 mm).

g. If the gap exceed 0.0078 in. (0.2 mm), replace the cover.

h. It is not possible to measure

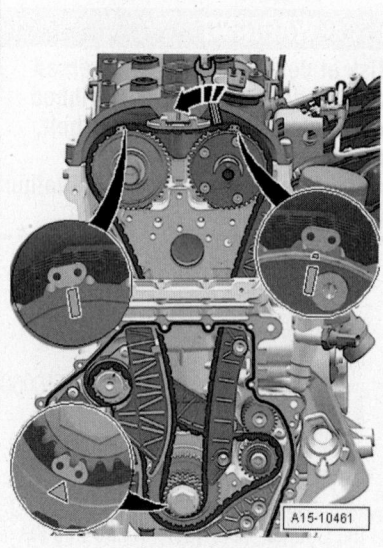

Fig. 116 Mount the timing chain on the exhaust camshaft and crankshaft

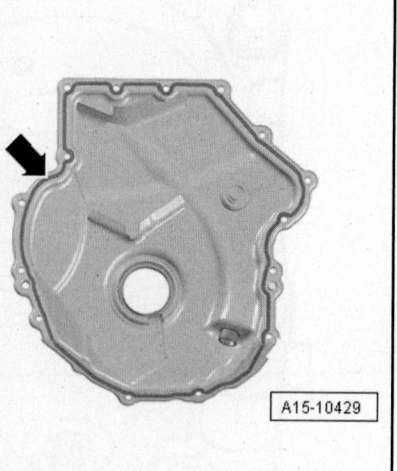

Fig. 117 Apply the silicone sealant D 174 003 A3 in a bead of 0.078–0.117 in. (2–3 mm) on the clean sealing surface of the cover as shown

between the cover the upper part of the oil pan, however check the sealing surface for evenness.

i. Make sure both alignment bushings for centering the cover are present.

j. Cut tube nozzle at front marking to approximately 0.117 in. (3 mm).

k. Apply the silicone sealant D 174 003 A3 in a bead of 0.078–0.117 in. (2–3 mm) on the clean sealing surface of the cover as shown.

l. The cover must be installed within 5 minutes after application of silicone sealant.

m. The sealant bead may not be thicker than specified, otherwise excess sealant could enter the oil pan and clog the oil intake tube.

n. Install the lid immediately and all the bolts.

o. Tighten the bolts 1 through 15 in 2 stages in the sequence shown:

• Tighten the bolts to 71 inch lbs. (8 Nm)

• Tighten the bolts an additional 90°

p. After installing cover, allow sealant to dry for approximately 30 minutes. Only after then may the engine oil be replenished.

25. Install timing chain upper cover.

a. Coat the sealing ring and the O-ring with engine oil.

b. Tighten the bolts 1 through 5 by hand in the illustrated sequence.

c. Tighten the bolt to 80 inch lbs. (9 Nm) by using the torque wrench V.A.G 1783 and the open end spanner insert AF 10 V.A.G 1783/1.

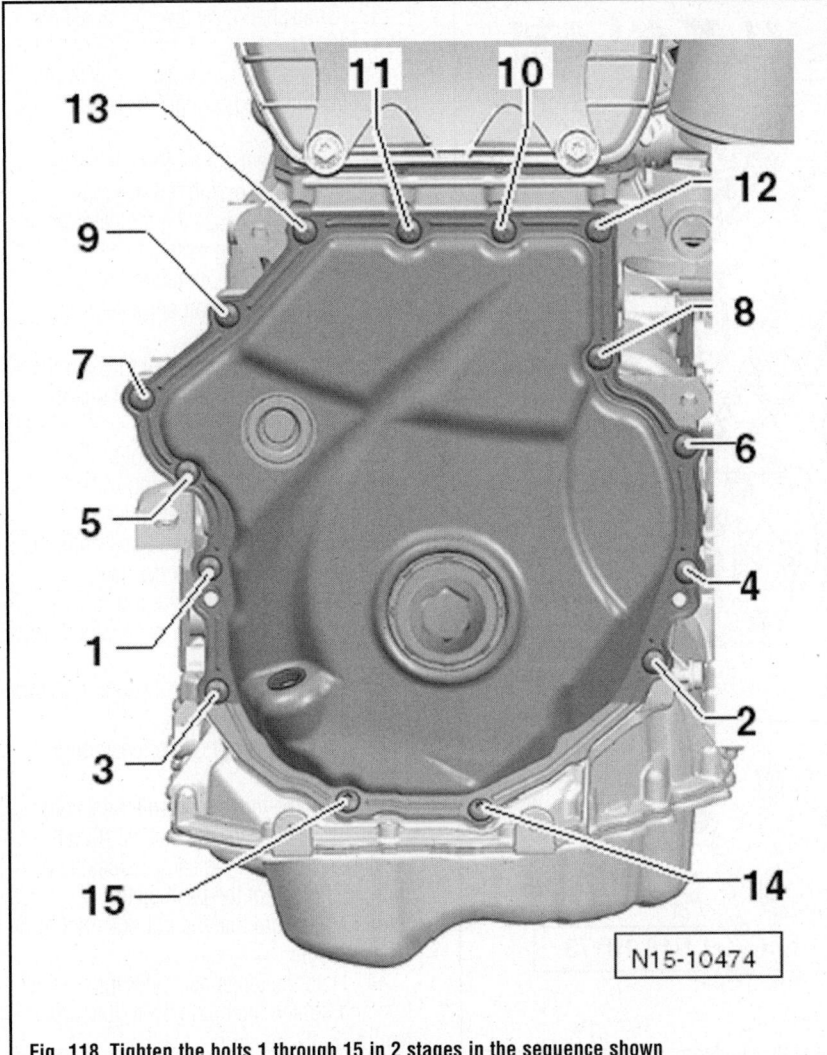

Fig. 118 Tighten the bolts 1 through 15 in 2 stages in the sequence shown

26. The rest of the assembly is basically a reverse of the disassembling sequence.
27. Fill the engine oil.
28. Check oil level.

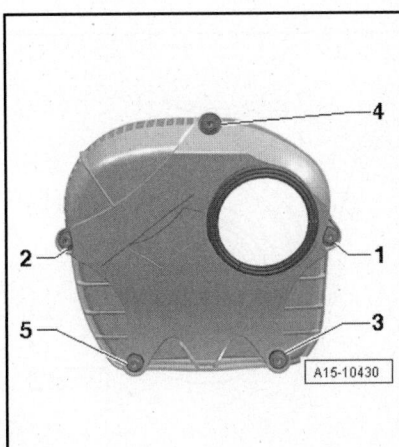

Fig. 119 Tighten the bolts 1 through 5 by hand in the illustrated sequence

2.0L TDI Engine

See Figures 120 through 124.

1. Before servicing the vehicle, refer to the precautions.
2. Remove engine cover.
   a. One piece engine cover, pull the one piece front engine cover upward with a quick jerk and then pull the lower mount forward.
   b. Two piece engine cover, first pull the outer cover upward with a quick jerk in the upper illustration, then pull the inner engine cover upward with a quick jerk in lower illustration.

✳✳ CAUTION

The temperature of the fuel lines as well as the fuel can, can be very hot on vehicles equipped with a TDI engine. Before opening any line connections, let the fuel cool down otherwise you could get burned. Wear protective gloves. Wear safety glasses.

3. Disconnect the fuel supply hose and the fuel return hose from the fuel lines.
4. Disconnect the coolant line.
5. Remove bolts.
6. Remove the connecting pipe between the charge air cooler and the intake connection; while doing this, slightly lift the clips.
7. Disconnect the fuel supply line and the fuel return line; while doing this pull the release buttons.
8. Remove fuel filter without the retaining plate.
   a. Release the clips and remove the fuel filter with the hoses still connected from the retaining plate.
9. Remove fuel filter with the retaining plate.
   a. Loosen the bolt one turn.
   b. Remove the bolt and the nut.
   c. Remove the fuel filter with the hoses still connected.
10. Remove the bolt on the fuel filler tube for the washer fluid reservoir.
11. Remove the retaining plate for the fuel filter, if equipped.
12. Disconnect the electrical connectors on the coolant expansion tank.
13. Remove coolant expansion tank with the hoses still connected. Lay it on the engine.
14. Remove ribbed belt.
15. Remove the ribbed belt tensioning element.
16. Remove the upper toothed belt guard; to do this, loosen the clips.
17. Remove front right wheel housing liner.
18. Remove vibration damper/belt pulley.
19. Remove the lower and center toothed belt guard.
20. Turn crankshaft to set cylinder 1 at TDC.
21. When doing so, turn the crankshaft so that the marking on the crankshaft toothed belt gear and the tooth segment of the camshaft gear are positioned upward. The marking on the rear toothed belt guard must align with the marking on the camshaft sensor wheel.
22. Lock the hub with the rig pin 3359. To do this, push the rig pin through the left-sided empty slot in the bore of the cylinder head.
23. Also, lock the toothed belt crankshaft sprocket with the crankshaft stop T10100. Push the crankshaft stop from the front side of the toothed belt sprocket into the teeth.
24. Markings on toothed belt crankshaft sprocket and the crankshaft stop must be

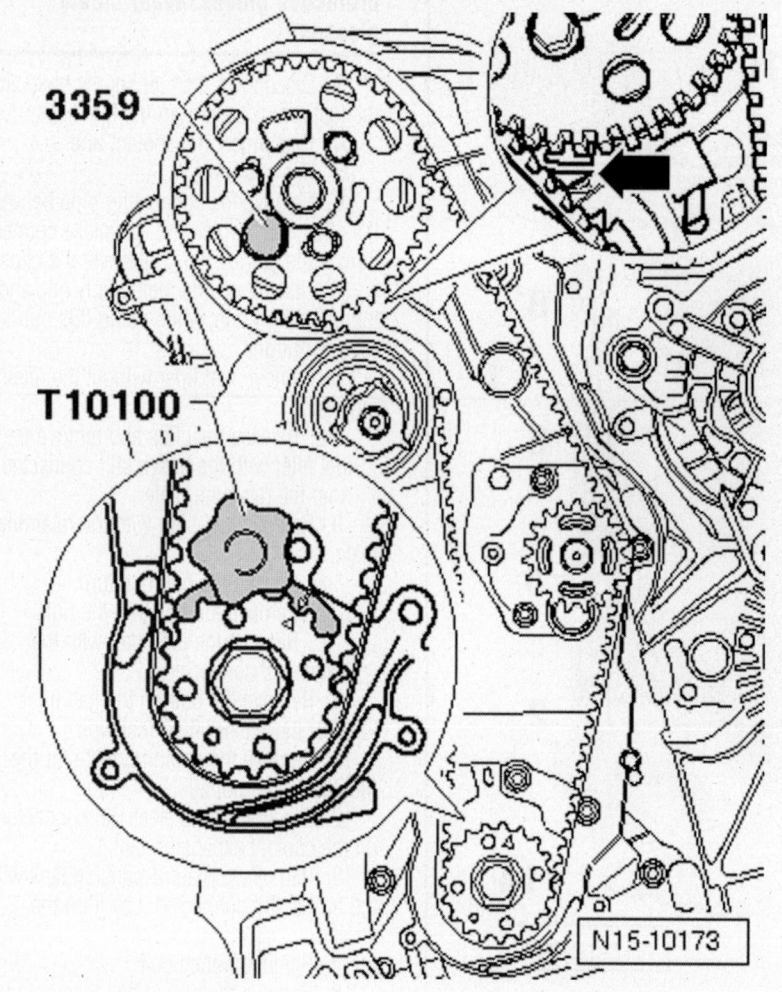

Fig. 120 Markings on toothed belt crankshaft sprocket and the crankshaft stop must be aligned. The tab of the crankshaft stop must engage in the bore of the sealing flange

aligned. The tab of the crankshaft stop must engage in the bore of the sealing flange.

25. Mark rotational direction of toothed belt.

26. Loosen the bolts of the camshaft sprockets, until the camshaft sprocket can be turned in the slots.

27. Loosen the nut of the tensioning roller.

28. Turn the tension roller eccentric pulley using socket wrench T10264 counterclockwise arrow, until the securing pin T10265 can lock the tension roller.

29. Now turn the tensioning roller eccentric pulley clockwise all the way and tighten the nut by hand.

30. First, take the toothed belt from the coolant pump and then from the remaining toothed belt gears.

Installing

31. Camshaft is secured with the rig pin 3359.

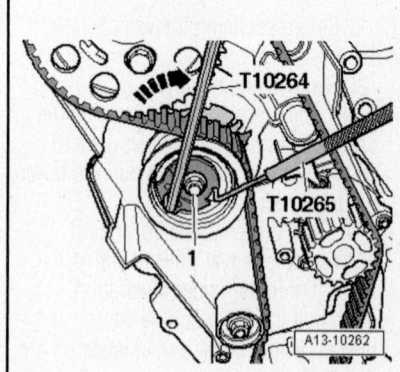

Fig. 121 Turn the tension roller eccentric pulley using socket wrench T10264 counterclockwise arrow, until the securing pin T10265 can lock the tension roller. Now turn the tensioning roller eccentric pulley clockwise all the way and tighten the nut by hand

32. Crankshaft locked with crankshaft stop T10100.

33. Tensioning roller secured with pin T10265 and seated on right stop with the nut.

34. Adjustments to toothed belt may generally only be performed when the engine is cold, because the indicator position of the tensioning element changes depending on engine temperature.

35. Turn the camshaft sprocket in its slots to middle position.

36. Install the toothed belt through the space between the engine mount and the engine.

37. Place the toothed belt onto the crankshaft sprocket, tensioning roller, camshaft sprocket and idler roller.

38. Lastly, lay the toothed belt onto the toothed belt coolant pump sprocket.

39. Make sure the tensioning roller is properly positioned in the rear toothed belt guard.

40. Pull the locking pin T10265 out from the tensioning roller.

41. Loosen the nut of the tensioning roller.

42. Turn the tensioning roller eccentric pulley using the socket wrench T10264 clockwise, until the indicator is located centrally in the gap of the base plate.

43. Make sure that the nut does not turn along with it.

44. Hold the tensioner roller in this position and tighten the nut to 15 ft. lbs. (20 Nm) plus 45° rotation.

45. Mount the counter-holder tool T10172 with the bolt T10172/4 as shown in the illustration, and hold the toothed belt tensioned by pushing in direction of.

46. Tighten the camshaft sprocket bolts to 19 ft. lbs. (25 Nm).

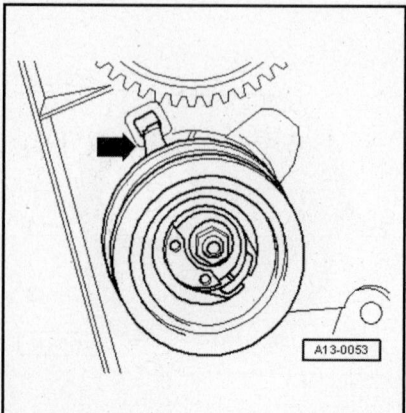

Fig. 122 Make sure the tensioning roller is properly positioned in the rear toothed belt guard (arrow)

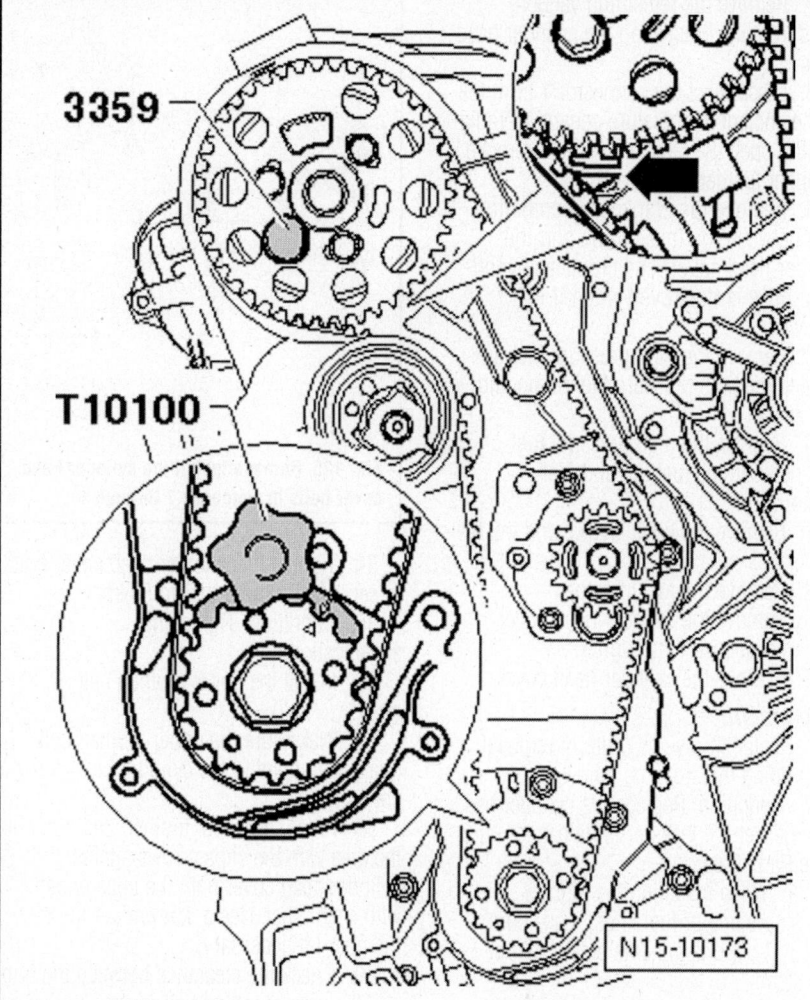

Fig. 123 Lock the hub with the rig pin 3359 and check if the crankshaft can be locked with the crankshaft stop T10100

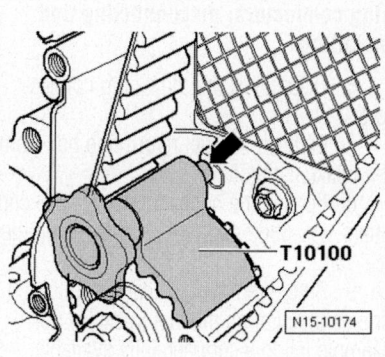

Fig. 124 Now turn the crankshaft in engine running direction until the crankshaft stop tab engages the sealing flange

47. Remove the rig pin 3359 and the crankshaft stop T10100.

48. Turn the crankshaft 2 turns in the direction of the engine, until the crankshaft is once again just in front of TDC.

49. Lock the hub with the rig pin 3359 from the rotating movement in engine rotation direction.

50. Check if the crankshaft can be locked with the crankshaft stop T10100.

51. If the crankshaft cannot be locked:

    a. Loosen the bolts of the camshaft sprocket.

    b. Turn the crankshaft against the engine running direction until the crankshaft stop tab is positioned shortly before the sealing flange bore.

    c. Now turn the crankshaft in engine running direction until the crankshaft stop tab engages the sealing flange.

52. Install the counter-holder T10172 with pins T10172/4 as shown. Push the

counter-holder T10172 in direction of and hold the camshaft sprocket pre-tensioned.

53. In this position, tighten the camshaft sprocket bolts 19 ft. lbs. (25 Nm).

54. Remove the rig pin 3359 and the crankshaft stop T10100.

55. Continue turning crankshaft two rotations in direction of engine rotation until the crankshaft is shortly before TDC for cylinder 1.

56. Repeat the inspection and adjust if necessary.

57. Install the lower and center toothed belt guard.

58. Install the vibration damper/belt pulley. Tightening specifications 89 inch lbs. (10 Nm) plus 90° rotation

59. Install ribbed belt.

60. Install upper toothed belt guard.

61. Install the connecting tube between the charge air cooler and intake connection.

62. Install the front right wheel housing liner.

63. Install the coolant expansion tank.

64. Install the fuel filter.

65. Tighten the filler tube for the windshield washer.

66. Install the engine cover.

TURBOCHARGER

REMOVAL & INSTALLATION

Refer to Exhaust Manifold.

VALVE COVERS

REMOVAL & INSTALLATION

See Figure 125.

➡When doing any repair work, especially in the engine compartment, pay attention to the following due to clearance issues:

➡Route all lines and wires in their original locations. For example, fuel, hydraulic, Evaporative Emission (EVAP), coolant, refrigerant, brake fluid and vacuum lines.

➡Ensure sufficient clearance to all moving or hot components.

1. Remove the engine cover.

2. Remove the protective strip.

3. Disconnect the connector from the fuel injectors A, the exhaust pressure sensor 1 G450 B and the fuel pressure sensor G247 C.

4. Remove the coolant line bolts arrows from the intake manifold and lay the line in front of the intake manifold.

5. Unclip the wiring harness for the glow plugs from the wiring guide.

➡**Always follow the procedure "glow plug connectors, disconnecting and installing".**

6. Disconnect the glow plug connectors.

7. Remove the fuel return line bolt from the intake manifold.

8. Loosen the hose clip using hose clip pliers VAS 6362 and remove the line on the fuel rail.

9. Before removing, clean the return line connection on the fuel injectors (for example using a commercially available detergent).

10. Cover the return line connections with a cloth.

11. Remove the fuel return line connections on the fuel injectors. Pull them upward to release them.

12. Follow the rules of cleanliness.

13. Do not let any dirt to get into the disconnected return lines or into the connections for the fuel injection units.

14. Loosen the hose clip using hose clip pliers VAS 6362 and remove the fuel return line.

15. Loosen the hose clip 4 using hose clip pliers VAS 6362 and remove the fuel return line at the high pressure fuel pump.

16. Seal the lines so that the fuel system is not contaminated by dirt, etc.

17. Remove the fuel return line and lay the lines in front of the intake manifold.

18. Disconnect the connector from the charge pressure actuator position sensor G581 at the turbocharger vacuum diaphragm and guide the line out of the retainers.

19. Disconnect the connector from the fuel pressure regulator valve N276.

20. Remove the line guide on the fuel rail and lay it aside.

21. Remove the vacuum hose from the cylinder head cover.

22. Remove the remaining vacuum hoses from the bracket on the cylinder head cover.

23. Disconnect the connector 1 from the engine coolant temperature sensor on radiator G83, open the clips arrows and remove the upper toothed belt guard.

24. Remove the crankcase ventilation hose between the intake tube and the cylinder head cover. The crankcase ventilation hose is destroyed when it is removed.

25. Remove the high pressure fuel line between the high pressure fuel pump and fuel rail.

26. Remove the high pressure fuel lines between the fuel rail and fuel injectors.

27. Remove the bolts arrows and the fuel rail.

28. Remove the fuel injectors.

29. Remove the cylinder head cover bolts in sequence 7 through 1.

30. Remove the cylinder head cover.

To install:

31. Install in reverse order of removal. When doing this note the following:

32. Condition: Replace the cylinder head cover gasket if it leaks or is damaged. Refer to the Parts Catalog.

  a. When installing the high pressure line or fuel lines, make sure no dirt or contaminants enter the fuel system.

  b. Only remove the sealing plugs right before installing the fuel lines.

  c. Do not change the angles of the high pressure lines

  d. Make sure line connections are securely fastened.

  e. Do not swap the supply and return lines.

33. First tighten the cylinder head cover bolts by hand in sequence 1 through 7.

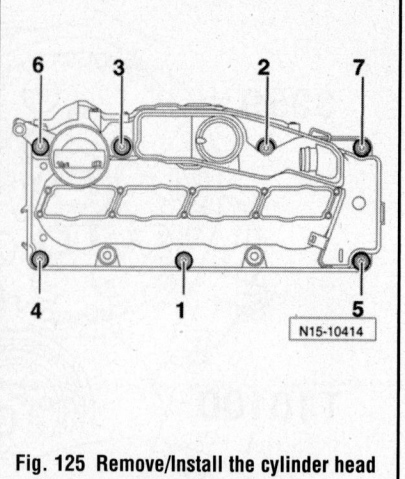

Fig. 125 Remove/Install the cylinder head cover bolts in sequence 7 through 1

34. Tighten the cylinder head cover bolts in sequence 1 through 7 to 5 Nm.

35. Condition: Tightening specifications.

36. Install the upper toothed belt guard.

37. Make sure the upper toothed belt guard is clipped to the cylinder head cover correctly.

38. Press the upper toothed belt guard in the area with the clips arrows against the cylinder head cover until the clips engage with each other. Use a screwdriver to press the guard if necessary.

39. Check the clearance between the hub and the upper toothed belt guard.

40. Tighten the high pressure line union nuts by hand.

41. Make sure the high pressure line is free of tension.

42. Use torque wrench (5-50 Nm) V.A.G 1331 with ratchet, reversible V.A.G 1331/1 and socket T40055 to tighten the high pressure line.

43. Fill the fuel system.

ENGINE PERFORMANCE & EMISSION CONTROLS

CAMSHAFT POSITION (CMP) SENSOR

REMOVAL & INSTALLATION

See Figures 126 and 127.

1. Remove the engine cover.
2. Remove the fuel filter and the auxiliary fuel pump V393 or fuel pump 2 V277.
3. Disconnect the connector from the Engine Coolant Temperature (ECT) sensor on radiator G83, open the clips arrows and remove the toothed belt guard.
4. Remove right front wheel housing liner.
5. Remove the ribbed belt.
6. Remove vibration damper.
7. Rotate the engine to Top Dead Center (TDC) and secure the crankshaft toothed belt gear using the crankshaft stop T10050. Push the crankshaft stop from the front side of the toothed belt gear into the teeth.
8. The camshaft toothed gear must be in the 12 o'clock position.
9. The marks on the crankshaft toothed belt gear 2 and the crankshaft stop T10050 1 must align. The pin on the crankshaft stop T10050 must engage in the hole on the sealing flange.
10. Loosen the bolts 1 for the camshaft sprocket.
11. Loosen the coolant pipe bolt 1 and then the high pressure pump toothed belt gear bolts 2.
12. Loosen the nut 1 for the tensioner.
13. Turn the tensioner eccentric pulley using the socket wrench T10264 counterclockwise arrow, until the locking tool T10265 can lock the tensioner.
14. Now, turn the tensioner eccentric pulley clockwise all the way and tighten the nut 1 by hand.
15. Remove the toothed belt from the idler roller and the high pressure pump gear.
16. Disconnect the CMP sensor connector.
17. Remove the connector from the mount.
18. Remove the CMP sensor.
19. Remove the ribs with a screwdriver and remove the cover for the repair opening arrows.
20. Remove the CMP sensor from the cylinder head and guide the connector through the opening in the toothed belt guard.

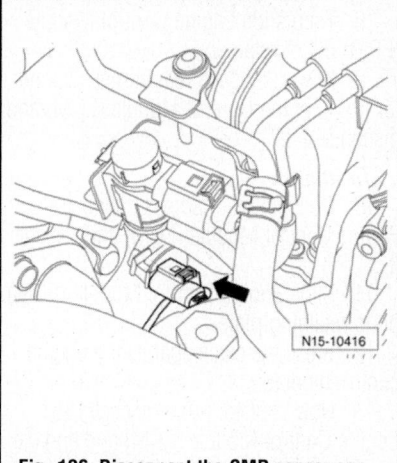

Fig. 126 Disconnect the CMP sensor connector (arrow)

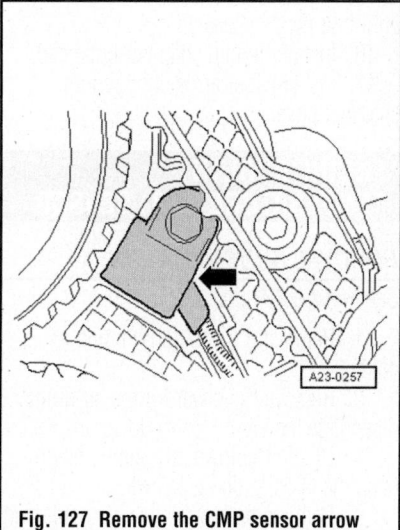

Fig. 127 Remove the CMP sensor arrow

To install:

21. Installation is performed in reverse order. When doing this note the following:
22. Seal off the opening in the toothed belt guard with a rubber plug. Refer to the Parts Catalog.
23. Install the toothed belt and adjust the valve timing.

CRANKSHAFT POSITION (CKP) SENSOR

LOCATION

See Figures 128 and 129.

The CKP sensor is the same as the Engine Speed Sensor (G28) and is mounted on the timing chain cover at the flywheel end—2.5L engine

Fig. 128 Crankshaft Position (CKP) sensor connector (1)—2.0L engine

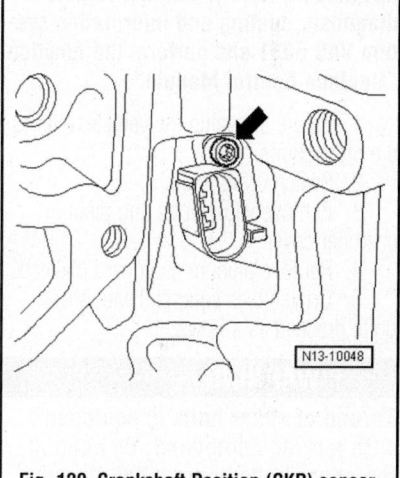

Fig. 129 Crankshaft Position (CKP) sensor connector (arrow)—2.0L TDI engine

REMOVAL & INSTALLATION

1. Before servicing the vehicle, refer to the precautions.
2. Unplug the connector.
3. Remove the screw and then the sensor

✷✷ WARNING

Cover the hole to prevent dirt from getting into the engine.

4. When installing, use a new seal as necessary.

ELECTRONIC CONTROL MODULE (ECM)

LOCATION

See Figure 130.

Fig. 130 ECM is location in the plenum chamber at the base of the windshield. Disengage harness (1) and pry up lock mechanism (2)

REMOVAL & INSTALLATION

➡**If it is desired to replace Engine Control Module (ECM), connect vehicle diagnosis, testing and information system VAS 5051 and perform the function "Replace Control Module".**

1. Before servicing the vehicle, refer to the precautions.
2. Switch off ignition.
3. Remove wiper arms and plenum chamber cover.
4. Remove plenum chamber bulkhead
5. On vehicles equipped with shear bolts proceed as follows:

❋❋ WARNING

Thread of shear bolts is equipped with locking compound. By heating the shear bolts using a hot air gun, inhibition effect of the locking compound is lowered.

➡**Cover wires, harness connectors and control modules in the close vicinity of Engine Control Module (ECM) to prevent damage from burning.**

a. Unscrew shear bolt using pliers on bolt head.

❋❋ WARNING

If screws cannot be removed, saw into heads of shear bolts so that two parallel surfaces are formed and then unscrew them.

b. Insert a screwdriver between protective housing and retaining plate.
c. Pry protective housing upward using screwdriver and pull it off sideways from retaining plate.
6. Disengage forward harness connec-

tor from Engine Control Module (ECM) and disconnect it.
7. Pry up locking mechanism slightly.
8. Then slide Engine Control Module (ECM) out of retainer.
9. Now disengage rear harness connector from Engine Control Module (ECM) and disconnect it.

To install:

10. Connect rear harness connector to Engine Control Module (ECM) and engage it.
11. Slide Engine Control Module (ECM) on to retaining plate.
12. Press the catch against the engine control module.
13. Now connect front connector to Engine Control Module (ECM) and engage it.
14. Slide protective housing on to retaining plate.
15. Tighten new shear bolts uniformly until bolt heads shear off.
16. Install plenum chamber bulkhead.
17. Install wiper arms and plenum chamber cover.

ENGINE COOLANT TEMPERATURE (ECT) SENSOR

REMOVAL & INSTALLATION

See Figures 131 and 132.

1. Removing Condition: Engine is cold.
2. Remove the cover for the air guide; disengage the side clips to do so arrows.
3. Unclip the lower air guide, disengage the clips to do so arrows.
4. Remove both the lower air guide and the air guide hose.
5. Vehicles with a Noise Generator: Remove the charge air pipe from the noise generator. Refer to Charge Air Pipe to Noise Generator.
6. Loosen the hose clamp.
7. Remove the bolt.
8. Disconnect the electrical connector.
9. Remove the noise insulation.
10. Loosen the clamps items and, remove the charge air hose and seal the charge air cooler with a clean cloth.
11. Remove the bolt and remove the charge air pipe downward.
12. Disconnect the electrical connector 1 from the throttle valve control module J338.
13. Remove the bolts arrows and remove the throttle valve control module.
14. Remove the intake manifold support; to do so, remove the nut and bolt.
15. Engine Coolant Temperature (ECT) Sensor with Clip

Fig. 131 Disconnect the electrical connector 1 from the ECT sensor and press latches (arrow)

a. Disconnect the electrical connector 1 from the ECT sensor.
b. Remove the clamp, to do so, press the latches.
c. Remove the ECT sensor.
d. Install the new ECT sensor with an O-ring as quickly as possible to prevent coolant from leaking out.
16. ECT Sensor with a Retaining Plate
a. Disconnect the electrical connector 2 from the ECT sensor.
b. Remove the bolts arrows and remove the retaining plate 1.
c. Remove the ECT sensor.
17. Install the new ECT sensor with an O-ring as quickly as possible to prevent coolant from leaking out.

To install:

18. Install in reverse order of removal. Note the following:
19. Replace the O-ring.
20. Check the coolant level.

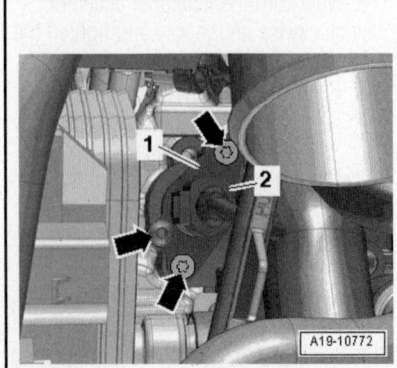

Fig. 132 Disconnect the electrical connector 2 from the ECT sensor. Remove the bolts arrows and remove the retaining plate 1

HEATED OXYGEN SENSOR (HO2S)

LOCATION

2.0L Engines

The primary oxygen sensor is on the exhaust pipe at the turbocharger outlet. The secondary sensor is behind the catalytic converter.

2.0L TDI Engine

The primary oxygen sensor is on the exhaust pipe at the turbocharger outlet.

2.5L Engines

The primary oxygen sensor is on the exhaust pipe. The secondary sensor is behind the catalytic converter.

REMOVAL & INSTALLATION

2.0L & 2.5L Engines

1. Before servicing the vehicle, refer to the precautions.
2. Unplug the connector.
3. Remove the sensor and cover the hole to prevent dirt from getting into the engine.

To install:

4. Installation is the reverse of removal.

➡**Thread of new oxygen sensors is coated with hot bolt paste.**

❊❊ WARNING

When re-using the previous oxygen sensor, grease only the threads with hot bolt paste G 052 112; the paste must not get into slots of oxygen sensor body

5. Tighten to 41 ft. lbs. (55 Nm).

2.0L TDI Engine

1. Before servicing the vehicle, refer to the precautions.
2. Unplug the connector.
3. Remove the sensor and cover the hole to prevent dirt from getting into the engine.

To install:

4. Installation is the reverse of removal.

➡**Thread of new oxygen sensors is coated with hot bolt paste.**

❊❊ WARNING

When re-using the previous oxygen sensor, grease only the threads with hot bolt paste G 052 112; the paste must not get into slots of oxygen sensor body

5. Tighten to 41 ft. lbs. (55 Nm).

INTAKE AIR TEMPERATURE (IAT) SENSOR

LOCATION

2.0L Engines

1. The IAT is mounted in the center of the intake manifold plenum near the throttle body.

2.5L Engine

The IAT is built into the Mass Airflow Sensor (MAF) and cannot be removed separately.

KNOCK SENSOR (KS)

LOCATION

The knock sensor 1 is located below the intake manifold behind the coolant pump.

REMOVAL & INSTALLATION

See Figure 133.

1. Remove the electrical connector 2 from the knock sensor 1.
2. Remove the coolant pump.
3. The knock sensor 1 is located below the intake manifold behind the coolant pump.
4. Remove the knock sensor 1.

To install:

5. Installation is performed in reverse order.

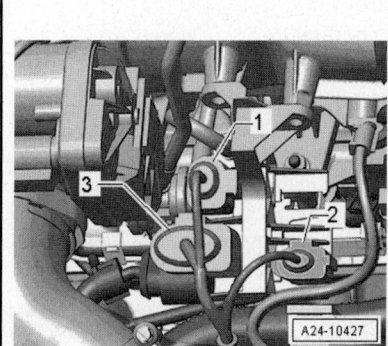

Fig. 133 Remove the electrical connector 2 from the knock sensor 1

MASS AIR FLOW (MAF) SENSOR

LOCATION

2.0L Engines

The MAF is mounted in the air filter housing assembly behind the opening for the oil filler cap.

2.0LTDI Engine

The MAF is mounted in the air filter housing assembly

2.5L Engine

The MAF is in the intake air tube next to the battery.

REMOVAL & INSTALLATION

2.0L & 2.5L Engines

1. Before servicing the vehicle, refer to the precautions.
2. Disconnect air intake hose from the air filter housing.
3. Disconnect electrical connector on Mass Air Flow (MAF) Sensor G70.
4. Remove both bolts from the Mass Air Flow (MAF) Sensor G70 and carefully remove the Mass Air Flow (MAF) Sensor G70 from the air filter housing guide.

To install:

5. Installation is the reverse of removal.
6. If the air filter element is very dirty or soaked, dirt particles or moisture may have contaminated the Mass Air Flow (MAF) Sensor G70 and may be causing false mass air flow values. This results in a reduction of power, since a lower injection quantity is calculated.
7. Always use an original equipment air filter element.
8. Use a lubricant (silicone-free) for installing the intake hose.
9. Secure all hose connections using hose clamps appropriate for the model type.
10. Check the MAF sensor and intake hose (intake air side) for salt residue, dirt, and leaves.
11. Check the intake ducting up to the air filter element for dirt. If any contaminants are discovered, clean the air filter housing (upper and lower parts) of salt residue, dirt and leaves (if necessary, clean by washing or vacuuming).
12. Tighten clamps/screws to 13 inch lbs. (1.5 Nm).

2.0L TDI Engine

1. Before servicing the vehicle, refer to the precautions.
2. Disconnect air intake hose from the air filter housing.
3. Disconnect electrical connector on Mass Air Flow (MAF) Sensor G70.
4. Remove both bolts from the Mass Air Flow (MAF) Sensor G70 and carefully remove the Mass Air Flow (MAF) Sensor G70 from the air filter housing guide.

To install:

5. Installation is the reverse of removal.
6. If the air filter element is very dirty or soaked, dirt particles or moisture may have contaminated the Mass Air Flow (MAF) Sensor G70 and may be causing false mass air flow values. This results in a reduction of power, since a lower injection quantity is calculated.
7. Always use an original equipment air filter element.
8. Use a lubricant (silicone-free) for installing the intake hose.
9. Secure all hose connections using hose clamps appropriate for the model type
10. Check the MAF sensor and intake hose (intake air side) for salt residue, dirt, and leaves.
11. Check the intake ducting up to the air filter element for dirt. If any contaminants are discovered, clean the air filter housing (upper and lower parts) of salt residue, dirt and leaves (if necessary, clean by washing or vacuuming).

THROTTLE POSITION SENSOR (TPS)

LOCATION

2.0L & 2.5L Engines

The Throttle Position Sensor (TPS) is built into the electronic throttle valve control module (throttle body).

2.0L TDI Engine

The Throttle Position Sensor (TPS) is built into the intake flap motor V157 (throttle body).

REMOVAL & INSTALLATION

2.0L & 2.5L Engines

See Figure 134.

1. Before servicing the vehicle, refer to the precautions.
2. Loosen the hose clamp.
3. Remove bolt.

4. Disconnect electrical connector.
5. Remove the noise insulation.
6. Remove the air guide pipe.
7. Remove the bolt and remove the air guide pipe downward.
8. Disconnect electrical connector on Throttle Valve Control Module J338.
9. Remove bolts and remove Throttle Valve Control Module J338.

To install:

10. Installation is performed in reverse order of removal, noting the following:
11. Clean O-ring sealing surface.
12. Replace the seal; when doing so, pay attention to the correct position of the service flag on the sealing ring.
13. Tighten bolts in criss-cross pattern to 31 inch lbs. (3.5 Nm).

✳✳ WARNING

If a new Throttle Valve Control Module J338 was installed, adapt the engine control module to the Throttle Valve Control Module J338.

2.0L TDI Engine

1. Before servicing the vehicle, refer to the precautions.

➡**When engine is switched off, the intake manifold flap is closed for approximately 3 seconds and then opens again. This reduces the stop jolt.**

2. Loosen the hose clamp.
3. Remove bolt.
4. Disconnect electrical connector.
5. Remove the noise insulation.
6. Remove the air guide pipe.
7. Remove the bolt and remove the air guide pipe downward.
8. Disconnect electrical connector on Intake flap motor V157.
9. Remove bolts and remove Intake flap motor V157.

To install:

10. Installation is performed in reverse order of removal, noting the following:
11. Clean O-ring sealing surface.
12. Replace the seal; when doing so, pay attention to the correct position of the service flag on the sealing ring.
13. Tighten bolts in criss-cross pattern to 89 inch lbs. (10 Nm).

✳✳ WARNING

If a new Intake flap motor V157 was installed, adapt the engine control module to the Intake flap motor V157.

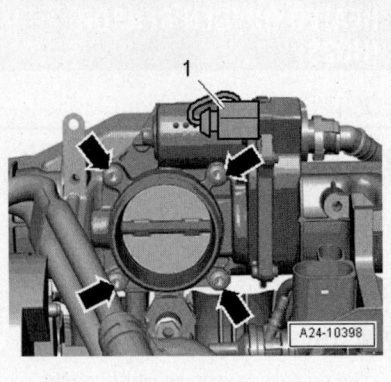

Fig. 134 Disconnect electrical connector (1) and remove Throttle Valve Control Module J338 bolts (arrow)

VEHICLE SPEED SENSOR (VSS)

REMOVAL & INSTALLATION

See Figure 135.

1. Remove the engine cover.
2. Open the air guide pipe hose clamp.
3. Disconnect the electrical harness connector.
4. Remove the noise insulation.
5. Remove the bolts and remove the charge air pipe downward from the throttle valve control module J338.
6. Remove the charge air hose from the charge air cooler and remove the charge air pipe downward.
7. Disconnect the electrical connector from engine speed sensor.
8. Remove the engine speed sensor bolt.
9. Install in reverse order of removal.

Fig. 135 Disconnect the electrical connector (1) from engine speed sensor

FUEL   **GASOLINE FUEL INJECTION SYSTEM**

FUEL SYSTEM SERVICE PRECAUTIONS

Safety is the most important factor when performing not only fuel system maintenance but any type of maintenance. Failure to conduct maintenance and repairs in a safe manner may result in serious personal injury or death. Maintenance and testing of the vehicle's fuel system components can be accomplished safely and effectively by adhering to the following rules and guidelines.

• To avoid the possibility of fire and personal injury, always disconnect the negative battery cable unless the repair or test procedure requires that battery voltage be applied.

• Always relieve the fuel system pressure prior to disconnecting any fuel system component (injector, fuel rail, pressure regulator, etc.), fitting or fuel line connection. Exercise extreme caution whenever relieving fuel system pressure to avoid exposing skin, face and eyes to fuel spray. Please be advised that fuel under pressure may penetrate the skin or any part of the body that it contacts.

• Always place a shop towel or cloth around the fitting or connection prior to loosening to absorb any excess fuel due to spillage. Ensure that all fuel spillage (should it occur) is quickly removed from engine surfaces. Ensure that all fuel soaked cloths or towels are deposited into a suitable waste container.

• Always keep a dry chemical (Class B) fire extinguisher near the work area.

• Do not allow fuel spray or fuel vapors to come into contact with a spark or open flame.

• Always use a back-up wrench when loosening and tightening fuel line connection fittings. This will prevent unnecessary stress and torsion to fuel line piping.

• Always replace worn fuel fitting O-rings with new Do not substitute fuel hose or equivalent where fuel pipe is installed.

Before servicing the vehicle, make sure to also refer to the precautions in the beginning of this section as well.

RELIEVING FUEL SYSTEM PRESSURE

1. Before servicing the vehicle, refer to the precautions.

✳✳ CAUTION

The fuel injection system is divided into a high pressure section (maximum approximately 1740 psi or 120 bar) and a low pressure system (approximately 87psi or 6 bar). Before opening high pressure area - e.g. removing high pressure pump, fuel rail, fuel injectors, fuel pipes or Fuel Pressure Sensor G247 - fuel pressure in high pressure area must be reduced to a residual pressure of approximately 87psi (6 bar).

2. Remove electrical connector from Fuel Pressure Regulator Valve N276 using the Assembly Tool T10118.

3. Allow engine to idle approximately 10 seconds.

a. When the Fuel Pressure Regulator Valve N276 electrical connector is disconnected during idle, pressure in high pressure area decreases to approximately 6 bar.

b. After high pressure has been released, high pressure system must be opened, otherwise the pressure increases again due to the warming of the fuel.

4. Switch off ignition.

✳✳ CAUTION

Fuel lines are pressurized! Wear protective goggles and protective clothing to prevent injuries and contact with skin. Before opening the high pressure system, place a cloth around the connection.

5. Place a clean cloth around the connection point and carefully open to release the residual pressure of approximately 87psi (6 bar). Escaping fuel must be absorbed.

6. To conclude work, check DTC memory of Engine Control Module (ECM), erase all DTC entries which may have occurred from removing the connector. If DTC memory was erased, generate readiness code.

FUEL FILTER

REMOVAL & INSTALLATION

See Figure 136.

1. Disconnect the fuel lines to the fuel tank:

a. A - Fuel supply line, black
b. B - Fuel return line, blue or with a blue mark

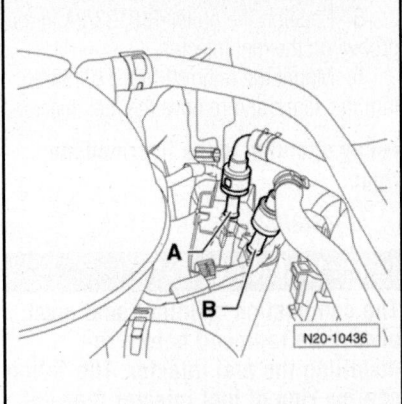

Fig. 136 A - Fuel supply line, black.
B - Fuel return line, blue or with a blue mark

2. Seal the lines so that the fuel system is not contaminated by dirt, etc.

3. Loosen the spring clips using spring clip pliers VAS 6362 and remove the fuel hoses items 6 and 7.

4. Seal the lines so that the fuel system is not contaminated by dirt, etc.

5. Remove the bolt and nut item 11.

6. Remove the fuel filter upward.

To install:

7. Install in reverse order of removal. When doing this note the following:

8. Route the fuel hoses free of kinks.

9. Ensure the fuel hoses are seated securely.

10. Do not interchange the supply and return lines (the return line is blue or has a blue mark, the supply line is white or has a white mark).

11. Clip the fuel hoses into the retainers.

12. Fill and bleed the fuel system

FUEL INJECTORS

REMOVAL & INSTALLATION

2.0L Engines

See Figure 137.

1. Before servicing the vehicle, refer to the precautions.

➡ **Puller T10133/2A is required to complete this operation.**

2. Remove the intake manifold with the fuel rail. If the injector valves remain attached in the fuel rail, then pull them out.

3. Cover the intake channels with a clean rag.

4. Remove the support element A downward and disconnect the connector from the fuel injectors.

5. Position the puller T10133/2A in the groove on the fuel injector.

6. Mount the removal tool T10133/16, turn the screw and remove the fuel injector.

➡ **Pay attention to the intermediate rings.**

To install:

✳✳ WARNING

The combustion chamber seal must always be replaced before re-installing the fuel injector. The Teflon sealing ring of fuel injector may not be oiled or greased.

➡ **If an opened intake valve hinders the cleaning, the engine must be turned further by hand using a screw wrench on the crankshaft.**

7. Thoroughly clean bores for high pressure fuel injectors in cylinder head using nylon brush T10133/4.

8. Replace O-ring and Teflon sealing ring of fuel injector Teflon Seal on Fuel Injector, Replacing.

9. Install the fuel injection with the intermediate ring again.

10. Use the Remover T10133/2A to push the fuel injector all the way into the hole in the cylinder head.

✳✳ WARNING

Make sure fuel injectors are positioned correctly in cylinder head.

11. Install the intake manifold with the fuel rail.

FUEL PUMP

REMOVAL & INSTALLATION

Bolt In High Pressure Pump

See Figures 138 through 140.

1. Before servicing the vehicle, refer to the precautions.

✳✳ CAUTION

Fuel system is under high pressure! Before opening the system, perform the procedure for releasing fuel pressure.

2. The removal and installation of the high-pressure fuel pump can only be performed on a cold engine.

3. Catch escaping fuel with a rag.

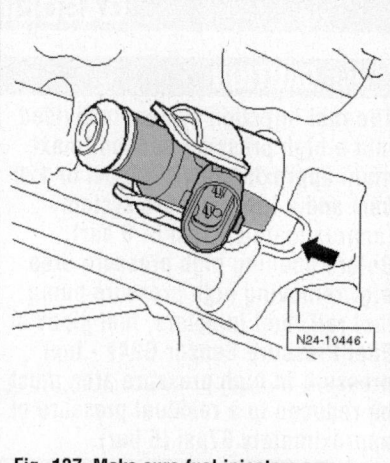

Fig. 137 Make sure fuel injectors are positioned correctly in cylinder head

4. Remove engine cover.

5. Disconnect the electrical connector from the Fuel Pressure Regulator Valve N276.

6. Open both fuel lines.

7. Remove the two bolts.

8. Carefully pull the high pressure fuel pump out. The roller tappet may stay in the cylinder head.

To install:

9. When installing the high-pressure fuel pump, make sure that no dirt enters the fuel system.

10. The O-ring must always be replaced.

11. High-pressure fuel lines must always be fastened free of tension.

12. Replace the O-ring for the high-pressure pump.

13. Carefully place high pressure pump with sleeve (pay attention to the groove) in opening in cylinder head (check sleeve for damage first).

14. Install new bolts and tighten by hand.

15. Before installing the fuel lines, check the torque of the connections on the high-pressure pump.

16. Tighten the bolts crosswise to 89 inch lbs. (10 Nm).

17. Hand tighten the fuel supply line union nut so that it is free of tension and then tighten it.

18. Connect the electrical connector from the Fuel Pressure Regulator Valve N276.

19. If the fuse was pulled, insert it again.

20. Check fuel system for leaks.

In Tank Lock Ring Pump

See Figures 141 through 143.

1. Condition: The fuel tank may be a maximum of 1/2 full.

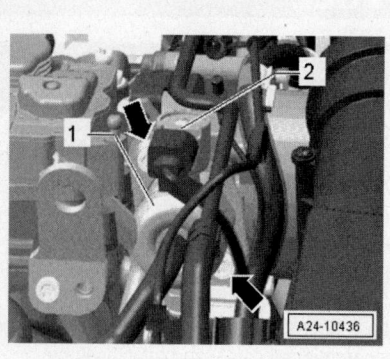

Fig. 138 Disconnect the electrical connector from the Fuel Pressure Regulator Valve N276

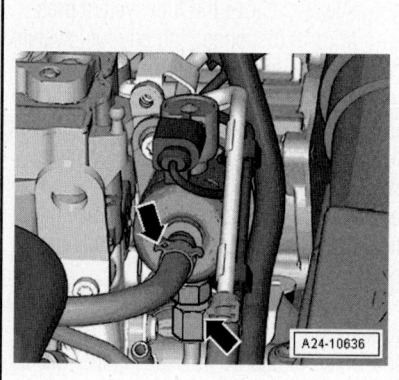

Fig. 139 Open both fuel lines

2. Empty the fuel tank if necessary using the fuel extracting device VAS 5190.

3. Turn off the ignition and disconnect the ground cable from the battery.

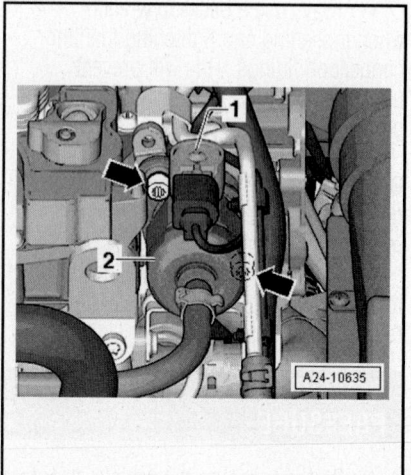

Fig. 140 Remove the two bolts

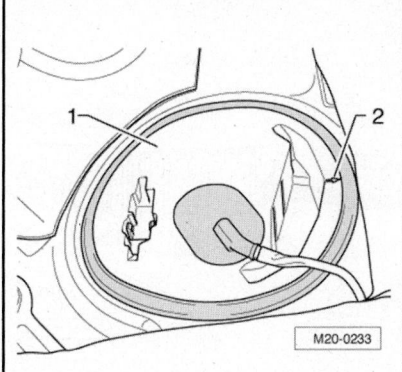

Fig. 141 Unclip the cover (1) for the fuel delivery unit. (2) points in direction of travel

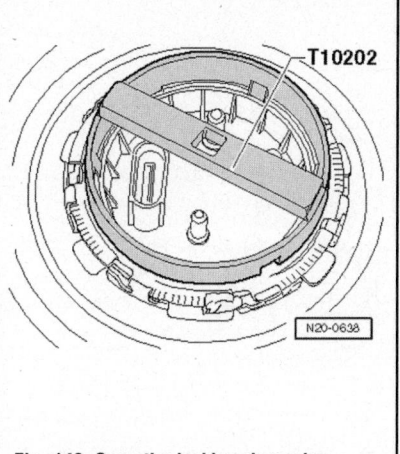

Fig. 143 Open the locking ring using wrench T10202

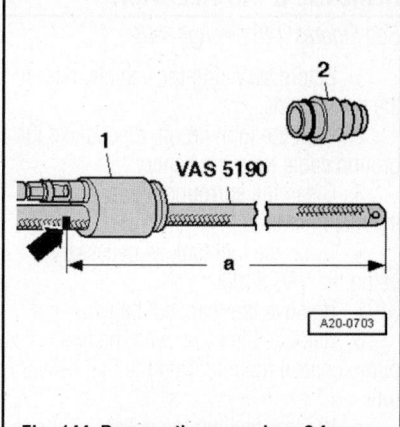

Fig. 144 Remove the cone piece 2 from the shaft piece 1 on the fuel extracting device VAS 5190

4. Remove the rear seat bench.
5. Unclip the cover for the fuel delivery unit. points in direction of travel.

➡**The fuel supply line is under pressure! Wear protective goggles and protective clothing to prevent injuries and contact with skin.**

➡**Before loosening the connection, place a cloth around the connection point. Then release pressure by carefully disconnecting the line.**

6. Disconnect the connector 1, the black supply line 2 and the blue return line 3.
7. Press in the securing ring to disengage the fuel lines.
8. Seal the lines so that the fuel system is not contaminated by dirt, etc.
9. Open the locking ring using wrench T10202.
10. Remove the fuel delivery unit and the seal from the opening in the fuel tank.

11. If the fuel delivery unit is to be replaced then drain the old delivery unit before disposal.
12. Follow disposal regulations.

To install:
13. Install in reverse order of removal. When doing this note the following:
14. Condition: Locking ring tightening specification: 110 Nm.
15. Do not bend the fuel level sensor G when inserting the fuel delivery unit.
16. Replace the fuel delivery unit seal if damaged and insert it in the fuel tank opening dry.
17. Lubricate the seal with fuel only for installing the fuel delivery unit.
18. Pay attention to the installed position of the fuel delivery unit flange. Tab on fuel delivery unit must lie between tabs.
19. Route the fuel lines free of kinks.
20. Do not interchange the supply and return lines (return line is blue, supply line is black).
21. Make sure the line connections are securely fastened.
22. Observe the notes after connecting the battery.

FUEL TANK

DRAINING

See Figures 144 and 145.

❉❉ CAUTION

Secure the fuel extracting device VAS 5190 ground strap to a bare area on the chassis.

1. Remove the cone piece from the shaft piece on the fuel extracting device VAS 5190.

2. Using insulating tape, apply a mark on the suction hose at a length of 1,500 mm (a) from the end of the hose.
3. Remove the cap from the fuel filler tube.
4. Install the shaft piece for the fuel extracting device VAS 5190 in on the fuel tank filler tube.
5. On vehicles equipped with a bayonet connection, the shaft piece of the fuel extracting device must be held accordingly.
6. Push the suction hose into the fuel tank until it reaches the mark on the suction hose made previously and extract the fuel. Refer to the operating instructions that come with the fuel extracting device VAS 5190.
7. A pressure point can be sensed after approximately 120 cm. The check valve in the fuel tank must be pushed open. Pull out the hose slightly and slide it in using a light jerk.
8. The fuel tank is drained almost completely.
9. Remove the hose the same way.

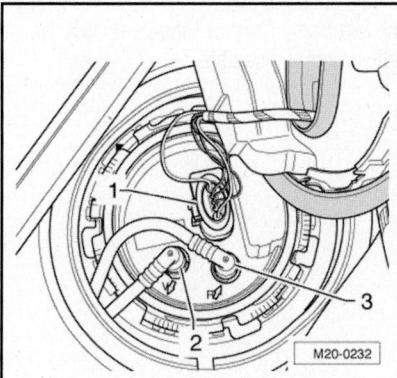

Fig. 142 Disconnect the connector 1, the black supply line 2 and the blue return line 3

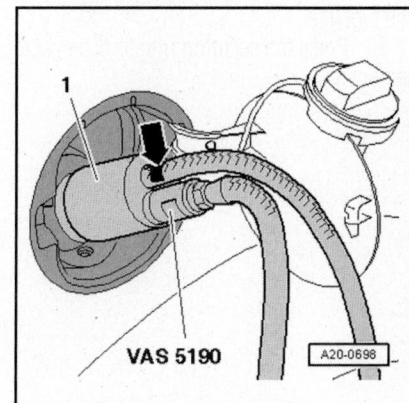

Fig. 145 Install the shaft piece 1 for the fuel extracting device VAS 5190 in on the fuel tank filler tube

REMOVAL & INSTALLATION

See Figures 146 through 148.

1. Before servicing the vehicle, refer to the precautions.

2. With the ignition off, disconnect the ground cable from the battery.

3. Clean the surrounding area around the fuel filler tube.

4. Drain the fuel tank as necessary using the VAS 5190.

5. Remove the rear seat bench.

6. Remove the cover with the fuel pump control module from the fuel delivery unit.

7. When installing the cover be sure to pay attention to the installed position: The points in the direction of vehicle travel.

8. Disconnect the electrical connector from the fuel delivery unit.

9. Remove the right rear wheel.

10. Remove the right rear wheel housing liner.

11. Remove the fuel tank door unit.

12. Disconnect the hoses.

13. Remove the fuel filler tube bolts from the body.

14. Unclip the wheel speed sensor wire from the filler tube bracket.

15. Remove the center and rear mufflers.

16. Remove the heat shield.

⁂ CAUTION

The fuel supply line is under pressure. Wear protective goggles and protective clothing to prevent injuries and contact with skin. Before disconnecting, place a cloth around the connection point. Then release pressure by carefully disconnecting the connection.

17. Disconnect the white vent line from the vent line and the black supply line from the fuel filter.

18. Press the securing ring to disengage the lines.

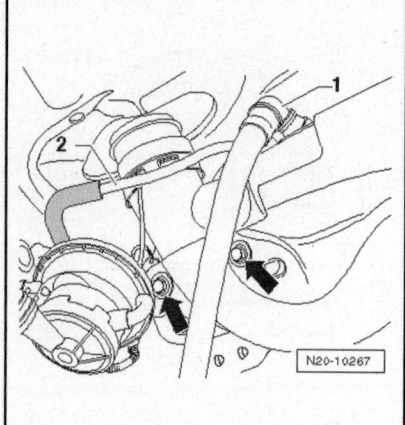

Fig. 146 Disconnect the hoses 1 and 2. Remove the fuel filler tube bolts (arrows)

19. Disconnect the green Leak Detection Pump (LDP) vacuum line as well.

20. Seal the lines so that the fuel system is not contaminated by dirt etc.

21. Remove the tensioning straps and bolts. Support the fuel tank using the VAG 1383A while doing so.

22. Lower the fuel tank.

To install:

23. Install in reverse order of removal.

24. Make sure the vent and fuel lines are not kinked.

25. Do not interchange the supply and return line (return line = blue, supply line = black).

26. Make sure the line connections are securely seated.

27. Check the ground connection for the fuel tank/chassis at the filler tube.

28. After installing the fuel tank, check to be sure the lines are still clipped to the fuel tank.

29. Observe the notes after connecting the battery.

30. Tighten bolts/nuts to specification as follows:

- Fuel tank to chassis (Replace bolts): 19 ft. lbs. (25 Nm)

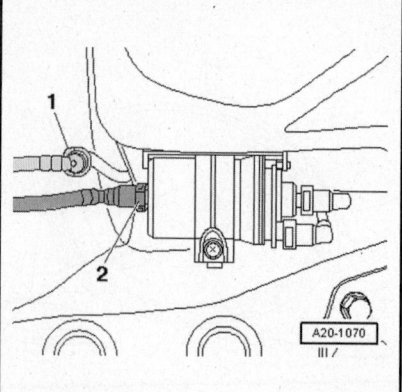

Fig. 147 Disconnect the white vent line (1) from the vent line and the black supply line (2) from the fuel filter

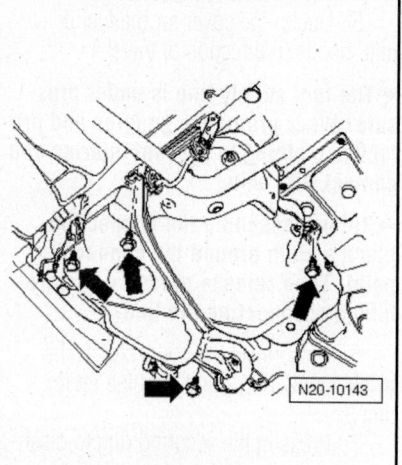

Fig. 148 Remove the tensioning straps and bolts

IDLE SPEED

ADJUSTMENT

Idle speed is automatically controlled by the Electronic Control Module (ECM). No adjustment is possible.

FUEL   **DIESEL FUEL INJECTION SYSTEM**

FUEL SYSTEM SERVICE PRECAUTIONS

Safety is the most important factor when performing not only fuel system maintenance but any type of maintenance. Failure to conduct maintenance and repairs in a safe manner may result in serious personal injury or death. Maintenance and testing of the vehicle's fuel system components can be accomplished safely and effectively by adhering to the following rules and guidelines.

• To avoid the possibility of fire and personal injury, always disconnect the negative battery cable unless the repair or test procedure requires that battery voltage be applied.

• Always relieve the fuel system pressure prior to disconnecting any fuel system component (injector, fuel rail, pressure regulator, etc.), fitting or fuel line connection. Exercise extreme caution whenever relieving fuel system pressure to avoid exposing skin, face and eyes to fuel spray. Please be advised that fuel under pressure may penetrate the skin or any part of the body that it contacts.

• Always place a shop towel or cloth around the fitting or connection prior to loosening to absorb any excess fuel due to spillage. Ensure that all fuel spillage (should it occur) is quickly removed from engine surfaces. Ensure that all fuel soaked cloths or towels are deposited into a suitable waste container.

• Always keep a dry chemical (Class B) fire extinguisher near the work area.

• Do not allow fuel spray or fuel vapors to come into contact with a spark or open flame.

• Always use a back-up wrench when loosening and tightening fuel line connection fittings. This will prevent unnecessary stress and torsion to fuel line piping.

• Always replace worn fuel fitting O-rings with new. Do not substitute fuel hose or equivalent where fuel pipe is installed.

Before servicing the vehicle, make sure to also refer to the precautions in the beginning of this section as well.

RELIEVING FUEL SYSTEM PRESSURE

Fuel pump is activated with switching on the ignition and by door contact switch of driver's door. For safety, disconnect the electrical connector from fuel delivery unit before opening fuel supply system, if the battery is not disconnected.

FUEL FILTER

REMOVAL & INSTALLATION

2.0L TDI Engine

See Figures 149 and 150.

1. Before servicing the vehicle, refer to the precautions.

✳✳ WARNING

Fuel pump is activated with switching on the ignition and by door contact switch of driver's door. For safety, disconnect the electrical connector from fuel delivery unit before opening fuel supply system, if the battery is not disconnected.

2. On fuel filter without the retaining plate, release the clips and remove the fuel filter with the hoses still connected from the retaining plate.

3. On fuel filter with the retaining plate
   a. Loosen the bolt one turn.
   b. Remove the bolt and the nut.
   c. Remove the fuel filter with the hoses still connected.

To install:

4. Installation is the reverse of removal.

FUEL SYSTEM PURGING

BLEEDING

1. Before servicing the vehicle, refer to the precautions.

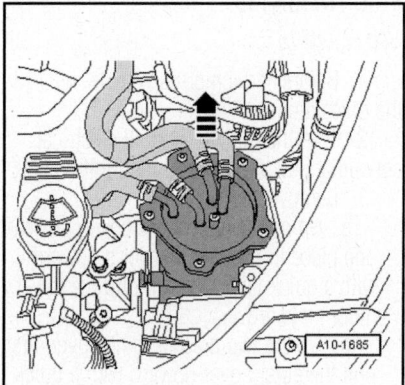

Fig. 149 On fuel filter without the retaining plate, release the clips and remove the fuel filter with the hoses still connected from the retaining plate (arrow)

2. Connect the diesel extractor VAS 5226 or the hand vacuum pump to the draining container V.A.G 1390/1 on the return hose.

3. Operate the diesel extractor VAS 5226 or the hand vacuum pump, until fuel comes out of the return hose. Make sure no fuel gets into the hand vacuum pump.

When installing the high pressure pump, make sure that no dirt enters the fuel system. Only remove the sealing plugs right before installing the fuel lines.

The fuel tank must be filled.

4. To fill the high pressure fuel pump with fuel, proceed as follows:
   a. Turn on the ignition.
   b. Connect the vehicle diagnostic tester and perform the "bleed fuel system" Guided Function.

5. The fuel pump is activated for 3 minutes.
   a. Then start the engine.
   b. After filling the fuel system, let the engine run at a moderate speed for a few minutes and then turn it off.
   c. Check fuel system for leaks.
   d. Check the Diagnostic Trouble Code (DTC) memory and erase any DTC memory entries if necessary.
   e. Take the vehicle on a 20 km road test using full throttle at least one time. Then check the high pressure area one more time for leaks.

6. If there is still air in the fuel system, the engine may switch to emergency mode during the road test. Turn off the engine and erase the DTC memory. Then continue the road test.

7. Check the DTC memory again.

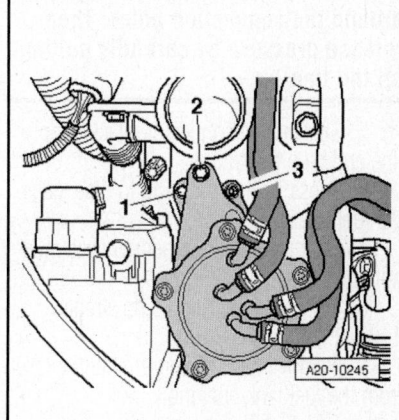

Fig. 150 Loosen the bolt (1) one turn, remove the bolt (2) and the nut (3)

INJECTION TIMING

ADJUSTMENT

Injection timing is automatically controlled by the Electronic Control Module (ECM). No adjustment is possible.

INJECTION LINES

REMOVAL & INSTALLATION

Refer to Intake Manifold.

INJECTORS

REMOVAL & INSTALLATION

Refer to Intake Manifold.

FUEL SUPPLY PUMP

REMOVAL & INSTALLATION

2.0L TDI Engine

See Figure 151.

➡The fuel tank may be a maximum of 1/2 full. Empty the fuel tank if necessary using the fuel extracting device VAS 5190Fuel Tank, Draining.

1. Before servicing the vehicle, refer to the precautions.
2. With the ignition switched off, disconnect Ground (GND) wire to the battery.
3. Remove seat bench.
4. Unclip cover for fuel delivery unit.

❋❋ CAUTION

The fuel supply line is under pressure. Wear protective goggles and protective clothing to prevent injuries and contact with skin. Before loosening line connections, place rags around the connection point. Then release pressure by carefully pulling off the line.

5. Disconnect connector, black supply line and blue return line.
6. Press in securing ring to disengage the fuel lines.
7. Seal lines so that the fuel system is not contaminated by dirt etc.
8. Open locking ring using wrench T10202.
9. Remove fuel delivery unit and gasket from the fuel tank opening.

➡If the fuel delivery unit is to be replaced then drain old delivery unit before disposal.

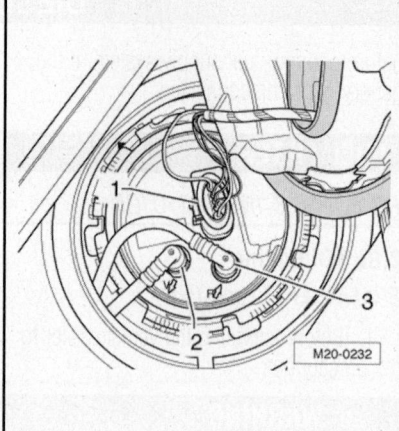

Fig. 151 Disconnect connector (1), black supply line (2) and blue return line (3)

To install:

10. Install in order of removal.
11. When inserting fuel delivery unit into fuel tank, be sure not to bend Fuel Level Sensor.
12. Replace fuel delivery unit gasket if damaged and insert it in the fuel tank opening dry.
13. Only coat seal with fuel when installing fuel delivery unit.
14. Note installation position of fuel delivery unit flange.
15. Route fuel lines kink-free.
16. Do not interchange supply and return line (return line blue, supply line black).
17. Make sure lines connections are securely fastened.
18. Observe notes after connecting the battery.

INJECTION PUMP

REMOVAL & INSTALLATION

2.0L TDI Engine

See Figure 152.

1. Before servicing the vehicle, refer to the precautions.
2. Turn the ignition and all electrical consumers off and remove the ignition key.
3. Remove engine cover.
   a. On one piece engine cover, pull the one piece front engine cover s upward with a quick jerk and then pull the lower mount forward.
   b. On the two piece engine cover, first pull the outer cover upward with a quick jerk s in the upper illustration, then pull the inner engine cover upward with a quick jerk s in lower illustration.
4. Disconnect electrical harness connector at Mass Air Flow (MAF) sensor G70.

5. Disconnect the ventilation hose and disengage it from the bracket.
6. Open the spring-type clip using spring-type clip pliers VAS 5024A and disconnect the intake hose from the Mass Air Flow (MAF) sensor G70.
7. Disconnect the intake manifold from the air guide.
8. Unfasten bolt and remove air filter housing and mass air flow sensor.
9. Carefully cut the cable tie.
10. Open the wiring bracket and disengage the wiring harness.
11. Remove both bolts s from the upper charge air pipe.
12. Remove noise insulation.
13. Remove the charge air pipe bolt from the oil pan.

❋❋ CAUTION

The fuel or fuel lines in fuel system can become very hot. In addition, the fuel system is under pressure. Before opening the system, place rags around the connection area and release pressure by carefully loosening the connection. Wear protective goggles and protective gloves when working on the fuel system.

14. Pull off the supply hose (white marking) and the return hose (blue marking) from the fuel filter.
15. Connect the diesel extractor VAS 5226 or the hand vacuum pump to the draining container V.A.G 1390/1 on the return hose.
16. Operate the diesel extractor VAS 5226 or the hand vacuum pump, until fuel stops coming out of the return hose. Make sure no fuel gets into the hand vacuum pump.
17. Disconnect vacuum line of brake booster from tandem pump.
18. Disconnect supply hose (white marking) and return hose (blue marking) from tandem pump.
19. Remove mounting bolts.
20. Remove tandem pump from cylinder head.

To install:

21. Installation is performed in reverse order.

❋❋ WARNING

Make sure that tandem pump coupling has proper seating in camshaft.

➡Tandem pump gasket must always be replaced.

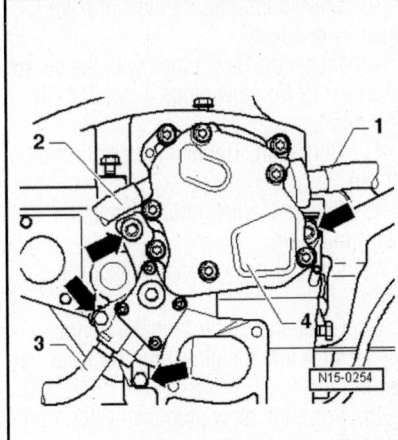

Fig. 152 Disconnect vacuum line of brake booster (1), disconnect supply hose (2) (white marking) and return hose (3) (blue marking) from tandem pump (4). Remove mounting bolts (arrows)

22. Install the tandem pump and tighten the upper bolts to 15 ft. lbs. (20 Nm).

23. Tighten the lower bolts to 89 inch lbs. (10 Nm).

24. Connect the return hose (blue marking) to the return connection on the tandem pump.

25. Connect the supply hose (white marking) to supply connection and the vacuum line from the brake booster to the tandem pump.

26. Connect the supply hose (white marking) to the fuel filter.

27. Connect the diesel extractor VAS 5226 or the hand vacuum pump to the draining container V.A.G 1390/1 on the return hose.

28. Operate the diesel extractor VAS 5226 or the hand vacuum pump, until fuel comes out of the return hose. Make sure no fuel gets into the hand vacuum pump.

29. Connect the return hose (blue marking) to the fuel filter.

INJECTION TIMING

2.0L TDI Engine

Injection timing is automatically controlled by the Electronic Control Module (ECM). No adjustment is possible.

GLOW PLUGS

REMOVAL & INSTALLATION

See Figures 153 through 155.

1. When removing the glow plugs, make sure no contaminants enter the fuel system and the glow plug duct.

2. Seal off the connections in the fuel system using the plugs from the engine bung set VAS 6122.

3. Requirements: Condition:
   a. Ignition turned off.
   b. Engine must be cold.

4. Remove the engine cover.

5. Remove the protective strip, if equipped.

6. Remove the connectors from the fuel injectors, the exhaust pressure sensor 1 G450 and the fuel pressure sensor G247.

7. Remove the coolant line bolts arrows from the intake manifold and lay the line in front of the intake manifold.

8. Remove the bolt on the intake manifold for the fuel return line.

9. Position the pliers 3314 with the groove on the upper collar of the connector and press together lightly.

➡**Position the pliers so they do not touch or damage the cable.**

10. Only use suitable tools.

11. Other unsuitable tools can damage the connector.

12. If the connector is damaged when removing it, replace the complete wiring harness including the connector (a connector cannot be replaced separately).

13. Carefully pull the connector off the glow plug in the direction of the with the pliers 3314.

➡**Do not pull abruptly on the connector.**

14. Do not damage the connector wire.

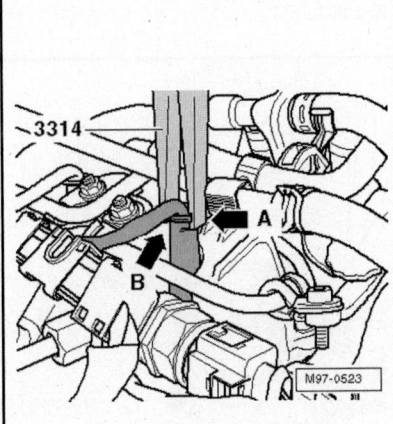

Fig. 153 Position the pliers 3314 with the groove A on the upper collar of the connector B

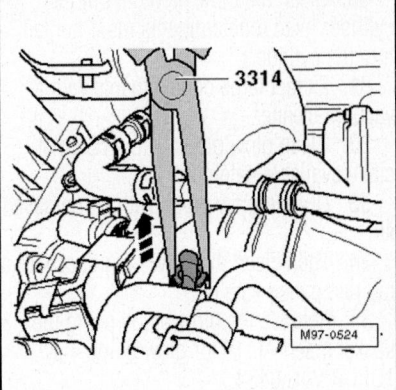

Fig. 154 Carefully pull the connector off the glow plug in the direction of the with the pliers 3314

15. Do not press the pliers together too firmly or the connector will be damaged.

16. The connector is surround by a protective sleeve. Replace the protective sleeve if it is damaged.

17. Loosen the hose clip using the hose clip pliers VAS 6362 and remove the line from the fuel rail.

18. Before removing, clean the return line connection on the fuel injectors (for example using a commercially available detergent).

19. Dry the return line connections.

20. Cover the return line connections with a cloth.

21. Remove the fuel return line connections from the fuel injectors. Pull them upward to release them.

22. Pay attention to cleanliness. Do not let any dirt to get into the disconnected return lines or into the connections for the fuel injection units.

23. Loosen the hose clip using the hose clip pliers VAS 6362 and remove the fuel return line.

24. Loosen the hose clip 4 using the hose clip pliers VAS 6362 and remove the fuel return line at the high pressure fuel pump.

25. Seal the lines so that the fuel system is not contaminated by dirt etc.

26. Remove the fuel return lines and lay them in front of the intake manifold.

27. Remove the glow plug wiring guide and lay it aside.

28. When cleaning the glow plug duct, make sure no contaminants or cleaning solutions enter the connector contacts on the glow plugs.

29. Do not clean the connectors with cleaning solutions or compressed air.

30. Clean the glow plug duct in the cylinder head (contaminants must not fall into the cylinder).

31. Extract large contaminants with a vacuum cleaner.

32. Clean glow plugs with a commercially available detergent.

33. Dry the glow plugs with compressed air.

34. Then clean the glow plug duct with a rag dampened with oil.

35. Remove the glow plugs using the socket insert AF 12 for glow plugs 4 cyl. TDI CR VAS 6454.

To install:

36. Install in reverse order of removal. When doing this note the following:

37. Condition: When installing the glow plugs, make sure no contaminants enter the fuel system and the glow plug duct.

38. Only remove the sealing plugs right before installing the fuel return line.

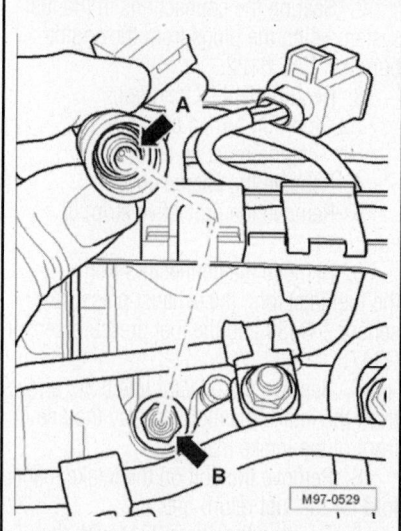

Fig. 155 Guide the center terminal on the connector A into the glow plug socket B by hand

39. Make sure lines connections are securely fastened.

40. Install the glow plugs with the socket insert AF 12 for glow plugs 4 cyl. TDI CR VAS 6454.

41. Condition: Tightening specification: 12 Nm.

42. Secure the fuel return line to the intake manifold.

43. Condition: Tightening specification: 8 Nm.

44. Guide the center terminal on the connector A into the glow plug socket B by hand.

45. Press the glow plug connector 1 on by hand until it engages.

46. Install the fuel return line.

47. Check the Engine Control Module (ECM) Diagnostic Trouble Code (DTC) memory and erase all DTC entries. Refer to "Guided Functions" in the vehicle diagnostic tester.

HEATING & AIR CONDITIONING SYSTEM

BLOWER MOTOR

REMOVAL & INSTALLATION

See Figures 156 and 157.

➡**Fresh Air Blower V2 is accessible from foot well on front passenger side.**

1. Remove partition from heating unit.
2. Unscrew plastic screws and remove partition.
3. Disconnect harness connector from Fresh Air Blower V2.
4. Remove screw for Fresh Air Blower V2.

5. Release catch and rotate Fresh Air Blower V2 in direction of.
6. Remove Fresh Air Blower V2 from heating unit.

To install:

7. Install in reverse order of removal.
8. Tighten bolts/nuts to specification as follows: fresh Air Blower: 9 inch lbs. (1 Nm)

HEATER CORE

REMOVAL & INSTALLATION

See Figures 158 through 161.

1. Before servicing the vehicle, refer to the precautions.

2. Remove facing wall in plenum chamber.
3. Place drip tray under the engine.

✱✱ CAUTION

Contact with hot engine coolant can cause severe scalding. Coolant temperature can be above 212° F (100° C) with a warm engine. The cooling system is under pressure. If necessary, reduce pressure and temperature before repairs.

4. Clamp off coolant hoses using hose clamps and disconnect coolant hoses to heater core.

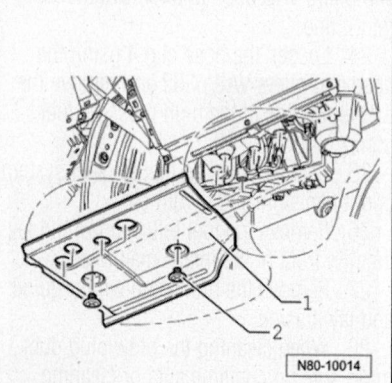

Fig. 156 Unscrew plastic screws (2) and remove partition (1)

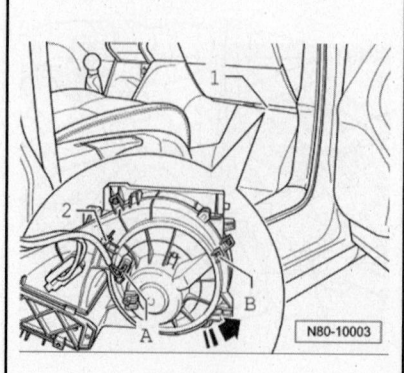

Fig. 157 Disconnect harness connector (A), remove screw (B) and release the catch (2)

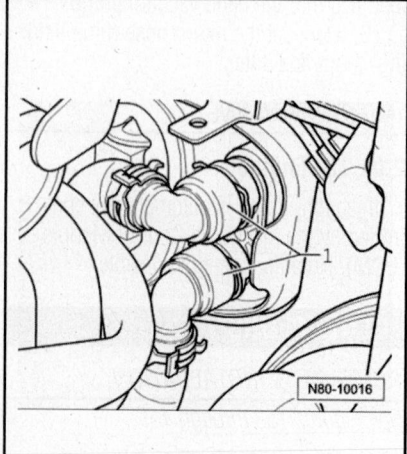

Fig. 158 Clamp off coolant hoses (1)

5. Connect a section of hose onto upper connection of heater core.

6. Hold a container under the lower connection.

7. Using a compressed air gun, carefully blow coolant out of heater core into container.

8. Loosen (do not unscrew completely) bolt out of connection flange between heater core connections.

9. This allows the coolant pipes to move for removing the heater core.

10. Remove driver side foot well trim.

11. Remove left foot well vent.

12. Remove screws and remove heater core trim.

13. Cover floor carpet in area below heater core with leak-proof foil and absorbent paper.

14. Open hose clamps A and disconnect coolant pipes.

15. Remove heater core from heating unit.

To install:

16. Installation is carried out in the reverse order.

17. Check seals installed on heater core, only install a heater core with undamaged seals.

18. An incorrectly glued seal can roll up into heating unit when sliding in the heater core.

19. Cold air may flow past heat exchanger if seal is damaged or not properly installed.

20. With the heater core removed, check heating unit for soiling (via heater core opening).

21. If necessary, remove dirt or coolant from heating unit, for example after removing leaky heater core.

22. Push heater core into heating unit.

23. Coat sealing rings with coolant before installing.

24. Insert sealing rings into connection on coolant pipe.

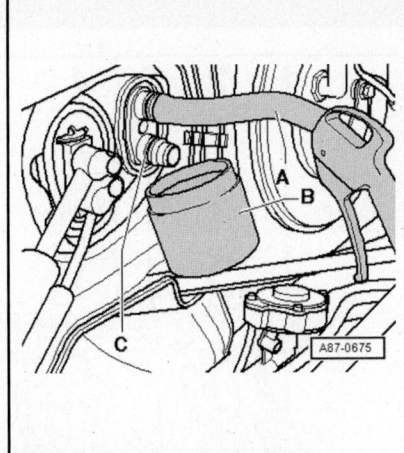

Fig. 159 Air gun (A), container (B) and lower connection (C)

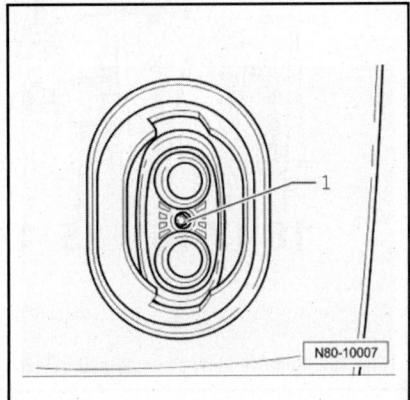

Fig. 160 Loosen (do not unscrew completely) bolt (1) out of connection flange

25. If hose clamps are deformed, replace them.

26. Connect coolant pipes.

27. Hose clamps must be able to be twisted slightly when installing onto the coolant pipes.

28. Tighten hose clamps.

29. Check seating of both clamps after tightening bolts, clamps must enclose the

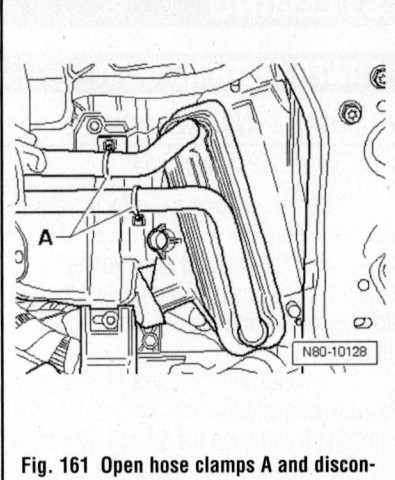

Fig. 161 Open hose clamps A and disconnect coolant pipes

flange on coolant pipe completely and must not touch other components.

30. Tighten the screw from the connecting flange between heater core connections.

31. Check position of grommet in bulkhead for proper seating.

32. Seal the flange for coolant pipes to heater core and for expansion valve (to evaporator, only in vehicles with A/C system) at pass-through of grommet with silicon adhesive sealant if necessary (to prevent water from penetrating).

33. Sealing rings must always be replaced.

34. If hose clamps are deformed, replace them.

35. After replacing heater core, coolant must be replaced completely.

36. Check coolant circuit for leaks, pay particular attention between coolant pipes and heater core.

37. Tighten bolts/nuts to specification as follows:

- Hose clamps: 18 inch lbs. (2.0 Nm)
- Heater core connections to: 18 inch lbs. (2.0 Nm)

STEERING

POWER STEERING GEAR

REMOVAL & INSTALLATION

See Figures 162 through 164.

1. Before servicing the vehicle, refer to the precautions.
2. Turn the steering wheel to the straight ahead position and remove the ignition key so that the steering wheel lock engages.
3. Vehicles with "Keyless Access" Keyless Locking and Starting System: Turn the ignition off and open the driver's door so the steering wheel lock locks.
4. Disconnect battery.
5. Remove foot well trim, remove nuts to do so.
6. Remove bolt and pull off universal joint from steering gear.
7. Remove front wheels.
8. Loosen tie rod end nut, but do not remove yet.

✲✲ WARNING

To protect thread, screw nut on pin a few turns.

9. Press tie rod end off of wheel bearing housing using Ball Joint Puller 3287A.
10. Remove lower noise insulation.
11. Remove pendulum support from transmission, remove bolts 14 to do so.
12. Remove bracket for exhaust system from subframe.
13. Remove bolts from heat shield.
14. Remove heat shield from subframe.
15. Now remove bolts 3, 6, 11 and 16 for the steering gear and stabilizer bar.
16. Locate subframe and brackets. Subframe and Brackets, Securing
17. Place Engine/Transmission Jack VAG1383A under subframe.
18. Place a block of wood , for example, between VAG 1383 A and the subframe.
19. Loosen bolts and lower subframe with brackets slightly. Observe electrical wires, when doing so.
20. Remove heat shield above steering gear.
21. Remove bolts.
22. Remove cable guide from subframe.
23. Unclip all other cable securing points on steering gear.
24. Disconnect all electrical connections from steering gear.

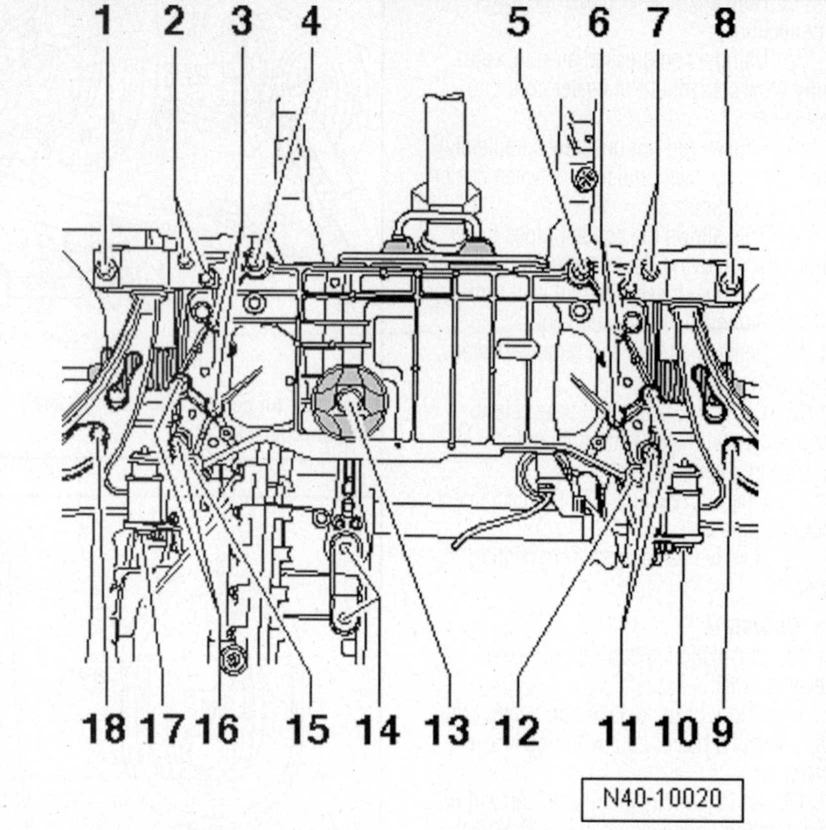

Fig. 162 Remove bolts as explained in text

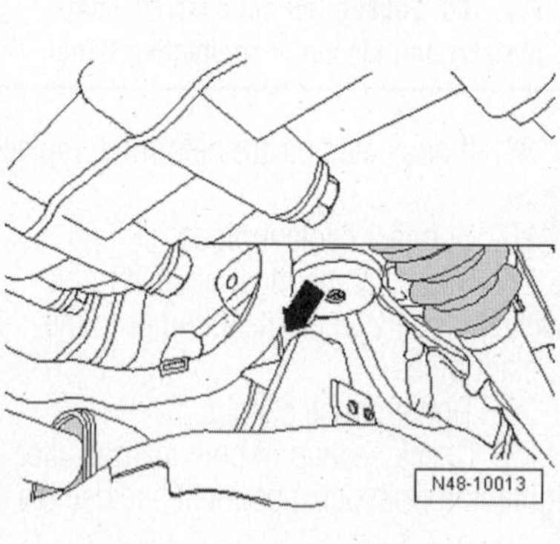

Fig. 163 Remove cable guide from subframe (arrow)

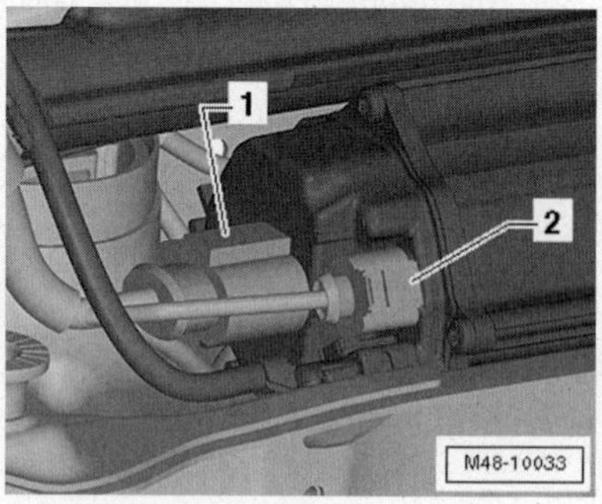

Fig. 164 Disconnect all electrical connections from steering gear

25. Lower subframe with the Engine/Transmission Jack V.A.G 1383 A until steering gear can be removed.
26. Lay steering gear aside. This avoids damages on control module.

To install:

27. Installation is in reverse order of removal.

✲✲ WARNING

The steering gear threaded sleeves must be seated in the bracket holes.

28. Coat seal on steering gear with lubricant, e.g. soft soap, before installing steering gear.
29. After attaching steering gear to drive

shaft, make sure that seal on steering gear is positioned to mounting plate without kinks and opening to foot well is sealed correctly. Ingress of water and/or noises may be the result.

30. Make sure sealing surfaces are clean.

Before fastening the bolts for subframe, position steering gear on subframe and fasten bolts for steering gear and stabilizer.

31. Clamp off electrical connections to the steering gear.

32. Install lower noise insulation.

33. Ensure that boot is not damaged or twisted.

34. Universal joint to steering gear.

35. Connect battery.

36. Perform Steering Angle Sensor G85 basic setting with the Vehicle Diagnosis, Testing and Information System VAS 5051

37. After installation, position of steering wheel must be checked with a road test.

38. If the steering wheel is crooked or new steering gear was installed, the toe on the front axle must be checked and adjusted if necessary.

39. Align vehicle. Alignment General Information

40. If new steering gear was installed, Power Steering Control Module J500 must be adapted using Vehicle Diagnosis, Testing and Information System VAS 5051.

41. Perform Power Steering Control Module J500 basic setting using Vehicle Diagnosis, Testing and Information System VAS 5051.

42. If parking assist is installed in the vehicle, the Power Steering Control Module J500 must be recoded after installing new steering gear.

43. Parking assist is only in installed vehicles with Generation II steering gear.

44. Tighten bolts/nuts to specification as follows:

- Subframe to body (Use new bolts): 52 ft. lbs. (70 Nm) plus 90° rotation
- Stabilizer bar to subframe (Use new bolts): 15 ft. lbs. (20 Nm) plus 90° rotation
- Stabilizer bar to connecting link (Use new bolts and counterhold at

joint pin inner multi-point fitting): 48 ft. lbs. (65 Nm)
- Ball joint to control arm (Use new nut): 44 ft. lbs. (60 Nm)
- Shield to subframe (M6 bolt is self-tapping) 53 inch lbs. (6 Nm)
- Steering gear to subframe (Use new bolts) 37 ft. lbs. (50 Nm) plus 90° rotation
- Universal joint to steering gear (Use new bolt): 22 ft. lbs. (30 Nm)
- Shield to steering gear (M6 bolt is self-tapping) 53 inch lbs. (6 Nm)
- Tie rod end to wheel bearing housing (Use new nut): 15 ft. lbs. (20 Nm) plus 90° rotation

POWER STEERING PUMP

REMOVAL & INSTALLATION

The power steering pump is electro-mechanical and is an integral part of the power steering gear.

SUSPENSION   FRONT SUSPENSION

LOWER BALL JOINT

REMOVAL & INSTALLATION

See Figure 165.

1. Before servicing the vehicle, refer to the precautions.

2. Loosen the drive axle to wheel hub bolt.

3. Remove the wheel.

4. Remove the ball joint nuts.

5. Pull the drive axle out of the wheel hub slightly.

6. Remove the ball joint from the control arm and at the same time swivel the wheel bearing housing to the outside.

7. Move the control arm downward as far as possible.

8. Install the VAG 3287A and press out the ball joint.

9. Place the VAG 1383A or similar, underneath (risk of accident if components fall off when pressing out ball joint).

➡ **To protect the ball joint threads, leave the nut on a few turns.**

To install:

10. Tighten bolts/nuts to specification as follows:

- Ball joint to steel control arm (Use new nuts): 44ft. lbs. (60 Nm)

- Ball joint to sheet steel or aluminum control arm (Use new nuts): 74 ft. lbs. (100 Nm)
- Ball joint to wheel bearing housing (Use new nut): 44 ft. lbs. (60 Nm)
- Drive axle to wheel hub "hex head bolt" (Use new bolt): 148 ft. lbs. (200 Nm) plus an additional 180° rotation
- Drive axle to wheel hub "12-point bolt" (Use new bolt): 52 ft. lbs. (70 Nm) plus an additional 90° rotation

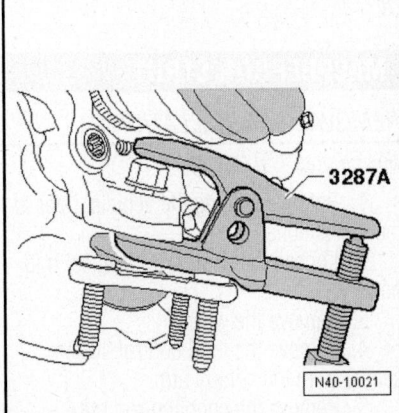

Fig. 165 Install the VAG 3287A and press out the ball joint

11. Pull the drive axle out of the wheel hub.

12. Install the ball joint into the wheel bearing housing.

13. Install a new self-locking nut, counter hold the stud using a T40 TORX®.

14. Install the drive axle to the wheel hub.

15. Install and tighten the ball joint nuts.

➡ **Make sure that the ball joint boot is not damaged or twisted.**

16. Install the wheel.

17. Tighten the drive axle to wheel hub bolt.

LOWER CONTROL ARM

REMOVAL AND & INSTALLATION

See Figure 166.

1. Before servicing the vehicle, refer to the precautions.

2. Remove the wheel.

3. Remove the lower noise insulation.

4. Remove the nuts from the control arm.

5. Separate the control arm from the ball joint and then turn the wheel bearing housing toward the outside to take the load off the control arm.

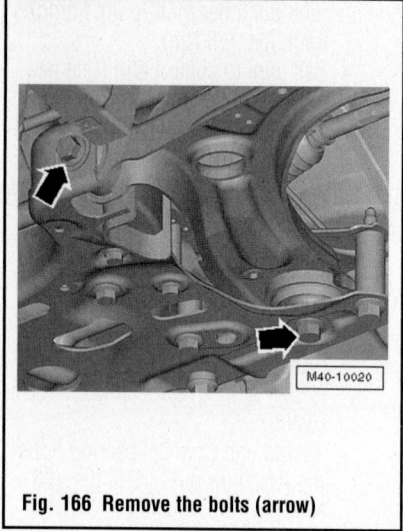

Fig. 166 Remove the bolts (arrow)

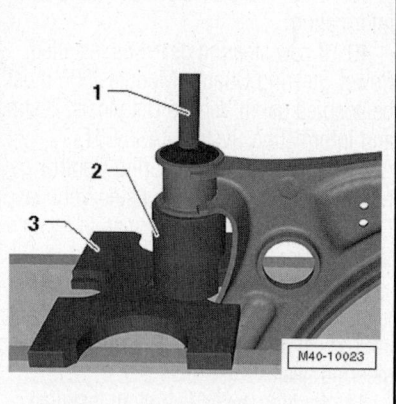

Fig. 167 Punch VW 411 (1), Tube T10219/1 (2) and Thrust plate VW 402 (3)

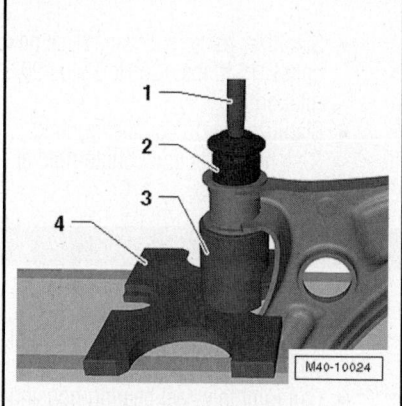

Fig. 168 Drift T10219/2 (1), Bonded rubber mount (2), Tube T10219/1 (3) and thrust plate (4)

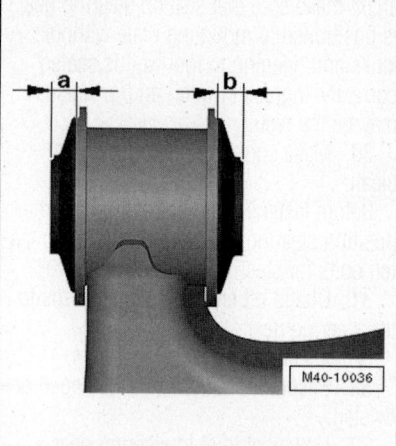

Fig. 169 Dimensions a and b must be identical

6. Remove the bolts arrows.

7. Swivel the control arm toward the rear and then remove it from the subframe in the direction of the.

To install:

8. Install in reverse order of removal. Note the following:

9. Install the control arm into the subframe in the direction of the and swivel it forward.

10. Install the front wheel and tighten the bolts. (Use new bolt and tighten bolts at normal ride height): 52 ft. lbs. (70 Nm) plus 180° rotation

11. Tighten the Ball joint to control arm (Use new nuts) to 44 ft. lbs. (60 Nm) plus 180° rotation

CONTROL ARM BUSHING REPLACEMENT

See Figures 167 through 169.

1. Remove the control arm, refer to one of the following:

2. Press out the bonded rubber bushings as shown in the illustration.

   a. Punch VW 411

   b. Tube T10219/1 (the hole must face the control arm)

   c. Thrust plate VW 402

To install:

3. Apply the assembly lubricant G 294 421 A1 onto the outside of the bonded rubber bushing.

4. Install the bonded rubber bushing as illustrated.

5. The bonded rubber bushing will be crooked for a short time at the beginning of the installation. Later it will straighten out. It will not be necessary to guide it.

6. Install the bonded rubber bushing

until the core 1 and the control arm hole 2 are at the same height.

7. Press back the bearing in the control arm slightly.

8. Dimensions a and b must be identical.

MACPHERSON STRUT

REMOVAL & INSTALLATION

See Figures 170 through 172.

1. Before servicing the vehicle, refer to the precautions.

2. Loosen the drive axle to wheel hub bolt.

3. Remove the wheel.

4. Remove the level control system sensor from the control arm.

5. Remove the coupling rod nut and remove the coupling rod from the strut.

6. Remove the ball joint nuts.

7. Remove the wheel bearing housing with ball joint from the control arm.

8. Remove the drive axle from the wheel hub.

9. Secure the drive axle to body using wire.

✳✳ WARNING

The drive axle must not hang down, otherwise the inner Constant Velocity (CV) joint may be damaged when bent too far.

10. Install the ball joint to the control arm again.

11. Secure the VAG 1383 with the T10149 to the wheel hub using one wheel bolt.

12. Remove the wheel bearing housing/strut pinch bolt nut.

13. Insert the 3424 into the slot in the wheel bearing housing.

14. Install a ratchet to the 3424 and turn it 90°, opening the slot in the wheel bearing housing, then remove the ratchet from the 3424.

15. Press the brake disc in the direction of the strut by hand.

Otherwise the strut tube may be tilted in the wheel bearing housing.

16. Pull the wheel bearing housing downward from the strut tube and lower using the VAG 1383A until the strut tube hangs free.

17. Secure the wheel bearing housing to the subframe with wire.

18. Remove the VAG 1383A from the below wheel bearing housing.

19. When removing the left strut, remove the wiper arms.

20. Remove the plenum chamber cover.

21. Remove the bolts from the strut dome and remove the strut.

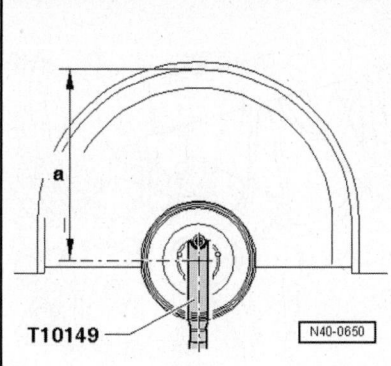

Fig. 170 Secure the VAG 1383 with the T10149 to the wheel hub using one wheel bolt

To install:

22. Secure the VAG 1383A with the T10149 to the wheel hub using one wheel bolt.

23. Install the strut to the wheel bearing housing and secure the strut using and a new pinch bolt and nut.

✳✳ WARNING

Bolt tip must point in direction of rotation vehicle travel.

24. Remove the 3424 from the wheel bearing housing.

✳✳ WARNING

One of two markings on the strut bearing must point in direction of rotation vehicle travel.

25. Remove the wire securing the wheel bearing housing.

26. Carefully lift the wheel bearing hous-

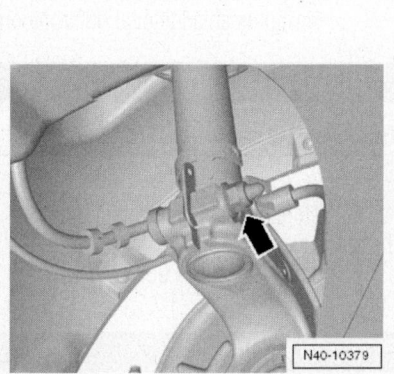

Fig. 171 Remove the wheel bearing housing/strut pinch bolt nut

ing using the VAG 1383A far enough until the bolts for the strut can be installed.

➡**If necessary, use ladder, for example VAS 5085 to install the bolts.**

27. Tighten the strut to strut dome bolts.
28. Remove the T10149.
29. Tighten the wheel bearing housing/strut pinch bolt nut.
30. Remove the ball joint nuts again.
31. Install the drive axle to the wheel hub.
32. Install the wheel bearing housing with ball joint to the control arm.
33. Install the ball joint to control arm nuts.

✳✳ WARNING

Make sure that the ball joint boot is not damaged or twisted.

34. Tighten the drive axle to wheel hub bolt.

✳✳ WARNING

When doing this, the vehicle must not rest on the ground, otherwise the wheel bearing could be damaged.

35. Install the plenum chamber cover.
36. Install the wiper arms, if required.
37. Install the wheel.
38. Tighten bolts/nuts to specification as follows:

- Strut to wheel bearing housing (Use new nut): 52 ft. lbs. (70 Nm) plus 90° additional rotation
- Strut to body (strut dome) (Use new bolts): 11 ft. lbs. (15 Nm) plus 90° additional rotation
- Ball joint to steel control arm (Use new nuts): 44 ft. lbs. (60 Nm)
- Coupling rod to strut (Use new nut and counter hold at inner joint multi point stud): 48 ft. lbs. (65 Nm)
- Drive axle to wheel hub "hex head bolt" (Use new bolt): 148 ft. lbs. (200 Nm) plus an additional 180° rotation
- Drive axle to wheel hub"12-point bolt"(Use new bolt): 52 ft. lbs. (70 Nm) plus an additional 90° rotation

OVERHAUL

1. Before servicing the vehicle, refer to the precautions.
2. Fit the strut into spring compressor V.A.G 1752/1 and compress the spring until upper axial groove ball bearing is free.

✳✳ CAUTION

First pre-load spring far enough so that tension is relieved on upper spring retainer!

3. Make sure that coil spring is seated correctly in the tool.
4. Remove hex nut from top of piston rod.
5. Remove components of suspension strut and coil spring.

To install:

6. Place coil spring with spring compressor V.A.G 1752/1 on lower spring plate. End of spring coil must rest against the stop in the spring seat.
7. Install a new self-locking hex nut onto piston rod and torque to 45 ft. lbs. (60 Nm).
8. Carefully relieve tension on spring compressor V.A.G 1752/1 and remove from coil spring.

STABILIZER BAR

REMOVAL & INSTALLATION

See Figure 162.

1. Before servicing the vehicle, refer to the precautions.
2. Remove front wheels.
3. Remove foot well trim, remove nuts to do so.
4. Remove bolt and pull off universal joint from steering gear.
5. Remove lower noise insulation.
6. Remove coupling rods from stabilizer.
7. Remove nuts.
8. Loosen tie rod end nut on both sides, but do not remove yet.

✳✳ WARNING

To protect thread, screw nut on pin a few turns.

9. Press off tie rod end from wheel bearing housing using ball joint puller 3287A.
10. Secure subframe with brackets Subframe and Brackets, Securing.
11. Remove stabilizer from subframe 11 and 16. See illustration for bolt locations.
12. Remove pendulum support from transmission, remove bolts 14 to do so.
13. Place engine/transmission jack V.A.G 1383 A below subframe.
14. Place, for example, a piece of wood between engine/transmission jack V.A.G 1383 A and subframe.
15. Loosen bolts and lower subframe with brackets slightly. Observe electrical wires, when doing so.

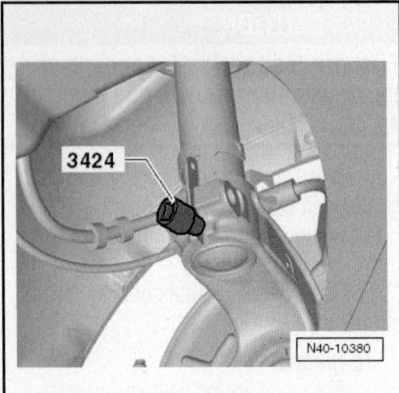

Fig. 172 Insert the 3424 into the slot in the wheel bearing housing

16. Now, lift stabilizer bar toward front, over bracket and down from subframe.

To install:

17. Installation is in reverse order of removal.

18. Coat seal on steering gear with lubricant, e.g. soft soap, before installing steering gear.

19. After attaching steering gear to drive axle, make sure that seal on steering gear is positioned to mounting plate without kinks and opening to foot well is sealed correctly. Ingress of water and/or noises may be the result.

20. Make sure sealing surfaces are clean.

21. Install lower noise insulation

22. Install front wheels.

23. Tighten bolts/nuts to specification as follows:

- Subframe to body (Use new bolts): 52 ft. lbs. (70 Nm) plus 90° rotation
- Bracket to body (Use new bolts): 52 ft. lbs. (70 Nm) plus 90° rotation
- Mounting bracket to body (Use new bolts): 52 ft. lbs. (70 Nm) plus 90° rotation
- Subframe to bracket (Use new bolts): 52 ft. lbs. (70 Nm) plus 90° rotation
- Ball joint to control arm (Use new nut): 44 ft. lbs. (60 Nm)
- Stabilizer bar to subframe (Use new bolts): 15 ft. lbs. (20 Nm) plus 90° rotation
- Stabilizer bar to connecting link (Use new bolts and counterhold at joint pin inner multi-point fitting): 48 ft. lbs. (65 Nm)
- Control arm to bracket (Use new bolts and tighten bracket in curb

weight position): 52 ft. lbs. (70 Nm) plus 90° rotation
- Steering gear to subframe (Use new bolts) 37 ft. lbs. (50 Nm) plus 90° rotation
- Universal joint to steering gear (Use new bolt): 22 ft. lbs. (30 Nm)

STEERING KNUCKLE

REMOVAL & INSTALLATION

See Figure 173.

1. Before servicing the vehicle, refer to the precautions.
2. Loosen drive axle bolt to wheel hub.

✼✼ WARNING

When doing this, vehicle must not stand on wheels, otherwise wheel bearing may be damaged.

3. Remove wheel.
4. Remove brake caliper and engage on body with wire.
5. Remove ABS wheel speed sensor.
6. Remove disc brake.
7. Remove cover plate from wheel bearing housing.
8. Loosen tie rod end nut, but do not remove yet.

✼✼ WARNING

To protect thread, screw nut on pin a few turns.

9. Press off tie rod end from wheel bearing housing with ball joint puller 3287A and then remove nut.
10. Press drive axle out of wheel hub (in direction of transmission) as far as possible.
11. Remove wheel bearing housing/suspension strut bolt connection.
12. Insert spreader 3424 into wheel bearing housing slot.
13. Turn ratchet around 90° and remove from spreader 3424.
14. Loosen nuts.
15. Place engine/transmission jack V.A.G 1383 beneath wheel bearing housing.
16. First, press off ball joint from control arm, then pull off wheel bearing housing from suspension strut.

To install:

17. Installation is reverse of removal, noting the following:
18. Tighten drive axle bolt to wheel hub. When doing this, vehicle must not stand on wheels, otherwise wheel bearing may be damaged.

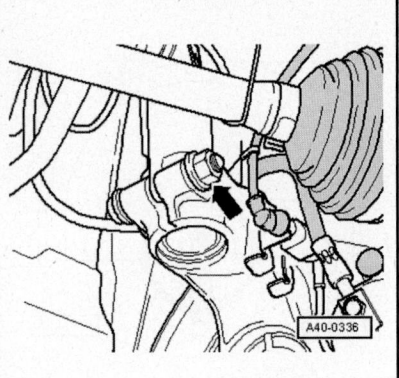

Fig. 173 Remove wheel bearing housing/suspension strut bolt connection (arrow)

✼✼ WARNING

If wheel bearing housing was replaced, vehicle alignment must be performed Alignment General Information.

19. Install wheel.
20. Tighten bolts/nuts to specification as follows:

- Strut to wheel bearing housing (Use new nut): 52 ft. lbs. (70 Nm) plus 90° additional rotation
- Ball joint to steel control arm (Use new nuts): 44 ft. lbs. (60 Nm)
- Tie rod end to wheel bearing housing (Use new nuts): 15 ft. lbs. (20 Nm) plus 90° additional rotation
- Drive axle to wheel hub "hex head bolt" (Use new bolt): 148 ft. lbs. (200 Nm) plus an additional 180° rotation
- Drive axle to wheel hub "12-point bolt" (Use new bolt): 52 ft. lbs. (70 Nm) plus an additional 90° rotation

WHEEL BEARINGS

REMOVAL & INSTALLATION

See Figure 174.

1. Before servicing the vehicle, refer to the precautions.
2. Loosen drive axle bolt to wheel hub.

✼✼ WARNING

When doing this, vehicle must not stand on wheels, otherwise wheel bearing may be damaged.

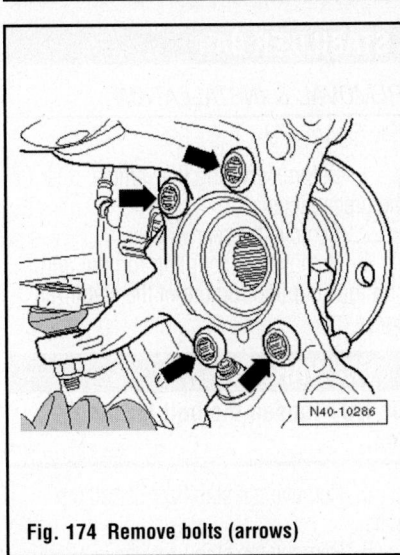

Fig. 174 Remove bolts (arrows)

3. Remove wheel.

4. Remove brake caliper and engage on body with wire.

5. Remove ABS wheel speed sensor.

6. Remove disc brake.

7. Press drive axle out of wheel hub (in direction of transmission) as far as possible.

8. Remove bolts.

9. Remove wheel bearing unit from wheel bearing housing.

To install:

10. Installation is in reverse order of removal.

11. Install brake caliper.

12. Tighten drive axle bolt to wheel hub.

13. When doing this, vehicle must not stand on wheels, otherwise wheel bearing may be damaged.

14. Install ABS wheel speed sensor.

15. Install wheel.

16. Tighten bolts/nuts to specification as follows:

- Drive axle to wheel hub "hex head bolt" (Use new bolt): 148 ft. lbs. (200 Nm) plus an additional 180° rotation
- Drive axle to wheel hub "12-point bolt" (Use new bolt): 52 ft. lbs. (70 Nm) plus an additional 90° rotation
- Wheel hub with wheel bearing to wheel bearing housing (Use new nut): 52 ft. lbs. (70 Nm) plus 90° additional rotation

SUSPENSION   REAR SUSPENSION

COIL SPRING

REMOVAL & INSTALLATION

See Figures 175 and 176.

1. Before servicing the vehicle, refer to the precautions.

2. Remove wheel.

3. Insert spring compressor.

※ CAUTION

Be sure coil spring is properly seated in spring holder V.A.G 1752/4 2.

4. Use wrench or ratchet for tightening spring compressor.

5. Compress coil spring until it can be removed.

6. Remove spring.

7. Spring holder V.A.G 1752/4

8. Adapter V.A.G 1752/9

9. Spring compressor V.A.G 1752/1

To install:

※ WARNING

The spring start must touch bottom of spring seat.

10. Install spring together with spring seat.

11. Lower spring support has a pin.

12. Insert this pin into hole of lower transverse link.

13. Then insert upper spring support into upper end of spring.

14. Release tension of spring, guiding upper spring support onto tab of body.

15. Remove spring tensioner.

16. Install wheel.

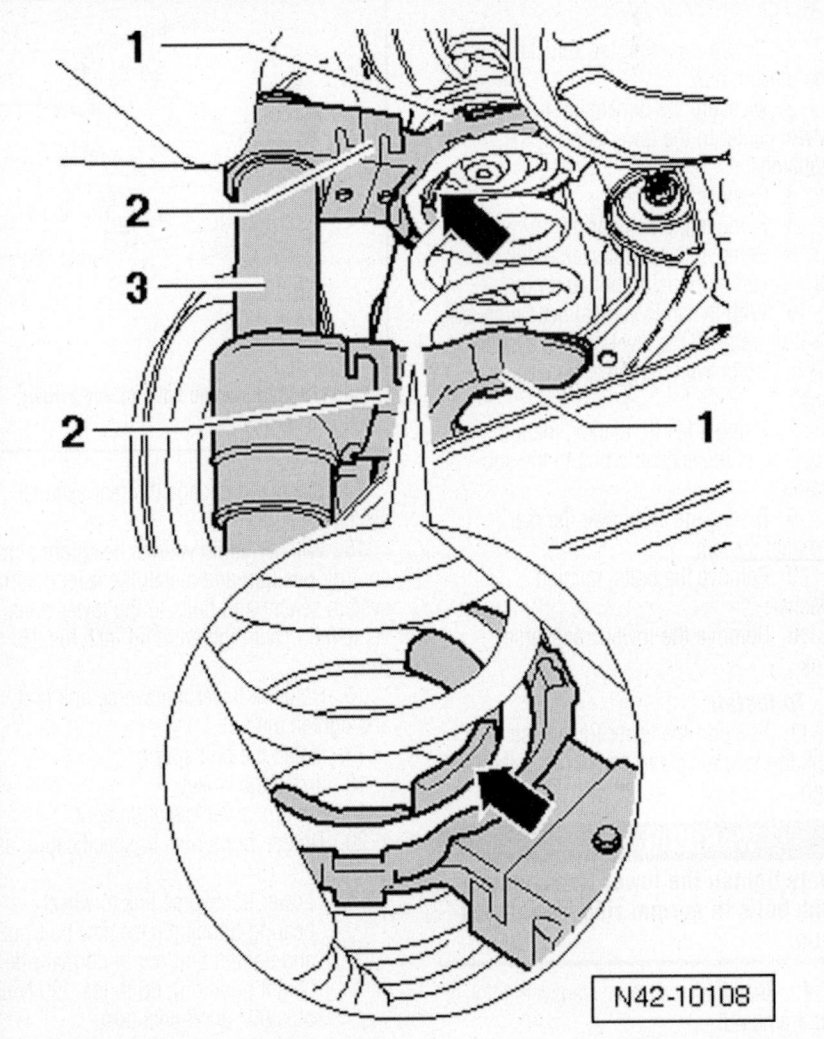

Fig. 175 Spring holder V.A.G 1752/4 (1), Adapter V.A.G 1752/9 (2) and Spring compressor V.A.G 1752/1 (3)

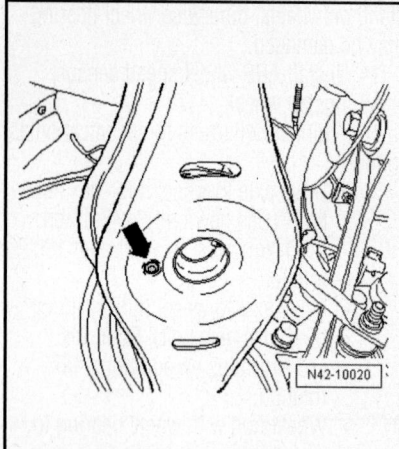

Fig. 176 The spring start must touch bottom of spring seat

LOWER CONTROL ARM

REMOVAL & INSTALLATION

See Figures 177 and 178.

1. Before servicing the vehicle, refer to the precautions.
2. Measure the dimension from the wheel center to the lower edge of the wheel housing.
3. Remove the wheel.
4. Remove the coil spring.
5. Remove lower transverse link to wheel bearing housing bolt and nut.
6. With dynamic vertical headlamp aim control, remove the level control system sensor bolts from the lower transverse link.
7. Using a felt tip marker, mark the position of the eccentric bolt to the subframe.
8. Disengage and lower the rear exhaust system.
9. Remove the bolts, nut and washer.
10. Remove the lower transverse link.

To install:

11. Position the lower transverse link to the vehicle and install the bolts hand tight.

✳✳ WARNING

Only tighten the lower transverse link bolts in normal ride height position.

12. Install a new upper transverse link to subframe nut.
13. Align the eccentric bolt to the previously made mark on the subframe and tighten the nut.

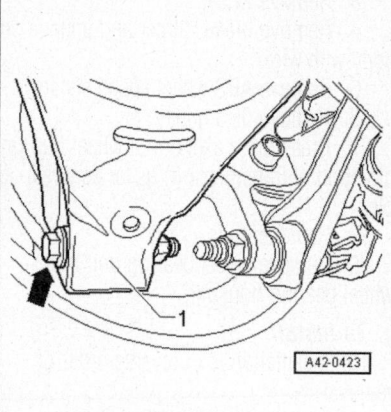

Fig. 177 Remove lower transverse link to wheel bearing housing bolt and nut

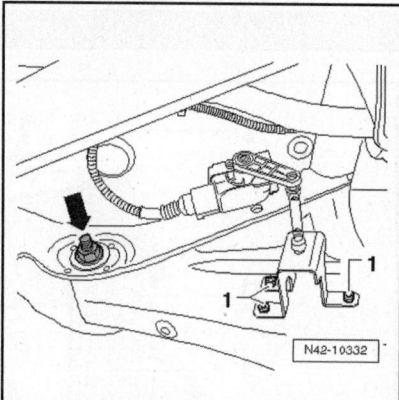

Fig. 178 Remove the bolts (1 and arrow), nut and washer

14. Raise and engage the rear exhaust system.
15. With dynamic vertical headlight aim control, position and install the level control system sensor and bolts to the lower transverse link. Then tighten to 44 inch lbs. (5 Nm).
16. Hold the lower transverse link bolt and tighten the nut.
17. Install the coil spring.
18. Install the wheel.
19. Perform a vehicle alignment.
20. Tighten bolts/nuts to specification as follows:

- Lower transverse link to wheel bearing housing (Use new bolt/nut and tighten bolt/nut in normal ride height position): 66 ft. lbs. (90 Nm) plus 90° additional turn
- Lower transverse link to subframe (Use new bolt/nut and tighten bolt/nut in normal ride height position): 70 ft. lbs. (95 Nm)

STABILIZER BAR

REMOVAL & INSTALLATION

See Figure 179.

1. Before servicing the vehicle, refer to the precautions.
2. Remove the rear wheels.
3. Remove the coupling rod nut and pull the coupling rod out of the stabilizer bar.

✳✳ WARNING

Do NOT loosen the bolt for the tie rod.

4. Remove the stabilizer bar clamp bolts.
5. Remove the stabilizer bar.

To install:

6. Tighten bolts/nuts to specification as follows:

- Stabilizer bar clamp to subframe (Use new bolts): 19 ft. lbs. (25 Nm) plus 45° additional turn
- Stabilizer bar to coupling rod (Use new nut): 33 ft. lbs. (45 Nm)

7. Install the stabilizer bar to the vehicle.
8. Tighten the stabilizer bar clamp bolts evenly.
9. Install the wheel.
10. Install the coupling rod to the stabilizer bar and tighten the nut.

SHOCK ABSORBER

REMOVAL & INSTALLATION

See Figures 180 and 181.

1. Before servicing the vehicle, refer to the precautions.
2. Remove wheel.
3. Remove wheel housing liner.

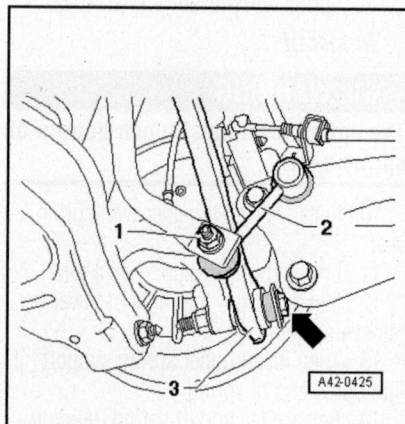

Fig. 179 Nut (1), coupling rod (2) and tie rod bolt (3)

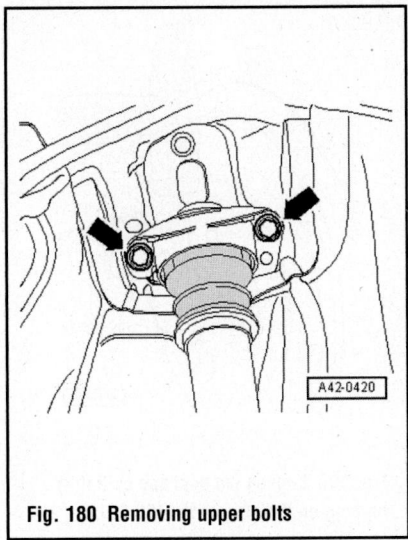

Fig. 180 Removing upper bolts

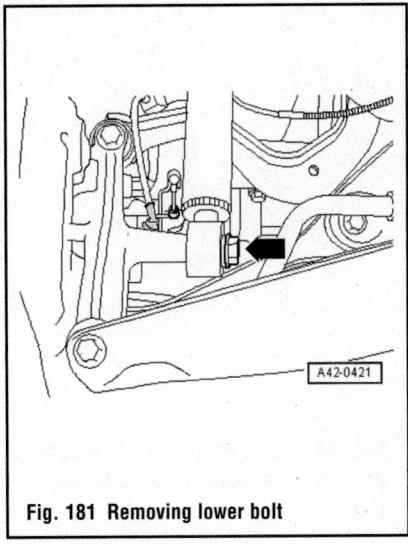

Fig. 181 Removing lower bolt

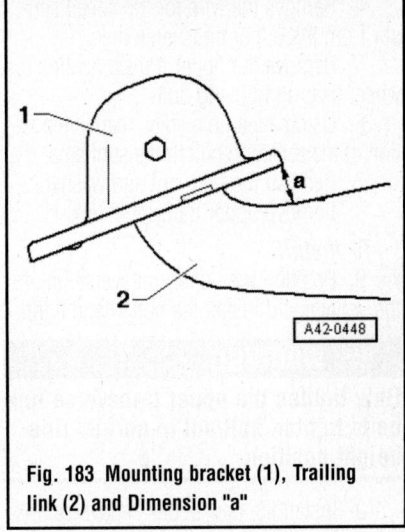

Fig. 183 Mounting bracket (1), Trailing link (2) and Dimension "a"

4. Remove coil spring.
5. Remove bolts.
6. Remove shock absorber.

To install:

7. Installation is in reverse order of removal.

➡**Only bolt on shock absorber to wheel bearing housing when vehicle is at normal ride height.**

8. Install shock absorber and tighten bolts.
9. Install coil spring.
10. Install wheel housing liner.
11. Install wheel.
12. Tighten bolts/nuts to specification as follows:
   - Shock absorber to body (Use new bolt): 37 ft. lbs. (50 Nm) plus 45° additional rotation
   - Shock absorber to wheel bearing housing: 133 ft. lbs. (180 Nm)

TRAILING ARM

REMOVAL & INSTALLATION

See Figures 182 and 183.

1. Remove the wheel.
2. Remove coil spring.
3. Remove the parking cable bracket by pressing out rivet inner pin.
4. Remove the coupling rod from trailing link and remove bolts.
5. Mark the installation position of mounting bracket on body.
6. Remove bolts.
7. Remove the trailing link with mounting bracket.

➡**If longitudinal control arm is being replaced, mounting bracket must be removed from trailing arm.**

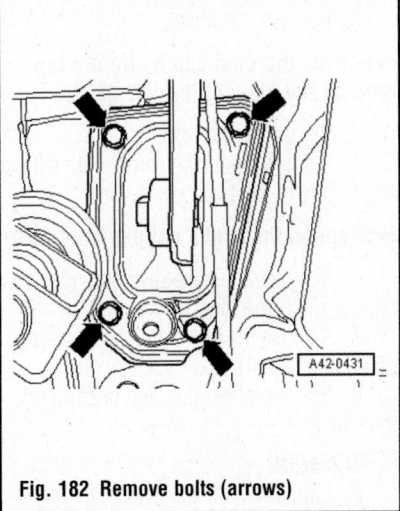

Fig. 182 Remove bolts (arrows)

Installation position of mounting bracket to trailing link must then be adjusted. Determining the Installation Position of Mounting Bracket Relative to Trailing Link. Dimension a is 34 ± 1 mm. Mounting bracket

8. When dimension "a" has been adjusted, tighten bolt.

To install:

9. Threaded connection of trailing link/wheel bearing housing must only be tightened when all other components (spring and strut always) of the respective wheel suspension have been already assembled. To tighten, suspension must be unloaded. Only now do the trailing link and wheel bearing housing move into the position required arrows.
10. Always follow the order of the following work steps!
11. Install trailing link and mounting bracket with bolts 2 on wheel bearing housing but do not yet tighten.

12. Insert coupling rod 3 in trailing link, do not tighten nut yet.
13. Raise wheel suspension using V.A.G 1383 A and T10149 until mounting bracket makes contact on body.
14. Tighten bolts arrows on old impression.
15. Let down wheel suspension again using V.A.G 1383 A and remove T10149 from wheel hub.
16. Fasten bolts 2 for trailing arm to torque specification, making sure of the required positioning of the components (dimension "a").
17. Connect the coupling rod 1 to the wheel bearing housing and stabilizer bar.
18. Install bracket 1 by pressing in new rivet inner pin.
19. Install coil spring.
20. Install wheel and tighten.
21. Perform vehicle alignment.
22. Tighten the following to specification using new bolts and/or nuts:
   - Trailing arm to wheel bearing housing: 66 ft. lbs. (90 Nm), plus 45° turn
   - Trailing arm to mounting bracket: 66 ft. lbs. (90 Nm), plus 90° turn
   - Mounting bracket to body: 37 ft. lbs. (50 Nm), plus 45° turn
   - Coupling rod to trailing arm: 33 ft. lbs. (45 Nm).

UPPER CONTROL ARM

REMOVAL & INSTALLATION

See Figure 184.

1. Before servicing the vehicle, refer to the precautions.
2. Remove the wheel.
3. Remove the coil spring.

4. Remove the wire for the speed sensor from the upper transverse link.

5. Remove the upper transverse link to wheel bearing housing bolt.

6. Using a felt tip marker, mark the position of the eccentric bolt to the subframe.

7. Remove the bolt, nut and washer.

8. Remove upper transverse link.

To install:

9. Position the upper transverse link to the vehicle and install the bolts hand tight.

✱✱ WARNING

Only tighten the upper transverse link bolts tighten bolt/nut in normal ride height position.

10. Install the new upper transverse link to subframe nut.

11. Align the eccentric bolt to the previously applied mark on the subframe and tighten the nut.

12. Tighten the new upper transverse link to wheel bearing housing bolt and nut.

✱✱ WARNING

Make sure that washer is installed between the bolt and wheel bearing housing.

13. Secure the wire for the speed sensor to the upper transverse link.

14. Install the coil spring.

15. Install the wheel.

16. Perform a vehicle alignment.

17. Tighten bolts/nuts to specification as follows:

- Upper transverse link to wheel bearing housing FWD (Use new bolt/nut and tighten bolt/nut in normal ride height position): 96 ft. lbs. (130 Nm) plus 90° ° additional turn
- Upper transverse link to subframe (Use new bolt/nut and tighten bolt/nut in normal ride height position): 70 ft. lbs. (95 Nm)

WHEEL BEARINGS

REMOVAL & INSTALLATION

See Figures 185 and 186.

1. Before servicing the vehicle, refer to the precautions.

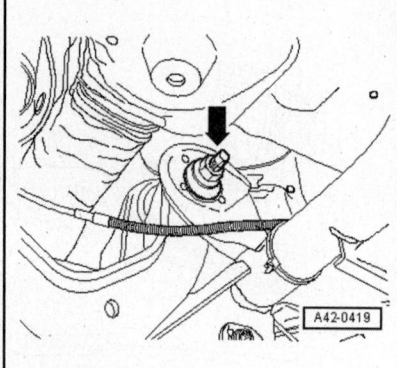

Fig. 184 Using a felt tip marker, mark the position of the eccentric bolt to the subframe

2. Raise the vehicle.

3. Remove the wheel.

➡**Loosen the dust cap by lightly tapping on the claw of the VW 637/2.**

4. Pry off the dust cap.

5. Remove the brake carrier with caliper and secure to the body using wire.

➡**Suspend the brake caliper from body.**

6. Remove the brake disc bolt and remove the brake disc.

7. Remove the wheel hub and bearing bolt using the T10162.

8. Pull the wheel hub and bearing off the stub axle.

To install:

9. Carefully slide the wheel hub and bearing onto the stub axle.

Make sure that wheel hub and bearing do not tilt!

10. Install a new wheel hub and bearing bolt and tighten.

➡**Tighten the bolt to specification using a torque wrench. Use a regular wrench for the additional torque angle.**

11. Install the dust cap using the 3241/4.

✱✱ WARNING

Always replace the dust cap. Damaged dust caps allow moisture to

Fig. 185 Loosen the dust cap by lightly tapping on the claw of the VW 637/2

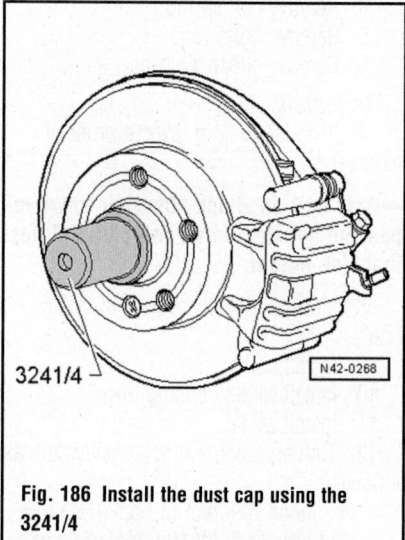

Fig. 186 Install the dust cap using the 3241/4

enter. Therefore, always use the tool shown.

12. Rest of the installation is the reverse of removal.

13. Install the wheel.

14. Tighten bolts/nuts to specification as follows:

- Wheel hub with bearing to wheel bearing housing (Use new bolt): 133 ft. lbs. (180 Nm) plus 180° additional rotation
- Brake disc to wheel bearing housing: 35 inch lbs. (4 Nm)

VOLKSWAGEN

6

Beetle

SPECIFICATIONS AND MAINTENANCE CHARTS

ENGINE AND VEHICLE IDENTIFICATION

		Engine						Model Year	
Eng Code	Liters (cc)	Cu. In.	Cyl.	Fuel Sys. ①	Engine Type	Eng. Mfg.		Code ②	Year
CBFA	2.0 (1984)	121	4	TFSI	DOHC	Volkswagen		C	2012
CCTA	2.0 (1984)	121	4	TFSI	DOHC	Volkswagen			
CBUA	2.5 (2480)	151	5	MFI	DOHC	Volkswagen			
CBTA	2.5 (2480)	151	5	MFI	DOHC	Volkswagen			

DOHC: Double Overhead Camshafts

① Bosch Motronic

② 10th digit of VIN

71105_VWNB_C0001

GENERAL ENGINE SPECIFICATIONS

Year	Model	Engine Displacement Liters	Engine ID/VIN	Net Horsepower @ rpm	Net Torque@rpm (ft. lbs.)	Bore x Stroke (in.)	Com- pression Ratio	Oil Pressure @ rpm
2012	Beetle	2.0 (1984)	①	200@5100	207@1700	3.20x3.70	9.6:1	36-65@2000
	Beetle	2.5 (2480)	①	170@5700	177@4250	3.25x3.64	9.5:1	36-65@2000

① Inspect timing cover for code.

71105_VWNB_C0002

GASOLINE ENGINE TUNE-UP SPECIFICATIONS

Year	Engine Displacement Liters	Engine ID/VIN	Spark Plug Gap (in.)	Ignition Timing (deg.) MT	Ignition Timing (deg.) AT	Fuel Pump (psi)	Idle Speed (rpm) MT	Idle Speed (rpm) AT	Valve Clearance Intake	Valve Clearance Exhaust
2012	2.0 (1984)	①	0.028-0.031	②	②	NS	②	②	HYD	HYD
	2.5 (2480)	①	0.039-0.043	②	②	NS	②	②	HYD	HYD

Note: The Vehicle Emission Control Information label reflects specification changes made during production.

NS: Not Specified

HYD: Hydraulic

① Inspect timing cover for code.

② Ignition timing/idle speed controlled electronically. Specification no longer provided.

71105_VWNB_C0003

CAPACITIES

Year	Model	Engine Displacement Liters	Engine ID/VIN	Engine Oil with Filter	Transmission Manual (pts.)	Transmission Auto. (qts.)	Fuel Tank (gal.)	Cooling System (qts.)
2012	Beetle	2.0 (1984)	①	4.9	4.9	NS	14.5	7.7
	Beetle	2.5 (2480)	①	5.9	4.1	NS	14.5	10.1

Note: All capacities are approximate. Add fluid gradually and check often to avoid overfilling or underfilling.

NS: Not Specified

① Inspect timing cover for code.

71105_VWNB_C0004

FLUID SPECIFICATIONS

Year	Model	Engine Displacement Liters	Engine ID/VIN	Engine Oil	Man. Trans.	Auto. Trans.	Brake Master Cylinder	Cooling System
2012	Beetle	2.0 (1984)	①	5W-40	Synthetic MTF 75W-90	Synthetic ATF	DOT4	LLC
	Beetle	2.5 (2480)	①	5W-40	Synthetic MTF 75W-90	Synthetic ATF	DOT4	LLC

DOT: Department Of Transpotation

LLC: Long Life Coolant

NA: Not Applicable

① Inspect timing cover for code.

71105_VWNB_C0005

VALVE SPECIFICATIONS

Year	Engine Displacement Liters	Engine ID/VIN	Seat Angle (deg.)	Face Angle (deg.)	Spring Test Pressure (lbs. @ in.)	Spring Installed Height (in.)	Stem-to-Guide Clearance (in.) Intake	Stem-to-Guide Clearance (in.) Exhaust	Stem Diameter (in.) Intake	Stem Diameter (in.) Exhaust
2012	2.0 (1984)	①	45	45	NS	NS	0.031	0.031	NS	NS
	2.5 (2480)	①	45	45	NS	NS	0.031	0.031	NS	NS

NS: Not Specified

① Inspect timing cover for code.

71105_VWNB_C0006

CRANKSHAFT AND CONNECTING ROD SPECIFICATIONS
All measurements are given in inches.

Year	Engine Disp. Liters	Engine ID/VIN	Main Brg. Journal Dia.	Main Brg. Oil Clearance	Shaft End-play	Thrust on No.	Connecting Rod		
							Journal Diameter	Oil Clearance	Side Clearance
2012	2.0	①	2.1260	0.0007-0.0015	0.0028-0.0090	3	1.8819	0.0008-0.0024	0.0039-0.0138
	2.5	①	2.2834	0.0007-0.0015	0.0007-0.0015	3	1.8819	0.0008-0.0024	0.0039-0.0138

① Inspect timing cover for code.

71105_VWNB_C0008

PISTON AND RING SPECIFICATIONS
All measurements are given in inches.

Year	Engine Disp. Liters	Engine ID/VIN	Piston Clearance	Ring Gap			Ring Side Clearance		
				Top Compression	Bottom Compression	Oil Control	Top Compression	Bottom Compression	Oil Control
2012	2.0	①	0.0177	0.008-0.016	0.008-0.016	0.010-0.020	0.0024-0.0035	0.0025-0.0042	0.0011-0.0027
	2.5	①	0.0177	0.008-0.016	0.008-0.016	0.010-0.020	0.0024-0.0035	0.0025-0.0042	0.0011-0.0027

① Inspect timing cover for code.

71105_VWNB_C0007

TORQUE SPECIFICATIONS
All readings in ft. lbs.

Year	Engine Displacement Liters	Engine ID/VIN	Cylinder Head Bolts	Main Bearing Bolts	Rod Bearing Bolts	Crankshaft Damper Bolt	Flywheel Bolts	Manifold		Spark Plugs	Oil Pan Drain Plug
								Intake	Exhaust		
2012	2.0	①	②	③	④	⑤	⑥	7	15 ⑦	18	22
	2.5	①	②	⑧	④	⑨	⑥	7	18 ⑦	18	22

① Inspect timing cover for code.
② Torque in three steps. Use new bolts.
  Step 1: 30 ft. lbs.
  Step 2: plus 90 degrees
  Step 3: plus 90 degrees
③ Two Steps. 66 ft. lbs. Plus 90 degrees. Use new bolt.

④ Two Steps. 22 ft. lbs. plus 90 degrees. Use new bolts.
⑤ Two Steps. 66 ft. lbs. Plus 90 degrees. Use new bolt.
⑥ Two Steps. 44 ft. lbs. plus 90 degrees. Use new bolts.
⑦ Use new bolts.
⑧ Two Steps. 30 ft. lbs. plus 90 degrees. Use new bolts.
⑨ Two Steps. 37 ft. lbs. plus 90 degrees. Use new bolts.

71105_VWNB_C0009

WHEEL ALIGNMENT

Year	Model		Caster Range (+/-Deg.)	Caster Preferred Setting (Deg.)	Camber Range (+/-Deg.)	Camber Preferred Setting (Deg.)	Toe-in (Deg.)
2012	Beetle	Front	0.50	+7.83	0.50	-0.58	1.67+/-0.33 ①
		Rear	—	—	0.50	-1.33	0.17+/-0.21 ②

① Toe differential angle with 20 deg. steering lock to left and right

② Total toe at specified camber.

71105_VWNB_C0010

TIRE, WHEEL AND BALL JOINT SPECIFICATIONS

Year	Model	OEM Tires Standard	OEM Tires Optional	Tire Pressures (psi) Front	Tire Pressures (psi) Rear	Wheel Size	Lug Nut (ft. lbs.)
2012	Beetle	P215/60R16	235/40R19	②	②	NS	89
		P235/45R18	215/60R16 ①	②	②	NS	89

NS: Not Specified

① Recommended winter tires

② See Vehicle Tire Information Sticker for correct inflation values.

71105_VWNB_C0011

BRAKE SPECIFICATIONS
All measurements in inches unless noted

Year	Model		Brake Disc Original Thickness	Brake Disc Minimum Thickness	Brake Disc Maximum Run-out	Drum Diameter Original Inside Diameter	Drum Diameter Maximum Machine Diameter	Minimum Lining Thickness	Brake Caliper Guide Pins (ft. lbs.)	Brake Caliper Mounting Bolts (ft. lbs.)
2012	Beetle	F	0.975	0.858	0.002	NS	NS	0.078	22	NS
		R	0.486	0.390	0.002	NS	NS	0.078	NS	35

NS: Not Specified

NOTE: Use minimum thickness noted on disc if different from specification.

Always use new bolts.

71105_VWNB_C0012

SCHEDULED MAINTENANCE INTERVALS
VOLKSWAGEN—Beetle

TO BE SERVICED	TYPE OF SERVICE	10	20	30	40	50	60	70	80	90	100	110	120
Auto Trans - fluid	R				✔				✔				✔
Battery - check	S/I		✔		✔		✔		✔		✔		✔
Body- inspect for corrosion	S/I		✔		✔		✔		✔		✔		✔
Brake Pad thickness - check	S/I	✔	✔	✔	✔	✔	✔	✔	✔	✔	✔	✔	✔
Brake system - inspection	S/I		✔		✔		✔		✔		✔		✔
Cooling System - level check	S/I				✔				✔				✔
CV Joints - leaks & damage	S/I				✔				✔				✔
Door Arresters - lubricate	S/I				✔				✔				✔
Engine Oil & Filter - replace	R	✔	✔	✔	✔	✔	✔	✔	✔	✔	✔	✔	✔
Engine Compartment - leaks & damage	S/I				✔				✔				✔
Exhaust System - inspection	S/I				✔				✔				✔
Headlights - Check and adjust	S/I				✔				✔				✔
Power Steering - level check	S/I				✔				✔				✔
Rotate wheels	S/I	✔	✔	✔	✔	✔	✔	✔	✔	✔	✔	✔	✔
Serpentine Belt - inspection	S/I				✔				✔				✔
Service Interval Display - reset	S/I	✔	✔	✔	✔	✔	✔	✔	✔	✔	✔	✔	✔
Spark Plugs (except 2.0L) - replace	R				✔				✔				✔
Spark Plugs (2.0L) - replace	R						✔						✔
Tie Rod Ends - play & boots	S/I				✔				✔				✔
Timing Belt - replace	R											✔	
Tires/Spare - inspection	S/I		✔		✔		✔		✔		✔		✔
Washer - clean nozzles	S/I	✔	✔	✔	✔	✔	✔	✔	✔	✔	✔	✔	✔
Wiper Blades - check	S/I	✔	✔	✔	✔	✔	✔	✔	✔	✔	✔	✔	✔
Air Cleaner - replace	Every 72 months												
Airbag System - inspect	Every 12 months												
Brake Fluid - replace	Every 24 months												
Cabin Air Filter - replace	Every 24 months												
Convertible roof latch - inspect	Every 24 months												
Spark Plugs - replace	Every 72 months												
Tire Filler Bottle - inspect	Every 24 months												
Tire Filler Bottle - replace	Every 48 months												
Tire Pressure Sensors - replace	Every 72 months												

R: Replace   S/I: Service or Inspect

71105_VWNB_C0013

PRECAUTIONS

Before servicing any vehicle, please be sure to read all of the following precautions, which deal with personal safety, prevention of component damage, and important points to take into consideration when servicing a motor vehicle:

• Never open, service or drain the radiator or cooling system when the engine is hot; serious burns can occur from the steam and hot coolant.

• Observe all applicable safety precautions when working around fuel. Whenever servicing the fuel system, always work in a well-ventilated area. Do not allow fuel spray or vapors to come in contact with a spark, open flame, or excessive heat (a hot drop light, for example). Keep a dry chemical fire extinguisher near the work area. Always keep fuel in a container specifically designed for fuel storage; also, always properly seal fuel containers to avoid the possibility of fire or explosion. Refer to the additional fuel system precautions later in this section.

• Fuel injection systems often remain pressurized, even after the engine has been turned **OFF**. The fuel system pressure must be relieved before disconnecting any fuel lines. Failure to do so may result in fire and/or personal injury.

• Brake fluid often contains polyglycol ethers and polyglycols. Avoid contact with the eyes and wash your hands thoroughly after handling brake fluid. If you do get brake fluid in your eyes, flush your eyes with clean, running water for 15 minutes. If eye irritation persists, or if you have taken brake fluid internally, IMMEDIATELY seek medical assistance.

• The EPA warns that prolonged contact with used engine oil may cause a number of skin disorders, including cancer. You should make every effort to minimize your exposure to used engine oil. Protective gloves should be worn when changing oil. Wash your hands and any other exposed skin areas as soon as possible after exposure to used engine oil. Soap and water, or waterless hand cleaner should be used.

• All new vehicles are now equipped with an air bag system, often referred to as a Supplemental Restraint System (SRS) or Supplemental Inflatable Restraint (SIR) system. The system must be disabled before performing service on or around system components, steering column, instrument panel components, wiring and sensors. Failure to follow safety and disabling procedures could result in accidental air bag deployment, possible personal injury and unnecessary system repairs.

• Always wear safety goggles when working with, or around, the air bag system. When carrying a non-deployed air bag, be sure the bag and trim cover are pointed away from your body. When placing a non-deployed air bag on a work surface, always face the bag and trim cover upward, away from the surface. This will reduce the motion of the module if it is accidentally deployed. Refer to the additional air bag system precautions later in this section.

• Clean, high quality brake fluid from a sealed container is essential to the safe and proper operation of the brake system. You should always buy the correct type of brake fluid for your vehicle. If the brake fluid becomes contaminated, completely flush the system with new fluid. Never reuse any brake fluid. Any brake fluid that is removed from the system should be discarded. Also, do not allow any brake fluid to come in contact with a painted surface; it will damage the paint.

• Never operate the engine without the proper amount and type of engine oil; doing so WILL result in severe engine damage.

• Timing belt maintenance is extremely important. Many models utilize an interference-type, non-freewheeling engine. If the timing belt breaks, the valves in the cylinder head may strike the pistons, causing potentially serious (also time-consuming and expensive) engine damage. Refer to the maintenance interval charts for the recommended replacement interval for the timing belt, and to the timing belt section for belt replacement and inspection.

• Disconnecting the negative battery cable on some vehicles may interfere with the functions of the on-board computer system(s) and may require the computer to undergo a relearning process once the negative battery cable is reconnected.

• When servicing drum brakes, only disassemble and assemble one side at a time, leaving the remaining side intact for reference.

• Only an MVAC-trained, EPA-certified automotive technician should service the air conditioning system or its components.

BRAKES

GENERAL INFORMATION

PRECAUTIONS

• Certain components within the ABS system are not intended to be serviced or repaired individually.

• Do not use rubber hoses or other parts not specifically specified for and ABS system. When using repair kits, replace all parts included in the kit. Partial or incorrect repair may lead to functional problems and require the replacement of components.

• Lubricate rubber parts with clean, fresh brake fluid to ease assembly. Do not use shop air to clean parts; damage to rubber components may result.

• Use only DOT 3 brake fluid from an unopened container.

• If any hydraulic component or line is removed or replaced, it may be necessary to bleed the entire system.

• A clean repair area is essential. Always clean the reservoir and cap thoroughly before removing the cap. The slightest amount of dirt in the fluid may plug an orifice and impair the system function. Perform repairs after components have been thoroughly cleaned; use only denatured alcohol to clean components. Do not allow ABS components to come into contact with any substance containing mineral oil; this includes used shop rags.

• The Anti-Lock control unit is a microprocessor similar to other computer units in

ANTI-LOCK BRAKE SYSTEM (ABS)

the vehicle. Ensure that the ignition switch is **OFF** before removing or installing controller harnesses. Avoid static electricity discharge at or near the controller.

• If any arc welding is to be done on the vehicle, the control unit should be unplugged before welding operations begin.

SPEED SENSORS

REMOVAL & INSTALLATION

Front

See Figure 1.

1. Raise the vehicle.
2. Separate speed sensor and speed sensor wiring connector.

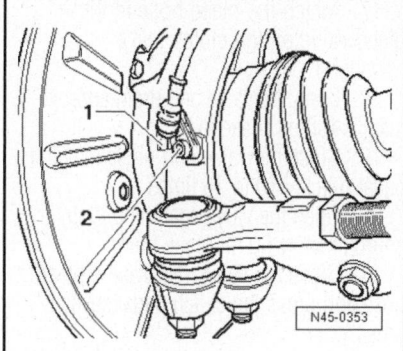

Fig. 1 Separate speed sensor and speed sensor wiring connector (1), Remove bolt (2)

3. Remove the bolt from wheel bearing housing.

4. Remove ABS speed sensor from wheel bearing housing.

Installing

5. Before inserting speed sensor, clean hole inner surface and coat speed sensor all-round with hot bolt paste G 052 112 A3.

6. Insert the speed sensor into the hole in the wheel bearing housing and tighten the bolt to 8 Nm.

7. Connect speed sensor to speed sensor wiring.

Rear

Disc

See Figure 2.

1. Raise vehicle.

2. Disconnect the connector.
3. Remove the bolt.
4. Remove the wheel speed sensor 1 from the wheel bearing housing.

To install:

5. Installation is performed in the reverse order of removal. Observe the following when doing so:

6. Clean the inside of the hole and coat it with hot bolt paste G 052 112 A3 before installing the wheel speed sensor.

7. Install the speed sensor into the hole in the rear axle and tighten it.

Drum

See Figure 3.

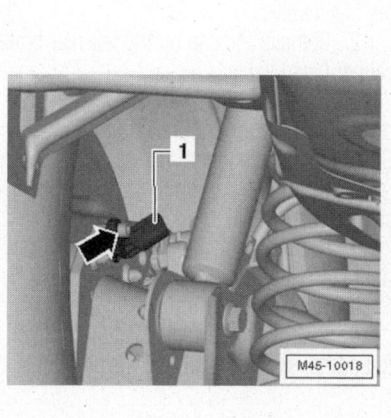

Fig. 2 Disconnect the connector (1), remove the bolt (arrow)

1. Raise the vehicle.
2. Disconnect the connector 1.
3. Remove the bolt.
4. Remove the wheel speed sensor 1 from the rear axle.

To install:

5. Installation is performed in the reverse order of removal. Observe the following when doing so:

6. Clean the inside of the hole and coat it with hot bolt paste G 052 112 A3 before installing the wheel speed sensor.

7. Install the wheel speed sensor into the hole in the rear axle and tighten it.

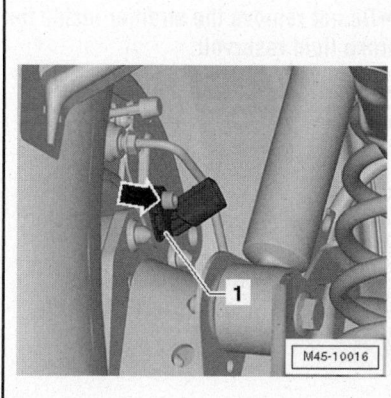

Fig. 3 Disconnect the connector (1), Remove the bolt (arrow)

BRAKES | BLEEDING THE BRAKE SYSTEM

BLEEDING PROCEDURE

BLEEDING PROCEDURE

1. Before servicing the vehicle, refer to the precautions.

✲✲ WARNING

Adhere strictly to work sequence when bleeding brake system.

2. Connect the brake charger/bleeder unit VAS 5234 or VAG 1869.

3. Open the bleeder valves in the prescribed sequence and bleed the brake calipers.
- Left front brake caliper
- Right front brake caliper
- Left rear brake caliper
- Right rear brake caliper

➡ **The bleeder hose must fit tightly on the bleeder valve so that no air can enter the brake system.**

4. With the bleeder bottle hose attached, leave the bleeder valve open long enough that brake fluid exits without bubbles.

5. Press the brake pedal forcefully and hold.

6. Open the bleeder valve at the brake caliper.

7. Press the brake pedal down until stopped.

8. Close the bleeder valve with the pedal pressed.

9. Release the brake pedal slowly.

✲✲ WARNING

This bleeding procedure must be performed 5 times per brake caliper.

10. Perform the bleeding sequence as follows:
- Left front brake caliper
- Right front brake caliper

- Left rear brake caliper
- Right rear brake caliper

✲✲ WARNING

A road test must be performed after bleeding. During this, at least one Anti-lock Brake System (ABS) stop must be performed!

POST BLEEDING

1. A second mechanic is required to assist:

a. Depress brake pedal forcefully and hold.

b. Open bleeder valve at brake caliper.

c. Press brake pedal down onto stop.

d. Close bleeder screw with pedal depressed.

e. Release brake pedal slowly.

2. This bleeding procedure must be performed 5 times per brake caliper.

3. Bleeding sequence:
   a. Front left brake caliper
   b. Front right brake caliper
   c. Left rear brake caliper
   d. Right rear brake caliper

4. A road test must be performed after bleeding. During this, at least one ABS regulation must be performed!

5. Install rear wheels.

FLUID CHANGE & FILL PROCEDURE

1. Remove the cap from the brake fluid reservoir.

2. Use the hose from the brake charger/bleeder unit VAS 5234 to extract as much brake fluid as possible.

➡**Do not remove the strainer inside the brake fluid reservoir.**

➡**Do not use extracted brake fluid again!**

3. Attach the adapter to the brake fluid reservoir.

4. Observe operating instructions for VAS 5234.

5. Set the correct pressure using a brake charger/bleeding unit VAS 5234.

6. Connect the hose from the brake charger/bleeding unit VAS 5234 to the adapter. Use a suitable bleed hose. It must seat tightly on the bleed valve so that no air can get into the brake system.

7. Remove the cap from the bleed valve on the left front brake caliper.

8. Connect collector bottle bleed hose to left front bleed valve. Then open the bleed valve and allow the corresponding quantity to flow out. Close the bleed valve.

9. Install the cap on the left front brake caliper bleed valve.

10. Repeat the same procedure on the right front side of the vehicle.

11. Remove both rear wheels to access the bleed valve.

12. Remove the cap on the left rear brake caliper bleed valve.

13. Open the bleed valve and let the corresponding amount of brake fluid flow out. Close the bleed valve.

14. Install the cap on the left rear brake caliper bleed valve.

15. Repeat the same procedure on the right rear side of the vehicle.

Manual Transmission

16. Remove the air filter housing. Refer to Engine, see Removal and Installation.

17. Attach the bleed hose to the bleed valve on the clutch slave cylinder 1.

18. Open the valve and drain approximately 100 ml brake fluid.

19. Close the value and press the clutch pedal quickly 10 to 15 times.

20. Open the valve again and drain approximately 50 ml brake fluid.

21. Close the valve, remove the bleed hose and press the clutch pedal several times.

22. Install the air filter housing in reverse order of removal.

23. Move filler lever on brake charger/bleeding unit VAS 5234 to "B" (see operating instructions).

24. Remove the filler hose from the adapter.

25. Remove the adapter from the brake fluid reservoir.

26. Check the brake fluid level and fill if necessary. It must be between 1 and 2.

27. Screw in cap for brake fluid reservoir.

28. Install the rear wheels, if necessary. Wheel Bolts, Tightening Specifications.

29. Perform a function test during the test drive.

BRAKES

FRONT DISC BRAKES

✳✳ CAUTION

Dust and dirt accumulating on brake parts during normal use may contain asbestos fibers from production or aftermarket brake linings. Breathing excessive concentrations of asbestos fibers can cause serious bodily harm. Exercise care when servicing brake parts. Do not sand or grind brake lining unless equipment used is designed to contain the dust residue. Do not clean brake parts with compressed air or by dry brushing. Cleaning should be done by dampening the brake components with a fine mist of water, then wiping the brake components clean with a dampened cloth. Dispose of cloth and all residue containing asbestos fibers in an impermeable container with the appropriate label. Follow practices prescribed by the Occupational Safety and Health Administration (OSHA) and the Environmental Protection Agency (EPA) for the handling, processing, and disposing of dust or debris that may contain asbestos fibers.

BRAKE CALIPER

REMOVAL & INSTALLATION

FN 3

See Figures 4 through 6.

Special Tools:
- Torque wrench V.A.G 1331
- Brake pedal depressor V.A.G 1869/2

➡**Work procedure applies only for replacing or when performing subsequent service work on brake caliper.**

1. Loosen wheel bolts.
2. Raise vehicle.
3. Remove wheel.
4. Pry the spring for the brake pads off the brake caliper with a screwdriver and remove it.
5. Remove the caps arrows.
6. Attach the bleeder bottle bleed hose to the brake caliper bleed valve.

7. Open the bleed valve.
8. Install the V.A.G 1869/2.
9. Close the bleed valve and remove the bleeder bottle.
10. Remove the brake hose threaded connection with the banjo bolt from the brake caliper.

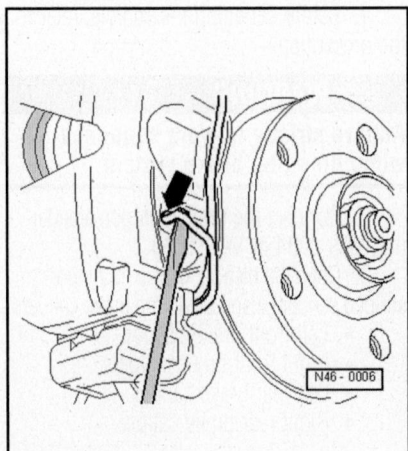

Fig. 4 Pry the spring for the brake pads off the brake caliper

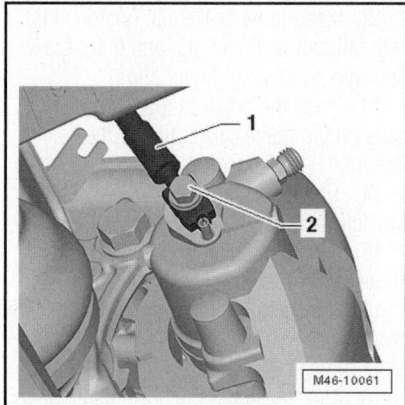

Fig. 5 Remove the brake hose threaded connection (1) with the banjo bolt (2)

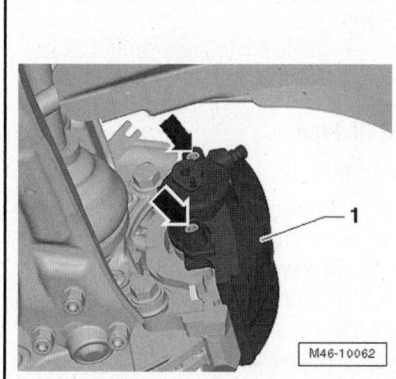

Fig. 6 Remove the guide pins arrows from the brake caliper 1

11. Seal off the brake line and the threaded hole immediately with plugs 1H0 698 311 A.

12. Remove the guide pins arrows from the brake caliper.

13. Remove the brake caliper from the brake carrier.

➡ **Do not blow brake system using compressed air, the dust produced is harmful to health!**

14. Cleaning: Clean brake caliper with mineral spirits exclusively.

To install:

15. Installation is performed in the reverse order of removal. Observe the following when doing so:

16. Before installing, clean carefully and check for wear and damage.

17. Thoroughly clean the contact surfaces on the brake carrier for the brake pads and remove any corrosion.

18. Condition: Piston is pressed back. Outer brake pad sits on brake carrier.

19. Insert inner brake pad with retaining spring in brake caliper (piston).

20. When installing brake caliper, make sure that brake pad is not affixed to brake caliper before the correct installation position has been reached.

21. Do not damage the adhesion surface.

22. Attach the brake caliper guide pins arrows and tighten them to 30 Nm.

23. Install both protective caps.

24. Attach the brake hose connection with the banjo bolt to the brake caliper and tighten it to 30 Nm.

25. Remove the V.A.G 1869/2.

26. Install the retaining spring in brake caliper.

27. Bleed the brake system. Refer to Brake System, Bleeding.

28. Install the wheel and tighten it.

29. Before moving vehicle, depress brake pedal several times firmly to properly seat brake pads in their normal operating position.

30. Check brake fluid level.

FS III

See Figures 7 through 9.

Special Tools:
- Torque wrench V.A.G 1331
- Brake pedal depressor V.A.G 1869/2

1. Work procedure applies only for replacing or when performing subsequent service work on brake caliper.

2. Loosen wheel bolts.

3. Raise vehicle.

4. Remove wheel.

5. Install the V.A.G 1869/2.

6. Attach the bleeder bottle bleed hose to the brake caliper bleed valve.

7. Open the bleed valve.

8. Close the bleed valve and remove the bleeder bottle.

9. Remove the caps arrows from the brake caliper bearing bushings.

10. Remove the brake hose connection with the banjo bolt from the brake caliper.

11. Seal off the brake line and the threaded hole immediately with plugs 1H0 698 311 A.

12. Loosen both guide pins arrows and remove them from the brake caliper.

13. Remove the brake caliper from the brake carrier.

14. Remove the brake pads from the brake caliper.

To install:

15. Installation is performed in the reverse order of removal. Observe the following when doing so:

16. Before installing, clean carefully and check for wear and damage.

17. Condition: Piston is pressed back.

18. Insert inner brake pad (piston side) and outer brake pad with retaining springs into brake caliper.

    a. Inside brake pad (piston side) with large 3-Finger clip.

    b. Outside brake pad with small 3-finger clip (black).

19. Install the brake caliper 1 with the brake pads 3 first at the bottom A of the brake carrier 2.

20. Condition: The pin B on the brake caliper 1 must be behind the brake carrier guide 2!

21. Attach the brake caliper to the brake carrier with both guide pins arrows and tighten.

22. Install both protective caps.

23. Attach the brake hose connection 1 with the banjo bolt 2 to the brake caliper.

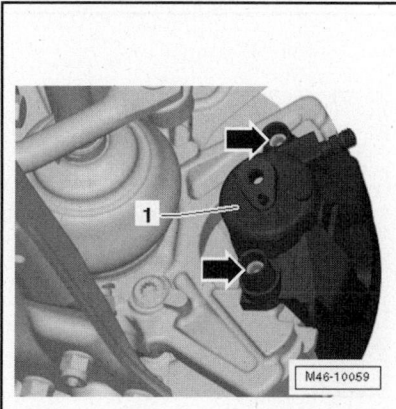

Fig. 7 Loosen both guide pins arrows and remove them from the brake caliper (1)

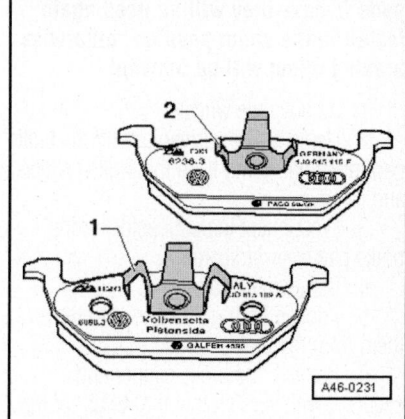

Fig. 8 Insert inner brake pad (piston side) (1) and outer brake pad (2)

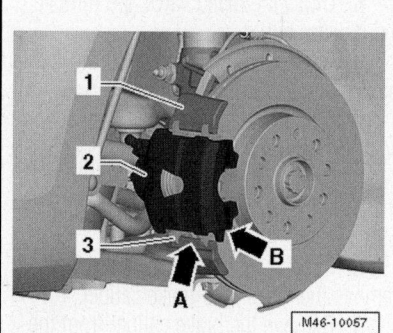

Fig. 9 Install the brake caliper (1) with the brake pads (3) first at the bottom (arrow A) of the brake carrier 2

24. Remove the V.A.G 1869/2.
25. Bleed the brake system. Refer to Brake System, Bleeding.
26. Install the wheels and tighten them.
27. Before moving vehicle, depress brake pedal several times firmly to properly seat brake pads in their normal operating position.
28. Check brake fluid level.
29. Tighten bolts/nuts to specification as follows:
- Guide pin to brake carrier (Use new bolts): 21 ft. lbs. (30 Nm)
- Brake line to brake caliper: 26 ft. lbs. (35 Nm)

DISC BRAKE PADS

REMOVAL & INSTALLATION

FN3 Type

See Figure 10.

➡**When removing, mark the brake pads in case they will be used again. Install in the same position, otherwise braking effect will be uneven!**

1. Remove the wheels.
2. Using a screwdriver, pry off the brake pad retaining spring from the brake caliper and remove.
3. Disconnect the connector for the brake pad wear indicator.
4. Remove the caps.
5. Loosen both guide pins and remove them from the brake caliper.
6. Remove the brake caliper and secure it with wire so that the weight of the caliper does not burden or damage the brake hose.
7. Remove the brake pads.

❋❋ CAUTION

Do not use compressed air to blow on the brake system components, the dust produced is harmful to health!

8. Thoroughly clean the contact surfaces for the brake pads at the brake carrier, removing any corrosion.
9. Clean the brake caliper, especially the adhesive contact surface for the brake pads, it must be free of residual adhesive and grease.

❋❋ WARNING

Use only appropriate solvents for cleaning the brake caliper.

To install:

❋❋ WARNING

Before pressing the piston into the cylinder bore, some brake fluid must be extracted from the brake fluid reservoir. Otherwise, especially if the reservoir has been topped off, fluid will overflow and cause damage.

10. Press the piston into the bore using the piston resetting tool T 10145.
11. If necessary, remove the protective foil on the backing plate of the outer brake pad. Install the outer brake pad to the brake carrier. Insert the inner brake pad with retaining spring in the brake caliper.

❋❋ WARNING

When installing the brake caliper, make sure that brake pad is not affixed to the brake caliper before the correct installation position has been reached. Do not damage the adhesion surface.

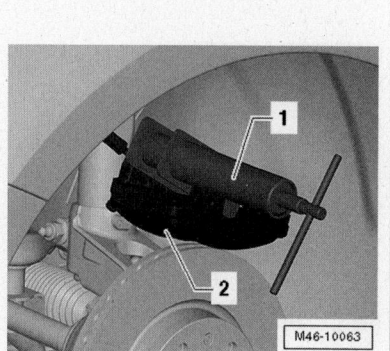

Fig. 10 Press the piston into the bore using the piston resetting tool T 10145

12. Insert inner brake pad (piston side) with large three finger clip and outer brake pad with small three finger clip.
13. Place the brake caliper with brake pads on the brake carrier first at the bottom.
14. Tighten guide pins and install both protective caps.
15. Install retaining spring to the brake caliper.
16. Connect the brake pad wear indicator connector.
17. Install the wheels.
18. After replacing the brake pads, press the brake pedal firmly several times with the vehicle stationary so that the brake pads are properly seated in their normal operating position.
19. Check the brake fluid level after replacing the brake pads.
20. Tighten bolts/nuts to specification as follows:
- Guide pin to brake carrier: 22 ft. lbs. (30 Nm)

FS III Type

See Figure 11.

1. Before servicing the vehicle, refer to the precautions.
2. Remove wheels.
3. Disconnect harness connector 1 on vehicles with brake pad wear indicator.
4. Remove protective caps.
5. Using screwdriver, pry off brake pad retaining spring from brake caliper housing and remove.
6. Unscrew and remove both guide pins from brake caliper housing.
7. Remove brake caliper housing and secure with wire so that the weight of the brake caliper housing does not stress or damage the brake hose.
8. Remove brake pads from brake caliper housing or from brake carrier.
9. Clean brake caliper housing, especially the adhesive surface for the brake pad, it must be free of residual adhesive and grease.

❋❋ WARNING

Use only appropriate solvents for cleaning brake caliper housing.

To install:

10. Press piston back into caliper housing using resetting tool before inserting new brake pads. Before pushing back the piston, siphon some of the brake fluid out of brake fluid reservoir. Otherwise, if reservoir has been topped off, fluid will overflow and cause damage.

11. Install the T10145 into the brake caliper and push the brake piston back.

12. Insert brake pads.

✳✳ WARNING

Brake pads are unidirectional. When installed, on the backing plate of brake pad must face downward. Make certain of this!

13. Install outer brake pad on brake carrier.

14. Remove protective foil on backing plate of outer brake pad.

15. Tighten brake caliper housing to brake carrier using both guide pins.

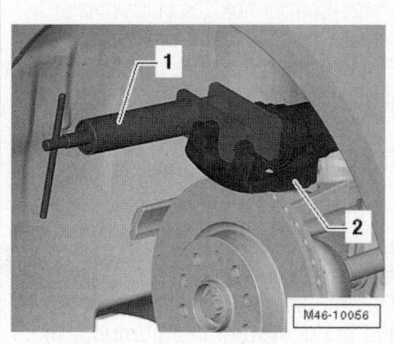

Fig. 11 Install the T10145 (1) into the brake caliper (2) and push the brake piston back

16. Install both protective caps.

17. Install retaining spring in brake caliper housing.

18. Insert connector for brake pad wear indicator into bracket at suspension strut.

19. Mount wheels.

20. After replacing brake pads and before moving vehicle, always depress brake pedal several times firmly to properly seat brake pads in their normal operating position.

21. Check brake fluid level after replacing brake pad.

22. Tighten bolts/nuts to specification as follows:

- Guide pin to brake carrier: 21–22 ft. lbs. (28–30 Nm)

BRAKES

✳✳ CAUTION

Dust and dirt accumulating on brake parts during normal use may contain asbestos fibers from production or aftermarket brake linings. Breathing excessive concentrations of asbestos fibers can cause serious bodily harm. Exercise care when servicing brake parts. Do not sand or grind brake lining unless equipment used is designed to contain the dust residue. Do not clean brake parts with compressed air or by dry brushing. Cleaning should be done by dampening the brake components with a fine mist of water, then wiping the brake components clean with a dampened cloth. Dispose of cloth and all residue containing asbestos fibers in an impermeable container with the appropriate label. Follow practices prescribed by the Occupational Safety and Health Administration (OSHA) and the Environmental Protection Agency (EPA) for the handling, processing, and disposing of dust or debris that may contain asbestos fibers.

BRAKE CALIPER

REMOVAL & INSTALLATION

C38 Type

See Figure 12.

➡**All other brake caliper types are similar in removal and installation.**

➡**When removing, mark the brake pads in case they will be used again. Install in the same position, otherwise braking effect will be uneven!**

1. Remove the wheels.
2. Unhook the brake cable from the lever on the brake caliper.
3. Remove the spring clip and pull the

REAR DISC BRAKES

brake cable from the holder on the brake caliper.

4. Connect the bleeder hose from the bleeder bottle to the bleeder valve on the brake caliper and then open the bleeder valve.

5. Install the brake pedal actuator VAG 1869/2.

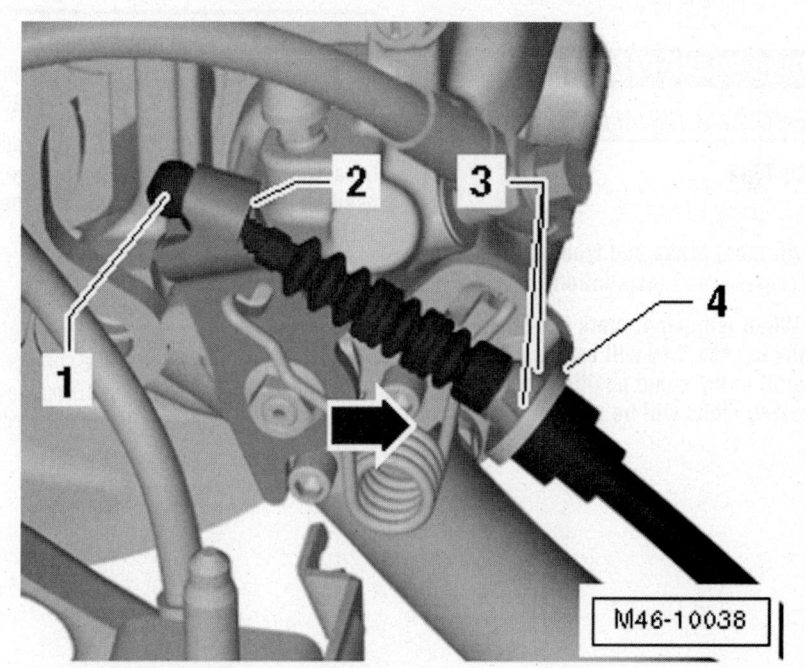

1. Parking brake cable
2. Brake caliper
3. Tabs
4. Bracket

Fig. 12 Push the lever on the brake caliper 2 in direction of.

6. Close the bleeder valve and remove the bleeder bottle.

7. Remove the brake line.

8. Remove both bolts from the brake caliper, counter hold on the guide pins when doing this.

9. Pull off the brake caliper from brake carrier.

To install:

10. Piston is pressed back into caliper.

11. Brake pads sit in the anti-rattle springs in the brake carrier.

12. Secure the brake caliper to the brake carrier using the new self-locking bolts.

13. Install the brake line to the brake caliper.

14. Bleed the brake system.

15. Hook in the brake cable and secure it to the holder with the spring clip.

16. Adjust the parking brake.

17. Install the wheels.

18. Before moving the vehicle, press the brake pedal firmly several times to properly seat the brake pads in their normal operating position.

19. Check the brake fluid level.

20. Tighten bolts/nuts to specification as follows:

- Bolt, brake caliper to brake carrier (Use new bolts): 26 ft. lbs. (35 Nm)
- Brake line to brake caliper: 26 ft. lbs. (35 Nm)

DISC BRAKE PADS

REMOVAL & INSTALLATION

C38 Type

See Figures 13 and 14.

➡All other brake pad types are similar in removal and installation.

➡When removing, mark the brake pads in case they will be used again. Install in the same position, otherwise braking effect will be uneven!

1. Remove the wheels.

2. Counter hold the guide pins and remove the bolts for the brake caliper.

3. Remove the brake caliper and secure it with wire so that the weight of the brake caliper does not burden or damage the brake hose.

4. Remove the brake pads and anti-rattle springs.

✳✳ CAUTION

Do not use compressed air to blow on the brake system components, the dust produced is harmful to health!

5. Contact surfaces between the brake pads and brake carrier must be cleaned, removing any corrosion.

6. Clean the brake caliper.

✳✳ WARNING

Use only appropriate solvents for cleaning brake caliper.

To install:

✳✳ WARNING

Before pressing the piston into the cylinder bore, some brake fluid must be extracted from the brake fluid reservoir. Otherwise, especially if the reservoir has been topped off, fluid will overflow and cause damage.

7. Press the piston into the bore using the resetting & extracting tool T 10165 and 1065/1. Do not damage the protective caps.

➡For pistons that are difficult to press in, a 13 mm open end wrench can be used on the resetting & extracting tool T 10165.

8. Insert the brake pad anti-rattle springs and brake pads to the brake carrier.

9. Make sure that the brake pads are located correctly in the anti-rattle springs.

10. Secure the brake caliper using the new self-locking bolts to 26 ft. lbs. (35 Nm)

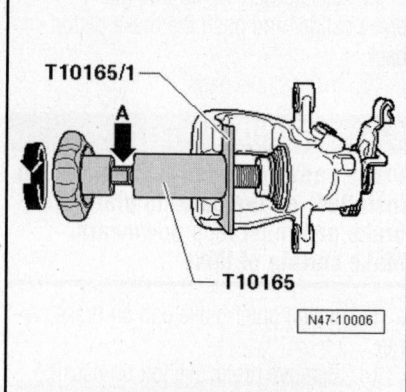

Fig. 13 Press the piston into the bore using the resetting & extracting tool T 10165 and 1065/1. Do not damage the protective caps

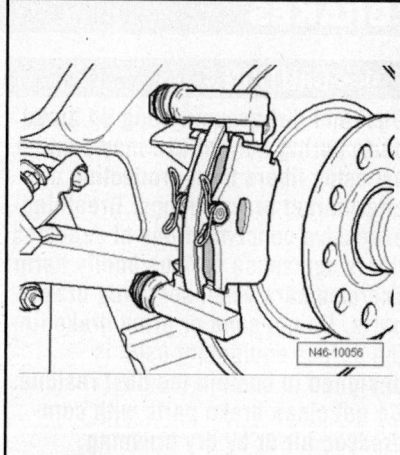

Fig. 14 Make sure that the brake pads are located correctly in the anti-rattle springs

11. Install the wheels.

12. After replacing the brake pads, press the brake pedal firmly several times with the vehicle stationary so that the brake pads are properly seated in their normal operating position.

13. Check the brake fluid level after replacing brake pad.

BRAKES

REAR DRUM BRAKES

BRAKE DRUM

REMOVAL & INSTALLATION

See Figure 15.

1. Loosen wheel bolts.
2. Raise vehicle.
3. Remove wheel.
4. Push the brake back with a screwdriver. Refer to Reset Brake, Rear Drum Brakes.

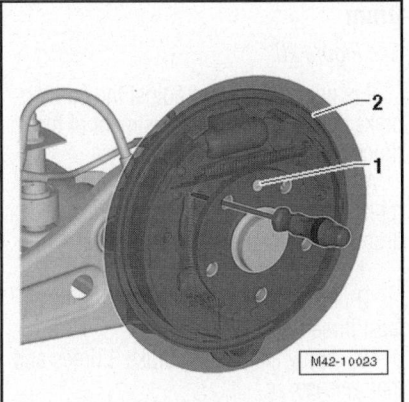

Fig. 15 Remove the bolt (1). Remove the brake drum (2)

5. Remove the bolt.
6. Remove the brake drum evenly.

➡**Do not blow brake system using compressed air, the dust produced is harmful to health!**

7. Use only appropriate solvents for cleaning brake system.

To install:

8. Installation is performed in the reverse order of removal. Observe the following when doing so:
9. Clean carefully and check for wear and damage, make sure the dimensions are correct and that the brake surface is perfect.
10. Install the brake drum evenly over the brake pads. Be careful not to tilt the brake drum.
11. Install the wheel and tighten it.
12. Adjust the parking brake. Refer to Parking Brake, Adjusting, with Rear Drum Brakes.

BRAKE SHOES

REMOVAL & INSTALLATION

See Figures 16 through 18.

After replacing the brake cylinder, the brake pads and the brake shoes, press the brake pedal once so that the brake shoes are properly seated.

Use the brake charger/bleeder unit VAS 5234 to extract the brake fluid form the brake fluid reservoir.

Before removing a brake cylinder, a brake carrier or disconnecting a brake hose from the brake cylinder, the brake pedal loading device V.A.G 1869/2 should be installed (relieve pressure).

- Bracket with spindle and hook 3438
- Torque wrench V.A.G 1331

Removing

1. Loosen wheel bolts.
2. Raise vehicle.
3. Remove wheel.
4. Reset the brake. Refer to Reset Brake, Rear Drum Brakes.
5. Remove the brake drum. Refer to Brake Drum.
6. Remove the spring plate and pressure springs.
7. Press against the spring and twist 90°.
8. Disengage the return spring downward using the special tool 3438.
9. Pry out the lower brake shoe with a screwdriver.

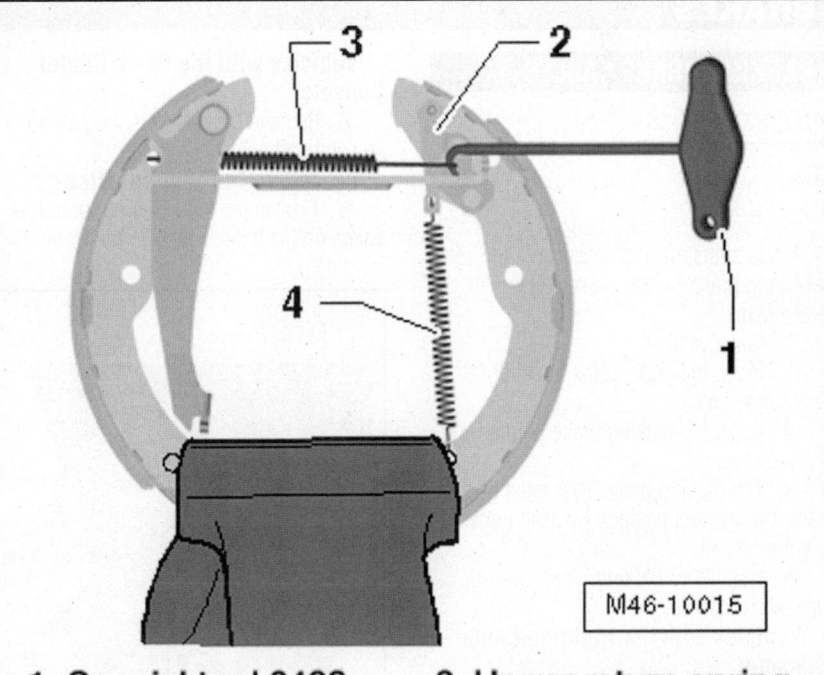

1. **Special tool 3438**
2. **Wedge**
3. **Upper return spring**
4. **Tension spring**

Fig. 16 Disassembling the brake pad assembly—Left pad

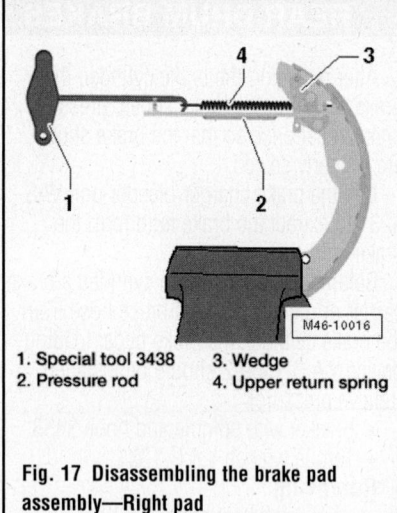

1. Special tool 3438   3. Wedge
2. Pressure rod   4. Upper return spring

Fig. 17 Disassembling the brake pad assembly—Right pad

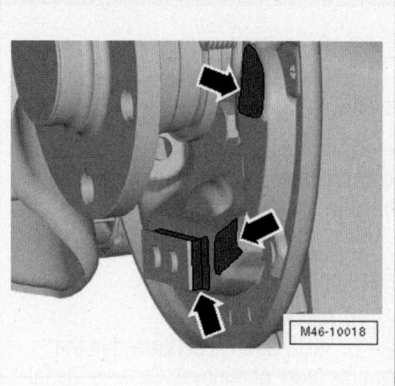

Fig. 18 Identifying lubrication contact surfaces

10. Lay the brake shoe on the support plate.

11. Disengage the parking brake cable.

12. Remove the brake shoes between the wheel hub and the brake carrier.

Disassembling

13. Clamp brake shoes into vise.

14. Remove the tension spring for the wedge.

15. Disengage the upper return spring.

16. Disengage the contact spring.

17. Remove the pressure rod and wedge from the brake shoe.

➡**Do not blow brake system using compressed air, the dust produced is harmful to health!**

18. Cleaning: Use only appropriate solvents for cleaning brake system.

To install:

19. Installation is performed in the reverse order of removal. Observe the following when doing so:

20. Hook the contact spring into the pressure rod.

21. Engage the wedge at the same time.

Installation position:

22. The elevation must be visible when installing.

23. Attach the brake shoe with the parking brake lever to the pressure rod.

24. Attach the return spring.

25. Engage the tension spring for the wedge. Lubricate the contact surfaces for the brake shoes on the support plate and on the brake carrier (distributed on the circumference; 6 places) with adhesive lubricating paste G 000 650.

26. Install the brake shoes between the wheel hub and the brake carrier.

27. Mount the brake shoes on the brake cylinder piston.

28. Attach the parking brake cable to the parking brake lever.

29. Install the return spring at the bottom using the 3438.

30. Pry the brake shoe behind the lower support.

31. Install the spring plate with the pressure spring and turn it 90°.

32. Install the brake drum.

33. Install the wheels and tighten them.

34. Adjust the parking brake. Refer to Parking Brake, Adjusting, with Rear Drum Brakes.

BRAKES

PARKING BRAKE CABLES

ADJUSTMENT

Disc

See Figure 19.

A new adjustment is necessary only after replacing brake cables, brake calipers or brake discs.

1. Raise vehicle.

2. Press the brake pedal forcefully at least three times.

3. Apply the parking brake 3 times and then release.

4. The parking brake lever must go back into the rest position by itself under the first detent.

5. Condition: Parking brake lever in released position.

Vehicles with the Highline Center Console

6. Open the cover on the rear storage compartment.

7. Remove the mat from the storage compartment.

Vehicles with the Basis Center Console

8. Remove the mat from the rear storage compartment.

Procedure for Both Vehicles

9. Tighten the adjusting nut until the levers on the brake calipers start to lift.

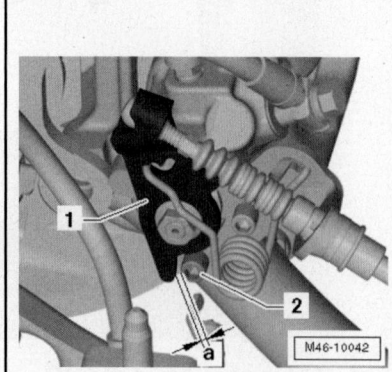

Fig. 19 The distance a between the lever 1 to the stop 2 on the left and right brake calipers may be ≤ 1.5 mm together

PARKING BRAKE

10. The distance a between the lever 1 to the stop 2 on the left and right brake calipers may be ≤ 1.5 mm together.

11. Check whether wheels turn freely.

12. Due to the automatic rear brake adjuster, there is no need to adjust the parking brake after making initial adjustment.

Drum

See Figure 20.

It is not necessary to adjust the parking brake due to automatic adjustment of the drum brakes on the rear axle.

An adjustment is necessary only after replacing parking brake cables, brake drums, brake carriers or brake pads.

1. Raise vehicle.

2. Press the brake pedal forcefully at least three times.

3. Apply the parking brake 3 times and then release.

4. The parking brake lever must go back into the rest position by itself under the first detent.

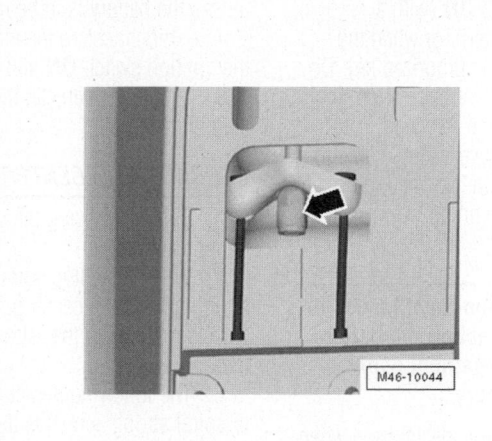

Fig. 20 Tighten the adjusting nut (arrow)

M46-10044

5. Condition: Parking brake lever in released position.

6. Engage parking brake 4 teeth.

Vehicles with the Highline Center Console

7. Open the cover on the rear storage compartment.

8. Remove the mat from the storage compartment.

Vehicles with the Basis Center Console

9. Remove the mat from the rear storage compartment.

Procedure for Both Vehicles

10. Tighten the adjusting nut enough until both wheels can only be moved with difficulty by hand.

11. Release the parking brake.

12. Condition: Parking brake lever in released position.

CHASSIS ELECTRICAL

AIR BAG (SUPPLEMENTAL RESTRAINT SYSTEM)

GENERAL INFORMATION

✳✳ CAUTION

These vehicles are equipped with an air bag system. The system must be disarmed before performing service on, or around, system components, the steering column, instrument panel components, wiring and sensors. Failure to follow the safety precautions and the disarming procedure could result in accidental air bag deployment, possible injury and unnecessary system repairs.

SERVICE PRECAUTIONS

Disconnect and isolate the battery negative cable before beginning any airbag system component diagnosis, testing, removal, or installation procedures. Allow system capacitor to discharge for two minutes before beginning any component service. This will disable the airbag system. Failure to disable the airbag system may result in accidental airbag deployment, personal injury, or death.

Do not place an intact undeployed airbag face down on a solid surface. The airbag will propel into the air if accidentally deployed and may result in personal injury or death.

When carrying or handling an undeployed airbag, the trim side (face) of the airbag should be pointing away from the body to minimize possibility of injury if accidental deployment occurs. Failure to do this may result in personal injury or death.

Replace airbag system components with OEM replacement parts. Substitute parts may appear interchangeable, but internal differences may result in inferior occupant protection. Failure to do so may result in occupant personal injury or death.

Wear safety glasses, rubber gloves, and long sleeved clothing when cleaning powder residue from vehicle after an airbag deployment. Powder residue emitted from a deployed airbag can cause skin irritation. Flush affected area with cool water if irritation is experienced. If nasal or throat irritation is experienced, exit the vehicle for fresh air until the irritation ceases. If irritation continues, see a physician.

Do not use a replacement airbag that is not in the original packaging. This may result in improper deployment, personal injury, or death.

The factory installed fasteners, screws and bolts used to fasten airbag components have a special coating and are specifically designed for the airbag system. Do not use substitute fasteners. Use only original equipment fasteners listed in the parts catalog when fastener replacement is required.

During, and following, any child restraint anchor service, due to impact event or vehicle repair, carefully inspect all mounting hardware, tether straps, and anchors for proper installation, operation, or damage. If a child restraint anchor is found damaged in any way, the anchor must be replaced. Failure to do this may result in personal injury or death.

Deployed and non-deployed airbags may or may not have live pyrotechnic material within the airbag inflator.

Do not dispose of driver/passenger/curtain airbags or seat belt tensioners unless you are sure of complete deployment. Refer to the Hazardous Substance Control System for proper disposal.

Dispose of deployed airbags and tensioners consistent with state, provincial, local, and federal regulations.

After any airbag component testing or service, do not connect the battery negative cable. Personal injury or death may result if the system test is not performed first.

If the vehicle is equipped with the Occupant Classification System (OCS), do not connect the battery negative cable before performing the OCS Verification Test using the scan tool and the appropriate diagnostic information. Personal injury or death may result if the system test is not performed properly.

Never replace both the Occupant Restraint Controller (ORC) and the Occupant Classification Module (OCM) at the same time. If both require replacement, replace one, then perform the Airbag System test before replacing the other.

Both the ORC and the OCM store Occupant Classification System (OCS) calibration data, which they transfer to one another when one of them is replaced. If both are replaced at the same time, an irreversible fault will be set in both modules and the OCS may malfunction and cause personal injury or death.

If equipped with OCS, the Seat Weight Sensor is a sensitive, calibrated unit and must be handled carefully. Do not drop or handle roughly. If dropped or damaged, replace with another sensor. Failure to do so may result in occupant injury or death.

If equipped with OCS, the front passenger seat must be handled carefully as well. When removing the seat, be careful when setting on floor not to drop. If dropped, the sensor may be inoperative, could result in occupant injury, or possibly death.

If equipped with OCS, when the passenger front seat is on the floor, no one should sit in the front passenger seat. This uneven force may damage the sensing ability of the seat weight sensors. If sat on and damaged, the sensor may be inoperative, could result in occupant injury, or possibly death.

DISARMING THE SYSTEM

➡ **The Anti-theft system must be deactivated before disconnecting the battery to avoid system engagement upon reconnecting the battery.**

The Anti-theft system is deactivated when the vehicle is unlocked via the unlock button on the key fob, or when the vehicle is

opened via Keyless Access, or when the ignition switch is turned **ON** (with a charged battery connected), or when the immobilizer registers an authorized key. Do not disconnect the positive battery terminal unless the battery is to be removed.

Disconnect the negative battery cable to disarm the airbag system. No waiting time is necessary before beginning work.

ARMING THE SYSTEM

➡ **The Anti-theft system must be deactivated before disconnecting the battery to avoid system engagement upon reconnecting the battery.**

The Anti-theft system is deactivated when the vehicle is unlocked via the unlock button on the key fob, or when the vehicle is opened via Keyless Access, or when the ignition switch is turned **ON** (with a charged battery connected), or when the immobilizer registers an authorized key. Do

not disconnect the positive battery terminal unless the battery is to be removed.

After reconnecting the airbag wiring, turn the ignition switch **ON** and make sure no one is inside the vehicle, then connect the battery cable.

CLOCKSPRING CENTERING

1. Before servicing the vehicle, refer to the precautions.

2. When installing spiral spring, spiral spring must be in center position and wheels must be in the "straight ahead position".

3. The following depicts center position of spiral spring, which is dependent on the manufacturer.

   a. The color marked (black square) band must be located in viewing window.

   b. The color marked (yellow) band must be located in viewing window.

DRIVE TRAIN

AUTOMATIC TRANSAXLE FLUID

DRAIN AND REFILL

See Figures 21 through 23.

Use the Direct Shift Gearbox (DSG) transmission fluid as a replacement part. Refer to the Parts Catalog. Short Description

First, the fluid temperature is read out. If it is higher than 122°F), then let the transmission cool down.

Turn off the engine, remove the overflow tube and drain any transmission fluid. Install the overflow tube and overfill the transmission fluid.

Start the engine and drain any excess fluid until the level has reached the overflow tube.

Tools:
• Vehicle Diagnosis, Testing and Information System VAS 5051B
• Oil Collecting and Extracting Device V.A.G 1782
• Adapter for Oil Filling VAS 6262 A

Requirements
• The engine is off.
• The vehicle is level and all hoist supports are the same height.
• The noise insulation is removed if necessary
• The selector level is in the "P" position.
• The vehicle diagnosis, testing and information system VAS 5051B is connected.

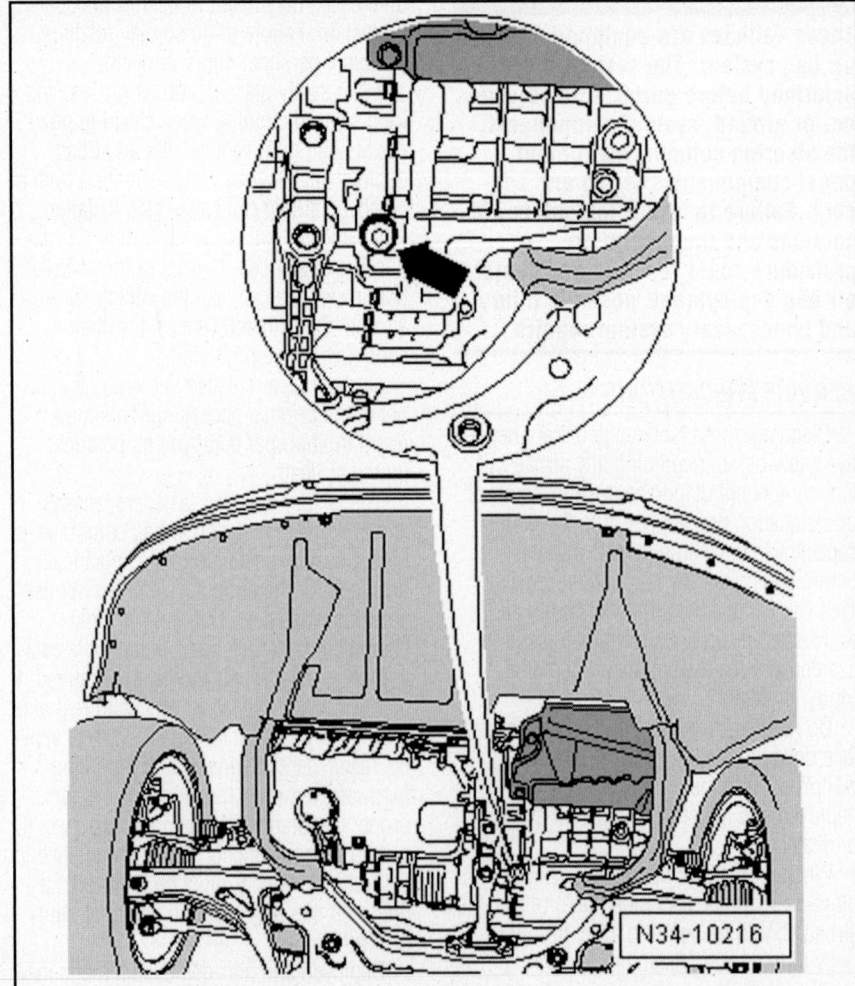

Fig. 21 Remove the drain plug (arrow) near the pendulum support

N34-10216

- The transmission fluid should not be warmer than 45°C (113°F) when starting the procedure.

Procedure

1. Follow the rules of cleanliness when working on the transmission.

2. Only use the transmission fluid for the DSG available as a replacement part. Other fluids can cause malfunctions or transmission failure.

➡**Risk of injury due to hot transmission fluid.**

3. Connect the vehicle diagnosis, testing and information system VAS 5051B and identify the vehicle in Guided Functions.

4. Select DSG transmission.

5. Select Check Fluid Level.

6. Let the transmission cool down if the fluid temperature is higher than 113°F.

➡**Do not start the engine if there is no transmission fluid in the transmission.**

7. Engine off - do not start!

8. Remove the drain plug near the pendulum support.

9. A black plastic overflow tube is located in this hole (with a 8 mm hex socket head). Its length determines the oil level in the transmission.

10. Remove the overflow tube and let the fluid drain.

➡**About 5 liters of fluid will drain out.**

11. Install the overflow tube and tighten it.

12. Install the adapter for oil filling VAS 6262 A into the hole hand tight.

13. Shake the bottle before opening.

14. Fill with 5.5 liters of fluid.

15. To change containers, close the shutoff lever or hold the adapter for oil fill-

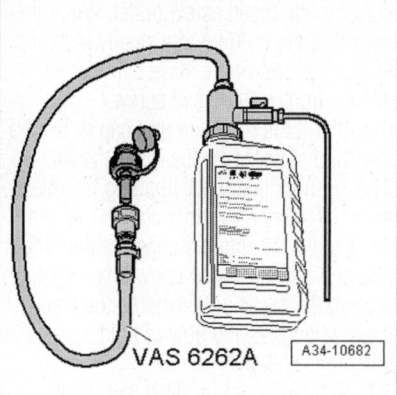

Fig. 23 Install the adapter for oil filling VAS 6262 A into the hole hand tight

ing VAS 6262 A higher than the transmission.

16. Install and tighten the drain plug hand tight.

17. Start the engine.

18. Press the brake pedal and select each selector lever position for approximately 3 seconds, then move the selector lever back into the "P" position.

19. Do not turn off the engine.

20. Check the fluid level and fill if necessary.

FILTER REPLACEMENT

See Figures 24 and 25.

When To Change the Oil Filter

The transmission fluid filter does not need to be changed in every case.

Do not replace the filter if:

1. The transmission oil cooler or its O-rings were replaced and no coolant has gotten into the fluid.

2. The selector shaft seal was replaced.

3. The flange or stub shaft seal was replaced.

4. Leaking Mechatronic covers, the multi-plate clutch or the oil pump were replaced.

5. The transmission input speed sensor G182 with clutch oil temperature sensor G509 was replaced.

The filter must be replaced if:

6. The 60,000 km maintenance interval was reached.

7. Coolant has entered the fluid.

8. Metal shavings were found in the fluid.

9. The clutch is burned or has a mechanical fault.

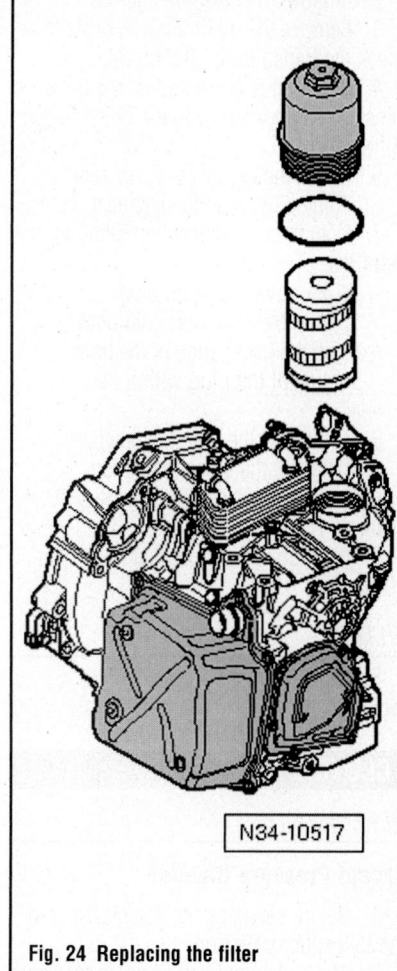

Fig. 24 Replacing the filter

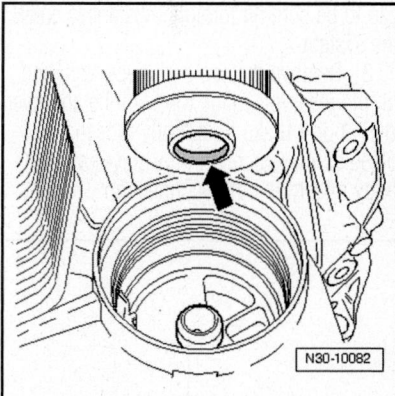

Fig. 25 Install the new filter with the seat facing downward and tighten the housing to 20 Nm

MANUAL TRANSAXLE FLUID

DRAIN AND REFILL

See Figure 26.

1. For the correct transmission fluid, refer to the Parts Catalog.

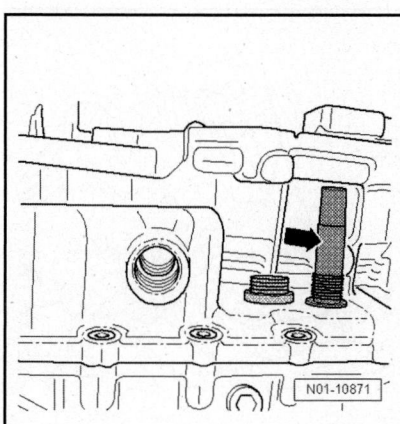

Fig. 22 Remove the overflow tube (arrow) and let the fluid drain

2. Remove the noise insulation.

3. Remove the oil fill plug in order to check the transmission fluid level.

4. The level is correct when the transmission fluid comes up to the bottom edge of hole.

5. Install the plug with a new seal.

6. Tighten the plug to specification.

7. Note the following when filling for the first time:

a. Remove the oil fill plug.

b. Add transmission fluid until it reaches the lower edge of the hole.

c. Install the plug with a new seal.

d. Tighten the plug to specification.

e. Install the noise insulation.

8. I - Plug with a multi-point socket head, 45 Nm

9. II - Plug with hex socket head, 30 Nm

FILTER

Refer to Automatic Transaxle filter replacement.

CLUTCH

BLEEDING

Except Pressure Bleeder

1. Before servicing the vehicle, refer to the Precautions Section.

2. The clutch and brakes share the same reservoir. Clean all dirt and grease from the cap to be sure no foreign substances enter the system.

3. Remove the cap and diaphragm and fill the reservoir to the top with the approved DOT 3 or 4 brake fluid. Fully loosen the bleed screw which is in the slave cylinder body next to the inlet connection.

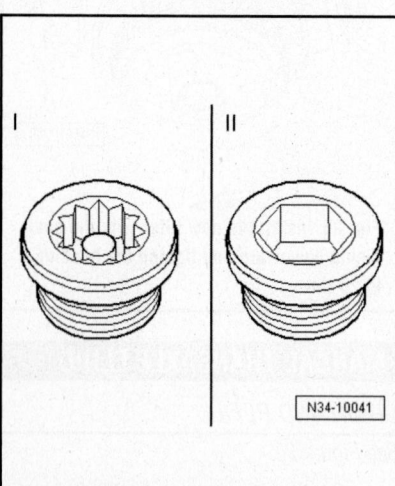

Fig. 26 Different Versions of the Oil Fill and Drain Plugs

4. At this point bubbles of air will appear at the bleed screw outlet. When the slave cylinder is full and a steady stream of fluid comes out of the slave cylinder bleeder, tighten the bleed screw.

5. Refill the reservoir and cap it. Exert a light load of about 20 lbs. (9 kg) to the slave cylinder piston by pushing the release lever towards the cylinder and loosen the bleed screw. Maintain a constant light load; fluid and any air that is left will be expelled through the bleed port. Tighten the bleed screw when a steady flow of fluid with no air is being expelled.

6. Fill the reservoir fluid level back to normal capacity, if necessary repeat Step 4.

7. Exert a light load to the release lever but do not open the bleeder screw as the piston in the slave cylinder will move slowly down the bore. Repeat this operation 2–3 times; the fluid movement will force any air left in the system into the reservoir. The hydraulic system should now be fully bled.

8. Check the operation of the clutch hydraulic system and repeat this procedure, if necessary.

Pressure Bleeder

1. Before servicing the vehicle, refer to the precautions.

2. Remove entire air filter housing if bleeder is not accessible through it.

3. Connect brake filler/bleeder unit VAS 5234 or V.A.G 1869.

➡ **If necessary, use bleeder hose (670 mm long) V.A.G 1238/B3 to bleed system.**

4. Connect bleeder hose to collector bottle of brake bleeder unit.

5. Connect bleeder hose to bleeder.

6. Pressurize the system to 29 psi (2 bar).

7. Open bleeder valve approximately 1/4 rotation.

8. Move the clutch pedal 15 to 20 times rapidly by hand from stop to stop.

9. Close bleeder valve and switch bleeder device off.

10. After completing the bleeding procedure, if a pressure of 29 psi (2 bar) has been released, operate brake pedal 10 times using the foot.

11. If removed, install entire air filter housing.

FLUID FILL PROCEDURE

Refer to Brakes.

FRONT HALFSHAFT

REMOVAL & INSTALLATION

See Figure 27.

1. Before servicing the vehicle, refer to the precautions.

2. Loosen drive axle bolt to wheel hub

3. When doing this, vehicle must not stand on wheels, otherwise wheel bearing may be damaged.

4. Remove wheel.

5. Remove lower noise insulation.

6. Remove nuts.

7. Pull wheel bearing housing with ball joint out of control arm.

8. Pull drive axle out of wheel hub and secure to body.

9. Attach wedge tool T10161 between transmission housing and triple roller joint.

10. Press inner joint out of transmission by tapping with hammer onto wedge tool T10161.

11. Remove drive axle.

To install:

12. Insert new securing ring into groove of joint piece pin.

13. Mesh outer and inner splines of joint piece and transmission.

14. Grasp drive axle by hand and slide into joint piece until stop.

15. Slide joint piece into transmission with a "jerk".

Sliding part in joint piece can be used for this "jerk". Do not pull drive axle out of joint piece too far when doing this.

16. Do not use hammer or other knocking tool under any circumstance!

17. Check drive axle in transmission for proper seating by pulling joint piece against resistance from circlip.

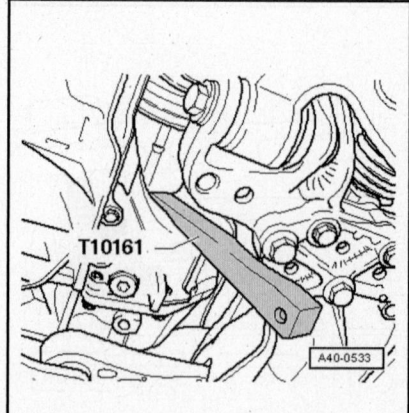

Fig. 27 Press inner joint out of transmission by tapping with hammer onto wedge tool T10161

➡**For this check, do not pull drive axle but pull joint piece only.**

18. Insert outer joint as far as possible into wheel hub splines.

19. Remove lower noise insulation.

20. Bolt on ball joint with control arm.

21. Ensure that boot is not damaged or twisted.

22. Tighten drive axle bolt to wheel hub.

23. When doing this, vehicle must not stand on wheels, otherwise wheel bearing may be damaged.

24. Install wheel.

25. Tighten bolts/nuts to specification as follows:

- Ball joint to control arm (Use new nut): 44 ft. lbs. (60 Nm)
- Drive axle to wheel hub "hex head bolt" (Use new bolt): 148 ft. lbs. (200 Nm) 180° additional rotation
- Drive axle to wheel hub" 12-point bolt" (Use new bolt): 52 ft. lbs. (70 Nm) plus 90° additional rotation
- Drive axle to wheel hub "hex head bolt" (Use new bolt): 148 ft. lbs. (200 Nm) 180° additional rotation
- Drive axle to wheel hub" 12-point bolt" (Use new bolt): 52 ft. lbs. (70 Nm) plus 90° additional rotation

FRONT FLANGE SHAFT SEAL

REMOVAL & INSTALLATION

Automatic Transaxle

See Figures 28 through 31.

➡**Transmission in vehicle.**

1. Only the left side is described here. Replacing the right side seal is almost the same.

2. On the right, the drive axle remains in the wheel bearing, use the T10177, on the left side, remove the drive axle and use the T10176.

3. Necessary tools:
- Drip tray V.A.G 1306
- PullerT10055
- Thrust pieceT10176

4. Remove the noise insulation.

5. Place the VAG 1306 underneath.

6. Remove the left ball joint lower nuts arrows from the control arm.

7. Press the drive axle out of the transmission.

Right Side

8. Place the right drive axle as far upward as possible and secure it in this position.

Left Side

➡**Do not set the vehicle on the floor.**

9. Press the brake in order to remove the left drive axle bolt.

10. Remove the left drive axle.

11. Seal the opening of the drive axle at the transmission using clean cloth.

12. Carefully drill a hole B (2 to 4 millimeters (mm) in size) into the outer metal ring C of the seal.

a. Grease the drill bit B so that the drill shavings remain held.

b. Drill only through the metal ring C, otherwise the transmission may be damaged.

13. Install a screw (approximately 4 mm in diameter) into the drilled hole in the seal. Do not install the screw too deeply to prevent damage to bearing lying behind it.

14. Pull out the seal using T10055 and T10055/2.

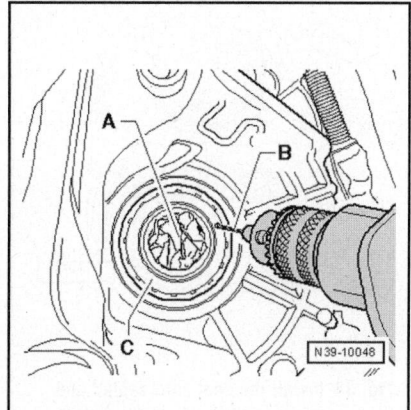

Fig. 28 Drill a hole (B) (2 to 4 millimeters (mm) in size) into the outer metal ring (C) of the seal

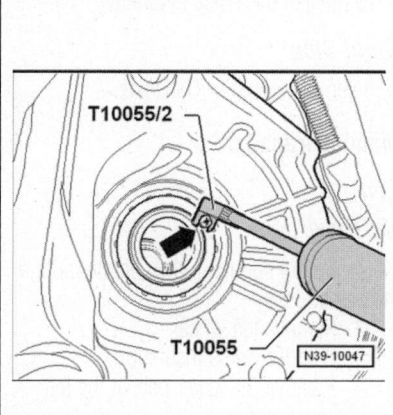

Fig. 29 Pull out the seal using T10055 and T10055/2

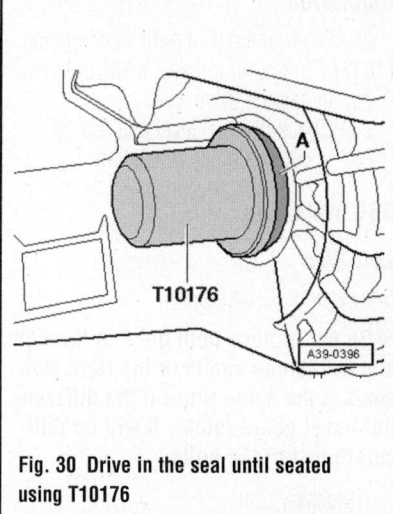

Fig. 30 Drive in the seal until seated using T10176

15. Remove the cloth and thoroughly clean the transmission and opening for the drive axle.

16. Metal shavings must not get into the transmission or into the opening for the drive axle, vacuum up the shavings if necessary.

17. If only the metal ring of the seal could be removed, carefully pry out the remaining seal using screwdriver.

To install:

18. Installation is performed in the reverse order of removal. Pay attention to the following:

19. Lubricate the outer circumference and sealing lips of the seal with Automatic Transmission Fluid (ATF).

20. Installed position: The open side of the seal faces the transmission.

21. Install the seal by hand as far as possible.

Left Side

Drive in the seal until seated using T10176, do not tilt the seal while doing this.

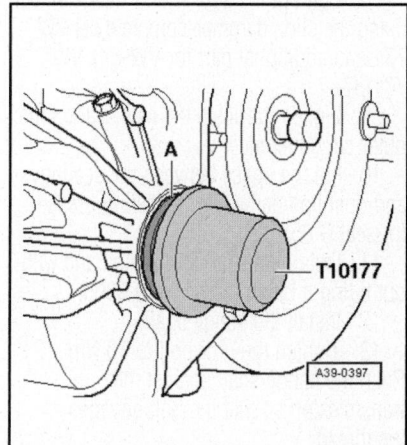

Fig. 31 Drive in the seal until seated using T10177

Right Side

22. Drive in the seal until seated using T10177, do not tilt the seal while doing this.
23. Install the drive axle.
24. Check the ATF level and top off.
25. Install the noise insulation.

DSG Transaxle

Left Side

See Figures 32 and 33.

➡**Do not remove both bolts in the right and left flange shafts or the right stub shaft at the same time. If the differential bevel gears rotate, it will be difficult to install the bolts.**

Necessary tools:
• Slide Hammer-Complete Set VW 771
• Additional Part for VW 771 VW 771/37
• Thrust Piece 3305
• Torque Wrench (5-50 Nm) V.A.G 1331
• Torque Wrench (40-200 Nm) V.A.G 1332
• Sealing Grease for Seal G 052 128 A1
• Drip Tray for VAS 6100 VAS 6208
1. Remove the left wheel.
2. Remove the noise insulation.
3. Remove the lower section of the left front wheel housing liner.
4. Remove the left drive axle.
5. Place the drip tray for VAS 6100 VAS 6208 under the transmission.
6. Remove bolt for the flange shaft, by installing two bolts into the flange and counter holding the flange shaft using a pry bar.
7. Remove the flange shaft together with the spring.
8. Pull out the seal for the flange shaft using the slide hammer-complete set VW 771 and additional part for VW 771 VW 771/37.
9. Lightly lubricate the new seal on the outer circumference.
10. Fill the space between the sealing and dust lips halfway with sealing grease for seal G 052 128.
11. Install the seal until seated and without tilting it using thrust piece 3305.
12. Install the flange shaft.
13. Tighten the new bolt to 30 Nm. Push the flange shaft against the transmission so that the bolt engages in the thread.
14. Install the left drive axle.
15. Install the left front wheel housing liner.

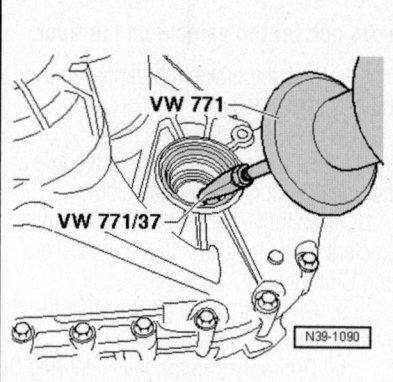

Fig. 32 Pull out the seal for the flange shaft using the slide hammer-complete set VW 771 and additional part for VW 771 VW 771/37

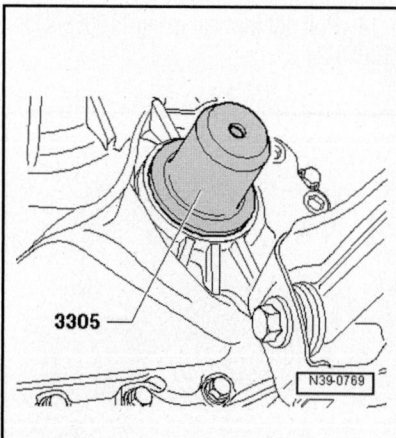

Fig. 33 Install the seal until seated and without tilting it using thrust piece 3305

16. Install the left wheel.
17. Check the transmission fluid level and fill if necessary.
18. Install the noise insulation.

Right Side

Refer to Automatic Transaxle.

Manual Transaxle

Left

See Figure 34.

1. Before servicing the vehicle, refer to the precautions.
2. Remove left wheel.
3. Remove noise insulation.
4. Remove the lower part of the left front wheel housing liner.
5. Remove left drive axle.
6. Place appropriate receptacle underneath transmission.

7. Remove bolts for flange shaft, by screwing two bolts into the flange and counter-holding flange shaft using a pry bar.
8. Pull out flange shaft with spring.
9. Pull out flange shaft oil seal.

To install:

10. Drive new seal in as far as the stop; be sure not to distort seal.
11. Fill area between sealing lip and dust lip halfway with sealing grease G 052 128 A1.
12. Insert flange shaft.
13. Secure flange shaft with countersunk bolt.
14. Install left drive axle.
15. Install lower section of the left front wheel housing liner.
16. Install wheel.
17. Check gear oil.
18. Install noise insulation.

Right

See Figure 34.

1. Before servicing the vehicle, refer to the precautions.
2. Remove noise insulation.
3. Remove drive axle heat shield from the engine, if equipped bolts 1.
4. Remove left drive axle from transmission and tie it up high.
5. On some engines, the drive axle cannot be tied up so that the flange shaft can be removed.
6. Remove drive axle.
7. Remove bolts for flange shaft, by installing two bolts into the flange and counter-holding flange shaft using a pry bar.
8. Place appropriate receptacle underneath transmission.
9. Pull out flange shaft with spring.

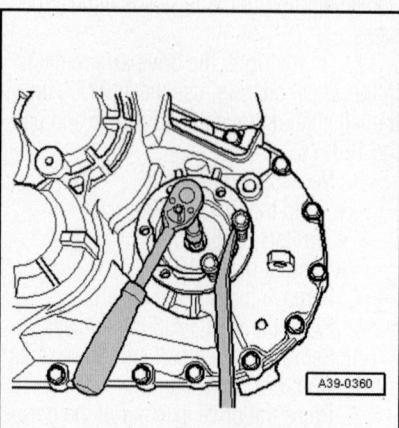

Fig. 34 Remove bolts for flange shaft, by screwing two bolts into the flange and counter-holding flange shaft using a pry bar

10. Pry out seal with a lever.

To install:

11. Drive new seal in as far as stop; be sure not to distort seal.

12. Fill area between sealing lip and dust lip halfway with sealing grease G 052 128 A1.

13. Secure flange shaft with countersunk bolt.

14. Install right drive axle.

15. Install drive axle heat shield to the engine, if equipped bolts.

16. Check gear oil.

17. Install noise insulation.

ENGINE COOLING

ENGINE COOLANT

DRAIN & REFILL PROCEDURE

2.0L Engine

See Figure 35.

Draining

1. Open the coolant expansion tank cap.

2. Remove the noise insulation.

3. Remove the coolant hose clip downward and remove the coolant hose from the radiator quick-release coupling.

4. In addition, to drain the coolant from the engine, disconnect the coolant hose at the oil cooler.

➡**Observe disposal regulations!**

➡**Only use tap water for mixing. Well water does not have the quality needed to ensure the coolant will function correctly.**

Filling

5. Only use coolant additive G 12 plus-plus that conforms to TL VW 774 G.

6. G 12 plus-plus prevents frost and corrosion damage, scaling and also raises the boiling point. The cooling system must be filled with coolant additive year-round.

7. Because of its high boiling point, the coolant improves engine reliability under heavy loads, particularly in countries with tropical climates.

8. Protection against frost must be assured down to approximately -13 °F (in arctic climatic countries down to approximately -31 °F).

9. The coolant concentration must not be reduced by adding water even in warmer seasons and in warmer countries. The coolant additive portion must be at least 40%.

10. The amount of G12 plus-plus can be increased if more freeze protection is needed. However, it may only be increased up to 60%, which provides freeze protection down to approximately -40 °F.

11. Otherwise the freeze protection and cooling effect are reduced.

12. If the radiator, heater core, cylinder head or cylinder head gasket is replaced, do not reuse the old coolant.

13. The refractometer T10007 is recommended for determining freeze protection density.

14. Install the lower coolant hose and secure with the retaining clamp.

15. Connect the coolant hoses to the oil cooler and to the engine coolant circulation pump 2.

16. Install the noise insulation.

17. Using Cooling System Filler Unit VAS 6096:

a. Install the adapter V.A.G 1274/8 onto the expansion tank.

b. Fill the coolant circuit using the cooling system filling unit VAS 6096. Refer to the operating instructions.

18. Without Cooling System Filler Unit VAS 6096:

a. Slowly fill the coolant up to the upper mark in the hatched area on the expansion tank.

b. Close the expansion tank.

19. Start the engine and maintain an engine speed of about 2000 RPM for approximately 3 minutes.

20. Let the engine run at idle until the coolant fan turns on.

21. Check the coolant level and fill if necessary. With the engine at operating temperature, the coolant level must be at the top mark, with the engine cold, it must be in the center of the hatched area.

2.5L Engine

Draining

Drained coolant must be stored in a clean container for disposal or reuse.

Follow all disposal regulations.

Risk of scalding due to hot steam and hot coolant.

The coolant system is under pressure when the engine is warm.

Wear protective goggles and protective clothing to prevent damage to eyes and scalding.

Reduce pressure by covering the coolant expansion tank cap with a cloth and carefully opening.

1. Open the coolant expansion tank cap.

2. Remove the noise insulation.

3. Place the drip tray under the radiator.

4. Open the spring clamp and remove the coolant hose.

Filling

5. Only use distilled water for mixing with G12 plus-plus. Using distilled water provides optimum corrosion protection.

6. Only use coolant additive G 12 plus-plus that conforms to TL VW 774 G.

7. Coolant additives with the note "conforming to TL VW 774 G" prevent frost, corrosion damage and scaling. They also increase the boiling point. For this reason the system must be filled all year round with frost and corrosion protection additives.

8. Because of its high boiling point, the coolant improves engine reliability under heavy loads, particularly in countries with tropical climates.

9. Protection against frost must be assured down to approximately -13 °F) (in arctic climatic countries down to approximately -31°F.

10. The coolant concentration must not be reduced by adding water even in warmer seasons and in warmer countries. The coolant additive portion must be at least 40%.

11. If a lower freeze protection is necessary due to the climatic conditions, increase

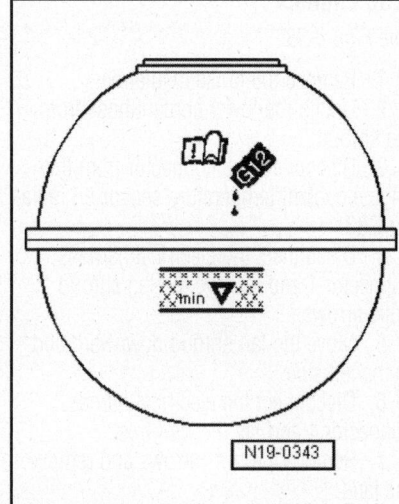

Fig. 35 Slowly fill the coolant up to the upper mark in the hatched area on the expansion tank

the amount of coolant additive. Increase the coolant additive only up to 60% (freeze protection down to approximately -40 °F). Otherwise the freeze protection and cooling effect are reduced.

12. The refractometer T10007 is recommended for determining freeze protection density.

13. If the radiator, heater core, cylinder head or cylinder head gasket is replaced, do not reuse the old coolant.

14. Using Cooling System Filler Unit VAS 6096:

   a. Install the adapter V.A.G 1274/8 onto the expansion tank.

   b. Fill the coolant circuit using the cooling system filling unit VAS 6096. Refer to the operating instructions.

15. Without Cooling System Filler Unit VAS 6096:

   a. Slowly fill the coolant up to the upper mark in the hatched area on the expansion tank.

   b. Close the expansion tank.

16. Turn off the heater and air conditioning.

17. Start the engine and maintain an engine speed of about 2000 RPM for approximately 3 minutes.

18. Let the engine run at idle until the coolant fan turns on.

19. Check the coolant level and fill if necessary. With the engine at operating temperature, the coolant level must be at the top mark, with the engine cold, it must be in the center of the hatched area.

ENGINE FAN

REMOVAL & INSTALLATION

2.0L Engines

See Figures 36 and 37.

1. Remove the bolts upper arrows at the top of the fan shroud.

2. Remove the noise insulation.

3. Remove the hot side hose for the charge air pipe. Loosen the hose clamp and lift the circlip.

4. Disconnect the connector.

5. Remove the bottom bolts lower arrows.

6. Remove the fan shroud and fans.

7. Disconnect the connector and (if equipped) and free up the wires.

8. Remove the nuts arrows and remove the fans.

9. Installation is performed in the reverse order of removal.

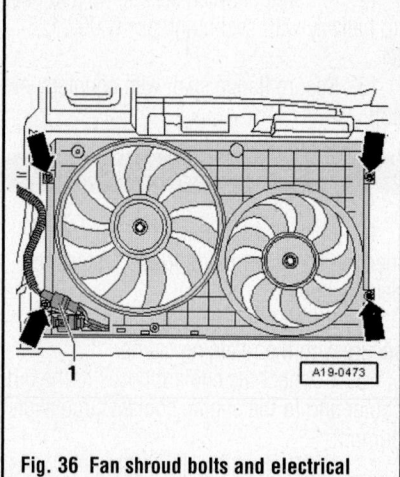

Fig. 36 Fan shroud bolts and electrical connector (1)

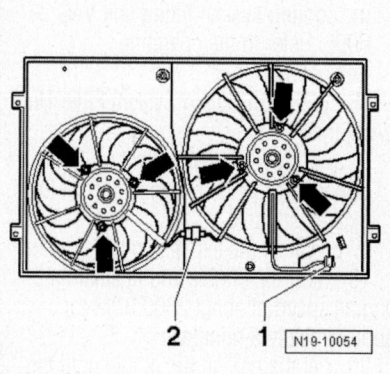

Fig. 37 Locating fan bolts and fan connectors (1 and 2)

2.5L Engines

See Figure 38.

1. Remove the noise insulation.

2. Unclip the lower coolant hose from fan shroud.

3. Disconnect the connector from the engine coolant temperature sensor on radiator G83.

4. Disconnect the electrical harness connector 1 and remove the fan shroud bolts arrows.

5. Move the fan shroud downward and to the left side.

6. Disconnect the electrical harness connector 1 and lay the wire free.

7. Remove the nuts arrows and remove the fans.

8. Installation is performed in the reverse order of removal.

Fig. 38 Locating fan bolts and fan connector (1)

RADIATOR

REMOVAL & INSTALLATION

2.0L Engine

See Figure 39.

1. Remove the air shroud with the radiator fans.

   a. Drain the coolant.

2. Open the spring clamps and remove the coolant hoses from the radiator.

3. Remove the front bumper cover.

4. Remove the air guides 3 at the bottom.

➡**To prevent damage to the condenser and the refrigerant lines, do not stretch, kink or bend the pipes and hoses.**

5. Remove the air guides 3 at the bottom.

6. Remove the bolts 1 from the condenser.

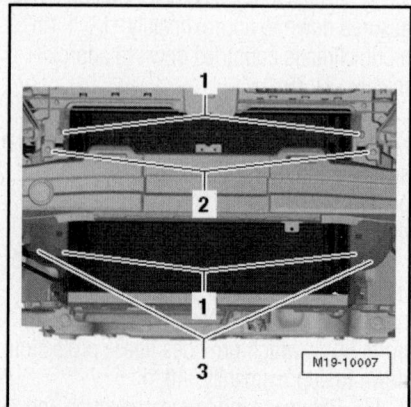

Fig. 39 Locating the bolts from the condenser (1), bolts from the radiator mounts and air guides (3)

7. Remove the bolts 2 from the radiator mounts.

8. Push the radiator to the rear and remove the radiator mounts.

9. Remove the radiator from its mounts in the lock carrier.

10. Installation is performed in the reverse order of removal. When doing this note the following:

11. Fill the coolant.

2.5L Engine

See Figures 40 and 41.

1. Remove the front bumper.
2. Remove the fan shroud.
3. Drain the coolant.
4. Disconnect the coolant hoses from radiator.

➡**To prevent damage to the condenser and the refrigerant lines, do not stretch, kink or bend the pipes and hoses.**

5. Remove the bolts arrows from the radiator brackets.

6. Move the radiator and condenser toward the rear and out of the lower support. While doing this, pull the lock carrier on the left support slightly downward.

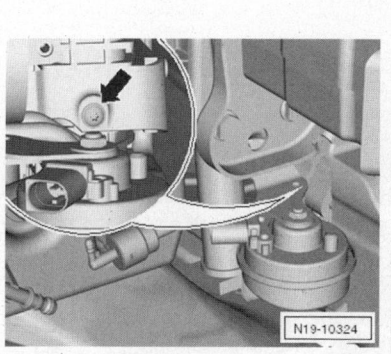

Fig. 41 Remove the bolts for the refrigerant lines on the right side of the radiator

7. Remove the bolts for the refrigerant lines on the right side of the radiator.

8. Remove the condenser bolts. Secure the condenser on the lock carrier using cable ties, for example.

9. Remove the radiator downward.

To install:

10. Install the radiator from below and secure it to the condenser.

11. Install the radiator and condenser in the lower supports.

12. Place the upper radiator mount on the radiator and secure it with the lock carrier arrows.

13. Install the front bumper.

14. Install the fan shroud.

15. Installation is performed in reverse order of removal. When doing this note the following:

16. Replace coolant if a new radiator was installed.

17. Fill with coolant.

THERMOSTAT

REMOVAL & INSTALLATION

2.0L Engines

See Figure 42.

1. Before servicing the vehicle, refer to the precautions.

2. Drain coolant.

3. Remove the cover for the air guide; disengage the side clips to do so.

4. Unclip the lower air guide, disengage the clips to do so.

5. Remove the lower air guide together with the air guide hose.

6. Loosen the hose clamp.

7. Remove bolt.

8. Disconnect electrical connector.

9. Remove the bolt and remove the air guide pipe downward.

10. Lay aside the coolant hose and electrical wiring harness.

11. Remove the bolt and remove bracket.

12. If installed, remove the bolt on the bracket for the After-Run Coolant Pump V51.

➡**The After-Run Coolant Pump V51 stays in the installation position.**

13. Remove the coolant hoses and lay them aside.

14. Loosen the nut, remove the bolt and move the support for the intake manifold to the right.

15. Remove bolts and remove connecting pieces. For the right bolt, the Multi-Point Socket T10058 is useful.

16. Remove the coolant thermostat.

To install:

17. Replace seals and O-rings.

18. Clean O-ring sealing surface.

19. Coat the O-ring with coolant G12 plus-plus.

20. Install the thermostat into the housing for the coolant pump and move it slightly forward.

21. Tighten the bolts to 80 inch lbs. (9 Nm).

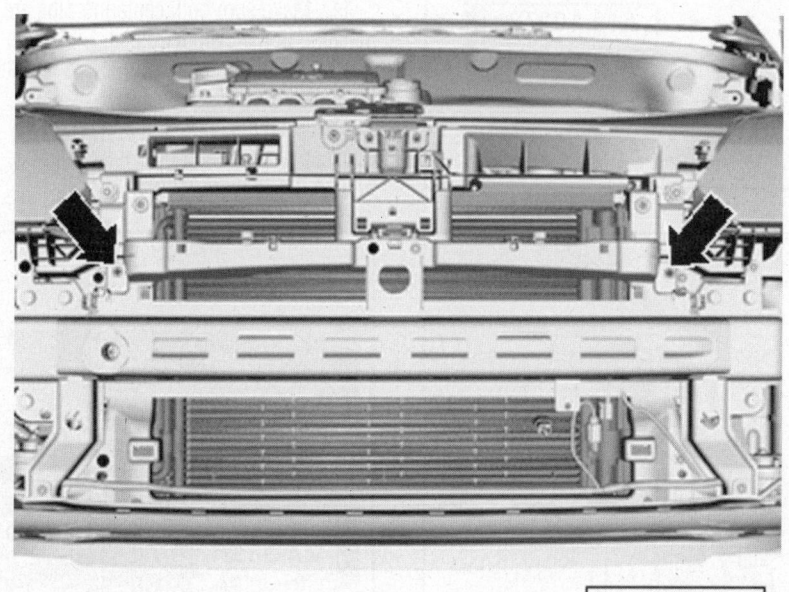

Fig. 40 Remove the bolts arrows from the radiator brackets

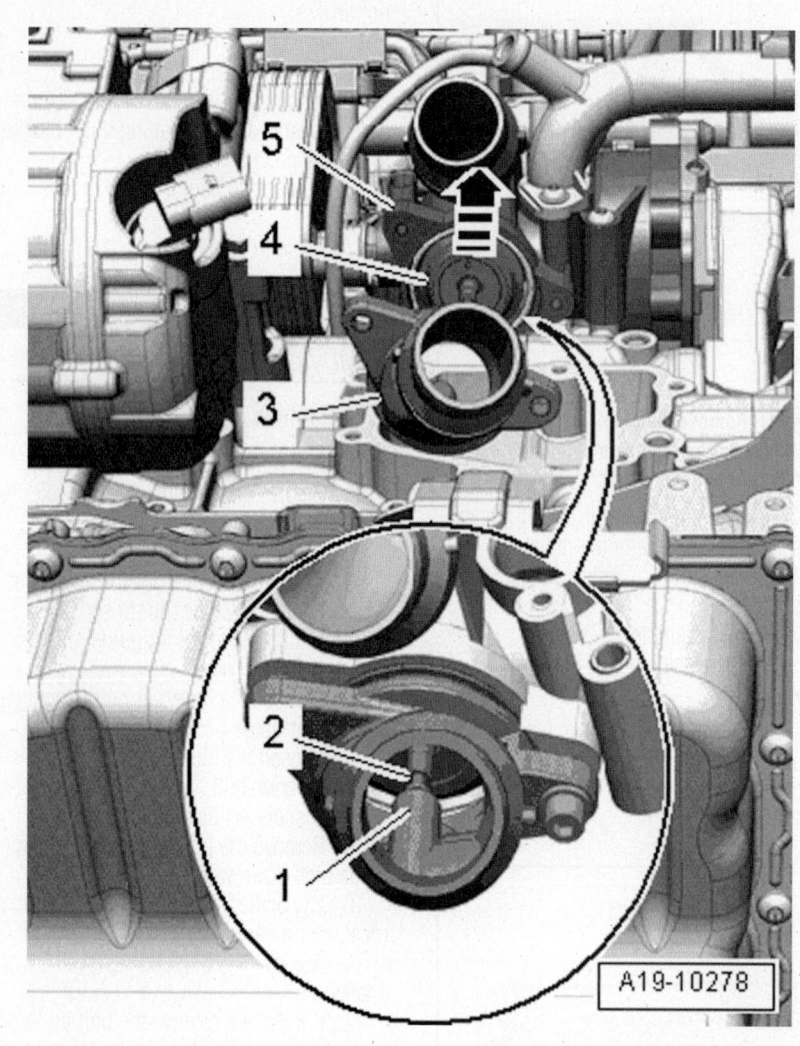

Fig. 42 Thermostat assembly

22. Carefully mount the connector; while doing so, insert the centering pin into the guide.

2.5L Engine

See Figure 43.

1. Drain the coolant.
2. Remove the engine cover with air filter.
3. Remove the intake manifold. Refer to Intake Manifold.
4. Insert the guide tube for the oil dipstick into the cylinder block again and secure it tightly so that no leaking coolant can run into the engine.
5. Place a suitable container under the coolant thermostat housing to catch coolant leaking out.
6. Remove the bolts arrows, the cover A and the thermostat

To install:

7. Installation is performed in the reverse order of removal. When doing this note the following:
8. Replace the seal and O-ring.

➡Note the installed position of the thermostat, the valve must point upward.

WATER PUMP

REMOVAL & INSTALLATION

2.0L Engines

See Figures 44 and 45.

1. Before servicing the vehicle, refer to the precautions.
2. Remove coolant pipes.
3. Remove the coolant pump toothed belt.
4. Disconnect electrical connector on Throttle Valve Control Module J338.
5. Remove bolts and remove Throttle Valve Control Module J338.
6. Disconnect the electrical connector on the engine coolant temperature (ECT) sensor G62.
7. Remove bolts.
8. Remove the coolant pump from the centering pin and remove the oil cooler.

To install:

9. Replace seals and O-rings.
10. Coat the O-rings with coolant.
11. Make sure both centering pins are installed in the cylinder block.
12. Install the connection piece into the oil cooler.
13. Push the coolant pump onto the connection piece and onto the centering pins in the cylinder block.

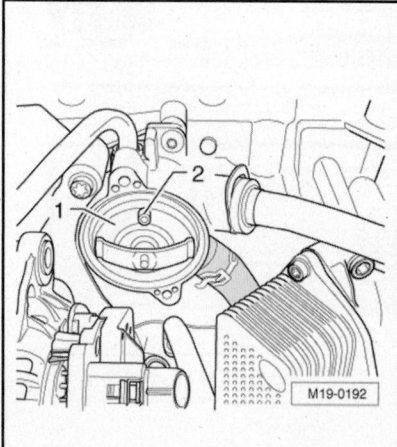

Fig. 43 Thermostat (1) and valve (2) installation orientation

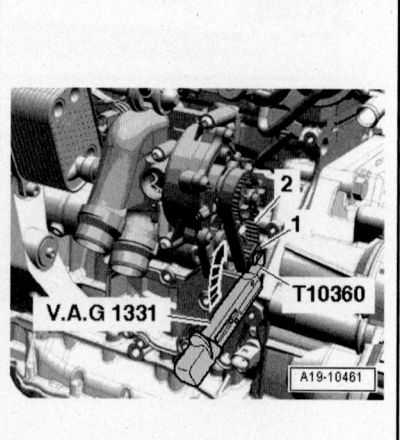

Fig. 44 Remove the coolant pump drive gear (1) and toothed belt (2)

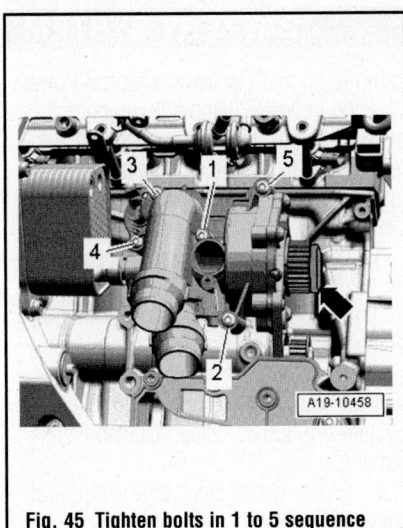

Fig. 45 Tighten bolts in 1 to 5 sequence

14. Tighten bolts in 1 to 5 sequence as shown.

15. If a new coolant pump was installed, then the protective cap must be removed.

16. The rest of the installation follows the reverse of the removal procedures.

2.5L Engine

See Figure 46.

➡**This procedure requires removal of the front engine mount. New bolts will be needed.**

1. Before servicing the vehicle, refer to the precautions.

2. Remove the engine cover/air filter assembly.

3. Remove the battery and battery box.

4. Drain the cooling system by disconnecting the bottom radiator hose.

5. Remove air inlet tube guide above the fans.

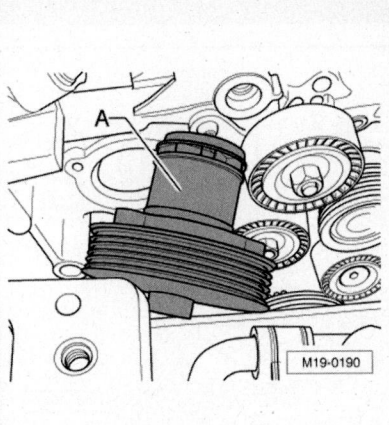

Fig. 46 Swivel the pump to remove it from the engine compartment—2.5L engine

6. Remove the air intake hose by disconnecting the smaller air hoses and removing the spring clamp.

7. Remove right inner fender.

8. Remove the coolant pump drive belt.

9. Disconnect the exhaust pipe from the manifold and remove the bracket bolts. Tie the pipe out of the way. The flex joint in the front exhaust pipe must not be bent more than 10 degrees, otherwise it may be damaged.

10. Remove the pendulum support (under car engine mount).

11. Disconnect the shift control cables at the transaxle.

12. Install engine support bridge 10-222A with adapters 10-222A/8 and support engine/transaxle assembly in installation position using adapter 10-222A/3 and shackle 10-222 A/12.

13. Remove the bolt that holds the windshield washer reservoir and move it towards the front.

14. Remove the coolant reservoir bolts and disconnect the wiring. Set the reservoir out of the way without disconnecting the hoses.

15. Remove the bolts to remove the front engine mount. The rear bolt in cylinder block is accessible above wheel housing liner.

16. Remove the two transaxle mount bolts.

17. Slide the engine as far as possible toward the front and left.

18. Remove the three mounting bolts and swivel the coolant pump out.

To install:

19. Install the pump and torque the bolts to 7 ft. lbs. (10 Nm).

20. Install the engine mounts using new bolts.

- Torque the two pendulum support bracket bolts to 30 ft. lbs. (40 Nm) plus 90°. Install a new pendulum support center bolt and torque it to 75 ft. lbs. (100 Nm) plus 90°.
- Install two new transaxle mount bolts and torque to 45 ft. lbs. (60 Nm) plus 90°.

21. Remove the engine support bridge and adapter brackets.

22. Connect the shift cables and adjust as necessary.

23. Connect the exhaust pipe and install the bracket bolts.

24. Install the remaining components and connect all wiring and hoses.

25. Refill the coolant reservoir with G 12 coolant and install the cap. Run the engine at 2000 rpm for three minutes or until the fan runs and check coolant level.

ENGINE ELECTRICAL

BATTERY SYSTEM

BATTERY

REMOVAL & INSTALLATION

See Figure 47.

1. Disconnect the battery.
2. Open the battery housing or the jacket in direction of and remove it from the battery.
3. Remove mounting screws and remove retaining bracket.
4. Fold handles arrows upward (if present) and take out battery.

➡️**If battery is not secured properly, the following risks are possible:**

- Shortened battery service life due to vibration damage (explosion hazard).
- If battery is not secured properly, the plates within the battery can be damaged.
- Damage to battery casing caused by bracket (possible electrolyte leakage, high subsequent costs).
- Reduced collision safety.

5. Install in reverse order of removal, noting the following:

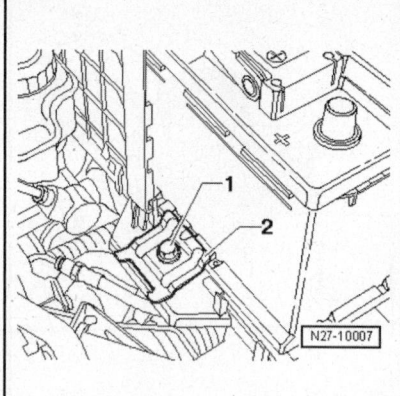

Fig. 47 Remove mounting screws (1) and remove retaining bracket (2)

6. Tighten the threaded connections.
7. After installing, verify battery is properly seated.
8. Connect battery.

BATTERY RECONNECT/RELEARN PROCEDURE

After connecting the battery and switching on the ignition, the ASR/ESP Control Lamp K155 and Electro-mechanical Power Steering Indicator Lamp light up continuously. The indicator lamps switch off automatically after driving straight ahead at 15 to 20 km/h. This activates Steering Angle Sensor G85.

Work steps required after connecting battery:

1. Switch on ignition using ignition key or start button and switch off again.
2. Read the DTC memory: using Vehicle Diagnosis, Testing & Information System VAS5051B, select "Guided Fault Finding".
3. Clock: Check clock time setting, set anew if necessary.
4. Electrical window regulators:
   a. Open and close windows to each end stop respectively.
   b. With window closed, then pull switch until relay switches audibly.
   c. Check comfort switching of power window. While comfort switching is operated, window must close without holding the switch.
5. Check function: all electrical consumers.

ENGINE ELECTRICAL

CHARGING SYSTEM

ALTERNATOR

REMOVAL & INSTALLATION

2.0L Engines

See Figure 48.

➡️**When disconnecting and connecting battery, the procedure must be followed as described in the repair manual.**

1. Disconnect battery.

✳️ WARNING

Before removing ribbed belt, mark the top side and direction of travel. When installing, pay attention to correct running direction and installation position. If the belt is installed in the opposite running direction or is positioned incorrectly, the belt will fail!

2. Remove the ribbed belt.
3. Disengage and disconnect harness connector.
4. Remove the oil pressure switch.

5. Remove the generator bolts.
6. Turn the generator slightly to the left in order to be able to access the connections on the back of the generator.
7. Release and disconnect DF wire connector.
8. Pry off protective cap.
9. Remove the nut and B+ wire below from generator connector threads.

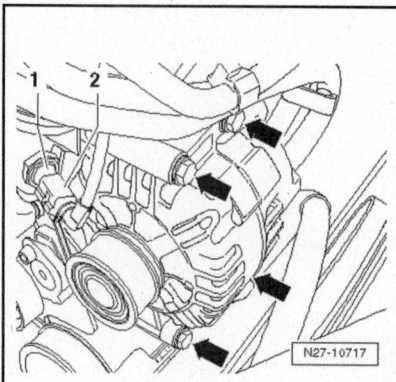

Fig. 48 Remove the connector (2) from oil pressure switch (1) and the generator bolts (arrows)

10. Remove both screws and move the pipes and the hose upward so that there is enough space to remove the generator.

➡️**The pipes and the hose can remain connected.**

11. Remove the generator upward and out of the vehicle.

To install:

12. Install in reverse order of removal, noting the following:

➡️**When installing an already used ribbed belt, note direction of travel marked when it was removed! Before installing the ribbed belt, make sure all components (generator, A/C compressor) are securely fastened. When installing the ribbed belt, make sure it is properly seated in the belt pulley!**

13. Tighten the threaded connections to the specification given in the assembly overview.

➡️**When disconnecting and connecting battery, the procedure must be followed as described in the repair manual.**

2.5L Engine

See Figures 49 and 50.

1. Before servicing the vehicle, refer to the precautions.
2. Disconnect the battery.
3. Pull off engine cover upward and forward.
4. Bring the lock carrier into the service position.
5. Remove ribbed belt.
6. Remove the A/C compressor, but do not disconnect the hoses.

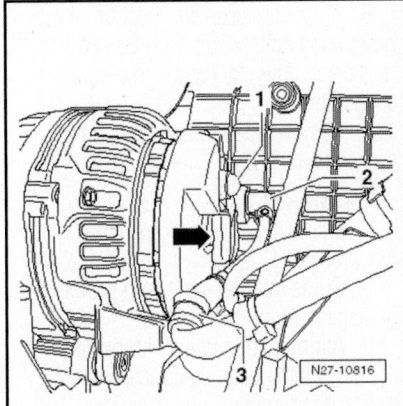

Fig. 49 Separate the connector for the DF-lead (2) and remove the protective cap (1), remove the B+ wire (arrow)

7. Remove the both bolts and then remove the lower idler roller from the auxiliary component bracket.
8. Remove the 3 bolts and then remove the upper idler roller from the auxiliary component bracket.
9. Separate the connector for the DF-lead and remove the protective cap.
10. Remove the B+ wire from the generator.

✳✳ WARNING

Before removing ribbed belt, mark the top side and direction of travel. When installing, pay attention to correct running direction and installation position. If the belt is installed in the opposite running direction or is positioned incorrectly, the belt will fail!

11. Remove the bolts and then remove the tensioning rollers
12. Remove the generator mounting bolts.
13. Remove the wire retainer from the generator.
14. Remove the generator upward.

To install:

15. Install in reverse order of removal.
16. Drive the threaded sleeves out of the generator housing approximately 4 mm.

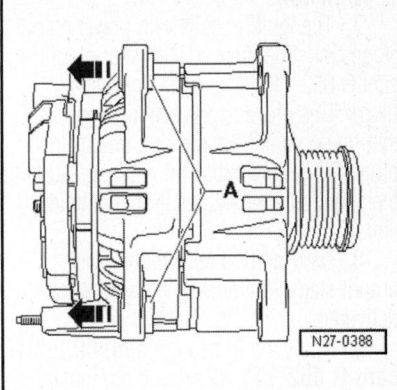

Fig. 50 Drive the threaded sleeves out of the generator housing approximately 4 mm

17. Install the wire retainer securely on the rear side of the generator in the 8 o'clock position.
18. Tighten mounting bolts to 19 ft. lbs. (25 Nm).

✳✳ WARNING

Observe notes for threaded connections of battery terminals.

19. Connect the Battery.
20. Start the engine and verify that the belt is running properly.
21. Turn off the engine.

ENGINE ELECTRICAL

FIRING ORDER

2.0L and 2.5 L engine firing order: 1–3–4–2 Distributorless ignition

IGNITION COIL

REMOVAL & INSTALLATION

2.0L & 2.5L Engines

See Figures 51 and 52.

1. Before servicing the vehicle, refer to the precautions.
2. To pull off spark plugs, place ignition coil puller T40039 on topmost thick rib of ignition coils with power output stages.

✳✳ WARNING

If lower ribs are used, these can be damaged

3. Remove engine covers.

➡Spark plugs are located under ignition coils with power output stages.

4. Remove both bolts.

➡Note installation position of ignition coils with power output stages.

5. Pull all ignition coils approximately 1.17 in (30 mm) out of cylinder head in direction of rotation using ignition coil puller T40039.

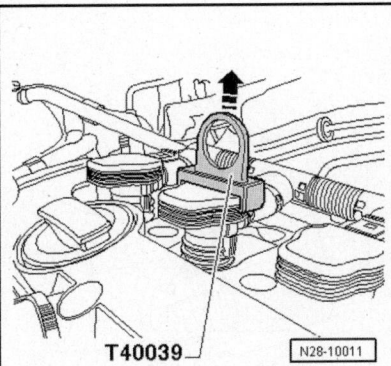

Fig. 51 To pull off spark plugs, place ignition coil puller T40039 on topmost thick rib of ignition coils with power output stages

IGNITION SYSTEM

6. Push connector in direction of rotation ignition coils with power output stages, press catch down by hand and disconnect connectors.

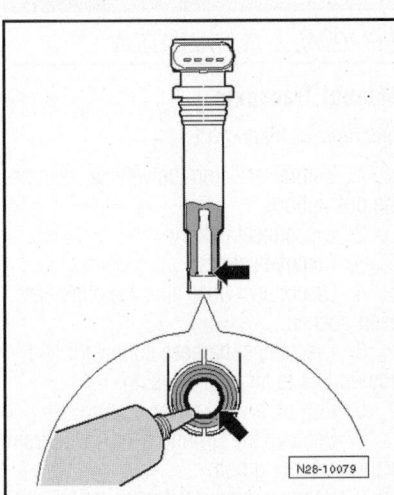

Fig. 52 Apply a thin bead of special lubricant G 052 141 A2 around the ignition sealing hose (arrow)

To install:

7. The ignition coils with power output stages must be greased with special lubricant G 052 141 A2 to install new spark plugs. This prevents the sealing hose on the ignition coil from sticking on the spark plug. The special lubricant must spread onto the spark plug when installing the ignition coil.

8. New ignition coils with power output stages are already greased when delivered.

9. Apply a thin bead of **special lubricant G 052 141 A2** around the ignition sealing hose. The bead must be 1 to 2 mm thick.

10. Guide ignition coils with power output stages into cylinder head.

11. Align ignition coils with power output stages into designated recesses of cylinder head cover.

12. Connect all connectors to ignition coils.

13. Press ignition coils with power output stages onto spark plugs by hand until stop. They must engage audibly.

14. Secure wiring using bolts.

15. Install engine cover.

IGNITION TIMING

ADJUSTMENT

All gasoline engines are equipped with a Distributorless Ignition System (DIS). No adjustment is necessary.

SPARK PLUGS

REMOVAL & INSTALLATION

2.0L & 2.5L Engines

See Figure 53.

1. Before servicing the vehicle, refer to the precautions.

2. To pull off spark plugs, place ignition coil puller T40039 on topmost thick rib of ignition coils with power output stages.

⁂ WARNING

If lower ribs are used, these can be damaged

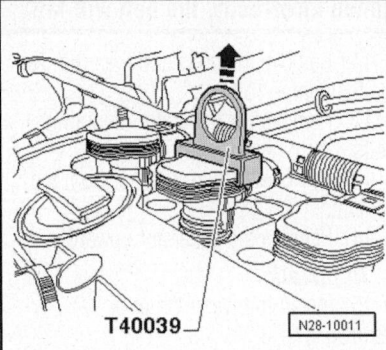

Fig. 53 To pull off spark plugs, place ignition coil puller T40039 on topmost thick rib of ignition coils with power output stages

3. Remove engine covers.

➡ **Spark plugs are located under ignition coils with power output stages.**

4. Remove both bolts.

➡ **Note installation position of ignition coils with power output stages.**

5. Pull all ignition coils approximately 1.17 in (30 mm) out of cylinder head in direction of rotation using ignition coil puller T40039.

6. Push connector in direction of rotation ignition coils with power output stages, press catch down by hand and disconnect connectors.

7. Remove spark plugs using spark plug wrench 3122 B.

To install:

8. Install new spark plugs using spark plug wrench 3122 B.

9. Guide ignition coils with power output stages into cylinder head.

10. Align ignition coils with power output stages into designated recesses of cylinder head cover.

11. Connect all connectors to ignition coils.

12. Press ignition coils with power output stages onto spark plugs by hand until stop. They must engage audibly.

13. Secure wiring using bolts.

14. Install engine cover.

ENGINE ELECTRICAL

STARTER

REMOVAL & INSTALLATION

Manual Transaxle

See Figures 54 and 55.

1. Before servicing the vehicle, refer to the precautions.

2. Disconnect battery.

3. Remove screws.

4. Disconnect hose after the clips have been opened.

5. Disconnect harness connector and free up line to air filter housing.

6. Pull off engine cover upward.

7. Remove the Ground (GND) wire from starter mounting bolt.

8. Remove upper starter mounting bolt.

9. Slide protective cap downward from magnetic switch.

10. Remove the positive wire and disconnect harness connector of terminal 50.

11. Remove noise insulation.

12. All hose connections for charge air system are secured by spring-type

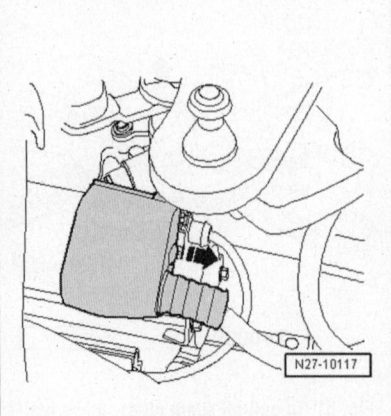

Fig. 54 Slide protective cap in direction of arrow

STARTING SYSTEM

clamps or by connector couplings. The following must be observed with connector couplings:

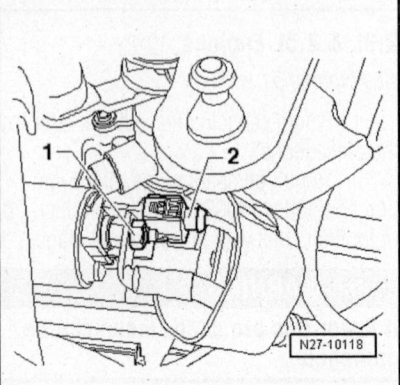

Fig. 55 Remove the positive wire and disconnect harness connector of terminal 50

13. Release the connection by pulling locking clip.

14. Disconnect hose/pipe without tools.

15. Open screw-type clamp and disconnect connector coupling.

16. Remove charge air hose from vehicle.

17. Remove the nut from lower mounting bolt of starter.

18. Remove wire retainer.

19. Remove lower starter mounting bolt

20. Remove the starter downward and out from the vehicle.

To install:

21. Install in reverse order of removal.

22. All hose connections for charge air system are secured by spring-type clamps or by connector couplings. The following must be observed with connector couplings:

23. Connect hose/pipe without tools.

24. Make sure retaining tabs lock securely.

25. Tighten bolts/nuts to specification as follows:

- Starter to transmission M12: 59 ft. lbs. (80 Nm)
- Starter to transmission M10: 30 ft. lbs. (40 Nm)

- Ground (GND) wire to starter mounting bolt M8: 11 ft. lbs. (15 Nm)
- Ground wire to transmission M8: 11 ft. lbs. (15 Nm)
- Wire retainer to starter mounting bolt M8: 11 ft. lbs. (15 Nm)
- Positive wire to starter solenoid switch M8: 11 ft. lbs. (15 Nm)
- Air filter housing to body: 89 inch lbs. (10 Nm)

Automatic Transaxle

1. Before servicing the vehicle, refer to the precautions.

2. Disconnect battery.

3. Pull off engine cover upward.

4. Disconnect harness connector, loosen spring-type clamp using Spring Type Clip Pliers VAS 5024 and disconnect vacuum hose.

5. Remove mounting bolt for air filter housing.

6. Release retaining tabs and remove cover.

7. Disconnect hose from air filter housing and remove it.

8. Pull off air filter housing upward out of brackets and remove it.

9. Slide protective cap in direction of downward from magnetic switch.

10. Remove the positive wire and disconnect harness connector of terminal 50.

11. Unclip wire from wiring harness.

12. Remove upper starter mounting bolt.

13. Remove lower mounting bolt for starter.

14. Remove starter upward and out of vehicle.

To install:

15. Install in reverse order of removal.

16. Tighten bolts/nuts to specification as follows:

- Starter to transmission M12: 59 ft. lbs. (80 Nm)
- Starter to transmission M10: 30 ft. lbs. (40 Nm)
- Ground (GND) wire to starter mounting bolt M8: 11 ft. lbs. (15 Nm)
- Ground wire to transmission M8: 11 ft. lbs. (15 Nm)
- Wire retainer to starter mounting bolt M8: 11 ft. lbs. (15 Nm)
- Positive wire to starter solenoid switch M8: 11 ft. lbs. (15 Nm)
- Air filter housing to body: 89 inch lbs. (10 Nm)

ENGINE MECHANICAL

➡**Disconnecting the negative battery cable may interfere with the functions of the on board computer systems and may require the computer to undergo a relearning process, once the negative battery cable is reconnected.**

ACCESSORY DRIVE BELTS

ACCESSORY BELT ROUTING

See Figures 56 and 57.

INSPECTION

1. Turn the engine at vibration damper/crankshaft pulley with a suitable socket wrench.

2. Raise the vehicle if necessary. Check the drive belt for:

    a. Sub-surface (deep) cracks

    b. Layer separation (top layer, cord strands)

    c. Traces of oil and grease

3. Replace the belt if any damage is found or if contaminated with oil or grease.

ADJUSTMENT

All models use an automatic (spring powered) tensioner. No adjustment is required.

REMOVAL & INSTALLATION

2.0L Engines

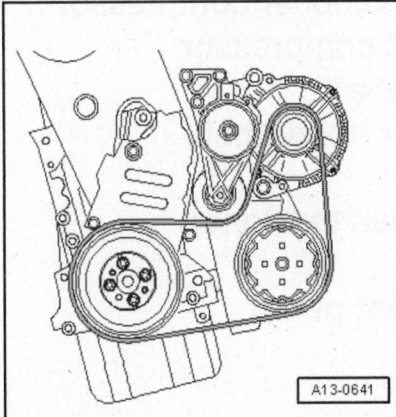

Fig. 56 Accessory drive belt routing: 2.0L Engine

1. Before servicing the vehicle, refer to the precautions.

❋❋ WARNING

Risk of destroying due to reversed running direction on a used ribbed belt. Before removing ribbed belt, marking running direction with chalk or felt-tip pen for reinstallation later.

2. Remove the noise insulation.

3. Remove the right air guide hose.

4. To release the tension on the ribbed belt, turn the tensioner in direction of rotation from underneath.

5. Secure tensioner with Drift T10060 A.

6. Remove ribbed belt.

To install:

7. Installation is performed in reverse order of removal.

❋❋ WARNING

Before installing ribbed belt, generator, A/C compressor must be securely installed.

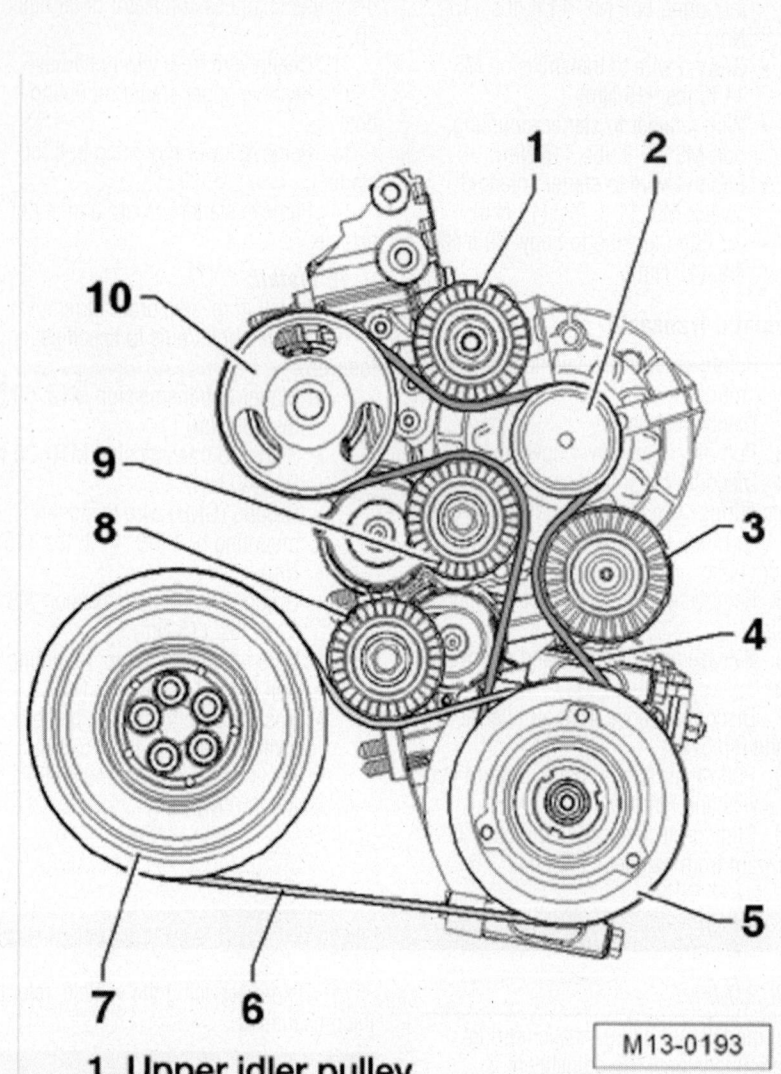

1. Upper idler pulley
2. Belt pulley - Generator
3. Lower idler pulley
4. Generator and coolant pump ribbed belt
5. Belt pulley - air conditioner compressor
6. Ribbed belt for A/C compressor
7. Belt pulley - crankshaft
8. Tensioning roller for ribbed belt for A/C compressor
9. Generator ribbed belt tensioner and coolant pump
10. Belt pulley - coolant pump

Fig. 57 Accessory drive belt routing: 2.5L Engine

8. First mount the ribbed belt on the crankshaft pulley, then on the A/C compressor and generator.

9. Turn the tensioner with a box-end wrench and remove the drift T10060 A.

10. Release tensioner.

11. Check whether ribbed belt is routed correctly.

12. Start engine and check whether ribbed belt runs correctly.

2.5L Engine

See Figure 58.

1. Before servicing the vehicle, refer to the precautions.

2. Raise and safely support the front of the vehicle.

3. Remove front part of right front inner fender.

4. Put a 15mm wrench on the A/C belt tensioner and push towards the rear of the vehicle.

5. Insert a pin to hold the wrench in place.

6. Remove the compressor belt and mark its running direction for installation. Do not leave the wrench and pin in place if moving on to other work.

7. Mark the running direction of the alternator belt.

8. Move the tensioner and insert a pin to hold it in place.

9. Remove the belt. Do not leave the wrench and pin in place if moving on to other work.

To install:

10. Place the alternator belt on the alternator and coolant pump pulleys, then lastly on the idler pulley.

11. Before releasing the tensioner, check ribbed for correct seating in the pulleys.

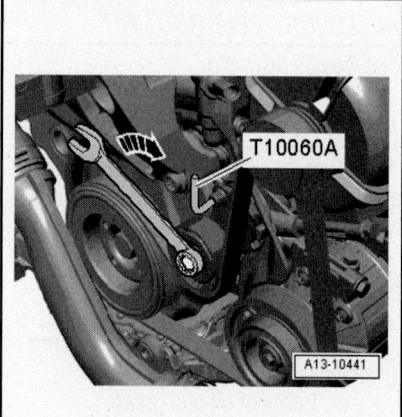

Fig. 58 Move the tensioner and insert a pin to hold it in place

12. Secure the other tensioner and install the A/C compressor belt. Be sure that it is seated correctly on pulley before releasing the tensioner.

13. Start engine and check belt running.

AIR CLEANER

REMOVAL & INSTALLATION

2.0L & 2.5L Gas Engines

See Figure 59.

1. Remove the cover for the air guide; disengage the side clips to do so.

2. Unclip the lower air guide, disengage the clips to do so.

3. Remove both the lower air guide and the air guide hose.

4. Engine Code CBFA: Disconnect the hose leading to the secondary air injection pump motor V101 from the air filter housing.

5. Loosen the bolt and pull the air filter housing upward out of the bracket.

6. Remove the air filter housing together with the Mass Airflow (MAF) sensor and connecting pipe.

7. Installation is performed in reverse order.

FILTER/ELEMENT REPLACEMENT

See Figure 60.

1. Removing for Engine Code CBFA: Disconnect the hose leading to the secondary air injection pump motor V101 from the air filter housing.

2. Remove the bolts from the upper air filter housing.

3. Lift the upper air filter housing and remove the air filter element.

To install:

4. Always use an original equipment air filter element.

5. Hose connections and charge air system hoses must be free of oil and grease before installing. When installing, do not use any lubricants containing silicone.

6. The air filter housing must be clean.

7. Secure all hose connections using hose clamps appropriate for the model type, refer to the Parts Catalog.

8. Note the following when blowing out the air filter housing with pressurized air: To prevent malfunctions, cover the critical air flow components such as the MAF sensor, air intake tubes, etc. with a clean cloth.

9. Observe disposal regulations!

10. Check the MAF sensor and intake hose (intake air side) for salt residue, dirt, and leaves.

11. Check the intake air guide from the air duct for dirt.

12. Remove the snow screen and clean it.

➡**The snow screen is not installed in all vehicles.**

13. Clean the water drain and the lower air filter housing.

14. Make sure that air filter is properly centered when placed in the mounting of the lower air filter housing.

15. Set the upper air filter housing onto the lower air filter housing, without using much force. When doing this, make sure that the upper air filter housing is not placed crooked onto the air filter element.

16. Check the sealing lip on the air filter element.

17. Further installation is performed in reverse order.

CAMSHAFT AND VALVE LIFTERS

REMOVAL & INSTALLATION

2.0L Engines

See Figures 61 through 68.

1. Before servicing the vehicle, refer to the precautions.

2. Remove the engine cover.

3. Remove the vacuum pump.

4. Remove the noise insulation.

5. Remove the front part of the right wheel housing liner and/or the front right wheel housing liner.

6. Remove bolts.

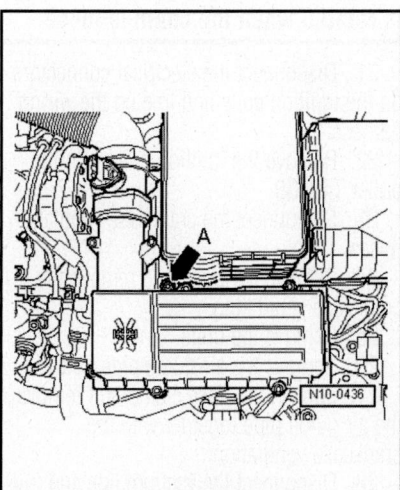

Fig. 59 Loosen the bolt (arrow A)

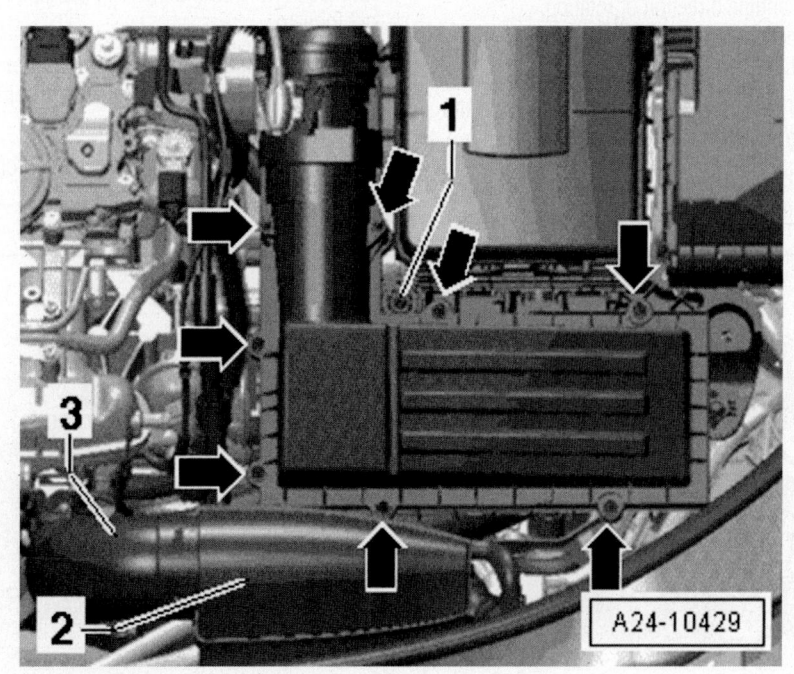

Fig. 60 Removing the upper air filter element housing bolts (arrows)

7. Remove the air guide pipe by lifting the clamps items.

8. Disconnect the connector from the Camshaft Adjustment Valve N205.

9. Remove the bolts and then the camshaft adjustment valve N205.

10. Remove the upper timing chain cover.

✳✳ WARNING

The control valve has a left thread.

11. Remove the control valve using Assembly Tool T10352 in the direction of.

12. Remove the bolts and remove the bearing bracket.

13. Rotate the vibration damper using the Counter Hold Tool T10355 into the "OT" position.

➡**The notch on the vibration damper must line up with the marking on the timing chain lower cover.**

14. Mark the drive chain/chain sprockets with a waterproof marker. These marks are necessary for reinstallation.

15. Remove the plug.

16. Lift the chain tensioner locking wedge by inserting a scriber or a suitable screwdriver into the hole in the chain tensioner direction.

17. Turn the crankshaft opposite the engine direction of rotation direction and secure it with a Securing Pin T40011.

➡**The intake camshaft switches in the engine direction of rotation.**

18. Remove the bolt and guide the tensioning rail downward.

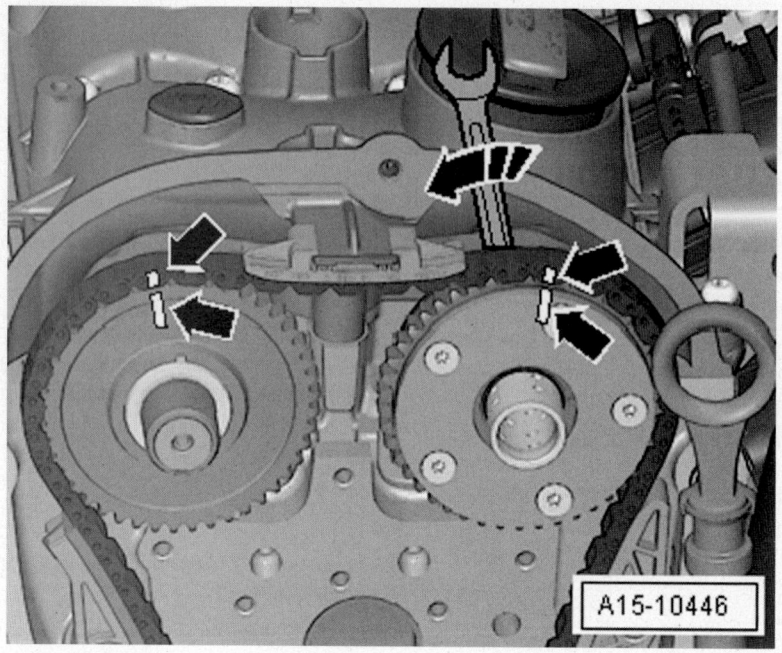

Fig. 62 Mark the drive chain/chain sprockets with a waterproof marker. These marks are necessary for reinstallation

19. Remove the upper guide rail by unlocking the latch (located in the center) with a screwdriver and pushing the guide rail forward.

➡**When the lower timing chain cover is installed, the loose chain on the crankshaft cannot jump off.**

20. Remove camshaft timing chain from chain sprockets.

✳✳ WARNING

If the camshaft timing chain was removed from the cylinder head, then the crankshaft may not be turn further. On this engine, when the valves are mounted, there is the danger that there are panels attached to the lower timing chain cover, which could fall and interfere with the chain; also a loose chain turned by the crankshaft can bend the panels. The panels can bend if the crankshaft is rotated when the chain is loose.

21. Disconnect the electrical connectors on the ignition coils and free up the wiring harness.

22. Remove the ignition coils with the puller T40039.

23. Disconnect the crankcase ventilation hoses.

24. Remove the bolts and remove the crankcase ventilation.

25. Remove the bolts.

26. Remove the air guide pipe bolt.

27. Loosen the hose clamp and remove the air guide pipe together with the crankcase ventilation.

28. Disconnect the vacuum line and free up the wire.

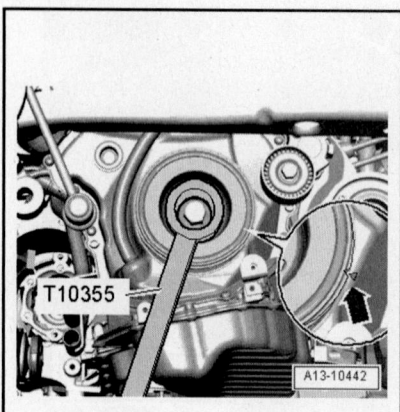

Fig. 61 Rotate the vibration damper using the Counter Hold Tool T10355 into the "OT" position

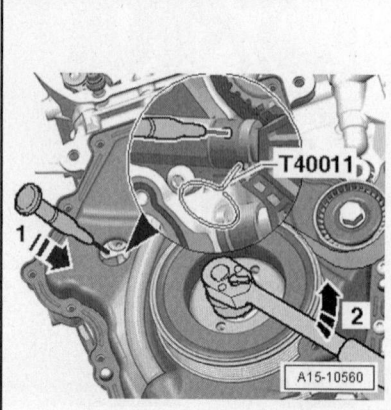

Fig. 63 Lift the chain tensioner locking wedge by inserting a scriber or a suitable screwdriver into the hole in the chain tensioner direction

29. Disconnect the electrical connector from the Camshaft Position (CMP) Sensor G40.

➡ The sealing surfaces of the lower cylinder head cover and on the upper cylinder head must not be reworked.

✳✳ WARNING

If the cylinder head cover was loosened, then the cover must be replaced.

✳✳ WARNING

The camshaft bearings are integrated in the cylinder head or cylinder head cover. The tension must be released from the camshaft timing chain before removing the cylinder head cover.

30. Remove the cylinder head cover bolts in 1 to 6 sequence.
31. Remove the cylinder head cover.
32. Remove the camshafts.
33. Prevent dirt and adhesive residue from entering cylinder head.

   To install:

➡ During installation, cable ties must be re-installed at the same location. Sealing surfaces must be completely free of oil and grease.

✳✳ WARNING

The pistons must not be positioned at TDC.

34. Make sure that all roller cam followers make contact correctly on valve stem ends.

✳✳ WARNING

The cover must be installed within 5 minutes after application of silicone sealant.

35. Remove any sealant residue on the cylinder head using the flat blade scraper.

✳✳ WARNING

Prevent dirt and adhesive residue from entering cylinder head.

36. Remove any seal out of the groove in the cylinder head cover as well as from any sealing surface using, for example, a rotating plastic brush.
37. Clean sealing surfaces, must be free of oil and grease.
38. Cut tube nozzle at front marking approximately 0.078 in. (2 mm).
39. Lubricate the running surfaces of both camshafts.
40. Place the camshaft into the cylinder head; the recesses must be perpendicular to each other.
41. Replace the cylinder head cover bolts.
42. Apply the silicone sealant D 154 103 A1 on the clean sealing surface of the cylinder head cover as shown. Thickness of sealant bead: 0.078–0.117 in. (2–3 mm).

✳✳ WARNING

The cylinder head cover must be installed within 5 minutes after application of silicone sealant. The sealant bead may not be thicker than specified, otherwise excess sealant could enter the oil pan and clog the oil intake tube.

43. Tighten bolts in several stages.

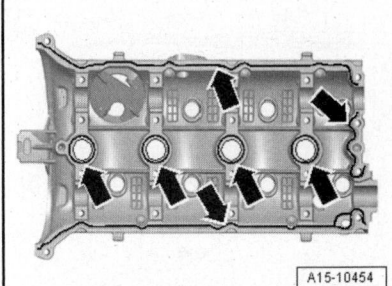

Fig. 66 Apply the silicone sealant D 154 103 A1 on the clean sealing surface of the cylinder head cover as shown. Thickness of sealant bead: 0.078–0.117 in. (2–3 mm)

- Replace bolts
- Hand-tighten bolts in several stages in 1 to 6 sequence
- Tighten the bolts in a 1 to 6 sequence to 71 inch lbs. (8 Nm) using a torque wrench
- Tighten the bolts an additional 90° using a rigid wrench in the sequence 1 to 6

✳✳ WARNING

Make sure the cylinder head cover is not tilted.

44. Insert the cover without sealing using Thrust Piece T10174. Measurement A should be 0.039–0.078 in. (1–2 mm).

✳✳ WARNING

When turning the crankshaft, make sure the timing chain cannot damage any other components.

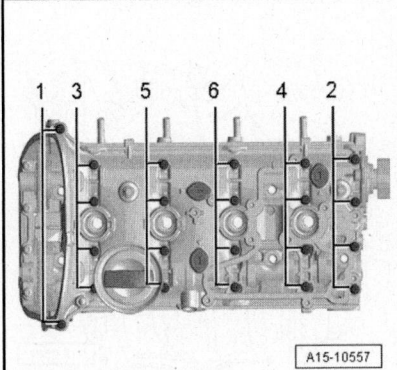

Fig. 64 Remove the cylinder head cover bolts in 1 to 6 sequence

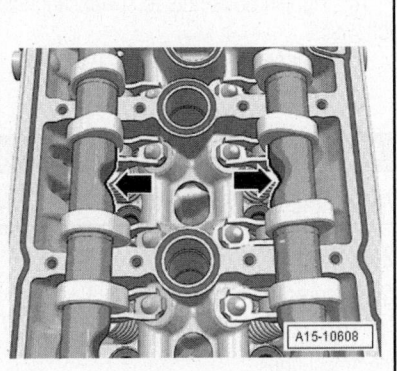

Fig. 65 Remove the cylinder head cover bolts in 1 to 6 sequence

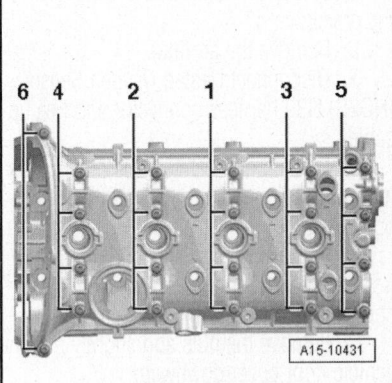

Fig. 67 Tighten bolts in several stages using the sequence shown

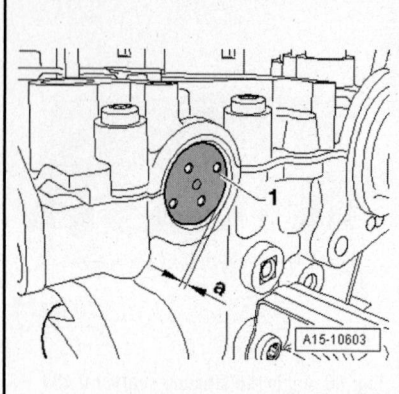

Fig. 68 Insert the cover without sealing using Thrust Piece T10174. Measurement A should be 0.039–0.078 in. (1–2 mm)

45. Rotate the vibration damper using the Counter Hold Tool T10355 into the "OT" position.

46. The notch on the vibration damper must line up with the marking on the timing chain lower cover.

47. The marked links of the timing chain must be positioned on the markings on the chain sprockets.

48. Mount the camshaft timing chain: The markings drive chain/chain sprockets must align.

49. Turn the intake camshaft using the wrench in the direction of the and mount the timing chain.

50. The rest of the assembly is basically a reverse of the disassembling sequence.

CATALYTIC CONVERTER

REMOVAL & INSTALLATION

2.0L & 2.5L Engines

See Figure 69.

1. Before servicing the vehicle, refer to the precautions.

2. Remove the air filter.

3. Disconnect Heated Oxygen Sensor (HO2S) G39 harness connector and free up cable.

4. From above, remove the nuts on the front exhaust pipe connection to the turbocharger.

5. Remove nuts accessible from below from front exhaust pipe to the turbocharger connection.

6. Remove the nuts and slightly pull the vehicle floor cover downward.

7. Disconnect the electrical connector on the right side of the underbody.

8. Remove the electrical connector out of the bracket and free up the electrical wire to the oxygen sensor.

Fig. 69 From above, remove the nuts on the front exhaust pipe connection to the turbocharger

9. Unclip the wires, remove the bracket and disconnect the connectors.

10. Remove exhaust system bracket.

11. Remove the front cross member for the vehicle floor.

> **✳✳ WARNING**
>
> **Risk of damaging decoupling elements. Do not bend decoupling element in front exhaust pipe more than 10°.**

12. Loosen clamping sleeve and push it rearward.

13. Remove the catalytic converters with the front exhaust pipe.

To install:

14. Installation is performed in the reverse order of removal.

15. Coat turbocharger stud bolts with hot bolt paste G 052 112 A3.

16. Replace gaskets and self-locking nuts.

17. Install exhaust system free of stress Exhaust System, Installing.

18. Tighten bolts/nuts to specification as follows:

- Tunnel bridge to body: 19 ft. lbs. (25 Nm)

CRANKSHAFT FRONT SEAL

REMOVAL & INSTALLATION

2.0L Engine

See Figures 70 through 72.

1. Before servicing the vehicle, refer to the precautions.

2. Remove toothed belt.

3. Remove toothed belt crankshaft sprocket. Secure toothed belt sprocket with the counterhold tool 3415

4. To guide seal remover 3203, install the center bolt manually into the crankshaft all the way.

5. Rotate inner section of the seal remover two turns, approximately 0.117 in. (3 mm), out of the outer section and secure it with the knurled bolt.

6. Lubricate threaded head of the seal remover.

7. Using considerable force, screw seal remover as far as possible into the seal.

8. Loosen knurled screw and turn inner portion against crankshaft until the oil seal is pulled out.

To install:

9. The sealing lip of the sealing ring may not be additionally oiled or greased.

10. Before installing, remove oil remains from end of crankshaft with a clean cloth.

11. Place guide sleeve T10053/1 on crankshaft pin.

12. Push seal over the guide sleeve onto the end of the crankshaft.

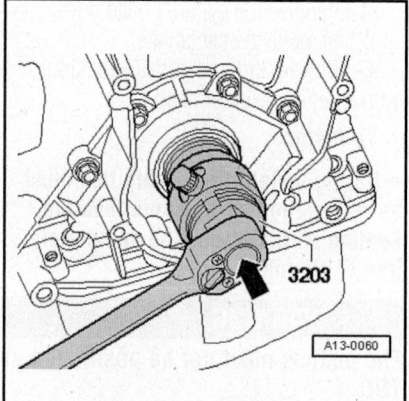

Fig. 70 To guide seal remover 3203, install the center bolt manually into the crankshaft all the way

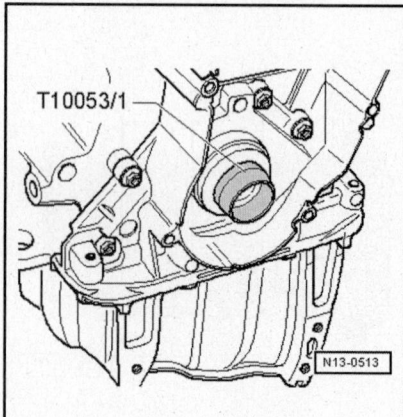

Fig. 71 Place guide sleeve T10053/1 on crankshaft pin

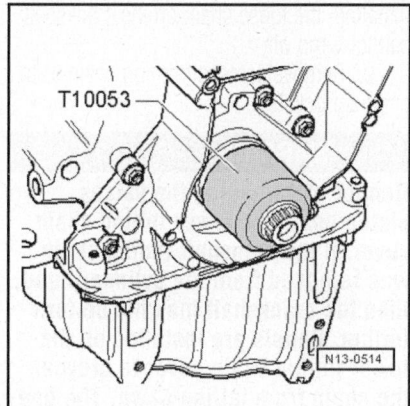

Fig. 72 Press seal in to the limit stop using the assembly tool T10053 and the center bolt

13. Press seal in to the limit stop using the assembly tool T10053 and the center bolt.

14. Install crankshaft toothed belt sprocket and tighten to 15 ft. lbs. (20 Nm).

2.5L Engine

See Figures 73 and 74.

1. Raise and safely support the vehicle and remove the engine undercover.

2. Remove the front part of the right inner fender.

3. Remove the A/C compressor drive belt. Mark the belt's direction of rotation for reinstallation.

4. Remove the belt tensioner.

5. Set the engine to TDC of cylinder No. 5 and insert the crankshaft locking tool at the rear of the engine block.

6. Remove the bolts that hold the front seal flange to the engine block.

7. Starting at the alignment pins, carefully pry off the sealing flange. Take care to prevent damaging the cylinder block. The sealing flange will be damaged while removing.

✳✳ WARNING

To prevent injuries from shavings, wear protective goggles and protective clothing.

8. Remove sealant from cylinder block. Make sure that no sealant residue enters the engine.

9. Clean sealing surface of cylinder block and the crankshaft; they must be clean and dry.

To install:

➡**The following steps must be followed so that the sealing lip of sealing flange**

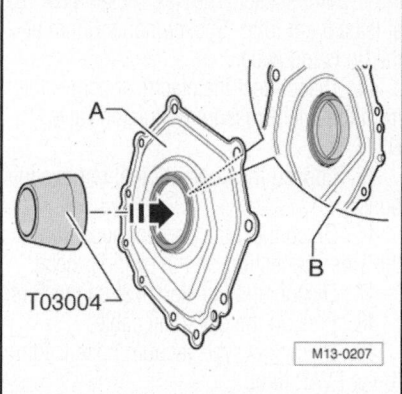

Fig. 73 Use the assembly sleeve to widen the seal enough to fit over the crankshaft–do not use any lubricants

does not roll itself up when installing. Do not use any lubricants!

10. Widen sealing lip of new sealing flange using the tapered end of assembly sleeve T03004.

11. After a short time, remove the assembly sleeve and insert the wide end into sealing ring. Assembly sleeve must protrude approximately 0.020 in. (3 mm) on the engine side of the seal.

12. Apply sealant bead into groove of sealing flange. Insert sealing flange sleeve T03004 over the crankshaft and press the flange plate uniformly into place.

13. Start all the bolts, then tighten uniformly in diagonal sequence. Torque to 7 ft. lbs. (10 Nm).

14. Install the crankshaft pulley and torque the bolt to 37 ft. lbs. (50 Nm) plus 90°.

15. Remove the crankshaft locking tool and install the plug.

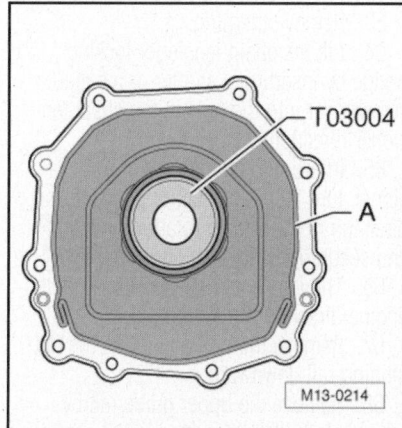

Fig. 74 Apply a bead of sealant and immediately install the sealing flange

16. Install the belt tensioner and A/C drive belt.

17. Install remaining components and run the engine to check for leaks.

CYLINDER HEAD

REMOVAL & INSTALLATION

2.0L & 2.5L Engines

See Figures 75 through 77.

1. Before servicing the vehicle, refer to the precautions.

2. Remove the engine cover.

3. Remove the air filter.

4. Loosen the hose clamp.

5. Remove bolt.

6. Disconnect the electrical connectors and free up the electrical wire.

✳✳ CAUTION

Reduce pressure by covering coolant reservoir cap with a cloth and carefully opening.

7. Open coolant reservoir cap.

8. Remove front exhaust pipe with catalytic converter

9. Remove the right front wheel.

10. Remove the noise insulation.

11. Remove the front right wheel housing liner.

12. Remove the air guide pipe items.

13. Drain coolant.

14. Remove the bolt and remove the air guide pipe downward.

15. Remove bolts.

16. Remove the air guide pipe by lifting the clamps.

17. Disconnect electrical connectors and free up electrical wire.

18. On vehicles with auxiliary heater remove the bolts and swivel the coolant tubs to the left.

19. On vehicles with all-wheel drive, remove the right axle shaft heat shield bolts using Socket AF 8 3247.

20. Remove bolts and remove the turbocharger support.

21. Remove the banjo bolt and move the coolant line to the side.

22. On vehicles with front wheel drive, remove the bolts on the oil return line.

23. On vehicles with all-wheel drive, remove the oil return line bolts on the crankcase.

24. Remove the bolt on the oil supply line.

25. Disconnect the connector from the Camshaft Adjustment Valve N205 1.

26. Disconnect the electrical connectors on the ignition coils and free up the wiring harness.

27. Remove the ignition coils with the puller T40039.

28. Remove the air guide pipe bolt.

29. Remove the air guide pipe; to do this, loosen the hose clamp.

30. Disconnect the hose for the crankcase ventilation.

31. Remove the bolts and remove the crankcase ventilation.

32. Disconnect the hose for the crankcase ventilation.

33. Remove the bolts.

34. Remove the air guide pipe bolt.

35. Loosen the hose clamp and remove the air guide pipe together with the crankcase ventilation.

➡ **Fuel supply line is under pressure! Wear protective goggles and protective clothing to prevent injuries and contact with skin. Before removing from hose connection wrap a cloth around the connection. Then release pressure by carefully pulling hose off connection.**

36. Disconnect the wires from the fuel transfer.

37. Disconnect the coolant line to the coolant reservoir.

38. Remove the coolant hoses from the coolant pipe.

39. Disconnect the ground wire (GND) and remove the bolt.

40. Disconnect the vacuum hoses.

41. Loosen the bolts and remove the heat shield together with the coolant pipe.

42. Disconnect the oil supply line from the turbocharger.

43. On 2.0L engines, remove the bolt from the heat shield using a 6 mm hex

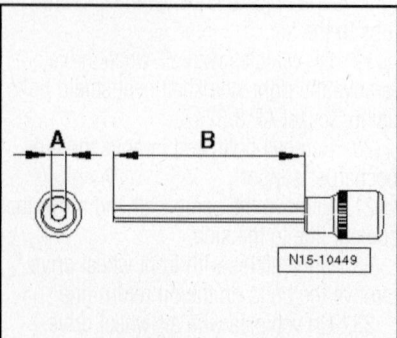

Fig. 75 On 2.0L engines, remove the bolt from the heat shield using a 6 mm hex multi-point socket. The hex socket must be at least 5 cm long. Socket that is 6 mm at the tip is too wide

multi-point socket. The hex socket must be at least 5 cm long. Socket that is 6 mm at the tip is too wide.

44. Disconnect the electrical connector from the Fuel Pressure Regulator Valve N276.

45. Loosen the coolant pipe; remove the bolts.

46. Disconnect the coolant hose from the side connection on the cylinder head.

47. Disconnect the electrical connectors.

48. Free up the electrical cable.

49. Disconnect the vacuum hose leading to the EVAP filter.

50. Disconnect the electrical connectors and pull the connectors out of the retainer.

51. Disconnect the electrical connectors.

52. Disconnect the coolant line from the intake manifold, when doing this, remove the bolts.

53. Remove the intake manifold bracket by removing the mounting nut.

54. Remove the oil filter.

55. Disconnect the coolant hoses and move them to the side.

56. Remove the bolts and remove Camshaft Adjustment Valve N205.

57. Remove timing chain upper cover.

➡ **The control valve has a left thread.**

58. Remove the control valve using Assembly Tool 10352 T10352 in the direction of.

59. Remove the bolts and remove the bearing bracket.

60. Rotate the vibration damper using the Counter Hold Tool T10355 into the "OT" position.

61. The notch on the vibration damper must line up with the marking on the timing chain lower cover.

62. Carefully mark the drive chain/chain sprockets with a waterproof marker. These marks are necessary for reinstallation.

63. Remove the plug.

64. Lift the chain tensioner locking wedge by inserting a scriber or a suitable screwdriver into the hole in the chain tensioner direction.

65. In order to tension the chain tensioner, turn the crankshaft opposite the direction of the engine rotation direction and secure it using Securing Pin T40011.

66. The intake camshaft switches in the engine direction of rotation.

67. Remove the bolt and guide the tensioning rail downward.

68. Remove the upper guide rail by unlocking the latch (located in the center) with a screwdriver and pushing the guide rail forward.

69. When the lower timing chain cover is

installed, the loose chain on the crankshaft cannot jump off.

70. Remove camshaft timing chain from chain sprockets.

✴✴ WARNING

Danger of damaging the valves, piston head and lower timing chain cover. If the camshaft timing chain was removed from the cylinder head, then the crankshaft may not be turn further. Panels are installed on the lower timing chain cover to prevent the chain from falling down. The panels can bend if the crankshaft is rotated when the chain is loose.

71. Turn the sealing plug counterclockwise 90° and remove it.

72. Remove the ball head.

73. Remove the oil filler cap.

74. Remove the bolts

75. Remove the cylinder head bolts in sequence 1 through 5 using Polydrive bit and drive socket T10070 until 2 are left.

76. To remove the cylinder head bolts, turn the camshaft with a wrench if necessary.

77. Make sure all wires and cables are disconnect!

78. Pay attention the tension and guide rails when lifting the cylinder head.

79. Install the Engine Support T10014 each of the two small and large washers.

80. Connect the Engine Sling 2024 in the Engine Support T10014 and in the front left lifting eye on the cylinder head.

81. Mount the Engine Sling 2024 into the workshop crane and gently lift the cylinder head.

82. Remove the last two cylinder head bolts.

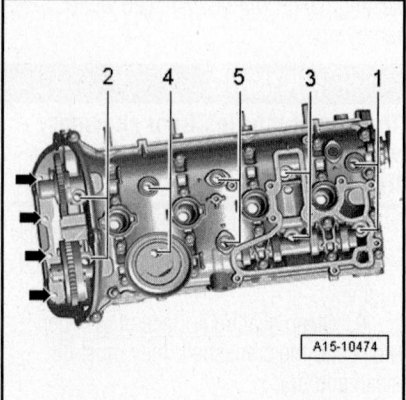

Fig. 76 Remove the cylinder head bolts in sequence 1 through 5 using Polydrive bit and drive socket T10070 until 2 are left

➡Carefully lift the cylinder head until the guide rail for the camshaft timing chain is free. The tension- and guide rail must not be damaged.

83. Lay the cylinder head on a soft surface, such as foam.

To install:

➡The sealing surfaces could be damaged. Carefully remove sealant residue from cylinder head and cylinder block. Make sure that no long scrapes or scratches result.

☀☀ WARNING

Risk of damaging cylinder block. There must be no oil or coolant in the blind holes for the cylinder head bolts in the cylinder block.

☀☀ WARNING

Risk of cylinder head seal leaking. Carefully remove all grinding and sanding residue. Only unpack new cylinder head gasket immediately prior to installation. To prevent cylinder head seal silicone layer and recessed area from being damaged, always handle seal extremely carefully.

☀☀ WARNING

Risk of damaging open valves. If a replacement cylinder is installed, only remove plastic base right before cylinder head is installed to protect open valves. Risk of damaging valves and piston heads after working on valvetrain. To ensure valves do not strike pistons when starting, carefully rotate engine at least 2 full revolutions.

84. Replace bolts which have been tightened to torque.

85. Replace sealing rings, seals and self-locking nuts.

86. Note different sealant for cylinder head sealing surfaces and bolts.

87. Secure all hose connections with hose clamps appropriate for the model.

88. When installing a replacement cylinder head, turn the camshaft to OT and mark the new chain sprockets exactly the same as on the old chain sprockets -arrows- (note the factory color marking on the chain sprockets).

89. If an exchange cylinder head is installed, all contact surfaces between bearing elements, roller rocker levers and

cam running surfaces of camshafts must be oiled before installing cylinder head cover.

90. The engine oil and coolant must be changed if the cylinder head or cylinder head seal are replaced.

91. Hang the cylinder head on the workshop crane and position it above the cylinder block.

➡Carefully lower the cylinder head. The tension- and guide rail must not be damaged. Pay attention to centering pins in cylinder block. Observe cylinder head seal location, identification: Replacement part number must be visible from intake side.

➡When turning the crankshaft, make sure the timing chain cannot damage any other components.

92. In the event the crankshaft has been rotated in the meantime: Set piston of cylinder 1 to TDC and turn crankshaft back again slightly.

93. Set cylinder head in place.

94. Insert cylinder head bolts and tighten by hand.

95. In order to be able to turn the cylinder head bolts, the intake camshaft must be turned with a wrench.

96. There is no requirement to retighten the cylinder head bolts after repairs.

97. Tighten cylinder head bolts in sequence to the following specification:
- Tighten the cylinder head bolts in 1 to 5 sequence.
- Tighten to 30 ft. lbs. (40 Nm) using a torque wrench
- Tighten further 90° using a rigid wrench
- Tighten further 90° using a rigid wrench

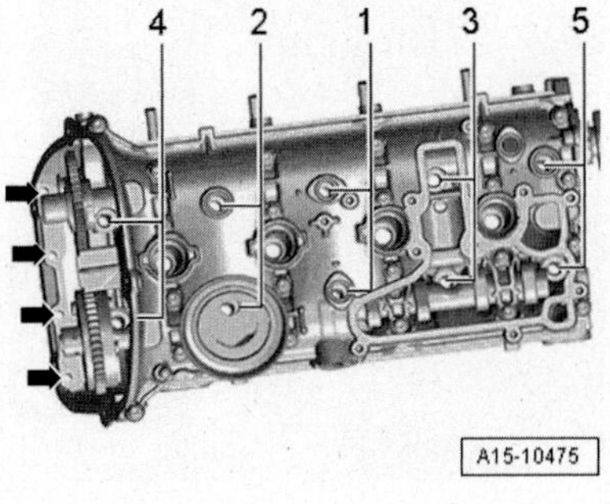

Fig. 77 Cylinder head bolt tightening sequence

- Pre-tighten the bolts (arrows) to 71 inch lbs. (8 Nm)
- Tighten the bolts (arrows) 90° further using a rigid wrench

➡When turning the crankshaft, make sure the timing chain cannot damage any other components.

98. Rotate the vibration damper using the Counter Hold Tool T10355 into the "OT" position.

99. The notch on the vibration damper must line up with the marking on the timing chain lower cover.

100. The marked links of the timing chain must be positioned on the markings on the chain sprockets.

101. Mount the camshaft timing chain: The markings drive chain/chain sprockets must align.

102. Turn the intake camshaft using the wrench and mount the timing chain.

103. The rest of the installation is performed in reverse order of removal, noting the following:

104. During installation, cable ties must be re-installed at the same location.

105. Change the engine oil

106. Replace coolant.

EXHAUST MANIFOLD

REMOVAL & INSTALLATION

2.0L Engine
See Figures 75 and 78.

1. Before servicing the vehicle, refer to the precautions.

☀☀ WARNING

If mechanical damage is found on exhaust turbocharger, e.g. a destroyed compression wheel, it is not enough to just replace the turbocharger. Perform the following steps to prevent subsequent damage. Check the air filter housing, the air filter insert and the intake hoses for contamination. Check entire charge air circuit and cooler for contamination. If contaminants are found in charge air circuit, circuit must be cleaned and cooler replaced if necessary.

2. Remove the air filter.
3. Remove the battery and battery tray.
4. Remove noise insulation.
5. Remove the front part of the right wheel housing liner and/or the front right wheel housing liner.

6. Drain the coolant.

7. Remove catalytic converters with front exhaust pipe.

8. Remove bolts.

9. Remove the air guide pipe by lifting the clamps items.

10. On vehicles with all-wheel drive remove the heat shield above the right driveshaft.

11. Disconnect electrical connectors and free up electrical wire.

12. On vehicles with auxiliary heater remove the bolts and swivel the coolant tubs to the left.

13. On vehicles with front wheel drive remove the right driveshaft heat shield.

14. Remove the bolt Socket XZN 10 T10154.

15. Remove the bolt.

16. Remove the banjo bolt and move the coolant line to the side.

17. On vehicles with front wheel drive remove the bolts on the oil return line.

18. On vehicles with all-wheel drive remove the oil return line bolts on the crankcase.

19. Remove the bolt on the oil supply line.

20. Remove engine cover.

21. Disconnect the connectors from the ignition coils and the wiring harness and lay them aside.

22. Disconnect the coolant line to the coolant reservoir.

23. Disconnect the vacuum line at the separating point and free up the wire.

24. Remove the coolant hoses from the coolant pipe.

25. Press the release buttons, remove the air guide hose and move them to the side.

26. Remove the air guide pipe bolt.

27. Remove the air guide pipe; to do this, loosen the hose clamp.

28. Remove the air guide pipe bolt.

29. Loose the hose clamp and lay the air guide pipe on the cylinder head.

30. Seal the turbocharger with the Engine bung set VAS 6122.

31. Remove the bolts and remove the heat shield together with the coolant pipe.

32. On 2.0L engines, remove the bolt from the heat shield with a 6 mm hex socket. The hex socket must be at least 5 cm long. A socket that is 6 mm at the tip is too wide.

33. Disconnect the oil supply line from the turbocharger.

34. Disconnect the coolant hose and move it to the side.

35. Remove the nuts.

36. Remove the turbocharger/exhaust manifold upward.

To install:

37. Installation is performed in the reverse order of removal, noting the following:

38. Always replace seals, gaskets and self-locking nuts.

39. Add oil to turbocharger through oil feed line connecting piece.

40. After installing turbocharger, let engine idle for approximately 1 minute to ensure adequate oil supply to the turbocharger.

41. Coolant return line must be installed together with turbocharger.

42. Hose connections and charge air system hoses must be free of oil and grease before installing. Sealing ring and sealing surfaces must only be lightly oiled with connector couplings.

43. Secure all hose connections using hose clamps appropriate for the model type.

44. Exhaust manifold/turbocharger to the cylinder head

- Tighten the bolts 1 through 5 in 4 stages as follows:
- Tighten the bolts to 44 inch lbs. (5 Nm)
- Tighten the bolts to 106 inch lbs. (12 Nm)
- Tighten the bolts to 12 ft. lbs. (16 Nm)
- Tighten the bolts to 19 ft. lbs. (25 Nm)

45. Tighten bolts/nuts to specification as follows:

- Oil supply line to exhaust turbocharger: 15 ft. lbs. (20 Nm) plus 45° additional rotation
- Oil return line to exhaust turbocharger: 80 inch lbs. (9 Nm)
- Coolant supply line to turbocharger: 15 ft. lbs. (20 Nm) plus 45° additional rotation

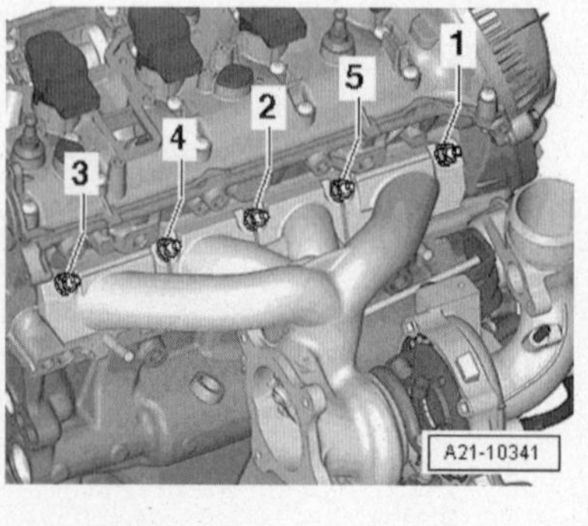

Fig. 78 Observe tightening sequence for exhaust manifold/turbocharger to the cylinder head

- Turbocharger bracket to cylinder block: 22 ft. lbs. (30 Nm)
- Turbocharger bracket to turbocharger: 22 ft. lbs. (30 Nm)
- Right charge air pipe to oil pan: 89 inch. lbs. (9 Nm)
- Heat shield to cylinder head (replace nuts and use hot bolt paste) M8 and M12: 15 ft. lbs. (20 Nm)

2.5L Engine

1. Before servicing the vehicle, refer to the precautions.

2. Remove the engine cover.

3. Remove the wiper arms.

4. Remove the outer plenum chamber cover and plenum chamber end plate.

5. Remove the heat shield.

6. Remove the protective cap for the right inner Constant Velocity (CV) joint from the engine.

7. Remove bolt and nut and remove the brace for the exhaust manifold.

8. Loosen the nuts for the double clamp.

9. Remove the nuts and bolts.

10. Remove the front exhaust pipe from the exhaust manifold and tie up firmly to the side.

11. The flex joint in the front exhaust pipe must not be bent more than 10°, otherwise it may be damaged.

12. Disconnect the electrical connector for the oxygen sensor.

13. Remove the heat shield at the top of the front exhaust pipe and free up the wiring harness of the oxygen sensor in the exhaust manifold.

14. Remove the exhaust manifold bolts and remove it downward.

To install:

15. Installation is performed in reverse order.

16. Gaskets and self-locking nuts must be replaced.

17. Install the exhaust manifold.

18. Install the front exhaust pipe with catalytic converter,

19. Check the Diagnostic Trouble code (DTC) memory of the Engine Control Module (ECM), repair any stored malfunctions and then erase the DTC memory.

20. Tighten bolts/nuts to specification as follows:

- Exhaust manifold nut: 19 ft. lbs. (25Nm)
- Heat shield bolt: 89 inch lbs. (10 Nm)
- Exhaust nut/bolt: 19 ft. lbs. (25Nm)

INTAKE MANIFOLD

REMOVAL & INSTALLATION

2.0L Engines

See Figure 79.

1. Before servicing the vehicle, refer to the precautions.

❋❋ WARNING

Fuel system is under pressure! Fuel pressure must be reduced to a residual pressure before opening high pressure area of injection system.

2. Remove the engine cover.
3. Clean the contact surface from the intake manifold to the cylinder head.
4. Remove the air filter.
5. Separate the vacuum line to the EVAP canister.
6. Disconnect the following electrical connections:

   - Intake Air Temperature Sensor G42
   - Throttle Valve Control Module J338
   - Evaporative Emission (EVAP) Canister Purge Regulator Valve N80
   - Camshaft Position sensor G40

7. Disconnect the vacuum line at the separating point and remove the crankcase ventilation hose.
8. Remove the bolts for the fuel supply line and lay the line to the side.
9. The fuel system must have no pressure.
10. Open the fuel line union nut lower.
11. Disconnect the vacuum line from the Intake Manifold Runner Control (IMRC) Valve N316.
12. Remove the bolts for the coolant line from the intake manifold.
13. Disconnect the electrical connector from the Fuel Pressure Sensor G247.
14. Loosen the hose clamp.
15. Remove bolt.
16. Disconnect electrical connector.
17. Remove the noise insulation.
18. Remove the air guide pipe items.
19. Remove the bolt and remove the air guide pipe downward.
20. Disconnect the electrical connectors and remove the bracket from the intake manifold.
21. Remove the intake manifold bracket by removing the mounting nut.
22. Remove the oil filter.
23. Loosen the wiring bracket.
24. Loosen the wire from the intake manifold.

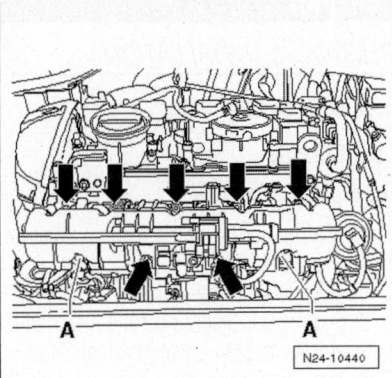

Fig. 79 Remove the nuts A and loosen the bolts from the intake manifold using the Multi-point socket T10347

25. Remove the nuts and loosen the bolts from the intake manifold using the Multi-point socket T10347.
26. Carefully pull the intake manifold and fuel rail away from the cylinder head just a little.
27. Disconnect the electrical connector from the Intake Manifold Runner Position Sensor G336 and remove the intake manifold.
28. Cover the intake channels with a clean rag.
29. The fuel injectors could remain stuck in the fuel rail.
30. Disconnect the fuel rail from the intake manifold.
31. To access the fuel injectors, the intake manifold and the fuel rail with intake manifold runner control valve must be removed. The fuel injectors sit in the cylinder head.

To install:

32. The combustion chamber seal (Teflon) and the O-ring must always be replaced.
33. Mount the intake manifold onto the cylinder head on the stud bolts (lower left and right).
34. Make sure the fuel injectors are installed correctly and pay attention to the wiring bracket when mounting the intake manifold (located under the intake manifold).
35. When installing the intake manifold, the manifold must be pulled out slightly and the fuel injectors will stick in the fuel rail. Pull the fuel injectors out of the fuel rail and insert them in the cylinder head again.
36. The rest of the installation follows the reverse of the removal procedures.
37. When attaching the wiring bracket onto the intake manifold, make sure it clips into both latches.

Tightening Specifications, Intake Manifold, Assembly Overview Intake Manifold, Assembly Overview.

Fuel Rail Tightening Specifications, Assembly Overview Fuel Rail, Assembly Overview

- High pressure pump bolts (Replace): 89 inch lbs. (10 Nm)
- Fuel high pressure line connection (Replace): 16 ft. lbs. (22 Nm)
- Fuel line to the fuel rail: 13 ft. lbs. (18 Nm)
- Bolt for the intake manifold support: 17 ft. lbs. (23 Nm)
- Nut for the intake manifold support: 89 inch lbs. (10 Nm)

2.5L Engine

See Figure 80.

1. Before servicing the vehicle, refer to the precautions.
2. First, check whether a coded radio is installed. If necessary, obtain the anti-theft coding.
3. Disconnect the negative battery cable.
4. Remove engine cover/air filter assembly.

❋❋ CAUTION

Fuel supply line is under pressure! Wear protective goggles and protective clothing to prevent injuries and contact with skin. Before loosening the fuel lines, place a rag around the connection point. Then release pressure by carefully pulling hose off connection.

5. Disconnect the three under-hood fuel lines. To release wires, press the circlip in. On the fuel supply line, the retainer must be pressed upward in the housing.
6. Disconnect connectors. Remove wiring harness from transport strap. Pull clamps and retaining ring out of locking mechanism. Remove bolts and remove transport strap.
7. Remove throttle valve control module (throttle body). The coolant hoses remain attached.
8. Disconnect manifold wiring and hose for crankcase ventilation.
9. Remove wiring harness by carefully pressing off clips.
10. Pull oil dipstick out and press dipstick tube retaining ring downward.
11. Raise and safely support the vehicle and remove the engine undercover.
12. Loosen bolts or nuts on the bottom side of the intake manifold.

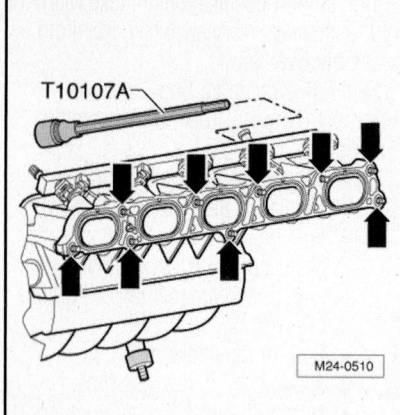

Fig. 80 This long multi point socket is needed to remove the manifold bolts

13. Loosen bolt for intake manifold support and dipstick tube. Lay tube aside.

14. Open clip on leak detection pump (LDP) vacuum hose.

15. Loosen intake manifold bolts using Tool T10107A. Bolts remain in intake manifold.

16. Remove intake manifold upward at an angle. Make sure that no bolts fall out.

17. Seal intake ports in cylinder head using a clean rag.

18. If manifold must be replaced:
- Remove fuel rail with injectors.
- Disconnect vacuum hose for Leak Detection Pump (LDP).
- Remove Manifold Absolute Pressure (MAP) sensor.

To install:

19. Make sure all sealing surfaces are clean and dry. Fit new sealing rings to the intake manifold runners.

20. If the injectors were removed, fit new O-rings, lubricate them with engine oil and install the injectors.

21. Replace oil dipstick tube seal.

22. Fit the manifold into place and torque the screws to 6 ft. lbs. (9 Nm) working from the middle and working towards the ends in a diagonal sequence.

23. Install mounting supports and torque bolts to 18 ft. lbs. (25 Nm).

24. Install the dipstick tube and insert the dipstick.

25. Install the throttle body.

26. Connect all wires, hoses and tubes using new seals or gaskets as needed.

27. Connect the battery

28. Bleed fuel supply system.

29. Run the engine to check for leaks.

OIL PAN

REMOVAL & INSTALLATION

2.0L & 2.5L Engines

LOWER PAN

See Figures 81 and 82.

1. Before servicing the vehicle, refer to the precautions.

2. Remove noise insulation.

3. If present, disconnect the electrical connector for the Oil Level Thermal Sensor G266.

4. Drain engine oil.

5. Remove the screws.

6. Remove oil pan, if necessary loosen by applying light strikes with a rubber hammer.

To install:

7. Remove sealant residue from upper part of the oil pan with a flat scraper.

8. Remove sealant residue on the lower part of the oil pan, e.g. with a rotating plastic brush.

9. Clean sealing surfaces, must be free of oil and grease.

10. Cut tube nozzle at front nozzle approximately 0.117 in. (3 mm).

11. Apply silicon sealant D 174 003 A2 to clean sealing surfaces of the oil pan (lower part) as shown in illustration.

❊❊ WARNING

The oil pan must be installed within 5 minutes after application of silicon sealant.

➡ **The sealant bead may not be thicker than 0.078–0.117 in. (2–3 mm), otherwise excess sealant could enter the oil pan and clog the oil intake tube.**

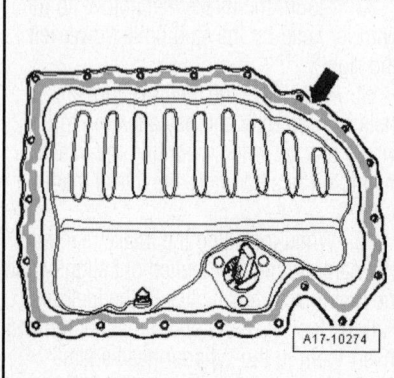

Fig. 81 Apply silicon sealant D 174 003 A2 to clean sealing surfaces of the oil pan (lower part) as shown in illustration

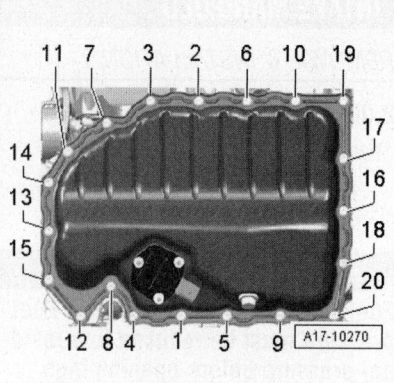

Fig. 82 Immediately mount the lower part of the oil pan and tighten the screws 1 through 20 in two steps as shown

12. Immediately mount the lower part of the oil pan and tighten the screws 1 through 20 in two steps as shown.

13. Tighten bolts/nuts to specification as follows:
- Tighten the bolts to 71 inch lbs. (8 Nm)
- Tighten the bolts an additional 90°

14. After installing oil pan, allow sealant to dry for approximately 30 minutes. Only after then may the engine oil be replenished.

15. Fill the engine oil, oil capacities Engine Oil.

16. The rest of the assembly is basically a reverse of the disassembling sequence.

OIL PUMP

REMOVAL & INSTALLATION

2.0L & 2.5L Engines

See Figures 83 and 84.

1. Before servicing the vehicle, refer to the precautions.

2. Remove the lower oil pan section.

3. Remove the oil baffle.

4. The following must be performed in one sequence; technicians are necessary.

5. Remove the oil pump bolts.

6. Pull back the chain tensioner using the Assembly Tool T10118 and have a second technician remove the oil pump.

To install:

7. Installation is performed in reverse order of removal.

8. Before installing the oil pump, make sure the screen in the supply line and the

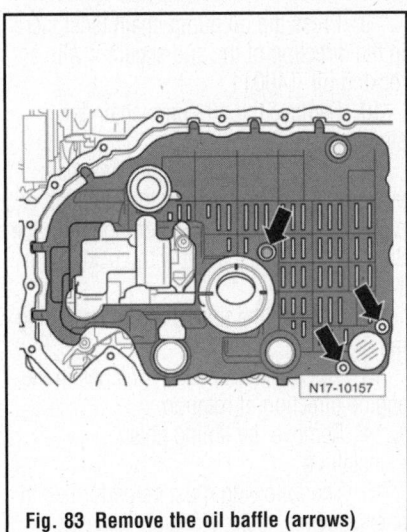

Fig. 83 Remove the oil baffle (arrows)

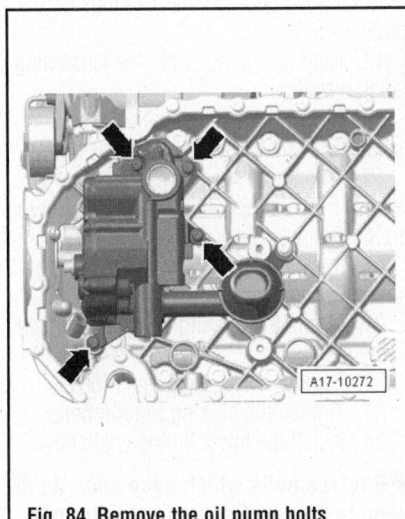

Fig. 84 Remove the oil pump bolts

oil passages in the upper part of the oil pan are clean.

9. Make sure both alignment bushings for centering the oil pump are in there.

10. Replace the baffle plate.

✳✳ WARNING

There are plastic ribs on the oil baffle that deform permanently when tightening. The plastic ribs ensure the oil baffle is not loosen and does not rattle. Because of this, always replace the oil baffle.

TIMING CHAIN, SPROCKETS, FRONT COVER AND SEAL

REMOVAL & INSTALLATION

2.0L & 2.5L Engines

See Figures 85 through 91.

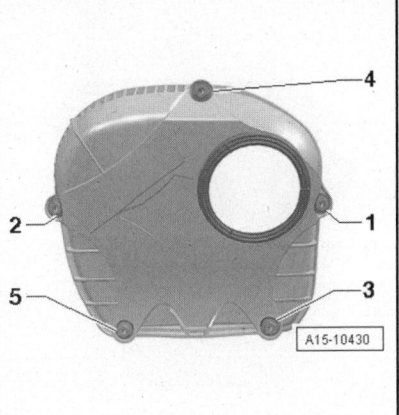

Fig. 85 Remove bolts 1 through 5 and remove the upper timing chain cover

1. Before servicing the vehicle, refer to the precautions.

2. Remove timing chain upper cover.

a. Remove the Camshaft Adjustment Valve N205.

b. Remove bolts 1 through 5 and remove the upper timing chain cover.

✳✳ WARNING

The control valve has a left thread.

3. Remove the control valve using Assembly Tool 10352 T10352 in the direction of.

4. Remove the bolts and remove the bearing bracket.

5. Rotate the vibration damper using the Counter Hold Tool T10355 into the "OT" position.

6. The notch on the vibration damper must line up with the marking on the timing chain lower cover.

7. The markings on the camshafts must point upward.

8. Remove the lower timing chain cover.

a. Remove the noise insulation.

b. Remove the front part of the right wheel housing liner.

c. Drain engine oil.

d. On vehicles with auxiliary heater, loosen the clamp, remove the bolt and remove the auxiliary heater muffler.

e. Remove bolts.

f. Remove the air guide pipe by lifting the clamps.

✳✳ WARNING

Risk of destroying due to reversed running direction on a used ribbed belt. Before removing ribbed belt, marking running direction with

chalk or felt-tip pen for reinstallation later.

g. Remove the right air guide hose.

h. To release the tension on the ribbed belt, turn the tensioner in direction of rotation from underneath.

i. Secure tensioner with Drift T10060 A.

j. Remove ribbed belt from vibration damper ribbed belt pulley.

k. Rotate the vibration damper using the Counter Hold Tool T10355 into the "OT" position.

l. The notch on the vibration damper must line up with the marking on the timing chain lower cover.

✳✳ WARNING

The engine could be destroyed. 1. In order not to change the valve timing, the crankshaft must not be moved out of the "OT" position when the vibration damper bolt is removed.

m. Remove vibration damper bolt using Counterhold T10355.

n. Remove the vibration damper.

✳✳ WARNING

To avoid damaging the splines, only use Thrust Piece T10368 to install the vibration damper bolt.

o. Install the vibration damper bolt and thrust piece T10368 again.

p. Mount the Engine Support Bridge 10 - 222 A.

q. Do not place the adapter 10 - 222 A /8 on the fender panels. They will be damaged.

r. The shackle 10 - 222 A /12 is needed to make sure the engine is lifted in the installation position and not tipped away.

s. Tension the engine with the spindle.

t. Remove the subframe bolts on the engine.

u. Remove the engine bracket subframe mount.

v. Lift the engine approximately 1.95 in. (50 mm) and loosen the upper bolt for the engine support.

w. Now lower the engine approximately 3.9 in. (100 mm).

x. Free up electrical wiring harness.

y. Remove the bolt and remove the ribbed belt tensioner from the accessory assembly bracket.

z. Remove the lower bolts for the engine support using Bits T10099.

aa. Remove the engine support and the bolts.

bb. Remove the bolts and pull the oil dipstick guide tube out of the lower timing chain cover.

cc. Disconnect the Wastegate Bypass Regulator Valve N75 from the turbocharger.

dd. Remove the turbocharger support.

ee. Remove the bolts 1 through 15.

✳✳ WARNING

The lower timing chain cover could be damaged. To avoid deformation, do not hold between the bolting points.

ff. Pry off the lower timing chain cover starting with bolts shown.

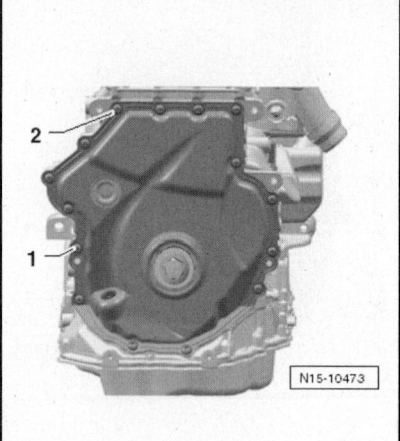

Fig. 87 Pry off the lower timing chain cover starting with bolts 1 & 2 as shown

9. Press the oil pump chain tensioner in the direction of the and secure it with a locking pin T40011.

10. Remove the oil pump chain tensioner.

11. Using a screwdriver, lift the chain tensioner locking wedge in the direction of, press the timing chain tensioning rail in the direction of and secure it with Locking Pin T40011.

12. Remove the timing chain tensioning rail.

13. The intake camshaft switches in the engine direction of rotation

14. Remove the timing chain.
Installing

15. The following must be performed in one sequence; technicians are necessary.

16. The painted links of the timing chain must be positioned on the markings on the chain sprockets.

17. Hold the wrench until the tensioning rail is installed.

18. Mount the timing chain on the exhaust camshaft and crankshaft as shown.

19. Turn the intake camshaft using the wrench in the direction of the and mount the timing chain.

20. Install the timing chain tensioning rail and tighten the bolt.

21. Mount the bearing bracket and hand tighten the bolts.

22. Remove the locking pin T40011.

23. Tighten the bearing bracket bolts

24. Install the lower timing chain cover.

➡**Replace bolts which have been tightened to torque. Replace sealing rings, seals and self-locking nuts.**

a. Remove any sealant residue on the engine block using the flat blade scraper.

b. Seal off both side of the seal with tape to prevent soiling

c. Remove residual sealant on the cover e.g. with a rotating plastic brush.

d. Clean sealing surfaces, must be free of oil and grease.

e. Install the cover using the old bolts and tighten to 71 inch lbs. (8 Nm).

f. Check between the cover and housing using a feel gauge; the gap must not exceed 0.0078 in. (0.2 mm).

g. If the gap exceed 0.0078 in. (0.2 mm), replace the cover.

h. It is not possible to measure between the cover the upper part of the oil pan, however check the sealing surface for evenness.

i. Make sure both alignment bushings for centering the cover are present.

j. Cut tube nozzle at front marking to approximately 0.117 in. (3 mm).

Fig. 86 Rotate the vibration damper using the Counter Hold Tool T10355 into the "OT" position

Fig. 88 Mount the timing chain on the exhaust camshaft and crankshaft

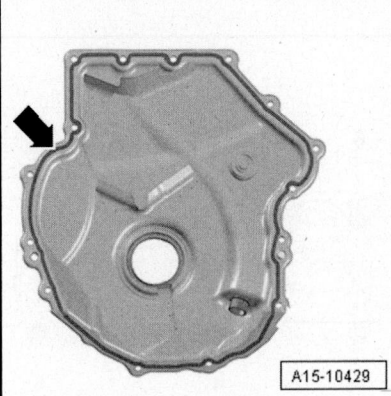

Fig. 89 Apply the silicone sealant D 174 003 A3 in a bead of 0.078–0.117 in. (2–3 mm) on the clean sealing surface of the cover as shown

k. Apply the silicone sealant D 174 003 A3 in a bead of 0.078–0.117 in. (2–3 mm) on the clean sealing surface of the cover as shown.

l. The cover must be installed within 5 minutes after application of silicone sealant.

m. The sealant bead may not be thicker than specified, otherwise excess sealant could enter the oil pan and clog the oil intake tube.

n. Install the lid immediately and all the bolts.

o. Tighten the bolts 1 through 15 in 2 stages in the sequence shown:
- Tighten the bolts to 71 inch lbs. (8 Nm)
- Tighten the bolts an additional 90°

p. After installing cover, allow sealant to dry for approximately 30 minutes.

Only after then may the engine oil be replenished.

25. Install timing chain upper cover.

a. Coat the sealing ring and the O-ring with engine oil.

b. Tighten the bolts 1 through 5 by hand in the illustrated sequence.

c. Tighten the bolt to 80 inch lbs. (9 Nm) by using the torque wrench V.A.G 1783 and the open end spanner insert AF 10 V.A.G 1783/1.

26. The rest of the assembly is basically a reverse of the disassembling sequence.

27. Fill the engine oil.

28. Check oil level.

TURBOCHARGER

REMOVAL & INSTALLATION

Refer to Exhaust Manifold.

VALVE COVERS

REMOVAL & INSTALLATION

See Figure 92.

➡**When doing any repair work, especially in the engine compartment, pay attention to the following due to clearance issues:**

➡**Route all lines and wires in their original locations. For example, fuel, hydraulic, Evaporative Emission (EVAP), coolant, refrigerant, brake fluid and vacuum lines.**

➡**Ensure sufficient clearance to all moving or hot components.**

1. Remove the engine cover.

2. Remove the protective strip.

3. Disconnect the connector from the fuel injectors A, the exhaust pressure sensor 1 G450 B and the fuel pressure sensor G247 C.

4. Remove the coolant line bolts arrows from the intake manifold and lay the line in front of the intake manifold.

5. Unclip the wiring harness for the glow plugs from the wiring guide.

➡**Always follow the procedure "glow plug connectors, disconnecting and installing".**

6. Disconnect the glow plug connectors.

7. Remove the fuel return line bolt from the intake manifold.

8. Loosen the hose clip using hose clip pliers VAS 6362 and remove the line on the fuel rail.

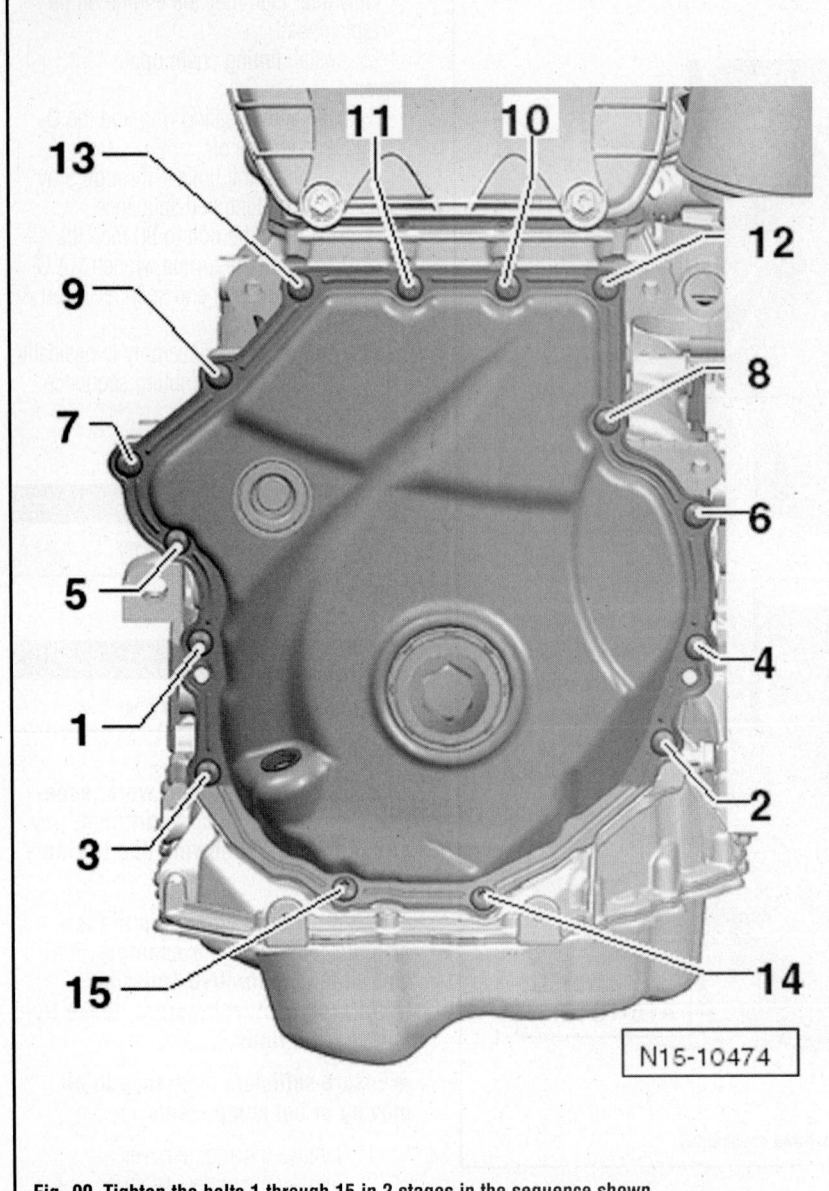

Fig. 90 Tighten the bolts 1 through 15 in 2 stages in the sequence shown

16. Seal the lines so that the fuel system is not contaminated by dirt, etc.

17. Remove the fuel return line and lay the lines in front of the intake manifold.

18. Disconnect the connector from the charge pressure actuator position sensor G581 at the turbocharger vacuum diaphragm and guide the line out of the retainers.

19. Disconnect the connector from the fuel pressure regulator valve N276.

20. Remove the line guide on the fuel rail and lay it aside.

21. Remove the vacuum hose from the cylinder head cover.

22. Remove the remaining vacuum hoses from the bracket on the cylinder head cover.

23. Disconnect the connector 1 from the engine coolant temperature sensor on radiator G83, open the clips arrows and remove the upper toothed belt guard.

24. Remove the crankcase ventilation hose between the intake tube and the cylinder head cover.

The crankcase ventilation hose is destroyed when it is removed.

25. Remove the high pressure fuel line between the high pressure fuel pump and fuel rail.

26. Remove the high pressure fuel lines between the fuel rail and fuel injectors.

27. Remove the bolts arrows and the fuel rail.

28. Remove the fuel injectors.

29. Remove the cylinder head cover bolts in sequence 7 through 1.

30. Remove the cylinder head cover.

To install:

31. Install in reverse order of removal. When doing this note the following:

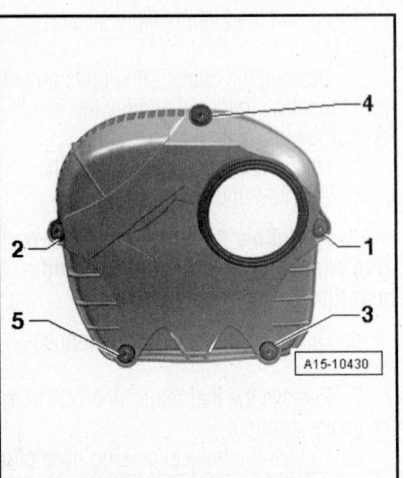

Fig. 91 Tighten the bolts 1 through 5 by hand in the illustrated sequence

9. Before removing, clean the return line connection on the fuel injectors (for example using a commercially available detergent).

10. Cover the return line connections with a cloth.

11. Remove the fuel return line connections on the fuel injectors. Pull them upward to release them.

12. Follow the rules of cleanliness.

13. Do not let any dirt to get into the disconnected return lines or into the connections for the fuel injection units.

14. Loosen the hose clip using hose clip pliers VAS 6362 and remove the fuel return line.

15. Loosen the hose clip 4 using hose clip pliers VAS 6362 and remove the fuel return line at the high pressure fuel pump.

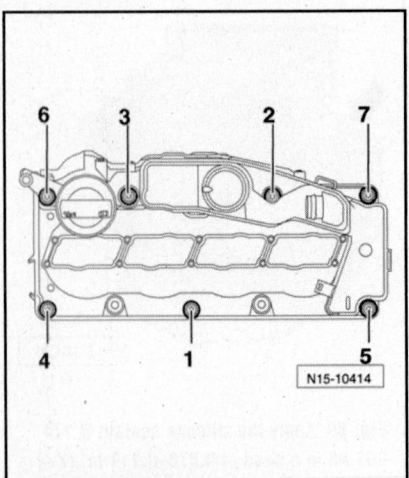

Fig. 92 Remove/Install the cylinder head cover bolts in sequence 7 through 1

32. Condition: Replace the cylinder head cover gasket if it leaks or is damaged. Refer to the Parts Catalog.

a. When installing the high pressure line or fuel lines, make sure no dirt or contaminants enter the fuel system.

b. Only remove the sealing plugs right before installing the fuel lines.

c. Do not change the angles of the high pressure lines

d. Make sure line connections are securely fastened.

e. Do not swap the supply and return lines.

33. First tighten the cylinder head cover bolts by hand in sequence 1 through 7.

34. Tighten the cylinder head cover bolts in sequence 1 through 7 to 5 Nm.

35. Condition: Tightening specifications.

36. Install the upper toothed belt guard.

37. Make sure the upper toothed belt guard is clipped to the cylinder head cover correctly.

38. Press the upper toothed belt guard in the area with the clips arrows against the cylinder head cover until the clips engage

with each other. Use a screwdriver to press the guard if necessary.

39. Check the clearance between the hub and the upper toothed belt guard.

40. Tighten the high pressure line union nuts by hand.

41. Make sure the high pressure line is free of tension.

42. Use torque wrench (5-50 Nm) V.A.G 1331 with ratchet, reversible V.A.G 1331/1 and socket T40055 to tighten the high pressure line.

43. Fill the fuel system.

ENGINE PERFORMANCE & EMISSION CONTROLS

CAMSHAFT POSITION (CMP) SENSOR

REMOVAL & INSTALLATION

See Figures 93 and 94.

1. Remove the engine cover.

2. Remove the fuel filter and the auxiliary fuel pump V393 or fuel pump 2 V277.

3. Disconnect the connector from the Engine Coolant Temperature (ECT) sensor on radiator G83, open the clips arrows and remove the toothed belt guard.

4. Remove right front wheel housing liner.

5. Remove the ribbed belt.

6. Remove vibration damper.

7. Rotate the engine to Top Dead Center (TDC) and secure the crankshaft toothed belt gear using the crankshaft stop T10050. Push the crankshaft stop from the front side of the toothed belt gear into the teeth.

8. The camshaft toothed gear must be in the 12 o'clock position.

9. The marks on the crankshaft toothed belt gear 2 and the crankshaft stop T10050 1 must align. The pin on the crankshaft stop T10050 must engage in the hole on the sealing flange.

10. Loosen the bolts 1 for the camshaft sprocket.

11. Loosen the coolant pipe bolt 1 and then the high pressure pump toothed belt gear bolts 2.

12. Loosen the nut 1 for the tensioner.

13. Turn the tensioner eccentric pulley using the socket wrench T10264 counterclockwise arrow, until the locking tool T10265 can lock the tensioner.

14. Now, turn the tensioner eccentric pulley clockwise all the way and tighten the nut 1 by hand.

15. Remove the toothed belt from the idler roller and the high pressure pump gear.

16. Disconnect the CMP sensor connector.

17. Remove the connector from the mount.

18. Remove the CMP sensor.

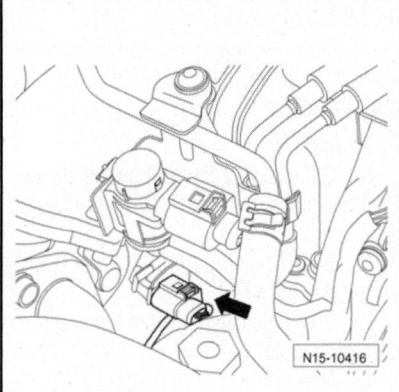

Fig. 93 Disconnect the CMP sensor connector (arrow)

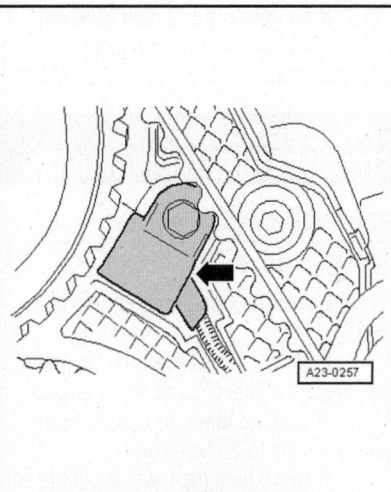

Fig. 94 Remove the CMP sensor arrow

19. Remove the ribs with a screwdriver and remove the cover for the repair opening arrows.

20. Remove the CMP sensor from the cylinder head and guide the connector through the opening in the toothed belt guard.

To install:

21. Installation is performed in reverse order. When doing this note the following:

22. Seal off the opening in the toothed belt guard with a rubber plug. Refer to the Parts Catalog.

23. Install the toothed belt and adjust the valve timing.

CRANKSHAFT POSITION (CKP) SENSOR

LOCATION

See Figure 95.

The CKP sensor is the same as the Engine Speed Sensor (G28) and is mounted on the timing chain cover at the flywheel end on the 2.5L engine

Fig. 95 Crankshaft position sensor connector (1)—2.0L engine

REMOVAL & INSTALLATION

1. Before servicing the vehicle, refer to the precautions.
2. Unplug the connector.
3. Remove the screw and then the sensor

⁂ **WARNING**

Cover the hole to prevent dirt from getting into the engine.

4. When installing, use a new seal as necessary.

ELECTRONIC CONTROL MODULE (ECM)

LOCATION

See Figure 96.

REMOVAL & INSTALLATION

➡️**If it is desired to replace Engine Control Module (ECM), connect vehicle diagnosis, testing and information system VAS 5051 and perform the function "Replace Control Module".**

1. Before servicing the vehicle, refer to the precautions.
2. Switch off ignition.
3. Remove wiper arms and plenum chamber cover.
4. Remove plenum chamber bulkhead
5. On vehicles equipped with shear bolts proceed as follows:

⁂ **WARNING**

Thread of shear bolts is equipped with locking compound. By heating the shear bolts using a hot air gun, inhibition effect of the locking compound is lowered.

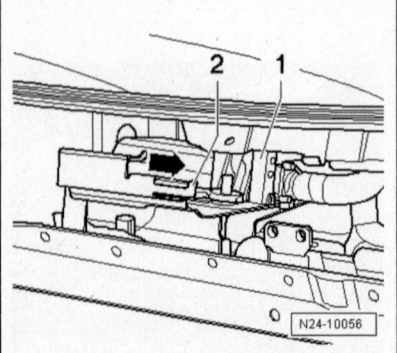

Fig. 96 ECM is location in the plenum chamber at the base of the windshield. Disengage harness (1) and pry up lock mechanism (2)

➡️**Cover wires, harness connectors and control modules in the close vicinity of Engine Control Module (ECM) to prevent damage from burning.**

a. Unscrew shear bolt using pliers on bolt head.

⁂ **WARNING**

If screws cannot be removed, saw into heads of shear bolts so that two parallel surfaces are formed and then unscrew them.

b. Insert a screwdriver between protective housing and retaining plate.
c. Pry protective housing upward using screwdriver and pull it off sideways from retaining plate.
6. Disengage forward harness connector from Engine Control Module (ECM) and disconnect it.
7. Pry up locking mechanism slightly.
8. Then slide Engine Control Module (ECM) out of retainer.
9. Now disengage rear harness connector from Engine Control Module (ECM) and disconnect it.

To install:

10. Connect rear harness connector to Engine Control Module (ECM) and engage it.
11. Slide Engine Control Module (ECM) on to retaining plate.
12. Press the catch against the engine control module.
13. Now connect front connector to Engine Control Module (ECM) and engage it.
14. Slide protective housing on to retaining plate.
15. Tighten new shear bolts uniformly until bolt heads shear off.
16. Install plenum chamber bulkhead.
17. Install wiper arms and plenum chamber cover.

ENGINE COOLANT TEMPERATURE (ECT) SENSOR

REMOVAL & INSTALLATION

See Figures 97 and 98.

1. Removing Condition: Engine is cold.
2. Remove the cover for the air guide; disengage the side clips to do so arrows.
3. Unclip the lower air guide, disengage the clips to do so arrows.
4. Remove both the lower air guide and the air guide hose.

5. Vehicles with a Noise Generator: Remove the charge air pipe from the noise generator.
6. Loosen the hose clamp.
7. Remove the bolt.
8. Disconnect the electrical connector.
9. Remove the noise insulation.
10. Loosen the clamps items and, remove the charge air hose and seal the charge air cooler with a clean cloth.
11. Remove the bolt and remove the charge air pipe downward.
12. Disconnect the electrical connector 1 from the throttle valve control module J338.
13. Remove the bolts arrows and remove the throttle valve control module.
14. Remove the intake manifold support; to do so, remove the nut and bolt.
15. Engine Coolant Temperature (ECT) Sensor with Clip
   a. Disconnect the electrical connector 1 from the ECT sensor.

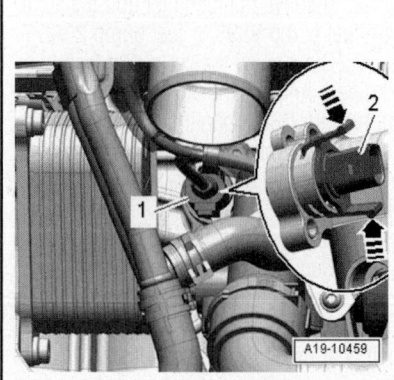

Fig. 97 Disconnect the electrical connector 1 from the ECT sensor and press latches (arrow)

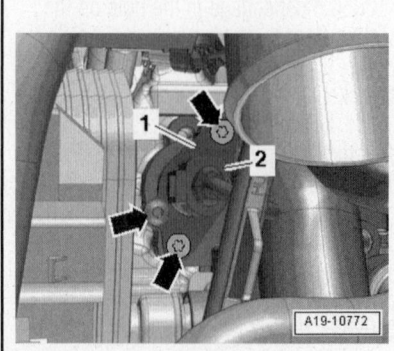

Fig. 98 Disconnect the electrical connector 2 from the ECT sensor. Remove the bolts arrows and remove the retaining plate 1

b. Remove the clamp, to do so, press the latches.

c. Remove the ECT sensor.

d. Install the new ECT sensor with an O-ring as quickly as possible to prevent coolant from leaking out.

16. ECT Sensor with a Retaining Plate

a. Disconnect the electrical connector 2 from the ECT sensor.

b. Remove the bolts arrows and remove the retaining plate 1.

c. Remove the ECT sensor.

17. Install the new ECT sensor with an O-ring as quickly as possible to prevent coolant from leaking out.

To install:

18. Install in reverse order of removal. Note the following:

19. Replace the O-ring.

20. Check the coolant level.

HEATED OXYGEN SENSOR (HO2S)

LOCATION

2.0L Engines

The primary oxygen sensor is on the exhaust pipe at the turbocharger outlet. The secondary sensor is behind the catalytic converter.

2.5L Engines

The primary oxygen sensor is on the exhaust pipe. The secondary sensor is behind the catalytic converter.

REMOVAL & INSTALLATION

2.0L & 2.5L Engines

1. Before servicing the vehicle, refer to the precautions.

2. Unplug the connector.

3. Remove the sensor and cover the hole to prevent dirt from getting into the engine.

To install:

4. Installation is the reverse of removal.

➡**Thread of new oxygen sensors is coated with hot bolt paste.**

❊❊ WARNING

When re-using the previous oxygen sensor, grease only the threads with hot bolt paste G 052 112; the paste must not get into slots of oxygen sensor body

5. Tighten to 41 ft. lbs. (55 Nm).

INTAKE AIR TEMPERATURE (IAT) SENSOR

LOCATION

2.0L Engines

1. The IAT is mounted in the center of the intake manifold plenum near the throttle body.

2.5L Engine

The IAT is built into the Mass Airflow Sensor (MAF) and cannot be removed separately.

KNOCK SENSOR (KS)

LOCATION

The knock sensor 1 is located below the intake manifold behind the coolant pump.

REMOVAL & INSTALLATION

See Figure 99.

1. Remove the electrical connector 2 from the knock sensor 1.

2. Remove the coolant pump.

3. The knock sensor 1 is located below the intake manifold behind the coolant pump.

4. Remove the knock sensor 1.

To install:

5. Installation is performed in reverse order.

MASS AIR FLOW (MAF) SENSOR

LOCATION

2.0L Engines

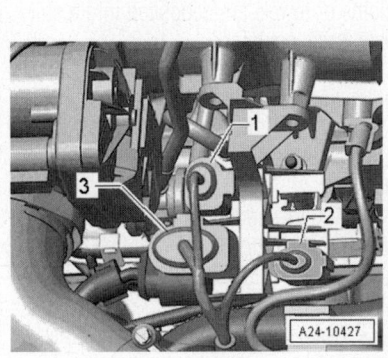

Fig. 99 Remove the electrical connector 2 from the knock sensor 1

The MAF is mounted in the air filter housing assembly behind the opening for the oil filler cap.

2.0L TDI Engine

The MAF is mounted in the air filter housing assembly

2.5L Engine

The MAF is in the intake air tube next to the battery.

REMOVAL & INSTALLATION

2.0L & 2.5L Engines

1. Before servicing the vehicle, refer to the precautions.

2. Disconnect air intake hose from the air filter housing.

3. Disconnect electrical connector on Mass Air Flow (MAF) Sensor G70.

4. Remove both bolts from the Mass Air Flow (MAF) Sensor G70 and carefully remove the Mass Air Flow (MAF) Sensor G70 from the air filter housing guide.

To install:

5. Installation is the reverse of removal.

6. If the air filter element is very dirty or soaked, dirt particles or moisture may have contaminated the Mass Air Flow (MAF) Sensor G70 and may be causing false mass air flow values. This results in a reduction of power, since a lower injection quantity is calculated.

7. Always use an original equipment air filter element.

8. Use a lubricant (silicone-free) for installing the intake hose.

9. Secure all hose connections using hose clamps appropriate for the model type.

10. Check the MAF sensor and intake hose (intake air side) for salt residue, dirt, and leaves.

11. Check the intake ducting up to the air filter element for dirt. If any contaminants are discovered, clean the air filter housing (upper and lower parts) of salt residue, dirt and leaves (if necessary, clean by washing or vacuuming).

12. Tighten clamps/screws to 13 inch lbs. (1.5 Nm).

THROTTLE POSITION SENSOR (TPS)

LOCATION

2.0L & 2.5L Engines

The throttle position sensor is built into the electronic throttle valve control module (throttle body).

REMOVAL & INSTALLATION

2.0L & 2.5L Engines

See Figure 100.

1. Before servicing the vehicle, refer to the precautions.
2. Loosen the hose clamp.
3. Remove bolt.
4. Disconnect electrical connector.
5. Remove the noise insulation.
6. Remove the air guide pipe.
7. Remove the bolt and remove the air guide pipe downward.

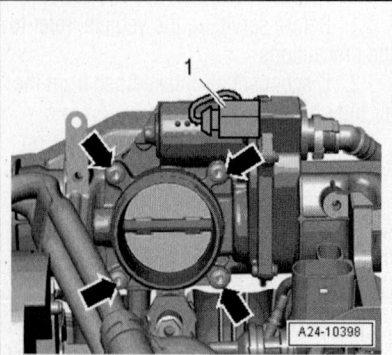

Fig. 100 Disconnect electrical connector (1) and remove Throttle Valve Control Module J338 bolts (arrow)

8. Disconnect electrical connector on Throttle Valve Control Module J338.
9. Remove bolts and remove Throttle Valve Control Module J338.

To install:

10. Installation is performed in reverse order of removal.
11. Clean O-ring sealing surface.
12. Replace the seal; when doing so, pay attention to the correct position of the service flag on the sealing ring.
13. Tighten bolts in criss-cross pattern to 31 inch lbs. (3.5 Nm).

> ⁑ **WARNING**
>
> **If a new Throttle Valve Control Module J338 was installed, adapt the engine control module to the Throttle Valve Control Module J338.**

VEHICLE SPEED SENSOR (VSS)

REMOVAL & INSTALLATION

See Figure 101.

1. Remove the engine cover.
2. Open the air guide pipe hose clamp.
3. Disconnect the electrical harness connector.
4. Remove the noise insulation.

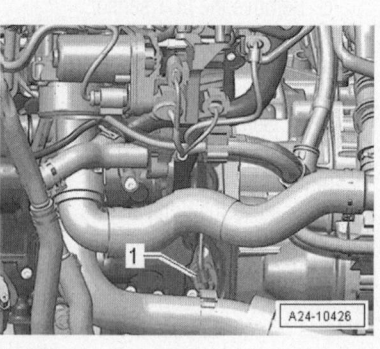

Fig. 101 Disconnect the electrical connector (1) from engine speed sensor

5. Remove the bolts and remove charge air pipe downward from the throttle valve control module J338.
6. Remove the charge air hose from the charge air cooler and remove the charge air pipe downward.
7. Disconnect the electrical connector from engine speed sensor.
8. Remove the engine speed sensor bolt.
9. Install in reverse order of removal.

FUEL   GASOLINE FUEL INJECTION SYSTEM

FUEL SYSTEM SERVICE PRECAUTIONS

Safety is the most important factor when performing not only fuel system maintenance but any type of maintenance. Failure to conduct maintenance and repairs in a safe manner may result in serious personal injury or death. Maintenance and testing of the vehicle's fuel system components can be accomplished safely and effectively by adhering to the following rules and guidelines.

• To avoid the possibility of fire and personal injury, always disconnect the negative battery cable unless the repair or test procedure requires that battery voltage be applied.

• Always relieve the fuel system pressure prior to disconnecting any fuel system component (injector, fuel rail, pressure regulator, etc.), fitting or fuel line connection. Exercise extreme caution whenever relieving fuel system pressure to avoid exposing skin, face and eyes to fuel spray. Please be advised that fuel under pressure may penetrate the skin or any part of the body that it contacts.

• Always place a shop towel or cloth around the fitting or connection prior to loosening to absorb any excess fuel due to spillage. Ensure that all fuel spillage (should it occur) is quickly removed from engine surfaces. Ensure that all fuel soaked cloths or towels are deposited into a suitable waste container.

• Always keep a dry chemical (Class B) fire extinguisher near the work area.

• Do not allow fuel spray or fuel vapors to come into contact with a spark or open flame.

• Always use a back-up wrench when loosening and tightening fuel line connection fittings. This will prevent unnecessary stress and torsion to fuel line piping.

• Always replace worn fuel fitting O-rings with new Do not substitute fuel hose or equivalent where fuel pipe is installed.

Before servicing the vehicle, make sure to also refer to the precautions in the beginning of this section as well.

RELIEVING FUEL SYSTEM PRESSURE

1. Before servicing the vehicle, refer to the precautions.

> ⁑ **CAUTION**
>
> **The fuel injection system is divided into a high pressure section (maximum approximately 1740 psi or 120 bar) and a low pressure system (approximately 87psi or 6 bar). Before opening high pressure area - e.g. removing high pressure pump, fuel rail, fuel injectors, fuel pipes or Fuel Pressure Sensor G247 - fuel pressure in high pressure area must be reduced to a residual pressure of approximately 87psi (6 bar).**

2. Remove electrical connector from Fuel Pressure Regulator Valve N276 using the Assembly Tool T10118.
3. Allow engine to idle approximately 10 seconds.

a. When the Fuel Pressure Regulator Valve N276 electrical connector is disconnected during idle, pressure in high pressure area decreases to approximately 6 bar.

b. After high pressure has been released, high pressure system must be opened, otherwise the pressure increases again due to the warming of the fuel.

4. Switch off ignition.

☀☀ CAUTION

Fuel lines are pressurized! Wear protective goggles and protective clothing to prevent injuries and contact with skin. Before opening the high pressure system, place a cloth around the connection.

5. Place a clean cloth around the connection point and carefully open to release the residual pressure of approximately 87psi (6 bar). Escaping fuel must be absorbed.

6. To conclude work, check DTC memory of Engine Control Module (ECM), erase all DTC entries which may have occurred from removing the connector. If DTC memory was erased, generate readiness code.

FUEL FILTER

REMOVAL & INSTALLATION

See Figure 102.

1. Disconnect the fuel lines to the fuel tank:

 a. A - Fuel supply line, black
 b. B - Fuel return line, blue or with a blue mark

2. Seal the lines so that the fuel system is not contaminated by dirt, etc.

3. Loosen the spring clips using spring

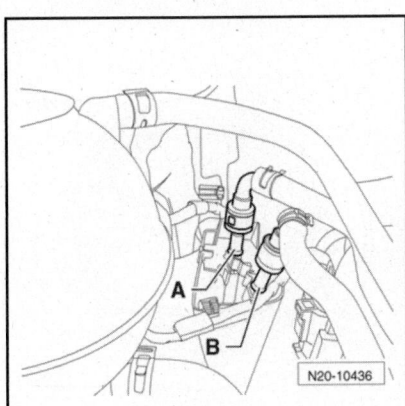

Fig. 102 A - Fuel supply line, black. B - Fuel return line, blue or with a blue mark

clip pliers VAS 6362 and remove the fuel hoses items 6 and 7.

4. Seal the lines so that the fuel system is not contaminated by dirt, etc.

5. Remove the bolt and nut item 11.

6. Remove the fuel filter upward.

To install:

7. Install in reverse order of removal. When doing this note the following:

8. Route the fuel hoses free of kinks.

9. Ensure the fuel hoses are seated securely.

10. Do not interchange the supply and return lines (the return line is blue or has a blue mark, the supply line is white or has a white mark).

11. Clip the fuel hoses into the retainers.

12. Fill and bleed the fuel system

FUEL INJECTORS

REMOVAL & INSTALLATION

2.0L Engines

See Figure 103.

1. Before servicing the vehicle, refer to the precautions.

➡**Puller T10133/2A is required to complete this operation.**

2. Remove the intake manifold with the fuel rail. If the injector valves remain attached in the fuel rail, then pull them out.

3. Cover the intake channels with a clean rag.

4. Remove the support element A downward and disconnect the connector from the fuel injectors.

5. Position the puller T10133/2A in the groove on the fuel injector.

6. Mount the removal tool T10133/16, turn the screw and remove the fuel injector.

➡**Pay attention to the intermediate rings.**

To install:

☀☀ WARNING

The combustion chamber seal must always be replaced before re-installing the fuel injector. The Teflon sealing ring of fuel injector may not be oiled or greased.

➡**If an opened intake valve hinders the cleaning, the engine must be turned further by hand using a screw wrench on the crankshaft.**

7. Thoroughly clean bores for high pressure fuel injectors in cylinder head using nylon brush T10133/4.

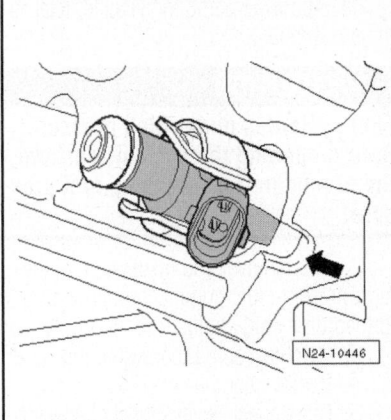

Fig. 103 Make sure fuel injectors are positioned correctly in cylinder head

8. Replace O-ring and Teflon sealing ring of fuel injector Teflon Seal on Fuel Injector, Replacing.

9. Install the fuel injection with the intermediate ring again.

10. Use the Remover T10133/2A to push the fuel injector all the way into the hole in the cylinder head.

☀☀ WARNING

Make sure fuel injectors are positioned correctly in cylinder head.

11. Install the intake manifold with the fuel rail.

FUEL PUMP

REMOVAL & INSTALLATION

Bolt In High Pressure Pump

See Figures 104 through 106.

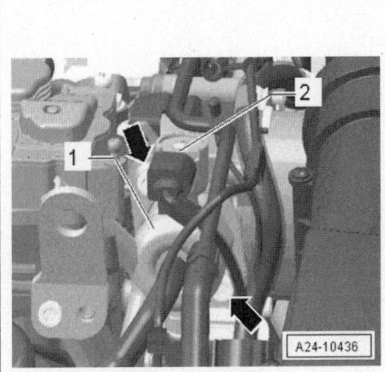

Fig. 104 Disconnect the electrical connector from the Fuel Pressure Regulator Valve N276

1. Before servicing the vehicle, refer to the precautions.

❈❈ CAUTION

Fuel system is under high pressure! Before opening the system, perform the procedure for releasing fuel pressure.

2. The removal and installation of the high-pressure fuel pump can only be performed on a cold engine.

3. Catch escaping fuel with a rag.

4. Remove engine cover.

5. Disconnect the electrical connector from the Fuel Pressure Regulator Valve N276.

6. Open both fuel lines.

7. Remove the two bolts.

8. Carefully pull the high pressure fuel pump out. The roller tappet may stay in the cylinder head.

To install:

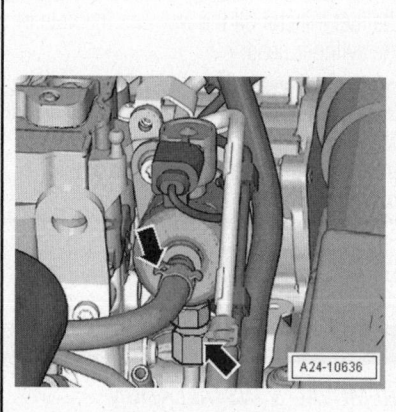

Fig. 105 Open both fuel lines

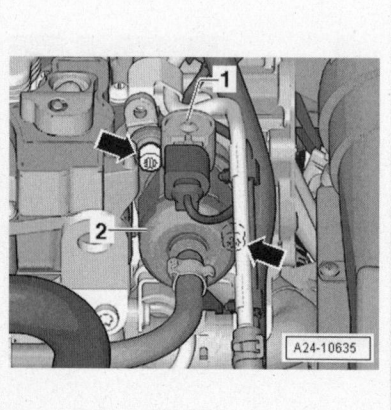

Fig. 106 Remove the two bolts

9. When installing the high-pressure fuel pump, make sure that no dirt enters the fuel system.

10. The O-ring must always be replaced.

11. High-pressure fuel lines must always be fastened free of tension.

12. Replace the O-ring for the high-pressure pump.

13. Carefully place high pressure pump with sleeve (pay attention to the groove) in opening in cylinder head (check sleeve for damage first).

14. Install new bolts and tighten by hand.

15. Before installing the fuel lines, check the torque of the connections on the high-pressure pump.

16. Tighten the bolts crosswise to 89 inch lbs. (10 Nm).

17. Hand tighten the fuel supply line union nut so that it is free of tension and then tighten it.

18. Connect the electrical connector from the Fuel Pressure Regulator Valve N276.

19. If the fuse was pulled, insert it again.

20. Check fuel system for leaks.

In Tank Lock Ring Pump

See Figures 107 through 109.

1. Condition: The fuel tank may be a maximum of 1/2 full.

2. Empty the fuel tank if necessary using the fuel extracting device VAS 5190.

3. Turn off the ignition and disconnect the ground cable from the battery.

4. Remove the rear seat bench.

5. Unclip the cover for the fuel delivery unit. points in direction of travel.

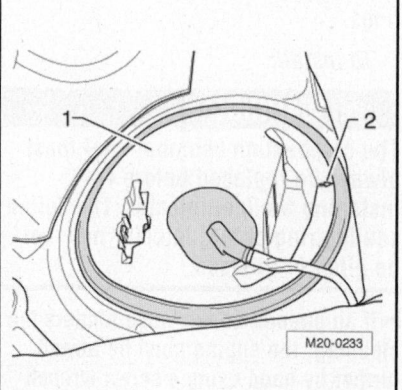

Fig. 107 Unclip the cover (1) for the fuel delivery unit. (2) points in direction of travel

➡The fuel supply line is under pressure! Wear protective goggles and protective clothing to prevent injuries and contact with skin.

➡Before loosening the connection, place a cloth around the connection point. Then release pressure by carefully disconnecting the line.

6. Disconnect the connector 1, the black supply line 2 and the blue return line 3.

7. Press in the securing ring to disengage the fuel lines.

8. Seal the lines so that the fuel system is not contaminated by dirt, etc.

9. Open the locking ring using wrench T10202.

10. Remove the fuel delivery unit and the seal from the opening in the fuel tank.

11. If the fuel delivery unit is to be replaced then drain the old delivery unit before disposal.

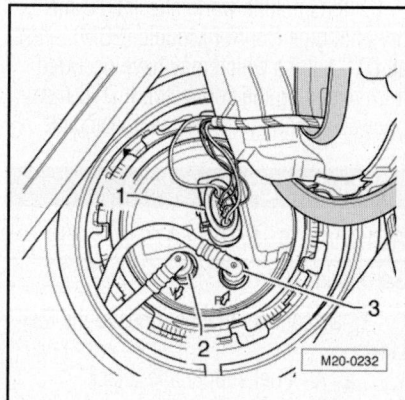

Fig. 108 Disconnect the connector 1, the black supply line 2 and the blue return line 3

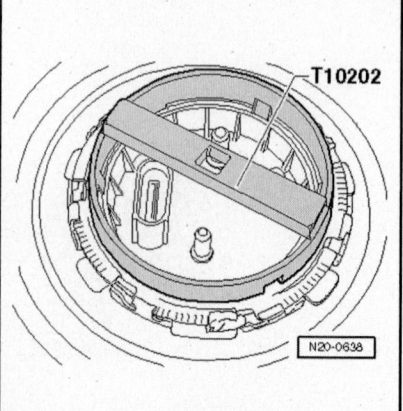

Fig. 109 Open the locking ring using wrench T10202

12. Follow disposal regulations.

To install:

13. Install in reverse order of removal. When doing this note the following:

14. Condition: Locking ring tightening specification: 110 Nm.

15. Do not bend the fuel level sensor G when inserting the fuel delivery unit.

16. Replace the fuel delivery unit seal if damaged and insert it in the fuel tank opening dry.

17. Lubricate the seal with fuel only for installing the fuel delivery unit.

18. Pay attention to the installed position of the fuel delivery unit flange. Tab on fuel delivery unit must lie between tabs.

19. Route the fuel lines free of kinks.

20. Do not interchange the supply and return lines (return line is blue, supply line is black).

21. Make sure the line connections are securely fastened.

22. Observe the notes after connecting the battery.

FUEL TANK

DRAINING

See Figures 110 and 111.

✳✳ CAUTION

Secure the fuel extracting device VAS 5190 ground strap to a bare area on the chassis.

1. Remove the cone piece from the shaft piece on the fuel extracting device VAS 5190.

2. Using insulating tape, apply a mark on the suction hose at a length of 1,500 mm (a) from the end of the hose.

3. Remove the cap from the fuel filler tube.

4. Install the shaft piece for the fuel extracting device VAS 5190 in on the fuel tank filler tube.

5. On vehicles equipped with a bayonet connection, the shaft piece of the fuel extracting device must be held accordingly.

6. Push the suction hose into the fuel tank until it reaches the mark on the suction hose made previously and extract the fuel. Refer to the operating instructions that come with the fuel extracting device VAS 5190.

7. A pressure point can be sensed after approximately 120 cm. The check valve in the fuel tank must be pushed open. Pull out the hose slightly and slide it in using a light jerk.

8. The fuel tank is drained almost completely.

9. Remove the hose the same way.

REMOVAL & INSTALLATION

See Figures 112 through 114.

1. Before servicing the vehicle, refer to the precautions.

2. With the ignition off, disconnect the ground cable from the battery.

3. Clean the surrounding area around the fuel filler tube.

4. Drain the fuel tank as necessary using the VAS 5190.

5. Remove the rear seat bench.

6. Remove the cover with the fuel pump control module from the fuel delivery unit.

7. When installing the cover be sure to pay attention to the installed position: The points in the direction of vehicle travel.

8. Disconnect the electrical connector from the fuel delivery unit.

9. Remove the right rear wheel.

10. Remove the right rear wheel housing liner.

11. Remove the fuel tank door unit.

12. Disconnect the hoses.

13. Remove the fuel filler tube bolts from the body.

14. Unclip the wheel speed sensor wire from the filler tube bracket.

15. Remove the center and rear mufflers.

16. Remove the heat shield.

✳✳ CAUTION

The fuel supply line is under pressure. Wear protective goggles and protective clothing to prevent injuries and contact with skin. Before disconnecting, place a cloth around the connection point. Then release pressure by carefully disconnecting the connection.

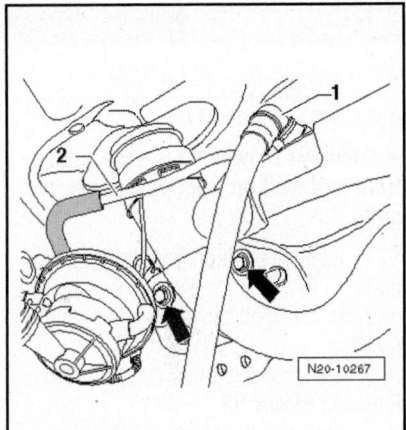

Fig. 112 Disconnect the hoses 1 and 2. Remove the fuel filler tube bolts (arrows)

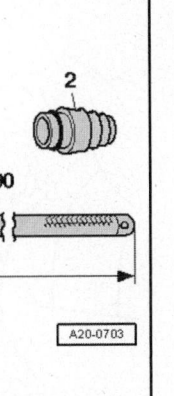
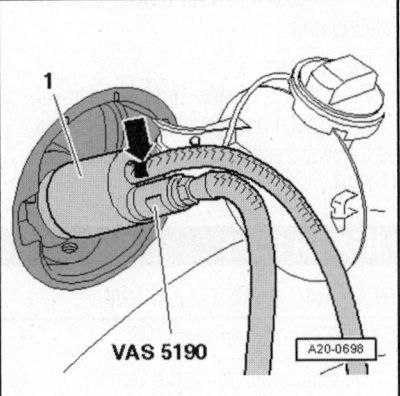

Fig. 110 Remove the cone piece 2 from the shaft piece 1 on the fuel extracting device VAS 5190

Fig. 111 Install the shaft piece 1 for the fuel extracting device VAS 5190 in on the fuel tank filler tube

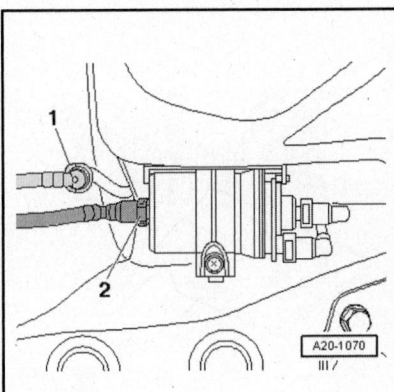

Fig. 113 Disconnect the white vent line (1) from the vent line and the black supply line (2) from the fuel filter

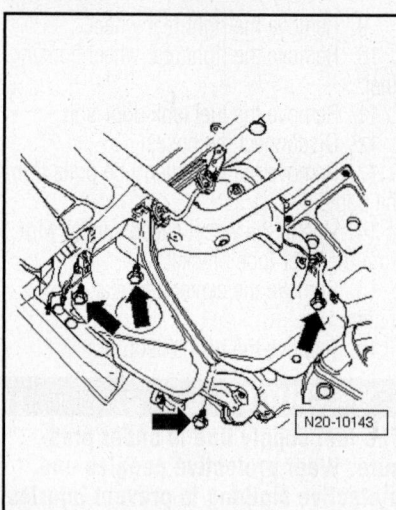

Fig. 114 Remove the tensioning straps and bolts

17. Disconnect the white vent line from the vent line and the black supply line from the fuel filter.

18. Press the securing ring to disengage the lines.

19. Disconnect the green Leak Detection Pump (LDP) vacuum line as well.

20. Seal the lines so that the fuel system is not contaminated by dirt etc.

21. Remove the tensioning straps and bolts. Support the fuel tank using the VAG 1383A while doing so.

22. Lower the fuel tank.

To install:

23. Install in reverse order of removal.

24. Make sure the vent and fuel lines are not kinked.

25. Do not interchange the supply and return line (return line = blue, supply line = black).

26. Make sure the line connections are securely seated.

27. Check the ground connection for the fuel tank/chassis at the filler tube.

28. After installing the fuel tank, check to be sure the lines are still clipped to the fuel tank.

29. Observe the notes after connecting the battery.

30. Tighten bolts/nuts to specification as follows:

- Fuel tank to chassis (Replace bolts): 19 ft. lbs. (25 Nm)

IDLE SPEED

ADJUSTMENT

Idle speed is automatically controlled by the Electronic Control Module (ECM). No adjustment is possible.

HEATING & AIR CONDITIONING SYSTEM

BLOWER MOTOR

REMOVAL & INSTALLATION

See Figures 115 and 116.

➡**Fresh Air Blower V2 is accessible from foot well on front passenger side.**

1. Remove partition from heating unit.

2. Unscrew plastic screws and remove partition.

3. Disconnect harness connector from Fresh Air Blower V2.

4. Remove screw for Fresh Air Blower V2.

5. Release catch and rotate Fresh Air Blower V2 in direction of.

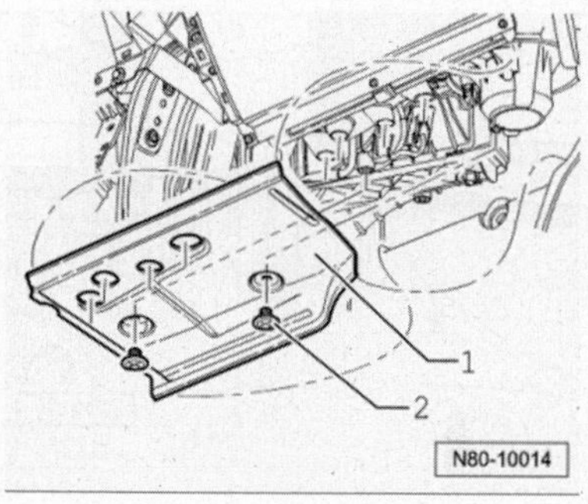

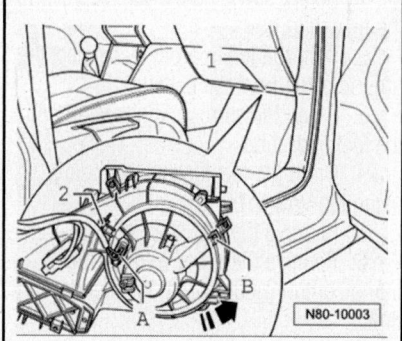

Fig. 116 Disconnect harness connector (A), remove screw (B) and release the catch (2)

6. Remove Fresh Air Blower V2 from heating unit.

To install:

7. Install in reverse order of removal.

8. Tighten bolts/nuts to specification as follows: fresh Air Blower: 9 inch lbs. (1 Nm)

HEATER CORE

REMOVAL & INSTALLATION

See Figures 117 through 120.

1. Before servicing the vehicle, refer to the precautions.

2. Remove facing wall in plenum chamber.

3. Place Drip tray under the engine.

✳✳ CAUTION

Contact with hot engine coolant can cause severe scalding. Coolant temperature can be above 212°F (100°C) with a warm engine. The cooling system is under pressure. If necessary, reduce pressure and temperature before repairs.

4. Clamp off coolant hoses using hose clamps and disconnect coolant hoses to heater core.

5. Connect a section of hose onto upper connection of heater core.

6. Hold a container under the lower connection.

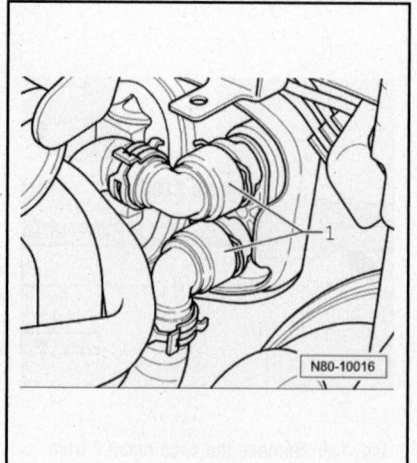

Fig. 117 Clamp off coolant hoses (1)

Fig. 115 Unscrew plastic screws (2) and remove partition (1)

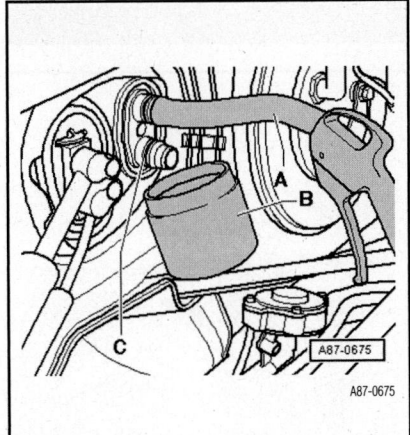

Fig. 118 Air gun (A), container (B) and lower connection (C)

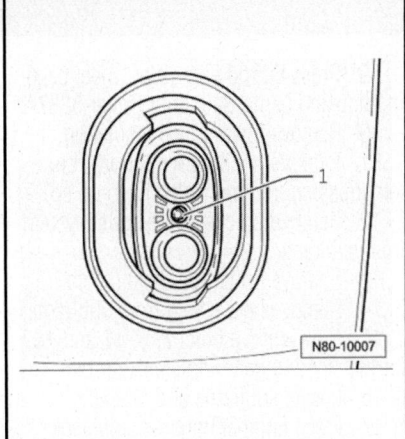

Fig. 119 Loosen (do not unscrew completely) bolt (1) out of connection flange

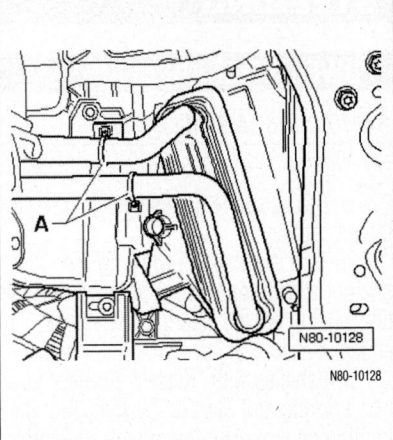

Fig. 120 Open hose clamps A and disconnect coolant pipes

7. Using a compressed air gun, carefully blow coolant out of heater core into container.

8. Loosen (do not unscrew completely) bolt out of connection flange between heater core connections.

9. This allows the coolant pipes to move for removing the heater core.

10. Remove driver side foot well trim.

11. Remove left foot well vent.

12. Remove screws and remove heater core trim.

13. Cover floor carpet in area below heater core with leak-proof foil and absorbent paper.

14. Open hose clamps A and disconnect coolant pipes.

15. Remove heater core from heating unit.

To install:

16. Installation is carried out in the reverse order.

17. Check seals installed on heater core, only install a heater core with undamaged seals.

18. An incorrectly glued seal can roll up into heating unit when sliding in the heater core.

19. Cold air may flow past heat exchanger if seal is damaged or not properly installed.

20. With the heater core removed, check heating unit for soiling (via heater core opening).

21. If necessary, remove dirt or coolant from heating unit, for example after removing leaky heater core.

22. Push heater core into heating unit.

23. Coat sealing rings with coolant before installing.

24. Insert sealing rings into connection on coolant pipe.

25. If hose clamps are deformed, replace them.

26. Connect coolant pipes.

27. Hose clamps must be able to be twisted slightly when installing onto the coolant pipes.

28. Tighten hose clamps.

29. Check seating of both clamps after tightening bolts, clamps must enclose the flange on coolant pipe completely and must not touch other components.

30. Tighten the screw from the connecting flange between heater core connections.

31. Check position of grommet in bulkhead for proper seating.

32. Seal the flange for coolant pipes to heater core and for expansion valve (to evaporator, only in vehicles with A/C system) at pass-through of grommet with silicon adhesive sealant if necessary (to prevent water from penetrating).

33. Sealing rings must always be replaced.

34. If hose clamps are deformed, replace them.

35. After replacing heater core, coolant must be replaced completely.

36. Check coolant circuit for leaks, pay particular attention between coolant pipes and heater core.

37. Tighten bolts/nuts to specification as follows:

- Hose clamps: 18 inch lbs. (2.0 Nm)
- Heater core connections to: 18 inch lbs. (2.0 Nm)

STEERING

POWER STEERING GEAR

REMOVAL & INSTALLATION

See Figures 121 through 123.

1. Before servicing the vehicle, refer to the precautions.

2. Turn the steering wheel to the straight ahead position and remove the ignition key so that the steering wheel lock engages.

3. Vehicles with "Keyless Access" Keyless Locking and Starting System: Turn the ignition off and open the driver's door so the steering wheel lock locks.

4. Disconnect battery.

5. Remove foot well trim, remove nuts to do so.

6. Remove bolt and pull off universal joint from steering gear.

7. Remove front wheels.

8. Loosen tie rod end nut, but do not remove yet.

❊❊ WARNING

To protect thread, screw nut on pin a few turns.

9. Press tie rod end off of wheel bearing housing using Ball Joint Puller 3287A.

10. Remove lower noise insulation.

11. Remove pendulum support from transmission, remove bolts 14 to do so.

12. Remove bracket for exhaust system from subframe.

13. Remove bolts from heat shield.

14. Remove heat shield from subframe.

15. Now remove bolts 3, 6, 11 and 16 for the steering gear and stabilizer bar.

16. Locate subframe and brackets.

17. Place Engine/Transmission Jack VAG1383A under subframe.

18. Place a block of wood , for example, between VAG 1383 A and the subframe.

19. Loosen bolts and lower subframe with brackets slightly. Observe electrical wires, when doing so.

20. Remove heat shield above steering gear.

21. Remove bolts.

22. Remove cable guide from subframe.

23. Unclip all other cable securing points on steering gear.

24. Disconnect all electrical connections from steering gear.

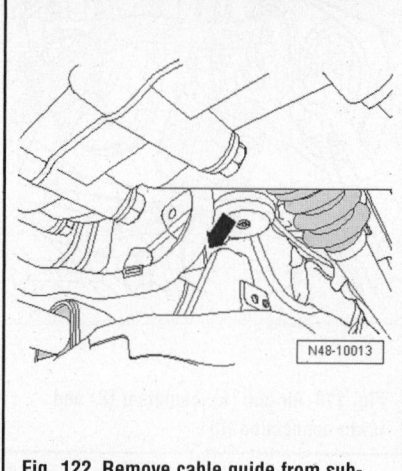

Fig. 122 Remove cable guide from subframe (arrow)

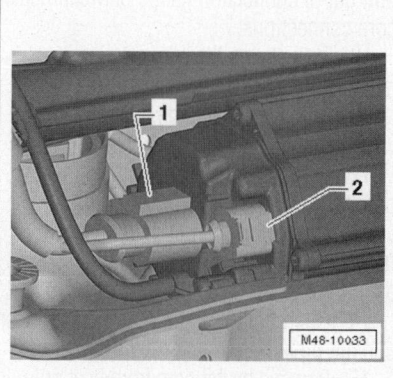

Fig. 123 Disconnect all electrical connections from steering gear

25. Lower subframe with the Engine/Transmission Jack V.A.G 1383 A until steering gear can be removed.

26. Lay steering gear aside. This avoids damages on control module.

To install:

27. Installation is in reverse order of removal.

❊❊ WARNING

The steering gear threaded sleeves must be seated in the bracket holes.

28. Coat seal on steering gear with lubricant, e.g. soft soap, before installing steering gear.

29. After attaching steering gear to drive shaft, make sure that seal on steering gear is positioned to mounting plate without kinks and opening to foot well is sealed

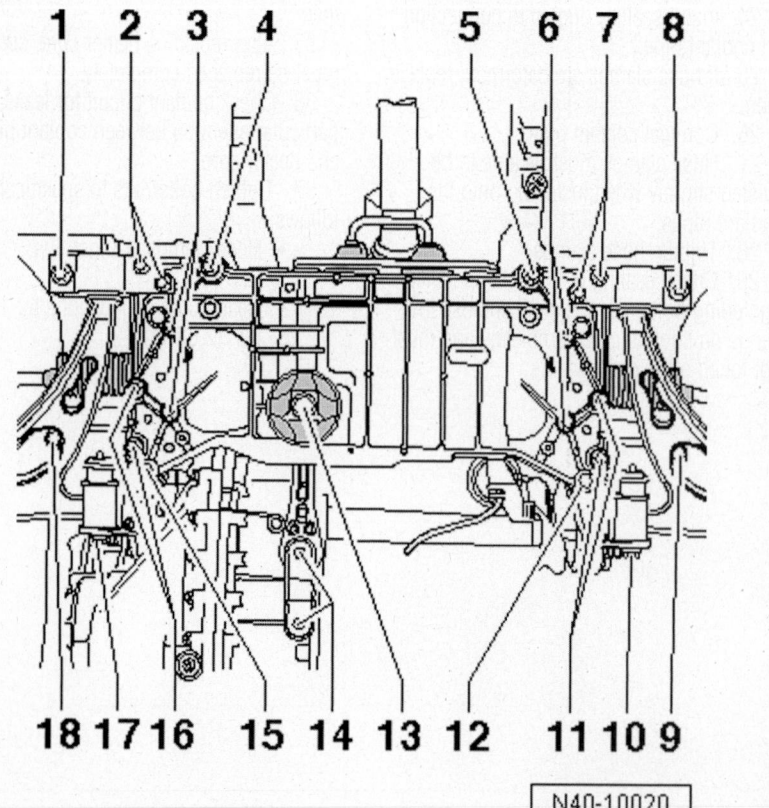

Fig. 121 Remove bolts as explained in text

correctly. Ingress of water and/or noises may be the result.

30. Make sure sealing surfaces are clean.

Before fastening the bolts for subframe, position steering gear on subframe and fasten bolts for steering gear and stabilizer.

31. Clamp off electrical connections to the steering gear.

32. Install lower noise insulation.

33. Ensure that boot is not damaged or twisted.

34. Universal joint to steering gear.

35. Connect battery.

36. Perform Steering Angle Sensor G85 basic setting with the Vehicle Diagnosis, Testing and Information System VAS 5051

37. After installation, position of steering wheel must be checked with a road test.

38. If the steering wheel is crooked or new steering gear was installed, the toe on the front axle must be checked and adjusted if necessary.

39. Align vehicle. Alignment General Information

40. If new steering gear was installed, Power Steering Control Module J500 must be adapted using Vehicle Diagnosis, Testing and Information System VAS 5051.

41. Perform Power Steering Control Module J500 basic setting using Vehicle Diagnosis, Testing and Information System VAS 5051.

42. If parking assist is installed in the vehicle, the Power Steering Control Module J500 must be recoded after installing new steering gear.

43. Parking assist is only in installed vehicles with Generation II steering gear.

44. Tighten bolts/nuts to specification as follows:

- Subframe to body (Use new bolts): 52 ft. lbs. (70 Nm) plus 90° rotation
- Stabilizer bar to subframe (Use new bolts): 15 ft. lbs. (20 Nm) plus 90° rotation
- Stabilizer bar to connecting link (Use new bolts and counterhold at

joint pin inner multi-point fitting): 48 ft. lbs. (65 Nm)
- Ball joint to control arm (Use new nut): 44 ft. lbs. (60 Nm)
- Shield to subframe (M6 bolt is self-tapping) 53 inch lbs. (6 Nm)
- Steering gear to subframe (Use new bolts) 37 ft. lbs. (50 Nm) plus 90° rotation
- Universal joint to steering gear (Use new bolt): 22 ft. lbs. (30 Nm)
- Shield to steering gear (M6 bolt is self-tapping) 53 inch lbs. (6 Nm)
- Tie rod end to wheel bearing housing (Use new nut): 15 ft. lbs. (20 Nm) plus 90° rotation

POWER STEERING PUMP

REMOVAL & INSTALLATION

The power steering pump is electro-mechanical and is an integral part of the power steering gear.

SUSPENSION

LOWER BALL JOINT

REMOVAL & INSTALLATION
See Figure 124.

1. Before servicing the vehicle, refer to the precautions.
2. Loosen the drive axle to wheel hub bolt.
3. Remove the wheel.
4. Remove the ball joint nuts.
5. Pull the drive axle out of the wheel hub slightly.
6. Remove the ball joint from the control arm and at the same time swivel the wheel bearing housing to the outside.
7. Move the control arm downward as far as possible.
8. Install the VAG 3287A and press out the ball joint.
9. Place the VAG 1383A or similar, underneath (risk of accident if components fall off when pressing out ball joint).

➥**To protect the ball joint threads, leave the nut on a few turns.**

To install:
10. Tighten bolts/nuts to specification as follows:
- Ball joint to steel control arm (Use new nuts): 44 ft. lbs. (ft. lbs. (60 Nm)

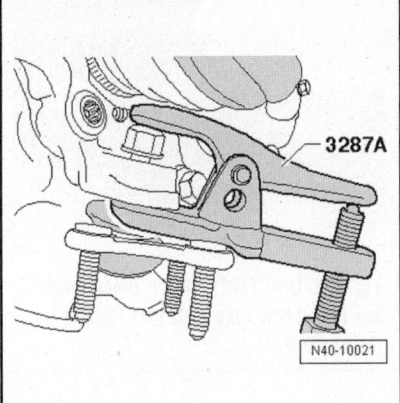

Fig. 124 Install the VAG 3287A and press out the ball joint

- Ball joint to sheet steel or aluminum control arm (Use new nuts): 74 ft. lbs. (100 Nm)
- Ball joint to wheel bearing housing (Use new nut): 44 ft. lbs. (60 Nm)
- Drive axle to wheel hub "hex head bolt" (Use new bolt): 148 ft. lbs. (200 Nm) plus an additional 180° rotation
- Drive axle to wheel hub "12-point bolt" (Use new bolt): 52 ft. lbs. (70 Nm) plus an additional 90° rotation
11. Pull the drive axle out of the wheel hub.

FRONT SUSPENSION

12. Install the ball joint into the wheel bearing housing.
13. Install a new self-locking nut, counter hold the stud using a T40 TORX®.
14. Install the drive axle to the wheel hub.
15. Install and tighten the ball joint nuts.

➥**Make sure that the ball joint boot is not damaged or twisted.**

16. Install the wheel.
17. Tighten the drive axle to wheel hub bolt.

LOWER CONTROL ARM

REMOVAL & INSTALLATION
See Figure 125.

1. Before servicing the vehicle, refer to the precautions.
2. Remove the wheel.
3. Remove the lower noise insulation.
4. Remove the nuts from the control arm.
5. Separate the control arm from the ball joint and then turn the wheel bearing housing toward the outside to take the load off the control arm.
6. Remove the bolts arrows.
7. Swivel the control arm toward the rear and then remove it from the subframe in the direction of the.

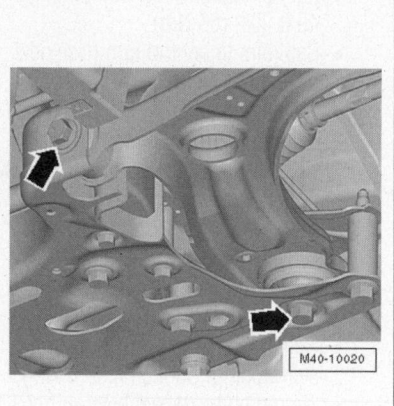

Fig. 125 Remove the bolts (arrow)

To install:

8. Install in reverse order of removal. Note the following:

9. Install the control arm into the subframe in the direction of the and swivel it forward.

10. Install the front wheel and tighten the bolts. (Use new bolt and tighten bolts at normal ride height): 52 ft. lbs. (70 Nm) plus 180° rotation

11. Tighten the Ball joint to control arm (Use new nuts) to 44 ft. lbs. (60 Nm) plus 180° rotation

CONTROL ARM BUSHING REPLACEMENT

See Figures 126 through 128.

1. Remove the control arm, refer to one of the following:

2. Press out the bonded rubber bushings as shown in the illustration.

   a. Punch VW 411

   b. Tube T10219/1 (the hole must face the control arm)

   c. Thrust plate VW 402

To install:

3. Apply the assembly lubricant G 294 421 A1 onto the outside of the bonded rubber bushing.

4. Install the bonded rubber bushing as illustrated.

5. The bonded rubber bushing will be crooked for a short time at the beginning of the installation. Later it will straighten out. It will not be necessary to guide it.

6. Install the bonded rubber bushing until the core 1 and the control arm hole 2 are at the same height.

7. Press back the bearing in the control arm slightly.

8. Dimensions a and b must be identical.

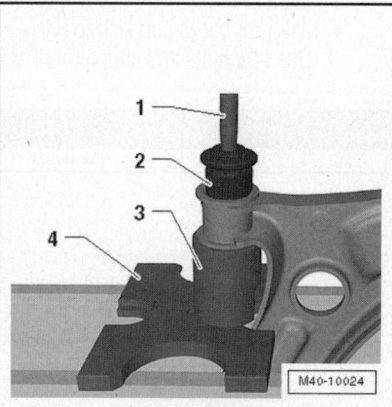

Fig. 127 Drift T10219/2 (1), Bonded rubber mount (2), Tube T10219/1 (3) and thrust plate (4)

MACPHERSON STRUT

REMOVAL & INSTALLATION

See Figures 129 through 131.

1. Before servicing the vehicle, refer to the precautions.

2. Loosen the drive axle to wheel hub bolt.

3. Remove the wheel.

4. Remove the level control system sensor from the control arm.

5. Remove the coupling rod nut and remove the coupling rod from the strut.

6. Remove the ball joint nuts.

7. Remove the wheel bearing housing with ball joint from the control arm.

8. Remove the drive axle from the wheel hub.

9. Secure the drive axle to body using wire.

✴✴ WARNING

The drive axle must not hang down, otherwise the inner Constant Velocity (CV) joint may be damaged when bent too far.

10. Install the ball joint to the control arm again.

11. Secure the VAG 1383 with the T10149 to the wheel hub using one wheel bolt.

12. Remove the wheel bearing housing/strut pinch bolt nut.

13. Insert the 3424 into the slot in the wheel bearing housing.

14. Install a ratchet to the 3424 and turn it 90°, opening the slot in the wheel bearing housing, then remove the ratchet from the 3424.

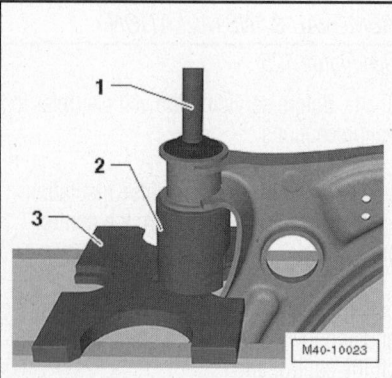

Fig. 126 Punch VW 411 (1), Tube T10219/1 (2) and Thrust plate VW 402 (3)

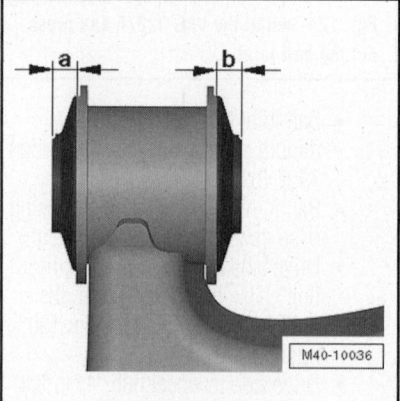

Fig. 128 Dimensions a and b must be identical

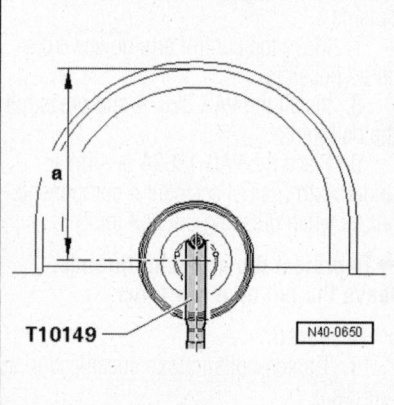

Fig. 129 Secure the VAG 1383 with the T10149 to the wheel hub using one wheel bolt

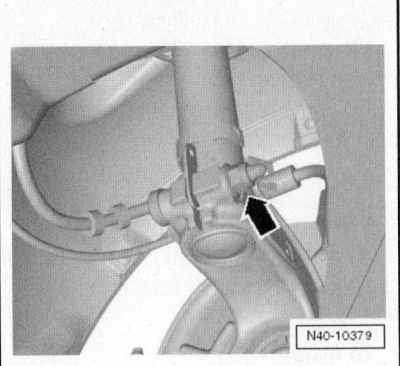

Fig. 130 Remove the wheel bearing housing/strut pinch bolt nut

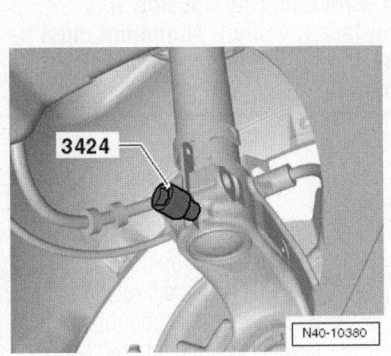

Fig. 131 Insert the 3424 into the slot in the wheel bearing housing

15. Press the brake disc in the direction of the strut by hand.

Otherwise the strut tube may be tilted in the wheel bearing housing.

16. Pull the wheel bearing housing downward from the strut tube and lower using the VAG 1383A until the strut tube hangs free.

17. Secure the wheel bearing housing to the subframe with wire.

18. Remove the VAG 1383A from the below wheel bearing housing.

19. When removing the left strut, remove the wiper arms.

20. Remove the plenum chamber cover.

21. Remove the bolts from the strut dome and remove the strut.

To install:

22. Secure the VAG 1383A with the T10149 to the wheel hub using one wheel bolt.

23. Install the strut to the wheel bearing housing and secure the strut using and a new pinch bolt and nut.

✳✳ WARNING

Bolt tip must point in direction of rotation vehicle travel.

24. Remove the 3424 from the wheel bearing housing.

✳✳ WARNING

One of two markings on the strut bearing must point in direction of rotation vehicle travel.

25. Remove the wire securing the wheel bearing housing.

26. Carefully lift the wheel bearing housing using the VAG 1383A far enough until the bolts for the strut can be installed.

➡ If necessary, use ladder, for example VAS 5085 to install the bolts.

27. Tighten the strut to strut dome bolts.

28. Remove the T10149.

29. Tighten the wheel bearing housing/strut pinch bolt nut.

30. Remove the ball joint nuts again.

31. Install the drive axle to the wheel hub.

32. Install the wheel bearing housing with ball joint to the control arm.

33. Install the ball joint to control arm nuts.

✳✳ WARNING

Make sure that the ball joint boot is not damaged or twisted.

34. Tighten the drive axle to wheel hub bolt.

✳✳ WARNING

When doing this, the vehicle must not rest on the ground, otherwise the wheel bearing could be damaged.

35. Install the plenum chamber cover.

36. Install the wiper arms, if required.

37. Install the wheel.

38. Tighten bolts/nuts to specification as follows:

- Strut to wheel bearing housing (Use new nut): 52 ft. lbs. (70 Nm) plus 90° additional rotation
- Strut to body (strut dome) (Use new bolts): 11 ft. lbs. (15 Nm) plus 90° additional rotation
- Ball joint to steel control arm (Use new nuts): 44 ft. lbs. (60 Nm)
- Coupling rod to strut (Use new nut and counter hold at inner joint multi point stud): 48 ft. lbs. (65 Nm)

- Drive axle to wheel hub "hex head bolt" (Use new bolt): 148 ft. lbs. (200 Nm) plus an additional 180° rotation
- Drive axle to wheel hub "12-point bolt" (Use new bolt): 52 ft. lbs. (70 Nm) plus an additional 90° rotation

OVERHAUL

1. Before servicing the vehicle, refer to the precautions.

2. Fit the strut into spring compressor V.A.G 1752/1 and compress the spring until upper axial groove ball bearing is free.

✳✳ CAUTION

First pre-load spring far enough so that tension is relieved on upper spring retainer!

3. Make sure that coil spring is seated correctly in the tool.

4. Remove hex nut from top of piston rod.

5. Remove components of suspension strut and coil spring.

To install:

6. Place coil spring with spring compressor V.A.G 1752/1 on lower spring plate. End of spring coil must rest against the stop in the spring seat.

7. Install a new self-locking hex nut onto piston rod and torque to 45 ft. lbs. (60 Nm).

8. Carefully relieve tension on spring compressor V.A.G 1752/1 and remove from coil spring.

STABILIZER BAR

REMOVAL & INSTALLATION

See Figure 121.

1. Before servicing the vehicle, refer to the precautions.

2. Remove front wheels.

3. Remove foot well trim, remove nuts to do so.

4. Remove bolt and pull off universal joint from steering gear.

5. Remove lower noise insulation.

6. Remove coupling rods from stabilizer.

7. Remove nuts.

8. Loosen tie rod end nut on both sides, but do not remove yet.

✳✳ WARNING

To protect thread, screw nut on pin a few turns.

9. Press off tie rod end from wheel bearing housing using ball joint puller 3287A.

10. Secure subframe with brackets.

11. Remove stabilizer from subframe 11 and 16. See illustration for bolt locations.

12. Remove pendulum support from transmission, remove bolts 14 to do so.

13. Place engine/transmission jack V.A.G 1383 A below subframe.

14. Place, for example, a piece of wood between engine/transmission jack V.A.G 1383 A and subframe.

15. Loosen bolts and lower subframe with brackets slightly. Observe electrical wires, when doing so.

16. Now, lift stabilizer bar toward front, over bracket and down from subframe.

To install:

17. Installation is in reverse order of removal.

18. Coat seal on steering gear with lubricant, e.g. soft soap, before installing steering gear.

19. After attaching steering gear to drive axle, make sure that seal on steering gear is positioned to mounting plate without kinks and opening to foot well is sealed correctly. Ingress of water and/or noises may be the result.

20. Make sure sealing surfaces are clean.

21. Install lower noise insulation

22. Install front wheels.

23. Tighten bolts/nuts to specification as follows:

- Subframe to body (Use new bolts): 52 ft. lbs. (70 Nm) plus 90° rotation
- Bracket to body (Use new bolts): 52 ft. lbs. (70 Nm) plus 90° rotation
- Mounting bracket to body (Use new bolts): 52 ft. lbs. (70 Nm) plus 90° rotation
- Subframe to bracket (Use new bolts): 52 ft. lbs. (70 Nm) plus 90° rotation
- Ball joint to control arm (Use new nut): 44 ft. lbs. (60 Nm)
- Stabilizer bar to subframe (Use new bolts): 15 ft. lbs. (20 Nm) plus 90° rotation
- Stabilizer bar to connecting link (Use new bolts and counterhold at joint pin inner multi-point fitting): 48 ft. lbs. (65 Nm)
- Control arm to bracket (Use new bolts and tighten bracket in curb

weight position): 52 ft. lbs. (70 Nm) plus 90° rotation
- Steering gear to subframe (Use new bolts) 37 ft. lbs. (50 Nm) plus 90° rotation
- Universal joint to steering gear (Use new bolt): 22 ft. lbs. (30 Nm)

STEERING KNUCKLE

REMOVAL & INSTALLATION

See Figure 132.

1. Before servicing the vehicle, refer to the precautions.

2. Loosen drive axle bolt to wheel hub.

✳✳ WARNING

When doing this, vehicle must not stand on wheels, otherwise wheel bearing may be damaged.

3. Remove wheel.

4. Remove brake caliper and engage on body with wire.

5. Remove ABS wheel speed sensor.

6. Remove disc brake.

7. Remove cover plate from wheel bearing housing.

8. Loosen tie rod end nut, but do not remove yet.

✳✳ WARNING

To protect thread, screw nut on pin a few turns.

9. Press off tie rod end from wheel bearing housing with ball joint puller 3287A and then remove nut.

10. Press drive axle out of wheel hub (in direction of transmission) as far as possible.

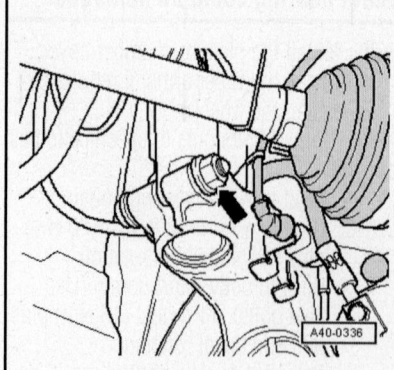

Fig. 132 Remove wheel bearing housing/suspension strut bolt connection (arrow)

11. Remove wheel bearing housing/suspension strut bolt connection.

12. Insert spreader 3424 into wheel bearing housing slot.

13. Turn ratchet around 90° and remove from spreader 3424.

14. Loosen nuts.

15. Place engine/transmission jack V.A.G 1383 beneath wheel bearing housing.

16. First, press off ball joint from control arm, then pull off wheel bearing housing from suspension strut.

To install:

17. Installation is reverse of removal.:

18. Tighten drive axle bolt to wheel hub. When doing this, vehicle must not stand on wheels, otherwise wheel bearing may be damaged.

✳✳ WARNING

If wheel bearing housing was replaced, vehicle alignment must be performed Alignment General Information.

19. Install wheel.

20. Tighten bolts/nuts to specification as follows:

- Strut to wheel bearing housing (Use new nut): 52 ft. lbs. (70 Nm) plus 90° additional rotation
- Ball joint to steel control arm (Use new nuts): 44 ft. lbs. (60 Nm)
- Tie rod end to wheel bearing housing (Use new nuts): 15 ft. lbs. (20 Nm) plus 90° additional rotation
- Drive axle to wheel hub "hex head bolt" (Use new bolt): 148 ft. lbs. (200 Nm) plus an additional 180° rotation
- Drive axle to wheel hub "12-point bolt" (Use new bolt): 52 ft. lbs. (70 Nm) plus an additional 90° rotation

WHEEL BEARINGS

REMOVAL & INSTALLATION

See Figure 133.

1. Before servicing the vehicle, refer to the precautions.

2. Loosen drive axle bolt to wheel hub.

✳✳ WARNING

When doing this, vehicle must not stand on wheels, otherwise wheel bearing may be damaged.

3. Remove wheel.

4. Remove brake caliper and engage on body with wire.

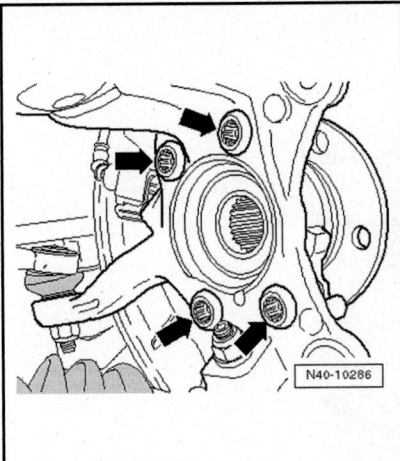

Fig. 133 Remove bolts (arrows)

5. Remove ABS wheel speed sensor.
6. Remove disc brake.
7. Press drive axle out of wheel hub (in direction of transmission) as far as possible.
8. Remove bolts.
9. Remove wheel bearing unit from wheel bearing housing.

To install:
10. Installation is in reverse order of removal.
11. Install brake caliper.
12. Tighten drive axle bolt to wheel hub.
13. When doing this, vehicle must not stand on wheels, otherwise wheel bearing may be damaged.

14. Install ABS wheel speed sensor.
15. Install wheel.
16. Tighten bolts/nuts to specification as follows:
- Drive axle to wheel hub "hex head bolt" (Use new bolt): 148 ft. lbs. (200 Nm) plus an additional 180° rotation
- Drive axle to wheel hub "12-point bolt"(Use new bolt): 52 ft. lbs. (70 Nm) plus an additional 90° rotation
- Wheel hub with wheel bearing to wheel bearing housing (Use new nut): 52 ft. lbs. (70 Nm) plus 90° additional rotation

SUSPENSION

COIL SPRING

REMOVAL & INSTALLATION
See Figures 134 and 135.

1. Before servicing the vehicle, refer to the precautions.
2. Remove wheel.
3. Insert spring compressor.

✳✳ CAUTION
Be sure coil spring is properly seated in spring holder V.A.G 1752/4 2.

4. Use wrench or ratchet for tightening spring compressor.
5. Compress coil spring until it can be removed.
6. Remove spring.
7. Spring holder V.A.G 1752/4
8. Adapter V.A.G 1752/9
9. Spring compressor V.A.G 1752/1

To install:

✳✳ WARNING
The spring start must touch bottom of spring seat.

10. Install spring together with spring seat.
11. Lower spring support has a pin.
12. Insert this pin into hole of lower transverse link.
13. Then insert upper spring support into upper end of spring.
14. Release tension of spring, guiding upper spring support onto tab of body.

15. Remove spring tensioner.
16. Install wheel.

SHOCK ABSORBER

REMOVAL & INSTALLATION

1. Before servicing the vehicle, refer to the precautions.
2. Remove wheel.
3. Remove wheel housing liner.
4. Remove coil spring.
5. Remove bolts.
6. Remove shock absorber.

To install:
7. Installation is in reverse order of removal.

➡**Only bolt on shock absorber to wheel bearing housing when vehicle is at normal ride height.**

8. Install shock absorber and tighten bolts.
9. Install coil spring.
10. Install wheel housing liner.
11. Install wheel.
12. Tighten bolts/nuts to specification as follows:
- Shock absorber to body (Use new bolt): 37 ft. lbs. (50 Nm) plus 45° additional rotation
- Shock absorber to wheel bearing housing: 133 ft. lbs. (180 Nm)

TRAILING ARM

REMOVAL & INSTALLATION
See Figures 136 and 137.

1. Remove the wheel.

REAR SUSPENSION

2. Remove coil spring.
3. Remove the parking cable bracket by pressing out rivet inner pin.
4. Remove the coupling rod from trailing link and remove bolts.
5. Mark the installation position of mounting bracket on body.
6. Remove bolts.
7. Remove the trailing link with mounting bracket.

➡**If longitudinal control arm is being replaced, mounting bracket must be removed from trailing arm. Installation position of mounting bracket to trailing link must then be adjusted. Determining the Installation Position of Mounting Bracket Relative to Trailing Link. Dimension a is 34 ± 1 mm. Mounting bracket**

8. When dimension a has been adjusted, tighten bolt.

To install:
9. Threaded connection of trailing link/wheel bearing housing must only be tightened when all other components (spring and strut always) of the respective wheel suspension have been already assembled. To tighten, suspension must be unloaded. Only now do the trailing link and wheel bearing housing move into the position required arrows.
10. Always follow the order of the following work steps!
11. Install trailing link and mounting bracket with bolts 2 on wheel bearing housing but do not yet tighten.
12. Insert coupling rod 3 in trailing link, do not tighten nut yet.

1
2
3
2
1
N42-10108

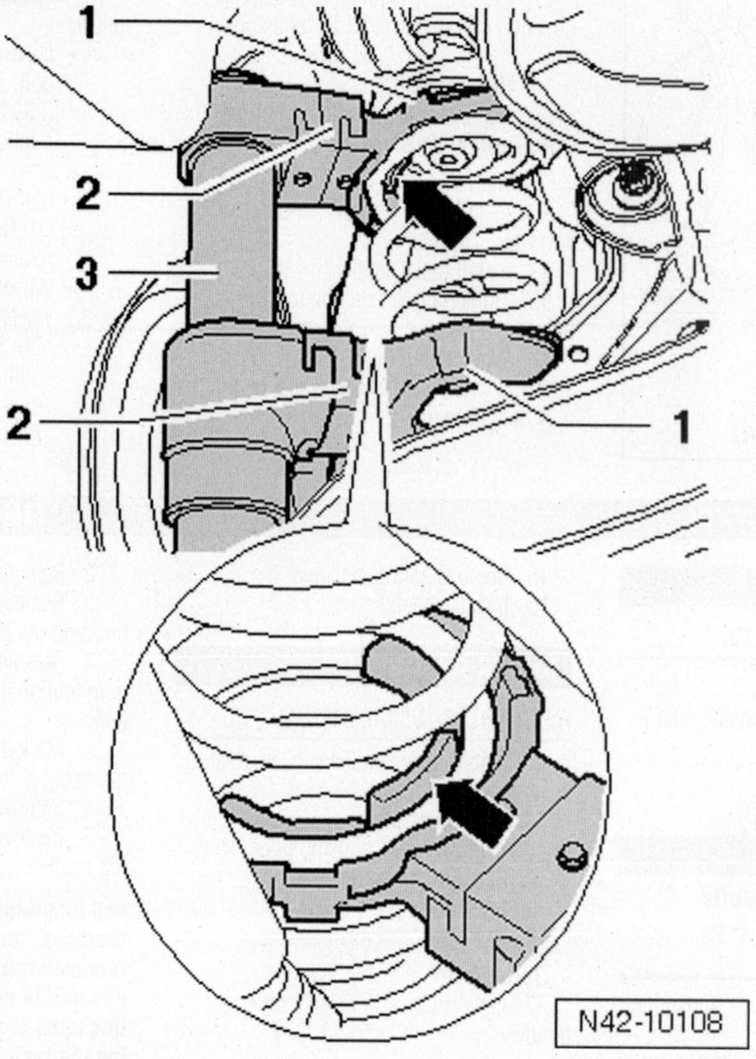

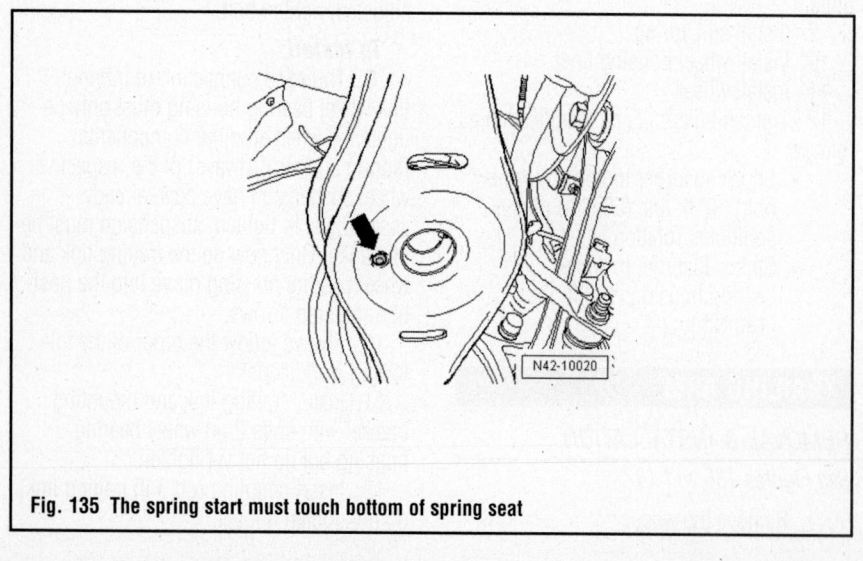

Fig. 134 Spring holder V.A.G 1752/4 (1), Adapter V.A.G 1752/9 (2) and Spring compressor V.A.G 1752/1 (3)

N42-10020

Fig. 135 The spring start must touch bottom of spring seat

A42-0431

Fig. 136 Remove bolts (arrows)

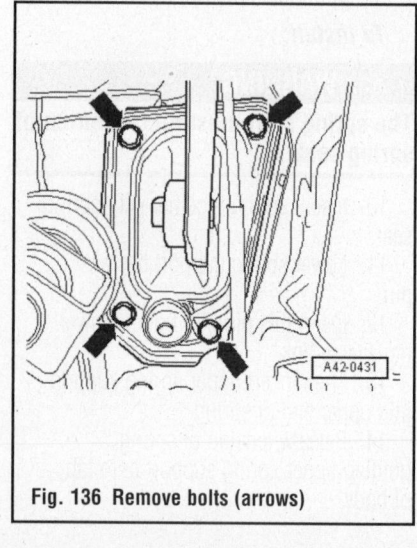

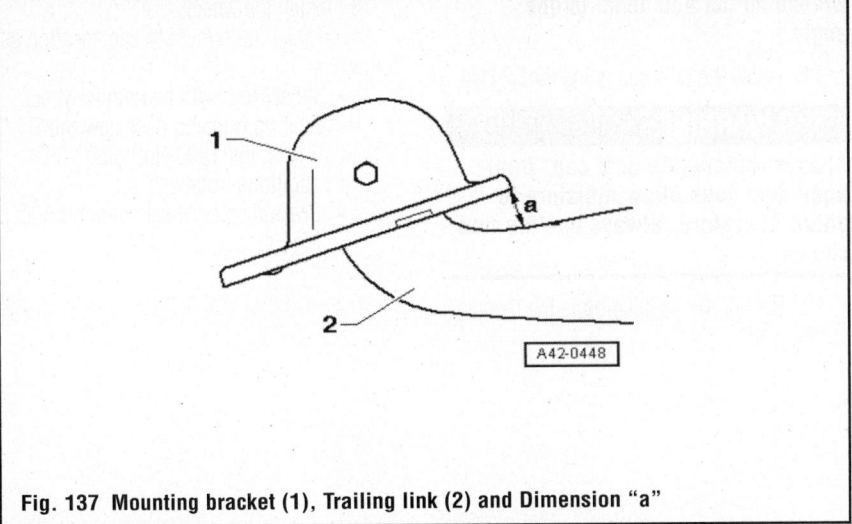

Fig. 137 Mounting bracket (1), Trailing link (2) and Dimension "a"

13. Raise wheel suspension using V.A.G 1383 A and T10149 until mounting bracket makes contact on body.

14. Tighten bolts arrows on old impression.

15. Let down wheel suspension again using V.A.G 1383 A and remove T10149 from wheel hub.

16. Fasten bolts 2 for trailing arm to torque specification, making sure of the required positioning of the components (dimension "a").

17. Connect the coupling rod 1 to the wheel bearing housing and stabilizer bar.

18. Install bracket 1 by pressing in new rivet inner pin.

19. Install coil spring.

20. Install wheel and tighten.

21. Perform vehicle alignment.

22. Tighten the following to specification using new bolts and/or nuts:

- Trailing arm to wheel bearing housing: 90 Nm plus 45° turn
- Trailing arm to mounting bracket: 90 Nm plus 90° turn
- Mounting bracket to body: 50 Nm plus 45° turn
- Coupling rod to trailing arm: 45 Nm

UPPER CONTROL ARM

REMOVAL & INSTALLATION

See Figure 138.

1. Before servicing the vehicle, refer to the precautions.

2. Remove the wheel.

3. Remove the coil spring.

4. Remove the wire for the speed sensor from the upper transverse link.

5. Remove the upper transverse link to wheel bearing housing bolt.

6. Using a felt tip marker, mark the position of the eccentric bolt to the subframe.

7. Remove the bolt, nut and washer.

8. Remove upper transverse link.

To install:

9. Position the upper transverse link to the vehicle and install the bolts hand tight.

✳✳ WARNING

Only tighten the upper transverse link bolts tighten bolt/nut in normal ride height position.

10. Install the new upper transverse link to subframe nut.

11. Align the eccentric bolt to the previously applied mark on the subframe and tighten the nut.

12. Tighten the new upper transverse link to wheel bearing housing bolt and nut.

✳✳ WARNING

Make sure that washer is installed between the bolt and wheel bearing housing.

13. Secure the wire for the speed sensor to the upper transverse link.

14. Install the coil spring.

15. Install the wheel.

16. Perform a vehicle alignment.

17. Tighten bolts/nuts to specification as follows:

- Upper transverse link to wheel bearing housing FWD (Use new bolt/nut and tighten bolt/nut in normal ride height position): 96 ft. lbs. (130 Nm) plus 90° additional turn
- Upper transverse link to subframe (Use new bolt/nut and tighten bolt/nut in normal ride height position): 70 ft. lbs. (95 Nm)

WHEEL BEARINGS

REMOVAL & INSTALLATION

1. Before servicing the vehicle, refer to the precautions.

2. Raise the vehicle.

3. Remove the wheel.

➡**Loosen the dust cap by lightly tapping on the claw of the VW 637/2.**

4. Pry off the dust cap.

5. Remove the brake carrier with caliper and secure to the body using wire.

➡**Suspend the brake caliper from body.**

6. Remove the brake disc bolt and remove the brake disc.

7. Remove the wheel hub and bearing bolt using the T10162.

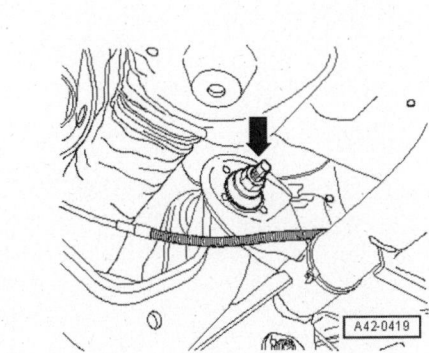

Fig. 138 Using a felt tip marker, mark the position of the eccentric bolt to the subframe

8. Pull the wheel hub and bearing off the stub axle.

To install:

9. Carefully slide the wheel hub and bearing onto the stub axle.

Make sure that wheel hub and bearing do not tilt!

10. Install a new wheel hub and bearing bolt and tighten.

➡**Tighten the bolt to specification using a torque wrench. Use a regular** wrench for the additional torque angle.

11. Install the dust cap using the 3241/4.

✳✳ WARNING

Always replace the dust cap. Damaged dust caps allow moisture to enter. Therefore, always use the tool shown.

---

12. Rest of the installation is the reverse of removal.

13. Install the wheel.

14. Tighten bolts/nuts to specification as follows:

- Wheel hub with bearing to wheel bearing housing (Use new bolt): 148 ft. lbs. (200 Nm) plus 180° additional rotation
- Brake disc to wheel bearing housing: 35 inch lbs. (4 Nm)

VOLKSWAGEN

CC • Passat

7

SPECIFICATIONS AND MAINTENANCE CHARTS

ENGINE AND VEHICLE IDENTIFICATION

Eng Code	Liters (cc)	Cu. In.	Cyl.	Fuel Sys.	Engine Type	Eng. Mfg.
CBFA	2.0 (1984)	121	4	MFI	DOHC	Volkswagen
CCTA	2.0 (1984)	121	4	MFI	DOHC	Volkswagen
CKRA	2.0 (1968)	120	4	TFI	DOHC	Volkswagen
CBTA	2.5 (2480)	151	5	MFI	DOHC	Volkswagen
CBUA	2.5 (2480)	151	5	MFI	DOHC	Volkswagen
BLV	3.6 (3580)	218	6	MFI	DOHC	Volkswagen
CCNA	3.6 (3580)	218	6	MFI	DOHC	Volkswagen
CDVB	3.6 (3580)	218	6	MFI	DOHC	Volkswagen

Model Year Code ①	Year
B	2011
C	2012

DOHC: Double Overhead Camshafts

SOHC: Single Overhead Camshaft

① 10th digit of VIN

71105_VWPA_C0001

GENERAL ENGINE SPECIFICATIONS

Year	Model	Engine Displacement Liters	Engine Code	Net Horsepower @ rpm	Net Torque@rpm (ft. lbs.)	Bore x Stroke (in.)	Com- pression Ratio	Oil Pressure @ rpm
2011	CC	2.0	CBFA/CCTA	200@5700	207@2000	3.25x3.65	10.5:1	39@2000
	CC	3.6	BLV/CCNA	280@6200	265@2800	3.25x3.40	12.0:1	43@2000
2012	CC	2.0	CBFA/CCTA	200@5700	207@2000	3.25x3.65	10.5:1	39@2000
	CC	3.6	CCNA	280@6200	265@2800	3.25x3.40	12.0:1	43@2000
	Passat	2.0 TDI	CKRA	140@4000	236@1500	3.19x3.74	16.5:1	29@2000
	Passat	2.5	CBTA/CBUA	170@5700	177@4250	3.25x3.65	9.5:1	39@2000
	Passat	3.6	CDVB	280@6200	265@2750	3.50x3.80	12.0:1	43@2000

① Inspect timing cover for code.

71105_VWPA_C0002

GASOLINE ENGINE TUNE-UP SPECIFICATIONS

Year	Engine Displacement Liters	Engine Code	Spark Plug Gap (in.)	Ignition Timing (deg.) MT	AT	Fuel Pump (psi)	Idle Speed (rpm) MT	AT	Valve Clearance Intake	Exhaust
2011	2.0	CBFA/CCTA	0.028-0.031	①	①	51-73 ②	620-800	620-800	HYD	HYD
	3.6	BLV/CCNA	0.039-0.043	①	①	81-87 ③	600-800	600-800	HYD	HYD
2012	2.0	CBFA/CCTA	0.028-0.031	①	①	51-73 ②	620-800	620-800	HYD	HYD
	2.5	CBTA/CBUA	0.039-0.043	①	①	NS	680	680	HYD	HYD
	3.6	CDVB/CNNA	0.039-0.043	①	①	81-87 ③	600-800	600-800	HYD	HYD

Note: The Vehicle Emission Control Information label reflects specification changes made during production.

The label figures must be used if they differ from those in this chart.

NS: Not specified

HYD: Hydraulic

① Ignition timing controlled electronically. Specification no longer provided.

② Engine OFF. Ignition ON. Fuel Pump connector pin 4 jumpered to harness pin 4. FP pin 1 jumpered to harness pin 3 with remote starter switch.

③ Keep Engine OFF. Cycle Ignition switch until fuel pressure no longer rises.

71105_VWPA_C0003

CAPACITIES

Year	Model	Engine Displacement Liters	Engine Code	Engine Oil with Filter	Transmission Manual (pts.)	Transmission Auto. (qts.)	Fuel Tank (gal.)	Cooling System (qts.)
2011	CC	2.0	CBFA/CCTA	4.5	4.9	7.4 ①	18.5	7.7
	CC	3.6	BLV	5.9	4.9	7.4 ①	18.5	8.5
2012	CC	2.0	CBFA/CCTA	4.5	4.9	7.4 ①	18.5	7.7
	CC	3.6	CCNA	5.9	4.9	7.4 ①	18.5	8.5
	Passat	2.0 TDI	CKRA	②	4.9	7.4 ①	18.5	7.7
	Passat	2.5	CBTA/CBUA	②	4.9	7.4 ①	18.5	8.5
	Passat	3.6	CDVB	4.5	4.9	7.4 ①	18.5	7.7

Note: All capacities are approximate. Add fluid gradually and check often to avoid overfilling or underfilling.

① Fill amount for new or rebuilt transmission. Be careful not to overfill.

② Carefully fill and check level on dipstick. Also see Owner's Manual.

71105_VWPA_C0004

FLUID SPECIFICATIONS

Year	Model	Engine Disp. Liters	Engine Code	Engine Oil	Man. Trans.	Auto. Trans.	Drive Axle Front	Drive Axle Rear	Transfer Case	Power Steering Fluid	Brake Master Cylinder	Cooling System
2011	CC	2.0	CBFA/CCTA	5W-40	NS	Synthetic ATF	NS	NS	NS	NS	DOT4	LLC
	CC	3.6	BLV	5W-40	NS	Synthetic ATF	NS	NS	NS	NS	DOT4	LLC
2012	CC	2.0	CBFA/CCTA	5W-40	NS	Synthetic ATF	NS	NS	NS	NS	DOT4	LLC
	CC	3.6	CCNA	5W-40	NS	Synthetic ATF	NS	NS	NS	NS	DOT4	LLC
	Passat	2.0 TDI	CKRA	①	NS	Synthetic ATF	NS	NS	NS	NS	DOT4	LLC
	Passat	2.5	CBTA/CBUA	5W-40	NS	Synthetic ATF	NS	NS	NS	NS	DOT4	LLC
	Passat	3.6	CDVB	5W-40	NS	Synthetic ATF	NS	NS	NS	NS	DOT4	LLC

DOT: Department Of Transpotation

LLC: Long Life Coolant

NS: Not specified; consult dealer information.

① Refer to Owner's Manual for proper oil type.

71105_VWPA_C0005

VALVE SPECIFICATIONS

Year	Engine Displacement Liters	Engine Code	Seat Angle (deg.)	Face Angle (deg.)	Spring Test Pressure (lbs. @ in.)	Spring Installed Height (in.)	Stem-to-Guide Clearance (in.) Intake	Stem-to-Guide Clearance (in.) Exhaust	Stem Diameter (in.) Intake	Stem Diameter (in.) Exhaust
2011	2.0	CBFA/CCTA	45	45	NS	NS	0.031	0.031	0.2354	0.2342
	3.6	BLV	45	45	NS	NS	0.031	0.031	0.2354	0.2350
2012	2.0	CBFA/CCTA	45	45	NS	NS	0.031	0.031	0.2354	0.2342
	2.0 TDI	CJAA	45	45	NS	NS	0.031	0.031	0.2354	0.2342
	2.5	CBTA/CBUA	45	45	NS	NS	0.031	0.031	0.2354	0.2342
	3.6	CDVB	45	45	NS	NS	0.031	0.031	0.2354	0.2350

NS: Not Specified

① Inspect timing cover for code.

71105_VWPA_C0006

CAMSHAFT AND BEARING SPECIFICATIONS

All measurements are given in inches.

Year	Engine Displacement Liters	Engine Code	Journal Diameter	Brg. Oil Clearance	Shaft End-play	Runout	Journal Bore	Lobe Lift Intake	Lobe Lift Exhaust
2011	2.0	CBFA/CCTA	NS	NS	NS	NS	NS	NS	NS
	3.6	BLV	NS	NS	0.016	NS	NS	NS	NS
2012	2.0	CBFA/CCTA	NS	NS	NS	NS	NS	NS	NS
	2.0 TDI	CJAA	NS	0.0014-0.0033	0.002-0.005	NS	NS	NS	NS
	2.5	CBTA/CBUA	NS	NS	NS	NS	NS	NS	NS
	3.6	CDVB	NS	NS	0.016	NS	NS	NS	NS

NS: Not specified

71105_VWPA_C0007

CRANKSHAFT AND CONNECTING ROD SPECIFICATIONS

All measurements are given in inches.

Year	Engine Disp. Liters	Engine Code ①	Crankshaft Main Brg. Journal Dia.	Crankshaft Main Brg. Oil Clearance	Crankshaft Shaft End-play	Crankshaft Thrust on No.	Connecting Rod Journal Diameter	Connecting Rod Oil Clearance	Connecting Rod Side Clearance
2011	2.0	CBFA/CCTA	2.1260	0.0009-0.0017 ②	0.0009-0.0017 ③	3	1.8819	0.0008-0.0024 ④	0.0039-0.0138 ⑤
	3.6	BLV	2.3605-2.3613	0.0008-0.0024 ⑥	0.0028-0.0091 ⑦	5	2.1243-2.1251	0.0008-0.0028 ⑥	0.0020-0.0122 ⑤
2012	2.0	CBFA/CCTA	2.1260	0.0009-0.0017 ②	0.0009-0.0017 ③	3	1.8819	0.0008-0.0024 ④	0.0039-0.0138 ⑤
	2.0 TDI	CJAA	2.1260	NS	0.003-0.007	NS	2.0040	NS	NS
	2.5	CNNA/CBUA	2.281-2.2830	NS	NS	NS	1.8804-1.8820	NS	NS
	3.6	CDVB	2.3605-2.3613	0.0008-0.0024 ⑥	0.0028-0.0091 ⑦	5	2.1243-2.1251	0.0008-0.0028 ⑥	0.0020-0.0122 ⑤

NS: Not specified.

① Inspect timing cover for code.

② Measurement with new parts. Wear limit is 0.0028 in.

③ Measurement with new parts. Wear limit is 0.0118 in.

④ Measurement with new parts. Wear limit is 0.0035 in.

⑤ Measurement with new parts. Wear limit is 0.0157 in.

⑥ Measurement with new parts. Wear limit is 0.0039 in.

⑦ Measurement with new parts. Wear limit is 0.0003 in.

71105_VWPA_C0009

PISTON AND RING SPECIFICATIONS

All measurements are given in inches.

Year	Engine Disp. Liters	Engine Code	Piston Clearance	Ring Gap ① Top Compression	Ring Gap ① Bottom Compression	Ring Gap ① Oil Control	Ring Side Clearance Top Compression	Ring Side Clearance Bottom Compression	Ring Side Clearance Oil Control
2011	2.0	CBFA/CCTA	0.0008 ①	0.008-0.016 ②	0.008-0.016 ②	0.010-0.020 ②	0.0024-0.0035 ②	0.0024-0.0035 ②	0.0012-0.0024 ②
	3.6	BLV	0.0026	0.008-0.016	0.008-0.016	0.010-0.020	0.0016-0.0035 ③	0.0012-0.0024 ③	0.0008-0.0024 ②
2012	2.0	CBFA/CCTA	0.0008 ①	0.008-0.016 ②	0.008-0.016 ②	0.010-0.020 ②	0.0024-0.0035 ②	0.0024-0.0035 ②	0.0012-0.0024 ②
	2.0 TDI	CJAA	0.0008 ①	0.008-0.015 ②	0.008-0.015 ②	0.010-0.020	0.002-0.003 ③	0.002-0.003 ③	0.001-0.002 ④
	2.5	CNNA/CBUA	0.0177 ①	0.008-0.016	0.008-0.016	0.010-0.020	0.002-0.003 ⑤	0.002-0.003 ⑤	0.001-0.002 ④
	3.6	CDVB	0.0026	0.008-0.016	0.008-0.016	0.010-0.020 ②	0.0016-0.0035 ④	0.0012-0.0024 ⑤	0.0008-0.0024 ②

① Measurement does not include graphite coating of new piston (0.0007 in.) Graphite coating wears off.

② Measurement with new parts. Wear limit is 0.0394 in.

③ Measurement with new parts. Wear limit is 0.010 in.

④ Measurement with new parts. Wear limit is 0.006 in.

⑤ Measurement with new parts. Wear limit is 0.008 in.

TORQUE SPECIFICATIONS

All readings in ft. lbs.

Year	Engine Disp. Liters	Engine Code ①	Cylinder Head Bolts	Main Bearing Bolts	Rod Bearing Bolts	Crankshaft Damper Bolt	Flywheel Bolts	Manifold Intake	Manifold Exhaust	Spark Plugs	Oil Pan Drain Plug
2011	2.0	CBFA/CCTA	②	③	④	⑤	⑥	7	15 ⑦	18	22
	3.6	BLV	⑧	⑨	④	⑩	⑥	6	18 ⑦	13	22
2012	2.0	CBFA/CCTA	②	③	④	⑤	⑥	7	15 ⑦	18	22
	2.0 TDI	CJAA	⑪	⑫	④	⑬	⑥	6	18 ⑦	13 ⑭	22
	2.5	CNNA/CBUA	⑮	⑯	④	⑰	⑥	7	17 ⑦	18	22
	3.6	CDVB	⑧	⑨	④	⑩	⑥	6	18 ⑦	13	22

① Inspect timing cover for code.

② Torque in three steps. Use new bolts.
   Step 1: 30 ft. lbs.
   Step 2: plus 90 degrees
   Step 3: plus 90 degrees

③ Two Steps. 66 ft. lbs. Plus 90 degrees. Use new bolt.

④ Two Steps. 22 ft. lbs. plus 90 degrees. Use new bolts.

⑤ Two Steps. 66 ft. lbs. Plus 90 degrees. Use new bolt.

⑥ Two Steps. 44 ft. lbs. plus 90 degrees. Use new bolts.

⑦ Use new bolts.

⑧ Torque in three steps. Use new bolts.
   Step 1: 11 ft. lbs.
   Step 2: 22 ft. lbs.
   Step 3: plus 180 degrees

⑨ Two Steps. 22 ft. lbs. plus 180 degrees. Use new bolts.

⑩ Two Steps. 74 ft. lbs. plus 180 degrees. Use new bolt.

⑪ Torque in four steps, using new bolts:
   Step 1: Tighten the bolts using a torque wrench, first time to 20 ft. lbs. (30 Nm)
   Step 2: Tighten the bolts using a torque wrench a second pass to 37 ft. lbs. (50 Nm).
   Step 3: Tighten each bolt in sequence, using a ratchet, an additional 90<deg.> (1/4 turn).
   Step 4: Repeat this process, tightening each bolt with a ratchet another 90<deg.> (1/4 turn).

⑫ 48 ft. lbs., plus 90 degrees. Use new bolts.

⑬ Torque setting unclear; contact dealer for information.

⑭ Glow plugs

⑮ Torque in three steps, using new bolts:
   Step 1: Using a torque wrench, tighten the bolts to 30 ft. lbs. (40 Nm).
   Step 2: Using a ratchet, tighten the bolts an additional 90<deg.> (1/4) turn.
   Step 3: Using a ratchet. tighten the bolts an additional 90<deg.> (1/4) turn.

⑯ 30 ft. lbs., plus 90 degrees. Use new bolts.

⑰ 37 ft. lbs., plus 90 degrees. Use new bolts.

WHEEL ALIGNMENT

Year	Model		Caster Range (+/-Deg.)	Caster Preferred Setting (Deg.)	Camber Range (+/-Deg.)	Camber Preferred Setting (Deg.)	Toe-in (Deg.)
2011	CC	Front	0.50	7.73	0.50	-0.68	1.33+/-0.33 ①
		Rear	—	—	0.50	-1.33	0.17+/-0.17 ②
2012	CC	Front	0.50	7.73	0.50	-0.68	1.33+/-0.33 ①
		Rear	—	—	0.50	-1.33	0.17+/-0.17 ②
	Passat	Front	0.50	7.53	0.50	-0.50	1.31+/-0.33 ①
		Rear	—	—	0.50	-1.33	0.17+/-0.17 ②

① Toe differential angle with 20 deg. steering lock to left and right

② Total toe at specified camber.

71105_VWPA_C0011

TIRE, WHEEL AND BALL JOINT SPECIFICATIONS

Year	Model	OEM Tires Standard	OEM Tires Optional	Tire Pressures (psi) Front	Tire Pressures (psi) Rear	Wheel Size	Lug Nut (ft. lbs.)
2011	CC	①	None	②	②	NS	89
2012	CC	①	None	②	②	NS	89
	Passat	③	None	②	②	NS	89

NS: Not Specified

① 235/45-17, 235/40-18, 235/35-19

② See Vehicle Tire Information Sticker for correct inflation values.

③ 235/45-17, 235/40-18

71105_VWPA_C0012

BRAKE SPECIFICATIONS

All measurements in inches unless noted

Year	Model		Brake Disc Original Thickness	Brake Disc Minimum Thickness	Maximum Run-out	Drum Diameter Original Inside Diameter	Drum Diameter Maximum Machine Diameter	Minimum Pad Thickness	Brake Caliper Ft. Guide Pins (ft. lbs.)	Brake Caliper Rear Guide Pins (ft. lbs.)
2011	CC (2.0L)	F	0.975	0.858	NS	—	—	0.078 ①	22	—
		R	0.468	0.390	NS	—	—	0.0472 ①	—	26 ②
	CC (3.6L)	F	1.170	1.053	NS	—	—	0.078 ①	22	—
		R	0.858	0.780	NS	—	—	0.0472 ①	—	26 ②
2012	CC (2.0L)	F	0.975	0.858	NS	—	—	0.078 ①	22	—
		R	0.468	0.390	NS	—	—	0.0472 ①	—	26 ②
	CC (3.6L)	F	1.170	1.053	NS	—	—	0.078 ①	22	—
		R	0.858	0.780	NS	—	—	0.0472 ①	—	26 ②
	Passat	F	0.984	0.866	0.002	—	—	0.078 ①	22	—
		R	0.468	0.394	0.002	—	—	0.0472 ①	—	26 ②

F: Front

R: Rear

NS: Not Specified

① Measurement does not include backing plate.

② Use new bolts.

71105_VWPA_C0013

SCHEDULED MAINTENANCE INTERVALS
VOLKSWAGEN—CC, PASSAT

TO BE SERVICED	TYPE OF SERVICE	10	20	30	40	50	60	70	80	90	100	110	120
Auto Trans - fluid	R				✔				✔				✔
Battery - check	S/I		✔		✔		✔		✔		✔		✔
Body- inspect for corrosion	S/I		✔		✔		✔		✔		✔		✔
Brake Pad thickness - check	S/I		✔	✔	✔	✔	✔	✔	✔	✔	✔	✔	✔
Brake system - inspection	S/I		✔		✔		✔		✔		✔		✔
Cooling System - level check	S/I				✔				✔				✔
CV Joints - leaks & damage	S/I				✔				✔				✔
Door Arresters - lubricate	S/I				✔				✔				✔
Engine Oil & Filter - replace	R		✔	✔	✔	✔	✔	✔	✔	✔	✔	✔	✔
Engine Compartment - leaks & damage	S/I				✔				✔				✔
Exhaust System - inspection	S/I				✔				✔				✔
Headlights - Check and adjust	S/I				✔				✔				✔
Power Steering - level check	S/I				✔				✔				✔
Rotate wheels	S/I	✔	✔	✔	✔	✔	✔	✔	✔	✔	✔	✔	✔
Serpentine Belt - inspection	S/I				✔				✔				✔
Service Interval Display - reset	S/I	✔	✔	✔	✔	✔	✔	✔	✔	✔	✔	✔	✔
Tie Rod Ends - play & boots	S/I				✔				✔				✔
Tires/Spare - inspection	S/I		✔		✔		✔		✔		✔		✔
Washer - clean nozzles	S/I	✔	✔	✔	✔	✔	✔	✔	✔	✔	✔	✔	✔
Wiper Blades - check	S/I	✔	✔	✔	✔	✔	✔	✔	✔	✔	✔	✔	✔
Air Cleaner - replace	Every 72 months												
Airbag System - inspect	Every 12 months												
Brake Fluid - replace	At 36 months, then every 24 months												
Cabin Air Filter - replace	Every 24 months												
Spark Plugs - replace	Every 72 months												
Tire Filler Bottle - inspect	Every 24 months												
Tire Filler Bottle - replace	Every 48 months												
Tire Pressure Sensors - replace	Every 72 months												

R: Replace   S/I: Service or Inspect

71105_VWPA_C0014

PRECAUTIONS

Before servicing any vehicle, please be sure to read all of the following precautions, which deal with personal safety, prevention of component damage, and important points to take into consideration when servicing a motor vehicle:

• Never open, service or drain the radiator or cooling system when the engine is hot; serious burns can occur from the steam and hot coolant.

• Observe all applicable safety precautions when working around fuel. Whenever servicing the fuel system, always work in a well-ventilated area. Do not allow fuel spray or vapors to come in contact with a spark, open flame, or excessive heat (a hot drop light, for example). Keep a dry chemical fire extinguisher near the work area. Always keep fuel in a container specifically designed for fuel storage; also, always properly seal fuel containers to avoid the possibility of fire or explosion. Refer to the additional fuel system precautions later in this section.

• Fuel injection systems often remain pressurized, even after the engine has been turned **OFF**. The fuel system pressure must be relieved before disconnecting any fuel lines. Failure to do so may result in fire and/or personal injury.

• Brake fluid often contains polyglycol ethers and polyglycols. Avoid contact with the eyes and wash your hands thoroughly after handling brake fluid. If you do get brake fluid in your eyes, flush your eyes with clean, running water for 15 minutes. If eye irritation persists, or if you have taken brake fluid internally, IMMEDIATELY seek medical assistance.

• The EPA warns that prolonged contact with used engine oil may cause a number of skin disorders, including cancer. You should make every effort to minimize your exposure to used engine oil. Protective gloves should be worn when changing oil. Wash your hands and any other exposed skin areas as soon as possible after exposure to used engine oil. Soap and water, or waterless hand cleaner should be used.

• All new vehicles are now equipped with an air bag system, often referred to as a Supplemental Restraint System (SRS) or Supplemental Inflatable Restraint (SIR) system. The system must be disabled before performing service on or around system components, steering column, instrument panel components, wiring and sensors. Failure to follow safety and disabling procedures could result in accidental air bag deployment, possible personal injury and unnecessary system repairs.

• Always wear safety goggles when working with, or around, the air bag system. When carrying a non-deployed air bag, be sure the bag and trim cover are pointed away from your body. When placing a non-deployed air bag on a work surface, always face the bag and trim cover upward, away from the surface. This will reduce the motion of the module if it is accidentally deployed. Refer to the additional air bag system precautions later in this section.

• Clean, high quality brake fluid from a sealed container is essential to the safe and proper operation of the brake system. You should always buy the correct type of brake fluid for your vehicle. If the brake fluid becomes contaminated, completely flush the system with new fluid. Never reuse any brake fluid. Any brake fluid that is removed from the system should be discarded. Also, do not allow any brake fluid to come in contact with a painted surface; it will damage the paint.

• Never operate the engine without the proper amount and type of engine oil; doing so WILL result in severe engine damage.

• Timing belt maintenance is extremely important. Many models utilize an interference)type, non)freewheeling engine. If the timing belt breaks, the valves in the cylinder head may strike the pistons, causing potentially serious (also time)consuming and expensive) engine damage. Refer to the maintenance interval charts for the recommended replacement interval for the timing belt, and to the timing belt section for belt replacement and inspection.

• Disconnecting the negative battery cable on some vehicles may interfere with the functions of the on)board computer system(s) and may require the computer to undergo a relearning process once the negative battery cable is reconnected.

• When servicing drum brakes, only disassemble and assemble one side at a time, leaving the remaining side intact for reference.

• Only an MVAC-trained, EPA-certified automotive technician should service the air conditioning system or its components.

BRAKES

ANTI)LOCK BRAKE SYSTEM (ABS)

GENERAL INFORMATION

PRECAUTIONS

• Certain components within the ABS system are not intended to be serviced or repaired individually.

• Do not use rubber hoses or other parts not specifically specified for and ABS system. When using repair kits, replace all parts included in the kit. Partial or incorrect repair may lead to functional problems and require the replacement of components.

• Lubricate rubber parts with clean, fresh brake fluid to ease assembly. Do not use shop air to clean parts; damage to rubber components may result.

• Use only DOT 3 brake fluid from an unopened container.

• If any hydraulic component or line is removed or replaced, it may be necessary to bleed the entire system.

• A clean repair area is essential. Always clean the reservoir and cap thoroughly before removing the cap. The slightest amount of dirt in the fluid may plug an orifice and impair the system function. Perform repairs after components have been thoroughly cleaned; use only denatured alcohol to clean components. Do not allow ABS components to come into contact with any substance containing mineral oil; this includes used shop rags.

• The Anti-Lock control unit is a microprocessor similar to other computer units in the vehicle. Ensure that the ignition switch is **OFF** before removing or installing controller harnesses. Avoid static electricity discharge at or near the controller.

• If any arc welding is to be done on the vehicle, the control unit should be unplugged before welding operations begin.

SPEED SENSORS

REMOVAL & INSTALLATION

Front

1. Raise the vehicle.
2. Release and remove the connector.

3. Remove bolt and remove the front speed sensor from the wheel bearing housing.

To install:

4. Install in reverse order of removal. Note the following:

a. Clean the inside of the hole and coat it with hot bolt paste (G 052 112 A3) before installing the front speed sensor.

b. Install the front speed sensor into

the hole in the wheel bearing housing and tighten it to 6 ft. lbs. (8 Nm).

Rear

1. Raise vehicle.
2. Separate speed sensor and speed sensor wiring connector.
3. Remove bolt from wheel bearing housing.
4. Remove ABS speed sensor from wheel bearing housing.

To install:

5. Before inserting speed sensor, clean hole inner surface and coat speed sensor all-round with hot bolt paste G 052 112 A3.

6. Insert the speed sensor into the hole in the wheel bearing housing and tighten the bolt to 6 ft. lbs. (8 Nm).

7. Connect speed sensor to speed sensor wiring.

BRAKES — BLEEDING THE BRAKE SYSTEM

BLEEDING PROCEDURE

BLEEDING PROCEDURE

➡ **The factory scan tool VAS 5051 or an equivalent bi-directional scan tool is required for this job.**

This procedure requires the use of brake filler and bleeder unit VAS 5234, or equivalent brake bleeding equipment. On ABS brakes, the valves must be driven open using a bi-directional scan tool to flush the valve body. Note the following important points about vehicles with ABS/EDL, ABS/EDL/ASR and ABS/EDL/ASR/ESP:

• When at least one chamber in the brake fluid reservoir is completely empty, the hydraulic unit must be bled with scan tool VAS 5051 in function "basic setting".

• Brakes must be bled in the proper sequence.

• After bleeding the brake system, perform a zero compensation of the brake pressure sender.

• Once the bleeding sequence is completed, carry out a test drive and perform at least one ABS application.

✳✳ CAUTION

Make sure that a filling pressure of 2 bar (29 psi) is not exceeded when filling brake fluid using brake filler and bleeder unit VAS 5234.

1. Connect the scan tool to the Data Link Connector (DLC) and turn it **ON**.
2. Turn the ignition switch **ON**.
3. On aftermarket tools, navigate to the ABS section and follow the directions on the screen for bleeding ABS brakes.
4. On the factory tool, touch "Guided Fault Finding" on the screen.
5. Select Brand, Model, Model year, Version, Engine identification. Confirm entered data.
6. Wait until tester has checked all control modules installed in the vehicle.
7. Press "Go" button and select "Function/component selection."
8. Select "Suspension" on the display.
9. Select "Bake system" on the display.
10. Select "01-On Board Diagnostic (OBD) capable system . . . " indicated on the display.
11. Select "Anti-lock Brake System (ABS) . . . " indicated on the display.
12. Select "Function" indicated on the display.
13. Now all possible functions of Anti-lock Brake System (ABS) installed in vehicle are displayed.

Select desired function on display.

14. Connect brake filler and bleeder unit VAS 5234.
15. If at least one chamber in the brake fluid reservoir is completely empty, pre-bleed the system:
   • Bleed both front brake calipers simultaneously
   • Bleed both rear brake calipers simultaneously
16. For normal bleeding, open bleeder screws in the following sequence:
   • Left front
   • Right front
   • Left rear
   • Right rear
17. A test drive must be carried out after bleeding brakes. When doing this an ABS application must be performed at least once.

✳✳ CAUTION

Brake fluid is poisonous. Brake fluid must not come into contact with paintwork as it is very corrosive. Brake fluid is hygroscopic, which means it absorbs moisture from the ambient air and should always be stored in air tight containers. Rinse off any spilled brake fluid using plenty of water.

BRAKES   **FRONT DISC BRAKES**

BRAKE CALIPER

REMOVAL & INSTALLATION

2.0L & 2.5L Engines

1. Remove wheels.
2. Using screwdriver, pry off brake pad retaining spring from brake caliper and remove.
3. Separate the connector for brake pad wear indicator.
4. Connect bleeder hose of bleeder bottle to bleeder valve of brake caliper and then open bleeder valve.
5. Insert brake pedal depressor V.A.G 1869/2.
6. Close bleeder valve and remove bleeder bottle.
7. Unscrew brake hose.
8. Pull both cover caps from bushings of brake caliper.
9. Loosen both guide pins and remove from brake caliper.
10. Pull off brake caliper from brake carrier.
11. Remove brake pads from brake caliper.

To install:
12. Press piston back into caliper.

13. Make sure outer brake pad sits on brake carrier.
14. Insert inner brake pad with retaining spring in brake caliper (piston).
15. Tighten brake caliper to brake carrier using both guide pins.
16. Install both protective caps.
17. Screw brake hose on brake caliper.
18. Tighten bolts/nuts to specification as follows:
   • Guide pin to brake carrier: 22 ft. lbs. (30 Nm)
   • Brake line to brake caliper: 26 ft. lbs. (35 Nm)
19. Remove brake pedal loading device V.A.G 1869/2.
20. Install retaining spring in brake caliper.
21. Connect brake pad wear indicator connector.
22. Bleed brake system.
23. Install wheels.
24. Before moving vehicle, depress brake pedal several times firmly to properly seat brake pads in their normal operating position.
25. Check brake fluid level.

3.6L Engine

1. Remove the wheels.
2. Pry brake caliper retaining spring out of brake pad retaining spring with screwdriver. To do this, place screwdriver between both retaining springs.
3. Secure brake caliper retaining spring with a cloth when doing this so that it cannot jump away.
4. Separate the connector for brake pad wear indicator.
5. Connect bleeder hose of bleeder bottle to bleeder valve of brake caliper and then open bleeder valve.
6. Insert brake pedal depressor V.A.G 1869/2.
7. Close bleeder valve and remove bleeder bottle.
8. Unscrew brake hose.
9. Pull both cover caps from bushings of brake caliper.
10. Loosen both guide pins and remove from brake caliper.
11. Pull off brake caliper from brake carrier.
12. Remove brake pads from brake caliper.

To install:
13. Press piston back into caliper.
14. Insert inner brake pad with retaining spring in brake caliper (piston).

15. Set outer brake pad with retaining springs into brake caliper.
16. Place brake caliper with brake pads on brake carrier.
17. Tighten brake caliper to brake carrier using both guide pins.
18. Install both protective caps.
19. Connect brake hose with brake caliper line.
20. Tighten bolts/nuts to specification as follows:
   • Guide pin to brake carrier: 22 ft. lbs. (30 Nm)
   • Brake hose to brake line: 10 ft. lbs. (14 Nm)
21. Remove brake pedal loading device V.A.G 1869/2.
22. Insert brake caliper retaining spring in brake pad retaining spring and press under brake carrier.
23. Connect brake pad wear indicator connector.
24. Bleed brake system.
25. Install the wheels.
26. Before moving vehicle, depress brake pedal several times firmly to properly seat brake pads in their normal operating position.
27. Check brake fluid level.

DISC BRAKE PADS

REMOVAL & INSTALLATION

2.0L & 2.5L Engines
See Figures 1 through 3.

➡**When removing, mark brake pads that will be used again. Install in the same position, otherwise braking effect will be uneven!**

1. Remove the wheels.
2. Using screwdriver, pry off brake pad retaining spring from brake caliper and remove.
3. Separate the connector for brake pad wear indicator.
4. Remove caps.
5. Loosen both guide pins and remove from brake caliper.
6. Remove brake caliper and secure with wire so that the weight of the brake caliper does not burden or damage the brake hose.
7. Remove brake pad from brake caliper or from brake carrier.

❋❋ CAUTION

Do not blow brake system using compressed air, the dust produced is harmful to health!

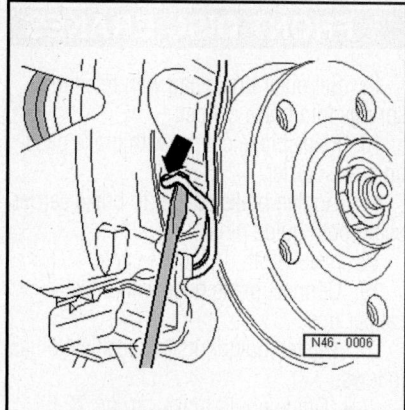

Fig. 1 Using screwdriver, pry off brake pad retaining spring from brake caliper and remove

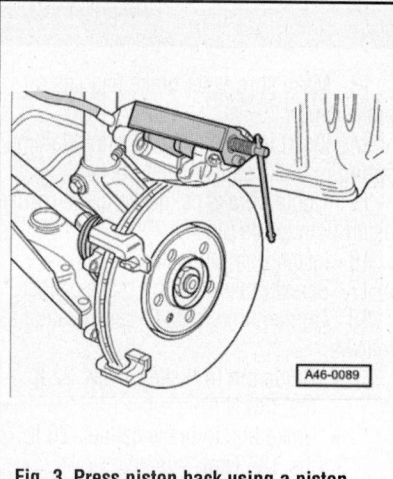

Fig. 3 Press piston back using a piston resetting tool T10145

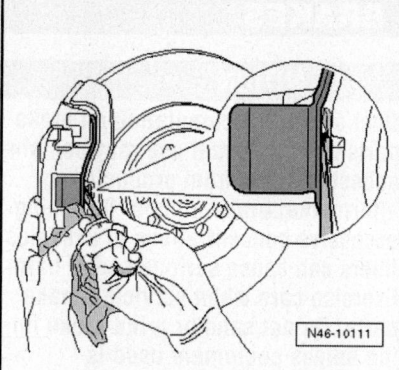

Fig. 4 Pry brake caliper retaining spring out of brake pad retaining spring with screwdriver. To do this, place screwdriver between both retaining springs close-up

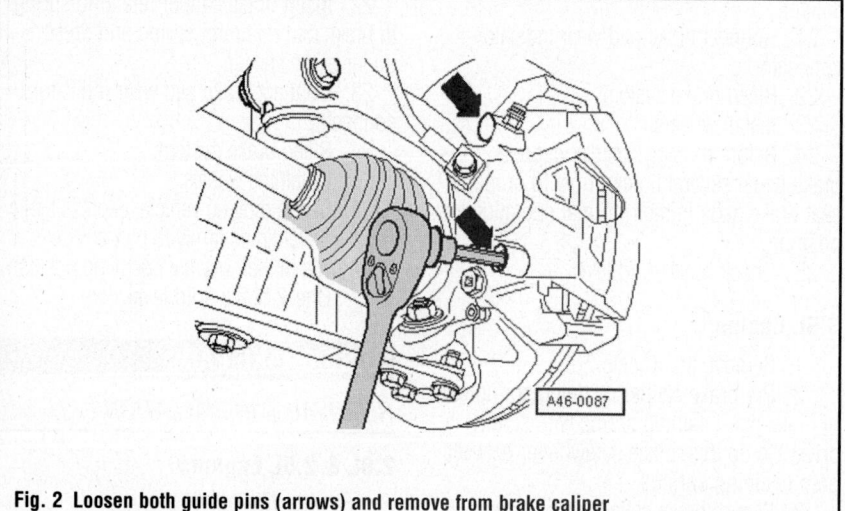

Fig. 2 Loosen both guide pins (arrows) and remove from brake caliper

8. Thoroughly clean contact surfaces for brake pads at brake carrier, remove corrosion.

9. Clean brake caliper.

❋❋ CAUTION

Use only appropriate solvents for cleaning brake caliper.

To install:

➡ Before pressing piston into cylinder using piston resetting tool, brake fluid must be extracted from brake fluid reservoir. Otherwise, especially if reservoir has been topped off, fluid will overflow and cause damage.

10. Press piston back using a piston resetting tool T10145.

11. Install outer brake pad on brake carrier.

12. Insert inner brake pad with retaining spring in brake caliper (piston).

13. Tighten brake caliper to brake carrier using both guide pins.

14. Tighten bolts/nuts to specification as follows:

- Guide pin to brake carrier: 22 ft. lbs. (30 Nm)

15. Install both protective caps.

16. Install retaining spring in brake caliper.

17. Connect brake pad wear indicator connector.

18. Install wheels.

19. After replacing brake pads, depress brake pedal firmly several times with vehicle stationary so that the brake pads are properly seated in their normal operating position.

20. Check brake fluid level after replacing brake pad.

3.6L Engine

See Figures 3 through 6.

➡ When removing, mark brake pads that will be used again. Install in the same position, otherwise braking effect will be uneven!

1. Remove wheels.

2. Pry brake caliper retaining spring out of brake pad retaining spring with screwdriver. To do this, place screwdriver between both retaining springs close-up.

3. Secure brake caliper retaining spring with a cloth when doing this so that it cannot fly away.

4. Separate the connector for brake pad wear indicator.

5. Remove caps.

6. Loosen both guide pins and remove from brake caliper.

7. Remove brake caliper and secure with wire so that the weight of the brake caliper does not burden or damage the brake hose.

8. Remove brake pads from brake caliper.

❋❋ CAUTION

Do not blow brake system using compressed air, the dust produced is harmful to health!

9. Thoroughly clean contact surfaces for brake pads at brake carrier, remove corrosion.

10. Clean brake caliper.

❋❋ CAUTION

Use only appropriate solvents for cleaning brake caliper.

To install:

➡ Before pressing piston into cylinder using piston resetting tool, brake fluid must be extracted from brake fluid reservoir. Otherwise, especially if reservoir has been topped off, fluid will overflow and cause damage.

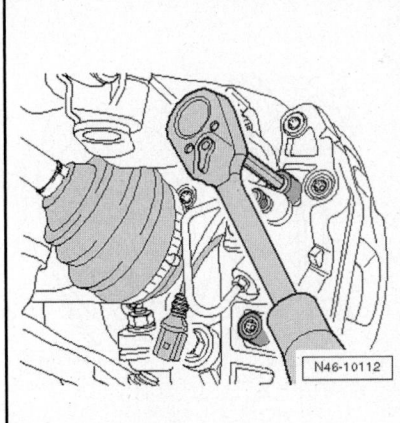

Fig. 5 Loosen both guide pins and remove from brake caliper

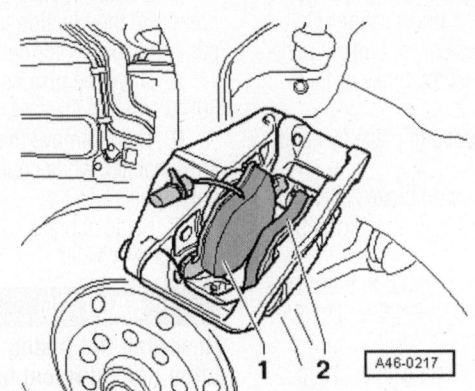

Fig. 6 Insert inner brake pad (1) with retaining spring in brake caliper (piston). Set outer brake pad (2) with retaining springs into brake caliper

11. Press piston back using piston resetting tool T 10145.

12. Insert inner brake pad with retaining spring in brake caliper (piston).

13. Set outer brake pad with retaining springs into brake caliper.

14. Place brake caliper with brake pads on brake carrier.

15. Tighten brake caliper to brake carrier using both guide pins.

16. Tighten bolts/nuts to specification as follows:
   • Guide pin to brake carrier: 22 ft. lbs. (30 Nm)

17. Install both protective caps.

18. Insert brake caliper retaining spring in brake pad retaining spring and press under brake carrier.

19. Connect brake pad wear indicator connector.

20. Install wheels.

21. After replacing brake pads, depress brake pedal firmly several times with vehicle stationary so that the brake pads are properly seated in their normal operating position.

22. Check brake fluid level after replacing brake pad.

BRAKES

REAR DISC BRAKES

✳✳ CAUTION

Dust and dirt accumulating on brake parts during normal use may contain asbestos fibers from production or aftermarket brake linings. Breathing excessive concentrations of asbestos fibers can cause serious bodily harm. Exercise care when servicing brake parts. Do not sand or grind brake lining unless equipment used is designed to contain the dust residue. Do not clean brake parts with compressed air or by dry brushing. Cleaning should be done by dampening the brake components with a fine mist of water, then wiping the brake components clean with a dampened cloth. Dispose of cloth and all residue containing asbestos fibers in an impermeable container with the appropriate label. Follow practices prescribed by the Occupational Safety and Health Administration (OSHA) and the Environmental Protection Agency (EPA) for the handling, processing, and disposing of dust or debris that may contain asbestos fibers.

BRAKE CALIPER

REMOVAL & INSTALLATION

✳✳ CAUTION

Do not disconnect the connectors from the parking brake motors.

1. Remove wheels.

The pistons of the parking brake must be driven back using the VAS 5051.

Before pressing piston back, draw off brake fluid from reservoir using a bleeder bottle. Otherwise, especially if reservoir has been topped off, fluid will overflow and cause damage.

2. VAS 5051, connecting and selecting functions VAS 5051.

3. Select the electromechanical parking brake and the function—"Moving piston of parking brake motor out and in".

4. Drive the pistons back using the VAS 5051.

5. Unscrew the parking brake motor, without disconnecting the connector.

6. Connect bleeder hose of bleeder bottle to bleeder valve of brake caliper and then open bleeder valve.

7. Insert brake pedal depressor V.A.G 1869/2.

8. Close bleeder valve and remove bleeder bottle.

9. Remove the brake line from the brake hose and brake caliper.

10. Unscrew both mounting bolts from brake caliper, counter hold on guide pin when doing this.

11. Pull off brake caliper from brake carrier.

To install:

➡**Brake pads sit in retaining springs on the brake carrier.**

12. Secure brake caliper on brake carrier using new self-locking bolts.

Ring groove and contact surface of parking brake motor must be clean.

13. Install new seal.

14. Turn the spindle back slightly the with help of a T45 Torx® bit, until the parking brake motor can be correctly positioned.

15. Carefully set the parking brake motor in place, paying attention to the seat of the seal.

16. Rotate the parking brake motor so far until the bolt hole and threads are aligned.

Make sure that the parking brake motor is seated flush against the brake caliper. Do not, under any circumstances, pull the parking brake motor against the brake caliper using the bolts.

17. Set the Torx® bolts in place by hand and then tighten.

18. Screw brake line on brake caliper.

19. Tighten bolts/nuts to specification as follows:

- Hex bolt, brake caliper to brake carrier (use new bolts): 26 ft. lbs. (35 Nm)
- Brake line to brake caliper: 10 ft. lbs. (14 Nm)
- Parking brake motor to brake caliper: 106 inch lbs. (12 Nm)

20. Bleed brake system.

After driving the pistons out with the VAS 5051, a basic setting of the brake system must be performed.

21. Perform the basic setting of the brake system with the VAS 5051.

22. Install wheels.

23. Check brake fluid level.

DISC BRAKE PADS

REMOVAL & INSTALLATION

See Figures 7 and 8.

➡When removing, mark brake pads that will be used again. Install in the same position, otherwise braking effect will be uneven!

1. Do not disconnect the connectors from the parking brake motors.

2. Make sure the parking brake is not actuated.

3. Remove wheels.

✳✳ CAUTION

The pistons of the parking brake must be driven back using the VAS 5051.

✳✳ CAUTION

Before pressing piston back, draw off brake fluid from reservoir using a bleeder bottle. Otherwise, especially if reservoir has been topped off, fluid will overflow and cause damage.

4. Select the electromechanical parking brake and the function—"Moving piston of parking brake motor out and in".

5. Drive the pistons back using the VAS 5051.

6. Then, remove the bolts from the brake caliper, while counter-holding the guide pins.

7. Remove brake caliper downward from brake carrier.

✳✳ CAUTION

Resetting the piston with VAS 5051 is often not sufficient but necessary! The pressure nut in the piston is a floating mount so the piston can only be pressed and cannot be pulled back. Only the spindle with the pressure nut is moved back.

8. The piston must first be reset with VAS 5051. Now, press piston all the way back with piston resetting tool T10145.

9. Secure brake caliper with wire so weight of caliper does not load or damage brake line.

10. Remove brake pads and anti-rattle springs.

➡**Do not blow brake system using compressed air, the dust produced is harmful to health!**

11. Thoroughly clean contact surfaces

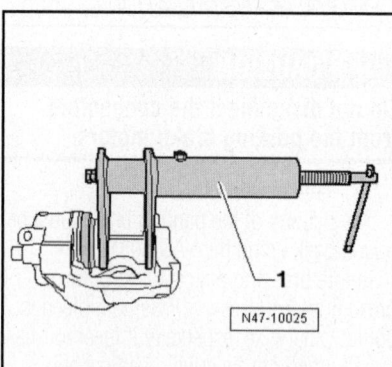

Fig. 7 The piston must first be reset with VAS 5051. Then press piston all the way back with piston resetting tool T10145

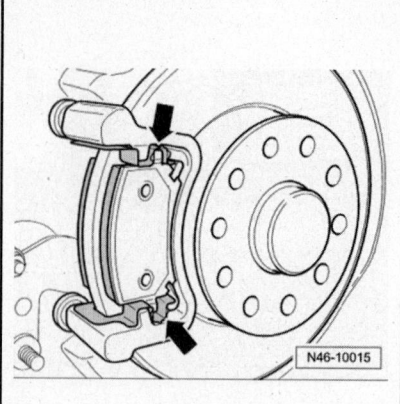

Fig. 8 Make sure that the brake pads are located correctly in the anti-rattle springs

for brake pads at brake carrier, remove corrosion.

12. Clean brake caliper.

Use only appropriate solvents for cleaning brake caliper.

Installing

13. Insert brake pad retention plates and brake pads in brake carrier.

14. Make sure that the brake pads are located correctly in the anti-rattle springs.

15. Secure brake caliper using new self-locking bolts.

16. Tighten bolts/nuts to specification as follows:

- Hex bolt, brake caliper to brake carrier (use new bolts): 26 ft. lbs. (35 Nm)

➡**The repair kit includes four self-locking hex bolts which must be installed in all cases.**

✳✳ CAUTION

After driving the pistons out with the VAS 5051, a basic setting of the brake system must be performed.

17. Perform the basic setting of the brake system with the VAS 5051.

18. Install wheels.

19. Check brake fluid level after replacing brake pad.

BRAKES **PARKING BRAKE**

PARKING BRAKE CABLES

ADJUSTMENT

See Figures 9 and 10.

1. Open the cover on the rear storage compartment inside the center console.

2. Remove the liner from the storage compartment:

   a. Release the tabs and open the service flap.

3. Remove the brake cable from the parking brake lever:

   a. Raise the vehicle.

   b. Push the brake pedal at least three times with force.

➡The parking brake lever must go back into the rest position by itself under the first detent. Parking brake lever in released position.

4. Install the brake cable:

   a. Set the parking brake one time, and then release the parking brake.

   b. Loosen the adjusting screw.

➡The brake cables will get tensioned through the quick adjustor.

   c. Tighten the adjusting screw to 18 ft. lbs. (25 Nm).

   d. Pull and loosen the parking brake three times.

   e. Loosen and tighten the adjusting screw.

➡The distance between the lever and the stop on the left and right brake calipers may be less than or equal to 0.050 in. (1.5 mm) together.

5. Check whether wheels turn freely.

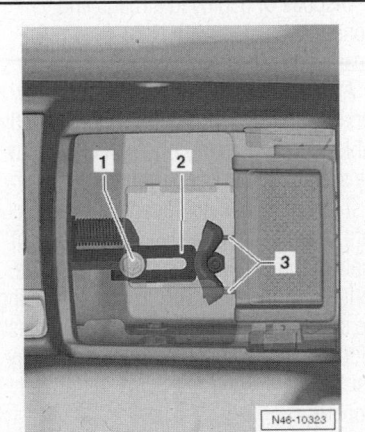

Fig. 9 Loosen the adjusting screw (1). The brake cables (3) will get tensioned through the quick adjustor (2).

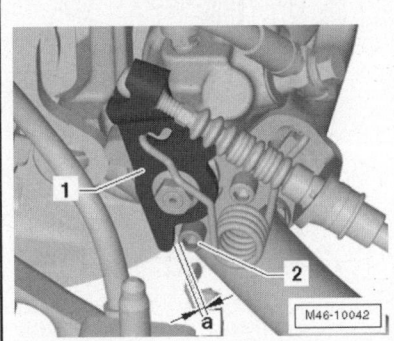

Fig. 10 The distance (a) between the lever (1) and the stop (2) on the left and right brake calipers may be less than or equal to 0.050 in. (1.5 mm) together.

➡Due to the automatic rear brake adjuster, there is no need to adjust the parking brake after making initial adjustment.

PARKING BRAKE LEVER

ADJUSTMENT

See Figure 11.

1. Loosen the adjusting screw 2 turns to adjust.

2. Ensure the brake cable is engaged at the compensator bracket.

3. Remove the brake cable, and replace if needed.

4. Tension the brake cable with the pressure spring.

PARKING BRAKE MOTOR

REMOVAL & INSTALLATION

See Figures 12 and 13.

➡This motor is used on CC models.

✳✳ CAUTION

Ignition must be switched off for at least 30 seconds before disconnecting the connector.

1. Remove connector off from parking brake motor.

2. Remove both Torx®bolts from the parking brake motor.

3. Remove parking brake motor from brake caliper.

4. Remove the seal.

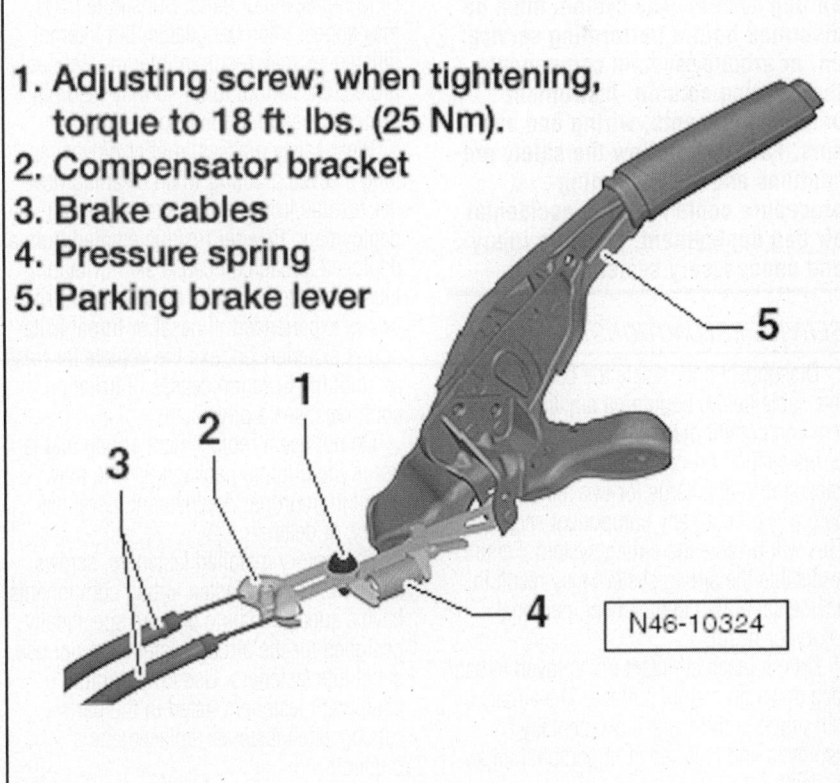

1. Adjusting screw; when tightening, torque to 18 ft. lbs. (25 Nm).
2. Compensator bracket
3. Brake cables
4. Pressure spring
5. Parking brake lever

Fig. 11 Showing the parking brake lever and cable components

❊❊ CAUTION

Make sure that the ring groove of the seal and the contact surface of the parking brake motor do not become damaged.

5. Clean the ring groove and the contact surface of the parking brake motor.
Installing
6. Lightly coat the new gasket with brake fluid and then install it.
7. Turn the spindle back slightly the with help of a T45 Torx® bit A, until the parking brake motor can be correctly positioned.

➡ **Do not remove the gasket when assembling the parking brake motor.**

8. Carefully set the parking brake motor in place, paying attention to the seat of the seal.
9. Rotate the parking brake motor so far until the bolt hole and threads are aligned.

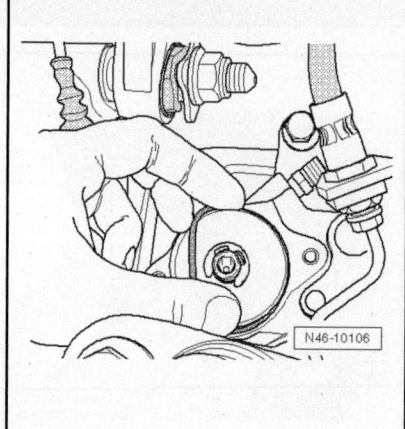

Fig. 12 Lightly coat the new gasket with brake fluid and then install it

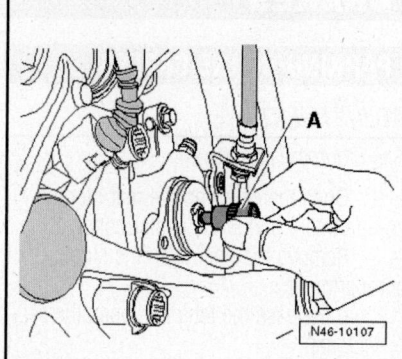

Fig. 13 Turn the spindle back slightly the with help of a T45 Torx® bit A, until the parking brake motor can be correctly positioned.

Make sure that the parking brake motor is seated flush against the brake caliper. Do not, under any circumstances, pull the parking brake motor against the brake caliper using the bolts.

10. Set the Torx® bolts in place by hand and then tighten.
11. Install connector.
12. Perform basic setting of brake system using VAS 5051.

CHASSIS ELECTRICAL
AIR BAG (SUPPLEMENTAL RESTRAINT SYSTEM)

GENERAL INFORMATION

❊❊ CAUTION

These vehicles are equipped with an air bag system. The system must be disarmed before performing service on, or around, system components, the steering column, instrument panel components, wiring and sensors. Failure to follow the safety precautions and the disarming procedure could result in accidental air bag deployment, possible injury and unnecessary system repairs.

SERVICE PRECAUTIONS

Disconnect and isolate the battery negative cable before beginning any airbag system component diagnosis, testing, removal, or installation procedures. Allow system capacitor to discharge for two minutes before beginning any component service. This will disable the airbag system. Failure to disable the airbag system may result in accidental airbag deployment, personal injury, or death.

Do not place an intact undeployed airbag face down on a solid surface. The airbag will propel into the air if accidentally deployed and may result in personal injury or death.

When carrying or handling an undeployed airbag, the trim side (face) of the airbag should be pointing away from the body to minimize possibility of injury if accidental deployment occurs. Failure to do this may result in personal injury or death.

Replace airbag system components with OEM replacement parts. Substitute parts may appear interchangeable, but internal differences may result in inferior occupant protection. Failure to do so may result in occupant personal injury or death.

Wear safety glasses, rubber gloves, and long sleeved clothing when cleaning powder residue from vehicle after an airbag deployment. Powder residue emitted from a deployed airbag can cause skin irritation. Flush affected area with cool water if irritation is experienced. If nasal or throat irritation is experienced, exit the vehicle for fresh air until the irritation ceases. If irritation continues, see a physician.

Do not use a replacement airbag that is not in the original packaging. This may result in improper deployment, personal injury, or death.

The factory installed fasteners, screws and bolts used to fasten airbag components have a special coating and are specifically designed for the airbag system. Do not use substitute fasteners. Use only original equipment fasteners listed in the parts catalog when fastener replacement is required.

During, and following, any child restraint anchor service, due to impact event or vehicle repair, carefully inspect all mounting hardware, tether straps, and anchors for proper installation, operation, or damage. If a child restraint anchor is found damaged in any way, the anchor must be replaced. Failure to do this may result in personal injury or death.

Deployed and non-deployed airbags may or may not have live pyrotechnic material within the airbag inflator.

Do not dispose of driver/passenger/curtain airbags or seat belt tensioners unless you are sure of complete deployment. Refer to the Hazardous Substance Control System for proper disposal.

Dispose of deployed airbags and tensioners consistent with state, provincial, local, and federal regulations.

After any airbag component testing or service, do not connect the battery negative cable. Personal injury or death may result if the system test is not performed first.

If the vehicle is equipped with the Occupant Classification System (OCS), do not connect the battery negative cable before performing the OCS Verification Test using the scan tool and the appropriate diagnostic information. Personal injury or death may result if the system test is not performed properly.

Never replace both the Occupant Restraint Controller (ORC) and the Occupant Classification Module (OCM) at the same time. If both require replacement, replace one, then perform the Airbag System test before replacing the other.

Both the ORC and the OCM store Occupant Classification System (OCS) calibration data, which they transfer to one another when one of them is replaced. If both are replaced at the same time, an irreversible fault will be set in both modules and the OCS may malfunction and cause personal injury or death.

If equipped with OCS, the Seat Weight Sensor is a sensitive, calibrated unit and must be handled carefully. Do not drop or handle roughly. If dropped or damaged, replace with another sensor. Failure to do so may result in occupant injury or death.

If equipped with OCS, the front passenger seat must be handled carefully as well. When removing the seat, be careful when setting on floor not to drop. If dropped, the sensor may be inoperative, could result in occupant injury, or possibly death.

If equipped with OCS, when the passenger front seat is on the floor, no one should sit in the front passenger seat. This uneven force may damage the sensing ability of the seat weight sensors. If sat on and damaged, the sensor may be inoperative, could result in occupant injury, or possibly death.

DISARMING THE SYSTEM

To disarm the airbag system, the battery Ground (GND) strap must be disconnected. No waiting time is necessary after disconnecting battery.

ARMING THE SYSTEM

To disarm the airbag system, connect the battery Ground (GND) strap.

☀☀ CAUTION

There must be no person present inside the vehicle when arming the airbag system.

CLOCKSPRING CENTERING

See Figure 14.

The Spiral Spring/Return Spring With Slip Ring is an integral part of the steering column switches.

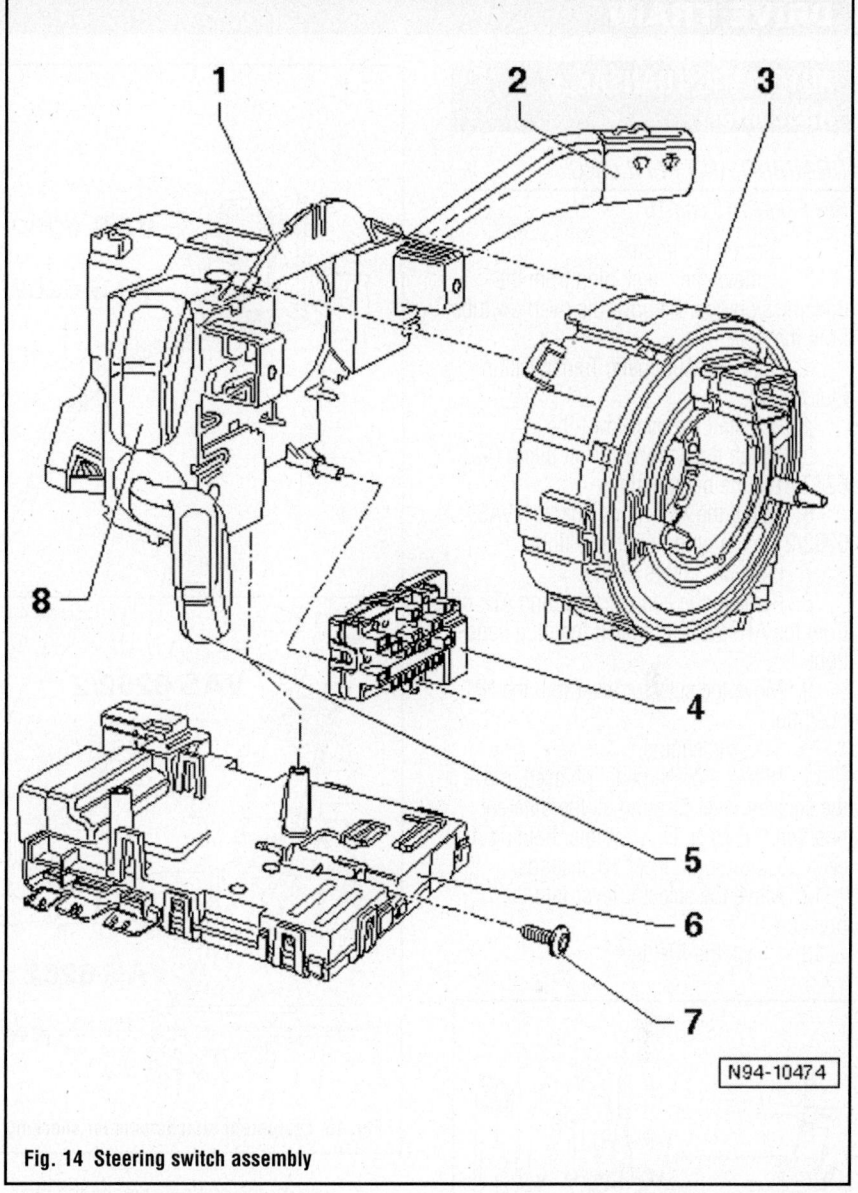

Fig. 14 Steering switch assembly

1. Disconnect battery.
2. Remove steering wheel.
3. Remove steering column trim.
4. Remove Steering Column Electronic Systems Control Module J527.
5. Remove Airbag Spiral Spring/Return Spring With Slip Ring.
6. Remove segment sensor for steering column sensor.

7. Remove both bolts on top side of Steering Column Combination Switch.
8. Pull off Steering Column Combination Switch E595 toward rear from steering column.

To install:
9. Install in reverse order of removal.
10. Tighten the threaded connections to 89 inch lbs. (10 Nm).

DRIVE TRAIN

AUTOMATIC TRANSAXLE ASSEMBLY

DRAINING AND REFILLING

See Figures 15 and 16.

1. Turn off the engine.
2. Remove the check plug from the transmission pan. Remove the overflow tube from the hole.
3. Drain the Automatic Transmission Fluid (ATF).
4. Reinstall the overflow tube.
5. Attach the adapter for oil filling (VAS 6262 A) to the oil container.
6. Install the ATF filling adapter (VAS 6262/2) to the plug hole hand-tight.
7. Fill with 3 liters of ATF.
8. Remove the adapter for filling ATF oil from the ATF pan and install the plug hand-tight.
9. Move the selector lever into the "P" position.
10. Start the engine.
11. With the brake pedal pressed, move the selector lever through all the different positions "P, R, N, D, S" at idle, holding it at each position for at least 10 seconds.
12. Move the selector lever into the "P" position.
13. Check the ATF level.

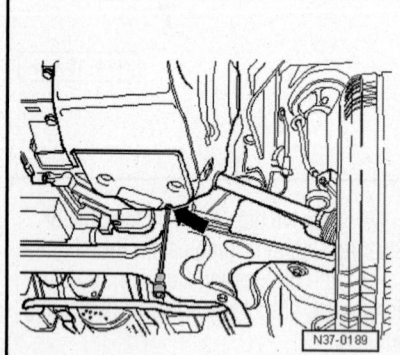

Fig. 15 Remove the check plug from the transmission pan. Remove the overflow tube (1) from the hole.

DIRECT SHIFT GEARBOX (DSG) AUTOMATIC TRANSAXLE ASSEMBLY

DRAINING AND REFILLING

See Figures 17 through 19.

1. Allow the transmission to cool down.

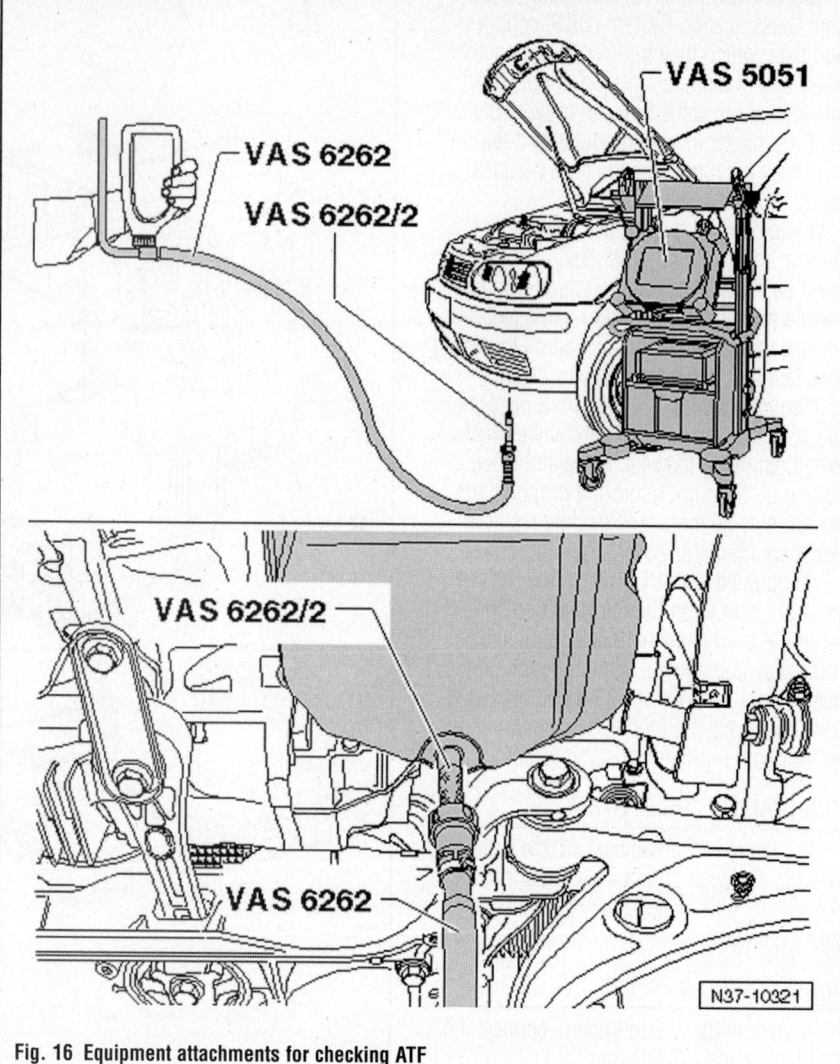

Fig. 16 Equipment attachments for checking ATF

2. Turn off the engine, remove the overflow tube and drain any oil.
3. Reinstall the overflow tube and "overfill" the oil.
4. Start the engine and drain any excess oil until the level has reached the overflow tube.
5. Turn the engine off.
6. Make sure the vehicle is level and all hoist supports are the same height.
7. The noise insulation is removed, if necessary.
8. The selector level is in the "P" position.
9. The vehicle diagnostic tester is connected.

➡️ **Only use the DSG®oil available as a replacement part. Other oils can cause malfunctions or transmission failure.**

10. Connect the vehicle diagnostic tester and identify the vehicle in "Guided Functions".
11. Select "DSG Transmission".
12. Select "Check Fluid Level".
13. Remove the oil drain and check plug.

➡️ **A black plastic overflow tube is located in the plug hole (with 8 mm hex socket head). Its length determines the oil level in the transmission.**

14. Remove the overflow tube and allow the oil to drain.

➡️ **About 5 liters of oil will drain out.**

15. Reinstall the overflow tube and tighten it to 2 ft. lbs. (3 Nm).
16. Install the quick release coupling from the adapter for oil filling (VAS 6262 A) into the plug hole hand-tight.

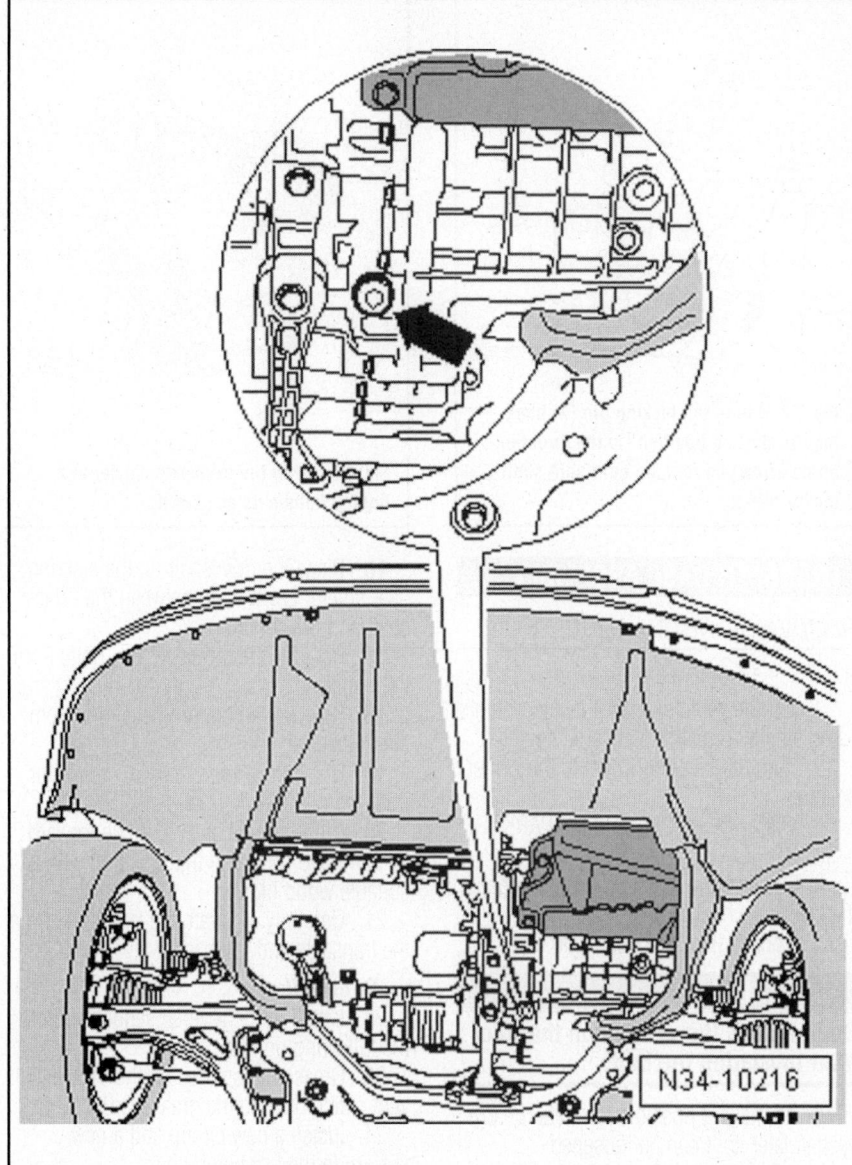

Fig. 17 Remove the oil drain and check plug.

Fig. 18 Remove the overflow tube and allow the oil to drain.

17. Shake the container before opening.

18. Connect the container to the adapter for oil filling. Connect the oil filler adapter to the quick release coupling.

19. Fill with 5.5 liters of oil.

20. To change containers, close the shut off valve or hold the adapter for oil filling higher than the transmission.

21. Install and tighten the oil drain and check plug hand-tight only.

22. Start the engine.

23. Press the brake pedal and select each selector lever position for approximately 3 seconds, then move the selector lever back into the "P" position.

24. Do not turn off the engine.

25. Check the oil level and add oil as necessary.

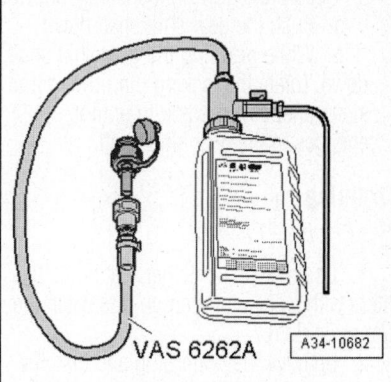

Fig. 19 Install the quick release coupling from the adapter for oil filling (VAS 6262 A) into the plug hole hand-tight.

MANUAL TRANSAXLE ASSEMBLY

DRAIN AND REFILL

Preparation

See Figure 20.

1. Turn off the ignition and disconnect the battery ground cable.

2. Remove the engine cover with air filter.

3. Remove the battery and the battery tray.

4. Remove the noise insulation.

➡**To drain the transaxle fluid, the journal for the shift forks in the transaxle must be removed.**

➡**To avoid changing the position of the shift forks, for example, by involuntarily operating the shift mechanism, the shift rod must be secured.**

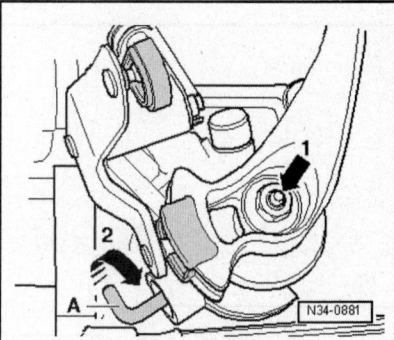

Fig. 20 Push the gear shift shaft down (in the direction of arrow 1). While pressing the gear shift shaft down, rotate the locking pin (A in the direction of arrow 2) upward and simultaneously press it in until it engages in the gear shift shaft.

5. Secure the gear shift shaft as follows:
   a. Push the gear shift shaft down.
   b. While pressing the gear shift shaft down, rotate the locking pin upward and simultaneously press it in until it engages in the gear shift shaft.

Draining

See Figures 21 and 22.

1. Use a clean container that holds 3 liters with a scale printed on it to catch the transaxle fluid.
2. Remove the drain plug and then the support pin and drain the transaxle fluid.
3. Install the support pin with a new O-ring. Tighten the support pin bolt.
4. Install the drain plug and tighten it to 26 ft. lbs. (35 Nm).
5. Rotate the locking pin back into its starting position so that the gear shift shaft moves freely.

Filling

1. Add 1.7 liters of fluid to the amount of transaxle fluid in the container.
2. Disconnect the backup lamp switch connector and remove the switch.
3. Insert a hose (approximately 600 mm long, outside diameter 10 mm) with a commercially available funnel into the hole backup lamp switch hole and fill the transaxle fluid.
4. Install the backup lamp switch and connect the connector.
5. Make sure the shift mechanism works correctly.
6. Install the battery tray and the battery.
7. Install the engine cover with air filter.
8. Connect the battery and follow the procedure regarding what to do after connecting the battery.
9. Install the noise insulation.

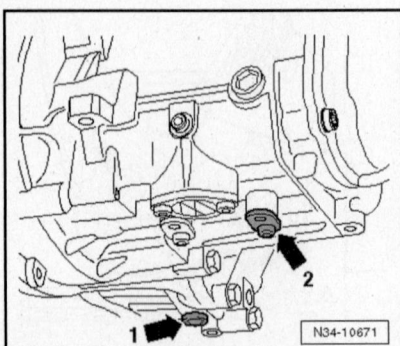

Fig. 21 Remove the drain plug (arrow 1) and then the support pin (arrow 2) and drain the transaxle fluid. Install the support pin with a new O-ring. Tighten the support pin bolt.

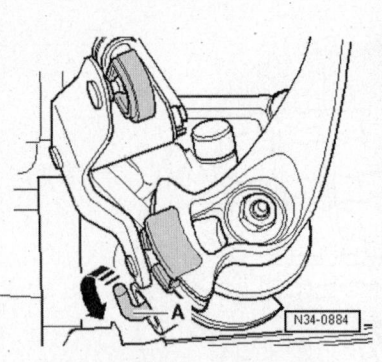

Fig. 22 Rotate the locking pin (A) back into its starting position (in the direction of the arrow) so that the gear shift shaft moves freely.

TRANSFER CASE ASSEMBLY

REMOVAL & INSTALLATION
See Figures 23 and 24.

1. Lift the vehicle, at all 4 take)up points using the lifting platform at same height.
2. Turn the steering wheel to the center position.
3. Place the shift lever in the PARK (P) position.
4. Remove the ignition key and engage the steering wheel lock.
5. Loosen the right drive axle bolt.

✸✸ CAUTION

Do not place the vehicle on the floor after loosening the bolt.

6. To make it possible to rotate the driveshaft later so it can be loosened:
   a. Place the shift lever in the NEUTRAL (N) position.
   b. Remove the ignition key and engage the steering wheel lock.
7. Remove the engine cover.
8. Remove the noise insulation below the engine/transaxle.
9. Remove the right drive axle.
10. Remove the pendulum support.
11. Remove the right drive axle heat shield bolts and shield from the bevel box.
12. Remove the transaxle carrier studs/bolts and carrier.
13. Mark the position of the driveshaft flexible disc to the bevel box output flange.
14. Remove the driveshaft bolts from the bevel box output flange.
15. Counterhold the rear final drive to loosen and tighten the driveshaft.

➡**To loosen the next bolt, rotate the driveshaft by turning the rear wheels.**

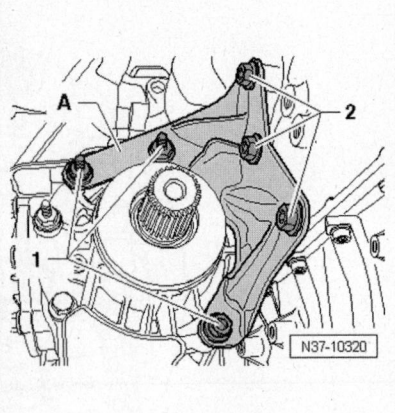

Fig. 23 Install the transaxle carrier and tighten bolts/nuts as shown

16. Place the driveshaft on the steering gear shield. Lay a cloth between the driveshaft and the shield.
17. Remove the top bevel box bolts from the transaxle.
18. Remove the bottom bevel box from the transaxle.
19. Disconnect the electrical connector from the oil level thermal sensor.
20. Press engine and transaxle forward by hand and secure in this position with a suitable wood block.
21. Carefully separate the bevel box from the transaxle and remove it.

To install:

22. Install in the reverse sequence; note the following points:
23. Grease the splines on the differential with clutch disc spline grease G 000 100.
24. Install a new circlip and a new O-ring on the right stub shaft.
25. Insert the bevel box and press it against the transaxle until it seats.
26. If the tooth position is incorrect (the bevel box cannot be pressed against the transaxle), rotate at the stub shaft.
27. If the tooth position is correct and it is centered, the bevel box slides against the transaxle until it seats.

➡**Do not pull the bevel box forcefully against the transaxle by tightening the bolts. The transaxle or bevel box could be damaged.**

28. Install and tighten by hand the new bevel box bolts, then tighten the bolts to 30 ft. lbs. (40 Nm), plus an additional 90° rotation.
29. Install the transaxle carrier and tighten bolts/nuts.
30. Check the gear oil in the bevel box, as necessary.

31. Install the right drive axle shield and bolts.

32. Position the driveshaft onto the bevel box by pressing the engine/transaxle forward as far as necessary.

> ✳✳ **CAUTION**
>
> **The seal in the driveshaft flange must not be damaged when removing and installing the transaxle. Replace the driveshaft if damaged.**

33. Press the engine and transaxle forward and remove the wood block.

34. Install the driveshaft onto the bevel box and install the bolts.

35. Tighten the pendulum support with new bolt.

36. Grease the stub shaft splines with grease G 000 100.

37. Install the right drive axle.

38. Install noise insulation.

FRONT DRIVESHAFT

REMOVAL & INSTALLATION

See Figures 24 and 25.

> ✳✳ **CAUTION**
>
> **Do not allow driveshaft to hang down when removing, always support. Always remove or install driveshaft horizontally on drive flange. Do not kink driveshaft, only store and move when fully extended.**

1. Before removing, mark the positions of all parts in relation to each other. Reinstall in the same position otherwise imbalance will be excessive; the bearings could be damaged causing rumbling noises.

2. Remove noise insulation.

3. Remove pendulum support bolts.

4. Press engine and transaxle forward and secure position with a suitable wood block.

5. Support the front part of the exhaust system using the engine and transaxle holder V.A.G 1383 A.

6. Disconnect the exhaust system at the clamping sleeve when removing the rear exhaust system components.

7. Remove the tunnel brace.

8. Loosen the bolts for the center bearing two turns.

9. Loosen the driveshaft front and rear bolts, but do not remove them.

10. Counterhold the rear final drive to loosen and tighten the driveshaft bolts. So that noises due to imbalance do not occur later:

11. If there are no markings present,

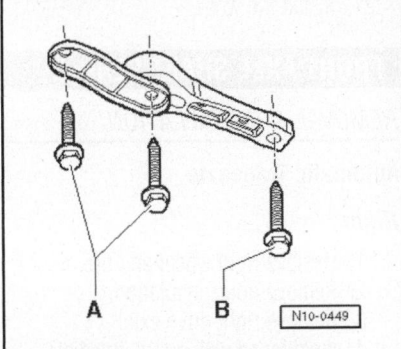

Fig. 24 Tighten the pendulum support with new bolts as shown

then mark the position of the driveshaft flexible disc to the rear final drive flange.

12. Also mark the position of the driveshaft flexible disc to the bevel box output flange.

13. Remove the driveshaft from the rear final drive and lower it onto the engine and transaxle holder V.A.G 1383 A.

14. When removing and installing the driveshaft, be careful not to damage the bushing.

> ➡ **Two technicians are needed to remove the driveshaft.**

15. Remove the driveshaft from the bevel box.

> ➡ **To prevent damaging the protective boot in the center bearing, remove and install the driveshaft in its fully extended position; likewise, store it in this position.**

16. Remove the center bearing and if possible, remove it to the rear in its fully extended length.

To install:

17. Install in reverse sequence; note the following points:

18. Install all parts marked to each other in original positions.

19. Tighten the driveshaft bolts.

20. Install the pendulum support with new bolts.

21. Install exhaust system.

22. Install noise insulation.

23. Install the tunnel brace.

FRONT HALFSHAFT

REMOVAL & INSTALLATION

1. Loosen the drive axle to wheel hub bolt.

2. Remove the wheel.

3. Remove the lower noise insulation.

4. Remove the ball joint nuts.

5. Remove the wheel bearing housing with ball joint from the control arm.

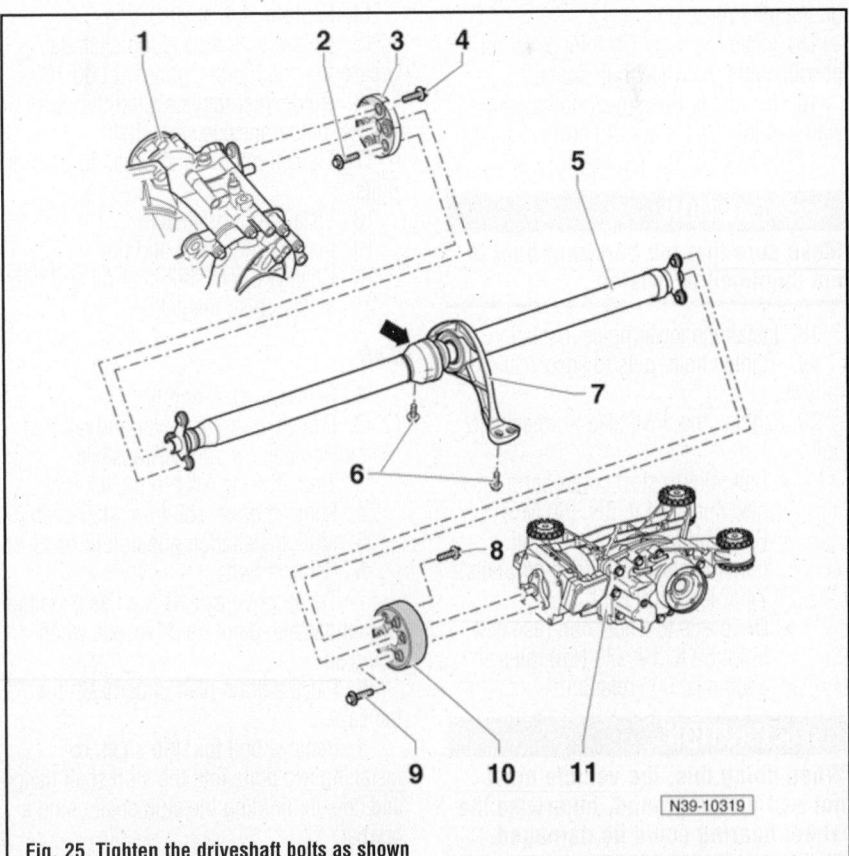

Fig. 25 Tighten the driveshaft bolts as shown

6. Remove the drive axle from the wheel hub and secure to body.

7. Install the T10161 between the transaxle housing and the inner Constant Velocity (CV) joint.

8. Pry the inner CV joint out of the transaxle by tapping the T10161 with a hammer.

9. Remove the drive axle.

To install:

10. Install a new circlip into the groove on the joint piece stub.

11. Align the outer splines of the joint piece with the inner splines of the transaxle.

12. Grasp the drive axle by hand and slide the joint piece in to the transaxle until seated.

13. Slide the joint piece into the transaxle with a jerking motion.

✳✳ CAUTION

Sliding part of the joint piece can be used for this jerking motion. Do not pull the drive axle out of the joint piece too far when doing this. Do not use a hammer or other tool under any circumstances!

14. Check the drive axle in the transaxle for proper seating by pulling the joint piece against the resistance of the circlip. For this check, do NOT pull the drive axle but pull on the joint piece only.

15. Insert the outer CV joint as far as possible into the wheel hub splines.

16. Install the wheel bearing housing with ball joint to the control arm.

17. Install the ball joint nuts.

✳✳ CAUTION

Make sure that the ball joint boot is not damaged or twisted.

18. Install the lower noise insulation.

19. Tighten bolts/nuts to specification as follows:

20. Tighten the drive axle to wheel hub bolt.

- Ball joint to steel control arm (use new nuts): 44 ft. lbs. (60 Nm)
- Ball joint to sheet steel or aluminum control arm (use new nuts): 74 ft. lbs. (100 Nm)
- Drive axle to wheel hub (use new bolt): 52 ft. lbs. (70 Nm), plus an additional 90° rotation

✳✳ CAUTION

When doing this, the vehicle must not rest on the ground, otherwise the wheel bearing could be damaged.

21. Install the wheel.

FRONT AXLE SHAFT SEAL

REMOVAL & INSTALLATION

Automatic Transaxle

Right

1. Remove right wheel and tire.
2. Remove noise insulation.
3. Remove right drive axle.
4. If equipped with an intermediate shaft, after removing right drive axle, remove intermediate shaft from bracket and pull off from transaxle stub shaft.
5. Place drain pan underneath transaxle.
6. Remove bolt for stub shaft.
7. Pull out stub shaft together with compression spring.
8. Pry out seal with a lever.

To install:

9. Lightly oil new seal on outer circumference.
10. Fill area between sealing lip and dust lip halfway with sealing grease G 052 128.
11. Drive new seal in until seated; be sure not to distort seal.
12. Insert stub shaft.
13. Install new bolt for securing stub shaft and tighten to 22 ft. lbs. (30 Nm).
14. Replace stub shaft O-ring.
15. Grease splines on stub shaft using grease for clutch disc splines G 000 100.
16. Guide intermediate shaft through bracket onto transaxle stub shaft.
17. Tighten intermediate shaft to bracket bolts.
18. Install right drive axle.
19. Install right wheel and tire.
20. Change direct shift gear oil and filter.
21. Install noise insulation.

Left

1. Remove wheel and tire.
2. If fitted, remove center and left part of insulation below engine/transaxle.
3. Turn steering fully to the left lock.
4. Remove drive axle from stub shaft.
5. Mark installation position of bolts.
6. Remove bolts.
7. Tie up drive axle as high as possible. Do not damage paint on drive axle when doing so.
8. Place a drain plan underneath the transaxle.
9. Remove bolt for stub shaft, by installing two bolts into the stub shaft flange and counter holding the stub shaft using a pry bar.
10. Pull out the stub shaft with spring.

11. Remove stub shaft seal with slide hammer VW771 and pulling hook VW 771/37.

To install:

12. Fill area between sealing lip and dust lip halfway with sealing grease G 052 128.
13. Drive new seal in until seated; be sure not to distort seal.
14. Insert the stub shaft.
15. Fasten stub shaft with countersunk bolt and tighten to 15 ft. lbs. (30 Nm).
16. Fasten ball joint and control arm to marks made during removal with new bolts.
17. Fasten left drive axle to stub shaft.
18. Install left front wheel housing liner.
19. Install left wheel and tire.
20. Check transaxle oil level.
21. Install underbody noise insulation.

Manual Transaxle

Right

1. Remove right wheel.
2. Install noise insulation tray below engine/transaxle, if equipped.
3. Remove drive axle heat shield, if equipped.
4. Remove right drive axle.
5. Place drip tray V.A.G 1306 underneath transaxle.
6. Remove right flange shaft mounting bolt with socket and key T10107 and installing 2 bolts in flange and counter hold flange shaft with pry bar.
7. Screw extractor T10037 onto right flanged shaft.
8. To remove right flange shaft, use puller T10037 to avoid damaging polygon bearing on flange shaft.
9. Place a spacer between transaxle carrier and knurled nut T10037/1.
10. Align puller parallel to flange with lower support.
11. Pull out right flange shaft.
12. Now assemble assembly tool T10047 as follows:
   a. Arrange both parts of the tool so that the marks "B" face each other.
   b. The sections must then be located under the bearing.
   c. Now install both halves together until they stop.
13. Pry out needle bearing circlip.
14. So that the bearing contact surface on shaft is not damaged, shaft must be rotated during the pressing procedure.
15. Remove seal from groove.

To install:

16. Coat seal with gear oil
17. Insert seal in flange shaft groove. Make sure seal is not tilted.

18. Assemble tensioning device, T10047.

19. So that the bearing contact surface on shaft is not damaged, shaft must be rotated during pressing procedure.

20. Secure needle bearing with a new circlip.

21. Carefully drive flanged shaft, turning while doing so.

22. Secure flange shaft with the countersunk bolt and tighten.

23. Install right drive axle.

24. Attach drive axle shield to bevel box

25. Install noise insulation, if equipped.

Left

1. Remove the noise insulation.

2. Set the drip tray for workshop crane VAS 6208 underneath.

3. Mark the position of the nuts securing lower control arm to the strut.

➡**Reestablish the position when reassembling.**

4. Separate the lower control arm from strut.

5. Press the drive axle off of the transaxle.

6. Remove the drive axle.

7. Secure the right drive axle as high as possible on the strut.

8. Seal the opening of drive axle at the transaxle using a clean cloth.

9. Grease the drill bit so that drill shavings remain held.

✳✳ CAUTION

Drill only through the metal ring, otherwise the transaxle may be damaged.

10. Carefully drill a hole 0.078–0.117 in. (2–4 mm in diameter) in the outer metal ring of the oil seal.

11. Install a small metal bolt of approximately 0.117 in. (4 mm) in diameter into the drilled hole of the oil seal.

✳✳ CAUTION

Do not install the bolt too deep in order to avoid damage to the bearing lying behind it.

12. Remove the seal using puller T10055 and adapter T10055/2.

13. Remove the cloth and clean this area.

✳✳ CAUTION

There must be no metal shavings in the transaxle of in the flange shaft, vacuum up any as necessary.

➡**If only the metal ring of the sealing ring could be pulled out, carefully pry out the remainder of the sealing ring using a screwdriver.**

To install:

14. Installation is performed in the reverse order of removal.

15. Lubricate the outer circumference and sealing lips of the seal with ATF.

➡**The open side of the sealing ring faces the transaxle.**

16. Press in the seal by hand evenly and as far as possible.

17. Drive in the seal until it seats using thrust piece T10105/6, do not tilt the thrust piece while doing this.

18. Install the drive axle.

19. Check the ATF level and top off, as necessary.

20. Install the noise insulation.

REAR AXLE SHAFT SEAL

REMOVAL & INSTALLATION

➡**Do not remove the rear final drive for this. This procedure applies to both sides.**

1. Remove the drive axle.

2. Place the drip tray under rear final drive.

3. Install the plate from the puller (T10037) on the flange and tighten the two M8 x 30 bolts 1 by hand.

➡**The sections for the larger flange diameter face outward.**

4. Tighten one turn each in an alternating sequence until the flange contacts the plate and then stop tightening.

➡**Wear gloves to get a good grip on the flange.**

5. Drive the flange out of the final drive by tapping lightly on the plate.

✳✳ CAUTION

Only use a plastic mallet so the final drive and tool are not damaged.

6. Pry out the flange shaft seal with the extractor lever VW 681.

To install:

7. Lightly lubricate the outer diameter of the new seal and drive in, without tilting until seated using the thrust piece T10049.

8. Fill the area between sealing lip and dust lip halfway with sealing grease (G 052 128 A1).

9. Clamp the flange shaft using jaw protectors in a vise.

10. Press the previous circlip out of flange shaft groove with the new circlip.

11. Drive in the flange shaft with a plastic hammer and a drift.

12. Install the drive axle.

13. Check the oil level in the rear final drive.

REAR HALFSHAFT

REMOVAL & INSTALLATION

1. Loosen the drive axle bolt.

2. Remove the wheel.

3. Remove the coil spring.

4. Remove the bolts for the lower transverse link and the tie rod from the wheel bearing housing.

5. Remove the shock absorber to wheel bearing housing bolt.

6. Loosen the drive axle to transaxle flange bolts.

7. Swing the wheel bearing housing upward and remove drive axle from the inner splines.

8. Remove drive axle.

To install:

9. Installation is the reverse of removal, with special attention to the following:

10. Place the drive axle inner Constant Velocity (CV) joint in position.

- Drive axle inner Constant Velocity (CV) joint: 30 ft. lbs. (40 Nm)
- Drive axle to wheel hub (use new bolt): 52 ft. lbs. (70 Nm), plus an additional 90° rotation
- Drive axle to rear final drive flange (use new bolt): 30 ft. lbs. (40 Nm)

REAR PINION SEAL

REMOVAL & INSTALLATION

1. Disconnect the exhaust system at the clamping sleeve when removing the rear exhaust system components.

✳✳ CAUTION

The flex joint of the exhaust system must not be bent more than 10 degrees, otherwise it may be damaged.

2. Remove the rear flexible disc.

3. Secure the vehicle on the hoist with the tensioning straps (T10038).

✳✳ CAUTION

If the vehicle is not secured, there is the risk that it could slip from the hoist.

4. Remove the rear final drive flange nut.

5. Remove the rear final drive flange. Use a slide hammer (Kukko 12/1) if it is difficult.

6. Remove rear final drive flange seal using the extractor lever (VW 681).

To install:

7. Before installing, lightly coat new seal on outside circumference and between sealing lips with high performance Haldex clutch oil.

8. Drive in new seal to until seated using thrust piece (T10019). Do not tilt seal when doing this.

9. Drive in rear final drive flange with sleeve (30 20).

10. Insert new nut with locking fluid (D 000 600) and tighten rear final drive flange nut 155 ft. lbs. (210 Nm).

11. Install the rear flexible disc.

12. Install the exhaust system and align it without tension.

13. Check the oil level in the Haldex clutch.

ENGINE COOLING

ENGINE COOLANT

DRAIN & REFILL PROCEDURE

1. Open the coolant expansion tank cap.

2. Remove the noise insulation.

3. Remove the coolant hose from the charge air cooling pump.

4. Release the clamp and remove coolant hose from the quick release coupling on the radiator for the air charge coolant circuit.

5. Release the coolant hose clamp and remove the coolant hose from the quick release couplings for the radiator.

6. In addition, to draining the coolant from the engine, remove the coolant hose from the engine oil cooler.

7. If equipped with an engine preheating element, loosen the spring clamps. Disconnect the coolant hoses from the engine preheating element. Allow any remaining coolant to drain.

➡ Coolant Notes:

- The water portion of the coolant influences the effectiveness of the coolant. Volkswagen has decided to define the water quality used in the cooling system based on the different mixtures and country and regional requirements. For this reason, we recommend using distilled water for older models when adding coolant or filling coolant for the first time. On newer models (from MY 2010), distilled water is required. Do not mix distilled water with coolant additives. Using distilled water provides optimum corrosion protection.

- Because of its high boiling point, the coolant improves engine reliability under heavy loads, particularly in countries with tropical climates.

- Protection against frost must be assured down to approximately (13° F (25° C); in arctic climatic counties down to approximately 31° F (35° C).

- The coolant concentration must not be reduced by adding water even in warmer seasons and in warmer countries. The coolant additive portion must be at least 40%.

- If a lower freeze protection is necessary due to the climatic conditions, increase the amount of coolant additives.

- Increase the ratio only up to 60%; freeze protection down to approximately 40° F (40° C). Otherwise the freeze protection and cooling effect are reduced.

- Do not use the old coolant again if replacing the radiator, heater core, cylinder head or cylinder head gasket.

- The refractometer (T10007) is recommended for determining freeze protection density.

8. Install the lower coolant hose and secure it with the retaining clamp.

9. Install the coolant hose to the radiator for the air charge coolant circuit and secure it with the clamp.

10. Connect the coolant hoses to the engine oil cooler and the charge air cooling pump.

11. Install the noise insulation.

Filling Using the Cooling System Charge Unit (VAS 6096)

1. Install the adapter (V.A.G 1274/8) onto the coolant expansion tank.

2. Fill the coolant circuit using the cooling system charge unit. Refer to the operating instructions.

Filling Without Using the Cooling System Charge Unit

1. Slowly add coolant until it reaches the upper mark on the expansion tank.

2. Install the expansion tank cap.

3. Start the engine and maintain an engine speed of approximately 2000 RPM for approximately 3 minutes.

4. Let the engine run at idle until the coolant fan turns on.

5. Check the coolant level and fill if necessary. With the engine at operating temperature, the coolant level must be at the top mark, with the engine cold, it must be in the center of hatched area.

ENGINE FAN

REMOVAL & INSTALLATION

2.0L & 3.6L Engines

See Figure 26.

1. Remove the cover for the air guide; disengage the side clips to do so.

2. Unclip the lower air guide, disengage the clips to do so.

3. Remove the lower air guide together with the air guide hose.

4. Remove the bolts from the top.

5. Remove noise insulation see: noise insulation.

6. Disconnect electrical connector.

7. Remove the bolts and remove the fan shroud downward.

8. Disconnect electrical connector.

9. Free up electrical wires.

10. Remove nuts and remove coolant fan.

To install:

11. Installation is performed in reverse order of removal.

12. Tightening radiator fan shroud to 44 inch lbs. (5 Nm).

2.0L TDI Engine

1. Remove the engine cover.

2. Remove the noise insulation.

3. Remove the cover for the air guide; disengage the side clips.

4. Release the left and right spring clips and disconnect the lower air guide.

5. Move the lower air guide slightly to the rear and disengage the lower air guide.

6. Disengage the air guide pipe from the lower air guide.

7. Remove the bolts from the lock carrier and remove the air guide.

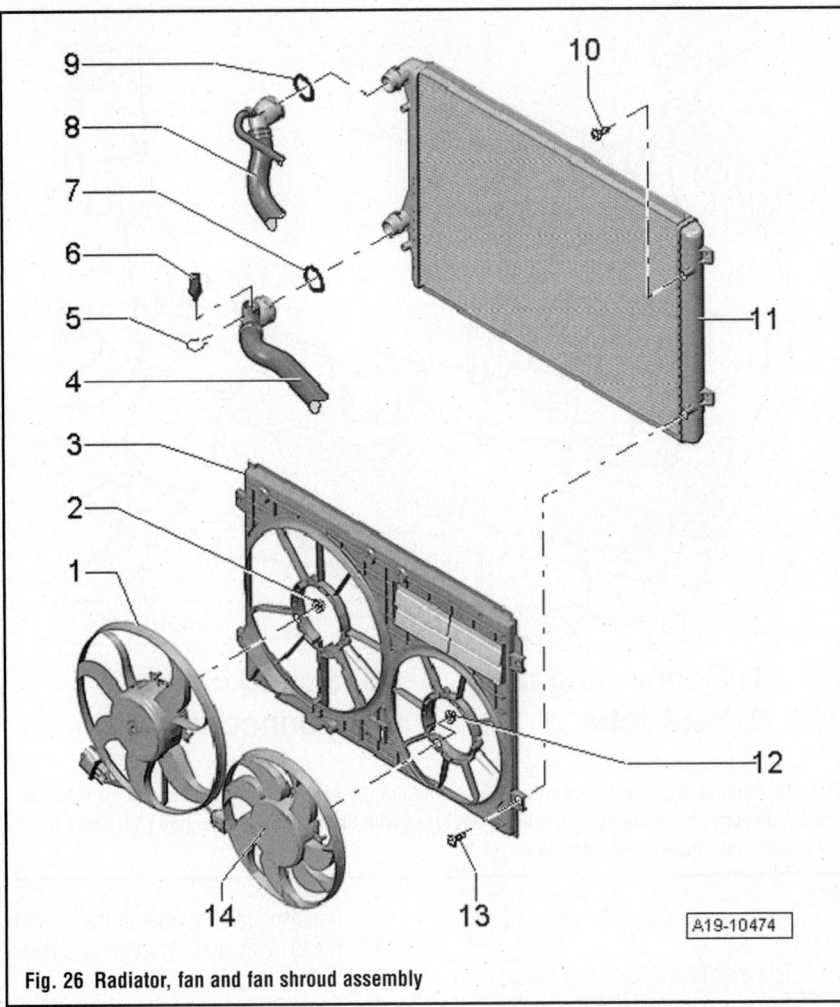

Fig. 26 Radiator, fan and fan shroud assembly

8. Remove the air filter housing with the Mass Airflow (MAF) sensor and connecting pipe. Release and disconnect the connector.

9. Remove the bolts and remove the fan shroud with the fans upward.

10. Free up the wire, then remove the nuts and the fan.

To install:

11. Install in reverse order of removal.

2.5L Engine

1. Remove the noise insulation.

2. Remove lower coolant hose from the clip on the fan shroud.

3. Disconnect the connector from the engine coolant temperature sensor on radiator outlet.

4. Disconnect the electrical connector and remove the fan shroud bolts.

5. Move the fan shroud downward on the left side.

6. Disconnect the electrical connector and lay the wire free.

7. Remove the fan nuts and remove the fans, if necessary.

To install:

8. Install in the reverse order of removal.

RADIATOR

REMOVAL & INSTALLATION

2.0L Engine

See Figure 26

1. Drain coolant.

2. Remove fan shroud.

3. Remove the upper coolant hose from the radiator.

4. Detach the air duct at the lock carrier and remove the air duct.

5. Remove the bolts and remove the radiator upward.

To install:

6. Installation is performed in reverse order.

7. Tightening radiator fasteners to 89 inch lbs. (10 Nm)

✴✴ CAUTION

When installing a new radiator, old coolant must not be reused.

8. Fill with coolant.

2.0L TDI Engine

Standard Coolant Radiator

1. Remove the noise insulation.

2. Drain the coolant.

3. Remove the fan shroud with the fans.

4. Remove the upper radiator coolant hose.

5. Remove the coolant hose from the right quick release couplings for the radiator.

6. Remove the radiator bolts and remove the radiator upward.

To install:

7. Install in reverse order of removal.

8. Fill the coolant.

Charge Air Cooler Radiator

See Figures 27 through 29.

1. Remove the noise insulation.

2. Drain the coolant.

3. Remove the fan shroud with the fans.

4. Remove the coolant radiator.

5. Remove the front bumper cover.

6. Drain the coolant from the charge air system by disconnecting the coolant hose from the lower connection point for the coolant auxiliary cooler.

7. Remove the hose.

8. Remove the bolts from the lock carrier.

9. Remove the Air Conditioning (A/C) condenser bolts.

10. Secure the A/C condenser to the lock carrier so A/C lines are not disconnected or stretched.

➡**Ensure that the coolant lines and hoses are not stretched, kinked or bent.**

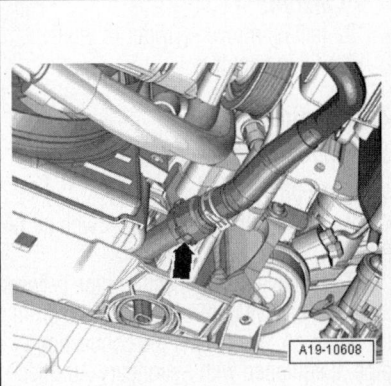

Fig. 27 Drain the coolant from the charge air system by disconnecting the coolant hose from the lower connection point for the coolant auxiliary cooler.

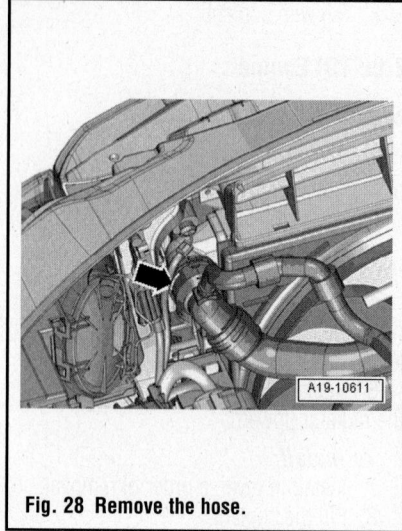

Fig. 28 Remove the hose.

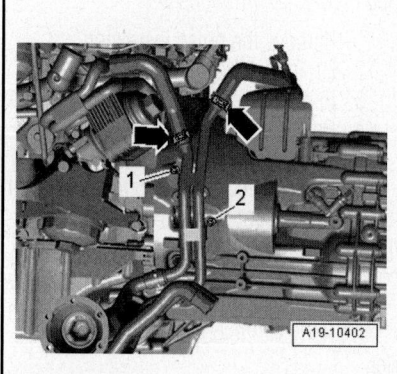

Fig. 29 Remove the bolts from the lock carrier.

11. Remove the radiator for the charged air coolant circuit from the bracket.

12. Remove the radiator for the charged air coolant circuit downward.

To install:

13. Install in reverse order of removal.

14. Fill the coolant.

2.5L Engine

See Figures 30 through 32.

1. Drain the coolant.

2. Remove the engine cover with air filter.

3. Remove the connecting pipe between the throttle valve control module and air filter. To do so, disconnect the connecting pipe, if equipped with Secondary Air Injection (AIR), and the vent tube and reposition the spring clamp.

4. Remove the air duct bolts and duct from the lock carrier.

5. Remove the fan shroud with fans.

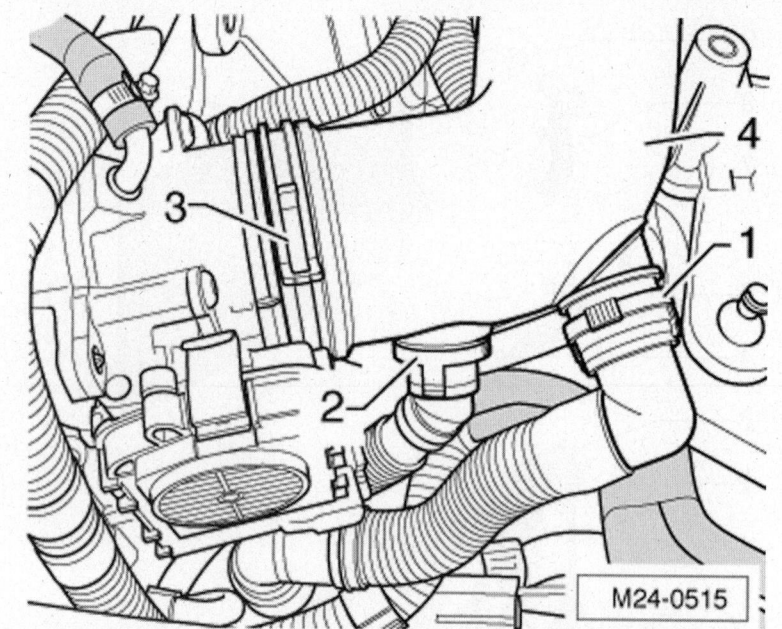

1. Connecting pipe   **3. Spring clamp**

2. Vent tube   **4. Connecting pipe**

Fig. 30 Remove the connecting pipe between the throttle valve control module and air filter. To do so, disconnect the connecting pipe, if equipped with Secondary Air Injection (AIR), and the vent tube and reposition the spring clamp.

6. Remove the coolant hoses from the radiator.

7. Remove the front bumper cover.

8. Remove the bolts and the center guide.

⁕⁕ CAUTION

To prevent damage to the Air Conditioning (A/C) condenser and the refrigerant lines, do not stretch, kink or bend the lines and hoses.

9. Remove the air guides at the bottom.

10. Remove the bolts from the A/C condenser.

11. Remove the bolts from the radiator mounts.

12. Push the radiator to the rear and remove the radiator mounts.

13. Remove the radiator from its mounts in the lock carrier.

To install:

14. Install in reverse order of removal.

15. Fill the coolant.

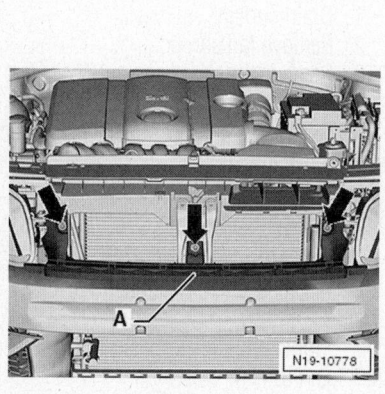

Fig. 31 Remove the bolts (arrows) and the center guide (A).

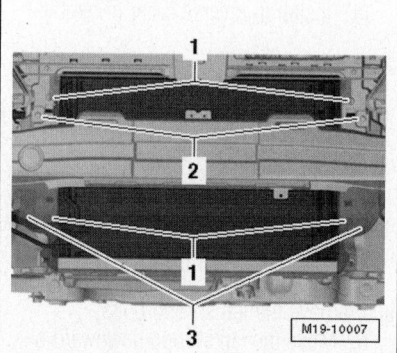

Fig. 32 Remove the air guides (3) at the bottom. Remove the bolts (1) from the A/C condenser. Remove the bolts (2) from the radiator mounts.

3.6L Engine

1. Remove noise insulation.
2. Drain coolant.
3. Disconnect all coolant hoses from radiator.
4. Remove intake air guide air filter.
5. Remove front bumper.
6. Remove radiator fan mount with fans.
7. Remove bolts from radiator bearing.
8. Move cooler and condenser toward the rear and out of the lower mount. While doing this, pull the lock carrier on the left mount slightly downward.
9. Push cooler and condenser to the left so that the right bolts are accessible. Remove bolts.
10. Push cooler and condenser to the right so that the left bolts are accessible. Remove bolts.
11. Remove radiator downward.

To install:

12. Install radiator and connect it to the condenser.
13. Install radiator and condenser into the lower mounts.
14. Move radiator and condenser forward and attach the radiator mount.
15. Further installation is performed in reverse order of removal.
16. Tighten bolts/nuts to specification as follows:
- Radiator mounting to lock carrier: 44 inch lbs. (5 Nm)
- Condenser to radiator: 44 inch lbs. (5 Nm)
- Fan mount to radiator: 44 inch lbs. (5 Nm)

✳✳ CAUTION

When installing a new radiator, old coolant must not be reused.

17. Fill with coolant.

THERMOSTAT

REMOVAL & INSTALLATION

2.0L Engine

See Figure 33.

1. Drain coolant.
2. Remove the cover for the air guide; disengage the side clips to do so.
3. Unclip the lower air guide, disengage the clips to do so.
4. Remove the lower air guide together with the air guide hose.
5. Loosen the hose clamp.
6. Remove bolt.
7. Disconnect electrical connector.

8. Remove the bolt and remove the air guide pipe downward.
9. Lay aside the coolant hose and electrical wiring harness.
10. Remove the bolt and remove bracket.
11. Remove the bolt on the bracket for the After-Run Coolant Pump.

➡ **The After-Run Coolant Pump stays in the installation position.**

12. Remove the coolant hoses and lay them aside.
13. Loosen the nut, remove the bolt and move the support for the intake manifold to the right.
14. Remove the oil separator
15. Remove bolts and remove connecting pieces. For the right bolt, the Multi-Point Socket (T10058) is useful.
16. Remove the coolant thermostat.

To install:

17. Replace seals and O-rings.
18. Clean O-ring sealing surface.
19. Coat the O-ring with coolant.
20. Install the thermostat into the housing for the coolant pump and move it slightly forward.
21. Tighten the bolts to 80 inch lbs. (9 Nm).
22. Carefully mount the connector; while doing so, insert the centering pin into the guide.

2.0L TDI Engine

See Figures 34 through 39.

➡ **The thermostat is located inside the 4/2-way valve. This procedure removes both components.**

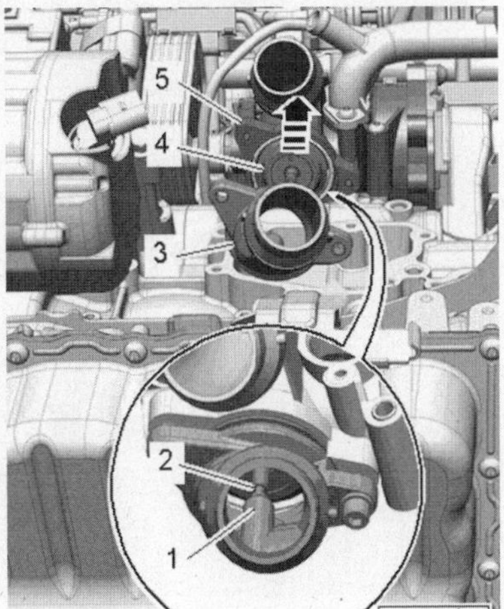

1. Remove the engine cover.
2. Drain the coolant.
3. Remove the generator.
4. Remove the charge air cooler.
5. Remove the nut for the coolant pipe.
6. Loosen the bolts and remove the support.
7. Remove the two bolts and remove the oil dipstick tube out of the cylinder block and move it to the side.
8. Remove the air filter housing with the mass air flow sensor and connecting pipe.
9. Remove the battery and tray.
10. Press the release buttons and remove the crankshaft housing ventilation hose from the cylinder head cover.
11. Disconnect the connector and remove it from the crankcase ventilation hose.

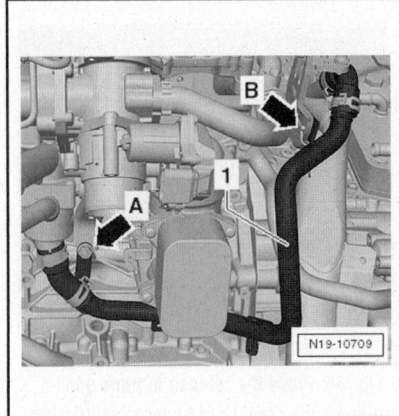

Fig. 34 Remove the nut (A) for the coolant pipe (1).

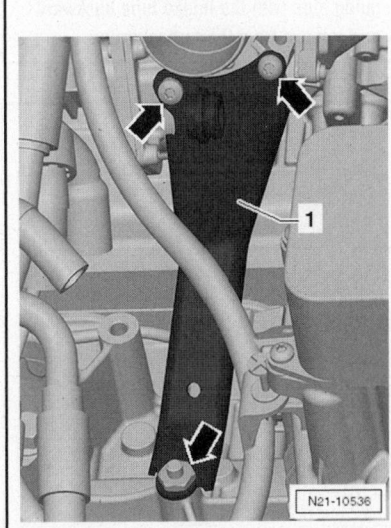

Fig. 35 Loosen the bolts and remove the support (1).

Fig. 33 Thermostat assembly—2.0L engine

12. Free up the vacuum hoses from the air guide pipe.

13. Remove the bolt and tilt the air guide pipe with the intake tube backward and remove from the turbocharger.

14. Remove the bolt and unclip the pre-heating pipe and remove it from the bracket.

15. If equipped with DSG transaxle, remove the coolant hoses from the transmission fluid cooler.

16. Remove the bolt and free up the electrical wires and the hoses on the left air guide pipe. Remove the air guide pipe.

17. Disconnect the coolant hoses from the 4/2-way valve.

18. Disconnect the connector for the camshaft position sensor from out of the mount.

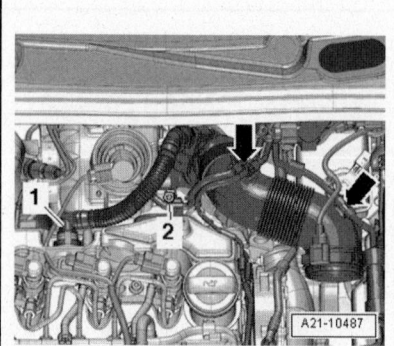

Fig. 36 Press the release buttons and remove the crankshaft housing ventilation hose (1) from the cylinder head cover. Disconnect the connector and remove it from the crankcase ventilation hose. Free up the vacuum hoses from the air guide pipe. Remove the bolt (2) and tilt the air guide pipe with the intake tube backward and remove from the turbocharger.

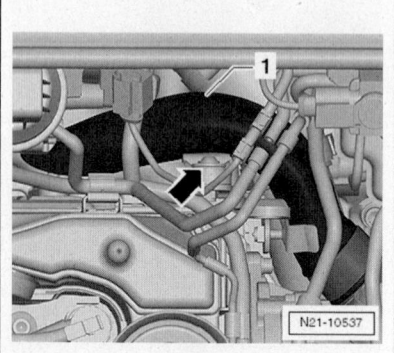

Fig. 37 Remove the bolt and unclip the preheating pipe (1) and remove it from the bracket.

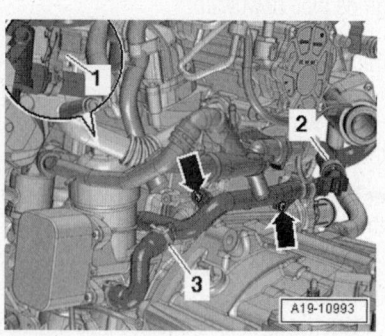

Fig. 38 Disconnect the connector (1) for the camshaft position sensor from out of the mount.

19. Remove the bolts and pull the coolant pipe with the wire bracket out of the connection for the 4/2-way valve.

20. Push the coolant pipe aside, do not remove it.

21. Disconnect the coolant hoses from the connection.

22. Disengage and disconnect the connector.

23. Remove the 4/2-way valve bolts.

Remove the 4/2-way valve from the cylinder block.

To install:

24. Install in reverse order of removal. When doing this, note the following:

    a. Replace the O-ring.

    b. Do not tilt the housing cover for the 4/2-way valve when positioning it and push it downward against the spring force.

25. Fill the coolant.

2.5L Engine

1. Drain the coolant.

2. Remove the engine cover with air filter.

3. Remove the connecting pipe between the throttle valve control module and air filter. To do so, disconnect the connecting pipe for the Secondary Air Injection (AIR), if equipped, and the vent tube and reposition the spring clamp.

4. Remove the intake manifold. See "ENGINE MECHANICAL" section.

5. Insert the guide tube for the oil dipstick into the cylinder block again and secure it tightly so that no leaking coolant can run into the engine.

6. Place a suitable container under the coolant thermostat housing to catch coolant leaking out.

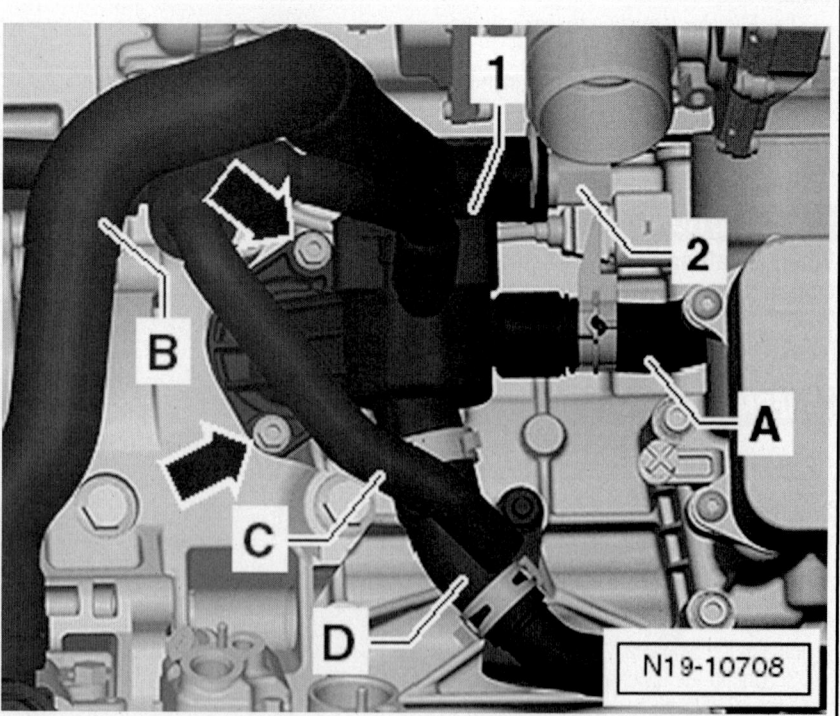

Fig. 39 Push the coolant pipe (A) aside, do not remove it. Disconnect the coolant hoses (B through D) from the connection. Disengage and disconnect the connector (2). Remove the 4/2-way valve bolts. Remove the 4/2-way valve (1) from the cylinder block.

7. Remove the bolts, the cover and remove the thermostat.

To install:

8. Install in the reverse order of removal. Note the following:

   a. Replace the seal and O-ring.

   b. Note the installed position of the thermostat. The valve must point upward.

9. Fill the coolant.

3.6L Engine

See Figure 40.

1. Remove noise insulation.
2. Drain coolant
3. Move connector A to the side.
4. Remove coolant hoses from the oil cooler and move them to the side.
5. Remove bolts and then remove the coolant connector and coolant hose.
6. Remove coolant thermostat from the coolant pipe.

To install:

7. Clean sealing ring surface.
8. Install coolant thermostat into the coolant pipe.

➡Edges on coolant thermostat and housing must align.

9. Coat new sealing with coolant and install it on the coolant connector.
10. Install coolant connector and sealing ring and tighten the bolts diagonally to 71 inch lbs. (8 Nm).
11. Install coolant hoses and connectors.
12. Fill with coolant.
13. Install noise insulation.

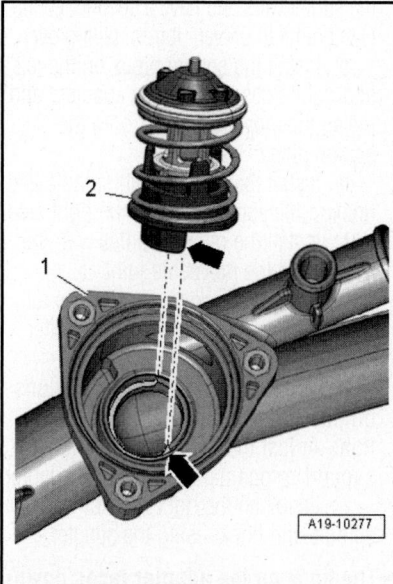

Fig. 40 Edges on coolant thermostat (2) and housing (1) must align

WATER PUMP

REMOVAL & INSTALLATION

2.0L Engine

See Figures 41 and 42.

1. Remove coolant pipes.
2. Remove the coolant pump toothed belt.
3. Disconnect electrical connector on Throttle Valve Control Module.
4. Remove bolts and remove Throttle Valve Control Module.
5. Disconnect the electrical connector on the Engine Coolant Temperature (ECT) sensor.
6. Remove bolts.
7. Remove the coolant pump from the centering pin and remove the oil cooler.

To install:

8. Replace seals and O-rings.
9. Coat the O-rings with coolant.
10. Make sure both centering pins are installed in the cylinder block.

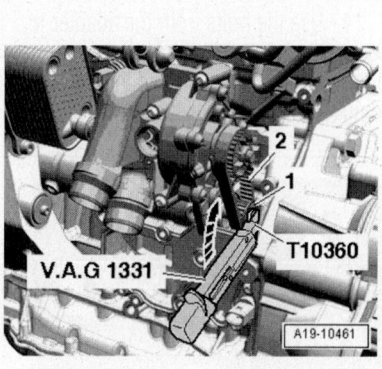

Fig. 41 Remove the coolant pump drive gear (1) and toothed belt (2)

Fig. 42 Tighten bolts in 1 to 5 sequence

11. Install the connection piece into the oil cooler.
12. Push the coolant pump onto the connection piece and onto the centering pins in the cylinder block.
13. Tighten bolts in sequence.
14. If a new coolant pump was installed, then the protective cap must be removed.
15. The rest of the installation follows the reverse of the removal procedures.

2.0L TDI Engine

See Figure 43.

1. Drain the coolant.
2. Remove the ribbed belt.
3. Remove the toothed belt.
4. Remove the coolant pump bolts and carefully remove the coolant pump.

To install:

5. Coat the new O-ring with coolant.
6. Insert the coolant pump into the cylinder block and tighten the bolts to 12 ft. lbs. (15 Nm).
7. The sealing plug on the coolant pump faces downward.
8. Install the toothed belt.
9. Install the ribbed belt.
10. Fill the coolant.

2.5L Engine

See Figures 44 and 45.

1. Remove the noise insulation.
2. Remove the exhaust system suspended-mount bolts from the subframe.
3. Remove the pendulum support bolts and remove the pendulum support.
4. Remove the engine cover with air filter.
5. Remove the connecting pipe between the throttle valve control module and air fil-

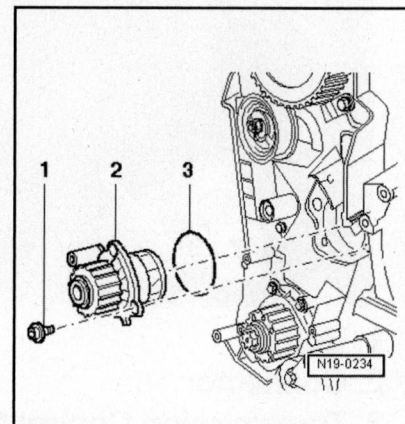

Fig. 43 Removing/installing the coolant pump bolts (1), coolant pump (2), and O-ring (3)

ter. To do so, disconnect connecting pipe, if equipped with Secondary Air Injection (AIR), and the vent tube and reposition the spring clamp.

6. If equipped with automatic transmission, do the following:

   a. Unclip the transmission control module from the bracket and remove it.

   b. Disconnect the transmission control module connector.

   c. Remove the bolts.

   d. Move the bracket with the power steering fluid reservoir to the side. Be careful of the wires.

➡**The hoses remain connected to the power steering fluid reservoir.**

7. Remove the battery, the battery tray bolts and tray.

8. Remove the plenum chamber cover.

9. Remove the wires from the transport strap.

10. Remove the transport strap from the engine and pull it out of the lifting eye. Attach the shackle to the lifting eye.

11. Remove the left and right sides of the lock carrier bracket bolts.

12. Remove the lower mount from the adapter and replace it with the other adapter.

13. Remove the bolts from the adapter.

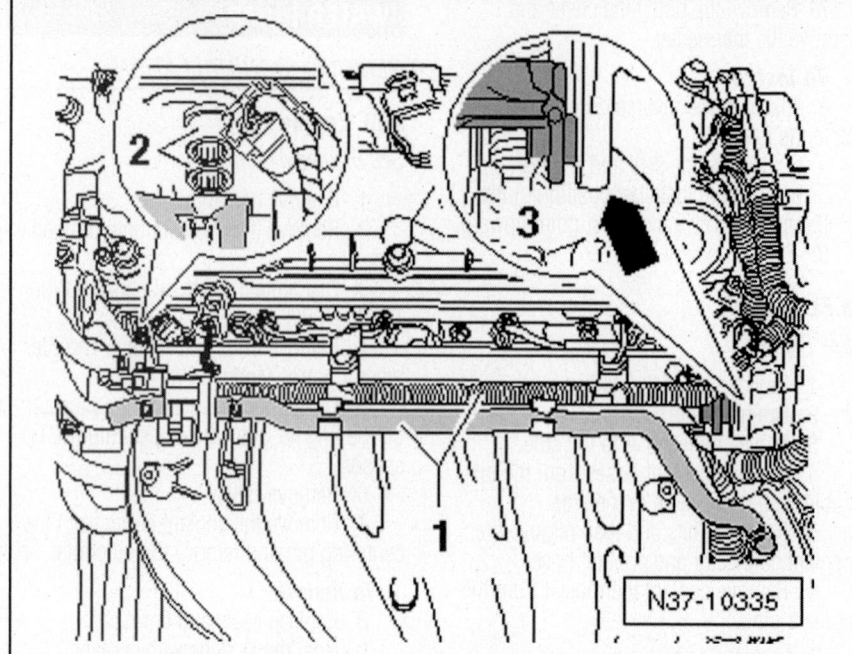

Fig. 45 Remove the wires (1) from the transport strap (3). Remove the transport strap from the engine (2) and pull it out of the lifting eye. Attach the shackle to the lifting eye.

14. Use the bolts from the adapter to secure the adapter to the lock carrier bracket. DO NOT use the bolts that were removed from the lock carrier bracket.

➡**A second technician is needed to install the engine support bridge to the vehicle in order to prevent the engine support bridge from tipping.**

15. Install the engine support bridge as follows:

   a. Install the moveable joint onto the engine support bridge square pipe.

   b. The moveable joint bolts, when installed on the engine support bridge face the direction of travel.

   c. Install the engine support bridge to the strut towers and have a second technician hold it to prevent it from falling over.

   d. Install the square pipes on the left and right sides through the adapters and install the moveable joints onto the square pipe.

   e. Install the bracket with spindle and hook to the square pipe on the right side.

   f. Install the rail with holes with the mount into the moveable joint.

   g. Insert the locking pin into the rail with holes and secure it with the cotter pins.

   h. Tighten all threaded connections on the engine support bridge hand tight. Adjust the height of the engine support bridge parallel over the adapter.

   i. Lengthen the right bracket with spindle and hook, using the adapter.

➡**The hook on the adapter faces downward and will be attached to the cylinder block later.**

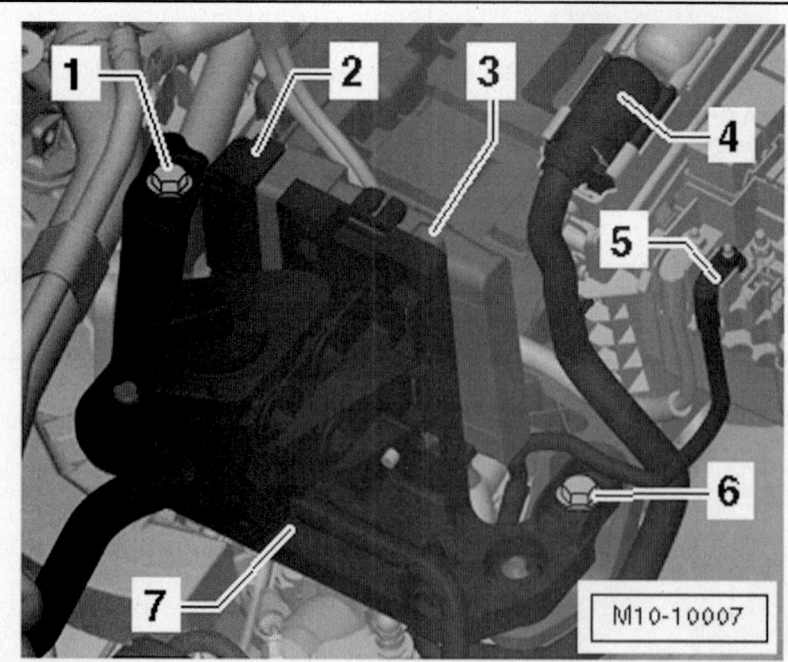

1. Bolt
2. Connector
3. Transmission Control Module (TCM)
4. Wiring
5. Wiring
6. Bolt
7. Bracket

Fig. 44 Removing the TCM and related components

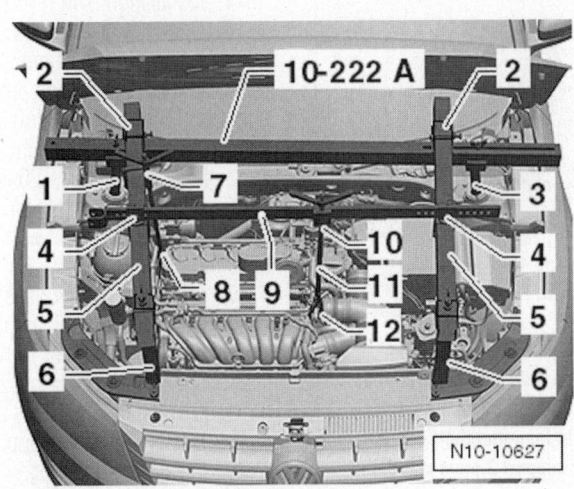

1. Adapter -10-222 A/31-2-
2. Moveable joint -T40091/3-
3. Adapter -10-222 A/31-1-
4. Moveable joint -T40093/4-
5. Square pipe -T40091/1-
6. Adapter -10-222 A/28- with adapter -10-222 A/28-2-
7. Bracket with spindle and hook -10-222 A/10-
8. Adapter -10-222 A/7-
9. Rail with holes -T40091/2-
10. Mount -T40093/5-
11. Spindle -10-222 A/11-
12. Shackle -10-222 A/12-

Fig. 46 Installing the engine support bridge

j. Attach the left spindle in the shackle.

k. Position the spindles and hold the engine and transmission. Do not lift.

16. Remove the bolt and move the windshield washer reservoir toward the front.

17. Remove the coolant expansion tank bolts and place the coolant expansion tank on top of the engine with the hoses connected.

18. Remove the bolts and remove the engine mount.

➡**The single bolt is accessible through a hole in the wheel housing.**

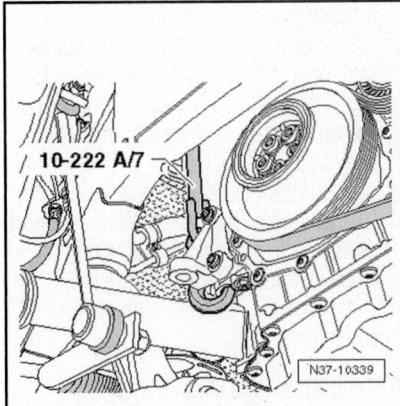

Fig. 47 Attach the left spindle in the shackle. Position the spindles and hold the engine and transmission. Do not lift.

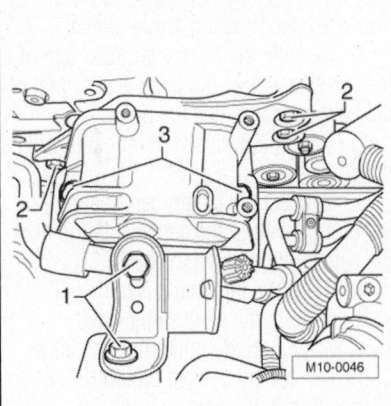

Fig. 48 Remove the bolts (1, 2, 3) and remove the engine mount.

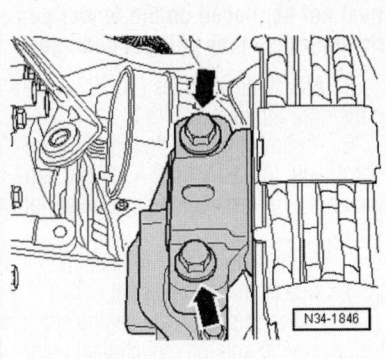

Fig. 49 Remove the transmission mount to transmission mount bracket bolts. Slide the engine as far as possible toward the left front.

Fig. 50 Remove the coolant pump bolts and rotate the coolant pump out.

19. Remove the transmission mount to transmission mount bracket bolts.

20. Slide the engine as far as possible toward the left front.

21. Remove the coolant pump bolts and rotate the coolant pump out.

To install:

22. Install in the reverse order of removal. Note the following:

a. Tighten the coolant pump retaining bolts to 7 ft. lbs. (10 Nm).

b. Note the installed position of the coolant pump. The seal in the housing points downward.

23. Fill the coolant.

3.6L Engine

See Figure 51.

1. Remove noise insulation.
2. Remove pendulum support.
3. Drain coolant.
4. Remove ribbed belt.

➡**The engine brackets (10 222 A /1) must not be placed on the fender panels otherwise they will get damaged.**

5. Attach the shackles (10 222 A /12) to the right lifting eye.

6. Assemble engine support bridge (10 222 A) with frame (10 222 A /1) and support engine in installation position at right lifting eyelet.

7. Remove bolts for subframe mount on engine side from engine mount.

8. Lower engine on the engine support bridge only far enough that coolant pump can be removed.

9. Remove belt pulley of coolant pump. To do so, counterhold belt pulley using a drift (standard).

10. Remove coolant pump bolts and then remove the coolant pump.

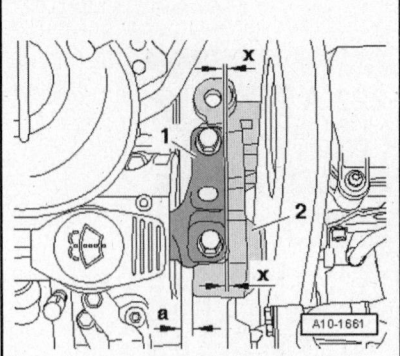

Fig. 51 There must be a distance a of at least 0.39 in (10 mm) between engine support and right long-member. Casting edge on engine support 2 must stand parallel to bracket.

To install:

11. Installation is in reverse of removal.

12. Coat new O-ring with coolant.

13. Install coolant pump.

14. Tighten mounting bolts for coolant pump to 71 inch lbs. (8 Nm).

15. Install belt pulley for coolant pump and tighten to 15 ft. lbs. (20 Nm)

16. Raise engine again with Engine Support Bridge and secure it with new bolts, tightening them by hand.

17. Align engine mount as follows:

18. Tighten new engine subframe mount and engine bracket bolts. Tightening specifications: 44 ft. lbs. (60 Nm), plus an additional 90° rotation.

19. Install pendulum support.

20. Install ribbed belt.

21. Fill with coolant.

ENGINE ELECTRICAL

BATTERY SYSTEM

BATTERY

DISCONNECTING & CONNECTING

Disconnecting

See Figures 52 and 53.

Service Notes:

• Deactivate the anti-theft alarm system first and then disconnect the battery.

• By removing the battery negative terminal clamp (current disruption), safe work on the electrical system is guaranteed.

• Disconnecting the battery positive (B+) terminal must only be performed as required to remove battery from vehicle, and must only be carried out after the negative (-) terminal is disconnected.

• Always follow the instructions for connecting the battery.

1. Turn off the ignition and all electrical consumers.

2. Remove the key.

3. Unclip the service cover off the side trim panel.

4. Disconnect the ground cable from the battery negative pole.

5. Open the terminal cover on the battery positive pole.

6. Disconnect the positive cable from the battery positive pole.

Connecting

After connecting the battery and switching on the ignition, the ASR/ESP Control Lamp and Electro-mechanical Power Steering Indicator Lamp light up continuously.

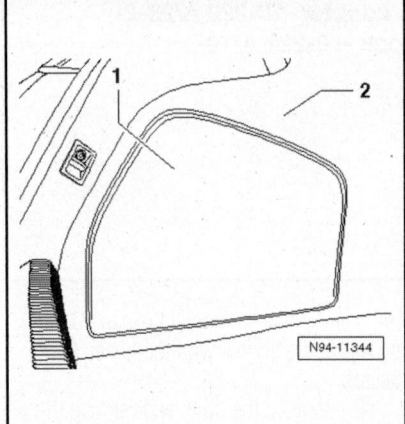

Fig. 52 Unclip the service cover (1) off the side trim panel (2).

The indicator lamps switch off automatically after driving straight ahead at 15 to 20 mph. This activates Steering Angle Sensor.

1. Connect the battery terminal clip of the positive wire to the positive terminal of the battery and tighten the bolt.

2. Turn positive cable/terminal in driving direction.

3. Connect the battery terminal clip of the ground wire to the negative terminal of the battery and tighten the bolt.

4. Close the terminal cover.

5. Perform the work steps listed:

   a. Turn on the ignition using either the key or start system button (E378) and then turn it off again.

   b. Read the DTC memory using the Vehicle Diagnostic Tester in "Guided Fault Finding".

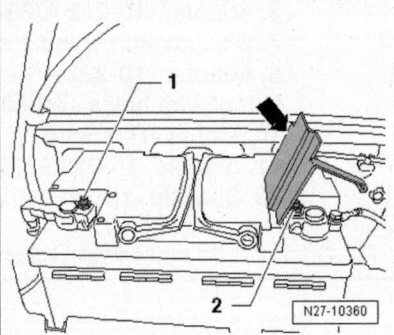

Fig. 53 Disconnect the ground cable (1) from the battery negative pole. Open the terminal cover on the battery positive pole. Disconnect the positive cable (2) from the battery positive pole.

   c. Check clock time setting, set anew if necessary.

   d. For the electrical window regulators, open and close all windows all the way. Then, with the windows closed, pull the window regulator switch until the relay audibly switches.

   e. Check the convenience switching for the window regulators. While comfort switching is operated, window must close without holding the switch.

   f. Check function of all electrical consumers.

REMOVAL & INSTALLATION

1. Disconnect the battery, as described above.

2. Remove the battery jacket.

3. Remove the bolt and clamping plate.

4. Fold the handles up (if equipped) and remove the battery.

To install:

⁂⁂ **CAUTION**

If the battery is not secured properly, the following risks are possible:

• Shortened battery service life due to vibration damage (explosion hazard).
• If the battery is not secured properly, the plates inside the battery can get damaged.
• Damage to battery casing caused by bracket (possible electrolyte leakage, high subsequent costs).

• Inadequate crash safety.
5. Install in reverse order of removal. Note the following:
　　a. Tighten the threaded connections.
　　b. Make sure the battery is secure after installing it.
　　c. Connect the battery.

ENGINE ELECTRICAL

GENERATOR

REMOVAL & INSTALLATION

2.0L Engine

See Figure 54.

➡**When disconnecting and connecting battery, the procedure must be followed as described in the repair manual.**

　1. Disconnect battery.

⁂⁂ **CAUTION**

Before removing ribbed belt, mark the top side and direction of travel. When installing, pay attention to correct running direction and installation position. If the belt is installed in the opposite running direction or is positioned incorrectly, the belt will fail!

　2. Remove the ribbed belt.
　3. Disengage and disconnect harness connector.
　4. Remove the oil pressure switch.
　5. Remove the generator bolts.
　6. Turn the generator slightly to the left in order to be able to access the connections on the back of the generator.
　7. Release and disconnect DF wire connector.

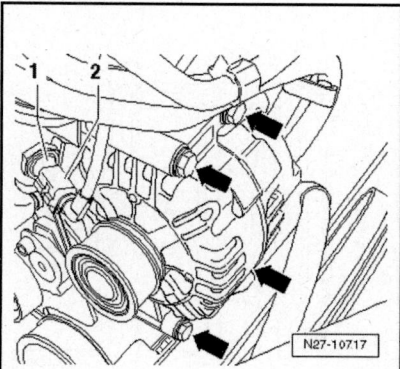

Fig. 54 Remove the connector (2) from oil pressure switch (1) and the generator bolts (arrows)

　8. Pry off protective cap.
　9. Remove the nut and B+ wire below from generator connector threads.
　10. Remove both screws and move the pipes and the hose upward so that there is enough space to remove the generator.

➡**The pipes and the hose can remain connected.**

　11. Remove the generator upward and out of the vehicle.

To install:
　12. Install in reverse order of removal, noting the following:

➡**When installing an already used ribbed belt, note direction of travel marked when it was removed! Before installing the ribbed belt, make sure all components (generator, A/C compressor) are securely fastened. When installing the ribbed belt, make sure it is properly seated in the belt pulley!**

　13. Tighten the threaded connections to the specification given in the assembly overview.

➡**When disconnecting and connecting battery, the procedure must be followed as described in the repair manual.**

2.0L TDI Engine

See Figure 55.

　1. Disconnect the battery.
　2. Remove the noise insulation.
　3. Remove the right front wheel housing liner.
　4. Mark the direction of travel of the ribbed belt.
　5. Swivel the tensioner in a counterclockwise direction, using a 16 mm wrench to release the tension.
　6. Lock the tensioner in place using T10060 A. Remove ribbed belt.
　7. Remove the A/C compressor from its mounting and tie to the body using wire. Do not disconnect the A/C lines.

CHARGING SYSTEM

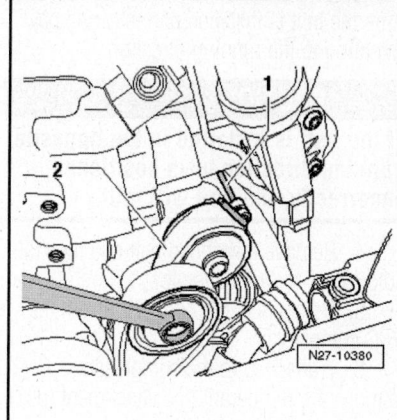

Fig. 55 Lock the tensioner (2) in place using T10060 A (1). Remove ribbed belt.

　8. Remove the nut from the wire holder on the back of the generator.
　9. Disconnect the other terminal connector.
　10. Remove the wire cap. Open the retainer and remove the line from the retainer.
　11. Remove the nut on the B+ wire from the generator and then move the B+ wire to the side.
　12. Remove the bolt from the tensioning roller and then remove the tensioning roller.
　13. Unscrew the mounting bolts of the generator and remove the generator downward from the vehicle.

To install:
　14. Installation is performed in the reverse order of removal. Note the following:
　　a. Drive the threaded sleeves out of the Generator housing approximately 2 mm to the rear.
　　b. Attach the wire holder on the back of the generator in the 9 o'clock position.
　　c. Install the idler roller and ribbed belt tensioning roller for the generator.
　　d. Tighten the nuts for the refrigerant lines on the longitudinal member to 7 ft. lbs. (10 Nm).
　　e. Install the ribbed belt.

f. Install the fan shroud.

g. Install the battery.

15. Start the engine and make sure the generator is running.

2.5L Engine

See Figures 56 and 57.

1. Disconnect the battery as described in this section.

2. Remove the fan shroud.

3. Mark the top of the ribbed belt and the running direction before removal. Make sure the belt is installed correctly and pay attention to the running direction.

❊❊ CAUTION

If the belt is installed in the opposite running direction or is positioned incorrectly, the belt will fail!

4. Remove the ribbed belt and then the idler roller for the generator.

5. Disconnect the connector from the A/C compressor.

6. If attached to the compressor, remove the refrigerant line attachment (do not disconnect the A/C lines).

7. Remove the A/C compressor bolts.

➡ **The hoses on the A/C compressor can remain connected.**

8. Tie the A/C compressor to a suitable place on the vehicle with wire until it is time to install it again. Make sure the hoses are not pulled off or kinked.

9. Release the connector (DF lead) and remove the cap.

10. Disconnect the B+ wire from the generator.

11. Remove the wire holder on the back of the generator.

12. Remove the bolts from the generator.

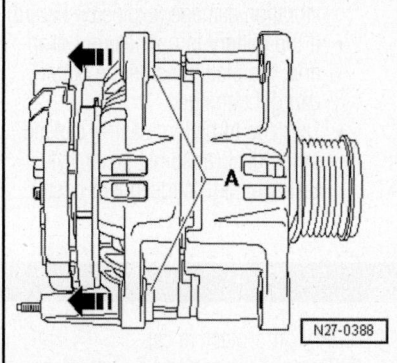

Fig. 57 Drive the threaded sleeves out of the Generator housing approximately 2 mm in direction of arrow.

13. Remove the generator.

To install:

14. Installation is performed in the reverse order of removal. Note the following:

a. Drive the threaded sleeves out of the Generator housing approximately 2 mm to the rear.

b. Attach the wire holder on the back of the generator in the 9 o'clock position.

15. Tighten the threaded connections.

a. Install the idler roller and ribbed belt tensioning roller for the generator.

b. Tighten the nuts for the refrigerant lines on the longitudinal member to 7 ft. lbs. (10 Nm).

c. Install the ribbed belt.

d. Install the fan shroud.

e. Install the battery.

16. Start the engine and make sure the generator is running.

3.6L Engine

See Figures 58 and 59.

❊❊ CAUTION

When disconnecting and connecting battery, the procedure must be followed as described in the repair manual.

1. Disconnect battery.

2. Remove noise insulation.

3. Remove the right front section of the wheel housing liner.

➡ **Before removing ribbed belt, mark the top side and direction of travel. When installing, pay attention to correct running direction and installation position. If the belt is installed in the**

opposite running direction or is positioned incorrectly, the belt will fail!

4. Mark running direction of ribbed belt.

5. Release tension on ribbed belt by swinging tensioning element using a 16 mm open-end wrench in direction of rotation.

6. Secure tensioning element using drift T10060 A.

7. Remove ribbed belt.

8. Remove the A/C compressor and secure it to body with suitable item (e.g. wire).

9. Remove the wiring bracket nut.

10. Release and disconnect the terminal connector.

11. Pull off protective cap.

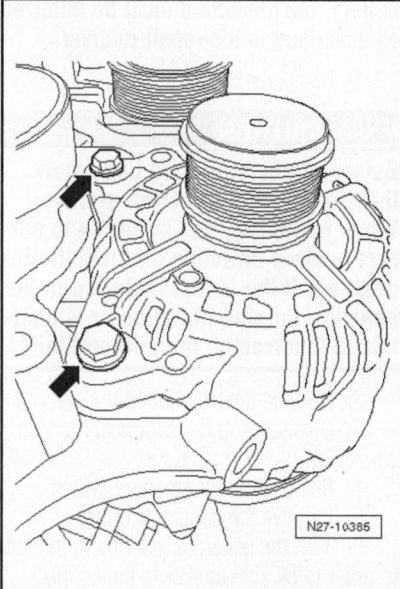

Fig. 58 Remove generator screws (arrows)

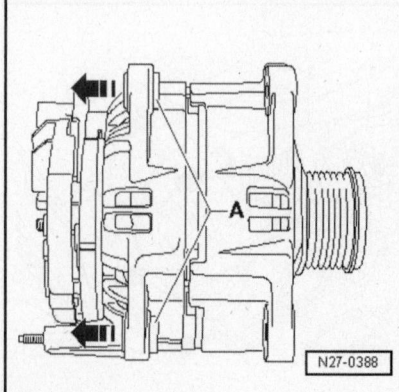

Fig. 59 Drive threaded sleeves (A) out of generator housing approximately 0.117 in. (4 mm) in direction of rotation

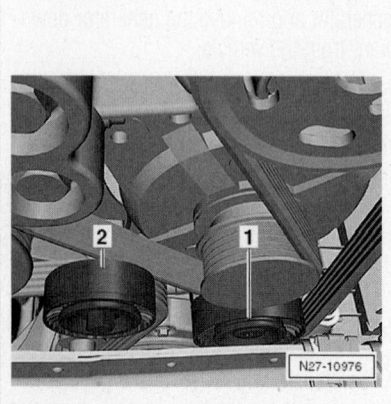

Fig. 56 Remove the idler roller (1) for the generator.

12. Open clip on plug and disengage wire from plug.

13. Remove the nut on the B+ wire from the generator and lay the B+ wire aside.

14. Remove the nut on the tensioner and remove the tensioner.

15. Remove generator screws as shown.

16. Remove generator downward from vehicle.

To install:

17. Install in reverse order of removal, noting the following.

➡**When installing an already used ribbed belt, note direction of travel marked when it was removed! Before installing the ribbed belt, make sure all components (generator, A/C compressor) are securely fastened. When installing the ribbed belt, make sure it is properly seated in the belt pulley!**

18. Drive threaded sleeves out of generator housing approximately 0.117 in. (4 mm) in direction of rotation.

19. Install wire retainer firmly to rear side of generator in 9 o'clock position.

20. Tighten all threaded connections to the specification.

➡**Observe notes for threaded connections of battery terminals.**

21. Reconnect battery.

22. Start the engine and verify that the belt is running properly.

23. Turn off the engine.

ENGINE ELECTRICAL

FIRING ORDER

2.0L & 2.0L TDI Engines

1–3–4–2

2.5L Engines

1–2–4–5–3

3.6L Engines

1–5–3–6–2–4

IGNITION COIL

REMOVAL & INSTALLATION

2.0L Engine

See Figure 60.

1. To pull off spark plugs, place ignition coil puller (T40039) on topmost thick rib of ignition coils with power output stages.

✳ CAUTION

If lower ribs are used, these can be damaged.

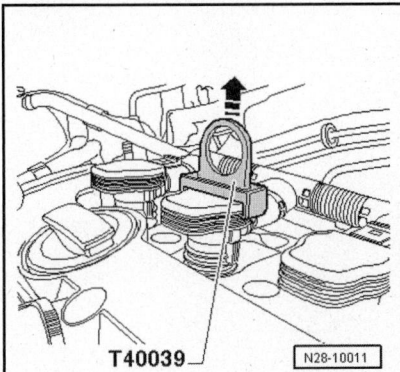

Fig. 60 To pull off spark plugs, place ignition coil puller on topmost thick rib of ignition coils with power output stages

2. Remove engine covers.

➡**Spark plugs are located under ignition coils with power output stages.**

3. Remove both bolts.

➡**Note installation position of ignition coils with power output stages.**

4. Pull all ignition coils approximately 1.17 in (30 mm) out of cylinder head in direction of rotation using ignition coil puller T40039.

5. Push connector in direction of rotation ignition coils with power output stages, press catch down by hand and disconnect connectors.

To install:

6. Guide ignition coils with power output stages into cylinder head.

7. Align ignition coils with power output stages into designated recesses of cylinder head cover.

8. Connect all connectors to ignition coils.

9. Press ignition coils with power output stages onto spark plugs by hand until stop. They must engage audibly.

10. Secure wiring using bolts.

11. Install engine cover.

2.5L Engine

See Figures 61 and 62.

1. Remove the engine cover with air filter.

2. Disconnect the connector from the Secondary Air Injection (AIR) solenoid valve, if equipped.

3. In order to prevent damage to the wire guide, remove the ignition coils with power output stages as follows:

a. Using the ignition coil puller (T40039), pull all the ignition coils out approximately 10 mm, starting with ignition coil No. 1. Then, pull all the ignition

---

IGNITION SYSTEM

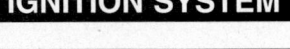

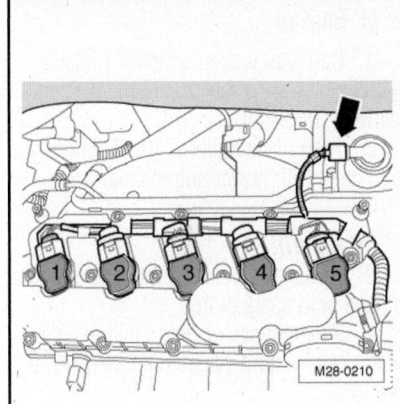

Fig. 61 Disconnect the connector (arrow) from the Secondary Air Injection (AIR) solenoid valve, if equipped.

coils out an additional 10 mm in the same sequence.

b. Disconnect all the connectors and pull them out just a little.

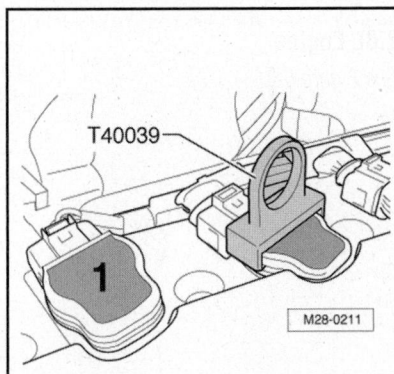

Fig. 62 Using the ignition coil puller, pull all the ignition coils out approximately 10 mm, starting with ignition coil No. 1. Then, pull all the ignition coils out an additional 10 mm in the same sequence.

c. Disconnect the connectors, starting with ignition coil No. 1.

d. Pull the ignition coils out of the spark plug shafts.

4. Remove the spark plugs, if necessary.

To install:

5. If removed, install the spark plugs. Tighten to 18 ft. lbs. (25 Nm).

6. Install all the ignition coils loosely into the spark plug shafts.

7. Align the ignition coils in the openings in the cylinder head cover and then connect all the connectors in reverse order.

8. Press the ignition coils down, evenly onto the spark plugs by hand.

3.6L Engine

1. Carefully loosen connector retainer with help of assembly tool (T10118) and remove connector.

2. Then place puller (T10095 A) on ignition coils with power output stages and remove them.

To install:

3. Press ignition coils with power output stages onto spark plugs.

4. Slide connector onto ignition coils with power output stages until it engages audibly.

IGNITION TIMING

ADJUSTMENT

All engines are equipped with a Distributorless Ignition System (DIS). No adjustment is necessary.

SPARK PLUGS

REMOVAL & INSTALLATION

2.0L Engine

See Figure 63.

1. To pull off spark plugs, place ignition coil puller (T40039) on topmost thick rib of ignition coils with power output stages.

✳✳ CAUTION

If lower ribs are used, these can be damaged.

2. Remove engine covers.

➡**Spark plugs are located under ignition coils with power output stages.**

3. Remove both bolts.

➡**Note installation position of ignition coils with power output stages.**

4. Pull all ignition coils approximately 1.17 in (30 mm) out of cylinder head in direction of rotation using ignition coil puller.

5. Push connector in direction of rota-

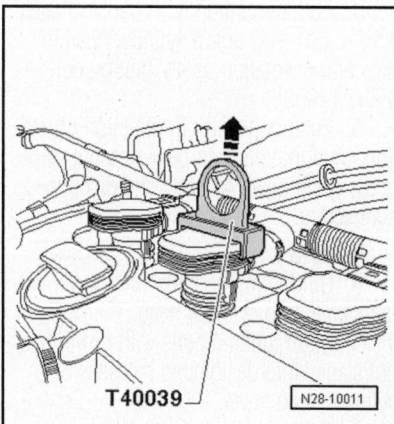

T40039 | N28-10011

Fig. 63 To pull off spark plugs, place ignition coil puller on topmost thick rib of ignition coils with power output stages

tion ignition coils with power output stages, press catch down by hand and disconnect connectors.

6. Remove spark plugs using spark plug wrench (3122 B).

To install:

7. Install new spark plugs using spark plug wrench.

8. Guide ignition coils with power output stages into cylinder head.

9. Align ignition coils with power output stages into designated recesses of cylinder head cover.

10. Connect all connectors to ignition coils.

11. Press ignition coils with power output stages onto spark plugs by hand until stop. They must engage audibly.

12. Secure wiring using bolts.

13. Install engine cover.

2.5L Engine

➡**See "Ignition Coils" in this section.**

3.6L Engine

1. Carefully loosen connector retainer with help of assembly tool (T10118) and remove connector.

2. Then place Puller (T10095 A) on ignition coils with power output stages and remove them.

3. Remove spark plugs using spark plug wrench.

To install:

4. Install new spark plugs using spark plug wrench (3122 B).

5. Press ignition coils with power output stages onto spark plugs.

6. Slide connector onto ignition coils with power output stages until it engages audibly.

STARTER

REMOVAL & INSTALLATION

Type 1

See Figure 64.

1. Disconnect battery.
2. Disconnect harness connector and loosen spring-type clamp using spring type clip pliers (VAS 5024A).
3. Remove mounting bolt for air filter housing.
4. Release retaining tabs and remove cover.
5. Disconnect hose from air filter housing and remove it.
6. Pull the air filter housing up out of the retainers and remove it from the vehicle.
7. Slide protective cap in direction of rotation downward from magnetic switch.
8. Remove positive wire and disconnect harness connector of terminal 50.
9. Remove the ground wire from the starter bolt.
10. Remove upper mounting bolt for starter.
11. Remove noise insulation.
12. Remove mounting nut from lower mounting bolt of starter.
13. Remove wire retainer.
14. Remove lower mounting bolt for starter.
15. Remove the starter downward and out from the vehicle.

To install:

16. Install in reverse order of removal.
17. Tighten bolts/nuts to specification as follows:
   - Mounting nut B+ wire to starter M8: 11 ft. lbs. (15 Nm)
   - Starter bolts M12: 56 ft. lbs. (75 Nm)
   - Wiring bracket nut M8: 17 ft. lbs. (23 Nm)

Type 2

See Figure 65.

1. Disconnect battery.
2. Loosen spring)type clamps using Spring Type Clip Pliers (VAS5024 A) and disconnect harness connector.
3. Disengage retaining lug and remove cover in direction of rotation.
4. Disengage retaining tabs and pull air duct forward direction of out of retainer.
5. Remove air filter housing mounting bolt.

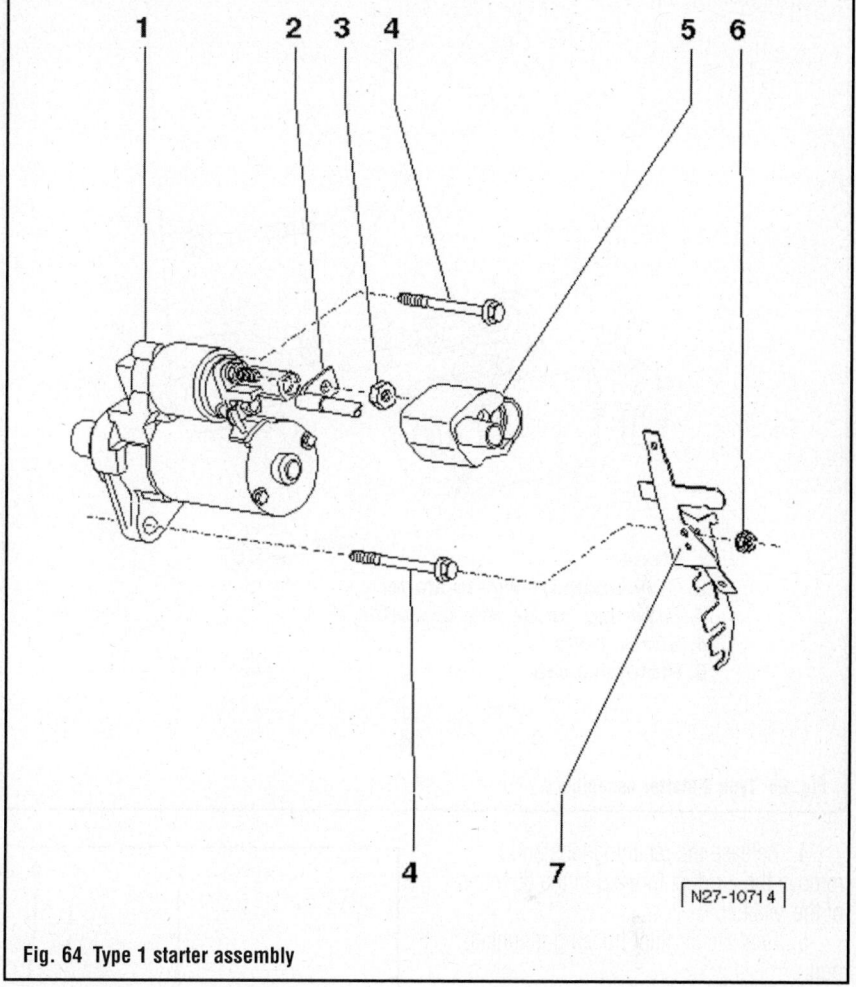

Fig. 64 Type 1 starter assembly

6. Pull the air filter housing up from the rubber mounting.
7. Remove air filter housing from vehicle.
8. Remove ground (GND) wire from transmission and set it aside.

❊❊ CAUTION

To prevent damage from corrosion, do not remove ground (GND) wire from GND point on body.

9. Remove the air filter housing bracket bolts.
10. Remove the air filter housing bracket from the vehicle.
11. Remove noise insulation.
12. Remove lower mounting bolt for starter.
13. Release and disconnect the connector and slide the protective cap downward from the solenoid switch in the direction of the.
14. Remove the nut and lay the positive wire aside.

15. Remove upper mounting bolt for starter.
16. Remove starter upward and out of vehicle.

To install:

17. Install in reverse order of removal, noting the following:
18. Tighten bolts/nuts to specification as follows:
   - Mounting nut B+ wire to starter M8: 11 ft. lbs. (15 Nm)
   - Starter bolts M12: 56 ft. lbs. (75 Nm)

Type 3

See Figure 66.

1. Disconnect battery.
2. Loosen spring clamp using spring clamp pliers (VAS 5024) and disconnect connector.
3. Disengage retaining lug and remove cover in direction of rotation.

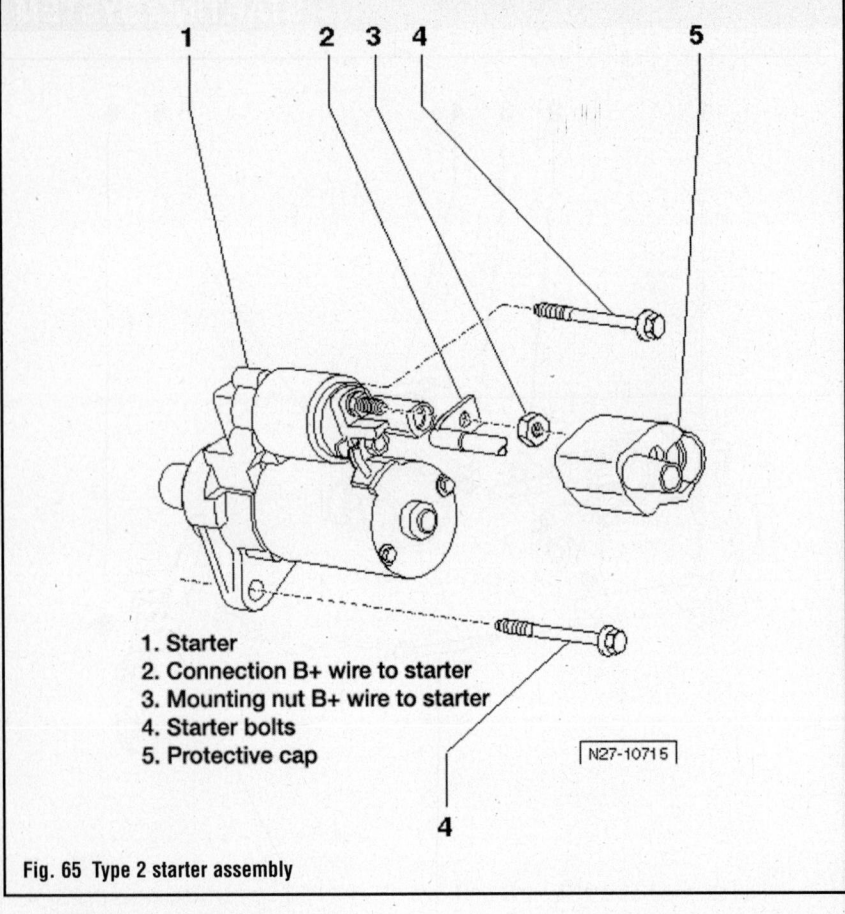

1. Starter
2. Connection B+ wire to starter
3. Mounting nut B+ wire to starter
4. Starter bolts
5. Protective cap

N27-10715

Fig. 65 Type 2 starter assembly

17. Remove the nut and the wiring bracket upward from the starter bolts.

18. Remove lower mounting bolt for starter.

19. Disengage harness connector and disconnect harness connector.

20. Remove the nut and move the ground wire aside.

✴✴ CAUTION

To prevent damage from corrosion, do not remove ground (GND) wire from GND point on body.

21. Remove upper mounting bolt for starter.

22. Remove starter upward and out of vehicle.

To install:

23. Install in reverse order of removal, noting the following:

24. Tighten bolts/nuts to specification as follows:

- Mounting nut B+ wire to starter M8: 11 ft. lbs. (15 Nm)
- Starter bolts M12: 56 ft. lbs. (75 Nm)
- Wiring bracket nut M8: 17 ft. lbs. (23 Nm)

4. Release the retaining tabs and remove the air duct forward in the direction of the retainer.

5. Remove air filter housing mounting bolt.

6. Pull the air filter housing up from the rubber mounting.

7. Remove air filter housing from vehicle.

8. Remove the air filter housing bracket bolts.

9. Remove the air filter housing bracket from the vehicle.

10. Disengage harness connector of terminal 50 and disconnect harness connector.

11. Slide protective cap in direction of rotation downward from magnetic switch.

12. Remove mounting nut and set aside the positive wire.

13. Unclip the cap on the wiring bracket and loosen the wire from the cap.

14. Remove mounting nut from upper mounting bolt of starter.

15. Remove noise insulation.

16. Unclip the cap on the wiring bracket and loosen the wire from the cap.

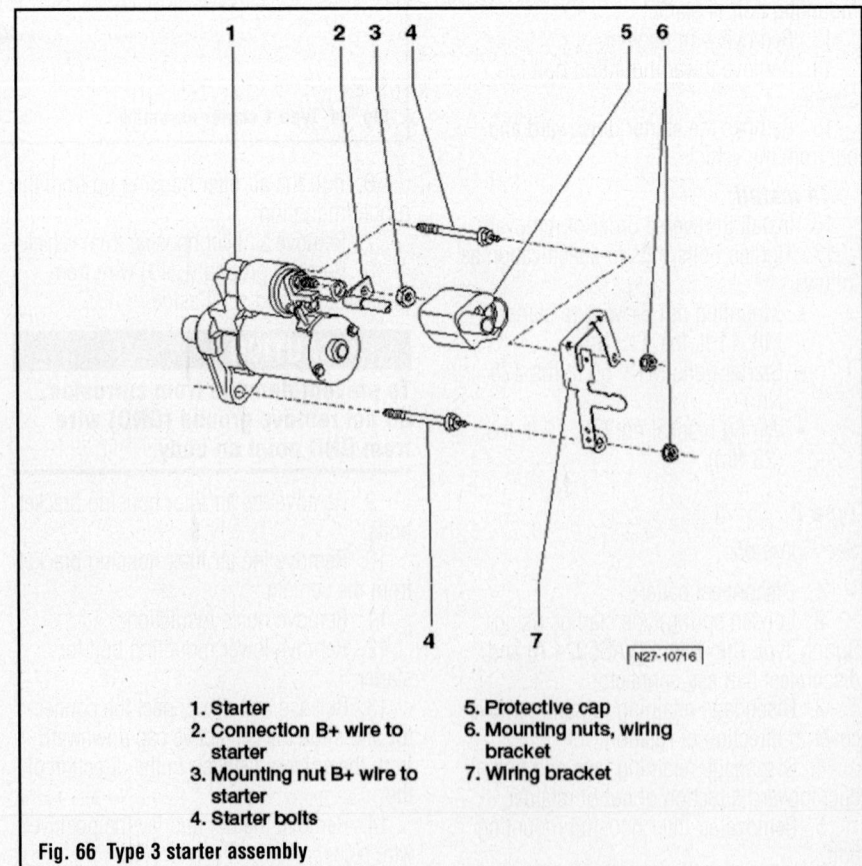

1. Starter
2. Connection B+ wire to starter
3. Mounting nut B+ wire to starter
4. Starter bolts
5. Protective cap
6. Mounting nuts, wiring bracket
7. Wiring bracket

N27-10716

Fig. 66 Type 3 starter assembly

ENGINE MECHANICAL

➡**Disconnecting the negative battery cable may interfere with the functions of the on board computer systems and may require the computer to undergo a relearning process, once the negative battery cable is reconnected.**

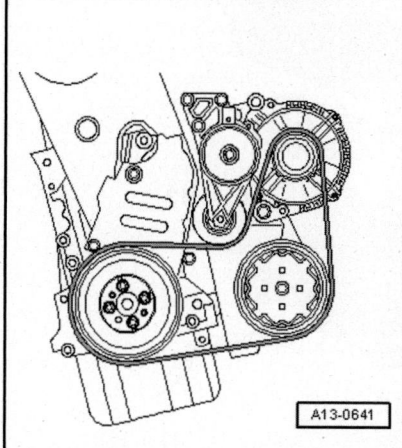

Fig. 67 Accessory drive belt routing— 2.0L Engine

ACCESSORY DRIVE BELTS

See Figures 67 through 70.

INSPECTION

1. Turn the engine at vibration damper/ crankshaft pulley with a suitable socket wrench.
2. Raise the vehicle if necessary. Check the drive belt for:
   a. Sub-surface (deep) cracks
   b. Layer separation (top layer, cord strands)
   c. Traces of oil and grease
3. Replace the belt if any damage is found or if contaminated with oil or grease.

ADJUSTMENT

All models use an automatic (spring powered) tensioner. No adjustment is required.

REMOVAL & INSTALLATION

2.0L Engine

✳✳ CAUTION

Risk of destroying due to reversed running direction on a used ribbed belt. Before removing ribbed belt, marking running direction with chalk or felt-tip pen for reinstallation later.

1. Remove the noise insulation.

2. Remove the right air guide hose.
3. To release the tension on the ribbed belt, turn the tensioner in direction of rotation from underneath.
4. Secure tensioner with Drift (T10060 A).
5. Remove ribbed belt.

To install:

6. Installation is performed in reverse order of removal.

✳✳ CAUTION

Before installing ribbed belt, generator, A/C compressor must be securely installed.

7. First mount the ribbed belt on the crankshaft pulley, then on the A/C compressor and generator.
8. Turn the tensioner with a box-end wrench and remove the drift (T10060 A).

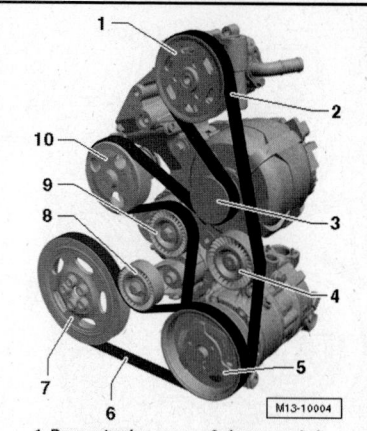

1. Power steering pump
2. Ribbed belt
3. Generator
4. Idler pulley
5. A/C compressor
6. Accessory belt
7. Crankshaft pulley
8. Idler
9. Starter
10. AIR pump

Fig. 69 Accessory drive belt and components—2.5L Engine

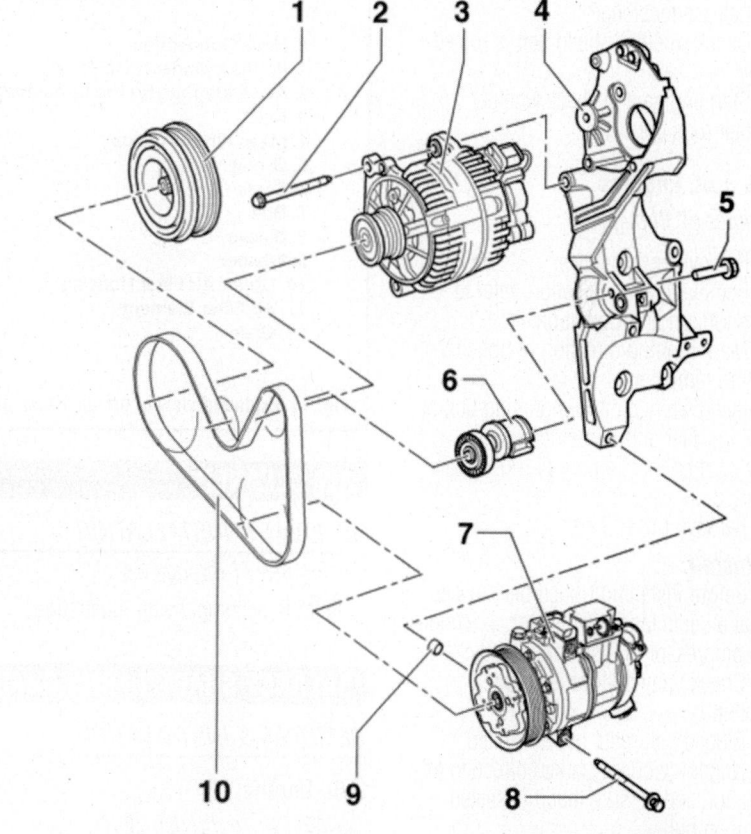

1. Vibration Damper
2. Bolt: 18 ft. lbs. (25 Nm)
3. Generator
4. Accessory Bracket
5. Bolt: 27 ft. lbs. (35 Nm)
6. Ribbed Belt Tensioner
7. A/C Compressor
8. Bolt
9. Alignment Sleeves
10. Ribbed Belt

Fig. 68 Accessory drive belt and components—2.0L TDI Engine

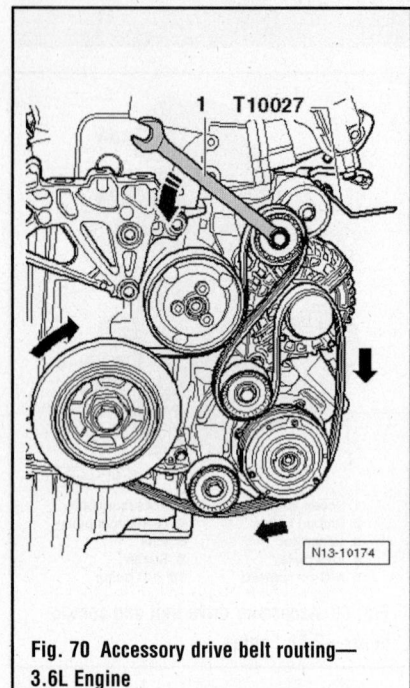

Fig. 70 Accessory drive belt routing—3.6L Engine

9. Release tensioner.
10. Check whether ribbed belt is routed correctly.
11. Start engine and check whether ribbed belt runs correctly.

2.5L & 3.6L Engines

See Figures 67 through 70.

1. Remove engine cover.
2. Remove noise insulation, refer to see: Description and Operation.
3. Mark running direction of ribbed V-belt before removing.
4. Insert wrench on to mounting bolt of tensioning roller and turn clockwise far enough until connecting pin (T10027) can be inserted on tensioning roller.
5. Remove ribbed belt.

To install:

6. Before installing ribbed belt, make sure that all ancillaries (generator, air conditioner compressor) are secured tightly.
7. Check relay pulleys for ease of movement
8. Ribbed belt must not be kinked.
9. Note previously marked direction of belt rotation and be sure that it is seated correctly on pulley.
10. Install ribbed belt.
11. Then press tensioning roller slightly in direction of rotation using wrench. This releases tension on connecting pin (T10027) in tensioning roller and it can be pulled out.
12. When finished, always perform the following work: start engine and check belt running.

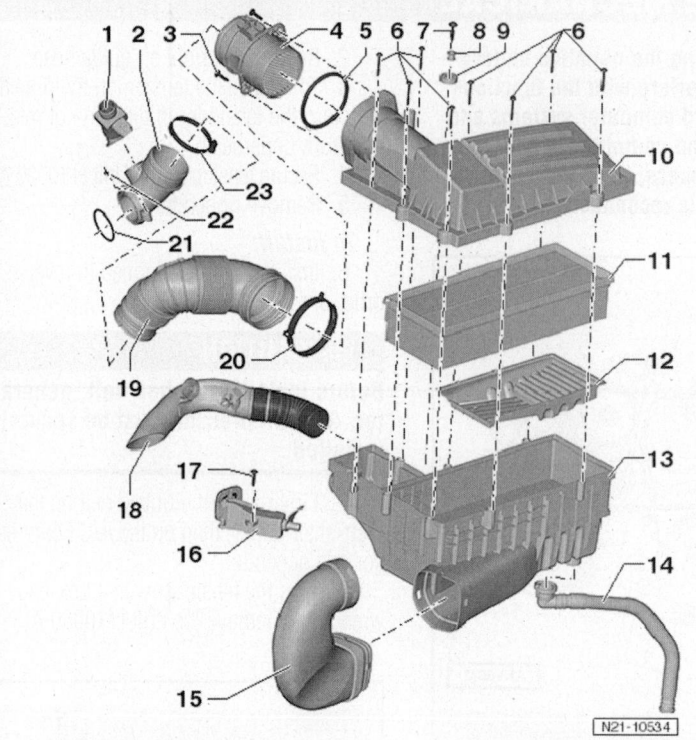

1. Hose Connection
   (to the cylinder head cover)
2. Air Guide Pipe (to the turbocharger)
3. Bolt
4. Mass Airflow Sensor
5. O-ring
6. Screw
7. Bolt
8. Sleeve
9. Washer
10. Upper Air Filter Housing
11. Air Filter Element
12. Grille
13. Lower Air Filter Housing
14. Water Drain Hose
   (with a shutter valve)
15. Intake Air Guide (to the lock carrier)
16. Adjusting Element
   (to the preheating change over)
17. Bolt
18. Preheating Intake Manifold
19. Connecting Hose
   (to the turbocharger)
20. Spring Clamps
21. Seal
22. Bolt
23. Hose Clamp

Fig. 71 Exploded view of the air intake and air cleaner assembly—2.0L TDI engine

AIR CLEANER

REMOVAL & INSTALLATION

See Figures 71 through 73.

Refer to accompanying illustrations.

BALANCE SHAFT TIMING CHAIN

REMOVAL & INSTALLATION

2.0L Engine

See Figures 74 through 77.

➡**Always replace the intermediate shaft sprocket. Otherwise the backlash will not adjust itself and it could result in engine damage. The new intermediate shaft sprocket has an anti-friction coating that wears off after a short period of use, which automatically adjusts the backlash.**

1. Remove timing chain upper cover.
2. Remove the lower timing chain cover.
3. Remove the camshaft timing chain.
4. Remove the balance shaft timing chain.
   a. Remove the guide rail for the camshaft timing chain.
   b. Remove chain tensioner for camshaft timing chain.
   c. Remove the balance shaft chain tensioner.
   d. Remove the tensioning rail.
   e. Remove the guide rail.
   f. Remove the guide rail.
   g. Remove the timing chain.
5. Remove the coolant pump toothed belt.
   a. Remove small coolant pipe.

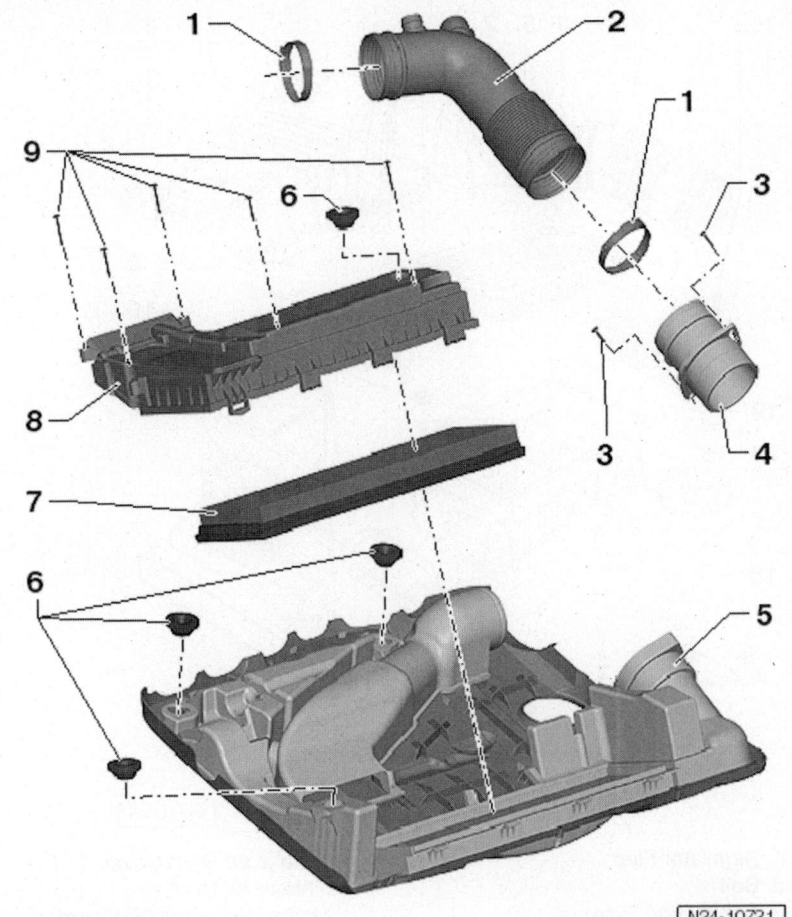

1. Spring Clamp
2. Connecting Pipe
3. Bolt
4. Connecting Piece
5. Engine Cover/Upper Air Filter Housing
6. Rubber bushing
7. Filter Element
8. Lower Air Filter Housing
9. Bolt

N24-10721

Fig. 72 Exploded view of the air intake and air cleaner assembly—2.5L engine

b. Lay aside the coolant hose and electrical wiring harness.

c. Remove the bolt and remove bracket.

d. Remove the bolt on the bracket for the After-Run Coolant Pump.

e. Remove the coolant hoses and lay them aside.

f. Remove the front right wheel housing liner.

g. Remove bolts.

h. Remove the air guide pipe by lifting the clamps items.

i. Pull off the Intake Manifold Runner Control (IMRC) Valve.

j. Remove the bolts and remove the toothed belt cover.

➡**The drive gear bolt has a left thread.**

k. Remove the bolt on the coolant pump drive gear using Torque Wrench (V.A.G 1331) clockwise and insert tool T10360; at the same time, counterhold the vibration damper.

l. Remove the drive gear and toothed belt.

6. Mark the tooth face on the intermediate sprocket.

7. Remove the intermediate sprocket.

8. Remove the intake camshaft balance shaft.

To install:

9. Lubricate the balance shaft bearing with engine oil.

10. Install the intake camshaft balance shaft.

11. Replace the O-ring and coat with engine oil.

12. Coat the bearing pin with engine oil and install it; the bearing pin must engage in the hole in the cylinder block.

13. Mark the tooth face on the intermediate sprocket.

14. Install the intermediate sprocket; the marking on the balance shaft must be between the markings on the tooth faces.

15. Tighten the chain sprocket bolt.

16. Check the markings on the intermediate shaft sprocket/balance shaft.

➡**Due to the ratio, the marking will align only every 7th turn.**

17. Replace the coolant pump drive seal.

18. Install the coolant pump toothed belt.

a. Replace the drive gear bolt.
b. Replace seals and O-rings.

➡**Drive gear installation position: The collar on the drive gear faces the transaxle.**

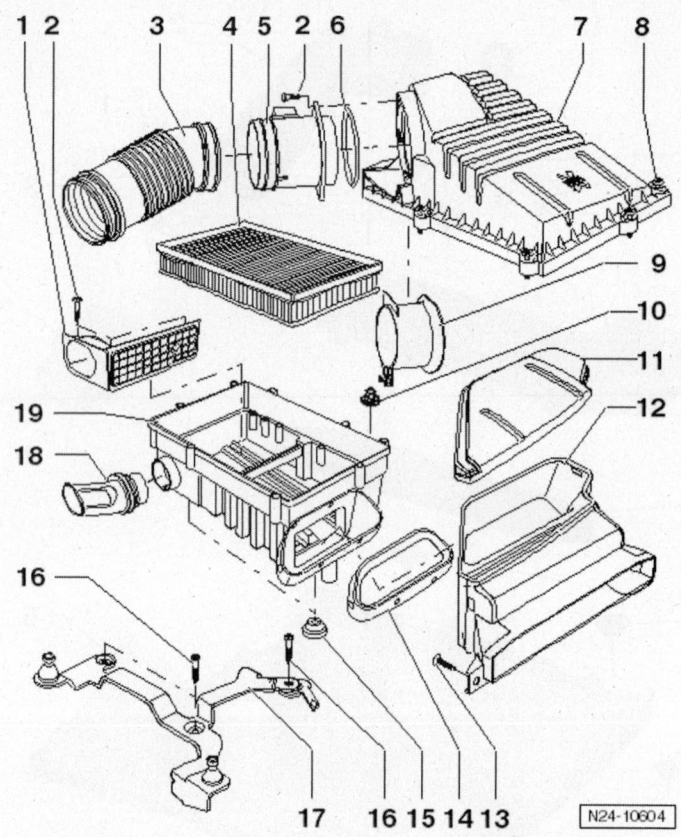

1. Regulator Flap
2. Bolt
3. Connecting Pipe
   (to the throttle valve control module)
4. Air Filter Element
5. Mass Airflow Sensor
6. Seal
7. Upper Air Filter Housing
8. Bolt
9. Connection (clipped into the
   upper air filter housing)
10. Nut
11. Intake Air Duct Cover
12. Intake Air Duct
    (attached to the lock carrier)
13. Bolt
14. Gasket
15. Rubber Bushing
16. Bolt (10 Nm)
17. Bracket
    (for the air filter housing)
18. Connection
    (not installed on all vehicles)
19. Lower Air Filter Housing

N24-10604

Fig. 73 Exploded view of the air intake and air cleaner assembly—3.6L engine

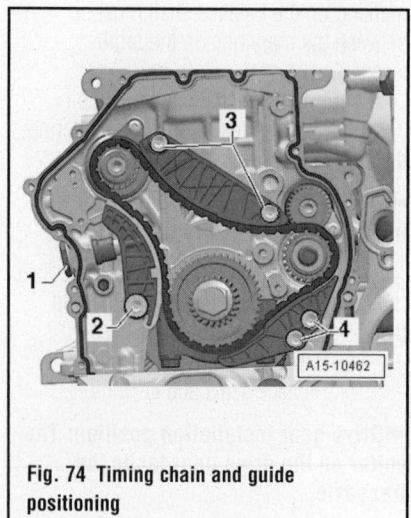

Fig. 74 Timing chain and guide positioning

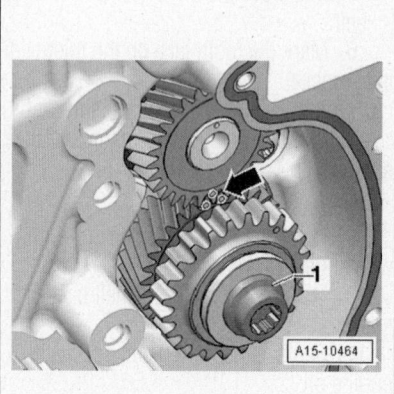

Fig. 75 Mark the tooth face on the intermediate sprocket (arrow)

19. Install the balance shaft timing chain.

   a. Turn the intermediate shaft sprocket/balance shaft to the marking.

   b. Mount the timing chain; the painted links of the timing chain must be positioned on the markings on the chain sprockets.

   c. Install the timing chain tensioning rail and tighten the bolt.

   d. Install the timing chain guide rail and tighten the bolts.

   e. Install the timing chain guide rail and tighten the bolts.

   f. Insert the timing chain tensioner with locking compound.

   g. Check this adjustment one more time.

Fig. 76 Install the intermediate sprocket; the marking on the balance shaft must be between the markings on the tooth faces (arrow)

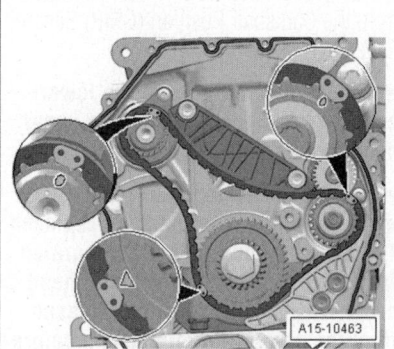

Fig. 77 Mount the timing chain; the painted links of the timing chain must be positioned on the markings on the chain sprockets

h. Check the markings on the intermediate shaft sprocket/balance shaft

20. The rest of the assembly is basically a reverse of the disassembling sequence.

CAMSHAFT AND VALVE LIFTERS

REMOVAL & INSTALLATION

2.0L Engine

See Figures 78 through 85.

1. Remove the engine cover.
2. Remove the vacuum pump.
3. Remove the noise insulation.
4. Remove the front part of the right wheel housing liner and/or the front right wheel housing liner.
5. Remove bolts.
6. Remove the air guide pipe by lifting the clamps items.
7. Disconnect the connector from the Camshaft Adjustment Valve.

Fig. 78 Rotate the vibration damper using the Counterhold Tool into the "OT" position

8. Remove the bolts and then the camshaft adjustment valve.
9. Remove the upper timing chain cover.

➡**The control valve has a left thread.**

10. Remove the control valve using Assembly Tool (T10352).
11. Remove the bolts and remove the bearing bracket.
12. Rotate the vibration damper using the Counterhold Tool (T10355) into the "OT" position.

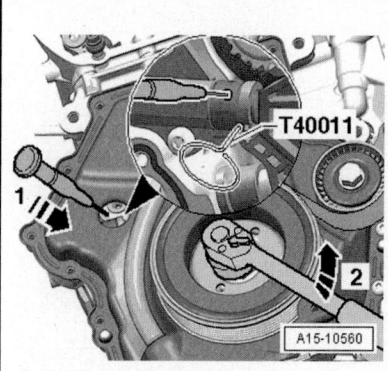

Fig. 80 Lift the chain tensioner locking wedge by inserting a scriber or a suitable screwdriver into the hole in the chain tensioner direction

➡**The notch on the vibration damper must line up with the marking on the timing chain lower cover.**

13. Mark the drive chain/chain sprockets with a waterproof marker. These marks are necessary for reinstallation.
14. Remove the plug.
15. Lift the chain tensioner locking wedge by inserting a scriber or a suitable screwdriver into the hole in the chain tensioner direction.

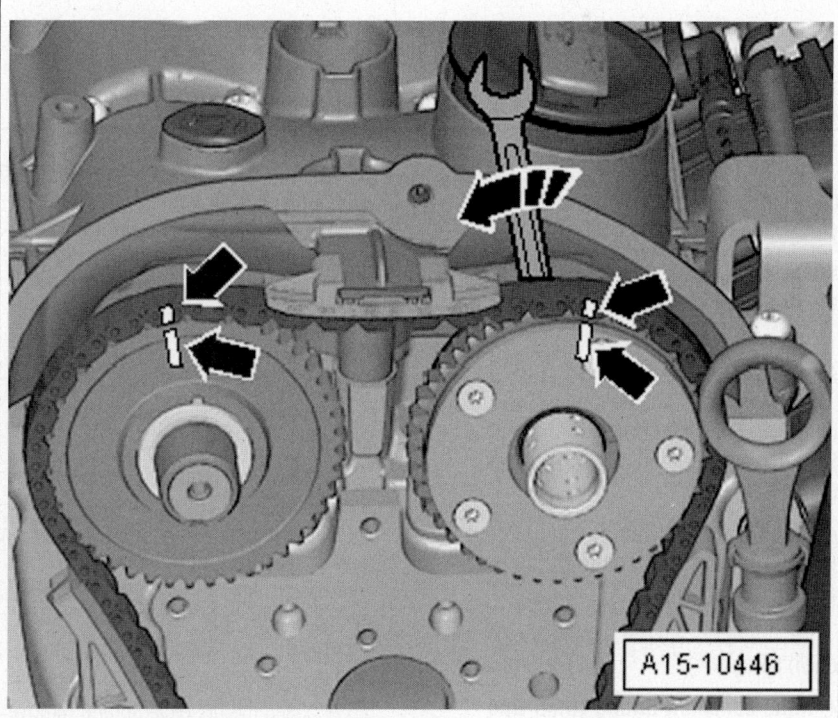

Fig. 79 Mark the drive chain/chain sprockets with a waterproof marker. These marks are necessary for reinstallation

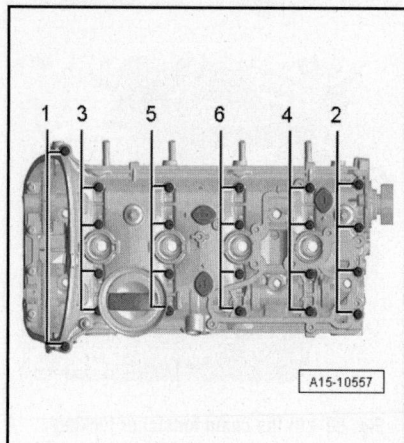

Fig. 81 Remove the cylinder head cover bolts in 1 to 6 sequence

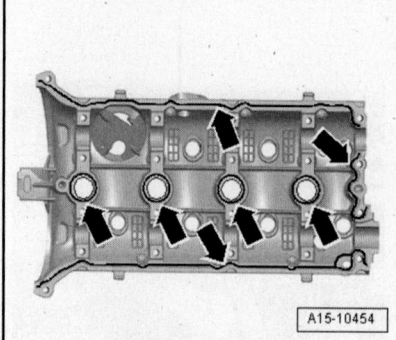

Fig. 83 Apply the silicone sealant D 154 103 A1 on the clean sealing surface of the cylinder head cover as shown. Thickness of sealant bead: 0.078–0.117 in. (2–3 mm)

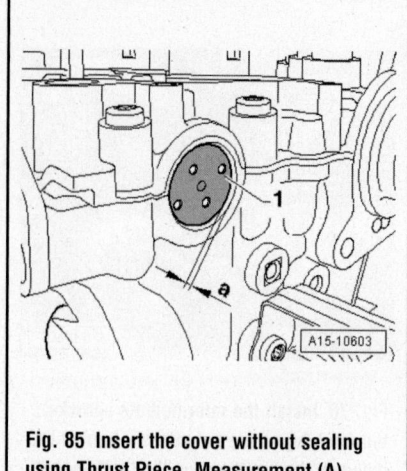

Fig. 85 Insert the cover without sealing using Thrust Piece. Measurement (A) should be 0.039–0.078 in. (1–2 mm)

Fig. 82 Remove the cylinder head cover bolts in 1 to 6 sequence

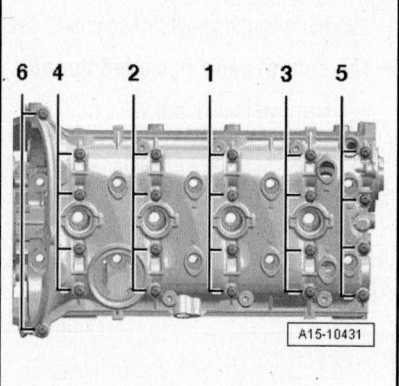

Fig. 84 Tighten bolts in several stages using the sequence shown

16. Turn the crankshaft opposite the engine direction of rotation direction and secure it with a Securing Pin (T40011).

➡**The intake camshaft switches in the engine direction of rotation.**

17. Remove the bolt and guide the tensioning rail downward.

18. Remove the upper guide rail by unlocking the latch (located in the center) with a screwdriver and pushing the guide rail forward.

➡**When the lower timing chain cover is installed, the loose chain on the crankshaft cannot jump off.**

19. Remove camshaft timing chain from chain sprockets.

➡**If the camshaft timing chain was removed from the cylinder head, then the crankshaft may not be turn further. On this engine, when the valves are mounted, there is the danger that there**

are panels attached to the lower timing chain cover, which could fall and interfere with the chain; also a loose chain turned by the crankshaft can bend the panels. The panels can bend if the crankshaft is rotated when the chain is loose.

20. Disconnect the electrical connectors on the ignition coils and free up the wiring harness.

21. Remove the ignition coils with the puller T40039.

22. Disconnect the crankcase ventilation hoses.

23. Remove the bolts and remove the crankcase ventilation.

24. Remove the bolts.

25. Remove the air guide pipe bolt.

26. Loosen the hose clamp and remove the air guide pipe together with the crankcase ventilation.

27. Disconnect the vacuum line and free up the wire.

28. Disconnect the electrical connector from the Camshaft Position (CMP) Sensor G40.

➡**The sealing surfaces of the lower cylinder head cover and on the upper cylinder head must not be reworked.**

➡**If the cylinder head cover was loosened, then the cover must be replaced. The camshaft bearings are integrated in the cylinder head or cylinder head cover. The tension must be released from the camshaft timing chain before removing the cylinder head cover.**

29. Remove the cylinder head cover bolts in sequence.

30. Remove the cylinder head cover.

31. Remove the camshafts.

32. Prevent dirt and adhesive residue from entering cylinder head.

To install:

➡**During installation, cable ties must be re-installed at the same location. Sealing surfaces must be completely free of oil and grease.**

➡**The pistons must not be positioned at TDC.**

33. Make sure that all roller cam followers make contact correctly on valve stem ends.

➡**The cover must be installed within 5 minutes after application of silicone sealant.**

34. Remove any sealant residue on the cylinder head using the flat blade scraper.

➡**Prevent dirt and adhesive residue from entering cylinder head.**

35. Remove any seal out of the groove in the cylinder head cover as well as from any

sealing surface using, for example, a rotating plastic brush.

36. Clean sealing surfaces, must be free of oil and grease.

37. Cut tube nozzle at front marking approximately 0.078 in. (2 mm).

38. Lubricate the running surfaces of both camshafts.

39. Place the camshaft into the cylinder head; the recesses must be perpendicular to each other.

40. Replace the cylinder head cover bolts.

41. Apply the silicone sealant D 154 103 A1 on the clean sealing surface of the cylinder head cover as shown. Thickness of sealant bead: 0.078–0.117 in. (2–3 mm).

✳✳ CAUTION

The cylinder head cover must be installed within 5 minutes after application of silicone sealant. The sealant bead may not be thicker than specified, otherwise excess sealant could enter the oil pan and clog the oil intake tube.

42. Tighten bolts in several stages.
*   Replace bolts
*   Hand-tighten bolts in several stages in sequence
*   Tighten the bolts in sequence to 71 inch lbs. (8 Nm) using a torque wrench
*   Tighten the bolts an additional 90° using a rigid wrench, in sequence.

✳✳ CAUTION

Make sure the cylinder head cover is not tilted.

43. Insert the cover without sealing using Thrust Piece (T10174). Measurement should be 0.039–0.078 in. (1–2 mm).

✳✳ CAUTION

When turning the crankshaft, make sure the timing chain cannot damage any other components.

44. Rotate the vibration damper using the Counterhold Tool (T10355) into the "OT" position.

45. The notch on the vibration damper must line up with the marking on the timing chain lower cover.

46. The marked links of the timing chain must be positioned on the markings on the chain sprockets.

47. Mount the camshaft timing chain: The markings drive chain/chain sprockets must align.

48. Turn the intake camshaft and mount the timing chain.

49. The rest of the assembly is basically a reverse of the disassembling sequence.

2.0L TDI Engines

See Figures 86 through 95.

Service Precautions:

*   There is a risk of damaging valves and piston heads after working on valve train.
*   The motor must not be started for about 30 minutes after installing camshafts because the hydraulic equalization elements must seat themselves.
*   To ensure valves do not strike pistons when starting, carefully rotate the crankshaft at least 2 turns.

1. Remove the engine cover.
2. Remove the fuel filter housing.
3. Remove the toothed belt from the camshaft sprocket and high-pressure pump.
4. Remove the cylinder head cover.
5. Remove the camshaft sprocket bolts and remove the camshaft sprocket from the hub.
6. Counterhold the hub with the camshaft gear counter-holder (T10051) and loosen the hub bolt.
7. Remove the hub bolt approximately 2 turns.
8. Attach the puller (T10052) and align it with the hub openings.
9. Tighten the bolts.
10. Steadily fasten the puller to the hub until the hub is loosened from the taper of the camshaft.
11. Remove the hub from the camshaft.
12. Remove the vacuum pump.
13. Remove the bearing frame bolts in sequence.

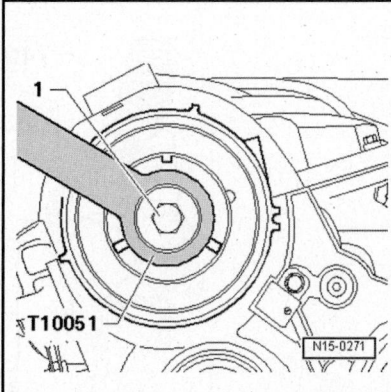

Fig. 86 Counterhold the hub with the camshaft gear counter-holder (T10051) and loosen the hub bolt (1).

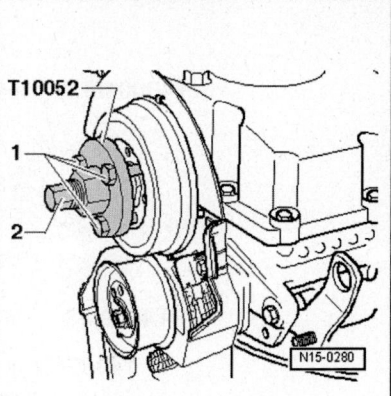

Fig. 87 Attach the puller (T10052) and align it with the hub openings. Tighten the bolts (1). Steadily fasten the puller (2) to the hub until the hub is loosened from the taper of the camshaft.

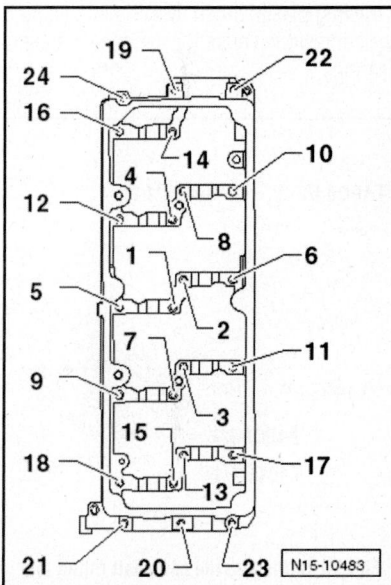

Fig. 88 Remove the bearing frame bolts, 24 through 1, in sequence.

14. Remove the bearing frame.
15. Carefully remove the camshaft.

To install:

➡ **At the appropriate step, seal the separating surfaces between the bearing frame and cylinder head with silicone adhesive sealant (D 176 501 A1).**

✳✳ CAUTION

The camshafts may only be installed using the camshaft fitting tool (T40094) as described. Otherwise the axial bearings inside the bearing frame will get permanently damaged and it will be necessary to replace the cylinder head.

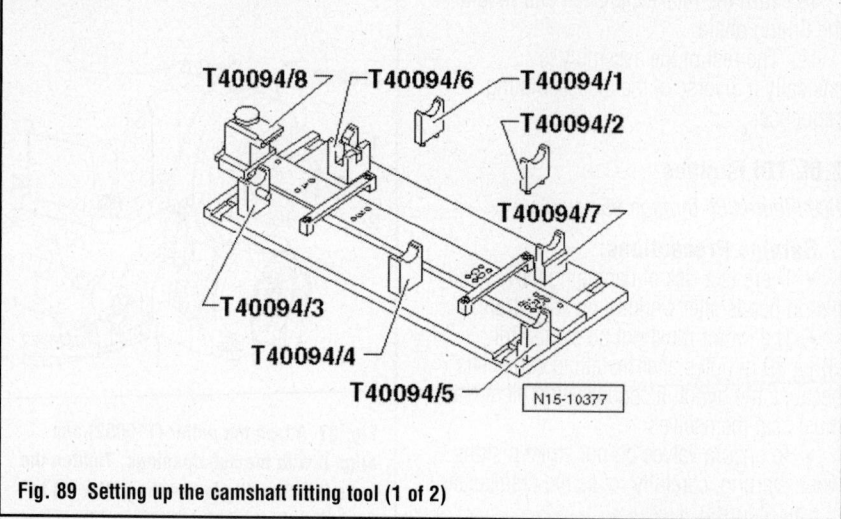

Fig. 89 Setting up the camshaft fitting tool (1 of 2)

16. Remove any sealant still on the cylinder head and on the bearing frame with a rotating plastic brush. Make sure that no sealant residue enters the cylinder head and bearings.

17. Clean the sealing surfaces.
18. The sealing surfaces must be free of oil and grease.
19. Oil the running surfaces of both camshafts.

20. Set up the camshaft fitting tool (T40094) for the camshaft as follows:

   a. Remove the mounts (T40094/3, T40094/4 and T40094/5) from the base plate. Loosen the lower bolts.

➡ **If the camshaft fitting tool (T40094) mounts are not marked, mark the removed mounts, for example, with numbers, to assure they can be assembled later.**

   b. Install the mounts (T40094/9 and T40094/10) in the empty outer locations.

   c. Install the mount (T40094/2) in position "A" and install the mount (T40094/1) in position "F".

21. Insert the intake camshaft. Make sure the indentation for the cylinder head bolt faces outward.

22. Position the 0.50 mm feeler gauge and slide the mount (T40094/8) into the groove on the intake camshaft.

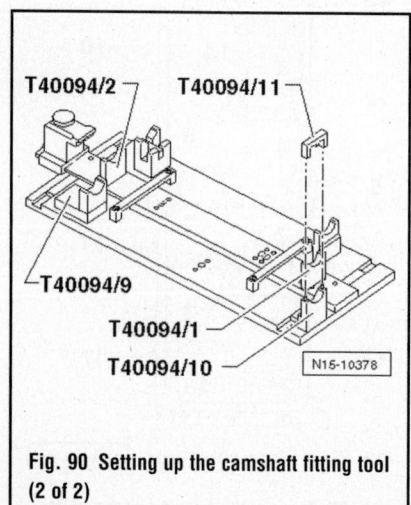

Fig. 90 Setting up the camshaft fitting tool (2 of 2)

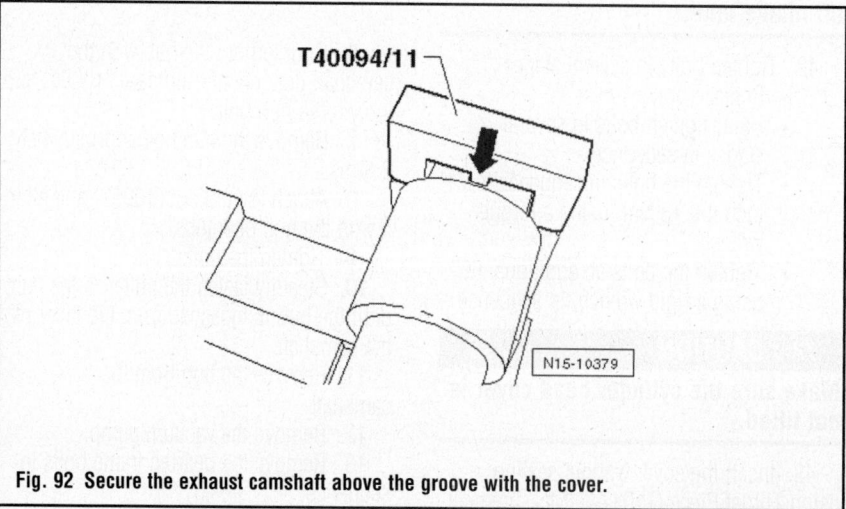

Fig. 92 Secure the exhaust camshaft above the groove with the cover.

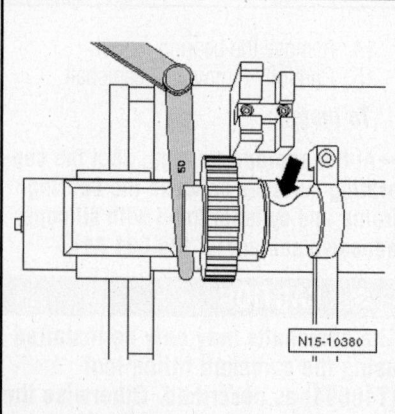

Fig. 91 Position the 0.50 mm feeler gauge and slide the mount into the groove on the intake camshaft.

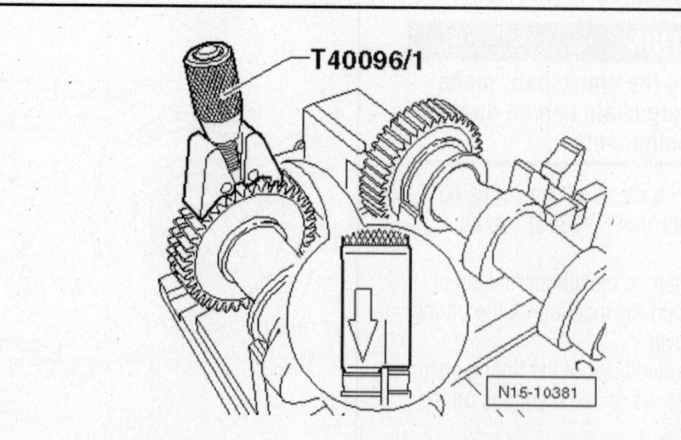

Fig. 93 Position the tensioning tool on the exhaust camshaft sprockets. Make sure the clamping jaw marked with an arrow is on the wider sprocket.

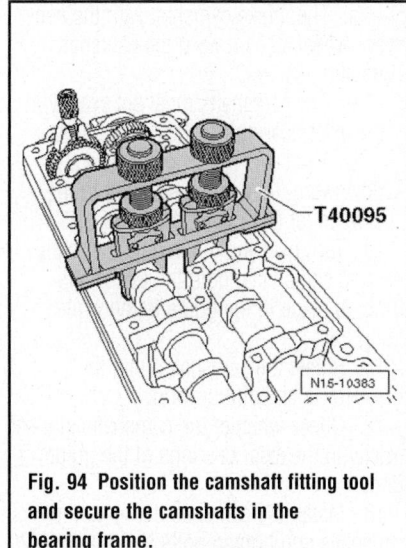

Fig. 94 Position the camshaft fitting tool and secure the camshafts in the bearing frame.

23. Secure the exhaust camshaft above the groove with the cover (T40094/11).

24. Position the tensioning tool (T40096/1) on the exhaust camshaft sprockets. Make sure the clamping jaw marked with an arrow is on the wider sprocket.

25. Tension the tensioning tool (T40096/1) with the thumb wheel until the tooth faces align. Use a 13 mm open end wrench if necessary.

26. Slide the intake camshaft toward the exhaust camshaft until the splines mesh.

27. Mount the bearing frame on the camshafts. All the camshaft bearings must align on the camshafts.

28. Position the camshaft fitting tool (T40095) and secure the camshafts in the bearing frame.

29. Remove the cover (T40094/11).

30. Remove the mount (T40094/8) from the intake camshaft groove.

31. Apply a bead of sealant (D 176 501 A1), approximately 2 to 3 mm, on the clean sealing surfaces of the cylinder head.

✳✳ CAUTION

The excess sealant could get on the camshaft bearings or seal off the oil supply holes.

➡**Do not apply the sealant bead thicker than indicated. Make sure that the excess sealant does not seal off the oil supply holes for the bearing frame.**

32. Remove the camshafts with the bearing frame and the camshaft fitting tool (T40095) from the camshaft fitting tool (T40094).

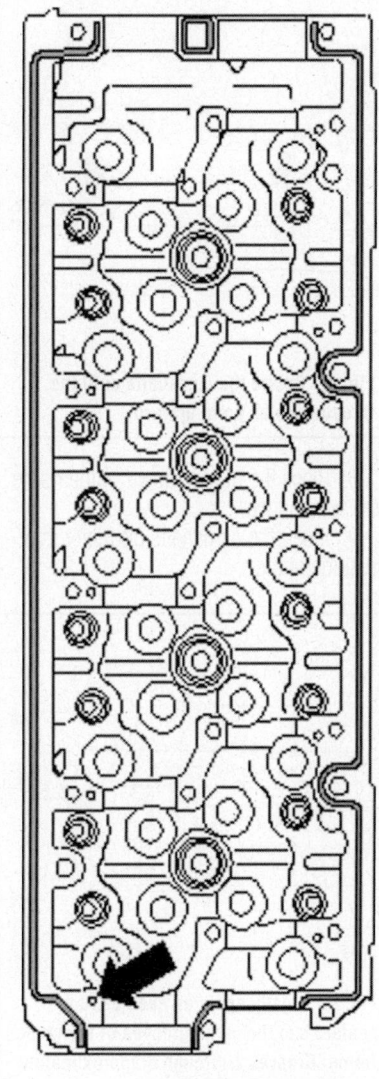

N15-10597

Fig. 95 Apply a bead of sealant, approximately 2 to 3 mm, on the clean sealing surfaces of the cylinder head as illustrated.

33. Carefully insert the camshafts and bearing frame in the cylinder head. Then, tighten the bearing frame bolts 1 through 24, by hand, in sequence.

➡**The guide frame must be touching the entire contact surface of the cylinder head.**

34. Tighten the bearing frame bolts to 7 ft. lbs. (10 Nm), following the same sequence as during removal.

35. Remove the camshaft fitting tool (T40095) and the tensioning tool (T40096/1).

36. Replace the camshaft seal. Install a new sealing cap onto the cylinder head with a suitable drift until it is flush.

37. Further installation is performed in the reverse order of removal, noting the following:

    a. There is considerable risk of damaging the valves and piston heads after working on valve train.

    • The engine must not be started for about 30 minutes after installing the camshafts because the hydraulic lash adjusters must seat themselves.

    • To ensure the valves do not strike the pistons when starting, carefully rotate the crankshaft at least 2 revolutions.

38. Place the hub on the camshaft. Tighten the hub bolt to 74 ft. lbs. (100 Nm). Use the camshaft gear counter-holder (T10051) to do so.

39. Push the camshaft sprocket onto the hub. The toothed segment of the camshaft sprocket must face upward.

40. Install the bolts into the camshaft sprocket by hand to eliminate play.

41. Secure the hub with the diesel injection pump locking pin (3359).

42. Install the toothed belt and adjust valve timing. Tighten the toothed belt sprocket bolt 15 ft. lbs. (20 Nm), plus an additional 45° (1/8 turn).

43. Install the vacuum pump.

44. Install the cylinder head cover.

45. Install the fuel filter housing.

2.5L Engine

See Figures 96 through 101.

Pre-Service Notes:

• The sealing surfaces on the bottom of the guide frame and the top of the cylinder head must not be reworked.

• Camshaft bearings are integrated in the cylinder head and the guide frame. Before removing the guide frame, the adjuster and sprocket on the camshafts must be removed.

• If the guide frame was loosened, the sealing plugs must be replaced.

1. Secure the camshafts with the clamping tool (T40070) and remove the adjuster and sprocket from the camshafts.

2. Then, remove the camshaft clamp.

3. Remove the guide frame bolts evenly working from the outside toward the inside and remove the CC guide frame.

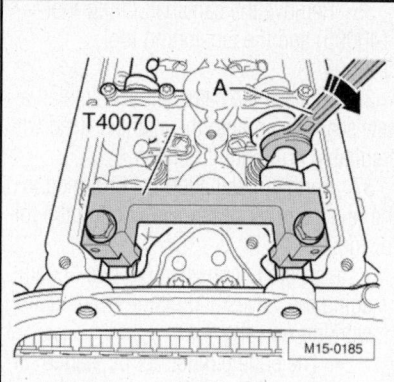

Fig. 96 Secure the camshafts with the clamping tool and remove the adjuster and sprocket from the camshafts.

4. Carefully remove the camshafts upward and place them on a clean surface.

To install:

5. Remove the remainder of the sealant from the guide frame (out of the grooves as well) and from the cylinder head using for example, a rotating plastic brush.

6. Clean the sealing surfaces, they must be free of oil and grease.

7. Oil the journal surfaces of the camshafts.

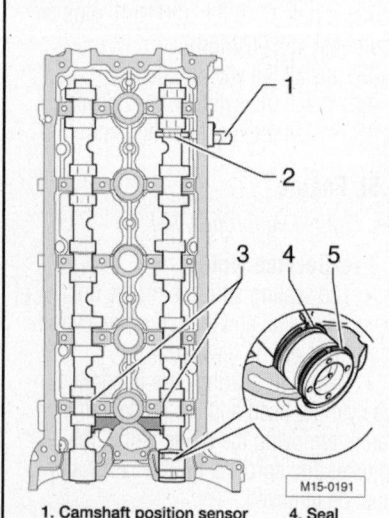

1. Camshaft position sensor
2. Sensor wheel
3. Axial bearings
4. Seal
5. Seal

Fig. 97 The intake camshaft with the sensor wheel faces toward the camshaft position sensor. The camshafts must set exactly in the axial bearings of the guide frame. The seals must point upward or downward, they must not point to the side under any circumstances.

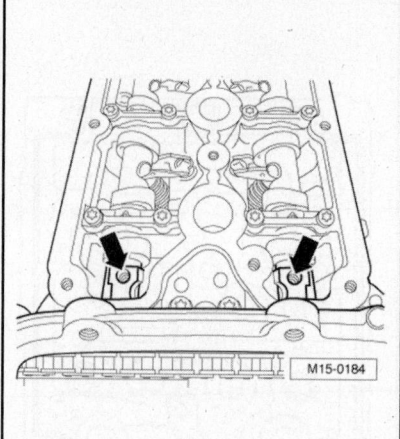

Fig. 98 Rotate the camshafts until the threaded holes point upward.

8. Place the upside down guide frame on a soft surface.

9. Insert the camshafts correctly into the guide frame.

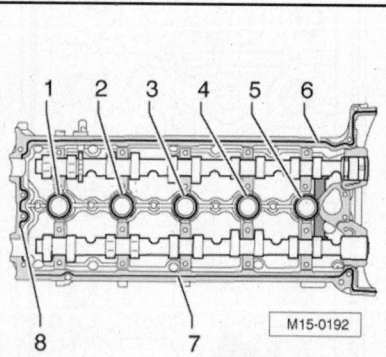

Fig. 99 Lightly apply an even bead of sealant into the clean grooves of the guide frame: Grooves 1 through 5 approximately 3.0 mm; Grooves 6 through 8 approximately 4.0 mm

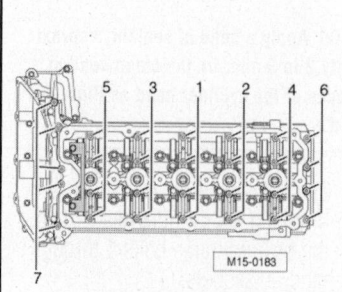

Fig. 100 Tighten the bolts 7 through 1 to 6 ft. lbs. (8 Nm) in sequence. After that, continue to tighten all the bolts, in the same sequence, an additional 90° (1/4) turn.

a. The intake camshaft with the sensor wheel faces toward the camshaft position sensor.

b. The camshafts must set exactly in the axial bearings of the guide frame.

c. The seals must point upward or downward, they must not point to the side under any circumstances.

10. Turn over the guide frame with the inserted camshafts, hold the camshafts firmly in place in the guide frame while doing this.

11. Rotate the camshafts until the threaded holes point upward.

12. Check whether the camshafts still set exactly in the axial bearings of the guide frame.

13. Install the camshaft clamp to the camshafts and tighten bolts to 15 ft. lbs. (20 Nm).

14. Turn over the guide frame again.

15. Lightly apply an even bead of sealant into the clean grooves of the guide frame:

a. Grooves 1 through 5 approximately 3.0 mm

b. Grooves 6 through 8 approximately 4.0 mm

➡**Sealant notes:**

• The sealant beads must be applied according to exact specifications; otherwise the excess sealant could get into the camshaft bearings.

• Installing and securing the guide frame should be performed without interruption because the sealant begins to harden immediately as soon as it contacts the sealing surfaces.

16. Install the guide frame onto the cylinder head immediately.

17. Gently tighten the bolts working from the inside toward the outside in several stages.

18. Then, tighten the bolts 7 through 1 to 6 ft. lbs. (8 Nm) in sequence.

19. After that, continue to tighten all the bolts, in the same sequence, an additional 90° (1/4) turn.

➡**Sealant must squeeze outward slightly, even in the area of the chain compartment.**

20. Wipe off any sealant on the timing chain cover sealing surface.

21. Carefully press in the sealing plugs until they reach the end of the chamfer.

➡**If the sealing plug was pressed in too far, it must be pressed through and pressed in again up to the mark.**

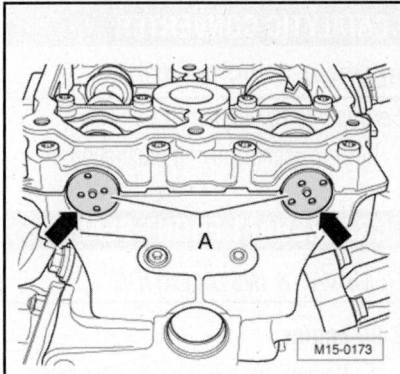

Fig. 101 If the sealing plug (A) was pressed in too far, it must be pressed through and pressed in again up to the mark.

22. The rest of the installation follows the reverse of the removal procedure.
    a. Remove the locking pin (T40069) from the rear of the cylinder block and install the plug and tighten to 20 ft. lbs. (30 Nm).
23. Fill the coolant.

3.6L Engine

See Figures 102 through 106.

> ☀ **CAUTION**
>
> **When doing any repair work, especially in the engine compartment, pay attention to the following due to clearance issues. Route lines of all types (e.g. for fuel, hydraulic, EVAP canister system, coolant and refrigerant, brake fluid, vacuum) and electrical wiring so that the original path is followed. Ensure sufficient clearance to all moving or hot components.**

1. Remove air filter housing.
2. Remove upper section of intake manifold.
3. Remove cylinder head cover.
4. Before disconnecting harness connectors, mark allocation to component.
5. Disconnect the following connectors:
    • Camshaft Position (CMP) sensor
    • Camshaft Adjustment Valve
    • Camshaft position (CMP) sensor
    • Camshaft Adjustment Valve (exhaust)
6. Free up the wiring harness.
7. Remove vacuum pump.
8. Remove top and bottom coolant pipes on cover piece.
9. Now remove cover piece on cylinder head.

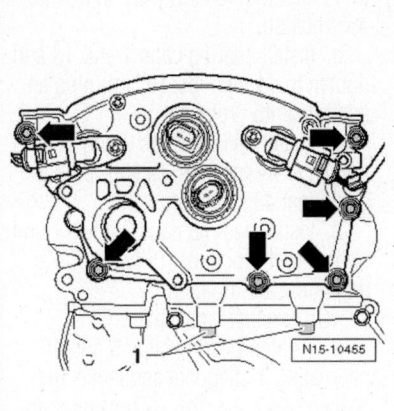

Fig. 102 Cover piece attaching bolts (arrows)

> ☀ **CAUTION**
>
> **Carefully cover lower chain compartment so no parts can fall in.**

10. Turn crankshaft in the engine direction of rotation to TDC No. 1 Cylinder mark. Use counter-holder (T10069).
11. It must be possible to insert camshaft bar (T10068) into both shaft grooves.
12. Also secure position of drive pinion for high-pressure pump using adjustment tool (T10363). Marking on high-pressure drive cams must be at top.
13. If vacuum pump drive pins are not vertical: Remove camshaft bar. Turn crankshaft in rotation direction until pins are vertical and camshaft bar can be inserted.
14. Remove chain tensioner for camshaft timing chain.
15. Only counter-hold at camshaft using 27 mm wrench. Camshaft bar must not be

Fig. 103 Turn crankshaft in the engine direction of rotation to TDC No. 1 Cylinder mark

inserted when tightening or loosening camshaft adjuster.
16. Loosen mounting bolts of camshaft adjusters.
17. Remove both camshaft adjusters.
18. Remove control housing with four mounting bolts from cylinder head and pull it down from camshafts in direction of rotation.
19. Lay timing chain to the side.
20. On Intake camshaft:
    a. First remove bearing caps 1 and 13.
    b. Remove bearing caps 3 and 11.
    c. Remove bearing cap 7.
    d. Loosen and remove bearing caps 5 and 9 in alternation and in diagonal sequence.
21. On Exhaust camshaft:
    a. First remove bearing caps 2 and 14.
    b. Remove bearing caps 4 and 12.
    c. Remove bearing cap 8.
    d. Loosen bearing caps 6 and 10 in alternation and in diagonal sequence.
22. Carefully remove camshafts and place on a clean surface.
23. Remove roller rocker lever together with support elements and place on a clean surface.
24. Ensure that the roller rocker levers and the support elements are not interchanged.

To install:

25. When installing the camshafts, the cam lobes for cylinder 1 must point upward.
26. Coat contact surface of bearing caps lightly with grease (G 052 723 A2) before installing.

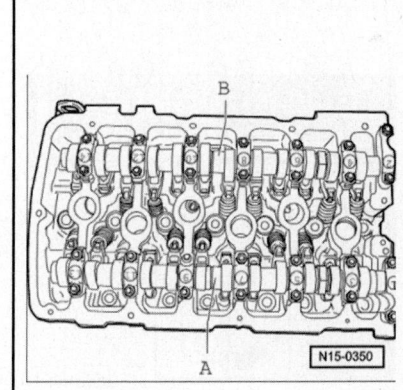

Fig. 104 Intake (A) and Exhaust (B) camshaft positions

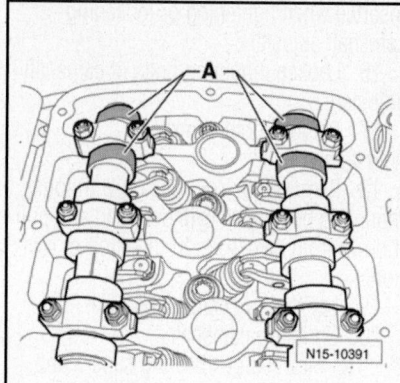

Fig. 105 When installing the camshafts, the cam lobes for cylinder 1 (A) must point upward

27. Insert support element in cylinder head and install roller rocker lever onto respective valve stem end and support element.

28. Make sure that all roller cam followers properly contact valve shaft tips and are clipped into the respective support elements.

29. Oil running surfaces of both camshafts.

30. Place respective camshaft carefully in camshaft bearings of cylinder head. While doing so, observe identification of camshafts.

31. Observe installed position of bearing caps. Points of intake and exhaust camshaft bearing caps face outwards.

32. On Intake camshaft:

   a. Tighten bearing caps 5 and 9 alternating in diagonal sequence and tighten

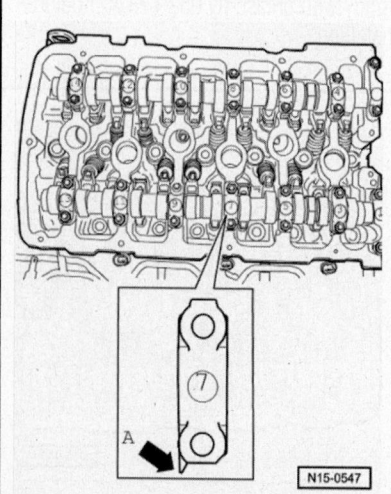

Fig. 106 Observe installed position of bearing caps. Points of intake and exhaust camshaft bearing caps (A) face outwards.

to 44 inch lbs. (5 Nm) plus an additional 45° rotation.

   b. Install bearing caps 1 and 13 and tighten to 44 inch lbs. (5 Nm) plus an additional 45° rotation

   c. Install bearing caps 7 and 13 and tighten to 44 inch lbs. (5 Nm) plus an additional 45° rotation

   d. Install bearing caps 3 and 11 and tighten to 44 inch lbs. (5 Nm) plus an additional 45° rotation

33. On Exhaust camshaft:

   a. Tighten bearing caps 6 and 10 alternating in diagonal sequence and tighten to 44 inch lbs. (5 Nm) plus an additional 45° rotation.

   b. Install bearing caps 2 and 14 and tighten to 44 inch lbs. (5 Nm) plus an additional 45° rotation

   c. Install bearing caps 8 and 13 and tighten to 44 inch lbs. (5 Nm) plus an additional 45° rotation

   d. Install bearing caps 4 and 12 and tighten to 44 inch lbs. (5 Nm) plus an additional 45° rotation

34. Insert the camshaft bar into both shaft grooves.

35. Before installing, check control housing strainer for contamination.

36. Before installing control housing, oil sealing rings for camshafts.

37. Oil contact surface of sealing rings in control housing and then slide control housing slowly over sealing rings for camshafts.

38. Install the control housing and mount the bolts using locking adhesive (D 000 600 A2). Tighten to 71 inch lbs. (8 Nm).

39. Install camshaft adjustor with timing chain for camshaft drive.

40. Clean sealing surface on cover piece as well as on cylinder head.

41. Coat sealing surface of cover piece with sealant (D 176 501 A1) and install immediately.

➡**Sealant hardens quickly.**

42. Tighten bolts/nuts to specification as follows:

   • First install all mounting bolts and tighten lightly
   • Then tighten mounting bolts to 71 inch lbs. (8 Nm)
   • Install the chain tensioner for the camshaft timing chain and tighten to 30 ft. lbs. (40 Nm)

43. Install the vacuum pump.

44. Install cylinder head cover.

45. Install intake manifold upper) section.

CATALYTIC CONVERTER

REMOVAL & INSTALLATION

See Figures 107 through 110.

Refer to accompanying illustrations.

CRANKSHAFT FRONT SEAL

REMOVAL & INSTALLATION

2.0L Engine

1. Remove the vibration damper and mount the Thrust Piece (T10368).
2. Pry out the sealing ring.

To install:

3. Clean running and sealing surface.
4. Disconnect the thrust piece.
5. Pull the sealing ring using the thrust piece and the vibration damper bolt in all the way.

➡**Replace the vibration damper bolt and O-ring.**

6. The rest of the assembly is basically a reverse of the disassembling sequence.

2.0L TDI Engine

See Figures 111 through 114.

1. Remove the toothed belt.
2. Remove the crankshaft toothed belt gear. Use the counter support (3415) to keep the toothed belt gear from moving.
3. To guide the seal remover (3203), thread the center bolt into the crankshaft by hand until it stops.
4. Unscrew the inner portion of the seal puller 2 rotations (approximately 3 mm) from the outer portion and secure with the knurled thumb screw.
5. Lubricate the seal remover threaded head.
6. Install the seal puller as far as possible into the seal.
7. Loosen the knurled thumb screw and turn the inner portion against the crankshaft until the seal is pulled out.

To install:

➡**The sealing lip of the seal may not be additionally oiled or greased.**

8. Remove any oil residue on the crankshaft journal using a clean cloth.
9. Position the guide sleeve (T10053/1) on the crankshaft.
10. Slide the seal over the guide sleeve onto the crankshaft.
11. Press the seal in all the way using the thrust sleeve (T10053) and the center bolt.

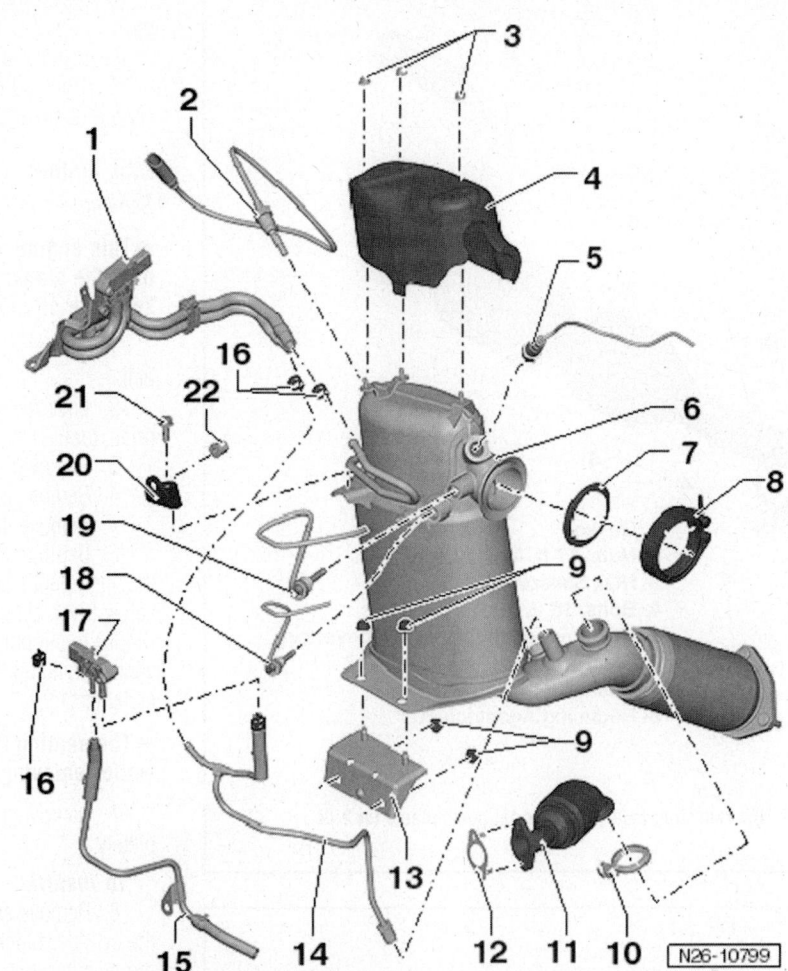

1. Differential Pressure Sensor
2. Exhaust Gas Temperature Sensor 4, 33 ft. lbs. (45 Nm)
3. Nut, 7 ft. lbs. (9 Nm)
4. Shield
5. Heated Oxygen Sensor, 37 ft. lbs. (50 Nm)
6. Front Exhaust Pipe with Particulate Filter
7. Gasket
8. Clamp
9. Nut, 18 ft. lbs. (25 Nm)
10. Clamp
11. Exhaust Gas Recirculation (EGR) Pipe
12. Gasket
13. Bracket
14. Control Line, 33 ft. lbs. (45 Nm)
15. Control Line
16. Clip
17. Exhaust Pressure Sensor 1
18. Exhaust Gas Temperature Sensor 3, 33 ft. lbs. (45 Nm)
19. Exhaust Gas Temperature Sensor 2, 33 ft. lbs. (45 Nm)
20. Bracket
21. Bolt, 17 ft. lbs. (23 Nm)
22. Nut, 17 ft. lbs. (23 Nm)

Fig. 107 Exploded view of the front exhaust pipe with particulate filter components for 2.0L TDI engine

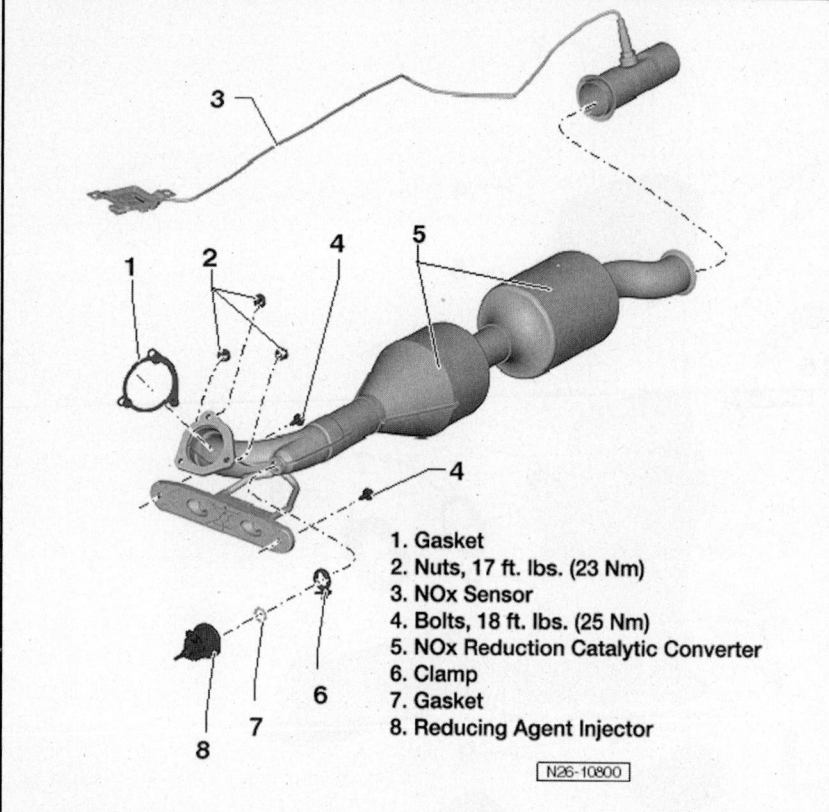

1. Gasket
2. Nuts, 17 ft. lbs. (23 Nm)
3. NOx Sensor
4. Bolts, 18 ft. lbs. (25 Nm)
5. NOx Reduction Catalytic Converter
6. Clamp
7. Gasket
8. Reducing Agent Injector

N26-10800

Fig. 108 Exploded view of the NOx reduction catalytic converter components for 2.0L TDI engine

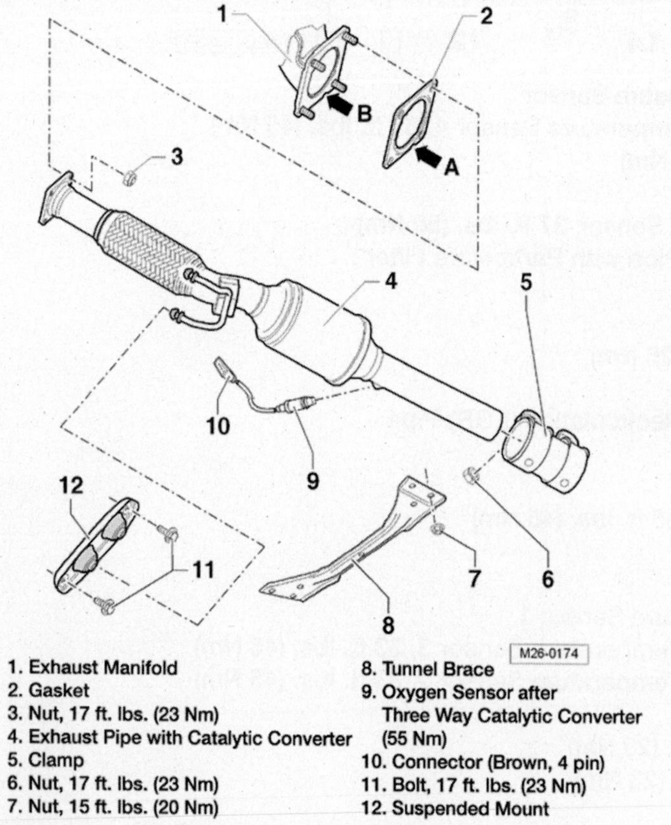

1. Exhaust Manifold
2. Gasket
3. Nut, 17 ft. lbs. (23 Nm)
4. Exhaust Pipe with Catalytic Converter
5. Clamp
6. Nut, 17 ft. lbs. (23 Nm)
7. Nut, 15 ft. lbs. (20 Nm)
8. Tunnel Brace
9. Oxygen Sensor after
   Three Way Catalytic Converter
   (55 Nm)
10. Connector (Brown, 4 pin)
11. Bolt, 17 ft. lbs. (23 Nm)
12. Suspended Mount

M26-0174

Fig. 109 Exploded view of the exhaust system components for 2.5L engine

12. Install the crankshaft toothed belt gear.
13. Install the toothed belt.
14. Tighten the camshaft bolt to (120 Nm), plus an additional 90° (1/4) turn.

2.5L Engine

See Figures 115 through 119.

➡This engine uses a sealing flange over the crankshaft end, instead of a separate oil seal.

1. Remove the A/C compressor ribbed belt.
2. Lock the crankshaft with an appropriate tool.
3. Remove the vibration damper.
4. Remove the belt tensioner.
5. Remove the sealing flange bolts.
6. Begin prying off the sealing flange at the alignment sleeves, using a suitable screwdriver. Use the trim removal wedge (3409) to support the screwdriver. This prevents damaging the sealing surface on the cylinder block.

➡The sealing flange will be damaged while removing.

7. Remove the sealing flange completely.

To install:

8. Remove any sealant remaining on the cylinder block; for example, use a rotating plastic brush.
9. Clean the sealing surface on the cylinder block and on the crankshaft. There must be no oil or grease on them.
10. Widen the sealing lip on the new sealing flange using the oil seal guide sleeve (T03004). Make sure surface "A" is the outer side.
11. Remove the oil seal guide sleeve (T03004) after a short while and push it into the seal rotated 180°.

➡The oil seal guide sleeve must stand out approximately 3 mm on the inner side. The surface "B" is the inner side (sealing surface).

➡The sealing flange for the sealing flange must be installed within 5 minutes after application of the sealant.

12. Apply the sealant bead into the groove of the sealing flange about 2.5–3.0 mm wide, and to a height of about 1 mm above the sealing surface.
13. Install the sealing flange using the oil seal guide sleeve on the crankshaft journal and press it uniformly onto the cylinder block.

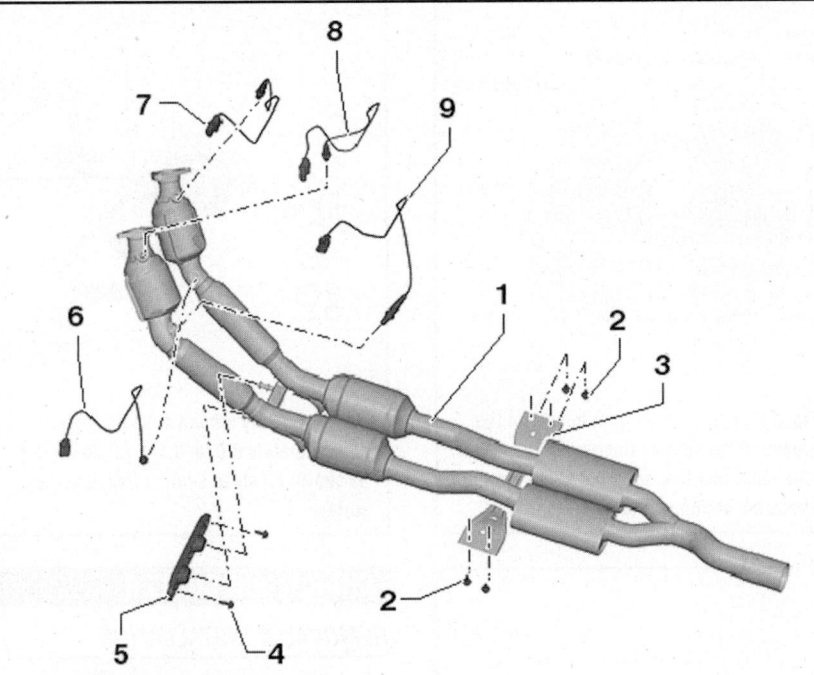

1. Exhaust Pipe with Converters
2. Bolt, 18 ft. lbs. (25 Nm)
3. Tunnel Brace
4. Bolt, 18 ft. lbs. (25 Nm)
5. Suspended Mount
6. Oxygen Sensor 1 After Catalytic Converter (Bank 1, Sensor 2), 37 ft. lbs. (50 Nm)
7. Heated Oxygen Sensor (Bank 1, Sensor 1), 37 ft. lbs. (50 Nm)
8. Heated Oxygen Sensor (Bank 2, Sensor 1), 37 ft. lbs. (50 Nm)
9. Oxygen Sensor 2 After Catalytic Converter (Bank 2, Sensor 2), 37 ft. lbs. (50 Nm)

Fig. 110 Exploded view of the exhaust system components for 3.6L engine

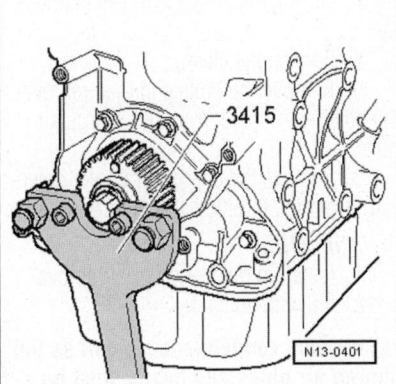

Fig. 111 Remove the crankshaft toothed belt gear. Use the counter support to keep the toothed belt gear from moving.

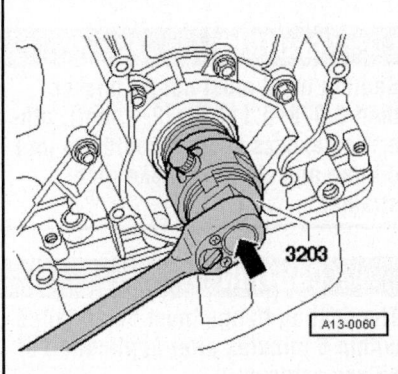

Fig. 112 To guide the seal remover, thread the center bolt into the crankshaft by hand until it stops.

14. Tighten the sealing flange bolts diagonally and evenly to 7 ft. lbs. (10 Nm).

15. The rest of the installation follows the reverse of the removal procedure.

16. Remove the locking pin (T40069) from the rear of the cylinder block and install the plug.

17. Tighten the new vibration damper to crankshaft bolt to 37 ft. lbs. (50 Nm), plus an additional 90° (1/4 turn).

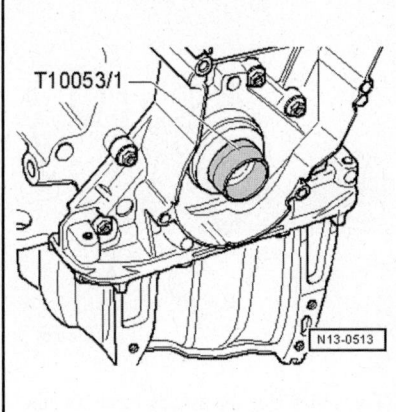

Fig. 113 Position the guide sleeve on the crankshaft.

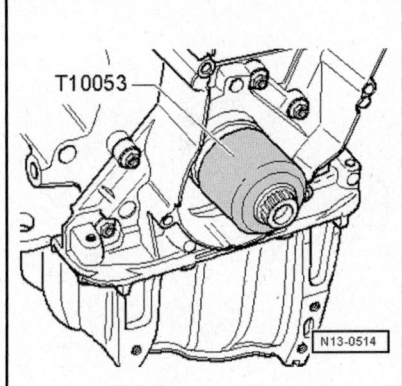

Fig. 114 Press the seal in all the way using the thrust sleeve and the center bolt.

18. Tighten the belt tensioner to accessory bracket to 22 ft. lbs. (35 Nm).

19. Tighten the plug to rear of cylinder block to 22 ft. lbs. (30 Nm).

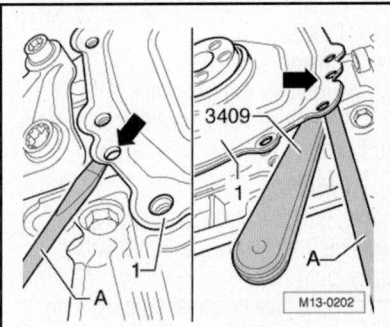

Fig. 115 Begin prying off the sealing flange (1) at the alignment sleeves, using a suitable screwdriver (A). Use the trim removal wedge to support the screwdriver. This prevents damaging the sealing surface on the cylinder block.

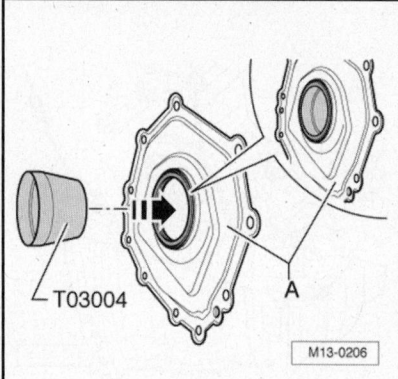

Fig. 116 Widen the sealing lip on the new sealing flange using the oil seal guide sleeve, as illustrated. Make sure surface "A" is the outer side.

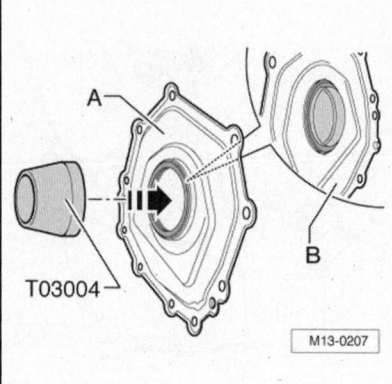

Fig. 117 Remove the oil seal guide sleeve after a short while and push it into the seal rotated 180°.

3.6L Engine

See Figure 120.

1. Remove ribbed belt.
2. Remove vibration damper. To do so, lock vibration damper using counter-holder tool (T10069).
3. Remove oil pan.
4. Remove sealing flange.
5. Remove sealant residue on sealing surfaces.

To install:

6. Before installing, remove oil remains from end of crankshaft with a clean cloth.
7. Cut tube nozzle at front marking approximately 0.117 in. (3 mm).
8. Apply a bead of sealant (D 176 501 A1) of approximately 0.078–0.117 in. (2–3 mm) on clean sealing flange sealing surface.
9. Cover sealing ring with a clean cloth before applying sealing bead.

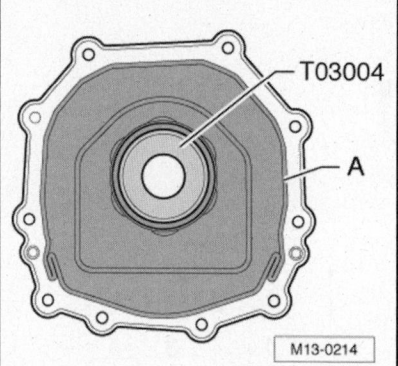

Fig. 118 Apply the sealant bead into the groove of the sealing flange about 2.5–3.0 mm wide, and to a height of about 1 mm above the sealing surface.

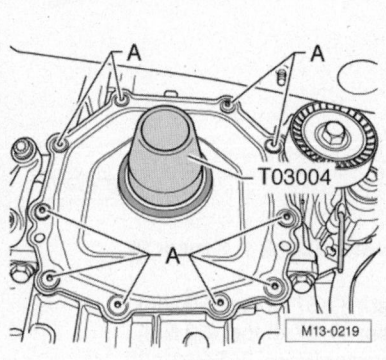

Fig. 119 Tighten the sealing flange bolts diagonally and evenly to 7 ft. lbs. (10 Nm).

✳✳ CAUTION

Sealant bead must not be thicker than 0.078–0.117 in. (2–3 mm), otherwise excess sealant could get into oil pan and clog oil intake pipe strainer.

✳✳ CAUTION

The sealing flange must be installed within 5 minutes after application of silicon sealant.

10. Insert guide sleeve (T10215/1) at front on to crankshaft pin.
11. Now slide sealing flange with sealing ring carefully over guide sleeve.
12. Tightly bolt sealing flange on cylinder crankshaft housing.
13. Install oil pan.
14. Install vibration damper.
15. Install ribbed belt.

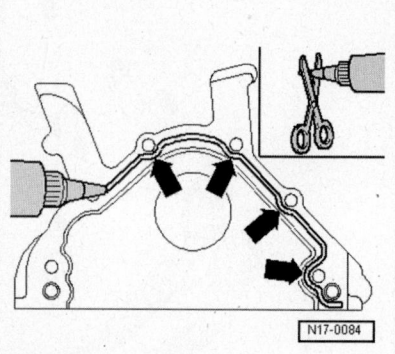

Fig. 120 Apply a bead of sealant of approximately 0.078–0.117 in. (2–3 mm) as shown on clean sealing flange sealing surface

CHARGE AIR COOLER

REMOVAL & INSTALLATION

2.0L TDI Engine

See Figure 121.

1. Remove the engine cover.
2. Remove the noise insulation.
3. Drain the coolant.
4. Remove the upper coolant hose from the radiator for the charged air coolant circuit by releasing the clip.
5. Remove coolant hoses from the charge air cooler by loosening the hose clamps.
6. Remove the bolt for the charge air cooler.
7. Disengage and disconnect connector.
8. Loosen the clamp.
9. Remove the bolts and then remove the charge air cooler from the charge air hose.
10. Remove the charge air cooler downward from the throttle valve control module.

To install:

11. Install in reverse order of removal.
12. Fill with coolant.

➤The hose connections as well as the charge air pipes and hoses must be free of oil and grease before installing.

CYLINDER HEAD

REMOVAL & INSTALLATION

2.0L Engine

See Figures 122 through 124.

1. Remove the engine cover.
2. Remove the air filter.
3. Loosen the hose clamp.

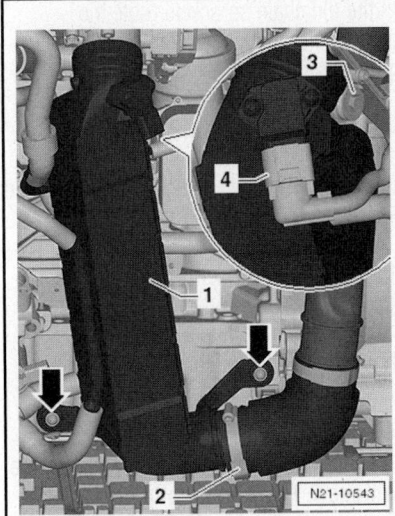

1. Charge air cooler 3. Bolt
2. Clamp   4. Connector

Fig. 121 Remove the charge air cooler downward from the throttle valve control module.

4. Remove bolt.

5. Disconnect the electrical connectors and free up the electrical wire.

✳✳ CAUTION

Reduce pressure by covering coolant reservoir cap with a cloth and carefully opening.

6. Open coolant reservoir cap.

7. Remove front exhaust pipe with catalytic converter

8. Remove the right front wheel.

9. Remove the noise insulation.

10. Remove the front right wheel housing liner.

11. Remove the air guide pipe items.

12. Drain coolant.

13. Remove the bolt and remove the air guide pipe downward.

14. Remove bolts.

15. Remove the air guide pipe by lifting the clamps.

16. Disconnect electrical connectors and free up electrical wire.

17. On vehicles with auxiliary heater remove the bolts and swivel the coolant tubs to the left.

18. On vehicles with all-wheel drive, remove the right axle shaft heat shield bolts using socket AF 8 3247.

19. Remove bolts and remove the turbocharger support.

20. Remove the banjo bolt and move the coolant line to the side.

21. On vehicles with front wheel drive, remove the bolts on the oil return line.

22. On vehicles with all-wheel drive, remove the oil return line bolts on the crankcase.

23. Remove the bolt on the oil supply line.

24. Disconnect the connector from the Camshaft Adjustment Valve (N205 1).

25. Disconnect the electrical connectors on the ignition coils and free up the wiring harness.

26. Remove the ignition coils with the puller (T40039).

27. Remove the air guide pipe bolt.

28. Remove the air guide pipe; to do this, loosen the hose clamp.

29. Disconnect the hose for the crankcase ventilation.

30. Remove the bolts and remove the crankcase ventilation.

31. Disconnect the hose for the crankcase ventilation.

32. Remove the bolts.

33. Remove the air guide pipe bolt.

34. Loosen the hose clamp and remove the air guide pipe together with the crankcase ventilation.

➡**Fuel supply line is under pressure! Wear protective goggles and protective clothing to prevent injuries and contact with skin. Before removing from hose connection wrap a cloth around the connection. Then release pressure by carefully pulling hose off connection.**

35. Disconnect the wires from the fuel transfer.

36. Disconnect the coolant line to the coolant reservoir.

37. Remove the coolant hoses from the coolant pipe.

38. Disconnect the ground wire (GND) and remove the bolt.

39. Disconnect the vacuum hoses.

40. Loosen the bolts and remove the heat shield together with the coolant pipe.

41. Disconnect the oil supply line from the turbocharger.

42. Remove the bolt 2 from the heat shield using a 6 mm hex multi-point socket. The hex socket must be at least 5 cm long. Socket that is 6 mm at the tip is too wide.

43. Disconnect the electrical connector from the Fuel Pressure Regulator Valve.

44. Loosen the coolant pipe; remove the bolts.

45. Disconnect the coolant hose from the side connection on the cylinder head.

46. Disconnect the electrical connectors.

47. Free up the electrical cable.

48. Disconnect the vacuum hose leading to the EVAP filter.

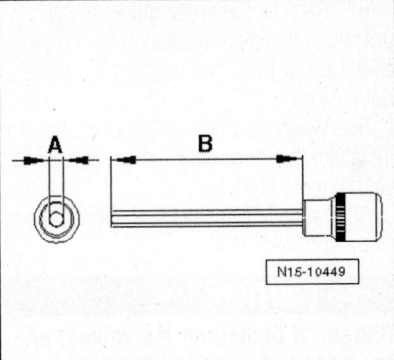

Fig. 122 Remove the bolt 2 from the heat shield using a 6 mm hex multi-point socket. The hex socket must be at least 5 cm long. Socket that is 6 mm at the tip is too wide

49. Disconnect the electrical connectors and pull the connectors out of the retainer.

50. Disconnect the electrical connectors.

51. Disconnect the coolant line from the intake manifold, when doing this, remove the bolts.

52. Remove the intake manifold bracket by removing the mounting nut.

53. Remove the oil filter.

54. Disconnect the coolant hoses and move them to the side.

55. Remove the bolts and remove Camshaft Adjustment Valve.

56. Remove timing chain upper cover.

➡**The control valve has a left thread.**

57. Remove the control valve using Assembly Tool (T10352).

58. Remove the bolts and remove the bearing bracket.

59. Rotate the vibration damper using the counter-hold tool (T10355) into the "OT" position.

60. The notch on the vibration damper must line up with the marking on the timing chain lower cover.

61. Carefully mark the drive chain/chain sprockets with a waterproof marker. These marks are necessary for reinstallation.

62. Remove the plug.

63. Lift the chain tensioner locking wedge by inserting a scriber or a suitable screwdriver into the hole in the chain tensioner direction.

64. In order to tension the chain tensioner, turn the crankshaft opposite the direction of the engine rotation direction and secure it using Securing Pin (T40011).

65. The intake camshaft switches in the engine direction of rotation.

66. Remove the bolt and guide the tensioning rail downward.

67. Remove the upper guide rail by unlocking the latch (located in the center) with a screwdriver and pushing the guide rail forward.

68. When the lower timing chain cover is installed, the loose chain on the crankshaft cannot jump off.

69. Remove camshaft timing chain from chain sprockets.

✳✳ CAUTION

Danger of damaging the valves, piston head and lower timing chain cover. If the camshaft timing chain was removed from the cylinder head, then the crankshaft may not be turn further. Panels are installed on the lower timing chain cover to prevent the chain from falling down. The panels can bend if the crankshaft is rotated when the chain is loose.

70. Turn the sealing plug counterclockwise 90° and remove it.

71. Remove the ball head.

72. Remove the oil filler cap.

73. Remove the bolts

74. Remove the cylinder head bolts in sequence using Polydrive bit and drive socket (T10070) until two are left.

75. To remove the cylinder head bolts, turn the camshaft with a wrench if necessary.

76. Make sure all wires and cables are disconnected!

77. Pay attention the tension and guide rails when lifting the cylinder head.

78. Install the Engine Support (T10014) each of the two small and large washers.

79. Connect the Engine Sling (2024) in the Engine Support and in the front left lifting eye on the cylinder head.

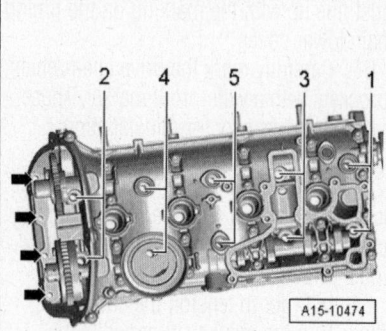

Fig. 123 Remove the cylinder head bolts in sequence 1 through 5 using Polydrive bit and drive socket until two are left

80. Mount the Engine Sling into the workshop crane and gently lift the cylinder head.

81. Remove the last two cylinder head bolts.

➡ **Carefully lift the cylinder head until the guide rail for the camshaft timing chain is free. The tensioner and guide rail must not be damaged.**

82. Lay the cylinder head on a soft surface, such as foam.

To install:

➡ **The sealing surfaces could be damaged. Carefully remove sealant residue from cylinder head and cylinder block. Make sure that no long scrapes or scratches result.**

✳✳ CAUTION

Risk of damaging cylinder block: There must be no oil or coolant in the blind holes for the cylinder head bolts in the cylinder block.

✳✳ CAUTION

Risk of cylinder head seal leaking: Carefully remove all grinding and sanding residue. Only unpack new cylinder head gasket immediately prior to installation. To prevent cylinder head seal silicone layer and recessed area from being damaged, always handle seal extremely carefully.

✳✳ CAUTION

Risk of damaging open valves: If a replacement cylinder is installed, only remove plastic base right before cylinder head is installed to protect open valves. Risk of damaging valves and piston heads after working on valve train: To ensure valves do not strike pistons when starting, carefully rotate engine at least 2 full revolutions.

83. Replace bolts which have been tightened to torque.

84. Replace sealing rings, seals and self-locking nuts.

85. Note different sealant for cylinder head sealing surfaces and bolts.

86. Secure all hose connections with hose clamps appropriate for the model.

87. When installing a replacement cylinder head, turn the camshaft to OT and mark the new chain sprockets exactly the same as

on the old chain sprockets (note the factory color marking on the chain sprockets).

88. If an exchange cylinder head is installed, all contact surfaces between bearing elements, roller rocker levers and cam running surfaces of camshafts must be oiled before installing cylinder head cover.

89. The engine oil and coolant must be changed if the cylinder head or cylinder head seal are replaced.

90. Hang the cylinder head on the workshop crane and position it above the cylinder block.

➡ **Carefully lower the cylinder head. The tension) and guide rail must not be damaged. Pay attention to centering pins in cylinder block. Observe cylinder head seal location, identification: Replacement part number must be visible from intake side.**

➡ **When turning the crankshaft, make sure the timing chain cannot damage any other components.**

91. In the event the crankshaft has been rotated in the meantime: Set piston of cylinder 1 to TDC and turn crankshaft back again slightly.

92. Set cylinder head in place.

93. Insert cylinder head bolts and tighten by hand.

94. In order to be able to turn the cylinder head bolts, the intake camshaft must be turned with a wrench.

95. There is no requirement to retighten the cylinder head bolts after repairs.

96. Tighten cylinder head bolts in sequence to the following specification:

- Tighten the cylinder head bolts in 1 to 5 sequence.
- Tighten to 30 ft. lbs. (40 Nm) using a torque wrench
- Tighten further 90° using a rigid wrench
- Tighten further 90° using a rigid wrench
- Pre-tighten the bolts (arrows) to 71 inch lbs. (8 Nm)
- Tighten the bolts (arrows) 90° further using a rigid wrench

➡ **When turning the crankshaft, make sure the timing chain cannot damage any other components.**

97. Rotate the vibration damper using the counter-hold tool into the "OT" position.

98. The notch on the vibration damper must line up with the marking on the timing chain lower cover.

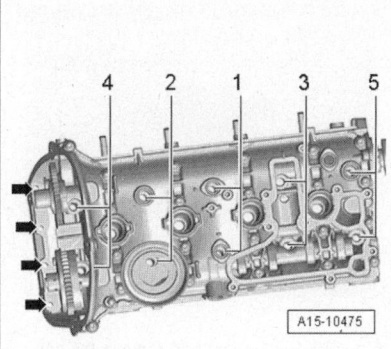

Fig. 124 Cylinder head bolt tightening sequence

99. The marked links of the timing chain must be positioned on the markings on the chain sprockets.

100. Mount the camshaft timing chain: The markings drive chain/chain sprockets must align.

101. Turn the intake camshaft using the wrench and mount the timing chain.

102. The rest of the installation is performed in reverse order of removal, noting the following:

103. During installation, cable ties must be re-installed at the same location.

104. Change the engine oil

105. Replace coolant.

2.0L TDI Engine

See Figures 125 through 149.

➡**Cylinder heads with cracks between the valve seats can continue to be used without reducing service life, as long as the tears have a width of maximum 0.5 mm.**

1. Remove the engine cover.
2. Remove the noise insulation. To perform this procedure, the ground cable must be disconnected from the battery. Check if a coded radio is installed. If so, obtain the anti)theft code beforehand.
3. Remove the battery and the battery tray.
4. Remove the air filter housing with the Mass Airflow (MAF) sensor and connecting pipe.
5. Drain the coolant.
6. Remove the charge air cooler.
7. Remove the cylinder head cover.
8. Remove the toothed belt.
9. Remove the camshaft sprocket and hub.

10. Remove the NOx reduction catalytic converter.
11. Remove the heated oxygen sensor and the oxygen sensor heater.
12. Remove the exhaust pressure sensor 1.
13. Remove the exhaust gas temperature sensors 2, 3 and 4.
14. Remove the EGR temperature sensor.
15. Disconnect the connector and remove it from the crankcase ventilation hose.
16. Free up the vacuum hose on the air guide pipe.
17. Remove the bolt and tilt the air guide pipe with the intake hose backward and remove it from the turbocharger.
18. Remove the pre-heater pipe from the bracket.
19. Remove the heat shield boot.
20. Remove the vacuum hose from the turbocharger vacuum diaphragm.
21. Release and disconnect the connector from the charge pressure actuator position sensor.
22. Remove the vacuum line from the brake booster.
23. Remove the vacuum line from the vacuum pump.
24. Remove the vacuum hose from the cylinder head cover.
25. Disconnect and remove the connector from the Wastegate bypass regulator valve.
26. Remove the nuts from the wastegate bypass regulator valve.
27. Set the vacuum line, vacuum hoses and wastegate bypass regulator valve aside.
28. Release and disconnect the connector and free up the wires.

29. If equipped with a Direct Shift Gearbox (DSG), remove the coolant hoses from the transmission fluid cooler.
30. Remove the bolt, and then unclip the wires and hoses using the pry lever from the air guide pipe. Remove the air guide pipe.
31. Remove the plug. Remove the engine lifting eye from the cylinder head.
32. Remove the pulsation damper.
33. Remove the bolts and then remove the connection on the cylinder head.
34. Mark and release the connectors from the cylinder head.
35. Release and disconnect the connector from the oil pressure switch.
36. Release and disconnect the connector from the Exhaust Gas Recirculation (EGR) cooler. Free up the wires near the cylinder head.
37. Loosen the clamp for the connection between the turbocharger and the particulate filter and remove it.
38. Remove the bolt on the upper particulate filter bracket.
39. Remove the nut and then remove the bracket on the upper cylinder head.
40. Remove the bolts holding the wiring around the turbocharger and free up the wires.
41. Release and disconnect the connectors on the EGR vacuum regulator solenoid valve and from the throttle valve control module.
42. Remove the upper bolt for the oil dipstick tube.
43. Remove the upper bolts from the side engine support.
44. Remove bolts and the connecting tube.
45. Release and disconnect the connector from the camshaft position sensor.

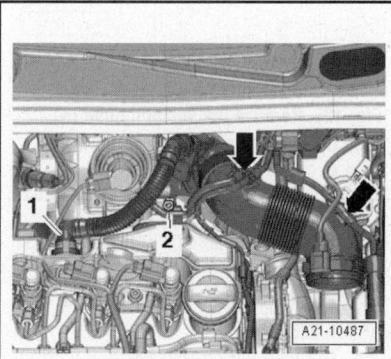

Fig. 125 Free up the vacuum hose (1) on the air guide pipe. Remove the bolt (2) and tilt the air guide pipe with the intake hose backward and remove it from the turbocharger.

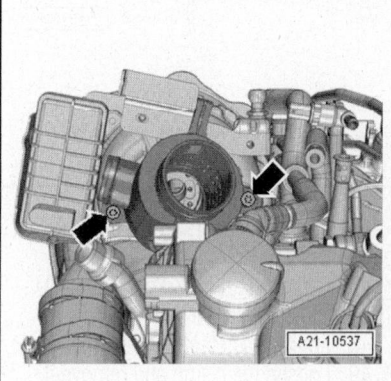

Fig. 126 Remove the pre-heater pipe (1) from the bracket.

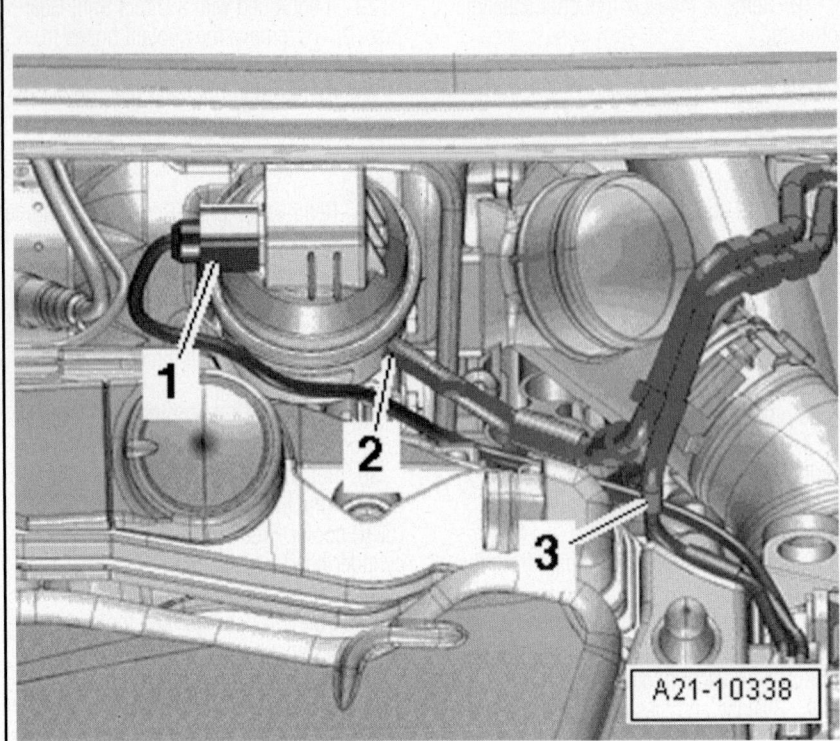

Fig. 127 Remove the heat shield boot from the connector. Remove the vacuum hose (2) from the turbocharger vacuum diaphragm. Release and disconnect the connector (1) from the charge pressure actuator position sensor.

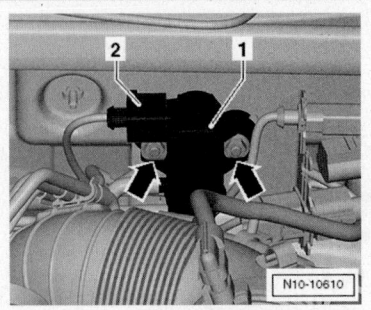

Fig. 130 Disconnect and remove the connector (2) from the Wastegate bypass regulator valve (1). Remove the nuts from the wastegate bypass regulator valve. Set the vacuum line, vacuum hoses and wastegate bypass regulator valve aside.

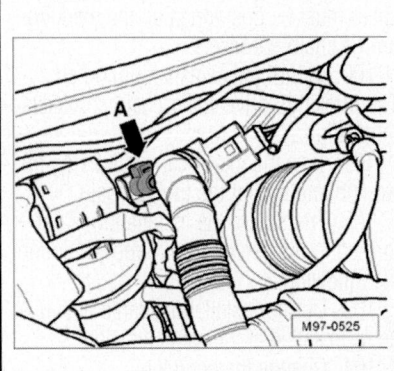

Fig. 131 Release and disconnect the connector (A) and free up the wires.

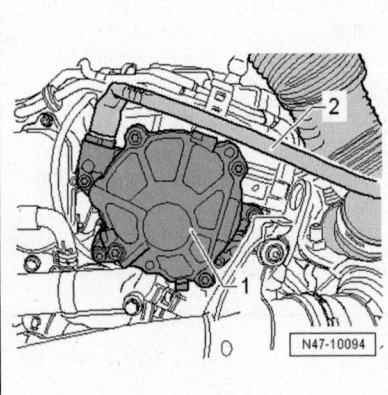

Fig. 128 Remove the vacuum line (2) from the vacuum pump (1).

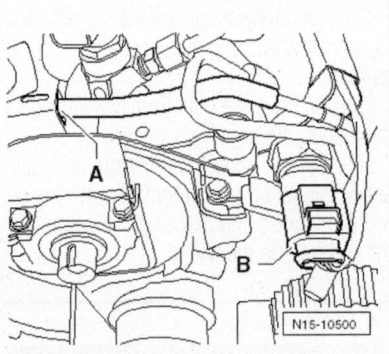

Fig. 129 Remove the vacuum hose (A) from the cylinder head cover (ignore item B).

bolt and then the toothed belt tensioning roller nut.

58. Remove the cylinder head bolts. Follow the sequence, 1 through 10, when loosening the cylinder head bolts.

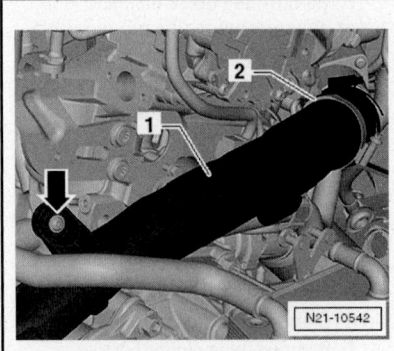

Fig. 132 Remove the bolt (2), and then unclip the wires and hoses using the pry lever from the air guide pipe (1). Remove the air guide pipe.

46. Unclip the connector on the coolant pipe.

47. Remove the right drive axle heat shield bolts and shield.

48. Loosen the clamp and remove it.

49. Loosen the clamp and remove it. Remove the bolts and remove the EGR pipe.

50. Loosen the nuts from the particulate filter bracket.

51. Remove the bolts and the nut.

52. Remove the sensor wire to the EGR pipe.

53. Remove the EGR pipe from the seal in the intake tube.

54. Remove the regular bolts and banjo bolts.

55. Loosen the fitting, then remove the oil supply line from the turbocharger.

56. Remove the oil line together with the turbocharger supports.

57. Remove the rear toothed belt guard

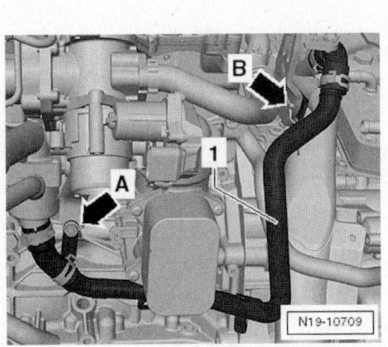

Fig. 133 Remove the plug (B). Remove the engine lifting eye from the cylinder head.

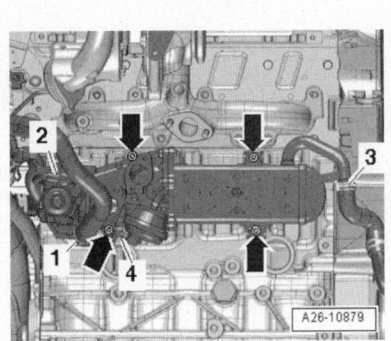

Fig. 136 Release and disconnect the connector (2) from the Exhaust Gas Recirculation (EGR) cooler. Free up the wires near the cylinder head (ignore 1, 3 and 4).

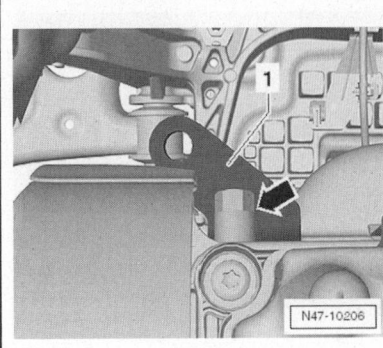

Fig. 138 Remove the nut and then remove the bracket (1) on the upper cylinder head.

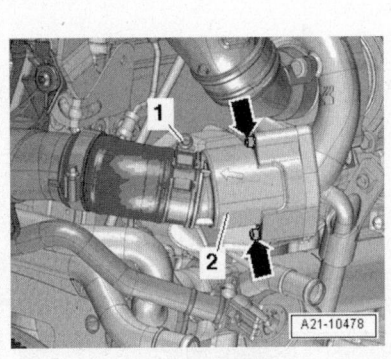

Fig. 134 Remove the pulsation damper (2; ignore item 1).

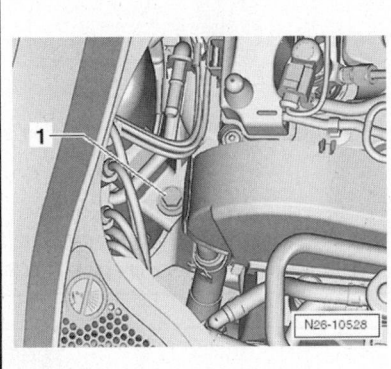

Fig. 137 Remove the bolt (1) on the upper particulate filter bracket.

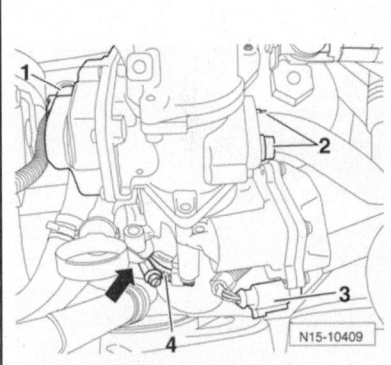

Fig. 139 Release and disconnect the connectors (1 and 3) on the EGR vacuum regulator solenoid valve and from the throttle valve control module.

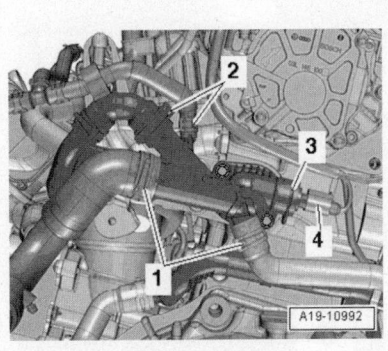

Fig. 135 Remove the bolts and then remove the connection (3) on the cylinder head. Mark and release the connectors (4) from the cylinder head (ignore 1 and 2).

Removal Notes:

• A second technician is needed when removing the cylinder head.
• The toothed belt tensioning roller is

pulled off the stud bolt when lifting the cylinder head out.
• Free up and remove the wires for the camshaft position sensor when removing the cylinder head.

59. First, lift the cylinder head on the transmission side and remove it from out of the toothed belt guard.

60. Be careful not to let the toothed belt tensioning roller fall.

61. Carefully lay the cylinder head down, on a piece of wood, if necessary.

To install:

Installation Notes:

• Always replace the cylinder head bolts.
• Carefully remove any sealant residue from the cylinder head and cylinder block. Make sure that no long scrapes or scratches result. When using sandpaper, the grit must not be below 100.
• Thoroughly remove all sanding and grinding residue.

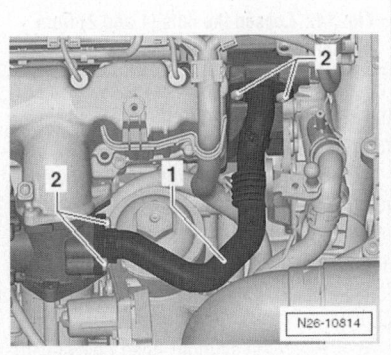

Fig. 140 Remove bolts (2) and the connecting tube (1)

• Only unpack the new cylinder head gasket immediately prior to installation.
• Handle the gasket carefully. Damage to

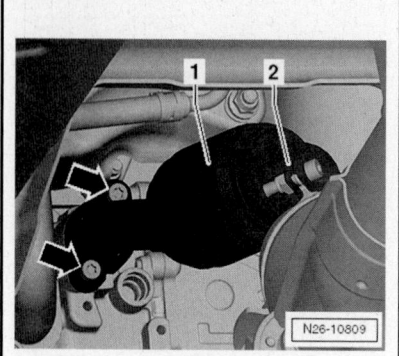

Fig. 141 Loosen the clamp (2) and remove it. Remove the bolts and remove the EGR pipe (1).

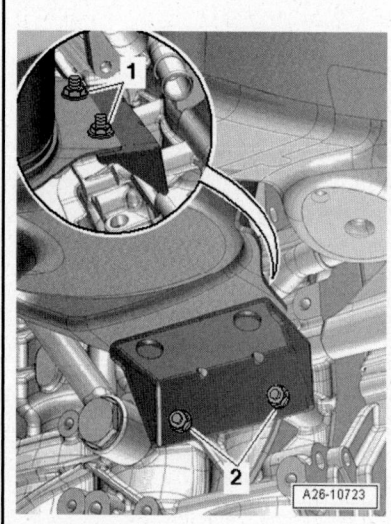

Fig. 142 Loosen the nuts (1 and 2) from the particulate filter bracket.

the silicone layer and in the areas of the recesses may result in leaks.

62. Before installing the cylinder head, remove the crankshaft stop (T10050) and rotate the crankshaft back opposite of the engine rotation direction until all of the pistons are nearly even under Top Dead Center (TDC).

63. Place the cylinder head gasket with the identification markings upward.

64. Slide the guide pins (3070) into the outer bores on the intake side.

➡**The tensioning roller must be placed on the stud bolt when positioning the cylinder head.**

65. Install the cylinder head, insert the eight cylinder head bolts and tighten them by hand, in sequence.

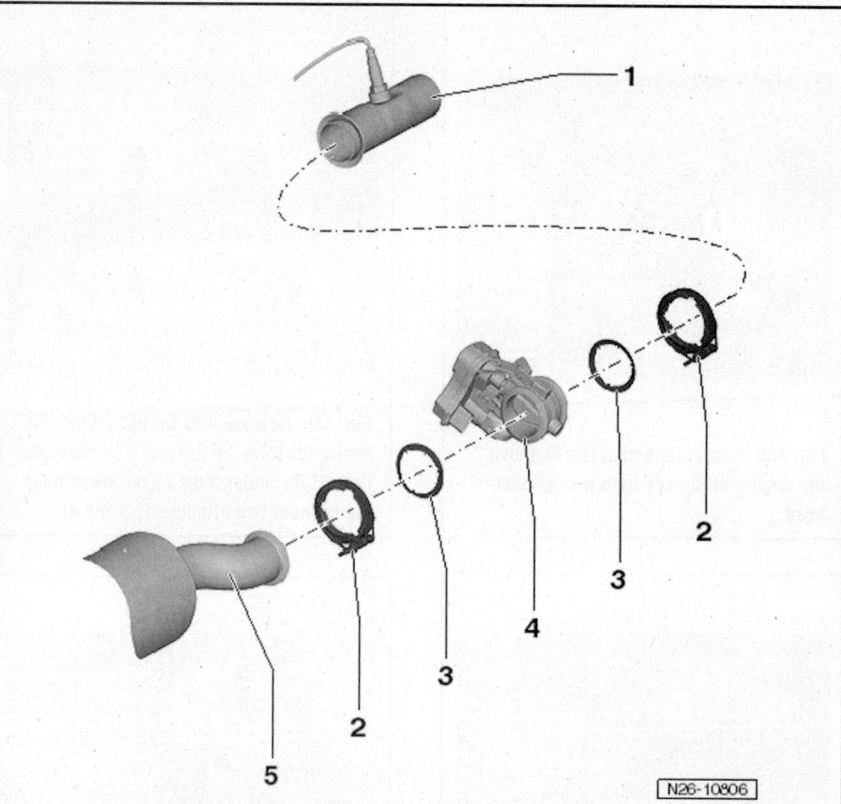

Fig. 143 Remove the bolts (A) and the nut (B). Remove the sensor wire (1) to the EGR pipe. Remove the EGR pipe from the seal (2) in the intake tube (3).

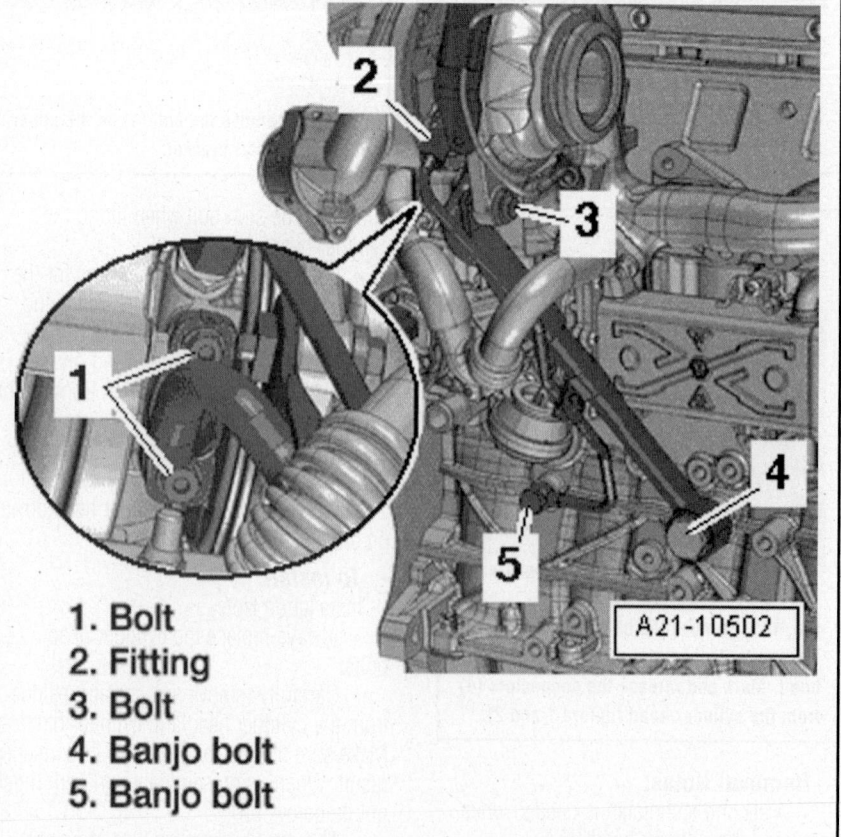

1. Bolt
2. Fitting
3. Bolt
4. Banjo bolt
5. Banjo bolt

Fig. 144 Remove the regular bolts (1 and 3) and banjo bolts (4 and 5).

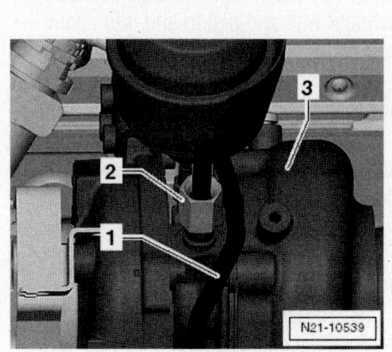

Fig. 145 Loosen the fitting (2), then remove the oil supply line (1) from the turbocharger (3).

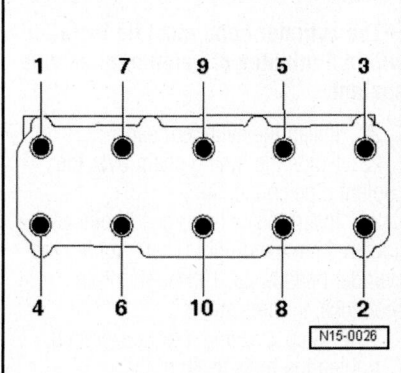

N15-0026

Fig. 146 Remove the cylinder head bolts. Follow the sequence, 1 through 10, when loosening the cylinder head bolts.

66. Remove the guide pins using the guide pin handle.

67. Install the 2 remaining cylinder head bolts hand tight in the outer opening on the intake side.

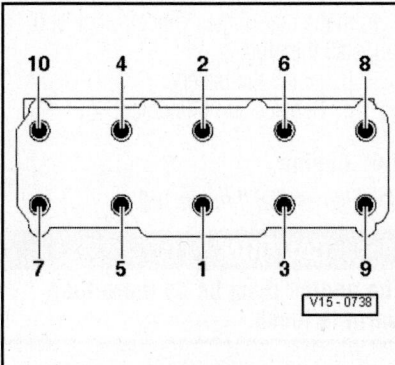

V15-0738

Fig. 147 Install the cylinder head, insert the eight cylinder head bolts and tighten them by hand, in sequence.

68. Tighten the cylinder head bolts in the sequence 1 through 10, in steps as follows:

a. Step 1: Tighten the bolts using a torque wrench, first time to 20 ft. lbs. (30 Nm)

b. Step 2: Tighten the bolts using a torque wrench a second pass to 37 ft. lbs. (50 Nm).

c. Step 3: Tighten the bolts using a ratchet, tightening each bolt, in sequence an additional 90° (1/4 turn).

d. Step 4: Repeat this process, tightening each bolt with a ratchet another 90° (1/4 turn).

69. Attach the rear toothed belt guard to the cylinder head.

70. Install the camshaft sprocket and the hub.

71. Lock the camshaft and the high-pressure pump using the diesel injection pump locking pin (3359).

72. Rotate the crankshaft in engine rotation direction to TDC and lock it with the crankshaft stop (T10050).

73. Install the toothed belt.

74. Replace the seals, self-locking nuts and the clamp for the particulate filter.

75. When installing the cable ties, try to bring them back to their original positions.

76. Make sure to follow the installation sequence when attaching the particulate filter:

a. Position the particulate filter on the turbocharger and then install the clamp so that is it still loose.

b. Loosely install the bolts and nuts 2 through 5 by hand. Ensure it is possible to slide the particulate filter and bracket back and forth.

c. Attach the EGR pipe, loosely secure the clamp.

d. Tighten the components as follows:

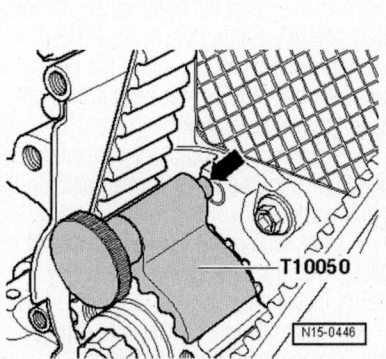

Fig. 148 Rotate the crankshaft in engine rotation direction to TDC and lock it with the crankshaft stop.

- Clamp (1) to 5 ft. lbs. (7 Nm)
- Nuts (5) to 17 ft. lbs. (23 Nm)
- Nuts (4) to 17 ft. lbs. (23 Nm)
- Nut (2) to 17 ft. lbs. (23 Nm)
- Bolts (3) to 17 ft. lbs. (23 Nm)
- Clamp (6) to 3 ft. lbs. (3.5 Nm)

77. Install the exhaust system free of stress.

78. Fill the coolant.

79. Perform a road test and then check all the Diagnostic Trouble code (DTC) memories.

2.5L Engine

See Figures 150 through 155.

➡**Note the following whenever working inside the engine compartment due to limited space:**

- Route all lines and wires in their original locations.
- Ensure sufficient clearance to all moving or hot components.

1. Drain the coolant.

2. Remove the engine cover with air filter.

3. Remove the connecting pipe between the throttle valve control module and air filter. To do so, disconnect the connecting pipe, if equipped with Secondary Air Injection (AIR) and the vent tube and reposition the spring clamp.

4. Remove the battery and the battery tray.

5. Remove the intake manifold. See "Intake Manifold" in this section.

6. Install the transport strap to the cylinder head again (following manifold removal) to hold the cylinder head when removing it.

7. Remove the timing chain cover.

8. Remove the cylinder head cover.

9. Secure the camshafts and remove the camshaft sprocket and adjuster.

10. Hold the timing chain and lay it under the coolant pipe connection.

11. Remove the four exhaust pipe with catalytic converter to exhaust manifold nuts and the exhaust system suspended mount bolts.

12. Remove the exhaust pipe with catalytic converter from the exhaust manifold and tie it to the side.

13. Disconnect the heated oxygen sensor connector at the plenum chamber bulkhead.

14. Remove the wire bracket from the AIR valve or cover (engines without AIR system).

15. Remove the cylinder head bolt, in sequence, 13 through 1.

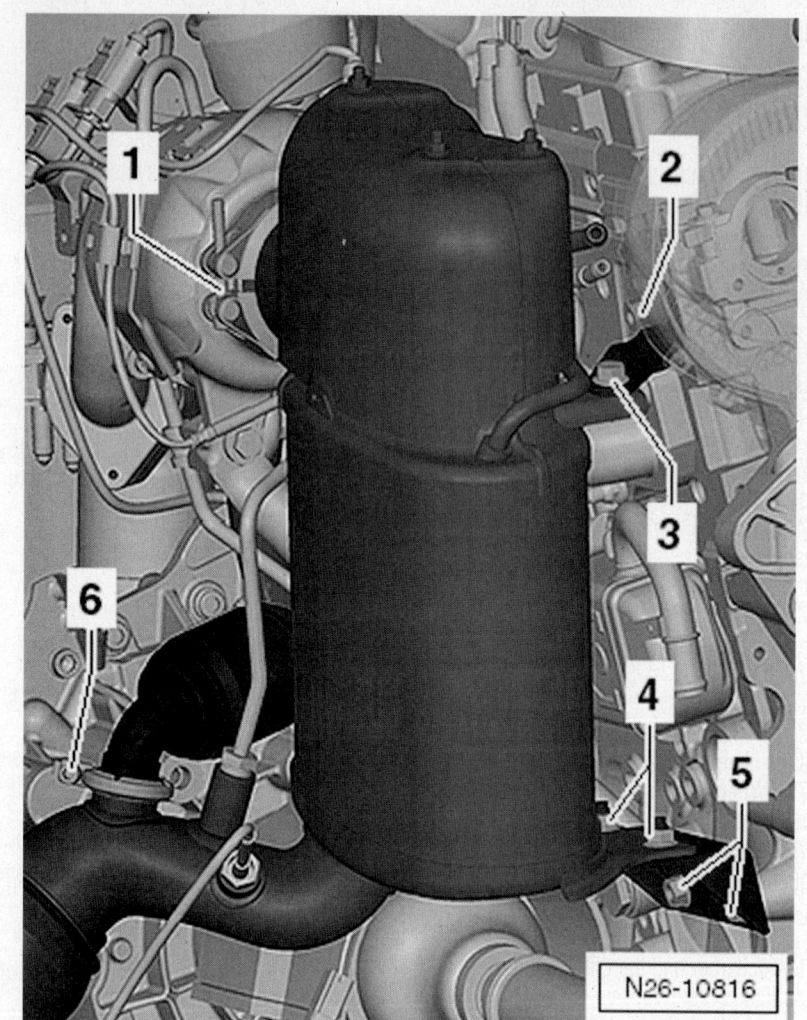

1. Clamp   4. Nuts
2. Nut   5. Nuts
3. Bolts   6. Clamp

Fig. 149 Installing the particulate filter

➡️**If the bolt "2" was not able to be pulled out using a magnet, loosen the camshaft clamp (T40070) bolts one rotation, slide the camshaft clamp toward the right front (as seen in the direction of travel) and tighten the bolts again.**

➡️**A second mechanic is required to remove and install the cylinder head.**

16. Carefully remove the cylinder head.

To install:
Installation Notes:
- Coat all contact surfaces between the hydraulic lash adjusters, the roller rocker arms and the lubricating surfaces on the camshaft with oil before installing a replacement cylinder head.
- Replace the cylinder head bolts.
- Only remove the plastic protectors installed to protect the open valves immediately before installing the cylinder head.
- It is necessary to replace the engine coolant when the cylinder head or cylinder head gasket are replaced.
- There must be no oil or coolant in the blind holes for the cylinder head bolts in the cylinder block.
- Only remove the new cylinder head gasket from its packaging immediately before installing.
- Handle the new gasket with extreme care. Damaging will lead to leaks.
- Replace the cylinder head bolts.
- Insert clean cloths into the cylinders and chain compartment so that no dirt or

abrasive powder can penetrate between the cylinder wall and piston and into chain compartment.
- Do not allow dirt or abrasive powder to get into the coolant either.

17. Carefully clean the cylinder head and cylinder block sealing surfaces. Avoid introducing scratches or scoring (do not use sandpaper with grit below 100).

18. Carefully remove any metal particles, emery remains and the cloths.

19. Apply a bead of sealant (front and rear) on the clean sealing surfaces. The sealant bead must be 2.0 to 2.5 mm thick.

20. Install the new cylinder head gasket. Note the centering pins in the cylinder block.

21. Then apply a bead of sealant, on the cylinder head gasket. The sealant bead must be 2.0 to 2.5 mm thick.

➡️**The cylinder head must be installed within 5 minutes of being applied with sealant.**

22. Install the cylinder head.

23. Guide the timing chain over the coolant pipe connection.

24. Insert the cylinder head bolts and tighten them hand tight. Then, tighten the cylinder head bolts, 1 through 12, in sequence, in three steps:
  a. Step 1: Using a torque wrench, tighten the bolts to 30 ft. lbs. (40 Nm).
  b. Step 2: Using a ratchet, tighten the bolts an additional 90° (1/4) turn.
  c. Step 3: Using a ratchet. tighten the bolts an additional 90° (1/4) turn.

25. Then tighten the bolts "13" to 7 ft. lbs. (10 Nm).

26. Wipe off any excess sealant, which has leaked out.

27. The rest of the installation follows the reverse of the removal procedure.
  a. Remove the locking pin (T40069) from the rear of the cylinder block and install the plug.
  b. Install the battery.
  c. Replace and fill coolant.

3.6L Engine
See Figures 156 through 160.

⁂ **CAUTION**

The engine must be no more than warm to touch.

⁂ **CAUTION**

When doing any repair work, especially in the engine compartment, pay attention to the following due to

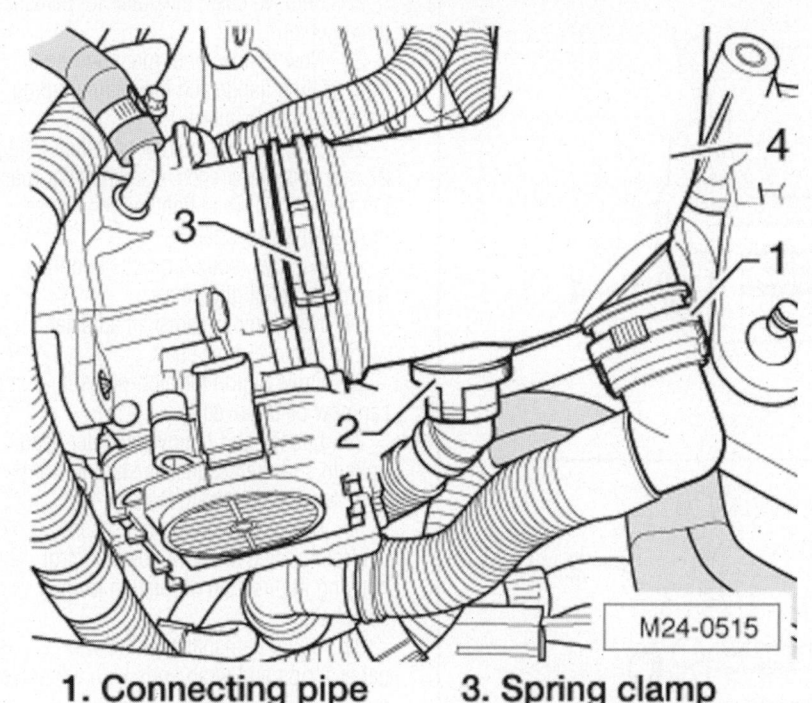

1. Connecting pipe
2. Vent tube
3. Spring clamp
4. Connecting pipe

Fig. 150 Remove the connecting pipe between the throttle valve control module and air filter. To do so, disconnect the connecting pipe, if equipped with Secondary Air Injection (AIR) and the vent tube and reposition the spring clamp.

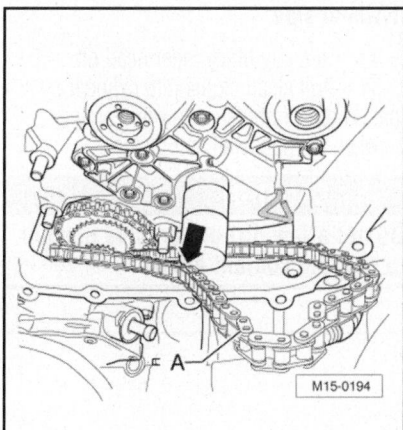

Fig. 151 Hold the timing chain (A) and lay it under the coolant pipe connection.

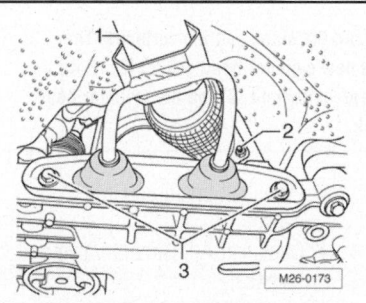

Fig. 152 Remove the four exhaust pipe with catalytic converter to exhaust manifold nuts (2) and the exhaust system suspended mount bolts (3). Remove the exhaust pipe with catalytic converter (1) from the exhaust manifold and tie it to the side.

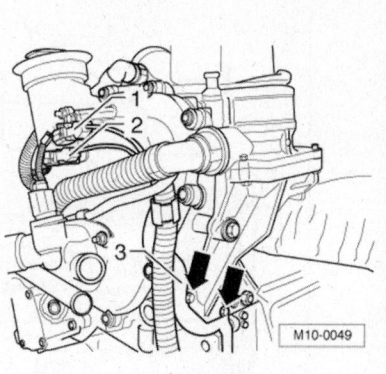

Fig. 153 Remove the wire bracket (3) from the AIR valve or cover (engines without AIR system). Ignore (1 and 2).

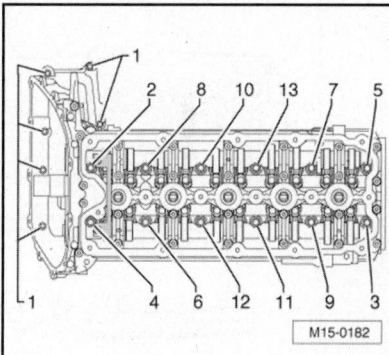

Fig. 154 Remove the cylinder head bolt, in sequence, 13 through 1.

※ **CAUTION**

Hot steam may escape when opening expansion tank. Wear protective goggles and protective clothing to prevent damage to eyes and scalding. Cover the cap with a rag and open very carefully.

4. Drain coolant.
5. Observe safety precautions before performing additional repair work.
6. Observe the rules for cleanliness.
   Pressure release in high-pressure area, refer to Releasing Pressure in High Pressure Area.

※ **CAUTION**

Fuel supply line is under pressure! Wear protective goggles and protective clothing to prevent injuries and contact with skin. Before removing from hose connection wrap a cloth around the connection. Then release pressure by carefully loosening union nut.

clearance issues. Route lines of all types (e.g. for fuel, hydraulic, EVAP canister system, coolant and refrigerant, brake fluid, vacuum) and electrical wiring so that the original path is followed. Ensure sufficient clearance to all moving or hot components.

➡To perform work sequence, the Ground (GND) cable must be disconnected from battery. Check whether a coded radio is installed. If so, obtain anti)theft coding beforehand.

➡All cable ties which are opened or cut open when removing, must be replaced in the same position when installing.

1. Disconnect battery Ground (GND) cable with the ignition switched off.
2. Remove noise insulation.
3. Remove air filter.

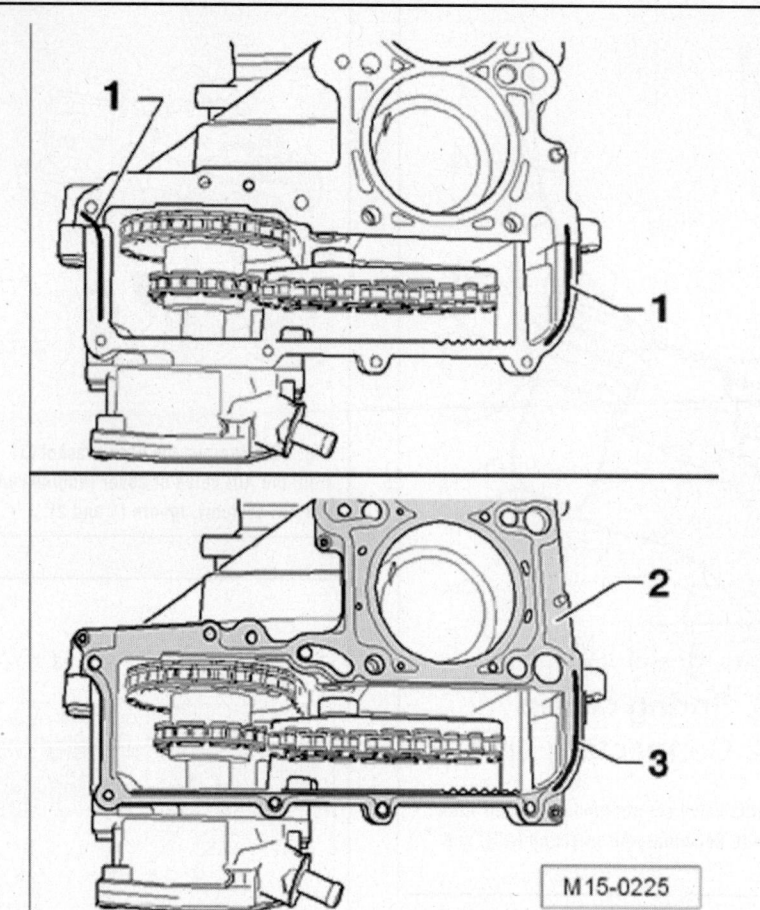

Fig. 155 Apply a bead of sealant (1 only at this time) on the clean sealing surfaces. The sealant bead must be 2.0 to 2.5 mm thick. Install the new cylinder head gasket (2). Note the centering pins in the cylinder block. Then, apply a bead of sealant (3), on the cylinder head gasket. The sealant bead must be 2.0 to 2.5 mm thick.

7. Disconnect fuel supply line and catch escaping fuel with a rag.

8. Press in securing ring to disengage the fuel lines.

> ❋❋ **CAUTION**
>
> **Seal the pipes so that the fuel system is not contaminated by dirt.**

9. Remove upper part of intake manifold.

10. Remove the lower section of the intake manifold and disconnect the connector.

11. Now remove heat shield with intake manifold support from cylinder head.

12. Unbolt front exhaust pipes from exhaust manifolds.

13. Remove high-pressure pump and pull out pump plunger.

14. Disconnect the following connectors:

- Camshaft Position (CMP) sensor
- Camshaft Adjustment Valve
- Camshaft position (CMP) sensor
- Camshaft Adjustment Valve (exhaust)

15. Pull off/disconnect all remaining electrical wires required from cylinder head and set aside.

16. Disconnect coolant hose at connection to heater core.

17. Remove top and bottom coolant pipes on cover piece of cylinder head.

18. Remove vacuum pump.

19. Remove three mounting bolts coolant connection.

20. Remove the cylinder head cover.

  a. Loosen the cylinder head cover bolts starting from the inside and working toward the outside, 17 through 1.

  b. Remove bolts and remove cylinder head cover.

21. Turn the crankshaft in the engine direction of rotation to TDC No. 1 Cylinder. Make sure cams of cylinder 1 must face each other.

22. Remove chain tensioner for camshaft timing chain.

23. Now remove both mounting bolts from sealing flange and then all mounting bolts from cover piece.

24. Only counter-hold at camshaft using 27 mm spanner wrench. Camshaft bar must not be inserted when tightening or loosening camshaft adjuster.

25. Remove mounting bolts and then remove bolts of glide track.

26. Now remove camshaft adjuster.

27. Remove drive shaft.

28. Drive pinion for high-pressure pump can now be removed.

29. Loosen and remove cylinder head bolts in specified sequence starting from outside working toward inside.

30. Remove mounting bolts from control housing and pull down control housing in direction of rotation from camshafts.

31. Cover camshafts with clean paper strips and wrap ends with adhesive tape.

32. Attach the lifting tackle 3033 as illustrated and carefully lift the cylinder head with the workshop crane (VAS 6100).

➡ **The lifting tackle (3033) items marked 1 through 12 face toward the flywheel side.**

33. Carefully lift cylinder head off.

34. Stuff clean cloths into cylinder so that no dirt or abrasive powder can get between cylinder wall and piston.

> ❋❋ **CAUTION**
>
> **Do not allow dirt or abrasive powder to get into coolant either.**

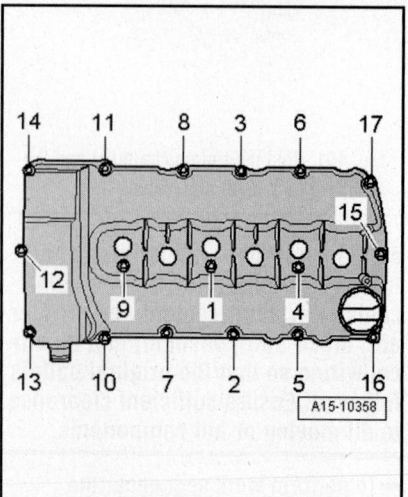

Fig. 156 Cylinder head bolt loosening/tightening sequence, 17 through 1

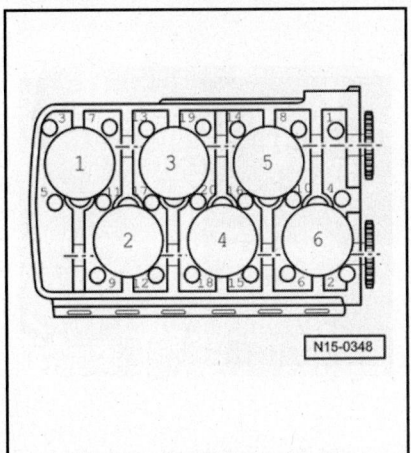

Fig. 157 Loosen and remove cylinder head bolts in specified sequence

35. Carefully clean cylinder head and cylinder block sealing surfaces. Avoid introducing scratches or scoring (do not use sandpaper with grit below 100).

36. Clean all threaded bores for cylinder head bolts.

37. Check cylinder head for warping.

To install:

38. Carefully remove metal particles, emery remains and cloths.

39. If the piston for cylinder 1 is not at TDC, turn the crankshaft in engine direction of rotation to TDC No. 1 Cylinder mark, while at the same time having a second technician guide the crankshaft timing chain by hand.

40. Make sure that alignment bushings are inserted in bore 12 and 20 in cylinder block.

41. Place a 0.078 in. (2 mm) thick sealant bead of sealant (D 176 501 A1) on to partition of cylinder block/sealing flange.

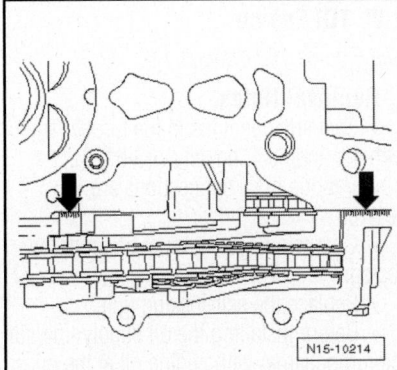

Fig. 158 Place a 0.078 in. (2 mm) thick sealant bead of sealant as shown (arrows) on to partition of cylinder block/sealing flange

42. Only remove the new cylinder head gasket from its packing immediately before installing.

43. Handle the new gasket with extreme care. Damaging will lead to leaks.

44. Immediately place new cylinder head gasket on. Text (replacement part number) must be visible.

45. Also fill some more sealant into both 0.117 (3 mm) bores, which lie on the sealant bead.

46. Position the camshafts in cylinder head to TDC No. 1 cylinder.

47. It must be possible to insert camshaft bar into both shaft grooves.

48. Install cylinder head.

49. Apply locking fluid (D 197 300 A2) on each cylinder head bolt in area and install the bolts.

✲✲ CAUTION

The longer cylinder head bolts must be inserted in the middle holes of cylinder head.

50. Tighten cylinder head bolts in specified sequence, starting from inside and working toward outside, as follows:
- Pre-tighten all the bolts to 11 ft. lbs. (15 Nm)
- Tighten all bolts to 22 ft. lbs. (30 Nm)

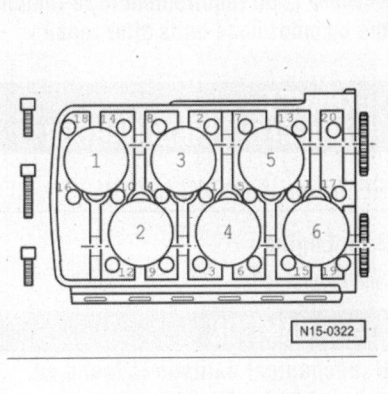

Fig. 160 Tighten cylinder head bolts in specified sequence, starting from inside and working toward outside

- Tighten all bolts with a rigid wrench an additional 90° rotation
- Tighten all bolts with a rigid wrench an additional 90° rotation

51. The rest of the assembly is basically a reverse of the disassembling sequence.

52. Install camshaft adjuster with timing chain.

53. Install cylinder head cover and tighten bolts in sequence to 89 inch lbs. (10 Nm).

54. Install intake manifold lower)section.

55. Install intake manifold upper)section.

56. Fill with new coolant.

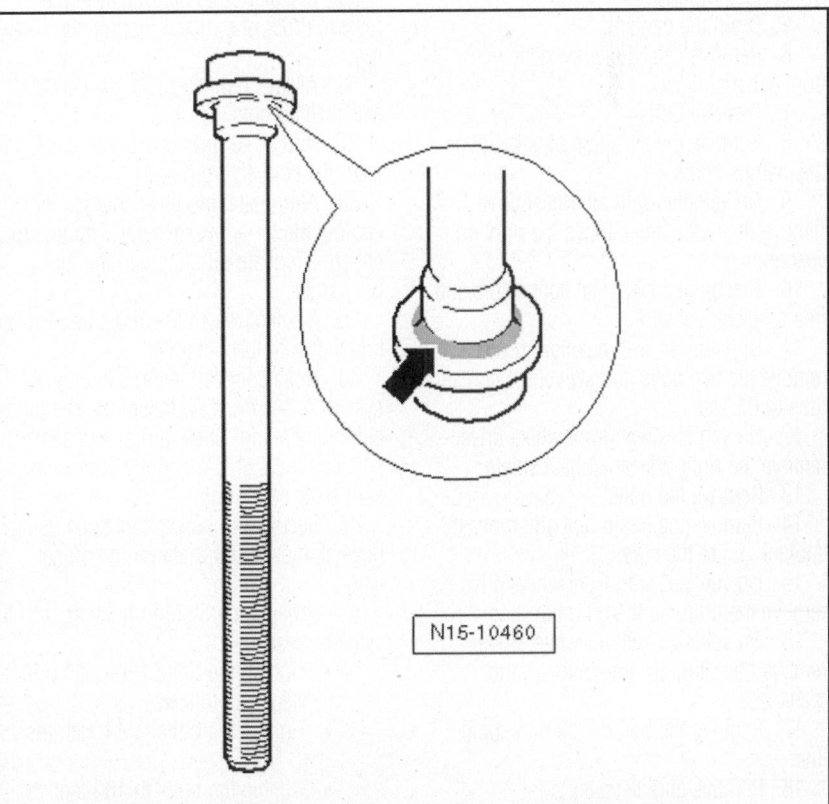

Fig. 159 Apply locking fluid on each cylinder head bolt in area and install the bolts

➡There is no requirement to re-tighten the cylinder head bolts after repairs.

EXHAUST MANIFOLD/TURBOCHARGER

REMOVAL & INSTALLATION

2.0L Engine

See Figure 161.

❄❄ CAUTION

If mechanical damage is found on exhaust turbocharger, e.g. a destroyed compression wheel, it is not enough to just replace the turbocharger. Perform the following steps to prevent subsequent damage. Check the air filter housing, the air filter insert and the intake hoses for contamination. Check entire charge air circuit and cooler for contamination. If contaminants are found in charge air circuit, circuit must be cleaned and cooler replaced if necessary.

1. Remove the air filter.
2. Remove the battery and battery tray.
3. Remove noise insulation.
4. Remove the front part of the right wheel housing liner and/or the front right wheel housing liner.
5. Drain the coolant.
6. Remove catalytic converters with front exhaust pipe.
7. Remove bolts.
8. Remove the air guide pipe by lifting the clamps items.
9. On vehicles with all-wheel drive remove the heat shield above the right driveshaft.
10. Disconnect electrical connectors and free up electrical wire.
11. On vehicles with auxiliary heater remove the two bolts and swivel the coolant tubs to the left.
12. On vehicles with front wheel drive remove the right driveshaft heat shield.
13. Remove the bolts.
14. Remove the banjo bolt and move the coolant line to the side.
15. On vehicles with front wheel drive remove the bolts on the oil return line.
16. On vehicles with all-wheel drive remove the oil return line bolts on the crankcase.
17. Remove the bolt on the oil supply line.
18. Remove engine cover.
19. Disconnect the connectors from the ignition coils and the wiring harness and lay them aside.
20. Disconnect the coolant line to the coolant reservoir.
21. Disconnect the vacuum line at the separating point and free up the wire.
22. Remove the coolant hoses from the coolant pipe.
23. Press the release buttons, remove the air guide hose and move them to the side.
24. Remove the air guide pipe bolt.
25. Remove the air guide pipe; to do this, loosen the hose clamp.
26. Remove the air guide pipe bolt.
27. Loose the hose clamp and lay the air guide pipe on the cylinder head.
28. Seal the turbocharger with the Engine bung set VAS 6122.
29. Remove the bolts and remove the heat shield together with the coolant pipe.
30. Remove the bolt 2 from the heat shield with a 6 mm hex socket. The hex socket must be at least 5 cm long. A socket that is 6 mm at the tip is too wide.
31. Disconnect the oil supply line from the turbocharger.
32. Disconnect the coolant hose and move it to the side.
33. Remove the nuts.
34. Remove the turbocharger/exhaust manifold upward.

To install:

35. Installation is performed in the reverse order of removal, noting the following:
36. Always replace seals, gaskets and self-locking nuts.
37. Add oil to turbocharger through oil feed line connecting piece.
38. After installing turbocharger, let engine idle for approximately 1 minute to ensure adequate oil supply to the turbocharger.
39. Coolant return line must be installed together with turbocharger.
40. Hose connections and charge air system hoses must be free of oil and grease before installing. Sealing ring and sealing surfaces must only be lightly oiled with connector couplings.
41. Secure all hose connections using hose clamps appropriate for the model type.
42. Exhaust manifold/turbocharger to cylinder head
   - Tighten the bolts 1 through 5 in 4 stages as follows:
   - Tighten the bolts to 44 inch lbs. (5 Nm)
   - Tighten the bolts to 106 inch lbs. (12 Nm)

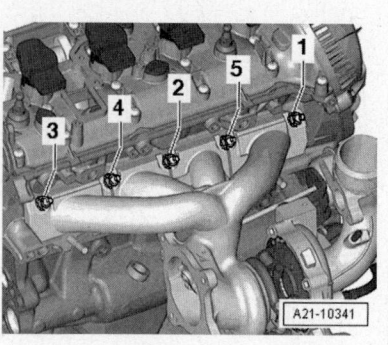

Fig. 161 Observe tightening sequence for exhaust manifold/turbocharger to the cylinder head

   - Tighten the bolts to 12 ft. lbs. (16 Nm)
   - Tighten the bolts to 19 ft. lbs. (25 Nm)
43. Tighten bolts/nuts to specification as follows:
   - Oil supply line to exhaust turbocharger: 15 ft. lbs. (20 Nm) plus 45° additional rotation
   - Oil return line to exhaust turbocharger: 80 inch lbs. (9 Nm)
   - Coolant supply line to turbocharger: 15 ft. lbs. (20 Nm) plus 45° additional rotation
   - Turbocharger bracket to cylinder block: 22 ft. lbs. (30 Nm)
   - Turbocharger bracket to turbocharger: 22 ft. lbs. (30 Nm)
   - Right charge air pipe to oil pan: 89 inch. lbs. (00 Nm)
   - Heat shield to cylinder head (replace nuts and use hot bolt paste) M8 and M12: 15 ft. lbs. (20 Nm)

2.0L TDI Engine

See Figures 162 through 172.

Removal Notes:
- Seal any openings in the turbocharger with the engine bung set (VAS 6122).
- Various hose connections are secured.
- Charge air system must be properly sealed.
- Replace the self-locking nuts.
- Before installing the oil supply line, fill the turbocharger with engine oil at the oil supply line connection.
- After installing the turbocharger, allow the engine idle for approximately 1 minute to ensure adequate oil supply to the turbocharger.

➥**If mechanical damage (such as a destroyed compression wheel) is found on the turbocharger, just replacing the turbocharger is not enough. To avoid damage later, perform the following steps:**

- Check the air filter housing, air filter element and air guide hoses for contamination.
- Check the entire charge air circuit and charge air cooler for foreign objects.
- If there are foreign objects in the charge air system, clean the charge air circuit and replace the charge air cooler, if necessary.

1. Remove the engine cover.

2. Drain the coolant.

3. Remove the NOx reduction catalytic converter.

4. Remove the heated oxygen sensor and the oxygen sensor heater.

5. Remove the exhaust pressure sensors 1, 2, 3 and 4.

6. Remove the particulate filter.

7. Remove rear coolant pipe.

8. Remove the air filter housing.

9. Remove the battery and tray.

10. Press the release buttons and remove the crankshaft housing ventilation hose from the cylinder head cover.

11. Remove the connector from the crankcase ventilation hose.

12. Free up the vacuum hose (arrows) on the air guide pipe.

13. Remove the bolt and tilt the air guide pipe with the intake manifold backward and remove from the turbocharger.

14. Unclip the preheating pipe and remove it from the bracket.

15. Remove the heat shield boot, then remove the vacuum hose from the turbocharger vacuum diaphragm. Disconnect the connector from the charge pressure actuator position sensor.

16. Release and disconnect the connector and free up the wires.

17. Remove the charge air pressure sensor from the charge air cooler by loosening the clamps.

18. If equipped with a Direct Shift Gearbox (DSG), remove the coolant hoses from the transmission fluid cooler.

19. Remove the bolt from the charge air pipe.

20. Loosen the hose clamp and unclip all the wires on the charge air pressure sensor.

21. Remove the charge air pipe from the charge air cooler and remove it.

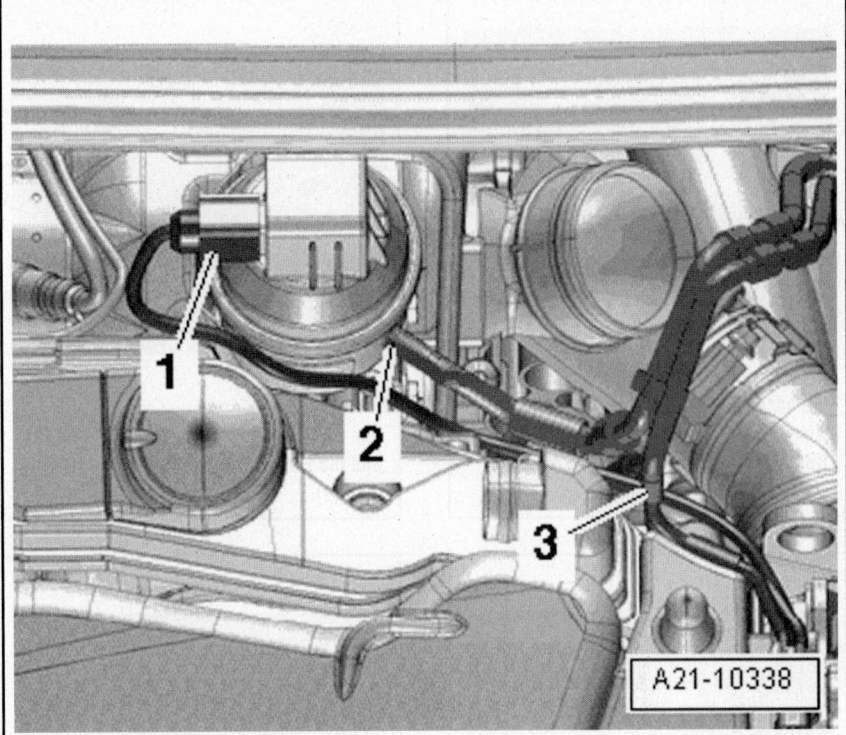

Fig. 162 Remove the heat shield boot, then remove the vacuum hose (2) from the turbocharger vacuum diaphragm. Disconnect the connector (1) from the charge pressure actuator position sensor. (Ignore item 3.)

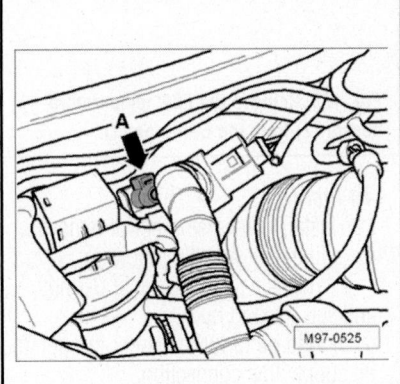

Fig. 163 Release and disconnect the connector (A) and free up the wires.

22. Remove the bolts, loosen the clamp and remove the pulsation damper.

23. Remove the bolts, free up the wire, and remove the exhaust gas temperature sensor 1.

24. Remove the Exhaust Gas Recirculation (EGR) pipe.

25. Remove the EGR temperature sensor from the EGR pipe.

26. Remove the bolts and the nut and remove the EGR pipe from the seal for the

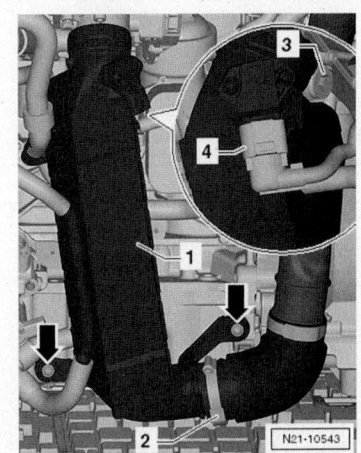

1. Charge air cooler 3. Bolt
2. Clamp 4. Connector

Fig. 164 Remove the charge air pressure sensor (2) from the charge air cooler (1) by loosening the clamps. Remove the two connectors.

intake tube, then remove the EGR pipe together with the sensor wire.

27. Remove the bolts indicated and unscrew the upper fitting.

28. Loosen the fitting and then remove the oil supply line (with the supports) from the turbocharger.

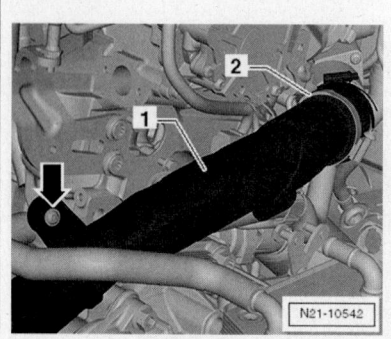

Fig. 165 Remove the bolt (arrow). Loosen the hose clamp (2) and unclip all the wires on the charge air pressure sensor. Remove the charge air pipe (1) from the charge air cooler and remove it.

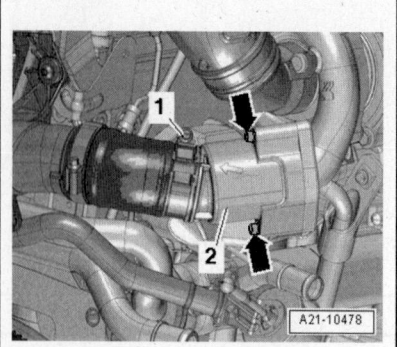

Fig. 166 Remove the bolts, loosen the clamp (1) and remove the pulsation damper (2).

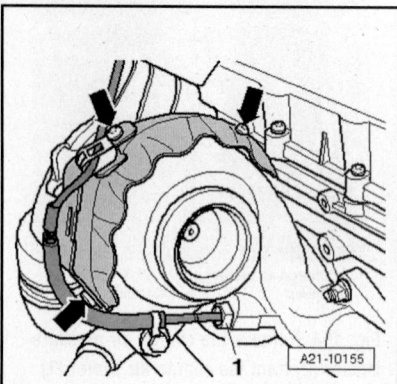

Fig. 167 Remove the bolts, free up the wire, and remove the exhaust gas temperature sensor 1 (1).

29. Remove the turbocharge heat shield.
30. Remove the turbocharger with the exhaust manifold from the cylinder head, removing it upward.

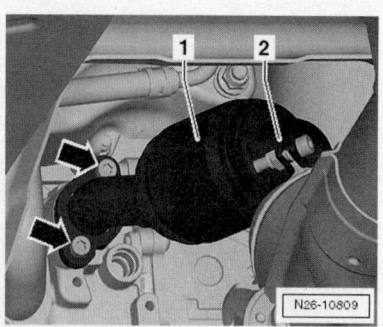

Fig. 168 Remove the bolts, the clamp (2) and the Exhaust Gas Recirculation (EGR) pipe (1).

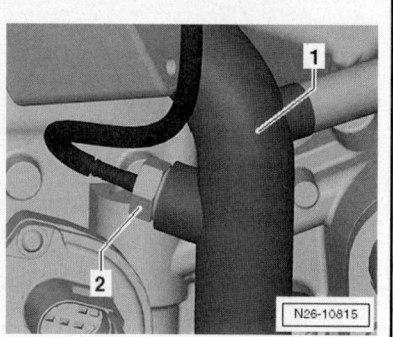

Fig. 169 Remove the EGR temperature sensor (2) from the EGR pipe (1).

To install:
31. Install in reverse order of removal. When doing this note the following:
　a. Replace seals, gaskets, O-rings and self-locking nuts.
　b. Add oil to turbocharger through the oil supply line connection.
　c. The hose connections as well as the charge air pipes and hoses must be free of oil and grease before installing.
　d. Secure hose connections with standard production clamps.
　e. To ensure the turbocharger is supplied with enough oil, allow the engine run at idle for approximately 1 minute after installing the turbocharger. Do not increase the engine speed during this time.
　f. When installing, install all heat shield boots back in the same positions.
32. Install the charge air hoses and screw-type clamps.

33. Install the EGR pipe.
34. Connect the vacuum hoses.
35. Electrical connectors and wiring routing.
36. Install the air filter housing.
37. Install the particulate filter.
38. Fill the coolant.

3.6L Engine

1. Remove upper part of intake manifold.
2. Remove coolant pipe from the heat shield. Remove the bolts and then remove the heat shield and intake manifold support.
3. Remove front exhaust pipe at exhaust manifolds and slide back slightly.

➡**Oxygen sensors remain installed.**

4. Remove upper and lower nuts on both exhaust manifolds.
5. Remove exhaust manifold toward back.

To install:
6. Installation is in reverse order of removal, note the following:
7. Replace gaskets and self-locking nuts.
8. Tighten bolts/nuts to specification as follows:
- Exhaust manifold to cylinder head (replace): 19 ft. lbs. (25 Nm)
- Front exhaust pipe to exhaust manifold (replace): 30 ft. lbs. (40 Nm)
- Exhaust manifold heat shield to cylinder head: 15 ft. lbs. (20 Nm)

INTAKE MANIFOLD

REMOVAL & INSTALLATION

2.0L Engine
See Figure 173.

❄❄ CAUTION

Fuel system is under pressure! Fuel pressure must be reduced to a residual pressure before opening high-pressure area of injection system.

1. Remove the engine cover.
2. Clean the contact surface from the intake manifold to the cylinder head.
3. Remove the air filter.
4. Separate the vacuum line to the EVAP canister.
5. Disconnect the following electrical connections:
- Intake Air Temperature Sensor
- Throttle Valve Control Module
- Evaporative Emission (EVAP) Canister Purge Regulator Valve
- Camshaft Position sensor

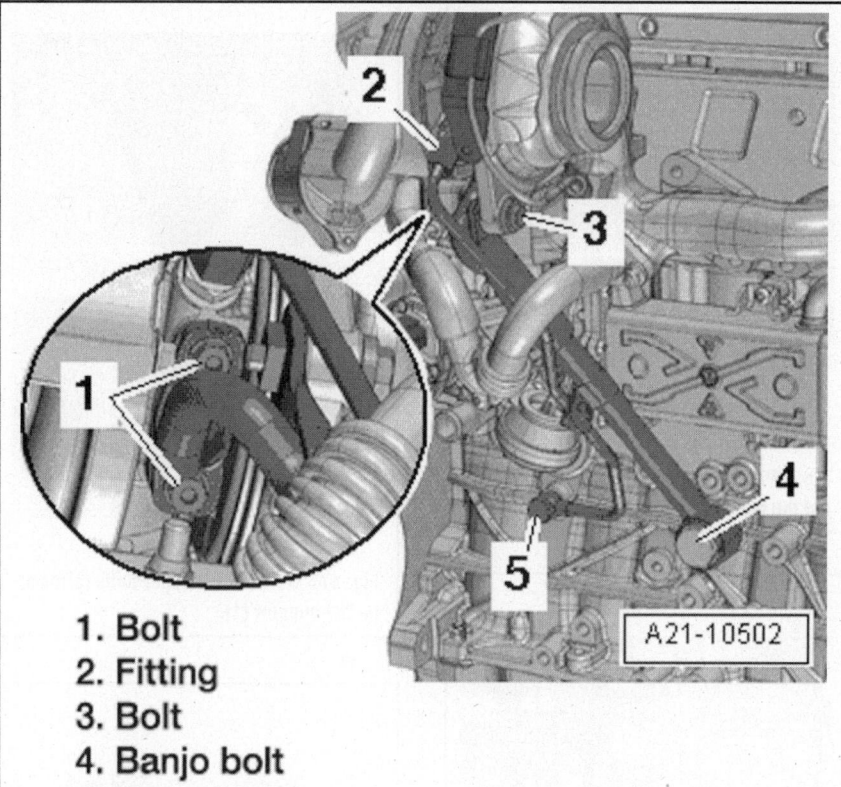

1. Bolt
2. Fitting
3. Bolt
4. Banjo bolt
5. Banjo bolt

Fig. 170 Remove the bolts indicated and unscrew the upper fitting.

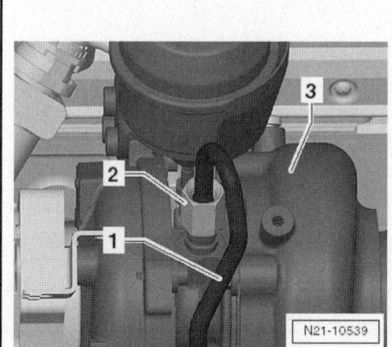

Fig. 171 Loosen the fitting (2) and then remove the oil supply line (1), with the supports, from the turbocharger (3).

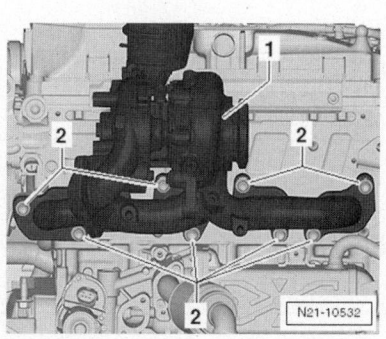

Fig. 172 Remove the turbocharger (1) with the exhaust manifold from the cylinder head, removing it upward.

6. Disconnect the vacuum line at the separating point and remove the crankcase ventilation hose.

7. Remove the bolts for the fuel supply line and lay the line to the side.

8. The fuel system must have no pressure.

9. Open the fuel line union nut lower.

10. Disconnect the vacuum line from the Intake Manifold Runner Control (IMRC) Valve.

11. Remove the bolts for the coolant line from the intake manifold.

12. Disconnect the electrical connector from the Fuel Pressure Sensor.

13. Loosen the hose clamp.

14. Remove bolt.

15. Disconnect electrical connector.

16. Remove the noise insulation.

17. Remove the air guide pipe items.

18. Remove the bolt and remove the air guide pipe downward.

19. Disconnect the electrical connectors and remove the bracket from the intake manifold.

20. Remove the intake manifold bracket by removing the mounting nut.

21. Remove the oil filter.

22. Loosen the wiring bracket.

23. Loosen the wire from the intake manifold.

24. Remove the nuts and loosen the bolts from the intake manifold using the multi-point socket (T10347).

25. Carefully pull the intake manifold and fuel rail away from the cylinder head just a little.

26. Disconnect the electrical connector from the Intake Manifold Runner Position Sensor and remove the intake manifold.

27. Cover the intake channels with a clean rag.

28. The fuel injectors could remain stuck in the fuel rail.

29. Disconnect the fuel rail from the intake manifold.

30. To access the fuel injectors, the intake manifold and the fuel rail with intake manifold runner control valve must be removed. The fuel injectors sit in the cylinder head.

To install:

31. The combustion chamber seal (Teflon) and the O-ring must always be replaced.

32. Mount the intake manifold onto the cylinder head on the stud bolts (lower left and right).

33. Make sure the fuel injectors are installed correctly and pay attention to the wiring bracket when mounting the intake manifold (located under the intake manifold).

34. When installing the intake manifold, the manifold must be pulled out slightly and

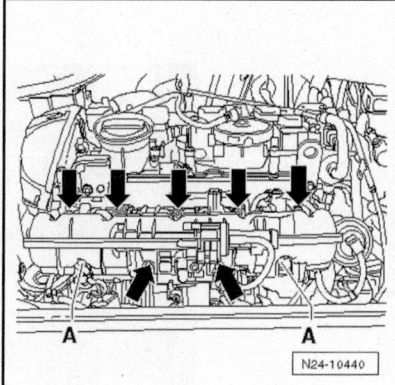

Fig. 173 Remove the nuts A and loosen the bolts from the intake manifold using the multi-point socket

the fuel injectors will stick in the fuel rail. Pull the fuel injectors out of the fuel rail and insert them in the cylinder head again.

35. The rest of the installation follows the reverse of the removal procedures.

36. When attaching the wiring bracket onto the intake manifold, make sure it clips into both latches.

37. Tightening specifications:
- High pressure pump bolts (replace): 89 inch lbs. (10 Nm)
- Fuel high-pressure line connection (replace): 16 ft. lbs. (22 Nm)
- Fuel line to the fuel rail: 13 ft. lbs. (18 Nm)
- Bolt for the intake manifold support: 17 ft. lbs. (23 Nm)
- Nut for the intake manifold support: 89 inch lbs. (10 Nm)

2.0L TDI Engine

See Figures 174 through 180.

1. Remove the engine cover.
2. Remove the noise insulation.
3. Remove the charge air cooler.
4. Disconnect the connectors for the glow plugs.
5. Remove the bolts and set the coolant supply line aside.
6. Remove the bolts and set the fuel return line aside.
7. Remove the bolt and union nuts, then remove the high-pressure line.
8. Remove the fuel rail.
9. Remove the bolts and remove the connecting tube from the manifold to the block.
10. Remove the upper bolts (arrows) for the support.
11. Release and disconnect the connector from on the EGR vacuum regulator solenoid valve.

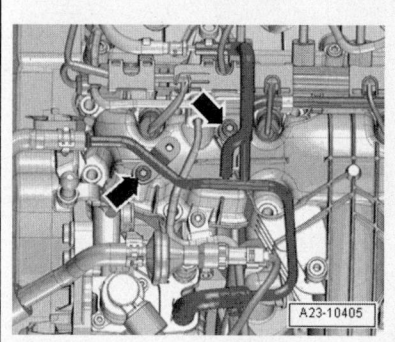

Fig. 175 Remove the bolts (arrows) and set the fuel return line aside.

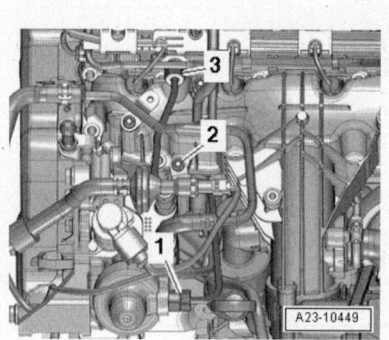

Fig. 176 Remove the bolt (2) and union nuts (1 and 3), then remove the high-pressure line.

12. Disconnect the connector.
13. Remove the bolt for the oil dipstick guide tube.

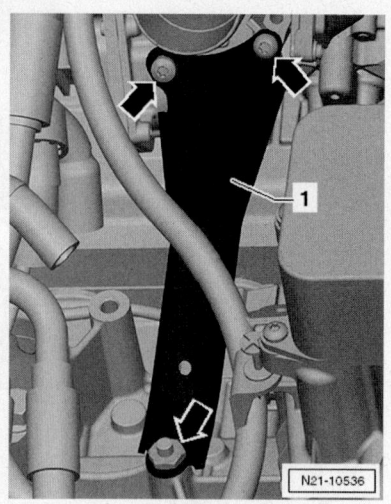

Fig. 177 Remove the upper bolts (arrows) for the support (1).

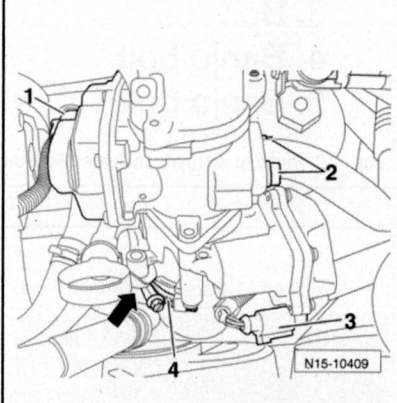

Fig. 178 Release and disconnect the connector (1) from on the EGR vacuum regulator solenoid valve.

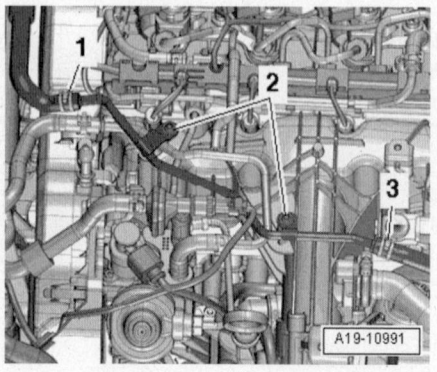

Fig. 174 Remove the bolts (2) and set the coolant supply line aside.

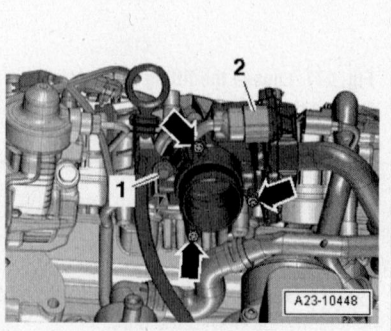

Fig. 179 Disconnect the connector (2). Remove the bolt (1) for the oil dipstick guide tube. Remove the upper bolt (arrow).

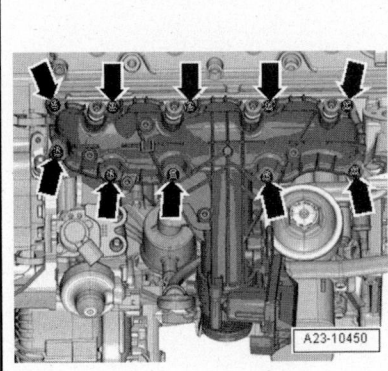

Fig. 180 Tighten the bolts for the intake manifold starting on the inside and working toward the outside, in a diagonal sequence.

4. Disconnect the fuel supply line and the vent line from the manifold. Seal the lines so that the fuel system is not contaminated by dirt, etc.

5. Disconnect the connectors.

6. Remove the wiring harness from the transport strap.

7. Pull the clamps and retaining ring out of the locking mechanism.

8. Remove the bolts and remove the transport strap.

9. Remove the throttle valve control module.

10. Disconnect the connector and the crankcase ventilation hose.

11. Remove the wiring harness. To do so, carefully press out the clips.

12. Pull the oil dipstick out and press the retaining ring downward.

13. Remove the noise insulation.

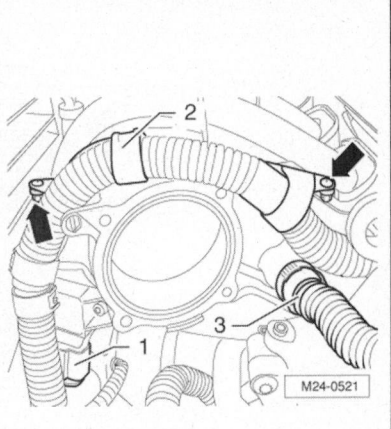

Fig. 182 Disconnect the connector (1) and the crankcase ventilation hose (3). Remove the wiring harness (2). To do so, carefully press out the clips (arrows).

14. Remove the upper bolt.

15. Remove the bolts (arrows) for the intake manifold with the socket (XZN 8, T40159) diagonally from the outside towards the inside.

16. Carefully remove the intake manifold.

To install:

17. Install in reverse order of removal. When doing this, note the following:

  a. Replace all seals.

  b. Tighten the bolts for the intake manifold starting on the inside and working toward the outside, in a diagonal sequence.

  c. Fill with coolant.

  d. Tightening specifications

- Intake manifold: 6 ft. lbs. (8 Nm)
- Oil dipstick: 7 ft. lbs. (10 Nm)
- Upper supports on the throttle valve control module: 7 ft. lbs. (10 Nm)
- Lower supports on the engine: 30 ft. lbs. (40 Nm)
- Connecting pipe: 15 ft. lbs. (20 Nm)

2.5L Engine

See Figures 181 through 185.

1. Disconnect the battery.

2. Remove the engine cover with air filter.

3. Remove the connecting pipe between the throttle valve control module and air filter. To do so, disconnect the connecting pipe, if equipped with Secondary Air Injection (AIR), and the vent tube and reposition the spring clamp.

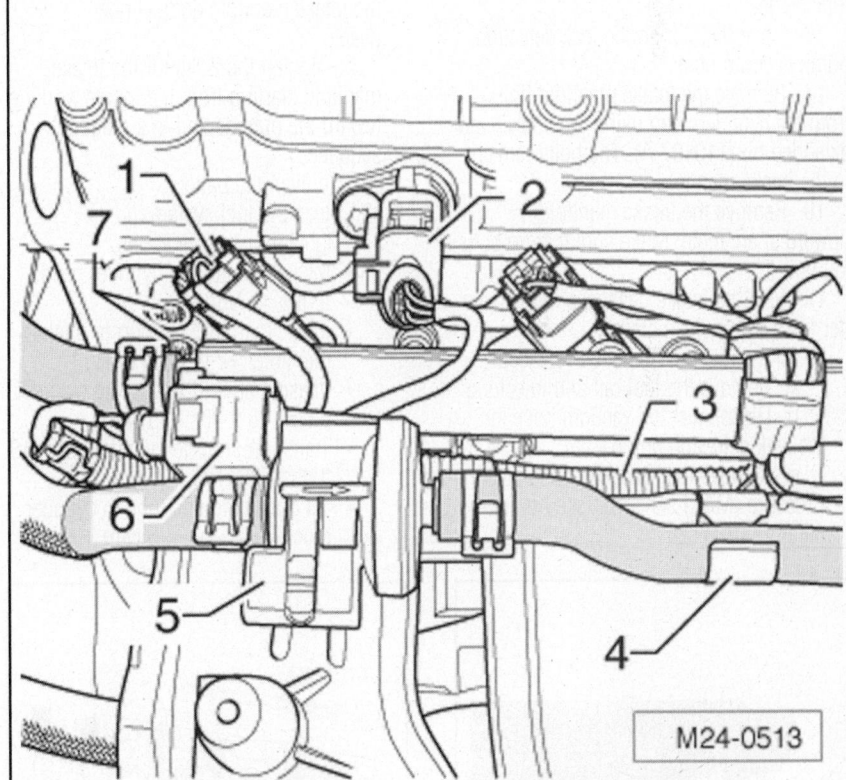

1. Connector	5. Retaining ring
2. Connector	6. Connector
3. Wiring harness	7. Bolts
4. Clamps	

Fig. 181 Disconnect the connectors. Remove the wiring harness from the transport strap. Pull the clamps and retaining ring out of the locking mechanism. Remove the bolts and remove the transport strap. Remove the throttle valve control module.

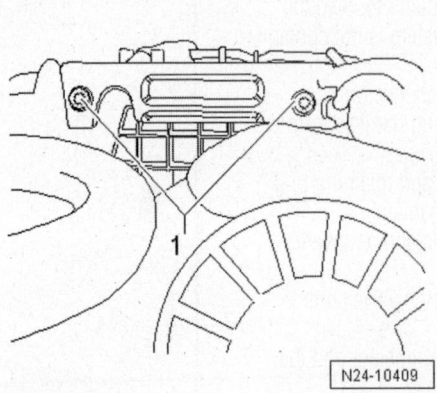

Fig. 183 Loosen the bolts or nuts (1) on the bottom side of the intake manifold.

Fig. 186 Upper/lower intake manifold bolt loosening/tightening sequence

14. Loosen the bolts or nuts on the bottom side of the intake manifold.

15. Loosen the lower bolt on the oil dipstick guide tube. Lay the oil dipstick guide tube aside.

16. Open the clip on the leak detection pump vacuum hose.

17. Remove the intake manifold bolts from the cylinder head using the socket and extended bit (T10107 A). The bolts remain in the intake manifold.

18. Remove the intake manifold upward at an angle. Make sure that no bolts fall out.

19. Seal the intake passages in the cylinder head using clean cloths.

20. If the manifold must be replaced:

a. Remove the fuel rail and injectors.

b. Disconnect the vacuum hose for the leak detection pump.

c. Remove the Manifold Absolute Pressure (MAP) sensor/Intake Air Temperature (IAT) sensor.

To install:

21. Install in the reverse order of removal. Note the following:

a. Replace the seals between the intake manifold and cylinder head.

b. Tighten the bolts for the intake manifold starting from the inside working toward the outside and in a diagonal sequence.

22. Connect the battery.

23. Bleed the fuel system.

24. Tightening specifications:

- Intake manifold to cylinder head: 7 ft. lbs. (9 Nm)
- Intake manifold support to intake manifold: 12 ft. lbs. (16 Nm)
- Intake manifold support to cylinder block: 18 ft. lbs. (25 Nm)
- Transport strap to cylinder head: 18 ft. lbs. (25 Nm)
- Oil dipstick guide tube to cylinder block: 18 ft. lbs. (25 Nm)

3.6L Engine

Upper Manifold

See Figures 186 and 187.

➡When doing any repair work, especially in the engine compartment, pay attention to the following due to clearance issues. Route lines of all types (e.g. for fuel, hydraulic, EVAP canister system, coolant and refrigerant, brake fluid, vacuum) and electrical wiring so that the original path is followed. To prevent damages to the lines, make sure there is sufficient clearance to all moving or hot components.

1. Remove ignition coil wiring harness cover strip.

2. Place assembly tool (T10118) against the release button, and carefully remove all the connectors from the ignition coil with power output stage.

3. Press cable duct upward using a

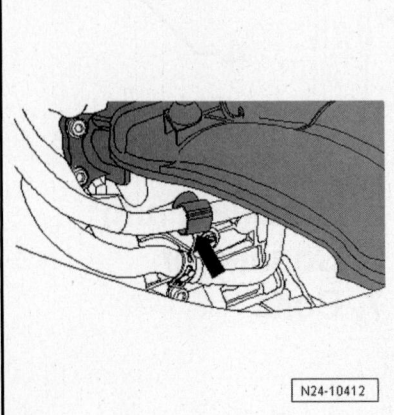

Fig. 184 Open the clip (arrow) on the leak detection pump vacuum hose.

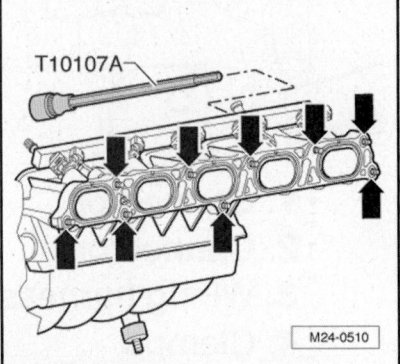

Fig. 185 Remove the intake manifold bolts (arrows) from the cylinder head using the socket and extended bit. The bolts remain in the intake manifold.

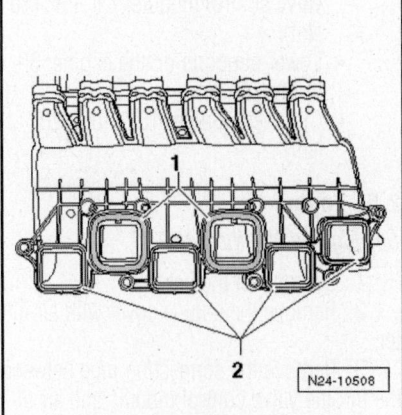

Fig. 187 Insert (1) large sealing rings (2) small gaskets in the intake manifold upper section and coat it lightly with engine oil.

screwdriver and move the connectors to the side.

4. Disconnect connectors, remove the intake hose and disconnect the connecting hose for the crankcase ventilation from the cylinder head cover.

5. Disconnect lines from the upper part of the intake manifold.

6. Remove mounting bolt for intake manifold support at rear.

7. Remove front intake manifold support bolt.

8. Remove bolts for the upper/lower intake manifold sections.

9. Lower upper section of the intake manifold and place it on a suitable surface.

10. Seal the intake channels in lower section of intake manifold using a clean rag.

To install:

11. Insert new gaskets in the intake manifold upper section and coat it lightly with engine oil.

12. Position the intake manifold upper section on the lower section.

13. Tighten the bolts connecting the upper and lower sections of the intake manifold to 89 inch lbs. (10 Nm) evenly from inside to outside.

14. Then tighten mounting bolts on intake manifold support.

15. The rest of the assembly is basically a reverse of the disassembling sequence.

Lower Manifold

See Figure 188.

> ※ **CAUTION**
>
> When doing any repair work, especially in the engine compartment, pay attention to the following due to clearance issues. Route lines of all types (e.g. for fuel, hydraulic, EVAP system, coolant and refrigerant, brake fluid, vacuum) and electrical

wiring so that the original path is followed. To prevent damages to the lines, make sure there is sufficient clearance to all moving or hot components.

> ※ **CAUTION**
>
> Follow safety measures for releasing fuel pressure in high-pressure area.

1. Disconnect battery ground (GND) cable with ignition switched off.

2. Remove noise insulation.

3. Remove upper part of intake manifold.

4. Remove high-pressure pump.

5. Remove fuel rail connecting pipe.

6. Remove intake manifold lower part/cylinder head bolts.

7. Remove mounting bolt from guide pipe for oil dipstick.

8. Remove bracket from the lower section of the intake manifold.

9. Remove bolts of fuel rail for cylinders 2, 4 and 6.

10. Carefully pull off fuel rail from fuel injectors.

11. Remove intake manifold lower section.

➡ **If a fuel injector is removed, Teflon sealing ring of combustion chamber as well as O-ring must always be replaced. Spring elements for fuel injectors must be also be replaced**

12. Seal the intake channels in cylinder head using a clean rag.

To install:

13. Installation is in reverse order of removal.

14. Tighten bolts/nuts to specification as follows:

- Intake manifold lower section to cylinder head: 71 inch lbs. (8 Nm)

- Fuel rail to cylinder head: 22 ft. lbs. (30 Nm) plus an additional 90° rotation
- High pressure pump to cylinder head: 89 inch lbs. (10 Nm)
- Union nuts for high-pressure fuel line: 21 ft. lbs. (28 Nm)
- Union nuts for connecting line of fuel rail: 21 ft. lbs. (28 Nm)

15. Replace O-rings between fuel injectors and fuel rail and coat them lightly with clean motor oil.

16. Replace spring elements at all fuel injectors.

17. Position intake manifold lower section with a new gasket.

18. Place fuel rail on and press evenly on to fuel injectors.

19. Insert all mounting bolts of intake manifold and of fuel rail by hand.

20. First evenly tighten fuel rail to cylinder head with new bolts from inside to outside.

21. Tighten the intake manifold lower section/cylinder head mounting bolts.

22. Install fuel rail connecting pipe.

23. Install high-pressure pump.

24. First, tighten connecting line union nuts by hand and then tighten to specification.

25. Install intake manifold upper section.

OIL PAN

REMOVAL & INSTALLATION

2.0L Engine

Lower Pan

See Figures 189 and 190.

1. Remove noise insulation.

2. If present, disconnect the electrical connector for the Oil Level Thermal Sensor G266.

3. Drain engine oil.

4. Remove the screws.

5. Remove oil pan.

To install:

6. Remove sealant residue from upper part of the oil pan with a flat scraper.

7. Remove sealant residue on the lower part of the oil pan, e.g. with a rotating plastic brush.

8. Clean sealing surfaces, must be free of oil and grease.

9. Cut tube nozzle at front nozzle approximately 0.117 in. (3 mm).

10. Apply silicon sealant (D 174 003 A2) to clean sealing surfaces of the oil pan (lower part).

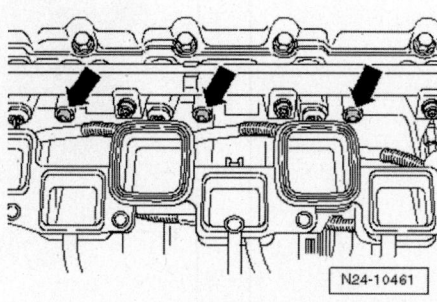

Fig. 188 Remove intake manifold lower part/cylinder head bolts (arrows)

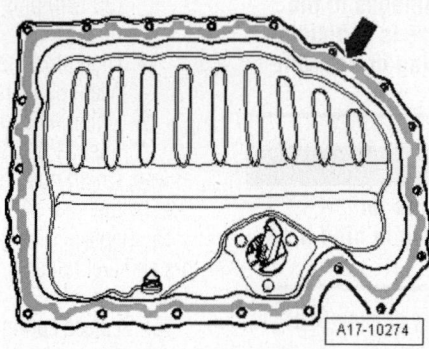

Fig. 189 Apply silicon sealant to clean sealing surfaces of the oil pan (lower part) as shown in illustration

❊❊ **CAUTION**

The oil pan must be installed within 5 minutes after application of silicon sealant.

➡ **The sealant bead may not be thicker than 0.078–0.117 in. (2–3 mm), otherwise excess sealant could enter the oil pan and clog the oil intake tube.**

11. Immediately mount the lower part of the oil pan and tighten the screws in two steps.

12. Tighten bolts/nuts to specification as follows:

- Tighten the bolts to 71 inch lbs. (8 Nm)
- Tighten the bolts an additional 90°

13. After installing oil pan, allow sealant to dry for approximately 30 minutes. Only after then may the engine oil be replenished.

14. Fill the engine oil.

15. The rest of the assembly is basically a reverse of the disassembling sequence.

Upper Pan

See Figures 191 through 193.

1. Remove the transaxle.
2. Remove the oil pump.
3. Remove the transaxle side sealing flange.
4. Remove the front right wheel housing liner.
5. Remove bolts.
6. Remove the air guide pipe by lifting the clamps.
7. Remove the two bolts.
8. Disconnect the wiring bracket mount next to the After-Run Coolant Pump from the upper part of the oil pan.

❊❊ **CAUTION**

To prevent leaks in the future, do not bend the lower timing chain cover

and do not reach between the mounting points.

❊❊ **CAUTION**

When removing the oil pan upper section, the chain tensioner spring for the oil pump motor will jump from the oil pan upper section to the lower timing chain cover. When removing the oil pan upper section, do not reach between the section and the lower timing chain cover.

9. Remove the bolts 1 through 14 and the upper section of the oil pan. When loosening, start on the transaxle side.

To install:

10. Mount the Assembly Tool (T10118) and pull the spring in the chain tensioner for the oil pump drive in the direction of the.

11. Secure the spring by inserting the gauge (VW 136) into the 2.2 mm hole.

12. Remove sealant residue from engine block with a flat scraper.

13. Remove the remaining sealant on the upper part of the oil an on the lower timing chain cover with a rotating plastic brush.

14. See if the timing chain cover is deformed. Then mount the top section of the oil pan without any sealant and check the gap between the cover and the top section. If a deformation is found, do not try to re)align it, replace the cover.

15. Clean sealing surfaces must be free of oil and grease.

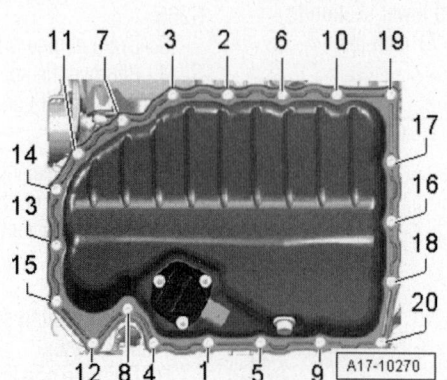

Fig. 190 Immediately mount the lower part of the oil pan and tighten the screws 1 through 20 in two steps as shown

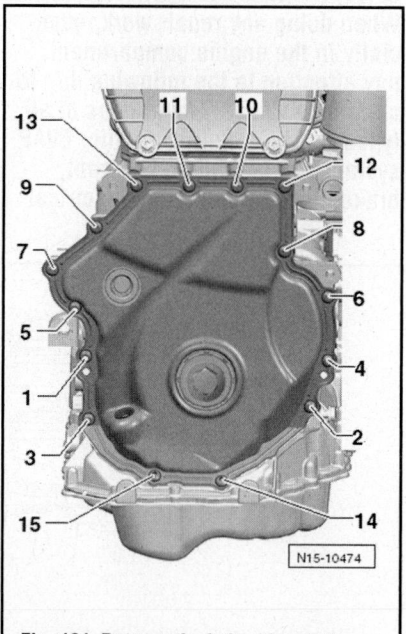

Fig. 191 Remove the bolts 14 and 15

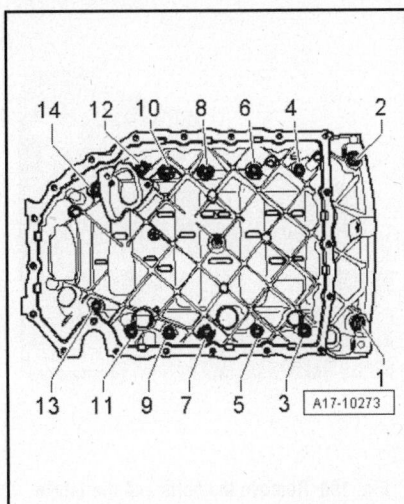

Fig. 192 Remove the bolts 1 through 15

16. Make sure the oil passages in the upper part of the oil pan and in the cylinder crankcase clean.

17. Cut tube nozzle at front to 0.117 in. (3 mm).

18. Apply the silicone sealant (D 174 003 A2) in a bead of 0.078–0.117 in. (2–3 mm) on the clean sealing surface of the upper oil pan section.

✳✳ CAUTION

The oil pan (upper part) must be installed within 5 minutes after application of silicone sealant.

➡**The sealant bead may not be thicker than specified, otherwise excess sealant could enter the oil pan and clog the oil intake tube.**

19. On the transaxle side, the upper part of the oil pan and the crankcase must align.

20. Immediately mount the upper part of

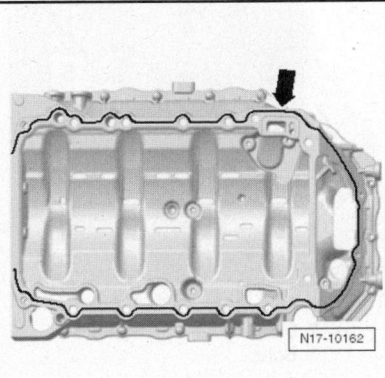

Fig. 193 Apply the silicone sealant in a bead of 0.078–0.117 in. (2–3 mm) on the clean sealing surface of the upper oil pan section as shown

the oil pan and tighten the screws 1 through 14 in two steps as follows:

21. Tighten bolts/nuts to specification as follows:
- Tighten the bolts to 11 ft. lbs. (15 Nm)
- Tighten the bolts an additional 90°
- Install the bolts 14 and 15

22. The rest of the assembly is basically a reverse of the disassembling sequence.

2.0L TDI Engine

See Figure 194.

1. Remove the noise insulation.
2. Drain the engine oil.
3. Remove the charge air cooler.
4. Remove the charge air cooling pump.
5. Loosen the fasteners and remove the oil pan noise insulation.
6. Remove the oil pan to transmission bolts.
7. Loosen and remove the oil pan bolts in a diagonal pattern.
8. Carefully loosen the oil pan.

To install:

9. Install in reverse order of removal.
10. Clean the oil pan mating surface.
11. Apply bead of sealant as illustrated to the clean sealing surface on the oil pan.
12. Install and tighten the oil pan bolts in a diagonal pattern.
13. Tighten the oil pan bolts as follows:
- Step 1: 1 through 20; tighten to 4 ft. lbs. (5 Nm) in a diagonal sequence
- Step 2 (arrows); tighten to 30 ft. lbs. (40 Nm)

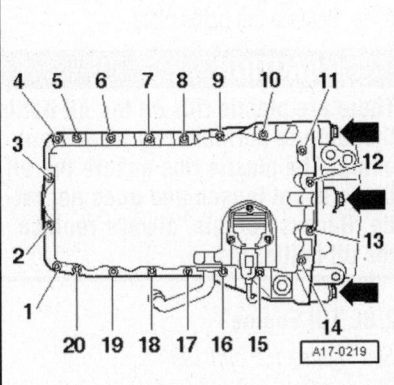

Fig. 194 Install and tighten the oil pan bolts in a diagonal pattern.

- Step 3: 1 through 20; tighten to 11 ft. lbs. (15 Nm) in a diagonal sequence

2.5L Engine

1. Remove noise insulation.
2. Drain engine oil.
3. Remove the screws, then pry oil pan, carefully, at equal points around the perimeter.
4. Remove oil pan.

To install:

5. Remove any sealant residue on the cylinder block and the upper oil pan
6. Apply sealant, in an even 1.5 to 2 mm bead, around the sealing surface of the oil pan mating.
7. Install the bolts and tighten them in a diagonal sequence to 7 ft. lbs. (10 Nm).
8. The rest of the installation follows the reverse of the removal procedure.
9. After installing the lower oil pan, the sealant must dry for approximately 30 minutes. Only after this may the engine oil be added.

3.6L Engine

See Figure 195.

1. Remove noise insulation.
2. Disconnect harness connector from the oil level thermal sensor.
3. Drain engine oil.
4. Remove oil pan.
5. Loosen oil pan with light blows of a rubber headed hammer if necessary.

To install:

6. Remove sealant residue from cylinder block with a flat scraper.
7. Remove remaining sealant at oil pan using a rotating brush, e.g. a drill with plastic brush attachment (wear protective glasses).
8. Clean sealing surfaces, they must be free of oil and grease.
9. Note the expiration date of the sealing compound.
10. The oil pan must be installed within 5 minutes after application of silicone sealant.
11. Cut tube nozzle to approximately 0.117 in. (3 mm).
12. Apply silicone sealing compound (D 176 501 A1) to clean oil pan sealing surface. The sealing compound bead must be 0.078–0.117 in. (2–4 mm in diameter) thick and run on inside of bolt holes.
13. Sealant bead must not be thicker than specified. Otherwise, excess sealant could get into oil pan and clog strainer in intake line of oil pump.

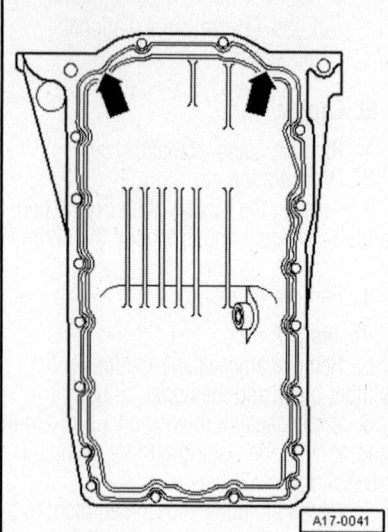

Fig. 195 Apply silicone sealing compound, as shown, to clean oil pan sealing surface. The sealing compound bead must be 0.078–0.117 in. (2–4 mm in diameter) thick and run on inside of bolt holes (arrows)

14. Apply sealant to clean sealing surface.

15. Install oil pan immediately and tighten all oil pan bolts lightly.
- Tighten oil pan bolts to 97 inch lbs. (11 Nm)
- Tighten oil pan/transaxle bolts to 33 ft. lbs. (45 Nm)

16. After installing oil pan, allow sealant to dry for approximately 30 minutes. Only after then may the engine oil be replenished.

17. The rest of the assembly is basically a reverse of the disassembling sequence.

OIL PUMP

REMOVAL & INSTALLATION

2.0L Engine

See Figures 196 and 197.

1. Remove the lower oil pan section.
2. Remove the oil baffle.
3. The following must be performed in one sequence; 2 technicians are necessary.
4. Remove the oil pump bolts.
5. Pull back the chain tensioner using the Assembly Tool (T10118) and have a second technician remove the oil pump.

To install:
6. Installation is performed in reverse order of removal.

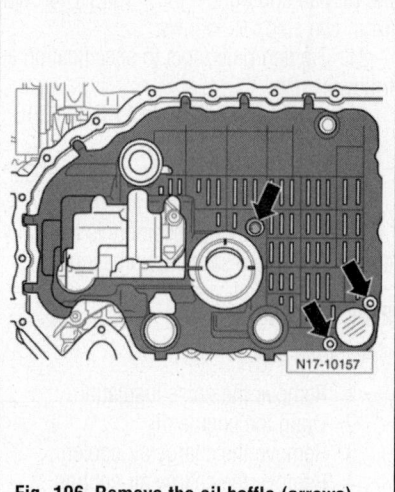

Fig. 196 Remove the oil baffle (arrows)

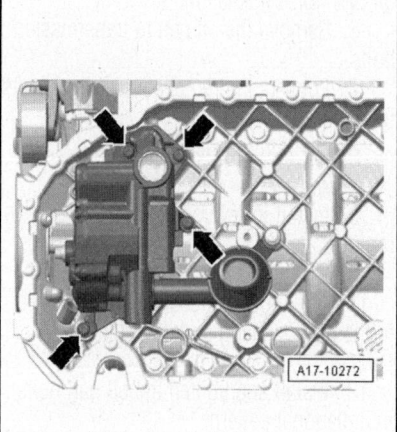

Fig. 197 Remove the oil pump bolts

7. Before installing the oil pump, make sure the screen in the supply line and the oil passages in the upper part of the oil pan are clean.

8. Make sure both alignment bushings for centering the oil pump are in place.

9. Replace the baffle plate.

✹✹ CAUTION

There are plastic ribs on the oil baffle that deform permanently when tightening. The plastic ribs ensure the oil baffle is not loosen and does not rattle. Because of this, always replace the oil baffle.

2.0L TDI Engine

See Figures 198 and 199.

➡If large quantities of metal particles or abraded material are detected during engine repairs, it may mean the crankshaft or rod bearings are dam-

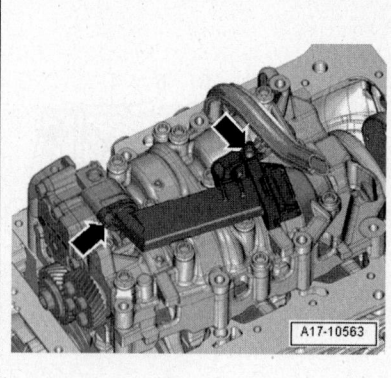

Fig. 198 Remove the bolts and the intake line from the oil pump.

aged. To prevent further damage, the following steps must be carried out after the repair: Oil passages must be cleaned carefully; replace the oil spray jets, the engine oil cooler and the oil filter element.

1. Remove the oil pan.
2. Remove the bolts and the intake line from the oil pump.
3. Remove the lock ring, using lock ring pliers.
4. Remove the driveshaft, with a magnet, from the oil pump.
5. Remove the bolts and remove the oil pump.

To install:
6. Install in reverse order of removal.
7. Replace the O-ring.

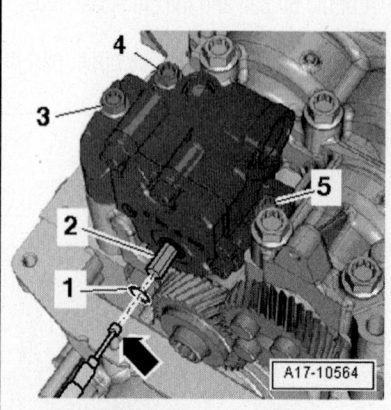

1. Lock ring   4. Bolts
2. Driveshaft   5. Bolts
3. Bolts

Fig. 199 Remove the lock ring, using lock ring pliers. Remove the driveshaft, with a magnet, from the oil pump. Remove the bolts and remove the oil pump.

8. Replace damaged or stretched lock rings.

9. The lock ring must lie in the base of the groove.

10. Replace any missing alignment sleeves for centering the oil pump on the balance shaft module.

11. Install the oil pan.

2.5L Engine

See Figures 200 through 205.

1. Remove the upper oil pan.

2. Tension the chain tensioner, secure it using the locking pin (T10115) and remove it.

3. Remove the oil pump sprocket bolt. Hold the sprocket (2) in place using the counterhold tool (T10172).

4. Remove the sprocket from the oil pump and unbolt the oil pump.

To install:

➡ **The crankshaft is secured**

5. Replace the O-ring.

6. Install the oil pump to the cylinder block hand tight.

7. Place the sprocket with the lettering facing outward onto the oil pump shaft and tighten it with a new bolt (drive chain not yet installed). Tighten to 15 ft. lbs. (20 Nm), plus an additional 90° (1/4) turn.

8. Loosen the three pump bolts (not the plate bolt).

➡ **The oil pump must be able to slide easily.**

9. Check the oil pump align plate (T03005). If there are still protective shields on the magnets, remove them.

10. Check that there are no shavings located on the magnets of the oil pump align plate.

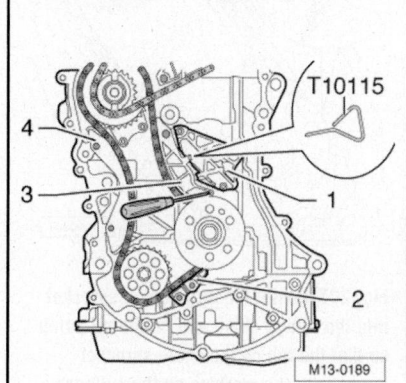

Fig. 200 Tension the chain tensioner (1), secure it using the locking pin and remove it. (Ignore 2, 3, 4.)

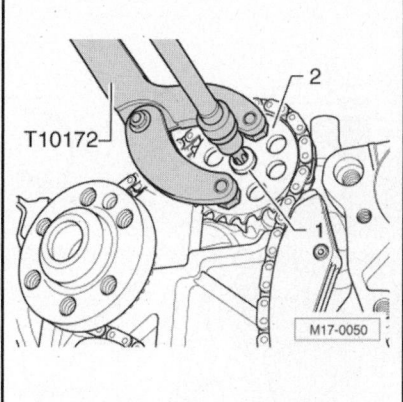

Fig. 201 Remove the oil pump sprocket bolt (1). Hold the sprocket (2) in place using the counterhold tool.

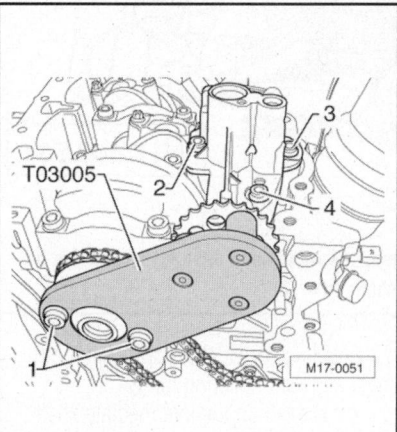

Fig. 202 Loosen the three pump bolts (2, 3, 4) (not the plate bolt).

➡ **The contact surfaces on the crankshaft, the tools and the sprocket must be clean.**

11. Place the oil pump shim (T03005/1) and the oil pump align plate on the crankshaft and secure both with two bolts from the vibration damper. Tighten the bolts to 22 ft. lbs. (30 Nm).

➡ **The oil pump is activated by magnets.**

12. Remove the locking pin (T40069). Remove the plug bolt and withdraw the pin.

13. Press the crankshaft in the axial bearing play toward the belt drive and secure it with a shim.

14. Press the oil pump lightly toward the chain drive.

15. In this condition, first tighten the bolts (2 and 3) and then the bolt (4) to 18 ft. lbs. (25 Nm).

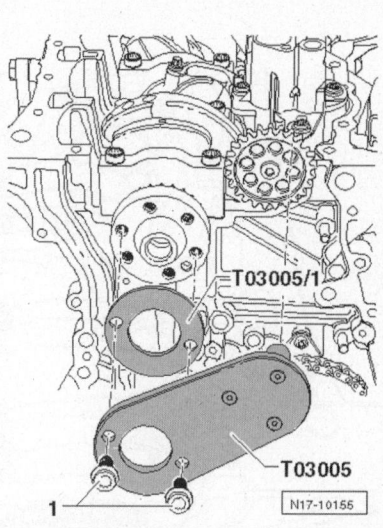

Fig. 203 Place the oil pump shim and the oil pump align plate on the crankshaft and secure both with two bolts (1) from the vibration damper. Tighten the bolts to 22 ft. lbs. (30 Nm).

16. Install the locking pin again. The crankshaft must only be rotated slightly around the Top Dead Center (TDC) point for this. Otherwise there is a risk the valves rest on the pistons.

17. Remove the oil pump align plate and the oil pump shim.

18. If a new oil pump is installed, fill the oil pump with some engine oil via the intake channel and rotate the oil pump several times through.

19. Place the drive chain onto the oil pump sprocket.

20. Install the upper oil pan.

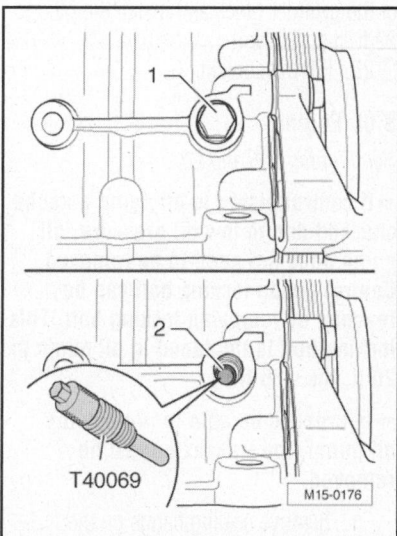

Fig. 204 Remove the locking pin. Remove the plug bolt (1) and withdraw the pin (2).

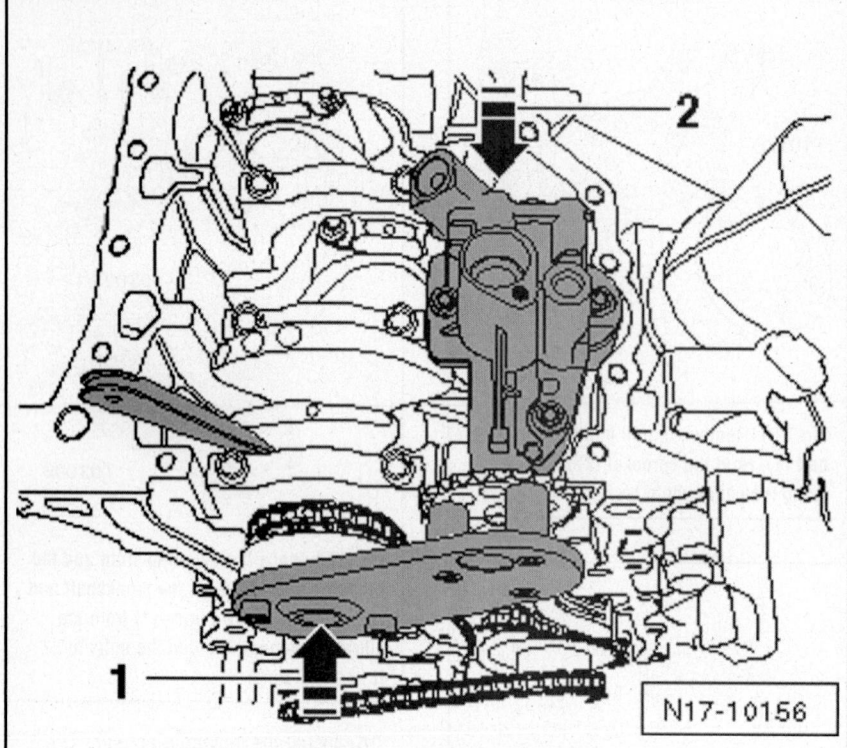

Fig. 205 Press the crankshaft in the axial bearing play toward the belt drive (1) and secure it with a shim. Press the oil pump lightly toward the chain drive (2).

21. Install the guide rail, relieve the tension on the chain tensioner and pull out the locking pin. Make sure that drive chain lies correctly in the guide rail and in the tensioning rail.

22. Adjust the valve timing.

23. The rest of the installation follows the reverse of the removal procedure.

24. Remove the locking pin from the rear of the cylinder block and install the plug to 22 ft. lbs. (30 Nm).

25. Fill the coolant.

3.6L Engine

See Figures 206 and 207.

➥If control piston in oil pump must be checked due to low oil pressure, oil pump does not need to be removed. Control piston locking bolt can be reached by removing locking bolt. This locking bolt is tightened in oil pump to 26 ft. lbs. (35 Nm).

➥In order to be able to remove the oil pump, the transaxle must be removed.

1. Remove sealing flange on the transaxle side.

2. Rotate engine by the vibration damper to the adjusting marking.

3. Milled drive chain sprocket tooth must align with bearing joint.

4. The tab on the intermediate shaft timing chain sprocket must align with the tab behind it.

5. This position is reached at every fourth turn.

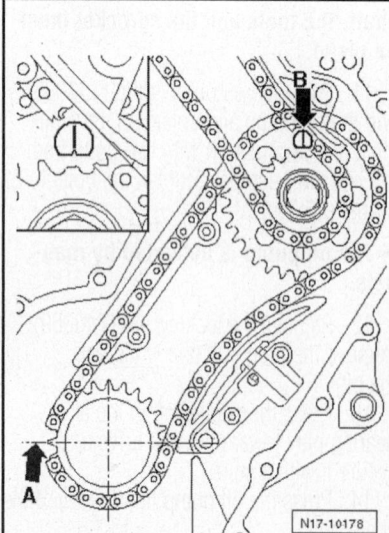

Fig. 206 Rotate engine by the vibration damper to the adjusting marking as shown

6. Loosen the chain sprocket bolt on the oil pump, but do not remove it. While doing that, counterhold the vibration damper using T10069.

7. Mark the position of the timing chain to the oil pump chain sprockets with a water resistant marker.

8. Remove chain tensioner for camshaft timing chain.

9. Remove tensioner for the oil pump drive chain.

10. Remove chain sprocket bolt and then remove the chain sprocket and timing chains from the oil pump.

11. Remove mounting bolts of oil pump.

12. Screw a threaded bolt M10x30 (standard) into oil pump shaft.

13. Screw extractor (T10055) with adapter (T10055/3) on to threaded bolt.

14. Pull oil pump out of cylinder block using light knocking motions.

To install:

15. Assembly is performed in reverse order.

16. Install oil pump and tighten the bolts.

17. O-ring as well as mounting bolts for oil pump and chain sprockets must always be replaced.

18. If the camshaft timing chain is to be replaced:

   a. Install the large chain sprocket into the timing chain and on the oil pump so

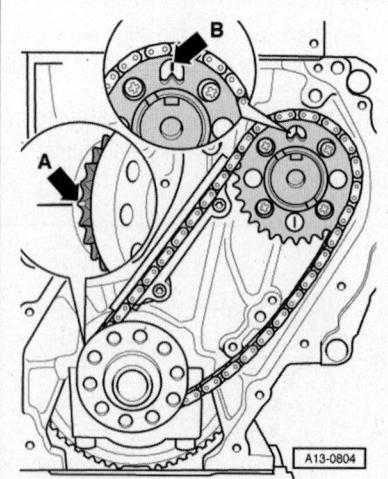

Fig. 207 Install the large chain sprocket into the timing chain and on the oil pump so that the tab on the chain sprocket aligns with the marking on the cylinder block (B). The markings made during removal must align. Milled drive chain sprocket tooth must align with bearing joint (A)

that the tab on the chain sprocket aligns with the marking on the cylinder block. The markings made during removal must align.

b. Milled drive chain sprocket tooth must align with bearing joint.

c. If large chain sprocket cannot be installed, rotate the oil pump slightly.

d. Insert small chain sprocket with installed chain into recess and bolt it on

hand-tight. The markings made during removal must align.

19. Now mount the chain tensioner.

20. Release locking splines of chain tensioner with a small screwdriver and tensioning rail pressed against chain tensioner.

21. Install the chain tensioner in this position and tighten to 71 inch lbs. (8 Nm).

22. Install chain tensioner for camshaft timing chain.

23. Tighten chain sprockets to 44 ft. lbs. (60 Nm) plus 90° additional rotation. To do so, lock vibration damper using counterholder tool. Only use bolts with strength category 10.9.

24. Install sealing flange.

PISTON AND RING

POSITIONING

See Figures 208 and 210.

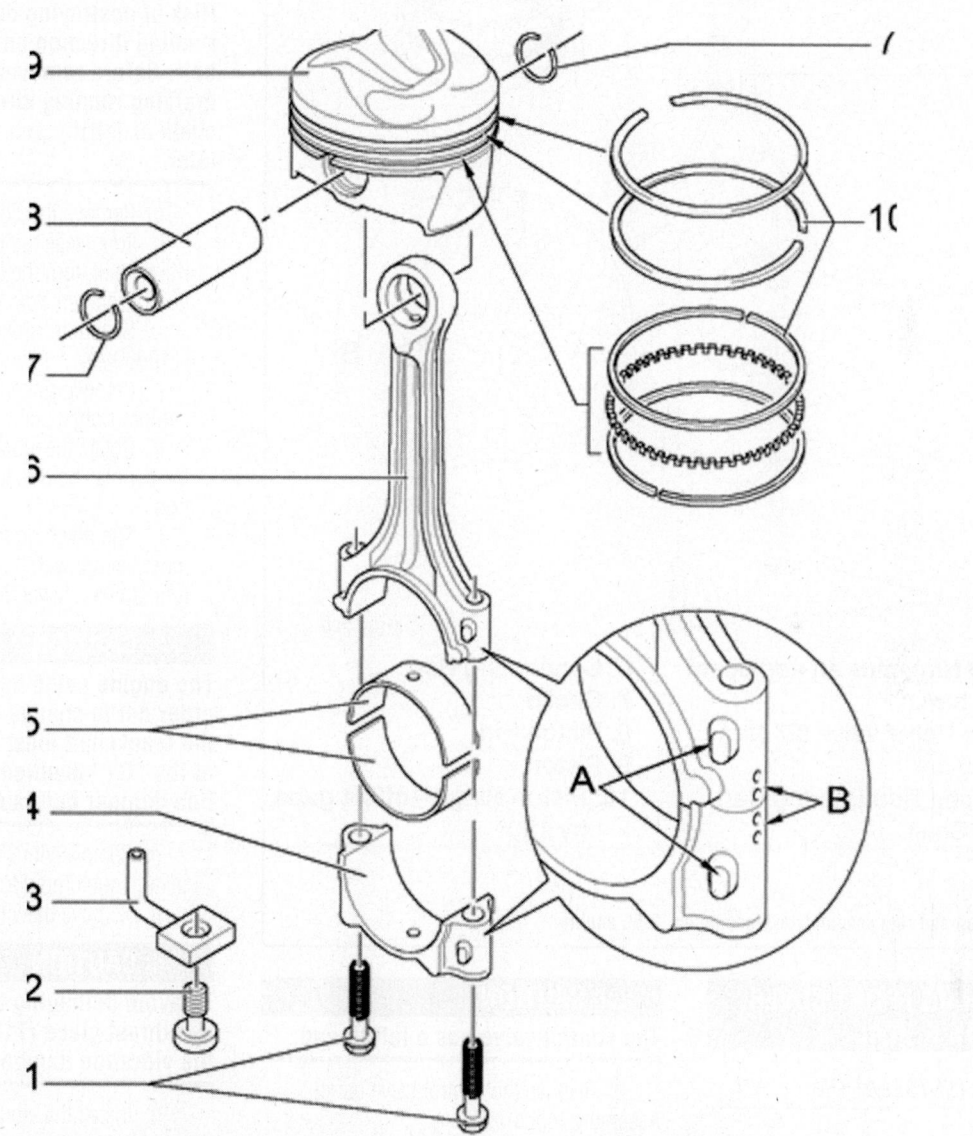

1. Connecting rod bolt
2. Bolt with pressure relief valve
3. Oil spray jet
4. Connecting rod bearing cap
5. Bearing shell
6. Connecting rod
7. Circlip
8. Piston pin
9. Piston
10. Piston rings

22205_VWCA_G0070

Fig. 208 Off set ring gaps by 120° –2.0L gasoline and 2.0L TDI engines

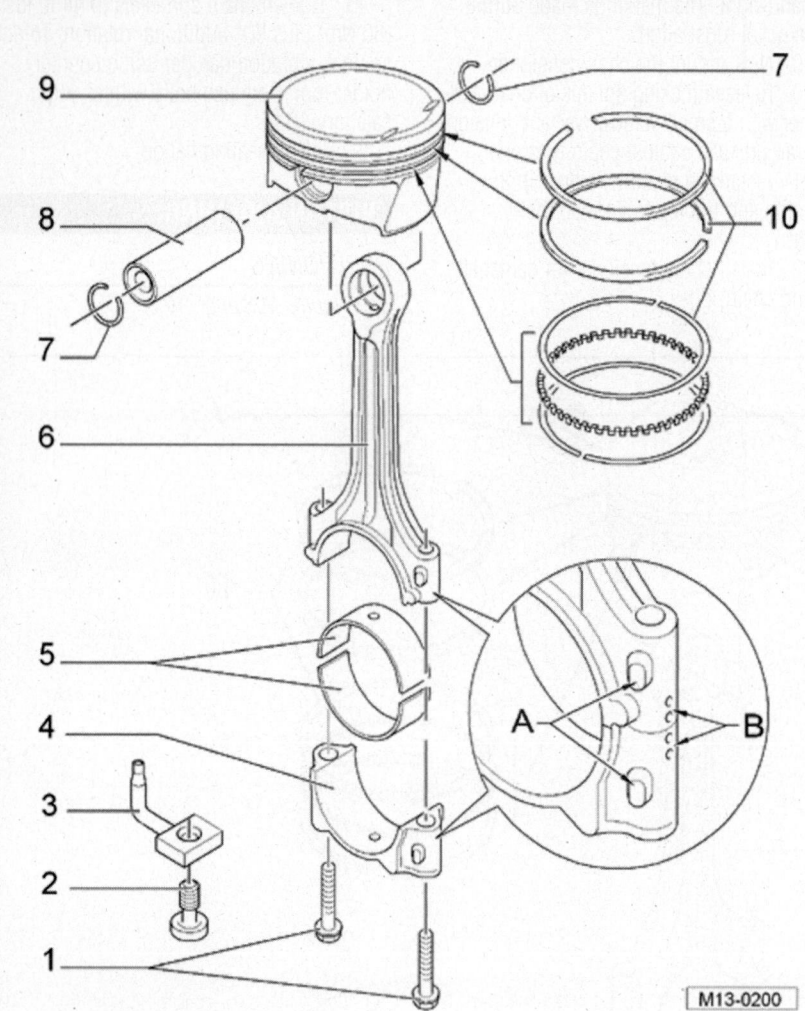

1. Bolt: (30 Nm), plus an additional 90° (1/4) turn.
2. Pressure Relief Valve (27 Nm)
3. Oil Spray Jet
4. Connecting Rod Bearing Cap
5. Bearing Shell
6. Connecting Rod
7. Circlip
8. Piston Pin
9. Piston
10. Piston Rings—offset gaps by 120°

Fig. 209 Piston and ring assembly exploded view–2.5L engine

TIMING CHAIN FRONT COVER, SPROCKETS & SEAL

REMOVAL & INSTALLATION

2.0L Engine

See Figures 211 through 217.

1. Remove the timing chain upper cover.
    a. Remove the Camshaft Adjustment Valve 1 N205.
    b. Remove bolts 1 through 5 and then remove the upper timing chain cover.

> ✻✻ **CAUTION**
>
> The control valve has a left thread.

2. Remove the control valve using Assembly Tool 10352.
3. Remove the bolts and remove the bearing bracket.
4. Rotate the vibration damper using the counter-hold tool T10355 into the "OT" position.
5. The notch on the vibration damper must line up with the marking on the timing chain lower cover.
6. The markings on the camshafts must point upward.

7. Remove the lower timing chain cover.
    a. Remove the noise insulation.
    b. Remove the front part of the right wheel housing liner.
    c. Drain engine oil.
    d. On vehicles with auxiliary heater, loosen the clamp, remove the bolt and remove the auxiliary heater muffler.
    e. Remove bolts.
    f. Remove the air guide pipe by lifting the clamps.

> ✻✻ **CAUTION**
>
> Risk of destroying due to reversed running direction on a used ribbed belt. Before removing ribbed belt, marking running direction with chalk or felt)tip pen for reinstallation later.

   g. Remove the right air guide hose.
   h. To release the tension on the ribbed belt, turn the tensioner in direction of rotation from underneath.
   i. Secure tensioner with drift (T10060 A).
   j. Remove ribbed belt from vibration damper ribbed belt pulley.
   k. Rotate the vibration damper using the counter-hold tool into the "OT" position.
   l. The notch on the vibration damper must line up with the marking on the timing chain lower cover.

> ✻✻ **CAUTION**
>
> The engine could be destroyed. In order not to change the valve timing, the crankshaft must not be moved out of the "OT" position when the vibration damper bolt is removed.

   m. Remove vibration damper bolt using counterhold tool.
   n. Remove the vibration damper.

> ✻✻ **CAUTION**
>
> To avoid damaging the splines, only use thrust piece (T10368) to install the vibration damper bolt.

   o. Install the vibration damper bolt and thrust piece again.
   p. Mount the engine support bridge (10 222 A).
   q. Do not place the adapter (10 222 A/8) on the fender panels. They will be damaged.
   r. The shackle 10 222 A /12 is needed to make sure the engine is lifted in the installation position and not tipped away.

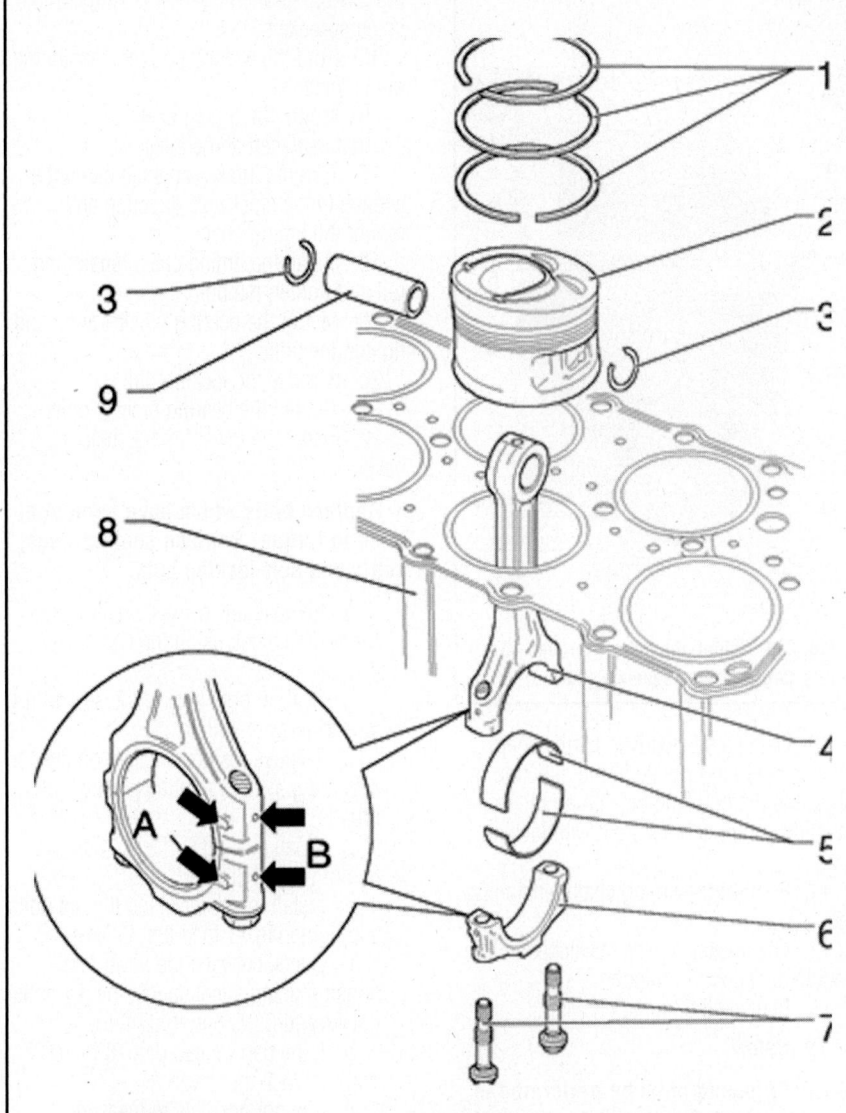

1. **Piston rings**
2. **Piston**
3. **Circlip**
4. **Connecting rod**
5. **Bearing shell**
6. **Connecting rod bearing cap**
7. **Rod bolts: always replace**
8. **Cylinder block**
9. **Piston pin**

22205_VWCA_G0206

Fig. 210 Off set ring gaps by 120° –3.6L engine

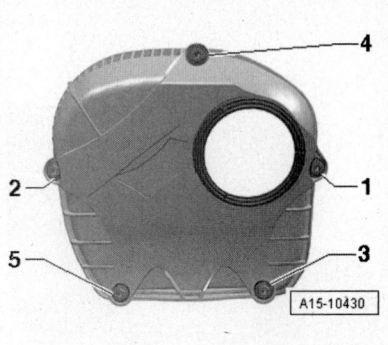

Fig. 211 Remove bolts 1 through 5 and remove the upper timing chain cover

Fig. 212 Rotate the vibration damper using the counter-hold tool T10355 into the "OT" position

Fig. 213 Pry off the lower timing chain cover starting with bolts 1 & 2 as shown

s. Tension the engine with the spindle.

t. Remove the subframe bolts on the engine.

u. Remove the engine bracket subframe mount.

v. Lift the engine approximately 1.95 in. (50 mm) and loosen the upper bolt for the engine support.

w. Now lower the engine approximately 3.9 in. (100 mm).

x. Free up electrical wiring harness.

y. Remove the bolt and remove the ribbed belt tensioner from the accessory assembly bracket.

z. Remove the lower bolts for the engine support using bits T10099.

aa. Remove the engine support and the bolts.

bb. Remove the bolts and pull the oil dipstick guide tube out of the lower timing chain cover.

cc. Disconnect the Wastegate Bypass Regulator Valve from the turbocharger.

dd. Remove the turbocharger support.

ee. Remove the bolts 1 through 15.

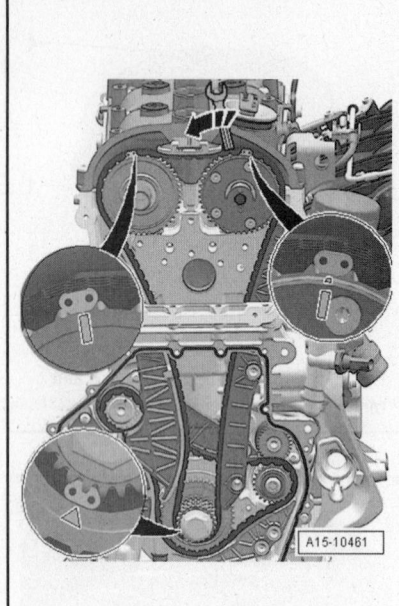

Fig. 214 Mount the timing chain on the exhaust camshaft and crankshaft

The lower timing chain cover could be damaged. To avoid deformation, do not hold between the bolting points.

ff. Pry off the lower timing chain cover.

8. Press the oil pump chain tensioner in the direction of the block side and secure it with a locking pin.

9. Remove the oil pump chain tensioner.

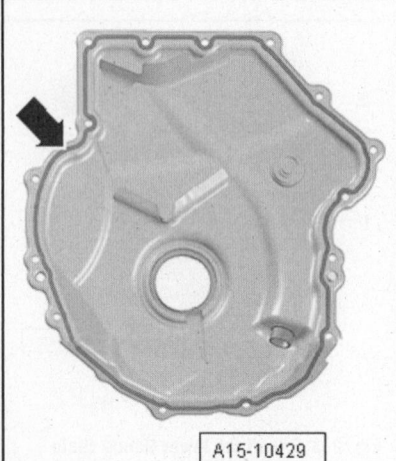

Fig. 215 Apply the silicone sealant in a bead of 0.078–0.117 in. (2–3 mm) on the clean sealing surface of the cover as shown

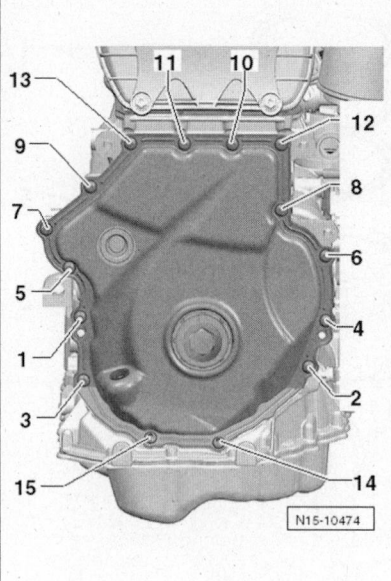

Fig. 216 Tighten the bolts 1 through 15 in 2 stages in the sequence shown

10. Using a screwdriver, lift the chain tensioner locking wedge in the direction of, press the timing chain tensioning rail in the direction of and secure it with locking pin.

11. Remove the timing chain tensioning rail.

12. The intake camshaft switches in the engine direction of rotation

13. Remove the timing chain.

To install:

➡ **The following must be performed in one sequence; 2 technicians are necessary.**

14. The painted links of the timing chain must be positioned on the markings on the chain sprockets.

15. Hold the wrench until the tensioning rail is installed.

16. Mount the timing chain on the exhaust camshaft and crankshaft.

17. Turn the intake camshaft using the wrench in the clockwise direction and mount the timing chain.

18. Install the timing chain tensioning rail and tighten the bolt.

19. Mount the bearing bracket and hand tighten the bolts.

20. Remove the locking pin.

21. Tighten the bearing bracket bolts

22. Install the lower timing chain cover.

➡ **Replace bolts which have been tightened to torque. Replace sealing rings, seals and self-locking nuts.**

a. Remove any sealant residue on the engine block using the flat blade scraper.

b. Seal off both side of the seal with tape to prevent soiling

c. Remove residual sealant on the cover; e.g., with a rotating plastic brush.

d. Clean sealing surfaces, must be free of oil and grease.

e. Install the cover using the old bolts and tighten to 71 inch lbs. (8 Nm).

f. Check between the cover and housing using a feel gauge; the gap must not exceed 0.0078 in. (0.2 mm).

g. If the gap exceed 0.0078 in. (0.2 mm), replace the cover.

h. It is not possible to measure between the cover the upper part of the oil pan, however check the sealing surface for evenness.

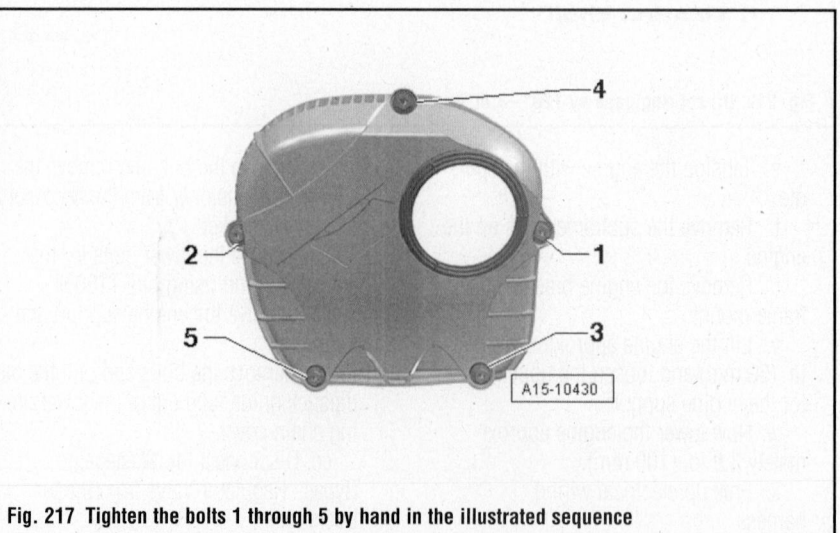

Fig. 217 Tighten the bolts 1 through 5 by hand in the illustrated sequence

i. Make sure both alignment bushings for centering the cover are present.

j. Cut tube nozzle at front marking to approximately 0.117 in. (3 mm).

k. Apply the silicone sealant (D 174 003 A3) in a bead of 0.078–0.117 in. (2–3 mm) on the clean sealing surface of the cover.

l. The cover must be installed within 5 minutes after application of silicone sealant.

m. The sealant bead may not be thicker than specified, otherwise excess sealant could enter the oil pan and clog the oil intake tube.

n. Install the lid immediately and all the bolts.

o. Tighten the bolts 1 through 15 in 2 stages in sequence:

- Tighten the bolts to 71 inch lbs. (8 Nm)
- Tighten the bolts an additional 90°

p. After installing cover, allow sealant to dry for approximately 30 minutes. Only after then may the engine oil be replenished.

23. Install timing chain upper cover.

a. Coat the sealing ring and the O-ring with engine oil.

b. Tighten the bolts 1 through 5 by hand in sequence.

c. Tighten the bolt to 80 inch lbs. (9 Nm) by using the torque wrench (V.A.G 1783) and the open end spanner insert (AF 10 V.A.G 1783/1).

24. The rest of the assembly is basically a reverse of the disassembling sequence.

25. Fill the engine oil.

26. Check oil level.

2.0L TDI Engine

See Figures 218 through 228.

1. Remove the dual mass flywheel.
2. Remove the intermediate plate.
3. Rotate the crankshaft to Top Dead Center (TDC) for cylinder 1.
4. Remove the oil pan.
5. Remove the engine speed sensor.
6. Remove the sealing flange bolts.

➡**The sealing flange and sensor wheel are pressed off the crankshaft using three M6 x 35 mm bolts.**

7. Install the three M6 x 35 mm bolts in the threaded holes on the sealing flange.

8. Tighten the bolts in an alternating sequence (maximum one turn 180° per bolt at a time) in the sealing flange and press the sealing flange and sensor wheel off the crankshaft.

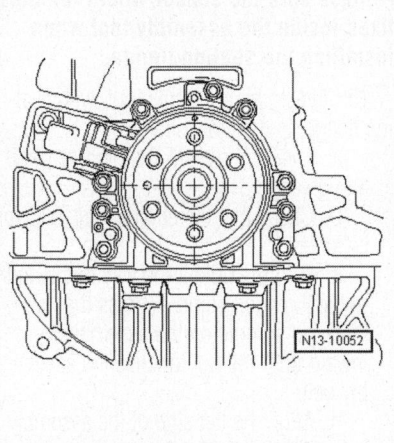

Fig. 218 Rotate the crankshaft to Top Dead Center (TDC) for cylinder 1.

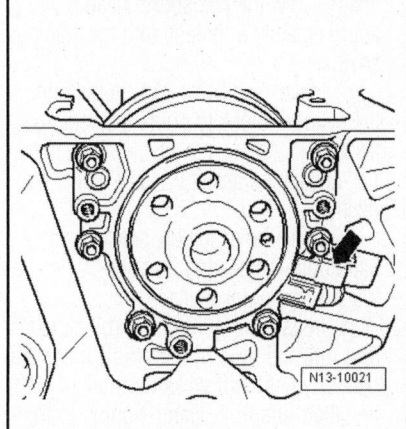

Fig. 219 Remove the engine speed sensor.

To install:
Installation Notes:
- The sealing flange with a Polytetrafluoroethylene (PTFE) seal is equipped with a

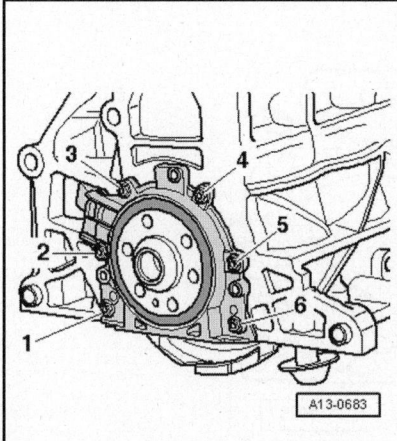

Fig. 220 Remove the sealing flange bolts.

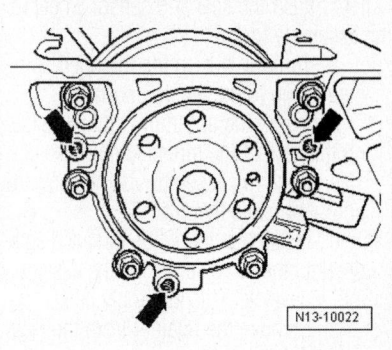

Fig. 221 Tighten the bolts in an alternating sequence (maximum one turn 180° per bolt at a time) in the sealing flange and press the sealing flange and sensor wheel off the crankshaft.

sealing lip support ring. This support ring serves the same function as a assembly sleeve and must not be removed before installation.

- The sealing flange and sensor wheel must not be separated or rotated after being removed from the replacement part packaging.

- The sensor wheel retains the installed position via being located on the locating pin of the assembly tool (T10134).

- The sealing flange and seal are one unit and may only be replaced together with the sensor wheel.

- The assembly tool retains the installed position to the crankshaft via a guide pin, which is guided into the bore of the crankshaft.

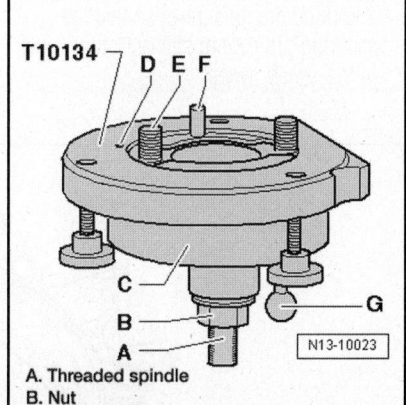

A. Threaded spindle
B. Nut
C. Assembly bell
D. Locating pin
E. Hex socket head bolt
F. Guide pin for diesel engines (black handle)
G. Guide pin for gas engines (red handle)

Fig. 222 The assembly tool retains the installed position to the crankshaft via a guide pin, which is guided into the bore of the crankshaft.

9. Attach the seal and sensor wheel to the assembly tool:

   a. Turn the nut on the threaded spindle just up to the tension surface.

   b. Install the assembly tool in a vise on the flats of the threaded spindle.

   c. Push the assembly bell downwards until it touches the nut.

   d. Install the nut on the threaded spindle until the inner section of the assembly tool is level with the assembly bell.

   e. Remove the retainer from the new sealing flange.

➡**The sensor wheel must not be removed from or rotated in the sealing flange.**

   f. The locating pin on the sensor wheel must align with the mark on the sealing flange.

   g. Place the sealing flange on a clean even surface with the front side facing up.

   h. Press the sealing lip support ring downward until it rests on the level surface.

   i. The upper edge of the sensor wheel and the front edge of the sealing flange must align.

   j. Install the sealing flange with the front side on the assembly tool so that the securing pin fits into the hole in the sensor wheel.

➡**Make sure the sealing flange is positioned flat on the assembly tool.**

   k. Press the sealing flange and the sealing lip support ring onto the surface of the assembly tool while tightening the 3 knurled thumb screws so that the securing pin cannot slip out of the hole in the sensor wheel.

➡**Make sure the sensor wheel remains fixed inside the assembly tool when installing the sealing flange.**

10. Attach the assembly tool, with sealing flange, to the crankshaft:

   a. Ensure the crankshaft is free of oil and grease.

   b. Check that the engine is at TDC for cylinder. 1.

   c. Turn the nut all the way to the end of the threaded spindle. Press the threaded spindle on the assembly tool inward until the nut touches the assembly bell.

   d. Align the flat side of the assembly bell with the oil pan side sealing surface of the crankcase.

   e. Secure the assembly tool with the hex socket head bolts to the crankshaft. Screw the hex socket head bolts approximately 5 threads into the crankshaft.

   f. Install two M7 x 35 mm bolts in the cylinder block to guide the sealing flange.

11. Fasten the assembly tool to the crankshaft:

   a. Slide the assembly bell inward by hand until the sealing lip support ring touches the crankshaft.

   b. Install the guide pins (black handle) into the hole in the crankshaft. The sensor wheel will be in its final installed position. Hand-tighten both hex socket head bolts of the assembly tool.

   c. Install the nut as far as possible on the threaded spindle by hand until the nut touches the assembly bell.

12. Install the sensor wheel on the crankshaft with the assembly tool:

   a. Tighten the nut for the assembly

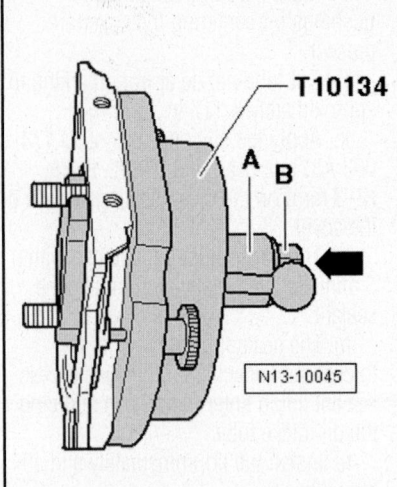

Fig. 224 Turn the nut (B) all the way to the end of the threaded spindle. Press the threaded spindle on the assembly tool inward until the nut touches the assembly bell (A).

tool using the torque wrench (5-50 Nm) (V.A.G 1331) and the tool insert (AF 24, V.A.G 1332/11) to 22 ft. lbs. (35 Nm).

   b. After tightening the nut, a minimal air gap must still be present between the cylinder block and sealing flange.

13. Check the sensor wheel installed position on the crankshaft:

   a. Install the nut all the way to the end of the threaded spindle.

   b. Remove the 2 bolts from the cylinder block.

   c. Remove the 3 knurled thumb screws from the sealing flange.

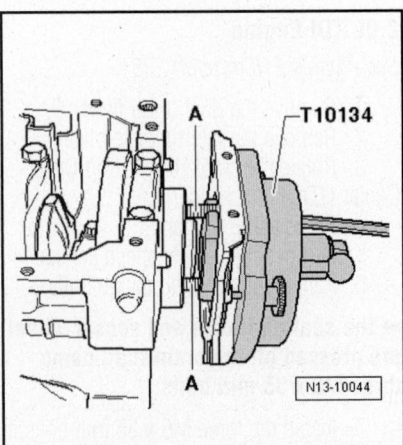

Fig. 225 Secure the assembly tool with the hex socket head bolts (A) to the crankshaft. Screw the hex socket head bolts approximately 5 threads into the crankshaft.

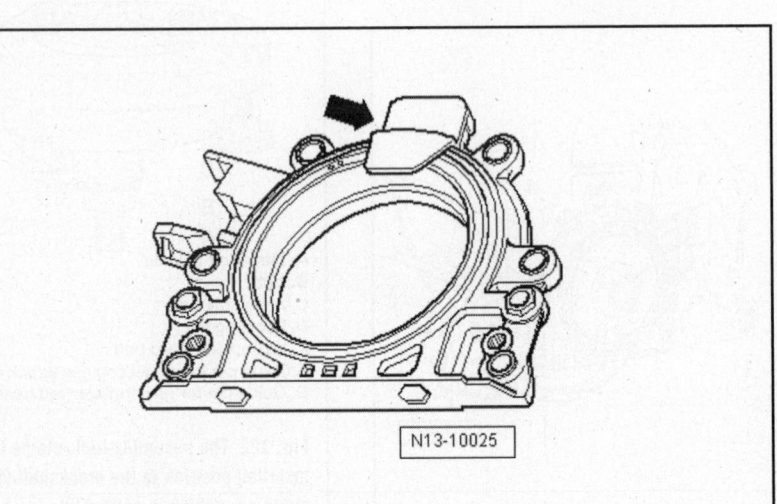

Fig. 223 Remove the retainer from the new sealing flange.

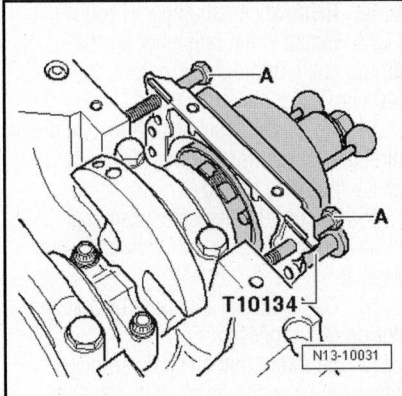

Fig. 226 Install two M7 x 35 mm bolts in the cylinder block to guide the sealing flange.

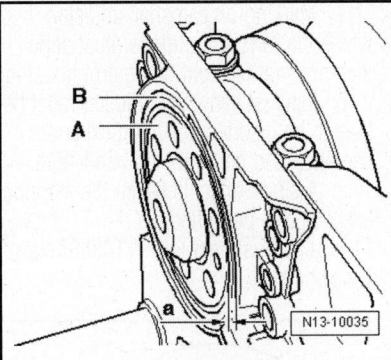

Fig. 227 The installed position of the sensor wheel on the crankshaft is exact if a gap of 0.5 mm (a) is present between the crankshaft flange (A) and sensor wheel (B).

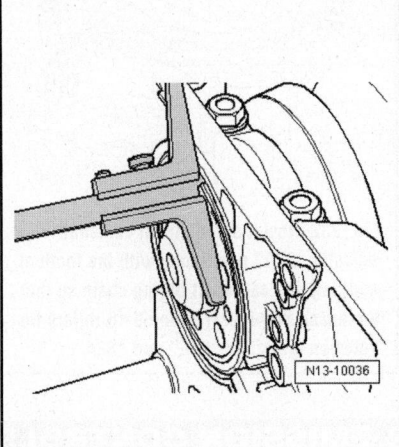

Fig. 228 Set a caliper gauge onto the crankshaft flange.

d. Remove the hex socket head bolt and remove the assembly tool.

e. Remove the sealing lip support ring.

f. The installed position of the sensor wheel on the crankshaft is exact if a gap of 0.5 mm is present between the crankshaft flange and sensor wheel.

g. Set a caliper gauge onto the crankshaft flange.

h. Measure the distance between the crankshaft flange and the sensor wheel. If dimension is too small, press on the sensor wheel.

i. If dimension is obtained, tighten the new sealing flange bolts alternating in a diagonal sequence to 11 ft. lbs. (15 Nm)

14. Install the engine speed sensor to 4 ft. lbs. (5 Nm).

15. Install the oil pan.

16. Install the intermediate plate.

17. Install the flywheel with new bolts.

3.6L Engine

See Figures 103, 229 through 232.

1. Removal is described in the camshaft removal & installation procedure.

2. Turn the crankshaft in engine direction of rotation to TDC No. 1 Cylinder.

3. Position camshafts in cylinder head to TDC of No. 1 cylinder.

➥**Cams of cylinder 1 must face each other.**

4. Insert the camshaft bar (T10068 A) into both shaft grooves. If necessary, slightly turn the camshaft back and forth using an open-end wrench.

5. Secure the position of the drive pinion for the high-pressure pump using the adjustment tool (T10363). Marking A on high-pressure drive cams must be at top.

6. First install camshaft adjuster for intake camshaft as follows:

a. Both camshaft adjusters (identification: "24E" on intake side and "32A" on exhaust side) can only bolted in one position on the camshaft mountings by an alignment pin.

b. Turn the sensor wheel on the intake camshaft adjuster clockwise in direction of rotation until it stops and hold the adjuster in this position.

c. If the intake camshaft adjuster is attached to the camshaft, the adjuster must be rotated left accordingly with the chain sprocket and then the camshaft timing chain must be routed.

7. Place the intake camshaft adjuster with the timing chain in place on the camshaft. Note the following:

a. The timing chain for the high-pressure pump drive train sprocket must not hang through.

b. It must be easy to mount the camshaft adjuster with the timing chain taut and can then be tighten by hand.

c. Arrow on camshaft adjuster "24E" must align with the right notch of control housing.

8. Now count exactly 16 rollers on timing chain, to the right, from the tooth with aligning notch. Mark this roller with a color marker. Exhaust camshaft adjuster is locked in the rest state. Therefore sensor wheel cannot be rotated when adjusting the valve timing. If locking mechanism in rest state is not engaged (locked) turn adjuster in both

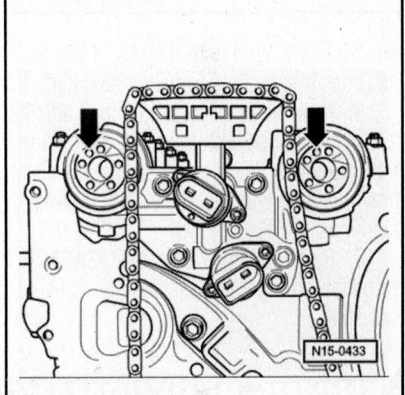

Fig. 229 Both camshaft adjusters (identification: "24E" on intake side and "32A" on exhaust side) can only bolted in one position on the camshaft mountings by an alignment pin

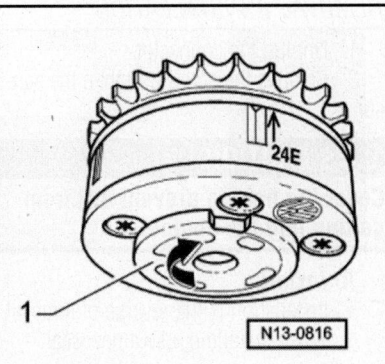

Fig. 230 Turn the sensor wheel 1 on the intake camshaft adjuster clockwise in direction of rotation until it stops and hold the adjuster in this position

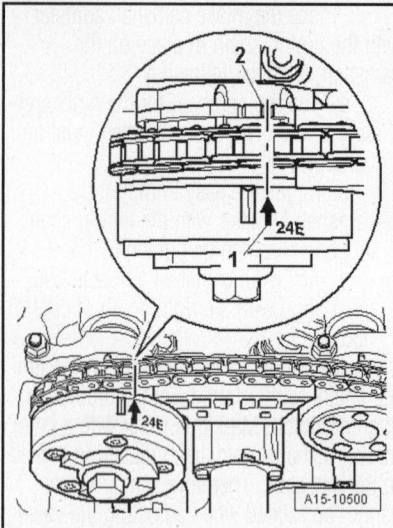

Fig. 231 Arrow on camshaft adjuster "24E" must align with the right notch of control housing.

directions by hand until it locks. If that is not possible, replace camshaft adjuster.

9. Now insert exhaust camshaft adjuster "32A" positioned with the tooth at marking into camshaft timing chain so that the exact, previously counted 16 rollers lie between markings "24E" and "32A".

10. Place camshaft adjuster "32A" with camshaft timing chain installed on exhaust camshaft.

a. Marking on camshaft adjuster which the "arrow" points to must align with notch at far right on control housing.

b. Exhaust camshaft adjuster must be able to be inserted easily on exhaust camshaft and be tightened hand-tight.

c. A small offset between the marking and notch is permitted.

11. Pull adjustment tool (T10363) out of bearing shaft.

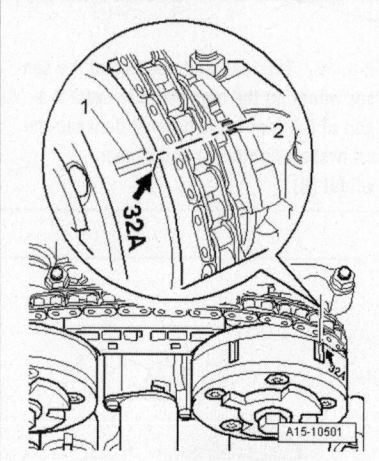

Fig. 232 Now insert exhaust camshaft adjuster "32A" positioned with the tooth at marking into camshaft timing chain so that the exact, previously counted 16 rollers lie between markings "24E" and "32A".

12. Remove camshaft bar (T10068).

13. Install chain tensioner for the timing chain and tighten to 30 ft. lbs. (40 Nm).

14. Rotate the crankshaft 2 revolutions in direction of rotation engine rotation and check the valve timing.

15. Secure the respective camshaft to be tightened using a 27 mm open-end wrench.

16. Camshaft bar must not be inserted during this process.

17. Be aware that all chain sprocket securing screws/bolts must be replaced.

18. Tighten the new mounting bolts for the intake and exhaust camshaft adjuster to 44 ft. lbs. (60 Nm) plus an additional 90° rotation.

19. Install sealing flange.

TURBOCHARGER

REMOVAL & INSTALLATION

➡**See "Exhaust Manifold/Turbocharger".**

VALVE LASH

ADJUSTMENT

➡**These engines use hydraulic valve lifters. No adjustment is necessary.**

ENGINE PERFORMANCE & EMISSION CONTROLS

CAMSHAFT POSITION (CMP) SENSOR

LOCATION

See Figures 233 through 235.

REMOVAL & INSTALLATION

1. Unplug the connector.
2. Remove the screw and then the sensor

✳ CAUTION

Cover the hole to prevent dirt from getting into the engine.

To install:

3. Installation is the reverse of removal.
4. When installing, use a new seal.

CRANKSHAFT POSITION (CKP) SENSOR

LOCATION

See Figures 236 and 237.

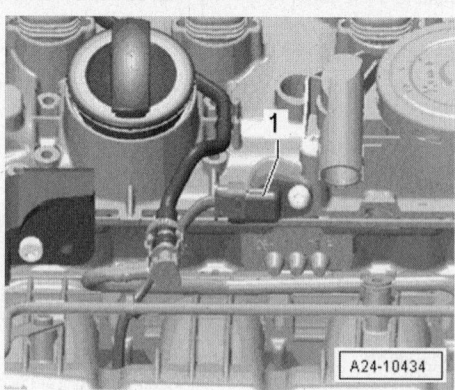

Fig. 233 Camshaft position sensor (1) with knock sensor (2) and fuel injector connector (3)— 2.0L engine

REMOVAL & INSTALLATION

1. Unplug the connector.
2. Remove the screw and then the sensor

➡**Cover the hole to prevent dirt from getting into the engine.**

3. When installing, use a new seal.

ELECTRONIC CONTROL MODULE (ECM)

LOCATION

See Figure 238.

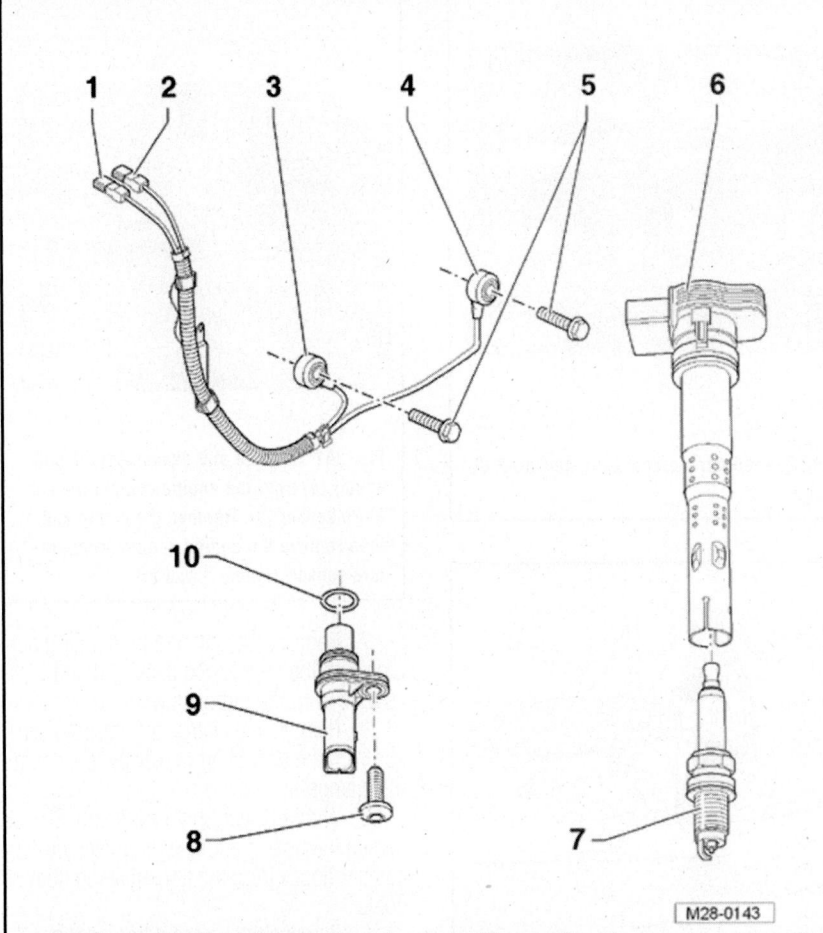

1. Knock sensor 2 connector (gray)
2. Knock sensor 1 connector (green)
3. Knock sensor 2
4. Knock sensor 1
5. Bolt: 15 ft. lbs. (20 Nm)
6. Ignition coil with power output stage
7. Spark plug
8. Bolt: 7 ft. lbs. (10 Nm)
9. Camshaft position sensor (CMP)
10. O-ring

Fig. 234 Camshaft position sensor with knock sensors and ignition coils—2.5L engine

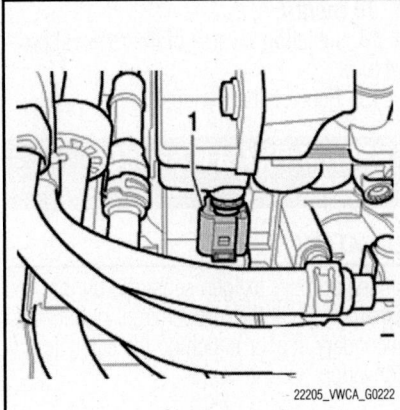

Fig. 235 Two CMP sensors are mounted on the front timing chain cover on either side of the camshaft timing control valves—3.6L Engine

Fig. 236 Crankshaft position sensor connector (1)—2.0L engine

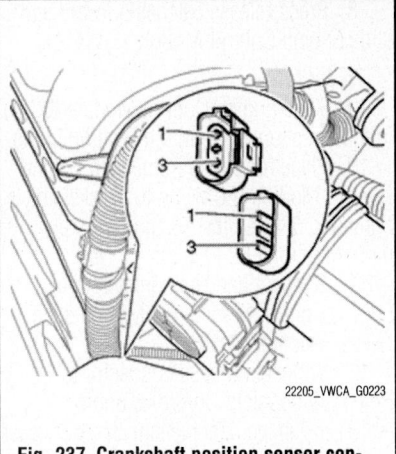

Fig. 237 Crankshaft position sensor connector—3.6L engine

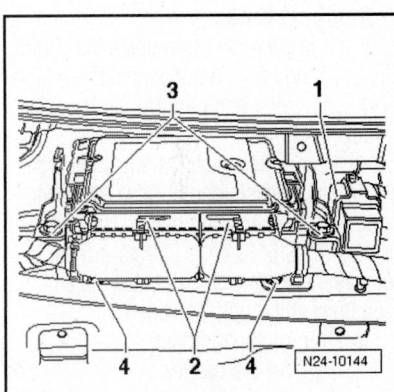

Fig. 238 ECM connector (1), catches (2), bolts (3) and nuts (4) location in the plenum chamber at the base of the windshield—Passat and Passat CC

REMOVAL & INSTALLATION

2011–12 CC Models and 2011 Passat Model

➡If it is desired to replace Engine Control Module (ECM), connect Vehicle Diagnosis, Testing and Information System (VAS 5051) and perform the guided function".

1. Switch off ignition.
2. Remove windshield wiper arms.
3. Remove the right plenum chamber cover.
4. Disconnect harness connector from Heated Windshield Control Module.
5. Slide connector release catches on Engine Control Module (ECM) outward and disconnect both harness connectors.
6. Unscrew mounting bolts.
7. Remove mounting frame with Engine Control Module (ECM) from plenum chamber.

8. Press release catches outward and slide Engine Control Module (ECM) off.

To install:

9. Slide Engine Control Module (ECM) in the direction of the into mounting frame.

10. Place mounting frame with Engine Control Module (ECM) on to bracket and tighten to 53 inch lbs. (6 Nm). Tighten mounting bolts 62 inch lbs. (7 Nm).

11. Connect harness connectors to Engine Control Module (ECM) and slide release catches inward.

12. Connect harness connector to Heated Windshield Control Module.

13. Install the right plenum chamber cover.

14. Install windshield wiper arms.

2012 Passat Model
Removal Notes:

• If it is necessary to replace the Engine Control Module (ECM), connect the vehicle diagnostic tester and perform the "Replace Control Module".

• Shear bolts attach the anti-theft brackets. It is not possible to remove the shear bolts without damaging them. Use axial grinder (VAS 6682) or a cutting grinder to remove the shear bolts. Replace the anti-theft bracket if it gets damaged.

1. Turn off the ignition.

2. Remove the battery.

3. Remove the E-box cover inside the engine compartment.

4. Free up the wiring harness and pull the ECM upward out of its mount. Push the locking mechanisms to the side.

5. Remove the shear bolts. Push the wiring harness as far as possible to the side. Remove the anti-theft bracket.

6. Unlock the connector and pull it off the ECM.

To install:

7. Install the ECM into the guides until it locks.

8. If the ECM was replaced, then attach the anti-theft bracket to the ECM with new shear bolts.

9. Tighten the shear bolts just enough until the bolt heads break off.

10. Connect the connectors to the ECM.

11. Install the anti-theft bracket with new shear bolts. Tighten the shear bolts just enough until the bolt heads break off.

12. Install the E-box cover.

13. Install the battery.

ENGINE COOLANT TEMPERATURE (ECT) SENSOR

LOCATION

See Figures 239 and 240.

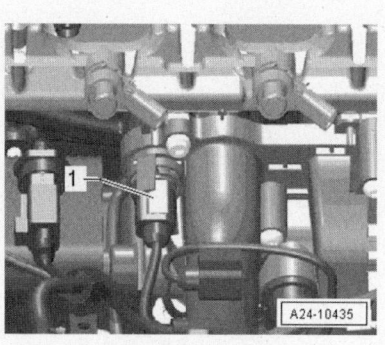

Fig. 239 Coolant temperature sensor–2.0L engine

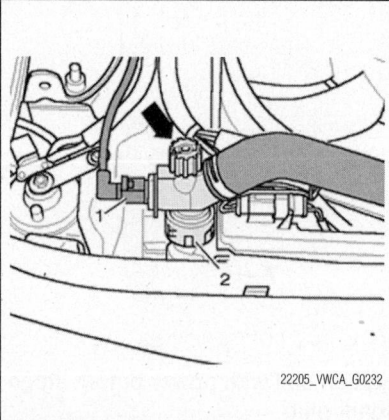

Fig. 240 Coolant temperature sensor–3.6L engine

REMOVAL & INSTALLATION

2.0L & 3.6L Engines

1. Drain the cooling system.
2. Unplug the connector.
3. Remove the sensor.

To install:

4. Installation is the reverse of removal.

5. When installing, use a new seal and/or retaining clip.

2.5L Engine

See Figure 241.

1. Remove the engine cover.
2. Remove the air filter housing.
3. Remove the noise insulation.
4. Press the release buttons and remove the crankshaft housing ventilation hose from the cylinder head cover.
5. Disconnect the connector from the crankshaft ventilation hose.
6. Free up the vacuum hoses -arrows- on the air guide pipe.

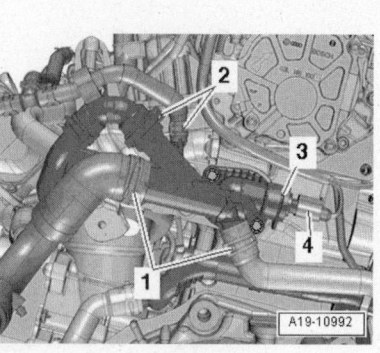

Fig. 241 Release and disconnect the connector (4) from the engine coolant temperature sensor (3). Remove the clamp and then remove the engine coolant temperature sensor. (Ignore 1 and 2.)

7. Remove the bolt and tilt the air guide pipe with the intake tube backward and remove from the turbocharger.

8. Remove the charge air pressure sensor from the charge air cooler by loosening the clamps.

9. With a Direct Shift Gearbox (DSG), loosen the hose clamps and remove the coolant hoses from the transmission fluid cooler.

10. Remove the bolt and free up the electrical wires and the hoses on the left air guide pipe.

11. Loosen the hose clamp and remove the air guide pipe.

12. Release and disconnect the connector from the engine coolant temperature sensor.

13. Remove the clamp and then remove the engine coolant temperature sensor.

To install:

14. Install in reverse of the removal procedure.

15. Replace the O-ring.

HEATED OXYGEN SENSOR (HO2S)

LOCATION

The primary oxygen sensor is on the exhaust pipe at the turbocharger outlet. The secondary sensor is behind the catalytic converter.

REMOVAL & INSTALLATION

1. Unplug the connector.
2. Remove the s sensor and cover the hole to prevent dirt from getting into the engine.

To install:

3. Installation is the reverse of removal.

➡ **Thread of new oxygen sensors is coated with hot bolt paste.**

✳✳ CAUTION

When re-using the previous oxygen sensor, grease only the threads with hot bolt paste G 052 112; the paste must not get into slots of oxygen sensor body

4. Tighten to 41 ft. lbs. (55 Nm).

INTAKE AIR TEMPERATURE (IAT) SENSOR

LOCATION

2.0L Engine

1. The IAT is mounted in the center of the intake manifold plenum near the throttle body.

3.6L Engine

The IAT is built into the Mass Airflow Sensor (MAF) and cannot be removed separately.

REMOVAL & INSTALLATION

2.0L Engine

1. Unplug the connector.
2. Remove the screw and the sensor and cover the hole to prevent dirt from getting into the engine.

To install:

3. Installation is the reverse of removal.
4. When installing, use a new seal.

KNOCK SENSOR (KS)

LOCATION

2.0L Engine

Knock sensor 1 is bolted to the cylinder block below the thermostat housing. Knock sensor 2 is bolted to the block below the oil filter bracket.

2.5L Engine

See Figure 242.

3.6L Engine

There are two knock sensors, one mounted on each side of the cylinder block.

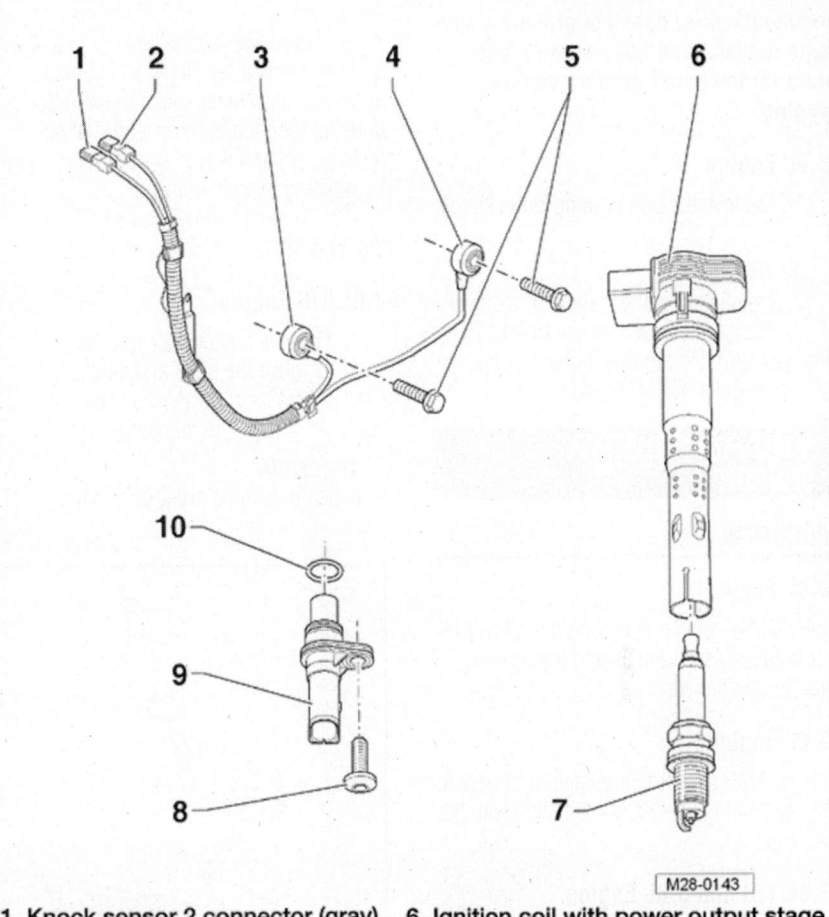

1. Knock sensor 2 connector (gray)
2. Knock sensor 1 connector (green)
3. Knock sensor 2
4. Knock sensor 1
5. Bolt: 15 ft. lbs. (20 Nm)
6. Ignition coil with power output stage
7. Spark plug
8. Bolt: 7 ft. lbs. (10 Nm)
9. Camshaft position sensor (CMP)
10. O-ring

M28-0143

Fig. 242 Showing the knock sensors on the 2.5L engine

REMOVAL & INSTALLATION

2.0L Engine

Knock Sensor 1

1. Drain the cooling system.
2. Remover the thermostat.
3. Remove the bolt to remove the knock sensor.

To install:

4. Installation is the reverse of removal.
5. Torque the knock sensor bolt to 15 ft. lbs. (20 Nm). Do not over-tighten or the sensor will not work properly.

Knock Sensor 2

1. Drain the cooling system.
2. Remove the intake manifold.
3. Disconnect the coolant hoses from the oil cooler.
4. Remove the oil cooler.
5. Disconnect the oil pressure switch.
6. Remove the four bolts to remove the oil filter bracket.
7. Remove the bolt to remove the knock sensor.

To install:

8. Install the sensor and torque the bolt to 15 ft. lbs. (20 Nm). Do not over-tighten or the sensor will not work properly.
9. Install the baffle plate, then install the oil filter bracket using new gaskets. Torque the bolts to 11 ft. lbs. (15 Nm).
10. Install oil cooler and connect coolant hoses.
11. Install the intake manifold.
12. Refill the cooling system and run the engine to check for leaks.

2.5L Engine

➡Manufacturer does not provide a specific removal and installation procedure for the knock sensors on this engine.

3.6L Engine

1. Remove the bolt to remove the knock sensor.

To install:

2. Installation is the reverse of removal.
3. Torque the knock sensor bolt to 15 ft. lbs. (20 Nm). Do not over-tighten or the sensor will not work properly.

MASS AIR FLOW (MAF) SENSOR

LOCATION

2.0L Engine

The MAF sensor is mounted in the air filter housing assembly behind the opening for the oil filler cap.

2.5L Engine

The MAF sensor is mounted in the intake air tube and is used in combination with the IAT sensor.

2.0L TDI and 3.6L Engine

The MAF sensor is mounted between the intake tube and the air filter housing.

REMOVAL & INSTALLATION

2.0L, 2.5L and 3.6L Engines

1. Disconnect air intake hose from the air filter housing.
2. Disconnect electrical connector 1 on Mass Air Flow (MAF) Sensor.
3. Remove both bolts from the Mass Air Flow (MAF) Sensor and carefully remove the Mass Air Flow (MAF) Sensor from the air filter housing guide.

To install:

4. Installation is the reverse of removal.
5. If the air filter element is very dirty or soaked, dirt particles or moisture may have contaminated the Mass Air Flow (MAF) Sensor and may be causing false mass air flow values. This results in a reduction of power, since a lower injection quantity is calculated.
6. Always use an original equipment air filter element.
7. Use a lubricant (silicone-free) for installing the intake hose.
8. Check the MAF sensor and intake hose (intake air side) for salt residue, dirt, and leaves.
9. Check the intake ducting up to the air filter element for dirt. If any contaminants are discovered, clean the air filter housing (upper and lower parts) of salt residue, dirt and leaves (if necessary, clean by washing or vacuuming).
10. Tighten clamps/screws to 13 inch lbs. (1.5 Nm).

2.0L TDI Engine

1. Remove the air filter housing.
2. Remove the bolts and carefully remove Mass Airflow (MAF) sensor out of guide on the air filter housing.

To install:

Install in reverse order of removal.

SECONDARY AIR INJECTION (AIR) SYSTEM

LOCATION

See Figure 243.

OPERATION

Secondary Air Injection (AIR) is an air pumping system consisting of the following:

- Secondary air injection pump motor
- Secondary air injection pump relay
- Secondary air injection solenoid valve
- Combination valves
- Air tubes
- Air inlet valves

The Engine Control Module (ECM) controls when the AIR system is activated by providing a ground to the AIR relay to turn on

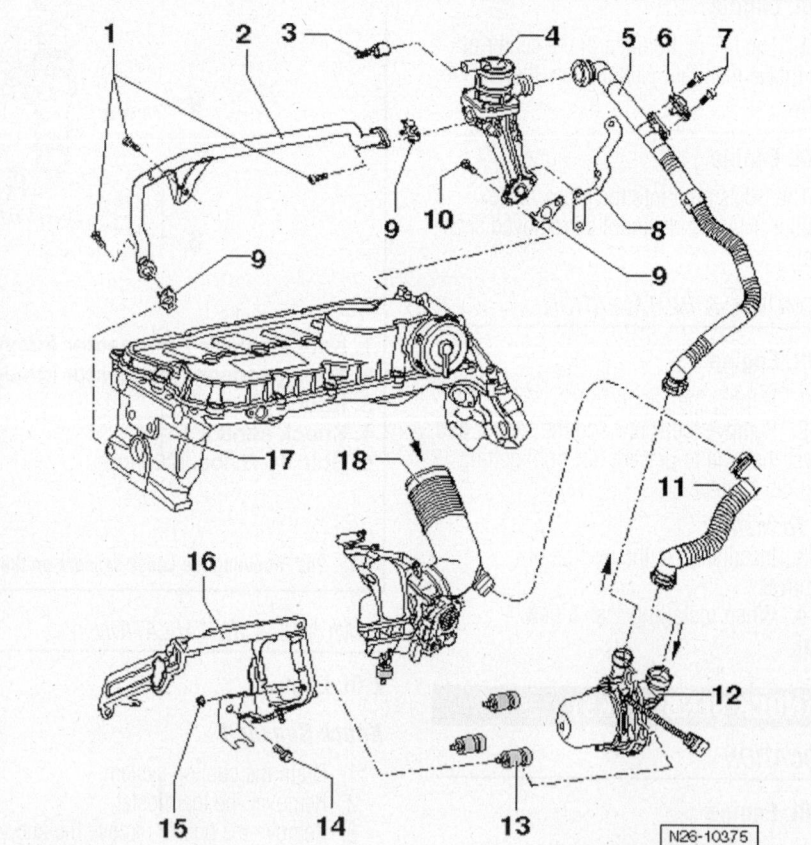

1. Bolt: 7 ft. lbs. (10 Nm)
2. Secondary Air Injection (AIR) Pipe
3. Connector
4. Secondary Air Injection Solenoid Valve -N112-
5. Connecting Pipe
6. Secondary Air Injection Sensor 1 -G609-
7. Screws
8. Bracket
9. Gasket
10. Bolt: 7 ft. lbs. (10 Nm)
11. Connecting Pipe
12. Secondary Air Injection Pump Motor -V101-
13. Rubber Bushing
14. Bolt: 18 ft. lbs. (25 Nm)
15. Nut: 7 ft. lbs. (10 Nm)
16. Bracket
17. Cylinder Head
18. Connecting Pipe

N26-10375

Fig. 243 Showing the AIR system component locations—2.5L engine

the pump motor. The AIR inlet valves (which are actually solenoids) controlled by the ECM, provide vacuum to open the combination valve. When vacuum is applied to the combination valves, pumped air is allowed to pass through to the exhaust manifolds. The purpose of the AIR system is to lower emissions during cold warm up by introducing oxygen into the exhaust manifolds to allow further combustion of unburned gasses resulting from cold enrichment.

It also has the added benefit of preheating the catalyst while the system is employed. The AIR system only runs during a cold start and the average run time is less that 2 minutes in cold weather. It will not run again unless the engine coolant temperature sensor and intake air temperature sensor readings match (usually within 4 Kelvin), indicating a cold start up.

REMOVAL & INSTALLATION

Secondary Air Injection Pump Motor

➡**Refer to the exploded view when servicing this and other components in the AIR system.**

1. Remove the nuts for the return line.

2. Remove the throttle valve control module.
3. Disconnect the connecting pipes.
4. Remove the noise insulation.
5. Disconnect the connectors.
6. Press out the wire guide clip.
7. Press out the wire clip at the top front mounting bolt.
8. Remove the Secondary Air Injection (AIR) pump motor bracket bolts from the intake manifold.
9. Remove the lower bolt from the AIR injection pump motor bracket.
10. Move the AIR injection pump motor bracket slightly to the side.
11. Remove the nuts and the AIR injection pump motor.

To install:

12. Install in reverse of the removal procedure.

THROTTLE POSITION SENSOR (TPS)

LOCATION

The throttle position sensor is built into the electronic throttle valve control module (throttle body).

REMOVAL & INSTALLATION

1. Loosen the hose clamp.
2. Remove bolt.
3. Disconnect electrical connector.
4. Remove the noise insulation.
5. Remove the air guide pipe.
6. Remove the bolt and remove the air guide pipe downward.
7. Disconnect electrical connector on Throttle Valve Control Module.
8. Remove bolts and remove Throttle Valve Control Module.

To install:

9. Installation is performed in reverse order of removal.:
10. Clean O-ring sealing surface.
11. Replace the seal; when doing so, pay attention to the correct position of the service flag on the sealing ring.
12. Tighten bolts in criss-cross pattern to 31 inch lbs. (3.5 Nm).

➡**If a new Throttle Valve Control Module was installed, adapt the engine control module to the Throttle Valve Control Module.**

FUEL

GASOLINE FUEL INJECTION SYSTEM

FUEL SYSTEM SERVICE PRECAUTIONS

Safety is the most important factor when performing not only fuel system maintenance but any type of maintenance. Failure to conduct maintenance and repairs in a safe manner may result in serious personal injury or death. Maintenance and testing of the vehicle's fuel system components can be accomplished safely and effectively by adhering to the following rules and guidelines.

• To avoid the possibility of fire and personal injury, always disconnect the negative battery cable unless the repair or test procedure requires that battery voltage be applied.

• Always relieve the fuel system pressure prior to disconnecting any fuel system component (injector, fuel rail, pressure regulator, etc.), fitting or fuel line connection. Exercise extreme caution whenever relieving fuel system pressure to avoid exposing skin, face and eyes to fuel spray. Please be advised that fuel under pressure may penetrate the skin or any part of the body that it contacts.

• Always place a shop towel or cloth around the fitting or connection prior to loosening to absorb any excess fuel due to spillage. Ensure that all fuel spillage

(should it occur) is quickly removed from engine surfaces. Ensure that all fuel soaked cloths or towels are deposited into a suitable waste container.

• Always keep a dry chemical (Class B) fire extinguisher near the work area.

• Do not allow fuel spray or fuel vapors to come into contact with a spark or open flame.

• Always use a back)up wrench when loosening and tightening fuel line connection fittings. This will prevent unnecessary stress and torsion to fuel line piping.

• Always replace worn fuel fitting O-rings with new Do not substitute fuel hose or equivalent where fuel pipe is installed.

Before servicing the vehicle, make sure to also refer to the precautions in the beginning of this section as well.

RELIEVING FUEL SYSTEM PRESSURE

❊❊ CAUTION

The fuel injection system is divided into a high-pressure section (maximum approximately 1740 psi or 120 bar) and a low pressure system (approximately 87psi or 6 bar).

Before opening high-pressure area e.g. removing high-pressure pump, fuel rail, fuel injectors, fuel pipes or Fuel Pressure Sensor fuel pressure in high-pressure area must be reduced to a residual pressure of approximately 87psi (6 bar).

1. Remove electrical connector from Fuel Pressure Regulator Valve using the Assembly Tool (T10118).
2. Allow engine to idle approximately 10 seconds.

a. When the Fuel Pressure Regulator Valve electrical connector is disconnected during idle, pressure in high-pressure area decreases to approximately 6 bar.

b. After high-pressure has been released, high-pressure system must be opened, otherwise the pressure increases again due to the warming of the fuel.

3. Switch off ignition.

❊❊ CAUTION

Fuel lines are pressurized! Wear protective goggles and protective clothing to prevent injuries and contact with skin. Before opening the high-pressure system, place a cloth around the connection.

4. Place a clean cloth around the connection point and carefully open to release the residual pressure of approximately 87psi (6 bar). Escaping fuel must be absorbed.

5. To conclude work, check DTC memory of Engine Control Module (ECM), erase all DTC entries which may have occurred from removing the connector. If DTC memory was erased, generate readiness code.

FUEL FILTER

REMOVAL & INSTALLATION

The fuel filter is located in-tank mounted to the fuel delivery unit.

FUEL INJECTORS

REMOVAL & INSTALLATION

2.0L Engine

See Figure 244.

➡**Puller T10133/2A is required to complete this operation.**

1. Remove the intake manifold with the fuel rail. If the injector valves remain attached in the fuel rail, then pull them out.
2. Cover the intake channels with a clean rag.
3. Remove the support element A downward and disconnect the connector from the fuel injectors.
4. Position the puller (T10133/2A) in the groove on the fuel injector.
5. Mount the removal tool (T10133/16), turn the screw and remove the fuel injector.

➡**Pay attention to the intermediate rings.**

To install:

✳✳ CAUTION

The combustion chamber seal must always be replaced before re-installing the fuel injector. The Teflon sealing ring of fuel injector may not be oiled or greased.

➡**If an opened intake valve hinders the cleaning, the engine must be turned further by hand using a screw wrench on the crankshaft.**

6. Thoroughly clean bores for high-pressure fuel injectors in cylinder head using nylon brush (T10133/4).
7. Replace O-ring and Teflon sealing ring of fuel injector.
8. Install the fuel injection with the intermediate ring again.

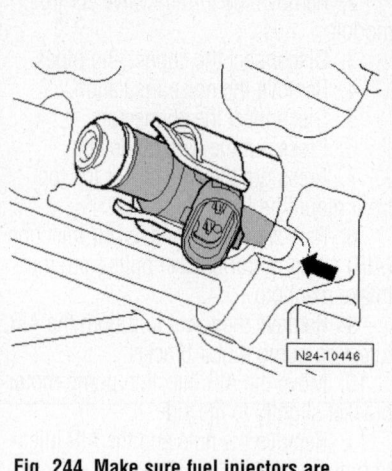

Fig. 244 Make sure fuel injectors are positioned correctly in cylinder head

9. Use the remover (T10133/2A) to push the fuel injector all the way into the hole in the cylinder head.

✳✳ CAUTION

Make sure fuel injectors are positioned correctly in cylinder head.

10. Install the intake manifold with the fuel rail.

2.5L Engine

See Figures 245 through 247.

1. Disconnect the battery.
2. Remove the engine cover with air filter.
3. Disconnect the fuel supply line and the vent line.

➡**Seal the lines so that the fuel system is not contaminated by dirt, etc.**

4. Disconnect the connectors.
5. Remove the wiring harness from the transport strap.
6. Pull the clamps and retaining ring out of the locking mechanism.
7. Remove the bolts and remove the transport strap.
8. Remove the bolts and pull the fuel rail with injectors evenly out of the intake manifold.
9. Seal or cover the openings in the intake manifold.
10. Pull of the retaining clips and then the fuel injectors.

To install:

11. Install new O-rings for the fuel injectors and coat them lightly with clean engine oil.
12. Press the fuel injectors into the fuel rail so that the tabs align.

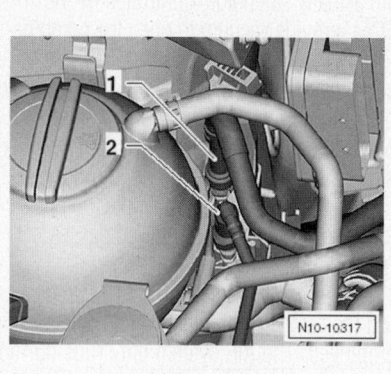

Fig. 245 Disconnect the fuel supply line (1) and the vent line (2).

13. Slide the retaining clip, into the groove of the fuel injector. The collar must be located correctly in the cutout of the retaining clip on both sides.
14. After assembling, check all fuel injectors for the correct fitting.
15. Attach the fuel rail with the secured fuel injectors onto the intake manifold and press it in uniformly.
16. Bolt the fuel rail to the intake manifold.
17. The rest of the installation follows the reverse of the removal procedure.
18. Connect the battery.
19. If the fuel injectors are replaced, erase the adaptation values and adapt the Engine Control Module (ECM) again. Refer to "Guided Functions" in the vehicle diagnostic tester.
20. Bleed the fuel system.

3.6L Engine

➡**The Teflon sealing ring on the fuel injector must be replaced each time the injector is removed. The long fuel injectors for cylinders 1, 3 and 5 must not be separated.**

1. Remove upper section of intake manifold.
2. Remove intake manifold lower section.
3. Remove fuel rail.
4. Push O-ring upward by hand and remove it from fuel injector.
5. Guide puller (T10133/15) onto the groove on the fuel injector.

➡**The spring element must not be removed prior to removing the injector valves.**

6. Carefully remove fuel injector.

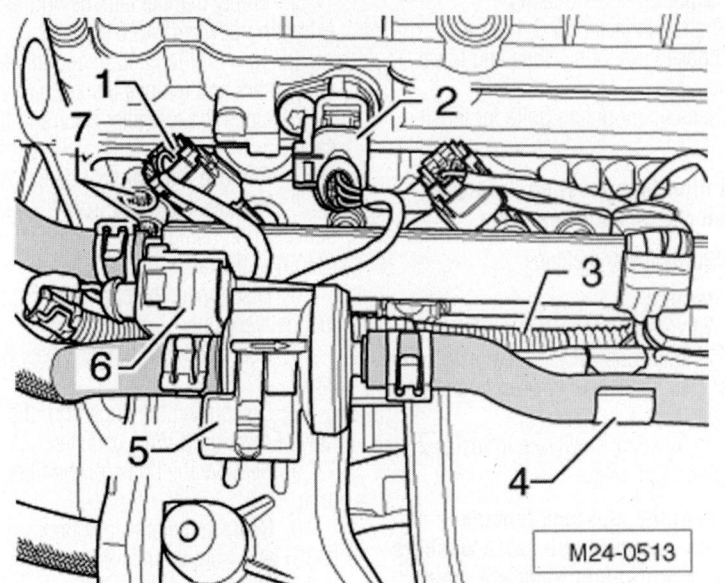

1. Connector
2. Connector
3. Wiring harness
4. Clamps
5. Retaining ring
6. Connector
7. Bolts

M24-0513

Fig. 246 Disconnect the connectors. Remove the wiring harness from the transport strap. Pull the clamps and retaining ring out of the locking mechanism. Remove the bolts and remove the transport strap.

To install:

7. Thoroughly clean bores for fuel injectors in cylinder head using nylon brush (T10133/4).

8. Check plastic support washer for damage and replace it if necessary.

9. Replace spring element and Teflon sealing ring each time fuel injector is removed.

10. Replace O-rings between fuel injectors and fuel rail and coat them lightly with clean motor oil.

11. Replace sealing ring at fuel injectors for cylinders 1, 3 and 5.

✳✳ CAUTION

The Teflon sealing ring of fuel injector may not be oiled or greased.

12. Press fuel injector by hand into cylinder head bore until it stops.

13. Check fuel injectors for correct seating and installation position in cylinder head.

14. Place fuel rail on and press evenly on to fuel injectors.

15. Tighten fuel rail with new bolts uniformly to 22 ft. lbs. (30 Nm) plus an additional 90° rotation.

16. Install intake manifolds.

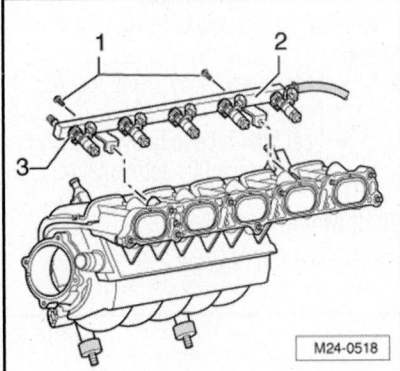

M24-0518

Fig. 247 Remove the bolts (1) and pull the fuel rail (2) with injectors evenly out of the intake manifold. Seal or cover the openings in the intake manifold. Pull of the retaining clips (3) and then the fuel injectors.

FUEL PUMP

REMOVAL & INSTALLATION

See Figures 248 and 249.

1. Empty the fuel tank.
2. Remove rear seat bench.
3. Remove cover with Fuel Pump (FP) Control Module from fuel delivery unit.

✳✳ CAUTION

Fuel supply line is under pressure! Wear protective goggles and protective clothing to prevent injuries and contact with skin. Before removing from hose connection wrap a cloth around the connection. Then release pressure by carefully pulling hose off connection.

4. Disconnect the 5-pin connector and disconnect the fuel line from flange.
   a. Press in securing ring to disengage the fuel line.
   b. On vehicles with auxiliary heater, harness connector and fuel line of Metering Pump must also be disconnected.

5. Open locking ring using wrench (T10202).

6. Lift the flange.

7. Disconnect coupling and remove suction jet pump. To do so, press tabs together.

8. Pull sealing ring and fuel delivery unit out of fuel tank opening.

➡ **If the delivery unit is to be replaced then drain old delivery unit before disposal.**

To install:

✳✳ CAUTION

Do not bend fuel level sensor floater arm when installing.

9. Insert delivery unit without suction jet pump into fuel tank.

10. Now install suction jet pump and connect coupling.

11. Install flange on to delivery unit.

➡ **Make sure hoses are correctly fastened.**

12. Now pull sealing ring over flange and insert it into fuel tank opening.

13. Coat sealing ring lightly with fuel and press flange into fuel tank.

14. Further installation is performed in reverse order.

15. Marking on flange must align with marking on fuel tank.

16. Tighten locking ring with wrench (T10202) so that locking ring is seated tightly.

17. Note the installation position of the cap. Mark on cover must point in direction of rotation travel.

18. Only coat sealing ring with fuel when installing flange

19. Route fuel lines kink-free.

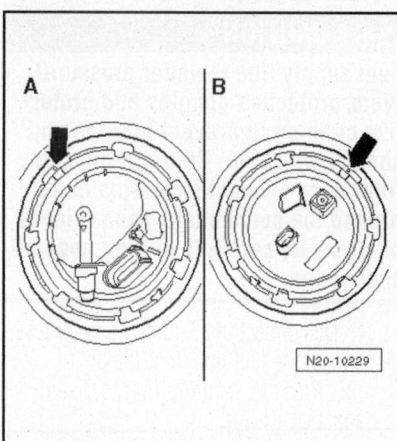

Fig. 248 Marking on flange must align with marking on fuel tank. FWD (A) and AWD (B)

20. Make sure lines connections are securely fastened.

FUEL TANK

REMOVAL & INSTALLATION

2011 Models

➡**Rear axle must be lowered to remove fuel tank.**

1. Empty the fuel tank.
2. Remove seat bench.
3. Remove cover with Fuel Pump (FP) Control Module from fuel delivery unit.
4. Disconnect 5-pin harness connector from flange.
5. Remove right rear wheel.
6. Remove right rear wheel housing liner.
7. Disconnect vent lines and vacuum line from EVAP canister.
8. Unclip electrical wire on fuel filler tube.
9. Remove mounting bolt for fuel flap unit and remove fuel flap unit.
10. Remove fuel filler tube from body.

⁕⁕ CAUTION

Fuel supply line is under pressure! Wear protective goggles and protective clothing to prevent injuries and contact with skin. Before removing from hose connection wrap a cloth around the connection. Then release pressure by carefully pulling hose off connection.

11. Press in securing ring to disengage the fuel lines.
12. Disconnect white vent line, green vacuum line and black fuel line at connection point.

13. Support rear axle using engine/transaxle jack (V.A.G 1383 A).
14. Loosen mounting bolts and lower rear axle.
15. Remove mounting bolts for tension straps.

➡**Fuel filler tube must be "removed" between chassis and rear axle.**

16. Slowly lower fuel tank.

To install:

17. With a second mechanic assisting, guide fuel filler tube between rear axle and chassis. Then place fuel tank on to engine and transaxle jack.
18. Lift fuel tank slowly up to installation position and secure it.

➡**To mount the fuel tank tension straps, only screws with loose washers may be used. If other bolts are used, the tensioning straps could twist when the bolts are tightened.**

19. Secure rear axle to chassis.
20. Further installation is performed in reverse order.
21. Make sure vent and fuel lines are not kinked.
22. Make sure lines connections are securely fastened.
23. Check ground (GND) connection of fuel tank/chassis at filler tube.
24. Tighten bolts/nuts to specification as follows:

- Fuel tank to body: 19 ft. lbs. (25 Nm)
- Fuel filler tube to body: 71 inch lbs. (8 Nm) plus 90° additional rotation

2012 Models

See Figures 250 through 256.

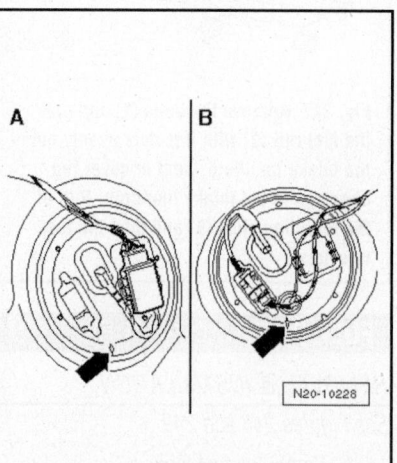

Fig. 249 Arrow on cover must point in direction of rotation travel. FWD (A) and AWD (B)

1. Empty the fuel tank using the fuel extracting device (VAS 5190).
2. Turn off the ignition and all electric consumers and remove the key.
3. Open the fuel filler door and the fuel cap.
4. Remove the rear seat bench.
5. Remove the cover from the fuel delivery unit using the trim removal wedge (3409) at the tabs.
6. Disconnect the connector from the fuel delivery unit.
7. Remove the right rear wheel housing liner.
8. Disconnect the lines from the Evaporative Emission (EVAP) canister.
9. Remove the bolts for the filler tube.
10. Remove the anti-lock brake system (ABS) wire from the retainers.
11. Loosen and lower the right rear underbody panel.

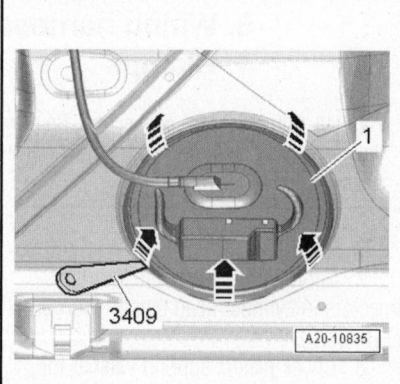

Fig. 250 Remove the cover from the fuel delivery unit using the trim removal wedge at the tabs.

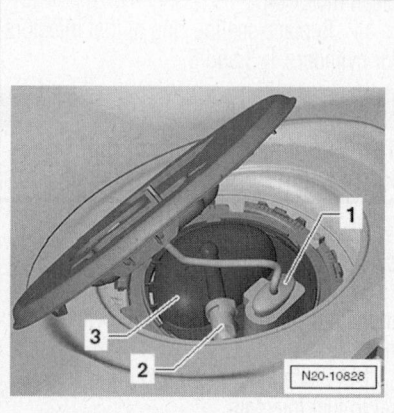

Fig. 251 Disconnect the connector (1) from the fuel delivery unit (2). Item (3) is a fuel line connection.

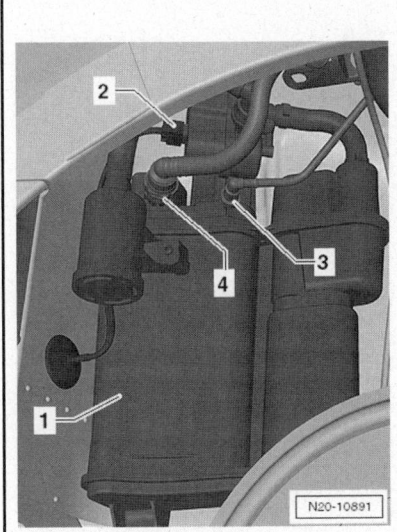

Fig. 252 Disconnect the lines (3, 4) from the Evaporative Emission (EVAP) canister (1). Ignore item (2).

12. Disconnect the black supply line and the white vent line.

13. Lower the rear subframe.

14. Loosen the bolts for the heat shield, if equipped, and then remove the heat shield.

15. Loosen the front exhaust clamping sleeve. Push the rear section of the exhaust system out of the retaining rings.

16. Remove the bolts, then remove the bumper cover outward and swivel the exhaust system downward.

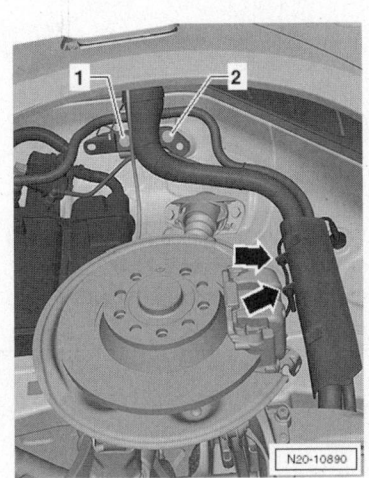

Fig. 253 Remove the bolts (1, 2) for the filler tube. Remove the anti-lock brake system (ABS) wire (arrows) from the retainers.

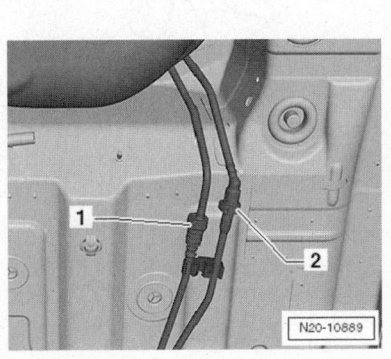

Fig. 254 Disconnect the black supply line (1) and the white vent line (2).

➡ **The exhaust system is then hanging by the rear subframe and the rear tunnel brace.**

17. Push the exhaust system as far as possible to the left.

18. Loosen the fuel tank heat shield nuts and remove the heat shield.

➡ **A second technician is required for the remainder of the procedure to help support the fuel tank.**

19. Remove the bolts from the straps. Have a second technician hold the fuel tank while doing this.

➡ **Pay attention to the installed position of the fuel tank tensioning straps. Mark them if necessary. Always make sure there is enough clearance for the filler tube to prevent damaging the fuel tank while removing it.**

20. Swivel the fuel tank downward and pull it as far as possible away from the rear

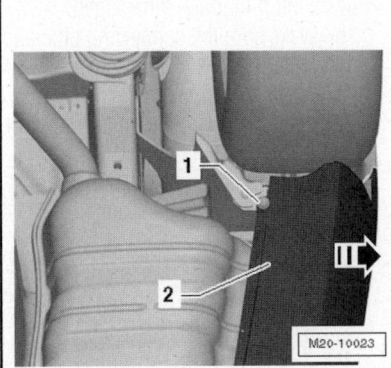

Fig. 255 Remove the bolts, then remove the bumper cover in the direction of the arrow and swivel the exhaust system downward.

subframe. Pay attention to the parking brake cable while doing this.

21. Move the fuel tank to the right and downward and then pull it forward.

22. Move the fuel tank downward once it is removed from the rear subframe. While doing this turn the fuel tank to the left.

23. Remove the fuel tank downward. While doing this turn the fuel tank slightly to the left. The filler tube can then be guided past the rear subframe.

To install:

24. Install in the reverse order of removal. Note the following:

   a. Make sure the vent and fuel lines are not kinked.

   b. Be careful not to confuse the supply line and the vent line (the supply line is black and the vent line is white).

   c. Make sure the line connections are securely fastened.

   d. Make sure the ground connection on the filler tube is secure.

   e. Make sure the lines are still attached to the fuel tank after installing the fuel tank.

   f. Install the heat shield and nuts to the fuel tank. Attach the heat shield to the rear subframe.

   g. Counter-hold the brake line bracket when tightening the bolts.

   h. Pay attention to the installed position of the fuel tank tensioning straps. Tighten the bolts to 15 ft. lbs. (20 Nm), plus an additional 90° (1/4) turn

25. Raise the rear subframe.

26. Bleed the fuel system.

IDLE SPEED

ADJUSTMENT

Idle speed is automatically controlled by the Electronic Control Module (ECM). No adjustment is possible.

THROTTLE BODY

REMOVAL & INSTALLATION

1. Loosen the hose clamp.
2. Remove bolt.
3. Disconnect electrical connector.
4. Remove the noise insulation.
5. Remove the air guide pipe.
6. Remove the bolt and remove the air guide pipe downward.
7. Disconnect electrical connector on Throttle Valve Control Module.
8. Remove bolts and remove Throttle Valve Control Module.

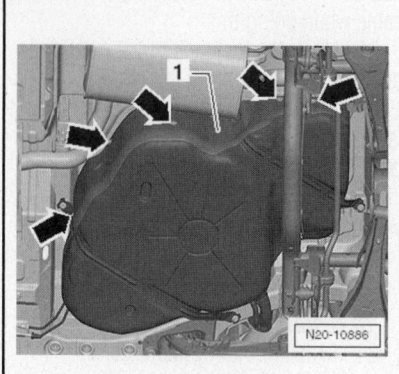

Fig. 256 Loosen the fuel tank heat shield (1) nuts and remove the heat shield.

To install:

9. Installation is performed in reverse order of removal.

10. Clean O-ring sealing surface.

11. Replace the seal; when doing so, pay attention to the correct position of the service flag on the sealing ring.

12. Tighten bolts in criss-cross pattern to 31 inch lbs. (3.5 Nm).

✳✳ CAUTION

If a new Throttle Valve Control Module was installed, adapt the engine control module to the Throttle Valve Control Module.

THROTTLE VALVE CONTROL MODULE

REMOVAL & INSTALLATION

2.5L Engine

See Figures 257 and 258.

1. Remove the engine cover with air filter.

2. Remove the connecting pipe between the throttle valve control module and air filter. To do so, disconnect the connecting pipe, if equipped with Secondary Air Injection (AIR), and the vent tube, then reposition the spring clamp.

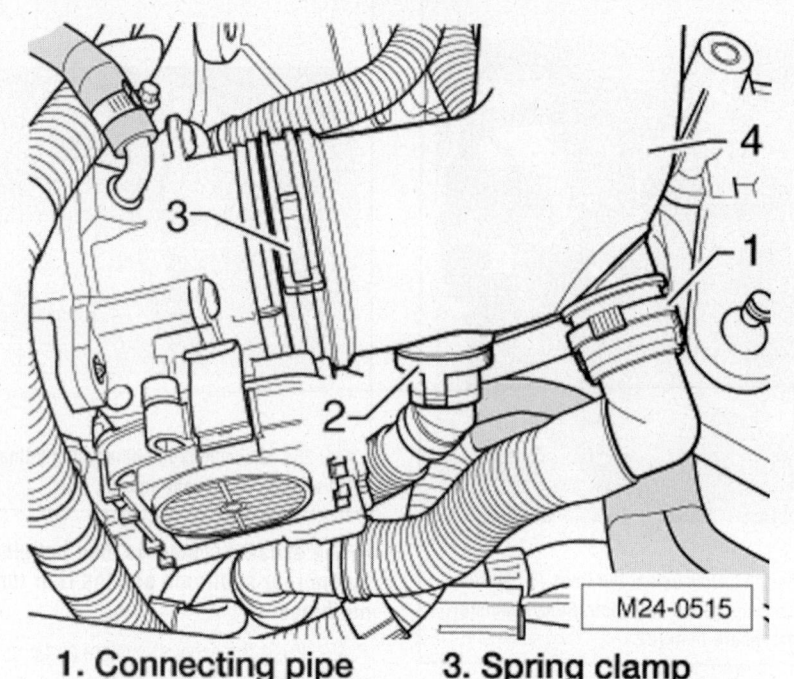

1. Connecting pipe   3. Spring clamp
2. Vent tube   4. Connecting pipe

Fig. 257 Remove the connecting pipe between the throttle valve control module and air filter. To do so, disconnect the connecting pipe, if equipped with Secondary Air Injection (AIR), and the vent tube and reposition the spring clamp.

3. Remove the air duct bolts and air duct from the lock carrier.

4. Disconnect the connector and vent hose.

5. Remove the bolts.

6. Remove the throttle valve control module.

7. Seal the intake passage in the intake manifold using a clean cloth.

To install:

8. Install in the reverse order of removal.

  a. Replace the seal for the throttle valve control module, if damaged.

  b. Make sure the connecting pipe and vent tube are securely connected.

  c. When replacing, erase the adaptation values and adapt the Engine Control Module (ECM) to the throttle valve control module. Refer to "Guided Functions" in the vehicle diagnostic tester.

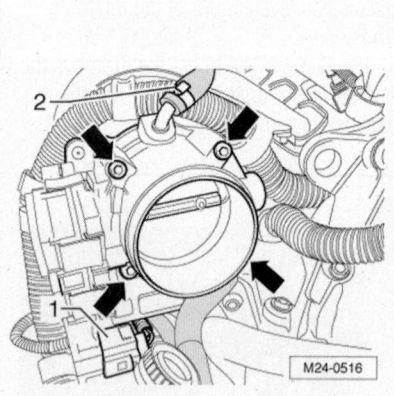

Fig. 258 Disconnect the connector (1) and vent hose (2), remove the bolts (arrows), and remove the throttle valve control module.

FUEL SYSTEM SERVICE PRECAUTIONS

Safety is the most important factor when performing not only fuel system maintenance but any type of maintenance. Failure to conduct maintenance and repairs in a safe manner may result in serious personal injury or death. Maintenance and testing of the vehicle's fuel system components can be accomplished safely and effectively by adhering to the following rules and guidelines.

• To avoid the possibility of fire and personal injury, always disconnect the negative battery cable unless the repair or test procedure requires that battery voltage be applied.

• Always relieve the fuel system pressure prior to disconnecting any fuel system component (injector, fuel rail, pressure regulator, etc.), fitting or fuel line connection. Exercise extreme caution whenever relieving fuel system pressure to avoid exposing skin, face and eyes to fuel spray. Please be advised that fuel under pressure may penetrate the skin or any part of the body that it contacts.

• Always place a shop towel or cloth around the fitting or connection prior to loosening to absorb any excess fuel due to spillage. Ensure that all fuel spillage (should it occur) is quickly removed from engine surfaces. Ensure that all fuel soaked cloths or towels are deposited into a suitable waste container.

• Always keep a dry chemical (Class B) fire extinguisher near the work area.

• Do not allow fuel spray or fuel vapors to come into contact with a spark or open flame.

• Always use a back)up wrench when loosening and tightening fuel line connection fittings. This will prevent unnecessary stress and torsion to fuel line piping.

• Always replace worn fuel fitting O-rings with new. Do not substitute fuel hose or equivalent where fuel pipe is installed.

Before servicing the vehicle, make sure to also refer to the precautions in the beginning of this section as well.

FUEL SYSTEM FILLING AND BLEEDING

FILLING & BLEEDING

✳✳ CAUTION

Allowing the high-pressure pump to run dry will destroy it. The high-pres-

sure pump must be filled with fuel before starting the engine for the first time. Do not allow the high-pressure pump to run dry.

1. When installing the high-pressure pump, make sure that no dirt enters the fuel system.

2. Only remove the sealing plugs right before installing the fuel lines.

➡**The fuel tank must be filled.**

3. To fill the high-pressure fuel pump with fuel, proceed as follows:

a. Turn on the ignition.

b. Connect the vehicle diagnostic tester and, depending on the software version, under Guided Functions, perform the "fuel system, bleeding" or "fuel system, filling/bleeding".

➡**The fuel pump is activated for 3 minutes.**

c. Start the engine.

d. After filling the fuel system, allow the engine to run at a moderate speed for a few minutes and then turn it off.

4. Check the fuel system for leaks.

5. Check the Diagnostic Trouble Code (DTC) memory and erase, if necessary. Refer to the vehicle diagnostic tester.

6. Then, perform a road test driving faster than 20 km and fully pressing the accelerator pedal at least one time. Then, check the high-pressure areas for leaks again.

➡**If there is still air in the fuel system, the engine may switch to emergency mode during the road test.**

7. Turn off the engine and erase the DTC memory. Then continue the road test.

8. Recheck the DTC memory.

FUEL PRESSURE REGULATOR VALVE

LOCATION & OPERATION

The fuel pressure regulator valve is located on the fuel rail and maintains a constant pressure inside the rail and in the fuel injector lines (fuel high-pressure circuit).

If the pressure in the fuel high-pressure circuit is too high, the regulator valve will open so that some of the fuel flows from the rail back into the fuel tank via a return line.

If the pressure in the fuel high-pressure circuit is too low, the fuel pressure regulator

valve closes and seals the high-pressure side from the low pressure side.

REMOVAL & INSTALLATION

➡**The fuel pressure regulator valve must always be replaced if removed.**

1. Remove the fuel rail.

2. Before removing the pressure regulator valve, clean the threaded area around the fuel pressure regulator valve (for example using commercially available coolant). Contamination must not enter the bore in the fuel rail. Dry the fuel pressure regulator valve.

3. Counter hold at the housing hex and loosen the union nut. Then remove it by hand.

4. Extract the contamination from the fuel rail bore (threads and sealing surface). Do not use mechanical tools.

5. Seal the fuel rail opening with a plug.

To install:

6. Install in reverse order of removal. When doing this note the following:

a. The fuel pressure regulator valve has a biting edge instead of a sealing ring and cannot be reused.

b. Check for damage to the sealing surfaces and threads for the new fuel pressure regulator valve.

c. Check the sealing surfaces on the fuel rail opening.

d. Coat the fuel pressure regulator valve threads and biting edge with diesel fuel.

e. Tighten the union nut by hand.

f. Align the new regulator valve so that the connection line is not taut after connecting the connector.

g. Counter hold the regulator valve at the housing hex in this position using an open end wrench or pliers (for example, water pump pliers).

h. Use a suitable torque wrench with a 30 mm open end wrench to tighten the union nut.

i. Install the fuel rail.

FUEL PRESSURE SENSOR

LOCATION

The fuel pressure sensor is located in the fuel rail. It measures the current fuel pressure in the high-pressure system and delivers a voltage signal to the Engine Control Module (ECM).

REMOVAL & INSTALLATION

See Figures 259 and 260.

1. Remove the engine cover.
2. Before removing, clean the threaded area around the fuel pressure sensor using a commercially available detergent.

➡**Dirt must not enter the bore. Clean carefully, the cleaner must not enter the connector.**

3. Open the wire strip and remove the connector for the glow plug. Set the wire set aside.
4. Dry the fuel pressure sensor.
5. Release and disconnect the connector for the fuel pressure sensor. Remove the fuel pressure sensor.
6. Extract the contamination from the fuel rail bore (threads and sealing surface). Do not use mechanical tools.
7. Seal the fuel rail opening with a plug.

To install:

8. Install in reverse order of removal. When doing this note the following:

   a. The fuel pressure sensor has a biting edge instead of a sealing ring.

   b. Check for damage to the sealing surfaces and threads for the fuel pressure sensor. If the sensor is OK, is it possible to reuse it.

   c. Check the sealing surfaces on the fuel rail opening.

   d. Coat the fuel pressure sensor threads and biting edge with diesel fuel.

9. Turn the fuel pressure sensor by hand, then tighten the fuel pressure sensor to 74 ft. lbs. (100 Nm).
10. After installing the fuel pressure sensor, turn on the engine and allow the engine run a few minutes at a moderate speed and

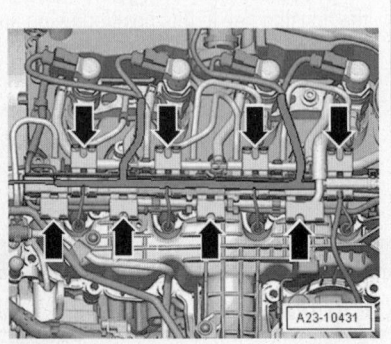

Fig. 259 Open the wire strip (arrows) and remove the connector for the glow plug. Set the wire set aside.

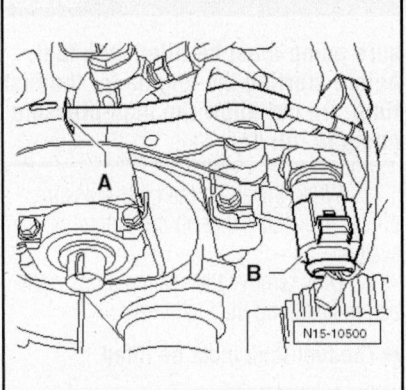

Fig. 260 Release and disconnect the connector (B) for the fuel pressure sensor. Remove the fuel pressure sensor.

then turn it off in order to bleed the fuel system.

➡**The high-pressure connections must not be opened; the fuel system bleeds itself.**

11. Check the Diagnostic Trouble Code (DTC) memory, and erase it if necessary. Refer to the vehicle diagnostic tester.
12. Turn off the ignition.
13. Carefully check the entire fuel system for leaks.
14. If there are leaks even though the correct tightening specification was used, replace the affected component.
15. Perform a road test where the accelerator pedal is pressed all the way down at least one time. Then check the high-pressure area again for leaks.
16. If there is still air in the fuel system, the engine may switch to emergency mode during the road test.
17. Turn off the engine and erase the DTC memory. Then continue the road test.
18. After the road test, check the DTC memory again.

FUEL RAIL

REMOVAL & INSTALLATION

See Figures 261 through 265.

➡**See illustrations under "Injectors" in this section for additional assistance.**

1. Remove the engine cover.
2. Disconnect the connector from the fuel pressure regulator valve.
3. Disconnect the fuel pressure sensor connector. Remove the vacuum hose from the cylinder head cover.
4. Loosen the hose clamps and remove the fuel hose from the fuel rail.

5. Open the retaining clips from the wiring harness.
6. Disconnect the connectors from the glow plug, using an appropriate grab tool.
7. Release and disconnect the connectors from the fuel injectors.
8. Remove the wires from the wiring guide.
9. Unclip the vacuum hose from the wiring guide.
10. Remove the bolt and union nuts, then remove the high-pressure line.
11. Remove the bolts and set the coolant supply line aside.
12. Remove the bolts and set the fuel return line aside.
13. Remove the wiring guide from the fuel rail and set it aside.
14. Open the four high-pressure line union nuts.
15. Place the high-pressure lines on a clean cloth.

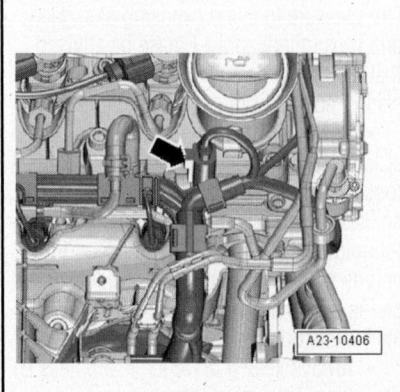

Fig. 261 Disconnect the connector (arrow) from the fuel pressure regulator valve.

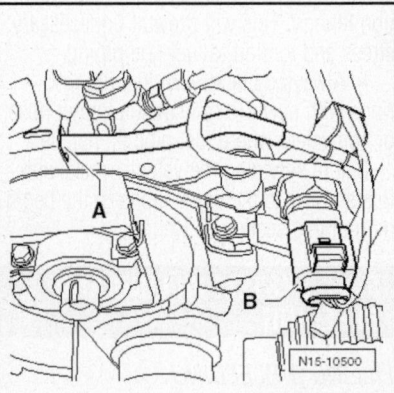

Fig. 262 Disconnect the fuel pressure sensor connector (B). Remove the vacuum hose (A) from the cylinder head cover.

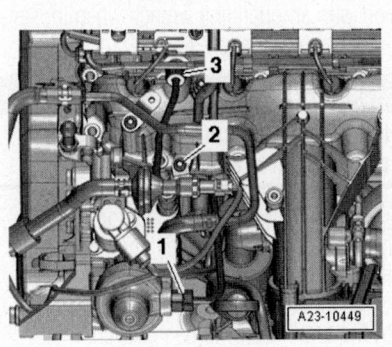

Fig. 263 Remove the bolt (2) and union nuts (1 and 3), then remove the high-pressure line.

16. Remove both bolts and then remove the fuel rail.

17. Seal the open connections with plugs.

To install:

18. Install in reverse order of removal. When doing this note the following:

   a. Install the high-pressure lines free of tension.

   b. When reusing the high-pressure lines again, pay attention to the cylinder marks.

   c. The high-pressure lines can be reused only after the following checks:

   - Check the sealing cone on each high-pressure line for deformation and cracks.
   - The bores for the lines must not be deformed, narrowed or damaged.
   - Do not use corroded lines again.

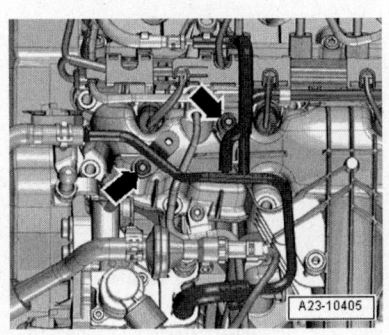

Fig. 264 Remove the bolts (arrows) and set the fuel return line aside.

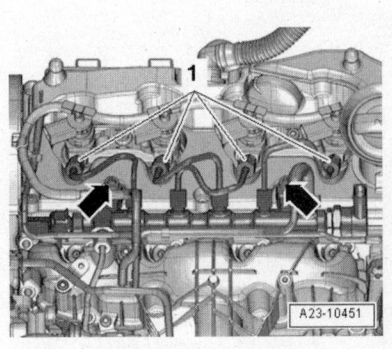

Fig. 265 Open the 4 high-pressure line union nuts (1). Remove both bolts (arrows) and then remove the fuel rail.

HIGH PRESSURE PUMP

REMOVAL & INSTALLATION

See Figures 266 through 270.

✳✳ CAUTION

Allowing the high-pressure pump to run dry will destroy it. The high-pressure pump must be filled with fuel before starting the engine for the first time. Do not allow the high-pressure pump to run dry.

1. Remove the toothed belt from the camshaft and the high-pressure pump.

2. Remove the bolts, then remove the toothed belt sprocket from the high-pressure pump.

3. Counterhold using the camshaft gear counter-holder (T10051) to remove the nut on the high-pressure pump hub.

4. Install the puller (T40064) with the pressure pad (T40064/1) and bolts (T40064/2), and remove the hub for the high-pressure pump. Counterhold with a 24mm open end wrench, if necessary.

5. Remove the bolts and set the coolant supply line aside.

6. Remove the bolts and set the fuel return line aside.

7. Remove the bolt and union nuts, then remove the high-pressure line.

8. Disconnect and remove the connectors. Disconnect the fuel supply hose and return hose.

9. If equipped with a high-pressure pump support, remove the nuts and bolt for the support and remove the support.

10. Remove the high-pressure pump bolts and carefully remove the high-pressure pump.

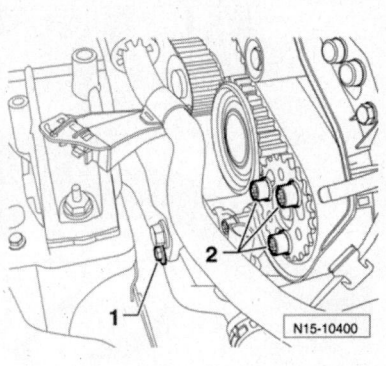

Fig. 266 Remove the bolts (2), then remove the toothed belt sprocket from the high-pressure pump.

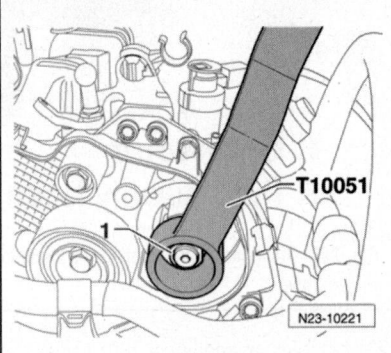

Fig. 267 Counterhold using the camshaft gear counter-holder to remove the nut (1) on the high-pressure pump hub.

To install:

11. Install in reverse order of removal. When doing this note the following:

12. Carefully install the high-pressure pump and tighten the bolts to 15 ft. lbs.

Fig. 268 Install the puller with the pressure pad and bolts, and remove the hub for the high-pressure pump. Counterhold with a 24mm open end wrench, if necessary.

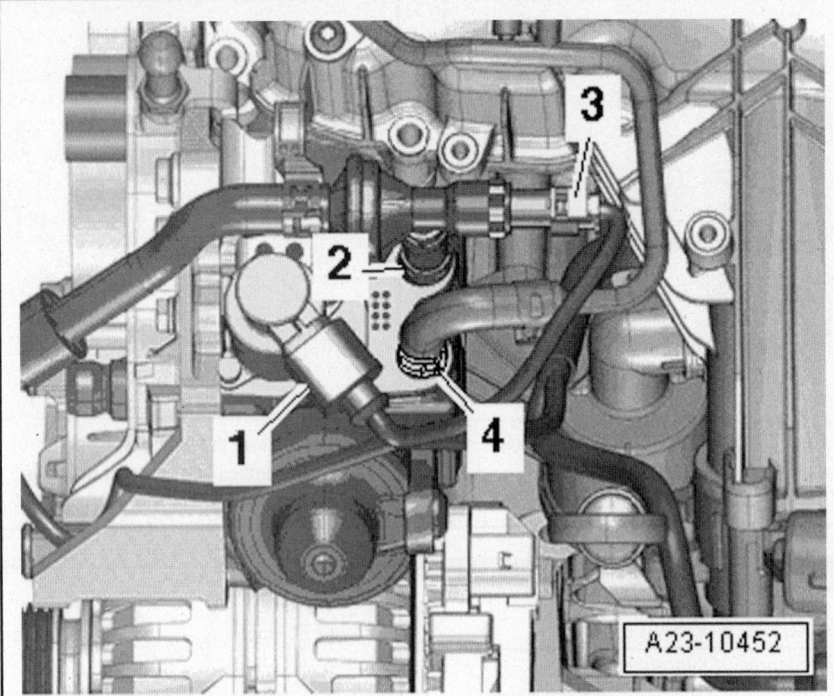

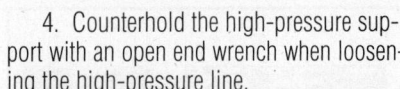

1. Connector
2. Fuel supply hose
3. Connector
4. Return hose

Fig. 269 Disconnect and remove the connectors. Disconnect the fuel supply hose and return hose.

(20 Nm), plus an additional 180° (1/2) turn.

13. Install the pump support. Install the stud bolt and tighten to 11 ft. lbs. (15 Nm), install the nuts only hand-tight, then install the support-to-engine bolt and tighten to 17 ft. lbs. (23 Nm). Now, tighten the nuts to 17 ft. lbs. (23 Nm).

14. When installing the pump hub, tighten the bolt to 70 ft. lbs. (95 Nm).

15. Install the toothed belt sprocket and tighten the bolts to 15 ft. lbs. (20 Nm).

FUEL INJECTORS

REMOVAL & INSTALLATION
See Figures 271 through 275.

1. Remove the engine cover.
2. Push both brackets down and at the same time pull the release upwards and remove the return line connection from the fuel injector.
3. Disconnect electrical connectors from all the fuel injectors.

4. Counterhold the high-pressure support with an open end wrench when loosening the high-pressure line.

✶✶ CAUTION
If the high-pressure supports are loosened, it may cause leaks.

5. Loosen the union nuts for each of the four high-pressure line and remove the high-pressure lines.
6. Remove the tensioning bracket bolt for the fuel injector to be removed.
7. Attach the puller (T10055) to the puller (T10415) and remove the injector upward using a knocking motion.
8. Remove the fuel injector with a turning motion in order to avoid damaging the sealing lip.
9. Place the injector on a clean cloth.

To install:

➡ **Important information on installing the fuel injector:**

- Replace the following components and seals or O-rings with each removal and installation: copper washer, injector shaft O-ring, injector return O-ring.
- The following components and seals and/or O-rings must be replaced whenever an fuel injector is replaced: tensioning bracket, copper washer, fuel injector shaft O-ring, fuel injector return O-ring.
- Lubricate all of the O-rings with assembly oil or engine oil before installing.
- When reusing the high-pressure line again, pay attention to the cylinder marks.

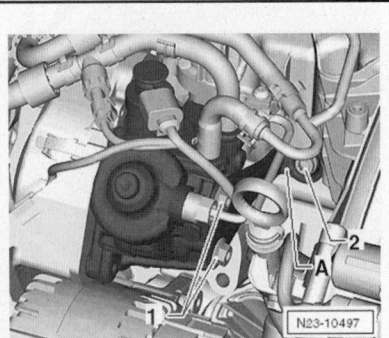

Fig. 270 If equipped with a high-pressure pump support, remove the nuts (1) and bolt (2) for the support (A) and remove the support.

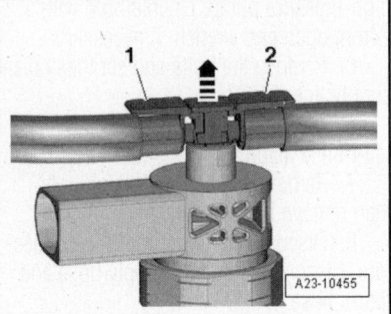

Fig. 271 Push both brackets (1 and 2) down and at the same time pull the release upwards (arrow) and remove the return line connection from the fuel injector.

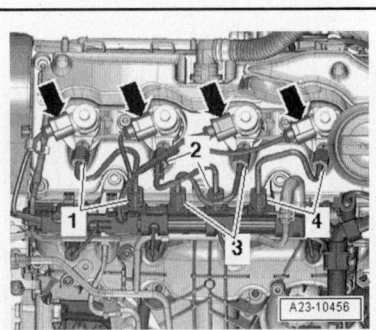

Fig. 272 Disconnect electrical connectors (arrows) from all the fuel injectors. Loosen the union nuts for each high-pressure line (1 through 4) and remove the high-pressure lines.

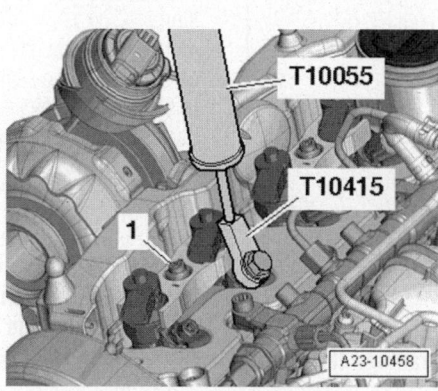

Fig. 273 Remove the tensioning bracket bolt (1) for the fuel injector to be removed. Attach the puller to the puller and remove the injector upward using a knocking motion.

10. To reuse the high-pressure line the following checks must be performed first:

a. Check the sealing cone on each high-pressure line for deformation and cracks.

b. The bores for the line must not be deformed, narrowed or damaged.

c. Do not reuse any corroded lines again.

11. To install a used fuel injector, perform the following:

a. Spray the tip of the fuel injector with a rust removing spray.

➡**Remove the rust or oil particles with a cloth after approximately 5 minutes.**

b. To remove the used copper washer from the fuel injector, clamp the washer

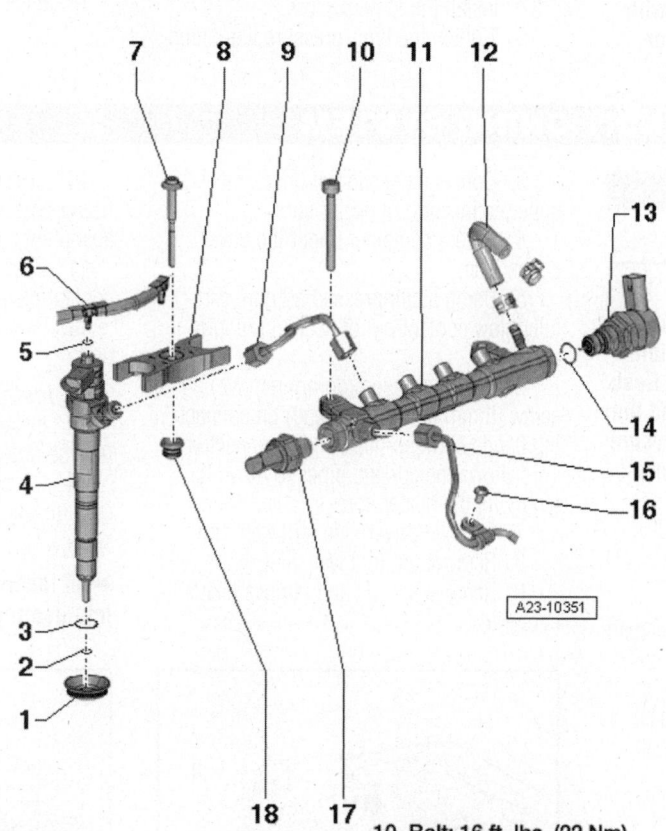

1. Seal
2. Copper Washer
3. O-ring
4. Fuel Injector
5. O-ring
6. Fuel Return Line (to the fuel tank)
7. Bolt: 6 ft. lbs. (8 Nm), plus an additional 180° (1/2) turn.
8. Tensioning Bracket
9. High Pressure Line: 21 ft. lbs. (28 Nm); between the fuel rail and the fuel injectors.
10. Bolt: 16 ft. lbs. (22 Nm)
11. Fuel Rail (High Pressure Reservoir)
12. Fuel Return Hose
13. Fuel Pressure Regulator Valve: 59 ft. lbs. (80 Nm)
14. O-ring
15. High Pressure Line: 21 ft. lbs. (28 Nm)
16. Bolt: 6 ft. lbs. (8 Nm)
17. Fuel Pressure Sensor: 74 ft. lbs. (100 Nm)
18. Grommet

Fig. 274 Exploded view of the fuel rail and injector assembly

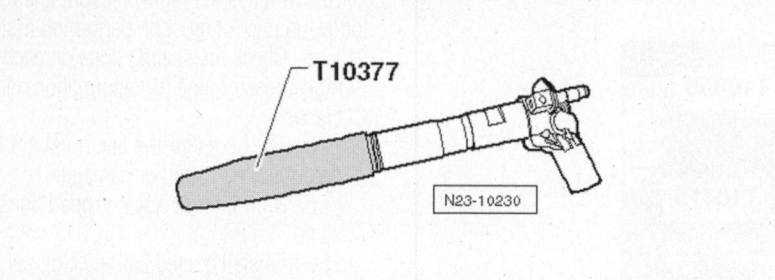

Fig. 275 Replace the fuel injector shaft seal using the guide sleeve.

carefully in a vise, until the clamping jaws on the vise prevent the washer from turning. Pull the fuel injector out of the copper washer by hand with a slight twisting and pulling motion.

➡**To remove rust particles on the fuel injector sealing surface, clean the fuel injector bore in the cylinder head with a cloth dampened with engine oil or** rust remover. **Do not damage the sealing flanges.**

12. Replace the fuel injector shaft seal using the guide sleeve (T10377).

13. Carefully slide the lubricated O-ring onto the fuel return line connection to prevent damaging it.

14. Install the fuel injectors.

15. Tighten the high-pressure line union nut by hand. Make sure it fits free of tension.

16. Press the return line connection carefully over the sealing ring onto the injector (check the sealing ring first for damage). The connection must engage audibly. Then press the release pin down carefully.

➡**The correction values for the new injectors must be must be programmed into the Engine Control Module (ECM) after replacing one or more injectors. Refer to the vehicle diagnostic tester.**

17. Check all the other injectors as well to make all their correction values have been entered correctly. If the correct comparison values have been stored in the ECM, then these comparison values must never be reentered.

18. Bleed the fuel system.

HEATING & AIR CONDITIONING SYSTEM

BLOWER MOTOR

REMOVAL & INSTALLATION

See Figure 276.

➡**The fresh air blower V2 and fresh air blower control module are accessible from the passenger foot well. The fresh air blower control module J126 and the fresh air blower are in a single housing together and cannot be replaced individually.**

1. Remove partition from heating unit.

2. Remove glove compartment.

3. Disconnect the connector on the fresh air blower and on the fresh air blower control module.

4. Disengage locking mechanism and then turn and remove the fresh air blower V2 and the fresh air blower control module.

To install:

5. Installation is performed in reverse order of removal.

HEATER CORE

REMOVAL & INSTALLATION

See Figure 277.

1. Place the drip tray under the motor.

2. Clamp off coolant hoses using hose clamps and disconnect coolant hoses to heater core.

3. Connect a section of hose onto upper connection of heater core.

4. Hold a container under the lower connection.

5. Using a compressed air gun, carefully blow coolant out of heater core into container.

6. Slightly loosen (do not remove) screw (6 mm hex socket head) on connecting flange between heater core connections. This allows the coolant pipes to move for removing the heater core.

7. Remove driver side foot well trim.

8. Remove left foot well vent.

9. Remove screws and remove heater core trim.

10. Cover floor carpet in area below heater core with leak-proof foil and absorbent paper.

11. Open hose clamps and disconnect coolant pipes from heater core.

12. Remove heater core from heating unit.

To install:

13. Installation is carried out in the reverse order.

14. Check seals installed on heater core, only install a heater core with undamaged seals.

➡**An incorrectly glued seal can roll up into heating unit when sliding in the**

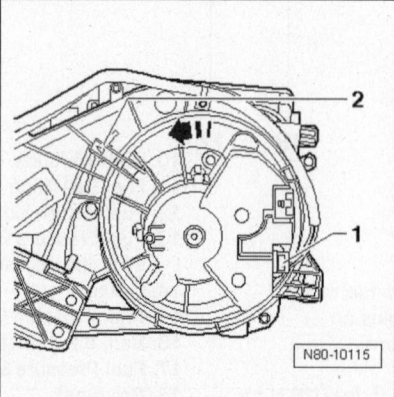

Fig. 276 Disengage locking mechanism (2) and then turn and remove the fresh air blower and the fresh air blower control module (1) in the direction of the arrow.

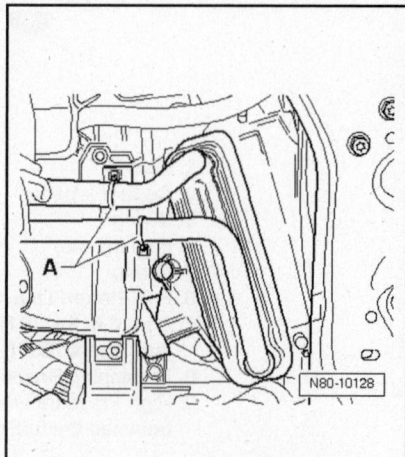

Fig. 277 Hose clamps must be installed as shown (A)

heater core. Cold air may flow past heat exchanger if seal is damaged or not properly fitted.

15. With the heater core removed, check heating unit for soiling (via heater core opening). If necessary remove dirt or coolant from heating unit, for example after removing leaky heater core.

16. Push heater core into heating unit.

➡The sealing rings must be replaced. Coat the sealing rings with coolant before installing. If hose clamps are deformed, replace them.

17. Connect coolant pipes to heater core.

18. Hose clamps must be able to be twisted slightly when installing onto the coolant pipes.

19. Hose clamps must be installed.

20. Tighten hose clamps to 18 inch lbs. (2.0 Nm).

21. Check seating of both clamps after tightening bolts, clamps must enclose the flange on heater core and coolant pipe completely and must not touch other components.

22. Tighten the screw from the connecting flange between heater core connections to 18 inch lbs. (2.0 Nm)m.

23. Check position of grommet in bulkhead for proper seating.

24. Seal the flange for coolant pipes to heater core and for expansion valve (to evaporator, only in vehicles with A/C system) at pass)through of grommet with silicon adhesive sealant if necessary (to prevent water from penetrating).

25. After replacing heater core, coolant must be replaced completely.

26. Check coolant circuit for leaks, pay particular attention between coolant hoses and heater core.

STEERING

ELECTRO-MECHANICAL POWER STEERING GEAR

REMOVAL & INSTALLATION

See Figures 278 through 285.

1. Turn the steering wheel to the straight-ahead position and remove the ignition key so that the steering wheel lock engages.

2. If equipped with "Keyless Access" keyless locking and starting system, switch the ignition off and open the driver door so the steering wheel lock locks.

3. Remove the bolts and remove the footwell trim panel.

4. Remove the screw from the universal joint. Then, remove the universal joint.

5. Raise the vehicle.

6. Remove the front wheels.

7. Remove the lower noise insulation.

8. Remove exhaust system bracket from subframe. Loosen the double clamp for the exhaust system.

9. Remove the left and right nut from the coupling rod. Remove the coupling rod from the stabilizer bar on the left and right sides.

10. Remove the control arm nuts on left and right side of vehicle. Remove the control arms from the ball joints.

11. Loosen nut of track rod ball joint, but do not unscrew yet.

12. Remove the tie rod end from the wheel bearing housing and remove the nut with the ball joint puller (T10187).

13. Remove the two bolts from the steering gear.

14. Remove the bolts and then remove the pendulum support from the transmission.

15. Secure the subframe.

16. Disconnect the connector for the service interval extension to the oil pan.

17. Move the engine and gearbox jack (V.A.G 1383 A) under the subframe.

18. Remove the bolts and lower the subframe slightly using the engine and gearbox

jack. Pay attention the electrical wiring while doing this.

19. Remove the bolts and the heat shield above the steering gear.

20. Remove cable guide from subframe.

21. Unclip all other cable mounting points on steering gear.

22. Disconnect the connectors from the steering gear.

23. Carefully lower subframe using the jack.

24. Lift the steering gear off the subframe and remove it downward.

✳✳ CAUTION

Avoid damage to the control module.

To install:

25. Install in reverse order of removal.

26. Always make sure the intermediate plate is installed between the subframe and the body. Insert the long side of the

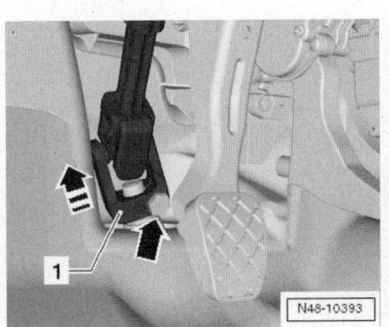

Fig. 278 Remove the screw (arrow) from the universal joint (1). Then, remove the universal joint (in direction of arrow).

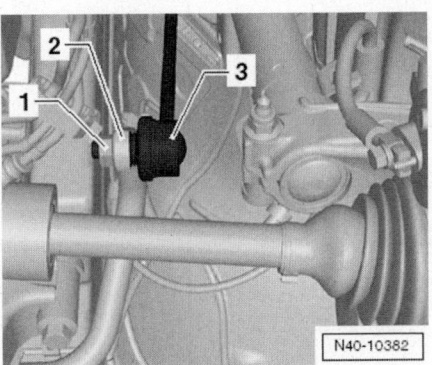

Fig. 279 Remove the left and right nut (1) from the coupling rod (3). Remove the coupling rod from the stabilizer bar (2) on the left and right sides.

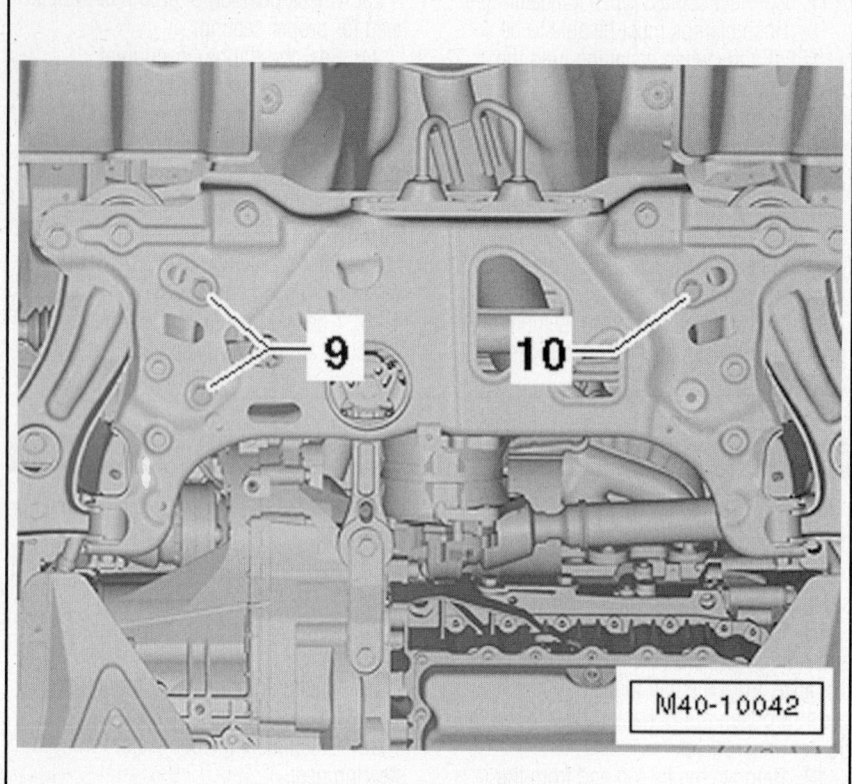

Fig. 280 Remove the two bolts (9 and 10) from the steering gear.

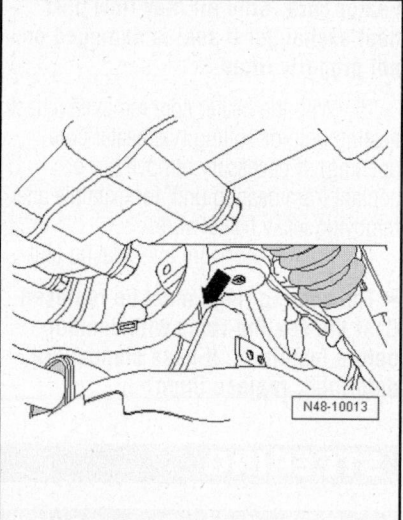

Fig. 283 Remove cable guide from subframe (arrow).

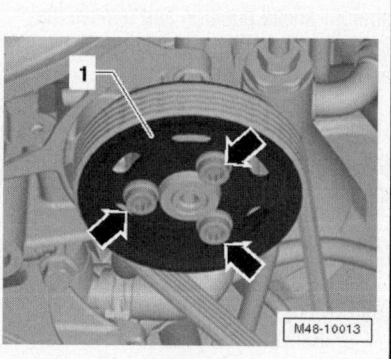

Fig. 284 Disconnect the connectors (1 and 2) from the steering gear.

intermediate plate so that it is perpendicular to direction of travel. The tabs fit into the subframe.

➡**The steering gear threaded sleeves must be seated in the console holes.**

27. Connect the connectors to the steering control module so that they audibly click into place.

28. Coat seal on steering gear with lubricant, e.g. soft soap, before installing steering gear.

29. After attaching steering gear to drive axle, make sure that seal on steering gear is positioned to mounting plate without kinks and opening to foot well is sealed correctly. Ingress of water and/or noises may be the result.

30. Make sure sealing surfaces are clean.

31. Before fastening the bolts for

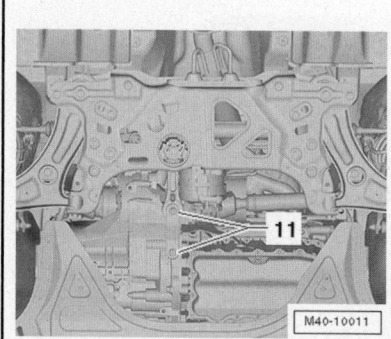

Fig. 281 Remove the bolts (11) and then remove the pendulum support from the transmission.

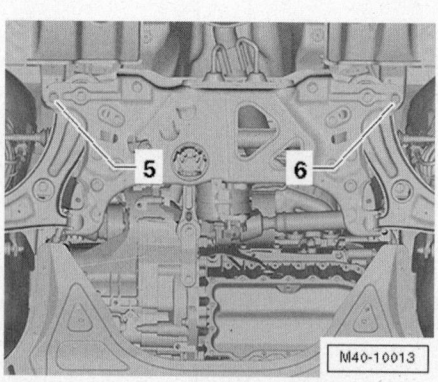

Fig. 282 Remove the bolts (5 and 6) and lower the subframe slightly using the engine and gearbox jack. Pay attention the electrical wiring while doing this.

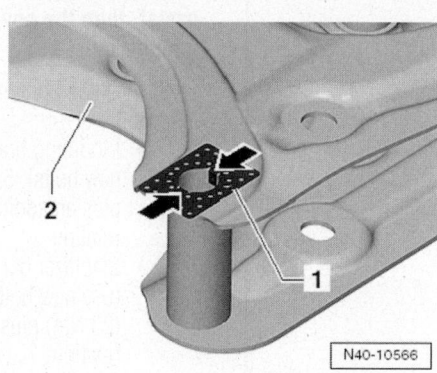

Fig. 285 Always make sure the intermediate plate (1) is installed between the subframe (2) and the body. Insert the long side of the intermediate plate so that it is perpendicular to direction of travel. The tabs fit into the subframe.

subframe, position steering gear on subframe and fasten bolts for steering gear and stabilizer. Install the steering gear to subframe bolts to 37 ft. lbs. (50 Nm), plus 90° (1/4) turn.

32. Clamp off the electrical connections to the steering gear.

33. Install the lower noise insulation.

34. Install the ball joint to control arm nuts to 74 ft. lbs. (100 Nm). Make sure that the ball joint boot is not damaged or twisted.

35. Install the subframe to body, tightening the bolts to 52 ft. lbs. (70 Nm), plus 180° (1/2) turn.

➡**For other suspension component tightening, refer to "SUSPENSION" section.**

36. Bolt the universal joint to steering gear to 20 ft. lbs. (30 Nm).

37. Connect battery.

38. Perform a basic setting on the steering angle sensor with Vehicle Diagnostic Tester Vehicle Diagnostic Tester.

39. It is necessary to adapt the electro-mechanical power steering with Vehicle Diagnostic Tester if a new steering gear was installed. Adapt the electro-mechanical power steering with Vehicle Diagnostic Tester, using this sequence:

- Chassis
- Electromechanical power steering
- 01—OBD-capable system
- Electro-mechanical power steering
- Functions
- Adapting electro-mechanical steering

40. After installation, position of steering wheel must be checked with a road test.

41. If steering wheel is at an angle or a new steering gear was installed, vehicle must be aligned.

42. Align vehicle.

HYDRAULIC POWER STEERING GEAR

REMOVAL & INSTALLATION

See Figures 286 and 287.

1. Disconnect the battery.

2. Remove the foot well trim, remove the nuts to do so.

3. Remove the universal joint bolt and remove the universal joint from the steering gear.

4. Remove the front wheels.

5. Loosen the tie rod nut, but do not remove yet.

➡**To protect the threads, leave the nut on the stud a few turns.**

6. Press the tie rod end off of the wheel bearing housing, then remove the nut.

7. Remove the lower noise insulation.

8. Remove the coupling rods from the stabilizer bar.

9. Remove the ball joint nuts.

10. Remove the pendulum support bolts from the transaxle.

11. Remove the exhaust system suspended mount bolts from the subframe.

12. Remove the heat shield bolts.

13. Remove the heat shield from the subframe.

14. Remove the steering gear.

15. Remove the stabilizer bar clamp bolts.

16. Secure the subframe.

17. Disconnect the electrical connector for the service interval extension to the oil pan.

18. Place the jack under the subframe.

19. Place a piece of wood between the jack and the subframe.

20. Remove the bolts and slightly lower the subframe. Pay attention the electrical wiring while doing this.

21. Remove the heat shield above the exhaust system.

22. Remove the bolts.

23. Remove the cable guide from the subframe.

24. Unclip all other wire mounting points on the steering gear.

25. Disconnect the electrical connectors from the steering gear.

26. Carefully lower the subframe using the jack.

27. Lift the stabilizer bar toward the front, over the subframe and down, slightly turn the stabilizer bar while doing so.

28. Lift the steering gear down from the subframe.

29. Lay the steering gear aside. This avoids damage to the control module.

To install:

30. Installation is the reverse of removal.

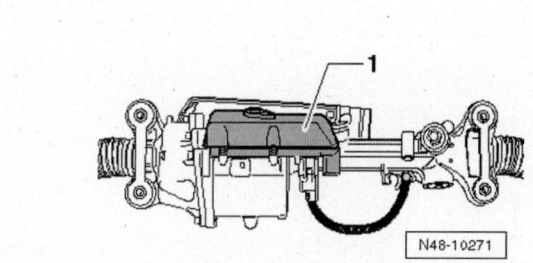

Fig. 286 Lay the steering gear aside as shown. This avoids damage to the control module (1)

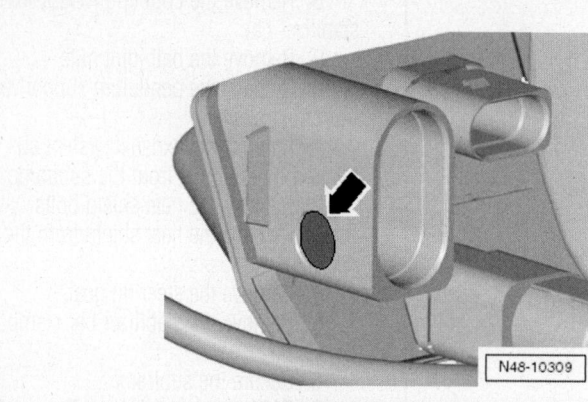

Fig. 287 Make sure the white pressure membrane is clean and not damaged

31. Make sure the white pressure membrane is clean and not damaged.

32. If necessary, carefully clean the pressure membrane. If the pressure membrane is damaged, then the steering gear must be replaced.

33. Connect the electrical connectors so that they audibly click into place.

34. The threaded sleeve must seat in the subframe hole.

35. Coat the seal on the steering gear with lubricant, for example soft soap, before installing the steering gear.

36. After installing the universal joint onto the steering gear, make sure that seal on the steering gear makes contact on the assembly plate without kinks and the opening to the foot well is correctly sealed. Ingress of water and/or noises may be the result.

37. Make sure sealing surfaces are clean.

38. Before attaching the subframe bolts, position the steering gear on the subframe and attach the steering gear bolts and stabilizer bar.

39. Install the lower noise insulation.

40. Tighten the universal joint to the steering gear.

41. Connect the battery.

42. Perform a basic setting on the steering angle sensor with the vehicle diagnosis, testing and information system (VAS 5051—diagnostic unit).

➡️**After installation, position of the steering wheel must be checked with a road test. If the steering wheel is crooked or a new steering gear was installed, a vehicle alignment must be performed.**

43. Perform a vehicle alignment.

➡️**If a new steering gear was installed, the power steering control module must be adapted using the vehicle diagnosis, testing and information system.**

44. Perform a power steering control module basic setting using the vehicle diagnosis, testing and information system.

➡️**If the vehicle is equipped with park assist, then the power steering control module must be re-coded.**

45. Tighten bolts/nuts to specification as follows:

- Mounting bracket to body (use new bolts): 52 ft. lbs. (70 Nm) plus an additional 180° rotation
- Stabilizer bar clamp to subframe (use new bolts): 15 ft. lbs. (20 Nm) plus an additional 90° rotation
- Coupling rod to stabilizer bar (use new nut): 48 ft. lbs. (65 Nm)
- Control arm to steel control arm (use new nuts): 44 ft. lbs. (60 Nm)
- Control arm to sheet steel or aluminum control arm (use new nuts): 74 ft. lbs. (100 Nm)
- Shield to subframe (M6 bolt is self-tapping): 53 inch lbs. (6 Nm)
- Steering gear to subframe (use new bolts): 37 ft. lbs. (50 Nm) plus an additional 90° rotation
- Universal joint to steering gear (use new bolt): 22 ft. lbs. (30 Nm)
- Shield to steering gear (M6 bolt is self-tapping): 53 inch lbs. (6 Nm)
- Tie rod end to wheel bearing housing (use new nut): Pre-tighten to 74 ft. lbs. (100 Nm), then loosen by 180° and tighten to 74 ft. lbs. (100 Nm) again

POWER STEERING PUMP

REMOVAL & INSTALLATION

The power steering pump is electromechanical and is an integral part of the power steering gear.

LOWER BALL JOINT

REMOVAL & INSTALLATION

1. Loosen the drive axle to wheel hub bolt.
2. Remove the wheel.
3. Remove the ball joint nuts.
4. Pull the drive axle out of the wheel hub slightly.
5. Remove the ball joint from the control arm and at the same time swivel the wheel bearing housing to the outside.
6. Move the control arm downward as far as possible.
7. Install the tool (VAG 3287A) and press out the ball joint.
8. Place the tool (VAG 1383A or similar), underneath (risk of accident if components fall off when pressing out ball joint).

➡ **To protect the ball joint threads, leave the nut on a few turns.**

To install:
9. Tighten bolts/nuts to specification as follows:
   - Ball joint to steel control arm (use new nuts): 44 ft. lbs. (60 Nm)
   - Ball joint to sheet steel or aluminum control arm (use new nuts): 74 ft. lbs. (100 Nm)
   - Ball joint to wheel bearing housing (use new nut): 44 ft. lbs. (60 Nm)
   - Drive axle to wheel hub (use new bolt): 52 ft. lbs. (70 Nm) plus an additional 90° rotation
10. Pull the drive axle out of the wheel hub.
11. Install the ball joint into the wheel bearing housing.
12. Install a new self-locking nut, counter hold the stud using a T40 Torx.
13. Install the drive axle to the wheel hub.
14. Install and tighten the ball joint nuts.

➡ **Make sure that the ball joint boot is not damaged or twisted.**

15. Install the wheel.
16. Tighten the drive axle to wheel hub bolt.

LOWER CONTROL ARM

REMOVAL & INSTALLATION

1. Remove the wheel.
2. Remove the lower noise insulation.

3. Remove the ball joint nuts.
4. Pull the wheel bearing housing with ball joint out of the control arm.
5. Secure the mounting bracket.
6. Replace the bolt on the left side or bolt on the right side and tighten to 15 ft. lbs. (20 Nm).

✳✳ CAUTION

The T10096 may only be tightened to a maximum of 15 ft. lbs. (20 Nm), since otherwise the threads of the locating bolts will be damaged.

7. Remove the control arm bolt on the right side or bolt on the left side.
8. Remove the mounting bracket bolts.
9. Remove the control arm with mounting bracket.

To install:
10. Position the control arm with mounting bracket to the subframe.
11. Insert bolts but do not tighten.
12. Insert bolts and tighten.
13. Now replace the T10096 with a new bolt and tighten it.
14. Install the control arm to the ball joint and tighten the nuts.
15. Tighten the control arm mounting bracket bolts to the subframe in curb weight position.
16. Further installation is in the reverse sequence to removal.
17. Install the lower noise insulation.

✳✳ CAUTION

Make sure that the ball joint boot is not damaged or twisted.

18. Tighten bolts/nuts to specification as follows:
   - Mounting bracket to body (use new bolts): 52 ft. lbs. (70 Nm) plus an additional 180° additional.
   - Mounting bracket to subframe (use new bolts): 37 ft. lbs. (50 Nm) 90° additional.
   - Ball joint to steel control arm (use new nuts): 44 ft. lbs. (60 Nm)
   - Ball joint to sheet steel or aluminum control arm (use new nuts): 74 ft. lbs. (100 Nm)
   - Control arm to subframe (use new bolt and tighten bolts at normal ride height): 52 ft. lbs. (70 Nm) plus 180° additional.

MACPHERSON STRUT

REMOVAL & INSTALLATION

1. Loosen the drive axle to wheel hub bolt.
2. Remove the wheel.
3. Remove the level control system sensor from the control arm.
4. Remove the coupling rod nut and remove the coupling rod from the strut.
5. Remove the ball joint nuts.
6. Remove the wheel bearing housing with ball joint from the control arm.
7. Remove the drive axle from the wheel hub.
8. Secure the drive axle to body using wire.

✳✳ CAUTION

The drive axle must not hang down; otherwise the inner Constant Velocity (CV) joint may be damaged when bent too far.

9. Install the ball joint to the control arm again.
10. Secure the removal tool (VAG 1383 A with the T10149) to the wheel hub using one wheel bolt.
11. Remove the wheel bearing housing/strut pinch bolt nut.
12. Insert the removal tool (3424) into the slot in the wheel bearing housing.
13. Install a ratchet to the tool and turn it 90 degrees, opening the slot in the wheel bearing housing, then remove the ratchet from the tool.
14. Press the brake disc in the direction of the strut by hand.
   Otherwise the strut tube may be tilted in the wheel bearing housing.
15. Pull the wheel bearing housing downward from the strut tube and lower using the puller until the strut tube hangs free.
16. Secure the wheel bearing housing to the subframe with wire.
17. Remove the puller from the below wheel bearing housing.
18. When removing the left strut, remove the wiper arms.
19. Remove the plenum chamber cover.
20. Remove the bolts from the strut dome and remove the strut.

To install:
21. Tighten bolts/nuts to specification as follows:

- Strut to wheel bearing housing (use new nut): 52 ft. lbs. (70 Nm), plus 90° additional rotation.
- Strut to body (strut dome) (use new bolts): 11 ft. lbs. (15 Nm), plus 90° additional rotation.
- Ball joint to steel control arm (use new nuts): 44 ft. lbs. (60 Nm).
- Ball joint to sheet steel or aluminum control arm (use new nuts): 74 ft. lbs. (100 Nm).
- Coupling rod to strut (use new nut and counter hold at inner joint multi point stud): 48 ft. lbs. (65 Nm).
- Drive axle to wheel hub (use new bolt): 52 ft. lbs. (70 Nm), plus 90° additional rotation.

22. Secure the tool set (VAG 1383A with the T10149) to the wheel hub using one wheel bolt.

23. Install the strut to the wheel bearing housing and secure the strut using and a new pinch bolt and nut.

※※ CAUTION

Bolt tip must point in direction of rotation vehicle travel.

24. Remove the 3424 from the wheel bearing housing.

※※ CAUTION

One of two markings on the strut bearing must point in direction of rotation vehicle travel.

25. Remove the wire securing the wheel bearing housing.

26. Carefully lift the wheel bearing housing using the VAG 1383A far enough until the bolts for the strut can be installed.

27. Tighten the strut to strut dome bolts.

28. Remove the T10149.

29. Tighten the wheel bearing housing/strut pinch bolt nut.

30. Remove the ball joint nuts again.

31. Install the drive axle to the wheel hub.

32. Install the wheel bearing housing with ball joint to the control arm.

33. Install the ball joint to control arm nuts.

※※ CAUTION

Make sure that the ball joint boot is not damaged or twisted.

34. Tighten the drive axle to wheel hub bolt.

※※ CAUTION

When doing this, the vehicle must not rest on the ground, otherwise the wheel bearing could be damaged.

35. Install the plenum chamber cover.
36. Install the wiper arms, if required.
37. Install the wheel.

OVERHAUL

1. Fit the strut into spring compressor (V.A.G 1752/1) and compress the spring until upper axial groove ball bearing is free.

※※ CAUTION

First pre-load spring far enough so that tension is relieved on upper spring retainer!

2. Make sure that coil spring is seated correctly in the tool.

3. Remove hex nut from top of piston rod.

4. Remove components of suspension strut and coil spring.

To install:

5. Place coil spring with spring compressor on lower spring plate. End of spring coil must rest against the stop in the spring seat.

6. Install a new self-locking hex nut onto piston rod and torque to 45 ft. lbs. (60 Nm).

7. Carefully relieve tension on spring compressor and remove from coil spring.

STABILIZER BAR

REMOVAL & INSTALLATION

1. Remove the nuts and remove the foot well trim.

2. Remove the universal joint bolt and remove the universal joint from the steering gear.

3. Remove the lower noise insulation.

4. Remove the coupling rods from the stabilizer bar.

5. Remove the ball joint nuts on both sides of the vehicle.

6. Loosen, but do not remove the tie rod nuts on both sides of the vehicle.

※※ CAUTION

To protect the threads, leave the nuts on the studs a few turns.

7. Press out the tie rod ends from the wheel bearing housings, then remove the nuts.

8. Secure the subframe.

9. Remove the stabilizer bar clamp bolts from the subframe.

10. Remove the pendulum support bolts from transaxle.

11. Place the jack under the subframe.

12. Place a block of wood between the jack and the subframe.

13. Remove the bolts, and lower the subframe slightly. Observe electrical wires when doing this.

14. Slide the stabilizer bar toward the right, as seen in direction of rotation vehicle travel.

15. Lift the stabilizer bar toward the front and over the subframe down, slightly turn the stabilizer bar while doing so.

To install:

16. Installation is performed in the reverse order of removal.

17. Install the lower noise insulation.

18. Coat the seal on the steering gear with lubricant, for example soft soap, before installing the universal joint.

19. After attaching the universal joint to the steering gear, make sure that seal on the steering gear is positioned to the mounting plate without kinks and the opening to the foot well is sealed correctly. Ingress of water and/or noises may be the result.

20. Make sure sealing surfaces are clean.

21. Tighten bolts/nuts to specification as follows:

- Mounting bracket to body (use new bolts): 52 ft. lbs. (70 Nm), plus an additional 180° rotation.
- Stabilizer bar to coupling rod (use new nut, counter hold at inner joint multi point stud): 48 ft. lbs. (65 Nm).
- Stabilizer bar clamp to subframe (use new bolts): 15 ft. lbs. (20 Nm), plus 90° additional turn.
- Ball joint to steel control arm (use new nuts): 37 ft. lbs. (50 Nm).
- Ball joint to sheet steel or aluminum control arm (use new nuts): 74 ft. lbs. (100 Nm).
- Control arm to subframe (use new bolt and tighten bolts at normal ride height): 52 ft. lbs. (70 Nm), plus 180° rotation.
- Tie rod end to wheel bearing housing (use new nut): Pre-tighten to 74 ft. lbs. (100 Nm), then loosen by 180° and tighten to 74 ft. lbs. (100 Nm) again.

- Universal joint to steering gear (use new bolt): 22 ft. lbs. (30 Nm).

22. After installing, perform the basic setting on the steering angle sensor.

STEERING KNUCKLE

REMOVAL & INSTALLATION

1. Loosen the drive axle to wheel hub bolt.
2. Remove the wheel.
3. Remove the brake caliper with brake carrier and secure to the body using wire.
4. Remove the wheel speed sensor.
5. Remove the disc brake.
6. Remove the cover plate from the wheel bearing housing.
7. Loosen, but do not remove the tie rod nut.

✷✷ CAUTION

To protect the threads, leave the nut on the stud a few turns.

8. Press out the tie rod end from the wheel bearing housing using the 3287A, then remove the nut.
9. Remove the drive axle from the wheel hub (in direction of rotation transaxle) as far as possible.
10. Remove the wheel bearing housing/strut pinch bolt nut and bolt.
11. Insert the 3424 in the slot in the wheel bearing housing.
12. Install a ratchet to the 3424 and turn it 90 degrees, opening the slot in the wheel bearing housing, then remove the ratchet from the 3424.
13. Loosen the ball joint nuts.
14. Place the jack under the wheel bearing housing.
15. Remove the control arm from the ball

joint studs, then remove the wheel bearing housing from the strut.

➡**If the wheel bearing housing is being replaced, then the ball joint must also be replaced. Use new nuts.**

To install:

16. Installation is the reverse of removal.
17. Tighten the drive axle to wheel hub bolt.

✷✷ CAUTION

When doing this, the vehicle must not rest on the ground, otherwise the wheel bearing could be damaged.

➡**If the wheel bearing housing was replaced, a vehicle alignment must be performed.**

18. Install the wheel.
19. Tighten bolts/nuts to specification as follows:

- Strut to wheel bearing housing (use new nut): 52 ft. lbs. (70 Nm), plus 90° additional turn.
- Ball joint to steel control arm (use new nuts): 44 ft. lbs. (60 Nm).
- Ball joint to sheet steel or aluminum control arm (use new nuts): 74 ft. lbs. (100 Nm).
- Tie rod end to wheel bearing housing (use new nut): Pre-tighten to 74 ft. lbs. (100 Nm), then loosen by 180° and tighten to 74 ft. lbs. (100 Nm) again.
- Drive axle to wheel hub (use new bolt): 52 ft. lbs. (70 Nm), plus 90° additional turn.

WHEEL BEARINGS

REMOVAL & INSTALLATION

1. Remove the drive axle to wheel hub bolt.

2. Remove the wheel.
3. Remove the brake caliper with brake carrier and secure to the body using wire.
4. Remove the wheel speed sensor.
5. Remove the brake disc.
6. Remove the ball joint nuts.
7. Remove the control arm from the ball joint studs.
8. Pull the drive axle out of the wheel hub.
9. Remove the bolts.
10. Remove the wheel hub with bearing from the wheel bearing housing.

To install:

11. Installation is performed in the reverse order of removal.
12. Install the brake caliper.
13. Tighten the drive axle to wheel hub bolt.

✷✷ CAUTION

When doing this, the vehicle must not rest on the ground, otherwise the wheel bearing could be damaged.

14. Install the wheel speed sensor.
15. Tighten bolts/nuts to specification as follows:

- Drive axle to wheel hub (use new bolt): 52 ft. lbs. (70 Nm), plus 90° additional turn
- Wheel hub with bearing to wheel bearing housing (use new bolts): 52 ft. lbs. (70 Nm), plus 90° additional turn
- Ball joint to steel control arm (use new nuts): 44 ft. lbs. (60 Nm)
- Ball joint to sheet steel or aluminum control arm (use new nuts): 74 ft. lbs. (100 Nm)

SUSPENSION

REAR SUSPENSION

COIL SPRING

REMOVAL & INSTALLATION

See Figure 288.

1. Remove the wheel.
2. Insert the spring compressor.

❋❋ CAUTION

Be sure the coil spring is properly seated in the VAG 1752/3A.

3. Use wrench or ratchet to tighten the spring compressor.
4. Compress the coil spring until it can be removed.
5. Remove the spring.

To install:

➡Observe the installed position. The end of the spring must rest against the stop on the lower spring support.

6. Install the spring together with the lower spring support.
7. Lower spring support has a pin.
8. Insert this pin into the hole in the lower transverse link.
9. Install the upper spring support to the top of the spring.
10. Release tension on the spring, guiding the upper spring support onto the tab on the body.
11. Remove spring compressor.
12. Install the wheel.

LOWER CONTROL ARM

REMOVAL & INSTALLATION

1. Measure the dimension from the wheel center to the lower edge of the wheel housing.
2. Remove the wheel.
3. Remove the coil spring.
4. Remove lower transverse link to wheel bearing housing bolt and nut.
5. With dynamic vertical headlamp aim control, remove the level control system sensor bolts from the lower transverse link.
6. Using a felt tip marker, mark the position of the eccentric bolt to the subframe.
7. Disengage and lower the rear exhaust system.
8. Remove the bolt, nut and washer.
9. Remove the lower transverse link.

To install:

10. Tighten bolts/nuts to specification as follows:
- Lower transverse link to wheel bearing housing (use new bolt/nut and tighten bolt/nut in normal ride height position): 66 ft. lbs. (90 Nm) plus 90° additional turn
- Lower transverse link to subframe (use new bolt/nut and tighten bolt/nut in normal ride height position): 70 ft. lbs. (95 Nm)

11. Position the lower transverse link to the vehicle and install the bolts hand tight.

❋❋ CAUTION

Only tighten the lower transverse link bolts in normal ride height position.

12. Install a new upper transverse link to subframe nut.
13. Align the eccentric bolt to the previously made mark on the subframe and tighten the nut.
14. Raise and engage the rear exhaust system.
15. With dynamic vertical headlight aim control, position and install the level control system sensor and bolts to the lower transverse link. Then tighten to 44 inch lbs. (5 Nm).
16. Hold the lower transverse link bolt and tighten the nut.
17. Install the coil spring.
18. Install the wheel.
19. Perform a vehicle alignment.

REAR VEHICLE LEVEL SENSOR

REMOVAL & INSTALLATION

See Figure 289.

➡This is applicable to vehicles with self-leveling suspension.

1. Disconnect the harness connector.
2. Remove the bolts from the lower transverse link.
3. Remove the bolts from the subframe.
4. Remove Left Rear Level Control System Sensor.

To install:

5. Install in reverse order of removal. Note the following:
   a. The lever on the left rear level control system sensor must point toward the outside of the vehicle.
6. Perform a basic setting on the headlamps after replacing them, refer to Vehicle diagnostic tester.

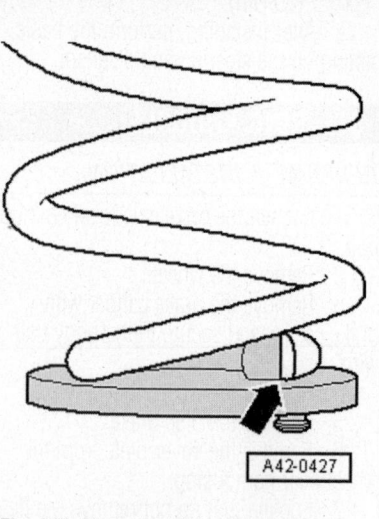

A42-0427

Fig. 288 The end of the spring must rest against the stop on the lower spring support

STABILIZER BAR

REMOVAL & INSTALLATION

FWD Vehicles

1. Remove the rear wheels.
2. Remove the coupling rod nut and pull the coupling rod out of the stabilizer bar.

❋❋ CAUTION

Do NOT loosen the bolt for the tie rod.

3. Remove the stabilizer bar clamp bolts.
4. Remove the stabilizer bar.

To install:

5. Tighten bolts/nuts to specification as follows:
- Stabilizer bar clamp to subframe (use new bolts): 19 ft. lbs. (25 Nm), plus 90° additional turn.
- Stabilizer bar to coupling rod (use new nut): 33 ft. lbs. (45 Nm).
6. Install the stabilizer bar to the vehicle.
7. Tighten the stabilizer bar clamp bolts evenly.
8. Install the wheel.
9. Install the coupling rod to the stabilizer bar and tighten the nut.

AWD Vehicles

1. Remove the rear wheels.
2. Remove the coupling rod nut and pull the coupling rod out of the stabilizer bar.

Do NOT loosen the bolt for the tie rod.

3. Remove the stabilizer bar clamp bolts.

4. If the upper bolts on the stabilizer bar clamp on the right side of the vehicle cannot be removed, then the following steps must be performed:

    a. Remove the right rear wheel.

    b. Secure the vehicle on both sides to the hoist lifting arm using the T10038.

If the vehicle is not secured, it could slide off of the hoist.

    c. Install the T10149 with a wheel bolt to the wheel hub.

    d. Lift the wheel hub far enough until it is possible to access the bolts on the right stabilizer bar clamp.

5. Remove the stabilizer bar.

To install:

6. Tighten bolts/nuts to specification as follows:

- Stabilizer bar clamp to subframe (use new bolts): 19 ft. lbs. (25 Nm), plus 90° additional turn
- Stabilizer bar to coupling rod (use new nut): 33 ft. lbs. (45 Nm)

7. Install the stabilizer bar to the vehicle.

8. Tighten the stabilizer bar clamp bolts evenly.

9. As necessary, lower the suspension back down using the VAG 1383A and remove the T10149 from the wheel hub. Remove the T10038.

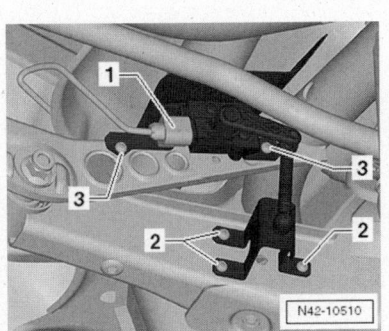

Fig. 289 Disconnect the harness connector (1), remove the bolts (2) from the lower transverse link, remove the bolts (3) from the subframe, then remove the Left Rear Level Control System Sensor.

10. Install the wheel.

11. Install the coupling rod to the stabilizer bar and tighten the nut.

STRUT & SPRING ASSEMBLY

REMOVAL & INSTALLATION

1. Remove the wheel.

2. Remove the coil spring.

3. Unclip the wire for the speed sensor from the upper transverse link.

4. Remove upper transverse link to wheel bearing housing bolt, nut and washers.

5. Using a felt tip marker, mark the position of the eccentric bolt to the subframe.

6. Remove the bolt and nut from the subframe.

7. Remove the upper transverse link.

To install:

8. Tighten bolts/nuts to specification as follows:

- Upper transverse link to wheel bearing housing FWD (use new bolt/nut and tighten bolt/nut in normal ride height position): 96 ft. lbs. (130 Nm), plus 90° additional turn.
- Upper transverse link to wheel bearing housing AWD (use new bolt/nut and tighten bolt/nut in normal ride height position): 111 ft. lbs. (150 Nm), plus 90° additional turn.
- Upper transverse link to subframe; use new bolt/nut and tighten bolt/nut in normal ride height position): 70 ft. lbs. (95 Nm).

9. Position the upper transverse link to the vehicle and install the bolts hand tight.

Only tighten the upper transverse link bolts tighten bolt/nut in normal ride height position.

10. Install the new upper transverse link to subframe nut.

11. Align the eccentric bolt to the previously applied mark on the subframe and tighten the nut.

12. Tighten the new upper transverse link to wheel bearing housing bolt and nut.

Make sure that the washers are installed between the bolt and the wheel bearing housing.

13. Clip the wire for the speed sensor to the upper transverse link.

14. Install the coil spring.

15. Install the wheel.

16. Perform a vehicle alignment.

UPPER CONTROL ARM

REMOVAL & INSTALLATION

1. Remove the wheel.

2. Remove the coil spring.

3. Remove the wire for the speed sensor from the upper transverse link.

4. Remove the upper transverse link to wheel bearing housing bolt.

5. Using a felt tip marker, mark the position of the eccentric bolt to the subframe.

6. Remove the bolt, nut and washer.

7. Remove upper transverse link.

To install:

8. Tighten bolts/nuts to specification as follows:

- Upper transverse link to wheel bearing housing FWD (use new bolt/nut and tighten bolt/nut in normal ride height position): 96 ft. lbs. (130 Nm), plus 90° additional turn.
- Upper transverse link to wheel bearing housing AWD (use new bolt/nut and tighten bolt/nut in normal ride height position): 111 ft. lbs. (150 Nm), plus 90° additional turn.
- Upper transverse link to subframe (use new bolt/nut and tighten bolt/nut in normal ride height position): 70 ft. lbs. (95 Nm).

9. Position the upper transverse link to the vehicle and install the bolts hand tight.

Only tighten the upper transverse link bolts tighten bolt/nut in normal ride height position.

10. Install the new upper transverse link to subframe nut.

11. Align the eccentric bolt to the previously applied mark on the subframe and tighten the nut.

12. Tighten the new upper transverse link to wheel bearing housing bolt and nut.

Make sure that washer is installed between the bolt and wheel bearing housing.

13. Secure the wire for the speed sensor to the upper transverse link.

14. Install the coil spring.

15. Install the wheel.
16. Perform a vehicle alignment.

WHEEL BEARINGS

REMOVAL & INSTALLATION

FWD Vehicles

1. Raise the vehicle.
2. Remove the wheel.

➡ **Loosen the dust cap by lightly tapping on the claw of the VW 637/2.**

3. Pry off the dust cap.
4. Remove the brake carrier with caliper and secure to the body using wire.

➡ **Suspend the brake caliper from body.**

5. Remove the brake disc bolt and remove the brake disc.
6. Remove the wheel hub and bearing bolt using the T10162.
7. Pull the wheel hub and bearing off the stub axle.

To install:

8. Carefully slide the wheel hub and bearing onto the stub axle.

Make sure that wheel hub and bearing do not tilt!

9. Install a new wheel hub and bearing bolt and tighten.

➡ **Tighten the bolt to specification using a torque wrench. Use a regular wrench for the additional torque angle.**

10. Install the dust cap using the 3241/4.

✻✻ CAUTION

Always replace the dust cap. Damaged dust caps allow moisture to enter. Therefore, always use the tool shown.

11. Rest of the installation is the reverse of removal.
12. Install the wheel.
13. Tighten bolts/nuts to specification as follows:

- Wheel hub with bearing to wheel bearing housing (use new bolt): 148 ft. lbs. (200 Nm), plus 180° additional rotation.
- Brake disc to wheel bearing housing: 35 inch lbs. (4 Nm).

AWD Vehicles

1. Remove the coil spring.
2. Remove the drive axle.
3. Remove the brake carrier and caliper and secure it to the body.

✻✻ CAUTION

Do not allow the brake caliper to hang from the brake line.

4. Remove the brake disc bolt and remove the brake disc.
5. Remove the wheel hub with bearing bolts.
6. Remove the wheel hub with bearing from the wheel bearing housing.

To install:

7. Installation is the reverse of removal.
8. Install a new twelve point drive axle bolt and tighten.
9. Tighten bolts/nuts to specification as follows:

- Wheel hub with bearing to wheel bearing housing (use new bolts): 52 ft. lbs. (70 Nm), plus 90° additional rotation
- Brake disc to wheel bearing housing: 35 inch lbs. (4 Nm).

VOLKSWAGEN

Routan

8

SPECIFICATIONS AND MAINTENANCE CHARTS

ENGINE AND VEHICLE IDENTIFICATION

VIN ①/VW Code	Liters	Cu. In.	Cyl.	Fuel Sys.	Engine Type	Eng. Mfg.	Code ②	Year
			Engine				Model Year	
G/CJRA	3.6	220	V6	MPFI	DOHC	Chrysler	B	2011
G/CJRA	3.6	220	V6	MPFI	DOHC	Chrysler	C	2012

DOHC: Dual Overhead Camshafts

MPFI: Multi-Port Fuel Injection

① 8th digit of VIN

② 10th digit of VIN

71105_VWR0_C0001

GENERAL ENGINE SPECIFICATIONS

Year	Model	Engine Displacement Liters	Engine Code VIN/VW	Net Horsepower @ rpm	Net Torque@rpm (ft. lbs.)	Bore x Stroke (in.)	Com- pression Ratio	Oil Pressure @ rpm
2011	Routan	3.6	G/ CJRA	283@6350	260@4400	3.78 x 3.27	10.2:1	①
2012	Routan	3.6	G/ CJRA	283@6350	260@4400	3.78 x 3.27	10.2:1	①

① Oil pressure specifications at normal operating temperatures:

5 psi (minimum)@curb idle speed. WARNING: If the oil pressure is zero at idle, do not run the engine at 3000 rpm.

5 (warm) - 139 (cold) psi@600 - 1200 rpm

30 (warm) - 139 (cold) psi@1201 - 3500 rpm

62 (warm) - 139 (cold) psi@3501 - 6400 rpm

71105_VWR0_C0002

ENGINE TUNE-UP SPECIFICATIONS

Year	Engine Displacement Liters	Engine Code VIN/VW	Spark Plug Gap (in.)	Ignition Timing (deg.)	Fuel Pump (psi)	Idle Speed (rpm)	Height of Valve Stem Tip- to- Aluminum Spring Seat Boss (in.) Intake	Exhaust
2011	3.6	G/CJRA	0.040	①	53-63	②	2.063-2.106	2.039-2.083
2012	3.6	G/CJRA	0.040	①	53-63	②	2.063-2.106	2.039-2.083

Note: The Vehicle Emission Control Information label reflects specification changes made during production.

The label figures must be used if they differ from those in this chart.

① The ignition timing is controlled by the Powertrain Control Module (PCM) and is not adjustable.

② The idle speed is controlled by the Powertrain Control Module (PCM). Idle speed is 640-760 rpm.

71105_VWR0_C0003

CAPACITIES

Year	Model	Engine Displacement Liters	Engine Code VIN/VW	Engine Oil with Filter	Automatic Transaxle Initial Fill (qts.)	Refill (qts.)	Fuel Tank (gal.)	Cooling System* (qts.)	Brake System (qts.)
2011	Routan	3.6	G/ CJRA	6.0	9.0	5.5	20.5	13.4	1.3
2012	Routan	3.6	G/ CJRA	6.0	9.0	5.5	20.5	13.4	1.3

Note: All capacities are approximate. Add fluid gradually and check often to avoid overfilling.

* If equipped with a rear heater, the capacity is 16.2 qts.

71105_VWRO_C0004

FLUID SPECIFICATIONS

Year	Model	Engine Displacement Liters	Engine Code VIN/VW	SAE Engine Oil*	Auto. Trans.	Power Steering Fluid	Brake Master Cylinder	Coolant
2011	Routan	3.6	G/CJRA	5W20 and 10W30	①	②	③	④
2012	Routan	3.6	G/CJRA	5W20 and 10W30	①	②	③	④

*WARNING! The Routan does not use synthetic oil.

① GUS 000 162 (VW ATF+4)

② VW Power Steering Fluid +4 or VW ATF +4

③ Use VW B 000 750 or DOT 3, SAE J1703. If DOT 3, SAE J1703 brake fluid is not available, then DOT 4 is acceptable. Use only recommended brake fluids.
   Note: Brake fluid MUST conform to VW norm VW 501.14.

④ VW GUS 012 001 01 or a 5 Year/100,000 Mile Formula HOAT (Hybrid Organic Additive Technology)

71105_VWRO_C0005

VALVE SPECIFICATIONS

Year	Engine Disp. Liters	Engine Code VIN/VW	Face Angle (deg.)	Spring Test Pressure (lbs. @ in.)	Spring Free Length (approx; in.)	Spring Installed Height (in.)	Stem-to-Guide Clearance (New) (in.) Intake	Exhaust	Stem Diameter (in.) Intake	Exhaust
2011	3.6	G/CJRA	45-45.5	63-69 @ 1.57	2.067	1.575	0.0009- 0.0024	0.0012- 0.0027	0.2346- 0.2354-	0.2343- 0.2351
2012	3.6	G/CJRA	45-45.5	63-69 @ 1.57	2.067	1.575	0.0009- 0.0024	0.0012- 0.0027	0.2346- 0.2354-	0.2343- 0.2351

71105_VWRO_C0006

CAMSHAFT AND BEARING SPECIFICATIONS CHART

All measurements are given in inches.

Year	Engine Displ. Liters	Engine Code VIN/VW	Journal Diameter	Bearing Oil Clearance	Shaft End-play	Runout	Bore Diameter	Lobe Height Intake	Lobe Height Exhaust
2011	3.6	G/ CJRA	①	0.00010-0.0026	0.003-0.010	NS	②	NS	NS
2012	3.6	G/ CJRA	①	0.00010-0.0026	0.003-0.010	NS	②	NS	NS

NS: Not Specified by VW

① No.1: 1.2589 -1.2596 in.

 No. 2, 3, and 4: 0.9440 - 0.9447 in

② No.1 Cam towers: 1.2606 - 1.2615 in.

 No. 2, 3, and 4 Cam towers: 0.9457 - 0.9465 in

71105_VWRO_C0006A

CRANKSHAFT AND CONNECTING ROD SPECIFICATIONS

All measurements are given in inches.

Year	Engine Disp. Liters	Engine Code VIN/VW	Crankshaft Main Brg. Journal Dia.	Crankshaft Main Brg. Oil Clearance	Crankshaft Shaft End-play	Crankshaft Thrust on No.	Connecting Rod Journal Diameter	Connecting Rod Brg. Clearance with crush	Connecting Rod Side Clearance
2011	3.6	G/ CJRA	2.8310-2.8380	0.0009-0.0020	0.0020-0.0114	2	2.3193-2.3263	0.0009-0.0025	0.0028-0.0146
2012	3.6	G/ CJRA	2.8310-2.8380	0.0009-0.0020	0.0020-0.0114	2	2.3193-2.3263	0.0009-0.0025	0.0028-0.0146

71105_VWRO_C0008

PISTON AND RING SPECIFICATIONS

All measurements are given in inches.

Year	Engine Disp. Liters	Piston Clearance (metal-to-metal)	Ring Gap (Top) No. 1	Ring Gap (Center) No. 2	Ring Gap (Steel Rails) Oil Control	Ring Side Clearance (Top) No. 1	Ring Side Clearance (Center) No. 2	Ring Side Clearance (Steel Rails) Oil Control
2011	3.6	0.0012-0.0020	0.010-0.016	0.012-0.018	0.006-0.026	0.0010-0.0033	0.0012-0.0031	0.0003-0.0068
2012	3.6	0.0012-0.0020	0.010-0.016	0.012-0.018	0.006-0.026	0.0010-0.0033	0.0012-0.0031	0.0003-0.0068

71105_VWRO_C0007

TORQUE SPECIFICATIONS

All readings in ft. lbs.

Year	Engine Disp. Liters	Engine Code VIN/VW	Cylinder Head Bolts	Main Bearing Bolts	Rod Bearing Bolts	Crankshaft Damper Bolt	Flexplate Bolts	Manifold Intake	Manifold Exhaust	Spark Plugs	Oil Pan Drain Plug
2011	3.6	G/CJRA	①	②	③	262	70	④	20	13	20
2012	3.6	G/CJRA	①	②	③	262	70	④	20	13	20

① Torque in nine steps:

Step 1: All to 22 ft. lbs.

Step 2: All to 33 ft. lbs.

Step 3: All plus 75 degrees, do not use a torque wrench for this step.

Step 4: For Nos. 2 and 3, plus 50 degrees (repair procedure illustation). Do not use a torque wrench for this

Step 5: Loosen all fasteners in the reverse order of the sequence shown in repair procedure illustration.

Step 6: All to 22 ft. lbs.

Step 7: All to 33 ft. lbs.

Step 8: All plus 60 degrees. Do not use a torque wrench for this step.

Step 9: All plus 70 degrees. Do not use a torque wrench for this step.

② Cap bolts: 16 ft. lbs. plus 90 degrees

(in sequence per repair procedure illustration)

③ Cap bolts: 15 ft. lbs. plus 90 degrees

④ Upper intake manifold bolt: 80 inch lbs.

Lower intake manifold bolt: 71 inch lbs.

71105_VWRO_C0009

WHEEL ALIGNMENT

Year	Model		Caster Range (+/-Deg.)	Caster Preferred Setting (Deg.)	Camber Range (+/-Deg.)	Camber Preferred Setting (Deg.)	Total Toe Range (+/-Deg.)	Total Toe Preferred Setting (Deg.)
2011	Routan	F	+1.50- +3.50	+2.50	①	①	+0.06- +0.46	+0.10
		R	NS	NS	-0.46- +0.34	-0.06	-0.15- +0.35	+0.26
2012	Routan	F	+1.50- +3.50	+2.50	①	①	+0.06- +0.46	+0.10
		R	NS	NS	-0.46- +0.34	-0.06	-0.15- +0.35	+0.26

NOTE: Alignment specifications are dependent on proper vehicle ride height. Caster, camber, and toe-in are for reference only; these are non-adjustable.

NS: Not Specified by VW

Total toe is the sum of both the left and right wheel toe settings. Total toe must be equally split between each front wheel to ensure the steering wheel is centered after setting toe. Positive toe is toe-in and negative toe is toe-out.

① Left camber preferred setting: +0.35 degrees and acceptable range: -0.05 to 0.75 degrees

Right camber preferred setting: +0.05 degrees and acceptable range: -0.35 to 0.45 degrees

71105_VWRO_C0010

TIRE, WHEEL AND BALL JOINT SPECIFICATIONS

Year	Model	OEM Tires Standard	Tire Pressures (psi) Front	Rear	Wheel Size	Lug Nut (ft. lbs.)
2011	Routan	P225/65-16 and P225/65-17	①	①	16 and 17 inch	100
2012	Routan	P225/65-16 and P225/65-17	①	①	16 and 17 inch	100

OEM: Original Equipment Manufacturer

PSI: Pounds Per Square Inch

① The proper tire pressure specification can be found on the tire and loading information label provided with the vehicle,
usually on the driver door opening B-pillar or rear frame of the driver's door.

71105_VWRO_C0011

BRAKE SPECIFICATIONS

All measurements in inches unless noted

Year	Model		Brake Disc Original Thickness	Minimum Thickness	Maximum Run-out	Minimum Lining Thickness	Brake Caliper Guide Pin Bolts (ft. lbs.)	Adapter Mounting Bolts (ft. lbs.)
2011	Routan	F	1.097-1.107	1.040	0.002	0.04	26	125
		R	0.463-0.482	0.409	0.002	0.04	26	74
2012	Routan	F	1.097-1.107	1.040	0.002	0.04	26	125
		R	0.463-0.482	0.409	0.002	0.04	26	74

F: Front

R: Rear

71105_VWRO_C0012

SCHEDULED MAINTENANCE INTERVALS
VOLKSWAGEN Routan

TO BE SERVICED	TYPE OF SERVICE	VEHICLE MILEAGE INTERVAL (x1000)																			
		6	12	18	24	30	36	42	48	54	60	66	72	78	84	90	96	102	108	114	120
Accessory drive belts	R																				✓
Air cleaner element (engine) ①	R					✓					✓					✓					✓
Air conditioner system	S/I	Inspect system operation annually																			
Automatic transaxle fluid	S/I	Once a month																			
Automatic transaxle fluid and filter	R																				✓
Battery (clean/tighten terminals)	S/I	Once a month																			
Brake fluid level	S/I	Once a month																			
Brake hoses/lines (incl. ABS)	S/I	✓	✓	✓	✓	✓	✓	✓	✓	✓	✓	✓	✓	✓	✓	✓	✓	✓	✓	✓	✓
Cabin air filter	R		✓		✓		✓		✓		✓		✓		✓		✓		✓		✓
CV joints	S/I		✓		✓				✓				✓			✓					✓
Engine coolant	R	60 months or 102,000 miles																			
Engine oil and filter ②	R	✓	✓	✓	✓	✓	✓	✓	✓	✓	✓	✓	✓	✓	✓	✓	✓	✓	✓	✓	✓
Engine oil and coolant levels	I	Inspect at each fuel stop																			
Exhaust system	S/I		✓		✓				✓				✓			✓					✓
Front and rear brake linings	S/I		✓		✓		✓		✓		✓		✓		✓		✓		✓		✓
Ignition cables	R																	✓			
Lights	S/I	Once a month																			
PCV valve	S/I														✓						
Power steering fluid level	S/I	Once a month																			
Rotate and inspect tires	S/I	✓	✓	✓	✓	✓	✓	✓	✓	✓	✓	✓	✓	✓	✓	✓	✓	✓	✓	✓	✓
Spark plugs	R																	✓			
Suspension components	S/I			✓					✓				✓				✓				✓
Timing belt (4.0L engine)	R																	✓			
Tire inflation and condition	S/I	Once a month																			
Windshield washer solvent level	I	Inspect at each fuel stop																			

R: Replace

S/I: Service or Inspect

If a vehicle is operated under any of the following conditions it is considered severe service:

- Extremely dusty areas.
- 50% or more of the vehicle operation is in 90°F (32°C) or higher temperatures, or constant operation in temperatures below 32°F (0°C).
- Prolonged idling (vehicle operation in stop and go traffic).
- Frequent short running periods (engine does not warm to normal operating temperatures).
- Police, taxi, delivery usage, or trailer towing usage.

Air cleaner element (engine) replace every 12,000 miles, if necessary

Automatic transmission fluid replace every 60,000 miles

Engine oil and filter replace every 3,000 miles

Front and rear axle fluid replace every 18,000 miles

Manual transmission replace every 60,000 miles

Transfer case fluid replace every 60,000 miles

① Inspect every 12,000 miles

② ENGINE OIL CHANGE RESET PROCEDURE:

The vehicle is equipped with an engine oil change indicator system. The "Oil Change Required" message flashes in the Electronic Vehicle Information Center (EVIC) display for approximately 10 seconds after a single chime has sounded, to indicate the next scheduled oil change interval. The engine oil change indicator system is duty cycle based, which means the engine oil change interval may fluctuate depending upon driving habits. Unless reset, this message continues to display each time the ignition switch is turned to the ON/RUN position. To turn off the message temporarily, press and release the Menu button.

To reset the oil change indicator system (after performing the scheduled maintenance), perform the following procedure:

1. Turn the ignition switch to the "ON" position. Do not start the engine.
2. Fully press the accelerator pedal slowly 3 times within 10 seconds.
3. Turn the ignition switch to the "LOCK" position.

NOTE: If the indicator message illuminates when starting the vehicle, the oil change indicator system did not reset. If necessary, repeat the above procedure.

71105_VWRO_C0014

PRECAUTIONS

Before servicing any vehicle, please be sure to read all of the following precautions, which deal with personal safety, prevention of component damage, and important points to take into consideration when servicing a motor vehicle:

• Never open, service or drain the radiator or cooling system when the engine is hot; serious burns can occur from the steam and hot coolant.

• Never work under a lifted vehicle unless it is solidly supported on stands designed for the purpose. Do not support a vehicle on cinder blocks, hollow tiles or other props that may crumble under continuous load. Never work under a vehicle that is supported solely by a jack. Never work under the vehicle while the engine is running.

• If you are going to work under a vehicle on the ground, make sure that the ground is level. Block the wheels to keep the vehicle from rolling. Disconnect the battery negative terminal (ground strap) to prevent others from starting the vehicle while you are under it.

• Do not attempt to work on your vehicle if you do not feel well. You increase the danger of injury to yourself and others if you are tired, upset, or have taken medicine or any other substances that may impair you or keep you from being fully alert.

• Never run the engine unless the work area is well ventilated. Carbon monoxide (CO) kills.

• Always observe good workshop practices. Wear goggles when you operate machine tools or work with acid. Wear goggles, gloves and other protective clothing whenever the job requires working with harmful substances.

• Tie long hair behind your head. Do not wear a necktie, a scarf, loose clothing, or a necklace when you work near machine tools or running engines. If your hair, clothing, or jewelry were to get caught in the machinery, severe injury could result.

• Do not reuse any fasteners that are worn or deformed in normal use. Some fasteners are designed to be used only once and are unreliable and may fail if used a second time. This includes, but is not limited to, nuts, bolts, washers, circlips and cotter pins. Always follow the recommendations in this manual — replace fasteners with new parts when indicated, and any other time it is deemed necessary based on inspection.

• Use pneumatic and electric tools only to loosen threaded parts and fasteners.

Never use these tools to tighten fasteners, especially on light alloy parts. Always use a torque wrench to tighten fasteners to the tightening torque listed.

• Remove finger rings so that they cannot create electrical shorts, get caught in running machinery, or be crushed by heavy parts.

• Illuminate the work area adequately but safely. Use a portable safety light for working inside or under the vehicle. Make sure the bulb is enclosed by a wire cage. The hot filament of an accidentally broken bulb can ignite spilled fuel or oil.

• Before starting a job, make certain that you have all the necessary tools and parts on hand. Read all the instructions thoroughly; do not attempt shortcuts. Use tools that are appropriate to the work and use only replacement parts meeting Volkswagen specifications. Makeshift tools, parts and procedures will not make good repairs.

• Keep sparks, lighted matches, and open flame away from the top of the battery. If escaping hydrogen gas is ignited, it will ignite gas trapped in the cells and cause the battery to explode.

• Disconnect the battery negative terminal (ground strap) whenever you work on the fuel system or the electrical system. Do not smoke or work near heaters or other fire hazards. Keep an approved fire extinguisher handy.

• Observe all applicable safety precautions when working around fuel. Whenever servicing the fuel system, always work in a well-ventilated area. Do not allow fuel spray or vapors to come in contact with a spark, open flame, or excessive heat (a hot drop light, for example). Keep a dry chemical fire extinguisher near the work area. Always keep fuel in a container specifically designed for fuel storage; also, always properly seal fuel containers to avoid the possibility of fire or explosion. Refer to the additional fuel system precautions later in this section.

• Fuel injection systems often remain pressurized, even after the engine has been turned **OFF**. Relieve the fuel system pressure before disconnecting any fuel lines. Failure to do so may result in fire and/or personal injury.

• Friction materials such as brake pads and clutch discs may contain asbestos fibers. Do not create dust by grinding, sanding, or by cleaning with compressed air. Avoid breathing asbestos fibers and

asbestos dust. Breathing asbestos can cause serious diseases such as asbestosis or cancer, and may result in death.

• Before doing any electrical welding on vehicles equipped with anti-lock brakes (ABS), disconnect the battery negative terminal (ground strap) and the ABS control module connector.

• Brake fluid often contains polyglycol ethers and polyglycols. Avoid contact with the eyes and wash your hands thoroughly after handling brake fluid. If you do get brake fluid in your eyes, flush your eyes with clean, running water for 15 minutes. If eye irritation persists, or if you have taken brake fluid internally, IMMEDIATELY seek medical assistance.

• Clean, high quality brake fluid from a sealed container is essential to the safe and proper operation of the brake system. You should always buy the correct type of brake fluid for your vehicle. If the brake fluid becomes contaminated, completely flush the system with new fluid. Never reuse any brake fluid. Any brake fluid that is removed from the system should be discarded. Also, do not allow any brake fluid to come in contact with a painted surface; it will damage the paint.

• Catch draining fuel, oil or brake fluid in suitable containers. Do not use empty food or beverage containers that might mislead someone into drinking from them. Store flammable fluids away from fire hazards. Wipe up spills at once, but do not store the oily rags, which can ignite and burn spontaneously.

• The EPA warns that prolonged contact with used engine oil may cause a number of skin disorders, including cancer. You should make every effort to minimize your exposure to used engine oil. Protective gloves should be worn when changing oil. Wash your hands and any other exposed skin areas as soon as possible after exposure to used engine oil. Soap and water, or waterless hand cleaner should be used.

• Be mindful of the environment and ecology. Before you drain the crankcase, find out the proper way to dispose of the oil. Do not pour oil onto the ground, down a drain, or into a stream, pond, or lake. Consult local ordinances that govern the disposal of wastes.

• Never operate the engine without the proper amount and type of engine oil; doing so WILL result in severe engine damage.

• The Routan is equipped with an air bag system, often referred to as a Supplemental Restraint System (SRS) system. The airbag is operated by an explosive device. The system must be disabled before performing service on or around system components, steering column, instrument panel components, wiring and sensors. Failure to follow safety and disabling procedures could result in accidental air bag deployment, possible personal injury and unnecessary system repairs.

• Always wear safety goggles when working with, or around, the air bag system. When carrying a non-deployed air bag, be sure the bag and trim cover are pointed away from your body. When placing a non-deployed air bag on a work surface, always face the bag and trim cover upward, away from the surface. This will reduce the motion of the module if it is accidentally deployed. Refer to the additional air bag system precautions later in this section.

• Never use a test light to conduct electrical tests of the airbag system. The system must only be tested by trained technicians using the VAG 1551 Scan Tool (ST) or an approved equivalent. The airbag unit must never be electrically tested while it is not installed in the vehicle.

• When driving or riding in an airbag-equipped vehicle, never hold test equipment in your hands or lap while the vehicle is in motion. Objects between you and the airbag can increase the risk of injury in an accident.

• Disconnecting the negative battery cable on some vehicles may interfere with the functions of the on-board computer system(s) and may require the computer to undergo a relearning process once the negative battery cable is reconnected. Any time the battery has been disconnected on an automatic transmission vehicle, it will be necessary to reestablish Transmission Control Module (TCM) basic settings using the VAG 1551 or a generic scantool. For vehicles equipped with an anti-theft radio, be sure of the correct radio activation code before disconnecting the battery or removing the radio. If the wrong code is entered when the power is restored, the radio may lock up and become inoperable, even if the correct code is used in a later attempt.

• Do not quick-charge the battery (for boost starting) for longer than one minute, and do not exceed 16.5 volts at the battery with the boosting cables attached. Wait at least one minute before boosting the battery a second time.

• When boost-charging the battery, first remove the fuses for the Engine Control Module (ECM), the Transmission Control Module (TCM), the ABS control module, and the trip computer. In cases where one or more of these components is not separately fused, disconnect the control module connector(s).

• The air-conditioning (A/C) system is filled with a chemical refrigerant that is hazardous. The A/C system should be serviced only by trained automotive service technicians using approved refrigerant recovery/recycling equipment, trained in related safety precautions, and familiar with regulations governing the discharging and disposal of automotive chemical refrigerants.

• Do not expose any part of the A/C system to high temperatures such as open flame. Excessive heat will increase system pressure and may cause the system to burst.

• Some aerosol tire inflators are highly flammable. Be extremely cautious when repairing a tire that may have been inflated using an aerosol tire inflator. Keep sparks, open flame or other sources of ignition away from the tire repair area. Inflate and deflate the tire at least four times before breaking the bead from the rim. Completely remove the tire from the rim before attempting any repair.

BRAKES

ANTI-LOCK BRAKE SYSTEM (ABS)

GENERAL INFORMATION

PRECAUTIONS

❄❄ CAUTION

Volkswagen does not manufacture any vehicles or replacement parts that contain asbestos. Aftermarket products may or may not contain asbestos. Refer to aftermarket product packaging for product information. Whether or not the product contains asbestos, dust and dirt can accumulate on brake parts during normal use. Follow practices prescribed by appropriate regulations for the handling, processing and disposing of dust and debris.

• The antilock brake module is designed to withstand normal current draws associated with vehicle operation. Take care to avoid overloading the circuits.

• In testing for open or short circuits, do not ground or apply voltage to any of the circuits unless instructed to do so for a diagnostic procedure.

• These circuits should only be tested using a high impedance multimeter or the proper scan tool. Power should never be removed or applied to any control module with the ignition in the ON position. Before removing or connecting battery cables, fuses, or connectors, always turn the ignition to the OFF position.

• The ABM 47-way connector should never be connected or disconnected with the ignition switch in the ON position.

• The Anti-Lock control unit is a microprocessor similar to other computer units in the vehicle. Ensure that the ignition switch is **OFF** before removing or installing controller harnesses. Avoid static electricity discharge at or near the controller.

• The Routan uses active wheel speed sensors. Do not apply voltage to wheel speed sensors at any time.

• Use only factory wiring harnesses. Do not cut or splice wiring to the brake circuits. The addition of aftermarket electrical equipment (car Phone, radar detector, citizen band radio, trailer lighting, trailer brakes, etc.) on a vehicle equipped with anti-lock brakes may affect the function of the anti-lock brake system.

• Do not apply a 12 volt power source to the ground circuit of the pump motor in the HCU when performing any service procedure on a vehicle equipped with ABS. Doing so will damage the pump motor and will require replacement of the entire HCU.

• An attempt to remove or disconnect certain system components may result in improper system operation. Only those components with approved removal and installation procedures should be serviced.

• Many components of the ABS are not serviceable and must be replaced as an assembly. Do not disassemble any component which is not designed to be serviced.

• If welding work is to be performed on the vehicle using an electric arc welder, the ABM connector should be disconnected during the welding operation.

• Brake fluid will damage painted surfaces. If brake fluid is spilled on any painted surface, wash off with water immediately.

• Only use the recommended jacking or hoisting positions for the Routan whenever it is necessary to lift the vehicle. Failure to raise a vehicle using the recommended lift points can result in damage to the vehicle.

• During service procedures, keep grease and any other foreign material off brake shoes and the braking surfaces of the brake rotor, and the external surfaces of the hub and bearing assembly.

• Brake rotor and caliper handling must be done in such a way as to avoid damage to the rotor, especially the machined surfaces, and to avoid scratching or nicking the brake linings.

• The brake fluid used in this vehicle must conform to specifications and SAE J1703 standards. No other type of brake fluid is recommended or approved for usage in the vehicle brake system. Use only brake fluid motor vehicle or equivalent from a tightly sealed container.

• If any hydraulic component or line is removed or replaced, it may be necessary to bleed the entire system.

• A clean repair area is essential. Always clean the reservoir and cap thoroughly before removing the cap. The slightest amount of dirt in the fluid may plug an orifice and impair the system function. Perform repairs after components have been thoroughly cleaned; use only denatured alcohol to clean components. Do not allow ABS components to come into contact with any substance containing mineral oil; this includes used shop rags.

• Lubricate rubber parts with clean, fresh brake fluid to ease assembly. Do not use shop air to clean parts, damage to rubber components may result.

SPEED SENSORS

REMOVAL & INSTALLATION

Front

See Figure 1.

1. Refer to the Precautions Section.
2. Raise and safely support the vehicle.
3. Remove the front brake rotor.
4. Remove the brake shield from the knuckle.
5. Disconnect the vehicle wiring harness from the wheel speed sensor connector.
6. Unclip the wheel speed sensor connector from the bracket on the frame rail.

7. Remove the wheel speed sensor grommet from the flex hose bracket on the frame rail.
8. Remove the screw fastening the wheel speed sensor routing bracket to the mounting flange on the strut.
9. Remove the screw fastening the wheel speed sensor routing bracket to the knuckle.

⁎⁎ WARNING

Prior to removal, clean the area around the sensor head to help prevent contaminants from entering the bearing when the sensor head is removed.

10. Remove the screw fastening the speed sensor head to the hub and bearing.
11. Remove the wheel speed sensor from the hub and bearing.

To install:
12. Apply the bearing grease supplied with the part to the sensor head shaft and O-ring.

⁎⁎ WARNING

Ensure that the sensor mounting surface on the bearing is clean before sensor installation.

13. Push the wheel speed sensor head into the mounting hole in the hub and bearing and align the mounting screw hole.
14. Install the new mounting screw. Tighten it to 55 inch lbs. (6 Nm).
15. Attach the wheel speed sensor routing bracket to the knuckle. Install and tighten the screw to 71 inch lbs. (8 Nm).
16. Attach the wheel speed sensor rout-

ing bracket to the mounting flange on the strut assembly. Install and tighten the screw to 89 inch lbs. (10 Nm).
17. Install the wheel speed sensor grommet into the flex hose bracket on the frame rail.
18. Clip the wheel speed sensor connector and routing clip to the bracket on the frame rail.
19. Connect the vehicle wiring harness to the wheel speed sensor connector.
20. Install the brake shield on the knuckle. Install and tighten the 3 mounting screws to 71 inch lbs. (8 Nm).
21. Install the brake rotor.
22. Verify that the speed sensor cable is properly routed and that it does not contact the rotor or other moving parts.
23. Perform the Diagnostic Verification Test and clear any faults.

Rear

See Figure 2.

1. Refer to the Precautions Section.
2. Raise and safely support the vehicle.
3. Remove the rear brake rotor.
4. Remove the exhaust heat shield above the exhaust system covering the wheel speed sensor wiring connector, if you are removing the sensor on the right side.
5. Disconnect the vehicle wiring harness from the wheel speed sensor connector.
6. Remove the wheel speed sensor from the routing clips along underbody of the vehicle.
7. Remove the wheel speed sensor from the routing clips along the brake flex hose.
8. Remove the wheel speed sensor routing clip from the rear axle.

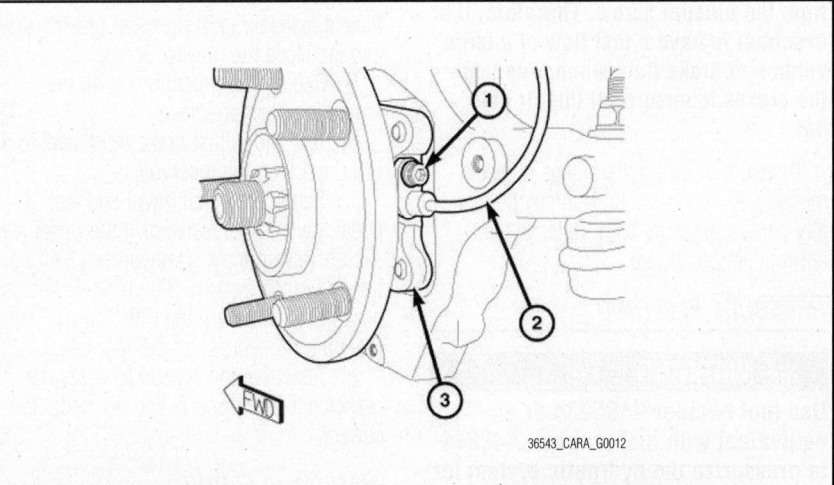

36543_CARA_G0012

Fig. 1 Remove the screw (1) fastening the speed sensor (2) head to the hub and bearing (3)

Prior to removal, clean the area around the sensor head to help prevent contaminants from entering the bearing when the sensor head is removed.

9. Remove the bolt fastening the speed sensor head to the hub and bearing.

10. Remove the wheel speed sensor from the hub and bearing.

To install:

11. Apply the bearing grease supplied with the part to the sensor head shaft and O-ring.

Ensure that the sensor mounting surface on the bearing is clean before installing the sensor.

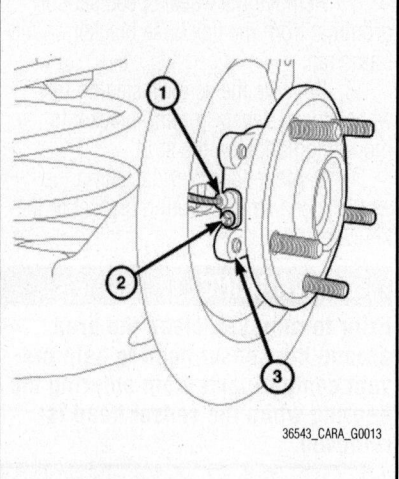

Fig. 2 Remove the bolt (2) fastening the rear wheel speed sensor head (1) to the hub and bearing (3)

12. Push the wheel speed sensor head into the mounting hole in the hub and bearing and align the mounting screw hole.

13. Install a NEW mounting bolt. Tighten the mounting bolt to 55 inch lbs. (6 Nm).

14. Install the wheel speed sensor routing clip into the hole in the rear axle.

15. Install the wheel speed sensor into the routing clips along the brake flex hose.

16. Install the wheel speed sensor into the routing clips along the underbody of the vehicle.

17. Connect the vehicle wiring harness to the wheel speed sensor connector.

18. Install the exhaust heat shield above the exhaust system covering the wheel speed sensor wiring connector, if installing the sensor on the right side only.

19. Install the rear brake rotor.

20. Perform the Diagnostic Verification Test and clear any faults.

BRAKES

BLEEDING THE BRAKE SYSTEM

BLEEDING PROCEDURE

Thoroughly clean the cap and master cylinder fluid reservoir before removing the master cylinder reservoir cap, to prevent dirt and other foreign matter from dropping into the master cylinder fluid reservoir.

➡Use this wheel sequence to ensure adequate removal of all trapped air from the brake hydraulic system: Left rear wheel, Right front wheel, Right rear wheel, and Left front wheel.

➡When bleeding the brake system, some air may be trapped in the brake lines far upstream, as much as ten feet from the bleeder screw. Therefore, it is essential to have a fast flow of a large volume of brake fluid when bleeding the brakes to ensure all the air gets out.

Pressure bleeding the brakes is recommended, although the brakes may be manually bled or pressure bled. Refer to the appropriate procedure.

PRESSURE BLEEDING

Use tool number VAS5234 or an equivalent with tool number J-48844 to pressurize the hydraulic system for bleeding. Follow the pressure bleeder manufacturer's instructions for use of the pressure bleeding equipment.

1. Install the brake bleeder adapter, part #J-48844, on the master cylinder fluid reservoir. Attach the fluid hose from the brake charger/bleeder unit #VAS5234 to the fitting on the brake bleeder adapter.

2. Attach a clear plastic hose to the bleeder screw and feed the hose into a clear jar containing enough fresh brake fluid to submerge the end of the hose. Refer to the illustration for manual bleeding.

3. Open the bleeder screw at least one full turn or more to obtain a steady stream of brake fluid.

4. After approximately 4 to 8 ounces (120 to 240 ml) of fluid have been bled through the brake circuit and an air-free flow is maintained in the clear plastic hose and jar, close the bleeder screw.

5. Repeat this procedure at all the remaining bleeder screws.

6. Test and adjust brake fluid level to the FULL mark on the reservoir.

7. Test brake pedal travel and feel. If pedal travel is excessive or if the pedal feels excessively spongy, some air may still be trapped in the system. Bleed the brakes as necessary including, the IPB Caliper Brake Bleeding Procedure, on the rear calipers.

8. Test drive the vehicle to verify the brakes operate properly and the pedal feel is correct.

MANUAL BLEEDING

See Figure 3.

➡To bleed the brakes manually, the aid of a helper will be required.

1. Attach a clear plastic hose to the bleeder screw and feed the hose into a clear jar containing enough fresh brake fluid to submerge the end of the hose.

2. Have a helper pump the brake pedal three or four times and hold it in the down position.

3. With the pedal in the down position, open the bleeder screw at least one full turn.

4. Once the brake pedal has dropped, close the bleeder screw. After the bleeder screw is closed, release the brake pedal.

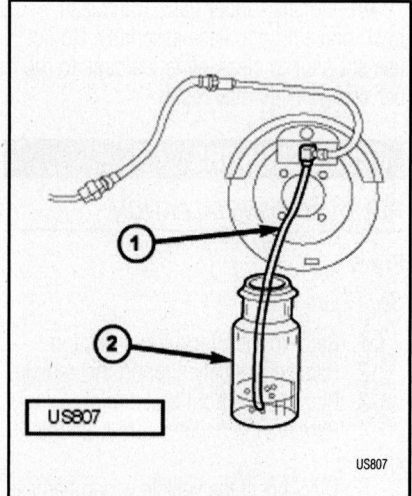

Fig. 3 Attach a clear plastic hose (1) to the bleeder screw and feed the hose into a clear jar (2) containing enough fresh brake fluid to submerge the end of the hose

5. Repeat the above steps until all trapped air is removed from that wheel circuit (usually four or five times).

6. Bleed the remaining wheel circuits in the same manner until all the air is removed from the brake system. Monitor the fluid level in the master cylinder reservoir to make sure it does not go dry.

7. Test and adjust brake fluid level to the FULL mark.

8. Test brake pedal travel and feel. If pedal travel is excessive or if the pedal feels excessively spongy, some air may still be trapped in the system. Bleed the brakes as necessary including, the IPB Caliper Brake Bleeding Procedure, on the rear.

9. Test drive the vehicle to verify the brakes operate properly and the pedal feel is correct.

MASTER CYLINDER BLEEDING

See Figure 4.

※※ WARNING

When clamping the master cylinder in vise, only clamp the master cylinder by its mounting flange. Do not clamp the master cylinder piston rod, reservoir, seal or body.

1. Clamp the master cylinder in a vise.

2. Thread the bleeder tubes, part #8358A, into each master cylinder outlet port. Tighten each tube to 120 inch lbs. (14 Nm). Flex the bleeder tubes and place the open ends into the mouth of the fluid reservoir as far down as possible to keep them lower than the fluid level while bleeding.

➡**Make sure open ends of the bleeder tubes stay below the surface of the brake fluid once the reservoir is filled to proper level.**

3. Fill the brake fluid reservoir with brake fluid conforming to specifications. Make sure the fluid level is higher than the tips of the bleeder tubes in the reservoir to ensure no air is ingested during bleeding.

4. Using a wooden dowel as a push rod, slowly depress the master cylinder pistons, then release pressure, allowing the pistons to return to the released position. Repeat several times until all air bubbles are expelled. Make sure the fluid level stays above the tips of the bleeder tubes in the reservoir while bleeding.

5. Remove the bleeder tubes from the master cylinder outlet ports, and then plug

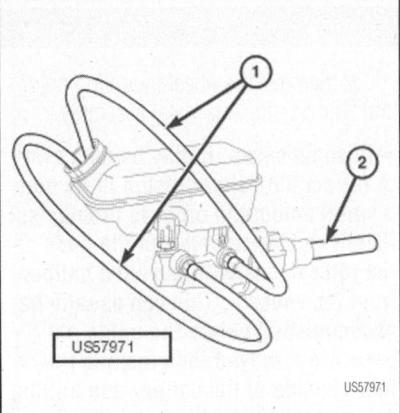

```
US57971
```

US57971

Fig. 4 Master cylinder bleeding using bleeder tubes, part #8358A (1) and a wooden dowel as a push rod (2)

the outlet ports and install the fill cap on the reservoir.

6. Remove the master cylinder from the vise.

7. Install the master cylinder on the vehicle.

ABS SYSTEM BLEEDING

Bleed the base brake hydraulic system anytime air enters the hydraulic system. Brake systems with ABS must be bled as two independent braking systems. Bleed the ABS portion of the brake system separately.

➡**During the brake bleeding procedure, be sure the brake fluid level remains close to the full level in the master cylinder fluid reservoir. Test the fluid level periodically during the bleeding procedure and add brake fluid as required.**

When bleeding the ABS system, follow the bleeding sequence to insure complete and adequate bleeding.

• Make sure all hydraulic fluid lines are installed and properly torqued.

• Connect the scan tool to the diagnostics connector. The diagnostic connector is located under the lower steering column cover to the left of the steering column.

• Using the scan tool, test to make sure the Antilock Brake Module (ABM) does not have any fault codes stored. If it does, clear them.

※※ WARNING

When bleeding the brake system wear safety glasses. A clear bleed tube must be attached to the bleeder screws and submerged in a clear container filled part way with clean

brake fluid. Direct the flow of brake fluid away from yourself and the painted surfaces of the vehicle. Brake fluid at high pressure may come out of the bleeder screws when opened.

➡**VW recommends bleeding the base brake system using pressure bleeding to ensure all the air is removed from the system. Manual bleeding may also be used, but additional time is needed to remove all air from the system.**

1. Bleed the base brake system.

2. Using the scan tool, select ECU VIEW, followed by ABS MISCELLANEOUS FUNCTIONS to access bleeding. Follow the instructions displayed. When finished, disconnect the scan tool and proceed.

3. Bleed the base brake system a second time. Test the brake fluid level in the reservoir periodically to prevent emptying, causing air to enter the hydraulic system.

4. Fill the master cylinder fluid reservoir to the FULL level.

5. Test drive the vehicle to be sure the brakes operate correctly and that the brake pedal does not feel spongy.

BRAKE FLUID LEVEL CHECKING

Test the level of the master cylinder reservoir fluid a minimum of twice annually. Fluid reservoirs are marked with the words MAX and MIN to indicate the proper brake fluid fill level of the master cylinder. If necessary, add brake fluid to bring the level to the bottom of the MAX mark on the side of the master cylinder fluid reservoir.

※※ WARNING

Use only the specified brake fluid or an equivalent from a tightly sealed container. See Specifications.

※※ CAUTION

DO NOT use brake fluid with a lower boiling point, as brake failure could result during prolonged hard braking.

※※ CAUTION

DO NOT use petroleum-based fluid because seal damage will result. Examples of petroleum-based fluids are items such as engine oil, transmission fluid, power steering fluid, etc.

✳✴ CAUTION

Volkswagen does not manufacture any vehicles or replacement parts that contain asbestos. Dust and dirt accumulating on brake parts during normal use may contain asbestos fibers from aftermarket brake linings. Breathing excessive concentrations of asbestos fibers can cause serious bodily harm. Exercise care when servicing brake parts. Do not sand or grind brake lining unless equipment used is designed to contain the dust residue. Do not clean brake parts with compressed air or by dry brushing. Cleaning should be done by dampening the brake components with a fine mist of water, then wiping the brake components clean with a dampened cloth. Dispose of cloth and all residue containing asbestos fibers in an impermeable container with the appropriate label. Follow practices prescribed by the Occupational Safety and Health Administration (OSHA) and the Environmental Protection Agency (EPA) for the handling, processing, and disposing of dust or debris that may contain asbestos fibers.

- During service procedures, keep grease and any other foreign material off brake shoes and the braking surfaces of the brake rotor, and the external surfaces of the hub and bearing assembly.
- Brake rotor and caliper handling must be done in such a way as to avoid damage to the rotor, especially the machined surfaces, and to avoid scratching or nicking the brake linings.
- Only use the recommended jacking or hoisting positions for the Routan whenever it is necessary to lift the vehicle. Failure to raise a vehicle using the recommended lift points can result in damage to the vehicle.

BRAKE CALIPER

REMOVAL & INSTALLATION

See Figure 5.

1. Refer to the Precautions.
2. Raise and safely support the vehicle.

3. Remove the wheel mounting nuts, and then the tire and wheel assembly.

➡ In some cases, it may be necessary to retract the caliper piston in its bore a small amount in order to provide sufficient clearance between the pads and the rotor to easily remove the caliper from the knuckle. This can usually be accomplished before the guide pin bolts are removed, by grasping the inboard side of the caliper and pulling outward working with the guide pins, thus retracting the piston. Never push on the piston directly as it may be damaged.

4. Remove the two bolts securing the disc brake caliper and the adapter bracket to the steering knuckle.
5. Remove the disc brake caliper and adapter bracket from the knuckle and rotor as an assembly. Hang the assembly out of the way using wire. Do not overextend the brake hose.

To install:

6. Install the disc brake caliper and adapter bracket assembly over the brake rotor and knuckle.
7. Install the mounting bolts securing the caliper adapter bracket to the knuckle. Tighten the bolts to 125 ft. lbs. (169 Nm).
8. Install the tire and wheel assembly.
9. Lower the vehicle.
10. Adjust the brake fluid level in the reservoir as necessary.
11. Pump the brake pedal several times to insure that the brake pedal is firm.
12. Road test the vehicle.

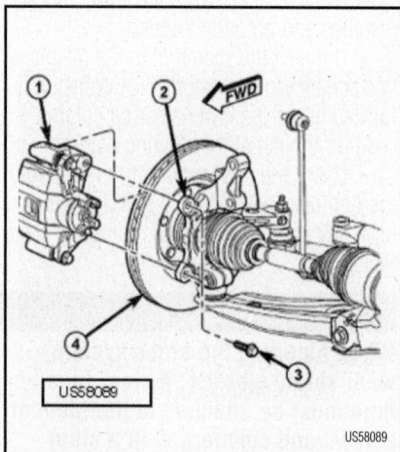

Fig. 5 Disc brake caliper and adapter bracket (1), steering knuckle (2), bolts (3), and rotor (4)

DISC BRAKE PADS

REMOVAL & INSTALLATION

See Figure 6.

1. Refer to the Precautions.
2. Raise and safely support the vehicle.
3. Remove the wheel mounting nuts, and then the tire and wheel assembly.

✳✴ WARNING

When removing or installing a caliper guide pin bolt, it is necessary to hold the guide pin stationary while turning the bolt. Hold the guide pin stationary using a wrench placed upon the pin's hex-shaped head.

4. Remove the 2 brake caliper guide pin bolts.
5. Remove the disc brake caliper from the disc brake adapter bracket and hang it out of the way using wire or a bungee cord. Use care not to over-extend the brake hose or the parking brake cable when doing this.
6. Remove the brake pads from the caliper adapter bracket.

To install:

➡ Make sure that the audible wear indicator (if equipped) is placed toward the top when the inboard brake pad is installed on each side of the vehicle.

➡ If the brake pads have a protective paper on the rear face of the brake pad plate, remove it before pad installation.

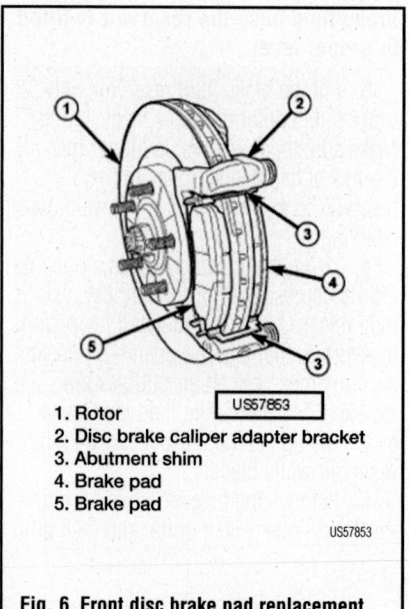

1. Rotor
2. Disc brake caliper adapter bracket
3. Abutment shim
4. Brake pad
5. Brake pad

Fig. 6 Front disc brake pad replacement

7. Place the brake pads in the abutment shims clipped into the disc brake caliper adapter bracket.

8. Place the pad with the wear indicator (if equipped) attached on the inboard side.

9. Completely retract the caliper piston back into the bore of the caliper.

✳✳ WARNING

Use care when installing the caliper onto the adapter bracket to avoid damaging the boots.

10. Install the disc brake caliper over the brake pads on the brake caliper adapter bracket.

➡**When removing or installing a caliper guide pin bolt, it is necessary to hold the guide pin stationary while turning the bolt. Hold the guide pin stationary using a wrench placed upon the pin's hex-shaped head.**

11. Align the caliper guide pin bolt holes with the adapter bracket. Install the upper and lower caliper guide pin bolts.

Tighten the guide pin bolts to 26 ft. lbs. (35 Nm).

12. Install the tire and wheel assembly.

13. Lower the vehicle.

14. Pump the brake pedal several times before moving the vehicle in order to set the pads to the brake rotor.

15. Check and adjust the brake fluid level in the reservoir, as necessary.

16. Road test the vehicle and make several stops to wear off any foreign material on the brakes and to seat the brake pads.

BRAKES

✳✳ CAUTION

Volkswagen does not manufacture any vehicles or replacement parts that contain asbestos. Dust and dirt accumulating on brake parts during normal use may contain asbestos fibers from aftermarket brake linings. Breathing excessive concentrations of asbestos fibers can cause serious bodily harm. Exercise care when servicing brake parts. Do not sand or grind brake lining unless equipment used is designed to contain the dust residue. Do not clean brake parts with compressed air or by dry brushing. Cleaning should be done by dampening the brake components with a fine mist of water, then wiping the brake components clean with a dampened cloth. Dispose of cloth and all residue containing asbestos fibers in an impermeable container with the appropriate label. Follow practices prescribed by the Occupational Safety and Health Administration (OSHA) and the Environmental Protection Agency (EPA) for the handling, processing, and disposing of dust or debris that may contain asbestos fibers.

• During service procedures, keep grease and any other foreign material off brake shoes and the braking surfaces of the brake rotor, and the external surfaces of the hub and bearing assembly.

• Brake rotor and caliper handling must be done in such a way as to avoid damage to the rotor, especially the machined surfaces, and to avoid scratching or nicking the brake linings.

• Only use the recommended jacking or hoisting positions for the Routan

whenever it is necessary to lift the vehicle. Failure to raise a vehicle using the recommended lift points can result in damage to the vehicle.

BRAKE CALIPER

REMOVAL & INSTALLATION

See Figure 7.

1. Refer to the Precautions.

2. Raise and safely support the vehicle.

3. Remove the wheel mounting nuts, and then the tire and wheel assembly.

4. Remove the screw securing the parking brake cable routing bracket to the axle.

5. Remove the two bolts securing the disc brake caliper and the adapter bracket to the axle.

6. Remove the disc brake caliper and adapter bracket from the axle and rotor as an assembly. Hang the assembly out of the way using wire. Do not overextend the brake hose.

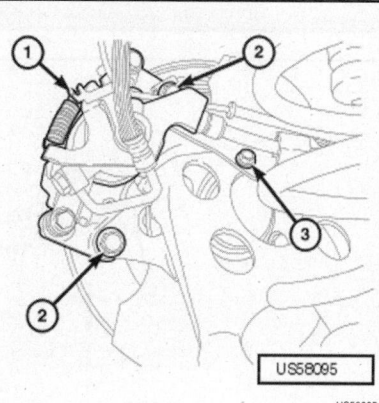

US58095

Fig. 7 Adapter bracket (1), the 2 bolts securing the disc brake caliper and adapter bracket to the axle (2), and the screw securing the parking brake cable routing bracket to the axle (3)

REAR DISC BRAKES

To install:

7. Install the disc brake caliper and adapter bracket over the axle and rotor as an assembly.

8. Install the 2 bolts securing the disc brake caliper and adapter bracket to the axle. Tighten the bolts to 74 ft. lbs. (100 Nm).

Position parking brake cable routing bracket to axle and install the screw securing it in place. Tighten the screw to 55 inch lbs. (6 Nm).

9. Install the tire and wheel assembly.

10. Lower the vehicle.

11. Adjust the brake fluid level as necessary.

12. Pump the brake pedal several times to insure that the brake pedal is firm.

13. Road test the vehicle.

DISC BRAKE PADS

REMOVAL & INSTALLATION

See Figure 8.

1. Refer to the Precautions.

2. Raise and safely support the vehicle.

3. Remove the wheel mounting nuts, and then the tire and wheel assembly.

✳✳ WARNING

When removing or installing a caliper guide pin bolt, it is necessary to hold the guide pin stationary while turning the bolt. Hold the guide pin stationary using a wrench placed upon the pin's hex-shaped head.

4. Remove the 2 brake caliper guide pin bolts.

5. Remove the disc brake caliper from the disc brake adapter bracket and hang it out of the way using wire or a bungee cord. Use care not to over-extend the brake hose when doing this.

6. Remove the brake pads from the caliper adapter bracket.

7. If the pads show signs of very uneven wear, and/or pads did not slide easily on adapter, replace the adapter bracket. Remove the 2 mounting bolts and then remove the bracket.

8. If pads do not show signs of very uneven wear remove and discard the old pad shims, and clean the abutments (the area behind the shims) of any debris or corrosion.

To install:

✳ CAUTION

Any time you replace the brake rotor or brake pads, the rear caliper piston must be seated (bottomed) to compensate for the new brake rotor or lining. Because the parking brake self-adjuster mechanism is attached to the piston, a special seating method is required. The only acceptable method is to rotate the piston back into the bore using the resetting and extracting tool #T10165 as described in the following. Any other seating method will damage the self-adjuster mechanism.

9. If necessary, seat (bottom) the caliper piston in the bore as follows:

   a. Insert the T10165 into the caliper.

10. Insert the lugs on the T10165 into the notches in the face of the caliper piston.

✳ CAUTION

Do not over tighten the screw-drive. Damage to the piston can occur.

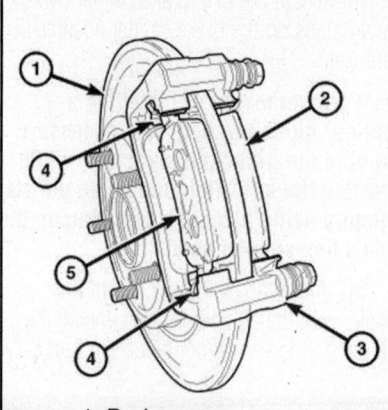

1. Brake rotor
2. Brake pad
3. Caliper adapter
4. Abutment shims
5. Brake pad

36543_CARA_G0021

Fig. 8 Rear disc brake pad replacement

11. Thread the T10165 until it is against the caliper piston.

12. Turn the T10165, rotating the piston in a clockwise direction until it is fully seated (bottomed) in the bore.

13. If caliper adapter was replaced, install the caliper adapter bolts and tighten them to 74 ft. lbs. (100 Nm.)

14. Make sure abutment shims are in place on both the upper and lower side abutments of the caliper adapter.

➡ **If the brake pads have a protective paper on the rear face of the brake pad**

plate, remove it before pad installation.

15. Place the brake pads in the abutment shims clipped into the disc brake caliper adapter bracket.

✳ WARNING

Use care when installing the caliper onto the adapter bracket to avoid damaging the guide pin boots.

16. Install the disc brake caliper over the brake pads on the brake caliper adapter bracket.

✳ WARNING

When removing or installing a caliper guide pin bolt, it is necessary to hold the guide pin stationary while turning the bolt. Hold the guide pin stationary using a wrench placed upon the pin's hex-shaped head.

17. Align the caliper guide pin bolt holes with the adapter bracket. Install the upper and lower caliper guide pin bolts. Tighten the guide pin bolts to 26 ft. lbs. (35 Nm).

18. Install the tire and wheel assembly.

19. Lower the vehicle.

20. Pump the brake pedal several times before moving the vehicle in order to set the pads to the brake rotor.

21. Check and adjust the brake fluid level, as necessary.

22. Road test the vehicle and make several stops to wear off any foreign material on the brakes and to seat the brake pads.

BRAKES   PARKING BRAKE

PARKING BRAKE CABLES

ADJUSTMENT

Automatic Adjuster Tension Release

See Figure 9.

1. Release the parking brake.

2. Raise the vehicle to a comfortable working position and support it safely.

3. Wipe the parking brake cable strands (front and both rear) clean where visible at the intermediate bracket.

✳ CAUTION

Do not use any type of sharp instrument to hold the cable strand in place. Damage to the cable strand or coating can occur.

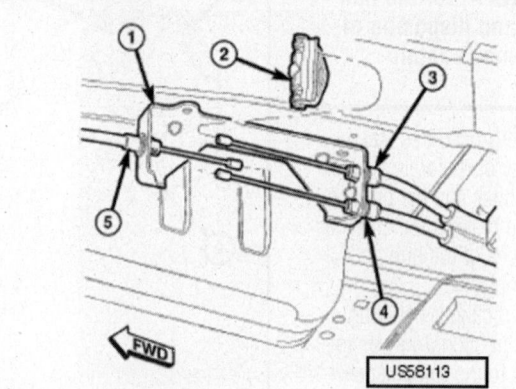

1. Intermediate bracket
2. Equalizer
3. Left rear cable
4. Right rear cable
5. Front cable

US58113

Fig. 9 Parking brake cable adjustment

4. Pull rearward on the equalizer until the front cable stops, then grasp the front cable strand and hold it in this position.

5. Disconnect the equalizer from the front cable strand.

6. Release the front cable strand allowing the lever automatic self-adjusting mechanism to pull the front cable strand forward. This action allows the adjuster mechanism to rotate around to its stop, removing tension from the adjuster and front parking brake cable.

Automatic Adjuster Tension Reset

1. Raise the vehicle to a comfortable working position and support it safely.

2. Wipe the front parking brake cable strand clean at the intermediate bracket area.

✳✳ WARNING

Do use any type of sharp instrument directly on the cable strand to hold it in place. Damage to the cable strand or coating can occur.

3. Clamp an appropriate pair of pliers on the front parking brake cable button (2) only and pull the cable strand rearward until it stops, then grasp the front cable strand and hold it in this position. Remove the pliers from the button.

4. While holding the front cable in this position, install the equalizer (attached to both rear cables) on the front parking brake cable.

5. Release the grasp on the front parking brake cable.

6. Lower the vehicle.

7. Apply and release the parking brake lever one time. This will seat the parking brake cables and allow the auto adjuster in the parking brake lever mechanism to correctly tension the parking brake cables.

CHASSIS ELECTRICAL

AIR BAG (SUPPLEMENTAL RESTRAINT SYSTEM)

GENERAL INFORMATION

✳✳ CAUTION

The Routan is equipped with an air bag system. Disarm the system before performing service on or around system components, the steering column, instrument panel components, wiring and sensors. Failure to follow the safety precautions and the disarming procedure could result in accidental air bag deployment, possible injury and unnecessary system repairs.

SERVICE PRECAUTIONS

• To avoid serious or fatal injury on vehicles equipped with the supplemental restraint system (SRS), never attempt to repair the electrically conductive circuits or wiring components related to the SRS. Such repairs can compromise the conductivity and current carrying capacity of those critical electrical circuits, which may cause SRS components not to deploy when required, or to deploy when not required. Any wire harness containing broken, cut, burned or otherwise damaged electrically conductive SRS wiring, terminals or connector components must be removed and replaced with an entire new wire harness. Only minor cuts or abrasions of wire and terminal insulation where the conductive material has not been damaged, or connector insulators where the integrity of the latching and locking mechanisms have not been compromised may be repaired using appropriate methods.

• To avoid serious or fatal injury during and following any seat belt or child

restraint anchor service, carefully inspect all seat belts, buckles, mounting hardware, retractors, tether straps, and anchors for proper installation, operation, or damage. Replace any belt that is cut, frayed, or torn. Straighten any belt that is twisted. Tighten any loose fasteners. Replace any belt that has a damaged or ineffective buckle or retractor. Replace any belt that has a bent or damaged latch plate or anchor plate. Replace any child restraint anchor or the unit to which the anchor is integral that has been bent or damaged. Never attempt to repair a seat belt or child restraint component. Always replace damaged or ineffective seat belt and child restraint components with the correct genuine Volkswagen part.

• To avoid serious or fatal injury on vehicles equipped with side curtain airbags, disable the SRS before attempting any occupant restraint controller diagnosis or service. The ORC contains a rollover sensor, which enables the system to deploy the side curtain airbags in the event of a vehicle rollover event. If an ORC is accidentally rolled during service while still connected to battery power, the side curtain airbags will deploy. Disconnect the negative battery cable, and then wait two minutes for the system capacitor to discharge before performing further diagnosis or service. This is the only sure way to disable the SRS. Failure to take the proper precautions could result in accidental airbag deployment.

• To avoid serious or fatal injury on vehicles equipped with airbags, disable the SRS before attempting any steering wheel, steering column, airbag, seat belt tensioner, impact sensor, or instrument panel component diagnosis or service. Disconnect the

negative battery cable, and then wait two minutes for the system capacitor to discharge before performing further diagnosis or service. This is the only sure way to disable the SRS. Failure to take the proper precautions could result in accidental airbag deployment.

• To avoid serious or fatal injury on vehicles equipped with airbags, before performing any welding operations disconnect the negative battery cable, and disconnect all wire harness connectors from the ORC. Failure to take the proper precautions could result in accidental airbag deployment and other possible damage to the SRS circuits and components.

• To avoid serious or fatal injury do not attempt to dismantle an airbag unit or tamper with its inflator. Do not puncture, incinerate or bring it into contact with electricity. Do not store at temperatures exceeding 93°C (200°F). An airbag inflator unit may contain sodium azide and potassium nitrate. These materials are poisonous and extremely flammable. Contact with acid, water, or heavy metals may produce harmful and irritating gases (sodium hydroxide is formed in the presence of moisture) or combustible compounds. An airbag inflator unit may also contain a gas canister pressurized to more than 2500 psi (17.24 kPa). Failure to follow these instructions may result in possible serious or fatal injury.

• To avoid serious or fatal injury when handling a seat belt tensioner retractor or buckle, keep fingers out from under the retractor or buckle cover and away from the seat belt webbing or cable where it exits from the retractor or buckle cover.

• To avoid serious or fatal injury, replace all SRS components with only

Volkswagen Genuine Parts. Substitute parts may appear interchangeable, but internal differences may result in inferior occupant protection. Failure to follow these instructions may result in possible serious or fatal injury.

• To avoid serious or fatal injury, the fasteners, screws, and bolts originally used for the SRS components must never be replaced with any substitutes. These fasteners have special coatings and are specifically designed for the SRS. Anytime a new fastener is needed, replace it with the correct fasteners provided in the service package or specified as a Volkswagen Genuine Part. Failure to follow these instructions may result in possible serious or fatal injury.

• To avoid serious or fatal injury when a steering column has an airbag unit attached, never place the column on the floor or any other surface with the steering wheel or airbag unit face down. Failure to follow these instructions may result in possible serious or fatal injury.

• When carrying or handling an undeployed airbag, point the trim side (face) of the airbag towards the body to minimize possibility of injury if accidental deployment occurs. Failure to do this may result in personal injury or death.

• Wear safety glasses, rubber gloves, and long sleeved clothing when cleaning powder residue from vehicle after an airbag deployment. Powder residue emitted from a deployed airbag can cause skin irritation. Flush affected area with cool water if irritation is experienced. If nasal or throat irritation is experienced, exit the vehicle for fresh air until the irritation ceases. If irritation continues, see a physician.

• Do not use a replacement airbag that is not in the original packaging. This may result in improper deployment, personal injury, or death.

• Deployed and non-deployed airbags may or may not have live pyrotechnic material within the airbag inflator.

• Do not dispose of driver/passenger/curtain airbags or seat belt tensioners unless you are sure of complete deployment. Refer to the Hazardous Substance Control System for proper disposal.

• Dispose of deployed airbags and tensioners consistent with state, provincial, local, and federal regulations.

• After any airbag component testing or service, do not connect the battery negative cable. Personal injury or death may result if the system test is not performed first.

DISARMING THE SYSTEM

1. Disconnect and isolate the negative battery cable.
2. Wait two minutes for the system capacitor to discharge before further service.

ARMING THE SYSTEM

1. Perform the SRS verification test procedure using a scantool.

CLOCKSPRING CENTERING

See Figure 10.

1. Place the front wheels in the straight ahead position.
2. Remove the clockspring from the steering column.
3. Rotate the clockspring rotor clockwise until a slight resistance is felt near the end of its travel. Do not apply excessive torque.

4. From the full clockwise rotation, rotate the rotor about two and one-half turns counterclockwise. The clockspring drive pin should end up near the bottom, and the airbag pigtail wires and connector receptacle should be near the top.
5. Turn the rotor slightly clockwise or counterclockwise as necessary so that the arrowheads on the rotor and the clockspring housing are in alignment.
6. The clockspring is now centered. Secure the clockspring rotor to the clockspring case using the original locking pin or adhesive tape to maintain clockspring centering until the steering wheel is reinstalled on the steering column.
7. The front wheels should still be in the straight-ahead position. Install the clockspring onto the steering column.

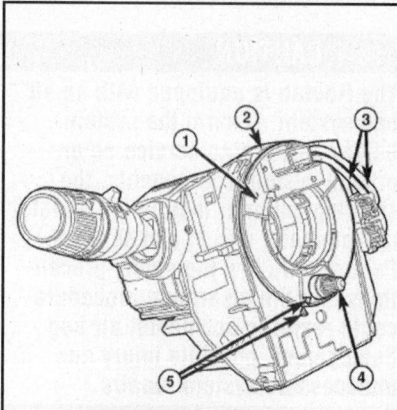

1. Clockspring rotor
2. Clockspring housing
3. Airbag pigtail wires
4. Clockspring drive pin
5. Arrowhead alignment marks

36543_CARA_G0026

Fig. 10 Clockspring centering

DRIVE TRAIN

AUTOMATIC TRANSAXLE FLUID

FLUID & FILTER

See Figure 11.

✳✳ WARNING

Use only fluids of the type labeled ATF+4. Change the filter at the time of the transmission oil change. Clean the magnet on the inside of the oil pan with a clean, dry cloth.

✳✳ WARNING

If the transaxle is disassembled for any reason, the fluid and filter should be changed.

1. Raise and suitably support the vehicle.
2. Place a drain pan with a large opening under the fluid filter oil pan.
3. Loosen the fluid filter oil pan bolts and tap the pan at one corner in order to loosen the pan, allowing the fluid to drain, and then remove the oil pan.
4. Remove the fluid filter nuts and remove the filter.
5. Install a new filter and nuts. Tighten the nuts to 44 inch lbs. (5 Nm).
6. Install the fluid filter oil pan; use a bead of RTV sealant.
7. Clean the oil pan and magnet. Install the pan using new silicone adhesive sealant. Tighten the oil pan bolts to 53 inch lbs. (6 Nm).

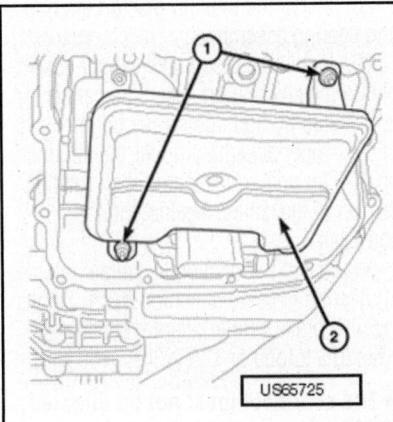

US65725

Fig. 11 Loosen the fluid filter oil pan bolts (1) and tap the pan (2) at one corner in order to loosen the pan allowing the fluid to drain

8. Pour four quarts of ATF+4 into the transaxle through the dipstick tube.
9. Start the engine and allow the engine to idle for at least one minute. Then, with the parking brake and brake pedal applied, move the shift lever momentarily to each gear position, ending in the park or neutral position.
10. Check the fluid level and add an appropriate amount in order to bring the fluid level to ⅛ inch (3 mm) below the lowest mark on the dipstick.
11. Check the fluid level after the normal operating temperature 180°F (82°C) has been reached. Refer to Fluid Level & Condition Check.
12. Prevent dirt from entering the transmission by making certain that the dipstick tube cap is fully seated into the dipstick tube.

FLUID LEVEL & CONDITION CHECK

1. Park the vehicle on a level surface.
2. Remove the dipstick tube cap.

✳✳ CAUTION

There is a risk of an accident from the vehicle moving when the engine is running. There is a risk of injury from contusions and burns if you place your hands in the engine compartment when it is started or when it is running. Secure the vehicle in order to prevent it from moving by itself. Wear properly fastened and close fitting work clothes. Do not touch hot or rotating parts.

3. Press the brake pedal and start engine, allow the engine to idle in the park position.
4. Shift through the transmission gears several times with the vehicle stationary and the engine idling.

➡**Excess insertion force when inserting transmission dipstick #9336A may cause the dipstick to slip past the stop bracket in the transmission oil pan. An approximate distance that the dipstick could be inserted into the fill tube is 16.69 inch (424 mm).**

5. Warm up the transmission, wait at least 2 minutes and check the fluid level with the engine running. Push the transmission dipstick into the transmission fill tube until the tip contacts the oil pan and pull out again, read the oil level, repeat if necessary.

➡**The transmission dipstick will protrude from the fill tube when installed.**

6. Check the transmission fluid temperature using the appropriate scan tool.
7. The transmission dipstick #9336A has indicator marks every 10 mm. Determine the height of the fluid level on the dipstick and using that height, and the transmission fluid temperature as viewed with the scan too, and the transmission fluid graph above, determine if the transmission fluid level is correct.
8. Add or remove fluid as necessary and recheck the level.
9. Once the level is correct, install the dipstick tube cap.

Fluid Condition

Along with the fluid level, it is important to check the condition of the fluid. When the fluid smells burnt, and is contaminated with metal or friction material particles, a complete transmission recondition is probably required. Be sure to examine the fluid on the dipstick closely. If there is any doubt about its condition, drain a sample for a double check.

ATF+4 when new, is red in color. The ATF is dyed red so it can be identified among the other fluids used in the vehicle such as engine oil, or engine coolant. The red color is not permanent and is not an indicator of fluid condition. As the vehicle is driven, the ATF will begin to look darker in color and may eventually become brown. This is normal. Also, the unique odor of ATF+4 may change with age. Consequently, odor and color cannot be used to indicate the fluid condition or the need for a fluid change.

Seat the dipstick tube cap fully to seal out water and dirt after the fluid has been checked.

FRONT DRIVE AXLE

REMOVAL & INSTALLATION

See Figures 12 and 13.

✳✳ WARNING

Never grasp the drive axle assembly by the inner or outer boots doing so may damage the boot.

1. Raise the vehicle.
2. Remove the wheel and tire assembly from the vehicle.
3. Apply the vehicle brakes to keep the hub from turning, and then loosen the drive axle nut.

4. Remove the nut from the drive axle.

5. Remove the two front disc brake caliper adapter to steering knuckle attaching bolts.

6. Remove the disc brake caliper assembly from the steering knuckle. Remove the caliper assembly by first rotating the top of the caliper assembly away from the steering knuckle and then removing the bottom of the assembly out from under the machined abutment on the steering knuckle.

✳✳ WARNING

Do not allow the brake caliper assembly to hang by the brake flex hose.

7. Support the disc brake caliper assembly by using a wire hook and suspending it from the strut assembly.

8. Remove the brake rotor from the hub and bearing assembly.

9. Remove the steering knuckle-to-strut attachment bolts from the steering knuckle.

10. Pull the steering knuckle from the strut clevis bracket.

✳✳ WARNING

Care must be taken not to separate the inner CV joint during this operation. Do not allow the drive axle to hang by the inner CV joint after removing the outer CV joint from the hub/bearing assembly in the steering knuckle, the end of the drive axle must be supported.

11. Pull the steering knuckle assembly down and away from the outer CV joint of the drive axle assembly while pulling the joint out of the hub bearing.

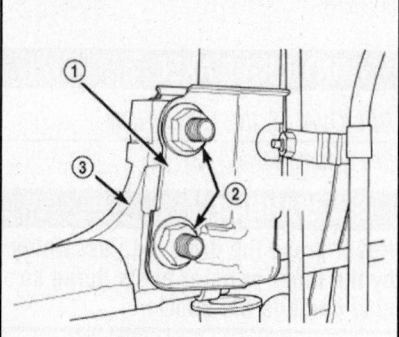

1. Strut
2. Attachment bolts
3. Steering knuckle

36543_CARA_G0066

Fig. 12 Remove the steering knuckle-to-strut attachment bolts (2) from the steering knuckle (3)

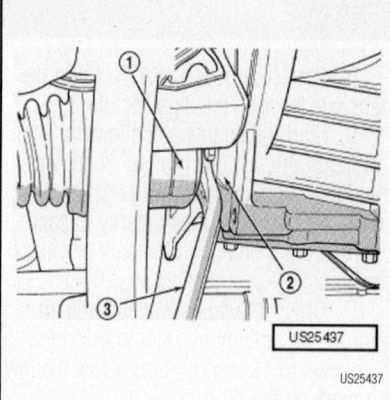

US25437

Fig. 13 Insert a pry bar (3) between the inner tripod joint (1) and the transmission case (2)

12. Support the outer end of the drive axle assembly. Insert a pry bar between the inner tripod joint and the transmission case. Pry against the inner tripod joint, until tripod joint retaining snap-ring is disengaged from the transmission side gear.

13. Pull the steering knuckle from the strut clevis bracket.

14. Pull the steering knuckle assembly down and away from the outer CV joint of the drive axle assembly while pulling the joint out of the intermediate shaft (if equipped) or the transmission.

15. Remove the bolts at the heat shield and remove the heat shield (if equipped).

16. Remove the 3 bolts holding the mid-shaft bearing to the block.

17. Remove the intermediate shaft from the transmission.

To install:

18. Install the intermediate shaft into the transmission.

19. Install the 3 bolts holding the mid-shaft bearing to the block and tighten them to 22 ft. lbs. (30 Nm).

20. Install the heat shield and bolts, and then tighten them to 40 inch lbs. (6 Nm; if equipped).

Outer CV Joint Inspection

✳✳ WARNING

A rubber-coated washer on the outer CV joint stem is used and should be in place during assembly.

21. Clean the tripod joint spline and oil seal sealing surface thoroughly. Lightly lubricate the oil seal sealing surface on the tripod joint with fresh clean transmission lubricant and install the rubber-coated washer.

---

22. Holding the drive axle assembly by the tripod joint and interconnecting shaft, install the tripod joint into the transmission side gear as far as possible by hand. Be sure to engage the splines prior to applying force.

23. Push the tripod joint onto the intermediate shaft forcefully, until the snap ring is engaged.

24. Clean all debris and moisture out of the steering knuckle, in the area where the outer CV joint will be installed into the steering knuckle.

25. Ensure that the front of the outer CV joint which fits against the face of the hub and bearing is free of debris and moisture before installing the outer CV joint into the hub and bearing assembly.

✳✳ WARNING

1.The steering knuckle-to-strut assembly attaching bolts are serrated and must not be turned during installation. Install the nuts while holding the bolts stationary in the steering knuckle. If the vehicle being serviced is equipped with eccentric strut assembly attaching bolts, the eccentric bolt must be installed in the bottom (slotted) hole on the strut clevis bracket.

26. Slide the drive axle back into the front hub and bearing assembly.

27. Install the steering knuckle in the clevis bracket of the strut damper assembly. Install the strut damper-to-steering knuckle attaching bolts. Tighten both bolts to a torque of 65 ft. lbs. (88 Nm) + 90° turn after the tightening specification is met.

28. Install the braking disc on the hub and bearing assembly.

29. Install the disc brake caliper assembly on the steering knuckle. The caliper is installed by first sliding the bottom of the caliper assembly under the abutment on the steering knuckle, and then rotating the top of the caliper against the top abutment.

30. Install the disc brake caliper adapter-to-steering knuckle attaching bolts. Tighten the disc brake caliper adapter attaching bolts to a torque of 125 ft. lbs. (169 Nm).

➡**The seal boot must not be dimpled, stretched, or out of shape in any way. If the seal boot is NOT shaped correctly, equalize pressure in the seal and shape it by hand.**

31. Clean all foreign matter from the threads of the outer CV joint. Install the drive axle to the hub/bearing assembly nut

on the drive axle and securely tighten the nut.

32. Install the front wheel and tire assembly. Install and tighten the wheel mounting stud nuts in proper sequence until all nuts are torqued to half the required specification. Then repeat the tightening sequence to the full specified torque of 100 ft. lbs. (135 Nm).

33. Lower the vehicle.

34. Apply the vehicle brakes to keep the hub from turning, and then tighten the hub nut to a torque of 118 ft. lbs. (160 Nm).

35. Check the fluid level in the transmission assembly. Refer to Fluid Level & Condition Check.

DIFFERENTIAL SEAL

REMOVAL & INSTALLATION

Right Side

See Figure 14.

1. Remove the drive axle.

➡**Some transmission fluid may spill when the transmission extension assembly is removed.**

2. Remove the transmission extension assembly bolts (1) and remove the assembly (2).

To install:

3. Clean the transmission case and apply VW RTV sealant.

4. Position the transmission extension assembly, install the bolts and tighten to 105 in. lbs. (12 Nm).

5. Install the drive axle.

6. Check the fluid level and adjust as necessary. Refer to the Automatic Transaxle Fluid section.

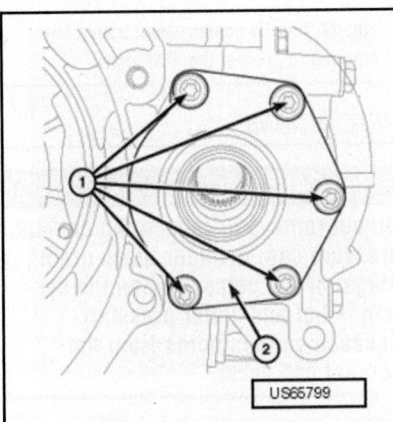

US65799

Fig. 14 Remove the transmission extension assembly bolts (1), and then remove the assembly (2)

Left Side

1. Remove the drive axle.

➡**Some transmission fluid may spill when the seal is removed.**

2. Remove the axle seal(s) by using a screw or hook style seal puller on a slide hammer.

To install:

3. Clean the axle shaft seal bores.

4. Install the seal using a seal installer, such as #C-3995-A and a universal driver handle, such as #C-4171.

5. Tap the seal into position until firmly seated against the transmission case.

6. Install the drive axle.

7. Check the fluid level and adjust as necessary. Refer to the Automatic Transaxle Fluid section.

REAR AXLE

REMOVAL & INSTALLATION

See Figure 15.

➡**Refer also to Front Suspension.**

1. Raise and support the vehicle.

2. On each side of vehicle, remove the wheel mounting nuts, and then remove the rear tire and wheel assembly.

3. Remove the screw securing the left rear parking brake cable to the left axle trailing arm.

4. Remove the screws securing the right rear parking brake cable to the front of the axle.

5. Remove the screw securing the parking brake cable routing bracket to the axle.

6. Remove the 2 bolts securing the disc brake caliper and adapter bracket to the axle.

7. Remove the disc brake caliper and adapter bracket from the axle and rotor as an assembly.

8. Hang the assembly out of the way using wire or a bungee cord. Use care not to overextend the brake hose when doing this.

9. Remove any retaining clips, and then slide the brake rotor off the hub and bearing.

➡**Prior to removal, clean the area around the sensor head to help prevent contaminants from entering the bearing when the sensor head is removed.**

10. Remove the wheel speed sensor routing clip from the rear axle.

11. Remove the screw fastening the speed sensor head to the hub and bearing.

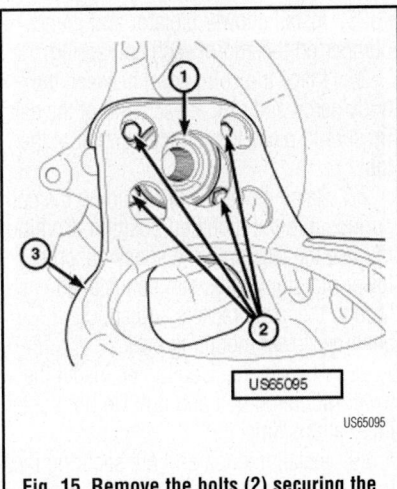

US65095

Fig. 15 Remove the bolts (2) securing the hub and bearing (1) to the axle (3)

12. Remove the wheel speed sensor from hub and bearing.

13. Remove the bolts securing the hub and bearing to the axle.

14. Remove hub and bearing and brake shield.

15. Position a transmission jack or its equivalent under the center of the axle raising it enough to support the axle.

16. Remove the bolt and nut securing the track bar to the axle.

17. On each side of vehicle, remove the lower mounting bolt and nut securing the shock absorber to the axle.

18. Lower the jack until each coil spring can be removed from the axle.

19. Remove both coil springs, jounce bumpers, and lower isolators.

20. On each side of vehicle, remove the nut and through-bolt fastening the axle trailing arm to the forward mounting bracket on the body.

21. Lower the jack and remove the axle from vehicle.

To install:

22. Center the axle beam on a transmission jack or equivalent standing at axle removal height.

23. Raise the jack as necessary, then swing the axle trailing arms upward aligning the bushings with the brackets mounted on the body.

24. At each trailing arm, install a through-bolt through the mounting bracket and bushing. Install a nut on the end of each through-bolt. Do not tighten at this time.

※※ WARNING

Although both ends of the coil spring may appear identical, they are not. Be sure to place the end with the tag upward.

25. Install a lower isolator and jounce bumper on the end of each coil spring.

26. Place the coil spring between the body perch and axle at each end of the axle. Be sure to place the jounce bumper at the top.

27. Raise the jack while guiding the coil springs into the mounted position. Continue to raise the jack until the shock absorber lower mounting bolts can be installed though the axle brackets and shock absorber lower mounting eyes.

28. At each shock absorber, install the lower mounting bolt and nut. Do not tighten them at this time.

29. Install the bolt and nut securing the track bar to the axle.

➡**Do not tighten at this time.**

30. Remove the jack from under the axle.

31. Install the hub and bearing and brake shield onto the end of the axle. Install the mounting bolts securing the hub and bearing to the axle. Tighten the mounting bolts to 41 ft. lbs. (55 Nm).

➡**Ensure that wheel speed sensor mounting surface on the bearing is clean before sensor installation.**

32. Push the wheel speed sensor head into the mounting hole in the hub and bearing and align the mounting screw hole.

33. Install a new mounting screw. Tighten the mounting screw to 55 inch lbs. (6 Nm).

34. Install the wheel speed sensor routing clip into the hole in the rear axle.

35. Install the brake rotor over the hub and bearing.

36. Install the disc brake caliper and adapter bracket over the axle and rotor as an assembly.

37. Install the 2 bolts securing the disc brake caliper and adapter bracket to the axle. Tighten the mounting bolts to 74 ft. lbs. (100 Nm).

38. Position the parking brake cable routing bracket to the axle and install the screw securing it in place. Tighten the screw to 55 inch lbs. (6 Nm).

39. Position the right rear parking brake

cable in front of the axle and install screws securing the cable in place. Tighten the screws to 55 inch lbs. (6 Nm).

40. Position the left rear parking brake cable routing clamp at the left axle trailing arm. Tighten the screw to 55 inch lbs. (6 Nm)

41. On each side of the vehicle, install the tire and wheel assembly. Install and tighten the wheel mounting nuts to 100 ft. lbs. (135 Nm).

42. Lower the vehicle.

43. Pump the brake pedal several times to ensure the vehicle has a firm brake pedal before moving the vehicle.

44. Position the vehicle on an alignment rack/drive-on lift. Raise the lift as necessary to access the rear suspension while keeping the vehicle at curb (riding) height.

45. Tighten both trailing arm mounting bracket pivot through-bolts to 129 ft. lbs. (175 Nm)

46. Tighten the shock absorber lower mounting bolt nut to 55 ft. lbs. (75 Nm).

47. Tighten the track bar lower mounting bolt nut to 60 ft. lbs. (81 Nm)

ENGINE COOLING

ENGINE COOLANT

DRAIN & FILLING PROCEDURE

Draining
See Figure 16.

1. Make sure the system is not pressurized. Without removing the radiator pressure cap, use a screwdriver to open the petcock. The petcock is located on the lower left side of radiator.

➡**DO NOT WASTE reusable coolant: If the solution is clean, drain the coolant** into a clean, labeled container for reuse.

2. After the coolant recovery/reserve container is empty, then remove the coolant pressure cap.

3. Remove the cylinder block drain plug(s).

Filling
See Figure 17.

1. Refer to Precautions.

2. Remove the radiator pressure cap and fill the system, use a 50/50 mixture of the appropriate coolant and distilled water. Refer to Specifications.

3. Continue filling the cooling system until it is full. Do not spill the coolant on the drive belt or the generator. For cooling system capacity refer to the Fluid Capacity table in Specifications.

4. Fill the coolant recovery reservoir to at least the MAX mark.

5. Recheck the coolant for a few days. It may be necessary to add coolant to the reservoir after three or four warm up/cool down cycles in order to maintain the coolant level between the MAX and MIN mark. This will allow trapped air to be removed from the cooling system.

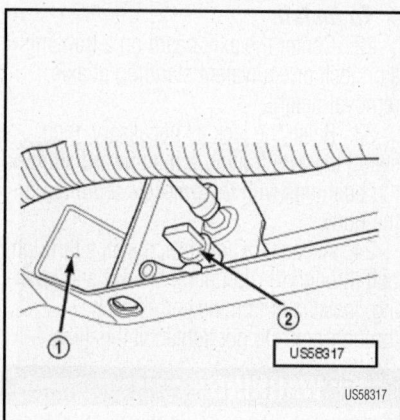

Fig. 16 Left side frame rail (1) and petcock (2)

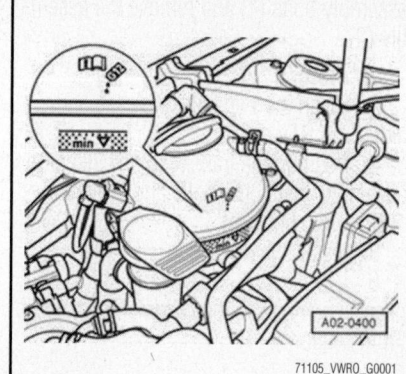

Fig. 17 Fill the coolant level above MIN marking to at least the MAX mark

PRECAUTIONS

✳✳ CAUTION

Do not remove or loosen the coolant pressure cap, cylinder block drain plugs, or the petcock when the system is hot and under pressure because serious burns from the coolant can occur.

✳✳ CAUTION

Hot Steam may escape when opening the expansion tank. Wear protective

goggles and protective clothing to prevent damage to eyes and scalding. Cover the expansion tank cap with a rag and open very carefully.

❊❊ CAUTION

Coolant is an ethylene glycol based coolant and is harmful if swallowed or inhaled. If swallowed, drink two glasses of water and induce vomiting. If inhaled, move to a fresh air area. Seek medical attention immediately. Do not store in open or unmarked containers. Wash skin and clothing thoroughly after coming in contact with ethylene glycol. Keep out of the reach of children and animals. Dispose of glycol base coolant properly; contact your dealer or government agency for the location of a collection center in your area.

❊❊ CAUTION

Avoid the radiator cooling fan when engine compartment related service is performed, personal injury can result.

❊❊ CAUTION

Store used coolant in compatible containers that are in good condition and labeled "Used Antifreeze Only" until you recycle it.

❊❊ CAUTION

Keep used coolant containers securely closed, except when emptying or filling, to minimize the potential for spillage.

❊❊ CAUTION

Clean up coolant spills immediately. Clean up the area well afterward and do not throw the rags in the trash. Dogs and cats dig through the garbage and can become exposed through contact with rags.

❊❊ CAUTION

Do not pour used coolant down a drain or on the ground. This is illegal and a danger to people and animals.

❊❊ WARNING

Volkswagen genuine parts antifreeze/coolant, 5 year 100,000

mile (160,000 km) formula (MS-9769) may not be mixed with any other type of antifreeze. Mixing of coolants other than specified (non-Hybrid Organic Additive Technology (HOAT) or other HOAT), may result in engine damage that may not be covered under the new vehicle warranty, and decreased corrosion protection.

❊❊ WARNING

Richer antifreeze mixtures cannot be measured with normal field equipment and can cause problems associated with 100 percent ethylene glycol.

❊❊ WARNING

Do not use coolant additives that are claimed to improve engine cooling.

REVERSE FLUSHING

1. Refer to the Cooling System Precautions as well as the following:

❊❊ CAUTION

The internal radiator pressure must not exceed 20 psi (138 kPa) as damage to radiator may result.

❊❊ CAUTION

On vehicles equipped with a heater water control valve, be sure the heater control valve is closed (heat off). This will prevent coolant flow with scale and other deposits from entering the heater core.

❊❊ CAUTION

Follow the manufacturer's instructions when using these flushing products.

Reverse Flushing

Reverse flushing the cooling system is the forcing of water through the cooling system. This is done using air pressure in the opposite direction of the normal coolant flow. It is usually only necessary with very dirty cooling systems with evidence of partial plugging.

Reverse Flushing the Radiator

1. Disconnect the radiator hoses from the radiator.

2. Attach a section of the radiator hose to the radiator outlet fitting and insert the flushing gun.
3. Connect a water supply hose and air supply hose to the flushing gun. Allow the radiator to fill with water.
4. When the radiator is filled, apply air in short blasts.
5. Allow the radiator to refill between blasts.
6. Continue this reverse flushing until clean water flows out through the rear of the radiator cooling tube passages.

Reverse Flushing the Engine

1. Drain the cooling system.
2. Remove the thermostat housing and thermostat.
3. Reinstall the thermostat housing.
4. Disconnect the upper radiator hose from the radiator and attach the flushing gun to the hose.
5. Disconnect the lower radiator hose from the water pump and attach a lead away hose to the water pump inlet fitting.
6. Connect the water supply hose and air supply hose to the flushing gun. Allow the engine to fill with water.
7. When the engine is filled, apply air in short blasts, allowing the system to fill between air blasts.
8. Continue until clean water flows through the lead away hose.
9. Remove the lead away hose, flushing gun, water supply hose and air supply hose.
10. Remove the thermostat housing and install the thermostat. Install the thermostat housing with a replacement gasket.
11. Reconnect the radiator hoses.
12. Refill the cooling system with the correct antifreeze/water mixture. Refer to Cooling System Draining and Filling,

Chemical Cleaning

In some instances, use a radiator cleaner before flushing. This will soften the scale and other deposits and aid the flushing operation.

ENGINE FAN

REMOVAL & INSTALLATION

See Figure 18.

1. Refer to Precautions.
2. Remove the engine cover.
3. Disconnect and isolate the negative battery cable. Refer to Engine Electrical, Battery.
4. Drain the cooling system partially—to below the upper radiator hose. Refer to Cooling System Draining & Filling.

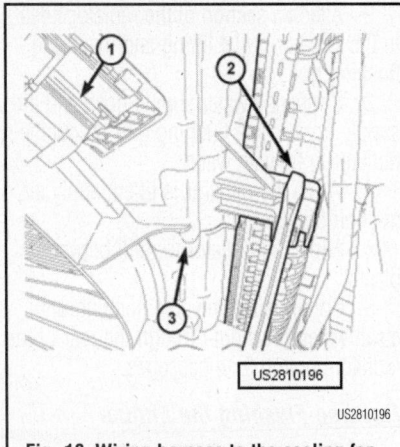

US2810196

Fig. 18 Wiring harness to the cooling fan assembly (1), radiator fan retaining clips (2), and radiator fan

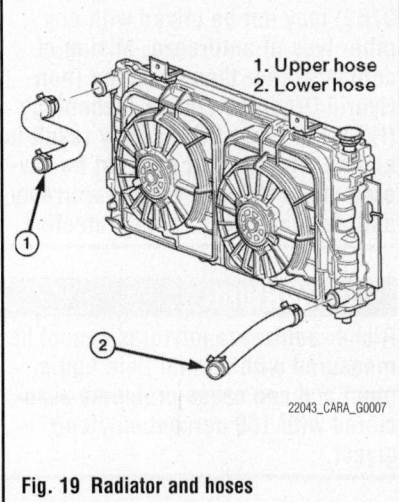

1. Upper hose
2. Lower hose

22043_CARA_G0007

Fig. 19 Radiator and hoses

5. Remove the overflow tubing.

6. Remove the coolant recovery reservoir.

7. Remove upper radiator hose and position it aside.

8. Disconnect the wiring harness to the cooling fan assembly and the low-speed resistor.

9. Remove the radiator fan by pressing the retaining clips in and lifting upwards to release it from the mounts.

To install:

10. Position the radiator cooling fan into the mounts and attaching clips on the radiator. Press down to lock it into place.

11. Connect the cooling fan electrical connectors.

12. Install the coolant recovery reservoir and overflow hose.

13. Install the upper radiator hose.

14. Install the engine cover.

15. Connect the negative battery cable.

16. Fill the cooling system. Refer to Cooling System Draining & Filling.

RADIATOR

REMOVAL & INSTALLATION

See Figure 19.

1. Refer to Precautions.

2. Disconnect the battery negative cable.

3. Drain the cooling system. Refer to Cooling System Draining & Filling.

4. Remove the coolant recovery container.

5. Remove the radiator fan.

6. Loosen and reposition the upper and lower radiator hose clamps at the radiator.

7. Remove the upper and lower radiator hoses.

8. Remove the grille.

9. Remove the radiator crossmember.

10. Remove the screw securing the air conditioning condenser taping block to the radiator located in the right corner of the engine compartment.

11. Disengage the condenser retaining tabs.

12. Disengage the radiator retaining tabs.

13. Lift the radiator out of vehicle.

To install:

➡Be sure the air seal is in position before the radiator is installed.

14. Slide the radiator down into position. Seat the radiator with the rubber isolators into the mounting holes provided, with 10 lbs of force.

15. Position the A/C condenser onto the radiator lower mounts and engage the upper mounting tabs.

16. Install the upper and lower radiator hoses.

17. Position and tighten the upper and lower radiator hose clamps at the radiator.

18. Install the grille.

19. Connect the coolant recovery hose.

20. Connect the vapor purge solenoid to the mounting bracket.

21. Install the radiator fan.

22. Install the radiator crossmember.

23. Install the coolant recovery container.

24. Fill the cooling system.

25. Connect the negative battery cable.

THERMOSTAT

REMOVAL & INSTALLATION

See Figure 20.

1. Refer to Precautions.

✳✳ WARNING

The Thermostat and housing is serviced as an assembly. Do not remove the thermostat from the housing, damage to the thermostat may occur.

➡Do not waste reusable coolant. If solution is clean, drain coolant into an appropriate clean, marked container for reuse.

➡If the thermostat is being replaced, be sure that the replacement is the specified thermostat for the vehicle model and engine type.

2. Disconnect the negative battery cable. Refer to see Removal and Installation.

3. Remove the air intake assembly. Refer to Air Cleaner Housing.

4. Drain the cooling system. Refer to Cooling System Draining and Filling.

5. Remove upper radiator hose clamp and upper radiator hose at thermostat housing.

6. Remove thermostat housing mounting bolts, thermostat housing and thermostat.

To install:

7. Clean the mating areas of the timing chain cover and thermostat housing.

8. Install a new gasket onto the thermostat housing.

9. Position the thermostat housing on the water crossover.

10. Install the two thermostat housing bolts. Tighten the bolts to 106 inch lbs. (12 Nm).

11. Install the upper radiator hose on the thermostat housing.

12. Fill the cooling system. Refer to Cooling System Draining & Filling.

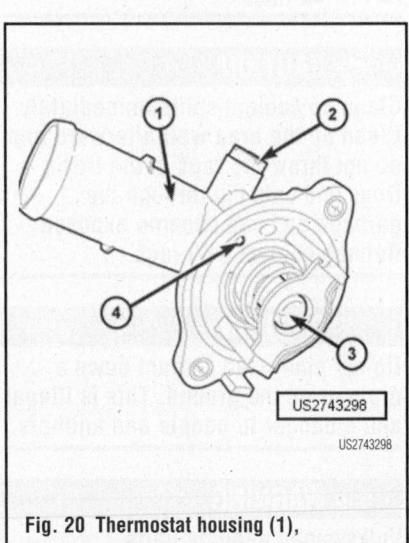

US2743298

Fig. 20 Thermostat housing (1), thermostat (3)

13. Install the air intake system.
14. Connect the negative battery cable.
15. Start and warm the engine. Check for leaks.

WATER PUMP

REMOVAL & INSTALLATION

See Figures 21 and 22.

1. Refer to Precautions.

➡**The water pump on 3.6L engines is bolted directly to the engine timing chain case cover.**

2. Disconnect negative battery cable from battery.

✳✳ CAUTION

Constant tension hose clamps are used on most cooling system hoses. When removing or installing, use only tools designed for servicing this type of clamp. Always wear safety glasses when servicing constant tension clamps.

✳✳ WARNING

A number or letter is stamped into the tongue of the constant tension clamps. If replacement is necessary, use only an original equipment

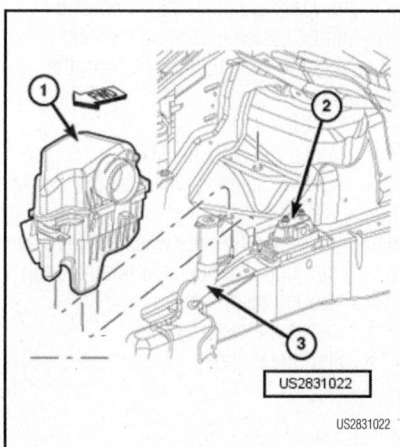

Fig. 21 Air filter housing assembly (1) and right side engine mount assembly (2)

US2831022

clamp with matching number or letter.

3. Support the engine with a jack.
4. Remove the air filter housing assembly and intake tube to throttle body.
5. Remove the power steering reservoir and position aside.
6. Remove the right side engine mount assembly.
7. Remove the engine mounting block from the water pump.
8. Raise the vehicle.

✳✳ WARNING

Do not pry on the water pump at the timing chain case/cover. The machined surfaces may be damaged resulting in leaks.

9. Remove the accessory drive belt. Refer to Accessory Drive Belt in the Engine Mechanical section.
10. Remove accessory drive belt idler pulley.
11. If equipped, remove the lower engine cover.
12. Drain the cooling system. Refer to Cooling System Draining & Filling.

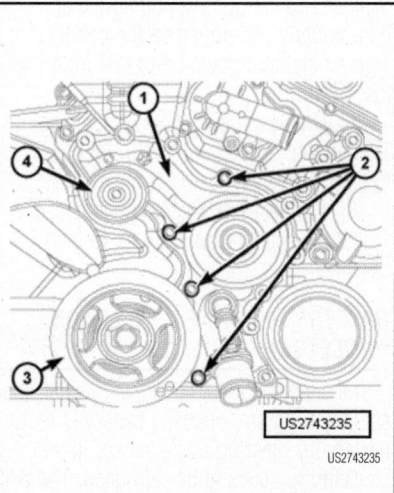

US2743235

Fig. 22 Water pump (1), the four water pump bolts (2) that mount directly to the timing chain cover, and the accessory drive belt idler pulley (4)

13. Remove right front wheel.
14. Remove the inner splash shield.
15. Remove the lower bypass hose and the lower radiator hose from the water pump and position it aside.
16. Remove the twelve water pump mounting bolts. Take note of the four water pump bolts that mount directly to the timing chain cover.
17. Remove the water pump and discard the seal.

To install:

18. Clean the mating surfaces.
19. Using a new seal, position the water pump and install the mounting bolts. Note the shorter bolts that bolt directly to the timing cover. Tighten the M6 water pump mounting bolts to 106 inch lbs. (12 Nm).
20. Spin the water pump to be sure that pump impeller does not rub against the timing chain case/cover.
21. Install the lower radiator hose and the bypass hose.
22. Install the idler pulley. Tighten the mounting bolt to 18 ft. lbs. (25 Nm).

✳✳ WARNING

When installing the serpentine accessory drive belt, the belt must be routed correctly. If not, the engine may overheat due to the water pump rotating in the wrong direction.

23. Install the accessory drive belt.
24. Install the right inner splash shield.
25. Install the right front wheel.
26. Lower the vehicle.
27. Position a jack under the engine.
28. Install the engine mount block. Tighten the M8 mounting bolt to 18 ft. lbs. (25 Nm). Tighten the M10 mounting bolt to 41 ft. lbs. (55 Nm).
29. Install the engine mount. Tighten the mounting bolt to the engine block to 45 ft. lbs. (61 Nm).
30. Install the air intake assembly.
31. Fill the cooling system. Refer to Cooling System Draining & Filling.
32. Connect negative battery cable.
33. Check the cooling system for leaks.

BATTERY

PRECAUTIONS

- To protect eyes from battery acid, wear a suitable pair of industrial grade safety glasses when removing or servicing a battery.
- To protect the hands from battery acid, wear a suitable pair of industrial grade heavy duty rubber gloves when removing or servicing a battery.
- Remove your metallic jewelry to avoid being injured by accidental arcing of battery current.
- If the battery shows signs of freezing, leaking or if it has loose posts, do not test, assist-boost, or charge it. The battery may arc internally and explode. Personal injury and/or vehicle damage may result.
- Explosive hydrogen gas forms in and around the battery. Do not smoke, use flame, or create sparks near the battery. Personal injury and/or vehicle damage may result.
- The battery contains sulfuric acid, which is poisonous and caustic. Avoid contact with the skin, eyes, or clothing. In the event of contact, flush with water and call a physician immediately. Keep out of the reach of children.
- Never exceed 14.4 volts when charging a spiral cell battery. Personal injury and/or battery damage may result.

➡Note the location of the positive and negative cables prior to service of the battery or related components.

REMOVAL & INSTALLATION

See Figure 23.

1. Before servicing the vehicle, refer to the Precautions Section.

➡Note the location of the positive and negative cables prior to service of the battery or related components.

2. Disconnect and isolate the battery negative cable.
3. Disconnect and isolate the battery positive cable.
4. Loosen the bolt and the retainer that hold the battery down to the tray.
5. Lift the battery out of the battery tray and remove it from the vehicle.
6. Remove the thermal guard from the battery, if equipped.

To install:

➡When replacing the battery, the thermal guard, if equipped, MUST be transferred to the new battery.

7. Install the battery into the vehicle making sure that the thermal guard, if equipped, is present and the battery is properly positioned on the battery tray.
8. Install the battery hold down retainer and the bolt making sure that it is properly positioned on the battery. Tighten the hold down bolt to 62 inch lbs. (7 Nm).
9. Connect the battery positive cable. Tighten the cable clamp nut to 45 inch lbs. (5 Nm).
10. Connect the battery negative cable. Tighten the cable clamp nut to 45 inch lbs. (5 Nm).

BATTERY RECONNECT/RELEARN PROCEDURE

If the vehicle is equipped with electronic stability program, once the battery is reconnected, the steering angle sensor in the clockspring needs to be calibrated. The SAS

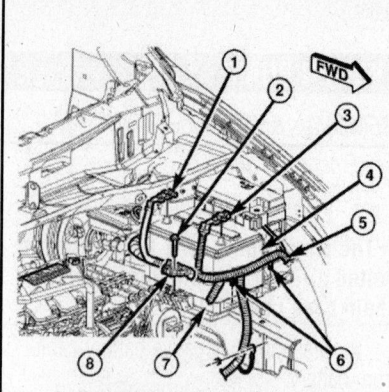

1. Positive cable connection
2. Hold down bolt
3. Negative cable connection
4. Battery
5. Battery cable
6. Cable fastener
7. Battery tray
8. Hold down retainer

36543_CARA_G0085

Fig. 23 Battery

requires calibration anytime the battery or an ABS/ESP component has been disconnected for any length of time. If the SAS is not calibrated following battery reconnecting, the ESP/BAS indicator lamp is illuminated following five ignition cycles indicating the need for calibration. To calibrate, perform the following:

1. Start the engine.
2. Center the steering wheel.
3. Turn the steering wheel all the way to the left until the internal stop in the steering gear is met, then turn the wheel all the way to the right until the opposite internal stop in the steering gear is met.
4. Center the steering wheel.
5. Stop the engine.

ENGINE ELECTRICAL
CHARGING SYSTEM

GENERATOR (ALTERNATOR)

REMOVAL & INSTALLATION
See Figure 24.

1. Disconnect the negative battery cable. Refer to Engine Electrical.
2. Remove the air cleaner body. Refer to Air Cleaner in the Engine Mechanical section.
3. Remove the cooling fan. Refer to Engine Cooling.
4. Remove the serpentine belt. Refer to Accessory Drive Belt in the Engine Mechanical section.
5. Disconnect the generator field electrical connector.
6. Remove the B+ retainer and remove the B+ cable.

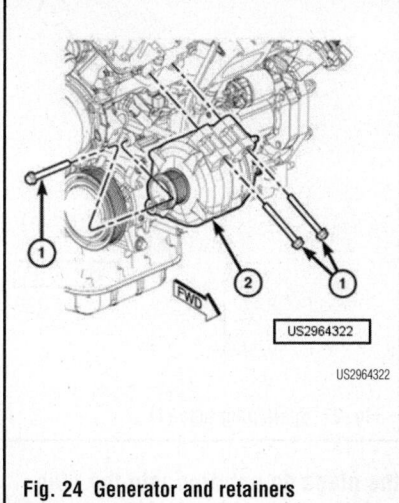

Fig. 24 Generator and retainers

7. Remove the generator retainers.
8. Remove the generator.

To install:

9. Place the generator on the engine and install the retainers.
10. Tighten the generator mounting retainers to 18 ft. lbs. (25 Nm).
11. Install the B+ cable and retainer.
12. Tighten the B+ retainer to 9.5 ft. lbs. (13 Nm).
13. Install the generator field connector.
14. Install the serpentine belt.
15. Install the cooling fan.
16. Install the air cleaner body.
17. Connect the negative battery cable.

ENGINE ELECTRICAL
IGNITION SYSTEM

FIRING ORDER

See Figure 25.

The firing order is 1–2–3–4–5–6.

IGNITION COIL

REMOVAL & INSTALLATION
See Figure 26.

1. Disconnect the negative battery.
2. If removing the ignition coils from cylinders 1 and 3 on the RH side of the engine, first remove the resonator. Refer to Air Cleaner Resonator.
3. If removing the ignition coils from cylinders 2, 4 or 6 on the LH side of the engine, first remove the upper intake manifold and insulator. Refer to Upper Intake Manifold.
4. Unlock and disconnect the electrical connector from the ignition coil.
5. Remove the ignition coil mounting bolt.
6. Pull the ignition coil from the cylinder head cover opening with a slight twisting action.

To install:

> ⁎⁎ **CAUTION**
> **Do not apply silicone-based grease to the ignition coil rubber boot. Silicone-based grease will absorb into the boot causing it to stick and tear.**

7. Using compressed air, blow out any dirt or contaminants from around the top of spark plug.
8. Check the condition of the ignition coil rubber boot.
9. Position the ignition coil into the cylinder head cover opening. Using a twisting action, push the ignition coil onto the spark plug.
10. Install the ignition coil mounting bolts and tighten them to 71 inch lbs. (8 Nm).
11. Connect and lock the electrical connector to the ignition coil.
12. If removed, install the insulator, upper intake manifold and resonator. Refer to Upper Intake Manifold.
13. Connect the negative battery cable.

IGNITION TIMING

ADJUSTMENT

All engines use a fixed ignition timing system. Basic ignition timing is not adjustable. Spark advance is determined by the Powertrain Control Module (PCM).

SPARK PLUGS

REMOVAL & INSTALLATION
See Figure 27.

1. Remove the ignition coil. Refer to Ignition Coil.
2. Prior to removing the spark plug, spray compressed air into the cylinder head opening. This will help prevent foreign

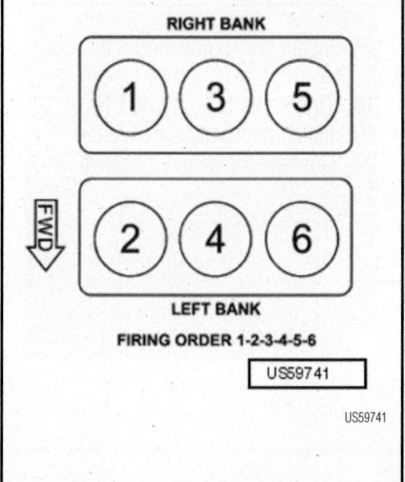

Fig. 25 Spark plug firing order

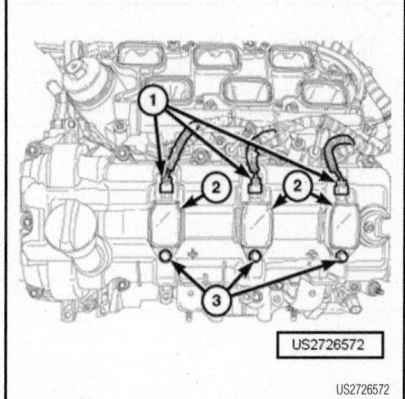

Fig. 26 Electrical connectors (1), ignition coils (2), and the ignition coil mounting bolts (3)

material from entering the combustion chamber.

> ✴✴ **WARNING**
>
> The spark plug tubes are a thin-wall design. Avoid damaging the spark plug tubes. Damage to the spark plug tube can result in oil leaks.

3. Remove the spark plug from the cylinder head using a quality thin-wall socket with a rubber or foam insert.

4. Inspect the spark plug condition.

To install:

5. Check and adjust the spark plug gap with a gap gauging tool.

> ✴✴ **WARNING**
>
> Special care should be taken when installing spark plugs into the cylinder head spark plug wells. Be sure

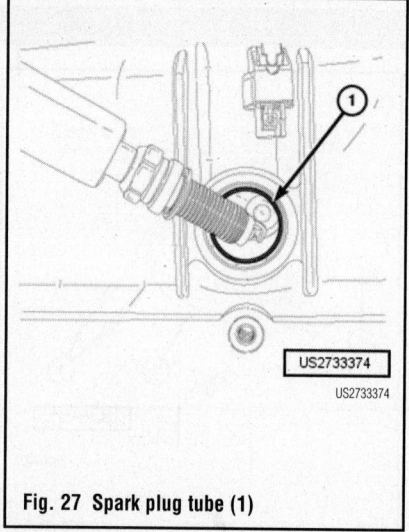

Fig. 27 Spark plug tube (1)

US2733374

the plugs do not drop into the plug wells as electrodes can be damaged.

> ✴✴ **WARNING**
>
> The spark plug tubes are a thin-wall design. Avoid damaging the spark plug tubes. Damage to the spark plug tube can result in oil leaks.

6. Start the spark plug into the cylinder head by hand to avoid cross threading.

> ✴✴ **WARNING**
>
> Spark plug torque is critical and must not exceed the specified value. Overtightening stretches the spark plug shell reducing its heat transfer capability resulting in possible catastrophic engine failure.

7. Tighten the spark plugs to 13 ft. lbs. (17.5 Nm).

8. Install the ignition coil.

ENGINE ELECTRICAL

STARTING SYSTEM

STARTER

REMOVAL & INSTALLATION

See Figures 28 and 29.

1. Disconnect the negative battery cable.

2. Remove the catalytic converter.

3. Remove the front engine mount through bolt.

4. Remove the retainers from the front engine mount bracket and remove the bracket.

5. Remove the field generator connector.

6. Remove the B+ retainer and B+ cable.

7. Remove the starter retainers.

8. Remove the starter.

To install:

9. Install the starter.

10. Install the starter retainers.
   a. Tighten to 40.5 ft. lbs. (55 Nm)

11. Install the B+ cable and retainer.

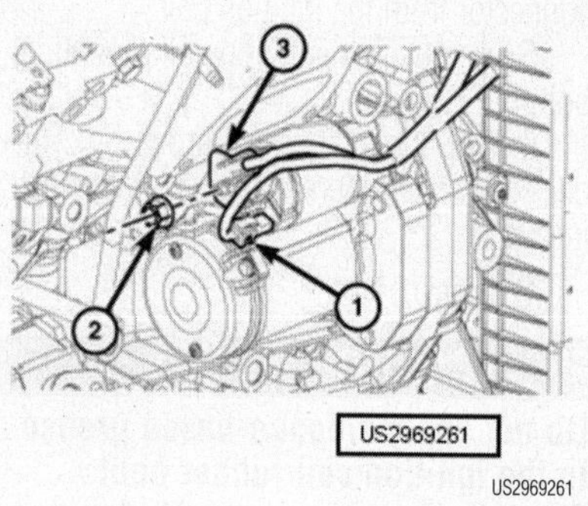

Fig. 28 Field generator connector (1), B+ retainer (2), and B+ cable (3)

US2969261

12. Tighten to 115 inch lbs. (13 Nm)

13. Install the field generator connector.

14. Install the engine mount bracket.

15. Install the engine mount bracket retainers.

16. Tighten to 41 ft. lbs. (55 Nm).

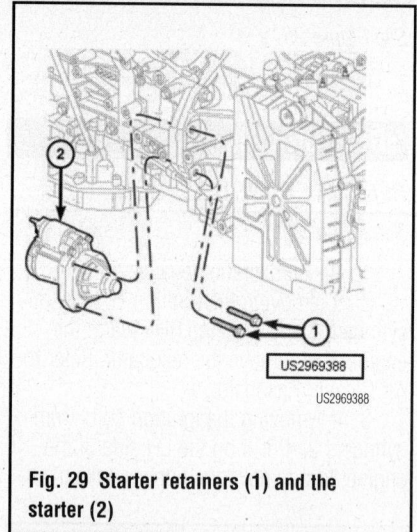

Fig. 29 Starter retainers (1) and the starter (2)

US2969388

17. Install the engine mount through bolt.

18. Tighten to 45 ft. lbs. (61 Nm).

19. Install the catalytic converter.

20. Connect the battery negative cable.

ENGINE MECHANICAL

➡**Disconnecting the negative battery cable may interfere with the functions of the on board computer systems and may require the computer to undergo a relearning process, once the negative battery cable is reconnected.**

ACCESSORY DRIVE BELTS

ACCESSORY BELT ROUTING
See Figure 30.

INSPECTION
See Figure 31.

Belt replacement under any or all of the following conditions is required:
• Excessive wear
• Frayed cords
• Severe glazing

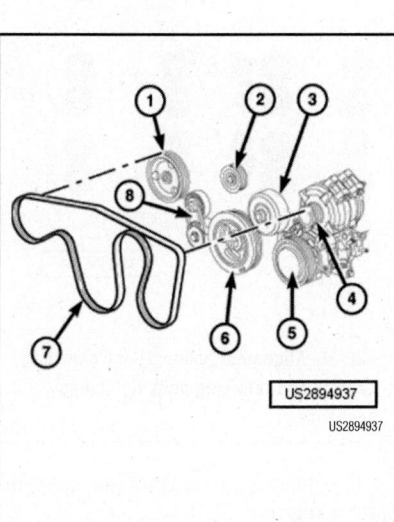

Fig. 30 Accessory drive belt routing

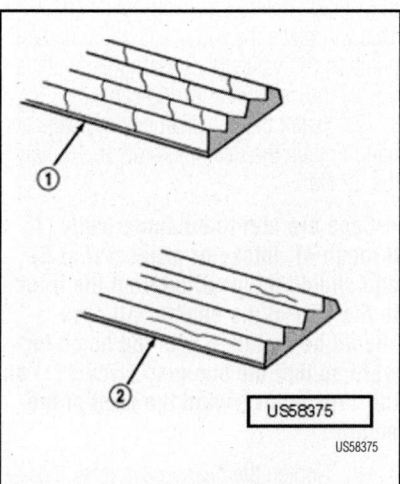

Fig. 31 Normal cracks—belt ok (1); not normal cracks—replace belt (2)

The poly-V Belt system may develop minor cracks across the ribbed side (due to reverse bending). These minor cracks are considered normal and acceptable. Parallel cracks are not.

✳✳ WARNING
Do not use any type of belt dressing or restorer on poly-V belts.

ADJUSTMENT

It is not necessary to adjust the accessory drive belt tension. These engines are equipped with an automatic belt tensioner. The tensioner maintains correct belt tension at all times; consequently, do not attempt to use a belt tension gauge on these engines.

REMOVAL & INSTALLATION
See Figure 32.

✳✳ CAUTION
Do not let the tensioner arm snap back to the free arm position, severe damage may occur to the tensioner.

1. Disconnect the negative battery cable from the battery.
2. Raise the vehicle.
3. Remove right front wheel.
4. Remove the inner splash shield.
5. Rotate the belt tensioner until it contacts its stop. Remove the belt, and then slowly rotate the tensioner into the free arm position.

To install:
6. Check the condition of all pulleys.

✳✳ CAUTION
When installing the serpentine accessory drive belt, the belt MUST be routed correctly. If not, the engine may overheat due to the water pump rotating in the wrong direction.

7. Install a new belt. Route the belt around all pulleys except the idler pulley. Rotate the tensioner arm until it contacts its stop position. Route the belt around the idler and slowly let the tensioner rotate into the belt. Make sure the belt is seated onto all pulleys.
8. Inspect the belt wear indicator with the drive belt installed. The gap between the tang and the housing stop (measurement A) must not exceed .94 inches (24 mm).
9. Install the inner splash shield.
10. Install the wheel.

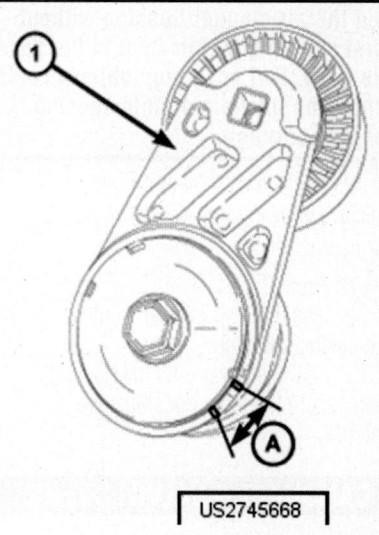

Fig. 32 Accessory drive belt tensioner (1); the gap between the tang and the housing stop (measurement A) must not exceed .94 inches

11. Lower the vehicle.
12. Connect the negative battery cable.

AIR CLEANER HOUSING

REMOVAL & INSTALLATION
See Figure 33.

FILTER/ELEMENT REPLACEMENT

1. Release the three air cleaner housing cover latches.
2. Lift the cover and remove the air cleaner element.

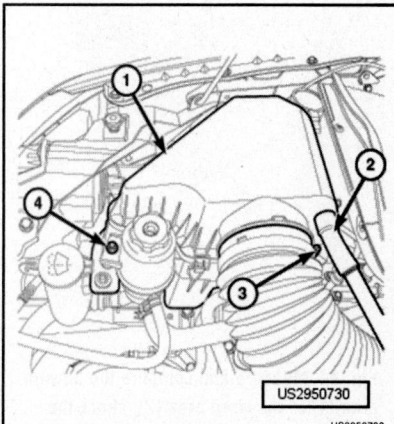

Fig. 33 Air cleaner housing (1), fresh air makeup hose (2) and clamp (3), and power steering fluid reservoir nut (4)

✳✳ WARNING

Do not use compressed air to clean out the air cleaner housing without first covering the air inlet to the throttle body. Dirt or foreign objects could enter the intake manifold causing engine damage.

3. Check the bottom of the air cleaner housing and remove any dirt or debris.

To install:

4. Install the air cleaner element into the air cleaner housing.

5. Seat the cover onto the housing and secure the three housing cover latches.

CAMSHAFT & VALVE LIFTERS

INSPECTION

See Figure 34.

1. Inspect the camshaft bearing journals for damage and binding. If journals are binding, check the cylinder head for damage. Also check cylinder head oil holes for clogging.

2. Check the surface of the cam lobes for abnormal wear. Measure and compare the unworn area to the worn area. Replace camshafts that are not within specification. Refer to Specifications.

REMOVAL & INSTALLATION

Left Camshafts

See Figures 35 through 37.

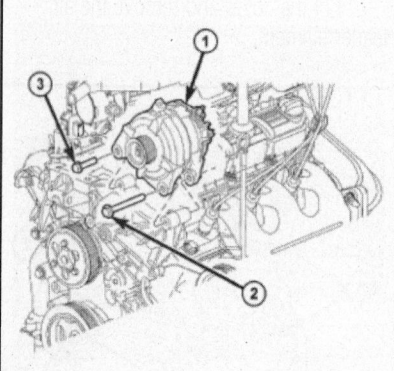

71105_VWRO_G0002

Fig. 34 Measure and compare the unworn area (1) to the worn area (2); check the surface of the cam lobes (5) for abnormal wear (3); check the camshaft bearing journals (4)—RH intake camshaft shown, other camshafts similar

✳✳ WARNING

The magnetic timing wheels must not come in contact with magnets (e.g., pickup tools, trays, etc.) or any other strong magnetic field. This will destroy the timing wheel's ability to correctly relay camshaft position to the camshaft position sensor.

✳✳ WARNING

When the timing chain is removed and the cylinder heads are still installed, do not forcefully rotate the camshafts or crankshaft independently of each other. Severe valve and/or piston damage can occur.

✳✳ WARNING

Do not stamp or strike the camshaft bearing caps. Severe damage will occur to the bearing caps.

1. Remove the upper intake manifold, all ignition coils, all spark plugs, the left cylinder head cover and the left cam phasers.

2. Rotate the camshafts counterclockwise to position the alignment holes approximately 30° before top-dead-center (BTDC). This places the camshafts in the neutral position (no valve load).

➡ Camshaft bearing caps should have been marked during engine manufacturing. For example, the number one exhaust camshaft bearing cap is marked "1E->." The caps should be installed with the notch forward.

3. Slowly loosen the camshaft bearing cap bolts in the sequence shown.

➡ When the camshaft is removed the rocker arms may slide downward, mark the rocker arms before removing the camshaft.

4. Remove the camshaft bearing caps and the camshafts.

To install:

✳✳ WARNING

The magnetic timing wheels must not come in contact with magnets (e.g., pickup tools, trays, etc.) or any other strong magnetic field. This will destroy the timing wheel's ability to correctly relay camshaft position to the camshaft position sensor.

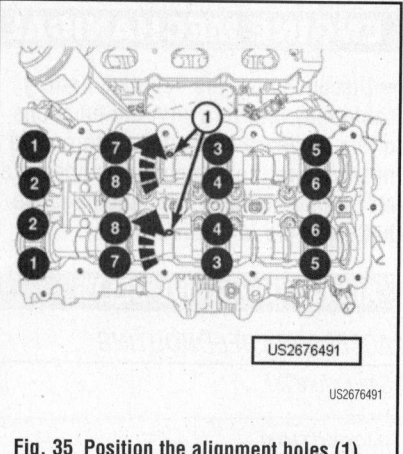

US2676491

Fig. 35 Position the alignment holes (1) to approximately 30° BTDC. Loosen in the sequence shown

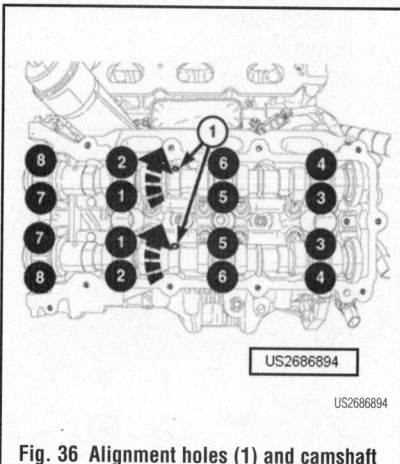

US2686894

Fig. 36 Alignment holes (1) and camshaft bearing cap retaining bolts tightening sequence

5. Lubricate the camshaft journals with clean engine oil.

6. Install the left side camshaft(s) with the alignment holes positioned approximately 30° before top-dead-center (BTDC). This will place the camshafts at the neutral position (no valve load) easing the installation of the camshaft bearing caps.

7. Install the camshaft bearing caps and hand tighten the retaining bolts to 18 inch lbs. (2 Nm).

➡ Caps are identified numerically (1 through 4), intake or exhaust (I or E) and should be installed from the front to the rear of the engine. All caps should be installed with the notch forward so that the stamped arrows (<) on the caps point toward the front of the engine.

8. Tighten the bearing cap retaining bolts in the sequence shown to 84 inch lbs. (9.5 Nm).

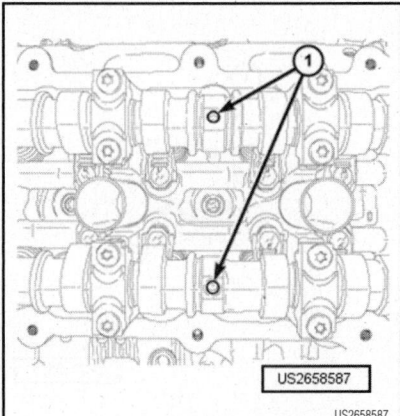

Fig. 37 Rotate the camshafts clockwise to TDC by positioning the alignment holes vertically

9. Rotate the camshafts clockwise to top-dead-center (TDC) by positioning the alignment holes vertically.

10. Install the left cam phasers, the cylinder head cover, the spark plugs, the ignition coils, and the upper intake manifold.

➡The Cam/Crank Variation Relearn procedure must be performed using the scan tool anytime there has been a repair/replacement made to a powertrain system, such as the flywheel, valvetrain, camshaft and/or crankshaft sensors or components.

Right Camshafts

See Figures 38 and 39.

❊❊ **WARNING**

The magnetic timing wheels must not come in contact with magnets (e.g., pickup tools, trays, etc.) or any other strong magnetic field. This will destroy the timing wheel's ability to correctly relay camshaft position to the camshaft position sensor.

❊❊ **WARNING**

When the timing chain is removed and the cylinder heads are still installed, do not forcefully rotate the camshafts or crankshaft independently of each other. Severe valve and/or piston damage can occur.

❊❊ **WARNING**

Do not stamp or strike the camshaft bearing caps. Severe damage will occur to the bearing caps.

1. Remove the upper intake manifold, all ignition coils, all spark plugs, the right cylinder head cover and the right cam phasers.

➡Camshaft bearing caps should have been marked during engine manufacturing. For example, the number one exhaust camshaft bearing cap is marked "1E->." The caps should be installed with the notch forward.

2. Slowly loosen the camshaft bearing cap bolts in the sequence shown.

➡When the camshaft is removed the rocker arms may slide downward, mark the rocker arms before removing the camshaft.

3. Remove the camshaft bearing caps and the camshafts.

To install:

❊❊ **WARNING**

The magnetic timing wheels must not come in contact with magnets (e.g., pickup tools, trays, etc.) or any other strong magnetic field. This will destroy the timing wheel's ability to correctly relay camshaft position to the camshaft position sensor.

4. Lubricate the camshaft journals with clean engine oil.

5. Install the right side camshaft(s) at TDC by positioning the alignment holes vertically. This will place the camshafts at the neutral position (no valve load) easing the installation of the camshaft bearing caps.

6. Install the camshaft bearing caps and hand tighten the retaining bolts to 18 inch lbs. (2 Nm).

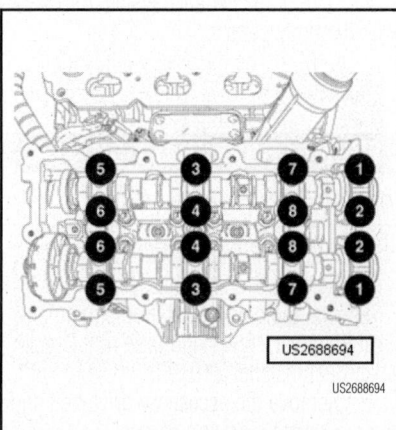

Fig. 38 Camshaft bearing caps loosening sequence

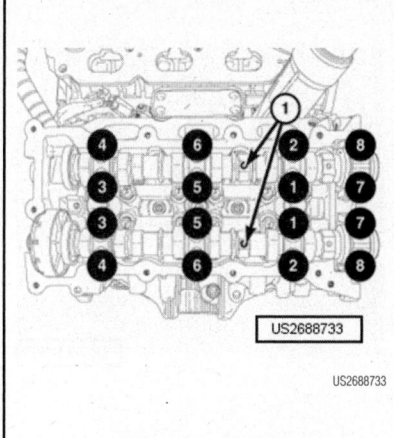

Fig. 39 Bearing cap retaining bolts tightening sequence

➡Caps are identified numerically (1 through 4), intake or exhaust (I or E) and should be installed from the front to the rear of the engine. All caps should be installed with the notch forward so that the stamped arrows (<) on the caps point toward the front of the engine.

7. Tighten the bearing cap retaining bolts in the sequence shown to 84 inch lbs. (9.5 Nm).

8. Install the right cam phasers, the cylinder head cover, the spark plugs, the ignition coils, and the upper intake manifold.

➡The Cam/Crank Variation Relearn procedure must be performed using the scan tool anytime there has been a repair/replacement made to a powertrain system, such as the flywheel, valvetrain, camshaft and/or crankshaft sensors or components.

Hydraulic Lifters

See Figure 40.

➡Refer also to Camshafts.

➡The LH cylinder head hydraulic lifters are shown; the RH cylinder head hydraulic lifters are similar.

1. Disconnect the negative battery cable.
2. Remove the camshaft(s).

➡If the rocker arms are to be reused, identify their positions so that they can be reassembled into their original locations.

3. Remove the rocker arm(s).

➡If the hydraulic lifters are to be reused, identify their positions so that they can be reassembled into their original locations.

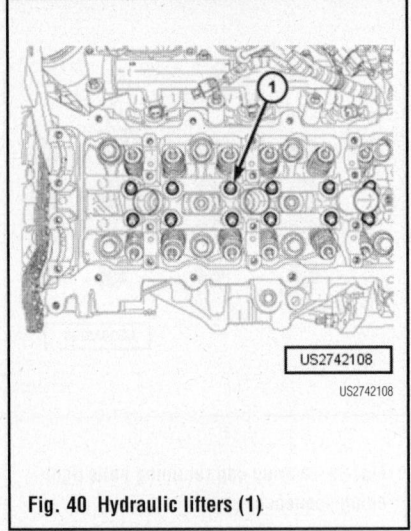

Fig. 40 Hydraulic lifters (1)

4. Remove the hydraulic lifter(s).

5. The hydraulic lifters should be at least partially full of oil, verify this. There should be little or no plunger travel when the hydraulic lifter is depressed.

6. Install the hydraulic lifter(s).

➡️**If the rocker arms are being reused reassemble them into their original locations.**

7. Install the rocker arm(s).

8. Install the camshaft(s), phasers, cylinder head cover(s) and upper intake manifold.

9. Connect the negative battery cable.

CATALYTIC CONVERTER

REMOVAL & INSTALLATION

1. Refer to Precautions.

✳️✳️ CAUTION

The normal operating temperature of the exhaust system is very high. Therefore, never attempt to service any part of the exhaust system until it is cooled. Take special care when working near the catalytic converter. The temperature of the converter rises to a high level after a short period of engine operation time.

✳️✳️ WARNING

Due to exterior physical similarities of some catalytic converters with pipe assemblies, extreme care should be taken with replacement parts. There are internal converter differences required in some parts of the country (particularly vehicles built for states with strict emission

requirements) and between model years.

2. Remove the cross-under pipe from the vehicle.

➡️**The lower bolts for the converter flange are used to hold a guide retainer plate. The retainer does not need to be removed. The catalytic converter is held in by the plate and upper bolts.**

3. Disconnect the temperature and oxygen sensor electrical connectors.

4. Remove the catalytic converter to exhaust manifold upper bolts.

5. Remove catalytic converter by lifting and sliding the flange up and away from the exhaust manifold.

6. Remove the temperature and oxygen sensors.

To install:

7. If the gaskets need replacing, position the new gasket onto the manifold flange and install the lower retainer plate. Then loosely install all four bolts to align the gasket. Tighten the lower retainer bolts to 27 ft. lbs. (37 Nm).

8. Position the catalytic converter against the exhaust manifold. Position the converter flange to the retainer.

9. Install the upper flange bolts. Tighten upper bolts to 27 ft. lbs. (37 Nm).

➡️**Be careful not to twist or kink the oxygen sensor wires.**

10. Install (if removed), connect the temperature and oxygen sensors' electrical connectors.

11. Install the cross-under pipe.

12. Start the engine and inspect for exhaust leaks. Repair exhaust leaks as necessary.

13. Check the exhaust system for contact with the body panels.

   a. Make the necessary adjustments, if needed.

FRONT CRANKSHAFT OIL SEAL

REMOVAL & INSTALLATION

See Figures 41 through 43.

1. Refer to Precautions.
Special tools and workshop equipment: Seal Remover #8511 and the Front Crankshaft Seal Installer #10199

2. Remove the accessory drive belt and the crankshaft vibration damper.

3. Install the sleeve from seal remover #8511 around the flywheel key and onto the nose of the crankshaft.

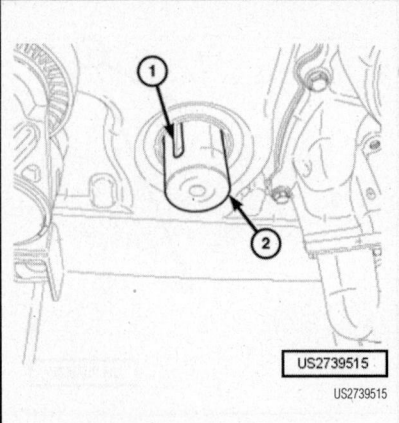

Fig. 41 Install the sleeve (2) from the seal remover #8511 around the flywheel key (1) and onto the nose of the crankshaft

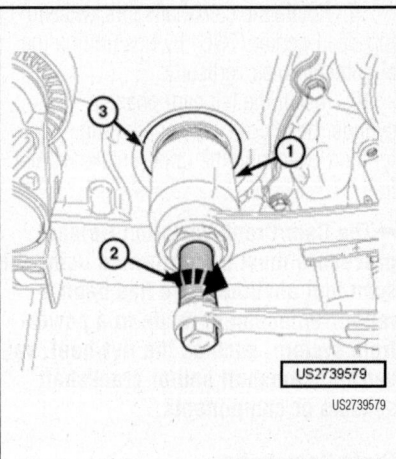

Fig. 42 Seal remover #8511 (1), extractor screw (2), and front crankshaft oil seal (3)

4. Screw seal remover #8511 into the front crankshaft oil seal.

5. Install the extractor screw into the seal remover #8511. Hold the seal remover stationary and tighten the extractor screw against the sleeve until the front crankshaft oil seal is removed from the engine timing cover.

To install:

6. Position the front crankshaft oil seal into place on the engine timing cover.

7. Align the front crankshaft seal installer #10199 to the flywheel key on the crankshaft and against the front crankshaft oil seal.

✳️✳️ CAUTION

Only tighten the crankshaft vibration damper bolt until the oil seal is seated in the cover. Overtightening of the bolt can crack the front timing cover.

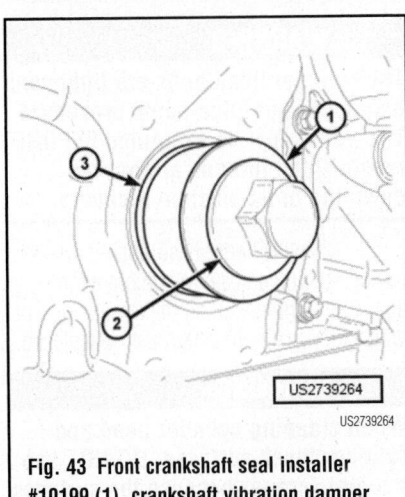

Fig. 43 Front crankshaft seal installer #10199 (1), crankshaft vibration damper bolt (2), and front crankshaft oil seal (3)

8. Install and tighten the crankshaft vibration damper bolt until the crankshaft oil seal is seated in the engine timing cover.

9. Install the crankshaft vibration damper and accessory drive belt.

CYLINDER HEAD

REMOVAL & INSTALLATION

Left Side

See Figures 44 through 48.

1. Refer to Precautions.
Special tools and workshop equipment: Tensioner Pin #8514 and Camshaft Phaser Lock #10202

✳✳ WARNING

The magnetic timing wheels must not come in contact with magnets (e.g., pickup tools, trays, etc.) or any other strong magnetic field. This will destroy the timing wheel's ability to correctly relay camshaft position to the camshaft position sensor. Refer to Camshafts.

2. Perform the fuel pressure release procedure. Refer to the Fuel System Pressure Release Procedure in the Fuel section.

3. Disconnect the negative battery cable.

4. Raise and support the vehicle.

5. Remove the belly pan.

6. Drain the cooling system. Refer to Cooling System Draining and Filling in the Engine Cooling section.

7. Drain the engine oil.

8. Lower the vehicle.

9. Remove the engine cover.

10. Recover the refrigerant from the refrigerant system.

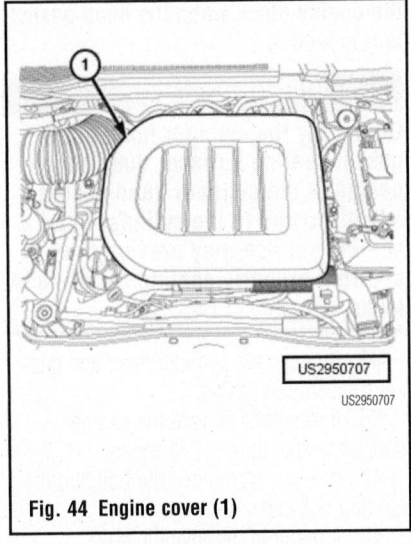

Fig. 44 Engine cover (1)

11. Remove the air cleaner body. Refer to Air Cleaner Housing.

12. Remove the resonator.

13. Disconnect the heater core return hose.

14. Disconnect the left upstream oxygen sensor connector from the main wire harness.

15. Disengage the 2 upper wire harness retainers from the intake manifold support brackets.

16. Disengage the 2 lower wire harness retainers from the intake manifold support brackets.

17. Remove the nut, bolt, and the heater core return tube.

18. Remove the bolt and the oil level indicator tube.

19. Remove the upper and lower intake manifolds and insulator. Refer to Lower Intake Manifold.

20. Remove the bolts and then remove the LH upper intake manifold support brackets.

21. Remove the accessory drive belt. Refer to Accessory Drive Belt.

22. Remove the generator. Refer to Engine Electrical.

23. Remove the A/C compressor from the engine compartment.

24. Disconnect the ignition coil capacitor electrical connector.

25. Disconnect the Engine Coolant Temperature (ECT) sensor connector.

26. Disconnect the main harness from the engine injection/ignition harness at the rear of the left cylinder head.

27. Disconnect the main harness from the engine oil pressure/temperature harness at the rear of the left cylinder head.

28. Remove the spark plugs. Refer to Spark Plugs in Engine Electrical.

29. Remove the cylinder head covers, lower and upper oil pans, crankshaft vibration damper and engine timing cover.

✳✳ WARNING

Rotate the engine by turning the crankshaft when aligning timing marks. Failure to do so will result in valve and/or piston damage.

30. Rotate the crankshaft counterclockwise (CW) to place the number one piston at TDC on the exhaust stroke by aligning the dimple on the crankshaft with the block/bearing cap junction. The left side cam phaser arrows should point toward each other and be parallel to the valve cover sealing surface. The right side cam phaser arrows should point away from each other and the scribe lines should be parallel to the valve cover sealing surface.

✳✳ WARNING

Always reinstall timing chains so that they maintain the same direction of rotation. Inverting a previously run chain on a previously run sprocket will result in excessive wear to both the chain and sprocket.

31. Mark the direction of rotation on the timing chain using a paint pen or equivalent to aid in reassembly.

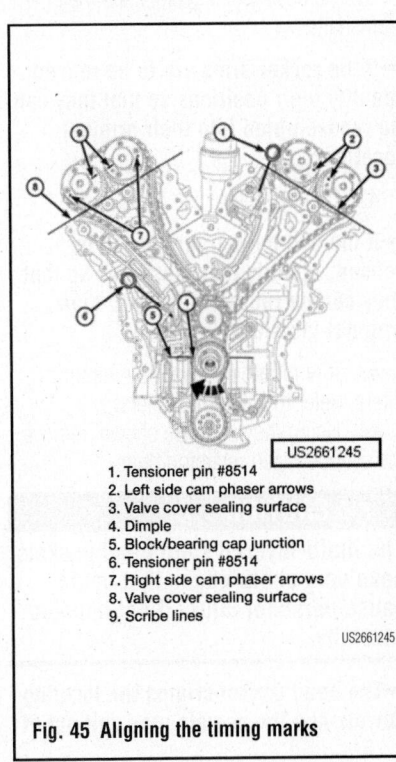

1. Tensioner pin #8514
2. Left side cam phaser arrows
3. Valve cover sealing surface
4. Dimple
5. Block/bearing cap junction
6. Tensioner pin #8514
7. Right side cam phaser arrows
8. Valve cover sealing surface
9. Scribe lines

Fig. 45 Aligning the timing marks

✳✳ WARNING

When the timing chains are removed and the cylinder heads are still installed, DO NOT rotate the camshafts or crankshaft without first locating the proper crankshaft position. Failure to do so will result in valve and/or piston damage.

32. Reset the LH cam chain tensioner by lifting the pawl, pushing back the piston, and installing tensioner pin #8514.

➡ **Minor rotation of a camshaft (a few degrees) may be required To Install the camshaft phaser lock. Refer To Installation for illustration of the tool.**

33. Install the LH camshaft phaser lock #10202.

34. Loosen both the intake oil control valve and exhaust oil control valve.

35. Remove the LH camshaft phaser lock #10202.

36. Remove the oil control valve from the left side exhaust cam phaser and then pull the phaser off of the camshaft.

37. Remove the oil control valve from the left side intake cam phaser and pull the phaser off of the camshaft.

38. Remove the LH cam chain tensioner arm.

39. Remove two T30 bolts and then remove the LH cam chain tensioner.

40. Remove two T30 bolts and then remove the LH cam chain guide.

41. Remove the left camshafts. Refer to Camshafts.

➡ **If the rocker arms are to be reused, identify their positions so that they can be reassembled into their original locations.**

42. Remove the rocker arms.

➡ **If the hydraulic lifters are to be reused, identify their positions so that they can be reassembled into their original locations.**

43. If required, remove the hydraulic lifters. Refer to Hydraulic Lifters.

44. Using the sequence shown, remove the cylinder head retaining bolts.

✳✳ CAUTION

The multi-layered steel head gaskets have very sharp edges that could cause personal injury if not handled carefully.

➡ **The head gasket crimps the locating dowels and the dowels may pull out of**

the engine block when the head gasket is removed.

✳✳ WARNING

Do not lay the cylinder head on its gasket sealing surface, due to the design of the cylinder head gasket, any distortion to the cylinder head sealing surface may prevent the gasket from properly sealing resulting in leaks.

45. Remove the cylinder head and gasket. Discard the gasket.

46. If required, remove the engine coolant temperature (ECT) sensor.

47. If required, remove the bolt and the ignition coil capacitor.

48. If required, remove the bolt and the engine wire harness retainer bracket.

To install:

✳✳ WARNING

The magnetic timing wheels must not come in contact with magnets (e.g., pickup tools, trays, etc.) or any other strong magnetic field. This will destroy the timing wheel's ability to correctly relay camshaft position to the camshaft position sensor.

49. If removed, install the Engine Coolant Temperature (ECT) sensor and tighten it to 97 inch lbs. (11 Nm).

50. If removed, install the ignition coil capacitor with an M6 bolt tightened to 89 inch lbs. (10 Nm).

51. If removed, install the engine wire harness retainer bracket with a T30 bolt tightened to 106 inch lbs. (12 Nm).

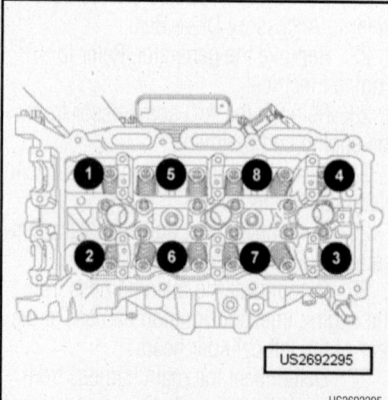

US2692295

Fig. 46 Cylinder head gasket retaining bolts removal sequence—Right head gasket shown, left head gasket similar

✳✳ WARNING

The cylinder head bolts are tightened using a torque-plus-angle procedure. The bolts must be examined BEFORE reuse. If the threads are necked down the bolts must be replaced.

52. Check cylinder head bolts for necking by holding a scale or straight edge against the threads. If all the threads do not contact the scale the bolt must be replaced.

✳✳ WARNING

When cleaning cylinder head and cylinder block surfaces, DO NOT use a metal scraper because the surfaces could be cut or ground. Use ONLY a wooden or plastic scraper.

53. Clean and prepare the gasket sealing surfaces of the cylinder head and block.

✳✳ WARNING

Non-compressible debris such as oil, coolant or RTV sealants that are not removed from bolt holes can cause the aluminum casting to crack when tightening the bolts.

54. Clean out the cylinder head bolt holes in the engine block.

✳✳ CAUTION

The multi-layered steel head gaskets have very sharp edges that could cause personal injury if not handled carefully.

✳✳ WARNING

The cylinder head gaskets are not interchangeable between the left and right cylinder heads and are clearly marked with "R" for right and "L" for left.

55. Position the new cylinder head gasket on the locating dowels.

56. Position the cylinder head onto the cylinder block. Make sure the cylinder head seats fully over the locating dowels.

➡ **Do not apply any additional oil to the bolt threads.**

57. Install the eight head bolts finger tight.

58. Tighten the cylinder head bolts in the sequence shown, following this 9-step torque-plus-angle method. Tighten according to the following torque values:
   a. Step 1: All to 22 ft. lbs. (30 Nm)
   b. Step 2: All to 33 ft. lbs. (45 Nm)

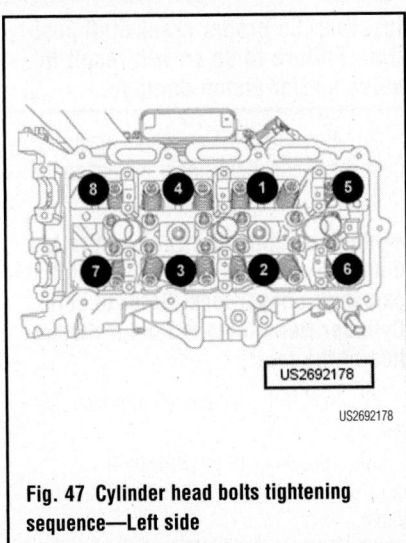

US2692178

US2692178

Fig. 47 Cylinder head bolts tightening sequence—Left side

c. Step 3: All + 75°Turn. Do not use a torque wrench for this step.

d. Step 4: (2) and (3) Additional + 50°Turn. Do not use a torque wrench for this step.

e. Step 5: Loosen all fasteners in reverse of the sequence shown

f. Step 6: All to 22 ft. lbs. (30 Nm)

g. Step 7: All to 33 ft. lbs. (45 Nm)

h. Step 8: All + 60° Turn. Do not use a torque wrench for this step.

i. Step 9: All + 70° Turn. Do not use a torque wrench for this step.

➡**If the hydraulic lifters are being reused, reassemble them into their original locations.**

59. If removed, install the hydraulic lifters.

➡**If the rocker arms are being reused reassemble them into their original locations.**

60. Install the rocker arms and camshafts.

61. Rotate the camshafts CW to TDC by positioning the alignment holes vertically.

62. Install the LH cam chain guide with 2 bolts. Tighten the T30 bolts to 106 inch lbs. (12 Nm).

63. Install the LH cam chain tensioner to the cylinder head with 2 bolts. Tighten the T30 bolts to 106 inch lbs. (12 Nm).

64. Reset the LH cam chain tensioner by lifting the pawl, pushing back the piston and installing the tensioner pin #8514.

65. Install the LH tensioner arm.

66. Press the LH intake cam phaser onto the intake camshaft. Install and hand tighten the oil control valve.

Always reinstall timing chains so that they maintain the same direction of rotation. Inverting a previously run chain on a previously run sprocket will result in excessive wear to both the chain and sprocket.

67. Drape the left side cam chain over the LH intake cam phaser and onto the idler sprocket so that the arrow is aligned with the plated link on the cam chain.

68. Route the cam chain around the exhaust and intake cam phasers while maintaining this alignment so that the plated links are aligned with the phaser timing marks. Position the left side cam phasers so that the arrows point toward each other and are parallel to the valve cover sealing surface. Press the exhaust cam phaser onto the exhaust cam, install and hand tighten the oil control valve.

➡**Minor rotation of a camshaft (a few degrees) may be required To Install the camshaft phaser or phaser lock.**

69. Install the LH camshaft phaser lock #10202 and tighten the oil control valves to 110 ft. lbs. (150 Nm).

70. Remove the LH camshaft phaser lock #10202.

71. Remove the tensioner pin #8514 from the LH cam chain tensioner.

72. Rotate the crankshaft CW two complete revolutions stopping when the dimple

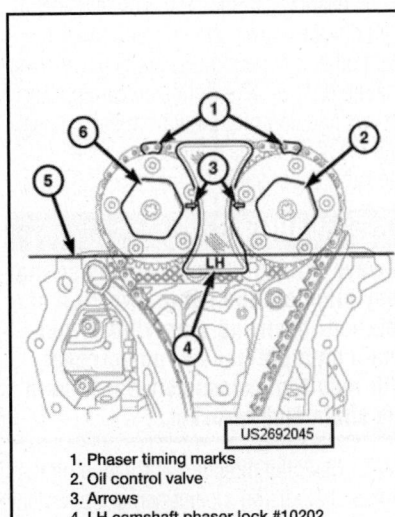

US2692045

1. Phaser timing marks
2. Oil control valve
3. Arrows
4. LH camshaft phaser lock #10202
5. Valve cover sealing surface
6. Oil control valve

US2692045

Fig. 48 Crankshaft and cam phaser positioning

on the crankshaft is aligned with the block/bearing cap junction.

73. While maintaining this alignment, verify that the arrows on the left side cam phasers point toward each other and are parallel to the valve cover sealing surface and that the right side cam phaser arrows point away from each other and the scribe lines are parallel to the valve cover sealing surface.

74. There should be 12 chain pins between the exhaust cam phaser triangle marking and the intake cam phaser circle marking.

75. If the engine timing is not correct, repeat this procedure.

76. Install the engine timing cover, crankshaft vibration damper, upper and lower oil pans and cylinder head covers.

77. Install the spark plugs.

78. Connect the main harness to the engine oil pressure/temperature harness at the rear of the left cylinder head.

79. Connect the main harness to the engine injection/ignition harness at the rear of the left cylinder head.

80. Connect the Engine Coolant Temperature (ECT) sensor connector.

81. Connect the ignition coil capacitor electrical connector.

82. Install the A/C compressor.

83. Install the generator.

84. Install the accessory drive belt.

85. Install the LH upper intake manifold support brackets.

86. Install the stud bolts loosely.

87. Install the lower and upper intake manifolds and insulator.

88. Install the oil level indicator tube and the bolt. Tighten the bolt to 106 inch lbs. (12 Nm).

89. Install the heater core return tube, the nut, and the bolt. Tighten the nut and bolt to 106 inch lbs. (12 Nm).

90. Engage the two lower wire harness retainers with the intake manifold support brackets.

91. Engage two upper wire harness retainers with the intake manifold support brackets.

92. Connect the left upstream oxygen sensor connector to the main wire harness.

93. Connect the heater core return hose.

94. Install the resonator and tighten the clamps to 35 inch lbs. (4 Nm).

95. Install the air cleaner housing.

96. Evacuate and charge the refrigerant system.

97. Install the engine cover.

98. If removed, install the oil filter and fill the engine crankcase with the proper oil to the correct level. Refer to Specifications.

99. Fill the cooling system.

100. Raise and support the vehicle.

101. Install the belly pan.

102. Lower the vehicle.

103. Connect the negative battery cable.

104. Run the engine until it reaches normal operating temperature.

105. Check the cooling system for correct fluid level.

➡The Cam/Crank Variation Relearn procedure must be performed using the scan tool anytime there has been a repair/replacement made to a powertrain system, for example: flywheel, valvetrain, camshaft and/or crankshaft sensors or components.

Right Side

See Figures 49 and 50.

1. Refer to Precautions.
2. Refer to Left Cylinder Head.

Special tools and workshop equipment: Tensioner Pin #8514 and Camshaft Phaser Lock #10202

❋❋ WARNING

The magnetic timing wheels must not come in contact with magnets (e.g., pickup tools, trays, etc.) or any other strong magnetic field. This will destroy the timing wheel's ability to correctly relay camshaft position to the camshaft position sensor. Refer to Camshafts.

3. Perform the fuel pressure release procedure. Refer to the Fuel System Pressure Release Procedure in the Fuel section.

4. Disconnect the negative battery cable.

5. Raise and support the vehicle.

6. Remove the belly pan.

7. Drain the cooling system. Refer to Cooling System Draining and Filling in the Engine Cooling section.

8. Drain the engine oil.

9. Lower the vehicle.

10. Remove the engine cover.

11. Recover the refrigerant from the refrigerant system.

12. Remove the air cleaner body. Refer to Air Cleaner Housing.

13. Remove the resonator.

14. Remove the upper and lower intake manifolds and insulator. Refer to Lower Intake Manifold.

15. Remove the bolts and then remove the LH upper intake manifold support brackets.

16. Remove the accessory drive belt. Refer to Accessory Drive Belt.

17. Remove 3 bolts and the power steering pump heat shield.

18. Disengage the wire harness retainer from the power steering pump.

19. Remove 3 bolts, and then reposition the power steering pump and bracket as an assembly. Do not disconnect the power steering lines from the pump.

20. Remove the two bolts and the heater core supply tube.

21. Disconnect the ignition coil capacitor electrical connector.

22. Disengage the wire harness retainer from the intake manifold support bracket.

23. Remove the stud bolt and remove the upper intake manifold support bracket.

24. Remove the spark plugs. Refer to Spark Plugs in Engine Electrical.

25. Remove the cylinder head covers, lower and upper oil pans, crankshaft vibration damper and engine timing cover.

❋❋ WARNING

Rotate the engine by turning the crankshaft when aligning timing marks. Failure to do so will result in valve and/or piston damage.

26. Rotate the crankshaft counterclockwise (CW) to place the number one piston at TDC on the exhaust stroke by aligning the dimple on the crankshaft with the block/bearing cap junction. The left side cam phaser arrows should point toward each other and be parallel to the valve cover sealing surface. The right side cam phaser arrows should point away from each other and the scribe lines should be parallel to the valve cover sealing surface.

❋❋ WARNING

Always reinstall timing chains so that they maintain the same direction of rotation. Inverting a previously run chain on a previously run sprocket will result in excessive wear to both the chain and sprocket.

27. Mark the direction of rotation on the timing chain using a paint pen or equivalent to aid in reassembly.

❋❋ WARNING

When the timing chains are removed and the cylinder heads are still installed, DO NOT rotate the camshafts or crankshaft without first

locating the proper crankshaft position. Failure to do so will result in valve and/or piston damage.

28. Reset the RH cam chain tensioner by pushing back the tensioner piston, and installing tensioner pin #8514.

➡Minor rotation of a camshaft (a few degrees) may be required To Install the camshaft phaser lock. Refer to Left Cylinder Head Installation for illustration of the tool.

29. Install the RH camshaft phaser lock #10202.

30. Loosen both the intake oil control valve and the exhaust oil control valve.

31. Remove the RH camshaft phaser lock #10202.

32. Remove the oil control valve from the right side intake cam phaser and then pull the phaser off of the camshaft.

33. Remove the oil control valve from the right side exhaust cam phaser and pull the phaser off of the camshaft.

34. Remove the RH cam chain tensioner arm.

35. Remove two T30 bolts and then remove the RH cam chain tensioner.

36. Remove two T30 bolts and then remove the RH cam chain guide.

37. Remove the right camshafts. Refer to Camshafts.

➡If the rocker arms are to be reused, identify their positions so that they can be reassembled into their original locations.

38. Remove the rocker arms.

➡If the hydraulic lifters are to be reused, identify their positions so that they can be reassembled into their original locations.

39. If required, remove the hydraulic lifters. Refer to Hydraulic Lifters.

40. Using the sequence shown, remove the cylinder head retaining bolts.

❋❋ CAUTION

The multi-layered steel head gaskets have very sharp edges that could cause personal injury if not handled carefully.

➡The head gasket crimps the locating dowels and the dowels may pull out of the engine block when the head gasket is removed.

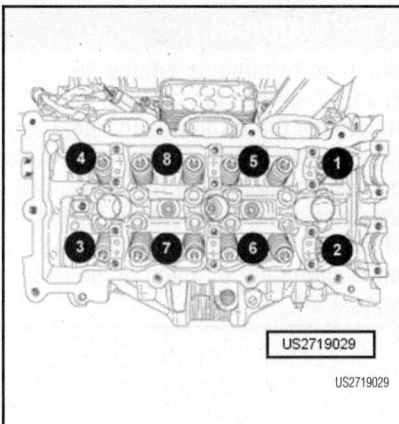

Fig. 49 Cylinder head retaining bolts removal sequence—Right side

✳✳ WARNING

Do not lay the cylinder head on its gasket sealing surface, due to the design of the cylinder head gasket, any distortion to the cylinder head sealing surface may prevent the gasket from properly sealing resulting in leaks.

41. Remove the cylinder head and gasket. Discard the gasket.
42. If required, remove the bolt and the ignition coil capacitor.

To install:

✳✳ WARNING

The magnetic timing wheels must not come in contact with magnets (e.g., pickup tools, trays, etc.) or any other strong magnetic field. This will destroy the timing wheel's ability to correctly relay camshaft position to the camshaft position sensor.

43. If removed, install the ignition coil capacitor with an M6 bolt tightened to 89 inch lbs. (10 Nm).

✳✳ WARNING

The cylinder head bolts are tightened using a torque-plus-angle procedure. The bolts must be examined BEFORE reuse. If the threads are necked down the bolts must be replaced.

44. Check cylinder head bolts for necking by holding a scale or straight edge against the threads. If all the threads do not contact the scale the bolt must be replaced.

✳✳ WARNING

When cleaning cylinder head and cylinder block surfaces, DO NOT use a metal scraper because the surfaces could be cut or ground. Use ONLY a wooden or plastic scraper.

45. Clean and prepare the gasket sealing surfaces of the cylinder head and block.

✳✳ WARNING

Non-compressible debris such as oil, coolant or RTV sealants that are not removed from bolt holes can cause the aluminum casting to crack when tightening the bolts.

46. Clean out the cylinder head bolt holes in the engine block.

✳✳ CAUTION

The multi-layered steel head gaskets have very sharp edges that could cause personal injury if not handled carefully.

✳✳ WARNING

The cylinder head gaskets are not interchangeable between the left and right cylinder heads and are clearly marked with "R" for right and "L" for left.

47. Position the new cylinder head gasket on the locating dowels.
48. Position the cylinder head onto the cylinder block. Make sure the cylinder head seats fully over the locating dowels.

➡ **Do not apply any additional oil to the bolt threads.**

49. Install the eight head bolts finger tight.
50. Tighten the cylinder head bolts in the sequence shown, following this 9-step torque-plus-angle method. Tighten according to the following torque values:
    a. Step 1: All to 22 ft. lbs. (30 Nm)
    b. Step 2: All to 33 ft. lbs. (45 Nm)
    c. Step 3: All + 75° Turn. Do not use a torque wrench for this step.
    d. Step 4: (2) and (3) Additional + 50° Turn. Do not use a torque wrench for this step.
    e. Step 5: Loosen all fasteners in reverse of the sequence shown
    f. Step 6: All to 22 ft. lbs. (30 Nm)
    g. Step 7: All to 33 ft. lbs. (45 Nm)
    h. Step 8: All + 60° Turn. Do not use a torque wrench for this step.

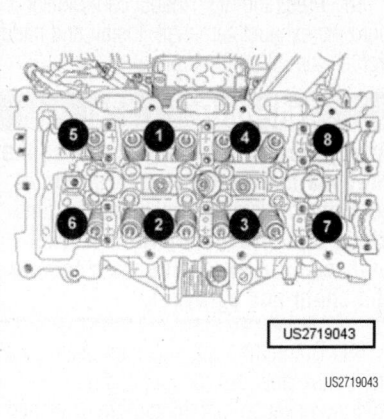

Fig. 50 Cylinder head bolts tightening sequence—Right side

    i. Step 9: All + 70° Turn. Do not use a torque wrench for this step.

➡ **If the hydraulic lifters are being reused, reassemble them into their original locations.**

51. If removed, install the hydraulic lifters.

➡ **If the rocker arms are being reused reassemble them into their original locations.**

52. Install the rocker arms and camshafts.

✳✳ WARNING

Do not rotate the camshafts more than a few degrees independently of the crankshaft. Valve to piston contact could occur resulting in possible valve damage. If the camshafts need to be rotated more than a few degrees, first move the pistons away from the cylinder heads by rotating the crankshaft counterclockwise to a position 30° BTDC. Once the camshafts are positioned at TDC rotate the crankshaft clockwise to return the crankshaft to TDC.

53. Verify that the camshafts are set at TDC by positioning the alignment holes vertically.
54. Install the RH cam chain guide with two bolts. Tighten the T30 bolts to 106 inch lbs. (12 Nm).
55. Install the RH cam chain tensioner to the engine block with two bolts. Tighten the T30 bolts to 106 inch lbs. (12 Nm).
56. Reset the RH cam chain tensioner by pushing back the tensioner piston and installing the tensioner pin #8514.
57. Install the RH tensioner arm.

58. Press the RH exhaust cam phaser onto the exhaust camshaft. Install and hand tighten the oil control valve.

✳✳ WARNING

Always reinstall timing chains so that they maintain the same direction of rotation. Inverting a previously run chain on a previously run sprocket will result in excessive wear to both the chain and sprocket.

59. Drape the right side cam chain over the RH exhaust cam phaser and onto the idler sprocket so that the dimple is aligned with the plated link on the cam chain.

60. Route the cam chain around the exhaust and intake cam phasers while maintaining this alignment so that the plated links are aligned with the phaser timing marks. Position the right side cam phasers so that the arrows point away from each other and the scribe lines are parallel to the valve cover sealing surface. Press the intake cam phaser onto the intake cam, install and hand tighten the oil control valve.

➡**Minor rotation of a camshaft (a few degrees) may be required To Install the camshaft phaser or phaser lock.**

61. Install the RH camshaft phaser lock #10202 and tighten the oil control valves to 110 ft. lbs. (150 Nm).

62. Remove the RH camshaft phaser lock #10202.

63. Remove the tensioner pin #8514 from the RH cam chain tensioner.

64. Rotate the crankshaft CW two complete revolutions stopping when the dimple on the crankshaft is aligned with the block/bearing cap junction.

65. While maintaining this alignment, verify that the arrows on the left side cam phasers point toward each other and are parallel to the valve cover sealing surface and that the right side cam phaser arrows point away from each other and the scribe lines are parallel to the valve cover sealing surface.

66. There should be 12 chain pins between the exhaust cam phaser triangle marking and the intake cam phaser circle marking.

67. If the engine timing is not correct, repeat this procedure.

68. Install the engine timing cover, crankshaft vibration damper, upper and lower oil pans and cylinder head covers.

69. Install the spark plugs.

70. Install the upper intake manifold support bracket with the stud bolt hand tight.

71. Engage the wire harness retainer with the intake manifold support brackets.

72. Connect the ignition coil capacitor electrical connector.

73. Install the heater core supply tube with one bolt tighten to 106 inch lbs. (12 Nm)

74. Reposition the power steering pump and bracket as an assembly and install 3 bolts. Tighten the bolts to 18 ft. lbs. (25 Nm)

75. Disengage the wire harness retainer from the power steering pump.

76. Install the power steering pump heat shield and three bolts. Tighten the bolts to 18 ft. lbs. (25 Nm)

77. Install the accessory drive belt.

78. Install the upper and lower manifolds and insulator.

79. Install the resonator and tighten the clamps to 35 inch lbs. (4 Nm).

80. Install the air cleaner body.

81. Evacuate and charge the refrigerant system.

82. Install the engine cover.

83. If removed, install the oil filter and fill the engine crankcase with the proper oil to the correct level. Refer to Specifications.

84. Fill the cooling system.

85. Raise and support the vehicle.

86. Install the belly pan.

87. Lower the vehicle.

88. Connect the negative battery cable.

89. Run the engine until it reaches normal operating temperature.

90. Check the cooling system for correct fluid level.

➡**The Cam/Crank Variation Relearn procedure must be performed using the scan tool anytime there has been a repair/replacement made to a powertrain system, for example: flywheel, valvetrain, camshaft and/or crankshaft sensors or components.**

ENGINE OIL & FILTER

REPLACEMENT

See Figure 51.

1. Refer to Precautions.

➡**Change the engine oil and filter at the mileage and time intervals indicated in the Maintenance Schedule. Refer to Maintenance.**

2. Run the engine until achieving normal operating temperature.

3. Position the vehicle on a level surface and turn the engine off.

4. Remove the engine cover.

✳✳ WARNING

When performing an engine oil change, remove the oil filter cap. Removing the oil filter cap releases oil held within the oil filter cavity and allows it to drain into the sump. Failure to remove the cap prior to reinstallation of the drain plug will not allow complete draining of the used engine oil.

5. Place an oil absorbent cloth around the oil filter housing at the base of the oil filter cap.

➡**The oil filter is attached to the oil filter cap.**

6. Rotate the oil filter cap counterclockwise and remove the cap and filter from the oil filter housing.

7. Raise and support the vehicle.

8. Place a suitable drain pan under the crankcase drain plug.

9. Remove the drain plug from the oil pan and allow the oil to drain into the pan. Inspect the drain plug threads for stretching or other damage. Replace the drain plug and gasket if there is damage.

10. Install the drain plug in the oil pan and tighten to 20 ft. lbs. (27 Nm).

11. Lower the vehicle.

12. Remove the oil filter from the oil filter cap.

13. Remove and discard the O-ring seal.

➡**It is not necessary to pre-oil the oil filter or to fill the oil filter housing.**

14. Lightly lubricate the new O-ring seal with clean engine oil.

15. Install the O-ring seal on the filter cap.

16. Install the new oil filter into the oil filter cap.

17. Thread the oil filter cap into the oil filter housing and tighten it to 18 ft. lbs. (25 Nm).

18. Remove the oil fill cap. Fill the crankcase with the specified type and amount of engine oil. Refer to Specifications.

19. Install the oil fill cap.

20. Start the engine and inspect for leaks.

21. Stop the engine and check the oil level.

22. Install the engine cover.

Oil Filter Specification: All engines are equipped with a high quality full flow, disposable-type oil filter. When replacing the oil filter, use a Volkswagen genuine parts filter or its equivalent.

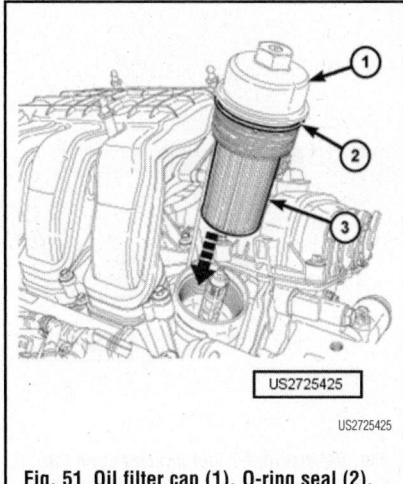

Fig. 51 Oil filter cap (1), O-ring seal (2), and oil filter (3)

EXHAUST MANIFOLD

REMOVAL & INSTALLATION

The exhaust manifolds are integrated into the cylinder heads for reduced weight. Refer also to Catalytic Converter.

INTAKE MANIFOLD

REMOVAL & INSTALLATION

Upper

See Figures 52 and 53.

1. Refer to Precautions.
2. Disconnect the negative battery cable. Refer to Engine Electrical.
3. Remove the engine cover.
4. Drain the engine cooling system. Refer to Engine Cooling.
5. Disengage the upper radiator hose retainer from the upper intake manifold.
6. Remove the engine cooling fan. Refer to Engine Cooling.
7. Remove the intake resonator.
8. Disconnect the electrical connectors from the Manifold Absolute Pressure (MAP) sensor and the Electronic Throttle Control (ETC).
9. Disengage the ETC harness from the clip on the throttle body. Disengage the wire harness retainers from the upper intake manifold near the MAP sensor and reposition the wire harness.
10. Disconnect the following hoses from the upper intake manifold:
    - Positive Crankcase Ventilation (PCV)
    - Vapor purge
    - Brake booster
11. Disengage the wire harness retainer from the upper intake manifold support bracket.

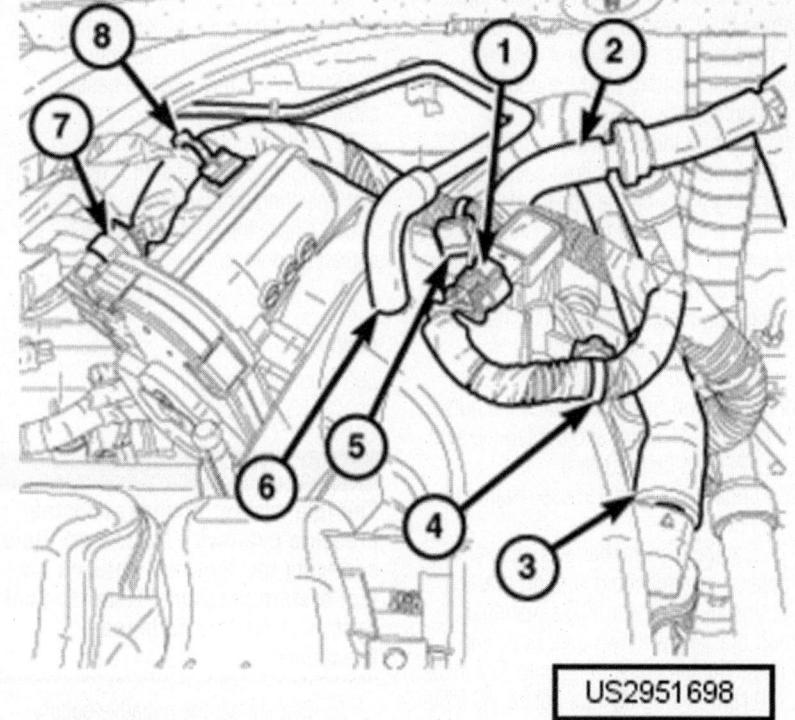

1. **Manifold Absolute Pressure (MAP) sensor**
2. **Brake booster hose**
3. **Positive Crankcase Ventilation ((PCV) hose**
4. **Wire harness retainer**
5. **Wire harness retainer**
6. **Vapor purge hose**
7. **Electronic Throttle Control (ETC)**
8. **Clip holding the ETC harness on the throttle body**

Fig. 52 Connectors and hoses

12. Disengage the wire harness retainer from the stud bolt.
13. Remove two nuts, loosen the stud bolt, and reposition the upper intake manifold support bracket.
14. Remove the nut from the support bracket of the heater core return tube.
15. Remove two nuts, loosen two stud bolts, and reposition the two upper intake manifold support brackets.

➡The upper intake manifold attaching bolts are captured in the upper intake manifold. Once loosened, the bolts will have to be lifted out of the lower intake manifold and held while removing the upper intake manifold.

16. Remove seven manifold attaching bolts and then remove the upper intake manifold.

17. Remove and discard the six upper to lower intake manifold seals.
18. Cover the open intake ports to prevent debris from entering the engine.
19. If required, remove the insulator from the LH cylinder head cover.

To install:
20. Clean and inspect the sealing surfaces. Install new upper to lower intake manifold seals.

➡Make sure the fuel injectors and wiring harnesses are in the correct position so that they don't interfere with the upper intake manifold installation.

21. If removed, install the insulator to the two alignment posts on top of the LH cylinder head cover.

22. Lift and hold the seven upper intake attaching bolts clear of the mating surface. Back the bolts out slightly or if required, use an elastic band to hold the bolts clear of the mating surface.

23. Position the upper intake manifold onto the lower intake manifold such that the two locating posts on the upper intake manifold align with corresponding holes in the lower intake manifold.

24. Install the seven upper intake manifold attaching bolts. Tighten the bolts in the sequence shown to 80 inch lbs. (9 Nm).

25. Install two nuts to the upper intake manifold support bracket. Tighten the nuts to 89 inch lbs. (10 Nm) and tighten the stud bolt to 177 inch lbs. (20 Nm).

26. Engage the wire harness retainer to the stud bolt.

27. Engage the wire harness retainer to the upper intake manifold support bracket.

28. Install two upper intake manifold support brackets with two stud bolts and two nuts. Tighten the stud bolts to 177 inch lbs. (20 Nm) and tighten the nuts to 89 inch lbs. (10 Nm).

29. Install the nut to the support bracket of the heater core return tube and tighten to 106 inch lbs. (12 Nm).

30. Connect the following hoses to the upper intake manifold:
- PCV
- Vapor purge
- Brake booster

31. Connect the electrical connectors to the MAP sensor and the ETC.

32. Secure the ETC harness to the clip on the throttle body and engage the wire harness retainers to the upper intake manifold near the MAP sensor.

33. Install the engine cooling fan and shroud assembly.

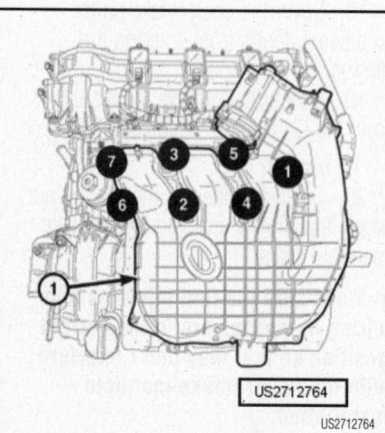

Fig. 53 Upper intake manifold attaching bolts tightening sequence

34. Engage the upper radiator hose retainer to the upper intake manifold.

35. Install the intake resonator.

36. Connect the negative battery cable.

37. Fill the cooling system.

38. Run the engine until it reaches normal operating temperature.

39. Check the cooling system for the correct fluid level.

40. Install the engine cover.

Lower

See Figures 54 and 55.

1. Refer to Precautions.

✷✷ CAUTION

The fuel system is under constant pressure even with engine off. Before servicing the fuel rail, release the fuel system pressure. Refer to Fuel System: Pressure Release Procedure.

2. Disconnect the negative battery cable. Refer to Engine Electrical.

3. Remove the air inlet hose and the upper intake manifold. Refer to Upper Intake Manifold.

4. Remove the insulator from the LH cylinder head cover.

5. Disconnect the fuel supply hose from the fuel rail.

6. Disconnect the fuel injector electrical connectors.

7. Disengage the injection/ignition harness retainer from the rear of the lower intake manifold.

8. Disengage the main wire harness retainer from the rear of the lower intake manifold.

9. Remove the eight lower intake manifold attaching bolts.

10. Remove the lower intake manifold with the fuel injectors and fuel rail.

11. Remove and discard the six lower intake manifold-to-cylinder head seals.

12. If required, remove the fuel rail and fuel injectors from the lower intake manifold.

To install:

13. Clean and inspect the sealing surfaces. Install new lower intake manifold-to-cylinder head seals.

14. If removed, install the fuel injectors and the fuel rail to the lower intake manifold. Tighten the four bolts in the sequence shown to 62 inch lbs. (7 Nm).

15. Position the lower intake manifold on the cylinder head surfaces.

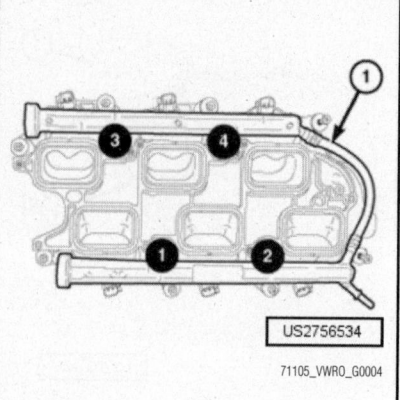

Fig. 54 Install the fuel injectors and the fuel rail (1) to the lower intake manifold and tighten the bolts in the sequence shown

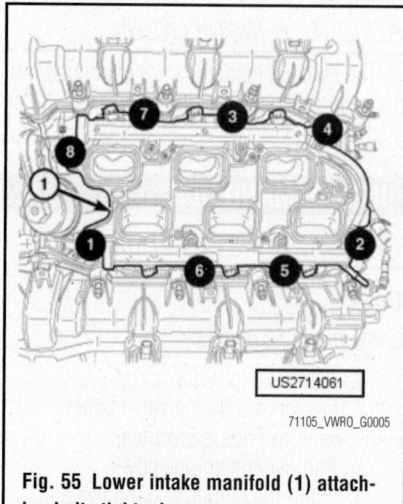

Fig. 55 Lower intake manifold (1) attaching bolts tightening sequence

16. Install the manifold attaching bolts and tighten in the sequence shown to 71 inch lbs. (8 Nm).

17. Engage the main wire harness retainer to the rear of the lower intake manifold.

18. Engage the injection/ignition harness retainer to the rear of the lower intake manifold.

19. Connect the fuel injector electrical connectors.

20. Connect the fuel supply hose to the fuel rail.

21. Install the insulator to the two alignment posts on top of the LH cylinder head cover.

22. Install the upper intake manifold, support brackets, and air inlet hose. Refer to Upper Intake Manifold.

23. Connect the negative battery cable.

24. Start the engine and check for leaks.

OIL PAN

REMOVAL & INSTALLATION

Lower Oil Pan

See Figure 56.

1. Refer to Precautions.
2. Raise and support the vehicle.
3. Drain the engine oil. Refer to Engine Oil & Filter Replacement.
4. Remove the belly pan.
5. Remove the inner splash shield.

→The lower oil pan must be removed to access all of the upper oil pan retaining bolts.

6. Remove fifteen bolts, two nuts, and two studs from the flange of the lower oil pan.

⁑ CAUTION

Do not pry on the lower oil pan flange. There are no designated pry points for lower oil pan removal. Prying on only one or a few locations could bend the flange and damage the pan.

7. Using a pry bar, apply a side force to the lower oil pan in order to shear the sealant bond and remove the pan.
8. Remove all residual sealant from the upper and lower oil pans.

To install:

9. Clean the upper and lower oil pan mating surfaces with isopropyl alcohol in preparation for sealant application.

⁑ WARNING

Engine assembly requires the use of a unique sealant that is compatible with the engine oil. Using a sealant other than Volkswagen genuine Engine RTV Sealant may result in engine fluid leakage.

⁑ WARNING

Following the application of Volkswagen genuine Engine RTV Sealant to the gasket surfaces, assemble the components within 20 minutes and tighten the attaching fasteners to specification within 45 minutes. Prolonged exposure to the air prior to assembly may result in engine fluid leakage.

10. Apply a 2 to 3 mm wide bead of Volkswagen genuine Engine RTV Sealant to the lower oil pan as shown.

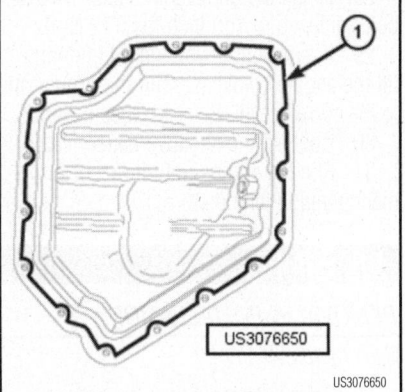

Fig. 56 Apply a 2 to 3 mm wide bead of Volkswagen genuine Engine RTV Sealant (1) to the lower oil pan as shown

11. Install two studs into the upper oil pan flange.
12. Install the lower oil pan to the upper oil pan with fifteen bolts and two nuts tightened to 97 inch lbs. (11 Nm).

⁑ WARNING

Following assembly, the Volkswagen genuine Engine RTV Sealant must be allowed to dry for 45 minutes prior to adding oil and operating the engine. Premature exposure to oil prior to drying may result in engine fluid leakage.

13. If removed, install the oil filter and fill the engine crankcase with the proper oil to the correct level. Refer to Specifications.
14. Run the engine until it reaches normal operating temperature.

Upper Oil Pan

See Figures 57 and 58.

1. Refer to Precautions.
2. Disconnect the negative battery cable. Refer to Engine Electrical.
3. Remove the bolt and the oil level indicator.
4. Raise and support the vehicle.
5. Remove the belly pan.
6. Drain the engine oil. Refer to Engine Oil & Filter Replacement.
7. Remove the cross-under pipe.

→The lower oil pan must be removed to access all of the upper oil pan retaining bolts.

8. Remove the lower oil pan. Refer to Lower Oil Pan.
9. Remove bolt securing the coolant tube to the oil pan.

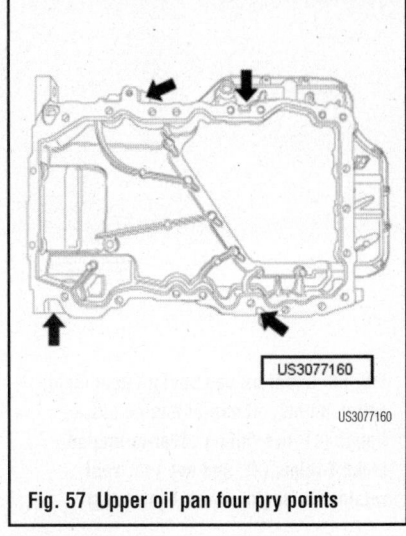

Fig. 57 Upper oil pan four pry points

10. Remove the oil pan-to-transmission bolts.
11. Remove two bolts from the rear oil seal retainer flange.
12. Remove nineteen oil pan mounting bolts.
13. Using the four indicated pry points, carefully remove the upper oil pan.
14. Remove all residual sealant from the upper and lower oil pans, timing chain cover, rear seal retainer and engine block mating surfaces.

To install:

15. Clean the upper and lower oil pans, timing chain cover, rear seal retainer and engine block mating surfaces with isopropyl alcohol in preparation for sealant application.

⁑ WARNING

Engine assembly requires the use of a unique sealant that is compatible with engine oil. Using a sealant other than Volkswagen genuine Engine RTV Sealant may result in engine fluid leakage.

⁑ WARNING

Following the application of Volkswagen genuine Engine RTV Sealant to the gasket surfaces, the components must be assembled within 20 minutes and the attaching fasteners must be tightened to specification within 45 minutes. Prolonged exposure to the air prior to assembly may result in engine fluid leaks.

16. Apply a 2 to 3 mm wide bead of Volkswagen genuine Engine RTV Sealant to

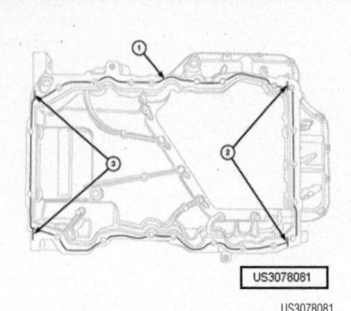

Fig. 58 Upper oil pan sealant bead application points: oil pan-to engine block flange (1), two timing cover-to-engine block T-joints (2), and two rear seal retainer-to-engine block T-joints (3)

the upper oil pan as shown in the following locations:

- Oil pan-to-engine block flange (1)
- Two timing cover-to-engine block T-joints (2)
- Two rear seal retainer-to-engine block T-joints (3)

✳✳ WARNING

Make sure that the rear face of the oil pan is flush to the transmission bell housing before tightening any of the oil pan mounting bolts. A gap between the oil pan and the transmission could crack the oil pan or transmission casting.

17. Install the oil pan to the engine block and flush to the transmission bellhousing. Secure the oil pan to the engine block with nineteen oil pan mounting bolts finger tight.

18. Install two bolts to the rear oil seal retainer flange and tighten finger tight.

19. Install the five oil pan-to-transmission bolts finger tight.

20. Tighten the nineteen previously installed oil pan mounting bolts to 18 ft. lbs. (25 Nm).

21. Install two bolts to the rear oil seal retainer flange and tighten them to 106 inch lbs. (12 Nm).

22. Tighten the five transmission-to-the engine oil pan bolts and tighten to 41 ft. lbs. (55 Nm).

23. Install the bolt securing the coolant tube to the oil pan and tighten it to 106 inch lbs. (12 Nm).

24. Install the lower oil pan. Refer to Lower Oil Pan.

25. Install the cross-under pipe.

26. Install the belly pan.

27. Lower the vehicle.

28. Install the oil level indicator with the bolt tightened to 106 inch lbs. (12 Nm).

29. If removed, install the oil filter and fill the engine crankcase with the proper oil to the correct level. Refer to Specifications.

30. Connect the negative battery cable.

31. Run the engine until it reaches normal operating temperature.

OIL PUMP

REMOVAL & INSTALLATION

See Figures 59 and 60.

1. Refer to Precautions.

2. Disconnect the negative battery cable. Refer to Engine Electrical.

3. Remove the upper oil pan. Refer to Upper Oil Pan.

4. Remove the oil pump pick-up.

5. Disconnect the engine wire harness from the oil pump solenoid electrical connector.

6. Depress the connector retention lock tab to disengage the oil pump solenoid electrical connector from the engine block.

7. Remove the bolts and then remove the timing gear splash shield.

8. Push the oil pump solenoid electrical connector into the engine block, rotate the connector slightly CW, push it past the primary chain tensioner mounting bolt and into the engine.

9. Push the oil pump chain tensioner back and insert a suitable retaining pin, such as a 3 mm Allen wrench.

✳✳ WARNING

Always reinstall timing chains so that they maintain the same direction of rotation. Inverting a previously run chain on a previously run sprocket will result in excessive wear to both the chain and sprocket.

10. Mark the direction of rotation on the oil pump chain and sprocket using a paint pen or equivalent to aid in reassembly.

➡**There are no timing marks on the oil pump gear or chain. Timing of the oil pump is not required.**

11. Remove the oil pump sprocket T45 retaining bolt and remove the oil pump sprocket.

12. Remove the retaining pin and disengage the oil pump chain tensioner spring from the dowel pin.

13. Remove the oil pump chain tensioner from the oil pump.

14. Remove the four oil pump bolts and remove the oil pump.

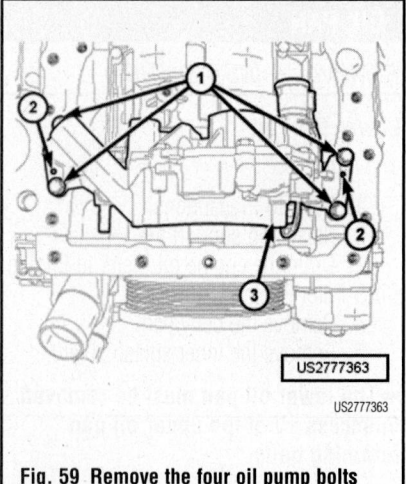

Fig. 59 Remove the four oil pump bolts and remove the oil pump

To install:

15. Align the locator pins with the engine block and install the oil pump with the four bolts. Tighten the bolts to 106 inch lbs. (12 Nm).

16. Install the oil pump chain tensioner on the oil pump.

17. Position the oil pump chain tensioner spring above the dowel pin.

18. Push the oil pump chain tensioner back and insert a suitable retaining pin, such as a 3 mm Allen wrench.

➡**There are no timing marks on the oil pump gear or chain. Timing of the oil pump is not required.**

✳✳ WARNING

Always reinstall timing chains so that they maintain the same direction of rotation. Inverting a previously run chain on a previously run sprocket will result in excessive wear to both the chain and sprocket.

19. Place the oil pump sprocket into the oil pump chain. Align the oil pump sprocket with the oil pump shaft and install the sprocket. Install the T45 retaining bolt and tighten it to 18 ft. lbs. (25 Nm).

20. Remove the retaining pin. Verify that the oil pump chain is centered on the tensioner and crankshaft sprocket.

21. Rotate the crankshaft CW one complete revolution to verify proper oil pump chain installation.

22. Position the oil pump solenoid electrical connector into the engine block. Rotate the connector so that it can be pushed past the primary chain tensioner mounting bolt. Then rotate the connector slightly CCW and push it into the engine block until it locks in place.

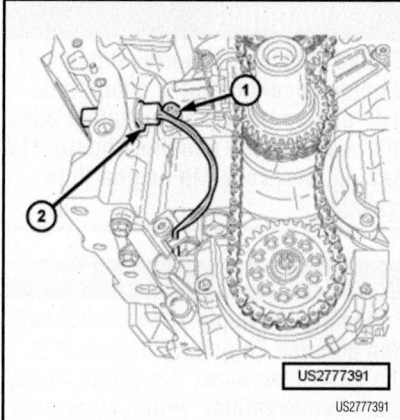

Fig. 60 Primary chain tensioner mounting bolt (1) and the oil pump solenoid electrical connector (2)

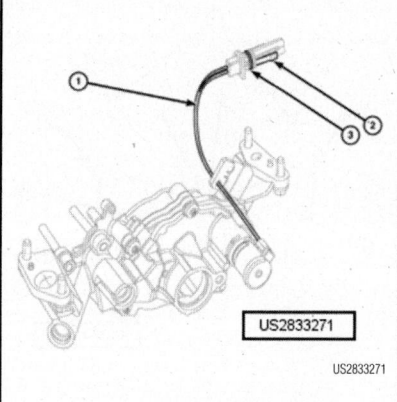

Fig. 61 Solenoid wires (1), connector retention lock tab (2), and connector O-ring seal (3)

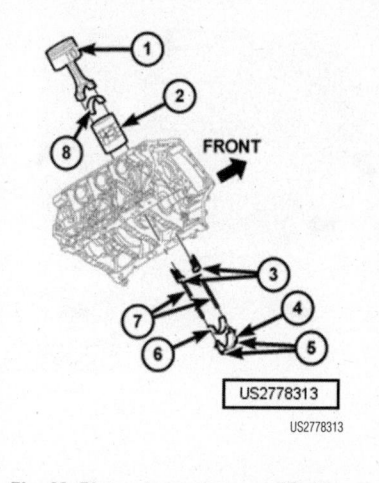

Fig. 63 Piston ring end-gap positioning

23. Install the timing gear splash shield. Tighten bolts to 35 inch lbs. (5 Nm).

24. Verify that the oil pump solenoid electrical connector retention lock tab is engaged to the engine block.

25. Connect the engine wire harness to the oil pump solenoid electrical connector.

26. Install the oil pump pick-up.

27. Install the oil pan. Refer to Upper Oil Pan.

28. If removed, install the oil filter and fill the engine crankcase with the proper oil to the correct level. Refer to Engine Oil & Filter Replacement.

29. Connect the negative battery cable.

❊❊ WARNING

A Malfunction Indicator Light (MIL) or low oil pressure indicator that remains illuminated for more than 2 seconds may indicate low or no engine oil pressure. Stop the engine and investigate the cause of the indication.

30. Start and run the engine until it reaches normal operating temperature.

INSPECTION

See Figure 61.

The 3.6L oil pump is released as an assembly. The assembly includes both the pump and the solenoid. There are no serviceable sub-assembly components. In the event the oil pump or solenoid are not functioning or out of specification they must be replaced as an assembly.

- Inspect the solenoid wires for cuts or chafing.
- Inspect the condition of the connector O-ring seal.

- Inspect the connector retention lock tab for fatigue or damage.

PISTON AND RING

POSITIONING

See Figures 62 through 64.

TIMING CHAIN COVER

REMOVAL & INSTALLATION

See Figures 65 through 67.

1. Refer to Precautions.

2. Disconnect the negative battery cable. Refer to Engine Electrical.

3. Drain the engine cooling system. Refer to Engine Cooling.

4. Remove the electric vacuum pump.

5. Remove the upper radiator hose and thermostat housing.

6. Remove the heater core return hose from the water pump housing.

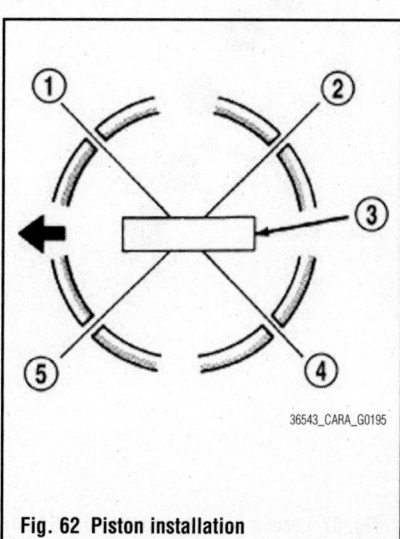

Fig. 62 Piston installation

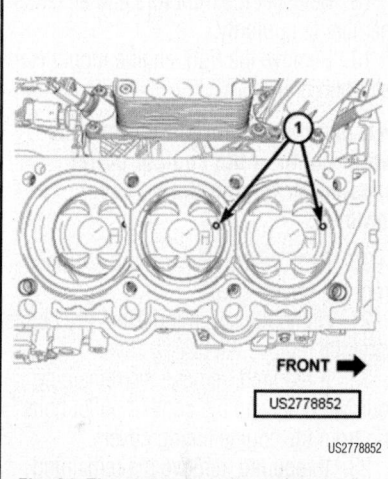

Fig. 64 The pistons crowns are stamped with a mark (1) indicating installation position. This mark must be positioned toward the front of engine on both cylinder banks

7. Remove the lower radiator hose from the water pump housing.

8. Remove the heater core supply hose from the coolant outlet housing.

9. Remove the bolt and reposition the heater core supply tube.

10. Remove the accessory drive belt.

11. Remove the accessory drive belt tensioner.

12. Remove the accessory idler pulley.

13. Remove the power steering pump pulley.

14. Remove the crankshaft vibration damper.

15. Remove the right and left cylinder head covers.

16. Remove the upper and lower oil pans. Refer to Oil Pan.

17. Remove the right engine mount bracket.

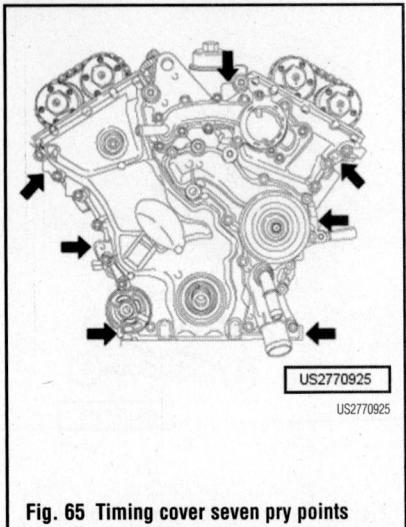

Fig. 65 Timing cover seven pry points

18. Reinstall the front fore and aft cross-member temporarily.

19. Remove the right engine mount isolator and bracket.

➡️It is not necessary to remove the water pump or the coolant outlet housing for engine timing cover removal.

20. Remove the twenty-three M6 bolts from the timing cover.

21. Using the seven indicated pry points, carefully remove the timing cover.

22. If required, remove the remaining four M6 bolts and the coolant outlet housing from the engine timing cover.

23. If required, remove the remaining four M6 bolts and the water pump from the engine timing cover.

☀️ WARNING

Do not use oil-based liquids, wire brushes, abrasive wheels or metal scrapers to clean the engine gasket surfaces. Use only isopropyl (rubbing) alcohol, along with plastic or wooden scrapers. Improper gasket surface preparation may result in engine fluid leakage.

24. Remove all residual sealant from the timing chain cover, cylinder head and engine block mating surfaces.

25. Remove and discard the coolant outlet housing gasket and the water pump gasket.

To install:

26. If removed, install the coolant outlet housing to the timing cover with a new gasket using only the four bolts tightened to 106 inch lbs. (12 Nm).

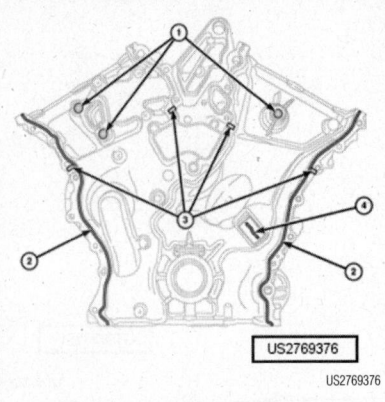

Fig. 66 Timing chain front cover sealant locations: Three cylinder head bosses (1), right and left flanges (2), four cylinder head to engine block T-joints (3), and cover-to-right cam chain tensioner gap (4)

27. If removed, install the water pump to the timing cover using only the four bolts. Refer to Water Pump.

28. Install the coolant outlet housing gasket and the water pump gasket.

29. Clean the engine timing cover, cylinder head and block mating surfaces with isopropyl alcohol in preparation for sealant application.

☀️ WARNING

Engine assembly requires the use of a unique sealant that is compatible with engine oil. Using a sealant other than Volkswagen genuine Engine RTV Sealant may result in engine fluid leakage.

☀️ WARNING

Following the application of Volkswagen genuine Engine RTV Sealant to the gasket surfaces, the components must be assembled within 20 minutes and the attaching fasteners must be tightened to specification within 45 minutes. Prolonged exposure to the air prior to assembly may result in engine fluid leakage.

30. Apply a 2 to 3 mm wide bead of Volkswagen genuine Engine RTV Sealant to the front cover as shown in the following locations:
- Three cylinder head bosses
- Right and left flanges
- Four cylinder head to engine block T-joints
- Cover-to-right cam chain tensioner gap

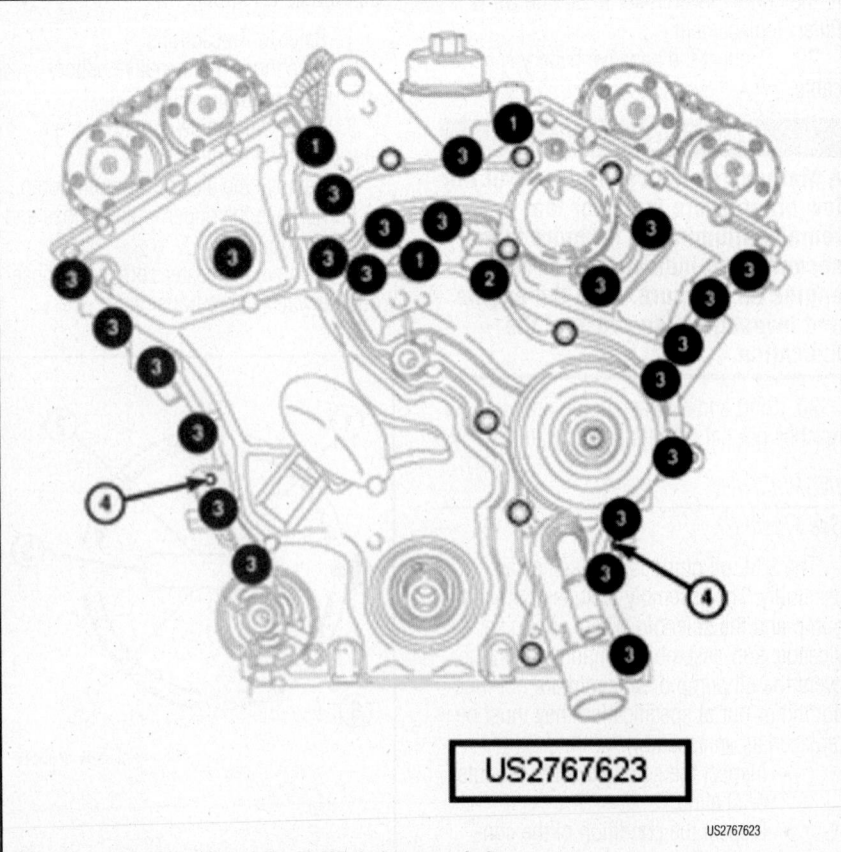

Fig. 67 Locator pins (4) and the 23 M6 timing cover bolts

31. Align the locator pins on the engine block to the engine timing cover and install the cover.

32. Install and tighten the twenty-three M6 timing cover bolts to 106 inch lbs. (12 Nm).

33. Install the right engine mount bracket and isolator.

34. Remove the temporarily installed front fore and aft crossmember.

35. Install the right engine mount bracket.

36. Install the upper and lower oil pans.

37. Install the right and left cylinder head covers.

38. Install the crankshaft vibration damper.

39. Install the power steering pump pulley.

40. Install the accessory idler pulley.

41. Install the accessory drive belt tensioner.

42. Install the accessory drive belt.

43. Install the heater core supply tube with one bolt tightened to 106 inch lbs. (12 Nm).

44. Install the heater core supply hose to the coolant outlet housing.

45. Install the lower radiator hose to the water pump housing.

46. Install the heater core return hose to the water pump housing.

47. Install the thermostat housing and upper radiator hose.

48. Install the electric vacuum pump.

49. If removed, install the oil filter and fill the engine crankcase with the proper oil to the correct level. Refer to Specifications.

50. Connect the negative battery cable.

51. Fill the cooling system.

52. Run the engine until it reaches normal operating temperature.

53. Check the cooling system for the correct fluid level.

TIMING CHAIN & SPROCKETS

REMOVAL & INSTALLATION

See Figures 68 through 70.

1. Refer to Precautions.
Special tools and workshop equipment:
• Camshaft Phaser Locks, Right Side #10202-1
• Camshaft Phaser Locks, Left Side #10202-2
• Tensioner Pin #8514

> ✳✳ **WARNING**
>
> **The magnetic timing wheels must not come in contact with magnets (e.g., pickup tools, trays, etc.) or any other strong magnetic field. This will destroy the timing wheel's ability to correctly relay camshaft position to the camshaft position sensor.**

> ✳✳ **WARNING**
>
> **When the timing chains are removed and the cylinder heads are still installed, DO NOT rotate the camshafts or crankshaft without first locating the proper crankshaft position. Failure to do so will result in valve and/or piston damage.**

➡ The Variable Valve Timing (VVT) assemblies (phasers) and Oil Control Valves (OCVs) can be serviced without removing the engine timing cover.

2. Disconnect the negative battery cable. Refer to Engine Electrical.

3. Remove the air cleaner housing assembly and upper intake manifold. Refer to Upper Intake Manifold.

4. Remove the cylinder head covers. Refer to Cylinder Head Cover.

5. Remove the spark plugs. Refer to Ignition in the Engine Electrical Section.

6. Raise and support the vehicle.

7. Drain the engine cooling system. Refer to Engine Cooling.

8. Remove the oil pan, accessory drive belts, crankshaft vibration damper and

---

engine timing cover. Refer to Engine Timing Cover.

➡ Take this opportunity to measure timing chain wear.

> ✳✳ **WARNING**
>
> **When aligning timing marks, always rotate the engine by turning the crankshaft. Failure to do so will result in valve and/or piston damage.**

9. Rotate the crankshaft clockwise (as viewed from the front) to place the number one cylinder piston at top-dead-center on the exhaust stroke by aligning the dimple on the crankshaft with the block/bearing cap junction.

10. While maintaining this alignment, verify that the arrows on the left side cam phasers point toward each other and are parallel to the cylinder head cover mounting surface and that the right side cam phaser arrows point away from each other and the scribe lines are parallel to the cylinder head cover mounting surface. (Refer to Left Cylinder Head Removal.)

➡ The phaser markings could align with either an external or internal chain link. Either alignment is acceptable as long as there are twelve chain pins between the markings.

11. There should be twelve chain pins between the exhaust cam phaser triangle marking and the intake cam phaser circle marking as viewed from either the front or rear of the cam phasers.

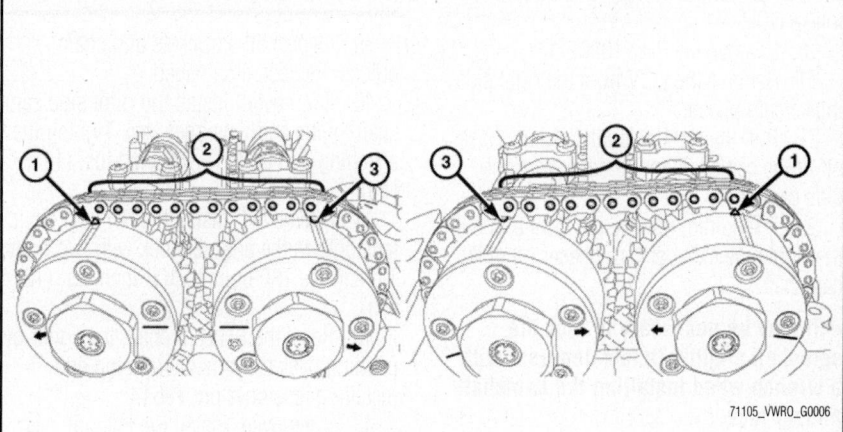

71105_VWRO_G0006

Fig. 68 There should be twelve chain pins (2) between the exhaust cam phaser triangle marking (1) and the intake cam phaser circle marking (3) as viewed from either the front or rear of the cam phasers

✳✳ WARNING

Always reinstall timing chains so that they maintain the same direction of rotation. Inverting a previously run chain on a previously run sprocket will result in excessive wear to both the chain and sprocket.

12. Mark the direction of rotation on the following timing chains using a paint pen or equivalent to aid in reassembly:

- Left side cam chain
- Right side cam chain
- Oil pump chain
- Primary chain

13. Reset the RH cam chain tensioner by pushing back the tensioner piston and installing #8514.

14. Reset the LH cam chain tensioner by lifting the pawl, pushing back the piston and installing #8514.

15. Remove the bolts and the timing gear splash shield.

16. Disengage the oil pump chain tensioner spring from the dowel pin and remove the oil pump chain tensioner.

17. Remove the oil pump sprocket T45 retaining bolt and remove the oil pump sprocket and oil pump chain.

➡It may be necessary to rock the camshaft slightly (a few degrees) with a wrench when installing the camshaft phaser lock. Refer to Left Cylinder Head Installation for an illustration of the tool.

18. Install the RH #10202-1 with the tool number facing up.

19. Loosen, but do not remove, the exhaust oil control valve (OCV) and the intake OCV.

20. Remove the RH #10202-1.

21. Remove the OCV from the right side intake cam phaser.

22. Pull the right side intake cam phaser off of the camshaft and remove the right side cam chain.

23. If required, remove the OCV and pull the right side exhaust cam phaser off of the camshaft.

➡It may be necessary to rock the camshaft slightly (a few degrees) with a wrench when installing the camshaft phaser lock.

24. Install the LH #10202-2 with the tool number facing up.

25. Loosen, but do not remove, the exhaust OCV and the intake OCV.

26. Remove the LH #10202-2.

27. Remove the OCV from the left side exhaust cam phaser.

28. Pull the left side exhaust cam phaser off of the camshaft and remove the left side cam chain.

29. If required, remove the OCV and pull the left side intake cam phaser off of the camshaft.

30. Reset the primary chain tensioner by pushing back the tensioner piston and installing #8514. Remove two T30 bolts and remove the primary chain tensioner.

31. Remove the T30 bolt and the primary chain guide.

32. Remove the idler sprocket T45 retaining bolt and washer.

33. Remove the primary chain, idler sprocket and crankshaft sprocket as an assembly.

34. If required, remove two T30 bolts and the LH cam chain tensioner.

35. If required, remove two T30 bolts and the LH cam chain guide and tensioner arm.

36. If required, remove two T30 bolts and the RH cam chain tensioner.

37. If required, remove three T30 bolts and the RH cam chain guide and tensioner arm.

38. Inspect all sprockets and chain guides. Replace if damaged.

To install:

✳✳ WARNING

The magnetic timing wheels must not come in contact with magnets (e.g., pickup tools, trays, etc.) or any other strong magnetic field. This will destroy the timing wheel's ability to correctly relay camshaft position to the camshaft position sensor.

39. Inspect all sprockets and chain guides. Replace if damaged.

40. If removed, install the right side cam chain guide and tensioner arm. Tighten the attaching T30 bolts to 106 inch lbs. (12 Nm).

41. If removed, install the RH cam chain tensioner to the engine block with two bolts. Tighten the T30 bolts to 106 inch lbs. (12 Nm).

42. Reset the RH cam chain tensioner by pushing back the tensioner piston and installing tensioner pin #8514.

43. If removed, install the left side cam chain guide and tensioner arm. Tighten the attaching T30 bolts to 106 inch lbs. (12 Nm).

44. If removed, install the LH cam chain tensioner to the cylinder head with two bolts. Tighten the T30 bolts to 106 inch lbs. (12 Nm).

45. Reset the LH cam chain tensioner by lifting the pawl, pushing back the piston and installing tensioner pin #8514.

46. Verify that the key is installed in the crankshaft.

✳✳ WARNING

Do not rotate the crankshaft more than a few degrees independently of the camshafts. Piston to valve contact could occur resulting in possible valve damage. If the crankshaft needs to be rotated more than a few degrees, first remove the camshafts. Refer to Camshaft.

47. Verify that the number one piston is positioned at TDC by aligning the dimple on the crankshaft with the block/bearing cap junction.

✳✳ WARNING

Do not rotate the camshafts more than a few degrees independently of the crankshaft. Valve to piston contact could occur resulting in possible valve damage. If the camshafts need to be rotated more than a few degrees, first move the pistons away from the cylinder heads by rotating the crankshaft counterclockwise to a position 30° BTDC. Once the camshafts are positioned at TDC rotate the crankshaft clockwise to return the crankshaft to TDC.

48. Verify that the camshafts are set at TDC by positioning the alignment holes vertically.

✳✳ WARNING

Always reinstall timing chains so that they maintain the same direction of rotation. Inverting a previously run chain on a previously run sprocket will result in excessive wear to both the chain and sprocket.

49. Place the primary chain onto the crankshaft sprocket so that the arrow is aligned with the plated link on the timing chain.

50. While maintaining this alignment, invert the crankshaft sprocket and timing chain and place the idler sprocket into the timing chain so that the dimple is aligned with the plated link on the timing chain.

51. While maintaining this alignment, lubricate the idler sprocket bushing with clean engine oil and install the sprockets

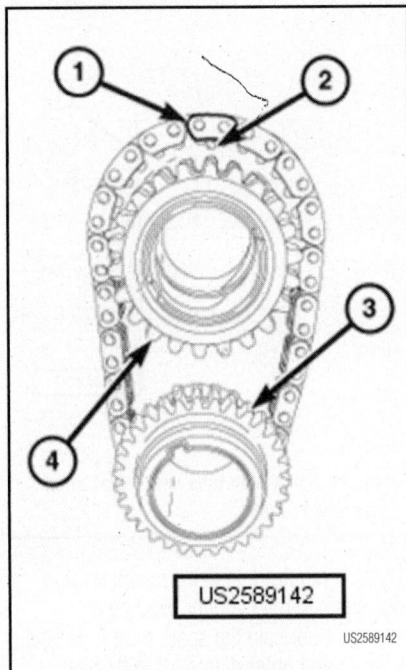

Fig. 69 Sprockets and timing chain installation

and timing chain on the engine. To verify that the timing is still correct, the timing chain plated link should be located at 12:00 when the dimple on the crankshaft is aligned with the block/bearing cap junction.

52. Install the idler sprocket retaining bolt and washer. Tighten the T45 bolt to 18 ft. lbs. (25 Nm).

53. Install the primary chain guide. Tighten attaching T30 bolt to 106 inch lbs. (12 Nm).

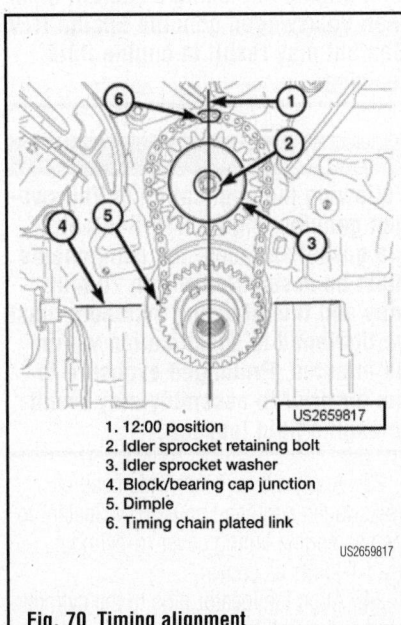

1. 12:00 position
2. Idler sprocket retaining bolt
3. Idler sprocket washer
4. Block/bearing cap junction
5. Dimple
6. Timing chain plated link

Fig. 70 Timing alignment

54. Reset the primary chain tensioner by pushing back the tensioner piston and installing #8514.

55. Install the primary chain tensioner to the engine block with two bolts. Tighten the T30 bolts to 106 inch lbs. (12 Nm) and remove the 8514.

56. Press the LH intake cam phaser onto the intake camshaft. Install and hand tighten the OCV.

➡ **The left side and right side cam chains are identical.**

✳✳ WARNING

Always reinstall timing chains so that they maintain the same direction of rotation. Inverting a previously run chain on a previously run sprocket will result in excessive wear to both the chain and sprocket.

57. Drape the left side cam chain over the left side intake cam phaser and onto the idler sprocket so that the arrow is aligned with the plated link on the cam chain.

58. While maintaining this alignment, route the cam chain around the exhaust and intake cam phasers so that the plated links are aligned with the phaser timing marks. Position the left side cam phasers so that the arrows point toward each other and are parallel to the cylinder head cover mounting surface. Press the exhaust cam phaser onto the exhaust cam, install and hand tighten the OCV.

➡ **Minor rotation of a camshaft (a few degrees) may be required To Install the camshaft phaser or phaser lock.**

59. Install the LH #10202-2 with the tool number facing up.

60. Tighten the OCV to 110 ft. lbs. (150 Nm).

61. Remove the Camshaft Phaser Lock.

62. Press the right side exhaust cam phaser onto the exhaust camshaft. Install and hand tighten the OCV.

✳✳ WARNING

Always reinstall timing chains so that they maintain the same direction of rotation. Inverting a previously run chain on a previously run sprocket will result in excessive wear to both the chain and sprocket.

63. Drape the right side cam chain over the right side exhaust cam phaser and onto the idler sprocket so that the dimple is aligned with the plated link on the cam chain.

64. While maintaining this alignment, route the cam chain around the exhaust and intake cam phasers so that the plated links are aligned with the phaser timing marks. Position the right side cam phasers so that the arrows point away from each other and the scribe lines are parallel to the cylinder head cover mounting surface. Press the intake cam phaser onto the intake cam, install and hand tighten the OCV.

➡ **Minor rotation of a camshaft (a few degrees) may be required To Install the camshaft phaser or phaser lock.**

65. Install the RH #10202-1 with the tool number facing up.

66. Tighten the OCV to 110 ft. lbs. (150 Nm).

67. Remove the Camshaft Phaser Lock.

➡ **There are no timing marks on the oil pump gear or chain.**

✳✳ WARNING

Always reinstall timing chains so that they maintain the same direction of rotation. Inverting a previously run chain on a previously run sprocket will result in excessive wear to both the chain and sprocket.

68. Place the oil pump sprocket into the oil pump chain. Place the oil pump chain onto the crankshaft sprocket while aligning the oil pump sprocket with the oil pump shaft. Tighten the T45 oil pump sprocket retaining bolt to 18 ft. lbs. (25 Nm).

69. Install the oil pump chain tensioner. Insure that the spring is positioned above the dowel pin.

70. Install the timing gear splash shield. Tighten the bolts to 35 inch lbs. (5 Nm).

71. Remove the #8514 from the RH and LH cam chain tensioners.

72. Rotate the crankshaft clockwise (as viewed from the front) two complete revolutions stopping when the dimple on the crankshaft is aligned with the block/bearing cap junction.

73. While maintaining this alignment, verify that the arrows on the left side cam phasers point toward each other and are parallel to the cylinder head cover mounting surface and that the right side cam phaser arrows point away from each other and the scribe lines are parallel to the cylinder head cover mounting surface.

74. There should be 12 chain pins between the exhaust cam phaser triangle marking and the intake cam phaser circle marking as viewed from either the front or rear of the cam phasers.

75. If the engine timing is not correct, repeat this procedure.

76. Install the engine timing cover, crankshaft vibration damper, accessory drive belts and oil pan.

77. Install the spark plugs.

78. Install the cylinder head covers.

79. Install the upper intake manifold and air cleaner housing assembly.

80. Fill the engine crankcase with the proper oil to the correct level. Refer to Specifications.

81. Connect the negative battery cable.

82. Fill the cooling system.

83. Operate the engine until it reaches normal operating temperature.

84. Check the cooling system for the correct fluid level.

➡ **The Cam/Crank Variation Relearn procedure must be performed using the scan tool anytime there has been a repair/replacement made to a powertrain system, such as the flywheel, valvetrain, camshaft and/or crankshaft sensors or components.**

VALVE (CYLINDER HEAD) COVERS

REMOVAL & INSTALLATION

Left Cylinder Head Cover

See Figures 71 through 73.

1. Refer to Precautions.

❊❊ **WARNING**

The magnetic timing wheels must not come in contact with magnets (e.g., pickup tools, trays, etc.) or any other strong magnetic field. This will destroy the timing wheel's ability to correctly relay camshaft position to the camshaft position sensor.

2. Disconnect the negative battery cable. Refer to Engine Electrical.

3. Remove the air cleaner body, resonator and upper intake manifold. Refer to Upper Intake Manifold.

4. Cover the open intake ports to prevent debris from entering the engine.

5. Remove the insulator from the LH cylinder head cover.

➡ **Mark the variable valve timing solenoid connectors with a paint pen or an equivalent so that they may be reinstalled in their original locations.**

6. Disconnect the electrical connectors from the variable valve timing solenoids on the left cylinder head cover.

7. Disengage the 3 wire harness retainers from the left cylinder head cover.

8. Mark the variable valve timing solenoids with a paint pen or an equivalent so that they may be reinstalled in their original locations.

9. Remove the variable valve timing solenoids.

10. Disconnect the left Camshaft Position (CMP) sensor.

11. Disengage one main wire harness retainer from the cylinder head cover and one main wire harness retainer from the cylinder head cover mounting stud.

➡ **Mark the sensors so they can be installed in their original locations.**

12. Remove the camshaft position sensor. Refer to Camshaft Position Sensor in the Engine Performance section.

13. Disengage the 2 injection/ignition harness retainers from the left cylinder head cover.

14. Remove the ignition coils. Refer to Ignition Coil in the Engine Electrical section.

15. Loosen the ten cylinder head cover mounting bolts and the two stud bolts and then remove the cylinder head cover.

16. Remove and discard the cylinder head cover gasket.

17. The spark plug tube seals can be reused if they are not damaged.

❊❊ **WARNING**

Do not use oil-based liquids, wire brushes, abrasive wheels or metal scrapers to clean the engine gasket surfaces. Use only isopropyl (rubbing) alcohol, along with plastic or wooden scrapers. Improper gasket surface preparation may result in engine fluid leakage.

18. Remove all residual sealant from the cylinder head, timing chain cover and cylinder head cover mating surfaces.

To install:

❊❊ **WARNING**

The magnetic timing wheels must not come in contact with magnets (e.g., pickup tools, trays, etc.) or any other strong magnetic field. This will destroy the timing wheel's ability to correctly relay camshaft position to the camshaft position sensor.

19. Install the cylinder head cover gasket.

20. The spark plug tube seals can be reused if they are not damaged.

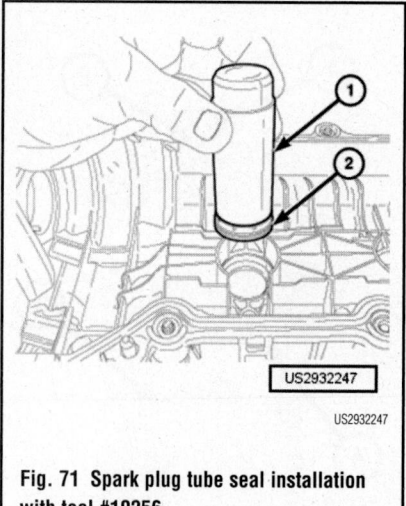

US2932247

Fig. 71 Spark plug tube seal installation with tool #10256

21. If required, install new spark plug tube seals in the cylinder head cover:

   a. Lubricate the spark plug tube seal inner and outer diameters with clean engine oil.

   b. Place the spark plug tube seal on the Cam Sensor/Spark Plug Tube Seal Installer #10256.

   c. Push the seal into the cylinder head cover until the base of the seal seats.

   d. Remove the tool.

22. Clean the timing engine timing cover, cylinder head and cylinder head cover mating surfaces with isopropyl alcohol in preparation for sealant application.

❊❊ **WARNING**

Engine assembly requires the use of a unique sealant that is compatible with engine oil. Using a sealant other than Volkswagen genuine Engine RTV Sealant may result in engine fluid leakage.

❊❊ **WARNING**

Following the application of Volkswagen genuine Engine RTV Sealant to the gasket surfaces, the components must be assembled within 20 minutes and the attaching fasteners must be tightened to specification within 45 minutes. Prolonged exposure to the air prior to assembly may result in engine fluid leakage.

23. Apply a 2 to 3 mm wide bead of Volkswagen genuine Engine RTV Sealant to the two engine timing cover-to-cylinder head T-joints as shown.

24. Align the locator pins to the cylinder head and install the cylinder head cover.

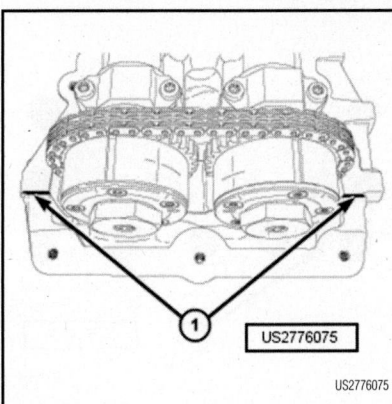

Fig. 72 The two engine timing cover-to-cylinder head T-joints sealant application locations

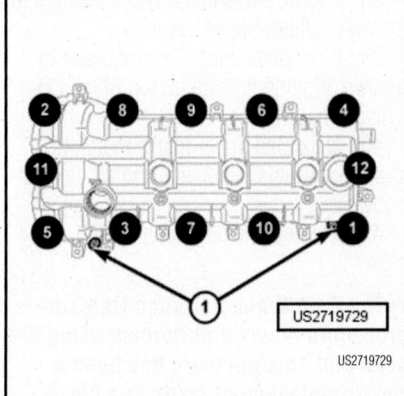

Fig. 73 Locator pins (1). Cylinder head cover bolts and double-ended studs tightening sequence

25. Tighten the cylinder head cover bolts and double ended studs in the sequence shown to 106 inch lbs. (12 Nm).
26. If removed, install the spark plugs.
27. Install the ignition coils.
28. Engage two injection/ignition harness retainers to the left cylinder head cover.

➡️**If both the RH and LH CMP sensors where removed, install them into their original locations.**

29. Install the camshaft position sensor.
30. Connect the electrical connector to the left CMP sensor.
31. Engage one main wire harness retainer to the cylinder head cover and one main wire harness retainer to the cylinder head cover mounting stud.
32. Refer to the markings made at disassembly and install the variable valve timing solenoids in their original locations.

33. Engage three wire harness retainers to the left cylinder head cover.
34. Connect the electrical connectors to the left variable valve timing solenoids.
35. Install the insulator to the two alignment posts on top of the LH cylinder head cover.
36. Install the upper intake manifold, support brackets, resonator and air cleaner body.
37. Fill the engine crankcase with the proper oil to the correct level. Refer to Specifications.
38. Connect the negative battery cable.

➡️**The Cam/Crank Variation Relearn procedure must be performed using the scan tool anytime there has been a repair/replacement made to a powertrain system, such as the flywheel, valvetrain, camshaft and/or crankshaft sensors or components.**

Right Cylinder Head Cover

See Figures 74 and 75.

1. Refer to Precautions.

⚡ WARNING

The magnetic timing wheels must not come in contact with magnets (e.g., pickup tools, trays, etc.) or any other strong magnetic field. This will destroy the timing wheel's ability to correctly relay camshaft position to the camshaft position sensor.

2. Disconnect the negative battery cable. Refer to Engine Electrical.
3. Remove the air cleaner body, resonator and upper intake manifold. Refer to Upper Intake Manifold.
4. Cover the open intake ports to prevent debris from entering the engine.
5. Remove the insulator from the LH cylinder head cover.

➡️**Mark the variable valve timing solenoid connectors with a paint pen or an equivalent so that they may be reinstalled in their original locations.**

6. Disconnect the electrical connectors from the variable valve timing solenoids on the right cylinder head.
7. Disengage the two wire harness retainers from the right cylinder head cover.
8. Mark the variable valve timing solenoids with a paint pen or an equivalent so that they may be reinstalled in their original locations.
9. Remove the variable valve timing solenoids.

10. Disengage three main wire harness retainers from the right cylinder head cover.
11. Disconnect the electrical connector for the right Camshaft Position (CMP) sensor.

➡️**If removing both the RH and LH CMP sensors, mark the sensors so they can be installed in their original locations.**

12. Remove the camshaft position sensor. Refer to Camshaft Position Sensor in the Engine Performance section.
13. Disengage the three injection/ignition harness retainers from the right cylinder head cover.
14. Remove the ignition coils. Refer to Ignition Coil in the Engine Electrical section.
15. Remove the PCV valve.
16. Remove the 2 resonator mounts from the stud bolts.
17. Loosen the 9 cylinder head cover mounting bolts and the three stud bolts and then remove the cylinder head cover.
18. Remove and discard the cylinder head cover gasket.
19. The spark plug tube seals can be reused if they are not damaged.

⚡ WARNING

Do not use oil-based liquids, wire brushes, abrasive wheels or metal scrapers to clean the engine gasket surfaces. Use only isopropyl (rubbing) alcohol, along with plastic or wooden scrapers. Improper gasket surface preparation may result in engine fluid leakage.

20. Remove all residual sealant from the cylinder head, timing chain cover and cylinder head cover mating surfaces.

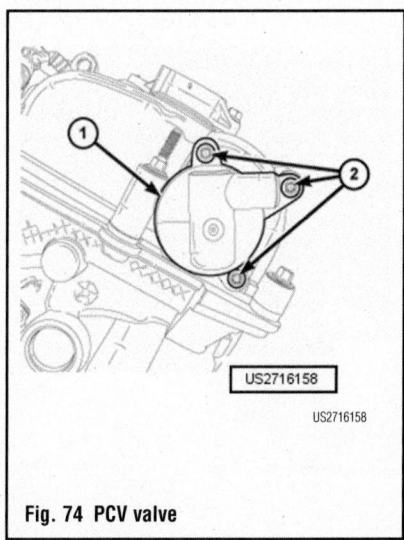

Fig. 74 PCV valve

To install:

> ⚜ **WARNING**
>
> The magnetic timing wheels must not come in contact with magnets (e.g., pickup tools, trays, etc.) or any other strong magnetic field.
> This will destroy the timing wheel's ability to correctly relay camshaft position to the camshaft position sensor.

21. Install the cylinder head cover gasket.

22. The spark plug tube seals can be reused if they are not damaged. Refer to Left Cylinder Head Cover installation illustration.

23. If required, install new spark plug tube seals in the cylinder head cover:

    a. Lubricate the spark plug tube seal inner and outer diameters with clean engine oil.

    b. Place the spark plug tube seal on the Cam Sensor/Spark Plug Tube Seal Installer #10256.

    c. Push the seal into the cylinder head cover until the base of the seal seats.

    d. Remove the tool.

24. Clean the timing engine timing cover, cylinder head and cylinder head cover mating surfaces with isopropyl alcohol in preparation for sealant application.

> ⚜ **WARNING**
>
> Engine assembly requires the use of a unique sealant that is compatible with engine oil. Using a sealant other than Volkswagen genuine Engine RTV Sealant may result in engine fluid leakage.

> ⚜ **WARNING**
>
> Following the application of Volkswagen genuine Engine RTV Sealant to the gasket surfaces, the components must be assembled within 20 minutes and the attaching fasteners must be tightened to specification within 45 minutes. Prolonged exposure to the air prior to assembly may result in engine fluid leaks.

25. Apply a 2 to 3 mm wide bead of Volkswagen genuine Engine RTV Sealant to the two engine timing cover-to-cylinder head T-joints as shown in the illustration for the Left Cylinder Head Cover installation.

26. Align the locator pins to the cylinder head and install the cylinder head cover.

27. Tighten the cylinder head cover bolts and double-ended studs in the sequence shown to 106 inch lbs. (12 Nm).

28. Install the two resonator mounts to the stud bolts.

29. Install the PCV valve.

30. If removed, install the spark plugs.

31. Install the ignition coils.

32. Engage three injection/ignition harness retainers to the right cylinder head cover.

➡ **If both the RH and LH CMP sensors where removed, install them into their original locations.**

33. Install the camshaft position sensor.

34. Connect the electrical connector to the right CMP sensor.

35. Engage three main wire harness retainers to the right cylinder head cover.

36. Refer to the markings made at disassembly and install the variable valve timing solenoids in their original locations.

37. Connect the electrical connectors to the variable valve timing solenoids on the right cylinder head.

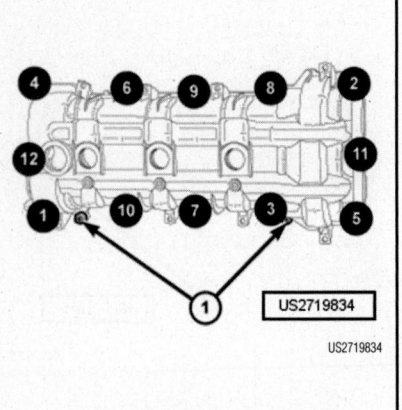

Fig. 75 Locator pins (1). Cylinder head cover bolts and double-ended studs tightening sequence

38. Engage two wire harness retainers to the right cylinder head cover.

39. If removed, install the insulator to the two alignment posts on top of the LH cylinder head cover.

40. Install the upper intake manifold, support brackets, resonator and air cleaner body.

41. Connect the negative battery cable.

➡ **The Cam/Crank Variation Relearn procedure must be performed using the scan tool anytime there has been a repair/replacement made to a powertrain system, such as the flywheel, valvetrain, camshaft and/or crankshaft sensors or components.**

VALVE LASH

ADJUSTMENT

The Routan 3.6L engine is equipped with hydraulic valve lifters. No valve clearance adjustments are necessary.

ENGINE PERFORMANCE & EMISSION CONTROLS

CAMSHAFT POSITION (CMP) SENSOR

LOCATION

There are two Camshaft Position (CMP) sensors on the 3.6L engine. The sensors are located on the top end of each valve cover, closest to the transmission side of the engine. CMP are mounted between the timing wheels.

REMOVAL & INSTALLATION

See Figures 76 and 77.

> ✳ **WARNING**
>
> **The magnetic timing wheels must not come in contact with magnets (pickup tools, trays, etc.) or any other strong magnetic field. This will destroy the timing wheels ability to correctly relay camshaft position to the Camshaft Position (CMP) Sensor.**

1. The Camshaft Position (CMP) sensors are located at the rear of the cylinder head covers and are bolted to the cylinder head.
2. Disconnect and isolate the negative battery cable.
3. Remove the air cleaner housing.
4. If removing the LH CMP sensor, first remove the upper intake manifold. Refer to Upper Intake Manifold in the Engine Mechanical section.

➡ **If removing both the RH and LH CMP sensors, mark the sensors so they can be installed in their original locations.**

5. Disconnect the electrical connector from the CMP sensor.
6. Loosen the sensor mounting bolt.
7. Pull the sensor and mounting bolt from the cylinder head cover.
8. The O-ring seal can be reused if it is not damaged.

To install:

> ✳ **WARNING**
>
> **The magnetic timing wheels must not come in contact with magnets (pickup tools, trays, etc.) or any other strong magnetic field. This will destroy the timing wheels ability to correctly relay camshaft position to the Camshaft Position (CMP) Sensor.**

9. Clean the CMP sensor mounting bolt hole in the cylinder head.
10. The CMP sensor seal can be reused if it is not damaged.
11. If required, install a new CMP sensor seal in the cylinder head cover:
12. Lubricate the CMP sensor seal inner and outer diameters with clean engine oil.
13. Place the CMP sensor seal on the Cam Sensor/Spark Plug Tube Seal Installer #10256. Refer to Left Cylinder Head Cover in the Engine Mechanical section.
14. Push the seal into the cylinder head cover until the base of the seal is seated.
15. Remove the tool.

➡ **A properly installed CMP sensor seal will have a 0.06–0.08 inch gap between the cylinder head cover and the seal upper flange.**

16. The sensor mounting bolt O-ring can be reused if it is not damaged.
17. Apply a small amount of engine oil to the sensor mounting bolt O-ring.

➡ **If both RH and LH CMP sensors were removed, install them into their original locations.**

18. Install the CMP sensor to the cylinder head. Tighten the mounting bolt to 80 inch lbs. (9 Nm).
19. Connect the electrical connector to the sensor.
20. Following installation of the LH CMP sensor, install the upper intake manifold as outlined in the Engine Mechanical Section.
21. Install the air cleaner housing.
22. Connect the negative battery cable.

➡ **The Cam/Crank Variation Relearn procedure must be performed using the scan tool anytime there has been a repair/replacement made to a powertrain system, for example: flywheel, valve train, camshaft and/or crankshaft sensors or components.**

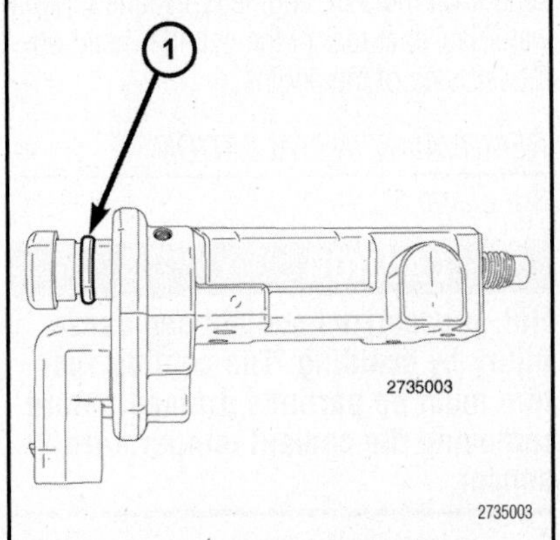

CRANKSHAFT POSITION (CKP) SENSOR

LOCATION

The Crankshaft Position (CKP) sensor is mounted into the right rear side of the cylinder block.

REMOVAL & INSTALLATION

See Figure 78.

1. Disconnect the negative battery cable. Refer to Engine Electrical.
2. Raise and support the vehicle.
3. Remove the front suspension skid plate.
4. Push back the heat shield from the Crankshaft Position (CKP) sensor.
5. Disconnect the electrical connector from the CKP sensor.
6. Remove the sensor mounting bolt.
7. Carefully twist the sensor from the cylinder block.
8. The CKP sensor O-ring can be reused if it is not damaged.

To install:

9. Apply a small amount of engine oil to the sensor O-ring.
10. Clean the CKP sensor mounting bolt hole in the engine block.

Fig. 76 Pull the sensor and mounting bolt from the cylinder head cover. The O-ring seal (1) can be reused if it is not damaged

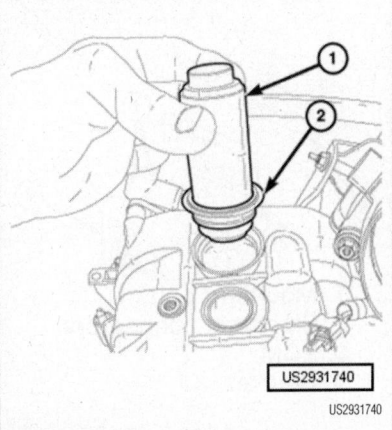

Fig. 77 Cam Sensor/Spark Plug Tube Seal Installer tool #10256 (1) and CMP sensor seal (2)

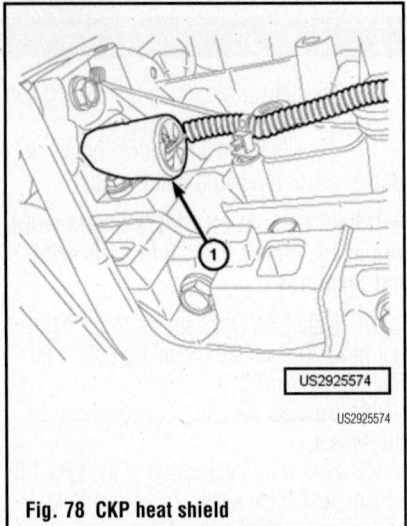

US2925574

Fig. 78 CKP heat shield

11. Install the sensor into the engine block with a slight rocking and twisting action.

❊❊ WARNING

Before tightening the CKP sensor mounting bolt, be sure the sensor is completely flush to the cylinder block. If the CKP sensor is not flush, damage to the sensor mounting tang may result.

12. Install the mounting bolt and tighten it to 106 inch lbs. (12 Nm).
13. Connect the electrical connector to the sensor.
14. Position the heat shield over the CKP sensor.
15. Install the front suspension skid plate.
16. Lower the vehicle.
17. Connect the negative battery cable.

➡**The Cam/Crank Variation Relearn procedure must be performed using the scan tool anytime there has been a repair/replacement made to a powertrain system, for example: flywheel, valve train, camshaft and/or crankshaft sensors or components.**

POWERTRAIN CONTROL MODULE (PCM)

LOCATION

The Powertrain Control Module (PCM) is located behind the left front wheelhouse liner.

REMOVAL & INSTALLATION

2011 Models
See Figure 79.

1. Before servicing the vehicle, refer to the Precautions Section.
2. Disconnect and isolate the negative battery cable.
3. Remove the left front wheelhouse liner.
4. Remove the wiring harness electrical connectors from the Powertrain Control Module (PCM).
5. Remove the bolts and then remove the PCM from the bracket.

To install:

6. Install the PCM and the bolts to the bracket. Tighten the bolts to 40 inch lbs. (4.5 Nm).
7. Install the electrical connectors to the PCM.
8. Install the left front wheelhouse liner.
9. Connect the negative battery cable.
10. Using a scan tool, program all the necessary information into the PCM.

2012 Models
See Figure 80.

1. Disconnect the negative battery cable. Refer to Engine Electrical.
2. Raise and support the vehicle.
3. Remove the push pin and reposition the PCM access cover.
4. Unlock and disconnect the electrical connectors from the PCM.
5. Remove the three bolts and the PCM.

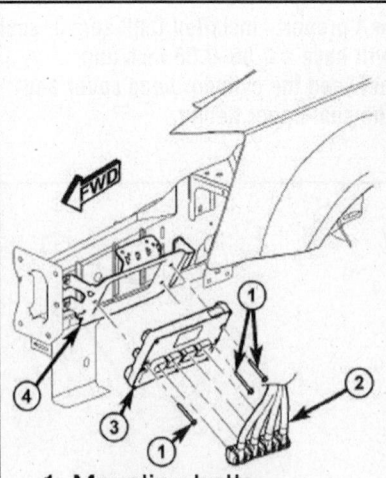

1. Mounting bolts
2. Electrical connectors
3. PCM
4. Bracket

36543_CARA_G0252

Fig. 79 Powertrain Control Module (PCM) replacement

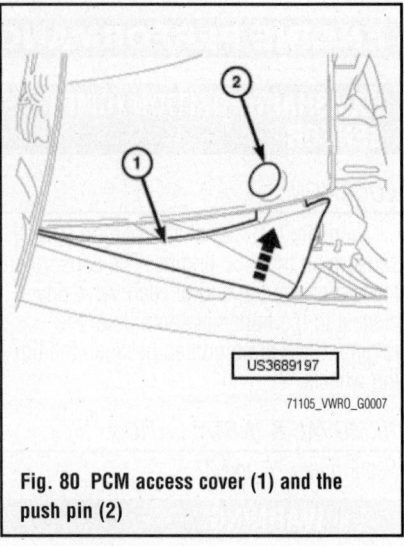

US3689197

71105_VWRO_G0007

Fig. 80 PCM access cover (1) and the push pin (2)

To install:

6. Install the PCM with the three bolts tightened to 40 inch lbs. (4.5 Nm).
7. Connect and lock the electrical connectors to the PCM.
8. Reposition the PCM access cover and install the push pin.
9. Lower the vehicle.
10. Connect the negative battery cable.

➡**If a new PCM is installed, it must be programmed with the original Vehicle Identification Number (VIN) and mileage. If this is not done, a Diagnostic Trouble Code (DTC) may set.**

11. If a new PCM is being installed, use a scan tool and program the new PCM with the original VIN and vehicle mileage.

ENGINE COOLANT TEMPERATURE (ECT) SENSOR

LOCATION

The Engine Coolant Temperature (ECT) sensor on the 3.6L engine is installed into a water jacket at rear of the cylinder head on the left side of the engine.

REMOVAL & INSTALLATION
See Figure 81.

❊❊ CAUTION

Hot, pressurized coolant can cause injury by scalding. The cooling system must be partially drained before removing the coolant temperature sensor.

❊❊ CAUTION

A small amount of antifreeze can kill human beings, pets and wildlife.

- Do not mix used antifreeze with any waste or other material such as solvents, cooling system flushes, used oil, or motor fuels.
- Store used antifreeze in compatible containers that are in good condition and labeled "Used Antifreeze Only" until you recycle it.
- Keep used antifreeze containers securely closed, except when emptying or filling, to minimize the potential for spillage.
- Clean up antifreeze spills immediately. Clean up the area well afterward and do not throw the rags in the trash. Dogs and cats dig through the garbage and can become exposed through contact with rags.
- Do not pour used coolant down a drain or on the ground. This is illegal and a danger to people and animals.

➡**Do not waste reusable coolant: if it is clean, drain the coolant for reuse.**

1. Drain the cooling system to a level below the engine coolant temperature sensor. Refer to Cooling System Draining and Filling in the Engine Cooling section.
2. Disconnect the wiring harness electrical connector from the ECT sensor.
3. Remove the ECT sensor.

To install:
4. Apply Volkswagen thread sealant with to the sensor threads.
5. Install the sensor to the cylinder head.
6. Tighten the sensor to 8 ft. lbs. (11 Nm) torque.
7. Connect the electrical connector to the sensor.
8. Fill the cooling system.

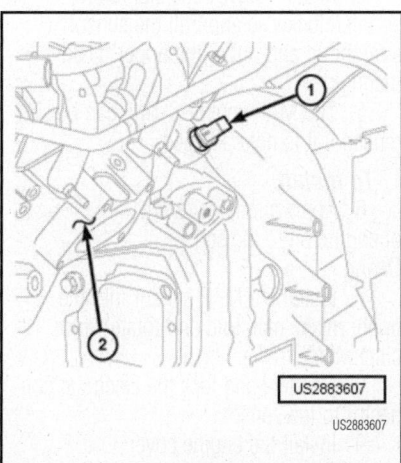

Fig. 81 ECT wiring harness electrical connector (1) and sensor (2)

HEATED OXYGEN (HO2S) SENSOR

LOCATION
See Figure 82.

REMOVAL & INSTALLATION

✳✳ CAUTION
The exhaust pipes and catalytic converter become very hot during engine operation. Allow the engine to cool before removing the oxygen sensors. Failure to allow the engine to cool before removal may result in personal injury caused by burns.

➡**Use an O2 sensor removal tool for this procedure.**

1. Disconnect the negative battery cable. Refer to Engine Electrical.
2. Raise and support the vehicle.

✳✳ WARNING
When disconnecting the oxygen sensor electrical connector, do not pull directly on the wire going into the sensor. The sensor wiring can be damaged resulting in sensor failure.

3. Disconnect the heated oxygen sensor electrical connector.
4. Remove the oxygen sensor.
5. Clean the exhaust pipe threads using an appropriate tap.

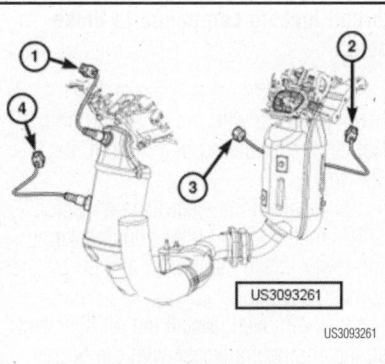

Fig. 82 The engine is equipped with four heated oxygen sensors: The right upstream or 1/1 oxygen sensor (1), the right downstream or 1/2 oxygen sensor (4), the left upstream or 2/1 oxygen sensor (3), and the left downstream or 2/2 oxygen sensor (2)

To install:
6. If reinstalling the original oxygen sensor, coat the sensor threads with an anti-seize compound. New sensors have compound on the threads and do not require an additional coating.

➡**Do not add any additional anti-seize compound to the threads of a new oxygen sensor.**

7. Install the oxygen sensor and tighten to:
   a. Left upstream oxygen sensor, 32 ft. lbs. (43 Nm)
   b. Left downstream oxygen sensor, 32 ft. lbs. (43 Nm)
   c. Right upstream oxygen sensor, 32 ft. lbs. (43 Nm)
   d. Right downstream oxygen sensor, 33 ft. lbs. (45 Nm)

✳✳ WARNING
Never apply any type of grease to the oxygen sensor electrical connector, or attempt any repair of the sensor wiring harness.

8. Connect the heated oxygen sensor electrical connector.
9. Lower the vehicle.
10. Connect the negative battery cable.

INTAKE AIR TEMPERATURE (IAT) SENSOR

LOCATION
The IAT sensor is installed on the air box.

REMOVAL & INSTALLATION
See Figure 83.

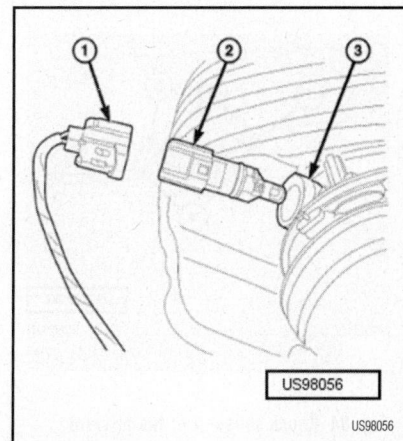

Fig. 83 IAT sensor electrical connector (1), sensor (2), and air box (3)

1. Disconnect and isolate the negative battery cable at the battery.

➡ **Clean the sensor area prior to removing it from the air cleaner housing.**

2. Disconnect the intake air temperature sensor electrical connector.

3. Remove the intake air temperature sensor from the air box by turning the sensor ¼ turn in the counter-clockwise direction.

To install:

4. Install the intake air temperature sensor to the air box by turning the sensor ¼ turn in the clockwise direction.

5. Connect the intake air temperature sensor electrical connector.

6. Connect the negative battery cable.

KNOCK SENSOR (KS)

LOCATION

Two Knock Sensors (KS) are located in the cylinder block valley.

REMOVAL & INSTALLATION

See Figure 84.

➡ **The forward sensor is known to the powertrain control module (PCM) as knock sensor 1. The rear sensor is known to the PCM as knock sensor 2.**

1. Perform the fuel pressure release procedure. Refer to the procedure in the Fuel section.

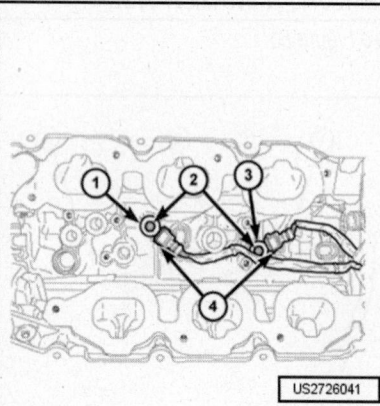

US2726041

Fig. 84 Knock sensor 1 or the forward sensor (1), mounting bolts (2), knock sensor 2 or the rear sensor (3), and the electrical connectors (4)

2. Disconnect and isolate the negative battery cable.

3. Drain the cooling system as outlined in the Engine Cooling section.

4. Remove the air cleaner housing assembly, upper and lower intake manifolds, and the oil filter housing. Refer to Lower Intake Manifold in the Engine Mechanical section.

5. Remove the electrical connector.

➡ **There may be a foam strip on the bolt threads. This foam is used only to retain the bolts to the sensors for plant assembly. It is not used as a sealant. Do not apply any adhesive, sealant, or thread locking compound to these bolts.**

6. Remove the mounting bolt and knock sensor 1 or knock sensor 2.

To install:

7. Clean the knock sensor mounting holes thoroughly.

➡ **Over or under tightening the sensor mounting bolts will affect knock sensor performance, possibly causing improper spark control. Always use the specified torque when installing the knock sensors. The torque specification for the knock sensor bolt is less than the typical 8 mm bolt.**

➡ **There may be a foam strip on the bolt threads. This foam is used only to retain the bolts to the sensors for plant assembly. It is not used as a sealant. Do not apply any adhesive, sealant, or thread locking compound to these bolts.**

8. Install the knock sensor 1 or knock sensor 2 with the mounting bolt. Tighten the mounting bolt to 16 ft. lbs. (22 Nm).

9. Connect the electrical connector.

10. Install the oil filter housing, upper and lower intake manifolds, and air cleaner housing assembly.

11. If removed, install the oil filter and fill the engine crankcase with the proper oil to the correct level. Refer to Specifications.

12. Connect the negative battery cable.

13. Fill the cooling system.

14. Operate the engine until it reaches normal operating temperature.

15. Check the cooling system for correct fluid level.

US2748730

Fig. 85 Rotate the MAP sensor ¼ turn counterclockwise and pull the sensor straight up and out of the upper intake manifold

MANIFOLD ABSOLUTE PRESSURE (MAP) SENSOR

LOCATION

The Manifold Air Pressure (MAP) sensor is attached directly to the upper intake manifold.

REMOVAL & INSTALLATION

See Figure 85.

1. Disconnect the negative battery cable. Refer to Battery in the Engine Electrical section.

2. Remove the engine cover. Refer to Left Cylinder Head Removal in the Engine Mechanical section.

3. Unlock and disconnect the electrical connector from the MAP sensor.

4. Rotate the MAP sensor ¼ turn counterclockwise and pull the sensor straight up and out of the upper intake manifold.

5. The MAP sensor O-ring can be reused if it is not damaged.

To install:

6. Apply a small amount of engine oil to the sensor O-ring.

7. Install the MAP sensor into the upper intake manifold and rotate ¼ turn clockwise.

8. Connect and lock the electrical connector to the sensor.

9. Install the engine cover.

10. Connect the negative battery cable.

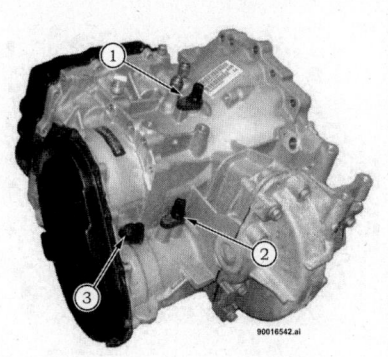

Fig. 86 Input speed sensor (1), output speed sensor (2), and transfer speed sensor (3)

OUTPUT SPEED SENSOR (OSS)

LOCATION

See Figure 86.

REMOVAL & INSTALLATION

1. Disconnect the output speed sensor electrical connector.
2. Remove the output speed sensor bolt.
3. Pull up and remove the output speed sensor.

To install:

4. Install a new O-ring (2) onto the output speed sensor.
5. Install the output speed sensor into the case.

6. Install the output speed sensor bolt. Tighten the bolt to 106 inch lbs. (12 Nm).
7. Connect the output speed sensor electrical connector.

THROTTLE POSITION SENSOR (TPS)

LOCATION

The TPS is an integral part of the throttle body.

REMOVAL & INSTALLATION

The throttle position sensor is not serviceable as a standalone part. If the throttle position sensor requires replacement, replace the throttle body. Refer to the Fuel section.

FUEL   GASOLINE FUEL INJECTION SYSTEM

FUEL SYSTEM SERVICE PRECAUTIONS

> ⁜ **CAUTION**
>
> The fuel system is under constant high pressure even with the engine off. Until the fuel pressure has been properly relieved from the system, do not attempt to open the fuel system. Do not smoke or use open flames/sparks when servicing the fuel system. Wear protective clothing and eye protection. Make sure the area in which the vehicle is being serviced is in a well-ventilated area and free of flames/sparks.

> ⁜ **CAUTION**
>
> Risk of poisoning from inhaling and swallowing fuel. Pour fuel only into appropriately marked OSHA approved containers. Wear protective clothing. There is a risk of injury to eyes and skin from contact with fuel.

- To avoid the possibility of fire and personal injury, always disconnect the negative battery cable unless the repair or test procedure requires that battery voltage be applied.
- Always relieve the fuel system pressure prior to disconnecting any fuel system component (injector, fuel rail, pressure regulator, etc.), fitting or fuel line connection. Exercise extreme caution whenever

relieving fuel system pressure to avoid exposing skin, face and eyes to fuel spray. Please be advised that fuel under pressure may penetrate the skin or any part of the body that it contacts.

- Always place a shop towel or cloth around the fitting or connection prior to loosening to absorb any excess fuel due to spillage. Ensure that all fuel spillage (should it occur) is quickly removed from engine surfaces. Ensure that all fuel soaked cloths or towels are deposited into a suitable waste container.
- Always keep a dry chemical (Class B) fire extinguisher near the work area.
- Always use a back-up wrench when loosening and tightening fuel line connection fittings. This will prevent unnecessary stress and torsion to fuel line piping.
- Always replace worn fuel fitting O-rings with new Do not substitute fuel hose or equivalent where fuel pipe is installed.

Before servicing the vehicle, make sure to also refer to the precautions in the beginning of the Routan section as well.

FUEL SYSTEM PRESSURE RELEASE PROCEDURE

See Figure 87.

1. Refer to Precautions.

> ⁜ **CAUTION**
>
> The fuel system is under constant high pressure even with engine off. Until the fuel pressure has been properly relieved from the system, do not attempt to open the fuel system. Do not smoke or use open flames/sparks when servicing the fuel system. Wear protective clothing and eye protection. Make sure the area in which the vehicle is being serviced is in a well-ventilated area and free of flames/sparks.

A separate fuel pump relay is no longer used. A circuit within the Totally Integrated Power Module (TIPM) is used to control the electric fuel pump located within the fuel pump module.

2. Remove the fuel fill cap.

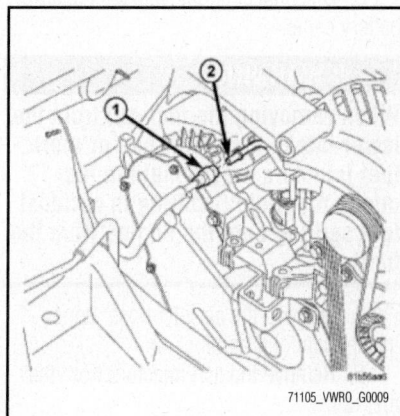

Fig. 87 Fuel line quick connect fitting (1) and fuel

3. Disconnect the fuel pump module electrical connector.

4. Start and run the engine until it stalls.

5. Attempt restarting engine until it will no longer run.

6. Turn the ignition key to the OFF position.

7. Place a rag or towel below the fuel line quick-connect fitting at the fuel rail.

8. Disconnect quick-connect fitting at the fuel rail.

➡️**After servicing the fuel system, one or more Diagnostic Trouble Codes (DTCs) may have been stored in the PCM memory due to disconnecting fuel pump module circuit. A diagnostic scan tool must be used to erase a DTC.**

FUEL FILTER

REMOVAL & INSTALLATION

The fuel filter is not serviceable as a standalone part. The fuel filter is integral to the fuel pump module located in the fuel tank.

FUEL INJECTORS

REMOVAL & INSTALLATION

1. Refer to Precautions.

❊ CAUTION

The fuel system is under constant pressure even with the engine off. Before servicing the fuel rail, the fuel system pressure must be released.

2. Release the fuel system pressure. Refer to Fuel System Pressure Release Procedure.

3. Disconnect and isolate the negative battery cable.

❊ WARNING

When removing the fuel rail from the lower intake manifold, one or more fuel injectors may remain in the intake manifold resulting in residual fuel spilling onto the engine from the fuel rail.

4. Remove the air inlet hose, upper intake manifold, and fuel rail.

5. Remove the fuel injectors from the fuel rail.

6. Remove the fuel injectors from the lower intake manifold.

7. Remove and discard all fuel injector O-ring seals.

To install:

8. Lubricate the new O-ring seals lightly with engine oil and install them on the fuel injector.

9. Install the fuel injectors to the fuel rail.

10. Install the fuel rail, upper inlet manifold and air inlet hose.

11. Connect the negative battery cable.

12. Start the engine and check for leaks.

FUEL PUMP MODULE

REMOVAL & INSTALLATION

See Figures 88 through 90.

Special tool: Fuel pump lock ring wrench #9340

1. Refer to Precautions.

2. Remove the fuel tank. Refer to Fuel Tank, removal & installation.

3. Disconnect the wiring harness electrical connector from the fuel pump module.

4. Disconnect the fuel line quick-connect from the fuel pump module.

❊❊ WARNING

Clean the area around the fuel pump module prior to removal. Make sure this area is free of dirt. Failure to clean the fuel pump area prior to removal may cause dirt to get into the fuel system causing damage to the fuel system and/or engine.

5. Clean the area around the fuel pump module with a suitable cleaner and dry with low pressure filtered compressed air.

6. Install the fuel pump module lock ring tool #9340 and turn counterclockwise

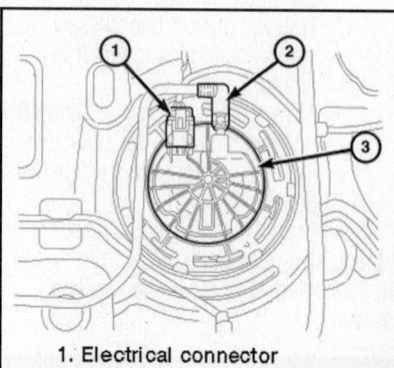

1. Electrical connector
2. Fuel line
3. Fuel pump module

36543_CARA_G0258

Fig. 88 Remove the connectors from the fuel pump module

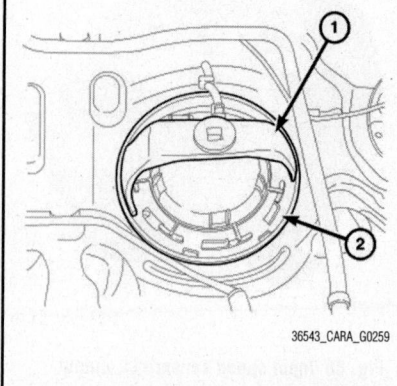

36543_CARA_G0259

Fig. 89 Install the fuel pump module lock ring tool 9340 (1) and turn counter-clockwise to remove the fuel pump module lock ring (2)

to remove the fuel pump module lock ring.

7. Remove the fuel pump module.

To install:

8. Install a new fuel pump module O-ring seal to the fuel tank.

❊❊ WARNING

The fuel pump module must be installed correctly to prevent damage to the fuel pump module.

9. Line the fuel pump module mounting tab up with the arrow on the fuel tank.

10. Install the fuel pump module lock ring.

11. Install the fuel pump module lock ring tool #9340 and turn clockwise until the fuel pump module lock ring is seated and locked into place.

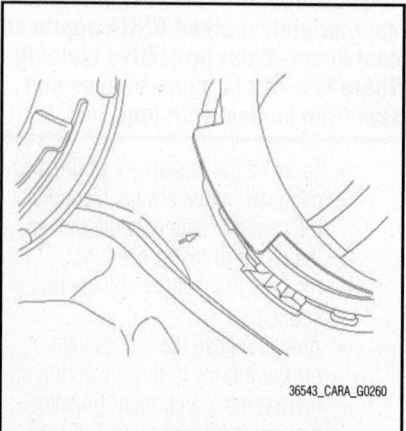

36543_CARA_G0260

Fig. 90 Line up the fuel pump module mounting tab with the arrow on the fuel tank

12. Connect the fuel line quick-connect to the fuel pump module.

13. Connect the wiring harness electrical connector to the fuel pump module.

14. Install the fuel tank.

FUEL TANK

DRAINING

1. Refer to Precautions.

➡**The tank cannot be drained at the fuel fill cap due to a one-way check valve installed into the fuel fill fitting at the tank.**

2. Disconnect the negative battery cable.

3. Raise and support the vehicle.

4. Remove the fuel tank. Refer to Fuel Tank.

5. Remove the fuel pump module. Refer to Fuel Pump Module.

6. Position a ⅜-inch hose into the fuel pump module opening of the fuel tank.

7. Attach the opposite end of this hose to an OSHA-approved fuel storage tank.

8. Drain the fuel from the fuel tank using approved siphoning equipment, store the drained fuel in an OSHA-approved fuel storage tank.

REMOVAL & INSTALLATION

See Figures 91 through 94.

❋❋ **CAUTION**

The fuel system is under constant pressure even with engine OFF. Before servicing any part of the fuel system, the pressure must be released.

1. Refer to Precautions.

2. Remove the fuel cap.

3. Release the fuel system pressure. Refer to the Fuel System Pressure Release Procedure.

4. Raise and safely support the vehicle.

5. Loosen and reposition the fuel fill hose clamp and then remove the fuel fill hose from the fuel tank.

6. Disconnect the body wiring harness electrical connector from the fuel pump.

7. Disconnect the fuel line quick connect fitting and the evaporator emission line quick connect fitting.

8. Disconnect the electrical connector from the Evaporative System Integrity Monitor (ESIM) switch.

9. Disconnect the fuel fill vapor hose from the fuel tank control valve hose.

10. Disconnect the fuel fill vapor hose from the ESIM switch.

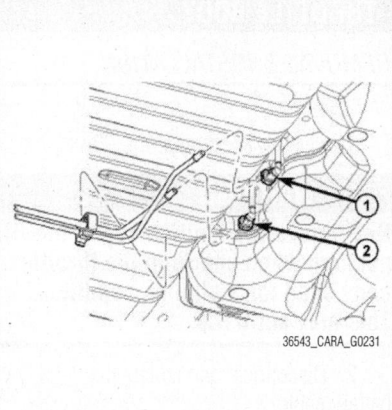

Fig. 91 Disconnect the fuel line quick connect fitting (1) and the evaporator emission line quick connect fitting (2)

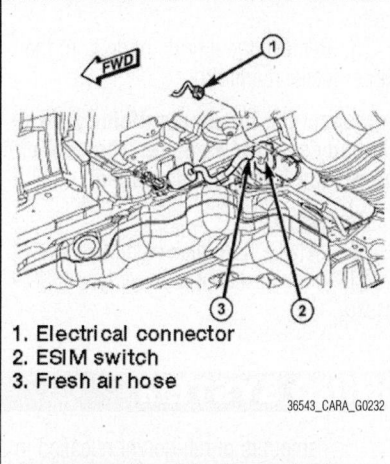

1. Electrical connector
2. ESIM switch
3. Fresh air hose

Fig. 92 Location of the Evaporative System Integrity Monitor (ESIM) switch

❋❋ **WARNING**

Support the fuel tank with a transmission jack, or equivalent. Use straps to secure the fuel tank to the jack. Failure to properly support and secure the fuel tank during removal may cause fuel to spill or the fuel tank to fall from the jack assembly.

11. Remove the fuel tank strap bolts and the straps.

12. Remove the EVAP canister bracket bolt.

13. Lower the fuel tank.

14. Disconnect the EVAP line quick connect fitting from the EVAP canister fitting.

15. Disconnect the EVAP canister quick connect fitting from the fuel tank control valve.

16. Remove the EVAP canister.

17. Remove the fuel pump module. Refer to Fuel Pump Module, removal & installation.

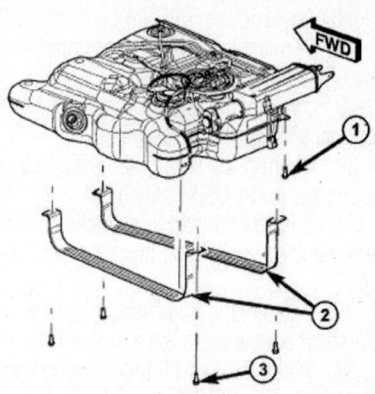

1. Vapor canister bracket bolt
2. Fuel tank straps
3. Fuel tank strap bolts

Fig. 93 Loosen the fuel tank strap bolts and remove the vapor canister bracket bolt

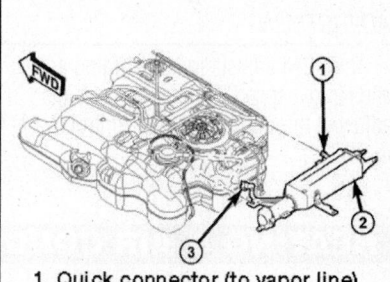

1. Quick connector (to vapor line)
2. EVAP vapor canister
3. Quick connector (to fuel tank control valve)

Fig. 94 Evaporative Emissions (EVAP) canister location

18. Remove all the fuel and EVAP lines from the fuel tank.

19. Drain any remaining fuel into an approved fuel storage container.

To install:

20. Install all the fuel and vapor lines to the fuel tank.

21. Install the fuel pump module.

22. Install the EVAP canister.

23. Connect the EVAP canister quick connect fitting to the fuel tank control valve.

24. Connect the EVAP line quick connect fitting to the EVAP canister fitting.

25. Position the fuel tank onto a transmission jack, or equivalent and raise the fuel tank into vehicle position.

26. Install the EVAP canister bracket bolt. Tighten to 41 ft. lbs. (55 Nm).

27. Install the fuel tank straps and bolts. Tighten to 41 ft. lbs. (55 Nm).

28. Connect the fuel fill vapor hose to the ESIM switch.

29. Connect the fuel fill vapor hose to the fuel tank control valve hose.

30. Connect the wiring harness electrical connector to the ESIM switch.

31. Connect the fuel line quick connect fitting and the EVAP line quick connect fitting.

32. Connect the body wiring harness electrical connector to the fuel pump.

33. Install the fuel-fill tube hose to the fuel tank.

34. Position and tighten the fuel fill hose clamp at the fuel tank.

35. Fill the fuel tank and install the fuel cap.

36. Use the scan tool auto shutdown fuel system test to pressurize the fuel system. Check for leaks.

IDLE SPEED

ADJUSTMENT

The PCM adjusts ignition timing and engine idle speed. Engine idle speed is adjusted through the idle air control motor.

THROTTLE BODY

REMOVAL & INSTALLATION

See Figure 95.

1. Refer to Precautions.

❊❊ WARNING

Never have the ignition key in the ON position when checking the throttle body shaft for a binding condition. This may set DTCs.

2. Disconnect and isolate the negative battery cable.

3. Remove the resonator.

4. Disconnect the Electronic Throttle Control (ETC) electrical connector and disengage the clip on the throttle body.

5. Remove the 4 throttle body mounting bolts.

6. Remove the throttle body from the upper intake manifold.

➥**Inspect the intake manifold-to-throttle body seal for damage. The seal can be reused if it is not damaged.**

To install:

7. Install a new intake manifold-to-throttle body gasket, if replacement is necessary.

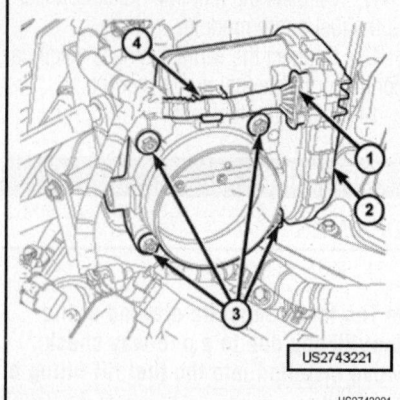

US2743221

Fig. 95 ETC electrical connector (1), ETC (2), throttle body mounting bolts (3), and ETC harness clip (4)

8. Clean the mating surfaces of the throttle body and intake manifold.

9. Position the throttle body to the intake manifold.

10. Install the 4 throttle body mounting bolts and tighten in a criss-cross sequence to 62 inch lbs. (7 Nm).

11. Connect the ETC electrical connector and secure the ETC harness to the clip.

12. Install the resonator and tighten the clamps to 35 inch lbs. (4 Nm).

13. Connect the negative battery cable.

HEATING & AIR CONDITIONING SYSTEM

PRECAUTIONS

- The A/C system contains refrigerant under high pressure. Repairs should only be performed by qualified service personnel. Serious or fatal injury may result from improper service procedures.
- Avoid breathing the refrigerant and refrigerant oil vapor or mist. Exposure may irritate the eyes, nose, and/or throat. Wear eye protection when servicing the A/C refrigerant system. Serious eye injury can result from direct contact with the refrigerant. If eye contact occurs, seek medical attention immediately.
- Do not expose the refrigerant to open flame. Poisonous gas is created when refrigerant is burned. An electronic leak detector is recommended. Serious or fatal injury may result from improper service procedures.
- If accidental A/C system discharge occurs, ventilate the work area before resuming service. Large

amounts of refrigerant released in a closed work area will displace the oxygen and cause suffocation and serious or fatal injury.
- The evaporation rate of R-134a refrigerant at average temperature and altitude is extremely high. As a result, anything that comes in contact with the refrigerant will freeze. Always protect the skin or delicate objects from direct contact with the refrigerant.
- The R-134a service equipment or the vehicle refrigerant system should not be pressure tested or leak tested with compressed air. Some mixtures of air and R-134a have been shown to be combustible at elevated pressures. These mixtures are potentially dangerous, and may result in fire or explosion causing property damage and serious or fatal injury.
- The engine cooling system is designed to develop internal pressures up to 145 kilopascals (21 pounds per square inch). Do not

remove or loosen the coolant pressure cap, cylinder block drain plugs, radiator drain, radiator hoses, heater hoses, or hose clamps while the engine cooling system is hot and under pressure. Allow the vehicle to cool for a minimum of 15 minutes before opening the cooling system for service. Failure to observe this warning can result in serious burns from the heated engine coolant.

Refrigerant Cautions

- Never add R-12 to a refrigerant system designed to use R-134a. Do not use R-12 equipment or parts on an R-134a A/C system. These refrigerants are not compatible and damage to the A/C system will result.
- Never use R-12 refrigerant oil in an A/C system designed to use R-134a refrigerant oil. These refrigerant oils are not compatible and damage to the A/C system will result.
- The use of A/C system sealers may result in damage to A/C refrigerant recovery/evacuation/recharging equipment and/or A/C system. Many federal, state/provincial

and local regulations prohibit the recharge of A/C systems with known leaks. Volkswagen recommends the detection of A/C system leaks through the use of approved leak detectors and fluorescent leak detection dyes. Vehicles found with A/C system sealers should be treated as contaminated and replacement of the entire A/C refrigerant system is recommended. A/C systems found to be contaminated with A/C system sealers, A/C stop-leak products or seal conditioners voids the warranty for the A/C system.

• Recover the refrigerant before opening any fitting or connection. Open the fittings with caution, even after the system has been discharged. Never open or loosen a connection before recovering the refrigerant.

• If equipped, do not remove the secondary retention clip from any spring-lock coupler connection while the refrigerant system is under pressure. Recover the refrigerant before removing the secondary retention clip. Open the fittings with caution, even after the system has been discharged. Never open or loosen a connection before recovering the refrigerant.

• The internal parts of the A/C system will remain stable as long as moisture-free refrigerant and refrigerant oil is used. Abnormal amounts of dirt, moisture or air can upset the chemical stability. This may cause operational troubles or even serious damage if present in more than very small quantities. Before disconnecting a component,

• Clean the outside of the fittings thoroughly to prevent contamination from entering the refrigerant system. Keep service tools and the work area clean. Do not open the refrigerant system or uncap a replacement component until you are ready to service the system. Immediately after disconnecting a component from the refrigerant system, seal the open fittings with a cap or plug. This will prevent contamination from entering the A/C system.

• Refrigerant oil will absorb moisture from the atmosphere if left uncapped. Do not open a container of refrigerant oil until you are ready to use it. Replace the cap on the oil container immediately after using. Store the refrigerant oil only in a clean, airtight, and moisture-free container.

• Do not overcharge the refrigerant system. Overcharging will cause excessive compressor head pressure and can cause compressor noise and A/C system failure.

BLOWER MOTOR

REMOVAL & INSTALLATION
See Figure 96.

✳✳ CAUTION

Disable the airbag system before attempting any steering wheel, steering column, or instrument panel component diagnosis or service. Disconnect and isolate the negative battery (ground) cable, then wait two minutes for the airbag system capacitor to discharge before performing further diagnosis or service. This is the only sure way to disable the airbag system. Failure to take the proper precautions may result in accidental airbag deployment and possible serious or fatal injury.

1. Disconnect and isolate the negative battery cable.
2. If equipped, remove the silencer from underneath the passenger side of the instrument panel.
3. Disconnect the wire harness connector from the blower motor.
4. Disengage the HVAC wire harness from the mounting bracket.
5. Remove the three screws that secure the blower motor to the front HVAC housing and remove the blower motor.

To install:

6. Position the blower motor into the front HVAC housing and install the three retaining screws. Tighten the screws to 10 inch lbs. (1.2 Nm).
7. Engage the wire harness to the mounting bracket.
8. Connect the wire harness connector to the blower motor.

9. If equipped, install the silencer underneath the passenger side of the instrument panel.
10. Reconnect the negative battery cable.

HEATER CORE

REMOVAL & INSTALLATION
See Figure 97.

✳✳ CAUTION

Disable the airbag system before attempting any steering wheel, steering column, or instrument panel component diagnosis or service. Disconnect and isolate the negative battery (ground) cable, then wait two minutes for the airbag system capacitor to discharge before performing further diagnosis or service. This is the only sure way to disable the airbag system. Failure to take the proper precautions may result in accidental airbag deployment and possible serious or fatal injury.

✳✳ CAUTION

Review the applicable warnings and cautions for this system before performing the following operation.

✳✳ WARNING

The heater core tubes are not serviced separately from the heater core. The heater core tubes should not be repositioned, loosened, or removed from the heater core. Failure to follow this warning may result in a coolant leak and possible serious or fatal injury.

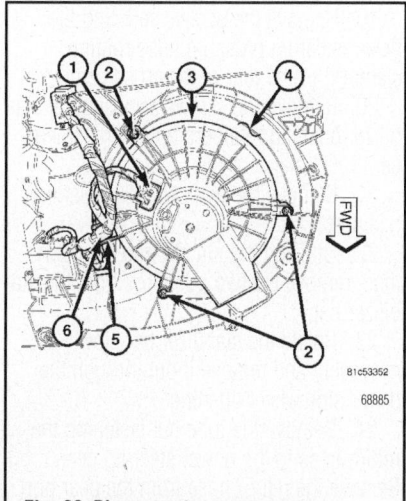

81c53352
68885

Fig. 96 Blower motor components

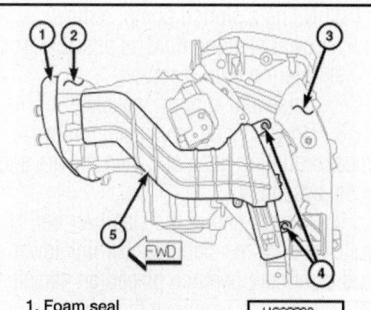

1. Foam seal
2. Front of the HVAC housing
3. Driver side of the air distribution housing
4. Heater core cover-to-air distribution housing screws (qty: 2)
5. Heater core cover

US68823

Fig. 97 Heater core cover replacement

1. Refer to the Precautions section

2. Disconnect and isolate the negative battery cable. Refer to Battery in the Engine Electrical section.

3. Drain the engine cooling system. Refer to Coolant in the Engine Cooling section.

4. Remove the left side instrument panel silencer, if equipped.

5. Remove the foam seal from the front of the HVAC housing.

6. Disengage the shift lever cable from the retaining clip located at the bottom of the heater core cover.

7. Remove the two screws that secure the heater core cover to the left side of air distribution housing.

8. Rotate and tilt the heater core cover as necessary to disengage the retaining tab that secures the cover to the front of the HVAC housing, near the foam seal and remove the cover.

➡**Take the proper precautions to protect the carpeting from engine coolant.**

Have absorbent toweling readily available to clean up any spills.

9. Remove the two clamps that secure the heater tubes to the heater core.

10. Disconnect the heater core tubes from the heater core and remove and discard the O-ring seals.

11. Install plugs in, or tape over the opened heater core tubes and heater core ports.

12. Pull the heater core out of the driver side of the air distribution housing—carefully.

To install:

➡**If the foam seal around the heater core is deformed or damaged, it must be replaced.**

13. Install the heater core into the driver side of the air distribution housing carefully.

14. Remove the tape or plugs from the heater core tubes and heater core ports.

15. Lubricate new rubber O-ring seals with clean engine coolant and install them onto the heater core tubes. Use only the

specified O-ring as they are made of a special material for the engine cooling system.

16. Connect the heater core tubes to the heater core.

17. Install the two clamps that secure the heater core tubes to the heater core. Tighten the screws on the clamps to 15 inch lbs. (1.7 Nm).

18. Position the heater core cover to the HVAC housing and engage the retaining tab that secures the cover to the housing, near the foam seal.

19. Install the heater core cover onto the air distribution housing and install the two retaining screws. Tighten the screws to 10 inch lbs. (1.2 Nm).

20. Engage the shift lever cable to the retaining clip located at the bottom of the heater core cover.

21. Install the left side instrument panel silencer, if equipped.

22. Connect the negative battery cable.

23. If the heater core is being replaced, flush the cooling system.

24. Refill the engine cooling system.

STEERING

POWER STEERING GEAR

REMOVAL & INSTALLATION

See Figures 98 through 100.

2. Place the front wheels of the vehicle in the STRAIGHT-AHEAD position.

3. Install the steering wheel holder locking steering wheel in the STRAIGHT-AHEAD position.

4. Remove the negative (-) battery cable from battery and isolate the cable.

5. Remove the cap from power steering fluid reservoir.

6. Using a siphon pump, remove as much power steering fluid as possible from power steering fluid reservoir.

7. Raise and support vehicle.

8. On each side of vehicle, remove wheel mounting nuts, and then the tire and wheel assembly.

9. At each end of the stabilizer bar, while holding the stabilizer bar link lower stud stationary (wrench placed on machined flats on the stud), remove the nut securing the link to the stabilizer bar.

10. If the outer tie rods need to be transferred to new gear, loosen tie rod jam nut on both sides of the vehicle.

11. On both sides of the vehicle, remove the nut attaching the outer tie rod to the knuckle by holding the rod end stud stationary while loosening and removing the nut with a wrench.

12. Release each outer tie rod end from the knuckle using a puller.

13. Remove the front engine mount through-bolt.

14. Remove the crossmember front mounting bolt.

15. Remove the four crossmember rear mounting bolts.

16. Remove the crossmember.

17. Remove the screws and push-pins securing the heat shield over the right side of the steering gear. Remove the heat shield.

18. Remove the rear engine mount.

19. Remove the screws securing the power steering pressure hose routing clamp(s) to the rear of the crossmember.

20. Remove the screws securing the stabilizer bushing retainers to the crossmember.

21. Remove the two stabilizer bushing retainers.

22. Utilizing the slit cut into the bushings, remove the two bushings from the stabilizer bar.

23. Rotate the stabilizer bar slowly as necessary and remove it out through the driver side wheel opening.

24. Remove the tube nut fastening the return hose to the power steering gear. Remove the return hose from the gear port.

25. Remove the tube nut fastening the

pressure hose to the power steering gear. Remove the pressure hose from the gear port.

26. Remove the bolts securing the steering gear to the crossmember.

27. Slide the dust shield upward exposing the pinch bolt securing the intermediate shaft extension to the steering gear shaft.

28. Remove the pinch bolt securing the intermediate shaft extension to the steering gear shaft.

29. Slide the intermediate shaft extension off the steering gear shaft.

30. Rotate the steering gear to the position shown, and then slide the steering gear out of the left wheel opening.

31. If necessary, remove the outer tie rods from the inner tie rod threads. Count how many rotations it takes to remove each outer tie rod for installation reference.

To install:

32. If necessary, install the outer tie rods onto the inner tie rod threads. As outer tie rods are installed, count out same number of rotations as were counted on tie rod removal. This will get the toe setting somewhat close to specification before the vehicle is aligned at end of this procedure. Snug the tie rod jam nuts on both ends of gear. Do not tighten at this time. Tighten tie rod jam nuts to specification while performing wheel alignment at end of this procedure.

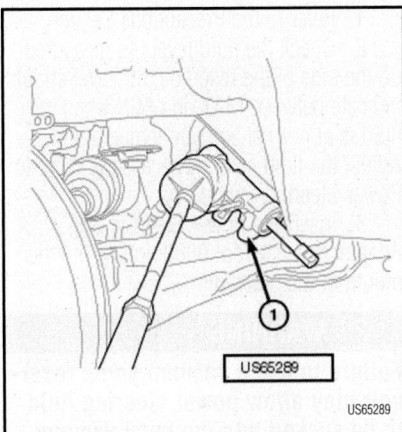

Fig. 98 Rotate the steering gear to the position shown, and then slide the steering gear out of the left wheel opening

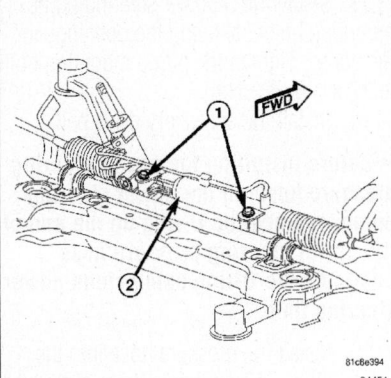

Fig. 100 Center the steering gear (2) mounting bosses over the mounting holes in the crossmember and install two steering gear mounting bolts (1).

33. Install the power steering gear carefully through left wheel opening using the reverse procedure of how it was removed, then set it up into mounted position.

34. Find the power steering gear's center of travel, then match the intermediate shaft extension with that on the steering gear shaft. Slide the extension onto the steering gear shaft.

35. Install the pinch bolt securing the intermediate shaft extension to extension shaft. Tighten the pinch bolt to 31 ft. lbs. (42 Nm).

36. Slide the dust shield down over the pinch bolt and steering gear shaft.

37. Center the steering gear mounting bosses over the mounting holes in the

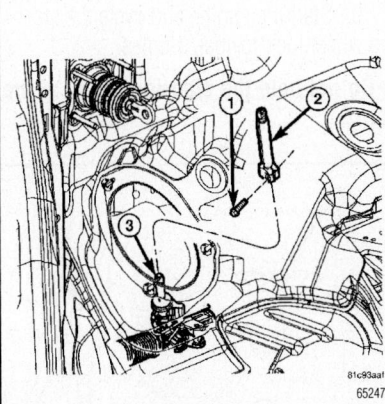

Fig. 99 Find the power steering gear's center of travel, and then match the intermediate shaft extension (2) with that on the steering gear shaft (3). Slide the extension onto the steering gear shaft. Install the pinch bolt (1) securing the intermediate shaft extension (2) to the extension shaft (3)

crossmember and install two steering gear mounting bolts. Tighten the mounting bolts to 55 ft. lbs. (75 Nm).

38. Install the return hose into the power steering gear port. Thread the return hose tube nut into the gear and tighten to 23 ft. lbs. (31 Nm).

39. Install the pressure hose into the power steering gear port. Thread the pressure hose tube nut into the gear and tighten to 23 ft. lbs. (31 Nm).

➡**Before stabilizer bar installation, inspect the cushions (bushings) and links for excessive wear, cracks, damage and distortion. Replace any pieces failing inspection.**

➡**Before installing the stabilizer bar, make sure the bar is not upside down. The stabilizer bar must be installed so that when in mounted position, the ends of the bar curve under the steering gear tie rods, up to the links.**

40. Install the stabilizer bar through the driver side wheel opening. Rotate the bar as necessary until it is centered over the suspension crossmember and the ends curve upward below the steering gear tie rods.

41. Install the two cushions (bushings) on the stabilizer bar utilizing the slit cut into the cushion sides.

42. Install the two stabilizer bushing retainers over the cushions.

43. Install the four screws securing the stabilizer bushing retainers to the crossmember. Tighten screws to 33 ft. lbs. (45 Nm).

44. Position the power steering pressure hose routing clamp(s) on the rear of the crossmember. Install and tighten the screw(s) to 71 inch lbs. (8 Nm).

45. Install the rear engine mount.

46. Position the heat shield over the steering gear. Install the mounting screws and push-pins. Tighten the screws to 71 inch lbs. (8 Nm).

47. Position the crossmember in the engine compartment and install the mounting bolts. Tighten the forward mounting bolt to 83 ft. lbs. (113 Nm). Tighten the rear mounting bolts at the suspension crossmember to 41 ft. lbs. (55 Nm).

48. Install the front engine mount through-bolt. Tighten bolt to 42 ft. lbs. (57 Nm).

49. On each side of vehicle, attach the outer tie rod to the knuckle. Start a NEW nut onto the outer tie rod stud. While holding the stud stationary, tighten the nut using a wrench. Using a crowfoot wrench on a torque wrench, tighten the nut to 55 ft. lbs. (75 Nm). Then, tighten nut an additional 245°turn after that torque is met.

50. Attach the stabilizer bar link at each end of the stabilizer bar. At each link, install and tighten the nut while holding the stabilizer bar link lower stud stationary. Tighten the nuts to 65 ft. lbs. (88 Nm).

51. On each side of vehicle, install tire and wheel assembly.

52. Tighten wheel mounting nuts in a star pattern to 100 ft. lbs. (135 Nm).

53. Lower the vehicle.

54. Connect the negative (-) battery cable on the negative battery post.

55. Remove the steering wheel holder.

56. Fill and bleed the power steering system.

57. Inspect for leaks

58. Perform wheel alignment, setting toe to specifications.

POWER STEERING PUMP

REMOVAL & INSTALLATION

See Figure 101.

✳✳ CAUTION

Power steering fluid, engine parts, and the exhaust system may be extremely hot if the engine has been running. Do not start the engine with any loose or disconnected hoses. Do not allow the hoses to touch a hot exhaust manifold or catalyst.

✳✳ CAUTION

The fluid level should be checked with the engine OFF to prevent personal injury from moving parts.

❋❋ WARNING

When the system is open, cap all open ends of the hoses, power steering pump fittings, or power steering gear ports to prevent entry of foreign material into the components.

❋❋ WARNING

When servicing power steering components do not pinch off the power steering hoses in any way to stop the fluid flow. Damage to the hoses may result.

1. Refer to the Precautions.
2. Remove the negative (-) battery cable from the battery and isolate the cable.
3. Remove the cap from the power steering fluid reservoir.
4. Using a siphon pump, remove as much power steering fluid as possible from the power steering fluid reservoir.
5. Remove the clamp, and then remove the supply hose from the pump.
6. Remove the tube nut and remove the pressure hose from the pump.
7. Remove the accessory drive belt. Refer to Accessory Drive Belts in the Engine Mechanical section.
8. Remove the 3 pump mounting bolts through the pump pulley.
9. Remove the power steering pump from the engine compartment.
10. Remove the power steering pump pulley if needed.

To install:

11. Install the power steering pump pulley if it was removed.
12. Position the power steering pump on the engine.

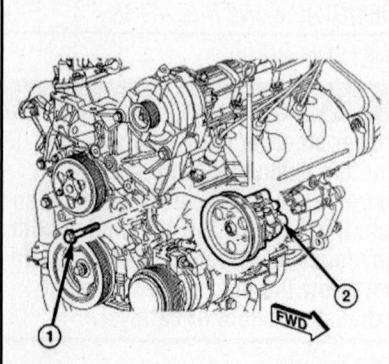

Fig. 101 Remove the pump mounting bolts (1) through the pump pulley and remove the pump (2)

13. Install the 3 power steering pump mounting bolts (1) using the openings in the pulley. Tighten the pump mounting bolts to 17 ft. lbs. (23 Nm).
14. Install the accessory drive belt.

➡**Before installing the power steering pressure hose on the power steering pump, replace the O-ring on the end of the power steering pressure hose. Lubricate the O-ring using clean power steering fluid.**

15. Install the pressure hose into the pump fitting. Thread the pressure hose tube nut into the pump and tighten to 23 ft. lbs. (31 Nm).
16. Slide the fluid supply hose onto the pump fitting and install the clamp securing it in place.
17. Connect the negative (-) battery cable on the negative battery post.
18. Fill and bleed the power steering system.
19. Inspect for leaks

BLEEDING

See Figure 102.

❋❋ CAUTION

Fluid level should be checked with the engine OFF to prevent personal injury from moving parts and to assure an accurate fluid level reading.

❋❋ CAUTION

Volkswagen genuine parts power steering fluid + 4 or Volkswagen genuine parts ATF+4 automatic transmission fluid is to be used in the power steering system. Both fluids have the same material standard specifications (MS-9602). No other power steering or automatic transmission fluid is to be used in the system. Damage may result to the power steering pump and system if another fluid is used. Do not overfill the system.

❋❋ WARNING

If the air is not purged from the power steering system correctly, pump failure could result.

Special tool used: Power Steering Cap Adapter #9688

➡**Be sure the vacuum tool used in the following procedure is clean and free of any fluids.**

1. Refer to the Precautions Section.
2. Check the fluid level. As measured on the side of the reservoir, the level should indicate between MAX and MIN when the fluid is at normal ambient temperature. Adjust the fluid level as necessary. Refer to Power Steering Fluid Level.
3. Insert the Power Steering Cap Adapter Special Tool 9688 tightly into the mouth of the reservoir.

❋❋ WARNING

Failure to use a vacuum pump reservoir may allow power steering fluid to be sucked into the hand vacuum pump.

4. Attach a hand vacuum with the reservoir attached, to the Power Steering Cap Adapter.

❋❋ WARNING

Do not run the vehicle while vacuum is applied to the power steering system. Damage to the power steering pump can occur.

➡**When performing the following step make sure the vacuum level is maintained during the entire time period.**

5. Using a hand vacuum pump, apply 20–25 inches Hg (68–85 kPa) of vacuum to the system for a minimum of 3 minutes.
6. Release the vacuum slowly and remove the Special Tools.
7. Adjust the fluid level as necessary.
8. Repeat above steps until the fluid no longer drops when vacuum is applied.
9. Start the engine and cycle the steering wheel lock-to-lock 3 times.

➡**Do not hold the steering wheel at the stops.**

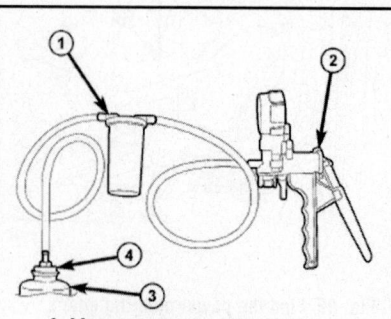

1. Vacuum pump reservoir
2. Hand vacuum pump
3. Reservoir
4. Power steering cap adaptor

36543_DAKO_G0210

Fig. 102 Hand Vacuum Pump, Special Tool C-4207 illustrated

10. Stop the engine and check for leaks at all connections.

11. Check for any signs of air in the reservoir and check the fluid level. If air is present, repeat the procedure as necessary.

✳ WARNING

Do not run a vehicle with foamy fluid for an extended period. This may cause pump damage.

FLUID FILL PROCEDURE

✳ CAUTION

Fluid level should be checked with the engine off to prevent personal injury from moving parts and to

assure an accurate fluid level reading.

✳ CAUTION

Volkswagen genuine parts power steering fluid + 4 or Volkswagen genuine parts ATF+4 automatic transmission fluid is to be used in the power steering system. Both fluids have the same material standard specifications (MS-9602). No other power steering or automatic transmission fluid is to be used in the system. Damage may result to the power steering pump and system if another fluid is used. Do not overfill the system.

➡**Although not required at specific intervals, the fluid level may be checked periodically. Check the fluid level anytime there is a system noise or fluid leak suspected.**

Power Steering Reservoir

The power steering fluid level can be viewed through the side of the power steering fluid reservoir. Compare the fluid level to the markings on the side of the reservoir. When the fluid is at normal ambient temperature, approximately 70°F to 80°F (21°C to 27°C), the fluid level should read between the MAX and MIN markings. When the fluid is hot, fluid level is allowed to read up to the MAX line.

SUSPENSION

PRECAUTIONS

➡**Volkswagen does not manufacture any vehicles or replacement parts that contain asbestos. Aftermarket products may or may not contain asbestos. Refer to aftermarket product packaging for product information.**

Whether or not the product contains asbestos, dust and dirt can accumulate on brake parts during normal use. Follow practices prescribed by appropriate regulations for the handling, processing and disposing of dust and debris.

✳ CAUTION

Do not remove the strut rod nut while strut assembly is installed in the vehicle or before the coil spring is compressed with a compression tool. The spring is held under high pressure.

➡**At no time when servicing a vehicle can a sheet metal screw, bolt, or other metal fastener be installed in the shock tower to take the place of an original plastic clip. It may come into contact with the strut or coil spring.**

✳ WARNING

Wheel bearing damage will result if after loosening the axle hub nut, the vehicle is rolled on the ground or the weight of the vehicle is allowed to be supported by the tires for any length of time.

✳ WARNING

Only frame contact or wheel lift hoisting equipment can be used on this vehicle. It cannot be hoisted using equipment designed to lift a vehicle by the rear axle. If this type of hoisting equipment is used, damage to rear suspension components will occur.

LOWER BALL JOINT

REMOVAL & INSTALLATION
See Figure 103.

Special tools: Ball joint press #C-4212F and Removers #8445-3 and 10140-3

1. Raise and support the vehicle.
2. Remove the wheel mounting nuts, then the tire and wheel assembly.
3. Remove the steering knuckle. Refer to Steering Knuckle.

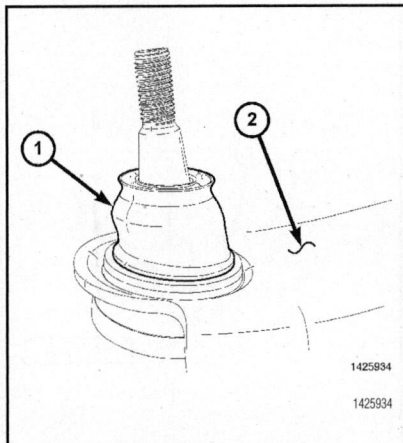

Fig. 103 Remove the ball joint dust boot (1).

FRONT SUSPENSION

4. Remove the ball joint dust boot.
5. Using the Ball Joint Press, and removers, press the ball joint out of the lower control arm.

To install:

6. Using Ball Joint Press, installer and receiver, press the ball joint into the lower control arm.
7. Install the steering knuckle, brake rotor and caliper.
8. Install the tire and wheel assembly.
9. Tighten the wheel mounting nuts to 100 ft. lbs. (135 Nm) in a star pattern.
10. Lower the vehicle.
11. Perform wheel alignment.

LOWER CONTROL ARM

REMOVAL & INSTALLATION
See Figure 104.

1. Raise and support the vehicle.
2. Remove the wheel mounting nuts, then tire and wheel assembly.
3. Remove the steering knuckle. Refer to Steering Knuckle.
4. If the left side lower control arm is being serviced, perform the following:
   a. Remove the front and rear engine mount through-bolts.
   b. Rotate the lower portion of the engine and transaxle forward.
   c. With the engine and transaxle in this position, perform the next step.
5. Remove the front bolt attaching the lower control arm to the crossmember.
6. Remove the rear bolt and nut attaching the lower control arm to the crossmember.
7. Remove the lower control arm.

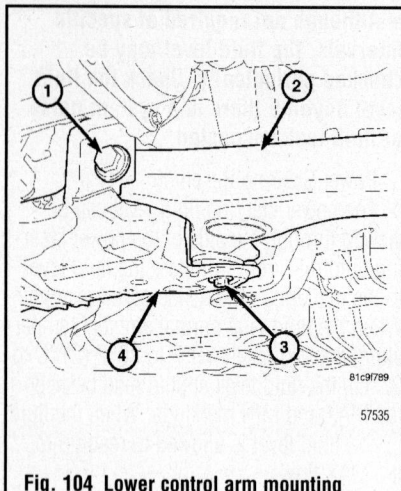

Fig. 104 Lower control arm mounting bolts (4)—front shown, rear similar

To install:

8. Position the lower control arm into the brackets on the suspension crossmember.

9. Install the front mounting bolt and rear mounting bolt and nut attaching the lower control arm to the crossmember. Do not tighten front bolt at this time. Tighten rear mounting bolt nut to 114 ft. lbs. (155 Nm).

10. If the left side lower control arm is being serviced, reinstall the front and rear engine mount through-bolts.

11. Install the steering knuckle, brake rotor and caliper.

12. Install the tire and wheel assembly.

13. Tighten the wheel mounting nuts to 100 ft. lbs. (135 Nm) in a star pattern.

14. Lower the vehicle.

15. Position the vehicle on alignment rack/drive-on hoist. Raise the hoist as necessary to access mounting bolts.

16. At curb height, tighten the front lower control arm mounting bolt to 148 ft. lbs. (200 Nm).

17. Perform wheel alignment.

CONTROL ARM BUSHING REPLACEMENT

See Figures 105 and 106.

1. Refer to Lower Control Arm.

2. Raise and support the vehicle.

3. Remove the wheel mounting nuts, and then remove the tire and wheel assembly.

4. While applying the vehicle's brakes to keep the hub from turning, loosen the drive axle nut.

5. Remove the nut from the drive axle to allow the drive axle to be pushed in.

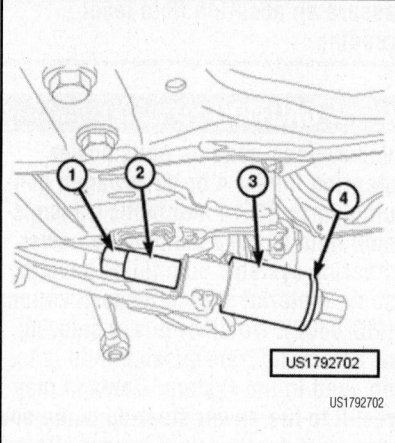

Fig. 105 Lower Control Arm Bushing Remover/Installer #10141 (1), adapters #10141-4, (2) #10141 2-1 (3), and #10141 2-2 (4), and screw assembly tool #8839

6. If the left side lower control arm bushing is being serviced, perform the following:

   a. Remove the front and rear engine mount through-bolts.

   b. Rotate the lower portion of the engine and transaxle forward.

   c. With the engine and transaxle in this position, perform the next step.

7. Remove the front bolt attaching the lower control arm to the crossmember.

8. Remove the rear bolt and nut attaching the lower control arm to the crossmember.

9. Remove the lower control arm from the engine cradle.

10. Using tool #10141 along with #8839 and adapters #10141-4, #10141 2-1, and #10141 2-2 press the bushing out of the lower control arm.

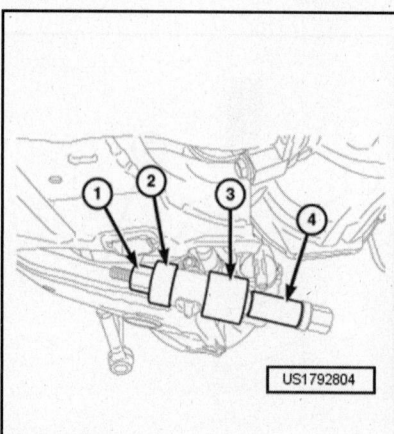

Fig. 106 Tools #10141- 1 (1), #10141-5 (2), #10141-1 (3), and #10141-3 (4)

To install:

➡**When installing the bushing in the tool #10141-1 use rubber bushing installation lube or an equivalent.**

11. Using tools #10141- 1, #10141-5, #10141-1, and #10141-3, install the bushing in the lower control arm.

12. Position the lower control arm into the brackets on the suspension crossmember.

13. Install front mounting bolt and the rear mounting bolt and nut attaching lower control arm to crossmember. Do not tighten the front bolt at this time. Tighten the rear mounting bolt nut to 114 ft. lbs. (155 Nm).

14. If the left side lower control arm is being serviced, reinstall the front and rear engine mount through-bolts.

✳✳ WARNING

Always install a new hub nut. The original hub nut is for one-time use only; discard it when removed.

15. Clean all foreign matter from the threads of the outer CV joint.

16. Install the drive axle to hub/bearing assembly nut on drive axle and securely tighten the nut.

17. Apply the vehicle's brakes to keep the hub from turning, and then tighten the hub nut to a torque of 118 ft. lbs. (160 Nm).

18. Install the tire and wheel assembly.

19. Tighten the wheel mounting nuts to 100 ft. lbs. (135 Nm) in a star pattern.

20. Lower the vehicle.

21. Position the vehicle on alignment rack/drive-on hoist. Raise the hoist as necessary to access mounting bolts.

22. At curb height, tighten the front lower control arm mounting bolt to 148 ft. lbs. (200 Nm).

23. Perform wheel alignment.

STABILIZER BAR

REMOVAL & INSTALLATION

See Figure 107.

1. Refer to Precautions.

2. Refer to Power Steering.

3. Raise and support the vehicle.

4. On each side of vehicle, remove wheel mounting nuts, and then remove the tire and wheel assembly.

5. At each end of the stabilizer bar, while holding the stabilizer bar link lower stud stationary (wrench placed on machined flats on the stud), remove the nut securing the link to the stabilizer bar.

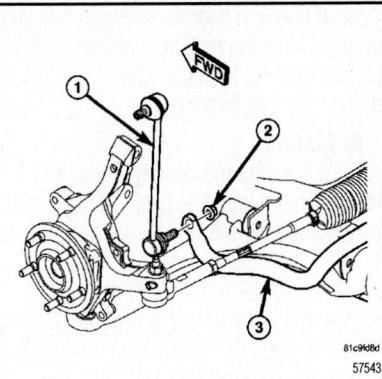

Fig. 107 At each end of the stabilizer bar, while holding the stabilizer bar link (1) lower stud stationary (wrench placed on machined flats on stud), remove the nut (2) securing the link to the stabilizer bar (3).

6. On both sides of vehicle, remove nut attaching the outer tie rod to the knuckle by holding the rod end stud stationary while loosening and removing the nut with a wrench.

7. Release each outer tie rod end from knuckle using the Ball Joint Remover #9360.

8. Remove the front engine mount through-bolt. Refer to Lower Control Arm.

9. Remove the fore-aft crossmember front mounting bolt.

10. Remove the four fore-aft crossmember rear mounting bolts.

11. Remove the fore-aft crossmember.

12. Remove the screws and push-pins securing the heat shield over the right side of the steering gear. Remove the heat shield.

13. Remove the rear engine mount.

14. Remove the fasteners securing the power steering pressure hose routing clamp(s) to the rear of the crossmember.

15. Remove the screws securing the stabilizer bushing retainers to the crossmember.

16. Remove the two stabilizer bushing retainers.

17. Utilizing the slit cut into the cushions (bushings), remove the two cushions from the stabilizer bar.

18. Slowly rotate the stabilizer bar as necessary and remove it out through the driver-side wheel opening.

To install:

➡**Before stabilizer bar installation, inspect the cushions and links for excessive wear, cracks, damage and distortion. Replace any pieces failing inspection.**

➡**Before installing the stabilizer bar, make sure the bar is not upside-down. The stabilizer bar must be installed so that when in mounted position, the ends of the bar curve under the steering gear tie rods, up to the links.**

19. Install the stabilizer bar through the driver side wheel opening. Rotate the bar as necessary until it is centered over the suspension crossmember and the ends curve upward below the steering gear tie rods.

20. Install the two bushings on the stabilizer bar utilizing the slit cut into the bushing sides.

21. Install the two stabilizer bushing retainers over the bushings.

22. Install the four screws securing the stabilizer bushing retainers to the crossmember. Tighten screws to 33 ft. lbs. (45 Nm).

23. Position the power steering pressure hose routing clamp(s) on the rear of the crossmember. Install and tighten the screw(s) to 71 inch lbs. (8 Nm).

24. Install the rear engine mount.

25. Position the heat shield over the steering gear. Install the mounting screws and push-pins. Tighten the screws to 71 inch lbs. (8 Nm).

26. Position the fore-aft crossmember in the engine compartment and install the mounting bolts. Tighten the forward mounting bolt to 83 ft. lbs. (113 Nm). Tighten the rear mounting bolts at the suspension crossmember to 41 ft. lbs. (55 Nm).

27. Install the front engine mount through-bolt. Tighten the bolt to 42 ft. lbs. (57 Nm).

28. On each side of the vehicle, attach the outer tie rod to the knuckle. Start a NEW nut onto the outer tie rod stud. While holding the stud stationary, tighten the nut using a wrench. Using a crowfoot wrench on a torque wrench, tighten the nut to 55 ft. lbs. (75 Nm).

29. Attach the stabilizer bar link at each end of the stabilizer bar. At each link, install and tighten the nut while holding the stabilizer bar link lower stud stationary. Tighten the nuts to 65 ft. lbs. (88 Nm).

30. On each side of vehicle, install the tire and wheel assembly.

31. Install the tire and wheel assembly and tighten the wheel mounting nuts in proper sequence to 100 ft. lbs. (135 Nm).

32. Lower the vehicle.

STEERING KNUCKLE

REMOVAL & INSTALLATION

See Figures 108 through 112.

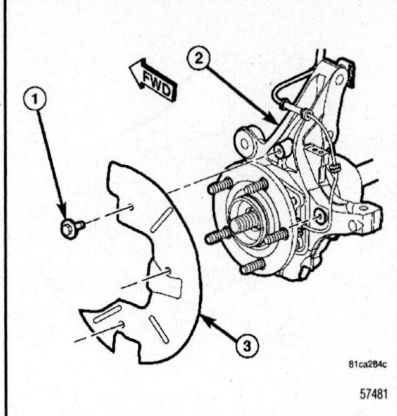

Fig. 108 Remove the screws (1) fastening the brake shield (3) to the knuckle (2), then remove the brake shield.

1. Raise and support the vehicle.

2. Remove the wheel mounting nuts, then tire and wheel assembly.

3. With aid of a helper applying brakes to keep front hub from turning, remove the hub nut from the drive axle stub shaft.

4. Push in on the end of the drive axle stub shaft, disengaging its splines from hub splines.

5. Access and remove the front brake rotor.

6. Remove the screws fastening the brake shield to the knuckle, then remove brake shield.

7. Disconnect the vehicle wiring harness from the wheel speed sensor connector.

8. Unclip the wheel speed sensor connector from the bracket on the frame rail.

9. Remove the screw fastening the wheel speed sensor routing bracket to the mounting flange on the strut.

10. Remove the screw fastening the wheel speed sensor routing bracket to the knuckle.

11. Remove the nut attaching the outer tie rod to the steering knuckle by holding the outer tie rod stud stationary while loosening and removing the nut with a wrench.

12. Remove the outer tie rod stud from steering knuckle using a puller.

✳✳ WARNING

The strut assembly-to-knuckle attaching bolts are serrated and must not be turned during removal. Proper removal is required. Refer to the following steps for the correct method.

13. If servicing left knuckle:
   a. While holding bolt heads stationary, remove two nuts from bolts attaching strut to knuckle.

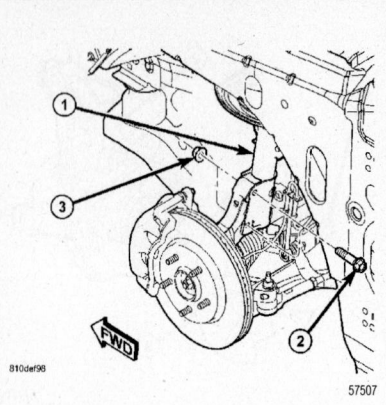

Fig. 109 While holding the bolt heads stationary, remove the two nuts (3) from the bolts (2) attaching the strut (1) to the knuckle. Remove the two bolts (2) attaching the strut (1) to the knuckle using a pin punch–Left Knuckle

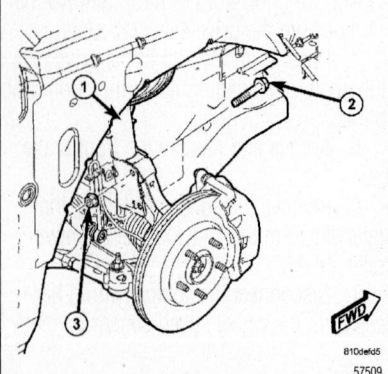

Fig. 110 While holding the bolt heads stationary, remove the two nuts (3) from the bolts (2) attaching the strut (1) to the knuckle. Remove the two bolts (2) attaching the strut (1) to the knuckle using a pin punch–Right Knuckle

   b. Remove the two bolts attaching strut to knuckle using a pin punch.

14. If servicing right knuckle:

   a. While holding bolt heads stationary, remove two nuts from bolts attaching strut to knuckle.

   b. Remove the two bolts attaching strut to knuckle using a pin punch.

15. Tip the knuckle outward at the top and remove the axle shaft stub shaft from the hub and bearing. Suspend the drive axle straight outward using a bungee cord or wire. Do not allow the drive shaft to hang by the inner joint.

16. Remove the ball joint nut using a power impact wrench. Because the tapered stud is held sufficiently in the knuckle at

this time, it is not necessary to hold the stud stationary to remove the nut.

17. Reinstall the ball joint nut until top of the nut is even with top of the ball joint stud. This action will keep stud from distorting while the stud is released from the knuckle in the following step.

✲✲ WARNING

Do not remove ball joint stud from the knuckle using a hammer. Damage to the ALUMINUM knuckle, ball joint or control arm will result.

18. Using the Press tool #C-4150A to release the ball joint:

   a. Lubricate the Press and the screw-drive threads before use to ease use and promote tool longevity.

➡To ease removal and installation, it may help to rotate the knuckle around so the inside of the knuckle faces outward.

   b. Place the Press tool over the ball joint stud and nut. Release the ball joint stud from the steering knuckle by tightening the tool screw-drive. To ease Remover installation and use, it may help to rotate knuckle around so inside of knuckle faces outward.

19. Remove the tool and nut from the top of the ball joint stud.

20. Remove the steering knuckle from the vehicle.

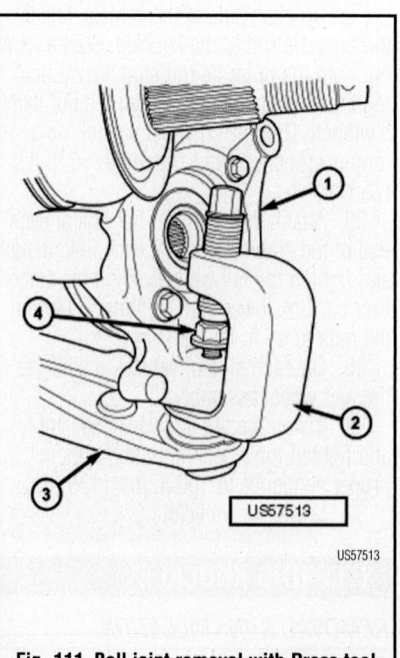

Fig. 111 Ball joint removal with Press tool

21. If hub and bearing needs to be transferred, remove the four bolts attaching the hub and bearing to the knuckle, and then remove hub and bearing.

To install:

22. If the hub and bearing needs to be installed in the knuckle, place the hub and bearing squarely into the center hole of the knuckle with the wheel speed sensor positioned toward the trailing end of the knuckle. Align the threaded mounting holes of the hub and bearing with the mounting holes in the steering knuckle, and then install the 4 mounting bolts. Progressively tighten the mounting bolts in a criss-cross pattern. Tighten the mounting bolts to 37 ft. lbs. (50 Nm).

✲✲ WARNING

Before installing the knuckle on the ball joint stud, wipe the ball joint stud and the knuckle contact area free of any grease or debris, otherwise damage to the knuckle can occur. Use a clean shop cloth with Volkswagen genuine parts Brake parts cleaner applied to it for proper cleaning. Do not spray the stud directly.

23. Place the knuckle on the ball joint stud.

24. Install a NEW steering knuckle-to-ball joint stud nut. Tighten the nut by holding the ball joint stud with a hex wrench while turning the nut with a wrench. Using a crowfoot wrench on a torque wrench, tighten the nut to 20 ft. lbs. (27 Nm), plus an additional 180° turn after the torque is met.

25. Slide the axle shaft stub shaft into the hub and bearing assembly.

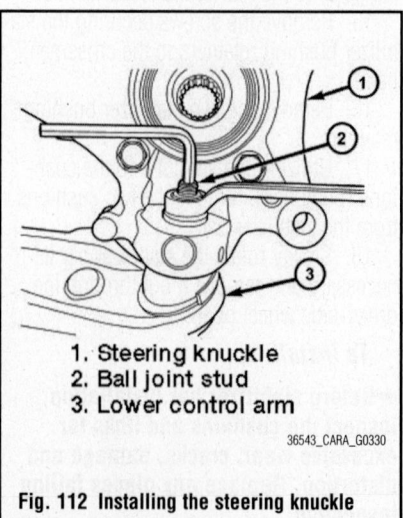

1. Steering knuckle
2. Ball joint stud
3. Lower control arm

Fig. 112 Installing the steering knuckle (1) on the ball joint stud (2)

❄❄ **WARNING**

The strut clevis-to-knuckle bolts are serrated and must not be turned during installation. Install the nuts while holding the bolts stationary in the steering knuckle. Refer to the following steps.

➡If the vehicle being serviced is equipped with eccentric cam strut attaching bolts, the eccentric cam bolt must be installed in the bottom (slotted) hole on the strut clevis bracket.

➡The strut clevis-to-knuckle bolts are installed differently on each side. The left hand side bolts are to be installed to the vehicle rear to front. The right side bolts are to be installed to the vehicle front to rear.

26. If servicing the left knuckle:
    a. Position the lower end of the strut assembly in line with the upper end of the knuckle, aligning the mounting holes. Install the 2 strut clevis-to-knuckle bolts.
    b. Install the strut clevis-to-knuckle nuts on the 2 bolts. While holding the bolts in place, tighten the strut clevis-to-knuckle nuts to 65 ft. lbs. (88 Nm), plus an additional 90° turn after the torque is met.
27. If servicing the right knuckle:
    a. Position the lower end of the strut assembly in line with the upper end of the knuckle, aligning the mounting holes. Install the 2 strut clevis-to-knuckle bolts.
    b. Install the strut clevis-to-knuckle nuts on the 2 bolts. While holding the bolts in place, tighten the strut clevis-to-knuckle nuts to 65 ft. lbs. (88 Nm), plus an additional 90° turn after the torque is met.

❄❄ **WARNING**

Before installing the tie rod stud in the knuckle steering arm, wipe the stud and the knuckle contact area free of any grease or debris, otherwise damage to the knuckle can occur. Use a clean shop cloth with Volkswagen genuine parts Brake parts cleaner applied to it for proper cleaning. Do not spray the stud directly.

28. Install the outer tie rod stud into the knuckle steering arm. Start the nut onto the tie rod stud. While holding the stud stationary, tighten the nut using a wrench. Using a crowfoot wrench on a torque wrench,

tighten the nut to 55 ft. lbs. (75 Nm), plus an additional 245° turn after the torque is met.
29. Attach the wheel speed sensor routing bracket to the knuckle. Install and tighten the screw to 71 inch lbs. (8 Nm).
30. Attach the wheel speed sensor routing bracket to the mounting flange on the strut assembly. Install and tighten the screw to 89 inch lbs. (10 Nm).
31. Clip the wheel speed sensor connector and the routing clip to the bracket on the frame rail.
32. Connect the vehicle wiring harness to the wheel speed sensor connector.
33. Install the brake shield on the knuckle. Install and tighten the 3 mounting screws (1) to 71 inch lbs. (8 Nm).
34. Install the brake rotor, and then install the disc brake caliper and the adapter assembly.
35. Verify that the wheel speed sensor is routed properly, not allowing the cable to come into contact with any moving parts.
36. Install the hub nut on the end of the axle shaft stub shaft. With the aid of a helper applying the brakes to keep the front hub from turning, tighten the hub nut to 118 ft. lbs. (160 Nm).
37. Install the tire and wheel assembly and tighten the wheel mounting nuts to 100 ft. lbs. (135 Nm) in a star pattern.
38. Lower the vehicle.
39. Pump the brake pedal several times to ensure the vehicle has a firm brake pedal before moving the vehicle.
40. Check and adjust the brake fluid level, as necessary.
41. Perform a wheel alignment.

STRUT ASSEMBLY

REMOVAL & INSTALLATION
See Figures 113 and 114.

❄❄ **CAUTION**

Do not remove the nut from strut rod while the strut assembly is installed in the vehicle or before the strut assembly spring is compressed.

1. Raise and support the vehicle.
2. Remove the wheel mounting nuts, and then remove the tire and wheel assembly.
3. If both strut assemblies are to be removed, mark the strut assemblies right or left according to which side of vehicle they were removed from to keep from mixing parts.

➡The left and right side wheel speed sensor routing brackets mount opposite each other on the strut making it necessary To Install the left side mounting screw from the rear and right side mounting screw from the front.

4. Remove the screw fastening wheel speed sensor routing bracket to mounting flange on the strut.

➡When removing the nut from the stud of the stabilizer bar link, do not allow the stud to rotate in its socket. Hold the stud from rotating by placing an open-end wrench on flat surface machined into the stud.

5. Remove the stabilizer bar link from bracket on strut assembly. To do so, place an open-end wrench on flat surface machined into the link's mounting stud, then remove the nut while holding the wrench in place. Push the stud out of the bracket.

❄❄ **WARNING**

The strut assembly-to-knuckle attaching bolts are serrated and must not be turned during removal. Proper removal is required. Refer to the following steps for the correct method.

6. If servicing the left strut:
    a. While holding the bolt heads stationary, remove the two nuts from the bolts attaching the strut to the knuckle.
    b. Remove the two bolts attaching the strut to the knuckle using a pin punch.

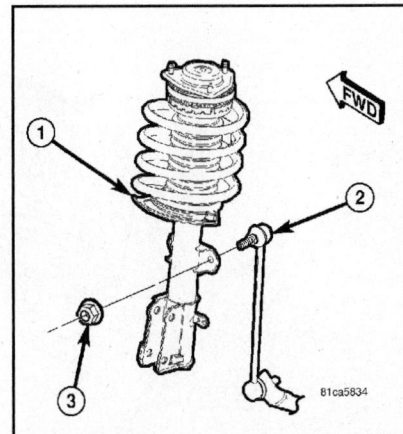

Fig. 113 Remove the stabilizer bar link (2) from the bracket on the strut assembly (1). To do so, place an open-end wrench on flat surface machined into the link's mounting stud, and then remove the nut (3) while holding the wrench in place. Push the stud out of the bracket.

7. If servicing the right strut:

a. While holding bolt heads stationary, remove the two nuts from the bolts attaching the strut to the knuckle.

b. Remove the two bolts attaching the strut to the knuckle using a pin punch.

8. Remove the wiper arms and cowl grille from the cowl plenum.

9. Remove the three nuts attaching the strut assembly upper mount to the strut tower, and then remove the strut assembly from the vehicle.

To install:

➡**Make sure the correct coil spring is used for that side of vehicle. Do not interchange the two sides when installing a strut assembly.**

10. Install the strut assembly into the strut tower, aligning and inserting three studs on the upper strut mount into the holes in the tower. Install the three mounting nuts. Tighten the nuts to 21 ft. lbs. (28 Nm).

11. Install the cowl grille and wiper arms.

❈❈ WARNING

The strut clevis-to-knuckle bolts are serrated and must not be turned during installation. Install the nuts while holding the bolts stationary in the

steering knuckle. Refer to the following steps.

➡**If vehicle being serviced is equipped with eccentric cam strut attaching bolts, eccentric cam bolt must be installed in bottom (slotted) hole on strut clevis bracket.**

➡**The strut clevis-to-knuckle bolts are installed differently on each side. Left hand side bolts are to be installed from vehicle rear to front. Right side bolts are to be installed from vehicle front to rear.**

12. If servicing the left strut:

a. Position the lower end of the strut assembly in line with the upper end of the knuckle, aligning the mounting holes. Install the two strut clevis-to-knuckle bolts.

b. Install the strut clevis-to-knuckle nuts on the two bolts. While holding the bolts in place, tighten the strut clevis-to-knuckle nuts to 65 ft. lbs. (88 Nm) plus an additional 90° turn after torque is met.

13. If servicing the right strut:

a. Position the lower end of the strut assembly in line with the upper end of the knuckle, aligning the mounting holes. Install the two strut clevis-to-knuckle bolts.

b. Install the strut clevis-to-knuckle nuts on the two bolts. While holding the bolts in place, tighten the strut clevis-to-knuckle nuts to 65 ft. lbs. (88 Nm) plus an additional 90° turn after torque is met.

14. Install the stabilizer bar link mounting stud through the rearmost hole in the bracket on the strut assembly.

➡**When installing the nut on the mounting stud of the stabilizer bar link, do not allow the stud to rotate in its socket. Hold the stud from rotating by placing an open-end wrench on a flat surface machined into the stud.**

15. Thread the nut on the end of the stabilizer bar link stud by hand. Place an open-end wrench on a flat surface machined into the link's mounting stud to hold stud from turning while tightening nut. Tighten nut to 65 ft. lbs. (88 Nm).

➡**The left and right side wheel speed sensor routing brackets mount opposite one another on the strut making it necessary To Install the left side mounting screw from the rear and right side mounting screw from the front.**

16. Attach the wheel speed sensor routing bracket to the mounting flange on the strut assembly. Install and tighten the screw to 89 inch lbs. (10 Nm).

17. Install the tire and wheel assembly.

18. Tighten the wheel mounting nuts to 100 ft. lbs. (135 Nm) in a star pattern.

19. Lower the vehicle.

20. Perform wheel alignment as necessary.

OVERHAUL

See Figures 115 through 118.

Special tool: Spring Tensioner #VAS 6046, Spring Retainers #KL-9001-13SP, and Strut Nut Wrench #9362

❈❈ CAUTION

Do not remove the strut rod nut before the coil spring is properly compressed. The coil spring is held under pressure. The coil spring must be compressed, removing spring tension from the upper mount and bearing, before the strut rod nut is removed.

1. Refer to the Precautions Section.

➡**The strut assembly must be removed from the vehicle for it to be disassembled and assembled.**

2. If both struts are being serviced at the same time, mark both the coil spring

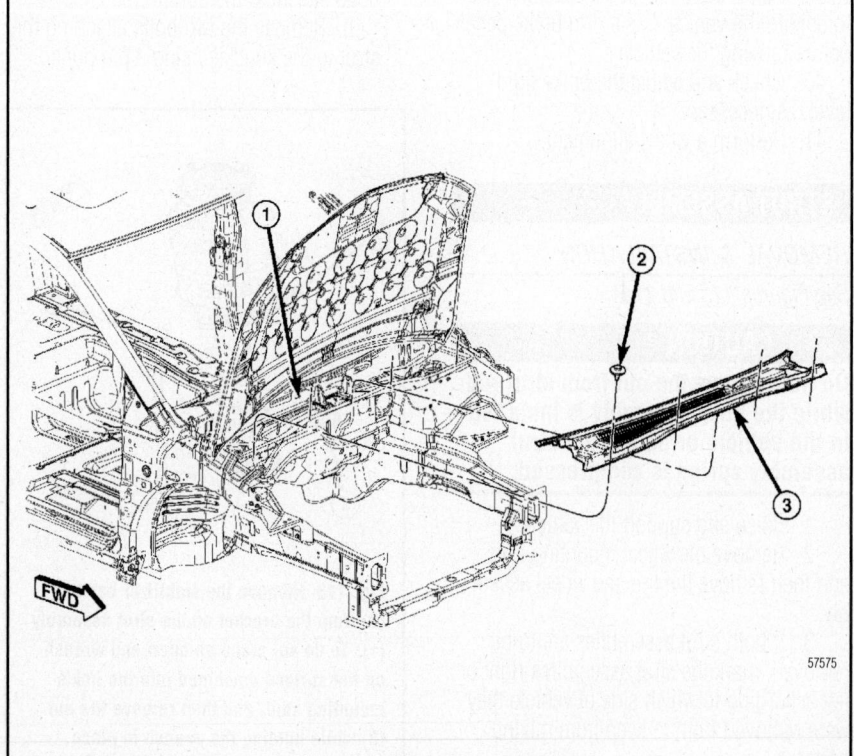

57575

Fig. 114 Remove wiper arms and cowl grille (3) from cowl plenum (1)

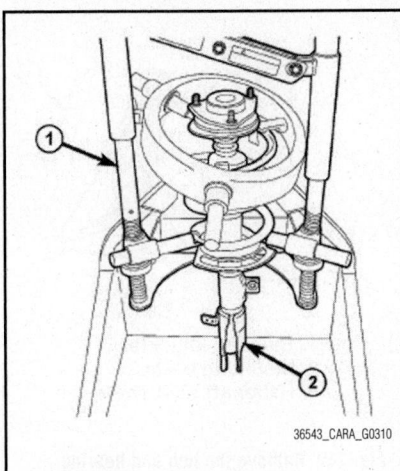

Fig. 115 View of strut coil spring compressor

and the strut assembly according to which side of the vehicle the strut is being removed from.

3. Position the strut assembly in the strut coil spring compressor #VAS6046, following the manufacturer's instructions, and set the lower and upper spring retainers (KL-9001-13SP) on the coil spring. Position the strut clevis bracket straight outward, away from the compressor.

4. Compress the coil spring until all the coil spring tension is removed from the upper mount and bearing.

✳✳ WARNING

Never use impact or high speed tools to remove the strut rod nut. Damage to the strut internal bearings can occur.

5. Once the spring is sufficiently compressed; install the Strut Nut Wrench Spe-

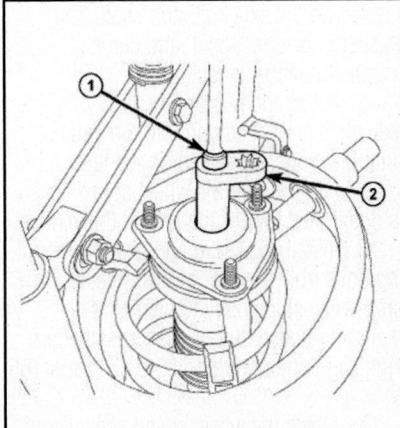

Fig. 116 Deep socket (1) and Strut Nut Wrench Special Tool 9362, on the strut rod nut

cial Tool #9362, on the strut rod nut. Next, install a deep socket on the end of the strut rod. While holding the strut rod from turning, remove the nut using the strut nut wrench.

6. Remove the clamp (if installed) from the bottom of the coil spring and remove the strut (damper) out through the bottom of the coil spring.

7. Remove the lower spring isolator from the strut seat.

8. Remove the dust shield and jounce bumper.

9. Remove the upper strut mount from the top of the bearing and upper spring seat.

10. Remove the upper spring seat and isolator from the top of the coil spring.

➥If the coil spring needs to be serviced, proceed with the next step.

11. Release the tension from the coil spring by backing off the compressor drive completely. Push back the compressor #KL-9001-13SP tool and remove the coil spring.

12. Inspect the strut assembly components for the following and replace as necessary:

a. Inspect the strut for shaft binding over the full stroke of the shaft.

b. Inspect the jounce bumper for cracks and signs of deterioration.

c. Inspect the dust shield for cracks and tears.

d. Check the upper mount for cracks and distortion and its retaining studs for any sign of damage.

e. Check the bearing and upper spring seat for any binding.

f. Inspect the upper and lower spring isolators for material deterioration and distortion.

g. Inspect the coil spring for any sign of damage to the coating

To assemble:

➥If the coil spring has been removed from the spring compressor, proceed with the next step.

➥When installing the coil spring in the spring compressor be sure to place the end with the tag closest to it upward.

13. Place the coil spring in the spring compressor following the manufacturer's instructions. Before compressing the spring, rotate the spring so the end of the bottom coil is at approximately the 9 o'clock position as viewed above (or to where the spring was when removed from

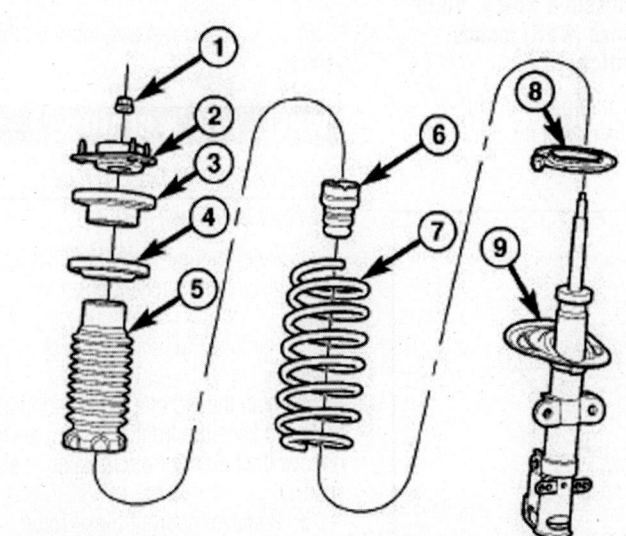

1. Strut nut
2. Upper strut mount
3. Upper spring seat
4. Isolator
5. Dust shield
6. Jounce bumper
7. Coil spring
8. Lower spring isolator
9. Strut (damper)

Fig. 117 Exploded view of strut components

the compressor). This action will allow the strut (damper) clevis bracket to be positioned outward, away from the compressor once installed.

14. Compress the coil spring slowly until enough room is available for the strut assembly reassembly.

15. Install the bearing and upper spring seat, and isolator, on top of the coil spring.

16. Install the upper mount on top of the bearing and upper spring seat.

17. Install the lower spring isolator on the spring seat on the strut (damper).

18. Slide the jounce bumper and dust shield onto the strut rod.

19. Install the strut up through the bottom of the coil spring and upper spring seat, mount, and bearing until the lower spring seat contacts the lower end of the coil spring. Rotate the strut as necessary until the end of the bottom coil comes in contact with the stop built into the lower spring isolator.

➥**Before installing the strut rod nut, make sure the hole in the upper mount faces away from the strut clevis bracket. Upon doing so, also make sure the bearing and upper spring seat is positioned so the notches in its top line with the studs located in the upper mount flange. This orientation is necessary to avoid possible Noise, Vibration, and Harshness (NVH) issues following installation.**

20. Hold the strut in position and install the nut on the end of the strut rod by hand.

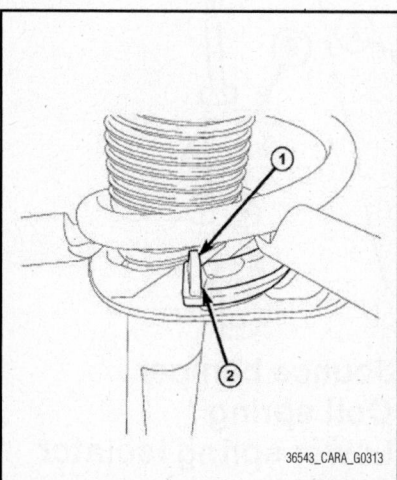

Fig. 118 Rotate the strut until the end of the bottom coil (2) comes in contact with the stop (1) built into the lower spring isolator

※ WARNING

Never use impact or high speed tools to remove the strut rod nut. Damage to the strut internal bearings can occur.

21. Install the Strut Nut Wrench, Special Tool #9362, on the strut rod nut. Next, install a deep socket on the end of the strut rod. While holding the strut rod from turning, tighten the strut rod nut to 48 ft. lbs. (65 Nm) using a torque wrench on the end of Special Tool 9362.

➥**Before releasing the tension from the coil spring by backing off the compressor drive, make sure the hole in the upper mount faces away from the strut clevis bracket. Upon doing so, also make sure the bearing and upper spring seat is positioned so the notches in its top line with the studs located in the upper mount flange. This orientation is necessary to avoid possible NVH issues following installation.**

22. Release the tension from the coil spring slowly by backing off the compressor drive completely. As the tension is relieved, make sure the upper mount and bearing align properly. Verify the upper mount does not bind when rotated.

23. Remove the strut assembly from the spring compressor.

24. Install the strut assembly on the vehicle.

WHEEL HUB & BEARINGS

REMOVAL & INSTALLATION

See Figures 119 and 120.

1. Refer to the Precautions Section.
2. Raise and safely support the vehicle.
3. Remove the tire and wheel assembly.
4. With the aid of a helper applying the brakes to keep the front hub from turning, remove the hub nut from the axle shaft stub shaft.
5. Remove the front brake rotor.
6. Remove the screws fastening the brake shield to the knuckle, and then remove the brake shield.
7. Disconnect the vehicle wiring harness from the wheel speed sensor connector.
8. Unclip the wheel speed sensor connector from the bracket on the frame rail.
9. Remove the screw fastening the wheel speed sensor routing bracket to the mounting flange on the strut.

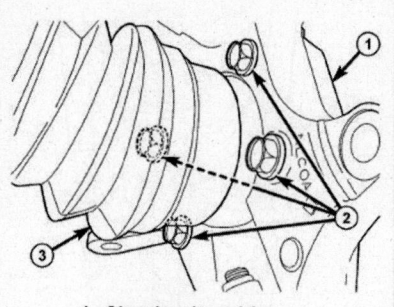

1. Steering knuckle
2. Mounting bolts
3. Halfshaft stub shaft

36543_CARA_G0064

Fig. 119 Remove the hub and bearing with the wheel speed sensor from the steering knuckle

10. Remove the screw fastening the wheel speed sensor routing bracket to the knuckle.

11. Push in on the end of the drive axle stub shaft, pushing its splines out of the hub splines.

12. Remove the 4 hub and bearing mounting bolts from the rear of the steering knuckle.

13. Remove the hub and bearing with the wheel speed sensor from the steering knuckle.

To install:

※ WARNING

The hub and bearing mounting surfaces on the knuckle and the stub shaft must be smooth and completely free of foreign material or nicks prior To Installing the hub and bearing assembly.

14. Make sure the isolation washer is located on the axle haft stub shaft. The washer is bi-directional, and can be installed in either direction.

15. Install the hub and bearing onto the axle shaft stub shaft and into the knuckle until it is squarely seated on the face of the knuckle. Make sure the wheel speed sensor is positioned toward the rear of the vehicle.

16. Install the 4 hub and bearing mounting bolts from the rear of the knuckle. Progressively and equally tighten all 4 mounting bolts using a crisscross pattern. Tighten the mounting bolts to 45 ft. lbs. (65 Nm).

17. Attach the wheel speed sensor routing bracket to the knuckle. Install and tighten the screw to 115 inch lbs. (13 Nm).

18. Attach the wheel speed sensor routing bracket to the mounting flange on the

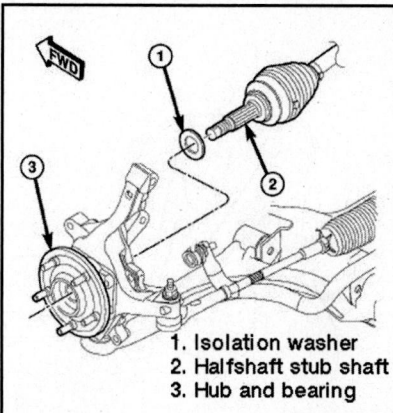

1. Isolation washer
2. Halfshaft stub shaft
3. Hub and bearing

36543_CARA_G0065

Fig. 120 Install the hub and bearing onto the axle shaft stub shaft and into the knuckle

strut assembly. Install and tighten the screw to 89 inch lbs. (10 Nm).

19. Clip the wheel speed sensor connector and routing clip to the bracket on the frame rail.

20. Connect the vehicle wiring harness to the wheel speed sensor connector.

21. Install the brake shield on the knuckle. Install and tighten the 3 mounting screws to 71 inch lbs. (8 Nm).

22. Install the brake rotor, and then install the disc brake caliper and adapter assembly.

23. Verify that the wheel speed sensor is routed properly. Do not allow the cable to come into contact with any moving parts.

24. Install the hub nut on the end of the axle shaft stub shaft. With the aid of a helper applying the brakes to keep the front hub from turning, tighten the hub nut to 118 ft. lbs. (160 Nm).

25. Install the tire and wheel assembly. Tighten the wheel mounting nuts to 100 ft. lbs. (135 Nm) in a star pattern.

26. Lower the vehicle.

27. Pump the brake pedal several times to ensure the vehicle has a firm brake pedal before moving the vehicle.

28. Check and adjust the brake fluid level, as necessary.

ADJUSTMENT

These models utilize a hub/bearing assembly which is not adjustable.

SUSPENSION

COIL SPRING & JOUNCE BUMPER

REMOVAL & INSTALLATION

See Figure 121.

1. Raise and support the vehicle.

2. On each side of the vehicle, remove the wheel mounting nuts, then remove the rear tire and wheel assembly.

3. Position a transmission jack or its equivalent under the center of the axle raising it enough to support the axle.

4. Remove the bolt and nut securing the track bar to the axle.

5. On each side of the vehicle, remove the lower mounting bolt and nut securing the shock absorber to the axle.

6. On each side of the vehicle, remove the screw fastening the rear brake flex hose bracket to the frame rail. Allow the bracket to hang free, but do not bend it downward, overextending the flex in the brake tubing.

7. Lower the jack until each coil spring can be removed from the axle.

8. Remove one side or remove both coil springs, jounce bumpers, and lower isolators.

9. Remove the jounce bumper and lower isolator from the spring as necessary.

To install:

✳✳ WARNING

Although both ends of the coil spring may appear identical, they are not. Be sure to place the end with the tag upward.

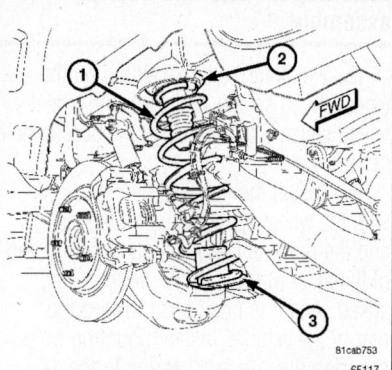

81cab753
65117

Fig. 121 Lower jack until each coil spring (1) can be removed from axle. Remove one side or both coil springs (1), jounce bumpers (2) and lower isolators (3). Remove jounce bumper (2) and lower isolator (3) from spring as necessary.

10. Install the lower isolator and jounce bumper on the end of the coil spring as necessary.

11. Place coil spring(s) between the body perch and axle at the end of the axle. Be sure to place jounce bumper end at top.

12. Raise the jack guiding the coil springs into the mounted position. Continue to raise the jack until the shock absorber lower mounting bolts can be installed though the axle brackets and shock absorber lower mounting eyes.

13. Install the lower mounting bolt and nut at each shock absorber. Do not tighten at this time.

14. Install the bolt and nut securing track bar to the axle. Do not tighten at this time.

15. Remove the jack from under the axle.

16. On each side of the vehicle, fasten

REAR SUSPENSION

the rear brake flex hose bracket to the frame rail.

17. On each side of the vehicle, install the tire and wheel assembly.

18. Tighten the wheel mounting nuts in a star pattern to 100 ft. lbs. (135 Nm).

19. Lower the vehicle.

20. Position the vehicle on an alignment rack/drive-on lift. Raise the lift as necessary to access the rear suspension while keeping vehicle at curb (riding) height.

21. Check for proper vehicle curb height.

22. Tighten the shock absorber lower mounting bolt nuts to 55 ft. lbs. (75 Nm).

23. Tighten the track bar lower mounting bolt nut to 60 ft. lbs. (81 Nm).

WHEEL HUB & BEARING

REMOVAL & INSTALLATION

See Figures 122 through 124.

1. Refer to the Precautions.

2. Raise and support the vehicle.

3. Remove the wheel mounting nuts, and then remove the rear tire and wheel assembly.

4. Right side only—Remove the exhaust heat shield above the exhaust system covering the wheel speed sensor wiring connector.

5. Disconnect the vehicle wiring harness from the wheel speed sensor connector.

6. Remove the wheel speed sensor from routing clips along the underbody of the vehicle.

7. Remove the wheel speed sensor from the routing clips along the brake flex hose.

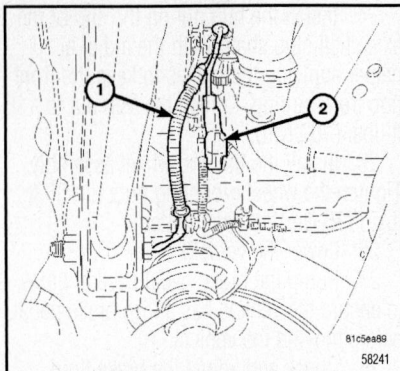

Fig. 122 Disconnect vehicle wiring harness (2) from wheel speed sensor (1) connector. Remove wheel speed sensor (1) from routing clips along underbody of vehicle.

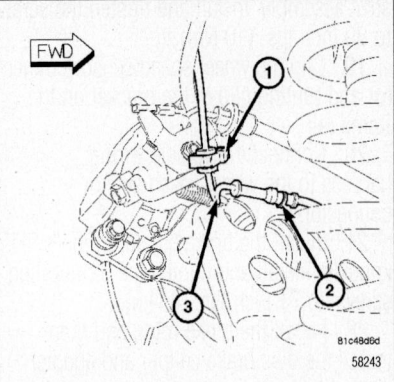

Fig. 123 Remove the wheel speed sensor (3) from the routing clips (1) along the brake flex hose. Remove the wheel speed sensor routing clip (2) from the rear axle

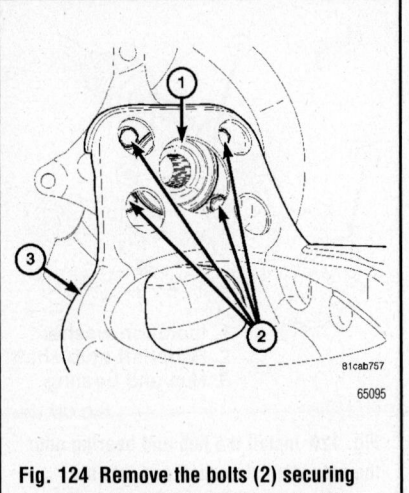

Fig. 124 Remove the bolts (2) securing the hub and bearing (1) to the axle (3)

8. Remove the wheel speed sensor routing clip from the rear axle.

9. Remove the screw securing parking the brake cable routing bracket to the axle.

10. Remove the two bolts securing the disc brake caliper and adapter bracket to the axle.

11. Remove the disc brake caliper and adapter bracket from the axle and rotor as an assembly. Hang the assembly out of the way using wire or a bungee cord. Use care not to overextend the brake hose when doing this.

12. Remove any retaining clips, and then slide the brake rotor off the hub and bearing.

13. Remove the bolts securing the hub and bearing to the axle. Remove the hub and bearing with the wheel speed sensor attached and the brake shield.

14. Separate the brake shield from the hub and bearing.

To install:

✳✳ WARNING

Hub and bearing mounting surfaces on the axle and brake shield must be smooth and completely free of foreign material or nicks prior To Installing the hub and bearing assembly.

15. Position the brake shield on the wheel speed sensor and route the wheel speed sensor cable through the access hole in the shield.

16. Install the hub and bearing with the wheel speed sensor attached and the brake shield squarely onto the end of the axle. Make sure the wheel speed sensor is positioned toward the rear of the vehicle. Install mounting bolts securing the hub and bearing to the axle. Tighten the mounting bolts to 41 ft. lbs. (55 Nm).

17. Install the brake rotor over the hub and bearing.

18. Install the disc brake caliper and adapter bracket over the axle and rotor as an assembly.

19. Install the two bolts securing the disc brake caliper and adapter bracket to the axle. Tighten the mounting bolts to 74 ft. lbs. (100 Nm).

20. Position the parking brake cable routing bracket to the axle and install the screw securing it in place. Tighten the screw to 55 inch lbs. (6 Nm).

21. Install the wheel speed sensor routing clip into hole in rear axle.

22. Install the wheel speed sensor into routing clips along brake flex hose.

23. Install the wheel speed sensor into routing clips along the underbody of the vehicle.

24. Connect vehicle wiring harness to wheel speed sensor connector.

25. Right side only—Install the exhaust heat shield above the exhaust system covering the wheel speed sensor wiring connector.

26. Install the tire and wheel assembly.

27. Tighten the wheel mounting nuts in a star pattern to 100 ft. lbs. (135 Nm).

28. Lower the vehicle.

29. Pump the brake pedal several times to ensure the vehicle has a firm brake pedal before moving the vehicle.

VOLKSWAGEN

Touareg

9

SPECIFICATIONS AND MAINTENANCE CHARTS

ENGINE AND VEHICLE IDENTIFICATION

Engine							Model Year	
Code	Liters	Cu. In.	Cyl.	Fuel Sys.	Engine Type	Eng. Mfg.	Code ②	Year
CATA	3.0	175	6	TDI	DOHC	Volkswagen	B	2011
CGRA	3.6	220	6	Motronic	DOHC	Volkswagen	C	2012
CGFA	3.0	183	6	Motronic	DOHC	Volkswagen		

DOHC: Double Overhead Camshafts

TDI: Turbo Direct Injection

71105_VWTO_C0001

GENERAL ENGINE SPECIFICATIONS

Year	Model	Engine Displacement Liters	Engine Code	Net Horsepower @ rpm	Net Torque@rpm (ft. lbs.)	Bore x Stroke (in.)	Com- pression Ratio	Oil Pressure @ rpm
2011	Touareg	3.0 TDI	CATA	240@4000	407@2000	3.30x3.50	16.8:1	58@2000
	Touareg	3.6	CGRA	280@6200	266@2500	3.50x3.80	12.0:1	44-80@2000
	Touareg	3.0	CGFA	380@5500	302@3200	3.33x3.66	10.5:1	44-80@2000
2012	Touareg	3.0 TDI	CATA	240@4000	407@2000	3.30x3.60	16.8:1	58@2000
	Touareg	3.6	CGRA	280@6200	266@2500	3.50x3.80	12.0:1	44-80@2000
	Touareg	3.0	CGFA	380@5500	302@3200	3.30x3.50	10.5:1	44-80@2000

71105_VWTO_C0002

GASOLINE ENGINE TUNE-UP SPECIFICATIONS

Year	Engine Displacement Liters	Engine Code	Spark Plug Gap (in.)	Ignition Timing (deg.) MT	AT	Fuel Pump (psi)	Idle Speed (rpm) MT	AT	Valve Clearance Intake	Exhaust
2011	3.6	CGRA	0.043	—	①	80 ②	—	670-730	HYD	HYD
	3.0	CGFA	0.043	—	①	58 ②	—	600-800	HYD	HYD
2012	3.6	CGRA	0.043	—	①	80 ②	—	670-730	HYD	HYD
	3.0	CGFA	0.043	—	①	58 ②	—	600-800	HYD	HYD

Note: The Vehicle Emission Control Information label reflects specification changes made during production.

The label figures must be used if they differ from those in this chart.

HYD: Hydraulic

NA: Information not available

① The ignition timing is controlled by the ECM and is not adjustable.

② System pressure at idle.

71105_VWTO_C0003

DIESEL ENGINE TUNE-UP SPECIFICATIONS

Year	Engine Displacement Liters	Engine Code	Valve Clearance		Intake Valve Opens (deg.)	Injection Pump Setting (deg.)	Injection Nozzle Pressure (psi)		Idle Speed (rpm)	Cranking Compression Pressure (psi)
			Intake (in.)	Exhaust (in.)			New	Used		
2011	3.0	CATA	HYD	HYD	NS	①	NS	NS	①	NS
2012	3.0	CATA	HYD	HYD	NS	①	NS	NS	①	NS

Note: The Vehicle Emission Control Information label reflects specification changes made during production.

NS: Not Specified

① Injection pump timing/idle speed controlled electronically. Specification no longer provided.

71105_VWTO_C0004

CAPACITIES

Year	Model	Engine Displacement Liters	Engine Code	Engine Oil with Filter	Transmission (qts.)		Final Drive (pts.)	Fuel Tank (gal.)	Cooling System (qts.)
					Manual	Automatic			
2011	Touareg	3.0 TDI	CATA	8.8	—	11-13 ①	②	26.4	16.3
	Touareg	3.6	CGRA	6.7	—	11-13 ①	②	26.4	18.0
	Touareg	3.0	CGFA	6.6	—	11-13 ①	②	21.7	18.0
2012	Touareg	3.0 TDI	CATA	8.8	—	11-13 ①	②	26.4	16.3
	Touareg	3.6	CGRA	6.7	—	11-13 ①	②	26.4	18.0
	Touareg	3.0	CGFA	6.6	—	11-13 ①	②	21.7	18.0

NOTE: All capacities are approximate. Add fluid gradually and check often to avoid overfilling.

① Initial Fill - Dependant on engine type

② Transfer case: 1.8 pts.; Front final drive: 1.6 pts..; Rear final drive w/o EDL: 2.6 pts.; Rear final drive w/ EDL: 3.4 pts

71105_VWTO_C0005

FLUID SPECIFICATIONS

Year	Model	Engine Displacement Liters	Engine Code	Engine Oil	Auto. Trans.	AC System Oil	Power Steering Fluid	Brake Master Cylinder
2011	Touareg	3.0 TDI	CATA	5W-30	VW ATF	PAG	①	DOT 4
	Touareg	3.6	CGRA	5W-40	VW ATF	PAG	①	DOT 4
	Touareg	3.0	CGFA	5W-40	VW ATF	PAG Hybrid	①	DOT 4
2012	Touareg	3.0 TDI	CATA	5W-30	VW ATF	PAG	①	DOT 4
	Touareg	3.6	CGRA	5W-40	VW ATF	PAG	①	DOT 4
	Touareg	3.0	CGFA	5W-40	VW ATF	PAG Hybrid	①	DOT 4

NA: Not Applicable

DOT: Department Of Transportation

① VW G002 000 (do not use ATF)

71105_VWTO_C0006

VALVE SPECIFICATIONS

Year	Engine Displacement Liters	Engine Code	Seat Angle (deg.)	Face Angle (deg.)	Spring Test Pressure (lbs. @ in.)	Spring Installed Height (in.)	Stem-to-Guide Clearance (in.) Intake	Exhaust	Stem Diameter (in.) Intake	Exhaust
2011	3.0 TDI	CATA	45	45	NS	NS	0.039	0.039	0.235-0.236	0.232-0.233
	3.6	CGRA	45	45	NS	NS	0.032	0.032	0.235	0.235
	3.0	CGFA	45	45	NS	NS	0.032	0.032	0.235-0.236	0.234-0.235
2012	3.0 TDI	CATA	45	45	NS	NS	0.039	0.039	0.235-0.236	0.232-0.233
	3.6	CGRA	45	45	NS	NS	0.032	0.032	0.235	0.235
	3.0	CGFA	45	45	NS	NS	0.032	0.032	0.235-0.236	0.234-0.235

NS: Not Specified

71105_VWTO_C0007

CAMSHAFT AND BEARING SPECIFICATIONS

All measurements are given in inches.

Year	Engine Displ. Liters	Engine Code	Journal Dia.	Brg. Oil Clearance	Shaft Axial-play	Runout	Journal Bore	Lobe Height Intake	Exhaust
2011	3.0 TDI	CATA	NS	NS	0.00047	NS	NS	NS	NS
	3.6	CGRA	NS	NS	0.0157	NS	NS	NS	NS
	3.0	CGFA	NS	NS	0.0358	NS	NS	NS	NS
2012	3.0 TDI	CATA	NS	NS	0.00047	NS	NS	NS	NS
	3.6	CGRA	NS	NS	0.0157	NS	NS	NS	NS
	3.0	CGFA	NS	NS	0.0358	NS	NS	NS	NS

NS: Not Specified

71105_VWTO_C0008

CRANKSHAFT AND CONNECTING ROD SPECIFICATIONS

All measurements are given in inches.

Year	Engine Displacement Liters	Engine Code	Crankshaft Main Brg. Journal Dia.	Main Brg. Oil Clearance	Shaft End-play	Thrust on No.	Connecting Rod Journal Diameter	Oil Clearance	Side Clearance
2011	3.0 TDI	CATA	2.5350	0.0007-0.0017	0.0035-0.0083	NS	2.3400	0.0006-0.0024	NS
	3.6	CGRA	2.3605	0.0007-0.0023	0.0027-0.0090	5	2.1243	0.0007-0.0027	0.0019-0.0122
	3.0	CGFA	2.558-2.5600	0.0007-0.0017	0.0035-0.0100	NS	2.1251-2.1276	0.0008-0.0027	NS
2012	3.0 TDI	CATA	2.5350	0.0007-0.0017	0.0035-0.0083	NS	2.3400	0.0006-0.0024	NS
	3.6	CGRA	2.3605	0.0007-0.0023	0.0027-0.0090	5	2.1243	0.0007-0.0027	0.0019-0.0122
	3.0	CGFA	2.558-2.5600	0.0007-0.0017	0.0035-0.0100	NS	2.1251-2.1276	0.0008-0.0027	NS

NS: Not Specified

71105_VWTO_C0010

PISTON AND RING SPECIFICATIONS
All measurements are given in inches.

Year	Engine Disp. Liters	Engine Code	Piston Clearance	Ring Gap			Ring Side Clearance		
				Top Compression	Bottom Compression	Oil Control	Top Compression	Bottom Compression	Oil Control
2011	3.0 TDI	CATA	0.0025-0.0026	0.010-0.014	0.027-0.035	0.0150	0.0047-0.0062	0.0008-0.0035	0.0008-0.0035
	3.6	CGRA	0.0025	0.008-0.015	0.008-0.015	0.009-0.019	0.0015-0.0035	0.0012-0.0024	0.0008-0.0024
	3.0	CGFA	0.0027	0.007-0.012	0.019-0.027	0.009-0.019	0.0015-0.0031	0.0011-0.0027	0.0007-0.0023
2012	3.0 TDI	CATA	0.0025-0.0026	0.010-0.014	0.027-0.035	0.0150	0.0047-0.0062	0.0008-0.0035	0.0008-0.0035
	3.6	CGRA	0.0025	0.008-0.015	0.008-0.015	0.009-0.019	0.0015-0.0035	0.0012-0.0024	0.0008-0.0024
	3.0	CGFA	0.0027	0.007-0.012	0.019-0.027	0.009-0.019	0.0015-0.0031	0.0011-0.0027	0.0007-0.0023

71105_VWTO_C0009

TORQUE SPECIFICATIONS
All readings in ft. lbs.

Year	Engine Disp. Liters	Engine Code	Cylinder Head Bolts	Main Bearing Bolts	Rod Bearing Bolts	Crankshaft Damper Bolt	Flywheel Bolts	Manifold		Spark Plugs	Oil Pan Drain Plug
								Intake	Exhaust		
2011	3.0L TDI	CATA	①	②	③	④	⑤	⑥	17	NA	22
	3.6	CGRA	⑦	⑧	⑨	⑩	⑪	⑫	NA	13	22
	3.0	CGFA	⑬	⑭	⑮	④	⑯	⑫	⑰	13	22
2012	3.0L TDI	CATA	①	②	③	④	⑤	⑥	17	NA	22
	3.6	CGRA	⑦	⑧	⑨	⑩	⑪	⑫	NA	13	22
	3.0	CGFA	⑬	⑭	⑮	④	⑯	⑫	⑰	13	22

NA: Not applicable

① Torque in four steps: (use new bolts)
  Step 1: 22 ft. lbs.
  Step 2: 44 ft. lbs.
  Step 3: plus 90 degrees
  Step 4: plus 90 degrees
② Torque in four steps: (use new bolts)
  Step 1: 22 ft. lbs.
  Step 2: 37 ft. lbs.
  Step 3: plus 90 degrees
  Step 4: plus 90 degrees
③ Use new bolts: 22 ft. lbs. plus 90 degrees
④ Use new bolts: 15 ft. lbs. plus 90 degrees
⑤ Use new bolts: 22 ft. lbs. plus 90 degrees
⑥ Upper intake manifold bolts: 7 ft. lbs.
  Lower intake manifold bolts: 6 ft. lbs.

⑦ Torque in four steps: (use new bolts)
  Step 1: 22 ft. lbs.
  Step 2: 37 ft. lbs.
  Step 3: plus 90 degrees
  Step 4: plus 90 degrees
⑧ Use new bolts: 22 ft. lbs. plus 180 degrees
⑨ Use new bolts: 22 ft. lbs. plus 90 degrees
⑩ Use new bolts: 74 ft. lbs. plus 90 degrees
⑪ Use new bolts: 44 ft. lbs. plus 90 degrees
⑫ Upper intake manifold bolts: 7 ft. lbs.
  Lower intake manifold bolts: 6 ft. lbs.
⑬ Torque in three steps: (use new bolts)
  Step 1: 29 ft. lbs.
  Step 2: plus 90 degrees
  Step 3: plus 90 degrees
⑭ Guide frame bolts 1-16
  Step 1: 36 ft. lbs.
  Step 2: plus 90 degrees (1/4 additional turn)
  Step 3: Guide frame bolts 17-31, 17 ft lbs.

⑮ Use new bolts: 37 ft. lbs. plus 90 degrees
⑯ Use new bolts: 44 ft. lbs. plus 90 degrees
⑰ Torque in two steps:
  Step 1: 11 ft. lbs.
  Step 2: 18 ft lbs

71105_VWTO_C0011

WHEEL ALIGNMENT

Year	Model		Caster Range (+/-Deg.)	Caster Preferred Setting (Deg.)	Camber Range (+/-Deg.)	Camber Preferred Setting (Deg.)	Toe-in (Deg.)
2011	Standard	F	0.16	8.16	0.33	0.00	0.04 +/- 0.04
	Suspension	R	—	—	0.33	1.00	0.16 +/- 0.08
	Sport	F	0.16	8.58	0.33	-0.16	0.08 +/- 0.04
	Suspension	R	—	—	0.33	1.00	0.16 +/- 0.08
	Air Springs	F	0.50	8.45	0.1	-0.20	0.10 +/- 0.30
	Suspension	R	—	—	0.2	-1.20	0.10 +/- 0.05
2012	Standard	F	0.16	8.16	0.33	0.00	0.04 +/- 0.04
	Suspension	R	—	—	0.33	1.00	0.16 +/- 0.08
	Sport	F	0.16	8.58	0.33	-0.16	0.08 +/- 0.04
	Suspension	R	—	—	0.33	1.00	0.16 +/- 0.08
	Air Springs	F	0.50	8.45	0.1	-0.20	0.10 +/- 0.30
	Suspension	R	—	—	0.2	-1.20	0.10 +/- 0.05

NOTE: Alignment specifications are dependent on proger vehicle ride height.

71105_VWTO_C0012

TIRE, WHEEL AND BALL JOINT SPECIFICATIONS

Year	Model	OEM Tires Standard	OEM Tires Optional	Tire Pressures (psi) Front	Tire Pressures (psi) Rear	Wheel Size	Lug Nut (ft. lbs.)
2011	Touareg 3.0L TDI	235/65 R 17,108V	①	33 ②	36 ②	7/ J x 17	133
	Touareg 3.6L	255/60 R 17,106V	①	33 ②	36 ②	7/ J x 17	133
	Touareg Hybrid	255/55 R 18,109V	265/50 R 19,110V	33 ②	36 ②	8/ J x 19	133
2012	Touareg 3.0L TDI	235/65 R 17,108V	①	33 ②	36 ②	7/ J x 17	133
	Touareg 3.6L	255/60 R 17,106V	①	33 ②	36 ②	7/ J x 17	133
	Touareg Hybrid	255/55 R 18,109V	265/50 R 19,110V	33 ②	36 ②	8/ J x 19	133

OEM: Original Equipment Manufacturer

PSI: Pounds Per Square Inch

① 255/55 R 18,109V, 265/50 R 19,110V, 275/45 R 20,110V, 275/40 R 21,107V

② All models equipped with TPMS; consult vehicle tag or owner's handbook for specific pressures.

71105_VWTO_C0013

BRAKE SPECIFICATIONS
All measurements in inches unless noted

Year	Model		Brake Disc			Minimum Lining Thickness	Brake Caliper	
			Original Thickness	Minimum Thickness	Maximum Run-out		Guide Pins (ft. lbs.)	Mounting Bolts (ft. lbs.)
2011	Touareg	F	①	③	NA	0.07	NA	⑤
		R	②	④	NA	0.07	NA	133
2012	Touareg	F	①	③	NA	0.07	NA	⑤
		R	②	④	NA	0.07	NA	133

NA: Not Applicable

① 17" 1LC, 1LE: 1.26"
   18" 1LF: 1.41"

② 17" 1KF, 1KQ: 1.10"

③ 17" 1LC, 1LE: 1.18"
   18" 1LF: 1.33"

④ 17" 1KF, 1KQ: 1.02"

⑤ 17" 1LC, 1LE: 199 ft. lbs."
   18" 1LF: 22 ft. lbs" plus 90 degrees

71105_VWTO_C0014

SCHEDULED MAINTENANCE INTERVALS
VOLKSWAGEN TOUAREG - 3.6L Engine

TO BE SERVICED	TYPE	VEHICLE MILEAGE INTERVAL (x1000)												
		5	10	20	30	40	50	60	70	80	90	100	110	120
Engine oil & filter	R	✓	✓	✓	✓	✓	✓	✓	✓	✓	✓	✓	✓	✓
Brake pad thickness	S/I		✓	✓	✓	✓	✓	✓	✓	✓	✓	✓	✓	✓
Dust seals, ball joints & tie rods	S/I			✓		✓		✓		✓		✓		✓
Battery	S/I			✓		✓		✓		✓		✓		✓
Body Corrosion	S/I					✓				✓				✓
Cooling system	S/I					✓				✓				✓
Driveshaft boots	S/I					✓				✓				✓
Engine (check for leaks)	S/I			✓		✓		✓		✓		✓		✓
Engine exhaust	S/I			✓		✓		✓		✓		✓	✓	✓
Exterior & interior lighting	S/I	✓	✓	✓	✓	✓	✓	✓	✓	✓	✓	✓	✓	✓
Power steering fluid level	S/I					✓				✓				✓
Service reminder (reset)	S/I	✓	✓	✓	✓	✓	✓	✓	✓	✓	✓	✓	✓	✓
Transmission fluid level	S/I					✓				✓				✓
Transmission Final drive	S/I					✓				✓				✓
Suspension system	S/I			✓		✓		✓		✓		✓		✓
Engine air cleaner element	S/I					✓				✓				✓
Air suspension (check for leaks)	S/I					✓				✓				✓
Lubricate locks, hinges, hood latch & sunroof frame	S/I					✓				✓				✓
Passenger compartment air filter (Cabin filter)	R			✓		✓		✓		✓		✓	✓	✓
Spark plugs	R							✓						✓
Tire rotation	R		✓	✓	✓	✓	✓	✓	✓	✓	✓	✓	✓	✓
Drive belts	S/I					✓				✓				✓
Wiper system	S/I		✓	✓	✓	✓	✓	✓	✓	✓	✓	✓	✓	✓

R: Replace   S/I: Service or Inspect

FREQUENT OPERATION MAINTENANCE (SEVERE SERVICE)

If a vehicle is operated under any of the following conditions it is considered severe service:

- Extremely dusty areas.

- 50% or more of the vehicle operation is in 32°C (90°F) or higher temperatures, or constant operation in temperatures below 0°C (32°F).

- Prolonged idling (vehicle operation in stop and go traffic).

- Frequent short running periods (engine does not warm to normal operating temperatures).

- Police, taxi, delivery usage or trailer towing usage.

Oil & oil filter change: change every 5000 miles.

Automatic transmission fluid & filter: replace every 40,000 miles.

Replace brake fluid every 24 months.

Inspect air bag system every 12 months.

Inspect tire filler bottle every 24 months.

71105_VWTO_C0015

SCHEDULED MAINTENANCE INTERVALS
VOLKSWAGEN TOUAREG - 3.0L Hybrid

TO BE SERVICED	TYPE	VEHICLE MILEAGE INTERVAL (x1000)												
		5	10	20	30	40	50	60	70	80	90	100	110	120
Engine oil & filter	R	✓	✓	✓	✓	✓	✓	✓	✓	✓	✓	✓	✓	✓
Brake pad thickness	S/I		✓	✓	✓	✓	✓	✓	✓	✓	✓	✓	✓	✓
Dust seals, ball joints & tie rods	S/I					✓				✓				✓
Battery (primary & secondary)	S/I					✓				✓				✓
Brake system	S/I		✓	✓	✓	✓	✓	✓	✓	✓	✓	✓	✓	✓
Body corrosion	S/I					✓				✓				✓
Cooling system	S/I					✓				✓				✓
Driveshaft boots	S/I					✓				✓				✓
Engine (check for leaks)	S/I			✓		✓		✓		✓		✓		✓
Hybrid components	S/I			✓		✓		✓		✓		✓		✓
Engine exhaust	S/I					✓				✓				✓
Power steering fluid level	S/I					✓				✓				✓
Transmission fluid level	S/I					✓				✓				✓
Transmission final drive	S/I					✓				✓				✓
Service reminder (reset)	S/I	✓	✓	✓	✓	✓	✓	✓	✓	✓	✓	✓	✓	✓
Engine air cleaner element	S/I					✓				✓				✓
Air suspension (check for leaks)	S/I					✓				✓				✓
Passenger compartment air filter	R		✓			✓		✓		✓		✓		✓
Lubricate locks, hinges, hood latch & sunroof frame	S/I					✓				✓				✓
Exterior & interior lighting	S/I	✓	✓	✓	✓	✓	✓	✓	✓	✓	✓	✓	✓	✓
Tire rotation	S/I		✓	✓	✓	✓	✓	✓	✓	✓	✓	✓	✓	✓
Windshield washer system & blades	S/I	✓	✓	✓	✓	✓	✓	✓	✓	✓	✓	✓	✓	✓
Spark plugs	R							✓						✓
Drive belts	S/I					✓				✓				✓

R: Replace   S/I: Service or Inspect

FREQUENT OPERATION MAINTENANCE (SEVERE SERVICE)

If a vehicle is operated under any of the following conditions it is considered severe service:

- **Extremely dusty areas.**
- **50% or more of the vehicle operation is in 32°C (90°F) or higher temperatures, or constant operation in temperatures below 0°C (32°F).**
- **Prolonged idling (vehicle operation in stop and go traffic).**
- **Frequent short running periods (engine does not warm to normal operating temperatures).**
- **Police, taxi, delivery usage or trailer towing usage.**

Oil & oil filter change: change every 5000 miles.

Air filter element: service or inspect every 80,000 miles.

Automatic transmission fluid & filter: replace every 40,000 miles.

Replace brake fluid every 24 months.

Inspect air bag system every 12 months.

Inspect tire filler bottle every 24 months.

71105_VWTO_C0016

SCHEDULED MAINTENANCE INTERVALS
VOLKSWAGEN TOUAREG - 3.0L TDI

TO BE SERVICED	TYPE	VEHICLE MILEAGE INTERVAL (x1000)												
		5	10	20	30	40	50	60	70	80	90	100	110	120
Engine oil & filter	R	✓	✓	✓	✓	✓	✓	✓	✓	✓	✓	✓	✓	✓
Brake pad thickness	S/I	✓	✓	✓	✓	✓	✓	✓	✓	✓	✓	✓	✓	✓
Dust seals, ball joints & tie rods	S/I			✓		✓		✓		✓		✓		✓
Battery's	S/I					✓				✓				✓
Brake system	S/I		✓	✓	✓	✓	✓	✓	✓	✓	✓	✓	✓	✓
Cooling system	S/I			✓		✓		✓		✓		✓		✓
Driveshaft boots	S/I			✓		✓		✓		✓		✓	✓	✓
Engine (check for leaks)	S/I			✓		✓		✓		✓		✓		✓
Engine exhaust	S/I			✓		✓		✓		✓		✓	✓	✓
Power steering fluid level	S/I					✓				✓				✓
Underbody	S/I					✓				✓				✓
Transmission fluid level	S/I					✓				✓				✓
Service reminder (reset)	S/I	✓	✓	✓	✓	✓	✓	✓	✓	✓	✓	✓	✓	✓
Lubricate locks, hinges, hood latch & sunroof frame	S/I					✓				✓				✓
Tire rotation	R		✓	✓	✓	✓	✓	✓	✓	✓	✓	✓	✓	✓
Exterior & interior lighting	S/I	✓	✓	✓	✓	✓	✓	✓	✓	✓	✓	✓	✓	✓
Suspension system	S/I			✓		✓		✓		✓		✓		✓
Transmission final drive	S/I					✓				✓				✓
Fuel filter	R					✓				✓				✓
Air cleaner fitler	S/I					✓				✓				✓
Air suspension (check for leaks)	S/I					✓				✓				✓
Passenger compartment air filter	R			✓		✓		✓		✓		✓	✓	✓
Service reminder (reset)	S/I	✓	✓	✓	✓	✓	✓	✓	✓	✓	✓	✓	✓	✓
Drive belts	S/I					✓				✓				✓
Water separator - drain	S/I	✓	✓	✓	✓	✓	✓	✓	✓	✓	✓	✓	✓	✓
Diesel particle filter	R													✓

R: Replace   S/I: Service or Inspect

① Replace every two years regardless of mileage.

FREQUENT OPERATION MAINTENANCE (SEVERE SERVICE)

If a vehicle is operated under any of the following conditions it is considered severe service:

- Extremely dusty areas.

- 50% or more of the vehicle operation is in 32°C (90°F) or higher temperatures, or constant operation in temperatures below 0°C (32°F).

- Prolonged idling (vehicle operation in stop and go traffic).

- Frequent short running periods (engine does not warm to normal operating temperatures).

- Police, taxi, delivery usage or trailer towing usage.

Oil & oil filter change: change every 5000 miles.

Air filter element: service or inspect every 80,000 miles.

Automatic transmission fluid & filter: replace every 40,000 miles.

Replace brake fluid every 24 months.

Inspect air bag system every 12 months.

Inspect tire filler bottle every 24 months.

PRECAUTIONS

Before servicing any vehicle, please be sure to read all of the following precautions, which deal with personal safety, prevention of component damage, and important points to take into consideration when servicing a motor vehicle:

- Never open, service or drain the radiator or cooling system when the engine is hot; serious burns can occur from the steam and hot coolant.

- Observe all applicable safety precautions when working around fuel. Whenever servicing the fuel system, always work in a well-ventilated area. Do not allow fuel spray or vapors to come in contact with a spark, open flame, or excessive heat (a hot drop light, for example). Keep a dry chemical fire extinguisher near the work area. Always keep fuel in a container specifically designed for fuel storage; also, always properly seal fuel containers to avoid the possibility of fire or explosion. Refer to the additional fuel system precautions later in this section.

- Fuel injection systems often remain pressurized, even after the engine has been turned **OFF**. The fuel system pressure must be relieved before disconnecting any fuel lines. Failure to do so may result in fire and/or personal injury.

- Brake fluid often contains polyglycol ethers and polyglycols. Avoid contact with the eyes and wash your hands thoroughly after handling brake fluid. If you do get brake fluid in your eyes, flush your eyes with clean, running water for 15 minutes. If eye irritation persists, or if you have taken brake fluid internally, IMMEDIATELY seek medical assistance.

- The EPA warns that prolonged contact with used engine oil may cause a number of skin disorders, including cancer. You should make every effort to minimize your exposure to used engine oil. Protective gloves should be worn when changing oil. Wash your hands and any other exposed skin areas as soon as possible after exposure to used engine oil. Soap and water, or waterless hand cleaner should be used.

- All new vehicles are now equipped with an air bag system, often referred to as a Supplemental Restraint System (SRS) or Supplemental Inflatable Restraint (SIR) system. The system must be disabled before performing service on or around system components, steering column, instrument panel components, wiring and sensors. Failure to follow safety and disabling procedures could result in accidental air bag deployment, possible personal injury and unnecessary system repairs.

- Always wear safety goggles when working with, or around, the air bag system. When carrying a non-deployed air bag, be sure the bag and trim cover are pointed away from your body. When placing a non-deployed air bag on a work surface, always face the bag and trim cover upward, away from the surface. This will reduce the motion of the module if it is accidentally deployed. Refer to the additional air bag system precautions later in this section.

- Clean, high quality brake fluid from a sealed container is essential to the safe and proper operation of the brake system. You should always buy the correct type of brake fluid for your vehicle. If the brake fluid becomes contaminated, completely flush the system with new fluid. Never reuse any brake fluid. Any brake fluid that is removed from the system should be discarded. Also, do not allow any brake fluid to come in contact with a painted surface; it will damage the paint.

- Never operate the engine without the proper amount and type of engine oil; doing so WILL result in severe engine damage.

- Timing belt maintenance is extremely important. Many models utilize an interference-type, non-freewheeling engine. If the timing belt breaks, the valves in the cylinder head may strike the pistons, causing potentially serious (also time-consuming and expensive) engine damage. Refer to the maintenance interval charts for the recommended replacement interval for the timing belt, and to the timing belt section for belt replacement and inspection.

- Disconnecting the negative battery cable on some vehicles may interfere with the functions of the on-board computer system(s) and may require the computer to undergo a relearning process once the negative battery cable is reconnected.

- When servicing drum brakes, only disassemble and assemble one side at a time, leaving the remaining side intact for reference.

- Only an MVAC-trained, EPA-certified automotive technician should service the air conditioning system or its components.

BRAKES   ANTI-LOCK BRAKE SYSTEM (ABS)

GENERAL INFORMATION

PRECAUTIONS

- Certain components within the ABS system are not intended to be serviced or repaired individually.
- Do not use rubber hoses or other parts not specifically specified for and ABS system. When using repair kits, replace all parts included in the kit. Partial or incorrect repair may lead to functional problems and require the replacement of components.
- Lubricate rubber parts with clean, fresh brake fluid to ease assembly.

- Do not use shop air to clean parts; damage to rubber components may result.
- Use only DOT 3 brake fluid from an unopened container.
- If any hydraulic component or line is removed or replaced, it may be necessary to bleed the entire system.
- A clean repair area is essential. Always clean the reservoir and cap thoroughly before removing the cap. The slightest amount of dirt in the fluid may plug an orifice and impair the system function. Perform repairs after components have been thoroughly cleaned; use only denatured alcohol to clean components.

- Do not allow ABS components to come into contact with any substance containing mineral oil; this includes used shop rags.
- The Anti-Lock control unit is a microprocessor similar to other computer units in the vehicle. Ensure that the ignition switch is **OFF** before removing or installing controller harnesses. Avoid static electricity discharge at or near the controller.
- If any arc welding is to be done on the vehicle, the control unit should be unplugged before welding operations begin.

SPEED SENSORS

REMOVAL & INSTALLATION

Front

See Figure 1.

1. Before servicing the vehicle, refer to the precautions.
2. Raise and support the vehicle.
3. Disconnect the speed sensor wiring connector.
4. Remove bolt from wheel bearing housing.
5. Remove ABS speed sensor from wheel bearing housing.

To install:

6. Before inserting wheel speed sensor, clean inner surface of bore hole and coat sensor completely with polycarbamide grease (G 052 142 A2).
7. Insert the speed sensor into the hole in the wheel bearing housing and tighten the bolt to 6 ft. lbs. (8 Nm).

8. Connect speed sensor to speed sensor wiring.

Rear

See Figure 2.

1. Before servicing the vehicle, refer to the precautions.
2. Disconnect the speed sensor wiring connector.
3. Remove bolt from wheel bearing housing.

4. Remove ABS speed sensor from wheel bearing housing.

To install:

5. Before inserting wheel speed sensor, clean inner surface of bore hole and coat sensor completely with polycarbamide grease (G 052 142 A2).
6. Insert the speed sensor into the hole in the wheel bearing housing and tighten the bolt to 8 Nm.
7. Connect speed sensor to speed sensor wiring.

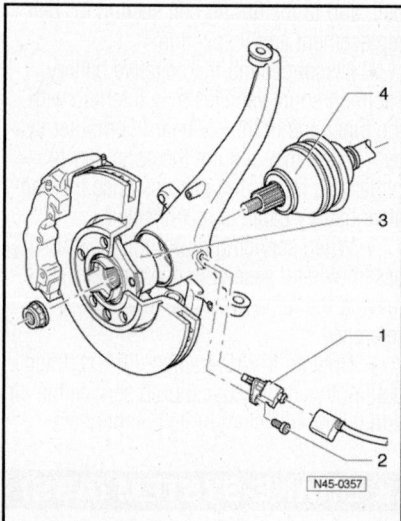

Fig. 1 Front wheel speed sensor assembly overview

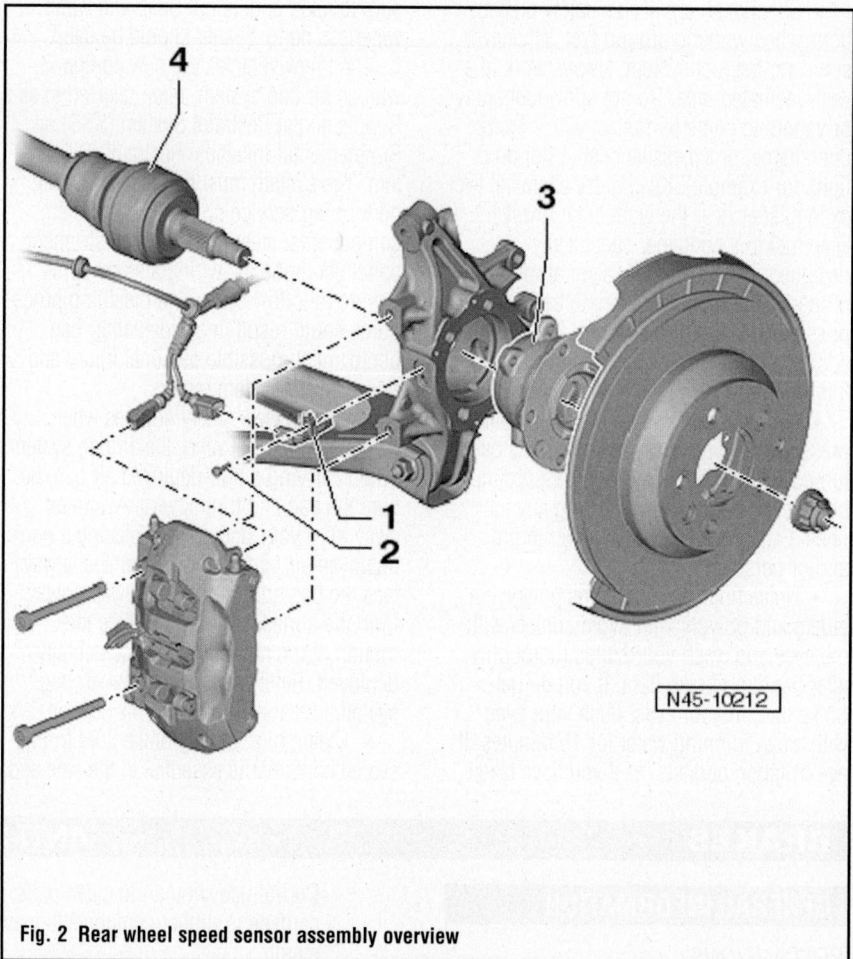

Fig. 2 Rear wheel speed sensor assembly overview

BRAKES

BLEEDING THE BRAKE SYSTEM

BLEEDING PROCEDURE

BLEEDING PROCEDURE

→If one chamber of the brake fluid reservoir has run completely empty (e.g. leak in the brake system), the brake system must be pre-bled first.

Pre-Bleeding

1. Before servicing the vehicle, refer to the precautions.

→There are two bleeder valves installed on Brembo brake calipers Always bleed at both bleeder valves.

2. Bleed at outer bleeder valve first.
3. Connect brake filling and bleeding tool (VAS 5234 or V.A.G 1869).
4. Note the bleeding sequence:
   - Bleed left front and right front brake caliper together simultaneously
   - Bleed left rear and right rear brake caliper together simultaneously
5. With bleeder bottle hoses attached, leave bleeder valves open long enough that brake fluid exits without bubbles.
6. Then hydraulic unit must be bled once more via function "Basic setting" using an approved tool (VAS 5051) or scan tool.

7. Initiate basic setting (to bleed brake system), then, brake system must be bled normally.
8. After bleeding brake system, basic setting for brake pressure sensor 1 (G201) must be performed.

Bleeding

1. Before servicing the vehicle, refer to the precautions.

→Adhere strictly to work sequence when bleeding the brake system. There are two bleeder valves installed on Brembo brake calipers. Always bleed at both bleeder valves.

2. Bleed at outer bleeder valve first.
3. Connect brake filling and bleeding tool (VAS 5234 or V.A.G 1869).
4. Open bleeder valves in the prescribed sequence and bleed brake caliper:
   - Right rear brake caliper
   - Left rear brake caliper
   - Front right brake caliper
   - Front left brake caliper
5. Use suitable bleeder hose. It must fit tightly on bleeder valve so that no air gets into brake system.

6. With bleeder bottle hose attached, leave bleeder valves open long enough that brake fluid exits without bubbles.

Post-Bleeding

1. Before servicing the vehicle, refer to the precautions.

→A second mechanic is required to assist.

2. Depress brake pedal forcefully and hold.
3. Open the bleeder valve at brake caliper.
4. Press brake pedal down onto stop.
5. Close bleeder valve with pedal depressed.
6. Release brake pedal slowly.

→This bleeding procedure must be performed 5 times per brake caliper.

7. Note the proper bleeding sequence:
   - Right rear brake caliper
   - Left rear brake caliper
   - Front right brake caliper
   - Front left brake caliper
8. A road test must be performed after bleeding. During this, at least one ABS regulation must be performed.

BRAKES

FRONT DISC BRAKES

❊❊ CAUTION

Dust and dirt accumulating on brake parts during normal use may contain asbestos fibers from production or aftermarket brake linings. Breathing excessive concentrations of asbestos fibers can cause serious bodily harm. Exercise care when servicing brake parts. Do not sand or grind brake lining unless equipment used is designed to contain the dust residue. Do not clean brake parts with compressed air or by dry brushing. Cleaning should be done by dampening the brake components with a fine mist of water, then wiping the brake components clean with a dampened cloth. Dispose of cloth and all residue containing asbestos fibers in an impermeable container with the appropriate label. Follow practices prescribed by the Occupational Safety and Health Administration (OSHA) and the Environmental Protection Agency (EPA) for the handling, processing, and disposing of

dust or debris that may contain asbestos fibers.

BRAKE CALIPER

REMOVAL & INSTALLATION

Brembo 17-inch
See Figure 3.

1. Before servicing the vehicle, refer to the precautions.
2. Remove the wheels.
3. Connect bleeder hose of bleeder bottle to bleeder valve of brake caliper and then open bleeder valve.
4. Insert a brake pedal depressor (V.A.G 1869/2).
5. Close bleeder valve and remove bleeder bottle.
6. Unscrew brake line from brake caliper.
7. Unscrew bracket from wheel bearing housing.
8. Remove the brake pads.
9. Remove brake caliper from wheel bearing housing.

To install:

10. Bolt brake caliper onto wheel bearing housing. Tighten the bolt to 199 ft. lbs. (270 Nm).
11. Install brake pads.
12. Install brake line on brake caliper. Tighten to 10 ft. lbs. (14 Nm).
13. Install bracket to wheel bearing housing. Tighten bolt to 7 ft. lbs. (9 Nm).
14. Remove brake pedal loading device.
15. Bleed brake system.
16. Install the wheels. Tighten the wheel nuts to 133 ft. lbs. (180 Nm).
17. Before moving vehicle, depress brake pedal several times firmly to properly seat brake pads in their normal operating position.
18. Check brake fluid level.

Brembo 18-inch
See Figure 4.

→Work procedure applies only for replacing or when performing subsequent service work on brake caliper.

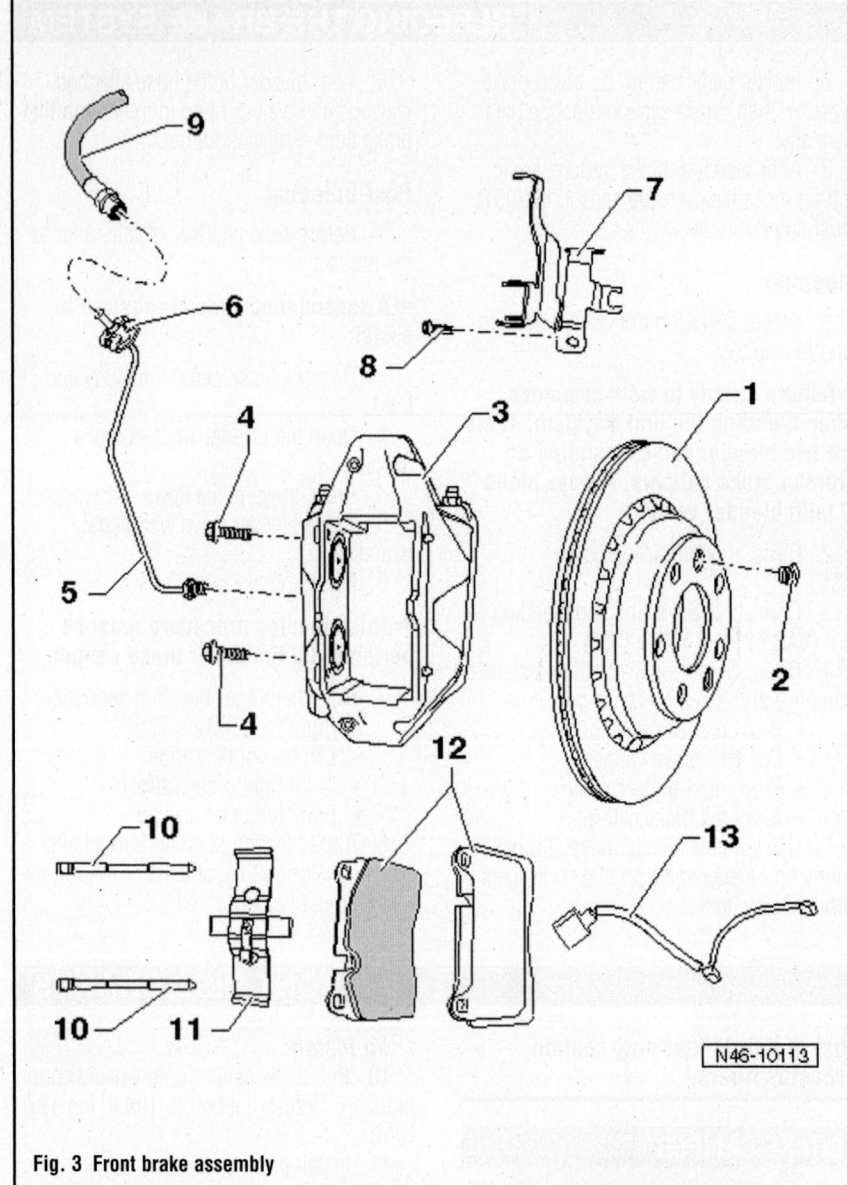

Fig. 3 Front brake assembly

1. Remove the wheels.
2. Connect bleeder hose of bleeder bottle to bleeder valve of brake caliper and then open bleeder valve.
3. Insert A brake pedal depressor (V.A.G 1869/2).
4. Close bleeder valve and remove bleeder bottle.
5. Unscrew bracket from wheel bearing housing.
6. Separate the connector for brake pad wear indicator.
7. Unfasten the brake hose from the brake caliper.
8. Remove brake caliper from wheel bearing housing.
9. Remove the brake pads.

To install:
10. Install brake pads.

11. Install brake caliper. Tighten to 22 ft. lbs. plus 90 degrees.
12. Install brake line on brake caliper. Tighten to 10 ft. lbs. (14 Nm).
13. Carefully install the brake pad wear indicator wire contact sensor in brake pads.
14. Install the wheels. Tighten the wheel nuts to 133 ft. lbs. (180 Nm).
15. Before moving vehicle, depress brake pedal several times firmly to properly seat brake pads in their normal operating position.
16. Check brake fluid level.

DISC BRAKE PADS

REMOVAL & INSTALLATION

Brembo 17-inch

1. Before servicing the vehicle, refer to the precautions.

2. Raise the vehicle and remove the wheels.
3. Unplug the connector for the brake pad wear indicator.
4. Remove the cotter pin on the inner side of the caliper from the pad retaining pin.
5. Press retaining spring down and remove pad retaining pin at the same time.
6. Pull the wire for the brake pad wear indicator out of the brake caliper housing and out of the retaining spring.
7. Remove the retaining spring.
8. Before pressing brake pads back, draw off brake fluid from reservoir using a bleeder bottle. Otherwise, especially if reservoir has been topped off, fluid will overflow and cause damage.
9. Press brake pads off brake disc and remove from brake caliper.
10. Carefully remove the contact sensor with the brake pad wear indicator wire from the brake pads and check for damage. (Reuse undamaged contact sensors and wires.)

To install:
11. Clean the brake caliper with mineral spirits of any adhesive residue. The surface must be dry and clean.
12. Before pressing the piston back in its bore to insert the new brake pads, draw off brake fluid from the reservoir with a bleeder bottle.
13. Push the piston back in its bore. Carefully install the brake pad wear indicator wire contact sensor in the new brake pads.
14. Insert the new brake pads into the caliper.
15. Insert retaining spring and install the wire for the brake pad wear indicator below the tab of the retaining spring and in the brake caliper housing.
16. Press the retaining spring down and press the pad retaining pin in until the stop.
17. Secure the pad retaining pin using securing cotter pin.
18. Connect connectors of the brake pad wear indicator in the bracket of brake caliper housing.
19. Install the wheels.
20. After replacing the brake pads, depress brake pedal firmly several times with the vehicle stationary so that the brake pads are properly seated in their normal operating position.
21. Check brake fluid level after replacing brake pad.

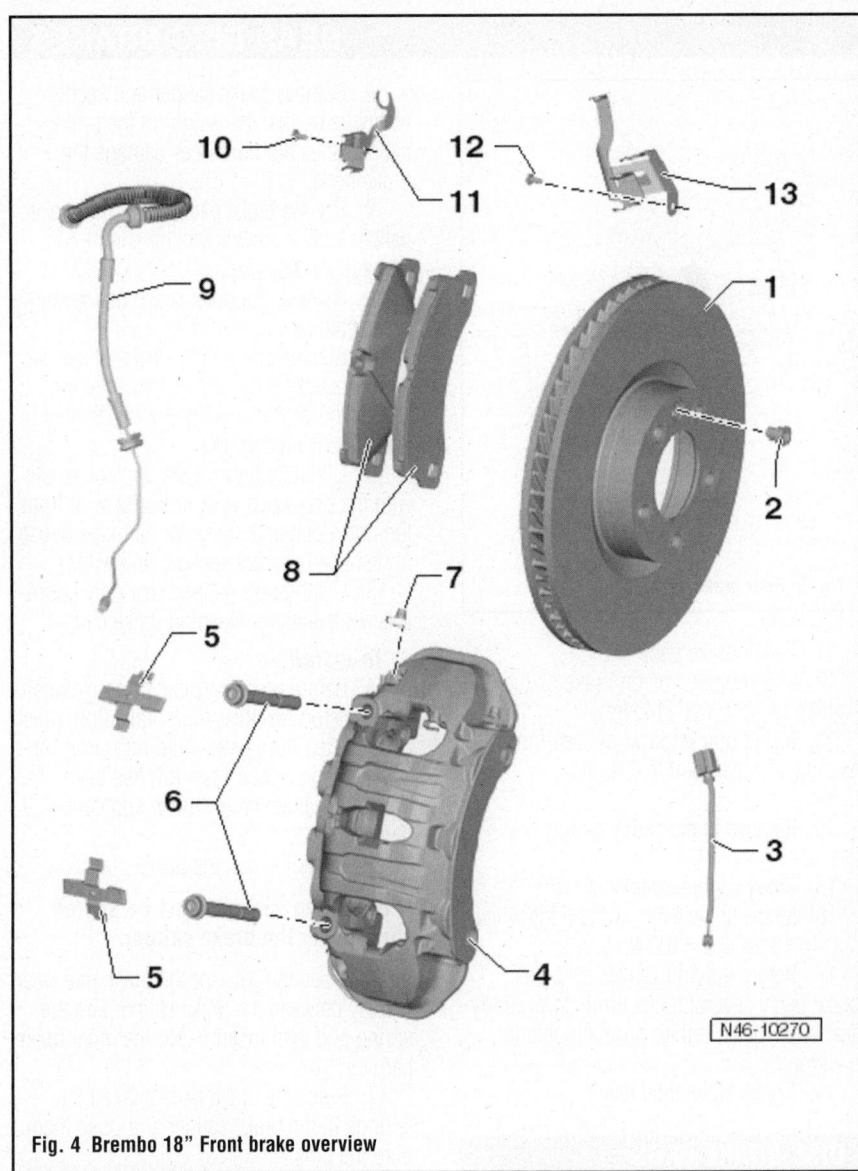

Fig. 4 Brembo 18" Front brake overview

Brembo 18-inch

➡ **When removing, mark brake pads that will be used again. Install in the same position, otherwise braking effect will be uneven!**

1. Remove the wheels.
2. Remove the upper brake hose bracket from the wheel bearing housing.
3. Disconnect the brake pad wear display connector and remove it from the bracket.
4. Remove the bolt and the lower brake hose bracket from the wheel bearing housing.
5. Remove the dust cap from the brake caliper bleed valve and the wire for the brake pad wear display.
6. Remove the wire for the brake pad wear display from the brake caliper.
7. Disconnect the connector from the speed sensor.
8. Press the brake pads off the brake rotor.
9. Remove the internal multi-point bolts from the brake caliper.
10. Install the caliper guide pins T10439.
11. Push the brake caliper as far forward as possible until the brake caliper locks into the T10439.

12. Pry the brake pads out of the brake caliper with a screwdriver; Be sure not to damage the dust caps.
13. Remove the brake pads from the brake caliper.
14. Carefully remove the contact sensor with the brake pad wear indicator wire from the brake pad and check for damage. Reuse undamaged contact sensors and wires.
15. Clean the brake caliper.

To install:

❊❊ WARNING

Before pressing piston into cylinder using piston resetting tool, brake fluid must be extracted from brake fluid reservoir. Otherwise, especially if reservoir has been topped off, fluid will overflow and cause damage.

16. Press pistons back.

➡ **The retaining springs must be seated correctly in the brake caliper.**

17. Mount the brake pads on the 4 contact surfaces of the brake retaining springs.
18. Install the brake pads onto the 4 pins.
19. Carefully place the brake caliper over the brake disc.
20. Remove the caliper guide pins T10439.
21. Install the internal multi-point bolts. Tighten to 22 ft. lbs. plus 90 degrees. (use new bolts)
22. Attach both brackets to the wheel bearing housing. Tighten bolt to 7 ft. lbs. (9 Nm).
23. Install the wire for the brake pad wear display in the brake caliper and under the dust cap.
24. Connect the connector for the brake pad wear display inside the bracket.
25. Reconnect the connector to the speed sensor.
26. Install the wheels. Tighten the wheel nuts to 133 ft. lbs. (180 Nm).
27. After replacing the brake pads, depress brake pedal firmly several times with the vehicle stationary so that the brake pads are properly seated in their normal operating position.
28. Check brake fluid level after replacing brake pad.

❊❊ CAUTION

Dust and dirt accumulating on brake parts during normal use may contain asbestos fibers from production or aftermarket brake linings. Breathing excessive concentrations of asbestos fibers can cause serious bodily harm. Exercise care when servicing brake parts. Do not sand or grind brake lining unless equipment used is designed to contain the dust residue. Do not clean brake parts with compressed air or by dry brushing. Cleaning should be done by dampening the brake components with a fine mist of water, then wiping the brake components clean with a dampened cloth. Dispose of cloth and all residue containing asbestos fibers in an impermeable container with the appropriate label. Follow practices prescribed by the Occupational Safety and Health Administration (OSHA) and the Environmental Protection Agency (EPA) for the handling, processing, and disposing of dust or debris that may contain asbestos fibers.

BRAKE CALIPER

REMOVAL & INSTALLATION

See Figure 5.

1. Before servicing the vehicle, refer to the precautions.
2. Remove the wheels.
3. Connect bleeder hose of bleeder bottle to bleeder valve of brake caliper and then open bleeder valve.
4. Insert A brake pedal depressor (V.A.G 1869/2).
5. Close bleeder valve and remove bleeder bottle.
6. Unscrew brake line from brake caliper.
7. Unscrew bracket from wheel bearing housing.
8. Remove the brake pads.
9. Remove brake caliper from wheel bearing housing.

To install:

10. Bolt brake caliper onto wheel bearing housing. Tighten to 22 ft. lbs. plus 90° (use new bolts)

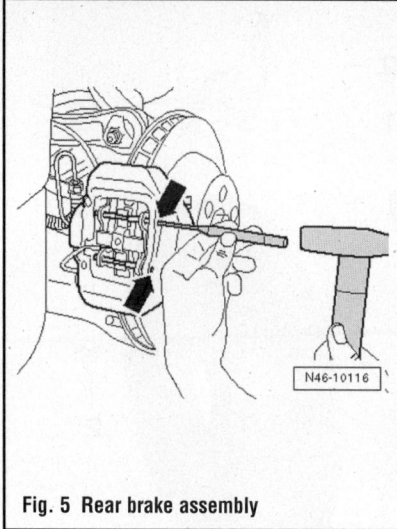

Fig. 5 Rear brake assembly

11. Install brake pads.
12. Install brake line on brake caliper. Tighten to 10 ft. lbs. (14 Nm).
13. Install bracket to wheel bearing housing. Tighten bolt to 7 ft. lbs. (9 Nm).
14. Remove brake pedal loading device.
15. Bleed brake system.
16. Install the wheels. Tighten the wheel nuts to 133 ft. lbs. (180 Nm).
17. Before moving vehicle, depress brake pedal several times firmly to properly seat brake pads in their normal operating position.
18. Check brake fluid level.

DISC BRAKE PADS

REMOVAL & INSTALLATION

1. Remove the wheels.
2. Separate the connector for brake pad wear indicator.
3. Disconnect the connector for brake pad wear indicator
4. Remove the wire for the brake pad wear display from the brake caliper.
5. Before pressing brake pads back, draw off brake fluid from reservoir using a bleeder bottle. Otherwise, especially if reservoir has been topped off, fluid will overflow and cause damage.
6. Press the brake pads off the brake rotor.
7. Remove brake caliper from wheel bearing housing.

8. Remove brake caliper and secure with wire so that the weight of the brake caliper does not burden or damage the brake hose.
9. Pry the brake pads out of the brake caliper with a screwdriver, be sure not to damage the dust caps.
10. Remove the outer brake pad from the brake caliper.
11. Remove the inner brake pad just far enough out of the brake caliper until the connector for the brake pad wear display wire touches the spring.
12. Carefully remove the contact sensor with the brake pad wear indicator wire from the brake pad and check for damage. Reuse undamaged contact sensors and wires.
13. Clean brake caliper. Use only appropriate solvents for cleaning brake caliper.

To install:

14. Before pressing piston into cylinder using piston resetting tool, brake fluid must be extracted from brake fluid reservoir. Otherwise, especially if reservoir has been topped off, fluid will overflow and cause damage.
15. Press the pistons back.

➡**Retaining springs must be seated correctly in the brake caliper.**

16. Place the wire for the brake pad wear display between the brake caliper and the spring and then insert it into the inner brake pad.
17. Press the brake pads against the springs in the brake caliper and push them onto the pins.
18. Carefully place the brake caliper over the brake disc.
19. Bolt brake caliper onto wheel bearing housing. Tighten to 22 ft. lbs. plus 90° (use new bolts)
20. Press the wire for the brake pad wear display into the opening in the brake caliper.
21. Install the brake pad wear display connector in the bracket on the brake caliper.
22. Install the wheels. Tighten the wheel nuts to 133 ft. lbs. (180 Nm).
23. Before moving vehicle, depress brake pedal several times firmly to properly seat brake pads in their normal operating position.
24. Check brake fluid level.

BRAKES

PARKING BRAKE

PARKING BRAKE CABLES

ADJUSTMENT

See Figures 5 through 6

✳✳ CAUTION

Adjustment must only be performed on both adjustment devices for rear wheels! Adjustment must never be performed at parking brake pedal or transfer module.

➡**Observe correct routing and guiding of parking brake cables.**

➡**If the brake shoes were replaced, adjust air gap to the 6th teeth. Then run in brake shoes by braking vehicle**

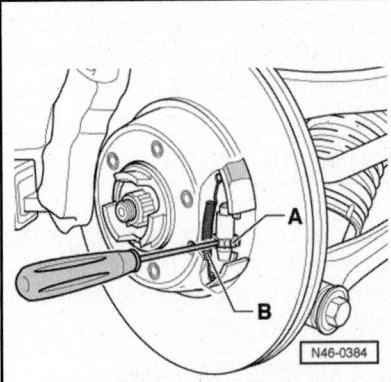

Fig. 6 Push screwdriver through hole and turn adjustment nut (A) against resistance of pull-spring (B) until brake disc can no longer be turned

in a single maneuver from a speed of approximately 50 km/h. Rear wheels must not lock up when doing so.

1. Park brake pedal in released position.
2. Remove rear wheels.
3. Brake discs must move freely. If necessary, press brake pads slightly back or move rear brake cables slightly to and fro.
4. Remove the locking bolt for adjustment nut of the parking brake.
5. Push screwdriver through hole in brake disc and turn adjustment nut against resistance of pull-spring until brake disc can no longer be turned.
6. Then loosen adjustment nut 6 teeth. Brake discs must move freely again.
7. Free play of foot operated parking brake lever must be checked again.
8. Install wheels

Pedal Parking Brake Lever, Checking Play

1. Actuate foot brake pedal 2 teeth, wheels must rotate freely without brake shoes dragging.
2. Actuate foot operated parking brake lever 5 to 7 teeth, wheels must be fixed. In case wheels can still be rotated, parking brake must be adjusted

PARKING BRAKE SHOES

REMOVAL & INSTALLATION

See Figure 5

1. Before servicing the vehicle, refer to the precautions.
2. Remove wheels.

3. Remove brake pads.
4. Pull wheel speed sensor wire out of bracket at brake caliper.
5. Remove the mounting bolts of brake caliper.
6. Remove brake caliper housing and secure with wire so that the weight of the brake caliper does not burden or damage the brake hose.
7. Remove locking bolt (arrow) for adjustment nut of parking brake.
8. With a proper adjusting tool inserted through the disk, turn the adjustment nut against resistance from the pull-spring.
9. Remove the brake disc.
10. Unhook the pull-springs.
11. Remove spring dowel sleeves with compression springs and remove brake shoes.

To install:

12. Install the brake shoes.
13. Install the spring dowel sleeves with the compression springs.
14. Hook the pull-spring to its original location.
15. Install the brake disc.
16. Install the brake caliper to the disc. Tighten to 22 ft. lbs. plus 90° (use new bolts)
17. Reposition the wheel speed sensor wire to the bracket.
18. Install the rear disc pads.
19. Install the wheels. Tighten the wheel nuts to 133 ft. lbs. (180 Nm).
20. Adjust the parking brake and lever.

CHASSIS ELECTRICAL

AIR BAG (SUPPLEMENTAL RESTRAINT SYSTEM)

GENERAL INFORMATION

✳✳ CAUTION

These vehicles are equipped with an air bag system. The system must be disarmed before performing service on, or around, system components, the steering column, instrument panel components, wiring and sensors. Failure to follow the safety precautions and the disarming procedure could result in accidental air bag deployment, possible injury and unnecessary system repairs.

SERVICE PRECAUTIONS

Disconnect and isolate the battery negative cable before beginning any airbag system component diagnosis, testing, removal, or installation procedures. Allow system capacitor to discharge for two minutes before beginning any component service. This will disable the airbag system. Failure to disable the airbag system may result in accidental airbag deployment, personal injury, or death.

Do not place an intact undeployed airbag face down on a solid surface. The airbag will propel into the air if accidentally deployed and may result in personal injury or death.

When carrying or handling an undeployed airbag, the trim side (face) of the airbag should be pointing away from the body to minimize possibility of injury if accidental deployment occurs. Failure to do this may result in personal injury or death.

Replace airbag system components with OEM replacement parts. Substitute parts may appear interchangeable, but internal differences may result in inferior occupant protection. Failure to do so may result in occupant personal injury or death.

Wear safety glasses, rubber gloves, and long sleeved clothing when cleaning powder residue from vehicle after an airbag deployment. Powder residue emitted from a deployed airbag can cause skin irritation.

Flush affected area with cool water if irritation is experienced. If nasal or throat irritation is experienced, exit the vehicle for fresh air until the irritation ceases. If irritation continues, see a physician.

Do not use a replacement airbag that is not in the original packaging. This may result in improper deployment, personal injury, or death.

The factory installed fasteners, screws and bolts used to fasten airbag components have a special coating and are specifically designed for the airbag system. Do not use substitute fasteners. Use only original equipment fasteners listed in the parts catalog when fastener replacement is required.

During, and following, any child restraint anchor service, due to impact event or vehicle repair, carefully inspect all mounting hardware, tether straps, and anchors for proper installation, operation, or damage. If a child restraint anchor is found damaged in any way, the anchor must be replaced. Failure to do this may result in personal injury or death.

Deployed and non-deployed airbags may or may not have live pyrotechnic material within the airbag inflator.

Do not dispose of driver/passenger/curtain airbags or seat belt tensioners unless you are sure of complete deployment. Refer to the Hazardous Substance Control System for proper disposal.

Dispose of deployed airbags and tensioners consistent with state, provincial, local, and federal regulations.

After any airbag component testing or service, do not connect the battery negative cable. Personal injury or death may result if the system test is not performed first.

If the vehicle is equipped with the Occupant Classification System (OCS), do not connect the battery negative cable before performing the OCS Verification Test using the scan tool and the appropriate diagnostic information. Personal injury or death may result if the system test is not performed properly.

Never replace both the Occupant Restraint Controller (ORC) and the Occupant Classification Module (OCM) at the same time. If both require replacement, replace one, then perform the Airbag System test before replacing the other.

Both the ORC and the OCM store Occupant Classification System (OCS) calibration data, which they transfer to one another when one of them is replaced. If both are replaced at the same time, an irreversible fault will be set in both modules and the OCS may malfunction and cause personal injury or death.

If equipped with OCS, the Seat Weight Sensor is a sensitive, calibrated unit and must be handled carefully. Do not drop or handle roughly. If dropped or damaged, replace with another sensor. Failure to do so may result in occupant injury or death.

If equipped with OCS, the front passenger seat must be handled carefully as well. When removing the seat, be careful when setting on floor not to drop. If dropped, the sensor may be inoperative, could result in occupant injury, or possibly death.

If equipped with OCS, when the passenger front seat is on the floor, no one should sit in the front passenger seat. This uneven force may damage the sensing ability of the seat weight sensors. If sat on and damaged, the sensor may be inoperative, could result in occupant injury, or possibly death.

DISARMING THE SYSTEM

✳✳ CAUTION

When working on the airbag system, the battery ground (GND) strap must be disconnected. No waiting time is necessary after disconnecting battery. When connecting the airbag system to a voltage source, there must be no person present inside the vehicle.

To avoid personal injury when working on vehicles equipped with an air bag, the negative battery cable must be disconnected before working on the system. Failure to do so may result in deployment of the air bag.

1. Before servicing the vehicle, refer to the precautions.
2. Turn the ignition switch to the **LOCK** position.
3. Disconnect the negative battery cable. Shield the cable by wrapping electrical tape around it. Work can begin immediately after disconnecting the battery, no waiting time is needed.

ARMING THE SYSTEM

After repairs are completed, the negative battery cable is properly reconnected to the battery. Ensure there are no additional personnel in the vehicle when reconnecting the negative battery cable.

CLOCKSPRING CENTERING

1. The airbag spiral spring/return spring with slip ring F138 is a construction-specific component of the steering column switches.

DRIVE TRAIN

AUTOMATIC TRANSMISSION FLUID

FILTER REPLACEMENT

See Figure 7.

1. Before servicing the vehicle, refer to the Precautions Section.
2. Lift the vehicle.
3. Remove the noise insulation for the transmission.
4. Place a drip pan underneath.
5. Remove the drain plug.
6. Unscrew the overflow tube.
7. Remove the transmission pan bolts.
8. Remove the transmission pan.
9. Remove the filter bolts.

10. Remove the transmission fluid filter.
11. Remove the filter seal from its seat in the valve body.

To install:

12. Clean all magnets in the oil pan recesses. Make sure the magnets touch the transmission pan completely.
13. First install the filter loosely. Then center it and press it into the valve body.
14. Lubricate the new seal with transmission fluid and install it on the suction collar. Position the filter loosely on the valve body but do not press it in.
15. Install the bolts approximately 3 turns (no more!) into the valve body.
16. The filter centers itself noticeably in the valve body seat.

17. Center the filter and press it into the valve body as far as the stop by pressing evenly on the corners. Hold it firmly in this position.
18. Counter turn the bolts by hand.
19. Tighten the transmission fluid filter bolts to 7 ft. lbs. (10 Nm).
20. Install the oil pan with a new gasket.
21. Tighten the oil pan bolts diagonally and in several steps to 6 ft. lbs. (6 Nm).
22. Install the overflow tube and tighten to 1.5 ft. lbs. (2 Nm).
23. Install the drain plug and tighten to 12 ft. lbs. (16 Nm).
24. After installation, fill with transmission fluid and check the level, add if necessary.

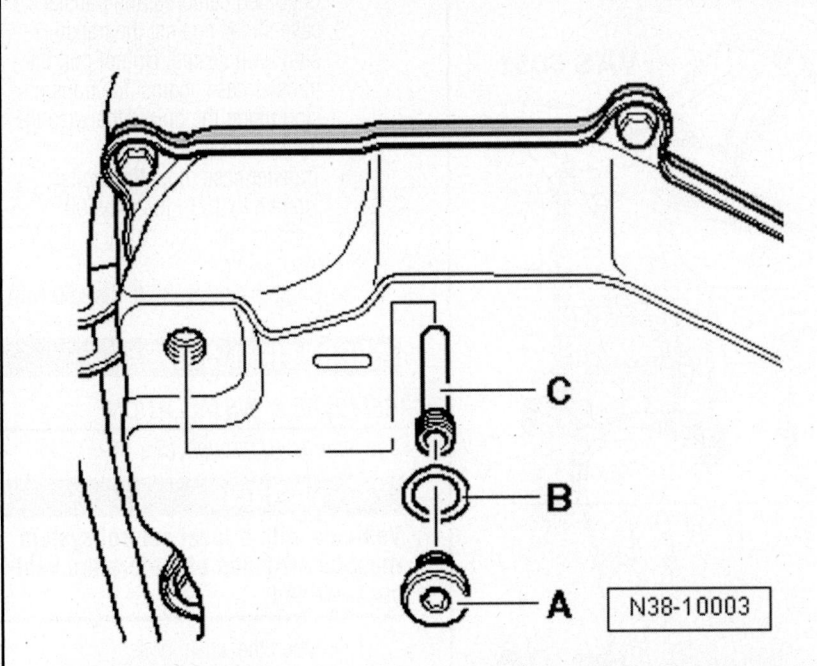

1. **Transfer case**
2. **Front and rear driveshaft**
3. **Rear final drive (axle)**
4. **Front final drive (axle)**

Fig. 7 Drain plug A, washer B, overflow tube C

TRANSMISSION FLUID BLEEDING

1. Check the transmission fluid level and add as necessary.

2. Perform a road test, the transmission fluid temperature must reach at least 212° F (100° C) to bleed the circuit.

3. When the air leaves the circuit, the transmission fluid level in the transmission decreases. Therefore, the fluid level must be checked again later after the fluid cools.

4. Let the fluid cool down to 86° F (30° C). Recheck the fluid level.

TRANSMISSION FLUID LEVEL CHECKING

The transmission fluid level is specified by a permanently installed overflow tube in the oil pan. Check the fluid level when the fluid is at a specific temperature and with the engine running. The fluid temperature is read out using the vehicle diagnosis, testing and information system VAS 5051 B scan tool. To check the fluid level, remove the plug in the oil pan once the test temperature has been reached.

1. Test Prerequisites Condition:

a. The transmission is not in the emergency operation mode, and the fluid temperature is not higher than 30°C (86 °F).

b. The vehicle must be horizontal.

c. The selector level is in the "P" position

d. All electrical consumers and the Air Conditioning (A/C) system must be turned off.

2. Connect the vehicle diagnostic tester and move through selections until it is ready for operation.

3. Press the right Guided Functions button.

4. Select the vehicle, the transmission and the Check ATF level button.

5. Press the button.

6. Press the brake pedal.

7. Start the engine.

8. Move the selector lever to each position for 2 seconds. Then move the selector lever to the "P" position.

9. Lift the vehicle.

10. Place a drip pan under the transmission.

11. Remove the plug from the transmission pan and check the fluid level.

➡**Even if the level of the transmission fluid is too low, at first a small amount of transmission fluid will leak out of the overflow tube, because it fills during operation.**

12. Drain any transmission fluid still in the overflow tube. If fluid continues to leak out of the hole, the fluid does not need to be topped off.

13. Install the plug (with a new seal) and tighten it to 12 ft. lbs. (16 Nm). The transmission fluid level test is now completed.

14. If no fluid leaks out of the hole, fill the transmission fluid

TRANSMISSION FLUID FILLING

See Figure 8.

1. With the engine running, install the adapter for filling ATF oil VAS 6262/2 to the pan hand tight.

2. Fill with 1 liter of transmission fluid.

3. Install the adapter for oil filling VAS 6262 to the quick release coupling on the adapter for filling ATF oil VAS 6262/2 and check. If fluid drips out of the hole, the fluid does not need to be topped off. Allow the fluid to drain until it drips stop.

4. If fluid does not drip out, add another liter of fluid.

✳✳ WARNING

Too little or too much transmission fluid will impair the transmission. If 2 liters are missing, you should check the transmission more closely. There is probably a larger leak.

TRANSFER CASE ASSEMBLY

REMOVAL & INSTALLATION

See Figure 9.

1. Before servicing the vehicle, refer to the Precautions Section.

2. Lift the vehicle.

3. Remove the noise insulation and bracket under the transmission

4. Remove the rear section of the exhaust system.

5. Remove the rear driveshaft.

6. Remove the front driveshaft.

7. Remove the exhaust system either from the transfer case support or from the transfer case, depending on the engine.

8. Position the engine/transmission jack V.A.G 1383/A and the transmission support 3282 under the transfer case and align them.

9. Secure the transmission support 3282 to the transfer case with bolts. Remove the chain balancer from the transfer case beforehand, if equipped.

10. Remove the transfer case support bolts from the underbody.

11. Remove both bracket bolts from the transfer case support.

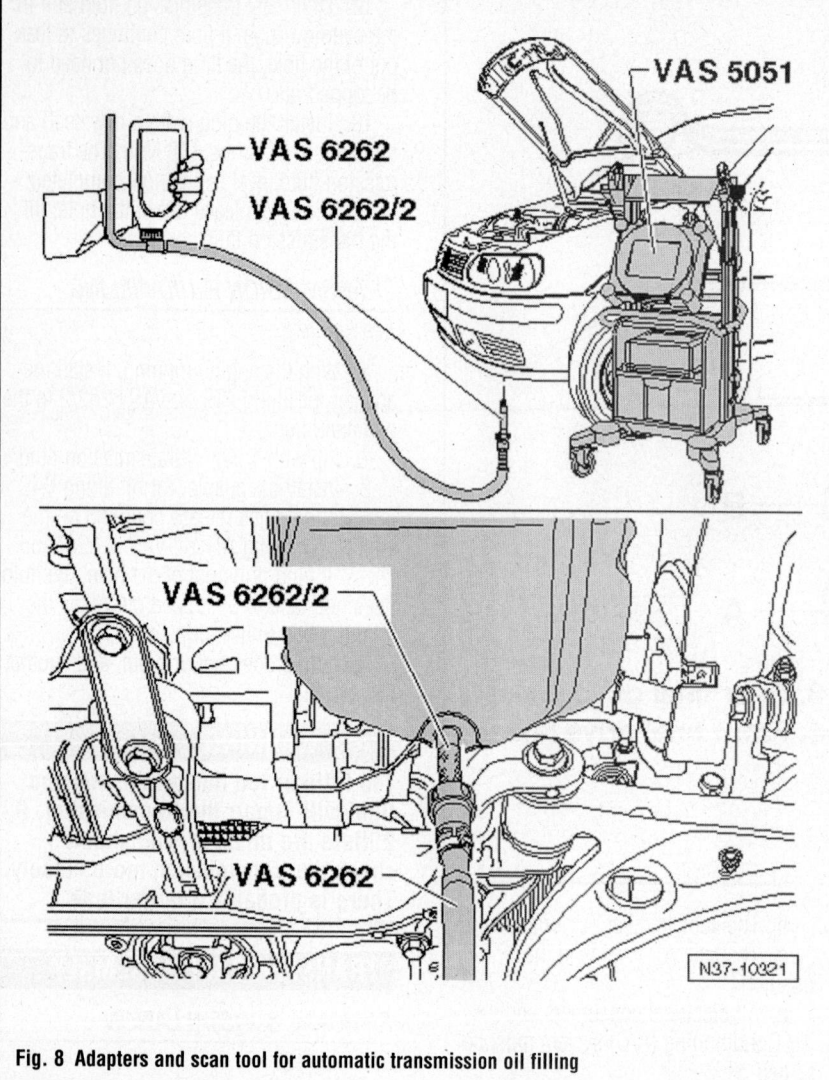

Fig. 8 Adapters and scan tool for automatic transmission oil filling

12. Remove the transfer case support and lay it down.

13. Remove the side and lower bolts that connect the transfer case to the transmission.

14. Lower the engine/transmission sub-assembly slightly using the engine/transmission jack V.A.G 1383/A, if necessary.

15. Secure the engine/transmission sub-assembly to the underbody using the transmission support VW 785/1B.

16. Apply the multipurpose grease to the contact surface of the pressure plate.

17. Mount the pressure pad on the thrust pad 3062. The smaller diameter on the thrust pad 3062 faces the pressure pad.

18. Place a block of wood A between the transfer case and the thrust pad 3062.

19. Remove the upper transfer case/transmission bolts.

20. Remove the transfer case from the transmission.

21. Lower the transfer case.

To install:

22. Installation is performed in the reverse order of removal while observing the following

- Make sure the alignment sleeves for centering the engine/transfer case are installed inside the transmission. Install them if necessary.
- Always replace the O-ring used for sealing the transfer case/transmission arrow and coat it lightly with oil.
- Always grease the splines on the transfer case and transmission driveshaft's with grease for clutch plate splines G 000 100.
- Push the transfer case all the way onto the transmission making sure the driveshaft splines/transfer case engage with the output shaft/transmission.
- If the tooth position is correct and it

is guided centered, the transfer case slides against the transmission until seated. Do not pull the transfer case against the transmission using the bolts otherwise the transfer case will tilt.

- Transfer case mounting bolts: Tighten to 15 ft. lbs. plus 90°
- Transfer case end balancer: 24 ft. lbs. (32 Nm)
- Chain balancer: 37 ft. lbs. (50 Nm)

FRONT FINAL DRIVE

REMOVAL & INSTALLATION

See Figures 10 through 13.

✳✳ WARNING

Vehicles with a level control system must be switched off before the vehicle is raised.

1. Loosen the wheel bolts.
2. Lift the vehicle.
3. Remove the front wheels.
4. Remove the left and right front wheel housing liners.
5. If the vehicle has air spring dampers installed, loosen the connection for the air line and let the air out. Retighten the connection.
6. Engage the tension hooks VW 552 in the upper opening in the wheel housing on both sides of the vehicle and into the upper control arm.
7. Lightly pretension the control arm so that the ball stud in the ball joint does not get damaged.
8. Remove the noise insulation underneath the engine/transmission.
9. Remove the impact guard under the front final drive, if equipped.
10. Remove the bracket for the noise insulation.
11. Remove the front driveshaft.
12. Remove the heat shield bolts and shield from the front final drive.
13. Remove the right and left drive axles. Use the bit T10099/1 to loosen the bolts.
14. Remove the heat shield from the steering gear (2 bolts), if equipped.
15. Remove the bolt for the steering gear for the universal joint and then remove the universal joint from the steering gear.
16. Remove the coolant pipes from the left longitudinal member, if equipped. Remove the nut and the bracket.
17. Engage the spindle 10-222 A/11 into the lifting eyes on the sub-frame on both the left and right sides of the vehicle.
18. Insert a block of wood, approxi-

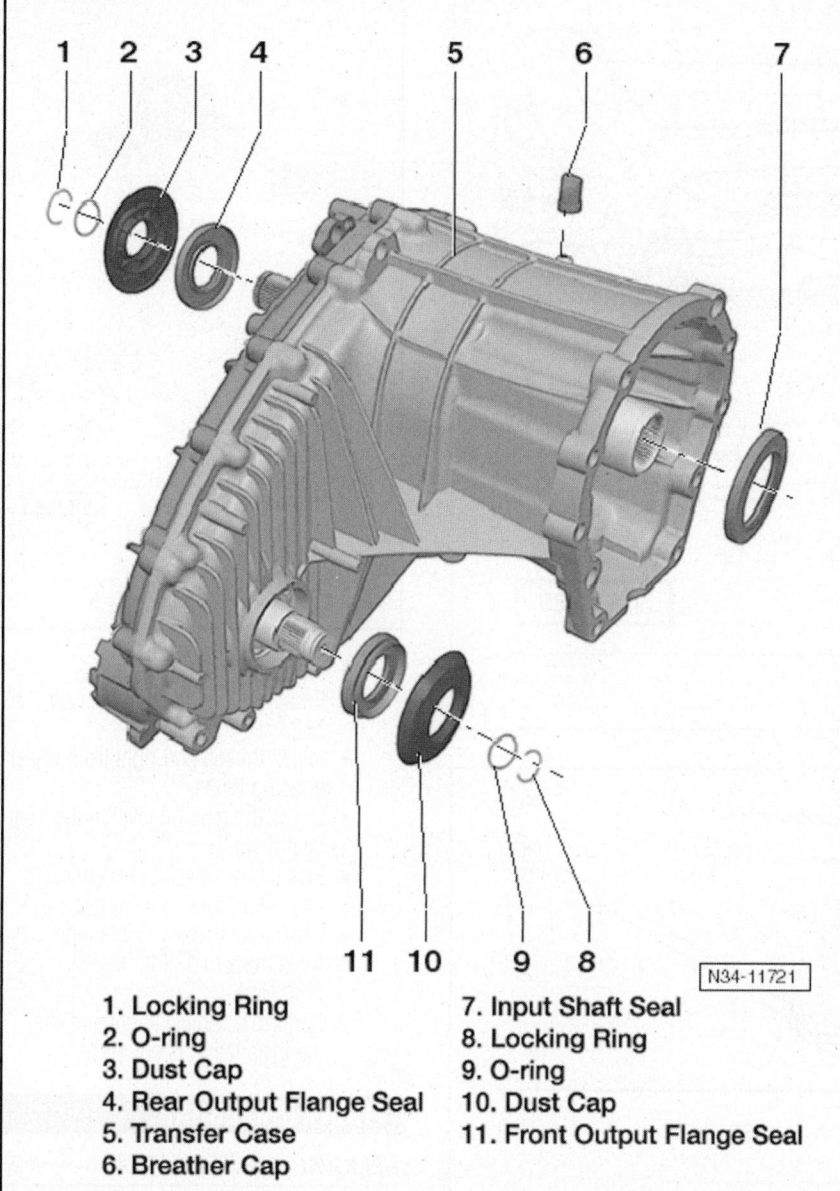

1. Locking Ring
2. O-ring
3. Dust Cap
4. Rear Output Flange Seal
5. Transfer Case
6. Breather Cap
7. Input Shaft Seal
8. Locking Ring
9. O-ring
10. Dust Cap
11. Front Output Flange Seal

N34-11721

Fig. 9 Transfer case overview

mately 300 mm long, into the spindle 10-222 A/11 bracket. The bracket must face toward the rear.

19. Tighten the wing nuts on the spindle. While doing this, the wood blocks must be supported on the sub-frame.

20. Place a floor jack on the N39-1225.

21. Position the engine/transmission jack V.A.G 1383 A under the sub-frame and lightly press against it.

22. Remove one of the rear bolts for the sub-frame.

23. Secure the sub-frame.

24. Remove the sub-frame bolts.

25. Remove the left and right coupling rods from the stabilizer bar.

26. Remove the air spring damper/strut to lower control arm bolts 2. Lower the sub-frame approximately 50 mm using the spindle 10-222 A/11 in the direction of the arrow to remove the bolt.

27. Install two M14 x 1.5 x 90 bolts, to secure the sub-frame to the left and right air spring damper/strut.

28. Remove the engine/transmission jack V.A.G 1383 A from under the sub-frame.

29. Place the engine/transmission jack V.A.G 1383 A along with the universal transmission support 1359/2 under the sub-frame and press against it lightly. Place the wooden block underneath the sub-frame and under the front final drive.

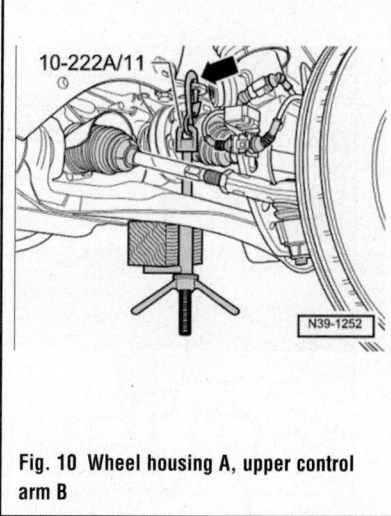

Fig. 10 Wheel housing A, upper control arm B

30. Secure the sub-frame using the belt from the universal transmission support V.A.G 1359/2.

31. Remove the spindle 10 - 222 A/11 from the sub-frame.

32. Carefully lower the sub-frame and the front final drive to approximately 200 mm.

33. Remove the bolts and nuts that attach the front final drive to the sub-frame.

➡**A second technician will be needed in order to remove the front final drive.**

34. Remove the front final drive 1 toward the rear between the sub-frame and the engine/transmission:

35. Tie up the left drive axle first.

36. The second technician can then remove the front final drive from the mounts inside the sub-frame.

37. Guide the right drive axle out of the flange shaft.

38. Lift the front final drive over the steering gear and guide it out toward the rear.

To install:

➡**A second technician will be needed to install the front final drive back into the mounts on the sub-frame.**

39. Installation is performed in the reverse order of removal while observing the following:

- Install the bolts and nuts that connect the front final drive to the sub-frame. Tighten to 66 ft. lbs. (90 Nm) plus 90°.
- Install sub-frame and sub-frame to body bolts. Tighten to 89 ft. lbs. (120 Nm) plus 120° turn.
- Attach the drive axles to the flange shafts

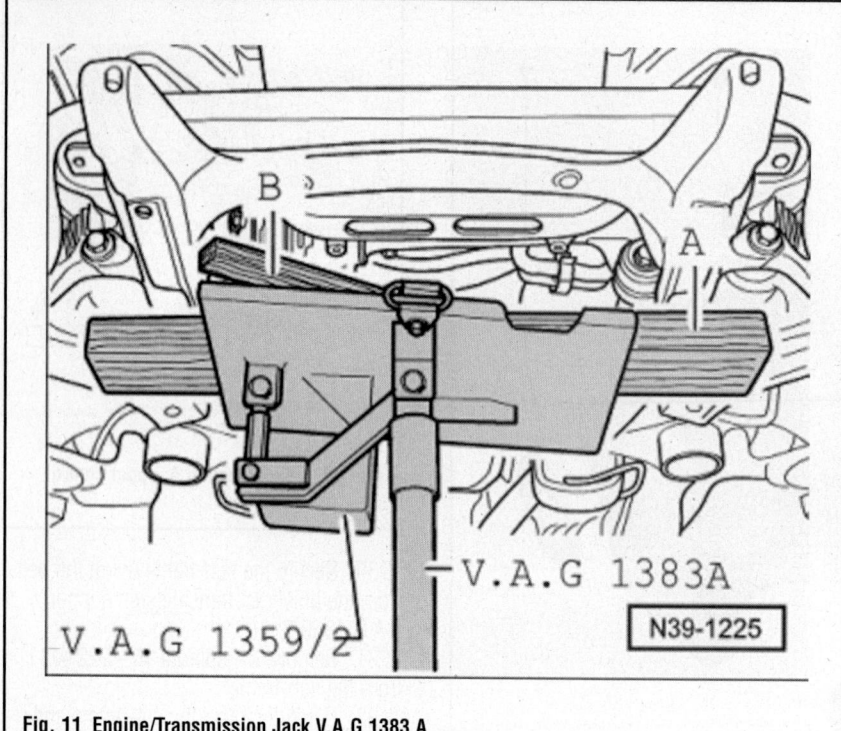

Fig. 11 Engine/Transmission Jack V.A.G 1383 A

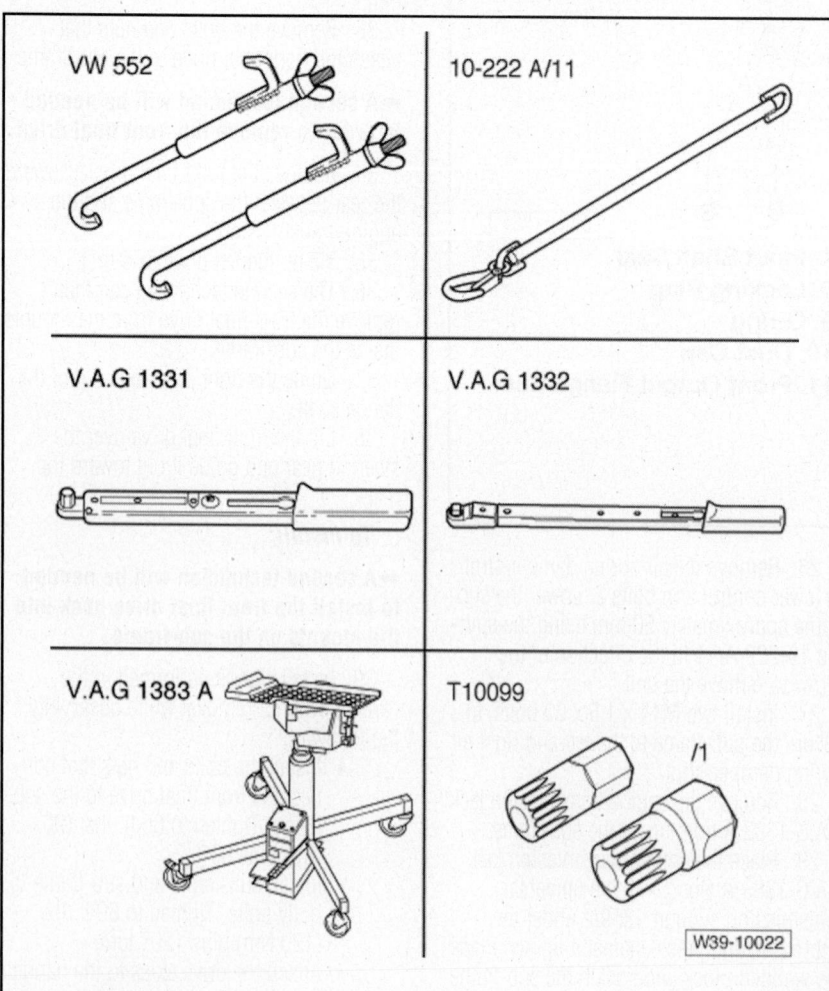

Fig. 12 Special tools required

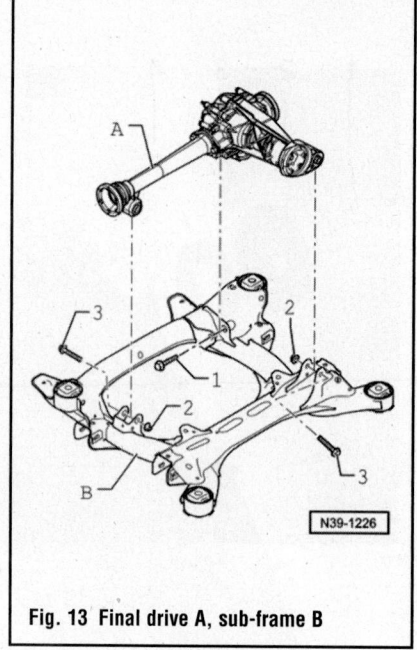

Fig. 13 Final drive A, sub-frame B

- Install the front driveshaft.
- Remove the tension hooks VW 552.
- Install the left and right front wheel housing liners.
- Check the gear oil level in the front final drive.
- Install the impact guard under the front final drive, if equipped.
- Install the wheels. Tighten the wheel nuts to 133 ft. lbs. (180 Nm).
- Perform a vehicle alignment after the installation is complete.

FRONT DRIVESHAFT

REMOVAL & INSTALLATION

See Figure 14.

1. Before servicing the vehicle, refer to the precautions.

2. A twin post hoist should be used when working on the front driveshaft.

❊❊ WARNING

Mark the position of all the parts to each other before removing them. Install them in the same position otherwise the imbalance will be excessive and the bearings could get damaged causing rumbling noises.

3. Lift the vehicle.

4. Remove the noise insulation and bracket under the transmission.

5. Remove the front muffler or the particulate filter depending on the type of engine.

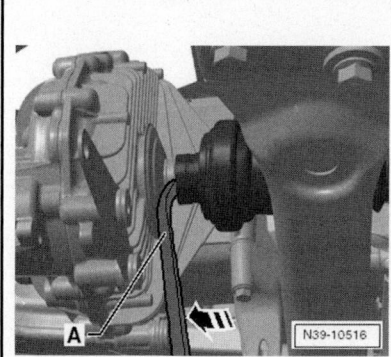

Fig. 14 Removing the driveshaft using a pry

6. Mark the installed position of the driveshaft to the transfer case and final drive.

7. Remove the driveshaft from the transfer case flange and front final drive using a pry bar.

➡**A locking ring secures the driveshaft to the flange, the driveshaft can be pulled off with a forceful pull.**

8. Guide the driveshaft downward and remove it.

To install:
Installation is performed in the reverse order of removal while observing the following:
- Always replace the locking ring and the O-ring on the transfer case flange and front final drive.
- Attach the front driveshaft to the flange and turn it so that it aligns with the mark made earlier.
- Install the driveshaft onto the flange with a quick push being careful not to tilt it. If it does not slide onto the flange, use a piece of wood. Pull on the driveshaft to make sure it is secure.
- Install the driveshaft onto the transfer case flange.
- Turn the driveshaft to the mark made earlier and install it onto the flange being careful not to tilt it. Pull the driveshaft to make sure it secure.

FRONT HALFSHAFT

REMOVAL & INSTALLATION

See Figures 15 through 17.

1. Before servicing the vehicle, refer to the precautions.

➡**For vehicles with an air spring shock absorber, the vehicle lift mode must be activated prior to lifting the vehicle with a jack or a hoist.**

✳✳ WARNING

The wheel bearing must not be under a load while the drive axle threaded connection on the wheel side is loose. If the wheel bearings are under the load of the vehicle's own weight, the wheel bearing will be damaged. This reduces the service life of the wheel bearings. The 12-point nut may only be loosened a maximum of 90° when the vehicle is resting on its wheels. Vehicles without a drive axle must not be moved, otherwise the wheel bearing will be damaged.

2. Loosen the 12-point nut for the drive axle on the wheel hub. Use the T10361 to loosen a maximum of 90°. Otherwise the wheel bearing will be damaged.

3. Lift the vehicle just enough so that the wheels are hanging free.

4. Press the brake pedal. A second technician will be needed.

5. Unscrew the 12-point nut axle nut.

6. Raise the vehicle and remove the wheel.

7. On vehicles with an air spring shock absorber, bleed the air spring shock absorber with the VAS 5051B.

8. Attach the VW 552 1 in the upper opening of the wheel housing and the upper control arm.

9. Slightly pretension the control arm so that the control arm ball stud is not damaged.

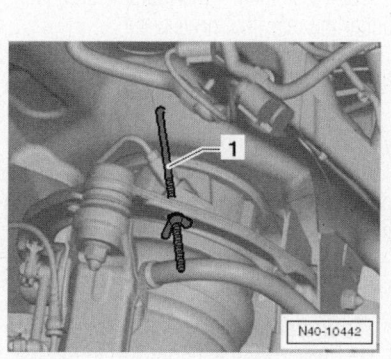

Fig. 15 VW 552 1 shown in the upper opening of the wheel housing and the upper control arm

10. Disconnect the drive axle from the front final drive.

11. Loosen nut of track rod ball joint, but do not unscrew yet.

12. Remove the tie rod from the wheel bearing housing and remove the nut.

13. Remove the upper brake line bracket from the wheel bearing housing.

14. Pull the harness connector and cable out of the bracket.

15. Remove the bolt and the lower line hose bracket from the wheel bearing housing.

16. Press out the drive axle using adapter plate T10103/1 T10103. During the pressing-out operation, ensure sufficient freedom of movement of the joints.

17. Turn wheel hub far enough until one of the holes for wheel bolts is on top, and install wheel bolt.

18. Loosen the nut on the upper control arm, but do not unscrew yet.

19. Press out the upper control arm from the wheel bearing housing and unscrew the nut.

20. Unscrew the bolt for the shock absorber on the control arm.

21. Unscrew the coupling rod bolt from the stabilizer bar, remove the bolt.

22. Lower the wheel bearing housing far enough so the drive axle can be removed.

23. Remove drive axle.

To install:

➡**Use new nuts and bolts.**

24. Install in reverse order of removal. Note the following:
- Insert outer joint as far as possible into wheel hub splines.
- Pull in drive axle until stop using T10206, remove the tool.

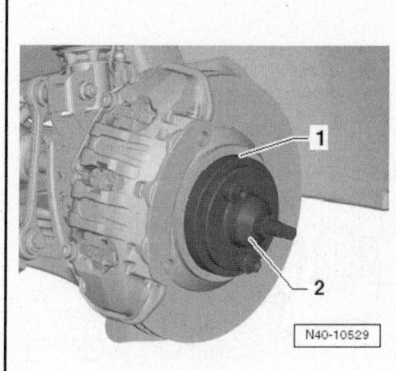

Fig. 16 Press out drive axle using the adapter plate T10103/1 T10103

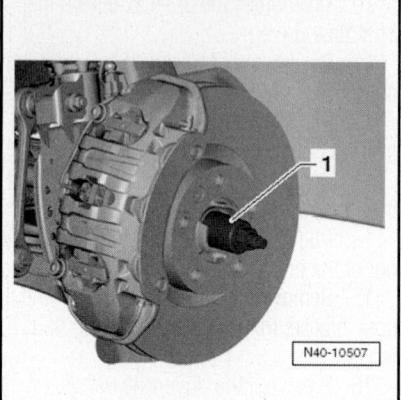

Fig. 17 Pulling the axle into the housing using the T10206

- Tighten the upper control arm nut to 63 ft. lbs. (85 Nm).
- Tighten the tie rod end to wheel bearing housing to 66 ft. lbs. (90 Nm).
- Tighten the shock absorber to the lower control arm to 111ft. lbs. (90 Nm) plus 90° turn.
- Press the brake pedal. A second technician will be needed.
- Pre-tighten the 12-point nut to 150 Nm.
- Lower the vehicle onto its wheels, and retighten the 12-point nut to 369 ft. lbs. (500 Nm).
- Install the wheels. Tighten the wheel nuts to 133 ft. lbs. (180 Nm).

REAR AXLE FLUID

DRAIN & REFILL

See Figure 18.

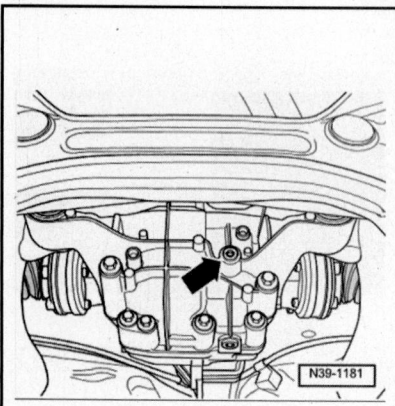

Fig. 18 Rear final drive fill plug shown

1. Before servicing the vehicle, refer to the precautions.
2. Raise the vehicle.
3. Install a drain pan under the rear final drive.
4. Remove the lower rear final drive drain plug and drain the fluid.

To refill:

5. Install the lower rear final drive drain plug and tighten to 26 ft. lbs. (35 Nm).
6. Remove the top fill plug and refill the unit. The level is correct when the rear final drive is filled up to the lower edge of the opening.
7. Install the top fill plug and tighten to 26 ft. lbs. (35 Nm).

REAR AXLE HOUSING

REMOVAL & INSTALLATION

See Figure 19.

1. Before servicing the vehicle, refer to the precautions.
2. Raise the vehicle.
3. If an underbody impact guard is located beneath the rear final drive, remove it.
4. Remove the rear part of the exhaust system.
5. Check whether there is a marking (colored marking) on rear driveshaft and on driveshaft flange at rear final drive. If no markings can be found, mark in color the position of the driveshaft flange to the rear final drive.
6. Remove the center support bolts. The tunnel brace is not removed.
7. Disconnect the rear driveshaft from the rear final drive and tie it up so it is properly supported.
8. If equipped, remove the differential lock motor.
9. Disconnect left and right drive axles and tie-up out of the way.
10. Place the engine/transmission jack under the rear final drive.
11. Remove the bolts and nuts for the rear final drive at sub-frame bolts (arrows).
12. Tip up the rear final drive so the driveshaft flange is upward.
13. Lower the rear final drive slightly and pull the breather line off the connection nipple.
14. Lower the rear final drive from the vehicle.

To install:

15. Installation is performed in reverse order of removal, noting the following:

   a. Always replace bolts for rear driveshaft.

   b. To prevent imbalance, the driveshaft flange and rear final drive must

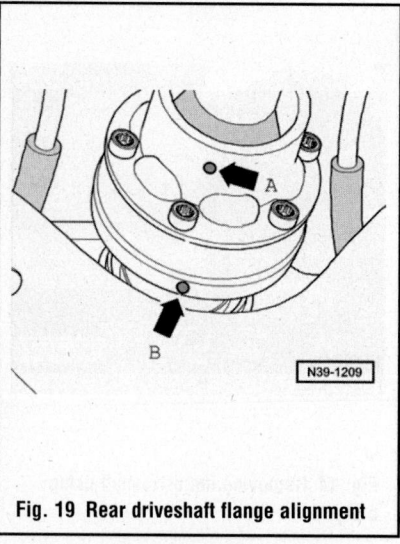

Fig. 19 Rear driveshaft flange alignment

be installed so that the colored markings from the factory or those subsequently made are in alignment.

   c. Tighten rear final drive to sub-frame bolts to specifications: 74 ft. lbs. (100 Nm), plus 180°.

   d. Fasten right and left drive axles at flange shafts.

   e. If equipped, install the differential lock motor.

   f. Connect the rear driveshaft to final drive. Use new bolts and nuts and tighten to 22 ft. lbs. (30 Nm), plus 90° turn.

   g. Install center bearing for driveshaft, so that it is free of stress. Tighten to 44 ft. lbs. (60 Nm).

   h. Check gear oil in the rear final drive.

   i. If an underbody impact guard is located beneath the rear final drive, install it.

   j. Install the rear part of the exhaust system

REAR AXLE SHAFT SEAL

REMOVAL & INSTALLATION

See Figures 20 and 21.

1. Before servicing the vehicle, refer to the precautions.
2. Raise the vehicle and remove the wheel.
3. Remove the rear final drive. Refer to Rear final drive.
4. Remove the flange shaft seal using the slide hammer and adapter

To install:

5. Install the new seal until seated using the installation tool.
6. Fill the space between the sealing and dust lips half way with sealing grease for seal.

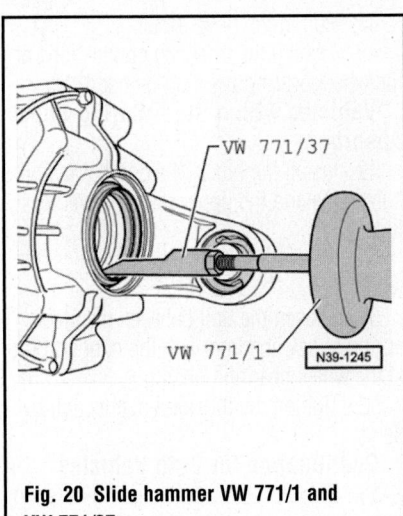

Fig. 20 Slide hammer VW 771/1 and VW 771/37.

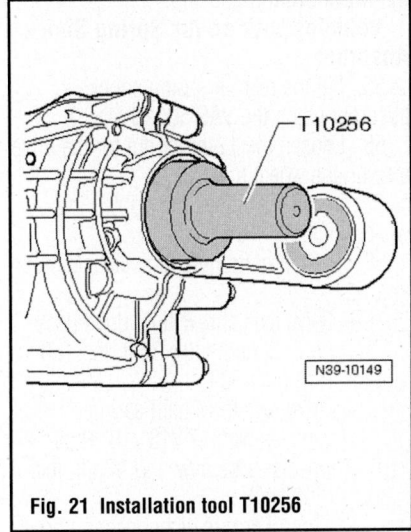

Fig. 21 Installation tool T10256

7. Install the rear final drive. Refer to Rear final drive.

8. Check the gear oil level in the rear final drive.

REAR DRIVESHAFT

REMOVAL & INSTALLATION

See Figure 22.

1. Before servicing the vehicle, refer to the precautions.

➡**A second technician will be needed to remove the driveshaft so that it does not get damaged.**

2. Select lever position "N" with the selector lever.

3. Insert brake pedal depressor.

4. Raise the vehicle.

5. Remove rear part of exhaust system.

6. If an underbody impact guard is located beneath the driveshaft, remove it. Remove the heat shield nuts, the heat

shield and the bracket from the tunnel support, if equipped. Reinstall the 2 nuts for the center bearing for the driveshaft hand tight.

7. Check whether there is a marking (colored marking) on rear driveshaft and on the rear final drive flange.

8. If this marking is not present, then mark in color the position of driveshaft flange to rear final drive.

9. Mark the position of the rear driveshaft to the transfer case output flange.

10. Remove the lower bolts for rear driveshaft at rear final drive.

11. Lower the vehicle.

12. Remove brake pedal depressor.

13. Raise the vehicle.

14. Rotate both rear wheels in the same direction at the same time so that the rear driveshaft rotates 1/2 turn (180 degrees).

15. Lower the vehicle.

16. Insert brake pedal depressor.

17. Raise the vehicle.

18. Remove the remaining bolts for rear driveshaft at rear final drive.

19. Remove bolts from rear driveshaft at transfer case. For this, counter hold the nuts using an open end wrench.

20. Place the engine and transmission holder VAG 1383 with universal transmission adapter 1359/2 under the subframe/rear axle.

21. Support the sub-frame using a wooden block.

22. Remove both front bolts on subframe.

23. Lower the sub-frame using the engine and transmission holder VAG 1383 by 1.95 in. (50 mm).

➡**To avoid damaging rear driveshaft, have a second technician assist in removing rear driveshaft.**

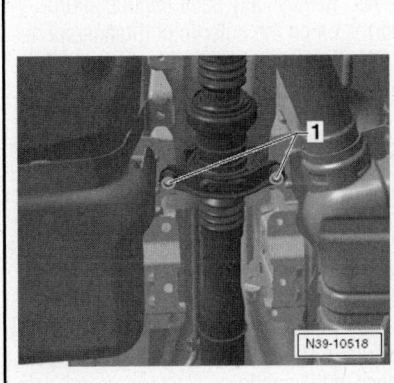

Fig. 22 Remove the center support bolts 1

24. Loosen the bolts for the center bearing at the bracket by approximately 2 turns.

25. Press off rear driveshaft from rear final drive and pivot it over the final drive flange.

26. Carefully pull off rear driveshaft from centering pin of output flange/transfer case.

27. Remove rear driveshaft.

28. Set aside rear driveshaft with center bearing bracket facing upwards.

To install:

➡**Always replace bolts for rear driveshaft.**

29. Further installation is performed in reverse order of removal, noting the following.

30. Always replace the locking ring and the O-ring on the transfer case flange and rear final drive

31. Markings must line up as much as possible.

32. Seal in rear driveshaft flange at flange/transfer case must not be damaged when removing and installing.

33. Replace rear driveshaft if damaged.

34. Do not tip rear driveshaft; push horizontally onto guide shaft.

35. Install and tighten bolts at subframe.

36. After installing rear driveshaft, install center bearing so that it is free of stress.

37. Install rear part of exhaust system:

38. Insert bolts for rear driveshaft and tighten to specifications.

39. If an underbody impact guard is located beneath the driveshaft, install it.

40. Tighten bolts/nuts to specification as follows:

- Rear driveshaft to rear final drive flange (Always replace the bolts) 22 ft. lbs. (30 Nm) plus 90°
- Center bearing bracket to body 44 ft. lbs. (60 Nm)

REAR HALFSHAFT

REMOVAL & INSTALLATION

See Figure 23.

1. Before servicing the vehicle, refer to the precautions.

2. Remove 12 point axle nut.

3. Only loosen and tighten 12 point nut when vehicle rests on its wheels (risk of accident!).

4. Do not move vehicle when 12 point nut is loosened. Otherwise, wheel bearing may be damaged.

5. If vehicle has to be moved with drive

axle removed, outer joint must be installed and tightened to 111 ft. lbs. (150 Nm).

For Vehicles with a Steel Spring Shock Absorbers

6. Loosen the wheel bolts.

7. Raise the vehicle and remove the wheel.

8. Loosen the threaded connection arrows between the steel spring shock absorber and the coupling rod at the wheel bearing housing.

9. Install the block of wood between the sub-frame and the upper rear transverse link.

10. Loosen the threaded connection arrows between the steel spring shock absorber and the coupling rod at the wheel bearing housing.

11. Install the block of wood between the sub-frame and the upper rear transverse link.

12. Press the axle down with a block of wood.

13. Remove the bolt.

For Vehicles with an Air Spring Shock Absorber

14. Activate the vehicle lift mode and place the vehicle on the lifting platform.

15. Bleed the rear air spring shock absorber with the VAS 5051B.

16. Loosen the wheel bolts.

17. Raise the vehicle.

18. Remove the wheel.

Continuation for Both Vehicles

19. Turn the wheel hub until one of the holes for the wheel bolts is on the bottom.

20. Support the wheel carrier.

21. Unscrew the threaded connection of the rear upper transverse link from the wheel bearing housing.

22. Release the connector from the parking brake motor of the electromechanical parking brake and disconnect.

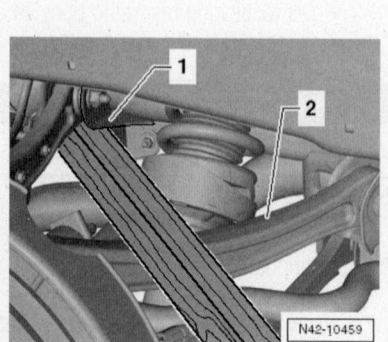

Fig. 23 Block of wood between the sub-frame 1 and the upper rear transverse link 2

23. Unscrew the tie rod from the wheel bearing housing.

For Vehicles with an Air Spring Shock Absorber

24. Unscrew the threaded connection between the air spring shock absorber and the coupling rod at the wheel bearing housing.

Continuation for Both Vehicles

25. Loosen the threaded connection of the upper front transverse link on the wheel bearing housing.

26. Loosen the bolt for the lower transverse link and remove.

27. Release the connector from the rear speed sensor and remove it.

28. Unscrew the threaded connection of the cable holder.

29. Detach the harness connector from the cable holder.

30. Release and remove the connector.

31. Place the wiring harness with the cable holder to the side.

32. Carefully tilt the wheel bearing housing upward.

33. Press the drive axle out of the internal gearing with the T10103/1. Ensure sufficient freedom of movement of the joints during the pressing-out operation by tilting the wheel bearing housing further upward.

34. Tilt the outer joint out of the wheel hub.

35. Secure the drive axle to keep it from falling.

36. Remove the drive axle at the transmission flange with a plastic-coated assembly lever.

37. Remove drive axle.

To install:

38. Installation is in the reverse order of removal. Note the following:

39. Before assembling, coat the outer joint gearing with assembly paste G 052 109 A2.

40. Remove any paint residue and/or corrosion on the outer joint threads/splines.

41. Insert a new securing ring into the groove of the inner CV joint.

42. Bring the outer and inner splines of joint piece and transmission into engagement.

43. Push the drive axle into the joint piece to the stop. Now push the joint piece with one jerk onto the transmission inner gearing. Never use a hammer or mallet!

44. Make sure the joint piece fits securely. The joint pulls against the resistance of the circlip.

45. Install the outer joint as far as possible into the wheel hub splines

46. Lower the wheel bearing housing.

47. Pull in the drive axle.

48. Tighten the threaded connections at the wheel bearing housing by hand.

Vehicles with a Steel Spring Shock Absorber

49. Install the block of wood between the sub-frame and the upper rear transverse link.

50. Press the axle down with a block of wood.

51. Loosen the bolt between the steel spring shock absorber and the coupling rod at the wheel bearing housing.

52. Tighten the threaded connection by hand.

Continuation for Both Vehicles

53. Only bolt the wheel bearing housing if the dimension "a" is reached.

54. Tighten the threaded connections on the wheel bearing housing.

Vehicles with an Air Spring Shock Absorber

55. Fill the rear air spring shock absorber using the VAS 5051B.

56. Loosen the 12-point nut for the drive axle on the wheel hub.

57. Install the wheel and tighten the wheel bolts.

58. Tighten bolts/nuts to specification as follows:

- Drive axle at rear final drive (Use new nut and bolt): 37 ft. lbs. (50 Nm) plus 90°
- Drive axle to wheel bearing on vehicles with 17"/18"/18" Plus wheels: (Use new nut) 370 ft. lbs. (500 Nm)
- Control arm to wheel bearing housing (Use new nut and bolt): 37 ft. lbs. (50 Nm) plus 90°
- Strut/coupling rod to wheel bearing housing (Use new nut and bolt): 67 ft. lbs. (90 Nm) plus 90°
- Clamp for stabilizer bar: 30 ft. lbs. (40 Nm)
- Separable stabilizer bar clamp: 37 ft. lbs. (50 Nm)
- Stabilizer bar to coupling rod (Use new nut): 74 ft. lbs. (100 Nm)
- Tie rod to wheel bearing housing (Use new nut and bolt): 37 ft. lbs. (50 Nm) plus 90°

REAR PINION SEAL

REMOVAL & INSTALLATION

See Figures 24 and 25.

1. Before servicing the vehicle, refer to the precautions.

2. Remove the rear final drive. Refer to rear final drive.

3. Lay the final drive on a workbench.

4. Remove the O-ring and the locking ring.

5. Punch two holes into the dust cap using a drift, then install the two 4 mm screws.

6. Remove the dust cap using the puller and adapter.

7. Punch two holes into the seal using a drift.

8. Install the 4 mm diameter screws into the seal. Be careful not to install the screw too deep otherwise the bearing underneath will get damaged.

9. Remove the seal using the puller and adapter.

To install:

10. Fill the space between the sealing and dust lips half way with sealing grease for seal G 052 128 A1.

11. Cover the splines on the input shaft with adhesive tape.

12. Install the new seal into the seal seat on the final drive.

13. Install the seal until seated using the assembly tool T10432. Be careful not to tilt it.

14. Remove the adhesive tape.

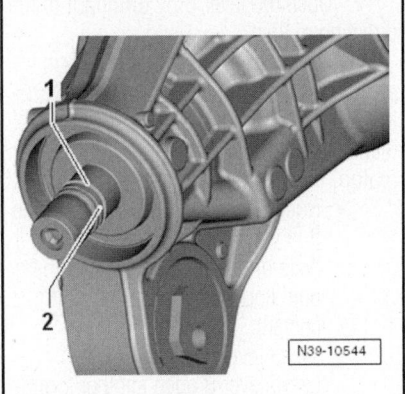

Fig. 24 Block of wood between the subframe 1 and the upper rear transverse link 2

15. Install the new dust cap using the assembly tool T10432/1.

16. Install the new O-ring and locking ring.

17. Install the rear final drive. Refer to rear final drive.

18. Check the gear oil level in the rear final drive

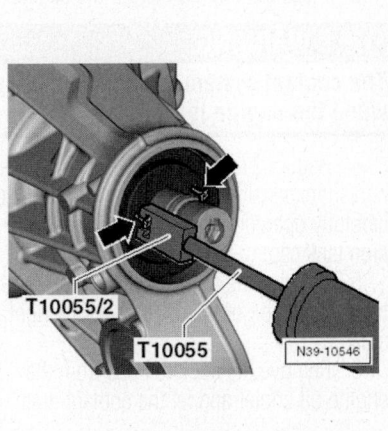

Fig. 25 Remove the dust cap & seal using the puller T10055 and adapter T10055/2

19. Tighten bolts/nuts to specification as follows:
- Refer to rear final drive for additional information.
- 12-point hub nut (use new): 369 ft. lbs. (500 Nm)
- Control arm bolt and nut (use new): 111 ft. lbs. (150 Nm) plus an additional 90° turn.

ENGINE COOLING

ENGINE COOLANT

DRAINING

3.0L TDI Engine

See Figures 26 and 27.

1. Before servicing the vehicle, refer to the precautions.

2. Remove the noise insulation cover.

3. Place the drip pan under the engine.

✳✳ WARNING

The coolant system is under pressure when the engine is warm. Risk of scalding due to hot steam and hot coolant.

4. Reduce pressure by covering the coolant expansion tank cap with a cloth and carefully opening.

5. Open the coolant expansion tank cap.

6. Remove the quick release arrow on the bottom connection of the radiator on the right side.

7. Open the clamps and remove the auxiliary heater coolant hoses.

3.6L Engine

1. Before servicing the vehicle, refer to the precautions.

2. Remove the noise insulation cover.

3. Place the drip pan under the engine.

✳✳ WARNING

The coolant system is under pressure when the engine is warm. Risk of scalding due to hot steam and hot coolant.

4. Reduce pressure by covering the coolant expansion tank cap with a cloth and carefully opening.

5. Open the coolant expansion tank cap.

6. Remove the quick release on the bottom connection of the radiator on the right side. Drain coolant.

3.0L Hybrid Engine

See Figure 28.

1. Before servicing the vehicle, refer to the precautions.

2. Remove the noise insulation cover.

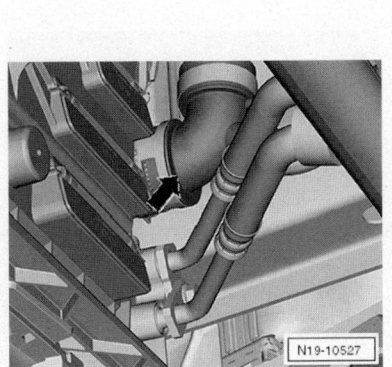

Fig. 26 Bottom connection of the radiator on the right side

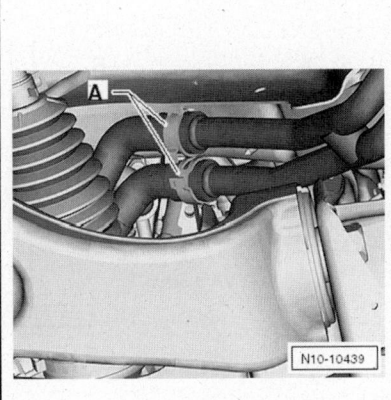

Fig. 27 Clamps A and auxiliary heater coolant hoses

3. Place the drip pan under the engine.

✳✳ WARNING

The coolant system is under pressure when the engine is warm.

4. Reduce pressure by covering the coolant expansion tank cap with a cloth and carefully opening. Open the coolant expansion tank cap.

5. Remove the quick release on the bottom connection of the radiator on the right side.

6. Remove the coolant hose from the engine oil cooler and let the coolant drain.

FILLING

See Figure 29.

➡ **Only use coolant additive G 12 plus-plus that conforms to TL VW 774 G.**

Use distilled water only. Recommended Mixture Ratio:

1. Fill the coolant reservoir on the cooling system charge unit with at least 17 liters of premixed coolant of the proper mixture ratio: 40%-50%.

2. Install the adapter V.A.G 1274/8 onto the coolant expansion tank.

3. Connect the cooling system charge unit to the adapter.

4. Place the air outlet in a small container. A small amount of coolant which should be collected is drawn off with the discharged air.

5. Close the levers A and B by turning the levers at a right angle to the direction of flow.

6. Connect hose to compressed air. Pressure: 87-145 psi. (6-10 bars) pressure.

7. Open the lever B by turning it in the direction of flow.

8. Condition: A further vacuum is created in the cooling system by the suction jet pump. The needle on the instrument display must travel into the green region.

- Briefly open the lever A by turning it in the direction of flow so that the hose on the cooling system charge unit, coolant reservoir fills with coolant.
- Close lever A again.
- Leave lever B open another 2 minutes.

Condition: A further vacuum is created in the cooling system by the suction jet pump. The needle on the instrument display must still remain in the green region.

- Close lever B.

9. Condition:

- The needle on display must remain in the green range. Only then is there enough vacuum in the coolant system for the filling. If the pressure falls, check the coolant system for leaks.
- Remove the pressurized air hose.
- Open the lever A slowly.

10. Coolant is extracted from the cooling system charge unit coolant reservoir by pressure in the coolant system and the system is filled.

11. Remove the cooling system charge unit from the adapter on the coolant expansion tank.

12. Check the coolant level inside the expansion tank. Either fill or extract to the "MAX" mark, if necessary.

ENGINE FAN

REMOVAL & INSTALLATION

3.0L TDI Engine

See Figure 30.

1. Before servicing the vehicle, refer to the precautions.

2. Drain the cooling system.

3. Open the clamp 2 and remove the hose from the left charge air pipe

4. Remove the charge air pipes and the coolant lines from the fan shroud.

5. Remove the upper charge air pipes from the left charge air cooler.

6. Disconnect the connector from the fan shroud and free up the wires.

7. Push the clips in on both sides of the shroud and remove the fan shroud upward.

To install:

8. Further installation is performed in reverse order of removal, noting the following:

- The coolant fan mount must engage into mounting points intended for it.
- Fill the cooling system.

3.6L Engine

See Figure 31.

1. Before servicing the vehicle, refer to the precautions.

2. Remove the insulation panel.

3. Remove the front coolant pipe from the fan mount.

4. Unclip the coolant hose from the lock carrier.

5. Remove the front bumper.

Fig. 28 Remove the coolant hose arrow

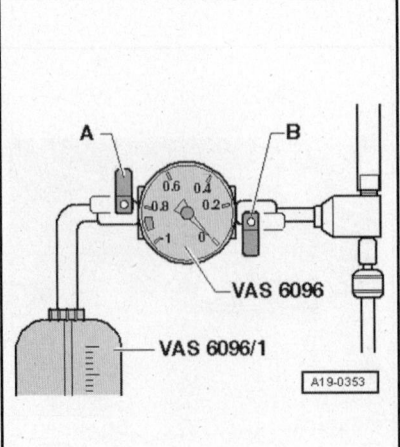

Fig. 29 Coolant charge unit VAS 6096, reservoir VAS 6096/1 and levers

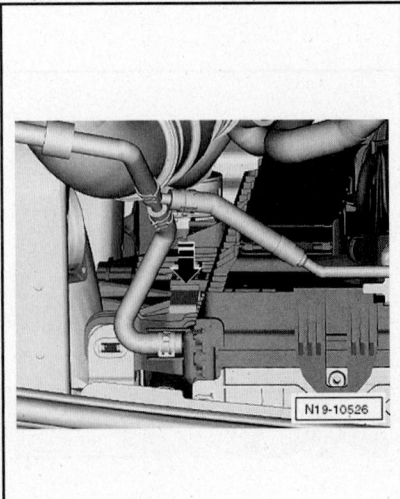

Fig. 30 Push the clips arrows in on both sides of the shroud

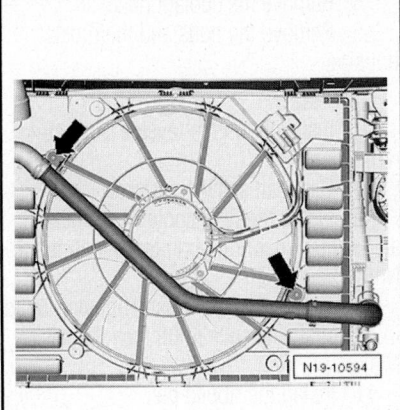

Fig. 31 Push the clips arrows in on both sides of the shroud

6. Bring the lock carrier into the service position.

7. Disconnect the fan connector and free up the wiring.

8. Loosen the fasteners and remove the fan support upward with the fans.

To install:

9. Installation is performed in the reverse of the removal procedure.

10. Fill the cooling system.

3.0L Hybrid Engine

See Figure 32.

1. Before servicing the vehicle, refer to the precautions

2. Loosen the low temperature coolant circuit coolant expansion tank 1, disconnect the connector 2 and lay the tank upward.

3. Remove the coolant pipe bolts 1 from the fan shroud. Disconnect the connector arrows and unclip the wire.

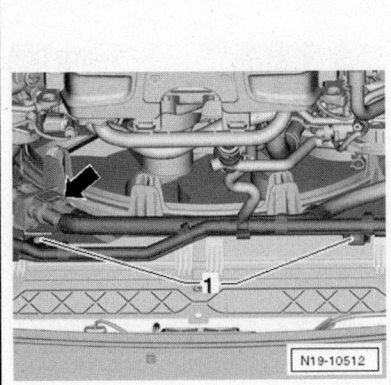

Fig. 32 Coolant pipe bolts 1, connector arrows

4. Push the clips arrows in on both sides of the shroud and remove the fan shroud upward.

5. Installation is performed in reverse order.

RADIATOR

REMOVAL & INSTALLATION

3.0L TDI Engine

1. Before servicing the vehicle, refer to the precautions.

2. Drain the cooling system.

3. Remove fan mount.

4. Remove the retaining clips on bumper carrier.

5. Disengage the securing clamps for Air Conditioning (A/C) system condenser and Automatic Transmission Fluid (ATF) oil cooler.

6. Remove upper radiator bolts and remove radiator upward.

To install:

7. Installation is performed in the reverse order of removal.

8. Fill the cooling system.

9. Check all electrical connections and routing.

10. Install front bumper.

11. Check headlight adjustment and correct, if necessary.

3.6L Engine

1. Before servicing the vehicle, refer to the precautions.

2. Remove the insulation panel.

3. Drain the coolant.

4. Disconnect all coolant hoses from the radiator.

5. Remove the front bumper.

6. Bring the lock carrier into the service position.

7. Remove the radiator fan support with fans.

To install:

8. Installation is in the reverse of removal.

3.0L Hybrid Engine

See Figures 33 through 36.

1. Before working on any part of the Hybrid high voltage system, refer to the precautions.

2. Remove the fan and shroud. Refer to fan removal

3. Evacuate the refrigerant in the A/C system.

4. Drain the coolant from the high temperature coolant circuit.

5. Place drain pan under the separating point on the transmission fluid cooler.

6. Remove the bolt and the connections on the transmission fluid cooler. Catch any fluid leaking out.

7. Remove the A/C pipe mounting bolts and pipes from the radiator module.

8. Remove the radiator grille.

9. Remove the license plate holder and the center air grille.

10. Remove the brackets and then remove the center radiator for the charge air cooling circuit from the radiator module. The coolant hoses remain connected.

11. Lift the retaining clip and remove the upper coolant hose from the radiator.

12. Remove the Secondary Air Injection (AIR) pump motor.

13. Open the air guide on both sides of the air guide opening and remove the bolts.

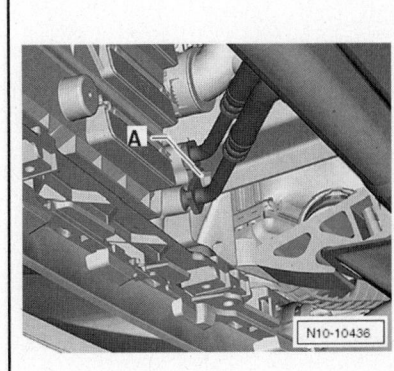

Fig. 33 Transmission fluid cooler mounting bolt A

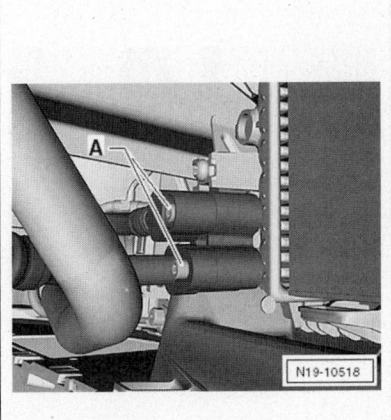

Fig. 34 A/C pipe mounting bolts A

14. Remove the lower radiator mounts from the radiator module over the longitudinal members.

15. Remove the bolts (quantity: 3) from the air guide through the lowest air grille.

16. Remove the bolt next to the left and right headlamps.

17. Push the radiator module toward the engine, open the clips on the upper air guide on the radiator and remove it.

18. Unlock the locking bolts on both upper radiator mounts by pushing them in and then pulling upward.

19. Remove both upper radiator mounts.

20. Remove the radiator module upward.

To install:

21. Install the radiator module.

22. Mount the upper radiator mount and tighten it.

23. Install the radiator module into the upper radiator mount and install the locking bolt.

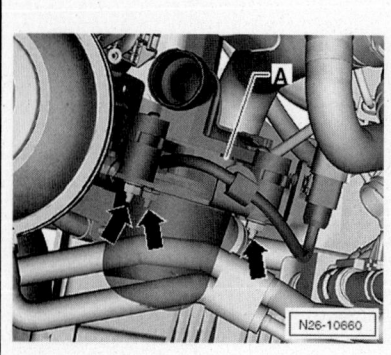

Fig. 35 Remove the nuts and AIR pump motor A

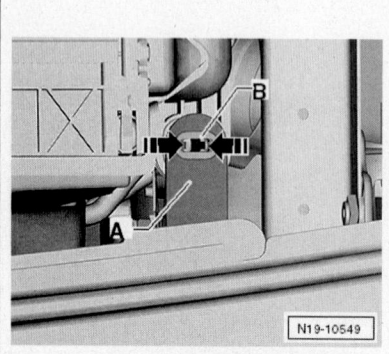

Fig. 36 Locking bolts B, upper radiator mounts A

24. Install the lower radiator mount into the radiator module and tighten it.

25. Push the clips on the upper air guide into the radiator.

26. Install the secondary air injection pump motor, tighten mounting nuts to 80 inch lbs. (9 Nm).

27. Install the radiator grille.

28. Install the license plate holder and the center air grille.

29. Further installation is performed in reverse order of removal, noting the following:

- Secure all the hose connections with hose clamps that are specific to that model. All the coolant must be changed if the radiator was replaced.
- Connect the coolant hoses with the connector coupling.
- Install the Automatic Transmission Fluid (ATF) lines.
- Drain the coolant system completely before filling.
- Fill the coolant for the high temperature coolant circuit.
- Check the ATF level.
- Install the noise insulation.

THERMOSTAT

REMOVAL & INSTALLATION

3.0L TDI Engine

See Figure 37.

1. Before servicing the vehicle, refer to the precautions.

2. Drain the coolant.

3. Remove ribbed belt from the tensioning element.

4. Remove the bolt and pull the Exhaust Gas Recirculation (EGR) cooler thermostat off of the connection.

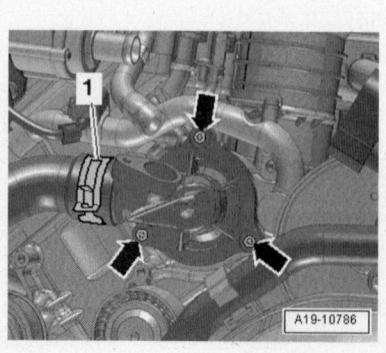

Fig. 37 3.0L TDI engine, bolts and thermostat housing

5. Remove the coolant hose.

6. Remove the bolts and thermostat housing.

To install:

7. Installation is in reverse order of removal.

8. Clean all sealing surface.

9. Install the EGR cooler thermostat, and tighten mounting bolt to 80 inch lbs. (9 Nm).

10. Tighten the thermostat housing bolts in diagonal sequence to 80 inch lbs. (9 Nm).

11. Install the ribbed belt.

12. Fill the system with coolant.

3.6L Engine

1. Before servicing the vehicle, refer to the precautions.

➡**The coolant thermostat housing is located in the lower part of oil filter housing.**

2. Drain the cooling system.

3. Separate the electrical connection at map controlled engine cooling thermostat F265.

4. Remove the coolant hoses from coolant thermostat housing.

5. Remove the bolts.

6. Remove map controlled engine cooling thermostat F265 housing.

To install:

7. Installation is performed in reverse order of removal.

8. Replace the seals and O-rings.

9. Tighten the coolant thermostat housing to 80 inch lbs. (9 Nm).

10. Secure all hose connections with hose clamps appropriate for the model.

11. Fill the cooling system.

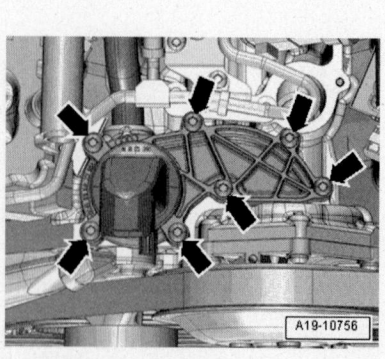

Fig. 38 3.0L Hybrid engine, bolts and the coolant thermostat

3.0L Hybrid Engine

See Figure 38.

1. Before working on any part of the Hybrid high voltage system, refer to the precautions.

2. Drain the coolant from the high temperature coolant circuit

3. Remove the supercharger.

4. Remove the front coolant pipe. Place a cloth underneath to catch any coolant leaking out.

5. Remove the bolts and the coolant thermostat with the connections.

To install:

6. Install the bolts and the coolant thermostat with the connections. Tighten to 80 inch lbs. (9 Nm).

7. Installation is performed in the reverse order of removal, noting the following:

8. Replace the seals, and install the front coolant pipe.

9. Install the supercharger.

10. Fill the coolant for the high temperature coolant circuit.

WATER PUMP

REMOVAL & INSTALLATION

3.0L TDI Engine

1. Before servicing the vehicle, refer to the precautions.

2. Drain the coolant.

3. Remove ribbed belt from the tensioning element.

4. Move toothed belt guard forward and disengage the pins at the bottom of the guard.

5. The toothed belt guard is shown with the upper section of the intake manifold removed.

6. Using an alignment fixture 3212 as a counter holder, remove the bolts and remove the coolant pump ribbed belt pulley.

7. Remove bolts and remove the coolant pump.

To install:

8. Installation is in reverse order of removal.

9. Clean all sealing surfaces.

10. Tighten coolant pump bolts in diagonal sequence to 80 inch lbs. (9 Nm).

11. Install ribbed belt.

12. Fill with engine coolant.

3.6L Engine

See Figure 39.

1. Before servicing the vehicle, refer to the precautions.

2. Remove the noise insulation.

3. Drain the coolant.

4. Remove the ribbed belt.

➡To remove the coolant pump, the pulley need not be removed.

5. Remove the coolant pump bolts through the holes in the belt pulley and remove coolant pump.

6. If the coolant pump must be replaced, remove the coolant pump belt pulley.

To install:

7. Installation is performed in the reverse of removal.

   a. Check sprayed-on coolant pump seal. If seal is damaged, coolant pump must be replaced.

   b. Install the coolant pump. Tighten coolant pump bolts to 6 ft. lbs. (8 Nm).

   c. Install the pulley for coolant pump. Tighten the bolts to 15 ft. lbs. (20 Nm).

   d. Install the ribbed belt.

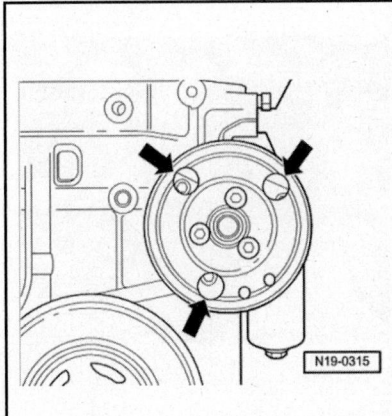

Fig. 39 3.6L engine, bolt through holes in the belt pulley

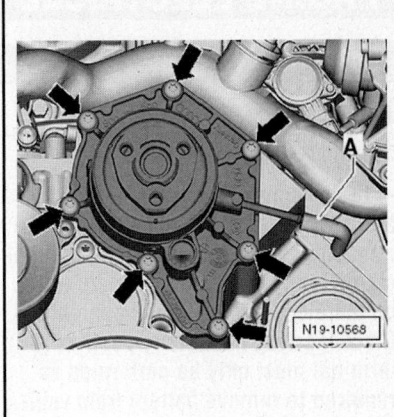

Fig. 40 3.0L Hybrid engine, bolts and hose A

   e. Fill the system with new coolant.

3.0L Hybrid Engine

See Figure 40.

1. Before working on any part of the Hybrid high voltage system, refer to the precautions.

2. Loosen the left front coolant pipes and move them to the side. The coolant hoses can remain connected.

3. Remove the supercharger drive belt.

4. Remove the accessory drive belt.

5. Remove the bolts for the coolant pump pulley, use tool to counter hold. Remove the pulley.

6. Remove the hose and the bolts. Remove the coolant pump.

To install:

7. Installation is performed in the reverse order of removal, noting the following:

8. Clean the sealing surfaces; they must be free of oil and grease.

9. Install and tighten coolant pump bolts to 80 inch lbs. (9 Nm).

10. Install the pulley for coolant pump. Tighten the bolts to 15 ft. lbs. (20 Nm).

11. Install the accessory drive belt.

12. Install the supercharger drive belt.

13. Install the left front coolant pipes.

14. Fill the coolant for the high temperature coolant circuit.

ENGINE ELECTRICAL   BATTERY SYSTEM

BATTERY

REMOVAL & INSTALLATION

See Figures 41 and 42.

➡ To disconnect battery, anti-theft alarm system must be deactivated. By removing the battery negative terminal clamp (current disruption), safe work on the electrical system is guaranteed. Disconnecting the battery positive (B+) terminal must only be performed as required to remove battery from vehicle, and must only be carried out after the negative (-) terminal is disconnected.

1. Turn off the ignition and all electrical consumers; remove the key.

2. If the seat is removed connect the airbag adapter to the wiring harness of the thorax airbag. If the battery only is serviced, leave the connectors plugged in and tilt the seat back.

3. Connect the airbag adapter to the wiring harness of the thorax airbag.

✳✳ WARNING

The airbag adapter must stay connected to the seat until the seat is reinstalled.

4. Remove the left front seat.

5. Cut open the carpet for access.

6. Fold back the carpet, open the latches on the battery case arrows and remove the cover.

7. Disconnect negative (-) terminal 1 from battery. Disconnect positive (B+) terminal 2 from battery.

8. Remove the mounting and retainer bracket, remove the battery.

To install:

9. Install the battery and mounting bracket, tighten the mounting bolt to 89 inch lbs. (10 Nm).

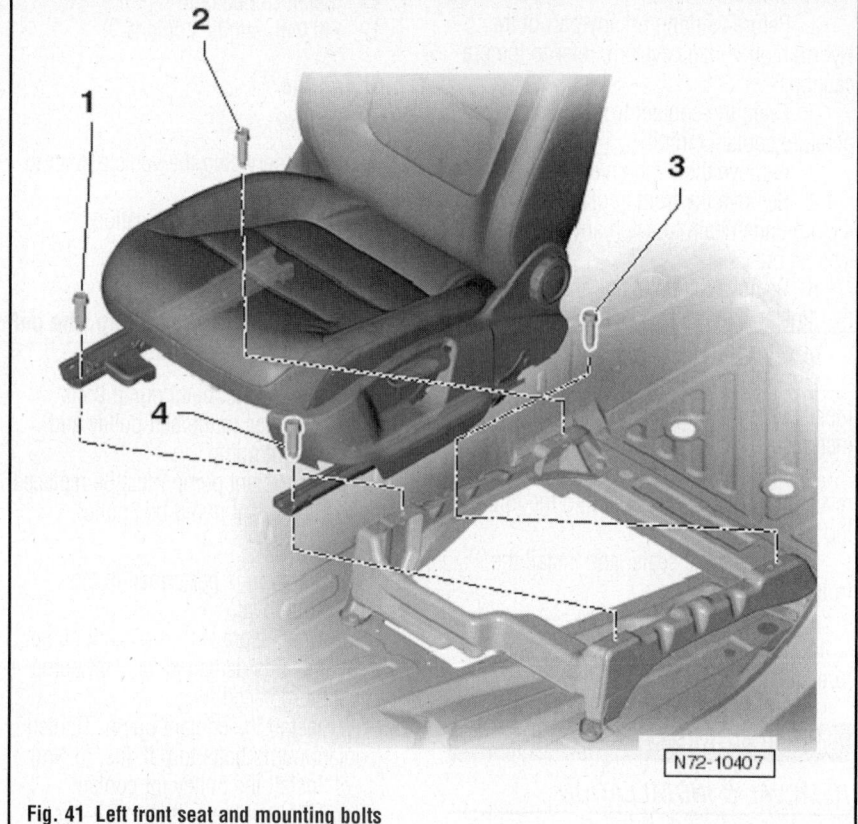

Fig. 41 Left front seat and mounting bolts

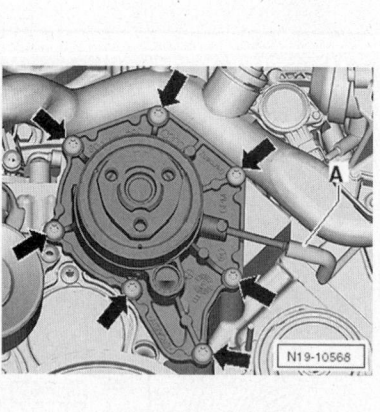

Fig. 42 Cut open the carpet where shown with arrows

10. Connect the battery positive clamp to the battery positive terminal.

11. Tighten bolt on the battery positive terminal to 80 inch lbs. (9 Nm).

12. Only after the positive (B+) terminal has been secured should negative (-) terminal clamp be installed.

13. Tighten the bolt on the battery negative terminal to 80 inch lbs. (9 Nm).

14. Tape the carpet together.

15. Install the left front seat, tighten mounting bolts to 37 ft. lbs. (50 Nm).

ALTERNATOR

REMOVAL & INSTALLATION

3.0L TDI Engine

See Figure 43.

1. Before servicing the vehicle, refer to the precautions.

2. With ignition switched off, disconnect battery Ground (GND) wire.

3. Carefully remove engine cover successively from the locking bolts.

❊❊ WARNING

Before removing ribbed belt, marking running direction with chalk or a felt-tip pen for reinstallation.

4. To release the tension the ribbed belt, move the tensioner in direction of using the T 60 Torx® socket T40087.

5. Remove both charge air pipe connecting hoses. This makes it easier to get to the generator.

6. Remove ribbed belt from tensioning roller.

7. Detach wiring harnesses from generator.

8. Free up electrical wiring harness.

9. Unscrew bolts and remove generator.

10. If alternator sticks in holder, install screw again down as far as the last 2 turns.

11. Carefully strike on bolt heads using flat side of hammer - doing this loosens sleeves of generator mount.

To install:

12. Installation is performed in the reverse order of removal, noting the following.

13. Replace all self-locking nuts.

14. Slightly drive back sleeves for retaining bolts in order for easier installation of generator.

15. Tight sleeves for generator mount must be made smooth-running, otherwise clamping force of sleeve is too little despite correct torque.

16. When installing ribbed belt, be sure that it is seated correctly on belt pulleys.

17. Tighten bolts to specification as follows:

- Alternator mounting bolts: 16 ft. lbs. (22 Nm)
- Terminal 30/B+ to generator: 12 ft. lbs. (16 Nm)

18. Connect the battery.

3.6L Engine

See Figure 44.

➡ **When disconnecting and connecting the battery, always perform the work procedure as described in the repair manual. Refer to Battery, Disconnecting and Connecting. Not adhering to sequence will result in the deactivation of Main Battery Switch -E74- and subsequent damage to electrical system components.**

1. Disconnect the negative cable terminal from the battery.

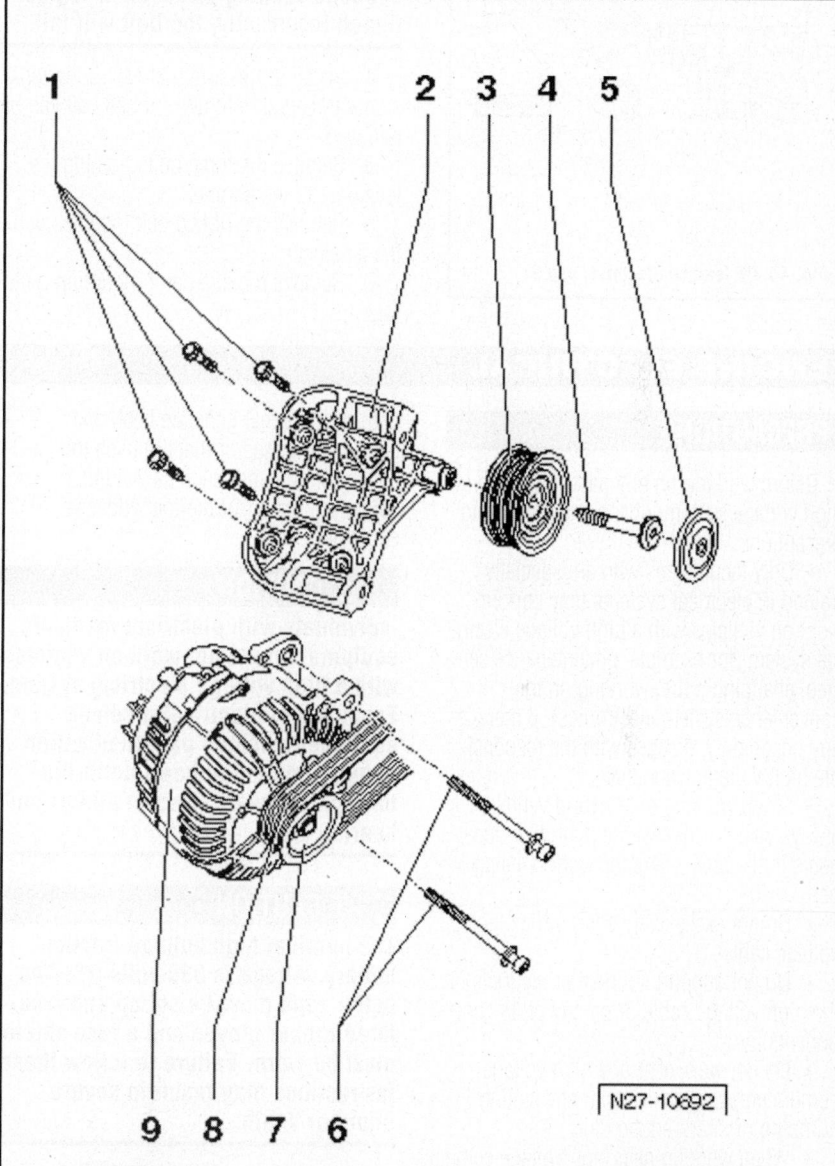

1. **Hex Head Combination Bolt**
2. **Bracket**
3. **Idler Pulley**
4. **Screw**
5. **Cap**
6. **Hex Flange Bolt**
7. **Ribbed Belt Pulley**
8. **Ribbed Belt**
9. **Generator**

N27-10692

Fig. 43 3.0L TDI engine, alternator overview

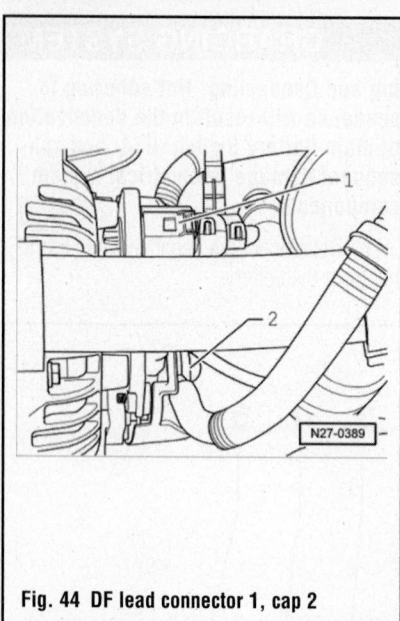

Fig. 44 DF lead connector 1, cap 2

2. Remove the protective cap of B+ wire.

3. Unscrew the B+ wire and disconnect the harness connector of the DF wire.

✳✳ WARNING

Before removing ribbed belt, mark the top side and direction of travel. When installing, pay attention to correct running direction and installation position. If the belt is installed in the opposite running direction or is positioned incorrectly, the belt will fail.

4. Install a pressure bolt M8_50 in tensioner threaded bore until ribbed belt can be removed.

5. Remove the three bolts holding the tensioner to the engine.

6. Remove the ribbed belt together with the tensioner.

7. Remove the alternator mounting bolts (M8 x 90) and remove the alternator from bracket.

To install:

8. Installation is in the reverse order of removal.

   a. Tighten the threaded connections to the specification.

   b. Remove pressure bolt M80 x 50 from tensioner.

   c. Tighten the fasteners to the following:

   - Socket head bolt (M8 x 30 mm): 15 ft. lbs. (20 Nm)
   - Fitting bolts (M8 x 1.10 in.): 15 ft. lbs. (20 Nm)
   - Torx® flat head bolt (M6 x 16 mm): 7 ft. lbs. (9 Nm)
   - Collar bolts (M8 x 3.54 in.): 15 ft. lbs. (20 Nm)
   - Bolt (M10 x 1.77 in.): 15 ft. lbs. (20 Nm)

ENGINE ELECTRICAL

HYBRID SYSTEM

PRECAUTIONS

Before working on any part of the Hybrid high voltage system, observe the following precautions:

- Only technicians who are specially trained in electrical systems may perform work on vehicles with a high voltage electrical system (for example a maintenance service, changing a tire, working on the convenience system electronics). If there is any uncertainty, discuss with the responsible high voltage technician.

- When working on a hybrid vehicle, always visually inspect the hybrid components in the area where the work is being performed.

- Do not excessively bend or flex high voltage cables.

- Do not support yourself or lay tools on the high voltage cable or on any of its components.

- Do not work near any high voltage components and cables with any cutting, crimping or sharp edged tools.

- When working near high voltage components and high voltage cables, do not use tools that generate heat, that have sharp edges or that are used for cutting or shaping, such as welding, soldering, hot air or thermal adhesive equipment.

- Always contact a high voltage technician or a high voltage expert specializing in electrical systems if anything unusual occurs or if anything is unclear.

- When working near high voltage components and high voltage cables, do not use tools that generate heat, that have sharp edges or that are used for cutting or shaping, such as welding, soldering, hot air or thermal adhesive equipment.

✳✳ CAUTION

Individuals with electrical medical equipment must not work on vehicles with a high voltage electrical system. Examples of electrical medical equipment include pain medication pumps, implanted heart defibrillators, pacemakers, insulin pumps and hearing aids.

✳✳ CAUTION

The nominal high voltage traction battery voltage is 330 volts DC. The buffer zone must be set up and insulated rubber gloves and a face shield must be worn. Failure to follow these instructions may result in severe injury or death.

✳✳ CAUTION

The high voltage traction battery and charging system contains high voltage components and wiring. High voltage insulated safety gloves and a face shield must be worn when carrying out any diagnostics on this vehicle. Failure to follow these instructions may result in severe personal injury or death.

✳✳ CAUTION

Before carrying out any removal and installation procedures of the high voltage traction battery system, the high voltage traction battery must be Disarmed. Failure to follow these instructions may result in severe personal injury or death.

✳✳ CAUTION

The rubber insulating gloves that are to be worn while working on the high voltage system should be of the appropriate safety and protection rating for use on the high voltage system. They must be inspected before use and must always be worn in conjunction with the leather outer gloves. Any hole in the rubber insulating glove is a potential entry point for high voltage. Failure to follow these instructions may result in severe personal injury or death.

➡The high voltage insulated safety gloves must be re-certified every 6 months to remain within Occupational Safety and Health Administration (OSHA) guidelines:

- Roll the glove up from the open end until the lower portion of the glove begins to balloon from the resulting air pressure. If the glove leaks any air, it must not be used.

- The gloves should not be used if they exhibit any signs of wear and tear.
- The leather gloves must always be worn over the rubber insulating gloves in order to protect them.
- The rubber insulating gloves must be class "00" and meet all of the American Society for Testing and Materials (ASTM) standards

※※ CAUTION

High voltage insulated safety gloves and a face shield must be worn when working with high voltage cables. The ignition switch must be OFF for a minimum of 5 minutes before removing high voltage cables. Failure to follow these instructions may result in severe personal injury or death.

※※ CAUTION

Establish a buffer zone before servicing the high voltage system. The buffer zone is required only when working with the high voltage system. See the text for buffer zone establishment. Failure to follow these instructions may result in severe personal injury or death. Do not allow any unauthorized personnel into the buffer zone during repairs involving the high voltage system. Only personnel trained for repair on the high voltage system are to be permitted in the buffer zone.

※※ CAUTION

Disarm the high voltage traction system before working on the high voltage system. See the text for the Disarming procedure. Failure to follow these instructions may result in severe personal injury or death.

BUFFER ZONE

1. Before servicing the vehicle, refer to the Precautions Section.

※※ CAUTION

Before proceeding, read and observe all of the High Voltage System Precautions.

2. Establish a buffer zone around the vehicle:
   a. Position the vehicle in the repair bay.

b. Position 4 orange cones at the corners of the vehicle to mark off a 1 m (3 ft.) perimeter around the vehicle.
   c. Do not allow any unauthorized personnel into the buffer zone during repairs involving the high voltage system. Only personnel trained for repair on the high voltage system are to be permitted in the buffer zone.

ARMING THE HIGH VOLTAGE SYSTEM

1. Connect the VAS 5051B scan tool.
2. Select "Guided Fault Finding" in the VAS 5051B.
3. Using the "Go To" button, select "Functions/Component selection" and the following menu options in sequence:
   - Body
   - Electrical Equipment
   - OBD capable systems
   - Hybrid battery management
   - Hybrid battery management functions
   - Restarting the high voltage system

DISARMING THE HIGH VOLTAGE SYSTEM

Read and follow the information below when disabling the high voltage electrical system to reduce the risk of fatal injury.

1. Only a qualified technician (high voltage technician) should disable the high voltage electrical system.
2. The high voltage technician makes sure the system is disabled and cannot turn on again.
3. The high voltage technician makes sure the system cannot turn on again by safekeeping the key, the service plug and the pilot line cable.
4. The high voltage technician puts a sign on the vehicle saying the voltage is disabled.
5. Only technicians who are specially trained in electrical systems may perform work on vehicles with a high voltage electrical system (for example a maintenance service, changing a tire, working on the convenience system electronics). If there is any uncertainty, discuss with the responsible high voltage technician.
6. A high voltage technician must disable the system before any work can be performed on the high voltage electrical system or any other service work to the body.
7. Only a High Voltage Expert (HVE) may perform repairs to the vehicle if it is not possible to disable the high voltage electrical system.

※※ CAUTION

Individuals with electrical medical equipment must not work on vehicles with a high voltage electrical system. Examples of electrical medical equipment include pain medication pumps, implanted heart defibrillators, pacemakers, insulin pumps and hearing aids.

8. Connect the VAS 5051B scan tool.
9. Select "Guided Fault Finding" in the VAS 5051B.
10. Using the "Go To" button, select "Functions/Component selection" and the following menu options in sequence:
   - Body
   - Electrical Equipment
   - OBD capable systems
   - Hybrid battery management
   - Hybrid battery management functions
   - Disabling the high voltage system

DECOUPLER PRESSURE ACTUATOR

REMOVAL & INSTALLATION
See Figures 45 through 47.

1. Read and follow the High Voltage Electrical System Precautions. Danger of electrocution! The following procedure requires working on the high voltage system. Disarm the high voltage system now.
2. Disable the high voltage system. Refer to High Voltage System, Disarming.
3. Remove the left front wheel.
4. Remove the left front wheel housing liner.

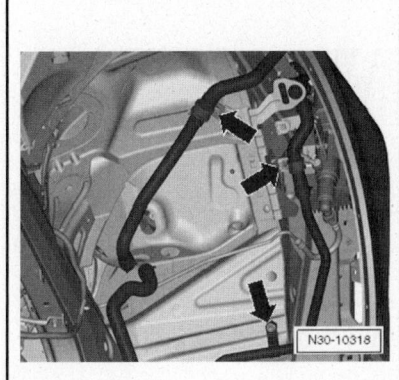

Fig. 45 Coolant pipe bracket bolts, arrows

5. Remove the coolant pipe bracket bolts and set the coolant pipe aside.

6. Clamp off the return hose using the hose clamps up to 25 mm dia. 3094 arrow.

7. Pry out the clips arrows using a screwdriver and disconnect the lines A and B from the actuator. Seal the lines with suitable plugs. Immediately wipe off any brake fluid that has leaked out.

8. Disconnect the harness connector from the actuator.

9. Remove the bolts and remove the actuator.

10. Installation is performed in the reverse order of removal while observing the following:

- Replace the O-rings for the lines.
- Install the coolant pipe brackets and tighten to 8 inch lbs. (10 Nm).
- Install the actuator bolts and tighten to 8 inch lbs. (10 Nm).

- Insert the lines into the actuator until seated and press in the clips until seated.
- Bleed the clutch mechanism. Connect the vehicle diagnostic tester, select function and follow the instructions.

HIGH VOLTAGE B+ CABLE & PROTECTOR

REMOVAL & INSTALLATION
See Figures 48 through 50.

1. Read and follow the High Voltage Electrical System Precautions. Danger of electrocution! The following procedure requires working on the high voltage system. Disarm the high voltage system now.

2. Disable the high voltage system. Refer to High Voltage System, Disarming.

3. Disconnect the 12 volt battery under the driver seat.

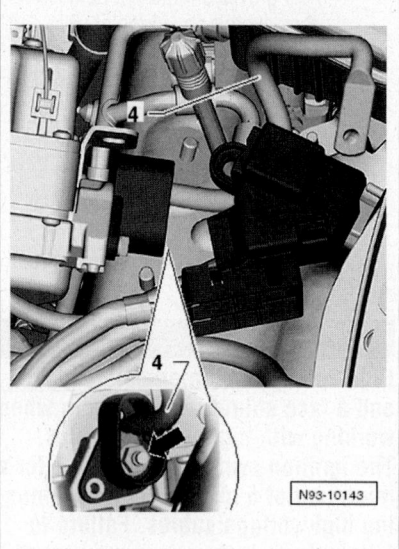

Fig. 50 High voltage B+ cable nut arrow and protector 4

4. Remove the cover plate for the high voltage connection on the Electric drive power and control electronics JX1.

5. Open the cap on the jump start point and remove the B+ cable nut.

6. Remove the B+ cable underneath from the threaded connector.

7. Remove the nuts. Remove the screws 1 and 2 and then remove the bracket 3 from the engine compartment.

8. Remove both nuts and lift the Electric drive power and control electronics JX1 from the rubber bushings inside the bracket just until the nut for the B+ cable is accessible.

9. Remove the nut. Remove the B+ cable and protector from the vehicle.

To install:

10. Installation is in the reverse order of removal.

- Tighten the high voltage B+ cable nut to 18 inch lbs. (20 Nm).
- Tighten nuts and screws to 8 inch lbs. (10 Nm).
- Restart the high voltage system and complete the required documentation.

HIGH VOLTAGE TRACTION BATTERY AX1

REMOVAL & INSTALLATION
See Figures 51 through 54.

1. Read and follow the High Voltage Electrical System Precautions. Danger of electrocution! The following procedure requires working on the high voltage sys-

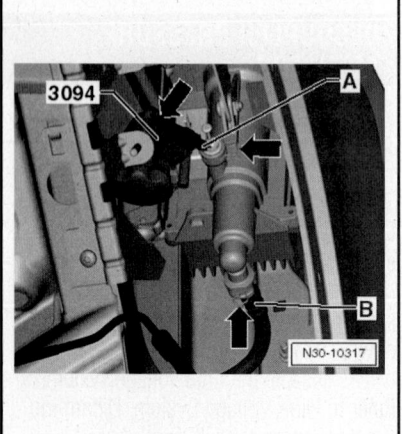

Fig. 46 Decoupler pressure actuator view

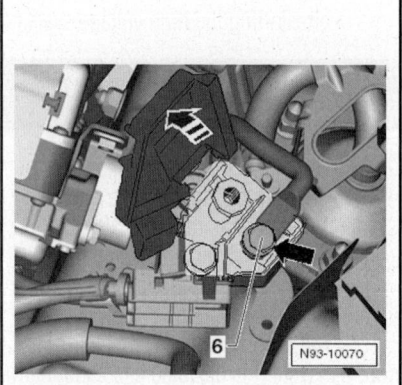

Fig. 48 High voltage B+ cable nut 6

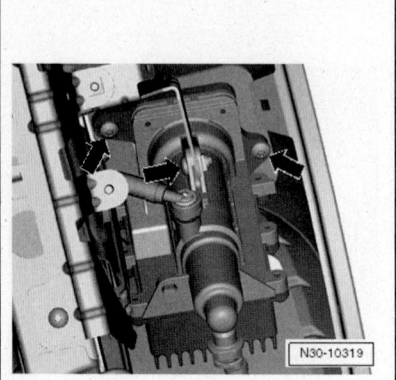

Fig. 47 Remove the actuator bolts arrows

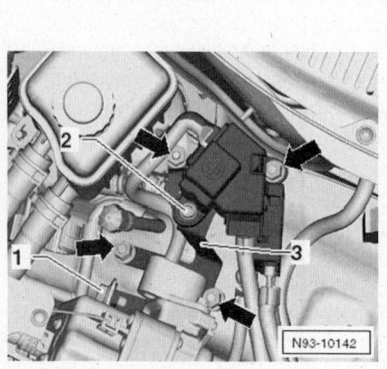

Fig. 49 Remove the nuts arrows, screws 1 and 2, then the bracket 3

tem. Disarm the high voltage system now. Refer to High Voltage System, Disarming.

2. Disable the high voltage system. Refer to High Voltage System, Disarming.

3. Remove the luggage compartment floor.

4. Remove the tire mobility kit and vehicle tools from the luggage compartment.

5. Disconnect the Battery regulation control module J840 connectors.

6. Disconnect the battery connectors.

7. Remove the bolt 1 from the hybrid battery unit and remove the potential equalization cable (ground cable).

8. Cut the cable tie and move the potential equalization cable (ground cable) to the side. Be careful not to damage the foam seals on the air guide channels when removing and installing the channels. Also, make sure the separating surfaces on the channels are completely sealed.

9. Pull the air guide channel toward the battery and upward out of its retainer1.

10. Lift the air guide channel and remove it from the mounts on the battery.

11. Remove the 8 bolts from the hybrid battery unit.

12. Remove the 4 bolts and then remove both brackets from the right side of the hybrid battery unit. To remove the hybrid battery unit, lift it up slightly first and then move it to the right. If not, then the Connection/conjunction box SX1 (E-box) will hit the left side of the battery as it is being removed from under the left luggage compartment trim panel.

13. Slightly lift the hybrid battery unit in the center using a short and a VAS 6100. Move the hybrid battery unit slightly to the right and lift it out with the help of a second technician to keep it stable.

To install:

➡ **Be careful not to get any wires or connectors caught under the battery**

when installing the hybrid battery unit back into the vehicle. Lift the hybrid battery unit in the center using a short lifting belt and the VAS 6100 back into the vehicle and align it with the holes in the body floor panel.

14. Install both brackets with the 4 bolts to the right side of the hybrid battery unit. Tighten the bolts to 17 ft. lbs. (23 Nm).

15. Install the 8 hybrid battery unit bolts.. Tighten the bolts to 17 ft. lbs. (23 Nm). Be careful not to damage the foam seals on the air guide channels when removing and installing the channels. Also, make sure the separating surfaces on the channels are completely sealed.

Insert the air guide channel into the mounts on the hybrid battery unit at the front and then lock it in the retainer.

a. Check the contact surfaces on the potential equalization cable before installation.

b. The contact surfaces must be clean. There must be no rust or grease on them.

c. If necessary, clean the contact surfaces using the contact surface cleaner.

16. Attach the potential equalization cable (ground cable) to the hybrid battery unit and install the bolt, tighten to 7 ft. lbs. (9 Nm)

17. Secure the potential equalization cable (ground cable) with a new cable tie arrow to the hybrid battery unit.

18. Connect both battery connectors and making sure they audibly engage.

19. Attach both Battery regulation control module J840 connectors and making sure they audibly engage.

20. Connect the connectors and to the mount on the hybrid battery unit and then press the wires into the wire holder.

21. Install the tire mobility kit and the vehicle tools.

22. Install the luggage compartment floor.

23. Restart the high voltage system and complete the required documentation.

HIGH VOLTAGE TRACTION BATTERY FANS

REMOVAL & INSTALLATION
See Figure 55.

1. Read and follow the High Voltage Electrical System Precautions. Danger of electrocution! The following procedure requires working on the high voltage

Fig. 51 Battery regulation control module J840 connectors 1 and 2

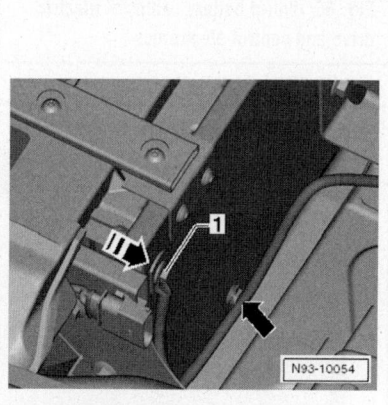

Fig. 53 Bolt 1 at the hybrid battery unit and ground cable

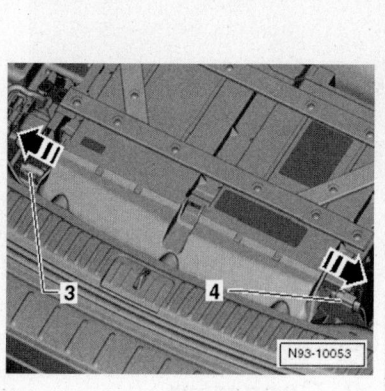

Fig. 52 Battery connectors 3and 4

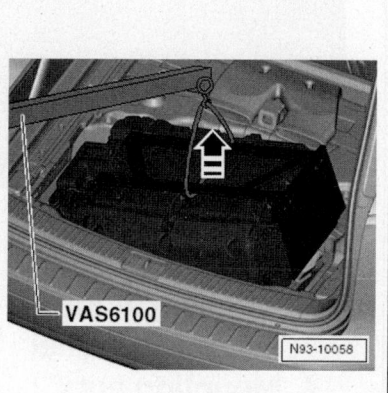

Fig. 54 Removing the hybrid battery unit

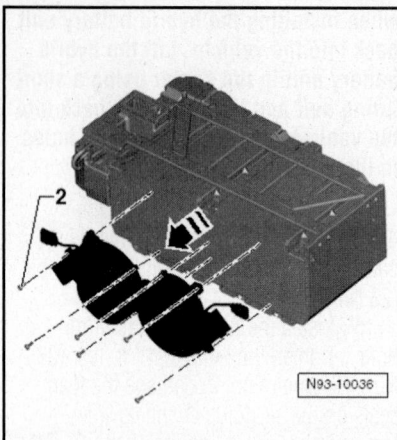

Fig. 55 Fan removal from the hybrid battery unit

system. Disarm the high voltage system now. Refer to High Voltage System, Disarming.

2. Disable the high voltage system. Refer to High Voltage System, Disarming.

3. Remove the Hybrid high voltage traction battery unit AX1. Refer to high voltage traction battery unit AX1.

4. Remove the 6 bolts and remove the ventilation guide.

5. Unclip the connector on the fan being removed from its retainer on the hybrid battery unit.

6. Remove the 3 bolts and then remove the fan from the hybrid high voltage traction battery unit battery unit.

To install:

7. Installation is in the reverse order of removal. Note the following:

- Use locking fluid when installing the fan and the ventilation guide bolts. Use new bolts when installing.
- Align the fan on the hybrid battery unit and tighten the 3 bolts.
- Install the fan bolts on the hybrid battery unit and tighten to 89 inch lbs. (10 Nm).
- Install the fan connectors into the retainer on the hybrid battery unit.
- Position the ventilation guide on the hybrid battery unit.
- Install the ventilation guide bolts on the hybrid battery unit and tighten to 89 inch lbs. (10 Nm).
- Install the hybrid battery unit. Refer to high voltage traction battery unit AX1.
- Restart the high voltage system and complete the required documentation

HIGH VOLTAGE CABLES

REMOVAL & INSTALLATION

See Figures 56 and 57.

1. Read and follow the High Voltage Electrical System Precautions. Danger of

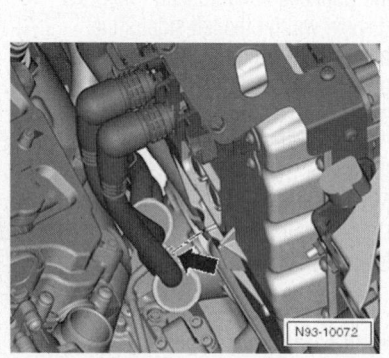

Fig. 56 Hybrid battery cables at electric drive and control electronics

electrocution! The following procedure requires working on the high voltage system. Disarm the high voltage system now. Refer to High Voltage System, Disarming.

2. Disable the high voltage system. Refer to high voltage system disarming.

3. Remove the front and rear noise insulation.

4. Remove the left underbody panel, and loosen the heat shield.

5. Remove both high voltage cable holders from the Electric drive power and control electronics JX1 housing.

6. Remove the 3 nuts from the harness protector.

7. Cut the cable tie, open the harness protector arrows and remove the hybrid battery high voltage wiring harness from the harness protector.

8. Remove the harness protector from the engine compartment.

9. Guide the high voltage cable set downward and out of the engine compartment.

1. Threaded pins
2. Bracket
3. Opening in the body floor panel
4. Mounting nuts
5. Cap
6. Hex Flange Bolt
7. Ribbed Belt Pulley
8. Ribbed Belt
9. Generator

Fig. 57 Hybrid battery high voltage cables

10. Open both clips, cut the cable tie and unclip the high voltage cable set.

➡ **Drain the fuel tank if it is more than 1/4 full, for removal. It may not be necessary to remove the fuel tank in order to remove and install the high voltage cable.**

11. Remove the lower protective cover and the mounting straps on the left side of the fuel tank.

12. Open and remove the 2 expanding rivets from the harness protector.

13. Remove the 2 expanding anchors from the holes in the body on the front harness protector.

14. Remove the 2 expanding anchors arrows from the holes in the body on the rear harness protector.

15. Open both clips and remove the high voltage cable set.

16. Remove the luggage compartment floor.

17. Remove the 3 nuts (9 Nm) 4 and remove the harness protector from the threaded pins.

18. Unclip the wiring guide and remove it downward through the body floor panel.

19. Guide both hybrid battery unit connectors through the opening in the body floor panel and remove the hybrid battery high voltage wiring harness downward from the vehicle.

To install:

20. Installation is in the reverse order of removal. Note the following:
- The hybrid battery high voltage wiring harness has a plastic loop near the harness protector inside the luggage compartment, which can be used to correctly position the length. This plastic loop must be mounted on the center thread pin on the harness protector inside the luggage compartment during installation.
- All cable ties opened or cut during removal must be reinstalled at the same locations during installation.
- Tighten all threaded connections to the tightening specifications.
- Make sure the wiring guide inside the luggage compartment floor is installed securely and sealed.
- Restart the high voltage system and complete the required documentation.

HIGH VOLTAGE ELECTRO DRIVE MOTOR & TRANSMISSION V141

REMOVAL & INSTALLATION

See Figures 58 through 60.

1. Read and follow the High Voltage Electrical System Precautions. Danger of electrocution! The following procedure requires working on the high voltage system. Disarm the high voltage system now.

2. Refer to High Voltage System, Disarming.

3. Remove the right and left front mufflers and the right and left catalytic converters

4. Remove the front driveshaft. Refer to removal and installation.

5. Remove the catalytic converter bracket bolts and bracket. Remove the bolt for the coolant pipe.

6. Remove the bolts and the plate. Remove the coolant hose.

7. Remove the bolt and nut.

8. Disconnect the vacuum hoses.

9. Remove the coolant hoses from the electro-drive drive motor and from the engine. Move the coolant hoses and pipes to the side.

10. Disconnect the connector and free up the breather pipe.

11. Remove the bolts and the Automatic Transmission Fluid (ATF) pipes. Seal off any open lines and connections with suitable plugs.

12. Free up the wiring harness for the transmission. Secure the hydraulic pipe for the clutch mechanism in its installed position using a cable tie.

13. Remove the right front ground cable from the engine and then install the articu-

lated joint support VAS 6131/13-7 inside the threaded hole.

14. Install the VAS 6131/13-7 to the VAS 6131 and tighten the bolt to 15 ft. lbs. (20 Nm). Attach the mounts VAS 6131/6-7 to the VAS 6131 as illustrated and support the transmission free of tension under the oil pan. The turning plates with the long spindles are needed.

15. Remove the 9 bolts and install the guide pins T10441. It is possible to remove the 9 bolts using the bit T10099/1.

16. Remove all the bolts from the electro-drive drive motor. Loosen the right and left clamping bolts on the VAS 6131. Separate the electro-drive drive motor and the transmission from the engine.

To install:

17. The engine and the transmission with the electro-drive drive motor are assembled on the VAS 6131A just as when they were separated.

18. Alignment sleeves are present inside the engine

19. Secure the hydraulic pipe for the clutch mechanism in its installed position using a cable ties.

20. Replace the pilot bearings in the crankshaft.

21. Lightly coat the splines on the input shaft with grease N 052 530. Lightly coat the bolt 1 with grease N 052 530.

22. Install the guide pin T10441 in the engine.

23. Line up the electro-drive drive motor with the centering pin. Make sure the input shaft is centered in front of the release bearing.

24. Push the electro-drive drive motor onto the engine. Correct the position of the transmission if necessary.

25. Secure the electro-drive drive motor to the engine evenly, follow the graphic.

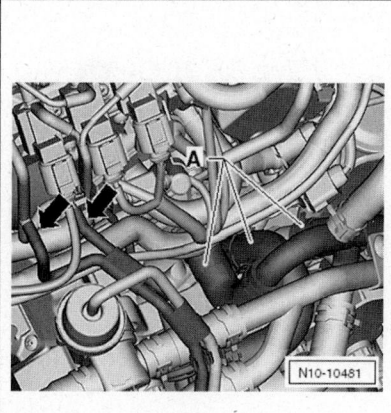

Fig. 58 Vacuum hoses arrows, coolant hoses A

Fig. 59 Guide pins T10441 in the engine

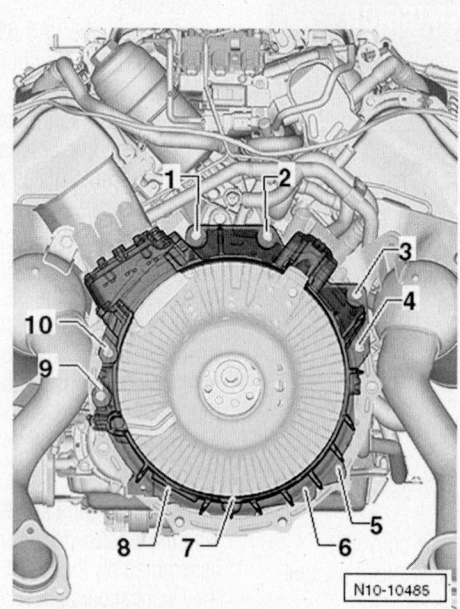

Item	Bolt	ft. lbs. **Nm**
1, 2, 3	M12 x 70	48 ft. lbs. (65 Nm)
4	M10 x 85 with nut	33 ft. lbs. (45 Nm)
5, 6, 7, 8	M10 x 60	15 ft. lbs. (20 Nm) + 90° (1/4) additional turn
9	M12 x 70	48 ft. lbs. (65 Nm)
10	M12 x 60 internal multipoint bolt	48 ft. lbs. (65 Nm)

Fig. 60 Tightening specifications, Electro-Drive Motor to engine

26. Further Installation is in the reverse order of removal. Note the following:

LOW TEMPERATURE CIRCUIT COOLANT PUMP

REMOVAL & INSTALLATION

See Figure 61.

1. Read and follow the High Voltage Electrical System Precautions. Danger of electrocution! The following procedure requires working on the high voltage system. Disarm the high voltage system now. Refer to High Voltage System, Disarming.

2. Drain the coolant from the low temperature coolant circuit.

3. Disconnect the connector and remove the coolant hoses.

4. Remove the bolts and remove the holding strap.

To install:

5. Installation is performed in the reverse order of removal, noting the following:

6. Install the holding straps and tighten coolant mounting bolts to 89 inch lbs. (10 Nm).

7. Fill the coolant for the low temperature coolant circuit.

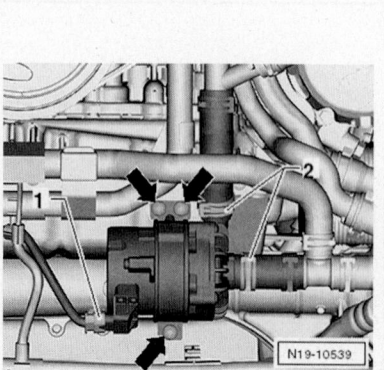

Fig. 61 Low temperature coolant pump, connector 1 and coolant hoses 2

8. Restart the high voltage system and complete the required documentation.

LOW TEMPERATURE CIRCUIT, COOLING SYSTEM DRAINING AND FILLING

DRAINING

See Figure 62.

✳✳ CAUTION

Risk of scalding due to hot steam and hot coolant.

1. Remove the coolant expansion tank cap.

2. Remove the noise insulation.

3. Install drain pan to catch the coolant. Drained coolant must be stored in a clean container for disposal or reuse.

4. Remove the coolant hoses arrows and drain the coolant.

FILLING

See Figures 63 and 64.

1. Fill the coolant reservoir on the cooling system charge unit with at least 5 liters of premixed coolant of the proper mixture ratio: 40%-50%.

2. Install the adapter V.A.G 1274/8 onto the coolant expansion tank.

3. Connect the cooling system charge unit to the adapter.

4. Place the air outlet in a small container. A small amount of coolant which should be collected is drawn off with the discharged air.

5. Close the levers A and B by turning the levers at a right angle to the direction of flow.

Fig. 62 Remove the coolant hoses (arrows) and drain the coolant

6. Connect hose to compressed air. Pressure: 87-145 psi. (6–10 bars) pressure.

7. Open the lever B by turning it in the direction of flow.

8. Condition: A further vacuum is created in the cooling system by the suction jet pump. The needle on the instrument display must travel into the green region.

- Briefly open the lever A by turning it in the direction of flow so that the hose on the cooling system charge unit, coolant reservoir fills with coolant.
- Close lever A again.
- Leave lever B open another 2 minutes.

Condition: A further vacuum is created in the cooling system by the suction jet pump. The needle on the instrument display must still remain in the green region.

- Close lever B.

9. Condition:

- The needle on display must remain in the green range. Only then is there enough vacuum in the coolant system for the filling. If the pressure falls, check the coolant system for leaks.
- Remove the pressurized air hose.
- Open the lever A slowly.

10. Coolant is extracted from the cooling system charge unit coolant reservoir by pressure in the coolant system and the system is filled.

11. Remove the cooling system charge unit from the adapter on the coolant expansion tank.

12. Check the coolant level inside the expansion tank. Either fill or extract to the "MAX" mark, if necessary. Coolant is extracted from the VAS 6096 coolant reservoir by pressure in the coolant system and the system is filled.

13. Remove the VAS 6096 from V.A.G 1274/8 on the expansion tank.

14. Install the V.A.G 1274/10 on the V.A.G 1274/8.

15. Fill the coolant until the V.A.G 1274/10 is full. Fill again during the bleeding procedure if necessary.

16. Remove the engine covers upward.

17. Place a cloth under the bleed valve to catch any leaking coolant.

18. Open the valve arrow until coolant starts to come out.

19. Close the valve.

20. Open the bleeder screws 1 and 2 one after the other until coolant starts to come out.

21. Close the bleeder screws.

22. Extract the coolant until the level is between the MIN and MAX marks.

23. Install the coolant expansion tank cap.

24. Install the noise insulation.

25. Note the following:

- Only use coolant additive G 12 plus-plus that conforms to TL VW 774 G.
- Use distilled water only.
- Coolant additives with the note "conforming to TL VW 774 G" prevent frost, corrosion damage and scaling. The boiling point will be raised. The cooling system must be filled with coolant additive year-round.

- Because of its high boiling point, the coolant improves engine reliability under heavy loads, particularly in countries with tropical climates.
- Freeze protection down to approximately -25°C (-13°F) must be guaranteed. Freeze protection down to approximately -35°C (-31°F) in cold climate countries
- The coolant concentration must not be reduced by adding water even in warmer seasons and in warmer countries. The coolant additive portion must be at least 40%.
- If a lower freeze protection is necessary due to the climatic conditions, increase the amount of coolant additive. Only up to 60% (freeze protection down to approximately -40°C (-40°F). Otherwise the freeze protection is lessened and the cooling effect will be diminished.
- Refractometer T10007 is recommended for determining freeze protection density.
- Do not use the old coolant if replacing the radiator or heater core.

RECIRCULATION PUMP V55

REMOVAL & INSTALLATION

See Figures 65 and 66.

1. Read and follow the High Voltage Electrical System Precautions. Danger of electrocution! The following procedure requires working on the high voltage system. Disarm the high voltage system now. Refer to High Voltage System, Disarming.

➡Recirculation pump V55 location: behind the right mount bracket Removing

2. Remove the coolant expansion tank cap.

3. Remove the noise insulation.

4. Drain the coolant from the high temperature coolant circuit.

5. Remove the right front wheel. Loosening the steering gear makes it easier to access.

6. Loosen the nut from the tie rod end, but do not remove it.

7. Remove the tie rod from the wheel bearing housing using and then remove the nut.

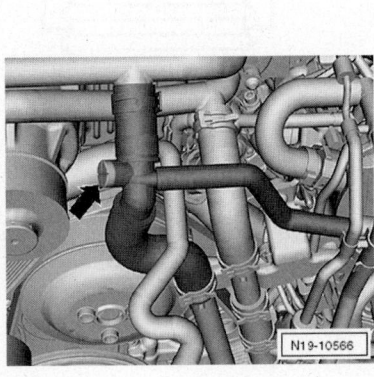

Fig. 63 Hybrid Low temperature circuit bleed valve

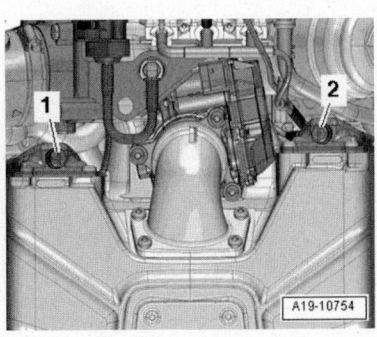

Fig. 64 Hybrid Low temperature circuit bleeder screws 1 and 2

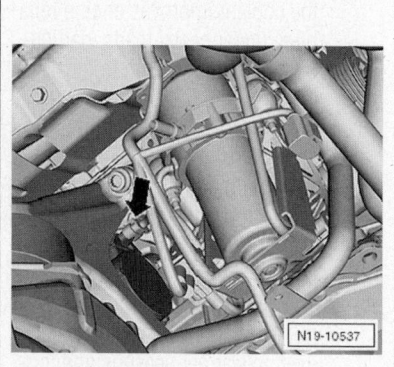

Fig. 65 Disconnect the connector arrow from the pump

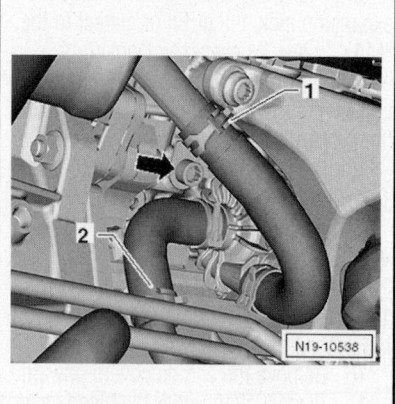

Fig. 66 Coolant hoses 1 and 2

8. Disconnect the connector from the pump.

9. Remove the bolt and the recirculation pump V55.

To install:

10. Installation is performed in the reverse order of removal, noting the following:

11. Tighten the recirculation pump mounting bolt to 30 ft. lbs. (40 Nm).

12. Fill the coolant for the high temperature coolant circuit.

13. Install the noise insulation.

14. Restart the high voltage system and complete the required documentation.

ENGINE ELECTRICAL

FIRING ORDER

3.0L TDI Engine

1–4–3–6–2–5

3.6L Engine

1–5–3–6–2–4

3.0L Hybrid Engine

1–4–3–6–2–5

IGNITION COIL

REMOVAL & INSTALLATION

3.6L Engine

See Figures 67 and 68.

1. Before servicing the vehicle, refer to the precautions.

2. Remove the ignition coil wiring harness cover strip.

3. Place assembly tool (T10118) on the locking button and carefully pull down on the harness connector.

4. Slide the puller tool for ignition coil (T10095 A) from the straight connector side, and then pull out the ignition coil with the power output stage.

To install:

5. To install, insert ignition coil with power output stage into corresponding spark plug shaft so that straight connector sides fit with each other.

6. Slide the puller for the ignition coil

IGNITION SYSTEM

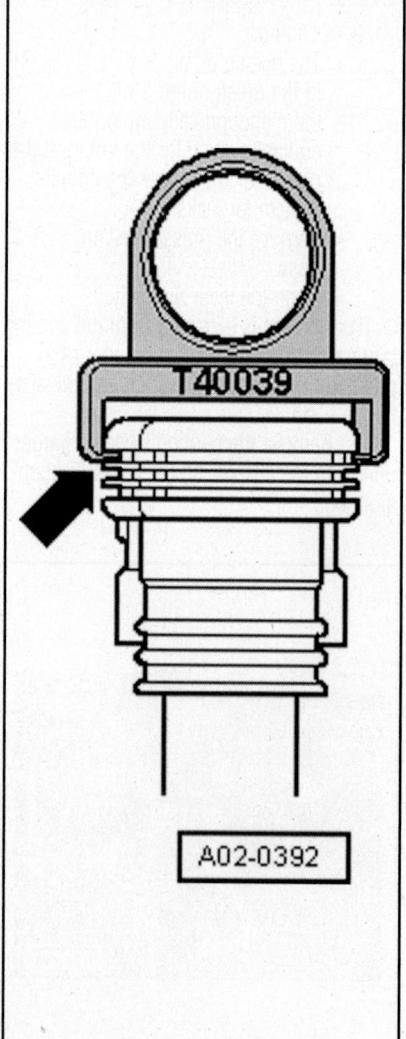

Fig. 69 To pull off spark plugs, place the T40039 on the top most thick rib arrow

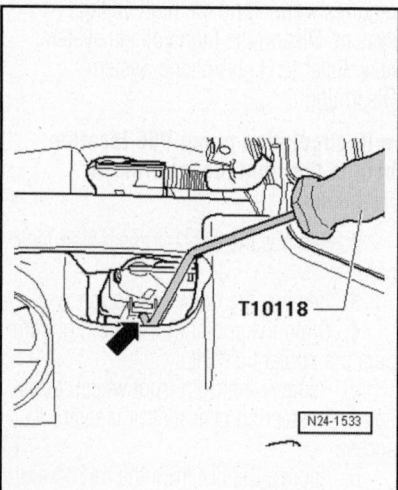

Fig. 67 Place assembly tool (T10118) on the locking button and carefully pull down

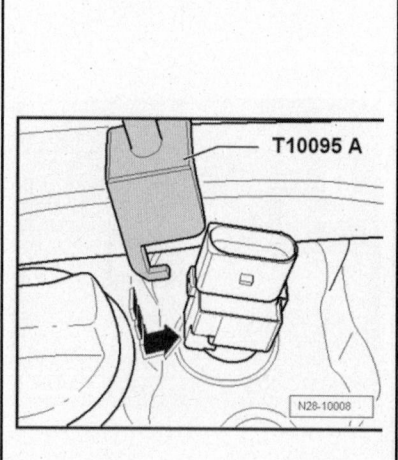

Fig. 68 Pulling out the ignition coil with tool T10095 A

(T10095) from straight connector side and press the ignition coil, with power output stage, onto the spark plugs.

3.0L Hybrid Engine

See Figures 69 through 74.

1. Read and follow the High Voltage Electrical System Precautions. Danger of electrocution! The following procedure requires working on the high voltage system. Disarm the high voltage system now. Refer to High Voltage System, Disarming.

➡ **To pull off spark plugs, place the T40039 on the top most thick rib of the ignition coil with power output stage. Lower ribs may be damaged if they are used.**

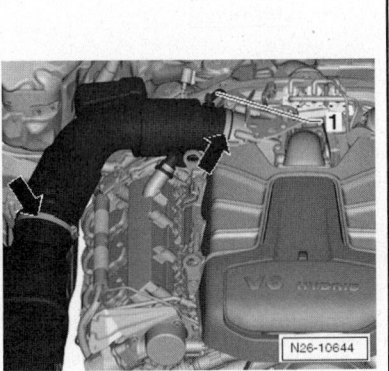

Fig. 70 Intake hose air guide, clamps N26-10644

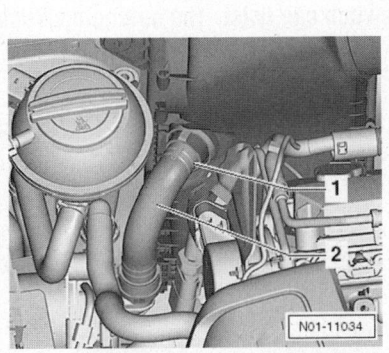

Fig. 71 Secondary Air Injection (AIR) hose 2

Removing the Right Ignition Coil with Power Output Stage (Bank 1):

2. Remove the intake hose air guide, the clamps and the air guide pipe.

3. Remove the engine compartment cover. Lift the engine cover upward.

4. Press the release buttons and remove the Secondary Air Injection (AIR) hose 2.

5. Open the clips and remove the upper air filter housing.

6. Remove the bolts arrows and disconnect the connectors from the ignition coils.

7. Remove the ignition coils using T40039.

Removing the Left Ignition Coil with Power Output Stage (Bank 2):

8. Unclip the high voltage cables.

9. Remove the bolts.

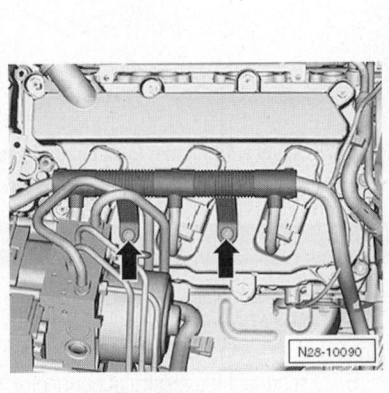

Fig. 72 Ignition coils harness mounting bolts (Bank 1)

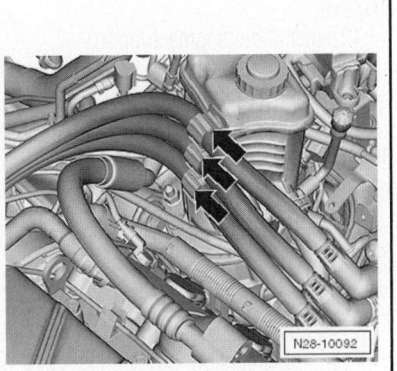

Fig. 73 Unclip the high voltage cables arrows.

10. Squeeze the connector retainers and disconnect the connectors from the ignition coils. If necessary, push the high voltage cables to the side and remove the ignition coils using T40039.

➡ **The ignition coils with power output stages must be greased with lubricating paste G 052 141 A2 to install new spark plugs. This prevents the sealing hose on the ignition coil from sticking on the spark plug. The lubricating paste must spread onto the spark plug when installing the ignition coil.**

New ignition coils with power output stages are already greased when delivered.

11. Apply a thin bead of lubricating paste G 052 141 A2 around the ignition coil sealing hose arrow. The bead must be 1 to 2 mm thick.

12. Install ignition coils loosely into the spark plug shaft. Line up the ignition coils and push them all the way onto the spark plugs.

13. Further installation is performed in reverse order of removal, noting the following:

- Ignition coil wire harness mounting bolts: tighten to 44 inch lbs. (5 Nm)

IGNITION TIMING

ADJUSTMENT

➡ **Ignition timing is electronically controlled and cannot be adjusted manually.**

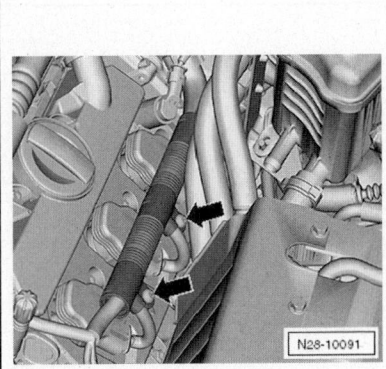

Fig. 74 Ignition coils harness mounting bolts (Bank 2)

SPARK PLUGS

REMOVAL & INSTALLATION

3.6L Engine

1. Remove the ignition coils. Refer to ignition coil Removal & Installation
2. Remove the spark plugs.
3. Install the spark plugs and tighten to 15 ft. lbs. (20 Nm).
4. Further installation is performed in reverse order of removal.

3.0L Hybrid Engine

See Figure 75.

1. Remove the ignition coils. Refer to ignition coil Removal & Installation
2. Remove the spark plugs.
3. Install the spark plugs and tighten to 37 ft. lbs. (50 Nm).

➡The ignition coils with power output stages must be greased with lubricating paste G 052 141 A2 to install new spark plugs.

4. Further installation is performed in reverse order of removal.

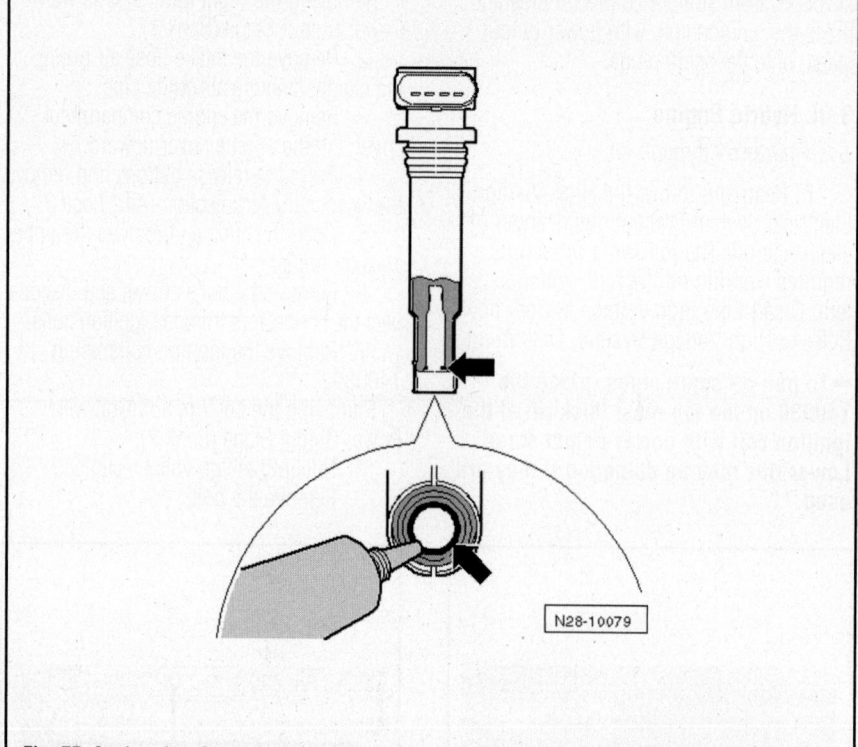

Fig. 75 Apply a 1 to 2 mm thick bead of paste around the ignition coil sealing hose arrow.

ENGINE ELECTRICAL

STARTING SYSTEM

STARTER

REMOVAL & INSTALLATION

3.0L TDI Engine

See Figure 76.

1. Before servicing the vehicle, refer to the precautions.
2. With ignition switched off, disconnect battery Ground (GND) wire.
3. Remove the generator.

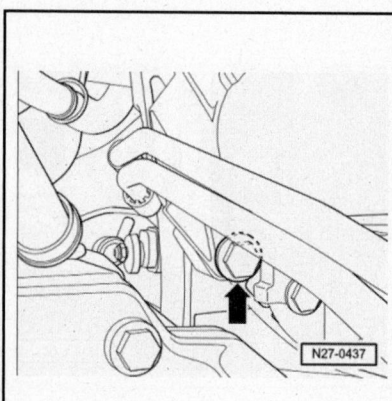

Fig. 76 Using the 16 mm open end wrench remove the bolt

4. Remove bolts.
5. Leave ATF line in installation location.
6. Disconnect the electrical connector.
7. Remove the B+ wire.
8. Remove engine support screw.
9. Remove the bolt using the 16 mm open end wrench T10388.
10. Remove the second bolt and remove the starter.

To install:

11. Installation is in the reverse order of removal.
12. Install the engine support.
13. Install generator
14. Connect the battery.
15. Tighten bolts/nuts to specification as follows:
   - Starter to transmission - lower bolt: 48 ft. lbs. (65 Nm)
   - B+ wire to starter: 12 ft. lbs. (16 Nm)
   - ATF line to Upper part of oil pan: 80 inch lbs. (9 Nm)
   - Transmission: 80 inch lbs. (9 Nm)

3.6L Engine

See Figure 77.

1. Before servicing the vehicle, refer to the precautions.

2. Disconnect the battery.
3. Remove the noise insulation.
4. Open the snaps and remove the starter solenoid heat shield mat.
5. Pry off the protective caps at the mounting nuts.
6. Remove the nut at solenoid positive (B+) terminal.
7. Remove the nut at solenoid terminal 50.

❊❊ CAUTION

Screw connections on magnetic switch can twist. The solenoid switch

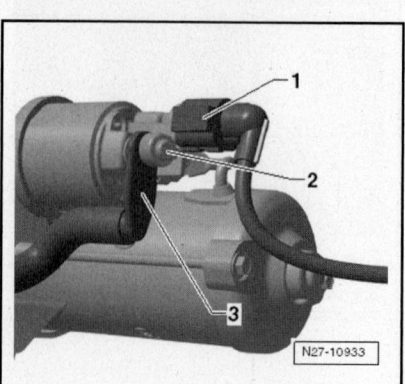

Fig. 77 Starter view with terminal 50 1, cap 2, (B+) cable 3

can be damaged. **When removing and installing nuts at positive terminal and terminal 50, counterhold the threaded connection at the solenoid switch using an open-end wrench.**

8. Remove the lower starter bolt (M12×60) on engine side.

9. Remove the bolt for the cable retainer and set aside. Remove the nuts to free the cable.

10. Remove the bolt for the exhaust system bracket from the engine side and remove the bracket.

11. Remove the bolt for the coolant pipe at engine sump.

12. Remove the upper bolt for the starter on the transmission side.

13. Remove the starter.

To install:

14. Install the starter.

15. Install and tighten the upper bolt for the starter on the transmission side.

16. Install and tighten the bolt for the coolant pipe at the engine sump.

17. Install the bolt for the exhaust system bracket from the engine side and remove the bracket.

18. Install the lower starter bolt (M12×60) on engine side. Tighten it to 55 ft. lbs. (75 Nm).

19. Install the remaining items in reverse of the removal procedure.

ENGINE MECHANICAL

➡**Disconnecting the negative battery cable may interfere with the functions of the on board computer systems and may require the computer to undergo a relearning process, once the negative battery cable is reconnected.**

ACCESSORY DRIVE BELTS

ACCESSORY BELT ROUTING

See Figures 78 through 80.

INSPECTION

1. Turn the engine at vibration damper/ crankshaft pulley with a suitable socket wrench.

2. Raise the vehicle if necessary. Check the drive belt for:

    a. Sub-surface (deep) cracks

    b. Layer separation (top layer, cord strands)

    c. Traces of oil and grease

3. Replace the belt if any damage is found or if contaminated with oil or grease.

ADJUSTMENT

All models use an automatic (spring powered) tensioner. No adjustment is required.

REMOVAL & INSTALLATION

3.0L TDI Engine

1. Before servicing the vehicle, refer to the precautions.

2. With ignition switched off, disconnect battery Ground (GND) wire.

3. Carefully remove engine cover successively from the locking bolts.

❋❋ WARNING

Before removing ribbed belt, marking running direction with chalk or a felt-tip pen for reinstallation.

4. To release the tension the ribbed belt, move the tensioner in direction of using the T 60 Torx socket T40087.

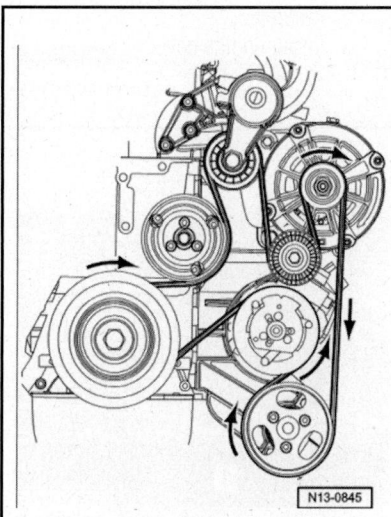

Fig. 79 Accessory belt routing—3.6L engine

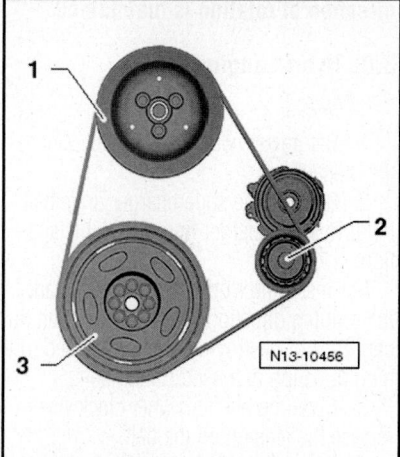

Fig. 80 Accessory belt routing—3.0L Hybrid engine

5. Remove ribbed belt from tensioning roller.

To install:

6. Install in the reverse order of removal.

7. Fit poly V-belt over pulleys as follows:

- Generator
- Idler pulley
- Idler pulley
- Coolant pump
- Idler pulley
- Power steering pump
- A/C Compressor
- Tensioner for ribbed belt
- Vibration damper

8. When installing the ribbed belt, be sure that it is seated correctly on belt pulleys.

➡**If reusing the same belt, ensure the direction of rotation is maintained.**

3.6L Engine

1. Before servicing the vehicle, refer to the precautions.

2. Install pressure bolt M8×50 in the tensioner threaded bore until ribbed belt can be removed.

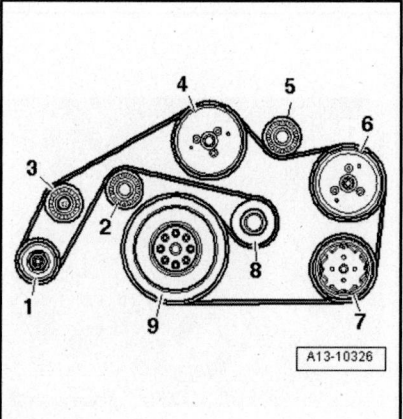

Fig. 78 Accessory belt routing—3.0L TDI engine

✳✳ CAUTION

Tensioner housing may be damaged. If hex bolt is threaded too far into tensioner housing, the housing may be damaged. Only screw the bolt in so far until the ribbed belt can be removed.

3. Remove bolts for the tensioner.
4. Remove the ribbed belt together with the tensioner.

To install:
5. Install and adjust tension.

➡️**If reusing the same belt, ensure the direction of rotation is maintained.**

3.0L Hybrid Engine
See Figure 81.

1. Before servicing the vehicle, refer to the precautions.
2. Remove the supercharger drive belt. Refer to supercharger Removal & Installation.

For installing ribbed belts again, mark the running direction with chalk or a felt tip pen. Risk of destroying due to reversed running direction of a used ribbed belt.

3. Pivot the belt tensioner clockwise to release the tension on the belt.
4. Remove the belt and release the tension on the tensioner.
5. Installation is performed in the reverse order of removal, noting the following:

- If installing ribbed belts again, mark the running direction with chalk or a felt tip pen.
- When installing the ribbed belt, ensure it is seated correctly on the pulleys.

- Install the supercharger drive belt.
- Start the engine and check the belt routing.

AIR CLEANER

FILTER/ELEMENT REPLACEMENT

3.0L TDI Engine
See Figure 82.

1. Before servicing the vehicle, refer to the precautions.
2. Remove engine cover.
3. Disconnect the connector for the throttle valve control module.
4. Remove bolts of throttle valve control module, then open the clamps.
5. Separate the air filter upper section from the lower section and pull it through the openings for the tabs. Observe installation position of air filter.
6. Remove the air filter. Clean the air filter housing if necessary, use compressed air.
7. Install the air filter and perform the following:

- Install the air filter upper section and secure it with the clamps.
- Make sure sealing surfaces on air filter housing are correctly positioned. Make sure that no cables or lines are pinched.
- Install the bolts for the throttle valve control module and tighten to 27 inch lbs. (3 Nm).
- Connect the connector 1 on the throttle valve control module. Make sure the connector is connected securely.
- Install engine cover.

3.6L Engine

1. Loosen the clamp and remove the connecting pipe.
2. Open the clamps.
3. Separate the air filter upper section, from the lower section and pull it through the openings for the tabs. Observe installation position of air filter
4. Remove the air filter.
5. Install the air filter and perform the following:

- Install the air filter upper section in the opening and lock it with the tensioner clamps.
- Make sure sealing surfaces on air filter housing are correctly positioned. Make sure that no cables or lines are pinched.
- Attach the connecting pipe to the connection and tighten the clamp.
- Install engine cover.

3.0L Hybrid Engine
See Figure 83.

1. Before servicing the vehicle, refer to the precautions.
2. Remove engine cover.
3. Unclip the coolant line from the connecting pipe and move it to the side.
4. Loosen the clamp and remove connecting pipe.
5. Loosen the intake line off the secondary air pump by compressing the locking ring and remove the line.
6. Open the clamps.
7. Separate the air filter upper section, from the lower section and pull it through the openings for the tabs. Observe installation position of air filter.
8. Remove the air filter.

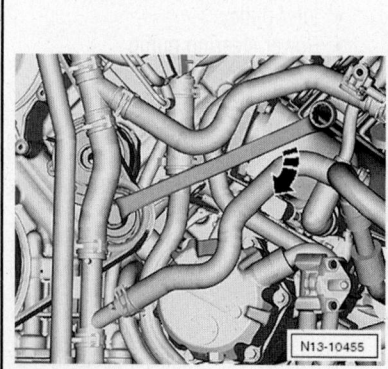

Fig. 81 Pivot the belt tensioner clockwise arrow

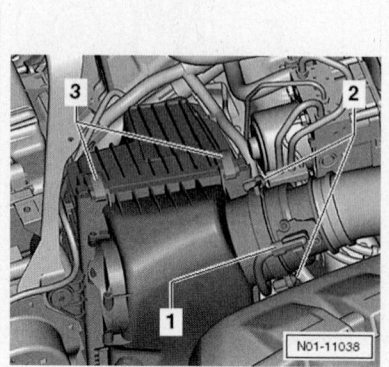

Fig. 82 Connector, mounting bolts 2 and clamps 3

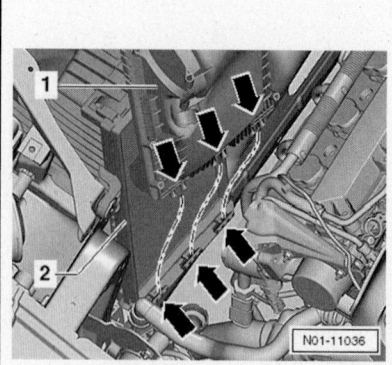

Fig. 83 Air filter upper section1, lower section 2

9. Install the air filter and perform the following:

- Install the air filter upper section in the opening and lock it with the tensioner clamps.
- Make sure sealing surfaces on air filter housing are correctly positioned. Make sure that no cables or lines are pinched.
- Attach the secondary air pump intake line 2 to the connection until it clicks. Gently pull on the intake line to make sure it is secure.
- Attach the connecting pipe to the connection and tighten the clamp.
- Install engine cover.

CAMSHAFT AND VALVE LIFTERS

REMOVAL & INSTALLATION

3.0L TDI Engine

See Figures 84 and 85.

1. Before servicing the vehicle, refer to the precautions.

2. Remove the affected camshaft timing chain from the camshafts.

3. On Left Cylinder Head:

a. Remove the upper intake manifold.

b. Remove the high pressure pump toothed belt.

c. Using the 3036, loosen the bolt 1 for the toothed belt drive sprocket approximately two turns.

d. Remove the toothed belt drive sprocket using the T10320.

4. Remove the left or right cylinder head cover.

5. Loosen the guide frame bolts and nuts in the sequence shown 18 through 1.

6. Be careful of the roller rocker levers and the adjusters when removing the camshafts.

7. Carefully remove the guide frame and the camshafts.

To install:

⁕⁕ WARNING

Only install the camshafts using the T40094 as described below. Otherwise the axial bearing in the guide frame will be destroyed and the cylinder head will have to be replaced.

8. Remove the sealant residue on the cylinder head and guide frame with a hand drill and rotating plastic brush.

⁕⁕ WARNING

Make sure that no sealant residue enters the cylinder head and bearings.

9. Clean the sealing surfaces, they must be free of oil and grease.

10. Oil the journal surfaces of the camshafts.

11. Assemble the T40094 as follows:

a. Left Cylinder Head, insert the bracket T40094/2 in location A and bracket T40094/1 in location D.

b. Right Cylinder Head, insert the bracket T40094/2 in location B and insert the bracket T40094/1 in location C.

12. The following procedure describes the left cylinder head.

13. The procedure is performed in the same order for the right cylinder head.

14. Insert the exhaust camshaft 1 in the T40094/1 and the T40094/2.

15. Rotate the camshaft so it can be secured in the Top Dead Center position with the straight edge.

16. Position the T40096 on the camshaft splines so each of the arms on the T40096 engages in half of the sprocket.

17. Tighten the T40096 with the knurled bolt until the tooth faces align.

18. Insert the intake camshaft 2 on the T40094.

19. The pin 3 must engage in the groove on the camshaft.

20. Slide the exhaust camshaft 1 toward the intake camshaft until the splines mesh.

21. Place the guide frame 1 on the camshafts.

22. All the camshaft bearings must lie on the camshafts.

23. Align the grips and tighten with the knurled nuts to install the T40095 on the camshafts.

⁕⁕ WARNING

Note that the intake and exhaust camshafts have different shapes.

24. Cut the tube nozzle at the front marking (diameter of nozzle approximately 1.5 mm).

25. The illustration shows the guide frame without the camshafts.

26. Turn the guide frame around.

27. Apply sealant beads on the clean sealing surfaces of the guide frame as shown in the illustration.

28. The grooves of the sealing surface must be completely filled with sealant.

29. The sealant beads must be 0.0585–0.078 in. (1.5–2.0 mm) above the sealing surface.

30. Sealant beads must not be thicker than specified, otherwise extra sealant can enter camshaft bearing.

31. The guide frame must be installed within 5 minutes after application of sealant.

32. Make sure all the roller rocker levers are seated correctly on the valve stem ends and the adjusters.

33. Place the guide frame on the cylinder head immediately with both camshafts and the T40095.

34. After installing the guide frame, sealant must dry for approximately 30 minutes.

35. Tighten the guide frame bolts by hand evenly in the sequence shown 1 through 18.

36. The guide frame must be in contact with the entire contact surface of the cylinder head.

37. Tighten the guide frame bolts in sequence 18 to 1 until they are fully seated.

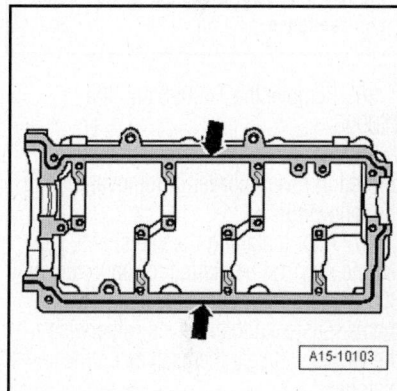

Fig. 84 Apply sealant beads on the clean sealing surfaces of the guide frame as shown in the illustration—3.0L TDI engine

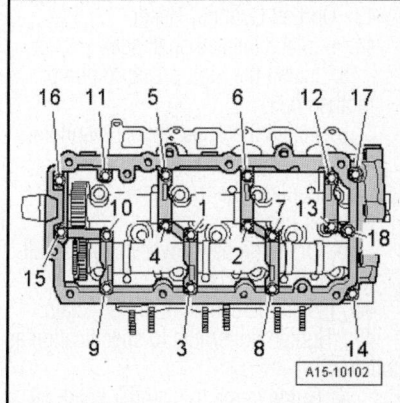

Fig. 85 Tighten the guide frame bolts in sequence 18 to 1 until they are fully seated—3.0L TDI engine

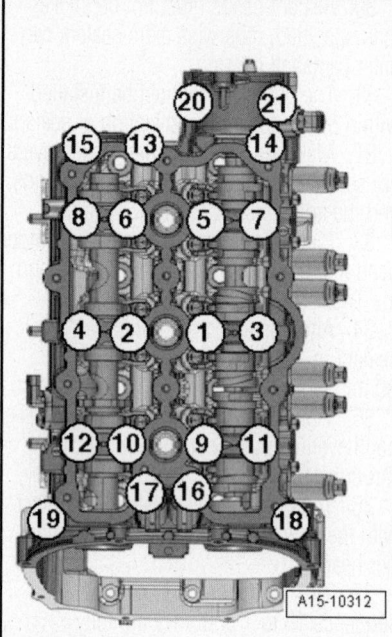

Fig. 86 3.0L Hybrid engine, guide frame bolt sequence

38. Remove the T40095 and the T40096.

39. The rest of the installation is performed in reverse order of removal, noting the following:

40. After installing the camshafts, the engine may not be started for approximately 30 minutes. The hydraulic adjusting elements must seat themselves (otherwise the valves will seat themselves on the pistons).

41. After working on the valvetrain, carefully rotate engine by hand at least 2 full revolutions to ensure that valves do not strike the pistons when starting.

42. Install the left or right cylinder head cover.

43. On Left Cylinder Head:

44. Replace the camshaft seal.

   a. Install the high pressure pump toothed belt.

   b. Install the upper intake manifold.

45. Right Cylinder Head:

   a. Replace the front cover on the cylinder head.

   b. Drive the new cover in with a suitable drift until it is flush.

46. Install the camshaft timing chain.

47. Tighten bolts/nuts to specification as follows:

   • Guide frame to cylinder head: 80 inch lbs. (9 Nm)

   • Toothed belt drive sprocket to camshaft: 56 ft. lbs. (75 Nm)

3.0L Hybrid Engine

See Figures 86 through 92.

1. Before servicing the vehicle, refer to the precautions.

2. Remove the camshaft timing chains from the camshafts.

3. To remove the camshafts from the left cylinder head, remove the vacuum pump.

4. To remove the camshafts from the right cylinder head, remove the high pressure pump and pump motor housing. Remove the bolt and remove the camshaft adjustment valve.

5. Disconnect the connector from the Camshaft Position (CMP) sensor.

6. Remove the ground wire bolt. Free up the vacuum hose on cylinder bank 2 (left).

7. Remove the bolts and remove the cover.

8. Loosen the guide frame bolts in sequence. Proceed in the same way with the right guide frame.

9. Remove the bolts, carefully loosen the guide frame from its bond and place it with the camshafts on a soft surface. Remove the bolts and the T40133.

10. Mark the camshafts, remove them and lay them on a clean surface.

To install:

11. Replace the seals and plugs.

12. Secure the crankshaft in the Top Dead Center (TDC) position using T40069. The hydraulic adjusting elements and roller rocker lever are inserted.

13. Remove the sealant residue on the cylinder head and guide frame and the upper oil pan, for example using a rotating plastic brush. Clean the sealing surfaces; they must be free of oil and grease.

14. Check the oil screen for dirt; clean it if necessary.

15. Lubricate the running surfaces of both camshafts.

16. Insert the camshafts in the guide frame. The placement of the camshafts must be exactly within the axial bearings arrows of the guide frame. The compression ring ends 1, 2 and 3 must face up or down. They must never face sideways.

17. Rotate the guide frame with the camshafts inserted while holding them securely in the frame.

18. Rotate the camshafts until the threaded holes face upward. Check if the camshafts still lie in the guide frame axial bearings.

   • Install the T40133 to both cylinder heads and tighten the bolts to 18 ft lbs. (25 Nm).

19. Rotate the guide frame again.

20. Apply sealant beads 4 through 8 to the clean sealing surfaces on the guide frame. Sealant bead thickness: 2.0 mm.

21. Apply sealant beads 1 through 3 to the clean sealing surfaces on the guide frame. Sealant bead thickness: 2.5 mm. The guide frame must be installed within 5 minutes after applying the sealant.

22. Place the guide frame on the cylinder head.

23. Insert the T40116 in the guide frame and cylinder head.

24. Tighten the t guide frame bolts. After installing the guide frame, let the sealant harden for approximately 30 minutes.

25. Clean the hole in the cylinder head of any oil and grease.

26. Lubricate the outside of the plug with sealant.

27. Drive in the sealing plugs until they are flush.

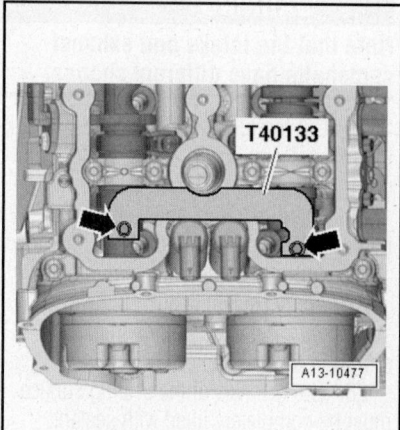

Fig. 87 3.0L Hybrid engine, bolts arrows and the T40133

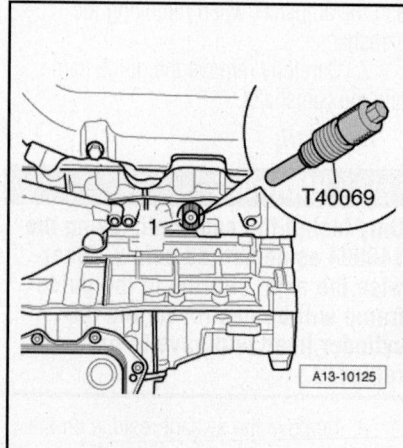

Fig. 88 Crankshaft 1 in the Top Dead Center (TDC) position using T40069

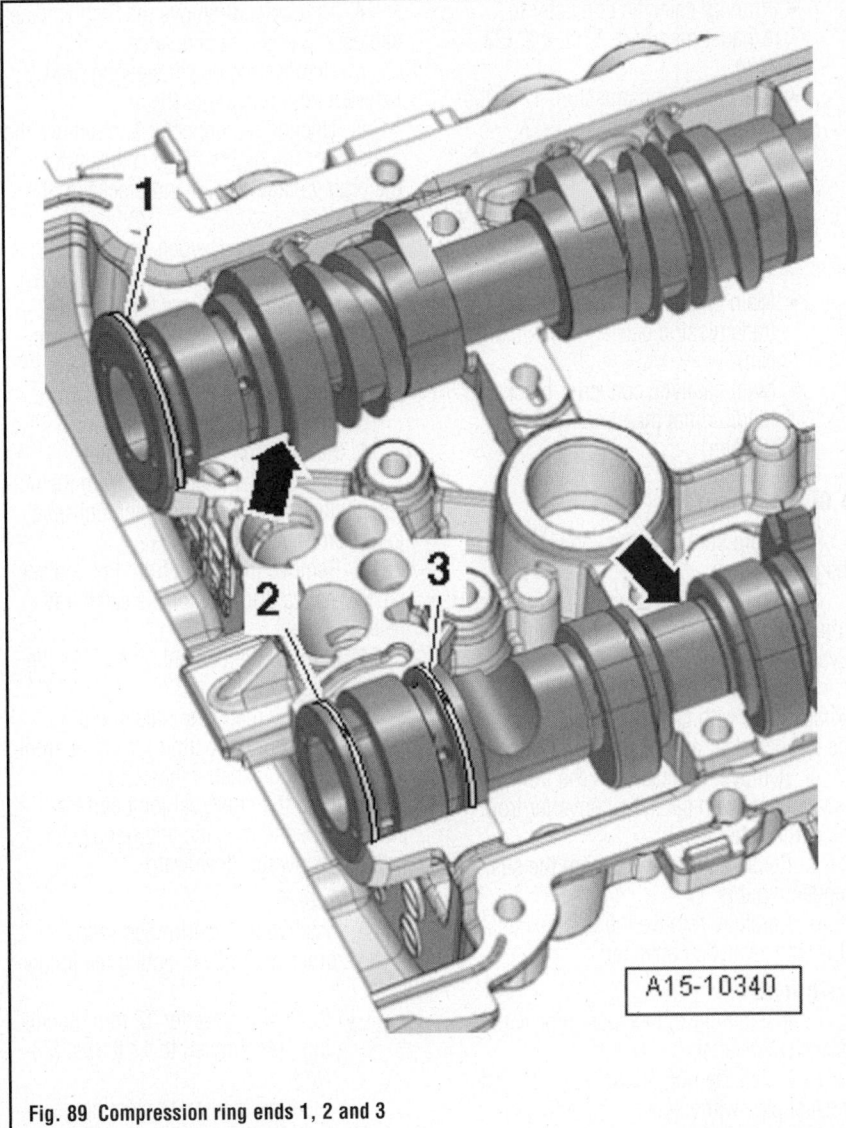

Fig. 89 Compression ring ends 1, 2 and 3

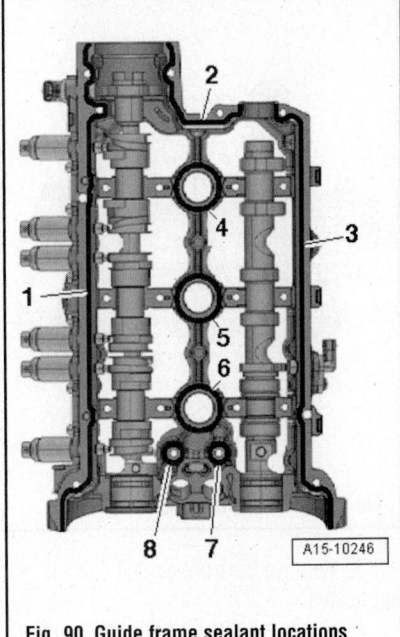

Fig. 90 Guide frame sealant locations

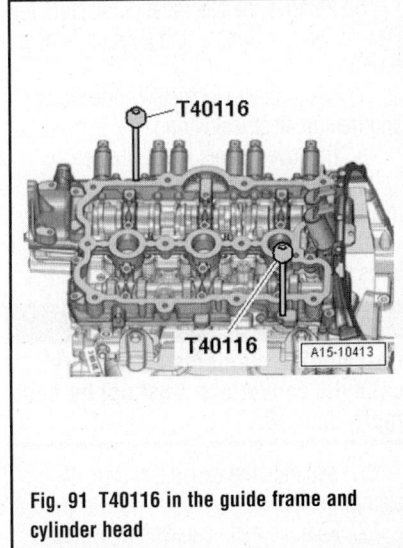

Fig. 91 T40116 in the guide frame and cylinder head

28. Remove the T40116 using T10133/3.

29. Further installation is performed in reverse order of removal, noting the following:
- Install the camshaft adjustment valves.
- Install the high pressure pump motor housing and the high pressure pump.
- Install the vacuum pump.
- Position the camshaft timing chain on the camshafts.
- Tighten wire bracket to right timing chain cover nut to 7 ft. lbs. (9 Nm).
- Tighten oil dipstick guide tube bolt to 7 ft. lbs. (9 Nm).

Tighten guide rail to cylinder block bolts to 8 ft. lbs. (10 Nm) plus an additional 90 degree turn
- Tighten camshaft position sensor to cylinder head bolt to 7 ft. lbs. (9 Nm).

- Tighten Intake camshaft adjuster to camshaft bolt to 59 ft. lbs. (80 Nm) plus an additional 90 degree turn.
- Tighten drive sprocket bearing plate to cylinder head bolt to 6 ft. lbs. (8 Nm) plus an additional 45 degree turn.
- Tighten left drive sprocket mounting pin to drive sprocket bearing plate bolt to 3. ft. lbs. (5 Nm).

✴✴ WARNING

Risk of damaging valves and piston heads after working on the valve-train. The motor must not be started for about 30 minutes after installing camshafts because the hydraulic equalization elements must seat themselves. To ensure valves do not strike pistons when starting, carefully rotate engine at least 2 full revolutions.

CATALYTIC CONVERTER

REMOVAL & INSTALLATION

3.6L Engine

Left and applicable right side catalytic converters are removed in a similar manner. Primary catalytic converters are located at the head of the exhaust pipe where it joins the exhaust manifold, while Main catalytic converters are located further down the exhaust pipe.

1. Remove the rear engine cover if applicable.

2. All cable ties opened or cut during engine removal must be reinstalled at the same locations during installation.

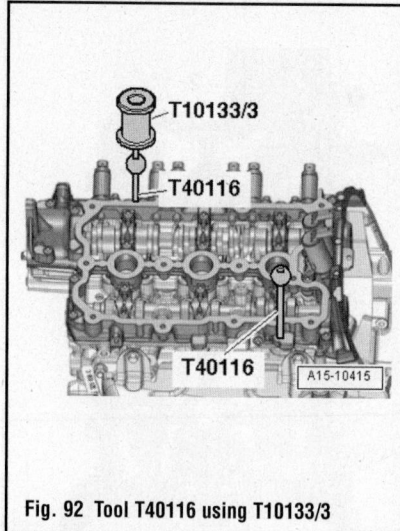

Fig. 92 Tool T40116 using T10133/3

3. Remove the front engine cover if applicable.

4. Remove entire air filter housing if applicable.

5. Remove air guide pipe.

6. Remove the electrical connectors for Heated Oxygen Sensor and Oxygen Sensor (O2S).

7. Disconnect electrical connections and free up electrical wiring.

8. Remove wheels if applicable.

9. Remove bolts and remove noise insulation.

10. Remove noise insulation bracket bolts and bracket.

✷✷ WARNING

De-coupling elements on primary catalytic converters must not be bent more than 10°.

11. Separate the exhaust system at clamping sleeve.

12. Remove main catalytic converter bracket bolts.

13. Remove nuts and remove right main catalytic converter.

14. Remove bolts at primary catalytic converter bracket.

15. Remove nuts and remove primary catalytic converter.

To install:

16. Installation is performed in reverse order of removal.

17. Replace the gaskets and self-locking nuts.

18. Secure all hose connections with hose clamps appropriate for the model.

19. During installation, all cable ties must be reinstalled at the same location.

20. Align exhaust system free of tension.

21. Replace nuts and tighten to specification as follows:

- Primary catalytic converter to exhaust manifold: 17 ft. lbs. (23 Nm)
- Bracket to Transmission: 17 ft. lbs. (23 Nm)
- Primary catalytic converter : 17 ft. lbs. (23 Nm)
- Main catalytic converter to primary catalytic converter: 17 ft. lbs. (23 Nm)
- Main catalytic converter bracket to transmission carrier : 17 ft. lbs. (23 Nm)
- Main catalytic converter bracket to longitudinal member: 17 ft. lbs. (23 Nm)

3.0L TDI Engine

1. Before servicing the vehicle, refer to the precautions.

2. Remove all the sensors and connections from the front exhaust pipe with catalytic converter.

3. Remove the nuts from the front exhaust pipe with catalytic converter from the turbocharger and push it toward the rear.

4. Remove the nuts from the front exhaust pipe with catalytic converter from the particulate filter.

5. Remove the exhaust from the suspended mounts.

6. Carefully remove the front exhaust pipe with catalytic converter.

To install:

7. Install the front exhaust pipe with catalytic converter.

8. Install the nuts to the front and rear exhaust pipe with catalytic converter, hand tighten.

9. Install the exhaust to the suspended mounts.

10. Install new nuts with hot bolt paste and tighten the front and rear exhaust pipe with catalytic converter nuts to 17 ft. lbs. (23 Nm)

3.0L Hybrid Engine

See Figures 93 through 94

Left Side TWC (Bank 2)

1. Read and follow the High Voltage Electrical System Precautions. Danger of electrocution! The following procedure requires working on the high voltage system. Disarm the high voltage system now. Refer to High Voltage System, Disarming.

2. Remove the engine compartment cover.

3. Unlock and remove the pilot line connector from the electric drive power and control electronics.

4. Unlock and remove the high voltage cables 2, 3 and 4 in sequence.

5. Remove the power steering fluid reservoir and move it to the side.

6. Unclip the connector and remove the bracket for the high voltage cables. Move the high voltage cables and bracket to the side.

7. Remove the Oxygen Sensor (O2S) 2 after Three Way Catalytic Converter (TWC).

8. Remove the top nut 2 accessible from the top using a joint socket, 12 mm.

9. Remove the catalytic converter support and the coolant pipe bolts arrows.

10. Remove the noise insulation.

11. Remove the left front muffler.

12. Remove the heat shield from the universal steering joint, remove the universal joint from the steering gear.

13. Remove the hoses from the coolant pipes. Have a drip tray for the catch tray nearby.

14. Remove the coolant pipes from the transmission.

15. Remove the lower nuts 1 and 3 (accessible from the bottom) from the front exhaust pipe to exhaust manifold.

16. Push the universal joint and the coolant pipes to the side and remove the catalytic converter downward.

To install:

17. Installation is performed in the reverse order of removal, noting the following:

- Catalytic converter 12 mm mounting nuts: tighten to 17 ft. lbs. (23 Nm).
- Steering column to steering gear bolt: tighten to 15 ft. lbs. (20 Nm) plus an additional 90°.
- During installation, all cable ties must be installed at the same location.
- Replace the gaskets and self-locking nuts.
- Install the exhaust system free of stress.
- Fill the coolant for the high temperature coolant circuit.
- Enable the high voltage system.

Right Side TWC (Bank 1)

1. Remove the engine compartment cover. Refer to Engine Compartment Cover.

2. Remove the Oxygen Sensor (O2S) after Three Way Catalytic Converter (TWC).

3. Remove the top nut 2 accessible from the top using a joint socket, 12 mm.

4. Remove the noise insulation and remove the right front muffler.

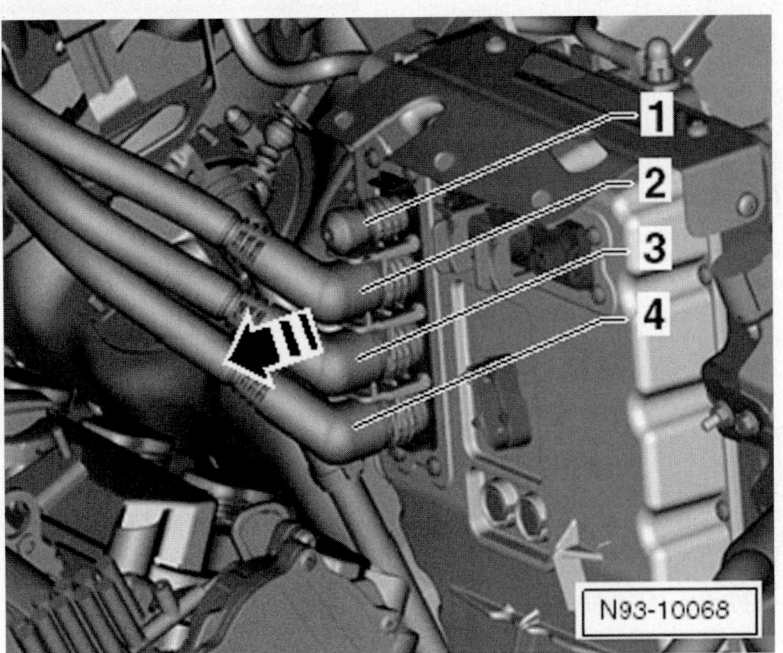

1. Pilot line connector
2. High voltage cable
3. High voltage cable
4. High voltage cable

Fig. 93 3.0L Hybrid engine—Electric drive power and control electronics

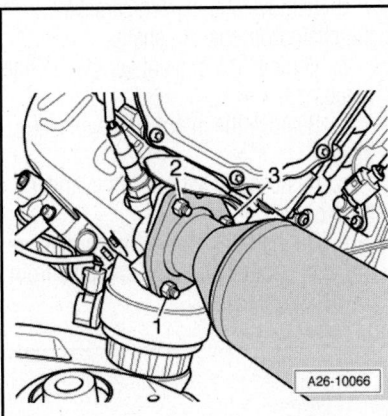

Fig. 94 3.0L Hybrid engine— Catalytic converter 12 mm mounting nuts

5. Remove the catalytic converter support bolt.

6. Remove the lower nuts 1 and 3 (accessible from the bottom) from the front exhaust pipe to exhaust manifold.

7. Remove the catalytic converter.

To install:

8. Installation is performed in the reverse order of removal, noting the following:

- Catalytic converter 12 mm mounting nuts: tighten to 17 ft. lbs. (23 Nm).
- Catalytic converter support bolt: tighten to 17 ft. lbs. (23 Nm).
- During installation, all cable ties must be installed at the same location.
- Replace the gaskets and self-locking nuts.
- Make sure the exhaust system is free of stress.

CRANKSHAFT FRONT SEAL

REMOVAL & INSTALLATION

3.0L TDI Engine

See Figures 95 through 97.

1. Before servicing the vehicle, refer to the precautions.

2. Remove the ribbed belt.

3. Remove the vibration damper.

4. Place the inner part of the T40019 flush with the outer part and secure using the knurled head screw.

5. Lubricate the threaded head of the T40019, place against the seal, and with strong force screw into the seal as far as possible.

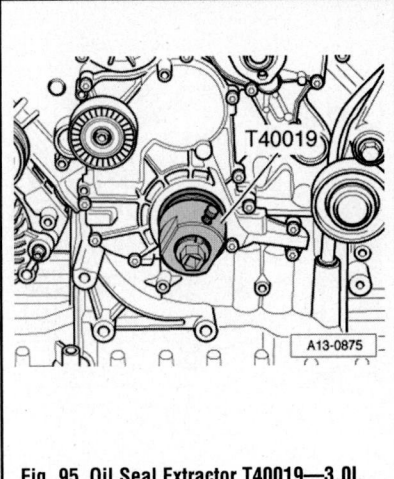

Fig. 95 Oil Seal Extractor T40019—3.0L TDI engine

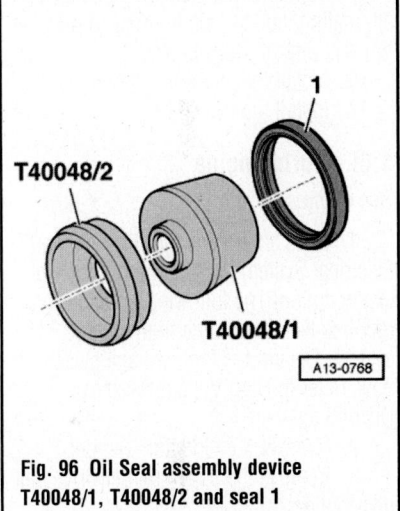

Fig. 96 Oil Seal assembly device T40048/1, T40048/2 and seal 1

6. Loosen the knurled thumb screw and turn the inner portion against the crankshaft until the seal is pulled out.

7. Secure the T40019 in a vice at the flat spots. Remove the seal using pliers

8. Clean the running and sealing surface.

To install:

9. Insert the T40048/1 onto the T40048/2 and slide the new seal 1 onto the T40048/2.

10. Remove the T40048/1.

11. Place the T40048/2 on the crankshaft and slide the seal 1 into the sealing surface on the engine.

12. The pull sleeve T40048/2 remains on the crankshaft for installation.

To install:

13. Install the T40048/4 to an installation depth of 0.195 (5 mm) to the crankshaft with M8 x 55 mm bolts.

14. Then tighten bolts by hand.

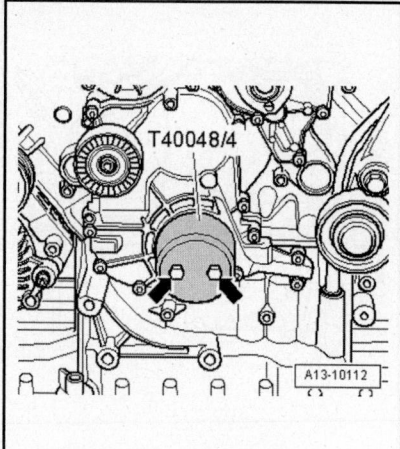

Fig. 97 Oil Seal assembly adapter T40048/4—3.0L TDI engine

15. Tighten bolts each 1/2 rotation by alternating side to side in order to press in the seal until it's fully seated.

16. Install the vibration damper.

17. Install the ribbed belt.

3.0L Hybrid Engine

See Figures 98 and 99.

1. Read and follow the High Voltage Electrical System Precautions. Danger of electrocution! The following procedure requires working on the high voltage system. Disarm the high voltage system now. Refer to High Voltage System, Disarming.

2. Remove the vibration damper.

3. Remove the supercharger drive belt idler pulley.

Fig. 98 Sealing flange bolts—3.0L Hybrid engine

4. Remove the bolts for the coolant pump pulley, use tool 3212 to counter-hold the pulley. Remove the pulley

5. Remove the sealing flange bolts and carefully loosen the sealing flange on the belt pulley side. Always replace the sealing flange.

To install:

6. Apply bead of sealant to the clean sealing surface of the sealing flange, approximately 2 mm. The lubrication system could be plugged with excess sealant. Do not apply a sealant bead thicker than indicated.

7. The groove in the sealing surface must be completely filled with sealant. The sealant bead must be 1.5 to 2.0 mm above the sealing surface.

8. The sealing flange must be installed within 5 minutes after applying the sealant.

9. Place the T40048/1 on the T40048/2 and slide the sealing flange onto the T40048.Remove the T40048.

10. Position the sealing flange with the T40048/2 installed on the crankshaft. Slide the sealing flange, without tilting, against the sealing surface on the engine.

11. Tighten the sealing flange bolts in a diagonal sequence in stages to 6.5 ft. lbs. (9 Nm).

12. Further installation is performed in reverse order of removal, noting the following:

- Install the coolant pump pulley, 15 ft. lbs. (20 Nm)
- Install the vibration damper, tighten bolt to 15 ft. lbs. (20 Nm) plus an additional 90° Always replace the bolt.

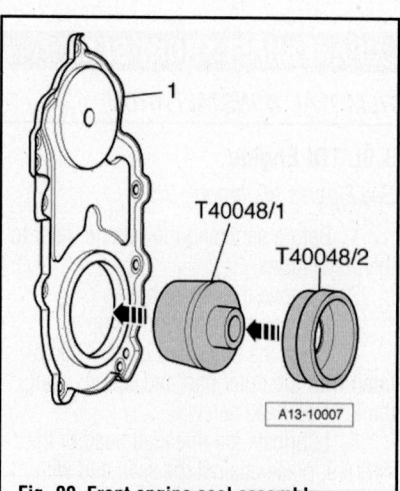

Fig. 99 Front engine seal assembly deviceT40048—3.0L Hybrid engine

CYLINDER HEAD

REMOVAL & INSTALLATION

3.0L TDI Engine

See Figures 100 through 103.

1. Before servicing the vehicle, refer to the precautions.

2. Drain the cooling system.

3. On Left Cylinder Head:

a. Remove the high pressure pump toothed belt.

b. Remove the high pressure pump toothed belt using T40064.

c. Using the 3036, loosen the bolt for the toothed belt drive sprocket approximately two turns.

d. Remove the toothed belt drive sprocket using T10320.

e. Remove the toothed belt drive sprocket with the toothed belt.

f. Remove the bolts and the rear toothed belt guard.

4. On Right Cylinder Head:

a. Remove the fuel supply line banjo bolt and line and the fuel return line banjo bolt and line from the high pressure pump and lay them aside.

b. Remove the upper intake manifold.

c. Remove the left or right lower intake manifold.

d. Remove the affected camshaft timing chain from the camshafts.

e. Remove the coolant ventilation line banjo bolt.

f. Remove the intermediate exhaust pipe,

g. Remove the left or right cylinder head cover.

h. On the right cylinder head, remove the right coolant pipe bolt and pipe from the cylinder head.

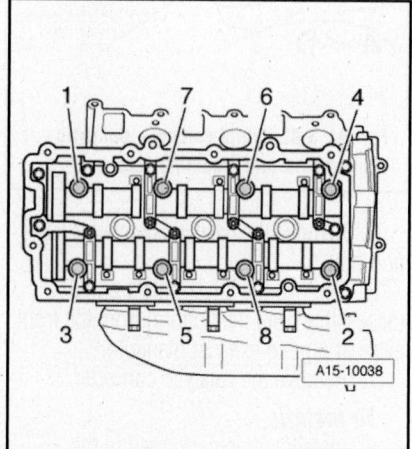

Fig. 100 Loosen the cylinder head bolts in the sequence shown—3.0L TDI engine

i. Loosen the cylinder head bolts in the sequence shown.

5. Remove the bolts and carefully remove the cylinder head.

❄❄ WARNING

Do not set the cylinder head down on the ends of the glow plug elements.

To install:

➡**Remanufacturing of diesel cylinder heads is not permitted.**

6. Replace the cylinder head bolts.

7. During assembly, replace the self-locking nuts and bolts.

8. Always replace the bolts that have been tightened to specifications as well as O-rings and gaskets.

9. Carefully remove sealant residue from the cylinder head and cylinder block. Make sure that no long scrapes or scratches result.

10. Carefully remove all grinding and sanding residue.

11. There must be no oil or coolant in the blind holes for the cylinder head bolts in the cylinder block.

12. Only unpack new cylinder head gasket immediately prior to installation.

13. Handle head gaskets carefully. Damages to the silicone layer and in areas of recesses may result in leaks.

14. Do not remove plastic bases protecting free up valves until immediately before the installing cylinder head.

15. When installing a replacement cylinder head with camshafts installed, lubricate the contact surfaces between the roller rocker lever and the cam running surfaces.

16. After working on the valvetrain and lifters, carefully rotate the crankshaft by hand at least 2 full revolutions before starting to be sure that the valves do not strike the pistons.

17. Secure all hose connections using hose clamps appropriate for the model type.

18. Hose connections and charge air system hoses must be free of oil and grease before installing.

19. Replace the coolant and engine oil when replacing the cylinder head or cylinder head gasket.

20. Installation is performed in reverse order of removal, noting the following:

21. Move the crankshaft and the camshafts to the Top Dead Center position before installing the cylinder head:

22. The 3242 must be installed in the TDC position for the crankshaft.

23. The camshafts on both cylinder head must be secured using the T40060.

24. If the cylinder head gasket or the cylinder head were replaced, select a new cylinder head gasket with the same number of holes as the old gasket.

25. If the crankshaft drive is replaced, measure the piston projection in TDC to determine the new cylinder head.

26. The cylinder head gaskets for the left and right cylinder head cannot be interchanged because they each have a different shape.

27. Install the cylinder head gasket.

28. Pay close attention to the alignment bushings in the cylinder blocks.

29. Pay attention to the installation position of the cylinder head gasket, marking "oben" or part number must face toward the cylinder head.

30. Install the cylinder head.

31. Insert new cylinder head bolts and tighten by hand.

32. Tighten the cylinder head bolts in the sequence 1 through 8 shown.

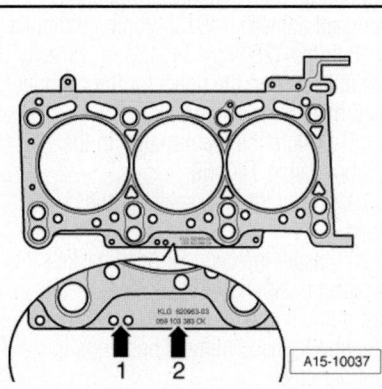

Fig. 101 The cylinder head gaskets for the left and right cylinder head cannot be interchanged because they each have a different shape

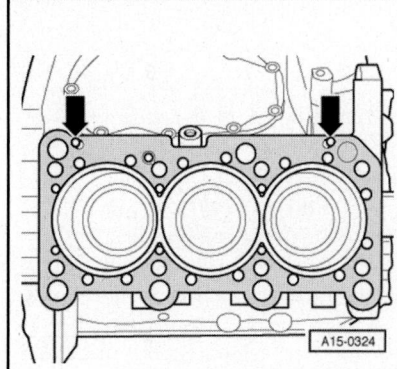

Fig. 102 Pay attention to the installation position of the cylinder head gasket, marking "oben" or part number must face toward the cylinder head

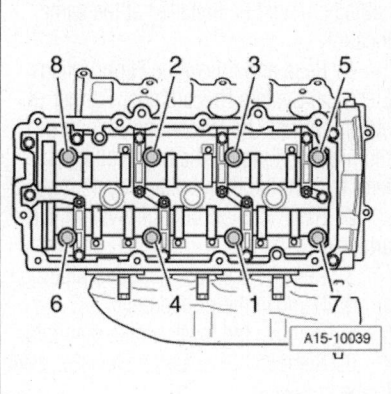

Fig. 103 Tighten the cylinder head bolts in the sequence shown

a. Using torque wrench, tighten the bolts to 26 ft. lbs. (35 Nm)

b. Using torque wrench, tighten the bolts to 44 ft. lbs. (60 Nm)

c. Using a Torx socket tighten an additional 90°

d. Using a Torx socket tighten an additional 90°

➡**The cylinder head bolts do not need to be tightened again after performing repairs.**

33. Install the left or right cylinder head cover.

34. Install the camshaft timing chains.

35. Install the intermediate exhaust pipe,

36. Install the left or right lower intake manifold.

37. Install the upper intake manifold.

38. On Left Cylinder Head, install the high pressure pump toothed belt.

39. Change the engine oil.

40. Replace the coolant.

41. Inspect the fuel system for leaks.

42. Tighten bolts/nuts to specification as follows:

- Coolant ventilation line to cylinder head: 11 ft. lbs. (15.5 Nm)
- Right coolant pipe to cylinder head: 80 inch lbs. (9 Nm)
- Toothed belt drive sprocket to camshaft: 56 ft. lbs. (75 Nm)
- Rear toothed belt guard to engine: 80 inch lbs. (9 Nm)
- Fuel supply and return line to high pressure pump: 19 ft. lbs. (25 Nm)

3.0L Hybrid Engine

See Figures 104 and 105.

The following describes removing both cylinder heads simultaneously. Only one cylinder head can be removed. Use the following description. During installation, all cable ties must be installed at the same location.

1. Read and follow the High Voltage Electrical System Precautions. Danger of electrocution! The following procedure requires working on the high voltage system. Disarm the high voltage system now.

2. Refer to High Voltage System, Disarming.

3. Remove the upper coolant pipe.

4. Remove the ribbed belt.

5. Remove the lower intake manifold.

6. Remove the catalytic converter, refer to the following:
- Left side, refer to Catalytic Converter, Left (Bank 2)
- Right side, refer to Catalytic Converter, Right (Bank 1)

7. Disconnect the left and right connectors from the fuel injectors.

8. Remove the camshaft timing chains from the camshafts. Refer to Camshaft Timing Chains, Removal & Installation.

9. Remove the T40071 from the left cylinder head.

10. Remove the 4 bolts and then remove the chain tensioner from the right cylinder head. The T40071 remains inserted.

11. Remove the ground wire bolts and connectors from the both cylinder heads. Move both electrical wiring harnesses to the side.

12. Remove the bolt and remove the oil dipstick and guide tube.

13. Open the clamp and remove the vacuum hose form the vacuum pump.

14. Remove the bolts for the rear of the cylinder heads. Left cylinder head: 3 bolts. Right cylinder head: 4 bolts.

15. Loosen the cylinder head bolts in sequence 1 through 8.

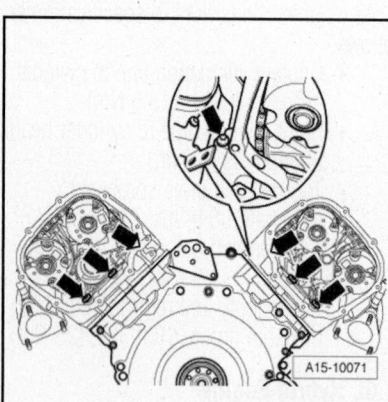

Fig. 104 Left cylinder head: 3 bolts. Right cylinder head: 4 bolts—3.0L Hybrid engine

16. Remove the bolts, remove the cylinder heads and place them on a soft surface.

To install:

➡Replace the bolts which have been tightened to a torque angle. Replace self-locking nuts, seals and O-rings. There are different cylinder head gaskets and bolts. Refer to the Parts Catalog. When installing a replacement cylinder head, coat the contact surfaces between the hydraulic adjusters, the roller rocker levers and the cam lubricating surfaces with oil before installing the cylinder head cover. Secure all hoses connections with hose clamps that are specific to that model. Refer to the Parts Catalog.

Change the coolant and engine oil whenever replacing the cylinder head or cylinder head gasket.

17. Secure the camshafts in the TDC position on both cylinder heads using camshaft adjuster T40133 tighten the bolts to 18 ft. lbs. (25 Nm). T40133 is correctly positioned when the holes for the cylinder head bolts remain free.

18. Secure the crankshaft 1 in the TDC position using T40069.

19. Install the new seals on the coolant pipes.

20. Install the cylinder head gaskets in place, position: the mark (top) or the part number must be legible. Pay close attention to the alignment bushings in cylinder block.

21. Carefully set the cylinder heads in place. Tighten the cylinder head bolts in sequence 1 through 8.

22. Tighten the bolts in 4 steps according to the tightening sequence:

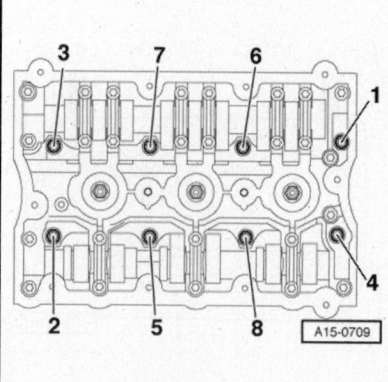

Fig. 105 Cylinder head bolt sequence 1 through 8—3.0L Hybrid engine

- Install the bolts by hand.
- Tighten to 30 ft. lbs. (40 Nm)
- Tighten an additional 90°
- Tighten an additional 90°

23. Tighten the guide frame bolts in 3 steps according to the tightening sequence 1 through 21.
- Install the bolts by hand. The guide frame must be in contact with the entire contact surface of the cylinder head.
- Tighten to 71 inch lbs. (8 Nm)
- Tighten an additional 90°

24. Tighten the bolts for the lower timing chain cover.

25. Further installation is performed in the reverse order of removal, noting the following:
- Install the oil dipstick and guide tube.
- Install the front coolant pipe.
- Install electrical connections check routing.
- Install the camshaft timing chains.
- Install the catalytic converters, refer to the following. Left side, refer to Catalytic Converter, Left (Bank 2). Right side, refer to Catalytic Converter, Right (Bank 1).
- Install the lower intake manifold. Refer to Intake Manifold, Lower Section.

26. Install the ribbed belt. Refer to Accessory Drive Belt.
- Install the upper coolant pipe.
- Change the engine oil.
- Fill cooling system with coolant.

ENGINE OIL & FILTER

REPLACEMENT

See Figure 106.

1. Before servicing the vehicle, refer to the precautions.

2. Remove the engine cover.

3. Cover the area surrounding the oil filter cover with an oil absorbent cloth.

4. Loosen the oil filter sealing cap using a 32 mm socket wrench.

5. Remove the sealing cap together with the oil filter element. Separate the oil filter element from the sealing cap.

6. Clean the sealing surfaces at cap and at oil filter housing.

7. Replace the oil filter element and install the sealing cap with new O-rings and tighten to 26 ft. lbs. (35 Nm).

8. Remove oil drain plug. Clean the M24 oil drain plug and install a new seal. The M14 oil drain plug with integrated seal must always be replaced.

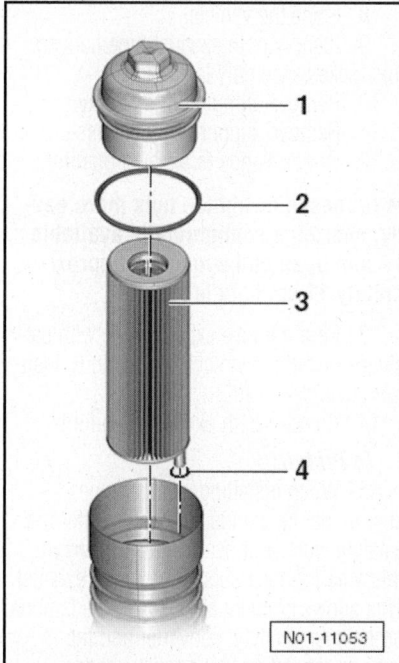

1. Oil filter housing sealing cap
2. Oil filter housing sealing cap o-ring
3. Oil filter element
4. Small o-ring

Fig. 106 Oil filter and housing

9. Let engine oil drain. Observe waste disposal regulations!

10. Install the new oil drain plug and seal hand-tight and then tighten to the tightening specification:
- Oil drain plug M14: 30 Nm
- Oil drain plug M24: 50 Nm

11. Fill the engine with oil, specifications:
- 3.0L TDI engine: 8.8 qts. (8.3 L)
- 3.6L engine: 6.7 qts. (6.3 L)
- 3.0L Hybrid engine: 6.6 qts. (6.2 L)

12. Start the engine and check drain plug and the oil filter housing for leaks.

13. Wait 3 minutes and then check the oil level. On some models there is no oil dipstick in the engine compartment. The actual engine oil level can be displayed in the Infotainment screen or using the oil level display tester T40178.

EXHAUST MANIFOLD

REMOVAL & INSTALLATION

3.0L TDI Engine

LEFT

See Figure 107.

1. Before servicing the vehicle, refer to the precautions.

2. Carefully remove the engine cover from the 4 studs one after the other.

3. Loosen the air guide hose clamps and remove the air guide hose.

4. Place a cloth under the separating point to catch any leaking hydraulic fluid.

5. Clamp off the power steering pump hydraulic hose.

6. Remove the hydraulic hose from the power steering pump.

7. Remove the banjo bolt and lay the pressure line aside.

8. Remove the power steering pump.

9. Remove the bolts 1 through 8 and remove the exhaust manifold.

To install:

10. Installation is performed in reverse order of removal, noting the following:

11. Replace seals, gaskets, O-rings and self-locking nuts.

12. Secure all hose connections using hose clamps appropriate for the model type.

13. Tighten the connection between the intermediate pipe and exhaust manifold as follows:

14. Tighten bolts/nuts to specification as follows:
- Tighten the nut to 89 inch lbs. (10 Nm)
- Tighten the nut to 22 ft. lbs. (30 Nm)
- Then, tighten the nut an additional 90°

15. Align the exhaust system so it is free of tension.

16. Check the power steering hydraulic fluid level.

17. Tighten bolts/nuts to specification as follows:
- Exhaust manifold to cylinder head: 18 ft. lbs. (25 Nm)
- Intermediate pipe to exhaust mani-

Fig. 107 3.0L TDI Exhaust manifold bolts 1–8

fold: 22 ft. lbs. (30 Nm) plus an additional 90°
- Pressure line banjo bolt to power steering pump: 37 ft. lbs. (50 Nm)
- Hose clamps 13 mm wide: 49 inch lbs. (5.5 Nm)

RIGHT

1. Before servicing the vehicle, refer to the precautions.

2. Carefully remove the engine cover from the studs one after the other.

3. Drain the cooling system.

4. Remove the differential ventilation hose from the upper air filter housing.

5. Disconnect the electrical connector for the Mass Air Flow sensor.

6. Loosen the air guide hose clamp at the turbocharger and remove the air guide hose from the turbocharger.

7. Release the clips and remove the upper air filter housing.

8. On vehicles with Air Suspension:
   a. If necessary, remove the electrical connector for the Heated Oxygen Sensor (HO2S) from the bracket at the right strut tower for better access.
   b. Press the circlip forward from the hose coupling.
   c. Press the release ring down and remove the ventilation hose from the upper air filter housing.

9. Remove the connector from the bracket and disconnect it.

10. Remove the connector bracket from the cylinder head cover.

11. Remove the coolant hose from the coolant reservoir.

12. Remove the bolts.

13. Remove the air duct pipe from the hoses and remove the pipe downward.

14. Remove the bolts 1 through 8 and the exhaust manifold.

15. Tighten bolts/nuts to specification as follows:
- Exhaust manifold to cylinder head: 18 ft. lbs. (25 Nm)
- Intermediate pipe to exhaust manifold: 22 ft. lbs. (30 Nm) plus an additional 90°
- Pressure line banjo bolt to power steering pump: 37 ft. lbs. (50 Nm)
- Hose clamps 13 mm wide: 49 inch lbs. (5.5 Nm)

To install:

16. Installation is performed in reverse order of removal, noting the following:

17. Replace the gaskets and self-locking nuts.

18. Hose connections and charge air system hoses must be free of oil and grease before installing.

19. Secure all hose connections using hose clamps appropriate for the model type.

20. Fill the cooling system.

3.6L Engine

See Figure 108.

1. Before servicing the vehicle, refer to the precautions.

2. If equipped with one-piece intake manifold:

　a. Remove the four vacuum hoses from intake manifold.

　b. Remove air filter housing with intake hose to throttle valve control module.

　c. Remove throttle valve control module from intake manifold.

3. If equipped with a two-piece intake manifold, remove the upper manifold.

4. Disconnect the four oxygen sensor connectors.

5. Using a ring spanner (3337), remove the Heated Oxygen sensors (HO2S) in front of catalytic converters.

6. Remove heat shield with intake manifold support.

7. Remove the oxygen sensor (O2S) behind both three-way catalytic (TWC) converters.

8. Raise the vehicle.

9. Identify both exhaust pipe flanges, this makes assembly later easier.

10. Remove all nuts on the flanges.

11. Remove support to transmission.

12. Unbolt flange to exhaust manifold.

➡ **To loosen or tighten nuts more easily, shorten a commercially available 16 mm open end wrench to approximately 11 cm handle length.**

13. First, remove exhaust pipe with catalytic converter from cylinders 4 to 6, then from cylinders 1 to 3.

14. Remove both exhaust manifolds.

　To install:

15. When installing exhaust pipes, ensure that the flange connection after the catalytic converter seals tightly. Leaks in this area produce pulsations in the exhaust. This allows ambient air to reach the lambda probe after catalytic converter and the lambda regulation will be disturbed.

16. Tighten the new exhaust manifold nuts to:

- M8: 18 ft. lbs. (25 Nm)
- M10: 30 ft. lbs. (40 Nm)

17. Adjust the exhaust system so that there is sufficient clearance to the transmission and subframe.

18. The rest of the assembly is basically a reverse of the disassembling sequence.

3.0L Hybrid Engine

Left

See Figure 109.

1. Before servicing the vehicle, refer to the precautions.

➡ **During installation, all cable ties must be installed at the same location.**

2. Remove the electric drive power and control electronics JX1.

3. Remove the power steering fluid reservoir and move it to the side.

4. Remove the left catalytic converter from the exhaust manifold, pull it slightly to the rear.

5. Remove the Heated Oxygen Sensor (HO2S).

6. Remove the bolts and the heat shield.

7. Remove the nuts and the heat shield bracket.

8. Remove the nuts 1 through 7 and the exhaust manifold.

　To install:

9. Install the exhaust manifold and gasket. Coat the nuts with hot bolt paste and install them.

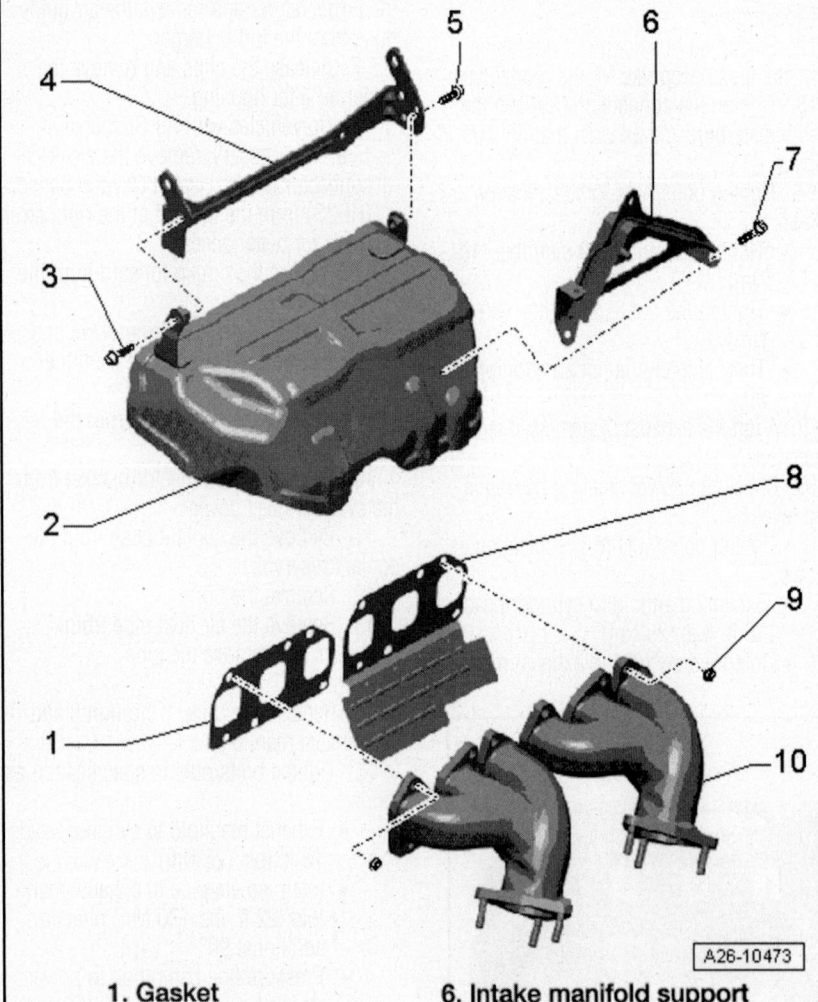

A26-10473

1. Gasket
2. Heat shield
3. Bolt
4. Intake manifold support
5. Bolt
6. Intake manifold support
7. Bolt
8. Gasket
9. Nut
10. Exhaust Manifold

Fig. 108 Exhaust manifolds—3.6L engine

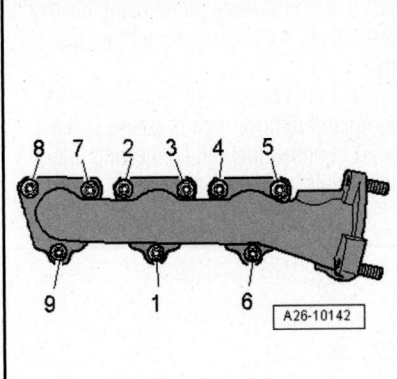

Fig. 109 Left exhaust manifold—3.0L Hybrid engine

10. Install the heat shield bracket and tighten the nuts to 88 inch lbs.(10 Nm).

11. Tighten the nuts in 3 stages and in sequence 1 through 9 as follows:
- Tighten nuts hand-tight.
- Tighten to 11 ft. lbs. (15 Nm).
- Tighten to 18 ft. lbs. (25 Nm).

RIGHT

See Figure 110.

1. Before servicing the vehicle, refer to the precautions.

2. Remove the right catalytic converter. Refer to Catalytic Converter, Right (Bank 1).

3. Remove the air filter housing. Refer to air filter.

4. Remove the Heated Oxygen Sensor (HO2S).

5. Remove the bolts 1 through 4 and remove the heat shield.

6. Remove the nuts and the heat shield bracket.

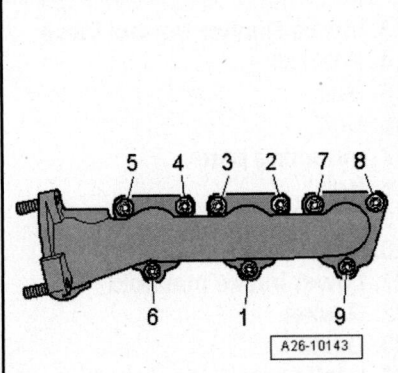

Fig. 110 Right exhaust manifold—3.0L Hybrid engine

7. Remove the nuts 1 through 7 and the exhaust manifold.

To install:

8. Install the exhaust manifold and gasket. Coat the nuts with hot bolt paste and install them.

9. Install the heat shield bracket and tighten the nuts to 88 inch lbs.(10 Nm).

10. Tighten the nuts in 3 stages and in sequence 1 through 9 as follows:
- Tighten nuts hand-tight.
- Tighten to 11 ft. lbs. (15 Nm).
- Tighten to 18 ft. lbs. (25 Nm).

INTAKE MANIFOLD

REMOVAL & INSTALLATION

3.0L TDI Engine

LOWER LEFT

1. Before servicing the vehicle, refer to the precautions.

2. Remove the upper intake manifold.

3. Carefully remove the intake flap motor connecting rod.

4. Disconnect the electrical connector.

5. Remove the bolts and then remove the intake flap motor.

6. Disconnect the glow plug connectors from cylinders 4, 5 and 6.

7. Remove the Exhaust Gas Recirculation cooler switch over valve 1 from the bracket.

8. Remove bolts.

9. Loosen the clamp and remove the EGR pipe.

10. Remove the lower left intake manifold.

11. Seal the intake channels in cylinder head using a clean cloth.

To install:

12. Installation is performed in reverse order of removal.

13. Replace seals and sealing rings.

14. Install the upper intake manifold.

15. Install the high pressure lines.

16. Inspect the fuel system for leaks.

17. Tighten bolts/nuts to specification as follows:
- Lower intake manifold bolt: 80 inch lbs. (9 Nm)
- Upper intake manifold bolt: 80 inch lbs. (9 Nm)

LOWER RIGHT

1. Before servicing the vehicle, refer to the precautions.

2. Remove the engine cover.

3. Remove the upper intake manifold.

4. Remove the bolts and the high pressure line protective plate.

5. Remove the union nuts and remove the high pressure line.

6. Disconnect the electrical connector from the exhaust gas recirculation cooler pump.

7. Remove bolts.

8. Remove the electrical connectors from the bracket.

9. Disconnect the electrical connector from the intake flap motor.

10. Remove bolts.

11. Disconnect the glow plug connectors for cylinders 1, 2 and 3.

12. Press the electrical wiring harness to the side.

13. Remove bolts.

14. Press the coolant pipe to the side and remove the lower right intake manifold.

15. Seal the intake channels in the cylinder head using a clean cloth.

To install:

16. Installation is performed in reverse order of removal, noting the following:

17. Replace the seals

18. Install the upper intake manifold.

19. Install the high pressure lines.

20. Inspect the fuel system for leaks.

21. Tighten bolts/nuts to specification as follows:
- Lower intake manifold bolt: 80 inch lbs. (9 Nm)
- Upper intake manifold bolt: 80 inch lbs. (9 Nm)

UPPER

1. Before servicing the vehicle, refer to the precautions.

2. Remove the engine cover.

3. Remove the oil dipstick from the guide tube.

4. Remove the coolant hose by loosening the hose clamp.

5. Remove the bolt 2 and disconnect the electrical connector.

6. Remove the Engine Coolant Temperature sensor.

7. Remove the bolts and remove the left front engine lifting eye.

8. Remove the bolts and the clamps.

9. Remove the union nuts and remove the high pressure line.

10. Remove the engine cover studs.

11. Remove the bolts and remove the upper intake manifold.

To install:

12. Installation is performed in reverse order of removal, noting the following:

13. Replace seals and sealing rings.

14. Hose connections and charge air system hoses must be free of oil and grease before installing.

15. Secure all hose connections using hose clamps appropriate for the model type.

16. To mount the charge hoses on their connectors securely, spray the bolts on the used clamps with rust remover before installing.

17. Install the high pressure line.

18. Tighten bolts/nuts to specification as follows:

- Upper intake manifold bolt: 80 inch lbs. (9 Nm)

3.6L Engine

See Figure 111.

1. Before servicing the vehicle, refer to the precautions.

➡**If a fuel injector is removed, Teflon sealing ring of combustion chamber as well as O-ring must always be replaced. If fuel rail is removed, spring elements for fuel injectors must be replaced.**

2. Disconnect battery ground (GND) strap with ignition switched off.

3. Drain the coolant.

4. Remove the coolant hoses from the straps on the intake manifold.

5. Remove bolt from oil dipstick guide tube. Remove guide tube with oil dipstick.

6. Remove accessory drive ribbed belt.

7. Remove ribbed belt tensioner.

8. Remove the alternator.

9. Remove the coolant hoses from coolant pipe on the intake manifold/cylinder head.

10. Remove vacuum hoses from Intake Manifold Runner Control (IMRC) valve.

11. Loosen bolts from coolant pipe approximately 1 turn, then remove bolt and remove coolant pipe from intake manifold.

12. Remove the connecting hose from the throttle valve control module.

13. Disconnect harness connector from throttle valve control module.

14. Disconnect harness connectors from ignition coil with power output stage.

15. Remove ignition coils with power output stage.

16. Remove wiring harness of ignition coils with power output stage from intake manifold.

❊❊ CAUTION

Fuel supply lines are under pressure! Wear protective goggles and protective clothing to prevent injuries and contact with skin. Before loosening the fuel lines, place a cloth around the connection point. Then release pressure by carefully loosening the union nuts.

17. Lay a cloth around threaded connection and loosen union nut from fuel supply hose. To do so, counter hold on fuel supply line using a wrench.

18. Disconnect high pressure line and low pressure line from high pressure pump. When doing this, counter hold on connec-

tion of high pressure pump using a wrench. Disconnect harness connectors in this area.

19. Remove bolts, of high pressure pump and remove high pressure pump.

20. Loosen fuel rail connecting line union nuts and remove the line.

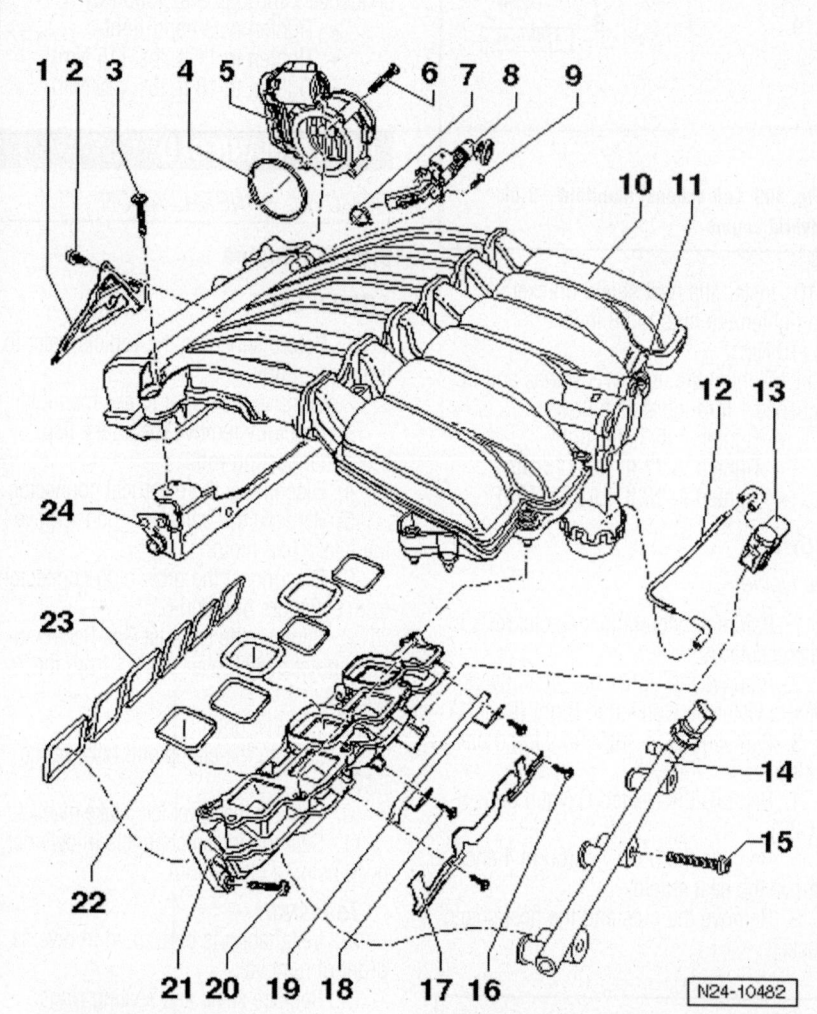

1. Intake Manifold Support
2. Bolt
3. Bolt
4. Gasket
5. Throttle valve control module
6. Bolt
7. Gasket
8. Vent hose
9. Bolt
10. Upper intake manifold
11. Bolt
12. Vacuum line
13. Intake Runner Control Valve
14. Fuel rail
15. Bolt
16. Bolt
17. mounting plate
18. Bolt
19. Coolant line
20. Bolt
21. Lower intake manifold
22. Gasket
23. Gasket
24. Intake manifold support

Fig. 111 Intake manifold overview—3.6L engine

21. Disconnect the connecting hose for the crankcase ventilation from the cylinder head cover.

22. Remove rear intake manifold support bolt.

23. Remove front intake manifold support bolt.

24. Disconnect lines from intake manifold. Remove right intake manifold support bolt.

25. Remove bolts for intake manifold/cylinder head.

26. Remove bolts of fuel rail for cylinders 2, 4 and 6.

27. Carefully pull off fuel rail from fuel injectors.

28. Remove intake manifold downward and set it down on a suitable surface.

➡**Seal the intake channels in intake manifold and in cylinder head using clean cloths.**

To install:

29. Installation is performed in the reverse order of removal.

  a. Replace O-rings between fuel injectors and fuel rail and coat them lightly with clean motor oil.

  b. Replace spring elements at all fuel injectors.

  c. Position the intake manifold on the cylinder head.

  d. Place fuel rail on and press evenly on to fuel injectors.

  e. Insert all bolts of intake manifold and of fuel rail by hand.

  f. Evenly tighten fuel rail to cylinder head with new bolts from inside to outside to 22 ft. lbs. (30 Nm), plus an additional 90°.

  g. Tighten intake manifold/cylinder head bolts, in an alternating pattern to 6 ft. lbs. (8 Nm).

  h. Tighten bolts on intake manifold support to 15 ft. lbs. (20 Nm).

  i. Install fuel rail connecting line, tighten union nuts. Tighten union nuts of connecting line first by hand and then tighten to 21 ft. lbs. (28 Nm).

  j. Check plunger in side of cylinder head, for damage; replace if necessary.

  k. Insert oiled lifter with guide perpendicularly into cylinder head.

  l. Rotate engine at vibration damper slowly in direction of engine rotation. When doing this, press plunger in until it reaches the deepest point in cylinder head.

  m. Install high pressure pump.

➡**O-ring of high pressure pump must always be replaced.**

  n. Before installing fuel lines, first tighten connection for fuel lines on high pressure pump. Tighten as follows:

- Connection for high pressure line: 30 ft. lbs. (40 Nm)
- Connection for low pressure line: 21 ft. lbs. (28 Nm)
- Tighten union nuts of fuel lines first by hand and then tighten to 21 ft. lbs. (28 Nm).
- Install ribbed belt tensioner.
- Install ribbed belt.
- Fill the system with coolant.

3.0L Hybrid Engine

LOWER SECTION WITH FUEL RAIL

See Figure 112.

The following removal and installation procedure is for the left intake manifold lower section. The procedure for the right side is identical.

1. Before servicing the vehicle, refer to the precautions.

2. Before opening the high pressure side of the fuel injection system, the fuel pressure must be relieved to a residual pressure

3. Reduce the high side fuel pressure.

4. Remove the supercharger.

5. Push the vacuum hoses to the side.

6. Disconnect the fuel pressure sensor.

7. Remove the union nut while counterholding the threaded connection.

8. Remove the bolts and nuts arrows and remove the lower intake manifold section and fuel rail.

9. Disconnect the connector on the intake manifold runner position sensor and disconnect the vacuum hose.

10. Cover the intake passages with a clean cloth to prevent small particles from getting into the engine through the intake passages in the cylinder heads.

To install:

11. Installation is performed in the reverse order of removal, noting the following:

- Replace O-rings. Lightly lubricate the fuel injector O-rings with clean engine oil.
- Move the intake manifold flaps using a vacuum hand pump so they are open when installing the intake manifold lower section. If the intake manifold flaps are not opened, they

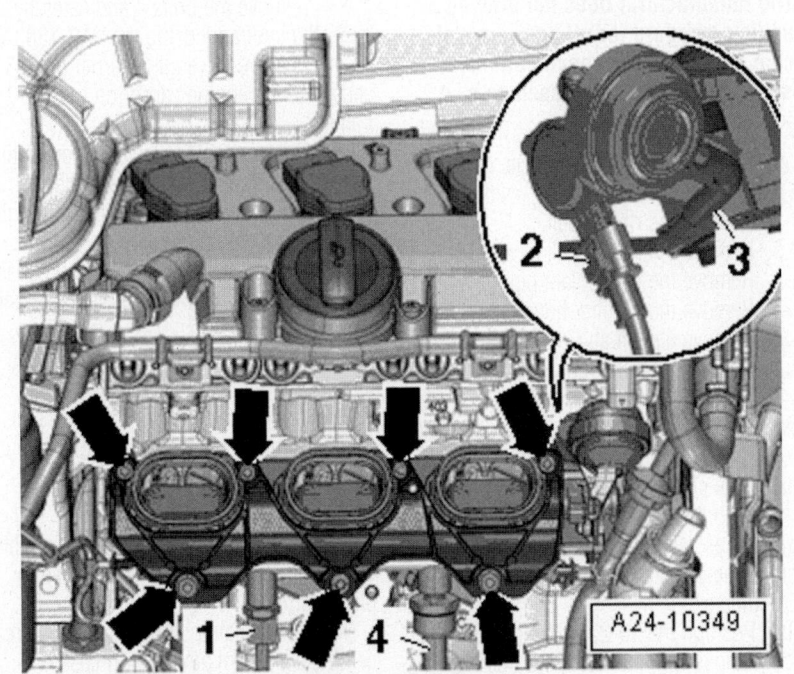

1. **High pressure line**
2. **Intake runner position sensor**
3. **Intake runner vacuum hose**
4. **Fuel pressure sensor connector**

Fig. 112 Lower intake manifold view—3.0L Hybrid engine

may get jammed when installing the intake manifold lower section on the cylinder head.

- Press the intake manifold lower section evenly onto the fuel injectors.
- Tighten the bolts and nuts diagonally on the intake manifold lower section to 88 inch lbs. (10 Nm).
- Remove the hand vacuum pump from the connection on the intake manifold runner control vacuum actuator.
- Connect the fuel pressure sensor connector.
- Counter-hold the threaded connection and tighten the fuel union nut to 20 ft. lbs. (27 Nm). Make sure the high pressure line does not have tension.
- Install the supercharger. Refer to Supercharger.

OIL PAN

REMOVAL & INSTALLATION

3.0L TDI Engine

LOWER

➡The manufacturer does not provide a specific procedure for oil pan removal. Except for the torque specifications, this procedure should be used as a guide only.

1. Before servicing the vehicle, refer to the precautions.
2. Remove the ribbed belt.
3. Remove the ribbed belt tensioner.
4. Remove the left coolant pipe.
5. Remove the air filter housing.
6. Remove the left and right engine mount bracket to engine mount nuts.
7. Remove the left front wheel housing liner.
8. Remove the nuts and bolts from the coolant line clamps.
9. With the nuts and bolts removed, the coolant lines can be moved aside slightly to position the 10-222 A /19 on the longitudinal members.
10. Position the 10-222A on the bolted fender flanges with the T40091/3 and two spindles.
11. The spindles are positioned forward.
12. Engage both spindles in both rear engine lifting eyes.
13. Install the additional parts of the 10-222A as shown in illustration. Position 10 - 222 A /19 on the notches in the longitudinal members.

14. Slide the support T40091/2 with the slide T40093/5 into both T40093/4.

15. Install the T10014 in the mounting hole for the ribbed belt tensioner.
16. Remove the 2024 A eyes.
17. Insert bolt 1 in the center bore of 2024 A again and secure with a cotter pin.
18. Engage the pins on the 2024 A in the front spindle on the 10-222A.
19. Install the 2024 A/1 on the left side of the 2024 A.
20. Engage the 2024 A in the right front engine lifting eye and on the T10014.

21. Raise engine until engine mount bracket are above threaded studs of the engine mounts and tension all spindles evenly to achieve even weight distribution.
22. Position the VAG 1383A on the bottom of the subframe.
23. Remove the bolts 4 and carefully lower the subframe using the VAG 1383A.
24. Remove the engine carrier bolts 3 and place the engine carrier on the subframe.
25. Disconnect the electrical connector item 1 for the oil level thermal sensor.
26. Place the VAG 1782 under the engine.
27. Drain the engine oil.
28. Remove the oil level thermal sensor.
29. Remove the lower oil pan bolts and pan.
30. Rotate the lower oil pan 180° and remove it toward the front.
31. When removing the lower oil pan, keep in mind that there is still some oil in it.

To install:
32. Replace the seals.
33. Remove any sealant residue on the upper and lower oil pans with a rotating plastic brush.
34. Clean sealing surfaces so they are completely free of any oil or grease.
35. Cut the tube nozzle at the front marking (nozzle diameter approximately 1.5 mm).
36. Apply the sealant bead on a clean sealing surface of the lower oil pan.
37. Apply the sealant in a 0.078 in (2 mm) bead on the lower oil pan so it seals corrected with the tapered base on the upper oil pan.

38. The sealant bead must not be thicker than specified or sealant could enter the oil pan and clog the oil pump strainer.
39. The lower oil pan must be installed within 5 minutes after application of sealant.
40. Position the lower oil pan and tighten all the bolts in a diagonal sequence to 44 inch lbs. (5 Nm).
41. Install the oil level thermal sensor.
42. Install the subframe.
43. If the subframe was not secured to the body, perform an alignment after installing.
44. Install the air filter housing.
45. Install the left coolant pipe.
46. Install the ribbed belt tensioner.
47. Install the ribbed belt.
48. Add engine oil and check the oil level.
49. Tighten bolts/nuts to specification as follows:

- Lower oil pan bolts: 71 inch lbs. (8 Nm)

3.6L Engine

See Figure 113.

1. Before servicing the vehicle, refer to the precautions.
2. Drain the engine oil.
3. Disconnect wire connection to air suspension compressor at air filter.
4. Completely remove air filter with the Mass Air Flow (MAF) sensor.
5. Remove all nuts on the right and left engine bracket.

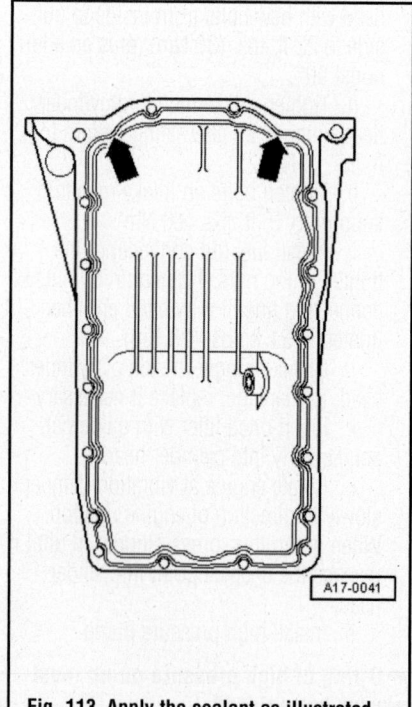

Fig. 113 Apply the sealant as illustrated

6. Position an engine support/lifting device to the engine.

7. With the lifting device in place, pre-tension engine slightly.

8. Remove the subframe.

9. Remove engine carrier. Engine mounts can remain attached to engine carrier.

10. Disconnect the 3-pin connector from the oil level thermal sensor.

11. Remove the oil pan.

12. Loosen oil pan with light blows of a rubber headed hammer if necessary.

13. Remove all sealant residue from cylinder block with a flat scraper.

14. Remove the sealant residue at oil pan using a rotating brush, e.g. a drill with plastic brush attachment (wear protective glasses).

15. Clean the sealing surfaces, they must be free of oil and grease.

To install:

➡**The oil pan must be installed within 5 minutes after application of silicone sealant.**

16. Apply the silicone sealant to clean sealing surfaces of oil pan. The sealing compound bead must be about 0.078–0.117 in. (2–3 mm) thick, and running on the inside of bolt holes.

➡**Sealant bead must not be thicker than specified. Otherwise, excess sealant could get into oil pan and clog strainer in intake line of oil pump.**

17. Apply the silicone sealant to a clean oil pan sealing surface.

18. Install oil pan immediately and tighten all oil pan bolts lightly.

19. Repeat the tightening sequence to 9 ft. lbs. (12 Nm).

20. After installing oil pan, allow the sealant to dry for approximately 30 minutes, before installing any new engine oil.

21. The rest of the assembly is basically a reverse of the disassembling sequence.

3.0L Hybrid Engine

UPPER

See Figure 114.

1. Read and follow the High Voltage Electrical System Precautions. Danger of electrocution! The following procedure requires working on the high voltage system. Disarm the high voltage system now.

2. Refer to High Voltage System, Disarming.

➡**The engine with transmission is removed downward with a scissor lift table.**

3. Drain the engine coolant, motor oil and evacuate the air conditioning system.

4. Remove the engine and Electro-Drive Drive Motor V141 and transmission. Place on proper engine/transmission holding system.

5. Remove the Air Conditioning (A/C) compressor from the engine.

6. Separate the engine from the Electro-Drive Drive Motor V141 and transmission.

7. Remove the lower timing chain cover.

8. Remove the oil pump.

9. Remove the bolts and remove the oil baffle downward.

10. Loosen the upper oil pan bolts 1 through 6 diagonally.

11. Carefully loosen the upper oil pan from its bond and press it off the cylinder block alignment bushings.

To install:

12. Remove any old sealant from the grooves on the upper oil pan as well as from the sealing surfaces.

Remove the sealant residue on the cylinder block and the upper oil pan, for example using a rotating plastic brush. Clean the sealing surfaces; they must be free of oil and grease.

13. Apply a sealant bead to a clean sealing surface on the upper oil pan. Completely fill the grooves on the sealing surfaces with sealant. The sealant bead must be 1.5 to 2.0 mm above the sealing surface. Install the upper oil pan within five minutes of applying the sealant.

14. Insert the seal and the O-ring in the guide frame.

15. Position the upper oil pan, paying attention to the alignment bushings, hand tighten the bolts.

16. Tighten the bolts in 2 stages as follows:
 - Tighten the bolts diagonally to 71 inch lbs. (8 Nm).
 - Turn an additional 90°

17. Further installation is performed in the reverse order of removal, noting the following:

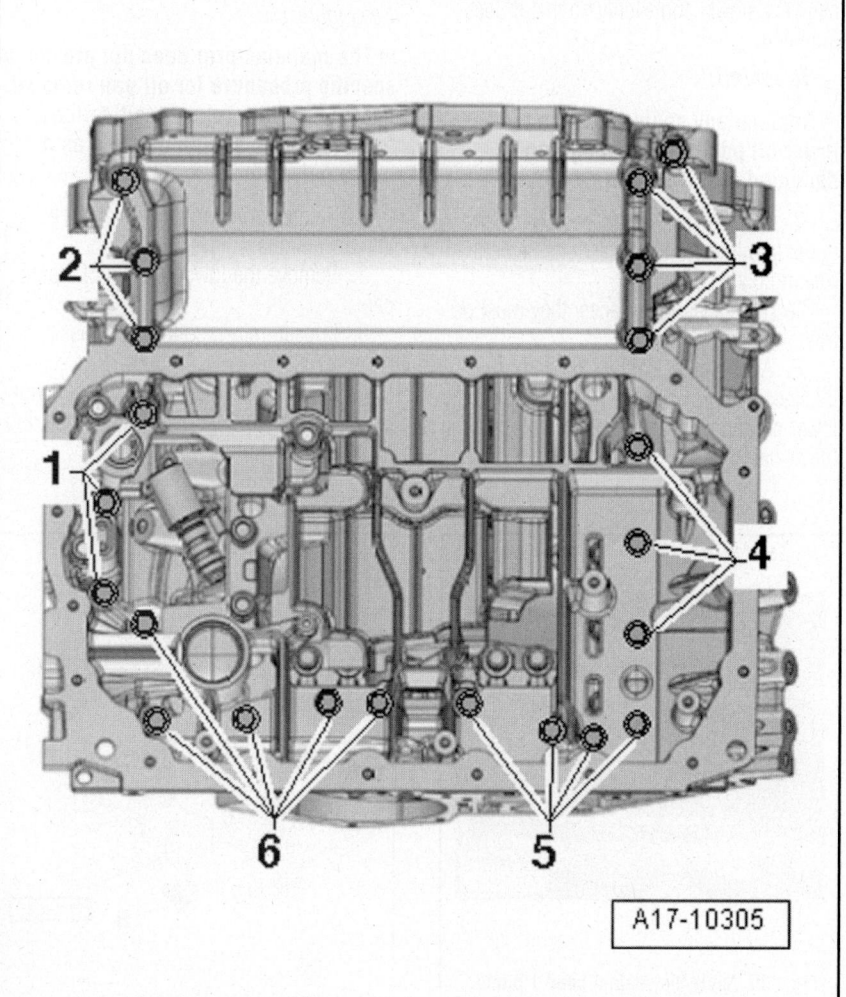

Fig. 114 Upper oil pan bolts 1 through 6—3.0L Hybrid engine

A17-10305

18. Install the oil pump. Refer to Oil Pump.

19. Install the lower timing chain cover. Refer to Lower Timing Chain Cover.

LOWER

See Figure 115.

1. Read and follow the High Voltage Electrical System Precautions. Danger of electrocution!

2. Drain the engine oil.

3. Remove the oil cooler from the engine and tie it to the side. The coolant hoses can remain connected.

4. Remove the 3 bolts for the Automatic Transmission Fluid (ATF) line bracket.

5. Disconnect the electrical connector from the oil level thermal sensor and free up the electrical wire.

6. Remove the bolts for the lower oil pan. Carefully loosen the lower oil pan from the sealant without bending it. The sealant for the oil pan is very strong. Pry off the oil pan very slowly and evenly so that it does not bend.

To install:

➡Replace any seals. Replace the lower oil pan if the coating on it is damaged or if it is bent.

7. Remove any sealant residue on the upper and lower oil pan sections using a rotating plastic brush.

Clean the sealing surfaces; they must be free of oil and grease.

8. Apply the sealant to the oil pan, thickness: approximately 1.5 mm. Install the lower oil pan within five minutes of applying the sealant.

✳✳ WARNING

Replace any bolts which have been tightened to a torque angle.

9. Position the lower oil pan and tighten the bolts in two stages as follows:

- Working diagonally, tighten the new oil pan bolts to 44 inch lbs. (5 Nm).
- Working diagonally, turn an additional 90°

10. Further installation is performed in the reverse order of removal, noting the following:

11. Install the oil cooler.

12. Install the ATF lines.

13. Fill the engine oil and check the oil level.

OIL PUMP

REMOVAL & INSTALLATION

3.0L TDI Engine

See Figure 116.

➡The manufacturer does not provide a specific procedure for oil pan removal. Except for the torque specifications, this procedure should be used as a guide only.

1. Before servicing the vehicle, refer to the precautions.

2. Remove the lower section of the oil pan.

3. Loosen return connections as shown.

4. To remove, slide slightly in direction of engine management side after loosening all mounts and remove.

To install:

➡During installation, replace all seals and O-rings.

5. Install the oil pump and tighten the bolts to 6 ft. lbs. (8 Nm), plus an additional 90°.

6. The rest of installation is in reverse order of removal, note the following:

7. Install lower section of oil pan.

8. Add engine oil and check oil level.

3.0L Hybrid Engine

See Figure 117.

1. Read and follow the High Voltage Electrical System Precautions. Danger of electrocution!

2. Drain the engine oil.

3. Remove the lower oil pan. Carefully loosen the lower oil pan from the sealant without bending it. The sealant for the oil pan is very strong. Pry off the oil pan very slowly and evenly so that it does not bend.

4. Remove the 3 mounting bolts from the oil pump. Carefully remove the oil pump forward from the input shaft.

To install:

5. Installation is performed in the reverse order of removal, noting the following:

6. Replace the gasket and O-ring.

7. Install the oil pump onto the driveshaft and tighten the 3 mounting bolts to 15 inch lbs. (20 Nm).

✳✳ WARNING

Replace any bolts which have been tightened to a torque angle.

8. Position the lower oil pan and tighten the bolts in two stages as follows:

- Working diagonally, tighten the new oil pan bolts to 44 inch lbs. (5 Nm).
- Working diagonally, turn an additional 90°
- Fill the engine oil and check the ATF and engine oil levels.

INSPECTION

Disassembly is not possible or recommended.

PISTON AND RING

POSITIONING

See Figures 118 through 120.

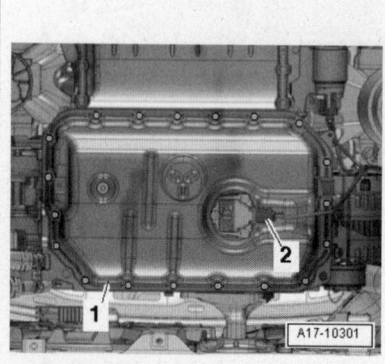

Fig. 115 Apply the sealant bead 1.5 mm. (arrow) to the surfaces of the lower oil pan as shown.

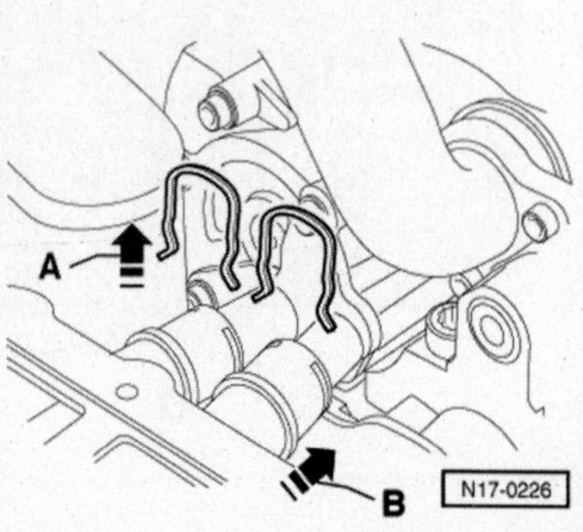

Fig. 116 Loosen return connections as shown

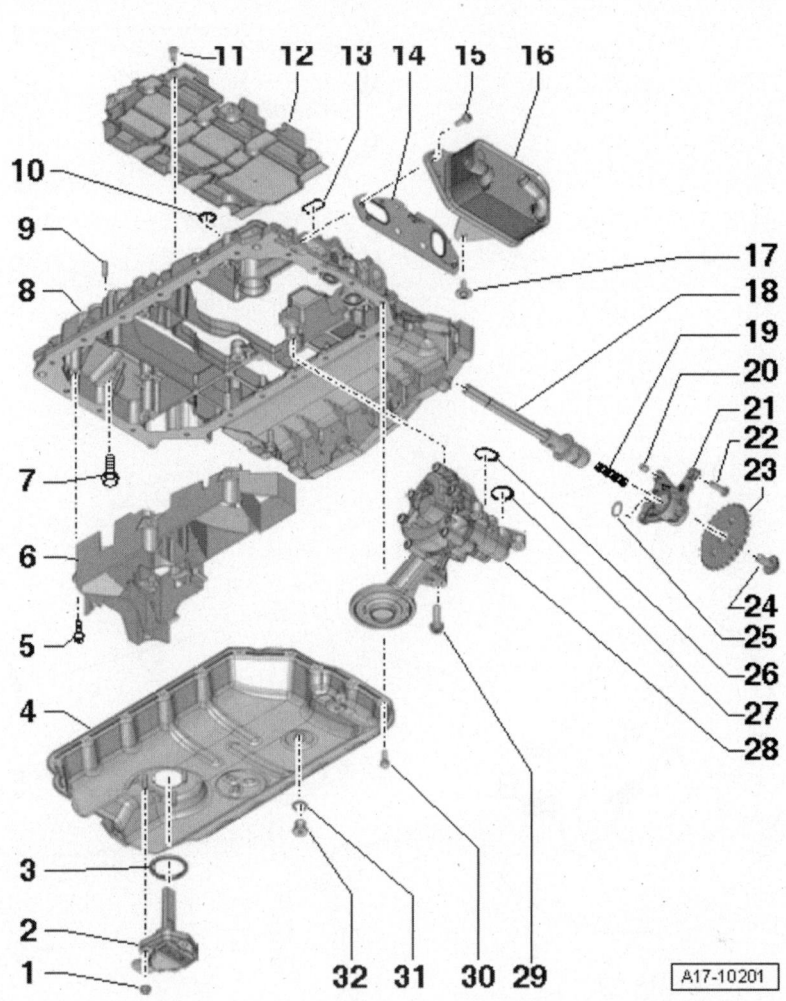

Fig. 117 Oil pan and pump overview—3.0L Hybrid engine

SUPERCHARGER

REMOVAL & INSTALLATION

3.0L Hybrid Engine

See Figure 121.

1. Before servicing the vehicle, refer to the precautions.

2. Remove the supercharger drive belt.

3. Place drain pan under the engine.

4. Open the clamps and disconnect the coolant hoses and remove them from the coolant pipes on the supercharger.

5. Remove the hose, the clamps and the air guide pipe.

6. Disconnect the electrical connector from the Evaporative Emission (EVAP) can-

ister purge regulator valve and disconnect the vacuum hose. Remove the EVAP canister purge regulator valve from the bracket and lay it aside with the hose connected.

7. Disconnect the connector from the throttle valve control module.

8. Disconnect the connector from the control valve control unit J808.

9. Disconnect the 3 remaining connectors. Disconnect and mark all the vacuum hoses for installation later.

10. Disconnect the connector from the Intake Air Temperature (IAT) sensor/Manifold Absolute Pressure (MAP) sensor.

11. Remove the left and right bolts and the cover. Free up the brake booster vacuum hose from the bracket.

12. Disconnect the 2 remaining electrical connectors.

13. Remove the nuts and remove the supercharger with the charge air coolers upward. Seal off the openings on the supercharger and on the charge air pipe using.

➡**Carefully cover or seal opened components, if repairs are not performed immediately.**

To install:

14. Installation is performed in the reverse order of removal, noting the following:

- Tighten the super charger mounting nuts to 16 ft. lbs. (22 Nm).
- Replace all the seals.
- The hose connections as well as the air guide pipes and hoses must be free of oil and grease before installing.

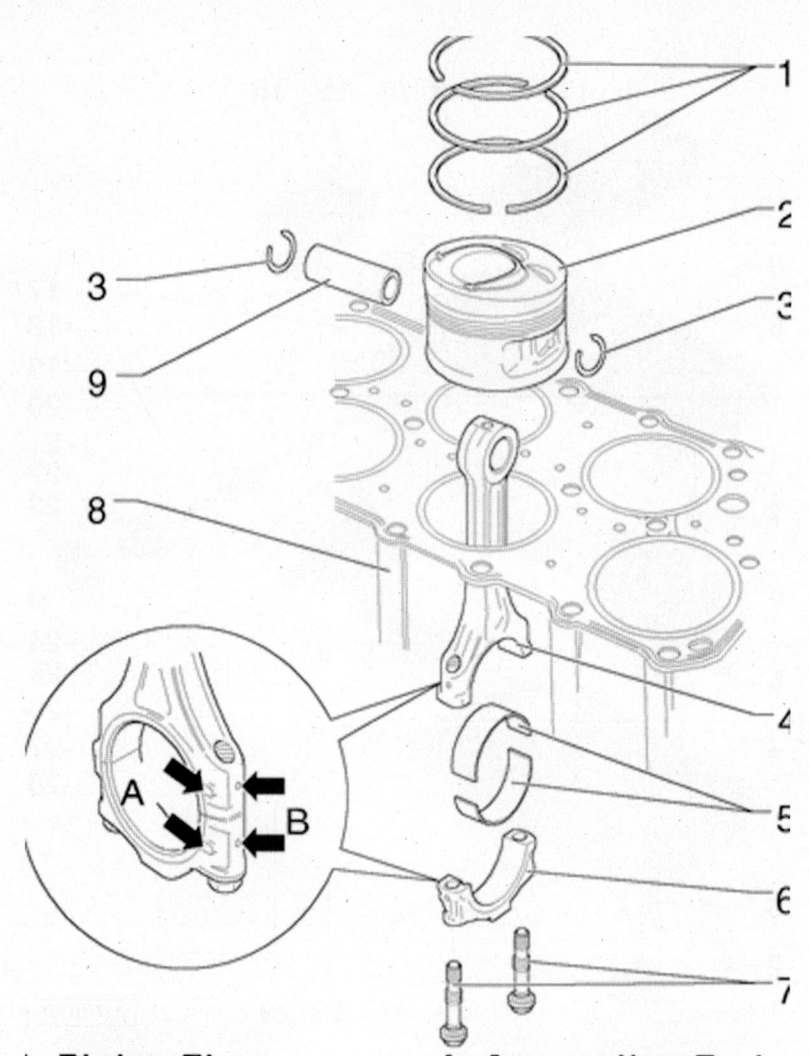

1. Piston Rings
2. Piston
3. Circlip
4. Connecting Rod
5. Bearing Shell
6. Connecting Rod
   Bearing Cap
7. Bearing Cap Bolts
8. Cylinder Block
9. Piston Pin

22205_TOUA_G0127

Fig. 118 Exploded view of the piston and rod assembly—note positions of ring end gaps on piston—3.6L engine

- Secure all the coolant hose connections with hose clamps that are specific to that model.
- In order to be able to securely mount the air guide hoses on their connectors, spray the bolts on the previously used clamps with a rust remover.
- Make sure the crankcase ventilation support is installed correctly when mounting the supercharger.
- Install the supercharger drive belt.
- Fill with coolant.

TURBOCHARGER

OVERVIEW

See Figure 122.

The following information is an overview of the turbocharger system.

- Hose connections are secured by clamps and retaining clips.
- The charge air system must be properly sealed.
- Replace the self-locking nuts.
- After installing the turbocharger, let the engine run at idle for approximately 1

minute, without increasing the engine speed. This ensures that the turbocharger is lubricated.

VALVE COVERS

REMOVAL & INSTALLATION

3.0L TDI Engine

The following removal and installation procedure is for the left cylinder head cover. The procedure for the opposite side is identical except for a few steps.

14. Loosen the cylinder head cover bolts diagonally, starting from the outside and working toward the inside. Remove the bolts and the cylinder head cover.

To install:

15. Installation is performed in the reverse order of removal, noting the following:

- Replace the cylinder head cover, if it is damaged.
- Replace all gaskets, seals and O-rings.
- Hose connections and charge air system hoses must be free of oil and grease before installing.
- Secure all the hose connections using hose clamps appropriate for the model type.
- Tighten the cylinder head cover bolts, diagonally and in steps, starting from the inside and working toward the outside: tighten to 80 inch lbs. (9 Nm).
- Make sure the injectors and their installed locations are clean before installing. Clean the injector shaft in the cylinder head with a clean cloth if necessary. Do not use any sharp tools and be careful not to damage it.
- Always use new seals. Coat all the seals with oil or assembly oil before installing.
- The fuel injectors must not be damaged. To remove the used copper sealing ring from the fuel injector, clamp the sealing ring carefully in a vise until the clamping jaws on the vise prevent the ring from turning. Pull the fuel injector out of the copper sealing ring by hand with a slight twisting and pulling motion.
- The injector line and tensioning plate must be replaced to replace the injector.
- When installing, the fuel injectors and injector lines may only be installed to the same cylinder as before.
- Carefully install the fuel injectors and tighten the sealing cap bolts to 49 inch lbs. (5.5 Nm).
- Tighten the tensioning plate to cylinder head nuts to 88 inch lbs. (10 Nm)
- Tighten the upper intake manifold bolts to 80 inch lbs. (9 Nm).
- Tighten all the high pressure line union nuts by hand, then tighten to 21 ft. lbs. (28 Nm).

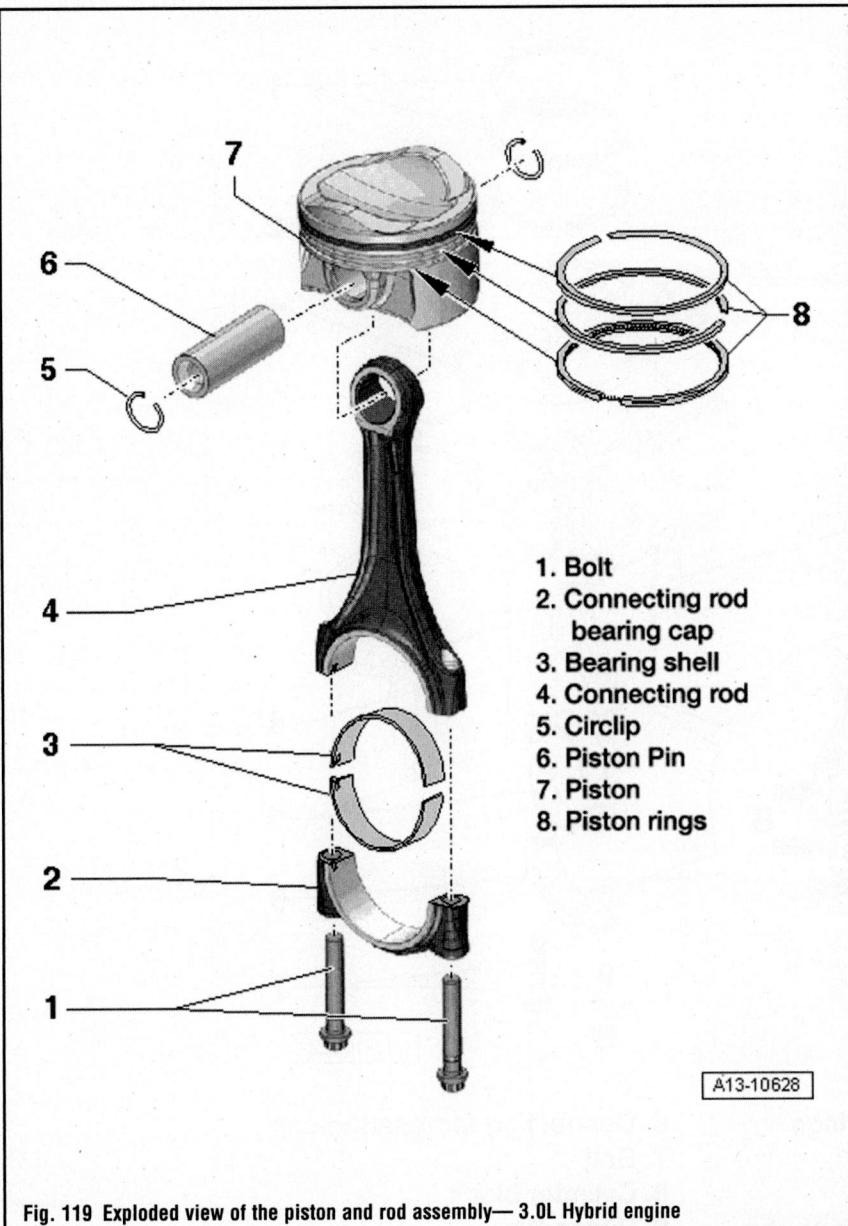

1. Bolt
2. Connecting rod bearing cap
3. Bearing shell
4. Connecting rod
5. Circlip
6. Piston Pin
7. Piston
8. Piston rings

A13-10628

Fig. 119 Exploded view of the piston and rod assembly— 3.0L Hybrid engine

1. Before servicing the vehicle, refer to the precautions.

2. Relieve the fuel system.

3. Disconnect the vacuum hose from the vacuum reservoir

4. Remove the fuel supply line.

5. Remove the high pressure fuel lines and the overflow oil line.

6. When removing Only the left cylinder head cover, remove the engine cover bracket, the bolts and the upper intake manifold.

7. Continuation for both sides, lift the tab and turn the oil filler tube counterclockwise and remove the tube.

8. Remove the wiring harness bracket bolt and bracket from the cylinder head cover.

9. Disconnect the connectors 1 through 4 from the fuel rail and injectors. Free up the wiring harness.

10. Pull the release pins upward and disconnect the return line connections from the injectors. Mark the high pressure lines to the injectors.

11. Loosen the high pressure line union nuts 1 through 6 using the tool insert AF 19 V.A.G 1331/5 or socket 14 mm 3150 and the socket T40055.

12. Remove the high pressure lines and then remove the sealing cap bolts. Pull the sealing cap upward and turn 90°.

13. Remove the tensioning plate nuts, remove the injectors using the puller T10055 and the adapter T10055/1.

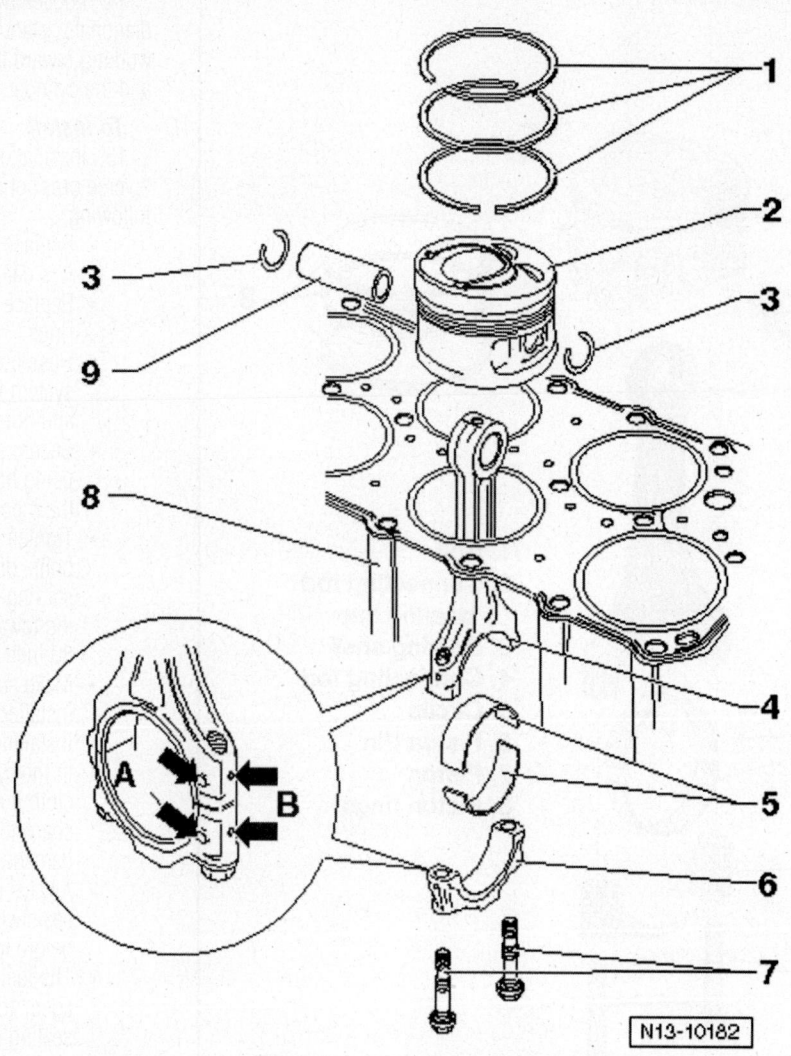

1. Piston rings
2. Piston
3. Circilp
4. Connecting rod
5. Bearing shell
6. Connecting rod bearing cap
7. Bolt
8. Cylinder block
9. Piston Pin

Fig. 120 Exploded view of the piston and rod assembly— 3.0L TDI engine

- Make sure the high pressure lines are seated free of stress.
- Inspect the fuel system for leaks.

3.6L Engine

See Figures 123 and 124.

1. Before servicing the vehicle, refer to the precautions.

2. Remove the ignition coils with power output stage.

3. Remove the upper intake manifold. Seal the intake passages in the intake manifold and in the cylinder head with clean cloths.

4. Remove the bolts and the bracket. Free up the wires on the rear of the cylinder head and remove the bracket bolts and bracket from the cylinder head cover.

5. Remove the crankcase housing ventilation hose from the cylinder head cover.

6. Loosen the cylinder head cover bolts 17 through 1 starting from the inside and working toward the outside. Remove the bolts and the cylinder head cover.

To install:

7. Apply sealant to the locations marked on the cover.

8. Install the cylinder head cover and tighten the bolts 1 through 17 evenly starting on the inside and working toward the outside: 88 inch lbs. (10 Nm).

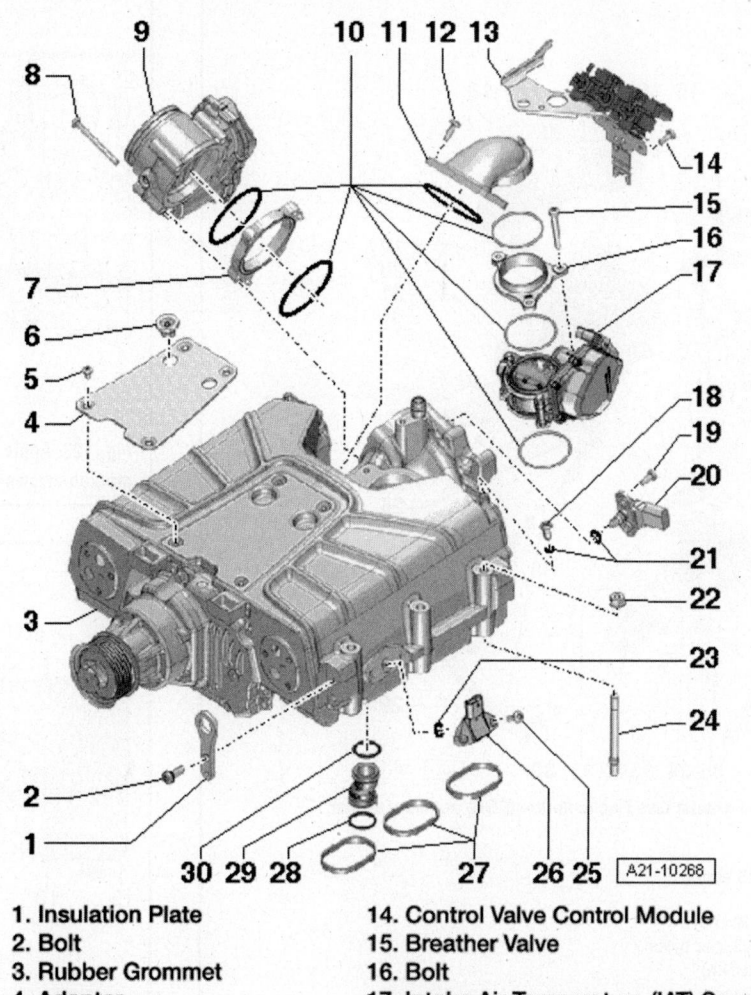

1. Insulation Plate
2. Bolt
3. Rubber Grommet
4. Adapter
5. Bolt
6. Throttle Valve Control Module
7. O-rings
8. Adapter
9. Bolt
10. Bracket
11. Bolt
12. Bolt
13. Adapter
14. Control Valve Control Module
15. Breather Valve
16. Bolt
17. Intake Air Temperature (IAT) Sensor
18. O-rings
19. Nut
20. O-ring
21. Pin
22. Bolt
23. Charge Air Pressure Sensor
24. Seals
25. O-ring
26. Connecting Piece
27. O-rings

Fig. 121 Super charger overview—3.0L Hybrid engine

9. Further installation is performed in reverse order of removal, noting the following:

- Replace the cylinder head cover if it is damaged or if there are leaks.
- First, bolt the intake manifold to the cylinder head. Then, tighten the bolts for the intake manifold support: 88 inch lbs. (10 Nm)
- Make sure the fuel hoses are secure.

- Check and fill with coolant, if necessary.

3.0L Hybrid Engine

LEFT VALVE COVER

See Figure 125.

✳✳ WARNING

Hybrid vehicles have a high voltage system! When performing the follow-ing work, it is also necessary to work on the high voltage system. Turn off the voltage in the high voltage system.

1. Remove the engine compartment cover.
2. Remove the bolts and the electric drive power and control electronics cover panel.
3. Unlock and remove the pilot connector 1 from the electric drive power and control electronics.

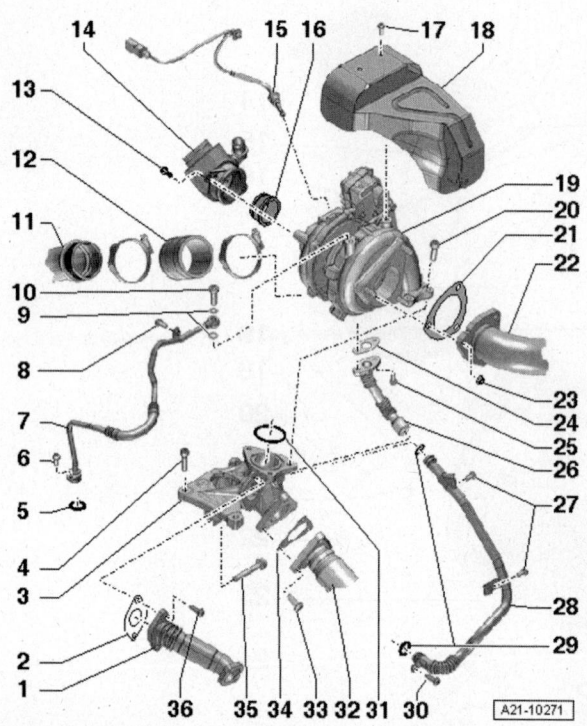

1. Pipe : By-pass valve for the Exhaust Gas Recirculation (EGR) auxiliary cooler.
2. Gasket : Always replace
3. Intermediate Flange
4. Bolt : tighten to 18 ft. lbs. (25 Nm)
5. O-ring: Always replace.
6. Bolt: tighten to 80 inch lbs. (9 Nm)
7. Oil Supply Line: From the cylinder block.
8. Bolt: tighten to 18 ft. lbs. (25 Nm)
9. Seals: Always replace.
10. Banjo Bolt: 11 ft. lbs. (15 Nm)
11. Right Charge Air Pipe
12. Pressure Hose: From the turbocharger to the right charge air pipe.
13. Bolt : tighten to 80 inch lbs. (9 Nm)
14. Damper: From the mass airflow sensor G70 to the turbocharger.
15. Exhaust Gas Temperature Sensor 1: tighten to 33 ft. lbs. (45 Nm).
16. Seal: Replace if damaged.
17. Bolt : tighten to 80 inch lbs. (9 Nm)
18. Turbocharger Heat Shield \
19. Turbocharger: With the turbocharger control module.
20. Bolt: tighten to 22 ft. lbs. (30 Nm) Plus an additional 90° (1/4) turn. Always replace bolt
21. Gasket: Always replace.
22. Primary Catalytic Converter
23. Nut: 17 ft. lbs. (23 Nm) Always replace.
24. Gasket : Always replace
25. Bolt: tighten to 80 inch lbs. (9 Nm.
26. Line from the turbocharger.
27. Bolt: tighten to 80 inch lbs. (9 Nm)
28. Line to the cylinder block.
29. O-rings: Always replace.
30. Bolt: tighten to 80 inch lbs. (9 Nm).
31. Gasket: Always replace.
32. Intermediate Pipe
33. Bolt: 30 Nm + 90° (1/4) turn.
34. Gasket: Always replace.
35. Bolt: tighten to 18 ft. lbs. (25 Nm).
36. Bolt: tighten to 80 inch lbs. (9 Nm).

Fig. 122 Turbocharger overview—3.0L TDI engine

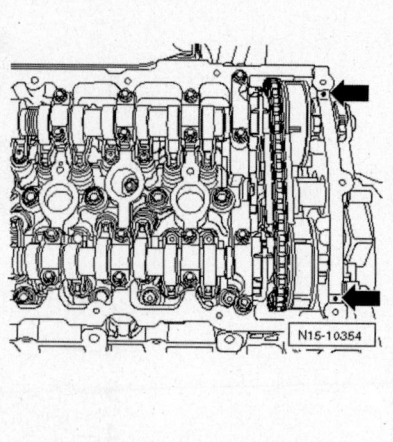

Fig. 123 Apply sealant at the locations marked arrows on the cover—3.6L engine

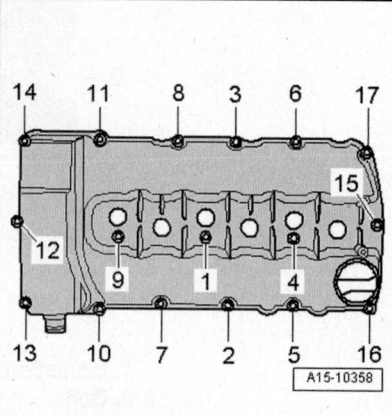

Fig. 124 Cylinder head cover bolts 1 through 17—3.6L engine

4. Unlock and remove the high voltage cables 2, 3 and 4 in sequence.

5. Unclip the high voltage cables and move them to the side.

6. Remove ignition coils. Remove the crankcase ventilation hose by pressing the release buttons.

7. Remove the bolts in sequence 12 through 1 and remove the left cylinder head cover.

To install:

8. Installation is performed in the reverse order of removal, noting the following:

- Replace the O-rings.
- Replace a damaged cylinder head cover seal. Replace the cylinder head cover bolts if the seal is damaged.
- Clean the sealing surfaces; they must be free of oil and grease.
- Tighten the left cylinder head cover bolts in sequence 1 through 12 to

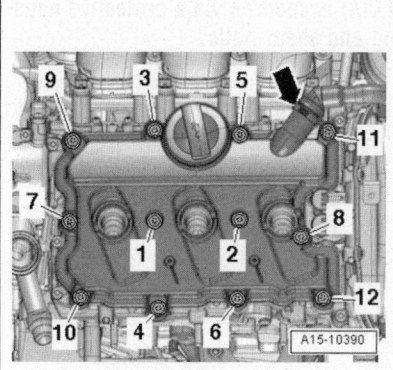

Fig. 125 Cylinder head cover bolts 1 through 12—3.0L Hybrid engine

30 ft. lbs. (40 Nm) Plus an additional 90°
- Install the ignition coils.
- Connect the high voltage cables.

- Bring the high voltage system back into operation.

RIGHT VALVE COVER

> ✳✳ **WARNING**
>
> **Hybrid vehicles have a high voltage system!**

1. Remove the engine compartment cover.
2. Remove the intake hose and the secondary air injection intake hose.
3. Open the clips and remove the upper air filter housing.
4. Remove ignition coils and loosen the fuel pipe clamps. Fuel lines remain connected.
5. Remove the crankcase ventilation hose by pressing the release buttons.
6. Remove the bolts in sequence 12 through 1 and remove the right cylinder head cover.

To install:

7. Installation is performed in the reverse order of removal, noting the following:

- Replace the O-rings.
- Replace a damaged cylinder head cover seal. Replace the cylinder head cover bolts if the seal is damaged.
- Clean the sealing surfaces; they must be free of oil and grease.
- Tighten the left cylinder head cover bolts in sequence 1 through 12 to 30 ft. lbs. (40 Nm) Plus an additional 90°
- Install the ignition coils.

VALVE LASH

ADJUSTMENT

Hydraulic lifters are used in these engines and do not require lash adjustment.

ENGINE PERFORMANCE & EMISSION CONTROLS

COMPONENT LOCATIONS

See Figures 126 through 129.

CAMSHAFT POSITION (CMP) SENSOR

LOCATION

See Figures 130 and 131.

REMOVAL & INSTALLATION

1. Before servicing the vehicle, refer to the precautions.
2. Unplug the connector.
3. Remove the screw and then the sensor.

> ✳✳ **WARNING**
>
> **Cover the hole to prevent dirt from getting into the engine.**

To install:

4. Installation is the reverse of removal.
5. When installing, use a new seal as necessary.
6. Tighten the CMP sensor mounting screws to 71 inch lbs. (8 Nm).

ELECTRONIC CONTROL MODULE (ECM)

LOCATION

See Figures 132 and 133.

REMOVAL & INSTALLATION

3.6L Engine

1. Before servicing the vehicle, refer to the precautions.
2. Switch off ignition.
3. Remove windshield wiper arms.
4. Remove plenum chamber cover.
5. Disengage connector from control module and then disconnect it.
6. Remove the old control unit and insert the new one.
7. Recode the control unit and adapt to electronic immobilizer and throttle valve control unit. If necessary, enable cruise control system "Guided Function", using scan tool.
8. Read fault memory of new engine control module and, if necessary, erase fault memory using scan tool.
9. Perform test drive.
10. Check control modules DTC memory again.

3.0L TDI Engine

1. Before servicing the vehicle, refer to the precautions.

➥ **When the Motronic Engine Control Module (ECM) electrical harness connectors are disconnected, the adaptation values are erased and the DTC memory content remains intact.**

2. Connect the scan tool.
3. Switch the ignition on.

4. Using the scan tool, select "Vehicle information".
5. Select "Calibration Identification" in vehicle information. The electronic control module identification number will be displayed, e.g.: 06A906032NA 4983.
6. Record the electronic control module identification number.
7. End diagnosis and switch the ignition off.
8. Switch the ignition on.
9. Actuate the touch-wipe function to allow the wipers to move to the end position.

➥ **The wiper arms will now move into the line of view on the windshield (service position).**

10. Remove the wiper arms caps.
11. Loosen the wiper arm nuts several turns.
12. Loosen the wiper arms from the wiper axle by rocking slightly.
13. Remove the wiper arms nuts and the wiper arms from the wiper axles.
14. Remove the spray nozzles.
15. Press the spray nozzles, with the water lines attached, through the plenum chamber opening.
16. Remove the rubber seal and the plenum chamber cover.

➥ **The threads of the shear bolts have been coated with a locking compound and must be heated to be removed.**

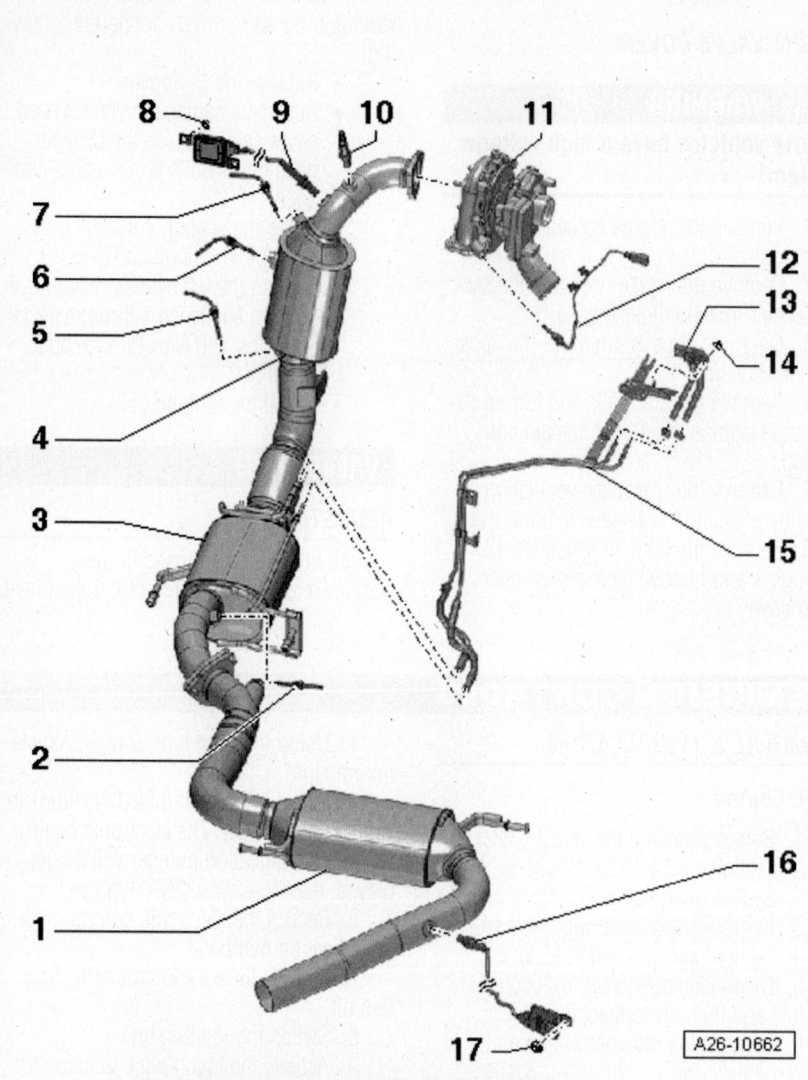

1. Rear Exhaust Pipe with Catalytic Converter
2. Exhaust Gas Temperature Sensor
3. Particulate Filter
4. Front Exhaust Pipe with Catalytic Converter
5. Exhaust Gas Temperature Sensor 3 G495
6. Catalyst Temperature Sensor 1 G20
7. Exhaust Gas Temperature Sensor 2 G448
8. Nut
9. NOx Sensor 1.
10. Heated Oxygen Sensor
11. Turbocharger
12. Exhaust Gas Temperature Sensor 1 G235
13. Differential Pressure Sensor G505
14. Nut
15. Control Line for the Differential Pressure Sensor
16. NOx Sensor 2
17. Nut

Fig. 126 Exhaust sensor overview—3.0L TDI engine

➡The Motronic Engine Control Module (ECM) is secured via a protective housing and shear bolts.

17. Using a heat gun set at its lowest setting, heat the shear bolt for approx. 20 to 25 seconds.

18. Remove the shear bolt with locking pliers. Discard the used shear bolts.

19. Repeat the previous steps for the second shear bolt.

20. Remove the protective housing from the Motronic Engine Control Module (ECM).

21. Remove the front electrical harness connector from the Motronic Engine Control Module (ECM).

22. Remove the Motronic Engine Control Module (ECM) from the retainer.

23. Remove the rear electrical harness connector from the Motronic Engine Control Module (ECM).

To install:

24. Installation is performed in reverse order of removal. Note the following:

   a. The Motronic Engine Control Module (ECM) must be installed with the protective housing.

   b. Use New shear bolts when installing the Motronic Engine Control Module (ECM).

   c. Motronic Engine Control Module (ECM) reprogramming is required.

   d. The new Engine Control Module (ECM) and immobilizer must be activated.

➡If scan tool does not have proper and complete software for this purpose, refer to an authorized dealer or to the Ebahn website for ECM and immobilizer activation instructions.

25. After repair work, the following work steps must be performed in the following sequence:

   • Check the DTC memory.
   • If necessary, erase the DTC memory.
   • If the DTC memory was erased, generate readiness code.

ENGINE COOLANT TEMPERATURE (ECT) SENSOR

LOCATION

3.6L Engine

The Engine Coolant Temperature (ECT) sensor is located between the intake manifold and the generator in the cylinder head.

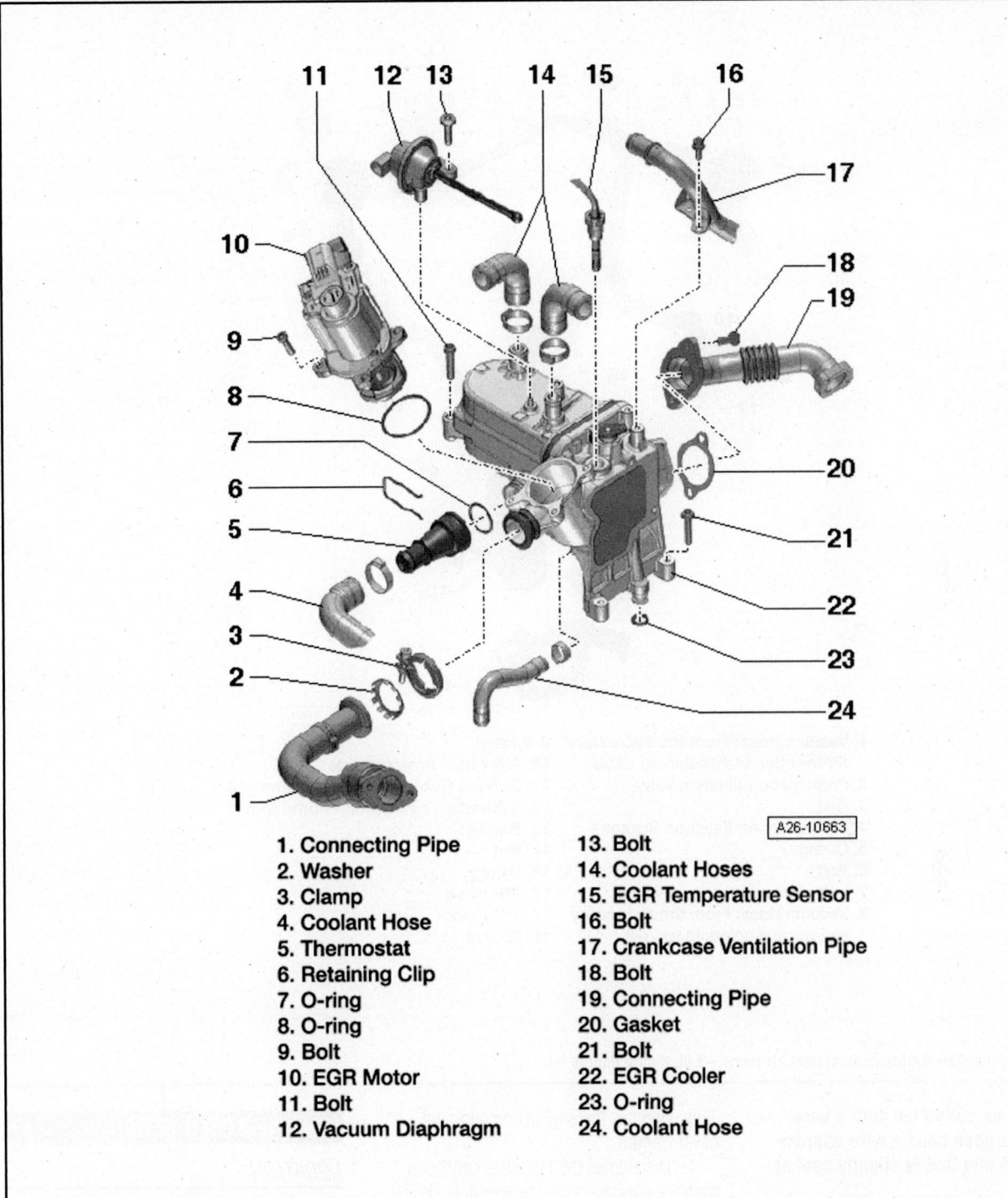

1. Connecting Pipe
2. Washer
3. Clamp
4. Coolant Hose
5. Thermostat
6. Retaining Clip
7. O-ring
8. O-ring
9. Bolt
10. EGR Motor
11. Bolt
12. Vacuum Diaphragm
13. Bolt
14. Coolant Hoses
15. EGR Temperature Sensor
16. Bolt
17. Crankcase Ventilation Pipe
18. Bolt
19. Connecting Pipe
20. Gasket
21. Bolt
22. EGR Cooler
23. O-ring
24. Coolant Hose

A26-10663

Fig. 127 EGR system overview—3.0L TDI engine

3.0L Hybrid Engine

The Engine Coolant Temperature (ECT) sensor is located on the rear coolant pipe.

REMOVAL & INSTALLATION

3.6L Engine

1. Before servicing the vehicle, refer to the precautions.
2. Use a suitable wrench to rotate the drive belt tensioner roller downward to release the belt tension.
3. Remove the 3 belt tensioner mounting bolts.
4. Disconnect the engine temperature control temperature sensor connector and expose the wire.

Remove the bolt for the engine temperature control temperature sensor using the hex ball socket T10058.

Pull the engine temperature control temperature sensor out of the cylinder head and remove it toward the front.

➡The O-ring and the support washer can get stuck in the cylinder head. Check whether the engine temperature control temperature sensor is complete. If the O-ring and the support washer are stuck in the cylinder head,

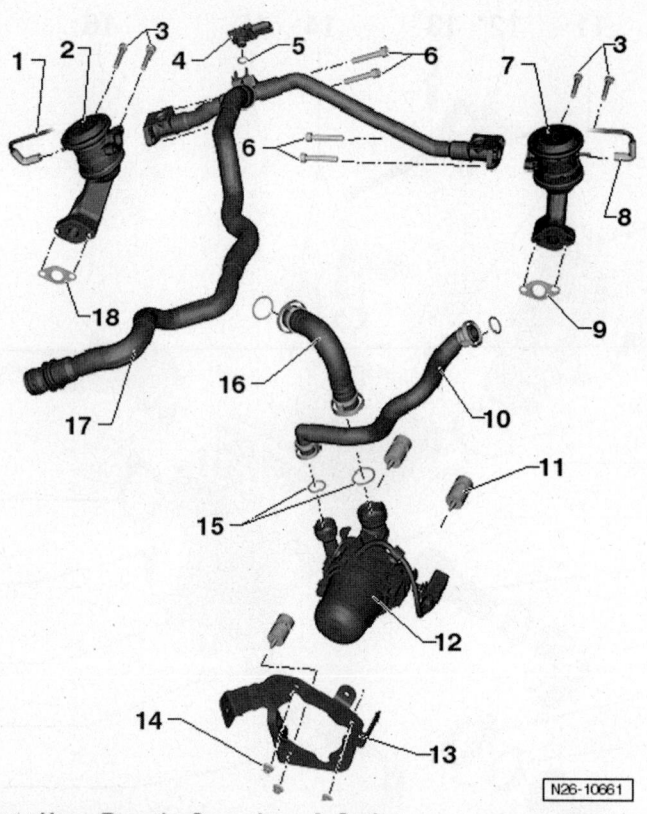

1. Vacuum Hose: From the Secondary Air Injection (AIR) solenoid valve
2. Right air combination Valve
3. Bolt
4. Secondary Air Injection Sensor 1
5. O-ring
6. Bolt
7. Left air combination valve
8. Vacuum Hose: From the secondary air injection solenoid valve 2
9. Gasket
10. AIR Hose: Pressure side
11. Bonded Rubber Bushing: Quantity: 3
12. Secondary Air Injection Pump Motor
13. Bracket
14. Nut
15. O-ring
16. AIR Hose
17. AIR Pipe
18. Gasket

Fig. 128 Secondary air injection system overview—3.0L Hybrid engine

they must be pulled out with a wire. For this purpose bend a wire approximately 1.5 mm that is slightly bent at the end.

To install:

5. Installation is the reverse of the removal procedure.

6. Tighten the ECT mounting bolt to 44 inch lbs. (5 Nm).

3.0L Hybrid Engine

1. Before servicing the vehicle, refer to the precautions.

2. Briefly open the coolant expansion tank cap to reduce the residual pressure in the coolant system.

3. Remove the engine compartment cover upward.

4. Disconnect the electrical connector from the engine coolant temperature (ECT) sensor. Place a cloth underneath to catch any coolant leaking out.

5. Remove the retaining clip and the ECT sensor.

To install:

6. Installation is performed in the reverse order of removal, noting the following:
   • Replace the O-ring.
   • To prevent coolant loss, immediately install the new ECT sensor into the connection.
   • Check the coolant level.

ENGINE SPEED SENSOR

LOCATION

3.0L Hybrid Engine

The engine speed sensor is located at the right side of the engine, just above the front final drive.

REMOVAL & INSTALLATION

3.0L Hybrid Engine

See Figure 132 through 134.

1. Before servicing the vehicle, refer to the precautions.

2. Remove the noise insulation.

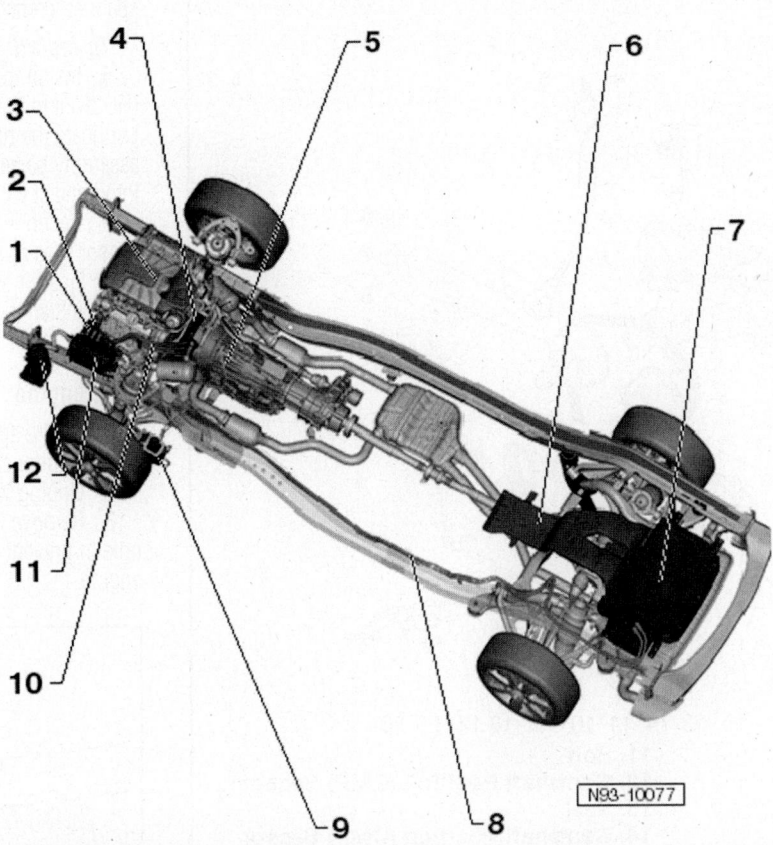

1. High Voltage Cable For The Electric A/C Compressor P3
2. Electric A/C compressor V470
3. 3.0L V6 TFSI Engine
4. Electro-Drive Drive Motor V141
5. Transmission Fluid Auxiliary Hydraulic Fluid Pump
6. Air Guide Channel For Hybrid Battery Cooling
7. Hybrid Battery Unit
8. High Voltage Cable Set For The Hybrid Battery
9. De-coupler Pressure Actuator
10. High Voltage Cable Set For The Engine PX2
11. Electric Drive Power and Control Electronics JX1
12. Electric Power Steering Pump V466

Fig. 129 Hybrid Components Overview—3.0L Hybrid engine

3. Disconnect the connector from the engine speed sensor.

4. Remove the bolt from the front final drive. Pry off the rubber cover.

5. Remove the bolt and remove the engine speed sensor.

To install:

6. Insert the engine speed sensor all the way into the opening in the engine.

7. Install the bolt for the engine speed sensor and tighten to 88 inch lbs. (10 Nm).

8. Reconnect the connector to the engine speed sensor.

9. Install the noise insulation.

HEATED OXYGEN (HO2S) SENSOR

LOCATION

See Figures 135 through 138.

REMOVAL & INSTALLATION

3.0L TDI Engine

1. Before servicing the vehicle, refer to the precautions.

2. Remove the engine compartment cover.

3. Remove the heated oxygen sensor connector from the bracket and disconnect it. Free up the heated oxygen sensor wiring from the guide.

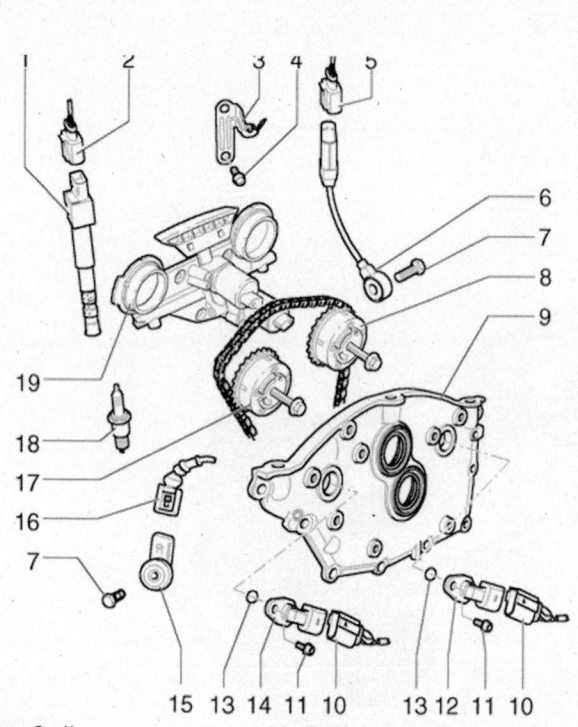

. Ignition Coil
. Connector
. Bracket
. Bolt
. Connector
. Knock Sensor 1
. Bolt
. Exhaust Camshaft Adjuster
. Cover

11. Bolt
12. Camshaft Position (CMP) Sensor
13. Seal
14. Camshaft Position (CMP) Sensor
15. Knock Sensor 2
16. Connector
17. Intake Camshaft Adjuster
18. Spark Plug
19. Control Housing

22205_TOUA_G0157

Fig. 130 CMP sensor (1) and CMP sensor (2) locations—3.6L engine

4. Remove the heated oxygen sensor and the oxygen sensor heater using a ring spanner wrench.

To install:

5. Install the Heated Oxygen Sensor (HO2S) and tighten to 41 ft. lbs. (55 Nm). Lubricate the new oxygen sensor with an assembly paste. This paste must not come into contact with the sensor slots.

6. Reconnect the harness connector. The sensor wire must always be attached at the same location when installing.

7. Install the engine compartment cover.

3.6L Engine

1. Before servicing the vehicle, refer to the precautions.

2. Unplug the connector.

3. Remove the sensor and cover the hole to prevent dirt from getting into the engine.

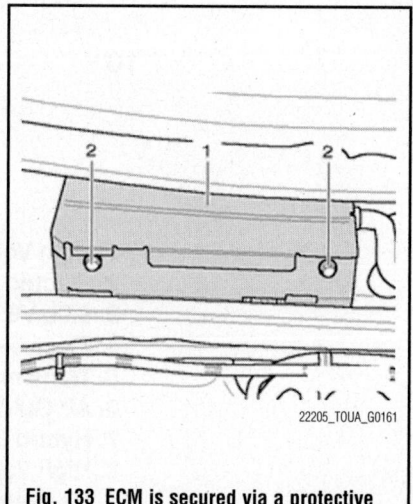

22205_TOUA_G0161

Fig. 133 ECM is secured via a protective housing—3.0L TDI

Fig. 131 CMP sensor connector (1) and (arrow) mounting bolt—3.0L Hybrid engine

N24-10280

Fig. 132 ECM is secured via a protective housing (1)—3.6L engine

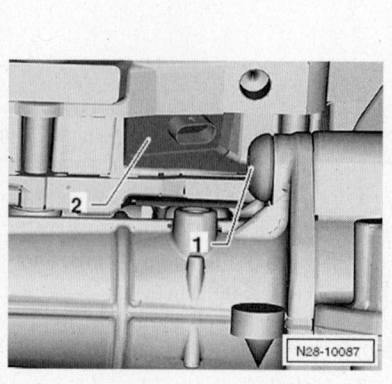

N28-10087

Fig. 134 Final drive bolt 1 and rubber cover 2.—3.0L Hybrid engine

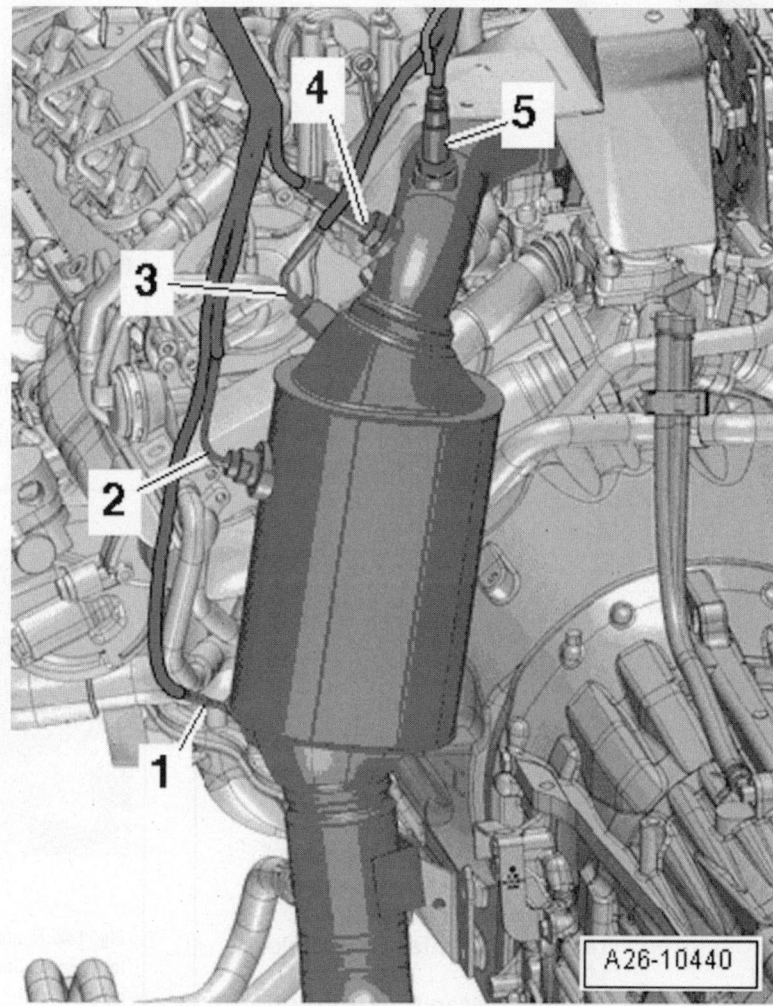

1. Exhaust Gas Temperature Sensor
2. Catalyst Temperature Sensor 1
3. Exhaust Gas Temperature Sensor 2
4. Nox sensor
5. Heated Oxygen Sensor

Fig. 135 Heated Oxygen (HO2S) sensors and Oxygen Sensors location—3.0L TDI engine

To install:
4. Installation is the reverse of removal.

→Thread of new oxygen sensors is coated with hot bolt paste.

✷✷ WARNING

When re-using the previous oxygen sensor, grease only the threads with hot bolt paste G 052 112; the paste must not get into slots of oxygen sensor body.

5. Tighten the oxygen sensors to 41 ft. lbs. (55 Nm).

3.0L Hybrid Engine

CYLINDER BANK 2 (LEFT)

1. Before servicing the vehicle, refer to the precautions.
2. Remove the engine compartment cover.
3. Disconnect the electrical connector for the Heated Oxygen Sensor (HO2S) and free up the wire.

4. Remove the Heated Oxygen Sensor (HO2S) and cover the hole to prevent dirt from getting into the engine.

To install:
5. Install the Heated Oxygen Sensor (HO2S) and tighten to 41 ft. lbs. (55 Nm).
6. Reconnect the harness connector. The sensor wire must always be attached at the same location when installing. This prevents the electric wire from touching the exhaust pipe.

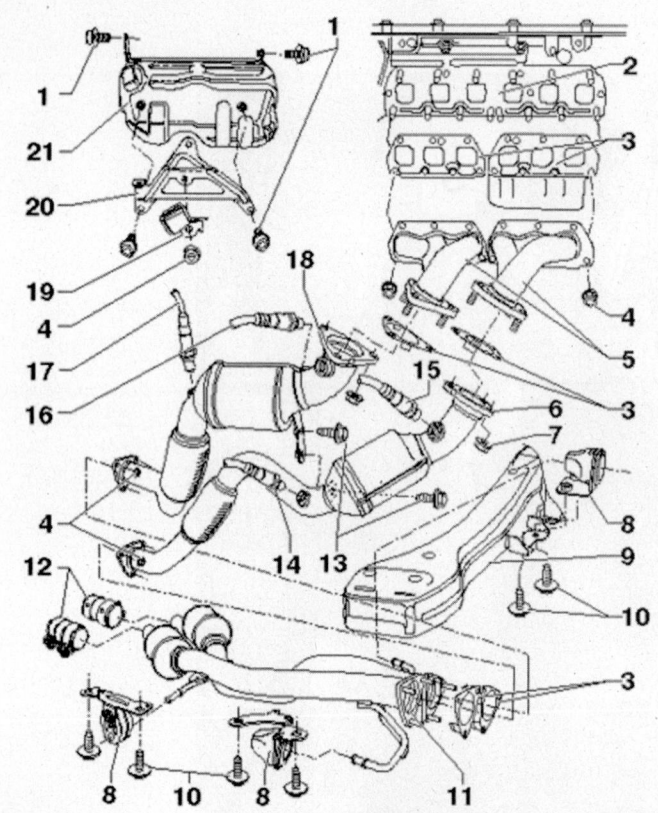

1. Bolt
2. Cylinder Head
3. Gasket
4. Nuts
5. Exhaust Manifold
6. Primary Catalytic Converter
7. Nuts
8. Suspended Mount
9. Transmission Bracket
10. Bolts
11. Catalytic Converters
12. Double Pipe Clamp
13. Bolts
14. Oxygen Sensor 1
15. Heated Oxygen Sensor 1
16. Heated Oxygen Sensor 2
17. Oxygen Sensor 2
18. Primary Catalytic Converter
19. Bracket
20. Intake Manifold Support
21. Heat Shield

22205_TOUA_G0165

Fig. 136 Heated Oxygen (HO2S) sensors and Oxygen Sensors location—3.6L engine

7. Install the engine compartment cover.

CYLINDER BANK 1 (RIGHT)

1. Before servicing the vehicle, refer to the precautions.

2. Remove the rear engine cover upward.

3. Remove the air intake hose.

4. Disconnect the electrical connector for the Heated Oxygen Sensor (HO2S) and free up the wire.

5. Remove the Heated Oxygen Sensor (HO2S) and cover the hole to prevent dirt from getting into the engine.

To install:

6. Install the Heated Oxygen Sensor (HO2S) and tighten to 41 ft. lbs. (55 Nm).

7. Reconnect the harness connector. The sensor wire must always be attached at the same location when installing. This prevents the electric wire from touching the exhaust pipe.

8. Install the air intake hose.

9. Install the engine compartment cover.

INTAKE AIR TEMPERATURE (IAT) SENSOR

LOCATION

The Mass Air Flow (MAF) sensor and the Intake Air Temperature (IAT) sensor are combined as a unit and are serviced as an assembly.

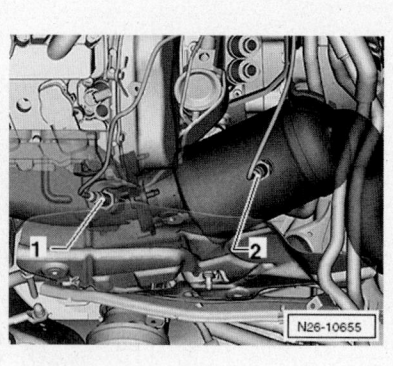

Fig. 137 Heated Oxygen (HO2S) sensor location, Cylinder Bank 2 (Left)—3.0L Hybrid engine

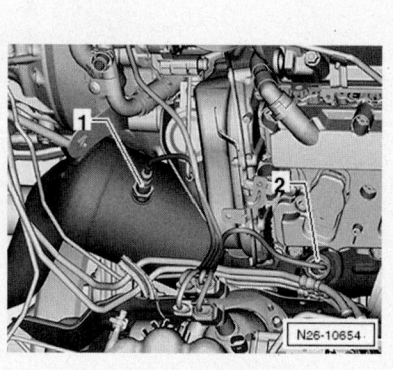

Fig. 138 Heated Oxygen (HO2S) sensor location, Cylinder Bank 1 (Right)—3.0L Hybrid engine

KNOCK SENSOR (KS)

LOCATION

3.6L Engine

Knock sensor 1 is located on the exhaust side of the cylinder block.

Knock sensor 2 is located on the intake side of the cylinder block. Sensor contacts and connector contacts are gold plated.

REMOVAL & INSTALLATION

3.6L Engine

1. Before servicing the vehicle, refer to the precautions.

2. Disconnect Knock Sensor (KS) 1 G61 electrical harness connector or Knock Sensor (KS) 2 G66 electrical harness connector.

3. Remove the screw and then the sensor.

Cover the hole to prevent dirt from getting into the engine.

To install:

4. Installation is the reverse of removal.

5. Tighten the knock sensor bolt to 16 ft. lbs. (22 Nm). Tightening specification affect the function of the knock sensor.

MASS AIR FLOW (MAF) SENSOR

LOCATION

The Mass Air Flow (MAF) sensor and the Intake Air Temperature sensor are combined as a unit and are serviced as an assembly. The MAF sensor is located at the air intake tubes for the air cleaner assembly.

REMOVAL & INSTALLATION

1. Before servicing the vehicle, refer to the precautions.

2. Disconnect air intake hose from the air filter housing.

3. Disconnect the electrical connector on the Mass Air Flow (MAF) Sensor.

4. Remove both bolts from the Mass Air Flow (MAF) Sensor and carefully remove the Mass Air Flow (MAF) Sensor from the air filter housing guide.

To install:

5. Installation is the reverse of removal. Tighten the mounting bolts to 71 inch lbs. (8 Nm).

6. If the air filter element is very dirty or soaked, dirt particles or moisture may have contaminated the Mass Air Flow (MAF) Sensor and may be causing false mass air flow values. This results in a reduction of power, since a lower injection quantity is calculated.

7. Always use an original equipment air filter element.

8. Use a lubricant (silicone-free) for installing the intake hose.

9. Secure all hose connections using hose clamps appropriate for the model type.

10. Check the MAF sensor and intake hose (intake air side) for salt residue, dirt, and leaves.

11. Check the intake ducting up to the air filter element for dirt. If any contaminants are discovered, clean the air filter housing (upper and lower parts) of salt residue, dirt and leaves (if necessary, clean by washing or vacuuming)

THROTTLE POSITION SENSOR (TPS)

LOCATION

The throttle position sensor is an integral part of the throttle body and is not serviced separately.

FUEL   GASOLINE FUEL INJECTION SYSTEM

FUEL SYSTEM SERVICE PRECAUTIONS

Safety is the most important factor when performing not only fuel system maintenance but any type of maintenance. Failure to conduct maintenance and repairs in a safe manner may result in serious personal injury or death. Maintenance and testing of the vehicle's fuel system components can be accomplished safely and effectively by adhering to the following rules and guidelines.

• To avoid the possibility of fire and personal injury, always disconnect the negative battery cable unless the repair or test procedure requires that battery voltage be applied.

• Always relieve the fuel system pressure prior to disconnecting any fuel system component (injector, fuel rail, pressure regulator, etc.), fitting or fuel line connection. Exercise extreme caution whenever relieving fuel system pressure to avoid exposing skin, face and eyes to fuel spray. Please be advised that fuel under pressure may penetrate the skin or any part of the body that it contacts.

• Always place a shop towel or cloth around the fitting or connection prior to loosening to absorb any excess fuel due to spillage. Ensure that all fuel spillage (should it occur) is quickly removed from engine surfaces. Ensure that all fuel soaked

cloths or towels are deposited into a suitable waste container.

• Always keep a dry chemical (Class B) fire extinguisher near the work area.

• Do not allow fuel spray or fuel vapors to come into contact with a spark or open flame.

• Always use a back-up wrench when loosening and tightening fuel line connection fittings. This will prevent unnecessary stress and torsion to fuel line piping.

• Always replace worn fuel fitting O-rings with new Do not substitute fuel hose or equivalent where fuel pipe is installed.

Before servicing the vehicle, make sure to also refer to the precautions in the beginning of this section as well.

RELIEVING FUEL SYSTEM PRESSURE

1. Before servicing the vehicle, refer to the precautions.

2. Remove electrical connector from fuel pressure regulator valve.

3. Allow engine to idle approximately 10 seconds.

➡ **When the fuel pressure regulator valve N276 electrical connector is disconnected during idle, pressure in high pressure area decreases to approximately 87 psi (6 bar).**

4. After high pressure has been released, high pressure system must be

opened immediately. Otherwise, the pressure increases again due to the warming of the fuel.

5. Switch off ignition.

Fuel lines are pressurized! Wear protective goggles and protective clothing to prevent injuries and contact with skin. Before opening the high pressure system, place a cloth around the connection.

6. Place a clean cloth around the connection point and carefully open to release the residual pressure of approximately 87 psi (6 bar). Escaping fuel must be absorbed.

7. To conclude work, check DTC memory of Engine Control Module (ECM), erase all DTC entries which may have occurred from removing the connector.

FUEL FILTER

REMOVAL & INSTALLATION

See Figure 139.

Fuel filter is located in left fuel tank opening, when viewed in direction of travel.

1. Before beginning work, read the "Fuel System Service Precautions" in this section.

2. Locate and remove fuel system fuses from fuse panel.

3. Drain the fuel tank.

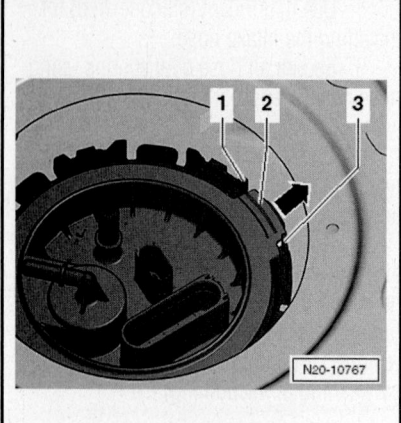

Fig. 139 Tab 2 must be between the tabs 1 and 3 on the fuel tank—Gas engines

4. Remove the rear seat bench.

5. Fold the carpet to the side.

6. Loosen the 4 nuts on the flange cover and remove the flange cover.

7. Disconnect the connector from the fuel filter flange.

➡**Mark installation position of filter cover, using colored felt tip marker pen.**

8. Remove the locking ring from the flange using the wrench T10202.

9. Drain the fuel if necessary. The ground wire can remain connected.

10. Remove the 2 fuel lines from the fuel filter housing. Squeeze the button on the line couplings.

11. Remove the fuel filter through the opening in the fuel tank. Drain the fuel filter housing.

To install:

12. Installation is performed in the reverse order of removal, noting the following:

- Replace the flange seal.
- Make sure the fuel level sensor connector, the ground wire and the fuel lines are secure.
- Install the fuel filter flange in the direction of travel arrow.
- The tab must be between the tabs on the fuel tank.
- Tighten the locking ring to 107 ft. lbs. (145 Nm) using the wrench T10202.

FUEL INJECTORS

REMOVAL & INSTALLATION

3.6L Engine

1. Before servicing the vehicle, refer to the precautions.

2. Remove the intake manifold.

3. If the fuel injectors for cylinders 1, 3 and 5 are to be removed, remove fuel rail.

4. Push the O-ring upward by hand and remove it from fuel injector.

5. Assemble a slide hammer/puller assembly (T10133/3 and T10133/15).

6. Guide the puller onto the groove on the fuel injector.

➡**The spring element must not be removed prior to removing the injector valves.**

7. Carefully remove fuel injector.

To install:

8. Thoroughly clean bores for fuel injectors in cylinder head using nylon brush T10133/4.

9. Check plastic support washer for damage, replace if necessary.

➡**Replace spring element and Teflon sealing ring each time fuel injector is removed.**

10. Replace O-rings between fuel injectors and fuel rail and coat them lightly with clean motor oil.

11. The Teflon sealing ring of fuel injector may not be oiled or greased.

12. Press fuel injector by hand into cylinder head bore until it stops.

13. Check fuel injectors for correct seating and installation position in cylinder head.

14. If fuel injectors for cylinders 1, 3 and 5 were removed, place fuel rail on and press evenly on to fuel injectors.

15. Tighten the fuel rail with new bolts, uniformly, to 22 ft. lbs. (30 Nm), plus an additional 90°.

16. Install the union nut for the fuel supply line tightly to supply line of fuel rail. To do so, counter hold on fuel supply line using a wrench. Tighten to 16 ft. lbs. (22 Nm).

17. Install the intake manifold.

3.0L Hybrid Engine

See Figure 140.

1. Before servicing the vehicle, refer to the precautions.

2. Reduce the fuel high side pressure.

3. Remove the supercharger.

4. Remove the affected intake manifold lower section.

5. Install the T10133/2A into the groove in the fuel injector.

6. Install T10133/16 to the T10133/2A, turn the bolt and remove the fuel injector.

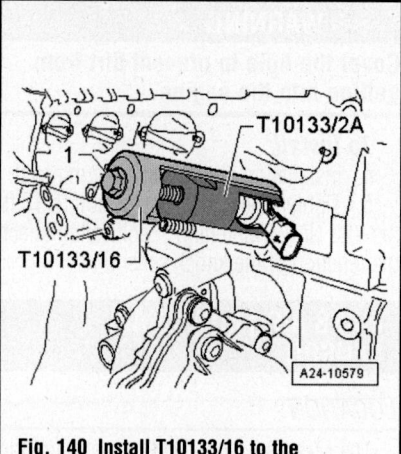

Fig. 140 Install T10133/16 to the T10133/2A, turn bolt and remove the fuel injector—3.0L Hybrid engine

To install:

7. Replace the combustion chamber seal and O-ring. Replace the spacer ring if damaged.

8. Lightly lubricate the fuel injector O-rings with clean engine oil.

9. Install the injector to the same cylinder. Clean the hole in the cylinder head using T10133/4.

Place the assembly cone T10133/5 with the new combustion chamber seal onto the injector.

Slide the combustion chamber seal with the assembly sleeve T10133/6 as far as possible onto the assembly cone T10133/5.

Turn the guide sleeve T10133/6 and the combustion chamber seal until they slide into the groove.

10. When pushing the combustion chamber seal onto the injector, the seal spreads open. Therefore after pushing it on, it must be tightened again in the steps, as follows:

- Press the sizing sleeve T10133/7 with a slight turning motion (approximately 180°) onto the injector until it stops.
- Turn the sizing sleeve T10133/7 in the opposite direction and remove it.
- Press the sizing sleeve T10133/8 with a slight turning motion (approximately 180°) onto the fuel injector until it stops.

11. Turn the sizing sleeve T10133/8 in the opposite direction and remove it.

12. Install the components from the repair kit onto the injector.

13. Lightly lubricate the new O-ring with clean engine oil before installing. The combustion chamber seal 8 must not be lubricated.

14. Slide the fuel injector into the cylinder head bore until seated using T10133/9.

➡**The fuel injector must not be difficult to install. If necessary, wait as the combustion chamber seal continues to pull itself together.**

15. The electrical connection for the injector must engage in the intended recess of the cylinder head.

16. Further installation is performed in reverse order of removal, noting the following:

17. Install the lower intake manifold section.

18. Install the supercharger.

FUEL PUMP

REMOVAL & INSTALLATION

1. Before beginning work, read the "Fuel System Service Precautions" in this section.

2. Locate and remove fuel system fuses from fuse panel.

3. Drain the fuel tank.

4. Remove the rear seat bench.

5. Fold the carpet to the side.

6. Loosen the 4 nuts on the flange cover and remove the flange cover.

7. Remove the vent line. Squeeze the button on the line couplings.

8. Place a cloth around the fuel supply line connection 2 and remove the hose coupling. Squeeze the button on the line couplings.

9. Disconnect the connector from the fuel level sensor and the connector from the fuel pump.

10. Remove the locking ring from the sensor flange using the wrench T10202. Carefully lift the sensor flange.

11. Disconnect the fuel pump connector from the flange.

12. Remove the fuel level sensor connector from the flange.

13. Remove the sensor flange.

14. Remove the sensor flange with the fuel filter fuel line through the right opening in the fuel tank.

15. Unclip the 2 black filler hoses from the fuel delivery unit housing. Remove the fuel line 3 for the suction jet pumps. Press in the securing ring to disengage the fuel line.

16. Remove the connecting line 4 from the fuel filter/fuel pump. To do this, press the red buttons on the hose coupling together. Use the assembly tool T10118 for this.

17. Rotate the fuel delivery unit approximately 15° to the left and remove it from the bottom of the fuel tank. The fuel delivery unit housing is filled with fuel. Fuel may run out if the housing is tipped or tilted.

18. Remove the fuel level sensor.

To install:

19. Installation is performed in reverse order of removal, noting the following:

- Replace the seals for the sensor flanges.
- Install the flanges in the direction of travel arrow.
- The tab on the flange must be between the tabs on the fuel tank.
- Tighten the locking ring to 107 ft. lbs. (145 Nm) using the wrench T10202.
- Make sure the connectors and the fuel hoses are secure.

FUEL TANK

DRAINING

1. Before beginning work, read the "Fuel System Service Precautions" in this section.

2. Locate and remove fuel system fuses from fuse panel.

3. Drain the fuel tank.

4. Remove the rear seat bench.

5. Fold the carpet to the side.

6. Loosen the 4 nuts on the flange cover and remove the flange cover.

7. Remove the vent line. Squeeze the button on the line couplings.

8. Place a cloth around the fuel supply line connection 2 and remove the hose coupling. Squeeze the button on the line couplings.

9. Disconnect the connector from the fuel level sensor and the connector from the fuel pump.

10. Remove the locking ring from the sensor flange using the wrench T10202. Carefully lift the sensor flange.

Insert a fuel extracting device with the suction hose as far as possible into the fuel tank and extract the fuel.

To install:

11. Installation is performed in the reverse order of removal, noting the following:

- Replace the seals for the sensor flanges.
- Install the flanges in the direction of travel arrow.
- The tab on the flange must be between the tabs on the fuel tank.

- Tighten the locking ring to 107 ft. lbs. (145 Nm) using the wrench T10202.
- Make sure the connectors and the fuel hoses are secure.

REMOVAL & INSTALLATION

1. Before servicing the vehicle, refer to the precautions.

✳✳ CAUTION

During all repair procedures on the fuel tank, be aware of the following:

- Route all the various lines (e.g. for fuel, EVAP system, or vacuum) and electrical wiring so that the original routing positions are restored.
- Make sure that the ground (-) strap between the fuel filler tube and body is securely fastened, to prevent electrostatic charging.
- Ensure sufficient clearance to all moving or hot components.

2. Drain the fuel tank.

3. Remove rear seat bench.

4. Cut open carpet on right side in pre-cut area (feel near seat bracket for fuel tank access panel before cutting).

5. Remove the nuts on the right side of the fuel delivery unit cover. If necessary, remove backrest support or mounting bracket.

✳✳ CAUTION

Fuel supply lines are under pressure! Wear protective goggles and protective gloves to avoid damage and contact with skin. Before removing from hose connection wrap a cloth around the connection. Then release pressure by carefully pulling hose off connection.

6. Remove fuel supply line, auxiliary heater fuel line, fuel pump connector, vent line, and fuel pump (FP) control module connector from fuel sending unit.

7. Press in on the securing ring to disengage the fuel line.

8. Remove the mufflers and mountings.

9. Remove the driveshaft.

10. Remove rear axle.

11. Open fuel flap and remove fuel tank cap.

12. Pull the rubber gasket off filler neck.

13. Remove bolts on filler neck and pull off ground wire.

14. Remove right rear wheel housing liner.

15. Unbolt fuel line cover plate.

16. Unclip fuel tank breather lines at securing clip attached on longitudinal member.

17. Remove bolts for filler pipe and EVAP canister in wheel housing.

18. Bend filler neck slightly downward and pull off breather line connections to EVAP canister.

➡ **Release the connection by pressing button on hose coupling.**

19. Disconnect ground wire clipped to EVAP canister and remove canister.

20. Separate fuel pump connectors, on left next to fuel tank.

21. Remove securing straps with covers on left and right below fuel tank.

22. Support fuel tank using engine/transmission jack, and remove securing strap at center of fuel tank.

23. Carefully lower fuel tank about 12 inches (30 cm).

24. Grab between fuel tank and vehicle floor and disconnect vent line from left sensor flange.

➡ **This step eliminates having to cut open the carpeting in the vehicle interior in the vicinity of sender flange cover.**

25. Lower the fuel tank.

To install:

26. Installation is performed in the reverse order of removal, noting the following:
- Connections for breather and fuel lines must engage audibly when joined.
- Make sure ventilation and fuel lines are not kinked when installed.
- The flange seal should be replaced each time it is opened.
- Secure fuel hoses with spring-type clamps.
- Ensure fuel hoses are seated securely.
- The ground strap at the fuel filler tube must be securely connected to the body.
- Before fastening the fuel tank, check that the supply and ventilation lines are still clipped onto the fuel tank.

IDLE SPEED

ADJUSTMENT

➡ **Idle speed is electronically controlled through the engine control module and is not manually adjustable.**

THROTTLE BODY

REMOVAL & INSTALLATION

3.6L Engine

1. Before servicing the vehicle, refer to the precautions.

2. Disconnect battery ground (GND) strap with ignition switched off.

3. Drain the coolant.

4. Remove the coolant hoses from the straps on the manifold.

5. Remove bolt from oil dipstick guide tube. Remove guide tube with oil dipstick.

6. Remove accessory drive ribbed belt.

7. Remove ribbed belt tensioner.

8. Remove the alternator.

9. Remove all coolant hoses from coolant pipe on the intake manifold/cylinder head.

10. Remove vacuum hoses from Intake Manifold Runner Control (IMRC) valve.

11. Loosen bolts from coolant pipe approximately 1 turn, then remove bolt and remove coolant pipe from intake manifold.

12. Remove the connecting hose to throttle valve control module.

13. Disconnect harness connector from throttle valve control module.

14. Remove throttle valve control module.

To install:

15. Installation is performed in the reverse order of removal.

16. Replace O-rings between fuel injectors and fuel rail and coat them lightly with clean motor oil.

17. Secure all hose connections with hose clamps appropriate for the model.

18. During the installation, all cable ties must be reinstalled at the same location.

3.0L Hybrid Engine

See Figure 141.

1. Before servicing the vehicle, refer to the precautions.

2. Remove the engine compartment cover.

3. Remove the rear engine cover 2 upward.

4. Remove the hose, the clamps and the air guide pipe.

5. Disconnect the connector.

6. Remove the bolts and remove the throttle valve control module with the adapter.

7. Cover the intake passage with a clean cloth to prevent small particles from getting into the supercharger

To install:

8. Installation is performed in the reverse order of removal, noting the following:
- Replace O-rings.
- Install the adapter and new O-rings into the supercharger.
- Install the throttle valve control module on the adapter and tighten the bolts to 88 inch lbs. (10 Nm).
- Adapt the Engine Control Module (ECM) if the throttle valve control module was replaced.

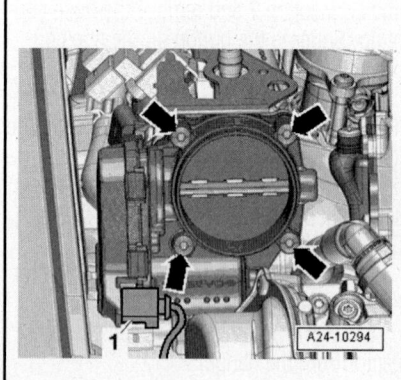

Fig. 141 Throttle body mounting bolts— 3.0L Hybrid engine

FUEL

DIESEL FUEL INJECTION SYSTEM

FUEL SYSTEM SERVICE PRECAUTIONS

Safety is the most important factor when performing not only fuel system maintenance but any type of maintenance. Failure to conduct maintenance and repairs in a safe manner may result in serious personal injury or death. Maintenance and testing of the vehicle's fuel system components can be accomplished safely and effectively by adhering to the following rules and guidelines.

• To avoid the possibility of fire and personal injury, always disconnect the negative battery cable unless the repair or test procedure requires that battery voltage be applied.

• Always relieve the fuel system pressure prior to disconnecting any fuel system component (injector, fuel rail, pressure regulator, etc.), fitting or fuel line connection. Exercise extreme caution whenever relieving fuel system pressure to avoid exposing skin, face and eyes to fuel spray. Please be advised that fuel under pressure may penetrate the skin or any part of the body that it contacts.

• Always place a shop towel or cloth around the fitting or connection prior to loosening to absorb any excess fuel due to spillage. Ensure that all fuel spillage (should it occur) is quickly removed from engine surfaces. Ensure that all fuel soaked cloths or towels are deposited into a suitable waste container.

• Always keep a dry chemical (Class B) fire extinguisher near the work area.

• Do not allow fuel spray or fuel vapors to come into contact with a spark or open flame.

• Always use a back-up wrench when loosening and tightening fuel line connection fittings. This will prevent unnecessary stress and torsion to fuel line piping.

• Always replace any worn fuel fitting O-rings with new. Do not substitute fuel hose or equivalent where fuel pipe is installed.

Before servicing the vehicle, make sure to also refer to the precautions in the beginning of this section as well.

RELIEVING FUEL SYSTEM PRESSURE

For the procedure, refer to "Guided Functions" in the vehicle diagnosis, testing and information system using a scan tool. Wear protective goggles and protective clothing

in order to avoid injury and contact with the skin. Wrap a cloth around the connection before disconnecting. Open the connection carefully and release the pressure.

FUEL FILTER

REMOVAL & INSTALLATION

See Figure 142.

The manufacturer does not provide a specific removal & installation procedure for this component. Refer to the illustration.

DRAINING WATER FROM THE SYSTEM

1. Remove the fuel filter and extract approximately 100 cm 3 of fluid using the hand vacuum pump VAG 1390 and draining container VAG 1390/1

FUEL SYSTEM PURGING

BLEEDING

※※ WARNING

After installing the high pressure pump, it must be filled with fuel before starting the engine. Do not run it when it is dry.

1. Connect the battery charger, if necessary.

2. Connect the vehicle diagnostic tester and perform the Guided Function "Activate Fuel Pump". The fuel pump now runs for 240 seconds.

3. Start the engine when the pump stops working.

4. Let the engine run a few minutes at a moderate speed and then turn it off.

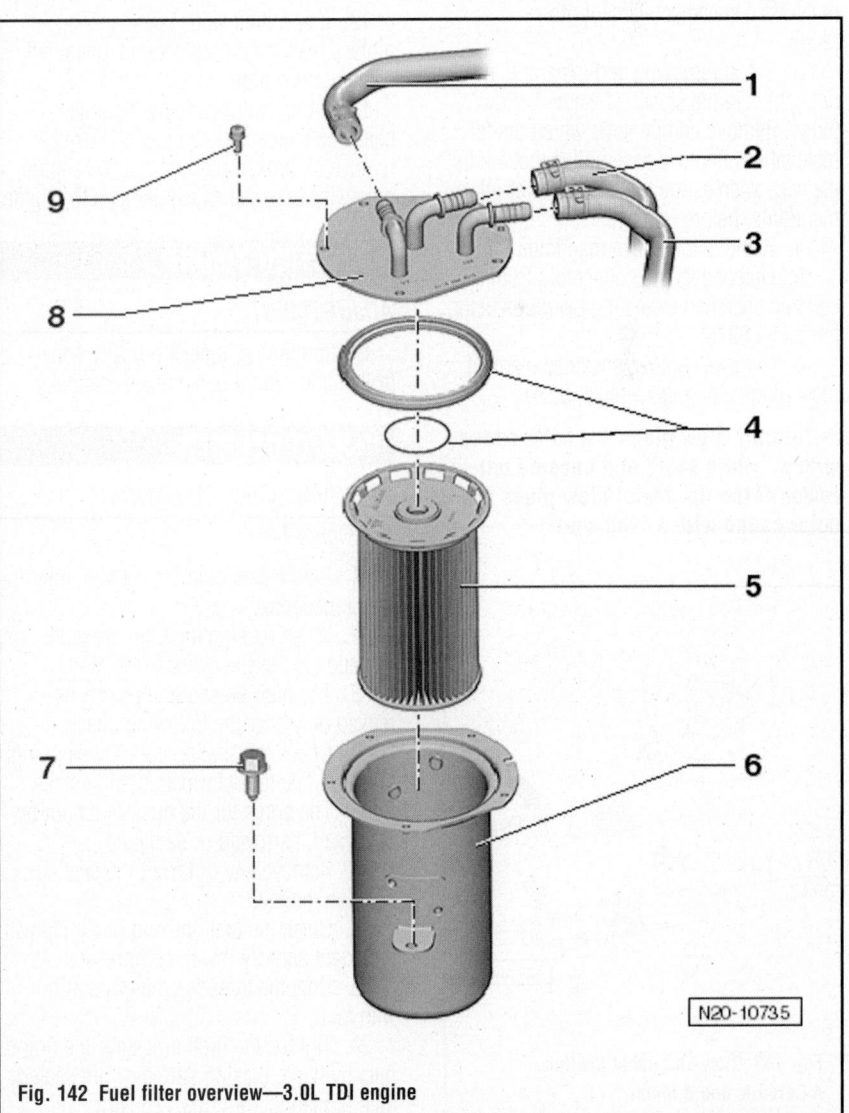

N20-10735

Fig. 142 Fuel filter overview—3.0L TDI engine

5. Check the fuel system for leaks.

6. Always follow all safety precautions when performing a road test. Perform a road test driving faster than 20 km and fully pressing the accelerator pedal at least one time.

7. Check the high pressure area for leaks again.

8. If there is still air in the fuel system, the engine may switch to emergency mode during the road test. In this case, turn off the engine and erase the Diagnostic Trouble Code (DTC) memory, refer to vehicle diagnosis, testing and information system VAS 5051. Then continue the road test.

GLOW PLUGS

REMOVAL & INSTALLATION

See Figure 143.

1. Before servicing the vehicle, refer to the precautions.

2. Observe visual characteristics of ceramic sheathed element glow plugs.

3. When removing and installing, do not cant ceramic sheathed element glow plugs. Remove components which hinder installation. Remove assemblies that are in the way, such as the upper and lower intake manifolds, before removal.

4. Remove the intake manifolds.

5. Disconnect the connectors from the ceramic sheathed element glow plugs using the pliers 6275.

6. Remove ceramic sheathed element glow plugs using flex wrench 3220.

➡Ceramic glow plugs are color coded with a "white seal" and become narrower at the tip. Metal glow plugs are color coded with a "red seal".

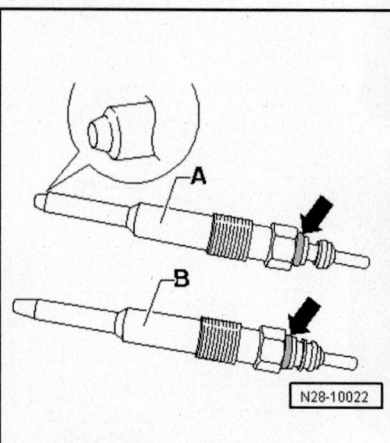

Fig. 143 Glow plug identification, A Ceramic and B Metal

To install:

7. Installation is performed in the reverse order of removal, noting the following:

8. Cylinder head bore and thread must be completely cleaned of deposits before installing.

9. Never oil or grease thread of bore in cylinder head and ceramic sheathed element glow plugs.

10. Install ceramic sheathed element glow plugs into cylinder head by hand using flex wrench 3220.

11. Then tighten 11 ft. lbs. (15 Nm) ceramic sheathed element glow plugs.

✳✳ WARNING

After installing and before first engine start with a cold engine, always perform a resistance test at all ceramic sheathed element glow plugs. Specified value: max.1.0 ohms.

12. If specified value is exceeded, replace malfunctioning ceramic sheathed element glow plug.

13. If the malfunctioning ceramic sheathed element glow plug is broken, remove all broken pieces from the engine, otherwise they can cause damage to engine.

INJECTION TIMING

ADJUSTMENT

Ignition timing is electronically controlled and cannot be adjusted manually.

INJECTION LINES

REMOVAL & INSTALLATION

See Figure 144.

1. Before servicing the vehicle, refer to the precautions.

2. When reusing the high pressure line, pay attention to the cylinder marking.

3. The high pressure lines can be reused only after the following checks:

4. Check the sealing cone on each high pressure line for deformation and cracks.

5. The bores for the lines must not be deformed, narrowed or damaged.

6. Remove any dirt from the sealing cone on the rail.

7. Clean the fuel line and line head with detergent and dry it with compressed air.

8. Coat the threads on the union nut with fuel.

9. Tighten the high pressure line union nuts by hand, making sure they are seated, then tighten to 19 ft. lbs. (25 Nm)

10. Tighten the high pressure lines using the VAG 1331 with the VAG 1331/1 and a T40055.

11. Tighten the high pressure lines using a VAG 1331 with the VAG 1331/6 or the VAG 1331/5.

12. Perform the fuel system leak test.

INJECTORS

REMOVAL & INSTALLATION

1. Before servicing the vehicle, refer to the precautions.

2. Remove the engine cover.

✳✳ WARNING

Mark the allocation of the injectors to the cylinder.

3. On cylinder bank 1, remove the upper air filter housing with the Mass Air Flow sensor.

4. Pull the release pins upward and remove the return line connections from the injectors.

5. Disconnect the electrical connector from the injector to be removed.

6. Loosen the union nuts for the injector lines at the injectors using the T40055.

7. Loosen the union nuts for the injector lines at the high pressure reservoir (rail element) using the 3150 or the VAG 1331/5.

8. Remove the fuel injector cover bolts and covers.

9. Pull the covers upward and turn them 1/4 turn.

10. Remove the fuel injector tensioning bracket nuts and brackets.

11. Remove the injectors using the T10055 and T10055/1.

12. Place the injectors on a clean cloth.

To install:

13. Replace the following components and seals or O-rings with each removal and installation
   - Copper washer
   - Injector shaft O-ring
   - Injector return O-ring

14. Replace the following components, seals and/or O-rings each time an injector is replaced.
   - Tensioning bracket
   - Injection line
   - Copper washer
   - Injector shaft O-ring
   - Injector return O-ring

15. When installing, the fuel injectors and injection lines may only be installed on the same cylinder as before.

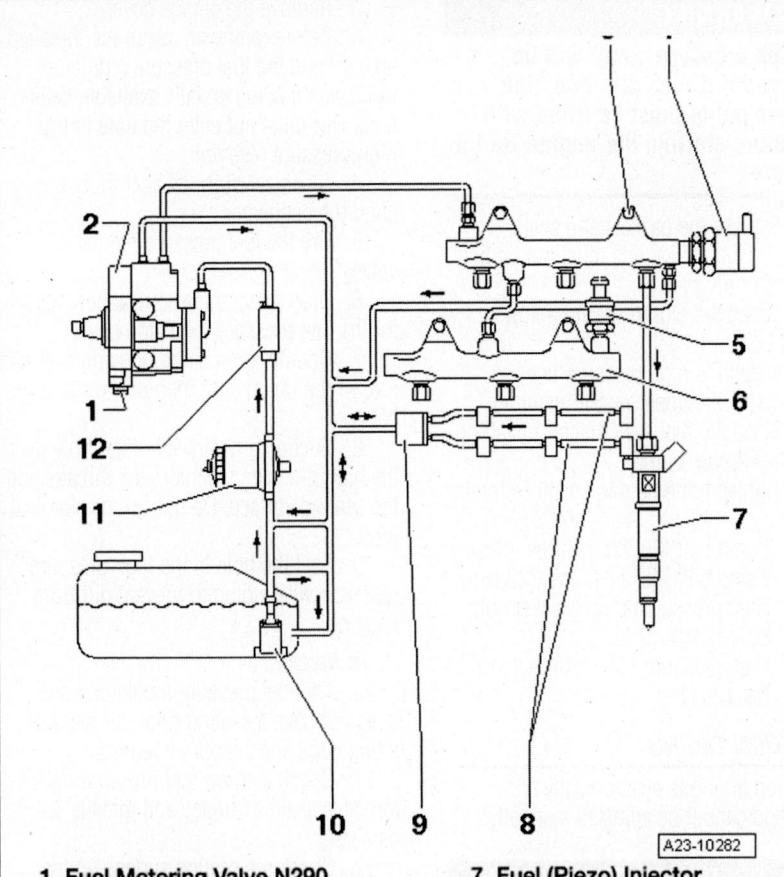

1. Fuel Metering Valve N290
2. High Pressure Pump
3. Fuel Rail (High Pressure Reservoir)
4. Fuel Pressure Regulator Valve N276
5. Fuel Pressure Sensor G247
6. Fuel Rail (High Pressure Reservoir)
7. Fuel (Piezo) Injector
8. Fuel Return Lines (Leak Lines)
9. Pressure Retention Valve
10. Fuel Tank
11. Fuel Filter
12. Auxiliary Fuel Pump V393

A23-10282

Fig. 144 Fuel system schematic overview—3.0L TDI engine

16. Check the fuel injectors and installation locations for contamination before assembling.

17. The fuel injectors must not have any damage.

18. Lubricate all of the O-rings with assembly oil or engine oil before installing.

19. If a used fuel injector is installed:

a. Spray the tip of the fuel injector with a rust removing spray. Remove the rust or oil particles with a cloth after approximately 5 minutes.

b. If an injector is very dirty, clean the tips of the injection around the copper sealing ring with a soft brush (do not let the brush come in contact with the holes for the jets).

c. To remove the used copper sealing ring from the fuel injector, clamp the sealing ring carefully in a vise until the clamping jaws on the vise prevent the

ring from turning. Pull the fuel injector out of the copper sealing ring by hand with slight twisting and pulling motions.

d. Use a scraper to remove any deposits under the copper sealing ring.

e. Install the new copper sealing ring with a plastic bushing.

f. To avoid damaging the O-ring, slide the new O-ring for the fuel return line connection over the assembly drift.

g. To remove rust particles on the fuel injector sealing surface, clean the fuel injector duct in the cylinder head with a cloth dampened with engine oil or rust remover. Do not damage the sealing flanges.

20. Install the fuel injectors.

21. First tighten the union nuts on the high pressure or injection lines by hand.

22. Make sure the lines are seated correctly without tension.

23. Tighten the high pressure lines to 19 ft. lbs. (25 Nm).

24. Press the return line connections carefully over the sealing ring onto the injector (check the sealing ring first for damage). The connection must engage audibly. Then press the release pin down carefully.

➡The "injector quantity calibration" and the "injection pressure calibration" for the new injectors must be must be programmed into the engine control module after replacing one or more injectors.

➡Check all the other injectors as well regarding their " injector quantity calibration" and "injection pressure calibration " to make sure all comparison values have been entered correctly. If the correct comparison value have been stored in the engine control module, then these comparison value must never be reentered.

25. Let the engine run a few minutes at idle and then stop it.

26. Switch off ignition.

27. Check the entire fuel system and the six return line connections for leaks.

If there are leaks despite correct tightening specifications, replace the affected component.

28. The return lines may only be replaced completely with the pressure retention valve.

29. Test drive the vehicle a minimum of 20 km/h and using full throttle at least one time. Then check the high pressure area one more time for leaks.

30. If there is still air in the fuel system, the engine may switch to emergency mode during the road test.

31. Stop the engine and erase the Diagnostic Trouble Code memory. Then continue the road test.

FUEL SUPPLY PUMP

REMOVAL & INSTALLATION

1. Before servicing the vehicle, refer to the precautions.

2. Drain the fuel tank.

3. Disconnect wires for the left and right sensor flanges.

4. Remove the locking rings for the left and right sensor flanges.

5. Read the safety precautions before beginning work.

6. Disconnect the electrical connectors and the fittings below the right sensor flange.

7. Remove the sensor flanges.

8. Unclip the black filler hose from the fuel delivery unit on the left and right sides of the fuel tank.

9. Remove the supply line to the suction jet pumps at the fuel delivery unit on the right and left sides of the fuel tank.

10. Disconnect the supply and return lines between both fuel delivery units on the left side of the fuel tank.

11. Rotate the fuel delivery unit approximately 90 degrees to the left and remove it from the bottom of the fuel tank.

❋❋ WARNING

The fuel delivery unit housing is filled with fuel. Fuel may run out if the housing is tipped or tilted.

12. Unclip the fuel level sensors on each side of fuel tank and pull them out.

13. Unclip the suction jet pumps from the bottom on each side and remove with a slight turn.

14. Pull out hose ends through left and right sensor openings.

To install:

❋❋ WARNING

After installing the high pressure pump, it must be filled with fuel before starting the engine. Do not run it when it is dry.

15. Installation is the reverse of removal.

16. Tighten fuel tank lock ring to 107 ft. lbs. (143 Nm).

INJECTION PUMP

REMOVAL & INSTALLATION

1. Before servicing the vehicle, refer to the precautions.

2. Remove the upper intake manifold.

3. Remove the high pressure pump toothed belt.

4. Remove the bolts and the high pressure line protective plate.

5. Remove the union nuts and free up the high pressure lines.

6. Disconnect the electrical connector.

7. Remove the fuel supply line and return line.

8. Remove the bolts and remove the high pressure pump.

To install:

9. Installation is performed in reverse order of removal, noting the following:

❋❋ WARNING

The high pressure pump will be destroyed if it runs dry. The high pressure pump must be filled with fuel before starting the engine for the first time.

10. Replace the gaskets and seals.

11. The fuel return line must not be bent, damaged or plugged

12. Install the high pressure pump toothed belt.

13. Install the high pressure lines.

14. Install the upper intake manifold.

15. Bleed the fuel system after installing the high pressure pump.

16. Tighten bolts/nuts to specification as follows:

- Pump bolt M6: 80 inch lbs. (9 Nm)
- Pump bolt M8: 17 ft. lbs. (23 Nm)
- High pressure pump bracket bolt: 80 inch lbs. (9 Nm)
- High pressure line union nut: 19 ft. lbs. (25 Nm)

INJECTION TIMING

Ignition timing is electronically controlled and cannot be adjusted manually.

FUEL PRESSURE REGULATOR

REMOVAL & INSTALLATION

➡The fuel pressure regulator valve is located in the right high pressure reservoir for cylinder bank 1 and maintains a constant pressure in the reservoir and the injector lines.

➡If the pressure in the fuel high pressure circuit is too high, the regulator valve will open so that some of the fuel flows from the rail back into the fuel tank via a return line.

➡If the pressure is too low, then the check valve closes and seals off the high pressure side from the low pressure side.

❋❋ WARNING

The fuel pressure regulator valve cannot be reused.

1. Before servicing the vehicle, refer to the precautions.

❋❋ WARNING

Follow the guidelines for clean working conditions when working on the fuel system.

2. Remove the engine cover.

3. Before removing, clean the threaded area around the fuel pressure regulator valve with a commercially available detergent. Dirt must not enter the hole in the high pressure reservoir.

4. Clean carefully, cleaner must not enter the connector.

5. Dry the fuel pressure regulator valve.

6. Disconnect the electrical connector for the fuel pressure regulator valve.

7. Counter hold at the housing bolt and loosen the union nut. Then remove it by hand.

8. Suction any dirt out of the hole in the high pressure reservoir, the threads and the sealing surface. Do not use mechanical tools.

9. Seal the hole in the high pressure reservoir with a plug to prevent dirt from entering.

To install:

10. The fuel pressure regulator valve does not have a sealing ring, but rather a biting edge and cannot be reused.

11. Check the new fuel pressure regulator valve sealing surface and threads for damage.

12. Check the sealing surface on the hole in the high pressure reservoir.

13. The threads on the fuel pressure regulator valve must be free of oil and grease.

14. Tighten the union nut by hand.

15. Align the fuel pressure regulator valve so the connecting line is not taut after connecting the connector.

16. Tighten the union nut in 2 steps:

- Step 1: 44 ft. lbs. (60 Nm), counter hold the housing bolt while doing this
- Then rotate the union nut back 1/4 turn while counter holding at the housing nut.
- Step 2: 59 ft. lbs. (80 Nm), counter hold the housing bolt while doing this

17. After installing, let the engine run at a moderate speed for a few minutes and then stop it.

18. Check the fuel system for leaks.

19. Check the Diagnostic Trouble Code memory.

20. Perform a road test where the accelerator pedal is pressed all the way down at least one time. Then check the high pressure area again for leaks.

21. Check the DTC memory again.

HEATING & AIR CONDITIONING SYSTEM

BLOWER MOTOR

REMOVAL & INSTALLATION

❊❊ CAUTION

The fan wheel can become deformed. Setting the front blower regulation motor down incorrectly causes the fan wheel to become unbalanced. Set the front blower regulation motor down so the fan wheel is not covered.

1. Before servicing the vehicle, refer to the precautions.
2. Remove the foot-well trim on front passenger side.
3. Remove blower mounting bolts, working under passenger side of instrument panel.
4. Disconnect the blower electrical connector.

➡**The blower motor and series resistor form a single unit and can only be replaced together.**

To install:
5. Installation is in the reverse order of removal.

HEATER CORE

REMOVAL & INSTALLATION

See Figure 145.

1. Before servicing the vehicle, refer to the precautions. Hybrid vehicles have a high voltage system. Danger of electrical shock! It will also be necessary to work on the high voltage system when performing the following procedures. Switch off the high voltage system.
2. Extract the refrigerant using A/C service equipment
3. Remove the instrument panel.
4. Remove the air intake shroud.
5. Remove the expansion valve.
6. Remove the air guides for the heater and A/C unit.
7. Place drip pan under the engine. Discharge the coolant circuit
8. Loosen the refrigerant lines at the bolts.

9. Loosen the coolant lines on the heat exchanger.
10. Remove the condensation water hose from the heater and air conditioner.
11. Disconnect the connectors from the heater and air conditioner.
12. Remove the sub-frame.
13. Loosen the nuts on the engine compartment side from the heating and A/C unit.
14. Remove the heating and A/C unit.

To install:
15. Installation is carried out in the reverse order, when doing this note the following:
   a. Always replace O-rings.
   b. Torque the coolant pipe screws to expansion valve to 88 inch lbs. (10 Nm).
   c. After installing retaining clips, make sure they are securely seated on the heater core.

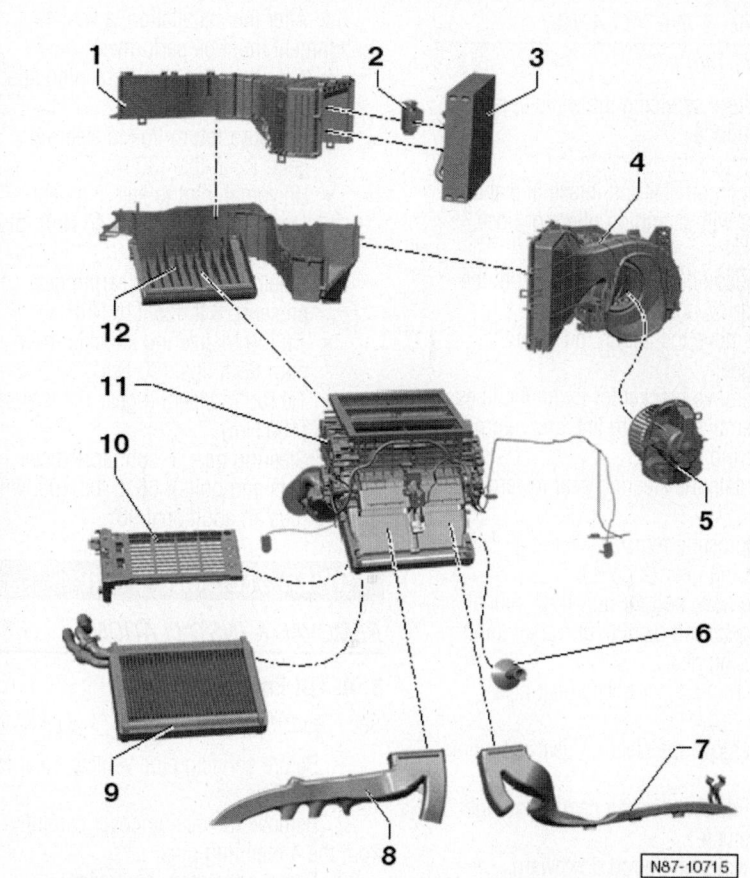

N87-10715

1. Upper Part Of The Distribution Box
2. Expansion Valve
3. Evaporator
4. Blower Housing
5. Fresh Air Blower
6. Condensate Drain Hose
7. Passenger Side Footwell Vent
8. Driver Side Footwell Vent
9. Heat Exchanger
10. Auxiliary Heater Heating Element
11. Junction Box
12. Lower Part Of The Distribution Box

Fig. 145 Heating and A/C unit overview

STEERING

POWER STEERING GEAR

REMOVAL & INSTALLATION

See Figure 146.

1. Before servicing the vehicle, refer to the precautions.
2. Remove front wheels.
3. Pinch off steering intake line and return line with clamping pliers or hose clamps.
4. Press off the tie rod ends from the wheel bearing housings.
5. Remove the left tie rod from the steering gear.
6. Remove bracket for hydraulic lines.
7. Remove pressure line and return line from steering gear.
8. Rotate the steering gear toward left until stop.
9. If present, remove shielding plate from steering gear (2 bolts).
10. Remove bolt for universal joint at steering gear and remove universal joint from steering gear.
11. Remove the steering gear heat shield.
12. Remove the steering gear mounting bolts.
13. Slide the steering gear to the right side of vehicle.
14. Swing left tie rod downward.
15. Remove the steering gear downward toward the left side of vehicle.

To install:

16. Installation is the reverse of removal. Note the following:
    a. Bleed the steering system.
    b. Check the steering system for leaks.

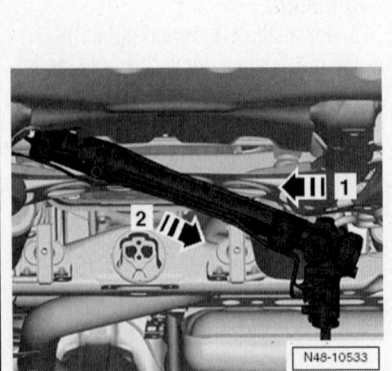

Fig. 146 Remove the steering gear downward toward the left side of vehicle

c. Check hydraulic fluid level and top off, if necessary.
d. After the installation, a vehicle alignment must be performed.
e. Note the following tightening specifications:

- Pressure/return line to steering gear: 22 ft. lbs. (30 Nm)
- Universal joint to steering gear (new bolt): 30 ft. lbs. (40 Nm), plus an additional 90°
- Shielding plate to steering gear (if present): 8 ft. lbs. (10 Nm)
- Tie rod to steering knuckle (new nut): 66 ft. lbs. (90 Nm)
- Tie rod to steering gear: 74 ft. lbs. (100 Nm)
- Steering gear to subframe (new nuts and bolts): 66 ft. lbs. (90 Nm), plus an additional 90°

POWER STEERING PUMP

REMOVAL & INSTALLATION

3.0L TDI Engine

See Figure 147.

1. Before servicing the vehicle, refer to the precautions.
2. Remove the design cover carefully from the 4 retaining pins.
3. Remove the air guide hose.
4. Clamp off intake hose using a pinching device.
5. Mark the ribbed belts running direction.
6. Loosen the bolts on the power steering pulley, then remove the drive belt.
7. Remove the steering pulley mounting bolts.
8. Remove the steering pressure hose and intake hose.
9. Remove the steering pump mounting bolts, and the pump assembly.

To install:

10. Installation is the reverse of removal, with special attention to the following:
11. Fill hydraulic oil into power steering pump. Fill oil at pump intake connection of vane pump.
12. Turn the hub by hand until oil runs out of the pressure side.
13. Install power steering pump.
14. Bleed the steering system.
15. Check the hydraulic fluid level.
16. Check the steering system for leaks.
17. Note the following tightening specifications:

- Power steering pump assembly to bracket: 16 ft. lbs. (22 Nm)
- Steering pulley to power steering pump: 16 ft. lbs. (22 Nm)
- Steering pressure hose banjo bolt to power steering pump: 80 inch. lbs. (9 Nm)

3.6L Engine

1. Before servicing the vehicle, refer to the precautions.
2. Remove engine noise insulation.
3. Mark ribbed belt running direction.
4. Thread bolt M8 x 50 into threaded hole of tensioning roller until ribbed belt is free of tension.
5. Remove ribbed belt pulley of power steering pump.
6. Remove the ribbed belt.

➡**When removing ribbed belt, observe adjustment shim located underneath. The shim is important for measurement and adjustment of power steering pump. Do not remove adjustment shim from power steering pump.**

7. Clamp off, the power steering intake hose.
8. Remove the connection banjo bolt.
9. Seal pressurized line using a plastic bag or something similar.
10. Open spring clip and pull intake hose off power steering pump.
11. Remove the power steering pump.

To install:

12. Installation is the reverse of removal, with special attention to the following:
13. Fill hydraulic oil into power steering pump. Fill oil at pump intake connection of vane pump.
14. Turn the hub by hand until oil runs out of the pressure side.
15. Install power steering pump.
16. Bleed the steering system.
17. Check the hydraulic fluid level.
18. Check the steering system for leaks.
19. Note the following tightening specifications:

- Power steering pump to bracket: 18 ft. lbs. (25 Nm)
- Belt pulley to power steering pump: 18 ft. lbs. (25 Nm)
- Banjo bolt to power steering pump: 30 ft. lbs. (40 Nm)

3.0L Hybrid Engine

See Figure 148.

1. Before servicing the vehicle, refer to the precautions.

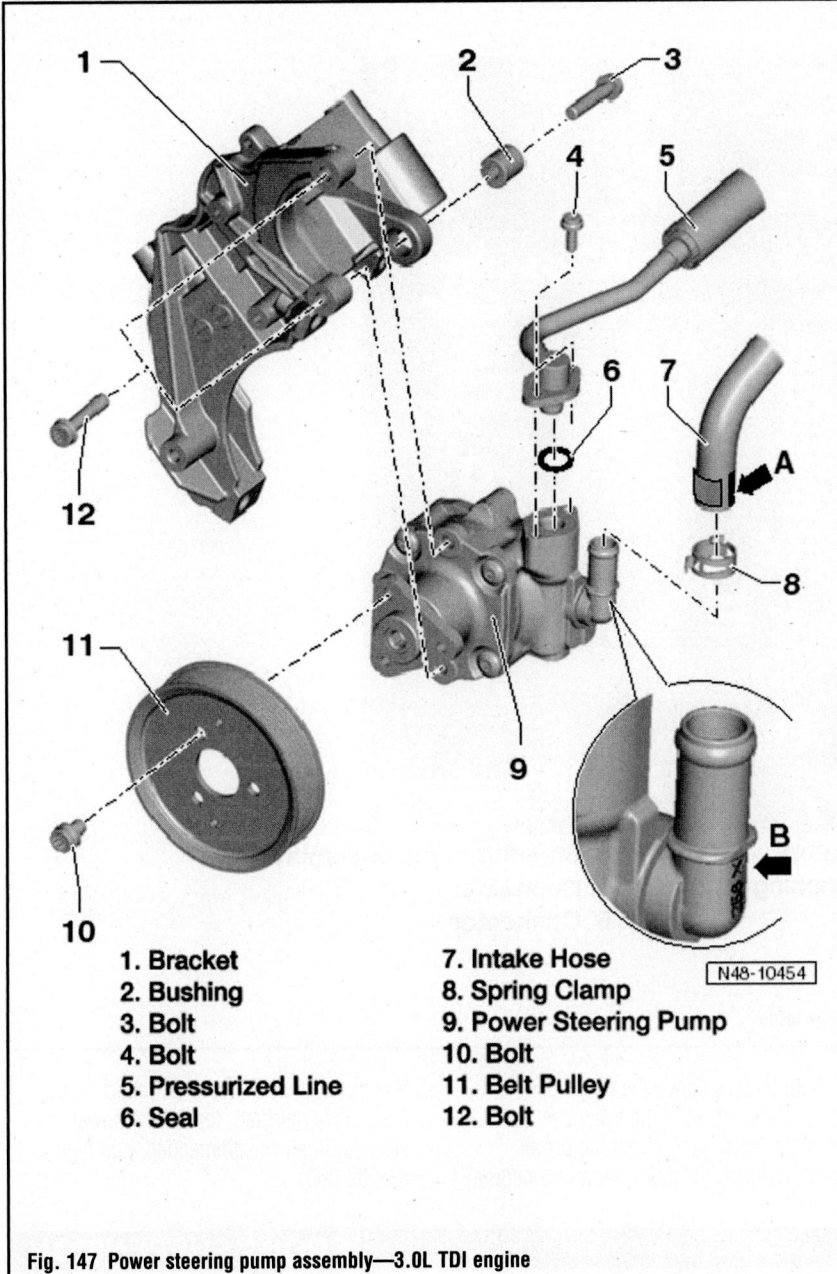

1. Bracket
2. Bushing
3. Bolt
4. Bolt
5. Pressurized Line
6. Seal
7. Intake Hose
8. Spring Clamp
9. Power Steering Pump
10. Bolt
11. Belt Pulley
12. Bolt

N48-10454

Fig. 147 Power steering pump assembly—3.0L TDI engine

- Pressure line union nut: 29 ft. lbs. (40 Nm).
- Bleed the steering system.
- Check the hydraulic fluid level and fill if necessary.
- Check the steering system for leaks.

BLEEDING

1. Before servicing the vehicle, refer to the precautions.

2. Inspect hydraulic oil level and top off as needed.

3. Raise the vehicle until front wheels are off the ground.

4. Start engine and let it run at idle for approximately 5 seconds.

5. Switch off engine and check hydraulic fluid level.

6. Repeat the procedure once more.

7. Start engine again and turn steering wheel 3 times from stop to stop at idle speed.

8. Switch off engine and check hydraulic fluid level, top off if necessary.

9. Repeat the procedure 2 times.

10. To dissipate gas of hydraulic fluid, let engine stand 2 to 3 minutes.

11. Lower the vehicle.

12. Now, once more, turn steering wheel 5 times from stop to stop at idle speed.

13. Steering system has been bled when air bubbles no longer rise to the surface in hydraulic fluid reservoir.

FLUID FILL PROCEDURE

1. Before servicing the vehicle, refer to the precautions.

2. With the engine OFF, move the front wheels into the straight ahead position.

3. Remove the reservoir cap arrow with the integrated dipstick.

4. Clean the dipstick with clean cloth.

5. Screw cap on hand-tight and remove again.

6. Check the power steering fluid level: the fluid level must be in area of MIN mark (up to 2 mm above or below mark). If oil level is above specified range, oil must be extracted off. If the fluid level is below the specified level, check the hydraulic system for leaks (repair measure). It is not sufficient just to add fluid.

7. If no leaks are detected, top off with hydraulic fluid.

8. Screw the cap in hand tight.

9. With the engine OFF, move the front wheels into the straight ahead position.

10. Unscrew the reservoir cap arrow with fitted dipstick.

11. Clean the dipstick with clean cloth.

2. Disconnect the battery ground strap with the ignition off.

3. For vehicles with an air spring shock absorber Activate the vehicle lift mode and place the vehicle on the lifting platform.

4. Loosen the wheel bolt.

5. Raise the vehicle and remove the wheel.

6. Remove the left front wheel housing liner.

7. Carefully pinch off the intake hose. (pinching tool 3094)

8. Open the clamp and remove the intake hose from the connector of the engine pump assembly.

9. Unplug the connectors from the engine pump assembly.

10. Disconnect the pressure line at the connection point.

11. Loosen but do not unscrew the securing nuts at the engine pump assembly.

12. Remove the engine pump assembly from the bracket.

To install:

13. Installation is in the reverse order of removal. Note the following:

- Replace the seals and gaskets.
- Hose supports and hoses must be free of oil and grease before installation.
- Secure all the hose connections with new hose clamps.
- Engine pump assembly bolts to the bracket: 71 inch lbs. (8Nm).

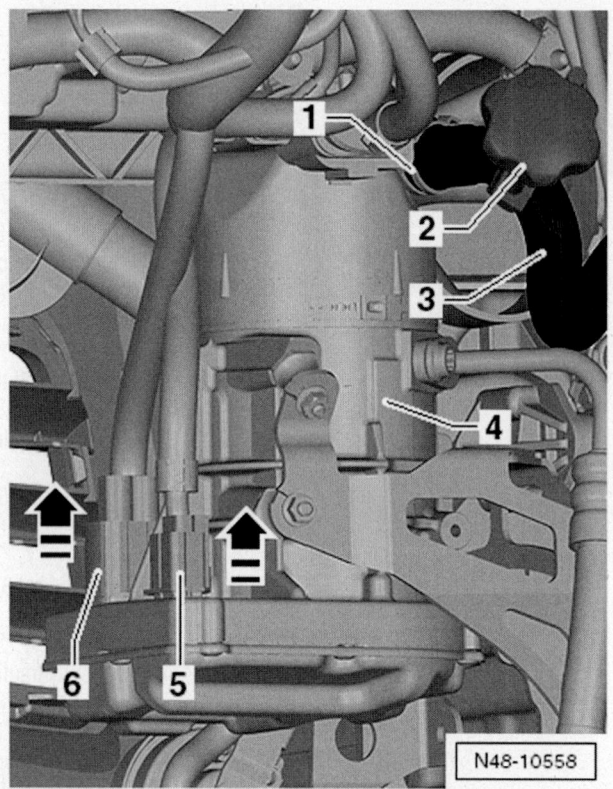

1. Intake hose clamp
2. Intake hose pinching tool 3094
3. Intake hose
4. Steering pump assembly
5. Connector
6. Connector

N48-10558

Fig. 148 Power steering pump assembly—3.0L Hybrid engine

12. Screw cap on hand-tight and remove again.

13. Check fluid level: the fluid level must be between the MIN and MAX markings. If the fluid level is above the MAX mark, siphon the fluid off. If the fluid level is below the MIN mark, check the power steering system for leaks (repair procedure). It is not sufficient just to add fluid. If no leaks were detected, top off the power steering fluid. Recommended fluid type (G 002 000)

SUSPENSION

See Figure 149.

COUPLING RODS

REMOVAL & INSTALLATION

See Figure 150.

1. Before servicing the vehicle, refer to the precautions.

For vehicles equipped with air suspension. Activate the vehicle lift mode and place the vehicle on the lifting platform.

2. Loosen the wheel bolts, raise the vehicle and remove the wheel.

3. Disconnect the drive axle from the final drive.

4. Remove the upper brake line bracket from the wheel bearing housing. Pull the harness connector and cable out of the bracket.

5. Remove the bolt and the lower line hose bracket from the wheel bearing housing.

6. Turn the wheel hub until one of the holes for the wheel bolts is on top.

7. Install the T10149 or equivalent this helps support the wheel bearing housing.

8. Support the wheel bearing housing.

9. Loosen the nut on the tie rod end, but do not unscrew yet.

10. Press out the tie rod end and unscrew the nut.

11. Tilt the wheel bearing housing outward.

12. Unscrew the top mounting bolt at the coupling rod.

FRONT SUSPENSION

13. Remove the bottom coupling rod mounting bolt at the stabilizer bar.

To install:

14. Installation is the reverse of removal. Perform a wheel alignment and observe the following torque specifications (use new hardware):

- Coupling rod to stabilizer bar: 81 ft. lbs. (110 Nm)
- Coupling rod to spring shock absorber: 81 ft. lbs. (110 Nm)
- Upper bracket for brake line to wheel bearing housing: 80 inch. lbs. (9 Nm)
- Lower bracket for brake line to wheel bearing housing: 15 ft. lbs. (20 Nm)

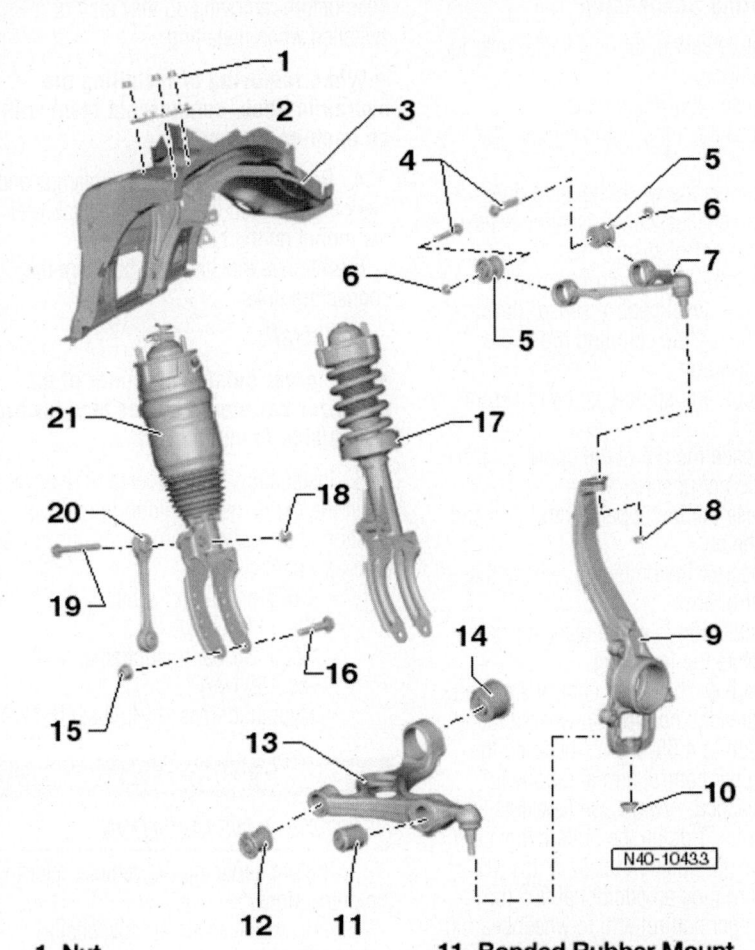

Fig. 149 Front suspension overview

1. Nut
2. Ring
3. Front Body
4. Bolts
5. Bonded Rubber Mount
6. Nut
7. Upper Control Arm
8. Nut
9. Wheel Bearing Housing (steering knuckle)
10. Nut

11. Bonded Rubber Mount
12. Bonded Rubber Mount
13. Lower Control Arm
14. Bonded Rubber Mount
15. Nut
16. Bolt
17. Steel Spring Shock Absorber
18. Nut
19. Bolt
20. Coupling Rod
21. Air Spring Shock Absorber

- Drive axle to front final drive: 37 ft. lbs (50 Nm) plus an additional 90° turn.
- Fill the air spring shock absorber using the VAS 5051B or equivalent scan tool.

LOWER BALL JOINT

REMOVAL & INSTALLATION

The ball joints are not replaceable. If necessary, the entire control arm must be replaced.

LOWER CONTROL ARM

REMOVAL & INSTALLATION

See Figure 151.

1. Before servicing the vehicle, refer to the precautions.

2. For vehicles with an air spring suspension activate the vehicle lift mode and place the vehicle on the lifting platform.

3. Measure the distance from the center of the wheel hub to the lip of the front fender.

4. Raise the vehicle and remove the wheel.

5. Remove the wheel housing liner.

6. Using hooks VW 552 or equivalent, secure the upper control arm to the upper opening of the wheel housing.

7. Raise the lower control arm slightly to preload it. This prevents damage to the stud of the ball joint.

8. Remove the suspension strut from the lower control arm.

9. Remove the ball joint nut from the lower control arm and press off the ball stud using a ball joint puller.

10. Remove the nuts, then remove the lower control arm in the direction of the arrow and thread out of the wheel bearing housing.

To install:

11. Installation is the reverse of removal. When installing the strut, tighten the strut in the normal ride height position. Perform a

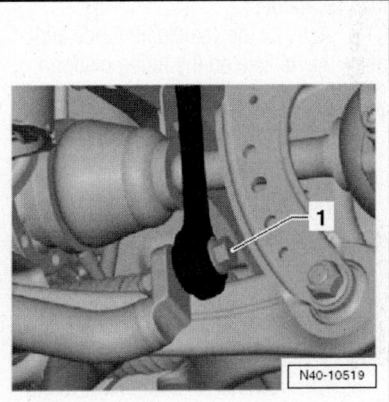

Fig. 150 Bottom coupling rod mounting bolt 1

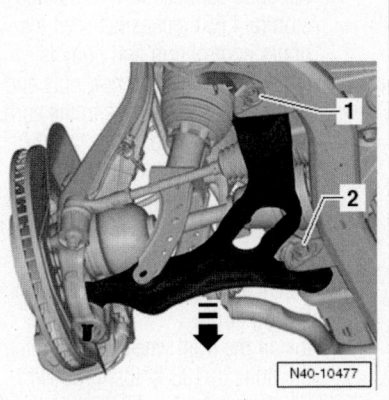

Fig. 151 Lower the lower control arm in the direction of the arrow

wheel alignment and observe the following torque specifications (use new hardware):

- Tighten the threaded connection of the lower control arm/sub-frame during the vehicle alignment.
- Lower control arm to sub-frame: 125 ft. lbs. (170 Nm)
- Suspension strut to lower control arm: 111 ft. lbs. (150 Nm) plus an additional 90° turn
- Lower control arm to steering knuckle 18" suspension (cast aluminum): 96 ft. lbs. (130 Nm). 17" suspension (cast steel): 81 ft. lbs. (110 Nm).
- Install the front wheels and tighten the bolts to 133 ft. lbs. (180 Nm).

UPPER CONTROL ARM

REMOVAL & INSTALLATION

Air Spring Suspension

1. Before servicing the vehicle, refer to the precautions.
2. Activate the vehicle lift mode and place the vehicle on the lifting platform.
3. Loosen the wheel bolts.
4. Raise the vehicle and remove the wheels.
5. Remove the wheel housing liner.
6. Pull the pin for the left front level control system sensor/right front level control sensor downward and unclip the coupling rod at the upper control arm.
7. Remove the air spring suspension damper. Refer to Air Spring strut.
8. Unscrew the bolts and remove the upper control arm.

To install:

9. Installation is in the reverse order of removal. Note the following:

- Tighten the upper control arm/body threaded connection when dimension (a 4.65) inches between the upper control arm and body is reached. Always use new nuts and bolts. Tighten the bolts in the curb weight position to: 37 ft. lbs. (50 Nm) plus an additional 90° turn.
- Upper control arm to wheel bearing housing: tighten the nut to 62 ft. lbs. (85 Nm).
- Install air spring strut. Refer to Air Spring strut.
- Install the front wheels and tighten the bolts to 133 ft. lbs. (180 Nm).
- Fill the air spring shock absorber using the VAS 5051B or equivalent scan tool.

Steel Spring Suspension

1. Before servicing the vehicle, refer to the precautions.
2. Loosen the wheel bolts.
3. Raise the vehicle and remove the wheels.
4. Remove the wheel housing liner.
5. For vehicles with a dynamic headlamp range control system. Pull the pin 2 for the left front level control system sensor/right front level control sensor downward and unclip the coupling rod at the upper control arm.
6. Secure the spindle and hub assembly.
7. Loosen the nut of the upper control arm, but do not unscrew yet.
8. Press out the upper control arm and unscrew the nut.
9. Unscrew the bolts and remove the upper control arm.
10. Installation is in the reverse order of removal. Note the following:

- Tighten the upper control arm/body threaded connection when dimension (a 4.65) inches between the upper control arm and body is reached. Always use new nuts and bolts. Tighten the bolts in the curb weight position to: 37 ft. lbs. (50 Nm) plus an additional 90° turn.
- Upper control arm to wheel bearing housing: tighten the nut to 62 ft. lbs. (85 Nm).
- Install steel spring strut. Refer to Steel Spring Strut.
- Install the front wheels and tighten the bolts to 133 ft. lbs. (180 Nm).

STABILIZER BAR

REMOVAL & INSTALLATION

1. Before servicing the vehicle, refer to the precautions.

❊❊ CAUTION

On vehicles with decouplable stabilizer bars, the stabilizer bars must be coupled in before proceeding. Otherwise, the risk of injury exists if the decoupled stabilizer bars become unintentionally coupled.

➡**The hydraulic system pressure must first be released using diagnostic tool VAS 5051. After installation, the system must be bled using this tool as well.**

2. Remove the underbody cover.
3. Disconnect the hydraulic lines and unplug the electrical connection. Label the lines before removing so they are not switched when installing.

➡**When removing or installing the hydraulic lines, counterhold them with an open-end wrench.**

4. Remove the stabilizer bar clamps and mark the installed location of the stabilizer bar mount on the bar.
5. Remove the stabilizer bar from the connecting links.

To install:

➡**The larger outside diameter of the stabilizer bar mount halves face toward the outside of vehicle.**

6. Installation is the reverse of removal. Align the markings made during removal. Observe the following torque specifications (use new hardware):

- Coupling rod to stabilizer bar: 81 ft. lbs. (110 Nm)
- Stabilizer bar to subframe: 44 ft. lbs. (60 Nm)
- Hydraulic lines: 11 ft. lbs. (15 Nm)

STEERING KNUCKLE

REMOVAL & INSTALLATION

1. Before servicing the vehicle, refer to the precautions.
2. For vehicles with air suspension activate the vehicle lift mode and place the vehicle on the lifting platform.
3. Loosen the 12-point nut for the drive axle on the wheel hub.

➡**The wheel bearing must not be under a load while the drive axle threaded connection on the wheel side is loose. If the wheel bearings are under the load of the vehicle's own weight, the wheel bearing will be damaged. This reduces the service life of the wheel bearings. The 12-point nut may only be loosened a maximum of 90° when the vehicle is resting on its wheels.**

Vehicles without a drive axle must not be moved, otherwise the wheel bearing will be damaged. If a vehicle must be moved, be sure to note the following:

- Install an outer joint in place of the drive axle.
- Tighten the outer joint to 110 ft. lbs. (150 Nm).

4. Loosen the wheel bolts.
5. Raise the vehicle and remove the wheel.
6. Loosen nut of track rod ball joint, but do not unscrew yet.

7. Remove the tie rod from the steering knuckle and remove the nut.

8. Remove the upper brake line bracket from the steering knuckle.

9. Pull the harness connector and cable out of the bracket.

10. Remove the bolt and the lower line hose bracket from the steering knuckle.

11. Remove brake caliper and engage on body with wire. Refer to Removal and Installation.

12. Remove ABS wheel speed sensor.

13. Remove the disc brake rotor.

14. Remove the cover plate.

15. Loosen the nut on the upper control arm conical pin, but do not unscrew yet.

16. Press out the upper control arm and unscrew the nut.

17. Unscrew the 12-point nut for the drive axle.

18. Press out drive axle. During the pressing-out operation, ensure sufficient freedom of movement of the joints.

19. Loosen the nut on the lower control arm conical pin, but do not unscrew yet.

20. Press out the lower control arm.

21. Unscrew the nut and remove the steering knuckle.

To install:

22. Installation is in the reverse order of removal. Note the following:

- Pull in the drive axle.
- Install the front wheels and tighten the bolts to 133 ft. lbs. (180 Nm).
- Replace the 12-point nut.
- Press the brake pedal. A second technician will be needed.
- Pre-tighten the 12-point nut to 110 ft. lbs. (150 Nm).
- Lower the vehicle onto its wheels.
- Tighten the 12-point nut to 369 ft. lbs. (500 Nm).
- Upper control arm to wheel bearing housing: tighten to 59 ft. lbs. (85 Nm).
- Lower control arm to the wheel bearing housing for 18" suspension (cast aluminum): 96 ft. lbs. (130 Nm).
- Lower control arm to the wheel bearing housing for 17" suspension (cast steel): 81 ft. lbs. (110 Nm).
- Tie rod end to wheel bearing housing: 66 ft. lbs. (90 Nm).

STRUT & SPRING ASSEMBLY

REMOVAL & INSTALLATION

Air Spring Suspension

1. Before servicing the vehicle, refer to the precautions.

2. Remove the wheel and raise the vehicle.

➡**During assembly work, make sure that no indentations form on the protective boot of the air spring shock absorber!**

3. Remove the engine compartment cover.

4. For the right air spring strut in vehicles with a diesel engine. Remove the fuel filter over the air spring shock absorber.

5. For the left air spring strut in vehicles with a hybrid drive. Unclip the lines from the brackets and remove the nuts.

6. For vehicles with air suspension activate the vehicle lift mode and place the vehicle on the lifting platform.

7. Disconnect the harness connector. Unscrew the strut top mounting nuts and remove the ring.

8. Loosen the wheel bolts and remove the wheel.

9. Bleed the air spring shock absorber with the VAS 5051B scan tool.

10. Using the VW 552 1, hook the upper control arm to the body and pretension it slightly.

11. Pull the pin for the left front level control system sensor/right front level control sensor downward and unclip the coupling rod at the upper control arm.

12. Remove the air line from the pressure-holding valve and seal both connections.

13. Disconnect the drive axle from the front final drive.

14. Remove the upper brake line bracket from the wheel bearing housing.

15. Pull the harness connector and cable out of the bracket.

16. Remove the bolt and the lower line hose bracket from the wheel bearing housing.

17. Turn the wheel hub until one of the holes for the wheel bolts is on top.

18. Support the wheel bearing housing.

19. Loosen the nut on the tie rod end, but do not unscrew yet.

20. Press out the tie rod end and unscrew the nut.

21. Tilt the wheel bearing housing outward, unscrew the threaded connection.

22. Unscrew the bolt for the air spring shock absorber on the control arm.

23. Press the upper control arm upward, press the air spring shock absorber together and remove.

To install:

24. Installation is the reverse of removal. Perform a wheel alignment and observe the

following torque specifications (use new hardware):

- Suspension strut to body nuts: 22 ft. lbs. (30 Nm)
- Suspension strut to lower control arm: 111 ft. lbs. (150 Nm) plus an additional 90° turn.
- Upper control arm to steering knuckle: 70 ft. lbs. (95 Nm)
- Tie rod to steering knuckle: 66 ft. lbs. (90 Nm)
- Install the front wheels and tighten the bolts to 133 ft. lbs. (180 Nm)
- Fill the air spring shock absorber using the VAS 5051B or equivalent scan tool.

Steel Spring Suspension

1. Before servicing the vehicle, refer to the precautions.

2. Remove the wheel and raise the vehicle.

➡**During assembly work, make sure that no indentations form on the protective boot of the air spring shock absorber!**

3. Remove the engine compartment cover.

4. For the right air spring strut in vehicles with a diesel engine. Remove the fuel filter over the air spring shock absorber.

5. For the left air spring strut in vehicles with a hybrid drive. Unclip the lines from the brackets.

6. Remove the nuts and press the bracket to the side.

7. Unscrew the strut top mounting nuts and remove the ring.

8. Loosen the wheel bolts and remove the wheel.

9. For vehicles with dynamic headlamp range control. Pull the pin for the left front level control system sensor/right front level control sensor downward and unclip the coupling rod at the upper control arm.

10. Disconnect the drive axle from the front final drive.

11. Remove the upper brake line bracket from the wheel bearing housing.

12. Pull the harness connector and cable out of the bracket.

13. Remove the bolt and the lower line hose bracket from the wheel bearing housing.

14. Turn the wheel hub until one of the holes for the wheel bolts is on top.

15. Support the wheel bearing housing.

16. Loosen the nut on the tie rod end, but do not unscrew yet.

17. Press out the tie rod end and unscrew the nut.

18. Tilt the wheel bearing housing outward, unscrew the threaded connection.

19. Unscrew the bolt for the air spring shock absorber on the control arm.

20. Press the upper control arm upward, press the air spring shock absorber together and remove.

To install:

21. Installation is the reverse of removal. Perform a wheel alignment and observe the following torque specifications (use new hardware):

- Suspension strut to body nuts: 22 ft. lbs. (30 Nm)
- Suspension strut to lower control arm: 111 ft. lbs. (150 Nm) plus an additional 90° turn.
- Upper control arm to steering knuckle: 70 ft. lbs. (95 Nm)
- Tie rod to steering knuckle: 66 ft. lbs. (90 Nm)
- Install the front wheels and tighten the bolts to 133 ft. lbs. (180 Nm).

OVERHAUL

See Figures 152 and 153.

1. Before servicing the vehicle, refer to the precautions.

2. Fit the strut into spring compressor V.A.G 1752/1 and compress the spring until upper axial groove ball bearing is free.

> ### ❋❋ CAUTION
>
> **First pre-load spring far enough so that tension is relieved on upper spring retainer!**

3. Make sure that coil spring is seated correctly in the tool.

4. Remove hex nut from top of piston rod.

5. Remove components of suspension strut and coil spring.

To install:

6. Place coil spring with spring compressor V.A.G 1752/1 on lower spring plate. End of spring coil must rest against the stop in the spring seat.

7. Install a new self-locking hex nut onto piston rod and tighten.

8. Carefully relieve tension on spring compressor V.A.G 1752/1 and remove from coil spring.

WHEEL BEARINGS

REMOVAL & INSTALLATION

17-inch Suspension

See Figures 154 and 155.

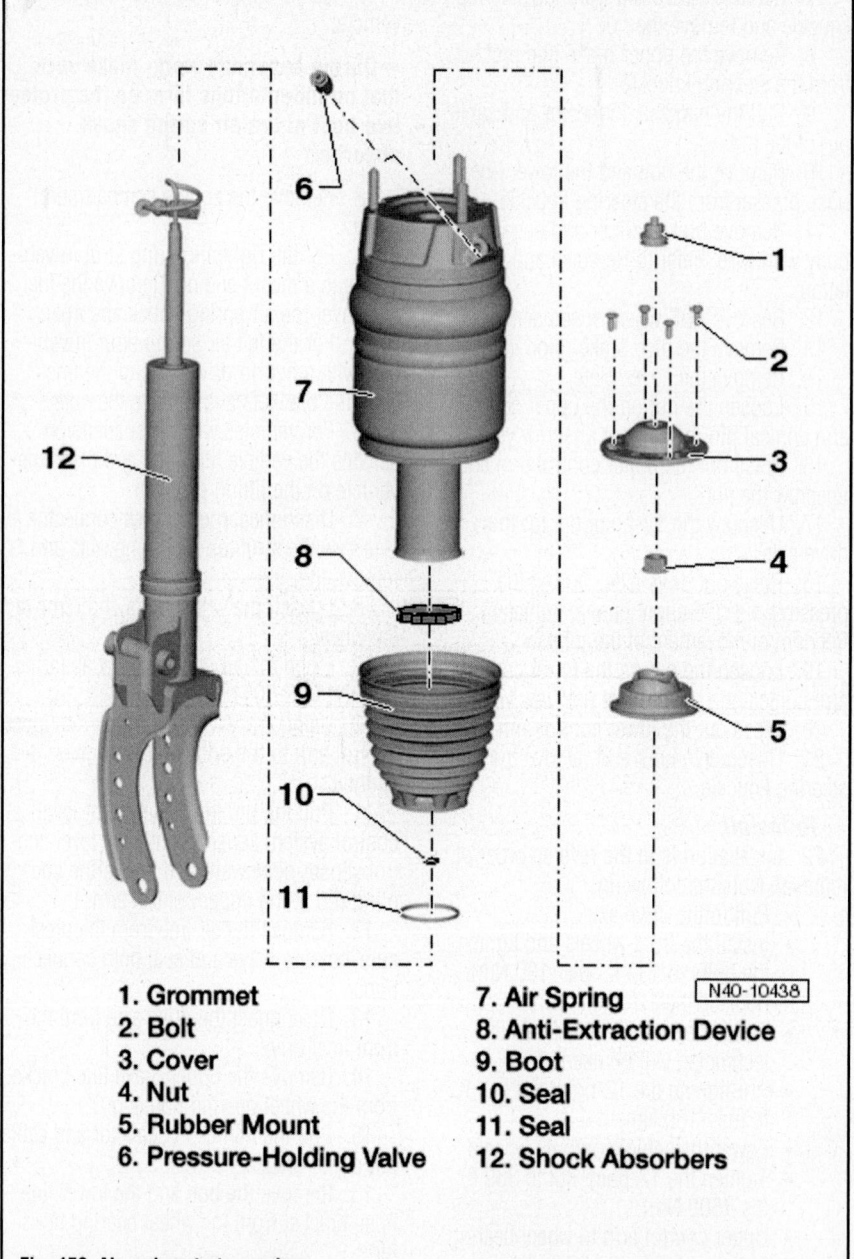

1. Grommet	7. Air Spring
2. Bolt	8. Anti-Extraction Device
3. Cover	9. Boot
4. Nut	10. Seal
5. Rubber Mount	11. Seal
6. Pressure-Holding Valve	12. Shock Absorbers

N40-10438

Fig. 152 Air spring strut overview

1. Before servicing the vehicle, refer to the Precautions Section.
   Remove drive axle.

2. Remove the upper control arm from wheel bearing housing.

3. Remove brake caliper and engage on body with wire.

4. Remove brake disc and backing plate.

5. Remove ABS wheel speed sensor.

6. To remove the wheel hub, secure the gripping pieces T10205/1 1 with the wheel bolts to the wheel hub. The wheel bolts must not protrude on the back side of the T10205/1 arrow.

➡**Before pressing out, place the V.A.G 1383 A with the universal mount under the cylinder since the cylinder may fall down at the end of the pressing out procedure. Hold the VAS 6178 during the pressing-out procedure.**

7. Pull out wheel hub, hold tool securely. Remove securing ring.

8. Offset of thrust piece T10205/6 must point toward rear final drive.

9. Pull out the wheel bearing while holding the device securely.

10. Install the separating tool behind the bearing inner ring. Beveled parts of blades face bearing inner ring.

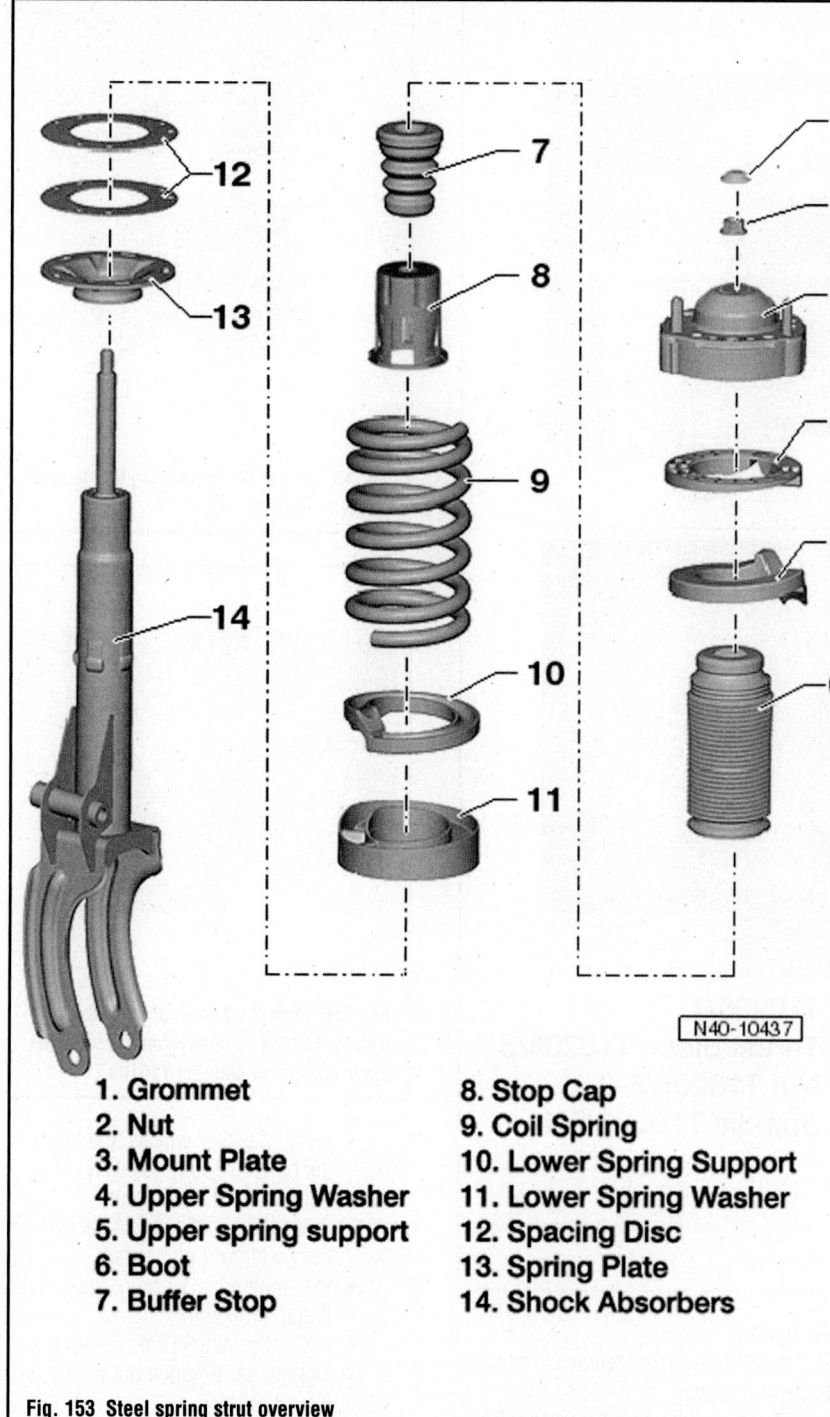

1. Grommet
2. Nut
3. Mount Plate
4. Upper Spring Washer
5. Upper spring support
6. Boot
7. Buffer Stop
8. Stop Cap
9. Coil Spring
10. Lower Spring Support
11. Lower Spring Washer
12. Spacing Disc
13. Spring Plate
14. Shock Absorbers

N40-10437

Fig. 153 Steel spring strut overview

11. Pull off the wheel hub from the bearing inner ring. Make sure that the rubberized ABS sensor ring faces the final drive. If no rubberized ring is visible, check for example with a paper clip, which of the two sides is magnetic. This side must face rear final drive when installed.

12. Mount the tools. Offset of thrust piece T10205/9 must point toward wheel bearing housing.

13. Press wheel bearing in until stop. Install circlip.

To install:

14. Install in reverse order of removal. Note the following:
- Install the drive axle.
- Install the brake disk and cover plate.
- Install brake caliper.
- Drive axle to front final drive: 37 ft. lbs. (50 Nm) plus an additional 90° turn
- Upper control arm to wheel bearing housing: 63 ft. lbs. (85 Nm).

- Spring shock absorber to the lower control arm: 110 ft. lbs. (150 Nm) plus an additional 90° turn
- Tie rod end to wheel bearing housing: 66 ft. lbs. (90 Nm).
- Upper bracket for brake line to wheel bearing housing: 80 inch lbs. (9 Nm).
- Lower bracket for brake line to wheel bearing housing: 15 ft. lbs. (20 Nm).
- Install the wheels and tighten the bolts to 133 ft. lbs. (180 Nm).

18 & 19-inch Suspension

See Figure 151

1. Before servicing the vehicle, refer to the Precautions Section.

2. For vehicles with an air spring suspension activate the vehicle lift mode and place the vehicle on the lifting platform.

3. Loosen the 12-point nut for the drive axle on the wheel hub.

➡**The wheel bearing must not be under a load while the drive axle threaded connection on the wheel side is loose.**

❊❊ WARNING

If the wheel bearings are under the load of the vehicle's own weight, the wheel bearing will be damaged. This reduces the service life of the wheel bearings.

➡**The 12-point nut may only be loosened a maximum of 90° when the vehicle is resting on its wheels.**

❊❊ WARNING

Vehicles without a drive axle must not be moved, otherwise the wheel bearing will be damaged. If a vehicle must be moved, be sure to note the following:

- Install an outer joint in place of the drive axle.
- Tighten the outer joint to 110 ft. lbs. (150 Nm).

4. Loosen the wheel bolts.

5. Raise the vehicle.

6. Remove the wheel.

7. Unscrew the brake caliper and push outward with the T10439.

8. Remove brake disc.

9. Remove ABS wheel speed sensor.

10. Press out the drive axle as far as possible

11. Unscrew the wheel bearing assembly bolts above and below the drive axle.

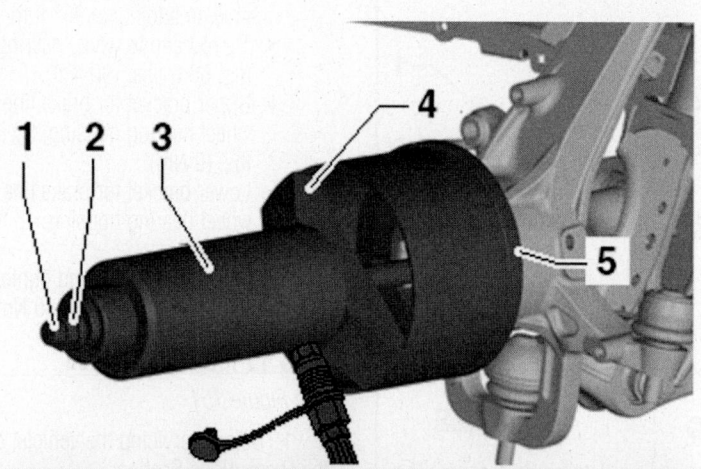

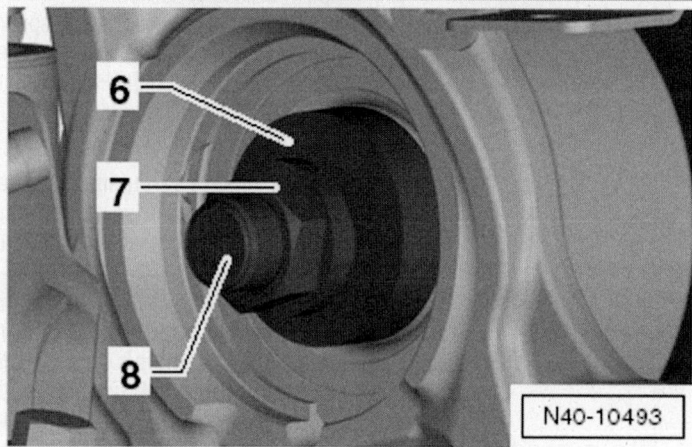

1. Spindle T10205/8-1
2. Nut T10205/8-2
3. VAS 6178 with T10205/13
4. Bell T10205/2

5. T10205/1
6. Thrust piece T10205/3
7. Nut T10205/8-2
8. Spindle T10205/8-1

Fig. 154 Mount the Hydraulic press as illustrated

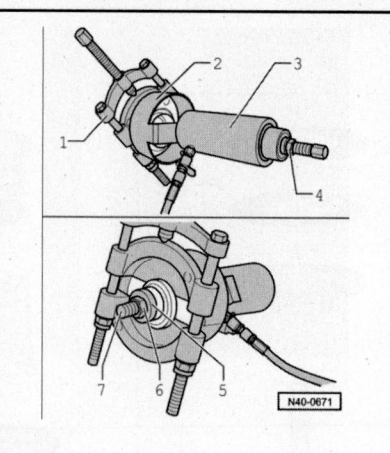

Fig. 155 Install the separating tool behind the bearing inner ring

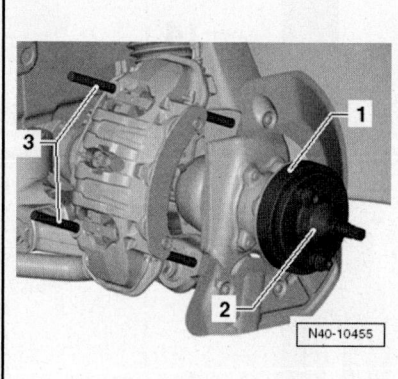

Fig. 156 Push the brake caliper outward with theT10439 3, remove the wheel bearing unit together with the T10103.

12. Remove the wheel bearing unit from the drive axle.

13. Remove the wheel bearing unit together with the T10103.

14. Always set the wheel bearing unit down on the wheel hub.

➠**The same procedure also applies to the wheel bearing without a wheel hub.**

To install:

15. Installation is the reverse of removal. Note the following:
- Position the wheel bearing unit on the gearing of the drive axle.
- Tighten the wheel bearing assembly bolts above and below the drive axle.
- Pull in the drive axle.
- Install the brake caliper and brake disk.

- Install the front wheels and tighten the bolts to 133 ft. lbs. (180 Nm).
- Replace the 12-point nut.
- Press the brake pedal. A second technician will be needed.
- Pre-tighten the 12-point nut to 110 ft. lbs. (150 Nm).
- Lower the vehicle onto its wheels.
- Tighten the 12-point nut to 369 ft. lbs. (500 Nm).
- Wheel bearing unit to wheel bearing housing: tighten to 59 ft. lbs. (80 Nm) plus an additional 120° turn
- Lower control arm ball joint nut (use a new one), tighten it to 77 ft. lbs. (105 Nm).

See Figure 157.

COUPLING ROD

REMOVAL & INSTALLATION

Air Spring Suspension

1. Before servicing the vehicle, refer to the Precautions Section.

2. Activate the vehicle lift mode and place the vehicle on the lifting platform.

3. Bleed the rear air spring shock absorber with the VAS 5051B or equivalent.

4. Loosen the wheel bolts, raise the vehicle and remove the wheels.

5. Turn the wheel hub until one of the holes for the wheel bolts is on top, secure the wheel hub assembly.

6. Release the harness connector at the electromechanical parking brake and disconnect.

7. Unscrew the bolt and remove the bracket with the lines.

8. Remove the bolt from lower air spring shock absorber and the coupling rod at the wheel bearing housing.

9. Remove the mounting nut and pull the top of the coupling rod out of the stabilizer bar. Wiggle the wheel bearing housing.

10. Remove the connecting link.

To install:

11. Install the coupling rod in the stabilizer bar and tighten the nut by hand.

12. Install the bolt between the air spring shock absorber and the coupling rod at the wheel bearing housing. Tighten the bolt by hand.

➡**All bolts at suspension parts with bonded rubber bushings must always be tightened in curb weight position (unloaded condition). Bonded rubber bushings can only be turned to a limited extent.**

Parts with bonded rubber bushings must therefore be brought into a position that corresponds to the position in driving mode before being tightened (curb weight position). Otherwise, the bonded rubber bushing will be stressed resulting in a shortened service life.

13. Observe the following torque specifications (use new hardware):

- Coupling rod to stabilizer bar: 74 ft. lbs. (100 Nm).
- Coupling rod with spring shock absorber to wheel bearing housing: 66 ft. lbs. (90 Nm) plus an additional 90°
- Cable bracket to the wheel bearing housing: 7 ft. lbs. (10 Nm).
- Wheels: tighten the bolts to 133 ft. lbs. (180 Nm).
- Fill the air spring shock absorber using the VAS 5051B or equivalent scan tool.

Steel Spring Suspension

1. Before servicing the vehicle, refer to the precautions.

2. Loosen the bottom mounting bolt from the steel spring shock absorber.

3. Insert a block of wood between the sub-frame and the upper rear transverse link, this is needed to press down on the axle. Press the axle down with a block of wood. Remove the mounting bolt.

4. Remove the mounting bolt.

5. Turn the wheel hub until one of the holes for the wheel bolts is on top, secure the wheel hub assembly.

6. Release the harness connector at the electromechanical parking brake and disconnect.

7. Unscrew the bolt and remove the bracket with the lines.

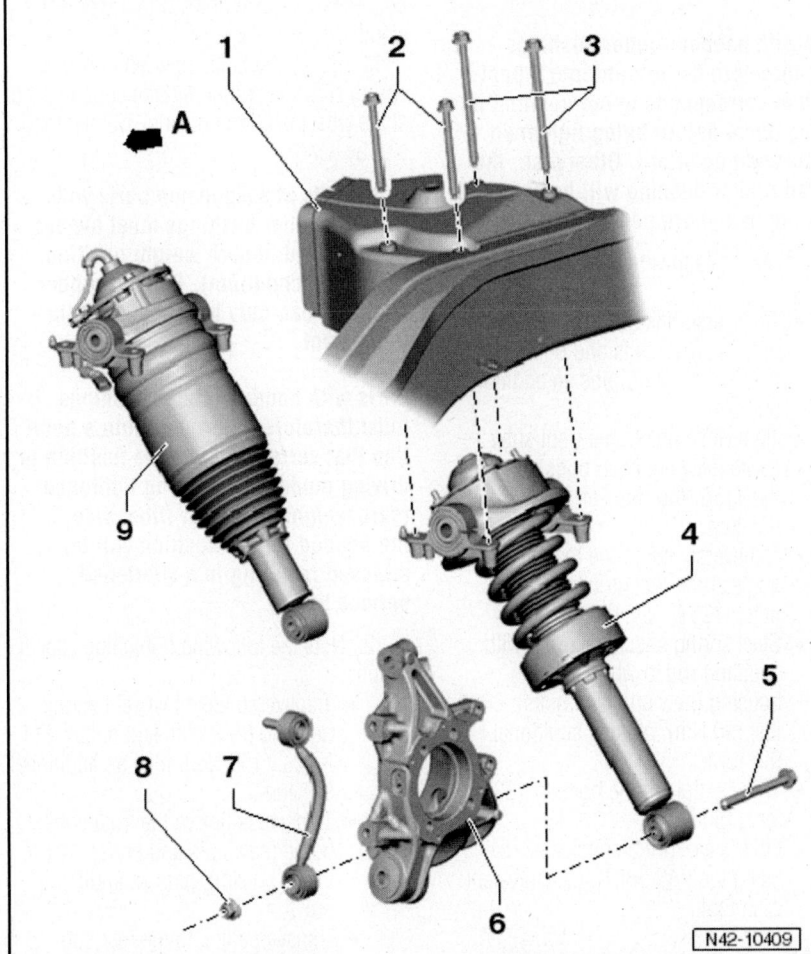

N42-10409

A. Direction of travel
1. Body
2. Bolt
3. Bolt
4. Steel Spring Shock Absorber
5. Bolt
6. Wheel Bearing Housing
7. Coupling Rod
8. Nut
9. Air Spring Shock Absorber

Fig. 157 Rear suspension overview

8. Remove the mounting nut and pull the top of the coupling rod out of the stabilizer bar. Wiggle the wheel bearing housing.

9. Remove the connecting link.

To install:

10. Install the coupling rod in the stabilizer bar and tighten the nut by hand.

11. Install the block of wood between the sub-frame and the upper rear transverse link. Press the axle down with a block of wood.

12. Install the bolt between the steel spring shock absorber and the coupling rod at the wheel bearing housing. Tighten the bolt by hand.

➡All bolts at suspension parts with bonded rubber bushings must always be tightened in curb weight position (unloaded condition). Bonded rubber bushings can only be turned to a limited extent.

Parts with bonded rubber bushings must therefore be brought into a position that corresponds to the position in driving mode before being tightened (curb weight position). Otherwise, the bonded rubber bushing will be stressed resulting in a shortened service life.

13. Observe the following torque specifications (use new hardware):
- Coupling rod to stabilizer bar: 74 ft. lbs. (100 Nm).
- Coupling rod with spring shock absorber to wheel bearing housing: 66 ft. lbs. (90 Nm) plus an additional 90°
- Cable bracket to the wheel bearing housing: 7 ft. lbs. (10 Nm).
- Wheels: tighten the bolts to 133 ft. lbs. (180 Nm).

LOWER TRANSVERSE LINK

REMOVAL & INSTALLATION

Air Spring Suspension

1. Before servicing the vehicle, refer to the precautions.

2. Activate the vehicle lift mode and place the vehicle on the lifting platform.

3. Bleed the rear air spring shock absorber with the VAS 5051B.

4. Loosen the wheel bolts, raise the vehicle and remove the wheels.

5. Support the wheel bearing housing.

6. Remove the nut to the lower transverse link on the wheel bearing housing, and remove the bolt.

7. Remove the bolts to the lower transverse link on the sub-frame.

8. Slide the transverse link inward to the sub-frame. Tilt the front transverse link on the wheel bearing housing downward to remove.

To install:

9. Insert the transverse link in the vehicle and tighten the bolts by hand.

10. Install the bolts between the air spring shock absorber and the coupling rod at the wheel bearing housing. Tighten the bolt by hand.

➡All bolts at suspension parts with bonded rubber bushings must always be tightened in curb weight position (unloaded condition). Bonded rubber bushings can only be turned to a limited extent.

Parts with bonded rubber bushings must therefore be brought into a position that corresponds to the position in driving mode before being tightened (curb weight position). Otherwise, the bonded rubber bushing will be stressed resulting in a shortened service life.

11. Note the following tightening specifications:
- Transverse link to wheel bearing housing (new nuts and bolts): 111 ft. lbs. (150 Nm), plus an additional 90° turn.
- Transverse link to the front sub-frame (new nuts and bolts): 111 ft. lbs. (150 Nm), plus an additional 90° turn.
- Transverse link to the rear sub-frame at the eccentric bolt (new nuts): 125 ft. lbs. (170 Nm).
- Steel spring shock absorber with coupling rod to wheel bearing housing (new nuts and bolts): 66 ft. lbs. (90 Nm), plus an additional 90° turn.
- Wheels: tighten the bolts to 133 ft. lbs. (180 Nm).
- Fill the air spring shock absorber using the VAS 5051B or equivalent scan tool.

Steel Spring Suspension

1. Before servicing the vehicle, refer to the precautions.

2. Loosen the wheel bolts, raise the vehicle and remove the wheels.

3. Loosen the threaded connection arrows between the steel spring shock absorber 1 and the coupling rod at the wheel bearing housing.

4. Install a block of wood between the sub-frame and the upper rear transverse link. Press the axle down with a block of wood. Remove the bolt.

5. Support the wheel bearing housing.

6. Remove the nut to the lower transverse link on the wheel bearing housing, and remove the bolt.

7. Remove the bolts to the lower transverse link on the sub-frame.

8. Slide the transverse link inward to the sub-frame. Tilt the front transverse link on the wheel bearing housing downward to remove.

To install:

9. Insert the transverse link in the vehicle and tighten the bolts by hand.

10. Install the block of wood between the sub-frame and the upper rear transverse link. Press the axle down with a block of wood.

11. Install the bolts between the steel spring shock absorber and the coupling rod at the wheel bearing housing. Tighten the bolt by hand.

➡All bolts at suspension parts with bonded rubber bushings must always be tightened in curb weight position (unloaded condition). Bonded rubber bushings can only be turned to a limited extent.

Parts with bonded rubber bushings must therefore be brought into a position that corresponds to the position in driving mode before being tightened (curb weight position). Otherwise, the bonded rubber bushing will be stressed resulting in a shortened service life.

12. Note the following tightening specifications:
- Transverse link to wheel bearing housing (new nuts and bolts): 111 ft. lbs. (150 Nm), plus an additional 90° turn.
- Transverse link to the front sub-frame (new nuts and bolts): 111 ft. lbs. (150 Nm), plus an additional 90° turn.
- Transverse link to the rear sub-frame at the eccentric bolt (new nuts): 125 ft. lbs. (170 Nm).
- Steel spring shock absorber with coupling rod to wheel bearing housing (new nuts and bolts): 66 ft. lbs. (90 Nm), plus an additional 90° turn.
- Wheels: tighten the bolts to 133 ft. lbs. (180 Nm).

STABILIZER BAR

REMOVAL & INSTALLATION

1. Before servicing the vehicle, refer to the precautions.

2. For air spring suspension, activate the vehicle lift mode and place the vehicle on the lifting platform.

3. Loosen the wheel bolts, raise the vehicle and remove the wheels.

4. Remove the mounting bolts for the stabilizer bar clamps on the sub-frame.

5. Remove the stabilizer bar clamps.

6. Remove the mounting nut and pull the coupling rod out of the stabilizer bar.

7. Remove the stabilizer bar.

To install:

➡**All bolts at suspension parts with bonded rubber bushings must always be tightened in curb weight position (unloaded condition). Bonded rubber bushings can only be turned to a limited extent.**

Parts with bonded rubber bushings must therefore be brought into a position that corresponds to the position in driving mode before being tightened (curb weight position). Otherwise, the bonded rubber bushing will be stressed resulting in a shortened service life.

8. Insert the stabilizer bar in the vehicle and hand tighten the mounting nuts and bolts.

9. Uniformly tighten the bolts for the stabilizer bar clamps on the sub-frame to 37 ft. lbs. (50 Nm).

10. Tighten the coupling rod on the stabilizer bar to 74 ft. lbs. (100 Nm).

11. Install the wheels and tighten the bolts to 133 ft. lbs. (180 Nm).

STRUT & SPRING ASSEMBLY

REMOVAL & INSTALLATION

Air Spring Suspension

1. Before servicing the vehicle, refer to the precautions.

2. Activate the vehicle lift mode and place the vehicle on the lifting platform.

3. Bleed the rear air spring shock absorber with the VAS 5051B or equivalent.

4. Remove the wheels and raise the vehicle.

✳✳ WARNING

During assembly work, make sure that no indentations form on the protective boot of the air spring shock absorber!

5. Remove the luggage compartment floor.

6. Remove the luggage compartment floor support.

7. Remove the plugs over the threaded connections of the air spring shock absorber.

8. Remove the mounting nuts from the top of the air spring shock absorber.

9. Remove the union nut of the air line from the air spring shock absorber and seal both connections.

10. Release and disconnect the harness connector for the damping adjustment valve.

11. Remove the lower mounting bolt from the bottom of the air spring shock absorber.

12. Remove the air spring shock absorber.

To install:

13. Insert the air spring shock absorber with the guide pins in the upper holes on the body.

14. Hand tighten all the mounting nuts and bolts, then tightening in sequence starting with the top air spring shock absorber mounting nuts.

15. Insert the air line until the end of the shrinkable tubing is in contact with the union nut. The end of the shrinkable tubing may be a maximum of 2 mm in front of the union nut.

16. Tighten the air line union nut at the air spring shock absorber.

17. Note the following tightening specifications:

- Steel spring shock absorber to body: 37 ft. lbs. (50 Nm) plus an additional 180 degree turn.
- Steel spring shock absorber to wheel bearing housing (new bolt and nut): 66 ft. lbs. (90 Nm), plus an additional 90 degree turn.
- Install the wheels and tighten the bolts to 133 ft. lbs. (180 Nm).
- Fill the air spring shock absorber using the VAS 5051B or equivalent scan tool.

Steel Spring Suspension

1. Before servicing the vehicle, refer to the precautions.

2. Remove the luggage compartment floor.

3. Remove the luggage compartment floor support.

4. Remove the plugs over the threaded connections of the steel spring shock absorber.

5. Remove the mounting nuts from the top of the steel spring shock absorber.

6. Loosen the bottom mounting bolt from the steel spring shock absorber.

7. Insert a block of wood between the sub-frame and the upper rear transverse link, this is needed to press down on the axle. Press the axle down with a block of wood. Remove the mounting bolt.

8. Remove the steel spring shock absorber.

To install:

9. Install the steel spring shock absorber with guide pins in the upper holes on the body.

10. Hand tighten all the mounting nuts and bolts, then tightening in sequence starting with the top steel spring shock absorber mounting nuts.

11. Note the following tightening specifications:

- Steel spring shock absorber to body: 37 ft. lbs. (50 Nm) plus an additional 180 degree turn.
- Steel spring shock absorber to wheel bearing housing (new bolt and nut): 66 ft. lbs. (90 Nm), plus an additional 90 degree turn.
- Install the wheels and tighten the bolts to 133 ft. lbs. (180 Nm).

UPPER FRONT TRANSVERSE LINK

REMOVAL & INSTALLATION

Air Spring Suspension

1. Before servicing the vehicle, refer to the precautions.

2. Activate the vehicle lift mode and place the vehicle on the lifting platform.

3. Bleed the rear air spring shock absorber with the VAS 5051B or equivalent.

4. Remove the wheels and raise the vehicle.

✳✳ WARNING

During assembly work, make sure that no indentations form on the protective boot of the air spring shock absorber!

5. For vehicles with dynamic headlamp range control. Remove the connection for the coupling rod from the rear level control system sensor at the transverse link.

6. Remove the threaded connection of the cable bracket. Remove the stone chip protective molding, if present.

7. Turn the wheel hub until one of the holes for the wheel bolts is on top. Support the wheel bearing housing.

8. Remove the nuts and bolts from the upper front transverse link.

9. Remove the upper front transverse link.

To install:

10. Insert the upper front transverse link in the vehicle and tighten the bolts by hand.

11. Install the bottom mounting bolt to the steel spring shock absorber.

➡ **All bolts at suspension parts with bonded rubber bushings must always be tightened in curb weight position (unloaded condition). Bonded rubber bushings can only be turned to a limited extent.**

Parts with bonded rubber bushings must therefore be brought into a position that corresponds to the position in driving mode before being tightened (curb weight position).

12. Note the following tightening specifications:

- Front upper transverse link to wheel bearing housing (new nuts and bolts): 111 ft. lbs. (150 Nm), plus an additional 90° turn.
- Steel spring shock absorber with coupling rod to wheel bearing housing 66 ft. lbs. (90 Nm), plus an additional 90° turn.
- Front upper transverse link to sub-frame (new nuts and bolts): 66 ft. lbs. (90 Nm), plus an additional 90° turn.
- Cable bracket to the front upper transverse link: 6 ft. lbs. (8 Nm).
- Coupling rod from the rear level control system to the front upper transverse link: 6 ft. lbs. (8 Nm).
- Wheels: tighten the bolts to 133 ft. lbs. (180 Nm).
- Fill the rear air spring shock absorber using the VAS 5051B or equivalent scan tool.

Steel Spring Suspension

1. Before servicing the vehicle, refer to the precautions.

2. Loosen the wheel bolts, raise the vehicle and remove the wheels.

3. Loosen the threaded connection between the steel spring shock absorber and the coupling rod at the wheel bearing housing.

4. Loosen the bottom mounting bolt from the steel spring shock absorber.

5. Insert a block of wood between the sub-frame and the upper rear transverse link, this is needed to press down on the axle. Press the axle down with a block of wood. Remove the mounting bolt.

6. For vehicles with dynamic headlamp range control. Remove the connection for the coupling rod from the rear level control system sensor at the transverse link.

7. Remove the threaded connection of the cable bracket. Remove the stone chip protective molding, if present.

8. Turn the wheel hub until one of the holes for the wheel bolts is on top. Support the wheel bearing housing.

9. Remove the nuts and bolts from the upper front transverse link.

10. Remove the upper front transverse link.

To install:

11. Insert the upper front transverse link in the vehicle and tighten the bolts by hand.

12. Insert the block of wood between the sub-frame and the upper rear transverse link. Press the axle down with a block of wood.

13. Install the bottom mounting bolt to the steel spring shock absorber.

➡ **All bolts at suspension parts with bonded rubber bushings must always be tightened in curb weight position (unloaded condition). Bonded rubber bushings can only be turned to a limited extent.**

Parts with bonded rubber bushings must therefore be brought into a position that corresponds to the position in driving mode before being tightened (curb weight position).

14. Note the following tightening specifications:

- Front upper transverse link to wheel bearing housing (new nuts and bolts): 111 ft. lbs. (150 Nm), plus an additional 90° turn.
- Steel spring shock absorber with coupling rod to wheel bearing housing 66 ft. lbs. (90 Nm), plus an additional 90° turn.
- Front upper transverse link to sub-frame (new nuts and bolts): 66 ft. lbs. (90 Nm), plus an additional 90° turn.
- Cable bracket to the front upper transverse link: 6 ft. lbs. (8 Nm).
- Coupling rod from the rear level control system to the front upper transverse link: 6 ft. lbs. (8 Nm).
- Wheels: tighten the bolts to 133 ft. lbs. (180 Nm).

UPPER REAR TRANSVERSE LINK

REMOVAL & INSTALLATION

Air Spring Suspension

1. Before servicing the vehicle, refer to the precautions.

2. Activate the vehicle lift mode and place the vehicle on the lifting platform.

3. Bleed the rear air spring shock absorber with the VAS 5051B or equivalent.

4. Remove the wheels and raise the vehicle.

❋ WARNING

During assembly work, make sure that no indentations form on the protective boot of the air spring shock absorber!

5. Turn the wheel hub until one of the holes for the wheel bolts is on top. Support the wheel bearing housing.

6. Remove the mounting bolts from the rear upper transverse link, and carefully remove the transverse link.

To install:

7. Insert the rear upper transverse link in the vehicle and tighten the bolts by hand. Insert the rear upper transverse link in the vehicle and tighten the bolts by hand. Tighten the bolt for the front upper transverse link on the wheel bearing housing by hand.

8. Note the following tightening specifications:

- Rear upper transverse link to wheel bearing housing (new nuts and bolts): 111 ft. lbs. (150 Nm), plus an additional 90° turn.
- Air spring shock absorber with coupling rod to wheel bearing housing 66 ft. lbs. (90 Nm), plus an additional 90° turn.
- Rear upper transverse link to sub-frame (new nuts and bolts): 66 ft. lbs. (90 Nm), plus an additional 90° turn.
- Front upper transverse link to sub-frame (new nuts and bolts): 66 ft. lbs. (90 Nm), plus an additional 90° turn.
- Wheels: tighten the bolts to 133 ft. lbs. (180 Nm).
- Fill the rear air spring shock absorber using the VAS 5051B or equivalent scan tool.

Steel Spring Suspension

1. Before servicing the vehicle, refer to the precautions.

2. Loosen the wheel bolts, raise the vehicle and remove the wheels.

3. Loosen the threaded connection between the steel spring shock absorber and the coupling rod at the wheel bearing housing.

4. Loosen the bottom mounting bolt from the steel spring shock absorber.

5. Insert a block of wood between the sub-frame and the upper rear transverse link, this is needed to press down on the axle. Press the axle down with a block of wood. Remove the mounting bolt.

6. Turn the wheel hub until one of the holes for the wheel bolts is on top. Support the wheel bearing housing.

7. Remove the mounting bolts from the rear upper transverse link, and carefully remove the transverse link.

To install:

8. Install the block of wood between the sub-frame and the upper rear transverse link. Press the axle down with a block of wood.

9. Insert the rear upper transverse link in the vehicle and tighten the bolts by hand. Insert the rear upper transverse link in the vehicle and tighten the bolts by hand. Tighten the bolt for the front upper transverse link on the wheel bearing housing by hand.

10. Install the bolts between the steel spring shock absorber and the coupling rod at the wheel bearing housing.

➡All bolts at suspension parts with bonded rubber bushings must always be tightened in curb weight position (unloaded condition). Bonded rubber bushings can only be turned to a limited extent.

Parts with bonded rubber bushings must therefore be brought into a position that corresponds to the position in driving mode before being tightened (curb weight position).

11. Note the following tightening specifications:
- Rear upper transverse link to wheel bearing housing (new nuts and bolts): 111 ft. lbs. (150 Nm), plus an additional 90° turn.
- Air spring shock absorber with coupling rod to wheel bearing housing 66 ft. lbs. (90 Nm), plus an additional 90° turn.
- Rear upper transverse link to sub-frame (new nuts and bolts): 66 ft. lbs. (90 Nm), plus an additional 90° turn.
- Front upper transverse link to sub-frame (new nuts and bolts): 66 ft. lbs. (90 Nm), plus an additional 90° turn.
- Wheels: tighten the bolts to 133 ft. lbs. (180 Nm).

WHEEL BEARINGS

REMOVAL & INSTALLATION

Steel Spring Suspension
See Figure 158.

1. Before servicing the vehicle, refer to the precautions.

2. Loosen the 12-point nut for the drive axle on the wheel hub.

3. Loosen the wheel bolts, raise the vehicle and remove the wheels.

4. Loosen the threaded connection between the steel spring shock absorber and the coupling rod at the wheel bearing housing.

5. Loosen the bottom mounting bolt from the steel spring shock absorber.

6. Insert a block of wood between the sub-frame and the upper rear transverse link, this is needed to press down on the axle. Press the axle down with a block of wood. Remove the mounting bolt.

7. Remove the brake caliper and brake disc. Secure the brake caliper to the body so that the weight of the caliper does not stress or damage the brake hose or brake line.

8. Remove the coupling rod. Refer to Coupling Rod.

9. Release the harness connector at the parking brake motor of the electromechanical parking brake and disconnect.

10. Release the connector from the rear speed sensor and remove it.

11. Remove the bolt and the bracket with the rear speed sensor lines.

12. Press the drive axle out of the wheel bearing housing to the stop.

13. Remove the top and bottom wheel bearing unit mounting bolts.

14. Remove the wheel bearing unit together with the T10103 bearing puller.

To install:

15. Insert the wheel bearing unit and mounting bolts, tighten by hand.

16. Tighten the wheel bearing unit mounting bolts to 60 ft. lbs. (80 Nm) plus an additional 120° turn

17. Carefully pull in the drive axle. Install the coupling rod.

18. Insert a block of wood between the sub-frame and the upper rear transverse link, this is needed to press down on the axle. Press the axle down with a block of wood. Remove the mounting bolt.

19. Install the brake caliper and brake disc.

20. Install the wheel and tighten the wheel bolts to 133 ft. lbs. (180 Nm).

21. Install the drive axle twelve-point nut and follow the tightening sequence:
   a. Replace the 12-point axle nut.
   b. Press the brake pedal. A second technician will be needed.
   c. Pre-tighten the 12-point nut to 110 ft. lbs. (150 Nm).
   d. Lower the vehicle onto its wheels.
   e. Tighten the 12-point axle nut to 369 ft. lbs. (500 Nm).

➡All bolts at suspension parts with bonded rubber bushings must always be tightened in curb weight position (unloaded condition). Bonded rubber bushings can only be turned to a limited extent.

Parts with bonded rubber bushings must therefore be brought into a position that corresponds to the position in driving mode before being tightened (curb weight position).

22. Note the following tightening specifications:
- Coupling rod to stabilizer bar (new nuts): 74 ft. lbs. (100 Nm).
- Steel spring shock absorber with coupling rod to wheel bearing housing 66 ft. lbs. (90 Nm), plus an additional 90° turn.
- Mounting bolts for the wheel bearing unit: 60 ft. lbs. (80 Nm) plus an additional 120° turn
- Bolt for the cable bracket on the wheel bearing housing: 7 ft. lbs. (10 Nm)

Air Spring Suspension

1. Before servicing the vehicle, refer to the precautions.

2. Activate the vehicle lift mode and place the vehicle on the lifting platform.

3. Loosen the 12-point nut for the drive axle on the wheel hub

4. Bleed the rear air spring shock absorber with the VAS 5051B or equivalent.

5. Remove the wheels and raise the vehicle.

6. Remove the brake caliper and brake disc. Secure the brake caliper to the body so that the weight of the caliper does not stress or damage the brake hose or brake line.

7. Remove the coupling rod. Refer to Coupling Rod.

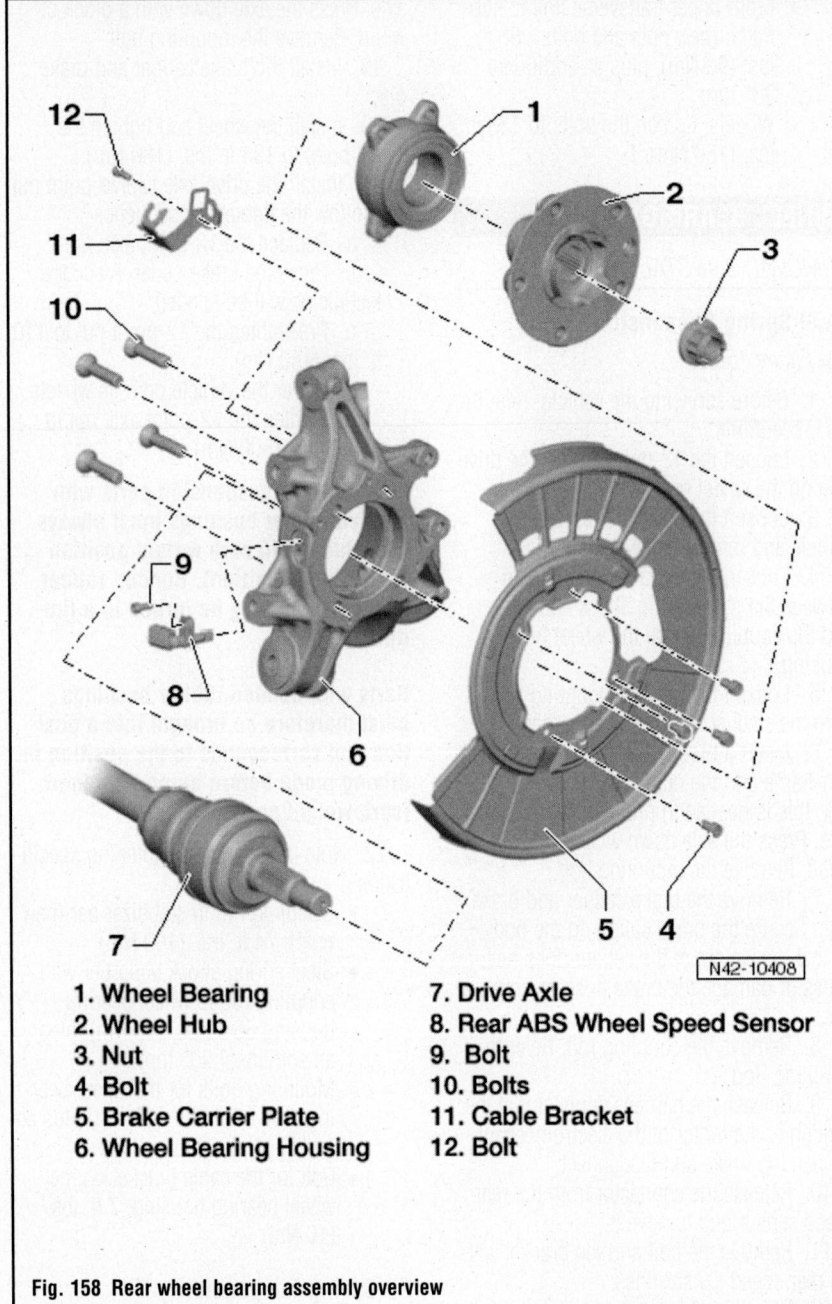

1. Wheel Bearing
2. Wheel Hub
3. Nut
4. Bolt
5. Brake Carrier Plate
6. Wheel Bearing Housing
7. Drive Axle
8. Rear ABS Wheel Speed Sensor
9. Bolt
10. Bolts
11. Cable Bracket
12. Bolt

N42-10408

Fig. 158 Rear wheel bearing assembly overview

To install:

14. Insert the wheel bearing unit and mounting bolts, tighten by hand.

15. Tighten the wheel bearing unit mounting bolts to 60 ft. lbs. (80 Nm) plus an additional 120° turn

16. Carefully pull in the drive axle. Install the coupling rod.

17. Install the brake caliper and brake disc.

18. Install the wheel and tighten the wheel bolts to 133 ft. lbs. (180 Nm).

19. Install the drive axle twelve-point nut and follow the tightening sequence:

   a. Replace the 12-point axle nut.

   b. Press the brake pedal. A second technician will be needed.

   c. Pre-tighten the 12-point nut to 110 ft. lbs. (150 Nm).

   d. Lower the vehicle onto its wheels.

   e. Tighten the 12-point axle nut to 369 ft. lbs. (500 Nm).

➡**All bolts at suspension parts with bonded rubber bushings must always be tightened in curb weight position (unloaded condition). Bonded rubber bushings can only be turned to a limited extent.**

Parts with bonded rubber bushings must therefore be brought into a position that corresponds to the position in driving mode before being tightened (curb weight position).

20. Note the following tightening specifications:

   • Coupling rod to stabilizer bar (new nuts): 74 ft. lbs. (100 Nm).

   • Steel spring shock absorber with coupling rod to wheel bearing housing 66 ft. lbs. (90 Nm), plus an additional 90° turn.

   • Mounting bolts for the wheel bearing unit: 60 ft. lbs. (80 Nm) plus an additional 120° turn

   • Bolt for the cable bracket on the wheel bearing housing: 7 ft. lbs. (10 Nm).

   • Fill the rear air spring shock absorber using the VAS 5051B or equivalent scan tool.

8. Release the harness connector at the parking brake motor of the electromechanical parking brake and disconnect.

9. Release the connector from the rear speed sensor and remove it.

10. Remove the bolt and the bracket with the rear speed sensor lines.

11. Press the drive axle out of the wheel bearing housing to the stop.

12. Remove the top and bottom wheel bearing unit mounting bolts.

13. Remove the wheel bearing unit together with the T10103 bearing puller.

VOLKSWAGEN

Diagnostic Trouble Codes

DIAGNOSTIC TROUBLE CODES

OBD II VEHICLE APPLICATIONS

VOLKSWAGEN

BEETLE
2011–2012
- 2.0L L4 TFSI..... Engine Code: CBFA
- 2.0L L4 TFSI..... Engine Code: CCTA
- 2.0L L4 TFSI..... Engine Code: CBFA
- 2.5L L5 MFI..... Engine Code: CBTA
- 2.5L L5 MFI.... Engine Code: CBUA

CC
2011–2012
- 2.0L L4 TFSI..... Engine Code: CBFA
- 2.0L L4 TFSI..... Engine Code: CCTA
- 2.0L L4 TFSI..... Engine Code: CBFA
- 3.6L L4 MFI.... Engine Code: CNNA

EOS
2011–2012
- 2.0L L4 TFSI..... Engine Code: CBFA
- 2.0L L4 TFSI..... Engine Code: CCTA

GTI
2011–2012
- 2.0L L4 TFSI..... Engine Code: CBFA
- 2.0L L4 TFSI..... Engine Code: CCTA

GOLF
2011–2012
- 2.0L L4 MFI..... Engine Code: CJAA
- 2.0L L4 MFI..... Engine Code: CRZA
- 2.0L L4 MFI..... Engine Code: CJAA
- 2.5L L5 MFI.... Engine Code: CBUA
- 2.5L L5 MFI..... Engine Code: CBTA

JETTA, GLI
2011–2012
- 2.0L L4 TFSI..... Engine Code: CBFA
- 2.0L L4 TFSI..... Engine Code: CCTA
- 2.0L L4 MFI..... Engine Code: CBPA
- 2.0L L4 MFI..... Engine Code: CJAA
- 2.5L L5 MFI..... Engine Code: CBTA
- 2.5L L5 MFI.... Engine Code: CBUA
- 2.5L L5 MFI.... Engine Code: CBUA

PASSAT
2011–2012
- 2.0L L4 MFI..... Engine Code: CKRA
- 2.0L L4 MFI..... Engine Code: CKRA
- 2.5L L5 MFI.... Engine Code: CBUA
- 2.5L L5 MFI..... Engine Code: CBTA
- 3.6L L4 MFI.... Engine Code: CDVB
- 3.6L L4 MFI..... Engine Code: CJRA

ROUTAN
2011–2012
- 3.6L L4 MFI..... Engine Code: CJRA

TIGUAN
2011–2012
- 2.0L L4 TFSI..... Engine Code: CCTA

TOUAREG
2011–2012
- 3.0L V6 TFSI.... Engine Code: CGFA
- 3.0L V6 MFI..... Engine Code: CATA
- 3.6L V6 FSI.... Engine Code: CGRA

OBD II Trouble Code List (P0XXX Codes)

DTC	Trouble Code Title and Conditions
DTC: P0001 **1T ECM, MIL: Yes** **Year:** 2011, 2012 **Model:** CC, Passat, Routan, Touareg **Engine:** 3.0L V6, 3.6L V6	**FUEL QUANTITY CONTROL CIRCUIT/OPEN:** With the ignition on and the ECM command of the Fuel Quantity Solenoid off. The ECM does not detect voltage on the Fuel Quantity Solenoid Control circuit for 0.2 seconds.
DTC: P0003 **1T ECM, MIL: Yes** **Year:** 2011, 2012 **Model:** CC, Passat, Routan, Touareg **Engine:** 3.0L V6, 3.6L V6	**FUEL QUANTITY CONTROL CIRCUIT LOW:** With the ignition on and the ECM command of the Fuel Quantity Solenoid off. The ECM detects that the Fuel Quantity Solenoid Control circuit voltage is shorted to ground for 0.2 seconds.
DTC: P0004 **1T ECM, MIL: Yes** **Year:** 2011, 2012 **Model:** CC, Passat, Routan, Touareg **Engine:** 3.0L V6, 3.6L V6	**FUEL QUANTITY CONTROL CIRCUIT HIGH:** With the ignition on and the ECM command of the Fuel Quantity Solenoid on. The ECM detects excessive current on the Fuel Quantity Solenoid Control circuit for 0.2 seconds.
DTC: P000A **2T ECM, MIL: Yes** **Year:** 2012 **Model:** Beetle, Eos, Golf, GTI, Jetta, Passat, Routan, Touareg **Engine:** 2.0L L4, 2.5L L5, V6	**BANK 1 CAMSHAFT (A or 1) POSITION SLOW RESPONSE:** The actual camshaft phasing position does not match the desired camshaft phasing position during camshaft phasing position changes. * Engine speed, 600 - 6320 RPM * Engine oil temp -48 to 180 °C * ECT -48 to 143 °C * Time after engine start > 1.5 to 3 Sec. * Number of checks 4
DTC: P000B **2T ECM, MIL: Yes** **Year:** 2011, 2012 **Model:** Beetle, Eos, Golf, GTI, Jetta, Passat, Routan, Touareg **Engine:** 2.0L L4, 2.5L L5, V6	**BANK 1 CAMSHAFT (B or 2) POSITION SLOW RESPONSE:** Variable Valve Timing (VVT) rationality is monitored under the following conditions: (1) Cam phasing is commanded off of the default (lock-pin) position; (2) Oil temperature is between -12° C to 139° C (10° F to 282° F); (3) Battery voltage is greater than 10 Volts; Engine speed is at least 650 to 1400 rpm, depending on oil temperature. (4) No CMP sensor, CKP sensor or OBDI plausibility errors. Before VVT can be enabled, reference adaptation must be completed. The actual camshaft phasing position does not match the desired camshaft phasing position during camshaft phasing position changes.
DTC: P000C **2T ECM, MIL: Yes** **Year:** 2011, 2012 **Model:** CC, Passat, Routan, Touareg **Engine:** 3.0L V6, 3.6L V6	**BANK 2 CAMSHAFT (A or 1) POSITION SLOW RESPONSE :** Variable Valve Timing (VVT) rationality is monitored under the following conditions: (1) Cam phasing is commanded off of the default (lock-pin) position; (2) Oil temperature is between -12° C to 139° C (10° F to 282° F); (3) Battery voltage is greater than 10 Volts; Engine speed is at least 650 to 1400 rpm, depending on oil temperature; (4) No CMP sensor, CKP sensor or OBDI plausibility errors. Before VVT can be enabled, reference adaptation must be completed. The actual camshaft phasing position does not match the desired camshaft phasing position during camshaft phasing position changes.
DTC: P000D **2T ECM, MIL: Yes** **Year:** 2011, 2012 **Model:** CC, Passat, Routan, Touareg **Engine:** 3.0L V6, 3.6L V6	**BANK 2 CAMSHAFT (B or 2) POSITION SLOW RESPONSE:** Variable Valve Timing (VVT) rationality is monitored under the following conditions: (1) Cam phasing is commanded off of the default (lock-pin) position; (2) Oil temperature is between -12° C to 139° C (10° F to 282° F); (3) Battery voltage is greater than 10 Volts; Engine speed is at least 650 to 1400 RPM, depending on oil temperature; (4) No CMP sensor, CKP sensor or OBDI plausibility errors. Before VVT can be enabled, reference adaptation must be completed. The actual camshaft phasing position does not match the desired camshaft phasing position during camshaft phasing position changes.
DTC: P000E **2T PCM, MIL: Yes** **Year:** 2011, 2012 **Model:** Golf, Jetta, Passat **Engine:** 2.0L L4	**Fuel Volume Regulator Control Exceeded Learning Limit:** Number of learning points at adaptation limits >= 8 of 64 Upper limit > 1.2 Monitoring Time Length: 100 m Sec.

DTC	Trouble Code Title and Conditions
DTC: P0010 **2T ECM, MIL: Yes** **Year:** 2011, 2012 **Model:** Beetle, CC, Eos, Golf, GTI, GLI, Jetta, Passat, Routan, Tiguan, Touareg **Engine:** 2.0L L4, 2.5L L5, 3.0L V6, 3.6L V6	**"A or 1" Camshaft Position Actuator Circuit / Open (Bank 1):** The Powertrain Control Module (PCM) detects that the actual state of the VVT Intake Solenoid does not match the intended state. * Camshaft valve, commanded off * Engine speed, >80 RPM
DTC: P0011 **2T ECM, MIL: Yes** **Year:** 2011, 2012 **Model:** Beetle, CC, Eos, Golf, GTI, GLI, Jetta, Passat, Routan, Tiguan, Touareg **Engine:** 2.0L L4, 2.5L L5, 3.0L V6, 3.6L V6	**"A or 1" Camshaft Position Timing - Over-Advanced (Bank 1):** * Time after engine start > 10 to 300 Sec. * Oil temperature -48 to 143.30 °C * Frequency 4 times * Frequency cold 2 times
DTC: P0012 **2T ECM, MIL: Yes** **Year:** 2011, 2012 **Model:** Beetle, CC, Eos, Golf, GTI, GLI, Jetta, Passat, Routan, Tiguan, Touareg **Engine:** 2.0L L4, 2.5L L5, 3.0L V6, 3.6L V6	**"A or 1" Camshaft Position Over-Retarded (Bank 1):** Engine started and driven at an engine speed of more than 400rpm; and the ECM detected the camshaft timing exceeded the minimum calibrated retarded value, or the camshaft remained in the retarded position during the CCM test. The valve timing did not change from the current valve timing or it remained fixed during the testing. **Note: The camshaft adjustment is load- and RPM dependant. The electrical camshaft adjustment valve 1 switches oil pressure onto camshaft adjuster (mechanical adjustment mechanism), which adjusts the camshaft.**
DTC: P0013 **2T ECM, MIL: Yes** **Year:** 2011, 2012 **Model:** Beetle, CC, Eos, Golf, GTI, GLI, Jetta, Passat, Routan, Tiguan, Touareg **Engine:** 2.0L L4, 2.5L L5, 3.0L V6, 3.6L V6	**"B or 2" Camshaft Position - Actuator Circuit Bank 1:** With the engine running and battery voltage greater than 10.4 Volts. The Powertrain Control Module (PCM) detects that the actual state of the VVT intake solenoid, does not match the intended state. • Battery voltage below 11.5 volts * Camshaft valve, Off * Engine speed, >80 RPM
DTC: P0014 **2T ECM, MIL: Yes** **Year:** 2011, 2012 **Model:** Beetle, CC, Eos, Golf, GTI, GLI, Jetta, Passat, Routan, Tiguan, Touareg **Engine:** 2.0L L4, 2.5L L5, 3.0L V6, 3.6L V6	**"B or 2" Camshaft Position - Timing Over-Advanced or System Performance Bank 1:** The Powertrain Control Module (PCM) detects that the CPS circuit is open, shorted to ground or shorted to power. * Time after engine start, >30 Sec. * Engine speed, 800-6400 RPM * Modeled oil Temperature, -10.5–105 °C * ECT -20.3–114.8 °C * Frequency, 3 times
DTC: P0016 **1T ECM, MIL: Yes** **Year:** 2011, 2012 **Model:** Beetle, CC, Eos, Golf, GTI, GLI, Jetta, Passat, Routan, Tiguan, Touareg **Engine:** 2.0L L4, 2.5L L5, 3.0L V6, 3.6L V6	**CRANKSHAFT/CAMSHAFT TIMING MISALIGNMENT:** Engine cranking and Engine running Powertrain Control Module (PCM) detects an error when the camshaft position is out of phase with the crankshaft position. One Trip Fault. Three good trips to turn off the MIL.
DTC: P0017 **1T ECM, MIL: Yes** **Year:** 2011, 2012 **Model:** Beetle, CC, Eos, Golf, GTI, GLI, Jetta, Passat, Routan, Tiguan, Touareg **Engine:** 2.0L L4, 2.5L L5, 3.0L V6, 3.6L V6	**Crankshaft Position – Camshaft Position Correlation Bank 1 Sensor (B or2):** The Powertrain Control Module (PCM) detects an error when the camshaft position is out of phase with the crankshaft position. One Trip Fault. Three good trips to turn off the MIL. * Engine speed, <1000 RPM * Engine load, <30% * ECT, -15–110° C * Time after engine start, >5 Sec.

DTC	Trouble Code Title and Conditions
DTC: P0018 **1T ECM, MIL: Yes** **Year:** 2011, 2012 **Model:** CC, Passat, Routan, Touareg **Engine:** 3.0L V6, 3.6L V6	**Crankshaft Position – Camshaft Position Correlation Bank 2 Sensor A:** The Powertrain Control Module (PCM) detects an error when the camshaft position is out of phase with the crankshaft position. One Trip Fault. Three good trips to turn off the MIL. * Engine speed, <1000 RPM * Engine load, <30% * ECT, -15–110° C * Time after engine start, >5 Sec.
DTC: P0019 **1T ECM, MIL: Yes** **Year:** 2011, 2012 **Model:** CC, Passat, Routan, Touareg **Engine:** 3.0L V6, 3.6L V6	**-CRANKSHAFT/CAMSHAFT TIMING MISALIGNMENT:** The Powertrain Control Module (PCM) detects an error when the camshaft position is out of phase with the crankshaft position. One Trip Fault. Three good trips to turn off the MIL. * Engine speed, <1000 RPM * Engine load, <30% * ECT, -15–110° C * Time after engine start, >5 Sec.
DTC: P0020 **Year:** 2011, 2012 **Model:** CC, Passat, Routan, Touareg **Engine:** 3.0L V6, 3.6L V6	**-BANK 2CAMSHAFT 1 POSITION ACTUATOR CIRCUIT OPEN:** With the engine running and battery voltage greater than 10.4 Volts. The Powertrain Control Module (PCM) detects that the actual state of the VVT Intake Solenoid does not match the intended state. * Engine speed, >550 RPM * ECT, -7.5° C * Time after engine start, >3.5 Sec. * Number of checks 3 * Time length for more than 1.5 Sec.
DTC: P0021 **1T ECM, MIL: Yes** **Year:** 2011, 2012 **Model:** CC, Passat, Routan, Touareg **Engine:** 3.0L V6, 3.6L V6	**Intake (A) Camshaft Position Timing - Over-Advanced (Bank 2):** The Powertrain Control Module (PCM) detects that the actual state of the VVT Intake Solenoid does not match the intended state. * Engine speed, >550 RPM * ECT, -7.5° C * Time after engine start, >3.5 Sec. * Number of checks 3 * Time length for more than 1.5 Sec.
DTC: P0023 **1T ECM, MIL: Yes** **Year:** 2011, 2012 **Model:** CC, Passat, Routan, Touareg **Engine:** 3.0L V6, 3.6L V6	**"B or 2" Camshaft Position - Actuator Circuit Bank 2:** With the engine running and battery voltage greater than 10.4 Volts. The Powertrain Control Module (PCM) detects that the actual state of the VVT Intake Solenoid does not match the intended state. * Camshaft valve, Off * Engine speed, >80 RPM
DTC: P0024 **1T ECM, MIL: Yes** **Year:** 2011, 2012 **Model:** CC, Passat, Routan, Touareg **Engine:** 3.0L V6, 3.6L V6	**"B" Camshaft Position - Timing Over-Advanced or System Performance Bank 2:** The Powertrain Control Module (PCM) detects that the actual state of the VVT Intake Solenoid does not match the intended state. * Engine speed, >550 RPM * ECT, -7.5° C * Time after engine start, >3.5 Sec. * Number of checks 3 * Time length for more than 1.5 Sec.
DTC: P0030 **1T ECM, MIL: Yes** **Year:** 2011, 2012 **Model:** Beetle, CC, Eos, Golf, GTI, GLI, Jetta, Passat, Routan, Tiguan, Touareg **Engine:** 2.0L L4, 2.5L L5, 3.0L V6, 3.6L V6	**HO2S Heater Control Circuit (Bank 1, Sensor 1):** With the ignition on and the Oxygen Sensor Heater command on. The ECM detects an implausible voltage on the bank 1, sensor 1heater control circuit for 2.0 seconds. * Heater, Commanded off * Time after engine start, >10 Sec.
DTC: P0031 **1T ECM, MIL: Yes** **Year:** 2011, 2012 **Model:** Beetle, CC, Eos, Golf, GTI, GLI, Jetta, Passat, Routan, Tiguan, Touareg **Engine:** 2.0L L4, 2.5L L5, 3.0L V6, 3.6L V6	**HO2S Heater Control Circuit Low (Bank 1, Sensor 1) Short to ground:** Continuously during O2 heater operation with battery voltage between 10.4 and 15.75 Volts. The Powertrain Control Module (PCM) detects that the O2 sensor heater element input is below the minimum acceptable voltage. One trip fault. Three good trips to turn off the MIL.

DTC	Trouble Code Title and Conditions
DTC: P0032 **1T ECM, MIL: Yes** **Year:** 2011, 2012 **Model:** Beetle, CC, Eos, Golf, GTI, GLI, Jetta, Passat, Routan, Tiguan, Touareg **Engine:** 2.0L L4, 2.5L L5, 3.0L V6, 3.6L V6	**HO2S Heater Control Circuit High (Bank 1, Sensor 1):** The Powertrain Control Module (PCM) detects that the O2 sensor heater element input is above the maximum acceptable voltage. One trip fault. Three good trips to turn off the MIL. * Continuously during O2 heater operation with battery voltage between 10.4 and 15.75 Volts. * Heater, Commanded On * Time after engine start, > 5 seconds
DTC: P0036 **2T ECM, MIL: Yes** **Year:** 2011, 2012 **Model:** Beetle, CC, Eos, Golf, GTI, Jetta, Passat, Tiguan **Engine:** 2.0L L4	**HO2S Heater Circuit (Bank 1, Sensor 3) Open Circuit** The Powertrain Control Module (PCM) detects that the O2 sensor heater element input is above the maximum acceptable voltage. * Engine speed, >80 RPM * Heater commanded off
DTC: P0036 **1T ECM, MIL: Yes** **Year:** 2011, 2012 **Model:** Beetle, CC, Eos, Golf, GTI, GLI, Jetta, Passat, Routan, Tiguan, Touareg **Engine:** 2.0L L4, 2.5L L5, 3.0L V6, 3.6L V6	**HO2S Heater Control Circuit (Bank 1, Sensor 2):** With the ignition on and the Oxygen Sensor Heater command on. The ECM detects an implausible voltage on the bank 1, sensor 2heater control circuit for 2.0 seconds. * Heater, Commanded off * Engine speed, >80 RPM
DTC: P0037 **1T ECM, MIL: Yes** **Year:** 2011, 2012 **Model:** Beetle, CC, Eos, Golf, GTI, GLI, Jetta, Passat, Routan, Tiguan, Touareg **Engine:** 2.0L L4, 2.5L L5, 3.0L V6, 3.6L V6	**O2 SENSOR 1⁄2 HEATER CIRCUIT LOW:** Continuously during O2 heater operation with battery voltage between 10.4 and 15.75 Volts. The Powertrain Control Module (PCM) detects that the O2 sensor heater element input is below the minimum acceptable voltage. One trip fault. Three good trips to turn off the MIL.
DTC: P0038 **1T ECM, MIL: Yes** **Year:** 2011, 2012 **Model:** Beetle, CC, Eos, Golf, GTI, GLI, Jetta, Passat, Routan, Tiguan, Touareg **Engine:** 2.0L L4, 2.5L L5, 3.0L V6, 3.6L V6	**HO2S Heater Control Circuit High (Bank 1, Sensor 2):** The Powertrain Control Module (PCM) detects that the O2 sensor heater element input is above the maximum acceptable voltage. One trip fault. Three good trips to turn off the MIL. Continuously during O2 heater operation with battery voltage between 10.4 and 15.75 Volts.
DTC: P0040 **2T PCM, MIL: Yes** **Year:** 2011, 2012 **Model:** CC, Passat, Routan, Touareg **Engine:** 3.0L V6, 3.6L V6	**O2 Sensor Signals Swapped Bank 1 Sensor 1/ Bank 2 Sensor 1:** The Powertrain Control Module (PCM) detects that the O2 sensor harness connectors are swapped or shorted. One trip fault. Three good trips to turn off the MIL. * Lambda control, Closed loop * VVT, Ready, no fault
DTC: P0042 **2T ECM, MIL: Yes** **Year:** 2011, 2012 **Model:** Beetle, CC, Eos. Golf, GTI, GLI, Passat, Tiguan **Engine:** 2.0L L4, 2.5L L5	**HO2S Heater Control Circuit (Bank 1 Sensor 3):** The Powertrain Control Module (PCM) detects that the O2 sensor signal circuit is shorted. One trip fault. Three good trips to turn off the MIL. * Heater, Commanded off * Engine speed, > 80 RPM
DTC: P0043 **Year:** 2011, 2012 **Model:** Beetle, CC, Eos. Golf, GTI, GLI, Passat, Tiguan **Engine:** 2.0L L4, 2.5L L5	**HO2S Heater Control Circuit Low Bank 1 Sensor 3:** The Powertrain Control Module (PCM) detects that the O2 sensor signal circuit is shorted. * Engine speed > 80 RPM * Heater commanded off

DTC	Trouble Code Title and Conditions
DTC: P0043 **2T PCM, MIL: Yes** **Year:** 2011, 2012 **Model:** CC, Passat, Routan, Touareg **Engine:** 3.0L V6, 3.6L V6	**HO2S Heater Control Circuit Low (Bank 1, Sensor 2) short to ground:** * SULEV Time after engine start, >5 Sec * Heater commanded off * ULEV engine speed >80 RPM * Heater, commanded off
DTC: P0044 **2T PCM, MIL: Yes** **Year:** 2011, 2012 **Model:** CC, Passat, Routan, Touareg **Engine:** 3.0L V6, 3.6L V6	**HO2S Heater Control Circuit High (Bank 1, Sensor 2) Short to B+:** With the ignition on and the Oxygen Sensor Heater command on. The ECM detects an implausible signal on the bank 1, sensor 2 control circuit for 2.0 seconds.
DTC: P0044 **2T ECM, MIL: Yes** **Year:** 2011, 2012 **Model:** Beetle, CC, Eos. Golf, GTI, GLI, Passat, Tiguan **Engine:** 2.0L L4, 2.5L L5	**HO2S Heater Control Circuit High (Bank 1 Sensor 3):** The Powertrain Control Module (PCM) detects that the O2 sensor control circuit is shorted.
DTC: P0045 **2T ECM, MIL: Yes** **Year:** 2011, 2012 **Model:** Beetle, Eos, Golf, GTI, Jetta, Passat, Touareg, Routan **Engine:** 2.0L L4, 2.5L L5, 3.6L V6 VIN G	**Turbocharger Boost Control Solenoid "A" Circuit Open:** With the ignition on and the Boost Pressure Servo Motor command off. The ECM detects that the Boost Pressure Servo Motor Control circuit is open for 0.5 second.
DTC: P0046 **2T ECM, MIL: Yes** **Year:** 2011, 2012 **Model:** Beetle, CC, Eos, Golf, GTI, GLI, Jetta, Passat, Routan, Tiguan, Touareg **Engine:** 2.0L L4, 2.5L L5, 3.0L V6, 3.6L V6	**TURBOCHARGER BOOST CONTROL CIRCUIT/EXCESSIVE CURRENT:** With the ignition on and the Boost Pressure Servo Motor command off. The Boost Pressure Servo Motor reports an internal error to the ECM. .
DTC: P0047 **2T ECM, MIL: Yes** **Year:** 2011, 2012 **Model:** Beetle, CC, Eos, Golf, GTI, GLI, Jetta, Passat, Routan, Tiguan, Touareg **Engine:** 2.0L L4, 2.5L L5, 3.0L V6, 3.6L V6	**Turbocharger Boost Control Solenoid "A" Circuit Low:** With the ignition on and the Boost Pressure Servo Motor command off. The ECM detects that the (K137) Boost Pressure Servo Motor Control circuit is shorted to ground for 0.5 second.
DTC: P0048 **2T ECM, MIL: Yes** **Year:** 2011, 2012 **Model:** Beetle, CC, Eos, Golf, GTI, GLI, Jetta, Passat, Routan, Tiguan, Touareg **Engine:** 2.0L L4, 2.5L L5, 3.0L V6, 3.6L V6	**Turbocharger Boost Control Solenoid "A" Circuit High:** With the ignition on and the Boost Pressure Servo Motor command on. The ECM detects that the Boost Pressure Servo Motor Control circuit is shorted to voltage for 0.5 second.
DTC: P0050 **2T ECM, MIL: Yes** **Year:** 2011, 2012 **Model:** Beetle, CC, Eos, Golf, GTI, GLI, Jetta, Passat, Routan, Tiguan, Touareg **Engine:** 2.0L L4, 2.5L L5, 3.0L V6, 3.6L V6	**HO2S Heater Control Circuit Bank 2 Sensor 1:** * Time after engine start, >5 Sec. * Heater, Commanded off

DTC	Trouble Code Title and Conditions
DTC: P0051 **2T ECM, MIL: Yes** **Year:** 2011, 2012 **Model:** Beetle, CC, Eos, Golf, GTI, GLI, Jetta, Passat, Routan, Tiguan, Touareg **Engine:** 2.0L L4, 2.5L L5, 3.0L V6, 3.6L V6	**HO2S SENSOR 2/1 HEATER CIRCUIT LOW:** Continuously during O2 heater operation with battery voltage between 10.4 and 15.75 Volts. The Powertrain Control Module (PCM) detects that the O2 sensor heater element input is below the minimum acceptable voltage. One trip fault. Three good trips to turn off the MIL.
DTC: P0052 **2T ECM, MIL: Yes** **Year:** 2011, 2012 **Model:** Beetle, CC, Eos, Golf, GTI, GLI, Jetta, Passat, Routan, Tiguan, Touareg **Engine:** 2.0L L4, 2.5L L5, 3.0L V6, 3.6L V6	**HO2S SENSOR 2/1 HEATER CIRCUIT HIGH:** Continuously during O2 heater operation with battery voltage between 10.4 and 15.75Volts. The Powertrain Control Module (PCM) detects that the O2 sensor heater element input is above the maximum acceptable voltage. One trip fault. Three good trips to turn off the MIL.
DTC: P0053 **2T ECM, MIL: Yes** **Year:** 2011, 2012 **Model:** Beetle, CC, Eos, Golf, GTI, GLI, Jetta, Passat, Routan, Tiguan, Touareg **Engine:** 2.0L L4, 2.5L L5, 3.0L V6, 3.6L V6	**HO2S SENSOR 1/1 HEATER RESISTANCE:** With the ignition on and the Oxygen Sensor Heater command on. The ECM detects an implausible voltage on the (K79) O2 1/1 Heater Control circuit for 2.0 seconds.
DTC: P0056 **2T ECM, MIL: Yes** **Year:** 2011, 2012 **Model:** Beetle, CC, Eos, Golf, GTI, GLI, Jetta, Passat, Routan, Tiguan, Touareg **Engine:** 2.0L L4, 2.5L L5, 3.0L V6, 3.6L V6	**HO2S Heater Control Circuit Bank 2 Sensor 2:** * Time after engine start, >5 Sec. * Heater, Commanded off
DTC: P0057 **2T ECM, MIL: Yes** **Year:** 2011, 2012 **Model:** Beetle, CC, Eos, Golf, GTI, GLI, Jetta, Passat, Routan, Tiguan, Touareg **Engine:** 2.0L L4, 2.5L L5, 3.0L V6, 3.6L V6	**HO2S SENSOR 2/2 HEATER CIRCUIT LOW:** Continuously during O2 heater operation with battery voltage between 10.4 and 15.75 volts. The Powertrain Control Module (PCM) detects that the O2 sensor heater element input is below the minimum acceptable voltage. One trip fault. Three good trips to turn off the MIL.
DTC: P0058 **2T ECM, MIL: Yes** **Year:** 2011, 2012 **Model:** Beetle, CC, Eos, Golf, GTI, GLI, Jetta, Passat, Routan, Tiguan, Touareg **Engine:** 2.0L L4, 2.5L L5, 3.0L V6, 3.6L V6	**HO2S SENSOR 2/2 HEATER CIRCUIT HIGH:** Continuously during O2 heater operation with battery voltage between 10.4 and 15.75 Volts. The Powertrain Control Module (PCM) detects that the O2 sensor heater element input is above the maximum acceptable voltage. One trip fault. Three good trips to turn off the MIL.
DTC: P0068 **2T ECM, MIL: Yes** **Year:** 2011, 2012 **Model:** Beetle, CC, Eos, Golf, GTI, GLI, Jetta, Passat, Routan, Tiguan, Touareg **Engine:** 2.0L L4, 2.5L L5, 3.0L V6, 3.6L V6	**MAP/MAF – Throttle Position Correlation:** * Fuel system monitor, running * Fuel adaptation, active, no fault * Lambda control, closed loop * Mass air flow, > 45 * Manifold to ambient pressure ratio, <0.82

DTC	Trouble Code Title and Conditions
DTC: P0069 **2T ECM, MIL: Yes** **Year:** 2011, 2012 **Model:** Beetle, CC, Eos, Golf, GTI, GLI, Jetta, Passat, Routan, Tiguan, Touareg **Engine:** 2.0L L4, 2.5L L5, 3.0L V6, 3.6L V6	**MANIFOLD PRESSURE/BAROMETRIC PRESSURE CORRELATION:** With the ignition on and at engine idle. There are no Sensor Reference Voltage DTC's. There are no other Boost Pressure related DTC's. There are no Inlet Pressure Sensor DTC's. The difference between the Boost Pressure Sensor Signal and the Inlet Pressure Sensor Signal is greater than 100 hpa (1.45 psi) for 4.0 seconds.
DTC: P0070 **2T ECM, MIL: Yes** **Year:** 2011, 2012 **Model:** Beetle, Eos, GTI, Jetta, Passat **Engine:** 2.0L L4	**Ambient Air Temp Sensor Short To B+:** * CAN active, Sensor signal circuit is shorted to B+
DTC: P0070 **2T ECM, MIL: Yes** **Year:** 2011, 2012 **Model:** Beetle, CC, Eos, Golf, GTI, GLI, Jetta, Passat, Routan, Tiguan, Touareg **Engine:** 2.0L L4, 2.5L L5, 3.0L V6, 3.6L V6	**Ambient Air Temperature:** * CAN active, signal circuit is shorted to ground or to sensor ground.
DTC: P0071 **2T ECM, MIL: Yes** **Year:** 2011, 2012 **Model:** Beetle, CC, Eos, Golf, GTI, GLI, Jetta, Passat, Routan, Tiguan, Touareg **Engine:** 2.0L L4, 2.5L L5, 3.0L V6, 3.6L V6	**Ambient Air Temperature Sensor Range/Performance:** Engine off time is greater than 480 minutes and the vehicle has been driven for one Minute, over 35 mph. Ambient temperature is greater than -64° C (-83°F). The PCM compares the ambient, engine coolant and intake air temperature sensor values. If engine coolant and intake air temperature sensors agree with each other, but ambient air temperature does not agree, the ambient air temperature sensor is declared as irrational. Two Trip Fault. Three good trips to turnoff the MIL.
DTC: P0072 **1T ECM, MIL: Yes** **Year:** 2011, 2012 **Model:** Beetle, CC, Eos, Golf, GTI, GLI, Jetta, Passat, Routan, Tiguan, Touareg **Engine:** 2.0L L4, 2.5L L5, 3.0L V6, 3.6L V6	**AMBIENT AIR TEMPERATURE SENSOR CIRCUIT LOW:** With the ignition on. Battery voltage greater than 10.4 volts. The Ambient Air Temperature (AAT) sensor circuit voltage at the TIPM is less than 0.078, of a volt for more than 2.8 seconds. One Trip Fault. Three good trips to clear the MIL.
DTC: P0073 **1 T ECM, MIL: Yes** **Year:** 2011, 2012 **Model:** Beetle, CC, Eos, Golf, GTI, GLI, Jetta, Passat, Routan, Tiguan, Touareg **Engine:** 2.0L L4, 2.5L L5, 3.0L V6, 3.6L V6	**AMBIENT AIR TEMPERATURE SENSOR CIRCUIT HIGH:** With the ignition on. Battery voltage greater than 10.4 volts. The Ambient Air Temperature (AAT) sensor circuit voltage at the TIPM is greater than 4.98 volts for more than 2.8 seconds. One Trip Fault. Three good trips to turn off the MIL.
DTC: P0087 **2T ECM, MIL: Yes** **Year:** 2011, 2012 **Model:** Beetle, CC, Eos, Golf, GTI, GLI, Jetta, Passat, Routan, Tiguan, Touareg **Engine:** 2.0L L4, 2.5L L5, 3.0L V6, 3.6L V6	**FUEL RAIL PRESSURE TOO LOW:** With the engine running. The ECM determines that the fuel rail pressure is too low for a given engine speed and load.

DTC	Trouble Code Title and Conditions
DTC: P0088 **2T ECM, MIL: Yes** **Year:** 2011, 2012 **Model:** Beetle, CC, Eos, Golf, GTI, GLI, Jetta, Passat, Routan, Tiguan, Touareg **Engine:** 2.0L L4, 2.5L L5, 3.0L V6, 3.6L V6	**FUEL RAIL PRESSURE TOO HIGH:** With the engine running. The ECM determines that the fuel rail pressure is too high for a given engine speed and load.
DTC: P0089 **2T ECM, MIL: Yes** **Year:** 2011, 2012 **Model:** Beetle, CC, Eos, Golf, GTI, GLI, Jetta, Passat, Routan, Tiguan, Touareg **Engine:** 2.0L L4, 2.5L L5, 3.0L V6, 3.6L V6	**Fuel Pressure Regulator 1 Performance:** * Time after engine start, 60 Sec. * Time after engine start, 60 Sec. * Fuel cut off, Not active * Time after fuel cut off, 20 Sec. * Time after engine start, 60 Sec.
DTC: P008A **2T ECM, MIL: Yes** **Year:** 2011, 2012 **Model:** Beetle, CC, Eos, Golf, GTI, GLI, Jetta, Passat, Routan, Tiguan, Touareg **Engine:** 2.0L L4, 2.5L L5, 3.0L V6, 3.6L V6	**Fuel System Pressure Sensor Low pressure system:** Actual pressure <40 kPa, monitoring time length 2 seconds.
DTC: P008B **2T ECM, MIL: Yes** **Year:** 2011, 2012 **Model:** Beetle, CC, Eos, Golf, GTI, GLI, Jetta, Passat, Routan, Tiguan, Touareg **Engine:** 2.0L L4, 2.5L L5, 3.0L V6, 3.6L V6	**Low Pressure Fuel System Pressure - Too High:** Actual pressure> 780 kPa, monitoring time length 2 seconds.
DTC: P0090 **2T ECM, MIL: Yes** **Year:** 2011, 2012 **Model:** Beetle, CC, Eos, Golf, GTI, GLI, Jetta, Passat, Routan, Tiguan, Touareg **Engine:** 2.0L L4, 2.5L L5, 3.0L V6, 3.6L V6	**FUEL PRESSURE 1 CONTROL CIRCUIT/OPEN:** With the ignition on and the Fuel Pressure Solenoid command off. The ECM detects that the (K370) Fuel Pressure Solenoid Control circuit is open for 0.28 seconds.
DTC: P0091 **2T ECM, MIL: Yes** **Year:** 2011, 2012 **Model:** Beetle, CC, Eos, Golf, GTI, GLI, Jetta, Passat, Routan, Tiguan, Touareg **Engine:** 2.0L L4, 2.5L L5, 3.0L V6, 3.6L V6	**-FUEL PRESSURE 1 CONTROL CIRCUIT LOW:** With the ignition on and the Fuel Pressure Solenoid command off. The ECM detects that the Fuel Pressure Solenoid Control circuit is shorted to ground for 0.22 seconds.
DTC: P0092 **2T ECM, MIL: Yes** **Year:** 2011, 2012 **Model:** Beetle, CC, Eos, Golf, GTI, GLI, Jetta, Passat, Routan, Tiguan, Touareg **Engine:** 2.0L L4, 2.5L L5, 3.0L V6, 3.6L V6	**Fuel Pressure Regulator 1 Control Circuit High:** With the ignition on and the Fuel Pressure Solenoid command on. The ECM detects excessive current on the Fuel Pressure Solenoid Control circuit for 0.28 seconds.

DTC	Trouble Code Title and Conditions
DTC: P0097 **2T ECM, MIL: Yes** **Year:** 2011, 2012 **Model:** Beetle, CC, Eos, Golf, GTI, GLI, Jetta, Passat, Routan, Tiguan, Touareg **Engine:** 2.0L L4, 2.5L L5, 3.0L V6, 3.6L V6	**Intake Air Temperature Sensor 2 Circuit Low:** * Time after engine start * Engine speed * No fuel cut off
DTC: P0098 **2T ECM, MIL: Yes** **Year:** 2011, 2012 **Model:** Beetle, CC, Eos, Golf, GTI, GLI, Jetta, Passat, Routan, Tiguan, Touareg **Engine:** 2.0L L4, 2.5L L5, 3.0L V6, 3.6L V6	**Intake Air Temperature Sensor 2 circuit high:** The ECM detects an Open in IAT sensor circuit. * Time after engine start * Engine speed * No fuel cut off
DTC: P00AF **2T ECM, MIL: Yes** **Year:** 2011, 2012 **Model:** Beetle, CC, Eos, Golf, GTI, GLI, Jetta, Passat, Routan, Tiguan, Touareg **Engine:** 2.0L L4, 2.5L L5, 3.0L V6, 3.6L V6	**Turbocharger Boost Control "A" Module Performance:** Boost pressure actuator stuck on or off. Control deviation > 15% or < -15% Time after engine start > 96000 m Sec
DTC: P00D1 **2T ECM, MIL: Yes** **Year:** 2011, 2012 **Model:** Beetle, CC, Eos, Golf, GTI, GLI, Jetta, Passat, Routan, Tiguan, Touareg **Engine:** 2.0L L4, 2.5L L5, 3.0L V6, 3.6L V6	**HO2S Bank 1 Sensor 1 Heater Output Warm Up Time Exceeded:** * Sensor temperature < 720 °C * Ambient temperature > -10 °C * Baro > 750 hPa * Battery voltage > 10.7 V * LSU heater control active, 20 min. up and down
DTC: P00D2 **2T ECM, MIL: Yes** **Year:** 2011, 2012 **Model:** Beetle, CC, Eos, Golf, GTI, GLI, Jetta, Passat, Routan, Tiguan, Touareg **Engine:** 2.0L L4, 2.5L L5, 3.0L V6, 3.6L V6	**HO2S Bank 1 Sensor 2 Heater Output Warm Up Time Exceeded:** * Sensor temperature < 720 °C * Ambient temperature > -10 °C * Baro > 750 hPa * Battery voltage > 10.7 V * LSU heater control active, 20 min. up and down
DTC: P00D5 **2T ECM, MIL: Yes** **Year:** 2011, 2012 **Model:** Beetle, CC, Eos, Golf, GTI, GLI, Jetta, Passat, Routan, Tiguan, Touareg **Engine:** 2.0L L4, 2.5L L5, 3.0L V6, 3.6L V6	**HO2S Bank 1 Sensor 1 to O2S Bank 1 Sensor 2 Implausible:** * Battery voltage > 10.7 V * LSU heater control active, modeled dew-point exceeded * Offset air fuel ratio > 0.05
DTC: P0100 **1 T ECM, MIL: Yes** **Year:** 2011, 2012 **Model:** Beetle, CC, Eos, Golf, GTI, GLI, Jetta, Passat, Routan, Tiguan, Touareg **Engine:** 2.0L L4, 2.5L L5, 3.0L V6, 3.6L V6	**Mass or Volume Air Flow A Circuit:** The ECM detects an open or short in the Mass Air Flow (MAF) sensor circuit. * Engine speed, >80 U/min * Battery voltage, >8 V

DTC	Trouble Code Title and Conditions
DTC: P0101 **1T ECM, MIL: Yes** **Year:** 2011, 2012 **Model:** Beetle, CC, Eos, Golf, GTI, GLI, Jetta, Passat, Routan, Tiguan, Touareg **Engine:** 2.0L L4, 2.5L L5, 3.0L V6, 3.6L V6	**Mass or Volume Air Flow A Circuit Range/Performance:** Mass air (Depending on engine speed, and throttle angle).>60.8-890 kg/h upper threshold map, <0-197 kg/h lower threshold map. Time after engine start, 150 Rev.
DTC: P0102 **1 T ECM, MIL: Yes** **Year:** 2011, 2012 **Model:** Beetle, CC, Eos, Golf, GTI, GLI, Jetta, Passat, Routan, Tiguan, Touareg **Engine:** 2.0L L4, 2.5L L5, 3.0L V6, 3.6L V6	**MASS AIR FLOW SENSOR CIRCUIT LOW:** No reference Voltage DTC's present. With the engine running and engine speed below 5100 rpm. The Mass Air Flow Sensor Signal is below the valid operating range for 0.5 Seconds.
DTC: P0103 **1 T ECM, MIL: Yes** **Year:** 2011, 2012 **Model:** Beetle, CC, Eos, Golf, GTI, GLI, Jetta, Passat, Routan, Tiguan, Touareg **Engine:** 2.0L L4, 2.5L L5, 3.0L V6, 3.6L V6	**MASS AIR FLOW SENSOR CIRCUIT HIGH:** No reference Voltage DTC's present. With the engine running and engine speed below 5100 rpm. The Mass Air Flow Sensor Signal is above the valid operating range for 0.5 seconds.
DTC: P0105 **1 T ECM, MIL: Yes** **Year:** 2011, 2012 **Model:** Beetle, CC, Eos, Golf, GTI, GLI, Jetta, Passat, Routan, Tiguan, Touareg **Engine:** 2.0L L4, 2.5L L5, 3.0L V6, 3.6L V6	**Manifold Absolute Pressure/Barometric Pressure Circuit:** Engine started, the temperature must be at least 185-degrees (F) and all electrical equipment (A/C, lights, etc) must be off. The ECM detected the BARO sensor was out of range during the test. Boost pressure sensor supply voltage 5.10 - 4.89 V, 480 m Sec.
DTC: P0106 **2T ECM** **Year:** 2011, 2012 **Model:** Golf **Engine:** 2.0L L4, 2.5L L5	**Manifold Absolute Pressure/Barometric Pressure Circuit Range/Performance:** * Engine speed, 0 RPM * Atm. pressure sensor, Not defective * Boost pres. sensor, Not defective
DTC: P0106 **1 T ECM, MIL: Yes** **Year:** 2011, 2012 **Model:** Beetle, CC, Eos, Golf, GTI, GLI, Jetta, Passat, Routan, Tiguan, Touareg **Engine:** 2.0L L4, 2.5L L5, 3.0L V6, 3.6L V6	**Manifold Absolute Pressure/BARO Sensor, range/performance:** * Time engine start, > 25 Revs * EVAP purge system, No fault * IAT, No fault * Ambient pressure sensor, No fault * Camshaft position sensor, No fault * Throttle, No fault * Time after engine start, 10 camshaft Revs
DTC: P0107 **1 T ECM, MIL: Yes** **Year:** 2011, 2012 **Model:** Beetle, CC, Eos, Golf, GTI, GLI, Jetta, Passat, Routan, Tiguan, Touareg **Engine:** 2.0L L4, 2.5L L5, 3.0L V6, 3.6L V6	**Manifold Absolute Pressure/Barometric Pressure Sensor Circuit Low Input:** Engine started, the temperature must be at least 185-degrees (F) and all electrical equipment (A/C, lights, etc) must be off. The ECM detected the BARO sensor was out of range during the CCM test. The BARO sensor signal should be in 4.5v. The BARO sensor is a variable capacitance unit used to detect altitude.

DTC	Trouble Code Title and Conditions
DTC: P0108 **1 T ECM, MIL: Yes** **Year:** 2011, 2012 **Model:** Beetle, CC, Eos, Golf, GTI, GLI, Jetta, Passat, Routan, Tiguan, Touareg **Engine:** 2.0L L4, 2.5L L5, 3.0L V6, 3.6L V6	**Manifold Absolute Pressure/Barometric Pressure Circuit High/Low Input:** Engine started, the temperature must be at least 185-degrees (F) and all electrical equipment (A/C, lights, etc) must be off. The ECM detected the BARO sensor was out of range during the test. The BARO sensor signal should be in 4.5v. The BARO sensor is a variable capacitance unit used to detect altitude.
DTC: P010B **1 T ECM, MIL: Yes** **Year:** 2011, 2012 **Model:** Beetle, CC, Eos, Golf, GTI, GLI, Jetta, Passat, Routan, Tiguan, Touareg **Engine:** 2.0L L4, 2.5L L5, 3.0L V6, 3.6L V6	**Mass or Volume Air Flow "B" Circuit Range/Performance:** * DTC P1009 (Map), Detected * Engine speed, 1400-4000 RPM * Throttle position, >15% * Vehicle speed, 19-75 MPH
DTC: P010C **1 T ECM, MIL: Yes** **Year:** 2011, 2012 **Model:** Beetle, CC, Eos, Golf, GTI, GLI, Jetta, Passat, Routan, Tiguan, Touareg **Engine:** 2.0L L4, 2.5L L5, 3.0L V6, 3.6L V6	**Mass or Volume Air Flow "B" Circuit Low:** * Engine speed, 1400-4000 RPM * Throttle position, >15% * Vehicle speed, 19-75 MPH
DTC: P010D **1 T ECM, MIL: Yes** **Year:** 2011, 2012 **Model:** Beetle, CC, Eos, Golf, GTI, GLI, Jetta, Passat, Routan, Tiguan, Touareg **Engine:** 2.0L L4, 2.5L L5, 3.0L V6, 3.6L V6	**Mass or Volume Air Flow "B" Circuit High:** * Engine speed, 1400-4000 RPM * Throttle position, >15% * Vehicle speed, 19-75 MPH
DTC: P0111 **2 T ECM, MIL: Yes** **Year:** 2011, 2012 **Model:** Beetle, CC, Eos, Golf, GTI, GLI, Jetta, Passat, Routan, Tiguan, Touareg **Engine:** 2.0L L4, 2.5L L5, 3.0L V6, 3.6L V6	**Intake Air Temperature Circuit Range/Performance:** The engine off time is greater than 480 minutes. Ambient Temperature if greater than -64° C (-83° F). Once the vehicle is soaked for a calibrated engine off time and then driven over calibrated speed and load conditions for some calibrated time, the PCM compares the ambient, engine coolant and intake air temperature sensor values. If engine coolant and ambient air temperature sensors agree with each other but intake air temperature does not agree with them, the intake air temperature sensor is declared as irrational. Two Trip Fault. Three good trips to turn off the MIL.
DTC: P0111 **2T** **Year:** 2011, 2012 **Model:** Beetle, Eos, GTI, Jetta, Passat **Engine:** 2.0L L4	**Intake Air Temperature Sensor 1 Circuit Low Input:** Key on or engine running, the temperature must be at least 185-degrees (F) and all electrical equipment (A/C, lights, etc) must be off; and the ECM detected the IAT sensor signal was less than the self-test minimum. This is a thermistor-type sensor with a variable resistance that changes when exposed to different temperatures. This means: the higher the temperature, the lower the resistance value.
DTC: P0112 **1 T ECM, MIL: Yes** **Year:** 2011, 2012 **Model:** Beetle, CC, Eos, Golf, GTI, GLI, Jetta, Passat, Routan, Tiguan, Touareg **Engine:** 2.0L L4, 2.5L L5, 3.0L V6, 3.6L V6	**INTAKE AIR TEMPERATURE SENSOR CIRCUIT LOW:** With the ignition on and battery voltage greater than 10.4 Volts. When the Inlet Air Temp Sensor Signal circuit voltage is less than the minimum acceptable value. One trip failure. Three good trips to clear the MIL.
DTC: P0112 **2T ECM, MIL: Yes** **Year:** 2011, 2012 **Model:** Beetle, Eos, Golf, GTI, Jetta, Passat **Engine:** 2.0L L4, 2.5L L5	**Intake Air Temperature Sensor 1 Circuit Low Input:** * Time after start, 180 sec. * Engine cranking range, 120 – 320 rpm * Fuel cutoff not active

DTC	Trouble Code Title and Conditions
DTC: P0113 **2 T ECM, MIL: Yes** **Year:** 2011, 2012 **Model:** Beetle, CC, Eos, Golf, GTI, GLI, Jetta, Passat, Routan, Tiguan, Touareg **Engine:** 2.0L L4, 2.5L L5, 3.0L V6, 3.6L V6	**Intake Air Temperature Sensor 1 Circuit high:** * Time after engine start 240 Sec * Engine speed, n.a. * Fuel cutoff, not active
DTC: P0113 **2T ECM, MIL: Yes** **Year:** 2012 **Model:** Beetle, Golf, GTI **Engine:** 2.0L L4, 2.5L L5	**Intake Air Temperature Sensor Circuit High Input:** Time after engine start 240 Sec. and no fuel cutoff. * * No fuel cut off
DTC: P0116 **2 T ECM, MIL: Yes** **Year:** 2011, 2012 **Model:** Beetle, CC, Eos, Golf, GTI, GLI, Jetta, Passat, Routan, Tiguan, Touareg **Engine:** 2.0L L4, 2.5L L5, 3.0L V6, 3.6L V6	**ENGINE COOLANT TEMPERATURE SENSOR CIRCUIT PERFORMANCE:** Engine off time is greater than 480 minutes and the vehicle has been driven for one minute over 35 mph. Ambient temperature is greater than -64° C (-83° F). Once the vehicle is soaked for a calibrated engine off time and then driven over calibrated speed and load conditions for some calibrated time, the PCM compares the ambient, engine coolant and intake air temperature sensor values. If ambient air and intake air temperature sensors agree with each other but engine coolant temperature does not agree with them, the engine coolant temperature sensor is declared as irrational. Two Trip Fault. Three good trips to turn off the MIL.
DTC: P0117 **1 T ECM, MIL: Yes** **Year:** 2011, 2012 **Model:** Beetle, CC, Eos, Golf, GTI, GLI, Jetta, Passat, Routan, Tiguan, Touareg **Engine:** 2.0L L4, 2.5L L5, 3.0L V6, 3.6L V6	**ENGINE COOLANT TEMPERATURE SENSOR CIRCUIT LOW:** With the ignition on. Battery voltage greater than 10.4 Volts. The Powertrain Control Module (PCM) detects that the Engine Coolant Temperature Sensor input voltage is below the minimum acceptable value. One Trip Fault. Three good trips to clear the MIL. The MIL and ETC light will illuminate if equipped.
DTC: P0118 **1 T ECM, MIL: Yes** **Year:** 2011, 2012 **Model:** Beetle, CC, Eos, Golf, GTI, GLI, Jetta, Passat, Routan, Tiguan, Touareg **Engine:** 2.0L L4, 2.5L L5, 3.0L V6, 3.6L V6	**ENGINE COOLANT TEMPERATURE SENSOR CIRCUIT HIGH:** With the ignition on. Battery voltage greater than 10.4 Volts. The Powertrain Control Module (PCM) detects that the Engine Coolant Temperature Sensor input voltage is above the maximum acceptable value. One Trip Fault. Three good trips to turn off the MIL. The MIL and ETC light will illuminate if equipped.
DTC: P0120 **1 T ECM, MIL: Yes** **Year:** 2011, 2012 **Model:** Beetle, CC, Eos, Golf, GTI, GLI, Jetta, Passat, Routan, Tiguan, Touareg **Engine:** 2.0L L4, 2.5L L5, 3.0L V6, 3.6L V6	**Throttle/Pedal Position Sensor (A) Circuit Malfunction:** Engine started, at idle, the temperature must be 80 degrees Celsius. The throttle position sensor supplies implausible signal to the ECM. The throttle valve activation occurs via an electric motor (throttle drive) in the throttle valve control module. It is activated by the Engine Control Module (ECM) according to specifications of the two sensors, Throttle Position (TP) Sensor and Accelerator Pedal Position Sensor 2.
DTC: P0121 **2 T ECM, MIL: Yes** **Year:** 2011, 2012 **Model:** Beetle, CC, Eos, Golf, GTI, GLI, Jetta, Passat, Routan, Tiguan, Touareg **Engine:** 2.0L L4, 2.5L L5, 3.0L V6, 3.6L V6	**THROTTLE POSITION SENSOR 1 PERFORMANCE:** Ignition on and No MAP Sensor DTCs set. The Powertrain Control Module (PCM) detects that the sensor input voltage does not fall within a valid range based on engine speed and load. Two Trip Fault. (Electronic Throttle Control) ETC light will illuminate.
DTC: P0121 **2T ECM, MIL: Yes** **Year:** 2011, 2012 **Model:** Beetle, Eos, Golf, GTI, Jetta, Passat **Engine:** 2.0L L4, 2.5L L5	**Throttle/Pedal Position Sensor A Circuit Range/Performance:** * Engine speed > 480 RPM

DTC	Trouble Code Title and Conditions
DTC: P0122 **1 T ECM, MIL: Yes** **Year:** 2011, 2012 **Model:** Beetle, CC, Eos, Golf, GTI, GLI, Jetta, Passat, Routan, Tiguan, Touareg **Engine:** 2.0L L4, 2.5L L5, 3.0L V6, 3.6L V6	**TPS/APP CIRCUIT LOW:** Continuously with the ignition on and engine running. This DTC will set if the monitored TPS voltage drops below .078 of a volt for the period of 0.48 of a second.
DTC: P0123 **1 T ECM, MIL: Yes** **Year:** 2011, 2012 **Model:** Beetle, CC, Eos, Golf, GTI, GLI, Jetta, Passat, Routan, Tiguan, Touareg **Engine:** 2.0L L4, 2.5L L5, 3.0L V6, 3.6L V6	**TPS/APP CIRCUIT HIGH:** Continuously with the ignition on and engine running. This DTC will set if the monitored TPS voltage rises above 4.94 volts for the period of 0.48 of a second.
DTC: P0123 **1T ECM, MIL: Yes** **Year:** 2012 **Model:** Beetle, Golf, GTI **Engine:** 2.0L L4, 2.5L L5	**Throttle/Pedal Position Sensor "A" Circuit High:** With the ignition on and battery voltage greater than 10 Volts. Throttle Position Sensor No.1 voltage is greater than 4.8 Volts for 25 ms. One Trip Fault. ETC light will illuminate.
DTC: P0124 **1 T ECM, MIL: Yes** **Year:** 2011, 2012 **Model:** Beetle, CC, Eos, Golf, GTI, GLI, Jetta, Passat, Routan, Tiguan, Touareg **Engine:** 2.0L L4, 2.5L L5, 3.0L V6, 3.6L V6	**TPS/APP INTERMITTENT:** Continuously with the ignition on and engine running. This DTC will set if the monitored TPS throttle angle is between 6° and 120° and the value changes by more than 5° in a period of 7.0 ms or less.
DTC: P0125 **2 T ECM, MIL: Yes** **Year:** 2011, 2012 **Model:** Beetle, CC, Eos, Golf, GTI, GLI, Jetta, Passat, Routan, Tiguan, Touareg **Engine:** 2.0L L4, 2.5L L5, 3.0L V6, 3.6L V6	**INSUFFICIENT COOLANT TEMP FOR CLOSED-LOOP FUEL CONTROL:** With battery voltage greater than 10.4 Volts and after engine is started. The engine temperature does not go above -10° C (15° F). Failure time depends on start-up coolant temperature and ambient temperature. (i.e. two minutes for a start temp of -10° C (15° F) or up to 10 minutes for a vehicle with a start-up temp of -28° C (5° F). Two Trip Fault. Three good trips to turn off the MIL.
DTC: P0128 **2 T ECM, MIL: Yes** **Year:** 2011, 2012 **Model:** Beetle, CC, Eos, Golf, GTI, GLI, Jetta, Passat, Routan, Tiguan, Touareg **Engine:** 2.0L L4, 2.5L L5, 3.0L V6, 3.6L V6	**Coolant Thermostat / Valve Temperature below control range:** With the engine running, ambient temperature between -8° C (17.6° F) and 50° C (122° F), start up coolant temperature less than 50° C (122° F) and average vehicle speed greater than 16 kph (10 mph) until coolant temperature reaches 85° C (185° F). The PCM detects that the actual engine coolant temperature falls too far below the predicted engine coolant temperature and the predicted coolant temperature reaches the predicted target value before the actual coolant temperature reaches the actual coolant temperature target value. Two trip fault. Three good trips to turn off the MIL.
DTC: P0129 **1 T ECM, MIL: Yes** **Year:** 2011, 2012 **Model:** Beetle, CC, Eos, Golf, GTI, GLI, Jetta, Passat, Routan, Tiguan, Touareg **Engine:** 2.0L L4, 2.5L L5, 3.0L V6, 3.6L V6	**BAROMETRIC PRESSURE OUT-OF-RANGE LOW:** With the ignition key on. No Cam or Crank signal within 75 ms. Engine speed less than 250 RPM. The Powertrain Control Module (PCM) senses the voltage from the MAP sensor to be less than 2.2 Volts but above 0.04 of a Volt for 300 milliseconds. One Trip Fault. Three good trips to turn off the MIL. MIL is illuminated and the ETC lamp will flash.
DTC: P0130 **2 T ECM, MIL: Yes** **Year:** 2011, 2012 **Model:** Beetle, CC, Eos, Golf, GTI, GLI, Jetta, Passat, Routan, Tiguan, Touareg **Engine:** 2.0L L4, 2.5L L5, 3.0L V6, 3.6L V6	**HO2S Sensor Circuit (Bank 1, Sensor 1):** * Modeled exhaust temp>300° C * Fuel cut-off not active * Heater control active

DTC	Trouble Code Title and Conditions
DTC: P0131 **2 T ECM, MIL: Yes** **Year:** 2011, 2012 **Model:** Beetle, CC, Eos, Golf, GTI, GLI, Jetta, Passat, Routan, Tiguan, Touareg **Engine:** 2.0L L4, 2.5L L5, 3.0L V6, 3.6L V6	**HO2S SENSOR 1/1 CIRCUIT LOW:** Engine running for less than 30 seconds and the O2 Sensor Heater Temperature is less than 251° C (484° F) with battery voltage greater 10.4 Volts. The Powertrain Control Module (PCM) detects that the 1/1 Oxygen Sensor signal voltage is below the minimum acceptable value. The DTC will set as Pending after one trip and Active after two trips. Three good trips to turn off the MIL.
DTC: P0132 **2 T ECM, MIL: Yes** **Year:** 2011, 2012 **Model:** Beetle, CC, Eos, Golf, GTI, GLI, Jetta, Passat, Routan, Tiguan, Touareg **Engine:** 2.0L L4, 2.5L L5, 3.0L V6, 3.6L V6	**HO2S Sensor Circuit, Bank 1 - Sensor 1 High Voltage:** With the ignition on and the O2 1/1 Sensor at operating temperature. The ECM detects a short to voltage on the (K902) O2 1/1 Negative Current Control circuit for 2.0 seconds.
DTC: P0133 **2 T ECM, MIL: Yes** **Year:** 2011, 2012 **Model:** Beetle, CC, Eos, Golf, GTI, GLI, Jetta, Passat, Routan, Tiguan, Touareg **Engine:** 2.0L L4, 2.5L L5, 3.0L V6, 3.6L V6	**HO2S Circuit Slow Response (Bank 1, Sensor 1):** With the ECT above 70° C (158° F), engine RPM between 1400 and 2300, vehicle speed between 64 and 96 kph (40 and 60 mph), and engine run time greater than three minutes. The Powertrain Control Module (PCM) detects that the oxygen sensor signal does not switch adequately during monitoring. Two Trip Fault. Three good trips to turn off the MIL.
DTC: P0134 **1 T ECM, MIL: Yes** **Year:** 2011, 2012 **Model:** Beetle, CC, Eos, Golf, GTI, GLI, Jetta, Passat, Routan, Tiguan, Touareg **Engine:** 2.0L L4, 2.5L L5, 3.0L V6, 3.6L V6	**HO2S (Bank 1 Sensor 1) Circuit No Activity:** Engine running, battery voltage 11.5, all electrical components off, ground between engine and chassis well connected and the exhaust system must be properly sealed between catalytic converter and the cylinder head. The ECM detected the HO2S signal failed to meet the maximum or minimum voltage levels (i.e., it failed the voltage range check).
DTC: P0135 **2 T ECM, MIL: Yes** **Year:** 2011, 2012 **Model:** Beetle, CC, Eos, Golf, GTI, GLI, Jetta, Passat, Routan, Tiguan, Touareg **Engine:** 2.0L L4, 2.5L L5, 3.0L V6, 3.6L V6	**HO2S SENSOR 1/1 HEATER PERFORMANCE:** Engine running and heater duty cycle greater than 0%. Battery voltage greater than 11.0 Volts. The Powertrain Control Module (PCM) detects no temperature change in the O2 sensor heater element when the heater circuit is active. The heater temperature is obtained by measuring the heater resistance and calculating the heater temperature. Two trip fault. Three good trips to turn off the MIL.
DTC: P0136 **2 T ECM, MIL: Yes** **Year:** 2011, 2012 **Model:** Beetle, CC, Eos, Golf, GTI, GLI, Jetta, Passat, Routan, Tiguan, Touareg **Engine:** 2.0L L4, 2.5L L5, 3.0L V6, 3.6L V6	**HO2S Circuit (Bank 1, Sensor 2) Malfunction:** * Battery voltage, >11 V * Engine speed, >25 RPM * O2S rear dew-point, Exceeded * O2S rear, fully heated up * Modeled exhaust gas temp. 200-800° C for 60 Sec. * Heater rear, Commanded on for >0.04 Sec.
DTC: P0137 **1 T ECM, MIL: Yes** **Year:** 2011, 2012 **Model:** Beetle, CC, Eos, Golf, GTI, GLI, Jetta, Passat, Routan, Tiguan, Touareg **Engine:** 2.0L L4, 2.5L L5, 3.0L V6, 3.6L V6	**HO2S SENSOR (Bank 1, Sensor 2) CIRCUIT LOW:** Engine running for less than 30 seconds and the O2 Sensor Heater Temperature is less than 251° C (484° F) with battery voltage greater 10.99 Volts The Powertrain Control Module (PCM) detects that the 1/2 Oxygen Sensor signal voltage is below minimum acceptable value. The DTC will set as Pending after one trip, and Active after two trips. Three good trips to turn off the MIL.

DTC	Trouble Code Title and Conditions
DTC: P0138 **1 T ECM, MIL: Yes** **Year:** 2011, 2012 **Model:** Beetle, CC, Eos, Golf, GTI, GLI, Jetta, Passat, Routan, Tiguan, Touareg **Engine:** 2.0L L4, 2.5L L5, 3.0L V6, 3.6L V6	**HO2S Circuit High Voltage (Bank 1, Sensor 2):** Continuously with the engine running, no O2 sensor heater DTCs present, 1/2 Oxygen Sensor heater temperature within a specific range and battery voltage greater than 10.4 Volts. The Powertrain Control Module (PCM) detects that the 1/2 Oxygen Sensor voltage is greater than the maximum acceptable value for a specific amount of time, based on O2 sensor heater temperature. The DTC will set as Pending after one trip and Active after two trips. Three good trips to turn off the MIL.
DTC: P0139 **1 T ECM, MIL: Yes** **Year:** 2011, 2012 **Model:** Beetle, CC, Eos, Golf, GTI, GLI, Jetta, Passat, Routan, Tiguan, Touareg **Engine:** 2.0L L4, 2.5L L5, 3.0L V6, 3.6L V6	**HO2S Circuit Slow Response (Bank 1, Sensor 2):** With the engine running, vehicle speed above 96 kph (60 mph), throttle open for a minimum of 120 seconds, ECT greater than 70° C (158° F), catalytic converter temperature greater than 600° C (1112° F) and downstream oxygen sensor in a rich state during a decel fuel shutoff event, the downstream oxygen sensor should switch from rich to lean within a specific time. The Powertrain Control Module (PCM) monitors the downstream O2 Sensor. If the PCM does not detect a rich to lean switch within a specific time during a decal, fuel shutoff event, the monitor will fail. One trip fault. Three good trips to turn off the MIL.
DTC: P013B **1T ECM, MIL: Yes** **Year:** 2011, 2012 **Model:** Golf, GTI, Jetta, Passat **Engine:** 2.0L L4, 2.5L L5	**O2 Sensor Bank 1 Sensor 2 Slow Response Lean to Rich:** * Regeneration demand for NOx trap = on * Adaptation of oxygen sensor pre and post NOx trap = realized * Dew point release oxygen sensor signals pre and post NOx trap = on * Temperature of upstream turbine < 850 °C * Fuel temp < 90 °C * APP > 1 and < 100%
DTC: P0140 **2 T ECM, MIL: Yes** **Year:** 2011, 2012 **Model:** Beetle, CC, Eos, Golf, GTI, GLI, Jetta, Passat, Routan, Tiguan, Touareg **Engine:** 2.0L L4, 2.5L L5, 3.0L V6, 3.6L V6	**HO2S Circuit No Activity Detected (Bank 1, Sensor 2):** With the engine running, vehicle speed between 32 and 88 kph (20 and 55 mph), throttle open for a minimum of 120 seconds, ECT greater than 70° C (158° F), Catalytic Converter Temperature greater than 600° C (1112° F) and EVAP Purge active. The Powertrain Control Module (PCM) detects that the oxygen sensor signal switches from lean to rich less than 16 times within 20 seconds during monitoring. Two Trip fault. Three good trips to turn off the MIL.
DTC: P0141 **2 T ECM, MIL: Yes** **Year:** 2011, 2012 **Model:** Beetle, CC, Eos, Golf, GTI, GLI, Jetta, Passat, Routan, Tiguan, Touareg **Engine:** 2.0L L4, 2.5L L5, 3.0L V6, 3.6L V6	**-O2 SENSOR 1/2 HEATER PERFORMANCE:** Continuously during O2 sensor heater operation with battery voltage between 10.4 and 15.75 Volts and no O2 sensor circuit DTCs present. The Powertrain Control Module (PCM) detects no temperature change in the O2 sensor heater element when the heater circuit is active. The heater temperature is obtained by measuring the heater resistance and calculating the heater temperature. Two trip fault. Three good trips to turn off the MIL.
DTC: P0142 **2T ECM, MIL: Yes** **Year:** 2011, 2012 **Model:** Beetle, CC, Eos, Golf, GTI, Jetta, Passat **Engine:** 2.0L L4, 2.5L L5	**O2 circuit Bank 1 Sensor 3 heater check:** * Modeled exhaust gas temp. 200-800° C * Dew-point exceeded and lower exhaust gas temp limit exceeded for 60 Sec.
DTC: P0143 **2T ECM, MIL: Yes** **Year:** 2011, 2012 **Model:** Beetle, CC, Eos, Golf, GTI, Jetta, Passat **Engine:** 2.0L L4, 2.5L L5	**O2 Sensor Circuit Low Voltage Bank 1 Sensor 3:** * Sensor voltage <= 0.40 V or 0.50 to 1.08 V * Modeled exhaust gas temp. 700 °C for > 10 Sec. * Heater power >= 50% for > 10 Sec.
DTC: P0144 **2T** **Year:** 2012 **Model:** Jetta **Engine:** 2.0L L4	**O2 Sensor Circuit High Voltage Bank 1 Sensor 3:** * Sensor voltage <= 0.40 V or 0.50 to 1.08 V * Modeled exhaust gas temp. 700 °C for > 10 Sec. * Heater power >= 50% for > 10 Sec.

DTC	Trouble Code Title and Conditions
DTC: P0145 **2 T ECM, MIL: Yes** **Year:** 2011, 2012 **Model:** Beetle, CC, Eos, Golf, GTI, GLI, Jetta, Passat, Routan, Tiguan, Touareg **Engine:** 3.0L V6, 3.6L V6	**O2 Circuit Slow Response (Bank 1, Sensor 2):** * Rich voltage, >=547.9 mV * Lean voltage <=152.3 mV * Max O2 mass flow (disable), >=6000 mg * HO2S rear, ready * Fuel cut-off, active * Front O2 sensor, lambda signal, >2.00 * Modeled exhaust gas temp. >400° C
DTC: P0145 **2T ECM, MIL: Yes** **Year:** 2011, 2012 **Model:** Beetle, CC, Eos, Golf, GTI, Jetta, Passat **Engine:** 2.0L L4, 2.5L L5	**O2 Sensor Circuit Slow Response Bank 1 Sensor 3:** * O2S rear, Fully heated up * Rich voltage enable > = 548 mV * Modeled exhaust temp. > 480 °C * No other O2 sensor faults set.
DTC: P0146 **2T ECM, MIL: Yes** **Year:** 2011, 2012 **Model:** Beetle, CC, Eos, Golf, GTI, Jetta, Passat **Engine:** 2.0L L4, 2.5L L5	**O2 Sensor Circuit No Activity Detected Bank 1 Sensor 3:** * Sensor voltage <= 0.40 V or 0.50 to 1.08 V * Modeled exhaust gas temp. 700 °C for > 10 Sec. * Heater power >= 50% for > 10 Sec.
DTC: P0147 **2T ECM, MIL: Yes** **Year:** 2011, 2012 **Model:** Beetle, CC, Eos, Golf, GTI, Jetta, Passat **Engine:** 2.0L L4, 2.5L L5	**O2 Sensor Heater Circuit Bank 1 Sensor 3:** * Modeled exhaust gas temp 250 - 650 °C * Engine shutoff time > 60 Sec. * Fuel cutoff not active * Heater commanded on
DTC: P0147 **2T ECM, MIL: Yes** **Year:** 2011, 2012 **Model:** Beetle, Eos, GTI, Jetta, Passat **Engine:** 2.0L L4	**O2 circuit Bank 1 Sensor 3 heater check SULEV:** * Modeled exhaust gas temp, 250-650.1° C * Engine shutoff time, >300 Sec. * Fuel cut-off not active * Heater commanded on
DTC: P014D **2T ECM, MIL: Yes** **Year:** 2011, 2012 **Model:** Beetle, CC, Eos, Golf, GTI, GLI, Jetta, Passat, Routan, Tiguan, Touareg **Engine:** 2.0L L4, 2.5L L5, 3.0L V6, 3.6L V6	**O2 Sensor Bank 1 Sensor 1 Slow Response Lean to Rich:** * Regeneration demand for NOx trap = on * Adaptation of oxygen sensor pre and post NOx trap = realized * Dew point release oxygen sensor signals pre and post NOx trap = on * Temperature of upstream turbine < 850 °C * Fuel temp < 90 °C * APP > 1 and < 100% * Gear = 2 * Engine run time > 240 Sec. * Exhaust gas flow > 100 and < 200 kg/h
DTC: P0150 **1T ECM, MIL: Yes** **Year:** 2011, 2012 **Model:** Beetle, CC, Eos, Golf, GTI, GLI, Jetta, Passat, Routan, Tiguan, Touareg **Engine:** 2.0L L4, 2.5L L5, 3.0L V6, 3.6L V6	**HO2S Sensor Circuit, Bank 2 Sensor 1 Low Voltage:** * Modeled exhaust gas temp, >170° C * Fuel cut off, Not active
DTC: P0151 **1T ECM, MIL: Yes** **Year:** 2011, 2012 **Model:** Beetle, CC, Eos, Golf, GTI, GLI, Jetta, Passat, Routan, Tiguan, Touareg **Engine:** 2.0L L4, 2.5L L5, 3.0L V6, 3.6L V6	**HO2S Sensor Circuit Low Voltage Bank 2 Sensor 1:** Engine running for less than 30 seconds and the O2 Sensor Heater Temperature is lessthan 251° C (484° F) with the battery voltage greater 10.99 Volts. The Powertrain Control Module (PCM) detects that the 2/1 Oxygen Sensor signal voltage is below the minimum acceptable value. The DTC will set as Pending after one trip and Active after two trips. Three good trips to turn off the MIL.

DTC	Trouble Code Title and Conditions
DTC: P0152 **2T ECM, MIL: Yes** **Year:** 2011, 2012 **Model:** Touareg **Engine:** 3.0L V6, 3.6L V6	**O2 Sensor Circuit High Voltage Bank 2 Sensor 1:** Engine speed, >25 RPM
DTC: P0152 **2T ECM, MIL: Yes** **Year:** 2011, 2012 **Model:** Routan, Toureg **Engine:** 3.0L V6, 3.6L V6	**HO2S Sensor Circuit High Voltage Bank 2 Sensor 1:** Continuously with the engine running, no O2 sensor heater DTCs present, 2/1 Oxygen Sensor heater temperature within a specific range and battery voltage greater than 10.4 Volts. The Powertrain Control Module (PCM) detects that the 2/1 Oxygen Sensor voltage is greater than the maximum acceptable value for a specific amount of time, based on O2 sensor heater temperature. The DTC will set as Pending after one trip and Active after two trips. Three good trips to turn off the MIL.
DTC: P0153 **2T ECM, MIL: Yes** **Year:** 2011, 2012 **Model:** Routan, Toureg **Engine:** 3.0L V6, 3.6L V6	**O2 Sensor Circuit Slow Response Bank 2 Sensor 1:** With the ECT above 70 °C (158 °F), engine RPM between 1400 and 2300, vehicle speed between 64 and 96 kph (40 and 60 mph) and engine run time greater than three minutes. The Powertrain Control Module (PCM) detects that the oxygen sensor signal does not switch adequately during monitoring. Two Trip Fault. Three good trips to turn off the MIL.
DTC: P0155 **2T** **Year:** 2011, 2012 **Model:** Eos, Golf **Engine:** 2.0L L4, 2.5L L5	**O2 Sensor Heater Circuit Bank 2 Sensor 1:** * Modeled exhaust gas temp., > 250 °C * Heater control, Active * ECT at start, >48 °C * Engine shut off time, >120 Sec. * During ECM keep alive time after ign off, <950 Sec.
DTC: P0155 **T** **Year:** 2011, 2012 **Model:** Routan **Engine:** 3.6L V6 VIN G	**O2 Sensor Heater Circuit Bank 2 Sensor 1:** Engine running and heater duty cycle greater than 0%. Battery voltage greater than 11.0 Volts. No sensor output is received when the Powertrain Control Module (PCM) powers up the sensor heater. Two trip fault. Three good trips to turn off the MIL.
DTC: P0156 **1T ECM, MIL: Yes** **Year:** 2011, 2012 **Model:** Beetle, CC, Eos, Golf, GTI, GLI, Jetta, Passat, Routan, Tiguan, Touareg **Engine:** 2.0L L4, 2.5L L5, 3.0L V6, 3.6L V6	**O2 Sensor Circuit Bank 2 Sensor 2:** * O2S rear, Ready * Modeled exhaust gas temp. 250-800 °C for >90 Sec. * Engine speed, >25 RPM
DTC: P0156 **2T ECM, MIL: Yes** **Year:** 2011, 2012 **Model:** Golf **Engine:** 2.5L L5	**O2 Sensor Circuit Bank 2 Sensor 2:** * Modeled exhaust gas temp. 250-700° C * Dew point exceeded and lower exhaust gas temp exceeded, 30 Sec.
DTC: P0157 **1T ECM, MIL: Yes** **Year:** 2011, 2012 **Model:** Beetle, CC, Eos, Golf, GTI, GLI, Jetta, Passat, Routan, Tiguan, Touareg **Engine:** 2.0L L4, 2.5L L5, 3.0L V6, 3.6L V6	**HO2S Sensor Circuit Low Voltage Bank 2 Sensor 2:** The Powertrain Control Module (PCM) detects that the 2/2 Oxygen Sensor signal voltage is below the minimum acceptable value. The DTC will set as Pending after one trip and Active after two trips. Three good trips to turn off the MIL.
DTC: P0158 **1T ECM, MIL: Yes** **Year:** 2011, 2012 **Model:** Beetle, CC, Eos, Golf, GTI, GLI, Jetta, Passat, Routan, Tiguan, Touareg **Engine:** 2.0L L4, 2.5L L5, 3.0L V6, 3.6L V6	**HO2S Sensor Circuit High Voltage Bank 2 Sensor 2:** Continuously with the engine running, no O2 sensor heater DTCs present, 2/2 Oxygen Sensor heater temperature within a specific range and battery voltage greater than 10.4 Volts. The Powertrain Control Module (PCM) detects that the 2/2 Oxygen Sensor voltage is greater than the maximum acceptable value for a specific amount of time, based on O2 sensor heater temperature. The DTC will set as Pending after one trip and Active after two trips. Three good trips to turn off the MIL.

DTC	Trouble Code Title and Conditions
DTC: P0159 **1T ECM, MIL: Yes** **Year:** 2011, 2012 **Model:** Beetle, CC, Eos, Golf, GTI, GLI, Jetta, Passat, Routan, Tiguan, Touareg **Engine:** 2.0L L4, 2.5L L5, 3.0L V6, 3.6L V6	**HO2S Sensor Circuit Slow Response Bank 2 Sensor 2:** With the engine running, vehicle speed above 96 kph (60 mph), throttle open for a minimum of 120 seconds, ECT greater than 70° C (158° F), catalytic converter temperature greater than 600° C (1112° F), and downstream oxygen sensor in a rich state. During a decel fuel shutoff event, the downstream oxygen sensor should switch from rich to lean within a specific time. The Powertrain Control Module (PCM) monitors the downstream O2 sensor. If the PCM does not detect a rich to lean switch within a specific time during a decel fuel shutoff event, the monitor will fail. One trip fault. Three good trips to turn off the MIL.
DTC: P0160 **2T ECM, MIL: Yes** **Year:** 2011, 2012 **Model:** Beetle, CC, Eos, Golf, GTI, GLI, Jetta, Passat, Routan, Tiguan, Touareg **Engine:** 2.0L L4, 2.5L L5, 3.0L V6, 3.6L V6	**HO2S Sensor Circuit No Activity Detected Bank 2 Sensor 2:** Vehicle is started and driven between 32 and 88.5 km/h (20 and 55 mph) with the Throttle open for a minimum of 120 seconds. Coolant greater than 70° C (158° F). Catalytic Converter Temp greater than 600° C (1112° F) and EVAP Purge are active. The oxygen sensor signal voltage switches less than 16 times from lean to rich within 20 seconds during monitoring. Two Trip Fault. Three good trips to turn off the MIL
DTC: P0161 **2T ECM, MIL: Yes** **Year:** 2011, 2012 **Model:** Beetle, CC, Eos, Golf, GTI, GLI, Jetta, Passat, Routan, Tiguan, Touareg **Engine:** 2.0L L4, 2.5L L5, 3.0L V6, 3.6L V6	**HO2S Sensor Heater Circuit Bank 2 Sensor 2 Malfunction:** Engine running and heater duty cycle greater than 0%. Battery voltage greater than 11.0 Volts. No sensor output is received when the Powertrain Control Module (PCM) powers up the sensor heater. Two trip fault. Three good trips to turn off the MIL.
DTC: P0169 **2T ECM, MIL: Yes** **Year:** 2011, 2012 **Model:** Beetle, Eos, Golf, GTI, Jetta, Passat **Engine:** 2.0L L4, 2.5L L5	**Incorrect Fuel Composition:** **NOTE: Use of a high concentration of ethanol may cause DTCs P0169. Other contamination such as water and salts may cause this DTC to set.** * Engine speed > 1200 RPM
DTC: P0170 **2T ECM, MIL: Yes** **Year:** 2011, 2012 **Model:** Beetle, Eos, GTI, Jetta, Passat **Engine:** 2.0L L4	**Fuel System Malfunction (Cylinder Bank 1):** The engine is running in a closed loop at a stable engine speed, and the ECM detected the lean or rich fuel trim correction valve was more than or less than a calibrated limit.
DTC: P0171 **1T ECM, MIL: Yes** **Year:** 2011, 2012 **Model:** Beetle, CC, Eos, Golf, GTI, GLI, Jetta, Passat, Routan, Tiguan, Touareg **Engine:** 2.0L L4, 2.5L L5, 3.0L V6, 3.6L V6	**-FUEL SYSTEM 1/1 LEAN:** With the engine running in closed loop mode, the ambient/battery temperature above -6.7°C (20°F) and altitude below 2590.8 m (8500 ft). If the Powertrain Control Module (PCM) multiplies short term compensation by long term adaptive and a certain percentage is exceeded for two trips, a freeze frame is stored, the MIL illuminates and a trouble code is stored. Two Trip Fault. Three good trips to turn off the MIL.
DTC: P0172 **2T ECM, MIL: Yes** **Year:** 2011, 2012 **Model:** Beetle, CC, Eos, Golf, GTI, GLI, Jetta, Passat, Routan, Tiguan, Touareg **Engine:** 2.0L L4, 2.5L L5, 3.0L V6, 3.6L V6	**System Too Rich (Bank 1):** With the engine running in closed loop mode, the ambient/battery temperature above -6.7°C (20°F) and altitude below 2590.8 m (8500 ft). If the Powertrain Control Module (PCM) multiplies short term compensation by long term adaptive and a purge fuel multiplier and the result is below a certain value for 30 seconds over two trips, a freeze frame is stored, the MIL illuminates and a trouble code is stored. Two Trip Fault. Three good trips to turn off the MIL.
DTC: P0174 **2T ECM, MIL: Yes** **Year:** 2011, 2012 **Model:** Beetle, CC, Eos, Golf, GTI, GLI, Jetta, Passat, Routan, Tiguan, Touareg **Engine:** 2.0L L4, 2.5L L5, 3.0L V6, 3.6L V6	**System Too Lean Bank 2:** With the engine running in closed loop mode, the ambient/battery temperature above -6.7°C (20°F) and altitude below 2590.8 m (8500 ft). If the Powertrain Control Module (PCM) multiplies short term compensation by long term adaptive and a certain percentage is exceeded for two trips, a freeze frame is stored, the MIL illuminates and a trouble code is stored. Two Trip Fault. Three good trips to turn off the MIL.

DTC	Trouble Code Title and Conditions
DTC: P0175 **2T ECM, MIL: Yes** **Year:** 2011, 2012 **Model:** Beetle, CC, Eos, Golf, GTI, GLI, Jetta, Passat, Routan, Tiguan, Touareg **Engine:** 2.0L L4, 2.5L L5, 3.0L V6, 3.6L V6	**System Too Rich Bank 2:** With the engine running in closed loop mode, the ambient/battery temperature above -6.7°C (20°F) and altitude below 2590.8 m (8500 ft). If the Powertrain Control Module (PCM) multiplies short term compensation by long term adaptive and a purge fuel multiplier and the result is below a certain value for 30 seconds over two trips, a freeze frame is stored, the MIL illuminates and a trouble code is stored. Two Trip Fault. Three good trips to turn off the MIL.
DTC: P0181 **2T ECM, MIL: Yes** **Year:** 2011, 2012 **Model:** Beetle, CC, Eos, Golf, GTI, GLI, Jetta, Passat, Routan, Tiguan, Touareg **Engine:** 2.0L L4, 2.5L L5, 3.0L V6, 3.6L V6	**Fuel Temperature Sensor A Circuit Range/Performance:** * Engine off time > 9 hr * Decrease of IAT and T2 < 5 °K at > 25 mph for 20 Sec. * Decrease of AAT after engine start < 5 °K for 60 Sec.
DTC: P0182 **2T ECM, MIL: Yes** **Year:** 2011, 2012 **Model:** Beetle, Golf, GTI, Jetta, Passat **Engine:** 2.0L L4, 2.5L L5	**Engine Fuel Temperature Sensor 'A' Circuit Low Input:** Key on or engine running; and the ECM detected the Engine Fuel Temperature (EFT) Sensor 'A' signal was under the required voltage in the self-test.
DTC: P0183 **2T ECM, MIL: Yes** **Year:** 2011, 2012 **Model:** Beetle, Golf, GTI, Jetta, Passat, Touareg **Engine:** 2.0L L4, 2.5L L5, 3.0L V6, 3.6L V6	**Fuel Temperature Sensor A Circuit High:** With the ignition on and engine running, the ECM detected the fuel temperature sensor was out of range.
DTC: P0190 **2T ECM, MIL: Yes** **Year:** 2011, 2012 **Model:** Beetle, CC, Eos, Golf, GTI, GLI, Jetta, Passat, Routan, Tiguan, Touareg **Engine:** 2.0L L4, 2.5L L5, 3.0L V6, 3.6L V6	**Fuel Rail Pressure Sensor A Circuit:** With the ignition on and engine running, the ECM detected the fuel temperature sensor was out of range. Malfunction Criteria and Threshold Value: 4.8V
DTC: P0191 **2T ECM, MIL: Yes** **Year:** 2011, 2012 **Model:** Beetle, CC, Eos, Golf, GTI, GLI, Jetta, Passat, Routan, Tiguan, Touareg **Engine:** 2.0L L4, 2.5L L5, 3.0L V6, 3.6L V6	**Fuel Rail Pressure Sensor Circuit Range/Performance:** With the ignition on and engine running, the ECM detected the fuel temperature sensor was out of range. * Time after engine start > 10 Sec. * Engine speed > 90 RPM
DTC: P0192 **2T ECM, MIL: Yes** **Year:** 2011, 2012 **Model:** Beetle, CC, Eos, Golf, GTI, GLI, Jetta, Passat, Routan, Tiguan, Touareg **Engine:** 2.0L L4, 2.5L L5, 3.0L V6, 3.6L V6	**Fuel Rail Pressure Sensor A Circuit Low Input:** With the ignition on and engine running, the ECM detected the fuel temperature sensor was out of range. Malfunction Criteria and Threshold Value: Signal voltage < 2.0 V.
DTC: P0193 **2T ECM, MIL: Yes** **Year:** 2011, 2012 **Model:** Beetle, CC, Eos, Golf, GTI, GLI, Jetta, Passat, Routan, Tiguan, Touareg **Engine:** 2.0L L4, 2.5L L5, 3.0L V6, 3.6L V6	**Fuel Rail Pressure Sensor Circuit High Input:** With the ignition on and engine running, the ECM detected the fuel temperature sensor was out of range. * Key On engine Off * Fuel temperature > 5 and < 60 °C * Fuel rail pressure set point > 500 hpa * Voltage deviation in pressure control valve < 2%

DTC	Trouble Code Title and Conditions
DTC: P0196 **2T ECM, MIL: Yes** **Year:** 2011, 2012 **Model:** Beetle, CC, Eos, Golf, GTI, GLI, Jetta, Passat, Routan, Tiguan, Touareg **Engine:** 2.0L L4, 2.5L L5, 3.0L V6, 3.6L V6	**ENGINE OIL TEMPERATURE SENSOR CIRCUIT PERFORMANCE:** With engine off time greater than 480 minutes and ambient temperature greater than -7°C (19.4°F). After a calibrated amount of cool down time, the Powertrain Control Module (PCM) compares the AAT, ECT and IAT Sensor values. If the general temperature rationality passes, the PCM compares the Oil Temperature Sensor value to a threshold based on the other temp sensor values. If the difference is greater than a calibrated value, the diagnostic fails.
DTC: P0197 **2T ECM, MIL: Yes** **Year:** 2011, 2012 **Model:** Beetle, CC, Eos, Golf, GTI, GLI, Jetta, Passat, Routan, Tiguan, Touareg **Engine:** 2.0L L4, 2.5L L5, 3.0L V6, 3.6L V6	**ENGINE OIL TEMPERATURE SENSOR CIRCUIT LOW:** With the ignition on. Battery voltage greater than 10.4 Volts. The Engine Oil Temperature sensor circuit voltage at the Powertrain Control Module (PCM) is less than the calibrated amount. One Trip Fault. Three good trips to clear the MIL.
DTC: P0198 **1T ECM, MIL: Yes** **Year:** 2011, 2012 **Model:** Beetle, CC, Eos, Golf, GTI, GLI, Jetta, Passat, Routan, Tiguan, Touareg **Engine:** 2.0L L4, 2.5L L5, 3.0L V6, 3.6L V6	**ENGINE OIL TEMPERATURE SENSOR CIRCUIT HIGH:** With the ignition on. Battery voltage greater than 10.4 Volts. The Engine Oil Temperature Sensor circuit voltage at the Powertrain Control Module (PCM) is greater than the calibrated amount. One Trip Fault. Three good trips to turn off the MIL.
DTC: P0201 **2T ECM, MIL: Yes** **Year:** 2011, 2012 **Model:** Beetle, CC, Eos, Golf, GTI, GLI, Jetta, Passat, Routan, Tiguan, Touareg **Engine:** 2.0L L4, 2.5L L5, 3.0L V6, 3.6L V6	**Injector Circuit / Open - Cylinder 1:** With battery voltage greater than 10 Volts. Auto Shutdown Relay energized. Engine speed less than 3000 RPM. The Powertrain Control Module (PCM) monitors the continuity of the injector circuits, as well as the voltage spike created by the collapse of the magnetic field in the injector coil. Any condition that reduces the maximum current flow or the magnitude of the voltage spike can cause this DTC to set.
DTC: P0202 **2T ECM, MIL: Yes** **Year:** 2011, 2012 **Model:** Beetle, CC, Eos, Golf, GTI, GLI, Jetta, Passat, Routan, Tiguan, Touareg **Engine:** 2.0L L4, 2.5L L5, 3.0L V6, 3.6L V6	**Injector Circuit / Open - Cylinder 2:** With battery voltage greater than 10 Volts. Auto Shutdown Relay energized. Engine speed less than 3000 RPM. The Powertrain Control Module (PCM) monitors the continuity of the injector circuits, as well as the voltage spike created by the collapse of the magnetic field in the injector coil. Any condition that reduces the maximum current flow or the magnitude of the voltage spike can cause this DTC to set.
DTC: P0203 **2T ECM, MIL: Yes** **Year:** 2011, 2012 **Model:** Beetle, CC, Eos, Golf, GTI, GLI, Jetta, Passat, Routan, Tiguan, Touareg **Engine:** 2.0L L4, 2.5L L5, 3.0L V6, 3.6L V6	**Injector Circuit / Open - Cylinder 3:** With battery voltage greater than 10 Volts. Auto Shutdown Relay energized. Engine speed less than 3000 RPM. The Powertrain Control Module (PCM) monitors the continuity of the injector circuits, as well as the voltage spike created by the collapse of the magnetic field in the injector coil. Any condition that reduces the maximum current flow or the magnitude of the voltage spike can cause this DTC to set.
DTC: P0204 **2T ECM, MIL: Yes** **Year:** 2011, 2012 **Model:** Beetle, CC, Eos, Golf, GTI, GLI, Jetta, Passat, Routan, Tiguan, Touareg **Engine:** 2.0L L4, 2.5L L5, 3.0L V6, 3.6L V6	**Injector Circuit / Open - Cylinder 4:** With battery voltage greater than 10 Volts. Auto Shutdown Relay energized. Engine speed less than 3000 RPM. The Powertrain Control Module (PCM) monitors the continuity of the injector circuits as well as the voltage spike created by the collapse of the magnetic field in the injector coil. Any condition that reduces the maximum current flow or the magnitude of the voltage spike can cause this DTC to set.

DTC	Trouble Code Title and Conditions
DTC: P0205 **2T ECM, MIL: Yes** **Year:** 2011, 2012 **Model:** Beetle, CC, Eos, Golf, GTI, GLI, Jetta, Passat, Routan, Tiguan, Touareg **Engine:** 2.5L L5, 3.0L V6, 3.6L V6	**Injector Circuit / Open - Cylinder 5:** With battery voltage greater than 10 Volts. Auto Shutdown Relay energized. Engine speed less than 3000 RPM. The Powertrain Control Module (PCM) monitors the continuity of the injector circuits as well as the voltage spike created by the collapse of the magnetic field in the injector coil. Any condition that reduces the maximum current flow or the magnitude of the voltage spike can cause this DTC to set.
DTC: P0206 **2T ECM, MIL: Yes** **Year:** 2011, 2012 **Model:** CC, Golf, GTI, Passat, Routan, Touareg **Engine:** 3.0L V6, 3.6L V6	**Injector Circuit / Open - Cylinder 6:** With battery voltage greater than 10 Volts. Auto Shutdown Relay energized. Engine speed less than 3000 RPM. The Powertrain Control Module (PCM) monitors the continuity of the injector circuits as well as the voltage spike created by the collapse of the magnetic field in the injector coil. Any condition that reduces the maximum current flow or the magnitude of the voltage spike can cause this DTC to set.
DTC: P020A **2T ECM, MIL: Yes** **Year:** 2011, 2012 **Model:** Golf, Jetta, Passat **Engine:** 2.0L L4	**Cylinder 1 Injection Timing:** * Engine running * ECM in closed loop * BARO pressure > 750 hPa * ECT > 50 °C * Time since engine start > 30 Sec. * Regeneration = off
DTC: P020B **2T ECM, MIL: Yes** **Year:** 2011, 2012 **Model:** Golf, Jetta, Passat **Engine:** 2.0L L4, 2.5L L5	**Cylinder 2 Injection Timing:** * Engine running * ECM in closed loop * ECT > 50 °C * Time since engine start > 30 Sec.
DTC: P020C **2T ECM, MIL: Yes** **Year:** 2011, 2012 **Model:** Golf, Jetta, Passat **Engine:** 2.0L L4	**Cylinder 3 Injection Timing:** * Engine running * ECM in closed loop * ECT > 50 °C * Time since engine start > 30 Sec.
DTC: P0216 **2T ECM, MIL: Yes** **Year:** 2011, 2012 **Model:** Jetta, Passat **Engine:** 2.0L L4	**Injector/Injection Timing Control Malfunction:** Engine started, and the ECM has detected a malfunction in the injector timing control.
DTC: P0218 **2T ECM, MIL: Yes** **Year:** 2011, 2012 **Model:** Routan **Engine:** 3.6L V6 VIN G	**-HIGH TEMPERATURE OPERATION ACTIVATED:** Whenever the engine is running. Immediately when an Overheat shift schedule is activated when the Transmission Oil Temperature reaches 115° C (240° F).
DTC: P0221 **2T ECM, MIL: Yes** **Year:** 2011, 2012 **Model:** Beetle, CC, Eos, Golf, GTI, GLI, Jetta, Passat, Routan, Tiguan, Touareg **Engine:** 2.0L L4, 2.5L L5, 3.0L V6, 3.6L V6	**Throttle/Pedal Position Sensor/Switch B Circuit Range/Performance:** Ignition on and No MAP Sensor DTCs set. The TP Sensor signals do not correlate to the MAP Sensor signal. Two Trip Fault. ETC light will illuminate. P2135 should set with this code. Engine speed, >1200 RPM.
DTC: P0222 **1T ECM, MIL: Yes** **Year:** 2011, 2012 **Model:** Beetle, CC, Eos, Golf, GTI, GLI, Jetta, Passat, Routan, Tiguan, Touareg **Engine:** 2.0L L4, 2.5L L5, 3.0L V6, 3.6L V6	**Throttle/Pedal Position Sensor/Switch B Circuit Low Input:** With the ignition on and the battery voltage greater than 10 Volts. Throttle Position Sensor voltage at the Powertrain Control Module (PCM) is less than 0.16 of a Volt for 0.7 of a second. One Trip Fault. Three good trips to turn off the MIL. ETC light will illuminate.

DTC	Trouble Code Title and Conditions
DTC: P0223 **1T ECM, MIL: Yes** **Year:** 2011, 2012 **Model:** Beetle, CC, Eos, Golf, GTI, GLI, Jetta, Passat, Routan, Tiguan, Touareg **Engine:** 2.0L L4, 2.5L L5, 3.0L V6, 3.6L V6	**Throttle/Pedal Position Sensor B Circuit High:** With the ignition on. Throttle Position Sensor No.2 Signal circuit voltage is greater than 4.9 Volts for 25ms. One Trip Fault. ETC light will illuminate.
DTC: P0225 **1T ECM, MIL: Yes** **Year:** 2011, 2012 **Model:** Beetle, Golf, GTI, Jetta, Passat **Engine:** 2.0L L4, 2.5L L5	**Throttle/Pedal Position Sensor/Switch "C" Circuit Voltage Supply:** Supply voltage for accelerator pedal position sensor -4.89 - 5.10 V.
DTC: P0226 **1T ECM, MIL: Yes** **Year:** 2011, 2012 **Model:** Beetle, Golf, GTI, Jetta, Passat **Engine:** 2.0L L4, 2.5L L5	**Throttle/Pedal Position Sensor/Switch "C" Circuit Range/Performance:** * Idle switch, idle * Idle switch, not idle
DTC: P0228 **1T ECM, MIL: Yes** **Year:** 2011, 2012 **Model:** Beetle Golf, GTI, Jetta, Passat **Engine:** 2.0L L4, 2.5L L5	**Throttle/Pedal Position Sensor/Switch "C" Circuit High:** Accelerator pedal position sensor voltage > 4.76 V.
DTC: P022A **2T ECM, MIL: Yes** **Year:** 2011, 2012 **Model:** Touareg **Engine:** 3.0L TDI V6	**Charge Air Cooler Bypass Control "A" Circuit Open:** * Power stage commanded Off * Ignition Off
DTC: P022B **2T ECM** **Year:** 2011, 2012 **Model:** Touareg **Engine:** 3.0L TDI V6	**Charge Air Cooler Bypass Control "A" Circuit Low:** * Power stage commanded Off * Ignition Off
DTC: P022C **2T ECM, MIL: Yes** **Year:** 2011, 2012 **Model:** Touareg **Engine:** 3.0L TDI V6	**Charge Air Cooler Bypass Control "A" Circuit High:** * Power stage commanded On
DTC: P0230 **2T ECM, MIL: Yes** **Year:** 2011, 2012 **Model:** Beetle, Eos, Golf, GTI, Jetta, Passat **Engine:** 2.0L TDI L4	**Fuel Pump Primary Circuit Malfunction:** Engine started, battery voltage at least 11.5v, all electrical components off, ground connections between engine and chassis well connected, coolant temperature at least 80-degrees celicius. The ECM detected high current in fuel pump or fuel shutoff valve (FSV) circuit, or it detected voltage with the valve off, or it did not detect voltage on the circuit. The circuit is used to energize the fuel pump relay at key on or while running. Fuel pressure value should be 3000 to 5000 kPa at idle.
DTC: P0234 **2T ECM, MIL: Yes** **Year:** 2011, 2012 **Model:** Touareg **Engine:** 3.0L TDI V6,	**Turbo Charger Over-boost Condition limit exceeded:** * Boost pressure control mode = closed loop * RPM > 1650* Fuel quantity > 15 mg/stroke
DTC: P0234 **2T ECM, MIL: Yes** **Year:** 2011, 2012 **Model:** Beetle, Eos, Golf, GTI, Jetta, Passat **Engine:** 2.0L TDI L4	**Turbocharger/Supercharger Over-boost Condition Rationality check high:** Malfunction Criteria and Threshold Value: * Negative system deviation high>300-1275 hPa * Engine speed > 2400 . . . 3000 RPM.

DTC	Trouble Code Title and Conditions
DTC: P0235 **1T ECM, MIL: Yes** **Year:** 2011, 2012 **Model:** Beetle, Eos, GTI, Jetta, Passat **Engine:** 2.0L TDI L4	**Turbocharger Boost Sensor (A) Circ Control Limit Not Reached:** Engine started, battery voltage at least 11.5v, all electrical components off, ground connections between engine and chassis well connected, coolant temperature at least 80-degrees celicius. The ECM detected an operating condition that could harm the engine or automatic transmission.
DTC: P0236 **2T ECM, MIL: Yes** **Year:** 2011, 2012 **Model:** Touareg **Engine:** 3.0L TDI V6	**Turbocharger Boost Sensor (A) Circuit Performance:** * Engine started, battery voltage at least 11.5v * Engine speed < 600 rpm
DTC: P0236 **1T ECM, MIL: Yes** **Year:** 2011, 2012 **Model:** Beetle, Eos, Golf, GTI, Jetta, Passat **Engine:** 2.0L TDI L4	**Turbocharger Boost Sensor (A) Circ Control Range/Performance:** Engine started, battery voltage at least 11.5v, all electrical components off, ground connections between engine and chassis well connected, coolant temperature at least 80-degrees Celicius. The ECM detected an operating condition that could harm the engine or automatic transmission.
DTC: P0237 **2T ECM, MIL: Yes** **Year:** 2011, 2012 **Model:** Beetle, Eos, Golf, GTI, Jetta, Passat **Engine:** 2.0L L4	**Turbocharger/Supercharger Boost Sensor A Circuit Low:** Malfunction Criteria and Threshold Value: * Signal voltage, < 0.2 V
DTC: P0238 **2T ECM, MIL: Yes** **Year:** 2011, 2012 **Model:** Beetle, Eos, Golf, GTI, Jetta, Passat **Engine:** 2.0L TDI L4	**Turbocharger/Supercharger Boost Sensor A Circuit High:** Malfunction Criteria and Threshold Value: * Short to battery + 4.88 V.
DTC: P0243 **2T ECM, MIL: Yes** **Year:** 2011, 2012 **Model:** Beetle, Eos, Golf, GTI, Jetta, Passat **Engine:** 2.0L TDI L4	**Turbocharger/Supercharger Wastegate Solenoid A:** * Charge pressure control valve, commanded off * Engine speed, > 80 RPM * Battery voltage, 9.04-16 V
DTC: P0245 **2T ECM, MIL: Yes** **Year:** 2011, 2012 **Model:** Beetle, Eos, Golf, GTI, Jetta, Passat **Engine:** 2.0L TDI L4	**Turbocharger/Supercharger Wastegate Solenoid A Low:** * Charge pressure control valve, commanded off * Engine speed, > 80 RPM
DTC: P0246 **2T ECM, MIL: Yes** **Year:** 2011, 2012 **Model:** Beetle, Eos, Golf, GTI, Jetta, Passat **Engine:** 2.0L TDI L4	**Turbocharger/Supercharger Wastegate Solenoid A High:** * Charge (boost) pressure control valve, commanded on * Engine speed, > 80 RPM
DTC: P025A **2T ECM, MIL: Yes** **Year:** 2011, 2012 **Model:** Beetle, Eos, Golf, GTI, Jetta, Passat, Touareg **Engine:** 2.0L TDI L4, 3.0L TDI V6	**Fuel Pump Module Control Circuit/Open:** * Engine speed, > 80 RPM
DTC: P025C **2T ECM, MIL: Yes** **Year:** 2011, 2012 **Model:** Beetle, Eos, Golf, GTI, Jetta, Passat, Touareg **Engine:** 2.0L TDI L4, 3.0L TDI V6	**Fuel Pump Module Control Circuit Low:** Engine speed, >40 RPM

DTC	Trouble Code Title and Conditions
DTC: P025D **2T ECM, MIL: Yes** **Year:** 2011, 2012 **Model:** Beetle, Eos, Golf, GTI, Jetta, Passat,Touareg **Engine:** 2.0L TDI L4, 3.0L TDI V6	**Fuel Pump Module Control Circuit High:** Engine speed, >40 RPM
DTC: P0261 **2T ECM, MIL: Yes** **Year:** 2011, 2012 **Model:** Beetle, CC, Eos, Golf, GTI, GLI, Jetta, Passat, Routan, Tiguan, Touareg **Engine:** 2.0L L4, 2.5L L5, 3.0L V6, 3.6L V6	**Cylinder 1 Injector Circuit Low:** With the engine cranking or running. The ECM detects a fault on a Fuel Injector Control circuit. * Engine speed,> 80 RPM * Injection valves, Switched off * High side signal current, > 4.20 A
DTC: P0262 **2T ECM, MIL: Yes** **Year:** 2011, 2012 **Model:** Beetle, CC, Eos, Golf, GTI, GLI, Jetta, Passat, Routan, Tiguan, Touareg **Engine:** 2.0L L4, 2.5L L5, 3.0L V6, 3.6L V6	**Cylinder 1 Injector Circuit High:** With the engine cranking or running. The ECM detects a fault on a Fuel Injector Control circuit. * Engine speed, > 80 RPM * Injection valve, switched on.
DTC: P0263 **2T ECM, MIL: Yes** **Year:** 2011, 2012 **Model:** Beetle, CC, Eos, Golf, GTI, GLI, Jetta, Passat, Routan, Tiguan, Touareg **Engine:** 2.0L L4, 2.5L L5, 3.0L V6, 3.6L V6	**Cylinder 1 Contribution/Balance:** With the engine cranking or running. The ECM detects a fault on a Fuel Injector Control circuit. * Engine speed > 1400 and < 2200 RPM * Fuel temperature > 0 and < 80 °C * Intake air temp > 0 °C * Coolant temp > 70 °C * Boost pressure > 80 hpa
DTC: P0264 **2T ECM, MIL: Yes** **Year:** 2011, 2012 **Model:** Beetle, CC, Eos, Golf, GTI, GLI, Jetta, Passat, Routan, Tiguan, Touareg **Engine:** 2.0L L4, 2.5L L5, 3.0L V6, 3.6L V6	**Cylinder 2 Injector Circuit Low:** With the engine cranking or running. The ECM detects a fault on a Fuel Injector Control circuit. * Injection valve, commanded OFF * Engine speed, > 80 RPM
DTC: P0265 **2T ECM, MIL: Yes** **Year:** 2011, 2012 **Model:** Beetle, CC, Eos, Golf, GTI, GLI, Jetta, Passat, Routan, Tiguan, Touareg **Engine:** 2.0L L4, 2.5L L5, 3.0L V6, 3.6L V6	**Cylinder 2 Injector Circuit High:** With the engine cranking or running. The ECM detects a fault on a Fuel Injector Control circuit. * Injection valve, Commanded on * Engine speed, > 80 RPM * Battery voltage, 9.04-16 V
DTC: P0266 **2T ECM, MIL: Yes** **Year:** 2011, 2012 **Model:** Beetle, CC, Eos, Golf, GTI, GLI, Jetta, Passat, Routan, Tiguan, Touareg **Engine:** 2.0L L4, 2.5L L5, 3.0L V6, 3.6L V6	**Cylinder 2 Contribution/Balance:** With the engine cranking or running. The ECM detects a fault on a Fuel Injector Control circuit. * Engine speed > 1600 and < 2500 RPM * Fuel temperature > 0 and < 80 °C * Intake air temp > 0 °C * Boost pressure > 90000 Pa * Gear > 2 * Fuel cutoff active

DTC	Trouble Code Title and Conditions
DTC: P0267 **2T ECM, MIL: Yes** **Year:** 2011, 2012 **Model:** Beetle, CC, Eos, Golf, GTI, GLI, Jetta, Passat, Routan, Tiguan, Touareg **Engine:** 2.0L L4, 2.5L L5, 3.0L V6, 3.6L V6	**Cylinder 3 Injector Circuit Low:** With the engine cranking or running. The ECM detects a fault on a Fuel Injector Control circuit. * Injection valve, commanded OFF * Engine speed, > 80 RPM
DTC: P0268 **2T ECM, MIL: Yes** **Year:** 2011, 2012 **Model:** Beetle, CC, Eos, Golf, GTI, GLI, Jetta, Passat, Routan, Tiguan, Touareg **Engine:** 2.0L L4, 2.5L L5, 3.0L V6, 3.6L V6	**Cylinder 3 Injector Circuit High:** With the engine cranking or running. The ECM detects a fault on a Fuel Injector Control circuit. * Injection valve, Commanded on * Engine speed, > 80 RPM
DTC: P0269 **2T ECM, MIL: Yes** **Year:** 2011, 2012 **Model:** Beetle, CC, Eos, Golf, GTI, GLI, Jetta, Passat, Routan, Tiguan, Touareg **Engine:** 2.0L L4, 2.5L L5, 3.0L V6, 3.6L V6	**Cylinder 3 Contribution/Balance:** With the ignition on. The Engine Control Module (ECM) is unable to stabilize fuel quantity in cylinder 3. * Engine speed > 1400 and < 2200 RPM * Fuel temperature > 0 and < 80 °C * Intake air temp > 0 °C * Coolant temp > 70 °C
DTC: P026A **2T ECM, MIL: Yes** **Year:** 2011, 2012 **Model:** Beetle, CC, Eos, Golf, GTI, GLI, Jetta, Passat, Routan, Tiguan, Touareg **Engine:** 2.0L L4, 2.5L L5, 3.0L V6, 3.6L V6	**Charge Air Cooler Efficiency Below Threshold:** * ECT > 60 °C * vehicle speed > 40 km/h * Ratio (boost pressure/baro) > 1.20 * Charge air flow rate > 50 and < 400 kg/h
DTC: P0270 **2T ECM, MIL: Yes** **Year:** 2011, 2012 **Model:** Beetle, CC, Eos, Golf, GTI, GLI, Jetta, Passat, Routan, Tiguan, Touareg **Engine:** 2.0L L4, 2.5L L5, 3.0L V6, 3.6L V6	**Cylinder 4 Injector Circuit Low:** With the engine cranking or running. The ECM detects a fault on a Fuel Injector Control circuit. * Injection valve, Commanded on * High pressure system current, >4.2 A * Engine speed, > 80 RPM
DTC: P0271 **2T ECM, MIL: Yes** **Year:** 2011, 2012 **Model:** Beetle, CC, Eos, Golf, GTI, GLI, Jetta, Passat, Routan, Tiguan, Touareg **Engine:** 2.0L L4, 2.5L L5, 3.0L V6, 3.6L V6	**Cylinder 4 Injector Circuit High:** With the engine cranking or running. The ECM detects a fault on a Fuel Injector Control circuit. * Injection valve, switched on * Engine speed > 80 RPM
DTC: P0272 **2T ECM, MIL: Yes** **Year:** 2011, 2012 **Model:** Beetle, CC, Eos, Golf, GTI, GLI, Jetta, Passat, Routan, Tiguan, Touareg **Engine:** 2.0L L4, 2.5L L5, 3.0L V6, 3.6L V6	**Cylinder 4 Contribution/Balance:** With the engine cranking or running. The ECM detects a fault on a Fuel Injector Control circuit. * Engine speed > 1600 and < 2500 RPM * Fuel temperature > 0 and < 80 °C * Intake air temp > 0 °C * Boost pressure > 90000 Pa * Gear > 2 * Fuel cutoff active

DTC	Trouble Code Title and Conditions
DTC: P0273 **2T ECM, MIL: Yes** **Year:** 2011, 2012 **Model:** Beetle, CC, Eos, Golf, GTI, GLI, Jetta, Passat, Routan, Tiguan, Touareg **Engine:** 2.5L L5, 3.0L V6, 3.6L V6	**Cylinder 5 Injector Circuit Low:** With the engine cranking or running. The ECM detects a fault on a Fuel Injector Control circuit. * Injection valve, switched off * Engine speed > 80 RPM
DTC: P0274 **2T ECM, MIL: Yes** **Year:** 2011, 2012 **Model:** Beetle, CC, Eos, Golf, GTI, GLI, Jetta, Passat, Routan, Tiguan, Touareg **Engine:** 2.5L L5, 3.0L V6, 3.6L V6	**Cylinder 5 Injector Circuit High:** With the engine cranking or running. The ECM detects a fault on a Fuel Injector Control circuit. * Engine speed,> 80 RPM * Injection valves, Switched on
DTC: P0275 **2T ECM, MIL: Yes** **Year:** 2011, 2012 **Model:** Beetle, CC, Eos, Golf, GTI, GLI, Jetta, Passat, Routan, Tiguan, Touareg **Engine:** 2.5L L5, 3.0L V6, 3.6L V6	**Cylinder 5 Contribution/Balance:** With the engine cranking or running. The ECM detects a fault on a Fuel Injector Control circuit. * Engine speed > 1600 and < 2500 RPM * Fuel temperature > 0 and < 80 °C * Intake air temp > 0 °C * Boost pressure > 90000 Pa * Gear > 2 * Fuel cutoff active
DTC: P0276 **2T ECM, MIL: Yes** **Year:** 2011, 2012 **Model:** CC, Passat, Routan, Touareg **Engine:** 3.0L V6, 3.6L V6	**Cylinder 6 Injector Circuit Low:** With the engine cranking or running. The ECM detects a fault on a Fuel Injector Control circuit. * Injection valve, Commanded on * High pressure system current, >4.2 A * Engine speed, > 80 RPM
DTC: P0277 **2T ECM, MIL: Yes** **Year:** 2011, 2012 **Model:** CC, Passat, Routan, Touareg **Engine:** 3.0L V6, 3.6L V6	**Cylinder 6- Injector Circuit High:** With the engine cranking or running. The ECM detects a fault on a Fuel Injector Control circuit. * Injection valve, Commanded on * Engine speed, > 80 RPM
DTC: P0278 **2T ECM, MIL: Yes** **Year:** 2011, 2012 **Model:** CC, Passat, Routan, Touareg **Engine:** 3.0L V6, 3.6L V6	**Cylinder 6 Contribution/Balance:** With the engine cranking or running. The ECM detects a fault on a Fuel Injector Control circuit. * Engine speed > 1600 and < 2500 RPM * Fuel temperature > 0 and < 80 °C * Intake air temp > 0 °C * Boost pressure > 90000 Pa * Gear > 2 * Fuel cutoff active
DTC: P0290 **2T ECM, MIL: Yes** **Year:** 2011, 2012 **Model:** Beetle, Eos, GTI, Passat **Engine:** 2.0L L4	**"B" Camshaft Position Actuator Control Circuit Low Bank 1:** * Camshaft valve, commanded off * Engine speed, >80 RPM
DTC: P0298 **2T ECM, MIL: Yes** **Year:** 2011, 2012 **Model:** Routan **Engine:** 3.6L V6 VIN G	**ENGINE OIL TEMPERATURE TOO HIGH:** The engine oil temperature has dropped below a calibrated value. Engine start up. The Engine Oil temperature rises faster than a calibrated modeled temperature. When the actual oil temperature exceeds the high boundary of the calibrated modeled temperature for three minutes the fault is set. Two trip fault. Three good trips to turn off the MIL.
DTC: P0299 **2T ECM, MIL: Yes** **Year:** 2011, 2012 **Model:** Beetle, Eos, Golf, GTI, Jetta, Passat **Engine:** 2.0L L4, 2.5L L5	**Turbocharger/Supercharger Under-boost:** * Difference of set value boost pressure vs. basic boost pressure value > 250 hPa * Engine speed, 2400-3000 RPM * Basic boost pressure * Ambient pressure, +450 hPa > 700 hPa

DTC	Trouble Code Title and Conditions
DTC: P0300 **2T ECM, MIL: Yes** **Year:** 2011, 2012 **Model:** Beetle, CC, Eos, Golf, GTI, GLI, Jetta, Passat, Routan, Tiguan, Touareg **Engine:** 2.0L L4, 2.5L L5, 3.0L V6, 3.6L V6	**Random Misfire Detected:** Engine running under positive torque conditions, and the ECM detected a misfire or uneven engine running in two or more cylinders. **NOTE: If the misfire is severe, the MIL will flash on/off on the first trip!** * Engine speed range, 440-6800 RPM * IAT, >-48° C * ECT at start, > 10.50° C * Fuel cutoff, Not active * rough road not detected * internal CAN no fault
DTC: P0301 **2T ECM, MIL: Yes** **Year:** 2011, 2012 **Model:** Beetle, CC, Eos, Golf, GTI, GLI, Jetta, Passat, Routan, Tiguan, Touareg **Engine:** 2.0L L4, 2.5L L5, 3.0L V6, 3.6L V6	**Cylinder 1 Misfire Detected:** Engine running under positive torque conditions, and the ECM detected a misfire or uneven engine function. **Note: If the misfire is severe, the MIL will flash on/off on the 1st trip!** * IAT, > -48° C * Time after engine start, Idle - 150 RPM * Engine torque, > 5.47-23.4% * Camshaft revolutions 1 * Engine speed range, 480-6800 RPM * Fuel cutoff, Not active * ECT at start, > -10.50 °C
DTC: P0302 **2T ECM, MIL: Yes** **Year:** 2011, 2012 **Model:** Beetle, CC, Eos, Golf, GTI, GLI, Jetta, Passat, Routan, Tiguan, Touareg **Engine:** 2.0L L4, 2.5L L5, 3.0L V6, 3.6L V6	**Cylinder 2 Misfire Detected:** Engine running under positive torque conditions, and the ECM detected a misfire or uneven engine function. **Note: If the misfire is severe, the MIL will flash on/off on the 1st trip!** * IAT, > -48° C * Time after engine start, Idle - 150 RPM * Engine torque, > 5.47-23.4% * Camshaft revolutions 1 * Engine speed range, 480-6800 RPM * Fuel cutoff, Not active * ECT at start, > -10.50 °C
DTC: P0303 **2T ECM, MIL: Yes** **Year:** 2011, 2012 **Model:** Beetle, CC, Eos, Golf, GTI, GLI, Jetta, Passat, Routan, Tiguan, Touareg **Engine:** 2.0L L4, 2.5L L5, 3.0L V6, 3.6L V6	**Cylinder 3 Misfire Detected:** Engine running under positive torque conditions, and the ECM detected a misfire or uneven engine function. **Note: If the misfire is severe, the MIL will flash on/off on the 1st trip!** * IAT, > -48° C * Time after engine start, Idle - 150 RPM * Engine torque, > 5.47-23.4% * Camshaft revolutions 1 * Engine speed range, 480-6800 RPM * Fuel cutoff, Not active * ECT at start, > -10.50 °C
DTC: P0304 **2T ECM, MIL: Yes** **Year:** 2011, 2012 **Model:** Beetle, CC, Eos, Golf, GTI, GLI, Jetta, Passat, Routan, Tiguan, Touareg **Engine:** 2.0L L4, 2.5L L5, 3.0L V6, 3.6L V6	**Cylinder 4 Misfire Detected:** Engine running under positive torque conditions, and the ECM detected a misfire or uneven engine function. **Note: If the misfire is severe, the MIL will flash on/off on the 1st trip!** * IAT, > -48° C * Time after engine start, Idle - 150 RPM * Engine torque, > 5.47-23.4% * Camshaft revolutions 1 * Engine speed range, 480-6800 RPM * Fuel cutoff, Not active * ECT at start, > -10.50 °C

DTC	Trouble Code Title and Conditions
DTC: P0305 **2T ECM, MIL: Yes** **Year:** 2011, 2012 **Model:** Beetle, CC, Eos, Golf, GTI, GLI, Jetta, Passat, Routan, Tiguan, Touareg **Engine:** 2.5L L5, 3.0L V6, 3.6L V6	**Cylinder 5 Misfire Detected:** Engine running under positive torque conditions, and the ECM detected a misfire or uneven engine function. **Note: If the misfire is severe, the MIL will flash on/off on the 1st trip!** * IAT, > -48° C * Time after engine start, Idle - 150 RPM * Engine torque, > 5.47-23.4% * Camshaft revolutions 1 * Engine speed range, 480-6800 RPM * Fuel cutoff, Not active * ECT at start, > -10.50 °C
DTC: P0306 **2T ECM, MIL: Yes** **Year:** 2011, 2012 **Model:** Beetle, CC, Eos, Golf, GTI, GLI, Jetta, Passat, Routan, Tiguan, Touareg **Engine:** 3.0L V6, 3.6L V6	**Cylinder Number 6 Misfire Detected:** Engine running under positive torque conditions, and the ECM detected a misfire or uneven engine function. **Note: If the misfire is severe, the MIL will flash on/off on the 1st trip!** * IAT, > -48° C * Time after engine start, Idle - 150 RPM * Engine torque, > 5.47-23.4% * Camshaft revolutions 1 * Engine speed range, 480-6800 RPM * Fuel cutoff, Not active * ECT at start, > -10.50 °C
DTC: P0315 **2T ECM, MIL: Yes** **Year:** 2011, 2012 **Model:** Beetle, CC, Eos, Golf, GTI, GLI, Jetta, Passat, Routan, Tiguan, Touareg **Engine:** 2.0L L4, 2.5L L5, 3.0L V6, 3.6L V6	**NO CRANK SENSOR LEARNED:** Under closed throttle decel and A/C off. ECT above 75° C (167° F). Engine start time is greater than 50 seconds. One of the CKP sensor target windows has more than 2% variance from the reference. One Trip Fault. Three good trips to turn off the MIL.
DTC: P0318 **2T ECM, MIL: Yes** **Year:** 2011, 2012 **Model:** Beetle, CC, Eos, Golf, GTI, GLI, Jetta, Passat, Routan, Tiguan, Touareg **Engine:** 2.0L L4, 2.5L L5, 3.0L V6, 3.6L V6	**Rough Road Sensor:** Engine running, and the ECM detected an implausible signal from the rough road sensor.
DTC: P0321 **2T ECM, MIL: Yes** **Year:** 2011, 2012 **Model:** Beetle, CC, Eos, Golf, GTI, GLI, Jetta, Passat, Routan, Tiguan, Touareg **Engine:** 2.0L L4, 2.5L L5, 3.6L V6	**Ignition/Distributor Engine Speed Input Circuit Range/Performance:** * Engine speed, >0 RPM * Crankshaft revolutions, 2 revs
DTC: P0322 **2T ECM, MIL: Yes** **Year:** 2011, 2012 **Model:** Beetle, CC, Eos, Golf, GTI, GLI, Jetta, Passat, Routan, Tiguan, Touareg **Engine:** 2.0L L4, 2.5L L5, 3.6L V6	**Ignition/Distributor Engine Speed Input Circuit No Signal:** * No engine speed signal but phase signals during 4.5 cam shaft revs. * Engine speed signal partly interrupted, Phase sensor, No DTC.
DTC: P0324 **2T ECM, MIL: Yes** **Year:** 2011, 2012 **Model:** Beetle, CC, Eos, Golf, GTI, GLI, Jetta, Passat, Routan, Tiguan, Touareg **Engine:** 2.0L L4, 2.5L L5, 3.0L V6, 3.6L V6	**Knock control System Error Malfunction:** * ECT >39° C * Knock control, Active * Engine load, >30% * Engine speed, 1200-5040 RPM

DTC	Trouble Code Title and Conditions
DTC: P0325 **2T ECM, MIL: Yes** **Year:** 2011, 2012 **Model:** Beetle, CC, Eos, Golf, GTI, GLI, Jetta, Passat, Routan, Tiguan, Touareg **Engine:** 2.0L L4, 2.5L L5, 3.0L V6, 3.6L V6	**Knock Sensor 1 Circuit Malfunction:** The Powertrain Control Module (PCM) detects that the Knock Sensor input voltage is: Above 4.0 Volts, less than or equal to 1.0 Volt with engine RPM at or above 2200 or equal to 0.0 Volts with engine RPM below 2200. Two Trip Fault. Three good trips to turn off the MIL.
DTC: P0327 **2T ECM, MIL: Yes** **Year:** 2011, 2012 **Model:** Beetle, CC, Eos, Golf, GTI, GLI, Jetta, Passat, Routan, Tiguan, Touareg **Engine:** 2.0L L4, 2.5L L5, 3.0L V6, 3.6L V6	**Knock Sensor 1 Circuit Low Input (Bank 1):** * Engine speed, > 2400 RPM * ECT, > 40.5 °C * Engine load, > 30% * Signal range check, No DTC
DTC: P0328 **2T ECM, MIL: Yes** **Year:** 2011, 2012 **Model:** Beetle, CC, Eos, Golf, GTI, GLI, Jetta, Passat, Routan, Tiguan, Touareg **Engine:** 2.0L L4, 2.5L L5, 3.0L V6, 3.6L V6	**Knock Sensor 1 Circuit High Input (Bank 1):** * Engine speed, > 1000 RPM * ECT > 40.5° C * Engine load > 35 - 60% * Engine speed > 2000 RPM
DTC: P0330 **2T ECM, MIL: Yes** **Year:** 2011, 2012 **Model:** Beetle, CC, Eos, Golf, GTI, GLI, Jetta, Passat, Routan, Tiguan, Touareg **Engine:** 2.0L L4, 2.5L L5, 3.0L V6, 3.6L V6	**-KNOCK SENSOR 2 CIRCUIT:** This monitor runs above 2000 RPM, under open throttle conditions. The Knock diagnostic does not run at idle or during decelerations. The high voltage test runs all the times the engine is running. The Powertrain Control Module (PCM) detects that the Knock Sensor input voltage is: Above 4.0 Volts, less than or equal to 1.0 Volt with engine RPM at or above 2200 or equal to 0.0 Volts with engine RPM below 2200. Two Trip Fault. Three good trips to turn off the MIL.
DTC: P0332 **2T ECM, MIL: Yes** **Year:** 2011, 2012 **Model:** Beetle, CC, Eos, Golf, GTI, GLI, Jetta, Passat, Routan, Tiguan, Touareg **Engine:** 2.5L L5, 3.0L V6, 3.6L V6	**Knock Sensor 2 Circuit Low Input (Bank 2):** * Signal or 5 V reference circuit > 1000 RPM * Signal range check > 2000 RPM * ECT > 40.5 °C * Engine load 30 to 33.8 %
DTC: P0333 **2T ECM, MIL: Yes** **Year:** 2011, 2012 **Model:** Beetle, CC, Eos, Golf, GTI, GLI, Jetta, Passat, Routan, Tiguan, Touareg **Engine:** 2.5L L5, 3.0L V6, 3.6L V6	**Knock Sensor 2 Circuit High Input (Bank 2):** * Signal or 5 V reference circuit > 1000 RPM * Signal range check > 2000 RPM * ECT > 40.5 °C * Engine load 30 to 33.8 %
DTC: P0335 **1T ECM, MIL: Yes** **Year:** 2011, 2012 **Model:** Beetle, CC, Eos, Golf, GTI, GLI, Jetta, Passat, Routan, Tiguan, Touareg **Engine:** 2.0L L4, 2.5L L5, 3.0L V6, 3.6L V6	**CRANKSHAFT POSITION SENSOR CIRCUIT:** With the engine cranking, No CKP signal is present during engine cranking and at least eight camshaft position sensor signals have occurred. One Trip Fault. Three good trips to turn off the MIL.

DTC	Trouble Code Title and Conditions
DTC: P0339 **1T ECM, MIL: Yes** **Year:** 2011, 2012 **Model:** Beetle, CC, Eos, Golf, GTI, GLI, Jetta, Passat, Routan, Tiguan, Touareg **Engine:** 2.0L L4, 2.5L L5, 3.0L V6, 3.6L V6	**CRANKSHAFT POSITION SENSOR INTERMITTENT:** While cranking the engine and with the engine running. When the CKP Sensor failure counter reaches 20. One Trip Fault. Three good trips to turn off the MIL.
DTC: P0340 **1T ECM, MIL: Yes** **Year:** 2011, 2012 **Model:** Beetle, CC, Eos, Golf, GTI, GLI, Jetta, Passat, Routan, Tiguan, Touareg **Engine:** 2.0L L4, 2.5L L5, 3.0L V6, 3.6L V6	**Camshaft Position Sensor A Circuit (Bank 1 or single sensor):** During engine cranking and with the engine running. Battery voltage greater than 10 Volts. At least five seconds or 2.5 engine revolutions have elapsed with crankshaft position sensor signals present but no camshaft position sensor signal. One Trip Fault. Three good trips to turn off the MIL.
DTC: P0341 **1T ECM, MIL: Yes** **Year:** 2011, 2012 **Model:** Beetle, CC, Eos, Golf, GTI, GLI, Jetta, Passat, Routan, Tiguan, Touareg **Engine:** 2.0L L4, 2.5L L5, 3.0L V6, 3.6L V6	**Camshaft Position Sensor A Circuit Range / Performance (Bank 1 or single sensor):** Signals compared to engine speed sensor signals. No alternating signal at reference gap.
DTC: P0342 **1T ECM, MIL: Yes** **Year:** 2011, 2012 **Model:** Beetle, CC, Eos, Golf, GTI, GLI, Jetta, Passat, Routan, Tiguan, Touareg **Engine:** 2.0L L4, 2.5L L5, 3.0L V6, 3.6L V6	**Camshaft Position Sensor A Circuit Low Input (Bank 1 or single sensor):** Irregular number of phase changes Incorrect for 12 crank revs. Engine speed signal and phase signal synchronized.
DTC: P0343 **1T ECM, MIL: Yes** **Year:** 2011, 2012 **Model:** Beetle, CC, Eos, Golf, GTI, GLI, Jetta, Passat, Routan, Tiguan, Touareg **Engine:** 2.0L L4, 2.5L L5, 3.0L V6, 3.6L V6	**Camshaft Position Sensor A Circuit High Input (Bank 1 or single sensor):** Irregular number of phase changes Incorrect for 12 crank revs. Engine speed signal and phase signal synchronized.
DTC: P0344 **1T ECM, MIL: Yes** **Year:** 2011, 2012 **Model:** Beetle, CC, Eos, Golf, GTI, GLI, Jetta, Passat, Routan, Tiguan, Touareg **Engine:** 2.0L L4, 2.5L L5, 3.0L V6, 3.6L V6	**CAMSHAFT POSITION SENSOR INTERMITTENT:** While cranking the engine and engine running. When the failure counter reaches 20. One Trip Fault. Three good trips to turn off the MIL.
DTC: P0345 **1T ECM, MIL: Yes** **Year:** 2011, 2012 **Model:** Beetle, CC, Eos, Golf, GTI, GLI, Jetta, Passat, Routan, Tiguan, Touareg **Engine:** 2.0L L4, 2.5L L5, 3.0L V6, 3.6L V6	**CAMSHAFT 1/3 POSITION SENSOR CIRCUIT:** During engine cranking and with the engine running. Battery voltage greater than 10 Volts. At least five seconds or 2.5 engine revolutions have elapsed with crankshaft position sensor signals present but no camshaft position sensor signal. One Trip Fault. Three good trips to turn off the MIL.

DTC	Trouble Code Title and Conditions
DTC: P0346 **1T ECM, MIL: Yes** **Year:** 2011, 2012 **Model:** Beetle, CC, Eos, Golf, GTI, GLI, Jetta, Passat, Routan, Tiguan, Touareg **Engine:** 2.5L L5, 3.0L V6, 3.6L V6	**Camshaft Position Sensor "A" Circuit Range/Performance Bank 2:** During engine cranking and with the engine running. Battery voltage greater than 10 Volts. At least five seconds or 2.5 engine revolutions have elapsed with crankshaft position sensor signals present but no camshaft position sensor signal. One Trip Fault. Three good trips to turn off the MIL.
DTC: P0347 **1T ECM, MIL: Yes** **Year:** 2011, 2012 **Model:** Beetle, CC, Eos, Golf, GTI, GLI, Jetta, Passat, Routan, Tiguan, Touareg **Engine:** 2.5L L5, 3.0L V6, 3.6L V6 I	**Camshaft Position Sensor "A" Circuit Low Bank 2:** During engine cranking and with the engine running. Battery voltage greater than 10 Volts. At least five seconds or 2.5 engine revolutions have elapsed with crankshaft position sensor signals present but no camshaft position sensor signal. One Trip Fault. Three good trips to turn off the MIL.
DTC: P0348 **1T ECM, MIL: Yes** **Year:** 2011, 2012 **Model:** Beetle, CC, Eos, Golf, GTI, GLI, Jetta, Passat, Routan, Tiguan, Touareg **Engine:** 2.5L L5, 3.0L V6, 3.6L V6 I	**Camshaft Position Sensor "A" Circuit High Bank 2:** During engine cranking and with the engine running. Battery voltage greater than 10 Volts. At least five seconds or 2.5 engine revolutions have elapsed with crankshaft position sensor signals present but no camshaft position sensor signal. One Trip Fault. Three good trips to turn off the MIL.
DTC: P0349 **1T ECM, MIL: Yes** **Year:** 2011, 2012 **Model:** Beetle, CC, Eos, Golf, GTI, GLI, Jetta, Passat, Routan, Tiguan, Touareg **Engine:** 2.0L L4, 2.5L L5, 3.0L V6, 3.6L V6	**-CAMSHAFT 1/3 POSITION SENSOR INTERMITTENT:** While cranking the engine and engine running. When the failure counter reaches 20. One Trip Fault. Three good trips to turn off the MIL.
DTC: P0351 **1T ECM, MIL: Yes** **Year:** 2011, 2012 **Model:** Beetle, CC, Eos, Golf, GTI, GLI, Jetta, Passat, Routan, Tiguan, Touareg **Engine:** 2.0L L4, 2.5L L5, 3.0L V6, 3.6L V6	**Ignition Coil A Primary/Secondary Circuit:** * Battery voltage, 9-16 V * Engine speed, 1400-7000 RPM * SW ignition counter diagnose, Not active
DTC: P0352 **1T ECM, MIL: Yes** **Year:** 2011, 2012 **Model:** Beetle, CC, Eos, Golf, GTI, GLI, Jetta, Passat, Routan, Tiguan, Touareg **Engine:** 2.0L L4, 2.5L L5, 3.0L V6, 3.6L V6	**Ignition Coil B Primary/Secondary Circuit:** * Battery voltage, 9-16 V * Engine speed, 1400-7000 RPM * SW ignition counter diagnose, Not active
DTC: P0353 **1T ECM, MIL: Yes** **Year:** 2011, 2012 **Model:** Beetle, CC, Eos, Golf, GTI, GLI, Jetta, Passat, Routan, Tiguan, Touareg **Engine:** 2.0L L4, 2.5L L5, 3.0L V6, 3.6L V6	**Ignition Coil C Primary/Secondary Circuit:** * Battery voltage, 9-16 V * Engine speed, 1400-7000 RPM * SW ignition counter diagnose, Not active

DTC	Trouble Code Title and Conditions
DTC: P0354 **1T ECM, MIL: Yes** **Year:** 2011, 2012 **Model:** Beetle, CC, Eos, Golf, GTI, GLI, Jetta, Passat, Routan, Tiguan, Touareg **Engine:** 2.0L L4, 2.5L L5, 3.0L V6, 3.6L V6	**Ignition Coil D Primary/Secondary Circuit:** * Battery voltage, 9-16 V * Engine speed, 1400-7000 RPM * SW ignition counter diagnose, Not active
DTC: P0355 **1T ECM, MIL: Yes** **Year:** 2011, 2012 **Model:** Beetle, CC, Eos, Golf, GTI, GLI, Jetta, Passat, Routan, Tiguan, Touareg **Engine:** 2.0L L4, 2.5L L5, 3.0L V6, 3.6L V6	**Ignition Coil "E" Primary/Secondary Circuit:** * Battery voltage, 9-16 V * Engine speed, 1400-7000 RPM * SW ignition counter diagnose, Not active
DTC: P0356 **1T ECM, MIL: Yes** **Year:** 2011, 2012 **Model:** Beetle, CC, Eos, Golf, GTI, GLI, Jetta, Passat, Routan, Tiguan, Touareg **Engine:** 2.5L L5, 3.0L V6, 3.6L V6	**Ignition Coil "F" Primary/Secondary Circuit:** * Battery voltage, 9-16 V * Engine speed, 1400-7000 RPM * SW ignition counter diagnose, Not active
DTC: P0365 **1T ECM, MIL: Yes** **Year:** 2011, 2012 **Model:** Beetle, CC, Eos, Golf, GTI, GLI, Jetta, Passat, Routan, Tiguan, Touareg **Engine:** 2.0L L4, 2.5L L5, 3.0L V6, 3.6L V6	**-CAMSHAFT 1/2 POSITION SENSOR CIRCUIT:** During engine cranking and with the engine running. Battery voltage greater than 10 volts. At least five seconds or 2.5 engine revolutions have elapsed with crankshaft position sensor signals present but no camshaft position sensor signal. One Trip Fault. Three good trips to turn off the MIL.
DTC: P0366 **2T ECM, MIL: Yes** **Year:** 2011, 2012 **Model:** Beetle, CC, Eos, Golf, GTI, GLI, Jetta, Passat, Routan, Tiguan, Touareg **Engine:** 2.0L L4, 2.5L L5, 3.0L V6, 3.6L V6	**Camshaft Position Sensor "B" Circuit Range/Performance Bank 1:** While cranking the engine and with the engine running. The ECM/PCM has detected an open or short in the circuit.
DTC: P0367 **2T ECM, MIL: Yes** **Year:** 2011, 2012 **Model:** Beetle, CC, Eos, Golf, GTI, GLI, Jetta, Passat, Routan, Tiguan, Touareg **Engine:** 2.0L L4, 2.5L L5, 3.0L V6, 3.6L V6	**Camshaft Position Sensor "B" Circuit Low Bank 1:** While cranking the engine and with the engine running. The ECM/PCM has detected an open or short in the circuit.
DTC: P0368 **2T ECM, MIL: Yes** **Year:** 2011, 2012 **Model:** Beetle, CC, Eos, Golf, GTI, GLI, Jetta, Passat, Routan, Tiguan, Touareg **Engine:** 2.0L L4, 2.5L L5, 3.0L V6, 3.6L V6	**Camshaft Position Sensor "B" Circuit High Bank 1:** While cranking the engine and with the engine running. The ECM/PCM has detected an open or short in the circuit.

DTC	Trouble Code Title and Conditions
DTC: P0369 **2T ECM, MIL: Yes** **Year:** 2011, 2012 **Model:** Beetle, CC, Eos, Golf, GTI, GLI, Jetta, Passat, Routan, Tiguan, Touareg **Engine:** 2.0L L4, 2.5L L5, 3.0L V6, 3.6L V6	**CAMSHAFT 1/2 POSITION SENSOR INTERMITTENT:** While cranking the engine and engine running. When the failure counter reaches 20. One Trip Fault. Three good trips to turn off the MIL.
DTC: P0381 **2T ECM, MIL: Yes** **Year:** 2011, 2012 Beetle, CC, Eos, Golf, GTI, GLI, Jetta, Passat, Touareg **Engine:** 2.0L TDI L4, 3.0L TDI V6	**Glow Plug/Heater Indicator Circuit:** While cranking the engine. The ECM/PCM has detected an open or short in the circuit. * Battery voltage > 9 V * Glow system active
DTC: P0383 **2T ECM, MIL: Yes** **Year:** 2011, 2012 Beetle, CC, Eos, Golf, GTI, GLI, Jetta, Passat, Touareg **Engine:** 2.0L TDI L4, 3.0L TDI V6	**Glow Plug Control Module Control Circuit Low:** While cranking the engine. The ECM/PCM has detected an open or short in the circuit. * Battery voltage > 9 V * Glow system active
DTC: P0384 **2T ECM, MIL: Yes** **Year:** 2011, 2012 Beetle, CC, Eos, Golf, GTI, GLI, Jetta, Passat, Touareg **Engine:** 2.0L TDI L4, 3.0L TDI V6	**Glow Plug Control Module Control Circuit High:** While cranking the engine. The ECM/PCM has detected an open or short in the circuit. * Battery voltage > 9 V * Glow system active
DTC: P0390 **1T ECM, MIL: Yes** **Year:** 2011, 2012 **Model:** Routan, Touareg **Engine:** 3.0L V6, 3.6L V6	**-CAMSHAFT 1/4 POSITION SENSOR CIRCUIT:** During engine cranking and with the engine running. Battery voltage greater than 10 Volts. At least five seconds or 2.5 engine revolutions have elapsed with crankshaft position sensor signals present but no camshaft position sensor signal. One Trip Fault. Three good trips to turn off the MIL.
DTC: P0391 **1T ECM, MIL: Yes** **Year:** 2011, 2012 **Model:** Routan, Touareg **Engine:** 3.0L V6, 3.6L V6	**Camshaft Position Sensor "B" Circuit Range/Performance Bank 2:** No camshaft position sensor signal detected.
DTC: P0392 **1T ECM, MIL: Yes** **Year:** 2011, 2012 **Model:** Routan, Touareg **Engine:** 3.0L V6, 3.6L V6	**Camshaft Position Sensor "B" Circuit Low Bank 2:** No camshaft position sensor signal detected.
DTC: P0393 **1T ECM, MIL: Yes** **Year:** 2011, 2012 **Model:** Routan, Touareg **Engine:** 3.0L V6, 3.6L V6	**Camshaft Position Sensor "B" Circuit High Bank 2:** No camshaft position sensor signal detected.
DTC: P0394 **1T ECM, MIL: Yes** **Year:** 2011, 2012 **Model:** Routan, Touareg **Engine:** 3.0L V6, 3.6L V6	**-CAMSHAFT 1/4 POSITION SENSOR INTERMITTENT:** While cranking the engine and engine running. When the failure counter reaches 20. One Trip Fault. Three good trips to turn off the MIL.
DTC: P0401 **2T ECM, MIL: Yes** **Year:** 2011, 2012 **Model:** Beetle, CC, Eos, Golf, GTI, GLI, Jetta, Passat, Routan, Tiguan, Touareg **Engine:** 2.0L L4, 2.5L L5, 3.0L V6, 3.6L V6	**Exhaust Gas Recirculation Flow Insufficient Detected:** Malfunction Criteria and Threshold Value: * EGR mode, closed loop * Fuel quantity, >6 mg/stroke * Fuel quantity, <22 mg/stroke * Engine speed, >1300 rpm * Engine speed, <2,000 rpm

DTC	Trouble Code Title and Conditions
DTC: P0402 **2T ECM, MIL: Yes** **Year:** 2011, 2012 **Model:** Beetle, CC, Eos, Golf, GTI, GLI, Jetta, Passat, Routan, Tiguan, Touareg **Engine:** 2.0L L4, 2.5L L5, 3.0L V6, 3.6L V6	**Exhaust Gas Recirculation Excessive Flow Detected:** Malfunction Criteria and Threshold Value: * EGR valve closed = 100% * Throttle valve signal > 94% * Engine speed, > 1100 - 2500 rpm * Boost pressure = 50 - 200 kPa * ECT = 60 - 110 °C * Ambient pressure > 50 kPa * Fuel quantity > 0.5 mg/stroke
DTC: P0403 **2T ECM, MIL: Yes** **Year:** 2011, 2012 **Model:** Beetle, CC, Eos, Golf, GTI, GLI, Jetta, Passat, Routan, Tiguan, Touareg **Engine:** 2.0L L4, 2.5L L5, 3.0L V6, 3.6L V6	**Exhaust gas recirculation valve -N18 Malfunction:** Power stage = On or Off (dependant on diagnostic run).
DTC: P0404 **2T ECM, MIL: Yes** **Year:** 2011, 2012 **Model:** Beetle, CC, Eos, Golf, GTI, GLI, Jetta, Passat, Routan, Tiguan, Touareg **Engine:** 2.0L L4, 2.5L L5, 3.0L V6, 3.6L V6	**Exhaust Gas Recirculation Contr. Circuit Range/Performance:** The ECM/PCM detected an unexpected low or high condition on the control circuit during testing. * Engine running 480 mSec.
DTC: P040B **2T ECM, MIL: Yes** **Year:** 2011, 2012 **Model:** Beetle, CC, Eos, Golf, GTI, GLI, Jetta, Passat, Routan, Tiguan, Touareg **Engine:** 2.0L L4, 2.5L L5, 3.0L V6, 3.6L V6	**Exhaust Gas Recirculation Temperature Sensor Circuit Range/Performance:** Condition 1: Engine run time > 3 min. ECT > 70 °C. Simulated sensor temp > 85 °C Elapsed time since EGR valve opens > 30 Sec. Condition 2: Engine off time > 32400 Sec. Decrease of intake air temp after engine start < 5 °K. Decrease of ambient air temp after engine start < 5°K
DTC: P040C **2T ECM, MIL: Yes** **Year:** 2011, 2012 **Model:** Beetle, CC, Eos, Golf, GTI, GLI, Jetta, Passat, Routan, Tiguan, Touareg **Engine:** 2.0L L4, 2.5L L5, 3.0L V6, 3.6L V6	**Exhaust Gas Recirculation Temperature Sensor Circuit Low:** The ECM/PCM detected an unexpected low condition on the control circuit during testing. * Signal sensor voltage < 0.06 V, * Engine running 480 mSec.
DTC: P040D **2T ECM, MIL: Yes** **Year:** 2011, 2012 **Model:** Beetle, CC, Eos, Golf, GTI, GLI, Jetta, Passat, Routan, Tiguan, Touareg **Engine:** 2.0L L4, 2.5L L5, 3.0L V6, 3.6L V6	**Exhaust Gas Recirculation Temperature Sensor Circuit High:** The ECM/PCM detected an unexpected high condition on the control circuit during testing.
DTC: P0410 **2T ECM, MIL: Yes** **Year:** 2011, 2012 **Model:** Beetle, Eos, Golf, GTI, Jetta, Passat **Engine:** 2.0L L4, 2.5L L5	**Secondary Air Injection System:** Malfunction Criteria and Threshold Value: * Mass airflow 7 to 120 kg/h * Delta engine load -10 to 10 % * ECT 5 to 108 °C * Altitude < 2700 m * IAT 5 to 100 °C * SAI pressure sensor - ready

DTC	Trouble Code Title and Conditions
DTC: P0411 **2T ECM, MIL: Yes** **Year:** 2011, 2012 **Model:** Beetle, Eos, Golf, GTI, Jetta, Passat **Engine:** 2.0L L4, 2.5L L5	**Secondary Air Injection System Upstream Flow Detected:** Engine started, battery voltage must be at least 11.5v, all electrical components must be off, parking brake must be engaged (to keep daytime driving lights off), automatic transmission selector must be in park and the ground between the engine and the chassis must be well connected. The ECM detected the Secondary AIR pump airflow was not diverted correctly when requested during the self-test. The pump is functioning but the quantity of air is recognized as insufficient by HO2S. **Note: The solenoid valve is closed when no voltage is present.**
DTC: P0412 **2T ECM, MIL: Yes** **Year:** 2011, 2012 **Model:** Beetle, Eos, Golf, GTI, Jetta, Passat **Engine:** 2.0L L4, 2.5L L5	**Secondary Air Injection Solenoid Circuit Malfunction:** Engine started, battery voltage must be at least 11.5v, all electrical components must be off, parking brake must be engaged (to keep daytime driving lights off), automatic transmission selector must be in park and the ground between the engine and the chassis must be well connected. The ECM detected an unexpected low or high voltage condition on the AIR solenoid control circuit during testing.
DTC: P0413 **2T ECM, MIL: Yes** **Year:** 2011, 2012 **Model:** Beetle, Eos, Golf, GTI, Jetta, Passat **Engine:** 2.0L L4, 2.5L L5	**Secondary Air Injection Solenoid Circuit Open:** Engine started, battery voltage must be at least 11.5v, all electrical components must be off, parking brake must be engaged (to keep daytime driving lights off), automatic transmission selector must be in park and the ground between the engine and the chassis must be well connected. The ECM detected an unexpected low or high voltage condition on the AIR solenoid control circuit during testing.
DTC: P0414 **2T ECM, MIL: Yes** **Year:** 2011, 2012 **Model:** Beetle, Eos, Golf, GTI, Jetta, Passat **Engine:** 2.0L L4, 2.5L L5	**Secondary Air Injection Solenoid Circuit Short:** Engine started, battery voltage must be at least 11.5v, all electrical components must be off, parking brake must be engaged (to keep daytime driving lights off), automatic transmission selector must be in park and the ground between the engine and the chassis must be well connected. The ECM detected an unexpected low or high voltage condition on the AIR solenoid control circuit during testing.
DTC: P0415 **2T ECM, MIL: Yes** **Year:** 2011, 2012 **Model:** Beetle, Eos, Golf, GTI, Jetta, Passat **Engine:** 2.0L L4, 2.5L L5	**Secondary Air Injection System Switching Valve "B" Circuit Malfunction:** The ECM/PCM detected an unexpected low or high voltage condition on the valve B control circuit during testing. * Engine started * Battery voltage must be at least 11.5v
DTC: P0416 **2T ECM, MIL: Yes** **Year:** 2011, 2012 **Model:** Beetle, Eos, Golf, GTI, Jetta, Passat **Engine:** 2.0L L4, 2.5L L5	**Secondary Air Injection System Switching Valve "B" Circuit Open:** The ECM/PCM detected an unexpected low or high voltage condition on the valve B control circuit during testing. * Engine started * Battery voltage must be at least 11.5v
DTC: P0417 **2T ECM, MIL: Yes** **Year:** 2011, 2012 **Model:** Beetle, Eos, Golf, GTI, Jetta, Passat **Engine:** 2.0L L4, 2.5L L5	**Secondary Air Injection System Switching Valve "B" Circuit Shorted:** The ECM/PCM detected an unexpected high voltage condition on the valve B control circuit during testing. * Air valve, commanded off * Engine speed, >80 RPM * Air valve, commanded on * Engine speed, >80 RPM
DTC: P0418 **2T ECM, MIL: Yes** **Year:** 2011, 2012 **Model:** Beetle, Eos, Golf, GTI, Jetta, Passat, Touareg **Engine:** 2.0L L4, 2.5L L5, 3.0L V6, 3.6L V6	**Secondary Air Injection Relay (A) Circuit Malfunction:** Engine started, battery voltage must be at least 11.5v, all electrical components must be off, parking brake must be engaged (to keep daytime driving lights off), automatic transmission selector must be in park and the ground between the engine and the chassis must be well connected. The ECM detected an unexpected low or high voltage condition on the AIR solenoid control circuit during testing.
DTC: P0420 **2T ECM, MIL: Yes** **Year:** 2011, 2012 **Model:** Beetle, CC, Eos, Golf, GTI, GLI, Jetta, Passat, Routan, Tiguan, Touareg **Engine:** 2.0L L4, 2.5L L5, 3.0L V6, 3.6L V6	**Catalyst System Efficiency (Bank 1) Below Threshold:** Engine started, battery voltage must be at least 11.5v, all electrical components must be off, parking brake must be engaged (to keep daytime driving lights off), automatic transmission selector must be in park, the exhaust system must be properly sealed between the catalytic converter and the cylinder head, coolant temperature must be at least 80 degrees Celsius and oxygen sensor heaters for oxygen sensors before the catalytic converter must be functioning properly and the ground between the engine and the chassis must be well connected. The ECM detected the switch rate of the rear HO2S-12 was close to the switch rate of front HO2S (it should be much slower).

DTC	Trouble Code Title and Conditions
DTC: P0421 **1T ECM, MIL: Yes** **Year:** 2011, 2012 **Model:** Beetle, CC, Eos, Golf, GTI, GLI, Jetta, Passat, Routan, Tiguan, Touareg **Engine:** 2.0L L4, 2.5L L5, 3.0L V6, 3.6L V6	**Warm Up Catalyst, Bank 1 Efficiency Below Threshold:** Malfunction Criteria and Threshold Value: * Catalyst temperature -385 - 665°C * engine start temperature-> -10°C * Misfire rate-< 2.3 %
DTC: P0422 **2T ECM, MIL: Yes** **Year:** 2011, 2012 **Model:** Beetle, CC, Eos, Golf, GTI, GLI, Jetta, Passat, Routan, Tiguan, Touareg **Engine:** 2.0L L4, 2.5L L5, 3.0L V6, 3.6L V6	**Main Catalyst (Bank 1) Efficiency Below Threshold:** Engine started, battery voltage must be at least 11.5v, all electrical components must be off, parking brake must be engaged (to keep daytime driving lights off), automatic transmission selector must be in park, the exhaust system must be properly sealed between the catalytic converter and the cylinder head, coolant temperature must be at least 80 degrees Celsius and oxygen sensor heaters for oxygen sensors before the catalytic converter must be functioning properly and the ground between the engine and the chassis must be well connected. The ECM detected the switch rate of the rear HO2S-12 was close to the switch rate of front HO2S (it should be much slower).
DTC: P0430 **2T ECM, MIL: Yes** **Year:** 2011, 2012 **Model:** Beetle, CC, Eos, Golf, GTI, GLI, Jetta, Passat, Routan, Tiguan, Touareg **Engine:** 2.0L L4, 2.5L L5, 3.0L V6, 3.6L V6	**Catalyst System Efficiency Below Threshold Bank 2:** The monitor will run at between 1400 and 2300 RPM and MAP vacuum between 40 to 70 kPa (15.0 and 21.0 (Hg)).If the final State of Change index is within the calibrated fail threshold. Two trip fault. Three good trips to turn off the MIL.
DTC: P0431 **2T ECM, MIL: Yes** **Year:** 2011, 2012 **Model:** Beetle, CC, Eos, Golf, GTI, GLI, Jetta, Passat, Routan, Tiguan, Touareg **Engine:** 2.0L L4, 2.5L L5, 3.0L V6, 3.6L V6	**Warm Up Catalyst, Bank 2 Efficiency Below Threshold:** Malfunction Criteria and Threshold Value: * Catalyst temperature -385 - 665°C * engine start temperature-> -10°C * Misfire rate-< 2.3 %
DTC: P0440 **2T ECM, MIL: Yes** **Year:** 2011, 2012 **Model:** Beetle, CC, Eos, Golf, GTI, GLI, Jetta, Passat, Routan, Tiguan, Touareg **Engine:** 2.0L L4, 2.5L L5, 3.0L V6, 3.6L V6	**EVAP System General Malfunction:** Engine running after a cold start with the difference between ECT and AAT is less than 10° C (19° F). Fuel Level between 12% and 88% full. Manifold vacuum greater than a calculated minimum value. Ambient Temperature between 4° C and 32° C (39° F and 89° F). When the monitor conditions are met, the Powertrain Control Module (PCM) will ramp in purge flow. If the PCM does not sense an ESIM Switch closure after a calculated amount of purge flow accumulation, an error is detected. Two Trip Fault. Three good trips to turn off the MIL.
DTC: P0441 **1T ECM, MIL: Yes** **Year:** 2011, 2012 **Model:** Beetle, CC, Eos, Golf, GTI, GLI, Jetta, Passat, Routan, Tiguan, Touareg **Engine:** 2.0L L4, 2.5L L5, 3.0L V6, 3.6L V6	**Evaporative Emission System Incorrect Purge Flow:** After the Evaporative System small leak test has passed, with the engine running, ambient temperature between 4° C (39° F) and 35° (95° F), with the engine at idle after a calibrated amount of drive time has accumulated. If the Powertrain Control Module (PCM) detects that the purge vapor ratio and the ESIM switch closed ratio are below a calculated value, the PCM commands the purge solenoid to flow at a specified rate to update the purge vapor ratio. If the ratio remains below a specified value, a one trip failure is recorded. Two Trip Fault. Three good trips to turn off the MIL.
DTC: P0442 **1T ECM, MIL: Yes** **Year:** 2011, 2012 **Model:** Beetle, CC, Eos, Golf, GTI, GLI, Jetta, Passat, Routan, Tiguan, Touareg **Engine:** 2.0L L4, 2.5L L5, 3.0L V6, 3.6L V6	**Evaporative Emission System Leak found (Small Leak):** Malfunction Criteria and Threshold Value: * Time after engine start, 5–1200 Sec. * ECT, 4.5-105.80° C * IAT, > 4.5-60.00° C * IAT drop after engine start, < 6.00 K * Intake manifold vacuum, >140 hPa * Altitude, <2700 m * Vehicle speed, 22 km/h * Selected gear, Any drive * Restart temperature difference, >45K * EVAP purge valve, Closed

DTC	Trouble Code Title and Conditions
DTC: P0443 **1T ECM, MIL: Yes** **Year:** 2011, 2012 **Model:** Beetle, CC, Eos, Golf, GTI, GLI, Jetta, Passat, Routan, Tiguan, Touareg **Engine:** 2.0L L4, 2.5L L5, 3.0L V6, 3.6L V6	**EVAP Vapor Management Valve Circuit Malfunction:** Engine started, battery voltage must be at least 11.5v, all electrical components must be off, parking brake must be engaged (to keep daytime driving lights off), automatic transmission selector must be in park, the exhaust system must be properly sealed between the catalytic converter and the cylinder head, coolant temperature must be at least 80 degrees Celsius and oxygen sensor heaters for oxygen sensors before the catalytic converter must be functioning properly and the ground between the engine and the chassis must be well connected. The ECM/PCM detected an unexpected high or low voltage condition on the Vapor Management Valve (VMV) circuit when the device was cycled On/Off during testing.
DTC: P0444 **1T ECM, MIL: Yes** **Year:** 2011, 2012 **Model:** Beetle, CC, Eos, Golf, GTI, GLI, Jetta, Passat, Routan, Tiguan, Touareg **Engine:** 2.0L L4, 2.5L L5, 3.0L V6, 3.6L V6	**Evaporative Emission System Purge Control Valve Circuit Open:** The ignition on or engine running. Battery voltage greater than 10 volts. The Powertrain Control Module (PCM) will set a trouble code if the actual state of the solenoid does not match the intended state. One Trip Fault. Three good trips to turn off the MIL. Malfunction Criteria and Threshold Value: * EVAP purge valve Commanded Off * Engine speed > 80 RPM
DTC: P0445 **1T ECM, MIL: Yes** **Year:** 2011, 2012 **Model:** Beetle, CC, Eos, Golf, GTI, GLI, Jetta, Passat, Routan, Tiguan, Touareg **Engine:** 2.0L L4, 2.5L L5, 3.0L V6, 3.6L V6	**Evaporative Emission System Purge Control Valve Circuit Shorted:** Engine started, battery voltage must be at least 11.5v, all electrical components must be off, parking brake must be engaged (to keep daytime driving lights off), automatic transmission selector must be in park, the exhaust system must be properly sealed between the catalytic converter and the cylinder head, coolant temperature must be at least 80 degrees Celsius and oxygen sensor heaters for oxygen sensors before the catalytic converter must be functioning properly and the ground between the engine and the chassis must be well connected. The ECM detected an unexpected voltage condition on the EVAP circuit when the device was cycled On/Off during testing.
DTC: P0449 **1T ECM, MIL: Yes** **Year:** 2011, 2012 **Model:** Beetle, CC, Eos, Golf, GTI, GLI, Jetta, Passat, Routan, Tiguan, Touareg **Engine:** 2.0L L4, 2.5L L5, 3.0L V6, 3.6L V6	**Evaporative Emission System Vent Valve/Solenoid Circuit:** Engine started, battery voltage must be at least 11.5v, all electrical components must be off, parking brake must be engaged (to keep daytime driving lights off), automatic transmission selector must be in park, the exhaust system must be properly sealed between the catalytic converter and the cylinder head, coolant temperature must be at least 80 degrees Celsius and oxygen sensor heaters for oxygen sensors before the catalytic converter must be functioning properly and the ground between the engine and the chassis must be well connected. The ECM detected an unexpected voltage condition on the EVAP circuit when the device was cycled On/Off during testing.
DTC: P0452 **2T ECM, MIL: Yes** **Year:** 2011, 2012 **Model:** Beetle, CC, Eos, Golf, GTI, GLI, Jetta, Passat, Routan, Tiguan, Touareg **Engine:** 2.0L L4, 2.5L L5, 3.0L V6, 3.6L V6	**EVAP PRESSURE SWITCH STUCK CLOSED:** Immediately after the ignition has been turned off. At key off, the Powertrain Control Module (PCM) energizes the Purge Solenoid for a calibrated amount of time (30 seconds maximum) and stores the state of the ESIM switch. The state is evaluated again at the next key on. If the PCM does not detect that the ESIM switch is open, an error is detected. Two Trip Fault. Three good trips to turn off the MIL.
DTC: P0455 **2T ECM, MIL: Yes** **Year:** 2011, 2012 **Model:** Beetle, CC, Eos, Golf, GTI, GLI, Jetta, Passat, Routan, Tiguan, Touareg **Engine:** 2.0L L4, 2.5L L5, 3.0L V6, 3.6L V6	**Evaporative Emission System Leak Detected (large leak/no flow):** With the engine running, during a cold start test with the fuel level above 12%, ambient temperature between 4° C and 32° C (39° F and 89° F) and the fuel system in closed loop. The test runs when the small leak test is maturing. The Powertrain Control Module (PCM) activates the Evap Purge solenoid to pull the Evaporative system into a vacuum to close the ESIM switch. Once the ESIM switch is closed, the PCM turns the Evap Purge solenoid off to seal the Evaporative system. If the ESIM switch reopens before the calibrated amount of time, a large leak error is detected. Two Trip Fault. Three good trips to turn off the MIL.
DTC: P0456 **1T ECM, MIL: Yes** **Year:** 2011, 2012 **Model:** Beetle, CC, Eos, Golf, GTI, GLI, Jetta, Passat, Routan, Tiguan, Touareg **Engine:** 2.0L L4, 2.5L L5, 3.0L V6, 3.6L V6	**Evaporative Emission System Leak Detected (very small leak):** With the ignition off, fuel level less than 88%, ambient temperature between 4° C and 43° C (39° F and 109° F) and the fuel system in closed loop. As temperatures change, a vacuum is created in the fuel tank and Evaporative system. With the Evaporative system sealed, the PCM monitors the ESIM Switch. If the ESIM Switch does not close within a calibrated time, an error is detected by the PCM. One Trip Fault. Three good trips to turn off the MIL.

DTC	Trouble Code Title and Conditions
DTC: P0457 **2T ECM, MIL: Yes** **Year:** 2011, 2012 **Model:** Beetle, CC, Eos, Golf, GTI, GLI, Jetta, Passat, Routan, Tiguan, Touareg **Engine:** 2.0L L4, 2.5L L5, 3.0L V6, 3.6L V6	**LOOSE FUEL CAP:** Ignition on. Ambient Temperature between 4° C and 32° C (39° F and 89° F) Close Loop fuel system. Test runs after the medium leak test is inconclusive and the PCM senses a fuel increase. If a leak greater than .090" is detected by the Powertrain Control Module (PCM) for two consecutive cold start trips after a significant fuel level change, this DTC will set. One good trip turns off the MIL.
DTC: P0458 **2T ECM, MIL: Yes** **Year:** 2011, 2012 **Model:** Beetle, CC, Eos, Golf, GTI, GLI, Jetta, Passat, Routan, Tiguan, Touareg **Engine:** 2.0L L4, 2.5L L5, 3.0L V6, 3.6L V6	**Evaporative Emission System Purge Control Valve Circuit Low:** The ECM detected an unexpected voltage condition on the EVAP circuit when the device was cycled On/Off during testing. * EVAP purge valve, Commanded off * Engine speed, >80 RPM
DTC: P0459 **2T ECM, MIL: Yes** **Year:** 2011, 2012 **Model:** Beetle, CC, Eos, Golf, GTI, GLI, Jetta, Passat, Routan, Tiguan, Touareg **Engine:** 2.0L L4, 2.5L L5, 3.0L V6, 3.6L V6	**Evaporative Emission System Purge Control Valve Circuit High:** The ECM detected an unexpected voltage condition on the EVAP circuit when the device was cycled On/Off during testing. * EVAP purge valve, Commanded on * Engine speed, >80 RPM
DTC: P045A **2T ECM, MIL: Yes** **Year:** 2011, 2012 **Model:** Golf, Jetta, Passat **Engine:** 2.0L L4, 2.5L L5	**Exhaust Gas Recirculation "B" Control Circuit:** With the engine running and the engine temperature at 120 °C. The ECM/PCM has detected an open or short in the control circuit.
DTC: P045B **2T ECM, MIL: Yes** **Year:** 2011, 2012 **Model:** Golf, Jetta, Passat **Engine:** 2.0L L4, 2.5L L5	**Exhaust Gas Recirculation "B" Control Circuit Range/Performance:** With the engine running and the engine temperature at 120 °C. The ECM/PCM has detected an open or short in the control circuit.
DTC: P045C **2T ECM, MIL: Yes** **Year:** 2011, 2012 **Model:** Golf, Jetta, Passat **Engine:** 2.0L L4, 2.5L L5	**Exhaust Gas Recirculation "B" Control Circuit Low:** With the engine running and the engine temperature at 120 °C. The ECM/PCM has detected an open or short in the control circuit.
DTC: P045D **2T ECM, MIL: Yes** **Year:** 2011, 2012 **Model:** Golf, Jetta, Passat **Engine:** 2.0L L4, 2.5L L5	**Exhaust Gas Recirculation "B" Control Circuit High:** With the engine running and the engine temperature at 120 °C. The ECM/PCM has detected an open or short in the control circuit.
DTC: P045E **2T ECM, MIL: Yes** **Year:** 2011, 2012 **Model:** Golf, Jetta, Passat **Engine:** 2.0L L4, 2.5L L5	**Exhaust Gas Recirculation "B" Control Stuck Open:** With the engine running and the engine temperature at 120 °C. The ECM/PCM has detected an open or short in the control circuit.
DTC: P0461 **2T ECM, MIL: Yes** **Year:** 2011, 2012 **Model:** Beetle, CC, Eos, Golf, GTI, GLI, Jetta, Passat, Routan, Tiguan, Touareg **Engine:** 2.0L L4, 2.5L L5, 3.0L V6, 3.6L V6	**FUEL LEVEL SENSOR 1 PERFORMANCE:** If the PCM does not see a difference in fuel level of greater than 0.1 Volt the test will fail. If the PCM does not see a change in the fuel level over a set amount of miles the test will fail. Two trip fault. Three good trips to turn off the MIL.

DTC	Trouble Code Title and Conditions
DTC: P0462 **1T ECM, MIL: Yes** **Year:** 2011, 2012 **Model:** Beetle, CC, Eos, Golf, GTI, GLI, Jetta, Passat, Routan, Tiguan, Touareg **Engine:** 2.0L L4, 2.5L L5, 3.0L V6, 3.6L V6	**FUEL LEVEL SENSOR 1 CIRCUIT LOW:** With the ignition on and battery voltage above 10.4 Volts. The fuel level sensor signal voltage goes below the minimum acceptable value. One Trip Fault. Three good trips to turn off the MIL.
DTC: P0463 **1T ECM, MIL: Yes** **Year:** 2011, 2012 **Model:** Beetle, CC, Eos, Golf, GTI, GLI, Jetta, Passat, Routan, Tiguan, Touareg **Engine:** 2.0L L4, 2.5L L5, 3.0L V6, 3.6L V6	**-FUEL LEVEL SENSOR 1 CIRCUIT HIGH:** With the ignition on and battery voltage above 10.4 Volts. The fuel level sensor input voltage is above the maximum acceptable value. One Trip Fault. Three good trips to turn off the MIL.
DTC: P046C **2T ECM, MIL: Yes** **Year:** 2011, 2012 **Model:** Touareg **Engine:** 3.0L V6, 3.6L V6	**Exhaust Gas Recirculation Sensor "A" Circuit Range/Performance:** * ECT > -20 °C
DTC: P0471 **2T ECM, MIL: Yes** **Year:** 2011, 2012 **Model:** Touareg **Engine:** 3.0L V6, 3.6L V6	**Exhaust Pressure Sensor "A" Range/Performance:** * ECT > 69.96 °C * Engine = after run * Engine run time > 720 Sec.
DTC: P0472 **2T ECM, MIL: Yes** **Year:** 2011, 2012 **Model:** Golf, GTI, Jetta, Passat **Engine:** 2.0L L4, 2.5L L5	**Exhaust Pressure Sensor A Low:** Exhaust Pressure Sensor A Low
DTC: P0473 **2T ECM, MIL: Yes** **Year:** 2011, 2012 **Model:** Golf, GTI, Jetta, Passat **Engine:** 2.0L L4, 2.5L L5	**Exhaust Pressure Sensor A High:** Exhaust Pressure Sensor A High
DTC: P0475 **2T ECM, MIL: Yes** **Year:** 2011, 2012 **Model:** Golf, GTI, Jetta, Passat **Engine:** 2.0L L4, 2.5L L5	**Exhaust Pressure Control Valve "A":** Engine Running
DTC: P0477 **2T ECM, MIL: Yes** **Year:** 2011, 2012 **Model:** Golf, GTI, Jetta, Passat **Engine:** 2.0L L4, 2.5L L5	**Exhaust Pressure Control Valve "A" Low:** Engine running
DTC: P0478 **2T ECM, MIL: Yes** **Year:** 2011, 2012 **Model:** Golf, GTI, Jetta, Passat **Engine:** 2.0L L4, 2.5L L5	**Exhaust Pressure Control Valve "A" High:** Engine running and circuit high.
DTC: P047C **2T ECM, MIL: Yes** **Year:** 2011, 2012 **Model:** Golf, GTI, Jetta, Passat **Engine:** 2.0L L4, 2.5L L5	**Exhaust Pressure Sensor "B" Low:** Engine running and circuit low.

DTC	Trouble Code Title and Conditions
DTC: P047D **2T ECM, MIL: Yes** **Year:** 2011, 2012 **Model:** Golf, GTI, Jetta, Passat **Engine:** 2.0L L4, 2.5L L5	**Exhaust Pressure Sensor "B" High:** Engine running and circuit high.
DTC: P047F **2T ECM, MIL: Yes** **Year:** 2011, 2012 **Model:** Golf, GTI, Jetta, Passat **Engine:** 2.0L L4, 2.5L L5	**Exhaust Pressure Control Valve "A" Stuck Open:** Engine running, control deviation > 10%
DTC: P0480 **1 T ECM, MIL: Yes** **Year:** 2011, 2012 **Model:** Beetle, CC, Eos, Golf, GTI, GLI, Jetta, Passat, Routan, Tiguan, Touareg **Engine:** 2.0L L4, 2.5L L5, 3.0L V6, 3.6L V6	**Cooling Fan 1 Control Circuit:** With the ignition on. Battery voltage greater than 10 Volts. The ECM/PCM) is requesting the Totally Integrated Power Module (TIPM) to turn on the Cooling Fan On and it is not operating.
DTC: P0481 **1 T ECM, MIL: Yes** **Year:** 2011, 2012 **Model:** Beetle, CC, Eos, Golf, GTI, GLI, Jetta, Passat, Routan, Tiguan, Touareg **Engine:** 2.0L L4, 2.5L L5, 3.0L V6, 3.6L V6	**Cooling Fan 2 Control Circuit:** With the ignition on. Battery voltage greater than 10 Volts. The ECM/PCM) is requesting the Totally Integrated Power Module (TIPM) to turn on the Cooling Fan On and it is not operating.
DTC: P048B **2T ECM, MIL: Yes** **Year:** 2011, 2012 **Model:** Golf, GTI, Jetta, Passat **Engine:** 2.0L L4, 2.5L L5	**Exhaust Pressure Control Valve Position Sensor Circuit Low:** Engine running
DTC: P048E **2T ECM, MIL: Yes** **Year:** 2011, 2012 **Model:** Golf, GTI, Jetta, Passat **Engine:** 2.0L L4, 2.5L L5	**Exhaust Pressure Control Valve Position Sensor Circuit High:** Engine running
DTC: P0491 **1 T ECM, MIL: Yes** **Year:** 2011, 2012 **Model:** Beetle, CC, Eos, Golf, GTI, GLI, Jetta, Passat, Routan, Tiguan, Touareg **Engine:** 2.0L L4, 2.5L L5, 3.0L V6, 3.6L V6	**Secondary Air Injection System Insufficient Flow:** * Mass air flow 7 to 120 kg/h * ECT 4.5 to 108 °C * IAT 4.5 to * Altitude < 2700
DTC: P0492 **1 T ECM, MIL: Yes** **Year:** 2011, 2012 **Model:** Beetle, CC, Eos, Golf, GTI, GLI, Jetta, Passat, Routan, Tiguan, Touareg **Engine:** 2.0L L4, 2.5L L5, 3.0L V6, 3.6L V6	**Secondary Air Injection System Insufficient Flow Bank 2:** * Mass air flow, 12–140 kg/h * ECT, 5.3–60° C * IAT, >5.3° C * Altitude, <2600 m
DTC: P0501 **2T ECM, MIL: Yes** **Year:** 2011, 2012 **Model:** Beetle, CC, Eos, Golf, GTI, GLI, Jetta, Passat, Routan, Tiguan, Touareg **Engine:** 2.0L L4, 2.5L L5, 3.0L V6, 3.6L V6	**Vehicle Speed Sensor A Range/Performance:** With the engine running, transmission not in park or neutral, brakes not applied. Engine rpm greater than 1500. This code will set if no vehicle speed signal is received from the ABS Module up to 120 seconds for two consecutive trips. Two Trip Fault. Three good trips to turn off the MIL.

DTC	Trouble Code Title and Conditions
DTC: P0503 **1 T ECM, MIL: Yes** **Year:** 2011, 2012 **Model:** Beetle, CC, Eos, Golf, GTI, GLI, Jetta, Passat, Routan, Tiguan, Touareg **Engine:** 2.0L L4, 2.5L L5, 3.0L V6, 3.6L V6	**Vehicle Speed Sensor "A" Intermittent/Erratic/High:** With the engine running, transmission not in park or neutral, brakes not applied. Engine rpm greater than 1500. This code will set if no vehicle speed signal is received from the ABS Module up to 120 seconds for two consecutive trips. Two Trip Fault. Three good trips to turn off the MIL.
DTC: P0504 **T** **Year:** 2011, 2012 **Model:** Routan **Engine:** 3.6L V6 VIN G	**-BRAKE SWITCH A/B CORRELATION:** With the ignition on. VSS indicates increasing and decreasing vehicle speed. APP Sensor indicates increasing and decreasing acceleration demand. The ECM determines that the brakes have been applied without the receiving an input from the Primary Brake Switch Signal and Secondary Brake Switches.
DTC: P0506 **1 T ECM, MIL: Yes** **Year:** 2011, 2012 **Model:** Beetle, CC, Eos, Golf, GTI, GLI, Jetta, Passat, Routan, Tiguan, Touareg **Engine:** 2.0L L4, 2.5L L5, 3.0L V6, 3.6L V6	**Idle Air Control System RPM Lower Than Expected:** Engine speed is 100 RPM or more below idle speed for 7 seconds. Two Trip Fault. Three good trips to turn off the MIL. * Engine speed, idle * Accelerator PP, 0% * Vehicle speed, 0 MPH * EVAP purge valve, Closed * Altitude, < 2600 m * IAT, >-7 °C * ECT, >60 °C
DTC: P0507 **2 T ECM, MIL: Yes** **Year:** 2011, 2012 **Model:** Beetle, CC, Eos, Golf, GTI, GLI, Jetta, Passat, Routan, Tiguan, Touareg **Engine:** 2.0L L4, 2.5L L5, 3.0L V6, 3.6L V6	**-IDLE SPEED PERFORMANCE HIGHER THAN EXCEPTED:** Engine speed is 200 RPM or more above idle speed for 7 seconds. Two Trip Fault. Three good trips to turn off the MIL. * Engine speed, idle * Vehicle speed 0 MPH * Altitude < 2700 m * IAT, > -48 °C * ECT, > -48 °C * Time after engine start > 0 Sec. * Lambda control active * EVAP purge adaptation < 22
DTC: P050A **2 T ECM, MIL: Yes** **Year:** 2011, 2012 **Model:** Beetle, CC, Eos, Golf, GTI, GLI, Jetta, Passat, Routan, Tiguan, Touareg **Engine:** 2.0L L4, 2.5L L5, 3.0L V6, 3.6L V6	**Cold Start Idle Air Control System Performance:** * Time after engine start > 0 Sec. * Driver torque demand - none * Veh speed 0 km/h * Altitude < 2700 m * IAT > -48.0 °C * Catalyst heating active * Man. trans engine load < 40 - 75% * Time after engine start > 0 Sec.
DTC: P050B **2 T ECM, MIL: Yes** **Year:** 2011, 2012 **Model:** Beetle, CC, Eos, Golf, GTI, GLI, Jetta, Passat, Routan, Tiguan, Touareg **Engine:** 2.0L L4, 2.5L L5, 3.0L V6, 3.6L V6	**-COLD START IGNITION TIMING PERFORMANCE:** Cold start condition. Ambient Air temperature between -7° C and 50° C (19.4° F and 122° F). Engine Coolant temperature between -7° C and 50° C (19.4° F and 122° F). The difference between the Ambient Air temp and ECT temp at Start is equal to and less than 10° C (50° F). Engine running at idle only. Engine RPM is 50 RPM or more (depending on vehicle specifications), below idle speed for at least 3 seconds and the average spark advance is above the threshold, too much spark advance, for a specified time limit. Two trip fault. Three good trips to turn off the MIL.
DTC: P0510 **2 T ECM, MIL: Yes** **Year:** 2011, 2012 **Model:** Beetle, CC, Eos, Golf, GTI, GLI, Jetta, Passat, Routan, Tiguan, Touareg **Engine:** 2.0L L4, 2.5L L5, 3.0L V6, 3.6L V6	**Closed Throttle Position Switch:** Throttle potentiometer – Engine is running at idle/coasting condition Throttle actuator potentiometer – Coasting condition /under load condition switch has to be open

DTC	Trouble Code Title and Conditions
DTC: P0513 **2 T ECM, MIL: Yes** **Year:** 2011, 2012 **Model:** Beetle, CC, Eos, Golf, GTI, GLI, Jetta, Passat, Routan, Tiguan, Touareg **Engine:** 2.0L L4, 2.5L L5, 3.0L V6, 3.6L V6	**INVALID SKIM KEY:** With the ignition on. The Engine Control Module (ECM) receives an invalid message from the Wireless Ignition Node (WIN).
DTC: P0520 **2 T ECM, MIL: Yes** **Year:** 2011, 2012 **Model:** Beetle, CC, Eos, Golf, GTI, GLI, Jetta, Passat, Routan, Tiguan, Touareg **Engine:** 2.0L L4, 2.5L L5, 3.0L V6, 3.6L V6	**ENGINE OIL PRESSURE SENSOR CIRCUIT:** Ignition on, engine not running. The Powertrain Control Module (PCM) senses the oil pressure is out of the calibrated range. Two Trip fault.
DTC: P0521 **1 T ECM, MIL: Yes** **Year:** 2011, 2012 **Model:** Beetle, CC, Eos, Golf, GTI, GLI, Jetta, Passat, Routan, Tiguan, Touareg **Engine:** 2.0L L4, 2.5L L5, 3.0L V6, 3.6L V6	**ENGINE OIL PRESSURE SENSOR PERFORMANCE:** Engine running. The Engine Oil pressure never reaches the calibrated specification with the engine RPM at 1250. One trip fault.
DTC: P0522 **2 T ECM, MIL: Yes** **Year:** 2011, 2012 **Model:** Beetle, CC, Eos, Golf, GTI, GLI, Jetta, Passat, Routan, Tiguan, Touareg **Engine:** 2.0L L4, 2.5L L5, 3.0L V6, 3.6L V6	**OIL PRESSURE SENSOR CIRCUIT LOW:** With the ignition key on and battery voltage above 10.4 Volts. The oil pressure sensor voltage at Powertrain Control Module (PCM) goes below the minimum acceptable value. One Trip Fault. Three good trips to turn off the MIL.
DTC: P0523 **1 T ECM, MIL: Yes** **Year:** 2011, 2012 **Model:** Beetle, CC, Eos, Golf, GTI, GLI, Jetta, Passat, Routan, Tiguan, Touareg **Engine:** 2.0L L4, 2.5L L5, 3.0L V6, 3.6L V6	**ENGINE OIL PRESSURE SENSOR CIRCUIT HIGH:** With the ignition on. Battery voltage greater than 10.4 Volts. The Engine Oil pressure signal is greater than the calibrated amount. One Trip Fault.
DTC: P0524 **1 T ECM, MIL: Yes** **Year:** 2011, 2012 **Model:** Beetle, CC, Eos, Golf, GTI, GLI, Jetta, Passat, Routan, Tiguan, Touareg **Engine:** 2.0L L4, 2.5L L5, 3.0L V6, 3.6L V6	**ENGINE OIL PRESSURE IS TOO LOW:** With the engine running. The Oil Pressure Sensor indicates low oil pressure for 5 seconds.
DTC: P052A **1 T ECM, MIL: Yes** **Year:** 2011, 2012 **Model:** Beetle, CC, Eos, Golf, GTI, GLI, Jetta, Passat, Routan, Tiguan, Touareg **Engine:** 2.0L L4, 2.5L L5, 3.0L V6, 3.6L V6	**Cold Start "A" Camshaft Position Timing Over-Advanced:** * Time after engine start >= 15 Sec. * Engine speed >= 0 RPM * Modeled oil temperature >= -13 °C * Catalyst heating active

DTC	Trouble Code Title and Conditions
DTC: P0532 **1 T ECM, MIL: Yes** **Year:** 2011, 2012 **Model:** Beetle, CC, Eos, Golf, GTI, GLI, Jetta, Passat, Routan, Tiguan, Touareg **Engine:** 2.0L L4, 2.5L L5, 3.0L V6, 3.6L V6	**-A/C PRESSURE SENSOR CIRCUIT LOW:** Engine running, AC is learned and AC Clutch Relay energized. The A/C pressure transducer signal voltage received by the PCM from the TIPM is below the minimum acceptable value. One Trip Fault. Three good trips to turn off the MIL.
DTC: P0533 **1 T ECM, MIL: Yes** **Year:** 2011, 2012 **Model:** Beetle, CC, Eos, Golf, GTI, GLI, Jetta, Passat, Routan, Tiguan, Touareg **Engine:** 2.0L L4, 2.5L L5, 3.0L V6, 3.6L V6	**A/C PRESSURE SENSOR CIRCUIT HIGH:** Engine running and the A/C Clutch Relay energized. The A/C pressure transducer signal the PCM received from the TIPM is above the maximum acceptable value. One trip Fault. Three good trips to turn off the MIL.
DTC: P0534 **2 T ECM, MIL: Yes** **Year:** 2011, 2012 **Model:** Beetle, CC, Eos, Golf, GTI, GLI, Jetta, Passat, Routan, Tiguan, Touareg **Engine:** 2.0L L4, 2.5L L5, 3.0L V6, 3.6L V6	**Vehicle Speed Sensor "A" Intermittent/Erratic/High:** * Engine speed 1500-4500 RPM
DTC: P053F **2 T ECM, MIL: Yes** **Year:** 2011, 2012 **Model:** Beetle, CC, Eos, Golf, GTI, GLI, Jetta, Passat, Routan, Tiguan, Touareg **Engine:** 2.0L L4, 2.5L L5, 3.0L V6, 3.6L V6	**Cold Start Fuel Pressure Performance:** * Time after engine start 3 Sec. * Fuel cutoff not active * Catalyst heating active
DTC: P0544 **2T** **Year:** 2011, 2012 **Model:** Golf, Jetta, Passat **Engine:** 2.0L L4, 2.5L L5	**Exhaust Gas Temperature Sensor Circuit - Bank 1:** Engine running
DTC: P0545 **2T** **Year:** 2011, 2012 **Model:** Golf, Jetta, Passat **Engine:** 2.0L L4, 2.5L L5	**Exhaust Gas Temperature Sensor Circuit - Bank 1 Low:** Engine running
DTC: P054A **2 T ECM, MIL: Yes** **Year:** 2011, 2012 **Model:** Beetle, CC, Eos, Golf, GTI, GLI, Jetta, Passat, Routan, Tiguan, Touareg **Engine:** 2.0L L4, 2.5L L5, 3.0L V6, 3.6L V6	**CAMSHAFT POSITION TIMING OVER - ADVANCED-BANK1:** Engine cranking and engine running If the Camshaft Position Signal (angular variation) is more than 15° of the Crankshaft Position Signal, this DTC is set.
DTC: P054C **2 T ECM, MIL: Yes** **Year:** 2011, 2012 **Model:** Beetle, CC, Eos, Golf, GTI, GLI, Jetta, Passat, Routan, Tiguan, Touareg **Engine:** 2.0L L4, 2.5L L5, 3.0L V6, 3.6L V6	**-CAMSHAFT POSITION TIMING OVER - ADVANCED-BANK 2:** Engine cranking and engine running If the Camshaft Position Signal (angular variation) is more than 15° of the Crankshaft Position Signal, this DTC is set.

DTC	Trouble Code Title and Conditions
DTC: P0562 **1 T ECM, MIL: Yes** **Year:** 2011, 2012 **Model:** Beetle, CC, Eos, Golf, GTI, GLI, Jetta, Passat, Routan, Tiguan, Touareg **Engine:** 2.0L L4, 2.5L L5, 3.0L V6, 3.6L V6	**BATTERY VOLTAGE LOW:** With the engine running and the PCM has commanded the TIPM to energize the Transmission Control Output. If the battery voltage of the Transmission Control Output Sense circuit(s) to the PCM is less than 10.0 volts for the period of 15 seconds.
DTC: P0563 **1 T ECM, MIL: Yes** **Year:** 2011, 2012 **Model:** Beetle, CC, Eos, Golf, GTI, GLI, Jetta, Passat, Routan, Tiguan, Touareg **Engine:** 2.0L L4, 2.5L L5, 3.0L V6, 3.6L V6	**BATTERY VOLTAGE HIGH:** With the ignition on. Engine RPM greater than 1000 RPM. With no other charging system codes set. Battery voltage is one Volt greater than desired voltage for more than 10 seconds. Battery voltage greater than 15.75 Volts. One Trip Fault. Three good trips to turn off the MIL.
DTC: P0568 **1 T ECM, MIL: Yes** **Year:** 2011, 2012 **Model:** Beetle, CC, Eos, Golf, GTI, GLI, Jetta, Passat, Routan, Tiguan, Touareg **Engine:** 2.0L L4, 2.5L L5, 3.0L V6, 3.6L V6	**Cruise Control Set Signal:** Engine running and vehicle speed above 8 mph.
DTC: P0571 **1 T ECM, MIL: Yes** **Year:** 2011, 2012 **Model:** Beetle, CC, Eos, Golf, GTI, GLI, Jetta, Passat, Routan, Tiguan, Touareg **Engine:** 2.0L L4, 2.5L L5, 3.0L V6, 3.6L V6	**-BRAKE SWITCH 1 PERFORMANCE:** With the gear selector in drive, vehicle speed above a minimum value, and battery voltage greater than 10.4 volts. The PCM detects that the actual state of Brake Signal 1 or Brake Signal 2 does not match the desired state during monitoring.
DTC: P0572 **1 T ECM, MIL: Yes** **Year:** 2011, 2012 **Model:** Beetle, CC, Eos, Golf, GTI, GLI, Jetta, Passat, Routan, Tiguan, Touareg **Engine:** 2.0L L4, 2.5L L5, 3.0L V6, 3.6L V6	**-BRAKE SWITCH 1 STUCK ON:** With the gear selector in drive, vehicle speed above a minimum value, and battery voltage greater than 10.4 volts. The PCM detects that the actual state of Brake Signal 1 or Brake Signal 2 does not match the desired state during monitoring.
DTC: P0573 **1 T ECM, MIL: Yes** **Year:** 2011, 2012 **Model:** Beetle, CC, Eos, Golf, GTI, GLI, Jetta, Passat, Routan, Tiguan, Touareg **Engine:** 2.0L L4, 2.5L L5, 3.0L V6, 3.6L V6	**BRAKE SWITCH STUCK OFF:** With the ignition on. VSS indicates increasing and decreasing vehicle speed. APP Sensor indicates increasing and decreasing acceleration demand. The ECM determines that the brakes have been applied without the receiving an input from the Primary Brake Switch Signal and Secondary Brake Switches.
DTC: P0579 **1 T ECM, MIL: Yes** **Year:** 2011, 2012 **Model:** Beetle, CC, Eos, Golf, GTI, GLI, Jetta, Passat, Routan, Tiguan, Touareg **Engine:** 2.0L L4, 2.5L L5, 3.0L V6, 3.6L V6	**SPEED CONTROL SWITCH 1 PERFORMANCE:** With the ignition switch on and no other S/C Switch DTCs present. The S/C Switch Signal 2 voltage is not within a valid switch signal range.

DTC	Trouble Code Title and Conditions
DTC: P0580 **1 T ECM, MIL: Yes** **Year:** 2011, 2012 **Model:** Beetle, CC, Eos, Golf, GTI, GLI, Jetta, Passat, Routan, Tiguan, Touareg **Engine:** 2.0L L4, 2.5L L5, 3.0L V6, 3.6L V6	**SPEED CONTROL SWITCH 1 CIRCUIT LOW:** With the ignition on and battery voltage greater than 10.4 Volts. The S/C Signal 1 voltage is below a calibrated threshold for 0.06 second.
DTC: P0581 **1 T ECM, MIL: Yes** **Year:** 2011, 2012 **Model:** Beetle, CC, Eos, Golf, GTI, GLI, Jetta, Passat, Routan, Tiguan, Touareg **Engine:** 2.0L L4, 2.5L L5, 3.0L V6, 3.6L V6	**SPEED CONTROL SWITCH 1 CIRCUIT HIGH:** With the ignition on. The S/C Signal 1 is above a calibrated threshold for 0.06 second.
DTC: P0585 **1 T ECM, MIL: Yes** **Year:** 2011, 2012 **Model:** Beetle, CC, Eos, Golf, GTI, GLI, Jetta, Passat, Routan, Tiguan, Touareg **Engine:** 2.0L L4, 2.5L L5, 3.0L V6, 3.6L V6	**SPEED CONTROL SWITCH 1/2 CORRELATION:** With the ignition on and no other S/C Switch DTCs present. The S/C Signal 1 and (V72) S/C Signal 2 do not indicate the same S/C Switch position.
DTC: P0591 **1 T ECM, MIL: Yes** **Year:** 2011, 2012 **Model:** Beetle, CC, Eos, Golf, GTI, GLI, Jetta, Passat, Routan, Tiguan, Touareg **Engine:** 2.0L L4, 2.5L L5, 3.0L V6, 3.6L V6	**SPEED CONTROL SWITCH 2 PERFORMANCE:** With the ignition on and battery voltage greater than 10.4 Volts. The Powertrain Control Module (PCM) detects that the Speed Control signal voltage is implausible.
DTC: P0592 **1 T ECM, MIL: Yes** **Year:** 2011, 2012 **Model:** Beetle, CC, Eos, Golf, GTI, GLI, Jetta, Passat, Routan, Tiguan, Touareg **Engine:** 2.0L L4, 2.5L L5, 3.0L V6, 3.6L V6	**SPEED CONTROL SWITCH 2 CIRCUIT LOW:** With the ignition on. The S/C Signal 2 voltage is below a calibrated threshold for 0.06 second.
DTC: P0593 **1 T ECM, MIL: Yes** **Year:** 2011, 2012 **Model:** Beetle, CC, Eos, Golf, GTI, GLI, Jetta, Passat, Routan, Tiguan, Touareg **Engine:** 2.0L L4, 2.5L L5, 3.0L V6, 3.6L V6	**SPEED CONTROL SWITCH 2 CIRCUIT HIGH:** With the ignition on. The S/C Signal 2 voltage is below a calibrated threshold for 0.06 second.
DTC: P0600 **1 T ECM, MIL: Yes** **Year:** 2011, 2012 **Model:** Beetle, CC, Eos, Golf, GTI, GLI, Jetta, Passat, Routan, Tiguan, Touareg **Engine:** 2.0L L4, 2.5L L5, 3.0L V6, 3.6L V6	**Serial Communication Link (Data Bus) Message Missing:** With the ignition on. Internal Bus communication failure between processors. One Trip Fault. Three good trips to clear. * Engine condition-running Battery voltage-> 9 V

DTC	Trouble Code Title and Conditions
DTC: P0601 **1 T ECM, MIL: Yes** **Year:** 2011, 2012 **Model:** Beetle, CC, Eos, Golf, GTI, GLI, Jetta, Passat, Routan, Tiguan, Touareg **Engine:** 2.0L L4, 2.5L L5, 3.0L V6, 3.6L V6	**INTERNAL MEMORY CHECKSUM INVALID:** With the ignition on. Internal checksum for software failed, it does not match the calculated value. One Trip Fault, Three Good Trips to clear.
DTC: P0602 **1 T ECM, MIL: Yes** **Year:** 2011, 2012 **Model:** Beetle, CC, Eos, Golf, GTI, GLI, Jetta, Passat, Routan, Tiguan, Touareg **Engine:** 2.0L L4, 2.5L L5, 3.0L V6, 3.6L V6	**CONTROL MODULE PROGRAMMING ERROR/NOT PROGRAMMED:** Check for generic software is made at power-up. If generic software is found , the MIL will light immediately. This DTC is designed to signal the technician that the controller still has generic software installed. * Re-programming not completed
DTC: P0604 **2 T ECM, MIL: Yes** **Year:** 2011, 2012 **Model:** Beetle, CC, Eos, Golf, GTI, GLI, Jetta, Passat, Routan, Tiguan, Touareg **Engine:** 2.0L L4, 2.5L L5, 3.0L V6, 3.6L V6	**Internal Control Module Random Access Memory (RAM) Error:** Internal logic and checksum control error. Write ability check, failed.
DTC: P0605 **2 T ECM, MIL: Yes** **Year:** 2011, 2012 **Model:** Beetle, CC, Eos, Golf, GTI, GLI, Jetta, Passat, Routan, Tiguan, Touareg **Engine:** 2.0L L4, 2.5L L5, 3.0L V6, 3.6L V6	**Internal Control Module Read Only Memory (ROM) Error:** ECM/PCM detected a ROM test error, Wrong check sum.
DTC: P0606 **2 T ECM, MIL: Yes** **Year:** 2011, 2012 **Model:** Beetle, CC, Eos, Golf, GTI, GLI, Jetta, Passat, Routan, Tiguan, Touareg **Engine:** 2.0L L4, 2.5L L5, 3.0L V6, 3.6L V6	**INTERNAL ECM/PCM PROCESSOR:** Engine running. When the ECM/PCM recognizes an internal failure to communicate with the ECM or the CMP and CKP Sensor count periods are too short. One trip fault. ETC light is flashing.
DTC: P0607 **2 T ECM, MIL: Yes** **Year:** 2011, 2012 **Model:** Beetle, CC, Eos, Golf, GTI, GLI, Jetta, Passat, Routan, Tiguan, Touareg **Engine:** 2.0L L4, 2.5L L5, 3.0L V6, 3.6L V6	**Control Module Performance:** * With the ignition ON * Fuel quantity-> 0 mg/stroke * Engine condition –running * Battery voltage-> 9 V
DTC: P060B **1 T ECM, MIL: Yes** **Year:** 2011, 2012 **Model:** Beetle, CC, Eos, Golf, GTI, GLI, Jetta, Passat, Routan, Tiguan, Touareg **Engine:** 2.0L L4, 2.5L L5, 3.0L V6, 3.6L V6	**ETC A/D GROUND PERFORMANCE:** When the Throttle Motor is powered. When A2D reading does not return to ground within a set period of time of test activation, this fault sets. The test typically runs a couple of times per second, and is the reason why APP2 signal spikes to ground a couple of times per second in normal running. Reprogramming the module may not always fix this fault. One trip fault. ETC lamp is illuminated.

DTC	Trouble Code Title and Conditions
DTC: P060D **1 T ECM, MIL: Yes** **Year:** 2011, 2012 **Model:** Beetle, CC, Eos, Golf, GTI, GLI, Jetta, Passat, Routan, Tiguan, Touareg **Engine:** 2.0L L4, 2.5L L5, 3.0L V6, 3.6L V6	**ETC LEVEL 2 APP PERFORMANCE:** Throttle motor is powered and no matured faults related to APP Sensors. When secondary software determines that APPS 1 and APPS 2 signals do not match for a period of time. One trip fault. ETC lamp will flash.
DTC: P060E **1 T ECM, MIL: Yes** **Year:** 2011, 2012 **Model:** Beetle, CC, Eos, Golf, GTI, GLI, Jetta, Passat, Routan, Tiguan, Touareg **Engine:** 2.0L L4, 2.5L L5, 3.0L V6, 3.6L V6	**ETC LEVEL 2 TPS PERFORMANCE:** Throttle motor is powered and no matured faults related to TP Sensors. When secondary software determines that TPS 1 and TPS 2 signals do not match for a period of time. One trip fault. ETC lamp will flash.
DTC: P060F **1 T ECM, MIL: Yes** **Year:** 2011, 2012 **Model:** Beetle, CC, Eos, Golf, GTI, GLI, Jetta, Passat, Routan, Tiguan, Touareg **Engine:** 2.0L L4, 2.5L L5, 3.0L V6, 3.6L V6	**ETC LEVEL 2 ECT PERFORMANCE:** Throttle motor is powered and no matured faults related to the Engine Coolant Temp Sensor. When secondary software determines that the Coolant Temperature is implausible for a period of time. One trip fault. ETC lamp will flash.
DTC: P0613 **2 T ECM, MIL: Yes** **Year:** 2011, 2012 **Model:** Beetle, CC, Eos, Golf, GTI, GLI, Jetta, Passat, Routan, Tiguan, Touareg **Engine:** 2.0L L4, 2.5L L5, 3.0L V6, 3.6L V6	**INTERNAL TRANSMISSION PROCESSOR:** After the ignition switch is turned to the run position and 60 seconds thereafter. The fault conditions occur 3 times in less than 590 milliseconds: * The watchdog line remains high after the watchdog test or the transmission relay coil is energized and remains on after the watchdog delay expires.
DTC: P0614 **2 T ECM, MIL: Yes** **Year:** 2011, 2012 **Model:** Beetle, CC, Eos, Golf, GTI, GLI, Jetta, Passat, Routan, Tiguan, Touareg **Engine:** 2.0L L4, 2.5L L5, 3.0L V6, 3.6L V6	**Transmission Control Module (TCM) Incorrect Software Version:** CAN communication valid. Replacement control module ID doesn't match old control module ID.
DTC: P061A **1 T ECM, MIL: Yes** **Year:** 2011, 2012 **Model:** Beetle, CC, Eos, Golf, GTI, GLI, Jetta, Passat, Routan, Tiguan, Touareg **Engine:** 2.0L L4, 2.5L L5, 3.0L V6, 3.6L V6	**ETC LEVEL 2 TORQUE PERFORMANCE:** Throttle motor is powered. When secondary software determines that the customer requested output is not being achieved by the engine for a period of time. One trip fault. ETC lamp will flash.
DTC: P061C **1 T ECM, MIL: Yes** **Year:** 2011, 2012 **Model:** Beetle, CC, Eos, Golf, GTI, GLI, Jetta, Passat, Routan, Tiguan, Touareg **Engine:** 2.0L L4, 2.5L L5, 3.0L V6, 3.6L V6	**ETC LEVEL 2 RPM PERFORMANCE:** Throttle motor is powered and no camshaft or crankshaft electrical signal related DTCs are set. When secondary software determines that the engine speed is implausible for a period of time. One trip fault. ETC lamp will flash.

DTC	Trouble Code Title and Conditions
DTC: P0622 **1 T ECM, MIL: Yes** **Year:** 2011, 2012 **Model:** Beetle, CC, Eos, Golf, GTI, GLI, Jetta, Passat, Routan, Tiguan, Touareg **Engine:** 2.0L L4, 2.5L L5, 3.0L V6, 3.6L V6	**GENERATOR FIELD CONTROL CIRCUIT:** With the ignition on and the engine running. The Powertrain Control Module (PCM) tries to regulate the generator field with no result during monitoring. One Trip Fault. Three good trips to turnoff the MIL.
DTC: P0627 **1 T ECM, MIL: Yes** **Year:** 2011, 2012 **Model:** Beetle, CC, Eos, Golf, GTI, GLI, Jetta, Passat, Routan, Tiguan, Touareg **Engine:** 2.0L L4, 2.5L L5, 3.0L V6, 3.6L V6	**FUEL PUMP RELAY CIRCUIT:** With the engine running and the battery voltage greater than 10.4 Volts. The Powertrain Control Module (PCM) detects that the actual state of the fuel pump control does not match the intended state.
DTC: P0629 **1 T ECM, MIL: Yes** **Year:** 2011, 2012 **Model:** Beetle, CC, Eos, Golf, GTI, GLI, Jetta, Passat, Routan, Tiguan, Touareg **Engine:** 2.0L L4, 2.5L L5, 3.0L V6, 3.6L V6	**Fuel Pump "A" Control Circuit High:** * Pump relay, Commanded on * Engine speed, >80 RPM * Faulty activation of Fuel Pump (FP) Relay
DTC: P062B **2T ECM, MIL: Yes** **Year:** 2011, 2012 **Model:** Beetle, CC, Eos, Golf, Jetta, Passat, Touareg **Engine:** 2.0L L4, 3.0L V6,	**Injector Valves Communication CPU:** Engine speed, >80 RPM
DTC: P062C **1 T ECM, MIL: Yes** **Year:** 2011, 2012 **Model:** Beetle, CC, Eos, Golf, GTI, GLI, Jetta, Passat, Routan, Tiguan, Touareg **Engine:** 2.0L L4, 2.5L L5, 3.0L V6, 3.6L V6	**ETC LEVEL 2 MPH PERFORMANCE:** Throttle motor is powered and no vehicle speed related DTCs have matured. When secondary software determines that the vehicle speed is implausible for a period of time. One trip fault. ETC lamp will flash.
DTC: P0630 **1 T ECM, MIL: Yes** **Year:** 2011, 2012 **Model:** Beetle, CC, Eos, Golf, GTI, GLI, Jetta, Passat, Routan, Tiguan, Touareg **Engine:** 2.0L L4, 2.5L L5, 3.0L V6, 3.6L V6	**VIN NOT PROGRAMMED IN PCM:** At initialization. The VIN has not been programmed into the PCM. One Trip Fault. Three good trips to turn off the MIL.
DTC: P0632 **1 T ECM, MIL: Yes** **Year:** 2011, 2012 **Model:** Beetle, CC, Eos, Golf, GTI, GLI, Jetta, Passat, Routan, Tiguan, Touareg **Engine:** 2.0L L4, 2.5L L5, 3.6L V6	**ODOMETER NOT PROGRAMMED IN PCM:** Ignition on. The Odometer is not programmed into the Powertrain Control Module (PCM). One Trip Fault. Three good trips to turn off the MIL.
DTC: P0632 **2 T ECM, MIL: Yes** **Year:** 2011, 2012 **Model:** Touareg **Engine:** 3.0L TDI V6	**ECM/PCM Injection Valves Communication:** Engine running. The ECM/PCM recognizes a communication failure with the injection valve circuit.

DTC	Trouble Code Title and Conditions
DTC: P0633 **2 T ECM, MIL: Yes** **Year:** 2011, 2012 **Model:** Beetle, CC, Eos, Golf, GTI, GLI, Jetta, Passat, Routan, Tiguan, Touareg **Engine:** 2.0L L4, 2.5L L5, 3.0L V6, 3.6L V6	**SKIM SECRET KEY NOT STORED IN PCM:** Ignition on. The Secret Key information has not been programmed into the Powertrain Control Module (PCM). One Trip Fault. Three good trips to turn off the MIL.
DTC: P0634 **2 T ECM, MIL: Yes** **Year:** 2011, 2012 **Model:** Beetle, CC, Eos, Golf, GTI, GLI, Jetta, Passat, Routan, Tiguan, Touareg **Engine:** 2.0L L4, 2.5L L5, 3.0L V6, 3.6L V6	**ECM Internal Temperature Too High:** Output driver On state OR not applicable.
DTC: P0638 **2 T ECM, MIL: Yes** **Year:** 2011, 2012 **Model:** Beetle, CC, Eos, Golf, GTI, GLI, Jetta, Passat, Routan, Tiguan, Touareg **Engine:** 2.0L L4, 2.5L L5, 3.0L V6, 3.6L V6	**Throttle Actuator Control Range/Performance - Bank 1:** * Ignition on * Engine speed 0 RPM * ECT > -20.3 to 114.8 °C * IAT > -20.3 to 143.3 °C * Vehicle speed 0 km/h * Engine shutoff time 5 Sec. * Number of checks = 2
DTC: P063A **1 T ECM, MIL: Yes** **Year:** 2011, 2012 **Model:** Beetle, CC, Eos, Golf, GTI, GLI, Jetta, Passat, Routan, Tiguan, Touareg **Engine:** 2.0L L4, 2.5L L5, 3.0L V6, 3.6L V6	**GENERATOR VOLTAGE SENSE CIRCUIT:** With the engine running and the speed greater than 1157 RPM. The Powertrain Control Module (PCM) recognizes the alternator output voltage is less than the Battery feed circuit voltage. One trip failure. The Generator light will illuminate. The fault will be checked again on the next key cycle.
DTC: P0641 **1 T ECM, MIL: Yes** **Year:** 2011, 2012 **Model:** Beetle, CC, Eos, Golf, GTI, GLI, Jetta, Passat, Routan, Tiguan, Touareg **Engine:** 2.0L L4, 2.5L L5, 3.0L V6, 3.6L V6	**Sensor Reference Voltage A Circuit/Open:** Threshold values depending on internal 5 V rev voltage. Internal communication failed.
DTC: P0642 **1 T ECM, MIL: Yes** **Year:** 2011, 2012 **Model:** Beetle, CC, Eos, Golf, GTI, GLI, Jetta, Passat, Routan, Tiguan, Touareg **Engine:** 2.0L L4, 2.5L L5, 3.0L V6, 3.6L V6	**SENSOR REFERENCE VOLTAGE 1 CIRCUIT LOW:** With the ignition on. The ECM detects low voltage on the Sensor Supply 1 circuit for 0.10 seconds.
DTC: P0643 **1 T ECM, MIL: Yes** **Year:** 2011, 2012 **Model:** Beetle, CC, Eos, Golf, GTI, GLI, Jetta, Passat, Routan, Tiguan, Touareg **Engine:** 2.0L L4, 2.5L L5, 3.0L V6, 3.6L V6	**SENSOR REFERENCE VOLTAGE 1 CIRCUIT HIGH:** Ignition on, the Powertrain Control Module (PCM) recognizes the Primary 5-Volt Supply circuit voltage is too high. One Trip Fault. ETC light is flashing.

DTC	Trouble Code Title and Conditions
DTC: P0645 **1 T ECM, MIL: Yes** **Year:** 2011, 2012 **Model:** Beetle, CC, Eos, Golf, GTI, GLI, Jetta, Passat, Routan, Tiguan, Touareg **Engine:** 2.0L L4, 2.5L L5, 3.0L V6, 3.6L V6	**A/C CLUTCH RELAY CIRCUIT:** With the ignition on. And the battery voltage greater than 10 Volts. The A/C is being requested. An open or shorted condition is detected in the A/C Clutch Relay control circuit. One Trip Fault. Three good trips to turn off the MIL.
DTC: P064C **2T ECM, MIL: Yes** **Year:** 2011, 2012 **Model:** Beetle Golf, Jetta, Passat, Touareg **Engine:** 2.0L TDI L4, 3.0L TDI V6	**Glow Plug Control Module:** Glow system = Active
DTC: P0651 **1 T ECM, MIL: Yes** **Year:** 2011, 2012 **Model:** Beetle, CC, Eos, Golf, GTI, GLI, Jetta, Passat, Routan, Tiguan, Touareg **Engine:** 2.0L L4, 2.5L L5, 3.0L V6, 3.6L V6	**Sensor Reference Voltage B Circuit/Open:** Internal communication failed. Faulty reference signal.
DTC: P0652 **1 T ECM, MIL: Yes** **Year:** 2011, 2012 **Model:** Beetle, CC, Eos, Golf, GTI, GLI, Jetta, Passat, Routan, Tiguan, Touareg **Engine:** 2.0L L4, 2.5L L5, 3.0L V6, 3.6L V6	**SENSOR REFERENCE VOLTAGE 2 CIRCUIT LOW:** Ignition on. When the Powertrain Control Module (PCM) recognizes the (K856) 5-Volt Supply circuit voltage is too low. One Trip Fault. ETC light is flashing.
DTC: P0653 **1 T ECM, MIL: Yes** **Year:** 2011, 2012 **Model:** Beetle, CC, Eos, Golf, GTI, GLI, Jetta, Passat, Routan, Tiguan, Touareg **Engine:** 2.0L L4, 2.5L L5, 3.0L V6, 3.6L V6	**SENSOR REFERENCE VOLTAGE 2 CIRCUIT HIGH:** Ignition on. When the Powertrain Control Module (PCM) recognizes the Auxiliary 5-Volt Supply circuit voltage is too high. One Trip Fault. ETC light is flashing.
DTC: P0657 **2 T ECM, MIL: Yes** **Year:** 2011, 2012 **Model:** Beetle, CC, Eos, Golf, GTI, GLI, Jetta, Passat, Routan, Tiguan, Touareg **Engine:** 2.0L L4, 2.5L L5, 3.0L V6, 3.6L V6	**Actuator Supply Voltage A Circuit / Open:** * Relay, commanded off * Engine speed, > 80 RPM * Battery voltage test counter, 9.04-16 V>3
DTC: P0658 **2 T ECM, MIL: Yes** **Year:** 2011, 2012 **Model:** Beetle, CC, Eos, Golf, GTI, GLI, Jetta, Passat, Routan, Tiguan, Touareg **Engine:** 2.0L L4, 2.5L L5, 3.0L V6, 3.6L V6	**Actuator Supply Voltage A Circuit Low:** * Relay, commanded off (Key on engine off) * Engine speed, < 80 RPM * Battery voltage test counter, 9.04-16 V>3

DTC	Trouble Code Title and Conditions
DTC: P0659 **2 T ECM, MIL: Yes** **Year:** 2011, 2012 **Model:** Beetle, CC, Eos, Golf, GTI, GLI, Jetta, Passat, Routan, Tiguan, Touareg **Engine:** 2.0L L4, 2.5L L5, 3.0L V6, 3.6L V6	**Actuator Supply Voltage "A" Circuit High:** * Relay, commanded off * Engine speed, < 80 RPM * Battery voltage test counter, 9.04-16 V>3
DTC: P065A **1 T ECM, MIL: Yes** **Year:** 2011, 2012 **Model:** Beetle, CC, Eos, Golf, GTI, GLI, Jetta, Passat, Routan, Tiguan, Touareg **Engine:** 2.0L L4, 2.5L L5, 3.0L V6, 3.6L V6	**GENERATOR PERFORMANCE:** With the engine running. The ECM detects that the Generator output is not within specifications.
DTC: P066A **2 T ECM, MIL: Yes** **Year:** 2011, 2012 **Model:** Beetle, CC, Eos, Golf, GTI, GLI, Jetta, Passat, Routan, Touareg **Engine:** 2.0L TDI, L4, 3.0L TDI V6	**CYLINDER 1 GLOW PLUG CIRCUIT LOW:** With the ignition on and the Glow Plug Module Glow Plug command on. The ECM detects an open or short to ground on the Cylinder 1 Glow Plug circuit for 0.5 second.
DTC: P066C **2 T ECM, MIL: Yes** **Year:** 2011, 2012 **Model:** Beetle, CC, Eos, Golf, GTI, GLI, Jetta, Passat, Routan, Touareg **Engine:** 2.0L TDI, L4, 3.0L TDI V6	**CYLINDER 2 GLOW PLUG CIRCUIT LOW:** With the ignition on and the Glow Plug Module Glow Plug command on. The ECM detects an open or short to ground on the Cylinder 2 Glow Plug circuit for 0.5 second.
DTC: P066E **2 T ECM, MIL: Yes** **Year:** 2011, 2012 **Model:** Beetle, CC, Eos, Golf, GTI, GLI, Jetta, Passat, Routan, Touareg **Engine:** 2.0L TDI, L4, 3.0L TDI V6	**CYLINDER 3 GLOW PLUG CIRCUIT LOW:** With the ignition on and the Glow Plug Module Glow Plug command off. The ECM detects an open or short to ground on the Cylinder 3 Glow Plug circuit.
DTC: P0670 **2 T ECM, MIL: Yes** **Year:** 2011, 2012 **Model:** Beetle, CC, Eos, Golf, GTI, GLI, Jetta, Passat, Routan, Touareg **Engine:** 2.0L TDI, L4, 3.0L TDI V6	**Glow Plug Module 1 Control Circuit electrical malfunction electrical circuit:** Open or short in glow plug control circuit * Glow system = not active * Glow system = active
DTC: P0671 **2 T ECM, MIL: Yes** **Year:** 2011, 2012 **Model:** Beetle, CC, Eos, Golf, GTI, GLI, Jetta, Passat, Routan, Touareg **Engine:** 2.0L TDI, L4, 3.0L TDI V6	**Cylinder 1 Glow Plug Circuit:** Key on, and the ECM detected an unexpected voltage condition on the Glow Plug Lamp circuit during the CCM test. The Glow Plug Lamp remains "on" for 1-12 seconds (depending on the Glow Plug relay on-time which can vary from 1 and 120 seconds).
DTC: P0672 **2 T ECM, MIL: Yes** **Year:** 2011, 2012 **Model:** Beetle, CC, Eos, Golf, GTI, GLI, Jetta, Passat, Routan, Touareg **Engine:** 2.0L TDI, L4, 3.0L TDI V6	**-CYLINDER 2 GLOW PLUG CIRCUIT:** With the ignition on and the Glow Plug Module Glow Plug command on. The ECM detects an open or short on the Cylinder 2 Glow Plug circuit for 0.5 second.
DTC: P0673 **2 T ECM, MIL: Yes** **Year:** 2011, 2012 **Model:** Beetle, CC, Eos, Golf, GTI, GLI, Jetta, Passat, Routan, Touareg **Engine:** 2.0L TDI, L4, 3.0L TDI V6	**-CYLINDER 3 GLOW PLUG CIRCUIT:** With the ignition on and the Glow Plug Module Glow Plug command off. The ECM detects an open or shorted on the Cylinder 3 Glow Plug circuit.

DTC	Trouble Code Title and Conditions
DTC: P0674 **2 T ECM, MIL: Yes** **Year:** 2011, 2012 **Model:** Beetle, CC, Eos, Golf, GTI, GLI, Jetta, Passat, Routan, Touareg **Engine:** 2.0L TDI, L4, 3.0L TDI V6	**CYLINDER 4 GLOW PLUG CIRCUIT:** With the ignition on and the Glow Plug Module Glow Plug command on. The ECM detects an open or short on the Cylinder 4 Glow Plug circuit for 0.5 seconds.
DTC: P0675 **2 T ECM, MIL: Yes** **Year:** 2011, 2012 **Model:** Passat, Touareg **Engine:** 3.0L TDI V6	**Cylinder 5 Glow Plug Circuit:** With the ignition on and the Glow Plug Module Glow Plug command on. The ECM detects an open or short on the Cylinder 5 Glow Plug circuit for 0.5 seconds.
DTC: P0676 **2 T ECM, MIL: Yes** **Year:** 2011, 2012 **Model:** Passat, Touareg **Engine:** 3.0L TDI V6	**Cylinder 6 Glow Plug Circuit:** With the ignition on and the Glow Plug Module Glow Plug command on. The ECM detects an open or short on the Cylinder 6 Glow Plug circuit for 0.5 seconds.
DTC: P067A **2 T ECM, MIL: Yes** **Year:** 2011, 2012 **Model:** Beetle, CC, Eos, Golf, GTI, GLI, Jetta, Passat, Routan, Touareg **Engine:** 2.0L TDI, L4, 3.0L TDI V6	**Cylinder 4 Glow Plug Control Circuit Low:** With the ignition on and the Glow Plug Module Glow Plug command on. The ECM detects an open or short on the Cylinder 4 Glow Plug circuit for 0.5 seconds.
DTC: P067C **2 T ECM, MIL: Yes** **Year:** 2011, 2012 **Model:** Passat, Touareg **Engine:** 3.0L TDI V6	**Cylinder 5 Glow Plug Control Circuit Low:** With the ignition on and the Glow Plug Module Glow Plug command on. The ECM detects an open or short on the Cylinder 5 Glow Plug circuit for 0.5 seconds.
DTC: P067E **2 T ECM, MIL: Yes** **Year:** 2011, 2012 **Model:** Passat, Touareg **Engine:** 3.0L TDI V6	**Cylinder 6 Glow Plug Control Circuit Low:** With the ignition on and the Glow Plug Module Glow Plug command on. The ECM detects an open or short on the Cylinder 6 Glow Plug circuit for 0.5 seconds.
DTC: P0684 **2T PCM, MIL: Yes** **Year:** 2011, 2012 **Model:** Golf, GTI, Jetta, Passat **Engine:** 2.0L L4	**Glow Plug Control Module to PCM Communication Circuit Range/Performance:** With the ignition on and the Glow Plug Module Glow Plug command on. The ECM detects an open or short in the Glow Plug circuit for 0.5 seconds.
DTC: P0685 **1 T ECM, MIL: Yes** **Year:** 2011, 2012 **Model:** Beetle, CC, Eos, Golf, GTI, GLI, Jetta, Passat, Routan, Tiguan, Touareg **Engine:** 2.0L L4, 2.5L L5, 3.0L V6, 3.6L V6	**AUTO SHUTDOWN RELAY CONTROL CIRCUIT OPEN:** With ignition on. Battery voltage above 10.0 Volts. The actual ASD state is not equal to the desired ASD state. One Trip Fault. Three good trips to turn off the MIL.
DTC: P0686 **1 T ECM, MIL: Yes** **Year:** 2011, 2012 **Model:** Beetle, CC, Eos, Golf, GTI, GLI, Jetta, Passat, Routan, Tiguan, Touareg **Engine:** 2.0L L4, 2.5L L5, 3.0L V6, 3.6L V6	**ECM/PCM Power Relay Control Circuit Low:** With ignition on. Battery voltage above 10.0 Volts. The power relay state is not equal to the desired state. One Trip Fault. Three good trips to turn off the MIL.

DTC	Trouble Code Title and Conditions
DTC: P0687 **1 T ECM, MIL: Yes** **Year:** 2011, 2012 **Model:** Beetle, CC, Eos, Golf, GTI, GLI, Jetta, Passat, Routan, Tiguan, Touareg **Engine:** 2.0L L4, 2.5L L5, 3.0L V6, 3.6L V6	**ECM/PCM Power Relay Control Circuit High:** With ignition on. Battery voltage above 10.0 Volts. The power relay state is not equal to the desired state. One Trip Fault. Three good trips to turn off the MIL. * Main relay, Commanded on * ECM keep alive time
DTC: P0688 **1 T ECM, MIL: Yes** **Year:** 2011, 2012 **Model:** Beetle, CC, Eos, Golf, GTI, GLI, Jetta, Passat, Routan, Tiguan, Touareg **Engine:** 2.0L L4, 2.5L L5, 3.0L V6, 3.6L V6	**ECM Power Relay Sense Circuit Open:** With ignition on. Battery voltage above 10.0 Volts. The power relay state is not equal to the desired state. One Trip Fault. Three good trips to turn off the MIL. * Main relay, Commanded on * Engine speed > 80 RPM
DTC: P068A **1 T ECM, MIL: Yes** **Year:** 2011, 2012 **Model:** Beetle, CC, Eos, Golf, GTI, GLI, Jetta, Passat, Routan, Tiguan, Touareg **Engine:** 2.0L L4, 2.5L L5, 3.0L V6, 3.6L V6	**ECM/PCM RELAY OFF TOO EARLY:** When the ignition is turned off, during after-run mode of operation. The internal ECM/PCM timer determines that the ASD Relay has shut off before the AFTER-RUN mode of operation has been completed.
DTC: P068B **1 T ECM, MIL: Yes** **Year:** 2011, 2012 **Model:** Beetle, CC, Eos, Golf, GTI, GLI, Jetta, Passat, Routan, Tiguan, Touareg **Engine:** 2.0L L4, 2.5L L5, 3.0L V6, 3.6L V6	**ECM/PCM RELAY OFF TOO LATE:** When the ignition is turned off, during AFTER-RUN mode of operation. The internal ECM timer determines that the ASD Relay remained on for 2.0 seconds once AFTER-RUN mode of operation has been completed.
DTC: P0691 **1 T ECM, MIL: Yes** **Year:** 2011, 2012 **Model:** Beetle, CC, Eos, Golf, GTI, GLI, Jetta, Passat, Routan, Tiguan, Touareg **Engine:** 2.0L L4, 2.5L L5, 3.0L V6, 3.6L V6	**COOLING FAN 1 CIRCUIT LOW:** With the engine running, battery voltage is greater than 10.4 volts, and the Cooling Fan 1 control is active. The Totally Integrated Power Module (TIPM) detects an open or shorted condition in the Cooling Fan 1 control circuit.
DTC: P0692 **1 T ECM, MIL: Yes** **Year:** 2011, 2012 **Model:** Beetle, CC, Eos, Golf, GTI, GLI, Jetta, Passat, Routan, Tiguan, Touareg **Engine:** 2.0L L4, 2.5L L5, 3.0L V6, 3.6L V6	**COOLING FAN 1 CIRCUIT HIGH:** With the engine running, battery voltage greater than 10.4 volts, and the Cooling Fan 1 control active. The Totally Integrated Power Module (TIPM) detects an open or shorted condition in the Cooling Fan 1 control circuit.
DTC: P0693 **1 T ECM, MIL: Yes** **Year:** 2011, 2012 **Model:** Beetle, CC, Eos, Golf, GTI, GLI, Jetta, Passat, Routan, Tiguan, Touareg **Engine:** 2.0L L4, 2.5L L5, 3.0L V6, 3.6L V6	**-COOLING FAN 2 CIRCUIT LOW - GAS:** With the engine running, battery-voltage greater than 10.4 volts, and the Cooling Fan 2 control is active. The Totally Integrated Power Module (TIPM) detects an open or shorted condition in the Cooling Fan 2 control circuit.

DTC	Trouble Code Title and Conditions
DTC: P0694 **1 T ECM, MIL: Yes** **Year:** 2011, 2012 **Model:** Beetle, CC, Eos, Golf, GTI, GLI, Jetta, Passat, Routan, Tiguan, Touareg **Engine:** 2.0L L4, 2.5L L5, 3.0L V6, 3.6L V6	**COOLING FAN 2 CIRCUIT HIGH:** With the engine running, battery voltage greater than 10.4 volts, and the Cooling Fan 2 control is active. The Totally Integrated Power Module (TIPM) detects an open or shorted condition in the Cooling Fan 2 control circuit.
DTC: P0697 **2 T ECM, MIL: Yes** **Year:** 2011, 2012 **Model:** Beetle, CC, Eos, Golf, GTI, GLI, Jetta, Passat, Routan, Tiguan, Touareg **Engine:** 2.0L L4, 2.5L L5, 3.0L V6, 3.6L V6	**Sensor Reference Voltage C Circuit Open:** With the ignition on. The ECM detects a low voltage on the sensor circuit for 0.10 seconds * Threshold values dep. on internal 5 V rev voltage.
DTC: P0698 **2 T ECM, MIL: Yes** **Year:** 2011, 2012 **Model:** Beetle, CC, Eos, Golf, GTI, GLI, Jetta, Passat, Routan, Tiguan, Touareg **Engine:** 2.0L L4, 2.5L L5, 3.0L V6, 3.6L V6	**SENSOR REFERENCE VOLTAGE 3 CIRCUIT LOW:** With the ignition on. The ECM detects a low voltage on the Sensor Supply 3 circuit for 0.10 seconds
DTC: P0699 **2 T ECM, MIL: Yes** **Year:** 2011, 2012 **Model:** Beetle, CC, Eos, Golf, GTI, GLI, Jetta, Passat, Routan, Tiguan, Touareg **Engine:** 2.0L L4, 2.5L L5, 3.0L V6, 3.6L V6	**SENSOR REFERENCE VOLTAGE 3 TOO HIGH:** With the ignition on. The ECM detects a short to voltage on the Sensor Supply 3 circuit for 0.10 seconds.
DTC: P06A3 **2T ECM** **Year:** 2011, 2012 **Model:** Golf, GTI, Jetta, Passat **Engine:** 2.0L L4, 2.5L L5	**Sensor Reference Voltage "D" Circuit/Open:** With the ignition on. The ECM detects an Open condition on the sensor voltage D circuit.
DTC: P06B9 **2 T ECM, MIL: Yes** **Year:** 2011, 2012 **Model:** Beetle, CC, Eos, Golf, GTI, GLI, Jetta, Passat, Routan, Touareg **Engine:** 2.0L TDI, L4, 3.0L TDI V6	**Cylinder 1 Glow Plug Circuit Range/Performance:** The ECM/PCM has detected an open or short in the glow plug control circuit. * Glow system active * Demand signal 8 - 95%
DTC: P06BA **2 T ECM, MIL: Yes** **Year:** 2011, 2012 **Model:** Beetle, CC, Eos, Golf, GTI, GLI, Jetta, Passat, Routan, Touareg **Engine:** 2.0L TDI, L4, 3.0L TDI V6	**Cylinder 2 Glow Plug Circuit Range/Performance:** The ECM/PCM has detected an open or short in the glow plug control circuit. * Glow system active * Demand signal 8 - 95%
DTC: P06BB **2 T ECM, MIL: Yes** **Year:** 2011, 2012 **Model:** Beetle, CC, Eos, Golf, GTI, GLI, Jetta, Passat, Routan, Touareg **Engine:** 2.0L TDI, L4, 3.0L TDI V6	**Cylinder 3 Glow Plug Circuit Range/Performance:** The ECM/PCM has detected an open or short in the glow plug control circuit. * Glow system active * Demand signal 8 - 95%

DTC	Trouble Code Title and Conditions
DTC: P06BC **2 T ECM, MIL: Yes** **Year:** 2011, 2012 **Model:** Beetle, CC, Eos, Golf, GTI, GLI, Jetta, Passat, Routan, Touareg **Engine:** 2.0L TDI, L4, 3.0L TDI V6	**Cylinder 4 Glow Plug Circuit Range/Performance:** The ECM/PCM has detected an open or short in the glow plug control circuit. * Glow system active * Demand signal 8 - 95%
DTC: P06BD **2 T ECM, MIL: Yes** **Year:** 2011, 2012 **Model:** Passat, Touareg **Engine:** 3.0L TDI V6	**Cylinder 5 Glow Plug Circuit Range/Performance:** The ECM/PCM has detected an open or short in the glow plug control circuit. * Glow system active * Demand signal 8 - 95%
DTC: P06BE **2 T ECM, MIL: Yes** **Year:** 2011, 2012 **Model:** Passat, Touareg **Engine:** 3.0L TDI V6	**Cylinder 6 Glow Plug Circuit Range/Performance:** The ECM/PCM has detected an open or short in the glow plug control circuit. * Glow system active * Demand signal 8 - 95%
DTC: P06C5 **2T ECM, MIL: Yes** **Year:** 2011, 2012 **Model:** Beetle, Golf, Jetta, Passat **Engine:** 2.0L TDI L4	**Cylinder 1 Glow Plug Incorrect:** * Glow System = active * ECT < 18 * ECU off time > or = to 900 Sec. * Demand signal = 95%
DTC: P06C6 **2T ECM, MIL: Yes** **Year:** 2011, 2012 **Model:** Beetle, Golf, Jetta, Passat **Engine:** 2.0L TDI L4	**Cylinder 2 Glow Plug Incorrect:** * Glow System = active * ECT < 18 * ECU off time > or = to 900 Sec. * Demand signal = 95%
DTC: P06C7 **2T ECM, MIL: Yes** **Year:** 2011, 2012 **Model:** Beetle, Golf, Jetta, Passat **Engine:** 2.0L TDI L4	**Cylinder 3 Glow Plug Incorrect:** * Glow System = active * ECT < 18 * ECU off time > or = to 900 Sec. * Demand signal = 95%
DTC: P06C8 **2T ECM, MIL: Yes** **Year:** 2011, 2012 **Model:** Beetle, Golf, Jetta, Passat **Engine:** 2.0L TDI L4	**Cylinder 4 Glow Plug Incorrect:** * Glow System = active * ECT < 18 * ECU off time > or = to 900 Sec. * Demand signal = 95%
DTC: P06DA **1T ECM, MIL: Yes** **Year:** 2011, 2012 **Model:** Routan **Engine:** 3.6L V6 VIN G	**DUAL STAGE OIL PUMP CIRCUIT:** With the battery voltage is between 11 and 18 Volts with the engine running. The Powertrain Control Module (PCM) detects that the actual voltage of the oil pump solenoid control circuit does not match the intended state. One Trip Fault. Three good trips to turn off the MIL.
DTC: P06DD **1T ECM, MIL: Yes** **Year:** 2011, 2012 **Model:** Routan **Engine:** 3.6L V6 VIN G	**-DUAL STAGE OIL PUMP STUCK LOW:** Based upon the engine oil temperature, the monitor runs when engine speed (RPM) is over a calibrated value. The cooler the engine oil, the lower is the enable engine speed (Minimum 1000rpm). To evaluate the dual stage oil pump, fully warm up the engine. To run DUAL STAGE OIL PUMP STUCK LOW (P06DD), drive vehicle with engine speed over 3500 rpm. The Powertrain Control Module (PCM) senses the oil pressure is less than a low Threshold for five (5) seconds. One Trip fault.
DTC: P06DE **1T ECM, MIL: Yes** **Year:** 2011, 2012 **Model:** Routan **Engine:** 3.6L V6 VIN G	**DUAL STAGE OIL PUMP STUCK HIGH:** Based upon Engine oil temperature, the monitor runs when engine speed (RPM) is over a calibrated value. The cooler the engine oil, the lower is the enable engine speed (Minimum 1000rpm). To evaluate dual stage oil pump, fully warm up the engine. To run DUAL STAGE OIL PUMP STUCK HIGH (P06DE), drive vehicle over 2500 rpm. The Powertrain Control Module (PCM) senses the oil pressure is more than a high threshold for (50) seconds . One Trip fault.

DTC	Trouble Code Title and Conditions
DTC: P0700 **2T ECM, MIL: Yes** **Year:** 2011, 2012 **Model:** Golf, Jetta, Passat **Engine:** 2.0L L4, 2.5L L5	**Transmission Control System (MIL Request):** With the battery voltage is between 11 and 18 Volts with the engine running. The ECM/PCM detects a malfunction
DTC: P0701 **2T ECM, MIL: Yes** **Year:** 2011, 2012 **Model:** Golf, Jetta, Passat **Engine:** 2.0L L4, 2.5L L5	**Transmission control system range/performance:** The TCM has detected a concern with the operational strategy.
DTC: P0702 **2T ECM, MIL: Yes** **Year:** 2011, 2012 **Model:** Golf, Jetta, Passat **Engine:** 2.0L L4, 2.5L L5	**Transmission control system electrical:** The TCM has detected a concern with the operational strategy. *Battery voltage > 9 V for more than 500 ms
DTC: P0703 **1 T ECM, MIL: Yes** **Year:** 2011, 2012 **Model:** Beetle, CC, Eos, Golf, GTI, GLI, Jetta, Passat, Routan, Tiguan, Touareg **Engine:** 2.0L L4, 2.5L L5, 3.0L V6, 3.6L V6	**BRAKE SWITCH 2 PERFORMANCE:** With the gear selector in drive, vehicle speed above a minimum value, and battery voltage greater than 10.4 volts. The PCM detects that the actual state of Brake Signal 1 or Brake Signal 2 does not match the desired state during monitoring.
DTC: P0705 **1 T ECM, MIL: Yes** **Year:** 2011, 2012 **Model:** Beetle, CC, Eos, Golf, GTI, GLI, Jetta, Passat, Routan, Tiguan, Touareg **Engine:** 2.0L L4, 2.5L L5, 3.0L V6, 3.6L V6	**Transmission Range Sensor Circuit Malfunction (PRNDL Input):** The DTC will set if an invalid PRNDL code exists for more than 100 milliseconds within one second of power-up
DTC: P0706 **1 T ECM, MIL: Yes** **Year:** 2011, 2012 **Model:** Beetle, CC, Eos, Golf, GTI, GLI, Jetta, Passat, Routan, Tiguan, Touareg **Engine:** 2.0L L4, 2.5L L5, 3.0L V6, 3.6L V6	**TRANSMISSION RANGE SENSOR RATIONALITY:** The DTC will set if an invalid PRNDL code exists for more than 100 milliseconds within one second of power-up or if the PRNDL code error does not correct itself when (or before) the shift lever is moved to a different position (P, R, N, or OD), or if the PCM sees the PRNDL code rapidly (within 7 ms) jump across more than three shift lever detent positions.
DTC: P0711 **1 T ECM, MIL: Yes** **Year:** 2011, 2012 **Model:** Beetle, CC, Eos, Golf, GTI, GLI, Jetta, Passat, Routan, Tiguan, Touareg **Engine:** 2.0L L4, 2.5L L5, 3.0L V6, 3.6L V6	**TRANSMISSION TEMPERATURE SENSOR PERFORMANCE:** This DTC will set when the transmission temperature does not reach a normal operating temperature within a given time frame. Time is variable due to ambient temperature. Approximate DTC set time is 10 to 35 minutes. The following are starting temperature to warm up times to set this DTC: starting temperature -40° C (-40° F) warm up time 35 minutes, starting temperature -28° C (-20° F) 25 minutes, starting temperature -6.6° C (20° F) 20 minutes, starting temperature 15.5 ° C (60° F) 10 minutes. When the fault is set, calculated temperature is substituted for measured temperature, however the DTC is stored only after three consecutive occurrences.
DTC: P0712 **1 T ECM, MIL: Yes** **Year:** 2011, 2012 **Model:** Beetle, CC, Eos, Golf, GTI, GLI, Jetta, Passat, Routan, Tiguan, Touareg **Engine:** 2.0L L4, 2.5L L5, 3.0L V6, 3.6L V6	**TRANSMISSION TEMPERATURE SENSOR LOW:** Continuously with the ignition on and engine running. The DTC will set when the monitored Temperature Sensor voltage drops below 0.078 of a volt for the period of 1.45 seconds. When the fault is set, calculated temperature is substituted for measured temperature, however the fault code is stored only after three consecutive occurrences of the fault.

DTC	Trouble Code Title and Conditions
DTC: P0713 **1 T ECM, MIL: Yes** **Year:** 2011, 2012 **Model:** Beetle, CC, Eos, Golf, GTI, GLI, Jetta, Passat, Routan, Tiguan, Touareg **Engine:** 2.0L L4, 2.5L L5, 3.0L V6, 3.6L V6	**TRANSMISSION TEMPERATURE SENSOR HIGH:** Continuously with the ignition on and engine running. The DTC will set when the monitored Temperature voltage rises above 4.94 volts for the period of 1.45 seconds. When the fault is set, calculated temperature is substituted for measured temperature, however the fault code is stored only after three consecutive occurrences of the fault.
DTC: P0714 **1 T ECM, MIL: Yes** **Year:** 2011, 2012 **Model:** Beetle, CC, Eos, Golf, GTI, GLI, Jetta, Passat, Routan, Tiguan, Touareg **Engine:** 2.0L L4, 2.5L L5, 3.0L V6, 3.6L V6	**TRANSMISSION TEMPERATURE SENSOR INTERMITTENT:** Continuously with the ignition on and engine running. The DTC will set when the monitored Temperature Sensor voltage fluctuates or changes abruptly within a predetermined period of time.
DTC: P0715 **2T TCM** **Year:** 2011, 2012 **Model:** Beetle, Eos, Golf, GTI, Jetta, Passat, Touareg **Engine:** 2.0L L4, 2.5L L5, 3.0L V6, 3.6L V6	**Input/Turbine Speed Sensor "A" Circuit:** Input sensor, No failure decision for input sensor no pulse failure.
DTC: P0716 **1 T ECM, MIL: Yes** **Year:** 2011, 2012 **Model:** Beetle, CC, Eos, Golf, GTI, GLI, Jetta, Passat, Routan, Tiguan, Touareg **Engine:** 2.0L L4, 2.5L L5, 3.0L V6, 3.6L V6	**Input Turbine/Speed Sensor (A) Circuit Range/Performance:** The transmission gear ratio is monitored continuously while the transmission is in gear. If there is an excessive change in the Input RPM in any valid gears this DTC will set.
DTC: P0720 **2 T ECM, MIL: Yes** **Model:** Beetle, CC, Eos, Golf, GTI, GLI, Jetta, Passat, Routan, Tiguan, Touareg **Engine:** 2.0L L4, 2.5L L5, 3.0L V6, 3.6L V6	**Output Speed Sensor Circuit:** Output sensor, No failure decision for output sensor no pulse.
DTC: P0721 **2 T ECM, MIL: Yes** **Model:** Beetle, CC, Eos, Golf, GTI, GLI, Jetta, Passat, Routan, Tiguan, Touareg **Engine:** 2.0L L4, 2.5L L5, 3.0L V6, 3.6L V6	**Output Speed Sensor Circuit Range/Performance:** The transmission gear ratio is monitored continuously while the transmission is in gear. If there is an excessive change in the Output rpm in any gear.
DTC: P0722 **2 T ECM, MIL: Yes** **Model:** Beetle, CC, Eos, Golf, GTI, GLI, Jetta, Passat, Routan, Tiguan, Touareg **Engine:** 2.0L L4, 2.5L L5, 3.0L V6, 3.6L V6	**Output Speed Sensor Circuit No Signal:** The transmission gear ratio is monitored continuously while the transmission is in gear. If there is an excessive change in the Output rpm in any gear. Comparison with reference voltage-VSS = 0 mph and U < 2.2 V.
DTC: P0725 **2T TCM** **Year:** 2011, 2012 **Model:** Beetle, Eos, Golf, GTI, Jetta, Passat, Touareg **Engine:** 2.0L L4, 2.5L L5, 3.0L V6, 3.6L V6	**Engine Speed Input Circuit:** Whenever the engine is running. The ECM detects a malfunction with the transmission input speed sensor.

DTC	Trouble Code Title and Conditions
DTC: P0726 **2 T ECM, MIL: Yes** **Year:** 2011, 2012 **Model:** Beetle, CC, Eos, Golf, GTI, GLI, Jetta, Passat, Routan, Tiguan, Touareg **Engine:** 2.0L L4, 2.5L L5, 3.0L V6, 3.6L V6	**Engine Speed Input Circuit Range/ Performance:** The Engine Speed (RPM) Sensor detects engine speed and reference marks. Without an engine speed signal, the engine will not start. If the engine speed signal fails while the engine is running, the engine will stop immediately.
DTC: P0729 **2 T TCM, MIL: Yes** **Year:** 2011, 2012 **Model:** Beetle, CC, Eos, Golf, GTI, GLI, Jetta, Passat, Routan, Tiguan, Touareg **Engine:** 2.0L L4, 2.5L L5, 3.0L V6, 3.6L V6	**GEAR RATIO ERROR IN 6TH:** The Transmission gear ratio is monitored continuously while the transmission is in gear. If the ratio of the Input RPM to the Output RPM does not match the current gear ratio when compared to the known gear ratio.
DTC: P0730 **2 T TCM, MIL: Yes** **Year:** 2011, 2012 **Model:** Beetle, CC, Eos, Golf, GTI, GLI, Jetta, Passat, Routan, Tiguan, Touareg **Engine:** 2.0L L4, 2.5L L5, 3.0L V6, 3.6L V6	**Gear Incorrect Ratio:** The Transmission gear ratio is monitored continuously while the transmission is in gear. If the ratio of the Input RPM to the Output RPM does not match the current gear ratio when compared to the known gear ratio.
DTC: P0731 **2 T TCM, MIL: Yes** **Year:** 2011, 2012 **Model:** Beetle, CC, Eos, Golf, GTI, GLI, Jetta, Passat, Routan, Tiguan, Touareg **Engine:** 2.0L L4, 2.5L L5, 3.0L V6, 3.6L V6	**Gear 1 incorrect ratio:** The Transmission gear ratio is monitored continuously while the transmission is in gear. If the ratio of the Input RPM to the Output RPM does not match the current gear ratio when compared to the known gear ratio.
DTC: P0732 **2 T TCM, MIL: Yes** **Year:** 2011, 2012 **Model:** Beetle, CC, Eos, Golf, GTI, GLI, Jetta, Passat, Routan, Tiguan, Touareg **Engine:** 2.0L L4, 2.5L L5, 3.0L V6, 3.6L V6	**Gear 2 incorrect ratio:** The Transmission gear ratio is monitored continuously while the transmission is in gear. If the ratio of the Input RPM to the Output RPM does not match the current gear ratio when compared to the known gear ratio.
DTC: P0733 **2 T TCM, MIL: Yes** **Year:** 2011, 2012 **Model:** Beetle, CC, Eos, Golf, GTI, GLI, Jetta, Passat, Routan, Tiguan, Touareg **Engine:** 2.0L L4, 2.5L L5, 3.0L V6, 3.6L V6	**Gear 3 Incorrect Ratio:** The Transmission gear ratio is monitored continuously while the transmission is in gear. If the ratio of the Input RPM to the Output RPM does not match the current gear ratio when compared to the known gear ratio.
DTC: P0734 **2 T TCM, MIL: Yes** **Year:** 2011, 2012 **Model:** Beetle, CC, Eos, Golf, GTI, GLI, Jetta, Passat, Routan, Tiguan, Touareg **Engine:** 2.0L L4, 2.5L L5, 3.0L V6, 3.6L V6	**Gear 4 Incorrect Ratio:** The Transmission gear ratio is monitored continuously while the transmission is in gear. If the ratio of the Input RPM to the Output RPM does not match the current gear ratio when compared to the known gear ratio.

DTC	Trouble Code Title and Conditions
DTC: P0735 **2 T TCM, MIL: Yes** **Year:** 2011, 2012 **Model:** Beetle, CC, Eos, Golf, GTI, GLI, Jetta, Passat, Routan, Tiguan, Touareg **Engine:** 2.0L L4, 2.5L L5, 3.0L V6, 3.6L V6	**Gear 5 Incorrect Ratio:** The Transmission gear ratio is monitored continuously while the transmission is in gear. If the ratio of the Input RPM to the Output RPM does not match the current gear ratio when compared to the known gear ratio.
DTC: P0736 **2 T TCM, MIL: Yes** **Year:** 2011, 2012 **Model:** Beetle, CC, Eos, Golf, GTI, GLI, Jetta, Passat, Routan, Tiguan, Touareg **Engine:** 2.0L L4, 2.5L L5, 3.0L V6, 3.6L V6	**GEAR RATIO ERROR IN REVERSE:** The Transmission gear ratio is monitored continuously while the transmission is in gear. If the ratio of the Input RPM to the Output RPM does not match the current gear ratio when compared to the known gear ratio.
DTC: P0740 **3T** **Year:** 2011, 2012 **Model:** Routan **Engine:** 3.6L V6 VIN G	**TCC OUT OF RANGE:** This DTC is set after the period of 10 seconds and three occurrences of either: FEMCC - with slip greater than 100 RPM or PEMCC - duty cycle greater than 85%.
DTC: P0743 **2 T TCM, MIL: Yes** **Year:** 2011, 2012 **Model:** Beetle, CC, Eos, Golf, GTI, GLI, Jetta, Passat, Routan, Tiguan, Touareg **Engine:** 2.0L L4, 2.5L L5, 3.0L V6, 3.6L V6	**Torque Converter Clutch Circuit Electrical Malfunction:** * Main Solenoid, ON * Linear feedback current, >23 mA (AD:15) < 1333 mA (AD:1000)
DTC: P0746 **2 T TCM, MIL: Yes** **Year:** 2011, 2012 **Model:** Beetle, CC, Eos, Golf, GTI, GLI, Jetta, Passat, Routan, Tiguan, Touareg **Engine:** 2.0L L4, 2.5L L5, 3.0L V6, 3.6L V6	**Pressure control solenoid A performance or stuck off:** * Desired pressure <= adapted clutch slipping point + 1 bar * Standing vehicle with accelerator pedal < 1.5% * Battery voltage > 9 V for more than 500 ms * Engine speed >600 RPM for more than 500 ms
DTC: P0747 **2 T TCM, MIL: Yes** **Year:** 2011, 2012 **Model:** Beetle, CC, Eos, Golf, GTI, GLI, Jetta, Passat, Routan, Tiguan, Touareg **Engine:** 2.0L L4, 2.5L L5, 3.0L V6, 3.6L V6	**Pressure Control Solenoid A (Stuck On):** Common high-side switch 1 on and not defective, gearbox subsystem 1 active Common high-side switches not deactivated by module 2 * Terminal 15 voltage >4 V for more than 500 ms
DTC: P0748 **2 T TCM, MIL: Yes** **Year:** 2011, 2012 **Model:** Beetle, CC, Eos, Golf, GTI, GLI, Jetta, Passat, Routan, Tiguan, Touareg **Engine:** 2.0L L4, 2.5L L5, 3.0L V6, 3.6L V6	**Pressure Control Solenoid "A" Electrical:** * Main Solenoid, ON * Linear feedback current, >23 mA (AD:15) < 1333 mA (AD:1000)
DTC: P0748 **2 T TCM, MIL: Yes** **Year:** 2011, 2012 **Model:** Beetle, CC, Eos, Golf, GTI, GLI, Jetta, Passat, Routan, Tiguan, Touareg **Engine:** 2.0L L4, 2.5L L5, 3.0L V6, 3.6L V6	**Pressure Control Solenoid 'A" Electrical:** * Main solenoid switch, On * Linear feedback current, > 23 mA (AD:15) < 1333 mA (AD:1000)

DTC	Trouble Code Title and Conditions
DTC: P0750 **2 T TCM, MIL: Yes** **Year:** 2011, 2012 **Model:** Beetle, CC, Eos, Golf, GTI, GLI, Jetta, Passat, Routan, Tiguan, Touareg **Engine:** 2.0L L4, 2.5L L5, 3.0L V6, 3.6L V6	**L/R SOLENOID CIRCUIT:** Initially at ignition on, then every 10 seconds thereafter. The solenoids will also be tested immediately after a gear ratio error or pressure switch error is detected. Three consecutive solenoid continuity test failures, or one failure if test is run in response to a gear ratio or pressure switches error.
DTC: P0751 **2 T TCM, MIL: Yes** **Year:** 2011, 2012 **Model:** Beetle, CC, Eos, Golf, GTI, GLI, Jetta, Passat, Routan, Tiguan, Touareg **Engine:** 2.0L L4, 2.5L L5, 3.0L V6, 3.6L V6	**Shift solenoid A performance or stuck off:** Common high-side switches 1 and 3 on and no defects gearbox subsystem 1 active. Common high-side switches not deactivated by module 2. Duty factor change of safety valve 1 (control of safety valve 1 is stable) <= 5% duty factor change of gearshift fork valve 2 (control of gearshift fork valve 2 is stable) <= 5% duty factor of control gearshift fork valve 1 >70% and steady state time >= 50 ms terminal 15 voltage > 4 V for more than 500 ms
DTC: P0753 **2 T TCM, MIL: Yes** **Year:** 2011, 2012 **Model:** Beetle, Golf, GTI, Jetta, Passat, Touareg **Engine:** 2.0L L4, 2.5L L5, 3.0L V6, 3.6L V6	**Shift Solenoid "A" Electrical:** Engine started, vehicle driven with the solenoid applied, and the ECM detected an unexpected voltage condition on the SS1/A solenoid circuit was incorrect during the test.
DTC: P0755 **2 T TCM, MIL: Yes** **Year:** 2011, 2012 **Model:** Beetle, CC, Eos, Golf, GTI, GLI, Jetta, Passat, Routan, Tiguan, Touareg **Engine:** 2.0L L4, 2.5L L5, 3.0L V6, 3.6L V6	**2/4 SOLENOID CIRCUIT:** Initially at ignition on, then every 10 seconds thereafter. The solenoids will also be tested immediately after a gear ratio error or pressure switch error is detected. Three consecutive solenoid continuity test failures, or one failure if test is run in response to a gear ratio or pressure switches error.
DTC: P0756 **2 T TCM, MIL: Yes** **Year:** 2011, 2012 **Model:** Beetle, Eos, Golf, GTI, Passat **Engine:** 2.0L L4, 2.5L L5	**Shift solenoid B performance or stuck off:** * Common high-side switch 1 and 3 on and no defects * Gearbox subsystem 1 active * Common high-side switches not deactivated by module 2 * Duty factor change of safety valve 1 (control of safety valve 1 is stable) <= 5% * Duty factor change of gearshift fork valve 1 (control of gearshift fork valve 1 is stable) <= 5%
DTC: P0758 **2 T TCM, MIL: Yes** **Year:** 2011, 2012 **Model:** Beetle, Eos, Golf, GTI, Passat **Engine:** 2.0L L4, 2.5L L5	**Shift Solenoid "B" Electrical:** Engine started, vehicle driven with the solenoid applied, and the ECM detected an unexpected voltage condition.
DTC: P075A **3 T TCM, MIL: Yes** **Year:** 2011, 2012 **Model:** Routan **Engine:** 3.6L V6 VIN G	**LC SOLENOID CIRCUIT:** Initially at ignition on, then every 10 seconds thereafter. The solenoids will also be tested immediately after a gear ratio error or pressure switch error is detected. Three consecutive solenoid continuity test failures, or one failure if test is run in response to a gear ratio or pressure switch error.
DTC: P0760 **3 T TCM, MIL: Yes** **Year:** 2011, 2012 **Model:** Routan **Engine:** 3.6L V6 VIN G	**OD SOLENOID CIRCUIT:** Initially at ignition on, then every 10 seconds thereafter. The solenoids will also be tested immediately after a gear ratio error or pressure switch error is detected. Three consecutive solenoid continuity test failures, or one failure if test is run in response to a gear ratio or pressure switches error.

DTC	Trouble Code Title and Conditions
DTC: P0761 **2 T TCM, MIL: Yes** **Year:** 2011, 2012 **Model:** Beetle, CC, Eos, Golf, GTI, GLI, Jetta, Passat, Routan, Tiguan, Touareg **Engine:** 2.0L L4, 2.5L L5, 3.0L V6, 3.6L V6	**Shift solenoid C performance or stuck off:** * Common high-side switch 2 and 3 on, and no defects * Gearbox subsystem 2 active * Common high-side switches not deactivated by module 2 * Duty factor change of safety valve 2 (control of safety valve 2 is stable) <= 5% * Duty factor change of gearshift fork valve 4 (control of gearshift fork valve 4 is stable) <= 5% * Duty factor of control gearshift fork valve 3 >70% and steady state time >= 50 ms * Terminal 15 voltage > 4 V for more than 500 ms
DTC: P0763 **2 T TCM, MIL: Yes** **Year:** 2011, 2012 **Model:** Beetle, CC, Eos, Golf, GTI, GLI, Jetta, Passat, Routan, Tiguan, Touareg **Engine:** 2.0L L4, 2.5L L5, 3.0L V6, 3.6L V6	**Shift Solenoid "C" Electrical:** Engine started, vehicle driven with the solenoid applied, and the ECM detected an unexpected voltage condition on the SS3/C solenoid circuit was incorrect during the test.
DTC: P0765 **2 T TCM, MIL: Yes** **Year:** 2011, 2012 **Model:** Beetle, CC, Eos, Golf, GTI, GLI, Jetta, Passat, Routan, Tiguan, Touareg **Engine:** 2.0L L4, 2.5L L5, 3.0L V6, 3.6L V6	**UD SOLENOID CIRCUIT:** Ignition on, then every 10 seconds thereafter. The solenoids will also be tested immediately after a gear ratio error or pressure switch error is detected. Three consecutive solenoid continuity test failures, or one failure if test is run in response to a gear ratio or pressure switches error.
DTC: P0766 **2 T TCM, MIL: Yes** **Year:** 2011, 2012 **Model:** Beetle, CC, Eos, Golf, GTI, GLI, Jetta, Passat, Routan, Tiguan, Touareg **Engine:** 2.0L L4, 2.5L L5, 3.0L V6, 3.6L V6	**Shift solenoid D performance or stuck off:** * Common high-side switch 2 and 3 on, and no defects * Gearbox subsystem 2 active * Common high-side switches not deactivated by module 2 * Duty factor change of safety valve 2 (control of safety valve 2 is stable) <= 5% * Duty factor change of gearshift fork valve 3 (control of gearshift fork valve 3 is stable) <= 5% * Duty factor of control gearshift fork valve 4 >70% and steady state time >= 50 ms * Terminal 15 voltage > 4 V for more than 500 ms
DTC: P0768 **2 T TCM, MIL: Yes** **Year:** 2011, 2012 **Model:** Beetle, CC, Eos, Golf, GTI, GLI, Jetta, Passat, Routan, Tiguan, Touareg **Engine:** 2.0L L4, 2.5L L5, 3.0L V6, 3.6L V6	**Shift Solenoid "D" Electrical:** Engine started, vehicle driven with the solenoid applied, and the ECM detected an unexpected voltage condition on the SS3/D solenoid circuit was incorrect during the test.
DTC: P076A-DC **3 T TCM, MIL: Yes** **Year:** 2011, 2012 **Model:** Routan, Touareg **Engine:** 3.6L V6 VIN G	**SOLENOID CIRCUIT:** With the ignition on, then every 10 seconds thereafter. The solenoids will also be tested immediately after a gear ratio error or pressure switch error is detected. Three consecutive solenoid continuity test failures, or one failure if test is run in response to a gear ratio or pressure switches error.
DTC: P0771 **1 T TCM, MIL: Yes** **Year:** 2011, 2012 **Model:** Beetle, CC, Eos, Golf, GTI, GLI, Jetta, Passat, Routan, Tiguan, Touareg **Engine:** 2.0L L4, 2.5L L5, 3.0L V6, 3.6L V6	**Shift solenoid E performance or stuck off:** * Common high-side switch 3 on and no defects * Common high-side switches not deactivated by module 2 * Multiplexer valve is controlled and steady state time (>= 50 ms) * Terminal 15 voltage >4 V for more than 500 ms

DTC	Trouble Code Title and Conditions
DTC: P0773 **1 T TCM, MIL: Yes** **Year:** 2011, 2012 **Model:** Beetle, CC, Eos, Golf, GTI, GLI, Jetta, Passat, Routan, Tiguan, Touareg **Engine:** 2.0L L4, 2.5L L5, 3.0L V6, 3.6L V6	**Shift Solenoid "E" Electrical:** Engine started, vehicle driven with the solenoid applied, and the ECM detected an unexpected voltage condition on the SS3/D solenoid circuit was incorrect during the test.
DTC: P0776 **1 T TCM, MIL: Yes** **Year:** 2011, 2012 **Model:** Beetle, CC, Eos, Golf, GTI, GLI, Jetta, Passat, Routan, Tiguan, Touareg **Engine:** 2.0L L4, 2.5L L5, 3.0L V6, 3.6L V6	**Pressure control solenoid B performance or stuck off:** * Desired pressure <= adapted clutch slipping point + 1 bar * Standing vehicle with accelerator pedal < 1.5% * Battery voltage > 9 V for more than 500 ms * Engine speed > 600 RPM for more than 500 ms
DTC: P0777 **1 T TCM, MIL: Yes** **Year:** 2011, 2012 **Model:** Beetle, CC, Eos, Golf, GTI, GLI, Jetta, Passat, Routan, Tiguan, Touareg **Engine:** 2.0L L4, 2.5L L5, 3.0L V6, 3.6L V6	**Pressure Control Solenoid B (Stuck On):** Common high-side switch 2 on and not defective gearbox subsystem 2 active common high-side switches not deactivated by module 2 terminal 15 voltage > 4 V for more than 500 ms.
DTC: P0781 **1 T TCM, MIL: Yes** **Year:** 2011, 2012 **Model:** Beetle, CC, Eos, Golf, GTI, GLI, Jetta, Passat, Routan, Tiguan, Touareg **Engine:** 2.0L L4, 2.5L L5, 3.0L V6, 3.6L V6	**1-2 shift:** * Control safety valve 1 (on) >=20% * Multiplexer position ==0 * desired main pressure > 2 bars * Terminal 15 V > 4 V for more than 500 ms * Battery voltage > 9 V for more than 500 ms * Engine speed > 600 RPM for more than 500 ms
DTC: P0782 **1 T TCM, MIL: Yes** **Year:** 2011, 2012 **Model:** Beetle, CC, Eos, Golf, GTI, GLI, Jetta, Passat, Routan, Tiguan, Touareg **Engine:** 2.0L L4, 2.5L L5, 3.0L V6, 3.6L V6	**2-3 shift:** * Control safety valve 1 (on) >=20% * Multiplexer position ==0 * desired main pressure > 2 bars * Terminal 15 V > 4 V for more than 500 ms * Battery voltage > 9 V for more than 500 ms * Engine speed > 600 RPM for more than 500 ms
DTC: P0783 **1 T TCM, MIL: Yes** **Year:** 2011, 2012 **Model:** Beetle, CC, Eos, Golf, GTI, GLI, Jetta, Passat, Routan, Tiguan, Touareg **Engine:** 2.0L L4, 2.5L L5, 3.0L V6, 3.6L V6	**3-4 shift:** * Control safety valve 1 (on) >=20% * Multiplexer position ==0 * desired main pressure > 2 bars * Terminal 15 V > 4 V for more than 500 ms * Battery voltage > 9 V for more than 500 ms * Engine speed > 600 RPM for more than 500 ms
DTC: P0784 **1 T TCM, MIL: Yes** **Year:** 2011, 2012 **Model:** Beetle, CC, Eos, Golf, GTI, GLI, Jetta, Passat, Routan, Tiguan, Touareg **Engine:** 2.0L L4, 2.5L L5, 3.0L V6, 3.6L V6	**4-5 shift:** * Control safety valve 2 (on) >=20% * Multiplexer position ==1 * Desired main pressure > 2 bars * Terminal 15 V > 4 V for more than 500 ms * Battery voltage > 9 V for more than 500 ms * Engine speed > 600 RPM for more than 500 ms

DTC	Trouble Code Title and Conditions
DTC: P0785 **1 T TCM, MIL: Yes** **Year:** 2011, 2012 **Model:** Beetle, CC, Eos, Golf, GTI, GLI, Jetta, Passat, Routan, Tiguan, Touareg **Engine:** 2.0L L4, 2.5L L5, 3.0L V6, 3.6L V6	**Shift/Timing Solenoid:** Engine running and vehicle driven, the ECM detected a malfunction within the transmission.
DTC: P0791 **1 T TCM, MIL: Yes** **Year:** 2011, 2012 **Model:** Routan **Engine:** 3.6L V6 VIN G	**RANSFER SPEED SENSOR CIRCUIT:** The transmission gear ratio is monitored continuously while the transmission is in gear. If there is an excessive change in the Transfer RPM in any gear.
DTC: P0792 **1 T TCM, MIL: Yes** **Year:** 2011, 2012 **Model:** Routan **Engine:** 3.6L V6 VIN G	**COMPOUNDER SPEED RATIO ERROR:** The transmission gear ratio is monitored continuously while the transmission is in gear. If there is an excessive change in the Output RPM in any gear.
DTC: P0797 **1 T TCM, MIL: Yes** **Year:** 2011, 2012 **Model:** Beetle, CC, Eos, Golf, GTI, GLI, Jetta, Passat, Routan, Tiguan, Touareg **Engine:** 2.0L L4, 2.5L L5, 3.0L V6, 3.6L V6	**Pressure control solenoid C stuck on:** * Common high-side switch 3 on and not defective * Common high-side switches not deactivated by module 2 * Terminal 15 voltage > 4 V for more than 500 ms
DTC: P0798 **1 T TCM, MIL: Yes** **Year:** 2011, 2012 **Model:** Beetle, CC, Eos, Golf, GTI, GLI, Jetta, Passat, Routan, Tiguan, Touareg **Engine:** 2.0L L4, 2.5L L5, 3.0L V6, 3.6L V6	**Pressure Control Solenoid "C" Electrical:** * Main Solenoid, ON * Linear feedback current, >23 mA (AD:15) < 1333 mA (AD:1000)
DTC: P0811 **1 T TCM, MIL: Yes** **Year:** 2011, 2012 **Model:** Beetle, CC, Eos, Golf, GTI, GLI, Jetta, Passat, Routan, Tiguan, Touareg **Engine:** 2.0L L4, 2.5L L5, 3.0L V6, 3.6L V6	**Excessive Clutch Slippage:** * Engine speed, 400 RPM * Shift lever, D or S * Engine speed, < 4000 RPM * Estimated engine torque, > 0 Nm * Revolution sensor, No back up condition * SLU target current, > 1000 mA* Model oil temp, > 20° C
DTC: P0811 **1 T TCM, MIL: Yes** **Year:** 2011, 2012 **Model:** Beetle, CC, Eos, Golf, GTI, GLI, Jetta, Passat, Routan, Tiguan, Touareg **Engine:** 2.0L L4, 2.5L L5, 3.0L V6, 3.6L V6	**Excessive Clutch Slippage:** * Engine speed, >400 RPM * Shift lever, D,S * Engine speed, < 4000 RPM * Estimated engine torque, >=0 Nm * Revolution sensor, No back up condition * SLU target current, > 1000 mA * Model oil temp, >=20° C
DTC: P0829 **1 T TCM, MIL: Yes** **Year:** 2011, 2012 **Model:** Beetle, CC, Eos, Golf, GTI, GLI, Jetta, Passat, Routan, Tiguan, Touareg **Engine:** 2.0L L4, 2.5L L5, 3.0L V6, 3.6L V6	**5-6 shift:** * Control safety valve 1 (on) >=20% * Multiplexer position ==1 * Desired main pressure > 2 bars * Terminal 15 V > 4 V for more than 500 ms * Battery voltage > 9 V for more than 500 ms * Engine speed > 600 RPM for more than 500 ms

DTC	Trouble Code Title and Conditions
DTC: P083A **1 T TCM, MIL: Yes** **Year:** 2011, 2012 **Model:** Routan **Engine:** 3.6L V6 VIN G	**LC HYDRAULIC PRESSURE TEST:** In any forward gear with engine speed above 1000 rpm, shortly after a shift and every minute thereafter. After a shift into a forward gear, with engine speed greater than 1000 rpm, the PCM momentarily turns on element pressure to the clutch circuits that don't have pressure to verify that the correct pressure switch closes. If the pressure switch does not close 2 times the DTC will set.
DTC: P083B **1 T TCM, MIL: Yes** **Year:** 2011, 2012 **Model:** Routan **Engine:** 3.6L V6 VIN G	**LC PRESSURE SWITCH RATIONALITY:** Whenever the engine is running. The DTC is set if one of the pressure switches is open or closed at the wrong time in a given gear. If the problem is identified for three successive key starts, the transmission will go into Limp-in mode and the MIL will turn on after 10 seconds of vehicle operation.
DTC: P0840 **1 T TCM, MIL: Yes** **Year:** 2011, 2012 **Model:** Beetle, CC, Eos, Golf, GTI, GLI, Jetta, Passat, Routan, Tiguan, Touareg **Engine:** 2.0L L4, 2.5L L5, 3.0L V6, 3.6L V6	**Transmission Fluid Pressure Sensor/Switch "A" Circuit:** * Engine speed, > 400 rpm * Shift Lever, D or S * Current Gear, 5th or 6th * Line pressure, > 6.0 kg/cm2 * Oil pressure No.1, No fault * Model oil temp, > 20°C * Common parameter, common condition
DTC: P0841 **1 T TCM, MIL: Yes** **Year:** 2011, 2012 **Model:** Beetle, CC, Eos, Golf, GTI, GLI, Jetta, Passat, Routan, Tiguan, Touareg **Engine:** 2.0L L4, 2.5L L5, 3.0L V6, 3.6L V6	**Transmission Fluid Pressure Sensor/Switch "A" Circuit Range/Performance:** Whenever the engine is running. The DTC is set if the L/R pressure switch is open or closed at the wrong time in a given gear. If the problem is identified for three successive key starts, the transmission will go into Limp-in mode and the MIL will turn on after 10 seconds of vehicle operation.
DTC: P0845 **1 T TCM, MIL: Yes** **Year:** 2011, 2012 **Model:** Beetle, CC, Eos, Golf, GTI, GLI, Jetta, Passat, Routan, Tiguan, Touareg **Engine:** 2.0L L4, 2.5L L5, 3.0L V6, 3.6L V6	**2/4 HYDRAULIC PRESSURE TEST:** In any forward gear with engine speed above 1000 RPM, shortly after a shift and every minute thereafter. After a shift into a forward gear, with engine speed greater than 1000 RPM, the Powertrain Control Module (PCM) momentarily turns on element pressure to the clutch circuits that don't have pressure to verify that the correct pressure switch closes. If the pressure switch does not close two times the DTC will set.
DTC: P0846 **1 T TCM, MIL: Yes** **Year:** 2011, 2012 **Model:** Beetle, CC, Eos, Golf, GTI, GLI, Jetta, Passat, Routan, Tiguan, Touareg **Engine:** 2.0L L4, 2.5L L5, 3.0L V6, 3.6L V6	**2/4 PRESSURE SWITCH RATIONALITY:** Whenever the engine is running. The DTC is set if the 2/4 pressure switch is open or closed at the wrong time in a given gear. If the problem is identified for three successive ignition starts, the transmission will go into Limp-in mode and the MIL will turn on after 10 seconds of vehicle operation.
DTC: P084A-DC **1 T TCM, MIL: Yes** **Year:** 2011, 2012 **Model:** Routan **Engine:** 3.6L V6 VIN G	**HYDRAULIC PRESSURE TEST:** In any forward gear with engine speed above 1000 rpm, shortly after a shift and every minute thereafter. After a shift into a forward gear, with engine speed greater than 1000 rpm, the PCM momentarily turns on element pressure to the clutch circuits that don't have pressure to verify that the correct pressure switch closes. If the pressure switch does not close 2 times the DTC sets
DTC: P084B-DC **1 T TCM, MIL: Yes** **Year:** 2011, 2012 **Model:** Routan **Engine:** 3.6L V6 VIN G	**PRESSURE SWITCH RATIONALITY:** Whenever the engine is running. The DTC is set if one of the pressure switches is open or closed at the wrong time in a given gear. If the problem is identified for 3 successive key starts, the transmission will go into Limp-in mode and the MIL will turn on after 10 seconds of vehicle operation.
DTC: P0850 **1 T TCM, MIL: Yes** **Year:** 2011, 2012 **Model:** Routan **Engine:** 3.6L V6 VIN G	**PARK/NEUTRAL SWITCH PERFORMANCE:** Continuously with the transmission in Park, Neutral, or Drive and not in Limp-in mode. This code will set if the Powertrain Control Module (PCM) detects an irrational Park/Neutral switch state. Two trip fault. Three good trips to turn off the MIL.

DTC	Trouble Code Title and Conditions
DTC: P0863 **1 T TCM, MIL: Yes** **Year:** 2011, 2012 **Model:** Beetle, CC, Eos, Golf, GTI, GLI, Jetta, Passat, Routan, Tiguan, Touareg **Engine:** 2.0L L4, 2.5L L5, 3.0L V6, 3.6L V6	**Communication to Transmission Control Module Electrical Malfunction:** CAN bus okay 500 mSec after ignition on.
DTC: P0864 **1 T TCM, MIL: Yes** **Year:** 2011, 2012 **Model:** Beetle, CC, Eos, Golf, GTI, GLI, Jetta, Passat, Routan, Tiguan, Touareg **Engine:** 2.0L L4, 2.5L L5, 3.0L V6, 3.6L V6	**Communication to Transmission Control Module Range Performance:** CAN bus okay 500 mSec after ignition on
DTC: P0865 **2T TCM** **Year:** 2011, 2012 **Model:** Beetle, CC, Eos, Golf, GTI, Jetta, Passat, Routan, Touareg **Engine:** 2.0L L4, 2.5L L5, 3.0L V6, 3.6L V6	**TCM Communication Circuit Low:** * Time, 500 ms after IGN on
DTC: P0868 **2T TCM** **Year:** 2011, 2012 **Model:** Beetle, CC, Eos, Golf, GTI, Jetta, Passat, Routan, Touareg **Engine:** 2.0L L4, 2.5L L5, 3.0L V6, 3.6L V6	**LINE PRESSURE LOW:** Continuously while driving in a forward gear. The Powertrain Control Module (PCM) continuously monitors Actual Line Pressure and compares it to Desired Line Pressure. If the Actual Line Pressure is more than 5 psi below Desired Line Pressure while the PCS duty cycle is at or near its minimum value, this DTC will set.
DTC: P0869 **2T TCM** **Year:** 2011, 2012 **Model:** Beetle, CC, Eos, Golf, GTI, Jetta, Passat, Routan, Touareg **Engine:** 2.0L L4, 2.5L L5, 3.0L V6, 3.6L V6	**LINE PRESSURE HIGH:** Continuously while driving in a forward gear. The Powertrain Control Module (PCM) continuously monitors Actual Line Pressure. If the Actual Line Pressure reading is greater than the highest Desired Line Pressure ever used in the current gear, while the Pressure Control Solenoid duty cycle is at or near its maximum value (which should result in minimum line pressure), the DTC will set.
DTC: P0870 **2T TCM** **Year:** 2011, 2012 **Model:** Beetle, CC, Eos, Golf, GTI, Jetta, Passat, Routan, Touareg **Engine:** 2.0L L4, 2.5L L5, 3.0L V6, 3.6L V6	**OD HYDRAULIC PRESSURE TEST:** In any forward gear with engine speed above 1000 RPM, shortly after a shift and every minute thereafter. After a shift into a forward gear, with engine speed greater than 1000 RPM, the Powertrain Control Module (PCM) momentarily turns on element pressure to the clutch circuits that don't have pressure to identify the correct pressure switch closes. If the pressure switch does not close two times the DTC sets.
DTC: P0871 **2T TCM** **Year:** 2011, 2012 **Model:** Beetle, CC, Eos, Golf, GTI, Jetta, Passat, Routan, Touareg **Engine:** 2.0L L4, 2.5L L5, 3.0L V6, 3.6L V6	**OD PRESSURE SWITCH RATIONALITY:** Whenever the engine is running. The DTC is set if the OD pressure switch is open or closed at the wrong time in a given gear. f the P0706 fault condition is also present, the transmission will go into Limp-in mode and the MIL will turn on.
DTC: P0882 **2T TCM** **Year:** 2011, 2012 **Model:** Beetle, CC, Eos, Golf, GTI, Jetta, Passat, Routan, Touareg **Engine:** 2.0L L4, 2.5L L5, 3.0L V6, 3.6L V6	**TCM POWER INPUT LOW:** When the ignition is turned from "OFF" position to "RUN" position and/or the ignition is turned from "START" position to "RUN" position. This DTC is set when there is less than 3.0 volts present at the transmission control output circuits located in the Powertrain Control Module (PCM) when the Transmission Control System request the power up of those circuits. **Note: Due to the integration of the Transmission Control Module and the Powertrain Control Module, both systems have their own power and ground circuits.**

DTC	Trouble Code Title and Conditions
DTC: P0883 **2T TCM** **Year:** 2011, 2012 **Model:** Beetle, CC, Eos, Golf, GTI, Jetta, Passat, Routan, Touareg **Engine:** 2.0L L4, 2.5L L5, 3.0L V6, 3.6L V6	**TCM POWER INPUT HIGH:** When the ignition is turned from "OFF" position to "RUN" position and/or the ignition is turned from "START" position to "RUN" position. This DTC is set if the Powertrain Control Module senses greater than 3.0 volts on the Transmission Control Relay Output circuits prior to a request from the PCM to TIPM to energize the Transmission Output circuits.
DTC: P0884 **2T TCM** **Year:** 2011, 2012 **Model:** Beetle, CC, Eos, Golf, GTI, Jetta, Passat, Routan, Touareg **Engine:** 2.0L L4, 2.5L L5, 3.0L V6, 3.6L V6	**POWER UP AT SPEED:** This DTC will set if the PCM powers up and senses the vehicle in a valid forward gear (no PRNDL DTCs) with an output speed above 800 rpm, approximately 32 km/h or 20 mph.
DTC: P0888 **2T TCM** **Year:** 2011, 2012 **Model:** Beetle, CC, Eos, Golf, GTI, Jetta, Passat, Routan, Touareg **Engine:** 2.0L L4, 2.5L L5, 3.0L V6, 3.6L V6	**TRANSMISSION RELAY ALWAYS OFF:** This DTC is set when there is less than 3.0 volts present at the transmission control output circuits located in the Powertrain Control Module (PCM) when the Transmission Control System request the power up of those circuits. **Note: Due to the integration of the Transmission Control Module and the Powertrain Control Module, both systems have their own power and ground circuits.**
DTC: P0890 **2T TCM** **Year:** 2011, 2012 **Model:** Beetle, Eos, Golf, GTI, Jetta, Passat **Engine:** 2.0L L4, 2.5L L5	**TCM Power Relay Sense Circuit Low:** Terminal 15 voltage > 4 V for more than 500 ms
DTC: P0890 **2T TCM** **Year:** 2011, 2012 **Model:** Beetle, CC, Eos, Golf, GTI, Jetta, Passat, Routan, Touareg **Engine:** 2.0L L4, 2.5L L5, 3.0L V6, 3.6L V6	**SWITCHED BATTERY:** One time after a reset (ignition key turned to the RUN position or after cranking engine). A fault is set if voltage greater than 4.5 volts is detected for 7 msec on any of the pressure switch circuits before the relay is energized. The transmission is placed in Limp-In. The MIL is on after 10 seconds of vehicle operation.
DTC: P0891 **2T TCM** **Year:** 2011, 2012 **Model:** Beetle, CC, Eos, Golf, GTI, Jetta, Passat, Routan, Touareg **Engine:** 2.0L L4, 2.5L L5, 3.0L V6, 3.6L V6	**TRANSMISSION RELAY ALWAYS ON:** When the ignition is turned from "OFF" position to "RUN" position and/or the ignition is turned from "START" position to "RUN" position. This DTC is set if the Powertrain Control Module senses greater than 3.0 volts on the Transmission Control Relay Output circuits prior to a request from the PCM to TIPM to energize the Transmission Output circuits.
DTC: P0892 **2T TCM** **Year:** 2011, 2012 **Model:** Beetle, CC, Eos, Golf, GTI, Jetta, Passat, Routan, Touareg **Engine:** 2.0L L4, 2.5L L5, 3.0L V6, 3.6L V6	**TCM Power Relay Sense Circuit Intermittent:** * Filtered battery voltage, > 7 V * High side and low side FET, enabled * Status counter initialization, 0 or 1
DTC: P0897 **2T TCM** **Year:** 2011, 2012 **Model:** Beetle, CC, Eos, Golf, GTI, Jetta, Passat, Routan, Touareg **Engine:** 2.0L L4, 2.5L L5, 3.0L V6, 3.6L V6	**TRANSMISSION FLUID DETERIORATED:** Each transition from full EMCC to partial EMCC for A/C bump prevention. DTC set if 20 occurrences of a turbine acceleration sum. Fault Set Time: 20 transitions from full EMCC to partial EMCC. Transmission will not use partial EMCC. Established for A/C bump prevention.

DTC	Trouble Code Title and Conditions
DTC: P0914 **2T TCM** **Year:** 2011, 2012 **Model:** Beetle, CC, Eos, Golf, GTI, Jetta, Passat, Routan, Touareg **Engine:** 2.0L L4, 2.5L L5, 3.0L V6, 3.6L V6	**Gear shift position circuit:** * Gear message for selector lever is transmittable and selector lever message is receivable * No failure of selector lever CAN messages * Terminal 15 voltage > 4 V for more than 500 ms
DTC: P0919 **2T TCM** **Year:** 2011, 2012 **Model:** Beetle, CC, Eos, Golf, GTI, Jetta, Passat, Routan, Touareg **Engine:** 2.0L L4, 2.5L L5, 3.0L V6, 3.6L V6	**Gear shift position control error:** * No failure of selector lever CAN messages * Terminal 15 voltage > 4 V for more than 500 ms * Battery voltage > 9 V for more than 500 ms
DTC: P0928 **2T TCM** **Year:** 2011, 2012 **Model:** Beetle, CC, Eos, Golf, GTI, Jetta, Passat, Routan, Touareg **Engine:** 2.0L L4, 2.5L L5, 3.0L V6, 3.6L V6	**BTSI CONTROL CIRCUIT:** When the ignition is in accessory, run or start position. This DTC will set if the WIN module detects a problem with the BTSI solenoid control circuit. The DTC will remain active until the WIN module no longer detects a failure of the BTSI control circuit.
DTC: P0929 **2T TCM** **Year:** 2011, 2012 **Model:** Beetle, CC, Eos, Golf, GTI, Jetta, Passat, Routan, Touareg **Engine:** 2.0L L4, 2.5L L5, 3.0L V6, 3.6L V6	**Gear shift lock solenoid control circuit range/performance:** * No failure of selector lever CAN messages * terminal 15 voltage > 4 V for more than 500 ms
DTC: P0932 **2T TCM** **Year:** 2011, 2012 **Model:** Beetle, CC, Eos, Golf, GTI, Jetta, Passat, Routan, Touareg **Engine:** 2.0L L4, 2.5L L5, 3.0L V6, 3.6L V6	**LINE PRESSURE SENSOR CIRCUIT:** Continuously with the ignition on, engine running, with the transmission in gear. The PCM continuously monitors Actual Line Pressure and compares it to Desired Line Pressure. If the Actual Line Pressure reading is more than 172.4 kPa (25 psi) higher than the Desired Line Pressure, but is less than the highest Line Pressure ever used in the current gear, the DTC sets.
DTC: P0934 **2T TCM** **Year:** 2011, 2012 **Model:** Beetle, CC, Eos, Golf, GTI, Jetta, Passat, Routan, Touareg **Engine:** 2.0L L4, 2.5L L5, 3.0L V6, 3.6L V6	**LINE PRESSURE SENSOR CIRCUIT LOW:** Continuously with the ignition on and engine running. This DTC will set when the monitored Line Pressure Sensor voltage is less than or equal to 0.35 of a volt for 0.18 of a second.
DTC: P0935 **2T TCM** **Year:** 2011, 2012 **Model:** Beetle, CC, Eos, Golf, GTI, Jetta, Passat, Routan, Touareg **Engine:** 2.0L L4, 2.5L L5, 3.0L V6, 3.6L V6	**LINE PRESSURE SENSOR CIRCUIT HIGH:** Continuously with ignition on and engine running. This DTC will set if the monitored Line Pressure Sensor voltage is greater than or equal to 4.75 volts for the period of 0.18 of a second.
DTC: P0944 **2T TCM** **Year:** 2011, 2012 **Model:** Beetle, CC, Eos, Golf, GTI, Jetta, Passat, Routan, Touareg **Engine:** 2.0L L4, 2.5L L5, 3.0L V6, 3.6L V6	**LOSS OF HYDRAULIC PUMP PRIME:** Every 350 msec If the transmission begins to slip in any forward gear, and the pressure switch or switches that should be closed for a given gear are open, a loss of prime test begins. All available elements (in 1st gear LR, 2/4 and OD, in 2nd, 3rd, and 4th gear 2/4 and OD) are turned on by the Powertrain Control Module (PCM) to see if pump prime exists. The code is set if none of the pressure switches respond. The PCM will continue to run the loss of prime test until pump pressure returns. The vehicle will not move or the transmission will slip. Normal operation will continue if pump prime returns.

DTC	Trouble Code Title and Conditions
DTC: P0957 **2T TCM** **Year:** 2011, 2012 **Model:** Beetle, CC, Eos, Golf, GTI, Jetta, Passat, Routan, Touareg **Engine:** 2.0L L4, 2.5L L5, 3.0L V6, 3.6L V6	**AUTOSTICK CIRCUIT LOW:** Whenever the engine is running. The transmission is not in the AutoStick® position and the up shift or downshift is reporting closed - below 0.71 of a volt or if both switches are reported closed at the same time.
DTC: P0992 **2T TCM** **Year:** 2011, 2012 **Model:** Beetle, CC, Eos, Golf, GTI, Jetta, Passat, Routan, Touareg **Engine:** 2.0L L4, 2.5L L5, 3.0L V6, 3.6L V6	**2/4/OD HYDRAULIC PRESSURE TEST:** In any forward gear with engine speed above 1000 RPM, shortly after a shift and every minute thereafter. After a shift into a forward gear, with engine speed greater than 1000 RPM, the Powertrain Control Module (PCM) momentarily turns on element pressure to the clutch circuits that do not have pressure to identify that the correct pressure switch closes. If the pressure switch does not close two times the DTC sets.

OBD II Trouble Code List (P1XXX Codes)

DTC	Trouble Code Title and Conditions
DTC: P1004 **2T ECM, MIL: Yes** **Year:** 2011, 2012 **Model:** Golf, GTI, Jetta, Passat **Engine:** 2.0L L4, 2.5L L5	**Torque difference cylinder 1 Limiting value exceeded:** * Engine running * ECM in closed loop * ECT > 50 °C * Time since engine start > 30 Sec.
DTC: P1005 **2T ECM, MIL: Yes** **Year:** 2011, 2012 **Model:** Golf, GTI, Jetta, Passat **Engine:** 2.0L L4, 2.5L L5	**Torque difference cylinder 2 Limiting value exceeded:** * Engine running * ECM in closed loop * ECT > 50 °C * Time since engine start > 30 Sec.
DTC: P1007 **2T ECM, MIL: Yes** **Year:** 2011, 2012 **Model:** Golf, GTI, Jetta, Passat **Engine:** 2.0L L4, 2.5L L5	**Torque difference cylinder 4 Limiting value exceeded:** * Engine running * ECM in closed loop * ECT > 50 °C * Time since engine start > 30 Sec.
DTC: P1009 **2T ECM, MIL: Yes** **Year:** 2011, 2012 **Model:** Touareg **Engine:** 3.0L V6, 3.6L V6	**Air mass meter 1/2 implausible signal from load detection:** * Time after engine start, 20 camshaft revs * Lambda control, Closed loop * Engine load, >14.25% * Throttle position, No fuel load * ECT, >59.25° C * Or Substitute ECT
DTC: P1026 **2T ECM, MIL: Yes** **Year:** 2011, 2012 **Model:** Jetta, Passat **Engine:** 2.0L L4, 2.5L L5	**Intake Manifold Flap For Air Stream Regulation (Short circuit to B+):** Output driver-ON state
DTC: P1027 **2T ECM, MIL: Yes** **Year:** 2011, 2012 **Model:** Jetta, Passat **Engine:** 2.0L L4, 2.5L L5	**Intake Manifold Flap For Air Stream Regulation Short circuit to (GND):** Output driver-OFF state
DTC: P1028 **2T ECM, MIL: Yes** **Year:** 2011, 2012 **Model:** Jetta, Passat **Engine:** 2.0L L4, 2.5L L5	**Activation intake manifold flap for air stream regulation Open circuit:** Output driver-OFF state

DTC	Trouble Code Title and Conditions
DTC: P1103 **2T ECM, MIL: Yes** **Year:** 2011, 2012 **Model:** Beetle, Eos, GTI, Jetta, Passat **Engine:** 2.0L L4	**O2 Sensor Circuit (Bank 1-Sensor 1) Output Too Low:** Engine started, battery voltage must be at least 11.5v, all electrical components must be off, the ground between the engine and the chassis must be well connected, the exhaust system must be properly sealed between the catalytic converter and the cylinder head, and the oxygen sensor heater for oxygen sensor before the catalytic converter must be properly functioning. The ECM detected a voltage on the O2 sensor circuit that was outside the parameters to function properly. **Note: For resistance testing of sensor heating, oxygen sensor should be cooled to ambient temperature. High temperatures at oxygen sensor may lead to inaccurate measurements.**
DTC: P1105 **2T ECM, MIL: Yes** **Year:** 2011, 2012 **Model:** Beetle, Eos, GTI, Jetta, Passat **Engine:** 2.0L L4	**O2 Sensor Circuit (Bank 1-Sensor 2) Short to B+:** Engine started, battery voltage must be at least 11.5v, all electrical components must be off, the ground between the engine and the chassis must be well connected, the exhaust system must be properly sealed between the catalytic converter and the cylinder head, and the oxygen sensor heater for oxygen sensor before the catalytic converter must be properly functioning. The ECM detected a voltage on the O2 sensor circuit that was outside the parameters to function properly. **Note: For resistance testing of sensor heating, oxygen sensor should be cooled to ambient temperature. High temperatures at oxygen sensor may lead to inaccurate measurements.**
DTC: P1111 **1T** **Year:** 2011, 2012 **Model:** Beetle, Eos, GTI, Jetta, Passat **Engine:** 2.0L L4	**O2 Control (Bank 1) System Too Lean:** Engine started, battery voltage must be at least 11.5v, all electrical components must be off, the ground between the engine and the chassis must be well connected, the exhaust system must be properly sealed between the catalytic converter and the cylinder head, and the oxygen sensor heater for oxygen sensor before the catalytic converter must be properly functioning. The ECM detected the measurement on the O2 sensor circuit that was outside the parameters to function properly. **Note: For resistance testing of sensor heating, oxygen sensor should be cooled to ambient temperature. High temperatures at oxygen sensor may lead to inaccurate measurements.**
DTC: P1112 **1T** **Year:** 2011, 2012 **Model:** Beetle, Eos, GTI, Jetta, Passat **Engine:** 2.0L L4	**O2 Control (Bank 1) System Too Rich:** Engine started, battery voltage must be at least 11.5v, all electrical components must be off, the ground between the engine and the chassis must be well connected, the exhaust system must be properly sealed between the catalytic converter and the cylinder head, and the oxygen sensor heater for oxygen sensor before the catalytic converter must be properly functioning. The ECM detected a measurement on the O2 sensor circuit that was outside the parameters to function properly. **Note: For resistance testing of sensor heating, oxygen sensor should be cooled to ambient temperature. High temperatures at oxygen sensor may lead to inaccurate measurements. When an O2S malfunction (P0131 to P0414) is also stored with this malfunction, the O2S malfunction(s) should be repaired first.**
DTC: P1113 **1T** **Year:** 2011, 2012 **Model:** Beetle, Eos, GTI, Jetta, Passat **Engine:** 2.0L L4	**O2 Control (Bank 1 Sensor 1) Internal Resistance Too High:** Engine started, battery voltage must be at least 11.5v, all electrical components must be off, the ground between the engine and the chassis must be well connected, the exhaust system must be properly sealed between the catalytic converter and the cylinder head, and the oxygen sensor heater for oxygen sensor before the catalytic converter must be properly functioning. The ECM detected a measurement on the O2 sensor circuit that was outside the parameters to function properly. **Note: For resistance testing of sensor heating, oxygen sensor should be cooled to ambient temperature. High temperatures at oxygen sensor may lead to inaccurate measurements.**
DTC: P1114 **2T ECM, MIL: Yes** **Year:** 2011, 2012 **Model:** Beetle, Eos, Golf, GTI, Jetta, Passat **Engine:** 2.0L L4, 2.5L L5	**Internal resistance too large (Bank 1, sensor 2):** * Battery voltage, 10.7-16.1 V * Modeled exhaust gas temp, 300-600° C * Engine shutoff time, 300 Sec. * IAT, >6.75° C
DTC: P1114 **1T** **Year:** 2011, 2012 **Model:** Beetle, Eos, GTI, Jetta, Passat **Engine:** 2.0L L4	**O2 Control (Bank 1 Sensor 2) Internal Resistance Too High:** Engine started, battery voltage must be at least 11.5v, all electrical components must be off, the ground between the engine and the chassis must be well connected, the exhaust system must be properly sealed between the catalytic converter and the cylinder head, and the oxygen sensor heater for oxygen sensor before the catalytic converter must be properly functioning. The ECM detected a measurement on the O2 sensor circuit that was outside the parameters to function properly. **Note: For resistance testing of sensor heating, oxygen sensor should be cooled to ambient temperature. High temperatures at oxygen sensor may lead to inaccurate measurements.**
DTC: P1115 **T** **Year:** 2011, 2012 **Model:** Routan, Touareg **Engine:** 3.6L V6 VIN G	**GENERAL TEMPERATURE RATIONALITY:** Engine off time is greater than 480 minutes and the vehicle has been driven for one minute over 35 mph. Ambient temperature is greater than -64° C (-83° F). Once the vehicle is soaked for a calibrated engine off time and then driven over calibrated speed and load conditions for some calibrated time, the PCM compares the ambient air, engine coolant, and intake air temperature sensor values. If the values of all the three sensors disagree with one another, a general temperature sensor irrationality is declared. Two Trip Fault. Three good trips to turn off the MIL.

DTC	Trouble Code Title and Conditions
DTC: P1115 **1T** **Year:** 2011, 2012 **Model:** Beetle, Eos, GTI, Jetta, Passat **Engine:** 2.0L L4	**O2 Control (Bank 1 Sensor 1) Short to Ground:** Engine started, battery voltage must be at least 11.5v, all electrical components must be off, the ground between the engine and the chassis must be well connected, the exhaust system must be properly sealed between the catalytic converter and the cylinder head, and the oxygen sensor heater for oxygen sensor before the catalytic converter must be properly functioning. The ECM detected a measurement on the O2 sensor circuit that was outside the parameters to function properly. **Note: For resistance testing of sensor heating, oxygen sensor should be cooled to ambient temperature. High temperatures at oxygen sensor may lead to inaccurate measurements. Or has failed**
DTC: P1116 **1T** **Year:** 2011, 2012 **Model:** Beetle, Eos, GTI, Jetta, Passat **Engine:** 2.0L L4	**O2 Control (Bank 1 Sensor 1) Open:** Engine started, battery voltage must be at least 11.5v, all electrical components must be off, the ground between the engine and the chassis must be well connected, the exhaust system must be properly sealed between the catalytic converter and the cylinder head, and the oxygen sensor heater for oxygen sensor before the catalytic converter must be properly functioning. The ECM detected a measurement on the O2 sensor circuit that was outside the parameters to function properly. **Note: For resistance testing of sensor heating, oxygen sensor should be cooled to ambient temperature. High temperatures at oxygen sensor may lead to inaccurate measurements.**
DTC: P1117 **1T** **Year:** 2011, 2012 **Model:** Beetle, Eos, GTI, Jetta, Passat **Engine:** 2.0L L4	**O2 Control (Bank 1 Sensor 2) Open:** Engine started, battery voltage must be at least 11.5v, all electrical components must be off, the ground between the engine and the chassis must be well connected, the exhaust system must be properly sealed between the catalytic converter and the cylinder head, and the oxygen sensor heater for oxygen sensor before the catalytic converter must be properly functioning. The ECM detected a measurement on the O2 sensor circuit that was outside the parameters to function properly. **Note: For resistance testing of sensor heating, oxygen sensor should be cooled to ambient temperature. High temperatures at oxygen sensor may lead to inaccurate measurements.**
DTC: P1118 **1T** **Year:** 2011, 2012 **Model:** Beetle, Eos, GTI, Jetta, Passat **Engine:** 2.0L L4	**O2 Sensor Heater Circ. (Bank 1-Sensor2) Open:** Engine started, battery voltage must be at least 11.5v, all electrical components must be off, the ground between the engine and the chassis must be well connected, the exhaust system must be properly sealed between the catalytic converter and the cylinder head, and the oxygen sensor heater for oxygen sensor before the catalytic converter must be properly functioning. The ECM detected a measurement on the O2 sensor circuit that was outside the parameters to function properly. **Note: For resistance testing of sensor heating, oxygen sensor should be cooled to ambient temperature. High temperatures at oxygen sensor may lead to inaccurate measurements.**
DTC: P1127 **2T ECM, MIL: Yes** **Year:** 2011, 2012 **Model:** Beetle, Eos, GTI, Jetta, Passat **Engine:** 2.0L L4	**Long Term Fuel Trim Add. Air. Bank 1 System Too Rich:** Engine started, battery voltage must be at least 11.5v, all electrical components must be off, the ground between the engine and the chassis must be well connected, the exhaust system must be properly sealed between the catalytic converter and the cylinder head, and the oxygen sensor heater for oxygen sensor before the catalytic converter must be properly functioning. The fuel mixture is so rich that the O2S control is on lean limit. **Note: After exhaust system repairs, make sure exhaust system is not under stress and that it has sufficient clearance from the bodywork. If necessary, loosen double clamps and align exhaust pipe so that sufficient clearance is maintained to the bodywork and support rings carry uniform loads. Do not use any silicone sealant. Traces of silicone components which are sucked into the engine are not burned there, and they damage the oxygen sensor.**
DTC: P1128 **2T ECM, MIL: Yes** **Year:** 2011, 2012 **Model:** Beetle, Eos, GTI, Jetta, Passat **Engine:** 2.0L L4	**Long Term Fuel Trim Add. Air. Bank 1 System Too Lean:** Engine started, battery voltage must be at least 11.5v, all electrical components must be off, the ground between the engine and the chassis must be well connected, the exhaust system must be properly sealed between the catalytic converter and the cylinder head, and the oxygen sensor heater for oxygen sensor before the catalytic converter must be properly functioning. The fuel mixture is so rich that the O2S control is on lean limit. **Note: After exhaust system repairs, make sure exhaust system is not under stress and that it has sufficient clearance from the bodywork. If necessary, loosen double clamps and align exhaust pipe so that sufficient clearance is maintained to the bodywork and support rings carry uniform loads. Do not use any silicone sealant. Traces of silicone components which are sucked into the engine are not burned there, and they damage the oxygen sensor.**
DTC: P1128 **2T ECM, MIL: Yes** **Year:** 2011, 2012 **Model:** Routan, Touareg **Engine:** 3.6L V6 VIN G	**CLOSED LOOP FUELING NOT ACHIEVED - BANK 1:** Engine running in closed loop mode. Enable conditions are met and the O2 sensor has not been in closed loop control at least once on each of the two consecutive trips, the MIL illuminates and the DTC is set. Two Trip Fault. Three good trips to turn off the MIL
DTC: P1129 **2T ECM, MIL: Yes** **Year:** 2011, 2012 **Model:** Routan, Touareg **Engine:** 3.6L V6 VIN G	**-LOSED LOOP FUELING NOT ACHIEVED - BANK 2:** Engine running in closed loop mode. Enable conditions are met and the O2 sensor has not been in closed loop control at least once on each of the two consecutive trips, the MIL illuminates and the DTC is set. Two Trip Fault. Three good trips to turn off the MIL

DTC	Trouble Code Title and Conditions
DTC: P1136 **2T ECM, MIL: Yes** **Year:** 2011, 2012 **Model:** Beetle, Eos, GTI, Jetta, Passat **Engine:** 2.0L L4	**Long Term Fuel Trim Add. Fuel, Bank 1 System Too Lean:** Engine started, battery voltage must be at least 11.5v, all electrical components must be off, the ground between the engine and the chassis must be well connected, the exhaust system must be properly sealed between the catalytic converter and the cylinder head, and the oxygen sensor heater for oxygen sensor before the catalytic converter must be properly functioning. The ECM detected the HO2S circuit was too lean, or that it could no longer change Fuel Trim because it was at its lean limit.
DTC: P1137 **2T ECM, MIL: Yes** **Year:** 2011, 2012 **Model:** Beetle, Eos, GTI, Jetta, Passat **Engine:** 2.0L L4	**Long Term Fuel Trim Add. Fuel, Bank 1 System Too Rich:** Engine started, battery voltage must be at least 11.5v, all electrical components must be off, the ground between the engine and the chassis must be well connected, the exhaust system must be properly sealed between the catalytic converter and the cylinder head, and the oxygen sensor heater for oxygen sensor before the catalytic converter must be properly functioning. The ECM detected the HO2S circuit was too rich, or that it could no longer change Fuel Trim because it was at its lean limit.
DTC: P113D **2T ECM, MIL: Yes** **Year:** 2011, 2012 **Model:** Routan, Touareg **Engine:** 3.6L V6 VIN G	**O2 SENSOR 1/1 SLOW RESPONSE (HIGH FREQUENCY):** With the Engine Coolant Temperature (ECT) at least 60° C (140° F), engine RPM between 1000 and 2750, minimum engine run time of 20 seconds and Manifold Absolute Pressure (MAP) reading is between 21 - 96 Kpa (6.2 - 28.3 inHg). The Powertrain Control Module (PCM) detects that the oxygen sensor signal does not switch adequately at high frequency. Two Trip Fault. Three good trips to turn off the MIL.
DTC: P113E **2T ECM, MIL: Yes** **Year:** 2011, 2012 **Model:** Routan **Engine:** 3.6L V6 VIN G	**-O2 SENSOR 2/1 SLOW RESPONSE (HIGH FREQUENCY):** With the ECT at least 60° C (140° F), engine RPM between 1000 and 2750, minimum engine run time of 20 seconds and Manifold Absolute Pressure (MAP) reading is between 21 - 96 Kpa (6.2 - 28.3 inHg). The Powertrain Control Module (PCM) detects that the oxygen sensor signal does not switch adequately at high frequency. Two Trip Fault. Three good trips to turn off the MIL.
DTC: P1141 **2T ECM, MIL: Yes** **Year:** 2011, 2012 **Model:** Beetle, Eos, GTI, Jetta, Passat **Engine:** 2.0L L4	**Load Calculation Cross Check Range/Performance:** Engine started, battery voltage must be at least 11.5v, all electrical components must be off, the ground between the engine and the chassis must be well connected, the exhaust system must be properly sealed between the catalytic converter and the cylinder head, and the oxygen sensor heater for oxygen sensor before the catalytic converter must be properly functioning. **Note: Vacuum in the intake system sucks in the leak detection spray with false air. Leak detection spray decreases ignition quality of the fuel mixture. This causes a drop in engine speed and changes the value produced by the Heated Oxygen Sensor.** **Note: Both the Throttle Position (TP) sensor and Sender 2 for accelerator pedal position are located at the accelerator pedal and communicate the driver's intentions to the ECM completely independently of each other. Both sensors are stored in one housing.**
DTC: P1143 **2T ECM, MIL: Yes** **Year:** 2011, 2012 **Model:** Beetle, Eos, GTI, Jetta, Passat **Engine:** 2.0L L4	**Load Calculation Cross Check Upper Limit:** Engine started, battery voltage must be at least 11.5v, all electrical components must be off, the ground between the engine and the chassis must be well connected, the exhaust system must be properly sealed between the catalytic converter and the cylinder head, and the oxygen sensor heater for oxygen sensor before the catalytic converter must be properly functioning. **Note: Vacuum in the intake system sucks in the leak detection spray with false air. Leak detection spray decreases ignition quality of the fuel mixture. This causes a drop in engine speed and changes the value produced by the Heated Oxygen Sensor.**
DTC: P1146 **2T ECM, MIL: Yes** **Year:** 2012 **Model:** Beetle, Golf, GTI **Engine:** 2.0L L4, 2.5L L5	**Air mass meter -G70 supply voltage:** Malfunction Criteria and Threshold Value: Airflow sensor supply voltage-4.89 - 5.10 V. Monitoring Time Length: 480 mSec.
DTC: P1149 **2T ECM, MIL: Yes** **Year:** 2011, 2012 **Model:** Beetle, Eos, GTI, Jetta, Passat **Engine:** 2.0L L4	**O2 Control (Bank 1) Out of Range:** Engine started, battery voltage must be at least 11.5v, all electrical components must be off, the ground between the engine and the chassis must be well connected, the exhaust system must be properly sealed between the catalytic converter and the cylinder head, and the oxygen sensor heater for oxygen sensor before the catalytic converter must be properly functioning. The ECM detected a voltage on the O2 sensor circuit that was outside the parameters to function properly. **Note: For resistance testing of sensor heating, oxygen sensor should be cooled to ambient temperature. High temperatures at oxygen sensor may lead to inaccurate measurements.**
DTC: P1160 **2T ECM, MIL: Yes** **Year:** 2012 **Model:** Beetle, Golf, GTI **Engine:** 2.0L L4, 2.5L L5	**Intake Air Temperature (IAT) Sensor Short circuit to Ground (GND):** Malfunction Criteria and Threshold Value: * Intake air temperature sensor voltage-< 0.14 V. * Monitoring Time Length: 480 mSec.
DTC: P1161 **2T ECM, MIL: Yes** **Year:** 2012 **Model:** Beetle, Golf, GTI **Engine:** 2.0L L4, 2.5L L5	**Intake Air Temperature (IAT) Sensor Open circuit/short circuit to B+:** Malfunction Criteria and Threshold Value: * Intake air temperature sensor voltage-> 4.87 V. * Monitoring Time Length: 480 mSec.

DTC	Trouble Code Title and Conditions
DTC: P1171 **2T ECM, MIL: Yes** **Year:** 2011, 2012 **Model:** Beetle, Eos, GTI, Jetta, Passat **Engine:** 2.0L L4	**Throttle Actuation Potentiometer Sign.2 Range/Performance:** Engine started, battery voltage must be at least 11.5v, all electrical components must be off, the ground between the engine and the chassis must be well connected, coolant temperature must be at least 80 degrees Celsius and the accelerator pedal must be properly adjusted. The ECM detected an incorrect signal from the throttle potentiometer. **Note: If the complete throttle valve control module is current-less (e.g. connector disconnected) the throttle valve moves into a particular, specified mechanical position, which signals an increased idle speed with an engine at operating temperature. If only the Throttle Position (TP) actuator is current-less, the throttle valve also moves into the specified mechanical position (emergency running gap), however, since Closed Throttle Position (CTP) switch can still be recognized, an "almost normal idle RPM" is reached via the respective ignition angle retardation.**
DTC: P1172 **2T ECM, MIL: Yes** **Year:** 2011, 2012 **Model:** Beetle, Eos, GTI, Jetta, Passat **Engine:** 2.0L L4	**Throttle Actuation Potentiometer Sign.2 Signal Too Low:** Engine started, battery voltage must be at least 11.5v, all electrical components must be off, the ground between the engine and the chassis must be well connected, coolant temperature must be at least 80 degrees Celsius and the accelerator pedal must be properly adjusted. The ECM detected an incorrect signal from the throttle potentiometer. **Note: If the complete throttle valve control module is current-less (e.g. connector disconnected) the throttle valve moves into a particular, specified mechanical position, which signals an increased idle speed with an engine at operating temperature. If only the Throttle Position (TP) actuator is current-less, the throttle valve also moves into the specified mechanical position (emergency running gap), however, since Closed Throttle Position (CTP) switch can still be recognized, an "almost normal idle RPM" is reached via the respective ignition angle retardation.**
DTC: P1173 **2T ECM, MIL: Yes** **Year:** 2011, 2012 **Model:** Beetle, Eos, GTI, Jetta, Passat **Engine:** 2.0L L4	**Throttle Actuation Potentiometer Sign.2 Signal Too High:** Engine started, battery voltage must be at least 11.5v, all electrical components must be off, the ground between the engine and the chassis must be well connected, coolant temperature must be at least 80 degrees Celsius and the accelerator pedal must be properly adjusted. The ECM detected an incorrect signal from the throttle potentiometer. **Note: If the complete throttle valve control module is current-less (e.g. connector disconnected) the throttle valve moves into a particular, specified mechanical position, which signals an increased idle speed with an engine at operating temperature. If only the Throttle Position (TP) actuator is current-less, the throttle valve also moves into the specified mechanical position (emergency running gap), however, since Closed Throttle Position (CTP) switch can still be recognized, an "almost normal idle RPM" is reached via the respective ignition angle retardation.**
DTC: P1176 **2T ECM, MIL: Yes** **Year:** 2011, 2012 **Model:** Beetle, Eos, GTI, Jetta, Passat **Engine:** 2.0L L4, 2.5L L4	**O2 Correction Behind Catalyst B1 Limit Attained:** Engine started, battery voltage must be at least 11.5v, all electrical components must be off, the ground between the engine and the chassis must be well connected, the exhaust system must be properly sealed between the catalytic converter and the cylinder head, the coolant temperature must be at least 80 degrees Celsius, and the oxygen sensor heater for oxygen sensor before the catalytic converter must be properly functioning. The ECM has detected a malfunction of the oxygen sensor. **Note: Vacuum in the intake system sucks in the leak detection spray with false air. Leak detection spray decreases ignition quality of the fuel mixture. This causes a drop in engine speed and changes the value produced by the Heated Oxygen Sensor (HO2S).**
DTC: P1177 **2T ECM, MIL: Yes** **Year:** 2011, 2012 **Model:** Beetle, Eos, GTI, Jetta, Passat **Engine:** 2.0L L4, 2.5L L4	**O2 Correction Behind Catalyst B2 Limit Attained:** Engine started, battery voltage must be at least 11.5v, all electrical components must be off, the ground between the engine and the chassis must be well connected, the exhaust system must be properly sealed between the catalytic converter and the cylinder head, the coolant temperature must be at least 80 degrees Celsius, and the oxygen sensor heater for oxygen sensor before the catalytic converter must be properly functioning. The ECM has detected a malfunction of the oxygen sensor. **Note: Vacuum in the intake system sucks in the leak detection spray with false air. Leak detection spray decreases ignition quality of the fuel mixture. This causes a drop in engine speed and changes the value produced by the Heated Oxygen Sensor (HO2S).**
DTC: P117A **2T ECM, MIL: Yes** **Year:** 2012 **Model:** Jetta **Engine:** 2.0L L4	**Bank 1 Lambda correction center sensor Control limit reached:** * Engine speed 1200 to 4000 RPM * Modeled exhaust gas temp 350 to 1000 °C * Engine load 24.8 to 99.8% * 1st, 2nd, 3rd lambda control in closed loop * O2S rear and heater ready, no faults
DTC: P117A **2T ECM, MIL: Yes** **Year:** 2011, 2012 **Model:** Beetle, Eos, Golf, GTI, Jetta, Passat **Engine:** 2.0L L4, 2.5L L5	**O2S (Bank 1, Sensor 3):** * Lambda control, closed loop 2nd lambda control, closed loop 3rd lambda control, closed loop * Modeled exhaust gas temp, >400° C * Engine speed, 1500-6300 RPM * Engine load, 14-120% * Electrical check, ready, no fault O2S heater rear 1, ready, no fault O2S heater rear 2, active

DTC	Trouble Code Title and Conditions
DTC: P1196 **2T ECM, MIL: Yes** **Year:** 2011, 2012 **Model:** Beetle, Eos, GTI, Jetta, Passat **Engine:** 2.0L L4	**O2 Sensor Heater Circuit (Bank 1-Sensor 1) Electrical Malfunction:** Engine started, battery voltage must be at least 11.5v, all electrical components must be off, the ground between the engine and the chassis must be well connected, the exhaust system must be properly sealed between the catalytic converter and the cylinder head, and the oxygen sensor heater for oxygen sensor before the catalytic converter must be properly functioning. **Note: For resistance testing of sensor heating, oxygen sensor should be cooled to ambient temperature. High temperatures at oxygen sensor may lead to inaccurate measurements. The ECM detected an open or shorted condition, or excessive current draw in the heater circuit.**
DTC: P1198 **2T ECM, MIL: Yes** **Year:** 2011, 2012 **Model:** Beetle, Eos, GTI, Jetta, Passat **Engine:** 2.0L L4	**O2 Sensor Heater Circuit (Bank 1-Sensor 2) Electrical Malfunction:** Engine started, battery voltage must be at least 11.5v, all electrical components must be off, the ground between the engine and the chassis must be well connected, the exhaust system must be properly sealed between the catalytic converter and the cylinder head, and the oxygen sensor heater for oxygen sensor before the catalytic converter must be properly functioning. **Note: For resistance testing of sensor heating, oxygen sensor should be cooled to ambient temperature. High temperatures at oxygen sensor may lead to inaccurate measurements. The ECM detected an open or shorted condition, or excessive current draw in the heater circuit.**
DTC: P1201 **1T ECM, MIL: Yes** **Year:** 2011, 2012 **Model:** Beetle, Eos, GTI, Jetta, Passat **Engine:** 2.0L L4	**Cylinder 1 Fuel Injection Circuit Electrical Malfunction:** Key on or engine running, fuses in the instrument panel and the E-box in the engine compartment must be functioning, and the ground connections between the engine and the chassis must be well connected; and the ECM detected an unexpected voltage condition on the injector circuit.
DTC: P1202 **1T ECM, MIL: Yes** **Year:** 2011, 2012 **Model:** Beetle, Eos, GTI, Jetta, Passat **Engine:** 2.0L L4	**Cylinder 2 Fuel Injection Circuit Electrical Malfunction:** Key on or engine running, fuses in the instrument panel and the E-box in the engine compartment must be functioning, and the ground connections between the engine and the chassis must be well connected; and the ECM detected an unexpected voltage condition on the injector circuit
DTC: P1203 **1T ECM, MIL: Yes** **Year:** 2011, 2012 **Model:** Beetle, Eos, GTI, Jetta, Passat **Engine:** 2.0L L4	**Cylinder 3 Fuel Injection Circuit Electrical Malfunction:** Key on or engine running, fuses in the instrument panel and the E-box in the engine compartment must be functioning, and the ground connections between the engine and the chassis must be well connected; and the ECM detected an unexpected voltage condition on the injector circuit.
DTC: P1204 **T1 ECM, MIL: Yes** **Year:** 2011, 2012 **Model:** Beetle, Eos, GTI, Jetta, Passat **Engine:** 2.0L L4	**Cylinder 4 Fuel Injection Circuit Electrical Malfunction:** Key on or engine running, fuses in the instrument panel and the E-box in the engine compartment must be functioning, and the ground connections between the engine and the chassis must be well connected; and the ECM detected an unexpected voltage condition on the injector circuit.
DTC: P1213 **1T ECM, MIL: Yes** **Year:** 2011, 2012 **Model:** Beetle, Eos, GTI, Jetta, Passat **Engine:** 2.0L L4	**Cylinder 1 Fuel Injection Circuit Short to B+:** Key on or engine running, fuses in the instrument panel and the E-box in the engine compartment must be functioning, and the ground connections between the engine and the chassis must be well connected; and the ECM detected an unexpected voltage condition on the injector circuit. Wiring or fuel injector has a short circuit to positive] supply.
DTC: P1213 **2T ECM, MIL: Yes** **Year:** 2012 **Model:** Beetle, Golf, GTI **Engine:** 2.0L L4, 2.5L L5	**Cylinder 1 Injector Circuit High:** Short to battery + Signal high before injection valves switched on.
DTC: P1214 **T** **Year:** 2011, 2012 **Model:** Beetle, Eos, GTI, Jetta, Passat **Engine:** 2.0L L4	**Cylinder 2 Fuel Injection Circuit Short to B+:** Key on or engine running, fuses in the instrument panel and the E-box in the engine compartment must be functioning, and the ground connections between the engine and the chassis must be well connected; and the ECM detected an unexpected voltage condition on the injector circuit. Wiring or fuel injector has a short circuit to positive supply.
DTC: P1214 **2T ECM, MIL: Yes** **Year:** 2012 **Model:** Beetle, Golf, GTI **Engine:** 2.0L L4, 2.5L L5	**Cylinder 2 Injector Circuit High:** Short to battery+ Signal high before injection valves switched on.

DTC	Trouble Code Title and Conditions
DTC: P1215 **1T** **Year:** 2011, 2012 **Model:** Beetle, Eos, GTI, Jetta, Passat **Engine:** 2.0L L4	**Cylinder 3 Fuel Injection Circuit Short to B+:** Key on or engine running, fuses in the instrument panel and the E-box in the engine compartment must be functioning, and the ground connections between the engine and the chassis must be well connected; and the ECM detected an unexpected voltage condition on the injector circuit. Wiring or fuel injector has a short circuit to positive supply.
DTC: P1215 **2T ECM, MIL: Yes** **Year:** 2012 **Model:** Beetle, Golf, GTI **Engine:** 2.0L L4, 2.5L L5	**Cylinder 3 Injector Circuit High:** Short to battery + Signal high before injection valves switched on.
DTC: P1216 **2T ECM, MIL: Yes** **Year:** 2012 **Model:** Beetle, Golf, GTI **Engine:** 2.0L L4, 2.5L L5	**Cylinder 4 Injector Circuit High:** Short to battery + Signal high before injection valves switched on.
DTC: P1216 **1T ECM, MIL: Yes** **Year:** 2011, 2012 **Model:** Beetle, Eos, GTI, Jetta, Passat **Engine:** 2.0L L4	**Cylinder 4 Fuel Injection Circuit Short to B+:** Key on or engine running, fuses in the instrument panel and the E-box in the engine compartment must be functioning, and the ground connections between the engine and the chassis must be well connected; and the ECM detected an unexpected voltage condition on the injector circuit. Wiring or fuel injector has a short circuit to positive supply.
DTC: P121A **2T ECM, MIL: Yes** **Year:** 2011, 2012 **Model:** Touareg **Engine:** 3.0L V6, 3.6L V6	**Fuel System Sensor high pressure side:** * Lambda control, Closed loop * EVAP purge valve, <23 * Fuel cut off, Not active
DTC: P1225 **1T** **Year:** 2011, 2012 **Model:** Beetle, Eos, GTI, Jetta, Passat **Engine:** 2.0L L4	**Cylinder 1 Fuel Injection Circuit Short to Ground:** Key on or engine running, fuses in the instrument panel and the E-box in the engine compartment must be functioning, and the ground connections between the engine and the chassis must be well connected; and the ECM detected an unexpected voltage condition on the injector circuit. Wiring or fuel injector has a short circuit to ground.
DTC: P1225 **2T ECM, MIL: Yes** **Year:** 2012 **Model:** Beetle, Golf, GTI **Engine:** 2.0L L4, 2.5L L5	**Cylinder 1 Injector Circuit Low:** Short to ground. Signal low while injection valves switched on.
DTC: P1226 **2T ECM, MIL: Yes** **Year:** 2011, 2012 **Model:** Beetle, Eos, GTI, Jetta, Passat **Engine:** 2.0L L4	**Cylinder 2 Fuel Injection Circuit Short to Ground:** Key on or engine running, fuses in the instrument panel and the E-box in the engine compartment must be functioning, and the ground connections between the engine and the chassis must be well connected; and the ECM detected an unexpected voltage condition on the injector circuit. Wiring or fuel injector has a short circuit to ground.
DTC: P1226 **2T ECM, MIL: Yes** **Year:** 2012 **Model:** Beetle, Golf, GTI **Engine:** 2.0L L4, 2.5L L5	**Cylinder 2 Injector Circuit Low:** Short to ground. Signal low while injection valves switched on.
DTC: P1227 **1T** **Year:** 2011, 2012 **Model:** Beetle, Eos, GTI, Jetta, Passat **Engine:** 2.0L L4	**Cylinder 3 Fuel Injection Circuit Short to Ground:** Key on or engine running, fuses in the instrument panel and the E-box in the engine compartment must be functioning, and the ground connections between the engine and the chassis must be well connected; and the ECM detected an unexpected voltage condition on the injector circuit. Wiring or fuel injector has a short circuit to ground.

DTC	Trouble Code Title and Conditions
DTC: P1227 **2T ECM, MIL: Yes** **Year:** 2012 **Model:** Beetle, Golf, GTI **Engine:** 2.0L L4, 2.5L L5	**Cylinder 3 Injector Circuit Low:** Short to ground. Signal low while injection valves switched on.
DTC: P1228 **2T ECM, MIL: Yes** **Year:** 2012 **Model:** Beetle, Golf, GTI **Engine:** 2.0L L4, 2.5L L5	**Cylinder 4 Injector Circuit Low:** Short to ground. Signal low while injection valves switched on.
DTC: P1228 **2T ECM, MIL: Yes** **Year:** 2011, 2012 **Model:** Beetle, Eos, GTI, Jetta, Passat **Engine:** 2.0L L4	**Cylinder 4 Fuel Injection Circuit Short to Ground:** Key on or engine running, fuses in the instrument panel and the E-box in the engine compartment must be functioning, and the ground connections between the engine and the chassis must be well connected; and the ECM detected an unexpected voltage condition on the injector circuit. Wiring or fuel injector has a short circuit to ground.
DTC: P122A 00 **T** **Year:** 2011, 2012 **Model:** Beetle, Eos, GTI, Passat **Engine:** 2.0L L4	**Cylinder 3 Injector Control Circuit Malfunction:** The engine is running. The ECM monitors for a condition once per camshaft revolution.
DTC: P1237 **1T** **Year:** 2011, 2012 **Model:** Beetle, Eos, GTI, Jetta, Passat **Engine:** 2.0L L4	**Cylinder 1 Fuel Injection Circuit Open Circuit:** Key on or engine running, fuses in the instrument panel and the E-box in the engine compartment must be functioning, and the ground connections between the engine and the chassis must be well connected; and the ECM detected an unexpected voltage condition on the injector circuit. Wiring or fuel injector has a short circuit that is open.
DTC: P1237 **2T ECM, MIL: Yes** **Year:** 2012 **Model:** Beetle, Golf, GTI **Engine:** 2.0L L4, 2.5L L5	**Cylinder 1 Injector, Open Circuit:** Open circuit Signal low while injection valves switched on.
DTC: P1238 **2T ECM, MIL: Yes** **Year:** 2012 **Model:** Beetle, Golf, GTI **Engine:** 2.0L L4, 2.5L L5	**Cylinder 2 Injector, Open Circuit:** Open circuit Signal low while injection valves switched on.
DTC: P1238 **2T ECM, MIL: Yes** **Year:** 2011, 2012 **Model:** Beetle, Eos, GTI, Jetta, Passat **Engine:** 2.0L L4	**Cylinder 2 Fuel Injection Circuit Open Circuit:** Key on or engine running, fuses in the instrument panel and the E-box in the engine compartment must be functioning, and the ground connections between the engine and the chassis must be well connected; and the ECM detected an unexpected voltage condition on the injector circuit. Wiring or fuel injector has a short circuit that is open.
DTC: P1239 **2T ECM, MIL: Yes** **Year:** 2011, 2012 **Model:** Routan **Engine:** 3.6L V6 VIN G	**ENGINE OIL TEMPERATURE TOO LOW:** The engine oil temperature has dropped below a calibrated temperature value. Engine start up. The Engine Oil temperature rises slower than a calibrated modeled temperature. When the actual oil temperature falls below the low boundary of the calibrated modeled temperature for three minutes the fault is set. Two trip fault. Three good trips to turn off the MIL.
DTC: P1239 **2T ECM, MIL: Yes** **Year:** 2012 **Model:** Beetle, Golf, GTI **Engine:** 2.0L L4, 2.5L L5	**Cylinder 3 Injector, Open Circuit:** Open circuit Signal low while injection valves switched on.

DTC	Trouble Code Title and Conditions
DTC: P1239 **2T ECM, MIL: Yes** **Year:** 2011, 2012 **Model:** Beetle, Eos, GTI, Jetta, Passat **Engine:** 2.0L L4	**Cylinder 3 Fuel Injection Circuit Open Circuit:** Key on or engine running, fuses in the instrument panel and the E-box in the engine compartment must be functioning, and the ground connections between the engine and the chassis must be well connected; and the ECM detected an unexpected voltage condition on the injector circuit. Wiring or fuel injector has a short circuit that is open.
DTC: P1240 **2T ECM, MIL: Yes** **Year:** 2011, 2012 **Model:** Beetle, Eos, Golf, GTI, Jetta, Passat **Engine:** 2.0L L4	**Cylinder 4 Fuel Injection Circuit Open Circuit:** Key on or engine running, fuses in the instrument panel and the E-box in the engine compartment must be functioning, and the ground connections between the engine and the chassis must be well connected; and the ECM detected an unexpected voltage condition on the injector circuit. Wiring or fuel injector has a short circuit that is open.
DTC: P1245 **2T ECM, MIL: Yes** **Year:** 2011, 2012 **Model:** Golf, GTI, Jetta, Passat **Engine:** 2.0L L4, 2.5L L5	**Needle Lift Sensor -G80- Short to ground:** Malfunction Criteria and Threshold Value: * Needle lift sensor voltage-< 0.30 V, Battery voltage->9 V. * Monitoring Time Length: 480 mSec.
DTC: P1246 **2T ECM, MIL: Yes** **Year:** 2011, 2012 **Model:** Golf, GTI, Jetta, Passat **Engine:** 2.0L L4, 2.5L L5	**Needle lift sender -G80 implausible signal:** * Battery voltage->9 V * Fuel quantity->8 mg/stroke * Engine speed- >1176 rpm * Engine speed sensor-not defective
DTC: P1247 **2T ECM, MIL: Yes** **Year:** 2011, 2012 **Model:** Golf, GTI, Jetta, Passat **Engine:** 2.0L L4, 2.5L L5	**Needle Lift Sensor -G80- Open circuit/ short circuit to B+:** Battery voltage- > 9 V
DTC: P1255 **2T ECM, MIL: Yes** **Year:** 2012 **Model:** Beetle, Golf, GTI **Engine:** 2.0L L4, 2.5L L5	**Engine Coolant Temperature (ECT) Sensor, Short to Ground:** Short to Ground>+268.3°F.
DTC: P1256 **2T ECM, MIL: Yes** **Year:** 2012 **Model:** Beetle, Golf, GTI **Engine:** 2.0L L4, 2.5L L5	**Engine Coolant Temperature (ECT) Sensor, Open circuit/short to B+:** Short to Battery+ <-47.7° F.
DTC: P1273 **2T ECM, MIL: Yes** **Year:** 2011, 2012 **Model:** Routan **Engine:** 3.6L V6 VIN G	**A/C CLUTCH CONTROL CIRCUIT 2 HIGH:** With the ignition on and the battery voltage greater than 10.4 volts. Air Conditioning (A/C) Switch on. A/C Compressor Clutch command on. The Totally Integrated Power Module (TIPM) detects the voltage on the A/C Clutch Driver circuit is higher than the calibrated level.
DTC: P1275 **2T ECM, MIL: Yes** **Year:** 2011, 2012 **Model:** Routan **Engine:** 3.6L V6 VIN G	**A/C CONTROL CIRCUIT 2 OVERCURRENT:** With the ignition on and the battery voltage greater than 10.4 volts. Air Conditioning (A/C) Switch on. A/C Compressor Clutch command on. The TIPM detects the current draw on the A/C Clutch Driver circuit is higher than the calibrated level.
DTC: P1296 **2T ECM, MIL: Yes** **Year:** 2011, 2012 **Model:** Beetle, Eos, Golf, GTI, Jetta, Passat **Engine:** 2.0L L4, 2.5L L4	**Cooling System Malfunction:** Key on, engine not running, the Engine Control Module (ECM) will use the intake air temperature as a replacement value for an engine start (start temperature replacement value) as soon as there is a Diagnostic Trouble Code (DTC) stored in DTC memory for the Engine Coolant Temperature (ECT) sensor. The temperature then rises according to a program stored in the ECM. When the engine has reached normal operating temperature a fixed replacement value will be displayed. This fixed value is also dependent upon the intake air temperature.
DTC: P129B **2T ECM, MIL: Yes** **Year:** 2011, 2012 **Model:** Touareg **Engine:** 3.0L V6, 3.6L V6	**Fuel Pressure Regulator 2 Control Circuit:** * Evap purge valve, Commanded off * Engine relay, Commanded on

DTC	Trouble Code Title and Conditions
DTC: P129C **2T ECM, MIL: Yes** **Year:** 2011, 2012 **Model:** Routan, Touareg **Engine:** 3.6L V6 VIN G	**INVERTER CONTROL CIRCUIT HIGH:** With the ignition on. Battery voltage greater than 10 volts. An open or shorted high condition has been detected in the Inverter Enable Switch Signal circuit by the Totally Integrated Power Module (TIPM).
DTC: P129C **2T ECM, MIL: Yes** **Year:** 2011, 2012 **Model:** Touareg, Routan **Engine:** 3.0L V6,	**Fuel Pressure Regulator 2 Control Circuit Low:** * Evap purge valve Commanded off * Engine relay, Commanded on
DTC: P129D **2T ECM, MIL: Yes** **Year:** 2011, 2012 **Model:** Touareg, Routan **Engine:** 3.0L V6,	**Fuel Pressure Regulator 2 Control Circuit High:** * Evap purge valve Commanded on * Engine relay, Commanded on
DTC: P129E **2T ECM, MIL: Yes** **Year:** 2011, 2012 **Model:** Routan, Touareg **Engine:** 3.6L V6 VIN G	**INVERTER CONTROL CIRCUIT OVERCURRENT:** With the ignition on. Battery voltage greater than 10.4 volts. An over current condition is detected in the (P805) Inverter Enable Switch Signal circuit.
DTC: P12A1 **2 T TCM, MIL: Yes** **Year:** 2011, 2012 **Model:** Beetle, CC, Eos, Golf, GTI, GLI, Jetta, Passat, Routan, Tiguan, Touareg **Engine:** 2.0L L4, 2.5L L5, 3.0L V6, 3.6L V6	**Fuel Rail Pressure Sensor Inappropriately Low:** * Mixture controller <0.8 * Output value rail pressure controller System deviation <-16.4-16.4 Mpa * Mixture controller <0 * Output value rail pressure controller System deviation >16.4 Mpa
DTC: P12A2 **2 T TCM, MIL: Yes** **Year:** 2011, 2012 **Model:** Beetle, CC, Eos, Golf, GTI, GLI, Jetta, Passat, Routan, Tiguan, Touareg **Engine:** 2.0L L4, 2.5L L5, 3.0L V6, 3.6L V6	**Fuel Rail Pressure Sensor Inappropriately High:** * Mixture controller <1.5 * Output value rail pressure controller <-0.14 MPa * System deviation <-16.4-16.4 Mpa * Mixture controller <16 * Output value rail pressure controller System deviation >16.4 Mpa
DTC: P12A4 **2 T TCM, MIL: Yes** **Year:** 2011, 2012 **Model:** Beetle, CC, Eos, Golf, GTI, GLI, Jetta, Passat, Routan, Tiguan, Touareg **Engine:** 2.0L L4, 2.5L L5, 3.0L V6, 3.6L V6	**Fuel Rail Pump Control Valve Stuck Closed:** * Mixture controller 1.15-0.9 * Output value rail pressure controller <-6 MPa * System deviation<16.4
DTC: P1300 **2T ECM, MIL: Yes** **Year:** 2011, 2012 **Model:** Beetle, Eos, Golf, GTI, Jetta **Engine:** 2.0L L4, 2.5L L4	**Misfire Detected Low Fuel:** Any misfire under low fuel conditions. Fuel level <15% of fuel capacity. Fuel level <15% of fuel capacity
DTC: P1325 **2T ECM, MIL: Yes** **Year:** 2011, 2012 **Model:** Beetle, Eos, Golf, GTI, Jetta **Engine:** 2.0L L4, 2.5L L4	**Cylinder 1-Knock Control Limit Attained:** Engine started, battery voltage at least 11.5v, all electrical components off, ground connections between engine and chassis well connected, and the ECM detected the Knock Sensor signal was more than the calibrated value.

DTC	Trouble Code Title and Conditions
DTC: P1326 **2T ECM, MIL: Yes** **Year:** 2011, 2012 **Model:** Beetle, Eos, Golf, GTI, Jetta **Engine:** 2.0L L4, 2.5L L4	**Cylinder 2-Knock Control Limit Attained:** Engine started, battery voltage at least 11.5v, all electrical components off, ground connections between engine and chassis well connected, and the ECM detected the Knock Sensor signal was more than the calibrated value.
DTC: P1327 **2T ECM, MIL: Yes** **Year:** 2011, 2012 **Model:** Beetle, Eos, Golf, GTI, Jetta **Engine:** 2.0L L4, 2.5L L4	**Cylinder 3-Knock Control Limit Attained:** Engine started, battery voltage at least 11.5v, all electrical components off, ground connections between engine and chassis well connected, and the ECM detected the Knock Sensor signal was more than the calibrated value.
DTC: P1335 **2T ECM, MIL: Yes** **Year:** 2011, 2012 **Model:** Beetle, Eos, Golf, GTI, Jetta **Engine:** 2.0L L4, 2.5L L4	**Engine Torque Monitoring 2 Control Limit Exceeded:** Engine cold, battery voltage at least 11.5v, all electrical components off, ground connections between engine and chassis well connected, the ECM detected a signal beyond the required limit.
DTC: P1336 **2T ECM, MIL: Yes** **Year:** 2011, 2012 **Model:** Beetle, Eos, Golf, GTI, Jetta **Engine:** 2.0L L4, 2.5L L4	**Engine Torque Monitoring Control Limit Exceeded:** Engine cold, battery voltage at least 11.5v, all electrical components off, ground connections between engine and chassis well connected, the ECM detected a signal beyond the required limit.
DTC: P1337 **2T ECM, MIL: Yes** **Year:** 2011, 2012 **Model:** Beetle, Eos, Golf, GTI, Jetta **Engine:** 2.0L L4, 2.5L L4	**Camshaft Position Sensor (Bank 1) Short to Ground:** Engine started, battery voltage at least 11.5v, all electrical components off, ground connections between engine and chassis well connected, and the ECM detected an unexpected low or high voltage condition on the camshaft position sensor circuit
DTC: P1338 **2T ECM, MIL: Yes** **Year:** 2011, 2012 **Model:** Beetle, Eos, Golf, GTI, Jetta **Engine:** 2.0L L4, 2.5L L4	**Camshaft Position Sensor (Bank 1) Open/Short to B+:** Engine started, battery voltage at least 11.5v, all electrical components off, ground connections between engine and chassis well connected, and the ECM detected an unexpected low or high voltage condition on the camshaft position sensor circuit
DTC: P1340 **2T ECM, MIL: Yes** **Year:** 2011, 2012 **Model:** Beetle, Eos, Golf, GTI, Jetta **Engine:** 2.0L L4, 2.5L L4	**Crankshaft Position/Camshaft Sensor Signal Out of Sequence:** Engine started, battery voltage at least 11.5v, all electrical components off, ground connections between engine and chassis well connected, and the ECM detected the crankshaft position sensor and the camshaft sensor were out of sequence with each other. **Note: The Engine Speed (RPM) Sensor detects engine speed and reference marks. Without an engine speed signal, the engine will not start. If the engine speed signal fails while the engine is running, the engine will stop immediately.**
DTC: P1355 **2T ECM, MIL: Yes** **Year:** 2011, 2012 **Model:** Beetle, Eos, Golf, GTI, Jetta **Engine:** 2.0L L4, 2.5L L4	**Cylinder 1 Ignition Circuit Open Circuit:** Key on or Engine started, battery voltage at least 11.5v, all electrical components off, ground connections between engine and chassis well connected, and the ECM detected the voltage of the ignition was outside the designed parameters.
DTC: P1356 **2T ECM, MIL: Yes** **Year:** 2011, 2012 **Model:** Beetle, Eos, Golf, GTI, Jetta **Engine:** 2.0L L4, 2.5L L4	**Cylinder 1 Ignition Circuit Short to B+:** Key on or Engine started, battery voltage at least 11.5v, all electrical components off, ground connections between engine and chassis well connected, and the ECM detected the voltage of the ignition was outside the designed parameters.

DTC	Trouble Code Title and Conditions
DTC: P1357 **2T ECM, MIL: Yes** **Year:** 2011, 2012 **Model:** Beetle, Eos, Golf, GTI, Jetta **Engine:** 2.0L L4, 2.5L L4	**Cylinder 1 Ignition Circuit Short to Ground:** Key on or Engine started, battery voltage at least 11.5v, all electrical components off, ground connections between engine and chassis well connected, and the ECM detected the voltage of the ignition was outside the designed parameters.
DTC: P1358 **2T ECM, MIL: Yes** **Year:** 2011, 2012 **Model:** Beetle, Eos, Golf, GTI, Jetta **Engine:** 2.0L L4, 2.5L L4	**Cylinder 2 Ignition Circuit Open Circuit:** Key on or Engine started, battery voltage at least 11.5v, all electrical components off, ground connections between engine and chassis well connected, and the ECM detected the voltage of the ignition was outside the designed parameters.
DTC: P1359 **2T ECM, MIL: Yes** **Year:** 2011, 2012 **Model:** Beetle, Eos, Golf, GTI, Jetta **Engine:** 2.0L L4, 2.5L L4	**Cylinder 2 Ignition Circuit Short to B+:** Key on or Engine started, battery voltage at least 11.5v, all electrical components off, ground connections between engine and chassis well connected, and the ECM detected the voltage of the ignition was outside the designed parameters.
DTC: P1360 **2T ECM, MIL: Yes** **Year:** 2011, 2012 **Model:** Beetle, Eos, Golf, GTI, Jetta **Engine:** 2.0L L4, 2.5L L4	**Cylinder 2 Ignition Circuit Short to Ground:** Key on or Engine started, battery voltage at least 11.5v, all electrical components off, ground connections between engine and chassis well connected, and the ECM detected the voltage of the ignition was outside the designed parameters.
DTC: P1361 **2T ECM, MIL: Yes** **Year:** 2011, 2012 **Model:** Beetle, Eos, Golf, GTI, Jetta **Engine:** 2.0L L4, 2.5L L4	**Cylinder 3 Ignition Circuit Open Circuit:** Key on or Engine started, battery voltage at least 11.5v, all electrical components off, ground connections between engine and chassis well connected, and the ECM detected the voltage of the ignition was outside the designed parameters.
DTC: P1362 **2T ECM, MIL: Yes** **Year:** 2011, 2012 **Model:** Beetle, Eos, Golf, GTI, Jetta **Engine:** 2.0L L4, 2.5L L4	**Cylinder 3 Ignition Circuit Short to B+:** Key on or Engine started, battery voltage at least 11.5v, all electrical components off, ground connections between engine and chassis well connected, and the ECM detected the voltage of the ignition was outside the designed parameters.
DTC: P1363 **2T ECM, MIL: Yes** **Year:** 2011, 2012 **Model:** Beetle, Eos, Golf, GTI, Jetta **Engine:** 2.0L L4, 2.5L L4	**Cylinder 3 Ignition Circuit Short to Ground:** Key on or Engine started, battery voltage at least 11.5v, all electrical components off, ground connections between engine and chassis well connected, and the ECM detected the voltage of the ignition was outside the designed parameters.
DTC: P1364 **2T ECM, MIL: Yes** **Year:** 2011, 2012 **Model:** Beetle, Eos, Golf, GTI, Jetta **Engine:** 2.0L L4, 2.5L L4	**Cylinder 4 Ignition Circuit Open Circuit:** Key on or Engine started, battery voltage at least 11.5v, all electrical components off, ground connections between engine and chassis well connected, and the ECM detected the voltage of the ignition was outside the designed parameters.
DTC: P1365 **2T ECM, MIL: Yes** **Year:** 2011, 2012 **Model:** Beetle, Eos, Golf, GTI, Jetta **Engine:** 2.0L L4, 2.5L L4	**Cylinder 4 Ignition Circuit Short to B+:** Key on or Engine started, battery voltage at least 11.5v, all electrical components off, ground connections between engine and chassis well connected, and the ECM detected the voltage of the ignition was outside the designed parameters.

DTC	Trouble Code Title and Conditions
DTC: P1366 **2T ECM, MIL: Yes** **Year:** 2011, 2012 **Model:** Beetle, Eos, Golf, GTI, Jetta **Engine:** 2.0L L4, 2.5L L4	**Cylinder 4 Ignition Circuit Short to Ground:** Key on or Engine started, battery voltage at least 11.5v, all electrical components off, ground connections between engine and chassis well connected, and the ECM detected the voltage of the ignition was outside the designed parameters.
DTC: P1386 **2T ECM, MIL: Yes** **Year:** 2011, 2012 **Model:** Beetle, Eos, Golf, GTI, Jetta **Engine:** 2.0L L4, 2.5L L4	**Internal Control Module, Knock Control Circuit Error:** Engine started, and the ECM detected a too high or too low voltage condition on the knock control circuits, or a miscommunication between the knock control and the ECM.
DTC: P1387 **2T ECM, MIL: Yes** **Year:** 2011, 2012 **Model:** Beetle, Eos, Golf, GTI, Jetta **Engine:** 2.0L L4, 2.5L L4	**Internal Control Module Altitude Sensor Error:** Ignition on, the ECM detected and altitude sensor error. To achieve optimal anti-theft protection for the vehicle, an anti-theft immobilizer is installed. The anti-theft immobilizer is a system for enabling and locking the Engine Control Module (ECM). So that this system cannot be circumvented, it is necessary to perform adaptation of the anti-theft immobilizer using the Vehicle Diagnostic and Information System VAS 5052 in the On Board Diagnostic (OBD) function. The great availability of equipment options makes it necessary to adapt the Engine Control Module (ECM) to the vehicle (e.g. throttle valve control module or cruise control system). This "writing" function is not possible with the generic scan tool.
DTC: P1388 **2T ECM, MIL: Yes** **Year:** 2011, 2012 **Model:** Beetle, Eos, Golf, GTI, Jetta **Engine:** 2.0L L4, 2.5L L4	**Internal Control Module Drive By Wire Error:** Ignition on, the ECM detected and drive by wire error. To achieve optimal anti-theft protection for the vehicle, an anti-theft immobilizer is installed. The anti-theft immobilizer is a system for enabling and locking the Engine Control Module (ECM). So that this system cannot be circumvented, it is necessary to perform adaptation of the anti-theft immobilizer using the Vehicle Diagnostic and Information System VAS 5052 in the On Board Diagnostic (OBD) function. The great availability of equipment options makes it necessary to adapt the Engine Control Module (ECM) to the vehicle (e.g. throttle valve control module or cruise control system). This "writing" function is not possible with the generic scan tool.
DTC: P13CE **2T ECM, MIL: Yes** **Year:** 2011, 2012 **Model:** Beetle, Eos, Golf, GTI, Jetta **Engine:** 2.0L L4, 2.5L L4	**Sensor for internal pressure of cylinder 1 Electrical malfunction:** Engine running
DTC: P13CF **2T ECM, MIL: Yes** **Year:** 2011, 2012 **Model:** Beetle, Eos, Golf, GTI, Jetta **Engine:** 2.0L L4, 2.5L L4	**Sensor for internal pressure of cylinder 1 Short circuit to ground:** Engine running
DTC: P13CF* **2T ECM, MIL: Yes** **Year:** 2011, 2012 **Model:** Beetle, Eos, Golf, GTI, Jetta **Engine:** 2.0L L4, 2.5L L4	**Sensor for internal pressure of cylinder 1 Short circuit to ground:** Engine running
DTC: P13D1 **2T ECM, MIL: Yes** **Year:** 2011, 2012 **Model:** Beetle, Eos, Golf, GTI, Jetta **Engine:** 2.0L L4, 2.5L L4	**Sensor for internal pressure of cylinder 2 Electrical malfunction:** Engine running
DTC: P13D4 **2T ECM, MIL: Yes** **Year:** 2011, 2012 **Model:** Beetle, Eos, Golf, GTI, Jetta **Engine:** 2.0L L4, 2.5L L4	**Sensor for internal pressure of cylinder 3 Electrical malfunction:** Engine running

DTC	Trouble Code Title and Conditions
DTC: P13D4* **2T ECM, MIL: Yes** **Year:** 2011, 2012 **Model:** Beetle, Eos, Golf, GTI, Jetta **Engine:** 2.0L L4, 2.5L L4	**Sensor for internal pressure of cylinder 3 Electrical malfunction:** Engine running
DTC: P1402 **2T ECM, MIL: Yes** **Year:** 2011, 2012 **Model:** Beetle, Eos, Golf, GTI, Jetta **Engine:** 2.0L L4, 2.5L L4	**EGR Vacuum Regulator Solenoid Valve -N18- Short circuit to B+:** Output driver-ON state
DTC: P1409 **2T ECM, MIL: Yes** **Year:** 2011, 2012 **Model:** Beetle, Eos, Golf, GTI, Jetta **Engine:** 2.0L L4, 2.5L L4	**Tank Ventilation Valve Circuit Malfunction Conditions:** Key on or engine running; and the ECM detected a too high or too low voltage level in the tank ventilation valve circuit.
DTC: P140C **2T ECM, MIL: Yes** **Year:** 2011, 2012 **Model:** Beetle, Eos, Golf, GTI, Jetta **Engine:** 2.0L L4, 2.5L L4	**Low Pressure EGR Sensor Position circuit high :**
DTC: P140E **2T ECM, MIL: Yes** **Year:** 2011, 2012 **Model:** Beetle, Eos, Golf, GTI, Jetta **Engine:** 2.0L L4, 2.5L L4	**Low Pressure EGR Sensor Position circuit Low:**
DTC: P1410 **2T ECM, MIL: Yes** **Year:** 2011, 2012 **Model:** Beetle, Eos, Golf, GTI, Jetta **Engine:** 2.0L L4, 2.5L L4	**Tank Ventilation Valve Circuit Short to B+::** Key on or engine running; and the ECM detected a too high or too low voltage level in the tank ventilation valve circuit.
DTC: P1410 **2T ECM, MIL: Yes** **Year:** 2011, 2012 **Model:** Beetle, Eos, Golf, GTI, Jetta **Engine:** 2.0L L4, 2.5L L4	**Evaporative Emission (EVAP) Canister Purge Regulator Valve Short to B+:** Short to battery+ Signal high.
DTC: P1419 **2T ECM** **Year:** 2011, 2012 **Model:** Touareg, Routan **Engine:** 3.0L V6, 3.6L V6	**Exhaust Gas Recirculation Cooler Switch-over Valve 2 Short circuit to Voltage:** Power stage = On state
DTC: P1420 **2T ECM, MIL: Yes** **Year:** 2011, 2012 **Model:** Beetle, Eos, Golf, GTI, Jetta **Engine:** 2.0L L4, 2.5L L4	**Secondary Air Injector Valve Circuit Electrical Malfunction:** The Engine Control Module activates the secondary air injection solenoid valve, but the Heated Oxygen Sensor (HO2S) does not detect secondary air injection. **Note: Solenoid valve is closed when no voltage is present.**
DTC: P1421 **2T ECM, MIL: Yes** **Year:** 2011, 2012 **Model:** Beetle, Eos, Golf, GTI, Jetta **Engine:** 2.0L L4, 2.5L L4	**Secondary Air Injector Valve Circuit Short to Ground:** The Engine Control Module detects a short circuit to ground when activating the secondary air injection solenoid valve. **Note: Solenoid valve is closed when no voltage is present.**

DTC	Trouble Code Title and Conditions
DTC: P1422 **2T ECM, MIL: Yes** **Year:** 2011, 2012 **Model:** Beetle, Eos, Golf, GTI, Jetta **Engine:** 2.0L L4, 2.5L L4	**Secondary Air Injector Valve Circuit Short to B+:** The Engine Control Module detects a short circuit to B+ when activating the secondary air injection solenoid valve. **Note: Solenoid valve is closed when no voltage is present.**
DTC: P1424 **2T ECM, MIL: Yes** **Year:** 2011, 2012 **Model:** Beetle, Eos, Golf, GTI, Jetta **Engine:** 2.0L L4, 2.5L L4	**Secondary Air Injector System (Bank 1) Leak Detected:** Ignition on or vehicle running, and the ECM detected a leak in the secondary air injector system.
DTC: P1425 **T2T ECM, MIL: Yes** **Year:** 2011, 2012 **Model:** Beetle, Eos, Golf, GTI, Jetta **Engine:** 2.0L L4, 2.5L L4	**Tank Ventilation Valve Short to Ground:** Ignition off. The Evaporative Emission (EVAP) canister purge regulator valve in the tank venting system or activation wire has a short circuit to ground. Engine started, engine running at a steady cruise speed, canister vent solenoid enabled, and the ECM detected an unexpected voltage condition on the Canister Vent solenoid circuit. **Note: Solenoid valve is closed when no voltage is present.**
DTC: P1425 **2T ECM, MIL: Yes** **Year:** 2011, 2012 **Model:** Beetle, Eos, Golf, GTI, Jetta **Engine:** 2.0L L4, 2.5L L4	**Evaporative Emission (EVAP) Canister Purge Regulator Valve Short to Ground:** Short to ground. Signal low.
DTC: P1426 **2T ECM, MIL: Yes** **Year:** 2011, 2012 **Model:** Beetle, Eos, Golf, GTI, Jetta **Engine:** 2.0L L4, 2.5L L4	**Tank Ventilation Valve Open:** Ignition off. The Evaporative Emission (EVAP) canister purge regulator valve in the tank venting system or activation wire has a short circuit to ground. Engine started, engine running at a steady cruise speed, canister vent solenoid enabled, and the ECM detected an unexpected voltage condition on the Canister Vent solenoid circuit.
DTC: P1426 **2T ECM, MIL: Yes** **Year:** 2011, 2012 **Model:** Beetle, Eos, Golf, GTI, Jetta **Engine:** 2.0L L4, 2.5L L4	**Evaporative Emission System Purge Control Valve Circuit Open:** Open circuit No activity/No signal
DTC: P1432 **2T ECM, MIL: Yes** **Year:** 2011, 2012 **Model:** Beetle, Eos, Golf, GTI, Jetta **Engine:** 2.0L L4, 2.5L L4	**Secondary Air Injection Valve Open:** The output Diagnostic Test Mode (DTM) can be activated only with the ignition switched on and the engine not running. The output DTM is interrupted if the engine is started, or if a rotary pulse from the ignition system is recognized.
DTC: P1433 **2T ECM, MIL: Yes** **Year:** 2011, 2012 **Model:** Beetle, Eos, Golf, GTI, Jetta **Engine:** 2.0L L4, 2.5L L4	**Secondary Air Injection System Pump Relay Circuit Open:** The output Diagnostic Test Mode (DTM) can be activated only with the ignition switched on and the engine not running. The output DTM is interrupted if the engine is started, or if a rotary pulse from the ignition system is recognized..
DTC: P1434 **2T ECM, MIL: Yes** **Year:** 2011, 2012 **Model:** Beetle, Eos, Golf, GTI, Jetta **Engine:** 2.0L L4, 2.5L L4	**Secondary Air Injection System Pump Relay Circuit Short to B+:** The output Diagnostic Test Mode (DTM) can be activated only with the ignition switched on and the engine not running. The output DTM is interrupted if the engine is started, or if a rotary pulse from the ignition system is recognized..
DTC: P1435 **2T ECM, MIL: Yes** **Year:** 2011, 2012 **Model:** Beetle, Eos, Golf, GTI, Jetta **Engine:** 2.0L L4, 2.5L L4	**Secondary Air Injection System Pump Relay Circuit Short to Ground:** The output Diagnostic Test Mode (DTM) can be activated only with the ignition switched on and the engine not running. The output DTM is interrupted if the engine is started, or if a rotary pulse from the ignition system is recognized..
DTC: P1436 **2T ECM, MIL: Yes** **Year:** 2011, 2012 **Model:** Beetle, Eos, Golf, GTI, Jetta **Engine:** 2.0L L4, 2.5L L4	**A/C Evaporator Temperature (ACET) Circuit Low Input:** Key on or engine running; and the ECM detected the ACET signal was less than the self-test minimum amount of in the self-test.

DTC	Trouble Code Title and Conditions
DTC: P1441 2T ECM, MIL: Yes **Year:** 2011, 2012 **Model:** Beetle, Eos, Golf, GTI, Jetta **Engine:** 2.0L L4, 2.5L L4	**EGR Valve Open Circuit/Short Circuit To Ground (GND):** Output driver-OFF state
DTC: P1471 2T ECM, MIL: Yes **Year:** 2011, 2012 **Model:** Beetle, Eos, Golf, GTI, Jetta **Engine:** 2.0L L4, 2.5L L4	**EVAP Emission Control Leak Detection Pump Circuit Short to B+:** Key on, KOEO Self-Test enabled, and the ECM detected an unexpected voltage condition on the EVAP emission control leak detection pump circuit.
DTC: P1471 2T ECM, MIL: Yes **Year:** 2011, 2012 **Model:** Beetle, Eos, Golf, GTI, Jetta **Engine:** 2.0L L4, 2.5L L4	**EVAP Emission Control LPD Circuit Short to B+:** Short to battery+. Signal always high.
DTC: P1472 2T ECM, MIL: Yes **Year:** 2011, 2012 **Model:** Beetle, Eos, Golf, GTI, Jetta **Engine:** 2.0L L4, 2.5L L4	**EVAP Emission Control Leak Detection Pump Circuit Short to Ground:** Key on, KOEO Self-Test enabled, and the ECM detected an unexpected voltage condition on the EVAP emission control leak detection pump circuit.
DTC: P1472 2T ECM, MIL: Yes **Year:** 2011, 2012 **Model:** Beetle, CC, Eos, Golf, GTI, Jetta, Passat **Engine:** 2.0L L4, 2.5L L4	**EVAP Emission Control LPD Circuit Short to Ground:** Short to ground. No signal after start.
DTC: P1473 2T ECM, MIL: Yes **Year:** 2011, 2012 **Model:** Beetle, CC, Eos, Golf, GTI, Jetta, Passat **Engine:** 2.0L L4, 2.5L L4	**EVAP Emission Control Leak Detection Pump Circuit Open:** Key on, KOEO Self-Test enabled, and the ECM detected an unexpected voltage condition on the EVAP emission control leak detection pump circuit.
DTC: P1473 2T ECM, MIL: Yes **Year:** 2011, 2012 **Model:** Beetle, CC, Eos, Golf, GTI, Jetta, Passat **Engine:** 2.0L L4, 2.5L L4	**Leak Diagnosis Pump - Tank Breather System Open Circuit:** Open circuit. No activity/No signal.
DTC: P1475 2T ECM, MIL: Yes **Year:** 2011, 2012 **Model:** Beetle, CC, Eos, Golf, GTI, Jetta, Passat **Engine:** 2.0L L4, 2.5L L4	**Leak diagnosis pump - tank breather system malfunction/no signal:** No signal Signal always low, EVAP purge check done or followed by EVAP purge check.
DTC: P1475 2T ECM, MIL: Yes **Year:** 2011, 2012 **Model:** Beetle, CC, Eos, Golf, GTI, Jetta, Passat **Engine:** 2.0L L4, 2.5L L4	**EVAP Emission Control LDP Circuit Malfunction/Signal Circuit Open:** Key on, KOEO Self-Test enabled, and the ECM detected an unexpected voltage condition on the EVAP emission control leak detection pump circuit.
DTC: P1475 2T ECM, MIL: Yes **Year:** 2011, 2012 **Model:** Beetle, CC, Eos, Golf, GTI, Jetta, Passat **Engine:** 2.0L L4, 2.5L L4	**Leak Detection Pump - (Tank breather system malfunction/no signal):** EVAP purge check done or followed by EVAP purge check

DTC	Trouble Code Title and Conditions
DTC: P1476 **2T ECM, MIL: Yes** **Year:** 2011, 2012 **Model:** Beetle, CC, Eos, Golf, GTI, Jetta, Passat **Engine:** 2.0L L4, 2.5L L4	**EVAP Emission Control LDP Circuit Malfunction/Insufficient Vacuum:** Key on, KOEO Self-Test enabled, and the ECM detected an unexpected voltage condition on the EVAP emission control leak detection pump circuit.
DTC: P1476 **2T ECM, MIL: Yes** **Year:** 2011, 2012 **Model:** Beetle, CC, Eos, Golf, GTI, Jetta, Passat **Engine:** 2.0L L4, 2.5L L4	**Leak Diagnosis Pump - Tank Breather System Malfunction/Vacuum To Low:** Contact unable to open Signal high> 0.5 sec. EVAP purge check done or followed by EVAP purge check.
DTC: P1476 **2T ECM, MIL: Yes** **Year:** 2011, 2012 **Model:** Beetle, CC, Eos, Golf, GTI, Jetta, Passat **Engine:** 2.0L L4, 2.5L L4	**Leak Detection Pump - (Tank breather system malfunction/vacuum to low):** EVAP purge check done or followed by EVAP purge check.
DTC: P1477 **2T ECM, MIL: Yes** **Year:** 2011, 2012 **Model:** Beetle, CC, Eos, Golf, GTI, Jetta, Passat **Engine:** 2.0L L4, 2.5L L4	**EVAP Emission Control LDP Circuit Malfunction:** Key on, KOEO Self-Test enabled, and the ECM detected an unexpected voltage condition on the EVAP emission control leak detection pump circuit.
DTC: P1478 **2T ECM, MIL: Yes** **Year:** 2011, 2012 **Model:** Beetle, CC, Eos, Golf, GTI, Jetta, Passat **Engine:** 2.0L L4, 2.5L L4	**EVAP Emission Control LDP Circuit Clamped Tube Detected:** Key on, KOEO Self-Test enabled, and the ECM detected an unexpected voltage condition on the EVAP emission control leak detection pump circuit.
DTC: P148F **2T ECM, MIL: Yes** **Year:** 2011, 2012 **Model:** Touareg, Routan **Engine:** 3.0L V6, 3.6L V6	**Exhaust Gas Recirculation (EGR) Cooler Switch-Over Valve 2 Electrical malfunction:** Power stage = Off state
DTC: P1499 **2T ECM, MIL: Yes** **Year:** 2011, 2012 **Model:** Touareg, Routan **Engine:** 3.0L V6, 3.6L V6	**Exhaust Gas Recirculation Cooler Switch-over Valve 2 Open circuit/short circuit to ground:** Power stage = Off state
DTC: P1500 **2T ECM, MIL: Yes** **Year:** 2011, 2012 **Model:** Beetle, CC, Eos, Golf, GTI, Jetta, Passat **Engine:** 2.0L L4, 2.5L L4	**Fuel Pump Relay Circuit Electrical Malfunction:** Engine running the ECM detected that the fuel pump relay signal was intermittent
DTC: P1500 **2T ECM, MIL: Yes** **Year:** 2011, 2012 **Model:** Beetle, CC, Eos, Golf, GTI, Jetta, Passat **Engine:** 2.0L L4, 2.5L L4	**Fuel Pump Primary Circuit Fault In Electrical Circuit:** No signal.
DTC: P1501 **2T ECM, MIL: Yes** **Year:** 2011, 2012 **Model:** Beetle, CC, Eos, Golf, GTI, Jetta, Passat **Engine:** 2.0L L4, 2.5L L4	**Fuel Pump Relay Circuit Electrical Short to Ground:** Engine running the ECM detected that the fuel pump relay signal was intermittent

DTC	Trouble Code Title and Conditions
DTC: P1502 **2T ECM, MIL: Yes** **Year:** 2011, 2012 **Model:** Beetle, CC, Eos, Golf, GTI, Jetta, Passat **Engine:** 2.0L L4, 2.5L L4	**Fuel Pump Relay Circuit Short to B+:** Engine running the ECM detected that the fuel pump relay signal was intermittent
DTC: P150A **2T ECM, MIL: Yes** **Year:** 2011, 2012 **Model:** Beetle, CC, Eos, Golf, GTI, Jetta, Passat, Touareg **Engine:** 2.0L L4, 2.5L L5, 3.0L V6, 3.6L V6	**Engine Off Timer Performance:** * Key on after ECM after run time active * Key on during ECM after run time active * CAN active
DTC: P1524 **1T ECM, MIL: Yes** **Year:** 2011, 2012 **Model:** Touareg, Routan **Engine:** 3.6L V6 VIN G	**OIL PRESSURE OUT OF RANGE - CAMSHAFT ADVANCE/RETARD DISABLED:** Engine running. RPM greater than or equal to 1100. Oil temperature less than or equal to 100°C (212°F). The engine oil pressure never reaches the calibrated specification to allow the VVT activation. One trip fault.
DTC: P1529 **2T ECM, MIL: Yes** **Year:** 2011, 2012 **Model:** Beetle, CC, Eos, Golf, GTI, Jetta, Passat, Touareg **Engine:** 2.0L L4, 2.5L L5, 3.0L V6, 3.6L V6	**Camshaft Control Circuit Short to B+:** Engine started and driven at an engine speed of more than 400rpm; and the ECM detected the camshaft timing exceeded the calibrated voltage levels. The valve timing did not change from the current valve timing or it remained fixed during the testing. **Note: The camshaft adjustment is load- and RPM dependant. The electrical camshaft adjustment valve 1 switches oil pressure onto camshaft adjuster (mechanical adjustment mechanism), which adjusts the camshaft.**
DTC: P1530 **2T ECM, MIL: Yes** **Year:** 2011, 2012 **Model:** Beetle, CC, Eos, Golf, GTI, Jetta, Passat, Touareg **Engine:** 2.0L L4, 2.5L L5, 3.0L V6, 3.6L V6	**Camshaft Control Circuit Short to Ground:** Engine started and driven at an engine speed of more than 400rpm; and the ECM detected the camshaft timing exceeded the calibrated levels. The valve timing did not change from the current valve timing or it remained fixed during the testing. **Note: The camshaft adjustment is load- and RPM dependant. The electrical camshaft adjustment valve 1 switches oil pressure onto camshaft adjuster (mechanical adjustment mechanism), which adjusts the camshaft.**
DTC: P1531 **2T ECM, MIL: Yes** **Year:** 2011, 2012 **Model:** Beetle, CC, Eos, Golf, GTI, Jetta, Passat, Touareg **Engine:** 2.0L L4, 2.5L L5, 3.0L V6, 3.6L V6	**Camshaft Control Circuit Open:** Engine started and driven at an engine speed of more than 400rpm; and the ECM detected the camshaft timing exceeded the calibrated levels. The valve timing did not change from the current valve timing or it remained fixed during the testing. **Note: The camshaft adjustment is load- and RPM dependant. The electrical camshaft adjustment valve 1 switches oil pressure onto camshaft adjuster (mechanical adjustment mechanism), which adjusts the camshaft.**
DTC: P1541 **2T ECM, MIL: Yes** **Year:** 2011, 2012 **Model:** Beetle, CC, Eos, Golf, GTI, Jetta, Passat, Touareg **Engine:** 2.0L L4, 2.5L L5, 3.0L V6, 3.6L V6	**Fuel Pump Relay Circuit Open:** The ECM detected an electrical malfunction on the fuel pump relay circuit
DTC: P1542 **2T ECM, MIL: Yes** **Year:** 2011, 2012 **Model:** Beetle, CC, Eos, Golf, GTI, Jetta, Passat, Touareg **Engine:** 2.0L L4, 2.5L L5, 3.0L V6, 3.6L V6	**Throttle Actuation Potentiometer Range/Performance:** Engine started, battery voltage must be at least 11.5v, all electrical components must be off, parking brake must be engaged (to keep daytime driving lights off), automatic transmission selector must be in park, the exhaust system must be properly sealed between the catalytic converter and the cylinder head, coolant temperature must be at least 80 degrees Celsius, and the ground between the engine and the chassis must be well connected. The signal from the Throttle Position Valve Module to the ECM detected was erratic, nonexistent or unreliable. **Note: If the complete throttle valve control module is current-less (e.g. connector disconnected) the throttle valve moves into a particular, specified mechanical position, which signals an increased idle speed with an engine at operating temperature. If only the Throttle Position (TP) actuator –V60- is current-less, the throttle valve also moves into the specified mechanical position (emergency running gap), however, since Closed Throttle Position (CTP) switch –F60- can still be recognized, an "almost normal idle RPM" is reached via the respective ignition angle retardation. If the Engine Control Module (ECM) detects a malfunction at Throttle Position (TP) sensor –G69-, Throttle Position (TP) actuator –V60- is switched current-less by the Engine Control Module (ECM) and the throttle valve moves into the specified mechanical position (emergency running gap) again.**

DTC	Trouble Code Title and Conditions
DTC: P1543 **2T ECM, MIL: Yes** **Year:** 2011, 2012 **Model:** Beetle, CC, Eos, Golf, GTI, Jetta, Passat, Touareg **Engine:** 2.0L L4, 2.5L L5, 3.0L V6, 3.6L V6	**Throttle Actuation Potentiometer Signal Too Low:** Engine started, battery voltage must be at least 11.5v, all electrical components must be off, parking brake must be engaged (to keep daytime driving lights off), automatic transmission selector must be in park, the exhaust system must be properly sealed between the catalytic converter and the cylinder head, coolant temperature must be at least 80 degrees Celsius, and the ground between the engine and the chassis must be well connected. The signal from the Throttle Position Valve Module to the ECM detected was erratic, nonexistent or unreliable. **Note: If the complete throttle valve control module is current-less (e.g. connector disconnected) the throttle valve moves into a particular, specified mechanical position, which signals an increased idle speed with an engine at operating temperature. If only the Throttle Position (TP) actuator –V60- is current-less, the throttle valve also moves into the specified mechanical position (emergency running gap), however, since Closed Throttle Position (CTP) switch –F60- can still be recognized, an "almost normal idle RPM" is reached via the respective ignition angle retardation. If the Engine Control Module (ECM) detects a malfunction at Throttle Position (TP) sensor –G69-, Throttle Position (TP) actuator –V60- is switched current-less by the Engine Control Module (ECM) and the throttle valve moves into the specified mechanical position (emergency running gap) again.**
DTC: P1543 **1T ECM, MIL: Yes** **Year:** 2011, 2012 **Model:** Beetle, CC, Eos, Golf, GTI, Jetta, Passat **Engine:** 2.0L L4, 2.5L L4	**Angle Sender 1 For Throttle Valve Drive, Signal Too Low:** Signal low <0.157 V.
DTC: P1544 **2T ECM, MIL: Yes** **Year:** 2011, 2012 **Model:** Beetle, CC, Eos, Golf, GTI, Jetta, Passat **Engine:** 2.0L L4, 2.5L L4	**Throttle Actuation Potentiometer Signal Too High:** Engine started, battery voltage must be at least 11.5v, all electrical components must be off, parking brake must be engaged (to keep daytime driving lights off), automatic transmission selector must be in park, the exhaust system must be properly sealed between the catalytic converter and the cylinder head, coolant temperature must be at least 80 degrees Celsius, and the ground between the engine and the chassis must be well connected. The signal from the Throttle Position Valve Module to the ECM detected was erratic, nonexistent or unreliable. **Note: If the complete throttle valve control module is current-less (e.g. connector disconnected) the throttle valve moves into a particular, specified mechanical position, which signals an increased idle speed with an engine at operating temperature. If only the Throttle Position (TP) actuator –V60- is current-less, the throttle valve also moves into the specified mechanical position (emergency running gap), however, since Closed Throttle Position (CTP) switch –F60- can still be recognized, an "almost normal idle RPM" is reached via the respective ignition angle retardation. If the Engine Control Module (ECM) detects a malfunction at Throttle Position (TP) sensor –G69-, Throttle Position (TP) actuator –V60- is switched current-less by the Engine Control Module (ECM) and the throttle valve moves into the specified mechanical position (emergency running gap) again.**
DTC: P1544 **1T ECM, MIL: Yes** **Year:** 2011, 2012 **Model:** Beetle, CC, Eos, Golf, GTI, Jetta, Passat **Engine:** 2.0L L4, 2.5L L4	**Angle Sender 1 For Throttle Valve Drive, Signal Too High:** Signal high >4.86 V.
DTC: P1545 **2T ECM, MIL: Yes** **Year:** 2011, 2012 **Model:** Beetle, CC, Eos, Golf, GTI, Jetta, Passat **Engine:** 2.0L L4, 2.5L L4	**Throttle Position Control Malfunction:** Engine started, battery voltage must be at least 11.5v, all electrical components must be off, parking brake must be engaged (to keep daytime driving lights off), automatic transmission selector must be in park, the exhaust system must be properly sealed between the catalytic converter and the cylinder head, coolant temperature must be at least 80 degrees Celsius, and the ground between the engine and the chassis must be well connected. The signal from the Throttle Position Valve Module to the ECM detected was erratic, nonexistent or unreliable. **Note: If the complete throttle valve control module is current-less (e.g. connector disconnected) the throttle valve moves into a particular, specified mechanical position, which signals an increased idle speed with an engine at operating temperature. If only the Throttle Position (TP) actuator is current-less, the throttle valve also moves into the specified mechanical position (emergency running gap), however, since Closed Throttle Position (CTP) switch – can still be recognized, an "almost normal idle RPM" is reached via the respective ignition angle retardation. If the Engine Control Module (ECM) detects a malfunction at Throttle Position (TP) sensor – Throttle Position (TP) actuator is switched current-less by the Engine Control Module (ECM) and the throttle valve moves into the specified mechanical position (emergency running gap) again.**
DTC: P1546 **2T ECM, MIL: Yes** **Year:** 2011, 2012 **Model:** Beetle, CC, Eos, Golf, GTI, Jetta, Passat **Engine:** 2.0L L4, 2.5L L4	**Boost Pressure Control Valve Short to B+:** Engine started, battery voltage at least 11.5v, all electrical components off, ground connections between engine and chassis well connected, coolant temperature at least 80-degrees Celicius. The ECM detected a short in the boost pressure control valve.

DTC	Trouble Code Title and Conditions
DTC: P1547 **2T ECM, MIL: Yes** **Year:** 2011, 2012 **Model:** Beetle, CC, Eos, Golf, GTI, Jetta, Passat **Engine:** 2.0L L4, 2.5L L4	**Boost Pressure Control Valve Short to Ground:** Engine started, battery voltage at least 11.5v, all electrical components off, ground connections between engine and chassis well connected, coolant temperature at least 80-degrees Celicius. The ECM detected an short in the boost pressure control valve.
DTC: P1548 **2T ECM, MIL: Yes** **Year:** 2011, 2012 **Model:** Beetle, CC, Eos, Golf, GTI, Jetta, Passat **Engine:** 2.0L L4, 2.5L L4	**Boost Pressure Control Valve Open:** Engine started, battery voltage at least 11.5v, all electrical components off, ground connections between engine and chassis well connected, coolant temperature at least 80-degrees Celicius. The ECM detected an short in the boost pressure control valve.
DTC: P1550 **2T ECM, MIL: Yes** **Year:** 2011, 2012 **Model:** Beetle, CC, Eos, Golf, GTI, Jetta, Passat **Engine:** 2.0L L4, 2.5L L4	**Charge Pressure Deviation:** Engine started, battery voltage at least 11.5v, all electrical components off, ground connections between engine and chassis well connected, coolant temperature at least 80-degrees Celicius. The ECM detected deviation from the normal operating parameters of the charge pressure sensor.
DTC: P1555 **2T ECM, MIL: Yes** **Year:** 2011, 2012 **Model:** Beetle, CC, Eos, Golf, GTI, Jetta, Passat **Engine:** 2.0L L4, 2.5L L4	**Charge Pressure Upper Limit Exceeded:** Engine started, battery voltage at least 11.5v, all electrical components off, ground connections between engine and chassis well connected, coolant temperature at least 80-degrees Celicius. The ECM detected deviation from the normal operating parameters of the charge pressure sensor.
DTC: P1556 **2T ECM, MIL: Yes** **Year:** 2011, 2012 **Model:** Beetle, CC, Eos, Golf, GTI, Jetta, Passat **Engine:** 2.0L L4, 2.5L L4	**Charge Pressure Control Negative Deviation:** Engine started, battery voltage at least 11.5v, all electrical components off, ground connections between engine and chassis well connected, coolant temperature at least 80-degrees Celicius. The ECM detected deviation from the normal operating parameters of the charge pressure sensor.
DTC: P1557 **2T ECM, MIL: Yes** **Year:** 2011, 2012 **Model:** Beetle, CC, Eos, Golf, GTI, Jetta, Passat **Engine:** 2.0L L4, 2.5L L4	**Charge Pressure Control Positive Deviation:** Engine started, battery voltage at least 11.5v, all electrical components off, ground connections between engine and chassis well connected, coolant temperature at least 80-degrees Celicius. The ECM detected deviation from the normal operating parameters of the charge pressure sensor.
DTC: P1558 **2T ECM, MIL: Yes** **Year:** 2011, 2012 **Model:** Beetle, CC, Eos, Golf, GTI, Jetta, Passat **Engine:** 2.0L L4, 2.5L L4	**Throttle Actuator Electrical Malfunction:** Engine started, battery voltage at least 11.5v, all electrical components off, ground connections between engine and chassis well connected, coolant temperature at least 80-degrees Celicius and the throttle valve must not be damaged or dirty; and the ECM detected the signal from the Throttle Position Valve Module to the ECM detected was erratic, nonexistent or unreliable (too high or too low).
DTC: P1559 **2T ECM, MIL: Yes** **Year:** 2011, 2012 **Model:** Beetle, CC, Eos, Golf, GTI, Jetta, Passat **Engine:** 2.0L L4, 2.5L L4	**Idle Speed Control Throttle Position Adaptation Malfunction:** Engine started, battery voltage at least 11.5v, all electrical components off, ground connections between engine and chassis well connected, coolant temperature at least 80-degrees Celicius and the throttle valve must not be damaged or dirty; and the ECM detected the signal from the Throttle Position Valve Module to the ECM detected was erratic, nonexistent or unreliable (too high or too low).
DTC: P1565 **2T ECM, MIL: Yes** **Year:** 2011, 2012 **Model:** Beetle, CC, Eos, Golf, GTI, Jetta, Passat **Engine:** 2.0L L4, 2.5L L4	**Throttle Valve Control Part, Lower Stop Not Reached:** Initialize of potentiometer adaptation — After ignition on, if adaptation has not been completed. Signal low <4.157 V.

DTC	Trouble Code Title and Conditions
DTC: P1565 **2T ECM, MIL: Yes** **Year:** 2011, 2012 **Model:** Beetle, CC, Eos, Golf, GTI, Jetta, Passat **Engine:** 2.0L L4, 2.5L L4	**Throttle Valve Control Lower Stop Not Reached:** Initialize of potentiometer adaptation – After ignition on, if adaptation has not been completed.
DTC: P1565 **2T ECM, MIL: Yes** **Year:** 2011, 2012 **Model:** Beetle, CC, Eos, Golf, GTI, Jetta, Passat **Engine:** 2.0L L4, 2.5L L4	**Idle Speed Control Throttle Position Lower Limit Not Attainted:** Engine started, battery voltage at least 11.5v, all electrical components off, ground connections between engine and chassis well connected, coolant temperature at least 80-degrees Celicius and the throttle valve must not be damaged or dirty; and the ECM detected the signal from the Throttle Position Valve Module to the ECM detected was erratic, nonexistent or unreliable (too high or too low).
DTC: P1568 **2T ECM, MIL: Yes** **Year:** 2011, 2012 **Model:** Beetle, CC, Eos, Golf, GTI, Jetta, Passat **Engine:** 2.0L L4, 2.5L L4	**Idle Speed Control Throttle Position Mechanical Malfunction:** Engine started, battery voltage at least 11.5v, all electrical components off, ground connections between engine and chassis well connected, coolant temperature at least 80-degrees Celicius and the throttle valve must not be damaged or dirty; and the ECM detected the signal from the Throttle Position Valve Module to the ECM detected was erratic, nonexistent or unreliable (too high or too low) suggesting a mechanical malfunction.
DTC: P1572 **2T ECM, MIL: Yes** **Year:** 2011, 2012 **Model:** Routan, Routan **Engine:** 3.6L V6 VIN G	**BRAKE PEDAL STUCK ON:** With the gear selector in drive, vehicle speed above a minimum value, and battery voltage greater than 10.4 volts. The PCM detects that the actual state of Brake Signal 1 or Brake Signal 2 does not match the desired state during monitoring.
DTC: P1573 **2T ECM, MIL: Yes** **Year:** 2011, 2012 **Model:** Routan, Routan **Engine:** 3.6L V6 VIN G	**-BRAKE PEDAL STUCK OFF:** With the gear selector in drive, vehicle speed above a minimum value, and battery voltage greater than 10.4 volts. The PCM detects that the actual state of Brake Signal 1 or Brake Signal 2 does not match the desired state during monitoring.
DTC: P1580 **2T ECM, MIL: Yes** **Year:** 2011, 2012 **Model:** Beetle, CC, Eos, Golf, GTI, Jetta, Passat **Engine:** 2.0L L4, 2.5L L4	**Throttle Valve Drive, Bank 1 Malfunction:** Comparison with throttle movement.
DTC: P1582 **2T ECM, MIL: Yes** **Year:** 2011, 2012 **Model:** Beetle, CC, Eos, Golf, GTI, Jetta, Passat **Engine:** 2.0L L4, 2.5L L4	**Idling Speed Regulation Adaption Limit Reached:** Signal low >4.571 V, Signal high <4.037 V, Potentiometer used in reversed logic (adaptive values).
DTC: P1593 **1T ECM, MIL: Yes** **Year:** 2011, 2012 **Model:** Routan, Touareg **Engine:** 3.6L V6 VIN G	**-SPEED CONTROL SWITCH 1/2 STUCK:** With the ignition on and battery voltage greater than 10.4 Volts. The Powertrain Control Module (PCM) detects that the (V37) S/C Signal 1 voltage does not match the (V38) S/C Signal 2 voltage.
DTC: P1602 **1T ECM, MIL: Yes** **Year:** 2011, 2012 **Model:** Beetle, CC, Eos, Golf, GTI, Jetta, Passat **Engine:** 2.0L L4, 2.5L L4	**Power Supply (B+) Terminal 15 Low Voltage:** Ignition on, the ECM detected a low voltage condition on the power supply terminal (15). To achieve optimal anti-theft protection for the vehicle, an anti-theft immobilizer is installed. The anti-theft immobilizer is a system for enabling and locking the Engine Control Module (ECM). So that this system cannot be circumvented, it is necessary to perform adaptation of the anti-theft immobilizer using the Vehicle Diagnostic and Information System VAS 5052 in the On Board Diagnostic (OBD) function. The great availability of equipment options makes it necessary to adapt the Engine Control Module (ECM) to the vehicle (e.g. throttle valve control module or cruise control system). This "writing" function is not possible with the generic scan tool.
DTC: P1603 **2T ECM, MIL: Yes** **Year:** 2011, 2012 **Model:** Beetle, CC, Eos, Golf, GTI, Jetta, Passat **Engine:** 2.0L L4, 2.5L L4	**Internal Control Module Malfunction:** Ignition on, the ECM detected a control module malfunction. To achieve optimal anti-theft protection for the vehicle, an anti-theft immobilizer is installed. The anti-theft immobilizer is a system for enabling and locking the Engine Control Module (ECM). So that this system cannot be circumvented, it is necessary to perform adaptation of the anti-theft immobilizer using the Vehicle Diagnostic and Information System VAS 5052 in the On Board Diagnostic (OBD) function. The great availability of equipment options makes it necessary to adapt the Engine Control Module (ECM) to the vehicle (e.g. throttle valve control module or cruise control system). This "writing" function is not possible with the generic scan tool.

DTC	Trouble Code Title and Conditions
DTC: P1604 **2T ECM, MIL: Yes** **Year:** 2011, 2012 **Model:** Beetle, CC, Eos, Golf, GTI, Jetta, Passat **Engine:** 2.0L L4, 2.5L L4	**Internal Control Module Driver Error:** Ignition on, the ECM detected a control module malfunction. To achieve optimal anti-theft protection for the vehicle, an anti-theft immobilizer is installed. The anti-theft immobilizer is a system for enabling and locking the Engine Control Module (ECM). So that this system cannot be circumvented, it is necessary to perform adaptation of the anti-theft immobilizer using the Vehicle Diagnostic and Information System VAS 5052 in the On Board Diagnostic (OBD) function. The great availability of equipment options makes it necessary to adapt the Engine Control Module (ECM) to the vehicle (e.g. throttle valve control module or cruise control system). This "writing" function is not possible with the generic scan tool.
DTC: P1607 **2T ECM, MIL: Yes** **Year:** 2011, 2012 **Model:** Beetle, CC, Eos, Golf, GTI, Jetta, Passat **Engine:** 2.0L L4, 2.5L L4	**-PCM INTERNAL SHUTDOWN TIMER SLOW RATIONALITY:** With the engine running after a cycle when a complete engine warm up was achieved, the difference between engine coolant temperature and ambient air temperature less than or equal to 10° C (50° F), and battery voltage greater than 10 volts. This DTC sets if the engine coolant temp does not drop enough or drops too much during engine off time. This DTC may also set if the controller timer is inaccurate. Two Trip Fault. Three good trips to turn off the MIL.
DTC: P1610 **2T ECM, MIL: Yes** **Year:** 2011, 2012 **Model:** Beetle, CC, Eos, Golf, GTI, Jetta, Passat **Engine:** 2.0L L4, 2.5L L4	**ECU Defective:** To achieve optimal anti-theft protection for the vehicle, an anti-theft immobilizer is installed. The anti-theft immobilizer is a system for enabling and locking the Engine Control Module (ECM). So that this system cannot be circumvented, it is necessary to perform adaptation of the anti-theft immobilizer using the Vehicle Diagnostic and Information System VAS 5052 in the On Board Diagnostic (OBD) function. The great availability of equipment options makes it necessary to adapt the Engine Control Module (ECM) to the vehicle (e.g. throttle valve control module or cruise control system). This "writing" function is not possible with the generic scan tool.
DTC: P1612 **2T ECM, MIL: Yes** **Year:** 2011, 2012 **Model:** Beetle, CC, Eos, Golf, GTI, Jetta, Passat **Engine:** 2.0L L4, 2.5L L4	**Electronic Control Module Incorrect Coding:** Ignition on, the ECM detected a control module malfunction. To achieve optimal anti-theft protection for the vehicle, an anti-theft immobilizer is installed. The anti-theft immobilizer is a system for enabling and locking the Engine Control Module (ECM). So that this system cannot be circumvented, it is necessary to perform adaptation of the anti-theft immobilizer using the Vehicle Diagnostic and Information System VAS 5052 in the On Board Diagnostic (OBD) function. The great availability of equipment options makes it necessary to adapt the Engine Control Module (ECM) to the vehicle (e.g. throttle valve control module or cruise control system). This "writing" function is not possible with the generic scan tool.
DTC: P1612 **2T ECM, MIL: Yes** **Year:** 2011, 2012 **Model:** Beetle, CC, Eos, Golf, GTI, Jetta, Passat **Engine:** 2.0L L4, 2.5L L4	**Engine Control Unit Incorrect Coding:** After engine has been started, If ECM is coded to manual transmission and TCM is available->ECM is wrong coded.
DTC: P1618 **1T ECM, MIL: Yes** **Year:** 2011, 2012 **Model:** Routan, Touareg **Engine:** 3.6L V6 VIN G	**-SENSOR REFERENCE VOLTAGE 1 CIRCUIT ERRATIC:** With the ignition on. The Powertrain Control Module (PCM) detects an excessive voltage variation on the 5-Volt supply circuit.
DTC: P1626 **1T ECM, MIL: Yes** **Year:** 2011, 2012 **Model:** Beetle, CC, Eos, Golf, GTI, Jetta, Passat **Engine:** 2.0L L4, 2.5L L4	**ECM missing message from TCM:** After engine has been started, Time since start->1 sec, Battery voltage->10.54 V
DTC: P1626 **1T ECM, MIL: Yes** **Year:** 2011, 2012 **Model:** Beetle, CC, Eos, Golf, GTI, Jetta, Passat **Engine:** 2.0L L4, 2.5L L4	**Data-Bus Drive Train Missing Message From Transmission Control Module:** After engine has been started. Time since start->1 sec. Battery voltage->10.54 V. Initialize failure and/or no acknowledge.
DTC: P1628 **1T ECM, MIL: Yes** **Year:** 2011, 2012 **Model:** Routan, Touareg **Engine:** 3.6L V6 VIN G	**-SENSOR REFERENCE VOLTAGE 2 CIRCUIT ERRATIC:** Ignition on. When the Powertrain Control Module (PCM) recognizes the Auxiliary 5-Volt Supply circuit voltage is varying too much too quickly. One Trip Fault. ETC light is flashing.

DTC	Trouble Code Title and Conditions
DTC: P1630 **1T ECM, MIL: Yes** **Year:** 2011, 2012 **Model:** Beetle, CC, Eos, Golf, GTI, Jetta, Passat **Engine:** 2.0L L4, 2.5L L4	**Acceleration Pedal Position Sensor 1 Signal Too Low:** Engine started, battery voltage at least 11.5v, all electrical components off, ground connections between engine and chassis well connected, the ECM detected that the accelerator pedal position sensor signal was too low. **Note: Both the Throttle Position (TP) Sensor and Accelerator Pedal Position Sensor 2 are located at the accelerator pedal module and communicate the driver's intentions to the ECM completely independently of each other. Both sensors are stored in one housing.**
DTC: P1631 **1T ECM, MIL: Yes** **Year:** 2011, 2012 **Model:** Beetle, CC, Eos, Golf, GTI, Jetta, Passat **Engine:** 2.0L L4, 2.5L L4	**Acceleration Pedal Position Sensor 1 Signal Too High:** Engine started, battery voltage at least 11.5v, all electrical components off, ground connections between engine and chassis well connected, the ECM detected that the accelerator pedal position sensor signal was too high. **Note: Both the Throttle Position (TP) Sensor and Accelerator Pedal Position Sensor 2 are located at the accelerator pedal module and communicate the driver's intentions to the ECM completely independently of each other. Both sensors are stored in one housing.**
DTC: P1633 **1T ECM, MIL: Yes** **Year:** 2011, 2012 **Model:** Beetle, CC, Eos, Golf, GTI, Jetta, Passat **Engine:** 2.0L L4, 2.5L L4	**Acceleration Pedal Position Sensor 2 Signal Too Low:** Engine started, battery voltage at least 11.5v, all electrical components off, ground connections between engine and chassis well connected, the ECM detected that the accelerator pedal position sensor signal was too low. **Note: Both the Throttle Position (TP) Sensor and Accelerator Pedal Position Sensor 2 are located at the accelerator pedal module and communicate the driver's intentions to the ECM completely independently of each other. Both sensors are stored in one housing.**
DTC: P1634 **1T ECM, MIL: Yes** **Year:** 2011, 2012 **Model:** Beetle, CC, Eos, Golf, GTI, Jetta, Passat **Engine:** 2.0L L4, 2.5L L4	**Acceleration Pedal Position Sensor 2 Signal Too High:** Engine started, battery voltage at least 11.5v, all electrical components off, ground connections between engine and chassis well connected, the ECM detected that the accelerator pedal position sensor signal was too high. **Note: Both the Throttle Position (TP) Sensor and Accelerator Pedal Position Sensor 2 are located at the accelerator pedal module and communicate the driver's intentions to the ECM completely independently of each other. Both sensors are stored in one housing.**
DTC: P1639 **1T ECM, MIL: Yes** **Year:** 2011, 2012 **Model:** Beetle, CC, Eos, Golf, GTI, Jetta, Passat **Engine:** 2.0L L4, 2.5L L4	**Accelerator Pedal Position Sensor 1+2 Range/Performance:** Engine started, battery voltage at least 11.5v, all electrical components off, ground connections between engine and chassis well connected, the ECM detected that the accelerator pedal position sensor signal was too high. **Note: Both the Throttle Position (TP) Sensor and Accelerator Pedal Position Sensor 2 are located at the accelerator pedal module and communicate the driver's intentions to the ECM completely independently of each other. Both sensors are stored in one housing.**
DTC: P1640 **1T ECM, MIL: Yes** **Year:** 2011, 2012 **Model:** Beetle, CC, Eos, Golf, GTI, Jetta, Passat **Engine:** 2.0L L4, 2.5L L4	**Internal Control Module (EEPROM) Error:** Ignition on, the ECM detected a control module malfunction (software). To achieve optimal anti-theft protection for the vehicle, an anti-theft immobilizer is installed. The anti-theft immobilizer is a system for enabling and locking the Engine Control Module (ECM). So that this system cannot be circumvented, it is necessary to perform adaptation of the anti-theft immobilizer using the Vehicle Diagnostic and Information System VAS 5052 in the On Board Diagnostic (OBD) function. The great availability of equipment options makes it necessary to adapt the Engine Control Module (ECM) to the vehicle (e.g. throttle valve control module or cruise control system). This "writing" function is not possible with the generic scan tool.
DTC: P1648 **1T ECM, MIL: Yes** **Year:** 2011, 2012 **Model:** Beetle, CC, Eos, Golf, GTI, Jetta, Passat **Engine:** 2.0L L4, 2.5L L4	**Data-Bus-driving gear faulty:** Time since start->1 sec. Battery voltage->10.54
DTC: P1648 **2T ECM, MIL: Yes** **Year:** 2011, 2012 **Model:** Beetle, CC, Eos, Golf, GTI, Jetta, Passat **Engine:** 2.0L L4, 2.5L L4	**Data-Bus-Driving Gear Faulty:** Time since start->1 sec. Battery voltage->10.54 V
DTC: P1648 **1T ECM, MIL: Yes** **Year:** 2011, 2012 **Model:** Beetle, CC, Eos, Golf, GTI, Jetta, Passat **Engine:** 2.0L L4, 2.5L L4	**Data Bus Powertrain Malfunction:** Ignition on, the ECM detected a data bus malfunction (software). To achieve optimal anti-theft protection for the vehicle, an anti-theft immobilizer is installed. The anti-theft immobilizer is a system for enabling and locking the Engine Control Module (ECM). So that this system cannot be circumvented, it is necessary to perform adaptation of the anti-theft immobilizer using the Vehicle Diagnostic and Information System VAS 5052 in the On Board Diagnostic (OBD) function. The great availability of equipment options makes it necessary to adapt the Engine Control Module (ECM) to the vehicle (e.g. throttle valve control module or cruise control system). This "writing" function is not possible with the generic scan tool.

DTC	Trouble Code Title and Conditions
DTC: P1649 **1T ECM, MIL: Yes** **Year:** 2011, 2012 **Model:** Beetle, CC, Eos, Golf, GTI, Jetta, Passat **Engine:** 2.0L L4, 2.5L L4	**Data Bus Powertrain Missing Message from ABS Control Module:** Ignition off, the ECU is missing general Data BUS information from the central electrical control. The Engine Control Module (ECM) communicates with all data bus-capable control modules via a CAN data bus. These data bus-capable control modules are connected via two data bus wires which are twisted together (CAN High and CAN Low), and exchange information (messages). Missing information on the data bus is recognized as a malfunction and stored. Trouble-free operation of the CAN-bus requires that it have a terminal resistance. This central terminal resistor is located in the Engine Control Module (ECM).
DTC: P1650 **2T ECM, MIL: Yes** **Year:** 2011, 2012 **Model:** Beetle, CC, Eos, Golf, GTI, Jetta, Passat **Engine:** 2.0L L4, 2.5L L4	**Data-bus-drive train missing message from instrument cluster:** Time since start->1 sec. Battery voltage->10.54 V
DTC: P1650 **1T ECM, MIL: Yes** **Year:** 2011, 2012 **Model:** Beetle, CC, Eos, Golf, GTI, Jetta, Passat **Engine:** 2.0L L4, 2.5L L4	**Data-bus-drive train missing message from instrument cluster:** Time since start->1 sec. Battery voltage->10.54 V.
DTC: P1676 **1T ECM, MIL: Yes** **Year:** 2011, 2012 **Model:** Beetle, CC, Eos, Golf, GTI, Jetta, Passat **Engine:** 2.0L L4, 2.5L L4	**Drive by Wire-MIL Circuit Electrical Malfunction:** Key on or engine running, the ECM detected an electrical malfunction regarding the drive-by-wire circuit. **Note: EPC" is an abbreviation and stands for Electronic Power Control and means "electronic engine load control". If malfunctions are recognized in the EPC system during operation of the engine, the Engine Control Module (ECM) switches on the EPC warning lamp. An entry is made in DTC memory at the same time. After a few seconds of the engine at idle, the EPC should extinguish itself.**
DTC: P1677 **1T ECM, MIL: Yes** **Year:** 2011, 2012 **Model:** Beetle, CC, Eos, Golf, GTI, Jetta, Passat **Engine:** 2.0L L4, 2.5L L4	**Drive by Wire-MIL Circuit Short to B+:** Key on or engine running, the ECM detected an electrical malfunction regarding the drive-by-wire circuit. **Note: EPC" is an abbreviation and stands for Electronic Power Control and means "electronic engine load control". If malfunctions are recognized in the EPC system during operation of the engine, the Engine Control Module (ECM) switches on the EPC warning lamp. An entry is made in DTC memory at the same time. After a few seconds of the engine at idle, the EPC should extinguish itself.**
DTC: P1681 **1T ECM, MIL: Yes** **Year:** 2011, 2012 **Model:** Beetle, CC, Eos, Golf, GTI, Jetta, Passat **Engine:** 2.0L L4, 2.5L L4	**Control Unit Programming Not Finished:** Reprogramming bit not set.
DTC: P1684 **1T ECM, MIL: Yes** **Year:** 2011, 2012 **Model:** Routan, Touareg **Engine:** 3.6L V6 VIN G	**BATTERY WAS DISCONNECTED:** After a reset (ignition turned to the RUN position). The checksum of the battery backed RAM does not match the stored checksum. Set Time: Less than 7 msec.
DTC: P1685 **1T ECM, MIL: Yes** **Year:** 2011, 2012 **Model:** Routan, Touareg **Engine:** 3.6L V6 VIN G	**SKIM SYSTEM:** With the ignition on. A communication error occurs between the ECM and SKREEM.
DTC: P1691 **1T ECM, MIL: Yes** **Year:** 2011, 2012 **Model:** Beetle, CC, Eos, Golf, GTI, Jetta, Passat **Engine:** 2.0L L4, 2.5L L4	**Malfunction Indication Light Open:** The exhaust Malfunction Indicator Lamp (MIL) lights up when exhaust relevant malfunctions are recognized by the Engine Control Module (ECM). The Malfunction Indicator Lamp (MIL) can blink or remain lit continuously. Blinking: There is a malfunction that causes damage to the catalytic converter in this driving condition. In this case, vehicle must only be driven at reduced power! Continuously lit: There is a malfunction that causes increased emissions. Check DTC memory for Motronic control module. DTC memory must still be checked if there are drivability problems or customer complaints and the MIL is not lit, since malfunctions can be stored without causing the MIL to light immediately.

DTC	Trouble Code Title and Conditions
DTC: P1692 **1T ECM, MIL: Yes** **Year:** 2011, 2012 **Model:** Beetle, CC, Eos, Golf, GTI, Jetta, Passat **Engine:** 2.0L L4, 2.5L L4	**Malfunction Indication Light Short to Ground:** The exhaust Malfunction Indicator Lamp (MIL) lights up when exhaust relevant malfunctions are recognized by the Engine Control Module (ECM). The Malfunction Indicator Lamp (MIL) can blink or remain lit continuously. Blinking: There is a malfunction that causes damage to the catalytic converter in this driving condition. In this case, vehicle must only be driven at reduced power! Continuously lit: There is a malfunction that causes increased emissions. Check DTC memory for Motronic control module. DTC memory must still be checked if there are drivability problems or customer complaints and the MIL is not lit, since malfunctions can be stored without causing the MIL to light immediately.
DTC: P1693 **1T ECM, MIL: Yes** **Year:** 2011, 2012 **Model:** Beetle, CC, Eos, Golf, GTI, Jetta, Passat **Engine:** 2.0L L4, 2.5L L4	**Malfunction Indication Light Short to B+:** The exhaust Malfunction Indicator Lamp (MIL) lights up when exhaust relevant malfunctions are recognized by the Engine Control Module (ECM). The Malfunction Indicator Lamp (MIL) can blink or remain lit continuously. Blinking: There is a malfunction that causes damage to the catalytic converter in this driving condition. In this case, vehicle must only be driven at reduced power! Continuously lit: There is a malfunction that causes increased emissions. Check DTC memory for Motronic control module. DTC memory must still be checked if there are drivability problems or customer complaints and the MIL is not lit, since malfunctions can be stored without causing the MIL to light immediately.
DTC: P1696 **1T ECM, MIL: Yes** **Year:** 2011, 2012 **Model:** Routan, Touareg **Engine:** 3.6L V6 VIN G	**EEPROM MEMORY WRITE DENIED/INVALID:** Continuously with the ignition on. An attempt to program/write to the internal EEPROM failed, Also checks at power down. One Trip Fault. Three good trips to turn off the MIL.
DTC: P1697 **1T ECM, MIL: Yes** **Year:** 2011, 2012 **Model:** Routan, Touareg **Engine:** 3.6L V6 VIN G	**EMR (SRI) MILEAGE NOT STORED:** Continuously with the ignition on. The PCM Odometer mileage has not been programmed into the PCM.
DTC: P1702 **2T ECM, MIL: Yes** **Year:** 2011, 2012 **Model:** Beetle, CC, Eos, Golf, GTI, Jetta, Passat **Engine:** 2.0L L4, 2.5L L4	**Malfunction cannot activate control module Replacement function, since another malfunction with equal priority is present:** Continuously with the ignition on.
DTC: P1702 **1T ECM, MIL: Yes** **Year:** 2011, 2012 **Model:** Beetle, CC, Eos, Golf, GTI, Jetta, Passat **Engine:** 2.0L L4, 2.5L L4	**Malfunction cannot activate control module Replacement function, since another malfunction with equal priority is present:** Continuously with the ignition on.
DTC: P1713 **1T ECM, MIL: Yes** **Year:** 2011, 2012 **Model:** Routan, Touareg **Engine:** 3.6L V6 VIN G	**-RESTRICTED MANUAL VALVE IN T2 RANGE:** Ignition on, engine running with the gear shift selector in a valid forward gear. This DTC sets whenever Transmission control system detects the manual valve is in the T2 range when it should be in OD. This is mainly an informational DTC.
DTC: P1718 **1T ECM, MIL: Yes** **Year:** 2011, 2012 **Model:** Routan, Touareg **Engine:** 3.6L V6 VIN G	**-EEPROM INTEGRITY FAILURE:** Continuously with the ignition on. An attempt to program/write to the internal EEPROM failed, Also checks at power down. One Trip Fault. Three good trips to turn off the MIL.
DTC: P1741 **1T ECM, MIL: Yes** **Year:** 2011, 2012 **Model:** Routan, Touareg **Engine:** 3.6L V6 VIN G	**-GEAR RATIO ERROR IN 4 PRIME:** The Transmission gear ratio is monitored continuously while the transmission is in gear. If the ratio of the Input RPM to the Output RPM does not match the current gear ratio when compared to the known gear ratio.
DTC: P1745 **1T ECM, MIL: Yes** **Year:** 2011, 2012 **Model:** Routan, Touareg **Engine:** 3.6L V6 VIN G	**-TRANSMISSION LINE PRESSURE TOO HIGH FOR TOO LONG:** Continuously with ignition on. If the transmission has been operating in an open-loop line pressure control for 3220 kilometers (2000 miles) or 1000 2-3 up shifts.

DTC	Trouble Code Title and Conditions
DTC: P1770 **1T ECM, MIL: Yes** **Year:** 2011, 2012 **Model:** Routan, Touareg **Engine:** 3.6L V6 VIN G	**-INADEQUATE ELEMENT VOLUME LR:** Whenever the engine is running. The LR Clutch Volume Index (CVI) is updated during a 3-1 or 2-1 manual downshift with throttle angle below 5 degrees. Transmission temperature must be at least 43° C (110° F). When the LR Clutch Volume Index (CVI) falls below a calibrated value.
DTC: P1771 **1T ECM, MIL: Yes** **Year:** 2011, 2012 **Model:** Routan, Touareg **Engine:** 3.6L V6 VIN G	**-INADEQUATE ELEMENT VOLUME 2/4:** Whenever the engine is running. The 2/4 Clutch Volume Index (CVI) is updated during a 3-1 or 2-1 manual downshift with throttle angle below 5 degrees. Transmission temperature must be at least 43° C (110° F). When the 2/4 Clutch Volume Index (CVI) falls below a calibrated value.
DTC: P1772 **1T ECM, MIL: Yes** **Year:** 2011, 2012 **Model:** Routan, Touareg **Engine:** 3.6L V6 VIN G	**INADEQUATE ELEMENT VOLUME OD:** Whenever the engine is running. The OD Clutch Volume Index (CVI) is updated during a 2-3 up shift with throttle angle between 10 and 54 degrees. Transmission temperature must be at least 43° C (110° F). When the OD CVI falls below a calibrated value.
DTC: P1775 **T ECM, MIL: Yes** **Year:** 2011, 2012 **Model:** Routan, Touareg **Engine:** 3.6L V6 VIN G	**SOLENOID SWITCH VALVE LATCHED IN TCC POSITION:** Prior to a shift into 1st gear. Transmission temperature must be hot. DTC is set after six unsuccessful attempts to shift into 1st gear.
DTC: P1776 **1T ECM, MIL: Yes** **Year:** 2011, 2012 **Model:** Routan, Touareg **Engine:** 3.6L V6 VIN G	**-SOLENOID SWITCH VALVE LATCHED IN LR POSITION:** Every 7 ms when doing PEMCC or FEMCC. Must be in partial or full EMCC. The DTC is set if L/R pressure is detected high for the fourth time.
DTC: P1778 **2T ECM, MIL: Yes** **Year:** 2011, 2012 **Model:** Beetle, CC, Eos, Golf, GTI, Jetta, Passat **Engine:** 2.0L L4, 2.5L L4	**Valve 7 Electrical Fault In Circuit:** Malfunction Criteria and Threshold Value: * Comparison of stored value with active level-switch off and U <2.1 V * Switch on and U > 1.6 V. Monitoring Time Length 0.3 Sec.
DTC: P1780 **2T ECM, MIL: Yes** **Year:** 2011, 2012 **Model:** Beetle, CC, Eos, Golf, GTI, Jetta, Passat **Engine:** 2.0L L4, 2.5L L4	**Torque Withdrawal Faulty:** Malfunction Criteria and Threshold Value: * Comparison with nominal values-switch off and U < 2.1 * Switch on and U > 1.6 V.
DTC: P1780 **2T ECM, MIL: Yes** **Year:** 2011, 2012 **Model:** Beetle, CC, Eos, Golf, GTI, Jetta, Passat **Engine:** 2.0L L4, 2.5L L4	**Torque withdrawal faulty:** Torque reduction requested by TCM.
DTC: P1790 **1T ECM, MIL: Yes** **Year:** 2011, 2012 **Model:** Routan, Touareg **Engine:** 3.6L V6 VIN G	**FAULT IMMEDIATELY AFTER SHIFT:** After a Gear Ratio Error code is stored. After a Gear Ratio Error DTC has already been set The DTC is set if the fault happened within 1.3 seconds of a shift. The DTC set time will vary from 1.214 seconds to 15 seconds.
DTC: P1794 **1T ECM, MIL: Yes** **Year:** 2011, 2012 **Model:** Routan, Touareg **Engine:** 3.6L V6 VIN G	**SPEED SENSOR GROUND ERROR:** Every 7ms after a controller reset with transmission in neutral. After a Powertrain Control Module (PCM) reset in neutral and Input and Output sensor ratio equals 2.50 to 1.0 ± 50.0 RPM.
DTC: P1797 **1T ECM, MIL: Yes** **Year:** 2011, 2012 **Model:** Routan, Touareg **Engine:** 3.6L V6 VIN G	**-MANUAL SHIFT OVERHEAT:** Continuously with engine running. If the Engine Temperature exceeds 123° C (255° F) or the Transmission Temperature exceeds 135° C (275° F) while in AutoStick® mode. **Note: Aggressive driving or driving in Low for extended periods of time will set this DTC.**

DTC	Trouble Code Title and Conditions
DTC: P1850 **2T ECM, MIL: Yes** **Year:** 2011, 2012 **Model:** Beetle, CC, Eos, Golf, GTI, Jetta, Passat **Engine:** 2.0L L4, 2.5L L4	**Data bus drive train missing message from engine control module:** CAN bus OK 500 mSec. after ign. on
DTC: P1850 **2T ECM, MIL: Yes** **Year:** 2011, 2012 **Model:** Beetle, CC, Eos, Golf, GTI, Jetta, Passat **Engine:** 2.0L L4, 2.5L L4	**Data-Bus Drive Train Missing Message From Engine Control Module:** No signal within 300 ms, CAN bus ok –500 ms after ign. ON.
DTC: P1854 **2T ECM, MIL: Yes** **Year:** 2012 **Model:** Beetle, Golf, GTI **Engine:** 2.0L L4, 2.5L L5	**Data-Bus Driving Gear Hardware Faulty:** Initialize failure and/or no acknowledge 2 attempts of initialize, 500 ms after ign. ON.
DTC: P1854 **2T ECM, MIL: Yes** **Year:** 2011, 2012 **Model:** Beetle, CC, Eos, Golf, GTI, Jetta, Passat **Engine:** 2.0L L4, 2.5L L4	**Data Bus driving gear Hardware faulty:** 500 mSec. after ign. on
DTC: P1855 **2T ECM, MIL: Yes** **Year:** 2011, 2012 **Model:** Beetle, CC, Eos, Golf, GTI, Jetta, Passat **Engine:** 2.0L L4, 2.5L L4	**Data-Bus-driving gear Software version monitoring.:** * CAN communication valid
DTC: P1866 **2T ECM, MIL: Yes** **Year:** 2011, 2012 **Model:** Beetle, CC, Eos, Golf, GTI, Jetta, Passat **Engine:** 2.0L L4, 2.5L L4	**Data-Bus-driving gear missing messages.:** * CAN bus ok 500 ms after ignition on

OBD II Trouble Code List (P2XXX Codes)

DTC	Trouble Code Title and Conditions
DTC: P2000 **2T ECM** **Year:** 2011, 2012 **Model:** Golf, GTI, Jetta, Passat **Engine:** 2.0L L4	**NOx Absorber Efficiency Bank 1 Below Threshold:** * Regeneration demand for NOx trap = On * Adaptation of oxygen sensor pre and post NOx trap = realized * Engine speed 1100 - 2700 RPM * Upstream turbine temperature 50 - 850 °C * Temperature of upstream NOx trap 250 - 410 °C * ECT 40 - 105 °C * Fuel temp < 70 °C * APP > 1% and < 100% * Engine run time > 220 Sec.
DTC: P2002 **5T ECM** **Year:** 2011, 2012 **Model:** Golf, GTI, Jetta, Passat **Engine:** 2.0L L4, 2.5L L5	**Particulate Trap Bank 1 Efficiency Below Threshold:** * Differential pressure = not defective * Exhaust gas volume flow > 160 mΔ 3/h * ECT > f (ambient temperature) * Particulate matter trap regeneration = not active * Time since PM trap regeneration > 300 Sec. * Calculated PM trap loading > 1 g

DTC	Trouble Code Title and Conditions
DTC: P2002 **2T ECM, MIL: Yes** **Year:** 2011, 2012 **Model:** Touareg **Engine:** 3.0L V6	**Particulate Trap Bank 1 Efficiency Below Threshold:** * Calculated temperature of diesel particulate filter between 250 - 450 °C * Calculated DPF loading > 11g * Exhaust gas flow rate < 300 (m3/h) * T ambient (T1) > -7 °C * Exhaust volumetric flow rate > 400 (m3/h) * Delta exhaust volumetric flow rate < (20) (m3/h)s * Within 1 Sec. time period
DTC: P2002* **5T** **Year:** 2011, 2012 **Model:** Golf, GTI, Jetta, Passat **Engine:** 2.0L L4, 2.5L L5	**Particulate Trap Bank 1 Efficiency Below Threshold:** * Exhaust gas temp. > 199.96 and < 499.96 °C * Exhaust gas volume flow > 160 and < 600mΔ 3/h * ECT > f (ambient temperature) * Time since engine start > 300 Sec. * Exhaust gas temp. before and after PM trap > 39.95 °C * Time since PM trap regeneration > 60 Sec. * ECT > 14.95 °C * Time since engine start > 300 Sec.
DTC: P2004 **2T ECM, MIL: Yes** **Year:** 2011, 2012 **Model:** Beetle, Eos, GTI, Jetta, Passat **Engine:** 2.0L L4, 2.5L L5	**Intake Manifold Runner Control Stuck Open Bank 1:** * ECM keep alive time Ignition, Off * Runner flaps, Commanded closed * Battery voltage, >10 V * ECT, -40.5-140 °C * IAT, -40.5-140 °C * Position sensor, No DTC * Actuator, No DTC
DTC: P2006* **2T ECM, MIL: Yes** **Year:** 2011, 2012 **Model:** Golf, GTI, Jetta, Passat **Engine:** 2.0L L4, 2.5L L5	**Intake Manifold Runner Control Bank 1 Stuck Closed:** Control deviation detected > 10% or < -10%
DTC: P2008 **2T ECM, MIL: Yes** **Year:** 2011, 2012 **Model:** Beetle, Eos, Golf, GTI, Jetta, Passat **Engine:** 2.0L L4, 2.5L L5	**Intake Manifold Runner Control Circuit/Open:** * Tumble flap commanded off * Engine speed > 80 RPM
DTC: P2008 **2T ECM, MIL: Yes** **Year:** 2011, 2012 **Model:** Beetle, Eos, GTI, Passat **Engine:** 2.0L L4	**Intake Manifold Runner Control Circuit/Open Bank 1:** * Duty cycle, >80% * deviation runner flap, >5% * Position vs. calculated position and ECM power stage, Failure * LBK adaption, Disabled
DTC: P2009 **2T ECM, MIL: Yes** **Year:** 2011, 2012 **Model:** Touareg **Engine:** 3.0L V6, 3.6L V6	**Intake Manifold Runner Control Circuit High Bank 1:** * Runner flaps, Commanded off * Engine speed, >40 RPM
DTC: P2009 **2T ECM, MIL: Yes** **Year:** 2011, 2012 **Model:** Beetle, Eos, GTI, Jetta, Passat **Engine:** 2.0L L4	**Intake Manifold Runner Control Circuit/Shorted Bank 1:** * Tumble flap, commanded off * Engine speed >80 RPM
DTC: P2009 **2T ECM, MIL: Yes** **Year:** 2011, 2012 **Model:** Beetle, Eos, Golf, GTI, Jetta, Passat **Engine:** 2.0L L4, 2.5L L5	**Intake Manifold Runner Control Circuit Low:** * Tumble flap commanded off * Engine speed > 80 RPM

DTC	Trouble Code Title and Conditions
DTC: P2010 **2T ECM, MIL: Yes** **Year:** 2011, 2012 **Model:** Passat, Touareg **Engine:** 3.0L V6, 3.6L V6	**Intake Manifold Runner Control Circuit High Bank 1:** * Runner flaps, Commanded on * Engine speed, >40 RPM
DTC: P2010 **2T ECM, MIL: Yes** **Year:** 2011, 2012 **Model:** Beetle, Eos, Golf, GTI, Jetta, Passat **Engine:** 2.0L L4, 2.5L L5	**Intake Manifold Runner Control Circuit High:** * Tumble flap commanded on * Engine speed > 80 RPM
DTC: P2010 **2T** **Year:** 2011, 2012 **Model:** Beetle, Eos, GTI, Jetta, Passat **Engine:** 2.0L L4	**Intake Manifold Runner Control Circuit/Shorted to B+ Bank 1:** * Tumble flap, commanded on * Engine speed >80 RPM
DTC: P2011 **2T ECM, MIL: Yes** **Year:** 2011, 2012 **Model:** Touareg **Engine:** 3.0L V6, 3.6L V6	**Intake Manifold Runner Bank 2 Control Circuit Stuck Open:** * Power stage = Off state * Power stage = On state
DTC: P2012 **2T ECM, MIL: Yes** **Year:** 2011, 2012 **Model:** Touareg **Engine:** 3.0L V6, 3.6L V6	**Intake Manifold Runner Bank 2 Control Circuit Low:** Power stage = On state
DTC: P2013 **2T ECM, MIL: Yes** **Year:** 2011, 2012 **Model:** Touareg **Engine:** 3.0L V6, 3.6L V6	**Intake Manifold Runner Bank 2 Control Circuit High:** Power stage = On state
DTC: P2014 **2T ECM, MIL: Yes** **Year:** 2011, 2012 **Model:** Beetle, Eos, Golf, GTI, Jetta, Passat, Touareg **Engine:** 2.0L L4, 2.5L L5, 3.0L V6, 3.6L V6	**Intake Manifold Runner Position Sensor/Switch Circuit Bank 1:** Signal voltage, >4.82 V.
DTC: P2015 **2T ECM, MIL: Yes** **Year:** 2011, 2012 **Model:** Beetle, Eos, Golf, GTI, Jetta, Passat **Engine:** 2.0L L4, 2.5L L5	**Intake Manifold Runner Position Sensor/Switch Circuit Range/Performance Bank 1:** * Intake manifold runner flaps position sensor, No DTC * ECM power stage, No failure
DTC: P2015 **2T ECM, MIL: Yes** **Year:** 2011, 2012 **Model:** Touareg **Engine:** 3.0L V6, 3.6L V6	**Intake Manifold Runner Position Sensor/Switch Circuit Range/Performance Bank 1:** * ECT, >-10° C, * Engine speed, >400 RPM
DTC: P2016 **2T ECM, MIL: Yes** **Year:** 2011, 2012 **Model:** Beetle, Eos, Golf, GTI, Jetta, Passat, Touareg **Engine:** 2.0L L4, 2.5L L5, 3.0L V6, 3.6L V6	**Intake Manifold Runner Position Sensor/Switch Circuit Low (Bank 1):** Signal voltage, <0.18 V.

DTC	Trouble Code Title and Conditions
DTC: P2017 **2T ECM, MIL: Yes** **Year:** 2011, 2012 **Model:** Beetle, Eos, Golf, GTI, Jetta, Passat, Touareg **Engine:** 2.0L L4, 2.5L L5, 3.0L V6, 3.6L V6	**Intake Manifold Runner Position Sensor/Switch Circuit High Bank 1:** Power stage = On state
DTC: P2017 **2T ECM, MIL: Yes** **Year:** 2011, 2012 **Model:** Golf, GTI, Jetta, Passat **Engine:** 2.0L L4, 2.5L L5	**Intake Manifold Runner Position Sensor Circuit High:** * Intake manifold runner flaps position sensor, No DTC * ECM power stage, No failure * Tumble flap commanded on * Engine speed > 80 RPM
DTC: P2019 **2T ECM, MIL: Yes** **Year:** 2011, 2012 **Model:** Touareg **Engine:** 3.0L V6, 3.6L V6	**Intake Manifold Runner Position Sensor/Switch Circuit Bank 2:** Power stage = On state
DTC: P2020 **2T ECM, MIL: Yes** **Year:** 2011, 2012 **Model:** Touareg **Engine:** 3.0L V6, 3.6L V6	**Intake Manifold Runner Position Sensor/Switch Circuit Range/Performance Bank 2:** * ECT, >-10° C * Engine speed, >400 RPM
DTC: P2022 **2T ECM, MIL: Yes** **Year:** 2011, 2012 **Model:** Touareg **Engine:** 3.0L V6, 3.6L V6	**Intake Manifold Runner Position Sensor/Switch Circuit High Bank 2:** Power stage = On state
DTC: P202A **2T ECM, MIL: Yes** **Year:** 2011, 2012 **Model:** Touareg **Engine:** 3.0L V6, 3.6L V6	**Reductant Tank Heater Control Circuit/Open:** * Heating = On
DTC: P202B **2T ECM, MIL: Yes** **Year:** 2011, 2012 **Model:** Touareg **Engine:** 3.0L V6, 3.6L V6	**Reductant Tank Heater Control Circuit Low:** * Time since engagement > 10 Sec.
DTC: P202C **2T ECM, MIL: Yes** **Year:** 2011, 2012 **Model:** Touareg **Engine:** 3.0L V6, 3.6L V6	**Reductant Tank Heater Control Circuit High:** * Time since engagement > 10 Sec.
DTC: P2031 **2T ECM, MIL: Yes** **Year:** 2011, 2012 **Model:** Golf, GTI, Jetta, Passat **Engine:** 2.0L L4, 2.5L L5	**Exhaust Gas Temperature Sensor 2 Circuit:** Ignition on.
DTC: P2032 **2T ECM, MIL: Yes** **Year:** 2011, 2012 **Model:** Golf, GTI, Jetta, Passat **Engine:** 2.0L L4, 2.5L L5	**Exhaust Gas Temperature Sensor 2 Circuit Low:** Ignition on.
DTC: P203A **2T ECM, MIL: Yes** **Year:** 2011, 2012 **Model:** CC, Passat, Touareg, Routan **Engine:** 3.0L V6, 3.6L V6	**Reductant Level Sensor Circuit:** * SCR tank temperature > -3 °C * If SCR tank temp < -3 °C then defrosting urea tank = done * Time until release of metering unit heating < 600 Sec.

DTC	Trouble Code Title and Conditions
DTC: P203B **2T ECM, MIL: Yes** **Year:** 2011, 2012 **Model:** CC, Passat, Touareg, Routan **Engine:** 3.0L V6, 3.6L V6	**Reductant Level Sensor Circuit Range/Performance:** * SCR tank temperature > -3 °C * If SCR tank temp < -3 °C then defrosting urea tank = done * Time until release of metering unit heating < 600 Sec.
DTC: P2047 **2T ECM, MIL: Yes** **Year:** 2011, 2012 **Model:** CC, Passat, Touareg, Routan **Engine:** 3.0L V6, 3.6L V6	**Reductant Injection Valve Circuit/Open Bank 1 Unit 1:** * Power stage = Off stat
DTC: P2048 **2T ECM, MIL: Yes** **Year:** 2011, 2012 **Model:** CC, Passat, Touareg, Routan **Engine:** 3.0L V6, 3.6L V6	**Reductant Injection Valve Circuit Low Bank 1 Unit 1:** * Power stage = Off state * Power stage = On state
DTC: P2049 **2T ECM, MIL: Yes** **Year:** 2011, 2012 **Model:** CC, Passat, Touareg, Routan **Engine:** 3.0L V6, 3.6L V6	**Reductant Injection Valve Circuit High Bank 1 Unit 1:** * Power stage = On state
DTC: P204D **2T ECM, MIL: Yes** **Year:** 2011, 2012 **Model:** CC, Passat, Touareg, Routan **Engine:** 3.0L V6, 3.6L V6	**Reductant Pressure Sensor Circuit High:** * T6 > 100 °C * Ambient temperature > -3 °C * Urea tank temperature > -7 °C * Engine speed > 800 rpm
DTC: P205B **2T ECM, MIL: Yes** **Year:** 2011, 2012 **Model:** CC, Passat, Touareg, Routan **Engine:** 3.0L V6, 3.6L V6	**Reductant Tank Temperature Sensor Circuit Range/Performance:** * Engine off time > 9 hr * Rising of urea temperature within 25 minutes < 1.5 °K
DTC: P2072 **T ECM, MIL: Yes** **Year:** 2011, 2012 **Model:** Routan **Engine:** 3.6L V6 VIN G	**ELECTRONIC THROTTLE CONTROL SYSTEM - ICE BLOCKAGE:** With the ignition on, the PCM recognizes the Throttle plate is stuck during extremely cold Ambient Temperature operation. The throttle plate goes through a de-icing procedure. If the throttle blade still doesn't move this fault sets. The MIL will not illuminate. The vehicle will be in Limp home condition, limiting rpm and vehicle speed.
DTC: P2080 **2T ECM, MIL: Yes** **Year:** 2011, 2012 **Model:** CC, Passat, Touareg, Routan **Engine:** 3.0L V6, 3.6L V6	**Exhaust Gas Temperature Sensor Circuit Range/Performance:** * Engine off time > 9 hr * Decrease of IAT and T2 < 5 °K at > 25 mph for 20 Sec. * Decrease of AAT after engine start < 5 °K for 60 Sec.
DTC: P2080 **2T** **Year:** 2011, 2012 **Model:** Golf, GTI, Jetta, Passat **Engine:** 2.0L L4, 2.5L L5	**Exhaust Gas Temperature Sensor Circuit Range/Performance:** * Engine run time > 3 mins. * ECT > 10 °C * Simulated sensor temp > 300 °C * Engine off time > 32400 Sec. * Decrease of IAT after engine start < 5 °K * Decrease of AAT after engine start < 5 °K
DTC: P2084 **2T ECM** **Year:** 2011, 2012 **Model:** Golf, GTI, Jetta, Passat **Engine:** 2.0L L4, 2.5L L5	**Exhaust Gas Temperature Sensor 2 Circuit Range/Performance:** * Engine run time > 3 mins. * ECT > 10 °C * Simulated sensor temp > 300 °C

DTC	Trouble Code Title and Conditions
DTC: P2084 **2T ECM, MIL: Yes** **Year:** 2011, 2012 **Model:** Touareg, Routan **Engine:** 3.0L V6, 3.6L V6	**Exhaust Gas Temperature Sensor 2 Circuit Range/Performance:** * Engine off time > 9 hr * Decrease of IAT and T2 < 5 °K at > 25 mph for 20 Sec. * Decrease of AAT after engine start < 5 °K for 60 Sec.
DTC: P2088 **2T ECM, MIL: Yes** **Year:** 2011, 2012 **Model:** Beetle, Eos, Golf, GTI, Passat, Touareg **Engine:** 2.0L L4, 2.5L L5, 3.0L V6, 3.6L V6	**A Camshaft Position Actuator Control Circuit Low Bank 1:** * Camshaft valve, commanded off * Engine speed, >80 RPM
DTC: P2089 **1 T ECM, MIL: Yes** **Year:** 2011, 2012 **Model:** Beetle, CC, Eos, Golf, GTI, GLI, Jetta, Passat, Routan, Tiguan, Touareg **Engine:** 2.0L L4, 2.5L L5, 3.0L V6, 3.6L V6	**A Camshaft Position Actuator Control Circuit High Bank 1:** * Camshaft valve, Commanded on * Engine speed, > 80 RPM
DTC: P208E **2T ECM, MIL: Yes** **Year:** 2011, 2012 **Model:** CC, Passat, Touareg, Routan **Engine:** 3.0L V6, 3.6L V6	**Reductant Injection Valve Stuck Closed Bank 1 Unit 1:** * Urea dosing = active * Ambient pressure = 700 - 1300 hPa * SCR urea pressure = 3500 - 6500 hPa * Dosing valve coil temperature = 10 - 20 °C
DTC: P2090 **2 T ECM, MIL: Yes** **Year:** 2011, 2012 **Model:** Beetle, CC, Eos, Golf, GTI, GLI, Jetta, Passat, Routan, Tiguan, Touareg **Engine:** 2.0L L4, 2.5L L5, 3.0L V6, 3.6L V6	**"B" Camshaft Position Actuator Control Circuit Low Bank 1:** * Camshaft valve, Off * Engine speed, >80 RPM
DTC: P2091 **2 T ECM, MIL: Yes** **Year:** 2011, 2012 **Model:** Beetle, CC, Eos, Golf, GTI, GLI, Jetta, Passat, Routan, Tiguan, Touareg **Engine:** 2.0L L4, 2.5L L5, 3.0L V6, 3.6L V6	**"B" Camshaft Position Actuator Control Circuit High Bank 1:** * Camshaft valve, Commanded on * Engine speed, > 80 RPM
DTC: P2091 **2 T ECM, MIL: Yes** **Year:** 2011, 2012 **Model:** Beetle, CC, Eos, Golf, GTI, GLI, Jetta, Passat, Routan, Tiguan, Touareg **Engine:** 2.0L L4, 2.5L L5, 3.0L V6, 3.6L V6	**"B" Camshaft Position Actuator Control Circuit High Bank 1:** * Camshaft valve, On * Engine speed, >80 RPM
DTC: P2092 **2T ECM, MIL: Yes** **Year:** 2011, 2012 **Model:** CC, Passat, Touareg, Routan **Engine:** 3.0L V6, 3.6L V6	**"A" Camshaft Position Actuator Control Circuit Low Bank 2:** * Camshaft valve, commanded on * Engine speed, >80 RPM

DTC	Trouble Code Title and Conditions
DTC: P2093 **2T ECM, MIL: Yes** **Year:** 2011, 2012 **Model:** CC, Passat, Touareg, Routan **Engine:** 3.0L V6, 3.6L V6	**"A" Camshaft Position Actuator Control Circuit High Bank 2:** * Camshaft valve, commanded on * Engine speed, >80 RPM
DTC: P2094 **2T ECM, MIL: Yes** **Year:** 2011, 2012 **Model:** CC, Passat, Touareg, Routan **Engine:** 3.0L V6, 3.6L V6	**"B" Camshaft Position Actuator Control Circuit Low Bank 2:** * Camshaft valve, Off * Engine speed, >80 RPM
DTC: P2095 **2T ECM, MIL: Yes** **Year:** 2011, 2012 **Model:** CC, Passat, Touareg, Routan **Engine:** 3.0L V6, 3.6L V6	**"B" Camshaft Position Actuator Control Circuit High Bank 2:** * Camshaft valve, On * Engine speed, >80 RPM
DTC: P2096 **1T ECM, MIL: Yes** **Year:** 2011, 2012 **Model:** Beetle, CC, Eos, Golf, GTI, GLI, Jetta, Passat, Routan, Tiguan, Touareg **Engine:** 2.0L L4, 2.5L L5, 3.0L V6, 3.6L V6	**DOWNSTREAM FUEL TRIM SYSTEM 1 LEAN:** With the engine running in closed loop mode, the ambient/battery temperature above -6.7° C (20° F) and altitude below 2590.8 m (8500 ft). The conditions that cause this diagnostic to fail is when the upstream O2 sensor becomes biased from an exhaust leak, O2 sensor contamination or some other extreme operating condition. The downstream O2 sensor is considered to be protected from extreme environments by the catalyst. The PCM monitors the downstream O2 sensor feedback control, called downstream fuel trim, to detect any shift in the upstream O2 sensor target voltage from nominal target voltage. The value of the downstream fuel trim is compared with the lean thresholds. Every time the value exceeds the calibrated threshold, a fail timer is incremented and mass flow through the exhaust is accumulated. If the fail timer and accumulated mass flow exceed the fail thresholds, the test fails and the diagnostic stops running for that trip. If the test fails on consecutive trips, a DTC is set.
DTC: P2097 **1T ECM, MIL: Yes** **Year:** 2011, 2012 **Model:** Beetle, CC, Eos, Golf, GTI, GLI, Jetta, Passat, Routan, Tiguan, Touareg **Engine:** 2.0L L4, 2.5L L5, 3.0L V6, 3.6L V6	**DOWNSTREAM FUEL TRIM SYSTEM 1 RICH:** With the engine running in closed loop mode, the ambient/battery temperature above -6.7°C (20°F) and altitude below 2590.8 m (8500 ft). The conditions that cause this diagnostic to fail is when the upstream O2 sensor becomes biased from an exhaust leak, O2 sensor contamination, or some other extreme operating condition. The downstream O2 sensor is considered to be protected from extreme environments by the catalyst. The PCM monitors the downstream O2 sensor feedback control, called downstream fuel trim, to detect any shift in the upstream O2 sensor target voltage from nominal target voltage. The value of the downstream fuel trim is compared with the rich thresholds. Every time the value exceeds the calibrated threshold, a fail timer is incremented and mass flow through the exhaust is accumulated. If the fail timer and accumulated mass flow exceed the fail thresholds, the test fails and the diagnostic stops running for that trip. If the test fails on consecutive trips, a DTC is set.
DTC: P2098 **1T ECM, MIL: Yes** **Year:** 2011, 2012 **Model:** Beetle, CC, Eos, Golf, GTI, GLI, Jetta, Passat, Routan, Tiguan, Touareg **Engine:** 2.0L L4, 2.5L L5, 3.0L V6, 3.6L V6	**-DOWNSTREAM FUEL TRIM SYSTEM 2 LEAN:** With the engine running in closed loop mode, the ambient/battery temperature above -6.7° C (20° F) and altitude below 2590.8 m (8500 ft). Fuel level greater than 15%. The conditions that cause this diagnostic to fail is when the upstream O2 sensor becomes biased from an exhaust leak, O2 sensor contamination or some other extreme operating condition. The downstream O2 sensor is considered to be protected from extreme environments by the catalyst. The PCM monitors the downstream O2 sensor feedback control, called downstream fuel trim, to detect any shift in the upstream O2 sensor target voltage from nominal target voltage. The value of the downstream fuel trim is compared with the lean thresholds. Every time the value exceeds the calibrated threshold, a fail timer is incremented and mass flow through the exhaust is accumulated. If the fail timer and accumulated mass flow exceed the fail thresholds, the test fails and the diagnostic stops running for that trip. If the test fails on consecutive trips, a DTC is set.
DTC: P2099 **1T ECM, MIL: Yes** **Year:** 2011, 2012 **Model:** Beetle, CC, Eos, Golf, GTI, GLI, Jetta, Passat, Routan, Tiguan, Touareg **Engine:** 2.0L L4, 2.5L L5, 3.0L V6, 3.6L V6	**-DOWNSTREAM FUEL TRIM SYSTEM 2 RICH:** With the engine running in closed loop mode, the ambient/battery temperature above -6.7°C (20°F) and altitude below 2590.8 m (8500 ft). The conditions that cause this diagnostic to fail is when the upstream O2 sensor becomes biased from an exhaust leak, O2 sensor contamination, or some other extreme operating condition. The downstream O2 sensor is considered to be protected from extreme environments by the catalyst. The PCM monitors the downstream O2 sensor feedback control, called downstream fuel trim, to detect any shift in the upstream O2 sensor target voltage from nominal target voltage. The value of the downstream fuel trim is compared with the lean thresholds. Every time the value exceeds the calibrated threshold, a fail timer is incremented and mass flow through the exhaust is accumulated. If the fail timer and accumulated mass flow exceed the fail thresholds, the test fails and the diagnostic stops running for that trip. If the test fails on consecutive trips, a DTC is set.

DTC	Trouble Code Title and Conditions
DTC: P20A0 **2T ECM, MIL: Yes** **Year:** 2011, 2012 **Model:** Touareg, Routan **Engine:** 3.0L V6, 3.6L V6	**Reductant Purge Control Valve Circuit Open:** * Power stage = Off state
DTC: P20A2 **2T ECM, MIL: Yes** **Year:** 2011, 2012 **Model:** Touareg, Routan **Engine:** 3.0L V6, 3.6L V6	**Reductant Purge Control Valve Circuit Low:** * Power stage = Off state
DTC: P20A3 **2T ECM, MIL: Yes** **Year:** 2011, 2012 **Model:** Touareg, Routan **Engine:** 3.0L V6, 3.6L V6	**Reductant Purge Control Valve Circuit High:** * Power stage = On state
DTC: P20B5 **2T ECM, MIL: Yes** **Year:** 2011, 2012 **Model:** Touareg, Routan **Engine:** 3.0L V6, 3.6L V6	**Reductant Metering Unit Heater Control Circuit/Open:** * Heating = On
DTC: P20B7 **2T ECM, MIL: Yes** **Year:** 2011, 2012 **Model:** Touareg, Routan **Engine:** 3.0L V6, 3.6L V6	**Reductant Metering Unit Heater Control Circuit Low:** * Time since engagement > 10 Sec.
DTC: P20B9 **2T ECM, MIL: Yes** **Year:** 2011, 2012 **Model:** Touareg, Routan **Engine:** 3.0L V6, 3.6L V6	**Reductant Heater "A" Control Circuit/Open:** * Power stage = Off state
DTC: P20BB **2T ECM, MIL: Yes** **Year:** 2011, 2012 **Model:** Touareg, Routan **Engine:** 3.0L V6, 3.6L V6	**Reductant Heater "A" Control Circuit Low:** * Power stage = Off state
DTC: P20BC **2T ECM, MIL: Yes** **Year:** 2011, 2012 **Model:** Touareg, Routan **Engine:** 3.0L V6, 3.6L V6	**Reductant Heater "A" Control Circuit High:** * Power stage = On state
DTC: P20BD **2T ECM, MIL: Yes** **Year:** 2011, 2012 **Model:** Touareg, Routan **Engine:** 3.0L V6, 3.6L V6	**Reductant Heater "B" Control Circuit/Open:** * Power stage = Off state
DTC: P20BF **2T ECM, MIL: Yes** **Year:** 2011, 2012 **Model:** Touareg **Engine:** 3.0L V6, 3.6L V6	**Reductant Heater "B" Control Circuit Low:** * Power stage = Off state
DTC: P20C0 **2T ECM, MIL: Yes** **Year:** 2011, 2012 **Model:** Touareg **Engine:** 3.0L V6, 3.6L V6	**Reductant Heater "B" Control Circuit High:** * Power stage = On state

DTC	Trouble Code Title and Conditions
DTC: P20D8 **2T ECM, MIL: Yes** **Year:** 2011, 2012 **Model:** Golf, GTI, Jetta, Passat **Engine:** 2.0L L4, 2.5L L5	**Exhaust After Treatment Fuel Supply Control Performance:** * Regeneration demand for NOx trap = On * Adaptation of oxygen sensor pre and post NOx trap = realized * Engine speed 1100 - 2700 RPM * Upstream turbine temperature 50 - 850 °C * Temperature of upstream NOx trap 250 - 410 °C * ECT 40 - 105 °C * Fuel temp < 70 °C * APP > 1% and < 100% * Engine run time > 220 Sec.
DTC: P20E8 **2T ECM, MIL: Yes** **Year:** 2011, 2012 **Model:** Touareg **Engine:** 3.0L V6, 3.6L V6	**Reductant Pressure Too Low:** * SCR system state = pressure control * SCR system state = metering control
DTC: P20E9 **2T ECM, MIL: Yes** **Year:** 2011, 2012 **Model:** Touareg **Engine:** 3.0L V6, 3.6L V6	**Reductant Pressure Too High:** * SCR system state = pressure reduction * SCR system state = metering control
DTC: P20EE **2T ECM, MIL: Yes** **Year:** 2011, 2012 **Model:** Touareg **Engine:** 3.0L V6, 3.6L V6	**SCR NOx Catalyst Efficiency Below Threshold Bank 1:** * Status NOx Sensor Downstream = ready * Status NOx Sensor Upstream = ready * Urea dosing = active * Adaptation = not active * DPF regeneration = not active * SCR Catalyst temp gradient < 0.2 to 0.34 K/s * SCR catalyst modeled temp. = 240 - 350 °C * NOx concentration upstream < 1500 ppm.
DTC: P2100 **2T ECM, MIL: Yes** **Year:** 2011, 2012 **Model:** Golf, GTI, Jetta, Passat **Engine:** 2.0L L4, 2.5L L5	**Throttle Actuator Control Motor Circuit/Open:** Output driver Off state
DTC: P2100 **1T ECM, MIL: Yes** **Year:** 2011, 2012 **Model:** Routan, Routan **Engine:** 3.6L V6 VIN G	**ELECTRONIC THROTTLE CONTROL MOTOR CIRCUIT:** With the ignition on and the ETC Motor is not in Limp Home mode. When the Powertrain Control Module (PCM) detects an internal error or a short between the ETC Motor - and ETC Motor + circuits in the ETC Motor Driver. One trip fault. ETC light is flashing.
DTC: P2100 **2T ECM, MIL: Yes** **Year:** 2011, 2012 **Model:** Touareg **Engine:** 3.0L V6, 3.6L V6	**Throttle Actuator Control Motor Circuit/Open:** Power stage = Off state
DTC: P2101 **2T ECM, MIL: Yes** **Year:** 2011, 2012 **Model:** Beetle, CC, Eos, Golf, GTI, GLI, Jetta, Passat, Routan, Tiguan, Touareg **Engine:** 2.0L L4, 2.5L L5, 3.0L V6, 3.6L V6	**Throttle Actuator Control Motor Circuit Range/Performance:** The ECM detected an unexpected low or high voltage condition on the Throttle Actuator Control Motor (TACM) circuit during the CCM test. **Note: The throttle valve activation occurs via an electric motor (throttle drive) in the throttle valve control module. It is activated by the Engine Control Module (ECM) according to specifications of the two sensors, Throttle Position (TP) Sensor and Sender 2 for accelerator pedal position. Duty cycle >80%, Throttle valve angle Δ max = 4.50 deviation %DK.**

DTC	Trouble Code Title and Conditions
DTC: P2102 **2T ECM, MIL: Yes** **Year:** 2011, 2012 **Model:** Beetle, CC, Eos, Golf, GTI, GLI, Jetta, Passat, Routan, Tiguan, Touareg **Engine:** 2.0L L4, 2.5L L5, 3.0L V6, 3.6L V6	**Throttle Actuator Control Motor Circuit Low:** Engine started, battery voltage must be at least 11.5v, all electrical components must be off, parking brake must be engaged (to keep daytime driving lights off), automatic transmission selector must be in park, the exhaust system must be properly sealed between the catalytic converter and the cylinder head, coolant temperature must be at least 80 degrees Celsius. The ECM detected an unexpected low or high voltage condition on the Throttle Actuator Control Motor (TACM) circuit during the CCM test. **Note: The throttle valve activation occurs via an electric motor (throttle drive) in the throttle valve control module. It is activated by the Engine Control Module (ECM) according to specifications of the two sensors, Throttle Position (TP) Sensor and Sender 2 for accelerator pedal position.**
DTC: P2103 **2T ECM, MIL: Yes** **Year:** 2011, 2012 **Model:** Beetle, CC, Eos, Golf, GTI, GLI, Jetta, Passat, Routan, Tiguan, Touareg **Engine:** 2.0L L4, 2.5L L5, 3.0L V6, 3.6L V6	**Throttle Actuator "A" Control Motor Circuit High:** Power stage = On state
DTC: P2106 **2T ECM, MIL: Yes** **Year:** 2011, 2012 **Model:** Beetle, CC, Eos, Golf, GTI, GLI, Jetta, Passat, Routan, Tiguan, Touareg **Engine:** 2.0L L4, 2.5L L5, 3.0L V6, 3.6L V6	**Throttle Actuator Control System - Forced Limited Power:** ECM power stage, Failure
DTC: P2107 **1T ECM, MIL: Yes** **Year:** 2011, 2012 **Model:** Beetle, CC, Eos, Golf, GTI, GLI, Jetta, Passat, Routan, Tiguan, Touareg **Engine:** 2.0L L4, 2.5L L5, 3.0L V6, 3.6L V6	**-ELECTRONIC THROTTLE CONTROL MODULE PROCESSOR:** With the ignition on and the ETC Motor is not in Limp Home mode. When the Powertrain Control Module (PCM) detects an internal error or a short between the ETC Motor - and ETC Motor + circuits in the ETC Motor Driver. One trip fault. ETC light is flashing.
DTC: P2108 **2T ECM, MIL: Yes** **Year:** 2011, 2012 **Model:** Beetle, CC, Eos, Golf, GTI, GLI, Jetta, Passat, Routan, Tiguan, Touareg **Engine:** 2.0L L4, 2.5L L5, 3.0L V6, 3.6L V6	**Throttle Actuator Control Module Performance:** * Ignition on * ECT > 5.3° C * Engine speed, 0 RPM * IAT, > 5.3° C * Vehicle speed, 0 Km/h
DTC: P2110 **1T ECM, MIL: Yes** **Year:** 2011, 2012 **Model:** Beetle, CC, Eos, Golf, GTI, GLI, Jetta, Passat, Routan, Tiguan, Touareg **Engine:** 2.0L L4, 2.5L L5, 3.0L V6, 3.6L V6	**ELECTRONIC THROTTLE CONTROL - FORCED LIMITED RPM:** Ignition on and ETC motor is working. When the Powertrain Control Module (PCM) requests to limit engine speed if PWM is too high for 25 seconds and before P2118 sets. One trip fault and the code will set within five seconds. ETC light is illuminated.
DTC: P2111 **1T ECM, MIL: Yes** **Year:** 2011, 2012 **Model:** Beetle, CC, Eos, Golf, GTI, GLI, Jetta, Passat, Routan, Tiguan, Touareg **Engine:** 2.0L L4, 2.5L L5, 3.0L V6, 3.6L V6	**-ELECTRONIC THROTTLE CONTROL - UNABLE TO CLOSE:** Ignition on and battery voltage greater than 10 Volts. Just after key on, the throttle is opened and closed to test the system. If the TP Sensor does not return to Limp Home Position at the end of this test, this DTC will set. One trip fault and the code will set within five seconds. ETC light is flashing.

DTC	Trouble Code Title and Conditions
DTC: P2112 **1T ECM, MIL: Yes** **Year:** 2011, 2012 **Model:** Beetle, CC, Eos, Golf, GTI, GLI, Jetta, Passat, Routan, Tiguan, Touareg **Engine:** 2.0L L4, 2.5L L5, 3.0L V6, 3.6L V6	**ELECTRONIC THROTTLE CONTROL - UNABLE TO OPEN:** Ignition on and battery voltage greater than 10 Volts. Just after key on, the throttle is opened and closed to test the system. If the TP Sensor does not return to Limp Home Position at the end of this test, this DTC will set. One trip fault and the code will set within five seconds. ETC light is flashing.
DTC: P2115 **2T ECM, MIL: Yes** **Year:** 2011, 2012 **Model:** Beetle, CC, Eos, Golf, GTI, GLI, Jetta, Passat, Routan, Tiguan, Touareg **Engine:** 2.0L L4, 2.5L L5, 3.0L V6, 3.6L V6	**ACCELERATOR PEDAL POSITION SENSOR 1 MINIMUM STOP PERFORMANCE:** Ignition on. During in plant mode the APP Sensors need to be checked to make sure that the idle and full pedal travel can be reached on both sensors. The test for P2115 is only enabled once test for P2166 has passed. APPS No.1 has failed to achieve the required minimum value during In Plant testing. One trip fault and the code will set within five seconds. Engine will only idle. ETC light is illuminated.
DTC: P2116 **2T ECM, MIL: Yes** **Year:** 2011, 2012 **Model:** Beetle, CC, Eos, Golf, GTI, GLI, Jetta, Passat, Routan, Tiguan, Touareg **Engine:** 2.0L L4, 2.5L L5, 3.0L V6, 3.6L V6	**-ACCELERATOR PEDAL POSITION SENSOR 2 MINIMUM STOP PERFORMANCE:** Ignition on. During in plant mode the APP Sensors need to be checked to make sure that idle and full pedal travel can be reached on both sensors. The test for P2116 is only enabled once test for P2167 has passed. APPS No.2 has failed to achieve the required minimum value during In Plant testing. One trip fault and the code will be stored within 5 seconds. Engine will only idle. ETC light is illuminated.
DTC: P2118 **2T ECM, MIL: Yes** **Year:** 2011, 2012 **Model:** Beetle, CC, Eos, Golf, GTI, GLI, Jetta, Passat, Routan, Tiguan, Touareg **Engine:** 2.0L L4, 2.5L L5, 3.0L V6, 3.6L V6	**-ELECTRONIC THROTTLE CONTROL MOTOR CIRCUIT:** With the ignition on and the ETC Motor is not in Limp Home mode. When the Powertrain Control Module (PCM) detects an internal error or a short between the ETC Motor- and ETC Motor + circuits in the ETC Motor Driver. One trip fault. ETC light is flashing.
DTC: P2122 **2T ECM, MIL: Yes** **Year:** 2011, 2012 **Model:** Beetle, CC, Eos, Golf, GTI, GLI, Jetta, Passat, Routan, Tiguan, Touareg **Engine:** 2.0L L4, 2.5L L5, 3.0L V6, 3.6L V6	**ACCELERATOR PEDAL POSITION SENSOR 1 CIRCUIT LOW:** With the ignition on and no other APPS No.1 DTCs present. When the APP Sensor No.1 voltage is too low. Engine will additionally idle if the brake pedal is pressed or has failed. Acceleration rate and Engine output are limited. One trip fault and the code will set within five seconds. ETC light is flashing.
DTC: P2123 **1T ECM, MIL: Yes** **Year:** 2011, 2012 **Model:** Beetle, CC, Eos, Golf, GTI, GLI, Jetta, Passat, Routan, Tiguan, Touareg **Engine:** 2.0L L4, 2.5L L5, 3.0L V6, 3.6L V6	**-ACCELERATOR PEDAL POSITION SENSOR 1 CIRCUIT HIGH:** With the ignition on and no other APPS No.1 DTCs present. When APP Sensor No.1 voltage is too high. Engine will additionally idle if the brake pedal is pressed or has failed. Acceleration rate and Engine output are limited. One trip fault and the code will set within five seconds. ETC light is flashing.
DTC: P2127 **T1T ECM, MIL: Yes** **Year:** 2011, 2012 **Model:** Beetle, CC, Eos, Golf, GTI, GLI, Jetta, Passat, Routan, Tiguan, Touareg **Engine:** 2.0L L4, 2.5L L5, 3.0L V6, 3.6L V6	**ACCELERATOR PEDAL POSITION SENSOR 2 CIRCUIT LOW:** With the ignition on and no other APPS No.2 DTCs present. When the APP Sensor No.2 voltage is too low. Engine will only idle if the brake pedal is pressed or has failed. Acceleration rate and Engine output are limited. One trip fault and the code will set within five seconds. ETC light is flashing.

DTC	Trouble Code Title and Conditions
DTC: P2128 **1T ECM, MIL: Yes** **Year:** 2011, 2012 **Model:** Beetle, CC, Eos, Golf, GTI, GLI, Jetta, Passat, Routan, Tiguan, Touareg **Engine:** 2.0L L4, 2.5L L5, 3.0L V6, 3.6L V6	**-ACCELERATOR PEDAL POSITION SENSOR 2 CIRCUIT HIGH:** With the ignition on and no other APPS No.2 DTCs present. When APP Sensor No.2 voltage is too high. Idle is additionally forced any time the brake is applied or failed. Acceleration rate and Engine output are limited. One trip fault and the code will set within five seconds. ETC light is flashing.
DTC: P2133 **1T ECM, MIL: Yes** **Year:** 2011, 2012 **Model:** Beetle, CC, Eos, Golf, GTI, GLI, Jetta, Passat, Routan, Tiguan, Touareg **Engine:** 2.0L L4, 2.5L L5, 3.0L V6, 3.6L V6	**Throttle/Pedal Position Sensor / Switch "F" Circuit High Input:** The Powertrain Control Module (PCM) recognizes TP Sensors No.1 and No.2 are not coherent. One trip fault and the code will set within five seconds. ETC light is illuminated.
DTC: P2135 **1T ECM, MIL: Yes** **Year:** 2011, 2012 **Model:** Beetle, CC, Eos, Golf, GTI, GLI, Jetta, Passat, Routan, Tiguan, Touareg **Engine:** 2.0L L4, 2.5L L5, 3.0L V6, 3.6L V6	**-THROTTLE POSITION SENSOR 1/2 CORRELATION:** With the ignition on and no other DTCs present for TP Sensor No.1 or No.2. The Powertrain Control Module (PCM) recognizes TP Sensors No.1 and No.2 are not coherent. One trip fault and the code will set within five seconds. ETC light is illuminated.
DTC: P2138 **1T ECM, MIL: Yes** **Year:** 2011, 2012 **Model:** Beetle, CC, Eos, Golf, GTI, GLI, Jetta, Passat, Routan, Tiguan, Touareg **Engine:** 2.0L L4, 2.5L L5, 3.0L V6, 3.6L V6	**-ACCELERATOR PEDAL POSITION SENSOR 1/2 CORRELATION:** With the ignition on and no APPS No.1 and APPS No.2 DTC present. APPS values No.1 and No.2 are not coherent. Idle is additionally forced when the brake pedal is pressed or failed. Acceleration rate and Engine output are limited. One trip fault and the code will set within five seconds. ETC light is flashing.
DTC: P2141 **1T ECM, MIL: Yes** **Year:** 2011, 2012 **Model:** Beetle, CC, Eos, Golf, GTI, GLI, Jetta, Passat, Routan, Tiguan, Touareg **Engine:** 2.0L L4, 2.5L L5, 3.0L V6, 3.6L V6	**EGR AIR FLOW CONTROL VALVE CIRCUIT LOW:** With the ignition on and the ECM EGR Air Flow Control Valve command off. The ECM detects a short ground on the EGR Air Flow Control Valve Control circuit for 0.5 second.
DTC: P2142 **1T ECM, MIL: Yes** **Year:** 2011, 2012 **Model:** Beetle, CC, Eos, Golf, GTI, GLI, Jetta, Passat, Routan, Tiguan, Touareg **Engine:** 2.0L L4, 2.5L L5, 3.0L V6, 3.6L V6	**EGR AIR FLOW CONTROL VALVE CIRCUIT HIGH:** With the ignition on and the ECM EGR Air Flow Control Valve command on. The ECM detects excessive current on the EGR Air Flow Control Valve Control circuit for 0.5 second.
DTC: P2146 **1T ECM, MIL: Yes** **Year:** 2011, 2012 **Model:** Beetle, CC, Eos, Golf, GTI, GLI, Jetta, Passat, Routan, Tiguan, Touareg **Engine:** 2.0L L4, 2.5L L5, 3.0L V6, 3.6L V6	**Fuel Injector Group A Supply Voltage Circuit / short to B+:** * Engine speed >80 RPM * low side signal current > 2.7 A

DTC	Trouble Code Title and Conditions
DTC: P2149 **1T ECM, MIL: Yes** **Year:** 2011, 2012 **Model:** Beetle, CC, Eos, Golf, GTI, GLI, Jetta, Passat, Routan, Tiguan, Touareg **Engine:** 2.0L L4, 2.5L L5, 3.0L V6, 3.6L V6	**Fuel Injector Group B Supply Voltage Circuit Open:** * Engine speed > 80 RPM * Low side signal current > 2.70 A
DTC: P2152 **2T ECM, MIL: Yes** **Year:** 2011, 2012 **Model:** Routan, Touareg **Engine:** 3.0L V6, 3.6L V6	**Fuel Injector Group "C" Supply Voltage Circuit/Open:** * Engine speed >80 RPM
DTC: P2155 **2T ECM, MIL: Yes** **Year:** 2011, 2012 **Model:** Routan, Touareg **Engine:** 3.0L V6, 3.6L V6	**Fuel Injector Group "D" Supply Voltage Circuit/Open:** * Injection valves, Commanded on * Engine speed >40 RPM * Low side signal current >2.7 A * Injection valve, commanded off * Engine speed >40 RPM
DTC: P2161 **12T ECM, MIL:** **Year:** 2011, 2012 **Model:** Routan, Touareg **Engine:** 3.0L V6, 3.6L V6	**VEHICLE SPEED SENSOR 2 ERRATIC:** Ignition on. The Powertrain Control Module (PCM) recognizes Vehicle speed input No.2 erratic or high. VSS No.2 is based on the average of the Front Wheel Speeds. One trip fault and the code will set within five seconds. No MIL and No ETC light. Cruise is disabled.
DTC: P2166 **1T ECM, MIL: Yes** **Year:** 2011, 2012 **Model:** Routan, Touareg **Engine:** 3.0L V6, 3.6L V6	**ACCELERATOR PEDAL POSITION SENSOR 1 MAXIMUM STOP PERFORMANCE:** Ignition on. During in plant mode the APP Sensors need to be checked to make sure that idle and full pedal travel can be reached on both sensors. APPS No.1 has failed to achieve the required maximum value during In Plant testing. One trip fault and the code will set within five seconds. Engine will only idle. ETC light will illuminate.
DTC: P2167 **1T ECM, MIL: Yes** **Year:** 2011, 2012 **Model:** Routan, Touareg **Engine:** 3.0L V6, 3.6L V6	**ACCELERATOR PEDAL POSITION SENSOR 2 MAXIMUM STOP PERFORMANCE:** Ignition on. During in plant mode the APP Sensors need to be checked to make sure that idle and full pedal travel can be reached on both sensors. APPS No.2 has failed to achieve the required maximum value during In Plant testing. One trip fault and the code will set within five seconds. Engine will only idle. ETC light will illuminate.
DTC: P2172 **1T ECM, MIL: Yes** **Year:** 2011, 2012 **Model:** Routan, Touareg **Engine:** 3.0L V6, 3.6L V6	**HIGH AIRFLOW/VACUUM LEAK DETECTED (INSTANTANEOUS ACCUMULATION):** Ignition on and engine running with no MAP Sensor DTCs. A large vacuum leak has been detected or the signal voltage for both TP Sensors is stuck at 2.5 volts and calculated MAP is less than actual MAP minus an offset value. One trip fault and the code will set within five seconds. ETC light will flash.
DTC: P2173 **1T ECM, MIL: Yes** **Year:** 2011, 2012 **Model:** Routan, Touareg **Engine:** 3.0L V6, 3.6L V6	**HIGH AIRFLOW/VACUUM LEAK DETECTED (SLOW ACCUMULATION):** Ignition on and engine running with no MAP Sensor DTCs. A large vacuum leak has been detected or the signal voltage for both TP Sensors is stuck at 2.5 Volts and calculated MAP is less than the Gas Flow Adaptation value. One trip fault; the DTC will set within five seconds. ETC light will flash.
DTC: P2174 **2T ECM, MIL: Yes** **Year:** 2011, 2012 **Model:** Routan, Touareg **Engine:** 3.0L V6, 3.6L V6	**LOW AIRFLOW/RESTRICTION DETECTED (INSTANTANEOUS ACCUMULATION):** Ignition on and engine running with no MAP Sensor DTCs. The Powertrain Control Module (PCM) detects that calculated MAP is greater than actual MAP plus an offset value. One trip fault and the code will set within 5 seconds. Three good trips to turn of the MIL. ETC light will flash.
DTC: P2175 **2T ECM, MIL: Yes** **Year:** 2011, 2012 **Model:** Routan, Touareg **Engine:** 3.0L V6, 3.6L V6	**LOW AIRFLOW/RESTRICTION DETECTED (SLOW ACCUMULATION):** Ignition on and engine running with no MAP Sensor DTCs. The Powertrain Control Module (PCM) detects that calculated MAP is greater than actual MAP plus an offset value. One trip fault and the code will set within 5 seconds. Three good trips to turn off the MIL. ETC light will flash.

DTC	Trouble Code Title and Conditions
DTC: P2177 **1T ECM, MIL: Yes** **Year:** 2011, 2012 **Model:** Beetle, CC, Eos, Golf, GTI, GLI, Jetta, Passat, Routan, Tiguan, Touareg **Engine:** 2.0L L4, 2.5L L5, 3.0L V6, 3.6L V6	**System too lean off idle, Bank 1:** * Engine speed 1280 - 6000 RPM * Engine load 20 - 100% * MAF 30 - 450 kg/h * ECT > 63 °C * IAT < 90 °C * Lambda control closed loop * EVAP purge closed
DTC: P2178 **2T ECM, MIL: Yes** **Year:** 2011, 2012 **Model:** Beetle, CC, Eos, Golf, GTI, GLI, Jetta, Passat, Routan, Tiguan, Touareg **Engine:** 2.0L L4, 2.5L L5, 3.0L V6, 3.6L V6	**System Too Rich off idle, Bank 1:** * Engine speed 1200 - 6000 RPM * Engine load 24 - 90% * Mass air flow 50 - 700 kg/h * ECT > 60 °C * IAT < 80 °C * Lambda control closed loop * EVAP purge valve closed
DTC: P2179 **2T ECM, MIL: Yes** **Year:** 2011, 2012 **Model:** Beetle, CC, Eos, Golf, GTI, GLI, Jetta, Passat, Routan, Tiguan, Touareg **Engine:** 2.0L L4, 2.5L L5, 3.0L V6, 3.6L V6	**System Too Lean off idle, Bank 2:** * Engine speed 1200 - 6000 RPM * Engine load 24 - 90% * Mass air flow 50 - 700 kg/h * ECT > 60 °C * IAT < 80 °C * Lambda control closed loop * EVAP purge valve closed * No low fuel signal
DTC: P2180 **2T ECM, MIL: Yes** **Year:** 2011, 2012 **Model:** Beetle, CC, Eos, Golf, GTI, GLI, Jetta, Passat, Routan, Tiguan, Touareg **Engine:** 2.0L L4, 2.5L L5, 3.0L V6, 3.6L V6	**System Too Rich off idle, Bank 2:** * Engine speed 1200 - 6000 RPM * Engine load 24 - 90% * Mass air flow 50 - 700 kg/h * ECT > 60 °C * IAT < 80 °C * Lambda control closed loop
DTC: P2181 **2T ECM, MIL: Yes** **Year:** 2011, 2012 **Model:** Beetle, CC, Eos, Golf, GTI, GLI, Jetta, Passat, Routan, Tiguan, Touareg **Engine:** 2.0L L4, 2.5L L5, 3.0L V6, 3.6L V6	**COOLING SYSTEM PERFORMANCE:** Ignition on, Engine running and no ECT DTCs present. The Powertrain Control Module (PCM) recognizes that the ECT Sensor has failed its self coherence test. The coolant temp should only change at a certain rate, if this rate is too slow or too fast this fault will set. Two trip fault. Three good trips to clear MIL. The MIL and ETC light will illuminate.
DTC: P2183 **2T ECM, MIL: Yes** **Year:** 2011, 2012 **Model:** Beetle, CC, Eos, Golf, GTI, GLI, Jetta, Passat, Routan, Tiguan, Touareg **Engine:** 2.0L L4, 2.5L L5, 3.0L V6, 3.6L V6	**Engine Coolant Temperature Sensor 2 Circuit Range/Performance:** * Engine off time > 32400 Sec. * IAT change after engine start < 5 °K * AAT change after engine start < 5 °K * Driving speed > 25 mph
DTC: P2183 **2T ECM, MIL: Yes** **Year:** 2011, 2012 **Model:** Beetle, CC, Eos, Golf, GTI, GLI, Jetta, Passat, Routan, Tiguan, Touareg **Engine:** 2.0L L4, 2.5L L5, 3.0L V6, 3.6L V6	**Engine Coolant Temperature Sensor 2 Circuit Range/Performance:** * Engine off time > 9 hr * Decrease of IAT and T2 < 5 °K at > 25 mph for 20 Sec. * Decrease of AAT after engine start < 5 °K for 60 Sec.

DTC	Trouble Code Title and Conditions
DTC: P2184 **2T ECM, MIL: Yes** **Year:** 2011, 2012 **Model:** Beetle, CC, Eos, Golf, GTI, GLI, Jetta, Passat, Routan, Tiguan, Touareg **Engine:** 2.0L L4, 2.5L L5, 3.0L V6, 3.6L V6	**Engine Coolant Temperature Sensor 2 Circuit Low:** ECT outlet >141 C.
DTC: P2185 **2T ECM, MIL: Yes** **Year:** 2011, 2012 **Model:** Beetle, CC, Eos, Golf, GTI, GLI, Jetta, Passat, Routan, Tiguan, Touareg **Engine:** 2.0L L4, 2.5L L5, 3.0L V6, 3.6L V6	**Engine Coolant Temperature Sensor 2 Circuit High:** * Engine off time > 9 hr * Decrease of IAT and T2 < 5 °K at > 25 mph for 20 Sec. * Decrease of AAT after engine start < 5 °K for 60 Sec.
DTC: P2187 **2T ECM, MIL: Yes** **Year:** 2011, 2012 **Model:** Beetle, CC, Eos, Golf, GTI, GLI, Jetta, Passat, Routan, Tiguan, Touareg **Engine:** 2.0L L4, 2.5L L5, 3.0L V6, 3.6L V6	**System too lean at idle, Bank 1:** * Engine load < 15% * Engine speed < 1000 RPM * Mass air flow < 50 kg/h * ECT > 60 °C * IAT < 80 °C * Delta part load adaptation ready * Lambda control, closed loop * EVAP purge valve closed * Low fuel signal not active
DTC: P2188 **2T ECM, MIL: Yes** **Year:** 2011, 2012 **Model:** Beetle, CC, Eos, Golf, GTI, GLI, Jetta, Passat, Routan, Tiguan, Touareg **Engine:** 2.0L L4, 2.5L L5, 3.0L V6, 3.6L V6	**System Too Rich On Idle Bank 1:** Engine started, battery voltage must be at least 11.5v, all electrical components must be off, the ground between the engine and the chassis must be well connected, the exhaust system must be properly sealed between the catalytic converter and the cylinder head, and the oxygen sensor heater for oxygen sensor before the catalytic converter must be properly functioning. ECM detected the system indicated a rich signal, or it could no longer control bank 1 because it was at its rich limit.
DTC: P2189 **2T ECM, MIL: Yes** **Year:** 2011, 2012 **Model:** CC, Passat, Routan, Touareg **Engine:** 3.0L V6, 3.6L V6	**System too lean at idle, Bank 2:** * Engine load < 15% * Engine speed < 1000 RPM * Mass air flow < 50 kg/h * ECT > 60 °C * IAT < 80 °C * Delta part load adaptation ready * Lambda control, closed loop * EVAP purge valve closed * Low fuel signal not active
DTC: P2190 **2T ECM, MIL: Yes** **Year:** 2011, 2012 **Model:** CC, Passat, Routan, Touareg **Engine:** 3.0L V6, 3.6L V6	**System too rich at idle, Bank 2:** * Engine load < 15% * Engine speed < 1000 RPM * Mass air flow < 50 kg/h * ECT > 60 °C * IAT < 80 °C * Delta part load adaptation ready * Lambda control, closed loop * EVAP purge valve closed * Low fuel signal not active

DTC	Trouble Code Title and Conditions
DTC: P2191 **2T ECM, MIL: Yes** **Year:** 2011, 2012 **Model:** Beetle, CC, Eos, Golf, GTI, GLI, Jetta, Passat, Routan, Tiguan, Touareg **Engine:** 2.0L L4, 2.5L L5, 3.0L V6, 3.6L V6	**System Too Lean at Higher Load; Bank 1:** * Part load adaptation range: * Engine speed – 1320-5000 RPM. * Engine load –20.25 - 80.25%. * Air mass – 35-150 k g/h. * Higher load adaptation range: Engine load ->54.75%. * Air mass – 200 kg /h
DTC: P2192 **2T ECM, MIL: Yes** **Year:** 2011, 2012 **Model:** Beetle, CC, Eos, Golf, GTI, GLI, Jetta, Passat, Routan, Tiguan, Touareg **Engine:** 2.0L L4, 2.5L L5, 3.0L V6, 3.6L V6	**System Too Rich at Higher Load; Bank 1:** * Part load adaptation range: * Engine speed – 1320-5000 RPM. * Engine load –20.25-80.25%. * Air mass – 35-150 k g/h. * Higher load adaptation range: Engine load ->54.75%. * Air mass – 200 kg /h
DTC: P2195 **2T ECM, MIL: Yes** **Year:** 2011, 2012 **Model:** Beetle, CC, Eos, Golf, GTI, GLI, Jetta, Passat, Routan, Tiguan, Touareg **Engine:** 2.0L L4, 2.5L L5, 3.0L V6, 3.6L V6	**O2 Sensor Signal Biased/Stuck Lean - Bank 1, Sensor 1:** * Modeled exhaust gas temp 400 - 880 °C * Delta engine load < 20% * Exh. gas mass flow 20 - 180 kg/h * Exhaust mass air integral 0.28 - 5.0kg * Lambda control, 2nd lambda control, closed loop * O2S front, rear and heaters ready - no fault * Fuel cutoff, catalyst heating, SAI - not active * 1st lambda control loop not at min or max * 2nd lambda control loop active
DTC: P2196 **2T ECM, MIL: Yes** **Year:** 2011, 2012 **Model:** Beetle, CC, Eos, Golf, GTI, GLI, Jetta, Passat, Routan, Tiguan, Touareg **Engine:** 2.0L L4, 2.5L L5, 3.0L V6, 3.6L V6	**O2 Sensor Signal Biased/Stuck Rich - Bank 1, Sensor 1:** * Lambda control, Closed loop * Lambda control post cat, Closed loop * O2S front, Ready, No DTC * O2S rear, Ready, No DTC * Engine load changes, >7% * Catalyst temp, 350–850° C * Mass air flow, 38–250 kg/h
DTC: P2197 **2T ECM, MIL: Yes** **Year:** 2011, 2012 **Model:** Beetle, CC, Eos, Golf, GTI, GLI, Jetta, Passat, Routan, Tiguan, Touareg **Engine:** 2.0L L4, 2.5L L5, 3.0L V6, 3.6L V6	**O2 Sensor Signal Stuck Lean Bank 2 Sensor 1:** * Exhaust temp, 300–900° C * Engine load, <9% * Exhaust gas mass flow, 15–140 kg/h * Number of interrupts by acceleration enrichment, >40 * Lambda control, Closed loop * 2nd Lambda control, Closed loop
DTC: P2198 **2T ECM, MIL: Yes** **Year:** 2011, 2012 **Model:** Beetle, CC, Eos, Golf, GTI, GLI, Jetta, Passat, Routan, Tiguan, Touareg **Engine:** 2.0L L4, 2.5L L5, 3.0L V6, 3.6L V6	**O2 Sensor Signal Stuck Rich Bank 2 Sensor 1:** * Modeled exhaust gas temp 350 - 870 °C * Delta engine load < 6% * Exh. gas mass flow 20 - 110 kg/h * Lambda control, 2nd lambda control, closed loop * O2S front, rear and heaters ready - no fault * Fuel cutoff, catalyst heating, SAI - not active * 1st lambda control loop not at min or max * 2nd lambda control loop active
DTC: P2199 **2T ECM, MIL: Yes** **Year:** 2011 **Model:** Beetle, Eos, Golf, GTI, Jetta, Passat **Engine:** 2.0L L4	**Intake Air Temperature Sensor 1 / 2 Correlation:** Cold start detected

DTC	Trouble Code Title and Conditions
DTC: P219A **2T ECM, MIL: Yes** **Year:** 2011, 2012 **Model:** Routan, Touareg **Engine:** 3.0L V6, 3.6L V6	**AIR-FUEL RATIO CYLINDER IMBALANCE BANK 1:** Engine Coolant Temperature (ECT) is greater than 70 °C (158 °F), Engine run time of 90 seconds, engine RPM 1000 - 2700, engine load 30 - 90% and in flex fuel vehicles the Fuel Adaptive Learned must be completed. P113D is not set and the high frequency content of the O2 sensor exceeds a calibrated amount. Two Trip Fault. Three good trips to turn off the MIL.
DTC: P219B **2T ECM, MIL: Yes** **Year:** 2011, 2012 **Model:** Routan, Touareg **Engine:** 3.0L V6, 3.6L V6	**AIR-FUEL RATIO CYLINDER IMBALANCE BANK 2:** Engine Coolant Temperature (ECT) is greater than 70 °C (158 °F), Engine run time of 90 seconds, engine RPM 1000 - 2700, engine load 30 - 90% and in flex fuel vehicles the Fuel Adaptive Learned must be completed. P113E is not set and the high frequency content of the O2 sensor exceeds a calibrated amount. Two Trip Fault. Three good trips to turn off the MIL.
DTC: P2201 **2T ECM, MIL: Yes** **Year:** 2011, 2012 **Model:** Routan, Touareg **Engine:** 3.0L V6, 3.6L V6	**NOx Sensor Circuit Range/Performance Bank 1 Sensor 1:** * NOx sensor heater control = active * Fuel cutoff = active * DPF regeneration = not active * Time since last DPF regeneration > 60 Sec. * Fuel quantity > 10 mg/stroke * Air mass = 250 - 450 mg/stroke * EGR sensor closed or position 70 - 90% * Engine speed 1300 - 1800 rpm * ECT > 65 °C * Exhaust gas temp upstream catalyst > 80 °C
DTC: P2202 **2T ECM, MIL: Yes** **Year:** 2011, 2012 **Model:** Routan, Touareg **Engine:** 3.0L V6, 3.6L V6	**NOx Sensor Bank 1 Sensor 1 Circuit Low:** * Dew point exceeded * NOx control = active
DTC: P2203 **2T ECM, MIL: Yes** **Year:** 2011, 2012 **Model:** Routan, Touareg **Engine:** 3.0L V6, 3.6L V6	**NOx Sensor Bank 1 Sensor 1 Circuit High:** * Dew point exceeded * NOx control = active
DTC: P2209 **2T ECM, MIL: Yes** **Year:** 2011, 2012 **Model:** Routan, Touareg **Engine:** 3.0L V6, 3.6L V6	**NOx Sensor Heater Sense Bank 1 Sensor 1 Circuit Range/Performance:** * Exhaust temperature upstream SCR = 100 - 600 °C * Dew point exceeded
DTC: P220A **2T ECM, MIL: Yes** **Year:** 2011, 2012 **Model:** Routan, Touareg **Engine:** 3.0L V6, 3.6L V6	**NOx Sensor Supply Voltage Bank 1 Sensor 1 Circuit:** * Dew point exceeded
DTC: P220B **2T ECM, MIL: Yes** **Year:** 2011, 2012 **Model:** Routan, Touareg **Engine:** 3.0L V6, 3.6L V6	**NOx Sensor Supply Voltage Bank 1 Sensor 2 Circuit:** * Dew point exceeded
DTC: P2231 **2T ECM, MIL: Yes** **Year:** 2011, 2012 **Model:** Beetle, CC, Eos, Golf, GTI, GLI, Jetta, Passat, Routan, Tiguan, Touareg **Engine:** 2.0L L4, 2.5L L5, 3.0L V6, 3.6L V6	**O2 Sensor Signal Circuit Shorted to Heater Circuit:** * Battery voltage, 10.7-16.1 V * Engine speed, >25 RPM * Modeled exhaust, <800° C * Temp. lambda control, Closed loop * Heater control, Active * Heater power, 20-80% * Desired lambda, =1 * Actual lambda value, 0-16%

DTC	Trouble Code Title and Conditions
DTC: P2234 **2T ECM, MIL: Yes** **Year:** 2011, 2012 **Model:** Beetle, CC, Eos, Golf, GTI, GLI, Jetta, Passat, Routan, Tiguan, Touareg **Engine:** 2.0L L4, 2.5L L5, 3.0L V6, 3.6L V6	**O2 Sensor Signal Circuit Shorted to Heater Circuit Bank 2 Sensor 1:** * Modeled exhaust gas temp, <800 °C * Heater duty cycle, >5% * Delta engine load, <3.0% * For at least, 0.5 Sec. * Catalyst heating, Not active * SAI, Not active
DTC: P2237 **2T ECM, MIL: Yes** **Year:** 2011, 2012 **Model:** Beetle, CC, Eos, Golf, GTI, GLI, Jetta, Passat, Routan, Tiguan, Touareg **Engine:** 2.0L L4, 2.5L L5, 3.0L V6, 3.6L V6	**O2 Sensor Positive Current Control Circuit / Open - Bank 1, Sensor 1:** * O2S ceramic temp, >715° C * Lambda control, Closed loop * Mass air integral, 0.8 kg * Lambda set value, 0.97 . . . 1.03 * O2S ceramic temp, >715 °C * electrical adjustment, not active * Heater control, active * EVAP purge valve, ready no fault * O2S ceramic temp, >715° C * Lambda modulation >0.02 * Lambda control, Closed loop *Heater control, active
DTC: P2238 **2T ECM, MIL: Yes** **Year:** 2011, 2012 **Model:** Beetle, CC, Eos, Golf, GTI, GLI, Jetta, Passat, Routan, Tiguan, Touareg **Engine:** 2.0L L4, 2.5L L5, 3.0L V6, 3.6L V6	**LSU Wire Signal Range Check Circuit Low (BEW Only):** * Virtual Mass (VM) < 2 V * Nernst voltage (UN) < 1.75 V * Adjustment voltage (IP) < 0.3 V
DTC: P2239 **2T ECM, MIL: Yes** **Year:** 2011, 2012 **Model:** Beetle, CC, Eos, Golf, GTI, GLI, Jetta, Passat, Routan, Tiguan, Touareg **Engine:** 2.0L L4, 2.5L L5, 3.0L V6, 3.6L V6	**O2 Sensor Positive Current Control Circuit High Bank 1 Sensor 1:** Engine started, battery voltage must be at least 11.5v, all electrical components must be off, parking brake must be engaged (to keep daytime driving lights off), and automatic transmission selector must be in park. The ECM detected an unexpected voltage condition, or it detected an unexpected current draw in the sensor circuit during the CCM test. **Note: Vehicle must be raised before connector for oxygen sensors is accessible.**
DTC: P2240 **2T ECM, MIL: Yes** **Year:** 2011, 2012 **Model:** Beetle, CC, Eos, Golf, GTI, GLI, Jetta, Passat, Routan, Tiguan, Touareg **Engine:** 2.0L L4, 2.5L L5, 3.0L V6, 3.6L V6	**O2 Sensor Positive Current Control Circuit/Open Bank 2 Sensor 1:** * O2S ceramic temperature, >720° C * Electrical adjustment, Not active * Heater control, Closed loop * EVAP purge valve, Ready, no fault * O2S ceramic temperature, >720° C * Lambda modulation, >0.017 * Lambda control, Closed loop * Heater control, Closed loop
DTC: P2243 **2T ECM, MIL: Yes** **Year:** 2011, 2012 **Model:** Beetle, CC, Eos, Golf, GTI, GLI, Jetta, Passat, Routan, Tiguan, Touareg **Engine:** 2.0L L4, 2.5L L5, 3.0L V6, 3.6L V6	**O2 Sensor Reference Voltage Circuit / Open - Bank 1, Sensor 1:** * Heater control active * Fuel cutoff

DTC	Trouble Code Title and Conditions
DTC: P2245 **2T ECM, MIL: Yes** **Year:** 2011, 2012 **Model:** Beetle, CC, Eos, Golf, GTI, GLI, Jetta, Passat, Routan, Tiguan, Touareg **Engine:** 2.0L L4, 2.5L L5, 3.0L V6, 3.6L V6	**O2 SENSOR 1/1, 2/1 REFERENCE VOLTAGE CIRCUIT LOW:** Continuously after 15 seconds of engine runtime, no O2 sensor heater DTCs present and battery voltage greater than 10.4 Volts. The Oxygen Sensor reference voltage is below 0.9 of a Volt for 60 seconds. The DTC will set as Pending after one trip and Active after two trips. Three good trips to turn off the MIL.
DTC: P2246 **2T ECM, MIL: Yes** **Year:** 2011, 2012 **Model:** Jetta, Passat **Engine:** 2.0L L4, 2.5L L5	**O2 Sensor Reference Voltage Circuit High Bank 1 Sensor 1:** Engine started, battery voltage must be at least 11.5v, all electrical components must be off, parking brake must be engaged (to keep daytime driving lights off), and automatic transmission selector must be in park. The ECM detected an unexpected voltage condition, or it detected an unexpected current draw in the sensor circuit during the CCM test.
DTC: P2246 **2T ECM, MIL: Yes** **Year:** 2012 **Model:** Beetle, Golf, GTI **Engine:** 2.0L L4, 2.5L L5	**LSU Wire Signal Range Check. Short To Battery (BEW Only):** * Virtual Mass (VM) > 3 V * Nernst voltage (UN) > 4 V * Adjustment voltage
DTC: P2246 **2T ECM, MIL: Yes** **Year:** 2011, 2012 **Model:** Beetle, CC, Eos, Golf, GTI, GLI, Jetta, Passat, Routan, Tiguan, Touareg **Engine:** 2.0L L4, 2.5L L5, 3.0L V6, 3.6L V6	**O2 SENSOR 1/1, 2/1 REFERENCE VOLTAGE CIRCUIT HIGH:** Engine running for 15 seconds, O2 Sensors at operating temperature and battery voltage greater 10.4 Volts. The PCM detects that the (K902) Reference Signal voltage is greater than 3.9 Volts for nine seconds.
DTC: P2247 **2T ECM, MIL: Yes** **Year:** 2011, 2012 **Model:** Beetle, CC, Eos, Golf, GTI, GLI, Jetta, Passat, Routan, Tiguan, Touareg **Engine:** 2.0L L4, 2.5L L5, 3.0L V6, 3.6L V6	**O2 Sensor Reference Voltage Circuit/Open Bank 2 Sensor 1:** Heater control, Active
DTC: P2251 **2T ECM, MIL: Yes** **Year:** 2011, 2012 **Model:** Beetle, CC, Eos, Golf, GTI, GLI, Jetta, Passat, Routan, Tiguan, Touareg **Engine:** 2.0L L4, 2.5L L5, 3.0L V6, 3.6L V6	**O2 Sensor Negative Current Control Circuit/Open (Bank 1, Sensor 1):** * Heater control, active * Modeled exhaust gas temp. < 750° C * No fuel cut off, >2 Sec
DTC: P2252 **2T ECM, MIL: Yes** **Year:** 2011, 2012 **Model:** Beetle, CC, Eos, Golf, GTI, GLI, Jetta, Passat, Routan, Tiguan, Touareg **Engine:** 2.0L L4, 2.5L L5, 3.0L V6, 3.6L V6	**O2 Sensor Negative Current Control Circuit Bank 1 Sensor 1 Low:** * Heater control, active * Modeled exhaust gas temp. < 750° C * No fuel cut off, >2 Sec
DTC: P2253 **2T ECM, MIL: Yes** **Year:** 2011, 2012 **Model:** Beetle, CC, Eos, Golf, GTI, GLI, Jetta, Passat, Routan, Tiguan, Touareg **Engine:** 2.0L L4, 2.5L L5, 3.0L V6, 3.6L V6	**O2 Sensor Negative Current Control Circuit Bank 1 Sensor 1 High:** * Heater control, active * Modeled exhaust gas temp. < 750° C * No fuel cut off, >2 Sec

DTC	Trouble Code Title and Conditions
DTC: P2254 **2T ECM, MIL: Yes** **Year:** 2011, 2012 **Model:** Beetle, CC, Eos, Golf, GTI, GLI, Jetta, Passat, Routan, Tiguan, Touareg **Engine:** 2.0L L4, 2.5L L5, 3.0L V6, 3.6L V6	**O2 Sensor Negative Current Control Circuit/Open Bank 2 Sensor 1:** * Heater control, Active * Modeled exhaust gas temp, N.A. * No fuel cut off, >2 Sec.
DTC: P2254 **2T ECM, MIL: Yes** **Year:** 2011, 2012 **Model:** Beetle, CC, Eos, Golf, GTI, GLI, Jetta, Passat, Routan, Tiguan, Touareg **Engine:** 2.0L L4, 2.5L L5, 3.0L V6, 3.6L V6	**O2 Sensor Negative Current Control Circuit/Open Bank 2 Sensor 1:** * Modeled exhaust temp, * No fuel cut off, >2 Sec. * Heater control, Active
DTC: P2257 **2T ECM, MIL: Yes** **Year:** 2011, 2012 **Model:** Beetle, Eos, GTI, Jetta, Passat, Touareg **Engine:** 2.0L L4, 3.0L V6, 3.6L V6	**Air pump relay. short to grnd. PZEV only:** * pump relay commanded off * engine speed >80 RPM
DTC: P2257 **2T ECM, MIL: Yes** **Year:** 2011, 2012 **Model:** Beetle, CC, Eos, Golf, GTI, GLI, Jetta, Passat, Routan, Tiguan, Touareg **Engine:** 2.0L L4, 2.5L L5, 3.0L V6, 3.6L V6	**Secondary Air Injection System Control "A" Circuit Low:** * Pump relay commanded OFF * Engine speed > 80 RPM
DTC: P2258 **2T ECM, MIL: Yes** **Year:** 2011, 2012 **Model:** Beetle, CC, Eos, Golf, GTI, GLI, Jetta, Passat, Routan, Tiguan, Touareg **Engine:** 2.0L L4, 2.5L L5, 3.0L V6, 3.6L V6	**Secondary Air Injection System Control "A" Circuit High:** * Pump relay commanded on * Engine speed > 80 mph
DTC: P2266 **2T ECM, MIL: Yes** **Year:** 2011, 2012 **Model:** Beetle, CC, Eos, Golf, GTI, GLI, Jetta, Passat, Routan, Tiguan, Touareg **Engine:** 2.0L L4, 2.5L L5, 3.0L V6, 3.6L V6	**-WATER IN FUEL (WIF) SENSOR VOLTAGE TOO LOW:** Ignition on. Low voltage detected at the Water In Fuel (WIF) Sensor Signal circuit at the ECM.
DTC: P2270 **2T ECM, MIL: Yes** **Year:** 2011, 2012 **Model:** Beetle, CC, Eos, Golf, GTI, GLI, Jetta, Passat, Routan, Tiguan, Touareg **Engine:** 2.0L L4, 2.5L L5, 3.0L V6, 3.6L V6	**O2 Sensor Signal Stuck Lean Bank 1 Sensor 2:** * Mass air flow 25 to 150 kg/h * Modeled exhaust gas temp > 350 °C * 2nd lambda control closed loop

DTC	Trouble Code Title and Conditions
DTC: P2271 **2T ECM, MIL: Yes** **Year:** 2011, 2012 **Model:** Beetle, CC, Eos, Golf, GTI, GLI, Jetta, Passat, Routan, Tiguan, Touareg **Engine:** 2.0L L4, 2.5L L5, 3.0L V6, 3.6L V6	**-O2 SENSOR 1/2 SIGNAL STUCK RICH:** With the engine running, vehicle speed above 96 kph (60 mph), throttle open for a minimum of 120 seconds, ECT greater than 70° C (158° F), catalytic converter temperature greater than 600° C (1112° F) and downstream oxygen sensor in a rich state. During a decel fuel shutoff event, the downstream oxygen sensor should switch from rich to lean within a specific time. The PCM monitors the downstream O2 sensor. If the PCM does not detect a rich to lean switch within a specific time during a decel fuel shutoff event, the monitor will fail. Two trip fault. Three good trips to turn off the MIL.
DTC: P2272 **2T ECM, MIL: Yes** **Year:** 2011, 2012 **Model:** Beetle, CC, Eos, Golf, GTI, GLI, Jetta, Passat, Routan, Tiguan, Touareg **Engine:** 2.5L L5, 3.0L V6, 3.6L V6	**O2 Sensor Signal Stuck Lean Bank 2 Sensor 2:** * Mass air flow, 30–60 kh/h * Modeled exhaust gas temp, >350° C * O2S rear readiness, >30 Sec. * 2nd Lambda control, Closed loop
DTC: P2273 **2T** **Year:** 2011, 2012 **Model:** Golf, GTI **Engine:** 2.0L L4, 2.5L L5	**O2 Sensor Signal Stuck Rich Bank 2 Sensor 2:** * Mass air flow, 30–160 kh/h * Exhaust gas temp, >350° C * O2S rear readiness, >10 Sec. * Fuel cut off, >5 Sec. * 2nd Lambda control, Closed loop
DTC: P2273 **2T ECM, MIL: Yes** **Year:** 2011, 2012 **Model:** Beetle, CC, Eos, Golf, GTI, GLI, Jetta, Passat, Routan, Tiguan, Touareg **Engine:** 2.5L L5, 3.0L V6, 3.6L V6	**-O2 SENSOR 2/2 SIGNAL STUCK RICH:** With the engine running, vehicle speed above 96 kph (60 mph), throttle open for a minimum of 120 seconds, ECT greater than 70 C (158 F), catalytic converter temperature greater than 600° C (1112° F) and downstream oxygen sensor in a rich state. During a decel fuel shutoff event, the downstream oxygen sensor should switch from rich to lean within a specific time. The Powertrain Control Module (PCM) monitors the downstream O2 sensor. If the PCM does not detect a rich to lean switch within a specific time during a decel fuel shutoff event, the monitor will fail. Two trip fault. Three good trips to turn off the MIL.
DTC: P2274 **2T ECM, MIL: Yes** **Year:** 2011, 2012 **Model:** Beetle, CC, Eos, Golf, GTI, Jetta, Passat, Tiguan **Engine:** 2.0L L4, 2.5L L5	**O2 Sensor Signal Stuck Lean Bank 1 Sensor 3:** * Mass air flow 22 to 120 kg/h * Modeled exhaust gas temp > 350 °C * O2S rear readiness > 10 Sec. * 2nd lambda control - closed loop
DTC: P2275 **2T ECM, MIL: Yes** **Year:** 2011, 2012 **Model:** Beetle, CC, Eos, Golf, GTI, Jetta, Passat, Tiguan **Engine:** 2.0L L4, 2.5L L5	**O2 Sensor Signal Stuck Rich Bank 1 Sensor 3:** * Rich voltage enable >= 548 mV * O2S rear ready * Modeled exhaust gas temp > 350 °C * 2nd lambda control closed loop
DTC: P2279 **2T ECM, MIL: Yes** **Year:** 2011, 2012 **Model:** Beetle, CC, Eos, Golf, GTI, GLI, Jetta, Passat, Routan, Tiguan, Touareg **Engine:** 2.5L L5, 3.0L V6, 3.6L V6	**Intake Air System Leak:** * Time after engine start > 0 Sec. * Engine load < 191.25% * Mass air flow < 655.40 kg/h * ECT > -48.00 °C * IAT < 143 °C * Lambda control value < -15% * Duration of measurement > 4 Sec. * Veh speed < 15 km/h * Lambda control active * Number of checks, 3
DTC: P2293 **2T ECM, MIL: Yes** **Year:** 2011, 2012 **Model:** Beetle, CC, Eos, Golf, GTI, GLI, Jetta, Passat, Routan, Tiguan, Touareg **Engine:** 2.5L L5, 3.0L V6, 3.6L V6	**Fuel Pressure Regulator 2 Performance:** Fuel pressure regulator output value malfunction. * Time after engine start 3 Sec.

DTC	Trouble Code Title and Conditions
DTC: P2294 **2T ECM, MIL: Yes** **Year:** 2011, 2012 **Model:** Beetle, CC, Eos, Golf, GTI, GLI, Jetta, Passat, Routan, Tiguan, Touareg **Engine:** 2.5L L5, 3.0L V6, 3.6L V6	**Fuel Pressure Regulator 2 Control Circuit:** * Fuel control valve, Commanded Off * Fuel pump, Commanded On
DTC: P2295 **2T ECM, MIL: Yes** **Year:** 2011, 2012 **Model:** Beetle, CC, Eos, Golf, GTI, GLI, Jetta, Passat, Routan, Tiguan, Touareg **Engine:** 2.5L L5, 3.0L V6, 3.6L V6	**Fuel Pressure Regulator 2 Control Circuit Low:** * Engine speed > 80 RPM * Fuel control valve, Commanded Off * Fuel pump commanded ON
DTC: P2296 **2T ECM, MIL: Yes** **Year:** 2011, 2012 **Model:** Beetle, CC, Eos, Golf, GTI, GLI, Jetta, Passat, Routan, Tiguan, Touareg **Engine:** 2.5L L5, 3.0L V6, 3.6L V6	**Fuel Pressure Regulator 2 Control Circuit High:** * Battery voltage, >7.5 V * Valve, Commanded on * Fuel pump, Commanded on
DTC: P2299 **1T ECM, MIL: Yes** **Year:** 2011, 2012 **Model:** Beetle, CC, Eos, Golf, GTI, GLI, Jetta, Passat, Routan, Tiguan, Touareg **Engine:** 2.5L L5, 3.0L V6, 3.6L V6	**-BRAKE PEDAL POSITION/ACCELERATOR PEDAL POSITION INCOMPATIBLE:** Ignition on. No Break or APPS faults present. The PCM recognizes a brake application following the APPS showing a fixed pedal opening. Temporary or permanent. Internally the PCM will reduce the throttle opening below driver demand. One trip fault and the code will be set within five seconds. ETC light will illuminate, the light will only stay illuminated while DTC is active.
DTC: P229E **2T ECM, MIL: Yes** **Year:** 2011, 2012 **Model:** Routan, Touareg **Engine:** 3.0L V6, 3.6L V6	**NOx Sensor Bank 1 Sensor 2 Circuit:** * Exhaust temperature upstream SCR 100 - 600 °C * Measured A/F ratio (O2S) > 1 * NOx control = 1st activation * Dew point exceeded * Steady state condition (actual filtered A/F ratio (O2S)) 0 - 0.2 for > 5 Sec.
DTC: P229F **2T ECM, MIL: Yes** **Year:** 2011, 2012 **Model:** Routan, Touareg **Engine:** 3.0L V6, 3.6L V6	**NOx Sensor Circuit Range/Performance Bank 1 Sensor 2:** * NOx sensor heaters = active * NOx sensor upstream rationality check = tested * Engine speed 1000 - 3500 rpm * Time since engine start = 120 Sec. * Calculated exhaust gas mass flow < 150 kg/hr * Measured NOx value upstream < 175 ppm stable for 1 Sec. * Calculated exhaust mass flow > 400 kg/hr * OR measured NOx value upstream > 600 ppm for 2.5 Sec. * Zero fuel calibration = not active
DTC: P22A0 **2T ECM, MIL: Yes** **Year:** 2011, 2012 **Model:** Routan, Touareg **Engine:** 3.0L V6, 3.6L V6	**NOx Sensor Bank 1 Sensor 2 Circuit Low:** * Dew point exceeded * NOx control = active
DTC: P22A1 **2T ECM, MIL: Yes** **Year:** 2011, 2012 **Model:** Routan, Touareg **Engine:** 3.0L V6, 3.6L V6	**NOx Sensor Bank 1 Sensor 2 Circuit High:** * Dew point exceeded * NOx control = active
DTC: P22A7 **2T ECM, MIL: Yes** **Year:** 2011, 2012 **Model:** Routan, Touareg **Engine:** 3.0L V6, 3.6L V6	**NOx Sensor Heater Sense Bank 1 Sensor 2 Circuit Range/Performance:** * Exhaust temperature upstream SCR = 100 - 600 °C * Dew point exceeded

DTC	Trouble Code Title and Conditions
DTC: P2300 **1T ECM, MIL: Yes** **Year:** 2011, 2012 **Model:** Beetle, CC, Eos, Golf, GTI, GLI, Jetta, Passat, Routan, Tiguan, Touareg **Engine:** 2.5L L5, 3.0L V6, 3.6L V6	**Ignition Coil 1 or A Primary Control Circuit Low:** Battery voltage, 9-16 V, engine speed, 1400-5000 RPM. SW ignition counter diagnose not active.
DTC: P2301 **1T ECM, MIL: Yes** **Year:** 2011, 2012 **Model:** Beetle, CC, Eos, Golf, GTI, GLI, Jetta, Passat, Routan, Tiguan, Touareg **Engine:** 2.0L L4, 2.5L L5, 3.6L V6	**Ignition Coil 1 or A Primary Control Circuit High:** * Battery voltage, 9-16 V * Engine speed, 1400-5000 RPM * SW ignition counter diagnose not active
DTC: P2302 **1T ECM, MIL: Yes** **Year:** 2011, 2012 **Model:** Beetle, CC, Eos, Golf, GTI, GLI, Jetta, Passat, Routan, Tiguan, Touareg **Engine:** 2.0L L4, 2.5L L5, 3.6L V6	**IGNITION COIL 1 or A SECONDARY CIRCUIT - INSUFFICIENT IONIZATION:** Engine running and battery voltage greater than 10.0 Volts. If the Powertrain Control Module (PCM) detects that the secondary ignition burn time is incorrect, too short or not present, an error is detected. One Trip Fault. Three good trips to turn off the MIL.
DTC: P2303 **1T ECM, MIL: Yes** **Year:** 2011, 2012 **Model:** Beetle, CC, Eos, Golf, GTI, GLI, Jetta, Passat, Routan, Tiguan, Touareg **Engine:** 2.0L L4, 2.5L L5, 3.6L V6	**Ignition Coil 2 or B Primary Control Circuit Low:** * Engine speed, > 80 RPM
DTC: P2304 **1T ECM, MIL: Yes** **Year:** 2011, 2012 **Model:** Beetle, CC, Eos, Golf, GTI, GLI, Jetta, Passat, Routan, Tiguan, Touareg **Engine:** 2.0L L4, 2.5L L5, 3.6L V6	**Ignition Coil 2 or B Primary Control Circuit High:** * Engine speed > 80 RPM
DTC: P2305 **1T ECM, MIL: Yes** **Year:** 2011, 2012 **Model:** Beetle, CC, Eos, Golf, GTI, GLI, Jetta, Passat, Routan, Tiguan, Touareg **Engine:** 2.0L L4, 2.5L L5, 3.6L V6	**IGNITION COIL 2 or B SECONDARY CIRCUIT - INSUFFICIENT IONIZATION:** Engine running and battery voltage greater than 10.0 Volts. If Powertrain Control Module (PCM) detects that the secondary ignition burn time is incorrect, too short, or not present, an error is detected. One Trip Fault. Three good trips to turn off the MIL.
DTC: P2306 **1T ECM, MIL: Yes** **Year:** 2011, 2012 **Model:** Beetle, CC, Eos, Golf, GTI, GLI, Jetta, Passat, Routan, Tiguan, Touareg **Engine:** 2.0L L4, 2.5L L5, 3.6L V6	**Ignition Coil 3 or C Primary Control Circuit Low:** * Engine speed, > 80 RPM
DTC: P2307 **1T ECM, MIL: Yes** **Year:** 2011, 2012 **Model:** Beetle, CC, Eos, Golf, GTI, GLI, Jetta, Passat, Routan, Tiguan, Touareg **Engine:** 2.0L L4, 2.5L L5, 3.6L V6	**Ignition Coil 3 or C Primary Control Circuit High:** * Battery voltage, 9-16 V * Engine speed, 1400-5000 RPM * SW ignition counter diagnose not active

DTC	Trouble Code Title and Conditions
DTC: P2308 **1T ECM, MIL: Yes** **Year:** 2011, 2012 **Model:** Beetle, CC, Eos, Golf, GTI, GLI, Jetta, Passat, Routan, Tiguan, Touareg **Engine:** 2.0L L4, 2.5L L5, 3.6L V6	**IGNITION COIL 3 or C SECONDARY CIRCUIT - INSUFFICIENT IONIZATION:** Engine running and battery voltage greater than 10.0 Volts. If the Powertrain Control Module (PCM) detects that the secondary ignition burn time is incorrect, too short, or not present, an error is detected. One Trip Fault. Three good trips to turn off the MIL.
DTC: P2309 **1T ECM, MIL: Yes** **Year:** 2011, 2012 **Model:** Beetle, CC, Eos, Golf, GTI, GLI, Jetta, Passat, Routan, Tiguan, Touareg **Engine:** 2.0L L4, 2.5L L5, 3.6L V6	**Ignition Coil 4 or D Primary Control Circuit Low:** Engine speed >80 RPM
DTC: P2310 **1T ECM, MIL: Yes** **Year:** 2011, 2012 **Model:** Beetle, CC, Eos, Golf, GTI, GLI, Jetta, Passat, Routan, Tiguan, Touareg **Engine:** 2.5L L5, 3.6L V6	**Ignition Coil 4 or D Primary Control Circuit High:** * Battery voltage, 9-16 V * Engine speed, 1400-5000 RPM * SW ignition counter diagnose not active
DTC: P2311 **1T ECM, MIL: Yes** **Year:** 2011, 2012 **Model:** Beetle, CC, Eos, Golf, GTI, GLI, Jetta, Passat, Routan, Tiguan, Touareg **Engine:** 2.5L L5, 3.6L V6	**IGNITION COIL 4 or D SECONDARY CIRCUIT - INSUFFICIENT IONIZATION:** Engine running and battery voltage greater than 10.0 Volts. If the Powertrain Control Module (PCM) detects that the secondary ignition burn time is incorrect, too short or not present, an error is detected. One Trip Fault. Three good trips to turn off the MIL.
DTC: P2312 **1T ECM, MIL: Yes** **Year:** 2011, 2012 **Model:** Beetle, CC, Eos, Golf, GTI, GLI, Jetta, Passat, Routan, Tiguan, Touareg **Engine:** 2.5L L5, 3.6L V6	**Ignition Coil 5 or E Primary Control Circuit Low:** * Engine speed, > 80 RPM
DTC: P2313 **1T ECM, MIL: Yes** **Year:** 2011, 2012 **Model:** Beetle, CC, Eos, Golf, GTI, GLI, Jetta, Passat, Routan, Tiguan, Touareg **Engine:** 2.5L L5, 3.6L V6	**Ignition Coil 5 or E Primary Control Circuit High:** Engine speed >80 RPM
DTC: P2314 **1T ECM, MIL: Yes** **Year:** 2011, 2012 **Model:** Beetle, CC, Eos, Golf, GTI, GLI, Jetta, Passat, Routan, Tiguan, Touareg **Engine:** 2.5L L5, 3.6L V6	**IGNITION COIL E or 5 SECONDARY CIRCUIT - INSUFFICIENT IONIZATION:** Engine running and battery voltage greater than 10.0 Volts. If the Powertrain Control Module (PCM) detects that the secondary ignition burn time is incorrect, too short or not present, an error is detected. One Trip Fault. Three good trips to turn off the MIL.
DTC: P2315 **1T ECM, MIL: Yes** **Year:** 2011, 2012 **Model:** Beetle, CC, Eos, Golf, GTI, GLI, Jetta, Passat, Routan, Tiguan, Touareg **Engine:** 2.5L, 3.6L V6	**Ignition Coil F or 6 Primary Control Circuit Low:** Engine speed >80 RPM

DTC	Trouble Code Title and Conditions
DTC: P2317 **1T ECM, MIL: Yes** **Year:** 2011, 2012 **Model:** Beetle, CC, Eos, Golf, GTI, GLI, Jetta, Passat, Routan, Tiguan, Touareg **Engine:** 2.5L, 3.6L V6	**IGNITION COIL F or 6 SECONDARY CIRCUIT- INSUFFICIENT IONIZATION:** Engine running and battery voltage greater than 10.0 Volts. If the Powertrain Control Module (PCM) detects that the secondary ignition burn time is incorrect, too short or not present, an error is detected. One Trip Fault. Three good trips to turn off the MIL.
DTC: P2400 **1T ECM, MIL: Yes** **Year:** 2011, 2012 **Model:** Beetle, CC, Eos, Golf, GTI, GLI, Jetta, Passat, Routan, Tiguan, Touareg **Engine:** 2.0L L4, 2.5L L5, 3.6L V6	**Evaporative Emission System Leak Detection Pump Control Circuit/Open:** * LDP Commanded off * Engine speed > 80 RPM
DTC: P2401 **1T ECM, MIL: Yes** **Year:** 2011, 2012 **Model:** Beetle, CC, Eos, Golf, GTI, GLI, Jetta, Passat, Routan, Tiguan, Touareg **Engine:** 2.0L L4, 2.5L L5, 3.6L V6	**Evaporative Emission System Leak Detection Pump Control Circuit Low:** * LDP Commanded Off * Engine speed, 80 RPM
DTC: P2401 **2T ECM, MIL: Yes** **Year:** 2011, 2012 **Model:** Beetle, CC, Eos, Golf, GTI, GLI, Jetta, Passat, Routan, Tiguan, Touareg **Engine:** 2.0L L4, 2.5L L5, 3.6L V6	**Evaporative Emission System Leak Detection Pump Control Circuit Low:** * Pump, Commanded off * Engine speed, 80 RPM * Time after engine start, 1 Sec. * Battery voltage, 9.04-16 V
DTC: P2402 **2T ECM, MIL: Yes** **Year:** 2011, 2012 **Model:** Beetle, CC, Eos, Golf, GTI, GLI, Jetta, Passat, Routan, Tiguan, Touareg **Engine:** 2.0L L4, 2.5L L5, 3.6L V6	**Evaporative Emission System Leak Detection Pump Control Circuit High:** * LDP Commanded On * Engine speed, 80 RPM
DTC: P2403 **2T ECM, MIL: Yes** **Year:** 2011, 2012 **Model:** Beetle, CC, Eos, Golf, GTI, GLI, Jetta, Passat, Routan, Tiguan, Touareg **Engine:** 2.0L L4, 2.5L L5, 3.6L V6	**Evaporative Emission System Leak Detection Pump Sense Circuit Open:** * Time after engine start 5.0 - 65530 * ECT 3.8 - 120 °C * ECT at start 3.8 - 50.3 °C * Engine off time > 21600 * Altitude < 2700 m * Integrated purge flow 12.1 g * Restart temp diff > 0 °K * Veh speed >= 0 km/h * Veh speed once > 40 km/h
DTC: P2404 **2T ECM, MIL: Yes** **Year:** 2011, 2012 **Model:** Beetle, CC, Eos, Golf, GTI, GLI, Jetta, Passat, Routan, Tiguan, Touareg **Engine:** 2.0L L4, 2.5L L5, 3.6L V6	**Evaporative Emission System Leak Detection Pump Sense Range/Performance:** * Time after engine start, 7–1200 Sec. * ECT, 4.5-105° C * IAT, > 4.5-95.3° C * Altitude, <2700 m * Intake manifold vacuum, >140 hPa * Restart temperature difference, >48 K * Vehicle speed, 1st time 15, afterwards 0 km/h * Evap purge valve, Closed, ready, no fault

DTC	Trouble Code Title and Conditions
DTC: P2413 **2T ECM, MIL: Yes** **Year:** 2011, 2012 **Model:** Beetle, CC, Eos, Golf, GTI, GLI, Jetta, Passat, Routan, Tiguan, Touareg **Engine:** 2.0L L4, 2.5L L5, 3.6L V6	**Exhaust Gas Recirculation System Performance:** * Battery voltage, 9-16 V * Engine speed, 1400-5000 RPM
DTC: P2414 **2T ECM, MIL: Yes** **Year:** 2011, 2012 **Model:** Beetle, CC, Eos, Golf, GTI, GLI, Jetta, Passat, Routan, Tiguan, Touareg **Engine:** 2.0L L4, 2.5L L5, 3.6L V6	**O2 Sensor Exhaust Sample Error Bank 1, Sensor 1:** * Lambda set value 1 * Fuel cut off, Not active * Heater control, closed loop * SAI not active * O2S ceramic temp > 715 °C * If low fuel signal then wait > 600 Sec.
DTC: P2415 **2T ECM, MIL: Yes** **Year:** 2011, 2012 **Model:** Beetle, CC, Eos, Golf, GTI, GLI, Jetta, Passat, Routan, Tiguan, Touareg **Engine:** 2.0L L4, 2.5L L5, 3.6L V6	**O2 Sensor Exhaust Sample Error Bank 2 Sensor 1:** * Lambda set value, <1.6 * O2S ceramic temperature, >715° C * Fuel cut off, Not active * Heater control, closed loop * SAI, Not active * Low fuel signal On Than wait, >600 Sec.
DTC: P2422 **2T ECM, MIL: Yes** **Year:** 2011, 2012 **Model:** Beetle, CC, Eos, Golf, GTI, GLI, Jetta, Passat, Routan, Tiguan, Touareg **Engine:** 2.0L L4, 2.5L L5, 3.6L V6	**Evaporative Emission System Vent Valve Stuck Closed:** * Purge valve, OPEN * LDP-Activated * Altitude-<2.500 m * IAT, >5° C * Ambient pressure, >6 hPa * Reduction of intake air start: no deep downhill driving-vehicle speed at low load (<2%)
DTC: P2425 **2T ECM, MIL: Yes** **Year:** 2011, 2012 **Model:** Jetta, Passat **Engine:** 2.0L L4, 2.5L L5	**Exhaust Gas Recirculation (EGR) Cooler Switch-over Valve Open:** Output driver = OFF state
DTC: P2426 **2T ECM, MIL: Yes** **Year:** 2011, 2012 **Model:** Touareg **Engine:** 3.0L V6, 3.6L V6	**Exhaust Gas Recirculation Cooling Valve Control Circuit Low:** Power stage = Off state
DTC: P2427 **2T ECM, MIL: Yes** **Year:** 2011, 2012 **Model:** Touareg **Engine:** 3.0L V6, 3.6L V6	**Exhaust Gas Recirculation Cooling Valve Control Circuit High:** Power stage = On state
DTC: P242A **2T ECM, MIL: Yes** **Year:** 2011, 2012 **Model:** Golf, GTI, Jetta, Passat **Engine:** 2.0L L4, 2.5L L5	**Exhaust Gas Temperature Sensor Circuit Bank 1 Sensor 3:** * Engine start, Completed * Fuel cut off, Not active
DTC: P242B **2T ECM, MIL: Yes** **Year:** 2011, 2012 **Model:** Golf, GTI, Jetta, Passat **Engine:** 2.0L L4, 2.5L L5	**Exhaust Gas Temperature Sensor Circuit Bank 1 Sensor 3 Range/Performance:** * Engine run time > 3 min. * ECT > 10 °C * Simulated sensor temp > 225 °C * Engine off time > 32400 Sec. * Decrease of IAT after engine start < 5 °K * Decrease of AAT after engine start < 5 °K

DTC	Trouble Code Title and Conditions
DTC: P242C **2T ECM, MIL: Yes** **Year:** 2011, 2012 **Model:** Golf, GTI, Jetta, Passat **Engine:** 2.0L L4, 2.5L L5	**Exhaust Gas Temperature Sensor Circuit Low Bank 1 Sensor 3:** * Engine run time > 3 min. * ECT > 10 °C * Simulated sensor temp > 225 °C * Engine off time > 32400 Sec. * Decrease of IAT after engine start < 5 °K * Decrease of AAT after engine start < 5 °K
DTC: P242F **2T ECM, MIL: Yes** **Year:** 2011, 2012 **Model:** Routan **Engine:** 3.6L V6 VIN G	**-DIESEL PARTICULATE FILTER RESTRICTION - ASH ACCUMULATION:** With the engine running. The Differential Pressure Sensor signal indicates partial clogging of the particulate filter due to the accumulation of ash or other debris.
DTC: P2431 **2T ECM, MIL: Yes** **Year:** 2012 **Model:** Beetle, Golf, GTI **Engine:** 2.0L L4, 2.5L L5	**Secondary Air Injection System Air Flow/Pressure Sensor Circuit Range/Performance:** * Secondary Air Injection - done
DTC: P2432 **2T ECM, MIL: Yes** **Year:** 2011, 2012 **Model:** Golf, GTI, Jetta, Passat **Engine:** 2.0L L4, 2.5L L5	**Secondary Air Injection Sensor Circuit Low:** SAI completed
DTC: P2433 **2T ECM, MIL: Yes** **Year:** 2011, 2012 **Model:** Golf, GTI, Jetta, Passat **Engine:** 2.0L L4, 2.5L L5	**Secondary Air Injection Sensor Circuit High:** SAI completed
DTC: P2440 **2T ECM, MIL: Yes** **Year:** 2012 **Model:** Jetta **Engine:** 2.0L L4	**Secondary Air Injection System Switching Valve Stuck Open:** * ECT 5 - 115 °C * IAT 5 - 100 °C * Altitude < 2700 m * SAI press sensor ready, no fault
DTC: P2440 **2T ECM, MIL: Yes** **Year:** 2011, 2012 **Model:** Beetle, Eos, GTI, Jetta, Passat **Engine:** 2.0L L4	**System Check After SAI PZEV Only:** * ECT, 5 . . . 39° C * IAT, 5 . . . 40° C * altitude, <2700m * SAI pressure sensor, ready no fault
DTC: P2442 **2T ECM, MIL: Yes** **Year:** 2011 **Model:** Eos **Engine:** 2.0L L4	**Secondary Air Injection System Switching Valve Stuck Open Bank 2:** * ECT, 3-40° C * IAT, 3-60° C * Altitude, <2700 m * SAI Pressure Sensor, ready, no faults
DTC: P244C **2T ECM, MIL: Yes** **Year:** 2011, 2012 **Model:** Touareg **Engine:** 3.0L V6	**Exhaust Temperature Too Low For Particulate Filter Regeneration Bank 1:** * T5 < 350 °C * Engine speed > 1500 rpm * Fuel mass > 15 mg/stroke * Regeneration with post injection = On
DTC: P2453 **2T ECM, MIL: Yes** **Year:** 2011, 2012 **Model:** CC, Golf, GTI, Jetta, Passat Touareg **Engine:** 2.0L L4, 3.0L TDI V6	**Diesel Particulate Filter Differential Pressure Sensor Circuit Range/Performance:** Engine Off

DTC	Trouble Code Title and Conditions
DTC: P2458 **2T ECM, MIL: Yes** **Year:** 2011, 2012 **Model:** CC, Golf, GTI, Jetta, Passat Touareg **Engine:** 2.0L L4, 3.0L TDI V6	**Diesel Particulate Filter Regeneration Duration:** * PM trap regeneration = active * PM trap regeneration has ended successfully = true
DTC: P2459 **2T ECM, MIL: Yes** **Year:** 2011, 2012 **Model:** CC, Golf, GTI, Jetta, Passat Touareg **Engine:** 2.0L L4, 3.0L TDI V6	**Diesel Particulate Filter Regeneration Frequency:** * PM trap regeneration = not active * PM trap regeneration has occurred successful = true * PM trap regeneration = starting
DTC: P245B **2T ECM, MIL: Yes** **Year:** 2011, 2012 **Model:** CC, Golf, GTI, Jetta, Passat Touareg **Engine:** 2.0L L4, 3.0L TDI V6	**Exhaust Gas Recirculation Cooler Bypass Control Circuit Range/Performance:** * Engine speed = 1200 - 2500 rpm * Delta engine speed = + -250 rpm * Fuel quantity = 9 - 80 mg/stroke * Delta fuel quantity = + -20 mg/stroke * EGR valve > 0 85% * Delta EGR valve = + -15% * EGR mass flow > 30 kg/hr * SCR temp > 150 °C * EGR temp < 300 °
DTC: P2463 **2T ECM, MIL: Yes** **Year:** 2011, 2012 **Model:** CC, Golf, GTI, Jetta, Passat Touareg **Engine:** 2.0L L4, 3.0L TDI V6	**Diesel Particulate Filter - Soot Accumulation:** * Engine speed > 680 RPM or greater
DTC: P246E **2T ECM, MIL: Yes** **Year:** 2011, 2012 **Model:** Golf, GTI, Jetta, Passat **Engine:** 2.0L L4, 2.5L L5	**Exhaust Gas Temperature Sensor Circuit Bank 1 Sensor 4:** * Engine run time > 3 min. * ECT > 10 °C * Simulated sensor temp > 200 °C * Engine off time > 32400 Sec. * Decrease of IAT after engine start < 5 °K * Decrease of AAT after engine start < 5 °K
DTC: P246F **2T ECM, MIL: Yes** **Year:** 2011, 2012 **Model:** Golf, GTI, Jetta, Passat **Engine:** 2.0L L4, 2.5L L5	**Exhaust Gas Temperature Sensor Circuit Bank 1 Sensor 4 Range/Performance:** * Engine run time > 3 min. * ECT > 10 °C * Simulated sensor temp > 200 °C * Engine off time > 32400 Sec. * Decrease of IAT after engine start < 5 °K * Decrease of AAT after engine start < 5 °K
DTC: P2470 **2T ECM, MIL: Yes** **Year:** 2011, 2012 **Model:** Golf, GTI, Jetta, Passat **Engine:** 2.0L L4, 2.5L L5	**Exhaust Gas Temperature Sensor Circuit Low Bank 1 Sensor 4:** * Engine run time > 3 min. * ECT > 10 °C * Simulated sensor temp > 200 °C * Engine off time > 32400 Sec. * Decrease of IAT after engine start < 5 °K * Decrease of AAT after engine start < 5 °K
DTC: P2478 **2T ECM, MIL: Yes** **Year:** 2011, 2012 **Model:** Touareg **Engine:** 3.0L V6, 3.6L V6	**Exhaust Gas Temperature Out of Range Bank 1 Sensor 1:** * Regeneration from PM trap = On * Upstream turbine temperature > 350 °C * Desired post injection > 1 mg/stroke * Fuel quantity > 3 mg/stroke * Engine speed 1250 - 4000 RPM

DTC	Trouble Code Title and Conditions
DTC: P247A **2T ECM, MIL: Yes** **Year:** 2011, 2012 **Model:** Touareg **Engine:** 3.0L V6, 3.6L V6	**Exhaust Gas Temperature Out of Range Bank 1 Sensor 3:** * Regeneration with post injection = On * Temperature controller set value > 90 or < 10% * Fuel mass > 6 mg/stroke * Engine speed > 1000 RPM
DTC: P2503 **1T ECM, MIL: Yes** **Year:** 2011, 2012 **Model:** Routan **Engine:** 3.6L V6 VIN G	**-CHARGING SYSTEM OUTPUT LOW:** The engine running. The engine RPM is high enough to assure sufficient generator current output to satisfy the electrical loads. The battery sensed voltage is less than the target charging voltage, during engine operation, for a calibrate able amount of time. One Trip Fault. Generator light will illuminate.
DTC: P2504 **1T ECM, MIL: Yes** **Year:** 2011, 2012 **Model:** Routan **Engine:** 3.6L V6 VIN G	**-CHARGING SYSTEM OUTPUT HIGH:** The engine running. The engine speed greater than 1157 RPM. The alternator B+ voltage sense circuit voltage reading exceeds the direct Battery B+ sense circuit. The Generator Output terminal is not connected to the Battery B+ post. One trip fault.
DTC: P2533 **2T ECM, MIL: Yes** **Year:** 2011, 2012 **Model:** Routan **Engine:** 3.6L V6 VIN G	**IGNITION SWITCH RUN/START POSITION CIRCUIT:** With the ignition on and the battery voltage greater than 10.4 Volts. The Powertrain Control Module (PCM) detects and open or shorted condition in the Ignition Switch Run/Start circuit.
DTC: P2539 **2T ECM, MIL: Yes** **Year:** 2011, 2012 **Model:** Beetle, Eos, Golf, GTI, Jetta, Passat **Engine:** 2.0L L4, 2.5L L5	**Low Pressure Fuel System Sensor Circuit:** Signal voltage 4.9 V.
DTC: P2539 **2T ECM, MIL: Yes** **Year:** 2011, 2012 **Model:** Touareg **Engine:** 3.0L V6, 3.6L V6	**Low Pressure Fuel System Sensor Circuit:** Signal voltage 4.9 V.
DTC: P2540 **2T ECM, MIL: Yes** **Year:** 2011, 2012 **Model:** Beetle, Eos, Golf, GTI, Jetta, Passat **Engine:** 2.0L L4, 2.5L L5	**Low Pressure Fuel System Sensor Circuit Range/Performance:** Actual pressure deviation < 800 kPa <80 kPa.
DTC: P2540 **2T ECM, MIL: Yes** **Year:** 2011, 2012 **Model:** Touareg **Engine:** 3.0L V6, 3.6L V6	**Low Pressure Fuel System Sensor Circuit Range/Performance:** Signal voltage 0.2 V.
DTC: P2541 **2T ECM, MIL: Yes** **Year:** 2011, 2012 **Model:** Touareg **Engine:** 3.0L V6, 3.6L V6	**Low Pressure Fuel System Sensor Circuit Low:** Signal voltage 0.2 V.
DTC: P2541 **2T ECM, MIL: Yes** **Year:** 2011, 2012 **Model:** Beetle, Eos, Golf, GTI, Jetta, Passat **Engine:** 2.0L L4, 2.5L L5	**Low Pressure Fuel System Sensor Circuit Low:** Signal voltage 0.2 V.
DTC: P2541 **2T ECM, MIL: Yes** **Year:** 2011, 2012 **Model:** Beetle, Eos, GTI, Passat **Engine:** 2.0L L4	**Low Pressure Fuel System Sensor Circuit Low Input:** Signal voltage < 0.2 V.

DTC	Trouble Code Title and Conditions
DTC: P2563 **2T ECM, MIL: Yes** **Year:** 2011, 2012 **Model:** Golf, GTI, Jetta, Passat **Engine:** 2.0L L4, 2.5L L5	**Turbocharger Boost Control Position Sensor Circuit Range/Performance:** Engine running, turbo boost control sensor is out of range
DTC: P2564 **2T ECM, MIL: Yes** **Year:** 2011, 2012 **Model:** Golf, GTI, Jetta, Passat **Engine:** 2.0L L4, 2.5L L5	**Turbocharger Boost Control Position Sensor Circuit Low:** Engine running, turbo boost control sensor is out of range
DTC: P2565 **2T ECM, MIL: Yes** **Year:** 2011, 2012 **Model:** Golf, GTI, Jetta, Passat **Engine:** 2.0L L4, 2.5L L5	**Turbocharger Boost Control Position Sensor Circuit High:** Engine running, turbo boost control sensor is out of range.
DTC: P2568 **2T ECM, MIL: Yes** **Year:** 2011, 2012 **Model:** Beetle, Eos, Golf, GTI, Jetta, Passat **Engine:** 2.0L L4, 2.5L L5	**Direct Ozone Reduction Catalyst Temperature Sensor Circuit Range/Performance:** * Engine speed > 400 RPM * ECT at engine start < 35.3 °C
DTC: P2569 **2T ECM, MIL: Yes** **Year:** 2011, 2012 **Model:** Beetle, Eos, GTI, Jetta, Passat **Engine:** 2.0L L4	**RIS Sensor signal low PZEV only:** * N/A
DTC: P2569 **2T ECM, MIL: Yes** **Year:** 2011, 2012 **Model:** Golf, GTI, Jetta, Passat **Engine:** 2.0L L4, 2.5L L5	**Direct Ozone Reduction Catalyst Temperature Sensor Circuit Low:** * Engine speed > 400 RPM * ECT at engine start < 35.3 °C
DTC: P2570 **2T ECM, MIL: Yes** **Year:** 2011, 2012 **Model:** Beetle, Eos, GTI, Jetta, Passat **Engine:** 2.0L L4	**RIS Sensor signal always high PZEV only:** * N/A
DTC: P2570 **2T ECM, MIL: Yes** **Year:** 2011, 2012 **Model:** Golf, GTI, Jetta, Passat **Engine:** 2.0L L4, 2.5L L5	**Direct Ozone Reduction Catalyst Temperature Sensor Circuit High:** * Engine speed > 400 RPM * ECT at engine start < 35.3 °C
DTC: P258A **2T ECM, MIL: Yes** **Year:** 2011, 2012 **Model:** Routan **Engine:** 3.6L V6 VIN G	**ELECTRIC VACUUM PUMP CIRCUIT:** With ignition on. Battery voltage above 10.0 Volts. The actual EVP state is not equal to the desired EVP state. One Trip Fault. Three good trips to turn off the MIL.
DTC: P258B **2T ECM, MIL: Yes** **Year:** 2011, 2012 **Model:** Routan **Engine:** 3.6L V6 VIN G	**ELECTRIC VACUUM PUMP PERFORMANCE:** With the ignition on and engine running. Minimum Manifold Absolute Pressure (MAP) reading is 15 kpa (4.4 inHg). EVP minimum vacuum is -35 kpa (-10 inHg) and the EVP cannot create 3 kpa (1 inHg) or the system cannot increase the vacuum from -35 kpa (-10 inHg) to -38 kpa (-11 inHg). Two trip fault. Three good trips to turn off the MIL.

DTC	Trouble Code Title and Conditions
DTC: P2600 **2T ECM, MIL: Yes** **Year:** 2011, 2012 **Model:** Beetle, CC, Eos, Golf, GTI, Passat, Routan< Touareg **Engine:** 2.0L L4, 2.5L L5, 3.0L V6, 3.6L V6	**Coolant Pump Control Circuit/Open:** Open circuit, signal voltage 4.55-5.00V
DTC: P2602 **2T ECM, MIL: Yes** **Year:** 2011, 2012 **Model:** Beetle, CC, Eos, Golf, GTI, Passat, Routan< Touareg **Engine:** 2.0L L4, 2.5L L5, 3.0L V6, 3.6L V6	**Coolant Pump Control Circuit Low:** Short to ground, signal voltage 3.0V
DTC: P2603 **2T ECM, MIL: Yes** **Year:** 2011, 2012 **Model:** Beetle, CC, Eos, Golf, GTI, Passat, Routan< Touareg **Engine:** 2.0L L4, 2.5L L5, 3.0L V6, 3.6L V6	**Coolant Pump Control Circuit High:** Short to battery (+), signal current 0.61.2A
DTC: P2610 **2T ECM, MIL: Yes** **Year:** 2011, 2012 **Model:** Routan, Touareg **Engine:** 3.6L V6 VIN G	**ECM/PCM INTERNAL SHUTDOWN TIMER RATIONALITY TOO FAST:** With the engine running after a cycle when a complete engine warm up was achieved, the difference between engine coolant temperature and ambient air temperature greater than 10° C (50° F), after a minimum temperature drop of 10° C (50° F) during ignition off and battery voltage greater than 10 Volts. The Powertrain Control Module (PCM) detects that the engine coolant temperature drops a specified amount during the measured engine off time. Two trip fault. Three good trips to turn off the MIL.
DTC: P261A **2T ECM, MIL: Yes** **Year:** 2011, 2012 **Model:** Beetle, CC, Eos, Golf, GTI, Passat, Routan< Touareg **Engine:** 2.0L L4, 2.5L L5, 3.0L V6, 3.6L V6	**Coolant Pump "B" Control Circuit/Open:** * Pump speed = 50 - 90%
DTC: P261C **2T ECM, MIL: Yes** **Year:** 2011, 2012 **Model:** Beetle, CC, Eos, Golf, GTI, Passat, Routan< Touareg **Engine:** 2.0L L4, 2.5L L5, 3.0L V6, 3.6L V6	**Coolant Pump "B" Control Circuit Low:** * Pump speed = 50 - 90%
DTC: P261D **2T ECM, MIL: Yes** **Year:** 2011, 2012 **Model:** Beetle, CC, Eos, Golf, GTI, Passat, Routan< Touareg **Engine:** 2.0L L4, 2.5L L5, 3.0L V6, 3.6L V6	**Coolant Pump "B" Control Circuit High:** * Pump speed = 50 - 90%
DTC: P2626 **2T ECM, MIL: Yes** **Year:** 2011, 2012 **Model:** Beetle, CC, Eos, Golf, GTI, Passat, Routan< Touareg **Engine:** 2.0L L4, 2.5L L5, 3.0L V6, 3.6L V6	**O2 Sensor Pumping Current Trim Circuit/Open Bank 1 Sensor 1:** * Modeled exhaust gas temp. < 700 °C * O2S ceramic temperature, >720 °C * Fuel cut off, Active * Heater control, Closed loop * Low fuel signal On

DTC	Trouble Code Title and Conditions
DTC: P2626 **2T ECM, MIL: Yes** **Year:** 2011, 2012 **Model:** Beetle, CC, Eos, Golf, GTI, Passat, Routan< Touareg **Engine:** 2.0L L4, 2.5L L5, 3.0L V6, 3.6L V6	**O2 Sensor Pumping Current Trim Circuit/Open Bank 1 Sensor 1:** * O2S ceramic temp > 720 °C * Modeled exhaust temp, < 750 °C * Fuel cut off, Active * Heater control - closed loop * No low fuel signal
DTC: P2629 **2T ECM, MIL: Yes** **Year:** 2011, 2012 **Model:** Beetle, CC, Eos, Golf, GTI, Passat, Routan< Touareg **Engine:** 2.0L L4, 2.5L L5, 3.0L V6, 3.6L V6	**O2 Sensor Pumping Current Trim Circuit/Open Bank 2 Sensor 1:** * O2S ceramic temperature, >685 °C * Modeled exhaust gas temp, < 750 °C * Fuel cut off, Active * Engine speed, >25 RPM * Low fuel signal, On Than wait >600 Sec.
DTC: P2632 **2T ECM, MIL: Yes** **Year:** 2011, 2012 **Model:** Beetle, CC, Eos, Golf, GTI, Passat, Routan< Touareg **Engine:** 2.0L L4, 2.5L L5, 3.0L V6, 3.6L V6	**Fuel Pump "B" Control Circuit Open:** Power stage = Off
DTC: P2633 **2T ECM, MIL: Yes** **Year:** 2011, 2012 **Model:** Beetle, CC, Eos, Golf, GTI, Passat, Routan< Touareg **Engine:** 2.0L L4, 2.5L L5, 3.0L V6, 3.6L V6	**Fuel Pump "B" Control Circuit Low:** Output driver Off
DTC: P2634 **2T ECM, MIL: Yes** **Year:** 2011, 2012 **Model:** Beetle, CC, Eos, Golf, GTI, Passat, Routan< Touareg **Engine:** 2.0L L4, 2.5L L5, 3.0L V6, 3.6L V6	**Fuel Pump "B" Control Circuit High:** Power stage = On
DTC: P2637 **2T ECM, MIL: Yes** **Year:** 2011, 2012 **Model:** Beetle, CC, Eos, Golf, GTI, Passat, Routan< Touareg **Engine:** 2.0L L4, 2.5L L5, 3.0L V6, 3.6L V6	**Torque management Feedback Signal "A":** * Ignition, on * CAN Bus, OK * DME CAN connection, OK
DTC: P2637 **2T ECM, MIL: Yes** **Year:** 2011, 2012 **Model:** Beetle, CC, Eos, Golf, GTI, Passat, Routan< Touareg **Engine:** 2.0L L4, 2.5L L5, 3.0L V6, 3.6L V6	**Engine Torque Signal A:** * CAN bus, active * ECU communication, active * ECU data update, active
DTC: P2714 **2T TCM, MIL: Yes** **Year:** 2011, 2012 **Model:** Beetle, Eos, Golf, GTI, Jetta, Passat, Touareg **Engine:** 2.0L L4, 2.5L L5, 3.0L V6, 3.6L V6	**Pressure Control Solenoid "D" Performance or Stuck off:** * Low side and high side FET, Activated * Power supply, > 9 V * Voltage drop at FET, < = 1 V * Solenoid supply, > 9 V

DTC	Trouble Code Title and Conditions
DTC: P2715 **2T TCM, MIL: Yes** **Year:** 2011, 2012 **Model:** Beetle, Eos, Golf, GTI, Jetta, Passat, Touareg **Engine:** 2.0L L4, 2.5L L5, 3.0L V6, 3.6L V6	**Pressure Control Solenoid "D" Stuck On:** * Low side and high side FET, Activated * Power supply, > 9 V * Voltage drop at FET, < = 1 V * Solenoid supply, > 9 V
DTC: P2716 **2T TCM, MIL: Yes** **Year:** 2011, 2012 **Model:** Beetle, Eos, Golf, GTI, Jetta, Passat, Touareg **Engine:** 2.0L L4, 2.5L L5, 3.0L V6, 3.6L V6	**Pressure Control Solenoid "D" Electrical:** * Main solenoid switch, On * Linear feedback current, > 23 mA (AD:15) < 1333 mA (AD:1000)
DTC: P2723 **2T TCM, MIL: Yes** **Year:** 2011, 2012 **Model:** Beetle, Eos, Golf, GTI, Jetta, Passat, Touareg **Engine:** 2.0L L4, 2.5L L5, 3.0L V6, 3.6L V6	**Pressure Control Solenoid "E" Performance or Stuck off:** * Low side and high side FET, Activated * Power supply, > 9 V * Voltage drop at FET, < = 1 V * Solenoid supply, > 9 V
DTC: P2724 **2T TCM, MIL: Yes** **Year:** 2011, 2012 **Model:** Beetle, Eos, Golf, GTI, Jetta, Passat, Touareg **Engine:** 2.0L L4, 2.5L L5, 3.0L V6, 3.6L V6	**Pressure Control Solenoid "E" Stuck On:** * Low side and high side FET, Activated * Power supply, > 9 V * Voltage drop at FET, < = 1 V * Solenoid supply, > 9 V
DTC: P2725 **2T TCM, MIL: Yes** **Year:** 2011, 2012 **Model:** Beetle, Eos, Golf, GTI, Jetta, Passat, Touareg **Engine:** 2.0L L4, 2.5L L5, 3.0L V6, 3.6L V6	**Pressure Control Solenoid "E" Electrical:** * Main solenoid switch, On * Linear feedback current, > 23 mA (AD:15) < 1333 mA (AD:1000)
DTC: P2725 **2T TCM, MIL: Yes** **Year:** 2011, 2012 **Model:** Beetle, Eos, Golf, GTI, Jetta, Passat, Touareg **Engine:** 2.0L L4, 2.5L L5, 3.0L V6, 3.6L V6	**Pressure Control Solenoid E Electrical:** Output sensor, No failure decision for output sensor no pulse.
DTC: P2732 **2T TCM, MIL: Yes** **Year:** 2011, 2012 **Model:** Beetle, Eos, Golf, GTI, Jetta, Passat, Touareg **Engine:** 2.0L L4, 2.5L L5, 3.0L V6, 3.6L V6	**Pressure Control Solenoid "F" Performance or Stuck off:** * Low side and high side FET, Activated * Power supply, > 9 V * Voltage drop at FET, < = 1 V * Solenoid supply, > 9 V
DTC: P2733 **2T TCM, MIL: Yes** **Year:** 2011, 2012 **Model:** Beetle, Eos, Golf, GTI, Jetta, Passat, Touareg **Engine:** 2.0L L4, 2.5L L5, 3.0L V6, 3.6L V6	**Pressure Control Solenoid "F" Stuck On:** * Low side and high side FET, Activated * Power supply, > 9 V * Voltage drop at FET, < = 1 V * Solenoid supply, > 9 V

DTC	Trouble Code Title and Conditions
DTC: P2734 **2T TCM, MIL: Yes** **Year:** 2011, 2012 **Model:** Beetle, Eos, Golf, GTi, Jetta, Passat, Touareg **Engine:** 2.0L L4, 2.5L L5, 3.0L V6, 3.6L V6	**Pressure Control Solenoid F Electrical:** Output sensor, No failure decision for output sensor no pulse.
DTC: P273A **2T TCM, MIL: Yes** **Year:** 2011, 2012 **Model:** Routan **Engine:** 3.6L V6 VIN G	**INADEQUATE ELEMENT VOLUME LC:** Whenever the engine is running. The LC Clutch Volume Index (CVI) is updated during a 3-1 or 2-1 manual downshift with throttle angle below 5 degrees. Transmission temperature must be at least 43° C (110° F). When the LC CVI falls below a calibrated value.
DTC: P273B **2T TCM, MIL: Yes** **Year:** 2011, 2012 **Model:** Routan **Engine:** 3.6L V6 VIN G	**INADEQUATE ELEMENT VOLUME DC:** Whenever the engine is running. The DC LC Clutch Volume Index (CVI) is updated during a 3-1 or 2-1 manual downshift with throttle angle below 5 degrees. Transmission temperature must be at least 43° C (110° F). When the DC CVI falls below a calibrated value.
DTC: P2763 **2T PCM, MIL: Yes** **Year:** 2011, 2012 **Model:** Routan **Engine:** 3.6L V6 VIN G	**Torque Converter Clutch Pressure Control Circuit High:** When Monitored: Battery voltage is greater than 7.0 volts. TCC duty cycle is greater than 42%. Torque converter is in lock up or partial lock up. Set Condition: The PCM detects the EMCC VFS voltage is more than a calibrated threshold for 1.785 seconds.
DTC: P2764 **2T ECM, MIL: Yes** **Year:** 2011, 2012 **Model:** Routan **Engine:** 3.6L V6 VIN G	**Torque Converter Clutch Pressure Control Circuit Low:** When Monitored: Battery voltage is greater than 7.0 volts. TCC duty cycle is less than 8%. Torque converter is not in lock up or partial lock up. Set Condition: The PCM detects the EMCC VFS voltage is less than a calibrated threshold for 357 ms.

SPECIFICATIONS AND MAINTENANCE CHARTS

ENGINE AND VEHICLE IDENTIFICATION

Engine							Model Year	
Code ①	Liters (cc)	Cu. In.	Cyl.	Fuel Sys.	Engine Type	Eng. Mfg.	Code ②	Year
R ③	1.4 (1368)	83.5	4	MFI	SOHC	Chrysler	C	2012
H ④	1.4 (1368)	83.5	4	MFI Turbo	SOHC	Chrysler		

① 8th position of VIN

② 10th position of VIN

③ EAJ: 1.4L 8V E100, EAB: 1.4L 16V MultiAir

④ EAF: 1.4L 16V Turbo

71105_F500_C0001

GENERAL ENGINE SPECIFICATIONS

All measurements are given in inches.

Year	Model	Engine Displacement Liters	Engine ID/VIN	Fuel System Type	Net Horsepower @ rpm	Net Torque @ rpm (ft. lbs.)	Bore x Stroke (in.)	Compression Ratio	Oil Pressure @ rpm
2012	500	1.4L 8V	R	MFI	NS	NS	2.83x3.31	NS	>61 @ 4,000
		1.4L 16V MultiAir	R	MFI	100 @ 6,500	93 @ 4,000	2.83x3.31	10.8:1	>58 @ 4,000
		1.4L 16V Turbo	H	MFI Turbo	135 @ 5,000	133 @ 1750	2.83x3.31	9.8:1	>58 @ 4,000

NS: Not Specified

71105_F500_C0002

CAPACITIES

Year	Model	Engine Displacement Liters	Engine ID/VIN	Engine Oil with Filter	Transaxle (pts.) ①		Fuel Tank (gal.)	Cooling System (qts.)
					Auto.	Manual		
2012	Fiat	1.4L 8V	R	4.0	3.6	—	10.5	4.6
		1.4L 16V MultiAir	R	4.0	13.2	3.6	10.5	4.6
		1.4L 16V Turbo	H	4.0	13.2	3.6	10.5	4.6

NOTE: All capacities are approximate. Add fluid gradually and ensure a proper fluid level is obtained.

① Capacity given is for drain and refill only.

71105_F500_C0004

FLUID SPECIFICATIONS

Year	Model	Engine Disp. Liters	Engine Oil	Manual Transaxle	Auto. Transaxle	Brake Master Cylinder	Cooling System
2012	500	1.4L 8V	5W-30 Engine Oil	—	Castrol BOT 350M3	DOT 3	①
		1.4L 16V MultiAir	5W-30 Engine Oil	Castrol BOT 350M3	MOPAR® AW1	DOT 3	①
		1.4L 16V Turbo	5W-40 Synthetic Oil	Castrol BOT 350M3	—	DOT 3	①

DOT: Department Of Transpotation

① MOPAR® Antifreeze/Coolant 10 Year 150,000 Mile Formula OAT (Organic Additive Technology)

71105_F500_C0005

VALVE SPECIFICATIONS

Year	Engine Displacement Liters	Engine VIN	Seat Angle (deg.)	Face Angle (deg.)	Spring Test Pressure (in. @ lbs.)	Spring Free-Length (in.)	Spring Installed Height (in.)	Stem-to-Guide Clearance (in.)		Stem Diameter (in.)	
								Intake	Exhaust	Intake	Exhaust
2012	1.4 8V	R	NS	NS	1.38 @ 35	1.665	NS	0.0009-0.0023	0.0012-0.0026	0.1968-0.1969	0.1958-0.1965
	1.4 16V MultiAir	R	NS	NS	1.39 @ 44-47	1.870	NA NS	0.0009-0.0023	0.0012-0.0026	0.2355-0.2362	0.2352-0.2359
	1.4L 16V Turbo	H	NS	NS	1.39 @ 44-47	1.870	NS	0.0009-0.0023	0.0012-0.0026	0.2355-0.2362	0.2352-0.2359

NS: Not Specifired

71105_F500_C0006

CAMSHAFT SPECIFICATIONS
All measurements in inches unless noted

Year	Engine Displacement Liters	Engine VIN	Journal Diameter	Brg. Oil Clearance	Shaft End-play	Runout	Journal Bore	Lobe Height	
								Intake	Exhaust
2012	1.4 8V	R	①	NS	NS	NS	NS	0.374	0.374
	1.4 16V MultiAir	R	1.0236-1.0242	NS	NS	NS	NS	0.0145	0.295
	1.4L 16V Turbo	H	1.0236-1.0242	NS	NS	NS	NS	NS	0.2950

NS: Not Specifired

① Bearing journal diameter - 1st: 0.9449-0.9455

Bearing journal diameter - 2nd: 0.9252-0.9258

Bearing journal diameter - 3rd: 1.2202-1.2208

71105_F500_C0007

CRANKSHAFT AND CONNECTING ROD SPECIFICATIONS

All measurements are given in inches.

Year	Engine Displacement Liters	Crankshaft			Connecting Rod		Connecting Rod Journal	
		Main Brg. Journal Dia.	Main Brg. Oil Clearance	Shaft End-play	Journal Bore Diameter	Bearing Clearance	Diameter	Bearing Clearance
2012	1.4 8V	①	0.0010-0.0016	0.0061-0.0140	1.7767-1.7771	0.0008-0.0024	1.6531-1.6539	0.0008-0.0024
	1.4 16V MultiAir	②	0.0010-0.0016	0.0061-0.0140	1.7767-1.7771	0.0009-0.0024	1.6531-1.6539	0.0009-0.0024
	1.4L 16V Turbo	②	0.0010-0.0016	0.0061-0.0140	1.7767-1.7771	0.0009-0.0024	1.6531-1.6539	0.0009-0.0024

① Diameter - Class A: 1.8896-1.8899

Diameter - Class B: 1.8893-1.8895

Diameter - Class C: 1.8890-1.8893

② Diameter - Class A: 1.8895-1.8898

Diameter - Class B: 1.8893-1.8895

Diameter - Class C: 1.8890-1.8893

71105_F500_C0008

PISTON AND RING SPECIFICATIONS

All measurements are given in inches.

Year	Engine Displacement Liters	Engine ID/VIN	Piston Clearance	Ring Gap			Ring Side Clearance		
				Top Compression	Bottom Compression	Oil Control	Top Compression	Bottom Compression	Oil Control
2012	1.4 8V	R	0.0012-0.0020	0.008-0.016	0.020-0.028	0.008-0.016	0.0012-0.0028	0.0008-0.0024	0.0008-0.0022
	1.4 16V MultiAir	R	0.0012-0.0020	0.008-0.014	0.016-0.024	0.008-0.016	0.0012-0.0028	0.0008-0.0024	0.0008-0.0022
	1.4L 16V Turbo	H	0.0012-0.0020	0.008-0.014	0.016-0.024	0.008-0.016	0.0012-0.0028	0.0008-0.0024	0.0008-0.0022

71105_F500_C0009

TORQUE SPECIFICATIONS
All readings in ft. lbs.

Year	Engine Disp. Liters	Engine ID/VIN	Cylinder Head Bolts	Main Bearing Bolts	Rod Bearing Bolts	Crankshaft Damper Bolts	Flywheel Bolts	Manifold Intake	Manifold Exhaust	Spark Plugs	Oil Pan Drain Plug
2012	1.4L 8V	R	①	②	③	19	44	18	15	13	33
	1.4L 16V MultiAir	R	④	②	③	19	44	11	15	12	20
	1.4L 16V Turbo	H	④	②	③	19	44	11	18	12	20

① Step 1: 22 ft. lbs.

Step 2: Plus 90 degrees (do NOT use a torque wrench)

Step 3: Plus 90 degrees (do NOT use a torque wrench)

② Step 1 (1-10): 15 ft. lbs.

Step 2 (11-20): 11 ft. lbs.

Step 3 (1-10): 15 ft. lbs.

Step 4 (1-10): Plus 80 degrees (do NOT use a torque wrench)

Step 5 (12-20): 27 ft. lbs.

③ Step 1: 15 ft. lbs.

Step 2: Plus 40 degrees (do NOT use a torque wrench)

④ Step 1: 15 ft. lbs.

Step 2: 22 ft. lbs.

Step 3: Plus 90 degrees (do NOT use a torque wrench)

Step 4: Plus 90 degrees (do NOT use a torque wrench)

71105_F500_C0010

WHEEL ALIGNMENT

Year	Model		Caster Range (+/-Deg.)	Caster Preferred Setting (Deg.)	Camber Range (+/-Deg.)	Camber Preferred Setting (Deg.)	Toe Range (+/-Deg.)	Toe Preferred Setting (Deg.)
2012	500 Pop, Lounge, Hatchback, Convertible	F	+2.00 - +3.00	+2.50	-0.60	-1.05 - -0.15	-0.25 - +0.25	0.0
		R	—	—	-1.40 - -0.40	-0.90	①	②
	500 Abarth	F	+2.15 - +3.15	+2.65	-2.50 - -1.00	-1.50	-0.25 - +0.25	0.0
		R	—	—	-2.20 - +0.40	-0.93	③	②

F: Front

R: Rear

① Toe - Individual

Range: -0.05-+0.55

Preferred Setting: +0.25

② Toe - Total

Range: +0.22-+0.78

Preferred Setting: +0.50

③ Toe - Individual

Range: -0.25-+0.50

Preferred Setting: +0.28

71105_F500_C0011

TIRE, WHEEL AND BALL JOINT SPECIFICATIONS

Year	Model	OEM Tires Standard	Tire Pressures (psi) Front	Rear	Wheel Size	Lug Nut (ft. lbs.)
2012	500 Pop	185/55 R15	①	①	15-inch x 6.0-inch	②
	500 Sport	195/45R16XL	①	①	16-inch x 6.5 inch	②
	500 Lounge	185/55 R15	①	①	15-inch x 6.0-inch	②
	500t	195/45R16XL	①	①	16-inch x 6.5 inch	②
	500c	185/55 R15	①	①	15-inch x 6.0-inch	②

OEM: Original Equipment Manufacturer

PSI: Pounds Per Square Inch

NA: Information not available

① Refer to the placard on the door jamb, or the owner's manual for tire pressure specification.

② Steel wheels: 63 ft. lbs.

   Aluminum wheels: 75 ft. lbs.

71105_F500_C0012

BRAKE SPECIFICATIONS

All measurements in inches unless noted

Year	Model		Brake Disc Original Thickness	Minimum Thickness	Max. Runout	Minimum Pad/Lining Thickness Front	Rear	Brake Caliper Adapter Bracket Bolts (ft. lbs.)	Guide Pin Bolts (ft. lbs.)
2012	500	Front	NS	①	NS	0.040	—	77	20
		Rear	NS	②	NS	—	0.040	42	25

NS: Information not specified

① The minimum thickness specification for the front brake rotor is located on the inside of the rotor.

② The minimum thickness specification for the rear brake rotor is located on the outside of the rotor.

71105_F500_C0013

SCHEDULED MAINTENANCE INTERVALS
FIAT 500

TO BE SERVICED	TYPE OF SERVICE	VEHICLE MILEAGE INTERVAL (x1000)											
		8	16	24	32	40	48	56	64	72	80	88	96
Engine oil & filter	R	✓	✓	✓	✓	✓	✓	✓	✓	✓	✓	✓	✓
Tires	Rotate	✓	✓	✓	✓	✓	✓	✓	✓	✓	✓	✓	✓
Brake system components	S/I		✓		✓		✓		✓		✓		✓
Exhaust system & heat shields	I		✓		✓		✓		✓		✓		✓
Inspect front suspension, tie rod ends & boot seals for cracks or leaks & all parts for damage, wear, improper looseness or end play.	I		✓		✓		✓		✓		✓		✓
CV Joints	I		✓		✓		✓		✓		✓		✓
Engine air filter	R				✓				✓				✓
Parking brake	I/A				✓				✓				✓
Engine coolant	R	At 152,000 miles											
Spark plugs	R				✓				✓				✓
PCV valve	S/I												✓
Transaxle fluid	S/I				✓				✓				✓
Accessory drive belt	R												
Battery	S/I		✓		✓		✓		✓		✓		✓
Horn, exterior lamps, turn signals and hazard warning light operation	I	✓	✓	✓	✓	✓	✓	✓	✓	✓	✓	✓	✓
Fluid levels (all)	Top off	✓	✓	✓	✓	✓	✓	✓	✓	✓	✓	✓	✓
Cabin air filter	R		✓		✓		✓		✓		✓		✓
Timing belt	R	At 152,000 miles											
Engine air filter	S/I		✓		✓		✓		✓		✓		✓
Sunroof glides	C/L		✓		✓		✓		✓		✓		✓

R: Replace   S/I: Inspect and service, if necessary   I: Inspect   L: Lubricate   A: Adjust   C: Clean

The maintenance schedule must be done at the times or mileages specified to

Protect your warranty and ensure the best vehicle performance and reliability.

More frequent maintenance may be needed for vehicles in severe operating conditions,

such as dusty areas and very short trip driving. Inspection and service should also be done anytime a malfunction is detected.

The oil change indictor system will remind you that it is time for scheduled maintenance.

Base on engine operation conditions the oil change indictor message will illuminate, this means that service is required for your vehicle.

Have your vehicle serviced as soon as possible, within the next 500 miles (805 km).

Note: the oil change indictor message will not monitor the time since the last oil change.

Change your vehicles oil if it has been 6 months since your last oil change even if the oil

Change indictor message is not illuminated.

1). Change your engine oil more often if drive your vehicle off-road for an extended period of time.

2). Under no circumstance should oil change intervals exceed 8,000 miles (13,000 km) or

6 months which ever comes first?

OIL INDICATOR RESET:

When a scheduled oil change is performed the message can be reset by turning the ignition switch to the on position (engine not running).

Fully depress the accelerator pedal slowly 3 times within 3 seconds.

Repeat the procedure if the indicator eliminates when you start the vehicle.

PRECAUTIONS

Before servicing any vehicle, please be sure to read all of the following precautions, which deal with personal safety, prevention of component damage, and important points to take into consideration when servicing a motor vehicle:

• Never open, service or drain the radiator or cooling system when the engine is hot; serious burns can occur from the steam and hot coolant.

• Observe all applicable safety precautions when working around fuel. Whenever servicing the fuel system, always work in a well-ventilated area. Do not allow fuel spray or vapors to come in contact with a spark, open flame, or excessive heat (a hot drop light, for example). Keep a dry chemical fire extinguisher near the work area. Always keep fuel in a container specifically designed for fuel storage; also, always properly seal fuel containers to avoid the possibility of fire or explosion. Refer to the additional fuel system precautions later in this section.

• Fuel injection systems often remain pressurized, even after the engine has been turned **OFF**. The fuel system pressure must be relieved before disconnecting any fuel lines. Failure to do so may result in fire and/or personal injury.

• Brake fluid often contains polyglycol ethers and polyglycols. Avoid contact with the eyes and wash your hands thoroughly after handling brake fluid. If you do get brake fluid in your eyes, flush your eyes with clean, running water for 15 minutes. If eye irritation persists, or if you have taken

brake fluid internally, IMMEDIATELY seek medical assistance.

• The EPA warns that prolonged contact with used engine oil may cause a number of skin disorders, including cancer. You should make every effort to minimize your exposure to used engine oil. Protective gloves should be worn when changing oil. Wash your hands and any other exposed skin areas as soon as possible after exposure to used engine oil. Soap and water, or waterless hand cleaner should be used.

• All new vehicles are now equipped with an air bag system, often referred to as a Supplemental Restraint System (SRS) or Supplemental Inflatable Restraint (SIR) system. The system must be disabled before performing service on or around system components, steering column, instrument panel components, wiring and sensors. Failure to follow safety and disabling procedures could result in accidental air bag deployment, possible personal injury and unnecessary system repairs.

• Always wear safety goggles when working with, or around, the air bag system. When carrying a non-deployed air bag, be sure the bag and trim cover are pointed away from your body. When placing a non-deployed air bag on a work surface, always face the bag and trim cover upward, away from the surface. This will reduce the motion of the module if it is accidentally deployed. Refer to the additional air bag system precautions later in this section.

• Clean, high quality brake fluid from a sealed container is essential to the safe and

proper operation of the brake system. You should always buy the correct type of brake fluid for your vehicle. If the brake fluid becomes contaminated, completely flush the system with new fluid. Never reuse any brake fluid. Any brake fluid that is removed from the system should be discarded. Also, do not allow any brake fluid to come in contact with a painted surface; it will damage the paint.

• Never operate the engine without the proper amount and type of engine oil; doing so WILL result in severe engine damage.

• Timing belt maintenance is extremely important. Many models utilize an interference-type, non-freewheeling engine. If the timing belt breaks, the valves in the cylinder head may strike the pistons, causing potentially serious (also time-consuming and expensive) engine damage. Refer to the maintenance interval charts for the recommended replacement interval for the timing belt, and to the timing belt section for belt replacement and inspection.

• Disconnecting the negative battery cable on some vehicles may interfere with the functions of the on-board computer system(s) and may require the computer to undergo a relearning process once the negative battery cable is reconnected.

• When servicing drum brakes, only disassemble and assemble one side at a time, leaving the remaining side intact for reference.

• Only an MVAC-trained, EPA-certified automotive technician should service the air conditioning system or its components.

BRAKES

ANTI-LOCK BRAKE SYSTEM (ABS)

GENERAL INFORMATION

PRECAUTIONS

• Certain components within the ABS system are not intended to be serviced or repaired individually.

• Do not use rubber hoses or other parts not specifically specified for and ABS system. When using repair kits, replace all parts included in the kit. Partial or incorrect repair may lead to functional problems and require the replacement of components.

• Lubricate rubber parts with clean, fresh brake fluid to ease assembly. Do not use shop air to clean parts; damage to rubber components may result.

• Use only DOT 3 brake fluid from an unopened container.

• If any hydraulic component or line is removed or replaced, it may be necessary to bleed the entire system.

• A clean repair area is essential. Always clean the reservoir and cap thoroughly before removing the cap. The slightest amount of dirt in the fluid may plug an orifice and impair the system function. Perform repairs after components have been thoroughly cleaned; use only denatured alcohol to clean components. Do not allow ABS components to come into contact with any substance containing mineral oil; this includes used shop rags.

• The Anti-Lock control unit is a microprocessor similar to other computer units in the vehicle. Ensure that the ignition switch is **OFF** before removing or installing con-

troller harnesses. Avoid static electricity discharge at or near the controller.

• If any arc welding is to be done on the vehicle, the control unit should be unplugged before welding operations begin.

• This vehicle utilizes active wheel speed sensors. Do not apply voltage to wheel speed sensors at any time.

• When performing any service procedure on a vehicle equipped with ABS, do not apply a 12-volt power source to the ground circuit of the pump motor in the HCU. Doing this will damage the pump motor and will require replacement of the entire HCU.

• Brake fluid will damage painted surfaces. If brake fluid is spilled on any painted surface, wash off with water immediately.

SPEED SENSORS

REMOVAL & INSTALLATION

Front

See Figures 1 and 2.

➥**Before proceeding, refer to Brake Warnings and Cautions.**

1. Raise and support the vehicle.
2. Disconnect the wheel speed sensor cable connector (1) from the wiring harness connector on the inner fender.
3. Separate sensor cable clips from retainers (2, 3).
4. Remove the speed sensor cable routing clips (1, 2, 3) from retainers.
5. Remove the mounting screw (1) fastening the wheel speed sensor head (2) to the knuckle. Pull the sensor head out of the knuckle and remove the wheel speed cable from the vehicle.

To install:

6. Install the wheel speed sensor head into the knuckle. Install the mounting screw (1) and tighten it to 62 inch lbs. (7 Nm).
7. Install the routing clip securing the wheel speed sensor cable to the knuckle.

❊❊ CAUTION

Failure to install speed sensor cables properly may result in contact with moving parts or an over

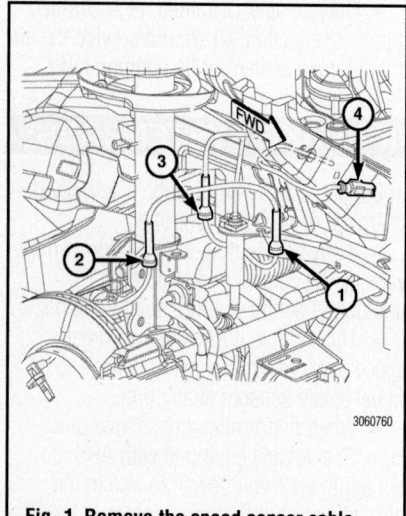

Fig. 1 Remove the speed sensor cable routing clips (1, 2, 3) from retainers

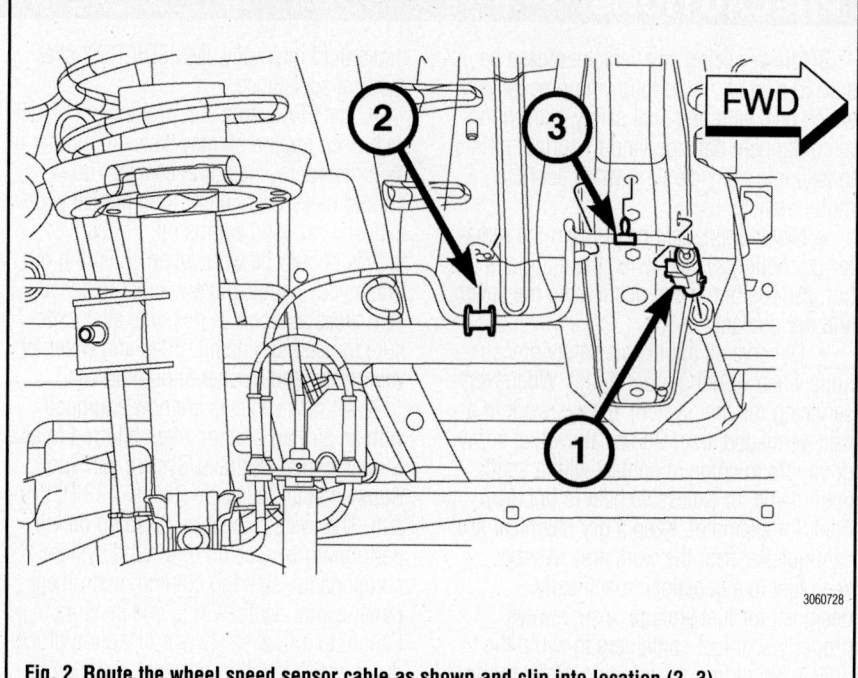

Fig. 2 Route the wheel speed sensor cable as shown and clip into location (2, 3).

extension of cables causing an open circuit. Be sure that cables are installed, routed, and clipped properly.

8. Route the wheel speed sensor cable as shown and clip into location (1, 2, & 3).
9. Route the wheel speed sensor cable as shown and clip into location (2, 3).
10. Connect wheel speed sensor cable (1) to wiring harness.
11. Lower the vehicle.
12. Perform the Diagnostic Verification Test and clear any faults

Rear

See Figure 3.

➥**Before proceeding, refer to Brake Warnings and Cautions.**

1. Raise and support the vehicle.
2. Disconnect the wheel speed sensor cable connector (1) from the body wiring harness.
3. Separate the wheels speed sensor cable from all retainers and clips.
4. Remove the screw (2) fastening the wheel speed sensor head in the spindle assembly. Remove the sensor from the vehicle

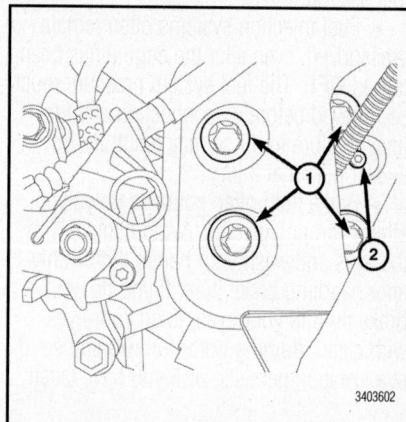

Fig. 3 Remove the screw (2) fastening the wheel speed sensor head in the spindle assembly.

To install:

5. Install the wheel speed sensor head into the rear of the hub and bearing.
6. Install the wheel speed sensor head mounting screw and tighten to 62 inch lbs. (7 Nm).
7. Route wheel speed sensor cable and snap into clips and retainers.
8. Connect wheel speed sensor cable connector to body wiring harness connector.
9. Lower the vehicle.

BRAKES   **BLEEDING THE BRAKE SYSTEM**

BLEEDING PROCEDURE

BLEEDING PROCEDURE

➡Do not pump the brake pedal at any time while having a bleeder screw open during the bleeding process. This will only increase the amount of air in the system and make additional bleeding necessary.

➡Do not allow the master cylinder reservoir to run out of brake fluid while bleeding the system. An empty reservoir will allow additional air into the brake system. Check the fluid level frequently and add fluid as needed.

The following wheel circuit sequence for bleeding the brake hydraulic system should be used to ensure adequate removal of all trapped air from the hydraulic system.
  a. Left rear wheel
  b. Right front wheel
  c. Right rear wheel
  d. Left front wheel

※※ CAUTION

Before removing the master cylinder cap, wipe it clean to prevent dirt and other foreign matter from dropping into the master cylinder reservoir.

※※ CAUTION

Use only Mopar® brake fluid or an equivalent from a fresh, tightly sealed container. Brake fluid must conform to DOT 3 specifications.

Manual
See Figure 4.

➡To bleed the brakes manually, the aid of a helper will be required.

1. Attach a clear plastic hose (1) to the bleeder screw and feed the hose into a clear jar (2) containing enough fresh brake fluid to submerge the end of the hose.
2. Have a helper pump the brake pedal three or four times and hold it in the down position.
3. With the pedal in the down position, open the bleeder screw at least one full turn.
4. Once the brake pedal has dropped, close the bleeder screw. After the bleeder screw is closed, release the brake pedal.
5. Repeat the above steps until all trapped air is removed from that wheel circuit (usually four or five times).

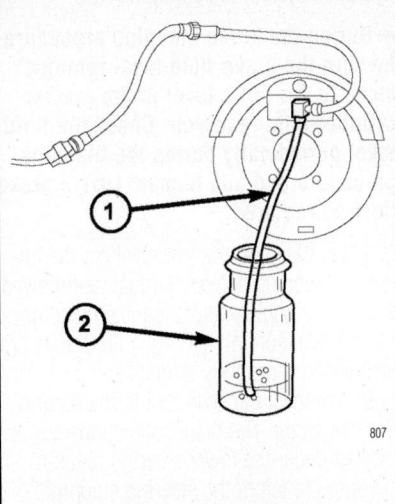

Fig. 4 Attach a clear plastic hose (1) to the bleeder screw and feed the hose into a clear jar (2) containing enough fresh brake fluid to submerge the end of the hose

Pressure Bleeding
See Figure 5.

➡Follow pressure bleeder manufacturer's instructions for use of pressure bleeding equipment.

1. Attach Master Cylinder Cap (2) in place of the filler cap on the master cylinder reservoir (3).
2. Attach Bleeder Tank C-3496-B (1) or an equivalent, to the Master Cylinder Cap (2).
3. Attach a clear plastic hose (1) to the bleeder screw and feed the hose into a clear jar (2) containing enough fresh brake fluid to submerge the end of the hose.
4. Open the bleeder screw at least one full turn or more to obtain a steady stream of brake fluid.
5. After approximately 120-240 ml (4-8 ounces) of fluid have been bled through the brake circuit and an air-free flow is maintained in the clear plastic hose and jar, close the bleeder screw.
6. Repeat this procedure at all the remaining bleeder screws.
7. Check and adjust brake fluid level to the FULL mark on the reservoir.
8. Check the brake pedal travel. If pedal travel is excessive or has not been improved, some air may still be trapped in the system. Re-bleed the brakes as necessary.
9. Test drive the vehicle to verify the brakes are operating properly and pedal feel is correct.

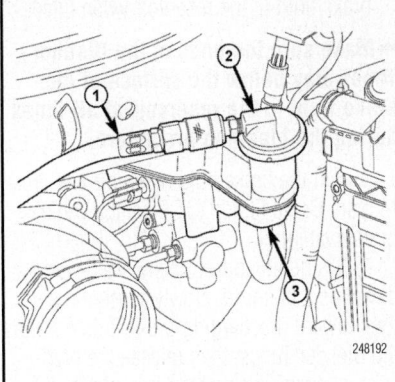

Fig. 5 Attach Master Cylinder Cap (2) in place of the filler cap on the master cylinder reservoir (3)

MASTER CYLINDER BLEEDING
See Figure 6.

➡On vehicles without ABS this procedure is designed to be performed with the proportioning valves installed in the master cylinder.

1. Clamp the master cylinder in a vise with soft-jaw caps.
2. Attach the special tools for bleeding the master cylinder in the following fashion:
    a. Thread Bleeder Tube Adapters (3), Special Tool, into the primary and secondary outlet ports of the master cylinder. Tighten Adapters to 1 lbs. (17 Nm).
    b. Thread a Bleeder Tube, Special Tool , into each Adapter. Tighten tube nuts to 13 ft. lbs. (17 Nm).
    c. Flex each Bleeder Tube and place the open ends into the neck of the master

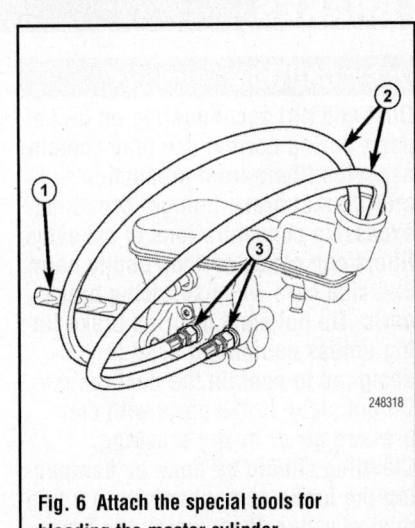

Fig. 6 Attach the special tools for bleeding the master cylinder

cylinder reservoir. Position the open ends of the tubes into the reservoir so their outlets are below the surface of the brake fluid in the reservoir when filled.

➡ **Make sure the ends of the Bleeder Tubes stay below the surface of the brake fluid in the reservoir at all times during the bleeding procedure.**

3. Fill the brake fluid reservoir with fresh Mopar® Brake Fluid DOT 3 Motor Vehicle, or equivalent.

4. Using an appropriately sized wooden dowel as a pushrod, slowly press the pistons inward discharging brake fluid through the Bleeder Tubes, then release the pressure, allowing the pistons to return to the released position. Repeat this several times until all air bubbles are expelled from the master cylinder bore and Bleeder Tubes.

5. Remove the Bleeder Tubes and Adapters from the master cylinder and plug the master cylinder outlet ports.

6. Install the fill cap on the reservoir.

7. Remove the master cylinder from the vise.

8. Install the master cylinder on the vehicle.

BLEEDING THE ABS SYSTEM

The base brake's hydraulic system must be bled anytime air enters the hydraulic system. The ABS must always be bled anytime it is suspected that the HCU has ingested air.

Brake systems with ABS must be bled as two independent braking systems. The non-ABS portion of the brake system with ABS is to be bled the same as any non-ABS system.

The ABS portion of the brake system must be bled separately. Use the following procedure to properly bleed the brake hydraulic system including the ABS.

➡ **During the brake bleeding procedure, be sure the brake fluid level remains close to the FULL level in the master cylinder fluid reservoir. Check the fluid level periodically during the bleeding procedure and add Mopar® DOT 3 brake fluid as required.**

When bleeding the ABS system, the following bleeding sequence must be followed to insure complete and adequate bleeding.

1. Make sure all hydraulic fluid lines are installed and properly torqued.

2. Connect the scan tool to the diagnostics connector. The diagnostic connector is located under the lower steering column cover to the left of the steering column.

3. Using the scan tool, check to make sure the ABM does not have any fault codes stored. If it does, clear them.

❊❊ WARNING

When bleeding the brake system wear safety glasses. A clear bleed tube must be attached to the bleeder screws and submerged in a clear container filled part way with clean brake fluid. Direct the flow of brake fluid away from yourself and the painted surfaces of the vehicle. Brake fluid at high pressure may come out of the bleeder screws when opened.

➡ **Pressure bleeding is recommended to bleed the base brake system to ensure all air is removed from system. Manual bleeding may also be used, but**

additional time is needed to remove all air from system.

4. Bleed the base brake system.

5. Using the scan tool, select ECU VIEW, followed by ABS MISCELLANEOUS FUNCTIONS to access bleeding. Follow the instructions displayed. When finished, disconnect the scan tool and proceed.

6. Bleed the base brake system a second time. Check brake fluid level in the reservoir periodically to prevent emptying, causing air to enter the hydraulic system.

7. Fill the master cylinder fluid reservoir to the FULL level.

8. Test drive the vehicle to be sure the brakes are operating correctly and that the brake pedal does not feel spongy.

FLUID FILL PROCEDURE

See Figure 7.

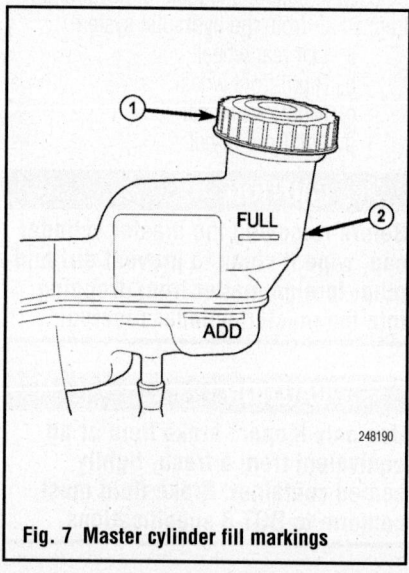

Fig. 7 Master cylinder fill markings

BRAKES

❊❊ CAUTION

Dust and dirt accumulating on brake parts during normal use may contain asbestos fibers from production or aftermarket brake linings. Breathing excessive concentrations of asbestos fibers can cause serious bodily harm. Exercise care when servicing brake parts. Do not sand or grind brake lining unless equipment used is designed to contain the dust residue. Do not clean brake parts with compressed air or by dry brushing. Cleaning should be done by dampening the brake components with a fine mist of water, then wiping the brake

components clean with a dampened cloth. Dispose of cloth and all residue containing asbestos fibers in an impermeable container with the appropriate label. Follow practices prescribed by the Occupational Safety and Health Administration (OSHA) and the Environmental Protection Agency (EPA) for the handling, processing, and disposing of dust or debris that may contain asbestos fibers.

BRAKE CALIPER

REMOVAL & INSTALLATION

See Figures 8 through 10.

FRONT DISC BRAKES

➡ **Before proceeding refer to Precautions.**

1. Using a brake pedal holding tool as shown, depress the brake pedal past its first 25 mm (1 inch) of travel and hold it in this position. This will isolate the master cylinder from the brake hydraulic system and will not allow the brake fluid to drain out of the master cylinder reservoir when the lines are opened.

2. Raise and support the vehicle

3. Remove the wheel mounting bolts, then the tire and wheel assembly.

4. Remove the banjo bolt (4) connecting the brake flex hose to the brake line connector.

5. Remove the clip and remove the brake hose (3) from the strut.

6. Remove brake hose connector (2) from brake caliper.

7. Remove the two brake caliper guide pin bolts.

8. Slide the disc brake caliper from the disc brake adapter bracket and remove.

To install:

✳✳ CAUTION

Use care when installing the caliper onto the adapter bracket to avoid damaging the guide pin boots.

9. Completely retract the caliper piston back into the bore of the caliper. Use a C-clamp to retract the piston. Place a wood block over the piston before installing the C-clamp to avoid damaging the piston.

10. Install the disc brake caliper over the brake pads on the brake caliper adapter bracket.

11. Align the caliper guide pin bolt holes with the adapter bracket. Install the caliper guide pin bolts (2) and tighten to 21 ft. lbs. (28 Nm)

12. Install the brake hose connector (2) to the brake caliper and tighten to 18 ft. lbs. (24 Nm).

13. Install brake hose fitting to brake line connector (4) and tighten to 18 ft. lbs. (24 Nm).

14. Install brake hose to mounting location on strut (3) and secure with the clip.

15. Install the tire and wheel assembly.

16. Lower the vehicle.

17. Remove the brake pedal holding tool.

18. Bleed the caliper as necessary.

19. Road test the vehicle and make several

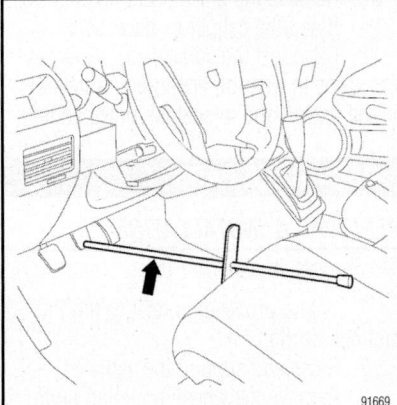

Fig. 8 Using a brake pedal holding tool as shown, depress the brake pedal past its first 25 mm (1 inch) of travel and hold it in this position.

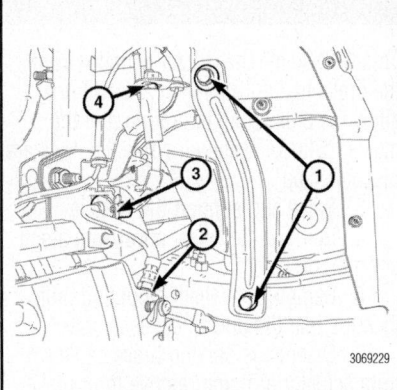

Fig. 9 Remove the banjo bolt (4) connecting the brake flex hose to the brake line connector

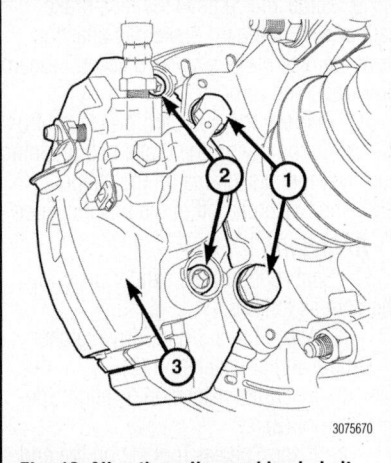

Fig. 10 Align the caliper guide pin bolt holes with the adapter bracket

stops to wear off any foreign material on the brakes and to seat the brake shoes.

DISC BRAKE PADS

REMOVAL & INSTALLATION
See Figure 11.

➡**Before proceeding refer to Precautions.**

1. Raise and support the vehicle.

2. Remove the wheel mounting bolts, then the tire and wheel assembly.

3. Remove brake pad clip from brake caliper.

4. Remove caps from caliper guide pin bolts, if equipped.

5. Remove the two brake caliper guide pin bolts.

6. Remove the disc brake caliper from the disc brake adapter bracket and hang it

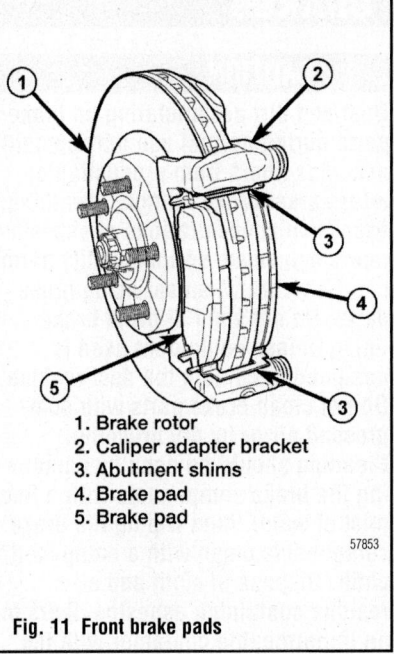

1. Brake rotor
2. Caliper adapter bracket
3. Abutment shims
4. Brake pad
5. Brake pad

Fig. 11 Front brake pads

out of the way using wire or a bungee cord. Use care not to overextend the brake hose when doing this.

7. Remove the brake pads (4, 5) from the caliper adapter bracket (2).

To install:

➡**Make sure that the audible wear indicators (if equipped) are placed toward the top when the inboard brake pads are installed on each side of the vehicle.**

8. Place the brake pads (4, 5) in the abutment shims (3) clipped into the disc brake caliper adapter bracket (2) as shown. Place the pad with the wear indicator attached on the inboard side.

9. Completely retract the caliper piston back into the bore of the caliper.

10. Install the disc brake caliper (3) over the brake pads on the brake caliper adapter bracket.

11. Align the caliper guide pin bolt holes with the adapter bracket. Install the caliper guide pin bolts (2) and tighten to 21 ft. lbs. (28 Nm).

12. Install brake pad retainer clip.

13. Install the tire and wheel assembly

14. Lower the vehicle.

15. Pump the brake pedal several times before moving the vehicle to set the pads to the brake rotor.

16. Check and adjust the brake fluid level in the reservoir as necessary.

17. Road test the vehicle and make several stops to wear off any foreign material on the brakes and to seat the brake pads.

BRAKES

✳✳ CAUTION

Dust and dirt accumulating on brake parts during normal use may contain asbestos fibers from production or aftermarket brake linings. Breathing excessive concentrations of asbestos fibers can cause serious bodily harm. Exercise care when servicing brake parts. Do not sand or grind brake lining unless equipment used is designed to contain the dust residue. Do not clean brake parts with compressed air or by dry brushing. Cleaning should be done by dampening the brake components with a fine mist of water, then wiping the brake components clean with a dampened cloth. Dispose of cloth and all residue containing asbestos fibers in an impermeable container with the appropriate label. Follow practices prescribed by the Occupational Safety and Health Administration (OSHA) and the Environmental Protection Agency (EPA) for the handling, processing, and disposing of dust or debris that may contain asbestos fibers.

BRAKE CALIPER

REMOVAL & INSTALLATION

See Figures 12 and 13.

1. Before proceeding refer to the Precautions section.
2. Using a brake pedal holding tool, depress the brake pedal past its first one inch of travel and hold it in this position.

This will isolate the master cylinder from the brake hydraulic system and will not allow the brake fluid to drain out of the master cylinder reservoir while the lines are disconnected.

3. Raise and support the vehicle
4. Remove the wheel cover with a soft prying tool.
5. Remove the wheel mounting bolts, then the rear tire and wheel assembly.
6. Disengage parking brake cable (2) from actuator arm and remove from brake caliper.
7. Unthread and remove the brake flex hose (3) from the brake caliper.
8. While holding guide pins from turning, remove caliper guide pin bolts (1).
9. Slide and remove the disc brake caliper with outboard brake pad attached from the disc brake adapter bracket, inboard brake pad and rotor.
10. Remove the outboard brake pad from the caliper by prying the brake pad retaining clip over the raised area on the caliper. Slide the brake pad off of the brake caliper.

To install:

11. Seat (bottom) the caliper piston in the bore as follows:

    a. Assemble a 3/8 in. drive ratchet handle and an extension (3).

    b. Insert the extension through Special Tool (2).

    c. Place Special Tool (1) on the end of the extension.

    d. Insert lugs on Special Tool into notches in face of caliper piston (5).

    e. Thread the screw drive on down until it contacts the top of which is against the caliper piston. Do not over

tighten the screw-drive. Damage to the piston can occur.

    f. Turn with the ratchet, rotating the piston in a clockwise direction until fully seated (bottomed) in the bore.

➡**There is a small post on the lower backside of the inboard pad. Make sure that this post lines up with one of the slots on the piston to ensure the pad interfaces with the piston correctly.**

12. Slide the outboard brake pad onto the caliper. Be sure the retaining clip is squarely seated in the depressed areas on the caliper beyond the raised retaining bead.

✳✳ CAUTION

Use care when installing the caliper onto the disc brake adapter to avoid damaging the guide pin boots.

13. Install the disc brake caliper with outboard brake pad attached over the inboard brake pad and rotor, onto the brake caliper adapter bracket.
14. Align the caliper guide pin bolt holes with the adapter bracket. Install the caliper guide pin bolts (1) and tighten the guide pin bolts to 25 ft. lbs. (34 Nm).
15. Install brake line fitting (3) and tighten to 13 ft. lbs. (17 Nm).
16. Insert parking brake cable through mounting hole in caliper and attach cable end (3) to parking brake actuator arm.
17. Install the tire and wheel assembly
18. Install wheel cover, if equipped.
19. Lower the vehicle.
20. Remove the brake pedal holding tool.
21. Bleed the caliper as necessary.
22. Road test the vehicle and make several stops to wear off any foreign material on the brakes and to seat the brake shoes.

DISC BRAKE PADS

REMOVAL & INSTALLATION

See Figures 14 and 15.

1. Before proceeding refer to the Precautions section.
2. Raise and support the vehicle
3. Remove the wheel mounting bolts, then the tire and wheel assembly.
4. While holding the slider pins stationary, remove the disc brake caliper guide pin bolts (1).

✳✳ CAUTION

Never allow the disc brake caliper to hang from the brake hose. Damage

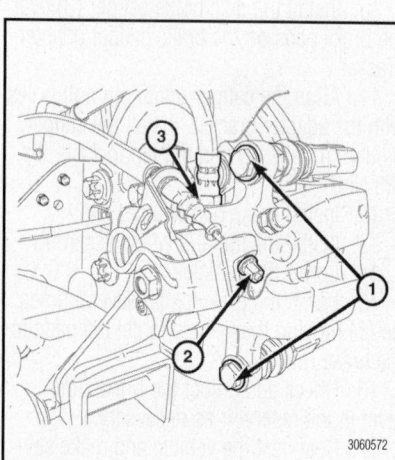

Fig. 12 Disengage parking brake cable (2) from actuator arm and remove from brake caliper

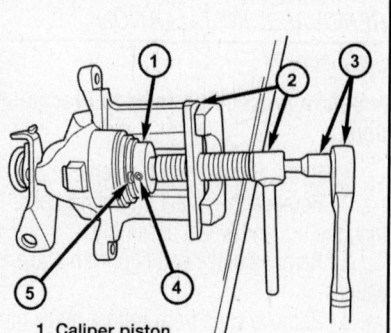

1. Caliper piston
2. Special tool
3. Ratchet and extension
4. Caliper piston
5. Notches in face of caliper piston

Fig. 13 Assemble a 3/8 in. drive ratchet handle and an extension (3).

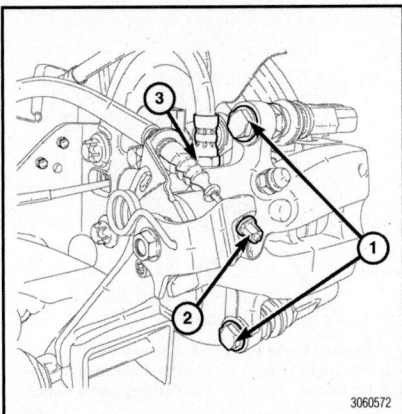

Fig. 14 While holding the slider pins stationary, remove the disc brake caliper guide pin bolts (1).

to the brake hose will result. Provide a suitable support to hang the caliper securely.

5. Remove the caliper from the caliper mounting bracket. Hang the caliper using wire or a bungee cord.

6. Remove the inboard brake pad (4) from the caliper adapter bracket (2).

7. Remove the outboard brake pad (3) from the caliper adapter bracket (2) by prying the brake pad outward until it clears the bracket and then remove the pad from the vehicle.

To install:

➡**If a rear caliper piston in this vehicle needs to be seated in its bore, Rear Caliper Piston Retractor must be used. If an attempt is made to force the piston back in the bore with a clamp or other method, dam-**

age will occur to the Integrated Park Brake.

8. Seat (bottom) the caliper piston in the bore as follows:

a. Assemble a 3/8 in. drive ratchet handle and an extension (3).

b. Insert the extension through Rear Caliper Piston Retractor (2).

c. Place Rear Caliper Piston Retractor (1) on the end of the extension.

d. Insert lugs on Rear Caliper Piston Retractor into notches in face of caliper piston (5).

e. Thread the screw drive on Rear Caliper Piston Retractor down until it contacts the top of Rear Caliper Piston Retractor which is against the caliper piston. Do not over tighten the screw-drive. Damage to the piston can occur.

f. Turn Rear Caliper Piston Retractor with the ratchet, rotating the piston in a **clockwise** direction until fully seated (bottomed) in the bore.

➡ **Place the brake pad with the audible wear indicator attached on the inboard side. The audible wear indicator should be positioned at the bottom when installed.**

9. Slide the outboard brake pad (3) in the abutment shims clipped into the caliper adapter bracket (2).

10. Place the inboard brake pad (4) in the abutment shims. Be sure that both pads are bottomed in their shims.

✳✳ CAUTION

Use care when installing the caliper onto the adapter bracket to avoid damaging the guide pin boot.

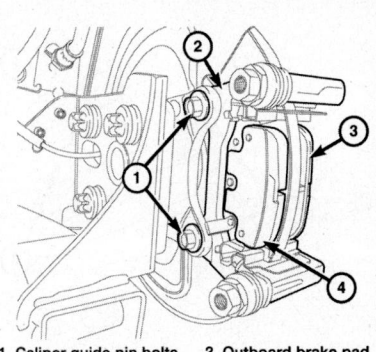

1. Caliper guide pin bolts   3. Outboard brake pad
2. Caliper adapter bracket   4. Inboard brake pad

Fig. 15 Remove the inboard brake pad (4) from the caliper adapter bracket (2)

➡ **There is a small post on the lower backside of the inboard pad. Make sure that this post lines up with one of the slots on the piston to ensure the pad interfaces with the piston correctly.**

11. Install the disc brake caliper over the brake rotor and caliper adapter.

12. Install the disc brake caliper guide pin bolts (1). While holding the slide pins stationary, tighten the guide pin bolts to 25 ft. lbs. (34 Nm).

13. Install the tire and wheel assembly.

14. Lower the vehicle.

15. Pump the brake pedal several times to ensure the vehicle has a firm brake pedal before moving the vehicle.

16. Road test the vehicle and make several stops to wear off any foreign material on the brakes and to seat the brake pads.

BRAKES   PARKING BRAKE

PARKING BRAKE CABLES

ADJUSTMENT

See Figures 16 through 20.

1. Remove the floor console.

a. Disconnect the negative battery cable.

b. Remove the screw (2) from the left side floor console panel (1).

c. Using trim stick, disengage the rear retaining tabs and remove the left side floor console panel (1).

d. Remove the screw (1) securing the front floor console to the lower instrument panel bezel. Repeat for the opposite side.

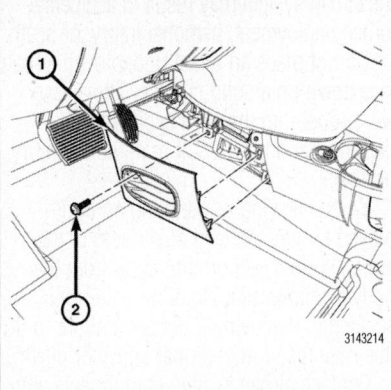

Fig. 16 Remove the screw (2) from the left side floor console panel (1).

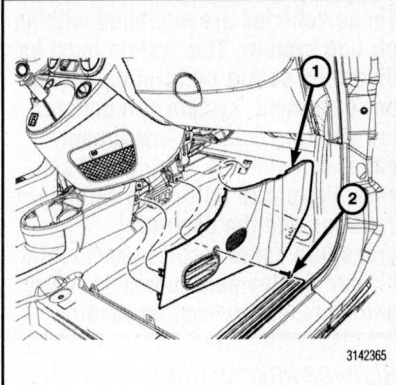

Fig. 17 Remove the screw (2) from the right side floor console panel (1)

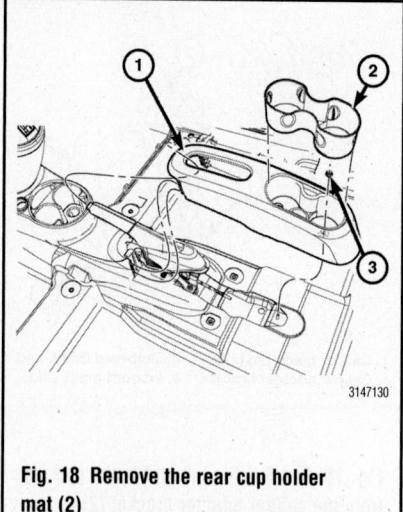

Fig. 18 Remove the rear cup holder mat (2)

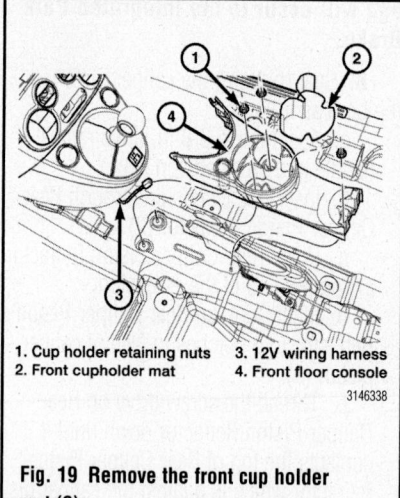

1. Cup holder retaining nuts
2. Front cupholder mat
3. 12V wiring harness
4. Front floor console

Fig. 19 Remove the front cup holder mat (2)

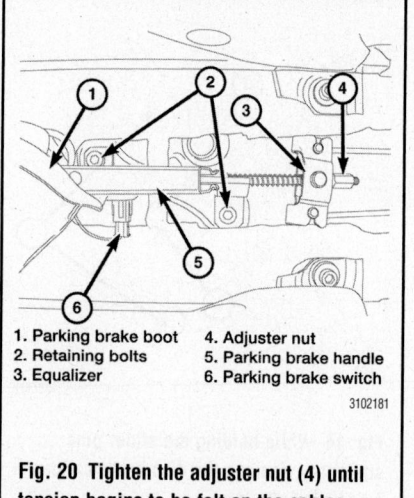

1. Parking brake boot
2. Retaining bolts
3. Equalizer
4. Adjuster nut
5. Parking brake handle
6. Parking brake switch

Fig. 20 Tighten the adjuster nut (4) until tension begins to be felt on the cables

e. Remove the screw (2) from the right side floor console panel (1).

f. Using trim stick, disengage the front floor console to floor console panel retaining clips.

g. Pull the floor console panel rearward to disengage the retaining clip in the floor.

h. Remove the right side floor console panel (1) from the vehicle.

i. Position the parking brake handle up fully.

j. Remove the rear cup holder mat (2).

k. Remove the rear retaining nut (3) located in the rear cup holder cavity.

l. Pull the rear floor console rearward to disengage the front to rear floor console retaining clips/tabs.

m. Slide the rear floor console (1) over the parking brake handle and remove from the vehicle.

n. Remove the front cup holder mat (2).

o. Remove the retaining nuts (1) located in the cup holder cavity and in the rear of the front floor console (4).

p. Pull the front floor console rearward slightly and disconnect the 12V power harness (3).

q. Remove the front floor console (4) from the vehicle.

2. Place the parking brake handle (5) in the completely lowered position.

3. Back the adjuster nut (4) off until

there is no tension on the parking brake cable.

4. Tighten the adjuster nut (4) until tension begins to be felt on the cables.

5. Look under vehicle and ensure that the parking brake actuating lever has not lifted off of the parking brake stop on both sides of the vehicle.

6. If lever is off of the stop, it will be necessary to go back inside the vehicle and loosen the adjuster nut.

7. Once there is tension on the parking brake cables and both actuating levers are still on their resting tabs, actuate the parking brake to ensure that it is functioning properly.

8. Install the floor console.

CHASSIS ELECTRICAL

AIR BAG (SUPPLEMENTAL RESTRAINT SYSTEM)

GENERAL INFORMATION

✳✳ CAUTION

These vehicles are equipped with an air bag system. The system must be disarmed before performing service on, or around, system components, the steering column, instrument panel components, wiring and sensors. Failure to follow the safety precautions and the disarming procedure could result in accidental air bag deployment, possible injury and unnecessary system repairs.

SERVICE PRECAUTIONS

Disconnect and isolate the battery negative cable before beginning any airbag system component diagnosis, testing, removal, or

installation procedures. Allow system capacitor to discharge for two minutes before beginning any component service. This will disable the airbag system. Failure to disable the airbag system may result in accidental airbag deployment, personal injury, or death.

Do not place an intact undeployed airbag face down on a solid surface. The airbag will propel into the air if accidentally deployed and may result in personal injury or death.

When carrying or handling an undeployed airbag, the trim side (face) of the airbag should be pointing away from the body to minimize possibility of injury if accidental deployment occurs. Failure to do this may result in personal injury or death.

Replace airbag system components with OEM replacement parts. Substitute parts may appear interchangeable, but internal differences may result in inferior occupant

protection. Failure to do so may result in occupant personal injury or death.

Wear safety glasses, rubber gloves, and long sleeved clothing when cleaning powder residue from vehicle after an airbag deployment. Powder residue emitted from a deployed airbag can cause skin irritation. Flush affected area with cool water if irritation is experienced. If nasal or throat irritation is experienced, exit the vehicle for fresh air until the irritation ceases. If irritation continues, see a physician.

Do not use a replacement airbag that is not in the original packaging. This may result in improper deployment, personal injury, or death.

The factory installed fasteners, screws and bolts used to fasten airbag components have a special coating and are specifically designed for the airbag system. Do not use substitute fasteners. Use only original equipment fasteners listed in the parts catalog when fastener replacement is required.

During, and following, any child restraint anchor service, due to impact event or vehicle repair, carefully inspect all mounting hardware, tether straps, and anchors for proper installation, operation, or damage. If a child restraint anchor is found damaged in any way, the anchor must be replaced. Failure to do this may result in personal injury or death.

Deployed and non-deployed airbags may or may not have live pyrotechnic material within the airbag inflator.

Do not dispose of driver/passenger/curtain airbags or seat belt tensioners unless you are sure of complete deployment. Refer to the Hazardous Substance Control System for proper disposal.

Dispose of deployed airbags and tensioners consistent with state, provincial, local, and federal regulations.

After any airbag component testing or service, do not connect the battery negative cable. Personal injury or death may result if the system test is not performed first.

If the vehicle is equipped with the Occupant Classification System (OCS), do not connect the battery negative cable before performing the OCS Verification Test using the scan tool and the appropriate diagnostic information. Personal injury or death may result if the system test is not performed properly.

Never replace both the Occupant Restraint Controller (ORC) and the Occupant Classification Module (OCM) at the same time. If both require replacement, replace one, then perform the Airbag System test before replacing the other.

Both the ORC and the OCM store Occupant Classification System (OCS) calibration data, which they transfer to one another when one of them is replaced. If both are replaced at the same time, an irreversible fault will be set in both modules and the OCS may malfunction and cause personal injury or death.

If equipped with OCS, the Seat Weight Sensor is a sensitive, calibrated unit and must be handled carefully. Do not drop or handle roughly. If dropped or damaged, replace with another sensor. Failure to do so may result in occupant injury or death.

If equipped with OCS, the front passenger seat must be handled carefully as well. When removing the seat, be careful when setting on floor not to drop. If dropped, the

sensor may be inoperative, could result in occupant injury, or possibly death.

If equipped with OCS, when the passenger front seat is on the floor, no one should sit in the front passenger seat. This uneven force may damage the sensing ability of the seat weight sensors. If sat on and damaged, the sensor may be inoperative, could result in occupant injury, or possibly death.

DISARMING THE SYSTEM

Disconnect and isolate the negative cable from the battery. Wait two minutes for the system capacitor to discharge before further service.

ARMING THE SYSTEM

Do not reconnect the negative cable to the battery at this time. The Supplemental Restraint System (SRS) Verification Test procedure should be performed following service of any SRS component

SRS VERIFICATION TEST

> ✳✳ **CAUTION**
>
> **To avoid serious or fatal injury on vehicles equipped with airbags, disable the Supplemental Restraint System (SRS) before attempting any steering wheel, steering column, airbag, seat belt tensioner, impact sensor or instrument panel component diagnosis or service. Disconnect and isolate the battery negative (ground) cable, then wait two minutes for the system capacitor to discharge before performing further diagnosis or service. This is the only sure way to disable the SRS. Failure to take the proper precautions could result in accidental airbag deployment.**

➡ **The following procedure should be performed using a diagnostic scan tool to verify proper Supplemental Restraint System (SRS) operation following the service or replacement of any SRS component. Refer to the appropriate diagnostic procedures.**

1. During the following test, the negative cable remains disconnected and isolated from the battery, as it was during the Supplemental Restraint System (SRS) component removal and installation procedures.
2. Be certain that the diagnostic scan tool contains the latest version of the proper diagnostic software. Connect the scan tool

to the 16-way Data Link Connector (DLC) (2). The DLC is located on the driver side lower edge of the instrument panel (1), near the cowl side inner panel (3).

3. Transition the status of the ignition switch to On and exit the vehicle with the scan tool.
4. Check to be certain that nobody is in the vehicle, then reconnect the negative cable to the battery.
5. Using the scan tool, read and record the active (current) Diagnostic Trouble Code (DTC) data.
6. Next, use the scan tool to read and record any stored (historical) DTC data.
7. If any DTC is found in Step 5 or Step 6, refer to the appropriate diagnostic information.
8. Use the scan tool to erase the stored DTC data. If any problems remain, the stored DTC data will not erase. Refer to the appropriate diagnostic information to diagnose any stored DTC that will not erase. If the stored DTC information is successfully erased, go to Step 9.
9. Transition the status of the ignition switch to Off for about 15 seconds, and then back to On. Observe the airbag indicator in the Instrument Panel Cluster (IPC). It should light for four to six seconds and then go out. This indicates that the SRS is functioning normally and that the repairs are complete. If the airbag indicator fails to light, or lights and stays On, there is still an active SRS fault or malfunction. Refer to the appropriate diagnostic information to diagnose the problem.

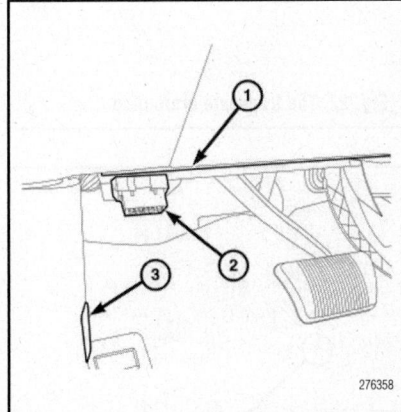

276358

Fig. 21 Connect the scan tool to the 16-way Data Link Connector (DLC) (2). The DLC is located on the driver side lower edge of the instrument panel (1), near the cowl side inner panel (3)

DRIVE TRAIN

AUTOMATIC TRANSAXLE FLUID

DRAIN AND REFILL

See Figures 22 and 23.

➡The vehicle must be level when checking the fluid level)

➡All C514 Transaxles require the use of Castrol BOT 350 M3.

1. The transaxle drain plug (1) is located on the lower left side of the transaxle differential housing. Tighten the drain plug to 13 ft. lbs. (18 Nm).

2. The transaxle fill plug (1) is located on the left side of the transaxle differential area. The fluid level should be even with the bottom of the transaxle fill hole. Tighten the fill plug to 18 lbs. ft. (25 Nm).

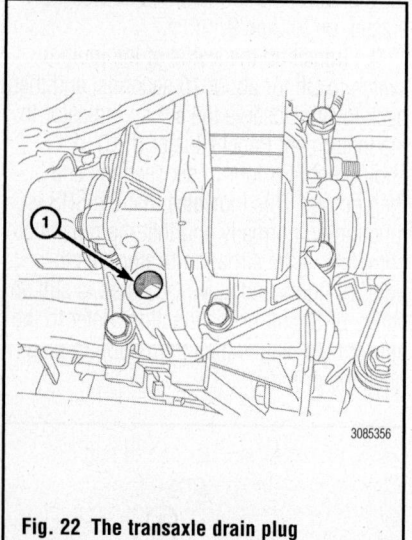

Fig. 22 The transaxle drain plug

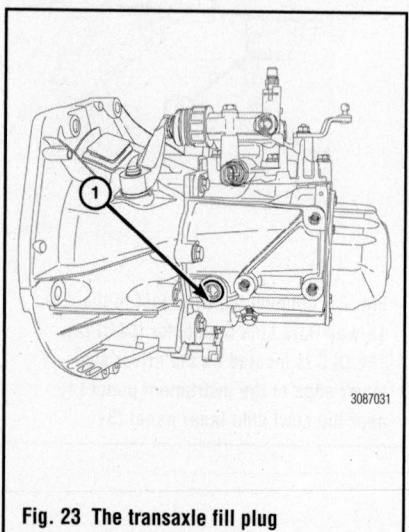

Fig. 23 The transaxle fill plug

MANUAL TRANSAXLE FLUID

DRAIN AND REFILL

See Figures 24 and 25.

➡The vehicle must be level when checking the fluid level.

➡All C510 transaxles require the use of Castrol BOT 350 M3.

1. The transaxle drain plug (1) is located on the lower left side of the transaxle differential housing. Tighten the drain plug to 13 ft. lbs. (18 Nm).

2. The transaxle fill plug (1) is located on the left side of the transaxle differential area. The fluid level should be even with the bottom of the transaxle fill hole. Tighten the fill plug to 18 ft. lbs. (25 Nm).

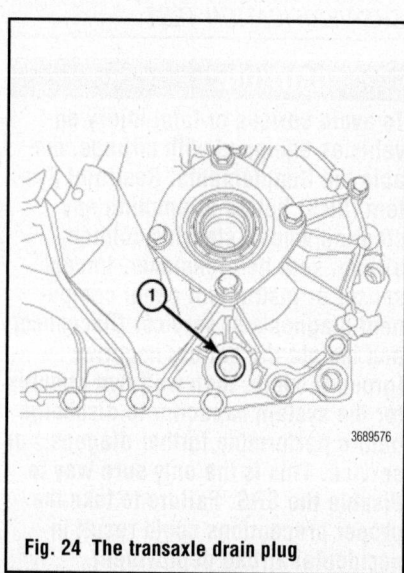

Fig. 24 The transaxle drain plug

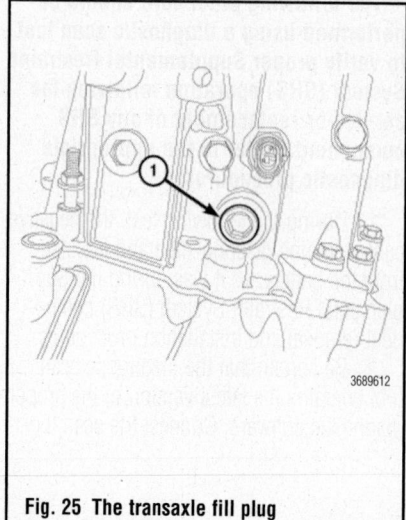

Fig. 25 The transaxle fill plug

CLUTCH

BLEEDING

Power Bleeding

1. Use Mopar® brake fluid, or an equivalent quality fluid meeting DOT 3 standards only. Use fresh, clean fluid from a sealed container at all times.

2. Follow the manufacturer's instructions carefully when using pressure equipment. Do not exceed the tank manufacturers pressure recommendations. The service filling machine should be pressurized between 2.0 and 2.5 bar (29 - 36 PSI).

3. Fill the bleeder tank with recommended fluid and purge air from the tank lines before bleeding.

4. Do not pressure bleed without a proper master cylinder adapter. The wrong adapter can lead to leakage, or drawing air back into the system.

5. Remove dust cap from bleeder valve and connect the transparent bleeder hose to bleeder valve.

➡Use a container to capture hydraulic fluid and a transparent bleeder hose to route fluid to the container.

➡The container must be at a lower level than the bleeder valve on the clutch slave cylinder.

6. Place the other end of hose in the bleeder container to capture the used fluid. The end of the hose MUST be submerged in the DOT 3 brake fluid.

7. Turn on the service filling machine.

➡While bleeding the system, do not allow the clutch fluid reservoir to completely empty out. If this happens, refill the clutch fluid reservoir, and repeat the procedure.

8. Open the bleeder valve on the clutch slave cylinder enough to allow fluid to flow from the clutch hydraulic system.

9. Allow fluid to flow out of bleed port until no more air bubbles can be seen in the transparent bleeder hose.

10. Once fluid is free of air bubbles; make 15 quick actuations between clutch pedal stop positions.

11. Close the bleeder valve at the clutch slave cylinder and disconnect the service filling machine.

12. Check clutch pedal to see if vehicle is properly bled.

13. If vehicle is not properly bled, repeat procedure.

14. Remove bleeder cap from the clutch fluid reservoir and replace reservoir cap.

15. Disconnect transparent bleeder hose from bleeder valve and replace dust cap.

Manual Bleeding

See Figure 26.

➡️**An assistant is required to perform this procedure**

1. Verify fluid level in clutch/brake cylinder. Top off with DOT 3 brake fluid as necessary. Leave cap off.

➡️**The container must be positioned at a lower level than the bleeder valve on the clutch slave cylinder**

2. Install suitable size and length of clear hose to the bleeder port (1) in order to monitor and divert fluid into a suitable container.

3. Have the assistant press down and hold the clutch pedal until it reaches the floor.

➡️**Do not allow clutch/brake fluid reservoir to run dry while fluid exits bleed port. If the reservoir runs dry during this procedure, it must be refilled. and this step must be repeated.**

➡️**Ensure the assistant does not release the clutch pedal from the floor while the bleed port on the clutch slave cylinder is open. Otherwise, air will enter the clutch hydraulic circuit.**

4. Open the bleed port on the clutch slave cylinder enough to allow hydraulic fluid to drain. Any air in the system will escape at this time.

5. Close the bleed port on the clutch slave cylinder, and have the assistant release the clutch pedal to the full up position.

6. Repeat steps 5 through 7 at least 15 times or until air bubbles are no longer present in the clutch hydraulic fluid.

7. Slowly actuate the clutch pedal 10 times between the full up and pedal stop position.

8. **Apply parking brake**. Start engine and verify clutch operation and pedal feel. If the clutch pedal feels fine and the transaxle can be easily shifted from neutral to any gear, the clutch is operating correctly. If pedal still feels spongy or clutch does not fully disengage, excessive air is still trapped within the system, most likely at the master cylinder.

9. Disconnect the hose from the bleed port on the clutch slave cylinder.

10. Top off brake master cylinder fluid level with DOT 3 brake fluid as necessary.

FRONT HALFSHAFT

REMOVAL & INSTALLATION

See Figures 27 through 29.

➡️**Never grasp the halfshaft assembly by the inner or outer boots doing so may damage to the boot.**

➡️**The inner tripod joints are designed with a retention feature that prevents the tripod rollers from coming out of the inner joint housing up to a specific load. If this feature is overcome and any of the rollers are pulled past the retention feature the joint will "lock-up" and no longer function properly. The entire halfshaft assembly must be replaced if this occurs.**

1. Before proceeding, review all Warnings and Cautions

2. Raise and support the vehicle

3. Remove the wheel and tire assembly

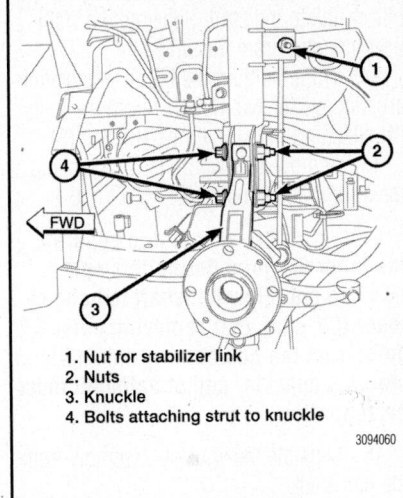

1. Nut for stabilizer link
2. Nuts
3. Knuckle
4. Bolts attaching strut to knuckle

3094060

Fig. 28 Remove the nut (1) attaching the stabilizer link to the strut

4. If equipped, remove the engine belly pan.

5. Remove the cross car cradle brace.

6. Drain the transmission fluid (manual transmissions only).

7. Remove the staking from the hub nut (2).

8. While a helper applies the brakes to keep the hub from rotating, use a 12 point thin-walled 36mm Craftsman® socket (or equivalent) to remove the hub nut and discard.

9. Disconnect the wheel speed sensor from the hub assembly.

10. Remove the nut attaching the outer tie rod to the knuckle.

11. Release the outer tie rod end (3) from the knuckle (2) using (1).

12. Remove the outer tie rod from the knuckle.

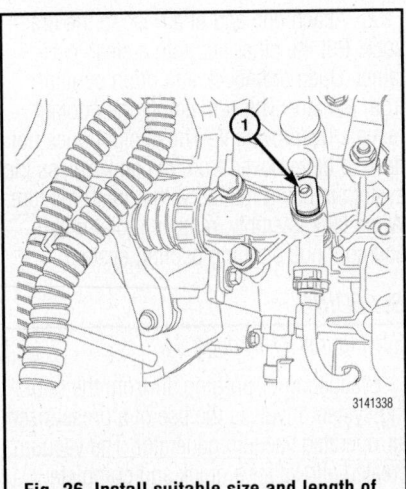

3141338

Fig. 26 Install suitable size and length of clear hose to the bleeder port (1)

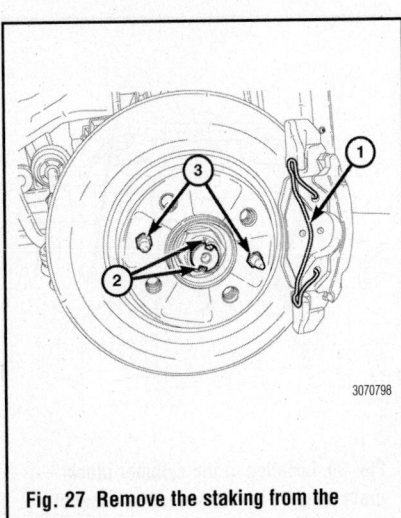

3070798

Fig. 27 Remove the staking from the hub nut

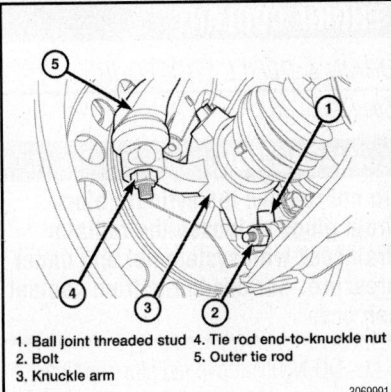

1. Ball joint threaded stud   4. Tie rod end-to-knuckle nut
2. Bolt   5. Outer tie rod
3. Knuckle arm

3069991

Fig. 29 Install the outer tie rod (5) ball stud into the hole in the knuckle (3) arm

13. Remove the nut (1) attaching the stabilizer link to the strut. Separate the stabilizer link stud from the strut.

14. While holding the bolt heads stationary, remove the two nuts (2) from the bolts (4) attaching the strut to the knuckle (3).

15. Remove the two bolts (2) attaching the strut to the knuckle (3).

➡ **Care must be taken not to separate the inner C/V joint during this operation. Do not allow halfshaft to hang by inner C/V Joint after removing outer C/V Joint from the hub/bearing assembly in steering knuckle, end of halfshaft must be supported**

16. Separate the knuckle assembly from the half shaft.

➡ **With manual transaxles some fluid might leak when the half shaft is removed from the transaxle.**

17. Supporting the outer end of the halfshaft assembly, insert a pry bar between the inner tripod joint and transaxle case). Pry against inner tripod joint until the retaining snap-ring is disengaged from transaxle side gear and remove half shaft from the vehicle.

To install:

➡ **The inner tripod joints are designed with a retention feature that prevents the tripod rollers from coming out of the inner joint housing up to a specific load. If this feature is overcome and any of the rollers are pulled past the retention feature the joint will "lock-up" and no longer function properly. The entire halfshaft assembly must be replaced if this occurs.**

18. Thoroughly clean the spline and oil seal sealing surface on tripod joint.

19. Lightly lubricate oil seal sealing surface on tripod joint with fresh clean transmission lubricant.

20. Holding halfshaft assembly by the tripod joint and interconnecting shaft, install tripod joint into transaxle side gear as far as possible by hand. Be sure to engage splines prior to applying force.

➡ **Attempt to remove tripod joint by hand to verify that the snap ring is fully engaged. If snap ring is fully engaged, tripod joint will not be removable from transmission by hand.**

21. Push the tripod joint into the transaxle side gear, until snap-ring is fully engaged.

22. Clean all debris and moisture at the bearing hub where the outer CV joint will be installed into steering knuckle assembly.

23. Install the outer CV joint to the bearing hub.

24. Slide half shaft back into front hub and bearing assembly.

➡ **Before tightening the bolts, press the knuckle toward the vehicle to achieve the most negative camber. If this is not done, it is possible to have positive camber which will negatively impact vehicle handling.**

25. Position the lower end of the strut assembly in line with the upper end of the knuckle (3), aligning the mounting holes. Install the two mounting bolts (4) from the front side of the vehicle.

26. Install the nuts (2) on the two bolts

(4). While holding the bolts in place, tighten the nuts to 55 ft. lbs. (75 Nm).

27. Install the outer tie rod (5) ball stud into the hole in the knuckle (3) arm. Start the tie rod end-to-knuckle nut (4) onto the stud. While holding the tie rod end stud with a wrench, tighten the nut with a wrench or crowfoot wrench to 30 ft. lbs. (40 Nm).

28. Install the wheel speed sensor head into the knuckle. Install the mounting screw and tighten it to 106 inch lbs. (12 Nm).

➡ **Always install a new hub nut. The original hub nut is one-time use only and must be discarded when removed.**

29. Clean all foreign matter from the threads of the halfshaft stub shaft.

30. Install a **NEW** hub nut on the end of the halfshaft stub shaft. While a helper applies the brakes to keep the hub from rotating, use a 12 point thin-walled 36mm Craftsman® socket (or equivalent) to tighten the hub nut to 229 ft. lbs. (310 Nm).

➡ **The hub nut must be staked so that it looks similar to Figure 1. The edge must be split and bent into the shape shown (3). The staking prevents the nut from coming off the vehicle while it is being operated. The staking must be in the opposite direction from the forward rotation of the wheel.**

31. Perform staking procedure.
32. Install the tire and wheel assembly
33. Install the cross car cradle brace. Tighten the bolts to 66 ft. lbs. (90 Nm).
34. Check for correct fluid level in transaxle assembly
35. If equipped, install the engine belly pan
36. Lower the vehicle.

ENGINE COOLING

ENGINE COOLANT

DRAIN & REFILL PROCEDURE
See Figure 30.

❋❋ CAUTION

Do not remove the cylinder block drain plugs or loosen the radiator draincock with system hot and under pressure. Serious burns from coolant can occur.

1. DO NOT remove radiator cap first. With engine cold, raise vehicle on a hoist and locate radiator draincock.

➡ **The radiator draincock is located on the right/lower side of radiator facing to rear of vehicle.**

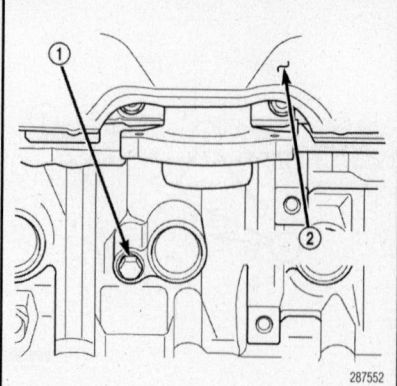

287552

Fig. 30 Location of the cylinder block drain plug (1) in relation to the exhaust manifold heat shield (2)

2. Attach one end of a hose to the draincock. Put the other end into a clean container. Open draincock and drain coolant from radiator. This will empty the coolant reserve/overflow tank. The coolant does not have to be removed from the tank unless the system is being refilled with a fresh mixture. When tank is empty, remove radiator cap and continue draining cooling system.

BLEEDING
See Figures 31 through 34.

Evacuating or purging air from the cooling system involves the use of a pressurized air operated vacuum generator. The vacuum created allows for a quick and complete coolant refilling while removing any airlocks present in the system components.

➡To avoid damage to the cooling system, ensure that no component would be susceptible to damage when a vacuum is drawn on the system.

❈❈ CAUTION

Antifreeze is an ethylene glycol base coolant and is harmful if swallowed or inhaled. If swallowed, drink two glasses of water and induce vomiting. If inhaled, move to fresh air area. Seek medical attention immediately. Do not store in open or unmarked containers. Wash skin and clothing thoroughly after coming in contact with ethylene glycol. Keep out of reach of children. Dispose of glycol based coolant properly. Contact your dealer or government agency for location of collection center in your area. Do not open a cooling system when the engine is at operating temperature or hot under pressure; personal injury can result. Avoid radiator cooling fan when engine compartment related service is performed; personal injury can result.

❈❈ CAUTION

Make sure to wear proper eye and hand protection when performing this procedure.

➡The service area where this procedure is performed should have a mini-mum shop air requirement of 80 PSI (5.5 bar) and should be equipped with an air dryer system.

➡For best results, the radiator should be empty. The vehicle's heater control should be set to the heat position (ignition may need to be turned to the on position but do not start the motor).

1. Refer to the Chrysler Pentastar Service Equipment (Chrysler PSE) Coolant Refiller #85-15-0650 or equivalent tool's operating manual for specific assembly steps.

2. Choose an appropriate adapter cone that will fit the vehicle's radiator filler neck or reservoir tank.

3. Attach the adapter cone (2) to the vacuum gauge (1).

4. Make sure the vacuum generator/venturi ball valve (3) is closed and attach an airline hose (2) (minimum shop air requirement of 80 PSI/5.5 bar) to the vacuum generator/venturi (1).

5. Position the adaptor cone/vacuum gauge assembly into the radiator filler neck or reservoir tank. Ensure that the adapter cone is sealed properly.

6. Connect the vacuum generator/venturi (2) to the positioned adaptor cone/vacuum gauge assembly (1).

7. Open the vacuum generator/venturi ball valve.

➡Do not bump or move the assembly as it may result in loss of vacuum. Some radiator overflow hoses may need to be clamped off to obtain vacuum.

8. Let the system run until the vacuum gauge shows a good vacuum through the cooling system. Refer to the tool's operating manual for appropriate pressure readings.

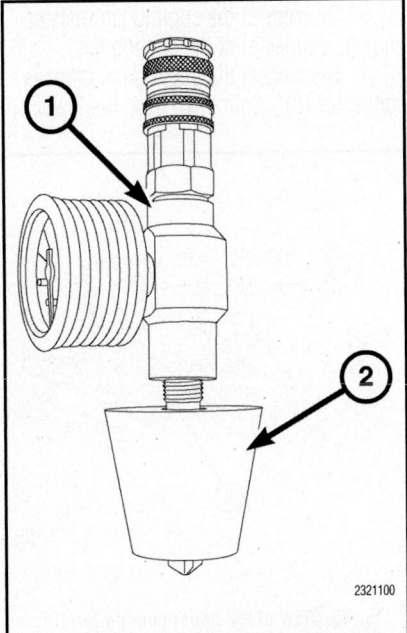

Fig. 31 Attach the adapter cone (2) to the vacuum gauge (1)

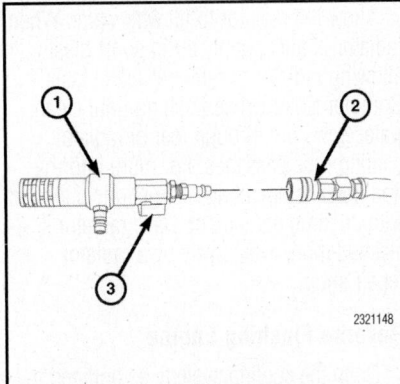

Fig. 32 Make sure the vacuum generator/venturi ball valve (3) is closed and attach an airline hose (2) (minimum shop air requirement of 80 PSI/5.5 bar) to the vacuum generator/venturi (1)

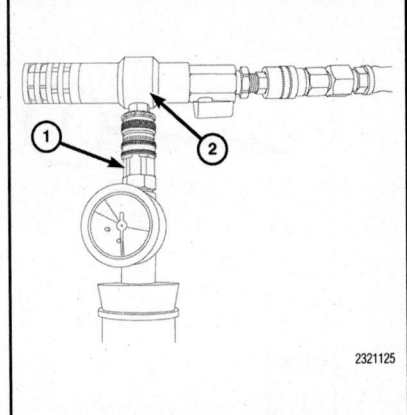

Fig. 33 Connect the vacuum generator/venturi (2) to the positioned adaptor cone/vacuum gauge assembly (1)

➡If a strong vacuum is being created in the system, it is normal to see the radiator hoses to collapse.

9. Close the vacuum generator/venturi ball valve.

10. Disconnect the vacuum generator/venturi and airline from the adaptor cone/vacuum gauge assembly.

11. Wait approximately 20 seconds, if the pressure readings do not move, the system has no leaks. If the pressure readings move, a leak could be present in the system and the cooling system should be checked for leaks and the procedure should be repeated.

12. Place the tool's suction hose into the coolant's container.

➡Ensure there is a sufficient amount of coolant, mixed to the required strength/protection level available for use. For best results and to assist the refilling procedure, place the coolant container at the same height as the radiator filler neck. Always draw more coolant than required. If the coolant level is too low, it will pull air into the cooling system which could result in airlocks in the system.

13. Connect the tool's suction hose (1) to the adaptor cone/vacuum gauge assembly (2).

14. Open the suction hose's ball valve to begin refilling the cooling system.

15. When the vacuum gauge reads zero, the system is filled.

➡On some remote pressurized tanks, it is recommended to stop filling when the proper level is reached.

16. Close the suction hose's ball valve and remove the suction hose from the adaptor cone/vacuum gauge assembly.

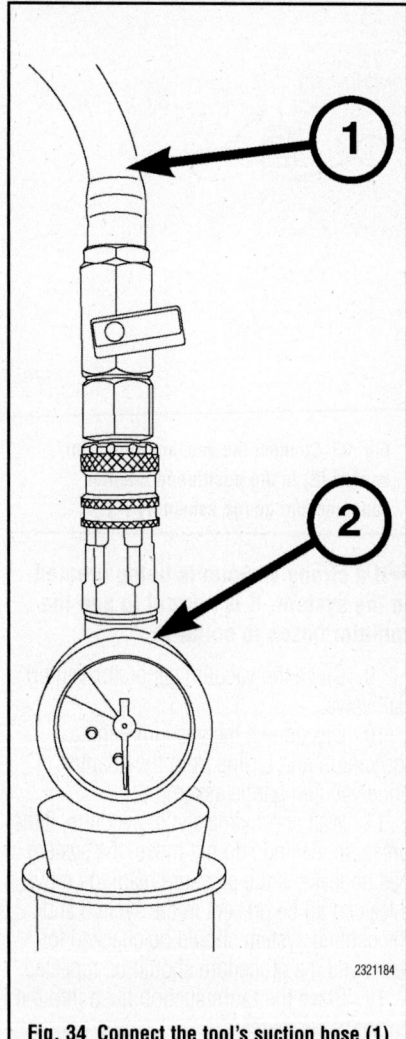

Fig. 34 Connect the tool's suction hose (1) to the adaptor cone/vacuum gauge assembly (2)

17. Remove the adaptor cone/vacuum gauge assembly from the radiator filler neck or reservoir tank.

18. With heater control unit in the HEAT position, operate engine with container cap in place.

After engine has reached normal operating temperature, shut engine off and allow it to cool. When engine is cooling down, coolant will be drawn into the radiator from the pressure container.

19. Add coolant to the recovery bottle/container as necessary. Only add coolant to the container when the engine is cold. Coolant level in a warm engine will be higher due to thermal expansion. Add necessary coolant to raise container level to the COLD MINIMUM mark after each cool down period.

20. Once the appropriate coolant level is achieved, attach the radiator cap or reservoir tank cap.

REVERSE FLUSHING

☀ WARNING

The cooling system normally operates at 97–124 kPa (14–18 psi) pressure. Exceeding this pressure may damage the radiator or hoses.

Reverse flushing of the cooling system is the forcing of water through the cooling system. This is done using air pressure in the opposite direction of normal coolant flow. It is usually only necessary with very dirty systems with evidence of partial plugging.

Chemical Cleaning

If visual inspection indicates the formation of sludge or scaly deposits, use a radiator cleaner (Mopar® Radiator Kleen or equivalent) before flushing. This will soften scale and other deposits and aid the flushing operation.

☀ WARNING

Make sure to follow the instructions on the container.

Reverse Flushing Radiator

Disconnect the radiator hoses from the radiator fittings. Attach a section of radiator hose to the radiator bottom outlet fitting and insert the flushing gun. Connect a water supply hose and air supply hose to the flushing gun.

☀ WARNING

The cooling system normally operates at 97-124 kPa (14-18 psi) pressure. Exceeding this pressure may damage the radiator or hoses.

Allow the radiator to fill with water. When radiator is filled, apply air in short blasts allowing radiator to refill between blasts. Continue this reverse flushing until clean water flows out through rear of radiator cooling tube passages. For more information, refer to operating instructions supplied with flushing equipment. Have radiator cleaned more extensively by a radiator repair shop.

Reverse Flushing Engine

Drain the cooling system, as outlined in this section. Remove the thermostat housing and thermostat. Install the thermostat housing. Disconnect the radiator upper hose from the radiator and attach the flushing gun to the hose. Disconnect the radiator lower hose from the water pump. Attach a lead away hose to the water pump inlet fitting.

☀ WARNING

Be sure that the heater control valve is closed (heat off). This is done to prevent coolant flow with scale and other deposits from entering the heater core.

Connect the water supply hose and air supply hose to the flushing gun. Allow the engine to fill with water. When the engine is filled, apply air in short blasts, allowing the system to fill between air blasts. Continue until clean water flows through the lead away hose. For more information, refer to operating instructions supplied with flushing equipment.

Remove the lead away hose, flushing gun, water supply hose and air supply hose. Remove the thermostat housing. Install the thermostat and housing with a replacement gasket. Connect the radiator hoses. Refill the cooling system with the correct antifreeze/water mixture.

ENGINE FAN

REMOVAL & INSTALLATION

See Figures 35 through 37.

➥**The cooling fan is removed from the bottom of the vehicle.**

1. Disconnect the negative battery cable.

2. Remove the engine cover and the air intake assembly.

3. Disconnect the cooling fan resistor harness connector at the cooling fan.

4. Disconnect the cooling fan harness connector (3). cooling fan from the lower

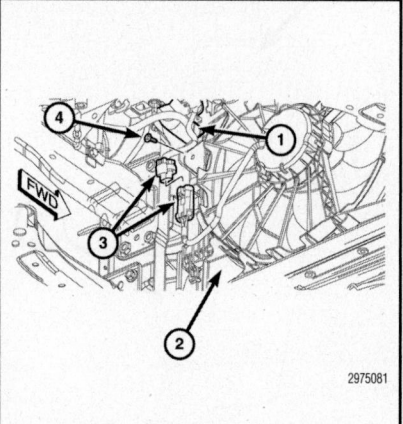

Fig. 35 View of the upper cooling fan (2), fan resistor harness connector (3) and mounting bolts (4)

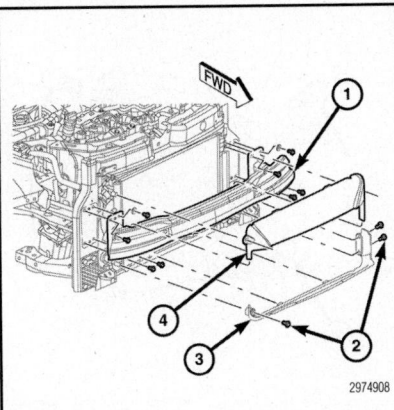

Fig. 36 Remove the upper (4) and lower (3) air seals. Remove the front bumper support beam (1)

mounting tabs at this time. Damage may occur to the fins of the radiator.

5. Remove the upper cooling fan (2) mounting bolts (4).

6. Raise vehicle.

7. Remove the front bumper fascia.

8. Remove the upper (4) and lower (3) air seals.

9. Remove the front bumper support beam (1).

10. Support the radiator and the A/C condenser with a suitable fixture.

11. Remove the lower radiator support brackets (2).

12. Use care when positioning the radiator and the A/C condenser aside.

13. Remove the cooling fan from the lower mounting tabs located on the radiator.

14. Remove the cooling fan from the vehicle through the bottom of the cooling module assembly.

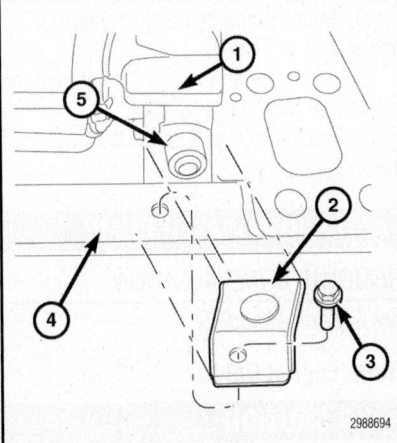

Fig. 37 Position the radiator into place and install the lower radiator support bracket (2) to the radiator mount (5), then tighten mounting bracket bolt (3)

To install:

15. Guide the cooling fan into position onto the radiator tabs through the bottom of the vehicle.

16. Position the radiator into place and install the lower radiator support bracket (2) to the radiator mount (5). Tighten mounting bracket bolt (3) to 70 inch lbs. (8 Nm).

17. Install the upper (4) and lower (3) air seals.

18. Install the from bumper support beam (1). Tighten mounting bolt to 30 ft. lbs. (40 Nm).

19. Install the front bumper fascia.

20. Lower vehicle.

21. Install the upper mounting screws for the cooling fan. Tighten mounting bolt to 70 inch lbs. (8 Nm).

22. Install the wire harness connectors to the cooling fan.

23. Connect the resistor harness connector at the cooling fan.

24. Install the engine cover and air intake assembly.

25. Reconnect the negative battery cable.

RADIATOR

REMOVAL & INSTALLATION

See Figures 35 through 37

1. Disconnect the negative battery cable.

2. Remove the engine cover and the air intake assembly.

3. Drain the cooling system.

➡**Do not remove the mounting bolts for the cooling fan. The fan is removed with the radiator.**

4. Remove the upper radiator hose.

5. Disconnect the cooling fan resistor.

6. Disconnect the cooling fan wire harness connector.

7. Raise the vehicle.

8. Remove the front bumper fascia.

9. Remove the lower radiator hose.

10. Partially lower the vehicle.

11. Remove the front bumper support.

12. Remove the upper seal.

13. Remove the lower seal.

14. If equipped, remove the turbo inter cooler.

15. Evacuate the A/C system.

16. Remove the A/C condenser from the cooling module.

17. Remove the lower radiator mounting bracket bolts from the lower cooling module support.

18. Remove the radiator from the vehicle.

19. Remove the mounting bolts (1) that

secure the cooling fan assembly (2) to the radiator.

To install:

20. Install the radiator cooling fan onto the lower mounting clips on the radiator.

21. Install the upper radiator cooling fan bolts. Tighten the radiator fan retaining screws to 70 inch lbs. (8 Nm).

22. Position the cooling module into the upper radiator supports.

23. Install the lower radiator bracket screws. Tighten the radiator screws to 70 inch lbs. (8 Nm).

24. Install the A/C condenser. Tighten the condenser retaining screws (2) to 70 inch lbs. (8 Nm).

25. Recharge the A/C system.

26. Install the upper and lower seals.

27. Install the front bumper. Tighten the bolts to 30 ft. lbs. (40 Nm).

28. Raise vehicle.

29. Install the lower radiator hose.

30. Install the front bumper fascia.

31. Lower vehicle.

32. Install the upper radiator hose

33. Install the wire harness connectors to the cooling fan.

✱✱ WARNING

The FIAT engines use a OAT coolant. OAT coolant CAN NOT be mixed with and other kinds of coolant. Heavy corrosion or damage may occur to the cooling system or engine, unless the proper coolant has been used.

34. Fill the cooling system with OAT coolant.

35. Install the engine cover and air intake assembly.

36. Reconnect the negative battery cable.

THERMOSTAT

REMOVAL & INSTALLATION

See Figures 38 through 40.

✱✱ CAUTION

Never loosen radiator draincock with system hot and pressurized. Serious burns from coolant can occur.

➡**The Thermostat and housing is serviced as an assembly. Do not remove the thermostat from the housing, damage to the thermostat may occur.**

1. Remove the engine cover.

2. Remove the air intake assembly.

3. Drain the cooling system.

4. Disconnect the negative and the positive battery cable.

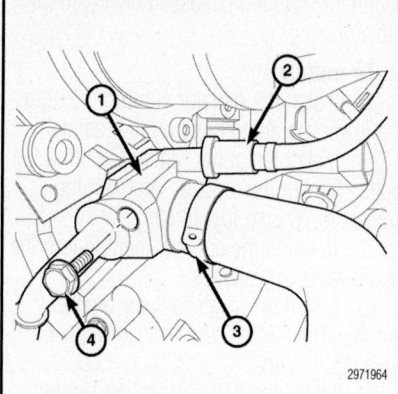

Fig. 38 Disconnect the coolant recovery bottle return hose (2), the lower radiator hose (3) and the oil cooler return hose (4)

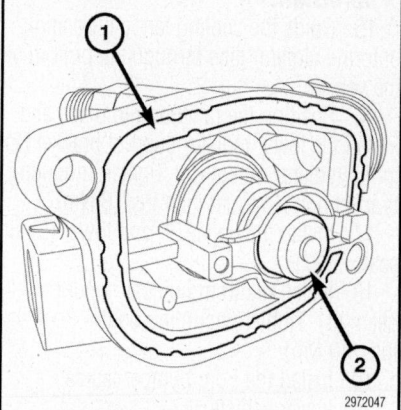

Fig. 40 Remove the thermostat (2) from the engine block and discard gasket seal (1)

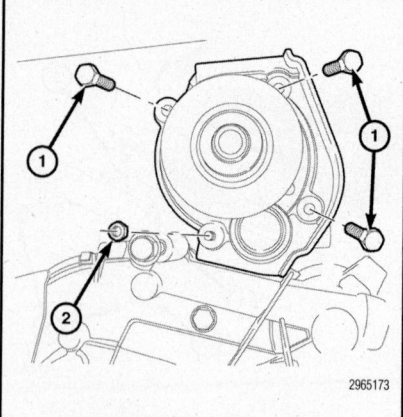

Fig. 41 Remove the screws (1) and the nut (2) securing the water pump to the engine block

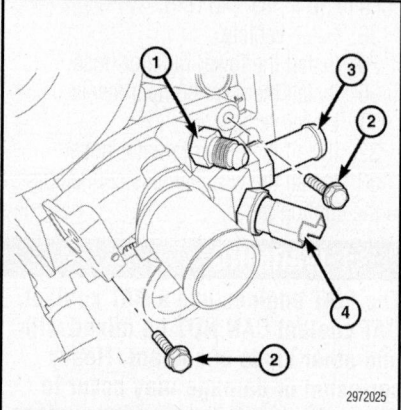

Fig. 39 Remove the Engine Coolant Temperature (ECT) sensor (4), then remove the thermostat mounting bolts (2)

18. Install new gasket seal onto the thermostat housing.

19. Install the Engine Coolant Temperature (ECT) sensor.

20. Install the thermostat housing mounting bolts. Tighten bolts to 80 inch lbs. (9 Nm).

21. Install the heater supply hose.

22. Connect the temperature sensor wire harness connector.

23. Install the coolant recovery bottle return hose.

24. Install the lower radiator hose.

25. Install the oil cooler hose. Tightened the bolt to 80 inch lbs. (9 Nm).

26. Install the battery tray. Tightened the nut and bolt to 9 ft. lbs. (12 Nm).

27. Install the battery. Tightened the nut to 62 inch lbs. (7 Nm).

28. Fill the cooling system.

29. Install the air intake.

30. Install the engine cover.

WATER PUMP

REMOVAL & INSTALLATION

See Figures 41 through 43.

1. Drain the cooling system.

2. Remove the timing belt, as outlined in the Engine Mechanical Section.

3. Remove the screws and the nut securing the water pump to the engine block.

4. Remove the water pump from the engine block by lightly prying at the upper tab located on the pump assembly.

To install:

5. Clean the mating surfaces.

6. Apply a strip of silicone sealant to the contact surfaces between the water pump and the engine block.

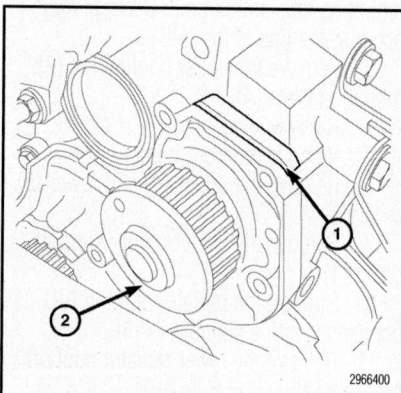

Fig. 42 Remove the water pump (2) from the engine block by lightly prying at the upper tab (1) located on the pump assembly

7. Position pump onto the engine block.

8. Install the mounting bolts and nut. Tighten to 89 inch lbs. (10 Nm).

9. Rotate pump by hand to check for freedom of movement.

10. Install the timing belt, as outlined in the Engine Mechanical Section.

11. Evacuate air and fill the cooling system.

AFTER RUN WATER PUMP

REMOVAL & INSTALLATION

See Figures 44 and 45.

Turbo Engine Only

※※ CAUTION

Hot, pressurized coolant can cause serious burns. Allow the system to cool down and decrease pressure prior to any service being performed.

5. Remove the battery hold down nut and remove the clamp.

6. Remove the battery.

7. Remove the battery tray bolt and nut and position the tray aside.

8. Remove the coolant recovery bottle return hose.

9. Remove the lower radiator hose.

10. Remove the oil cooler return hose.

11. Disconnect the Engine Coolant Temperature (ECT) sensor harness connector.

12. Remove the heater supply hose.

13. Remove the Engine Coolant Temperature (ECT) sensor (4).

14. Remove the thermostat mounting bolts (2).

15. Remove the thermostat from the engine block and discard gasket seal.

16. Remove the temperature sensor.

To install:

17. Clean the mating surfaces on the engine block and thermostat housing.

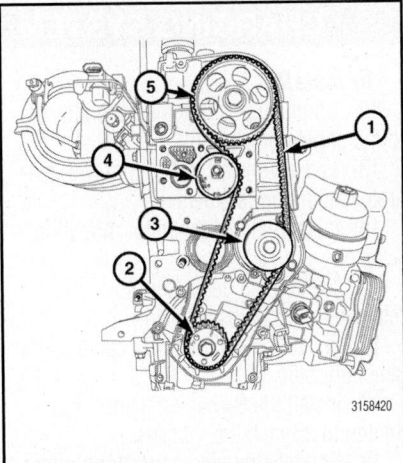

Fig. 43 Installed view of the timing belt (1) and related components

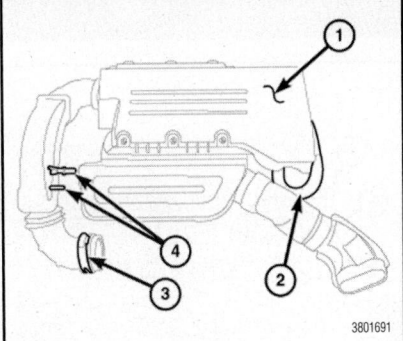

Fig. 44 Disconnect the two vacuum fittings (4), loosen the clamp (3) at the air to turbocharger inlet tube. Disconnect he fresh air intake hose (2). Remove the air cleaner assembly (1)

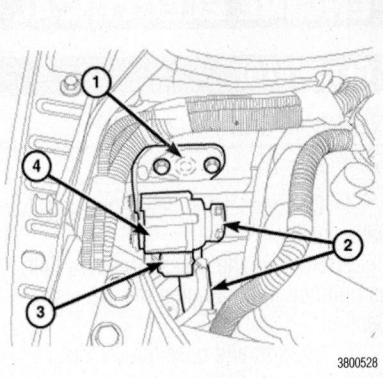

Fig. 45 View of the two bracket bolts (1), hoses (2), electrical connector (3), and after-run pump—turbo engines only

✳✳ CAUTION

The after-run pump can activate without warning for up to 10 minutes after engine shutdown.

1. Disconnect and isolate the negative battery cable.
2. Raise and support vehicle.
3. If equipped, remove the belly pan.
4. Drain out enough coolant to bring the level below the pump.
5. Disconnect the two vacuum fittings, loosen the clamp at the air to turbocharger inlet tube.
6. Disconnect he fresh air intake hose.

7. Remove the air cleaner assembly.
8. Remove the nut and bolt at the degas bottle and set the bottle aside.
9. Disconnect the after-run electrical connector.
10. Using suitable hose clamp pliers, release and reposition the hose clamps to allow for hose removal.
11. Disconnect the hoses from the pump.
12. Remove the two bracket bolts.

To install:

13. Position the pump and install the two bracket bolts.
14. Tighten the bolts to 80 inch lbs. (9 Nm).

15. Attach the two hoses to the pump.
16. Using suitable hose clamp pliers, reposition the hose clamps to the proper position and activate the clamps to tension.
17. Connect the pump electrical connector.
18. Install the nut and bolt at the degas bottle and tighten to 53 inch lbs. (6 Nm).
19. Install the air cleaner and hoses. Tighten clamp.
20. Attach the clean air hose and two vacuum hoses.
21. Top off the coolant.
22. Start the engine and check for leaks.

ENGINE ELECTRICAL

BATTERY SYSTEM

BATTERY

REMOVAL & INSTALLATION

See Figures 46 and 47.

1. Remove the positive battery terminal cover.
2. Disconnect the negative battery cable (2).
3. Disconnect the positive battery cable (1).
4. Remove the battery thermo cover.
5. Remove the battery hold-down retainer.
6. Remove the battery (2) from the vehicle.

To install:

7. Install the battery into the vehicle.
8. Install the battery hold-down retainer.
9. Install the battery thermo cover.

10. Connect the positive battery cable.
11. Connect the negative battery cable.

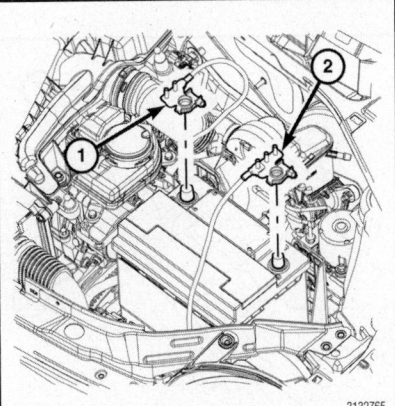

Fig. 46 Disconnect the negative battery cable (2), and then the positive battery cable (1)

12. Install the positive battery terminal cover.

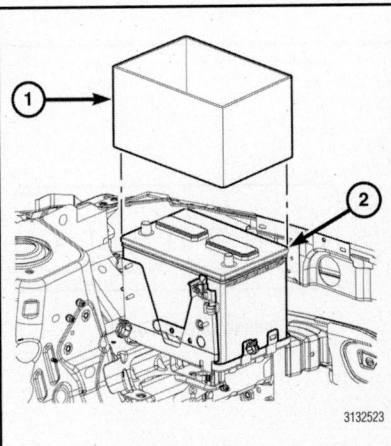

Fig. 47 View of the battery thermo cover (1) and the battery (2)

ENGINE ELECTRICAL

GENERATOR

REMOVAL & INSTALLATION

See Figure 48.

1. Disconnect and isolate the negative battery cable.
2. Remove the accessory drive belt, as outlined in the Engine Mechanical Section.
3. Support and raise the vehicle.
4. Remove the belly pan covering the bottom side of the engine compartment.
5. Remove the right side axle shaft.
6. Disconnect the field generator harness connector.
7. Remove the generator B+ cable retainer.
8. Remove the cable from the generator stud.
9. Remove the top generator mounting bolt. This bolt is located between the generator and the a/c compressor.

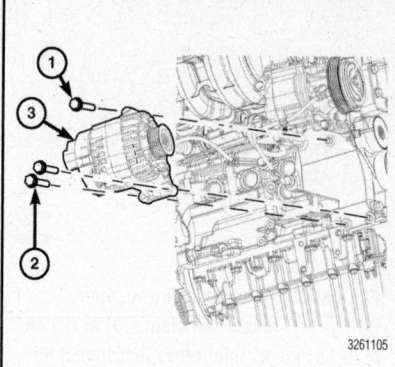

Fig. 48 View of the top generator mounting bolt (1), two bottom bolts (2) and generator (3)

10. Remove the bottom two generator mounting bolts.
11. Carefully remove the generator.

CHARGING SYSTEM

To install:

12. Carefully position the generator up to the engine block.
13. Loosely install the bottom two generator mounting retainers.
14. Install the top generator mounting retainer.
15. Tighten the generator mounting retainers to 18 ft. lbs. (25 Nm).
16. Install the generator B+ cable on the generator stud.
17. Install the B+ cable retainer, and tighten to 36 inch lbs. (4 Nm).
18. Connect the field generator harness connector.
19. Install the right side axle shaft.
20. Install the belly pan covering the bottom side of the engine compartment.
21. Lower the vehicle.
22. Install the accessory drive belt.
23. Connect the negative battery cable.
24. Start the engine and verify the generator is operating properly.

ENGINE ELECTRICAL

FIRING ORDER

See Figure 49.

The firing order is 1–3–4–2.

IGNITION COIL

REMOVAL & INSTALLATION

1.4L 8V Engine

See Figure 50.

1. Disconnect and isolate the negative battery cable.

2. Remove the air cleaner assembly.
3. Disconnect the spark plug cables from the ignition coil.
4. Unlock and disconnect the electrical connector from the ignition coil.
5. Remove the ignition coil mounting bolts and the ignition coil from the cylinder head cover.

To install:

6. Install the ignition coil on the cylinder head cover with bolts tightened to 80 inch lbs. (9 Nm).

IGNITION SYSTEM

7. Connect and lock the electrical connector to the ignition coil.
8. Connect the spark plug cables to the ignition coil.
9. Install the air cleaner assembly.
10. Connect the negative battery cable and tighten nut to 45 inch lbs. (5 Nm).

1.4L 16V MultiAir Engine

See Figures 51 and 52.

1. Disconnect and isolate the negative battery cable.
2. Remove the engine cover.

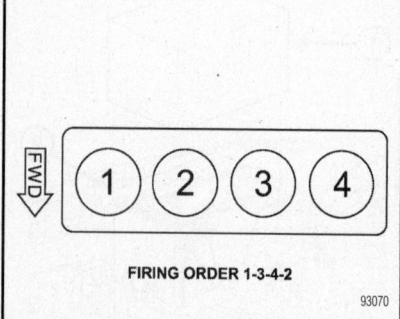

Fig. 49 Engine firing order and cylinder identification

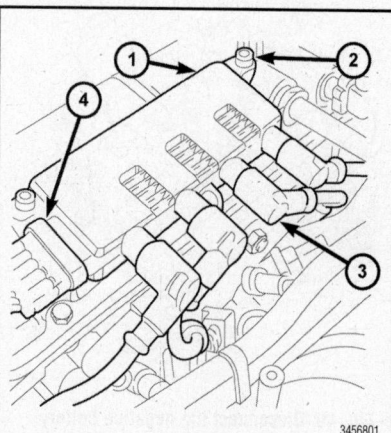

Fig. 50 View of the ignition coil (1), mounting bolts (2), spark plug wires (3) and electrical connector (4)

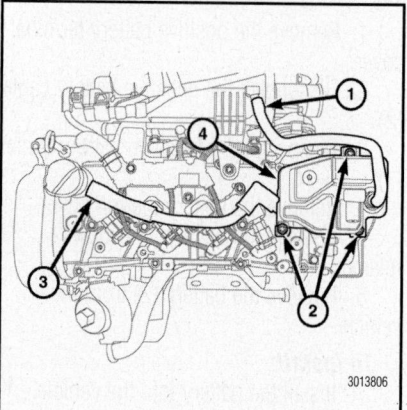

Fig. 51 View of the PCV hose (1), vent hose (3), three bolts (2) and oil separator housing (4)

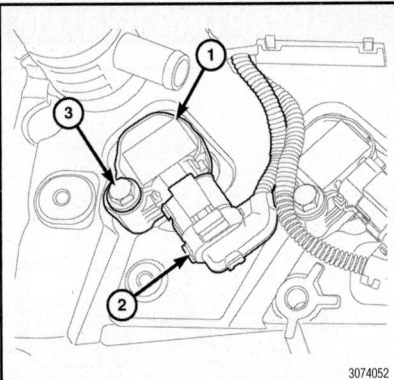

Fig. 52 Unlock and disconnect the electrical connector (2) from the ignition coil. Remove the ignition coil mounting bolt (3). Pull the ignition coil (1) from cylinder head cover opening with a slight twisting action

3. Remove the air cleaner assembly.

4. Disconnect the PCV hose from the intake manifold.

5. Disconnect the vent hose from the oil filler neck.

6. Remove the three bolts and remove the oil separator housing from the cylinder head cover.

➡**The No. 1 cylinder ignition coil is shown, others similar.**

7. Unlock and disconnect the electrical connector (2) from the ignition coil.

8. Remove the ignition coil mounting bolt (3).

9. Pull the ignition coil (1) from cylinder head cover opening with a slight twisting action.

To install:

10. Using compressed air, blow out any dirt or contaminants from around the top of spark plug.

11. The ignition coil seal can be reused if not damaged.

12. Check the condition of the ignition coil rubber boot. To aid in ignition coil installation, apply a silicone based grease such as Mopar® Dielectric Grease # J8126688 into the spark plug end of the rubber boot.

13. Position the ignition coil into the cylinder head cover opening. Using a twisting action, push the ignition coil onto the spark plug.

14. Install the ignition coil mounting bolt and tighten to 80 inch lbs. (9 Nm).

15. Connect and lock the electrical connector to the ignition coil.

16. Install the oil separator housing to the cylinder head cover with three bolts tightened to 115 inch lbs. (13 Nm).

17. Connect the vent hose to the oil filler neck.

18. Connect the PCV hose to the intake manifold.

19. Install the air cleaner assembly.

20. Install the engine cover.

21. Connect the negative battery cable and tighten nut to 45 inch lbs. (5 Nm).

SPARK PLUGS

REMOVAL & INSTALLATION

1.4L 8V Engine

See Figure 53.

1. Disconnect and isolate the negative battery cable.

2. Remove the air cleaner assembly.

3. Disconnect the spark plug cable from the spark plug.

4. Remove the spark plug from the cylinder head using a quality thin wall socket with a rubber or foam insert.

5. Inspect the spark plug condition.

To install:

6. Check and adjust the spark plug gap. Proper gap is: 0.040 in. (1mm).

7. Start the spark plug (1) into the cylinder head by hand to avoid cross threading.

8. Tighten the spark plug to 13 ft. lbs. (18 Nm).

9. Connect the spark plug cable (2) to the spark plug.

10. Install the air cleaner assembly.

11. Connect the negative battery cable and tighten nut to 45 inch lbs. (5 Nm).

1.4L 16V MultiAir & Turbo Engine

See Figure 54.

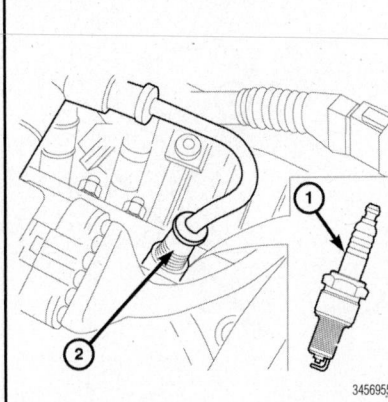

Fig. 53 Disconnect the spark plug cable (2) from the spark plug, then remove the spark plug (1)

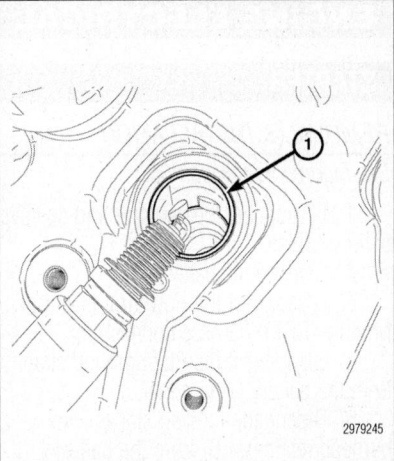

Fig. 54 The spark plug tubes (1) are a thin wall design. Avoid damaging the spark plug tubes. Damage to the spark plug tube can result in oil leaks

➡**The No. 1 cylinder ignition coil is shown, others similar.**

1. Remove the ignition coil, as outlined in this section.

2. Prior to removing the spark plug, spray compressed air into the cylinder head opening. This will help prevent foreign material from entering the combustion chamber.

⁂ **WARNING**

The spark plug tubes (1) are a thin wall design. Avoid damaging the spark plug tubes. Damage to the spark plug tube can result in oil leaks

3. Remove the spark plug from the cylinder head using a quality thin wall socket with a rubber or foam insert.

4. Inspect the spark plug condition.

To install:

5. Check and adjust the spark plug gap. Proper gap is: 0.040 in. (1mm) for the non-turbo engine, and 0.025 in. (0.635mm) for the turbo engine.

⁂ **WARNING**

Special care should be taken when installing spark plugs into the cylinder head spark plug wells. Be sure the plugs do not drop into the plug wells as electrodes can be damaged.

6. Start the spark plug into the cylinder head by hand to avoid cross threading. Tighten the spark plugs to 12 ft. lbs. (16 Nm).

7. Install the ignition coil.

STARTER

REMOVAL & INSTALLATION

See Figures 55 through 58.

1. Disconnect the negative and positive battery cables.
2. Remove the battery.
3. Disconnect the Powertrain Control Module (PCM) harness connectors.
4. Disconnect the PCM ground strap from the battery (-) terminal.
5. Disengage the two starter wire harness retainers (6) from the battery tray (3).
6. Disengage the engine wire harness connector (2) from the battery tray (3) and reposition.
7. Remove the nut (5) and two bolts (1).
8. Open the two wire harness retainers (3) and reposition the wire harness.
9. Remove the battery tray keeping the PCM attached.
10. Remove the engine cover.
11. Remove the air cleaner assembly.
12. Remove the starter bolt access plug located on the back side of the transmission bellhousing to gain access to the top starter bolt.
13. Remove the starter bolt through the access hole in the transmission bellhousing.
14. Support and raise the vehicle.
15. Remove the belly pan covering the bottom side of the engine compartment.

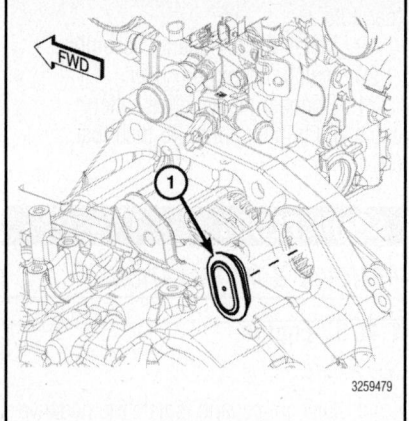

Fig. 56 Remove the starter bolt access plug (1) located on the back side of the transmission bellhousing to gain access to the top starter bolt

16. Remove the lower cradle brace retainers.
17. Remove the lower cradle brace.
18. Remove the retainer (1) from the starter solenoid (3).
19. Disconnect the starter solenoid harness connector (2).
20. Remove the starter retainers (4).
21. Remove the starter assembly (5).

To install:

22. Install the starter assembly into the transmission bellhousing while lining up the alignment pin.

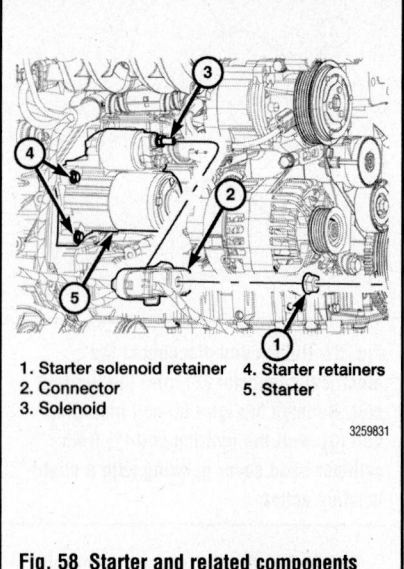

1. Starter solenoid retainer 4. Starter retainers
2. Connector 5. Starter
3. Solenoid

Fig. 58 Starter and related components

23. Install the starter retainers. Tighten to 19 ft. lbs. (26 Nm).
24. Connect the starter solenoid harness.
25. Install the starter solenoid retainer. Tighten to 80 inch lbs. (9 Nm).
26. Install the lower cradle brace and retainers.
27. Install the belly pan covering the bottom side of the engine compartment.
28. Lower the vehicle.
29. Install the starter bolt through the access panel in the transmission bellhousing and tighten to 19 ft. lbs. (26 Nm).
30. Install the starter bolt access plug located on the back side of the transmission bellhousing. Be careful not to push the plug in too far.
31. Install the air cleaner assembly.
32. Install the engine cover.
33. Install the battery tray and PCM as an assembly.
34. Position wire harness inside the two wire harness retainers.
35. Install the nut and two bolts.
36. Position the engine wire harness connector to the battery tray.
37. Engage the two starter wire harness retainers to the battery tray.
38. Connect the PCM ground strap to the battery terminal.
39. Connect the PCM harness connectors.
40. Install the battery and connect the battery cables.
41. Start the engine to verify the starter functions properly.

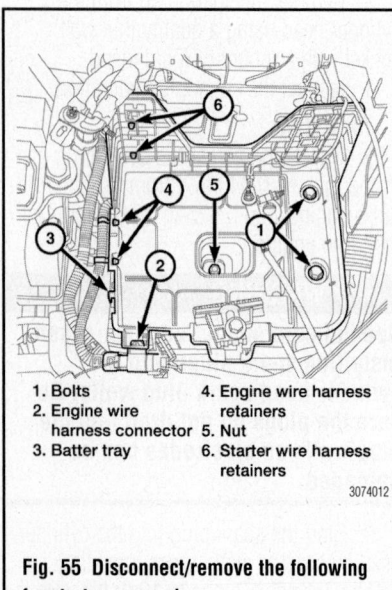

1. Bolts 4. Engine wire harness
2. Engine wire   retainers
   harness connector 5. Nut
3. Batter tray 6. Starter wire harness
       retainers

Fig. 55 Disconnect/remove the following for starter removal

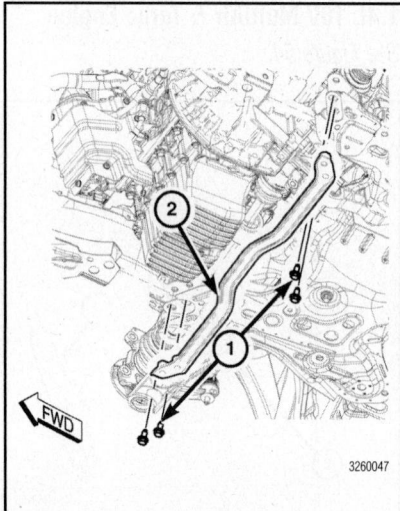

Fig. 57 Remove the lower cradle brace retainers (1) and the lower cradle brace (2)

ENGINE MECHANICAL

➡ **Disconnecting the negative battery cable may interfere with the functions of the on board computer systems and may require the computer to undergo a relearning process, once the negative battery cable is reconnected.**

ACCESSORY DRIVE BELTS

REMOVAL & INSTALLATION

With A/C

See Figure 59.

1. Remove the air cleaner assembly, as outlined in this section.
2. Release the serpentine belt tensioner (1) by rotating the pulley center bolt (2) counterclockwise.
3. Remove the accessory drive belt (3).
4. Remove the accessory drive belt (3)

To install:

✳✳ WARNING

Do not let the tensioner arm snap back to the freearm position, severe damage may occur to the tensioner.

5. Position the serpentine belt (3) around the pulleys.
6. Rotate the tensioner center bolt (2) counterclockwise
7. Position the belt around the tensioner pulley.
8. Verify the belt is properly positioned around all of the pulleys.
9. Install the air cleaner assembly.

Without A/C

See Figures 60 through 63.

✳✳ CAUTION

Care must be used when removing the accessory drive belt. Always wear appropriate eye and hand protection and use extreme caution when working with the belt.

1. Disconnect the negative battery cable.
2. Hoist the vehicle.
3. Remove the right front wheel.
4. Remove the inner splash shield.

➡ **The drive belt is a one-time use only. Any time the belt is removed for repairs, it MUST be replaced with a new belt.**

5. Using care. Cut the belt (1) and discard.

To install:

✳✳ CAUTION

Always wear appropriate eye and hand protection and use extreme caution when working with the belt.

➡ **A supplied belt installer tool must be used to aid in proper installation of the belt. Failure to use the tool may result in damage to the belt.**

6. Install the accessory drive belt (1) around the alternator (4).
7. Position the belt onto the vibration dampener (3).

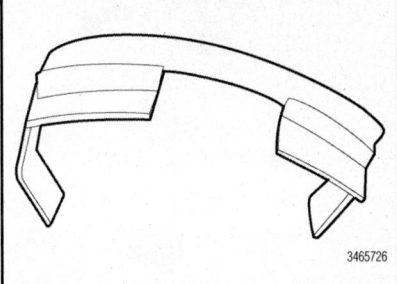

Fig. 61 A supplied belt installer tool must be used to aid in proper installation of the belt. Failure to use the tool may result in damage to the belt

8. Position the belt installer tool (2) between the belt and vibration dampener.
9. Rotate the crankshaft clockwise until the belt is properly seated onto the vibration dampener.
10. Install the inner wheel splash shield.
11. Install the right front wheel.
12. Lower vehicle.
13. Connect the negative battery cable.

AIR CLEANER

REMOVAL & INSTALLATION

1.4L 8V Engine

See Figure 64.

1. Disengage the air inlet hose (4) from the cover of the air cleaner assembly (1).
2. Loosen the clamp (2) and remove the oil vapor hose from the air cleaner assembly (1).

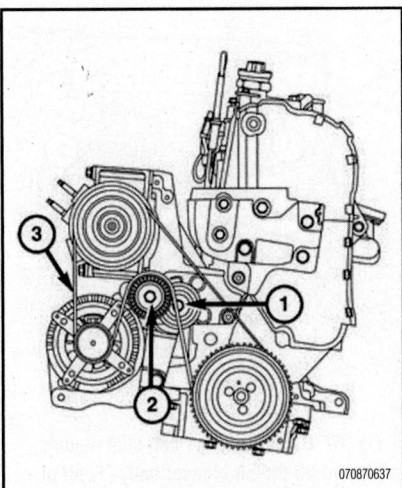

Fig. 59 Release the serpentine belt tensioner (1) by rotating the pulley center bolt (2) counterclockwise.

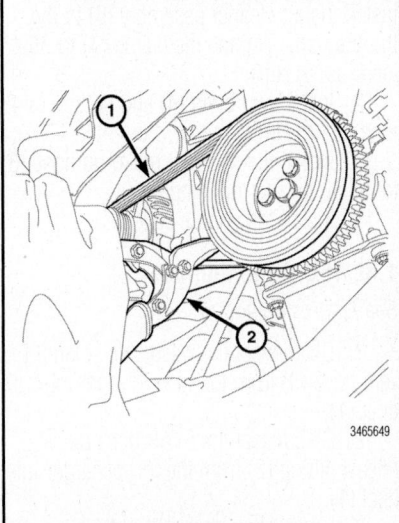

Fig. 60 Using a suitable tool (2), cut the drive belt and discard it

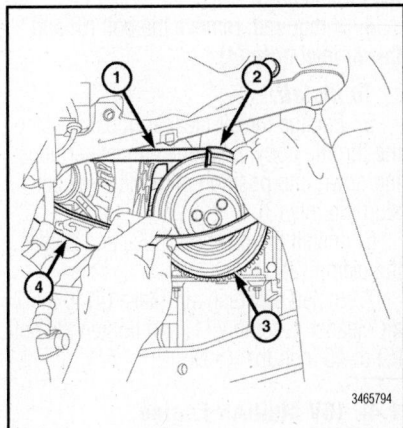

Fig. 62 Install the accessory drive belt (1) around the alternator (4). Position the belt onto the vibration dampener (3). Position the belt installer tool (2) between the belt and vibration dampener

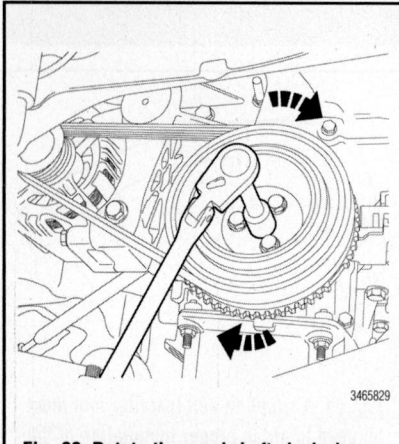

Fig. 63 Rotate the crankshaft clockwise until the belt is properly seated onto the vibration dampener

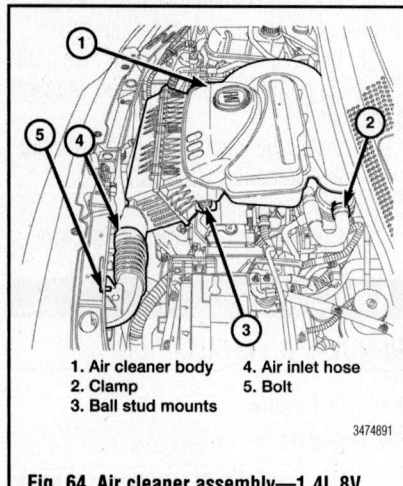

1. Air cleaner body
2. Clamp
3. Ball stud mounts
4. Air inlet hose
5. Bolt

3474891

Fig. 64 Air cleaner assembly—1.4L 8V engine

3. Disengage three ball stud mounts (3) and lift the air cleaner assembly (1) off of the throttle body.

4. If required, remove the bolt (5) and the air inlet hose (4).

To install:

5. Engage the air cleaner housing (1) to the throttle body, push the air cleaner housing down into position onto the three ball stud mounts (3).

6. Install the oil vapor hose and tighten the clamp (2).

7. Install the fresh air intake (4) to the air cleaner assembly (1) and tighten the bolt (5) to 45 inch lbs. (5 Nm).

1.4L 16V MultiAir Engine

See Figure 65.

1. Remove the engine cover.
2. Loosen the clamp (1) at the throttle body.
3. Remove the fresh air make-up hose (3) from the air cleaner housing.

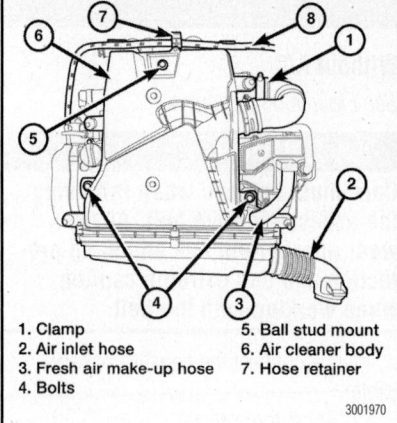

1. Clamp
2. Air inlet hose
3. Fresh air make-up hose
4. Bolts
5. Ball stud mount
6. Air cleaner body
7. Hose retainer

3001970

Fig. 65 Air cleaner assembly—1.4L 16V MultiAir engine

4. Remove the two bolts (4)
5. Disengage the air inlet hose (2) from the air cleaner cover.
6. Disengage the ball stud mount (5) and lift the air cleaner assembly (6) off of the intake manifold.
7. Open the hose retainer (7), reposition the coolant hose (8) and remove the air cleaner assembly (6) form the vehicle.

To install:

8. Lubricate the rubber mount socket (5) on the air cleaner assembly (6) with Mopar® Rubber Bushing Installation Lube.

9. Install the coolant line (8) to the air cleaner housing and close the hose retainer (7).

10. Push the air cleaner assembly (6) down onto the locating pin (5) on the intake manifold until the rubber mount socket is fully seated.

11. Engage the air inlet hose (2) and install the air cleaner assembly (6) to the throttle body. Tighten the clamp (1) to 35 inch lbs. (4 Nm).

12. Install two bolts (4) and tighten to 45 inch lbs. (5 Nm).

13. Install the fresh air make-up hose (3) to the air cleaner housing.

14. Install the engine cover.

1.4L 16V Turbo Engine

See Figures 66 and 67.

1. Disconnect the wastegate solenoid vent hose (3) from the turbocharger inlet duct (1).

2. Disconnect the EVAP hose quick release fitting (2) from the turbocharger inlet duct (1).

3. Loosen the clamp (6) at the turbocharger inlet duct (1) and remove the duct from the hose.

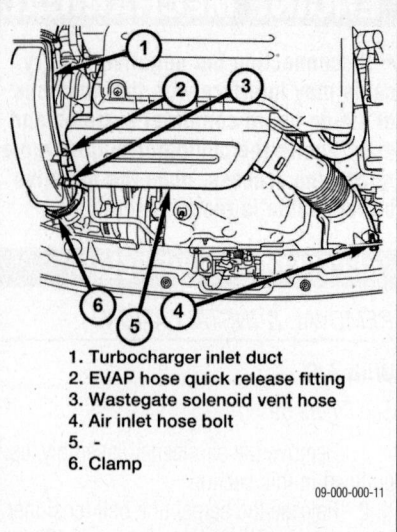

1. Turbocharger inlet duct
2. EVAP hose quick release fitting
3. Wastegate solenoid vent hose
4. Air inlet hose bolt
5. -
6. Clamp

09-000-000-11

Fig. 66 Items to be disconnected/removed for air cleaner assembly removal

4. Remove the bolt (4) from the air inlet hose.

5. Disengage four ball stud mounts (3) and lift the air cleaner body (1) off of the engine.

6. Remove the fresh air make-up hose (2) from the oil separator housing and remove the air cleaner housing from the vehicle.

To install:

7. Lubricate the rubber mount sockets on the air cleaner body (1) with Mopar® Rubber Bushing Installation Lube.

8. Install the fresh air make-up hose (2) to the oil separator housing.

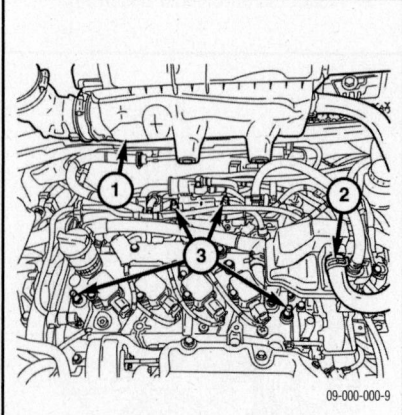

09-000-000-9

Fig. 67 Disengage four ball stud mounts (3) and lift the air cleaner body (1) off of the engine. Remove the fresh air make-up hose (2) from the oil separator housing and remove the air cleaner housing from the vehicle

9. Align the air cleaner body (1) and press down onto the four ball stud mounts (3) to engage the rubber mount sockets.

10. Install the air inlet hose retaining bolt (4) and tighten to 80 inch lbs. (9 Nm).

11. Install the turbocharger inlet duct (1) to the hose and tighten the clamp (6) to 35 inch lbs. (4 Nm).

12. Connect the EVAP hose quick release fitting (2) to the turbocharger inlet duct (1).

13. Connect the wastegate solenoid vent hose (3) to the turbocharger inlet duct (1).

FILTER/ELEMENT REPLACEMENT

1.4L 8V Engine

See Figure 68.

1. Disengage the air inlet hose from the air cleaner assembly cover.

2. Release the spring clamps and remove the air cleaner assembly cover.

3. Remove the air cleaner element from the air cleaner assembly cover.

To install:

4. Install the air cleaner element to the air cleaner assembly cover.

5. Install the air cleaner assembly cover and lock the spring clamps.

6. Install the fresh air intake to the air cleaner assembly cover.

1.4L 16V MultiAir & 1.4L 16V Turbo Engines

1. Remove the engine cover, if necessary.

2. Remove the three screws and remove the air cleaner assembly cover

3. Remove the air cleaner element from the air cleaner housing.

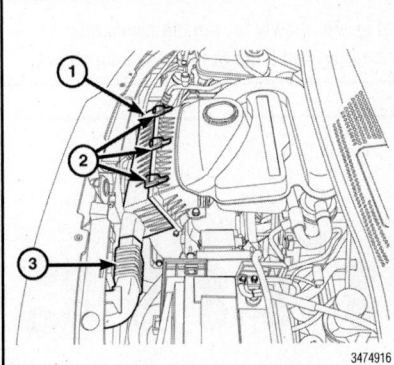

Fig. 68 Disengage the air inlet hose (3) from the air cleaner assembly cover (1). Release the spring clamps (2) and remove the air cleaner assembly cover (1)

To install:

4. Install the air cleaner element to the air cleaner housing.

5. Install the air cleaner assembly cover with three screws, and tighten to 35 inch lbs. (4 Nm).

6. If removed, install the engine cover.

CAMSHAFT AND VALVE LIFTERS

INSPECTION

See Figure 69.

1. Inspect the camshaft bearing journals (4) for damage and binding. If the journals are binding, check the camshaft bearing housing for damage. Also check the oil supply holes for clogging.

2. Check the surface of the cam lobes (5) for abnormal wear (1). Measure and compare the unworn area (3) to the worn area (2). Replace the camshaft if it is not within specification

REMOVAL & INSTALLATION

1.4L 8V Engine

See Figures 70 and 71.

1. Disconnect and isolate the negative battery cable.

2. Remove the air cleaner assembly.

3. Remove the ignition coil(s).

4. Remove the upper timing belt cover.

5. Remove the accessory drive belt.

6. Remove the crankshaft vibration damper.

7. Remove the lower timing belt cover.

8. Remove the right engine mount insulator and right engine mount bracket.

9. Remove the timing belt.

10. Remove the cylinder head cover.

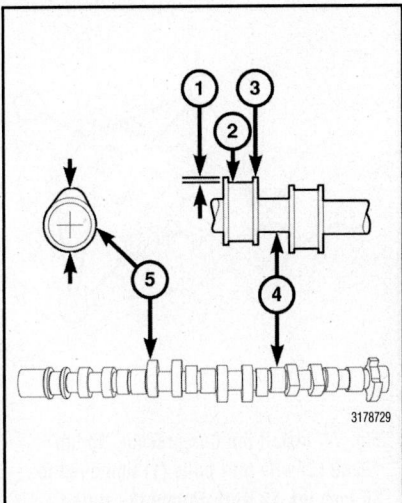

Fig. 69 Inspecting the camshaft

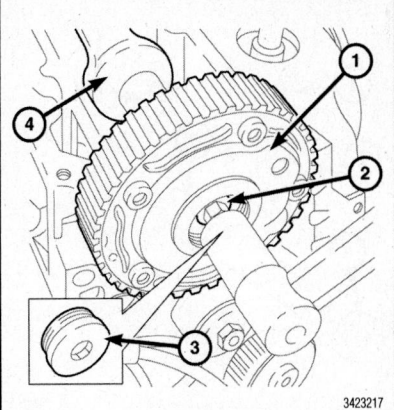

Fig. 70 Unscrew and remove the camshaft pulley cap (3). Hold the camshaft against rotation with a wrench (4) and remove the camshaft pulley bolt (2). Remove the camshaft pulley (1) from the camshaft.

11. Unscrew and remove the camshaft pulley cap (3).

12. Hold the camshaft against rotation with a wrench (4) and remove the camshaft pulley bolt (2). Remove the camshaft pulley (1) from the camshaft.

➡**Camshaft bearing caps (2) are marked during engine manufacturing. The markings on the caps (2) should align with the markings on the cylinder head.**

❋❋ WARNING

Do not stamp or strike the camshaft bearing caps. Severe damage will occur to the bearing caps.

13. Slowly loosen the camshaft bearing cap bolts (1) and remove the bearing caps (2).

14. Remove the camshaft (3) from cylinder head.

15. Remove the camshaft oil seal (4) from the cylinder head.

To install:

16. Lubricate the camshaft journals with clean engine oil.

17. Install the camshaft (3) on the cylinder head.

18. Install the camshaft oil seal (4) over the camshaft end and on the cylinder head.

19. Install the camshaft bearing caps (2) and tighten the bolts (1) to 15 ft. lbs. (20 Nm).

20. Install the timing belt and camshaft pulley.

21. Install the cylinder head cover.

22. Install the right engine mount bracket and insulator.

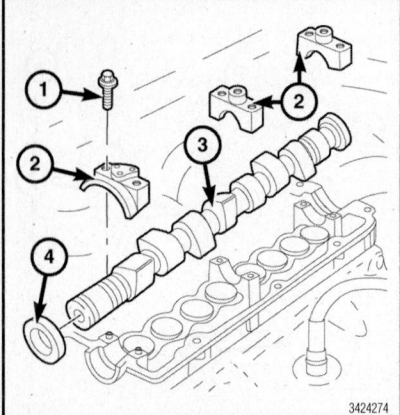

Fig. 71 View of the camshaft bearing cap bolts (1), bearing caps (2), camshaft (3) and camshaft oil seal (4)

23. Install the lower timing belt cover.
24. Install the crankshaft vibration damper.
25. Install the accessory drive belt.
26. Install the upper timing belt cover.
27. Install the ignition coil(s).
28. Install the air cleaner assembly.

➡**The Cam/Crank Variation Relearn procedure must be performed using the scan tool anytime there has been a repair/replacement made to a powertrain system, for example: flywheel, valvetrain, camshaft and/or crankshaft sensors or components.**

1.4L 16V MultiAir & 1.4L 16V Turbo Engines

See Figures 72 through 77.

1. Remove the cylinder head cover.
2. Remove the timing belt.

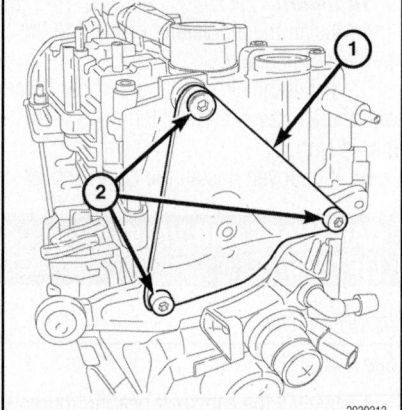

Fig. 73 Remove the three bolts (2) and the Tool, Camshaft Timing Locking 10277 (1)

3. Use the Holder, Camshaft Sprocket 6847 (2) and remove the bolt (1) and the camshaft sprocket (3).
4. Remove the three bolts (2) and the Tool, Camshaft Timing Locking 10277 (1).
5. Install the Compressor, Spring 10259 (2) with four bolts (1) tightened to 80 inch lbs. (9 Nm).
Rotate the spring compressors (3) CCW until fully seated.

➡**Camshaft bearing caps are marked during engine manufacturing. For example, the center camshaft bearing cap is marked "C". The markings on the caps (1) should align with the markings on the camshaft housing (2).**

6. Slowly loosen the camshaft bearing cap bolts in the sequence shown. Remove the camshaft bearing caps and the camshaft.

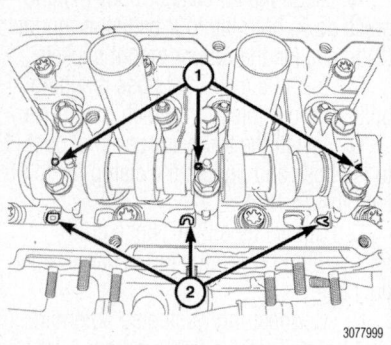

Fig. 75 Camshaft bearing caps are marked during engine manufacturing. For example, the center camshaft bearing cap is marked "C". The markings on the caps (1) should align with the markings on the camshaft housing (2)

To install:

➡**Following the installation of each camshaft bearing cap, visually verify that the camshaft has some endplay.**

7. Lubricate camshaft journals with clean engine oil.

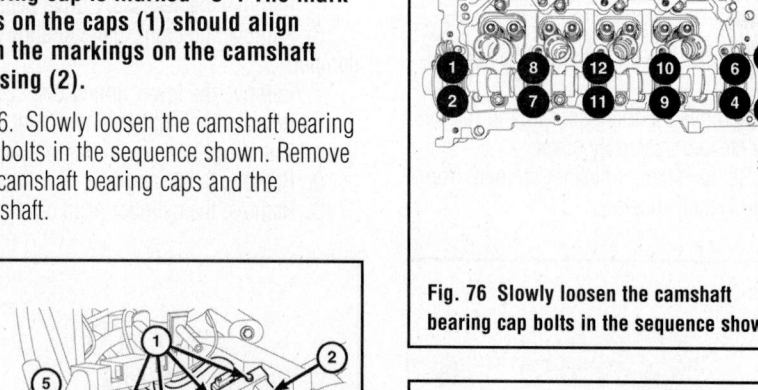

Fig. 76 Slowly loosen the camshaft bearing cap bolts in the sequence shown

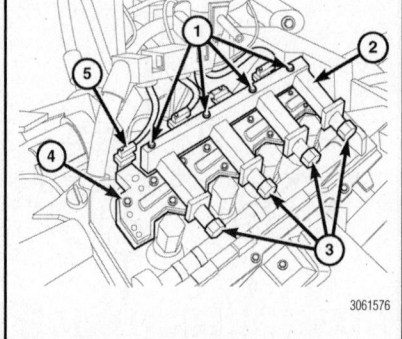

Fig. 72 Use the Holder, Camshaft Sprocket 6847 (2) and remove the bolt (1) and the camshaft sprocket

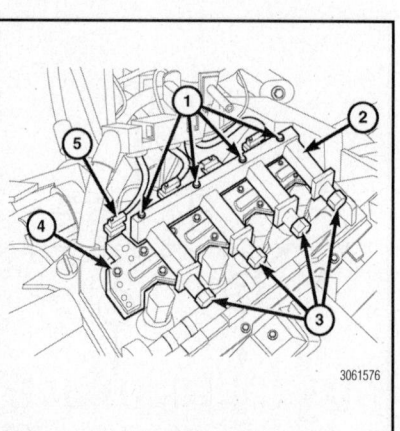

Fig. 74 Install the Compressor, Spring 10259 (2) with four bolts (1) tightened to 80 inch lbs. (9 Nm). Rotate the spring compressors (3) CCW until fully seated

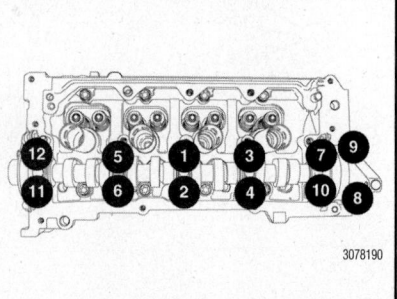

Fig. 77 Tighten the twelve camshaft bearing cap bolts in two steps following the sequence shown

8. Apply a seam of Anaerobic Loc-tite®518 Sealant on the camshaft housing in the contact area of the front and rear camshaft caps.

9. Install the camshaft and camshaft bearing caps. Tighten the twelve bolts in two steps following the sequence shown:

   a. Step 1: All to 44 inch lbs. (5 Nm).
   b. Step 2: All to 89 inch lbs. (10 Nm).

10. Loosen the spring compressors, remove the four bolts and the spring compressor.

11. If required, install a new camshaft seal.

12. Install the camshaft sprocket and timing belt.

13. Install the cylinder head cover.

➡ The Cam/Crank Variation Relearn procedure must be performed using the scan tool anytime there has been a repair/replacement made to a powertrain system, for example: flywheel, valvetrain, camshaft and/or crankshaft sensors or components.

CATALYTIC CONVERTER

REMOVAL & INSTALLATION

1. Disconnect and isolate the negative battery cable.

2. Disconnect the two vacuum fittings, loosen the clamp at the air to turbocharger inlet tube, if equipped.

3. Disconnect the fresh air intake hose.

4. Remove the air cleaner assembly.

5. Remove the upper heat shield bolts. Remove and discard the nuts.

6. Remove the Charge Air Cooler (CAC) supply hose from the turbocharger, if equipped.

7. Remove the catalytic converter heat shield.

8. Disconnect the upstream and downstream oxygen sensor connectors.

9. Loosen the catalytic converter clamp at the turbocharger, if equipped..

10. Raise and support vehicle.

11. If equipped, remove the belly pan.

12. Remove the front exhaust pipe support bolt.

13. Remove the exhaust flange nuts.

14. Remove the nuts that secure the cross under pipe to the catalytic converter.

15. Remove the front exhaust pipe and flange gasket.

16. Remove the converter mount bolts.

17. Remove the catalytic converter lower support mount.

18. Carefully lower the catalytic converter down and out of the vehicle.

19. Remove the catalytic converter gasket ring.

To install:

20. Install the new converter to turbo seal ring.

21. Install the catalytic converter assembly.

22. Position the exhaust manifold shield and install the 2 bolts and one new nut.

23. Tighten the shield bolts and nut to 80 inch lbs. (9 Nm).

✳✳ WARNING

Band clamps should never be tightened such that the two sides of the clamps are bottomed out against the hourglass shaped center block. Once this occurs, the clamp has lost clamping force and must be replaced.

24. install the catalytic converter v-clamp at the turbocharger. Tighten clamp to 71 inch lbs. (8 Nm).

25. Connect the oxygen sensor connector.

26. Install the catalytic converter lower support bracket.

27. Install and tighten the bracket bolts to 41 ft. lbs. (56 Nm).

28. Install a new converter to pipe gasket.

29. Install the front exhaust pipe.

30. Install the front exhaust pipe gasket. Install the front exhaust pipe nuts to the converter outlet.

31. Tighten the front exhaust pipe nuts to 41 ft. lbs. (56 Nm).

32. Install the front exhaust pipe support bolt. Tighten to 41 ft. lbs. (56 Nm).

33. Install the exhaust flange gasket and nuts. Tighten the nuts to 51 ft. lbs. (69 Nm).

34. Install the Charge Air Cooler (CAC) supply hose to the turbocharger.

35. Install the CAC hose clamp and tighten.

36. Install the catalytic converter heat shield.

37. Tighten the nuts and bolts to 71 inch lbs. (8 Nm). Care must be taken when tightening the shield bolts. If torque value is not correct, noise will occur.

38. Connect the upstream and downstream oxygen sensor connectors.

39. Install the air cleaner assembly.

40. Connect he fresh air intake hose.

41. Connect the two vacuum fittings, tighten the clamp at the air to turbocharger inlet tube.

42. Connect the negative battery cable.

CRANKSHAFT FRONT OIL SEAL

REMOVAL & INSTALLATION

See Figures 78 through 81.

1. Remove the crankshaft pulley or sprocket, as applicable. Refer to the Timing Chain procedure for more information.

✳✳ WARNING

When the timing belt is removed and the cylinder head is still installed, DO NOT rotate the camshaft or crankshaft without first locating the proper crankshaft position. Failure to do so will result in valve and/or piston damage.

2. Remove the front crankshaft seal.

To install:

3. Apply engine oil to the seal pilot diameter of the Crankshaft front oil seal installer (1), and to the inside diameter of the front crankshaft oil seal (2)

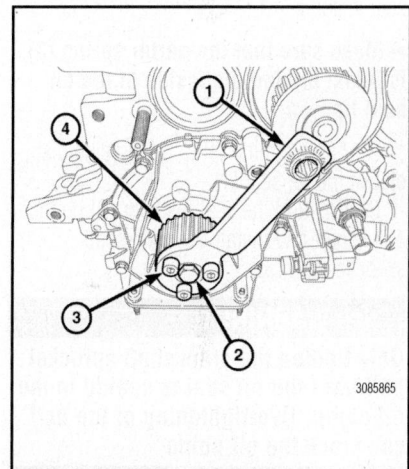

Fig. 78 Remove the crankshaft sprocket (4)

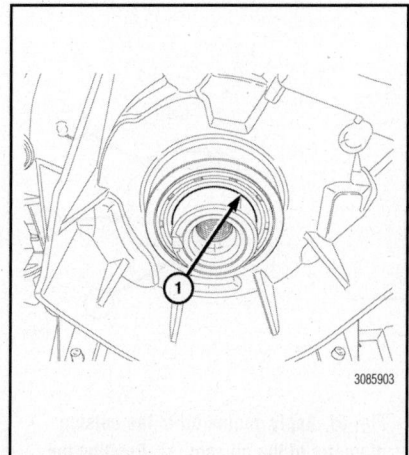

Fig. 79 Remove the front crankshaft seal (1)

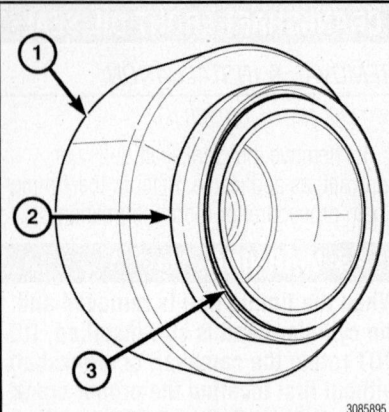

Fig. 80 Apply engine oil to the seal pilot diameter of the Crankshaft front oil seal installer (1), and to the inside diameter of the front crankshaft oil seal (2). Make sure that the garter spring (3) is intact around the inside of the oil seal lip

4. Carefully install the oil seal onto the seal installer.

➡**Make sure that the garter spring (3) is intact around the inside of the oil seal lip.**

5. Apply engine oil to the outside diameter of the oil seal (1).

6. Position the seal installer (2) on the crankshaft and install the crankshaft sprocket bolt (3).

✴✴ WARNING

Only tighten the crankshaft sprocket bolt until the oil seal is seated in the oil pump. Overtightening of the bolt can crack the oil pump

7. Tighten the crankshaft sprocket bolt

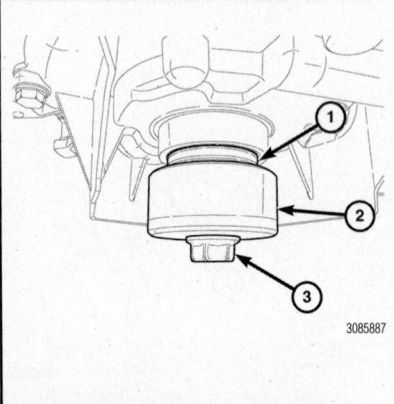

Fig. 81 Apply engine oil to the outside diameter of the oil seal (1). Position the seal installer (2) on the crankshaft and install the crankshaft sprocket bolt (3)

(3) until the crankshaft oil seal is seated in the oil pump.

8. Verify that the oil seal is uniformly seated and that the seal lip (1) is not curled inward toward the engine.

9. Install the timing belt and sprockets/crankshaft pulley, as applicable.

CRANKSHAFT VIBRATION DAMPER

REMOVAL & INSTALLATION

See Figures 82 and 83.

1. Raise and support the vehicle.
2. Remove the right front wheel and tire assembly.
3. Remove two bolts and the right vertical brace.
4. Remove two screws from the front wheelhouse splash shield.
5. Remove three screws and the frame splash shield.
6. Remove the accessory drive belt, as outlined in this section.
7. Remove the three bolts and the vibration damper.

To install:

8. Align the locator pin on the crankshaft sprocket with the hole in the vibration damper. Install the vibration damper with three bolts tightened to 19 ft. lbs. (25 Nm).

9. Install the accessory drive belt.
10. Install the frame splash shield with three screws.
11. Install two screws to the front wheelhouse splash shield.
12. Install the right vertical brace with two bolts tightened to 33 ft. lbs. (45 Nm).
13. Install the right front wheel and tire assembly.

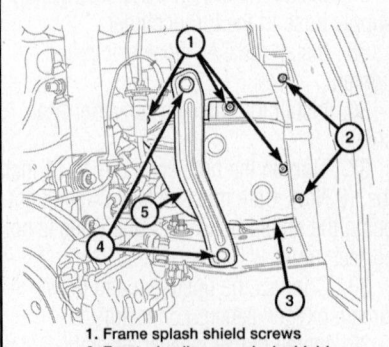

1. Frame splash shield screws
2. Front wheelhouse splash shield
3. Frame splash shield
4. Bolts
5. Right vertical brace

Fig. 82 Right vertical brace and splash shields

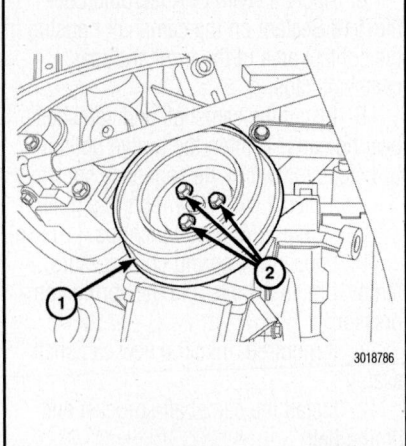

Fig. 83 Remove the three bolts (2) and the vibration damper (1)

➡**The Cam/Crank Variation Relearn procedure must be performed using the scan tool anytime there has been a repair/replacement made to a powertrain system, for example: flywheel, valvetrain, camshaft and/or crankshaft sensors or components.**

CYLINDER HEAD

REMOVAL & INSTALLATION

1.4L 8V Engine

See Figures 84 through 89.

1. Perform the fuel pressure release procedure.
2. Disconnect and isolate the negative battery cable.
3. Remove the air cleaner assembly.
4. Remove the ignition coil(s).
5. Remove the upper timing belt cover.
6. Remove the exhaust maniverter.
7. Drain the engine coolant.

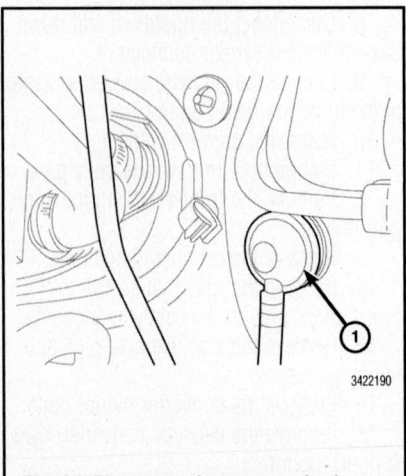

Fig. 84 Disconnect the vacuum check valve (1) from the brake booster

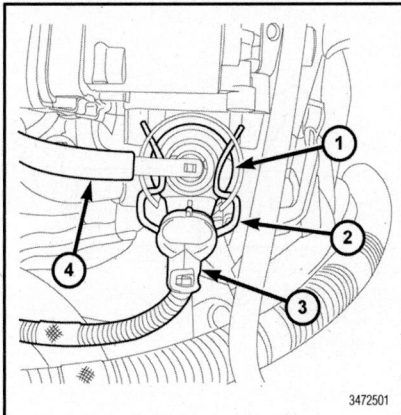

Fig. 85 Unlock and disconnect the fuel vapor purge solenoid electrical connector (3). Disconnect the fuel vapor purge hose (4) from the fuel vapor purge solenoid (1).

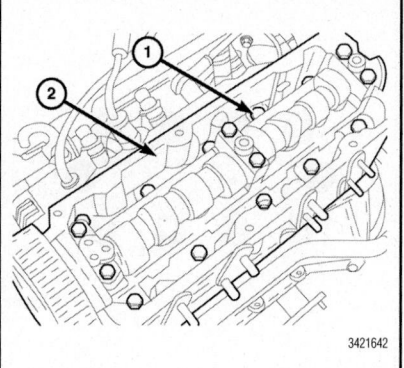

Fig. 87 Remove the cylinder head retaining bolts (1) and remove the cylinder head (2) with the camshaft and intake manifold attached

Overhaul Mounting 1860470000 (2) and position the fixture in a bench vice.

29. Remove the nuts (3) and bolts (4) and remove the intake manifold (1) from the cylinder head.

30. If required, remove the camshaft from the cylinder head.

31. If required, remove the thermostat housing and thermostat from the cylinder head.

To install:

32. If removed, install the camshaft on the cylinder head.

33. If removed, install the thermostat and thermostat housing on the cylinder head.

34. Install the intake manifold to the cylinder head with nuts and bolts tightened to 18 ft. lbs. (25 Nm).

8. Remove the accessory drive belt.

9. Remove the crankshaft vibration damper.

10. Remove the lower timing belt cover.

11. Remove the right engine mount insulator and right engine mount bracket.

12. Remove the timing belt.

13. Remove the cylinder head cover.

14. Support the engine with a floor jack positioned under the oil pan.

15. Disconnect the vacuum check valve (1) from the brake booster.

16. Unlock and disconnect the fuel vapor purge solenoid electrical connector (3).

17. Disconnect the fuel vapor purge hose (4) from the fuel vapor purge solenoid (1).

18. Unlock and disconnect the electrical connector from the IAT/MAP sensor.

19. Unlock and disconnect the fuel injection harness electrical connector.

20. Unlock and disconnect the electronic throttle control (ETC) electrical connector.

21. Disconnect the fuel line from the fuel rail.

22. Unlock and disconnect the engine coolant temperature (ECT) sensor electrical connector (2).

23. Loosen the clamp (5) and remove the upper radiator hose (4) from the thermostat housing.

24. Loosen the clamp (3) and remove the heater core inlet hose (1) from the thermostat housing.

25. Disconnect the coolant recovery bottle return hose (6) from the thermostat housing.

26. Remove the cylinder head retaining bolts (1) and remove the cylinder head (2) with the camshaft and intake manifold attached.

27. Remove the cylinder head gasket.

28. Install the cylinder head on Head

✳✳ WARNING

When cleaning cylinder head and cylinder block surfaces, DO NOT use a metal scraper because the surfaces could be cut or ground. Use ONLY a wooden or plastic scraper.

35. Clean and prepare the gasket sealing surfaces of the cylinder head and block.

36. Position the new cylinder head gasket on the cylinder block.

37. Position the cylinder head onto the cylinder block.

38. Install the ten head bolts finger tight.

39. Tighten the cylinder head bolts in the sequence shown, following this 3 step torque plus angle method. Tighten according to the following torque values:

   a. Step 1: All to 22 ft. lbs. (30 Nm).

   b. Step 2: All + 90° turn. Do not use a torque wrench for this step.

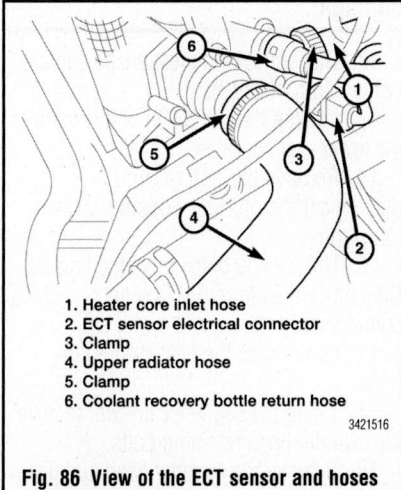

1. Heater core inlet hose
2. ECT sensor electrical connector
3. Clamp
4. Upper radiator hose
5. Clamp
6. Coolant recovery bottle return hose

Fig. 86 View of the ECT sensor and hoses to be disconnected

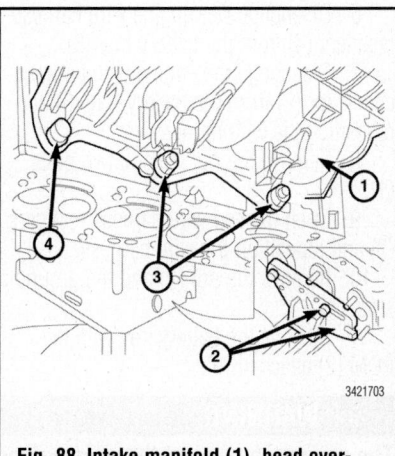

Fig. 88 Intake manifold (1), head overhaul mounting tool (2), nuts (3) and bolts (4)

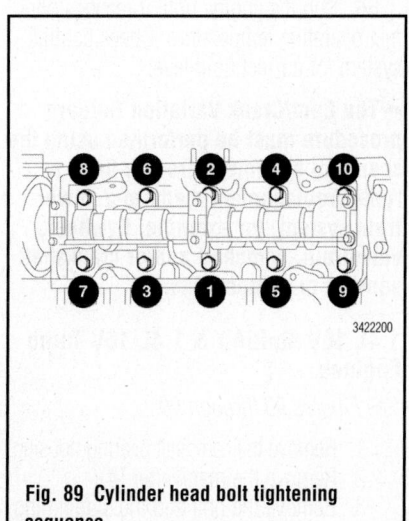

Fig. 89 Cylinder head bolt tightening sequence

c. Step 3: All an additional + 90°
turn. Do not use a torque wrench for this
step.

40. Connect the coolant recovery bottle
return hose to the thermostat housing.

41. Install the heater core inlet hose to
the thermostat housing and tighten the
clamp.

42. Install the upper radiator hose to the
thermostat housing and tighten the clamp.

43. Connect and lock the engine coolant
temperature (ECT) sensor electrical connector.

44. Connect the fuel line to the fuel rail.

45. Connect and lock the electronic
throttle control (ETC) electrical connector.

46. Connect and lock the fuel injection
harness electrical connector.

47. Connect and lock the IAT/MAP sensor electrical connector

48. Connect the fuel vapor purge hose to
the fuel vapor purge solenoid.

49. Connect and lock the fuel vapor
purge solenoid electrical connector.

50. Connect the vacuum check valve to
the brake booster.

51. Install the cylinder head cover.

52. Install the timing belt.

53. Install the right engine mount
bracket and insulator.

54. Install the lower timing belt cover.

55. Install the crankshaft vibration damper.

56. Install the accessory drive belt.

57. Install the exhaust maniverter.

58. Install the upper timing belt cover.

59. Install the ignition coil(s).

60. Install the air cleaner assembly.

61. If removed, install the oil filter and
fill the engine crankcase with the proper oil
to the correct level.

62. Fill the cooling system.

63. Connect the negative battery cable
and tighten nut to 45 inch lbs. (5 Nm).

64. Run the engine until it reaches normal operating temperature. Check cooling
system for correct fluid level.

➡**The Cam/Crank Variation Relearn
procedure must be performed using the
scan tool anytime there has been a
repair/replacement made to a powertrain system, for example: flywheel,
valvetrain, camshaft and/or crankshaft
sensors or components.**

1.4L 16V MultiAir & 1.4L 16V Turbo Engines

See Figures 90 through 99.

1. Remove the camshaft bearing housing.
2. Remove the maniverter (4).
3. Remove the bolt and the side timing
belt cover.

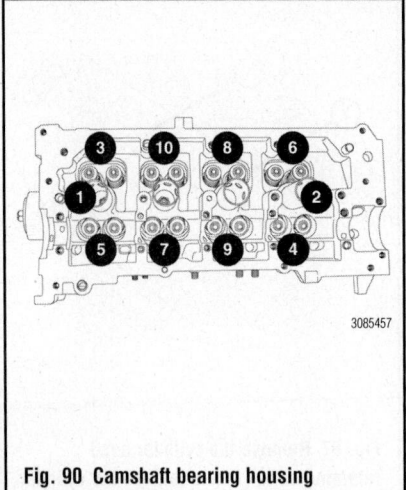

**Fig. 90 Camshaft bearing housing
removal sequence**

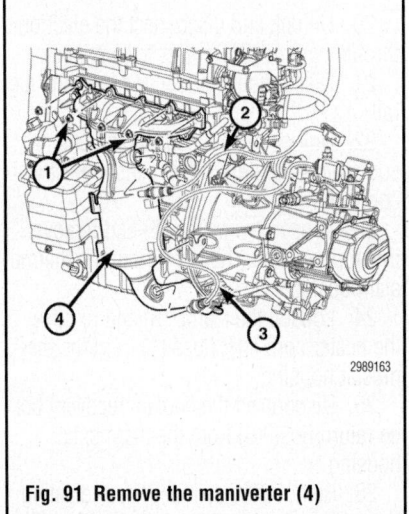

Fig. 91 Remove the maniverter (4)

4. Unlock and disconnect the Powertrain Control Module (PCM) harness connectors (1 and 2).

5. Disengage two starter wire harness
retainers (6) from the battery tray (3).

6. Disengage two engine wire harness
retainers (4) from the battery tray (3).

7. Disengage the engine wire harness
connector (2) from the battery tray (3) and
reposition the wire harness.

8. Remove the nut (5) and two bolts
(1).

9. Open the two wire harness retainers
(3) and reposition the wire harness.

10. Remove the nut (1) and the ground
strap (4).

11. Remove the battery tray with the
PCM (2) attached.

⁂ WARNING

**The vacuum hose and the pressurized
coolant bottle return hose have the
same quick-connect fitting end. If**

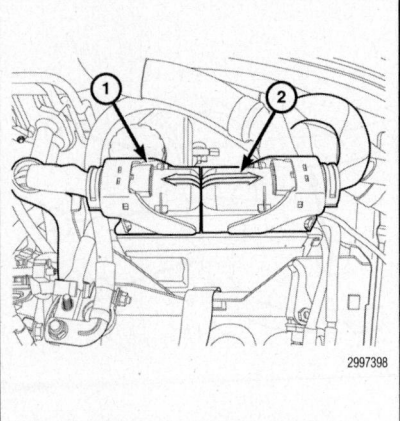

**Fig. 92 Unlock and disconnect the Power-
train Control Module (PCM) harness connectors (1 and 2)**

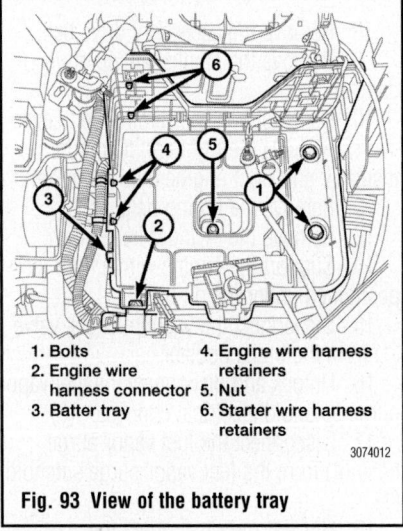

1. Bolts
2. Engine wire
   harness connector
3. Batter tray
4. Engine wire harness
   retainers
5. Nut
6. Starter wire harness
   retainers

Fig. 93 View of the battery tray

**removing both hoses, it is recom-
mended that the hoses be marked at
disassembly to avoid an incorrect
installation. Failure to properly
install the hoses can result in engine
damage.**

12. Disconnect the pressurized coolant
bottle return hose (2).

13. Loosen the clamp (3) and disconnect
the lower radiator hose.

14. Remove the bolt (4) and
disconnect the oil filter housing coolant
return hose.

15. Unlock and disconnect the Engine
Coolant Temperature (ECT) sensor electrical
connector (2).

16. Disconnect the heater core inlet
hose.

17. Using the sequence shown, remove
the cylinder head retaining bolts.

18. Remove the cylinder head and gasket. Discard the gasket.

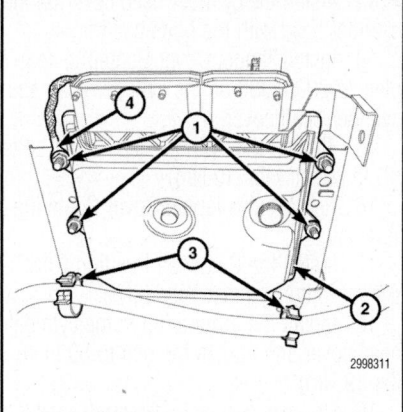

Fig. 94 View of the nut (1), PCM (2), wire harness retainers (3) and ground strap (4)

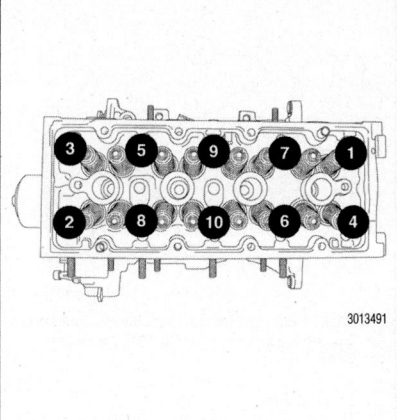

Fig. 96 Cylinder head bolt loosening sequence

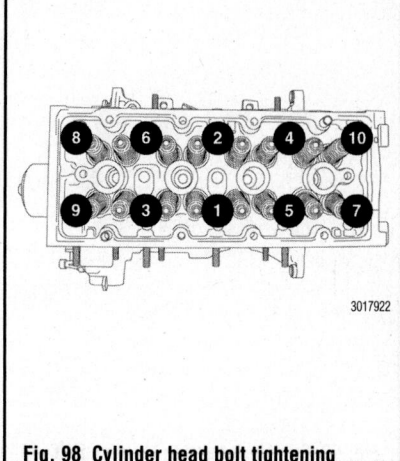

Fig. 98 Cylinder head bolt tightening sequence

19. If required, remove the bolts and the thermostat housing from the cylinder head.

20. If required, remove the tensioner lock nut (1) and the tensioner (2) from the cylinder head.

To install:

21. If removed, install the tensioner mounting stud to the cylinder head and tighten to 97 inch lbs. (11 Nm).

22. If removed, install new exhaust maniverter mounting studs.

23. If removed, install the thermostat housing and gasket with bolts (2) tightened to 89 inch lbs. (10 Nm).

❋❋ WARNING

The cylinder head bolts are tightened using a torque plus angle procedure. The bolts must be examined BEFORE reuse. If the threads are necked down the bolts must be replaced.

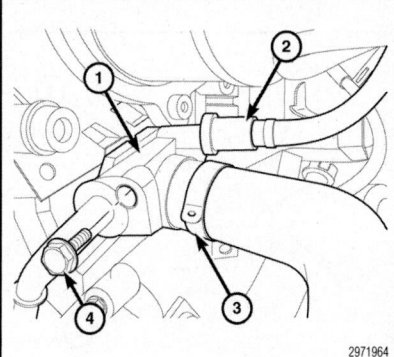

Fig. 95 Disconnect the pressurized coolant bottle return hose (2). Loosen the clamp (3) and disconnect the lower radiator hose. Remove the bolt (4) and disconnect the oil filter housing coolant return hose

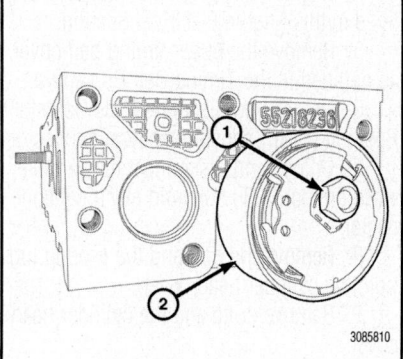

Fig. 97 If required, remove the tensioner lock nut (1) and the tensioner (2) from the cylinder head

24. Check cylinder head bolts for necking by holding a scale or straight edge against the threads. If all the threads do not contact the scale the bolt must be replaced.

❋❋ WARNING

When cleaning cylinder head and cylinder block surfaces, DO NOT use a metal scraper because the surfaces could be cut or ground. Use ONLY a wooden or plastic scraper.

25. Clean and prepare the gasket sealing surfaces of the cylinder head and block.

26. Install two cylinder head locating dowels.

27. Position the new cylinder head gasket on the locating dowels.

28. Position the cylinder head onto the cylinder block. Make sure the cylinder head seats fully over the locating dowels.

29. Install the ten head bolts finger tight.

30. Tighten the cylinder head bolts in the

sequence shown, following this 4 step torque plus angle method. Tighten according to the following torque values:

a. Step 1: All to 15 ft. lbs. (20 Nm).

b. Step 2: All to 22 ft. lbs. (30 Nm).

c. Step 3: All + 90° turn. Do not use a torque wrench for this step.

d. Step 4: All an additional + 90° turn. Do not use a torque wrench for this step.

31. Connect the heater core inlet hose.

32. Connect and lock the engine coolant temperature (ECT) sensor electrical connector.

33. Apply engine oil to the oil filter housing coolant return hose O-ring.

34. Install the oil filter housing coolant return hose to the thermostat housing. Tighten the bolt to 80 inch lbs. (9 Nm).

❋❋ WARNING

The vacuum hose and the pressurized coolant bottle return hose have the same quick-connect fitting end. Verify that the hoses are correctly installed. Failure to properly install the hoses can result in engine damage.

35. Connect the pressurized coolant bottle return hose.

36. Connect the lower radiator hose and tighten the clamp.

37. Install the side timing belt cover with bolt tightened to 18 ft. lbs. (25 Nm).

38. If equipped with a manual transmission, install the maniverter.

39. If equipped with an automatic transmission, install the maniverter gasket and maniverter.

40. Lower the vehicle.

41. Position the battery tray and PCM in the vehicle. Route the wire harness and close the wire harness retainers.

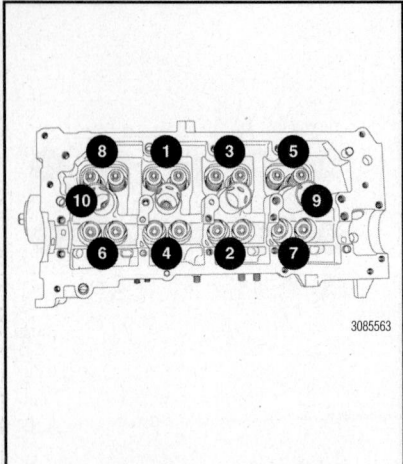

Fig. 99 Camshaft bearing housing bolt tightening sequence

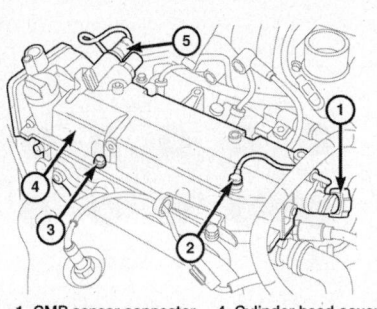

1. CMP sensor connector
2. Ground lug bolts
3. Bolts
4. Cylinder head cover
5. VVT connector

Fig. 100 View of components necessary to removal cylinder head cover

42. Install the battery tray with one nut and two bolts tightened to 18 ft. lbs. (25 Nm).

43. Engage the engine wire harness connector to the battery tray.

44. Engage two engine wire harness retainers to the battery tray.

45. Engage two starter wire harness retainers to the battery tray.

46. Connect the powertrain control module (PCM) electrical connectors.

47. Install the camshaft bearing housing.

48. If removed, install the oil filter and fill the engine crankcase with the proper oil to the correct level.

49. Fill the cooling system.

50. Install the engine cover.

51. Connect the negative battery cable and tighten nut to 45 inch lbs. (5 Nm).

52. Run the engine until it reaches normal operating temperature. Check cooling system for correct fluid level.

➡ **The Cam/Crank Variation Relearn procedure must be performed using the scan tool anytime there has been a repair/replacement made to a powertrain system, for example: flywheel, valvetrain, camshaft and/or crankshaft sensors or components.**

CYLINDER HEAD (VALVE) COVER

REMOVAL & INSTALLATION

1.4L 8V Engine

See Figures 100 and 101.

1. Disconnect and isolate the negative battery cable.

2. Remove the air cleaner assembly.

3. Remove the battery and battery tray.

4. Remove the ignition coil(s), as outlined in this Engine Electrical Section.

5. Remove the upper timing belt cover, as outlined in the Timing Belt Procedure.

6. Unlock and disconnect the Camshaft Position (CMP) sensor electrical connector.

7. Unlock and disconnect the variable valve timing (VVT) solenoid electrical connector.

8. Remove the bolt and the ground lug from the cylinder head cover.

9. Remove bolts and the cylinder head cover.

10. Remove the bolt and the Camshaft Position (CMP) sensor from the cylinder head cover.

To install:

11. Apply a strip of Loctite® 5900 or equivalent silicone sealant, over the four corners of the contact surface with the cylinder head cover.

12. Install the cylinder head cover gasket.

13. Install the cylinder head cover on the cylinder head with the bolts hand tight.

14. Install Tappet Cover Centering Template 2000004300 on the cylinder head and cylinder head cover.

15. Tighten the cylinder head cover bolts (2) to 80 inch lbs. (9 Nm).

16. Remove the Tappet Cover Centering Template.

17. Install the Camshaft Position (CMP) sensor to the cylinder head cover.

18. Install the ground lug to the cylinder head cover and tighten the bolt to 80 inch lbs. (9 Nm).

19. Connect and lock the variable valve timing (VVT) solenoid electrical connector.

20. Connect and lock the Camshaft Position (CMP) sensor electrical connector.

21. Install the upper timing belt cover.

22. Install the ignition coil(s).

23. Install the battery tray and battery.

24. Install the air cleaner assembly..

25. Install the negative battery cable and tighten nut to 45 inch lbs. (5 Nm).

➡ **The Cam/Crank Variation Relearn procedure must be performed using the scan tool anytime there has been a repair/replacement made to a powertrain system, for example: flywheel, valvetrain, camshaft and/or crankshaft sensors or components.**

1.4L 16V MultiAir Engine

See Figures 102 through 113.

1. Perform the fuel pressure release procedure.

2. Disconnect and isolate the negative battery cable.

3. Recover the refrigerant from the refrigerant system.

4. Remove the engine cover.

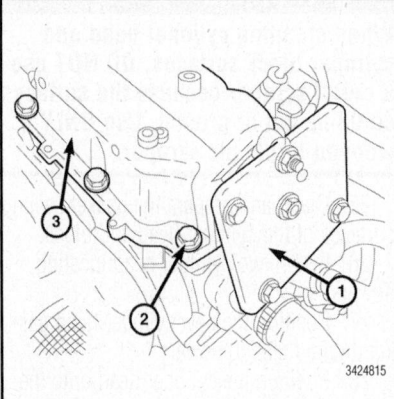

Fig. 101 Tappet Cover Centering template (1), cover bolts (2), and cylinder head cover (3)

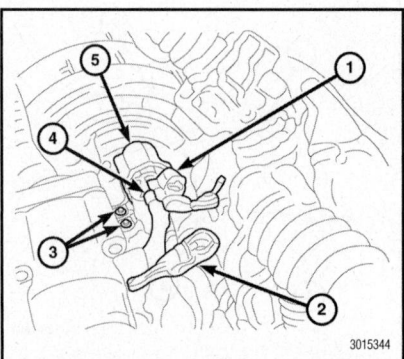

Fig. 102 Unlock and disconnect the evaporative emissions purge solenoid electrical connector (1), then unlock and disconnect the fuel injector wire harness electrical connector (2)

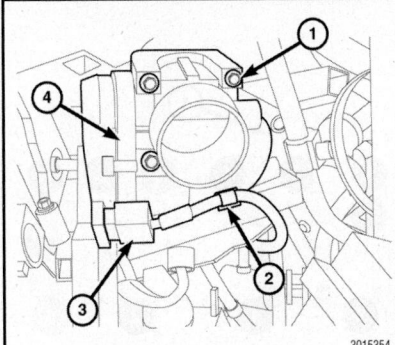

Fig. 103 Unlock and disconnect the electrical connector (3) from the Electronic Throttle Control (ETC) (4) and disengage the ETC harness from the clip (2) on the throttle body

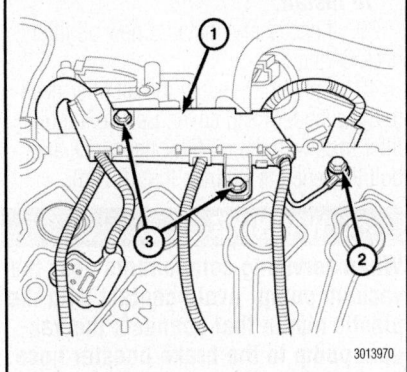

Fig. 105 Remove the bolt (2) and the ground lug from the cylinder head cover. Remove two bolts (3) and reposition the wire harness duct (1)

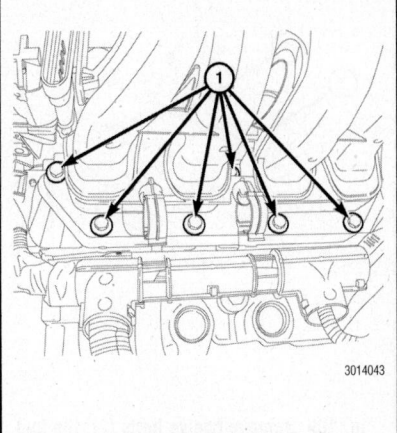

Fig. 107 Remove six of the seven intake manifold flange bolts (1)

5. Remove the air cleaner assembly.

6. Disconnect the PCV hose from the intake manifold.

7. Disconnect the vent hose from the oil filler neck.

8. Remove three bolts and remove the oil separator housing from the cylinder head cover.

9. Disconnect the fuel vapor purge hose from the intake manifold.

10. Open the hose retainer and disconnect the fuel line from the fuel rail.

11. Unlock and disconnect the IAT/MAP sensor electrical connector.

12. Unlock and disconnect the evaporative emissions purge solenoid electrical connector.

13. Unlock and disconnect the fuel injector wire harness electrical connector.

14. Unlock and disconnect the electrical connector from the Electronic Throttle Control (ETC) and disengage the ETC harness from the clip on the throttle body.

✳✳ WARNING

When servicing components near the vacuum pump, avoid contact with the plastic nipple that connects the vacuum pump to the brake booster hose. It is possible to crack the plastic nipple resulting in a brake booster vacuum leak.

15. Disconnect the vacuum line from the vacuum pump.

16. Remove two bolts, nut and reposition the oil separator housing bracket.

17. Remove the ignition coils, as outlined in the Engine Electrical Section.

18. Remove the bolt and the ground lug from the cylinder head cover.

19. Remove two bolts and reposition the wire harness duct.

20. Raise and support the vehicle.

21. Remove the belly pan.

22. Remove two bolts and the right vertical brace.

23. Remove two screws from the front wheelhouse splash shield.

24. Remove three screws and the frame splash shield.

25. Remove the accessory drive belt.

26. Remove the A/C compressor.

27. Open the two wire harness retainers and reposition the wire harness.

28. Remove six of the seven intake manifold flange bolts.

29. Lower the vehicle.

30. Remove the remaining intake manifold flange bolt, the intake manifold support bolt and reposition the intake manifold.

31. Remove and discard the four intake manifold seals.

32. Cover the open intake ports to prevent debris from entering the engine.

33. Remove the bolt from the upper timing belt cover.

34. Remove twelve bolts, the fuel rail blocker and the cylinder head cover.

35. Remove and discard the cylinder

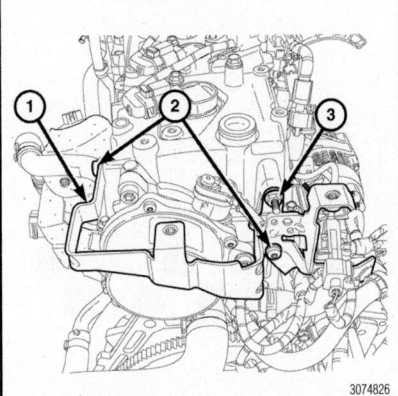

Fig. 104 Remove two bolts (2), nut (3) and reposition the oil separator housing bracket (1)

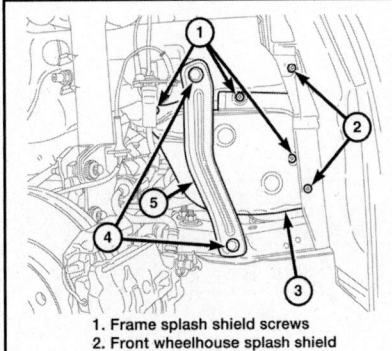

1. Frame splash shield screws
2. Front wheelhouse splash shield
3. Frame splash shield
4. Bolts
5. Right vertical brace

Fig. 106 Right vertical brace and splash shields

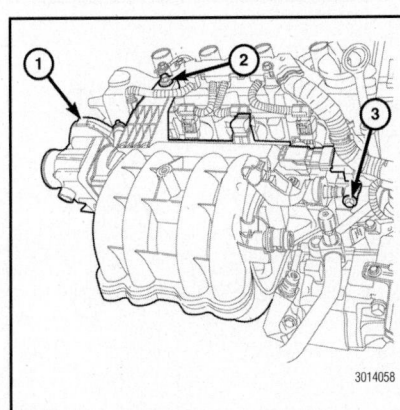

Fig. 108 Remove the remaining intake manifold flange bolt (3), the intake manifold support bolt (2) and reposition the intake manifold (1)

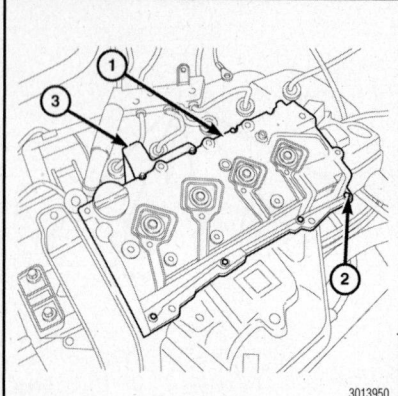

Fig. 109 Remove twelve bolts (2), the fuel rail blocker (3) and the cylinder head cover (1)

head cover gasket. The spark plug tube seals can be reused if not damaged.

✳✳ WARNING

Never use oil based liquids, wire brushes, abrasive wheels or metal scrapers to clean the engine gasket surfaces. Use only isopropyl (rubbing) alcohol, along with plastic or wooden scrapers. Improper gasket surface preparation may result in engine fluid leakage.

36. Remove all residual sealant from the variable valve actuator assembly, camshaft caps, camshaft housing and cylinder head cover mating surfaces.

37. If required, remove the bolt, oil filler neck lock and the oil filler neck from the cylinder head cover.

38. The oil filler neck O-ring can be reused if not damaged.

To install:

39. If necessary, install a new oil filler neck O-ring.

40. If required, install the oil filler neck to the cylinder head cover. Secure the oil filler neck with the oil filler neck lock and bolt tightened to 80 inch lbs. (9 Nm).

✳✳ WARNING

When servicing components near the vacuum pump, avoid contact with the plastic nipple that connects the vacuum pump to the brake booster hose. It is possible to crack the plastic nipple resulting in a brake booster vacuum leak.

41. Install the cylinder head cover gasket. The spark plug tube seals can be reused if not damaged.

42. Clean the variable valve actuator assembly, camshaft caps, camshaft housing and cylinder head cover mating surfaces with isopropyl alcohol in preparation for sealant application.

✳✳ WARNING

Engine assembly requires the use of a unique sealant that is compatible with engine oil. Using a sealant other than Mopar® Engine RTV GEN II may result in engine fluid leakage.

✳✳ WARNING

Following the application of Mopar® Engine RTV GEN II to the gasket surfaces, the components must be assembled within 10 minutes and the attaching fasteners must be tightened to specification within the next 10

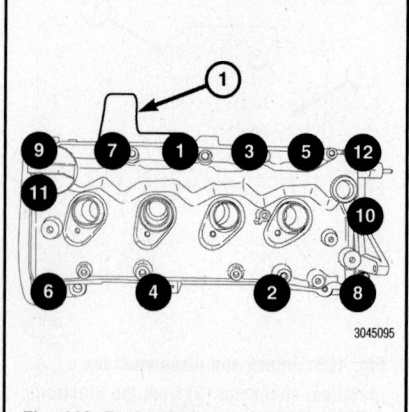

Fig. 112 Fuel rail blocker (1) and cylinder head cover bolt tightening sequence (black shaded circles)

minutes. Prolonged exposure to the air prior to assembly may result in engine fluid leakage.

43. Apply a 2–3 mm wide bead of Mopar® Engine RTV GEN II sealant (1) to the cylinder head cover T-joints as shown.

44. Install the cylinder head cover and fuel rail blocker with twelve bolts. Tighten the twelve bolts in two steps following the sequence shown:
   a. Step 1: All to 44 inch lbs. (5 Nm).
   b. Step 2: All to 80 inch lbs. (9 Nm).

45. Install the upper timing belt cover with two bolts tightened to 80 inch lbs. (9 Nm).

46. Install four new intake manifold seals.

47. Loosely install an intake manifold flange bolt and the support bolt) to hold the intake manifold in position.

48. Raise and support the vehicle.

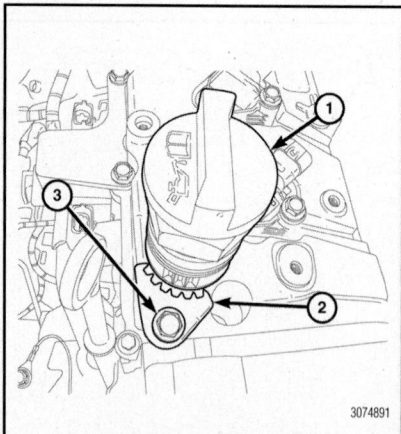

Fig. 110 If required, remove the bolt (3), oil filler neck lock (2) and the oil filler neck (1) from the cylinder head cover

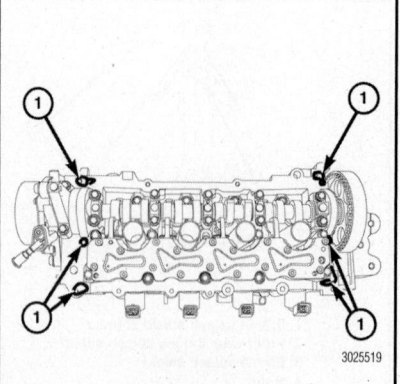

Fig. 111 Apply a 2 to 3 mm wide bead of Mopar® Engine RTV GEN II sealant (1) to the cylinder head cover T-joints

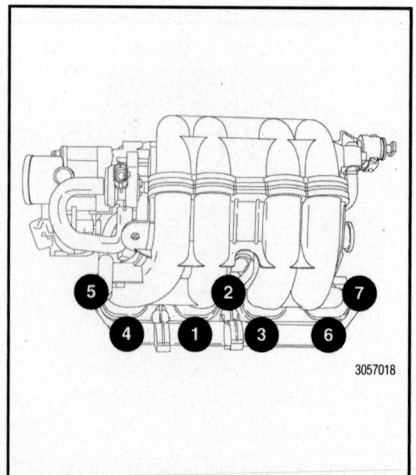

Fig. 113 Intake manifold flange bolt tightening sequence

49. Install the remaining six of the seven intake manifold flange bolts (1). Tighten all seven intake manifold flange bolts in the sequence shown to 11 ft. lbs. (15 Nm).

50. Position the wire harness and close the two wire harness retainers.

51. Lower the vehicle.

52. Tighten the intake manifold support bolt to 80 inch lbs. (9 Nm).

53. Install the A/C compressor.

54. Install the accessory drive belt.

55. Install the frame splash shield with three screws.

Install two screws to the front wheelhouse splash shield.

Install the right vertical brace with two bolts tightened to 33 ft. lbs. (45 Nm).

56. Install the belly pan.

57. Install the wiring harness duct to the cylinder head cover with two bolts tightened to 80 inch lbs. (9 Nm).

58. Install the ground lug to the cylinder head cover and tighten the bolt to 80 inch lbs. (9 Nm).

59. Install the ignition coils..

60. Install the oil separator housing bracket with two bolts and one nut. Tighten the three fasteners to 115 inch lbs. (13 Nm).

61. Connect the vacuum line to the vacuum pump.

62. Connect and lock the electrical connector to the Electronic Throttle Control (ETC) and engage the ETC harness to the clip on the throttle body.

63. Connect and lock the fuel injector wire harness electrical connector.

64. Connect and lock the evaporative emissions purge solenoid electrical connector.

65. Connect and lock the IAT/MAP sensor electrical connector.

66. Connect the fuel vapor purge hose to the intake manifold.

67. Connect the fuel line to the fuel rail and close the hose retainer.

68. Install the oil separator housing to the cylinder head cover with three bolts tightened to 115 inch lbs. (13 Nm).

69. Connect the vent hose to the oil filler neck.

70. Connect the PCV hose to the intake manifold.

71. Install the air cleaner assembly.

72. Evacuate and charge the refrigerant system.

73. Install the negative battery cable and tighten nut to 45 inch lbs. (5 Nm).

74. Install the engine cover.

75. Run the engine until it reaches normal operating temperature. Check cooling system for correct fluid level.

1.4L 16V Turbo Engine

See Figures 114 through 124.

1. Perform the fuel pressure release procedure.

2. Disconnect and isolate the negative battery cable.

3. Remove the air cleaner assembly.

4. Remove two bolts, nut, and the turbocharger support bracket.

5. Disconnect the PCV hose from the intake manifold.

6. Disconnect the vent hose from the cylinder head cover.

7. Remove three bolts and remove the oil separator housing from the cylinder head cover.

8. Open the hose retainer and disconnect the fuel vapor purge hose.

9. Disconnect the fuel line from the fuel rail.

10. Disengage and reposition the purge flow control solenoid from the bracket.

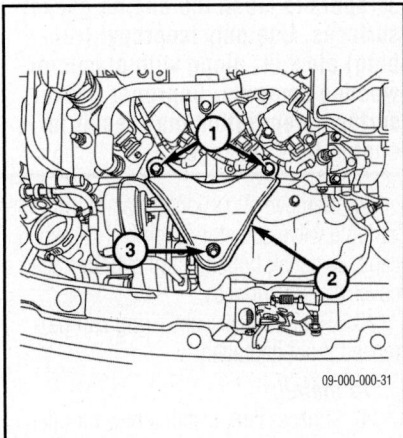

Fig. 114 Remove two bolts (1), nut (3), and the turbocharger support bracket (2)

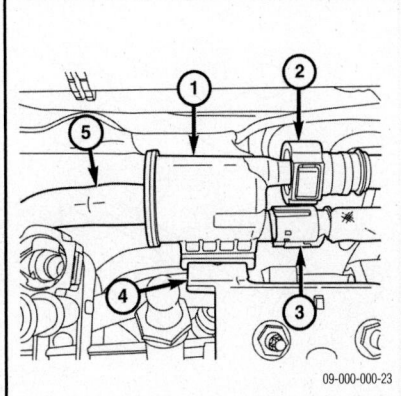

Fig. 115 Disengage and reposition the purge flow control solenoid (1) from the bracket (4)

When servicing components near the vacuum pump, avoid contact with the plastic nipple that connects the vacuum pump to the brake booster hose. It is possible to crack the plastic nipple resulting in a brake booster vacuum leak.

11. Disconnect the vacuum line from the vacuum pump.

12. Remove the nuts, bolt and bracket.

13. Disengage the retainer from the support bracket.

14. Remove the nut, bolt and support bracket.

15. Remove two bolts, nut and reposition the oil separator housing bracket.

16. Remove the ignition coils, as outlined in the Engine Electrical Section.

17. Remove the bolt and the ground lug from the cylinder head cover.

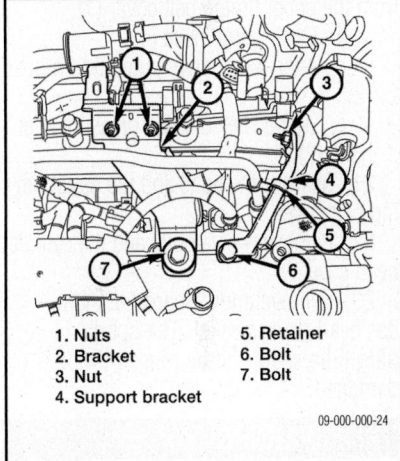

1. Nuts 5. Retainer
2. Bracket 6. Bolt
3. Nut 7. Bolt
4. Support bracket

09-000-000-24

Fig. 116 View of the support bracket and retainers

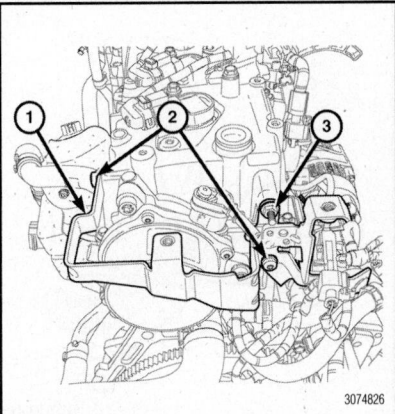

Fig. 117 Remove two bolts (2), nut (3) and reposition the oil separator housing bracket (1)

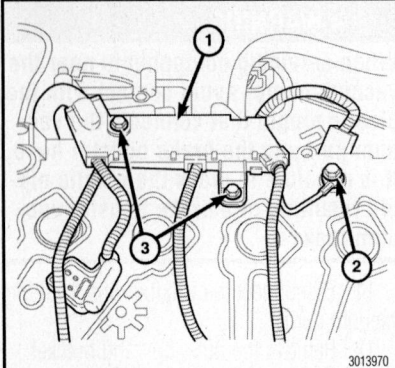

Fig. 118 Remove the bolt (2) and the ground lug from the cylinder head cover. Remove two bolts (3) and reposition the wire harness duct (1)

18. Remove two bolts and reposition the wire harness duct.

19. Remove the bolt and reposition the turbocharger wastegate solenoid.

20. Disengage the following retainers from the upper timing belt cover (1):

   a. EVAP purge hose (4).

   b. After-run coolant pump return hose (3).

   c. Wastegate solenoid pressure inlet hose (2).

21. Remove the bolts and the upper timing belt cover.

22. Remove twelve bolts and the cylinder head cover.

23. Remove and discard the cylinder head cover gasket. The spark plug tube seals can be reused if not damaged.

✳✳ WARNING

Do not use oil based liquids, wire brushes, abrasive wheels or metal

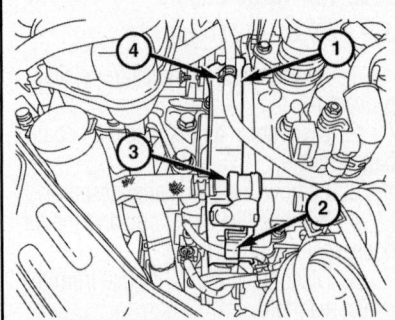

1. Upper timing belt cover
2. Wastegate solenoid pressure inlet hose
3. After-run coolant pump return hose
4. EVAP emissions purge hose

Fig. 120 Upper timing belt cover (1), wastegate solenoid pressure inlet hose (2), after-run coolant pump return hose (3) and EVAP purge hose (4)

scrapers to clean the engine gasket surfaces. Use only isopropyl (rubbing) alcohol, along with plastic or wooden scrapers. Improper gasket surface preparation may result in engine fluid leakage.

24. Remove all residual sealant from the variable valve actuator assembly, camshaft caps, camshaft housing and cylinder head cover mating surfaces.

25. The oil filler neck O-ring can be reused if not damaged.

To install:

26. If necessary, install a new oil filler neck O-ring.

27. If required, install the oil filler neck to the cylinder head cover. Secure

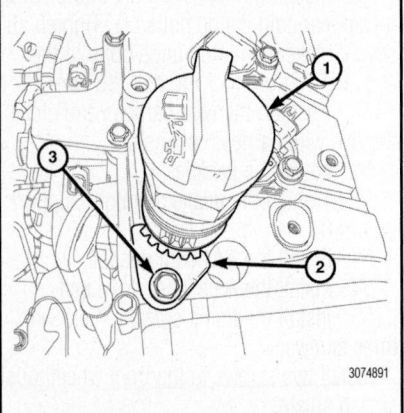

Fig. 122 If required, remove the bolt (3), oil filler neck lock (2) and the oil filler neck (1) from the cylinder head cover

the oil filler neck with the oil filler neck lock and bolt tightened to 80 inch lbs. (9 Nm).

✳✳ WARNING

When servicing components near the vacuum pump, avoid contact with the plastic nipple that connects the vacuum pump to the brake booster hose. It is possible to crack the plastic nipple resulting in a brake booster vacuum leak.

28. Install the cylinder head cover gasket. The spark plug tube seals can be reused if not damaged.

29. Clean the variable valve actuator assembly, camshaft caps, camshaft housing and cylinder head cover mating surfaces with isopropyl alcohol in preparation for sealant application.

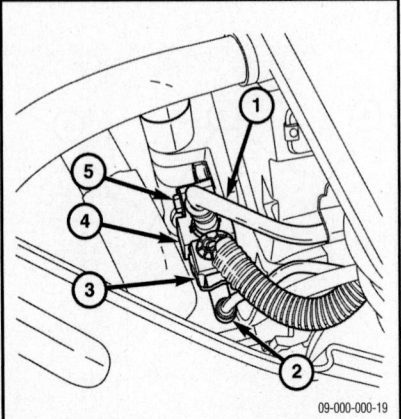

Fig. 119 Remove the bolt (5) and reposition the turbocharger wastegate solenoid (4)

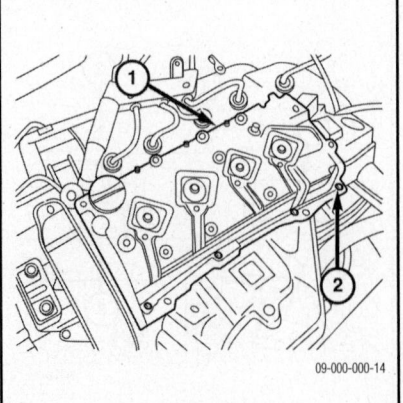

Fig. 121 Remove twelve bolts (2) and the cylinder head cover (1)

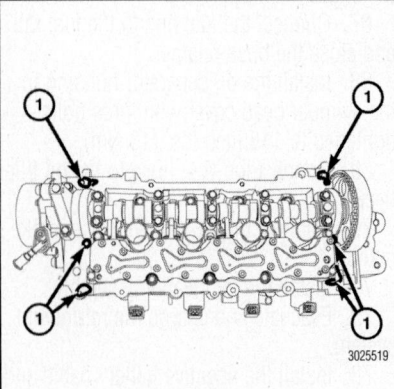

Fig. 123 Apply a 2 to 3 mm wide bead of Mopar® Engine RTV GEN II sealant (1) to the cylinder head cover T-joints

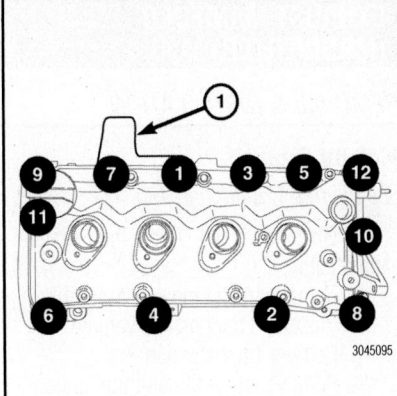

Fig. 124 Fuel rail blocker (1) and cylinder head cover bolt tightening sequence (black shaded circles)

> ✳✳ **WARNING**
>
> **Engine assembly requires the use of a unique sealant that is compatible with engine oil. Using a sealant other than Mopar® Engine RTV GEN II may result in engine fluid leakage.**

> ✳✳ **WARNING**
>
> **Following the application of Mopar® Engine RTV GEN II to the gasket surfaces, the components must be assembled within 10 minutes and the attaching fasteners must be tightened to specification within the next 10 minutes. Prolonged exposure to the air prior to assembly may result in engine fluid leakage.**

30. Apply a 2–3 mm wide bead of Mopar® Engine RTV GEN II sealant (1) to the cylinder head cover T-joints as shown.

31. Install the cylinder head cover and fuel rail blocker with twelve bolts. Tighten the twelve bolts in two steps following the sequence shown:

    a. Step 1: All to 44 inch lbs. (5 Nm).

    b. Step 2: All to 80 inch lbs. (9 Nm).

32. Install the upper timing belt cover with two bolts tightened to 80 inch lbs. (9 Nm).

33. Engage the following retainers from the upper timing belt cover:

    a. Wastegate solenoid pressure inlet hose.

    b. After-run coolant pump return hose.

    c. EVAP purge hose

34. Reposition and install the turbocharger wastegate solenoid. Tighten bolt to 71 inch lbs. (8 Nm).

35. Install the wiring harness duct to the cylinder head cover with two bolts tightened to 80 inch lbs. (9 Nm).

36. Install the ground lug to the cylinder head cover and tighten the bolt to 80 inch lbs. (9 Nm).

37. Install the ignition coils.

38. Install the oil separator housing bracket with two bolts and one nut. Tighten the three fasteners to 115 inch lbs. (13 Nm).

39. Install the support bracket. Tighten Nut, Bolt to 80 inch lbs. (9 Nm).

40. Engage the retainer to the support bracket.

41. Install the bracket. Tighten Nut, Bolt to 80 inch lbs. (9 Nm).

42. Connect the vacuum line to the vacuum pump.

43. Position and engage the purge flow control solenoid to the bracket.

44. Connect the fuel line to the fuel rail and close the hose retainer.

45. Connect the fuel line to the fuel rail.

46. Connect the fuel vapor purge hose to the intake manifold.

47. Install the oil separator housing to the cylinder head cover with three bolts tightened to 115 inch lbs. (13 Nm).

48. Connect the vent hose to the cylinder head cover.

49. Connect the PCV hose to the intake manifold.

50. Install the turbocharger support bracket. Tighten one nut, two bolts to 18 ft. lbs. (25 Nm).

51. Install the air cleaner assembly.

52. Connect the negative battery cable.

53. Run the engine until it reaches normal operating temperature and check for leaks.

ENGINE OIL & FILTER

REPLACEMENT

1.4L 8V Engine

See Figure 125.

> ✳✳ **CAUTION**
>
> **New or used engine oil can be irritating to the skin. Avoid prolonged or repeated skin contact with engine oil. Contaminants in used engine oil, caused by internal combustion, can be hazardous to your health. Thoroughly wash exposed skin with soap and water. Do not wash skin with gasoline, diesel fuel, thinner, or solvents, health problems can result. Do not pollute, dispose of used engine oil properly. Contact your dealer or government agency for location of collection center in your area.**

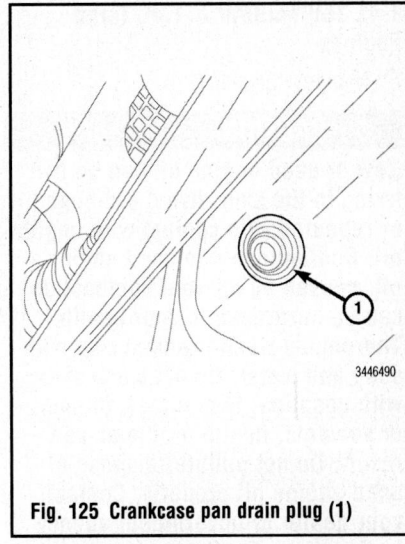

Fig. 125 Crankcase pan drain plug (1)

➡**Change the engine oil and filter at mileage and time intervals described in the Maintenance Schedule.**

1. Run the engine until achieving normal operating temperature.

2. Remove the engine oil fill cap from the cylinder head cover.

3. Raise and support the vehicle.

4. Place a suitable drain pan under the crankcase drain plug.

5. Remove the crankcase oil drain plug from oil pan and allow the oil to drain into the pan. Inspect the drain plug threads for stretching or other damage. Replace the drain plug and gasket if damaged.

6. Place a suitable drain pan under the engine oil filter.

7. Remove the oil filter from the oil pump housing.

8. Remove and discard the oil filter gasket.

9. Install the drain plug in the oil pan and tighten to 33 ft. lbs. (45 Nm).

10. Lightly lubricate the new oil filter gasket with clean engine oil.

11. Install the new oil filter onto the oil filter housing and tighten by hand.

12. Lower the vehicle.

13. Position the vehicle on a level surface.

14. Fill the crankcase with the specified type and amount of engine oil. Refer to the Capacities specification chart in this section.

15. Check the oil level using the dipstick.

16. Install the oil fill cap.

17. Start and run the engine for at least two minutes.

18. Stop the engine, wait several minutes then check the oil level and inspect for leaks.

1.4L 16V MultiAir & 1.4L Turbo Engines

See Figures 126 and 127.

✳✳ CAUTION

New or used engine oil can be irritating to the skin. Avoid prolonged or repeated skin contact with engine oil. Contaminants in used engine oil, caused by internal combustion, can be hazardous to your health. Thoroughly wash exposed skin with soap and water. Do not wash skin with gasoline, diesel fuel, thinner, or solvents, health problems can result. Do not pollute, dispose of used engine oil properly. Contact your dealer or government agency for location of collection center in your area.

➡Change the engine oil and filter at mileage and time intervals described in the Maintenance Schedule.

1. Run the engine until achieving normal operating temperature.
2. Position the vehicle on a level surface and turn the engine off.
3. Remove the engine cover.

✳✳ WARNING

When performing an engine oil change, the oil filter cap must be removed. Removing the oil filter cap releases oil held within the oil filter cavity and allows it to drain into the sump. Failure to remove the cap prior to reinstallation of the drain plug will not allow complete draining of the used engine oil.

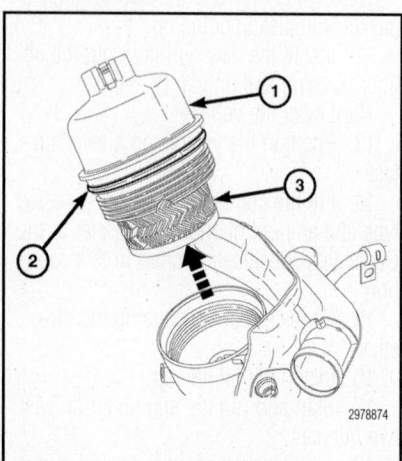

Fig. 126 View of the oil filter cap (1), O-ring seal (2), and oil filter (3)

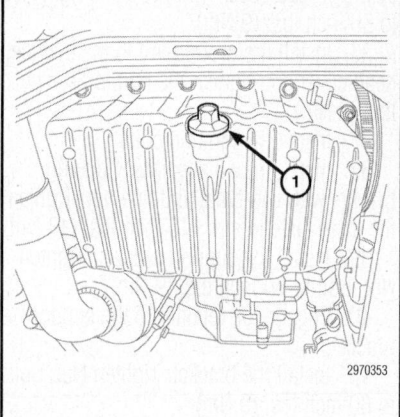

Fig. 127 Location of the oil pan drain plug (1)

4. Place an oil absorbent cloth around the oil filter housing at the base of the oil filter cap.

➡The oil filter is attached to the oil filter cap.

5. Rotate the oil filter cap counterclockwise and remove the cap and filter from the oil filter housing.
6. Raise and support the vehicle.
7. Place a suitable drain pan under the crankcase drain plug.
8. Remove the drain plug from oil pan and allow the oil to drain into the pan. Inspect the drain plug threads for stretching or other damage. Replace the drain plug and gasket if damaged.
9. Install the drain plug in the oil pan and tighten to 20 ft. lbs. (27 Nm).
10. Lower the vehicle.
11. Remove the oil filter from the oil filter cap.
12. Remove and discard the O-ring seal.

➡It is not necessary to pre-oil the oil filter or fill the oil filter housing.

13. Lightly lubricate the new O-ring seal with clean engine oil.
14. Install the O-ring seal on the filter cap.
15. Install the new oil filter into the oil filter cap.
16. Thread the oil filter cap into the oil filter housing and tighten to 18 ft. lbs. (25 Nm).
17. Remove the oil fill cap. Fill the crankcase with the specified type and amount of engine oil. Refer to the Capacities Specification chart in this section.
18. Install the oil fill cap.
19. Start the engine and inspect for leaks.
20. Stop the engine and check the oil level.
21. Install the engine cover.

EXHAUST MANIFOLD (MANIVERTER)

REMOVAL & INSTALLATION

1.4L 8V Engine

See Figures 128 through 130.

1. Disconnect and isolate the negative battery cable.
2. Remove the air cleaner assembly.
3. Raise and support the vehicle.
4. Remove the belly pan.
5. Remove four bolts and the tunnel support brace.
6. Remove the exhaust flange nuts.
7. Remove the maniverter pipe extension support bolt.
8. Unlock and disconnect the downstream oxygen sensor connector.

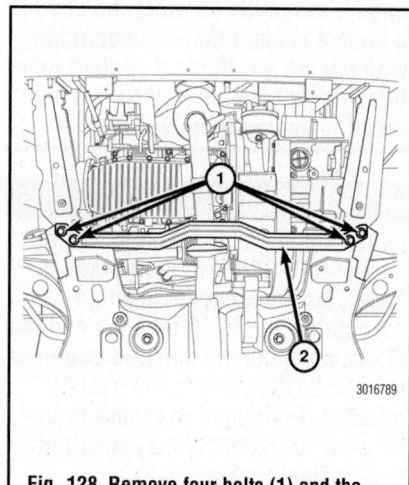

Fig. 128 Remove four bolts (1) and the tunnel support brace (2)

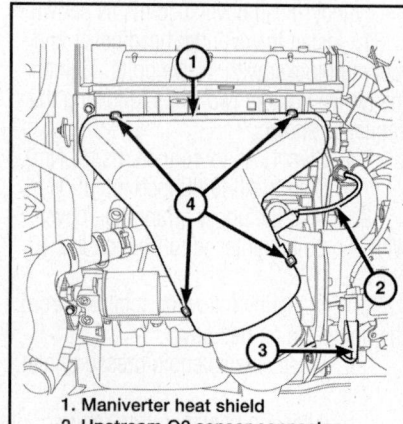

1. Maniverter heat shield
2. Upstream O2 sensor connector
3. Downstream O2 sensor connector
4. Maniverter bolts

Fig. 129 Heat shield, O2 sensors and maniverter bolts

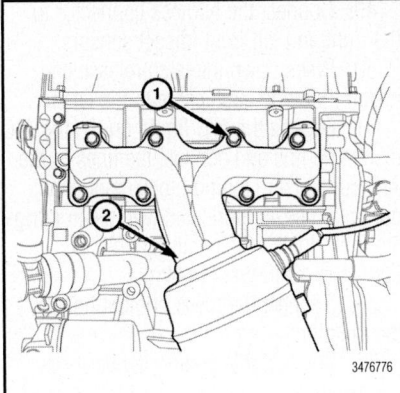

Fig. 130 Remove eight nuts (1) and remove the maniverter (2) from the cylinder head

9. Lower the vehicle.

10. Unlock and disconnect the upstream oxygen sensor connector.

11. Remove four bolts and the maniverter heat shield.

12. Remove eight nuts (1) and remove the maniverter (2) from the cylinder head. Lower the maniverter down through the engine compartment and remove the maniverter from the vehicle.

13. Remove and discard the maniverter gasket.

14. If required, remove the oxygen sensors from the maniverter.

To install:

15. If removed, install the oxygen sensors to the maniverter.

16. Clean the mating surfaces of the cylinder head and the maniverter flange.

17. Install a new maniverter gasket on the cylinder head.

18. Raise and support the vehicle.

19. Guide the maniverter up into place onto the studs.

20. Lower the vehicle.

21. Install and tighten the eight nuts to 15 ft. lbs. (20 Nm).

22. Install the maniverter heat shield with four bolts tightened to 80 inch lbs. (9 Nm).

23. Connect and lock the upstream oxygen sensor connector.

24. Raise and support the vehicle.

25. Connect and lock the downstream oxygen sensor connector.

26. Install the muffler flexible intake pipe to the maniverter flange with two nuts. Tighten the nuts to 18 ft. lbs. (25 Nm).

27. Install the maniverter pipe extension support to the structural collar. Tighten the bolt to 37 ft. lbs. (50 Nm).

28. Install the tunnel support brace with four bolts tightened to 60 ft. lbs. (90 Nm).

29. Install the belly pan.

30. Lower the vehicle.

31. Install the air cleaner assembly.

32. Connect the negative battery cable and tighten nut to 45 inch lbs. (5 Nm).

1.4L 16V MultiAir Engine

See Figures 128, 131 through 135.

1. Recover the refrigerant from the refrigerant system.

2. Disconnect and isolate the negative battery cable.

3. Remove the engine cover.

4. Remove the air cleaner assembly.

5. Raise and support the vehicle.

6. Remove the belly pan.

7. Drain the cooling system.

8. Remove four bolts and the tunnel support brace. Reinstall the four bolts to maintain alignment of the frame extensions. Tighten the bolts to 60 ft. lbs. (90 Nm).

9. Remove both front tire and wheel assemblies.

10. Remove both front inner wheel well splash shields.

11. Remove the front fascia.

12. Remove the right and left headlamp units .

13. Disconnect the upper coolant hose from the radiator.

14. Disconnect the harness connector from the cooling fan resistor.

15. Disconnect the lower coolant hose from the radiator.

16. Disconnect the cooling fan harness connector.

17. Remove the bolt and disconnect the

1. A/C liquid line
2. A/C compressor discharge line
3. A/C condenser tapping block
4. Bolt

3065473

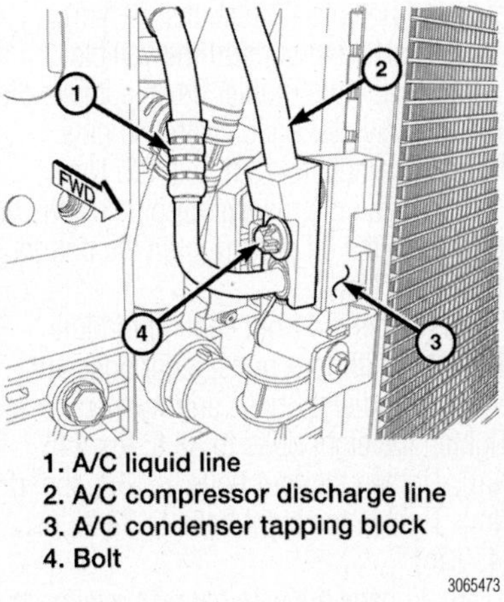

Fig. 131 Remove the bolt (4) and disconnect the A/C liquid line (1) and the A/C discharge line (2) from the A/C condenser tapping block (3)

A/C liquid line and the A/C discharge line from the A/C condenser tapping block.

18. Separate the A/C liquid line from the A/C discharge line. Remove and discard the dual plain seals.

Install plugs in, or tape over, the opened refrigerant line fittings and condenser ports.

19. Press down the latch release and remove the hood latch cable from the latch.

20. Disconnect the harness connector from the right and left front impact sensors.

21. Disconnect the harness connector from the horn.

22. Disengage the harness connector from the bumper reinforcement.

23. Disengage the harness retainer from the bottom of the bumper reinforcement.

24. Remove four bolts, eight bolts and washers, eight bolts and washers and the cooling module assembly from the vehicle.

25. Remove the exhaust flange nuts.

26. Remove the maniverter pipe extension support bolt.

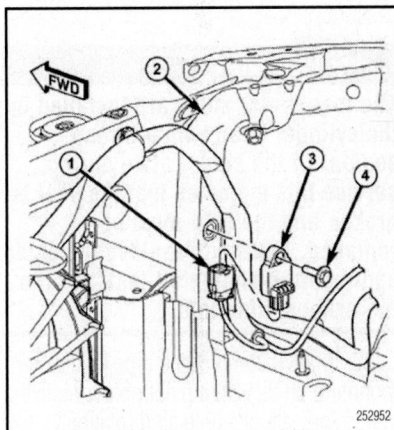

252952

Fig. 132 Disconnect the harness connector (1) from the right and left front impact sensors (3)

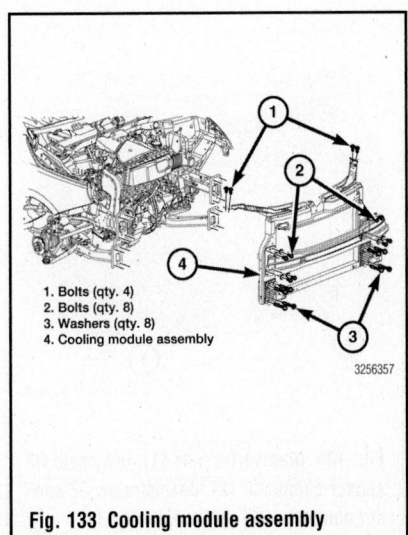

1. Bolts (qty. 4)
2. Bolts (qty. 8)
3. Washers (qty. 8)
4. Cooling module assembly

3256357

Fig. 133 Cooling module assembly

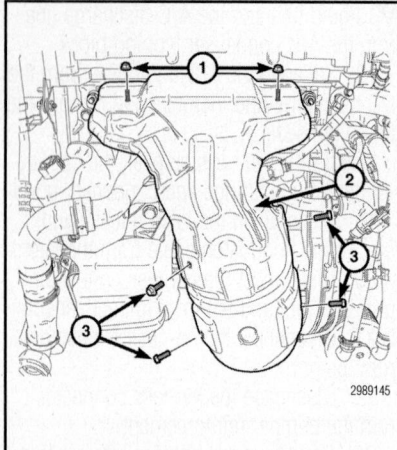

Fig. 134 Remove two nuts (1), four bolts (3) and the maniverter heat shield (2)

27. Remove two nuts (1), four bolts (3) and the maniverter heat shield (2).

28. Disengage the wire harness retainers and disconnect the electrical connectors from the upstream and downstream oxygen sensors.

✲✲ WARNING

The maniverter studs are installed in the cylinder head with a thread sealant. If the studs rotate during service this indicates that the seal is broken and the stud must be replaced. Failure to replace the studs can result in engine oil leaking onto the exhaust manifold.

29. Mark the end of the nine maniverter mounting studs with a paint pen or equivalent to indicate possible stud rotation.

30. Remove nine nuts and remove the maniverter from the cylinder head.

31. Check the markings on the studs for

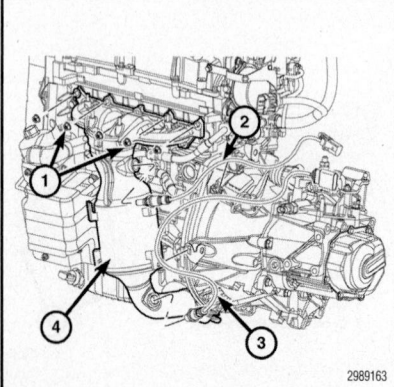

Fig. 135 Maniverter nuts (1), upstream O2 sensor connector (2), downstream O2 sensor connector (3) and maniverter (4)

indication of rotation. If there is evidence of stud rotation, replace the stud.

32. Remove and discard the maniverter gasket.

33. If required, remove the upstream and downstream oxygen sensors from the maniverter.

To install:

34. If removed, install the upstream and downstream oxygen sensor(s) to the maniverter.

35. Clean the mating surfaces of the cylinder head and the maniverter flange.

36. Install a new maniverter gasket on the cylinder head.

✲✲ WARNING

The maniverter studs are installed in the cylinder head with a thread sealant. If the studs rotate during service this indicates that the seal is broken and the stud must be replaced. Failure to replace the studs can result in engine oil leaking onto the exhaust manifold.

37. Mark the end of the nine maniverter mounting studs with a paint pen or equivalent to indicate possible stud rotation.

38. Guide the maniverter into place onto the studs. Install and tighten the nine nuts to 15 ft. lbs. (20 Nm).

39. Check the markings on the studs for indication of rotation. If there is evidence of stud rotation, replace the stud.

40. Engage the wire harness retainers and connect the upstream and downstream oxygen sensor electrical connectors.

41. Install the maniverter heat shield with four bolts and two nuts. Tighten the nuts and bolts to 80 inch lbs. (9 Nm).

42. Raise and support the vehicle..

43. Install the muffler flexible intake pipe to the maniverter flange with two nuts. Tighten the nuts to 18 ft. lbs. (25 Nm).

44. Install the maniverter pipe extension support to the oil pan. Tighten the bolt to 37 ft. lbs. (50 Nm).

45. Install the front cooling module assembly with four bolts, eight bolts and washers and eight bolts and washers. Tighten the eight bolts to 33 ft. lbs. (45 Nm). Tighten the four bolts to 18 ft. lbs. (24 Nm). Tighten the eight bolts to 33 ft. lbs. (45 Nm).

46. Engage the wire harness retainer to the bottom of the bumper reinforcement.

47. Engage the wire harness connector to the bumper reinforcement.

48. Connect the harness connector to the horn.

49. Connect the harness connector to the right and left front impact sensors.

50. Press down the latch release and install the hood latch cable to the latch.

51. Engage the A/C liquid line to the A/C discharge line and connect the lines to the A/C condenser tapping block using new dual plain seals lubricated with clean refrigerant oil. Install the retaining bolt and tighten to 10 ft. lbs. (14 Nm).

52. Connect the lower coolant hose to the radiator.

53. Connect the cooling fan harness connector.

54. Connect the upper coolant hose to the radiator.

55. Connect the harness connector to the cooling fan resistor.

56. Install the right and left headlamp units.

57. Install the front fascia.

58. Install both front inner wheel well splash shields.

59. Install both front tire and wheel assemblies.

60. Remove the four bolts and install the tunnel support brace. Reinstall the four bolts and tighten to 60 ft. lbs. (90 Nm).

61. Install the belly pan.

62. Lower the vehicle.

63. Install the air cleaner assembly.

64. Fill the cooling system.

65. Connect the negative battery cable. Tighten nut to 45 inch lbs. (5 Nm).

66. Evacuate and charge the refrigerant system.

67. Install the engine cover.

68. Run the engine until it reaches normal operating temperature. Check cooling system for correct fluid level.

1.4L 16V Turbo Engine

See Figures 136 and 137.

➡**The turbocharger and exhaust manifold must be removed from the cylinder head as an assembly.**

1. Remove the turbocharger, as outlined in this section.

2. Remove and discard the four nuts.

3. Lift the manifold up and off of the turbocharger. Remove and discard the gasket.

To install:

4. Install a new gasket onto the manifold/turbocharger mating surface.

5. Set the manifold onto the turbocharger studs and install four new nuts by hand.

6. Tighten the four nuts to 18 ft. lbs. (24 Nm).

7. Install the turbocharger and exhaust

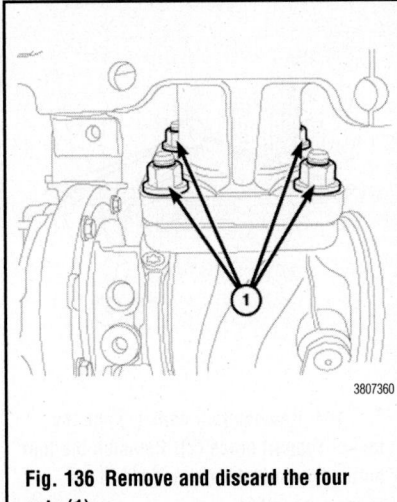

Fig. 136 Remove and discard the four nuts (1)

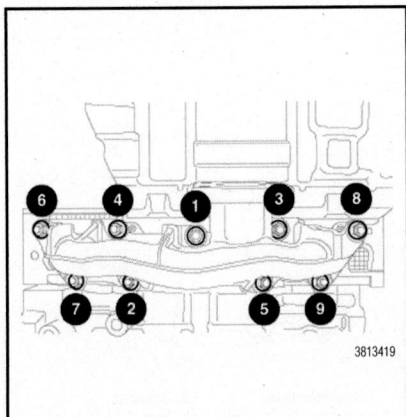

Fig. 137 Turbocharger and exhaust manifold-to-cylinder head bolt tightening sequence

manifold to the cylinder head. Refer to the Turbocharger procedure in this section.

INTAKE MANIFOLD

REMOVAL & INSTALLATION

1.4L 8V Engine

See Figures 138 and 139.

1. Perform the fuel pressure release procedure, as outlined in the Fuel System Section.

2. Disconnect and isolate the negative battery cable.

3. Remove the air cleaner assembly.

4. Disconnect the vacuum check valve from the brake booster.

5. Unlock and disconnect the fuel vapor purge solenoid electrical connector.

6. Disconnect the fuel vapor purge hose from the fuel vapor purge solenoid.

7. Unlock and disconnect the electrical connector from the IAT/MAP sensor.

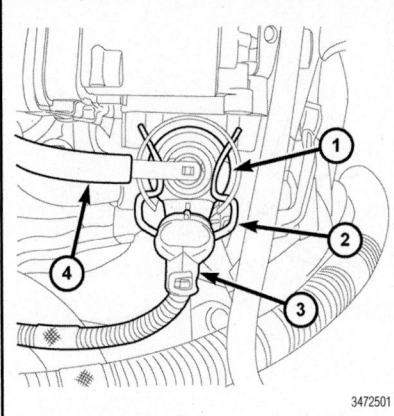

Fig. 138 View of the fuel vapor purge solenoid (1), electrical connector (3) and hose (4)

8. Unlock and disconnect the fuel injection harness electrical connector.

9. Unlock and disconnect the electronic throttle control (ETC) electrical connector.

10. Remove the fuel rail with fuel injectors. Refer to the Fuel System Section for more information.

11. Disconnect the spark plug wires from the spark plugs.

12. Remove the nuts (1) and bolts and remove the intake manifold (3).

13. Cover the open intake ports to prevent debris from entering the engine.

14. If required, remove the following components from the intake manifold:

　a. Throttle body

　b. Evaporative emissions purge solenoid

　c. Inlet Air Temperature/Manifold Air Pressure (IAT/MAP) sensor

To install:

15. If required, install the following components on the intake manifold:

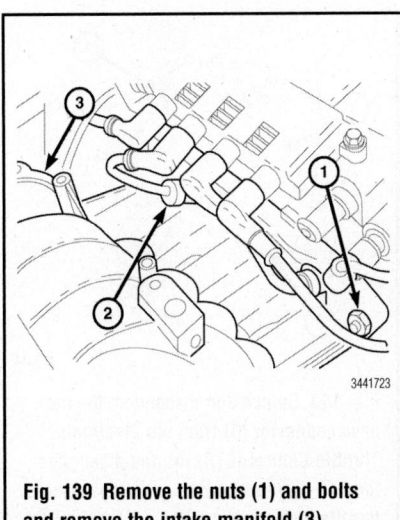

Fig. 139 Remove the nuts (1) and bolts and remove the intake manifold (3)

　a. Throttle body

　b. Evaporative emissions purge solenoid

　c. Inlet Air Temperature/Manifold Air Pressure (IAT/MAP) sensor

16. Install the intake manifold to the cylinder head with nuts and bolts tightened to 18 ft. lbs. (25 Nm).

17. Connect the spark plug wires to the spark plugs.

18. Install the fuel rail with fuel injectors.

19. Connect the fuel line to the fuel rail.

20. Connect and lock the electronic throttle control (ETC) electrical connector.

21. Connect and lock the fuel injection harness electrical connector.

22. Connect and lock the IAT/MAP sensor electrical connector.

23. Connect the fuel vapor purge hose to the fuel vapor purge solenoid.

24. Connect and lock the fuel vapor purge solenoid electrical connector.

25. Connect the vacuum check valve to the brake booster.

26. Install the air cleaner assembly.

27. Connect the negative battery cable and tighten nut to 45 inch lbs. (5 Nm).

1.4L 16V MultiAir Engine

See Figures 140 through 154.

1. Perform the fuel pressure release procedure, as outlined in the Fuel System Section.

2. Recover the refrigerant from the refrigerant system.

3. Remove the engine cover.

4. Remove the air cleaner assembly.

5. Disconnect the PCV hose from the intake manifold.

6. Disconnect the vent hose from the oil filler neck.

7. Remove three bolts and remove the

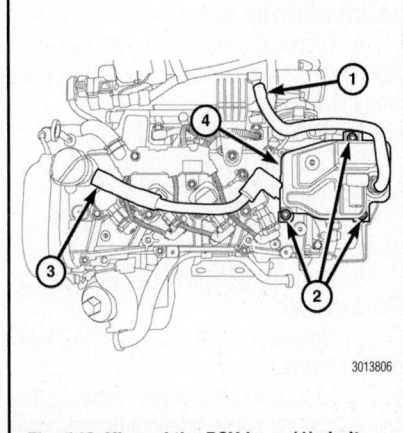

Fig. 140 View of the PCV hose (1), bolts (2), vent hose (3), and oil separator housing (4)

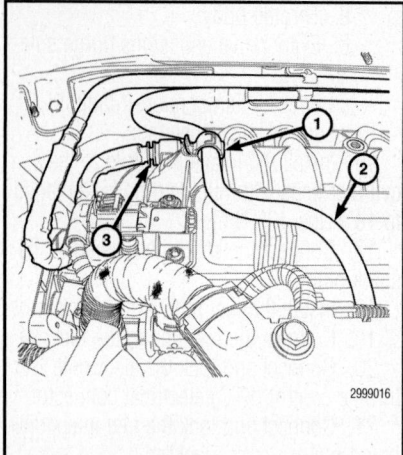

Fig. 141 View of the hose retainer (1), fuel line (2) and fuel vapor purge hose (3)

oil separator housing from the cylinder head cover.

8. Disconnect the fuel vapor purge hose from the intake manifold.

9. Open the hose retainer and disconnect the fuel line from the fuel rail.

☼ WARNING

When servicing components near the vacuum pump, avoid contact with the plastic nipple that connects the vacuum pump to the brake booster hose. It is possible to crack the plastic nipple resulting in a brake booster vacuum leak.

10. Disconnect and remove the battery. Refer to Engine Electrical for more information.

11. Unlock and disconnect the Powertrain Control Module (PCM) harness connectors.

12. Disengage two starter wire harness retainers from the battery tray

13. Disengage two engine wire harness retainers from the battery tray.

14. Disengage the engine wire harness connector from the battery tray and reposition the wire harness.

15. Remove the nut and two bolts.

16. Open the two wire harness retainers and reposition the wire harness.

17. Remove the nut and the ground strap.

18. Remove the battery tray with the PCM attached.

19. Unlock and disconnect the IAT/MAP sensor harness connector.

20. Unlock and disconnect the evaporative emissions purge solenoid harness connector (1).

21. Unlock and disconnect the fuel injector harness connector (2).

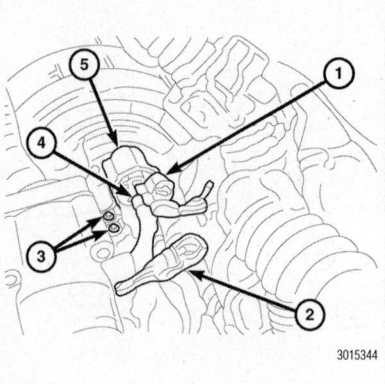

Fig. 142 View of the EVAP purge solenoid harness connector (1) and fuel injector harness connector (2)

22. Unlock and disconnect the harness connector from the Electronic Throttle Control (ETC) and disengage the ETC harness from the clip on the throttle body.

23. Remove two bolts, nut and reposition the oil separator housing bracket.

24. Disconnect the vacuum line from the vacuum pump.

25. Raise and support the vehicle.

26. Remove the belly pan.

27. Drain the cooling system.

28. Remove four bolts and the tunnel support brace. Reinstall the four bolts to maintain alignment of the frame extensions. Tighten the bolts to 60 ft. lbs. (90 Nm).

29. If equipped with a manual transmission, remove the rear engine mount bracket bolt and nut, loosen the isolator bolt and reposition the rear engine mount isolator away from the bracket.

30. If equipped with an automatic transmission, remove two bolts from the rear

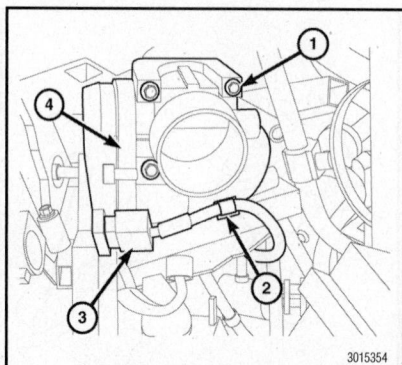

Fig. 143 Unlock and disconnect the harness connector (3) from the Electronic Throttle Control (ETC) (4) and disengage the ETC harness from the clip (2) on the throttle body

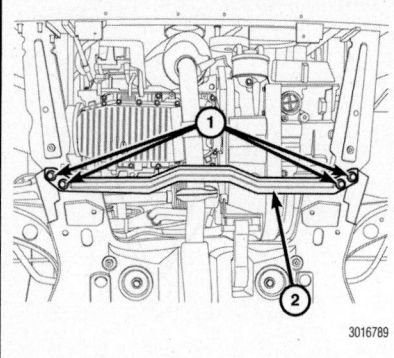

Fig. 144 Remove four bolts (1) and the tunnel support brace (2). Reinstall the four bolts (1) to maintain alignment of the frame extensions

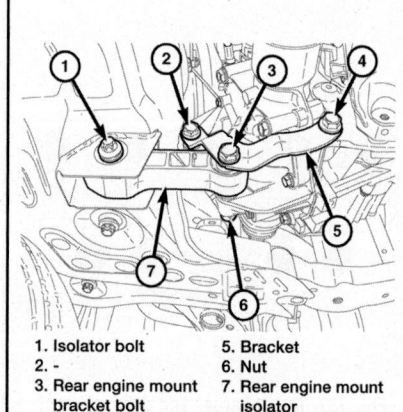

1. Isolator bolt	5. Bracket
2. -	6. Nut
3. Rear engine mount bracket bolt	7. Rear engine mount isolator
4. -	

Fig. 145 If equipped with a manual transmission, reposition the rear engine mount isolator away from the bracket

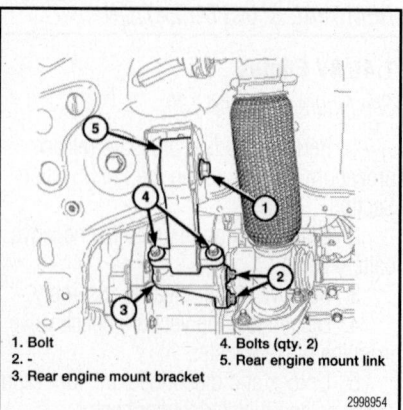

1. Bolt	4. Bolts (qty. 2)
2. -	5. Rear engine mount link
3. Rear engine mount bracket	

Fig. 146 If equipped with an automatic transmission, reposition the rear engine mount link away from the bracket

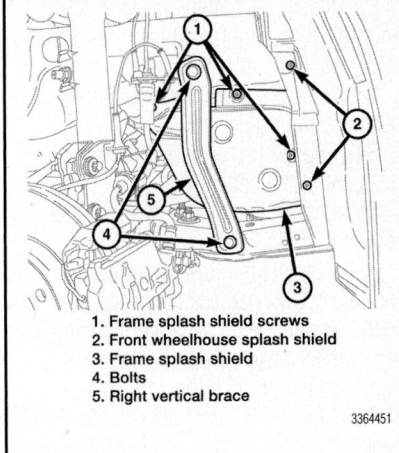

1. Frame splash shield screws
2. Front wheelhouse splash shield
3. Frame splash shield
4. Bolts
5. Right vertical brace

3364451

Fig. 147 Right vertical bracket and splash shields

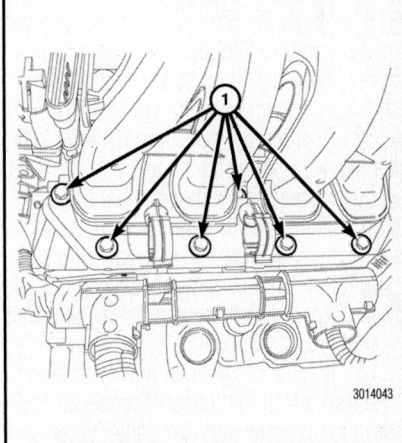

3014043

Fig. 149 Remove six of the seven intake manifold flange bolts (1)

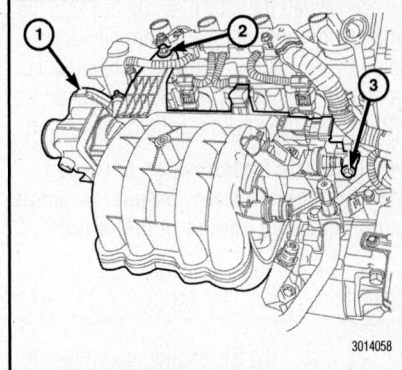

3014058

Fig. 151 Remove the remaining intake manifold flange bolt (3), the intake manifold support bolt (2) and remove the intake manifold (1) from the vehicle through the space normally occupied by the battery

engine mount bracket, loosen the bolt and reposition the rear engine mount link away from the bracket.

31. Remove the engine cooling fan.

32. Remove two bolts and the right vertical brace.

33. Remove two screws from the front wheelhouse splash shield.

34. Remove three screws and the frame splash shield.

35. Remove the accessory drive belt.

36. Remove the A/C compressor.

37. Disconnect the heater core outlet hose and inlet hose from the heater core.

38. Open the two wire harness retainers and reposition the wire harness.

39. Remove six of the seven intake manifold flange bolts.

40. Disconnect the lower coolant hose from the radiator.

41. Reposition the coolant recovery bottle.

42. Support the engine with a floor jack positioned under the oil pan.

43. Remove six bolts and the RH engine mount isolator.

44. Slowly lower the engine so that it rolls forward and down.

45. Remove the remaining intake manifold flange bolt, the intake manifold support bolt and remove the intake manifold from the vehicle through the space normally occupied by the battery.

46. Remove and discard the four intake manifold seals.

47. Cover the open intake ports to prevent debris from entering the engine.

48. If required, remove the following components from the intake manifold:

   a. Throttle body

   b. Fuel rail

   c. Fuel injector(s)

   d. Evaporative emissions purge solenoid

   e. IAT/MAP sensor

To install:

49. If required, install the following components on the intake manifold:

   a. Throttle body

   b. Fuel rail

   c. Fuel injector(s)

   d. Evaporative emissions purge solenoid

   e. IAT/MAP sensor

50. Install four new intake manifold seals.

❉❉❉ WARNING

When servicing components near the vacuum pump, avoid contact with the plastic nipple that connects the vacuum pump to the brake booster hose. It is possible to crack the plastic nipple resulting in a brake booster vacuum leak.

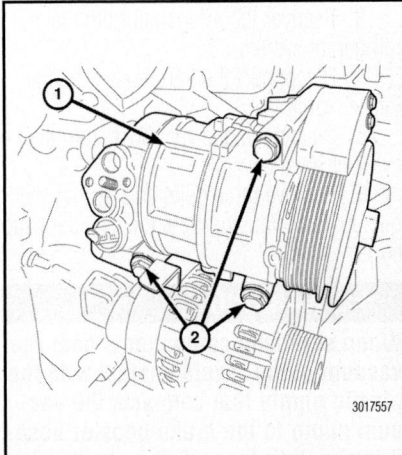

3017557

Fig. 148 Remove the bolts (2), then the A/C compressor (1)

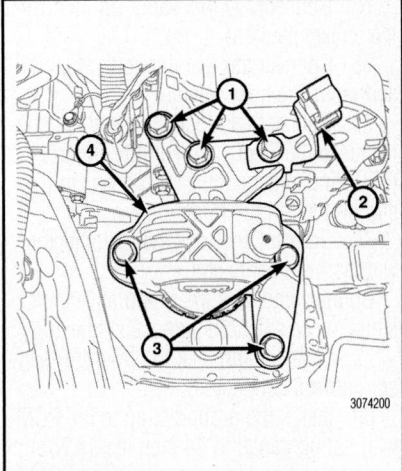

3074200

Fig. 150 Remove six bolts (1 and 3) and the RH engine mount isolator (4)

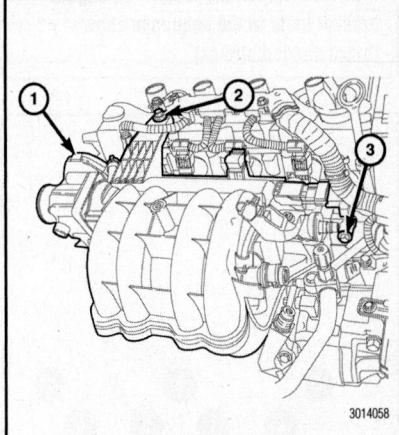

3014058

Fig. 152 Install the intake manifold (1) to the engine through the space normally occupied by the battery. Loosely install an intake manifold flange bolt (3) and the support bolt (2) to hold the intake manifold in position

51. Install the intake manifold (1) to the engine through the space normally occupied by the battery. Loosely install an intake manifold flange bolt (3) and the support bolt (2) to hold the intake manifold in position.

➡ **Automatic transmission equipped engine mount shown, manual transmission equipped engine mount similar.**

52. Slowly raise the engine so that the RH engine mount isolator (3) can be reinstalled.

53. Install the RH engine mount isolator (3) and support bracket (1) to the engine mount bracket with three bolts. Tighten the isolator to engine bracket bolts in the sequence shown to 44 ft. lbs. (60 Nm).

Install the RH engine mount isolator (3) to the body with three bolts (2). Tighten the isolator to body bolts (2) to 44 ft. lbs. (60 Nm).

54. Connect the lower coolant hose to the radiator.

55. Install the pressurized coolant bottle.

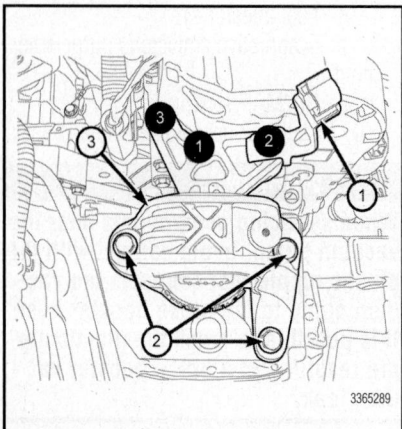

Fig. 153 Tighten the isolator to engine bracket bolts in the sequence shown (black shaded circles)

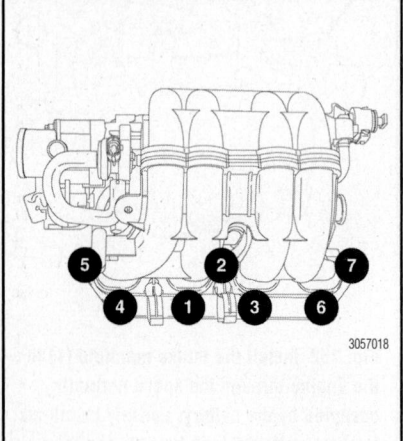

Fig. 154 Intake manifold bolt tightening sequence

56. Raise and support the vehicle.

57. Install the remaining six of the seven intake manifold flange bolts. Tighten all seven intake manifold flange bolts in the sequence shown to 11 ft. lbs. (15 Nm).

58. Position the wire harness and close the two wire harness retainers.

59. If equipped with a manual transmission, install the rear engine mount isolator to the transmission with the rear engine mount bracket bolt and nut tightened to 59 ft. lbs. (80 Nm) and tighten the isolator bolt to 96 ft. lbs. (130 Nm).

60. If equipped with an automatic transmission, install the rear engine mount isolator in the bracket with two bolts tighten to 44 ft. lbs. (60 Nm). Install the isolator bolt and tighten to 96 ft. lbs. (130 Nm).

61. Lower the vehicle.

62. Tighten the previously installed intake manifold support bolt to 90 inch lbs. (8 Nm).

63. Connect the heater core outlet hose and inlet hose to the heater core.

64. Install the A/C compressor.

65. Install the accessory drive belt.

66. Install the frame splash shield with three screws.

67. Install two screws to the front wheelhouse splash shield.

68. Install the right vertical brace with two bolts tightened to 33 ft. lbs. (45 Nm).

69. Install the engine cooling fan.

70. Raise and support the vehicle.

71. Remove four bolts and install the tunnel support brace. Reinstall the bolts and tighten to 60 ft. lbs. (90 Nm).

72. Install the belly pan.

73. Connect the vacuum supply line to the pump.

74. Install the oil separator housing bracket with two bolts and one nut. Tighten the three fasteners to 115 inch lbs. (13 Nm).

75. Connect the fuel vapor purge hose to the intake manifold.

76. Connect the fuel line to the fuel rail and close the hose retainer.

77. Connect and lock the electrical connector to the Electronic Throttle Control (ETC) and engage the ETC harness to the clip on the throttle body.

78. Connect and lock the fuel injector wire harness connector.

Connect and lock the evaporative emissions purge solenoid harness connector.

79. Connect and lock the IAT/MAP sensor harness connector.

80. Install the ground strap to the PCM with nut tightened to 44 inch lbs. (5 Nm).

81. Position the battery tray and PCM in the vehicle. Route the wire harness and close the wire harness retainers.

82. Install the battery tray with one nut and two bolts. Tighten all three fasteners to 18 ft. lbs. (25 Nm).

83. Engage the engine wire harness connector to the battery tray.

84. Engage two engine wire harness retainers to the battery tray.

85. Engage two starter wire harness retainers to the battery tray.

86. Connect the Powertrain Control Module (PCM) harness connectors.

87. Install the oil separator housing to the cylinder head cover with three bolts tightened to 115 inch lbs. (13 Nm).

88. Connect the vent hose to the oil filler neck.

89. Connect the PCV hose to the intake manifold.

90. Install the air cleaner assembly.

91. Fill the cooling system.

✳✳ WARNING

When servicing components near the vacuum pump, avoid contact with the plastic nipple that connects the vacuum pump to the brake booster hose. It is possible to crack the plastic nipple resulting in a brake booster vacuum leak.

92. Install and connect the battery.

93. Evacuate and charge the refrigerant system.

94. Install the engine cover.

95. Run the engine until it reaches normal operating temperature. Check cooling system for correct fluid levels.

1.4L 16V Turbo Engine

See Figures 155 through 161.

1. Perform the fuel pressure release procedure.

2. Remove the engine cover assembly.

3. Recover the refrigerant from the refrigerant system.

4. Disconnect the PCV hose from the intake manifold.

5. Disconnect the vent hose from the cylinder head cover.

6. Remove three bolts and remove the oil separator housing from the cylinder head cover.

✳✳ WARNING

When servicing components near the vacuum pump, avoid contact with the plastic nipple that connects the vacuum pump to the brake booster hose. It is possible to crack the plastic nipple resulting in a brake booster vacuum leak.

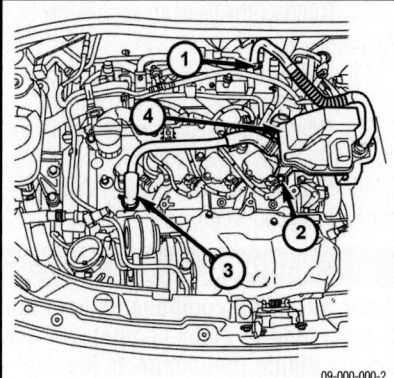

Fig. 155 Disconnect the PCV hose (1) from the intake manifold. Disconnect the vent hose (3) from the cylinder head cover. Remove three bolts (2) and remove the oil separator housing (4) from the cylinder head cover

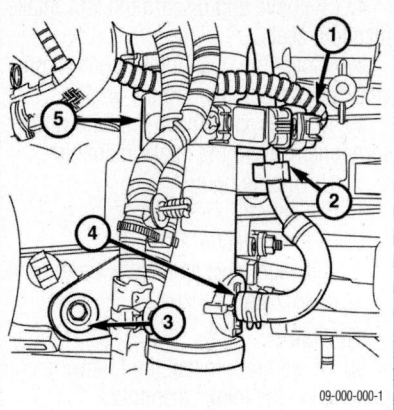

Fig. 157 Disengage the EVAP purge hose (4) from the retaining clip (2) and remove the hose from the charge air cooler outlet hose (5).

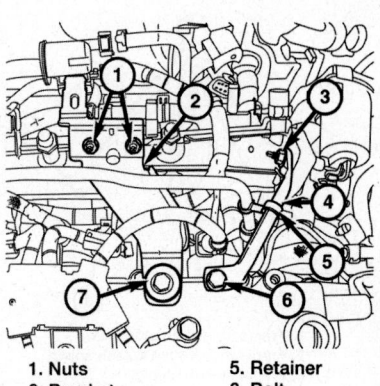

1. Nuts   5. Retainer
2. Bracket   6. Bolt
3. Nut   7. Bolt
4. Support bracket

Fig. 158 Remove two nuts (1), bolt (7), and the bracket (2). Disengage the retainers (5) from the support bracket (4). Remove the nut (3), bolt (6), and the support bracket (4).

7. Disconnect and remove the battery, as outlined in the Engine Electrical section.

8. Unlock and disconnect the Power-train Control Module (PCM) harness connectors.

9. Disengage two engine wire harness retainers from the battery tray.

10. Disengage the engine wire harness connector from the battery tray and reposition the wire harness.

11. Remove the nut and two bolts securing battery tray.

12. Remove the battery tray with the PCM attached.

13. Unlock and disconnect the harness connector from the Electronic Throttle Control (ETC).

14. Disconnect the EVAP purge hose from the retaining clip.

15. Loosen the clamp securing the charge air cooler outlet hose to throttle body.

16. Remove two bolts, nut and reposition the oil separator housing bracket

17. Disengage the EVAP purge hose from the retaining clip and remove the hose from the charge air cooler outlet hose.

18. Disconnect the boost pressure sensor wire harness connector.

19. Remove the bolts from the charge air cooler outlet hose.

20. Disconnect the charge air cooler outlet hose from the charge air outlet manifold and remove the hose from the vehicle.

21. Open hose retainer and disconnect the fuel vapor purge hose.

22. Disconnect the fuel line from the fuel rail.

❋❋ WARNING

When servicing components near the vacuum pump, avoid contact with the plastic nipple that connects the vacuum pump to the brake booster hose. It is possible to crack the plastic nipple resulting in a brake booster vacuum leak.

23. Disconnect the vacuum line from the vacuum pump.

24. Unlock and disconnect the IAT/MAP sensor harness connector.

25. Unlock and disconnect the fuel injector wire harness connector.

26. Disengage and reposition the purge flow control solenoid from the bracket.

27. Remove two nuts, bolt, and the bracket.

28. Disengage the retainers from the support bracket.

29. Remove the nut, bolt, and the support bracket.

30. Raise and support the vehicle.

31. Remove the belly pan.

32. Drain the cooling system.

33. Remove four bolts (1) and the tunnel support brace (2).

34. Remove both front wheels and tires.

35. Remove two bolts and the right vertical brace.

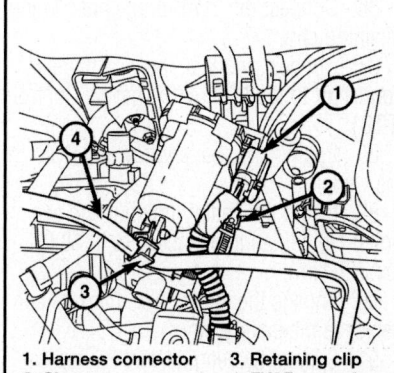

1. Harness connector   3. Retaining clip
2. Clamp   4. EVAP purge hose

Fig. 156 Unlock and disconnect the harness connector (1) from the Electronic Throttle Control (ETC). Disconnect the EVAP purge hose (4) from the retaining clip (3). Loosen the clamp (2) securing the charge air cooler outlet hose to throttle body

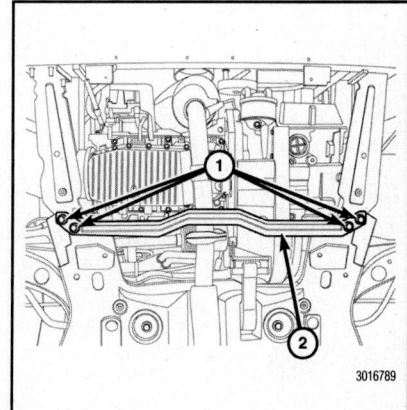

Fig. 159 Remove four bolts (1) and the tunnel support brace (2)

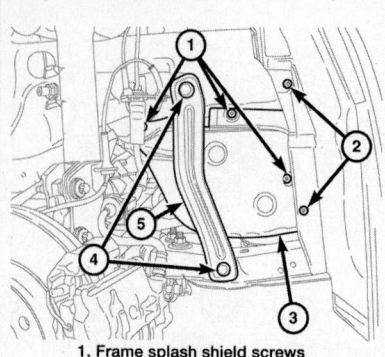

1. Frame splash shield screws
2. Front wheelhouse splash shield
3. Frame splash shield
4. Bolts
5. Right vertical brace

3364451

Fig. 160 Remove two bolts (4) and the right vertical brace (5). Remove two screws (2) from the front wheelhouse splash shield, then remove three screws (1) and the frame splash shield (3)

36. Remove two screws from the front wheelhouse splash shield.

37. Remove three screws and the frame splash shield.

38. Remove the accessory drive belt.

39. Lower the vehicle.

40. Remove the A/C compressor.

41. Disconnect the heater core outlet hose and inlet hose from the heater core.

42. Raise and support the vehicle.

43. Open the two wire harness retainers and reposition the wire harness.

44. Lower the vehicle.

45. Remove the bolt securing the hose retainer to the intake manifold.

46. Remove the seven intake manifold flange bolts and remove the intake manifold from vehicle.

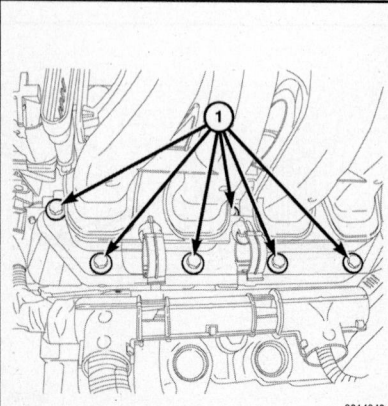

3014043

Fig. 161 Remove the seven intake manifold flange bolts (1) and remove the intake manifold from vehicle

47. Remove and discard the four intake manifold seals.

48. Cover the open intake ports to prevent debris from entering the engine.

49. If required, remove the following components from the intake manifold:
    a. Throttle body
    b. Fuel rail
    c. Fuel injector(s)
    d. Evaporative emissions purge valve
    e. IAT/MAP sensor

To install:

50. If required, install the following components on the intake manifold:
    a. Throttle body
    b. Fuel rail
    c. Fuel injector(s)
    d. Evaporative emissions purge valve
    e. IAT/MAP sensor

51. Install four new intake manifold seals.

52. Install the intake manifold to the engine through the space normally occupied by the battery.

53. Loosely install an intake manifold flange bolt and the support bolt to hold the intake manifold in position.

54. Install the remaining six of the seven intake manifold flange bolts. Tighten all seven intake manifold flange bolts to 11 ft. lbs. (15 Nm).

55. Install the bolt securing the hose retainer to the intake manifold and securely tighten.

56. Raise and support the vehicle.

57. Position the wire harness into the two wire harness retainers and close retainers.

58. Lower the vehicle.

59. Connect the heater core outlet hose and inlet hose to the heater core.

60. Install the A/C compressor.

61. Raise and support the vehicle.

62. Install the accessory drive belt.

63. Install the frame splash shield with three screws.

64. Install two screws to the front wheelhouse splash shield.

65. Install the right vertical brace with two bolts tightened to 33 ft. lbs. (45 Nm).

66. Install both front wheels and tires.

67. Install the tunnel support brace. Tighten bolts to 74 ft. lbs. (100 Nm).

68. Install the belly pan.

69. Lower the vehicle.

70. Install the support bracket, nut, bolt, and tighten to 80 inch lbs. (9 Nm).

71. Engage the retainers to the support bracket.

72. Install the bracket, two nuts, bolt, and tighten to 80 inch lbs. (9 Nm).

73. Connect the vacuum supply line to the pump.

74. Reposition and engage the purge flow control solenoid to the bracket.

75. Connect and lock and the fuel injector wire harness connector.

76. Connect and lock the IAT/MAP sensor harness connector.

❋❋ WARNING

When servicing components near the vacuum pump, avoid contact with the plastic nipple that connects the vacuum pump to the brake booster hose. It is possible to crack the plastic nipple resulting in a brake booster vacuum leak.

77. Connect the vacuum line to the vacuum pump.

78. Connect the fuel vapor purge hose and close the hose retainer.

79. Connect the fuel line to the fuel rail.

80. Install the hose and connect the charge air cooler outlet hose to the charge air outlet manifold.

81. Install the bolts to the charge air cooler outlet hose and securely tighten.

82. Connect the boost pressure sensor wire harness connector.

83. Install the hose to the charge air cooler outlet hose and engage the EVAP purge hose to the retaining clip.

84. Install the oil separator housing bracket with two bolts and one nu. Tighten the three fasteners to 115 inch lbs. (13 Nm).

85. Tighten the clamp securing the charge air cooler outlet hose to throttle body.

86. Connect the EVAP purge hose to the retaining clip.

87. Connect and lock the wire harness connector to the Electronic Throttle Control (ETC).

88. Position the battery tray and PCM in the vehicle.

89. Install the battery tray nut and two bolts. Tighten all three fasteners to 18 ft. lbs. (25 Nm).

90. Engage the engine wire harness connector to the battery tray.

91. Engage two engine wire harness retainers to the battery tray.

92. Connect the Powertrain Control Module (PCM) harness connectors.

93. Install the oil separator housing to the cylinder head cover with three bolts tightened to 115 inch lbs. (13 Nm).

94. Connect the vent hose to the cylinder head cover.

95. Connect the PCV hose to the intake manifold.

96. Install the engine cover assembly.

97. Evacuate and charge the refrigerant system.

98. Fill the cooling system.

99. Install and connect the battery.

100. Run the engine until it reaches normal operating temperature. Check cooling system for correct fluid level.

OIL PAN

REMOVAL & INSTALLATION

1.4L 16V MultiAir Engine

With Manual Transmission

See Figures 162 through 167.

1. Disconnect and isolate the negative battery cable.

2. Raise and support the vehicle.

3. Remove the belly pan.

4. Drain the engine oil.

5. Remove the viscosity sensor.

6. Remove the maniverter. Refer to Exhaust Manifold in this section.

7. Raise and support the vehicle.

8. Remove the rear engine mount bracket bolt and nut.

9. Remove two bolts and remove the rear engine mount bracket.

10. Remove two bolts and the blocker plate from the oil pan.

11. Remove the two bolts from the flywheel dust cover.

➡**The flywheel dust cover is bolted to the oil pan and cannot be removed at this time.**

12. Remove the two lower transmission bell housing bolts (3).

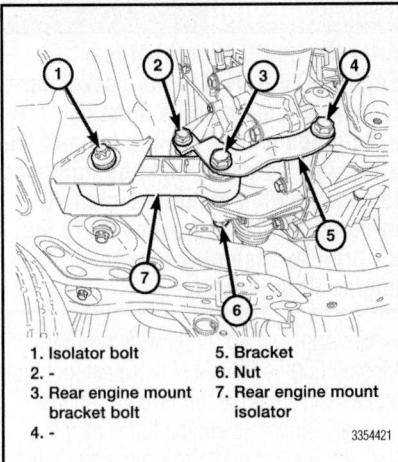

1. Isolator bolt
2. -
3. Rear engine mount bracket bolt
4. -
5. Bracket
6. Nut
7. Rear engine mount isolator

3354421

Fig. 162 Remove the rear engine mount bracket bolt (3) and nut (6). Remove two bolts (2 and 4) and remove the rear engine mount bracket (5)

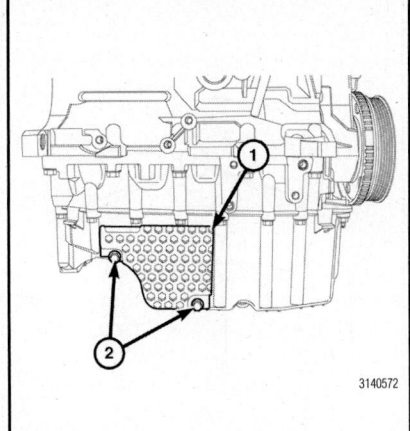

3140572

Fig. 163 Remove two bolts (2) and the blocker plate (1) from the oil pan

13. Remove fourteen bolts, two nuts and two studs from the flange of the oil pan. Using the four indicated pry points, carefully remove the oil pan and flywheel dust cover.

14. Remove the bolt and the flywheel dust cover from the oil pan.

15. Remove all residual sealant from the oil pan, engine block, oil pump and rear seal retainer

To install:

16. Clean the oil pan, engine block, oil pump and rear seal retainer mating surfaces with isopropyl alcohol in preparation for sealant application.

※※ **WARNING**

Engine assembly requires the use of a unique sealant that is compatible with engine oil. Using a sealant other than Mopar® Engine RTV GEN II may result in engine fluid leakage.

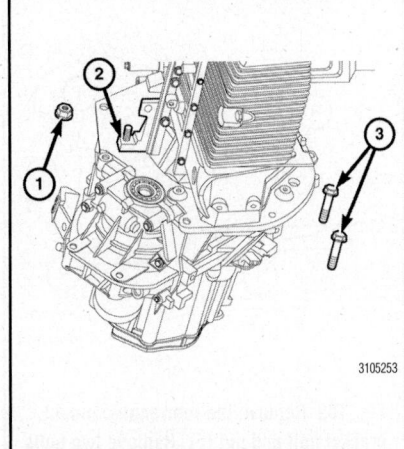

3105253

Fig. 164 Remove the two lower transmission bell housing bolts (3)

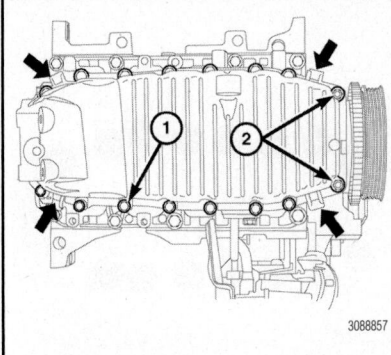

3088857

Fig. 165 Remove fourteen bolts (1), two nuts and two studs (2) from the flange of the oil pan. Using the four indicated pry points (arrows), carefully remove the oil pan and flywheel dust cover.

※※ **WARNING**

After the application of Mopar® Engine RTV GEN II to the gasket surfaces, the components must be assembled within 10 minutes and the attaching fasteners must be tightened to specification within the next 10 minutes. Prolonged exposure to the air prior to assembly may result in engine fluid leakage.

17. Apply a 2 to 3 mm wide bead of Mopar® Engine RTV GEN II sealant to the oil pan as shown in the following locations:

a. Oil pan to engine block flange

b. Two oil pump to engine block T-joints

c. Two rear seal retainer to engine block T-joints

18. Install the flywheel dust cover to the oil pan. Tighten the bolt to 80 inch lbs. (9 Nm).

19. Install the oil pan with fourteen bolts, two studs and two nuts hand tight.

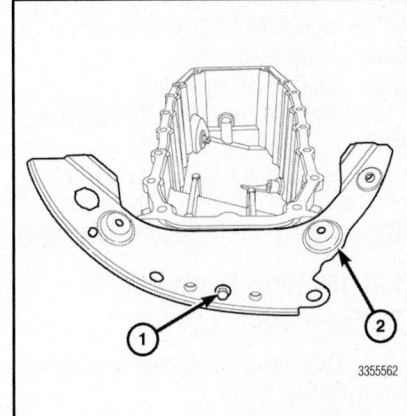

3355562

Fig. 166 Remove the bolt (1) and the flywheel dust cover (2) from the oil pan

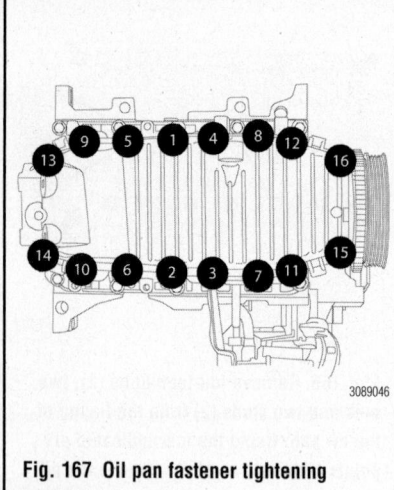

Fig. 167 Oil pan fastener tightening sequence

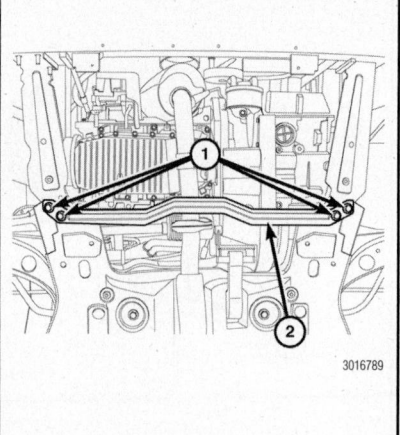

Fig. 168 Remove the four bolts (1) and the tunnel support brace (2)

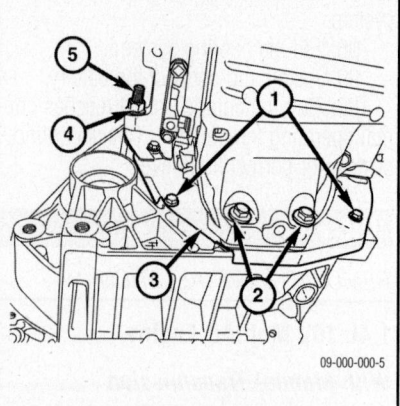

Fig. 170 Remove three bolts (1) from the flywheel dust cover. Remove the two lower transmission bell housing bolts (2)

20. Install the two lower transmission bell housing bolts and tighten to 30 ft. lbs. (40 Nm).

21. Tighten the sixteen oil pan fasteners in two steps following the sequence shown:
   a. Step 1: All to 35 inch lbs. (4 Nm).
   b. Step 2: All to 80 inch lbs. (9 Nm).

22. Install the two bolts to the flywheel dust cover and tighten to 80 inch lbs. (9 Nm).

23. Install the blocker plate with two bolts tightened to 80 inch lbs. (9 Nm).

24. Install the rear engine mount bracket with bolt and nut and bolt. Tighten the fasteners to 59 ft. lbs. (80 Nm).

25. Install the rear engine mount isolator to the transmission with the rear engine mount bracket bolt and nut tightened to 59 ft. lbs. (80 Nm).

26. Tighten the isolator bolt to 96 ft. lbs. (130 Nm).

27. Install the maniverter, cooling module and front fascia.

28. Install the viscosity sensor.

29. Install the belly pan.

30. If removed, install the oil filter and fill the engine crankcase with the proper oil to the correct level.

31. Fill the cooling system.

32. Evacuate and charge the refrigerant system.

33. Start and run the engine until it reaches normal operating temperature. Check cooling system for correct fluid level.

1.4L 16V Turbo Engine

See Figures 168 through 172.

1. Disconnect and isolate the negative battery cable.

2. Raise and support the vehicle.

3. Remove the belly pan.

4. Remove the four bolts and the tunnel support brace.

5. Drain the engine oil.

6. Remove the front exhaust pipe support bolt.

7. Remove the exhaust flange nuts.

8. Remove the nuts that secure the front exhaust pipe to the catalytic converter.

9. Remove the front exhaust pipe and gasket.

10. Remove the rear engine mount bracket bolt and nut.

11. Remove two bolts and remove the rear engine mount bracket.

12. Remove three bolts (1) from the flywheel dust cover.

13. Remove the two lower transmission bell housing bolts (2).

➡ **The flywheel dust cover is bolted to the oil pan and cannot be removed at this time.**

14. Remove fourteen bolts, two nuts and two studs from the flange of the oil pan.

15. Using the four indicated pry points,

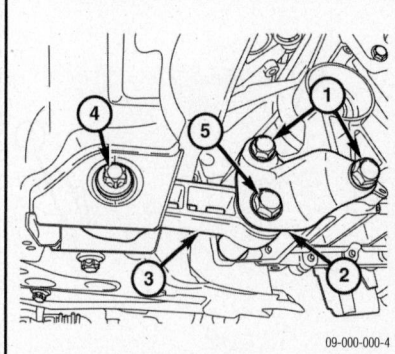

Fig. 169 Remove the rear engine mount bracket bolt and nut (5). Remove two bolts (1) and remove the rear engine mount bracket (2)

carefully remove the oil pan and flywheel dust cover.

16. Remove the bolt and the flywheel dust cover from the oil pan.

17. Remove all residual sealant from the oil pan, engine block, oil pump and rear seal retainer.

To install:

18. Clean the oil pan, engine block, oil pump and rear seal retainer mating surfaces with isopropyl alcohol in preparation for sealant application.

✳✳ WARNING

Engine assembly requires the use of a unique sealant that is compatible with engine oil. Using a sealant other than Mopar® Engine RTV GEN II may result in engine fluid leakage.

✳✳ WARNING

After the application of Mopar® Engine RTV GEN II to the gasket surfaces, the components must be assembled within 10 minutes and the attaching fasteners must be tightened to specification within the next 10 minutes. Prolonged exposure to the air prior to assembly may result in engine fluid leakage.

19. Apply a 2 to 3 mm wide bead of Mopar® Engine RTV GEN II sealant to the oil pan as shown in the following locations:
   a. Oil pan to engine block flange
   b. Two oil pump to engine block T-joints
   c. Two rear seal retainer to engine block T-joints

20. Install the flywheel dust cover to the oil pan. Tighten the bolt to 80 inch lbs. (9 Nm).

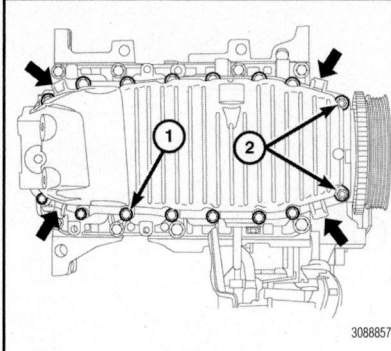

Fig. 171 Remove fourteen bolts (1), two nuts and two studs (2) from the flange of the oil pan. Using the four indicated pry points (arrows, carefully remove the oil pan and flywheel dust cover

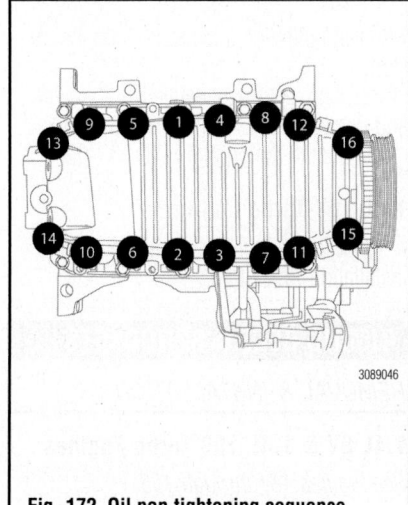

Fig. 172 Oil pan tightening sequence

21. Install the oil pan with fourteen bolts, two studs and two nuts hand tight.

22. Install the two lower transmission bell housing bolts and tighten to 30 ft. lbs. (40 Nm).

23. Install the three bolts to the flywheel dust cover and tighten to 80 inch lbs. (9 Nm).

24. Tighten the sixteen oil pan fasteners in two steps following the sequence shown:
    a. Step 1: All to 35 inch lbs. (4 Nm).
    b. Step 2: All to 80 inch lbs. (9 Nm).

25. Install the rear engine mount bracket with two bolts tightened to 59 ft. lbs. (80 Nm).

26. Install the rear engine mount isolator to the transmission with the rear engine mount bracket bolt and nut tightened to 59 ft. lbs. (80 Nm).

27. Tighten the isolator bolt to 96 ft. lbs. (130 Nm).

28. Install a new catalytic converter to front exhaust pipe gasket.

29. Install the front exhaust pipe to the catalytic converter with two nuts tightened to 41 ft. lbs. (56 Nm).

30. Install the front exhaust pipe support bolt and tighten to 41 ft. lbs. (56 Nm).

31. Install the exhaust flange nuts and tighten to 51 ft. lbs. (69 Nm).

32. Install the tunnel support brace with four bolts tightened to 60 ft. lbs. (90 Nm).

33. Install the belly pan.

34. If removed, install the oil filter and fill the engine crankcase with the proper oil to the correct level.

35. Connect the negative battery cable and tighten nut to 45 inch lbs. (5 Nm).

36. Start and run the engine until it reaches normal operating temperature.

OIL PUMP

REMOVAL & INSTALLATION

1.4L 16V MultiAir & 1.4L Turbo Engines

See Figures 173 and 174.

1. Disconnect and isolate the negative battery cable.

2. Remove the oil pan, as outlined in this section.

3. Remove the bolts (2) from the oil pick-up tube and remove the oil pick-up tube from the oil pump.

4. Remove and discard the O-ring seal from the oil pump.

To install:

5. Lightly lubricate the new O-ring seal with clean engine oil and install on the oil pump.

6. Install the oil pick-up tube with two bolts. Tighten the bolts to 89 inch lbs. (10 Nm).

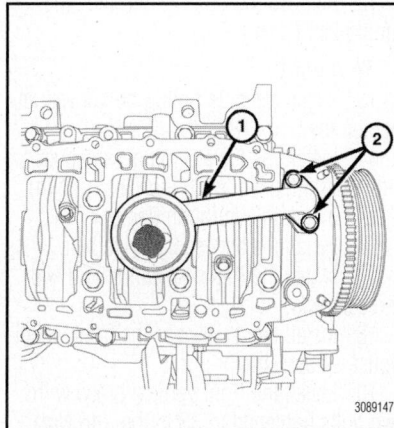

Fig. 173 Remove the bolts (2) from the oil pick-up tube and remove the oil pick-up tube (1) from the oil pump

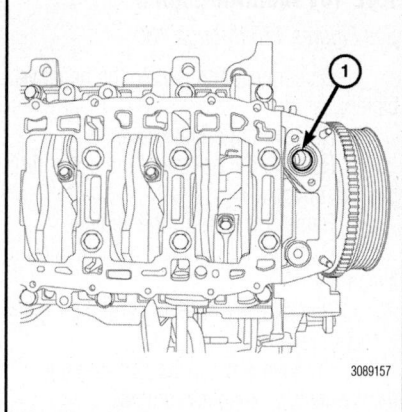

Fig. 174 Remove and discard the O-ring seal (1) from the oil pump

7. Install the oil pan, as outlined in this section.

8. If removed, install the oil filter and fill the engine crankcase with the proper oil to the correct level.

9. Connect the negative battery cable and tighten nut to 45 inch lbs. (5 Nm).

10. Run the engine until it reaches normal operating temperature.

PISTON AND RING

POSITIONING
See Figure 175.

TIMING BELT FRONT COVER

REMOVAL & INSTALLATION

1.4L 8V Engine

Refer to the Timing Belt Removal & Installation Procedure.

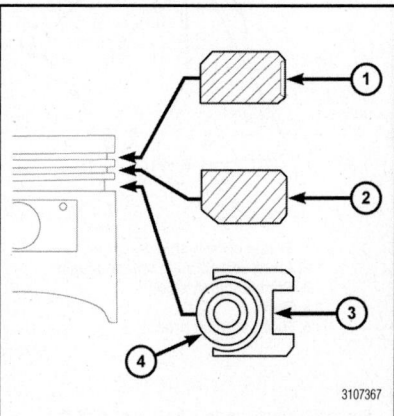

Fig. 175 No. 1 (upper) piston ring (1), No. 2 (intermediate) piston ring (2), Oil control ring (3), & Oil control ring expander (4)

1.4L 16V MultiAir Engine

See Figures 176 through 180.

1. Disconnect and isolate the negative battery cable.

2. Remove the engine cover.

3. Remove the bolts and the upper timing belt cover.

4. Raise and support the vehicle.

5. Remove the right front wheel and tire assembly.

6. Remove two bolts (4) and the right vertical brace (5).

7. Remove two screws (2) from the front wheelhouse splash shield.

8. Remove three screws (1) and the frame splash shield (3).

9. Remove the accessory drive belt, as outlined in this section.

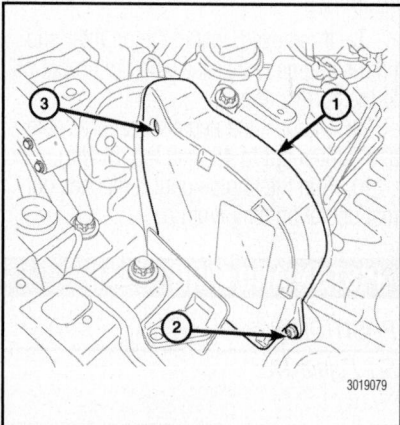

Fig. 176 Remove the bolts (2 and 3) and the upper timing belt cover (1)

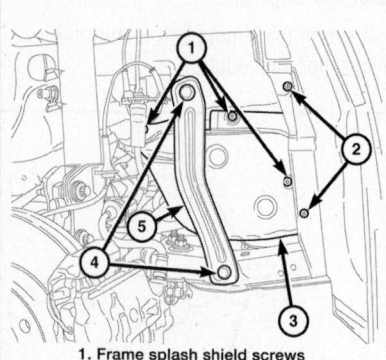

1. Frame splash shield screws
2. Front wheelhouse splash shield
3. Frame splash shield
4. Bolts
5. Right vertical brace

Fig. 177 Remove two bolts (4) and the right vertical brace (5). Remove two screws (2) from the front wheelhouse splash shield, then remove three screws (1) and the frame splash shield (3)

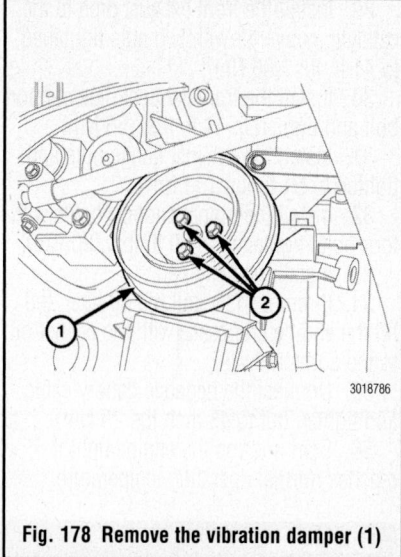

Fig. 178 Remove the vibration damper (1)

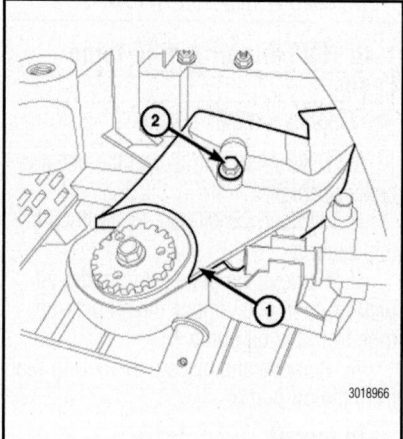

Fig. 179 Remove the bolt (2) and the lower timing belt cover (1)

10. Remove the vibration damper.

11. Remove the bolt and the lower timing belt cover.

12. Remove the bolt (2) and the side timing belt cover (1).

To install:

13. Install the side timing belt cover, and tighten the bolts 18 ft. lbs. (25 Nm).

14. Install the lower timing belt cover with bolt tightened to 80 inch lbs. (9 Nm).

15. Install the vibration damper.

16. Install the accessory drive belt.

17. Install the frame splash shield with three screws.

18. Install two screws to the front wheelhouse splash shield.

19. Install the right vertical brace with two bolts tightened to 33 ft. lbs. (45 Nm).

20. Install the right front wheel and tire assembly.

21. Lower the vehicle.

22. Install the upper timing belt cover

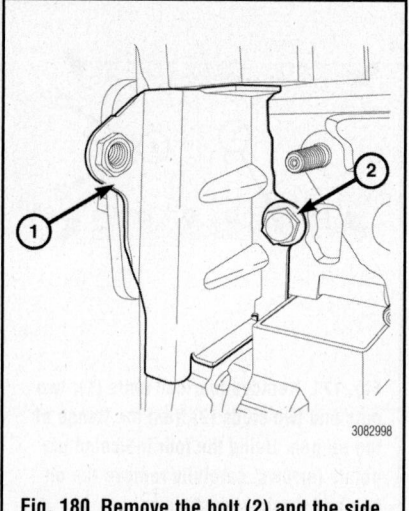

Fig. 180 Remove the bolt (2) and the side timing belt cover (1)

with two bolts tightened to 80 inch lbs. (9 Nm).

23. Connect the negative battery cable and tighten nut to 45 inch lbs. (5 Nm).

24. Install the engine cover.

1.4L 16V Turbo Engine

Refer to the Timing Belt Removal & Installation Procedure.

TIMING BELT & SPROCKETS

REMOVAL & INSTALLATION

1.4L 8V & 1.4L 16V Turbo Engines

See Figures 181 through 196.

1. Disconnect and isolate the negative battery cable.

2. Remove the air cleaner assembly.

3. Disconnect the PCV hose from the intake manifold.

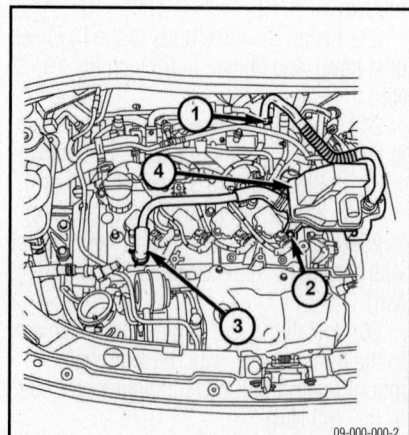

Fig. 181 View of the PCV hose (1), bolts (2), vent hose (3) and oil separator housing (4)

4. Disconnect the vent hose from the cylinder head cover.

5. Remove three bolts and remove the oil separator housing from the cylinder head cover.

When servicing components near the vacuum pump, avoid contact with the plastic nipple that connects the vacuum pump to the brake booster hose. It is possible to crack the plastic nipple resulting in a brake booster vacuum leak.

6. Remove the vacuum pump.

7. Install the Camshaft Timing Locking Tool 10277 to the rear of the camshaft.

Rotate the crankshaft vibration damper clockwise to align the tool with the vacuum pump mounting. Install three bolts and tighten to 15 ft. lbs. (20 Nm).

8. Raise and support the vehicle.

9. Remove the belly pan.

10. Drain the cooling system.

11. Remove four bolts and the tunnel support brace.

12. Remove the rear engine mount bracket bolt and nut, loosen the isolator bolt and reposition the rear engine mount isolator away from the bracket.

13. Remove the vibration damper, as outlined in this section.

14. Lower the vehicle.

15. Disconnect the coolant hose from the pressurized coolant bottle.

16. Remove the two bolts and reposition the pressurized coolant bottle.

17. Support the engine with a floor jack positioned under the oil pan.

18. Remove six bolts and the right engine mount isolator.

19. On Turbo engines, remove the bolt (5) and reposition the turbocharger wastegate solenoid (4).

20. Disengage the following retainers from the upper timing belt cover:

   a. Evaporative emissions purge hose.

   b. After run coolant pump return hose.

   c. Wastegate solenoid pressure inlet hose.

21. Remove the bolts and the upper timing belt cover.

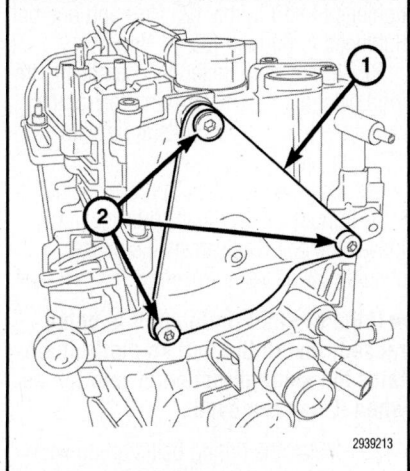

Fig. 182 Install the Camshaft Timing Locking Tool 10277 (1) to the rear of the camshaft. Rotate the crankshaft vibration damper clockwise to align the tool with the vacuum pump mounting. Install three bolts (2) and tighten 15 ft. lbs.

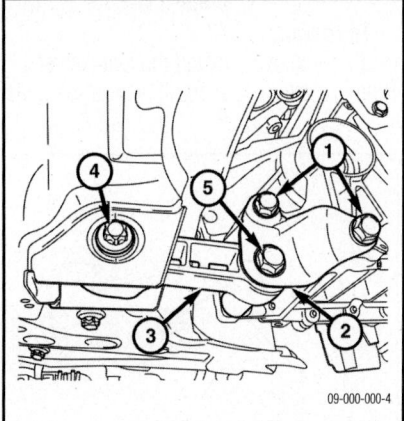

Fig. 184 Remove the rear engine mount bracket bolt and nut (5), loosen the isolator bolt (4) and reposition the rear engine mount isolator (3) away from the bracket (2)

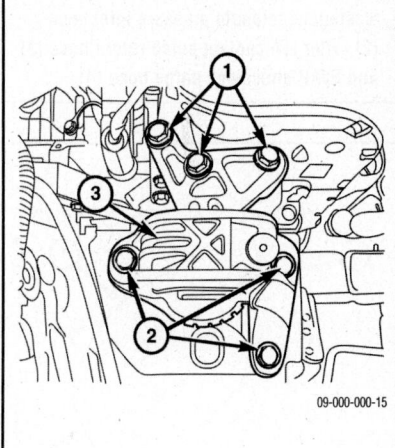

Fig. 186 With a floor jack positioned under the oil pan to support the oil pan, remove six bolts (1 and 2) and the right engine mount isolator (3)

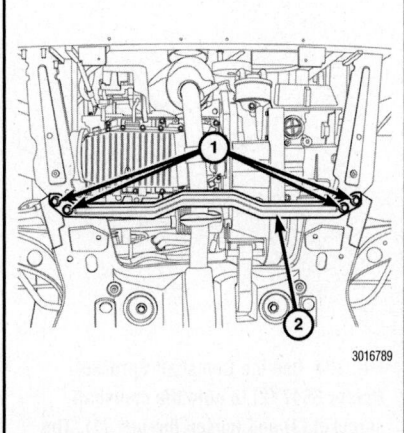

Fig. 183 Remove four bolts (1) and the tunnel support brace (2)

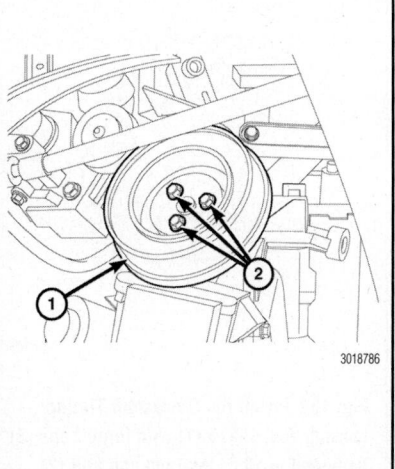

Fig. 185 Remove the vibration damper (1)

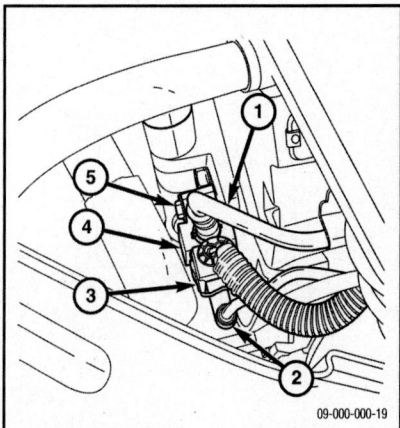

Fig. 187 On Turbo engines, remove the bolt (5) and reposition the turbocharger wastegate solenoid (4)

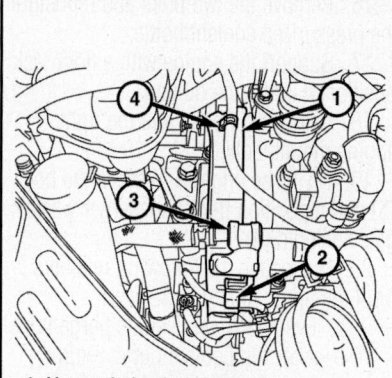

1. Upper timing belt cover
2. Wastegate solenoid pressure inlet hose
3. After-run coolant pump return hose
4. EVAP emissions purge hose

09-000-000-33

Fig. 188 Upper timing belt cover (1), wastegate solenoid pressure inlet hose (2), after run coolant pump return hose (3) and EVAP emissions purge hose (4)

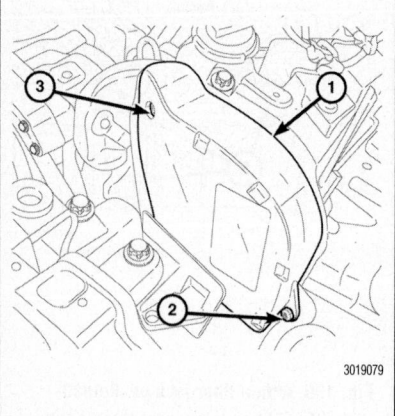

3019079

Fig. 189 Remove the bolts (2 and 3) and the upper timing belt cover (1)

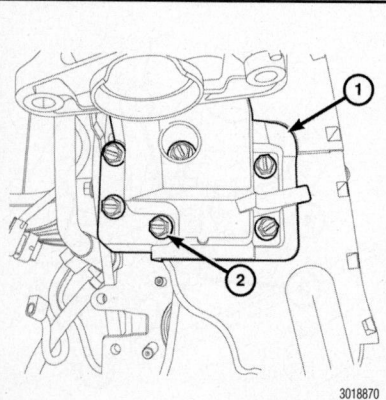

3018870

Fig. 190 Carefully raise the front of the engine and remove the six bolts (2) and the right engine mount bracket (1)

22. Carefully raise the front of the engine and remove the six bolts and the right engine mount bracket.

23. Remove the bolt and the lower timing belt cover.

24. Install the Crankshaft Timing Locking Tool 10276 with three bolts tightened to 18 ft. lbs. (25 Nm) and one bolt tightened to 80 inch lbs. (9 Nm).

➡️ **If the bolt (2) does not align with the lower timing belt cover mounting boss, the camshaft timing is not correct.**

➡️ **If the timing belt is to be reused, mark the direction of rotation using a paint pen or equivalent to aid in reassembly.**

25. Loosen the tensioner lock nut (3) and remove the timing belt (1).

To install:

26. If removed, install the Crankshaft Timing Locking Tool 10276 with three bolts

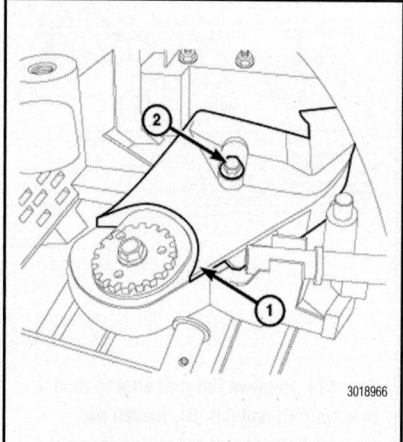

3018966

Fig. 191 Remove the bolt (2) and the lower timing belt cover (1)

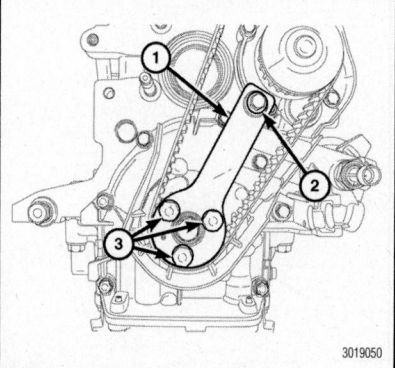

3019050

Fig. 192 Install the Crankshaft Timing Locking Tool 10276 (1) with three bolts (3) tightened to 18 ft. lbs. and one bolt (2) tightened to 80 inch lbs.

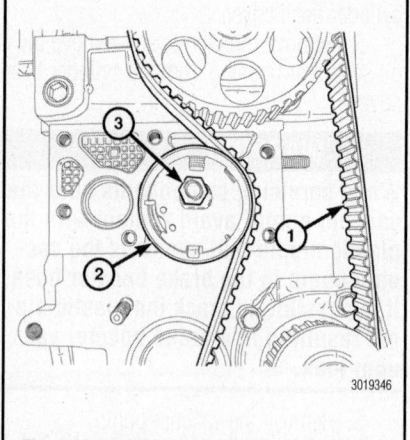

3019346

Fig. 193 Loosen the tensioner lock nut (3) and remove the timing belt (1)

tightened to 18 ft. lbs. (25 Nm) and one bolt tightened to 80 inch lbs. (9 Nm).

27. If removed, install the Camshaft Timing Locking Tool 10277 to the rear of the camshaft. Install three bolts and tighten to 15 ft. lbs. (20 Nm).

28. Use the Camshaft Sprocket Holder 6847 to hold the camshaft sprocket and loosen the bolt. The camshaft sprocket should now be free to rotate on the camshaft.

➡️ **If the original timing belt is being reused, install the belt so that it maintains the same direction of rotation as when it was removed.**

29. Install the timing belt starting with the crankshaft sprocket, then the water pump sprocket, finishing with the camshaft sprocket.

30. Rotate and adjust the timing tensioner so that the silver tab is centered in the middle of the window. Tighten the lock nut to 21 ft. lbs. (28 Nm).

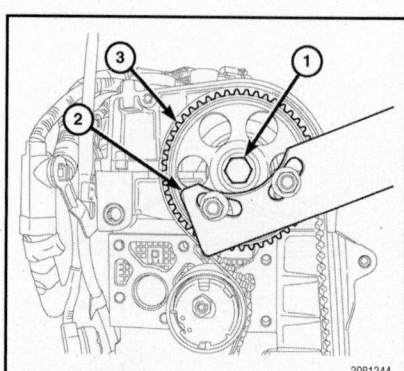

3081344

Fig. 194 Use the Camshaft Sprocket Holder 6847 (2) to hold the camshaft sprocket (3) and loosen the bolt (1). The camshaft sprocket (3) should now be free to rotate on the camshaft

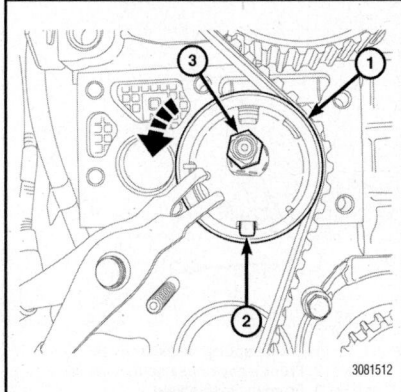

Fig. 195 Rotate and adjust the timing tensioner (1) so that the silver tab (2) is centered in the middle of the window. Tighten the lock nut (3) to 21 ft. lbs. (28 Nm)

31. Use the Camshaft Sprocket Holder 6847 to hold the camshaft sprocket and tighten the camshaft sprocket bolt to 88 ft. lbs. (120 Nm).

32. Remove the Camshaft Timing Locking Tool 10277 and the Crankshaft Timing Locking Tool 10276.

Rotate the crankshaft clockwise at least two complete revolutions to center the timing belt on the sprockets.

33. Verify that the silver tab is still centered in the middle of the window. If required, loosen the tensioner lock nut, readjust the timing belt tensioner and tighten the lock nut to 21 ft. lbs. (28 Nm).

➡ **Reinstall the timing locking tools to verify correct camshaft timing.**

34. Install the Camshaft Timing Locking Tool 10277 to the rear of the camshaft. Install three bolts and tighten to 15 ft. lbs. (20 Nm).

35. Install the Crankshaft Timing Locking Tool 10276 with three bolts tightened to 18 ft. lbs. (25 Nm) and one bolt tightened to 80 inch lbs. (9 Nm).

➡**If the bolt does not align with the lower timing belt cover mounting boss, the camshaft timing is not correct. Loosen the tensioner lock nut and the camshaft sprocket bolt and repeat this procedure.**

36. Remove the Camshaft Timing Locking Tool 10277 and the Crankshaft Timing Locking Tool 10276.

37. Install the lower timing belt cover with bolt tightened to 80 inch lbs. (9 Nm).

38. Install the right engine mount bracket with six bolts tightened to 18 ft. lbs. (25 Nm).

39. Install the upper timing belt cover

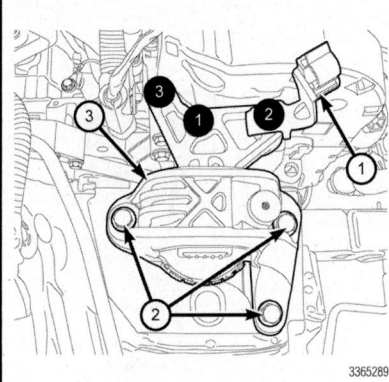

Fig. 196 View of the right engine mounting insulator (3) bolt tightening sequence (black shaded circles)

with two bolts tightened to 80 inch lbs. (9 Nm).

40. Engage the following retainers to the upper timing belt cover:

　a. Wastegate solenoid pressure inlet hose

　b. After run coolant pump return hose

　c. Evaporative emissions purge hose

41. Position the turbocharger wastegate solenoid. Install the bolt and tighten to 80 inch lbs. (9 Nm).

42. Install the right engine mount isolator to the engine mount bracket with three bolts. Tighten the isolator to engine bracket bolts in the sequence shown to 44 ft. lbs. (60 Nm).

43. Install the right engine mount isolator to the body with three bolts. Tighten the isolator to body bolts to 44 ft. lbs. (60 Nm).

44. Remove the floor jack supporting the engine.

45. Install the pressurized coolant bottle. Tighten bolts to 71 inch lbs. (8 Nm).

46. Connect the coolant hose to the pressurized coolant bottle.

47. Raise and support the vehicle.

48. Install the vibration damper.

49. Raise and support the vehicle.

50. Position the rear engine mount isolator to bracket. Install the rear engine mount bracket bolt and nut and tighten to 59 ft. lbs. (80 Nm). Tighten the isolator bolt to 96 ft. lbs. (130 Nm).

51. Install the tunnel support brace with four bolts tightened to 74 ft. lbs. (100 Nm).

52. Install the belly pan.

53. Lower the vehicle.

✳✳ **WARNING**

When servicing components near the vacuum pump, avoid contact with the plastic nipple that connects the vac-

uum pump to the brake booster hose. It is possible to crack the plastic nipple resulting in a brake booster vacuum leak.

54. Install the vacuum pump.

55. Install the oil separator housing to the cylinder head cover with three bolts tightened to 115 inch lbs. (13 Nm).

56. Connect the vent hose to the cylinder head cover.

57. Connect the PCV hose to the intake manifold.

58. Install the air cleaner assembly.

59. Fill cooling system.

60. Connect the battery negative cable and tighten nut to 45 inch lbs. (5 Nm).

61. Start and run the engine until it reaches normal operating temperature. Check cooling system for correct fluid level.

➡**The Cam/Crank Variation Relearn procedure must be performed using the scan tool anytime there has been a repair/replacement made to a powertrain system, for example: flywheel, valvetrain, camshaft and/or crankshaft sensors or components**

1.4L 16V MultiAir Engine

See Figures 197 through 215.

1. Perform the fuel pressure release procedure, as outlined in the Fuel System Section.

2. Disconnect and isolate the negative battery cable.

3. Remove the engine cover.

4. Remove the air cleaner assembly.

5. Disconnect the PCV hose from the intake manifold.

6. Disconnect the vent hose from the oil filler neck.

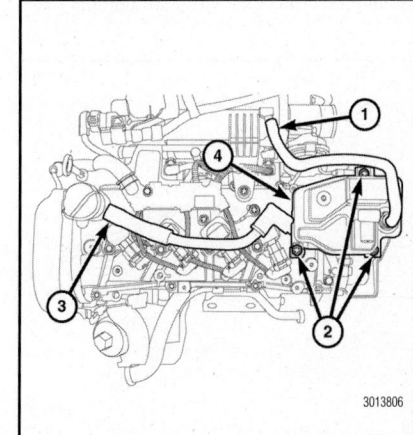

Fig. 197 PCV hose (1), bolts (2), vent hose (3) and oil separator housing (4)

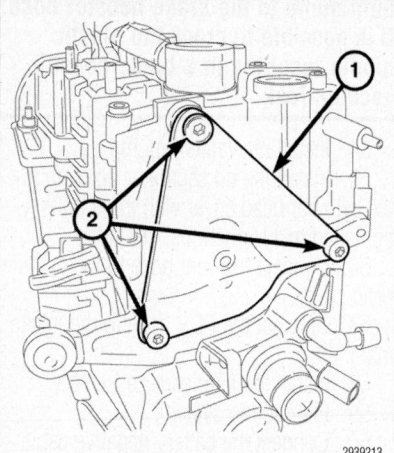

Fig. 198 Install the Camshaft Timing Locking Tool 10277 (1) to the rear of the camshaft. Rotate the crankshaft vibration damper clockwise to align the tool with the vacuum pump mounting. Install three bolts (2) and tighten 15 ft. lbs.

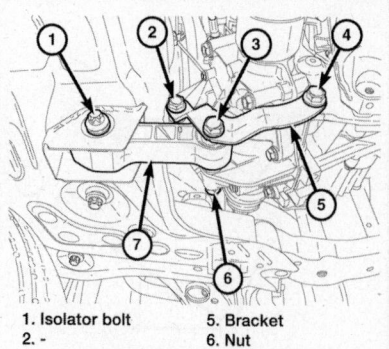

1. Isolator bolt
2. -
3. Rear engine mount bracket bolt
4. -
5. Bracket
6. Nut
7. Rear engine mount isolator

Fig. 200 If equipped with a manual transmission, remove the rear engine mount bracket bolt (3) and nut (6), loosen the isolator bolt (1) and reposition the rear engine mount isolator (7) away from the bracket (5)

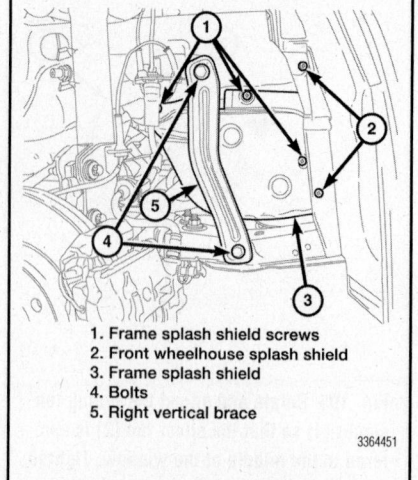

1. Frame splash shield screws
2. Front wheelhouse splash shield
3. Frame splash shield
4. Bolts
5. Right vertical brace

Fig. 202 Remove two bolts (4) and the right vertical brace (5). Remove two screws (2) from the front wheelhouse splash shield, then remove three screws (1) and the frame splash shield (3)

7. Remove three bolts and remove the oil separator housing from the cylinder head cover.

8. Disconnect the fuel vapor hose from the intake manifold.

9. Open the hose retainer and disconnect the fuel line from the fuel rail.

✳✳ WARNING

When servicing components near the vacuum pump, avoid contact with the plastic nipple that connects the vacuum pump to the brake booster hose. It is possible to crack the plastic nipple resulting in a brake booster vacuum leak.

10. Remove the vacuum pump.

11. Install the Camshaft Timing Locking Tool 10277 to the rear of the camshaft. Rotate the crankshaft vibration damper

clockwise to align the tool with the vacuum pump mounting. Install three bolts and tighten to 15 ft. lbs. (20 Nm).

12. Raise and support the vehicle.

13. Remove the belly pan.

14. Remove four bolts and the tunnel support brace.

15. If equipped with a manual transmission, remove the rear engine mount bracket bolt and nut, loosen the isolator bolt and reposition the rear engine mount isolator away from the bracket.

16. If equipped with an automatic transmission, remove two bolts (4) from the rear engine mount bracket (3), loosen the bolt (1) and reposition the rear engine mount link (5) away from the bracket (3).

17. Remove the right front wheel and tire assembly.

18. Remove two bolts and the right vertical brace.

19. Remove two screws from the front wheelhouse splash shield.

20. Remove three screws and the frame splash shield

21. Remove the accessory drive belt.

22. Remove the vibration damper, as outlined in this section.

23. Lower the vehicle.

24. Reposition the coolant recovery bottle.

25. Support the engine with a floor jack positioned under the oil pan.

26. Remove six bolts and the RH engine mount isolator.

27. Remove the bolts and the upper timing belt cover.

28. Carefully raise the front of the engine and remove the six bolts and the right engine mount bracket.

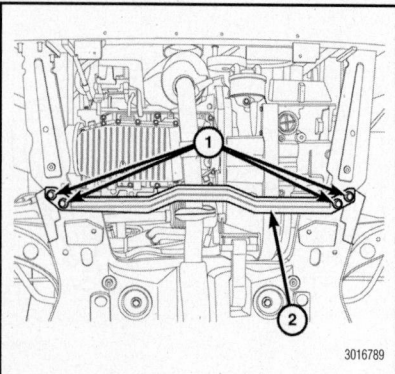

Fig. 199 Remove four bolts (1) and the tunnel support brace (2)

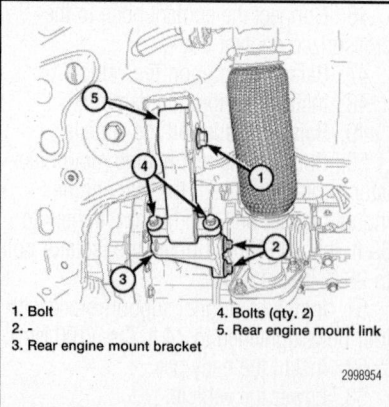

1. Bolt
2. -
3. Rear engine mount bracket
4. Bolts (qty. 2)
5. Rear engine mount link

Fig. 201 If equipped with an automatic transmission, remove two bolts (4) from the rear engine mount bracket (3), loosen the bolt (1) and reposition the rear engine mount link (5) away from the bracket (3)

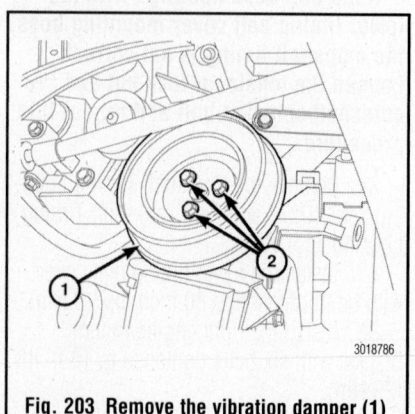

Fig. 203 Remove the vibration damper (1)

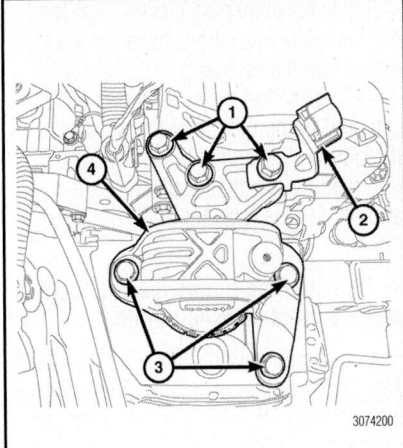

Fig. 204 With a floor jack positioned under the oil pan to support the engine, remove six bolts (1 and 3) and the right engine mount isolator (4)

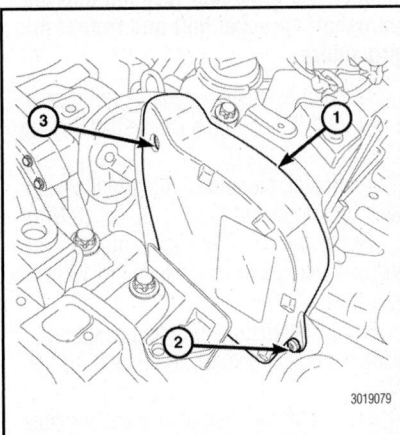

Fig. 205 Remove the bolts (2 and 3) and the upper timing belt cover (1)

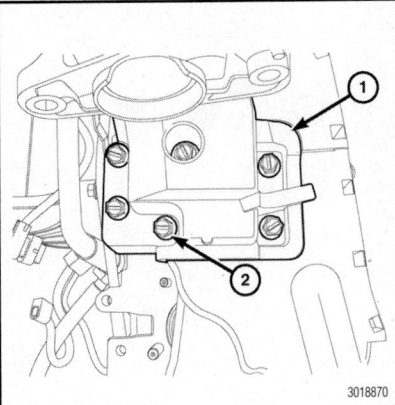

Fig. 206 Carefully raise the front of the engine and remove the six bolts (2) and the right engine mount bracket (1)

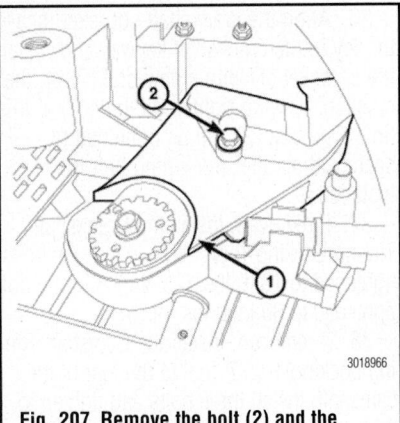

Fig. 207 Remove the bolt (2) and the lower timing belt cover (1)

29. Remove the bolt and the lower timing belt cover.

30. Install the Crankshaft Timing Locking Tool 10276 with three bolts tightened to 18 ft. lbs. (25 Nm) and one bolt tightened to 80 inch lbs. (9 Nm).

➡ **If the bolt (2) does not align with the lower timing belt cover mounting boss, the camshaft timing is not correct.**

➡ **If the timing belt is to be reused, mark the direction of rotation using a paint pen or equivalent to aid in reassembly.**

31. Loosen the tensioner lock nut (3) and remove the timing belt (1).

To install:

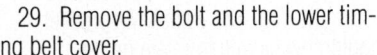

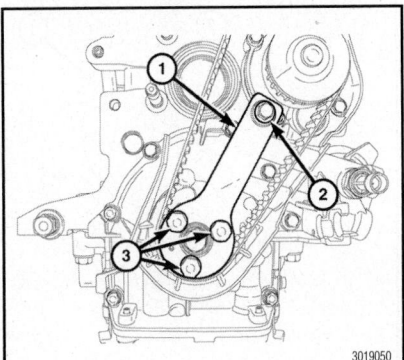

Fig. 208 Install the Crankshaft Timing Locking Tool 10276 (1) with three bolts (3) tightened to 18 ft. lbs. and one bolt (2) tightened to 80 inch lbs.

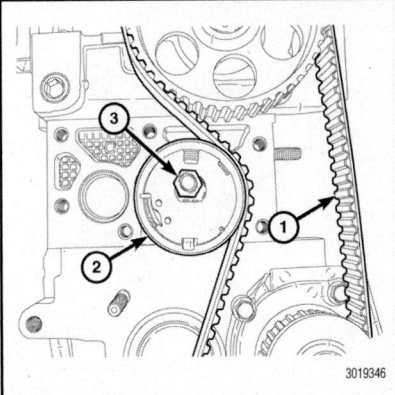

Fig. 209 Loosen the tensioner lock nut (3) and remove the timing belt (1)

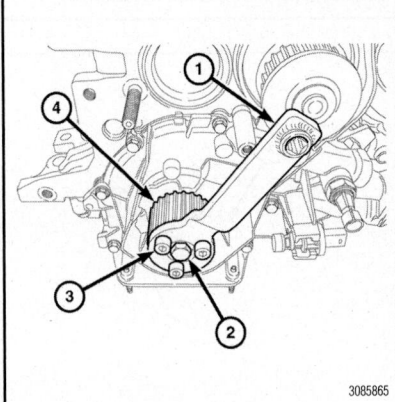

Fig. 210 Crankshaft sprocket holder tool (1), sprocket bolt (2), bolts (3) and sprocket (4)

will result in valve and/or piston damage.

32. Raise and support the vehicle.

33. If required, remove the crankshaft sprocket:

    a. Install the Crankshaft Sprocket Holder 10307 with three bolts tightened to 18 ft. lbs. (25 Nm).

    b. Remove the bolt and the crankshaft sprocket.

    c. Discard the bolt.

34. Lower the vehicle.

35. If required, use Camshaft Sprocket Holder 6847 and remove the bolt and the camshaft sprocket.

To install:

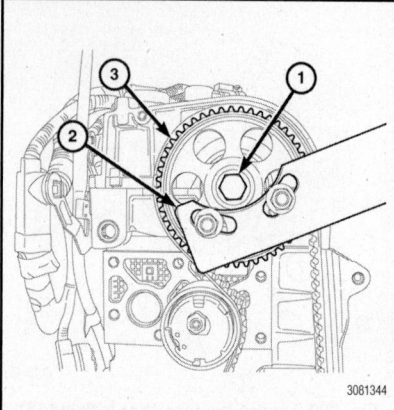

Fig. 211 If required, use Camshaft Sprocket Holder 6847 (2) and remove the bolt (1) and the camshaft sprocket (3)

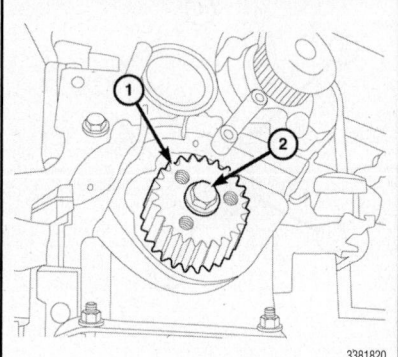

Fig. 212 Align the crankshaft sprocket locator key to the crankshaft keyway and install the sprocket (1) with a new bolt (2) on the crankshaft. Hand tighten the bolt (2) at this time. The bolt (2) will be tightened to specification after the timing belt is installed

36. Align the crankshaft sprocket locator key to the crankshaft keyway and install the sprocket (1) with a new bolt (2) on the crankshaft. Hand tighten the bolt (2) at this time. The bolt (2) will be tightened to specification after the timing belt is installed.

37. If removed, install the Crankshaft Timing Locking Tool 10276 with three bolts tightened to 18 ft. lbs. (25 Nm) and one bolt tightened to 80 inch lbs. (9 Nm).

38. If removed, install the Camshaft Timing Locking 10277 Tool to the rear of the camshaft. Install three bolts and tighten to 15 ft. lbs. (20 Nm).

39. Use the Camshaft Sprocket Holder 6847 to hold the camshaft sprocket and loosen the bolt. The camshaft sprocket should now be free to rotate on the camshaft.

➡ **If the original timing belt is being reused, install the belt so that it maintains the same direction of rotation as when it was removed.**

40. Install the timing belt starting with the crankshaft sprocket, then the water pump sprocket, finishing with the camshaft sprocket.

41. Rotate and adjust the timing tensioner so that the silver tab is centered in the middle of the window. Tighten the lock nut to 21 ft. lbs. (28 Nm).

42. Use the Camshaft Sprocket Holder 6847 to hold the camshaft sprocket and tighten the camshaft sprocket bolt to 88 ft. lbs. (120 Nm).

43. Remove the Camshaft Timing Locking Tool 10277 and the Crankshaft Timing Locking Tool 10276.

Rotate the crankshaft clockwise at least two complete revolutions to center the timing belt on the sprockets.

44. Verify that the silver tab is still centered in the middle of the window. If required, loosen the tensioner lock nut, readjust the timing belt tensioner and tighten the lock nut to 21 ft. lbs. (28 Nm).

➡ **Reinstall the timing locking tools to verify correct camshaft timing.**

45. Install the Camshaft Timing Locking Tool 10277 to the rear of the camshaft. Install three bolts and tighten to 15 ft. lbs. (20 Nm).

46. Install the Crankshaft Timing Locking Tool 10276 with three bolts tightened to 18 ft. lbs. (25 Nm) and one bolt tightened to 80 inch lbs. (9 Nm).

➡ **If the bolt does not align with the lower timing belt cover mounting boss, the camshaft timing is not correct. Loosen the tensioner lock nut and the camshaft sprocket bolt and repeat this procedure.**

47. Remove the Camshaft Timing Locking Tool 10277 and the Crankshaft Timing Locking Tool 10276.

48. Install the lower timing belt cover with bolt tightened to 80 inch lbs. (9 Nm).

49. Install the right engine mount bracket with six bolts tightened to 18 ft. lbs. (25 Nm).

50. Install the upper timing belt cover with two bolts tightened to 80 inch lbs. (9 Nm).

51. Install the right engine mount isolator to the engine mount bracket with three

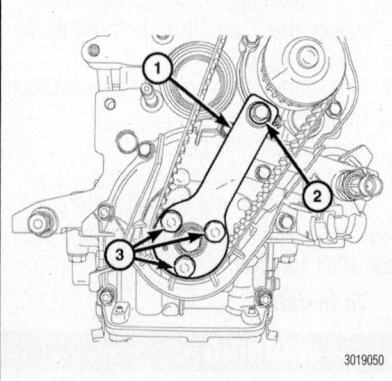

Fig. 213 If removed, install the Crankshaft Timing Locking Tool 10276 (1) with three bolts (3) tightened to 18 ft. lbs. (25 Nm) and one bolt (2) tightened to 80 inch lbs. (9 Nm)

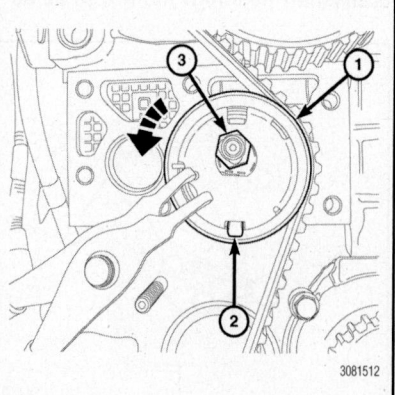

Fig. 214 Rotate and adjust the timing tensioner (1) so that the silver tab (2) is centered in the middle of the window. Tighten the lock nut (3) to 21 ft. lbs. (28 Nm)

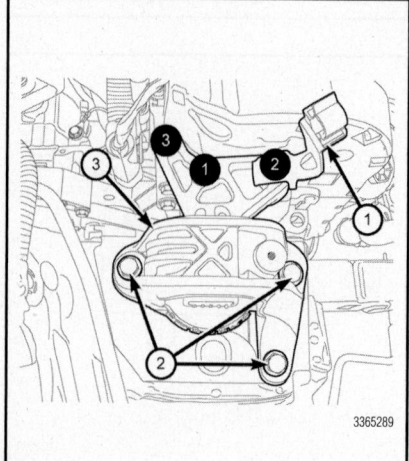

Fig. 215 View of the right engine mounting insulator (3) bolt tightening sequence (black shaded circles)

bolts. Tighten the isolator to engine bracket bolts in the sequence shown to 44 ft. lbs. (60 Nm).

52. Install the right engine mount isolator to the body with three bolts. Tighten the isolator to body bolts to 44 ft. lbs. (60 Nm).

53. Install the pressurized coolant bottle.

54. Raise and support the vehicle.

55. Install the vibration damper.

56. Install the accessory drive belt.

57. Install the frame splash shield with three screws.

58. Install two screws to the front wheel-house splash shield.

59. Install the right vertical brace with two bolts tightened to 33 ft. lbs. (45 Nm).

60. Install the right front wheel and tire assembly.

61. Raise and support the vehicle.

62. Install the tunnel support brace with four bolts tightened to 60 ft. lbs. (90 Nm).

63. If equipped with a manual transmission, install the rear engine mount isolator to the transmission with the rear engine mount bracket bolt and nut tightened to 59 ft. lbs. (80 Nm) and tighten the isolator bolt to 96 ft. lbs. (130 Nm).

64. If equipped with an automatic transmission, install the rear engine mount isolator in the bracket with two bolts tighten to 44 ft. lbs. (60 Nm). Install the isolator bolt and tighten to 96 ft. lbs. (130 Nm).

65. Install the belly pan.

66. Lower the vehicle.

67. Connect the fuel vapor purge hose to the intake manifold.

68. Connect the fuel line to the fuel rail and close the hose retainer.

69. Install the vacuum pump.

70. Install the oil separator housing to the cylinder head cover with three bolts tightened to 115 inch lbs. (13 Nm).

71. Connect the vent hose to the oil filler neck.

72. Connect the PCV hose to the intake manifold.

73. Install the air cleaner assembly.

74. Connect the negative battery cable. Tighten nut to 45 inch lbs. (5 Nm).

75. Install the engine cover.

76. Start and run the engine until it reaches normal operating temperature. Check cooling system for correct fluid level.

➡️**The Cam/Crank Variation Relearn procedure must be performed using the scan tool anytime there has been a repair/replacement made to a powertrain system, for example: flywheel, valvetrain, camshaft and/or crankshaft sensors or components**

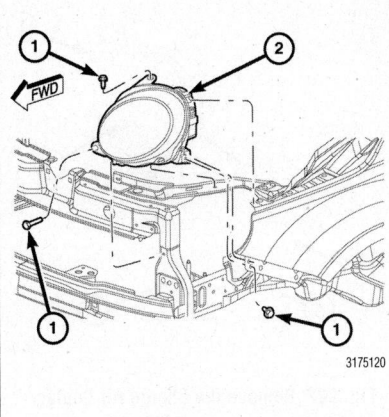

Fig. 216 Exploded view of the headlamp unit (2) mounting

TURBOCHARGER

REMOVAL & INSTALLATION

See Figures 216 through 226.

1. Disconnect and isolate the negative battery cable.

2. Remove the front fascia.

3. Remove the right and left headlamp units.

4. Disconnect the upper coolant hose from the radiator.

5. Disconnect the electrical connector from the cooling fan resistor located on the cooling fan shroud.

6. Disconnect the cooling fan electrical connector (3).

7. Disconnect the lower coolant hose from the radiator.

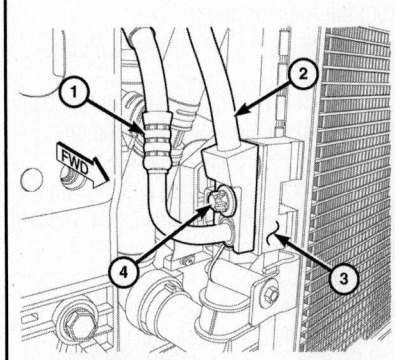

1. A/C liquid line
2. A/C compressor discharge line
3. A/C condenser tapping block
4. Bolt

Fig. 217 Remove the bolt (4) and disconnect the A/C liquid line (1) and the A/C compressor discharge line (2) from the A/C condenser tapping block (3)

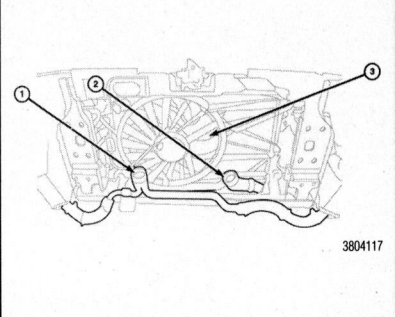

Fig. 218 Disconnect the throttle body inlet hose (1) and turbocharger outlet hose (2) at the lower quick disconnects located behind the cooling fan (3)

8. Recover the refrigerant from the refrigerant system.

9. Remove the bolt and disconnect the A/C liquid line and the A/C compressor discharge line from the A/C condenser tapping block.

10. Separate the A/C liquid line from the A/C compressor discharge line. Remove and discard the dual plane seals.

11. Install plugs in, or tape over, the opened refrigerant line fittings and condenser ports.

12. Press down the latch release and remove the hood latch cable from the latch.

13. Disconnect the wire harness connector from the right and left front impact sensors. It is not necessary to unbolt the sensor from the frame.

14. Disconnect the wire harness connector from the horn.

15. Disengage the wire harness from the bumper reinforcement.

16. Disengage the block heater wire harness retainer from the upper core support.

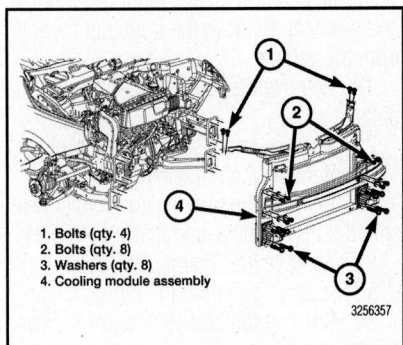

1. Bolts (qty. 4)
2. Bolts (qty. 8)
3. Washers (qty. 8)
4. Cooling module assembly

Fig. 219 Remove the four upper bolts (1), eight center bolts and washers (2), eight lower bolts and washers (3). Remove the front end module (4) from the vehicle.

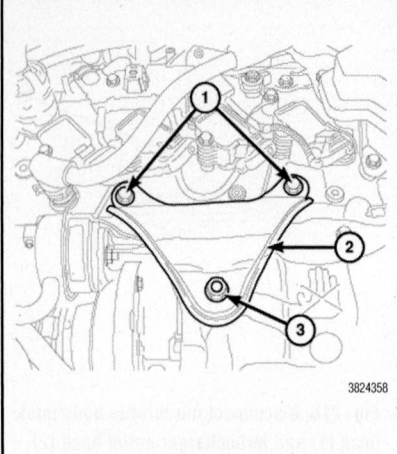

Fig. 220 View of the turbocharger bracket bolts (1), bracket (2) and nut (3)

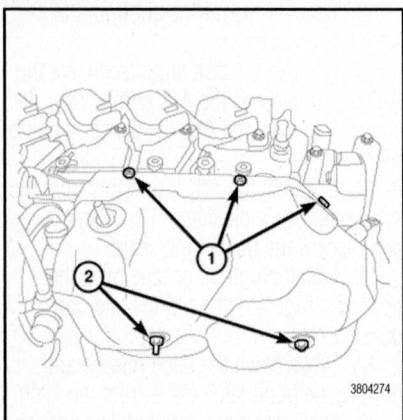

Fig. 221 Remove the turbocharger upper heat shield bolts (1). Remove and discard the nuts (2)

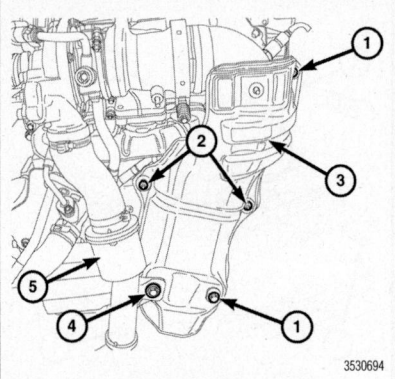

Fig. 222 Remove the Charge Air Cooler (CAC) supply hose (5) from the turbocharger. Remove the catalytic converter heat shield (3).

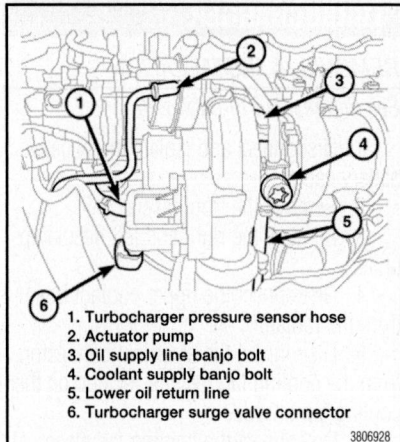

1. Turbocharger pressure sensor hose
2. Actuator pump
3. Oil supply line banjo bolt
4. Coolant supply banjo bolt
5. Lower oil return line
6. Turbocharger surge valve connector

Fig. 223 Various components must be disconnected from the turbocharger

install the surge valve onto the new turbocharger assembly.

32. Raise and support vehicle.
33. Remove the exhaust flange nuts.
34. Remove the front exhaust pipe support bolt.
35. Remove the nuts that secure the cross under pipe to the catalytic converter.
36. Remove the front exhaust pipe and flange gasket.
37. Remove the lower catalytic converter support mount.
38. Lower the vehicle.
39. Disconnect the upstream oxygen sensor connector.
40. Loosen the catalytic converter clamp at the turbocharger and remove the converter assembly from vehicle.
41. Remove and discard the converter to turbo seal ring.

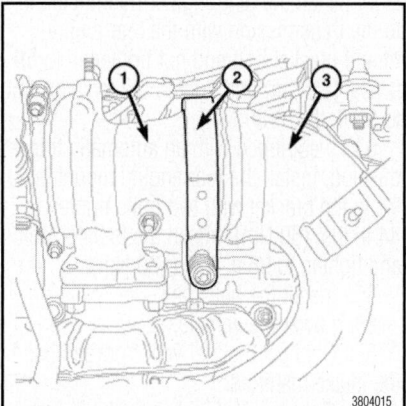

Fig. 224 Loosen the catalytic converter clamp (2) at the turbocharger (1) and remove the converter assembly from vehicle

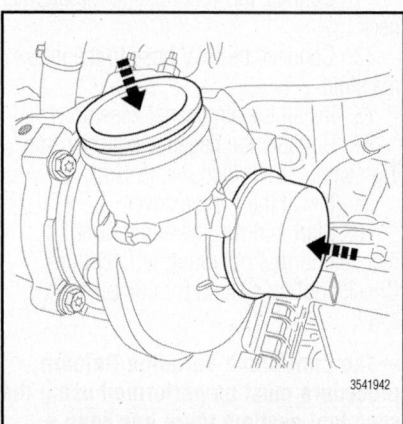

Fig. 225 Install the Universal Protective Cap Set (10368) into the open bores on the turbo to prevent any foreign material from entering the turbocharger

17. Disconnect the throttle body inlet hose and turbocharger outlet hose at the lower quick disconnects located behind the cooling fan.
18. Remove the four upper bolts eight center bolts and washers, eight lower bolts and washers. Remove the front end module from the vehicle.
19. Remove the turbocharger bracket bolts.
20. Remove and discard the bracket nut.
21. Remove the turbocharger bracket.
22. Remove the turbocharger upper heat shield bolts. Remove and discard the nuts.
23. Remove the Charge Air Cooler (CAC) supply hose from the turbocharger.
24. Remove the catalytic converter heat shield.

※※ WARNING

The oil supply and return lines MUST be replaced whenever the lines are loosened or removed.

25. Disconnect the wastegate supply line from the actuator pump.
26. Disconnect the turbocharger pressure sensor hose.
27. Remove the coolant return line banjo bolt located on the rear side of the turbocharger. Discard the banjo washers.
28. Remove the coolant supply banjo bolt (4) and position the line aside. Discard the banjo washers.
29. Remove the oil supply line banjo bolt (3). Remove the line as an assembly. The oil supply and return lines must be replaced. The oil line banjo bolts and banjo washers must be replaced.
30. Remove the lower oil return line (5). The oil supply and return lines must be replaced. The oil line banjo bolts and banjo washers must be replaced.
31. Disconnect the turbocharger surge valve connector (6).

➡ Remove the surge valve from the turbocharger. It will be necessary to

➡️**Install the Universal Protective Cap Set (10368) into the open bores on the turbo to prevent any foreign material from entering the turbocharger.**

42. Remove the two bolts that secure the shield to the exhaust manifold. Remove and discard the nut .

43. Remove the shield.

44. Remove and discard the nine exhaust manifold nuts. Remove the nine washers.

45. Remove and discard the nine exhaust manifold studs.

➡️**The exhaust manifold nuts and studs must be replaced. The washers can be reused. The exhaust manifold gasket and the turbocharger to manifold gasket must be replaced.**

46. With the manifold removed, invert the manifold and turbocharger as an assembly. Remove and discard the four nuts. The mounting nuts MUST be replaced.

47. Lift the manifold up and off of the turbocharger. Remove and discard the gasket.

To install:

> ❊❊ **WARNING**
>
> **The oil supply and return lines MUST be replaced whenever the lines are loosened or removed.**

48. With the manifold removed, invert the manifold and turbocharger.

49. Install a new gasket onto the manifold/turbocharger mating surface.

50. Set the manifold onto the turbocharger studs and install four new nuts by hand. Tighten the four nuts to 18 ft. lbs. (24 Nm).

51. After the nuts are tightened to 18 ft. lbs. (24 Nm) once, repeat the step to be sure that all nuts are at the proper torque.

➡️**Replace any stud that loosens during removal. If a stud is to be replaced, tighten the new stud to 97 inch lbs. (11 Nm). Age of the vehicle and environment impact how many of the studs come out. Any that stay in the head also need to be checked for the 97 inch lbs. (11 Nm).**

➡️**When screwing the studs into the head, install them dry. Do not apply any lubricants, adhesives, sealants or the like to the threads. The new studs have a locking adhesive impregnated into the threads**

52. Install new manifold studs. Tighten the studs to 97 inch lbs. (11 Nm).

53. Install a new manifold gasket/shield assembly.

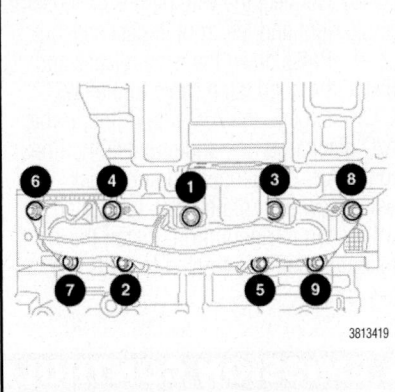

Fig. 226 Manifold/Turbocharger assembly tightening sequence—note that the turbocharger has been removed for clarity

54. Set the manifold and turbocharger assembly onto the cylinder head studs.

55. Install the nine exhaust manifold washers and new nuts (1). Tighten in sequence, as follows:

    a. Tighten to 11 ft. lbs. (15 Nm) in order from 1 to 9.

    b. Retighten to 11 ft. lbs. (15 Nm) in order from 1 to 4 only.

    c. Add additional 30 degrees (one 1/8 of a turn) of clockwise rotation to all in order from 1 to 9.

56. Position the exhaust manifold shield and install the two bolts and one new nut. Tighten the shield bolts to 80 inch lbs. (9 Nm).

> ❊❊ **WARNING**
>
> **Band clamps should never be tightened such that the two sides of the clamps are bottomed out against the hourglass shaped center block. Once this occurs, the clamp has lost clamping force and must be replaced.**

57. Install the new converter to turbo seal ring.

58. Install the catalytic converter assembly.

59. Install the catalytic converter v-clamp at the turbocharger. Tighten clamp to 71 inch lbs. (8 Nm).

60. Connect the O2 sensor connector.

61. Install the catalytic converter lower support bracket.

62. Install and tighten the bracket bolts to 41 ft. lbs. (56 Nm).

63. Install a new converter to pipe gasket.

64. Install the front exhaust pipe.

65. Install the nuts that secure the cross under pipe to the catalytic converter.

66. Tighten the front exhaust pipe nuts to 41 ft. lbs. (56 Nm).

67. Install the front exhaust pipe support bolt. Tighten to 41 ft. lbs. (56 Nm).

68. Install the exhaust flange nuts. Tighten to 51 ft. lbs. (69 Nm).

➡️**Banjo bolts and banjo bolt gaskets must be replaced during assembly. Also, the oil supply and return lines must be replaced during assembly or ANY TIME the fittings are loosened to prevent turbine bearing failure due to debris.**

69. Connect the wastegate supply hose to the actuator pump.

70. Connect the turbocharger pressure sensor hose.

71. Install the coolant return line with new washers located on the rear side of the turbocharger. Tighten to 28 ft. lbs. (38 Nm).

72. Install the coolant supply banjo bolt and new washers. Tighten to 28 ft. lbs. (38 Nm).

73. Install the new oil supply line, banjo bolts and washers. Tighten to 22 ft. lbs. (30 Nm).

74. Install the lower new oil return line and new upper gasket. Tighten the bolt to 124 inch lbs. (14 Nm).

75. Install the previously removed surge valve and tighten the bolts to 80 inch lbs. (9 Nm)

76. Connect the turbocharger surge valve connector.

77. Install the Charge Air Cooler (CAC) supply hose to the turbocharger.

78. Install the CAC hose clamp and tighten.

79. Install the catalytic converter heat shield. Install the bolts and new nuts. Tighten the nuts and bolts to 71 inch lbs. (8 Nm).

80. Install the upper heat shield. Install the three bolts and the two new nuts. Tighten the bolts and the nuts to 80 inch lbs. (9 Nm). Care must be taken when tightening the shield bolts. If torque value is not correct, noise will occur.

81. Connect the upstream and downstream oxygen sensor connectors.

82. Install the turbocharger bracket, bolts and new nut.

83. Tighten the bolts and nut to 18 ft. lbs. (25 Nm).

84. Position the Front End Module onto the front of the vehicle.

85. Install the front end module assembly with four bolts, eight bolts and washers and eight bolts and washers. Tighten the eight bolts to 33 ft. lbs. (45 Nm). Tighten the four bolts to 18 ft. lbs. (24 Nm). Tighten the eight bolts to 33 ft. lbs. (45 Nm).

86. Connect the throttle body inlet hose and turbocharger outlet hose at the lower quick disconnects located behind the cooling fan.

87. Engage the block heater wire harness retainer at the upper core support.

88. Connect the wire harness connector to the horn.

89. Engage the wire harness connector to the bumper reinforcement.

90. Connect the wire harness connector to the right and left front impact sensors.

91. Press down the latch release and install the hood latch cable to the latch.

92. Engage the A/C liquid line to the A/C discharge line and connect the lines to the A/C condenser tapping block using new dual plain seals lubricated with clean refrigerant oil. Install the retaining bolt and tighten to 10 ft. lbs. (14 Nm).

93. Connect the cooling fan electrical connector.

94. Install the upper and lower radiator hoses and clamps. Tighten the clamps.

95. Recharge the AC system to specifications.

96. Connect the electrical connector to the cooling fan resistor.

97. Install the right and left headlamp units.

98. Install the fascia assembly.

ENGINE PERFORMANCE & EMISSION CONTROLS

ACCELERATOR PEDAL POSITION SENSOR (APPS)

LOCATION

See Figure 227

The Accelerator Pedal Position Sensor (APPS) (2) is attached to the accelerator pedal assembly under the instrument panel.

The APPS and the accelerator pedal (2) assembly must be replaced as a unit.

REMOVAL & INSTALLATION

See Figure 227.

➡The Accelerator Pedal Position Sensor (APPS) and the accelerator pedal is serviced as a complete assembly including the bracket.

1. Disconnect electrical connector (1) at the APPS (2).

2. Remove the three accelerator pedal retaining bracket nuts (3) and remove the accelerator pedal assembly (4) from the mounting studs (5).

To install:

3. Position the accelerator pedal assembly onto the three mounting studs (5).

4. Install the three accelerator pedal retaining bracket nuts (3) and tighten to 9 ft. lbs. (12 Nm).

5. Connect the accelerator pedal electrical connector (1) to the APPS (2).

6. Use a scan tool to learn electrical parameters. Go to the Miscellaneous menu, and then select ETC Learn.

7. If the previous step is not performed, a Diagnostic Trouble Code (DTC) may set.

8. If necessary, also use a scan tool to erase any Diagnostic Trouble Codes (DTC's) from the PCM.

9. Before starting the engine, operate the accelerator pedal to check for any binding.

CAMSHAFT POSITION (CMP) SENSOR

LOCATION

The Camshaft Position (CMP) sensor is located on the camshaft bearing housing and faces the camshaft.

REMOVAL & INSTALLATION

1.4L 8V Engine

See Figure 228.

1. Disconnect and isolate the negative battery cable.

2. Remove the air cleaner assembly.

3. Unlock and disconnect the Camshaft Position (CMP) sensor electrical connector.

4. Remove the mounting bolt (1) and Camshaft Position (CMP) sensor (2).

➡The Camshaft Position (CMP) sensor O-ring can be reused if not damaged.

To install:

5. Apply a small amount of clean engine oil to the sensor O-ring.

6. Install the Camshaft Position (CMP) sensor with mounting bolt tightened to 80 inch lbs. (9 Nm).

7. Connect and lock the Camshaft Position (CMP) sensor electrical connector.

8. Install the air cleaner assembly.

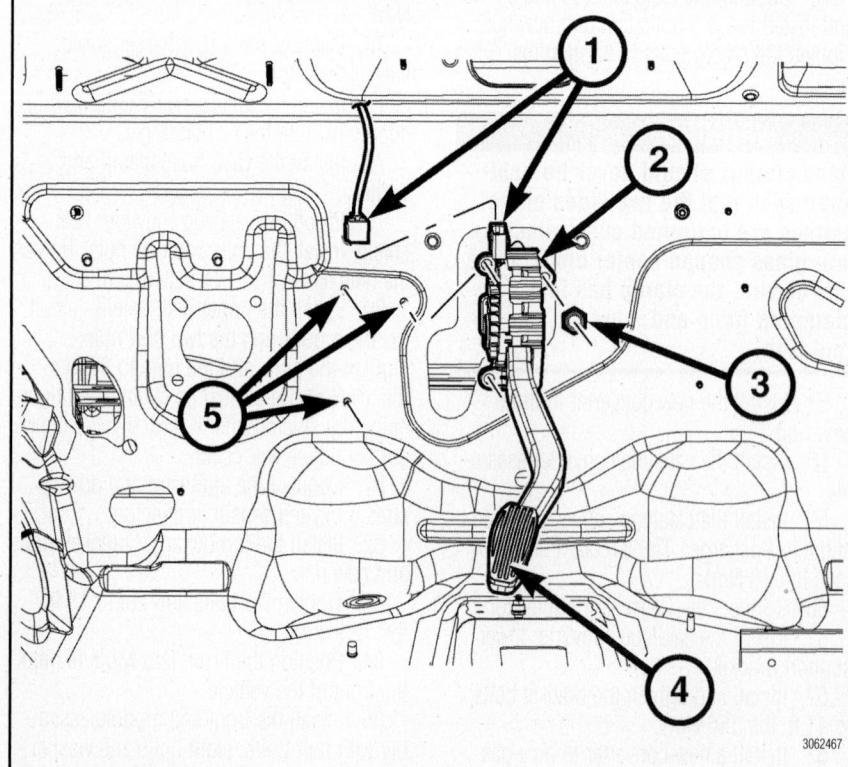

3062467

Fig. 227 Disconnect electrical connector (1) at the APPS (2). Remove the three accelerator pedal retaining bracket nuts (3) and remove the accelerator pedal assembly (4) from the mounting studs (5).

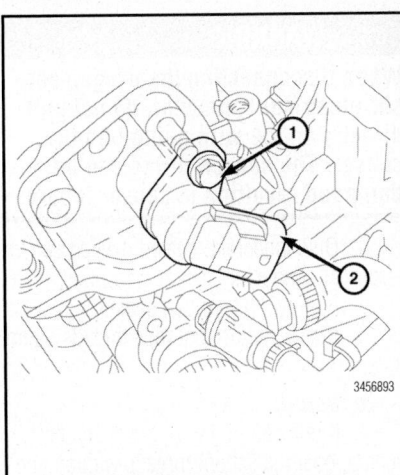

Fig. 228 Remove the mounting bolt (1) and Camshaft Position (CMP) sensor (2)

9. Install the negative battery cable and tighten nut to 45 inch lbs. (5 Nm).

➡️**The Cam/Crank Variation Relearn procedure must be performed using the scan tool anytime there has been a repair/replacement made to a power-train system, for example: flywheel, valvetrain, camshaft and/or crankshaft sensors or components.**

1.4L 16V MultiAir & 1.4L 16V Turbo Engines

See Figures 229 and 230.

1. Disconnect and isolate the negative battery cable.
2. Remove the engine cover.
3. Remove the air cleaner assembly.
4. Disconnect the PCV hose from the intake manifold.
5. Disconnect the vent hose from the oil filler neck.
6. Remove three bolts and remove the

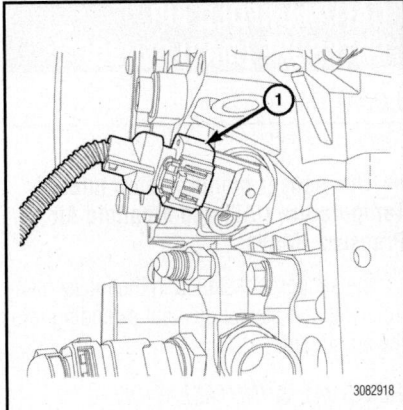

Fig. 229 Unlock and disconnect the Camshaft Position (CMP) sensor electrical connector (1)

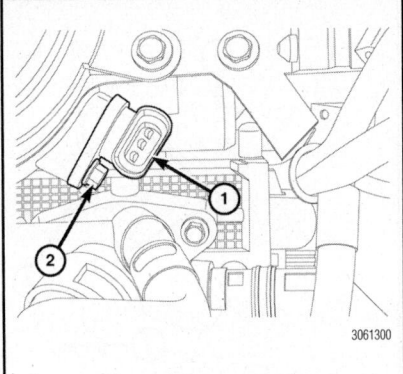

Fig. 230 Remove the mounting bolt (2) and Camshaft Position (CMP) sensor (1)

oil separator housing from the cylinder head cover.

7. Unlock and disconnect the Camshaft Position (CMP) sensor electrical connector.
8. Remove the mounting bolt and Camshaft Position (CMP) sensor.

➡️**The Camshaft Position (CMP) sensor O-ring (1) can be reused if not damaged.**

To install:

9. Apply a small amount of engine oil to the sensor O-ring.
10. Install the Camshaft Position (CMP) sensor with mounting bolt). Tighten the mounting bolt to 80 inch lbs. (9 Nm).
11. Connect and lock the Camshaft Position (CMP) sensor electrical connector.
12. Install the oil separator housing to the cylinder head cover with three bolts tightened to 115 inch lbs. (13 Nm).
13. Connect the vent hose to the oil filler neck.
14. Connect the PCV hose to the intake manifold.
15. Install the air cleaner assembly.
16. Install the negative battery cable and tighten nut to 45 inch lbs. (5 Nm).
17. Install the engine cover.

➡️**The Cam/Crank Variation Relearn procedure must be performed using the scan tool anytime there has been a repair/replacement made to a power-train system, for example: flywheel, valvetrain, camshaft and/or crankshaft sensors or components.**

CRANKSHAFT POSITION (CKP) SENSOR

LOCATION

The Crankshaft Position (CKP) sensor is mounted into the left side of the cylinder block at the front of the engine. It is posi-

tioned to read the tonewheel mounted on the vibration damper.

REMOVAL & INSTALLATION

See Figure 231.

1. Disconnect and isolate the negative battery cable.
2. Raise and support the vehicle.
3. Remove the belly pan.
4. Remove the Crankshaft Position (CKP) sensor electrical connector.
5. Remove the mounting bolt and the Crankshaft Position (CKP) sensor.

To install:

6. Install the Crankshaft Position (CKP) sensor with mounting bolt. Tighten the mounting bolt to 80 inch lbs. (9 Nm).
7. Connect the electrical connector.
8. Install the belly pan.
9. Lower the vehicle.
10. Connect the negative battery cable and tighten nut to 45 inch lbs. (5 Nm).

➡️**The Cam/Crank Variation Relearn procedure must be performed using the scan tool anytime there has been a repair/replacement made to a power-train system, for example: flywheel, valvetrain, camshaft and/or crankshaft sensors or components.**

ENGINE COOLANT TEMPERATURE (ECT) SENSOR

REMOVAL & INSTALLATION

See Figure 232.

❄️❄️ **CAUTION**

Do not remove cylinder block drain plugs, pressure caps, or loosen radiator draincock with system hot and under pressure. Serious burns from coolant can occur.

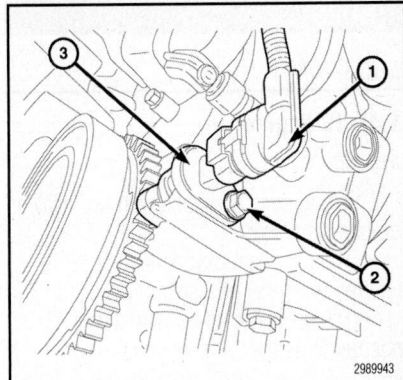

Fig. 231 CKP electrical connector (1), mounting bolt (2) and CKP sensor (3)

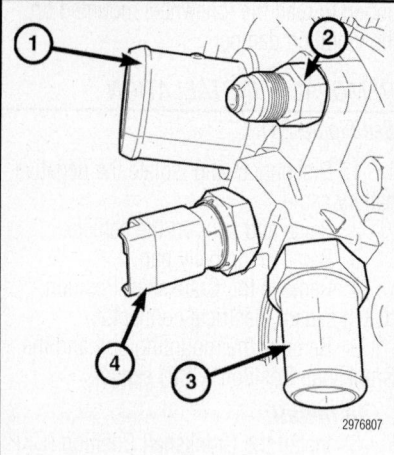

Fig. 232 Remove the ECT sensor (4) from the thermostat housing

1. Drain the cooling system.
2. Disconnect the negative, then the positive battery cables.
3. Remove the nut for the battery hold down clamp and remove battery.
4. Remove the engine cover.
5. Remove the air intake assembly.
6. Disconnect the Engine Coolant Temperature (ECT) sensor harness connector.
7. Remove the Engine Coolant Temperature (ECT) sensor from the thermostat housing.

To install:
8. Install the Engine Coolant Temperature (ECT) sensor into the thermostat housing.
9. Connect the wire harness connector.
10. Install the battery and the hold-down clamp. Tighten the nut to 40 ft. lbs. (50 Nm).
11. Install the air intake assembly.
12. Fill the cooling system.
13. Connect the positive and negative battery cable.

HEATED OXYGEN SENSOR (HO2S)

LOCATION

1.4L 8V Engine
See Figure 233.

This engine is equipped with two heated oxygen sensors:
- The upstream oxygen sensor (2) is referred to as the 1/1 sensor.
- The downstream oxygen sensor (3) is referred to as the 1/2 sensor.

1.4L 16V MultiAir & 1.4L Turbo Engines
See Figure 234.

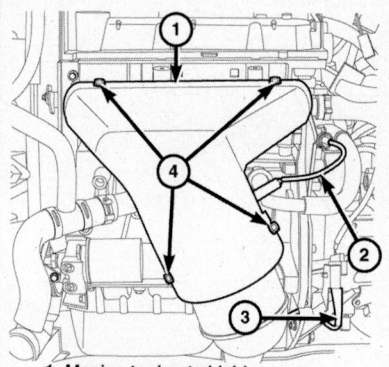

1. Maniverter heat shield
2. Upstream O2 sensor connector
3. Downstream O2 sensor connector
4. Maniverter bolts

Fig. 233 Upstream Oxygen 1/1 Sensor (2) & Downstream Oxygen 1/2 Sensor (3)

This engine is equipped with two heated oxygen sensors:
- The upstream oxygen sensor (1) is referred to as the 1/1 sensor.
- The downstream oxygen sensor (2) is referred to as the 1/2 sensor.

REMOVAL & INSTALLATION

※※ CAUTION
The exhaust pipes and catalytic converter become very hot during engine operation. Allow the engine to cool before removing the oxygen sensor.

1. Disconnect and isolate the negative battery cable.
2. Raise and support the vehicle.
3. Remove the belly pan.

Fig. 234 Upstream Oxygen 1/1 Sensor (1) & Downstream Oxygen 1/2 Sensor (2)

※※ WARNING
When disconnecting the oxygen sensor electrical connector, do not pull directly on the wire going into the sensor. The sensor wiring can be damaged resulting in sensor failure.

4. Disconnect the heated oxygen sensor electrical connector.
5. Remove the oxygen sensor.
6. Clean the exhaust pipe threads using an appropriate tap.

To install:
7. If reinstalling the original oxygen sensor, coat the sensor threads with an anti-seize compound such as Loctite® 771- 64 or equivalent. New sensors have compound on the threads and do not require an additional coating. Do not add any additional anti-seize compound to the threads of a new oxygen sensor.
8. Install the oxygen sensor and tighten to 33 ft. lbs. (45 Nm).

※※ WARNING
Never apply any type of grease to the oxygen sensor electrical connector, or attempt any repair of the sensor wiring harness.

9. Connect the heated oxygen sensor electrical connector.
10. Install the belly pan.
11. Lower the vehicle.
12. Connect the negative battery cable and tighten nut to 45 inch lbs. (5 Nm).

➡The Oxygen Sensor Relearn procedure must be performed using a suitable scan tool following replacement of any oxygen sensor.

INLET AIR TEMPERATURE (IAT)/MANIFOLD AIR PRESSURE (MAP) SENSOR

LOCATION
See Figure 235.

➡ This sensor monitors both Inlet Air Temperature (IAT) and Manifold Air Pressure (MAP).

The sensor is installed in the intake manifold with the sensor element extending into the air stream.

REMOVAL & INSTALLATION
See Figure 236.

➡ This sensor monitors both Inlet Air Temperature (IAT) and Manifold Air Pressure (MAP).

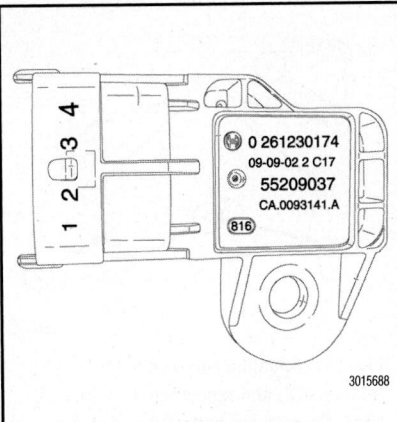

Fig. 235 This sensor monitors both Inlet Air Temperature (IAT) and Manifold Air Pressure (MAP)

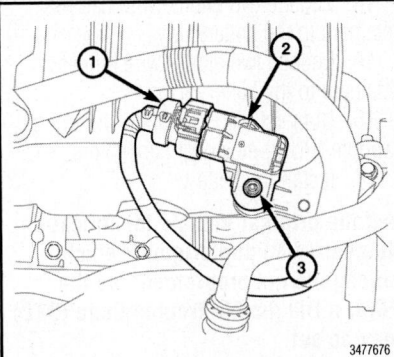

Fig. 236 Unlock and disconnect the electrical connector (1) from the IAT/MAP sensor. Remove the bolt (3) and the IAT/MAP sensor (2) from the intake manifold—non-Turbo engines shown, Turbo is similar

1. Disconnect and isolate the negative battery cable.
2. Remove the engine cover, if necessary
3. Remove the air cleaner assembly.
4. Unlock and disconnect the electrical connector (1) from the IAT/MAP sensor.
5. Remove the bolt (3) and the IAT/MAP sensor (2) from the intake manifold.
6. The IAT/MAP sensor O-ring can be reused if not damaged.

To install:
7. Apply a small amount of engine oil to the sensor O-ring.
8. Install the IAT/MAP sensor into the intake manifold with the bolt tightened to 80 inch lbs. (9 Nm).
9. Connect and lock the electrical connector to the sensor.
10. Install the air cleaner assembly.
11. Connect the negative battery cable and tighten nut to 45 inch lbs. (5 Nm).

KNOCK SENSOR (KS)

REMOVAL & INSTALLATION
See Figure 237.

1. Disconnect and isolate the negative battery cable.
2. Raise and support the vehicle.
3. Remove the belly pan.
4. Remove the knock sensor electrical connector
5. Remove the mounting bolt and knock sensor.
6. Discard the mounting bolt, it cannot be reused.

To install:

➡**Over or under tightening the knock sensor mounting bolt will affect knock sensor performance, possibly causing improper spark control. Always use the specified torque when installing the knock sensor. Do not apply any adhesive, sealant or thread locking compound to the bolt.**

7. Install the knock sensor with a new mounting bolt. Tighten the mounting bolt to 18 ft. lbs. (25 Nm).
8. Connect the electrical connector.
9. Install the belly pan.
10. Lower the vehicle.
11. Connect the negative battery cable and tighten nut to 45 inch lbs. (5 Nm).

POWERTRAIN CONTROL MODULE (PCM)

LOCATION

1.8L 8V Engine
See Figure 239

The Powertrain Control Module (PCM) (1) is located in the engine compartment on the side of the battery tray.

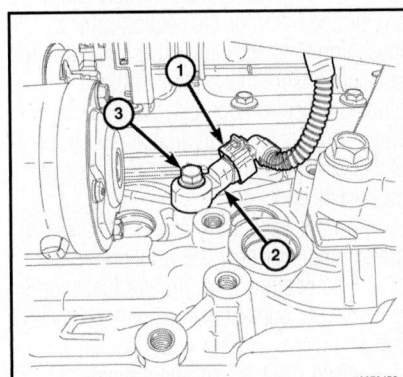

Fig. 237 Knock Sensor (KS) electrical connector (1), sensor (2) and mounting bolt (3)

1.4L 16V MultiAir & 1.4L 16V Turbo Engines
See Figure 94.

The Powertrain Control Module (PCM) (2) is located in the engine compartment on the back of the battery tray.

REMOVAL & INSTALLATION

1.8L 8V Engine
See Figures 238 and 239.

1. Disconnect and remove the battery, as outlined in the Engine Electrical Section.
2. Disconnect the Powertrain Control Module (PCM) electrical connectors.
3. Remove the four nuts with ground strap and remove the PCM from the battery tray.

To install:
4. Install the Powertrain Control Module (PCM) to the battery tray with four nuts and

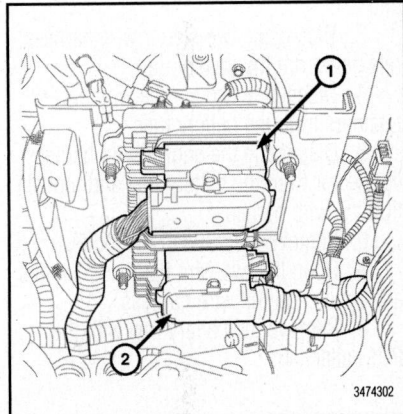

Fig. 238 Disconnect the Powertrain Control Module (PCM) electrical connectors (1 and 2)

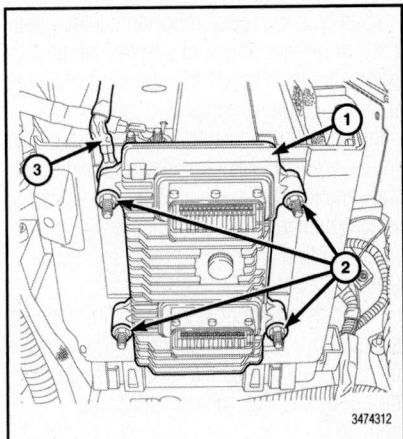

Fig. 239 Remove the four nuts (2) with ground strap (3) and remove the PCM (1) from the battery tray

ground strap (3). Tighten nuts to 44 inch lbs. (5 Nm).

5. Connect the Powertrain Control Module (PCM) electrical connectors.

6. Install the battery.

➡️If the original Vehicle Identification Number (VIN) and original vehicle mileage is not programed into the PCM, a Diagnostic Trouble Code (DTC) may be set.

7. If installing a new PCM, use a diagnostic scan tool to reprogram the new PCM with the vehicles original VIN and mileage.

1.4L 16V MultiAir & 1.4L 16V Turbo Engines

See Figures 240 and 241.

1. Disconnect and remove the battery, as outlined in the Engine Electrical Section.

2. Disconnect the Powertrain Control Module (PCM) electrical connectors (1 and 2).

3. Disengage two starter wire harness retainers from the battery tray.

4. Disengage two engine wire harness retainers from the battery tray.

5. Disengage the engine wire harness connector from the battery tray and reposition the wire harness.

6. Remove the nut and two bolts.

7. Open the two wire harness retainers and reposition the wire harness.

8. Remove the battery tray with the PCM attached.

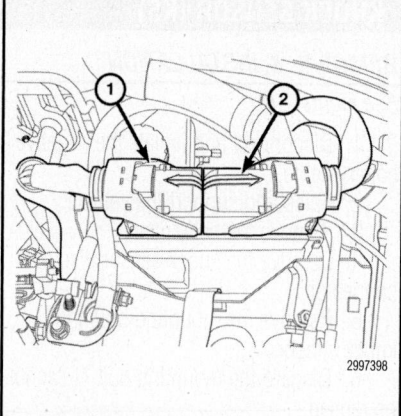

Fig. 240 Disconnect the Powertrain Control Module (PCM) electrical connectors (1 and 2)

9. Remove the four nuts with ground strap and remove the PCM from the battery tray.

To install:

10. Install the PCM to the battery tray with four nuts and ground strap. Tighten nuts to 44 inch lbs. (5 Nm).

11. Position the battery tray and PCM in the vehicle. Route the wire harness and close the wire harness retainers.

12. Install the battery tray with one nut and two bolts. Tighten all three fasteners to 18 ft. lbs. (25 Nm).

13. Engage the engine wire harness connector to the battery tray.

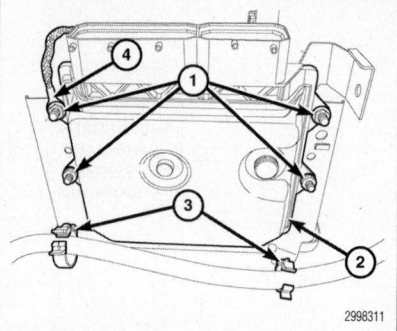

Fig. 241 Open the two wire harness retainers (3) and reposition the wire harness. Remove the battery tray with the PCM (2) attached. Remove the four nuts (1) with ground strap (4) and remove the PCM (2) from the battery tray

14. Engage two engine wire harness retainers to the battery tray.

15. Engage two starter wire harness retainers to the battery tray.

16. Connect the Powertrain Control Module (PCM) electrical connectors.

17. Install the battery

➡️If the original Vehicle Identification Number (VIN) and original vehicle mileage is not programed into the PCM, a Diagnostic Trouble Code (DTC) may be set.

18. If installing a new PCM, use a diagnostic scan tool to reprogram the new PCM with the vehicles original VIN and mileage.

FUEL

GASOLINE FUEL INJECTION SYSTEM

FUEL SYSTEM SERVICE PRECAUTIONS

Safety is the most important factor when performing not only fuel system maintenance but any type of maintenance. Failure to conduct maintenance and repairs in a safe manner may result in serious personal injury or death. Maintenance and testing of the vehicle's fuel system components can be accomplished safely and effectively by adhering to the following rules and guidelines.

• To avoid the possibility of fire and personal injury, always disconnect the negative battery cable unless the repair or test procedure requires that battery voltage be applied.

• Always relieve the fuel system pressure prior to disconnecting any fuel system component (injector, fuel rail, pressure regulator, etc.), fitting or fuel line connection. Exercise extreme caution whenever relieving

fuel system pressure to avoid exposing skin, face and eyes to fuel spray. Please be advised that fuel under pressure may penetrate the skin or any part of the body that it contacts.

• Always place a shop towel or cloth around the fitting or connection prior to loosening to absorb any excess fuel due to spillage. Ensure that all fuel spillage (should it occur) is quickly removed from engine surfaces. Ensure that all fuel soaked cloths or towels are deposited into a suitable waste container.

• Always keep a dry chemical (Class B) fire extinguisher near the work area.

• Do not allow fuel spray or fuel vapors to come into contact with a spark or open flame.

• Always use a back-up wrench when loosening and tightening fuel line connection fittings. This will prevent unnecessary stress and torsion to fuel line piping.

• Always replace worn fuel fitting O-rings with new Do not substitute fuel hose or equivalent where fuel pipe is installed.

Before servicing the vehicle, make sure to also refer to the precautions in the beginning of this section as well.

RELIEVING FUEL SYSTEM PRESSURE

1. Remove the fuel fill cap.

2. Remove the fuel pump fuse from the Power Distribution Center (PDC). For location of the fuel pump fuse, refer to label on the underside of the PDC cover.

3. Start and run the engine until it stalls.

4. Attempt restarting the engine until it will no longer run.

5. Turn the ignition key to the OFF position.

6. Return the fuel pump fuse to the PDC.

➡One or more Diagnostic Trouble Codes (DTC) may have been stored in the PCM memory due to fuel pump fuse removal. A diagnostic scan tool must be used to erase a DTC.

FUEL INJECTORS

REMOVAL & INSTALLATION

1.4L 8V Engine
See Figure 242.

✸✸ WARNING

The fuel system is under constant pressure even with engine off. Before servicing fuel injector(s), fuel system pressure must be released.

➡To remove one or more fuel injectors, the fuel rail assembly must be removed from engine.

1. Perform the fuel system pressure release procedure.
2. Remove the fuel rail assembly.
3. Remove the fuel injector retaining clip(s) (2) from the fuel rail.
4. Remove the injector(s) (1) from the fuel rail assembly.

To install:
5. Apply a small amount of engine oil to each fuel injector O-ring. This will help with the fuel rail installation.
6. Install the fuel injector(s) (1) into the fuel rail and install the retainer clip(s) (2).
7. Install the fuel rail assembly.
8. Start the engine and check for leaks.

1.4L 16V MultiAir & 1.4L 16V Turbo Engines
See Figure 243.

✸✸ WARNING

The fuel system is under constant pressure even with engine off. Before servicing fuel injector(s), fuel system pressure must be released.

➡To remove one or more fuel injectors, the fuel rail assembly must be removed from engine.

1. Perform the fuel system pressure release procedure.
2. Remove the fuel rail assembly.
3. Remove the fuel injector retaining clip(s) (2) from the fuel rail (1).
4. Remove the injector(s) (3) from the fuel rail assembly.

To install:
Check the condition of the O-rings before installing the injectors. Replace if any damage or abnormal wear is found.
5. Apply a small amount of engine oil to each fuel injector O-ring. This will help with the fuel rail installation.
6. Install the fuel injector(s) (3) into the fuel rail and install the retainer clip(s) (2).
7. Install the fuel rail assembly.

✸✸ CAUTION

When servicing components near the vacuum pump, avoid contact with the plastic nipple that connects the vacuum pump to the brake booster hose. It is possible to crack the plastic nipple resulting in a brake booster vacuum leak.

8. Install the intake manifold.
9. Start the engine and check for leaks.

FUEL PUMP

REMOVAL & INSTALLATION
See Figures 244 and 245.

✸✸ WARNING

The fuel system may be under a constant pressure (even with the engine off). Before servicing the fuel pump module, the fuel system pressure must be released.

1. Perform the fuel pressure release procedure.
2. Disconnect and isolate the negative battery cable.
To gain access to the fuel pump use one of the following procedures:
   a. Tilt the middle seat forward to gain access to the fuel pump
   b. Remove the middle seat molded carpet. It will be necessary to spread the carpet open at the prop rods and the seat latch anchors.
   c. Or, Remove the rear lower seat mounting bolts
   d. Carefully remove the cushion (1) assembly past the seat belt latches.
3. Remove the fuel pump module access cover (1) by removing the screws (2).
4. Disconnect the fuel pump module wiring connector (4).
5. Disconnect the fuel lines.
6. Remove the fuel pump module locking ring using SAE Fuel Pump Lock Ring Wrench.
7. Remove the fuel pump module (4) from the fuel tank and discard the seal (gasket).

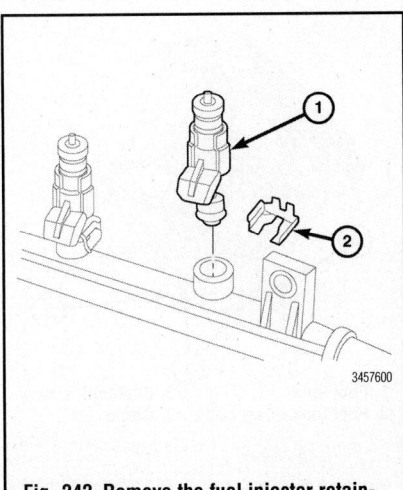

Fig. 242 Remove the fuel injector retaining clip(s) (2) from the fuel rail

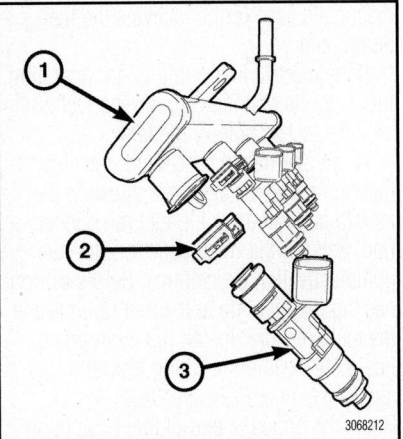

Fig. 243 Remove the fuel injector retaining clip(s) (2) from the fuel rail (1)

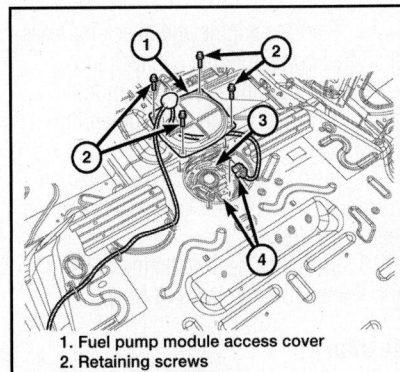

1. Fuel pump module access cover
2. Retaining screws
3. Fuel pump module
4. Fuel pump module wring connector

Fig. 244 Remove the fuel pump module access cover (1) by removing the screws

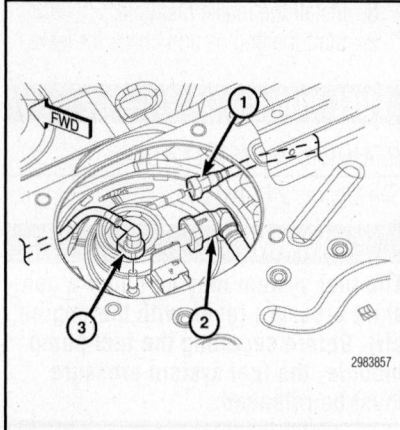

Fig. 245 Connect the return (1), fuel supply (2), and vapor (3) lines to the fuel pump module

To install:

8. Align the fuel pump module to the alignment tabs for proper sending unit float operation.

9. Using a new seal (gasket), install the fuel pump module into the fuel tank opening.

10. Position the lockring over top of fuel pump module.

11. Install the fuel pump module locking ring using SAE Fuel Pump Lock Ring Wrench

   a. Position the tool into the locking ring and turn the ring till the tabs are locked into the notches.

12. Connect the return (1), fuel supply (2), and vapor (3) lines to the fuel pump module.

13. Connect the fuel pump module wiring harness connector.

14. Connect the negative battery cable and tighten nut to 45 in. lb. (5 Nm).

➡ **Allow time for air to purge from the fuel lines.**

15. Start the engine and check for leaks at all fuel pump module connections.

16. Position the fuel pump module cover (1) into position and tighten the screws (2).

17. Install the rear lower seat cushion (1). Guide the seat belt latches through the rear of the seat.

18. Install the seat mounting bolts (3) and tighten to 30 ft. lbs. (40 Nm).

Auxiliary

See Figure 246.

1. Disconnect and isolate the negative battery cable.

2. Remove the auxiliary fuel tank.

3. Disengage the auxiliary fuel pump (1)

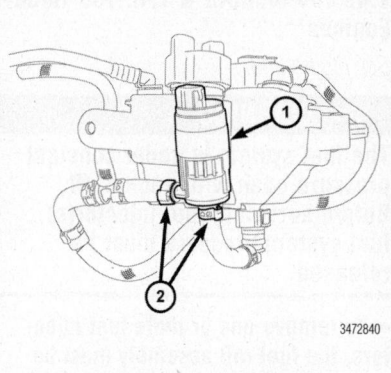

Fig. 246 Disengage the auxiliary fuel pump (1) from the auxiliary fuel tank and disconnect the fuel hoses (2) from the pump.

from the auxiliary fuel tank and disconnect the fuel hoses (2) from the pump.

To install:

4. Connect the fuel hoses (2) to the auxiliary fuel pump (1) and install the pump to the auxiliary fuel tank.

5. Install the auxiliary fuel tank.

6. Connect the negative battery cable and tighten nut to 45 inch lbs. (5 Nm).

FUEL TANK

DRAINING

✳✳ WARNING

The fuel system may be under constant fuel pressure even with the engine off. This pressure must be released before servicing the fuel tank.

Two different procedures may be used to drain the fuel tank; through the fuel pump module access hole on the tank, or using a diagnostic scan tool to activate the fuel pump relay.

If the electric fuel pump is not operating, fuel must be drained through the fuel pump module access hole in the tank

As an alternative procedure, the electric fuel pump may be activated allowing the tank to be drained at the fuel rail connection. Refer to the diagnostic tool for fuel pump activation procedures. Before disconnecting the fuel line at the fuel rail, release the fuel pressure. Install the appropriate Fuel Line Adapters / Fitting from the Gas and Diesel Fuel Pressure/Decay Tester. Route the opposite end of this hose to an approved gasoline draining station. Activate the fuel pump and drain the tank until empty.

REMOVAL & INSTALLATION

See Figure 247.

1. Disconnect and isolate the negative battery cable.

2. Remove the fuel pump module.

3. Remove the fuel from the fuel tank.

4. Replace the fuel access hole cover to reduce fuel odor.

5. Raise and support the vehicle.

6. Remove the muffler (2) and resonator (3)

7. Remove the fuel filler connector (5) from the fuel tank (3).

➡ **The heat shield and the fuel tank support straps are part of the fuel tank and do not require being removed from the tank. If the fuel tank is being replaced. The new tank will have the support straps and heat shield mounted.**

8. Using a suitable jack. Support the fuel tank.

9. Remove the fuel tank (1) from the vehicle.

To install:

10. Install the fuel pump module.

11. Position the fuel tank on a suitable stand to be raised into the vehicle. Tighten the fuel tank strap bolts (2) to 26 ft. lbs. (35 Nm).

12. Install the fuel filler connector tube onto the fuel tank.

13. Install the muffler and resonator.

14. Lower the vehicle.

15. Connect the fuel lines and vapor lines.

16. Connect the fuel pump module electrical connector.

17. Install the access cover. Tighten screws.

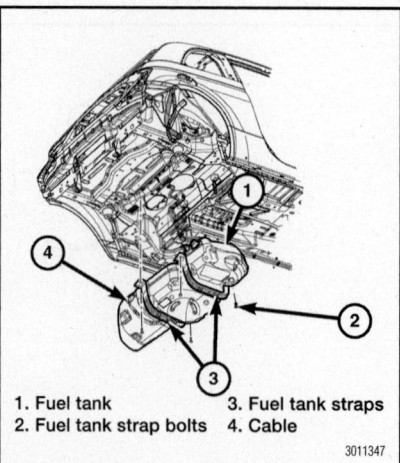

1. Fuel tank	3. Fuel tank straps
2. Fuel tank strap bolts	4. Cable

Fig. 247 Remove the fuel tank (1) from the vehicle

18. Install the lower rear seat .
19. Fill tank with fuel and install fuel fill cap.
20. Connect the negative battery cable.
21. Run vehicle. Inspect for leaks.

Auxiliary

See Figures 248 and 249.

1. Disconnect and isolate the negative battery cable.
2. Disconnect the electrical connectors (2) from the auxiliary fuel level sensor.
3. Disconnect the electrical connector (3) from the auxiliary fuel pump.
4. Reposition the pressurized coolant bottle.
5. Remove the bolt (2) and disengage the auxiliary fuel tank (1) from the grommets.
6. If necessary, remove the auxiliary fuel tank cap and drain the fuel from the tank.
7. If required, remove the auxiliary fuel pump from the auxiliary fuel tank.
8. If required, remove the auxiliary fuel level sensor from the auxiliary fuel tank.

To install:

9. If removed, install the auxiliary fuel level sensor to the auxiliary fuel tank.
10. If removed, install the auxiliary fuel pump to the auxiliary fuel tank.
11. Engage the auxiliary fuel tank (1) to the grommets and install the bolt (2).
12. Install the pressurized coolant bottle.
13. Connect the electrical connector (3) to the auxiliary fuel pump.
14. Connect the electrical connectors (2) to the auxiliary fuel level sensor.
15. Connect the negative battery cable and tighten nut to 45 inch lbs. (5 Nm).

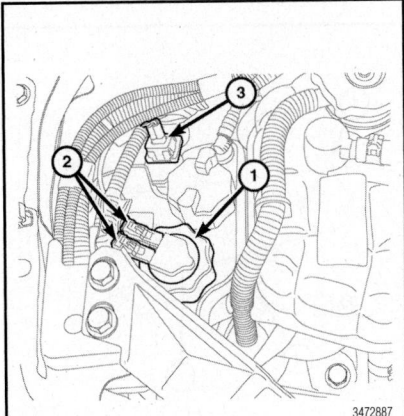

Fig. 248 Disconnect the electrical connectors (2) from the auxiliary fuel level sensor

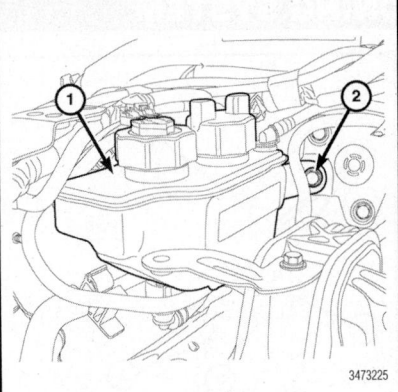

Fig. 249 Remove the bolt (2) and disengage the auxiliary fuel tank (1) from the grommets

THROTTLE BODY

REMOVAL & INSTALLATION

1.4L 8V Engine

> ※※ **CAUTION**
>
> **Never have the ignition key in the ON position when checking the throttle body shaft for a binding condition. This may set DTC's.**

1. Disconnect and isolate the negative battery cable.
2. Remove the air cleaner assembly.
3. Disconnect the electrical connector from the Electronic Throttle Control (ETC) and disengage the ETC harness from the clip on the throttle body.
4. Remove four throttle body mounting bolts and remove the throttle body from the intake m
5. Check the condition of the throttle body-to-intake manifold seal. The seal can be reused if not damaged.

To install:

6. Check the condition of the throttle body-to-intake manifold seal. The seal can be reused if not damaged.
7. Clean the mating surfaces of the throttle body and intake manifold.
8. Install the throttle body and tighten the mounting bolts in a criss-cross pattern sequence to 80 inch lbs. (9 Nm).
9. Connect the electrical connector (1) to the Electronic Throttle Control (ETC) and secure the ETC harness to the clip on the throttle body.
10. Install the air cleaner assembly.
11. Connect the negative battery cable and tighten nut to inch lbs. (5 Nm).

1.4L 16V MultiAir & 1.4L 16V Turbo Engines

See Figure 250.

➡**Never have the ignition key in the ON position when checking the throttle body shaft for a binding condition. This may set DTC's.**

1. Disconnect and isolate the negative battery cable.
2. Remove the engine cover.
3. Remove the air cleaner assembly.
4. Disconnect the electrical connector (3) from the Electronic Throttle Control (ETC) (4) and disengage the ETC harness from the clip (2) on the throttle body.
5. Remove four throttle body mounting bolts and remove the throttle body from the intake manifold.
6. Check the condition of the throttle body-to-intake manifold seal. The seal can be reused if not damaged.

To install:

7. Check the condition of the throttle body-to-intake manifold seal. The seal can be reused if not damaged.
8. Clean the mating surfaces of the throttle body and intake manifold.
9. Position the throttle body to the intake manifold.
10. Install the throttle body mounting bolts and tighten in a criss-cross pattern sequence to 80 inch lbs. (9 Nm).
11. Connect the electrical connector to the Electronic Throttle Control (ETC) and secure the ETC harness to the clip on the throttle body.
12. Install the air cleaner assembly.
13. Install the engine cover.
14. Connect the negative battery cable and tighten nut to 45 inch lbs. (5 Nm).

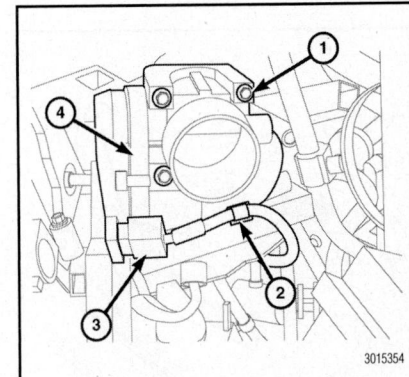

Fig. 250 Disconnect the electrical connector (3) from the Electronic Throttle Control (ETC) (4) and disengage the ETC harness from the clip (2) on the throttle body

HEATING & AIR CONDITIONING SYSTEM

BLOWER MOTOR

REMOVAL & INSTALLATION
See Figures 251 and 252.

✳✳ WARNING

Disable the airbag system before attempting any steering wheel, steering column or instrument panel component diagnosis or service. Disconnect and isolate the negative battery (ground) cable. Wait two minutes for the airbag system capacitor to discharge before performing further diagnosis or service. This is the only sure way to disable the airbag system. Failure to follow these instructions may result in possible serious or fatal injury.

✳✳ WARNING

The blower motor power module may get very hot during normal operation. If the blower motor was turned on prior to servicing the power module, wait at least five minutes to allow the module heat sink to cool before performing diagnosis or service. Failure to take this precaution may result in possible serious injury.

1. Disconnect and isolate the negative battery cable.
2. Remove the passenger side silencer panel
3. Remove the screw (2) that secures the passenger side console closeout cover (1).
4. Disengage the console closeout cover rear retaining clips.

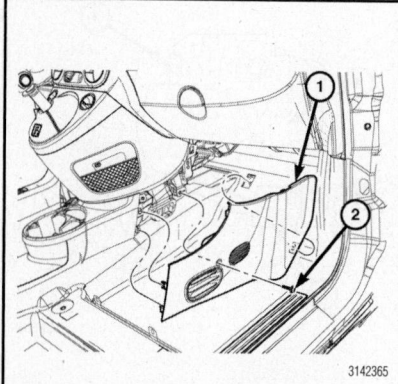

Fig. 251 Remove the screw (2) that secures the passenger side console closeout cover (1).

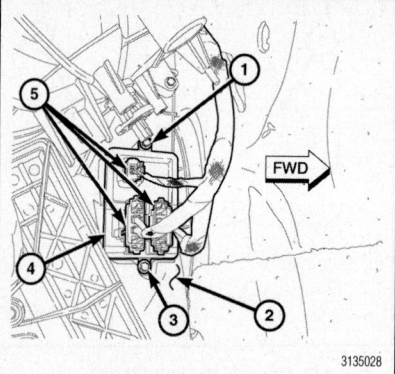

Fig. 252 Disconnect the three wire harness connectors (5) from the blower motor power module (4), located at the right front of the HVAC housing (2)

5. Pull the console closeout cover rearward to disengage the front retaining tab and remove the cover.
6. Remove the recirculation door actuator
7. Disconnect the three wire harness connectors (5) from the blower motor power module (4), located at the right front of the HVAC housing (2).
8. Remove the two screws (1 and 3) that secure the blower motor power module to the HVAC housing and remove the power module.

To install:

9. Install the blower motor power module to the right side of the HVAC housing (2) and install the two retaining screws. Tighten the screws to 7 inch lbs. (0.8 Nm)
10. Connect the three wire harness connectors to the blower motor power module.
11. Install the recirculation door actuator
12. Position the passenger side console closeout cover and engage the front retaining tab.
13. Carefully engage the console closeout cover rear retaining clips and install the screw. Tighten the screw securely.
14. Install the passenger side silencer panel
15. Reconnect the negative battery cable.

HEATER CORE

REMOVAL & INSTALLATION
See Figures 253 and 254.

✳✳ WARNING

Disable the airbag system before attempting any steering wheel, steering column or instrument panel com-

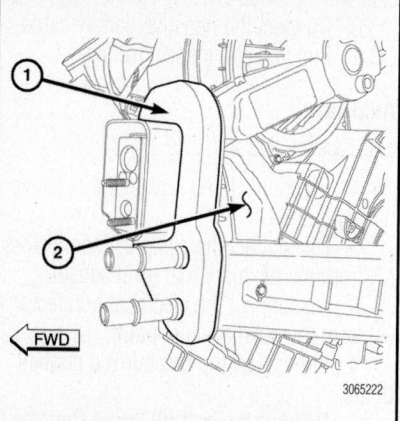

Fig. 253 Remove the foam seal (1) from the flange at the front of the HVAC housing (2)

ponent diagnosis or service. Disconnect and isolate the negative battery (ground) cable, then wait two minutes for the airbag system capacitor to discharge before performing further diagnosis or service. This is the only sure way to disable the airbag system. Failure to follow these instructions may result in accidental airbag deployment and possible serious or fatal injury.

1. Remove the HVAC housing and place it on a workbench.

➡ **If the foam seal at the front of the HVAC housing is deformed or damaged, it must be replaced.**

2. Remove the foam seal (1) from the flange at the front of the HVAC housing (2).
3. Remove the three screws (1 and 2)

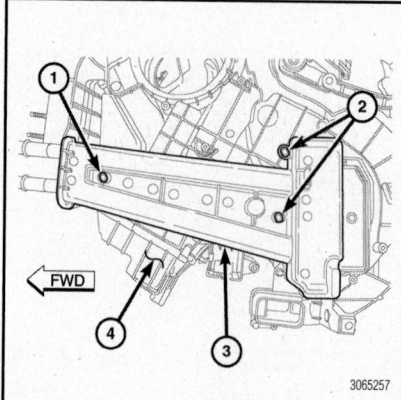

Fig. 254 Remove the three screws (1 and 2) that secure the heater core cover (3) to the left side of the HVAC housing.

that secure the heater core cover (3) to the left side of the HVAC housing.

4. Remove the heater core cover from the HVAC housing.

5. Carefully pull the heater core out of the left side of the HVAC housing.

To install:

✳✳ WARNING

Use care when removing the heater core. Do not apply excessive force to the heater core tubes. Failure to follow these instructions can result in a possible engine coolant leak and serious or fatal injury.

➡ **If the foam seal around the heater core is deformed or damaged, it must be replaced.**

6. Carefully install the heater core into the left side of the HVAC housing. Do not force the heater core into the housing. Do not push on the heater core tubes. Apply pressure on the heater core side tank only.

7. Install the heater core cover onto the left side of the HVAC housing.

8. Install the three screws that secure the heater core cover to the HVAC housing. Tighten the screws to 7 inch lbs. (0.8 Nm).

➡ **If the foam seal at the front of the HVAC housing is deformed or damaged, it must be replaced.**

9. Install the foam seal onto the flange at the front of the HVAC housing.

10. Install the HVAC housing.

11. If the heater core is being replaced, flush the cooling system.

STEERING

POWER STEERING GEAR

REMOVAL & INSTALLATION

See Figures 255 through 258 and 263.

1. Using a steering wheel holder, lock the steering wheel in place to keep it from rotating. This keeps the clockspring in the proper orientation.

2. Remove pinch bolt (3) and separate intermediate shaft (2) from steering gear shaft.

3. Raise and support the vehicle.

4. Remove the wheel mounting bolts (1), then the tire and wheel assembly.

5. Remove the nut (2) and pinch bolt clamping the ball joint stud (1) to the knuckle (3).

6. Remove the nut (4) attaching the outer tie rod (5) to the knuckle (3).

7. On each side of the steering gear, separate the tie rod end from the knuckle using a ball joint remover tool or equivalent.

8. If equipped, remove the engine belly pan.

✳✳ CAUTION

Use care when separating the ball joint stud from the knuckle, so the ball joint seal does not get cut or compressed excessively.

9. Using the ball joint remover tool, separate the ball joint stud from the knuckle.

10. While holding the link stud stationary, remove the nut attaching the stabilizer link to the strut. Separate the stabilizer link stud from the strut.

11. At each end of the stabilizer bar, while holding the stabilizer bar link lower stud stationary, remove the nut securing the link to the stabilizer bar.

12. Remove the rear engine isolator.

13. Remove the exhaust pipe.

14. Remove four bolts (1) and the tunnel support brace (2).

➡ **The steering gear bolts must be removed before attempting to lower the front crossmember so that the crossmember can be moved rearward to dis-**
engage it from the front support beams. If the steering gear mounting bolts are not removed before trying to move the crossmember rearward, the steering gear pinion shaft will hit the body.

15. Remove steering gear bolts.

➡ **Before removing the front suspension crossmember from the vehicle, the location of the crossmember must be marked on the body of the vehicle. Do this so the crossmember can be relocated, upon reinstallation, against the body of vehicle in the same location as before removal. If the front suspension crossmember is not reinstalled in exactly the same location as before removal, the preset front wheel alignment settings (caster and camber) may be lost.**

16. Mark the location of the front crossmember on the body near each mounting bolt using a marker or crayon.

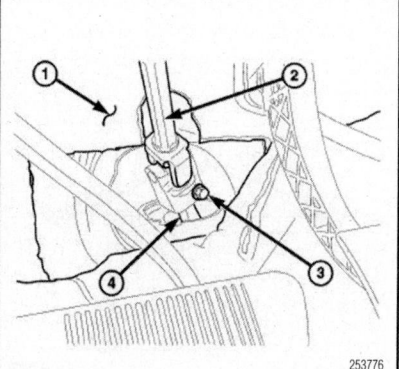

253776

Fig. 255 Remove pinch bolt (3) and separate intermediate shaft (2) from steering gear shaft

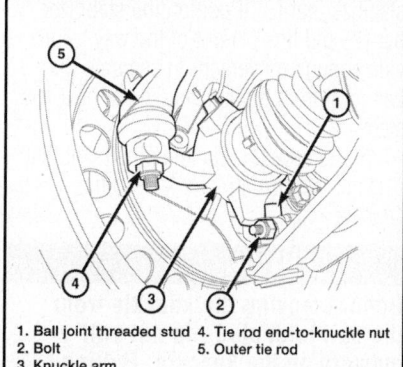

1. Ball joint threaded stud 4. Tie rod end-to-knuckle nut
2. Bolt   5. Outer tie rod
3. Knuckle arm

3069991

Fig. 256 Remove the nut (2) and pinch bolt clamping the ball joint stud (1) to the knuckle (3)

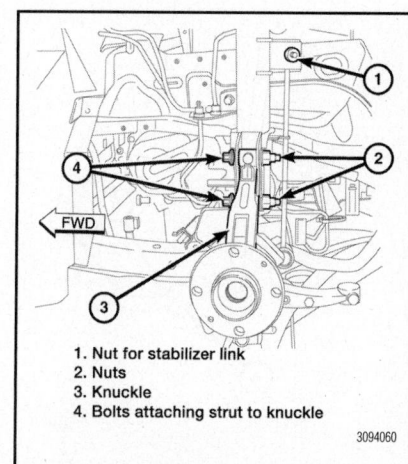

1. Nut for stabilizer link
2. Nuts
3. Knuckle
4. Bolts attaching strut to knuckle

3094060

Fig. 257 remove the nut (1) attaching the stabilizer link to the strut.

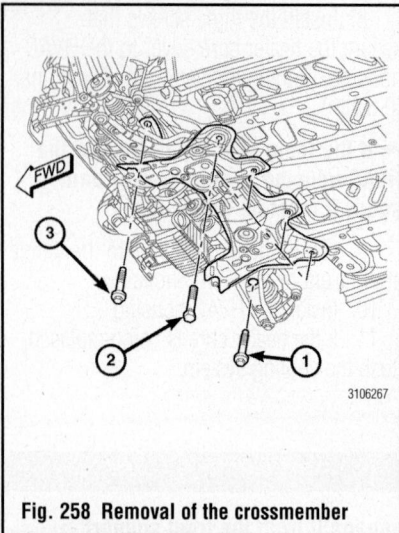

Fig. 258 Removal of the crossmember

17. Remove the bolts securing the stabilizer bushing retainers to the crossmember and discard the bolts.

18. Support the front crossmember with a transmission jack.

19. Remove the four mounting bolts (2) securing the front crossmember to the body.

20. Remove the two bolts (1, 3) securing the front crossmember to the body.

21. Move the jack and crossmember rearward to disengage the crossmember from the front support beams.

22. Slowly lower the crossmember until there is enough space present to remove the steering gear between the crossmember and the body.

23. Remove the steering gear from the crossmember.

To install:

➡ **While raising the crossmember, pay close attention to the steering rack pinion shaft so that it properly fits up and into the dash panel boot between the rack and body.**

24. Rotate the stabilizer bar up and install the steering gear on the crossmember.

25. Slowly raise the crossmember into mounted position using the transmission jack matching the crossmember to the marked locations on the body made during removal. Ensure that the steering rack pinion shaft is aligned with the dash panel boot opening.

26. Install four NEW stabilizer bushing retainer bolts and tighten to 18 ft. lbs. (25 Nm)

27. Install the four mounting bolts securing the front crossmember to the body. Tighten the crossmember mounting bolts to 122 ft. lbs. (165 Nm).

28. Install two mounting bolts securing the front crossmember to the body. Tighten the bolts to 92 ft. lbs. (125 Nm)

29. Remove the transmission jack.

30. Install tunnel support brace. Install mounting bolts and tighten to 74 ft. lbs. (100 Nm).

31. Install the rear engine mount.

32. Install the exhaust pipe.

33. Attach the upper stabilizer link at the strut on each side of the vehicle. While holding the link stud stationary, install and tighten each nut to 37 ft. lbs. (50 Nm).

34. Attach the stabilizer bar link at each end of the stabilizer bar . At each link, install and tighten the nut while holding the stabilizer bar link lower stud stationary. Tighten the nuts to 37 ft. lbs. (50 Nm).

35. Install outer tie rod end to knuckle. Install nut and tighten to 30 ft. lbs. (40 Nm).

36. Install lower ball joint stud to knuckle and install retaining nut . Tighten nut to 48 ft. lbs. (65 Nm).

37. If equipped, install the engine belly pan.

38. On each side of the vehicle, install the tire and wheel assembly.

39. Lower the vehicle.

40. Verify the front wheels of vehicle are in the straight-ahead position.

41. Install intermediate shaft to steering rack pinion shaft. Install a new pinch bolt and tighten to 40 ft. lbs. (55 Nm).

42. Perform wheel alignment as necessary.

SUSPENSION

LOWER CONTROL ARM

REMOVAL & INSTALLATION

See Figures 259 through 262.

➡ **Before proceeding, refer to the precautions.**

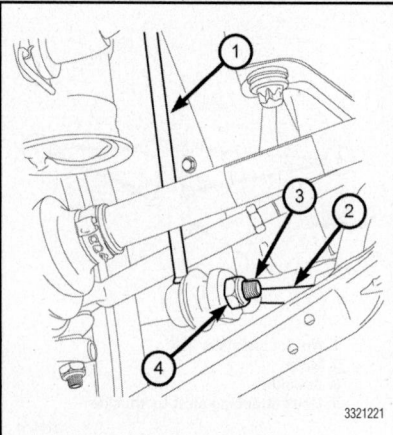

Fig. 259 Removal of the stabilizer bolts and link studs.

1. Remove front fascia.

2. Raise and support the vehicle.

3. Remove the wheel mounting bolts, then the tire and wheel assembly.

4. Remove the lower stabilizer link nut (4) on each side of the vehicle by holding each link stud (3) stationary. Separate the link stud (3) from the stabilizer bar (2). Position the stabilizer bar (2) and link (1) out of the way to provide enough movement to separate the ball joint from the knuckle in the next few steps.

5. Remove the nut and pinch bolt that is clamping the ball joint stud to the knuckle.

✳ CAUTION

Upon removing the knuckle from the ball joint stud, do not pull outward on the knuckle. Pulling the knuckle outward at this point can separate the inner C/V joint on the halfshaft thus damaging it.

FRONT SUSPENSION

✳ CAUTION

Use care when separating the ball joint stud from the knuckle, so the ball joint seal does not get cut or compressed excessively.

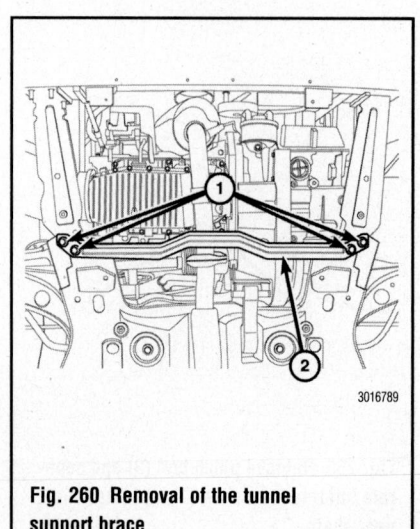

Fig. 260 Removal of the tunnel support brace

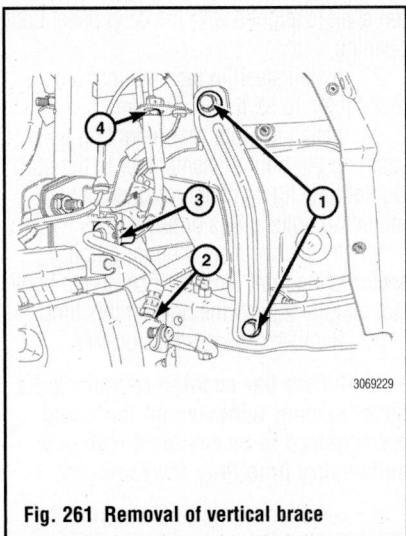

Fig. 261 Removal of vertical brace

6. Using a ball joint removal tool or equivalent, separate the ball joint stud from the knuckle.

7. Remove the belly pan.

8. Remove four bolts (1) and the tunnel support brace (2).

9. Remove two mounting bolts (1) and remove vertical brace from vehicle.

10. Remove front fascia support beams.

11. Remove the rear bolt and nut attaching the lower control arm to the front suspension crossmember. The nut and bolt are one-time use and must be discarded after removal.

12. Remove the front bolt (1) attaching the lower control arm (2) to the front suspension crossmember. The bolt is one-time use and must be discarded after removal.

13. Remove the lower control arm from the crossmember.

To install:

14. Place the lower control arm into the front suspension crossmember.

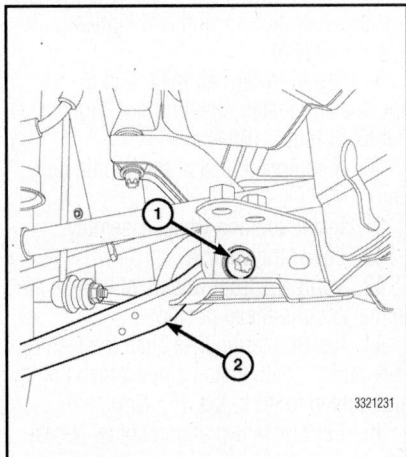

Fig. 262 Removal of the lower control arm

15. Insert a new rear bolt up through the crossmember and lower control arm. Install a new nut on the rear bolt but do not fully tighten.

➡ **The front lower control arm pivot bolt must be tightened to specification before the rear mounting bolt is tightened to specification.**

16. Insert a new lower control arm front pivot bolt but do not fully tighten the bolt.

17. Partially lower the hoist and place a floor jack under the control arm. Raise the floor jack until the lower control arm is at approximate ride height.

18. Tighten the lower control arm front pivot bolt to 80 ft. lbs. plus 45° additional rotation (110 Nm plus 45°).

19. Tighten the lower control arm rear mounting bolt while holding the nut to 80 ft. lbs. plus 45° additional rotation (110 Nm plus 45°).

20. Remove floor jack and return hoist to fully lifted position.

21. Install front support beams into front suspension crossmember.

22. Install tunnel support brace. Install mounting bolts and tighten to 74 ft. lbs. (100 Nm).

23. Install vertical brace and mounting bolts. Tighten bolts to 33 ft. lbs. (45 Nm).

24. Install the ball joint stud into the knuckle, aligning the bolt hole in the knuckle boss with the groove formed in the side of the ball joint stud.

25. Install a new ball joint stud pinch bolt and nut. Tighten the nut to 48 ft. lbs. (65 Nm).

➡ **Perform the following two steps on each side of the vehicle.**

26. Place stabilizer bar in position and install link stud to stabilizer bar.

27. Install stabilizer link nut and tighten to 37 ft. lbs. (50 Nm) while holding the link stud stationary.

28. Install the tire and wheel assembly.

29. Lower the vehicle.

30. Install the front fascia.

STABILIZER BAR

REMOVAL & INSTALLATION
See Figures 263 through 266.

➡ **Before proceeding, refer to the precautions.**

1. Using a steering wheel holder, lock the steering wheel in place to keep it from rotating. This keeps the clockspring in the proper orientation.

2. Remove pinch bolt (3) and separate

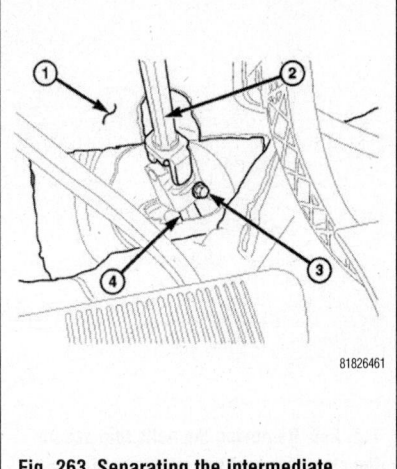

Fig. 263 Separating the intermediate shaft (2) from the steering gear shaft.

intermediate shaft (2) from steering gear shaft.

3. Raise and support the vehicle.

4. Remove wheel mounting bolts, then the tire and wheel assembly.

5. Remove the nut and pinch bolt clamping the ball joint stud to the knuckle.

6. Remove the nut attaching the outer tie rod to the knuckle.

7. On each side of the steering gear, separate the tie rod end from the knuckle using a tie rod removal tool or equivalent.

8. If equipped, remove the engine belly pan.

✳✳ CAUTION

Use care when separating the ball joint stud from the knuckle, so the ball joint seal does not get cut or compressed excessively.

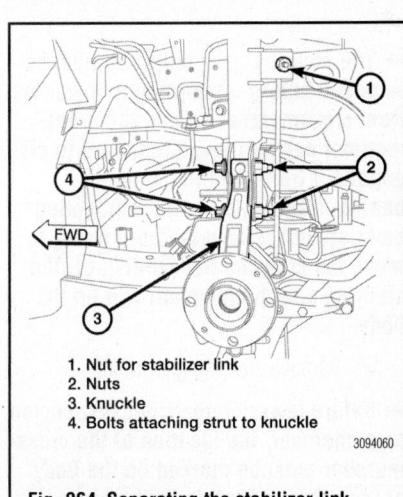

1. Nut for stabilizer link
2. Nuts
3. Knuckle
4. Bolts attaching strut to knuckle

Fig. 264 Separating the stabilizer link stud from the strut.

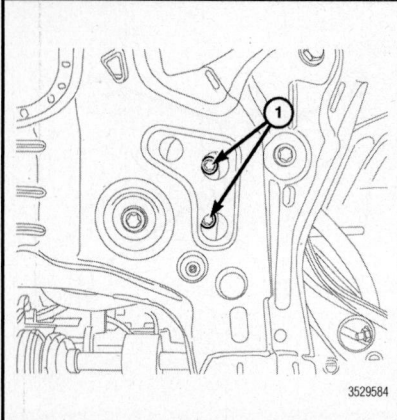

Fig. 265 Removing the bolts that secure the stabilizer bushing retainers (right side shown, left side similar)

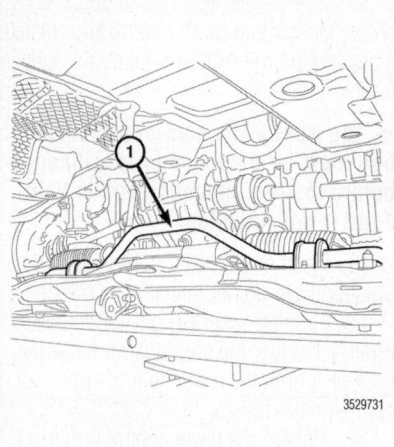

Fig. 266 Removing the stabilizer bar from the crossmember

9. Using a ball joint removal tool or equivalent, separate the ball joint stud from the knuckle.

10. While holding the stabilizer stud stationary, remove the nut (1) attaching the stabilizer link to the strut. Separate the stabilizer link stud from the strut.

11. At each end of the stabilizer bar, while holding the stabilizer bar link lower stud stationary, remove the nut securing the link to the stabilizer bar.

12. Remove rear engine mount insulator.

13. Remove the exhaust pipe .

14. Remove four bolts and the tunnel support brace.

15. Remove the right side bolts (1) securing the stabilizer bushing retainers to the crossmember. Discard these bolts, as they have a fastener adhesive on them and are one-time use.

16. Remove the left side bolts securing the stabilizer bushing retainers to the crossmember. Discard these bolts, as they have a fastener adhesive on them and are one-time use.

➡ **The steering gear bolts (2) must be removed before attempting to lower the front crossmember so that the crossmember can be moved rearward to disengage it from the front support beams. If the steering gear mounting bolts are not removed before trying to move the crossmember rearward, the steering gear pinion shaft will hit the body.**

17. Remove steering gear bolts.

➡ **Before lowering the front suspension crossmember, the location of the crossmember must be marked on the body of the vehicle. Do this so the crossmember can be relocated, upon rein-**

stallation, against the body of vehicle in the same location as before removal. If the front suspension crossmember is not reinstalled in exactly the same location as before removal, the preset front wheel alignment settings (caster and camber) may be lost.

18. Mark the location of the front crossmember on the body near each mounting bolt.

19. Support the crossmember with a transmission jack.

20. Remove the four rear mounting bolts (2) securing the front crossmember to the body.

21. Remove the two front bolts (1, 3) securing the front crossmember to the body.

22. Move the jack and crossmember rearward to disengage the crossmember from the front support beams.

23. Slowly lower the crossmember until there is enough space present to remove the stabilizer bar between the crossmember and the body.

24. Remove the stabilizer bar (1) from the crossmember.

To install:

➡ **While raising the crossmember, pay close attention to the steering rack pinion shaft so that it properly fits up and into the dash boot between the rack and body.**

25. Install the stabilizer bar, link ends first, over top of the crossmember. Curve the ends of the bar over the steering gear.

26. Slowly raise the crossmember into mounted position using the transmission jack, matching the crossmember to the marked locations on the body made during removal. Ensure that the steering rack pin-

ion shaft is aligned with the dash panel boot opening.

27. Install steering rack mounting bolts and tighten to 55 ft. lbs. (75 Nm).

28. Install the four rear mounting bolts securing the front crossmember to the body. Do not fully tighten the crossmember mounting bolts at this time.

29. Install two front mounting bolts securing the front crossmember to the body. Do not fully tighten the bolts at this time.

30. Remove the transmission jack.

➡ **Stabilizer bar cushion retainer bolts have fastener adhesive on them and are required to be replaced with new bolts every time they are removed.**

31. Install four new bolts securing the stabilizer bushing retainers to the crossmember. Tighten the right side stabilizer bar cushion retainer bolts to 18 ft. lbs. (25 Nm).

32. Tighten the left side stabilizer bar cushion retaining bolts to 18 ft. lbs. (25 Nm).

➡ **Ensure that the front support beams are inserted into the crossmember front clevis prior to installing the tunnel support brace bolts in the next step.**

33. Install tunnel support brace. Install mounting bolts and tighten to (74 ft. lbs.100 Nm).

34. Install rear engine mount insulator.

35. Install the exhaust pipe.

36. Attach the upper stabilizer link at the strut on each side of the vehicle. While holding the stabilizer stud stationary, install and tighten each nut to 37 ft. lbs. (50 Nm).

37. Attach the stabilizer bar link at each end of the stabilizer bar . At each link, install and tighten the nut while holding the stabilizer bar link lower stud stationary. Tighten the nuts to (37 ft. lbs.50 Nm).

38. Install outer tie rod end to knuckle. Install nut on tie rod stud and tighten to 30 ft. lbs. (40 Nm).

39. Install lower ball joint stud to knuckle and install retaining nut. Tighten nut to 48 ft. lbs. (65 Nm).

40. If equipped, install the engine belly pan.

41. Install tire and wheel assembly.

42. Lower the vehicle.

43. Verify the front wheels of vehicle are in the straight-ahead position.

44. Install intermediate shaft to steering rack pinion shaft. Install a new pinch bolt and tighten to 40 ft. lbs. (55 Nm).

45. Perform wheel alignment as necessary.

46. After the alignment has been performed, tighten four rear mounting bolts to

122 ft. lbs. (165 Nm) and tighten two front mounting bolts to 92 ft. lbs. (125 Nm).

STEERING KNUCKLE

REMOVAL & INSTALLATION

See Figures 267 and 268.

➡ **Before proceeding, refer to the precautions.**

1. Raise and support the vehicle.
2. Remove the wheel mounting bolts, then the tire and wheel assembly.
3. Remove retaining clip from hub nut.
4. While keeping the hub from rotating, use a 12 point 36mm socket or equivalent to remove the hub nut and discard.
5. Access and remove the front brake rotor.
6. Remove the screw (1) fastening the wheel speed sensor head to the knuckle. Pull the sensor head out of the knuckle.
7. Remove the nut and pinch bolt clamping the ball joint stud to the knuckle.
8. Remove the nut attaching the outer tie rod to the knuckle.
9. Release the outer tie rod end from the knuckle using a tie rod remover tool or equivalent
10. Remove the outer tie rod from the knuckle.
11. While holding the stabilizer stud stationary, remove the nut (1) attaching the stabilizer link to the strut. Separate the stabilizer link stud from the strut.
12. While holding the bolt heads stationary, remove the two nuts (2) from the bolts (4) attaching the strut to the knuckle (3).
13. Remove the two bolts (4) attaching the strut to the knuckle (3).

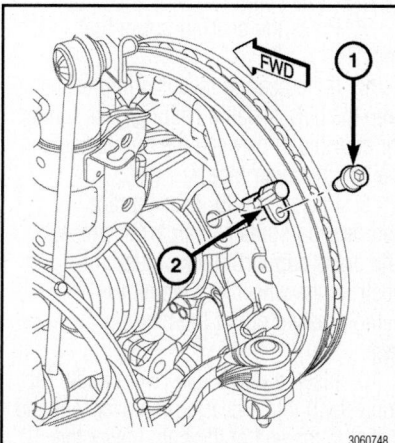

Fig. 267 Removing the wheel speed sensor nut

※ **CAUTION**

Use care when separating the ball joint stud from the knuckle, so the ball joint seal does not get cut or compressed excessively.

14. Using a ball joint remover tool or equivalent, separate the ball joint stud from the knuckle.

➡ **Do not allow the half shaft to hang by the inner C/V joint; it must be supported to keep the joint from separating during this operation.**

15. Pull the knuckle off the half shaft outer C/V joint splines and remove the knuckle from the vehicle.

To install:
16. Slide the hub of the knuckle onto the splines of the halfshaft outer C/V joint.
17. Install the knuckle onto the ball joint stud aligning the bolt hole in the knuckle boss with the groove formed into the side of the ball joint stud.
18. Install a new ball joint stud pinch bolt and nut. Tighten the nut to 48 ft. lbs. (65 Nm).

➡ **Before tightening the bolts, press the knuckle toward the vehicle to achieve the most negative camber. If this is not done, it is possible to have positive camber which will negatively impact vehicle handling.**

19. Position the lower end of the strut assembly in line with the upper end of the knuckle, aligning the mounting holes. Install the two mounting bolts from the front side of the vehicle.
20. Install the nuts on the two bolts. Press the knuckle inward towards the vehicle, and tighten the nuts to 55 ft. lbs. (75 Nm).
21. Install the outer tie rod ball stud into the hole in the knuckle arm. Start the tie rod end-to-knuckle nut on the stud. While holding the tie rod end stud with a wrench, tighten the nut with a wrench or crowfoot wrench to 30 ft. lbs. (40 Nm).
22. Install the wheel speed sensor head into the knuckle. Install the mounting screw and tighten it to 62 inch lbs. (7 Nm).
23. Install the brake rotor, disc brake caliper, and adapter.

➡ **Always install a new hub nut. The original hub nut is one-time use only and must be discarded when removed**

24. Clean all foreign matter from the threads of the halfshaft stub shaft.

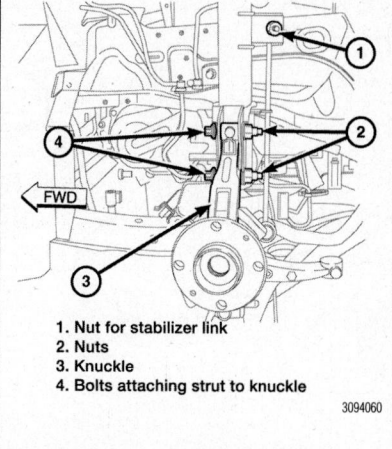

1. Nut for stabilizer link
2. Nuts
3. Knuckle
4. Bolts attaching strut to knuckle

Fig. 268 Removing the strut from the knuckle

25. Install a new hub nut on the end of the halfshaft stub shaft. While a helper applies the brakes to keep the hub from rotating, use a 12-point 36mm socket (or equivalent) to tighten the hub nut to 229 ft. lbs. (310 Nm).
26. Perform staking procedure described in the next step.

➡ **The hub nut must be staked. Both edges must be split and bent into the shape shown. The staking must be in the opposite direction from the forward rotation of the wheel**

27. Stake the hub nut as shown.
28. Install the tire and wheel assembly.
29. Lower the vehicle.

STRUT & SPRING ASSEMBLY

REMOVAL & INSTALLATION

See Figures 269 through 271.

➡ **Before proceeding, refer to the precautions.**

➡ **If both strut assemblies are to be removed, mark the strut assemblies right or left and keep the parts separated to avoid mix-up. Not all parts of the strut assembly are interchangeable side-to-side.**

1. Raise and support the vehicle.
2. Remove the wheel mounting bolts, then the tire and wheel assembly.
3. Separate the speed sensor cable from the strut.
4. While holding the stabilizer bar link stud stationary, remove the nut securing the link to the strut.
5. While holding the bolt heads stationary, remove the two nuts from the bolts attaching the strut to the knuckle.

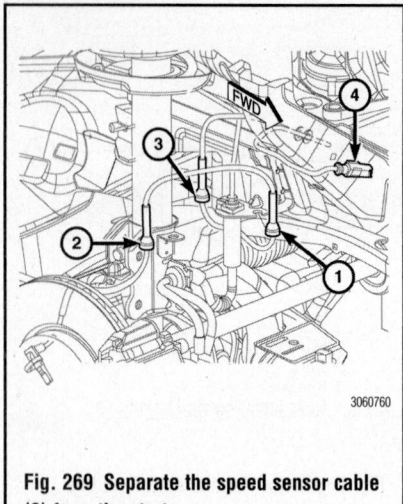

Fig. 269 Separate the speed sensor cable (2) from the strut

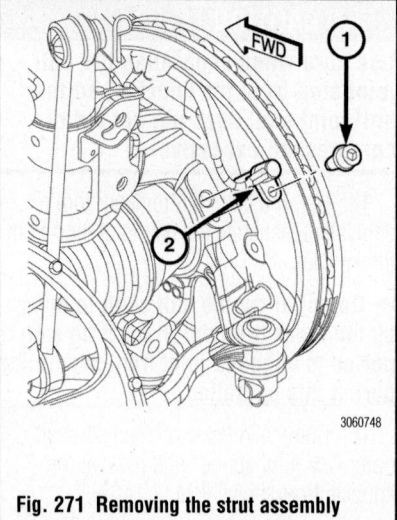

Fig. 271 Removing the strut assembly

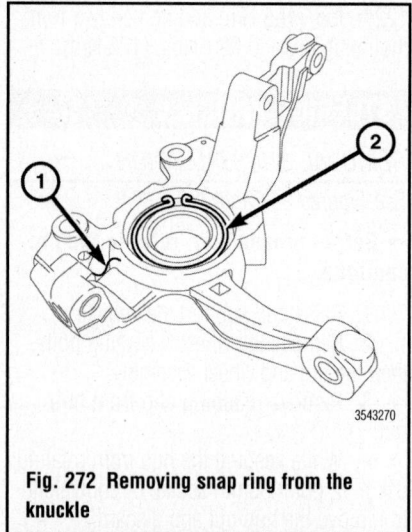

Fig. 272 Removing snap ring from the knuckle

6. Remove the two bolts attaching the strut to the knuckle.

7. Lower the vehicle just enough to open the hood without allowing the tires to touch the floor.

8. Remove the strut cap (1) from the top of the strut mount (2) and discard. A new strut cap will be required for installation.

➡ **The internal hex of the strut rod must be held stationary while removing the strut mounting nut. Failure to do so will cause internal damage to the strut.**

9. While holding the internal hex of the strut rod stationary, remove the nut (1) attaching the strut assembly (3) upper mount to the strut tower.

10. Remove the rebound plate (2) and strut assembly (3) from the vehicle.

To install:

➡ **The internal hex of the strut rod must be held stationary while tighten-**

ing the mounting nut on the strut. Failure to do so will cause internal damage to the strut.

11. Raise the strut assembly into the strut tower, aligning the stud on the strut assembly upper mount with the hole in strut tower. Install the rebound plate and a new mounting nut on the stud. While holding the inner hex of the strut rod stationary, tighten the nut to 33 ft. lbs. (45 Nm).

12. Install a new strut cap on the top of the strut mounting location.

➡ **Before tightening the bolts, press the knuckle toward the vehicle to achieve the most negative camber. If this is not done, it is possible to have positive camber which will negatively impact vehicle handling.**

13. Position the lower end of the strut assembly in line with the upper end of the knuckle, aligning the mounting holes. Install the two attaching bolts from the front side of the vehicle and install the nuts.

14. Press the knuckle inward towards the vehicle, and tighten the nuts to 55 ft. lbs. (75 Nm).

15. Attach the stabilizer bar link to the strut. Install and tighten the nut while holding the stabilizer bar link stud stationary. Tighten the nut to 37 ft. lbs. (50 Nm).

16. Secure the wheel speed sensor to the strut.

17. Install the tire and wheel assembly.

18. Lower the vehicle.

WHEEL BEARINGS

REMOVAL & INSTALLATION

See Figure 272.

➡ **Before proceeding, refer to the precautions.**

➡ **The removal and installation of the wheel bearing and hub from the knuckle is only to be done with the knuckle removed from the vehicle.**

1. Remove the steering knuckle from the vehicle.

2. Remove the three dust shield mounting bolts and remove the dust shield.

3. Install knuckle into an arbor press, making sure the knuckle is level and supported by spacer blocks.

4. Press the hub out of the knuckle using driver handle or equivalent and bearing remover

5. Remove the snap ring (2) from the knuckle (1) using an appropriate pair of snap ring pliers.

6. Install knuckle into the press, making sure the knuckle is level and supported by spacer blocks.

7. Press the bearing out of the knuckle.

8. If the bearing race is still pressed onto the hub, install a bearing/gear splitter (or equivalent) between the hub flange and the bearing inner race.

9. Place the hub, bearing race and bearing splitter in an arbor press. The press support blocks must not obstruct the wheel hub while it is being pressed out of the bearing race.

10. Insert a universal driver handle (or equivalent) into a bearing remover tool and install in the end of the hub. Lower the arbor press ram and remove the hub from the bearing race.

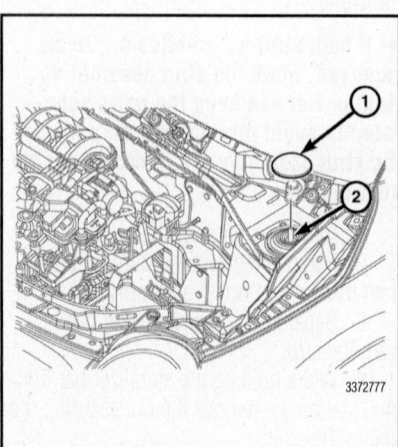

Fig. 270 strut cap (1) from the top of the strut mount (2)

To install:

✷✷ CAUTION

When installing the wheel bearing in the knuckle it is important to place the side of bearing with the wheel speed sensor magnetic encoder ring (dark band) facing inboard. Otherwise, the wheel speed sensor will not operate correctly.

11. Place the knuckle into arbor press, making sure that it is level on the press blocks.

12. Place the new wheel bearing into the bore of the knuckle so that the magnetic encoder ring is visible (facing up). Be sure the wheel bearing is placed squarely into the bore.

13. Install the wheel bearing into the knuckle using a suitable tool until the bearing is bottomed in the bore of the knuckle.

14. Install a new snap ring in the

knuckle using an appropriate pair of snap ring pliers. Make sure the snap ring is fully seated.

15. Place the knuckle in an arbor press supporting the knuckle from underneath

16. Place the hub in the wheel bearing making sure it is square with the bearing inner race.

17. Install hub until it is bottomed in the bore of the knuckle.

18. Remove the knuckle and tools from the arbor press.

SUSPENSION

SHOCK ABSORBER

REMOVAL & INSTALLATION

See Figure 273.

➡ **Before proceeding, refer to the precautions.**

1. Raise and support the vehicle.

2. Remove the wheel mounting bolts, then the rear tire and wheel assembly.

3. Position a transmission jack or equivalent under the center of the axle raising it enough to support the axle.

4. Remove the shock absorber lower mounting bolt (4).

5. Remove the shock absorber upper mounting bolt (2), then remove the shock absorber (3) from the vehicle.

To install:

6. Install the shock absorber by first attaching the top shock absorber eye to the body using the upper mounting bolt. Do not fully tighten the bolt at this time.

7. Raise or lower the jack as necessary until the shock absorber lower mounting

bolt can be inserted through the axle flange and the shock absorber lower mounting eye.

8. Tighten the lower mounting bolt to 74 ft. lbs. (100 Nm).

9. Tighten the upper shock absorber mounting bolt to 52 ft. lbs. (70 Nm).

10. Remove the jack.

11. Install tire and wheel assembly.

12. Lower the vehicle.

SPRINGS

REMOVAL & INSTALLATION

➡ **Before proceeding, refer to the precautions.**

1. Raise and support the vehicle.

2. On both sides of the vehicle, remove the wheel mounting bolts, then the rear tire and wheel assembly.

3. Position a transmission jack or equivalent under the center of the axle, raising it enough to support the axle.

4. On each side, remove the lower mounting bolt securing the shock absorber to the axle.

5. Lower the transmission jack until the coil springs can be removed from the axle.

6. Remove the coil springs and rubber isolators.

To install:

➡ **The part tag on the coil spring has a specific color and pattern which indicate different load ratings. When replacing coil springs, the new coil spring must have the same part tag as the spring that was removed. Also, the part tag must be installed to the top mount.**

7. Place the coil springs on top of the axle spring perches, ensuring that the part tag is on the end facing up and the bottom "D" shape of the coil spring matches the "D" shape in the lower isolator.

REAR SUSPENSION

8. Raise the transmission jack guiding the coil springs into the spring mounting brackets on the body of the vehicle. Raise the jack until the shock absorber lower mounting bolts can be installed though the axle brackets and shock absorber lower mounting eyes.

9. With the axle at approximate ride height, tighten the lower mounting bolts to 74 ft. lbs. (100 Nm).

10. Remove the transmission jack.

11. On both sides of the vehicle, install the tire and wheel assembly.

12. Lower the vehicle.

13. Check for proper vehicle curb height.

WHEEL BEARINGS

REMOVAL & INSTALLATION

See Figures 274 and 275.

➡ **Before proceeding, refer to the precautions.**

1. Raise and support the vehicle.

2. Remove the wheel mounting bolts (1), then the rear tire and wheel assembly.

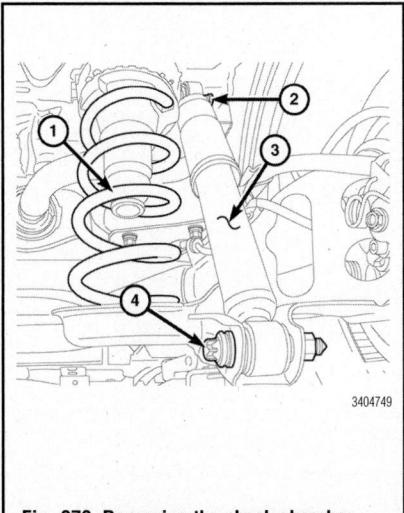

Fig. 273 Removing the shock absorber

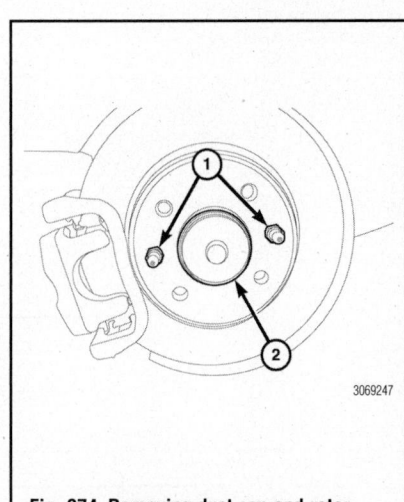

3069247

Fig. 274 Removing dust cap and rotor mounting pins

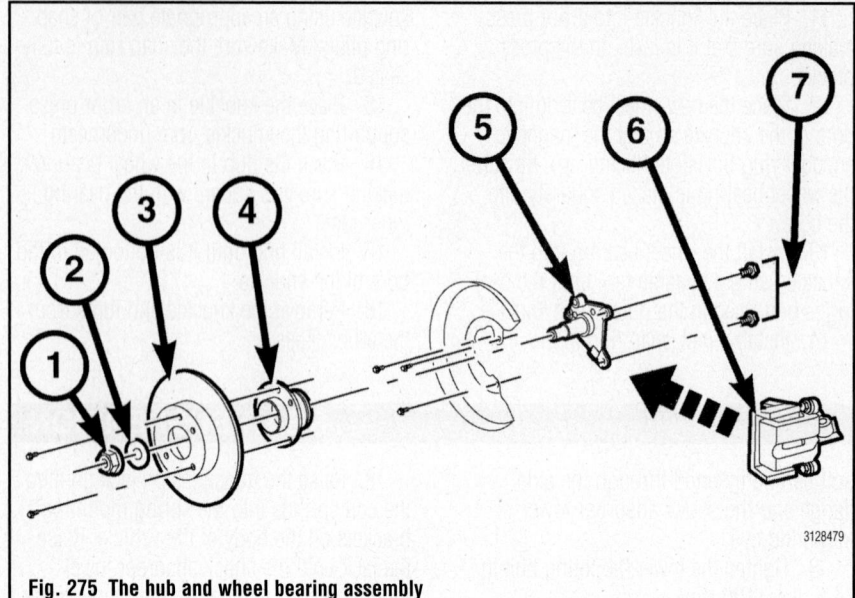

Fig. 275 The hub and wheel bearing assembly

3. Remove the hub and bearing dust cap (2).

4. Remove the rotor mounting pins (1).

5. Remove caliper mounting bolts (7) and remove the caliper and mounting bracket (6) as an assembly. Support the assembly with a bungee cord or wire. Do not allow the caliper to hang by the flex hose; damage to the hose may occur.

6. Remove the brake rotor (3).

7. Remove the hub nut (1) and washer (2), then remove the hub and bearing (4).

To install:

8. Slide the hub and bearing onto the spindle.

9. Install a washer and a new hub nut on the spindle. Tighten the nut to 207 ft. lbs. (280 Nm).

10. Install the brake rotor and caliper assembly. Install and tighten the caliper adapter mounting bolts to 42 ft. lbs. (57 Nm).

11. Install the hub and bearing dust cap.

12. Install rotor mounting pins and tighten to 106 inch lbs. (12 Nm).

13. Install tire and wheel assembly.

14. Lower the vehicle.

15. Pump the brake pedal several times to ensure the vehicle has a firm brake pedal before moving the vehicle.

FIAT

Diagnostic Trouble Codes

DIAGNOSTIC TROUBLE CODES

OBD II VEHICLE APPLICATIONS

FIAT

500

2012

- 1.4L 8V . . . . . Engine VIN/Code: R/EAF
- 1.4L 16V . . . . . Engine VIN/Code: R/EAB
- 1.4L 16V Turbo . . Engine VIN/Code: H/EAF

OBD II Trouble Code List (P0XXX Codes)

DTC	Trouble Code Title and Conditions
DTC: P0009-64 **Year:** 2012 **Model:** 500 **Engine:** 1.4L L4	**VVT BLOCKED TO REPOSE:** Powertrain Control Module (PCM) detects an error when the camshaft position is out of phase with the crankshaft position. One Trip Fault. Three good trips to turn off the MIL.
DTC: P0010-11 **Year:** 2012 **Model:** 500 **Engine:** 1.4L L4	**ELECTROVALVE VVT CIRCUIT SHORT TO GROUND:** The PCM detects that the CMP 1/1 Position Solenoid Control voltage is below the minimum acceptable value.
DTC: P0010-12 **Year:** 2012 **Model:** 500 **Engine:** 1.4L L4	**VVT ELECTROVALVE SHORT TO BATTERY:** The Powertrain Control Module (PCM) detects that the Camshaft 1/1 Position Solenoid input voltage is above the maximum acceptable value.
DTC: P0010-13 **Year:** 2012 **Model:** 500 **Engine:** 1.4L L4	**ELECTROVALVE VVT CIRCUIT OPEN:** The PCM detects that the actual state of the VVT Intake Solenoid does not match the intended state.
DTC: P0011-64 **Year:** 2012 **Model:** 500 **Engine:** 1.4L L4	**POSITION ERROR VVT:** The actual camshaft phasing position is not moving towards the desired camshaft phasing position during steady state operation.
DTC: P0012-66 **Year:** 2012 **Model:** 500 **Engine:** 1.4L L4	**VVT SPEED TO HIGH:** When the Powertrain Control Module (PCM) recognizes a problem with the Solenoid control circuit. One trip fault.
DTC: P0012-84 **Year:** 2012 **Model:** 500 **Engine:** 1.4L L4	**VVT SPEED TO LOW:** When the Powertrain Control Module (PCM) recognizes a problem with the Solenoid control circuit. One trip fault.
DTC: P0016 **Year:** 2012 **Model:** 500 **Engine:** 1.4L L4	**CRANKSHAFT/CAMSHAFT TIMING MISALIGNMENT:** Powertrain Control Module (PCM) detects an error when the camshaft position is out of phase with the crankshaft position. One Trip Fault. Three good trips to turn off the MIL.
DTC: P0016 **Year:** 2012 **Model:** 500 **Engine:** 1.4L L4	**CRANKSHAFT/CAMSHAFT TIMING MISALIGNMENT:** Powertrain Control Module (PCM) detects an error when the camshaft position is out of phase with the crankshaft position. One Trip Fault. Three good trips to turn off the MIL.
DTC: P0031 **Year:** 2012 **Model:** 500 **Engine:** 1.4L L4	**O2 SENSOR 1/1 HEATER CIRCUIT LOW:** The Powertrain Cotrol Module (PCM) detects that the O2 sensor heater element input is below the minimum acceptable voltage. One trip fault. Three good trips to turn off the MIL.
DTC: P0032 **Year:** 2012 **Model:** 500 **Engine:** 1.4L L4	**O2 SENSOR 1/1 HEATER CIRCUIT HIGH:** The Powertrain Control Module (PCM) detects that the O2 sensor heater element input is above the maximum acceptable voltage. One trip fault. Three good trips to turn off the MIL.
DTC: P0037 **Year:** 2012 **Model:** 500 **Engine:** 1.4L L4	**O2 SENSOR 1/2 HEATER CIRCUIT LOW:** The Powertrain Control Module (PCM) detects that the O2 sensor heater element input is below the minimum acceptable voltage. One trip fault. Three good trips to turn off the MIL.
DTC: P0038 **Year:** 2012 **Model:** 500 **Engine:** 1.4L L4	**O2 SENSOR 1/2 HEATER CIRCUIT HIGH:** The Powertrain Control Module (PCM) detects that the O2 sensor heater element input is above the maximum acceptable voltage. One trip fault. Three good trips to turn off the MIL.

DTC	Trouble Code Title and Conditions
DTC: P0054 **Year:** 2012 **Model:** 500 **Engine:** 1.4L L4	**O2 SENSOR 1/2 HEATER RESISTANCE:** No sensor output is received when the PCM powers up the sensor heater. Two trip fault. Three good trips to turn off the MIL.
DTC: P0054-62 **Year:** 2012 **Model:** 500 **Engine:** 1.4L L4	**O2 SENSOR HEATER 1/2 RESISTANCE:** No sensor output is received when the PCM powers up the sensor heater. Two trip fault. Three good trips to turn off the MIL.
DTC: P0069 **Year:** 2012 **Model:** 500 **Engine:** 1.4L L4	**MANIFOLD PRESSURE/BAROMETRIC PRESSURE CORRELATION:** At PCM power-up, the manifold pressure is compared with barometric pressure. If the two do not correlate and it cannot be determined which sensor is faulty,then this code is reported. One Trip Fault. Three good trips to turn off the MIL.
DTC: P0069-62 **Year:** 2012 **Model:** 500 **Engine:** 1.4L L4	**MANIFOLD PRESSURE/BAROMETRIC PRESSURE CORRELATION:** At PCM power-up, the manifold pressure is compared with barometric pressure. If the two do not correlate and it cannot be determined which sensor is faulty, then this code is reported. One Trip Fault. Three good trips to turn off the MIL.
DTC: P0071 **Year:** 2012 **Model:** 500 **Engine:** 1.4L L4	**AMBIENT AIR TEMPERATURE SENSOR PERFORMANCE:** The PCM compares the ambient, engine coolant and intake air temperature sensor values. If engine coolant and intake air temperature sensors agree with each other but ambient air temperature does not agree, the ambient air temperature sensor is declared as irrational. Two Trip Fault. Three good trips to turn off the MIL.
DTC: P0072 **Year:** 2012 **Model:** 500 **Engine:** 1.4L L4	**AMBIENT AIR TEMPERATURE SENSOR CIRCUIT LOW:** Ambient Temperature Sensor is less than the minimum acceptable value. One Trip Fault. Three good trips to turn off the MIL.
DTC: P0073 **Year:** 2012 **Model:** 500 **Engine:** 1.4L L4	**AMBIENT AIR TEMPERATURE SENSOR CIRCUIT HIGH:** The Ambient Temperature Sensor voltage is greater than the maximum acceptable value. OneTrip Fault. Three good trips to turn off the MIL.
DTC: P0101-62 **Year:** 2012 **Model:** 500 **Engine:** 1.4L L4	**HIGH AIRFLOW/VACUUM LEAK DETECTED (INSTANTANEOUS ACCUMULATION):** A large vacuum leak has been detected or both of the TP Sensors have failed based on their position being 2.5 Volts and the calculated MAP value is less than the actual MAP minus an Offset value. One trip fault and the code will set within five seconds. ETC light will flash.
DTC: P0105 **Year:** 2012 **Model:** 500 **Engine:** 1.4L L4	**MANIFOLD ABSOLUE PRESSURE SENSOR / BAROMETRIC PRESSURE SENSOR CIRCUIT:** The MAP Sensor Signal is above 4.8 Volts or below 0.19 of a Volt for 0.3 of a second.
DTC: P0105-12 **Year:** 2012 **Model:** 500 **Engine:** 1.4L L4	**MANIFOLD ABSOLUTE PRESSURE SENSOR CIRCUIT HIGH:** The MAP sensor signal voltage is greater than the maximum acceptable value. One trip fault. Three good trips to turn off the MIL. MIL will illuminate and the ETC light will flash if equipped.
DTC: P0105-14 **Year:** 2012 **Model:** 500 **Engine:** 1.4L L4	**MANIFOLD ABSOLUTE PRESSURE SENSOR CIRCUIT LOW:** The MAP sensor signal voltage is below the minimum acceptable value. One Trip Fault. Three good trips to turn off the MIL. MIL will illuminate and the ETC light will flash if equipped.
DTC: P0106-26 **Year:** 2012 **Model:** 500 **Engine:** 1.4L L4	**MANIFOLD ABSOLUTE PRESSURE SENSOR PERFORMANCE SIGNAL RATE OF CHANGE BELOW THRESHOLD:** The PCM detects an implausible voltage on the MAP Sensor circuit.
DTC: P0106-27 **Year:** 2012 **Model:** 500 **Engine:** 1.4L L4	**MANIFOLD ABSOLUTE PRESSURE SENSOR PERFORMANCE SIGNAL RATE OF CHANGE ABOVE THRESHOLD:** The PCM detects an implausible voltage on the MAP Sensor circuit.
DTC: P0107 **Year:** 2012 **Model:** 500 **Engine:** 1.4L L4	**MANIFOLD ABSOLUTE PRESSURE SENSOR CIRCUIT LOW:** The MAP sensor signal voltage is below the minimum acceptable value. One Trip Fault. Three good trips to turn off the MIL. MIL will illuminate and the ETC light will flash if equipped.

DTC	Trouble Code Title and Conditions
DTC: P0108 **Year:** 2012 **Model:** 500 **Engine:** 1.4L L4	**MANIFOLD ABSOLUTE PRESSURE SENSOR CIRCUIT HIGH:** The MAP sensor signal voltage is greater than the maximum acceptable value. Onetrip fault. Three good trips to turn off the MIL. MIL will illuminate and the ETC light will flash if equipped.
DTC: P0110-11 **Year:** 2012 **Model:** 500 **Engine:** 1.4L L4	**INTAKE AIR TEMPERATURE SENSOR 1 CIRCUIT LOW:** When the Inlet Air Temp Sensor Signal circuit voltage is less than the minimum acceptable value. One trip failure. Three good trips to clear the MIL.
DTC: P0110-15 **Year:** 2012 **Model:** 500 **Engine:** 1.4L L4	**INTAKE AIR TEMPERATURE SENSOR 1 CIRCUIT HIGH:** The Intake Air Temperature (IAT) Sensor circuit voltage at the PCM goes above the maximum acceptable value. One Trip Fault. Three good trips to turn off the MIL.
DTC: P0110-3A **Year:** 2012 **Model:** 500 **Engine:** 1.4L L4	**INTAKE AIR TEMPERATURE SENSOR ERRATIC:** No circuit short high or circuit short low fault present for the IAT Sensor. The IAT Sensor value is greater than 140° C (284° F) or less than −50° C (−58° F) for a calibrated period of time. One Trip Fault. Three good trips to turn off the MIL.
DTC: P0111 **Year:** 2012 **Model:** 500 **Engine:** 1.4L L4	**INTAKE AIR TEMPERATURE SENSOR RATIONALITY:** Once the vehicle is soaked for a calibrated engine off time and then driven over calibrated speed and load conditions for some calibrated time, the PCM compares the ambient, engine coolant and intake air temperature sensor values. If engine coolant and ambient air temperature sensors agree with each other but intake air temperature does not agree with them, the intake air temperature sensor is declared as irrational. Two Trip Fault. Three good trips to turn off the MIL.
DTC: P0111-62 **Year:** 2012 **Model:** 500 **Engine:** 1.4L L4	**INTAKE AIR TEMPERATURE SENSOR 1 CIRCUIT PERFORMANCE:** No circuit short high or circuit short low fault present for the IAT Sensor. The IAT Sensor value is greater than 140° C (284° F) or less than -50° C (-58° F) for a calibrated period of time. One Trip Fault. Three good trips to turn off the MIL.
DTC: P0112 **Year:** 2012 **Model:** 500 **Engine:** 1.4L L4	**INTAKE AIR TEMPERATURE SENSOR CIRCUIT LOW:** When the Inlet Air Temp Sensor Signal circuit voltage is less than the minimum acceptable value. One trip failure. Three good trips to clear the MIL.
DTC: P0113 **Year:** 2012 **Model:** 500 **Engine:** 1.4L L4	**INTAKE AIR TEMPERATURE SENSOR CIRCUIT HIGH:** The Intake Air Temperature (IAT) Sensor circuit voltage at the PCM goes above the maximum acceptable value. One Trip Fault. Three good trips to turn off the MIL.
DTC: P0114 **Year:** 2012 **Model:** 500 **Engine:** 1.4L L4	**INTAKE AIR TEMPERATURE SENSOR INTERMITTENT:** No circuit short high or circuit short low fault present for the IAT Sensor. The IAT Sensor value is greater than 140° C (284° F) or less than -50° C (-58° F) for a calibrated period of time. One Trip Fault. Three good trips to turn off the MIL.
DTC: P0115-11 **Year:** 2012 **Model:** 500 **Engine:** 1.4L L4	**ENGINE COOLANT TEMPERATURE SENSOR 1 CIRCUIT LOW:** The Powertrain Control Module (PCM) detects that the Engine Coolant Temperature Sensor input voltage is below the minimum acceptable value. One Trip Fault. Three good trips to clear the MIL. The MIL and ETC light will illuminate if equipped.
DTC: P0115-15 **Year:** 2012 **Model:** 500 **Engine:** 1.4L L4	**ENGINE COOLANT TEMPERATURE SENSOR 1 CIRCUIT HIGH:** The Powertrain Control Module (PCM) detects that the Engine Coolant Temperature Sensor input voltage is above the maximum acceptable value. One Trip Fault. Three good trips to turn off the MIL. The MIL and ETC light will illuminate if equipped.
DTC: P0115-3A **Year:** 2012 **Model:** 500 **Engine:** 1.4L L4	**ENGINE COOLANT TEMPERATURE SENSOR 1 CIRCUIT INTERMITTANT:** Once the vehicle is soaked for a calibrated engine off time and then driven over calibrated speed and load conditions for some calibrated time, the PCM compares the ambient, engine coolant and intake air temperature sensor values. If ambient air and intake air temperature sensors agree with each other but engine coolant temperature does not agree with them, the engine coolant temperature sensor is declared as irrational. Two Trip Fault. Three good trips to turn off the MIL.
DTC: P0116 **Year:** 2012 **Model:** 500 **Engine:** 1.4L L4	**ENGINE COOLANT TEMPERATURE SENSOR CIRCUIT PERFORMANCE:** Once the vehicle is soaked for a calibrated engine off time and then driven over calibrated speed and load conditions for some calibrated time, the PCM compares the ambient, engine coolant and intake air temperature sensor values. If ambient air and intake air temperature sensors agree with each other but engine coolant temperature does not agree with them, the engine coolant temperature sensor is declared as irrational. Two Trip Fault. Three good trips to turn off the MIL.

DTC	Trouble Code Title and Conditions
DTC: P0116-62 **Year:** 2012 **Model:** 500 **Engine:** 1.4L L4	**ENGINE COOLANT TEMPERATURE SENSOR 1 CIRCUIT PERFORMANCE:** Once the vehicle is soaked for a calibrated engine off time and then driven over calibrated speed and load conditions for some calibrated time, the PCM compares the ambient, engine coolant and intake air temperature sensor values. If ambient air and intake air temperature sensors agree with each other but engine coolant temperature does not agree with them, the engine coolant temperature sensor is declared as irrational. Two Trip Fault. Three good trips to turn off the MIL.
DTC: P0117 **Year:** 2012 **Model:** 500 **Engine:** 1.4L L4	**ENGINE COOLANT TEMPERATURE SENSOR CIRCUIT LOW:** The Powertrain Control Module (PCM) detects that the Engine Coolant Temperature Sensor input voltage is below the minimum acceptable value. One Trip Fault. Three good trips to clear the MIL. The MIL and ETC light will illuminate if equipped.
DTC: P0118 **Year:** 2012 **Model:** 500 **Engine:** 1.4L L4	**ENGINE COOLANT TEMPERATURE SENSOR CIRCUIT HIGH:** The Powertrain Control Module (PCM) detects that the Engine Coolant Temperature Sensor input voltage is above the maximum acceptable value. One Trip Fault. Three good trips to turn off the MIL. The MIL and ETC light will illuminate if equipped.
DTC: P0118 **Year:** 2012 **Model:** 500 **Engine:** 1.4L L4	**ENGINE COOLANT TEMPERATURE SENSOR CIRCUIT HIGH:** The Powertrain Control Module (PCM) detects that the Engine Coolant Temperature Sensor input voltage is above the maximum acceptable value. One Trip Fault. Three good trips to turn off the MIL. The MIL and ETC light will illuminate if equipped.
DTC: P0120-12 **Year:** 2012 **Model:** 500 **Engine:** 1.4L L4	**ACCELERATOR PEDAL POSITION SENSOR 1 CIRCUIT HIGH:** When APP Sensor No.1 voltage is too high. Engine will additionally idle if the brake pedal is pressed or has failed. Acceleration rate and Engine output are limited. One trip fault and the code will set within five seconds. ETC light is flashing.
DTC: P0120-14 **Year:** 2012 **Model:** 500 **Engine:** 1.4L L4	**ACCELERATOR PEDAL POSITION SENSOR 1 CIRCUIT LOW:** When the APP Sensor No.1 voltage is too low. Engine will additionally idle if the brake pedal is pressed or has failed. Acceleration rate and Engine output are limited. One trip fault and the code will set within five seconds. ETC light is flashing.
DTC: P0121-11 **Year:** 2012 **Model:** 500 **Engine:** 1.4L L4	**THROTTLE POSITION SENSOR 1 CIRCUIT LOW:** Throttle Position Sensor (TPS) voltage at the Powertrain Control Module (PCM) is less than 0.16 of a Volt for 0.7 of a second. One Trip Fault. Three good trips to turn off the MIL. ETC light will illuminate.
DTC: P0121-15 **Year:** 2012 **Model:** 500 **Engine:** 1.4L L4	**THROTTLE POSITION SENSOR 1 CIRCUIT HIGH:** Throttle Position Sensor 1 voltage is greater than 4.8 Volts for 25 ms. One Trip Fault. ETC light will illuminate.
DTC: P0122 **Year:** 2012 **Model:** 500 **Engine:** 1.4L L4	**THROTTLE POSITION SENSOR 1 CIRCUIT LOW:** Throttle Position Sensor (TPS) voltage at the Powertrain Control Module (PCM) is less than 0.16 of a Volt for 0.7 of a second. One Trip Fault. Three good trips to turn off the MIL. ETC light will illuminate.
DTC: P0123 **Year:** 2012 **Model:** 500 **Engine:** 1.4L L4	**THROTTLE POSITION SENSOR 1 CIRCUIT HIGH:** Throttle Position Sensor 1 voltage is greater than 4.8 Volts for 25 ms. One Trip Fault. ETC light will illuminate.
DTC: P0128 **Year:** 2012 **Model:** 500 **Engine:** 1.4L L4	**THERMOSTAT RATIONALITY:** The PCM detects that the actual engine coolant temperature falls too far below the predicted engine coolant temperature and the predicted coolant temperature reaches the predicted target value before the actual coolant temperature reaches the actual coolant temperature target value. Two trip fault. Three good trips to turn off the MIL.
DTC: P0130 **Year:** 2012 **Model:** 500 **Engine:** 1.4L L4	**O2 SENSOR 1/1 CIRCUIT:** The oxygen sensor signal voltage is greater than 2.20 volts for a calibrated period of time. Two Trip Fault. Three good trips to turn off the MIL.
DTC: P0130-01 **Year:** 2012 **Model:** 500 **Engine:** 1.4L L4	**O2 SENSOR 1/1 CIRCUIT LOW:** The oxygen sensor signal voltage is greater than 2.20 volts for a calibrated period of time. Two Trip Fault. Three good trips to turn off the MIL.
DTC: P0133 **Year:** 2012 **Model:** 500 **Engine:** 1.4L L4	**O2 SENSOR 1/1 SLOW RESPONSE:** The Powertrain Control Module (PCM) detects that the oxygen sensor signal does not switch adequately during monitoring. Two Trip Fault. Three good trips to turn off the MIL.

DTC	Trouble Code Title and Conditions
DTC: P0133-26 **Year:** 2012 **Model:** 500 **Engine:** 1.4L L4	**O2 SENSOR 1/1 SLOW RESPONSE:** The Powertrain Control Module (PCM) detects that the oxygen sensor signal does not switch adequately during monitoring. Two Trip Fault. Three good trips to turn off the MIL.
DTC: P0135 **Year:** 2012 **Model:** 500 **Engine:** 1.4L L4	**O2 SENSOR 1/1 HEATER PERFORMANCE:** The Powertrain Control Module (PCM) detects no temperature change in the O2 sensor heater element when the heater circuit is active. The heater temperature is obtained by measuring the heater resistance and calculating the heater temperature. Two trip fault. Three good trips to turn off the MIL.
DTC: P0136-23 **Year:** 2012 **Model:** 500 **Engine:** 1.4L L4	**O2 SENSOR 1/2 CIRCUIT LOW:** The Powertrain Control Module (PCM) detects that the 1/2 Oxygen Sensor signal voltage is below minimum acceptable value. The DTC will set as Pending after one trip and Active after two trips. Three good trips to turn off the MIL.
DTC: P0136-24 **Year:** 2012 **Model:** 500 **Engine:** 1.4L L4	**O2 SENSOR 1/2 SLOW RESPONSE:** The Powertrain Control Module (PCM) monitors the downstream O2 Sensor. If the PCM does not detect a rich to lean switch within a specific time during a decel fuel shutoff event, the monitor will fail. One trip fault. Three good trips to turn off the MIL.
DTC: P0137 **Year:** 2012 **Model:** 500 **Engine:** 1.4L L4	**O2 SENSOR 1/2 CIRCUIT LOW:** The Powertrain Control Module (PCM) detects that the 1/2 Oxygen Sensor signal voltage is below minimum acceptable value. The DTC will set as Pending after one trip and Active after two trips. Three good trips to turn off the MIL.
DTC: P0138 **Year:** 2012 **Model:** 500 **Engine:** 1.4L L4	**O2 SENSOR 1/2 CIRCUIT HIGH:** The Powertrain Control Module (PCM) detects that the 1/2 Oxygen Sensor voltage is greater than the maximum acceptable value for a specific amount of time, based on O2 sensor heater temperature. The DTC will set as Pending after one trip and Active after two trips. Three good trips to turn off the MIL.
DTC: P0138-12 **Year:** 2012 **Model:** 500 **Engine:** 1.4L L4	**O2 SENSOR 1/2 CIRCUIT HIGH:** The Powertrain Control Module (PCM) detects that the 1/2 Oxygen Sensor voltage is greater than the maximum acceptable value for a specific amount of time, based on O2 sensor heater temperature. The DTC will set as Pending after one trip and Active after two trips. Three good trips to turn off the MIL.
DTC: P0139 **Year:** 2012 **Model:** 500 **Engine:** 1.4L L4	**O2 SENSOR 1/2 SLOW RESPONSE:** The Powertrain Control Module (PCM) monitors the downstream O2 Sensor. If the PCM does not detect a rich to lean switch within a specific time during a decel fuel shutoff event, the monitor will fail. One trip fault. Three good trips to turn off the MIL.
DTC: P0140 **Year:** 2012 **Model:** 500 **Engine:** 1.4L L4	**O2 SENSOR 1/2 NO ACTIVITY DETECTED:** The Powertrain Control Module (PCM) detects that the oxygen sensor signal switches from lean to rich less than 16 times within 20 seconds during monitoring. Two Trip Fault. Three good trips to turn off the MIL.
DTC: P0141 **Year:** 2012 **Model:** 500 **Engine:** 1.4L L4	**O2 SENSOR 1/2 HEATER PERFORMANCE:** The Powertrain Control Module (PCM) detects no temperature change in the O2 sensor heater element when the heater circuit is active. The heater temperature is obtained by measuring the heater resistance and calculating the heater temperature. Two trip fault. Three good trips to turn off the MIL.
DTC: P0141-12 **Year:** 2012 **Model:** 500 **Engine:** 1.4L L4	**O2 SENSOR 1/2 HEATER CIRCUIT HIGH:** The Powertrain Control Module (PCM) detects that the O2 sensor heater element input is above the maximum acceptable voltage. One trip fault. Three good trips to turn off the MIL.
DTC: P0141-14 **Year:** 2012 **Model:** 500 **Engine:** 1.4L L4	**O2 SENSOR 1/2 HEATER CIRCUIT LOW:** The Powertrain Control Module (PCM) detects that the O2 sensor heater element input is below the minimum acceptable voltage. One trip fault. Three good trips to turn off the MIL.
DTC: P0171 **Year:** 2012 **Model:** 500 **Engine:** 1.4L L4	**FUEL SYSTEM 1/1 LEAN:** If the Powertrain Control Module (PCM) multiplies short term compensation by long term adaptive and a certain percentage is exceeded for two trips, a freeze frame is stored, the MIL illuminates and a trouble code is stored. Two Trip Fault. Three good trips to turn off the MIL.
DTC: P0172 **Year:** 2012 **Model:** 500 **Engine:** 1.4L L4	**FUEL SYSTEM 1/1 RICH:** If the Powertrain Control Module (PCM) multiplies short term compensation by long term adaptive and a purge fuel multiplier and the result is below a certain value for 30 seconds over two trips, a freeze frame is stored, the MIL illuminates and a trouble code is stored. Two Trip Fault. Three good trips to turn off the MIL.

DTC	Trouble Code Title and Conditions
DTC: P0195 **Year:** 2012 **Model:** 500 **Engine:** 1.4L L4	**ENGINE OIL TEMPERATURE SENSOR CIRCUIT:** • IAT correlation test passed this ignition cycle. ECT range/performance test, EOT range/performance test passed this ignition cycle. IAT sensor start temperature exceeds EOT sensor start temperature by more than 20° C (68° F) and the difference between IAT sensor start temperature and ECT sensor start temperature is less than 10° C (50° F). IAT sensor start temperature is above the temperature threshold to detect that the block heater is switched off (-17.8° C - 0.0° F) and IAT sensor start temperature exceeds ECT start temperature by less than 10° C (50° F) and EOT sensor start temperature exceeds IAT sensor start temperature by more than 20° C (68° F). Two trip fault, three good trips required to reset the MIL.
DTC: P0195-11 **Year:** 2012 **Model:** 500 **Engine:** 1.4L L4	**ENGINE OIL TEMPERATURE SENSOR CIRCUIT LOW:** The Engine Oil Temperature sensor circuit voltage at the Powertrain Control Module (PCM) is less than the calibrated amount. One Trip Fault. Three good trips to clear the MIL.
DTC: P0195-15 **Year:** 2012 **Model:** 500 **Engine:** 1.4L L4	**ENGINE OIL TEMPERATURE SENSOR CIRCUIT HIGH:** The Engine Oil Temperature Sensor circuit voltage at the Powertrain Control Module (PCM) is greater than the calibrated amount. One Trip Fault. Three good trips to turn off the MIL.
DTC: P0196 **Year:** 2012 **Model:** 500 **Engine:** 1.4L L4	**ENGINE OIL TEMPERATURE SENSOR CIRCUIT PERFORMANCE:** After a calibrated amount of cool down time, the Powertrain Control Module (PCM) compares the AAT, ECT and IAT Sensor values. If the general temperature rationality passes, the PCM compares the Oil Temperature Sensor value to a threshold based on the other temp sensor values. If the difference is greater than a calibrated value, the diagnostic fails.
DTC: P0197 **Year:** 2012 **Model:** 500 **Engine:** 1.4L L4	**ENGINE OIL TEMPERATURE SENSOR CIRCUIT LOW:** The Engine Oil Temperature sensor circuit voltage at the Powertrain Control Module (PCM) is less than the calibrated amount. One Trip Fault. Three good trips to clear the MIL.
DTC: P0198 **Year:** 2012 **Model:** 500 **Engine:** 1.4L L4	**ENGINE OIL TEMPERATURE SENSOR CIRCUIT HIGH:** The Engine Oil Temperature Sensor circuit voltage at the Powertrain Control Module (PCM) is greater than the calibrated amount. One Trip Fault. Three good trips to turn off the MIL.
DTC: P0201 **Year:** 2012 **Model:** 500 **Engine:** 1.4L L4	**FUEL INJECTOR 1 CIRCUIT OPEN:** The Powertrain Control Module (PCM) detects an open in the Fuel Injector 1 circuit.
DTC: P0201 **Year:** 2012 **Model:** 500 **Engine:** 1.4L L4	**11 FUEL INJECTOR 1 CIRCUIT LOW:** The Powertrain Control Module (PCM) tests the injector circuit and determines the
DTC: P0201-12 **Year:** 2012 **Model:** 500 **Engine:** 1.4L L4	**FUEL INJECTOR 1 CIRCUIT HIGH:** The Powertrain Control Module (PCM) tests the injector circuit internally and determines the circuit is shorted to voltage. One trip fault and MIL.
DTC: P0201-13 **Year:** 2012 **Model:** 500 **Engine:** 1.4L L4	**FUEL INJECTOR 1 CIRCUIT OPEN:** The Powertrain Control Module (PCM) detects an open in the Fuel Injector 1 circuit.
DTC: P0202 **Year:** 2012 **Model:** 500 **Engine:** 1.4L L4	**FUEL INJECTOR 2 CIRCUIT OPEN:** The Powertrain Control Module (PCM) detects an open in the Fuel Injector 2 circuit.
DTC: P0202-11 **Year:** 2012 **Model:** 500 **Engine:** 1.4L L4	**FUEL INJECTOR 2 CIRCUIT LOW:** The Powertrain Control Module (PCM) tests the injector circuit internally and determines the circuit is shorted to ground. One trip fault and MIL.
DTC: P0202-12 **Year:** 2012 **Model:** 500 **Engine:** 1.4L L4	**FUEL INJECTOR 2 CIRCUIT HIGH:** The Powertrain Control Module (PCM) tests the injector circuit internally and determines the circuit is shorted to voltage. One trip fault and MIL.

DTC	Trouble Code Title and Conditions
DTC: P0202-13 **Year:** 2012 **Model:** 500 **Engine:** 1.4L L4	**FUEL INJECTOR 2 CIRCUIT OPEN:** The Powertrain Control Module (PCM) detects an open in the Fuel Injector 2 circuit.
DTC: P0203 **Year:** 2012 **Model:** 500 **Engine:** 1.4L L4	**FUEL INJECTOR 3 CIRCUIT OPEN:** The Powertrain Control Module (PCM) detects an open in the Fuel Injector 3 circuit.
DTC: P0203-11 **Year:** 2012 **Model:** 500 **Engine:** 1.4L L4	**FUEL INJECTOR 3 CIRCUIT LOW:** The Powertrain Control Module (PCM) tests the injector circuit internally and determines the circuit is shorted to ground. One trip fault and MIL.
DTC: P0203-12 **Year:** 2012 **Model:** 500 **Engine:** 1.4L L4	**FUEL INJECTOR 3 CIRCUIT HIGH:** The Powertrain Control Module (PCM) tests the injector circuit internally and determines the circuit is shorted to voltage. One trip fault and MIL.
DTC: P0203-13 **Year:** 2012 **Model:** 500 **Engine:** 1.4L L4	**FUEL INJECTOR 3 CIRCUIT OPEN:** The Powertrain Control Module (PCM) detects an open in the Fuel Injector 3 circuit.
DTC: P0204 **Year:** 2012 **Model:** 500 **Engine:** 1.4L L4	**FUEL INJECTOR 4 CIRCUIT OPEN:** The Powertrain Control Module (PCM) detects an open in the Fuel Injector 4 circuit.
DTC: P0204-11 **Year:** 2012 **Model:** 500 **Engine:** 1.4L L4	**FUEL INJECTOR 4 CIRCUIT LOW:** The Powertrain Control Module (PCM) tests the injector circuit internally and determines the circuit is shorted to ground. One trip fault and MIL.
DTC: P0204-12 **Year:** 2012 **Model:** 500 **Engine:** 1.4L L4	**FUEL INJECTOR 4 CIRCUIT HIGH:** The Powertrain Control Module (PCM) tests the injector circuit internally and determines the circuit is shorted to voltage. One trip fault and MIL.
DTC: P0204-13 **Year:** 2012 **Model:** 500 **Engine:** 1.4L L4	**FUEL INJECTOR 4 CIRCUIT OPEN:** The Powertrain Control Module (PCM) detects an open in the Fuel Injector 4 circuit.
DTC: P0219 **Year:** 2012 **Model:** 500 **Engine:** 1.4L L4	**ENGINE OVERSPEED:** The Powertrain Control Module (PCM) detects that engine speed is above 6000 RPM for 0.64 of a second.
DTC: P0219-66 **Year:** 2012 **Model:** 500 **Engine:** 1.4L L4	**ENGINE OVERSPEED:** The Powertrain Control Module (PCM) detects that engine speed is above 6000 RPM for 0.64 of a second.
DTC: P0220-12 **Year:** 2012 **Model:** 500 **Engine:** 1.4L L4	**ACCELERATOR PEDAL POSITION SENSOR 2 CIRCUIT HIGH:** When APP Sensor No.2 voltage is too high. Idle is additionally forced any time the brake is applied or failed. Acceleration rate and Engine output are limited. One trip fault and the code will set within five seconds. ETC light is flashing.
DTC: P0220-14 **Year:** 2012 **Model:** 500 **Engine:** 1.4L L4	**ACCELERATOR PEDAL POSITION SENSOR 2 CIRCUIT LOW:** When the APP Sensor No.2 voltage is too low. Engine will only idle if the Brake pedal is Pressed or has failed. Acceleration rate and Engine output are limited. One trip fault and the code will set within five seconds. ETC light is flashing.
DTC: P0221-11 **Year:** 2012 **Model:** 500 **Engine:** 1.4L L4	**THROTTLE POSITION SENSOR 2 CIRCUIT LOW:** Throttle Position Sensor voltage at the Powertrain Control Module (PCM) is less than 0.16 of a Volt for 0.7 of a second. One Trip Fault. Three good trips to turn off the MIL. ETC light will illuminate.

DTC	Trouble Code Title and Conditions
DTC: P0221-15 **Year:** 2012 **Model:** 500 **Engine:** 1.4L L4	**THROTTLE POSITION SENSOR 2 CIRCUIT HIGH:** Throttle Position Sensor 2 Signal circuit voltage is greater than 4.9 Volts for 25 ms. One Trip Fault. ETC light will illuminate.
DTC: P0222 **Year:** 2012 **Model:** 500 **Engine:** 1.4L L4	**THROTTLE POSITION SENSOR 2 CIRCUIT LOW:** Throttle Position Sensor voltage at the Powertrain Control Module (PCM) is less than 0.16 of a Volt for 0.7 of a second. One Trip Fault. Three good trips to turn off the MIL. ETC light will illuminate.
DTC: P0223 **Year:** 2012 **Model:** 500 **Engine:** 1.4L L4	**THROTTLE POSITION SENSOR 2 CIRCUIT HIGH:** Throttle Position Sensor 2 Signal circuit voltage is greater than 4.9 Volts for 25 ms. One Trip Fault. ETC light will illuminate.
DTC: P0230-11 **Year:** 2012 **Model:** 500 **Engine:** 1.4L L4	**FUEL PUMP CONTROL CIRCUIT LOW:** The Powertrain Control Module (PCM) detects that the fuel pump control circuit is low.
DTC: P0230-12 **Year:** 2012 **Model:** 500 **Engine:** 1.4L L4	**FUEL PUMP CONTROL CIRCUIT HIGH:** The Powertrain Control Module (PCM) detects that the fuel pump control circuit is high.
DTC: P0230-13 **Year:** 2012 **Model:** 500 **Engine:** 1.4L L4	**FUEL PUMP RELAY CIRCUIT OPEN:** The Powertrain Control Module (PCM) detects that the actual state of the fuel pump control does not match the intended state.
DTC: P0261 **Year:** 2012 **Model:** 500 **Engine:** 1.4L L4	**INJECTOR 1 CONTROL CIRCUIT LOW:** The Powertrain Control Module (PCM) tests the injector circuit and determines the circuit is shorted to ground. One trip fault and MIL.
DTC: P0262 **Year:** 2012 **Model:** 500 **Engine:** 1.4L L4	**INJECTOR 1 CONTROL CIRCUIT HIGH:** The Powertrain Control Module (PCM) tests the injector circuit internally and determines the circuit is shorted to voltage. One trip fault and MIL.
DTC: P0264 **Year:** 2012 **Model:** 500 **Engine:** 1.4L L4	**INJECTOR 2 CONTROL CIRCUIT LOW:** The Powertrain Control Module (PCM) tests the injector circuit internally and determines the circuit is shorted to ground. One trip fault and MIL.
DTC: P0265 **Year:** 2012 **Model:** 500 **Engine:** 1.4L L4	**INJECTOR 2 CONTROL CIRCUIT HIGH:** The Powertrain Control Module (PCM) tests the injector circuit internally and determines the circuit is shorted to voltage. One trip fault and MIL.
DTC: P0267 **Year:** 2012 **Model:** 500 **Engine:** 1.4L L4	**INJECTOR 3 CONTROL CIRCUIT LOW:** The Powertrain Control Module (PCM) tests the injector circuit internally and determines the circuit is shorted to ground. One trip fault and MIL.
DTC: P0268 **Year:** 2012 **Model:** 500 **Engine:** 1.4L L4	**INJECTOR 3 CONTROL CIRCUIT HIGH:** The Powertrain Control Module (PCM) tests the injector circuit internally and determines the circuit is shorted to voltage. One trip fault and MIL.
DTC: P0270 **Year:** 2012 **Model:** 500 **Engine:** 1.4L L4	**INJECTOR 4 CONTROL CIRCUIT LOW:** The Powertrain Control Module (PCM) tests the injector circuit internally and determines the circuit is shorted to ground. One trip fault and MIL.
DTC: P0271 **Year:** 2012 **Model:** 500 **Engine:** 1.4L L4	**INJECTOR 4 CONTROL CIRCUIT HIGH:** The Powertrain Control Module (PCM) tests the injector circuit internally and determines the circuit is shorted to voltage. One trip fault and MIL.

DTC	Trouble Code Title and Conditions
DTC: P0298 **Year:** 2012 **Model:** 500 **Engine:** 1.4L L4	**ENGINE OIL TEMPERATURE TOO HIGH:** The Engine Oil temperature rises faster than a calibrated modeled temperature. When the actual oil temperature exceeds the high boundary of the calibrated modeled temperature for three minutes the fault is set. Two trip fault. Three good trips to turn off the MIL.
DTC: P0300 **Year:** 2012 **Model:** 500 **Engine:** 1.4L L4	**MULTIPLE CYLINDER MISFIRE:** The threshold to set the fault is application specific; it is tied to the level of misfire that will cause emissions to increase to 1.5 times the standard or in some cases 1%. It is always a two trip fault above the calibrated RPM. It takes one fail to set a Pending Fault and two trips to set the MIL. Three good trips to turn off the MIL.
DTC: P0300-92 **Year:** 2012 **Model:** 500 **Engine:** 1.4L L4	**MULTIPLE CYLINDER MISFIRE PERFORMANCE OR INCORRECT OPERATION:** The threshold to set the fault is application specific; it is tied to the level of misfire that will cause emissions to increase to 1.5 times the standard or in some cases 1%. It is always a two trip fault above the calibrated RPM. It takes one fail to set a Pending Fault and two trips to set the MIL. Three good trips to turn off the MIL.
DTC: P0300-98 **Year:** 2012 **Model:** 500 **Engine:** 1.4L L4	**MULTIPLE CYLINDER MISFIRE COMPONENT OR SYSTEM IN OVER TEMP:** The threshold to set the fault is application specific; it is tied to the level of misfire that will cause emissions to increase to 1.5 times the standard or in some cases 1%. It is always a two trip fault above the calibrated RPM. It takes one fail to set a Pending Fault and two trips to set the MIL. Three good trips to turn off the MIL.
DTC: P0301 **Year:** 2012 **Model:** 500 **Engine:** 1.4L L4	**CYLINDER 1 MISFIRE:** The threshold to set the fault is application specific; it is tied to the level of misfire that will cause emissions to increase to 1.5 times the standard or in some cases 1%. It is always a two trip fault above the calibrated RPM. It takes one fail to set a Pending Fault and two trips to set the MIL. Three good trips to turn off the MIL.
DTC: P0301-92 **Year:** 2012 **Model:** 500 **Engine:** 1.4L L4	**CYLINDER 1 MISFIRE PERFORMANCE OR INCORRECT OPERATION:** The threshold to set the fault is application specific; it is tied to the level of misfire that will cause emissions to increase to 1.5 times the standard or in some cases 1%. It is always a two trip fault above the calibrated RPM. It takes one fail to set a Pending Fault and two trips to set the MIL. Three good trips to turn off the MIL.
DTC: P0301-98 **Year:** 2012 **Model:** 500 **Engine:** 1.4L L4	**CYLINDER 1 MISFIRE COMPONENT OR SYSTEM IN OVER TEMP:** The threshold to set the fault is application specific; it is tied to the level of misfire that will cause emissions to increase to 1.5 times the standard or in some cases 1%. It is always a two trip fault above the calibrated RPM. It takes one fail to set a Pending Fault and two trips to set the MIL. Three good trips to turn off the MIL.
DTC: P0302 **Year:** 2012 **Model:** 500 **Engine:** 1.4L L4	**CYLINDER 2 MISFIRE:** The threshold to set the fault is application specific; it is tied to the level of misfire that will cause emissions to increase to 1.5 times the standard or in some cases 1%. It is always a two trip fault above the calibrated RPM. It takes one fail to set a Pending Fault and two trips to set the MIL. Three good trips to turn off the MIL.
DTC: P0302-92 **Year:** 2012 **Model:** 500 **Engine:** 1.4L L4	**CYLINDER 2 MISFIRE PERFORMANCE OR INCORRECT OPERATION:** The threshold to set the fault is application specific; it is tied to the level of misfire that will cause emissions to increase to 1.5 times the standard or in some cases 1%. It is always a two trip fault above the calibrated RPM. It takes one fail to set a Pending Fault and two trips to set the MIL. Three good trips to turn off the MIL.
DTC: P0302-98 **Year:** 2012 **Model:** 500 **Engine:** 1.4L L4	**CYLINDER 2 MISFIRE COMPONENT OR SYSTEM IN OVER TEMP:** The threshold to set the fault is application specific; it is tied to the level of misfire that will cause emissions to increase to 1.5 times the standard or in some cases 1%. It is always a two trip fault above the calibrated RPM. It takes one fail to set a Pending Fault and two trips to set the MIL. Three good trips to turn off the MIL.
DTC: P0303 **Year:** 2012 **Model:** 500 **Engine:** 1.4L L4	**CYLINDER 3 MISFIRE:** The threshold to set the fault is application specific; it is tied to the level of misfire that will cause emissions to increase to 1.5 times the standard or in some cases 1%. It is always a two trip fault above the calibrated RPM. It takes one fail to set a Pending Fault and two trips to set the MIL. Three good trips to turn off the MIL.
DTC: P0303-92 **Year:** 2012 **Model:** 500 **Engine:** 1.4L L4	**CYLINDER 3 MISFIRE PERFORMANCE OR INCORRECT OPERATION:** The threshold to set the fault is application specific; it is tied to the level of misfire that will cause emissions to increase to 1.5 times the standard or in some cases 1%. It is always a two trip fault above the calibrated RPM. It takes one fail to set a Pending Fault and two trips to set the MIL. Three good trips to turn off the MIL.
DTC: P0303-98 **Year:** 2012 **Model:** 500 **Engine:** 1.4L L4	**CYLINDER 3 MISFIRE COMPONENT OR SYSTEM IN OVER TEMP:** The threshold to set the fault is application specific; it is tied to the level of misfire that will cause emissions to increase to 1.5 times the standard or in some cases 1%. It is always a two trip fault above the calibrated RPM. It takes one fail to set a Pending Fault and two trips to set the MIL. Three good trips to turn off the MIL.
DTC: P0304 **Year:** 2012 **Model:** 500 **Engine:** 1.4L L4	**CYLINDER 4 MISFIRE:** The threshold to set the fault is application specific; it is tied to the level of misfire that will cause emissions to increase to 1.5 times the standard or in some cases 1%. It is always a two trip fault above the calibrated RPM. It takes one fail to set a Pending Fault and two trips to set the MIL. Three good trips to turn off the MIL.

DTC	Trouble Code Title and Conditions
DTC: P0304-92 **Year:** 2012 **Model:** 500 **Engine:** 1.4L L4	**CYLINDER 4 MISFIRE PERFORMANCE OR INCORRECT OPERATION:** The threshold to set the fault is application specific; it is tied to the level of misfire that will cause emissions to increase to 1.5 times the standard or in some cases 1%. It is always a two trip fault above the calibrated RPM. It takes one fail to set a Pending Fault and two trips to set the MIL. Three good trips to turn off the MIL.
DTC: P0304-98 **Year:** 2012 **Model:** 500 **Engine:** 1.4L L4	**CYLINDER 4 MISFIRE COMPONENT OR SYSTEM IN OVER TEMP:** The threshold to set the fault is application specific; it is tied to the level of misfire that will cause emissions to increase to 1.5 times the standard or in some cases 1%. It is always a two trip fault above the calibrated RPM. It takes one fail to set a Pending Fault and two trips to set the MIL. Three good trips to turn off the MIL.
DTC: P0315 **Year:** 2012 **Model:** 500 **Engine:** 1.4L L4	**NO CRANK SENSOR LEARNED:** One of the CKP sensor target windows has more than 2% variance from the reference. One Trip Fault. Three good trips to turn off the MIL.
DTC: P0324 **Year:** 2012 **Model:** 500 **Engine:** 1.4L L4	**KNOCK CONTROL SYSTEM:** The Powertrain Control Module detects the that knock sensor capacitance is less than a calibrated value.
DTC: P0325 **Year:** 2012 **Model:** 500 **Engine:** 1.4L L4	**KNOCK SENSOR 1 CIRCUIT:** During engine operation in a speed/load range that does not exhibit engine knock but only engine noise, the knock sensor noise voltage is accumulated over a calibrated number of engine events. If after the calibrated number of engine events the accumulated noise voltage is less than a calibratable threshold the knock sensor output is considered low and P0325 will set. Two Trip Fault. Three good trips to turn off the MIL.
DTC: P0325-12 **Year:** 2012 **Model:** 500 **Engine:** 1.4L L4	**KNOCK SENSOR 1 CIRCUIT:** The Powertrain Control Module (PCM) detects that the Knock Sensor input voltage is: Above 4.0 Volts, less than or equal to 1.0 Volt with engine RPM at or above 2200 or equal to 0.0 Volts with engine RPM below 2200. Two Trip Fault. Three good trips to turn off the MIL.
DTC: P0326 **Year:** 2012 **Model:** 500 **Engine:** 1.4L L4	**KNOCK SENSOR 1 CIRCUIT PERFORMANCE:** The Powertrain Control Module detects the that knock sensor capacitance is greater than a calibrated value.
DTC: P0327 **Year:** 2012 **Model:** 500 **Engine:** 1.4L L4	**KNOCK SENSOR 1 CIRCUIT LOW:** The Powertrain Control Module detects the that knock sensor voltage is less than a calibrated value.
DTC: P0328 **Year:** 2012 **Model:** 500 **Engine:** 1.4L L4	**KNOCK SENSOR 1 CIRCUIT HIGH:** The Powertrain Control Module detects the that knock sensor voltage is greater than a calibrated value.
DTC: P0335 **Year:** 2012 **Model:** 500 **Engine:** 1.4L L4	**CRANKSHAFT POSITION SENSOR CIRCUIT:** No CKP signal is present during engine cranking and at least eight camshaft position sensor signals have occurred. One Trip Fault. Three good trips to turn off the MIL.
DTC: P0335-62 **Year:** 2012 **Model:** 500 **Engine:** 1.4L L4	**CRANKSHAFT POSITION SENSOR CIRCUIT:** No CKP signal is present during engine cranking and at least eight camshaft position sensor signals have occurred. One Trip Fault. Three good trips to turn off the MIL.
DTC: P0339 **Year:** 2012 **Model:** 500 **Engine:** 1.4L L4	**CRANKSHAFT POSITION SENSOR INTERMITTENT:** When the CKP Sensor failure counter reaches 20. One Trip Fault. Three good trips to turn off the MIL.
DTC: P0340 **Year:** 2012 **Model:** 500 **Engine:** 1.4L L4	**CAMSHAFT POSITION SENSOR CIRCUIT:** The Powertrain Control Module (PCM) detects an implausible Camshaft Position Sensor signal during eight consecutive crankshaft revolutions. One Trip Fault. Three good trips to turn off the MIL.
DTC: P0340-11 **Year:** 2012 **Model:** 500 **Engine:** 1.4L L4	**CAMSHAFT POSITION SENSOR 1/1 CIRCUIT LOW:** The Powertrain Control Module (PCM) detects an implausible Camshaft Position Sensor signal during eight consecutive crankshaft revolutions. One Trip Fault. Three good trips to turn off the MIL.

DTC	Trouble Code Title and Conditions
DTC: P0340-15 **Year:** 2012 **Model:** 500 **Engine:** 1.4L L4	**CAMSHAFT POSITION SENSOR 1/1 CIRCUIT HIGH:** The Powertrain Control Module (PCM) detects an implausible Camshaft Position Sensor signal during eight consecutive crankshaft revolutions. One Trip Fault. Three good trips to turn off the MIL.
DTC: P0340-62 **Year:** 2012 **Model:** 500 **Engine:** 1.4L L4	**CAMSHAFT POSITION SENSOR CIRCUIT BANK 1 SENSOR 1:** The Powertrain Control Module (PCM) detects an implausible Camshaft Position Sensor signal during eight consecutive crankshaft revolutions. One Trip Fault. Three good trips to turn off the MIL.
DTC: P0342 **Year:** 2012 **Model:** 500 **Engine:** 1.4L L4	**CAMSHAFT POSITION SENSOR CIRCUIT LOW:** The Powertrain Control Module (PCM) detects an implausible Camshaft Position Sensor signal during eight consecutive crankshaft revolutions. One Trip Fault. Three good trips to turn off the MIL.
DTC: P0343 **Year:** 2012 **Model:** 500 **Engine:** 1.4L L4	**CAMSHAFT POSITION SENSOR CIRCUIT HIGH:** The Powertrain Control Module (PCM) detects an implausible Camshaft Position Sensor signal during eight consecutive crankshaft revolutions. One Trip Fault. Three good trips to turn off the MIL.
DTC: P0351 **Year:** 2012 **Model:** 500 **Engine:** 1.4L L4	**IGNITION COIL 1 PRIMARY CIRCUIT:** Peak current is not achieved with battery based dwell plus 1.5 ms of diagnostic offset. It takes less than three (3) seconds during cranking or up to six (6) seconds while running to set.
DTC: P0351-12 **Year:** 2012 **Model:** 500 **Engine:** 1.4L L4	**IGNITION COIL 1 CIRCUIT HIGH:** If the Powertrain Control Module (PCM) detects a short to voltage on the Ignition Coil 1 Control circuit for more than 15 coil change requests, it will set this DTC.
DTC: P0351-14 **Year:** 2012 **Model:** 500 **Engine:** 1.4L L4	**IGNITION COIL 1 CIRCUIT:** Peak current is not achieved with battery based dwell plus 1.5 ms of diagnostic offset. It takes less than three (3) seconds during cranking or up to six (6) seconds while running to set.
DTC: P0352 **Year:** 2012 **Model:** 500 **Engine:** 1.4L L4	**IGNITION COIL 2 PRIMARY CIRCUIT:** Peak current is not achieved with battery based dwell plus 1.5 ms of diagnostic offset. It takes less than threee (3) seconds during cranking or up to six (6) seconds while running to set.
DTC: P0352-12 **Year:** 2012 **Model:** 500 **Engine:** 1.4L L4	**IGNITION COIL 2 CIRCUIT HIGH:** If the Powertrain Control Module (PCM) detects a short to voltage on the Ignition Coil 2 Control circuit for more than 15 coil change requests, it will set this DTC.
DTC: P0352-14 **Year:** 2012 **Model:** 500 **Engine:** 1.4L L4	**IGNITION COIL 2 CIRCUIT:** Peak current is not achieved with battery based dwell plus 1.5 ms of diagnostic offset. It takes less than threee (3) seconds during cranking or up to six (6) seconds while running to set.
DTC: P0353 **Year:** 2012 **Model:** 500 **Engine:** 1.4L L4	**IGNITION COIL 3 PRIMARY CIRCUIT:** Peak current is not achieved with battery based dwell plus 1.5 ms of diagnostic offset. It takes less than three (3) seconds during cranking or up to six (6) seconds while running to set.
DTC: P0353-12 **Year:** 2012 **Model:** 500 **Engine:** 1.4L L4	**IGNITION COIL 3 CIRCUIT HIGH:** The Powertrain Control Module (PCM) detects that the Coil 3 Control voltage is above the maximum acceptable value.
DTC: P0353-14 **Year:** 2012 **Model:** 500 **Engine:** 1.4L L4	**IGNITION COIL 3 CIRCUIT:** Peak current is not achieved with battery based dwell plus 1.5 ms of diagnostic offset. It takes less than three (3) seconds during cranking or up to six (6) seconds while running to set.
DTC: P0354 **Year:** 2012 **Model:** 500 **Engine:** 1.4L L4	**IGNITION COIL 4 PRIMARY CIRCUIT:** Peak current is not achieved with battery based dwell plus 1.5 ms of diagnostic offset. It takes less than three (3) seconds during cranking or up to six (6) seconds while running to set.

DTC	Trouble Code Title and Conditions
DTC: P0354-12 **Year:** 2012 **Model:** 500 **Engine:** 1.4L L4	**IGNITION COIL 4 CIRCUIT HIGH:** The Powertrain Control Module (PCM) detects that the Coil 4 Control voltage is above the maximum acceptable value.
DTC: P0354-14 **Year:** 2012 **Model:** 500 **Engine:** 1.4L L4	**IGNITION COIL 4 CIRCUIT:** Peak current is not achieved with battery based dwell plus 1.5 ms of diagnostic offset. It takes less than three (3) seconds during cranking or up to six (6) seconds while running to set.
DTC: P0420 **Year:** 2012 **Model:** 500 **Engine:** 1.4L L4	**CATALYST EFFICIENCY (BANK 1):** If the final State of Change index is within the calibrated fail threshold. Two trip fault. Three good trips to turn off the MIL.
DTC: P0420-62 **Year:** 2012 **Model:** 500 **Engine:** 1.4L L4	**CATALYST EFFICIENCY (BANK 1):** If the final State of Change index is within the calibrated fail threshold. Two trip fault. Three good trips to turn off the MIL.
DTC: P0440 **Year:** 2012 **Model:** 500 **Engine:** 1.4L L4	**GENERAL EVAP SYSTEM FAILURE:** When the monitor conditions are met, the Powertrain Control Module (PCM) will ramp in purge flow. If the PCM does not sense an ESIM Switch closure after a calculated amount of purge flow accumulation, an error is detected. Two Trip Fault. Three good trips to turn off the MIL.
DTC: P0441 **Year:** 2012 **Model:** 500 **Engine:** 1.4L L4	**EVAP PURGE SYSTEM PERFORMANCE:** If the Powertrain Control Module (PCM) detects that the purge vapor ratio and the ESIM switch closed ratio are below a calculated value, the PCM commands the purge solenoid to flow at a specified rate to update the purge vapor ratio. If the ratio remains below a specified value, a one trip failure is recorded. Two Trip Fault. Three good trips to turn off the MIL.
DTC: P0443-11 **Year:** 2012 **Model:** 500 **Engine:** 1.4L L4	**EVAP PURGE 1 CONTROL CIRCUIT LOW:** If the Powertrain Control Module (PCM) detects an shorted circuit in the Purge Solenoid or in the circuit, a one trip fault is set and the MIL is illuminated.
DTC: P0443-12 **Year:** 2012 **Model:** 500 **Engine:** 1.4L L4	**EVAP PURGE 1 CONTROL CIRCUIT HIGH:** If the Powertrain Control Module (PCM) detects a short to ground in the Purge Solenoid or in the circuit, a one trip fault is set and the MIL is illuminated.
DTC: P0443-13 **Year:** 2012 **Model:** 500 **Engine:** 1.4L L4	**EVAP PURGE 1 CONTROL CIRCUIT OPEN:** If the PCM detects an open circuit in the Purge Solenoid or in the circuit, a one trip fault is set and the MIL is illuminated.
DTC: P0444 **Year:** 2012 **Model:** 500 **Engine:** 1.4L L4	**EVAP PURGE SOLENOID CIRCUIT OPEN:** If the PCM detects an open circuit in the Purge Solenoid or in the circuit, a one trip fault is set and the MIL is illuminated.
DTC: P0451 **Year:** 2012 **Model:** 500 **Engine:** 1.4L L4	**FUEL TANK PRESSURE SENSOR PERFORMANCE:** Low limit: The Fuel Tank Pressure Sensor voltage is less than 0.1 Volt for 10 seconds. High limit: The Fuel Tank Pressure Sensor voltage is greater than 4.7 Volts for 10 seconds. Signal curve: The Fuel Tank Pressure Sensor Performance code will be set if the signal remains constant.
DTC: P0452 **Year:** 2012 **Model:** 500 **Engine:** 1.4L L4	**EVAP PRESSURE SWITCH STUCK CLOSED:** At key off, the Powertrain Control Module (PCM) energizes the Purge Solenoid for a calibrated amount of time (30 seconds maximum) and stores the state of the ESIM switch. The state is evaluated again at the next key on. If the PCM does not detect that the ESIM switch is open, an error is detected. Two Trip Fault. Three good trips to turn off the MIL.
DTC: P0455 **Year:** 2012 **Model:** 500 **Engine:** 1.4L L4	**EVAP PURGE SYSTEM LARGE LEAK:** The Powertrain Control Module (PCM) activates the Evap Purge Solenoid to pull the Evaporative system into a vacuum to close the ESIM Switch. Once the ESIM Switch is closed, the PCM turns the Evap Purge solenoid off to seal the Evaporative System. If the ESIM Switch reopens before the calibrated amount of time, a large leak error is detected. Two Trip Fault. Three good trips to turn off the MIL.
DTC: P0456 **Year:** 2012 **Model:** 500 **Engine:** 1.4L L4	**EVAP PURGE SYSTEM SMALL LEAK:** As temperatures change, a vacuum is created in the fuel tank and Evaporative system. With the Evaporative system sealed, the PCM monitors the ESIM Switch. If the ESIM Switch does not close within a calibrated time, an error is detected by the PCM. One Trip Fault. Three good trips to turn off the MIL.

DTC	Trouble Code Title and Conditions
DTC: P0457 **Year:** 2012 **Model:** 500 **Engine:** 1.4L L4	**LOOSE FUEL CAP:** If a leak greater than .090" is detected by the Powertrain Control Module (PCM) for three consecutive cold start trips after a significant fuel level change, this DTC will set. One good trip turns off the MIL.
DTC: P0458 **Year:** 2012 **Model:** 500 **Engine:** 1.4L L4	**EVAP PURGE CONTROL CIRCUIT LOW:** If the Powertrain Control Module (PCM) detects an shorted circuit in the Purge Solenoid or in the circuit, a one trip fault is set and the MIL is illuminated.
DTC: P0459 **Year:** 2012 **Model:** 500 **Engine:** 1.4L L4	**EVAP PURGE CONTROL CIRCUIT HIGH:** If the Powertrain Control Module (PCM) detects a short to ground in the Purge Solenoid or in the circuit, a one trip fault is set and the MIL is illuminated.
DTC: P0460-86 **Year:** 2012 **Model:** 500 **Engine:** 1.4L L4	**FUEL LEVEL SENSOR 1:** TEST No.1: If the PCM does not see a difference in fuel level of greater than 0.1 Volt the test will fail. TEST No.2: If the PCM does not see a change in the fuel level over a set amount of miles the test will fail. Two trip fault. Three good trips to turn off the MIL.
DTC: P0461 **Year:** 2012 **Model:** 500 **Engine:** 1.4L L4	**FUEL LEVEL SENSOR 1 PERFORMANCE:** TEST No.1: If the PCM does not see a difference in fuel level of greater than 0.1 Volt the test will fail. TEST No.2: If the PCM does not see a change in the fuel level over a set amount of miles the test will fail. Two trip fault. Three good trips to turn off the MIL.
DTC: P0462 **Year:** 2012 **Model:** 500 **Engine:** 1.4L L4	**FUEL LEVEL SENSOR 1 CIRCUIT LOW:** The fuel level sensor signal voltage goes below the minimum acceptable value. One Trip Fault. Three good trips to turn off the MIL.
DTC: P0463 **Year:** 2012 **Model:** 500 **Engine:** 1.4L L4	**FUEL LEVEL SENSOR 1 CIRCUIT HIGH:** The fuel level sensor signal voltage at the Powertrain Control Module (PCM) goes above the maximum acceptable value. One Trip Fault. Three good trips to turn off the MIL.
DTC: P0480 **Year:** 2012 **Model:** 500 **Engine:** 1.4L L4	**COOLING FAN 1 CONTROL CIRCUIT:** An open or shorted circuit is detected in the Low Rad Fan Control circuit. One Trip Fault. Three good trips to turn off the MIL.
DTC: P0480-11 **Year:** 2012 **Model:** 500 **Engine:** 1.4L L4	**COOLING FAN 1 CONTROL CIRCUIT LOW:** The DTC is set if the Low Speed Fan Relay Control circuit is shorted to ground.
DTC: P0480-12 **Year:** 2012 **Model:** 500 **Engine:** 1.4L L4	**COOLING FAN 1 CONTROL CIRCUIT HIGH:** The DTC is set if the Low Speed Fan Relay Control circuit is open or shorted high.
DTC: P0480-13 **Year:** 2012 **Model:** 500 **Engine:** 1.4L L4	**COOLING FAN 1 CONTROL CIRCUIT OPEN:** An open or shorted circuit is detected in the Low Rad Fan Control circuit. One Trip Fault. Three good trips to turn off the MIL.
DTC: P0481 **Year:** 2012 **Model:** 500 **Engine:** 1.4L L4	**COOLING FAN 2 CONTROL CIRCUIT:** An open or shorted circuit is detected in the High Speed Rad Fan Control circuit. One Trip Fault. Three good trips to turn off the MIL.
DTC: P0481-11 **Year:** 2012 **Model:** 500 **Engine:** 1.4L L4	**COOLING FAN 2 CONTROL CIRCUIT LOW:** The DTC is set if the High Speed Fan Relay Control circuit is shorted to ground.
DTC: P0481-12 **Year:** 2012 **Model:** 500 **Engine:** 1.4L L4	**COOLING FAN 2 CONTROL CIRCUIT HIGH:** The DTC is set if the High Speed Fan Relay Control circuit is open or shorted high.

DTC	Trouble Code Title and Conditions
DTC: P0481-13 **Year:** 2012 **Model:** 500 **Engine:** 1.4L L4	**COOLING FAN 2 CONTROL CIRCUIT OPEN:** An open or shorted circuit is detected in the High Speed Rad Fan Control circuit. One Trip Fault. Three good trips to turn off the MIL.
DTC: P0500 **Year:** 2012 **Model:** 500 **Engine:** 1.4L L4	**NO VEHICLE SPEED SENSOR SIGNAL:** The DTC will set if multiple ABS wheel speed signals are invalid.
DTC: P0500-64 **Year:** 2012 **Model:** 500 **Engine:** 1.4L L4	**VEHICLE SPEED SENSOR "A" INTERMITTENT/ERRATIC/HIGH:** This code will set if no vehicle speed signal is received from the ABS Module up to 120 seconds for two consecutive trips. Two Trip Fault. Three good trips to turn off the MIL.
DTC: P0500-68 **Year:** 2012 **Model:** 500 **Engine:** 1.4L L4	**VEHICLE SPEED SENSOR 1 CIRCUIT:** The DTC will set if multiple ABS wheel speed signals are invalid.
DTC: P0501 **Year:** 2012 **Model:** 500 **Engine:** 1.4L L4	**VEHICLE SPEED SENSOR 1 PERFORMANCE:** This code will set if no vehicle speed signal is received from the ABS Module up to 120 seconds for two consecutive trips. Two Trip Fault. Three good trips to turn off the MIL.
DTC: P0504 **Year:** 2012 **Model:** 500 **Engine:** 1.4L L4	**BRAKE SWITCH A/B CORRELATION:** The Powertrain Control Module (PCM) detects a plausibility error is present in the brake information received from the ABS Module.
DTC: P0504-13 **Year:** 2012 **Model:** 500 **Engine:** 1.4L L4	**BRAKE PEDAL NOT PLAUSIBLE BLS/RBS CIRCUIT OPEN:** When the Powertrain Control Module (PCM) recognizes Brake Switch No.1 is stuck in the high/off position. Two Trip Fault. Three good trips to turn off the MIL.
DTC: P0504-62 **Year:** 2012 **Model:** 500 **Engine:** 1.4L L4	**BRAKE PEDAL SIGNAL COMPARE FAILURE:** The Primary Brake Switch Signal and Secondary Brake Switch Signal inputs to the Powertrain Control Module (PCM) do not agree.
DTC: P0504-67 **Year:** 2012 **Model:** 500 **Engine:** 1.4L L4	**BRAKE PEDAL NOT PLAUSIBLE BLS/RBS SIGNAL INCORRECT AFTER EVENT:** The Powertrain Control Module (PCM) recognizes the Brake Pedal could not electrically indicate the applied (On) position with both switch inputs. One trip fault.
DTC: P0504-86 **Year:** 2012 **Model:** 500 **Engine:** 1.4L L4	**BRAKE PEDAL NOT PLAUSIBLE BLS/RBS SIGNAL INVALID:** If the output of Brake Switch No.1 signal to the Powertrain Control Module (PCM) looks like it is not applied, while Brake Lamp Switch Output circuit to the BCM is applied, the fault will mature in 60ms. One Trip Fault.
DTC: P0506 **Year:** 2012 **Model:** 500 **Engine:** 1.4L L4	**IDLE SPEED PERFORMANCE LOWER THAN EXCEPTED:** Engine speed is 100 RPM or more below idle speed for seven (7) seconds. Two Trip Fault. Three good trips to turn off the MIL.
DTC: P0507 **Year:** 2012 **Model:** 500 **Engine:** 1.4L L4	**IDLE SPEED PERFORMANCE HIGHER THAN EXCEPTED:** Engine speed is 200 RPM or more above idle speed for 7 seconds. Two Trip Fault. Three good trips to turn off the MIL.
DTC: P050B **Year:** 2012 **Model:** 500 **Engine:** 1.4L L4	**COLD START IGNITION TIMING PERFORMANCE:** Engine RPM is 50 RPM or more (depending on vehicle specifications), below idle speed for at least 3 seconds and the average spark advance is above the threshold, too much spark advance, for a specified time limit. Two trip fault. Three good trips to turn off the MIL.
DTC: P0513 **Year:** 2012 **Model:** 500 **Engine:** 1.4L L4	**INVALID SKIM KEY:** The Powertrain Control Module (PCM) detects an invalid Secret key. One Trip Fault.

DTC	Trouble Code Title and Conditions
DTC: P0520 **Year:** 2012 **Model:** 500 **Engine:** 1.4L L4	**ENGINE OIL PRESSURE SENSOR CIRCUIT:** The Powertrain Control Module (PCM) senses the oil pressure is out of the calibrated range. One Trip fault.
DTC: P0520-67 **Year:** 2012 **Model:** 500 **Engine:** 1.4L L4	**ENGINE OIL PRESSURE SENSOR CIRCUIT:** The Powertrain Control Module (PCM) senses the oil pressure is out of the calibrated range. One Trip fault.
DTC: P0530-12 **Year:** 2012 **Model:** 500 **Engine:** 1.4L L4	**A/C PRESSURE SENSOR CIRCUIT HIGH:** The A/C pressure transducer signal the PCM is above the maximum acceptable value. One trip Fault. Three good trips to turn off the MIL.
DTC: P0530-14 **Year:** 2012 **Model:** 500 **Engine:** 1.4L L4	**A/C PRESSURE SENSOR CIRCUIT LOW:** The A/C pressure transducer signal voltage received by the PCM is below the minimum acceptable value. One Trip Fault. Three good trips to turn off the MIL.
DTC: P0532 **Year:** 2012 **Model:** 500 **Engine:** 1.4L L4	**A/C PRESSURE SENSOR CIRCUIT LOW:** The A/C pressure transducer signal voltage received by the PCM is below the minimum acceptable value. One Trip Fault. Three good trips to turn off the MIL.
DTC: P0533 **Year:** 2012 **Model:** 500 **Engine:** 1.4L L4	**A/C PRESSURE SENSOR CIRCUIT HIGH:** The A/C pressure transducer signal the PCM is above the maximum acceptable value. One trip Fault. Three good trips to turn off the MIL.
DTC: P0560 **Year:** 2012 **Model:** 500 **Engine:** 1.4L L4	**BATTERY VOLTAGE:** TCM detects incorrect battery voltage.
DTC: P0560-16 **Year:** 2012 **Model:** 500 **Engine:** 1.4L L4	**BATTERY/SYSTEM VOLTAGE LOW:** Battery voltage is less than 6 Volts. One Trip Fault.
DTC: P0560-17 **Year:** 2012 **Model:** 500 **Engine:** 1.4L L4	**BATTERY/SYSTEM VOLTAGE HIGH:** Battery voltage is 1 Volt greater than desired voltage for more than 10 seconds. Battery voltage greater than 15.75 Volts. One Trip Fault. Three good trips to turn off the MIL.
DTC: P0561 **Year:** 2012 **Model:** 500 **Engine:** 1.4L L4	**BATTERY VOLTAGE:** TCM detects incorrect battery voltage.
DTC: P0561 **Year:** 2012 **Model:** 500 **Engine:** 1.4L L4	**SYSTEM VOLTAGE UNSTABLE:** Battery voltage is below 10.5 volts, but greater than 9 volts.
DTC: P0562 **Year:** 2012 **Model:** 500 **Engine:** 1.4L L4	**BATTERY/SYSTEM VOLTAGE LOW:** Battery voltage is below 9.0 volts.
DTC: P0562 **Year:** 2012 **Model:** 500 **Engine:** 1.4L L4	**BATTERY VOLTAGE LOW:** Battery voltage is less than 6 Volts. One Trip Fault.
DTC: P0563 **Year:** 2012 **Model:** 500 **Engine:** 1.4L L4	**BATTERY VOLTAGE HIGH:** Battery voltage is 1 Volt greater than desired voltage for more than 10 seconds. Battery voltage greater than 15.75 Volts. One Trip Fault. Three good trips to turn off the MIL.

DTC	Trouble Code Title and Conditions
DTC: P0563 **Year:** 2012 **Model:** 500 **Engine:** 1.4L L4	**SYSTEM VOLTAGE HIGH:** Battery voltage is above 18.0 volts.
DTC: P0564 **Year:** 2012 **Model:** 500 **Engine:** 1.4L L4	**SPEED CONTROL SWITCH 1:** The S/C Switch 1 Signal is below 0.60 volt for 1.0 second.
DTC: P0564-92 **Year:** 2012 **Model:** 500 **Engine:** 1.4L L4	**SPEED CONTROL SWITCH 1:** The S/C Switch1 Signal is below 0.60 volt for 1.0 second.
DTC: P0571 **Year:** 2012 **Model:** 500 **Engine:** 1.4L L4	**BRAKE SWITCH 1 PERFORMANCE:** If the output of Brake Switch No.1 signal to the Powertrain Control Module (PCM) looks like it is not applied, while Brake Lamp Switch Output circuit to the BCM is applied, the fault will mature in 60ms. One Trip Fault.
DTC: P0571 **Year:** 2012 **Model:** 500 **Engine:** 1.4L L4	**SERVICE BRAKE SWITCH (FROM CAN):** TCM detects incorrect brake switch state.
DTC: P0572 **Year:** 2012 **Model:** 500 **Engine:** 1.4L L4	**BRAKE SWITCH 1 STUCK ON:** When the Powertrain Control Module (PCM) recognizes Brake Switch No.1 is mechanically stuck in the low/on position. Two Trip Fault. Three good trips to clear.
DTC: P0573 **Year:** 2012 **Model:** 500 **Engine:** 1.4L L4	**BRAKE SWITCH 1 STUCK OFF:** When the Powertrain Control Module (PCM) recognizes Brake Switch No.1 is stuck in the high/off position. Two Trip Fault. Three good trips to turn off the MIL.
DTC: P0576-62 **Year:** 2012 **Model:** 500 **Engine:** 1.4L L4	**SPEED CONTROL DISABLED DUE TO EXCESSIVE DECELERATION:** The vehicle speed is above 250 kph for 0.5 of a second.
DTC: P0579-62 **Year:** 2012 **Model:** 500 **Engine:** 1.4L L4	**SPEED CONTROL DISABLED DUE TO HIGH ACCELERATION:** The vehicle speed is above 250 kph for 0.5 of a second.
DTC: P0601 **Year:** 2012 **Model:** 500 **Engine:** 1.4L L4	**INTERNAL CONTROL MODULE MEMORY CHECKSUM ERROR:** When the value of check sum calculated after Ignition ON is different from the correct check sum value stored in flash ROM.
DTC: P0601 **Year:** 2012 **Model:** 500 **Engine:** 1.4L L4	**INTERNAL MEMORY CHECKSUM INVALID:** Internal checksum for software failed, does not match calculated value. One trip fault, three good trips to clear.
DTC: P0601-44 **Year:** 2012 **Model:** 500 **Engine:** 1.4L L4	**INTERNAL MEMORY CHECKSUM ERROR:** Internal checksum for software failed, does not match calculated value. One trip fault, three good trips to clear.
DTC: P0603 **Year:** 2012 **Model:** 500 **Engine:** 1.4L L4	**INTERNAL CONTROL MODULE KEEP ALIVE MEMORY (KAM) ERROR:** When the calculated check sum in RAM is different from check sum value in EEPROM.
DTC: P0604 **Year:** 2012 **Model:** 500 **Engine:** 1.4L L4	**CONTROL UNIT FAULTY (MICROPROCESSOR):** When the TCM cannot correctly write to, or read from the RAM.

DTC	Trouble Code Title and Conditions
DTC: P0604 **Year:** 2012 **Model:** 500 **Engine:** 1.4L L4	**INTERNAL CONTROL MODULE RANDOM ACCESS MEMORY (RAM) ERROR:** When the TCM cannot correctly write to, or read from the RAM.
DTC: P0604 **Year:** 2012 **Model:** 500 **Engine:** 1.4L L4	**INTERNAL CONTROL MODULE RAM ERROR:** Internal Powertrain Control Module software error. One trip failure illuminates the MIL and three good trips to turn off the MIL.
DTC: P0604 **Year:** 2012 **Model:** 500 **Engine:** 1.4L L4	**CONTROL UNIT FAULTY (MICROPROCESSOR):** The TCM has deteted a problem with the lever switch 1 sensor.
DTC: P0604-62 **Year:** 2012 **Model:** 500 **Engine:** 1.4L L4	**INTERNAL CONTROL MODULE RAM ERROR:** Internal Powertrain Control Module software error. One trip failure illuminates the MIL and three good trips to turn off the MIL.
DTC: P0605 **Year:** 2012 **Model:** 500 **Engine:** 1.4L L4	**INTERNAL CONTROL MODULE ROM:** Whenever the Powertrain Control Module (PCM) detects an internal controller problem.
DTC: P0605-41 **Year:** 2012 **Model:** 500 **Engine:** 1.4L L4	**INTERNAL CONTROL MODULE EEPROM:** The Powertrain Control Module (PCM) detects an internal failure.
DTC: P0605-49 **Year:** 2012 **Model:** 500 **Engine:** 1.4L L4	**INTERNAL CONTROL MODULE ROM:** Whenever the Powertrain Control Module (PCM) detects an internal controller problem.
DTC: P0606 **Year:** 2012 **Model:** 500 **Engine:** 1.4L L4	**INTERNAL ECM PROCESSOR:** When the Powertrain Control Module (PCM) recognizes an internal failure. One trip fault. Three good trip to clear. ETC light is flashing.
DTC: P0606-47 **Year:** 2012 **Model:** 500 **Engine:** 1.4L L4	**INTERNAL ECM PROCESSOR:** When the Powertrain Control Module (PCM) recognizes an internal failure. One trip fault. Three good trip to clear. ETC light is flashing.
DTC: P0606-92 **Year:** 2012 **Model:** 500 **Engine:** 1.4L L4	**ECU INTERNAL PERFORMANCE:** The Powertrain Control Module (PCM) detects an internal failure.
DTC: P0607 **Year:** 2012 **Model:** 500 **Engine:** 1.4L L4	**ECU INTERNAL PERFORMANCE:** The Powertrain Control Module (PCM) detects an internal failure.
DTC: P060B **Year:** 2012 **Model:** 500 **Engine:** 1.4L L4	**ETC A/D GROUND PERFORMANCE:** When A2D reading does not return to ground within a set period of time of test activation, this fault sets. The test typically runs a couple of times per second and is the reason why APP2 signal spikes to ground a couple of times per second in normal running. Reprogramming the module may not always fix this fault. One trip fault. ETC lamp is illuminated.
DTC: P060B-49 **Year:** 2012 **Model:** 500 **Engine:** 1.4L L4	**INTERNAL CONTROL MODULE A/D PROCESSING PERFORMANCE:** When A2D reading does not return to ground within a set period of time of test activation, this fault sets. The test typically runs a couple of times per second and is the reason why APP2 signal spikes to ground a couple of times per second in normal running. Reprogramming the module may not always fix this fault. One trip fault. ETC lamp is illuminated.
DTC: P060C **Year:** 2012 **Model:** 500 **Engine:** 1.4L L4	**CONTROL UNIT FAULTY (MICROPROCESSOR):** When the TCM cannot correctly write to, or read from the RAM.

DTC	Trouble Code Title and Conditions
DTC: P060C **Year:** 2012 **Model:** 500 **Engine:** 1.4L L4	**INTERNAL CONTROL MODULE MAIN PROCESSOR PERFORMANCE:** Internal checksum for software failed, does not match calculated value. One trip fault, three good trips to clear.
DTC: P0613 **Year:** 2012 **Model:** 500 **Engine:** 1.4L L4	**CONTROL UNIT FAULTY (MICROPROCESSOR):** When the TCM cannot correctly write to, or read from the RAM.
DTC: P0615 **Year:** 2012 **Model:** 500 **Engine:** 1.4L L4	**STARTER CONTROL CIRCUIT OPEN:** The Powertrain Control Module (PCM) detects an open condition in the starter relay control circuit.
DTC: P0616 **Year:** 2012 **Model:** 500 **Engine:** 1.4L L4	**STARTER CONTROL CIRCUIT LOW:** The Powertrain Control Module (PCM) detects an open condition in the starter relay control circuit.
DTC: P0617 **Year:** 2012 **Model:** 500 **Engine:** 1.4L L4	**STARTER CONTROL CIRCUIT HIGH:** The Powertrain Control Module (PCM) detects an shorted high condition in the starter relay control circuit.
DTC: P0621-11 **Year:** 2012 **Model:** 500 **Engine:** 1.4L L4	**GENERATOR FIELD CONTROL CIRCUIT LOW:** The PCM detects that the Generator Field Control circuit is shorted to ground.
DTC: P0621-15 **Year:** 2012 **Model:** 500 **Engine:** 1.4L L4	**GENERATOR FIELD CONTROL CIRCUIT HIGH:** The PCM detects that the Generator Field Control circuit is open or shorted to voltage.
DTC: P0625 **Year:** 2012 **Model:** 500 **Engine:** 1.4L L4	**GENERATOR FIELD CONTROL CIRCUIT LOW:** The PCM detects that the Generator Field Control circuit is shorted to ground.
DTC: P0626 **Year:** 2012 **Model:** 500 **Engine:** 1.4L L4	**GENERATOR FIELD CONTROL CIRCUIT HIGH:** The PCM detects that the Generator Field Control circuit is open or shorted to voltage.
DTC: P0627 **Year:** 2012 **Model:** 500 **Engine:** 1.4L L4	**FUEL PUMP RELAY CIRCUIT:** The Powertrain Control Module (PCM) detects that the actual state of the fuel pump control does not match the intended state.
DTC: P0628 **Year:** 2012 **Model:** 500 **Engine:** 1.4L L4	**FUEL PUMP CONTROL CIRCUIT LOW:** The Powertrain Control Module (PCM) detects that the fuel pump control circuit is low.
DTC: P0629 **Year:** 2012 **Model:** 500 **Engine:** 1.4L L4	**FUEL PUMP CONTROL CIRCUIT HIGH:** The Powertrain Control Module (PCM) detects that the fuel pump control circuit is high.
DTC: P062F **Year:** 2012 **Model:** 500 **Engine:** 1.4L L4	**INTERNAL CONTROL MODULE EEPROM ERROR:** The Powerterain Control Module (PCM) detects an internal failure.
DTC: P0630-51 **Year:** 2012 **Model:** 500 **Engine:** 1.4L L4	**VIN NOT PROGRAMMED IN PCM:** The VIN has not been programmed into the PCM. One Trip Fault. Three good trips to turn off the MIL.

DTC	Trouble Code Title and Conditions
DTC: P0633 **Year:** 2012 **Model:** 500 **Engine:** 1.4L L4	**SKIM SECRET KEY NOT STORED IN PCM:** The Secret Key information has not been programmed into the Powertrain Control Module (PCM). One Trip Fault. Three good trips to turn off the MIL.
DTC: P0638-11 **Year:** 2012 **Model:** 500 **Engine:** 1.4L L4	**ELECTRONIC THROTTLE CONTROL MOTOR CIRCUIT LOW:** When the Powertrain Control Module (PCM) detects an internal error or a short to ground in the ETC Motor - and ETC Motor + circuits. One trip fault. ETC light is flashing.
DTC: P0638-12 **Year:** 2012 **Model:** 500 **Engine:** 1.4L L4	**ELECTRONIC THROTTLE CONTROL MOTOR CIRCUIT HIGH:** When the Powertrain Control Module (PCM) detects an internal error or a short to voltage in the ETC Motor - and ETC Motor + circuits. One trip fault. ETC light is flashing.
DTC: P0638-13 **Year:** 2012 **Model:** 500 **Engine:** 1.4L L4	**ELECTRONIC THROTTLE CONTROL MOTOR CIRCUIT OPEN BANK 1:** When the Powertrain Control Module (PCM) detects an internal error or a short between the ETC Motor - and ETC Motor + circuits in the ETC Motor Driver. One trip fault. ETC light is flashing.
DTC: P0638-61 **Year:** 2012 **Model:** 500 **Engine:** 1.4L L4	**ELECTRONIC THROTTLE CONTROL MOTOR PERFORMANCE:** The Powertrain Control Module (PCM) recognizes too large of an error between the actual position of the Throttle Plate and the Set Point position. One trip fault and the code will set within five seconds. Three good trips to turn off the MIL ETC light is flashing.
DTC: P0641 **Year:** 2012 **Model:** 500 **Engine:** 1.4L L4	**SENSOR REFERENCE VOLTAGE 1 CIRCUIT:** The Powertrain Control Module (PCM) detects that the voltage on the 5-Volt Sensor Supply 1 circuit is below 4.7 Volts or above 5.3 Volts for 0.16 of a second.
DTC: P0641 **Year:** 2012 **Model:** 500 **Engine:** 1.4L L4	**SENSOR POWER SUPPLY:** The TCM has deteted a problem with the sensor power supply.
DTC: P0641-49 **Year:** 2012 **Model:** 500 **Engine:** 1.4L L4	**SENSOR REFERENCE VOLTAGE 1 CIRCUIT:** The Powertrain Control Module (PCM) detects that the voltage on the 5-Volt Sensor Supply 1 circuit is below 4.7 Volts or above 5.3 Volts for 0.16 of a second.
DTC: P0645 **Year:** 2012 **Model:** 500 **Engine:** 1.4L L4	**A/C CLUTCH RELAY CIRCUIT:** An open or shorted condition is detected in the A/C Clutch Relay control circuit. One Trip Fault. Three good trips to turn off the MIL.
DTC: P0645-11 **Year:** 2012 **Model:** 500 **Engine:** 1.4L L4	**A/C CONTROL CIRCUIT LOW:** The PCM detects that the A/C Compressor control circuit voltage is below the minimum acceptable value.
DTC: P0645-12 **Year:** 2012 **Model:** 500 **Engine:** 1.4L L4	**A/C CLUTCH RELAY CONTROL CIRCUIT HIGH:** The Powertrain Control Module senses voltage on the A/C Clutch Relay Control circuit when A/C is not being requested. One Trip Fault. Three good trips to turn off the MIL.
DTC: P0645-13 **Year:** 2012 **Model:** 500 **Engine:** 1.4L L4	**A/C CLUTCH RELAY CIRCUIT:** An open or shorted condition is detected in the A/C Clutch Relay control circuit. One Trip Fault. Three good trips to turn off the MIL.
DTC: P0646 **Year:** 2012 **Model:** 500 **Engine:** 1.4L L4	**A/C CONTROL CIRCUIT LOW:** The PCM detects that the A/C Compressor control circuit voltage is below the minimum acceptable value.
DTC: P0647 **Year:** 2012 **Model:** 500 **Engine:** 1.4L L4	**A/C CLUTCH RELAY CONTROL CIRCUIT HIGH:** The Powertrain Control Module senses voltage on the A/C Clutch Relay Control circuit when A/C is not being requested. One Trip Fault. Three good trips to turn off the MIL.

DTC	Trouble Code Title and Conditions
DTC: P0651 **Year:** 2012 **Model:** 500 **Engine:** 1.4L L4	**SENSOR REFERENCE VOLTAGE 2 CIRCUIT:** The PCM detects low voltage on the Sensor Supply 2 circuit for 0.16 second
DTC: P0651-49 **Year:** 2012 **Model:** 500 **Engine:** 1.4L L4	**SENSOR REFERENCE VOLTAGE 2 CIRCUIT:** The PCM detects low voltage on the Sensor Supply 2 circuit for 0.16 second
DTC: P0657 **Year:** 2012 **Model:** 500 **Engine:** 1.4L L4	**ACTUATOR SUPPLY VOLTAGE "A" CIRCUIT/OPEN:** TCM detects an internal Linear solenoid drive error.
DTC: P0657-16 **Year:** 2012 **Model:** 500 **Engine:** 1.4L L4	**ACTUATOR SUPPLY VOLTAGE "A" CIRCUIT LOW:** The Powertrain Control Module (PCM) detects low voltage on the ASD Relay Output circuits.
DTC: P0657-17 **Year:** 2012 **Model:** 500 **Engine:** 1.4L L4	**ACTUATOR SUPPLY VOLTAGE "A" CIRCUIT HIGH:** The Powertrain Control Module (PCM) detects high voltage on the ASD Relay Output circuits.
DTC: P0658 **Year:** 2012 **Model:** 500 **Engine:** 1.4L L4	**ACTUATOR SUPPLY VOLTAGE "A" CIRCUIT LOW:** The Powertrain Control Module (PCM) detects low voltage on the ASD Relay Output circuits.
DTC: P0659 **Year:** 2012 **Model:** 500 **Engine:** 1.4L L4	**ACTUATOR SUPPLY VOLTAGE "A" CIRCUIT HIGH:** The Powertrain Control Module (PCM) detects high voltage on the ASD Relay Output circuits.
DTC: P0685 **Year:** 2012 **Model:** 500 **Engine:** 1.4L L4	**ASD/MAIN CONTROL CIRCUIT:** The actual ASD state is not equal to the desired ASD state. One Trip Fault. Three good trips to turn off the MIL.
DTC: P0685-11 **Year:** 2012 **Model:** 500 **Engine:** 1.4L L4	**MAIN CONTROL CIRCUIT LOW:** The actual ASD state is not equal to the desired ASD state. One Trip Fault. Three good trips to turn off the MIL.
DTC: P0685-12 **Year:** 2012 **Model:** 500 **Engine:** 1.4L L4	**MAIN CONTROL CIRCUIT HIGH:** If the Powertrain Control (PCM) detects high voltage on the ASD Relay Control circuit for more than 3.5 seconds, it will set this DTC.
DTC: P0685-13 **Year:** 2012 **Model:** 500 **Engine:** 1.4L L4	**ASD/MAIN CONTROL CIRCUIT:** The actual ASD state is not equal to the desired ASD state. One Trip Fault. Three good trips to turn off the MIL.
DTC: P0686 **Year:** 2012 **Model:** 500 **Engine:** 1.4L L4	**ASD/MAIN CONTROL CIRCUIT LOW:** The actual ASD state is not equal to the desired ASD state. One Trip Fault. Three good trips to turn off the MIL.
DTC: P0687 **Year:** 2012 **Model:** 500 **Engine:** 1.4L L4	**ASD/MAIN CONTROL CIRCUIT HIGH:** If the Powertrain Control (PCM) detects high voltage on the ASD Relay Control circuit for more than 3.5 seconds, it will set this DTC.
DTC: P0691 **Year:** 2012 **Model:** 500 **Engine:** 1.4L L4	**COOLING FAN 1 CONTROL CIRCUIT LOW:** The DTC is set if the Low Speed Fan Relay Control circuit is shorted to ground.

DTC	Trouble Code Title and Conditions
DTC: P0692 **Year:** 2012 **Model:** 500 **Engine:** 1.4L L4	**COOLING FAN 1 CONTROL CIRCUIT HIGH:** The DTC is set if the Low Speed Fan Relay Control circuit is open or shorted high.
DTC: P0693 **Year:** 2012 **Model:** 500 **Engine:** 1.4L L4	**COOLING FAN 2 CONTROL CIRCUIT LOW:** The DTC is set if the High Speed Fan Relay Control circuit is shorted to ground.
DTC: P0694 **Year:** 2012 **Model:** 500 **Engine:** 1.4L L4	**COOLING FAN 2 CONTROL CIRCUIT HIGH:** The DTC is set if the High Speed Fan Relay Control circuit is open or shorted high.
DTC: P0697 **Year:** 2012 **Model:** 500 **Engine:** 1.4L L4	**SENSOR REFERENCE VOLTAGE 3 CIRCUIT:** The Powertrain Control Module (PCM) detects a low voltage on the Sensor Supply 3 circuit for 0.10 second.
DTC: P0697-49 **Year:** 2012 **Model:** 500 **Engine:** 1.4L L4	**SENSOR REFERENCE VOLTAGE 3 CIRCUIT:** The Powertrain Control Module (PCM) detects a low voltage on the Sensor Supply 3 circuit for 0.10 second.
DTC: P0700-62 **Year:** 2012 **Model:** 500 **Engine:** 1.4L L4	**TRANSMISSION CONTROL SYSTEM (MIL REQUEST):** An active DTC is stored in the Transmission Control Module. This is a one trip fault. Three good trips to turn off the MIL Lamp.
DTC: P0703 **Year:** 2012 **Model:** 500 **Engine:** 1.4L L4	**BRAKE SWITCH 2 PERFORMANCE:** When the Brake Switch No.2 signal the PCM recieves from the BCM does not match the status the Brake Switch No.1 supplies to the PCM. This could be a normal condition. If this condition is seen repeatedly by the PCM the fault is set. Cruise will not work for the rest of the key cycle.
DTC: P0704 **Year:** 2012 **Model:** 500 **Engine:** 1.4L L4	**CLUTCH SWITCH INPUT CIRCUIT:** The Powertrain Control Module (PCM) receives a signal from the Clutch Upstop Switch indicating that the clutch pedal is depressed while the vehicle is driven.
DTC: P0704-23 **Year:** 2012 **Model:** 500 **Engine:** 1.4L L4	**CLUTCH PEDAL SWITCH 1 CIRCUIT LOW:** The Powertrain Control Module (PCM) receives a signal from the Clutch Interlock Switch indicating that the clutch pedal is not depressed when the vehicle is started.
DTC: P0704-24 **Year:** 2012 **Model:** 500 **Engine:** 1.4L L4	**CLUTCH PEDAL SWITCH 1 CIRCUIT HIGH:** The Powertrain Control Module (PCM) receives a signal from the Clutch Interlock Switch indicating that the clutch pedal is depressed while the vehicle is driven.
DTC: P0704-87 **Year:** 2012 **Model:** 500 **Engine:** 1.4L L4	**CLUTCH SWITCH INPUT CIRCUIT:** The Powertrain Control Module (PCM) receives a signal from the Clutch Upstop Switch indicating that the clutch pedal is depressed while the vehicle is driven.
DTC: P0705 **Year:** 2012 **Model:** 500 **Engine:** 1.4L L4	**TRANSMISSION RANGE SENSOR "A" CIRCUIT (PRNDL INPUT):** When position sensor is below 0.12 of a volt for 100 ms for two consecutive checks.
DTC: P0707 **Year:** 2012 **Model:** 500 **Engine:** 1.4L L4	**TRANSMISSION RANGE SENSOR "A" CIRCUIT LOW:** When position sensor is below 0.12 of a volt for 100 ms for two consecutive checks.
DTC: P0708 **Year:** 2012 **Model:** 500 **Engine:** 1.4L L4	**TRANSMISSION RANGE SENSOR "A" CIRCUIT HIGH:** When position sensor is above 4.87 volts for 100 ms for two consecutive checks.

DTC	Trouble Code Title and Conditions
DTC: P0710 **Year:** 2012 **Model:** 500 **Engine:** 1.4L L4	**TEMPERATURE (FROM CAN):** TCM detects incorrect temperature.
DTC: P0711 **Year:** 2012 **Model:** 500 **Engine:** 1.4L L4	**TRANSMISSION FLUID TEMPERATURE SENSOR "A" CIRCUIT RANGE/PERFORMANCE:** Change in Transmission Oil Temperature is less than a calibrated value over time (slow to hange). Or, Change in Transmission Oil Temperature is greater that a calibrated value (rapid change).Or, Transmission Oil Temperature is less than expected after a calibrated time (little or no change). Or, Transmission Oil Temperature is greater than Engine Coolant temperature by a calibrated value (skewed or shifted sensor reading).
DTC: P0712 **Year:** 2012 **Model:** 500 **Engine:** 1.4L L4	**TRANSMISSION FLUID TEMPERATURE SENSOR "A" CIRCUIT LOW:** The Diagnostic Trouble Code (DTC) will set if the monitored Transmission Temperature Sensor Signal circuit is greater than 200° C (392° F) for more than 10 seconds.
DTC: P0713 **Year:** 2012 **Model:** 500 **Engine:** 1.4L L4	**TRANSMISSION FLUID TEMPERATURE SENSOR "A" CIRCUIT HIGH:** The Diagnostic Trouble Code (DTC) will set if the monitored Transmission Temperature Sensor Signal circuit is less than -40° C (-40° F) for more than one second.
DTC: P0715 **Year:** 2012 **Model:** 500 **Engine:** 1.4L L4	**INPUT/TURBINE SPEED SENSOR "A" CIRCUIT:** 500 consecutive Output Speed sensor pulses without Input Speed sensor pulses.
DTC: P0715 **Year:** 2012 **Model:** 500 **Engine:** 1.4L L4	**CLUTCH DISK SPEED:** The TCM has deteted a problem with the clutch speed.
DTC: P0717 **Year:** 2012 **Model:** 500 **Engine:** 1.4L L4	**INPUT/TURBINE SPEED SENSOR "A" CIRCUIT NO SIGNAL:** Input Speed sensor voltage is less than 0.206 of a volt or greater than 2.727 volts for 100 msec.
DTC: P0720 **Year:** 2012 **Model:** 500 **Engine:** 1.4L L4	**VEHICLE SPEED:** TCM detects incorrect vehicle speed.
DTC: P0720 **Year:** 2012 **Model:** 500 **Engine:** 1.4L L4	**OUTPUT SPEED SENSOR CIRCUIT:** 500 consecutive tests without Output Speed sensor pulses.
DTC: P0722 **Year:** 2012 **Model:** 500 **Engine:** 1.4L L4	**OUTPUT SPEED SENSOR CIRCUIT NO SIGNAL:** 500 consecutive tests without Output Speed sensor pulses.
DTC: P0725 **Year:** 2012 **Model:** 500 **Engine:** 1.4L L4	**ENGINE SPEED:** TCM detects incorrect engine speed.
DTC: P0729 **Year:** 2012 **Model:** 500 **Engine:** 1.4L L4	**GEAR 6 INCORRECT RATIO:** If the calculated ratio does not match the predetermined ratio for the current gear for more than 1.0 second, five consecutive times, this DTC will set.
DTC: P072D **Year:** 2012 **Model:** 500 **Engine:** 1.4L L4	**STUCK IN GEAR 2:** If the calculated ratio does not match the predetermined ratio for the current gear for more than 1.0 second, five consecutive times, this DTC will set.
DTC: P072E **Year:** 2012 **Model:** 500 **Engine:** 1.4L L4	**STUCK IN GEAR 3:** If the calculated ratio does not match the predetermined ratio for the current gear for more than 1.0 second, five consecutive times, this DTC will set.

DTC	Trouble Code Title and Conditions
DTC: P072F **Year:** 2012 **Model:** 500 **Engine:** 1.4L L4	**STUCK IN GEAR 4:** If the calculated ratio does not match the predetermined ratio for the current gear for more than 1.0 second, five consecutive times, this DTC will set.
DTC: P0731 **Year:** 2012 **Model:** 500 **Engine:** 1.4L L4	**GEAR 1 INCORRECT RATIO:** If the calculated ratio does not match the predetermined ratio for the current gear for more than 1.0 second, fjive consecutive times, this DTC will set.
DTC: P0732 **Year:** 2012 **Model:** 500 **Engine:** 1.4L L4	**GEAR 2 INCORRECT RATIO:** If the calculated ratio does not match the predetermined ratio for the current gear for more than 1.0 second, five consecutive times, this DTC will set.
DTC: P0733 **Year:** 2012 **Model:** 500 **Engine:** 1.4L L4	**GEAR 3 INCORRECT RATIO:** If the calculated ratio does not match the predetermined ratio for the current gear for more than 1.0 second, five consecutive times, this DTC will set.
DTC: P0734 **Year:** 2012 **Model:** 500 **Engine:** 1.4L L4	**GEAR 4 INCORRECT RATIO:** If the calculated ratio does not match the predetermined ratio for the current gear for more than 1.0 second, five consecutive times, this DTC will set.
DTC: P0735 **Year:** 2012 **Model:** 500 **Engine:** 1.4L L4	**GEAR 5 INCORRECT RATIO:** If the calculated ratio does not match the predetermined ratio for the current gear for more than 1.0 second, five consecutive times, this DTC will set.
DTC: P073A **Year:** 2012 **Model:** 500 **Engine:** 1.4L L4	**STUCK IN GEAR 5:** If the calculated ratio does not match the predetermined ratio for the current gear for more than 1.0 second, five consecutive times, this DTC will set.
DTC: P073B **Year:** 2012 **Model:** 500 **Engine:** 1.4L L4	**STUCK IN GEAR 6:** If the calculated ratio does not match the predetermined ratio for the current gear for more than 1.0 second, five consecutive times, this DTC will set.
DTC: P0741 **Year:** 2012 **Model:** 500 **Engine:** 1.4L L4	**TORQUE CONVERTER CLUTCH CIRCUIT PERFORMANCE/STUCK OFF:** Engine speed minus Input speed is greater than or equal to 100 rpm for two seconds for two consecutive ignition cycles.
DTC: P0742 **Year:** 2012 **Model:** 500 **Engine:** 1.4L L4	**TORQUE CONVERTER CLUTCH CIRCUIT STUCK ON:** Engine speed drops below 100 rpm with no TCC slip detected.
DTC: P0748 **Year:** 2012 **Model:** 500 **Engine:** 1.4L L4	**PRESSURE CONTROL SOLENOID "A" ELECTRICAL:** Line Pressure Control solenoid current is greater than 0.05 of an amp for more than 1 second or the TCM detected Line Pressure Control solenoid amperage exceeded 20 amps.
DTC: P0777 **Year:** 2012 **Model:** 500 **Engine:** 1.4L L4	**PRESSURE CONTROL SOLENOID "B" STUCK ON:** The TCM detects a clutch error during shifting.
DTC: P0778 **Year:** 2012 **Model:** 500 **Engine:** 1.4L L4	**PRESSURE CONTROL SOLENOID "B" ELECTRICAL:** C1 Pressure Control Linear solenoid current is greater than 0.05 of an amp for more than 1 second or the TCM detected C1 Pressure Control Linear solenoid amperage exceeded 20 amps.
DTC: P0797 **Year:** 2012 **Model:** 500 **Engine:** 1.4L L4	**PRESSURE CONTROL SOLENOID "C" STUCK ON:** The TCM detects a clutch error during shifting.

DTC	Trouble Code Title and Conditions
DTC: P0798 **Year:** 2012 **Model:** 500 **Engine:** 1.4L L4	**PRESSURE CONTROL SOLENOID "C" ELECTRICAL:** C2 Pressure Control Linear solenoid current is greater than 0.05 of an amp for more than 1 second or the TCM detected C2 Pressure Control Linear solenoid amperage exceeded 20 amps.
DTC: P0831 **Year:** 2012 **Model:** 500 **Engine:** 1.4L L4	**CLUTCH PEDAL SWITCH 1 CIRCUIT LOW:** The Powertrain Control Module (PCM) receives a signal from the Clutch Interlock Switch indicating that the clutch pedal is not depressed when the vehicle is started.
DTC: P0832 **Year:** 2012 **Model:** 500 **Engine:** 1.4L L4	**CLUTCH PEDAL SWITCH 1 CIRCUIT HIGH:** The Powertrain Control Module (PCM) receives a signal from the Clutch Interlock Switch indicating that the clutch pedal is depressed while the vehicle is driven.
DTC: P0850 **Year:** 2012 **Model:** 500 **Engine:** 1.4L L4	**PARK/NEUTRAL SWITCH PERFORMANCE:** This code will set if the PCM detects an incorrect Park/Neutral switch state for a given mode of vehicle operation. Two trip fault. Three good trips to turn off the MIL.
DTC: P0856 **Year:** 2012 **Model:** 500 **Engine:** 1.4L L4	**VDC MESSAGES (FROM CAN):** TCM detects incorrect VDC message.
DTC: P0857 **Year:** 2012 **Model:** 500 **Engine:** 1.4L L4	**VDC MESSAGES (FROM CAN):** TCM detects incorrect VDC message.
DTC: P0867 **Year:** 2012 **Model:** 500 **Engine:** 1.4L L4	**TRANSMISSION FLUID PRESSURE:** TCM detects a neutral condition based on engine rpm, input rpm and output rpm with low or no line pressure while the shifter is in drive.
DTC: P0868 **Year:** 2012 **Model:** 500 **Engine:** 1.4L L4	**TRANSMISSION FLUID PRESSURE LOW:** The TCM detects a clutch error during shifting with low line pressure.
DTC: P0880 **Year:** 2012 **Model:** 500 **Engine:** 1.4L L4	**KEY SIGNAL (+15) RECEIVED ON CAN IRREGULAR:** TCM detects incorrect key signal.
DTC: P0881 **Year:** 2012 **Model:** 500 **Engine:** 1.4L L4	**ECO LEVER SWITCH STUCK:** The TCM has detected a problem with the ECO lever switch.
DTC: P0949 **Year:** 2012 **Model:** 500 **Engine:** 1.4L L4	**AUTO SHIFT MANUAL ADAPTIVE LEARNING NOT COMPLETE:** Neutral position has not been learned.
DTC: P0962 **Year:** 2012 **Model:** 500 **Engine:** 1.4L L4	**PRESSURE CONTROL SOLENOID "A" CONTROL CIRCUIT LOW:** Line Pressure Control solenoid current is less than 0.02 of an amp for more than 0.1 of a second for 5 consecutive tests.
DTC: P0963 **Year:** 2012 **Model:** 500 **Engine:** 1.4L L4	**PRESSURE CONTROL SOLENOID "A" CONTROL CIRCUIT HIGH:** Line Pressure Control solenoid current is greater than 1.38 of an amps for more than 0.1 of a second for five consecutive tests.
DTC: P0965 **Year:** 2012 **Model:** 500 **Engine:** 1.4L L4	**PRESSURE CONTROL SOLENOID "B" CONTROL CIRCUIT RANGE/PERFORMANCE:** TCM detects a neutral condition based on engine rpm, input rpm and output rpm while the shifter is in drive.

DTC	Trouble Code Title and Conditions
DTC: P0966 **Year:** 2012 **Model:** 500 **Engine:** 1.4L L4	**PRESSURE CONTROL SOLENOID "B" CONTROL CIRCUIT LOW:** C1 Pressure Control Linear solenoid current is less than 0.02 of an amp for more than 0.1 of a second for five consecutive tests.
DTC: P0967 **Year:** 2012 **Model:** 500 **Engine:** 1.4L L4	**PRESSURE CONTROL SOLENOID "B" CONTROL CIRCUIT HIGH:** C1 Pressure Control Linear Solenoid current is greater than 1.38 of an amps for more than 0.1 of a second for five consecutive tests.
DTC: P0970 **Year:** 2012 **Model:** 500 **Engine:** 1.4L L4	**PRESSURE CONTROL SOLENOID "C" CONTROL CIRCUIT LOW:** C2 Pressure Control Linear solenoid current is less than 0.02 of an amp for more than 0.1 of a second for five consecutive tests.
DTC: P0971 **Year:** 2012 **Model:** 500 **Engine:** 1.4L L4	**PRESSURE CONTROL SOLENOID "C" CONTROL CIRCUIT HIGH:** C2 Pressure Control Linear solenoid current is greater than 1.38 of an amps for more than 0.1 of a second for five consecutive tests.
DTC: P0973 **Year:** 2012 **Model:** 500 **Engine:** 1.4L L4	**SHIFT SOLENOID "A" CONTROL CIRCUIT LOW:** TCM detects the (S1) Shift Solenoid No. 1 feedback state is OFF for five consecutive tests.
DTC: P0974 **Year:** 2012 **Model:** 500 **Engine:** 1.4L L4	**SHIFT SOLENOID "A" CONTROL CIRCUIT HIGH:** TCM detects the (S1) Shift Solenoid No. 1 feedback state is ON for five consecutive tests.
DTC: P0976 **Year:** 2012 **Model:** 500 **Engine:** 1.4L L4	**SHIFT SOLENOID "B" CONTROL CIRCUIT LOW:** TCM detects the (S2) Shift Solenoid No. 2 feedback state is OFF for five consecutive tests.
DTC: P0977 **Year:** 2012 **Model:** 500 **Engine:** 1.4L L4	**SHIFT SOLENOID "B" CONTROL CIRCUIT HIGH:** TCM detects the (S2) Shift Solenoid No. 2 feedback state is ON for five consecutive tests.

OBD II Trouble Code List (P1XXX Codes)

DTC	Trouble Code Title and Conditions
DTC: P101A **Year:** 2012 **Model:** 500 **Engine:** 1.4L L4	**CYLINDER 1 OIL SUPPLY SOLENOID VALVE RETURN RETURN CONTROL CIRCUIT:** When the Powertrain Control Module (PCM) recognizes a problem with the Solenoid return control circuit. One trip fault.
DTC: P101B **Year:** 2012 **Model:** 500 **Engine:** 1.4L L4	**CYLINDER 2 OIL SUPPLY SOLENOID VALVE RETURN CONTROL CIRCUIT:** When the Powertrain Control Module (PCM) recognizes a problem with the Solenoid return control circuit. One trip fault.
DTC: P101C **Year:** 2012 **Model:** 500 **Engine:** 1.4L L4	**CYLINDER 3 OIL SUPPLY SOLENOID VALVE RETURN CONTROL CIRCUIT:** When the Powertrain Control Module (PCM) recognizes a problem with the Solenoid return control circuit. One trip fault.
DTC: P101D **Year:** 2012 **Model:** 500 **Engine:** 1.4L L4	**CYLINDER 4 OIL SUPPLY SOLENOID VALVE RETURN CONTROL CIRCUIT:** When the Powertrain Control Module (PCM) recognizes a problem with the Solenoid return control circuit. One trip fault.
DTC: P1021 **Year:** 2012 **Model:** 500 **Engine:** 1.4L L4	**VVA CYLINDER 1 COMPONENT DAMAGE:** If the PCM microprocessor internal watchdog detects an error.

DTC	Trouble Code Title and Conditions
DTC: P1022 **Year:** 2012 **Model:** 500 **Engine:** 1.4L L4	**VVA CYLINDER 2 COMPONENT DAMAGE:** If the PCM microprocessor internal watchdog detects an error.
DTC: P1022 **Year:** 2012 **Model:** 500 **Engine:** 1.4L L4	**VVA CYLINDER 2 COMPONENT DAMAGE:** If the PCM microprocessor internal watchdog detects an error.
DTC: P1023 **Year:** 2012 **Model:** 500 **Engine:** 1.4L L4	**VVA CYLINDER 3 COMPONENT DAMAGE:** If the PCM microprocessor internal watchdog detects an error.
DTC: P1023 **Year:** 2012 **Model:** 500 **Engine:** 1.4L L4	**VVA CYLINDER 3 COMPONENT DAMAGE:** If the PCM microprocessor internal watchdog detects an error.
DTC: P1024 **Year:** 2012 **Model:** 500 **Engine:** 1.4L L4	**VVA CYLINDER 4 COMPONENT DAMAGE:** If the PCM microprocessor internal watchdog detects an error.
DTC: P1024 **Year:** 2012 **Model:** 500 **Engine:** 1.4L L4	**VVA CYLINDER 4 COMPONENT DAMAGE:** If the PCM microprocessor internal watchdog detects an error.
DTC: P1025 **Year:** 2012 **Model:** 500 **Engine:** 1.4L L4	**VVA ASIC CYLINDER 1 UNDER VOLTAGE:** When the Powertrain Control Module (PCM) recognizes a problem with the Solenoid control circuit. One trip fault.
DTC: P1025 **Year:** 2012 **Model:** 500 **Engine:** 1.4L L4	**VVA ASIC CYLINDER 1 UNDER VOLTAGE:** When the Powertrain Control Module (PCM) recognizes a problem with the Solenoid control circuit. One trip fault.
DTC: P1026 **Year:** 2012 **Model:** 500 **Engine:** 1.4L L4	**VVA ASIC CYLINDER 1 OVER VOLTAGE:** When the Powertrain Control Module (PCM) recognizes a problem with the Solenoid Return control circuit. One trip fault.
DTC: P1026 **Year:** 2012 **Model:** 500 **Engine:** 1.4L L4	**VVA ASIC CYLINDER 1 OVER VOLTAGE:** When the Powertrain Control Module (PCM) recognizes a problem with the Solenoid Return control circuit. One trip fault.
DTC: P1027 **Year:** 2012 **Model:** 500 **Engine:** 1.4L L4	**VVA ASIC CYLINDER 2 UNDER VOLTAGE:** When the Powertrain Control Module (PCM) recognizes a problem with the Solenoid control circuit. One trip fault.
DTC: P1027 **Year:** 2012 **Model:** 500 **Engine:** 1.4L L4	**VVA ASIC CYLINDER 2 UNDER VOLTAGE:** When the Powertrain Control Module (PCM) recognizes a problem with the Solenoid control circuit. One trip fault.
DTC: P1028 **Year:** 2012 **Model:** 500 **Engine:** 1.4L L4	**VVA ASIC CYLINDER 2 OVER VOLTAGE:** When the Powertrain Control Module (PCM) recognizes a problem with the Solenoid return control circuit. One trip fault.
DTC: P1028 **Year:** 2012 **Model:** 500 **Engine:** 1.4L L4	**VVA ASIC CYLINDER 2 OVER VOLTAGE:** When the Powertrain Control Module (PCM) recognizes a problem with the Solenoid return control circuit. One trip fault.

DTC	Trouble Code Title and Conditions
DTC: P1029 **Year:** 2012 **Model:** 500 **Engine:** 1.4L L4	**VVA ASIC CYLINDER 3 UNDER VOLTAGE:** When the Powertrain Control Module (PCM) recognizes a problem with the Solenoid control circuit. One trip fault.
DTC: P1029 **Year:** 2012 **Model:** 500 **Engine:** 1.4L L4	**VVA ASIC CYLINDER 3 UNDER VOLTAGE:** When the Powertrain Control Module (PCM) recognizes a problem with the Solenoid control circuit. One trip fault.
DTC: P102A **Year:** 2012 **Model:** 500 **Engine:** 1.4L L4	**VVA ASIC CYLINDER 3 OVER VOLTAGE:** When the Powertrain Control Module (PCM) recognizes a problem with the Solenoid Return circuit. One trip fault.
DTC: P102A **Year:** 2012 **Model:** 500 **Engine:** 1.4L L4	**VVA ASIC CYLINDER 3 OVER VOLTAGE:** When the Powertrain Control Module (PCM) recognizes a problem with the Solenoid Return circuit. One trip fault.
DTC: P102B **Year:** 2012 **Model:** 500 **Engine:** 1.4L L4	**VVA ASIC CYLINDER 4 UNDER VOLTAGE:** When the PCM recognizes a problem with the Solenoid control circuit. One trip fault.
DTC: P102B **Year:** 2012 **Model:** 500 **Engine:** 1.4L L4	**VVA ASIC CYLINDER 4 UNDER VOLTAGE:** When the PCM recognizes a problem with the Solenoid control circuit. One trip fault.
DTC: P102C **Year:** 2012 **Model:** 500 **Engine:** 1.4L L4	**VVA ASIC CYLINDER 4 OVER VOLTAGE:** When the Powertrain Control Module (PCM) recognizes a problem with the Solenoid Return Control circuit. One trip fault.
DTC: P102C **Year:** 2012 **Model:** 500 **Engine:** 1.4L L4	**VVA ASIC CYLINDER 4 OVER VOLTAGE:** When the Powertrain Control Module (PCM) recognizes a problem with the Solenoid Return Control circuit. One trip fault.
DTC: P1031 **Year:** 2012 **Model:** 500 **Engine:** 1.4L L4	**WWA POWERSTAGE CYLINDER 1 PLAUSIBILITY ERROR:** When the Powertrain Control Module (PCM) recognizes a problem with the Solenoid Control or Return circuit. One trip fault. Three good trips to turn the MIL off.
DTC: P1032 **Year:** 2012 **Model:** 500 **Engine:** 1.4L L4	**WWA POWERSTAGE CYLINDER 2 PLAUSIBILITY ERROR:** When the Powertrain Control Module (PCM) recognizes a problem with the Solenoid Control or Return circuit. One trip fault. Three good trips to turn the MIL off.
DTC: P1033 **Year:** 2012 **Model:** 500 **Engine:** 1.4L L4	**WWA POWERSTAGE CYLINDER 3 PLAUSIBILITY ERROR:** When the Powertrain Control Module (PCM) recognizes a problem with the Solenoid Control or Return circuit. One trip fault. Three good trips to turn the MIL off.
DTC: P1034 **Year:** 2012 **Model:** 500 **Engine:** 1.4L L4	**WWA POWERSTAGE CYLINDER 4 PLAUSIBILITY ERROR:** When the Powertrain Control Module (PCM) recognizes a problem with the Solenoid Control or Return circuit. One trip fault. Three good trips to turn the MIL off.
DTC: P1035 **Year:** 2012 **Model:** 500 **Engine:** 1.4L L4	**VVA POWERSTAGE CYLINDER 1 OPEN:** When the Powertrain Control Module (PCM) recognizes a problem with the Solenoid Control or Return circuit. One trip fault. Three good trips to turn the MIL off.
DTC: P1036 **Year:** 2012 **Model:** 500 **Engine:** 1.4L L4	**VVA POWERSTAGE CYLINDER 1 SHORTED TO BATTER VOLTAGE:** When the Powertrain Control Module (PCM) recognizes a short to voltage in the Solenoid Control or Return circuit. One trip fault. Three good trips to turn the MIL off.

DTC	Trouble Code Title and Conditions
DTC: P1037 **Year:** 2012 **Model:** 500 **Engine:** 1.4L L4	**VVA POWERSTAGE CYLINDER 1 SHORTED TO GROUND:** When the Powertrain Control Module (PCM) recognizes a short to ground with the Solenoid Control or Return circuit. One trip fault. Three good trips to turn the MIL off.
DTC: P1038 **Year:** 2012 **Model:** 500 **Engine:** 1.4L L4	**VVA POWERSTAGE CYLINDER 2 OPEN:** When the Powertrain Control Module (PCM) recognizes a problem with the Solenoid Control or Return circuit. One trip fault. Three good trips to turn the MIL off.
DTC: P1039 **Year:** 2012 **Model:** 500 **Engine:** 1.4L L4	**VVA POWERSTAGE CYLINDER 2 SHORTED TO BATTERY VOLTAGE:** When the Powertrain Control Module (PCM) recognizes a short to voltage in the Solenoid Control or Return circuit. One trip fault. Three good trips to turn the MIL off.
DTC: P103A **Year:** 2012 **Model:** 500 **Engine:** 1.4L L4	**VVA POWERSTAGE CYLINDER 2 SHORTED TO GROUND:** When the Powertrain Control Module (PCM) recognizes a short to ground in the Solenoid Control or Return circuit. One trip fault. Three good trips to turn the MIL off.
DTC: P103B **Year:** 2012 **Model:** 500 **Engine:** 1.4L L4	**VVA POWERSTAGE CYLINDER 3 OPEN:** When the Powertrain Control Module (PCM) recognizes a problem with the Solenoid Control or Return circuit. One trip fault. Three good trips to turn the MIL off.
DTC: P103C **Year:** 2012 **Model:** 500 **Engine:** 1.4L L4	**VVA POWERSTAGE CYLINDER 3 SHORTED TO BATTERY VOLTAGE:** When the Powertrain Control Module (PCM) recognizes a short to voltage in the Solenoid Control or Return circuit. One trip fault. Three good trips to turn the MIL off.
DTC: P103D **Year:** 2012 **Model:** 500 **Engine:** 1.4L L4	**VVA POWERSTAGE CYLINDER 3 SHORTED TO GROUND:** When the Powertrain Control Module (PCM) recognizes a short to ground in the Solenoid Control or Return circuit. One trip fault. Three good trips to turn the MIL off.
DTC: P103E **Year:** 2012 **Model:** 500 **Engine:** 1.4L L4	**VVA POWERSTAGE CYLINDER 4 OPEN:** When the Powertrain Control Module (PCM) recognizes a problem with the Solenoid Control or Return circuit. One trip fault. Three good trips to turn the MIL off.
DTC: P103F **Year:** 2012 **Model:** 500 **Engine:** 1.4L L4	**VVA POWERSTAGE CYLINDER 4 SHORTED TO BATTERY VOLTAGE:** When the Powertrain Control Module (PCM) recognizes a short to voltage in the Solenoid Control or Return circuit. One trip fault. Three good trips to turn the MIL off.
DTC: P1040 **Year:** 2012 **Model:** 500 **Engine:** 1.4L L4	**VVA POWERSTAGE CYLINDER 4 SHORTED TO GROUND:** When the Powertrain Control Module (PCM) recognizes a short to ground in the Solenoid Control or Return circuit. One trip fault. Three good trips to turn the MIL off.
DTC: P1041 **Year:** 2012 **Model:** 500 **Engine:** 1.4L L4	**VVA CURRENT SENSING CYLINDER 1 CURRENT SENSING:** When the Powertrain Control Module (PCM) recognizes a problem with the Solenoid Control or Return circuit. One trip fault. Three good trips to turn the MIL off.
DTC: P1042 **Year:** 2012 **Model:** 500 **Engine:** 1.4L L4	**VVA CURRENT SENSING CYLINDER 2 CURRENT SENSING:** When the Powertrain Control Module (PCM) recognizes a problem with the Solenoid Control or Return circuit. One trip fault. Three good trips to turn the MIL off.
DTC: P1043 **Year:** 2012 **Model:** 500 **Engine:** 1.4L L4	**VVA CURRENT SENSING CYLINDER 3 CURRENT SENSING:** When the Powertrain Control Module (PCM) recognizes a problem with the Solenoid Control or Return circuit. One trip fault. Three good trips to turn the MIL off.
DTC: P1044 **Year:** 2012 **Model:** 500 **Engine:** 1.4L L4	**VVA CURRENT SENSING CYLINDER 4 CURRENT SENSING:** When the Powertrain Control Module (PCM) recognizes a problem with the Solenoid Control or Return circuit. One trip fault. Three good trips to turn the MIL off.

DTC	Trouble Code Title and Conditions
DTC: P1061 **Year:** 2012 **Model:** 500 **Engine:** 1.4L L4	**CYLINDER 1 SOLENOID VALVE STUCK:** When the Powertrain Control Module (PCM) recognizes a problem with the Solenoid Control circuit.
DTC: P1105-62 **Year:** 2012 **Model:** 500 **Engine:** 1.4L L4	**THROTTLE ACTUATOR CONTROL SYSTEM HIGH AIR FLOW DETECTED:** A large vacuum leak has been detected or both of the TP Sensors have failed based on their position being 2.5 Volts and the calculated MAP value is less than the Gas Flow Adaptation value is too high. One trip fault the code will set within five seconds. ETC light will flash.
DTC: P1106-62 **Year:** 2012 **Model:** 500 **Engine:** 1.4L L4	**INTAKE AIR SYSTEM LEAK:** The Powertrain Control Module (PCM) compares the current MAP reading with a theoretical MAP value based on EGR rate. This DTC is logged if the current value is deemed to be implausible to the theoretical value for 6.5 seconds.
DTC: P1115 **Year:** 2012 **Model:** 500 **Engine:** 1.4L L4	**GENERAL TEMPERATURE RATIONALITY:** Once the vehicle is soaked for a calibrated engine off time and then driven over calibrated speed and load conditions for some calibrated time, the PCM compares the ambient air, engine coolant and intake air temperature sensor values. If the values of all the three sensors disagree with one another, a general temperature sensor irrationality is declared. Two Trip Fault. Three good trips to turn off the MIL.
DTC: P1120-61 **Year:** 2012 **Model:** 500 **Engine:** 1.4L L4	**TPS CONTROL SIGNAL CALCULATION:** The Powertrain Control Module (PCM) detects that the sensor input voltage does not fall within a valid range based on engine speed and load. Two Trip Fault. (Electronic Throttle Control) ETC light will illuminate. P2135 should set with this code also.
DTC: P1121-62 **Year:** 2012 **Model:** 500 **Engine:** 1.4L L4	**THROTTLE POSITION SENSOR 1/2 CORRELATION:** The Powertrain Control Module (PCM) recognizes TP Sensors No.1 and No.2 are not coherent. One trip fault and the code will set within five seconds. ETC light is illuminated.
DTC: P1128 **Year:** 2012 **Model:** 500 **Engine:** 1.4L L4	**CLOSED LOOP FUELING NOT ACHIEVED BANK 1:** Enable conditions are met and the O2 sensor has not been in closed loop control at least once on each of the two consecutive trips, the MIL illuminates and the DTC is set. Two Trip Fault. Three good trips to turn off the MIL
DTC: P1212 **Year:** 2012 **Model:** 500 **Engine:** 1.4L L4	**ENGINE OIL TEMPERATURE HIGH RPM LIMITED:** The engine oil temperature rises faster than a calibrated modeled temperature. When the actual oil temperature exceeds the calibrated modeled temperature for three minutes the fault is set.
DTC: P1215 **Year:** 2012 **Model:** 500 **Engine:** 1.4L L4	**DRIVERS DOOR (FROM CAN):** TCM detects incorrect drivers door signal.
DTC: P1220-62 **Year:** 2012 **Model:** 500 **Engine:** 1.4L L4	**ACCELERATOR PEDAL POSITION SENSOR 1/2 CORRELATION:** APPS values No.1 and No.2 are not coherent. Idle is additionally forced when the brake pedal is pressed or failed. Acceleration rate and Engine output are limited. One trip fault and the code will set within five seconds. ETC light is flashing.
DTC: P1239 **Year:** 2012 **Model:** 500 **Engine:** 1.4L L4	**ENGINE OIL TEMPERATURE TOO LOW:** The Engine Oil temperature rises slower than a calibrated modeled temperature. When the actual oil temperature falls below the low boundary of the calibrated modeled temperature for three minutes the fault is set. Two trip fault. Three good trips to turn off the MIL.
DTC: P1300-55 **Year:** 2012 **Model:** 500 **Engine:** 1.4L L4	**FLYWHEEL SELFLEARNING NOT PERFORMED:** One of the CKP sensor target windows has more than 2% variance from the reference. One Trip Fault. Three good trips to turn off the MIL.
DTC: P1325 **Year:** 2012 **Model:** 500 **Engine:** 1.4L L4	**64KNOCK SENSOR 1 CIRCUIT PERFORMANCE TOO FEW TRANSITIONS:** The Powertrain Control Module (PCM) detects that the Knock Sensor input voltage is: Above 4.0 Volts, less than or equal to 1.0 Volt with engine RPM at or above 2200 or equal to 0.0 Volts with engine RPM below 2200. Two Trip Fault. Three good trips to turn off the MIL.
DTC: P1325-11 **Year:** 2012 **Model:** 500 **Engine:** 1.4L L4	**KNOCK SENSOR 1 CIRCUIT LOW:** The Powertrain Control Module (PCM) detects that the Knock Sensor input voltage is: Above 4.0 Volts, less than or equal to 1.0 Volt with engine RPM at or above 2200 or equal to 0.0 Volts with engine RPM below 2200. Two Trip Fault. Three good trips to turn off the MIL.

DTC	Trouble Code Title and Conditions
DTC: P1325-12 Year: 2012 Model: 500 Engine: 1.4L L4	**KNOCK SENSOR 1 CIRCUIT HIGH:** The Powertrain Control Module (PCM) detects that the Knock Sensor 1 Signal circuit is shorted high.
DTC: P1325-49 Year: 2012 Model: 500 Engine: 1.4L L4	**KNOCK SENSOR 1 CIRCUIT PERFORMANCE TOO MANY TRANSITIONS:** If the PCM detects an error with the controllers internal watchdog.
DTC: P1456 Year: 2012 Model: 500 Engine: 1.4L L4	**FUEL TANK PRESSURE SENSOR CIRCUIT LOW:** The Powertrain Control Module (PCM) detects that the Fuel Tank Pressure (FTP) sensor input voltage is below the minimum acceptable value. One Trip Fault. Three good trips to turn off the MIL.
DTC: P1457 Year: 2012 Model: 500 Engine: 1.4L L4	**FUEL TANK PRESSURE SENSOR CIRCUIT HIGH:** The Fuel Tank Pressure (FTP) sensor signal voltage is greater than the maximum allowable voltage. One trip fault. Three good trips to turn off the MIL.
DTC: P1523 Year: 2012 Model: 500 Engine: 1.4L L4	**VCM HIGH PRESSURE OIL ABSENT:** The engine oil pressure never reaches the calibrated specification to allow the VVA activation. One trip fault.
DTC: P1524 Year: 2012 Model: 500 Engine: 1.4L L4	**OIL PRESSURE OUT OF RANGE CAMSHAFT ADVANCE/RETARD DISABLED:** The engine oil pressure never reaches the calibrated specification to allow the VVA activation. One trip fault.
DTC: P1524-79 Year: 2012 Model: 500 Engine: 1.4L L4	**ANTIFOULING SPARK FUNCTION MECHANICAL LINKAGE:** The engine oil pressure never reaches the calibrated specification to allow the VVA activation. One trip fault.
DTC: P1572 Year: 2012 Model: 500 Engine: 1.4L L4	**BRAKE PEDAL STUCK ON:** The Powertrain Control Module (PCM) recognizes the Brake Pedal could not electrically indicate the applied (On) position with both switch inputs. One trip fault.
DTC: P1573 Year: 2012 Model: 500 Engine: 1.4L L4	**BRAKE PEDAL STUCK OFF:** The Powertrain Control Module (PCM) recognizes the Brake Pedal could not electronically indicate the released (Off) position with both switches. If P1572 sets, P1573 will also set. One trip fault.
DTC: P1593 Year: 2012 Model: 500 Engine: 1.4L L4	**SPEED CONTROL SWITCH 1/2 STUCK:** Fault signifies when the switch voltage does not register a valid cruise position.
DTC: P1607 Year: 2012 Model: 500 Engine: 1.4L L4	**PCM INTERNAL SHUTDOWN TIMER RATIONALITY TOO SLOW:** This DTC sets if the engine coolant temp does not drop enough or drops too much during engine off time. This DTC may also set if the controller timer is inaccurate. Two Trip Fault. Three good trips to turn off the MIL.
DTC: P161C Year: 2012 Model: 500 Engine: 1.4L L4	**OIL VISCOSITY SENSOR PERFORMANCE:** The Powertrain Control Module (PCM) detects an implausible Oil Viscosity Signal.
DTC: P1680-77 Year: 2012 Model: 500 Engine: 1.4L L4	**ETC MOTOR SELFLEARNING (SPRING CLOSURE):** Just after key on, the throttle is opened and closed to test the system. If the TP Sensor does not return to Limp Home Position at the end of this test, this DTC will set. One trip fault and the code will set within five seconds. ETC light is flashing.
DTC: P1681-77 Year: 2012 Model: 500 Engine: 1.4L L4	**ETC MOTOR SELF LEARNING (SPRING OPENING):** Just after key on, the throttle is opened and closed to test the system. If the TP Sensor does not return to Limp Position at the end of this test, this DTC will set. One trip fault and the code will set within five seconds. ETC light is flashing.

DTC	Trouble Code Title and Conditions
DTC: P1683-77 **Year:** 2012 **Model:** 500 **Engine:** 1.4L L4	**ETC MOTOR SELFLEARNING (LIMP HOME POSITION):** The Powertrain Control Module (PCM) detects the Throttle Position Sensor voltage readings are out of spec for Limp Home Position. One trip failure and three good trips to clear the MIL.
DTC: P1684-94 **Year:** 2012 **Model:** 500 **Engine:** 1.4L L4	**ETC MOTOR SELFLEARNING (UNEXPECTED OPERATION):** When the Powertrain Control Module (PCM) detects a short or grounded condition in either the ETC Motor - or ETC Motor + circuits. One trip fault. ETC light is flashing.
DTC: P1686-92 **Year:** 2012 **Model:** 500 **Engine:** 1.4L L4	**ETC MOTOR SELFLEARNING (LOW LIMIT PERFORMANCE/INCORRECT OPERATION):** The Throttle Body Self Learn procedure was not able to run because the Intake Air temperature and Engine Coolant temperatrue are either too high or too low, the vehicle is moving, or the engine is started.
DTC: P1687-94 **Year:** 2012 **Model:** 500 **Engine:** 1.4L L4	**ETC MOTOR SELFLEARNING (STOP UNEXPECTED OPERATION):** Just after key on, the throttle is opened and closed to test the system. If the TP Sensor does not return to Limp Home Position at the end of this test, this DTC will set. One trip fault and the code will set within five seconds. ETC light is flashing.
DTC: P16A0 **Year:** 2012 **Model:** 500 **Engine:** 1.4L L4	**ETC MOTOR ERROR POSITION:** When the Powertrain Control Module (PCM) detects a short or grounded condition in either the ETC Motor - or ETC Motor + circuits. One trip fault. ETC light is flashing.
DTC: P16A1 **Year:** 2012 **Model:** 500 **Engine:** 1.4L L4	**ETC SELF LEARNING (BATTERY):** The Powertrain Control Module (PCM) detects that the battery voltage is too low while performing the Throttle Body Self Learn with the scan tool.
DTC: P16A2 **Year:** 2012 **Model:** 500 **Engine:** 1.4L L4	**ETC MOTOR SELFLEARNING (LIMP HOME POSITION):** The Powertrain Control Module (PCM) detects the Throttle Position Sensor voltage readings are out of spec for Limp Home Position. One trip failure and three good trips to clear the MIL.
DTC: P16A3 **Year:** 2012 **Model:** 500 **Engine:** 1.4L L4	**ETC MOTOR SELFLEARNING (MECHANICAL THROTTLE CLOSURE):** Just after key on, the throttle is opened and closed to test the system. If the TP Sensor does not return to Limp Home Position at the end of this test, this DTC will set. One trip fault and the code will set within five seconds. ETC light is flashing.
DTC: P16A4 **Year:** 2012 **Model:** 500 **Engine:** 1.4L L4	**ETC MOTOR SELFLEARNING (SPRING CLOSURE):** Just after key on, the throttle is opened and closed to test the system. If the TP Sensor does not return to Limp Home Position at the end of this test, this DTC will set. One trip fault and the code will set within five seconds. ETC light is flashing.
DTC: P16A5 **Year:** 2012 **Model:** 500 **Engine:** 1.4L L4	**ETC MOTOR SELF LEARNING (SPRING OPENING):** Just after key on, the throttle is opened and closed to test the system. If the TP Sensor does not return to Limp Position at the end of this test, this DTC will set. One trip fault and the code will set within five seconds. ETC light is flashing.
DTC: P16AA **Year:** 2012 **Model:** 500 **Engine:** 1.4L L4	**CRUISE CONTROL SYSTEM VEHICLE SPEED TOO HIGH:** The vehicle speed is above 250 kph for 0.5 of a second.
DTC: P16AB **Year:** 2012 **Model:** 500 **Engine:** 1.4L L4	**CRUISE CONTROL SYSTEM VEHICLE SPEED TOO LOW:** The vehicle speed is above 250 kph for 0.5 of a second.
DTC: P1741 **Year:** 2012 **Model:** 500 **Engine:** 1.4L L4	**ENGAGEMENT SENSOR:** The TCM has deteted a problem with the engagement sensor.
DTC: P1742 **Year:** 2012 **Model:** 500 **Engine:** 1.4L L4	**SELECTION SENSOR:** The TCM has deteted a problem with the selection sensor.

DTC	Trouble Code Title and Conditions
DTC: P1743 Year: 2012 Model: 500 Engine: 1.4L L4	**CLUTCH SENSOR:** The TCM has deteted a problem with the clutch sensor.
DTC: P1744 Year: 2012 Model: 500 Engine: 1.4L L4	**HYDRAULIC CIRCUIT PRESSURE SENSOR:** The TCM has deteted a problem with the hydraulic pressure sensor.
DTC: P1745 Year: 2012 Model: 500 Engine: 1.4L L4	**LEVER SWITCH 0:** The TCM has deteted a problem with the lever switch 0 sensor.
DTC: P1747 Year: 2012 Model: 500 Engine: 1.4L L4	**LEVER SWITCH 2:** The TCM has deteted a problem with the lever switch 2 sensor.
DTC: P1748 Year: 2012 Model: 500 Engine: 1.4L L4	**LEVER SWITCH 3:** The TCM has deteted a problem with the lever switch 3 sensor.
DTC: P1749 Year: 2012 Model: 500 Engine: 1.4L L4	**LEVERS ON STEERING WHEEL:** The TCM has deteted a problem with the steering wheel lever switches.
DTC: P1750 Year: 2012 Model: 500 Engine: 1.4L L4	**SOLENOID VALVE SELECTION:** The TCM has deteted a problem with the solenoid valve.
DTC: P1752 Year: 2012 Model: 500 Engine: 1.4L L4	**PUMP RELAY:** The TCM has deteted a problem with the pump relay.
DTC: P1755 Year: 2012 Model: 500 Engine: 1.4L L4	**STARTUP RELAY:** The TCM has deteted a problem with the start-up relay.
DTC: P1756 Year: 2012 Model: 500 Engine: 1.4L L4	**ODD SPEEDS ENGAGEMENT:** The TCM detects a problem engaging the odd gears.
DTC: P1757 Year: 2012 Model: 500 Engine: 1.4L L4	**EVEN SPEEDS ENGAGEMENT:** The TCM detects a problem engaging the even gears.
DTC: P1758 Year: 2012 Model: 500 Engine: 1.4L L4	**CLUTCH SV CURRENT:** The TCM has deteted a problem with the solenoid valve.
DTC: P1760 Year: 2012 Model: 500 Engine: 1.4L L4	**BRAKE SWITCH:** The TCM has deteted a problem with the brake switch.
DTC: P1765 Year: 2012 Model: 500 Engine: 1.4L L4	**CONTROL UNIT GROUNDS:** The TCM detects a control unit ground fault.

DTC	Trouble Code Title and Conditions
DTC: P1768 **Year:** 2012 **Model:** 500 **Engine:** 1.4L L4	**OIL TANK EMPTY:** The TCM detects the oil tank is low or empty.
DTC: P1769 **Year:** 2012 **Model:** 500 **Engine:** 1.4L L4	**PUMP DRIVING RELAY STUCK:** The TCM has deteted a problem with the pump relay.
DTC: P1770 **Year:** 2012 **Model:** 500 **Engine:** 1.4L L4	**NO ACCELERATOR PEDAL INFORMATION:** TCM detects incorrect accelerator pedal signal.
DTC: P1771 **Year:** 2012 **Model:** 500 **Engine:** 1.4L L4	**LEAKS IN HYDRAULIC GROUP:** The TCM detects the oil tank is low or empty.
DTC: P1772 **Year:** 2012 **Model:** 500 **Engine:** 1.4L L4	**GEARSHIFT LEVER SWITCHES (ONE OF 4):** The TCM has deteted a problem with the gear shift lever switch sensor.
DTC: P1773 **Year:** 2012 **Model:** 500 **Engine:** 1.4L L4	**HYDRAULIC CIRCUIT PRESSURE:** The TCM has deteted a problem with the hydraulic pressure sensor.
DTC: P1774 **Year:** 2012 **Model:** 500 **Engine:** 1.4L L4	**ROBOTISED GEARBOX ANOMALOUS USE:** TCM detects an gearbox error..
DTC: P1810 **Year:** 2012 **Model:** 500 **Engine:** 1.4L L4	**CLUTCH SYSTEM:** The TCM detects a problem with the clutch system.
DTC: P1818 **Year:** 2012 **Model:** 500 **Engine:** 1.4L L4	**GEARCHANGE CONTROL:** The TCM detects a problem in the gear change system.
DTC: P1819 **Year:** 2012 **Model:** 500 **Engine:** 1.4L L4	**ENGINE TORQUE (FROM CAN):** TCM detects incorrect engine torque signal.
DTC: P1880 **Year:** 2012 **Model:** 500 **Engine:** 1.4L L4	**CONTROL UNIT POWER SUPPLY:** The TCM detects a control unit power supply fault.
DTC: P1C4F **Year:** 2012 **Model:** 500 **Engine:** 1.4L L4	**ESM DTC PRESENT:** TCM receives an ESM error message from the BCM.
DTC: P1C50 **Year:** 2012 **Model:** 500 **Engine:** 1.4L L4	**INCORRECT TRANSMISSION:** TCM receives an configuration message from the PCM that does not indicate automatic transmission.
DTC: P1C51 **Year:** 2012 **Model:** 500 **Engine:** 1.4L L4	**GEAR 1 INCORRECT RATIO DURING ENGINE BRAKING:** If the calculated ratio does not match the predetermined ratio for the current gear for more than 1.0 second, five consecutive times, this DTC will set.

DTC	Trouble Code Title and Conditions
DTC: P1C52 **Year:** 2012 **Model:** 500 **Engine:** 1.4L L4	**PRESSURE CONTROL SOLENOID "C" STUCK ON DURING GEAR 1 ENGINE BRAKING:** If the calculated ratio does not match the predetermined ratio for the current gear for more than 1.0 second, five consecutive times, this DTC will set.
DTC: P1C53 **Year:** 2012 **Model:** 500 **Engine:** 1.4L L4	**PRESSURE CONTROL SOLENOID "D" OR "E" STUCK ON DURING GEAR 1 ENGINE BRAKING:** If the calculated ratio does not match the predetermined ratio for the current gear for more than 1.0 second, five consecutive times, this DTC will set.
DTC: P1C57 **Year:** 2012 **Model:** 500 **Engine:** 1.4L L4	**REDUCTANT CONTROL MODULE SHUTDOWN CRASH EVENT DETECTED:** The Airbag Control Module reported a crash event to the Powertrain Control Module (PCM).
DTC: P1C5F **Year:** 2012 **Model:** 500 **Engine:** 1.4L L4	**OIL VISCOSITY SENSOR CIRCUIT OVERTEMPERATURE:** When the Powertrain Control Module (PCM) detect an overtemperature condition with the Oil Viscosity Sensor.
DTC: P1C5F **Year:** 2012 **Model:** 500 **Engine:** 1.4L L4	**OIL VISCOSITY SENSOR CIRCUIT LOW:** When the Powertrain Control Module (PCM) recognizes the Oil Viscosity signal is shorted to ground.
DTC: P1C60 **Year:** 2012 **Model:** 500 **Engine:** 1.4L L4	**OIL VISCOSITY SENSOR CIRCUIT HIGH:** When the Powertrain Control Module (PCM) recognizes the Oil Viscosity signal is open or shorted high.
DTC: P1D30 **Year:** 2012 **Model:** 500 **Engine:** 1.4L L4	**OIL VISCOSITY TOO LOW:** When the Powertrain Control Module (PCM) recognizes the Oil Viscosity is too low for proper engine operation. The eninge will not be allowed to start.
DTC: P1D31 **Year:** 2012 **Model:** 500 **Engine:** 1.4L L4	**OIL VISCOSITY TOO HIGH:** When the Powertrain Control Module (PCM) recognizes the Oil Viscosity is too high for proper engine operation. The eninge will not be allowed to start.
DTC: P1D52 **Year:** 2012 **Model:** 500 **Engine:** 1.4L L4	**INTERNAL CONTROL MODULE CRUISE CONTROL ERROR:** The Powertrain Control Module (PCM) detects an internal failure.
DTC: P1D7F **Year:** 2012 **Model:** 500 **Engine:** 1.4L L4	**ETC SELFLEARNING FAILURE:** The Throttle Body Self Learn procedure was not able to run because the Intake Air temperature and Engine Coolant temperatrue are either too high or too low, the vehicle is moving, or the engine is started.
DTC: P1D80 **Year:** 2012 **Model:** 500 **Engine:** 1.4L L4	**INTERNAL CONTROL MODULE EEPROM ERROR:** The control module has detected an internal malfunction.
DTC: P1D83 **Year:** 2012 **Model:** 500 **Engine:** 1.4L L4	**IMPLAUSABLE ENGINE OIL TEMPERATURE SIGNAL RECIEVED:** After a calibrated amount of cool down time, the Powertrain Control Module (PCM) compares the AAT, ECT and IAT Sensor values. If the general temperature rationality passes, the PCM compares the Oil Temperature Sensor value to a threshold based on the other temp sensor values. If the difference is greater than a calibrated value, the diagnostic fails.
DTC: P1D84 **Year:** 2012 **Model:** 500 **Engine:** 1.4L L4	**ETC SYSTEM FAILURE:** TCM receives an ETC error message from the PCM.

OBD II Trouble Code List (P2XXX Codes)

DTC	Trouble Code Title and Conditions
DTC: P2096 **Year:** 2012 **Model:** 500 **Engine:** 1.4L L4	**DOWNSTREAM FUEL TRIM SYSTEM 1 LEAN:** The conditions that cause this diagnostic to fail is when the upstream O2 sensor becomes biased from an exhaust leak, O2 sensor contamination or some other extreme operating condition. The downstream O2 sensor is considered to be protected from extreme environments by the catalyst. The PCM monitors the downstream O2 sensor feedback control, called downstream fuel trim, to detect any shift in the upstream O2 sensor target voltage from nominal target voltage. The value of the downstream fuel trim is compared with the lean thresholds. Every time the value exceeds the calibrated threshold, a fail timer is incremented and mass flow through the exhaust is accumulated. If the fail timer and accumulated mass flow exceed the fail thresholds, the test fails and the diagnostic stops running for that trip. If the test fails on consecutive trips, a DTC is set.
DTC: P2097 **Year:** 2012 **Model:** 500 **Engine:** 1.4L L4	**DOWNSTREAM FUEL TRIM SYSTEM 1 RICH:** The conditions that cause this diagnostic to fail is when the upstream O2 sensor becomes biased from an exhaust leak, O2 sensor contamination or some other extreme operating condition. The downstream O2 sensor is considered to be protected from extreme environments by the catalyst. The PCM monitors the downstream O2 sensor feedback control, called downstream fuel trim, to detect any shift in the upstream O2 sensor target voltage from nominal target voltage. The value of the downstream fuel trim is compared with the rich thresholds. Every time the value exceeds the calibrated threshold, a fail timer is incremented and mass flow through the exhaust is accumulated. If the fail timer and accumulated mass flow exceed the fail thresholds, the test fails and the diagnostic stops running for that trip. If the test fails on consecutive trips, a DTC is set.
DTC: P2100 **Year:** 2012 **Model:** 500 **Engine:** 1.4L L4	**ELECTRONIC THROTTLE CONTROL MOTOR CIRCUIT:** When the Powertrain Control Module (PCM) detects an internal error or a short between the ETC Motor - and ETC Motor + circuits in the ETC Motor Driver. One trip fault. ETC light is flashing.
DTC: P2101 **Year:** 2012 **Model:** 500 **Engine:** 1.4L L4	**ELECTRONIC THROTTLE CONTROL MOTOR PERFORMANCE:** The Powertrain Control Module (PCM) recognizes too large of an error between the actual position of the Throttle Plate and the Set Point position. One trip fault and the code will set within five seconds. Three good trips to turn off the MIL ETC light is flashing.
DTC: P2102 **Year:** 2012 **Model:** 500 **Engine:** 1.4L L4	**ELECTRONIC THROTTLE CONTROL MOTOR CIRCUIT LOW:** When the Powertrain Control Module (PCM) detects an internal error or a short to ground in the ETC Motor - and ETC Motor + circuits. One trip fault. ETC light is flashing.
DTC: P2103 **Year:** 2012 **Model:** 500 **Engine:** 1.4L L4	**ELECTRONIC THROTTLE CONTROL MOTOR CIRCUIT HIGH:** When the Powertrain Control Module (PCM) detects an internal error or a short to voltage in the ETC Motor - and ETC Motor + circuits. One trip fault. ETC light is flashing.
DTC: P2115 **Year:** 2012 **Model:** 500 **Engine:** 1.4L L4	**ACCELERATOR PEDAL POSITION SENSOR 1 MINIMUM STOP PERFORMANCE:** APPS No.1 has failed to achieve the required minimum value during In Plant testing. One trip fault and the code will set within five seconds. Engine will only idle. ETC light is illuminated.
DTC: P2116 **Year:** 2012 **Model:** 500 **Engine:** 1.4L L4	**ACCELERATOR PEDAL POSITION SENSOR 2 MINIMUM STOP PERFORMANCE:** APPS No.2 has failed to achieve the required minimum value during In Plant testing. One trip fault and the code will be stored within 5 seconds. Engine will only idle. ETC light is illuminated.
DTC: P2122 **Year:** 2012 **Model:** 500 **Engine:** 1.4L L4	**ACCELERATOR PEDAL POSITION SENSOR 1 CIRCUIT LOW:** When the APP Sensor No.1 voltage is too low. Engine will additionally idle if the brake pedal is pressed or has failed. Acceleration rate and Engine output are limited. One trip fault and the code will set within five seconds. ETC light is flashing.
DTC: P2123 **Year:** 2012 **Model:** 500 **Engine:** 1.4L L4	**ACCELERATOR PEDAL POSITION SENSOR 1 CIRCUIT HIGH:** When APP Sensor No.1 voltage is too high. Engine will additionally idle if the brake pedal is pressed or has failed. Acceleration rate and Engine output are limited. One trip fault and the code will set within five seconds. ETC light is flashing.
DTC: P2127 **Year:** 2012 **Model:** 500 **Engine:** 1.4L L4	**ACCELERATOR PEDAL POSITION SENSOR 2 CIRCUIT LOW:** When the APP Sensor No.2 voltage is too low. Engine will only idle if the Brake pedal is Pressed or has failed. Acceleration rate and Engine output are limited. One trip fault and the code will set within five seconds. ETC light is flashing.
DTC: P2128 **Year:** 2012 **Model:** 500 **Engine:** 1.4L L4	**ACCELERATOR PEDAL POSITION SENSOR 2 CIRCUIT HIGH:** When APP Sensor No.2 voltage is too high. Idle is additionally forced any time the brake is applied or failed. Acceleration rate and Engine output are limited. One trip fault and the code will set within five seconds. ETC light is flashing.

DTC	Trouble Code Title and Conditions
DTC: P2135 **Year:** 2012 **Model:** 500 **Engine:** 1.4L L4	**THROTTLE POSITION SENSOR 1/2 CORRELATION:** The Powertrain Control Module (PCM) recognizes TP Sensors No.1 and No.2 are not coherent. One trip fault and the code will set within five seconds. ETC light is illuminated.
DTC: P2138 **Year:** 2012 **Model:** 500 **Engine:** 1.4L L4	**ACCELERATOR PEDAL POSITION SENSOR 1/2 CORRELATION:** APPS values No.1 and No.2 are not coherent. Idle is additionally forced when the brake pedal is pressed or failed. Acceleration rate and Engine output are limited. One trip fault and the code will set within five seconds. ETC light is flashing.
DTC: P2166 **Year:** 2012 **Model:** 500 **Engine:** 1.4L L4	**ACCELERATOR PEDAL POSITION SENSOR 1 MAXIMUM STOP PERFORMANCE:** APPS No.1 has failed to achieve the required maximum value during In Plant testing. One trip fault and the code will set within five seconds. Engine will only idle. ETC light will illuminate.
DTC: P2167 **Year:** 2012 **Model:** 500 **Engine:** 1.4L L4	**ACCELERATOR PEDAL POSITION SENSOR 2 MAXIMUM STOP PERFORMANCE:** APPS No.2 has failed to achieve the required maximum value during In Plant testing. One trip fault and the code will set within five seconds. Engine will only idle. ETC light will illuminate.
DTC: P2172 **Year:** 2012 **Model:** 500 **Engine:** 1.4L L4	**HIGH AIRFLOW/VACUUM LEAK DETECTED (INSTANTANEOUS ACCUMULATION):** A large vacuum leak has been detected or both of the TP Sensors have failed based on their position being 2.5 Volts and the calculated MAP value is less than the actual MAP minus an Offset value. One trip fault and the code will set within five seconds. ETC light will flash.
DTC: P2226 **Year:** 2012 **Model:** 500 **Engine:** 1.4L L4	**BAROMETRIC PRESSURE SENSOR:** The Powertrain Control Module (PCM) detects that the Barometric pressure value differs from the other pressure sensors by a calibrated amount.
DTC: P2226-12 **Year:** 2012 **Model:** 500 **Engine:** 1.4L L4	**BAROMETRIC PRESSURE CIRCUIT HIGH:** The circuit voltage to the Powertrain Control Module (PCM) is too high.
DTC: P2226-14 **Year:** 2012 **Model:** 500 **Engine:** 1.4L L4	**BAROMETRIC PRESSURE CIRCUIT LOW:** The PCM detects the baro pressure signal is too low.
DTC: P2226-62 **Year:** 2012 **Model:** 500 **Engine:** 1.4L L4	**BAROMETRIC PRESSURE CIRCUIT PERFORMANCE:** The Powertrain Control Module (PCM) detects that the Barometric pressure value differs from the other pressure sensors by a calibrated amount.
DTC: P2227 **Year:** 2012 **Model:** 500 **Engine:** 1.4L L4	**BAROMETERIC PRESSURE SENSOR RATIONALITY:** The Powertrain Control Module (PCM) detects that the Barometric pressure value differs from the other pressure sensors by a calibrated amount.
DTC: P2228 **Year:** 2012 **Model:** 500 **Engine:** 1.4L L4	**BAROMETRIC PRESSURE CIRCUIT LOW:** The PCM detects the baro pressure signal is too low.
DTC: P2229 **Year:** 2012 **Model:** 500 **Engine:** 1.4L L4	**BAROMETRIC PRESSURE CIRCUIT HIGH:** The circuit voltage to the Powertrain Control Module (PCM) is too high.
DTC: P222A **Year:** 2012 **Model:** 500 **Engine:** 1.4L L4	**BAROMETRIC PRESSURE SENSOR 1 CIRCUIT:** The Powertrain Control Module (PCM) detects that the Barometric pressure value differs from the other pressure sensors by a calibrated amount.
DTC: P2231-12 **Year:** 2012 **Model:** 500 **Engine:** 1.4L L4	**O2 SENSOR 1/1 HEATER CIRCUIT HIGH:** The Powertrain Control Module (PCM) detects that the O2 sensor heater element input is above the maximum acceptable voltage. One trip fault. Three good trips to turn off the MIL.

DTC	Trouble Code Title and Conditions
DTC: P2231-14 **Year:** 2012 **Model:** 500 **Engine:** 1.4L L4	**O2 SENSOR 1/1 HEATER CIRCUIT LOW:** The Powertrain Cotrol Module (PCM) detects that the O2 sensor heater element input is below the minimum acceptable voltage. One trip fault. Three good trips to turn off the MIL.
DTC: P2244 **Year:** 2012 **Model:** 500 **Engine:** 1.4L L4	**O2 SENSOR REFERENCE VOLTAGE PERFORMANCE BANK 1 SENSOR 1:** The Powertrain Control Module (PCM) detects that the oxygen sensor signal does not switch adequately during monitoring. Two Trip Fault. Three good trips to turn off the MIL.
DTC: P2244-92 **Year:** 2012 **Model:** 500 **Engine:** 1.4L L4	**O2 SENSOR REFERENCE VOLTAGE PERFORMANCE BANK 1 SENSOR 1:** The Powertrain Control Module (PCM) detects that the oxygen sensor signal does not switch adequately during monitoring. Two Trip Fault. Three good trips to turn off the MIL.
DTC: P2271 **Year:** 2012 **Model:** 500 **Engine:** 1.4L L4	**O2 SENSOR 1/2 SIGNAL STUCK RICH:** The PCM detects that the sensor does not output a voltage greater than a calibrated high voltage value and less than a calibrated low voltage value within a specific time period. If the voltage pass values are not achieved after the total accumulated test time, a pending fault will be set. An active fault is matured on a second trip failure. Three good trips will turn off the MIL.
DTC: P2279 **Year:** 2012 **Model:** 500 **Engine:** 1.4L L4	**INTAKE AIR SYSTEM LEAK:** The Powertrain Control Module (PCM) compares the current MAP reading with a theoretical MAP value based on EGR rate. This DTC is logged if the current value is deemed to be implausible to the theoretical value for 6.5 seconds.
DTC: P2299 **Year:** 2012 **Model:** 500 **Engine:** 1.4L L4	**BRAKE PEDAL POSITION/ACCELERATOR PEDAL POSITION INCOMPATIBLE:** The Powertrain Control Module (PCM) recognizes a brake application following the APPS showing a fixed pedal opening. Temporary or permanent. Internally the PCM will reduce throttle opening below driver demand. One trip fault and the code will be set within five seconds. ETC light will illuminate, the light will only stay illuminated while DTC is active.
DTC: P2299-62 **Year:** 2012 **Model:** 500 **Engine:** 1.4L L4	**BRAKE PEDAL POSITION/ACCELERATOR PEDAL POSITION INCOMPATIBLE:** The Powertrain Control Module (PCM) recognizes a brake application following the APPS showing a fixed pedal opening. Temporary or permanent. Internally the PCM will reduce throttle opening below driver demand. One trip fault and the code will be set within five seconds. ETC light will illuminate, the light will only stay illuminated while DTC is active.
DTC: P2301 **Year:** 2012 **Model:** 500 **Engine:** 1.4L L4	**IGNITION COIL 1 CIRCUIT HIGH:** If the Powertrain Control Module (PCM) detects a short to voltage on the Ignition Coil 1 Control circuit for more than 15 coil change requests, it will set this DTC.
DTC: P2304 **Year:** 2012 **Model:** 500 **Engine:** 1.4L L4	**IGNITION COIL 2 CIRCUIT HIGH:** If the Powertrain Control Module (PCM) detects a short to voltage on the Ignition Coil 2 Control circuit for more than 15 coil change requests, it will set this DTC.
DTC: P2307 **Year:** 2012 **Model:** 500 **Engine:** 1.4L L4	**IGNITION COIL 3 CIRCUIT HIGH:** The Powertrain Control Module (PCM) detects that the Coil 3 Control voltage is above the maximum acceptable value.
DTC: P2310 **Year:** 2012 **Model:** 500 **Engine:** 1.4L L4	**IGNITION COIL 4 CIRCUIT HIGH:** The Powertrain Control Module (PCM) detects that the Coil 4 Control voltage is above the maximum acceptable value.
DTC: P2610 **Year:** 2012 **Model:** 500 **Engine:** 1.4L L4	**PCM INTERNAL SHUTDOWN TIMER RATIONALITY TOO FAST:** The Powertrain Control Module (PCM) detects that the engine coolant temperature drops a specified amount during the measured engine off time. Two trip fault. Three good trips to turn off the MIL.
DTC: P2715 **Year:** 2012 **Model:** 500 **Engine:** 1.4L L4	**PRESSURE CONTROL SOLENOID "D" STUCK ON:** The TCM detects a clutch error during shifting.
DTC: P2716 **Year:** 2012 **Model:** 500 **Engine:** 1.4L L4	**PRESSURE CONTROL SOLENOID "D" ELECTRICAL:** C3 Pressure Control Linear solenoid current is greater than 0.05 of an amp for more than 1 second or the TCM detected C3 Pressure Control Linear solenoid amperage exceeded 20 amps.

DTC	Trouble Code Title and Conditions
DTC: P2719 **Year:** 2012 **Model:** 500 **Engine:** 1.4L L4	**PRESSURE CONTROL SOLENOID "D" CONTROL CIRCUIT RANGE/PERFORMANCE:** TCM detects a neutral condition based on engine rpm, input rpm and output rpm while the shifter is in reverse.
DTC: P2720 **Year:** 2012 **Model:** 500 **Engine:** 1.4L L4	**PRESSURE CONTROL SOLENOID "D" CONTROL CIRCUIT LOW:** C3 Pressure Control Linear solenoid current is less than 0.02 of an amps for more than 0.1 of a second for five consecutive tests.
DTC: P2721 **Year:** 2012 **Model:** 500 **Engine:** 1.4L L4	**PRESSURE CONTROL SOLENOID "D" CONTROL CIRCUIT HIGH:** C3 Pressure Control Linear solenoid current is greater than 1.38 of an amps for more than 0.1 of a second for five consecutive tests.
DTC: P2724 **Year:** 2012 **Model:** 500 **Engine:** 1.4L L4	**PRESSURE CONTROL SOLENOID "E" STUCK ON:** The TCM detects a clutch error during shifting.
DTC: P2727 **Year:** 2012 **Model:** 500 **Engine:** 1.4L L4	**PRESSURE CONTROL SOLENOID "E" CONTROL CIRCUIT/OPEN:** B1 Pressure Control Linear solenoid current is greater than 0.05 of an amp for more than 1 second or the TCM detected B1 Pressure Control Linear solenoid amperage exceeded 20 amps.
DTC: P2729 **Year:** 2012 **Model:** 500 **Engine:** 1.4L L4	**PRESSURE CONTROL SOLENOID "E" CONTROL CIRCUIT LOW:** B1 Pressure Control Linear solenoid current is less than 0.02 of an amps for more than 0.1 of a second for five consecutive tests.
DTC: P2730 **Year:** 2012 **Model:** 500 **Engine:** 1.4L L4	**PRESSURE CONTROL SOLENOID "E" CONTROL CIRCUIT HIGH:** B1 Pressure Control Linear solenoid current is greater than 1.38 of an amps for more than 0.1 of a second for five consecutive tests.
DTC: P2761 **Year:** 2012 **Model:** 500 **Engine:** 1.4L L4	**TORQUE CONVERTER CLUTCH PRESSURE CONTROL SOLENOID CONTROL CIRCUIT/OPEN:** L-UP Linear solenoid current is greater than 0.05 of an amp for more than one second or the TCM detected L-UP Linear solenoid amperage exceeded 20 amps.
DTC: P2763 **Year:** 2012 **Model:** 500 **Engine:** 1.4L L4	**TORQUE CONVERTER CLUTCH PRESSURE CONTROL SOLENOID CONTROL CIRCUIT :** L-UP Linear solenoid current is greater than 1.38 of an amps for more than 0.1 of a second for five consecutive tests.
DTC: P2764 **Year:** 2012 **Model:** 500 **Engine:** 1.4L L4	**TORQUE CONVERTER CLUTCH PRESSURE CONTROL SOLENOID CONTROL CIRCUIT LOW:** L-UP Linear solenoid current is less than 0.02 of an amp for more than 0.1 of a second for five consecutive tests.
DTC: P290D **Year:** 2012 **Model:** 500 **Engine:** 1.4L L4	**END OF LINE/SERVICE SELFCALIBRATION:** The TCM is in self calibration mode.
DTC: P290E **Year:** 2012 **Model:** 500 **Engine:** 1.4L L4	**CLUTCH SELFCALIBRATION ENABLE:** The TCM is in clutch self calibration mode.
DTC: P290F **Year:** 2012 **Model:** 500 **Engine:** 1.4L L4	**SIDE ACCELER./YAW NODE (NYL):** TCM detects incorrect side acceleration/yaw signal.
DTC: P2910 **Year:** 2012 **Model:** 500 **Engine:** 1.4L L4	**CLUTCH SUBSYSTEM:** The TCM detects a problem in the clutch system.

DTC	Trouble Code Title and Conditions
DTC: P2911 **Year:** 2012 **Model:** 500 **Engine:** 1.4L L4	**CLUTCH SUBSYSTEM:** The TCM detects a problem in the clutch system.
DTC: P2912 **Year:** 2012 **Model:** 500 **Engine:** 1.4L L4	**CLUTCH SUBSYSTEM:** The TCM detects a problem in the clutch system.
DTC: P2914 **Year:** 2012 **Model:** 500 **Engine:** 1.4L L4	**GEARBOX SUBSYSTEM:** The TCM detects a problem in the gearbox.
DTC: P2915 **Year:** 2012 **Model:** 500 **Engine:** 1.4L L4	**GEARBOX SUBSYSTEM:** The TCM detects a problem in the gearbox.
DTC: P2916 **Year:** 2012 **Model:** 500 **Engine:** 1.4L L4	**GEARBOX SUBSYSTEM:** The TCM detects a problem in the gearbox.
DTC: P2917 **Year:** 2012 **Model:** 500 **Engine:** 1.4L L4	**GEARBOX SUBSYSTEM:** The TCM detects a problem in the gearbox.

MINI

Cooper

SPECIFICATIONS AND MAINTENANCE CHARTS

ENGINE AND VEHICLE IDENTIFICATION

Engine								Model Year	
Code ① ②	Liters (cc)	Cu. In.	Cyl.	Fuel Sys.	Engine Type	Eng. Mfg.		Code ③	Year
N14B16C	1.6 (1598)	97.5	4	SFI	DOHC	BMW		B	2011
N16B16A	1.6 (1598)	97.5	4	SFI	DOHC	BMW		C	2012
N18B16A	1.6 (1598)	97.5	4	DI	DOHC	BMW			

NS: Not Specified

DOHC: Dual Overhead Camshaft

SFI: Sequential Fuel Injection

DI: Direct Injection

① Mini uses an engine numbering system

② N14B16C turbocharged. N16B16A non turbocharged. N18B16A turbocharged.

③ 10th position of VIN

71105_MINI_C0001

GENERAL ENGINE SPECIFICATIONS

Year	Model	Series	Engine Displacement Liters (ID)	Net Horsepower @ rpm	Net Torque @ rpm (ft. lbs.)	Bore x Stroke (in.)	Compression Ratio	Oil Pressure @ rpm
2011	Clubman, S, JCW	R55	1.6 (N14B16C)	181@5500	177@1600-5000	3.38x3.03	10.5:1	16.7-93.5@3000
	Clubman, S, JCW	R55	1.6 (N16B16A)	121@6000	114@4250	3.38x3.03	11.0:1	16.7-93.5@3000
	Clubman, S, JCW	R55	1.6 (N18B16A)	181@5500	177@1600-5000	3.38x3.03	10.5:1	16.7-93.5@3000
	Base, S, JCW	R56	1.6 (N14B16C)	181@5500	177@1600-5000	3.38x3.03	10.5:1	16.7-93.5@3000
	Base, S, JCW	R56	1.6 (N16B16A)	121@6000	114@4250	3.38x3.03	11.0:1	16.7-93.5@3000
	Base, S, JCW	R56	1.6 (N18B16A)	181@5500	177@1600-5000	3.38x3.03	10.5:1	16.7-93.5@3000
	Base, S, JCW	R57	1.6 (N14B16C)	181@5500	177@1600-5000	3.38x3.03	10.5:1	16.7-93.5@3000
	Base, S, JCW	R57	1.6 (N16B16A)	121@6000	114@4250	3.38x3.03	11.0:1	16.7-93.5@3000
	Base, S, JCW	R57	1.6 (N18B16A)	181@5500	177@1600-5000	3.38x3.03	10.5:1	16.7-93.5@3000
	Countryman, S, ALL4	R60	1.6 (N14B16C)	181@5500	177@1600-5000	3.38x3.03	10.5:1	16.7-93.5@3000
	Countryman, S, ALL4	R60	1.6 (N16B16A)	121@6000	114@4250	3.38x3.03	11.0:1	16.7-93.5@3000
	Countryman, S, ALL4	R60	1.6 (N18B16A)	181@5500	177@1600-5000	3.38x3.03	10.5:1	16.7-93.5@3000
2012	Clubman, S, JCW	R55	1.6 (N14B16C)	181@5500	177@1600-5000	3.38x3.03	10.5:1	16.7-93.5@3000
	Clubman, S, JCW	R55	1.6 (N16B16A)	121@6000	114@4250	3.38x3.03	11.0:1	16.7-93.5@3000
	Clubman, S, JCW	R55	1.6 (N18B16A)	181@5500	177@1600-5000	3.38x3.03	10.5:1	16.7-93.5@3000
	Base, S, JCW	R56	1.6 (N14B16C)	181@5500	177@1600-5000	3.38x3.03	10.5:1	16.7-93.5@3000
	Base, S, JCW	R56	1.6 (N16B16A)	121@6000	114@4250	3.38x3.03	11.0:1	16.7-93.5@3000
	Base, S, JCW	R56	1.6 (N18B16A)	181@5500	177@1600-5000	3.38x3.03	10.5:1	16.7-93.5@3000
	Base, S, JCW	R57	1.6 (N14B16C)	181@5500	177@1600-5000	3.38x3.03	10.5:1	16.7-93.5@3000
	Base, S, JCW	R57	1.6 (N16B16A)	121@6000	114@4250	3.38x3.03	11.0:1	16.7-93.5@3000
	Base, S, JCW	R57	1.6 (N18B16A)	181@5500	177@1600-5000	3.38x3.03	10.5:1	16.7-93.5@3000
	Coupe, S, JCW	R58	1.6 (N14B16C)	181@5500	177@1600-5000	3.38x3.03	10.5:1	16.7-93.5@3000
	Coupe, S, JCW	R58	1.6 (N16B16A)	121@6000	114@4250	3.38x3.03	11.0:1	16.7-93.5@3000
	Coupe, S, JCW	R58	1.6 (N18B16A)	181@5500	177@1600-5000	3.38x3.03	10.5:1	16.7-93.5@3000
	Roadster, S, JCW	R59	1.6 (N14B16C)	181@5500	177@1600-5000	3.38x3.03	10.5:1	16.7-93.5@3000
	Roadster, S, JCW	R59	1.6 (N16B16A)	121@6000	114@4250	3.38x3.03	11.0:1	16.7-93.5@3000
	Roadster, S, JCW	R59	1.6 (N18B16A)	181@5500	177@1600-5000	3.38x3.03	10.5:1	16.7-93.5@3000
	Countryman, S, ALL4	R60	1.6 (N16B16A)	121@6000	114@4250	3.38x3.03	11.0:1	16.7-93.5@3000
	Countryman, S, ALL4	R60	1.6 (N18B16A)	181@5500	177@1600-5000	3.38x3.03	10.5:1	16.7-93.5@3000

JCW: John Cooper Works

71105_MINI_C0002

ENGINE TUNE-UP SPECIFICATIONS

Year	Model	Series	Engine Displacement Liters (ID)	Spark Plug Gap (in.)	Ignition Timing (deg.)	Fuel Pump (psi)	Idle Speed (rpm)	Valve Clearance In.	Ex.
2011	Clubman, S, JCW	R55	1.6 (N14B16C)	0.044	①	NA	②	HYD	HYD
	Clubman, S, JCW	R55	1.6 (N16B16A)	0.044	①	NA	②	HYD	HYD
	Clubman, S, JCW	R55	1.6 (N18B16A)	0.044	①	NA	②	HYD	HYD
	Base, S, JCW	R56	1.6 (N14B16C)	0.044	①	NA	②	HYD	HYD
	Base, S, JCW	R56	1.6 (N16B16A)	0.044	①	NA	②	HYD	HYD
	Base, S, JCW	R56	1.6 (N18B16A)	0.044	①	NA	②	HYD	HYD
	Base, S, JCW	R57	1.6 (N14B16C)	0.044	①	NA	②	HYD	HYD
	Base, S, JCW	R57	1.6 (N16B16A)	0.044	①	NA	②	HYD	HYD
	Base, S, JCW	R57	1.6 (N18B16A)	0.044	①	NA	②	HYD	HYD
	Countryman, S, ALL4	R60	1.6 (N14B16C)	0.044	①	NA	②	HYD	HYD
	Countryman, S, ALL4	R60	1.6 (N16B16A)	0.044	①	NA	②	HYD	HYD
	Countryman, S, ALL4	R60	1.6 (N18B16A)	0.044	①	NA	②	HYD	HYD
2012	Clubman, S, JCW	R55	1.6 (N14B16C)	0.044	①	NA	②	HYD	HYD
	Clubman, S, JCW	R55	1.6 (N16B16A)	0.044	①	NA	②	HYD	HYD
	Clubman, S, JCW	R55	1.6 (N18B16A)	0.044	①	NA	②	HYD	HYD
	Base, S, JCW	R56	1.6 (N14B16C)	0.044	①	NA	②	HYD	HYD
	Base, S, JCW	R56	1.6 (N16B16A)	0.044	①	NA	②	HYD	HYD
	Base, S, JCW	R56	1.6 (N18B16A)	0.044	①	NA	②	HYD	HYD
	Base, S, JCW	R57	1.6 (N14B16C)	0.044	①	NA	②	HYD	HYD
	Base, S, JCW	R57	1.6 (N16B16A)	0.044	①	NA	②	HYD	HYD
	Base, S, JCW	R57	1.6 (N18B16A)	0.044	①	NA	②	HYD	HYD
	Coupe, S, JCW	R58	1.6 (N14B16C)	0.044	①	NA	②	HYD	HYD
	Coupe, S, JCW	R58	1.6 (N16B16A)	0.044	①	NA	②	HYD	HYD
	Coupe, S, JCW	R58	1.6 (N18B16A)	0.044	①	NA	②	HYD	HYD
	Roadster, S, JCW	R59	1.6 (N14B16C)	0.044	①	NA	②	HYD	HYD
	Roadster, S, JCW	R59	1.6 (N16B16A)	0.044	①	NA	②	HYD	HYD
	Roadster, S, JCW	R59	1.6 (N18B16A)	0.044	①	NA	②	HYD	HYD
	Countryman, S, ALL4	R60	1.6 (N16B16A)	0.044	①	NA	②	HYD	HYD
	Countryman, S, ALL4	R60	1.6 (N18B16A)	0.044	①	NA	②	HYD	HYD

NOTE: The Vehicle Emission Control Information label often reflects specification changes made during production. The label figures must be used if they differ from those in this chart.

NA: Not available

HYD: Hydraulic

JCW: John Cooper Works

① Ignition timing is regulated by the Electronic Control Module (ECM), and cannot be adjusted.

② Idle speed is controled by the Electronic Control Module (ECM), and cannot be adjusted.

CAPACITIES

Year	Model	Series	Engine Displacement Liters (ID)	Engine Oil with Filter (qts.)	Automatic Transaxle (qts.)	Manual Transaxle (qts.)	Fuel Tank (gal.)	Cooling System (qts.)
2011	Clubman, S, JCW	R55	1.6 (N14B16C)	4.44	5.3	①	13.2	②
	Clubman, S, JCW	R55	1.6 (N16B16A)	4.44	5.3	①	13.2	②
	Clubman, S, JCW	R55	1.6 (N18B16A)	4.44	5.3	①	13.2	②
	Base, S, JCW	R56	1.6 (N14B16C)	4.44	5.3	①	13.2	②
	Base, S, JCW	R56	1.6 (N16B16A)	4.44	5.3	①	13.2	②
	Base, S, JCW	R56	1.6 (N18B16A)	4.44	5.3	①	13.2	②
	Base, S, JCW	R57	1.6 (N14B16C)	4.44	5.3	①	13.2	②
	Base, S, JCW	R57	1.6 (N16B16A)	4.44	5.3	①	13.2	②
	Base, S, JCW	R57	1.6 (N18B16A)	4.44	5.3	①	13.2	②
	Countryman, S, ALL4	R60	1.6 (N14B16C)	4.44	5.3	①	13.2	②
	Countryman, S, ALL4	R60	1.6 (N16B16A)	4.44	5.3	①	13.2	②
	Countryman, S, ALL4	R60	1.6 (N18B16A)	4.44	5.3	①	13.2	②
2012	Clubman, S, JCW	R55	1.6 (N14B16C)	4.44	5.3	①	13.2	②
	Clubman, S, JCW	R55	1.6 (N16B16A)	4.44	5.3	①	13.2	②
	Clubman, S, JCW	R55	1.6 (N18B16A)	4.44	5.3	①	13.2	②
	Base, S, JCW	R56	1.6 (N14B16C)	4.44	5.3	①	13.2	②
	Base, S, JCW	R56	1.6 (N16B16A)	4.44	5.3	①	13.2	②
	Base, S, JCW	R56	1.6 (N18B16A)	4.44	5.3	①	13.2	②
	Base, S, JCW	R57	1.6 (N14B16C)	4.44	5.3	①	13.2	②
	Base, S, JCW	R57	1.6 (N16B16A)	4.44	5.3	①	13.2	②
	Base, S, JCW	R57	1.6 (N18B16A)	4.44	5.3	①	13.2	②
	Coupe, S, JCW	R58	1.6 (N14B16C)	4.44	5.3	①	13.2	②
	Coupe, S, JCW	R58	1.6 (N16B16A)	4.44	5.3	①	13.2	②
	Coupe, S, JCW	R58	1.6 (N18B16A)	4.44	5.3	①	13.2	②
	Roadster, S, JCW	R59	1.6 (N14B16C)	4.44	5.3	①	13.2	②
	Roadster, S, JCW	R59	1.6 (N16B16A)	4.44	5.3	①	13.2	②
	Roadster, S, JCW	R59	1.6 (N18B16A)	4.44	5.3	①	13.2	②
	Countryman, S, ALL4	R60	1.6 (N16B16A)	4.44	5.3	①	13.2	②
	Countryman, S, ALL4	R60	1.6 (N18B16A)	4.44	5.3	①	13.2	②

NOTE: If information in chart disagrees with owners manual, use information in owners manual

JCW: John Cooper Works

① 1.8 quarts for GS6-55 BG unit. 2.0 quarts for GS6-53 BG/DG unit.

② 5.81 quarts with manual transaxle. 6.34 quarts with automatic transaxle.

71105_MINI_C0004

FLUID SPECIFICATIONS

Year	Body Type	Model	Engine Displ. Liters (ID)	Engine Oil	Man. Trans.	Auto. Trans.	Rear Drive Axle	Transfer Case	Power Steering Fluid	Brake Master Cylinder	Cooling System
2011	Clubman, S, JCW	R55	1.6 (N14B16C)	5W-30	Dexron II	①	②	②	Dexron III	DOT 4	LLC
	Clubman, S, JCW	R55	1.6 (N16B16A)	5W-30	Dexron II	①	②	②	Dexron III	DOT 4	LLC
	Clubman, S, JCW	R55	1.6 (N18B16A)	5W-30	Dexron II	①	②	②	Dexron III	DOT 4	LLC
	Base, S, JCW	R56	1.6 (N14B16C)	5W-30	Dexron II	①	②	②	Dexron III	DOT 4	LLC
	Base, S, JCW	R56	1.6 (N16B16A)	5W-30	Dexron II	①	②	②	Dexron III	DOT 4	LLC
	Base, S, JCW	R56	1.6 (N18B16A)	5W-30	Dexron II	①	②	②	Dexron III	DOT 4	LLC
	Base, S, JCW	R57	1.6 (N14B16C)	5W-30	Dexron II	①	②	②	Dexron III	DOT 4	LLC
	Base, S, JCW	R57	1.6 (N16B16A)	5W-30	Dexron II	①	②	②	Dexron III	DOT 4	LLC
	Base, S, JCW	R57	1.6 (N18B16A)	5W-30	Dexron II	①	②	②	Dexron III	DOT 4	LLC
	Countryman, S, ALL4	R60	1.6 (N14B16C)	5W-30	Dexron II	①	②	②	Dexron III	DOT 4	LLC
	Countryman, S, ALL4	R60	1.6 (N16B16A)	5W-30	Dexron II	①	②	②	Dexron III	DOT 4	LLC
	Countryman, S, ALL4	R60	1.6 (N18B16A)	5W-30	Dexron II	①	②	②	Dexron III	DOT 4	LLC
2012	Clubman, S, JCW	R55	1.6 (N14B16C)	5W-30	Dexron II	①	②	②	Dexron III	DOT 4	LLC
	Clubman, S, JCW	R55	1.6 (N16B16A)	5W-30	Dexron II	①	②	②	Dexron III	DOT 4	LLC
	Clubman, S, JCW	R55	1.6 (N18B16A)	5W-30	Dexron II	①	②	②	Dexron III	DOT 4	LLC
	Base, S, JCW	R56	1.6 (N14B16C)	5W-30	Dexron II	①	②	②	Dexron III	DOT 4	LLC
	Base, S, JCW	R56	1.6 (N16B16A)	5W-30	Dexron II	①	②	②	Dexron III	DOT 4	LLC
	Base, S, JCW	R56	1.6 (N18B16A)	5W-30	Dexron II	①	②	②	Dexron III	DOT 4	LLC
	Base, S, JCW	R57	1.6 (N14B16C)	5W-30	Dexron II	①	②	②	Dexron III	DOT 4	LLC
	Base, S, JCW	R57	1.6 (N16B16A)	5W-30	Dexron II	①	②	②	Dexron III	DOT 4	LLC
	Base, S, JCW	R57	1.6 (N18B16A)	5W-30	Dexron II	①	②	②	Dexron III	DOT 4	LLC
	Coupe, S, JCW	R58	1.6 (N14B16C)	5W-30	Dexron II	①	②	②	Dexron III	DOT 4	LLC
	Coupe, S, JCW	R58	1.6 (N16B16A)	5W-30	Dexron II	①	②	②	Dexron III	DOT 4	LLC
	Coupe, S, JCW	R58	1.6 (N18B16A)	5W-30	Dexron II	①	②	②	Dexron III	DOT 4	LLC
	Roadster, S, JCW	R59	1.6 (N14B16C)	5W-30	Dexron II	①	②	②	Dexron III	DOT 4	LLC
	Roadster, S, JCW	R59	1.6 (N16B16A)	5W-30	Dexron II	①	②	②	Dexron III	DOT 4	LLC
	Roadster, S, JCW	R59	1.6 (N18B16A)	5W-30	Dexron II	①	②	②	Dexron III	DOT 4	LLC
	Countryman, S, ALL4	R60	1.6 (N16B16A)	5W-30	Dexron II	①	②	②	Dexron III	DOT 4	LLC
	Countryman, S, ALL4	R60	1.6 (N18B16A)	5W-30	Dexron II	①	②	②	Dexron III	DOT 4	LLC

NOTE: If information in chart disagrees with owners manual, use information in owners manual

DOT: Department Of Transpotation

LLC: Long Life Coolant

① GACVT16Z: Esso EZL-799A

   GA6F21WA: AFF JWS-3309

② BMW differential oil SAF-XO/OSP

VALVE SPECIFICATIONS

Year	Engine Displacement Liters (ID)	Seat Angle (deg.)	Face Angle (deg.)	Spring Test Pressure (lbs. @ in.)	Spring Installed Height (in.)	Stem-to-Guide Clearance (in.)		Stem Diameter (in.)	
						Intake	Exhaust	Intake	Exhaust
2011	1.6 (N14B16C)	①	45	NS	NS	② 0.0197	② 0.0197	0.0234-0.0235	0.0234-0.0235
	1.6 (N16B16A)	①	45	NS	NS	②	②	0.0234-0.0235	0.0234-0.0235
	1.6 (N18B16A)	①	45	NS	NS	②	②	0.0234-0.0235	0.0234-0.0235
2012	1.6 (N14B16C)	①	45	NS	NS	② 0.0197	② 0.0197	0.0234-0.0235	0.0234-0.0235
	1.6 (N16B16A)	①	45	NS	NS	②	②	0.0234-0.0235	0.0234-0.0235
	1.6 (N18B16A)	①	45	NS	NS	②	②	0.0234-0.0235	0.0234-0.0235

NS: Not specified by the manufacturer

① Valve seat angle: 45 degrees

Correction angle outside: 15 degrees

② To measure: Insert a new valve into guide

with end of valve flush with end of guide.

Use a dial indicator to measure axial valve head movement.

71105_MINI_C0006

CAMSHAFT SPECIFICATIONS

All measurements in inches unless noted

Year	Engine Displacement Liters (ID)	Journal Dia.	Brg. Oil Clearance	Shaft End-play	Circle Runout	Lobe Height	
						Intake	Exhaust
2011	1.6 (N14B16C)	NS	NS	0.0015-0.0035	0.0014-0.0028	NS	NS
	1.6 (N16B16A)	NS	NS	0.0015-0.0035	0.0014-0.0028	NS	NS
	1.6 (N18B16A)	NS	NS	0.0015-0.0035	0.0014-0.0028	NS	NS
2012	1.6 (N14B16C)	NS	NS	0.0015-0.0035	0.0014-0.0028	NS	NS
	1.6 (N16B16A)	NS	NS	0.0015-0.0035	0.0014-0.0028	NS	NS
	1.6 (N18B16A)	NS	NS	0.0015-0.0035	0.0014-0.0028	NS	NS

NS: Not specified by the manufacturer

71105_MINI_C0007

CRANKSHAFT AND CONNECTING ROD SPECIFICATIONS

All measurements are given in inches.

Year	Engine Displacement Liters (ID)	Crankshaft				Connecting Rod		
		Main Brg. Journal Dia.	Main Brg. Oil Clearance	Shaft End-play	Thrust on No.	Journal Diameter	Oil Clearance	Side Clearance
2011	1.6 (N14B16C)	1.7542-1.7550	0.0010-0.0016	0.0058-0.0019	NS	1.5980-1.5986	0.0008-0.0025	NS
	1.6 (N16B16A)	1.7542-1.7550	0.0010-0.0016	0.0058-0.0019	NS	1.5980-1.5986	0.0008-0.0025	NS
	1.6 (N18B16A)	1.7542-1.7550	0.0010-0.0016	0.0058-0.0019	NS	1.5980-1.5986	0.0008-0.0025	NS
2012	1.6 (N14B16C)	1.7542-1.7550	0.0010-0.0016	0.0058-0.0019	NS	1.5980-1.5986	0.0008-0.0025	NS
	1.6 (N16B16A)	1.7542-1.7550	0.0010-0.0016	0.0058-0.0019	NS	1.5980-1.5986	0.0008-0.0025	NS
	1.6 (N18B16A)	1.7542-1.7550	0.0010-0.0016	0.0058-0.0019	NS	1.5980-1.5986	0.0008-0.0025	NS

NS: Not specified by the manufacturer

37698_MINI_C0008

PISTON AND RING SPECIFICATIONS

All measurements are given in inches

Year	Engine Displacement Liters (ID)	Piston Clearance	Ring Gap			Ring Side Clearance		
			Top Compression	Bottom Compression	Oil Control	Top Compression	Bottom Compression	Oil Control
2011	1.6 (N14B16C)	NS	0.0097-0.0136	0.0136-0.0195	0.0039-0.0136	0.0011-0.0027	0.0011-0.0027	0.0011-0.0027
	1.6 (N16B16A)	NS	0.0097-0.0136	0.0136-0.0195	0.0039-0.0136	0.0011-0.0027	0.0011-0.0027	0.0011-0.0027
	1.6 (N18B16A)	NS	0.0097-0.0136	0.0136-0.0195	0.0039-0.0136	0.0011-0.0027	0.0011-0.0027	0.0011-0.0027
2012	1.6 (N14B16C)	NS	0.0097-0.0136	0.0136-0.0195	0.0039-0.0136	0.0011-0.0027	0.0011-0.0027	0.0011-0.0027
	1.6 (N16B16A)	NS	0.0097-0.0136	0.0136-0.0195	0.0039-0.0136	0.0011-0.0027	0.0011-0.0027	0.0011-0.0027
	1.6 (N18B16A)	NS	0.0097-0.0136	0.0136-0.0195	0.0039-0.0136	0.0011-0.0027	0.0011-0.0027	0.0011-0.0027

NS: Not specified by the manufacturer

71105_MINI_C0009

TORQUE SPECIFICATIONS
All readings in ft. lbs.

Year	Model	Series	Engine Displacement Liters (ID)	Cylinder Head Bolts	Main Bearing Bolts	Rod Bearing Bolts	Crankshaft Damper Bolts	Flywheel Bolts	Manifold Intake	Manifold Exhaust	Spark Plugs	Oil Pan Drain Plug
2011	Clubman, S, JCW	R55	1.6 (N14B16C)	①	②	③	NS	④	⑤	18	14-20	22
	Clubman, S, JCW	R55	1.6 (N16B16A)	①	②	③	NS	④	⑤	18	14-20	22
	Clubman, S, JCW	R55	1.6 (N18B16A)	①	②	③	NS	④	⑤	18	14-20	22
	Base, S, JCW	R56	1.6 (N14B16C)	①	②	③	NS	④	⑤	18	14-20	22
	Base, S, JCW	R56	1.6 (N16B16A)	①	②	③	NS	④	⑤	18	14-20	22
	Base, S, JCW	R56	1.6 (N18B16A)	①	②	③	NS	④	⑤	18	14-20	22
	Base, S, JCW	R57	1.6 (N14B16C)	①	②	③	NS	④	⑤	18	14-20	22
	Base, S, JCW	R57	1.6 (N16B16A)	①	②	③	NS	④	⑤	18	14-20	22
	Base, S, JCW	R57	1.6 (N18B16A)	①	②	③	NS	④	⑤	18	14-20	22
	Countryman, S, ALL4	R60	1.6 (N14B16C)	①	②	③	NS	④	⑤	18	14-20	22
	Countryman, S, ALL4	R60	1.6 (N16B16A)	①	②	③	NS	④	⑤	18	14-20	22
	Countryman, S, ALL4	R60	1.6 (N18B16A)	①	②	③	NS	④	⑤	18	14-20	22
2012	Clubman, S, JCW	R55	1.6 (N14B16C)	①	②	③	NS	④	⑤	18	14-20	22
	Clubman, S, JCW	R55	1.6 (N16B16A)	①	②	③	NS	④	⑤	18	14-20	22
	Clubman, S, JCW	R55	1.6 (N18B16A)	①	②	③	NS	④	⑤	18	14-20	22
	Base, S, JCW	R56	1.6 (N14B16C)	①	②	③	NS	④	⑤	18	14-20	22
	Base, S, JCW	R56	1.6 (N16B16A)	①	②	③	NS	④	⑤	18	14-20	22
	Base, S, JCW	R56	1.6 (N18B16A)	①	②	③	NS	④	⑤	18	14-20	22
	Base, S, JCW	R57	1.6 (N14B16C)	①	②	③	NS	④	⑤	18	14-20	22
	Base, S, JCW	R57	1.6 (N16B16A)	①	②	③	NS	④	⑤	18	14-20	22
	Base, S, JCW	R57	1.6 (N18B16A)	①	②	③	NS	④	⑤	18	14-20	22
	Coupe, S, JCW	R58	1.6 (N14B16C)	①	②	③	NS	④	⑤	18	14-20	22
	Coupe, S, JCW	R58	1.6 (N16B16A)	①	②	③	NS	④	⑤	18	14-20	22
	Coupe, S, JCW	R58	1.6 (N18B16A)	①	②	③	NS	④	⑤	18	14-20	22
	Roadster, S, JCW	R59	1.6 (N14B16C)	①	②	③	NS	④	⑤	18	14-20	22
	Roadster, S, JCW	R59	1.6 (N16B16A)	①	②	③	NS	④	⑤	18	14-20	22
	Roadster, S, JCW	R59	1.6 (N18B16A)	①	②	③	NS	④	⑤	18	14-20	22
	Countryman, S, ALL4	R60	1.6 (N16B16A)	①	②	③	NS	④	⑤	18	14-20	22
	Countryman, S, ALL4	R60	1.6 (N18B16A)	①	②	③	NS	④	⑤	18	14-20	22

NS: Not specified by the manufacturer

① Step 1: Bolts 1 through 10 (M10): 22 ft. lbs.
  Step 2: Bolts 1 through 10 (M10) tighten an additional 90 degrees
  Step 3: Bolts 1 through 10 (M10) tighten an additional 90 degrees
  Step 4: Bolts 11 through 12 (M8): 11 ft. lbs.
  Step 5: Bolts 11 through 12 (M8) tighten an additional 90 degrees
  Step 6: Bolts 11 through 12 (M8) tighten an additional 90 degrees
  Step 7: Screw replaced and tightened to 22 ft. lbs.

② Inner (M9) bolts: 22 ft. lbs. plus 150 degrees
  Outer (M6) bolts: 7 ft. lbs.

③ Step 1: 44 inch lbs.
  Step 2: 132 inch lbs.
  Step 3: Plus 90 degrees

④ Step 1: 72 inch lbs.
  Step 2: 22 ft.lbs.
  Step 3: Plus 90 degrees

⑤ M8 bolts: 11 ft.lbs.
  Hexagon nut: 15 ft. lbs.

71105_MINI_C0010

WHEEL ALIGNMENT

Year	Model	Series		Caster Range (+/-Deg.)	Caster Preferred Setting (Deg.)	Camber Range (+/-Deg.)	Camber Preferred Setting (Deg.)	Toe-in (Deg.)
2011	Clubman, S, JCW	R55	F	0.25	①	0.42	-0.50	0.2+/-0.17
			R	—	—	0.33	-1.75	0.4+/-0.13
	Base, S, JCW	R56	F	0.25	①	0.42	-0.50	0.2+/-0.17
			R	—	—	0.33	-1.75	0.4+/-0.13
	Base, S, JCW	R57	F	0.25	①	0.42	-0.50	0.2+/-0.17
			R	—	—	0.33	-1.75	0.4+/-0.13
	Countryman, S, ALL4	R60	F	NS	NS	NS	NS	NS
			R	—	—	NS	NS	NS
2012	Clubman, S, JCW	R55	F	0.25	①	0.42	-0.50	0.2+/-0.17
			R	—	—	0.33	-1.75	0.4+/-0.13
	Base, S, JCW	R56	F	0.25	①	0.42	-0.50	0.2+/-0.17
			R	—	—	0.33	-1.75	0.4+/-0.13
	Base, S, JCW	R57	F	0.25	①	0.42	-0.50	0.2+/-0.17
			R	—	—	0.33	-1.75	0.4+/-0.13
	Countryman, S, ALL4	R60	F	NS	NS	NS	NS	NS
			R	—	—	NS	NS	NS

NOTE: Refer to an authorized BMW alignment tool for individual specifications by engine, model and series identification

NS: Not specified by the manufacturer

① Difference between left/right max. 0.5 degrees

71105_MINI_C0011

TIRE, WHEEL AND BALL JOINT SPECIFICATIONS

Year	Model	Series	OEM Tires Standard	OEM Tires Optional	Tire Pressures (psi) Front	Tire Pressures (psi) Rear	Wheel Size	Ball Joint	Lug Nut (ft. lbs)
2011	Clubman, S, JCW	R55	①	①	②	②	③	NS	96-110
	Base, S, JCW	R56	①	①	②	②	③	NS	96-110
	Base, S, JCW	R57	①	①	②	②	③	NS	96-110
	Countryman, S, ALL4	R60	①	①	②	②	③	NS	96-110
2012	Clubman, S, JCW	R55	①	①	②	②	③	NS	96-110
	Base, S, JCW	R56	①	①	②	②	③	NS	96-110
	Base, S, JCW	R57	①	①	②	②	③	NS	96-110
	Countryman, S, ALL4	R60	①	①	②	②	③	NS	96-110

OEM: Original Equipment Manufacturer

PSI: Pounds Per Square Inch

① 175/65R15, 195/55R16, 205/45R17, 205/55R17, 225/45R18

② See specification in owners manual, or vehicle placard on driver's inside door area.

③ 15X5.5J, 16X6.5J, 17X7.5J, 18X8.5J

71105_MINI_C0012

BRAKE SPECIFICATIONS

All measurements in inches unless noted

Year	Series		Brake Disc			Brake Drum Diameter			Min. Lining Thick-ness	Brake Caliper	
			Original Thickness	Minimum Thickness	Maximum Run-out	Original Inside Diameter	Max. Wear Limit	Maximum Machine Diameter		Bracket Bolts (ft. lbs.)	Mounting Bolts (ft. lbs.)
2011	R55	F	NA	①	NA	NA	NA	NA	NA	②	②
		R	NA	①	NA	NA	NA	NA	NA	③	③
	R56	F	NA	①	NA	NA	NA	NA	NA	②	②
		R	NA	①	NA	NA	NA	NA	NA	③	③
	R57	F	NA	①	NA	NA	NA	NA	NA	②	②
		R	NA	①	NA	NA	NA	NA	NA	③	③
	R60	F	NA	①	NA	NA	NA	NA	NA	②	②
		R	NA	①	NA	NA	NA	NA	NA	③	③
2012	R55	F	NA	①	NA	NA	NA	NA	NA	②	②
		R	NA	①	NA	NA	NA	NA	NA	③	③
	R56	F	NA	①	NA	NA	NA	NA	NA	②	②
		R	NA	①	NA	NA	NA	NA	NA	③	③
	R57	F	NA	①	NA	NA	NA	NA	NA	②	②
		R	NA	①	NA	NA	NA	NA	NA	③	③
	R58	F	NA	①	NA	NA	NA	NA	NA	②	②
		R	NA	①	NA	NA	NA	NA	NA	③	③
	R59	F	NA	①	NA	NA	NA	NA	NA	②	②
		R	NA	①	NA	NA	NA	NA	NA	③	③
	R60	F	NA	①	NA	NA	NA	NA	NA	②	②
		R	NA	①	NA	NA	NA	NA	NA	③	③

F: Front

R: Rear

NA: Not available

① Minimum thickness is stamped in the brake disc shell

② Brake disc to wheel hub: Except R60 20 . R60 12.

Brake caliper to steering knuckle: Except R60 81. R60 37, than 90 degrees. New screw must be tightened to specification within 5 minutes of installation.

③ Brake disc to wheel hub: Except R60 20 . R60 12.

Brake caliper to wheel carrier: Except R60 48. R60 74.

71105_MINI_C0013

SCHEDULED MAINTENANCE INTERVALS
MINI

MINI vehicles follow a maintenance schedule as programmed into the vehicle called the Condition Based Service (CBS) system. Calculation of oil changes is determined by the CBS system and the remainder of maintenance services are determined by the CBS system. Mileage based maintenance intervals are not used. The only exceptions are as follows:

Brake Fluid: Every two years
Air Filter: Every 2nd oil change
Spark plugs: Every 2nd oil change
Spark plugs (John Cooper Works): Every oil change
Passenger compartment microfilter: Every oil change

RESET PROCEDURE

The following sequence must be observed if you are resetting with the trip meter reset button:
Switch on terminal 15.
Press and hold the trip meter reset button for approx. 10 seconds until the 1st maintenance service appears in the LCD display.
The upper display in the speedometer is lit up by a symbol (example: an oil can is the symbol for an oil change).
The lower display in the speedometer shows the time or distance remaining until the next service is due (example: 14000).
Scroll by repeatedly pressing the on-board computer button.
To reset, press the on-board computer button on the turn-signal/main-bean switch and hold it until the word "RESET" appears in the display.
Pressing the on-board computer button again will reset the service shown n the upper display.
Repeat this procedure for every service that is to be reset.
Change year with rocker switch on direction indicator/main-beam switch.
Press on-board computer button to confirm.

37698_BMW3_C0014

PRECAUTIONS

Before servicing any vehicle, please be sure to read all of the following precautions, which deal with personal safety, prevention of component damage, and important points to take into consideration when servicing a motor vehicle:

• Never open, service or drain the radiator or cooling system when the engine is hot; serious burns can occur from the steam and hot coolant.

• Observe all applicable safety precautions when working around fuel. Whenever servicing the fuel system, always work in a well-ventilated area. Do not allow fuel spray or vapors to come in contact with a spark, open flame, or excessive heat (a hot drop light, for example). Keep a dry chemical fire extinguisher near the work area. Always keep fuel in a container specifically designed for fuel storage; also, always properly seal fuel containers to avoid the possibility of fire or explosion. Refer to the additional fuel system precautions later in this section.

• Fuel injection systems often remain pressurized, even after the engine has been turned **OFF**. The fuel system pressure must be relieved before disconnecting any fuel lines. Failure to do so may result in fire and/or personal injury.

• Brake fluid often contains polyglycol ethers and polyglycols. Avoid contact with the eyes and wash your hands thoroughly after handling brake fluid. If you do get brake fluid in your eyes, flush your eyes with clean, running water for 15 minutes. If eye irritation persists, or if you have taken brake fluid internally, IMMEDIATELY seek medical assistance.

• The EPA warns that prolonged contact with used engine oil may cause a number of skin disorders, including cancer. You should make every effort to minimize your exposure to used engine oil. Protective gloves should be worn when changing oil. Wash your hands and any other exposed skin areas as soon as possible after exposure to used engine oil. Soap and water, or waterless hand cleaner should be used.

• All new vehicles are now equipped with an air bag system, often referred to as a Supplemental Restraint System (SRS) or Supplemental Inflatable Restraint (SIR) system. The system must be disabled before performing service on or around system components, steering column, instrument panel components, wiring and sensors. Failure to follow safety and disabling procedures could result in accidental air bag deployment, possible personal injury and unnecessary system repairs.

• Always wear safety goggles when working with, or around, the air bag system. When carrying a non-deployed air bag, be sure the bag and trim cover are pointed away from your body. When placing a non-deployed air bag on a work surface, always face the bag and trim cover upward, away from the surface. This will reduce the motion of the module if it is accidentally deployed. Refer to the additional air bag system precautions later in this section.

• Clean, high quality brake fluid from a sealed container is essential to the safe and proper operation of the brake system. You should always buy the correct type of brake fluid for your vehicle. If the brake fluid becomes contaminated, completely flush the system with new fluid. Never reuse any brake fluid. Any brake fluid that is removed from the system should be discarded. Also, do not allow any brake fluid to come in contact with a painted surface; it will damage the paint.

• Never operate the engine without the proper amount and type of engine oil; doing so WILL result in severe engine damage.

• Timing belt maintenance is extremely important. Many models utilize an interference-type, non-freewheeling engine. If the timing belt breaks, the valves in the cylinder head may strike the pistons, causing potentially serious (also time-consuming and expensive) engine damage. Refer to the maintenance interval charts for the recommended replacement interval for the timing belt, and to the timing belt section for belt replacement and inspection.

• Disconnecting the negative battery cable on some vehicles may interfere with the functions of the on-board computer system(s) and may require the computer to undergo a relearning process once the negative battery cable is reconnected.

• When servicing drum brakes, only disassemble and assemble one side at a time, leaving the remaining side intact for reference.

• Only an MVAC-trained, EPA-certified automotive technician should service the air conditioning system or its components.

BRAKES

GENERAL INFORMATION

PRECAUTIONS

• Certain components within the ABS system are not intended to be serviced or repaired individually.

• Do not use rubber hoses or other parts not specifically specified for and ABS system. When using repair kits, replace all parts included in the kit. Partial or incorrect repair may lead to functional problems and require the replacement of components.

• Lubricate rubber parts with clean, fresh brake fluid to ease assembly. Do not use shop air to clean parts; damage to rubber components may result.

• Use only DOT 3 brake fluid from an unopened container.

• If any hydraulic component or line is removed or replaced, it may be necessary to bleed the entire system.

• A clean repair area is essential. Always clean the reservoir and cap thoroughly before removing the cap. The slightest amount of dirt in the fluid may plug an orifice and impair the system function. Perform repairs after components have been thoroughly cleaned; use only denatured alcohol to clean components. Do not allow ABS components to come into contact with any substance containing mineral oil; this includes used shop rags.

• The Anti-Lock control unit is a microprocessor similar to other computer units in the vehicle. Ensure that the ignition switch is **OFF** before removing or installing controller harnesses. Avoid static electricity discharge at or near the controller.

• If any arc welding is to be done on the vehicle, the control unit should be unplugged before welding operations begin.

ANTI-LOCK BRAKE SYSTEMS (ABS)

SPEED SENSORS

REMOVAL & INSTALLATION

Front

1. Before servicing the vehicle, refer to the Precautions Section.
2. Disconnect the negative battery cable.
3. Raise and safely support the vehicle.
4. Remove the tire and wheel assembly.
5. Disconnect the electrical connector.

6. Remove the cable from the holder.
7. Remove the retaining screw.
8. Remove the component from its mounting.

➡**Do not allow the sensor to drop to the ground or hang by its cable.**

To install:

➡**Be sure to use new fasteners, as required.**

9. Installation is the reverse of the removal procedure.

Rear

1. Before servicing the vehicle, refer to the Precautions Section.
2. Disconnect the negative battery cable.
3. Raise and safely support the vehicle.
4. Remove the tire and wheel assembly, as necessary.
5. Partially detach the rear underbody paneling.
6. Disconnect the electrical connector.
7. Disengage the cable from the shock.
8. Remove the cable from the holder.

9. Remove the retaining screw.
10. Remove the component from its mounting.

➡**Do not allow the sensor to drop to the ground or hang by its cable.**

To install:

➡**Be sure to use new fasteners, as required.**

11. Installation is the reverse of the removal procedure.

BRAKES

BLEEDING THE BRAKE SYSTEM

BLEEDING PROCEDURE

BLEEDING PROCEDURE

ABS/ASC+T

1. Before servicing the vehicle, refer to the precautions.
2. Connect pressurized brake bleeder to the reservoir.

✳✳ CAUTION

Charging pressure should not exceed 2 bar (29 psi)

Front

1. Connect bleeder hose and collecting container to the right front brake.
2. Open the bleeder valve.
3. Fully depress brake pedal at least 12 times until brake fluid emerges clear and without air bubbles.
4. Hold the brake pedal down.
5. Close the bleeder valve
6. Repeat for the left front brake.
7. Remove the pressurized brake bleeder.
8. Test for proper brake operation.
9. Connect bleeder hose and collecting container to the right front brake.
10. Open the bleeder valve.
11. Fully depress brake pedal at least 12 times until brake fluid emerges clear and without air bubbles.
12. Hold the brake pedal down.
13. Close the bleeder valve
14. Repeat for the left front brake.
15. Remove the pressurized brake bleeder.
16. Test for proper brake operation.

Rear

1. Connect bleeder hose and collecting container to the right rear brake.

2. Open the bleeder valve and flush until clear brake fluid emerges with no air bubbles.
3. Close the bleed valve.
4. Repeat for the left rear brake.
5. Connect bleeder hose and collecting container to the right rear brake.
6. Open the bleeder valve and flush until clear brake fluid emerges with no air bubbles.
7. Close the bleed valve.
8. Repeat for the left rear brake.

DSC

➡**This procedure requires the use of a factory or equivalent scan tool. Refer to scan tool documentation.**

1. Before servicing the vehicle, refer to the precautions.
2. Connect the scan tool and set for service function 'Bleeding ABS/DSC Hydraulics'.
3. Connect pressurized brake bleeder to the reservoir.

✳✳ CAUTION

Charging pressure should not exceed 2 bar (29 psi).

Front

1. Connect bleeder hose and collecting container to the right front brake.
2. Open the bleeder valve.
3. Run the scan tool bleeding routine.
4. Press the brake pedal 5 times. Clear and bubble-free fluid must flow out.
5. Close the bleed valve.
6. Repeat for left front brake.
7. Remove the pressurized brake bleeder.
8. Test for proper brake operation.

9. Connect bleeder hose and collecting container to the right front brake.
10. Open the bleeder valve.
11. Run the scan tool bleeding routine.
12. Press the brake pedal 5 times. Clear and bubble-free fluid must flow out.
13. Close the bleed valve.
14. Repeat for left front brake.
15. Remove the pressurized brake bleeder.
16. Test for proper brake operation.

Rear

1. Connect bleeder hose and collecting container to the right rear brake.
2. Open the bleeder valve.
3. Run the scan tool bleeding routine.
4. Press the brake pedal 5 times. Clear and bubble-free fluid must flow out.
5. Close the bleed valve.
6. Repeat for left rear brake.
7. Connect bleeder hose and collecting container to the right rear brake.
8. Open the bleeder valve.
9. Run the scan tool bleeding routine.
10. Press the brake pedal 5 times. Clear and bubble-free fluid must flow out.
11. Close the bleed valve.
12. Repeat for left rear brake.

FLUID FILL PROCEDURE

➡**Immediately wash off any brake fluid that comes into contact with any painted surfaces. Depressing the brake pedal with the reservoir cap removed will cause the fluid to spray. When bleeding, maintain the amount of fluid in the reservoir between the MIN. and MAX. lines indicated on the master cylinder. When filling the master cylinder be sure to use the proper type of brake fluid.**

BRAKES   FRONT DISC BRAKES

Dust and dirt accumulating on brake parts during normal use may contain asbestos fibers from production or aftermarket brake linings. Breathing excessive concentrations of asbestos fibers can cause serious bodily harm. Exercise care when servicing brake parts. Do not sand or grind brake lining unless equipment used is designed to contain the dust residue. Do not clean brake parts with compressed air or by dry brushing. Cleaning should be done by dampening the brake components with a fine mist of water, then wiping the brake components clean with a dampened cloth. Dispose of cloth and all residue containing asbestos fibers in an impermeable container with the appropriate label. Follow practices prescribed by the Occupational Safety and Health Administration (OSHA) and the Environmental Protection Agency (EPA) for the handling, processing, and disposing of dust or debris that may contain asbestos fibers.

BRAKE CALIPER

REMOVAL & INSTALLATION

See Figures 1 and 2.

1. Before servicing the vehicle, refer to the precautions.
2. Remove front left or right wheel.
3. Press clutch pedal down to floor and secure with pedal support. The pedal sup-

port may only be released when the brake lines are reconnected. This prevents brake fluid from emerging from the expansion tank and air from entering the system when the brake lines are opened.

4. Pull brake hose out of holder. Grip brake hose at square head to prevent connecting piece from turning in retaining bracket.
5. Disconnect brake hose from brake line.
6. Detach brake hose from brake caliper.
7. Pull brake lining wear sensor out of brake lining (left side only).
8. Unscrew guide bolts.
9. Detach brake caliper in direction of arrow.

To install:

10. Install in the reverse order.
11. Replace guide screws.
12. Never twist brake hose when installing it and avoid all contact with parts attached rigidly to the body.
13. First tighten brake hose on brake caliper.
14. Tighten bolts/nuts to specification as follows:
15. Brake line screw: 10 ft. lbs. (14 Nm)
16. Brake hose to caliper: 10 ft. lbs. (14 Nm)
17. Guide screws (hexagon): 26 ft. lbs. (35 Nm)
18. Move wheels into straight-ahead position.
19. Insert brake hose in bracket and screw onto brake pipe.
20. Bleed the brake system.

DISC BRAKE PADS

REMOVAL & INSTALLATION

See Figure 3.

1. Before servicing the vehicle, refer to the precautions.
2. Remove front wheels.
3. Remove brake pad wear sensor. After removal it must be replaced (brake pad wear sensor loses its. retention capability in the break pad).
4. Pull brake pad wear sensor towards front out of pad (left side only).
5. Release guide screw.
6. If necessary, grip at hexagon head.
7. Feed brake hose out of holder.
8. Tilt brake caliper upwards.
9. Remove brake pads in direction of arrow from brake console. Mark any worn brake pads.
10. If replacing brake pads, remove pad retaining springs. Retaining spring for vehicles older than 48 months it is recommended to replace the retaining spring!.

To install:

11. Install in the reverse order.
12. In the event of one-sided brake pad wear, do not change brake pads round. Observe minimum thickness of brake pads.
13. Clean brake pads. So as not to damage the surface coating, if possible do not mechanically clean the. guide surfaces for the brake pads on the brake caliper mounting bracket. Instead, clean with brake cleaner BMW part no. 83 19 2 154 780 and apply a thin coating of brake pad paste BMW part no. 81 22 9 407 103.
14. Do not apply grease to brake pad back plate.

37698_MINI_G0060

Fig. 1 Pull brake hose out of holder (1). Grip brake hose at square head (3) to prevent connecting piece from turning in retaining bracket. Disconnect brake hose from brake line (2)

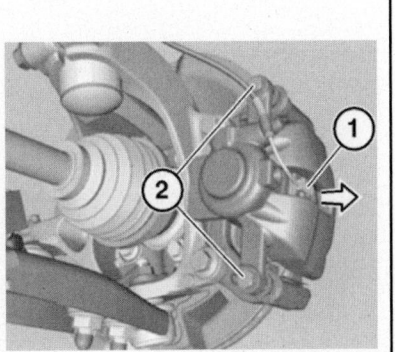

37698_MINI_G0062

Fig. 2 Pull brake lining wear sensor (1) out of brake lining (left side only). Unscrew guide bolts (2)

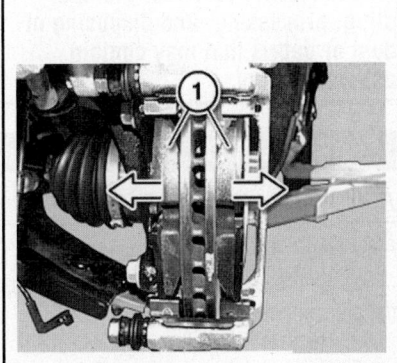

37698_MINI_G0064

Fig. 3 Remove brake pads (1) in direction of arrow from brake console

15. Check minimum brake disc thickness. Position special tool 34 1 280 at three measuring points in area and measure. Compare measurement result and lowest value with set point value . New brake pads may only be fitted if the brake disc thickness is greater than the minimum brake disc thickness (MIN TH).

16. Press brake piston fully back with special tool 34 1 050 . When pressing piston back, note brake fluid level in expansion tank. Overflowing brake fluid will damage the paintwork.

17. Check dust boot for damage and replace if necessary.

18. Clean contact surface of brake piston with brake cleaner and apply a thin coating of brake pad paste. Dust boot must not come into contact with brake pad paste as this may cause the dust boot to swell.

19. Clean contact surface of brake caliper with brake cleaner and apply a thin coating of brake pad paste. So as not to damage the surface coating, if possible do not mechanically clean pad guides.

20. So as not to damage the surface coating, if possible do not mechanically clean the guide surfaces for the brake pads on the brake caliper holder. Instead, clean with brake cleaner and apply a thin coating of Never Sees Compound brake pad paste.

21. Brake pad with indentation is intended for accommodating the brake pad wear sensor and must be fitted on the piston side.

22. Replace guide screw and tighten to 26 ft. lbs. (35 Nm).

23. When installing new brake pads at front and rear axles, brake fluid level must be brought up to "MAX" marking.

24. Fully depress brake pedal several times so that brake pads contact brake discs.

25. If necessary, when replacing pads, reset CBS display in accordance with factory specification.

BRAKES

REAR DISC BRAKES

❋❋ CAUTION

Dust and dirt accumulating on brake parts during normal use may contain asbestos fibers from production or aftermarket brake linings. Breathing excessive concentrations of asbestos fibers can cause serious bodily harm. Exercise care when servicing brake parts. Do not sand or grind brake lining unless equipment used is designed to contain the dust residue. Do not clean brake parts with compressed air or by dry brushing. Cleaning should be done by dampening the brake components with a fine mist of water, then wiping the brake components clean with a dampened cloth. Dispose of cloth and all residue containing asbestos fibers in an impermeable container with the appropriate label. Follow practices prescribed by the Occupational Safety and Health Administration (OSHA) and the Environmental Protection Agency (EPA) for the handling, processing, and disposing of dust or debris that may contain asbestos fibers.

BRAKE CALIPER

REMOVAL & INSTALLATION

See Figures 4 and 5.

1. Before servicing the vehicle, refer to the precautions.

2. Remove front left or right wheel.

3. Press clutch pedal down to floor and secure with pedal support. The pedal support may only be released when the brake lines are reconnected. This prevents brake fluid from emerging from the expansion

tank and air from entering the system when the brake lines are opened.

4. Detach locking clip in direction of arrow.

5. Disengage parking brake Bowden cable from actuating lever at brake caliper.

6. Feed out parking brake Bowden cable downwards.

7. Grip brake hose at square head so that connecting piece cannot rotate in retaining bracket.

8. Disconnect brake hose from brake line.

9. Disengage brake hose from holder.

10. Detach brake hose from brake caliper.

11. Pull brake lining wear sensor out of brake lining (right side only).

12. Unscrew guide bolts.

13. If necessary, grip at hexagon head.

14. Remove brake caliper.

To install:

15. Install in the reverse order.

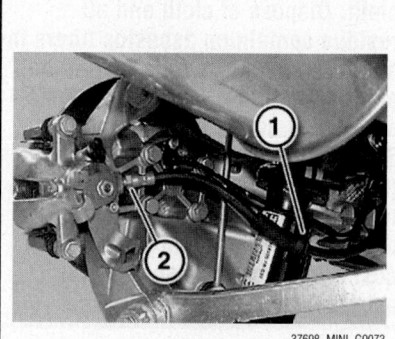

37698_MINI_G0073

Fig. 5 Disengage brake hose from holder (1). Detach brake hose (2) from brake caliper

16. Never twist brake hose when installing it and avoid all contact with parts attached.

17. rigidly to the body.

18. First tighten brake hose on brake caliper.

19. Insert brake hose in bracket and screw onto brake pipe.

20. Replace guide screws.

21. Tighten bolts/nuts to specification as follows:

22. Brake line screw: 10 ft. lbs. (14 Nm)

23. Brake hose to caliper: 10 ft. lbs. (14 Nm)

24. Guide screws (hexagon): 26 ft. lbs. (35 Nm)

DISC BRAKE PADS

REMOVAL & INSTALLATION

See Figures 6 and 7.

1. Before servicing the vehicle, refer to the precautions.

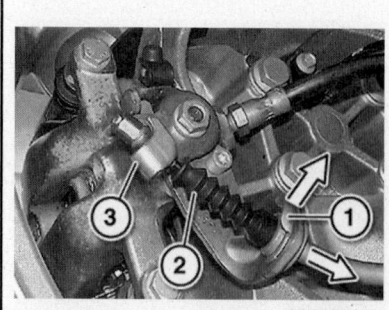

37698_MINI_G0071

Fig. 4 Detach locking clip (1) in direction of arrow. Disengage parking brake Bowden cable (2) from actuating lever (3) at brake caliper

2. Remove front left or right wheel.

3. Detach locking clip in direction of arrow.

4. Disengage parking brake Bowden cable from actuating lever at brake caliper.

5. Feed out parking brake Bowden cable downwards.

6. Both guide bolts must be released and then the brake caliper detached towards the rear!.

7. The springs may be bent when only one bolt is released and the brake caliper is folded up!.

8. Unscrew guide bolts. If necessary, grip at hexagon head.

9. Mark any worn brake pads. In the event of one-sided brake pad wear, do not change brake pads round.

10. Remove brake pads in direction of arrow from brake console. Observe minimum thickness of brake pads. Clean brake pads. Do not apply grease to brake pad back plate.

11. Remove lining springs and replace.

12. Check minimum brake disc thickness. Position special tool 34 1 280 at three measuring points in area and measure. Compare measurement result and lowest value with set point value .

13. New brake pads may only be fitted if the brake disc thickness is greater than the minimum brake disc thickness (MIN TH).

14. Screw brake piston with special tools 34 6 309, 34 6 306, 34 6 307, 34 6 308 into brake caliper. When pressing piston back, note brake fluid level in expansion tank. Overflowing brake fluid will damage the paintwork.

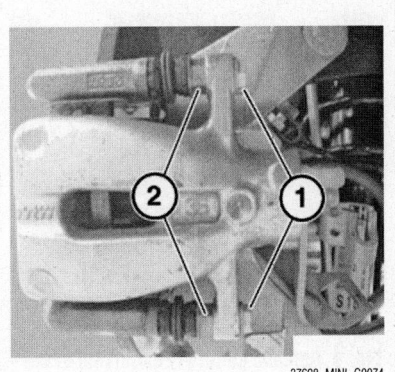

Fig. 6 **Unscrew guide bolts (1). If necessary, grip at hexagon head (2)**

37698_MINI_G0074

Fig. 7 **Check minimum brake disc thickness**

37698_MINI_G0075

15. Check dust boot for damage and replace if necessary.

16. Clean contact surface of brake piston with brake cleaner and apply a thin coating of brake.

17. pad paste. Dust boot must not come into contact with brake pad paste as this may cause the dust boot to swell.

18. Clean contact surface of brake caliper with brake cleaner and apply a thin coating of brake pad paste.

19. Brake pad with indentation is intended for accommodating the brake pad wear sensor and must be fitted on the piston side.

20. So as not to damage the surface coating, if possible do not mechanically clean pad guides. Instead, clean with brake cleaner and apply a thin coating of brake pad paste.

21. When installing new brake pads at front and rear axles, brake fluid level must be brought up to "MAX" marking.

22. Replace guide screw and tighten to 26 ft. lbs. (35 Nm).

23. Fully depress brake pedal several times so that brake pads contact brake discs.

24. If necessary, when replacing pads, reset CBS display in accordance with factory specification.

BRAKES

PARKING BRAKE CABLES

REMOVAL & INSTALLATION

See Figure 8.

1. Before servicing the vehicle, refer to the precautions.

2. Remove bracket on centre console.

3. Release heat shield and slide over exhaust system.

4. Release adjusting fixture for parking brake Bowden cable.

5. Detach both parking brake Bowden cables from balance arm.

6. Attach special tool 34 6 330 to parking brake Bowden cable.

7. Slide special tool 34 6 330 in direction of arrow onto barbs of parking brake Bowden cable until barbs are free.

8. Push parking brake Bowden cable towards rear.

9. Release cable assemblies from clips on fuel tank.

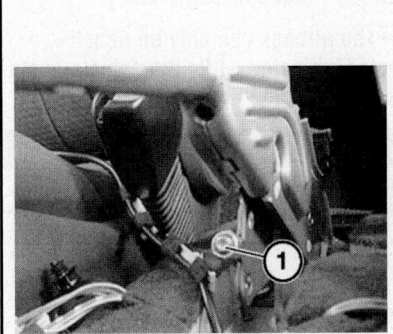

Fig. 8 **Release adjusting fixture (1) for parking brake Bowden cable**

37698_MINI_G0079

PARKING BRAKE

10. Release screws and remove bracket from control arm at top.

11. After completing tasks, adjust handbrake.

ADJUSTMENT

See Figure 9.

1. Before servicing the vehicle, refer to the precautions.

2. When 1st ratchet is engaged, no braking force should be exerted.

3. The difference in wheel circumferential forces between the left and right wheels may deviate by max. 30% from the greater value (measured on brake analyzer).

4. In event of larger deviations of wheel circumferential force: readjust parking brake.

5. Braking with locked wheels must be possible with the parking brake.

6. The parking brake must be reset if the actuation stroke is greater than 6 teeth.

7. Accurate adjustment of the parking brake is only possible if the parking brake Bowden cables and all moving parts on the parking brake move easily and function correctly.

8. Release gaiter of parking brake lever from clip.

9. Release self-locking nut until the load on the Bowden cable has been relieved completely.

10. Remove rear brake pads.

11. Insert brake piston into brake caliper with special tools 34 6 309, 34 6 306, 34 6 307, 34 6 308.

12. Install brake pads.

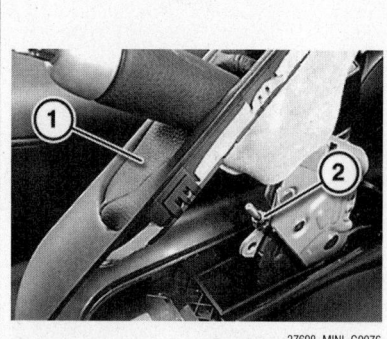

37698_MINI_G0076

Fig. 9 Release gaiter (1) of parking brake lever from clip. Release self-locking nut (2) until the load on the Bowden cable has been relieved completely

13. Screw in adjusting nut on parking brake lever until a gap of 0.5-1.5 mm between parking brake actuating lever and stop is set at brake calipers.

14. Release adjusting nut on parking brake lever completely.

15. Remove brake pads.

16. Insert brake piston into brake caliper.

17. Install brake pads.

18. Adjust adjusting nut on parking brake lever as shown above.

19. Apply parking brake lever three times.

20. Press brake pedal to floor at least three times so that air gap can be set.

21. Carry out operational check.

CHASSIS ELECTRICAL

GENERAL INFORMATION

✳✳ CAUTION

These vehicles are equipped with an air bag system. The system must be disarmed before performing service on, or around, system components, the steering column, instrument panel components, wiring and sensors. Failure to follow the safety precautions and the disarming procedure could result in accidental air bag deployment, possible injury and unnecessary system repairs.

SERVICE PRECAUTIONS

✳✳ CAUTION

Disconnect and isolate the battery negative cable before beginning any airbag system component diagnosis, testing, removal, or installation procedures. Wait at least 90 seconds after the ignition switch is turned off and the negative (-) terminal cable is disconnected from the battery before starting the operation. The SRS is equipped with a backup power source, so if work is started within 90 seconds after disconnecting the negative (-) terminal cable from the battery, the SRS may be deployed. Failure to disable the airbag system may result in accidental airbag

deployment, personal injury, or death.

DISARMING THE SYSTEM

➡️**If procedure in owners manual differs with this procedure, use the procedure listed in the owner's manual.**

1. Before servicing the vehicle, refer to the precautions.

2. Place the ignition switch in the **OFF**-position.

3. Disconnect the negative battery terminal and cover the battery terminal to prevent accidental contact.

4. Once the battery has been disconnected, wait for a period of approximately 10 minutes allowing the capacitor in the control unit to discharge.

➡️**The following airbags are deactivated simultaneously with the ignition key switch. Front passenger side, side airbag (front passenger side), knee airbag (front passenger side).**

➡️**The airbags can only be deactivated/activated while the vehicle is stationary and the door open.**

✳✳ CAUTION

The head airbag remains active.

5. Turn the key switch with ignition key to OFF position.

➡️**Deactivatable airbags on front passenger side out of operation. Head**

AIR BAG (SUPPLEMENTAL RESTRAINT SYSTEM)

airbag on front passenger side remains active. All airbags on driver's side remain active.

6. To activate, turn key switch with ignition key to ON position.

➡️**All airbags in the vehicle are activated and are triggered in appropriate situations.**

When the ignition key is turned in the ignition lock, the function of the airbag system is checked and the indicator light in the center console lights up for several seconds. The indicator light is permanently ON when the front passenger airbags are deactivated. The indicator light goes out after a few seconds when the front passenger airbags are activated.

ARMING THE SYSTEM

When repairs are completed, connect the negative battery cable.

CLOCKSPRING CENTERING

1. If unauthorized rotation of volute spring cassette cannot be ruled out, it is essential to return volute spring cassette to centre position.

2. Turn volute spring counterclockwise as far as it will go.

3. Turn volute spring clockwise as far as it will go.

4. Turn volute spring back to centre position and secure so that centering pin is at bottom position.

DRIVE TRAIN

AUTOMATIC TRANSMISSION FLUID

DRAIN AND REFILL

See Figures 10 and 11.

1. Before servicing the vehicle, refer to the precautions.

> ❋❋ **WARNING**
>
> **Use only the approved automatic transmission fluid in this automatic transmission. Failure to comply with this requirement will result in serious damage to the automatic transmission.**

2. Remove underbody protection.
3. Remove heat shield from hydraulic steering gear.
4. Move selector lever to "P" position.
5. The vehicle must be horizontal and secured against rolling off.
6. Connect BMW Diagnosis and Information System to vehicle.
7. Release filler plug with special tool 24 4 240 .
8. Remove M10 oil drain plug from transmission sump.
9. Pour in automatic transmission fluid through filler plug until fluid emerges at oil drain plug.
10. Start engine and run at idle speed.
11. Check whether ATF emerges at M10 oil drain plug.
12. If not, continue to add ATF.
13. Actuate brake pedal and at idle shift through all gears "P" to "D" twice for more than 2 seconds.
14. Then move switch to "P" position.

15. Again check whether ATF emerges at M10 oil drain plug.
16. Interrogate temperature of automatic transmission fluid with DIS Tester.
17. Increase temperature of automatic transmission fluid to 95–113°F (35–45°C).
18. Top up automatic transmission fluid until it flows over.
19. Screw in filler plug and oil drain plug.
20. Replace sealing rings.

CHECKING FLUID LEVEL

1. Before servicing the vehicle, refer to the precautions.

> ❋❋ **WARNING**
>
> **Use only the approved automatic transmission fluid in this automatic transmission. Failure to comply with this requirement will result in serious damage to the automatic transmission.**

➡ **Fluid temperature must be between 95–113°F (35–45°C).**

2. Remove underbody protection.
3. Remove heat shield from hydraulic steering gear.
4. Move selector lever to "P" position.
5. The vehicle must be horizontal and secured against rolling off.
6. Connect BMW Diagnosis and Information System to vehicle.
7. Release filler plug with special tool 24 4 240 .
8. Slacken M10 oil drain plug from transmission sump.

9. Start engine and run at idle speed.
10. Unscrew oil drain plug.
11. Check whether ATF emerges at oil drain plug.
12. If not, pour in ATF up to filler plug.
13. Top up automatic transmission fluid until it overflows at oil drain plug.
14. Actuate brake pedal and at idle shift through all gears "P" to "D" twice for more than 2 seconds.
15. Move switch to "P" position.
16. Check ATF level again.
17. Seal plugs when the fluid emerges slightly from the drain plug.

MANUAL TRANSMISSION FLUID

DRAIN AND REFILL

1. Before servicing the vehicle, refer to precautions.
2. Raise and safely support vehicle.
3. Make sure gearbox is at normal operation temperature.
4. Unscrew oil drain plug (1) and allow oil to flow out completely.
5. Clean oil drain plug and reinstall; tighten to 32 ft. lbs. (43 Nm)
6. Unscrew filler/fill level monitoring plug (2) and fill gearbox until oil overflows.
7. Allow excess oil to drain and reinstall filler/fill level monitoring plug; tighten to 32 ft. lbs. (43 Nm)

HALFSHAFTS

REMOVAL & INSTALLATION

See Figures 12 and 13.

1. Before servicing the vehicle, refer to the precautions section.
2. Remove front wheel.
3. Remove front wheel hub nut.
4. Drain transmission.
5. Remove brake caliper from disc (tie out of way; hose connected).
6. Remove tie rod ball joint from steering knuckle.
7. Remove ABS sensor from steering knuckle.
8. Remove control arm from steering knuckle.
9. On right side driveshaft only, remove bolts holding the intermediate shaft housing to the bracket.
10. Pull the driveshaft from transmission (discard snap ring).

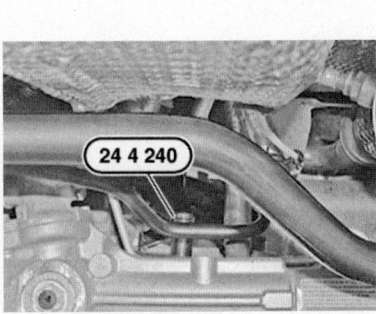

37698_MINI_G0112

Fig. 10 Release filler plug with special tool 24 4 240

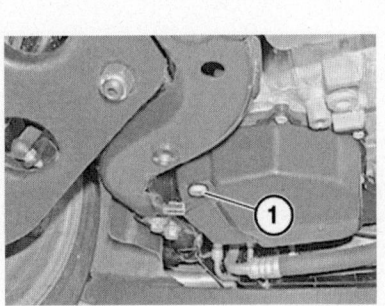

37698_MINI_G0113

Fig. 11 Remove M10 oil drain plug from transmission sump

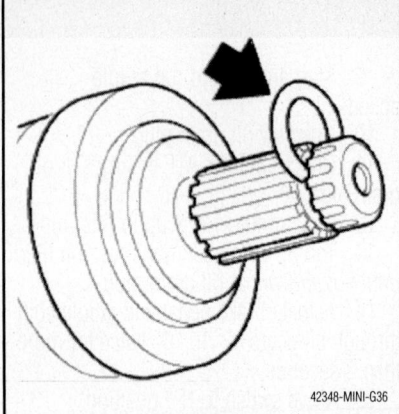

Fig. 12 Installing a new snap ring on driveshaft inner spline

Fig. 13 Showing special seal protector tool installed in transmission

Fig. 14 Rear axle fill plug (1)

11. Remove the bolt holding the steering knuckle to the McPherson strut, then lift the steering knuckle out with the driveshaft.

To install:

12. Install in the reverse order.

13. Install a new snap ring on the end of the driveshaft inner spline.

14. Install a special seal protector tool, 24-8-120, into side of transmission.

15. Position the driveshaft to the transmission and insert into to seal. Pull on the special tool handle to remove once the driveshaft is in position.

16. Push in output shaft over the resistance of the retaining ring until it snaps in place.

17. Install the steering knuckle to the McPherson strut. Torque the retaining bolt to 60 ft. lbs. (81 Nm).

18. Install the intermediate shaft housing to the bracket. Torque the retaining bolts to 18 ft. lbs. (25 Nm).

19. Tighten bolts/nuts to specification as follows:

- Control arm to steering knuckle; torque new nut to 41 ft. lbs. (56 Nm)
- ABS sensor to steering knuckle; torque to 6 ft. lbs. (8 Nm)
- Tie rod to steering knuckle; torque new ball joint nut to 38 ft. lbs. (52 Nm)
- Brake caliper to disc; torque caliper guide bolts to 23 ft. lbs. (31 Nm)
- Front wheel hub nut; torque new nut to 134 ft. lbs. (182 Nm)
- Front wheel

20. Refill the transmission.

REAR AXLE FLUID

DRAIN & REFILL

See Figure 14.

At this time the manufacturer does not provide service procedures for this component. The following procedure is a guideline.

1. Before servicing the vehicle, refer to the Precautions Section.

2. Raise and safely support the vehicle.

3. Position a drain pan under the component.

4. Remove the drain plug and drain the fluid. Be sure to properly dispose of used fluid.

5. Discard the O-ring.

To install:

➡ **Be sure to use new fasteners, as required.**

6. Be sure to use a new O-ring.

7. Tighten the drain plug to 60 Nn.

8. Fill the unit with the proper grade and type fluid.

9. Check for leaks and correct as required.

ENGINE COOLING

ENGINE COOLANT

DRAIN & REFILL PROCEDURE

See Figure 15.

1. Before servicing the vehicle, refer to precautions.
2. Unscrew cap on coolant expansion tank.
3. Release spring strap on lower coolant hose with special tool 17 2 051 .
4. Detach coolant hose.
5. Drain, catch and dispose of coolant.
6. Release vent screw.
7. Before filling, turn on ignition and set heating control to maximum temperature.
8. Set fan to slow setting.
9. Pour in coolant slowly.
10. Pour in special coolant through expansion tank filler neck until bubble-free coolant emerges at vent screw.
11. Observe filling capacities and mixture ratio .
12. Continue topping up coolant in expansion tank to max. level.
13. Start engine and run at idle speed.
14. If the level drops, top up coolant until the level no longer drops.
15. Switch off engine and if necessary top up coolant to max. level.
16. Close expansion tank.
17. Close vent screw and tighten to 18 inch lbs. (2 Nm).

ENGINE FAN

REMOVAL & INSTALLATION

See Figure 16.

1. Before servicing the vehicle, refer to the precautions.

2. Disconnect the negative battery cable.
3. Unlock plug and remove.
4. Release screw.
5. Unlock fan cowl duct in direction of arrow and remove.

To install:
6. Install in the reverse order.

RADIATOR

REMOVAL & INSTALLATION

See Figures 17 through 19.

1. Before servicing the vehicle, refer to the precautions.
2. Disconnect the negative battery cable.
3. Drain the cooling system.
4. Remove the front bumper trim.
5. Remove the outside air temperature sensor cable, if applicable.

6. Remove the front bumper trim carrier.
7. Remove oil cooler, if equipped.
8. Remove the upper radiator hose.

➡ **It is not necessary to discharge the air conditioning system.**

9. Detach the condenser and lift it free of the retaining lugs.
10. Remove lower radiator hose.
11. Remove the radiator retaining pins.
12. Tilt the radiator forward and disconnect the fan relay wiring harness.
13. Remove the radiator.

To install:
14. Install the radiator.
15. Install the fan relay wiring harness.
16. Install the lower radiator hose.
17. Set the condenser in place and attach.
18. Install the upper radiator hose.

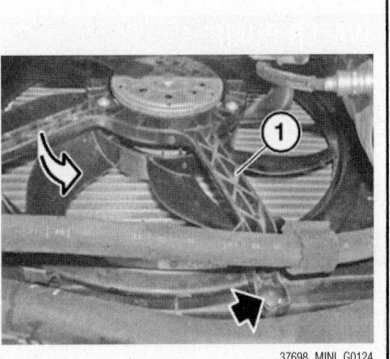

Fig. 16 Unlock fan cowl duct (1) in direction of arrow and remove

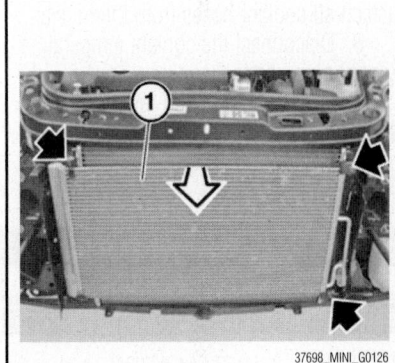

Fig. 18 Detach the condenser and lift it free of the retaining lugs

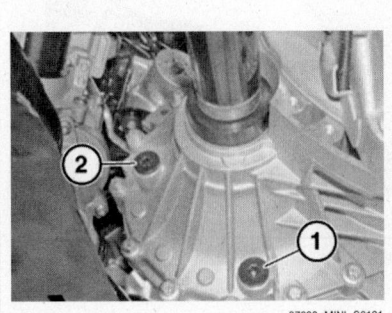

Fig. 15 Release spring strap on lower coolant hose with special tool 17 2 051

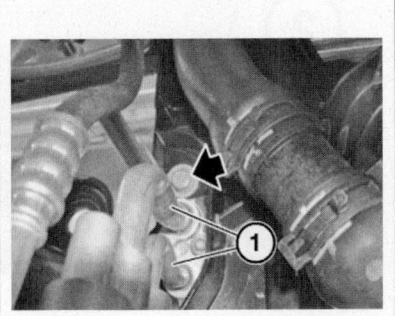

Fig. 17 Release retaining screws for refrigerant lines (1) on front panel

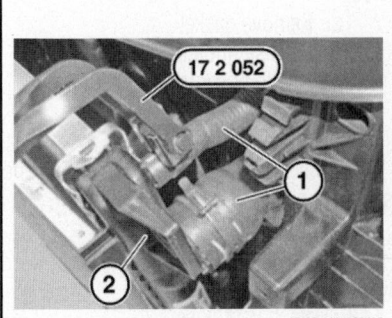

Fig. 19 Detach coolant hoses (1), carefully feed out radiator (2) towards top and remove

19. Install the oil cooler, if equipped.
20. Install the front bumper trim carrier.
21. Install the outside air temperature sensor cable.
22. Install the front bumper trim.
23. Fill and vent the cooling system.
24. Start the engine and check for leaks.

THERMOSTAT

REMOVAL & INSTALLATION

See Figure 20.

1. Before servicing the vehicle, refer to precautions.
2. Disconnect the negative battery cable.
3. Drain coolant.
4. Remove the intake air manifold, as required.
5. Release lock on coolant pipe in direction of arrow.
6. Disconnect the thermostat plug connection.
7. Using Special Tool No. 17 2 050, detach all coolant hoses from thermostat.
8. Disconnect the coolant temperature sensor plug connection.
9. Loosen the nut and remove the screws.
10. Remove the seal.

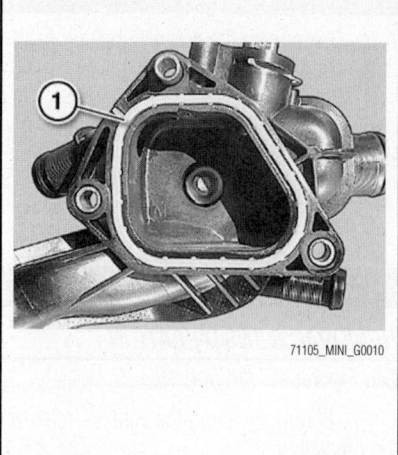

71105_MINI_G0010

Fig. 20 Thermostat gasket (1) positioning

To install:
11. Install in reverse order.
12. Replace seal.
13. Tighten thermostat housing to 71 inch lbs. (8 Nm).

WATER PUMP

REMOVAL & INSTALLATION

See Figure 21.

1. Before servicing the vehicle, refer to precautions.

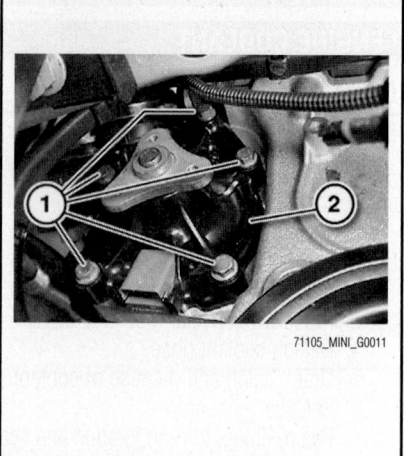

71105_MINI_G0011

Fig. 21 Water pump (2) and bolts (1)

2. Disconnect the negative battery cable.
3. Remove drive belt tensioner.
4. Remove screws.
5. Remove seal.

To install:
6. Install in the reverse order.
7. Replace seal.
8. Clean sealing surfaces.
9. Bleed the cooling system, using BMW cooling system bleeding tool or equivalent.

ENGINE ELECTRICAL

CHARGING SYSTEM

BATTERY

REMOVAL & INSTALLATION

See Figures 22 and 23.

1. Before servicing the vehicle, refer to precautions.
2. Disconnect the negative battery cable.
3. Remove right cowl panel cover.
   a. Remove gasket.
   b. Release nut and screw.
   c. Unclip cover towards top from retaining strip and feed out.
4. Loosen nut. Tighten.
5. Disconnect battery negative lead and secure at side.
6. Loosen nut.
7. Remove battery positive lead.
8. Detach vent hose.
9. Release screw and remove with holder.
10. Lift out battery.

To install:
11. Install in the reverse order.

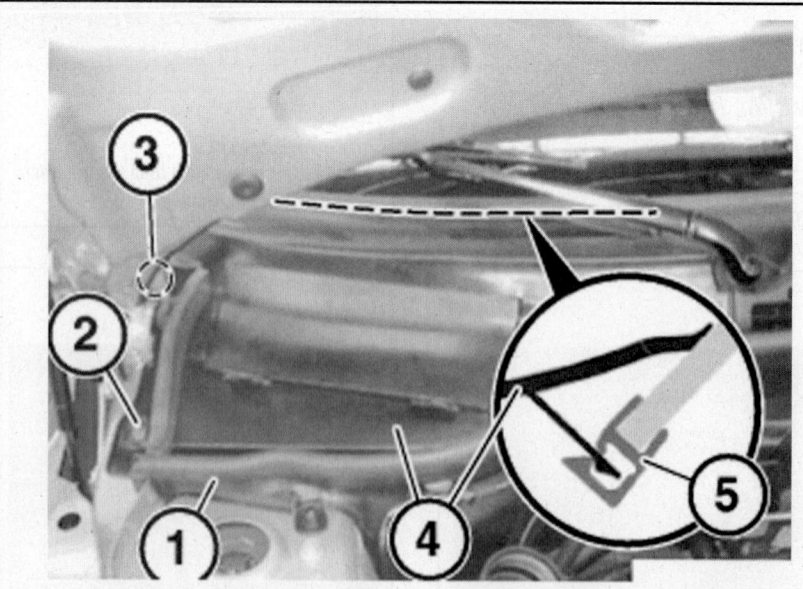

1. Gasket
2. Nut
3. Screw
4. Cover
5. Retaining strip

37698_MINI_G0130

Fig. 22 Removing right cowl panel cover

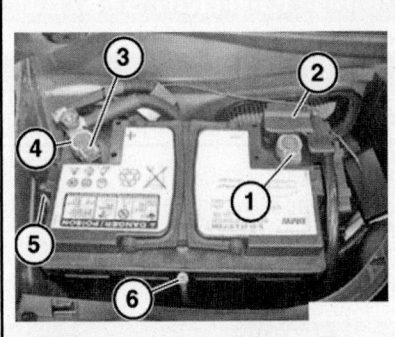

1. Nut
2. Battery negative lead
3. Nut
4. Battery positive lead
5. Vent hose
6. Screw

37698_MINI_G0129

Fig. 23 Battery and related components

12. Tighten bolts/nuts to specification as follows:

- Retaining bracket: 53 inch lbs. (6 Nm)
- Battery terminals: 44 inch lbs. (5 Nm)

13. Make sure battery is correctly seated in associated fixture.

14. Read out fault memory, clear if necessary.

15. On vehicles with IBS (intelligent battery sensor) register battery replacement.

BATTERY RECONNECT/RELEARN PROCEDURE

All MINI programming is performed by reading the fault memory of control unit using the BMW Diagnosis and Information System (DIS) and if necessary, working through procedures contained in the diagnosis tool.

➡Be sure to read to the information listed in the Engine Mechanical section of this section.

ALTERNATOR

REMOVAL & INSTALLATION

See Figures 24 and 25.

1. Before servicing the vehicle, refer to the precautions.

2. Check for stored fault codes, then erase fault code memory.

3. Switch off ignition.

4. Disconnect the battery.

5. Move the front panel into assembly position.

6. On N14 and N18 engines, remove the bolt, then remove the bracket and place to one side.

7. Bring belt tensioner with wrench into assembly position and hold.

8. Secure assembly position of belt tensioner by sliding locating pin in direction of arrow.

37698_MINI_G0131

Fig. 24 For N14 and N18 engines, remove the bolt, then remove the bracket and place to one side

❋❋ CAUTION

Remove wrench again from belt tensioner.

9. Unlock connector and remove.

10. Release nut and remove battery positive lead.

11. Release screws and remove the belt tensioner.

12. Release screw with joint extension.

13. Remove alternator.

To install:

14. Install in the reverse order.

15. Tighten bolts/nuts to specification as follows:

- Alternator to crankcase: 15 ft. lbs. (20 Nm)
- Battery positive lead to alternator: 10 ft. lbs. (13.5 Nm)
- Friction gear to crankcase: 71 inch lbs. (8 Nm)

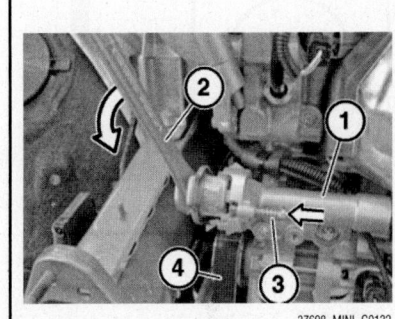

37698_MINI_G0132

Fig. 25 Secure assembly position of belt tensioner (1) by sliding locating pin (3) in direction of arrow. Remove wrench (2). Remove drive belt (4) from alternator

FIRING ORDER

See Figure 26.

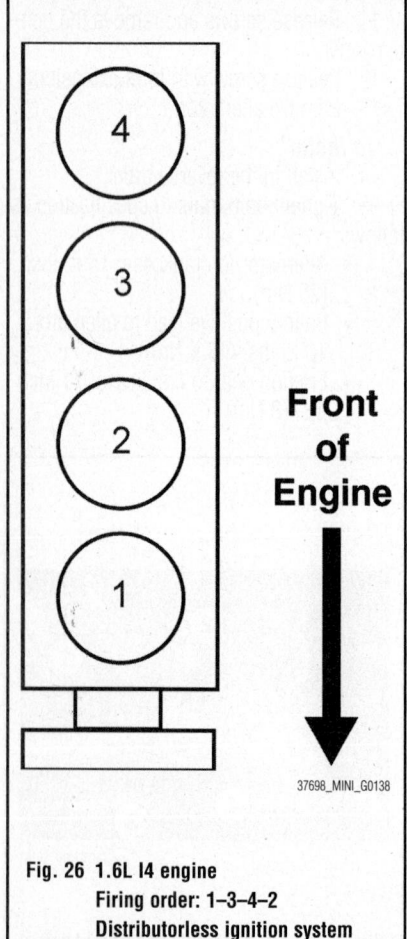

Fig. 26 1.6L I4 engine
Firing order: 1–3–4–2
Distributorless ignition system

IGNITION COIL

REMOVAL & INSTALLATION

See Figures 27 and 28.

1. Before servicing the vehicle, refer to the precautions section.
2. Disconnect the negative battery cable.
3. Check for stored fault codes.
4. Turn ignition off.
5. Remove upper engine cover.

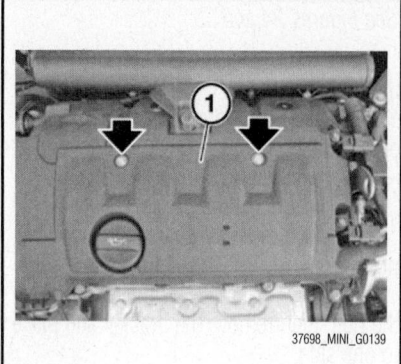

Fig. 27 Remove upper engine cover (1)

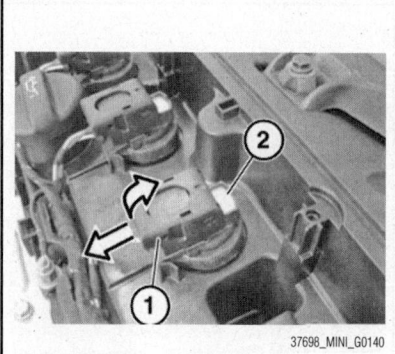

Fig. 28 Unlock plug retainer (1) of ignition coil (2) and disconnect plug

6. Unlock the plug retainer of ignition coil and disconnect the plug.
7. Pull the ignition coil up and out.

To install:

8. Installation is the reverse of removal.

IGNITION TIMING

ADJUSTMENT

The ignition timing is controlled by the Powertrain Control Module (PCM). No adjustment is necessary or possible.

SPARK PLUGS

REMOVAL & INSTALLATION

See Figure 29.

1. Before servicing the vehicle, refer to the precautions section.
2. Disconnect the negative battery cable.

❊❊ WARNING

Spark plugs must be replaced with the same type/number spark plug as the original. If another spark plug is substituted, damage may result.

➡ Allow engine to cool completely prior to starting this procedure.

3. Turn off ignition.
4. Remove ignition coils.
5. Unscrew and remove spark plugs with Special Tools 12 1 172 and 12 1 220.

To install:

6. Install and tighten spark plugs, using special tools 12 1 220 in conjunction with special tool 12 1 172.
7. If special tool 12 1 172 is not used, tighten spark plugs to 15 to 19 ft. lbs. (20 to 26 Nm).
8. Reinstall the ignition coils.

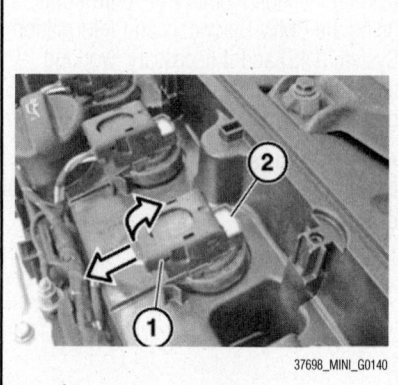

Fig. 29 Unscrew and remove spark plugs with Special Tool 12 1 172 and 12 1 220

ENGINE ELECTRICAL

STARTER

REMOVAL & INSTALLATION

See Figures 30 and 31.

1. Before servicing the vehicle, refer to the precautions section.
2. Turn ignition off.
3. Disconnect the negative battery cable.
4. Remove intake filter housing.
5. For N16 engine, remove the tank venting valve.
6. Remove the right wheel.
7. For N14 and N16 engines, remove the bolts and lay the vacuum tank to one side.
8. Release screw.
9. Unlock plug and remove.
10. Release nut and remove battery positive lead.
11. Release screws.
12. Remove bracket and starter motor.

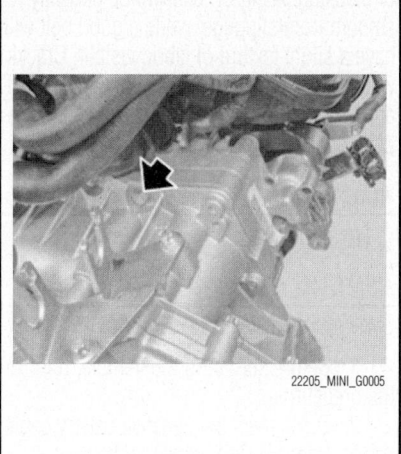

22205_MINI_G0005

Fig. 30 Remove starter screw

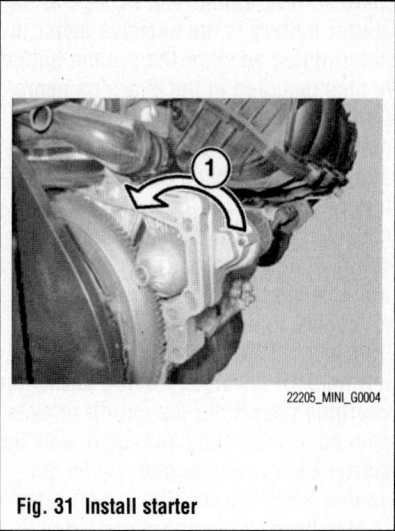

22205_MINI_G0004

Fig. 31 Install starter

To install:
13. Install in reverse order.
14. Install starter and fit screws.

15. Press starter in direction of arrow and tighten down.

ENGINE MECHANICAL

➡Disconnecting the negative battery cable may interfere with the functions of the on board computer systems and may require the computer to undergo a relearning process, once the negative battery cable is reconnected.

➡Before disconnecting battery, refer to the BMW diagnostic tool or equivalent for user documentation and further information on vehicle-specific deactivation/activation procedures. Turn off the ignition and other electrical loads/consumers to prevent sparking when reconnecting. If the ignition is not turned off when the battery is disconnected, fault memories may be set in some control units. There is a danger of mixing up battery cables: If the battery positive and negative leads are the same colour and you are in doubt, follow the polarity to the battery, then mark and cover the leads. On vehicles with radio code: After disconnecting the battery, the radio code must be reentered. Therefore obtain the radio code card. Note stored stations and restore them after connecting the battery. Stored settings of the on-board computer and clock will also be lost. All available central keys must be recoded for cars with first generation infrared transmitter locking systems.

➡If the vehicle is equipped with Intelligent Battery Sensor (IBS) on battery negative terminal, do not under any circumstances pull/lever off pole shoes by force. Do not under any circumstances release socket-head cap screw of IBS. The IBS wiring can be destroyed by mechanical strain upon battery replacement be careful. The size (capacity) of the battery required for the car is coded in the Car Access System (CAS). Use the battery size (capacity) installed as standard upon battery replacement. Recode the CAS when installing a battery with a different capacity. Register battery replacement via service functions in the diagnosis system. Delete fault code entries in the Digital Engine Electronics (DME) associated with battery replacement. After connecting battery, some systems may be restricted after a power supply interruption. Likewise, individual settings may be lost. Settings or activations must be carried out, depending on the equipment specification. Refer to the BMW diagnostic tool or equivalent for user documentation and further information on vehicle-specific activation procedures. If the vehicle is equipped with engine start-stop function (MSA), the MSA function is active only after a learning period (vehicle must not be

woken for a period of approx. 6 hours). Using BMW diagnostic tool or equivalent, E46 Perform (four-wheel drive) / E53 / E83: steering angle sensor adjustment. If equipped, activate slide/tilt sunroof. If equipped, activate power windows. If equipped, activate mirror with compass. Only E60, E61, E63, E64, E70, E71, E90, E91, E92, E93: mount steering angle.

➡On vehicles equipped with a two battery system (Starter and system battery) please note the following. A two battery system has a starter battery circuit and a system battery circuit An auxiliary control unit monitors both battery circuits. Depending on the situation, the battery circuits are connected to or isolated from the auxiliary control unit via a cut-off relay. These batteries must not under any circumstances be charged with a voltage in excess of 14.8 V. Rapid programs must not be used either. The engine can be jump-started with an external voltage supply via the jump start terminal on the right side of the engine compartment. The starter battery is isolated from the alternators when the engine hood is open. Giving starting assistance via the jump start terminal is thus limited by the capacity of the starter battery when the engine hood is open. The starter battery is charged as a matter of priority with a charger connected to the jump start terminal. The voltage at the starter battery is the decisive factor in determining whether the system battery is also included in the charging operation. The auxiliary control unit automatically detects a charging operation at a charging voltage at the starter battery of ≥ 13.5 V. The cut-off relay is closed and thus the system battery is connected in parallel. Both batteries are now charged. Prerequisite to this procedure is as follows: Terminal 61 inactive and Terminal 15 inactive. If terminal 15 becomes ACTIVE during the charging operation, the cut-off relay is opened immediately and again only the starter battery is charged. When the engine hood is open, the cut-off relay is also opened in normal operation when the engine is running. A special mode can be set by means of diagnosis for workshop/garage operation (see BMW diagnostic tool or equivalent information). The cut-off relay is closed from terminal R in this operating mode. This mode is automatically reset once a distance of 5 km has been driven.

➡On vehicles equipped with automatic engine start-stop function (MSA). If the engine hood contact is pulled upwards (workshop mode), the information "switch closed" is output. The automatic engine start-stop function is active. An automatic engine start is possible.

➡Before working on a vehicle equipped with MSA, always ensure that the MSA functionality is deactivated so as to prevent automatic engine starting while work is being carried out in the engine compartment.

1. To deactivate the MSA function, press button (1) in passenger compartment. Open seat buckle and driver's door.
2. Open engine hood and ensure that engine hood contact is not in workshop mode. Workshop mode A = 10 mm. Basic setting (engine hood open) B = 7 mm. To make sure that the engine hood contact is at the basic setting; if necessary press the hood contact up to the limit position before starting work and slowly release.

ACCESSORY DRIVE BELTS

ACCESSORY BELT ROUTING

See Figure 32.

INSPECTION

Inspect the drive belt for signs of glazing or cracking. A glazed belt will be perfectly smooth from slippage, while a good belt will have a slight texture of fabric visible. Cracks will usually start at the inner edge of the belt and run outward. All worn or damaged drive belts should be replaced immediately.

ADJUSTMENT

No adjustment is possible.

REMOVAL & INSTALLATION

See Figures 32 and 33.

1. Before servicing the vehicle, refer to the precautions.
2. Disconnect the negative battery cable.
3. Remove right wheel arch cover.
4. Remove right headlight.
5. Remove lock bridge.
6. Bring belt tensioner with wrench into assembly position.

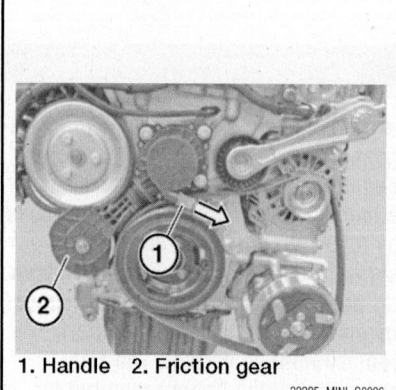

1. Handle   2. Friction gear

22205_MINI_G0006

Fig. 32 Drive belt routing

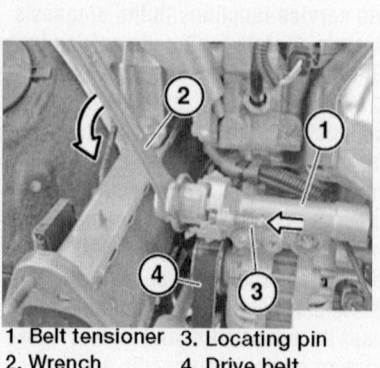

1. Belt tensioner   3. Locating pin
2. Wrench   4. Drive belt

22205_MINI_G0003

Fig. 33 Drive belt removal

7. Secure assembly position of belt tensioner by sliding locating pin in direction of arrow.

✲✲ CAUTION

Remove wrench again from belt tensioner.

8. Remove drive belt from alternator.
9. Move friction wheel into servicing position.
10. In order to release the frictional connection between crankshaft and coolant pump, it is necessary to move the friction gear into the servicing position.
11. Firmly pull the handle in direction of arrow until friction gear is separated from belt pulley.
12. To secure friction gear in servicing position, suspend pull cable on housing.

To install:
13. Installation is the reverse of the removal procedure.

AIR CLEANER

REMOVAL & INSTALLATION

N16 Engine

See Figure 34.

1. Before servicing the vehicle, refer to the Precautions Section.
2. Disconnect the negative battery cable.
3. Pull the intake ports off the intake air silencer housing.
4. Unlock the intake silencer housing with rotational movement from the resonance body.
5. Remove the housing.

To install:
6. Installation is the reverse of the removal procedure.

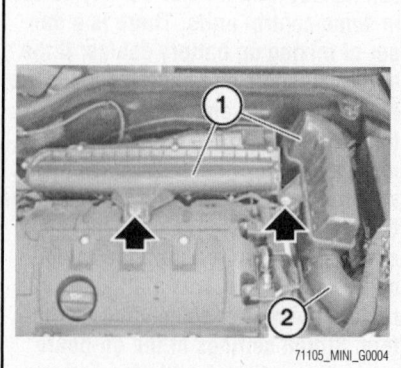

71105_MINI_G0004

Fig. 34 Air cleaner housing (1) and intake port (2)—N16 engine

➡Make sure the silencer housing rubber mounts and bearing journal are correctly seated.

N14 and N18 Engines

See Figure 35.

1. Before servicing the vehicle, refer to the Precautions Section.
2. Disconnect the negative battery cable.
3. Loosen the clamp and detach the gaiter from the housing.
4. Remove the housing.

➡If equipped with hot film air sensor meter, disconnect plug connection.

To install:
5. Installation is the reverse of the removal procedure.

AIR FILTER ELEMENT REPLACEMENT

1. Before servicing the vehicle, refer to the Precautions Section.
2. Disconnect the negative battery cable.
3. Loosen the screws and remove the lid.
4. Remove the element.

To install:
5. Installation is the reverse of the removal procedure.

CAMSHAFT AND VALVE LIFTERS

REMOVAL & INSTALLATION

N16 Engine

Intake

See Figures 36 through 38.

1. Before servicing the vehicle, refer to the precautions.

2. Disconnect the negative battery cable.
3. Remove cylinder head cover.
4. Remove adjusting unit for intake camshaft.
5. Remove intermediate lever.
6. Remove exhaust camshaft.

✳✳ WARNING

The screws of the bearing bridge must not be opened. Releasing the bearing bridge will result in damage to the cylinder head.

➡The bearing cap marked 5 is a thrust bearing.

7. Release screws of bearing caps 1 to 5.
8. Set all bearing caps down in special tool No. 11 4 481.
9. Remove camshaft.

To install:
10. Install in reverse order.
11. Clean all bearing points and lubricate with oil.
12. Check plain compression rings for damage and replace if necessary.
13. The plain compression rings have catches at the joint. Press plain compression rings apart upwards and downwards and remove towards front, being careful as they can break easily. Make sure they can move freely.

✳✳ WARNING

Both camshafts have different identifications. Mixing up the two camshafts will result in engine damage.

14. Insert camshaft so that "IN" marking points upwards.

15. Position inlet camshaft so that cams point upwards at an angle.
16. Attach special tool No. 11 9 551 to twin surface.
17. Make sure plain compression rings cable can move freely.
18. All bearing caps are identified from 5 to 10.
19. Tighten bearing caps from inside outwards. Tighten to 7 ft. lbs. (10 Nm).
20. Adjust valve timing.

Exhaust

See Figures 39 through 43.

1. Before servicing the vehicle, refer to the precautions.
2. Disconnect the negative battery cable.
3. Remove cylinder head cover.
4. Remove vacuum pump.
5. Remove exhaust adjusting unit for exhaust camshaft.

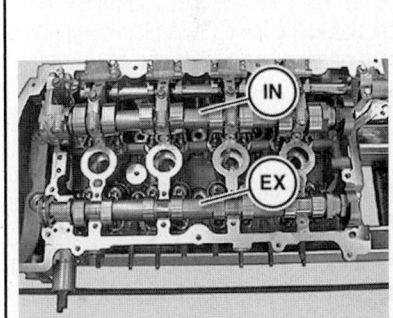

EX: Exhaust camshaft
IN: Intake camshaft

22205_MINI_G0023

Fig. 37 Camshaft identification

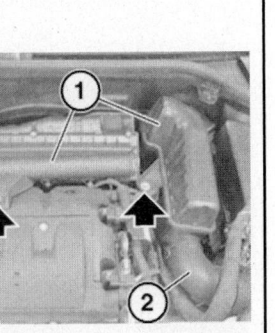

71105_MINI_G0004

Fig. 35 Air cleaner gaiter (1) suction line (2) and air cleaner housing (3)—N14 and N18 engines

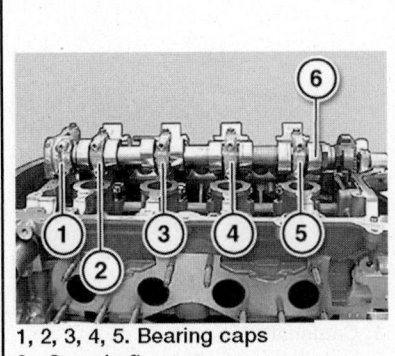

1, 2, 3, 4, 5. Bearing caps
6. Camshaft

22205_MINI_G0021

Fig. 36 Remove camshaft

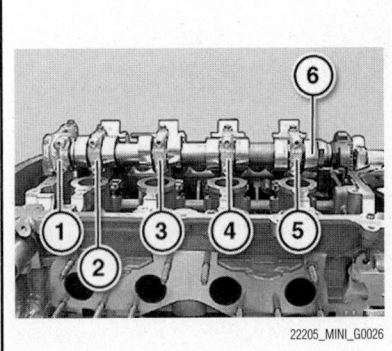

22205_MINI_G0026

Fig. 38 Bearing cap tightening sequence

6. Release central bolt of intake adjustment unit.

> ※ **WARNING**
>
> **The screws of the bearing bridge must not be opened. Releasing the bearing bridge will result in damage to the cylinder head.**

> ※ **WARNING**
>
> **Risk of damage to spark plug bores. Check special tool No. 11 9 652 for damage.**

7. Secure special tool No. 11 9 650 on cylinder head with screws in spark plug holes.

8. With special tool No. 11 9 650 installed, release bearing caps from 10 to 1.

9. Set all bearing caps down in special tool No. 11 4 480.

10. Check plain compression rings for damage and replace if necessary.

11. The plain compression rings have catches at the joint. Press plain compression rings apart upwards and downwards and remove towards front, being careful as they can break easily. Make sure they can move freely.

➡**Removal on engine: Block engine with special tool No. 11 9 590.**

➡**Removed cylinder head: When using special tool No. 11 9 000, it will be necessary to remove the aluminum profile insert.**

To install:

12. Install in reverse order.

13. Before installing exhaust camshaft, make sure roller rocker arm is correctly seated HVCA element and valve.

14. Lubricate all bearing points with engine oil.

15. Insert camshaft, paying close attention to installation position.

> ※ **WARNING**
>
> **Both camshafts have different identifications. Mixing up the two camshafts will result in engine damage.**

16. Make sure plain compression rings can move freely.

17. Align plain compressing rings in downward direction.

18. Lubricate all bearing points with engine oil.

19. Secure special tool No. 11 9 650 on cylinder head with screws in spark plug holes.

20. Fit all bearing bridges from 0 to 4.

21. Secure screws in sequence 1 to 10. Tighten to 7 ft. lbs. (10 Nm).

22. Adjust valve timing.

N14 and N18 Engines

See Figures 44 through 49.

1. Before servicing the vehicle, refer to the precautions section.

2. Disconnect the negative battery cable.

3. Remove cylinder head cover.

4. Check timing.

5. Remove chain tensioner.

6. To release central bolts, always use special tool No. 11 9 551 of exhaust camshaft.

7. Position special tool No. 11 9 551 on twin surface of exhaust camshaft.

8. Secure special tool No. 11 9 551 with a screw.

➡**Check function of adjustment unit locking by rotating camshaft.**

9. Mount special tool No. 11 9 551 on inlet and exhaust camshafts.

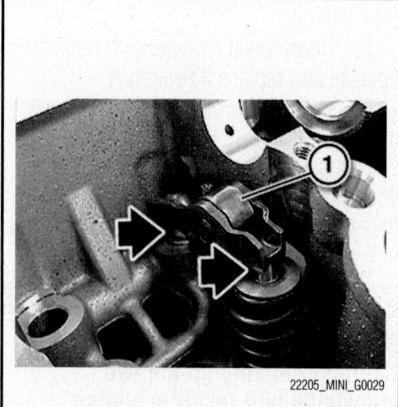

Fig. 40 Rocker arm positioning

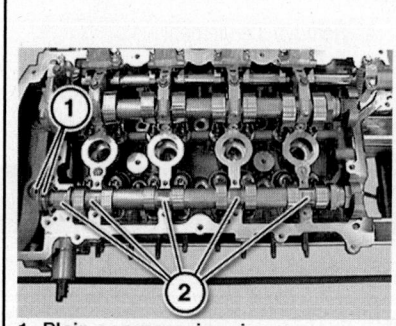

1. Plain compression rings
2. Bearing points

Fig. 42 Positioning plain compression rings

Fig. 39 Release bearing caps (shown without special tool for clarity)

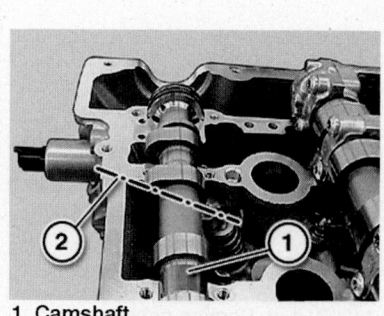

1. Camshaft
2. Installation position

Fig. 41 Camshaft positioning

Fig. 43 Bearing bridge locations from 0 to 4

10. Screw in special tool No. 11 9 552 on cylinder head with a screw.

11. To release central bolts, always use special tool No. 11 9 551.

12. Release screws.

13. Remove clamping rail.

14. Release screw.

15. Release central bolt.

16. Feed out sprocket wheel from timing chain towards front.

17. Release central bolt.

18. For exhaust camshaft, do not remove VANOS unit.

19. For intake camshaft, set down VANOS adjustment unit on special tool No. 11 4 480.

➡**With the cylinder head removed, it will be necessary to remove the aluminum profile insert when using special tool No. 11 9 000.**

20. Screw special tool No. 11 9 661 with special tool No. 11 9 662 into spark plug holes.

21. For intake camshaft, turn eccentric shaft in direction of ring and lock.

22. Release all screws on bearing caps.

23. Bearing cap No. 1 is a thrust bearing and has the number 0.

24. Bearing cap No. 2 is a thrust bearing and has the number 5.

25. All intake bearing caps are identified with numbers from 6 to 9.

26. All exhaust bearing caps are identified with numbers from 1 to 4.

27. Intake camshaft is identified with designation (IN), and exhaust camshaft is identified with the designation (EX).

28. Insert camshafts so that designations (IN and EX) can be read from above.

To install:

29. Install in reverse order.

30. Position intake camshaft so that cam of the intake camshaft points upward at an angle.

31. Position exhaust camshaft so that cam of exhaust camshaft points inward at an angle.

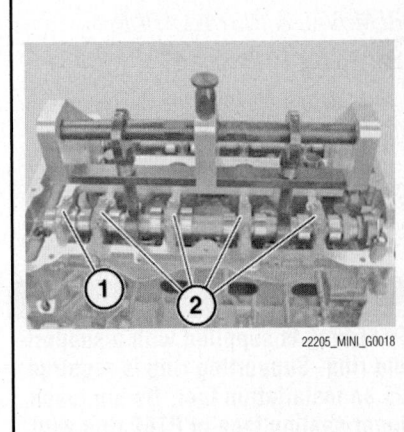

Fig. 48 Exhaust camshaft bearing caps

32. Tighten to bearing caps to 7 ft. lbs. (10 Nm).

33. Adjust valve timing.

CATALYTIC CONVERTER

REMOVAL & INSTALLATION

N14 and N18 Engines

1. Before servicing the vehicle, refer to the Precautions Section.

2. Disconnect the negative battery cable.

3. Move the front panel into working position.

4. Remove the control sensor.

5. Remove the monitoring sensor.

6. Remove the upper heat shield.

7. Remove the lower heat shield.

8. Remove the exhaust manifold and converter assembly.

To install:

9. Install in reverse order.

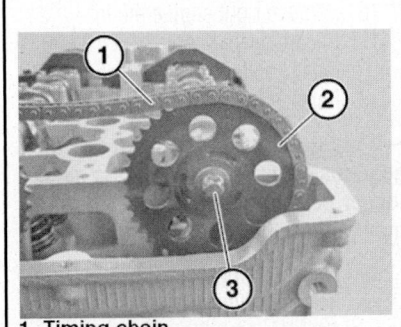

1. Timing chain
2. Sprocket wheel
3. Central bolt

Fig. 44 Removing camshaft sprocket

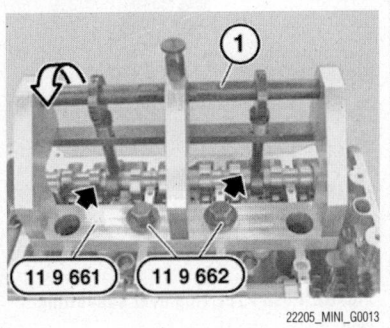

Fig. 46 Screw special tool into spark plug holes and turn intake camshaft eccentric shaft

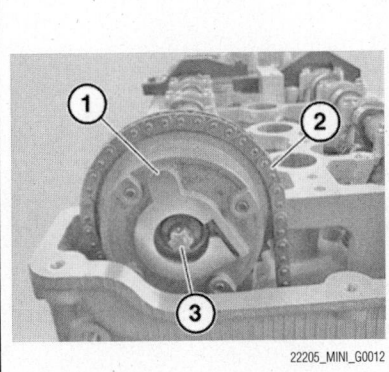

Fig. 45 Set down VANOS adjustment

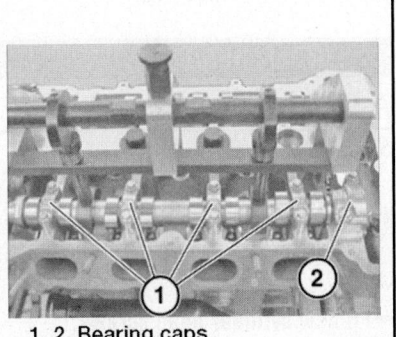

1, 2. Bearing caps

Fig. 47 Intake camshaft bearing caps

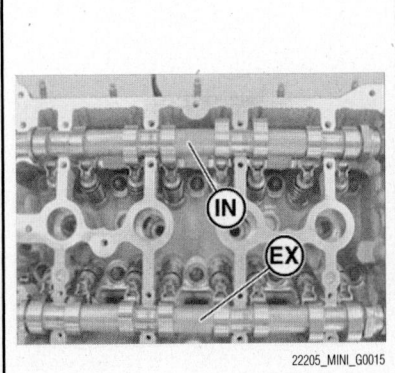

Fig. 49 Identifying intake and exhaust camshafts

CRANKSHAFT FRONT SEAL

REMOVAL & INSTALLATION

See Figures 50 through 52.

1. Before servicing the vehicle, refer to the precautions section.
2. Disconnect the negative battery cable.
3. Remove A/C line from compressor.
4. Remove vibration damper.

> **✼✼ WARNING**
>
> **PTFE ring is supplied with a supporting ring. Supporting ring is required as an installation tool. Do not touch inner sealing face of PTFE ring with fingers (risk of damage).**

> **✼✼ WARNING**
>
> **Do not release central bolt. If the central bolt is released, the sprocket wheels of the timing chain and the oil pump will no longer be non-positively connected to the crankshaft. The camshafts to the crankshaft can warp (risk of damage).**

5. Drive PTFE ring inwards with a drift until PTFE ring tilts outwards at bottom. Do not allow PTFE ring to slip inward.
6. Secure special tool No. 11 9 601 with screws to crankshaft and tighten to 11 ft. lbs. (15 Nm).

To install:

7. Install in reverse order.
8. Apply a light coating of oil to special tool No. 11 9 601.
9. Position PTFE ring with supporting ring on special tool No. 11 9 601.
10. Push PTFE ring over supporting ring in direction of arrow up to crankcase.

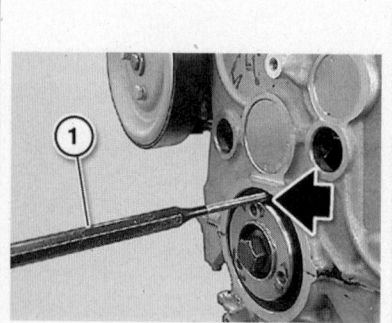

Fig. 50 Push PTFE ring in until it tilts out at the bottom

22205_MINI_G0066

Fig. 51 Install special tool on crankshaft

22205_MINI_G0067

Fig. 52 Push PTFE ring over supporting ring

11. Remove supporting ring from special tool No. 11 9 601. Supporting ring is no longer needed.
12. Draw in PTFE ring with special tool No. 11 9 602 in conjunction with special tool No. 11 9 603 until flush.

CYLINDER HEAD

REMOVAL & INSTALLATION

See Figure 53.

1. Before servicing the vehicle, refer to the precautions.
2. Disconnect the negative battery cable.

➡ **Fit new cylinder head screws.**

➡ **Do not wash off bolt coating.**

➡ **There must not be any coolant, water or oil present in the pocket holes (risk of corrosion and cracking).**

3. Remove exhaust system.
4. Drain coolant.
5. Drain engine oil.
6. Remove exhaust manifold.
7. Remove intake air manifold.
8. Remove oil dipstick.
9. Detach coolant hoses from cylinder head.
10. Remove cylinder head cover.
11. Remove inlet and exhaust adjustment unit.
12. Secure crankshaft with special tool No. 11 9 590.

➡ **Remove and install cylinder head in installed state.**

13. Suspend engine with engine crane.

➡ **Remove and install cylinder head in installed state.**

14. Move front panel into assembly position.
15. Release upper alternator screws, do not remove alternator.
16. Remove right engine mount.
17. Secure special tool No. 11 9 630 with standard bolts.
18. Release bolts.

➡ **If the timing chain is stowed in the gear case, the crankshaft must no longer be rotated. The timing chain may jam on the crankshaft gear.**

19. Release screw.
20. Release cylinder head bolts with special tool No. 11 2 250.
21. Release cylinder head bolts from outside inward (10 to 1).

➡ **Remove shims with a magnet.**

➡ **Do not use any metal-cutting tools for gasket removal.**

22205_MINI_G0037

Fig. 53 Cylinder head bolts (illustration shows camshafts removed)

22. Use special tool No. 11 4 471 to remove coarse gasket remnants from sealing faces of cylinder head and crankcase.

23. Remove fine gasket remnants with special tool No. 11 4 472.

➡ **There must not be any coolant, water or oil present in the pocket holes (risk of corrosion and cracking).**

24. Clean all pocket holes.

To install:
25. Install in reverse order.
26. Replace cylinder head gasket.

➡ **Fit new cylinder head screws. Do not wash off bolt coating. Attach shims to cylinder head bolts.**

❊❊ WARNING

Do not allow shims to drop into engine.

27. Secure cylinder head bolts from inside outward (1 to 10), using the following sequence:
- Step 1: Tighten to 22 ft. lbs. (30 Nm)
- Step 2: Turn angle 90°
- Step 3: Turn angle 90°

28. Secure bolts, using the following sequence:
- Step 1: Tighten to 11 ft. lbs. (15 Nm)
- Step 2: Turn angle 90°
- Step 3: Turn angle 90°

29. Tighten the screw to 22 ft. lbs. (30 Nm).

ENGINE OIL & FILTER

REPLACEMENT

See Figures 54 and 55.

1. Before servicing the vehicle, refer to the precautions.
2. Disconnect the negative battery cable.

❊❊ WARNING

It is essential to adhere to the exact filling capacities specified. Overfilling the engine with engine oil will result in engine damage.

3. Slowly open oil filter cap at hexagon catch escaping engine oil in a cloth.
4. Remove and insert oil filter element in direction of arrow.
5. Replace O-ring.
6. Remove engine oil drain plug.

To install:.
7. Lubricate O-ring with engine oil and tighten oil filter cap to 19 ft. lbs. (25 Nm).

8. Replace sealing ring and tighten oil filter housing to 89 inch lbs. (10 Nm).
9. Fill engine with oil.
10. Check engine oil level with vehicle parked on a horizontal surface.

EXHAUST MANIFOLD

REMOVAL & INSTALLATION

N14 Engine

See Figures 56 through 58.

1. Before servicing the vehicle, refer to the precautions.
2. Disconnect the negative battery cable.

❊❊ WARNING

The oxygen sensors are in danger of being damaged when the exhaust manifolds are removed and installed.

3. Remove control sensor.
4. Remove monitoring sensor.

37698_MINI_G0144

Fig. 54 Slowly open oil filter cap (1) at hexagon (2)

37698_MINI_G0145

Fig. 55 Remove and insert oil filter element (1) in direction of arrow and replace O-ring (2)

5. Release screws and remove upper heat shield.
6. Release screws and remove lower heat shield.
7. Release screws.
8. Unfasten clip.
9. Release nuts and remove exhaust manifold.

To install:
10. Install in the reverse order.
11. Replace seal and nuts.
12. Clean sealing surfaces.
13. Apply a thin coat of copper paste to thread.
14. Tighten bolts/nuts to specification as follows:
15. Heat shield: 36 inch lbs. (4 Nm)
16. Catalytic converter to crankcase: 19 ft. lbs. (25 Nm)
17. Exhaust system to catalytic converter clamp: 19 ft. lbs. (25 Nm)

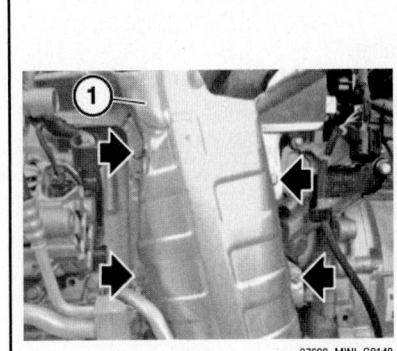

37698_MINI_G0148

Fig. 56 Release screws (arrows)

37698_MINI_G0149

Fig. 57 Unfasten clip (arrow)

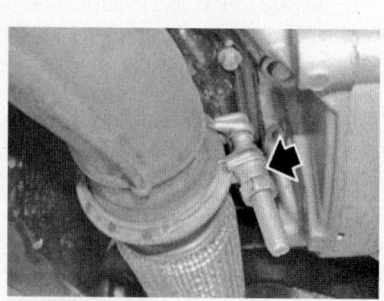

Fig. 58 Release nuts and remove exhaust manifold (1)

18. Exhaust manifold to cylinder head: 19 ft. lbs. (25 Nm)

N14 and N18 Engines

1. Before servicing the vehicle, refer to the Precautions Section.
2. Disconnect the negative battery cable.
3. Drain coolant. Remove coolant expansion tank.
4. Remove catalytic converter.
5. Detach charge air duct. Remove air intake pipe.
6. Separate turbocharger from mounting.
7. Remove manifold retaining nuts.
8. Remove manifold and turbocharger assembly.
9. Separate turbocharger from exhaust manifold.

To install:

10. Install in the reverse order.
11. Be sure to replace all gaskets.

➡ The following components must be checked when installing the turbocharger. Engine oil and coolant screw connection, air filter and proper functioning of the PCV system

INTAKE MANIFOLD

REMOVAL & INSTALLATION

N14 Engine

See Figures 59 through 62.

1. Before servicing the vehicle, refer to the precautions section.
2. Disconnect the negative battery cable.
3. Remove suction filter housing.

---

4. Remove engine cover.
5. Unfasten engine wiring harness on intake manifold.
6. Disconnect plug connection.
7. Disconnect plug connection on tank vent valve.
8. Disconnect plug connection.
9. Release tank vent valve.
10. Disconnect plug connection on solenoid valve.
11. Release engine breathers and hold to one side.
12. Loosen nut.
13. Disconnect plug connection.
14. Unfasten engine wiring harness on intake manifold.
15. Release cable at intake manifold holder.
16. Release screws.
17. Take off holder.
18. Release screw.
19. Unscrew nuts.

1. Engine wiring harness
2. Plug connection
3. Plug connection on tank valve.

22205_MINI_G0041

Fig. 59 Disconnect wiring harness and plug connections

1. Plug connection
2. Engine wiring harness

22205_MINI_G0044

Fig. 60 Unfasten engine wiring harness

To install:

20. Install in reverse order.
21. Replace all seals.
22. Torque the intake manifold to cylinder head to 11 ft. lbs. (15 Nm).

N14 and N18 Engines

See Figures 63 through 65.

1. Before servicing the vehicle, refer to the precautions section.
2. Disconnect the negative battery cable.
3. Remove suction filter housing.
4. Disconnect vacuum lines on vacuum connection.
5. Disconnect plug connection at EPPC.
6. Disconnect plug connection on tank vent valve.
7. Detach hose from tank vent valve.
8. Unscrew nuts.

To install:

9. Install in reverse order.

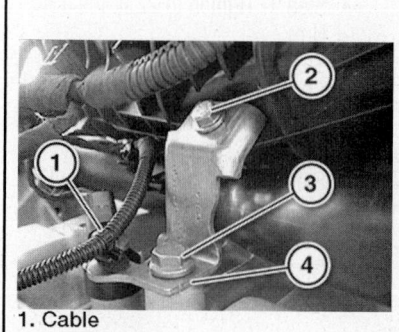

1. Cable
2, 3. Screws
4. Holder

22205_MINI_G0045

Fig. 61 Release cable, screws, and take off holder

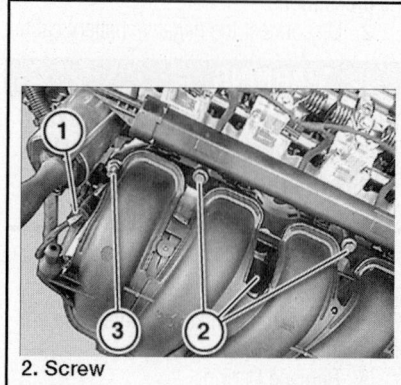

2. Screw
3. Nuts

22205_MINI_G0046

Fig. 62 Release screw and nuts

➡OUT connector on EPPC is identified with a green ring, vacuum line is fitted with a green ring (OUT) and vacuum line without green ring (VAC).

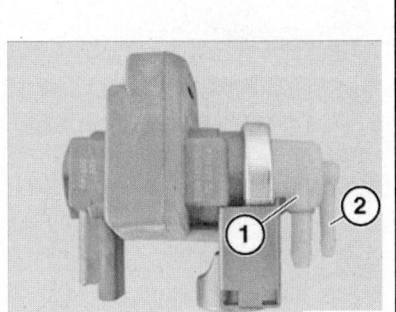

1,2. Vacuum lines

22205_MINI_G0047

Fig. 63 Disconnect plug connection at EPPC (picture shows EPPC removed)

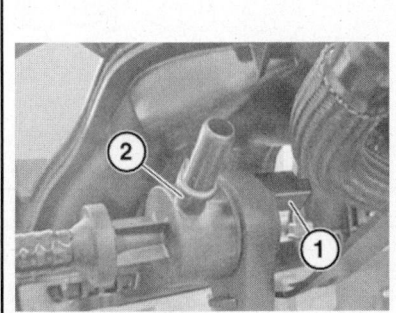

1. Plug connection
2. Tank vent valve

22205_MINI_G0048

Fig. 64 Detach hose from tank vent valve

1. Nuts

22205_MINI_G0049

Fig. 65 Unscrew nuts

10. Replace all seals.
11. Torque the intake manifold to cylinder head to 11 ft. lbs. (15 Nm).

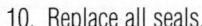
OIL PAN

REMOVAL & INSTALLATION
See Figure 66.

1. Before servicing the vehicle, refer to the precautions.
2. Disconnect the negative battery cable.
3. Drain engine oil.
4. Release oil pan bolts in area of line.
5. Release screw over exhaust manifold with special tools No. 11 9 582 and No. 11 9 581.
6. Clean sealing face with special tool No. 11 4 470.
7. Remove protruding or surplus sealing beads with a suitable tool.

To install:
8. Install in reverse order.

➡A metal substrate gasket is available for repairs. Do not use adhesive sealing bead or liquid seal.

9. Tighten oil pan bolts to 9 ft. lbs. (11 Nm).

OIL PUMP

REMOVAL & INSTALLATION

N14 Engine
See Figures 67 through 69.

1. Before servicing the vehicle, refer to the precautions.
2. Disconnect the negative battery cable.
3. Remove oil pan.
4. Pull off cover in direction of arrow.
5. Release screw.

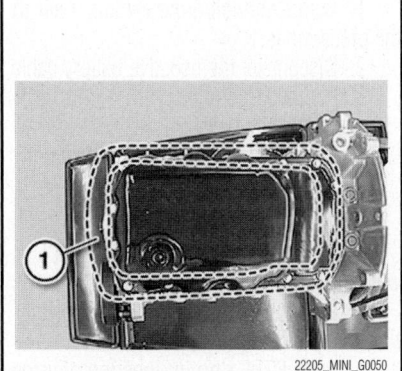

22205_MINI_G0050

Fig. 66 Oil pan bolts

6. Grip central bolt to release central bolt.
7. Release screws.

37698_MINI_G0152

Fig. 67 Pull off cover (1) in direction of arrow—N14 engine

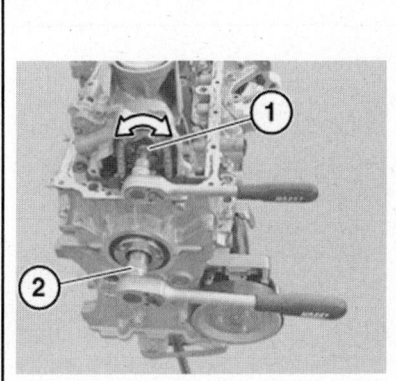

37698_MINI_G0153

Fig. 68 Grip central bolt (2) to release central bolt (1).—N14 engine

37698_MINI_G0154

Fig. 69 Release screws (1)—N14 engine

To install:

8. Install in reverse order.
9. Replace cover.
   - Oil pump to bedplate: 19 ft. lbs. (25 Nm)
   - Sprocket to oil pump: 44 inch lbs. (5 Nm) pus an additional 90° rotation

N16 and N18 Engines

See Figures 70 through 72.

1. Before servicing the vehicle, refer to the Precautions Section.
2. Disconnect the negative battery cable.
3. Remove the oil pan.
4. Remove the chain cover.
5. Release the screw. Counter hold crankshaft center bolt to release center bolt.
6. Release screw. Remove sealing plate. Disconnect plug connection. Unclip cable from cable clip.
7. Press out counter support with cable. Feed cable thru bore hole. Unfasten screws.
8. Remove oil pump from mounting.

Fig. 70 Pull off cover (1) in direction of arrow—N14 and N18 engines

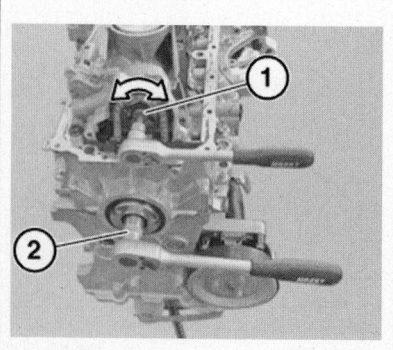

Fig. 71 Grip central bolt (2) to release central bolt (1)—N14 and N18 engines

Fig. 72 Release screws (1)—N14 and N18 engines

To install:

➡**Be sure to use new fasteners, as required.**

9. Installation is the reverse of the removal procedure.

INSPECTION

At this time the manufacturer does not provide Inspection procedures for this component.

PISTON AND RING

POSITIONING

See Figures 73 through 75.

➡**Offset position of ring end gaps by 120° from each other, but not above piston pin boss.**

REAR MAIN SEAL

REMOVAL & INSTALLATION

See Figures 76 through 80.

1. Before servicing the vehicle, refer to the precautions.
2. Disconnect the negative battery cable.
3. Remove transmission.
4. Remove flywheel.
5. Break off PTFE ring with a drift.

To install:

6. Install in reverse order.
7. Secure special tool No. 11 9 611 with supplied screws to crankshaft.
8. Position PTFE ring with supporting ring on special tool No. 11 9 611.
9. Push PTFE ring in direction of arrow over supporting ring onto crankshaft.
10. Attach special tool No. 11 9 612.
11. Draw in PTFE ring with special tool No. 11 9 613.

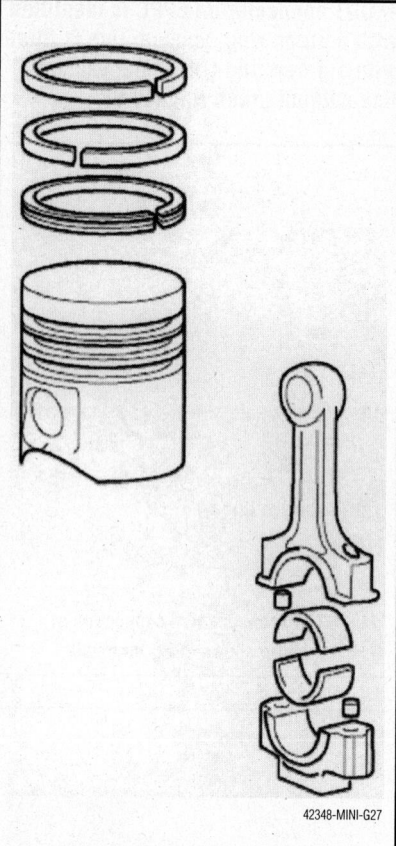

Fig. 73 Showing orientation of piston, rings and connecting rod

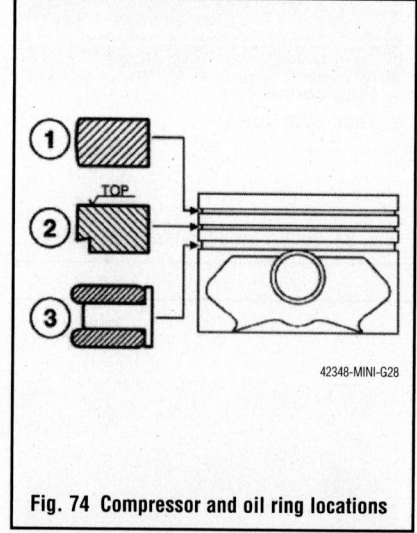

Fig. 74 Compressor and oil ring locations

12. Screw in special tool No. 11 9 612 up to engine block.

TIMING CHAIN & SPROCKETS

REMOVAL & INSTALLATION

See Figures 81 through 86.

1. Before servicing the vehicle, refer to the precautions.

2. Disconnect the negative battery cable.

➡**Procedure is modified for timing adjustment.**

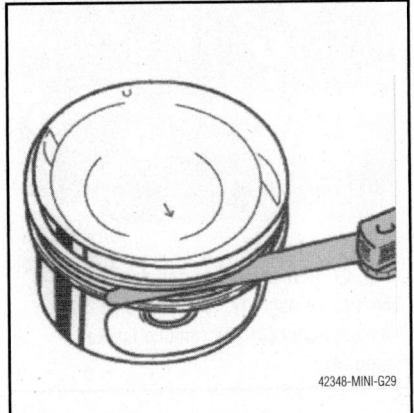

Fig. 75 Showing piston positioning arrow pointing toward front of block

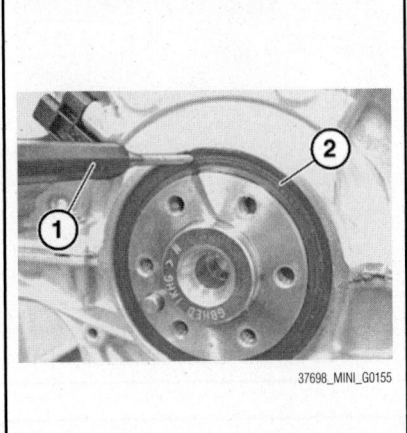

Fig. 76 Brake off PTFE ring (2) with a drift (1)

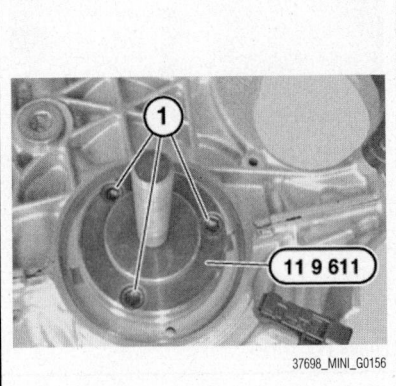

Fig. 77 Secure special tool No. 11 9 611 with supplied screws (1) to crankshaft

➡**The timing is not determined at firing TDC of cylinder No. 1.**

➡**All pistons are in the 90° position.**

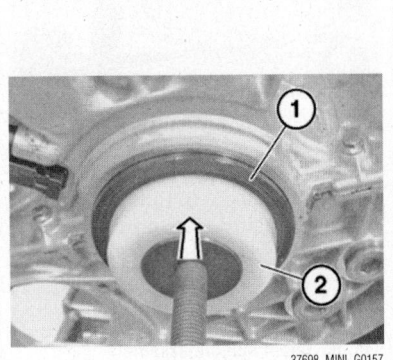

Fig. 78 Push PTFE ring (1) in direction of arrow over supporting ring (2) onto crankshaft

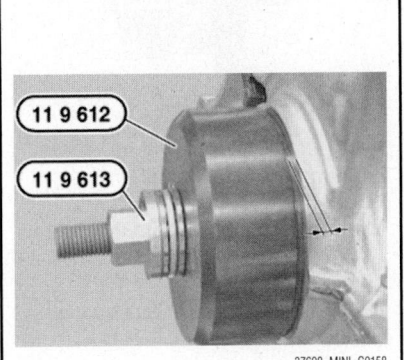

Fig. 79 Attach special tool No. 11 9 612. Draw in PTFE ring with special tool No. 11 9 613

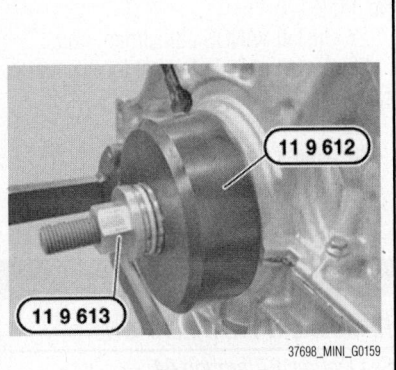

Fig. 80 Screw in special tool No. 11 9 612 up to engine block

3. Before servicing the vehicle, refer to the precautions section.

4. Remove cylinder head cover.

5. Remove all spark plugs.

6. Remove vibration damper.

7. Remove chain tensioner.

8. Remove both VANOS adjustment units.

9. Remove PTFE ring at front.

10. Remove belt tensioner.

11. Position crankshaft with special tool No. 11 9 590. Do not remove special tool No. 11 9 590 during repair work. Do not remove special tool No. 11 9 540.

12. Fit special tool No. 11 9 280 on hub for vibration damper with screws.

➡**You will need another person for gripping when releasing the central bolt.**

13. Release central bolt in direction of arrow.

14. Release bearing pins.

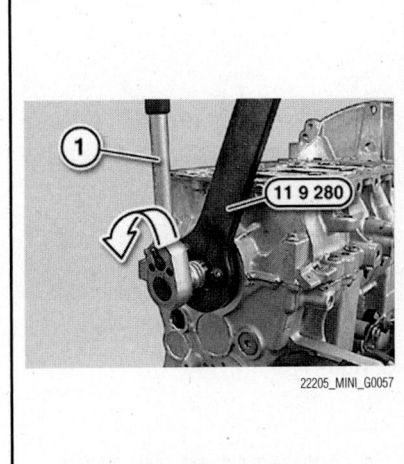

Fig. 81 Release central bolt

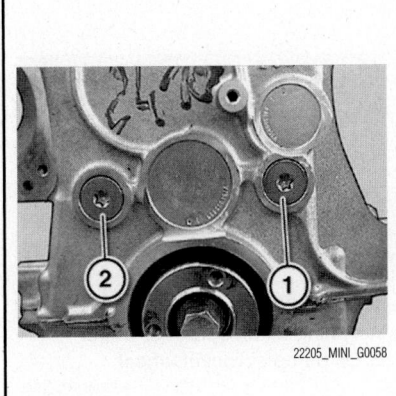

Fig. 82 Bearing pins

15. Remove hub towards front.

16. Remove chain module with timing chain.

17. Using a hook, pull oil pump chain upwards.

To install:

18. Secure chain module with rubber bands to facilitate assembly.

19. Pull timing chain upwards until sprocket wheel rests against chain guide.

20. Install timing chain and sprocket wheel in this position.

➡**Always keep timing chain tensioned; it is possible for timing chain to jam on chain module.**

21. Attach oil pump sprocket wheel in direction of arrow to crankshaft.

22. Insert chain module with timing chain and secure.

23. Attach crankshaft hub.

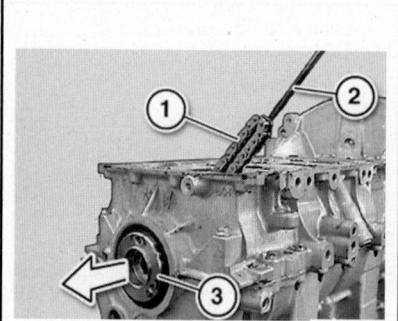

1. Oil pump chain
2. Hook
3. Hub

22205_MINI_G0059

Fig. 83 Remove hub and chain module with timing chain

1. Timing chain sprocket wheel
2. Oil pump sprocket wheel

22205_MINI_G0060

Fig. 84 Sprocket wheels

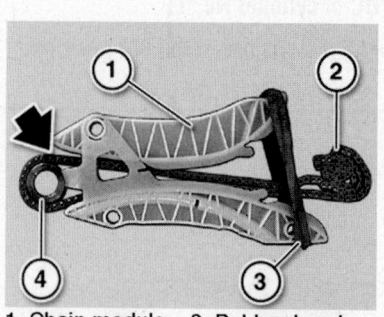

1. Chain module   3. Rubber bands
2. Timing chain   4. Sprocket wheel

22205_MINI_G0061

Fig. 85 Chain module assembly

1. Oil pump sprocket wheel
2. Timing chain guide rail
3. Hub on crankshaft
4. Timing chain sprocket wheel

22205_MINI_G0062

Fig. 86 Install position of both sprocket wheels

24. Screw in central bolt. Central bolt torque: 37 ft. lbs. (50 Nm), plus torque angle: 100°.

25. Remove special tool No. 11 9 280 from hub.

26. Secure central bolt with special tool No. 00 9 120.

27. Install VANOS adjustment units.

28. Install sprocket wheel for exhaust camshaft.

29. Crank engine twice.

30. Check timing.

31. Install PTFE ring.

32. Assemble engine.

TURBOCHARGER

REMOVAL & INSTALLATION

See Figures 87 through 94.

1. Before servicing the vehicle, refer to the precautions.

2. Disconnect the negative battery cable.

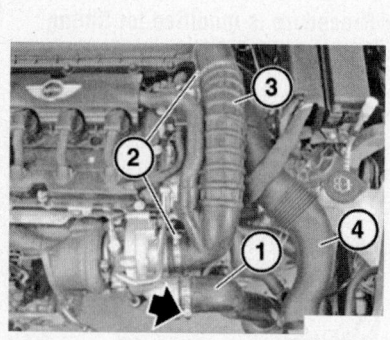

37698_MINI_G0163

Fig. 87 Release clamp and detach charge-air duct (1), release clamps (2), detach gaiter (3) and remove intake pipe (4)

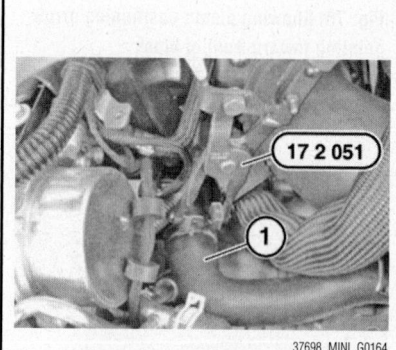

17 2 051

37698_MINI_G0164

Fig. 88 Release spring strap with special tool 17 2 051 and detach coolant hose (1)

37698_MINI_G0165

Fig. 89 Release screws and detach lines (1)

3. Drain coolant.

4. Remove coolant expansion tank.

5. Remove catalytic exhaust-gas converter.

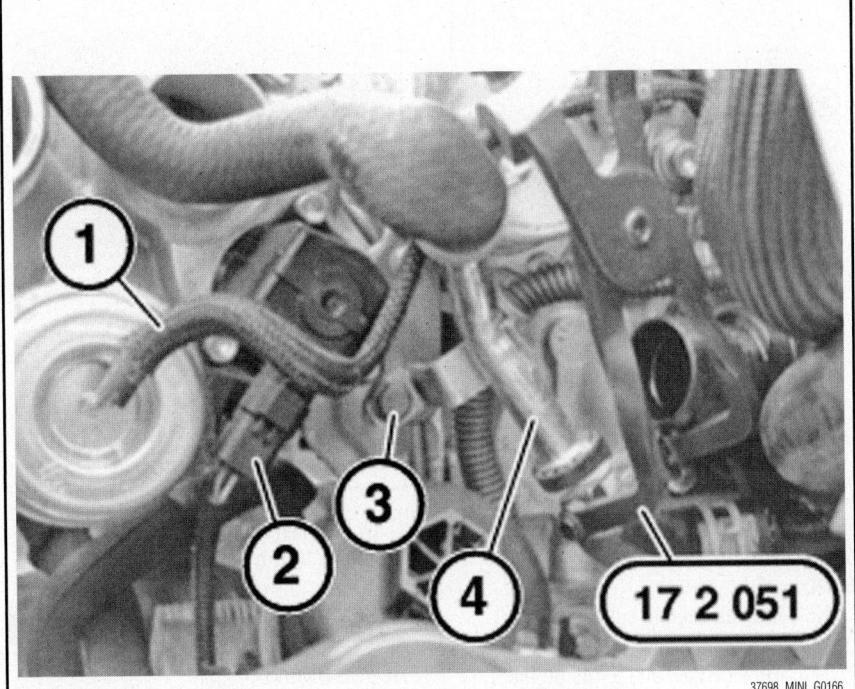

Fig. 90 Pull off hose (1), unlock connector (2), unscrew bolt (3), release spring strap and detach line (4)

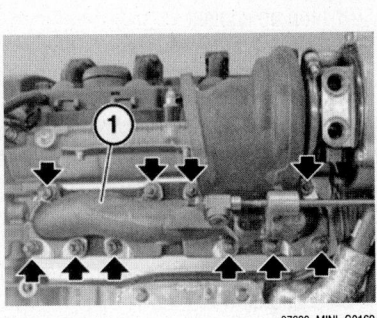

Fig. 93 Release nuts and remove exhaust manifold (1)

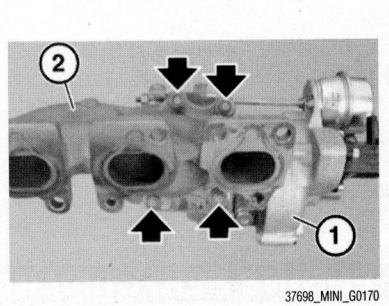

Fig. 94 Release nuts and remove turbocharger (1) from exhaust manifold (2)

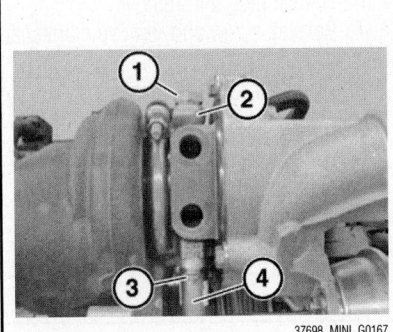

Fig. 91 Release screw (1 & 3) and detach line (2 & 4)

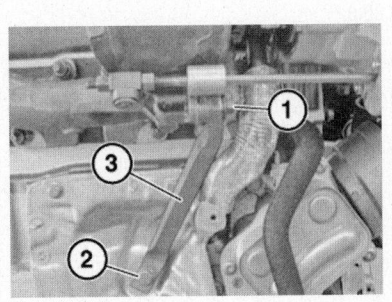

Fig. 92 Release screws (1 & 2) and remove holder (3)

6. Release clamp and detach charge-air duct.

7. Release clamps and detach gaiter.

8. Remove intake pipe.

9. Release spring strap with special tool 17 2 051 and detach coolant hose.

10. Release screws and detach lines.

11. Pull off hose.

12. Unlock connector and remove.

13. Unscrew bolt.

14. Release spring strap with special tool 17 2 051.

15. Detach line and remove.

16. Release screw and detach line.

17. Release screws and remove holder.

18. Release nuts and remove exhaust manifold.

19. Release nuts and remove turbocharger from exhaust manifold.

To install:

20. Install in the reverse order.

21. Tighten bolts/nuts to specification as follows:

- Turbocharger to exhaust manifold: 15 ft. lbs. (20 Nm)
- Bracket to turbocharger: 19 ft. lbs. (25 Nm)
- Oil feed to turbocharger: 22 ft. lbs. (30 Nm)
- Oil return to turbocharger: 71 inch lbs. (8 Nm)
- Bracket to crankcase: 14 ft. lbs. (19 Nm)
- Coolant inlet and outlet lines to turbocharger: 26 ft. lbs. (35 Nm)
- Exhaust manifold to cylinder head: 19 ft. lbs. (25 Nm)

22. Replace sealing ring.

23. Replace seals and nuts.

24. Clean sealing surfaces.

25. Apply a thin coat of copper paste to exhaust manifold nut thread.

26. Install gaiter and charge-air duct dry and free from grease.

27. Fitting on turbocharger must be dry and free from grease.
28. Top up coolant.
29. Check engine oil level.
30. Clear DME fault memory.

VALVE COVERS

REMOVAL & INSTALLATION

See Figures 95 and 96.

1. Before servicing the vehicle, refer to the precautions.
2. Disconnect the negative battery cable.
3. Unclip ignition wiring harness on cylinder head.
4. Remove rod-type ignition coils .
5. Remove suction filter housing .
6. Unclip engine wiring harness with holders.
7. Unclip engine wiring harness holder.
8. Release oxygen sensors on cylinder head.
9. Detach earth cable at bolt connection.
10. Undo cylinder head cover bolts in the sequence 13 to 1.

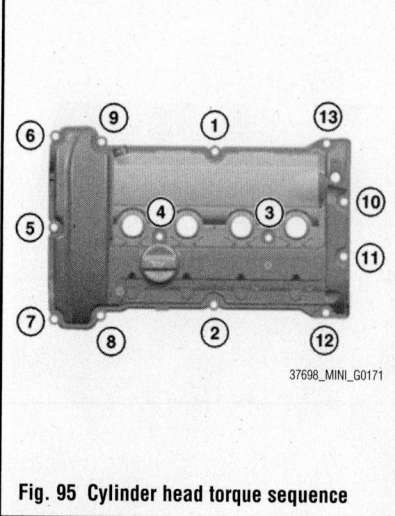

Fig. 95 Cylinder head torque sequence

To install:
11. Install in the reverse order.
12. Clean all sealing surfaces.
13. Replace all seals.
14. Seal all edges and joints on the cylinder head with sealing compound Drei Bond 1209.
15. Secure bolts for cylinder head cover in sequence 1 to 13.

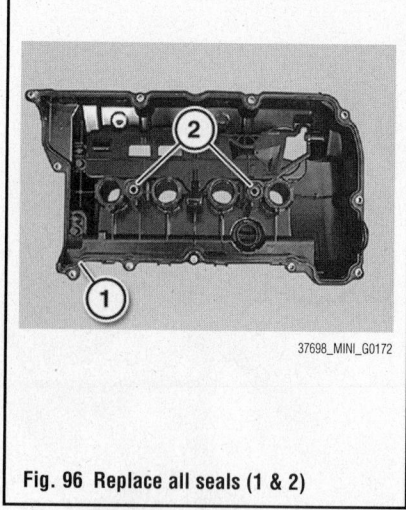

Fig. 96 Replace all seals (1 & 2)

16. Tighten cylinder head cover to 89 inch lbs. (10 Nm).

VALVE LASH

ADJUSTMENT

All engines are equipped with hydraulic valve lash adjusters. This design does not permit adjustments nor are adjustments possible.

ENGINE PERFORMANCE & EMISSION CONTROLS

CAMSHAFT POSITION (CMP) SENSOR

LOCATION

See Figure 97.

REMOVAL & INSTALLATION

1. Before servicing the vehicle, refer to precautions.

2. Disconnect the negative battery cable.
3. Switch off ignition.
4. Read out fault memory of DME control unit.
5. Check stored fault messages.
6. Unlock and remove plug.
7. Release screw and camshaft sensor.

To install:
8. Install in reverse order.
9. Replace sealing ring and coat with antiseize agent.
10. Clear the fault memory.

CRANKSHAFT POSITION (CKP) SENSOR

LOCATION

See Figure 98.

REMOVAL & INSTALLATION

1. Before servicing the vehicle, refer to the precautions.
2. Disconnect the negative battery cable.
3. Switch off ignition.
4. Read out fault memory of DME control unit.
5. Remove cover.

6. Unlock plug and remove.
7. Release screw and remove crankshaft position sensor.
8. Check stored fault messages.

To install:
9. Replace sealing ring.
10. The remainder of installation is the reverse of removal.
11. Clear the fault memory.

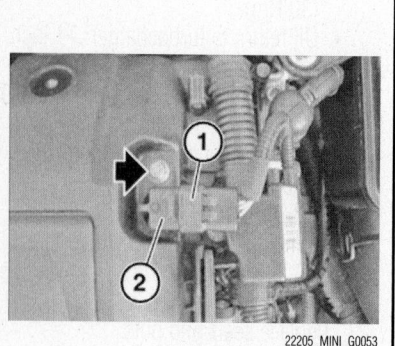

Fig. 97 CMP sensor location

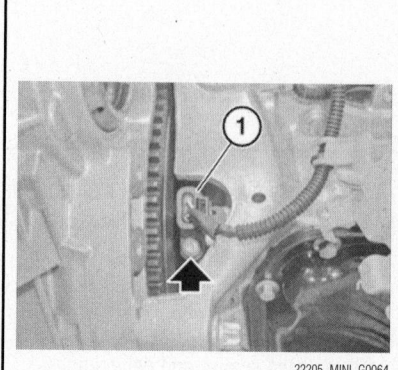

Fig. 98 CKP sensor location

DIGITAL MOTOR ELECTRONIC (DME) CONTROL UNIT

LOCATION

See Figure 99.

REMOVAL & INSTALLATION

See Figure 100.

1. Before servicing the vehicle, refer to precautions.

When replacing the DME/DDE control unit, observe the following: In each case read out the hardware/software status of the relevant control unit using the BMW diagnosis system. Comply with the instructions of the DIS diagnosis system on the steps pertaining to coding and programming. On vehicles with electronic vehicle immobilization, comply with the instructions of the BMW diagnosis system. Each control unit is programmed with certain basic values, which serve as mean values. The control unit receives different input values, depending on engine condition, which are compared with the stored values. The adaptive system compares the input values with the stored map values. The control commands are routed to the relevant actuators.

If the DME control unit is without current for a long time (more than one hour), its adaptive system loses the stored values. When a cleared control unit is restarted or a new control unit is installed, the adaptive system must read in and store the input values of the associated engine as new basic values itself.

This procedure could lead to erratic idling and disturbed overrunning of the engine after starting. Depending on the engine it could require some time before all values are adapted to the engine condition.

Therefore observe the following procedure before replacing or reinstalling a DME/DDE control unit:

If possible before exchanging control unit, run engine up to operating temperature. Exchange control units and run the vehicle at alternating engine speeds.

✳✳ WARNING

Before beginning, always make sure to communicate with the fault memory with a BMW DIS (or equivalent OBD-II scan tool) for existing faults. It may be helpful to print out the results. Once the installation is complete, rerun the scan and correct the remaining faults.

✳✳ WARNING

Make sure that all electrical accessories are off and the ignition is switched off.

2. Disconnect the negative battery cable.

✳✳ WARNING

Take precautions against electrostatic damage.

3. Connect diagnosis system.
4. Read fault memory.
5. Check stored fault messages.
6. Rectify faults.
7. Clear fault memory.
8. Unlock and remove cover
9. Unlock plug and remove
   - Press locks in direction of arrow and remove control unit towards top (Locks are accessible through bores)

To install:

10. Installation is the reverse of removal.
11. Check stored fault messages.
12. Clear fault memory.

ENGINE COOLANT TEMPERATURE (ECT) SENSOR

LOCATION

See Figure 101.

REMOVAL & INSTALLATION

✳✳ WARNING

There is a danger of scalding so only perform this task on an engine that has completely cooled down.

1. Before servicing the vehicle, refer to the precautions.
2. Disconnect the negative battery cable.
3. Read out fault memory of DME control unit.
4. Check stored fault messages.
5. Switch off ignition.

➡**Coolant can escape when temperature sensor is being replaced. Catch and dispose of coolant.**

6. Release screw or clamps, as applicable.
7. Pull intake muffler towards top and detach clean air pipe.
8. Detach intake muffler from air filter housing and remove.
9. Remove clean air pipe.
10. Unlock and detach plugs.
11. Unlock and disconnect line.
12. Carefully pull cable duct upwards slightly.
13. Unlock plug and remove.

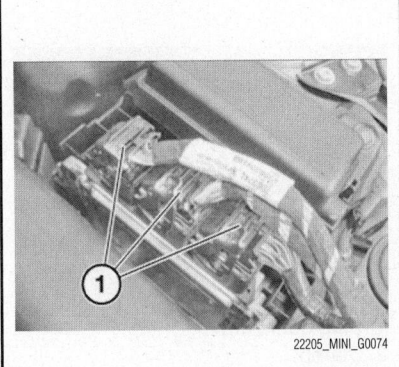

22205_MINI_G0074

Fig. 99 DME location

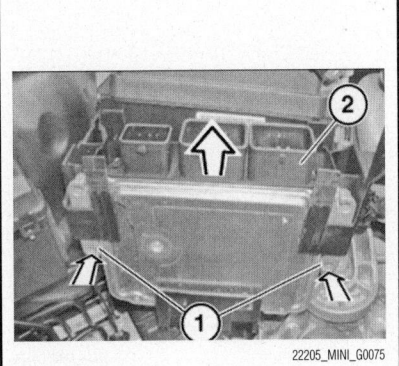

22205_MINI_G0075

Fig. 100 Removing DME

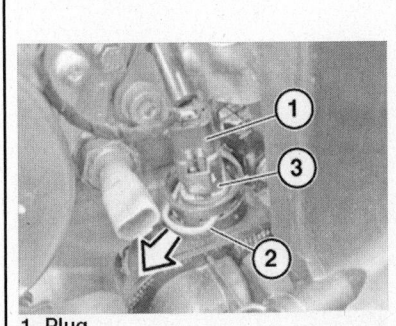

1. Plug
2. Lock
3. Coolant temperature sensor

22205_MINI_G0068

Fig. 101 ECT location

14. Detach lock and remove temperature sensor.

To install:

15. Install in reverse order.
16. Replace sealing ring.
17. If necessary, add coolant.
18. Check cooling system for leaks.
19. Clear the fault memory.

HEATED OXYGEN (HO2S) SENSOR

LOCATION

See Figure 102.

REMOVAL & INSTALLATION

1. Before servicing the vehicle, refer to the precautions section.
2. Disconnect the negative battery cable.
3. Read fault memory.

➡If an oxygen sensor is to be reused, only apply a thin and uniform coat of Never Sees Compound (refer to BMW Parts Service) to thread.

➡The part of the oxygen control sensor which projects into the exhaust system branch (sensor ceramic) must not be cleaned or come into contact with lubricant.

4. Disconnect plug connection for lambda control sensor.
5. Release oxygen sensor with special tool No. 11 7 020.

To install:

6. Installation is reverse of removal.
7. Check function of DME.

KNOCK SENSOR (KS)

LOCATION

See Figure 103.

REMOVAL & INSTALLATION

1. Before servicing the vehicle, refer to precautions.
2. Disconnect the negative battery cable.

❋❋ CAUTION

Before beginning, always make sure to communicate with the fault memory with a BMW DIS (or equivalent OBD-II scan tool) for existing faults. It may be helpful to print out the results. Once the installation is complete, rerun the scan and correct the remaining faults.

❋❋ CAUTION

Make sure that all electrical accessories are off and the ignition is switched off.

3. Remove the intake air manifold and as necessary the exhaust turbocharger.
4. Unlock and disconnect the Knock (KS) sensor plug connection.
5. Unscrew the KS screw and remove knock sensor.

To install:

6. Install in reverse order.
7. Clean the surface of knock sensors where they contact the engine block.
8. Observe the position of the KS in relation to the engine block. It should be positioned at an angle of 20 degrees to the perpendicular of the engine block.
9. Replace the KS and knock sensor screw.

10. Connect and lock the KS plug connection.
11. Clear the fault memory.

MASS AIR FLOW (MAF) SENSOR

LOCATION

See Figure 104.

REMOVAL & INSTALLATION

1. Before servicing the vehicle, refer to the precautions.
2. Disconnect the negative battery cable.
3. Read out fault memory of DME control unit.
4. Check stored fault messages.
5. Switch off ignition.
6. Disconnect plug connection.
7. Release clamp.
8. Release screws.
9. Remove air-mass sensor in direction of arrow.

To install:

10. Installation is the reverse of removal.
11. Check stored fault messages.
12. Clear the fault memory.

THROTTLE POSITION SENSOR (TPS)

LOCATION

See Figures 105 and 106.

REMOVAL & INSTALLATION

N16 Engine

1. Before servicing the vehicle, refer to the precautions section.

Fig. 102 O2 sensor location

Fig. 103 KS sensor (2) and plug (1) location

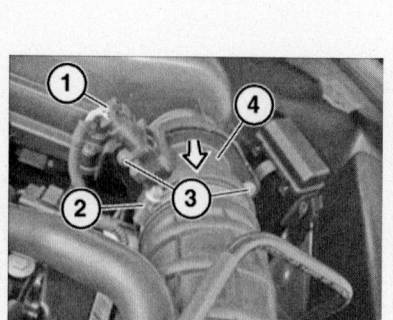

1. Plug connection
2. Clamp
3. Screws

Fig. 104 MAF location

1. Throttle valve assembly

22205_MINI_G0071

Fig. 105 Throttle body assembly—N16 engine

22205_MINI_G0072

Fig. 106 Throttle body assembly—N14 and N18 engines

2. Disconnect the negative battery cable.

3. Read out fault memory of DME control unit.

4. Check stored fault messages.

5. Switch off ignition.

6. Unfasten screws.

7. Carefully feed out throttle valve assembly towards top until plug for cable connection is accessible.

8. Unlock connector and remove.

9. Remove throttle valve assembly.

To install:

10. Replace sealing ring.

11. The remainder of installation is the reverse of removal.

12. Clear the fault memory.

N14 and N18 Engines

1. Before servicing the vehicle, refer to the precautions section.

2. Disconnect the negative battery cable.

3. Read out fault memory of DME control unit.

4. Check stored fault messages.

5. Switch off ignition.

6. Remove sound generator.

7. Release clamps and detach air intake hose.

8. Release screws and carefully feed out throttle valve assembly towards top until plug is accessible.

9. Unlock plug and disconnect.

10. Detach cable ties.

11. Remove throttle valve assembly.

To install:

12. Install in reverse order.

13. Replace sealing ring.

14. Clear the fault memory.

FUEL   GASOLINE FUEL INJECTION SYSTEM

FUEL SYSTEM SERVICE PRECAUTIONS

Safety is the most important factor when performing not only fuel system maintenance but any type of maintenance. Failure to conduct maintenance and repairs in a safe manner may result in serious personal injury or death. Maintenance and testing of the vehicle's fuel system components can be accomplished safely and effectively by adhering to the following rules and guidelines.

• To avoid the possibility of fire and personal injury, always disconnect the negative battery cable unless the repair or test procedure requires that battery voltage be applied.

• Always relieve the fuel system pressure prior to disconnecting any fuel system component (injector, fuel rail, pressure regulator, etc.), fitting or fuel line connection. Exercise extreme caution whenever relieving fuel system pressure to avoid exposing skin, face and eyes to fuel spray. Please be advised that fuel under pressure may penetrate the skin or any part of the body that it contacts.

• Always place a shop towel or cloth around the fitting or connection prior to

loosening to absorb any excess fuel due to spillage. Ensure that all fuel spillage (should it occur) is quickly removed from engine surfaces. Ensure that all fuel soaked cloths or towels are deposited into a suitable waste container.

• Always keep a dry chemical (Class B) fire extinguisher near the work area.

• Do not allow fuel spray or fuel vapors to come into contact with a spark or open flame.

• Always use a back-up wrench when loosening and tightening fuel line connection fittings. This will prevent unnecessary stress and torsion to fuel line piping.

• Always replace worn fuel fitting O-rings with new Do not substitute fuel hose or equivalent where fuel pipe is installed.

Before servicing the vehicle, make sure to also refer to the precautions in the beginning of this section as well.

RELIEVING FUEL SYSTEM PRESSURE

See Figure 107.

1. Install special tool, 13-5-220.

2. Fit a suitable length of hose onto the special tool and route the hose into a fuel container.

3. Screw in check valve (1) of the special tool to release the fuel pressure from the injector rail.

4. Hold an absorbent cloth around the special tool and remove the hose and tool.

✳✳ WARNING

Other parts of the fuel system may have some residual pressure. Always open fittings slowly and be prepared to catch any fuel.

42348-MINI-G30

Fig. 107 Using special tool to relieve fuel rail pressure

FUEL FILTER

REMOVAL & INSTALLATION

See Figures 108 through 111.

1. Before servicing the vehicle, refer to the precautions.
2. Disconnect the negative battery cable.
3. Remove fuel filter with fuel level sensor.
4. Disconnect lines.
5. Release line from hooks.
6. Release retaining hook and pull off sensor in downward direction.
7. Release cap on fuel filter housing by one turn counterclockwise (bayonet lock).
8. Pull off cap towards top.
9. Pull off fuel filter towards top. If necessary, twist fuel filter in so doing.

To install:
10. Install in the reverse order.

11. Clean inside of fuel filter housing.
12. Replace sealing rings.
13. Pay attention to fitting of spring.

FUEL RAIL AND INJECTOR

REMOVAL & INSTALLATION

See Figures 112 through 115.

1. Before servicing the vehicle, refer to the precautions.
2. Disconnect the negative battery cable.
3. Read out fault memory of DME control unit.
4. Switch off ignition.
5. Remove intake filter housing.
6. Fuel escapes when fuel line is detached. Catch and dispose of escaping fuel.
7. Remove protective cap from compressed air valve.
8. Connect compressed air line to compressed air valve.

9. Blow fuel back into tank with a short blast of compressed air (max. 3 bar).
10. Unlock and detach fuel line.
11. Seal off fuel line with special tool 13 5 281.
12. Release bolts.
13. Detach fuel rail from cylinder head.
14. Unlock plug and remove.
15. Remove fuel rail.
16. Lever out retainers.
17. Pull fuel injectors out of injection pipe.

To install:
18. Install in reverse order.
19. Replace sealing rings on fuel injectors and coat with anti-friction rubber coating.
20. Tighten bolts/nuts to specification as follows:
- Injection pipe to cylinder head (N12): 71 inch lbs. (8 Nm)
- Injection pipe to cylinder head (N14): 14 ft. lbs. (19 Nm)

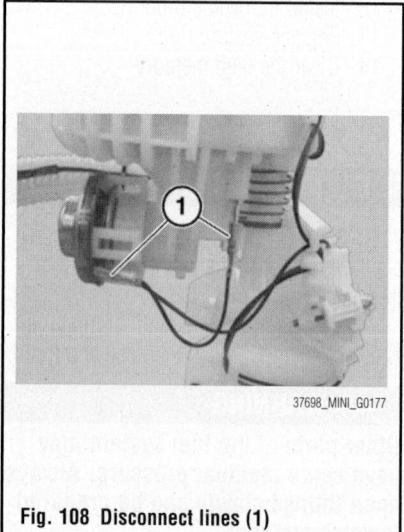

Fig. 108 Disconnect lines (1)

Fig. 110 Release cap (1) on fuel filter housing (2) by one turn counterclockwise (bayonet lock).

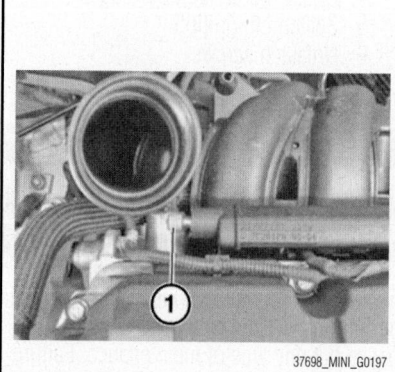

Fig. 112 Remove protective cap (1) from compressed air valve

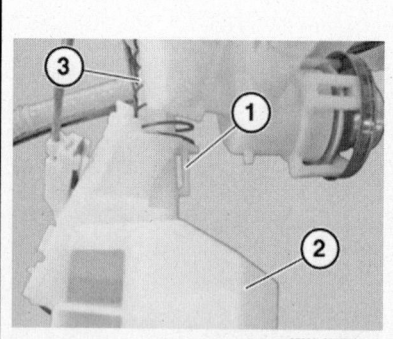

Fig. 109 Release retaining hook (1) and pull off sensor (2) in downward direction. Pay attention to fitting of spring (3)

Fig. 111 Pull off fuel filter (1) towards top. Clean inside of fuel filter housing (2)

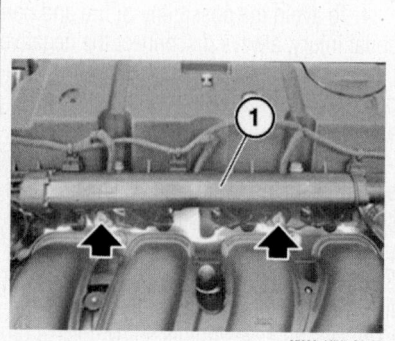

Fig. 113 Detach fuel rail (1) from cylinder head

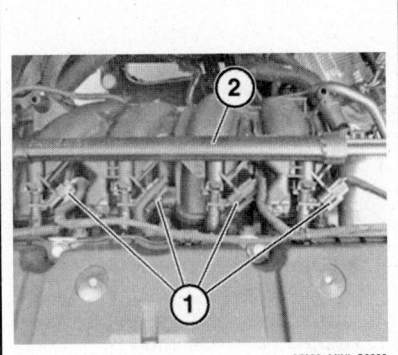

Fig. 114 Unlock plug (1) and remove. Remove fuel rail (2)

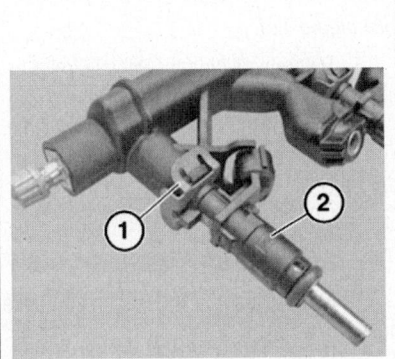

Fig. 115 Lever out retainers (1) and remove fuel injectors (2)

FUEL PUMP MODULE

REMOVAL & INSTALLATION

See Figures 116 through 118.

1. Before servicing the vehicle, refer to the precautions.
2. Disconnect the negative battery cable.
3. Draw off fuel from fuel tank.
4. Remove rear seat.
5. Push trim panel forward.
6. Disconnect plug connection.
7. Release screw cap with special tool 16 1 020.
8. Raise unit.
9. To improve installation, secure cable and lines with cord.
10. Disconnect plug connection.
11. Unlock line at quick-release fastener and detach.
12. Unclip line.
13. Carefully lift fuel pump with fuel level sensor out of fuel tank. Replace rubber seal.

To install:

14. Install in the reverse order.
15. Tighten bolts/nuts to specification as follows:

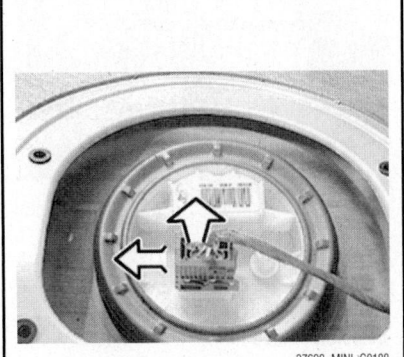

Fig. 116 Disconnect plug connection (arrows)

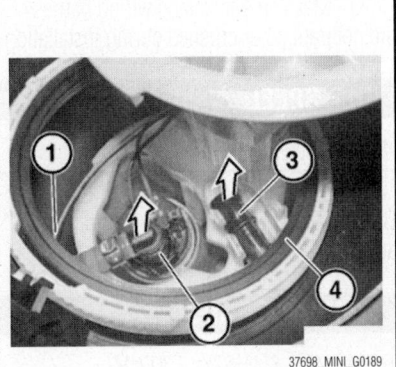

Fig. 117 Secure cable (1) and lines (2 and 3) with cord and replace rubber seal (4)

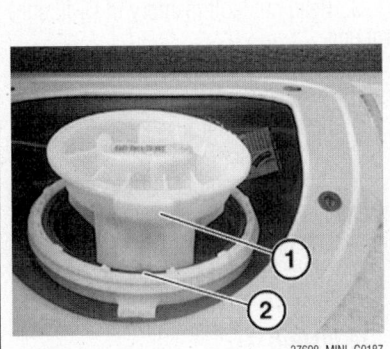

Fig. 118 When installing fuel filter, make sure lug engages in recess on tank

- Service cover to body: 53 inch lbs. (39 Nm)
- Locking ring (metal): 33 ft. lbs. (45 Nm)

16. Replace rubber seal.
17. When installing fuel filter, make sure lug engages in recess on tank.

FUEL TANK

DRAINING

1. Start engine and allow to run. The electric fuel pump runs.

➡ **The pump delivers fuel via the suction jet pump and the tank expansion line from the left to the right side of the fuel tank. Fuel can be drawn off from the left and right tank halves through the fuel filler pipe down to a small residual amount. This residual amount is drawn off after removal of the sensors for the fuel gauge (right/left).**

2. Feed suction hose of extractor unit into filler pipe. In so doing, turn hose slightly if necessary.
3. Insert to a length of 35 inches (90 cm).
4. Draw off fuel with suction extractor unit as far as possible.
5. Observe the fuel gauge in the instrument cluster while extracting fuel.

REMOVAL & INSTALLATION

See Figures 119 through 122.

1. Before servicing the vehicle, refer to the precautions.
2. Disconnect the negative battery cable.
3. Drain the fuel tank.
4. Remove the muffler.

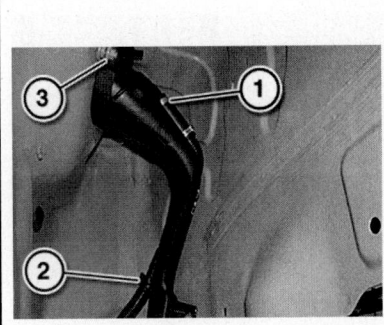

Fig. 119 Release hose clamp (1) and disengage filler vent line from holder (2)

Fig. 120 Release hose clamp (1) and remove filler hose from fuel tank

5. Remove the exhaust heat shield.

6. Remove the rear storage compartment bracket.

7. Remove the parking brake cables.

8. Remove the rear seat.

9. Remove trim panels.

10. Remove the left wheel arch trim.

11. Disconnect the fuel level sensor and wiring harness.

12. Remove the fuel tank filler hose.

13. Remove the vent hose from the fuel filler pipe.

14. Release hose clamp and remove filler hose from fuel tank.

15. Unlock quick-release fasteners on carbon canister and detach.

16. Remove expansion rivets. Release screws and lower fuel tank a little.

17. Disconnect plug connection. Unlock quick-release fastener and detach fuel feed line.

18. Remove the fuel tank.

19. Pass filler vent line through body and slowly lower fuel tank.

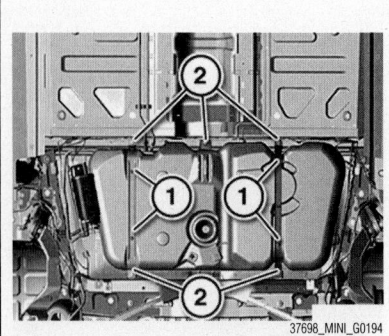

Fig. 121 Remove expansion rivets (1). Release screws (2) and lower fuel tank a little

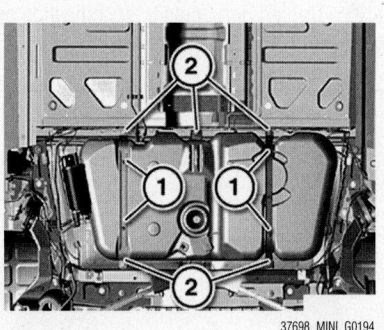

Fig. 122 Disconnect plug connection (1). Unlock quick-release fastener (2) and detach fuel feed line.

To install:

20. Install in reverse order.

21. Tighten tank to rear axle carrier and body to 14 ft. lbs. (19 Nm).

22. Make sure that quick-release fastener is correctly engaged.

23. Make sure lines and wiring harness are not trapped or crushed during installation

IDLE SPEED

ADJUSTMENT

Idle speed is controlled by the Electronic Control Module (ECM), and cannot be adjusted.

THROTTLE BODY

REMOVAL & INSTALLATION

N16 Engine

See Figure 123.

1. Before servicing the vehicle, refer to the precautions section.

2. Disconnect the negative battery cable.

3. Read out fault memory of DME control unit.

4. Check stored fault messages.

5. Switch off ignition.

6. Remove the air intake hose.

7. Unfasten screws.

8. Carefully feed out throttle valve assembly towards top until plug for cable connection is accessible.

9. Unlock connector and remove.

10. Remove throttle valve assembly.

To install:

11. Replace sealing ring.

12. The remainder of installation is the reverse of removal.

13. Clear the fault memory.

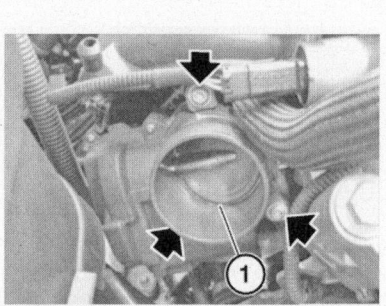

1. Throttle valve assembly

Fig. 123 Removing throttle body assembly

N14 and N18 Engines

See Figure 124.

1. Before servicing the vehicle, refer to the precautions section.

2. Disconnect the negative battery cable.

3. Read out fault memory of DME control unit.

4. Check stored fault messages.

5. Switch off ignition.

6. Remove sound generator.

7. Release clamps and detach air intake hose.

8. Release screws and carefully feed out throttle valve assembly towards top until plug is accessible.

9. Unlock plug and disconnect.

10. Detach cable ties.

11. Remove throttle valve assembly.

To install:

12. Install in reverse order.

13. Replace sealing ring.

14. Clear the fault memory.

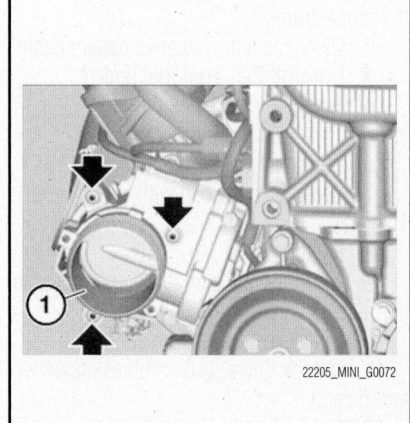

Fig. 124 Removing throttle body assembly

HEATING & AIR CONDITIONING COMPONENTS

BLOWER MOTOR

REMOVAL & INSTALLATION

See Figures 125 and 126.

1. Before servicing the vehicle, refer to the precautions.
2. Disconnect the negative battery cable.
3. Remove trim for instrument panel at bottom left (driver's side).
4. Release screws and remove cover.
5. Disconnect plug connection.
6. Release screws and feed out blower.

To install:
7. Install in the reverse order.

HEATER CORE

REMOVAL & INSTALLATION

See Figures 127 through 130.

Fig. 127 Unlock and detach coolant lines (1)

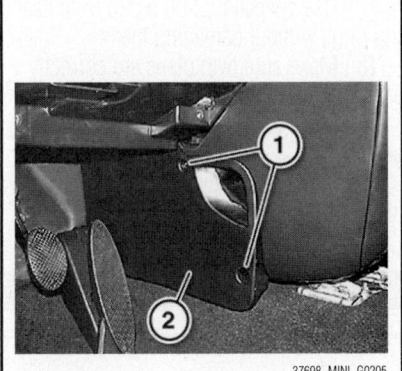

Fig. 125 Release screws (1) and remove cover (2).

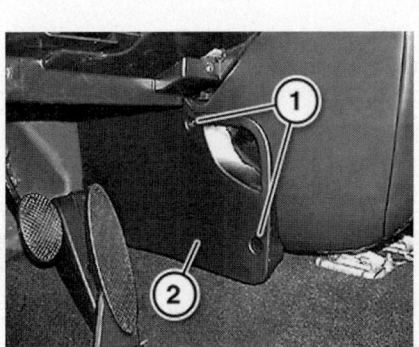

Fig. 128 Release screws (1) and feed out cover (2) towards bottom

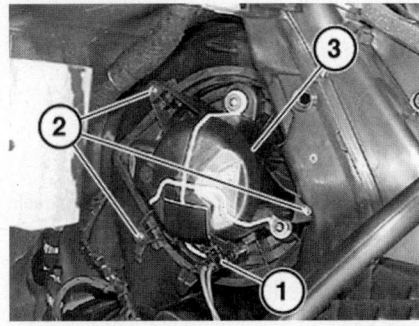

Fig. 126 Disconnect plug connection (1). Release screws (2) and feed out blower (3)

1. Before servicing the vehicle, refer to the precautions.
2. Disconnect the negative battery cable.
3. Remove intake filter housing.
4. Unlock and detach coolant lines.
5. Carefully blow through twin pipes to remove remaining coolant from heater core.
6. Remove trim for instrument panel at bottom left.
7. Release screws and feed out cover towards bottom.
8. Release screws and pull out heater core approximately 0.39 in (10 mm).
9. Release screw.
10. Unclip holder and remove.

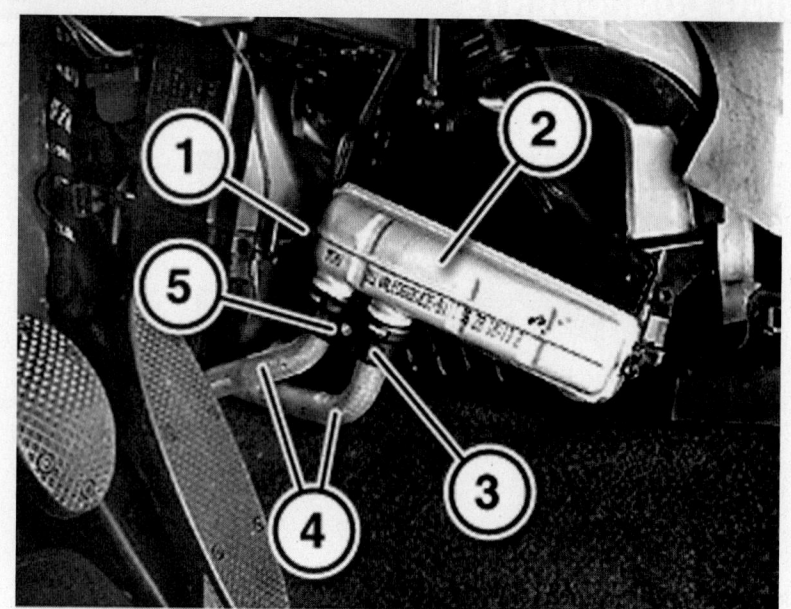

1. Screws
2. Heater core
3. Holder

4. Pipes
5. Screw

37698_MINI_G0219

Fig. 129 Carefully disconnect and pull out heater core

11. Carefully pull twin pipes out of heater core and if necessary catch escaping coolant.

12. Carefully pull out heater core.

To install:
13. Install in the reverse order.

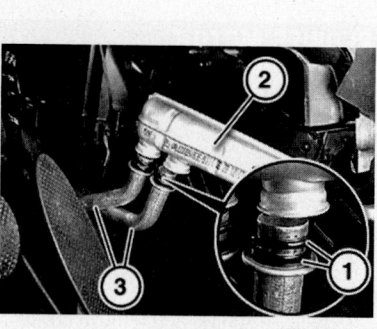

37698_MINI_G0220

Fig. 130 Replace sealing rings (1) and make sure twin pipes (3) are correctly seated on heater core (2)

14. Fins of heater core must not be damaged.

15. Make sure heater core is correctly seated.

16. Replace sealing rings.

17. Use special tool 00 9 030 to fit sealing rings without damaging them.

18. Make sure twin pipes are correctly seated on heater core.

19. Make sure coolant lines are correctly seated.

20. Vent cooling system and check for leaks.

STEERING

POWER RACK & PINION STEERING GEAR

REMOVAL & INSTALLATION

See Figure 131.

1. Before servicing the vehicle, refer to the precautions section.

2. Disconnect the negative battery cable.

➡These vehicles are fitted with electronic power steering and do not use the typical hydraulic fluid and pump.

✳✳ WARNING

Steering gear: Check connection of steering gear for corrosion, clean contacts if necessary. The steering gear must be replaced if the corrosion is too far advanced.

✳✳ WARNING

Connecting cable: In the event of moisture/corrosion inside the two plug connections, check the insulation of the connecting cable. If the insulation reveals any noticeable/striking features, it will be necessary to replace the part. Otherwise it will be sufficient to replace the contacts or plug housing.

3. Disconnect the negative battery cable.

4. Remove both tie rod ends from swivel bearing.

5. Replacement: Remove both tie rod ends from steering gear.

6. Lower front axle support.

7. Release screws.

✳✳ WARNING

Do not allow the control head of the steering gear to strike other components. This may result in damage to the steering gear.

8. First swing steering gear in direction of travel to right and then remove towards front.

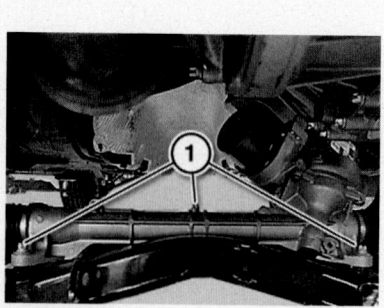

22205_MINI_G0077

Fig. 131 Electronic power steering

To install:

➡For replacement: On cars with 18" tires, it will be necessary to replace steering stop limiters.

➡Deformation elements must point to steering gear.

9. The remainder of installation is the reverse of removal.

10. After installation, check alignment.

11. For replacement: Carry out programming/coding.

12. For models with Dynamic Stability Control (DSC): Carry out steering angle sensor adjustment.

➡Only cars with DSC are fitted with a steering angle sensor (integrated in the steering column switch cluster).

SUSPENSION   FRONT SUSPENSION

LOWER BALL JOINT

REMOVAL & INSTALLATION

The lower ball joint is an integral part of the lower control arm assembly.

LOWER CONTROL ARM

REMOVAL & INSTALLATION

See Figures 132 through 135.

1. Before servicing the vehicle, refer to the precautions.

2. Disconnect the negative battery cable.

3. Remove front wheel.

4. On vehicles equipped with Dynamic Stability Control, release screw on left side at ride-height sensor and remove bracket from control arm.

5. Unfasten nut.

6. Press control arm off swivel bearing with special tool 31 2 310.

7. Unscrew nuts.

8. Screw special tool 31 1 040 onto joint.

9. Strike joint from below to release it from taper in front axle carrier.

10. Lower front axle support.

11. Remove stabilizer from front axle carrier and tie up.

12. Remove control arm with bracket from front axle carrier.

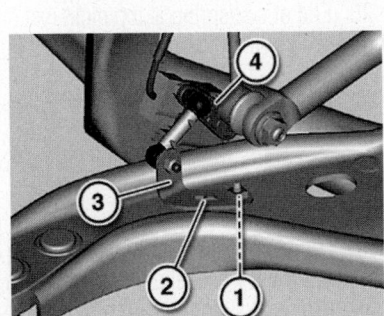

Fig. 132 Release screw (1) and remove bracket (3) from control arm. Sensor lever (4) must point from ride-height sensor to left front wheel. Align bracket (3) by way of lug (2) to corresponding opening in control arm

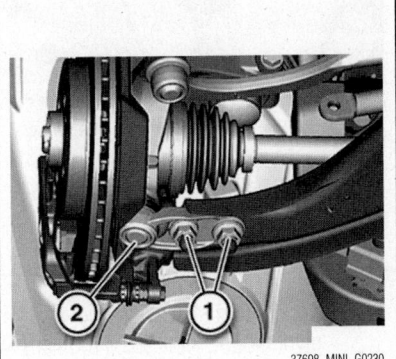

Fig. 133 Unscrew nuts (1). Keep wheel control joint (2) to control arm

Fig. 134 Screw special tool 31 1 040 onto joint. Strike joint from below to release it from taper in front axle carrier

To install:

13. Install in the reverse order.

14. Tighten bolts/nuts to specification as follows:

- Wheel guide joint to control arm: 129.5 ft. lbs. (175 Nm)
- Wheel guide joint to swivel bearing: 52 ft. lbs. (70 Nm) plus an additional 90° rotation
- Ball joint to front axle carrier: 52 ft. lbs. (70 Nm) plus an additional 90° rotation
- Bracket to control arm: 53 inch lbs. (6 Nm)

15. Replace self-locking nuts.

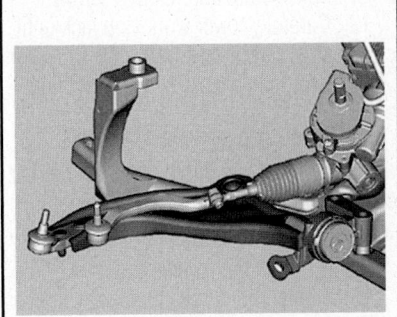

Fig. 135 Remove control arm with bracket from front axle carrier

16. Sensor lever must point from ride-height sensor to left front wheel.

17. Align bracket by way of lug to corresponding opening in control arm.

18. Keep wheel guide joint to swivel bearing connection clean and free from oil and grease.

19. Keep wheel control joint to control arm connection clean and free from oil and grease.

20. Keep control arm to front axle carrier connection clean and free from oil and grease.

21. On vehicles equipped with Dynamic Stability Control, carry out steering angle sensor adjustment.

MACPHERSON STRUT

REMOVAL & INSTALLATION

See Figures 136 through 138.

1. Before servicing the vehicle, refer to the precautions.

2. Disconnect the negative battery cable.

3. If the centering pin is missing from the support bearing, the position of the studs to the wheel arch must be parked so that the original camber is approximately maintained.

4. Only one nut may ever be released for marking.

5. Remove front wheel.

6. Remove tie rod end from swivel bearing.

7. Remove stabilizer link from spring strut.

8. Disengage brake hose from spring strut.

9. Secure special tool 31 5 220 with wheel bolts to wheel bearing and support swivel bearing with workshop jack.

10. Disengage pulse generator from spring strut.

11. Release nut and remove screw.

12. Carefully lower workshop jack until spring strut can be removed.

13. Secure spring strut against falling out.

14. Unscrew nuts.

15. Remove spring strut downwards out of wheel arch.

To install:

16. Install in the reverse order.

17. Tighten bolts/nuts to specification as follows:

  • Spring strut support bearing to body: 25 ft. lbs. (34 Nm)

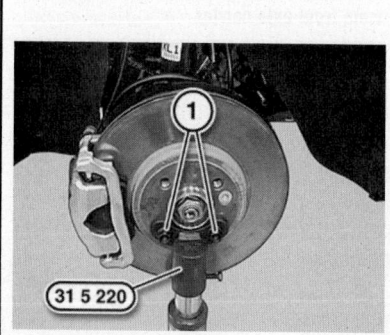

Fig. 136 Secure special tool 31 5 220 with wheel bolts (1) to wheel bearing and support swivel bearing with workshop jack

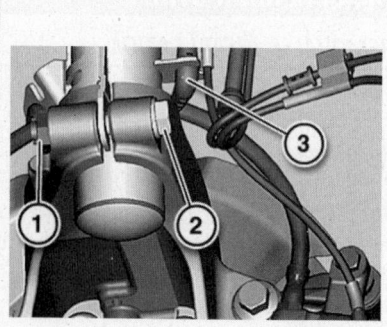

Fig. 137 Disengage pulse generator (3) from spring strut. Release nut (1) and remove screw (2)

Fig. 138 Unscrew nuts (1)

  • Spring strut shock absorber to pivot mount: 74 ft. lbs. (100 Nm)

18. Keep press fit of swivel gearing and spring strut in lower area clean and free from oil and grease.

19. Replace self-locking nuts.

20. Tightening permitted by means of screw only.

21. Centering pin missing: Make position of studs in relation to wheel arch.

22. Clean contact surface in spring strut dome.

23. Align spring strut using centering pin to bore in wheel arch or studs to markings on wheel arch.

24. Replace self-locking nuts.

25. Carry out wheel alignment check if a spring strut with support bearing was or has been installed without centering pin.

OVERHAUL

1. Before servicing the vehicle, refer to the precautions.

2. Remove front spring strut.

3. Clamp special tool 31 3 341 with guide in vice.

4. Fit special tools 31 3 351 from above on special tool 31 3 341 until locking pins can be felt and heard to snap into place.

5. Check seating of special tools 31 3 351, correct if necessary.

6. Coils of coil spring must be located completely in recesses of special tools 31 3 351 when tensioned!.

7. Compress coil spring until stress on piston rod is relieved.

8. Clean coil spring to remove all coarse dirt and mount on special tools 31 3 351.

9. Turn spring strut until end of coil spring points upwards.

10. Compress coil spring until stress on piston rod is relieved.

11. Nut may only be released when the upper and lower coils of the coil spring are located completely in the recess of the spring holder!.

12. Take off cap.

13. Release nut with special tool 31 2 210; if necessary, grip piston rod with wrench.

14. Remove support bearing, shim and upper spring cup.

15. Remove spring strut with auxiliary damper and protective tube sideways from tensioned coil spring.

16. Remove auxiliary damper with protective tube and lower spring pad from shock absorber.

To install:.

17. Check auxiliary damper, protective tube and lower spring pad for damage, replace if necessary.

18. Attach lower spring pad to spring plate.

19. Attach auxiliary damper with protective tube to piston rod.

20. Make sure rubber knob is correctly positioned in spring cup bore.

21. Insert spring strut in tensioned coil spring.

22. Check upper spring pad for damage, replace if necessary.

23. Connect upper spring cup, shim and support bearing to piston rod.

24. Mount shim and dust sleeve correctly between support bearing and upper spring cup.

25. Replace nut, screw onto piston rod and tighten down with special tool 31 2 210.

26. Tighten spring strut support bearing to 47 ft. lbs. (64 Nm).

27. Fit cover cap.

28. End of coil spring at top must rest on indentation in upper spring cup and spring pad.

29. Check installation position of protective tube, correct if necessary.

30. End of lower coil spring must rest on stop of spring pad.

31. Align all components correctly to each other and relive tension on coil spring.

32. Carry out wheel alignment check if a spring strut with support bearing was or has been installed without centering pin.

STEERING KNUCKLE

REMOVAL & INSTALLATION

See Figures 139 and 140.

1. Before servicing the vehicle, refer to the precautions.

2. Disconnect the negative battery cable.

3. Remove front wheel.

4. Expand turning lock sufficiently to avoid damaging thread when releasing collar nut.

5. Release collar nut, press brake pedal to floor for this purpose.

6. Remove brake disc.

7. Remove pulse generator from swivel bearing and expose line up to engine carrier.

8. To avoid damaging the stabilizer link, remove the stabilizer link from the stabilizer.

9. Remove tie rod end from swivel bearing.

10. Remove wheel guide joint from swivel bearing.

11. Press swivel bearing outwards and remove output shaft from wheel bearing.

12. Disengage brake hose from holder.

13. Support swivel bearing with workshop jack.

Fig. 139 Release collar nut (1), press brake pedal to floor for this purpose. Secure collar nut on flattened area (2) of drive shaft by positive peening

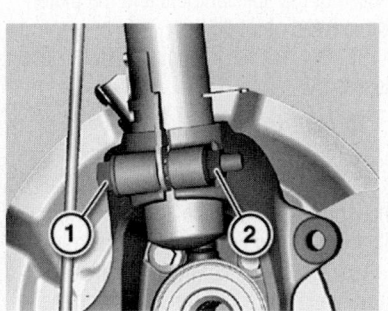

Fig. 140 Slacken nut (2). Pull out screw (1) towards rear and remove swivel bearing

14. Slacken nut.

15. Pull out screw towards rear and remove swivel bearing.

To install:

16. Install in the reverse order.

17. Tighten bolts/nuts to specification as follows:

- Output shaft to angular contact ball bearing: 135 ft. lbs. (182 Nm)
- Spring strut shock absorber to pivot mount: 74 ft. lbs. (100 Nm)

18. Tightening to torque must be effected by means of the screw.

19. Note insertion direction of screw.

20. Replace self-locking nuts.

21. Replace collar nut, oil collar nut/wheel bearing contact surface only and tighten down.

22. No oil permitted on thread of shaft journal or collar nut.

23. Secure collar nut on flattened area of drive shaft by positive peening.

24. Keep swivel bearing to spring strut connection clean and free from oil and grease.

25. Perform chassis alignment check.

STABILIZER BAR

REMOVAL & INSTALLATION

See Figures 141 and 142.

1. Before servicing the vehicle, refer to the precautions.

2. Disconnect the negative battery cable.

3. Lower front axle support.

4. Release nut; if necessary, grip dihedron or hexagon socket.

5. Release left and right screws.

6. Remove stabilizer from control arm bracket.

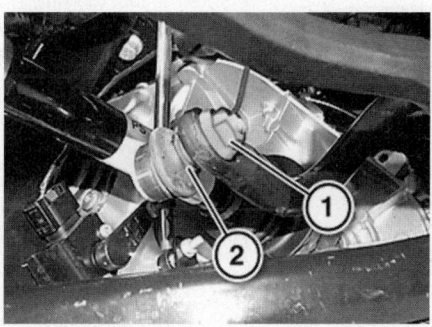

Fig. 141 Release nut (1); if necessary, grip dihedron (2) or hexagon socket.

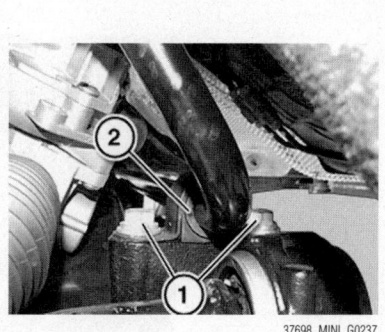

Fig. 142 Release left and right screws (1). Remove stabilizer (2) from control arm bracket

To install:

7. Install in the reverse order.

8. Replace self-locking nut.

9. Replace rubber mount for stabilizer.

10. Tighten bolts/nuts to specification as follows:

- Stabilizer link to stabilizer: 41 ft. lbs. (56 Nm)
- Bracket, control arm rubber mount to front axle carrier: 122 ft. lbs. (165 Nm)

11. On vehicles with Dynamic Stability Control, carry out steering angle sensor adjustment.

WHEEL HUB & BEARING

REMOVAL & INSTALLATION

See Figures 139 and 143.

1. Before servicing the vehicle, refer to the precautions.

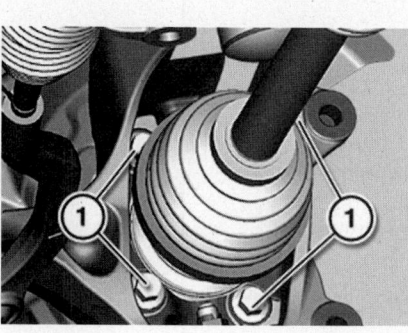

Fig. 143 Release screws (1) and remove bearing from output shaft

2. Disconnect the negative battery cable.

3. Remove front wheel.

4. Expand turning lock sufficiently to avoid damaging thread when releasing collar nut.

5. Release collar nut, press brake pedal to floor for this purpose.

6. Remove brake disc.

7. Remove pulse generator from swivel bearing and expose line up to engine carrier

8. Release screws (1) and remove bearing from output shaft.

To install:

9. Replace microencapsulated screws.

10. Tighten wheel bearing to swivel bearing: 15 ft. lbs. (20 Nm)

SUSPENSION

MACPHERSON STRUTS

REMOVAL & INSTALLATION

See Figures 144 and 145.

1. Before servicing the vehicle, refer to the precautions.

2. Disconnect the negative battery cable.

3. Remove rear wheel.

4. Remove lead for pulse generator and brake hose from spring strut.

5. Support trailing arm from underneath using a workshop jack.

6. Secure spring strut against falling out.

7. Release screw and tie up spring strut.

8. Release screws and remove spring strut.

Fig. 144 Release screw (1) and tie up spring strut

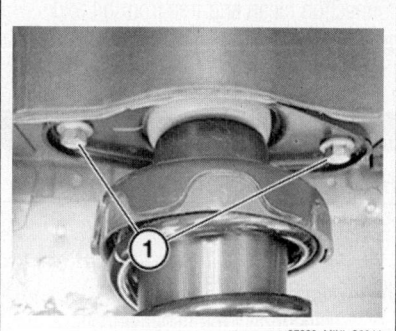

Fig. 145 Release screws (1) and remove spring strut

To install:

9. Install in the reverse order.

10. Tighten bolts/nuts to specification as follows:

11. Spring strut support bearing to body: 41 ft. lbs. (56 Nm)

12. Spring strut shock absorber to trailing arm: 122 ft. lbs. (165 Nm)

13. Replace screws.

14. Blow out chips in thread of trailing arm with compressed air (caused by initial screwing with.

15. self-tapping screw).

16. Make sure rubber grommets are correctly seated.

17. Secure upper spring strut in body.

18. Align shock absorber to swivel bearing by turning shock absorber.

OVERHAUL

See Figure 146.

REAR SUSPENSION

1. Before servicing the vehicle, refer to the precautions.

2. Remove rear spring strut shock absorber.

3. Clamp special tool 31 3 341 at guide in vice.

4. Fit special tools 31 3 357 from above on special tool 31 3 341 until locking pins can be felt and heard to snap into place.

5. Check seating of special tools 31 3 357, correct if necessary.

6. Do not damage protective tube.

7. Clean coil spring to remove all coarse dirt and mount on special tools 31 3 357.

8. Coils of coil spring must be located completely in recesses of special tools 31 3 357 when tensioned!.

9. Compress coil spring until stress on piston rod is relieved.

10. Nut may only be release when the spring coil is located completely in the recess of the special tools and the piston rod is freed of load!.

11. Release nut, gripping piston rod if necessary.

To install:

12. Install in the reverse order.

13. Insert coil spring in special tools so that spring end with the smaller spring diameter points downwards in the middle.

14. Make sure spring end contacts spring pad correctly. The locator on the spring pad must rest in the recess of the spring cup.

15. Make sure that the correct support bearing is installed on each side of the vehicle and it is aligned correctly corresponding to the line holder.

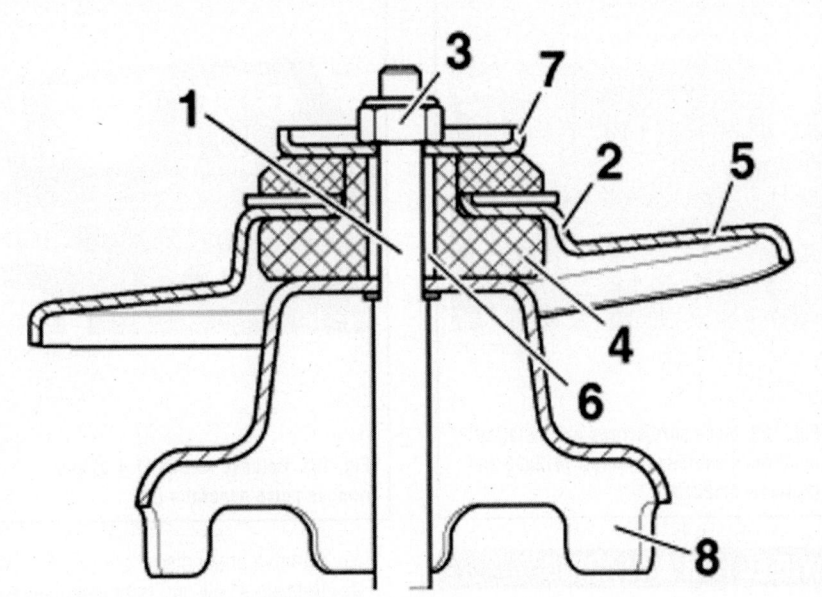

1. Shock absorber piston rod
2. Thrust bearing
3. Hexagon nut
4. Elastomer seal
5. Position of stud (upper mount to body)
6. Inner sleeve (steel insert)
7. Plate
8. Spring retainer

37698_MINI_G0242

Fig. 146 Make sure that the correct support bearing is installed on each side of the vehicle and it is aligned correctly corresponding to the line holder

16. Replace self-locking nut.
17. Tighten spring strut support bearing nut to 22 ft. lbs. (30 Nm).

STABILIZER BAR

REMOVAL & INSTALLATION

See Figures 147 through 150.

1. Before servicing the vehicle, refer to the precautions.
2. Disconnect the negative battery cable.
3. On R55, R56 and R58 Series, remove underbody paneling on left and right.
4. On R57 and R59 Series remove floor plate cruciform reinforcement.
5. Remove rear left and right spring strut shock absorbers.
6. Release nut on left and right; if necessary,.
7. grip hexagon socket or dihedron.

8. Disengage exhaust rubber at rear.
9. Release screws and nuts.
10. Remove heat shield in rear area from body.
11. Remove brake line from holders. Brake line is located on right side of floor plate in front of tank.
12. Support rear axle support with special tools 31 5 250, 31 5 252 and 31 5 253.
13. Release screws on left and right.
14. Lower axle support by a maximum of 1.56 in. (40 mm).
15. Release left and right screws.
16. Remove retaining bar and rubber mount on left and right.
17. Turn stabilizer bar and feed out sideways.
18. Keep rubber mount and stabilizer clean and free from oil and grease.

To install:
19. Install in the reverse order.
20. Tighten bolts/nuts to specification as follows:
- Rear axle carrier to body: 74 ft. lbs. (100 Nm)
- Stabilizer link to stabilizer: 41 ft. lbs. (56 Nm)
- Retaining bracket, stabilizer bar to rear axle support: 14 ft. lbs. (19 Nm)
21. Replace self-locking nut.
22. Replace damaged holders.
23. Make sure brake line is correctly seated in holders.
24. Replace microencapsulated screws.
25. Make sure screws are installed in correct positions.

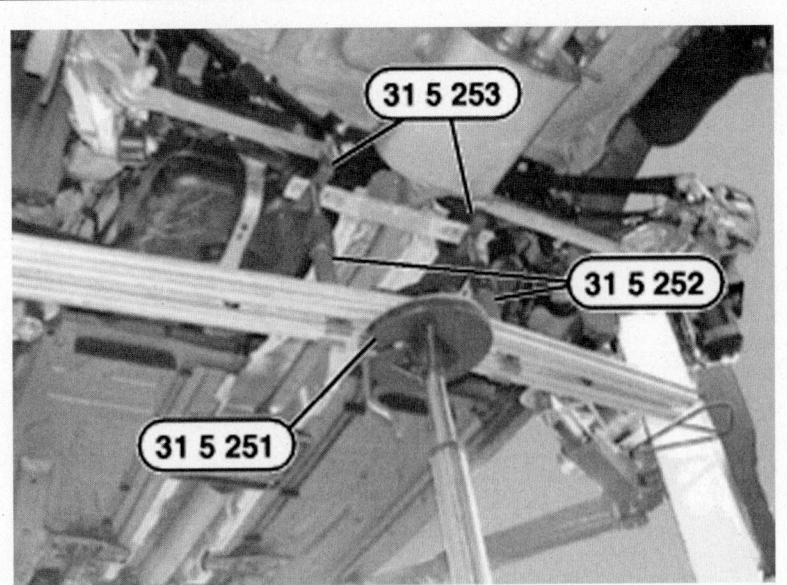

37698_MINI_G0251

Fig. 147 Support rear axle support with special tools 31 5 250, 31 5 252 and 31 5 253

Fig. 148 Lower axle support by a maximum of 1.56 in. (40 mm)

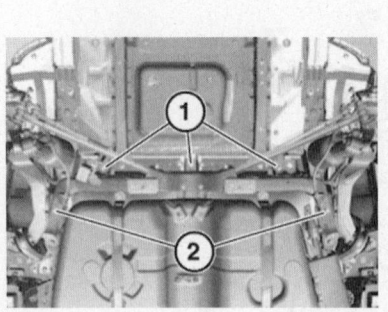

Fig. 150 Make sure screws are installed in correct positions (1)Screw M12x62 and (2)Screw M12x132

Fig. 151 Release screws (1 & 3) and remove pulse generator (2)

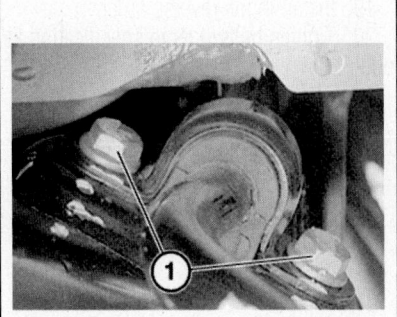

Fig. 149 Release left and right screws (1)

WHEEL HUB & BEARING

REMOVAL & INSTALLATION

See Figure 151.

1. Before servicing the vehicle, refer to the precautions.
2. Raise and safely support the vehicle.
3. Remove the tire and wheel assembly.
4. Activate the parking brake and release the collar nut.

➡**On AWD, expand the anti-twist lock sufficiently to avoid damaging thread when releasing collar nut.**

5. Remove brake disc.
6. Release screw and remove pulse generator.
7. Release screws and remove wheel hub.

To install:

8. Install in the reverse order.
9. Tighten bolts/nuts to specification as follows:
10. Pulse generator to steering knuckle/frame side member: 71 inch lbs. (8 Nm)
11. Wheel bearing to trailing arm: 41 ft. lbs. (56 Nm)

MINI

Diagnostic Trouble Codes

DIAGNOSTIC TROUBLE CODES

OBD II VEHICLE APPLICATIONS

MINI

Base
2011–2012
- 1.6L I4 SFI . . . Engine Code: N14B16C
- 1.6L I4 SFI . . . Engine Code: N16B16A
- 1.6L I4 SFI . . . Engine Code: N18B16A

Clubman
2011–2012
- 1.6L I4 SFI . . . Engine Code: N14B16C

- 1.6L I4 SFI . . . Engine Code: N16B16A
- 1.6L I4 SFI . . . Engine Code: N18B16A

Countryman
2011–2012
- 1.6L I4 SFI . . . Engine Code: N14B16C
- 1.6L I4 SFI . . . Engine Code: N16B16A
- 1.6L I4 SFI . . . Engine Code: N18B16A

Coupe
2012
- 1.6L I4 SFI . . . Engine Code: N14B16C
- 1.6L I4 SFI . . . Engine Code: N16B16A
- 1.6L I4 SFI . . . Engine Code: N18B16A

Roadster
2012
- 1.6L I4 SFI . . . Engine Code: N14B16C
- 1.6L I4 SFI . . . Engine Code: N16B16A
- 1.6L I4 SFI . . . Engine Code: N18B16A

OBD II Trouble Code List (P0XXX Codes)

DTC	Trouble Code Title and Conditions
DTC: P0010 T **Year:** 2011, 2012 **Model:** Cooper, Cooper Countryman **Engine:** 1.6L L4	**"A" Camshaft Position Actuator Circuit (Bank 1):** Key on or engine running; and the DME detected an unexpected high voltage or low voltage condition on the camshaft position sensor. The relative position between the camshaft and crankshaft needs to be optimal so the engine has better torque, fuel economy and emissions. **NOTE: The camshaft adjustment is load- and RPM-dependant. The electrical camshaft adjustment valve 1 switches oil pressure onto camshaft adjuster (mechanical adjustment mechanism), which adjusts the camshaft.**
DTC: P0011 T **Year:** 2011, 2012 **Model:** Cooper, Cooper Countryman **Engine:** 1.6L L4	**"A" Camshaft Position Timing Over-Advanced (Bank 1):** Engine started and driven at an engine speed of more than 400rpm; and the DME detected the camshaft timing exceeded the maximum calibrated advance value, or the camshaft remained in an advanced position during the CCM test. The valve timing did not change from the current valve timing or it remained fixed during the testing. **NOTE: The camshaft adjustment is load- and RPM-dependant. The electrical camshaft adjustment valve 1 switches oil pressure onto camshaft adjuster (mechanical adjustment mechanism), which adjusts the camshaft.**
DTC: P0012 T **Year:** 2011, 2012 **Model:** Cooper, Cooper Countryman **Engine:** 1.6L L4	**"A" Camshaft Position Over-Retarded (Bank 1):** Engine started and driven at an engine speed of more than 400rpm; and the DME detected the camshaft timing exceeded the minimum calibrated retarded value, or the camshaft remained in an retarded position during the CCM test. The valve timing did not change from the current valve timing or it remained fixed during the testing. **NOTE: The camshaft adjustment is load- and RPM dependant. The electrical camshaft adjustment valve 1 switches oil pressure onto camshaft adjuster (mechanical adjustment mechanism), which adjusts the camshaft.**
DTC: P0013 T **Year:** 2011, 2012 **Model:** Cooper, Cooper Countryman **Engine:** 1.6L L4	**"B" Camshaft Position Actuator Circuit (Bank 1):** Key on or engine running; and the DME detected an unexpected high voltage or low voltage condition on the camshaft position sensor. The relative position between the camshaft and crankshaft needs to be optimal so the engine has better torque, fuel economy and emissions. **NOTE: The camshaft adjustment is load- and RPM dependant. The electrical camshaft adjustment valve 1 switches oil pressure onto camshaft adjuster (mechanical adjustment mechanism), which adjusts the camshaft.**
DTC: P0014 T **Year:** 2011, 2012 **Model:** Cooper, Cooper Countryman **Engine:** 1.6L L4	**"B" Camshaft Position Timing Over-Advanced (Bank 1):** Engine started and driven at an engine speed of more than 400rpm; and the DME detected the camshaft timing exceeded the maximum calibrated advance value, or the camshaft remained in an advanced position during the CCM test. The valve timing did not change from the current valve timing or it remained fixed during the testing. The VANOS is in the end position. **NOTE: The camshaft adjustment is load- and RPM dependant. The electrical camshaft adjustment valve 1 switches oil pressure onto camshaft adjuster (mechanical adjustment mechanism), which adjusts the camshaft.**
DTC: P0015 T **Year:** 2011, 2012 **Model:** Cooper, Cooper Countryman **Engine:** 1.6L L4	**"B" Camshaft Position Over-Retarded (Bank 1):** Engine started and driven at an engine speed of more than 400rpm; and the DME detected the camshaft timing exceeded the minimum calibrated retarded value, or the camshaft remained in an retarded position during the CCM test. The valve timing did not change from the current valve timing or it remained fixed during the testing. **NOTE: The camshaft adjustment is load- and RPM dependant. The electrical camshaft adjustment valve 1 switches oil pressure onto camshaft adjuster (mechanical adjustment mechanism), which adjusts the camshaft.**
DTC: P0017 T **Year:** 2011, 2012 **Model:** Cooper, Cooper Countryman **Engine:** 1.6L L4	**Crankshaft Position - Camshaft Position Correlation Bank 1 Sensor B:** Engine started, engine running, and the DME detected a deviation between the crankshaft position sensor signal and the camshaft position sensor. A rationality error has been detected for camshaft position out of phase with crankshaft.
DTC: P0031 T **Year:** 2011, 2012 **Model:** Cooper, Cooper Countryman **Engine:** 1.6L L4	**HO2S Heater (Bank 1 Sensor 1) Circuit Low Input:** Engine started, battery voltage must be at least 11.5v, all electrical components must be off, the ground between the engine and the chassis must be well connected, the exhaust system must be properly sealed between the catalytic converter and the cylinder head, the coolant temperature must be 80 degrees Celsius, and the oxygen sensor heater for oxygen sensor before the catalytic converter must be properly functioning. The DME detected the HO2S signal was in a negative voltage range referred to as "character shift downward". This code sets when the HO2S signal remains in a low state. In effect, it does not switch properly in the closed loop operation. The HO2S (before the three-way catalytic converter) has a short circuit to ground that has lasted longer than 200 seconds.
DTC: P0032 T **Year:** 2011, 2012 **Model:** Cooper, Cooper Countryman **Engine:** 1.6L L4	**HO2S Heater (Bank 1 Sensor 1) Circuit High Input:** Engine started, battery voltage must be at least 11.5v, all electrical components must be off, the ground between the engine and the chassis must be well connected, the exhaust system must be properly sealed between the catalytic converter and the cylinder head, the coolant temperature must be 80 degrees Celsius, and the oxygen sensor heater for oxygen sensor before the catalytic converter must be properly functioning. The DME detected the HO2S signal remained in a high state. **NOTE: The HO2S signal circuit may be shorted to the heater power circuit due to tracking inside of the HO2S connector. Remove the connector and visually inspect the connector for signs of oil or water.**

DTC	Trouble Code Title and Conditions
DTC: P0036 **T** **Year:** 2011, 2012 **Model:** Cooper, Cooper Countryman **Engine:** 1.6L L4	**HO2S Heater (Bank 1 Sensor 2) Control Circuit Malfunction:** Engine started, battery voltage must be at least 11.5v, all electrical components must be off, the ground between the engine and the chassis must be well connected, the exhaust system must be properly sealed between the catalytic converter and the cylinder head, the coolant temperature must be 80 degrees Celsius, and the oxygen sensor heater for oxygen sensor before the catalytic converter must be properly functioning. The DME detected the HO2S signal was in a negative voltage range referred to as "character shift downward". This code sets when the HO2S signal remains in a low state.
DTC: P0037 **T** **Year:** 2011, 2012/ **Model:** Cooper, Cooper Countryman **Engine:** 1.6L L4	**HO2S Heater (Bank 1 Sensor 2) Circuit Low Input:** Engine started, battery voltage must be at least 11.5v, all electrical components must be off, the ground between the engine and the chassis must be well connected, the exhaust system must be properly sealed between the catalytic converter and the cylinder head, the coolant temperature must be 80 degrees Celsius, and the oxygen sensor heater for oxygen sensor before the catalytic converter must be properly functioning. The DME detected the HO2S signal was in a negative voltage range referred to as "character shift downward". This code sets when the HO2S signal remains in a low state. In effect, it does not switch properly in the closed loop operation. The HO2S (before the three-way catalytic converter) has a short circuit to ground that has lasted longer than 200 seconds.
DTC: P0038 **T** **Year:** 2011, 2012 **Model:** Cooper, Cooper Countryman **Engine:** 1.6L L4	**HO2S Heater (Bank 1 Sensor 2) Circuit High Input:** Engine started, battery voltage must be at least 11.5v, all electrical components must be off, the ground between the engine and the chassis must be well connected, the exhaust system must be properly sealed between the catalytic converter and the cylinder head, the coolant temperature must be 80 degrees Celsius, and the oxygen sensor heater for oxygen sensor before the catalytic converter must be properly functioning. The DME detected the HO2S signal remained in a high state. **NOTE: The HO2S signal circuit may be shorted to the heater power circuit due to tracking inside of the HO2S connector. Remove the connector and visually inspect the connector for signs of oil or water.**
DTC: P0053 **2T** **Year:** 2011, 2012 **Model:** Cooper, Cooper Countryman **Engine:** 1.6L L4	**HO2S Heater (Bank 1 Sensor 1) Control Circuit Malfunction:** Engine started, battery voltage must be at least 10.96v, all electrical components must be off, the ground between the engine and the chassis must be well connected, the exhaust system must be properly sealed between the catalytic converter and the cylinder head, and the coolant temperature must be 80 degrees Celsius. The DME detected the HO2S signal was in a negative voltage range referred to as "character shift downward". The resistance is out of limits. The engine speed is less than 7008rpm (6208 for A/T) and the exhaust temperatures are between 350.006 and 649.995 degrees Celsius.
DTC: P0054 **2T** **Year:** 2011, 2012 **Model:** Cooper, Cooper Countryman **Engine:** 1.6L L4	**HO2S Heater (Bank 1 Sensor 2) Circuit High Input:** Engine started, battery voltage must be at least 11.5v, all electrical components must be off, the ground between the engine and the chassis must be well connected, the exhaust system must be properly sealed between the catalytic converter and the cylinder head, the coolant temperature must be 80 degrees Celsius, and the oxygen sensor heater for oxygen sensor before the catalytic converter must be properly functioning. The DME detected the HO2S signal remained in a high state. The resistance is out of limits. The engine speed is less than 7008rpm (6208 for A/T) and the exhaust temperatures are between 350.006 and 649.995 degrees Celsius. **NOTE: The HO2S signal circuit may be shorted to the heater power circuit due to tracking inside of the HO2S connector. Remove the connector and visually inspect the connector for signs of oil or water.**
DTC: P0100 **1T , MIL: Yes** **Year:** 2011, 2012 **Model:** Cooper, Cooper Countryman **Engine:** 1.6L L4	**Mass Airflow Sensor Circuit Continuity Monitoring (short circuit):** This diagnostic function monitors for circuit continuity malfunction by comparing the MAF sensor signal period duration to the upper calibrated threshold value and to the lower calibrated threshold value to detect an intermitted contact. A short circuit malfunction is detected when the period duration equals 0. When the MAF sensor signal period duration equals 0 for a calibrated period of time, a short circuit malfunction is detected and an the DTC P0100 set.
DTC: P0102 **1T** **Year:** 2011, 2012 **Model:** Cooper, Cooper Countryman **Engine:** 1.6L L4	**Mass Airflow Sensor Circuit Continuity Monitoring (high frequency):** This diagnostic function monitors for circuit continuity malfunction by comparing the MAF sensor signal period duration to the upper calibrated threshold value and to the lower calibrated threshold value to detect an intermitted contact. When the MAF sensor signal period duration is below the lower calibrated threshold value for a calibrated period of time, an intermitted contact (high frequency) malfunction is detected and the DTC P0102 set.
DTC: P0103 **1T , MIL: Yes** **Year:** 2011, 2012 **Model:** Cooper, Cooper Countryman **Engine:** 1.6L L4	**Mass Airflow Sensor Circuit Continuity Monitoring (low frequency):** This diagnostic function monitors for circuit continuity malfunction by comparing the MAF sensor signal period duration to the upper calibrated threshold value and to the lower calibrated threshold value to detect an intermitted contact. When the MAF sensor signal period duration exceeds the upper calibrated threshold value for a calibrated period of time, an intermitted contact (low frequency) malfunction is detected and the DTC P0103 is set.
DTC: P0107 **2T** **Year:** 2011, 2012 **Model:** Cooper, Cooper Countryman **Engine:** 1.6L L4	**Manifold Pressure Sensor Circuit Low:** Engine started, battery voltage must be at least 11v, and the differential pressure sensor detected a control deviation at the minimum limit. The closed loop control of the differential pressure in the intake manifold is suspended and replaced by a direct specification. The MAP was too low (less than 105.0016kPa); engine stopped.

DTC	Trouble Code Title and Conditions
DTC: P0108 **2T** **Year:** 2011, 2012 **Model:** Cooper, Cooper Countryman **Engine:** 1.6L L4	**Manifold Pressure Sensor Circuit Short to Battery:** Engine started, battery voltage must be at least 11v, and the differential pressure sensor detected a control deviation at the minimum limit. The closed loop control of the differential pressure in the intake manifold is suspended and replaced by a direct specification. The MAP was too low (less than 105.0016kPa); engine stopped.
DTC: P0112 **T** **Year:** 2011, 2012 **Model:** Cooper, Cooper Countryman **Engine:** 1.6L L4	**Intake Air Temperature Sensor Circuit Low Input:** Key on or Engine running, the temperature must beat least 185-degrees (F) and all electrical equipment (A/C, lights, etc) must be off; and the DME detected the IAT sensor signal was less than the self-test minimum. This is a thermistor-type sensor with a variable resistance that changes when exposed to different temperatures. This means: the higher the temperature, the lower the resistance value.
DTC: P0113 **T** **Year:** 2011, 2012 **Model:** Cooper, Cooper Countryman **Engine:** 1.6L L4	**Intake Air Temperature Sensor Circuit High Input:** Key on or engine running, the temperature must beat least 185-degrees (F) and all electrical equipment (A/C, lights, etc) must be off; and the DME detected the IAT sensor signal was more than the self-test maximum. This is a thermistor-type sensor with a variable resistance that changes when exposed to different temperatures. This means: the higher the temperature, the lower the resistance value.
DTC: P0114 **2T** **Year:** 2011, 2012 **Model:** Cooper, Cooper Countryman **Engine:** 1.6L L4	**Intake Air Temperature Sensor Circuit Intermittent Failure:** Key on or engine running, the temperature must beat least 185-degrees (F) and all electrical equipment (A/C, lights, etc) must be off; and the DME detected the IAT sensor signal was more than the self-test maximum. This is a thermistor-type sensor with a variable resistance that changes when exposed to different temperatures. This means: the higher the temperature, the lower the resistance value. The gradient between filtered and current intake air sensor values exceeds 9.75 degrees Celsius.
DTC: P0117 **T** **Year:** 2011, 2012 **Model:** Cooper, Cooper Countryman **Engine:** 1.6L L4	**ECT Sensor Circuit Low Input:** Engine started (cold) for 10 seconds, battery voltage must be 11.5, and all equipment must be off. The DME detected the ECT sensor signal was less than the self-test minimum. This is a thermistor-type sensor with a variable resistance that changes when exposed to different temperatures
DTC: P0118 **T** **Year:** 2011, 2012 **Model:** Cooper, Cooper Countryman **Engine:** 1.6L L4	**ECT Sensor Circuit High Input:** Engine started (cold) for 10 seconds, battery voltage must be 11.5, and all equipment must be off. The DME detected the ECT sensor signal was more than the self-test maximum. This is a thermistor-type sensor with a variable resistance that changes when exposed to different temperatures
DTC: P0119 **T** **Year:** 2011, 2012 **Model:** Cooper, Cooper Countryman **Engine:** 1.6L L4	**ECT Sensor Circuit Continuity:** Engine started (cold) for 10 seconds, battery voltage must be 11.5, and all equipment must be off. The DME detected the ECT sensor signal was out of the specified range. This is a thermistor-type sensor with a variable resistance that changes when exposed to different temperatures
DTC: P0122 **T** **Year:** 2011, 2012 **Model:** Cooper, Cooper Countryman **Engine:** 1.6L L4	**Throttle/Pedal Position Sensor Circuit Low Input:** Engine started, at idle, the temperature must be at least 80 degrees Celsius. The throttle position sensor supplies implausible signal to the DME.
DTC: P0123 **T** **Year:** 2011, 2012 **Model:** Cooper, Cooper Countryman **Engine:** 1.6L L4	**TP Sensor Circuit High Input:** Engine started, at idle, the temperature must be at least 80 degrees Celsius. The DME detected the TP sensor signal was more than the self-test maximum during testing.

DTC	Trouble Code Title and Conditions
DTC: P0125 T **Year:** 2011, 2012 **Model:** Cooper, Cooper Countryman **Engine:** 1.6L L4	**ECT Sensor Insufficient for Closed Loop Fuel Control:** Engine started (cold), battery voltage must be 11.5, and all equipment must be off. The DME detected the ECT sensor exceeded the required calibrated value, or the engine is at idle and doesn't reach operating temperature quickly enough; the Catalyst, Fuel System, HO2S and Misfire Monitor did not complete, or the timer expired. Testing completion of procedure, the engine's temperature must rise uniformly during idle.
DTC: P0128 T **Year:** 2011, 2012 **Model:** Cooper, Cooper Countryman **Engine:** 1.6L L4	**Coolant Thermostat (Coolant Temperature Below Thermostat Regulating Temperature):** The engine's warm up performance is monitored by comparing measured coolant temperature with the modeled coolant temperature to detect a defective coolant thermostat. The engine temperature must be less than 65 degrees Celsius, engine speed greater than 800rpm (with the vehicle speed greater than 10 but less than 90km/h) and the ambient temperature greater than -8 degrees Celsius. The thermostat should be wide open when cold, but is in error if it opens below desired control temperature.
DTC: P0130 2T **Year:** 2011, 2012 **Model:** Cooper, Cooper Countryman **Engine:** 1.6L L4	**O2 Sensor Circuit Bank 1 Sensor 1:** Engine running, battery voltage 11.5, all electrical components off, ground between engine and chassis well connected and the exhaust system must be properly sealed between catalytic converter and the cylinder head. The DME detected the HO2S signal was implausible or not detected. The engine speed is less than 8000 rpm.
DTC: P0131 2T **Year:** 2011, 2012 **Model:** Cooper, Cooper Countryman **Engine:** 1.6L L4	**HO2S (Bank 1 Sensor 1) Circuit Low Input:** Engine running, battery voltage 11.5, all electrical components off, ground between engine and chassis well connected and the exhaust system must be properly sealed between catalytic converter and the cylinder head. The DME detected the HO2S signal was in a negative voltage range referred to as "character shift downward". This code sets when the HO2S signal remains in a low state for a measured period of time. In effect, it does not switch properly in the closed loop operation. Engine speed is less than 8000rpm.
DTC: P0132 T **Year:** 2011, 2012 **Model:** Cooper, Cooper Countryman **Engine:** 1.6L L4	**HO2S (Bank 1 Sensor 1) Circuit High Input:** Engine running, battery voltage 11.5, all electrical components off, ground between engine and chassis well connected and the exhaust system must be properly sealed between catalytic converter and the cylinder head. The DME detected the HO2S signal was in a high state. This code sets when the HO2S signal remains in a high state for a measured period of time. In effect, it does not switch properly in the closed loop operation. **NOTE: The HO2S signal circuit may be shorted to the heater power circuit due to tracking inside of the HO2S connector. Remove the connector and visually inspect the connector for signs of oil or water.**
DTC: P0133 2T **Year:** 2011, 2012 **Model:** Cooper, Cooper Countryman **Engine:** 1.6L L4	**HO2S (Bank 1 Sensor 1) Circuit Slow Response:** Engine running, battery voltage 11.5, all electrical components off, ground between engine and chassis well connected and the exhaust system must be properly sealed between catalytic converter and the cylinder head. The DME detected the HO2S amplitude and frequency were out of the normal range (e.g., the HO2S rich to lean switch) during the HO2S Monitor test. The engine speed is 1984 to 3488rpm (1888 to 3296 for A/T), the coolant temperature is greater than 80.25 degrees Celsius and the vehicle speed is between 24.85 and 68.35mph. The ambient pressure is greater than 75.00114kPa.
DTC: P0135 2T **Year:** 2011, 2012 **Model:** Cooper, Cooper Countryman **Engine:** 1.6L L4	**HO2S (Bank 1 Sensor 1) Heater Circuit Malfunction:** Engine running, battery voltage is between 11 and 16 volts, all electrical components off, ground between engine and chassis well connected and the exhaust system must be properly sealed between catalytic converter and the cylinder head. The DME detected an unexpected voltage condition, or it detected excessive current draw in the heater circuit during the CCM test. The engine load is 25 to 160kg/h. The exhaust gas temperature is between 450 and 700 degrees Celsius.
DTC: P0136 2T **Year:** 2011, 2012 **Model:** Cooper, Cooper Countryman **Engine:** 1.6L L4	**HO2S (Bank 1 Sensor 2) Circuit Malfunction:** Engine running, battery voltage 11.5, all electrical components off, ground between engine and chassis well connected and the exhaust system must be properly sealed between catalytic converter and the cylinder head. The DME detected the HO2S signal failed to meet the maximum or minimum voltage levels (i.e., it failed the voltage range check). The heater has been on for less than 90 seconds, the fuel system status is in fuel cut-off, the output voltage is between 400mV and 500mV and it is 120 seconds after engine start up. The engine speed is less than 8000rpm.
DTC: P0137 T **Year:** 2011, 2012 **Model:** Cooper, Cooper Countryman **Engine:** 1.6L L4	**HO2S (Bank 1 Sensor 2) Circuit Low Input:** Engine running, battery voltage 11.5, all electrical components off, ground between engine and chassis well connected and the exhaust system must be properly sealed between catalytic converter and the cylinder head. The DME detected the HO2S signal remained in a high state. **NOTE: The HO2S signal circuit may be shorted to the heater power circuit due to "tracking inside of the HO2S connector. Remove the connector and visually inspect the connector for signs of oil or water.**

DTC	Trouble Code Title and Conditions
DTC: P0138 **T** **Year:** 2011, 2012 **Model:** Cooper, Cooper Countryman **Engine:** 1.6L L4	**HO2S (Bank 1 Sensor 2) Circuit High Input:** Engine running, battery voltage 11.5, all electrical components off, ground between engine and chassis well connected and the exhaust system must be properly sealed between catalytic converter and the cylinder head. The DME detected the HO2S signal remained in a high state. **NOTE: The HO2S signal circuit may be shorted to the heater power circuit due to "tracking inside of the HO2S connector. Remove the connector and visually inspect the connector for signs of oil or water.**
DTC: P0141 **T** **Year:** 2011, 2012 **Model:** Cooper, Cooper Countryman **Engine:** 1.6L L4	**HO2S (Bank 1 Sensor 2) Malfunction:** Engine running, battery voltage 11.5, all electrical components off, ground between engine and chassis well connected and the exhaust system must be properly sealed between catalytic converter and the cylinder head. The DME detected the HO2S signal failed to meet the maximum or minimum voltage levels (i.e., it failed the voltage range check). The engine speed is greater than 40rpm, the battery voltage must be between 10.7 and 15.5 volts, and the fault occurs 200 seconds after engine start up.
DTC: P0153 **T** **Year:** 2011, 2012 **Model:** Cooper, Cooper Countryman **Engine:** 1.6L L4	**HO2S (Bank 2 Sensor 1) Circuit Slow Response:** Engine running, battery voltage 11.5, all electrical components off, ground between engine and chassis well connected and the exhaust system must be properly sealed between catalytic converter and the cylinder head. The DME detected the HO2S amplitude and frequency were out of the normal range during the HO2S Monitor test. For the 1999 M62: The idle speed variation is between 1400 and 2600rpm, the engine load variation is between 20 and 54 while the catalyst temperature should be greater than 360 degrees Celsius.
DTC: P0154 **T** **Year:** 2011, 2012 **Model:** Cooper, Cooper Countryman **Engine:** 1.6L L4	**HO2S (Bank 2 Sensor 1) Circuit No Activity:** Engine running, battery voltage 11.5, all electrical components off, ground between engine and chassis well connected and the exhaust system must be properly sealed between catalytic converter and the cylinder head. The DME detected the HO2S signal failed to meet the maximum or minimum voltage (i.e., it failed the voltage check).
DTC: P0171 **2T** **Year:** 2011, 2012 **Model:** Cooper, Cooper Countryman **Engine:** 1.6L L4	**Fuel System Too Lean (Cylinder Bank 1):** Key on or engine running, all electrical components off and coolant temperature at least 80 degrees Celsius; and the DME detected the Bank 1 Adaptive Fuel Control System reached its rich correction limit (a lean A/F condition). The fuel status is in a closed loop pattern, the coolant temperature is greater than 7 degrees Celsius, and the engine speed is less than 1400rpm.
DTC: P0172 **2T** **Year:** 2011, 2012 **Model:** Cooper, Cooper Countryman **Engine:** 1.6L L4	**Fuel System Too Rich (Cylinder Bank 1):** Key on or engine running, all electrical components off and coolant temperature at least 80 degrees Celsius; and the DME detected the Bank 1 Adaptive Fuel Control System reached its rich correction limit (a rich A/F condition). The fuel status is in a closed loop pattern, the coolant temperature is greater than 7 degrees Celsius, and the engine speed is less than 1400rpm.
DTC: P0201 **T** **Year:** 2011, 2012 **Model:** Cooper, Cooper Countryman **Engine:** 1.6L L4	**Cylinder 1 Injector Circuit Malfunction:** Engine started, and the DME detected the fuel injector "1" control circuit was in a high state when it should have been low, or in a low state when it should have been high (wiring harness & injector okay). The battery voltage should be between 9.5 and 17 volts while the engine speed is less than 40rpm.
DTC: P0202 **T** **Year:** 2011, 2012 **Model:** Cooper, Cooper Countryman **Engine:** 1.6L L4	**Cylinder 2 Injector Circuit Malfunction:** Engine started, and the DME detected the fuel injector "2" control circuit was in a high state when it should have been low, or in a low state when it should have been high (wiring harness & injector okay). The battery voltage should be between 9.5 and 17 volts while the engine speed is less than 40rpm.
DTC: P0203 **T** **Year:** 2011, 2012 **Model:** Cooper, Cooper Countryman **Engine:** 1.6L L4	**Cylinder 3 Injector Circuit Malfunction:** Engine started, and the DME detected the fuel injector "3" control circuit was in a high state when it should have been low, or in a low state when it should have been high (wiring harness & injector okay). The battery voltage should be between 9.5 and 17 volts while the engine speed is less than 40rpm.

DTC	Trouble Code Title and Conditions
DTC: P0204 T **Year:** 2011, 2012 **Model:** Cooper, Cooper Countryman **Engine:** 1.6L L4	**Cylinder 4 Injector Circuit Malfunction:** Engine started, and the DME detected the fuel injector "4" control circuit was in a high state when it should have been low, or in a low state when it should have been high (wiring harness & injector okay). The battery voltage should be between 9.5 and 17 volts while the engine speed is less than 40rpm.
DTC: P0218 T **Year:** 2011, 2012 **Model:** Cooper, Cooper Countryman **Engine:** 1.6L L4	**Engine Oil Over Temperature:** The oil temperature difference of greater than 100 degrees within one second. The ignition must be on. The DME detected an error in the Engine Oil Temperature sensor. This occurs during attempted start value calibration.
DTC: P0222 T **Year:** 2011, 2012 **Model:** Cooper, Cooper Countryman **Engine:** 1.6L L4	**Throttle Position Sensor 'B' Circuit Low Input:** Engine started, battery voltage at least 11.5v, all electrical components off, ground connections between engine and chassis well connected, coolant temperature at least 80-degrees Celsius and the throttle valve must not be damaged or dirty; and the DME detected the TP Sensor 'B' circuit was out of its normal operating range during a condition with the throttle wide open, or with it completely closed. The throttle valve activation occurs via an electric motor (throttle drive) in the throttle valve control module. It is activated by the DME according to specifications of the two sensors, Throttle Position Sensor and Accelerator Pedal Position Sensor 2. Slowly depress accelerator pedal up to Wide Open Throttle (WOT) stop while observing the percentage display on the PID data function of the scan tool. The percentage display must increase uniformly.
DTC: P0223 T **Year:** 2011, 2012 **Model:** Cooper, Cooper Countryman **Engine:** 1.6L L4	**Throttle Position Sensor 'B' Circuit High Input:** Engine started, battery voltage at least 11.5v, all electrical components off, ground connections between engine and chassis well connected, coolant temperature at least 80-degrees Celsius and the throttle valve must not be damaged or dirty; and the DME detected the TP Sensor 'B' circuit was out of its normal operating range during a condition with the throttle wide open, or with it completely closed. The throttle valve activation occurs via an electric motor (throttle drive) in the throttle valve control module. It is activated by the DME according to specifications of the two sensors, Throttle Position Sensor and Accelerator Pedal Position Sensor 2. Slowly depress accelerator pedal up to Wide Open Throttle (WOT) stop while observing the percentage display on the PID data function of the scan tool. The percentage display must increase uniformly.
DTC: P0261 T **Year:** 2011, 2012 **Model:** Cooper, Cooper Countryman **Engine:** 1.6L L4	**Cylinder 1 Injector Circuit Low Input/Short to Ground:** Key on or engine running, fuses in the instrument panel and the E-box in the engine compartment must be functioning, and the ground connections between the engine ad the chassis must be well connected; and the DME detected an unexpected voltage condition on the injector circuit.
DTC: P0262 T **Year:** 2011, 2012 **Model:** Cooper, Cooper Countryman **Engine:** 1.6L L4	**Cylinder 1 Injector Circuit Low Input/Short to B+:** Key on or engine running, fuses in the instrument panel and the E-box in the engine compartment must be functioning, and the ground connections between the engine ad the chassis must be well connected; and the DME detected an unexpected voltage condition on the injector circuit.
DTC: P0264 T **Year:** 2011, 2012 **Model:** Cooper, Cooper Countryman **Engine:** 1.6L L4	**Cylinder 2 Injector Circuit Low Input/Short to Ground:** Key on or engine running, fuses in the instrument panel and the E-box in the engine compartment must be functioning, and the ground connections between the engine ad the chassis must be well connected; and the DME detected an unexpected voltage condition on the injector circuit.
DTC: P0265 T **Year:** 2011, 2012 **Model:** Cooper, Cooper Countryman **Engine:** 1.6L L4	**Cylinder 2 Injector Circuit Low Input/Short to B+:** Key on or engine running, fuses in the instrument panel and the E-box in the engine compartment must be functioning, and the ground connections between the engine ad the chassis must be well connected; and the DME detected an unexpected voltage condition on the injector circuit.
DTC: P0267 T **Year:** 2011, 2012 **Model:** Cooper, Cooper Countryman **Engine:** 1.6L L4	**Cylinder 3 Injector Circuit Low Input/Short to Ground:** Key on or engine running, fuses in the instrument panel and the E-box in the engine compartment must be functioning, and the ground connections between the engine ad the chassis must be well connected; and the DME detected an unexpected voltage condition on the injector circuit.

DTC	Trouble Code Title and Conditions
DTC: P0268 T **Year:** 2011, 2012 **Model:** Cooper, Cooper Countryman **Engine:** 1.6L L4	**Cylinder 3 Injector Circuit Low Input/Short to B+:** Key on or engine running, fuses in the instrument panel and the E-box in the engine compartment must be functioning, and the ground connections between the engine ad the chassis must be well connected; and the DME detected an unexpected voltage condition on the injector circuit.
DTC: P0270 T **Year:** 2011, 2012 **Model:** Cooper, Cooper Countryman **Engine:** 1.6L L4	**Cylinder 4 Injector Circuit Low Input/Short to Ground:** Key on or engine running, fuses in the instrument panel and the E-box in the engine compartment must be functioning, and the ground connections between the engine ad the chassis must be well connected; and the DME detected an unexpected voltage condition on the injector circuit.
DTC: P0271 T **Year:** 2011, 2012 **Model:** Cooper, Cooper Countryman **Engine:** 1.6L L4	**Cylinder 4 Injector Circuit Low Input/Short to B+:** Key on or engine running, fuses in the instrument panel and the E-box in the engine compartment must be functioning, and the ground connections between the engine ad the chassis must be well connected; and the DME detected an unexpected voltage condition on the injector circuit.
DTC: P0300 2T **Year:** 2011, 2012 **Model:** Cooper, Cooper Countryman **Engine:** 1.6L L4	**Random/Multiple Misfire Detected:** Engine running at an RPM greater than 600 but less than 7000 the DME detected a misfire or uneven engine running in two or more cylinders within 1000 engine revolutions. The sum of misfires caused an increase in emissions for the first 1000 revolutions after start up, or the sum of misfires caused catalyst damage after the first 200 engine revolutions. Time after start less than one second. **NOTE: If the misfire is severe, the MIL will flash on/off on the first trip!**
DTC: P0301 2T **Year:** 2011, 2012 **Model:** Cooper, Cooper Countryman **Engine:** 1.6L L4	**Cylinder Number 1 Misfire Detected:** Engine running at an RPM greater than 600 but less than 7000 the DME detected a misfire or uneven engine running in two or more cylinders within 1000 engine revolutions. The sum of misfires caused an increase in emissions for the first 1000 revolutions after start up, or the sum of misfires caused catalyst damage after the first 200 engine revolutions. Time after start less than one second. **NOTE: If the misfire is severe, the MIL will flash on/off on the first trip!**
DTC: P0302 2T **Year:** 2011, 2012 **Model:** Cooper, Cooper Countryman **Engine:** 1.6L L4	**Cylinder Number 2 Misfire Detected:** Engine running at an RPM greater than 600 but less than 7000 the DME detected a misfire or uneven engine running in two or more cylinders within 1000 engine revolutions. The sum of misfires caused an increase in emissions for the first 1000 revolutions after start up, or the sum of misfires caused catalyst damage after the first 200 engine revolutions. Time after start less than one second. **NOTE: If the misfire is severe, the MIL will flash on/off on the 1st trip!**
DTC: P0303 2T **Year:** 2011, 2012 **Model:** Cooper, Cooper Countryman **Engine:** 1.6L L4	**Cylinder Number 3 Misfire Detected:** Engine running at an RPM greater than 600 but less than 7000 the DME detected a misfire or uneven engine running in two or more cylinders within 1000 engine revolutions. The sum of misfires caused an increase in emissions for the first 1000 revolutions after start up, or the sum of misfires caused catalyst damage after the first 200 engine revolutions. Time after start less than one second. **NOTE: If the misfire is severe, the MIL will flash on/off on the 1st trip!**
DTC: P0304 2T **Year:** 2011, 2012 **Model:** Cooper, Cooper Countryman **Engine:** 1.6L L4	**Cylinder Number 4 Misfire Detected:** Engine running at an RPM greater than 600 but less than 7000 the DME detected a misfire or uneven engine running in two or more cylinders within 1000 engine revolutions. The sum of misfires caused an increase in emissions for the first 1000 revolutions after start up, or the sum of misfires caused catalyst damage after the first 200 engine revolutions. Time after start less than one second. **NOTE: If the misfire is severe, the MIL will flash on/off on the 1st trip!**
DTC: P0313 2T **Year:** 2011, 2012 **Model:** Cooper, Cooper Countryman **Engine:** 1.6L L4	**Misfire Detected with Low Fuel:** Engine running under positive torque conditions, and the DME detected a misfire or uneven engine function as well as an indication of low fuel level when another misfire was detected. **NOTE: If the misfire is severe, the MIL will flash on/off on the 1st trip!**

DTC	Trouble Code Title and Conditions
DTC: P0324 T **Year:** 2011, 2012 **Model:** Cooper, Cooper Countryman **Engine:** 1.6L L4	**Knock Control System Error:** Engine started, vehicle driven, and the DME detected the Knock Sensor 1 (KS1) signal was too low or not recognized by the DME
DTC: P0326 2T **Year:** 2011, 2012 **Model:** Cooper, Cooper Countryman **Engine:** 1.6L L4	**Knock Sensor Circuit Malfunction:** Engine started, vehicle driven at 1520rpm for 3 seconds or to a temperature of 40 degrees Celsius, and the DME detected the Knock Sensor 1 (KS1) signal was not recognized. The engine speed is greater than 2016rpm and the coolant temperature is greater than 50.25 degrees Celsius. The difference between raw and filtered knock sensor signal is less than 0.0499 to 0.0698 volts.
DTC: P0335 2T **Year:** 2011, 2012 **Model:** Cooper, Cooper Countryman **Engine:** 1.6L L4	**Camshaft Position Sensor "A" Circ Malfunction:** Engine started, battery voltage must be at least 11.5v, all electrical components must be off, parking brake must be engaged (to keep daytime driving lights off), automatic transmission selector must be in park and the ground between the engine and the chassis must be well connected. The DME detected the CMP sensor signal was implausible or missing. Engine speed is greater than 500rpm, and the fault is tolerable as long as there are no misfired occurring at the same time.
DTC: P0336 T **Year:** 2011, 2012 **Model:** Cooper, Cooper Countryman **Engine:** 1.6L L4	**Camshaft Position Sensor "A" Circ Range/Performance:** Engine started (and engine speed is less than 25rpm), battery voltage must be at least 11.5v, all electrical components must be off, parking brake must be engaged (to keep daytime driving lights off), automatic transmission selector must be in park and the ground between the engine and the chassis must be well connected. The DME detected the CMP sensor signal was implausible.
DTC: P0340 T **Year:** 2011, 2012 **Model:** Cooper, Cooper Countryman **Engine:** 1.6L L4	**Camshaft Position Sensor Circuit Malfunction:** Engine started, battery voltage must be at least 11.5v, all electrical components must be off, parking brake must be engaged (to keep daytime driving lights off), automatic transmission selector must be in park and the ground between the engine and the chassis must be well connected. The DME detected the CMP sensor signal was missing or it was erratic. There is no signal or an invalid one, and the engine speed is greater than 200rpm for two cycles.
DTC: P0341 T **Year:** 2011, 2012 **Model:** Cooper, Cooper Countryman **Engine:** 1.6L L4	**Camshaft Position Sensor Circ Range/Performance:** Engine started, battery voltage must be at least 11.5v, all electrical components must be off, parking brake must be engaged (to keep daytime driving lights off), automatic transmission selector must be in park and the ground between the engine and the chassis must be well connected. The DME detected the CMP sensor signal was implausible.
DTC: P0351 T **Year:** 2011, 2012 **Model:** Cooper, Cooper Countryman **Engine:** 1.6L L4	**Ignition Coilpack A Primary/Secondary Circuit Malfunction:** Engine started, battery voltage must be at least 11.5v, all electrical components must be off, parking brake must be engaged (to keep daytime driving lights off), automatic transmission selector must be in park and the ground between the engine and the chassis must be well connected. The DME did not receive any valid pulses from the ignition module for the Ignition Coilpack A primary circuit. **NOTE: Ignition coils and power output stages are one component and cannot be replaced individually.**
DTC: P0352 2T **Year:** 2011, 2012 **Model:** Cooper, Cooper Countryman **Engine:** 1.6L L4	**Ignition Coilpack A Primary/Secondary Circuit Malfunction:** Engine started, battery voltage must be at least 11.5v, all electrical components must be off, parking brake must be engaged (to keep daytime driving lights off), automatic transmission selector must be in park and the ground between the engine and the chassis must be well connected. The DME did not receive any valid pulses from the ignition module for the Ignition Coilpack A primary circuit. **NOTE: Ignition coils and power output stages are one component and cannot be replaced individually.**
DTC: P0420 T **Year:** 2011, 2012 **Model:** Cooper, Cooper Countryman **Engine:** 1.6L L4	**Catalyst System Efficiency (Bank 1) Below Threshold:** Engine started for longer than one second, battery voltage must be at least 11.5v, all electrical components must be off, parking brake must be engaged (to keep daytime driving lights off), automatic transmission selector must be in park, the exhaust system must be properly sealed between the catalytic converter and the cylinder head, coolant temperature must be at least 80 degrees Celsius and oxygen sensor heaters for oxygen sensors before the catalytic converter must be functioning properly and the ground between the engine and the chassis must be well connected. The DME detected the switch rate of the rear HO2S-12 was close to the switch rate of front HO2S (it should be much slower). The coolant temperature is greater than 80.25 degrees Celsius. The fuel system is in closed loop. The vehicle speed is between 28 and 80.8mph. The engine speed is between 1984 and 3648rpm. Exhaust gas temperature is between 450 and 700 degrees Celsius. Ambient pressure is 75.001kPa.

DTC	Trouble Code Title and Conditions
DTC: P0440 **2T , MIL: Yes** **Year:** 2011, 2012 **Model:** Cooper, Cooper Countryman **Engine:** 1.6L L4	**EVAP System Canister Purge Valve Monitoring (CPV stuck closed):** When the cut-off valve has been diagnosed as being fully functional, it is reopened and the EVAP CPV is closed. The EVAP CPV is then reopened when a certain DMTL pump current value is reached. When the current then decreases by a certain amount, the system is diagnosed as being in working order, or when the current then continues to increase, a malfunction is present in the EVAP CPV, in the cut-off valve, or in Line 1.
DTC: P0441 **2T** **Year:** 2011, 2012 **Model:** Cooper, Cooper Countryman **Engine:** 1.6L L4	**EVAP Control System Incorrect Purge Flow:** ECT sensor is cold during startup, engine started, battery voltage must be at least 11.5v, all electrical components must be off. The coolant temperature is less than 60 degrees Celsius, and the ambient pressure is greater than 76.2994kPa. The air intake temperature at start is between 9.04 and 16.04 degrees Celsius. The change in barometric pressure since engine start is less than 0.9998kPa. The vehicle speed is less than 74.56mph, and the purge valve has opened enough on previous driving cycle. The DME detected the switch rate of the rear HO2S-12 was close to the switch rate of front HO2S (it should be much slower). DME detected a problem in the EVAP system during the EVAP System Monitor test.
DTC: P0442 **2T** **Year:** 2011, 2012 **Model:** Cooper, Cooper Countryman **Engine:** 1.6L L4	**EVAP Control System Small Leak Detected:** Engine started, battery voltage must be at least 11.5v, all electrical components must be off. The DME detected a leak in the EVAP system as small as 0.040 inches during the EVAP Monitor Test. The coolant temperature is less than 60 degrees Celsius, and the ambient pressure is greater than 76.2994kPa. The air intake temperature at start is between 9.04 and 16.04 degrees Celsius. The change in barometric pressure since engine start is less than 0.9998kPa. The vehicle speed is less than 74.56mph, and the purge valve has opened enough on previous driving cycle.
DTC: P0443 **T** **Year:** 2011, 2012 **Model:** Cooper, Cooper Countryman **Engine:** 1.6L L4	**EVAP Vapor Management Valve Circuit Malfunction:** Engine started, battery voltage must be at least 11.5v, all electrical components must be off, parking brake must be engaged (to keep daytime driving lights off), automatic transmission selector must be in park, the exhaust system must be properly sealed between the catalytic converter and the cylinder head, coolant temperature must be at least 80 degrees Celsius and oxygen sensor heaters for oxygen sensors before the catalytic converter must be functioning properly and the ground between the engine and the chassis must be well connected. The DME detected an unexpected high or low voltage condition on the Vapor Management Valve (VMV) circuit when the device was cycled On/Off during testing.
DTC: P0444 **T** **Year:** 2011, 2012 **Model:** Cooper, Cooper Countryman **Engine:** 1.6L L4	**Evaporative Emission System Purge Control Valve Circuit Open:** Engine started, battery voltage must be at least 11.5v, all electrical components must be off, parking brake must be engaged (to keep daytime driving lights off), automatic transmission selector must be in park, the exhaust system must be properly sealed between the catalytic converter and the cylinder head, coolant temperature must be at least 80 degrees Celsius and oxygen sensor heaters for oxygen sensors before the catalytic converter must be functioning properly and the ground between the engine and the chassis must be well connected. The DME detected an unexpected voltage condition on the EVAP circuit when the device was cycled On/Off during testing.
DTC: P0445 **T** **Year:** 2011, 2012 **Model:** Cooper, Cooper Countryman **Engine:** 1.6L L4	**Evaporative Emission System Purge Control Valve Circuit Shorted:** Engine started, battery voltage must be at least 11.5v, all electrical components must be off, parking brake must be engaged (to keep daytime driving lights off), automatic transmission selector must be in park, the exhaust system must be properly sealed between the catalytic converter and the cylinder head, coolant temperature must be at least 80 degrees Celsius and oxygen sensor heaters for oxygen sensors before the catalytic converter must be functioning properly and the ground between the engine and the chassis must be well connected. The DME detected an unexpected voltage condition on the EVAP circuit when the device was cycled On/Off during testing.
DTC: P0455 **2T** **Year:** 2011, 2012 **Model:** Cooper, Cooper Countryman **Engine:** 1.6L L4	**EVAP Control System Large Leak Detected:** Engine started, battery voltage must be at least 11.5v, all electrical components must be off. The coolant temperature is less than 60 degrees Celsius, and the ambient pressure is greater than 76.2994kPa. The air intake temperature at start is between 9.04 and 16.04 degrees Celsius. The change in barometric pressure since engine start is less than 0.9998kPa. The vehicle speed is less than 74.56mph, and the purge valve has opened enough on previous driving cycle. The DME detected multiple small fuel vapor leaks; or it detected a large leak in the system during the leak test.
DTC: P0456 **2T** **Year:** 2011, 2012 **Model:** Cooper, Cooper Countryman **Engine:** 1.6L L4	**EVAP Control System Small Leak Detected:** Engine started, battery voltage must be at least 11.5v, all electrical components must be off. The coolant temperature is less than 60 degrees Celsius, and the ambient pressure is greater than 76.2994kPa. The air intake temperature at start is between 9.04 and 16.04 degrees Celsius. The change in barometric pressure since engine start is less than 0.9998kPa. The vehicle speed is less than 74.56mph, and the purge valve has opened enough on previous driving cycle. The DME detected multiple small fuel vapor leaks; or it detected a large leak in the system during the leak test.
DTC: P0462 **2T** **Year:** 2011, 2012 **Model:** Cooper, Cooper Countryman **Engine:** 1.6L L4	**Fuel Level Sensor Electrical Monitoring (Resistance is too low):** Both fuel level sensor signal lines are monitored for electrical faults by measuring the resistance in the signal lines. When the resistance is too low, a minimum fault code is set (P0462 for Fuel Level Sensor 1 or P2067 for Fuel Level Sensor 2). **NOTE: The fuel level sensor signal is transmitted via CAN-Bus and is monitored for both electrical and rationality faults.**

DTC	Trouble Code Title and Conditions
DTC: P0463 **2T** **Year:** 2011, 2012 **Model:** Cooper, Cooper Countryman **Engine:** 1.6L L4	**Fuel Level Sensor Electrical Monitoring:** Both fuel level sensor signal lines are monitored for electrical faults by measuring the resistance in the signal lines. When the resistance is too high, a maximim fault code is set (P0463 for Fuel Level Sensor 1 or P2068 for Fuel Level Sensor 2).
DTC: P0500 **2T** **Year:** 2011, 2012 **Model:** Cooper, Cooper Countryman **Engine:** 1.6L L4	**Vehicle Speed Sensor "A" Malfunction:** Engine started; engine speed above the TCC stall speed, and the DME detected a loss of the VSS signal over a period of time or the signal is not usable. **NOTE: The DME receives vehicle speed data from the VSS, TCSS, ABS module, CTM or GEM controller, depending up the application. Speed Signal from DSC too high because of possible tampering. Check DSC and wires.**
DTC: P0506 **2T** **Year:** 2011, 2012 **Model:** Cooper, Cooper Countryman **Engine:** 1.6L L4	**Idle Air Control System RPM Lower Than Expected:** Engine started, battery voltage must be at least 10.96v, all electrical components must be off, parking brake must be engaged (to keep daytime driving lights off), automatic transmission selector must be in park, the exhaust system must be properly sealed between the catalytic converter and the cylinder head, coolant temperature must be between 80.25 and 110.25 degrees Celsius and oxygen sensor heaters for oxygen sensors before the catalytic converter must be functioning properly and the ground between the engine and the chassis must be well connected. The DME detected it could not control the idle speed correctly, as it is constantly more than 100 rpm less than specification.
DTC: P0507 **2T** **Year:** 2011, 2012 **Model:** Cooper, Cooper Countryman **Engine:** 1.6L L4	**Idle Air Control System RPM Higher Than Expected:** Engine started, battery voltage must be at least 10.96v, all electrical components must be off, parking brake must be engaged (to keep daytime driving lights off), automatic transmission selector must be in park, the exhaust system must be properly sealed between the catalytic converter and the cylinder head, coolant temperature must be between 80.25 and 110.25 degrees Celsius and oxygen sensor heaters for oxygen sensors before the catalytic converter must be functioning properly and the ground between the engine and the chassis must be well connected. The DME detected it could not control the idle speed correctly, as it is constantly more than 200 rpm more than specification.
DTC: P0571 **T** **Year:** 2011, 2012 **Model:** Cooper, Cooper Countryman **Engine:** 1.6L L4	**Cruise/Brake Switch (A) Circuit Malfunction:** Engine started, battery voltage must be at least 11.5v, all electrical components must be off, parking brake must be engaged (to keep daytime driving lights off), automatic transmission selector must be in park, and the ground between the engine and the chassis must be well connected. The DME has detected a voltage value that is implausible or erratic.
DTC: P0601 **T** **Year:** 2011, 2012 **Model:** Cooper, Cooper Countryman **Engine:** 1.6L L4	**Internal Control Module Memory Check Sum Error:** Key on, the DME has detected a programming error. The RAM and ROM check displays an invalid check-sum at power up/down.
DTC: P0603 **T** **Year:** 2011, 2012 **Model:** Cooper, Cooper Countryman **Engine:** 1.6L L4	**DME Keep Alive Memory Test Error:** Key on, and the DME detected an internal memory fault. This code will set if KAPWR to the DME is interrupted (at the initial key on). Watchdog on.
DTC: P0604 **T** **Year:** 2011, 2012 **Model:** Cooper, Cooper Countryman **Engine:** 1.6L L4	**Internal Control Module Random Access Memory (RAM) Error:** Key on, and the DME detected an internal memory fault. This code will set if KAPWR to the DME is interrupted (at the initial key on). Watchdog on.
DTC: P0704 **T** **Year:** 2011, 2012 **Model:** Cooper, Cooper Countryman **Engine:** 1.6L L4	**Clutch Switch Input Circuit Malfunction:** Engine started, battery voltage must be at least 11.5v, all electrical components must be off, parking brake must be engaged (to keep daytime driving lights off), automatic transmission selector must be in park, and the ground between the engine and the chassis must be well connected. The DME detected a voltage outside the normal performance range to allow the system to properly function.

DTC	Trouble Code Title and Conditions
DTC: P0705 **T** **Year:** 2011, 2012 **Model:** Cooper, Cooper Countryman **Engine:** 1.6L L4	**TR Sensor Circuit Malfunction:** Engine started, battery voltage must be at least 11.5v, all electrical components must be off, parking brake must be engaged (to keep daytime driving lights off), automatic transmission selector must be in park, and the ground between the engine and the chassis must be well connected. The DME detected a voltage or signal outside the normal performance range to allow the system to properly function. The engine speed is between 200 and 440rpm.
DTC: P0712 **T** **Year:** 2011, 2012 **Model:** Cooper, Cooper Countryman **Engine:** 1.6L L4	**Oil Temperature Sensor Circuit Low Input:** Engine started, battery voltage must be at least 11.5v, all electrical components must be off, parking brake must be engaged (to keep daytime driving lights off), automatic transmission selector must be in park, and the ground between the engine and the chassis must be well connected. The DME detected the oil temperature sensor was less than its minimum self-test range in the test.
DTC: P0713 **T** **Year:** 2011, 2012 **Model:** Cooper, Cooper Countryman **Engine:** 1.6L L4	**Oil Temperature Sensor Circuit High Input:** Engine started, battery voltage must be at least 11.5v, all electrical components must be off, parking brake must be engaged (to keep daytime driving lights off), automatic transmission selector must be in park, and the ground between the engine and the chassis must be well connected. The DME detected the oil temperature sensor was more than its maximum self-test range in the test.
DTC: P0721 **T** **Year:** 2011, 2012 **Model:** Cooper, Cooper Countryman **Engine:** 1.6L L4	**A/T Output Shaft Speed Sensor Noise Interference:** Engine started, VSS signal more than 1 mph, and the DME detected "noise" interference on the Output Shaft Speed (OSS) sensor circuit. The calculation of the road speed impossible, as the indicated speed is less than the minimum road speed value and the timer expired.

OBD II Trouble Code List (P1XXX Codes)

DTC	Trouble Code Title and Conditions
DTC: P1106 **2T** **Year:** 2011, 2012 **Model:** Cooper, Cooper Countryman **Engine:** 1.6L L4	**Manifold Pressure Too Low at Full Load for Low Engine Speed:** Engine started, battery voltage must be at least 11v, and the differential pressure sensor detected a control deviation at the minimum limit. The closed loop control of the differential pressure in the intake manifold is suspended and replaced by a direct specification. The engine speed is less than 4000rpm. The manifold pressure is less than 600hPa.
DTC: P1107 **2T** **Year:** 2011, 2012 **Model:** Cooper, Cooper Countryman **Engine:** 1.6L L4	**Manifold Pressure Too Low at Idle:** Engine started, battery voltage must be at least 11v, and the differential pressure sensor detected a control deviation at the minimum limit. The closed loop control of the differential pressure in the intake manifold is suspended and replaced by a direct specification. The engine speed is less than 1504rpm. The manifold pressure is less than 120hPa.
DTC: P1108 **2T** **Year:** 2011, 2012 **Model:** Cooper, Cooper Countryman **Engine:** 1.6L L4	**Manifold Pressure Too Low at Stable and in Full Load for Low Engine Speed:** Engine started, battery voltage must be at least 11v, and the differential pressure sensor detected a control deviation at the minimum limit. The closed loop control of the differential pressure in the intake manifold is suspended and replaced by a direct specification. The engine speed is less than 4000rpm. The manifold pressure is less than 600hPa.
DTC: P1109 **2T** **Year:** 2011, 2012 **Model:** Cooper, Cooper Countryman **Engine:** 1.6L L4	**Manifold Pressure Too High During Deceleration:** Engine started, battery voltage must be at least 11v, and the differential pressure sensor detected a control deviation at the minimum limit. The closed loop control of the differential pressure in the intake manifold is suspended and replaced by a direct specification. The engine speed is greater than 1696rpm. The manifold pressure is greater than 600hPa.
DTC: P1122 **2T** **Year:** 2011, 2012 **Model:** Cooper, Cooper Countryman **Engine:** 1.6L L4	**Accelerator Pedal Position Sensor 'D' Circuit Low Input:** Engine started, battery voltage at least 11.5v, all electrical components off, ground connections between engine and chassis well connected, the DME detected that the accelerator pedal position sensor signal was outside the parameters to function normally. **NOTE: Both the Throttle Position (TP) Sensor and Accelerator Pedal Position Sensor are located at the accelerator pedal module and communicate the driver's intentions to the DME completely independently of each other. Both sensors are stored in one housing.**

DTC	Trouble Code Title and Conditions
DTC: P1123 2T **Year:** 2011, 2012 **Model:** Cooper, Cooper Countryman **Engine:** 1.6L L4	**Accelerator Pedal Position Sensor 'D' Circuit High Input:** Engine started, battery voltage at least 11.5v, all electrical components off, ground connections between engine and chassis well connected, the DME detected that the accelerator pedal position sensor signal was outside the parameters to function normally. **NOTE: Both the Throttle Position (TP) Sensor and Accelerator Pedal Position Sensor are located at the accelerator pedal module and communicate the driver's intentions to the DME completely independently of each other. Both sensors are stored in one housing.**
DTC: P1125 2T **Year:** 2011, 2012 **Model:** Cooper, Cooper Countryman **Engine:** 1.6L L4	**Throttle/Pedal Position Sensor Circuit Plausibility Error:** Engine started, at idle, the temperature must be at least 80 degrees Celsius. The throttle position sensor supplies implausible signal to the DME. The difference between the TPS1 and the TPS2 is greater than five percent.
DTC: P1126 2T **Year:** 2011, 2012 **Model:** Cooper, Cooper Countryman **Engine:** 1.6L L4	**Throttle/Pedal Position Sensor Circuit Large Plausibility Error:** Engine started, at idle, the temperature must be at least 80 degrees Celsius. The throttle position sensor supplies implausible signal to the DME. The difference between the TPS1 and the TPS2 is greater than five percent.
DTC: P1143 2T **Year:** 2011, 2012 **Model:** Cooper, Cooper Countryman **Engine:** 1.6L L4	**O2 Sensor Signal Stuck Lean Bank 1 Sensor 2:** Engine started, battery voltage must be at least 11.5v, all electrical components must be off, parking brake must be engaged (to keep daytime driving lights off), automatic transmission selector must be in park. The DME detected an unexpected voltage condition, or it detected an unexpected current draw in the heater circuit during the CCM test. Coolant temperature must been at least 80.25 degrees Celsius. The vehicle speed is greater than 27.96 and less than 80.76. The engine speed is between 1984 and 3647rpm. Ambient pressure is greater than 75.001kPa and the engine stability load is 6.94g/s. **NOTE: Vehicle must be raised before connector for oxygen sensors is accessible.**
DTC: P1144 2T **Year:** 2011, 2012 **Model:** Cooper, Cooper Countryman **Engine:** 1.6L L4	**O2 Sensor Signal Stuck Rich Bank 1 Sensor 2:** Engine started, battery voltage must be at least 11.5v, all electrical components must be off, parking brake must be engaged (to keep daytime driving lights off), automatic transmission selector must be in park. The DME detected an unexpected voltage condition, or it detected an unexpected current draw in the heater circuit during the CCM test. Coolant temperature must been at least 80.25 degrees Celsius. The vehicle speed is greater than 27.96 and less than 80.76. The engine speed is between 1984 and 3647rpm. Ambient pressure is greater than 75.001kPa and the engine stability load is 6.94g/s. **NOTE: Vehicle must be raised before connector for oxygen sensors is accessible.**
DTC: P115C 1T , MIL: Yes **Year:** 2011, 2012 **Model:** Cooper, Cooper Countryman **Engine:** 1.6L L4	**Mass Air Flow Rationality and Range Monitoring:** The MAF rate into the cylinder is calculated and is dependant on the engine speed, valve-lift, the intake CMP, the exhaust CMP, and the manifold pressure. This calculated MAF rate is also corrected, which depends on the IAT, the ECT, and the manifold pressure. The ratio between the measured MAF and the calculated MAF needs to remain within adjustable minimum and maximum threshold values. When these threshold values are exceeded, a time counter is incremented. When this counter reaches its threshold value within one diagnostic cycle, a MAF meter malfunction is detected.
DTC: P115D 1T , MIL: Yes **Year:** 2011, 2012 **Model:** Cooper, Cooper Countryman **Engine:** 1.6L L4	**Mass Air Flow Rationality and Range Monitoring:** The MAF rate into the cylinder is calculated and is dependant on the engine speed, valve-lift, the intake CMP, the exhaust CMP, and the manifold pressure. This calculated MAF rate is also corrected, which depends on the IAT, the ECT, and the manifold pressure. The ratio between the measured MAF and the calculated MAF needs to remain within adjustable minimum and maximum threshold values. When these threshold values are exceeded, a time counter is incremented. When this counter reaches its threshold value within one diagnostic cycle, a MAF meter malfunction is detected.
DTC: P1222 2T **Year:** 2011, 2012 **Model:** Cooper, Cooper Countryman **Engine:** 1.6L L4	**Accelerator Pedal Position Sensor 'E' Circuit Low Input:** Engine started, battery voltage at least 11.5v, all electrical components off, ground connections between engine and chassis well connected, the DME detected that the accelerator pedal position sensor signal was outside the parameters to function normally. **NOTE: Both the Throttle Position (TP) Sensor and Accelerator Pedal Position Sensor are located at the accelerator pedal module and communicate the driver's intentions to the DME completely independently of each other. Both sensors are stored in one housing.**
DTC: P1223 2T **Year:** 2011, 2012 **Model:** Cooper, Cooper Countryman **Engine:** 1.6L L4	**Accelerator Pedal Position Sensor 'E' Circuit High Input:** Engine started, battery voltage at least 11.5v, all electrical components off, ground connections between engine and chassis well connected, the DME detected that the accelerator pedal position sensor signal was outside the parameters to function normally. **NOTE: Both the Throttle Position (TP) Sensor and Accelerator Pedal Position Sensor are located at the accelerator pedal module and communicate the driver's intentions to the DME completely independently of each other. Both sensors are stored in one housing.**

DTC	Trouble Code Title and Conditions
DTC: P1224 2T **Year:** 2011, 2012 **Model:** Cooper, Cooper Countryman **Engine:** 1.6L L4	**Throttle Position Sensor D/E Voltage Correlation:** Engine started, battery voltage must be at least 11.5v, all electrical components must be off, parking brake must be engaged (to keep daytime driving lights off), automatic transmission selector must be in park; and the DME detected the Throttle Position 'D' (TPD) and Throttle Position 'B' (TPE) sensors disagreed, or that the TPD sensor should not be in its detected position, or that the TPE sensor should not be in its detected position during testing. **NOTE: Both the Throttle Position (TP) Sensor and Accelerator Pedal Position Sensor are located at the accelerator pedal module and communicate the driver's intentions to the DME completely independently of each other. Both sensors are stored in one housing.**
DTC: P1229 2T **Year:** 2011, 2012 **Model:** Cooper, Cooper Countryman **Engine:** 1.6L L4	**Throttle/Pedal Position Sensor Adaptation Outside Tolerance:** Engine started, at idle, the temperature must be at least 80 degrees Celsius. The throttle position sensor supplies implausible signal to the DME and is outside the specified tolerance. The measured max/min TPS values within the limits is greater than 0.0244 volts.
DTC: P1320 2T **Year:** 2011, 2012 **Model:** Cooper, Cooper Countryman **Engine:** 1.6L L4	**Misfire Detected Crankshaft Segment Adaptation:** Engine running under positive torque conditions, and the DME detected a misfire or uneven engine function as well as the crankshaft adaptation at its limit. **NOTE: If the misfire is severe, the MIL will flash on/off on the 1st trip!**
DTC: P1321 2T **Year:** 2011, 2012 **Model:** Cooper, Cooper Countryman **Engine:** 1.6L L4	**Misfire Crank Wheel Tooth Count:** Engine running under positive torque conditions, and the DME detected a misfire or uneven engine function as well as a tooth error of plus or minus one or two teeth during the count. **NOTE: If the misfire is severe, the MIL will flash on/off on the 1st trip!**
DTC: P1366 2T **Year:** 2011, 2012 **Model:** Cooper, Cooper Countryman **Engine:** 1.6L L4	**Ignition Coilpack A Primary/Secondary Circuit Malfunction Open Circuit/Short to Ground:** Engine started, battery voltage must be at least 11.5v, all electrical components must be off, parking brake must be engaged (to keep daytime driving lights off), automatic transmission selector must be in park and the ground between the engine and the chassis must be well connected. The DME did not receive any valid pulses from the ignition module for the Ignition Coilpack A primary circuit. **NOTE: Ignition coils and power output stages are one component and cannot be replaced individually.**
DTC: P1367 2T **Year:** 2011, 2012 **Model:** Cooper, Cooper Countryman **Engine:** 1.6L L4	**Ignition Coilpack A Primary/Secondary Circuit Malfunction Open Circuit/Short to Ground:** Engine started, battery voltage must be at least 11.5v, all electrical components must be off, parking brake must be engaged (to keep daytime driving lights off), automatic transmission selector must be in park and the ground between the engine and the chassis must be well connected. The DME did not receive any valid pulses from the ignition module for the Ignition Coilpack A primary circuit. **NOTE: Ignition coils and power output stages are one component and cannot be replaced individually.**
DTC: P1436 2T **Year:** 2011, 2012 **Model:** Cooper, Cooper Countryman **Engine:** 1.6L L4	**EVAP Leak Detection Pump (LDP) Control Circuit Open:** Engine started, battery voltage must be at least 11.5v, all electrical components must be off, parking brake must be engaged (to keep daytime driving lights off), automatic transmission selector must be in park, the exhaust system must be properly sealed between the catalytic converter and the cylinder head, coolant temperature must be at least 80 degrees Celsius and oxygen sensor heaters for oxygen sensors before the catalytic converter must be functioning properly and the ground between the engine and the chassis must be well connected. The DME detected voltage irregularity in the leak detection pump control circuit.
DTC: P1437 2T **Year:** 2011, 2012 **Model:** Cooper, Cooper Countryman **Engine:** 1.6L L4	**EVAP Emission Control LDP Circuit Malfunction Pump Problem:** Key on, KOEO Self-Test enabled, and the DME detected an unexpected voltage condition on the EVAP emission control leak detection pump circuit. The reed switch level stays low after activation of solenoids within the time threshold of more than 1 second. The coolant temperature is less than 60 degrees Celsius, and the ambient pressure is greater than 76.2994kPa. The air intake temperature at start is between 9.04 and 16.04 degrees Celsius. The change in barometric pressure since engine start is less than 0.9998kPa. The vehicle speed is less than 74.56mph, and the purge valve has opened enough on previous driving cycle.
DTC: P1439D 2T , MIL: Yes **Year:** 2011, 2012 **Model:** Cooper, Cooper Countryman **Engine:** 1.6L L4	**EVAP System Canister Purge Valve Monitoring (Cut-off valve stuck open):** When the current value remains above the threshold value, the system DMTL pump continues to pump pressure into the EVAP System. When a certain current value is achieved, the cut-off valve is monitored by closing the cut-off valve and opening the EVAP CPV. The system is diagnosed as being in working order when the current continues to increase. When the current decreases by a certain amount, however, a stuck open cut-off valve is detected (P149D).

DTC	Trouble Code Title and Conditions
DTC: P143F **2T** **Year:** 2011, 2012 **Model:** Cooper, Cooper Countryman **Engine:** 1.6L L4	**EVAP System Canister Purge Valve Monitoring (CPV Malfunction):** After the DMTL Leak Detection Monitor has been executed, the cut-off valve is closed and the EVAP CPV is opened. When the current decreases by a certain amount, the EVAP CPV and Line 2 are diagnosed as being in working order. When the current does not decrease, a malfunction is detected in the EVAP CPV or in Line 2.
DTC: P1442 **2T** **Year:** 2011, 2012 **Model:** Cooper, Cooper Countryman **Engine:** 1.6L L4	**EVAP Leak Detection Pump Control Circuit Low:** Engine started, battery voltage must be at least 11.5v, all electrical components must be off, parking brake must be engaged (to keep daytime driving lights off), automatic transmission selector must be in park, the exhaust system must be properly sealed between the catalytic converter and the cylinder head, coolant temperature must be at least 80 degrees Celsius and oxygen sensor heaters for oxygen sensors before the catalytic converter must be functioning properly and the ground between the engine and the chassis must be well connected. The DME detected voltage irregularity in the leak detection pump control circuit.
DTC: P1443 **2T** **Year:** 2011, 2012 **Model:** Cooper, Cooper Countryman **Engine:** 1.6L L4	**EVAP Leak Detection Pump Control Circuit High:** Engine started, battery voltage must be at least 11.5v, all electrical components must be off, parking brake must be engaged (to keep daytime driving lights off), automatic transmission selector must be in park, the exhaust system must be properly sealed between the catalytic converter and the cylinder head, coolant temperature must be at least 80 degrees Celsius and oxygen sensor heaters for oxygen sensors before the catalytic converter must be functioning properly and the ground between the engine and the chassis must be well connected. The DME detected voltage irregularity in the leak detection pump control circuit.
DTC: P144B **2T** **Year:** 2011, 2012 **Model:** Cooper, Cooper Countryman **Engine:** 1.6L L4	**Fuel Level Sensor Rationality Monitoring:** The rationality of the fuel level sensors is monitored by comparing the calculated fuel consumption value during the current DC to the measured fuel level change value. The error condition is fulfilled when this deviation exceeds the calibrated threshold value. This monitor can be performed over the duration of several consecutive DCs, since a significant change in the measured fuel level or in the calculated fuel level needs to occur in order for the diagnostic result to be reliable. When this change in the measured fuel level reaches or exceeds the calirbrated threshold value and the error condition explained in the paragraph above has been fulfilled, a fuel level sensor rationality fault is set. The diagnostic is reset when re-fueling or de-fueling is detected or when a diagnostic result has been achieved, i.e. achieving a passing result or setting a fault code. **NOTE: The fuel level sensor signal is transmitted via CAN-Bus and is monitored for both electrical and rationality faults.**
DTC: P1475 **2T** **Year:** 2011, 2012 **Model:** Cooper, Cooper Countryman **Engine:** 1.6L L4	**EVAP Emission Control LDP Circuit Malfunction:** Key on, KOEO Self-Test enabled, and the DME detected an unexpected voltage condition on the EVAP emission control leak detection pump circuit. The reed switch level stays high after activation of solenoids within the time threshold of more than 0.5 seconds. The coolant temperature is less than 60 degrees Celsius, and the ambient pressure is greater than 76.2994kPa. The air intake temperature at start is between 9.04 and 16.04 degrees Celsius. The change in barometric pressure since engine start is less than 0.9998kPa. The vehicle speed is less than 74.56mph, and the purge valve has opened enough on previous driving cycle.
DTC: P1476 **2T** **Year:** 2011, 2012 **Model:** Cooper, Cooper Countryman **Engine:** 1.6L L4	**EVAP Emission Control LDP Circuit Malfunction/Insufficient Vacuum:** Key on, KOEO Self-Test enabled, and the DME detected an unexpected voltage condition on the EVAP emission control leak detection pump circuit. There is a clamped tube during the time period of any of the five first pump cycles. The coolant temperature is less than 60 degrees Celsius, and the ambient pressure is greater than 76.2994kPa. The air intake temperature at start is between 9.04 and 16.04 degrees Celsius. The change in barometric pressure since engine start is less than 0.9998kPa. The vehicle speed is less than 74.56mph, and the purge valve has opened enough on previous driving cycle.
DTC: P1477 **2T** **Year:** 2011, 2012 **Model:** Cooper, Cooper Countryman **Engine:** 1.6L L4	**EVAP Emission Control LDP Circuit Malfunction:** Key on, KOEO Self-Test enabled, and the DME detected an unexpected voltage condition on the EVAP emission control leak detection pump circuit. The reed switch level stays continuously low after activation of solenoids within the time threshold of more than 1 second. The coolant temperature is less than 60 degrees Celsius, and the ambient pressure is greater than 76.2994kPa. The air intake temperature at start is between 9.04 and 16.04 degrees Celsius. The change in barometric pressure since engine start is less than 0.9998kPa. The vehicle speed is less than 74.56mph, and the purge valve has opened enough on previous driving cycle.
DTC: P1600 **2T** **Year:** 2011, 2012 **Model:** Cooper, Cooper Countryman **Engine:** 1.6L L4	**Internal Control Module Random Access Memory (RAM) Error:** Key on, and the DME detected an internal memory fault. This code will set if KAPWR to the DME is interrupted (at the initial key on). Watchdog on.
DTC: P1607 **2T** **Year:** 2011, 2012 **Model:** Cooper, Cooper Countryman **Engine:** 1.6L L4	**CAN Bus Error:** Engine started, VSS over 1 mph, and the DME detected a problem in the CAN Bus system during the self-test.

DTC	Trouble Code Title and Conditions
DTC: P1611 **2T** **Year:** 2011, 2012 **Model:** Cooper, Cooper Countryman **Engine:** 1.6L L4	**MIL Call-Up Circuit, Transmission Control Module Short to Ground:** Engine started, VSS over 1 mph, and the DME detected a problem in the Transmission Control system during the self-test.
DTC: P1612 **2T** **Year:** 2011, 2012 **Model:** Cooper, Cooper Countryman **Engine:** 1.6L L4	**INSTR Module Error:** Engine started, VSS over 1 mph, and the DME detected a problem in the INSTR Module system during the self-test.
DTC: P1613 **2T** **Year:** 2011, 2012 **Model:** Cooper, Cooper Countryman **Engine:** 1.6L L4	**ASC Error:** Engine started, VSS over 1 mph, and the DME detected a problem in the ASC system during the self-test.
DTC: P1615 **2T** **Year:** 2011, 2012 **Model:** Cooper, Cooper Countryman **Engine:** 1.6L L4	**SPI-Bus Error:** Engine started, VSS over 1 mph, and the DME detected a problem in the SPI Bus system during the self-test.
DTC: P1679 **1T** **Year:** 2011, 2012 **Model:** Cooper, Cooper Countryman **Engine:** 1.6L L4	**Monitoring of Torque Losses:** Key on, engine running, the DME has detected that there is an error in the torque loss calculation. The limit was exceeded in the threshold map during the first 360 ms of operation.
DTC: P1680 **1T** **Year:** 2011, 2012 **Model:** Cooper, Cooper Countryman **Engine:** 1.6L L4	**Monitoring of A to D Conversion:** Key on, engine running to at least 1200rpm, the DME has detected that the PVS ratio differences exceeds the threshold greater than 0.273 volts.
DTC: P1681 **1T** **Year:** 2011, 2012 **Model:** Cooper, Cooper Countryman **Engine:** 1.6L L4	**Monitoring of Engine Speed:** Key on, engine running to at least 1200rpm, the DME has detected that the engine speed difference exceeds the threshold of 576rpm
DTC: P1682 **1T** **Year:** 2011, 2012 **Model:** Cooper, Cooper Countryman **Engine:** 1.6L L4	**Idle Speed Control, Monitoring of the Proportional Derivative:** Key on, engine running to at least 1200rpm, the DME has detected that there is an error in the torque demand from the proportional derivative part. The maximum limit has been exceeded.
DTC: P1683 **1T** **Year:** 2011, 2012 **Model:** Cooper, Cooper Countryman **Engine:** 1.6L L4	**Idle Speed Control, Monitoring of the Integral Part:** Key on, engine running to at least 1200rpm, the DME has detected that there is an error in the torque demand from the integral part is greater than 25NM.

DTC	Trouble Code Title and Conditions
DTC: P1684 1T **Year:** 2011, 2012 **Model:** Cooper, Cooper Countryman **Engine:** 1.6L L4	**Monitoring of Minimum Torque at Clutch:** Key on, engine running, the DME has detected that there is an error in the minimum torque at the clutch calculation. The limit was exceeded in the threshold map.
DTC: P1685 1T **Year:** 2011, 2012 **Model:** Cooper, Cooper Countryman **Engine:** 1.6L L4	**Monitoring of Maximum Torque at Clutch:** Key on, engine running, the DME has detected that there is an error in the maximum torque at the clutch calculation. The limit was exceeded in the threshold map.
DTC: P1686 1T **Year:** 2011, 2012 **Model:** Cooper, Cooper Countryman **Engine:** 1.6L L4	**Monitoring of Pedal Values:** Key on, engine running, the DME has detected that there is an error in pedal value checks. The difference exceeds the threshold map by 15.23 to 28.91 percent.
DTC: P1687 1T **Year:** 2011, 2012 **Model:** Cooper, Cooper Countryman **Engine:** 1.6L L4	**Monitoring of Throttle Position:** Key on, engine running, the DME has detected that there is an error in the throttle position sensor ratio calculation by greater than 0.313 volts.
DTC: P1688 1T **Year:** 2011, 2012 **Model:** Cooper, Cooper Countryman **Engine:** 1.6L L4	**Monitoring of Mass Airflow:** Key on, engine running, the DME has detected that there is an error in the MAF calculation. The limit was exceeded in the threshold map by 0.044 to 0.218g/rev.
DTC: P1689 1T **Year:** 2011, 2012 **Model:** Cooper, Cooper Countryman **Engine:** 1.6L L4	**Monitoring of Actual Indicated Engine Torque:** Key on, engine running, the DME has detected that there is an error in the maximum torque at the clutch calculation. The limit was exceeded in the threshold map by 30 to 38NM.
DTC: P1691 1T **Year:** 2011, 2012 **Model:** Cooper, Cooper Countryman **Engine:** 1.6L L4	**Monitoring of Engine Speed Limit in Limp Home:** Key on, engine running, the DME has detected that monitoring of the engine speed limit in limp home condition exceeds the threshold map by greater than 2656rpm.
DTC: P1692 1T **Year:** 2011, 2012 **Model:** Cooper, Cooper Countryman **Engine:** 1.6L L4	**Monitoring of Processor Calculations:** Key on, engine running, the DME has detected that there is an error in the for the final request for disabled power stages of MTC and IV.
DTC: P1693 1T **Year:** 2011, 2012 **Model:** Cooper, Cooper Countryman **Engine:** 1.6L L4	**Monitoring of Processor Calculations:** Key on, engine running, the DME has detected that there is an error in the for the temporary request for disabled power stages of MTC and IV.

DTC	Trouble Code Title and Conditions
DTC: P1698 **1T** **Year:** 2011, 2012 **Model:** Cooper, Cooper Countryman **Engine:** 1.6L L4	**ECU Functionality Incorrect:** The ECU Functionality is in error as there are internal errors. This test is performed by the GIB (Gearbox Interface Box), a system dedicated to low level control of the transmission control unit.
DTC: P1699 **1T** **Year:** 2011, 2012 **Model:** Cooper, Cooper Countryman **Engine:** 1.6L L4	**EPROM Checksum Incorrect:** The EPROM Checksum is incorrect. This test is performed by the GIB (Gearbox Interface Box), a system dedicated to low level control of the transmission control unit.
DTC: P1705 **2T** **Year:** 2011, 2012 **Model:** Cooper, Cooper Countryman **Engine:** 1.6L L4	**LED Drives Plausibility:** Key on or engine running; and the DME detected an implausible signal (fault performed by the Gearbox Interface Box). The battery voltage is greater than 9 volts and the CAN Bus is operational.
DTC: P1706 **2T** **Year:** 2011, 2012 **Model:** Cooper, Cooper Countryman **Engine:** 1.6L L4	**LED Drives Short Circuit:** Key on or engine running; and the DME detected short circuit (fault performed by the Gearbox Interface Box). The battery voltage is greater than 9 volts and the CAN Bus is operational.
DTC: P1739 **2T** **Year:** 2011, 2012 **Model:** Cooper, Cooper Countryman **Engine:** 1.6L L4	**Clutch Solenoid Circuit Communication Error:** The clutch solenoid circuit signal is implausible or missing. This test is performed by the GIB (Gearbox Interface Box), a system dedicated to low level control of the transmission control unit.
DTC: P1741 **2T** **Year:** 2011, 2012 **Model:** Cooper, Cooper Countryman **Engine:** 1.6L L4	**Clutch Solenoid Circuit Open Circuit:** The clutch solenoid circuit continuity is in error. This test is performed by the GIB (Gearbox Interface Box), a system dedicated to low level control of the transmission control unit.
DTC: P1742 **2T** **Year:** 2011, 2012 **Model:** Cooper, Cooper Countryman **Engine:** 1.6L L4	**Clutch Solenoid Circuit Short Circuit:** The clutch solenoid circuit continuity is in error. This test is performed by the GIB (Gearbox Interface Box), a system dedicated to low level control of the transmission control unit.

OBD II Trouble Code List (P2XXX Codes)

DTC	Trouble Code Title, Conditions, Possible Causes
DTC: P2067 **2T** **Year:** 2011, 2012 **Model:** Cooper, Cooper Countryman **Engine:** 1.6L L4	**Fuel Level Sensor Electrical Monitoring (Resistance is too low):** Both fuel level sensor signal lines are monitored for electrical faults by measuring the resistance in the signal lines. When the resistance is too low, a minimum fault code is set (P0462 for Fuel Level Sensor 1 or P2067 for Fuel Level Sensor 2).
DTC: P2068 **2T** **Year:** 2011, 2012 **Model:** Cooper, Cooper Countryman **Engine:** 1.6L L4	**Fuel Level Sensor Electrical Monitoring:** When the resistance is too high, a maximim fault code is set (P0463 for Fuel Level Sensor 1 or P2068 for Fuel Level Sensor 2). **NOTE: The fuel level sensor signal is transmitted via CAN-Bus and is monitored for both electrical and rationality faults.**

DTC	Trouble Code Title, Conditions, Possible Causes
DTC: P2096 **2T** **Year:** 2011, 2012 **Model:** Cooper, Cooper Countryman **Engine:** 1.6L L4	**Post Catalyst Fuel Trim System Too Lean (Bank 1):** Engine started, battery voltage must be at least 11.5v, all electrical components must be off, the ground between the engine and the chassis must be well connected, the exhaust system must be properly sealed between the catalytic converter and the cylinder head, and the oxygen sensor heater for oxygen sensor before the catalytic converter must be properly functioning. The DME detected a problem with the fuel mixture. Trim control 1 segment (precision controller with oxygen sensor behind cat.) below delta lambda threshold of less than -1.56. Coolant temperature greater than 45 degrees Celsius. O2 heaters ready, fuel system in a closed loop, but the rear O2 sensor is in voltage outside the parameters. **NOTE: For resistance testing of sensor heating, oxygen sensor should be cooled to ambient temperature. High temperatures at oxygen sensor may lead to inaccurate measurements.**
DTC: P2097 **2T** **Year:** 2011, 2012 **Model:** Cooper, Cooper Countryman **Engine:** 1.6L L4	**Post Catalyst Fuel Trim System Too Rich (Bank 1):** Engine started, battery voltage must be at least 11.5v, all electrical components must be off, the ground between the engine and the chassis must be well connected, the exhaust system must be properly sealed between the catalytic converter and the cylinder head, and the oxygen sensor heater for oxygen sensor before the catalytic converter must be properly functioning. The DME detected a problem with the fuel mixture. Trim control 1 segment (precision controller with oxygen sensor behind cat.) below delta lambda threshold of less than -1.56. Coolant temperature greater than 45 degrees Celsius. O2 heaters ready, fuel system in a closed loop, but the rear O2 sensor is in voltage outside the parameters. **NOTE: For resistance testing of sensor heating, oxygen sensor should be cooled to ambient temperature. High temperatures at oxygen sensor may lead to inaccurate measurements.**
DTC: P2122 **T** **Year:** 2011, 2012 **Model:** Cooper, Cooper Countryman **Engine:** 1.6L L4	**Accelerator Pedal Position Sensor 'D' Circuit Low Input:** Engine started, battery voltage at least 11.5v, all electrical components off, ground connections between engine and chassis well connected, the DME detected that the accelerator pedal position sensor signal was outside the parameters to function normally. **NOTE: Both the Throttle Position (TP) Sensor and Accelerator Pedal Position Sensor are located at the accelerator pedal module and communicate the driver's intentions to the DME completely independently of each other. Both sensors are stored in one housing.**
DTC: P2123 **T** **Year:** 2011, 2012 **Model:** Cooper, Cooper Countryman **Engine:** 1.6L L4	**Accelerator Pedal Position Sensor 'D' Circuit High Input:** Engine started, battery voltage at least 11.5v, all electrical components off, ground connections between engine and chassis well connected, the DME detected that the accelerator pedal position sensor signal was outside the parameters to function normally. **NOTE: Both the Throttle Position (TP) Sensor and Accelerator Pedal Position Sensor are located at the accelerator pedal module and communicate the driver's intentions to the DME completely independently of each other. Both sensors are stored in one housing.**
DTC: P2127 **T** **Year:** 2011, 2012 **Model:** Cooper, Cooper Countryman **Engine:** 1.6L L4	**Accelerator Pedal Position Sensor 'E' Circuit Low Input:** Engine started, battery voltage at least 11.5v, all electrical components off, ground connections between engine and chassis well connected, the DME detected that the accelerator pedal position sensor signal was outside the parameters to function normally. **NOTE: Both the Throttle Position (TP) Sensor and Accelerator Pedal Position Sensor are located at the accelerator pedal module and communicate the driver's intentions to the DME completely independently of each other. Both sensors are stored in one housing.**
DTC: P2128 **T** **Year:** 2011, 2012 **Model:** Cooper, Cooper Countryman **Engine:** 1.6L L4	**Accelerator Pedal Position Sensor 'E' Circuit High Input:** Engine started, battery voltage at least 11.5v, all electrical components off, ground connections between engine and chassis well connected, the DME detected that the accelerator pedal position sensor signal was outside the parameters to function normally. **NOTE: Both the Throttle Position (TP) Sensor and Accelerator Pedal Position Sensor are located at the accelerator pedal module and communicate the driver's intentions to the DME completely independently of each other. Both sensors are stored in one housing.**
DTC: P2138 **T** **Year:** 2011, 2012 **Model:** Cooper, Cooper Countryman **Engine:** 1.6L L4	**Throttle Position Sensor D/E Voltage Correlation:** Engine started, battery voltage must be at least 11.5v, all electrical components must be off, parking brake must be engaged (to keep daytime driving lights off), automatic transmission selector must be in park; and the DME detected the Throttle Position 'D' (TPD) and Throttle Position 'B' (TPE) sensors disagreed, or that the TPD sensor should not be in its detected position, or that the TPE sensor should not be in its detected position during testing. **NOTE: Both the Throttle Position (TP) Sensor and Accelerator Pedal Position Sensor are located at the accelerator pedal module and communicate the driver's intentions to the DME completely independently of each other. Both sensors are stored in one housing.**

DTC	Trouble Code Title, Conditions, Possible Causes
DTC: P2177 **2T , MIL: Yes** **Year:** 2011, 2012 **Model:** Cooper, Cooper Countryman **Engine:** 1.6L L4	**Fuel System Monitoring-Lambda Adaptation:** The fuel system diagnostic utilizes two separate monitors. The first monitor assesses the percentage of the long-term fuel adaptation. The second monitor assesses the percentage of the short-term FT's physical limits. The short-term FT monitor is enabled in every engine state except for DFCO. The long-term FT monitor is enabled during its learning process and is inhibited during EVAP canister purge phases. Therefore, an additional learning process can be initiated when large short-term FT deviations occur and the assessment can be executed. Separate counters are started for both assessments. When neither a lean condition nor a rich condition is detected, the end diagnostic counter is decremented from a calibratable value to zero and a passing decision is made. When a lean condition is present and the total fuel control exceeds the calibrated threshold value, a time counter is incremented. When the time counter exceeds the calibrated threshold value, a lean error is set. When a rich condition is present and the total fuel control falls below the calibrated threshold value, a time counter is incremented. When the time counter exceeds the calibrated threshold value, a rich error is set. The time counters are incremented while the "lambda controller" or the "lambda adaptation" exceeds minimum or maximum threshold values. A malfunction is detected as soon as one of the time counters reaches its respective maximum value.
DTC: P2178 **1T , MIL: Yes** **Year:** 2011, 2012 **Model:** Cooper, Cooper Countryman **Engine:** 1.6L L4	**Fuel System Monitoring-Lambda Adaptation:** The fuel system diagnostic utilizes two separate monitors. The first monitor assesses the percentage of the long-term fuel adaptation. The second monitor assesses the percentage of the short-term FT's physical limits. The short-term FT monitor is enabled in every engine state except for DFCO. The long-term FT monitor is enabled during its learning process and is inhibited during EVAP canister purge phases. Therefore, an additional learning process can be initiated when large short-term FT deviations occur and the assessment can be executed. Separate counters are started for both assessments. When neither a lean condition nor a rich condition is detected, the end diagnostic counter is decremented from a calibratable value to zero and a passing decision is made. When a lean condition is present and the total fuel control exceeds the calibrated threshold value, a time counter is incremented. When the time counter exceeds the calibrated threshold value, a lean error is set. When a rich condition is present and the total fuel control falls below the calibrated threshold value, a time counter is incremented. When the time counter exceeds the calibrated threshold value, a rich error is set. The time counters are incremented while the "lambda controller" or the "lambda adaptation" exceeds minimum or maximum threshold values. A malfunction is detected as soon as one of the time counters reaches its respective maximum value.
DTC: P2270 **2T** **Year:** 2011, 2012 **Model:** Cooper, Cooper Countryman **Engine:** 1.6L L4	**O2 Sensor Signal Stuck Lean Bank 1 Sensor 2:** Engine started, battery voltage must be at least 11.5v, all electrical components must be off, parking brake must be engaged (to keep daytime driving lights off), automatic transmission selector must be in park. The DME detected an unexpected voltage condition, or it detected an unexpected current draw in the heater circuit during the CCM test. Coolant temperature must been at least 80.25 degrees Celsius. The vehicle speed is greater than 27.96 and less than 80.76. The engine speed is between 1984 and 3647rpm. Ambient pressure is greater than 75.001kPa and the engine stability load is 6.94g/s. **NOTE: Vehicle must be raised before connector for oxygen sensors is accessible.**
DTC: P2271 **2T** **Year:** 2011, 2012 **Model:** Cooper, Cooper Countryman **Engine:** 1.6L L4	**O2 Sensor Signal Stuck Rich Bank 1 Sensor 2:** Engine started, battery voltage must be at least 11.5v, all electrical components must be off, parking brake must be engaged (to keep daytime driving lights off), automatic transmission selector must be in park. The DME detected an unexpected voltage condition, or it detected an unexpected current draw in the heater circuit during the CCM test. Coolant temperature must been at least 80.25 degrees Celsius. The vehicle speed is greater than 27.96 and less than 80.76. The engine speed is between 1984 and 3647rpm. Ambient pressure is greater than 75.001kPa and the engine stability load is 6.94g/s. **NOTE: Vehicle must be raised before connector for oxygen sensors is accessible.**
DTC: P2300 **2T** **Year:** 2011, 2012 **Model:** Cooper, Cooper Countryman **Engine:** 1.6L L4	**Ignition Coilpack A Primary/Secondary Circuit Malfunction Open Circuit/Short to Ground:** Engine started, battery voltage must be at least 11.5v, all electrical components must be off, parking brake must be engaged (to keep daytime driving lights off), automatic transmission selector must be in park and the ground between the engine and the chassis must be well connected. The DME did not receive any valid pulses from the ignition module for the Ignition Coilpack A primary circuit. **NOTE: Ignition coils and power output stages are one component and cannot be replaced individually.**
DTC: P2301 **2T** **Year:** 2011, 2012 **Model:** Cooper, Cooper Countryman **Engine:** 1.6L L4	**Ignition Coilpack A Primary/Secondary Circuit Malfunction Short to Battery:** Engine started, battery voltage must be at least 11.5v, all electrical components must be off, parking brake must be engaged (to keep daytime driving lights off), automatic transmission selector must be in park and the ground between the engine and the chassis must be well connected. The DME did not receive any valid pulses from the ignition module for the Ignition Coilpack A primary circuit. **NOTE: Ignition coils and power output stages are one component and cannot be replaced individually.**
DTC: P2303 **2T** **Year:** 2011, 2012 **Model:** Cooper, Cooper Countryman **Engine:** 1.6L L4	**Ignition Coilpack A Primary/Secondary Circuit Malfunction Open Circuit/Short to Ground:** Engine started, battery voltage must be at least 11.5v, all electrical components must be off, parking brake must be engaged (to keep daytime driving lights off), automatic transmission selector must be in park and the ground between the engine and the chassis must be well connected. The DME did not receive any valid pulses from the ignition module for the Ignition Coilpack A primary circuit. **NOTE: Ignition coils and power output stages are one component and cannot be replaced individually.**

DTC	Trouble Code Title, Conditions, Possible Causes
DTC: P2304 **2T** **Year:** 2011, 2012 **Model:** Cooper, Cooper Countryman **Engine:** 1.6L L4	**Ignition Coilpack A Primary/Secondary Circuit Malfunction Short to Battery:** Engine started, battery voltage must be at least 11.5v, all electrical components must be off, parking brake must be engaged (to keep daytime driving lights off), automatic transmission selector must be in park and the ground between the engine and the chassis must be well connected. The DME did not receive any valid pulses from the ignition module for the Ignition Coilpack A primary circuit. **NOTE: Ignition coils and power output stages are one component and cannot be replaced individually.**
DTC: P2400 **T** **Year:** 2011, 2012 **Model:** Cooper, Cooper Countryman **Engine:** 1.6L L4	**EVAP Leak Detection Pump (LDP) Control Circuit Open:** Engine started, battery voltage must be at least 11.5v, all electrical components must be off, parking brake must be engaged (to keep daytime driving lights off), automatic transmission selector must be in park, the exhaust system must be properly sealed between the catalytic converter and the cylinder head, coolant temperature must be at least 80 degrees Celsius and oxygen sensor heaters for oxygen sensors before the catalytic converter must be functioning properly and the ground between the engine and the chassis must be well connected. The DME detected voltage irregularity in the leak detection pump control circuit.
DTC: P2401 **T** **Year:** 2011, 2012 **Model:** Cooper, Cooper Countryman **Engine:** 1.6L L4	**EVAP Leak Detection Pump Control Circuit Low:** Engine started, battery voltage must be at least 11.5v, all electrical components must be off, parking brake must be engaged (to keep daytime driving lights off), automatic transmission selector must be in park, the exhaust system must be properly sealed between the catalytic converter and the cylinder head, coolant temperature must be at least 80 degrees Celsius and oxygen sensor heaters for oxygen sensors before the catalytic converter must be functioning properly and the ground between the engine and the chassis must be well connected. The DME detected voltage irregularity in the leak detection pump control circuit.
DTC: P2402 **T** **Year:** 2011, 2012 **Model:** Cooper, Cooper Countryman **Engine:** 1.6L L4	**EVAP Leak Detection Pump Control Circuit High:** Engine started, battery voltage must be at least 11.5v, all electrical components must be off, parking brake must be engaged (to keep daytime driving lights off), automatic transmission selector must be in park, the exhaust system must be properly sealed between the catalytic converter and the cylinder head, coolant temperature must be at least 80 degrees Celsius and oxygen sensor heaters for oxygen sensors before the catalytic converter must be functioning properly and the ground between the engine and the chassis must be well connected. The DME detected voltage irregularity in the leak detection pump control circuit.
DTC: P2404 **2T** **Year:** 2011, 2012 **Model:** Cooper, Cooper Countryman **Engine:** 1.6L L4	**EVAP Emission Control LDP Circuit Malfunction Pump Problem:** Key on, KOEO Self-Test enabled, and the DME detected an unexpected voltage condition on the EVAP emission control leak detection pump circuit. The reed switch level stays low after activation of solenoids within the time threshold of more than 1 second. The coolant temperature is less than 60 degrees Celsius, and the ambient pressure is greater than 76.2994kPa. The air intake temperature at start is between 9.04 and 16.04 degrees Celsius. The change in barometric pressure since engine start is less than 0.9998kPa. The vehicle speed is less than 74.56mph, and the purge valve has opened enough on previous driving cycle.
DTC: P2421 **2T , MIL: Yes** **Year:** 2011, 2012 **Model:** Cooper, Cooper Countryman **Engine:** 1.6L L4	**EVAP System Canister Purge Valve Monitoring:** This diagnostic is similar to the "EVAP System DMTL Diagnostic". The solenoid valve in DMTL is closed and the pump is activated in this diagnostic process. When a stable reference current value has been achieved, the DMTL solenoid valve is opened. When the current value falls below the threshold value, a stuck open EVAP CPV is detected (P2421).

OBD II Trouble Code List (P3XXX Codes)

DTC	Trouble Code Title and Conditions
DTC: P306D **2T , MIL: Yes** **Year:** 2011, 2012 **Model:** Cooper, Cooper Countryman **Engine:** 1.6L L4	**Fuel System Monitoring-Lambda Adaptation:** The fuel system diagnostic utilizes two separate monitors. The first monitor assesses the percentage of the long-term fuel adaptation. The second monitor assesses the percentage of the short-term FT's physical limits. The short-term FT monitor is enabled in every engine state except for DFCO. The long-term FT monitor is enabled during its learning process and is inhibited during EVAP canister purge phases. Therefore, an additional learning process can be initiated when large short-term FT deviations occur and the assessment can be executed. Separate counters are started for both assessments. When neither a lean condition nor a rich condition is detected, the end diagnostic counter is decremented from a calibratable value to zero and a passing decision is made. When a lean condition is present and the total fuel control exceeds the calibrated threshold value, a time counter is incremented. When the time counter exceeds the calibrated threshold value, a lean error is set. When a rich condition is present and the total fuel control falls below the calibrated threshold value, a time counter is incremented. When the time counter exceeds the calibrated threshold value, a rich error is set. The time counters are incremented while the "lambda controller" or the "lambda adaptation" exceeds minimum or maximum threshold values. A malfunction is detected as soon as one of the time counters reaches its respective maximum value.

DTC	Trouble Code Title and Conditions
DTC: P306E **1T , MIL: Yes** **Year:** 2011, 2012 **Model:** Cooper, Cooper Countryman **Engine:** 1.6L L4	**Fuel System Monitoring-Lambda Adaptation:** The fuel system diagnostic utilizes two separate monitors. The first monitor assesses the percentage of the long-term fuel adaptation. The second monitor assesses the percentage of the short-term FT's physical limits. The short-term FT monitor is enabled in every engine state except for DFCO. The long-term FT monitor is enabled during its learning process and is inhibited during EVAP canister purge phases. Therefore, an additional learning process can be initiated when large short-term FT deviations occur and the assessment can be executed. Separate counters are started for both assessments. When neither a lean condition nor a rich condition is detected, the end diagnostic counter is decremented from a calibratable value to zero and a passing decision is made. When a lean condition is present and the total fuel control exceeds the calibrated threshold value, a time counter is incremented. When the time counter exceeds the calibrated threshold value, a lean error is set. When a rich condition is present and the total fuel control falls below the calibrated threshold value, a time counter is incremented. When the time counter exceeds the calibrated threshold value, a rich error is set. The time counters are incremented while the "lambda controller" or the "lambda adaptation" exceeds minimum or maximum threshold values. A malfunction is detected as soon as one of the time counters reaches its respective maximum value.

GLOSSARY

ABS: Anti-lock braking system. An electro-mechanical braking system which is designed to minimize or prevent wheel lock-up during braking.

ABSOLUTE PRESSURE: Atmospheric (barometric) pressure plus the pressure gauge reading.

ACCELERATOR PUMP: A small pump located in the carburetor that feeds fuel into the air/fuel mixture during acceleration.

ACCUMULATOR: A device that controls shift quality by cushioning the shock of hydraulic oil pressure being applied to a clutch or band.

ACTUATING MECHANISM: The mechanical output devices of a hydraulic system, for example, clutch pistons and band servos.

ACTUATOR: The output component of a hydraulic or electronic system.

ADVANCE: Setting the ignition timing so that spark occurs earlier before the piston reaches top dead center (TDC).

ADAPTIVE MEMORY (ADAPTIVE STRATEGY): The learning ability of the TCM or PCM to redefine its decision-making process to provide optimum shift quality.

AFTER TOP DEAD CENTER (ATDC): The point after the piston reaches the top of its travel on the compression stroke.

AIR BAG: Device on the inside of the car designed to inflate on impact of crash, protecting the occupants of the car.

AIR CHARGE TEMPERATURE (ACT) SENSOR: The temperature of the airflow into the engine is measured by an ACT sensor, usually located in the lower intake manifold or air cleaner.

AIR CLEANER: An assembly consisting of a housing, filter and any connecting ductwork. The filter element is made up of a porous paper, sometimes with a wire mesh screening, and is designed to prevent airborne particles from entering the engine through the carburetor or throttle body.

AIR INJECTION: One method of reducing harmful exhaust emissions by injecting air into each of the exhaust ports of an engine. The fresh air entering the hot exhaust manifold causes any remaining fuel to be burned before it can exit the tailpipe.

AIR PUMP: An emission control device that supplies fresh air to the exhaust manifold to aid in more completely burning exhaust gases.

AIR/FUEL RATIO: The ratio of air-to-gasoline by weight in the fuel mixture drawn into the engine.

ALDL (assembly line diagnostic link): Electrical connector for scanning ECM/PCM/TCM input and output devices.

ALIGNMENT RACK: A special drive-on vehicle lift apparatus/measuring device used to adjust a vehicle's toe, caster and camber angles.

ALL WHEEL DRIVE: Term used to describe a full time four wheel drive system or any other vehicle drive system that continuously delivers power to all four wheels. This system is found primarily on station wagon vehicles and SUVs not utilized for significant off road use.

ALTERNATING CURRENT (AC): Electric current that flows first in one direction, then in the opposite direction, continually reversing flow.

ALTERNATOR: A device which produces AC (alternating current) which is converted to DC (direct current) to charge the car battery.

AMMETER: An instrument, calibrated in amperes, used to measure the flow of an electrical current in a circuit. Ammeters are always connected in series with the circuit being tested.

AMPERAGE: The total amount of current (amperes) flowing in a circuit.

AMPLIFIER: A device used in an electrical circuit to increase the voltage of an output signal.

AMP/HR. RATING (BATTERY): Measurement of the ability of a battery to deliver a stated amount of current for a stated period of time. The higher the amp/hr. rating, the better the battery.

AMPERE: The rate of flow of electrical current present when one volt of electrical pressure is applied against one ohm of electrical resistance.

ANALOG COMPUTER: Any microprocessor that uses similar (analogous) electrical signals to make its calculations.

ANODIZED: A special coating applied to the surface of aluminum valves for extended service life.

ANTIFREEZE: A substance (ethylene or propylene glycol) added to the coolant to prevent freezing in cold weather.

ANTI-FOAM AGENTS: Minimize fluid foaming from the whipping action encountered in the converter and planetary action.

ANTI-WEAR AGENTS: Zinc agents that control wear on the gears, bushings, and thrust washers.

ANTI-LOCK BRAKING SYSTEM: A supplementary system to the base hydraulic system that prevents sustained lock-up of the wheels during braking as well as automatically controlling wheel slip.

ANTI-ROLL BAR: See stabilizer bar.

ARC: A flow of electricity through the air between two electrodes or contact points that produces a spark.

ARMATURE: A laminated, soft iron core wrapped by a wire that converts electrical energy to mechanical energy as in a motor or relay. When rotated in a magnetic field, it changes mechanical energy into electrical energy as in a generator.

ATDC: After Top Dead Center.

ATF: Automatic transmission fluid.

ATMOSPHERIC PRESSURE: The pressure on the Earth's surface caused by the weight of the air in the atmosphere. At sea level, this pressure is 14.7 psi at 32°F (101 kPa at 0°C).

ATOMIZATION: The breaking down of a liquid into a fine mist that can be suspended in air.

AUXILIARY ADD-ON COOLER: A supplemental transmission fluid cooling device that is installed in series with the heat exchanger (cooler), located inside the radiator, to provide additional support to cool the hot fluid leaving the torque converter.

AUXILIARY PRESSURE: An added fluid pressure that is introduced into a regulator or balanced valve system to control valve movement. The auxiliary pressure itself can be either a fixed or a variable value. (See balanced valve; regulator valve.)

AWD: All wheel drive.

AXIAL FORCE: A side or end thrust force acting in or along the same plane as the power flow.

AXIAL PLAY: Movement parallel to a shaft or bearing bore.

AXLE CAPACITY: The maximum load-carrying capacity of the axle itself, as specified by the manufacturer. This is usually a higher number than the GAWR.

AXLE RATIO: This is a number (3.07:1, 4.56:1, for example) expressing the ratio between driveshaft revolutions and wheel revolutions. A low numerical ratio allows the engine to work easier because it doesn't have to turn as fast. A high numerical ratio means that the engine has to turn more rpm's to move the wheels through the same number of turns.

BACKFIRE: The sudden combustion of gases in the intake or exhaust system that results in a loud explosion.

BACKLASH: The clearance or play between two parts, such as meshed gears.

BACKPRESSURE: Restrictions in the exhaust system that slow the exit of exhaust gases from the combustion chamber.

BAKELITE®: A heat resistant, plastic insulator material commonly used in printed circuit boards and transistorized components.

BALANCED VALVE: A valve that is positioned by opposing auxiliary hydraulic pressures and/or spring force. Examples include mainline regulator, throttle, and governor valves. (See regulator valve.)

BAND: A flexible ring of steel with an inner lining of friction material. When tightened around the outside of a drum, a planetary member is held stationary to the transmission/transaxle case.

BALL BEARING: A bearing made up of hardened inner and outer races between which hardened steel balls roll.

BALL JOINT: A ball and matching socket connecting suspension components (steering knuckle to lower control arms). It permits rotating movement in any direction between the components that are joined.

BARO (BAROMETRIC PRESSURE SENSOR): Measures the change in the intake manifold pressure caused by changes in altitude.

BAROMETRIC MANIFOLD ABSOLUTE PRESSURE (BMAP) SENSOR: Operates similarly to a conventional MAP sensor; reads intake manifold pressure and is also responsible for determining altitude and barometric pressure prior to engine operation.

BAROMETRIC PRESSURE: (See atmospheric pressure.)

BALLAST RESISTOR: A resistor in the primary ignition circuit that lowers voltage after the engine is started to reduce wear on ignition components.

BATTERY: A direct current electrical storage unit, consisting of the basic active materials of lead and sulfuric acid, which converts chemical energy into electrical energy. Used to provide current for the operation of the starter as well as other equipment, such as the radio, lighting, etc.

BEAD: The portion of a tire that holds it on the rim.

BEARING: A friction reducing, supportive device usually located between a stationary part and a moving part.

BEFORE TOP DEAD CENTER (BTDC): The point just before the piston reaches the top of its travel on the compression stroke.

BELTED TIRE: Tire construction similar to bias-ply tires, but using two or more layers of reinforced belts between body plies and the tread.

BEZEL: Piece of metal surrounding radio, headlights, gauges or similar components; sometimes used to hold the glass face of a gauge in the dash.

BIAS-PLY TIRE: Tire construction, using body ply reinforcing cords which run at alternating angles to the center line of the tread.

BI-METAL TEMPERATURE SENSOR: Any sensor or switch made of two dissimilar types of metal that bend when heated or cooled due to the different expansion rates of the alloys. These types of sensors usually function as an on/off switch.

BLOCK: See Engine Block.

BLOW-BY: Combustion gases, composed of water vapor and unburned fuel, that leak past the piston rings into the crankcase during normal engine operation. These gases are removed by the PCV system to prevent the buildup of harmful acids in the crankcase.

BOOK TIME: See Labor Time.

BOOK VALUE: The average value of a car, widely used to determine trade-in and resale value.

BOOST VALVE: Used at the base of the regulator valve to increase mainline pressure.

BORE: Diameter of a cylinder.

BRAKE CALIPER: The housing that fits over the brake disc. The caliper holds the brake pads, which are pressed against the discs by the caliper pistons when the brake pedal is depressed.

BRAKE HORSEPOWER (BHP): The actual horsepower available at the engine flywheel as measured by a dynamometer.

BRAKE FADE: Loss of braking power, usually caused by excessive heat after repeated brake applications.

BRAKE HORSEPOWER: Usable horsepower of an engine measured at the crankshaft.

BRAKE PAD: A brake shoe and lining assembly used with disc brakes.

BRAKE PROPORTIONING VALVE: A valve on the master cylinder which restricts hydraulic brake pressure to the wheels to a specified amount, preventing wheel lock-up.

BREAKAWAY: Often used by Chrysler to identify first-gear operation in D and 2 ranges. In these ranges, first-gear operation depends on a one-way roller clutch that holds on acceleration and releases (breaks away) on deceleration, resulting in a freewheeling coast-down condition.

BRAKE SHOE: The backing for the brake lining. The term is, however, usually applied to the assembly of the brake backing and lining.

BREAKER POINTS: A set of points inside the distributor, operated by a cam, which make and break the ignition circuit.

BRINNELLING: A wear pattern identified by a series of indentations at regular intervals. This condition is caused by a lack of lube, overload situations, and/or vibrations.

BTDC: Before Top Dead Center.

BUMP: Sudden and forceful apply of a clutch or band.

BUSHING: A liner, usually removable, for a bearing; an anti-friction liner used in place of a bearing.

CALIFORNIA ENGINE: An engine certified by the EPA for use in California only; conforms to more stringent emission regulations than Federal engine.

CALIPER: A hydraulically activated device in a disc brake system,

which is mounted straddling the brake rotor (disc). The caliper contains at least one piston and two brake pads. Hydraulic pressure on the piston(s) forces the pads against the rotor.

CAPACITY: The quantity of electricity that can be delivered from a unit, as from a battery in ampere-hours, or output, as from a generator.

CAMBER: One of the factors of wheel alignment. Viewed from the front of the car, it is the inward or outward tilt of the wheel. The top of the tire will lean outward (positive camber) or inward (negative camber).

CAMSHAFT: A shaft in the engine on which are the lobes (cams) which operate the valves. The camshaft is driven by the crankshaft, via a belt, chain or gears, at one half the crankshaft speed.

CAPACITOR: A device which stores an electrical charge.

CARBON MONOXIDE (CO): A colorless, odorless gas given off as a normal byproduct of combustion. It is poisonous and extremely dangerous in confined areas, building up slowly to toxic levels without warning if adequate ventilation is not available.

CARBURETOR: A device, usually mounted on the intake manifold of an engine, which mixes the air and fuel in the proper proportion to allow even combustion.

CASTER: The forward or rearward tilt of an imaginary line drawn through the upper ball joint and the center of the wheel. Viewed from the sides, positive caster (forward tilt) lends directional stability, while negative caster (rearward tilt) produces instability.

CATALYTIC CONVERTER: A device installed in the exhaust system, like a muffler, that converts harmful byproducts of combustion into carbon dioxide and water vapor by means of a heat-producing chemical reaction.

CENTRIFUGAL ADVANCE: A mechanical method of advancing the spark timing by using flyweights in the distributor that react to centrifugal force generated by the distributor shaft rotation.

CENTRIFUGAL FORCE: The outward pull of a revolving object, away from the center of revolution. Centrifugal force increases with the speed of rotation.

CETANE RATING: A measure of the ignition value of diesel fuel. The higher the cetane rating, the better the fuel. Diesel fuel cetane rating is roughly comparable to gasoline octane rating.

CHECK VALVE: Any one-way valve installed to permit the flow of air, fuel or vacuum in one direction only.

CHOKE: The valve/plate that restricts the amount of air entering an engine on the induction stroke, thereby enriching the air/fuel ratio.

CHUGGLE: Bucking or jerking condition that may be engine related and may be most noticeable when converter clutch is engaged; similar to the feel of towing a trailer.

CIRCLIP: A split steel snapring that fits into a groove to hold various parts in place.

CIRCUIT BREAKER: A switch which protects an electrical circuit from overload by opening the circuit when the current flow exceeds a pre-determined level. Some circuit breakers must be reset manually, while most reset automatically.

CIRCUIT: Any unbroken path through which an electrical current can flow. Also used to describe fuel flow in some instances.

CIRCUIT, BYPASS: Another circuit in parallel with the major circuit through which power is diverted.

CIRCUIT, CLOSED: An electrical circuit in which there is no interruption of current flow.

CIRCUIT, GROUND: The non-insulated portion of a complete circuit used as a common potential point. In automotive circuits, the ground is composed of metal parts, such as the engine, body sheet metal, and frame and is usually a negative potential.

CIRCUIT, HOT: That portion of a circuit not at ground potential. The hot circuit is usually insulated and is connected to the positive side of the battery.

CIRCUIT, OPEN: A break or lack of contact in an electrical circuit, either intentional (switch) or unintentional (bad connection or broken wire).

CIRCUIT, PARALLEL: A circuit having two or more paths for current flow with common positive and negative tie points. The same voltage is applied to each load device or parallel branch.

CIRCUIT, SERIES: An electrical system in which separate parts are connected end to end, using one wire, to form a single path for current to flow.

CIRCUIT, SHORT: A circuit that is accidentally completed in an electrical path for which it was not intended.

CLAMPING (ISOLATION) DIODES: Diodes positioned in a circuit to prevent self-induction from damaging electronic components.

CLEARCOAT: A transparent layer which, when sprayed over a vehicle's paint job, adds gloss and depth as well as an additional protective coating to the finish.

CLUTCH: Part of the power train used to connect/disconnect power to the rear wheels.

CLUTCH, FLUID: The same as a fluid coupling. A fluid clutch or coupling performs the same function as a friction clutch by utilizing fluid friction and inertia as opposed to solid friction used by a friction clutch. (See fluid coupling.)

CLUTCH, FRICTION: A coupling device that provides a means of smooth and positive engagement and disengagement of engine torque to the vehicle powertrain. Transmission of power through the clutch is accomplished by bringing one or more rotating drive members into contact with complementing driven members.

COAST: Vehicle deceleration caused by engine braking conditions.

COEFFICIENT OF FRICTION: The amount of surface tension between two contacting surfaces; identified by a scientifically calculated number.

COIL: Part of the ignition system that boosts the relatively low voltage supplied by the car's electrical system to the high voltage required to fire the spark plugs.

COMBINATION MANIFOLD: An assembly which includes both the intake and exhaust manifolds in one casting.

COMBINATION VALVE: A device used in some fuel systems that routes fuel vapors to a charcoal storage canister instead of venting them into the atmosphere. The valve relieves fuel tank pressure and allows fresh air into the tank as the fuel level drops to prevent a vapor lock situation.

COMBUSTION CHAMBER: The part of the engine in the cylinder head where combustion takes place.

COMPOUND GEAR: A gear consisting of two or more simple gears with a common shaft.

COMPOUND PLANETARY: A gearset that has more than the three elements found in a simple gearset and is constructed by combining members of two planetary gearsets to create additional gear ratio possibilities.

COMPRESSION CHECK: A test involving removing each spark plug and inserting a gauge. When the engine is cranked, the gauge will record a pressure reading in the individual cylinder. General operating condition can be determined from a compression check.

COMPRESSION RATIO: The ratio of the volume between the piston and cylinder head when the piston is at the bottom of its stroke (bottom dead center) and when the piston is at the top of its stroke (top dead center).

COMPUTER: An electronic control module that correlates input data according to prearranged engineered instructions; used for the management of an actuator system or systems.

CONDENSER: An electrical device which acts to store an electrical charge, preventing voltage surges.

2. A radiator-like device in the air conditioning system in which refrigerant gas condenses into a liquid, giving off heat.

CONDUCTOR: Any material through which an electrical current can be transmitted easily.

CONNECTING ROD: The connecting link between the crankshaft and piston.

CONSTANT VELOCITY JOINT: Type of universal joint in a halfshaft assembly in which the output shaft turns at a constant angular velocity without variation, provided that the speed of the input shaft is constant.

CONTINUITY: Continuous or complete circuit. Can be checked with an ohmmeter.

CONTROL ARM: The upper or lower suspension components which are mounted on the frame and support the ball joints and steering knuckles.

CONVENTIONAL IGNITION: Ignition system which uses breaker points.

CONVERTER: (See torque converter.)

CONVERTER LOCKUP: The switching from hydrodynamic to direct mechanical drive, usually through the application of a friction element called the converter clutch.

COOLANT: Mixture of water and anti-freeze circulated through the engine to carry off heat produced by the engine.

CORROSION INHIBITOR: An inhibitor in ATF that prevents corrosion of bushings, thrust washers, and oil cooler brazed joints.

COUNTERSHAFT: An intermediate shaft which is rotated by a mainshaft and transmits, in turn, that rotation to a working part.

COUPLING PHASE: Occurs when the torque converter is operating at its greatest hydraulic efficiency. The speed differential between the impeller and the turbine is at its minimum. At this point, the stator freewheels, and there is no torque multiplication.

CRANKCASE: The lower part of an engine in which the crankshaft and related parts operate.

CRANKSHAFT: Engine component (connected to pistons by connecting rods) which converts the reciprocating (up and down) motion of pistons to rotary motion used to turn the driveshaft.

CURB WEIGHT: The weight of a vehicle without passengers or payload, but including all fluids (oil, gas, coolant, etc.) and other equipment specified as standard.

CURRENT: The flow (or rate) of electrons moving through a circuit. Current is measured in amperes (amp).

CURRENT FLOW CONVENTIONAL: Current flows through a circuit from the positive terminal of the source to the negative terminal (plus to minus).

CURRENT FLOW, ELECTRON: Current or electrons flow from the negative terminal of the source, through the circuit, to the positive terminal (minus to plus).

CV-JOINT: Constant velocity joint.

CYCLIC VIBRATIONS: The off-center movement of a rotating object that is affected by its initial balance, speed of rotation, and working angles.

CYLINDER BLOCK: See engine block.

CYLINDER HEAD: The detachable portion of the engine, usually fastened to the top of the cylinder block and containing all or most of the combustion chambers. On overhead valve engines, it contains the valves and their operating parts. On overhead cam engines, it contains the camshaft as well.

CYLINDER: In an engine, the round hole in the engine block in which the piston(s) ride.

DATA LINK CONNECTOR (DLC): Current acronym/term applied to the federally mandated, diagnostic junction connector that is used to monitor ECM/PC/TCM inputs, processing strategies, and outputs including diagnostic trouble codes (DTCs).

DEAD CENTER: The extreme top or bottom of the piston stroke.

DECELERATION BUMP: When referring to a torque converter clutch in the applied position, a sudden release of the accelerator pedal causes a forceful reversal of power through the drivetrain (engine braking), just prior to the apply plate actually being released.

DELAYED (LATE OR EXTENDED): Condition where shift is expected but does not occur for a period of time, for example, where clutch or band engagement does not occur as quickly as expected during part throttle or wide open throttle apply of accelerator or when manually downshifting to a lower range.

DETENT: A spring-loaded plunger, pin, ball, or pawl used as a holding device on a ratchet wheel or shaft. In automatic transmissions, a detent mechanism is used for locking the manual valve in place.

DETENT DOWNSHIFT: (See kickdown.)

DETERGENT: An additive in engine oil to improve its operating characteristics.

DETONATION: An unwanted explosion of the air/fuel mixture in the combustion chamber caused by excess heat and compression, advanced timing, or an overly lean mixture. Also referred to as "ping".

DEXRON®: A brand of automatic transmission fluid.

DIAGNOSTIC TROUBLE CODES (DTCs): A digital display from the control module memory that identifies the input, processor, or output device circuit that is related to the powertrain emission/driveability malfunction detected. Diagnostic trouble codes can be read by the MIL to flash any codes or by using a handheld scanner.

DIAPHRAGM: A thin, flexible wall separating two cavities, such as in a vacuum advance unit.

DIESELING: The engine continues to run after the car is shut off; caused by fuel continuing to be burned in the combustion chamber.

DIFFERENTIAL: A geared assembly which allows the transmission of motion between drive axles, giving one axle the ability to rotate faster than the other, as in cornering.

DIFFERENTIAL AREAS: When opposing faces of a spool valve are acted upon by the same pressure but their areas differ in size, the face with the larger area produces the differential force and valve movement. (See spool valve.)

DIFFERENTIAL FORCE: (See differential areas)

DIGITAL READOUT: A display of numbers or a combination of numbers and letters.

DIGITAL VOLT OHMMETER: An electronic diagnostic tool used to measure voltage, ohms and amps as well as several other functions, with the readings displayed on a digital screen in tenths, hundredths and thousandths.

DIODE: An electrical device that will allow current to flow in one direction only.

DIRECT CURRENT (DC): Electrical current that flows in one direction only.

DIRECT DRIVE: The gear ratio is 1:1, with no change occurring in the torque and speed input/output relationship.

DISC BRAKE: A hydraulic braking assembly consisting of a brake disc, or rotor, mounted on an axle shaft, and a caliper assembly containing, usually two brake pads which are activated by hydraulic pressure. The pads are forced against the sides of the disc, creating friction which slows the vehicle.

DISPERSANTS: Suspend dirt and prevent sludge buildup in a liquid, such as engine oil.

DOUBLE BUMP (DOUBLE FEEL): Two sudden and forceful applies of a clutch or band.

DISPLACEMENT: The total volume of air that is displaced by all pistons as the engine turns through one complete revolution.

DISTRIBUTOR: A mechanically driven device on an engine which is responsible for electrically firing the spark plug at a pre-determined point of the piston stroke.

DOHC: Double overhead camshaft.

DOUBLE OVERHEAD CAMSHAFT: The engine utilizes two camshafts mounted in one cylinder head. One camshaft operates the exhaust valves, while the other operates the intake valves.

DOWEL PIN: A pin, inserted in mating holes in two different parts allowing those parts to maintain a fixed relationship.

DRIVELINE: The drive connection between the transmission and the drive wheels.

DRIVE TRAIN: The components that transmit the flow of power from the engine to the wheels. The components include the clutch, transmission, driveshafts (or axle shafts in front wheel drive), U-joints and differential.

DRUM BRAKE: A braking system which consists of two brake shoes and one or two wheel cylinders, mounted on a fixed backing plate, and a brake drum, mounted on an axle, which revolves around the assembly.

DRY CHARGED BATTERY: Battery to which electrolyte is added when the battery is placed in service.

DVOM: Digital volt ohmmeter

DWELL: The rate, measured in degrees of shaft rotation, at which an electrical circuit cycles on and off.

DYNAMIC: An application in which there is rotating or reciprocating motion between the parts.

EARLY: Condition where shift occurs before vehicle has reached proper speed, which tends to labor engine after upshift.

EBCM: See Electronic Control Unit (ECU).

ECM: See Electronic Control Unit (ECU).

ECU: Electronic control unit.

ELECTRODE: Conductor (positive or negative) of electric current.

ELECTROLYSIS: A surface etching or bonding of current conducting transmission/transaxle components that may occur when grounding straps are missing or in poor condition.

ELECTROLYTE: A solution of water and sulfuric acid used to activate the battery. Electrolyte is extremely corrosive.

ELECTROMAGNET: A coil that produces a magnetic field when current flows through its windings.

ELECTROMAGNETIC INDUCTION: A method to create (generate) current flow through the use of magnetism.

ELECTROMAGNETISM: The effects surrounding the relationship between electricity and magnetism.

ELECTROMOTIVE FORCE (EMF): The force or pressure (voltage) that causes current movement in an electrical circuit.

ELECTRONIC CONTROL UNIT: A digital computer that controls engine (and sometimes transmission, brake or other vehicle system) functions based on data received from various sensors. Examples used by some manufacturers include Electronic Brake Control Module (EBCM), Engine Control Module (ECM), Powertrain Control Module (PCM) or Vehicle Control Module (VCM).

ELECTRONIC IGNITION: A system in which the timing and firing of the spark plugs is controlled by an electronic control unit, usually called a module. These systems have no points or condenser.

ELECTRONIC PRESSURE CONTROL (EPC) SOLENOID: A specially designed solenoid containing a spool valve and spring assembly to control fluid mainline pressure. A variable current flow, controlled by the ECM/PCM, varies the internal force of the solenoid on the spool valve and resulting mainline pressure. (See variable force solenoid.)

ELECTRONICS: Miniaturized electrical circuits utilizing semiconductors, solid-state devices, and printed circuits. Electronic circuits utilize small amounts of power.

ELECTRONIFICATION: The application of electronic circuitry to a mechanical device. Regarding automatic transmissions, electrification is incorporated into converter clutch lockup, shift scheduling, and line pressure control systems.

ELECTROSTATIC DISCHARGE (ESD): An unwanted, high-voltage electrical current released by an individual who has taken on a static charge of electricity. Electronic components can be easily damaged by ESD.

ELEMENT: A device within a hydrodynamic drive unit designed with a set of blades to direct fluid flow.

ENAMEL: Type of paint that dries to a smooth, glossy finish.

END BUMP (END FEEL OR SLIP BUMP): Firmer feel at end of shift when compared with feel at start of shift.

END-PLAY: The clearance/gap between two components that allows for expansion of the parts as they warm up, to prevent binding and to allow space for lubrication.

ENERGY: The ability or capacity to do work.

ENGINE: The primary motor or power apparatus of a vehicle, which converts liquid or gas fuel into mechanical energy.

ENGINE BLOCK: The basic engine casting containing the cylinders, the crankshaft main bearings, as well as machined surfaces for the mounting of other components such as the cylinder head, oil pan, transmission, etc.

ENGINE BRAKING: Use of engine to slow vehicle by manually downshifting during zero-throttle coast down.

ENGINE CONTROL MODULE (ECM): Manages the engine and incorporates output control over the torque converter clutch solenoid. (Note: Current designation for the ECM in late model vehicles is PCM.)

ENGINE COOLANT TEMPERATURE (ECT) SENSOR: Prevents converter clutch engagement with a cold engine; also used for shift timing and shift quality.

EP LUBRICANT: EP (extreme pressure) lubricants are specially formulated for use with gears involving heavy loads (transmissions, differentials, etc.).

ETHYL: A substance added to gasoline to improve its resistance to knock, by slowing down the rate of combustion.

ETHYLENE GLYCOL: The base substance of antifreeze.

EXHAUST MANIFOLD: A set of cast passages or pipes which conduct exhaust gases from the engine.

FAIL-SAFE (BACKUP) CONTROL: A substitute value used by the PCM/TCM to replace a faulty signal from an input sensor. The temporary value allows the vehicle to continue to be operated.

FAST IDLE: The speed of the engine when the choke is on. Fast idle speeds engine warm-up.

FEDERAL ENGINE: An engine certified by the EPA for use in any of the 49 states (except California).

FEEDBACK: A circuit malfunction whereby current can find another path to feed load devices.

FEELER GAUGE: A blade, usually metal, of precisely predetermined thickness, used to measure the clearance between two parts.

FILAMENT: The part of a bulb that glows; the filament creates high resistance to current flow and actually glows from the resulting heat.

FINAL DRIVE: An essential part of the axle drive assembly where final gear reduction takes place in the powertrain. In RWD applications and north-south FWD applications, it must also change the power flow direction to the axle shaft by ninety degrees. (Also see axle ratio).

FIRING ORDER: The order in which combustion occurs in the cylinders of an engine. Also the order in which spark is distributed to the plugs by the distributor.

FIRM: A noticeable quick apply of a clutch or band that is considered normal with medium to heavy throttle shift; should not be confused with harsh or rough.

FLAME FRONT: The term used to describe certain aspects of the fuel explosion in the cylinders. The flame front should move in a controlled pattern across the cylinder, rather than simply exploding immediately.

FLARE (SLIPPING): A quick increase in engine rpm accompanied by momentary loss of torque; generally occurs during shift.

FLAT ENGINE: Engine design in which the pistons are horizontally opposed. Porsche, Subaru and some old VW are common examples of flat engines.

FLAT RATE: A dealership term referring to the amount of money paid to a technician for a repair or diagnostic service based on that particular service versus dealership's labor time (NOT based on the actual time the technician spent on the job).

FLAT SPOT: A point during acceleration when the engine seems to lose power for an instant.

FLOODING: The presence of too much fuel in the intake manifold and combustion chamber which prevents the air/fuel mixture from firing, thereby causing a no-start situation.

FLUID: A fluid can be either liquid or gas. In hydraulics, a liquid is used for transmitting force or motion.

FLUID COUPLING: The simplest form of hydrodynamic drive, the fluid coupling consists of two look-alike members with straight radial varies referred to as the impeller (pump) and the turbine. Input torque is always equal to the output torque.

FLUID DRIVE: Either a fluid coupling or a fluid torque converter. (See hydrodynamic drive units.)

FLUID TORQUE CONVERTER: A hydrodynamic drive that has the ability to act both as a torque multiplier and fluid coupling. (See hydrodynamic drive units; torque converter.)

FLUID VISCOSITY: The resistance of a liquid to flow. A cold fluid (oil) has greater viscosity and flows more slowly than a hot fluid (oil).

FLYWHEEL: A heavy disc of metal attached to the rear of the crankshaft. It smoothes the firing impulses of the engine and keeps the crankshaft turning during periods when no firing takes place. The starter also engages the flywheel to start the engine.

FOOT POUND (ft. lbs., lbs. ft. or sometimes, ft. lb.): The amount of energy or work needed to raise an item weighing one pound, a distance of one foot.

FREEZE PLUG: A plug in the engine block which will be pushed out if the coolant freezes. Sometimes called expansion plugs, they protect the block from cracking should the coolant freeze.

FRICTION: The resistance that occurs between contacting surfaces. This relationship is expressed by a ratio called the coefficient of friction (CL).

FRICTION, COEFFICIENT OF: The amount of surface tension between two contacting surfaces; expressed by a scientifically calculated number.

FRONT END ALIGNMENT: A service to set caster, camber and toe-in to the correct specifications. This will ensure that the car steers and handles properly and that the tires wear properly.

FRICTION MODIFIER: Changes the coefficient of friction of the fluid between the mating steel and composition clutch/band surfaces during the engagement process and allows for a certain amount of intentional slipping for a good "shift-feel".

FRONTAL AREA: The total frontal area of a vehicle exposed to air flow.

FUEL FILTER: A component of the fuel system containing a porous paper element used to prevent any impurities from entering the engine through the fuel system. It usually takes the form of a canister-like housing, mounted in-line with the fuel hose, located anywhere on a vehicle between the fuel tank and engine.

FUEL INJECTION: A system replacing the carburetor that sprays fuel into the cylinder through nozzles. The amount of fuel can be more precisely controlled with fuel injection.

FULL FLOATING AXLE: An axle in which the axle housing extends through the wheel giving bearing support on the outside of the housing. The front axle of a four-wheel drive vehicle is usually a full floating axle, as are the rear axles of many larger (1 ton and over) pick-ups and vans.

FULL-TIME FOUR-WHEEL DRIVE: A four-wheel drive system that continuously delivers power to all four wheels. A differential between the front and rear driveshafts permits variations in axle speeds to control gear wind-up without damage.

FULL THROTTLE DETENT DOWNSHIFT: A quick apply of accelerator pedal to its full travel, forcing a downshift.

FUSE: A protective device in a circuit which prevents circuit overload by breaking the circuit when a specific amperage is present. The device is constructed around a strip or wire of a lower amperage rating than the circuit it is designed to protect. When an amperage higher than that stamped on the fuse is present in the circuit, the strip or wire melts, opening the circuit.

FUSIBLE LINK: A piece of wire in a wiring harness that performs the same job as a fuse. If overloaded, the fusible link will melt and interrupt the circuit.

FWD: Front wheel drive.

GAWR: (Gross axle weight rating) the total maximum weight an axle is designed to carry.

GCW: (Gross combined weight) total combined weight of a tow vehicle and trailer.

GARAGE SHIFT: initial engagement feel of transmission, neutral to reverse or neutral to a forward drive.

GARAGE SHIFT FEEL: A quick check of the engagement quality and responsiveness of reverse and forward gears. This test is done with the vehicle stationary.

GEAR: A toothed mechanical device that acts as a rotating lever to transmit power or turning effort from one shaft to another. (See gear ratio.)

GEAR RATIO: A ratio expressing the number of turns a smaller gear will make to turn a larger gear through one revolution. The ratio is found by dividing the number of teeth on the smaller gear into the number of teeth on the larger gear.

GEARBOX: Transmission

GEAR REDUCTION: Torque is multiplied and speed decreased by the factor of the gear ratio. For example, a 3:1 gear ratio changes an input torque of 180 ft. lbs. and an input speed of 2700 rpm to 540 Ft. lbs. and 900 rpm, respectively. (No account is taken of frictional losses, which are always present.)

GEARTRAIN: A succession of intermeshing gears that form an assembly and provide for one or more torque changes as the power input is transmitted to the power output.

GEL COAT: A thin coat of plastic resin covering fiberglass body panels.

GENERATOR: A device which produces direct current (DC) necessary to charge the battery.

GOVERNOR: A device that senses vehicle speed and generates a hydraulic oil pressure. As vehicle speed increases, governor oil pressure rises.

GROUND CIRCUIT: (See circuit, ground.)

GROUND SIDE SWITCHING: The electrical/electronic circuit control switch is located after the circuit load.

GVWR: (Gross vehicle weight rating) total maximum weight a vehicle is designed to carry including the weight of the vehicle, passengers, equipment, gas, oil, etc.

BM-6 GLOSSARY

HALOGEN: A special type of lamp known for its quality of brilliant white light. Originally used for fog lights and driving lights.

HARD CODES: DTCs that are present at the time of testing; also called continuous or current codes.

HARSH(ROUGH): An apply of a clutch or band that is more noticeable than a firm one; considered undesirable at any throttle position.

HEADER TANK: An expansion tank for the radiator coolant. It can be located remotely or built into the radiator.

HEAT RANGE: A term used to describe the ability of a spark plug to carry away heat. Plugs with longer nosed insulators take longer to carry heat off effectively.

HEAT RISER: A flapper in the exhaust manifold that is closed when the engine is cold, causing hot exhaust gases to heat the intake manifold providing better cold engine operation. A thermostatic spring opens the flapper when the engine warms up.

HEAVY THROTTLE: Approximately three-fourths of accelerator pedal travel.

HEMI: A name given an engine using hemispherical combustion chambers.

HERTZ (HZ): The international unit of frequency equal to one cycle per second (10,000 Hertz equals 10,000 cycles per second).

HIGH-IMPEDANCE DVOM (DIGITAL VOLT-OHMMETER): This styled device provides a built-in resistance value and is capable of limiting circuit current flow to safe milliamp levels.

HIGH RESISTANCE: Often refers to a circuit where there is an excessive amount of opposition to normal current flow.

HORSEPOWER: A measurement of the amount of work; one horsepower is the amount of work necessary to lift 33,000 lbs. one foot in one minute. Brake horsepower (bhp) is the horsepower delivered by an engine on a dynamometer. Net horsepower is the power remaining (measured at the flywheel of the engine) that can be used to turn the wheels after power is consumed through friction and running the engine accessories (water pump, alternator, air pump, fan etc.)

HOT CIRCUIT: (See circuit, hot; hot lead.)

HOT LEAD: A wire or conductor in the power side of the circuit. (See circuit, hot.)

HOT SIDE SWITCHING: The electrical/electronic circuit control switch is located before the circuit load.

HUB: The center part of a wheel or gear.

HUNTING (BUSYNESS): Repeating quick series of up-shifts and downshifts that causes noticeable change in engine rpm, for example, as in a 4-3-4 shift pattern.

HYDRAULICS: The use of liquid under pressure to transfer force of motion.

HYDROCARBON (HC): Any chemical compound made up of hydrogen and carbon. A major pollutant formed by the engine as a by-product of combustion.

HYDRODYNAMIC DRIVE UNITS: Devices that transmit power solely by the action of a kinetic fluid flow in a closed recirculating path. An impeller energizes the fluid and discharges the high-speed jet stream into the turbine for power output.

HYDROMETER: An instrument used to measure the specific gravity of a solution.

HYDROPLANING: A phenomenon of driving when water builds up under the tire tread, causing it to lose contact with the road. Slowing down will usually restore normal tire contact with the road.

HYPOID GEARSET: The drive pinion gear may be placed below or above the centerline of the driven gear; often used as a final drive gearset.

IDLE MIXTURE: The mixture of air and fuel (usually about 14:1) being fed to the cylinders. The idle mixture screw(s) are sometimes adjusted as part of a tune-up.

IDLER ARM: Component of the steering linkage which is a geometric duplicate of the steering gear arm. It supports the right side of the center steering link.

IMPELLER: Often called a pump, the impeller is the power input (drive) member of a hydrodynamic drive. As part of the torque converter cover, it acts as a centrifugal pump and puts the fluid in motion.

INCH POUND (inch lbs.; sometimes in. lb. or in. lbs.): One twelfth of a foot pound.

INDUCTANCE: The force that produces voltage when a conductor is passed through a magnetic field.

INDUCTION: A means of transferring electrical energy in the form of a magnetic field. Principle used in the ignition coil to increase voltage.

INITIAL FEEL: A distinct firmer feel at start of shift when compared with feel at finish of shift.

INJECTOR: A device which receives metered fuel under relatively low pressure and is activated to inject the fuel into the engine under relatively high pressure at a predetermined time.

INPUT: In an automatic transmission, the source of power from the engine is absorbed by the torque converter, which provides the power input into the transmission. The turbine drives the input(turbine)shaft.

INPUT SHAFT: The shaft to which torque is applied, usually carrying the driving gear or gears.

INTAKE MANIFOLD: A casting of passages or pipes used to conduct air or a fuel/air mixture to the cylinders.

INTERNAL GEAR: The ring-like outer gear of a planetary gearset with the gear teeth cut on the inside of the ring to provide a mesh with the planet pinions.

ISOLATION (CLAMPING) DIODES: Diodes positioned in a circuit to prevent self-induction from damaging electronic components.

IX ROTARY GEAR PUMP: Contains two rotating members, one shaped with internal gear teeth and the other with external gear teeth. As the gears separate, the fluid fills the gaps between gear teeth, is pulled across a crescent-shaped divider, and then is forced to flow through the outlet as the gears mesh.

IX ROTARY LOBE PUMP: Sometimes referred to as a gerotor type pump. Two rotating members, one shaped with internal lobes and the other with external lobes, separate and then mesh to cause fluid to flow.

JOURNAL: The bearing surface within which a shaft operates.

JUMPER CABLES: Two heavy duty wires with large alligator clips used to provide power from a charged battery to a discharged battery mounted in a vehicle.

JUMPSTART: Utilizing the sufficiently charged battery of one vehicle to start the engine of another vehicle with a discharged battery by the use of jumper cables.

KEY: A small block usually fitted in a notch between a shaft and a hub to prevent slippage of the two parts.

KICKDOWN: Detent downshift system; either linkage, cable, or electrically controlled.

KILO: A prefix used in the metric system to indicate one thousand.

KNOCK: Noise which results from the spontaneous ignition of a portion of the air-fuel mixture in the engine cylinder caused by overly advanced ignition timing or use of incorrectly low octane fuel for that engine.

KNOCK SENSOR: An input device that responds to spark knock, caused by over advanced ignition timing.

LABOR TIME: A specific amount of time required to perform a certain repair or diagnostic service as defined by a vehicle or after-market manufacturer.

LACQUER: A quick-drying automotive paint.

LATE: Shift that occurs when engine is at higher than normal rpm for given amount of throttle.

LIGHT-EMITTING DIODE (LED): A semiconductor diode that emits light as electrical current flows through it; used in some electronic display devices to emit a red or other color light.

LIGHT THROTTLE: Approximately one-fourth of accelerator pedal travel.

LIMITED SLIP: A type of differential which transfers driving force to the wheel with the best traction.

LIMP-IN MODE: Electrical shutdown of the transmission/ transaxle output solenoids, allowing only forward and reverse gears that are hydraulically energized by the manual valve. This permits the vehicle to be driven to a service facility for repair.

LIP SEAL: Molded synthetic rubber seal designed with an outer sealing edge (lip) that points into the fluid containing area to be sealed. This type of seal is used where rotational and axial forces are present.

LITHIUM-BASE GREASE: Chassis and wheel bearing grease using lithium as a base. Not compatible with sodium-base grease.

LOAD DEVICE: A circuit's resistance that converts the electrical energy into light, sound, heat, or mechanical movement.

LOAD RANGE: Indicates the number of plies at which a tire is rated. Load range B equals four-ply rating; C equals six-ply rating; and, D equals an eight-ply rating.

LOAD TORQUE: The amount of output torque needed from the transmission/transaxle to overcome the vehicle load.

LOCKING HUBS: Accessories used on part-time four-wheel drive systems that allow the front wheels to be disengaged from the drive train when four-wheel drive is not being used. When four-wheel drive is desired, the hubs are engaged, locking the wheels to the drive train.

LOCKUP CONVERTER: A torque converter that operates hydraulically and mechanically. When an internal apply plate (lockup plate) clamps to the torque converter cover, hydraulic slippage is eliminated.

LOCK RING: See Circlip or Snapring.

MAGNET: Any body with the property of attracting iron or steel.

MAGNETIC FIELD: The area surrounding the poles of a magnet that is affected by its attraction or repulsion forces.

MAIN LINE PRESSURE: Often called control pressure or line pressure, it refers to the pressure of the oil leaving the pump and is controlled by the pressure regulator valve.

MALFUNCTION INDICATOR LAMP (MIL): Previously known as a check engine light, the dash-mounted MIL illuminates and signals the driver that an emission or driveability problem with the powertrain has been detected by the ECM/PCM. When this occurs, at least one diagnostic trouble code (DTC) has been stored into the control module memory.

MANIFOLD ABSOLUTE PRESSURE (MAP) SENSOR: Reads the amount of air pressure (vacuum) in the engine's intake manifold system; its signal is used to analyze engine load conditions.

MANIFOLD VACUUM: Low pressure in an engine intake manifold formed just below the throttle plates. Manifold vacuum is highest at idle and drops under acceleration.

MANIFOLD: A casting of passages or set of pipes which connect the cylinders to an inlet or outlet source.

MANUAL LEVER POSITION SWITCH (MLPS): A mechanical switching unit that is typically mounted externally to the transmission/transaxle to inform the PCM/ECM which gear range the driver has selected.

MANUAL VALVE: Located inside the transmission/transaxle, it is directly connected to the driver's shift lever. The position of the manual valve determines which hydraulic circuits will be charged with oil pressure and the operating mode of the transmission.

MANUAL VALVE LEVER POSITION SENSOR (MVLPS): The input from this device tells the TCM what gear range was selected.

MASS AIR FLOW (MAF) SENSOR: Measures the airflow into the engine.

MASTER CYLINDER: The primary fluid pressurizing device in a hydraulic system. In automotive use, it is found in brake and hydraulic clutch systems and is pedal activated, either directly or, in a power brake system, through the power booster.

MacPherson STRUT: A suspension component combining a shock absorber and spring in one unit.

MEDIUM THROTTLE: Approximately one-half of accelerator pedal travel.

MEGA: A metric prefix indicating one million.

MEMBER: An independent component of a hydrodynamic unit such as an impeller, a stator, or a turbine. It may have one or more elements.

MERCON: A fluid developed by Ford Motor Company in 1988. It contains a friction modifier and closely resembles operating characteristics of Dexron.

METAL SEALING RINGS: Made from cast iron or aluminum, their primary application is with dynamic components involving pressure sealing circuits of rotating members. These rings are designed with either butt or hook lock end joints.

METER (ANALOG): A linear-style meter representing data as lengths; a needle-style instrument interfacing with logical numerical increments. This style of electrical meter uses relatively low impedance internal resistance and cannot be used for testing electronic circuitry.

METER (DIGITAL): Uses numbers as a direct readout to show values. Most meters of this style use high impedance internal resistance and must be used for testing low current electronic circuitry.

MICRO: A metric prefix indicating one-millionth (0.000001).

MILLI: A metric prefix indicating one-thousandth (0.001).

MINIMUM THROTTLE: The least amount of throttle opening required for upshift; normally close to zero throttle.

MISFIRE: Condition occurring when the fuel mixture in a cylinder fails to ignite, causing the engine to run roughly.

MODULE: Electronic control unit, amplifier or igniter of solid state or integrated design which controls the current flow in the ignition primary circuit based on input from the pick-up coil. When the module opens the primary circuit, high secondary voltage is induced in the coil.

MODULATED: In an electronic-hydraulic converter clutch system (or shift valve system), the term modulated refers to the pulsing of a solenoid, at a variable rate. This action controls the buildup of oil pressure in the hydraulic circuit to allow a controlled amount of clutch slippage.

MODULATED CONVERTER CLUTCH CONTROL (MCCC): A pulse width duty cycle valve that controls the converter lockup apply pressure and maximizes smoother transitions between lock and unlock conditions.

MODULATOR PRESSURE (THROTTLE PRESSURE): A hydraulic signal oil pressure relating to the amount of engine load, based on either the amount of throttle plate opening or engine vacuum.

MODULATOR VALVE: A regulator valve that is controlled by engine vacuum, providing a hydraulic pressure that varies in relation to engine torque. The hydraulic torque signal functions to delay the shift pattern and provide a line pressure boost. (See throttle valve.)

MOTOR: An electromagnetic device used to convert electrical energy into mechanical energy.

MULTIPLE-DISC CLUTCH: A grouping of steel and friction lined plates that, when compressed together by hydraulic pressure acting upon a piston, lock or unlock a planetary member.

MULTI-WEIGHT: Type of oil that provides adequate lubrication at both high and low temperatures.

needed to move one amp through a resistance of one ohm.

MUSHY: Same as soft; slow and drawn out clutch apply with very little shift feel.

MUTUAL INDUCTION: The generation of current from one wire circuit to another by movement of the magnetic field surrounding a current-carrying circuit as its ampere flow increases or decreases.

NEEDLE BEARING: A bearing which consists of a number (usually a large number) of long, thin rollers.

NITROGEN OXIDE (NOx): One of the three basic pollutants found in the exhaust emission of an internal combustion engine. The amount of NOx usually varies in an inverse proportion to the amount of HC and CO.

NONPOSITIVE SEALING: A sealing method that allows some minor leakage, which normally assists in lubrication.

O2 SENSOR: Located in the engine's exhaust system, it is an input device to the ECM/PCM for managing the fuel delivery and ignition system. A scanner can be used to observe the fluctuating voltage readings produced by an O2 sensor as the oxygen content of the exhaust is analyzed.

O-RING SEAL: Molded synthetic rubber seal designed with a circular cross-section. This type of seal is used primarily in static applications.

OBD II (ON-BOARD DIAGNOSTICS, SECOND GENERATION): Refers to the federal law mandating tighter control of 1996 and newer vehicle emissions, active monitoring of related devices, and standardization of terminology, data link connectors, and other technician concerns.

OCTANE RATING: A number, indicating the quality of gasoline based on its ability to resist knock. The higher the number, the better the quality. Higher compression engines require higher octane gas.

OEM: Original Equipment Manufactured. OEM equipment is that furnished standard by the manufacturer.

OFFSET: The distance between the vertical center of the wheel and the mounting surface at the lugs. Offset is positive if the center is outside the lug circle; negative offset puts the center line inside the lug circle.

OHM'S LAW: A law of electricity that states the relationship between voltage, current, and resistance. Volts = amperes x ohms

OHM: The unit used to measure the resistance of conductor-to-electrical flow. One ohm is the amount of resistance that limits current flow to one ampere in a circuit with one volt of pressure.

OHMMETER: An instrument used for measuring the resistance, in ohms, in an electrical circuit.

ONE-WAY CLUTCH: A mechanical clutch of roller or sprag design that resists torque or transmits power in one direction only. It is used to either hold or drive a planetary member.

ONE-WAY ROLLER CLUTCH: A mechanical device that transmits or holds torque in one direction only.

OPEN CIRCUIT: A break or lack of contact in an electrical circuit, either intentional (switch) or unintentional (bad connection or broken wire).

ORIFICE: Located in hydraulic oil circuits, it acts as a restriction. It slows down fluid flow to either create back pressure or delay pressure buildup downstream.

OSCILLOSCOPE: A piece of test equipment that shows electric impulses as a pattern on a screen. Engine performance can be analyzed by interpreting these patterns.

OUTPUT SHAFT: The shaft which transmits torque from a device, such as a transmission.

OUTPUT SPEED SENSOR (OSS): Identifies transmission/transaxle output shaft speed for shift timing and may be used to calculate TCC slip; often functions as the VSS (vehicle speed sensor).

OVERDRIVE: (1.) A device attached to or incorporated in a transmission/transaxle that allows the engine to turn less than one full revolution for every complete revolution of the wheels. The net effect is to reduce engine rpm, thereby using less fuel. A typical overdrive gear ratio would be .87:1, instead of the normal 1:1 in high gear. (2.) A gear assembly which produces more shaft revolutions than that transmitted to it.

OVERDRIVE PLANETARY GEARSET: A single planetary gearset designed to provide a direct drive and overdrive ratio. When coupled to a three-speed transmission/transaxle configuration, a four-speed/overdrive unit is present.

OVERHEAD CAMSHAFT (OHC): An engine configuration in which the camshaft is mounted on top of the cylinder head and operates the valve either directly or by means of rocker arms.

OVERHEAD VALVE (OHV): An engine configuration in which all of the valves are located in the cylinder head and the camshaft is located in the cylinder block. The camshaft operates the valves via lifters and pushrods.

OVERRUNCLUTCH: Another name for a one-way mechanical clutch. Applies to both roller and sprag designs.

OVERSTEER: The tendency of some vehicles, when steering into a turn, to over-respond or steer more than required, which could result in excessive slip of the rear wheels. Opposite of under-steer.

OXIDATION STABILIZERS: Absorb and dissipate heat. Automatic transmission fluid has high resistance to varnish and sludge buildup that occurs from excessive heat that is generated primarily in the torque converter. Local temperatures as high as 6000F (3150C) can occur at the clutch plates during engagement, and this heat must be absorbed and dissipated. If the fluid cannot withstand the heat, it burns or oxidizes, resulting in an almost immediate destruction of friction materials, clogged filter screen and hydraulic passages, and sticky valves.

OXIDES OF NITROGEN: See nitrogen oxide (NOx).

OXYGEN SENSOR: Used with a feedback system to sense the presence of oxygen in the exhaust gas and signal the computer which can use the voltage signal to determine engine operating efficiency and adjust the air/fuel ratio.

PARALLEL CIRCUIT: (See circuit, parallel.)

PARTS WASHER: A basin or tub, usually with a built-in pump mechanism and hose used for circulating chemical solvent for the purpose of cleaning greasy, oily and dirty components.

PART-TIME FOUR WHEEL DRIVE: A system that is normally in the two wheel drive mode and only runs in four-wheel drive when the system is manually engaged because more traction is desired. Two or four wheel drive is normally selected by a lever to engage the front axle, but if locking hubs are used, these must also be manually engaged in the Lock position. Otherwise, the front axle will not drive the front wheels.

PASSIVE RESTRAINT: Safety systems such as air bags or automatic seat belts which operate with no action required on the part of the driver or passenger. Mandated by Federal regulations on all vehicles sold in the U.S. after 1990.

PAYLOAD: The weight the vehicle is capable of carrying in addition to its own weight. Payload includes weight of the driver, passengers and cargo, but not coolant, fuel, lubricant, spare tire, etc.

PCM: Powertrain control module.

PCV VALVE: A valve usually located in the rocker cover that vents crankcase vapors back into the engine to be reburned.

PERCOLATION: A condition in which the fuel actually "boils," due to excessive heat. Percolation prevents proper atomization of the fuel causing rough running.

PICK-UP COIL: The coil in which voltage is induced in an electronic ignition.

PING: A metallic rattling sound produced by the engine during acceleration. It is usually due to incorrect ignition timing or a poor grade of gasoline.

PINION: The smaller of two gears. The rear axle pinion drives the ring gear which transmits motion to the axle shafts.

PINION GEAR: The smallest gear in a drive gear assembly.

PISTON: A disc or cup that fits in a cylinder bore and is free to move. In hydraulics, it provides the means of converting hydraulic pressure into a usable force. Examples of piston applications are found in servo, clutch, and accumulator units.

PISTON RING: An open-ended ring which fits into a groove on the outer diameter of the piston. Its chief function is to form a seal between the piston and cylinder wall. Most automotive pistons have three rings: two for compression sealing; one for oil sealing.

PITMAN ARM: A lever which transmits steering force from the steering gear to the steering linkage.

PLANET CARRIER: A basic member of a planetary gear assembly that carries the pinion gears.

PLANET PINIONS: Gears housed in a planet carrier that are in constant mesh with the sun gear and internal gear. Because they have their own independent rotating centers, the pinions are capable of rotating around the sun gear or the inside of the internal gear.

PLANETARY GEAR RATIO: The reduction or overdrive ratio developed by a planetary gearset.

PLANETARY GEARSET: In its simplest form, it is made up of a basic assembly group containing a sun gear, internal gear, and planet carrier. The gears are always in constant mesh and offer a wide range of gear ratio possibilities.

PLANETARY GEARSET (COMPOUND): Two planetary gearsets combined together.

PLANETARY GEARSET (SIMPLE): An assembly of gears in constant mesh consisting of a sun gear, several pinion gears mounted in a carrier, and a ring gear. It provides gear ratio and direction changes, in addition to a direct drive and a neutral.

PLY RATING: A. rating given a tire which indicates strength (but not necessarily actual plies). A two-ply/four-ply rating has only two plies, but the strength of a four-ply tire.

POLARITY: Indication (positive or negative) of the two poles of a battery.

PORT: An opening for fluid intake or exhaust.

POSITIVE SEALING: A sealing method that completely prevents leakage.

POTENTIAL: Electrical force measured in volts; sometimes used interchangeably with voltage.

POWER: The ability to do work per unit of time, as expressed in horsepower; one horsepower equals 33,000 ft. lbs. of work per minute, or 550 ft. lbs. of work per second.

POWER FLOW: The systematic flow or transmission of power through the gears, from the input shaft to the output shaft.

POWER-TO-WEIGHT RATIO: Ratio of horsepower to weight of car.

POWERTRAIN: See Drivetrain.

POWERTRAIN CONTROL MODULE (PCM): Current designation for the engine control module (ECM). In many cases, late model vehicle control units manage the engine as well as the transmission. In other settings, the PCM controls the engine and is interfaced with a TCM to control transmission functions.

Ppm: Parts per million; unit used to measure exhaust emissions.

PREIGNITION: Early ignition of fuel in the cylinder, sometimes due to glowing carbon deposits in the combustion chamber. Preignition can be damaging since combustion takes place prematurely.

PRELOAD: A predetermined load placed on a bearing during assembly or by adjustment.

PRESS FIT: The mating of two parts under pressure, due to the inner diameter of one being smaller than the outer diameter of the other, or vice versa; an interference fit.

PRESSURE: The amount of force exerted upon a surface area.

PRESSURE CONTROL SOLENOID (PCS): An output device that provides a boost oil pressure to the mainline regulator valve to control line pressure. Its operation is determined by the amount of current sent from the PCM.

PRESSURE GAUGE: An instrument used for measuring the fluid pressure in a hydraulic circuit.

PRESSURE REGULATOR VALVE: In automatic transmissions, its purpose is to regulate the pressure of the pump output and supply the basic fluid pressure necessary to operate the transmission. The regulated fluid pressure may be referred to as mainline pressure, line pressure, or control pressure.

PRESSURE SWITCH ASSEMBLY (PSA): Mounted inside the transmission, it is a grouping of oil pressure switches that inputs to the PCM when certain hydraulic passages are charged with oil pressure.

PRESSURE PLATE: A spring-loaded plate (part of the clutch) that transmits power to the driven (friction) plate when the clutch is engaged.

PRIMARY CIRCUIT: The low voltage side of the ignition system which consists of the ignition switch, ballast resistor or resistance wire, bypass, coil, electronic control unit and pick-up coil as well as the connecting wires and harnesses.

PROFILE: Term used for tire measurement (tire series), which is the ratio of tire height to tread width.

PROM (PROGRAMMABLE READ-ONLY MEMORY): The heart of the computer that compares input data and makes the engineered program or strategy decisions about when to trigger the appropriate output based on stored computer instructions.

PULSE GENERATOR: A two-wire pickup sensor used to produce a fluctuating electrical signal. This changing signal is read by the controller to determine the speed of the object and can be used to measure transmission/transaxle input speed, output speed, and vehicle speed.

PSI: Pounds per square inch; a measurement of pressure.

PULSE WIDTH DUTY CYCLE SOLENOID (PULSE WIDTH MODULATED SOLENOID): A computer-controlled solenoid that turns on and off at a variable rate producing a modulated oil pressure; often referred to as a pulse width modulated (PWM) solenoid. Employed in many electronic automatic transmissions and transaxles, these solenoids are used to manage shift control and converter clutch hydraulic circuits.

PUSHROD: A steel rod between the hydraulic valve lifter and the valve rocker arm in overhead valve (OHV) engines.

PUMP: A mechanical device designed to create fluid flow and pressure buildup in a hydraulic system.

QUARTER PANEL: General term used to refer to a rear fender. Quarter panel is the area from the rear door opening to the tail light area and from rear wheel well to the base of the trunk and roof-line.

RACE: The surface on the inner or outer ring of a bearing on which the balls, needles or rollers move.

RACK AND PINION: A type of automotive steering system using a pinion gear attached to the end of the steering shaft. The pinion meshes with a long rack attached to the steering linkage.

RADIAL TIRE: Tire design which uses body cords running at right angles to the center line of the tire. Two or more belts are used to give tread strength. Radials can be identified by their characteristic sidewall bulge.

RADIATOR: Part of the cooling system for a water-cooled engine, mounted in the front of the vehicle and connected to the engine with rubber hoses. Through the radiator, excess combustion heat is dissipated into the atmosphere through forced convection using a water and glycol based mixture that circulates through, and cools, the engine.

RANGE REFERENCE AND CLUTCH/BAND APPLY CHART: A guide that shows the application of clutches and bands for each gear, within the selector range positions. These charts are extremely useful for understanding how the unit operates and for diagnosing malfunctions.

RAVIGNEAUX GEARSET: A compound planetary gearset that features matched dual planetary pinions (sets of two) mounted in a single planet carrier. Two sun gears and one ring mesh with the carrier pinions.

REACTION MEMBER: The stationary planetary member, in a planetary gearset, that is grounded to the transmission/transaxle case through the use of friction and wedging devices known as bands, disc clutches, and one-way clutches.

REACTION PRESSURE: The fluid pressure that moves a spool valve against an opposing force or forces; the area on which the opposing force acts. The opposing force can be a spring or a combination of spring force and auxiliary hydraulic force.

REACTOR, TORQUE CONVERTER: The reaction member of a fluid torque converter, more commonly called a stator. (See stator.)

REAR MAIN OIL SEAL: A synthetic or rope-type seal that prevents oil from leaking out of the engine past the rear main crankshaft bearing.

RECIRCULATING BALL: Type of steering system in which recirculating steel balls occupy the area between the nut and worm wheel, causing a reduction in friction.

RECTIFIER: A device (used primarily in alternators) that permits electrical current to flow in one direction only.

REDUCTION: (See gear reduction.)

REGULATOR VALVE: A valve that changes the pressure of the oil in a hydraulic circuit as the oil passes through the valve by bleeding off (or exhausting) some of the volume of oil supplied to the valve.

REFRIGERANT 12 (R-12) or 134 (R-134): The generic name of the refrigerant used in automotive air conditioning systems.

REGULATOR: A device which maintains the amperage and/or voltage levels of a circuit at predetermined values.

RELAY: A switch which automatically opens and/or closes a circuit.

RELAY VALVE: A valve that directs flow and pressure. Relay valves simply connect or disconnect interrelated passages without restricting the fluid flow or changing the pressure.

RELIEF VALVE: A spring-loaded, pressure-operated valve that limits oil pressure buildup in a hydraulic circuit to a predetermined maximum value.

RELUCTOR: A wheel that rotates inside the distributor and triggers the release of voltage in an electronic ignition.

RESERVOIR: The storage area for fluid in a hydraulic system; often called a sump.

RESIN: A liquid plastic used in body work.

RESIDUAL MAGNETISM: The magnetic strength stored in a material after a magnetizing field has been removed.

RESISTANCE: The opposition to the flow of current through a circuit or electrical device, and is measured in ohms. Resistance is equal to the voltage divided by the amperage.

RESISTOR SPARK PLUG: A spark plug using a resistor to shorten the spark duration. This suppresses radio interference and lengthens plug life.

RESISTOR: A device, usually made of wire, which offers a preset amount of resistance in an electrical circuit.

RESULTANT FORCE: The single effective directional thrust of the fluid force on the turbine produced by the vortex and rotary forces acting in different planes.

RETARD: Set the ignition timing so that spark occurs later (fewer degrees before TDC).

RHEOSTAT: A device for regulating a current by means of a variable resistance.

RING GEAR: The name given to a ring-shaped gear attached to a differential case, or affixed to a flywheel or as part of a planetary gear set.

ROADLOAD: grade.

ROCKER ARM: A lever which rotates around a shaft pushing down (opening) the valve with an end when the other end is pushed up by the pushrod. Spring pressure will later close the valve.

ROCKER PANEL: The body panel below the doors between the wheel opening.

ROLLER BEARING: A bearing made up of hardened inner and outer races between which hardened steel rollers move.

ROLLER CLUTCH: A type of one-way clutch design using rollers and springs mounted within an inner and outer cam race assembly.

ROTARY FLOW: The path of the fluid trapped between the blades of the members as they revolve with the rotation of the torque converter cover (rotational inertia).

ROTOR: (1.) The disc-shaped part of a disc brake assembly, upon which the brake pads bear; also called, brake disc. (2.) The device mounted atop the distributor shaft, which passes current to the distributor cap tower contacts.

ROTARY ENGINE: See Wankel engine.

RPM: Revolutions per minute (usually indicates engine speed).

RTV: A gasket making compound that cures as it is exposed to the atmosphere. It is used between surfaces that are not perfectly machined to one another, leaving a slight gap that the RTV fills and in which it hardens. The letters RTV represent room temperature vulcanizing.

RUN-ON: Condition when the engine continues to run, even when the key is turned off. See dieseling.

SEALED BEAM: A automotive headlight. The lens, reflector and filament from a single unit.

SEATBELT INTERLOCK: A system whereby the car cannot be started unless the seatbelt is buckled.

SECONDARY CIRCUIT: The high voltage side of the ignition system, usually above 20,000 volts. The secondary includes the ignition coil, coil wire, distributor cap and rotor, spark plug wires and spark plugs.

SELF-INDUCTION: The generation of voltage in a current-carrying wire by changing the amount of current flowing within that wire.

SEMI-CONDUCTOR: A material (silicon or germanium) that is neither a good conductor nor an insulator; used in diodes and transistors.

SEMI-FLOATING AXLE: In this design, a wheel is attached to the axle shaft, which takes both drive and cornering loads. Almost all solid axle passenger cars and light trucks use this design.

SENDING UNIT: A mechanical, electrical, hydraulic or electromagnetic device which transmits information to a gauge.

SENSOR: Any device designed to measure engine operating conditions or ambient pressures and temperatures. Usually electronic in nature and designed to send a voltage signal to an on-board computer, some sensors may operate as a simple on/off switch or they may provide a variable voltage signal (like a potentiometer) as conditions or measured parameters change.

SERIES CIRCUIT: (See circuit, series.)

SERPENTINE BELT: An accessory drive belt, with small multiple v-ribs, routed around most or all of the engine-powered accessories such as the alternator and power steering pump. Usually both the front and the back side of the belt comes into contact with various pulleys.

SERVO: In an automatic transmission, it is a piston in a cylinder assembly that converts hydraulic pressure into mechanical force and movement; used for the application of the bands and clutches.

SHIFT BUSYNESS: When referring to a torque converter clutch, it is the frequent apply and release of the clutch plate due to uncommon driving conditions.

SHIFT VALVE: Classified as a relay valve, it triggers the automatic shift in response to a governor and a throttle signal by directing fluid to the appropriate band and clutch apply combination to cause the shift to occur.

SHIM: Spacers of precise, predetermined thickness used between parts to establish a proper working relationship.

SHIMMY: Vibration (sometimes violent) in the front end caused by misaligned front end, out of balance tires or worn suspension components.

SHORT CIRCUIT: An electrical malfunction where current takes the path of least resistance to ground (usually through damaged insulation). Current flow is excessive from low resistance resulting in a blown fuse.

SHUDDER: Repeated jerking or stick-slip sensation, similar to chuggle but more severe and rapid in nature, that may be most noticeable during certain ranges of vehicle speed; also used to define condition after converter clutch engagement.

SIMPSON GEARSET: A compound planetary gear train that integrates two simple planetary gearsets referred to as the front planetary and the rear planetary.

SINGLE OVERHEAD CAMSHAFT: See overhead camshaft.

SKIDPLATE: A metal plate attached to the underside of the body to protect the fuel tank, transfer case or other vulnerable parts from damage.

SLAVE CYLINDER: In automotive use, a device in the hydraulic clutch system which is activated by hydraulic force, disengaging the clutch.

SLIPPING: Noticeable increase in engine rpm without vehicle speed increase; usually occurs during or after initial clutch or band engagement.

SLUDGE: Thick, black deposits in engine formed from dirt, oil, water, etc. It is usually formed in engines when oil changes are neglected.

SNAP RING: A circular retaining clip used inside or outside a shaft or part to secure a shaft, such as a floating wrist pin.

SOFT: Slow, almost unnoticeable clutch apply with very little shift feel.

SOFTCODES: DTCs that have been set into the PCM memory but are not present at the time of testing; often referred to as history or intermittent codes.

SOHC: Single overhead camshaft.

SOLENOID: An electrically operated, magnetic switching device.

SPALLING: A wear pattern identified by metal chips flaking off the hardened surface. This condition is caused by foreign particles, overloading situations, and/or normal wear.

SPARK PLUG: A device screwed into the combustion chamber of a spark ignition engine. The basic construction is a conductive core inside of a ceramic insulator, mounted in an outer conductive base. An electrical charge from the spark plug wire travels along the conductive core and jumps a preset air gap to a grounding point or points at the end of the conductive base. The resultant spark ignites the fuel/air mixture in the combustion chamber.

SPECIFIC GRAVITY (BATTERY): The relative weight of liquid (battery electrolyte) as compared to the weight of an equal volume of water.

SPLINES: Ridges machined or cast onto the outer diameter of a shaft or inner diameter of a bore to enable parts to mate without rotation.

SPLIT TORQUE DRIVE: In a torque converter, it refers to parallel paths of torque transmission, one of which is mechanical and the other hydraulic.

SPONGY PEDAL: A soft or spongy feeling when the brake pedal is depressed. It is usually due to air in the brake lines.

SPOOLVALVE: A precision-machined, cylindrically shaped valve made up of lands and grooves. Depending on its position in the valve bore, various interconnecting hydraulic circuit passages are either opened or closed.

SPRAG CLUTCH: A type of one-way clutch design using cams or contoured-shaped sprags between inner and outer races. (See one-way clutch.)

SPRUNG WEIGHT: The weight of a car supported by the springs.

SQUARE-CUT SEAL: Molded synthetic rubber seal designed with a square- or rectangular-shaped cross-section. This type of seal is used for both dynamic and static applications.

SRS: Supplemental restraint system

STABILIZER (SWAY) BAR: A bar linking both sides of the suspension. It resists sway on turns by taking some of added load from one wheel and putting it on the other.

STAGE: The number of turbine sets separated by a stator. A turbine set may be made up of one or more turbine members. A three-element converter is classified as a single stage.

STALL: In fluid drive transmission/transaxle applications, stall refers to engine rpm with the transmission/transaxle engaged and the vehicle stationary; throttle valve can be in any position between closed and wide open.

STALL SPEED: In fluid drive transmission/transaxle applications, stall speed refers to the maximum engine rpm with the transmission/transaxle engaged and vehicle stationary, when the throttle valve is wide open. (See stall; stall test.)

STALL TEST: A procedure recommended by many manufacturers to help determine the integrity of an engine, the torque converter stator, and certain clutch and band combinations. With the shift lever in each of the forward and reverse positions and with the brakes firmly applied, the accelerator pedal is momentarily pressed to the wide open throttle (WOT) position. The engine rpm reading at full throttle can provide clues for diagnosing the condition of the items listed above.

STALL TORQUE: The maximum design or engineered torque ratio of a fluid torque converter, produced under stall speed conditions. (See stall speed.)

STARTER: A high-torque electric motor used for the purpose of starting the engine, typically through a high ratio geared drive connected to the flywheel ring gear.

STATIC: A sealing application in which the parts being sealed do not move in relation to each other.

STATOR (REACTOR): The reaction member of a fluid torque converter that changes the direction of the fluid as it leaves the turbine to enter the impeller vanes. During the torque multiplication phase, this action assists the impeller's rotary force and results in an increase in torque.

STEERING GEOMETRY: Combination of various angles of suspension components (caster, camber, toe-in); roughly equivalent to front end alignment.

STRAIGHT WEIGHT: Term designating motor oil as suitable for use within a narrow range of temperatures. Outside the narrow temperature range its flow characteristics will not adequately lubricate.

STROKE: The distance the piston travels from bottom dead center to top dead center.

SUBSTITUTION: Replacing one part suspected of a defect with a like part of known quality.

SUMP: The storage vessel or reservoir that provides a ready source of fluid to the pump. In an automatic transmission, the sump is the oil pan. All fluid eventually returns to the sump for recycling into the hydraulic system.

SUN GEAR: In a planetary gearset, it is the center gear that meshes with a cluster of planet pinions.

SUPERCHARGER: An air pump driven mechanically by the engine through belts, chains, shafts or gears from the crankshaft. Two general types of supercharger are the positive displacement and centrifugal type, which pump air in direct relationship to the speed of the engine.

SUPPLEMENTAL RESTRAINT SYSTEM: See air bag.

SURGE: Repeating engine-related feeling of acceleration and deceleration that is less intense than chuggle.

SWITCH: A device used to open, close, or redirect the current in an electrical circuit.

SYNCHROMESH: A manual transmission/transaxle that is equipped with devices (synchronizers) that match the gear speeds so that the transmission/transaxle can be downshifted without clashing gears.

SYNTHETIC OIL: Non-petroleum based oil.

TACHOMETER: A device used to measure the rotary speed of an engine, shaft, gear, etc., usually in rotations per minute.

TDC: Top dead center. The exact top of the piston's stroke.

TEFLON SEALING RINGS: Teflon is a soft, durable, plastic-like material that is resistant to heat and provides excellent sealing. These rings are designed with either scarf-cut joints or as one-piece rings. Teflon sealing rings have replaced many metal ring applications.

TERMINAL: A device attached to the end of a wire or cable to make an electrical connection.

TEST LIGHT, CIRCUIT-POWERED: Uses available circuit voltage to test circuit continuity.

TEST LIGHT, SELF-POWERED: Uses its own battery source to test circuit continuity.

THERMISTOR: A special resistor used to measure fluid temperature; it decreases its resistance with increases in temperature.

THERMOSTAT: A valve, located in the cooling system of an engine, which is closed when cold and opens gradually in response to engine heating, controlling the temperature of the coolant and rate of coolant flow.

THERMOSTATIC ELEMENT: A heat-sensitive, spring-type device that controls a drain port from the upper sump area to the lower sump. When the transaxle fluid reaches operating temperature, the port is closed and the upper sump fills, thus reducing the fluid level in the lower sump.

THROTTLE POSITION (TP) SENSOR: Reads the degree of throttle opening; its signal is used to analyze engine load conditions. The ECM/PCM decides to apply the TCC, or to disengage it for coast or load conditions that need a converter torque boost.

THROTTLE PRESSURE/MODULATOR PRESSURE: A hydraulic signal oil pressure relating to the amount of engine load, based on either the amount of throttle plate opening or engine vacuum.

THROTTLE VALVE: A regulating or balanced valve that is controlled mechanically by throttle linkage or engine vacuum. It sends a hydraulic signal to the shift valve body to control shift timing and shift quality. (See balanced valve; modulator valve.)

THROW-OUT BEARING: As the clutch pedal is depressed, the throwout bearing moves against the spring fingers of the pressure plate, forcing the pressure plate to disengage from the driven disc.

TIE ROD: A rod connecting the steering arms. Tie rods have threaded ends that are used to adjust toe-in.

TIE-UP: Condition where two opposing clutches are attempting to apply at same time, causing engine to labor with noticeable loss of engine rpm.

TIMING BELT: A square-toothed, reinforced rubber belt that is driven by the crankshaft and operates the camshaft.

TIMING CHAIN: A roller chain that is driven by the crankshaft and operates the camshaft.

TIRE ROTATION: Moving the tires from one position to another to make the tires wear evenly.

TOE-IN (OUT): A term comparing the extreme front and rear of the front tires. Closer together at the front is toe-in; farther apart at the front is toe-out.

TOP DEAD CENTER (TDC): The point at which the piston reaches the top of its travel on the compression stroke.

TORQUE: Measurement of turning or twisting force, expressed as foot-pounds or inch-pounds.

TORQUE CONVERTER: A turbine used to transmit power from a driving member to a driven member via hydraulic action, providing changes in drive ratio and torque. In automotive use, it links the driveplate at the rear of the engine to the automatic transmission.

TORQUE CONVERTER CLUTCH: The apply plate (lockup plate) assembly used for mechanical power flow through the converter.

TORQUE PHASE: Sometimes referred to as slip phase or stall phase, torque multiplication occurs when the turbine is turning at a slower speed than the impeller, and the stator is reactionary (stationary). This sequence generates a boost in output torque.

TORQUE RATING (STALL TORQUE): The maximum torque multiplication that occurs during stall conditions, with the engine at wide open throttle (WOT) and zero turbine speed.

TORQUE RATIO: An expression of the gear ratio factor on torque effect. A 3:1 gear ratio or 3:1 torque ratio increases the torque input by the ratio factor of 3. Input torque (100 ft. lbs.) x 3 = output torque (300 ft. lbs.)

TRACTION: The amount of usable tractive effort before the drive wheels slip on the road contact surface.

TORSION BAR SUSPENSION: Long rods of spring steel which take the place of springs. One end of the bar is anchored and the other arm (attached to the suspension) is free to twist. The bars' resistance to twisting causes springing action.

TRACK: Distance between the centers of the tires where they contact the ground.

TRACTION CONTROL: A control system that prevents the spinning of a vehicle's drive wheels when excess power is applied.

TRACTIVE EFFORT: The amount of force available to the drive wheels, to move the vehicle.

TRANSAXLE: A single housing containing the transmission and differential. Transaxles are usually found on front engine/front wheel drive or rear engine/rear wheel drive cars.

TRANSDUCER: A device that changes energy from one form to another. For example, a transducer in a microphone changes sound energy to electrical energy. In automotive air-conditioning controls used in automatic temperature systems, a transducer changes an electrical signal to a vacuum signal, which operates mechanical doors.

TRANSMISSION: A powertrain component designed to modify torque and speed developed by the engine; also provides direct drive, reverse, and neutral.

TRANSMISSION CONTROL MODULE (TCM): Manages transmission functions. These vary according to the manufacturer's product design but may include converter clutch operation, electronic shift scheduling, and mainline pressure.

TRANSMISSION FLUID TEMPERATURE (TFT) SENSOR: Originally called a transmission oil temperature (TOT) sensor, this input device to the ECM/PCM senses the fluid temperature and provides a resistance value. It operates on the thermistor principle.

TRANSMISSION INPUT SPEED (TIS) SENSOR: Measures turbine shaft (input shaft) rpm's and compares to engine rpm's to determine torque converter slip. When compared to the transmission output speed sensor or VSS, gear ratio and clutch engagement timing can be determined.

TRANSMISSION OIL TEMPERATURE (TOT) SENSOR: (See transmission fluid temperature (TFT) sensor.)

TRANSMISSION RANGE SELECTOR (TRS) SWITCH: Tells the module which gear shift position the driver has chosen.

TRANSFER CASE: A gearbox driven from the transmission that delivers power to both front and rear driveshafts in a four-wheel drive system. Transfer cases usually have a high and low range set of gears, used depending on how much pulling power is needed.

TRANSISTOR: A semi-conductor component which can be actuated by a small voltage to perform an electrical switching function.

TREAD WEAR INDICATOR: Bars molded into the tire at right angles to the tread that appear as horizontal bars when 1/16 in. of tread remains.

TREAD WEAR PATTERN: The pattern of wear on tires which can be "read" to diagnose problems in the front suspension.

TUNE-UP: A regular maintenance function, usually associated with the replacement and adjustment of parts and components in the electrical and fuel systems of a vehicle for the purpose of attaining optimum performance.

TURBINE: The output (driven) member of a fluid coupling or fluid torque converter. It is splined to the input (turbine) shaft of the transmission.

TURBOCHARGER: An exhaust driven pump which compresses intake air and forces it into the combustion chambers at higher than atmospheric pressures. The increased air pressure allows more fuel to be burned and results in increased horsepower being produced.

TURBULENCE: The interference of molecules of a fluid (or vapor) with each other in a fluid flow.

TYPE F: Transmission fluid developed and used by Ford Motor Company up to 1982. This fluid type provides a high coefficient of friction.

TYPE 7176: The preferred choice of transmission fluid for Chrysler automatic transmissions and transaxles. Developed in 1986, it closely resembles Dexron and Mercon. Type 7176 is the recommended service fill fluid for all Chrysler products utilizing a lockup torque converter dating back to 1978.

U-JOINT (UNIVERSAL JOINT): A flexible coupling in the drive train that allows the driveshafts or axle shafts to operate at different angles and still transmit rotary power.

UNDERSTEER: The tendency of a car to continue straight ahead while negotiating a turn.

UNIT BODY: Design in which the car body acts as the frame.

UNLEADED FUEL: Fuel which contains no lead (a common gasoline additive). The presence of lead in fuel will destroy the functioning elements of a catalytic converter, making it useless.

UNSPRUNG WEIGHT: The weight of car components not supported by the springs (wheels, tires, brakes, rear axle, control arms, etc.).

UPSHIFT: A shift that results in a decrease in torque ratio and an increase in speed.

VACUUM: A negative pressure; any pressure less than atmospheric pressure.

VACUUM ADVANCE: A device which advances the ignition timing in response to increased engine vacuum.

VACUUM GAUGE: An instrument used for measuring the existing vacuum in a vacuum circuit or chamber. The unit of measure is inches (of mercury in a barometer).

VACUUM MODULATOR: Generates a hydraulic oil pressure in response to the amount of engine vacuum.

VALVES: Devices that can open or close fluid passages in a hydraulic system and are used for directing fluid flow and controlling pressure.

VALVE BODY ASSEMBLY: The main hydraulic control assembly of the transmission/transaxle that contains numerous valves, check balls, and other components to control the distribution of pressurized oil throughout the transmission.

VALVE CLEARANCE: The measured gap between the end of the valve stem and the rocker arm, cam lobe or follower that activates the valve.

VALVE GUIDES: The guide through which the stem of the valve passes.

The guide is designed to keep the valve in proper alignment.

VALVE LASH (clearance): The operating clearance in the valve train.

VALVE TRAIN: The system that operates intake and exhaust valves, consisting of camshaft, valves and springs, lifters, pushrods and rocker arms.

VAPOR LOCK: Boiling of the fuel in the fuel lines due to excess heat. This will interfere with the flow of fuel in the lines and can completely stop the flow. Vapor lock normally only occurs in hot weather.

VARIABLE DISPLACEMENT (VARIABLE CAPACITY) VANE PUMP: Slipper-type vanes, mounted in a revolving rotor and contained within the bore of a movable slide, capture and then force fluid to flow. Movement of the slide to various positions changes the size of the vane chambers and the amount of fluid flow. **Note:** GM refers to this pump design as variable displacement, and Ford terms it variable capacity.

VARIABLE FORCE SOLENOID (VFS): Commonly referred to as the electronic pressure control (EPC) solenoid, it replaces the cable/linkage style of TV system control and is integrated with a spool valve and spring assembly to control pressure. A variable computer-controlled current flow varies the internal force of the solenoid on the spool valve and resulting control pressure.

VARIABLE ORIFICE THERMAL VALVE: Temperature-sensitive hydraulic oil control device that adjusts the size of a circuit path opening. By altering the size of the opening, the oil flow rate is adapted for cold to hot oil viscosity changes.

VARNISH: Term applied to the residue formed when gasoline gets old and stale.

VCM: See Electronic Control Unit (ECU).

VEHICLE SPEED SENSOR (VSS): Provides an electrical signal to the computer module, measuring vehicle speed, and affects the torque converter clutch engagement and release.

VESPEL SEALING RINGS: Hard plastic material that produces excellent sealing in dynamic settings. These rings are found in late versions of the 4T60 and in all 4T60-E and 4T80-E transaxles.

VISCOSITY: The ability of a fluid to flow. The lower the viscosity rating, the easier the fluid will flow. 10 weight motor oil will flow much easier than 40 weight motor oil.

VISCOSITY INDEX IMPROVERS: Keeps the viscosity nearly constant with changes in temperature. This is especially important at low temperatures, when the oil needs to be thin to aid in shifting and for cold-weather starting. Yet it must not be so thin that at high temperatures it will cause excessive hydraulic leakage so that pumps are unable to maintain the proper pressures.

VISCOUS CLUTCH: A specially designed torque converter clutch apply plate that, through the use of a silicon fluid, clamps smoothly and absorbs torsional vibrations.

VOLT: Unit used to measure the force or pressure of electricity. It is defined as the pressure needed to move one amp through the resistance of one ohm.

VOLTAGE: The electrical pressure that causes current to flow. Voltage is measured in volts (V).

VOLTAGE, APPLIED: The actual voltage read at a given point in a circuit. It equals the available voltage of the power supply minus the losses in the circuit up to that point.

VOLTAGE DROP: The voltage lost or used in a circuit by normal loads such as a motor or lamp or by abnormal loads such as a poor (high-resistance) lead or terminal connection.

VOLTAGE REGULATOR: A device that controls the current output of the alternator or generator.

VOLTMETER: An instrument used for measuring electrical force in units called volts. Voltmeters are always connected parallel with the circuit being tested.

VORTEX FLOW: The crosswise or circulatory flow of oil between the blades of the members caused by the centrifugal pumping action of the impeller.

WANKEL ENGINE: An engine which uses no pistons. In place of pistons, triangular-shaped rotors revolve in specially shaped housings.

WATER PUMP: A belt driven component of the cooling system that mounts on the engine, circulating the coolant under pressure.

WATT: The unit for measuring electrical power. One watt is the product of one ampere and one volt (watts equals amps times volts). Wattage is the horsepower of electricity (746 watts equal one horsepower).

WHEEL ALIGNMENT: Inclusive term to describe the front end geometry (caster, camber, toe-in/out).

WHEEL CYLINDER: Found in the automotive drum brake assembly, it is a device, actuated by hydraulic pressure, which, through internal pistons, pushes the brake shoes outward against the drums.

WHEEL WEIGHT: Small weights attached to the wheel to balance the wheel and tire assembly. Out-of-balance tires quickly wear out and also give erratic handling when installed on the front.

WHEELBASE: Distance between the center of front wheels and the center of rear wheels.

WIDE OPEN THROTTLE (WOT): Full travel of accelerator pedal.

WORK: The force exerted to move a mass or object. Work involves motion; if a force is exerted and no motion takes place, no work is done. Work per unit of time is called power. Work = force x distance = ft. lbs. 33,000 ft. lbs. in one minute = 1 horsepower

ZERO-THROTTLE COAST DOWN: A full release of accelerator pedal while vehicle is in motion and in drive range.

ENGLISH TO METRIC CONVERSION: TORQUE

To convert foot-pounds (ft. lbs.) to Newton-meters (Nm), multiply the number of ft. lbs. by 1.36

To convert Newton-meters (Nm) to foot-pounds (ft. lbs.), multiply the number of Nm by 0.7376

ft. lbs.	Nm	ft. lbs.	Nm	ft. lbs.	Nm	ft. lbs.	Nm
0.1	0.1	34	46.2	76	103.4	118	160.5
0.2	0.3	35	47.6	77	104.7	119	161.8
0.3	0.4	36	49.0	78	106.1	120	163.2
0.4	0.5	37	50.3	79	107.4	121	164.6
0.5	0.7	38	51.7	80	108.8	122	165.9
0.6	0.8	39	53.0	81	110.2	123	167.3
0.7	1.0	40	54.4	82	111.5	124	168.6
0.8	1.1	41	55.8	83	112.9	125	170.0
0.9	1.2	42	57.1	84	114.2	126	171.4
1	1.4	43	58.5	85	115.6	127	172.7
2	2.7	44	59.8	86	117.0	128	174.1
3	4.1	45	61.2	87	118.3	129	175.4
4	5.4	46	62.6	88	119.7	130	176.8
5	6.8	47	63.9	89	121.0	131	178.2
6	8.2	48	65.3	90	122.4	132	179.5
7	9.5	49	66.6	91	123.8	133	180.9
8	10.9	50	68.0	92	125.1	134	182.2
9	12.2	51	69.4	93	126.5	135	183.6
10	13.6	52	70.7	94	127.8	136	185.0
11	15.0	53	72.1	95	129.2	137	186.3
12	16.3	54	73.4	96	130.6	138	187.7
13	17.7	55	74.8	97	131.9	139	189.0
14	19.0	56	76.2	98	133.3	140	190.4
15	20.4	57	77.5	99	134.6	141	191.8
16	21.8	58	78.9	100	136.0	142	193.1
17	23.1	59	80.2	101	137.4	143	194.5
18	24.5	60	81.6	102	138.7	144	195.8
19	25.8	61	83.0	103	140.1	145	197.2
20	27.2	62	84.3	104	141.4	146	198.6
21	28.6	63	85.7	105	142.8	147	199.9
22	29.9	64	87.0	106	144.2	148	201.3
23	31.3	65	88.4	107	145.5	149	202.6
24	32.6	66	89.8	108	146.9	150	204.0
25	34.0	67	91.1	109	148.2	151	205.4
26	35.4	68	92.5	110	149.6	152	206.7
27	36.7	69	93.8	111	151.0	153	208.1
28	38.1	70	95.2	112	152.3	154	209.4
29	39.4	71	96.6	113	153.7	155	210.8
30	40.8	72	97.9	114	155.0	156	212.2
31	42.2	73	99.3	115	156.4	157	213.5
32	43.5	74	100.6	116	157.8	158	214.9
33	44.9	75	102.0	117	159.1	159	216.2

METRIC TO ENGLISH CONVERSION: TORQUE

To convert foot-pounds (ft. lbs.) to Newton-meters (Nm), multiply the number of ft. lbs. by 1.36
To convert Newton-meters (Nm) to foot-pounds (ft. lbs.), multiply the number of Nm by 0.7376

Nm	ft. lbs.	Nm	ft. lbs.	Nm	ft. lbs.	Nm	ft. lbs.	Nm	ft. lbs.
0.1	0.1	34	25.0	76	55.9	118	86.8	160	117.6
0.2	0.1	35	25.7	77	56.6	119	87.5	161	118.4
0.3	0.2	36	26.5	78	57.4	120	88.2	162	119.1
0.4	0.3	37	27.2	79	58.1	121	89.0	163	119.9
0.5	0.4	38	27.9	80	58.8	122	89.7	164	120.6
0.6	0.4	39	28.7	81	59.6	123	90.4	165	121.3
0.7	0.5	40	29.4	82	60.3	124	91.2	166	122.1
0.8	0.6	41	30.1	83	61.0	125	91.9	167	122.8
0.9	0.7	42	30.9	84	61.8	126	92.6	168	123.5
1	0.7	43	31.6	85	62.5	127	93.4	169	124.3
2	1.5	44	32.4	86	63.2	128	94.1	170	125.0
3	2.2	45	33.1	87	64.0	129	94.9	171	125.7
4	2.9	46	33.8	88	64.7	130	95.6	172	126.5
5	3.7	47	34.6	89	65.4	131	96.3	173	127.2
6	4.4	48	35.3	90	66.2	132	97.1	174	127.9
7	5.1	49	36.0	91	66.9	133	97.8	175	128.7
8	5.9	50	36.8	92	67.6	134	98.5	176	129.4
9	6.6	51	37.5	93	68.4	135	99.3	177	130.1
10	7.4	52	38.2	94	69.1	136	100.0	178	130.9
11	8.1	53	39.0	95	69.9	137	100.7	179	131.6
12	8.8	54	39.7	96	70.6	138	101.5	180	132.4
13	9.6	55	40.4	97	71.3	139	102.2	181	133.1
14	10.3	56	41.2	98	72.1	140	102.9	182	133.8
15	11.0	57	41.9	99	72.8	141	103.7	183	134.6
16	11.8	58	42.6	100	73.5	142	104.4	184	135.3
17	12.5	59	43.4	101	74.3	143	105.1	185	136.0
18	13.2	60	44.1	102	75.0	144	105.9	186	136.8
19	14.0	61	44.9	103	75.7	145	106.6	187	137.5
20	14.7	62	45.6	104	76.5	146	107.4	188	138.2
21	15.4	63	46.3	105	77.2	147	108.1	189	139.0
22	16.2	64	47.1	106	77.9	148	108.8	190	139.7
23	16.9	65	47.8	107	78.7	149	109.6	191	140.4
24	17.6	66	48.5	108	79.4	150	110.3	192	141.2
25	18.4	67	49.3	109	80.1	151	111.0	193	141.9
26	19.1	68	50.0	110	80.9	152	111.8	194	142.6
27	19.9	69	50.7	111	81.6	153	112.5	195	143.4
28	20.6	70	51.5	112	82.4	154	113.2	196	144.1
29	21.3	71	52.2	113	83.1	155	114.0	197	144.9
30	22.1	72	52.9	114	83.8	156	114.7	198	145.6
31	22.8	73	53.7	115	84.6	157	115.4	199	146.3
32	23.5	74	54.4	116	85.3	158	116.2	200	147.1
33	24.3	75	55.1	117	86.0	159	116.9	201	147.8

ENGLISH/METRIC CONVERSION: TEMPERATURE

To convert Fahrenheit (F°) to Celsius (C°), take F° temperature and subtract 32, multiply the result by 5 and divide the result by 9
To convert Celsius (C°) to Fahrenheit (F°), take C° temperature and multiply it by 9, divide the result by 5 and add 32

F°	C°	F°	C°	C°	F°	C°	F°
-40	-40.0	150	65.6	-38	-36.4	46	114.8
-35	-37.2	155	68.3	-36	-32.8	48	118.4
-30	-34.4	160	71.1	-34	-29.2	50	122
-25	-31.7	165	73.9	-32	-25.6	52	125.6
-20	-28.9	170	76.7	-30	-22	54	129.2
-15	-26.1	175	79.4	-28	-18.4	56	132.8
-10	-23.3	180	82.2	-26	-14.8	58	136.4
-5	-20.6	185	85.0	-24	-11.2	60	140
0	-17.8	190	87.8	-22	-7.6	62	143.6
1	-17.2	195	90.6	-20	-4	64	147.2
2	-16.7	200	93.3	-18	-0.4	66	150.8
3	-16.1	205	96.1	-16	3.2	68	154.4
4	-15.6	210	98.9	-14	6.8	70	158
5	-15.0	212	100.0	-12	10.4	72	161.6
10	-12.2	215	101.7	-10	14	74	165.2
15	-9.4	220	104.4	-8	17.6	76	168.8
20	-6.7	225	107.2	-6	21.2	78	172.4
25	-3.9	230	110.0	-4	24.8	80	176
30	-1.1	235	112.8	-2	28.4	82	179.6
35	1.7	240	115.6	0	32	84	183.2
40	4.4	245	118.3	2	35.6	86	186.8
45	7.2	250	121.1	4	39.2	88	190.4
50	10.0	255	123.9	6	42.8	90	194
55	12.8	260	126.7	8	46.4	92	197.6
60	15.6	265	129.4	10	50	94	201.2
65	18.3	270	132.2	12	53.6	96	204.8
70	21.1	275	135.0	14	57.2	98	208.4
75	23.9	280	137.8	16	60.8	100	212
80	26.7	285	140.6	18	64.4	102	215.6
85	29.4	290	143.3	20	68	104	219.2
90	32.2	295	146.1	22	71.6	106	222.8
95	35.0	300	148.9	24	75.2	108	226.4
100	37.8	305	151.7	26	78.8	110	230
105	40.6	310	154.4	28	82.4	112	233.6
110	43.3	315	157.2	30	86	114	237.2
115	46.1	320	160.0	32	89.6	116	240.8
120	48.9	325	162.8	34	93.2	118	244.4
125	51.7	330	165.6	36	96.8	120	248
130	54.4	335	168.3	38	100.4	122	251.6
135	57.2	340	171.1	40	104	124	255.2
140	60.0	345	173.9	42	107.6	126	258.8
145	62.8	350	176.7	44	111.2	128	262.4

LENGTH CONVERSION

To convert inches (in.) to millimeters (mm), multiply the number of inches by 25.4

To convert millimeters (mm) to inches (in.), multiply the number of millimeters by 0.04

Inches	Millimeters	Inches	Millimeters	Inches	Millimeters	Inches	Millimeters
0.0001	0.00254	0.005	0.1270	0.09	2.286	4	101.6
0.0002	0.00508	0.006	0.1524	0.1	2.54	5	127.0
0.0003	0.00762	0.007	0.1778	0.2	5.08	6	152.4
0.0004	0.01016	0.008	0.2032	0.3	7.62	7	177.8
0.0005	0.01270	0.009	0.2286	0.4	10.16	8	203.2
0.0006	0.01524	0.01	0.254	0.5	12.70	9	228.6
0.0007	0.01778	0.02	0.508	0.6	15.24	10	254.0
0.0008	0.02032	0.03	0.762	0.7	17.78	11	279.4
0.0009	0.02286	0.04	1.016	0.8	20.32	12	304.8
0.001	0.0254	0.05	1.270	0.9	22.86	13	330.2
0.002	0.0508	0.06	1.524	1	25.4	14	355.6
0.003	0.0762	0.07	1.778	2	50.8	15	381.0
0.004	0.1016	0.08	2.032	3	76.2	16	406.4

ENGLISH/METRIC CONVERSION: LENGTH

To convert inches (in.) to millimeters (mm), multiply the number of inches by 25.4
To convert millimeters (mm) to inches (in.), multiply the number of millimeters by 0.04

Inches		Millimeters	Inches		Millimeters	Inches		Millimeters
Fraction	Decimal	Decimal	Fraction	Decimal	Decimal	Fraction	Decimal	Decimal
1/64	0.016	0.397	11/32	0.344	8.731	11/16	0.688	17.463
1/32	0.031	0.794	23/64	0.359	9.128	45/64	0.703	17.859
3/64	0.047	1.191	3/8	0.375	9.525	23/32	0.719	18.256
1/16	0.063	1.588	25/64	0.391	9.922	47/64	0.734	18.653
5/64	0.078	1.984	13/32	0.406	10.319	3/4	0.750	19.050
3/32	0.094	2.381	27/64	0.422	10.716	49/64	0.766	19.447
7/64	0.109	2.778	7/16	0.438	11.113	25/32	0.781	19.844
1/8	0.125	3.175	29/64	0.453	11.509	51/64	0.797	20.241
9/64	0.141	3.572	15/32	0.469	11.906	13/16	0.813	20.638
5/32	0.156	3.969	31/64	0.484	12.303	53/64	0.828	21.034
11/64	0.172	4.366	1/2	0.500	12.700	27/32	0.844	21.431
3/16	0.188	4.763	33/64	0.516	13.097	55/64	0.859	21.828
13/64	0.203	5.159	17/32	0.531	13.494	7/8	0.875	22.225
7/32	0.219	5.556	35/64	0.547	13.891	57/64	0.891	22.622
15/64	0.234	5.953	9/16	0.563	14.288	29/32	0.906	23.019
1/4	0.250	6.350	37/64	0.578	14.684	59/64	0.922	23.416
17/64	0.266	6.747	19/32	0.594	15.081	15/16	0.938	23.813
9/32	0.281	7.144	39/64	0.609	15.478	61/64	0.953	24.209
19/64	0.297	7.541	5/8	0.625	15.875	31/32	0.969	24.606
5/16	0.313	7.938	41/64	0.641	16.272	63/64	0.984	25.003
21/64	0.328	8.334	21/32	0.656	16.669	1/1	1.000	25.400
			43/64	0.672	17.066			

CHILTON LABOR GUIDE

Chilton's labor times are so trusted, even a competing publisher uses them!

The *Chilton 2013 Labor Guide* features new models and new labor operations in order to stay current with new technologies. Labor times have also been refined for normal and severe maintenance schedules, if applicable. The 2013 edition Labor Guide Manuals provide repair times for 1990-current import and domestic vehicles and the 2013 edition Labor Guide CD-ROM provides repair times for 1981-current import and domestic vehicles. Chilton's editors consider warranty times, component locations, component type, the environment in which technicians work, the training they receive, and the tools they use when calculating a labor time. To allow for vehicle age, operating conditions, and type of service, the *Chilton 2013 Labor Guide* provides standard and severe service times, plus OEM warranty times. Vehicle makes and models conform to current Automotive Aftermarket Industry Association (AAIA) standards.

Chilton 2013 Labor Guide Manual Set (Domestic & Import) ISBN 978-1-2851-9293-2, Part No. 209293

Chilton 2013 Labor Guide CD-ROM (Domestic & Import) ISBN 978-1-2851-9296-3, Part No. 209296

CD-ROM FEATURES

- ❑ Access labor times for 1981- current import and domestic vehicle models.
- ❑ Save time with automatically calculated labor charges, taxes, & parts as total job is estimated.
- ❑ Create professional estimates for your customer and worksheets for your technicians, printing them whenever needed.
- ❑ Keep track of customers, prior estimates, and your own parts or package jobs with less paper.
- ❑ Choose part names for estimates from an industry standard database to reduce typing.
- ❑ Estimate and track your work status with improved forms.
- ❑ Communicate easily with customers using re-designed printouts which show all labor and parts in an easy-to-read format.
- ❑ Simplify adding parts to your estimate or work order with a helpful parts list.
- ❑ Locate information quick with a keyword search engine.
- ❑ Quickly locate work requests by day, week and month using the calendar feature.

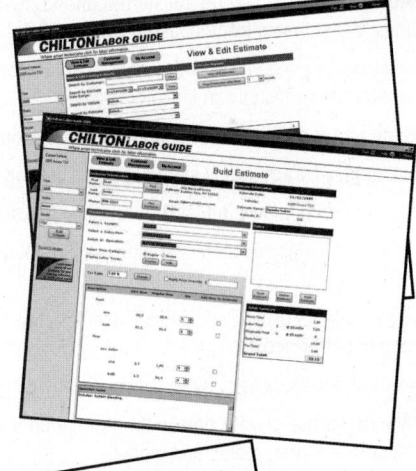

Manual FEATURES

- ❑ Nearly 4,000 pages of updated Chilton labor times split into two volumes includes vehicle information from 1990 to current models.
- ❑ Trusted by more service professionals than any other labor guide.
- ❑ Less flipping though pages with separate domestic and imported vehicle manuals and more specific vehicle groups.
- ❑ Convenient tabs display contents by manufacturer and model.
- ❑ Easy-to-find manufacturers are arranged alphabetically within each volume.
- ❑ Search using two-indexes - labor operations and systems - in each model group.
- ❑ Page numbers include manufacturer code so you know where you are in the book.

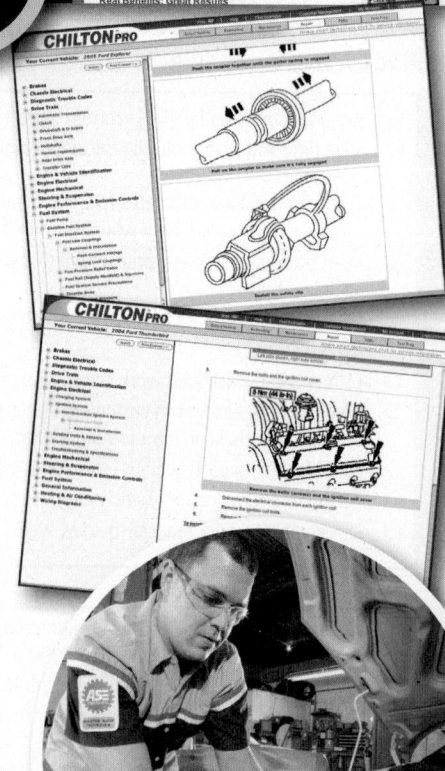

CHILTON®ESTIMATING

Proudly Partnered With:

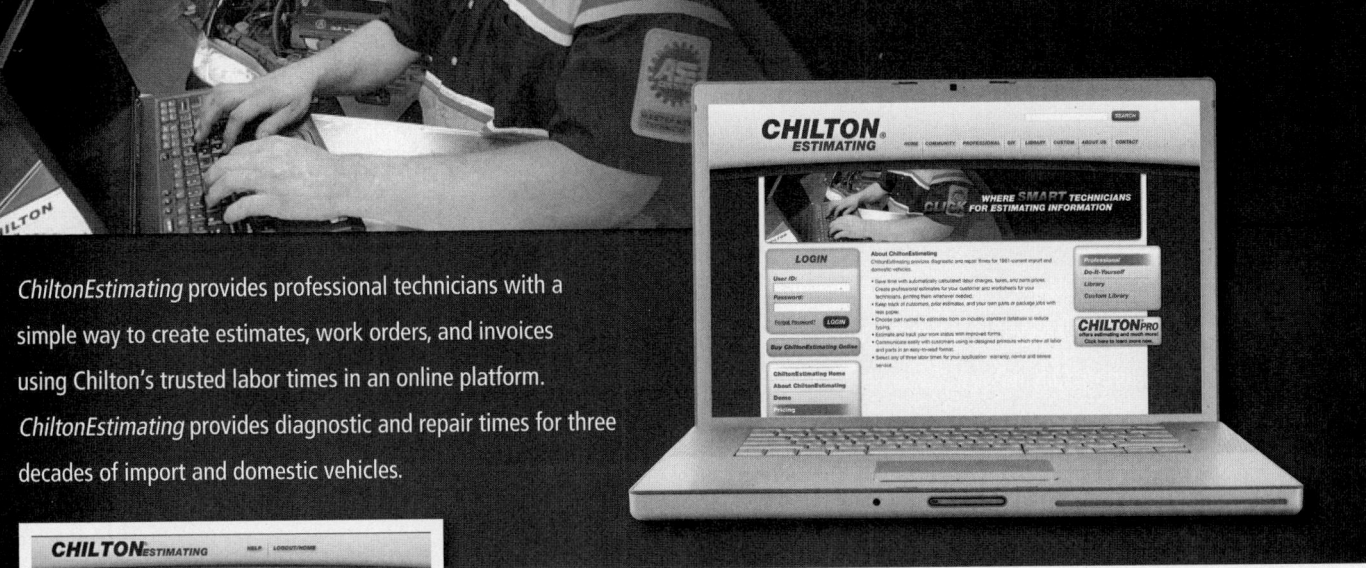

ChiltonEstimating provides professional technicians with a simple way to create estimates, work orders, and invoices using Chilton's trusted labor times in an online platform. *ChiltonEstimating* provides diagnostic and repair times for three decades of import and domestic vehicles.

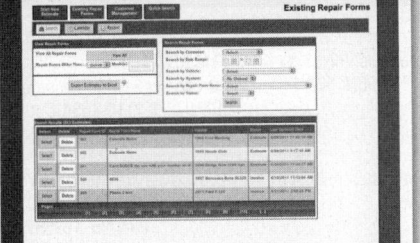

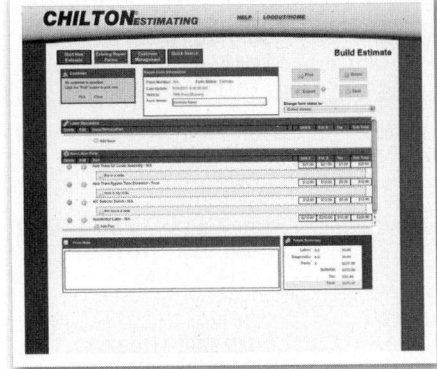

System Requirements:
Web browser

- Internet Explorer 7.0 or above (recommended)
- Firefox 3.6 or 4 or Safari
- High-speed internet connection
- Adobe Flash Player
- Adobe Reader
- Windows XP or above

○ Access up-to-date information immediately. *ChiltonEstimating* is continuously updated!

○ Enjoy a hassle-free product with nothing to download and nothing to install.

○ Never fret over lost or damaged software or books again.

○ Secure your valuable customer data on our server, which won't be lost if your computer crashes.

○ Easily access the program from any web-enabled computer.

○ Work on more than one job at a time using *ChiltonEstimating's* two shop-user accounts.

○ Download all customer contact information easily for marketing purposes.

○ Cancel your subscription at any time by going to the "My Account" tab. No contract or obligation required. Customer data will be available to download for up to six months after a subscription has expired.

○ Save time with automatically calculated labor charges, taxes, and parts prices. Create professional estimates for your customer and worksheets for your technicians, printing them whenever needed.

○ Keep track of customers, prior estimates, and your own parts or package jobs with less paper.

○ Choose part names for estimates from an industry standard database to reduce typing.

○ Estimate and track your work status with improved forms.

○ Communicate easily with customers using re-designed printouts which show all labor and parts in an easy-to-read format.

○ Select any of three labor times for your application: warranty, normal and severe service.

ONLINE **www.chilton.cengage.com**   TO PLACE AN ORDER CALL **1-800-347-7707**

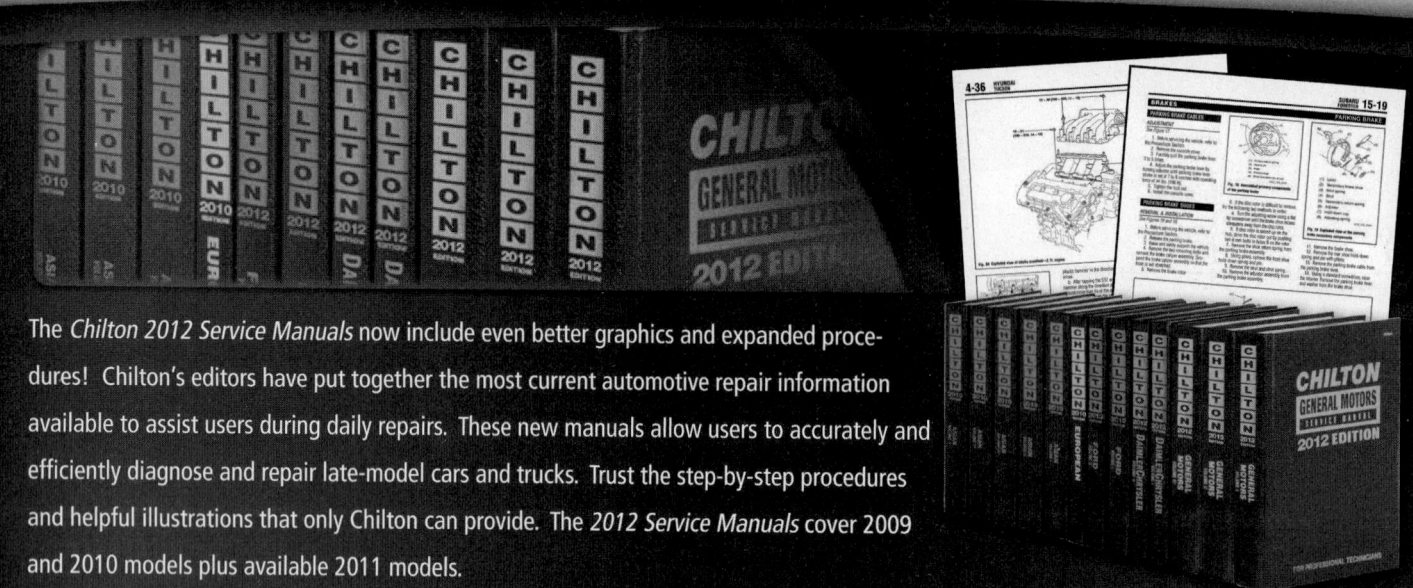

CHILTON SERVICE MANUALS

The *Chilton 2012 Service Manuals* now include even better graphics and expanded procedures! Chilton's editors have put together the most current automotive repair information available to assist users during daily repairs. These new manuals allow users to accurately and efficiently diagnose and repair late-model cars and trucks. Trust the step-by-step procedures and helpful illustrations that only Chilton can provide. The *2012 Service Manuals* cover 2009 and 2010 models plus available 2011 models.

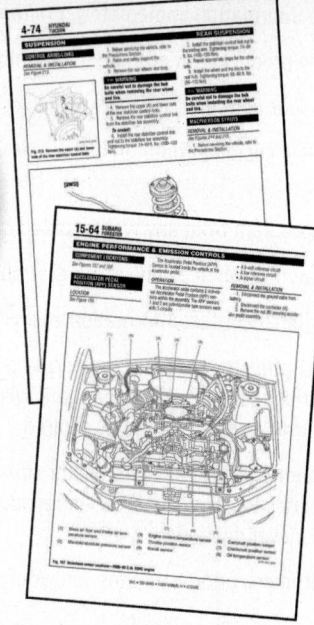

KEY FEATURES
- Organized by vehicle manufacturer.
- Provides thousands of pages of expertly written content.
- Access new year, make, and model information without repeating previous edition's content.
- Comprehensive, technically detailed content, including exploded view illustrations, diagnostics and specification charts, arranged alphabetically by model group for quick, easy access.

2012 EDITIONS

2012 Chrysler Service Manuals Vols. 1 & 2   ISBN: 978-1-1336-2576-6
Part No. 222576

2012 Ford Service Manuals Vols. 1 & 2
ISBN: 978-1-1336-2575-9
Part No. 222575

2012 General Motor Service Manuals Vols. 1 & 2
ISBN: 978-1-1336-2574-2
Part No. 222574

2012 Asian Service Manual Vol. 1
ISBN 978-1-2854-7105-1
Part No. 207105

2012 Asian Service Manual Vol. 2
ISBN 978-1-2854-7106-8
Part No. 207106

2012 Asian Service Manual Vol. 3
ISBN 978-1-2854-7107-5
Part No. 207107

2012 Asian Service Manual Vol. 4
ISBN 978-1-2854-7108-2
Part No. 207108

2012 Asian Service Manual Vol. 5
ISBN 978-1-2854-7109-9
Part No. 207109

2012 European Service Manuals Vols. 1 & 2
ISBN 978-1-2854-7112-9
Part No. 207112

2010 EDITIONS

2010 Chrysler Service Manuals, Vols. 1 & 2
ISBN 978-1-1110-3654-6
Part No. 163654

2010 Ford Service Manuals, Vols. 1 & 2
ISBN 978-1-1110-3657-7
Part No. 163657

2010 General Motors Service Manuals, Vols. 1, 2, & 3
ISBN 978-1-111-03661-4
Part No. 163661

2010 Asian Service Manual Vol. 1
ISBN 978-1-1110-3764-2
Part No. 163764

2010 Asian Service Manual Vol. 2
ISBN 978-1-1110-3765-9
Part No. 163765

2010 Asian Service Manual Vol. 3
ISBN 978-1-1110-3766-6
Part No. 163766

2010 Asian Service Manual Vol. 4
ISBN 978-1-1110-3767-3
Part No. 163767

2010 Asian Service Manual Vol. 5
ISBN 978-1-1110-3768-0
Part No. 163768

2010 European Service Manual
ISBN 978-1-1110-3769-7
Part No. 163769